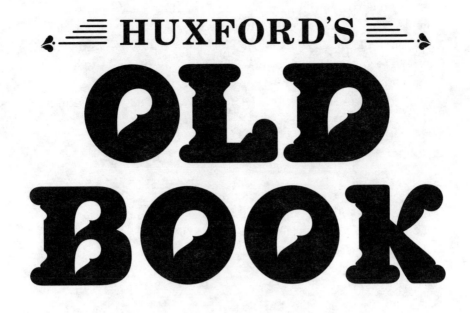

HUXFORD'S
OLD BOOK
VALUE GUIDE
Eighth Edition

COLLECTOR BOOKS
A Division of Schroeder Publishing Co., Inc.

The current values in this book should be used only as a guide. They are not intended to set prices, which vary from one section of the country to another. Auction prices as well as dealer prices vary greatly and are affected by condition as well as demand. Neither the Author nor the Publisher assumes responsibility for any losses that might be incurred as a result of consulting this guide.

Searching For A Publisher?

We are always looking for knowledgeable people considered to be experts within their fields. If you feel that there is a real need for a book on your collectible subject and have a large comprehensive collection, contact Collector Books.

On the Cover:

Nasibova, Aida. *The Faceted Chamber in the Moscow Kremlin.* 1978. Leningrad. Aurora Art Publishers. 1st edition. F/F. $65.00.

Nichols, Beverly. *Sunlight on the Lawn.* 1956. NY. E.P. Dutton. 1st edition. F/F. $30.00.

Shakespeare, William. *The Complete Oxford Shakespeare.* 1987. Oxford University Press. 3 volumes. VG/VG slipcase. $22.00.

Books featured on cover courtesy of:
David & Nancy Haines
Vintage Books
181 Hayden Rowe St.
Hopkington, MA 01748
(508)435-3499

Additional copies of this book may be ordered from:

COLLECTOR BOOKS
P.O. Box 3009
Paducah, KY 42002-3009

@ $19.95. Add $2.00 for postage and handling.

Copyright: Schroeder Publishing Co., Inc. 1996

INTRODUCTION

This book was compiled to help the owner of old books evaluate his holdings and find a buyer for them. Most of us have a box, trunk, stack, or bookcase of old books. Chances are they are not rare books, but they may have value. Two questions that we are asked most frequently are 'Can you tell me the value of my old books?' and 'Where can I sell them?' *Huxford's Old Book Value Guide* will help answer both of these questions. Not only does this book place retail values on nearly 25,000 old books, it also lists scores of buyers along with the type of material each is interested in purchasing. Note that we list retail values (values that an interested party would be willing to pay to obtain possession of the book). These prices are taken from dealers' selling lists that have been issued within the past year. All of the listings are coded (A1, S7, etc.) before the price. This coding refers to a specific dealer's listing for that book. When two or more dealers have listed the same book, their codes will be listed alphabetically in the description line. Please refer to the section titled 'Book Sellers' for codes.

If you were to sell your books to a dealer, you should expect to receive no more than 50% of the values listed in this book, unless the dealer has a specific buyer in mind for some of your material. In many cases, a dealer will pay less than 50% of retail for a book to stock.

Do not ask a dealer to evaluate your old books unless you intend to sell them to him. Most antiquarian book dealers in the larger cities will appraise your books and ephemera for a fee that ranges from a low of $10.00 per hour to $50.00 per hour (or more). If you have an extensive library of rare books, the $50.00-an-hour figure would be money well spent (assuming, of course, the appraiser to be qualified and honest).

Huxford's Old Book Value Guide places values on the more common holdings that many seem to accumulate. You will notice that the majority of the books listed are in the $10.00 to $40.00 range. Many such guides list only the rare, almost non-existent books that the average person will never see. The format is very simple: listings are alphabetized first by the name of the author, translator, editor, or illustrator; if more than one book is listed for a particular author, each title is listed alphabetically under his or her name. When pseudonyms are known, names have been cross-referenced. (Please also see the section titled 'Pseudonyms' for additional information.) Dust jackets or wrappers are noted when present, and sizes (when given) are approximate. Condition is usually noted as well.

Fine condition refers to books that are perfect, in as-issued condition with no defects. Books in near-fine condition are perfect, but not as crisp as those graded fine. Near-fine condition books show only a little wear from reading (such as very small marks on binding); they are not as crisp as those graded fine, but they still have no major defects. Books rated very good may show wear but must have no tears on pages, binding, or dust jacket (if issued). A rating of good applies to an average used book that has all of its pages and yet may have small tears and other defects. The term reading copy (some dealers also use 'poor') describes a book having major defects; however, its text must be complete. Ex-library books are always indicated as such; they may be found in any condition. This rule also applies to any Book Club edition. Some of our booksellers indicate intermediate grades with a + or ++, or VG-EX. We have endeavored to use the grade that best corresponded to the description of condition as given in each dealer's listing. If you want to check further on the condition of a specific book, please consult the bookseller indicated. Please note that the condition stated in the description is for the book and then the dust jacket. (Dust jackets on many modern first editions may account for up to 80% of their value.)

In the back of the book we have listed buyers of books and book-related material. When you correspond with these dealers, be sure to enclose a self-addressed, stamped envelope if you want a reply. Please do not send lists of books for an appraisal. If you wish to sell your books, quote the price that you want or negotiate price only on the items the buyer is interested in purchasing. When you list your books, do so by author, full title, publisher and place, date, and edition. Indicate condition, noting any defects on cover or contents.

When shipping your books, first wrap each book in paper such as brown kraft or a similar type of material. Never use newspaper for the inner wrap, since newsprint tends to rub off. (It may, however be used as a cushioning material within the outer carton.) Place your books in a sturdy corrugated box and use a good shipping tape to seal it. Tape reinforced with nylon string is preferable, as it will not tear. Books shipped by parcel post may be sent at a special fourth class book rate, which may be lower than regular parcel post zone rates.

LISTING OF STANDARD ABBREVIATIONS

/ ....and, also, with, or indicates dual-title book
ACS ....advance copy slip
aeg ....all edge gilt
AJA.......American Jewish Archives
AJC ......American Jewish Congress
AJHS...American Jewish Historical Society
Am ....American
AP ..proof, advance proof, advance uncorrected proof, or galley
ARC .....advance reading or review copy
bdg..........................binding, bound
decor............decoration, decorated
b&w ....black & white
bl ....blue
blk ....black
BC ....any book club edition
BOMC............Book of Month Club
brd...boards
c ....copyright
ca ....circa
cbdg...........................comb binding
chip ....chipped
clip ....clipped price
CMG....Coward McCann Geoghegan
dk ....dark
dj...............................dust jacket
DSP ....Duell Sloan Pearce
dtd...............................dated
E ....east, eastern
edit...................................editor
ed ....edition
emb.............embossed, embossing
Eng....................England, English
ep ....end pages
ES.............................errata slip
ERB ....Edgar Rice Burroughs Inc.
F ....fine
fld.........................folding, folder
ftspc...........................frontispiece
FSC..........Farrar, Straus & Cudahy
FSG ....Farrar, Straus & Giroux
fwd.................................forward
G ....good
GPO...Government Printing Office

gr ....green
HBJ .....Harcourt Brace Jovanovich, Inc.
HBW.............Harcourt Brace World
hist ....history
hc ....hard cover
HRW ....Holt Rinehart Winston
ils ....illustrated
imp................................imprint
intl..................................initialed
inscr ....inscribed
Inst.................................Institute
Internat ....International
intro............................introduction
LEC..............Limited Edition Club
lg ....large
Lib ....library
lt ....light
ltd...................................limited
mc ....multicolor
MIT .....MA Institute of Technology
MTI ....movie tie-in
MOMA.....Museum of Modern Art
MPA ....Museum of Primitive Art
mtd...............................mounted
Mus..................................museum
N.....................north, northern
NAL ....New American Library
Nat ....national
NEL..............New English Library
nd ....no date
ne ....no edition given
NF ....near fine
NGS..National Geographic Society
np..............................no place given
NYGS ...New York Graphic Society
obl ....oblong
orig ....original
p....................................page, pages
pc ....piece
pb ....paperback
pict ....pictorial
pl ....plate, plates
Pr ....press
pref ....preface
pres................................presentation
promo.............................promotion

prt...............................print, printing
pub ....publisher, publishing
rem mk..................remainder mark
repro ....reproduction
rpr ....repair
rpt...................................reprint
RS.............................review slip
S ....south, southern
swrp ....shrink wrap
sans ....none issued
sbdg.........................spiral binding
sc ....softcover
SF ....science fiction
sgn...............signature, signed
sm ....small
sq ....square
stp ....stamp or stamped
supp ....supplement
TB.................................textbook
teg ....top edge gilt
trans ....translated
TVTI ....TV tie-in
U ....University
unp ....unpaged
UP.....................uncorrected proof
VG ....very good
W.................west, western
w/...with, indicates laid in material
wht ....white
wrp...............................wrappers
xl...................................ex-library
yel.................................yellow
#d ....numbered
12mo ....about 7" tall
16mo ....6" to 7" tall
24mo ....5" to 6" tall
32mo ....4" to 5" tall
48mo.......................less than 4" tall
64mo ....about 3" tall
sm 8vo ....7½" to 8" tall
8vo...............................8" to 9" tall
sm 4to ....about 10" tall, quarto
4to.................between 11" to 13" tall
folio ....13" or larger
elephant folio ....23" or larger
atlas folio ....25"
double elephant folio..larger than 25"

A

AALL, Herman Harris. *Neutral Investigation of Causes of Wars.* 1923. Kristiania, Norway. biblio. VG/wrp. A17. $15.00

AARONS, Edward S. *Death Is My Shadow.* 1957. Mystery House. 1st ed. F/clip. M15. $45.00

ABBATE, Francesco. *Egyptian Art.* 1972. Octopus. 1st Eng ed. F/F. W1. $9.00

ABBATE, Francesco. *Precolumbian Art.* 1972. London. Octopus. 12mo. ils. VG/dj. N2. $7.50

ABBEY, Edward. *Abbey's Road.* 1979. Dutton. 1st ed. 1/2500. F/clip. B4. $450.00

ABBEY, Edward. *Abbey's Road.* 1979. NY. simultaneous wrps issue. sgn. F/8vo wrp. A11. $175.00

ABBEY, Edward. *Black Sun.* 1971. Simon Schuster. 1st ed. NF/NF. B3. $225.00

ABBEY, Edward. *Brave Cowboy.* 1993. Dream Garden. 1/500. sgn Kirk Douglas. 280p. orange cloth. M/dj. A18/H5. $100.00

ABBEY, Edward. *Confessions of a Barbarian: Selections From Journals of...* 1994. Little Brn. 1st prt. edit/sgn David Peterson. F/F. B3. $35.00

ABBEY, Edward. *Desert Images.* 1979. HBJ. 1st ed. photos David Muench. NF/NF dj/case. B3. $250.00

ABBEY, Edward. *Desert Solitaire.* 1968. NY. 1st ed. VG/VG. B5. $100.00

ABBEY, Edward. *Earth Apples.* 1994. St Martin. 1st ed. edit/sgn Dave Peterson. F/F. B3. $20.00

ABBEY, Edward. *Fool's Progress.* 1988. Holt. 1st ed. inscr. F/NF. B2. $125.00

ABBEY, Edward. *Fool's Progress.* 1988. NY. AP. F/wrp. C2. $75.00

ABBEY, Edward. *Hidden Canyon.* 1977. Viking. 1st ed. photos John Blaustein. F/VG. B3. $225.00

ABBEY, Edward. *Jonathan Troy.* 1954. Dodd Mead. 1st ed. 8vo. 374p. yel stp blk cloth. xl. dj. H5. $750.00

ABBEY, Edward. *Jonathan Troy.* 1954. Dodd Mead. 1st ed/author's 1st book. F/rpr tear. S9. $1,250.00

ABBEY, Edward. *Journey Home.* 1977. Dutton. 1st ed. F/F. B3. $95.00

ABBEY, Edward. *Monkey Wrench Gang.* 1975. Lippincott. 1st ed. F/F. B4. $500.00

ABBEY, Edward. *Monkey Wrench Gang.* 1985. Dream Garden. Special Ltd/10th Anniversary ed. 1/250. sgn. M/case. A18. $900.00

ABBEY, Edward. *Monkey Wrench Gang.* 1990. Dream Garden. revised ils ed/1st prt. M/M. A18. $50.00

ABBEY, Edward. *Sliprock.* 1971. Sierra Club. 1st ed. ils Philip Hyde. F/NF. B3. $200.00

ABBEY, Sue. *Francis Cummings Lockwood, 1864-1948.* 1990. Westernlore. 183p. F/F. B19. $25.00

ABBEY & ASPRIN. *Catwoman.* 1992. Warner. 1st hc ed. F/SF BC issue. F4. $20.00

ABBIE, A.A. *Original Australians.* 1970. Am Elsevier Pub. 263p. VG/dj. K4. $9.00

ABBOT, Anthony. *Shudders.* 1943. Farrar Rinehart. VG. P3. $20.00

ABBOTT, Berenice. *World of Atget.* 1964. Horizon. 180 photo pl. 180p. NF/chip. A17. $100.00

ABBOTT, Bernice. *World of Atget.* 1964. NY. 1st ed. VG/VG. B5. $90.00

ABBOTT, Bruce. *Sign of the Scorpion.* 1970. Grove. 1st ed. F/F. P3. $20.00

ABBOTT, G.F. *Macedonian Folklore.* 1903. Cambridge. 1st ed. 8vo. cloth/leather label. uncut. O2. $85.00

ABBOTT, G.F. *Turkey in Transition.* 1909. London. pres. 370p. cloth. F. O2. $75.00

ABBOTT, Isabelle A. *Pacific Seaweed Aquaculture.* 1980. La Jolla. 4to. ils. 228p. sc. B26. $15.00

ABBOTT, Jacob. *Franconia Stories.* 1923. Putnam. 1st ed. 8vo. ils Helen M Armstrong. gilt bl cloth. NF. D6. $40.00

ABBOTT, Jacob. *Gentle Measures in Management & Training of the Young.* 1872. NY. ils. 330p. cloth. B14. $95.00

ABBOTT, Jacob. *Harper Establishment; or, How Story Books Are Made.* 1956 (1855). np. ils. 160p. F. A4. $45.00

ABBOTT, Jacob. *Jacob Learning To Read; or, Easy Stories for Young Children.* 1845. Phil/Boston. 180p. morocco/marbled brd. B14. $95.00

ABBOTT, John. *Exposition of Principles of Abbott's Hydrolic Engine...* 1835. Boston. Hart. 1st ed. 7 pl. 132p. cloth. VG. H10. $150.00

ABBOTT, John. *Life of General Ulysses S Grant.* 1868. Boston. Russell. VG. M20. $35.00

ABBOTT, John. *Peter Stuyvesant: Last Dutch Governor of New Amsterdam.* 1873. Dodd Mead. 1st ed. 12mo. 362p. brn cloth. VG. B11. $30.00

ABBOTT, John. *Rollo's Tour in Europe.* 1864. Sheldon. 10 vol set. ils. gilt red emb bdg. VG. P2. $125.00

ABBOTT, Lee K. *Living After Midnight: Novella & Stories.* 1991. Putnam. 1st ed. F/F. A14. $25.00

ABBOTT, Lee K. *Strangers in Paradise.* 1986. Putnam. 1st ed. sgn. F/F. B4. $75.00

ABBOTT, Newton Carl. *Montana in the Making.* 1934. np. 4th prt. xl. poor. B34. $10.00

ABBOTT & DICKINSON. *Guide to Reading.* 1925. Doubleday. G+. P3. $13.00

ABBOTT & STIX. *Shell: 500 Years of Inspired Design.* 1968. NY. 1st ed. F/F. A9. $50.00

ABD AL-RAHIM, Muddathir. *Imperialism & Nationalism in the Sudan.* 1969. Oxford. 1st ed. 275p. xl. VG. W1. $22.00

ABDEL-MALEK, Anouar. *Contemporary Arab Political Thought.* 1983. London. Zed. 1st Eng ed. sm 8vo. VG. W1. $15.00

ABDILL, George. *Civil War Railroads.* 1961. ils. 190+p. dj. O8. $18.50

ABDUL-HAK, Selim. *Treasures of the National Museum of Damascus.* ca 1950. Damascus. 2nd ed. 69 pl. pict wrp. O2. $30.00

ABDULLA, Ramjoo. *Ramjoo's Diaries: 1922-1929...* 1979. Walnut Creek. Sufism Reoriented. VG/VG. B33. $25.00

ABDULLAH, King. *Memoirs of King Abdullah of Transjordan.* 1950. London. 1st ed. 280p. gilt red cloth. VG/VG. M7. $75.00

ABDULLAH & BALDWIN *Broadway Interlude.* 1929. Payson Clarke. 7th ed. VG. P3. $15.00

ABE, Kobo. *Ruined Map.* 1969. Knopf. 1st ed. VG/VG. P3. $25.00

ABE, Kobo. *Secret Rendezvous.* 1979. Knopf. 1st Am ed. F/F. B4. $50.00

ABE, Kobo. *Woman in the Dunes.* 1964. Knopf. 1st Am ed. F/NF. N3. $10.00

ABEEL, David. *Journal of a Residence in China.* 1836. NY. Williamson. 2nd ed. 12mo. 378p. orig cloth. K1. $100.00

ABEL, Annie H. *Am Indian As Slaveholder & Secessionist. Vol 1.* ca 1970. Scholarly. reprint. biblio/index. 394p. VG. A17. $25.00

ABEL, Annie H. *Tabeau's Narrative of Loisel's Expedition to Upper MS.* 1968. OK U. 2nd prt. F/F. B34. $45.00

ABEL, Charles. *Commercial Photographic Lightings.* 1948. Greenberg. ils/photos, 272 p. VG. A17. $15.00

ABEL, Ernest. *Ancient Views on the Origins of Life.* 1973. NY. Rutherford. 1st ed. 93p. dj. A13. $30.00

ABELL, Westcott. *Shipwright's Trade.* 1962. NY. Caravan. 8vo. 218p. VG. T7. $50.00

ABELLS, Chana Byers. *Children We Remember.* 1986. Greenwillow. 1st ed. ils Yad Vashem. F/F. C8. $25.00

ABERCROMBIE, John. *Inquiries Concerning Intellectual Powers & Investigation...* 1836. Boston. full leather. VG. B30. $60.00

ABERCROMBIE, John. *Inquiries Concerning Intellectual Powers...* 1833 (1830). Harper. 12mo. prt brd. NF. G1. $50.00

ABERCROMBIE, M.L. Johnson. *Anatomy of Judgment.* 1960. Basic. 141p. VG/dj. K4. $9.00

ABERNETHY, James. *Hunterian Oration for Year 1819...Royal College Surgeons...* 1819. London. 66p. new marble brd. G7. $75.00

ABERNETHY, John. *Surgical & Physiological Works of...* 1830. London. Longman. 4 vol. G. G7. $250.00

ABERNETHY, John. *Surgical Observations on Injuries of the Head.* 1811. Phil. Dobson. ils. 162p. brd. uncut. K1. $150.00

ABODAHER, David J. *Youth in the Middle East: Voices of Despair.* 1990. Franklin Watts. 112p. VG/dj. W1. $18.00

ABRAHAMS, Israel. *By-Paths in Hebraic Bookland.* 1920. Phil. 8vo. ils. 371p. cloth. O2. $30.00

ABRAMS, Albert. *Transactions of the Antiseptic Club.* 1895. NY. 1st ed. 205p. VG. A13. $100.00

ABRAMS, Alexander St. Clair. *Trials of Soldier's Wife: Tale of 2nd Am Revolution.* 1864. Atlanta, GA. Intelligencer Steam Power Presses. 1st ed. lacks wrp. M1. $1,250.00

ABRAMSON, Harold A. *Problems of Consciousness.* 1951. NY. Foundation. 199p. VG/dj. K4. $15.00

ABRAMSON, Una. *Crafts Canada: The Useful Arts.* 1974. Tor. 191 p. VG/torn. A17. $25.00

ABRO, Ben. *Assassination.* 1963. Jonathan Cape. 1st ed. VG/VG. P3. $20.00

ABU-LUGHOD, Ibrahim. *Arab-Israeli Confrontation of June 1967: Arab Perspective.* 1970. Evanston. Northwestern. 1st ed. VG. W1. $18.00

ABURISH, Said K. *St George Hotel Bar.* 1989. London. Bloomsbury. 8vo. 8 pl. 214p. NF/dj. W1. $18.00

ACHENBAUM, W.A. *Images of Old of Old Age in Am 1790 to Present.* 1982. Ann Arbor. revised. 4to. VG/wrp. A17. $10.00

ACHESONEN, Edward. *Grammarian's Funeral.* nd. Grosset Dunlap. VG. P3. $15.00

ACHINSTEIN, Peter. *Concepts of Science.* 1968. Baltimore. Johns Hopkins. 266p. brn cloth. VG/dj. G1. $30.00

ACIER, Marcel. *From Spanish Trenches: Recent Letters From Spain.* 1937. Modern Age. 1st ed. VG/G. V4. $25.00

ACKER, Kathy. *In Memoriam to Identity.* 1990. Grove Weidenfeld. ARC. RS. w/photo. F/F. B3. $25.00

ACKERMAN, Nathan W. *Psychodynamics of Family Life.* 1958. Basic. 344p. VG. K4. $9.00

ACKERMAN, Phyllis. *Guide to Exhibition of Persian Art.* 1940. NY. Iranian Inst. 8vo. 562p. VG/stiff wrp. G1. $8.00

ACKROYD, Peter. *Dickens.* 1991. Harper Collins. F/F. P3. $35.00

ACKROYD, Peter. *Notes for a New Culture: Essay on Modernism.* 1976. Barnes Noble. 1st ed. inscr. F/NF. B4. $250.00

ACKWORTH, Robert C. *Dr Kildare Assigned to Trouble.* 1963. Whitman. VG. P3. $10.00

ACOSTA, Karen. *Three Little Pigs, a Carousel Book.* nd. Los Angeles. Intervisual Communications. lg 16mo. VG+. C8. $50.00

ADAIR, Douglas. *Fame & the Founding Fathers.* 1974. Williamsburg, VA. Inst Early Am Hist. 1st ed. 315p. F/VG. B11. $25.00

ADAM, Colin Forbes. *Life of Lord Lloyd.* 1948. London. Macmillan. 1st ed. 318p. gilt bl cloth. G. M7. $22.00

ADAM, Paul. *Exceptional Corpse.* 1993. London. Harper Collin. 1st ed. F/F. S6. $25.00

ADAM, Paul. *Les Eches de TE Lawrence.* 1962. private prt. 1st French ed. 199p. gray cloth. M7. $90.00

ADAM & FABIAN. *Masters of Early Travel Photography.* 1983. NY. Vendome. 1st ed. intro Sam Wagstaff. NF/NF. S9. $235.00

ADAMIC, Louis. *Native's Return. Am Immigrant Visits Yugoslavia...* 1934. Harper. 1st ed. 8vo. 32 pl. 370p. VG. O2/W1. $10.00

ADAMS, A. *Account of Manners & Customs of Romans/Antiquities.* 1823. np. 500p. full leather. E5. $35.00

ADAMS, A. *Log of a Cowboy.* 1982 (1903). np. 387p. full leather. VG. E5. $35.00

ADAMS, Adrienne. *Day We Saw the Sun Come Up.* 1962. Scribner. 1st ed. VG+/G. A3. $30.00

ADAMS, Alice. *Beautiful Girl.* 1979. Knopf. 1st ed. 8vo. 242p. gilt cream cloth. rem mk. F/F. H5. $75.00

ADAMS, Andy. *Brazilian Gold Mine Mystery.* 1960. Grosset Dunlap. VG. P3. $8.00

ADAMS, Andy. *Mystery of the Chinese Ring.* 1960. Grosset Dunlap. VG. P3. $8.00

ADAMS, Andy. *Trail Drive.* 1965. Holiday. 1st ed. F/dj. A18. $25.00

ADAMS, Ansel. *Eloquent Light.* 1963. San Francisco. Sierra Club. 1st ed. folio. VG+/VG+. S9. $125.00

ADAMS, Ansel. *Letter & Images 1916-1984.* 1988. Little Brn. 4to. 402p. blk cloth. M/dj. F1. $35.00

ADAMS, Ansel. *Negative: Exposure & Development.* 1948. NY. Morgan Lester. 1st ed. ils. 120p. VG/worn. A17. $20.00

ADAMS, Ansel. *Photographs of the Southwest.* 1976. Boston. NYGS. 1st ed. sgn. F/F. S9. $150.00

ADAMS, Ansel. *Print.* 1968. NY. Morgan. 1st ed thus. sm 4to. VG+/VG. S9. $35.00

ADAMS, Ansel. *These We Inherit.* 1962. San Francisco. Sierra Club. 1st ed. B5/F1. $75.00

ADAMS, Charles Francis. *Charles Francis Adams by Himself. An Autobiography.* 1916. 1st ed. index. 224p. F. O8. $12.50

ADAMS, Charles M. *Randall Jarrell: A Bibliography.* 1958. Chapel Hill. 1st ed. 8vo. 72p. F. C6. $30.00

ADAMS, Cleve F. *Contraband.* nd. BC. VG/G. P3. $8.00

ADAMS, Clifton. *Hassle & the Medicine Man.* nd. BC. VG/G. P3. $5.00

ADAMS, Daniel. *Medical & Agricultural Register...* 1806-1807. Boston. Manning Loring. 378p. half leather. VG. H10. $185.00

ADAMS, Douglas. *Dirk Gently's Holistic Detective Agency.* 1987. Simon Schuster. 1st ed. F/F. P3. $20.00

ADAMS, Douglas. *Dirk Gently's Holistic Detective Agency.* 1987. Simon Schuster. 1st ed. 247p. NF/NF. M20. $15.00

ADAMS, Douglas. *Life, the Universe & Everything.* 1982. Harmony. 1st ed. F/F. P3. $20.00

ADAMS, Douglas. *Long Dark Tea-Time of the Soul.* 1988. Simon Schuster. 1st ed. sgn. F/F. B3. $25.00

ADAMS, Douglas. *Long Dark Tea-Time of the Soul.* 1988. Stoddart. 1st ed. VG/VG. P3. $20.00

ADAMS, Douglas. *Mostly Harmless.* 1992. Heinemann. 1st ed. VG/VG. P3. $25.00

ADAMS, Douglas. *Restaurant at the End of the Universe.* nd. Harmony. 4th ed. F/F. P3. $15.00

ADAMS, Douglas. *So Long, & Thanks for All the Fish.* 1984. Pan. 1st ed. F/F. P3. $20.00

ADAMS, E.C.L. *Pottee's Gal. A Drama of Negro Life Near Big Congaree Swamp.* 1929. Columbia, SC. ltd sgn ed. 12mo. 49p. maroon cloth. B11. $95.00

ADAMS, Eustace L. *Death Charter.* nd. Coward McCann. 2nd ed. VG. P3. $13.00

ADAMS, Eustace L. *Fifteen Days in the Air.* nd. Grosset Dunlap. VG/G. P3. $10.00

ADAMS, Eustace L. *Pirates of the Air.* 1929. Grosset Dunlap. VG/G. P3. $15.00

ADAMS, Eustace L. *Racing Around the World.* nd. Grosset Dunlap. VG. P3. $10.00

ADAMS, Eustace L. *Wings of the Navy.* nd. Grosset Dunlap. VG/VG. P3. $20.00

ADAMS, F.U. *John Henry Smith: A Humorous Romance of Outdoor Life.* 1905. NY. 1st ed. ils. NF. C2. $75.00

ADAMS, Frank. *Mother Goose.* nd. Dodge. 4to. inscr/dtd 1916. VG. M5. $55.00

ADAMS, Harold. *Man Who Missed the Party.* 1989. Mysterious. 1st ed. F/F. P3. $17.00

ADAMS, Harold. *Man Who Missed the Party.* 1989. Mysterious. 1st ed. sgn. F/F. $25.00

ADAMS, Herbert. *Mystery & Minette.* 1934. Lippincott. 1st ed. VG. P3. $35.00

ADAMS, Herbert. *Rogues Fall Out.* 1928. Lippincott. 1st Am ed. VG/rpr. M15. $50.00

ADAMS, J. Howe. *Hist of the Life of D Hayes Agnew, MD, LLD.* 1892. Phil. 13 pl. 376p. cloth. G. G7. $35.00

ADAMS, James Truslow. *Adams Family.* 1930. NY. Literary Guild. 8vo. 364p. F. B11. $20.00

ADAMS, James. *Financing of Terror: How Groups...Get Money To Do It.* 1986. Simon Schuster. 1st ed. 8vo. 293p. NF/dj. W1. $20.00

ADAMS, Jill. *Wild Flowers of Northern Cape.* 1976. Cape Town. ils. 152p. F. B26. $25.00

ADAMS, John Quincy. *Address of the Convention for Framing New Constitution...* 1780. Boston. Wht Adams. 1st ed. 12mo. 18p. sewn. M1. $650.00

ADAMS, John Quincy. *Lectures on Rhetoric & Oratory...* 1810. Cambridge. 1st ed. orig brd/rebacked/new labels. VG. A9. $250.00

ADAMS, John Quincy. *Lectures on Rhetoric & Oratory...* 1810. Hilliard Metcalf. 2 vol. 1st ed. 8vo. contemporary full tree calf. F. M1. $425.00

ADAMS, Maryline Poole. *Punch & Judy. The Tragical Comedy or Comical Tragedy.* 1988. Berkeley. Poole. 72x55mm. 1/45. inscr. movables. book/box/metal clasps. B24. $400.00

ADAMS, Nathaniel. *Annals of Portsmouth.* 1825. Portsmouth. self pub. 400p. orig mottled calf/gr spine label. K1. $100.00

ADAMS, Percy G. *Travelers & Travel Liars 1660-1800.* 1962. Berkeley. 8vo. pres. 292p. cloth. O2. $40.00

ADAMS, Ramon F. *Rampaging Herd.* 1982. np. 482p. F/F. A4. $75.00

ADAMS, Ramon F. *Six-Guns & Saddle Leather.* nd. Zubal. rpt. M. A18. $35.00

ADAMS, Ramon F. *Six-Guns & Saddle Leather.* 1954. OK U. 1st ed. F/clip. A18. $100.00

ADAMS, Ramon F. *Six-Guns & Saddle Leather.* 1969. np. revised/enlarged ed/1st prt. 833p. F/VG. A4. $150.00

ADAMS, Richard. *Day Gone By.* 1990. Hutchinson. 1st ed. P3. $30.00

ADAMS, Richard. *Girl in a Swing.* 1980. Knopf. 1st ed. VG/VG. P3. $18.00

ADAMS, Richard. *Iron Wolf & Other Stories.* 1980. Allen Lane. 1st ed. F/F. P3. $25.00

ADAMS, Richard. *Maia.* 1985. Knopf. 1st ed. F/F. F4. $20.00

ADAMS, Richard. *Maia.* 1985. Knopf. 1st ed. VG/G. P3. $15.00

ADAMS, Richard. *Plague Dogs.* 1977. Allen Lane. 1st ed. F/F. P3. $20.00

ADAMS, Richard. *Plague Dogs.* 1978. Knopf. 1st ed. VG/VG. P3. $18.00

ADAMS, Richard. *Shardik.* 1974. Simon Schuster. 1st ed. F/F. P3. $25.00

ADAMS, Richard. *Watership Down.* 1974. Macmillan. 1st Am ed. VG/VG clip. M21. $20.00

ADAMS, Robert. *Evolution of Urban Society.* 1966. Chicago. Aldine. 1st ed. 191p. VG. F3. $20.00

ADAMS, Samuel Hopkins. *Night Bus.* 1951. Avon. 1st ed. F/stapled wrp. B4. $150.00

ADAMS, Samuel. *Oration Delivered at the State House, in Phil...* 1776. London. E Johnson. 1st ed. 8vo. 42p. later leather. M1. $750.00

ADAMS, Sherred Willcox. *Five Little Friends.* 1947. Macmillan. 20th prt. ils. G. B10. $12.00

ADAMS & CARWARDINE. *Last Chance To See.* 1991. Harmony. 1st ed. sgn. F/F. S9. $45.00

ADAMS & CORLE. *Death Valley.* 1962. LA. 1st ed. VG/VG. B5. $90.00

ADAMS & LLOYD. *Deeper Meaning of Life: A Dictionary of Things.* 1990. London. Pan Books. 1st ed. NF. B3. $20.00

ADAMS & MCKAY. *Threads of Life: Mayan Clothing From Guatemala...* 1993. Kauffman Mus. 39p. VG/wrp. F3. $15.00

ADAMS & MONTAGUE. *Contemporary Am Philosophy: Personal Statements.* 1930. Macmillan. 2 vol. 1st Am ed. cloth. VG. G1. $50.00

ADAMS & RAINEY. *Shoot-Em-Ups.* 1978. Arlington. 1st ed. VG/chip. P3. $50.00

ADAMS & SAMPSON. *Massachusetts Register for 1862.* 1862. Boston. Adams Sampson. 430p. O8. $35.00

ADAMSON, Ewart. *Hero of the Big Snows: A Story of the Frozen North...* 1926. NY. Jacobsen Hodgkinson. 1st ed. 135p. VG. very scarce. R2. $75.00

ADAMSON, James B. *James: Man & His Message.* 1989. Eerdmans. 553p. M. VG. B29. $11.00

ADAMSON, Robert. *Development of Modern Philosophy & Other Lectures...* 1903. Edinburgh. Blackwood. 2 vol. bl-gr cloth. VG. G1. $85.00

ADDAMS, Charles. *Mother Goose.* 1967. Windmill. probable 1st ed. sm 4to. F/F. C8. $100.00

ADDAMS, Charles. *Nightcrawlers.* 1957. Simon Schuster. 1st ed. sm 4to. VG/VG. C8. $75.00

ADDISON, Charles G. *Damascus & Palmyra.* 1838. London. 2 vol. 9 (of 10) hand-colored pl. quarter leather. VG+. O2. $450.00

ADE, George. *Fables in Slang/More Fables.* 1900. Chicago. Herbert Stone. 2 vol (both inscr). ils Clyde J Newman. VG/custom case. F1. $425.00

ADE, George. *Old-Time Saloon, Not Wet — Not Dry/Just History.* 1931. Ray Long/Richard Smith. ltd ed. sgn. F. Q1. $125.00

ADELMAN & ADELMAN. *Bound for the Stars.* 1981. Prentice Hall. 4to. ils/diagrams. 335p. xl. G. K5. $16.00

ADHEMAR, J. *Toulouse-Lautrec: His Complete Lithographs & Drypoints.* nd. np. VG/VG. M17. $45.00

ADLER, Bill. *Dear Beatles.* 1966. Wonder. VG. P3. $5.00

ADLER, Bill. *Kennedy Wit.* 1964. Citadel. ils. 83p. VG/dj. M10. $4.50

ADLER, Irving. *Man-Made Moons: Earth Satellites & What They Tell Us.* 1957. John Day. 8vo. ils Ruth Adler. 128p. K5. $15.00

ADLER, Mortimer J. *Angels & Us.* 1982. Macmillan. 205p. VG/VG. B29. $5.50

ADLER. *How To Read a Book: Art of Getting Liberal Education.* 1940. np. 407p. NF. A4. $15.00

ADLINGTON, John Henry. *Cyclopaedia of Law; or, Correct British Lawyer...* 1826. London. Kelly. 8vo. pls. contemporary mottled calf/rebacked orig spine. D3. $250.00

ADNAN, Abdulhak. *La Science Chez les Turcs Ottomans.* 1939. Paris. 8vo. 174p. cloth. O2. $20.00

ADOMEIT, Ruth E. *Miniature Book Collector, Vol I & II.* 1960s. Worcester. St Onge. 16mo. complete run of 8 issues. deluxe gilt gr leather. B24. $350.00

ADRAIN, E.D. *Basis of Sensation. Action of the Sense Organs.* 1928. Norton. 1st ed. 122p. G7. $35.00

AERO CLUB OF AMERICA. *Navigating the Air.* 1907. NY. 1st ed. ils/photos. 259p. VG. B18. $295.00

AESOP. *Aesop's Fables, a New Version...by Rev Thomas James.* 1848. London. Murray. 1st ed thus. ils John Tenniel. morocco. F. B24. $400.00

AESOP. *Aesop's Fables.* 1971. Hallmark. 12mo. ils Fritz Kredel. F/F. B17. $12.50

AESOP. *Fables d'Esope.* 1913. Paris. Hachette. 1/55 on Japon paper. ils/sgn Rackham. gilt vellum. F. F1. $1,325.00

AESOP. *Selected Fables of (A)Esop & Other Fabulists.* 1764. Brimingham. Bakersville. 2nd ed. 8vo. 186p. morocco/rpr hinge. F. F1. $550.00

AESOP. *Twelve Fables of Aesop.* 1954. MOMA. 1/975. sgn author/ils/printer. F/case. B24. $250.00

AFANASEV, Aleksandr. *Russian Fairy Tales.* 1943. Pantheon. 2nd ed. ils. 651p. NF. S12. $35.00

AGASSIZ, Alexander. *Three Cruises on US Coast & Geodetic Survey Steamer Blake...* 1888. Boston. Riverside. 2 vol. brd. G7. $125.00

AGASSIZ, Louis. *Twelve Lectures on Comparative Embryology.* 1849. Boston. ils. 104p. F/wrp. B14. $100.00

AGEE, Helene Barret. *Facets of Goochland County's History.* 1962. Richmond, VA. Dietz. 1st ed. 8vo. 227p. F/VG. B11. $18.00

AGEE, James. *Last Letter of James Agee to Father Flye.* 1969. Boston. Godine. 1st ed. 1/500. F/wrp. B4. $65.00

AGEE, James. *Let Us Now Praise Famous Men.* 1941. Houghton Mifflin. Riverside. ils. NF/NF. Q1. $600.00

AGNON, S.Y. *Bridal Canopy.* 1967. Schocken. 1st ed. F/NF. B4. $55.00

AGRAWALA, Vasudeva S. *Indian Art: History of Indian Art From Earlist Times...* 1965. Varanasi, India. Prithivi Prakashan. 1st ed. 4to. 389p. VG/dj. F1. $40.00

AGRICOLA, Georgius. *De Re Metallica.* 1912. London. trans/pres from 1st Latin ed by Herbert Hoover. H4. $750.00

AGUIRRE, Lily. *Land of Eternal Spring.* 1949. NY. Patio. 1st ed. 253p. VG/dj. F3. $20.00

AGUIRRE, Lowry Walker. *Lope Aguirre: The Wanderer.* (1952). NY. Bookman Assoc. 1st ed. 78p. VG. F3. $15.00

AHAMAD, Feroz. *Turkish Experiment in Democracy 1950-1975.* 1977. London. 8vo. 474p. cloth. O2. $60.00

AHEARN & AHEARN. *Collected Books: Guide to Values.* 1991. Putnam. 2nd prt. M/dj. A18. $50.00

AHERN, Allen. *Book Collecting: A Comprehensive Guide.* 1989. Putnam. 320p. VG/VG. A10. $18.00

AHMED, Jamal Mohamed. *Stories of Serra East.* 1985. Khartoum. 1st ed. uvo. 89p. VG/stiff wrp. W1. $15.00

AICKMAN, Robert. *Model.* 1987. Arbor. 1st ed. VG/VG. P3. $20.00

AICKMAN, Robert. *Night Voices: Strange Stories.* 1985. London. Gollancz. 1st ed. fwd Barry Humphries. F/F. T2. $35.00

AICKMAN, Robert. *Wine-Dark Sea.* 1988. Arbor/Morrow. 1st ed. intro Peter Straub. F/F. T2. $28.00

AIKEN, Conrad. *Divine Pilgrim.* 1949. GA U. 1st ed. w/2 sgn typed p notes & corrections. F/G+. V1. $65.00

AIKEN, Conrad. *Skylight One.* 1951. London. Lehmann. 1st Eng ed. 8vo. 63p. NF. H5. $75.00

AIKEN, Joan. *Beware of the Bouquet.* 1966. Doubleday. 1st ed. NF/NF. O4. $15.00

AIKEN, Joan. *Black Hearts in Battersea.* 1964. Doubleday. 1st Am ed. VG/VG. C8. $22.50

AIKEN, Joan. *Castle Barebane.* 1976. Viking. 1st ed. VG/VG. P3. $15.00

AIKEN, Joan. *Cluster of Separate Sparks.* 1972. Doubleday. 1st ed. F/NF clip. O4. $15.00

AIKEN, Joan. *Fortune Hunters.* 1965. Doubleday. 1st ed. VG/VG. O4. $15.00

AIKEN, Joan. *Foul Matter.* 1983. BC. 1st ed. VG/VG. P3. $13.00

AIKEN, John. *Biographical Memoirs of Medicine in Great Britain...* 1780. London. Johnson. 338p. rebound contemporary full calf. G7. $495.00

AIKMAN, Lonnelle. *Nature's Healing Arts: From Folk Medicine to Modern Drugs.* 1977. WA. 1st ed. ils. 199p. A13. $25.00

AIMES, Hubert H.S. *History of Slavery in Cuba 1511-1868.* 1967. NY. Octagon. rpt of 1907 ed. 8vo. 298p. gr cloth. VG. B11. $30.00

AINSWORTH, Edward Maddin. *Beckoning Desert.* 1962. Prentice Hall. special author/contributor sgn ed. 8vo. 264p. F/VG. A8. $100.00

AINSWORTH, William Harrison. *Historial Romances.* nd. Phil. Barrie. 2 vol. lib ed. ils. 329p. S12. $125.00

AINSWORTH, William Harrison. *Rookwood.* 1851. London. Chapman Hall. ils Cruikshank. gilt bl cloth. VG. B14. $65.00

AIRD, Catherine. *Going Concern.* 1993. London. Macmillan. 1st ed. F/F. S6. $30.00

AIRD, Catherine. *Parting Breath.* 1977. Collins Crime Club. 1st ed. G/VG. P3. $13.00

AITKEN, Will. *Visit Home.* 1992. Simon Schuster. 1st ed. rem mk. NF/F. B3. $15.00

AJAMI, Fouad. *Vanished Imam: Musa Al Sadr & the Shia of Lebanon.* 1986. Cornell. 1st ed. 228p. VG/dj. G1. $18.00

AKERS, F. *Boy Fortune Hunters in the South Seas.* 1911. Chicago. 1st ed. G. B5. $150.00

AKOMINATOS, Niketas. *La Historia de Gli Imperatori Greci...* 1562. Venice. sm 4to. contemporary vellum. O2. $1,200.00

AKUTAGAWA, Ryunosuke. *Kirishtohoro Shouin-Den (St Kirishtohoro).* 1983. Bijou Hoshino. 25x25mm. 1/50 (200 total). goatskin/18k Christ figure. F/case. B24. $450.00

AKUTAGAWA, Ryunosuke. *Kumo-No-Ito (Spider's Thread).* 1982. Bijou Hoshino. 19x21mm. 1/40 (190 total). teg. F/god's face onlay on case. B24. $550.00

ALACON, Francisco. *Body in Flames/Cuerpo en Llamas.* 1990. San Francisco. Chronicle. 4to. 107p. wrp. F3. $10.00

ALAMAN, Mohammed. *Arabia Unified.* 1982. London. Hutchinson. revised ed. photos/maps. 328p. F/F. M7. $35.00

ALAUX, Jean-Paul. *L'Histoire Merveilleuse de Christophe Columb.* 1924. Paris. ils Gustave Alaux. 243p. VG/wrp. M20. $75.00

ALBEE, Edward. *Play: The Ballad of the Sad Cafe.* 1963. Boston. 1st ed. sgn. F/8vo wrp. A11. $45.00

ALBERS, Annie. *On Weaving.* 1965. np. cloth. VG. G2. $50.00

ALBERS, Betty. *Macrame.* 1971. np. VG/wrp. G2. $2.00

ALBERT, James W. *Through the Country of the Comanche Indians in Year 1845.* 1970. San Francisco. Howell. 1/5000. gilt cloth. NF. P4. $125.00

ALBERT, Virginia. *Peter Rabbit & Sammy Squirrel.* 1918. Saalfield. B Potter imitation. pict brd. VG. M5. $48.00

ALBERTI, Rafael. *Spectre Is Haunting Europe.* 1936. Critics Group. 1st ed. VG/wrp. B2. $25.00

ALBERTSON, Chris. *Bessie.* 1972. London. Barrie Jenkins. 1st ed. F/NF. B2. $35.00

ALBERTSON, Chris. *Bessie.* 1972. Stein Day. 1st ed. NF/NF. B2. $35.00

ALBION, Robert Greenhalgh. *Makers of Naval Policy 1798-1947.* 1980. Naval Inst. index. 737p. F. A17. $15.00

ALBOTT, Kenneth. *Poems.* 1938. Hogarth. 1st ed. sgn. F/NF. V1. $55.00

ALBRAND, Martha. *Manhattan North.* 1971. CMG. 1st ed. VG/VG. P3. $20.00

ALBRAND, Martha. *Mask of Alexander.* 1955. Random. 1st ed. VG/VG. P3. $20.00

ALBRAND, Martha. *Remembered Anger.* 1946. Little Brn. 2nd ed. G/VG. P3. $10.00

ALCOCK, Leslie. *Was This Camelot: Excavations at Cadbury Castle 1966-1970.* 1972. Stein Day. 1st ed. VG/dj. N2. $15.00

ALCOHOLICS ANON. *Alcoholics Anonymous Comes of Age.* 1980. AA World Services. 9th prt. 333p. free ep removed. fair. A8. $5.00

ALCOHOLICS ANON. *Alcoholics Anonymous.* nd. AA World Services. 1st ed/16th prt. 575p. red bdg. VG/chip. A8. $225.00

ALCOHOLICS ANON. *Alcoholics Anonymous.* 1967. AA World Services. 2nd ed/9th prt. 575p. VG. A8. $35.00

ALCOHOLICS ANON. *Alcoholics Anonymous.* 1972. AA World Services. 2nd ed/13th prt. 575p. VG. A8. $20.00

ALCOHOLICS ANON. *In All Our Affairs.* 1990. Al Anon Family Group HQ. 1st ed. 245p. F/F. A8. $8.00

ALCOHOLICS ANON. *Lois Remembers.* 1979. Canada. TH Best. 1st prt. 8vo. 203p. cream cloth. VG/VG. A8. $20.00

ALCOHOLICS ANON. *Twelve Steps & Twelve Traditions.* nd. Al Anon Family Group HQ. 1st ed/11th prt. 192p. gray bdg. VG/VG bl dj. A8. $5.00

ALCOHOLICS ANON. *Twelve Steps & Twelve Traditions.* nd. Al Anon Family Group HQ. 1st ed/7th prt. 142p. gr bdg. F/F gr & wht dj. A8. $5.00

ALCOHOLICS ANON. *Twelve Steps & Twelve Traditions.* 1981. Al Anon Family Group HQ. 192p. bl bdg. F/F bl dj. A8. $12.00

ALCORN, Robert Hayden. *Riding High.* 1953. NY. Putnam. 1st Am ed. sgn pres. ils Michael Lyne. VG. O3. $45.00

ALCOTT, Louisa May. *Behind a Mask.* nd. BC. VG. P3. $10.00

ALCOTT, Louisa May. *Candy Country.* 1900 (1885). Little Brn. 8vo. 52p. gilt taupe cloth. G+. D6. $22.00

ALCOTT, Louisa May. *Eight Cousins.* nd. World. VG. P3. $12.00

ALCOTT, Louisa May. *Hidden Louisa May Alcott.* 1984. Avenel. VG/VG. P3. $15.00

ALCOTT, Louisa May. *Jo's Boys.* 1886. Roberts Bros. 1st ed. 365p/18p ads. VG. P2. $125.00

ALCOTT, Louisa May. *Life, Letters & Journals.* 1889. Boston. 1st ed. VG. B5. $60.00

ALCOTT, Louisa May. *Little Women.* 1904. Boston. ils. gr cloth. VG. M5. $35.00

ALCOTT, Louisa May. *Little Women.* 1922. Boston. ils Jessie Willcox Smith. blk cloth. VG. M5. $60.00

ALCOTT, Louisa May. *Little Women.* 1922. Little Brn. rpt. 8vo. ils JW Smith. pict bdg. G. B17. $12.50

ALCOTT, Louisa May. *Little Women.* 1969. Collins. BC. ils Tasha Tudor. F/damaged. M5. $60.00

ALCOTT, Louisa May. *Lulu's Library. Vol II.* 1902. Boston. stp bl cloth. VG. M5. $35.00

ALCOTT, Louisa May. *May Flowers.* 1899 (1887). Little Brn. 8vo. 4 pl. 56p. gilt taupe cloth. NF. D6. $25.00

ALCOTT, Louisa May. *Rose in Bloom.* 1933. Winston. ils Clara Burd. gilt gr cloth. NF/dj. M5. $38.00

ALCOTT, Louisa May. *Rose in Bloom.* 1955. Whitman. VG. P3. $10.00

ALCOTT, Louisa May. *Silver Pitchers & Independence. A Centenniel Love Story.* 1876. Boston. 1st ed. blk stp red cloth. fair. scarce. M5. $25.00

ALCOTT, Louisa May. *Work: A Story of Experience.* 1873. Boston. 1st ed. ils Sol Eytinge. gilt gr cloth. VG. scarce. M5. $175.00

ALDANOV, Mark. *For Thee the Best.* 1945. Scribner. 1st ed. VG/G. P3. $15.00

ALDEN, Carroll Storrs. *George Hamilton Perkins, Commodore USN.* 1914. Houghton Mifflin. VG. N2. $25.00

ALDEN, Isabella M. *Memories of Yesterdays.* 1931. Lippincott. 1st ed. photos. cloth. VG. M5. $20.00

ALDEN, John Richard. *Robert Dinwiddie, Servant to the Crown.* 1973. Colonial Williamsburg. 8vo. 126p. brn cloth. VG/VG. B11. $20.00

ALDEN, Raymond MacDonald. *Reading in English Prose of the 19th Century.* 1917. Houghton Mifflin. 695p. NF. S12. $35.00

ALDIN, Cecil. *Cecil Aldin Book.* 1932. Eyre Spottiswoode. 1st ed. front ep missing. G+. O3. $40.00

ALDIN, Cecil. *Ratcatcher to Scarlet.* 1927. Eyre Spottiswoode. 2nd imp. sm 4to. G+. O3. $45.00

ALDIN, Cecil. *Romance of the Road.* 1986. London. Bracken Books, facsimile of 1st ed. F/F. O3. $45.00

ALDING, Peter. *Man Condemned.* 1981. Walker. 1st ed. VG/VG. P3. $15.00

ALDINGTON, Richard. *AE Housman & WB Yeats: Two Lectures.* 1955. Peacocks. 1st ed. sgn. 1/360. Sangorski Sutcliffe bdg. F/cb case. H5. $350.00

ALDINGTON, Richard. *Der Fall TE Lawrence. Ein Kritische Biographie.* nd. Germany. Hermann Rinn. 1st German ed. 349p. brn oatmeal cloth. NF. M7. $125.00

ALDINGTON, Richard. *Lawrence l'Imposteur.* 1954. Paris. Amoit-Dumont. 1st French ed. 332p. VG. M7. $85.00

ALDINGTON, Richard. *Lawrence of Arabia.* 1954. London. Collins. AP/1st ed. 447p. VG/brn wrp/bl-gr label. M7. $500.00

ALDINGTON, Richard. *Lawrence of Arabia.* 1955. London. Collins. 1st ed. 448p. VG+/fair clip. M7. $45.00

ALDINGTON, Richard. *Lawrence of Arabia.* 1971. Eng/Australia. Penguin. 1st ed thus. 504p. pict bdg. M7. $30.00

ALDINGTON, Richard. *Love & the Luxembourg.* 1930. Covici Friede. 1/475. sgn. F. B2. $75.00

ALDINGTON & DURRELL. *Literary Lifelines.* 1981. Viking. 1st ed. 236p. gilt red cloth/blk brd. F/NF. M7. $24.50

ALDISS, Brian W. *...And the Lurid Glare of the Comet: Articles & Autobio...* 1986. Seattle. Serconia. 1st ed. F/F. T2. $15.00

ALDISS, Brian W. *Barefoot in the Head.* 1970. Doubleday. 1st Am ed. F/NF. N3. $10.00

ALDISS, Brian W. *Billion Year Spree.* 1973. BC. P3. $18.00

ALDISS, Brian W. *Canopy of Time.* 1961. British SF BC. VG/torn. P3. $10.00

ALDISS, Brian W. *Dracula Unbound.* 1991. Harper Collins. 1st ed. F/F. P3. $19.00

ALDISS, Brian W. *Earthworks.* 1966. BC. 1st ed. VG/VG. P3. $35.00

ALDISS, Brian W. *Enemies of the System.* 1978. Harper Row. 1st ed. xl. dj. P3. $10.00

ALDISS, Brian W. *Frankenstein Unbound.* 1973. Random. 1st Am ed. NF/dj. M2. $30.00

ALDISS, Brian W. *Helliconia Spring.* 1982. Jonathan Cape. 2nd ed. F/dj. P3. $15.00

ALDISS, Brian W. *Helliconia Summer.* 1983. Atheneum. 1st ed. F/F. N3. $25.00

ALDISS, Brian W. *Helliconia Winter.* 1985. Jonathan Cape. 1st ed. F/dj. P3. $30.00

ALDISS, Brian W. *Last Orders.* 1977. Jonathan Cape. 1st ed. F/dj. P3. $28.00

ALDISS, Brian W. *Last Orders.* 1989. NY. Carroll Graf. 1st Am ed. F/F. P8. $14.00

ALDISS, Brian W. *Life in the West.* 1980. London. Weidenfeld Nicolson. 1st ed. NF/clip. B3. $45.00

ALDISS, Brian W. *Malacia Tapestry.* 1977. Harper Row. 1st ed. F/dj. P3. $30.00

ALDISS, Brian W. *Man in His Time: Best SF Stories of Brian W Aldiss.* 1989. Atheneum. 1st Am ed. F/F. T2. $16.00

ALDISS, Brian W. *New Arrivals, Old Encounters.* 1979. Jonathan Cape. 1st ed. F/dj. P3. $25.00

ALDISS, Brian W. *Report on Probability A.* 1969. BC. 1st ed. VG/VG. P3. $25.00

ALDISS, Brian W. *Romance of the Equator...* 1990. Atheneum. 1st ed. F/F. N3. $15.00

ALDISS, Brian W. *Rude Awakening.* 1978. Random. 1st ed. VG/VG. P3. $25.00

ALDISS, Brian W. *Rude Awakening.* 1978. Weidenfeld Nicolson. 1st ed. VG/dj. P3. $25.00

ALDISS, Brian W. *Ruins.* 1987. Hutchinson. 1st ed. F/dj. P3. $15.00

ALDISS, Brian W. *Soldier Erect.* 1971. Weidenfeld Nicolson. 1st ed. VG/VG. P3. $35.00

ALDISS, Brian W. *Year Before Yesterday.* 1987. Watts. 1st ed/ F/dj. P3. $17.00

ALDISS & HARRISON. *Decade the 1940s.* 1975. Macmillan. 1st ed. NF/dj. P3. $20.00

ALDISS & WILKS. *Pile.* 1979. HRW. F/Sans. P3. $15.00

ALDRED, Cryil. *Egyptians.* 1961. Thames Hudson. 1st ed. ils/photos. 268p. xl. G. W1. $10.00

ALDRICH, Ann; see Meaker, Marijane.

ALDRICH, Bess Streeter. *Drum Goes Dead.* 1941. NY. 1st ed. VG/VG. B5. $25.00

ALDRICH, Bess Streeter. *Miss Bishop.* 1933. Appleton Century. 1st ed. F/dj. A18. $40.00

ALDRICH, Bess Streeter. *Song of Years.* 1943. NY. 1st ed. VG/VG. B5. $20.00

ALDRICH, Bess Streeter. *Spring Came on Forever.* 1935. Appleton Century. 1st ed. F/chip. A18. $40.00

ALDRICH, Bess Streeter. *White Bird Flying.* 1931. Appleton. 1st ed. F/VG. A18. $40.00

ALDRICH, Mrs. Thomas Bailey. *Crowning Memories.* 1920. Houghton Mifflin. 1st ed. photos. 295p. gr cloth. G+. S11. $12.00

ALDRICH, Thomas Bailey. *Young Folks Library, Selections From Choicest Literature...* 1901. Boston. Hall Locke. 20 vol. 8vo. ils Edward Lear/H Granville Fell. NF. D6. $225.00

ALDRIDGE, Alan. *Beatles Illustrated Lyrics.* 1972. Dell. 1st ed. inscr pres G Harrison/Ringo/J Lennon/Yoko/Aldridge. H4. $550.00

ALDRIDGE, James. *Heroes of the Empty View.* 1954. Knopf. 1st ed. 432p. copper stp maroon cloth. NF/VG. M7. $55.00

ALDRIDGE, James. *Marvelous Mongolian.* 1974. Boston. Little Brn. VG/G. O3. $15.00

ALDRIDGE, James. *Sporting Propositon.* 1973. Little Brn. BC. VG. O3. $10.00

ALEMAN, Mateo. *Life of Guzman d'Alfarache; or, The Spanish Rogue.* 1708. London. Bonwick. 2 vol. ils Gaspar Bouttats. Cecil/Larkins bdg. VG. F1. $325.00

ALEXANDER, Archibald. *Biographical Sketches of Founder & Principal Alumni...* 1851. Phil. 279p. gilt cloth. VG. M20. $30.00

ALEXANDER, David. *Most Men Don't Kill.* 1951. Random. 1st ed. VG/G. P3. $15.00

ALEXANDER, David. *Pennies From Hell.* 1960. Lippincott. 1st ed. VG/dj. P3. $25.00

ALEXANDER, Edward. *Crime of Vengeance: Armenian Struggle for Justice.* 1991. Free Pr. 1st ed. 218p. NF/dj. W1. $20.00

ALEXANDER, Franz. *Criminal, the Judge, & the Public: A Psychological Analysis.* 1956. Glencoe. Free Pr. M11. $35.00

ALEXANDER, Karl. *Time After Time.* 1979. Delacorte. 1st ed. F/F. F4. $30.00

ALEXANDER, Lloyd. *Fortune-Tellers.* 1992. Dutton. 1st ed. inscr/dtd 1992. ils/inscr Hyman. M/M. C8. $50.00

ALEXANDER, Lloyd. *Kestrel.* 1982. Dutton. 1st ed. NF/dj. F4. $25.00

ALEXANDER, Peter. *Selected Poems of Roy Campbell.* 1932. Oxford. 1st ed. 131p. F/F. M7. $30.00

ALEXANDER, Ruth. *Ghost Train.* 1928. Readers Library. 8th ed. NF/dj. P3. $18.00

ALEXANDER, Samuel. *Beauty & Other Forms of Value.* 1933. London. Macmillan. 1st prt. bl cloth. NF/VG. G1. $85.00

ALEXANDER, Samuel. *Space, Time & Diety: Gifford Lectures at Glasgow.* 1916-1918. London. Macmillan. 2 vol. pebbled crimson cloth. VG. G1. $100.00

ALEXANDER, Samuel. *Spinoza: Address in Commemoration of Tercentennary...* 1933. Manchester U. 90p. VG/prt gr wrp. w/1 leaf sgn holograph letter. G1. $185.00

ALEXANDER, William. *Recreations With the Muses.* 1637. Harper. folio. 326p. early calf/rebacked. K1. $650.00

ALEXANDER & ALEXANDER. *Eerdman's Handbook to the Bible.* 1984. Guideposts. 680p. VG/dj. B29. $10.50

ALEXANDER & FRENCH. *Studies in Psychosomatic Medicine.* 1948. Ronald Pr. VG. K4. $15.00

ALEXANDER & SELESNICK. *History of Psychiatry: Evaluation of Psychiatric Thought...* 1849. NY. 1st ed. 471p. A13. $30.00

ALEXANDER. *Decorated Letter.* 1978. Braziller. 4to. 199p. F/F. A4. $65.00

ALEXIE, Sherman. *Lone Ranger & Tonto Fistfight in Heaven.* 1993. Atlantic Monthly. 1st ed. sgn. F/F. B3. $40.00

ALFANGE, Dean. *Supreme Court & the National Will.* 1937. Doubleday Doran. 1st ed. 297p. VG. D3. $25.00

ALFORD, J.G. *Alford Family Notes, Ancient & Modern.* 1908. London. VG. A9. $50.00

ALGER, Edwin. *Luke Walton.* nd. Hurst. brd. VG. P3. $20.00

ALGER, Horatio Jr. *Ben, the Luggage Boy; or, Among the Wharves.* 1870. Boston. Loring. 1st ed. 12mo. 290p. cloth. VG. M1. $150.00

ALGER, Horatio Jr. *Fame & Fortune; or, Progress of Richard Hunter.* 1868. Boston. Loring. 1st ed/1st state. 12mo. 279p. VG. M1. $400.00

ALGREN, Nelson. *Chicago: City on the Make.* 1951. Doubleday. 1st ed. F/NF. B2. $100.00

ALGREN, Nelson. *De Man Met de Gouden Arm.* 1956. Baarn. Uitgave Hollandia. 1st Dutch ed. F/F. w/catalog. B2. $100.00

ALGREN, Nelson. *Nacht Ohne Morgen.* 1956. Hamburg. Rowohlt. 1st German ed. F/NF. B2. $85.00

ALGREN, Nelson. *Neon Wilderness.* 1947. Doubleday. 1st ed. F/NF. B2. $150.00

ALGREN, Nelson. *Never Come Morning.* (1942). NY. 1st ed/author's 2nd book. F/dj. A9. $300.00

ALGREN, Nelson. *Somebody in Boots.* 1935. Vanguard. 1st ed/author's 1st book. xl. G. B2. $65.00

ALGREN, Nelson. *Walk on the Wild Side.* 1956. FSC. 1st ed. 8vo. 346p. yel/bl brd. NF/NF. H5. $75.00

ALGREN & DONOHUE. *Conversations With Nelson Algren.* 1964. Hill Wang. 1st ed. inscr Donohue. F/NF. B2. $60.00

ALINGTON, Charles. *Field Trials & Judging.* 1929. London. Kennel Gazette. 1st ed. 109p. cloth. VG+. R2. $30.00

ALINSKY, Saul. *John L Lewis: An Unauthorized Bibliography.* 1949. Putnam. 1st ed. F/G. V4. $25.00

ALIREZA, Marianne. *At the Drop of a Veil.* 1971. Houghton Mifflin. 1st ed. 275p. VG/dj. W1. $22.00

ALKEN, Henry. *Art & Practice of Etching.* 1849. London. Fuller. 1st ed. 12mo. 9 pl. cloth. M1. $325.00

ALLA, Ogal. *Blue Eye: Story of People of the Plains.* 1905. Portland. 1st/only ed. emb bdg. VG. E5. $35.00

ALLAN, Iris. *White Sioux: Story of Major Walsh of the Mounted Police.* 1969. np. 1st ed. VG/G. B34. $30.00

ALLAN, John B.; see Westlake, Donald E.

ALLAN. *Book Hunter at Home.* 1920. np. 399p. VG. scarce. A4. $75.00

ALLAN. *Story of the Book.* 1952. np. ils. 230p. F/F. A4. $15.00

ALLAND, Alexander Jr. *Human Imperative.* 1972. Columbia. 185p. cloth. VG/dj. G1. $22.50

ALLARD, Harry. *Bumps in the Night.* 1979. Doubleday. 1st ed. ils/inscr James Marshall. M/M. C8. $60.00

ALLARD, William A. *Vanishing Breed: Photographs of the Cowboy & the West.* 1983. NYGS/Little Brn. obl 8vo. photos. VG/VG. w/photo pl & card. B11. $20.00

ALLBEURY, Ted. *Alpha List.* 1979. General. 1st ed. VG/dj. P3. $20.00

ALLBEURY, Ted. *Children of Tender Years.* 1985. Beaufort. 1st ed. NF/dj. P3. $15.00

ALLBEURY, Ted. *Choice of Enemies.* 1972. St Martin. 1st ed (precedes Eng ed)/author's 1st novel. NF/NF. M15. $85.00

ALLBEURY, Ted. *Seeds of Treason.* 1986. London. NEL. 1st ed. F/F. S6. $30.00

ALLBEURY, Ted. *Snowball.* 1974. Lippincott. 1st ed. VG/G. P3. $20.00

ALLBEURY, Ted. *Wilderness of Mirrors.* 1988. London. NEL. ARC/1st ed. w/promo material. F/F. S6. $27.50

ALLBEURY, Ted. *Wilderness of Mirrors.* 1988. Stoddart. 1st ed. F/dj. P3. $20.00

ALLEGRETTO, Michael. *Blood Stone.* 1988. Scribner. 1st ed. F/dj. P3. $17.00

ALLEGRETTO, Michael. *Blood Stone.* 1989. London. Macmillan. ARC/1st ed. RS. NF/NF. S6. $22.50

ALLEGRETTO, Michael. *Suitor.* 1993. Simon Schuster. 1st ed. sgn. F/F. B3. $20.00

ALLEGRETTO, Michael. *Watchmen.* 1991. Simon Schuster. 1st ed. sgn. VG/NF. B3. $25.00

ALLEN, Betsy. *Connie Blair: Clue in Blue (#1).* 1948. Grosset Dunlap. VG/dj. M20. $12.00

ALLEN, Betsy. *Connie Blair: Green Island Mystery (#5).* 1949. Grosset Dunlap. lists to #11. VG/dj. M20. $25.00

ALLEN, Betsy. *Connie Blair: Peril In Pink (#10).* 1955. Grosset Dunlap. lists to #11. VG/VG. M20. $50.00

ALLEN, Betsy. *Connie Blair: Puzzle in Purple (#3).* 1948. Grosset Dunlap. lists to #9. VG/clip. M20. $20.00

ALLEN, Betsy. *Connie Blair: Riddle in Red (#2).* 1948. Grosset Dunlap. lists to #7. VG/dj. M20. $15.00

ALLEN, Betsy. *Connie Blair: Secret of Black Cat Gulch (#4).* 1948. Grosset Dunlap. lists to #6. VG/VG. M20. $20.00

ALLEN, Dave. *Little Night Reading.* 1974. Roger Schlesinger. 1st ed. F/dj. P3. $20.00

ALLEN, E.L. *Self & Its Hazards: Guide to Thought of Karl Jaspers.* 1951. Philosophical Lib. 12mo. 45p. prt 2-toned gr wrp. G1. $22.50

ALLEN, Edward. *Straight Through the Night.* 1989. NY. Soho. 1st ed/author's 1st book. F/F. A14. $25.00

ALLEN, Fletcher. *Wayfarer in North Africa: Tunisia & Algeria.* 1931. Houghton Mifflin. sm 8vo. 16 pl. VG. W1. $10.00

ALLEN, Francis H. *Men of Concord & Some Others As Portrayed in Journal...* 1936. Houghton Mifflin. 1st ed. 8vo. 255p. gr brd. B11. $120.00

ALLEN, Frank. *Universe From Crystal Spheres to Relativity.* 1931. London. Nicholson Watson. 1st ed. 146p. VG/VG-. B33. $27.00

ALLEN, Hervey. *Action at Aquila.* 1938. Farrar Rinehart. 1st ed. 369p. cloth. NF/VG. B14. $45.00

ALLEN, Hugh. *Goodyear Aircraft.* 1947. Cleveland. 1st ed. inscr. 159p. G. B18. $35.00

ALLEN, Ida Bailey. *Dainty Desserts.* ca 1920. Volland. ils Carrie Dudley. 58p. VG. S11. $20.00

ALLEN, Ira. *Narrative of Transactions Relative to Capture of Am Ship...* 1804. Phil? 1st ed of Vol II. 368p. M1. $1,250.00

ALLEN, Ivan. *Atlanta From the Ashes.* 1928. Atlanta. sgn. 114p. G. B18. $22.50

ALLEN, James Egert. *Negro in NY.* 1964. Exposition. 1st ed. 94p. G/VG. H1. $15.00

ALLEN, James Lane. *Kentucky Cardinal.* 1899. Harper. ils. 12mo. 138p. G. H1. $6.50

ALLEN, Jay. *Forty Carets.* 1969. Random. 1st ed. F/NF. B4. $75.00

ALLEN, Jean. *Synopsis Universae Medicinae Practicae: Sive...De Morbis...* 1762. Venetiis. Balilium. 2 vol in 1. contemporary calf. G7. $75.00

ALLEN, Jerry. *Adventures of Mark Twain.* 1955. Little Brn. 359p. F/dj. M10. $6.50

ALLEN, John Houghton. *Southwest.* 1952. Lippincott. ARC. inscr/sgn pres. F/NF. B19. $15.00

ALLEN, John L. *Passage Through the Garden.* 1975. Urbana, IL. 412p. M/dj. A10. $40.00

ALLEN, Leslie. *Liberty: Statue & the American Dream.* 1985. NY. Ellis Island Found. sq 8vo. ils. 304p. VG/VG. B11. $25.00

ALLEN, Lewis F. *Rural Architecture: Farm Houses, Cottages & Out Buildings.* 1852. NY. ils/plans. G+. M17. $60.00

ALLEN, Lewis. *Airship Almanac: Little Light Literature on High Life...* 1909. Boston. ils DC Bartholomew. 79p. G. B18. $95.00

ALLEN, Malcolm. *Medievalism of Lawrence of Arabia.* 1991. PA State. 1st ed. 224p. gilt bl-gr cloth. F/NF. M7. $28.50

ALLEN, R.G.D. *Mathematical Analysis for Economics.* 1953. London. Macmillan. 541p. VG/dj. K4. $15.00

ALLEN, Richard Sanders. *Revolution in the Sky.* 1988. NY. revised ed. 253p. B18. $27.50

ALLEN, Steve. *Murder in Manhattan.* 1990. Zebra. 1st ed. F/dj. P3. $19.00

ALLEN, Steve. *Murder in Vegas.* 1991. NY. Zebra. 1st ed. sgn. F/F. S6. $35.00

ALLEN, V.C. *Rhea & Meigs Counties (TN) in the Confederate War.* 1909. np. 1st ed. 12mo. 126p. gray cloth. NF. C6. $150.00

ALLEN, Walter C. *Hendersonia: Music of Fletcher Henderson.* 1973. Highland Park. Allen. 1st ed. NF. B2. $125.00

ALLEN, Warner. *Uncounted Hour.* 1936. Constable. 1st ed. VG. P3. $30.00

ALLEN, William C. *Son of the Morning: Incidents in Life of Richard Davies.* 1894. Porter Coates. 24mo. 94p. VG. V3. $10.00

ALLEN, William. *Life of William Allen With Selections From Correspondence.* 1902. Phil. Longstreth. 2 vol. 8vo. fair. V3. $40.00

ALLEN & MONTELL. *From Memory to Hist: Using Oral Sources...Research.* 1981. Nashville, TN. Am Assn for State. 172p. F/dj. M10. $8.50

ALLEN & YEN. *Intro to Measurement Theory.* 1979. Brooks/Cole. 273p. VG. K4. $15.00

ALLENDE, Isabel. *Infinite Plan.* 1993. Harper Collins. ARC/1st Am ed. F/wrp. L3. $40.00

ALLENDE, Isabel. *Of Love & Shadows.* 1987. Knopf. 1st ed/author's 2nd book. w/postcard. F/F. B3. $45.00

ALLER, Lawrence H. *Atoms, Stars & Nebulae.* 1971. Cambridge. Harvard. revised ed. sm 4to. 351p. VG/worn. K5. $20.00

ALLIBONE, S.A. *Prose Quotations From Socrates to Macaulay.* 1876. Phil. calf. NF. A9. $45.00

ALLING, Edward. *Law of Karma & Its Solvent.* 1907. Chicago. Barnard Miller. 20p. stapled wrp. M11. $35.00

ALLINGHAM, Cedric. *Flying Saucers From Mars.* 1955. British Book Centre. VG/fair. P3. $20.00

ALLINGHAM, Margery. *China Governess.* 1963. Chatto Windus. 1st ed. VG. P3. $25.00

ALLINGHAM, Margery. *Deadly Duo.* 1949. BC. VG. P3. $15.00

ALLINGHAM, Margery. *Estate of the Beckoning Lady.* 1955. BC. 1st ed. VG. P3. $40.00

ALLINGHAM, Margery. *Mind Readers.* 1965. Morrow. 3rd ed/ VG+/dj. P3. $15.00

ALLINGHAM, Margery. *Pearls Before Swine.* 1945. Crime Club. 1st ed. VG. P3. $15.00

ALLINGHAM, Margery. *Tether's End.* 1958. Doubleday. 1st Am ed. F/NF. M15. $45.00

ALLISON, Dorothy. *Bastard Out of Carolina.* 1992. NY. 1st ed/author's 1st novel. F/F. C2. $90.00

ALLISON, Sally. *Climbing & Rambling Rose. A Guide for Cultivation.* 1994. Milford, Auckland. sm 4to. ils. 128p. sc. M. B26. $19.00

ALLISON, Sam. *Wells Fargo & Danger Station.* 1958. Whitman. TVTI. G. P3. $10.00

ALLISON, William Henry. *Baptist Councils of America.* 1906. Chicago. Kazlitt. 1st ed. 115p. half leather/cloth brd. w/pres card. VG. M8. $37.50

ALLPORT, Gordon W. *Personality: A Psychological Interpretation.* 1937. Holt. 566p. G. K4. $9.00

ALLSTON, Washington. *Outlines & Sketches.* 1850. Boston. 1st ed. obl folio. cloth/rebacked leather. M1. $250.00

ALLSTON, Washington. *Sylphs of the Seasons, With Other Poems.* 1813. Boston. 1st Am ed. 12mo. 168p. plain brd. VG. M1. $200.00

ALLWRIGHT, Michael. *Neighbors.* 1968. Walker. 1st ed/author's 1st book. F/dj. F4. $20.00

ALMOND, Philip C. *Rudolf Otto: Intro to His Philosophical Theology.* 1984. NC U. 172p. blk cloth. F/dj. G1. $22.50

ALOUF, Michel M. *Hist of Baalbek.* 1951. Beirut. Am Pr. 122p. VG/wrp. W1. $12.00

ALQUIE, Ferdinand. *Philosophy of Surrealism.* 1965. Ann Arbor. 1st ed. F/F. B2. $40.00

ALSAR, Vital. *La Balsa: The Longest Raft Voyage in History.* 1973. Dutton. 1st ed. VG/dj. N2. $7.50

ALSON, Lawrence. *Leave It to Beaver.* 1959. Little Golden Book. TVTI. G+. P3. $12.00

ALSOP, Richard. *Narrative of Adventures & Sufferings of John R Jewitt...* 1815. Middletown. Seth Richards. 1st ed. 12mo. 204p. calf/leather label. M1. $750.00

ALTER, Robert Edmond. *Shovel Nose & the Gator Grabbers.* 1963. Putnam. VG. P3. $35.00

ALTERTON & CRAIG. *Edgar Allan Poe.* 1935. Am Book. 12mo. biblio/index. 563p. G. A17. $10.00

ALTHAMER, Andreas. *Diallage, Hoc Est, Conciliatio Locorum Scripturae...* 1527. Nuremberg. Fridericus Peypus. 8vo. tan marbled brd. VG. K1. $450.00

ALTMAN, Joseph. *Organic Foundations of Animal Behavior.* 1966. HRW. 469p. VG/dj. K4. $25.00

ALTMANN, Alexander. *Essays in Jewish Intellectual Hist.* 1981. Hanover. Brandeis U. 324p. blk cloth. G1. $30.00

ALTOUNYAN, E.H.R. *Ornament of Honour.* 1937. Cambridge. 1st ed. 131p. rust cloth/red spine. G. M7. $35.00

ALTROCCHI. *Sleuthing in the Stacks.* 1944. Harvard. ils. 297p. VG/VG. A4. $85.00

ALTSHELER, Joseph A. *Sun of Saratoga.* 1897. NY. Appleton. 1st ed/author's 1st book. F/wrp. Q1. $200.00

ALVAREZ, Julia. *In the Time of the Butterflies.* 1994. Algonquin. ARC. NF/wrp. B2. $30.00

ALVAREZ, Julia. *In the Time of the Butterflies.* 1994. Algonquin. 1st ed. sgn. F/F. B3. $30.00

ALVERSON, Charles. *Not Sleeping, Just Dead.* 1977. Houghton Mifflin. F. P3. $13.00

ALVORD, Clarence W. *Laws of the Territory of IL 1809-1811.* 1906. Springfield, IL. 1st ed. 34p. new wrp. D3. $25.00

AMADO, Jorge. *Morte e a Morte de Quincas Berro Dagua.* 1962. Brazil. Bibliofilos do Brasil. ils Di Cavalcanti. brd. VG. F1. $350.00

AMADO, Jorge. *Show Down.* 1988. Bantam. 1st ed. F/F. B3. $25.00

AMANZHOLOV, Altai S. *Clagol'Noe Upravlenie V Iazke Drevnetiurskikh Pamiatnikov.* 1969. Moscow. 101p. VG. G1. $8.00

AMARAL, A. *Will James: Gilt-Edged Cowboy.* 1967. LA. 1st ed. VG/VG. B5. $60.00

AMAYA, Jesus. *Ameca: Protofundacio Mexicana...* 1951. Mexico. Editorial Lumen. 4to. 200p. G. F3. $20.00

AMAZING, Randi & Sugar. *Houdini, His Life and Art.* 1978. Grosset Dunlap. VG. P3. $15.00

AMBEKDAR, B.R. *What Congress & Gandhi Have Done to the Untouchables.* 1945. Bombay. Thacker. 1st ed. 368p. VG. A17. $20.00

AMBLER, Charles. *Reports of Cases Argued & Determined in High Court...* 1790. London. Strahan & Woodfall for T Whieldon. modern buckram. M11. $250.00

AMBLER, Eric. *Background to Danger.* 1937. Knopf. 1st Am ed. 8vo. 280p. blk stp orange cloth. VG/dj. H5. $500.00

AMBLER, Eric. *Care of Time.* 1981. FSG. 1st ed. VG/VG. P3. $15.00

AMBLER, Eric. *Dark Frontier.* 1990. Mysterious. 1st ed. F/F. P3. $19.00

AMBLER, Eric. *Dirty Story.* 1967. Atheneum. 1st ed. sgn. F/F. S9. $60.00

AMBLER, Eric. *Dirty Story.* 1967. Bodley Head. 1st ed. VG/G. P3. $20.00

AMBLER, Eric. *Doctor Frigo.* 1974. Atheneum. 1st ed. VG/VG. P3. $20.00

AMBLER, Eric. *Eric Ambler.* 1978. Heinemann/Octopus. F/F. P3. $15.00

AMBLER, Eric. *Here Lies Eric Ambler.* 1986. NY. 1st Am ed. 234p. F/F. A17. $10.00

AMBLER, Eric. *Intercom Conspiracy.* 1969. Atheneum. 1st ed. VG/VG. P3. $25.00

AMBLER, Eric. *Intrigue.* 1960. Knopf. VG/VG. P3. $20.00

AMBLER, Eric. *Kind of Anger.* 1964. Bodley Head. 1st ed. VG/G. P3. $30.00

AMBLER, Eric. *Passage of Arms.* 1960. Rpt Soc. VG/VG. P3. $8.00

AMBLER, Eric. *Siege of the Villa Lipp.* 1977. Random. 1st ed. VG/VG. P3. $15.00

AMEDEO, Luigi. *On the Polar Star in the Arctic Sea.* 1903. London. Hutchinson. 2 vol in 1. 1st ed. ils/pl/maps/diagrams. VG. P4. $325.00

AMERICAN CRAYON CO. *Two Famous Classics: Peter Pan...Racketty-Packetty House...* 1946. Sandusky, OH. VG/G. C8. $25.00

AMERICAN KENNEL CLUB. *Complete Dog Book.* 1939. NY. Halcyon. revised/updated ed. ils. cloth. M/dj. R2. $35.00

AMERICAN KENNEL CLUB. *Purebred Dogs. The Breeds & Standards As Recognized by...* 1935. NY. Watt. 1st ed. ils. 640p. cloth. G+. R2. $45.00

AMES, C.E. *Pioneering the Union Pacific.* (1969). NY. later prt. VG/dj. C11. $37.50

AMES, Delano. *Corpse Diplomatique.* 1950. Hodder Stoughton. 1st ed. VG/VG. P3. $20.00

AMES, Delano. *Murder, Maestro, Please.* 1952. Hodder Stoughton. VG. P3. $15.00

AMES, Evelyn. *My Brother Bird.* 1954. Dodd Mead. 1st ed. 125p. VG+/G+. P2. $25.00

AMES, Jennifer. *Flight Into Fear.* 1954. Collins. 1st ed. VG/VG. P3. $20.00

AMES & CORRELL. *Orchids of Guatemala & Belize.* 1985. Dover. 3 vol in 1. rpt of 1952/1965 ed. 779p. VG/wrp. F3. $20.00

AMIDON, R.W. *Effect of Willed Muscular Movements on Temperature of Head.* 1880. Putnam. pres. 57p. stiff wrp. G7. $295.00

AMIS, Kingsley. *Alteration.* 1977. Viking. NF/NF. P3. $35.00

AMIS, Kingsley. *Anti-Death League.* 1966. HBW. 1st Am ed. 8vo. 307p. blk stp gr cloth. F/dj. H5. $75.00

AMIS, Kingsley. *Colonel Sun: A James Bond Adventure.* 1968. NY. Harper. 1st AM ed. F/F. S6. $30.00

AMIS, Kingsley. *Girl.* 1971. Jonathan Cape. 1st ed. VG/VG. P3. $20.00

AMIS, Kingsley. *Girl.* 1972. HBJ. 1st ed. VG/G. P3. $15.00

AMIS, Kingsley. *I Want It Now.* 1968. Jonathan Cape. 1st ed. VG/VG. P3. $23.00

AMIS, Kingsley. *Jake's Thing.* 1978. Hutchinson. 1st ed. F/F. P3. $18.00

AMIS, Kingsley. *James Bond Dossier.* (1965). NAL. 1st Am ed. F/NF clip. N3. $20.00

AMIS, Kingsley. *One Fat Englishman.* 1963. Gollancz. 1st ed. VG/VG. P3. $30.00

AMIS, Kingsley. *Rudyard Kipling & His World.* 1975. London. Thames Hudson. 1st ed. photos. F/F. T2. $12.00

AMIS, Kingsley. *Russian Hide & Seek.* 1980. Hutchinson. 1st ed. VG/VG. P3. $20.00

AMIS, Kingsley. *Take a Girl Like You.* 1960. Gollancz. 2nd ed. NF/NF. P3. $25.00

AMIS, Martin. *Dead Babies.* 1975. Knopf. 1st ed. NF/NF. P3. $75.00

AMIS, Martin. *Dead Babies.* 1975. London. Cape. 1st ed/author's 2nd book. sgn. F/NF. B4. $400.00

AMIS, Martin. *Einstein's Monsters.* 1987. NY. Harmony. 1st Am ed. sgn. F/F. B2. $75.00

AMIS, Martin. *Invasion of the Space Invaders.* 1982. London. Hutchinson. 1st ed. 4to. F/wrp. L3. $100.00

AMIS, Martin. *London Fields.* 1989. Harmony. 1st ed. F/F. B3. $25.00

AMIS, Martin. *Moronic Inferno. And Other Visits to America.* 1986. London. 1st ed. sgn. F/F. A11. $55.00

AMIS, Martin. *Success.* 1987. Harmony. 1st Am ed. F/F. B4. $45.00

AMIS, Martin. *Time's Arrow.* 1991. Harmony. 1st ed. inscr. F/F. B2. $45.00

AMIS, Martin. *Time's Arrow.* 1991. NY. Harmony. AP. F/wrp. B2. $45.00

AMIS & CONQUEST. *Egyptologists.* 1966. Random. 1st ed. VG/G. P3. $23.00

AMORY, Copley Jr. *Persian Days.* 1929. Houghton Mifflin. 1st ed. 230p. G. W1. $14.00

AMORY, Robert. *Treatise on Electrolysis & Its Applications...* 1886. NY. Wood. Wood Lib 307p. NF. G7. $65.00

AMOS, Alan. *Borderline Murder.* 1947. Crime Club. 1st ed. VG. P3. $12.00

AMOS, Alan. *Fatal Harvest.* 1957. Crime Club. 1st ed. VG/G. P3. $18.00

AMOS, Sheldon. *Political & Legal Remedies for War.* 1880. Franklir Sq, NY. Harper. brd. M11. $250.00

AMOS, William. *Originals: A-Z of Fiction's Real-Life Characters.* 1985. np. 40 photos. 634p. F/NF. A4. $65.00

AMOSOFF, N. *Notes From the Future.* (1970). Simon Schuster. 1st Eng-language ed. F/VG+. N3. $10.00

AMRAM. *Makers of Hebrew Books in Italy...* 1963. np. ils. 434p. F/F. A4. $65.00

AMUNDSEN, Bjornstad. *Kirkenesferda 1942.* 1946. oslo. fld chart/photos/maps. 464p. VG/worn. A17. $35.00

AMUNDSEN & ELLSWORTH. *Den Forste Flukt Over Polhavet.* 1926. Oslo. Glydendal Norsk. F/chip. B2. $250.00

AMUNDSEN & ELLSWOTH. *First Crossing of the Polar Sea.* 1928. Doubleday Doran. 8vo. ils/fld map. 324p. VG. T7. $65.00

ANAGNOSTOU, Manos D. *Samos. Postal History & Stamps 1800-1915.* 1992. Nicosia. 8vo. ils/maps. 220p. pict brd. O2. $60.00

ANASTASI, Anne. *Differential Psychology.* 1958. Macmillan. 3rd ed. 664p. VG. K4. $15.00

ANBUREY, Thomas. *Journal d'un Voyage Fait Dans l'Interier de l'Amerique...* 1793. Paris. 2 vol in 1. 3rd French ed. 8vo. vellum-backed brd. M1. $350.00

ANDERS, E. *Practical Macrame.* 1971. np. VG/wrp. G2. $4.95

ANDERS, Max. *Good Life: Living With Meaning in Never-Enough World.* 1993. Word. 296p. F/djn. B29. $7.50

ANDERSEN, Hans Christian. *Andersen's Fairy Tales.* nd. London. ils Jiri Trnka. cloth. F/torn. M5. $60.00

ANDERSEN, Hans Christian. *Complete Andersen Fairy Tales, 6 Volumes.* 1949. LEC. 1/1500. ils/sgn Kredel. trans/sgn Hersholt. F/NF case. C8. $360.00

ANDERSEN, Hans Christian. *Fairy Tales.* ca 1934. London. Ward Lock. ils Margaret Tarrant. gr cloth/prt brd. F/VG-. F1. $125.00

ANDERSEN, Hans Christian. *Hans Andersen's Fairy Tales.* nd. Nister. ils ES Hardy. aeg. pict cloth. VG. M5. $95.00

ANDERSEN, Hans Christian. *Hans Andersen's Fairy Tales.* nd. Stokes. ils Cecile Walton. cloth/triangular mc pl. VG. M5. $60.00

ANDERSEN, Hans Christian. *Hans Andersen's Fairy Tales...for Little Folks.* nd. London. Blackie. folio. ils Helen Stratton. VG. D6. $100.00

ANDERSEN, Hans Christian. *Kate Greenaway's Original Drawings for the Snow Queen.* 1981. Schocken. 1st ed. Not For Resale stp. VG/VG. S11. $18.00

ANDERSEN, Hans Christian. *Red Shoes.* 1982. Bijou Hoshino. 29x28mm. 1/40 (190 total). English/Japanese text. teg. F/case. B24. $325.00

ANDERSEN, Hans Christian. *Stories From...* 1911. Hodder Stoughton. ils Edmond Dulac/28 mtd pl. 250p. VG+. P2. $275.00

ANDERSEN, Hans Christian. *Ugly Duckling.* 1955. Macmillan. 1st ed thus. ils Larsen. M/M. C8. $25.00

ANDERSEN, Hans Christian. *Wild Swans.* 1986. Hyattsville, MD. Rebecca. 74x57mm. ils/sgn Chamberlain. fore-edge painting. box. B24. $1,500.00

ANDERSEN, Lis. *Lis Sails the Atlantic.* 1936. NY. Dutton. 1st ed. 8vo. ils. 240p. VG. T7. $25.00

ANDERSEN, Richard. *Muckaluck.* 1980. Delacorte. 1st ed. F/F. P8. $17.50

ANDERSON, Alan Ross. *Entailment: Logic of Revelance & Necessity.* 1975. Princeton. 542p. blk cloth. VG/dj. G1. $40.00

ANDERSON, Anne. *Nursery Zoo.* nd. Nelson. 4 books in 1. possible 1st ed thus. 47 pl. VG. M5. $95.00

ANDERSON, Archer. *Campaign & Battle of Chickamauga.* 1881. Richmond. Wm Ellis. 1st ed. 8vo. G/prt wrp. C6. $150.00

ANDERSON, Barry C. *Lifeline to the Yukon: Hist of Yukon River Navigation.* 1983. Seattle. Superior. 1st ed. 152p. F/F. A17. $25.00

ANDERSON, Bernhard W. *Understanding the Old Testament.* 1962. Prentice Hall. 551p. VG/worn. B29. $7.50

ANDERSON, Bernice G. *Topsy Turvy & the Easter Bunny.* 1939. Rand McNally #269. unp. pict brd. VG. A3. $40.00

ANDERSON, C.L.G. *Old Panama & Castilla del Oro.* 1914 (1911). Page. 559p. teg. pict cloth. VG. F3. $40.00

ANDERSON, C.W. *Afraid To Ride.* 1966. Scholastic BC rpt. G/wrp. O3. $10.00

ANDERSON, C.W. *Billy & Blaze.* 1946. Macmillan. later prt. VG/G+. O3. $30.00

ANDERSON, C.W. *Blaze & the Forest Fire.* 1947. Macmillan. late prt. VG/VG. O3. $45.00

ANDERSON, C.W. *Blaze & the Gypsies.* 1945. Macmillan. later prt. VG/VG. O3. $25.00

ANDERSON, C.W. *Blaze & Thunderbolt.* 1956. Macmillan. 2nd prt. 4to. 46p. VG/VG. A3. $25.00

ANDERSON, C.W. *Blaze Finds Forgotten Roads.* 1970. NY. 1st ed. VG/VG. B5. $25.00

ANDERSON, C.W. *Blind Connemara*. 1971. Macmillan. 1st ed. 8vo. F/VG. B17. $12.50

ANDERSON, C.W. *Bobcat*. 1949. Macmillan. 1st ed. VG/G. O3. $45.00

ANDERSON, C.W. *Crooked Colt*. 1956. Macmillan. 3rd prt. 4to. VG/VG. A3. $17.50

ANDERSON, C.W. *Deep Through the Heart. Profiles of Twenty Valiant Horses*. 1940. Macmillan. 1st ed. obl 4to. VG/G. A3. $22.50

ANDERSON, C.W. *Heads Up, Heels Down*. 1944. Macmillan. 1st ed. ils. cloth. VG. M5. $10.00

ANDERSON, C.W. *Heads Up, Heels Down*. 1944. NY. 1st ed. F/F. R2. $15.00

ANDERSON, C.W. *Thoroughbreds*. 1942. Macmillan. 1st ed. VG. P2. $16.00

ANDERSON, C.W. *Tomorrow's Champion*. 1946. Macmillan. 1st ed. ils. cloth. VG+. M5. $16.00

ANDERSON, C.W. *Touch of Greatness*. 1945. Macmillan. 1st ed. 46p. NF/VG. P2. $35.00

ANDERSON, Christopher. *Annals of the English Bible*. 1845. London. Pickering. 2 vol. 1st ed. 6 pl. full leather. H10. $100.00

ANDERSON, Dwight G. *Abraham Lincoln: The Quest for Immortality*. 1982. Knopf. 1st ed. 271p. F/dj. M10. $15.00

ANDERSON, Edgar. *Introgressive Hypridization*. 1949. NY. ils. 109p. VG. B26. $22.50

ANDERSON, Eugene N. *First Moroccan Crisis*. 1966. Hamden, CT. 2nd prt. 420p. VG. W1. $15.00

ANDERSON, Fannie. *Doctors Under Three Flags*. 1951. Detroit. 1st ed. 185p. VG. A13. $40.00

ANDERSON, Frederick. *Selected Mark Twain-Howell Letters 1872-1910*. 1967. Harvard. 453p. F/dj. M10. $15.00

ANDERSON, Isabel. *Circling South America*. 1928. Boston. Marshall Jones. 1st ed. 8vo. photos/pl. 214p. orange brd. dj. B11. $60.00

ANDERSON, Isabel. *Great Sea Horse*. 1909. Little Brn. 1st ed. 4to. 251p. NF. D6. $155.00

ANDERSON, Isabel. *Yacht in Mediterranean Seas*. 1930. Boston. Marshall Jones. 428p. cloth. dj. W1. $45.00

ANDERSON, Jack. *Fiasco*. 1983. Time Books. 1st ed. 386p. VG/dj. W1. $25.00

ANDERSON, James. *Assault & Matrimony*. 1980. London. Muller. 1st ed. NF/NF. S6. $22.50

ANDERSON, James. *Murder, She Wrote*. nd. BC. TVTI. VG/VG. P3. $10.00

ANDERSON, Janice. *Marilyn Monroe*. 1983. Royce. 1st ed. VG/VG. P3. $25.00

ANDERSON, Jim. *Billarooby*. 1988. Ticknor Fields. ARC. VG/pict wrp. B3. $25.00

ANDERSON, John E. *Psychological Aspects of Aging*. 1956. Am Psychological Assn. 289p. VG/dj. K4. $15.00

ANDERSON, John R.L. *Death in the Caribbean*. 1977. London. Gollancz. 1st ed. NF/VG. O4. $20.00

ANDERSON, John R.L. *Death in the Channel*. 1976. Stein Day. 1st Am ed. NF/VG. O4. $15.00

ANDERSON, John R.L. *Death in the City*. 1982. Scribner. 1st Am ed. F/F. O4. $15.00

ANDERSON, John R.L. *Death in the Thames*. 1975. Stein Day. 1st Am ed. NF/VG. O4. $15.00

ANDERSON, Ken. *Tom Huntner: Sophomore Pitcher*. 1947. Zondervan. 1st ed. VG+/VG+. P8. $40.00

ANDERSON, Paul. *Brain Wave*. 1969. Walker. 1st Am hc ed. VG/dj. M2. $75.00

ANDERSON, Poul. *Agent of the Terran Empire*. 1979. Gregg. F/F. P3. $20.00

ANDERSON, Poul. *Avatar*. 1978. Berkley Putnam. 1st ed. F/F. P3 $20.00

ANDERSON, Poul. *Circus of Hells*. 1979. Gregg. F/F. P3. $20.00

ANDERSON, Poul. *Harvest of Stars*. 1993. Tor. 1st ed. F/F. P3. $23.00

ANDERSON, Poul. *Infinite Voyage*. 1969. Crowell Collier. 1st ed. VG. P3. $25.00

ANDERSON, Poul. *Let the Spacemen Beware!* 1969. London. Dobson. 1st hc ed. sgn. F/F clip. T2. $38.00

ANDERSON, Poul. *Merman's Children*. 1979. Berkley Putnam. 1st ed. F/F. P3. $20.00

ANDERSON, Poul. *Orion Shall Rise*. 1983. Phantasia. 1st ed. sgn. 1/600 #d. F/box. P3. $45.00

ANDERSON, Poul. *Perish by the Sword*. 1959. Macmillan. 1st ed. sgn. F/VG. O4. $135.00

ANDERSON, Poul. *Rebel Worlds*. 1979. Gregg. sgn. F/F. P3. $30.00

ANDERSON, Poul. *Shield of Time*. 1990. Tor. 1st ed. F/F. T2. $20.00

ANDERSON, Poul. *Shield of Time*. 1990. Tor. 1st ed. sgn. F/dj. F4. $30.00

ANDERSON, Poul. *Three Worlds To Conquer*. 1982. Sidgwick Jackson. F/F. P3. $22.00

ANDERSON, Poul. *Trader to the Stars*. nd. BC. VG/VG. P3. $8.00

ANDERSON, Poul. *Vault of the Ages*. 1967. HRW. 4th ed. VG/VG. P3. $30.00

ANDERSON, Poul. *Virgin Planet*. 1959. Avalon. 1st ed. F/dj. M2. $100.00

ANDERSON, Poul. *Year of the Ransom*. 1988. Walker. 1st ed. ils Paul Rivoche. F/F. T2. $20.00

ANDERSON, R.C. *Rigging of Ships in Days of Spritsail Topmast 1600-1720*. 1927. Marine Research Soc. gilt bl cloth. NF. F1. $85.00

ANDERSON, R.C. *Rigging of Ships in Days of Spritsail Topmast 1600-1720*. 1927. Marine Research Soc. 278p. VG/dj. M20. $90.00

ANDERSON, Robert Gordon. *Seven-O'Clock Stories*. 1920. Putnam. 1st ed. ils E Boyd Smith. 180p. G. D6. $35.00

ANDERSON, Roy. *White Star*. 1964. Prescott, Eng. Stephenson. 8vo. 58 photos/fld pl. 236p. VG/dj. T7. $35.00

ANDERSON, Sherwood. *Alice/The Lost Novel*. 1929. London. Mathews Marrot. Woburn Book Series. 1/500. sgn. NF/NF. L3. $150.00

ANDERSON, Sherwood. *Buck Fever Papers*. 1971. Charlottesville. 1st ed. VG/VG. B5. $25.00

ANDERSON, Sherwood. *Certain Things Last...* 1992. NYC. 1st ed. 359p. VG. B18. $15.00

ANDERSON, Sherwood. *Dark Laughter*. 1925. Boni Liveright. 1st ed. NF/NF. Q1. $175.00

ANDERSON, Sherwood. *Home Town*. 1940. NY. Alliance Book Corp. 1st ed. inscr. VG/clip. Q1. $350.00

ANDERSON, Sherwood. *Memoirs*. 1942. Harcourt Brace. 1st ed. 507p. cloth. VG/dj. M20. $60.00

ANDERSON, Sherwood. *Mid-American Chants*. 1918. NY. John Lane. 1st ed. sgn pres. 82p. gr/gilt stp yel buckram. NF/dj. H5. $600.00

ANDERSON, Sherwood. *New Testament*. 1927. NY. Boni Liveright. 1st ed. 12mo. 118p. gilt/red stp bl cloth. F/NF. H5. $85.00

ANDERSON, Sherwood. *Return to Winesburg*. 1967. NC U. 1st ed. 223p. VG/worn. M20. $25.00

ANDERSON, Sherwood. *Story Tellers Story*. 1924. NY. 1st ed. VG/VG. B5. $125.00

ANDERSON, Sherwood. *Tar, a Midwest Childhood*. 1926. Boni Liveright. 1st ed. 346p. VG/chip. M20. $75.00

ANDERSON, Terry A. *Den of Lions: Memoirs of Seven Years*. 1993. Crown. 1st ed. 356p. NF/dj. W1. $20.00

ANDERSON, Verily. *Friends of Relations: Three Centuries of Quaker Families*. 1980. Hodder Stoughton. 1st ed. 8vo. 320p. VG. V3. $16.00

ANDERSON & AUSUBEL. *Readings in Psychology of Cognition.* 1965. HRW. 676p. VG. K4. $15.00

ANDERSON & BEASON. *Assemblers of Infinity.* 1993. Bantam Spectra. 1st ed. F/F. F4. $16.00

ANDERSON & BLAIR. *Nautilus 90 North.* 1959. Cleveland. 1st ed. 251p. map ep. VG/torn. B18. $22.50

ANDERSON & DICKSON. *Earthman's Burden.* 1957. Gnome. 1st ed. F/F. M2. $100.00

ANDERSON & DICKSON. *Earthman's Burden.* 1957. Gnome. 1st ed. VG/VG. P3. $75.00

ANDERSON & FERBER. *Albert Bierstadt Art & Enterprise.* 1990. Brooklyn Mus. 1st ed. 327 p. VG/glossy wrp/dj. A17. $25.00

ANDERSON & WRIGHT. *Tales of Teeny-Wee.* nd. Whitman. ils/6 mc pl. 248p. G. P2. $45.00

ANDERSON. *Ils Hist of Herbals.* 1977. Columbia. 110 ils. 284p. F. A4. $55.00

ANDOR, L.E. *Aptitudes & Abilities of Black Man in Sub-Saharan Africa.* 1966. Johannesburg. 174p. VG. K4. $15.00

ANDRADE, E.N. *Isaac Newton.* 1950. London. Parrish. photos/ils. 111p. G/dj. K5. $15.00

ANDRE, Richard. *Babes in the Wood.* 1988. McLoughlin. 4to. 6 chromolithographs. G+. D6. $50.00

ANDREW, Christopher. *KGB: The Inside Story.* 1990. Hodder Stoughton. 1st ed. P3. $35.00

ANDREW, Felicia; see Grant, Charles L.

ANDREWS, Allen. *Pig Plantagenet.* 1981. Viking. 1st ed. VG/G. P3. $15.00

ANDREWS, Bart. *Story of I Love Lucy.* nd. BC. TVTI. VG/VG. P3. $8.00

ANDREWS, C.L. *Story of Stika: Historic Outpost of the Northwest Coast.* ca 1922. Seattle. Lowman Hanford. 1st ed. 108p. VG. P4. $85.00

ANDREWS, Edward D. *Community Industries of the Shakers.* 1933. Albany, NY. 1st ed. 322p. NF/wrp. B2. $40.00

ANDREWS, James. *Citizen Christian.* 1968. Sheed Ward. 190p. VG/dj. B29. $3.50

ANDREWS, Kenneth R. *Nook Farm: Mark Twain's Hartford Circle.* 1950. Harvard. 1st ed. ils. 288p. G/chip. M10. $15.00

ANDREWS, Lynn V. *Woman of Wyrrd.* 1990. Harper. 1st ed. F/F. B3. $20.00

ANDREWS, Mary Raymond Shipman. *Perfect Tribute.* 1908 (1906). Scribner. ils. 74p. G. H1. $6.00

ANDREWS, Nigel. *Horror Films.* 1985. Gallery Books. F. P3. $20.00

ANDREWS, Stephen Pearl. *Discoveries in Chinese or Symbolism of Primitive Characters.* 1854. NY. 1st ed. 12mo. 137p. cloth. xl. M1. $150.00

ANDREWS, Stephen Pearl. *Love, Marriage, & Divorce...* 1853. NY. Stringer Townsend. 1st ed. 12mo. M1. $550.00

ANDREWS, V.C. *Fallen Hearts.* 1988. Poseidon. 1st ed. VG/VG. P3. $20.00

ANDREWS, V.C. *Flowers in the Attic.* 1979. Simon Schuster. 1st ed. VG/VG. P3. $25.00

ANDREWS, Wayne. *Autobiography of Carl Schurz.* 1961. 1st ed. 331p. O8. $12.50

ANDREWS, William Given. *Hist of Christ Episcopal Church in Guilford, CT.* 1895. Guilford. Echo. 1st ed. 73p. cloth. VG. M8. $45.00

ANDREWS, William. *Doctor in History, Literature, Folk-Lore, Etc.* 1896. London. 1st ed. 287p. very scarce. A13. $175.00

ANDREWS & BOYLE. *Phonographic Reader: Complete Course of Inductive Reading...* 1845. Boston. 1st ed. 16mo. 36p. plain wrp. M1. $125.00

ANDREWS & KARLINS. *Gomorrah.* 1974. Doubleday. 1st ed. NF/NF. P3. $13.00

ANDREWS. *Work & Workshop Among the Shakers.* 1982. np. ils. 224p. VG. E5. $35.00

ANDRIC, Ivo. *Devil's Yard.* 1962. NY. 1st ed. 8vo. 137p. dj. O2. $35.00

ANDRIST, Ralph K. *Long Death: Last Days of the Plains Indians.* 1964. Macmillan. 2nd ed. 371p. VG/dj. B34. $25.00

ANGELL, Roger. *Summer Game.* 1972. Viking. UP. NF/wrp. L3. $225.00

ANGELO, Valenti. *Nino.* 1938. NY. 1st ed. ils. 244p. NF/worn. A17. $10.00

ANGELONI, Francesco. *History of Augustus From Julius Ceasar to Constantine...* 1641. Rome. 1st ed. folio. 70 pl of medals. 396p. tooled leather. H3. $400.00

ANGELOU, Maya. *Heart of a Woman.* 1981. Random. 1st ed. inscr. 272p. NF/dj. C6. $100.00

ANGELOU, Maya. *Just Give Me a Cool Drink of Water.* 1971. Random. 1st ed. F/NF. V1. $65.00

ANGELOU, Maya. *Shaker, Why Don't You Sing.* 1983. Random. 1st ed. F/F. B3. $55.00

ANGELOU, Maya. *Wouldn't Take Nothing for My Journey Now.* 1993. Random. special ltd ed. sgn. 1/500. special bdg. F/case. Q1. $75.00

ANGELOU, Maya. *Wouldn't Take Nothing for My Journey Now.* 1993. Random. 1st ed. F/F. B3. $30.00

ANGERMEYER, Johanna. *My Father's Land. A Galapagos Quest.* 1989. London. Viking. 1st ed. 16 pl/2 maps. 303p. map ep. bl cloth. F/F. B11. $20.00

ANGLE, Paul M. *Portrait of Abraham Lincoln in Letters by His Oldest Son.* 1968. Chicago Hist Soc. ARC. 92p. F/dj. M10. $22.50

ANGLE, Paul. *Bloody Williamson.* 1952. NY. 1st ed. sgn pres. VG/VG. B5. $32.50

ANGLE, Paul. M. *Lincoln Reader.* 1947. BOMC. biblio/index. VG/chip. A17. $9.50

ANGLO, Michael. *Nostalgia Spotlight on the Fifties.* 1977. Jupiter. F/F. P3. $20.00

ANGLO. *Penny Dreadfuls & Other Victorian Horrors.* 1977. London. 4to. 125p. F/F. A4. $35.00

ANGLUND, Joah Walsh. *Mother Goose ABC, in a Pumpkin Shell.* 1960. HBW. later pt. 8vo. VG. B17. $10.00

ANGLUND, Joan Walsh. *Book of Good Things.* 1965. Harcourt Brace. 1st ed. F/F. C8. $30.00

ANGLUND, Joan Walsh. *Childhood Is a Time of Innocence.* 1964. Harcourt. stated 1st ed. ils. VG+/G. M5. $25.00

ANGLUND, Joan Walsh. *Christmas Is a Time of Giving.* 1961. Harcourt Brace. 1st ed. pict cloth. F/F. C8. $26.00

ANGLUND, Joan Walsh. *Circle of the Spirit.* 1983. Random. 1st ed. 12mo. cloth. F/F. C8. $25.00

ANGLUND, Joan Walsh. *Joan Walsh Anglund Story Book.* 1978. Random. 1st prt. VG/G. C8. $35.00

ANGLUND, Joan Walsh. *Morning Is a Little Child.* 1969. Harcourt. ils. cloth. F. M5. $18.00

ANGLUND, Joan Walsh. *Pocket Full of Proverbs.* 1964. Harcourt Brace. possible 1st ed. F/F/NF slipcase. C8. $30.00

ANGLUND, Joan Walsh. *Pook of Poetry.* 1987. Random. 1st ed. 4to. VG. B17. $15.00

ANGLUND, Joan Walsh. *Slice of Snow.* 1970. Harcourt Brace. 1st ed. sm 12mo. cloth. M/M. C8. $35.00

ANGLUND, Joan Walsh. *Spring Is a New Beginning.* 1963. Harcourt. stated 1st ed. ils. F/VG. M5. $25.00

ANGLUND, Joan Walsh. *What Color Is Love?* 1966. Harcourt. stated 1st ed. NF/VG. M5. $25.00

ANGLUND, Joan Walsh. *Year Is Round.* 1966. Harcourt Brace. 1st ed. 24mo. VG/VG. C8. $35.00

ANGOLD, Michael. *Byzantine Government in Exile.* 1975. Oxford. 8vo. 2 maps. 332p. dj. O2. $35.00

ANIOL, Claude B. *San Antonio: City of Missions.* 1942. Hastings. 1st ed. NF/VG. B19. $15.00

ANNAN, David. *Movie Fantastic: Beyond the Dream...* 1974. Bounty. VG. P3. $10.00

ANNO, Mitsumasa. *Anno's Counting House.* 1982. Philomel. 1st Am ed. sm 4to. M/M. C8. $45.00

ANNO, Mitsumasa. *Anno's Medieval World.* 1979-80. Philomel. 1st revised ed. F/VG. C8. $40.00

ANOBILE, Richard J. *Godfrey Daniels!* 1975. Crown. VG/VG. P3. $15.00

ANOBILE, Richard J. *Why a Duck?* nd. Darien. 8th ed. VG/VG. P3. $15.00

ANON. *Affecting Hist of Captivity & Sufferings of Mrs Mary Velnet.* 1804? Boston. Wm Crary. 1st ed. 16mo. 96p. contemporary brd. M1. $475.00

ANON. *Agnes Arlington: Life, Times, Troubles, Tribulations...* 1854. Baltimore/Phil/NY/ Buffalo. AR Orton. 1st ed. 8vo. M1. $750.00

ANON. *American Bee: Collection of Entertaining Histories...* 1797. Leominster, MA. Prentiss. 12mo. 249p. full contemporary tree calf. M1. $550.00

ANON. *Betty Lee & Her Pals.* ca 1940s. Whitehall. 1 moveable. VG+. M5. $18.00

ANON. *Beyond the Stars.* 1986. Cathay. brd. F. P3. $10.00

ANON. *BJ & the Bear Annual.* 1981. Grandreams. TVTI. VG. P3. $20.00

ANON. *Brudder Bones 4-11-44 Joker.* 1897. Chicago. 12mo. 30p. prt wrp. M1. $75.00

ANON. *Charlie Chaplain Annual.* 1974. Brown Watson. MTI. VG. P3. $20.00

ANON. *Date With Danger.* 1984. Octopus. F. P3. $15.00

ANON. *Death in the Air.* 1936. London. Heinemann. 2nd ed. photos. gilt blk linen. VG. M7. $50.00

ANON. *Doctor Who Annual 1976.* 1976. World. TVTI. VG. P3. $20.00

ANON. *Gone With the Wind Cookbook.* 1991. Abbeville. 2nd ed. VG. P3. $8.00

ANON. *Granny's Birds: A Story of Russia.* 1947. Saalfield 448. dj. K2. $30.00

ANON. *Grocer's Guide: Being a Directory for Making...Liquors...* 1820. NY. 1st ed. 8vo.202p. disbound. M1. $475.00

ANON. *Luke Darrell, the Chicago Newsboy.* 1866. Chicago. Tomlinson. 12mo. 377p. cloth. M1. $125.00

ANON. *Manners & Customs of the Jews & Other Nations...* 1831. London. 12mo. ils. 176p. cloth/leather label. O2. $65.00

ANON. *Miranda; or, The Discovery. A Tale.* 1800. Norwich, CT. Trumbull. 1st ed. 12mo. 108p. calf/wood brd. M1. $750.00

ANON. *Mother Goose ABC Book.* 1907. JW Bevans. letters on spokes form a fan. G. very scarce. M5. $50.00

ANON. *Mother Goose Jingles.* 1904. Saalfield Muslin Books. 18p. VG. M5. $40.00

ANON. *Parliaments & Councils of England.* 1839. London. Murray. 1st ed. 8vo. 603p. rebound. F. D3. $150.00

ANON. *Principles of Quakerism: A Collection of Essays.* 1909. Friends Bookstore. revised ed. 12mo. 217p. VG. V3. $14.00

ANON. *Rosie-Posie Book.* ca 1920. London. Thomas Nelson. lg 8vo. 12 mc pl. pict cloth w/label. VG+. C8. $130.00

ANON. *Rowan & Martin's Laugh-In.* 1969. World. TVTI. VG. P3. $20.00

ANON. *Space Wars, Fact & Fiction.* 1980. Octopus. 1st ed. VG. P3. $15.00

ANON. *Star Trek Annual 1971.* 1970. World. TVTI. VG. P3. $30.00

ANON. *Stories by American Authors.* 1902. Scribner. 10 vol. VG. P3. $125.00

ANON. *Stories for Bedtime.* 1952. Saalfield 4201. K2. $5.00

ANON. *Temperance Cook Book: Being a Collection of Receipts...* 1841. Phil. Gihon Kucher. 1st ed. 18mo. 159p. G. M1. $650.00

ANON. *Wanderings Over Bible Lands & Seas.* 1866. London. 8vo. 301p. gilt cloth. O2. $135.00

ANSCOMBE, G.E.M. *Ethics, Religion & Politics.* 1981. MN U. 161p. VG. G1. $25.00

ANSHEN, Ruth Nanda. *Language: Enquiry Into Its Meaning & Function.* 1957. Harper. 366p. brn cloth. G1. $27.50

ANSHEN, Ruth Nanda. *Our Emergent Civilization.* 1947. Harper. 340p. VG/dj. G1. $25.00

ANSON, Jay. *666.* 1981. Simon Schuster. 1st ed. F/dj. F4. $20.00

ANSON, Jay. *666.* 1981. Simon Schuster. 1st ed. VG/VG. P3. $15.00

ANSON, P. *Mariners of Brittany.* 1931. London/NY. 1st ed. G. C11. $35.00

ANSTED, D.T. *Ionian Islands in the Year 1863.* 1863. London. 8vo. maps/ils. 480p. new half brn calf/red & gr labels. O2. $550.00

ANSTEY, F. *Vice Versa.* 1911. Smith Elder. 40th prt. VG/VG. P3. $20.00

ANTHOLOGY. *Bits of Silver: Vignettes of the Old West.* 1961. Hastings. VG/dj. B34. $22.50

ANTHOLOGY. *Carriers of the Dream Wheel: Contemporary Native Am Poetry.* 1973. NY. 1st ed. F/F. C2. $100.00

ANTHOLOGY. *Collision Course.* 1968. Random. ARC. sgn contributors. RS. F/F. B4. $150.00

ANTHOLOGY. *Contemporary American Photography Part 1.* 1986. Tokyo. 1st ed. sm 4to. VG+. S9. $60.00

ANTHOLOGY. *Counterpoint.* 1965. London. Allen Unwin. 1st ed. VG/VG. S9. $30.00

ANTHOLOGY. *Delphinium Blossoms.* 1990. Delphinium Books. 1st ed. rem mk. F/F. A14. $25.00

ANTHOLOGY. *Gauntlet 2.* 1991. Baltimore. 1st ed. 1/500. 32 contributor sgns. F/F/case. C2. $100.00

ANTHOLOGY. *Juden in Deutschen Literatur. Essays Uber Zeitgenossiche...* 1922. Berlin. Welt. 359p. cloth. VG. B14. $60.00

ANTHOLOGY. *Lifted Veil.* 1992. Carroll Graf. 1st Am ed. F/F. M21. $30.00

ANTHOLOGY. *Man To Send Rain Clouds: Contemporary Stories by Am Indians.* 1974. Viking. 1st ed. edit Kenneth Rosen. NF/NF. B4. $150.00

ANTHOLOGY. *Modern Poets: An American-British Anthology.* 1963. McGraw Hill. 1st ed. sgn contributors. F/F. B4. $125.00

ANTHOLOGY. *Prize Stories 1961: The O Henry Awards.* 1961. Doubleday. 1st ed. edit Richard Poirier. F/NF. B4. $85.00

ANTHOLOGY. *Queen's Gift Book.* nd. London. Hodder Stoughton. ne. pl. 160p. G+. S11. $35.00

ANTHOLOGY. *Sparrow 37-48.* 1975-1976. Blk Sparrow. 1/50. sgn most contributors. unp. brn cloth. F. H5. $250.00

ANTHOLOGY. *Statments: New Fiction From the Fiction Collective.* 1975. Braziller. 1st wrp ed. inscr contributors. F/wrp. B4. $85.00

ANTHOLOGY. *Stony Brook Holographs 1968.* 1968. Stony Brook Poetics. 1st ed. sgns. 1/10 sets of 7 broadside poems. B4. $2,500.00

ANTHOLOGY. *Thirty Favorite Paintings by American Artists.* 1908. NY. Collier. obl folio. ils Remington/Parrish/Smith/ Christy, etc. NF. D6. $125.00

ANTHOLOGY. *Treasury of Scripture Knowledge.* 1982. MacDonald. VG. B20. $9.50

ANTHOLOGY. *Tribute to Jim Lowell.* 1967. Cleveland. Ghost. 1st ed. NF/wrp. B2. $100.00

ANTHOLOGY. *Wayside Willow: Prose & Verse.* 1945. Trenton. Wht Eagle. 1st ed. intro/sgn MacInnes. F/VG. B4. $125.00

ANTHOLOGY. *Who Took the Weight?* 1972. Little Brn. 1st ed. F/chip. B2. $30.00

ANTHOLOGY. *Wings From the Wind.* 1964. Lippincott. 1st ed. ils Tasha Tudor. 119p. brd/cloth spine. VG/VG. A3. $40.00

ANTHONY, Earl of Shaftesbury. *Character- istics of Men, Manners, Opinions, Times.* 1714. London. 3 vol. 2nd ed. VG. A15. $225.00

ANTHONY, Evelyn. *Albatross.* 1982. Hutchinson. 1st ed. VG/VG. P3. $20.00

ANTHONY, Evelyn. *Anne Boleyn.* 1986. Century. VG/VG. P3. $15.00

ANTHONY, Evelyn. *Company of Saints.* 1983. Hutchinson. 1st ed. F/dj. P3. $20.00

ANTHONY, Evelyn. *Grave of Truth.* 1979. Hutchinson. 1st ed. F/F. P3. $18.00

ANTHONY, Evelyn. *Janus Imperative.* 1980. Coward McCann. 1st ed. VG/torn. P3. $13.00

ANTHONY, Evelyn. *Mission to Malaspiga.* 1974. CMG. 1st ed. VG/VG. P3. $20.00

ANTHONY, Evelyn. *Persian Price.* 1975. CMG. 1st ed. VG/VG. P3. $15.00

ANTHONY, Evelyn. *Scarlet Thread.* 1990. Harper Row. 1st ed. F/F. P3. $19.00

ANTHONY, Evelyn. *Silver Falcon.* 1977. Coward McCann. 1st ed. VG/VG. P3. $12.00

ANTHONY, Evelyn. *Voices on the Wind.* 1985. Hutchinson. 1st ed. VG/dj. P3. $15.00

ANTHONY, Gordon. *Ballet, Camera Stud- ies.* 1937. London. Bles. 1st ed. 96 tipped-in pl. gilt wht/red cloth. NF. F1. $175.00

ANTHONY, John. *About Tunisia.* 1961. London. Bles. inscr pres. 221p. cloth. VG/dj. W1. $15.00

ANTHONY, Katharine. *Susan B Anthony: Her Personal History & Her Era.* 1954. Dou- bleday. 1st ed. 8vo. 521p. VG. V3. $15.00

ANTHONY, Piers. *And Eternity.* 1990. Mor- row. 1st ed. F/F. F4. $17.00

ANTHONY, Piers. *Bearing an Hourglass.* 1984. Del Rey. 1st ed. F/F. P3. $20.00

ANTHONY, Piers. *Demons Don't Dream.* 1993. Tor. 1st ed. F/F. P3. $20.00

ANTHONY, Piers. *For Love of Evil.* 1988. Morrow. 1st ed. F/F. F4. $17.00

ANTHONY, Piers. *Fractal Mode.* 1992. Ace Putnam. 1st ed. F/F. F4. $16.00

ANTHONY, Piers. *Ghost.* 1986. Tor. 1st ed. F/F. P3. $15.00

ANTHONY, Piers. *Hard Sell.* 1990. Tafford. 1st ed. F/F. F4. $18.00

ANTHONY, Piers. *Isle of Woman.* 1993. Tor. 1st ed. NF/dj. P3. $24.00

ANTHONY, Piers. *On a Pale Horse.* 1983. Del Rey. 1st ed. F/F. P3. $22.00

ANTHONY, Piers. *Out of Phaze.* 1987. Ace Putnam. 1st ed. F/F. P3. $18.00

ANTHONY, Piers. *Pornucopia.* 1989. Tafford. 1st ed. F/dj. M2. $35.00

ANTHONY, Piers. *Shade of the Tree.* 1986. Tor. 1st ed/ F/F. P3. $16.00

ANTHONY, Piers. *Unicorn Point.* 1989. Ace Putnam. 1st ed. F/F. P3. $16.00

ANTHONY, Piers. *Wielding a Red Sword.* 1986. Del Rey. 1st ed. F/F. P3. $17.00

ANTHONY, Piers. *With a Tangled Skein.* 1985. Del Rey. 1st ed. F/F. P3. $20.00

ANTHONY & KORNWISE. *Through the Ice.* 1989. Underwood Miller. 1st ed. F/dj. M2. $35.00

ANTON, Ferdinand. *Art of Ancient Peru.* 1972. Putnam. 1st Am ed. sm folio. 368p. VG. F3. $125.00

ANTON, Ferdinand. *Art of the Maya.* 1970. NY. Putnam. 1st Am ed. 344p. NF/VG. P4. $75.00

ANTONGINI, Tom. *D'Annunzio.* 1938. Boston. 1st Am ed. photos/index. 583p. NF. A17. $15.00

ANTONIADI, E.M. *Planet Mercury.* 1974. Devon, UK. 8vo. trans Patrick Moore. 83p. VG. K5. $30.00

ANTUNANO, J.A. Sanchez. *Practical Edu- cation of the Bird Dog.* 1965 (1931). Chicago. Am Field. 9th prt. ils. 164p. VG/wrp. R2. $15.00

ANVIL, Christopher. *Strangers in Paradise.* 1976. Herbert Jenkins. 1st ed. F/F. P3. $20.00

APPEL, Benjamin. *We Were There in the Klondike Gold Rush.* ca 1956. Grosset Dun- lap. 8vo. 175p. VG/worn. P4. $25.00

APPEL. *Fantastic Mirror, SF Across the Ages.* 1969. np. ils. 139p. VG/G. A4. $30.00

APPELBAUM, David. *Contact & Attention: Anatomy...Metaphysical Method.* 1986. WA, DC. Center Advanced Research Phe- nomenology. F. G1. $14.00

APPLE, Max. *Three Stories.* 1983. Dallis. 1/226. sgn. gr cloth/prt labels. F/clear acetate. A11. $45.00

APPLEBY. John. *Bad Summer.* 1958. Wash- burn. 1st ed. VG. P3. $10.00

APPLEGARTH, Margaret T. *Mission Messen- ger.* 1967. St Louis. 192p. VG/dj. B29. $4.00

APPLEGARTH, Margaret T. *Twelve Baskets Full.* 1957. Harper. 245p. VG/torn. B29. $4.00

APPLEGATE, Frank G. *Native Tales of NM.* 1932. Lippincott. 1st ed. intro Mary Austin. 263p. NF. B19. $55.00

APPLEGATE, Jesse A. *Day With the Cow Column.* 1990. Ye Galleon. 1st ed thus. new intro. pict ep/bdg. M. A18. $17.50

APPLETON, Victor. *Desert of Mystery.* 1953. Children's Pr. 1st ed. VG/VG. P3. $15.00

APPLETON, Victor. *Movie Boys Under Fire (#9).* 1926 (1918). Garden City. lists 17 titles. 218p. NF. M20. $25.00

APPLETON, Victor. *Tom Swift & Big Dirigi- ble (#33).* 1930. Grosset Dunlap. 1st ed. lists to #32. 214p. VG/dj. M20. $65.00

APPLETON, Victor. *Tom Swift & His Atomic Earth Blaster.* nd. Grosset Dunlap. VG. P3. $8.00

APPLETON, Victor. *Tom Swift & His Big Tunnel (#19).* 1916. Grosset Dunlap. lists to #33. 218p. VG/dj. M20. $30.00

APPLETON, Victor. *Tom Swift & His Chest of Secrets (#28).* 1925. Grosset Dunlap. lists to #29. 219p. VG/dj. M20. $50.00

APPLETON, Victor. *Tom Swift & His Elec- tric Locomotive (#25).* 1922. Grosset Dunlap. lists to #33. 212p. VG/dj. M20. $45.00

APPLETON, Victor. *Tom Swift & His Elec- tronic Retroscop.* nd. Grosset Dunlap. VG. P3. $10.00

APPLETON, Victor. *Tom Swift & His Giant Robot.* nd. Grosset Dunlap. VG. P3. $8.00

APPLETON, Victor. *Tom Swift & His Jetma- rine.* 1954. Grosset Dunlap. VG/G. C8. $20.00

APPLETON, Victor. *Tom Swift & His Motor Cycle.* nd. Grosset Dunlap. G/VG. P3. $15.00

APPLETON, Victor. *Tom Swift & His Motorboat (#2).* 1910. Grosset Dunlap. lists to #22. VG/2 djs. M20. $35.00

APPLETON, Victor. *Tom Swift & His Ocean Airport (#37).* 1934. Grosset Dunlap. 214p. orange cloth. VG. M20. $40.00

APPLETON, Victor. *Tom Swift & His Out- post in Space.* 1955. Grosset Dunlap. 12mo. VG/VG. C8. $20.00

APPLETON, Victor. *Tom Swift & His Planet Stone (#38?).* 1935. Grosset Dunlap. 203p. orange cloth. VG. M20. $65.00

APPLETON, Victor. *Tom Swift & His Space Solartron.* nd. Grosset Dunlap. VG. P3. $10.00

APPLETON, Victor. *Tom Swift & His Spec- tromarine Select.* nd. Grosset Dunlap. VG. P3. $10.00

APPLETON, Victor. *Tom Swift & His Sub- marine Boat (#4).* 1910. Grosset Dunlap. lists to #28. VG/dj. M20. $50.00

APPLETON, Victor. *Tom Swift & His Talk- ing Pictures.* nd. Whitman. VG. P3. $10.00

APPLETON, Victor. *Tom Swift & His Ultra- sonic Cycloplan.* nd. Grosset Dunlap. VG. P3. $8.00

APPLETON, Victor. *Tom Swift & His 3-D Telejector.* nd. Grosset Dunlap. VG. P3. $15.00

APPLETON, Victor. *Tom Swift & the Land of Wonders (#20).* 1917. Grosset Dunlap. lists to #36. 218p. VG/VG. M20. $45.00

APPLETON, Victor. *Tom Swift in the Caves of Ice.* nd. Grosset Dunlap. VG. P3. $15.00

APPLETON, Victor. *Tom Swift Jr & His Jetmarine.* 1954. Grosset Dunlap. VG/frayed. M2. $15.00

APPLETON. *Typological Tally: 1300 Writings in Eng Prt Hist...* 1973. np. 1/1250. 95p. F/VG. A4. $35.00

APSLEY, Lady. *Bridleways Through History.* 1936. London. Hutchinson. later prt. VG. O3. $40.00

ARAGO, M. *Analyse de la Vie et Des Travaus de Sir Wm Herschel.* 1843. Paris. Bachelier. 367p. VG. B14. $85.00

ARASTEH, A. Reza. *Rumi: The Persian, the Sufi.* 1974. London. Routledge. 1st ed. 196p. cloth. VG/dj. G1. $27.50

ARBERRY, A.J. *Discourses of Rumi.* 1961. London. Murray. 1st ed. 276p. cloth. VG/dj. W1. $45.00

ARBERRY, A.J. *More Tales From the Masnavi.* 1963. London. Allen Unwin. 1st ed. 8vo. cloth. VG/dj. W1. $35.00

ARBERRY, A.J. *Mystical Poems of Rumi.* 1968. Chicago/London. 202p. cloth. VG. W1. $28.00

ARBERRY, A.J. *Sufi Martyr.* 1969. London. Allen Unwin. 1st ed. 8vo. VG. W1. $25.00

ARBUS, Diane. *Magazine Work.* 1984. Millerton. Aperture. 1st ed. 4to. NF/NF. S9. $75.00

ARBUTHNOT, J. *Works...* 1770. London. 2 vol. new ed. VG-. A15. $120.00

ARBUTHNOT, May Hill. *Children & Books.* 1947. Scott Foresman. ils. 626p. VG. M10. $8.50

ARCH, E.L. *Bridge to Yesterday.* 1963. Avalon. 1st ed. F/F. P3. $20.00

ARCHER, Jeffrey. *First Among Equals.* 1984. Hodder Stoughton. 1st ed. F/F. P3. $20.00

ARCHER, Jeffrey. *First Among Equals.* 1984. Linden Pr. 1st ed. F/F. P3. $18.00

ARCHER, Jeffrey. *Prodigal Daughter.* nd. BC. VG/G. P3. $6.00

ARCHER, Jeffrey. *Shall We Tell the President?* 1977. Viking. 1st ed. VG/VG. P3. $20.00

ARCHIBALD, Joe. *Cather's Choice.* 1958. MacRae Smith. later prt. xl. G/G. P8. $10.00

ARCHIBALD, William. *Day in the Life of a Clown.* 1963. Stein Day. probable 1st ed. lg 4to. F/G. C8. $25.00

ARCIERI, John. *Circulation of Blood in Andrea Cesalpino of Arezzo.* 1945. NY. 1st ed. 193p. A13. $75.00

ARD, William. *.38.* 1952. Rinehart. 1st ed. F/NF. B2. $25.00

ARDEN, William. *Goliath Scheme.* 1971. Dodd Mead. 1st ed. VG/VG. P3. $15.00

ARDIES, Tom. *Palm Springs.* 1978. Doubleday. 1st ed. 8vo. F/F. A8. $22.50

ARDIZZONE, Edward. *Book for Eleanor Farjeon. A Tribute to Her Life & Work...* 1966. NY. Henry Walck. 1st Am ed. 8vo. 184p. VG/G+. A3. $25.00

ARDIZZONE, Edward. *Funnybone Alley.* 1927. NY. 1st ed. 7 mtd pl. VG+. M5. $90.00

ARDIZZONE, Edward. *Nicholas & the Fast-Moving Diesel.* 1959. Walck. 1st ed thus. ils. cloth. F/VG. M5. $35.00

ARDIZZONE, Edward. *Tim & Ginger.* 1965. Walck. ils. unp. VG/dj. M20. $30.00

ARDIZZONE, Tony. *Evening News.* 1986. Athens, GA. 1st ed. sgn. F/F. A11. $30.00

ARDIZZONE, Tony. *Heart of the Order.* 1986. Holt. 1st ed. M/M. P8. $15.00

ARDREY, Robert. *Territorial Imperative: Personal Inquiry...* 1966. Atheneum. 1st ed. ils Berdine Ardrey. 390p. VG/VG. S11. $20.00

ARDREY, Robert. *Worlds Beginning.* 1944. DSP. 2nd ed. VG/VG. P3. $20.00

ARENDT, Hannah. *Human Condition.* 1958. Chicago. 1st prt. 332p. VG/dj. G1. $45.00

ARFA, Hassan. *Kurd: Hist & Political Study.* 1966. Oxford. 1st ed. pl/maps. 178p. NF/dj. W1. $26.00

ARGAN, Guilio Carlo. *Henry Moore.* nd (1972). Abrams. sq 4to. gilt brn cloth. VG/dj. F1. $75.00

ARGENTI, Philip P. *Expedition of Colonel Favier to Chios.* 1933. London. 8vo. pres. ils/maps. 383p. uncut. O2. $200.00

ARGYLL, Duke of. *Intimate Society Letters of the 18th Century.* 1910. London. Stanley Paul. 2 vol. 8vo. teg. Riviere gr crushed morocco. NF. F1. $165.00

ARIETI, Silvano. *American Handbook of Psychiatry. Vol 1.* 1959. Basic. G. K4. $15.00

ARIOSTO, Lodovico. *Il Negromate Comedia di Mes.* 1535. np. 12mo. 66p. wrp. H4. $125.00

ARIOSTO, Ludovico. *Orlando Furioso...* 1596. Venice. Misserino. ils. unp. VG. H10. $125.00

ARISHIMA, Takeo. *Chiisaki-Mono-E (To Little Children).* 1984. Tokyo. Bijou. 30x27mm. 1/50 (200 total). 127p. teg. gr paper brd. F/case. B24. $300.00

ARISTOPHANES. *Frogs.* 1937. Holland. LEC. ils/sgn John Austen. F/case. M19. $75.00

ARISTOTLE. *De Poetica Liber.* 1760. Oxford. Typographeo Clarendoniano. 132p. calf. VG. K1. $175.00

ARISTOTLE. *On Parts of Animals. Trans, With an Intro & Notes by W Ogle.* 1882. London. 1st Eng trans. 263p. A13. $200.00

ARISTOTLE. *Works of...Trans Into Eng Under Editorship WD Ross.. Vol 7.* 1927. Clarendon. unp. 390p. F/torn. G1. $65.00

ARKIN, Arthur M. *Mind in Sleep: Psychology & Psychophysiology.* 1978. Lawrence Erlbaum Assoc. 565p. dj. K4. $20.00

ARKIN, Stephen. *Venetian Masks.* 1989. Mill Valley. Figment. 68x74mm. 1/75. sgn printer/Diane Weiss. 30p. M. B24. $225.00

ARLEN, Michael J. *Passage to Ararat.* 1975. FSG. 4th prt. 293p. cloth. NF/dj. W1. $10.00

ARMATAGE. *Horse.* 1894. London. 1st ed. 272p. G+. R2. $20.00

ARMBRUSTER, Wally. *It's Still Lion Vs Christian in Corporate Arena.* 1979. Concordia. 116p. G/torn. B29. $3.50

ARMBRUSTER & TAYLOR. *Astronaut Training.* 1990. Franklin Watts. 64p. laminated pict brd. VG. K5. $10.00

ARMER, Laura Adams. *Cactus.* 1934. NY. ils. 102p. VG/torn. B26. $34.00

ARMER, Laura Adams. *Forest Pool.* 1938. Longman Gr. 1st ed. 40p. NF/G. P2. $75.00

ARMES, George A. *Ups & Downs of an Army Officer.* 1900. WA, DC. lg 8vo. 784p. silver stp brn cloth. scarce. K1. $250.00

ARMITAGE, Angus. *John Kepler.* 1966. London. Faber. 8vo. 194p. VG/VG. K5. $30.00

ARMITAGE, Flora. *Desert & the Stars.* 1955. Holt. 2nd prt. 318p. gilt brn brd. NF/NF. M7. $18.00

ARMITAGE, Merle. *Accent on America.* 1944. NY. Wyehe. 1st ed. sgn. 1/325. NF. S9. $125.00

ARMITAGE, Merle. *Brett Weston Photographs.* 1956. NY. 1st ed. VG/VG. B5. $100.00

ARMITAGE, Merle. *Dance Memoranda.* 1946. DSP. 2nd ed. inscr/dtd 1950. gilt bl cloth/prt brd. NF/gray dj. F1. $125.00

ARMITAGE, Merle. *Homage to the Santa Fe.* 1973. Manzanita. 1st ed. photos. 141p. NF/NF. B19. $50.00

ARMOUR, George Denholm. *Bridle & Brush: Reminiscences of Artist Sportsman.* nd. Eyre Spottiswoode/Scribner. 1st ed. 4 pl. VG. O3. $45.00

ARMOUR, Margaret. *Eerie Book.* 1981. Castle. VG/VG. P3. $13.00

ARMOUR, Richard. *It All Started With Hippocrates*. 1966. NY. ils. 136p. dj. G7. $15.00

ARMSTRONG, Campbell. *Mambo*. 1990. NY. Harper. ARC/1st ed. sgn. F/NF. S6. $35.00

ARMSTRONG, Charlotte. *Balloon Man*. nd. BC. VG. P3. $8.00

ARMSTRONG, Charlotte. *Black-Eyed Stranger*. 1952. Peter Davies. 1st ed. G/VG. P3. $10.00

ARMSTRONG, Charlotte. *Charlotte Armstrong Treasury*. 1972. McCann Geoghegan. BC. VG/G+. M21. $5.00

ARMSTRONG, Charlotte. *Chocolate Cobweb*. 1948. Coward McCann. 1st ed. inscr. F/VG. M15. $35.00

ARMSTRONG, D.M. *Bodily Sensations*. 1962. London. Kegan Paul. 128p. VG/dj. K4. $10.00

ARMSTRONG, H.C. *Grey Wolf, Mustafa Kemal*. May 1938. Harmondsmith. Penguin. 4th imp. sc. VG/VG. M7. $11.50

ARMSTRONG, H.C. *Lord of Arabia*. 1939. Harmondsworth. Penguin. 2nd prt. 247p. VG. M7. $10.00

ARMSTRONG, Margaret. *Blue Santo Murder Mystery*. 1941. Random House. 1st ed. VG. P3. $30.00

ARMSTRONG, Margaret. *Fanny Kemble: Passionate Victorian*. 1938. Macmillan. 1st ed. 387p. xl. G+. H1. $3.50

ARMSTRONG, Margaret. *Five Generations, Life & Letters of an American Family*. 1930. Harper. 1st ed. photos. 425p. VG. S11. $30.00

ARMSTRONG, Martin. *Saint Hercules & Other Stories*. 1927. London. Fleuron. 1/310. tall 4to. 65p. patterned cloth brd. F. B24. $375.00

ARMSTRONG, William Clinton. *Patriotic Poems of New Jersey*. 1906. NJ Soc Sons of Am Revolution. 8vo. 248p. VG. B11. $60.00

ARMSTRONG, William H. *Barefoot in the Grass: Story of Grandma Moses*. 1970. Doubleday. 1st ed. ils. 96p. VG/G. A3. $15.00

ARMSTRONG & ARMSTRONG. *Prayer Poems*. 1942. Abingdon Cokesbury. 256p. G. B29. $3.50

ARNALDUS, De Villa Nova. *Opera Utilissima...* (1548). Venice. Tramezino. 8vo. 136p. 18th-C bdg. K1. $500.00

ARNEMAN, J. *Magazin fur die Wundarzneiwissenschaft...* 1797. Gottingen. 116p. limp wrp. G7. $60.00

ARNOLD, Edmund C. *Ink on Paper: Handbook of the Graphic Arts*. 1963. NY. ils/index. 323 p. VG. A17. $15.00

ARNOLD, Edwin L. *Phra the Phoenician*. 1917. Putnam. VG. P3. $35.00

ARNOLD, Edwin. *Japonica. With Ils by Robert Blum*. 1891. Scribner. 1st ed. 4to. 128p. pict cloth. VG. M1. $150.00

ARNOLD, H.J.P. *Man in Space: Ils Hist of Spaceflight*. 1993. Smithmark, NY. 240p. F/F. K5. $30.00

ARNOLD, James. *Farm Wagons & Carts*. 1978. Newton Abbott. 2nd prt. obl sm 4to. VG/VG. O3. $45.00

ARNOLD, Janis. *Daughters of Memory*. 1991. Algonquin. 1st ed/author's 1st book. NF/NF. A14. $25.00

ARNOLD, Josias Lyndon. *Poems*. 1797. Providence. Carter Wilkinson. 12mo. contemporary calf. VG. K1. $125.00

ARNOLD, Julian B. *Giants in Dressing Gowns*. 1942. Chicago. Argus. 1st ed. 242p. gilt bl cloth. F. M7. $45.00

ARNOLD, Magda B. *Emotion & Personality*. 1960. Columbia. 2 vol. VG/dj. K4. $50.00

ARNOLD, William Harris. *First Report of a Book-Collector...* 1898. Dodd Mead. 2nd ed. 12mo. 143p. cloth. M1. $150.00

ARNOLD, William Harris. *Ventures in Book Collecting*. 1923. Scribner. G+. N2. $17.50

ARNOW, H. *Hunter's Horn*. 1949. NY. 1st ed. VG/VG. B5. $35.00

ARNTZEN & RAINWATER. *Guide to the Literature of Art History*. 1980. np. 4to. 634p. VG. A4. $80.00

ARONICA, MCCARTHY & STOUT. *Full Spectrum 2* 1989. BC. 1st ed. F/F. P3. $20.00

ARRILAGA, Francisco C. *Cardiacos Negros*. 1912. Buenos Aires. orig thesis bdg w/6 additional rpts. half calf. G7. $295.00

ARTAUD, Antonin. *Artaud Le Momo*. 1947. Lyon. Bordas. 1st ed. sgn. 1/300 on Johannot. F/wrp/dj. B4. $1,500.00

ARTELT, Walter. *Einfuhrung in die Medizinhistorik*. 1949. Stuttgart. Enke. 240p. G7. $65.00

ARTHUR, Elizabeth. *Antarctic Navigation*. 1994. Knopf. ARC. F/pict wrp. B3. $35.00

ARTHUR, R.A. *3rd Marine Division*. 1948. WA. 1st ed. VG. C11. $75.00

ARTHUR, Robert. *Mystery of the Talking Skull*. 1969. Random. G/VG. P3. $7.00

ARTHUR, Stanley Clisby. *Jean Laffite, Gentleman Rover*. 1952. New Orleans. Harmanson. 8vo. 3 pl. 282p. VG/stiff wrp. T7. $35.00

ARTHUR, T.S. *Orange Blossoms, Fresh & Faded*. ca 1885. Phil. Porter Coates. early Alta Ed rpt. 8vo. 415p. VG/rare dj. C6. $85.00

ARTHUR, T.S. *Stories for Good Boys*. 1830s. NY. Cozans. 64p. pict brd. G. B14. $150.00

ARTZYBASHEFF, Boris. *Seven Simeons*. 1937. Viking. 1st ed. VG/G. P2. $75.00

ARVIDSON, Lloyd A. *Hamlin Garland: Centennial Tributes & Checklist...* 1962. CA U Lib Bulletin 9. 1st ed. sc. F. A18. $17.50

ASBURY, H. *French Quarter. An Informal Hist of New Orleans Underworld*. 1938. Garden City. 8vo. ils. 462p. VG/G. B11. $15.00

ASBURY, H. *Suckers Progress*. 1938. NY. 1st ed. VG/VG. B5. $35.00

ASCH, Sholem. *Apostle*. 1943. Putnam. 1st ed. 754p. VG/dj. W1. $10.00

ASCHNER, Bernhard. *Die Krise der Medizin Konstitutionstherapie...* 1928. Stuttgart. 562p. G7. $35.00

ASCHOFF, Ludwig. *Lectures on Pathology Delivered in the US*. 1959. NY. Hoeber. 365p. G7. $45.00

ASCHOFF & DIEPGEN. *Kurze Ubersichtstabelle zur Geschichte der Medizin*. 1920. Munchen. 37p. prt wrp. G7. $35.00

ASH, Edward C. *New Book of the Dog*. 1938. London. Cassell. 1st ed. ils. 534p. cloth. F. R2. $45.00

ASH & LAKE. *Bizarre Books*. 1985. St Martin. ils. 180p. F/F. A4. $45.00

ASH & LAKE. *Bizarre Books*. 1985. St Martin. 1st ed. 180p. VG/VG. S11. $25.00

ASHBERY, John. *Self-Portrait in Convex Mirror*. 1975. Viking. 1st ed. 8vo. 83p. NF/clip. C6. $95.00

ASHBERY, John. *Some Trees*. 1956. Yale. Series Younger Poets. 1st ed. sgn. NF/VG. V1. $225.00

ASHBROOK, H. *Murder of Steven Kester*. 1931. Coward McCann. G/VG. P3. $20.00

ASHDOWN, Clifford. *From a Surgeon's Diary*. 1977. Phil. Oswald Train. 1st ed. ils Wm Dixon. F/F. T2. $15.00

ASHDOWN, Clifford. *Queen's Treasure*. 1975. Phil. Oswald Train. 1st ed. F/F. T2. $15.00

ASHE, Gordon; see Creasey, John.

ASHE, Sydney W. *Electric Railways*. 1907. Van Nostrand. 2nd ed. 285p. G. N2. $20.00

ASHFORD, Jeffrey. *Double Run*. 1973. Walker. 1st ed. VG/VG. P3. $20.00

ASHFORD, Jeffrey. *Honourable Detective*. 1988. St Martin. 1st ed. VG/VG. P3. $15.00

ASHFORD, Jeffrey. *Question of Principle*. 1986. St Martin. 1st ed. VG/VG. P3. $15.00

ASHFORD, Jeffrey. *Recipe for Murder*. 1980. Walker. F/F. P3. $13.00

ASHLEY, Bernard. *Weather Men*. 1974 (1970). London. Allman. 8vo. 120p. VG. K5. $14.00

ASHLEY, Clifford W. *Ashley Book of Knots.* ca 1944. Doubleday. rpt. ils of knots. 620p. VG. T7. $30.00

ASHLEY, Maurice. *John Wildman: Plotter & Postmaster.* 1947. New Haven. Yale. VG. N2. $10.00

ASHRAF PAHLAVI, Princess. *Faces in a Mirror: Memoirs From Exile.* 1980. Prentice Hall. 1st ed. 8vo. 32pl. VG/dj. W1. $18.00

ASHTON, James M. *Ice-Bound.* 1928. Putnam. 1st ed. ils/fld map. 235p. VG. P4. $50.00

ASHWAL, Stephen. *Founders of Child Neurology.* 1990. San Francisco. 935p. G7. $105.00

ASIMOV, GREENBERG & WAUGH. *Science-Fictional Solar System.* 1979. Harper Row. 1st ed. F/VG+. M21. $20.00

ASIMOV, GREENBERG & WAUGH. *Short Science Fiction Novels.* 1985. Bonanza. VG/VG. P3. $15.00

ASIMOV, GREENBERG & WAUGH. *7 Deadly Sins of Science Fiction.* nd. BC. VG/VG. P3. $8.00

ASIMOV, Isaac. *Alternate Asimovs.* 1986. Doubleday. 1st ed. F/F. P3. $20.00

ASIMOV, Isaac. *Asimov Chronicles.* 1989. Dark Harvest. ltd ed. sgn. 1/500. F/case. M2. $100.00

ASIMOV, Isaac. *Asimov Chronicles.* 1989. Dark Harvest. 1st ed. F/F. P3. $22.00

ASIMOV, Isaac. *Asimov on Astronomy.* 1974. Doubleday. VG. P3. $20.00

ASIMOV, Isaac. *Asimov's Sherlockian Limericks.* 1978. Mysterious. 1st ed. F/frayed. M2. $25.00

ASIMOV, Isaac. *Before the Golden Age Trilogy.* 1988. Blk Cat. F/F. P3. $20.00

ASIMOV, Isaac. *Before the Golden Age.* 1974. Doubleday. 1st ed. VG/VG. P3. $25.00

ASIMOV, Isaac. *Choice of Catastrophes.* 1979. Simon Schuster. 1st ed. VG. P3. $23.00

ASIMOV, Isaac. *Clock We Live On.* 1959. Abelard Schuman. 8vo. ils. 160p. G/dj. K5. $10.00

ASIMOV, Isaac. *Collapsing Universe: Story of Black Holes.* nd (1977). NY. Walker. 6th prt. VG/dj. K5. $12.00

ASIMOV, Isaac. *Counting the Eons.* 1984. Granada. 1st ed. VG. P3. $20.00

ASIMOV, Isaac. *Double Planet.* 1967. Abelard Schuman. VG. P3. $20.00

ASIMOV, Isaac. *Edge of Tomorrow.* 1985. Tor. 1st ed. F/F. P3. $16.00

ASIMOV, Isaac. *Extraterrestrial Civilizations.* 1979. Crown. 1st ed. F/F. T2. $15.00

ASIMOV, Isaac. *Fantastic Voyage II.* 1987. Doubleday. 1st ed. VG/VG. P3. $19.00

ASIMOV, Isaac. *Foundation & Earth.* 1986. Doubleday. 1st ed. F/F. P3. $20.00

ASIMOV, Isaac. *Foundation's Edge.* 1982. Doubleday. UP. NF/prt wrp. B3. $85.00

ASIMOV, Isaac. *Foundation's Edge.* 1982. Whispers. 1st ed. 1/1000. F/sans. P3. $85.00

ASIMOV, Isaac. *In the Beginning.* 1981. Crown. 1st ed. F/F. F4. $20.00

ASIMOV, Isaac. *Jupiter, the Largest Planet.* 1973. Lothrop Lee Shepard. sm 4to. 224p. xl. dj. K5. $7.00

ASIMOV, Isaac. *Lucky Starr & Pirates of Asteroids.* 1978. Gregg. 1st ed. VG/VG. P3. $20.00

ASIMOV, Isaac. *Lucky Starr & the Rings of Saturn.* 1978. Gregg. VG/VG. P3. $18.00

ASIMOV, Isaac. *Murder at the ABA.* 1976. Doubleday. 1st ed. F/VG. M15. $30.00

ASIMOV, Isaac. *Opus 100.* 1969. Houghton Mifflin. 1st ed. VG/VG. P3. $50.00

ASIMOV, Isaac. *Opus 200.* 1979. Houghton Mifflin. 1st ed. NF/NF. P3. $20.00

ASIMOV, Isaac. *Robots & Empire.* 1985. Doubleday. 1st ed. F/F. P3. $17.00

ASIMOV, Isaac. *Robots of Dawn.* 1983. Doubleday. 1st ed. F/F. P3. $8.00

ASIMOV, Isaac. *Satellites in Outer Space.* 1960. Random. sm 4to. 79p. VG/dj. K5. $12.00

ASIMOV, Isaac. *Satellites in Outer Space.* 1960. Random. 1st ed. NF/VG+. M21. $45.00

ASIMOV, Isaac. *Short Fantasy Novels.* 1984. Greenwich. 1st ed. VG/VG. P3. $15.00

ASIMOV, Isaac. *Today & Tomorrow &...* 1973. Doubleday. 1st ed. VG/G. P3. $30.00

ASIMOV, Isaac. *Universe, From Flat Earth to Quasar.* 1966. NY. Walker. lg 8vo. 308p. xl. dj. K5. $14.00

ASIMOV & GREENBERG. *Visions of Fantasy.* 1989. Doubleday. 1st ed. F/F. P3. $15.00

ASIMOV & LAURANCE. *Who Done It?* 1980. Boston. Houghton. 1st ed. sgn Ball/Davis/Hoch/Moyes/Pronzini. F/F. S6. $40.00

ASIMOV & SILVERBERG. *Positronic Man.* 1993. Doubleday. 1st ed. F/F. P3. $22.00

ASIMOV & SILVERBERG. *Ugly Little Boy.* 1992. Doubleday. 1st ed. F/F. $23.00

ASINOF, E. *Eight Men Out.* 1963. NY. 1st ed. VG/G. B5. $35.00

ASMOUS, Vladimir. *Fontes Historiae Botanicae Rossicae.* 1947. Chronica Botanica. 28p. bl wrp/protective sleeve. A10. $25.00

ASPRIN, Robert L. *Bug Wars.* 1979. St Martin. 1st ed. VG/VG. P3. $20.00

ASQUITH, Cynthia. *This Mortal Coil.* 1947. Arkham. 1st ed. F/dj. M2. $110.00

ASQUITH, Cynthia. *This Mortal Coil.* 1947. Arkham. 1st ed. NF/NF. P3. $80.00

ASQUITH & EARL OF OXFORD. *Fifty Years of British Parliament.* 1926. Little Brn. 590p. VG. M20. $18.00

ASTAIRE, Fred. *Steps in Time.* 1959. NY. ARC/1st ed. sgn. VG/VG. B5. $125.00

ATATURK, Mustapha Kemal. *Speech Delivered by Ghazi...October 1927.* 1929. Leipzig. 8vo. Harry Howard's copy. buckram. O2. $60.00

ATENBERG, Peter. *Evocations of Love.* 1960. Simon Schuster. 1st ed thus. ils Alexander King. copper cloth. F/case. F1. $25.00

ATGET, Eugene. *Vision of Paris.* 1963. NY. Macmillan. 1st ed. photos/inscr/dtd Berenice Abbott. VG+/VG. S9. $400.00

ATHEARN, Robert G. *High Country Empire, the High Plains & Rockies.* 1960. NE U. ils/photos. G. B34. $8.00

ATHEARN, Robert G. *Mythic West in 20th-Century America.* 1986. KS U. 1st ed. ils/index. F/dj. A18. $30.00

ATHELING, William. *Issue at Hand.* 1964. Advent. 1st ed. VG. P3. $45.00

ATHERTON, Gertrude. *Conqueror.* (1902). Macmillan. 4th prt. 546p. G. H1. $7.00

ATHERTON, Gertrude. *Splendid Idle Forties.* 1903. np. VG. B19. $20.00

ATHERTON, Nancy. *Aunt Dimity & the Duke.* 1994. Viking. 1st ed. sgn. F/F. B3. $30.00

ATKINS, Fred C. *Mushroom Growing Today.* 1956 (1950). London. 3rd ed. ils/photos. 200p. dj. B26. $10.00

ATKINSON, Linda. *Mother Jones: The Most Dangerous Woman in America.* 1978. NY. Crown. photos. G. V4. $8.00

ATKINSON, Minnie. *Hist of First Religious Soc in Newburyport, MA.* 1933. Newburyport. 1st ed. 104p. cloth. NF. M8. $37.50

ATKINSON, Oriana. *Big Eyes.* 1949. NY. 1st ed. VG/dj. A17. $10.00

ATLA-ULLAH, Mohammed. *Citizen of 2 Worlds.* 1960. Harper. 285p. cloth. VG/torn. W1. $12.00

ATLEE, Philip; see Philips, James Atlee.

ATLEE, Samuel Yorke. *Religion of the Sun, a Posthumous Poem of Thomas Paine...* 1826. Phil. 1st ed. 12mo. 2-toned brd. uncut. M1. $175.00

ATTANASIO, A.A. *Beast Marks.* 1984. Ziesing. 1st ed. sgn. F/F. P3. $45.00

ATTANASIO, A.A. *Hunting the Ghost Dancer.* 1991. Harper Collins. 1st ed. F/F. P3. $22.00

ATTANASIO, A.A. *In Other Worlds.* 1984. Morrow. 1st ed. VG/VG. P3. $20.00

ATTANASIO, A.A. *Wyvern.* 1988. Ticknor Fields. 1st ed. F/F. P3. $25.00

ATTAR, Farid Ud-Din. *Conference of Birds.* 1954. London. Janus. 1st ed. 147p. NF/dj. W1. $22.00

ATTORPS, Gosta. *De Tre Musketorerna och Andra Essayer.* 1938. Stockholm. 1st Swedish ed. 159p. NF/tan wrp. uncut. M7. $45.00

ATTWATER, Donald. *Christian Churches of the East...* 1962. Milwaukee. 8vo. ils. 260p. dj. O2. $20.00

ATTWATER, Donald. *Dictionary of Popes From Peter to Pius XII.* (1939). London. Catholic BC. 337p. H10. $15.00

ATWATER, George Parkin. *Annals of a Parrish: Chronicle of Founding & Growth...* 1928. np. 1st ed. 67p. cloth. NF. M8. $37.50

ATWATER, Mary. *Shuttle-Craft Book of American Hand-Weaving.* 1961. Macmillan. 1st revised ed. 341p. VG/dj. F3. $15.00

ATWOOD, Margaret. *Bluebeard's Egg.* 1983. McClelland Stewart. 1st ed. F/F. P3. $25.00

ATWOOD, Margaret. *Bodily Harm.* 1982. Simon Schuster. 1st ed. sgn. F/VG. B3. $40.00

ATWOOD, Margaret. *Cat's Eye.* 1989. London. Bloomsbury. 1st ed. sgn. F/F. B4. $85.00

ATWOOD, Margaret. *Dancing Girls & Other Stories.* 1977. McClelland Stewart. 1st Canadian ed. F/NF. B3. $75.00

ATWOOD, Margaret. *Good Bones.* 1992. London. Bloomsbury. 1st ed. NF/F. B3. $45.00

ATWOOD, Margaret. *Handmaid's Tale.* 1985. McClelland Stewart. 1st ed. VG/VG. P3. $30.00

ATWOOD, Margaret. *Journals of Susanna Moodie.* 1970. Toronto. Oxford. 1st ed. sgn. VG/wrp. L3. $100.00

ATWOOD, Margaret. *Life Before Man.* 1979. McClelland Stewart. 2nd ed. VG/VG. P3. $15.00

ATWOOD, Margaret. *Life Before Man.* 1979. Simon Schuster. 1st ed. sgn. F/VG. B3. $40.00

ATWOOD, Margaret. *Power Politics.* 1971. Harper. ARC/1st Am ed. RS. NF/dj. B4. $125.00

ATWOOD, Margaret. *Robber Bride.* 1993. Doubleday. 1st ed. sgn. F/F. B3. $25.00

ATWOOD, Margaret. *Robber Bride.* 1993. Toronto. McClelland Stewart. 1st ed. sgn. F/F. B4. $85.00

ATWOOD & STOLOROW. *Structures of Subjectivity.* 1984. Hillsdale, NJ. Erlbaum. later prt. 132p. VG/dj. G1. $22.50

AUBIN, N. *Cheats & Illusions of Romanish Priests & Exorcists.* 1703. Lonodn. 1st/only Eng ed. no spine label. VG. A15. $225.00

AUBREY, Edward. *Sherlock Holmes in Dallas.* 1980. Dodd. 1st Am ed. F/NF. S6. $25.00

AUCHINCLOSS, Louis. *Edith Wharton: A Woman in Her Time.* 1971. NY. 1st ed. sgn. F/VG clip. A11. $40.00

AUCHINCLOSS, Louis. *Motiveless Malignity.* 1969. Houghton Mifflin. 1st ed. F/NF. B4. $75.00

AUCHINCLOSS, Louis. *Narcissa & Other Fables.* 1983. Houghton Mifflin. UP/1st ed. 213p. F/wrp. C6. $30.00

AUCHINCLOSS, Louis. *Pioneers & Caretakers: Study of 9 Am Women Novelists.* 1965. Minneapolis. 1st ed. F/VG. B4. $75.00

AUCHINCLOSS, Louis. *Venus in Sparta.* 1958. Houghton Mifflin. 1st ed. F/NF. B4. $85.00

AUDEMARS, Pierre. *And One for the Dead.* 1981. Walker. VG/VG. P3. $13.00

AUDEN, W.H. *Another Time.* 1940. London. Faber. 1st ed. NF/G. V1. $65.00

AUDEN, W.H. *Biography of Humphrey Carpenter.* 1981. Houghton Mifflin. 1st ed. F/VG. V1. $20.00

AUDEN, W.H. *City Without Walls.* 1969. London. Faber. 1st ed. sgn. F/NF. V1. $45.00

AUDEN, W.H. *Collected Poetry of...* 1958. Random. 13th prt. sgn. F/F. B2. $95.00

AUDEN, W.H. *Dyer's Hand.* 1962. NY. 1st ed. VG. A17. $15.00

AUDEN, W.H. *Dyer's Hand.* 1962. Random. 1st ed. NF/NF. S9. $45.00

AUDEN, W.H. *Epistle to a Godson.* 1972. Random. 1st ed. sgn. F/VG+. V1. $25.00

AUDEN, W.H. *For the Time Being.* 1944. Random. 1st Am ed. sgn. NF/VG. V1. $65.00

AUDEN, W.H. *Look Stranger.* 1936. London. Faber. 1st ed. sgn. NF/VG. V1. $50.00

AUDEN, W.H. *On This Island.* 1937. Random. 1st ed. sgn. NF/VG. V1. $65.00

AUDEN, W.H. *Poems (Second Edition With Some New Poems).* 1933. London. Faber. 1st ed. VG/dj. Q1. $150.00

AUDEN, W.H. *Selected Poems.* 1938. London. Faber. 1st ed. sgn. NF/VG. V1. $100.00

AUDEN, W.H. *Shield of Achilles.* 1955. Random. 1st ed. F/NF. B4. $85.00

AUDEN & ISHERWOOD. *Ascent of F6: Tragedy in 2 Acts.* 1937. Random. 1st Am ed. 8vo. 123p. beige cloth. VG. C6. $275.00

AUDEN & ISHERWOOD. *Dog Beneath the Skin.* 1935. NY. 1st ed. NF/sm tear. V1. $145.00

AUDEN & ISHERWOOD. *Tragedy in 2 Acts: Ascent of F6.* 1936. London. Faber. 1st ed. 123p. gilt bl cloth. VG. M7. $45.00

AUDIN. *Le Livre Francais.* 1929. Paris. 60 pl. 80p. VG. A4. $40.00

AUDLJO, John. *Journal of Visit to Constantinople...1833.* 1835. London. 1st ed. 8vo. 259p. recent half morocco. VG. W1. $165.00

AUDOUIN-DUBREUIL & HAARDT. *Le Raid Citreon. La Premiere Traversee du Sahara Automobile.* 1924. Paris. 4to. sgns. ils Movel. full maroon leather. F/gilt case. F1. $600.00

AUEL, Jean M. *Clan of the Cave Bear.* 1980. Crown. 1st ed. VG/VG. P3. $40.00

AUEL, Jean M. *Clan of the Cave Bear.* 1980. NY. Crown. UP. VG/wrp. B4. $250.00

AUEL, Jean M. *Mammoth Hunters.* 1985. Crown. 1st ed. VG/VG. P3. $20.00

AUEL, Jean M. *Mammoth Hunters.* 1985. NY. UP. VG+/wrp. A15. $40.00

AUEL, Jean M. *Plains of Passage.* 1990. Crown. 1st ed. NF/NF. P3. $25.00

AUEL, Jean M. *Valley of the Horses.* 1982. NY. Crown. 1st ed. F/clip. B3. $40.00

AUGUR, Helen. *Zapotec.* 1954. Doubleday. 1st ed. 279p. VG/dj. F3. $20.00

AUGUST, John. *Advance Agent.* 1944. Tower. 2nd ed. G+/dj. P3. $8.00

AUGUSTINOS, Gerasimos. *Greeks of Asia Minor.* 1992. NY. 8vo. frontis map. 270p. cloth. dj. O2. $30.00

AUGUSTINOS, Olga. *French Odysseys. Greece in French Travel Literature...* 1994. Baltimore. 8vo. 345p. cloth. dj. O2. $36.00

AUGUSTUS, Albert Jr.; see Neutzel, Charles.

AURAND, A. Monroe Jr. *Hist Account of Mollie Maguires & James McKenna McParlan.* 1940. Harrisburg. Aurand. 1st ed. NF/wrp. B2. $75.00

AURELIUS ANTONIUS, Marcus. *Dei Seipso et ad Seipsum Libri XII.* 1643. London. Flesher. 2 parts in 1. 8vo. contemporary vellum. K1. $350.00

AUSTER, Paul. *Disappearances.* 1988. Overlook. 1st ed. 8vo. 126p. beige brd. F/clip. H5. $40.00

AUSTER, Paul. *Ghosts.* 1986. Los Angeles. 1st ed. sgn. F/F. A11. $50.00

AUSTER, Paul. *In the Country of Last Things.* 1987. Viking. 1st ed. VG/VG. P3. $16.00

AUSTER, Paul. *Invention of Solitude.* 1982. NY. 1st ed. sgn. F/8vo wrp. A11. $55.00

AUSTER, Paul. *Leviathan.* 1992. Viking. ARC. F. B2. $40.00

AUSTER, Paul. *Leviathan.* 1992. Viking. 1st ed. inscr. F/F. B2. $45.00

AUSTER, Paul. *Moon Palace.* 1989. London. Faber. 1st ed. VG/clip. B3. $35.00

AUSTER, Paul. *Moon Palace.* 1989. Viking. 1st ed. sgn. F/F. B4. $85.00

AUSTER, Paul. *Mr Vertigo.* 1994. Viking. ARC. F/wrp. B2. $40.00

AUSTIN, Alicia. *Age of Dreams.* 1978. Donald Grant. 1st ed. F/dj. M2. $40.00

AUSTIN, Alicia. *Age of Dreams.* 1978. Donald Grant. 1st ed. VG/VG. P3. $35.00

AUSTIN, Anne. *Murder at Bridge.* nd. Grosset Dunlap. VG. P3. $10.00

AUSTIN, Cyril. *Edward Buttoneye & His Adventures.* early 1900s. Nister. ils Hilda Austin. pict brd. VG. M5. $60.00

AUSTIN, Hugh. *Murder of a Matriarch.* 1936. Crime Club. 1st ed. VG. P3. $30.00

AUSTIN, Margot. *Trumpet.* 1943. Dutton. 1st ed. ils. VG+/G. M5. $40.00

AUSTIN, Mary. *Flock.* 1906. Houghton Mifflin. 1st ed. ils E Boyd Smith. teg. pict bdg. VG. A18. $75.00

AUSTIN, Mary. *Literary America 1903-1934: The Mary Austin Letters.* 1979. Greenwood. 1st ed. M/sans. A18. $15.00

AUSTIN, Mary. *Western Trails: Collecton of Short Stories by...* 1987. NV U. 1st ed. M/dj. A18. $25.00

AUSTIN, R.B. *Early American Medical Imprints 1668-1820.* 1977. Boston. 240p. G7. $15.00

AUSTING, G.R. *World of Red-Tailed Hawk.* 1964. Phil. 1st ed. VG/VG. B5. $25.00

AUSUBEL, David P. *Theory & Problems of Child Development.* 1958. Grune Stratton. 607p. dj. K4. $25.00

AVALLONE, Michael. *Blue Leader.* 1979. Arbor. VG/VG. P3. $15.00

AVALLONE, Michael. *Dead Game.* 1954. Holt. 1st ed. author's agent's copy. VG/VG. P8. $125.00

AVALLONE, Michael. *Spitting Image.* 1953. Henry Holt. 1st ed. G+/dj. P3. $25.00

AVALLONE, Michael. *Splitting Image.* 1953. Henry Holt. 1st ed. 2nd Ed Noon novel. xl. VG/VG. A17. $10.00

AVALLONE, Michael. *Time of Reckoning.* 1977. Playboy. 1st ed. VG/VG. P3. $18.00

AVALLONE, Michael. *Viper Three.* 1971. Macmillan. 1st ed. VG/VG. P3. $20.00

AVEDON, Richard. *In the American West.* 1985. Abrams. 1st ed. folio. photos. NF. photo ils cloth. NF. S9. $150.00

AVEDON, Richard. *Observations. Photographs by Richard Avedon.* 1959. Simon Schuster. 1st ed. folio. prt brd. F/glassine/case. B24. $300.00

AVEDON, Richard. *Portraits.* 1976. NY. 1st ed. VG/VG. B5. $90.00

AVENARIUS, Johann. *Hoc Est, Liber Radicum seu Lexicon Ebraicum...* 1589. Wittenberg. 2nd ed. Hebrew/Latin text. 860p. contemporary pigskin. K1. $1,250.00

AVENI, Anthony. *Archeoastronomy in Pre-Columbian America.* 1977 (1975). TX U. 2nd ed. gray cloth. G. K5. $30.00

AVENI, Anthony. *Native American Astronomy.* 1979 (1977). TX U. 2nd ed. 4to. ils. 286p. gray cloth. G. K5. $35.00

AVERILL, Esther. *Captains of the City Streets.* 1972. Harper Row. 1st ed. 147p. VG/VG. P2. $35.00

AVERILL, Esther. *Flash, the Story of a Horse, Coach Dog & Gypsies.* May 1934. London. Faber. possible 1st ed. VG. C8. $35.00

AVERILL, Esther. *How the Brothers Joined the Cat Club.* 1959 (1953). Kingswood Surrey. 1st UK ed. pict brd. NF/NF. C8. $35.00

AVERILL, Esther. *Voyages of Jacques Cartier.* (1937). NY. Domino. ltd ed. 1/3000. ils Rojankovsky. rusty-red cloth. NF/VG. D6. $75.00

AVERILL, Naomi. *Whistling-Two-Teeth & Forty-Nine Buffalos.* 1939. Grosset Dunlap. 1st ed. ils. VG+/G+. P2. $100.00

AVERY, David. *Poem on the Origin & Suppression of Late Rebellion.* 1865. Willimantic. 1st ed. 12mo. 24p. prt wrp. M1. $125.00

AVERY, Karen. *Beauty & the Beast.* 1976. Intervisual Communications. mechanical pop-up. F. C8. $50.00

AVERY, Karen. *Beauty & the Beast.* 1976. Chatto Windus. Peepshow Book. mechanical pop-up. F. C8. $60.00

AVERY, Samuel P. *Short List of Microscopic Books in Lib of Grolier Club.* 1911. NY. sm 8vo. 30p. biographical listing of 176 titles. F/wrp. B24. $150.00

AVERY, V. *Big Book of Applique.* 1978. np. VG/wrp. G2. $12.95

AVI. *Man From the Sky.* 1992. Morrow Jr Books. 1st ed. 120p. F/F. A3. $13.00

AXELSON & COMISKEY. *Commy.* 1919. Chicago. 1st ed. VG/VG photocopy. B5. $175.00

AXFORD, Joseph Mack. *Around Western Campfires.* 1964. NY. 1st ed. inscr. 262p. G/dj. B18. $45.00

AXTON, David; see Koontz, David R.

AYE, Lillian. *Iran Caboose.* 1952. Hollywood. House Waarven. 2nd prt. 190p. NF/dj. W1. $12.00

AYER, Alfred Jules. *Foundations of Empirical Knowledge.* 1953. London. Macmillan. 4th prt. 276p. bl cloth. VG. G1. $35.00

AYER, Alfred Jules. *Metaphysics & Common Sense.* 1970. San Francisco. Freeman Cooper. 267p. ES. VG/dj. G1. $28.50

AYER, Alfred Jules. *Revolution in Philosophy.* 1956. London. Macmillan. 2nd prt. 12mo. VG/VG. G1. $27.50

AYRES, Atlee B. *Mexican Architecture: Domestic, Civil & Ecclesiastical...* (1926). NY. Helburn. folio. 150 pl. gilt gr cloth. VG. K1. $150.00

AYRES, Paul; see Aarons, Edward S.

AYRES, Ruby M. *Planter of the Tree.* (1927). Grosset Dunlap. 298p. VG/G. H1. $3.50

AYRTON, Michael. *Testament of Daedalus.* 1962. London. Methuen. 1st ed. 8vo. bl cloth/brd. F/NF. F1. $30.00

AYSCOUGH, Florence. *Autobiography of a Chinese Dog.* 1926. Houghton Mifflin. 1st ed. 105p. VG+. R2. $60.00

AZAIIS, Pierre Hyacinthe. *Compensations Dans les Destinees Humaines.* 1818. Paris. 3 vols. 3rd revised/enlarged ed. VG. G1. $125.00

B

B.F.; see Goffstein, Brooke.

BAAKLINI, Abdo I. *Legislative & Political Development: Lebanon, 1842-1972.* 1976. Durham. Duke. M11. $25.00

BABBITT, John G. *Babbitt Brothers Trading Company.* 1967. private prt. sgn. F. B19. $50.00

BABCOCK, Philip H. *Falling Leaves.* 1937. Derrydale. 1/950. F. H4. $150.00

BABSON, Marian. *Death Warmed Up.* 1982. NY. Walker. 1st Am ed. sgn. F/F. S6. $35.00

BABSON, Marian. *Murder, Murder, Little Star.* 1977. Collins Crime Club. 1st ed. VG/VG. P3. $20.00

BABSON, Marian. *Pretty Lady.* 1990. Walker. 1st ed. F/F. P3. $16.00

BABSON, Marian. *There Must Be Some Mistake.* nd. St Martin. 1st ed. F/F. P3. $14.00

BABSON, Naomi L. *I Am Lidian.* 1960. np. VG/dj. B34. $25.00

BABULA, William. *St John & the Seven Veils.* 1991. Birch Lane. 1st ed. F/F. P3. $16.00

BACH, Richard. *Bridge Across Forever.* 1984. Morrow. 1st ed. VG/VG. P3. $20.00

BACHE, Richard Meade. *American Wonderland.* 1871. Phil. Claxton Remsen Haffelfinger. 1st ed. G. M20. $45.00

BACHE & BACHE. *When Mother Lets Us Make Candy.* 1915. NY. Moffat Yard. G+. H7. $30.00

BACHELARD, Gaston. *Study of Husserl's Formal & Transcental Logic.* 1968. NW U. 1st Eng-language ed. russet cloth. G1. $22.50

BACHMAN, Richard; see King, Stephen.

BACHMANN, Alberto. *Encyclopedia of the Violin.* 1929. NY. Appleton. 470p. gilt gr cloth. VG. F1. $85.00

BACHMANN, Lawrence. *Lorelei.* 1957. Crime Club. VG/torn. P3. $8.00

BACK, Joe. *Horses, Hitches & Rocky Trails.* 1959. Sage Books. 8th prt. VG/dj. B34. $30.00

BACKEBERG, Curt. *Wunderwelt Kakteen.* 1961. Jena. 1st ed. ils. 242p. red lettered yel cloth. VG. B26. $125.00

BACKEBERG & KNUTH. *Kaktus — ABC.* 1935. Copenhagen. pres. Danish text. photos. 432p. new brn buckram. F. B26. $125.00

BACKES, Magnus. *Art of Dark Ages.* 1969. Abram. ils. 263p. VG. M10. $15.00

BACKHOUSE, James. *Memoir...by His Sister.* 1877. Wm Sessions. 2nd ed. 16mo. 191p. cloth. V3. $22.00

BACON, Francis. *Essays of Francis Bacon.* 1944. LEC. ils/sgn Bruce Rogers. F/box. M19. $75.00

BACON, Francis. *Novum Organum.* 1902. Am Home Lib. 290p. G. H1. $4.50

BACON, Francis. *Novum Organum; or, True Suggestions Intrepretation Nature.* 1850. London. Pickering. 16mo. 323p. ochre cloth. VG. G1. $35.00

BACON, Francis. *Of Gardens.* 1959. Northampton. Gehenna. 1/200. ils/sgn Baskin. F/floral wrp. B24. $350.00

BACON, Francis. *Sylva Sylvarum; or, Natural Historie.* 1635. London. William Lee. folio. old calf. K1. $475.00

BACON, Frank. *Lightnin'.* nd. Grosset Dunlap. photoplay ed. VG. P3. $25.00

BACON, Frank. *Lightnin'.* 1920. Grosset Dunlap. 282p. VG/dj. M20. $40.00

BACON, George W. *Bacon's Guide to American Politics; or, A Complete View...* 1863. London. Sampson Low/Bacon. 12mo. 94p. bl pebbled cloth. H9. $500.00

BACON, Gertrude. *Balloons, Airships & Flying Machines.* 1905. NY. 1st Am ed. ils. 124p. pict cloth. xl. G. B18. $75.00

BACON, John. *Liber Regis, del Thesaurus Rerum Ecclesiaticarum.* 1786. London. Nichols. contemporary paper-backed brd. untrimmed. M11. $150.00

BACON, Leonard. *Christian Unity: A Sermon...* 1845. New Haven. 1st ed. 43p. VG/prt wrp. M8. $15.00

BACON, Margaret Hope. *Rebellion at Christiana.* 1975. NY. Crown. 2nd prt. 8vo. 216p. G/dj. V3. $12.00

BACON & GODWYN. *Hist of Reigns of Henry VII, Henry VIII, Edward VI...* 1676. London. Scot Basset. folio. 202p. calf. K1. $350.00

BADCOCK, G. *Hist of Transport Services of Egyptian Expeditionary Force.* 1925. London. Hugh Rees. 1st ed. ils/diagrams/charts/fld map. bl cloth. VG. M7. $65.00

BADDELEY, John F. *Rugged Flanks of Caucasus.* 1940. Oxford. 2 vol. 1st ed. 4to. 38 pl. rebound half calf/red label. O2. $650.00

BADDELEY, John F. *Russian Conquest of the Caucasus.* 1908. London. 4to. maps/plans. 518p. cloth. extremely scarce. O2. $275.00

BADEEB, Saeed M. *Saudi-Egyptian Conflict Ove North Yemen.* 1986. Boulder, CO. Westview. 148p. NF/dj. W1. $20.00

BADER, Barbara. *American Picture Books From Noah's Ark to Beast Within.* 1976. Macmillan. ils. 615p. F/dj. F1. $100.00

BAEDEKER. *Austria.* 1929. Leipzig. 12th ed. F. O2. $40.00

BAEDEKER. *Austria.* 1929. np. VG. M17. $20.00

BAEDEKER. *Deutschland Nebst Theilen Angrenzenden Lander Strassburg...* 1862. Coblenz. 10th ed. O2. $225.00

BAEDEKER. *Die Rheinlande.* 1862. Coblenz. 12th ed. loose front cover. O2. $225.00

BAEDEKER. *Holland.* 1927. Leipzig. 26th ed. F. O2. $50.00

BAEDEKER. *Mediterranean Sea Port & Sea Routes...* 1911. Baedeker. 1st ed. 38 maps/49 plans. 607p. VG. W1. $75.00

BAEDEKER. *Palestine & Syria.* 1894. Leipzig. 3rd ed. very scarce. O2. $100.00

BAEDEKER. *Rhine.* 1911. np. VG/VG. M17. $50.00

BAEDEKER. *Southern Italy & Sicily.* 1876. Leipzig. 6th ed. lg map (rpr). O2. $75.00

BAEDEKER. *Spain & Portugal.* 1901. Leipzig. 2nd ed. 12mo. 608p. G. W1. $30.00

BAEDEKER. *Switzerland & Adjacent Portions of Italy, Savoy & Tyrol.* 1869. Coblenz. 4th ed. split in rear hinge. O2. $150.00

BAENSCH, Ulrich. *Tropical Aquarium.* 1983. Tetra. VG. P3. $6.00

BAER, Dallas C. *Messages of the Prophets to Their Day & Ours.* 1940. Pulpit. 152p. G. B29. $4.00

BAER & WOODRUFF. *Commodity Exchanges.* 1935. Harper. red cloth. VG. M11. $45.00

BAEZ, Joan. *And a Voice To Sing With.* 1987. Summit. 1st ed. VG/dj. N2. $10.00

BAGBY, George. *Murder on the Nose.* 1938. Doubleday Crime Club. 1st ed. NF/NF. M15. $40.00

BAGBY, George. *Starting Gun.* 1948. Crime Club. 1st ed. G/VG. P3. $12.00

BAGBY, George. *Tough Get Going.* 1977. Crime Club. 1st ed. VG. P3. $13.00

BAGLEY, David T. *Reports of Cases Determined in Supreme Court of State CA.* 1862. Sacramento. self pub. vol 19 in series. contemporary sheep. M11. $75.00

BAGLEY, Desmond. *Bahama Crisis.* 1981. BC Assoc. VG. P3. $10.00

BAGLEY, Desmond. *Enemy.* 1978. BC. 1st ed. VG. P3. $18.00

BAGLEY, Desmond. *Juggernaut.* 1985. Collins. 1st ed. VG. P3. $20.00

BAGLEY, Desmond. *Spoilers.* 1969. Collins. 1st ed. F. P3. $23.00

BAGLEY, Desmond. *Tightrope Men.* 1973. Collins. 1st ed. VG. P3. $25.00

BAGLEY, Helen. *Sand in My Shoe.* 1980. Homestead. 1st ed. 8vo. 268p. F/F. A8. $40.00

BAHR, Edith-Jane. *Nice Neighbourhood.* 1973. Collins Crime Club. 1st ed. VG. P3. $15.00

BAIKIE, James. *Through the Telescope.* 1906. London. Blk. 8vo. ils. 292p. gilt bl cloth. G. K5. $40.00

BAILEY, Alice A. *Reappearance of the Christ.* 1948. NY. Lucis. 1st ed. 189p. bl cloth. VG. B33. $18.00

BAILEY, Alice Cooper. *Kimo: The Whistling Boy. A Story of Hawaii.* nd. Wise Parslow. ils Lucille Holling. 96p. G+. A3. $12.50

BAILEY, Bernadine. *Iceland in Story & Pictures.* 1942. Chicago. ils Kurt Wiese. pict bl cloth. F. B14. $45.00

BAILEY, Bernadine. *Pictured Geography: Venezuela in Story & Pictures.* 1942. Chicago. 1st ed. ils Kurt Wiese. cloth. F/F. B14. $45.00

BAILEY, Brian. *Almshouses.* 1988. London. 1st ed. 208p. VG/dj. A13. $35.00

BAILEY, Chris. *200 Years of American Clocks & Watches.* 1975. Prentice Hall. 4to. 255p. F/G+. A8. $40.00

BAILEY, H.C. *Case for Mr. Fortune.* 1932. Canada. Doubleday Doran. VG/VG. P3. $45.00

BAILEY, H.C. *Meet Mr. Fortune.* 1942. Book League. VG. P3. $22.00

BAILEY, H.C. *Mr Clunk's Text.* 1939. Crime Club. 1st ed. F/NF. F4. $45.00

BAILEY, H.C. *Sullen Sky Mystery.* 1935. Crime Club. 1st ed. G/VG. P3. $25.00

BAILEY, H.J. *Reminiscences of a Christian Life.* 1885. Portland, ME. Hoyt Fogg Donham. 3rd ed. 12mo. 419p. pres slip. V3. $12.00

BAILEY, Hamilton. *Emergency Surgery.* 1930. Wood. 2 vol. NF. G7. $50.00

BAILEY, J.O. *Pilgrims Through Time & Space.* 1947. Argus. 1st ed. NF/NF. M2. $40.00

BAILEY, L.H. *Garden-Making.* 1906 (1898). NY. 11th ed. ils. 417p. VG. B26. $27.50

BAILEY, L.H. *Standard Cyclopedia of Horticulture.* 1943. NY. 3 vol. corrected ed. ils/pl/engravings. VG+/dj. B26. $175.00

BAILEY, Richard. *Neither Carpetbaggers Nor Scalawags.* 1991. Montgomery. 1st ed. 500p. F/NF. B2. $30.00

BAILEY, Samuel. *Letters on Philosophy of Human Mind.* 1855. London. Longman Brn Gr. 8vo. w/catalog. VG. G1. $285.00

BAILEY, Temple. *Adventures in Girlhood.* 1925. Phil. ils Clara Peck. F/F. A17. $7.50

BAILEY, Thomas A. *Diplomatic Hist of Am People.* 1941. NY. 3rd prt. 806p. VG. A17. $10.00

BAILEY, Thomas John. *Ordinum Sacrorum in Ecclesia Anglicana Defensio...* 1870. London. Parker. 1st ed. folio. VG. H10. $95.00

BAILEY, William Whitman. *My Boyhood at West Point.* 1891. Providence, RI. 1st ed. 1/250. prt wrp. M8. $45.00

BAILEY & BUCHANAN. *Intracranial Tumors of Infancy & Childhood.* 1948. Chicago. 2nd imp. 23 pl. 598p. G. G7. $85.00

BAILLIE, G.H. *Watchmakers & Clockmakers of the World.* 1976. London. NAG Pr. 8vo. 373p. VG. A8. $20.00

BAILLIE, John. *Belief in Progress.* 1951 (1950). London. Cumberlege. 2nd prt. 12mo. VG/clip. G1. $22.50

BAILLY, Jean Sylvain. *Lettres sur l'Origine des Sciences...* 1777. London. Elmesly. 1st ed. 348p. contemporary calf. K1. $150.00

BAILYN & BAILYN. *Massachusetts Shipping 1697-1714.* 1959. Cambridge. Harvard. 1st ed. 148p. burgundy cloth. VG/VG. P4. $35.00

BAIN, Alexander. *Logic. Part First: Deduction; Part Second: Induction.* 1870. London. Longman Gr Reader Dyer. 2 vols. 12mo. VG. G1. $175.00

BAIN, Alexander. *Mental & Moral Science: Compendium of Psychology & Ethics.* 1883 (1868). London. Longman Gr. 3rd revised ed/later prt. ruled mauve cloth. VG. M20. $65.00

BAIN, Alexander. *Mental Science: Compendium of Psychology & Hist Philosophy.* 1973. Arno. Classics Psychology Series. 428p. prt gray cloth. G1. $35.00

BAINBRIDGE, George C. *Fly Fisher's Guide, Ils by Coloured Plates...* 1816. Liverpool. 1st ed. 8vo. 150p. calf. M1. $550.00

BAINBRIDGE, William Sims. *Dimensions of Science Fiction.* 1986. Harvard. 1st ed. P3. $20.00

BAIRD, William Raimond. *American College Fraternities.* 1890. NY. James P Downs. 4th ed. VG. N2. $20.00

BAK & BAK. *On Top of This...* 1968. Chicago. 2nd/revised ed. sgn. 50 full-p linoleum cuts. VG+. F1. $60.00

BAKER, Carol. *Boy & the Lion on the Wall.* 1969. Franklin Watts. 4to. F/VG. B17. $10.00

BAKER, Cecily Mary. *Little Book of Old Rhymes.* nd. Blackie. 12 mc pl. bl/wht ep. checkered-pattern brd. NF/dj. M5. $75.00

BAKER, Clyde. *Modern Gunsmithing.* 1933. Samworth. VG/G+. A1. $50.00

BAKER, David. *Conquest: Hist of Space Achievements...* 1984. London. Holland Clark. pb. ils. 191p. K5. $20.00

BAKER, Denys Val. *Family at Sea.* 1981. William Kimber. 1st ed. F. P3. $20.00

BAKER, Denys Val. *Phantom Lovers.* 1984. William Kimber. 1st ed. VG. P3. $20.00

BAKER, Denys Val. *When Cornish Skies Are Smiling.* 1984. William Kimber. 1st ed. VG. P3. $20.00

BAKER, Don. *Fresh New Look at God.* 1986. Multnomah. sgn. 153p. VG/dj. B29. $4.50

BAKER, George. *Opuscula Medica, Iterrum Edita.* 1771. London. Hughs. 228p. orig full polished calf/morocco label. G7. $145.00

BAKER, Henry. *Employment for the Microscope, in Two Parts.* 1764. London. 2nd ed. 450p. VG. B14. $350.00

BAKER, Henry. *Microscope Made Easy; or, Nature, Uses & Magnifying Powers.* 1754. London. Dodsley. 4th ed. 309p. sheepskin. VG. B14. $250.00

BAKER, Houston Jr. *Long Black Song. Essays in Black Am Literature & Culture.* 1972. Charlottesville, VA. 1st ed/author's 1st solo book. F/NF. B2. $60.00

BAKER, Houston Jr. *No Matter Where You Travel, You Still Be Black.* 1979. Detroit. Lotus. 1st ed. F/wrp. B2. $40.00

BAKER, Houston Jr. *Singers of Daybreak.* 1974. WA, DC. 1st ed. F/NF. B2. $45.00

BAKER, James Robert. *Tim & Peter.* 1993. Simon Schuster. 1st ed. rem mk. F/F. A14. $25.00

BAKER, James. *Turkey.* 1877. NY. tall 8vo. 495p. rebacked/orig spine. xl. O2. $150.00

BAKER, Jean-Claude. *Josephine: The Hungry Heart.* 1993. Random. 1st ed. F/F. S9. $30.00

BAKER, Kevin. *Sometimes You See It Coming.* 1993. NY. Crown. 1st ed/author's 1st book. rem mk. F/F. A14. $25.00

BAKER, Margaret. *Little Girl Who Curtsied to the Owl.* nd (1925). London. Werner Laurie. silhouette ils Mary Baker. VG. P2. $25.00

BAKER, Michael. *Doyle Diary.* 1978. Paddington. VG. P3. $12.00

BAKER, Nicholson. *Mezzanine.* 1988. NY. 1st ed/author's 1st book. F/clip. B3. $100.00

BAKER, Nicholson. *Mezzanine.* 1988. NY. 1st ed/author's 1st novel. sgn. F/F. A11. $125.00

BAKER, Nicholson. *Mezzanine.* 1989. London. Granta/Penguin. 1st ed/author's 1st book. NF/F. A14. $30.00

BAKER, Nicholson. *Vox.* 1992. London. 1st UK ed. sgn. F/gilt wrp. A11. $50.00

BAKER, Nicholson. *Vox.* 1992. Random. AP. F/wrp. B2. $100.00

BAKER, Nicholson. *Vox.* 1992. Random. 1st ed. NF/NF. A14. $45.00

BAKER, Richard M. *Death Stops the Rehearsal.* 1937. Scribner. 1st ed. VG. P3. $35.00

BAKER, Robert H. *Astronomy.* 1964. Van Nostrand. 8th ed. 8vo. 557p. gr cloth. G. K5. $12.00

BAKER, Robert H. *Universe Unfolding: Story of Man's Increasing Comprehension.* 1932. Baltimore. Williams Wilkins. 8vo. 140p. bl cloth. G. K5. $8.00

BAKER, Robert L. *Oil, Blood & Sand: States & Strategy in Middle East.* 1942. Appleton Century. 1st ed. 300p. VG/tattered. W1. $20.00

BAKER, Roger. *Marilyn Monroe.* 1990. Portland. VG. P3. $25.00

BAKER, S. *Permissible Lie.* 1968. Cleveland. 236p. NF. D3. $12.50

BAKER, S.W. *Exploration of Nile Tributaries of Abyssinia.* 1868. Hartford. OD Case. 1st Am ed. 608p. gilt plum cloth. F. F1. $185.00

BAKER, T. Lindsay. *Water for the SW.* 1973. Am Soc Civil Engineers. 1st ed. ils/notes/index. 204p. NF/wrp. B19. $35.00

BAKER, Victor R. *Channels of Mars.* 1982. TX. 1st ed. 198p. VG/dj. B18. $35.00

BAKER, Willard F. *Bob Dexter & the Storm Mountain Mystery (#3).* 1925. Cupples Leon. lists to this title. 250p. VG/worn. M20. $20.00

BAKER, Willard F. *Boy Ranchers (#1).* 1921. Cupples Leon. 1st ed. lists 3 titles. 210p. VG/VG. M20. $12.00

BAKER, William A. *Sloops & Shallops.* 1966. Barre, MA. ils. 174p. dj. T7. $35.00

BAKER & BAKER. *Doctor Who-Ultimate Foe.* 1988. WH Allen. TVTI. F. P3. $14.00

BAKER & BAKER. *Water Elf & the Miller's Child.* 1928. Duffield. 1st ed. ils/silhouettes. cloth. VG/G. M5. $75.00

BAKER & MERLEN. *America's First Woman Astronomer, Maria Mitchell.* 1962. NY. Messner. 3rd prt. ils. 192p. VG/dj. K5. $25.00

BAKER. *Bibliography of British Book Ils 1860-1900.* 1978. np. 1/1000. ils. 197p. F/VG. A4. $125.00

BAKEWELL, Charles M. *Plato the Republic.* 1928. Scribner. 426p. red cloth. G1. $22.50

BAKHASH, Shaul. *Reign of the Ayatollahs.* 1984. NY. Basic Books. 1st ed. 276p. VG/dj. W1. $20.00

BALCHIN, Nigel. *Seen Dimly Before Dawn.* 1964. Rpt Soc. VG. P3. $8.00

BALDERSTON. *Census of Manuscripts of Oliver Goldsmith.* 1926. Brick Row Book Shop. 73p. VG/case. A4. $95.00

BALDICK, Robert. *Pages From the Goncourt Journal.* 1962. Oxford. 1st Eng ed. 434p. F/F. A17. $17.50

BALDWIN, Alfred L. *Theories of Child Development.* 1967. Wiley. 599p. VG. K4. $15.00

BALDWIN, Caleb C. *Manual of the Foochow Dialect.* 1871. Foochow. Methodist Episcopal Mission. 1st ed. 8vo. 256p. M1. $175.00

BALDWIN, Ernest. *Dynamic Aspects of Biochemistry.* 1949. Cambridge. 164p. G/dj. K4. $6.00

BALDWIN, James Mark. *Individual & Soc; or, Psychology & Sociology.* 1911. London. Rebman Ltd. 1st Eng ed. 12mo. 210p. rose cloth. scarce. G1. $50.00

BALDWIN, James. *If Beale Street Could Talk.* 1974. Dial. AP. VG/wrp. B2. $65.00

BALDWIN, James. *Tell Me How Long the Train's Been Gone.* 1968. Dial. 1st ed. F/NF. B2. $50.00

BALDWIN, Joseph G. *Flush Times of AL & MS: Series of Sketches.* 1853. Appleton. 1st ed. 330p. VG. E5. $85.00

BALDWIN, L. *Keelboat Age on Western Waters.* 1941. Pittsburgh. 1st ed. VG/VG. B5. $45.00

BALDWIN, Louis. *Hon Politician, Mike Mansfield of MT.* 1979. np. F/F. B34. $10.00

BALDWIN, Marshall W. *Mediaeval Church.* 1963. Ithaca. 8th prt. 8vo. 124p. VG. W1. $8.00

BALDWIN, Oliver. *Oasis.* 1936. London. Grayson. 2nd imp. 8vo. 320p. VG. W1. $20.00

BALDWIN, Ruth. *100 19th-Century Rhyming Alphabets...from Lib R Baldwin.* 1972. np. 4to. 296p. F/VG. A4. $45.00

BALDWIN & MEAD. *Rap on Race.* 1971. Lippincott. 1st ed. NF/NF. B2. $35.00

BALDWIN. *Nigerian Literature: Bibliography of Criticism.* 1980. np. 163p. NF. A4. $25.00

BALET, Jan. *Amos & the Moon.* 1948. Oxford. 1st ed. ils. VG/VG. P2. $35.00

BALFOUR, Arthur James. *Foundations of Belief: Being Notes...Theology.* 1895. London. Longman. 1st ed. 356p. w/sgn letter. H10. $125.00

BALFOUR, Michael. *Stonehenge & Its Mysteries.* 1980. Scribner. sm 4to. ils/photos. 189p. VG/VG. K5. $25.00

BALFOUR. *Opinions & Arguments From Speeches & Addresses 1910-1927.* 1928. Doubleday Doran. 1st ed. 301p. VG. H1. $9.50

BALKIN. *Writer's Guide to Book Publishing.* 1977. np. 250p. VG/G. A4. $25.00

BALL, Alice E. *Bird Biographies.* 1924. Dodd Mead. 2nd prt. 56 mc pl. 295p. VG. H1. $22.50

BALL, John. *Cop Cade.* 1978. Crime Club. 1st ed. VG. P3. $15.00

BALL, John. *Eyes of Buddah.* 1976. Boston. Little Brn. 1st ed. inscr. F/F. S6. $37.50

BALL, John. *Eyes of Buddah.* 1976. Little Brn. 1st ed. G+/G+. O4. $20.00

BALL, John. *Five Pieces of Jade.* 1972. Little Brn. 1st ed. G+/G+. O4. $10.00

BALL, John. *Five Pieces of Jade.* 1972. London. Michael Joseph. 1st Eng ed. inscr pres. F/F. S6. $37.50

BALL, John. *Johnny Get Your Gun.* 1969. Little Brn. 1st ed. F/VG. P8. $50.00

BALL, John. *Kiwi Target.* 1989. Carroll Graf. 1st ed. F. P3. $16.00

BALL, John. *Mark One: The Dummy.* 1974. Little Brn. 1st ed. VG/G. O4. $10.00

BALL, John. *Mystery Story.* 1976. Del Mar. 1st ed. F/F. B2. $35.00

BALL, John. *Singapore.* nd. Dodd Mead. 2nd ed. VG. P3. $15.00

BALL, Richard A. *Brussels Griffon Primer.* 1984. Nat Brussels Griffon Club. 1st ed. 94p. M/wrp. R2. $12.00

BALL, Richard. *Hounds Will Meet.* 1921. Country Life/Scribner. ils Lionel Edwards. VG/G. O3. $45.00

BALL, Robert S. *Primer of Astronomy.* 1912 (1900). Cambridge. ils/11 pl/2 fld maps. 228p. gr cloth. G. K5. $15.00

BALL, Terence. *Civil Disobedience & Civil Deviance.* 1973. Beverly Hills. 49p. VG/wrp. D3. $15.00

BALL & BREEN. *Murder, California Style.* 1987. St Martin. 1st ed. F/F. P3. $18.00

BALL & BREEN. *Murder California Style.* 1987. NY. St Martin. ARC/1st ed. RS. sgn 10 contributors. F/F. S6. $40.00

BALLANTYNE, Robert. *Robber Kitten.* 1904. Altemus. 24mo. ils JR Neill. 94p. NF. D6. $40.00

BALLARD, J.G. *Concrete Island.* 1974. FSG. 1st ed. VG. P3. $30.00

BALLARD, J.G. *Day of Creation.* 1988. Farrar. 1st Am ed. sgn. F/dj. F4. $25.00

BALLARD, J.G. *Empire of the Sun.* 1984. Simon Schuster. 1st Am ed. 8vo. 279p. beige cloth. NF. H5. $50.00

BALLARD, J.G. *Hello America.* 1988. Carroll Graf. 1st ed. F. P3. $18.00

BALLARD, J.G. *Kindness of Women.* 1991. FSG. 1st ed. F. P3. $20.00

BALLARD, J.G. *Memories of the Space Age.* 1988. Arkham. 1st ed. F/F. T2. $17.00

BALLARD, J.G. *Myths of the Near Future.* 1982. Jonathan Cape. 1st ed. F. P3. $25.00

BALLARD, J.G. *Running Wild.* 1988. Hutchinson. 1st ed. F. P3. $30.00

BALLARD, J.G. *Unlimited Dream Company.* 1979. HRW. 1st ed. VG/VG. P3. $25.00

BALLARD, J.G. *Venus Hunters.* 1986. Gollancz. 1st ed. F. P3. $20.00

BALLARD, J.G. *Wind From Nowhere.* 1967. London. 1st UK ed/PBO/author's 1st novel. inscr. VG+/wrp. A11. $145.00

BALLEM, John. *Judas Conspiracy.* 1976. Musson. VG. P3. $13.00

BALLENTINE, Bill. *Clown Alley.* 1982. Boston. 1st ed. F/F. B5. $40.00

BALLIETT, Whitney. *Dinosaurs in the Morning.* 1962. Lippincott. 1st ed/author's 2nd book. F/NF. B2. $125.00

BALLIETT, Whitney. *Sound of Surprise.* 1959. Dutton. 1st ed/author's 1st book. F/F. B2. $125.00

BALLINGER, Bill S. *Bill S Ballinger Triptych.* nd. Sherbourne. 1st ed. VG/dj. P3. $20.00

BALLINGER, Bill S. *Corsican.* 1974. Dodd Mead. 1st ed. VG/VG. P3. $15.00

BALLINGER, Bill S. *Darkening Door.* 1952. Harper. 1st ed. VG/VG. P3. $20.00

BALLINGER, Bill S. *Doom-Maker.* 1959. Boardman. 1st ed. VG. P3. $15.00

BALLINGER, John. *Williamsburg Forgeries.* 1989. St Martin. sgn. 276p. VG/VG. A10. $15.00

BALLINGER, W.A. *Rebellion.* 1967. Howard Baker. 1st ed. F/F. P3. $15.00

BALLOU, Adin. *After Readin Thoreau. Sonnets by Adin Ballou.* 1979. Seal Harbor, ME. High Loft. 1/140. 8vo. 59p. F. B24. $125.00

BALLOU, Adin. *Christian Non-Resistance in All Its Important Bearings.* 1910. Universal Peace Union. 12mo. 278p. VG. V3. $18.00

BALLOU, Aldin. *Exposition of Views Respecting the Principal Facts...* 1850s. Boston. Bela Marsh. 2nd ed. 258p. cloth. VG. M1. $150.00

BALLOU, Aldin. *Towpath.* 1966. NY. Uphill. 1/120. 8vo. 13p. cloth/marbled brd. F/glassine wrp. B24. $50.00

BALLOU, Daniel Ross. *Military Services of Maj-Gen Ambrose Everett Burnside...* 1914. Providence, RI. 1st ed. 1/250. prt wrp. M8. $65.00

BALLOU, Hosea. *Treatise on Atonement.* 1805. Randolph. Wright. 1st ed. 216p. VG. H10. $225.00

BALLS, Edward K. *Early Uses of California Plants.* 1962. Berkeley. ils/16 mc photos. 103p. sc. M. B26. $10.00

BALMER, Randall H. *Perfect Babel of Confusion: Dutch Religion & Eng Culture...* 1989. Oxford. 258p. M/dj. B29. $14.00

BALMER & WYLIE. *When Worlds Collide.* 1933. Lippincott. 1st ed. VG. M21. $30.00

BALTZELL, E. Digby. *Puritan Boston & Quaker Phil.* 1979. NY. Free Pr. 1st ed. 8vo. 585p. VG/VG. V3. $15.00

BALZER, Robert Lawrence. *Beyond Conflict.* 1963. Bobbs Merrill. 1st ed. inscr. 352p. VG. A8. $35.00

BAMM, Peter. *Kingdoms of Christ From the Days of the Apostles...* 1959. McGraw Hill. ils. 367p. VG/dj. M10. $15.00

BANCROFT, Alberta. *Goblins of Haubert.* 1933 (1925). Jr Literary Guild. ils Harold Sichel. 117p. VG. P2. $10.00

BANCROFT, Emery H. *Elemental Theology: Doctrinal & Conservative.* 1945. Zondervan. 326p. G/worn. B29. $5.50

BANCROFT, George. *California: Inter Pocula.* 1888. San Francisco. Works by Bancroft Vol 25. 828p. O8. $27.50

BANCROFT, George. *Plea for Constitution of the US of America...* 1886. Harper. 16mo. 95p. new wrp/orig wrp bdg in. D3. $25.00

BANCROFT, Hubert Howe. *Hist of Mexico.* 1914. Bancroft. 1st ed. 581p. VG. F3. $20.00

BANCROFT, Hubert Howe. *History of Mexico 1516-1887.* 1883-1888. San Francisco. Bancroft. 6 vol set. 1st ed. maps. full leather. G+. P4. $200.00

BANCROFT, Hubert Howe. *Literary Industries, a Memoir.* 1891. np. 477p. VG. A4. $65.00

BANCROFT, Hubert Howe. *Native Races of the Pacific States of N Am, Vol I...* (1874). np. 8vo. fld maps. full leather. A8. $50.00

BANDELL, Betty. *Sing the Lord's Song in Strange Land: Life of Justin Morgan.* 1981. Fairleigh Dickinson. 287p. VG. M10. $5.00

BANDINI, Ralph. *Veiled Horizons: Stories of Big Game Fish of the Sea.* 1939. Derrydale. 1/950. F. H4. $185.00

BANGS, John Kendrick. *Enchanted Typewriter.* 1899. Harper. VG. P3. $65.00

BANGS, John Kendrick. *House-Boat on the Styx.* 1896. Harper. VG. P3. $50.00

BANGS, John Kendrick. *Mr Bonaparte of Corsica.* (1895). Harper. 12mo. ils. emb pict bdg. G. H1. $12.00

BANGS, John Kendrick. *Songs of Cheer.* 1910. Boston. Sherman French. 1st ed. inscr/dtd 1911. 64p. F/dj. C6. $150.00

BANISTER, Manly. *Bookbinding As a Handcraft.* 1981. NY. Bell. 160p. VG/torn. A10. $12.00

BANKOFF, George. *Story of Plastic Surgery.* 1952. London. 1st ed. 224p. VG. A13. $125.00

BANKS, Carolyn. *Darkroom.* 1980. Viking. 1st ed. F/F. P3. $15.00

BANKS, Iain M. *State of the Art.* 1989. Mark Ziesing. 1st ed. F/F. P3. $25.00

BANKS, Lynne Reid. *L-Shaped Room.* 1960. Chatto Windus. correct 1st ed. VG/VG. L3. $150.00

BANKS, Russell. *Family Life.* 1975. NY. Avon Equinox. 1st ed/PBO/author's 1st novel. sgn. F/8vo wrp. A11. $60.00

BANKS & READ. *Complete Hist of San Francisco Disaster...* 1906. CE Thomas. ils. red cloth. VG. M10. $15.00

BANKS & READ. *History of the San Francisco Disaster & Mount Vesuvius...* 1906. Beaver Springs, PA. Am Pub. 8vo. ils/photos. 464p. pict red cloth. G. B11. $30.00

BANKS & TAVELSTAD. *Boy Who Talks to Horses.* 1970. NY. Vantage. 1st ed. VG/fair. O3. $18.00

BANNERMAN, Helen. *Black Sambo/Little Red Hen/Peter Rabbit.* 1944. Racine, WI. Whitman. sm 4to. VG/rpr. C8. $48.00

BANNERMAN, Helen. *Little Black Mingo.* nd. rpt. 24mo. pict cloth. G. C8. $40.00

BANNERMAN, Helen. *Little Black Mingo.* 1901. London. 2nd (stated) ed. 32mo. pict cloth. G. C8. $340.00

BANNERMAN, Helen. *Little Black Sambo, a Surprise Book.* 1950. Dell. sm obl 12mo. F/wrp. C8. $30.00

BANNERMAN, Helen. *Little Black Sambo.* Aug 1966. np. 2nd prt. VG/VG. C8. $85.00

BANNERMAN, Helen. *Little Black Sambo.* 1932. Platt Munk #3100-B. ils Eulalie. unp. VG. A3. $25.00

BANNERMAN, Helen. *Little Black Sambo.* 1942. Akron, OH. Saalfield. lg 4to. pict paper brd. VG. C8. $60.00

BANNERMAN, Helen. *Little Black Sambo.* 1943. Am Crayon Co. ils FB Peat. bl stp red bdg. VG-. A3. $50.00

BANNERMAN, Helen. *Little Black Sambo.* 1948. Samuel Gabriel. 4to. VG. C8. $50.00

BANNERMAN, Helen. *Little Black Sambo.* 1950. Whitman Tell-A-Tale. ils Suzanne. unp. pict brd. VG. A3. $15.00

BANNERMAN, Helen. *Little Black Sambo.* 1959. Whitman. glazed pict paper brd. M. C8. $75.00

BANNERMAN, Helen. *Little Black Sambo.* 1976 (1961). Golden/Western. 2nd prt. VG. C8. $75.00

BANNERMAN, Helen. *Little White Squibba.* 1966. London. Chatto Windus. 1st ed. lg 24mo. F/NF. C8. $95.00

BANNERMAN, Helen. *Peter Rabbit & Black Sambo Painting Book.* 1908. Reilly Britton. sm 12mo. pict paper brd. VG. C8. $40.00

BANNERMAN, Helen. *Sambo & the Twins, a New Adventure of Little Black Sambo.* 1936. NY. Stokes. 1st Am ed. sm 8vo. 90p. F/dj. B24. $185.00

BANNERMAN, Helen. *Story of Little Black Sambo, by..., 1899.* 1983. Berkeley. Poole. 63x49mm. 1/25 (100 total) on Japan. ils MP Adams. F/case. B24. $275.00

BANNERMAN, Helen. *Story of Little Black Sambo.* Nov 1899. London. Grant Richards. 2nd ed. 32mo. pict cloth. VG. C8. $1,400.00

BANNERMAN, Helen. *Story of Little Black Sambo.* 1900. Stokes. very early ed. 24mo. pict label/paper brd. VG. C8. $350.00

BANNERMAN, Helen. *Story of Little Black Sambo.* 1905 (1899). Chicago. Christmas Stocking Series. pict label/cloth. VG. C8. $200.00

BANNERMAN, Helen. *Story of Little Black Sambo.* 1908. Chicago. Reilly Britton. ils Neill. G. C8. $100.00

BANNERMAN, Helen. *Story of Sambo & the Twins.* 1936. Stokes. 1st ed. 24mo. VG+/partial dj. C8. $250.00

BANNERMAN, Helen. *Story of Sambo & the Twins.* 1971 (1936). Chatto Windus. 32mo. pict paper brd. VG. C8. $40.00

BANNING, Evelyn I. *Helen Hunt Jackson.* 1973. Vanguard. 1st ed. 248p. VG/clip. N2. $7.50

BANNION, Della; see Sellers, Con(nie Leslie).

BANNON, John. *Indian Labor in Spanish Indies.* 1966. Heath. 1st ed. 105p. VG/wrp. F3. $15.00

BANNON, Laura. *Horse on a Houseboat.* 1951. Whitman. 8vo. pict cloth. VG. C8. $17.50

BANTA, Martha. *Imaging American Women...* 1987. Columbia. 884p. VG/dj. K4. $25.00

BANVILLE, John. *Nightspawn.* 1971. Norton. 1st Am ed/author's 2nd book. NF/VG. B2. $45.00

BARATZ, Joseph. *Village by the Jordan.* 1957. Sharon Books. 1st ed. 16 pl. 175p. VG. W1. $8.00

BARATZ, Joseph. *Village by the Jordan. Story of Degania.* 1960. Tel Aviv. 8vo. inscr. 174p. cloth. VG/dj. O2. $20.00

BARBA, Simone Della. *Nuova Spositione del Sonetto...* 1554. Florence. Torrentino. sm 8vo. 44p. modern navy calf. K1. $300.00

BARBER, E.A. *Majolica of Mexico.* 1908. Phil. VG. A1. $75.00

BARBER, E.A. *Pottery & Porcelain of the US.* 1893. NY. rebound bl cloth. VG. C11. $75.00

BARBER, J.W. *Connecticut Historical Collections.* (1838). New Haven. 1st ed. pl/map. leather/lacks labels. A9. $50.00

BARBER, Jonathan. *Practical Treatise on Gesture, Chiefly Abstracted...* 1831. Cambridge, MA. Hilliard Brn. 1st ed. 12mo. 13 full-p pl. cloth. M1. $200.00

BARBER, Noel. *Sultans.* 1973. Simon Schuster. 304p. VG/dj. W1. $12.00

BARBER, Noel. *White Desert.* 1958. London. Hodder Stoughton. 207p. VG/worn. A17. $15.00

BARBER, Ohio C. *Anna Dean Farm, Barberton, OH.* 1975. Barberton. 105p. VG. B18. $25.00

BARBER, Red. *Rhubarb in Cat Bird Seat.* 1968. NY. 1st ed. VG/VG. B5. $27.50

BARBER, Richard. *Reign of Chivalry.* 1980. St Martin. 4to. ils. 208p. NF/dj. M10. $18.50

BARBER, Theodore Xenophon. *LSD, Marijuana, Joga & Hypnosis.* 1970. Aldine. 312p. VG/dj. K4. $20.00

BARBES, John. *Orbital Resonance.* 1991. Tor. 1st ed. F/F. P3. $18.00

BARBOUR, Ralph Henry. *Double Play.* 1909. Appleton. 1st ed. G+/sans. P8. $25.00

BARBOUR, Ralph Henry. *Junior Trophy.* 1913. Appleton. 1st ed. 310p. red cloth. VG/VG. M20. $35.00

BARBOUR, Ralph Henry. *Lovell Leads Off.* 1928. Appleton. 1st ed. VG. P8. $45.00

BARBOUR, Ralph Henry. *Right Tackle Todd.* 1924. Dodd Mead. 1st ed. 291p. brn cloth. VG. M20. $12.00

BARCLAY, John. *Euphormionis Lusinini.* 1634. Oxford. Cripps. 12mo. 782p. contemporary calf. K1. $200.00

BARCLAY, John. *John Barclay, His Argensis...* 1628. London. Kyngston. 1st ed/new trans. 490p. mottled calf/rebacked. K1. $450.00

BARCLAY, Robert. *Apology for the True Christian Divinity.* 1843. Providence. Knowles Vose. 8vo. 587p. full leather. G. V3. $45.00

BARCLAY, Robert. *Apology for True Christian Divinity...Quakers...* 1729. Newport. James Franklin. 574p. ornate tooled calf. H10. $285.00

BARCYNSKA, Countess. *Yesterday Is Tomorrow.* 1950. Rich Cowan. VG/torn. P3. $10.00

BARDI, P.M. *Lasar Segall.* 1952. Sao Paulo. sm 4to. Italian text. 200p. prt brd. G/poor. F1. $40.00

BARICH, Bill. *Hart To Be Good.* 1987. NY. 1st short story collection. sgn. F/F. A11. $25.00

BARICHILION, Jacques. *Perrault's Tales of Mother Goose.* 1956. NY. Pierpont Morgan Lib. 2 vol. 1/250 by Stinehour Pr. beige cloth/brd. case. K1. $125.00

BARING, Maurice. *Glass Mender & Other Tales.* 1910. London. Nesbit. 1st ed. 8vo. gilt bl cloth. VG. D6. $55.00

BARING-GOULD, William S. *Annotated Sherlock Holmes.* 1972. Potter. 2nd ed/8th prt. M/F/VG case. H1. $65.00

BARING-GOULD, William S. *Sherlock Holmes.* 1962. Hart Davis. 1st ed. VG/VG. P3. $75.00

BARJAVEL, Rene. *Immortals.* 1974. Morrow. 1st ed. VG/VG. P3. $20.00

BARKER, Cicely Mary. *Book of the Flower Fairies.* nd. London. Blackie. 12mo. 72 mc pl. gilt gr cloth. NF. C8. $300.00

BARKER, Cicely Mary. *Fairies of the Trees.* nd. London. Blackie. 24 mc pl. VG+/clip. C8. $80.00

BARKER, Cicely Mary. *Flower Fairies — Autumn.* nd. London. Blackie. pre-ISBN ed/Mod rpt. 16mo. M/M. C8. $15.00

BARKER, Cicely Mary. *Flower Fairies of the Autumn.* nd. London. Blackie. Beautiful Color Book ed. 24 mc pl. F/VG+. C8. $100.00

BARKER, Cicely Mary. *Flower Fairies of the Spring.* nd. London. Blackie. pre-ISBN ed/Mod rpt. F/NF. C8. $15.00

BARKER, Cicely Mary. *Flower Fairies of the Spring.* nd. London. Blackie. Tiny Tots Srs ed. 24 mc pl. NF/VG. C8. $85.00

BARKER, Cicely Mary. *Flower Fairies of the Winter.* 1985. London. Bedrick/Blackie. 1st US ed thus. Mod rpt. M/M. C8. $15.00

BARKER, Cicely Mary. *Flower Fairy Alphabet.* nd. London. Blackie. Beautiful Color Book ed. 24 mc pl. G+/VG. C8. $80.00

BARKER, Cicely Mary. *Little Book of Old Rhymes.* 1976 (1936). London. Blackie. NF/F. C8. $15.00

BARKER, Cicely Mary. *Lord of the Rishie River.* 1976 (1938). London. Blackie. lg 16mo. pict paper brd. VG/VG+. C8. $10.00

BARKER, Cicely Mary. *Rhyming Rainbow.* 1977. London. Blackie. NF/NF. C8. $15.00

BARKER, Clive. *Books of Blood Volume 1.* 1991. Macdonald. F/F. P3. $25.00

BARKER, Clive. *Books of Blood.* 1991. Dorset. 1st ed thus. F/M. M21. $15.00

BARKER, Clive. *Cabal.* 1988. Poseidon. 1st ed. F/F. P3. $25.00

BARKER, Clive. *Damnation Game.* 1985. Weidenfeld Nicolson. 1st ed. F/F. P3. $30.00

BARKER, Clive. *Great & Secret Show.* 1990. Harper. 1st ed. F/F. M2/P3. $20.00

BARKER, Clive. *Imajica.* 1991. Harper Collins. 1st ed. VG/VG. P3. $23.00

BARKER, Clive. *In the Flesh.* 1986. Poseidon. 1st ed/author's 2nd book. F/F. B3/T2. $25.00

BARKER, Clive. *Inhuman Condition: Tales of Terror.* 1986. Poseidon. 1st Am ed. sgn. F/F. T2. $25.00

BARKER, Clive. *Thief of Always.* 1992. Harper Collins. ARC. inscr. F/wrp. L3. $45.00

BARKER, Clive. *Weaveworld.* 1987. Collins. 1st ed. F/F. P3. $25.00

BARKER, Ernest. *Greek Political Theory: Plato & His Predecessors.* 1918. London. Methuen. 404p. emb bl cloth. VG. G1. $50.00

BARKER, Ernest. *Social & Political Thought in Byzantium.* 1957. Oxford. 1st ed. 8vo. 239p. cloth. O2. $35.00

BARKER, Fordyce. *On Sea-Sickness.* 1870. Appleton. 36p. aeg. limp brd. scarce. G7. $65.00

BARKER, Rodney. *Hiroshima Maidens.* 1985. Viking. 1st ed. 8vo. 240p. VG/VG. V3. $14.00

BARKER, Samuel W. *Cast Up by the Sea.* 1869. NY. Harper. ils. 419p. T7. $50.00

BARKER, William P. *Everyone in the Bible.* 1966. Revell. 370p. VG. B29. $9.00

BARKER & ROBBINS. *Hist of London Transport.* 1963. London. 2 vol. ils. VG/G+. M17. $45.00

BARKER. *Treasures of British Library.* 1989. np. ils/photos. 272p. F/F. A4. $50.00

BARKHUUS, Arne. *Medical Geography.* 1945. np. 32p. VG/wrp. A13. $25.00

BARKLEY, Henry C. *Between the Danube & the Black Sea; or, 5 Years in Bulgaria.* 1876. London. 8vo. 313p. half gr calf/red label. O2. $110.00

BARKMAN, Carl. *Ambassador in Athens.* 1989. London. 8vo. 297p. cloth. dj. O2. $30.00

BARKUS, Homer A. *Know the Escapement.* 1945. San Diego, CA. revised ed. 12mo. sgn. 130p. blk cloth. A8. $40.00

BARLOW, Boris V. *Astronomical Telescope.* 1975. London. Wykeham. 8vo. ils/photos/diagrams. 213p. pb. K5. $25.00

BARLOW, Joel. *Letter Addressed to the People of Piedmont...* 1795. NY. Columbian Pr. 1st Am ed. 12mo. lib cloth. M1. $125.00

BARLOW, Robert. *Annals of the Jinns.* 1978. Necronomicon. 1st ed. F/wrp. M2. $10.00

BARLOW, Theodore. *Justice of Peace: A Treatise Containing Power & Duty...* 1745. London. Henry Lintot. contemporary calf. VG. M11. $450.00

BARLOW, Walter. *God So Loved: Spiritual Basis of Evangelism.* 1962. Revell. 159p. VG. B29. $3.00

BARLOW, William. *Looking Up at Down.* 1989. Phil. Temple U. 1st ed. F/F. B2. $25.00

BARLOW & BRYAN. *Elementary Mathematical Astronomy...* 1903 (1892). London. Tutorial Pr. sm 8vo. ils. 442p. blk cloth. G. K5. $24.00

BARMAN, Christian. *Bridge.* 1926. London. Bodley Head. 1st ed. ils Frank Brangwyn. gilt brn cloth. G. F1. $40.00

BARNARD, John. *Present for an Apprentice; or, A Sure Guide...* 1788. Phil. John Dobson. 18mo. 80p. w/Dobson booklist. contemporary calf. M1. $175.00

BARNARD, Robert. *Bodies.* 1986. Scribner. 1st ed. VG/VG. P3. $14.00

BARNARD, Robert. *Cherry Blossom Corpse.* 1987. Scribner. 1st ed. VG/VG. P3. $15.00

BARNARD, Robert. *City of Strangers.* 1990. Scribner. 1st ed. sgn. F/F. T2. $22.00

BARNARD, Robert. *Corpse in a Gilded Cage.* 1984. London. Collins. 1st ed. F/dj. M15. $35.00

BARNARD, Robert. *Corpse in a Gilded Cage.* 1984. Scribner. 1st ed. F/VG. P3. $15.00

BARNARD, Robert. *Death in Purple Prose.* 1987. London. Collins. ARC/1st ed. RS. F/F. S6. $30.00

BARNARD, Robert. *Death of a Salesperson.* 1989. Scribner. 1st ed. F/F. B3. $20.00

BARNARD, Robert. *Death of the Chaste Apprentice.* 1989. Scribner. 1st ed. sgn. F/F. T2. $22.00

BARNARD, Robert. *Fete Fatale.* 1985. Scribner. 1st ed. F/F. P3. $14.00

BARNARD, Robert. *Political Suicide.* 1986. London. Collins. 1st ed. sgn. F/F. S6. $40.00

BARNARD, Robert. *Political Suicide.* 1986. Scribner. 1st ed. sgn. F/F. T2. $25.00

BARNARD, Robert. *Political Suicide.* 1986. Scribner. 1st ed. VG/VG. P3. $14.00

BARNARD, Robert. *Talent To Deceive: Appreciation of Agatha Christie.* 1980. Collins. 1st ed. VG. P3. $25.00

BARNARD, Robert. *Talent To Deceive: Appreciation of Agatha Christie.* 1980. London. Collins. 1st ed. sgn. F/F. S6. $40.00

BARNARD, Robert. *To Die Like a Gentleman.* 1993. London. Macmillan. 1st ed. F/F. S6. $27.50

BARNES, Arthur K. *Interplanetary Hunter.* 1956. Gnome. 1st ed. NF/dj. M2. $25.00

BARNES, Djuna. *Book.* 1923. Boni Liveright. 1st ed/author's 2nd book. NF. B2. $125.00

BARNES, Djuna. *Creatures in an Alphabet.* 1982. NY. Dial. 1st ed. 8vo. bl cloth/wht brd. F/NF. H5. $60.00

BARNES, Harry E. *New Horizons in Criminology...* 1950. NY. revised ed. 1069p. VG. D3. $25.00

BARNES, James M. *Picture Analysis of Golf Strokes.* 1919. Lippincott. 4th imp. gr cloth. VG. M20. $125.00

BARNES, John. *Man Who Pulled Down the Sky.* 1986. Congdon Weed. 1st ed. VG/VG. P3. $16.00

BARNES, John. *Million Open Doors.* 1992. Tor. 1st ed. F/F. P3. $20.00

BARNES, John. *Sin of Origin.* 1988. Congdon Weed. 1st ed. F/F. P3. $16.00

BARNES, Joseph. *Medical & Surgical History of War of the Rebellion.* 1875. WA. 3 vol. G. B5. $600.00

BARNES, Julian; see Kavanagh, Dan.

BARNES, Linda. *Bitter Finish.* 1983. St Martin. 1st ed. F/NF. M15. $35.00

BARNES, Linda. *Coyote.* nd. BC. VG/VG. P3. $10.00

BARNES, Linda. *Hardware.* 1994. Delacorte. ARC. sgn. NF/wrp. B3. $15.00

BARNES, Linda. *Snake Tattoo.* nd. BC. VG/VG. P3. $8.00

BARNES, Linda. *Snake Tattoo.* 1989. St Martin. ARC/1st ed. sgn. w/photo material & photo. F/F. S6. $40.00

BARNES, Linda. *Snake Tattoo.* 1989. St Martin. 1st ed. F/F. M15. $35.00

BARNES, Margaret Ayer. *Westward Passage.* 1931. Houghton Mifflin. 1st ed. sgn. VG/shabby dj. H4. $22.00

BARNES, Nellie. *American Indian Love Lyrics & Other Verse.* 1925. Macmillan. 1st ed. 190p. NF/dj. B19. $35.00

BARNES, Thomas Garden. *Hastings College of the Law, the First Century.* 1978. San Francisco. Hastings College of the Law Pr. M11. $35.00

BARNES, Winston H. *Philosophical Predicament.* 1950. Boston. Beacon. 1st Am ed. 184p. cloth. G1. $22.50

BARNES & BLAKE. *120 Needlepoint Design Projects.* 1974. np. VG/wrp. G2. $6.95

BARNES. *Authors, Publishers & Politicians...* 1974. np. 325p. F/F. A4. $25.00

BARNETT, Albert E. *New Testament: Its Making & Meaning.* 1946. Abingdon Cokesbury. 304p. G. B29. $5.50

BARNETT, Albert E. *Understanding the Parables of Our Lord.* 1954. Allenson. 223p. VG. B29. $4.00

BARNETT, Lincoln. *Treasure of Our Tongue.* 1964. Knopf. 304p. cloth. VG/dj. M20. $15.00

BARNEY, Maginel Wright. *Valley of God Almighty Joneses.* 1965. NY. 1st ed. VG/G. B5. $35.00

BARNHART, Peter. *Wounded Duck.* 1979. Scribner. 1st ed. ils Adrienne Adams. F/F. P2. $28.00

BAROFSKY, Seymour. *In Grandpa's House.* 1985. NY. 1st ed. ils/inscr Sendak. F/F. A11. $70.00

BARON, Roger. *Science et Sagesse Chez Hugues de Saint-Victor.* 1957. Paris. Lethielleux. 280p. VG/wrp. G1. $35.00

BARONIUS, Caesar. *Martyrologium Romanum, ad Novam Kalendarii Rationem...* 1589. Antwerp. Plantin. 2nd ed. folio. later plain brd. 576p. H10. $350.00

BARR, Amelia E. *Border Shepherdess.* (1887). Dodd Mead. 16mo. 325p. VG. H1. $6.00

BARR, Ken. *Lone Ranger.* 1981. NY. Random. 1st prt. pop-up. glazed pict brd. VG+. C8. $65.00

BARR, Nevada. *Superior Death.* 1994. Putnam. 1st ed. sgn. F/F. T2. $45.00

BARR, Nevada. *Track of the Cat.* 1993. Putnam. 1st ed. sgn. Anna Pigeon Series #1. F/F. T2. $125.00

BARR, Thele Elaine. *His Majesty the King, Our Baby's Biography.* 1902. Hill. silhouettes. red cloth. VG+. M5. $65.00

BARRE, M.L. *Herculanum et Pompei Recueil General des Peintures Bronzes.* 1840. Paris. 7 vol. 1st ed. lg 8vo. half red morocco. NF. C6. $425.00

BARRETT, Andrea. *Forms of Water.* 1993. Pocket. 1st ed. NF/NF. A14. $30.00

BARRETT, Cyril S.J. *Collected Papers on Aesthetics.* 1965. Oxford. Basil Blackwell. sm 8vo. bl cloth. G1. $28.50

BARRETT, Ezra. *Sabbath School Psalmody...* 1820. Richardson Lord Holbrook. 2nd ed. 56p. wrp. scarce. B14. $65.00

BARRETT, John. *Panama Canal, What It Is, What It Means.* 1913. Pan Am Union. 1st ed. slim 8vo. tri-fld map. VG. B11. $50.00

BARRETT, Joseph O. *Barbarities of the Rebels, As Shown in Their Cruelty...* 1863. Providence. 1st ed. 8vo. 40p. prt wrp. M1. $150.00

BARRETT, Joseph O. *Hist of Old Abe, the Live War Eagle of 8th Regiment...* 1865. Chicago. Sewell. 1st ed. ils/map. prt wrp. M1. $300.00

BARRETT, N.S. *Picture World of Space Voyages.* 1990. Franklin Watts. 4to. 29p. laminated pict brd. F. K5. $12.00

BARRETT, Neal. *Hereafter Gang.* 1991. Shingletown. Ziesing. 1st ed. F/F. P3/T2. $25.00

BARRETT, Neal. *Slightly Off Center.* 1992. Austin. Swan. 1st ed. sgn. intro/sgn JR Lansdale. F/wrp. T2. $15.00

BARRETT, Richard Carter. *Popular American Ruby-Stained Pattern Glass.* 1969. Manchester, VT. 2nd prt. unp. sbdg. F. H1. $22.50

BARRETT, S.M. *Geronimo's Story of His Life.* 1915 (1906). Duffield. photos. 216p. F/G. H1. $42.00

BARRETT, William. *Irrational Man: Study in Existential Philosophy.* 1958. NY. Doubleday Anchor. later prt. cream cloth. G1. $25.00

BARRETT & DEHN. *How To Draw & Print Lithographs.* 1950. Am Artists Group. ARC/1st ed. ils. wht/gilt stp gr cloth. F/F. F1. $135.00

BARRIE, James M. *Peter Pan, a Stand-Up Story Especially for You.* nd. Hallmark. ils Gayle Bergman. VG. C8. $35.00

BARRIE, James M. *Peter Pan in Kensington Gardens.* 1906. Hodder Stoughton. 1/500. ils/sgn Arthur Rackham. teg. gilt stp vellum. F. B24. $4,500.00

BARRIE, James M. *Peter Pan in Kensington Gardens.* 1906. London. Hodder Stoughton. 1st ed. sm 4to. pict cloth. VG+. C8. $750.00

BARRIE, James M. *Peter Pan.* 1911. Grosset Dunlap. photoplay ed. 220p. cloth. VG/ragged. M20. $25.00

BARRIE, James M. *Peter Pan.* 1987. Holt. 1st ed. ils Michael Hague. F/F. B17. $20.00

BARRIE, James M. *Quality Street.* 1901. London. 4to. 1/1000. ils/sgn Hugh Thomson. gilt full vellum. custom case. H4. $350.00

BARRIE, James M. *Story of Peter Pan.* 1930. Phil. Altemus. ils Alice B Woodward. 95p. NF. D6. $40.00

BARRINGTON, P.V. *Night of Violence.* 1959. Hammond. lacks front ep. VG. P3. $10.00

BARROW, George. *Fire of Life.* 1940s. London. Hutchinson. 2nd prt. 256p. wht lettered red cloth. VG. M7. $60.00

BARROW, John. *Voyages of Discovery & Reasearch Within Arctic Regions...* 1846. NY. Harper. 12mo. ils/2 maps. 359p. T7. $275.00

BARROWS, Angela. *Donkey Keeping & Breeding.* 1977. Claverdon. Old Barn. 1st ed. VG/G+. O3. $38.00

BARROWS, Marjorie. *Ezra the Elephant.* 1934. Grosset Dunlap. 1st ed. ils Nell Stolp Smock. VG/G. P2. $25.00

BARROWS, Samuel J. *Isles & Shrines of Greece.* 1898. Boston. 8vo. ils. 389p. uncut. O2. $60.00

BARRUEL, A.A. *Memoirs, Ils History of Jacobinism.* 1797-1798. London. Burton. 4 vol. old calf/rebacked/gilt red spine labels. K1. $175.00

BARRUEL, A.A. *Memoirs, Ils History of Jacobinism.* 1799. Hartford. Hudson Goodwin. 2 vol in 1. worn half leather. H10. $125.00

BARRY, Jerome. *Extreme License.* 1958. Crime Club. 1st ed. G/G. P3. $8.00

BARRY, John Evarts. *Skeleton in Concrete.* nd. BC. VG/VG. P3. $8.00

BARRY, Jonathan; see Strieber, Whitley.

BART, Barry. *It's Story Time.* ca 1940. np. 12 ils fairy tales. unp. pict brd. VG+. A3. $12.50

BARTH, Alan. *Loyalty of Free Men.* 1951. Viking. fwd Zechariah Chafee jr. M11. $35.00

BARTH, John. *End of the Road.* 1958. Doubleday. 1st ed/author's 2nd book. 8vo. 230p. VG/dj. C6. $250.00

BARTH, John. *Floating Opera.* 1956. Appleton Century. 1st ed/author's 1st book. sgn. F/NF. B4. $450.00

BARTH, John. *Last Voyage of Somebody the Sailor.* 1991. Little Brn. ARC. VG/pict wrp. B3. $45.00

BARTH, John. *Sot-Weed Factor.* 1960. Doubleday. 1st ed. 8vo. 806p. yel/bl bdg. VG/VG. H5. $400.00

BARTH, John. *Tidewater Tales.* 1987. Putnam. 1st ed. F/NF. B3. $25.00

BARTH, John. *Tidewater Tales.* 1987. Putnam. 1st ed. sgn. F/NF. A11. $40.00

BARTH, Richard. *Rag Bag Clan.* 1983. London. Gollancz. 1st ed. F/F. S6. $20.00

BARTHEL, Joan. *Death in CA.* 1981. NY. 1st ed. F/F. A17. $10.00

BARTHELEMY-MADAULE, Madeleine. *Lamarck the Mythical Precursor: Study of Relations...* 1982. Cambridge. MIT. 1st Eng-language ed. sm 8vo. 174p. gray cloth. VG/dj. G1. $25.00

BARTHELME, Donald. *Amateurs.* 1976. FSG. ARC/1st ed. RS. w/pub material. F/F. B4. $85.00

BARTHELME, Donald. *Guilty Pleasures.* 1974. NY. 1st ed. sgn. F/F. A11. $35.00

BARTHELME, Donald. *Slightly Irregular Fire Engine.* 1971. FSG. 1st ed. inscr/sgn. F/F. scarce. B4. $350.00

BARTHELME, Donald. *Snow White.* 1967. Atheneum. 1st ed/author's 2nd book. F/NF clip. L3. $125.00

BARTHELME, Frederick. *Rangoon.* 1970. NY. Winter House. 1st ed/author's 1st book. VG/wrp. L3. $50.00

BARTHLOTT, Wilhelm. *Cacti.* 1979. Cheltenham. photos. 249p. F/dj. B26. $27.50

BARTHOLIN, Caspar the Younger. *De Tibiis Veterum & Earum Antiquo USU.* 1677. Rome. Pauli Monetae. 1st ed. 3 fld pl. contemporary vellum. K1. $500.00

BARTHOLOMEW & SINCLAIR. *Lemon Fruit: Its Composition, Physiology & Products.* 1951. Berkeley. ils/index. 163p. F/dj. B26. $27.50

BARTLETT, Arthur C. *Sea Dog.* 1927. Boston. Wilde. 1st ed. 299p. cloth. G/worn. R2. $35.00

BARTLETT, Arthur C. *Spunk: Leader of the Dog Team.* 1926. Boston. Wilde. 1st ed. 311p. cloth. VG. R2. $10.00

BARTLETT, Elisha. *History, Diagnosis & Treatment of Fevers of the US.* 1990. Birmingham. facsimile of 1847 ed. 546p. full leather. A13. $50.00

BARTLETT, John Russell. *Bartlett's West: Drawing the Mexican Boundary.* 1968. Yale. 1st ed. ils/index. 155p. F/tattered. B19. $45.00

BARTLETT, John Russell. *Personal Narrative of Explorations & Incidents in TX.* 1965. Rio Grande Pr. 2 vol. rpt. F/sans. B19. $135.00

BARTLETT, John. *Familiar Quotations.* 1892. Boston. 9th ed. 1158p. teg. quarter leather/raised bands. VG. H3. $50.00

BARTLETT, Lee. *Sun Is But a Morning Star.* 1989. Albuquerque. 1st ed. F/F. B3. $15.00

BARTLETT, Napier. *Soldier's Story of the War...* 1874. New Orleans. Clark Hofeline. 1st ed. 8vo. 252p. bl cloth. G. C6. $350.00

BARTLETT, Percy W. *Barrow Cadbury: A Memory.* 1960. London. Bannisdale. 1st ed. 8vo. 159p. M/F. V3. $14.00

BARTLETT, W.H. *Plates From Willis' Canadian Scenery & Am Scenery.* ca 1840. London. 2 vol. lg 4to. contemporary full red morocco. C6. $500.00

BARTLEY, R. *Joy of Machine Embroidery.* 1976. np. VG/wrp. G2. $6.00

BARTOL, C. *Criminal Behavior. A Psychosocial Approach.* 1980. Prentice Hall. 434p. brd. VG. D3. $15.00

BARTON, Benjamin Smith. *Collections for Essay Towards a Materia Medica of US.* 1900. Cincinnati. 2 parts in 1. half morocco. VG+. B14. $75.00

BARTON, D. Plunket. *Story of Our Inns of Court.* 1924. London. 1st ed. 17 pl. 320p. buckram. VG. D3. $25.00

BARTON, Frank Townend. *Non-Sporting Dogs: Their Points & Management.* 1905. London. Everett. 1st ed. ils. 251p. cloth. scarce. R2. $125.00

BARTON, Fred B. *Let Yourself Go.* 1937. NY. 1st ed. inscr. G. B18. $12.50

BARTON, James L. *Daybreak in Turkey.* 1908. Boston. 8vo. 204p. cloth. O2. $45.00

BARTON, James L. *Story of Near East Relief (1915-1930).* 1930. NY. 1st ed. pres. cloth. O2. $40.00

BARTON, Julia. *Art of Embroidery.* 1990. np. cloth. VG. G2. $30.00

BARTON, Phyllis S. *Annotated Bibliography Honoring Eulalie Banks...* 1992. Pictus Orbis. ltd sgn ed. 1/100. 40p. M. S11. $25.00

BARTON & CAPOBIANO. *Iris.* 1990. Doubleday. 1st ed/ F/F. P3. $20.00

BARTRAM, George. *Job Abroad.* 1975. Macmillan. 1st ed. VG/VG. P3. $20.00

BARUSS, Imants. *Personal Nature of Notions of Consciousness...* 1990. Lanham. U Pr of Am. 217p. bl cloth. G1. $27.50

BARZMAN, Ben. *Twinkle, Twinkle, Little Star.* nd. BC. VG/VG. P3. $8.00

BARZUN & GRAFF. *Modern Researcher.* 1957. Harcourt Brace. 386p. VG/dj. K4. $9.00

BASCOM, William. *Crest of the Wave: Adventues in Oceanography.* 1988. Harper Row. 1st ed. dj. N2. $7.50

BASHO. *982 Haiku Poems.* 1985. Bijou Hoshino. 40x31mm. 1/75 (225 total). teg. morocco/inlay. M/case/box. B24. $400.00

BASKETT, John. *Horse in Art.* 1980. Boston. NY Graphic Soc. 1st Am ed. obl 4to. VG/case. O3. $85.00

BASKIN, John. *New Burlington: Life & Death of an American Village.* 1976. Norton. 1st ed. 8vo. 260p. VG/VG. V3. $12.00

BASKIN, Leonard. *Ars Anatomica, a Medical Fantasia.* 1972. NY. Medicina Rara. 1/2800. ils/sgn Baskin. cloth/brd portfolio. F/case. F1. $200.00

BASKIN, Leonard. *Hosie's Zoo.* 1981. Viking. 1st ed. sm 4to. F/F. C8. $30.00

BASKIN, Leonard. *Poppy & Other Deadly Plants.* 1967. Delacorte. 1st ed. sm 4to. F/F. C8. $75.00

BASLER & BRUMMER. *L'Art Precolombien.* 1947 (1928). Paris. Librairie Grund. rpt. 63p. orig wrp rebound in cloth. F3. $65.00

BASNAGE, Jacques. *Hist of the Jews, From Jesus Christ to Present Time.* 1708. London. 1st Eng-language ed. folio. VG. C6. $400.00

BASS, Rick. *Deer Pasture.* 1985. College Station. 1st ed. sgn. ils/sgn Elizabeth Hughes. F/F. B3. $125.00

BASS, Rick. *Ninemile Wolves.* 1992. Livingston. Clark City. 1/125. sgn. F/case. B3. $125.00

BASS, Rick. *Watch.* 1989. NY. ARC. NF/wrp. A15. $25.00

BASS, Rick. *Wild to the Heart.* 1987. Stackpole. 1st ed. ils/sgn Elizabeth Hughes. F/F. B3. $75.00

BASS, T.J. *Godwhale.* 1975. Eyre Methuen. 1st ed. NF/NF. P3. $40.00

BASS & BERG. *Objective Approaches to Personality Assessment.* 1959. Van Nostrand. 233p. G/dj. K4. $20.00

BASSANI, Giorgio. *Garden of the Finzi-Continis.* 1965. Atheneum. 1st ed. F/NF. B2. $35.00

BASSET, Bernard. *Born for Friendship: Spirit of Sir Thomas Moore.* 1965. NY. Sheed Ward. 220p. VG/VG. B33. $14.00

BASSETT, Sara Ware. *Within the Harbor.* 1948. NY. 1st ed. VG/VG. A17. $8.50

BASSIOUNI & FISHER. *Storm Over the Arab World.* 1972. Chicago. Follett. 1st ed. 8vo. VG/dj. W1. $12.00

BASTABLE, Bernard; see Barnard, Robert.

BATES, Charles F. *Custer's Indian Battles.* nd. Ft Collins, CO. ils/maps. 36p. VG/dj. B18. $37.50

BATES, D.R. *Space Research & Exploration.* 1957. Eyre Spottiswoode. 8vo. ils. 224p. xl. dj. K5. $25.00

BATES, Ernest Sutherland. *Bible Designed To Be Read As Literature.* 1937. London. Heinemann. 1237p. map ep. burgundy cloth. VG/VG. B33. $75.00

BATES, H.E. *Down the River.* 1937. Holt. ARC. 151p. VG/dj. M20. $150.00

BATES, H.E. *Poacher.* 1935. Macmillan. 1st Am ed. NF/F. B2. $50.00

BATES, Marston. *Ifalik, Lonely Paradise of the South Seas.* 1956. NGS. sm map/photos. F/stiff wrp/cloth spine. P4. $8.50

BATES, William. *Harmony of the Divine Attributes...* 1674. London. Ranew Robinson. 1st ed. 502p. calf. front hinge cracked. H10. $225.00

BATESON, V. *Woven Fashion.* 1982. np. cloth. VG. G2. $25.50

BATH, Order of. *Statutes of the Most Honourable Order of the Bath.* 1744. London. np. sm 4to. ils. 64p. later maroon morocco/red cloth. K1. $150.00

BATH, Virginia. *Needlework in America.* 1979. np. cloth. VG. G2. $40.00

BATRES, Leopoldo. *Archaelogical Explorations in Escalerillas Street...* 1902. Mexico. J Aguilar Vera. 4to. photos/fld plan. 59p. gilt cloth. VG. H4. $135.00

BATSON, BRIDGES & INGE. *Atlas of Mars.* 1979. WA, DC. NASA SP-438. ils. 146p. glk cloth. VG. K5. $75.00

BATTELL, Joseph. *American Stallion Register.* 1901-1911. Middlebury, VT. 2 vol. 1st ed. tall 8vo. gilt leather/raised bands. F. H3. $175.00

BATTEN, Jack. *Crang Plays the Ace.* 1987. Macmillan of Canada. 1st ed. F/F. P3. $20.00

BATTEN, Jack. *Straight No Chaser.* 1989. Macmillan of Canada. 1st ed. F/F. P3. $20.00

BATTERBERRY & BATTERBERRY. *Mirror, Mirror: A Social History of Fashion.* 1977. np. ils. VG/VG. M17. $45.00

BATTERSBY, W.J. *Brother Potamian, Educator & Scientist.* 1953. London. 182p. G7. $25.00

BATTEUX, Charles. *Historie des Causes Premieres...* 1769. Paris. Chez Saillant. 452p. contemporary leather. G1. $150.00

BAUDELAIRE, Charles. *Les Paradis Artificiels.* 1860. Paris. Poulet-Malassis et de Broise. NF. B4. $1,500.00

BAUDET, Henti. *Paradise on Earth.* 1965. Yale. 1st ed. cloth. VG/dj. W1. $15.00

BAUDUY, Jerome K. *Diseases of the Nervous System.* 1892. Lippincott. 2nd ed. 352p. recased orig cloth. G7. $150.00

BAUER, Elisabeth. *Armenie. Son Histoire et Son Present.* 1977. Paris. 4to. 180p. cloth. dj. O2. $30.00

BAUER, Raymond A. *Some Views on Soviet Psychology.* 1962. Am Psychological Assn. 276p. G/dj. K4. $25.00

BAUER. Steven. *Satyrday.* 1980. Berkley Punam. 1st ed. NF/NF. P3. $15.00

BAUM, L. Frank. *Dorothy & the Wizard in Oz.* 1908. Reilly Britton. 1st ed/1st state. 4to. 256p. bl cloth. F. B24. $750.00

BAUM, L. Frank. *Dorothy & the Wizard in Oz.* 1920. Reilly Lee. G/VG. P3. $75.00

BAUM, L. Frank. *Emerald City of Oz.* 1910. Reilly Britton. 1st ed. 8vo. ils JR Neill. bl cloth. VG. D6. $600.00

BAUM, L. Frank. *Emerald City of Oz.* 1920. Reilly Lee. ils Neill. 295p. pict tan cloth. G. A3. $100.00

BAUM, L. Frank. *Emerald City of Oz.* 1939. Rand McNally. G. P3. $10.00

BAUM, L. Frank. *Enchanted Island of Yew...* 1903. Bobbs Merrill. 1st ed/2nd prt. ils FY Cory. 242p. VG. D6. $125.00

BAUM, L. Frank. *Glinda of Oz.* 1920. Reilly Lee. 1st ed (lists 13 titles). ils Neill. 279p. tan cloth. G. A3. $250.00

BAUM, L. Frank. *Land of Oz.* ca 1920s. Reilly Lee. VG. P3. $90.00

BAUM, L. Frank. *Land of Oz: A Sequel to Wizard of Oz.* 1925. Reilly Lee. Popular ed. ils Neill. 286p. pict gr cloth. G. A3. $75.00

BAUM, L. Frank. *Land of Oz: A Sequel to Wizard of Oz.* 1939. Reilly Lee. words Popular Ed deleted. 286p. pict yel cloth. G. A3. $40.00

BAUM, L. Frank. *Lost Princess of Oz.* ca 1920. Reilly Lee. early rpt. 4to. ils Neill. 312p. bl cloth. G. A3. $95.00

BAUM, L. Frank. *Lost Princess of Oz.* 1941. Reilly Lee. VG/F. P3. $100.00

BAUM, L. Frank. *Magic of Oz.* 1920. Reilly Lee. 1st ed/3rd state. ils Neill. 266p. pict gr cloth. G. A3. $150.00

BAUM, L. Frank. *Magic of Oz.* 1931. Reilly Lee. VG/F. P3. $125.00

BAUM, L. Frank. *Magical Monarch of Mo & His People.* 1903. Chicago. Donohue. 2nd ed/1st state. ils Frank VerBeck. bl cloth. VG. D6. $110.00

BAUM, L. Frank. *Magical Monarch of Mo.* ca 1920s. Bobbs Merrill. VG. P3. $100.00

BAUM, L. Frank. *Mother Goose in Prose.* 1986. Bounty. VG/VG. P3. $15.00

BAUM, L. Frank. *Rinkitink in Oz.* ca 1920s. Reilly Lee. NF/chip. P3. $125.00

BAUM, L. Frank. *Road to Oz.* ca 1965. Reilly Lee. ils Neill. 268p. pict wht cloth. VG. A3. $17.50

BAUM, L. Frank. *Road to Oz.* 1909. Chicago. Reilly Britton. 1st ed/1st ed. pict gr cloth. NF. B24. $750.00

BAUM, L. Frank. *Road to Oz.* 1941. Reilly Lee. VG/F. P3. $120.00

BAUM, L. Frank. *Scarecrow of Oz.* ca 1923 (1915). Reilly Lee. 12 mc pl. 288p. VG. P2. $125.00

BAUM, L. Frank. *Sea Fairies.* 1911. Reilly Britton. 1st ed. 4to. 240p. VG+. D6. $350.00

BAUM, L. Frank. *Sky Island.* 1912. Reilly Britton. 1st ed. ils JR Neill. 288p. VG+. D6. $300.00

BAUM, L. Frank. *Tik-Tok of Oz.* 1920. Reilly Lee. ils Neill. 271p. pict bl cloth. G. A3. $85.00

BAUM, L. Frank. *Tin Woodman of Oz...an Original Story.* nd (ca 1955). Reilly Lee. ils Dale Ulrey. 262p. cloth. VG/G+. A3. $20.00

BAUM, L. Frank. *Wizard of Oz.* ca 1920-30 (1899). Bobbs Merrill. 5th ed/2nd state. 8 pl. VG+. P2. $150.00

BAUM, L. Frank. *Wizard of Oz.* 1939. Grosset Dunlap. ils Osker Lebeck. F/VG. P3. $35.00

BAUM, L. Frank. *Wizard of Oz.* 1944. Akron. Saalfield. 8vo. animator Julian Wehr. pict brd/sbdg. VG-. D6. $85.00

BAUM, L. Frank. *Wizard of Oz.* 1991. Jelly Bean. 1st ed thus. ils Charles Santore. F/VG. B17. $8.50

BAUM, L. Frank. *Wonderful Wizard of Oz.* 1900. Chicago. George M Hill. 1st ed. 24 mc pl/Denslow. red/gr stp lt gr cloth. case. H5. $4,500.00

BAUM, Vicki. *Martin's Summer.* 1931. Cosmopolitan. 1st ed. NF/NF. B2. $40.00

BAUMANN, Hans. *World of the Pharaohs.* 1960. Pantheon. 1st ed. photos. 256p. xl. VG. W1. $15.00

BAUMBACH, Jonathan. *Landscape of Nightmare.* nd. np. 1st ed/author's 1st book. sgn. NF/VG+. A11. $50.00

BAUR, John I. *Revolution & Tradition in Modern American Art.* 1951. Cambridge. ARC/1st ed. 8vo. ils. 170p. gr cloth. F/VG. F1. $75.00

BAUSCH, Richard. *Violence.* 1992. Houghton Mifflin. 1st ed. VG/pict wrp. B3. $25.00

BAVINK, Berhard. *Natural Sciences: Intro to Scientific Philosophy of Today.* 1932. NY. Century. 1st Eng-language ed/Am issue. 12 halftones. 684p. G1. $42.00

BAWDEN, Nina. *Odd Flamingo.* 1980. Collins Crime Club. 2nd ed. VG/VG. P3. $17.00

BAXANDALL, D. *Calculating Machines & Instruments.* 1975 (1926). London. Science Mus. sm 4to. ils. 102p. laminated wrp. K5. $16.00

BAXT, George. *Affair at Royalties.* 1971. London. Macmillan. 1st ed (precedes Am ed). F/NF. M15. $35.00

BAXT, George. *I! Said the Demon.* 1969. Random. 2nd ed. xl. dj. P3. $6.00

BAXT, George. *Neon Graveyard.* 1979. St Martin. 1st ed. VG/VG. P3. $30.00

BAXTER, Charles. *Relative Stranger: Stories.* 1990. Norton. 1st ed. F/F. A14. $45.00

BAXTER, Charles. *Shadow Play.* 1993. Norton. 1st ed. sgn. F/F. S9. $75.00

BAXTER, Charles. *Through the Safety Net.* 1985. Viking. 1st ed. sgn/dtd 1993. F/NF. B2. $75.00

BAXTER, Charles. *Through the Safety Net.* 1985. Viking. 1st ed/author's 2nd book. F/VG. B3. $45.00

BAXTER, John. *New & Impartial History of England.* ca 1800. London. HD Symonds. sm folio. 45 pl. 830p. contemporary calf/rebacked. K1. $350.00

BAXTER, Lorna. *Eggchild.* 1979. Dutton. 1st ed. VG/VG. P3. $18.00

BAXTER, Richard. *Guilty Women.* 1943. Quality Press. 7th ed. VG/F. P3. $9.00

BAXTER, W.M. *Sun & the Amateur Astronomer.* 1963. Norton. 8vo. ils/pl. 158p. G/dj. K5. $22.00

BAY, J. Christian. *Handful of Western Books.* 1925. Torch. 1/350. ils. F. A4. $45.00

BAYER, Oliver Weld. *An Eye for An Eye.* 1946. Tower. VG/G. P3. $15.00

BAYER, William. *Peregrine.* 1981. Congdon Lattes. 1st ed. F/F. P3. $20.00

BAYER, William. *Peregrine.* 1981. NY. Congdon Lattes. 1st ed. sgn. F/dj. M15. $30.00

BAYER, William. *Punish Me With Kisses.* 1980. Congdon Lattes. 1st ed. VG/F. P3. $20.00

BAYER, William. *Tangier.* 1978. Dutton. 1st ed. VG/VG. P3. $20.00

BAYLE, Pierre. *Dictionary Historical & Critical...Life of the Author.* 1734-1738. London. 5 vol. 2nd ed. folio. contemporary calf. G7. $1,500.00

BAYLE, Pierre. *Historical & Critical Dictionary.* 1710. London. 4 vol set. 1st Eng ed. VG. A15. $240.00

BAYLEY, Barington J. *Soul of the Robot.* 1974. Doubleday. 1st ed. VG/VG. P3. $15.00

BAYLOR, Byrd. *Best Town in the World.* 1983. Scribner. 1st ed. inscr. lg 8vo. pict paper brd. VG+. C8. $35.00

BAYLOR, George. *Bull Run to Bull Run.* 1900. Richmond. Johnson. 1st ed. 8vo. 412p. NF. C6. $300.00

BAZZONI, Charles. *Energy & Matter.* 1934. NY. U Soc. 1st trade ed. ils/diagrams. red cloth. G. K5. $9.00

BEACH, Alfred E. *Science Record for 1872: A Compendium...* 1872. NY. half leather/marbled brd. VG. B30. $100.00

BEACH, Frank A. *Neuropsychology of Lashley.* 1960. McGraw Hill. 564p. G/dj. K4. $20.00

BEACH, S.A. *Apples of New York.* 1905. NY. 2 vol. 1st ed. VG. B5. $135.00

BEACH, Sylvia. *Shakespeare & Company.* 1959. NY. Harcourt Brace. 1st ed. 230 p. VG/rpr. A17. $25.00

BEACH, Sylvia. *Shakespeare & Company.* 1960. London. 39 photos. 248p. NF/VG. A4. $45.00

BEACHY, Stephen. *Whistling Song.* 1991. Norton. 1st ed/author's 1st book. F/F. A14. $35.00

BEADLE, George W. *Genetics & Modern Biology.* 1963. Phil. 72p. dj. G7. $25.00

BEADLE, J.H. *Das Leben in Utah...* 1870. Phil. Nat Pub. 1st Am German-language ed. 8vo. 544p. cloth. M1. $350.00

BEADLE, J.H. *Life in Utah; or, Mysteries & Crimes of Mormonism.* 1870. Phil. Nat Pub. 1st ed/1st issue. 8vo. 540p. emb full leather. NF. P4. $185.00

BEAGLE, Peter S. *Fantasy Worlds of Peter Beagle.* 1978. Viking. 1st ed. VG/F. P3. $20.00

BEAGLE, Peter S. *Folk of the Air.* 1986. Del Rey. VG/F. P3. $17.00

BEAHM, George. *Stephen King Story.* 1991. Andrews McMeel. 1st ed. VG. P3. $17.00

BEAL, Merrill D. *Story of Man in Yellowstone.* 1949. Caxton. 1st ed. sgn. map ep. F/dj. A18. $40.00

BEALE, J.H. *Picturesque Sketches of Am Progress.* 1889. NY. gilt cloth. VG. A17. $15.00

BEALE, R. *Lawns for Sports: Their Construction & Upkeep.* 1924. London. 1st ed. cloth. VG. C11. $85.00

BEALS, Art. *Beyond Hunger: Biblical Mandate for Social Responsibility.* 1985. Multnomah. 221p. F/dj. B29. $5.50

BEALS, Carleton. *Brimstone & Chili.* 1927. Knopf. 1st ed. VG. F3. $15.00

BEAMONT, William. *Diary of a Journey From Warrington to the East.* 1855. Warrington. 1st ed. 8vo. 268p. new quarter calf. O2. $175.00

BEANEY, Jan. *Art of the Needle, Designed in Fabric & Thread.* 1988. np. cloth. VG. G2. $28.00

BEAR, Greg. *Anvil of Stars.* 1992. Warner. 1st ed. F/F. T2. $16.00

BEAR, Greg. *Blood Music.* 1985. Arbor. 1st ed. F/F. T2. $75.00

BEAR, Greg. *Eternity.* 1988. Warner. 1st ed. F/F. P3/T2. $17.00

BEAR, Greg. *Forge of God.* 1987. Tor. 1st ed. VG/VG. P3. $18.00

BEAR, Greg. *Queen of Angels.* 1990. Warner. 1st ed. F/F. P3. $20.00

BEAR, Greg. *Venging.* 1992. Legend. 1st ed. F/F. P3. $35.00

BEARD, Dan. *Hardly a Man Is Now Alive.* 1939. NY. 1st ed. VG/G. B5. $60.00

BEARD, Patten. *Tucked-In Tales.* 1939 (1929). Rand McNally. ils Clarence Biers. VG. P2. $20.00

BEARDSLEY, Aubrey. *Selected Drawings.* 1967. Grove. 1st prt thus. 4to. silvered blk cloth. VG/VG. F1. $25.00

BEARDSLEY & GLASSCO. *Under the Hill.* 1959. NY. 1st ed. ils. VG/VG. A17. $10.00

BEARSE, Austin. *Reminiscences of Fugitive-Slave Law Days in Boston.* 1880. Boston. Warren Richardson. 41p. sewn wrp. M11. $250.00

BEASLEY, Conger. *Hidalgo's Beard.* 1979. Andrews McMeel. 1st ed. VG/VG. P3. $20.00

BEATLY & SARGENT. *Basic Rug Hooking.* 1977. np. VG/wrp. G2. $15.00

BEATON, Cecil. *Beaton.* 1980. Viking. 1st ed. text James Dazinger. 200+ full-p pl. VG+/VG+. S9. $50.00

BEATON, Cecil. *Face of the World: Internat Scrapbook of People & Places.* nd. John Day. 1st Am ed. 240p. VG. H1. $18.00

BEATON, Cecil. *Face of the World: Internat Scrapbook of People & Places.* nd. NY. John Day. VG/VG. B5. $35.00

BEATTIE, Ann. *Chilly Scenes of Winter.* 1976. Doubleday. UP. w/pub sheet detached. NF/tall wrp. B4. $275.00

BEATTIE, Ann. *Chilly Scenes of Winter.* 1976. Doubleday. 1st ed/author's 1st novel. 280p. F/clip. C6. $75.00

BEATTIE, Ann. *Jacklighting.* 1981. Worcester. Metacom. 1st ed. 1/26 hc. sgn. brn linen. M/dj. B24. $125.00

BEATTIE, Ann. *Spectacles.* 1985. Workman. 1st ed/1st prt. lg 8vo. F/F. C8. $35.00

BEATTIE, James. *Essay on Nature & Immutability of Truth.* 1809. Phil. Wieatt. 1st Am ed. full calf. G+. H7. $50.00

BEATTIE, James. *Essays: On Poetry & Music, As They Affect the Mind...* 1778. London. Wm Creech. 555p. marbled brd/modern calf. VG. G1. $325.00

BEATTY, Richmond Croom. *Vanderbilt Miscellany 1919-1944.* 1944. Nashville. Vanderbilt. 1st ed. sgn. ils/sgn Marion Junkin. 397p. NF/worn. C6. $50.00

BEAUMONT, Charles. *Intruder.* 1959. Putnam. 1st ed. xl. dj. P3. $30.00

BEAUMONT, William. *Experiments & Observations on Gastric Juice...* 1833. Plattsburgh. 1st ed. 3 engraved pl. 280p. G/orig brd/clamshell box. G7. $1,275.00

BEAVER & BEAVER. *All About the Saint Bernard.* 1980. London. Pelham. 1st ed. 176p. cloth. M/dj. R2. $15.00

BECHDOLT, Jack. *Torch.* 1948. Prime. 1st ed. F/dj. M2. $15.00

BECHWOURTH, James P. *Life & Adventures of...* 1931. NY. 1st ed thus. 405p. VG. A17. $40.00

BECK, Adams L. *Garden of Vision.* 1929. Copp Clark. 1st ed. VG/VG. P3. $40.00

BECK, Adams L. *Treasure of Ho.* 1926. Collins. 2nd ed. VG. P3. $20.00

BECK, Frank O. *Study of Boys in Municipal Court of Chicago.* 1919. Chicago. 15 tables (some fld). 31p. lib brd. wrp. D3. $12.50

BECK, James M. *May It Please the Court.* 1930. Atlanta, GA. 1st ed. inscr. 511p. VG. D3. $35.00

BECK, Joseph C. *Applied Pathology in Diseases of Nose, Throat & Ear.* 1923. St Louis. ils/pls. 280p. G7. $45.00

BECK, K.K. *Amateur Night.* 1993. Mysterious. 1st ed. F/F. O4. $15.00

BECK, K.K. *Peril Under the Palms.* 1989. Walker. 1st ed. sgn. F/F. O4. $15.00

BECK, K.K. *Unwanted Attentions.* 1988. Walker. 1st ed. sgn. F/F. O4. $20.00

BECK, Richard. *Icelandic Lyrics: Originals & Translations.* 1930. Reykjavik. Bjarnarson. 1st ed. 269p. VG. A17. $30.00

BECK, Samuel J. *Rorschach's Test.* 1944. Grune Stratton. 2 vol. G. K4. $50.00

BECK, William. *Friends: Who They Are — What They Have Done.* 1893. London. Edward Hicks. 16mo. 277p. VG. V3. $12.00

BECK & MOLISH. *Reflexes to Intelligence.* 1960. Glencoe, IL. Free Pr. 2nd ed. 669p. dj. K4. $15.00

BECKER, Carl. *Heavenly City of the 18th-Century Philosophers.* 1932. Yale. sm 8vo. 168p. maroon cloth. G1. $30.00

BECKER, Ernest. *Angel in Armor: Post-Freudian Perspective on Nature of Man.* 1969. Braziller. cloth. VG/dj. G1. $25.00

BECKER, Peter. *Dingane: King of the Zulu 1828-1840.* 1964. London. Crowell. 1st ed. 8vo. 283p. F/NF. P4. $45.00

BECKER, Stephen. *Dog Tags.* 1973. Random. 1st ed. VG/VG. P3. $25.00

BECKER, Stephen. *When the War Is Over.* 1969. Random. 1st ed. VG/VG. P3. $25.00

BECKER, Theodore L. *Political Trials.* 1971. Bobbs Merrill. M11. $35.00

BECKER & LANDES. *Essays in Economics of Crime & Punishment.* 1974. NY. 268p. NF. D3. $15.00

BECKETT, Edmund. *Clocks, Watches & Bells.* 1975. Yorkshire, Eng. 1st ed/9th prt. 12mo. 404p. F/VG. A8. $25.00

BECKETT, Oliver. *JF Herring & Sons.* 1981. London. Allen. 1st ed. VG/VG. O3. $58.00

BECKETT, Samuel. *Dream of Fair to Middling Women.* 1992. Dublin. Blk Cat. 1st ed. F/F. S9. $40.00

BECKETT, Samuel. *Echo's Bones & Other Precipates.* 1935. Paris. Europa. 1/327. sgn. 36p. F/tan wrp. H5. $500.00

BECKFORD, William. *Vathek.* 1928. John Day. 1st Am ed. ils Mahlon Blaine. 229p. NF/ragged. M20. $65.00

BECLARD, P.A. *Elements of General Anatomy: Trans From Last Ed of French...* 1830. Edinburgh. pres. 399p. brd. worn. G7. $195.00

BEDELL, Clyde. *Concordex of the Urantia Book.* 1974. Santa Barbara. Urantia Found. hc. sgn. 438p. VG/VG. B33. $25.00

BEDFORD, Annie North. *Disneyland on the Air.* 1955. Mickey Mouse Club Book. TVTI. VG. P3. $20.00

BEDFORD, John. *Bristol & Other Coloured Glass.* (1964). Walker. 3rd prt. 64p. F/G. H1. $16.00

BEDFORD, Sybille. *Aldous Huxley Volume 1.* 1973. Chatto Windus. P3. $25.00

BEDINI, Silvio A. *Life of Benjamin Banneker.* 1972. Scribner. 8vo. 434p. VG/chip. K5. $50.00

BEDWELI, C.E.A. *Catalog of Prt Books in Lib of Honorable Soc Middle Temple.* 1914-1925. Glasgow. 4 vol. cloth. G. M11. $350.00

BEE, Clair. *Championship Ball.* 1948. Grosset Dunlap. later prt. VG/G+. P8. $25.00

BEE, Clair. *Home Run Feud.* 1964. Grosset Dunlap. Chip Hilton Series #22. VG. P8. $110.00

BEE, Clair. *Triple-Threat Trouble.* 1960. Grosset Dunlap. 1st ed. last title printed. VG/VG. M20. $50.00

BEEBE, L. *Central Pacific & Southern Pacific.* 1966. Berkley. 3rd ed. VG/VG. B5. $50.00

BEEBEE, Chris. *Hub.* 1987. Macdonald. F/F. P3. $22.00

BEEBEE, Elizabeth. *Roy Rogers on the Double-R Ranch.* 1951. Simon Schuster. VG. P3. $15.00

BEECHER & STOWE. *New Housekeeper's Manual...* 1873. NY. Ford. new revised ed. cloth. F. B14. $75.00

BEECHING, Jack. *Dakota Project.* 1968. Delacorte. 1st ed. F/F. F4. $16.00

BEEDING, Francis. *Death Walks in Eastrepps.* 1931. Mystery League. 1st ed. G/VG. P3. $15.00

BEEDING, Francis. *Spellbound.* 1945. Tower. MTI. VG/VG. P3. $20.00

BEEDING, Francis. *There Are Thirteen.* 1946. Harper. 1st ed. VG. P3. $18.00

BEEDING, Francis. *12 Disguises.* 1946. Books Inc. G/VG. P3. $15.00

BEEM, Frances. *Foxy Squirrel in the Garden.* 1933. Rand McNally Jr Elf Book 121. K2. $7.00

BEER, Eileene Harrison. *Scandinavian Design, Objects of a Life Style.* 1975. FSG. 1st ed. 4to. 214p. silvered purple cloth. F/G. F1. $65.00

BEER, Thomas. *Mauve Decade, American Life at End of 19th Century.* 1926. np. VG. A4. $20.00

BEERBOHM, Max. *And Even Now.* 1920. London. Heinemann. 1st ed. 8vo. yel cloth. VG. M7. $65.00

BEERBOHM, Max. *Poets' Corner.* 1904. Dodd Mead. 1st Am ed. folio. 22 sheets. VG/stitched wrp. H5. $225.00

BEERBOHM, Max. *Rossetti & His Circle.* 1922. London. Heinemann. sm 4to. 22 tipped-in pl. gilt bl cloth. VG+. F1. $95.00

BEERS, Fannie A. *Memories: Record of Personal Experience...* 1891. Lippincott. 2nd ed. 8vo. 336p. brn cloth. xl. VG. C6. $45.00

BEESON, John. *Plea for the Indians With Facts & Features of the Late War.* 1858. NY. Beeson. 3rd ed. 12mo. 143p. prt wrp. M1. $200.00

BEET, Ernest Agar. *Astronomy Old & New.* 1967. London. Bell. 8vo. ils. 198p. VG/dj. K5. $16.00

BEGBIE, Harold. *Cage.* nd. Hodder Stoughton. VG. P3. $8.00

BEGLEY, Louis. *Man Who Was Late.* 1993. Knopf. 1st ed. F/F. A14. $45.00

BEGLEY, Louis. *Wartime Lies.* 1991. Knopf. 1st ed/author's 1st book. F/F. A14. $75.00

BEHANAN, Kovoor T. *Yoga: A Scientific Evaluation.* 1937. Macmillan. not 1st ed. G+. N2. $6.00

BEHBEHANI, Hashim S.H. *China's Foreign Policy in the Arab World 1955-1975.* 1985. London/Boston. 1st pb ed. 426p. VG. W1. $10.00

BEHN, Jack. *'45-70' Rifles.* 1956. Stackpole. 1st ed. 137p. VG/dj. M20. $40.00

BEHRENS, Charles. *Atomic Medicine.* 1949. NY. 416p. VG. A13. $150.00

BEHRMAN, S.N. *Worchester Account.* 1954. NY. 1st ed. inscr/dtd 1954. F/NF. A11. $35.00

BEIER, Lucinda. *Sufferers & Healers: Experience of Illness in 17th-C Eng.* 1987. London. 1st ed. 314p. dj. A13. $40.00

BEINHART, Larry. *American Hero.* 1993. Pantheon. ARC. F/pict wrp. B3. $20.00

BEINHART, Larry. *No One Rides for Free.* 1986. Morrow. 1st ed. sgn. F/dj. M15. $45.00

BEIRNE, F. *War of 1812.* 1949. NY. ARC/1st ed. w/photos. VG/VG. B5. $30.00

BELANTEUR, Said. *Les Chevaux de Diar el Mahcoul.* ca 1974. Diffusion. 1st ed. 222p. VG. W1. $9.00

BELDECOS, George John. *Hellenic Orders, Decorations & Medals.* 1991. Athens. ils. 169p. O2. $30.00

BELFOUR, Stanton. *Centennial Hist of Shadyside Presbyterian Church.* 1966. Pittsburgh. 1st ed. 154p. cloth. VG. M8. $37.50

BELFRAGE, Cedric. *Frightened Giant.* 1957. London/NY. Weekly Guardian/S&W. 1st ed. F/NF. B2. $35.00

BELFRAGE, Cedric. *Seeds of Destruction: Truth About US Occupation of Germany.* 1954. NY. Cameron Kahn. 1st ed. 232p. NF/wrp. B2. $30.00

BELIAEV, Alexander. *Professor Dowell's Head.* 1980. Macmillan. 1st ed. VG. P3. $15.00

BELINSKII, V.A. *Dynamic Meteorology.* 1961. Jerusalem. sm 4to. 591p. VG/dj. K5. $30.00

BELKNAP, Jeremy. *Hist of NH. Comprehending Events of One Complete Century...* 1812. Dover, NH. Mann Remick. 3 vol. 8vo. fld map. 2-toned brd. uncut. M1. $275.00

BELL, A.E. *Christian Huygens & Development of Science in 17th C.* 1947. NY. Longman Gr. 8vo. 220p. G/chip. K5. $40.00

BELL, Archie. *Spell of Caribbean Islands.* 1926. Boston. 1st ed. VG. B14. $20.00

BELL, Charles. *Institutes of Surgery: Arranged in Order of Lectures...* 1840. Phil. Waldie. 446p. contemporary quarter sheep/brd. G7. $145.00

BELL, Charles. *Letters Concerning Diseases of the Urethra.* 1811. Boston. 6 pl. modern polished calf. G7. $250.00

BELL, Charles. *Manuscript of Drawings of the Arteries.* 1970. Editions Medicina Rare. 1/2500. pl. F/case. G7. $65.00

BELL, Clare. *Ratha's Creature.* 1983. Atheneum. 1st ed. F/F. P3. $11.00

BELL, Clive. *Legend of Monte Della Sibilla.* 1923. Hogarth. 1/400. wht pict brd. F/blk prt wht dj. Q1. $650.00

BELL, Gertrude. *Letters of...* 1928. Boni Liveright. 2 vol. 8th ed. VG/dj. W1. $65.00

BELL, Gertrude. *Poems From the Divan of Hafiz.* 1928. London. Heinemann. 2nd ed. 12mo. VG/dj. W1. $65.00

BELL, Gertrude. *Teachings of Hafiz.* 1979. London. Octagon. sm 8vo. VG/dj. W1. $25.00

BELL, Gordon B. *Golden Troubadour.* 1980. McGraw Hill. F/F. P3. $13.00

BELL, Josephine. *In the King's Absence.* 1973. Bles. 1st ed. F/F. P3. $20.00

BELL, Josephine. *New People at the Hollies.* 1961. Macmillan. 1st ed. VG/VG. P3. $25.00

BELL, Josephine. *No Escape.* 1966. Macmillan. 1st ed. VG/rpr. P3. $13.00

BELL, Josephine. *Pigeon Among the Cats.* 1977. Stein Day. 1st ed. VG/VG. P3. $18.00

BELL, Josephine. *Wolf! Wolf!* 1980. Walker. 1st ed. VG/VG. P3. $15.00

BELL, Linda A. *Sartre's Ethics of Ambiguity.* 1989. Tuscaloosa/London. sm 8vo. 224p. bl cloth. VG/dj. G1. $18.50

BELL, Madison Smartt. *Doctor Sleep.* 1992. London. Bloomsbury. 1st ed. F/F. B3. $20.00

BELL, Madison Smartt. *Waiting for the End of the World.* 1985. NY. 1st ed/author's 2nd novel. sgn. F/F. A11. $45.00

BELL, Madison Smartt. *Waiting for the End of the World.* 1985. World. 1st ed/author's 2nd book. F/torn. A15. $30.00

BELL, Madison Smartt. *Zero DB & Other Stories.* 1987. Ticknor Fields. 1st ed. NF/VG. B3. $20.00

BELL, Millicent. *Marquand: An American Life.* 1979. Little Brn. 1st ed. 537p. F/dj. M10. $5.00

BELL, Pauline. *Feast Into Mourning.* 1991. London. Macmillan. 1st ed. F/F. S6. $25.00

BELL, T. *Out of This Furnace.* 1941. Boston. 1st ed. VG/VG. B5. $30.00

BELL, Whitfield J. Jr. *Colonial Physician.* 1975. NY. Science Hist Pub. 1st/ltd ed. 230p. F/wrp. B11. $25.00

BELL, Whitfield J. Jr. *Early American Science Needs & Opportunities for Study.* 1955. Williamsburg, VA. Inst Early Am Hist & Culture. 85p. VG. B11. $75.00

BELL, William Dixon. *Moon Colony.* 1937. Goldsmith. VG. P3. $10.00

BELL, William Gardner. *Will James: Life & Works of a Lone Cowboy.* 1987. Northland. 1st ed. 13 pl. M/dj. A18. $40.00

BELL & WOODCOCK. *Diversity of Green Plants.* 1969. Reading, MA. ils. 374p. VG. B26. $25.00

BELLAH, James Warner. *Sons of Cain.* 1928. Appleton. 1st prt. 248p. blk cloth. G/G. S11. $10.00

BELLAH, Robert Neelly. *Tokugawa Religion: Values of Pre-Industrial Japan.* 1957. Glencoe, IL. 1st ed. 249p. cloth. F/VG. M8. $30.00

BELLAIRS, John. *Animal Babies.* 1949. Donohue. ils Jacob Bates Abbott. VG/G. B17. $8.00

BELLAIRS, John. *Dark Secret of Weatherend.* 1984. Dial. 1st ed. VG/dj. P3. $15.00

BELLAIRS, John. *Pedant & the Shuffly.* 1968. Macmillan. 1st ed. ils Mariyn Fitschen. F/F. B17. $20.00

BELLAMY, Edward. *Equality.* 1897. Appleton. 3rd ed. xl. G+. N2. $10.00

BELLAMY, Joe David. *Olympic Gold Medalist.* 1978. Cedar Falls, IA. N Am Review. 1st ed/author's 1st book. F/wrp. B4. $45.00

BELLEM, Robert L. *Blue Murder.* 1987. Dennis McMillan. 1st ed thus. F/wrp. M2. $10.00

BELLI, Melvin. *Blood Money.* 1956. NY. 1st ed/author's 1st book. F/F. A17. $15.00

BELLI & JONES. *Belli Looks at Life & Law in Japan.* 1960. Bobbs Merrill. pref Toshio Irie. M11. $35.00

BELLIN, Mildred. *Jewish Cook Book According to...Dietary Laws...* 1945. NY. 455p. red cloth. VG. B14. $35.00

BELLINGHAM, Ellen. *Bibliography of Industrial Hygiene 1900-1933.* 1945. WA. 1st ed. 95p. wrp. A13. $100.00

BELLOC, Hilaire. *Bad Child's Book of Beasts.* nd. London. Duckworth. very early ed. lg 8vo. F. C8. $45.00

BELLOC, Hilaire. *Cautionary Verses.* (1941). Knopf. Ils Album ed/6th (8/59) prt. VG+/VG+. C8. $37.50

BELLOC, Hilaire. *Cruise of the Nona.* 1955. Westminster, MD. Newman. 347p. dj. T7. $20.00

BELLOC, Hilaire. *Emerald of Catherine the Great.* 1926. London. Arrowsmith. 1st ed. F/NF. M15. $250.00

BELLOC, Hilaire. *More Beasts for Worse Children.* nd. London. Duckworth. very early ed. lg 8vo. F. C8. $45.00

BELLOC, Hilaire. *New Cautionary Tales.* 1930. Harper. 1st ed. sm 8vo. VG. C8. $95.00

BELLONI, Gian Guido. *Prehistoric to Classical Painting.* 1962. London. Hamlyn. 1st ed. folio. pl. VG. W1. $12.00

BELLOW, Saul. *Dangling Man.* 1944. Vanguard. 1st ed/author's 1st book. pres. 191p. VG. H9. $1,000.00

BELLOW, Saul. *Herzog.* 1966. Paris. Gallimard. 1st French ed. 1/26. F/wrp. B4. $200.00

BELLOW, Saul. *Humboldt's Gift.* 1975. Viking. ARC/author's 8th novel. NF/wrp. L3. $125.00

BELLOW, Saul. *Mosby's Memoirs & Other Stories.* 1968. Viking. ARC. RS. w/promo material. F/VG. B4. $85.00

BELLOW, Saul. *Mr. Sammler's Planet.* 1970. Viking. 1st ed. VG. P3. $15.00

BELLOW, Saul. *Nobel Lecture.* 1979. NY. Targ. ltd ed. sgn. 1/350. F/F. A9. $150.00

BELLOW, Saul. *Nobel Lecture.* 1979. Targ. ARC. sgn. 1/350. mk Hors de Commerce. F/wrp. B4. $175.00

BELLOW, Saul. *Theft.* 1989. Secker Warburg. 1st Eng/1st hc ed. F/F clip. L3. $85.00

BELLOW, Saul. *Victim.* 1947. Vanguard. 1st ed. F/VG. B2. $100.00

BELLOWS, H.W. *Historical Sketch of Col Benjamin Bellows...* 1855. NY. rebound. xl. A9. $45.00

BELM & BELM. *Two Is a Team.* (1945). HBW. 9th prt. ils Ernest Crichlow. unp. cloth. VG/dj. A3. $15.00

BELMONT, Bob; see Reynolds, Mack.

BELOFF, Max. *Foreign Policy & the Democratic Process.* 1955. Johns Hopkins. 1st ed. sm 8vo. xl. VG. W1. $8.00

BELOTE & BELOTE. *Typhoon of Steel: Battle for Okinawa.* 1970. NY. BC. 384p. F/F. A17. $7.50

BELTING, Natalia. *Christmas Folk.* 1969. Holt Rinehart. 1st ed. M/M. C8. $60.00

BEMELMANS, Ludwig. *Hansi.* 1934. Viking. 1st ed/author's 1st book. ils. pict bl cloth. NF. D6. $125.00

BEMELMANS, Ludwig. *Madeline's Rescue.* nd (1953). London. Derek Verschoyle. probable 1st UK ed. 4to. NF/VG. C8. $175.00

BEMELMANS, Ludwig. *My Life in Art.* 1958. Harper. possible 1st ed. pls w/2 tipped-in pl. VG/G+. P2. $85.00

BEMMANN, Hans. *Stone & the Flute.* 1986. Viking. 1st ed. VG/VG. P3. $20.00

BENCHLEY, Nathaniel. *One To Grow On.* 1958. McGraw Hill. 1st ed/author's 1st novel. inscr. F/NF. B4. $125.00

BENCHLEY, Peter. *Girl of the Sea of Cortez.* 1982. Andre Deutsch. 1st ed. F/F. P3. $20.00

BENCHLEY, Peter. *Island.* 1979. BC. 1st ed. VG/VG. P3. $18.00

BENCHLEY, Peter. *Jaws.* 1974. London. Deutsch. 1st ed. F/F. B4. $100.00

BENCHLEY, Robert. *20,000 Leagues Under the Sea; or, David Copperfield.* 1946. Bl Ribbon. 233p. VG. H1. $4.00

BENDER, Lionel. *Telescopes.* 1991. Gloucester. 4to. ils. 31p. pict brd. F. K5. $10.00

BENDIX, Reinhard. *Max Weber: Intellectual Portrait.* 1960. Doubleday. 480p. blk cloth. VG/worn. G1. $27.50

BENEDICT, Howard. *NASA: The Journey Continues.* 1989. Houston, TX. Pioneer Pub. 4to. ils. 303p. VG/dj. K5. $25.00

BENEDICT, Pickney. *Dogs of God.* 1994. London. Secker Warburg. ARC/author's 1st novel. F/wrp. B3. $40.00

BENEDICTUS, David. *Fourth of June.* 1962. London. 1st ed/author's 1st novel. inscr. NF/VG+ clip. A11. $45.00

BENEKE, Friedrich Eduard. *Erfahrungslehre Grundlage Alles Wissens Ihren Hauptzugen.* 1820. Berlin. Ernst Siegfried Mittler. sm 8vo. 172p. VG. G1. $225.00

BENET, Stephen Vincent. *James Shore's Daughter.* 1934. Doubleday Doran. 1st ed. sgn. 1/307 #d. 277p. F/glassine wrp/pub case. H5. $85.00

BENET, William Rose. *Adolphus; or, The Adopted Dolphin.* 1941. Houghton Mifflin. 1st ed. sm 4to. VG+/G+. C8. $60.00

BENET, William Rose. *Famous Heritage Ed of Mother Goose.* 1943 (1936). Heritage. new ed. ils Roger Duvoisin. VG/VG. C8. $50.00

BENFORD, Gregory. *Across the Sea of Suns.* 1984. Timescape. 1st ed. F/F. P3. $18.00

BENFORD, Gregory. *Against Infinity.* 1983. Timescape. 1st ed. F/F. P3. $25.00

BENFORD, Gregory. *Artifact.* 1985. Tor. 1st ed. F/F. P3. $17.00

BENFORD, Gregory. *In Alien Flesh.* 1986. Tor. 1st ed. F/F. P3. $15.00

BENFORD, Gregory. *Jupiter Project.* 1975. Thomas Nelson. 1st ed. VG/dj. M20. $35.00

BENFORD, Gregory. *Tides of Light.* 1989. Bantam. 1st ed. F/F. P3. $18.00

BENFORD & BRIN. *Heart of the Comet.* 1986. Bantam. 1st ed. VG/VG. P3. $20.00

BENFORD & EKLUND, *If the Stars Are Gods.* 1977. Berkley. 1st ed. F/F. P3. $23.00

BENGTSSON, F.G. *Folk Som Sjong och Andre Essayer.* 1955. Stockholm. Norstedt. 1st ed. 320p. VG+/tan wrp. uncut. M7. $45.00

BENJAMIN, Asher. *Architect; or, Practical House Carpenter.* 1839. Boston. Mussey. 6th ed. 119p. contemporary sheepskin. B14. $425.00

BENJAMIN, M.D.; see Block, Lawrence.

BENJAMIN, Mary A. *Autographs: A Key to Collecting.* 1948. NY. Bowker. 1/3000. 305p. VG. A10. $18.00

BENJAMIN, Paul; see Auster, Paul.

BENJAMIN, Robert Spiers. *Call to Adventure.* 1934. World. VG/VG. P3. $20.00

BENNETT, Alan R. *Horsewoman: The Extraordinary Mrs D (Louie Dingwall).* 1979. Dorset. 1st UK ed. 207p. gilt bl cloth. VG/VG. M7. $26.50

BENNETT, Arnold. *Imperial Palace.* (1931). Doubleday Doran. 769p. VG/VG. H1. $4.00

BENNETT, Arnold. *Loot of Cities.* 1972. Oswald Train. 1st Am ed. F/dj. M2. $10.00

BENNETT, Charles H. *Bennett's Fables. From Aesop & Others.* 1978. Viking. 1st ed thus/rpt of 1857 ed. 54p. VG/VG. A3. $10.00

BENNETT, Dorothy. *Golden Encyclopedia.* 1946. Simon Schuster. ils Cornelius DeWitt. pict brd. G. A17. $15.00

BENNETT, Estelline. *Old Deadwood Days.* 1928. NY. JH Sears. 1st ed. 12mo. 300p. VG. B11. $25.00

BENNETT, Ira E. *Hist of the Panama Canal...* 1915. WA, DC. 1st ed. 543p. G. B18. $65.00

BENNETT, Joan. *Virginia Woolf: Her Art As a Novelist.* 1945. Harcourt Brace. 1st ed. VG+/VG+. S9. $30.00

BENNETT, O.P. *Collie.* 1924. WA, IL. 2nd ed. ils. 334p. cloth. scarce. R2. $125.00

BENNETT, Peter. *Ils Child.* 1979. Putnam. 1st ed. 4to. ils. gr cloth. VG/VG. S11. $35.00

BENNETT, Ralph. *Ultra & Mediterranean Strategy.* 1989. NY. 1st ed. 496p. VG/dj. B18. $15.00

BENNETT, Richard. *Skookum & Sandy.* 1935. Doubleday Doran. 1st ed. VG. P2. $17.50

BENNETT, Rowena. *Runner for the King.* 1944. Chicago. apparent 1st ed. ils Fiore Mastri. F/torn. M5. $22.00

BENNETT, Whitman. *Practical Guide to American 19th-Century Color Plate Books.* 1980. NY. Haydn Found. 1940p. cloth. VG. A10. $40.00

BENNETTS, Pamela. *Death of the Red King.* 1976. St Martin. ARC of 1st Am ed. RS. F/dj. F4. $25.00

BENOIT, Hubert. *Metaphysique et Psychanalyse...* 1949. Paris. La Colombe. sq 8vo. 151p. prt tan wrp. G1. $30.00

BENOIT, Hubert. *Supreme Doctrine: Psychological Studies in Zen Thought.* 1955. London. Kegan Paul. 248p. xl. VG/VG. B33. $25.00

BENSMAN, David. *Practice of Solidarity: American Hat Finishers...* 1985. Urbana. M/VG. V4. $12.50

BENSON, A.C. *Edward Fitzgerald.* 1905. Macmillan. 1st ed. sm 8vo. 207p. gilt bl cloth. G. F1. $15.00

BENSON, A.C. *Thread of Gold.* 1907. Dutton. 1st ed. VG. P3. $2.00

BENSON, Allan L. *Way To Prevent War.* 1915. Girard. Appeal to Reason. gilt bl cloth. F. B2. $65.00

BENSON, Ben. *Ninth Hour.* 1956. Mill. VG/G. P3. $25.00

BENSON, Egbert. *Vindication of the Captors of Major Andre.* 1817. NY. Kirk Mercein. 1st ed. 12mo. 99p. prt brd. worn spine. M1. $225.00

BENSON, Elizabeth. *Conference of Chavin.* 1971. WA, DC. 1st ed. 124p. VG. F3. $25.00

BENSON, Lyman. *Cacti of Arizona.* 1940. Tucson. 1st ed. photos/pl/maps. red cloth. F. B26. $30.00

BENSON, Lyman. *Native Cacti of CA.* 1969. Stanford. ils/photos/maps. 243p. VG+/dj. B26. $25.00

BENSON, Raymond. *James Bond Companion: All About the World According to 007.* 1984. Dodd Mead. 1st ed. ils. F/wrp. S6. $22.50

BENT, Arthur C. *Life Histories of North American Gulls & Terns.* 1947. Dodd Mead. 1st ed thus. 333p. gray cloth. VG. B14. $30.00

BENT, George P. *Pioneer's Historical Sketches...* nd. Chicago. ils. 381p. G. B18. $22.50

BENTLEY, E.C. *Elephant's Work.* 1950. Knopf. 1st ed. VG/VG. P3. $25.00

BENTLEY, E.C. *Trent's Last Case.* nd. Nelson. VG/G. P3. $25.00

BENTLEY, Nicolas. *Inside Information.* 1974. London. Deutsch. 1st ed. F/F. M15. $30.00

BENTLEY, Nicolas. *Nicolas Bentley's Book of Birds.* 1965. London. Deutsch. 1st ed. lg 8vo. F/F. C8. $35.00

BENTLEY. *Blake Books, Annotated Catalogues of Wm Blake's Writings...* 1977. Oxford. 1091p. F/F. A4. $250.00

BENTLEY. *Vanished Society: Essays in Am Hist.* 1962. Friends of Princeton Lib. ils. 94p. F. A4. $30.00

BENTON, Joel. *Life of Hon Phineas T Barnum.* (1891). Edgewood. lg 12mo. VG+. C8. $25.00

BENWELL, H. *History of Yankee Division in WWI.* 1919. Boston. 1st ed. 272p. VG. B5. $40.00

BENZ, Francis E. *On to Suex! Story of DeLesseps & the Canal.* 1939. Dodd Mead. 1st ed. 238p. G. W1. $10.00

BERCKMAN, Evelyn. *Finger to Her Lips.* 1971. BC. 1st ed. xl. dj. P3. $5.00

BERCOVICI, Konrad. *For a Song.* 1931. Dodd Mead. ARC. RS. F/VG. F4. $45.00

BERCOVICI, Konrad. *It's the Gypsy in Me.* 1941. Prentice Hall. 1st ed. 8vo. xl. G+. C8. $15.00

BERDYAEV, Nicholas. *Dream & Reality.* 1950. London. Bles. 1st Eng-language ed. 332p. bl cloth. VG/dj. G1. $38.00

BERENDT, John. *Midnight in the Garden of Good & Evil.* 1994. Random. 1st ed/author's 1st book. F/F. S9. $45.00

BERENSON, Mary. *Modern Pilgrimage.* 1933. Appleton. 1st ed. 8vo. 355p. VG. W1. $12.00

BERESFORD, Elisabeth. *Wombles.* 1969. Meredith. 1st Am ed. 183p. VG/dj. M20. $18.00

BERG, Elizabeth. *Durable Goods.* 1993. Random. 1st ed/author's 1st novel. F/F. A14. $30.00

BERG, Gertrude. *Molly & Me.* 1961. McGraw Hill. 1st ed. 246p. F/F. B14. $35.00

BERGAUST, Erik. *Russians in Space.* 1969. Putnam. photos/diagrams. 95p. pict cloth. xl. K5. $15.00

BERGAUST, Erik. *Wernher von Braun.* 1976. Nat Space Inst. 1st ed. 589p. VG/dj. B18. $25.00

BERGE & WYSHAM. *Pearl Diver: Adventuring Over & Under Southern Seas.* ca 1930. Garden City. 8vo. 368p. blk cloth. VG. P4. $20.00

BERGER, Erick. *Honey of the Nile.* 1938. Oxford. 1st ed. 8vo. 225p. NF. W1. $8.00

BERGER, Gaston. *Cogito Dans la Philosophie de Husserl.* 1941. Paris. Aubier. 1st prt. 156p. VG/wrp. G1. $37.00

BERGER, Melvin. *Early Humans, a Prehistoric World.* 1988. Putnam. obl 8vo. rem mk. F. B17. $7.50

BERGER, Sidney. *Design of Bibliographies: Observations, References...* 1992. np. 4to. 208p. F. A4. $95.00

BERGER, Thomas. *Houseguest.* 1988. Little Brown. 1st ed. VG/VG. P3. $17.00

BERGER, Thomas. *Nowhere.* 1985. Delacourt/Lawrence. 1st ed. VG/G+. N2. $7.50

BERGERON, A. *Confederate Mobile (Alabama).* 1991. MS U. 271p. VG. E5. $30.00

BERGET, Alphonse. *Conquest of the Air.* 1909. NY. 1st Am ed. 295p. VG. B19. $175.00

BERGLER, Edmund. *Battle of the Conscience.* 1948. WA Inst Medicine. 296p. G. K4. $6.00

BERGMAN, Andrew. *Big Kiss-Off of 1944.* 1974. HRW. 1st ed. VG/VG. P3. $25.00

BERGMAN, Andrew. *Hollywood & Levine.* 1975. Holt. 1st ed. F/NF. B2. $30.00

BERGMAN, Jules. *Ninety Seconds to Space: The X-15 Story.* 1960. Garden City. Hanover. 4to. 224p. cloth. xl. K5. $20.00

BERGMAN, Ray. *Trout.* 1949. Knopf. 13th prt. pl. VG/dj. B34. $50.00

BERGMANN, Peter G. *Riddle of Gravitation.* 1968. Scribner. 8vo. 270p. VG/dj. K5. $30.00

BERGSLAND, Knut. *Aleut Dialects of Atka & Attu.* 1959. Am Philosophical Soc. ils/maps. VG/brn wrp. P4. $65.00

BERGSMA, Daniel. *Clinical Cytogenetics & Genetics.* 1974. NY/London. Stratton Intercontiental Medical Books. 194p. VG. K4. $15.00

BERGSON, Henri Louis. *Creative Evolution.* 1911. Holt. later prt. 408p. bl cloth. G1. $25.00

BERGSON, Henri Louis. *Essay sur les Donnees de la Conscience.* 1901. London. Germer Bailliere. 3rd prt. inscr. F/bl wrp. G1. $200.00

BERGSON, Henri Louis. *Evolution Creatrice.* 1962. Paris. later prt. 372p. rebound bl buckram. G1. $25.00

BERGSON, Henri Louis. *Matter & Memory.* 1978. NY. Humanities Pr. rpt. 339p. bl cloth. VG. G1. $27.50

BERGSON, Henri Louis. *Two Sources of Morality & Religion.* 1935. Holt. 1st Eng-language ed. 308p. russet cloth. VG. G1. $35.00

BERILLON, Edgar. *Voltaire.* 1891 (1890). Paris. Bureaux Revue de l'Hypnotisme. 36p. rare. G1. $35.00

BERJEAU, Charles. *Horses of Antiquity, Middle Ages & Renaissance...* 1864. London. Dulau. 1st Eng-language ed. ils. VG. O3. $125.00

BERKEBILE, Don. *Carriage Terminology.* 1979. Smithsonian. 3rd prt. 4to. F/sans. O3. $65.00

BERKELEY, Anthony. *Silk Stocking Murders.* nd. Canada. Doubleday Doran. 1st ed. VG. P3. $35.00

BERKELEY, Anthony. *Trial & Error.* 1965. Hodder Stoughton. VG/G. P3. $20.00

BERKELEY, Edmund C. *Computer Revolution.* 1962. Doubleday. 194p. VG/dj. K4. $15.00

BERKELEY, George. *Alciphron; or, Minute Philosopher.* 1803. New Haven. For Increase Cooke & Co. 1st Am ed. 388p. VG. G1. $150.00

BERKELEY, George. *New Theory of Vision & Other Select Philosophical Writings.* 1910. London. Dent. later prt. 16mo. 304p. bl cloth. G1. $25.00

BERKELEY, George. *Philosophical Commentaries Generally Called Commonplace...* 1944. London. Nelson. 1/400. 485p. yel cloth/leather spine label. VG/dj. G1. $85.00

BERKELEY, George. *Works..., Late Bishop of Cloyne in Ireland...* 1784. Dublin. John Exshaw. 2 vols. lg 4to. later quarter morocco/raised bands. G1. $850.00

BERKELEY, Grentley F. *Reminiscences of a Huntsman.* 1897. London. Sportsman's Lib. VG. O3. $65.00

BERKELEY & BERKELEY. *Yankee Botanist in the Carolinas.* 1986. Berlin. Cramer. pb. 242p. M. A10. $35.00

BERKIN & LOVETT. *Women, War & Revolution.* 1980. NY. Holmes Meier. M/M. V4. $15.00

BERKMAN & KARROW. *Index to Maps in Catalogue of Everett D Graff Collection...* 1972. np. index to 860 maps. F/wrp. A4. $15.00

BERLE & DE CAMP. *Inventions & Their Management.* 1948. Scranton. Internat TB Co. M11. $45.00

BERLIN, Jean V. *Confederate Nurse 1860-1865: Being Diary of Ada W Bacot.* 1994. index. 199p. dj. O8. $12.50

BERLIN, Sven. *Alfred Wallis, Primitive.* 1949. London. Nicholson Watson. ils. 122p. dj. T7. $45.00

BERLITZ, Charles. *Atlantis: Lost Continent Revealed.* 1984. Macmillan. 1st ed. VG. P3. $15.00

BERLO, Janet. *Art, Ideology, & City of Teotihuacan.* 1992. WA, DC. 1st ed. 442p. VG. F3. $40.00

BERMAN, Eugene. *Graphic Work of...* 1971. NY. Clarkson Potter. 1st ed. ils. gilt bl cloth. rem mk. VG/VG. F1. $45.00

BERMAN, Louis. *Religion Called Behaviorism.* 1927. Boni Liveright. 153p. G. K4. $15.00

BERMAN, Wallace. *Retrospective.* 1978. LA. Fellows of Contemporary Art. 1st ed. 4to. F/wrp. S9. $45.00

BERNARD, Claude. *Intro to Study of Experimental Medicine.* 1927. Macmillan. 1st Eng-language ed. ruled gr cloth. VG. G1. $50.00

BERNARD, Claude. *Lecons sur la Physiologie et la Pathologie Systeme Nerveux.* 1858. Paris. Bailliere. 2 vol. G7. $895.00

BERNARD, Claude. *Lecons sur les Effects Substances Toxiques Medicamenteuses.* 1857. Paris. Bailliere. ils. 388p. xl. new cloth. G7. $250.00

BERNARD, Robert. *Deadly Meeting.* nd. BC. VG/VG. P3. $8.00

BERNAYS, Jacob. *Grundzuge der Verlorenen Abhandlung des Aristoteles...* 1857. Breslau. Verlag. 1st separate ed. VG/wrp. rare. G1. $185.00

BERNHARD, Thomas. *Wittgenstein's Nephew.* 1989. Knopf. 1st Am ed. rem mk. F/F. A14. $20.00

BERNIER, Jane. *American Birds.* 1979 & 1982. Cleveland Hgts. 2 vol. 1/300. sgn. full bl leather. F. B24. $150.00

BERNSTORFF, Count. *My 3 Years in Am.* 1920. NY. 1st ed. 428p. G. A17. $8.50

BERQUE, Jacques. *Arab Rebirth: Pain & Ecstasy.* 1983. London. Alsaqi Books. 1st ed. 138p. F. M7. $25.00

BERQUIN, Arnaud. *Children's Friend. Trans From the French...* 1794? Newbury-Ort. John Mycall. 16mo. 354p. M1. $200.00

BERRA & FERDENZI. *Behind the Plate.* 1962. Argonaut. 1st ed. VG/F. P8. $45.00

BERRA. *William Beebe: Annotated Bibliography.* 1977. np. 157p. F/F. A4. $30.00

BERREY, Lester. *Treasury of Biblical Quotations.* 1950. Garden City. 240p. VG. B29. $4.00

BERRY, Carole. *Year of the Monkey.* 1988. St Martin. 1st ed. F/F. P3. $17.00

BERRY, Don. *Moontrap.* 1962. Viking. 1st ed. F/VG+. A18. $50.00

BERRY, Erick. *Humbo the Hippo.* 1938. Grosset Dunlap. lg 8vo. F/F. C8. $75.00

BERRY, Erick. *Mom Du Jos: The Story of a Little Black Doll.* 1931. Doubleday Doran. 1st ed. ils. 116p. F/VG. P2. $100.00

BERRY, Erick. *Pinky Pup & the Empty Elephant.* 1922. Volland. 1st revised ed. VG. M5. $75.00

BERRY, John. *Krishna Fluting.* 1959. Macmillan. VG. P3. $8.00

BERRY, Mike; see Malzberg, Barry.

BERRY, Ray. *Spiritual Athlete: A Primer for the Inner Life.* 1992. Olema. Joshua. pb. 352p. M. B33. $15.00

BERRY, Richard. *Build Your Own Telescope.* nd (1985). Scribner. photos/plans/diagrams. 276p. VG/VG. K5. $25.00

BERRY, Wendell. *Clearing.* 1977. HBJ. 1st ed. F/2 djs. V1. $35.00

BERRY, Wendell. *Findings.* 1969. Prairie Pr. 1st ed. F/NF. B4. $150.00

BERRY, Wendell. *Home Economics.* 1987. Berkeley. UP. VG/prt pink wrp. B4. $30.00

BERRY, Wendell. *Nathan Coulter.* 1985. Northpoint. 2nd ed. inscr. F/F. B2. $45.00

BERRY, Wendell. *Openings.* 1968. HBW. 1st ed. sgn. F/NF. V1. $75.00

BERRY, Wendell. *Standing by Words.* 1983. Northpoint. UP. F/wrp. B4. $75.00

BERRY, Wendell. *Traveling at Home.* 1989. Northpoint. 1st ed. sgn. F/sans. B3. $50.00

BERRY, Wendell. *Unforseen Wilderness, KY's Red River Gorge.* 1991. Northpoint. UP. NF/prt gr wrp. B3. $40.00

BERRY, Wendell. *Wheel.* 1982. Northpoint. 1st ed. inscr. F/F. B2. $75.00

BERRY, Wendell. *Wild Birds: 6 Stories of Port William Membership.* 1986. Northpoint. 1st ed. inscr. F/F. B2. $65.00

BERRY & DASEN. *Culture & Cognition: Readings in Cross-Cultural Psychology.* 1974. London. Methuen. 427p. VG/dj. K4. $12.50

BERRYMAN, John. *Disposed.* 1948. Wm Sloane. 1st ed. sgn. F/VG. V1. $200.00

BERRYMAN, John. *His Toy, His Dream, His Rest.* 1968. NY. 1st ed. F/F. w/pub card. A15. $45.00

BERRYMAN, John. *Homage to Mistress Bradstreet.* 1956. NY. 1st ed. F/VG+. A9. $90.00

BERRYMAN, John. *Homage to Mistress Bradstreet.* 1956. NY. 1st ed. ils Ben Shahn. F/NF. Q1. $150.00

BERRYMAN, John. *77 Dream Songs.* 1964. FSG. 1st ed. sgn. F/VG. V1. $100.00

BERTEAUT, Simone. *Piaf: A Biography.* 1972. Harper Row. 1st Am ed. VG/dj. N2. $7.50

BERTHOFF, Warner. *Edmund Wilson.* 1968. MN U. 47p. VG. A17. $7.50

BERTIN, Jack. *Brood of Helios.* 1966. Arcadia. 1st ed. VG/VG. P3. $13.00

BERTO, Hazel. *North to Alaska's Shining River.* 1959. Indianapolis. 1st ed. 224p. map ep. VG/VG. A17. $10.00

BERTOLINI, Dewey M. *Back to the Heart of Youth Work.* 1989. Victor. 210p. M/M. B29. $7.50

BERTON, Pierre. *Arctic Grail: Quest for the NW Passage & N Pole.* 1989. NY. biblio/index. rem mk. 672p. F. A17. $10.00

BERTON & WU. *Contemporary China: A Research Guide.* 1967. Stanford. 4to. 724p. xl. VG. A4. $65.00

BERTRAM, Ernst. *Nietzsche: Essai de Mythologie.* 1932. Paris. Rieder. 1st French ed. 468p. prt buff wrp. G1. $27.50

BERTRAM, James G. *Harvest of the Sea.* 1865. London. 519p. cloth. VG. B14. $95.00

BESANT, Annie. *Study in Consciousness: Contribution to Science Psychology.* 1918. London. Theosophical Pub. 3rd ed. 460p. VG. B33. $22.00

BESANT & LEADBEATER. *Thought Forms.* 1961. Adyar. Theosophical Pub. 66p. VG/VG. B33. $30.00

BESCHKE, William. *Dreadful Sufferings & Thrilling Adventures...* 1850. St Louis. Barclay. 1st ed (1st issue?). 8vo. 60p. pict wrp. M1. $5,000.00

BESCHLOSS, Michael R. *Crisis Years: Kennedy & Krushchev 1960-1963.* 1991. NY. Burlinghame. 1st ed. ils. F/dj. M10. $15.00

BESKOW, Elsa. *Pelle's New Suit.* nd. Harper. lg obl 4to. pict paper brd/cloth spine. VG+. C8. $25.00

BESKOW, Elsa. *Tant Gron, Tant Brun Och Tant Gredelin.* 1949. Stockholm. Albert Bonniers. Swedish text. G+. P2. $35.00

BESSE, Joseph. *Collection of Sufferings of People Called Quakers...* 1753. London. Luke Hinde. folio. 638 tables. 767p. leather. G. V3. $350.00

BESSIE, Alvah. *Inquisition in Eden.* 1965. Macmillan. 1st ed. F/NF. B2. $35.00

BESSIE, Alvah. *Men in Battle: Story of Americans in Spain.* 1954. NY. Veterans of Abraham Lincoln Brigade. VG. V4. $25.00

BEST, Harry. *Blindness & the Blind in the US.* 1934. NY. 1st ed. 714p. A13. $40.00

BEST, Jim. *Scribner Ils Classic.* 1983. Scribner. 1st ed. sgn. 24p. M/pict wrp. B18. $9.50

BESTER, Alfred. *Demolished Man.* 1953. Shasta. 1st ed. sgn subscriber copy. F/F. M2. $450.00

BESTER, Alfred. *Light Fantastic.* 1977. Gollancz. ARC. RS. VG/dj. P3. $25.00

BESTER, Alfred. *Star Light, Star Bright.* 1976. Berkley Putman. 1st ed. VG/F. P3. $20.00

BESTERMAN, Theodore. *Agriculture: A Bibliography of Bibliographies.* 1971. Rowan Littlefield. F. O3. $18.00

BESTERMAN, Theodore. *Periodical Publications: Bibliography of Bibliographies.* 1971. np. 2 vol. F. A4. $20.00

BESTERMAN, Theodore. *World Bibliogrphy of African Bibliographies.* 1975. Totowa. Rowman Littlefield. 241p. bl cloth. NF. P4. $35.00

BESTOR, Art. *Three Presidents & Their Books.* 1963 (1955). Urbana, IL. 129p. VG. A10. $5.00

BETANCOURT, J. Gregory. *Preformance Art.* 1992. Wildside. 1st ed. sgn. 1/100. F. M2. $15.00

BETJEMAN, John. *Ring of Bells.* 1963. Houghton Mifflin. 1st ed. sgn. F/2 sm tears. V1. $40.00

BETT, W.R. *History & Conquest of Common Diseases.* 1954. Norman, OK. 1st ed. 334p. A13. $75.00

BETTERTON, Thomas. *Life of Mr Thomas Betterton, the Last Eminent Tragedian...* 1710. London. Gosling. 2 parts in 1. sm 8vo. rebound. K1. $200.00

BETTMANN, Otto. *Delights of Reading: Quotes, Notes & Anecdotes.* 1987. np. ils. 152p. F/F. A4. $35.00

BETTS, Wilbur W. *Bear Chief's War Shirt.* 1984. Mountain Pr. ils Glen Speaker. M. B34. $12.00

BEUCHAMP, Loren; see Silverberg, Robert.

BEUCHNER, Thomas. *Norman Rockwell: Artist & Ils.* 1970. Abrams. 1st ed. 328 p. F/F. A17. $60.00

BEURDELEY, Cecile. *L'Amour Bleu.* 1978. NY. Rizzoli. 1st ed. folio. trans Michael Taylor. bl cloth. F/dj/case. F1. $125.00

BEURDELEY & HINZ. *Thai Forms.* 1980. NY. lg 4to. photos. F/dj/slipcase. A17. $25.00

BEVERIDGE, W.I.B. *Art of Scientific Investigation.* 1951. Norton. 171p. cloth. VG. A10. $15.00

BEVINS, Winfred. *Charbonneau: Man of Two Dreams.* 1975. Nash. 1st ed. sgn. map ep. F/F. A18. $40.00

BEVINS, Winfred. *Misadventures of Silk & Shakespeare.* 1985. Jameson. 1st ed. sgn. M/M. A18. $15.00

BEVIS, H.U. *Alien Abductors.* 1971. Lenox Hill. G/VG. P3. $10.00

BEWICK, John. *Children's Miscellany.* 1804. London. early ed. full leather/detached front. VG/fld/case. F1. $375.00

BEWICK, Thomas. *Memoir of Thomas Bewick Written by Himself.* 1961. London. Cresset. ils. gilt bl cloth. F/NF. F1. $30.00

BEYER, August. *Index Librovm Selectorvm Theologici Potissimvm...* nd. np. 126p. VG. A4. $240.00

BEYER, H. *Hist of Norwegian Literature.* 1956. NYU. 1st ed. 370 p. F/F. A17. $15.00

BEYER, Wiliam Gray. *Minions of the Moon.* 1950. Gnome. 1st ed. VG/dj. P3. $30.00

BEYER, William H. *Standard Mathematical Tables.* 1976 (1964). Cleveland, OH. CRC. 24th ed. 656p. xl. K5. $8.00

BHATIA, S.L. *Greek Medicine in Asia & Other Essays.* 1970. Bangalore. 226p. cloth. M/dj. G7. $45.00

BIANCO, Margery. *Winterbound.* 1936. Viking. 1st ed. decor Kate Seredy. VG/dj. M20. $45.00

BIANCO, Pamela. *Beginning With A.* 1947. Oxford. 1st ed. lacks front ep. VG. A3. $3.00

BIANCO & BOWMAN. *Tales From a Finnish Tupa.* 1936. Whitman. 1st ed. ils Laura Bannon. VG. P2. $20.00

BIBBY, Geoffrey. *Four Thousand Years Ago. World Panorama of Life...* 1961. Knopf. 1st ed. 8vo. xl. VG/dj. W1. $12.00

BIBBY, Geoffrey. *Looing for Dilmun.* 1969. Knopf. 1st ed. 383p. VG+/dj. M20. $18.00

BIBBY, Geoffrey. *Testimony of the Space.* 1956. Knopf. 414p. VG/dj. K4. $15.00

BIBESCO, Marthe Lucie. *Alexandre Asiatique...* 1927. Paris. Marcelle Lesage. 1/300. 4to. ils. 94p. prt wrp. K1. $175.00

BIBLE. *Bible in Miniature; or, Concise Hist...* 1780. London. Newbery. 1st ed/3rd state. 45x30mm. 14 pl. gilt brn leather. NF. B24. $400.00

BIBLE. *Bible of Every Land: A Hist of Sacred Scriptures...* ca 1851. London. Bagster. 1st ed. 4to. emb morocco. 406p. H10. $175.00

BIBLE. *Bible Pictures.* 1972. Enkhuizen. 25x19mm. ils JR Levien. aeg. gilt bl morocco. F. B24. $200.00

BIBLE. *Biblia; or, Practical Summary of Ye Old & New Testaments.* 1727. London. P Wilkin. 43x27mm. 16 pl. 278p. aeg. 18th-C red morocco. F. B24. $1,200.00

BIBLE. *Book of Psalms. Trans From the Hebrew...* 1815. London. Rivington. 2 vol. calf/marbled brd/gilt spine. K1. $150.00

BIBLE. *Child's Bible.* 1970. Enkhuizen, Holland. 36x26mm. aeg. ils. full gr morocco/metal clasp. F. B24. $250.00

BIBLE. *Chumosh.* ca 1925. Chicago. Meites. 25x17mm. Hebrew/Pentateuch text. 500p. leather/locket. F. B24. $950.00

BIBLE. *Columbian Family & Pulpit Bible.* 1822. Boston. Teal. corrected/improved Am ed. folio. calf. H10. $165.00

BIBLE. *Daniel D Smith's Stereotype Edition. The Holy Bible...* 1823. NY. Smith. lg/thick 4to. ils. 770p. orange ep. red morocco. M1. $750.00

BIBLE. *Das Neue Testament...* 1795. Germantaun. Billmeyer. 8vo. 537p. tooled leather. H10. $95.00

BIBLE. *Everyday Bible.* 1988. Guideposts. 1128p. VG/dj. B29. $5.50

BIBLE. *General Epistle of James.* 1837. Ceylon. Jaffna Auxiliary Bible Soc. 68x54mm. Tamil text. 48p. B24. $200.00

BIBLE. *Guideposts Parallel Bible.* 1983. Guideposts. comparing 4 popular trans. 3193p. VG. B29. $10.00

BIBLE. *History of the Bible.* 1924. Lansingburgh. Stratton. 52x36mm. 15 woodcuts. 256p. gilt leather. B24. $350.00

BIBLE. *Holy Bible Containing Old & New Testaments: Improved Ed.* 1913. Am Baptist Pub Soc. 1086p. VG. B29. $7.50

BIBLE. *Holy Bible New International Version.* 1978. Zondervan. 1156p. F. B29. $5.50

BIBLE. *Holy Bible.* ca 1890. Joseph Horner Co. ils Gustave Dore. VG. M19. $125.00

BIBLE. *Holy Bible.* 1961. Kenedy. OT Douay Version/NT Confraternity Version. VG. B29. $10.00

BIBLE. *Holy Bible.* 1975. Falwell Ministries. Am Bicentennial ed. VG. B29. $10.50

BIBLE. *Holy Bible.* 1976. Regence. Giant Prt ed. 1855p. VG. B29. $10.50

BIBLE. *Illuminated Bible, Containing Old & New Testaments...* 1846. Harper. 1st ed. ils JA Adams/JG Chapman. aeg. contemporary gilt morocco. M1. $750.00

BIBLE. *Ke Kauoha Hou...* 1871. NY. Am Bible Soc. 2nd ed. 1/797. 339p. emb blk leather. G. H10. $125.00

BIBLE. *Koran, Commonly Called the Alcoran of Mahomet.* 1806. Springfield, MA. Isaiah Thomas. 8vo. 524p. old calf/leather label. VG. M1. $300.00

BIBLE. *Layman's Parallel Bible.* 1980. Zondervan. 3037p. VG/dj. B29. $17.00

BIBLE. *Les Pseumes de David, Mis en Vers Francois...* 1730. Amstedam. Henri Dusauzet. Nouvelle ed. aeg. full gr morocco. F. B24. $550.00

BIBLE. *Living Book of Moses.* 1969. Tyndale. 531p. VG/dj. B29. $5.00

BIBLE. *Living Psalms & Proverbs With the Major Prophets.* 1967. Tyndale. Billy Graham edit. VG/dj. B29. $5.00

BIBLE. *Megillah (The Book of Esther).* ca 1880. E Europe. 67x67mm. Hebrew text. 24p. emb cloth brd. cb sleeve. B24. $650.00

BIBLE. *New American Bible.* 1970. Catholic Book Pub. pb. 348p. VG. B29. $3.00

BIBLE. *New American Standard Bible.* 1971. Creation House. VG/torn. B29. $12.00

BIBLE. *New Eng Bible With Apocrypha.* 1970. Oxford. 1502p. VG. B29. $10.50

BIBLE. *New Open Bible.* 1982. Nelson. KJV. lg prt. 1568p. G. B29. $15.50

BIBLE. *New Testament from 26 Trans.* 1967. Zondervan. 1237p. VG/dj. B29. $8.50

BIBLE. *New Testament.* ca 1864. type carried by Civil War soldiers. blk bdg. VG. O8. $12.50

BIBLE. *New Testament.* nd. Am Bible Soc. 260p. VG. B29. $6.50

BIBLE. *New Testament. Revised Standard Version.* 1946. Nelson. 521p. G/worn. B29. $3.50

BIBLE. *New Version of the Psalms of David...* 1766. Boston. Perkins. hymns/appendix. 276p. old worn leather. H10. $95.00

BIBLE. *Novum Jesu Christi Testamentum a Sebastiano Castalione...* 1682. London. Mearne. 12mo. 367p. calf. H10. $85.00

BIBLE. *Novum Testamentum Domini Nostri Jesu Christi...* 1698. Amsterdam. Gallet. 2 vol. folio. old calf. H10. $85.00

BIBLE. *Novum Testamentum Graece & Latine...* 1543. Paris. Joannem Roigny. 2 parts in 1. laks free ep. 18th-C brd. K1. $650.00

BIBLE. *Novum Testamentum...* 1814. Boston. Thomas. 2nd ed. 478p. sheep. H10. $145.00

BIBLE. *Old Testament.* 1966. Doubleday. 3rd prt. ils Marguerite de Angeli. 264p. VG/dj. W1. $15.00

BIBLE. *Polychrome Bible: Book of Prophet Ezekiel.* 1899. London. Clark. trans/ils CH Toy. 208p. gilt bl cloth. B33. $50.00

BIBLE. *Psalm (sic) of David in Metre...Used in Kirk of Scotland.* 1779. Edinburgh. WIlliamson. 76x46mm. 253p. aeg. full red morocco. B24. $475.00

BIBLE. *Rarotonga. Te au Buka a Mose Kiritiia ei Tuatua Rarotonga.* 1838. Rarotonga. Missionari Societi I Lonedona. 12mo. red leather. H10. $1,800.00

BIBLE. *Reader's Digest Bible.* 1982. Reader's Digest. 799p. VG/torn. B29. $7.00

BIBLE. *Solomon's Song of Songs.* 1991. Dallas. Jan Sobota. 63x42mm. 1/30. F/velvet & paper-lined pigskin box. B24. $450.00

BIBLE. *Song of Songs of Solomon.* 1985. Utrecht. Catharijne. 63x43mm. 1/12 (total of 167). teg. gilt full vellum. F. B24. $350.00

BIBLE. *The Holy Bible.* 1924-1927. London. Nonesuch. 5 vol. 1/1000 sets. cream brd. VG. F1. $325.00

BIBLE. *Wesley Bible: Personal Study Bible for Holy Living.* 1990. Nelson. F/dj. B29. $15.50

BIBLE. *Woteninwaste Topa ga Psalm Wowapi Kin, Dakota Lapi En.* 1890. London. Sare. Sioux text. 133p. VG. H10. $75.00

BICHAT, Xavier. *Traite des Membranes en General et de Diverse Membranes...* 1900. Paris. Chez Richard. 326p. G7. $995.00

BICKEL, Alexander M. *Politics & the Warren Court.* 1965. NY. Harper. M11. $45.00

BICKHAM, Warren Stone. *Operative Surgery Covering Operative Technic...* 1930. Phil. Saunders. 6 vol. 1st rpt. cloth. G7. $150.00

BICKHAM, William D. *From OH to the Rocky Mtns.* 1879. Dayton, OH. Journal Book/Job Prt House. 8vo. pres. 178p. morocco. K1. $275.00

BIDDLE, George. *Green Island.* 1930. Coward McCann. 1st ed. ils. 177p. dk gr stp gr cloth. VG/G+. F1. $150.00

BIDDLE, Nicholas. *Journals of Expedition Under Command...Lewis & Clark...* 1962. Heritage. 2 vol. ils. F/box. B34. $160.00

BIDDLE, Tyrrel E. *Corinthian Yachtsman.* 1881. London. ils. xl. G+. M17. $45.00

BIDDLECOMBE, George. *Art of Rigging, Containing Explanation of Terms & Phrases...* 1925. Salem. Marine Research. ils. gilt gr cloth. NF. F1. $75.00

BIDWELL, John. *Echoes of the Past About CA.* 1928. Lakeside. 377 p. gilt red cloth. VG. M20. $35.00

BIEBER, Edmund Ellis. *Springfield Church: A Brief Hist of Trinity...Lutheran...* 1953. Easton, PA. 1st ed. 207p. cloth. NF. M8. $37.50

BIELY, Audrey. *St Petersburg.* 1959. Grove. trans Cournos. 310p. F/worn. A17. $10.00

BIER, Jesse. *Year of the Cougar.* 1976. np. 1st ed. F/F. B34. $40.00

BIERCE, Ambrose. *Black Beetles in Amber.* 1892. San Francisco/NY. Western Authors Pub. 1st ed. 8vo. 280p. 2-part box. F. M1. $950.00

BIERCE, Ambrose. *Collected Works of...* 1909-1912. NY. Neale. 12 vol. teg. cream cloth/brd/paper label. K1. $250.00

BIERCE, Ambrose. *Collected Writings of Ambrose Bierce.* 1952. Citadel. 3rd ed. G/VG. xl. P3. $20.00

BIERCE & DANZIGER. *Monk & the Hangman's Daughter.* 1892. Chicago. Schulte. 1st ed. 166p. cloth. VG. B18. $195.00

BIESTERVELD, Betty. *Peter's Wagon.* 1968. Whitman. lg 32mo. pict brd. M. C8. $20.00

BIGELOW, John Jr. *Campaign of Chancellorsville: A Strategic & Tactical Study.* 1910. New Haven. Yale. 1st ed. maps/sketches/plans. 528p. later cloth. xl. M8. $150.00

BIGGERS, Earl Derr. *Charlie Chan Carries On.* 1930. Bobbs Merrill. 1st ed. G/VG. P3. $20.00

BIGGERS, Earl Derr. *Chinese Parrot.* 1931. Harrap. 3rd ed. G/VG. P3. $15.00

BIGGERS, Earl Derr. *Keeper of the Keys.* 1932. Bobbs Merrill. VG. P3. $30.00

BIGGERS, Earl Derr. *Keeper of the Keys.* 1932. McClelland Stewart. 1st Canadian ed. VG. P3. $35.00

BIGGERS, Earl Derr. *Seven Keys to Baldpate.* 1913. Bobbs Merrill. 1st ed. ftspc missing. G. P3. $12.00

BIGGERS, Earl Derr. *Seven Keys to Baldpate.* 1913. McLeod Allen. 1st Canadian ed. G/VG. P3. $30.00

BIGGERS & RITCHIE. *Inside the Lines.* 1915. Bobbs Merrill. 1st ed. VG. P3. $35.00

BIGGLE, Jacob. *Biggle Health Book: A Family Monitor & Guide to Good Health.* 1904. Phil. index. 184p. bl cloth. F. B14. $45.00

BIGGLE, Jacob. *Biggle Pet Book.* 1900. Phil. 110 ils. 144p. bl cloth. F. B14. $45.00

BIGGLE, Lloyd. *Fury Out of Time.* 1966. Dobson. 1st ed. VG/G. P3. $25.00

BIGGLE, Lloyd. *Light That Never Was.* 1974. Elmfield. VG/F. P3. $17.00

BIGGLE, Lloyd. *Monument.* 1975. NEL. F/F. P3. $17.00

BIGGLE, Lloyd. *Watchers of the Dark.* 1966. Rapp Whiting. 1st ed. VG/VG. P3. $20.00

BIJOU. *Bijou Almanack 1853.* 1852. London. Rock Bros/Payne. 30x26mm. ftspc/pict title/ils. gilt flexible morocco. B24. $475.00

BIJOU. *Bijou Illustrations of the United States.* ca 1845. London. Rock Bros/Payne. 31x25mm. 32 lithos. aeg. gilt limp blk leather. F/case. B24. $650.00

BIJOU. *Bijou Language of Flowers.* ca 1840. London. Harris. 47x32mm. 106p+6 ad p. aeg. gilt red leather. F. B24. $350.00

BILEZIKIAN, Gilbert. *Christianity 101: Your Guide to 8 Basic Christian Beliefs.* 1993. Zondervan. 287p. F/F. B29. $6.50

BILLINGS & HURD. *Hospitals, Dispensaries & Nursing.* 1984. NY. facsimile of 1894 ed. 719p. A13. $125.00

BILLINGSLEY, K.L. *Seductive Image: Christian Critique of World of Film.* 1989. Crossway Books. 236p. M/M. B29. $9.00

BILLINGTON, Jill. *Architectural Foliage.* 1991. London. ils. 128p. M. B26. $22.95

BILLINGTON, Ray A. *Genesis of the Frontier Thesis: A Study...* 1971. Huntington Lib. 1st ed. M/glassine. A18. $20.00

BINDER, Leonard. *Iran: Political Development in Changing Society.* 1962. Berkeley. 8vo. xl. cloth. G. W1. $12.00

BINFORD, Gurney. *As I Remember It: Forty-Three Years in Japan.* 1950. np. 8vo. 228p. VG/VG. V3. $12.50

BINGHAM, Clifton. *Funny Favorites.* nd. London. Nister. ils Louis Wain. 44p. VG. D6. $150.00

BINGHAM, John A. *Trail of Conspirators for Assassination President Lincoln...* 1865. GPO. 122p. VG/rear wrp missing. E5. $75.00

BINGHAM, John. *Good Old Charlie.* 1968. Simon Schuster. 1st xl ed. P3. $6.00

BINGHAM, Rebecca Saady. *Conclave Cookbook.* 1992. Berkeley/Hyattsville. 75x55mm. 1/35 (125 total). sgn. damask. F/lucite box. B24. $225.00

BINGHAM & WEEDON. *Pretty Pets.* nd. NY. Nister. enlarged ed. 4to. ils W Foster. G+. D6. $65.00

BINNS, Archie. *Land Is Bright.* 1992. OR State U. 1st ed thus. sc. M. A18. $12.00

BINNS. *Intro to Historical Bibliography.* 1962. London. Lib Assn. 2nd ed. 396p. VG/VG. A4. $65.00

BINYON, Mrs. Laurence. *Paths of Peace, Book II.* nd. Oxford. 16mo. 170p. limp cloth. G. V3. $9.00

BIOCCA, Ettore. *Yanoama: Narrative of a White Girl Kidnapped...* 1970. Dutton. 2nd prt. 382p. VG/dj. F3. $15.00

BIRBECK, Morris. *Letters From Illinois.* 1818. Phil/Dublin. rebacked leather. H4. $150.00

BIRBECK, Morris. *Notes on a Journey in America From Coast of Virginia...IL.* 1818. London. 4th ed. rebacked leather. H4. $125.00

BIRCH, Jonathan. *Fifty-One Original Fables With Morals & Ethical Index.* 1833. London. Hamilton Adams. 1st ed. ils Cruickshank. 251p. aeg. Tout bdg. F. B24. $475.00

BIRCHALL, M. Joyce. *King Charles Spaniel.* 1988. London. Foyle. 8th ed. 77p. glossy brd. M. R2. $12.00

BIRD, Alan. *Hist of Russian Painting.* 1987. Oxford. Phaidon. 1st ed. 4to. VG/dj. N2. $17.50

BIRD, Brandon. *Death in Four Colors.* 1950. Dodd Mead. ARC/1st ed. RS. F/dj. M15. $30.00

BIRD, Herbert S. *Theology of Seventh-Day Adventism.* 1961. Eerdmans. 137p. VG/dj. B29. $7.00

BIRD, Isabella. *Lady's Life in the Rocky Mountains.* nd. Dutton. 7th ed. VG. B34. $35.00

BIRD, Isabella. *Lady's Life in the Rocky Mountains.* 1966 (1960). OK U. new ed/4th prt. F. B34. $20.00

BIRD, Sarah. *Alamo House.* 1986. Norton. 1st ed/author's 1st book. F/F. B3. $65.00

BIRD, Sarah. *Virgin of the Rodeo.* 1993. Doubleday. 1st ed. inscr. F/F. B3. $40.00

BIRDSONG, James C. *Brief Sketches of NC State Troops in War Between States.* 1894. Raleigh. Josephus Daniels. 1st ed. 8vo. 213p. NF/wrp. C6. $350.00

BIRKEN, Andreas. *Philatelic Atlas of the Ottoman Empire.* 1992. Limassol. 95 maps. 334p. O2. $70.00

BIRKENHEAD. *Famous Trials of History.* (1924). Garden City. 319p. G. H1. $7.50

BIRKLEY, Dolan. *Unloved.* 1965. Crime Club. 1st ed. VG/VG. P3. $18.00

BIRNBAUM, Alfred. *Monkey Brain Sushi.* 1991. Kodansha Internat. 1st ed. F/F. P3. $19.00

BIRNBAUM, Uriel. *Der Kaiser und Der Arkitekt Wien.* 1924. np. 4to. pl. cloth. VG. M5. $30.00

BIRNEY, Hoffman. *Roads to Roam.* 1930. Al Burt. ils Charles Hargens. NF/dj. B34. $60.00

BIRO, Frederick. *Perfect Circus.* nd. BC. F/F. P3. $8.00

BIRREN, Faber. *Creative Color.* 1961. NY. Reinhold. sm 4to. 128p. orange cloth. VG. F1. $30.00

BIRREN, Faber. *Selling With Color.* 1945. London/NY. McGraw Hill. 2nd imp. 244p. G+. N2. $7.50

BISCHOF, Ledford J. *Interpreting Personality Theories.* 1964. Harper Row. 670p. VG. K4. $15.00

BISCHOF, Werner. *Werner Bischof.* 1966. NY. Paragraphic. 1st ed. 16mo. NF/wrp. S9. $35.00

BISE, Gabriel. *Illuminated Manuscripts: Medieval Hunting Scenes.* 1978. Fribourg. Liber. 1st ed. 4to. ils. VG. W1. $20.00

BISHER, Furman. *Strange But True Baseball Stories.* 1966. Random. VG. P3. $8.00

BISHOP, Ada L. *All About the Collie.* 1971. London. Pelham. 1st ed. ils. 136p. cloth. M/dj. R2. $32.00

BISHOP, Claire Huchet. *Pancakes-Paris.* 1947. Viking. 1st ed. ils Georges Schreiber. cloth. VG. M5. $10.00

BISHOP, Claire Huchet. *Pancakes-Paris.* 1947. Viking. 1st ed. ils Georges Schreiber. 62p. VG+/VG. P2. $35.00

BISHOP, Claire Huchet. *Twenty & Ten.* 1952. Viking. 1st ed. ils Wm Pene Du Bois. VG/VG. C8. $35.00

BISHOP, Curtis. *Little League Amigo.* 1964. Lippincott. 1st ed. VG/G. P8. $17.50

BISHOP, Curtis. *Little League Little Brother.* 1968. Lippincott. 1st ed. pict bdg. G+. P8. $12.50

BISHOP, Curtis. *Little League Victory.* 1967. Lippincott. 1st ed. xl. G/G. P8. $10.00

BISHOP, Edward. *Debt We Owe.* 1989. Shrewsbury. 1st ed. 216p. gilt bl bdg. F/F. M7. $35.00

BISHOP, Elizabeth. *Ballad of the Burglar of Babylon.* 1968. FSG. 1st ed. F/2 sm tears. V1. $100.00

BISHOP, Elizabeth. *Collected Prose.* 1984. FSG. 1st ed. NF/NF. E3. $30.00

BISHOP, Elizabeth. *Complete Poems.* 1969. FSG. 1st ed. sgn. F/NF. V1. $100.00

BISHOP, Elizabeth. *Memorial Tribute.* 1982. Albondocani. ltd ed. edit/sgn Richard Wilburt. F/wrp/dj. V1. $65.00

BISHOP, Elizabeth. *North & South, a Cold Spring.* 1955. Houghton Mifflin. 1st ed. sgn. F/sm tears. V1. $145.00

BISHOP, Elizabeth. *Poems: North & South/A Cold Spring.* 1955. Houghton Mifflin. 1st ed. NF/NF. B4. $250.00

BISHOP, John Peale. *Collected Poems.* 1948. Scribner. 1st ed. sgn. F/sm tears. V1. $35.00

BISHOP, John Peale. *Green Fruit.* 1917. Boston. Sherman French. 1st ed/author's 1st book. VG. Q1. $200.00

BISHOP, Michael. *Blooded on Arachne.* 1982. Arkham. 1st ed. ils G Tutor. F/F. T2. $15.00

BISHOP, Michael. *Close Encounters With the Diety.* 1986. Atlanta. Peachtree. 1st ed. fwd Isaac Asimov. F/F. T2. $20.00

BISHOP, Michael. *Little Knowledge.* 1977. Berkley Putnam. 1st ed. F/F. P3. $25.00

BISHOP, Michael. *One Winter in Eden.* 1984. Arkham. 1st ed. fwd TM Disch. F/F. T2. $35.00

BISHOP, Michael. *Stolen Faces.* 1977. Harper Row. 1st ed. F/F. P3. $15.00

BISHOP, Michael. *Strange at Ecbatan the Trees.* 1976. Harper Row. 1st ed. F/F. P3. $15.00

BISHOP, Michael. *Transfigurations.* 1980. Gollancz. 1st ed. VG/VG. P3. $20.00

BISHOP & KEOGH. *Essays Offered to Herbert Putnam by His Colleagues...* 1967 (1929). np. 567p. NF. A4. $35.00

BISSELL, Richard. *My Life on the Mississippi.* 1973. Little Brn. 1st ed. ils. 240p. dj. T7. $24.00

BISSET, James. *Tramps & Ladies.* 1959. NY. 1st ed. VG/VG. B5. $25.00

BISSETT, Clark Prescott. *Mussolini & Fascismo.* 1925. Seattle. Art Prt Co. pres. 48p. half bl calf/bl brd/red morocco label. K1. $85.00

BISSON & MCCONAUGHY. *Madame X.* nd. Grosset Dunlap. MTI. G/VG. P3. $20.00

BITSCHAI & BRODNEY. *History of Urology in Egypt.* 1956. Cambridge, MA. 1st ed. 122p. A13. $35.00

BIXBY, William. *Forgotten Village of Charles Wilkes.* 1966. McKay. VG/dj. N2. $7.50

BIXBY, William. *Universe of Galileo & Newton.* 1964. NY. Am Heritage. 4to. 153p. pict cloth. G. K5. $12.00

BLACK, Archibald. *Transport Aviation.* 1929. NY. 2nd ed. 348p. VG. B18. $125.00

BLACK, Baxter. *Coyote Cowboy Poetry.* 1986. np. ils Don Gill. VG/dj. B34. $15.00

BLACK, Baxter. *Croutons on a Cowpie, Vol II.* 1992. Denver. Coyote Cowboy Co. 1st ed. F/F. B3. $20.00

BLACK, Campbell. *Brainfire.* 1979. Morrow. 1st ed. VG/VG. P3. $15.00

BLACK, Campbell. *Letters From the Dead.* 1985. Villard. 1st ed. NF/dj. P3. $16.00

BLACK, Claudia. *It Will Never Happen to Me.* 1982. Denver. 8vo. 178p. wrp. A8. $7.00

BLACK, David. *Carl Linnaeus: Travels.* 1979. NY. sm 4to. ils. 108p. VG/dj. B26. $19.00

BLACK, Donald. *Behavior of Law.* 1976. NY. Academic. M11. $35.00

BLACK, Gavin. *Bitter Tea.* 1971. Harper Row. 1st ed. xl. dj. P3. $6.00

BLACK, Gavin. *Dragon For Christmas.* 1963. Harper Row. 1st ed. xl. dj. P3. $8.00

BLACK, Gavin. *Golden Cockatrice.* 1975. Harper Row. 1st ed. VG/VG. P3. $20.00

BLACK, Gavin. *You Want To Die, Johnny?* 1966. Harper Row. 1st ed. VG/VG. P3. $20.00

BLACK, John Logan. *Crumbling Defenses...* 1960. Macon, GA. McSwain. 1st ed. ils/facsimiles. 133p. gray cloth. F. C6. $75.00

BLACK, Lionel. *Breakaway.* 1970. Collins Crime Club. NF/dj. P3. $15.00

BLACK, Lionel. *Flood.* 1971. Stein Day. VG/VG. P3. $13.00

BLACK, Lionel. *Life & Death of Peter Wade.* 1974. Stein Day. 1st ed. VG/VG. P3. $13.00

BLACK, Mary. *Summerfield Farm.* 1951. Viking. 1st ed. ils Wesley Dennis. VG/G. O3. $25.00

BLACK, Max. *Philosophy in Am.* 1967. Ithaca. 2nd prt. 307p. bl cloth. VG/dj. G1. $30.00

BLACK, Michael. *Literature of Fidelity.* 1975. Barnes Noble. VG/dj. N2. $10.00

BLACK, Veronica. *Vow of Chastity.* nd. BC. F/F. P3. $8.00

BLACK, W.G. *Folk-Medicine: A Chapter in Hist of Culture.* 1970. NY. Franklin. facsimile of 1883 ed. 226p. VG. G7. $45.00

BLACKBURN, Bill. *What You Should Know About Suicide.* 1984. World. 154p. F/dj. B29. $4.50

BLACKBURN, Graham. *Overlook Illustrated Dictionary of Nautical Terms.* 1981. Overlook. ils. 349p. dj. T7. $25.00

BLACKBURN, Henry. *Randolph Caldecott. His Early Art Career.* 1887. London. Sampson Low. 4th ed. gilt gr cloth. G+. M20. $55.00

BLACKBURN, John. *Cyclops Gambit.* 1977. Jonathan Cape. 1st ed. F/F. M21. $35.00

BLACKBURN, John. *Gaunt Woman.* 1962. Mill Morrow. 1st ed. VG/VG. P3. $30.00

BLACKBURN, Paul. *Nets.* 1961. Trobar. 1st ed/author's 3rd book. F/wrp. B2. $60.00

BLACKBURN, Tom W. *Range War.* nd. Sampson Low. VG/G. P3. $10.00

BLACKER, Irwin R. *Irregulars, Partisans, Guerillas.* 1954. Simon Schuster. 1st ed. 487p. VG/VG. M7. $55.00

BLACKER, Irwin R. *Old West in Fiction.* 1961. Ivan Obolensky. 1st ed. F/dj. A18. $25.00

BLACKER, Irwin. *Cortes & the Aztec Conquest.* 1965. Am Heritage. 1st ed. 153p. VG. F3. $15.00

BLACKER, J.F. *ABC of Collecting Old Continental Pottery.* 1913. London. Paul Stanley. 1st ed. free ep missing. F. F1. $45.00

BLACKFORD, Susan Leigh. *Letters From Lee's Army; or, Memoirs of Life...* 1947. Scribner. 1st trade ed. cloth. NF/VG. M8. $65.00

BLACKFORD & NEWCOMB. *Job, Man, Boss.* (1920). Doubleday Page. 266p. VG+. H1. $8.50

BLACKHAM, H.J. *Objections to Humanism.* 1963. Lippincott. 128p. VG/dj. B29. $3.00

BLACKMAN, E.C. *History of Susquehanna County, PA.* 1873. Phil. 1st ed. 4 fld maps. 640p. VG. H7. $100.00

BLACKMON, Anita. *Murder a La Richelieu.* 1937. Crime Club. 1st ed. VG. P3. $30.00

BLACKMORE, R.D. *Lorna Doone.* (1921). Springfield. 1st ed. ils Harold Brett. 351p. blk cloth. VG. H3. $35.00

BLACKMORE, R.D. *Lorna Doone.* nd. Winston. 18mo. teg. 640p. G. S11. $20.00

BLACKMORE, R.D. *Slain by the Doones.* 1895. Dodd Mead. 1st Am ed/later issue. 244p. gr cloth. VG. M20. $20.00

BLACKMUR, R.P. *Second World.* 1942. Cummington. 1/300. cloth brd. F. Q1. $175.00

BLACKSTOCK, Lee. *All Men Are Murderers.* 1958. Doubleday Crime Club. 1st ed. F/NF. S6. $22.50

BLACKSTOCK, Lee. *All Men Are Murderers.* 1958. Doubleday Crime Club. 1st ed. VG/VG. P3. $15.00

BLACKSTONE, Bernard. *Consecrated Urn: Interpretation of Keats...* 1959. Longman Gr. 1st ed. 426p. VG/dj. M10. $7.50

BLACKSTONE, Harry. *Blackstone Book of Magic & Illusion.* 1985. Newmarket. 1st ed. VG/VG. P3. $23.00

BLACKSTONE, William. *Anaylsis of the Laws of England.* 1759. Clarendon. 4th ed. 8vo. 189p. contemporary calf. VG. D3. $250.00

BLACKWELL, B.H. *Blackwell's Byzantine Hand List.* 1938. Oxford. 8vo. 67p. cloth. xl. F. O2. $25.00

BLACKWELL, Leslie. *African Occasions. Reminiscences of 30 Years of Bar, Bench.* 1970. Westport. rpt of 1938 ed. 8vo. red cloth. M/sans. P4. $17.50

BLACKWOOD, Algernon. *Best Supernatural Tales of Blackwood.* 1973. Causeway. VG/VG. P3. $30.00

BLACKWOOD, Algernon. *Dance of Death.* 1928. Dial. 1st ed. VG. M2. $75.00

BLACKWOOD, Algernon. *Dudley & Gilderoy.* 1929. Dutton. 1st ed. VG/VG. P3. $75.00

BLACKWOOD, Algernon. *Tales of the Mysterious & Macabre.* 1967. Spring Books. VG/fair. P3. $18.00

BLADES, William. *Books in Chains & Other Bibliographcial Papers.* 1968. np. 270p. F. A4. $30.00

BLAGG, Mary A. *Collated List of Lunar Formations.* 1913. Edinburgh. 4to. 182p. VG. K5. $85.00

BLAGOWIDOW, George. *Last Train From Berlin.* 1977. Doubleday. 1st ed. VG/VG. P3. $13.00

BLAIKLOCK, E.M. *Pictorial Bible Atlas.* 1981. Zondervan. 459p. VG/dj. B29. $5.50

BLAINE, James G. *Twenty Years of Congress.* 1884. 2 vol. 1st ed. ils. F. O8. $21.50

BLAINE, John. *Egyptian Cat Mystery.* nd. Grosset Dunlap. VG/VG. P3. $15.00

BLAINE, John. *Electronic Mind Reader.* nd. Grosset Dunlap. VG. P3. $10.00

BLAINE, John. *Magic Talisman.* 1989. Manuscript. 1st ed. brd. VG. P3. $25.00

BLAINE, John. *Veiled Raiders.* 1965. Grosset Dunlap. 178p. lists to this title. VG. M20. $50.00

BLAIR, Anne Denton. *Where's Rachel? Another Adventure of Arthur...* 1978. Acropolis. 4to. F/VG. B17. $12.50

BLAIR, Hugh. *Lectures on Rhetoric...* 1784. Phil. Robert Aitkin. 1st Am ed. 4to. 454p. VG. M1. $125.00

BLAIR, John. *Poetic Art (WH Auden).* 1965. Princeton. 1st ed. F/VG+. V1. $25.00

BLAIR, Walter. *Mark Twain's West: Author's Memoirs About His Boyhood...* 1983. Lakeside. 12mo. 450p. F. M10. $20.00

BLAISDALE, Silas. *First Lessons in Intellectual Philosophy...* 1829. Boston. Lincoln Edmands. 12mo. 358p. orig calf. G1. $125.00

BLAKE, Michael. *Airman Mortensen.* 1991. Los Angeles. Seven Wolves. 1st ed. sgn. F/F. S9. $40.00

BLAKE, Neil. *World of Show Jumping.* 1967. Doubleday. 1st Am ed. VG/G. O3. $28.00

BLAKE, Nicholas. *End of the Chapter.* 1957. Collins Crime Club. 1st ed. VG/VG. P3. $20.00

BLAKE, William. *Vala or the Four Zoas.* 1963. Clarendon. facsimile. folio. VG/G. F1. $185.00

BLAKE, William. *Visions of Daughters of Albion.* 1957. Pawlet. Banyan. 1/180. folio. loose as issued/marbled paper fld. F. B24. $175.00

BLAKEY, George C. *Gambler's Companion.* 1979. Paddington. 1st ed. NF/NF. P3. $20.00

BLAKEY, Robert. *Hist of Moral Science.* 1833. London. Duncan. 2 vol. mauve cloth/paper spine label. G1. $100.00

BLANC, Louis. *Letters on England.* 1866. Sampson Low. 2 vol. 1st ed. VG. B2. $150.00

BLANC, Suzanne. *Rose Window.* 1968. Cassell. VG/VG. P3. $15.00

BLANCHARD, F.S. *Block Island to Nantucket: Their Harbors, Yacht Clubs...* 1961. NY. 1st ed. VG/G. B5. $50.00

BLANCHARD, Jean Pierre. *First Air Voyage in America.* 1943. Phil. Penn Mutual Life. G. B18. $15.00

BLANCHARD. *First Editions of John Buchan: Collector's Bibliography.* 1981. np. 295p. F. A4. $85.00

BLAND, Eleanor Taylor. *Dead Time.* 1992. St Martin. 1st ed. F/F. P3. $18.00

BLANK, Clair. *Beverly Gray, Reporter.* 1940. Grosset Dunlap. 1st ed. last title on list. 239p. VG/VG. M20. $25.00

BLANK, Clair. *Beverly Gray's Quest.* 1942. Grosset Dunlap. 1st ed. 220p. gr cloth. VG/VG. M20. $40.00

BLANK, Clair. *Beverly Gray's Scoop.* 1954. McLoughlin. 184p. VG. M20. $15.00

BLANK, Clair. *Beverly Gray's Surprise.* 1955. McLoughlin. last title in series. 182p. glossy pict brd. G+. M20. $20.00

BLANTON, Wyndham. *Medicine in Virginia in the 17th Century.* 1972. NY. facsimile of 1930 ed. 337p. A13. $40.00

BLASHVIELD, Jean. *Iolanthe.* 1967 (1966). Franklin Watts. 1st Am ed. NF/VG+. C8. $17.50

BLASHVIELD, Jean. *Pirates of Penzance.* 1966 (1965). Franklin Watts. 1st Am ed. NF/VG. C8. $17.50

BLATTY, William Peter. *Exorcist.* 1971. Harper Row. 1st ed. VG/VG. Q1. $75.00

BLATTY, William Peter. *Exorcist.* 1971. NY. 1st ed. sgn. NF/F. A11. $90.00

BLATTY, William Peter. *Legion.* 1983. Simon Schuster. 1st ed. VG/VG. P3. $15.00

BLATTY, William Peter. *Ninth Configuration.* 1979. Harper Row. 1st ed. F/F. T2. $30.00

BLATTY, William Peter. *Which Way to Mecca, Jack?* 1958. NY. 1st ed/author's 1st novel. sgn. NF/NF clip. A11. $50.00

BLAU, Eric. *Beggar's Cup.* 1993. Knopf. 1st ed. F/F. A14. $25.00

BLAUSTEIN, John. *Hidden Canyon.* 1977. Viking. 1st ed. intro Martin Litton. 135p. F/NF. B19. $100.00

BLAVATSKII, Vladimir D. *Antichnaia Arkheologiia i Istoriia.* 1985. Moscow. 1st ed. 8vo. 279p. VG. W1. $15.00

BLAYLOCK, James P. *Last Coin.* 1988. Ace. 1st ed. VG/G. P3. $18.00

BLEECK, Oliver; see Thomas, Ross.

BLEILER, Everett F. *Checklist of Fantastic Literature.* 1972. Starmont. 1st ed thus. F/dj. M2. $50.00

BLESH, Rudi. *Combo.* 1971. Chilton. 1st ed. rem mk. F/NF. B2. $40.00

BLEVINS, William L. *Care & Maintenance for the Christian Life.* 1979. World. 114p. VG. B29. $3.50

BLEVINS, Winfred. *Charbonneau: Man of Two Dreams.* 1975. Nash. 1st ed. sgn. map ep. F/VG. A18. $50.00

BLEVINS, Winfred. *Dictionary of the American West.* 1993. Facts on File. 1st ed. sgn. M/dj. A18. $35.00

BLEVINS, Winfred. *Misadventures of Silk & Shakespeare.* 1985. Jameson Books. 1st ed. sgn. M/dj. A18. $17.50

BLEW, Mary Clarman. *All But the Waltz.* 1991. Viking. 1st ed. rem mk. NF/F. B3. $15.00

BLICHFELDT, E.H. *Mexican Journey.* 1913. Crowell. 1st ed. 280p. teg. pict cloth. VG. F3. $30.00

BLIGH, Captain W. *Log of HMS Providence 1791-1793.* 1976. Guildford. Genesis. ltd ed. 1/500. 951p. F/case. P4. $750.00

BLINDLOSS, Harold. *Mystery Reef.* 1928. NY. Stokes. 1st Am ed. F/F. M15. $35.00

BLINDLOSS, Harold. *Prescott of Saskatchewan.* Aug 1913. Stokes. 1st ed. 346p. F. H1. $12.00

BLINKLEY, Luther J. *Conflict of Ideals: Changing Values in W Society.* 1969. Van Nostrand. 340p. VG. B29. $7.50

BLISH, James. *Doctor Mirabilis.* 1971. Dodd Mead. 1st ed. NF/NF. P3. $75.00

BLISH, James. *Frozen Year.* 1957. Ballantine. 1st ed. VG/G. P3. $75.00

BLISH, James. *Jack of Eagles.* 1952. Greenberg. 1st ed. VG/VG. P3. $85.00

BLISH, James. *Seedling Stars.* 1957. Faber. 1st ed. F/dj. F4. $40.00

BLISH, James. *Seedling Stars.* 1957. Gnome. stated 1st ed. VG/VG. M17. $25.00

BLISH, James. *Star Dwellers.* 1961. Putnam. 1st ed. F/NF. F4. $58.00

BLISH, James. *Star Trek Reader II.* 1977. Dutton. 1st prt thus. F/clip. N3. $25.00

BLISH, James. *Star Trek Reader III.* 1977. Dutton. 1st ed. VG/VG. P3. $25.00

BLISH, James. *Tale That Wags the God.* 1987. Advent. 1st ed. F/dj. M2. $17.00

BLISHEN, Edward. *Oxford Book of Poetry for Children.* 1963. Watts. 1st Am ed. ils Brian Wildsmith. VG/dj. M20. $27.00

BLISS, E. *Blood-Thirsty Turk in Armenia, Crete & Greece.* 1897. np. ils. 600+p. VG. E5. $45.00

BLISS, Ronald G. *Indian Softball Summer.* 1974. Dodd Mead. 1st ed. VG+/VG. P8. $20.00

BLISS. *Autos Across America: Bibliography of Transcontinental...* 1982. np. 2nd ed. 112p. F. A4. $125.00

BLOCH, Robert. *Blood Runs Cold.* 1961. Simon Schuster. 1st ed. F/dj. M2. $100.00

BLOCH, Robert. *Dragons & Nightmares.* 1968. Baltimore. Mirage. 1st ed. sgn. 1/1000. ils David prosser. F/F. T2. $90.00

BLOCH, Robert. *Eighth Stage of Fandom.* 1962. Advent. 1st ed. F/wrp. M2. $50.00

BLOCH, Robert. *Lori.* 1989. Tor. 1st ed. F/F. P3. $20.00

BLOCH, Robert. *Lost in Time & Space With Lefty Feep.* 1987. Pacifica. Creatures at Large. 1st ed. sgn. 1/250. F/F/F case. T2. $65.00

BLOCH, Robert. *Midnight Pleasures.* 1987. Doubleday. 1st ed. F/F. P3. $25.00

BLOCH, Robert. *Opener of the Way.* 1974. Neville Spearman. VG/VG. P3. $30.00

BLOCH, Robert. *Out of My Head.* 1986. Cambridge. 1st ed. sgn. ils John Stewart. F/F. T2. $45.00

BLOCH, Robert. *Out of the Mouths of Graves.* 1978. Mysterious. 1st ed. sgn. 1/250 #d. F/F/F case. P3. $100.00

BLOCH, Robert. *Pleasant Dreams — Nightmares.* 1960. Arkham. 1st ed. NF/NF. P3. $100.00

BLOCH, Robert. *Psycho House.* 1990. Tor. 1st ed. F/F. T2. $20.00

BLOCH, Robert. *Psycho II.* 1982. Whispers. 1st hc ed. sgn. pub/sgn Stuart Schiff. 1/750. F/F/case. F4/T2. $50.00

BLOCH, Robert. *Psycho: The 35th Anniversary Edition.* 1994. Springfield. Gauntlet. 1st ed. sgn. intro/sgn Richard Matheson. F/F/case. T2. $75.00

BLOCH, Robert. *Strange Eons.* 1978. Whispers. 1st ed. sgn. F/F. T2. $45.00

BLOCH, Robert. *Unholy Trinity.* 1986. Scream. 1st combined ed. sgn. ils Harry O Morris. F/F. T2. $65.00

BLOCH, Robert. *Yours Truly, Jack the Ripper.* 1991. Pulphouse Short Story. sgn. hc. F. P3. $20.00

BLOCH & MUNGER. *Angel.* 1977. Ward Ritchie. F/F. P3. $8.00

BLOCH & NORTON. *Jekyll Legacy.* 1990. Tor. 1st ed. F/F. P3. $20.00

BLOCK, Lawrence. *Ariel.* 1980. Arbor. 1st ed. NF/NF. P3. $25.00

BLOCK, Lawrence. *Ariel.* 1980. Arbor. 1st ed. sgn. F/VG. O4. $35.00

BLOCK, Lawrence. *Burglar Who Liked To Quote Kipling.* 1979. Random. 1st ed. sgn. F/dj. F4. $30.00

BLOCK, Lawrence. *Burglar Who Painted Like Mondrain.* 1983. Arbor. 1st ed. sgn. F/dj. F4. $30.00

BLOCK, Lawrence. *Burglar Who Traded Ted Williams.* 1994. Dutton. ARC. sgn. 1/650. F/wrp/band. B2. $45.00

BLOCK, Lawrence. *Dance at the Slaughterhouse.* 1991. NY. Morrow. ARC/1st ed. sgn. w/promo material. F/F. S6. $40.00

BLOCK, Lawrence. *Devil Knows You're Dead.* 1993. Morrow. 1st ed. sgn. F/F. B3. $30.00

BLOCK, Lawrence. *Into the Night.* 1987. Mysterious. 1st ed. sgn. F/F. T2. $16.00

BLOCK, Lawrence. *Like a Lamb to Slaughter.* 1984. Arbor. 1st ed. F/NF. T2. $25.00

BLOCK, Lawrence. *Like a Lamb to Slaughter.* 1984. Arbor. 1st ed. NF/dj. F4. $20.00

BLOCK, Lawrence. *Like a Lamb To Slaughter.* 1984. NY. Arbor. 1st ed. sgn. F/F. S6. $40.00

BLOCK, Lawrence. *Me Tanner, You Jane.* 1970. Macmillan. 1st ed. VG/VG. P3. $40.00

BLOCK, Lawrence. *Some Days You Get the Bear.* 1993. Morrow. 1st ed. sgn. F/F. T2. $25.00

BLOCK, Lawrence. *Ticket to the Boneyard.* 1990. Morrow. 1st ed. sgn. F/F. T2. $20.00

BLOCK, Lawrence. *Walk Among the Tombstones.* 1992. Morrow. 1st ed. F/F. P3. $17.00

BLOCK, Lawrence. *Walk Among the Tombstones.* 1992. Morrow. 1st ed. sgn. F/F. T2. $20.00

BLOCK, Lawrence. *When the Sacred Gin Mill Closes.* 1986. Arbor. 1st ed. F/F. F4. $30.00

BLOCK, Lawrence. *When the Sacred Gin Mill Closes.* 1986. Arbor. 1st ed. F/NF. B3. $25.00

BLOCK, Thomas H. *Airship Nine.* 1984. Putnam. 1st ed. VG/VG. P3. $17.00

BLOCK & KING. *Code of Arms.* 1981. Marek. 1st ed. F/F. F4. $35.00

BLOCKMAN, Lawrence G. *Bombay Mail.* 1934. Little Brn. 1st ed. VG/VG. M15. $45.00

BLOCKMAN, Lawrence G. *Midnight Sailing.* 1938. Harcourt Brace. 1st ed. VG. P3. $28.00

BLOFELD, John. *Tantric Mysticism of Tibet: A Practical Guide.* 1970. Dutton. 1st ed. 257p. VG/VG. B33. $38.00

BLOMBERG, Nancy J. *Navajo Textiles: William Randolph Hearst Collection.* 1988. AZ U. 1st ed. ils/index. 257p. F/NF. B19. $75.00

BLOMBERY & RODD. *Palms: Informative, Practical Guide to Palms of the World.* 1992 (1982). Pymble, NSW. photos. 201p. M/dj. B26. $35.00

BLOODGOOD, Lida Fleitmann. *Saddle of Queens.* 1959. London. Allen. 1st ed. VG/G. O3. $68.00

BLOODSTONE, John; see Byrne, Stuart.

BLOOM, Amy. *Come to Me.* 1993. Harper Collins. 1st ed/author's 1st book. sgn. F/F. L3. $85.00

BLOOM, Sol. *Story of the Constitution.* 1937. Sesquicentennial Comm. ils HC Christy. 192p. G. H1. $15.00

BLOOMFIELD & MENDELSON. *WH Auden: Bibliography 1924-1969.* 1972. np. 2nd ed. 436p. F. A4. $45.00

BLOSIUS, Ludovicus. *Book of Spiritual Instruction.* 1955. London. Burns Oates. 143p. VG/VG. B33. $18.00

BLOTNER, Joseph. *Uncollected Stories of William Faulkner.* 1979. Franklin Lib. ltd 1st ed. gilt leather. F. M21. $55.00

BLOUNT, Thomas. *Nomo-Lexicon: Law Dictionary...* 1970. Los Angeles. facsimile of 1670 London ed. 285p. buckram. M. D3. $35.00

BLOWER, Arthur H. *Akron at the Turn of the Century, 1890-1913.* 1962. Akron. 2nd ed. VG. B18. $7.50

BLUCHER, Evelyn. *Eng Wife in Berlin.* 1920. NY. index. 336p. VG. A17. $8.50

BLUHM, Heinz. *Essays in History & Literature Presented by Fellows...* 1965. Newberry Lib. 231p. F. M10. $9.50

BLUM, Daniel. *Pict Hist of Am Theatre 1900-1956.* 1956. NY. 4to. ils/index. 320 p. VG/dj. A17. $22.50

BLUM & BLUM. *Dangerous Hour. Lore of Crisis & Mystery in Rural Greece.* 1970. London. 8vo. 410p. cloth. dj. O2. $45.00

BLUMBERG, Fannie Burgheim. *Roweena Teena Tot & the Blackberries.* 1938. Whitman. 2nd prt. ils Mary Grosjean. hot pink cloth. F/VG. M5. $95.00

BLUME, Judy. *It's Not the End of the World.* 1979. London. Heinemann. 1st ed. VG/VG. B3. $20.00

BLUMENTHAL, Joseph. *Art of the Printed Book 1455-1955.* 1973. NY. Morgan Lib. 4to. 70 facsimile pl. 192p. M/F. B24. $85.00

BLUMENTHAL, Joseph. *Printed Book in America.* 1977. np. Godine. ils. 4to. 266p. F/NF. A4. $80.00

BLUMENTHAL, Walter Hart. *American Panorama: Pattern of the Past & Womanhood...* 1962. Worcester, MA. Achille St Onge. 1st ed. 47p. VG. M10. $20.00

BLUMLEIN, Michael. *Movement of Mountains.* 1987. St Martin. 1st ed. F/F. P3. $18.00

BLUNDELL, Nigel. *World's Greatest Crooks & Conmen.* 1982. Octopus. 1st ed. F/F. P3. $13.00

BLUNT, Wilfred Scawen. *Cockerell: Sydney Carlyle Cockerell, Friend of Ruskin...* 1965. Knopf. 1st Am ed. 385p. gilt bl cloth. F/NF. M7. $65.00

BLUNT, Wilfred Scawen. *My Diaries.* 1932. Knopf. 3rd/1st 1-vol ed. 383p. gilt bl bdg. G. M7. $18.00

BLUNT & STEARN. *Art of Botanical Ils.* 1951. NY. ils/pl. 304p. VG/dj. B26. $87.50

BLY, Robert. *Sea & the Honeycomb.* 1971. Beacon. 1st ed. F/clip. B3. $30.00

BLY, Robert. *Traveller Who Repeats His Cry.* 1982. Red Ozier. 1st ed. sgn. 1/160. purple/blk prt text. F/prt wrp. H5. $150.00

BLY, Robert. *Whole Moisty Night.* 1983. NY. Red Ozier. 1/300. sgn. ils Barry Moser. F/prt wrp. B24. $150.00

BLYTON, Enid. *Be Brave Little Noddy.* 1956. London. Sampson Low. Little Noddy Book #13/post-ISBN prt. NF/NF. C8. $20.00

BLYTON, Enid. *Brer Rabbit Again.* 1963. London. Dean. 1st ed. 12mo. cloth. VG/VG. C8. $20.00

BLYTON, Enid. *Brer Rabbit's a Rascal.* 1965. London. Dean. 1st ed. 12mo. cloth. VG/VG. C8. $20.00

BLYTON, Enid. *Do Look Out Noddy.* 1957. London. Sampson Low. Little Noddy Book #15/post-ISBN prt. NF/NF. C8. $20.00

BLYTON, Enid. *Enid Blyton's Big Noddy Book.* 1976 (1956). Purnell Maidenhead. sm 4to. glazed pict brd. F. C8. $17.50

BLYTON, Enid. *Hurray for Little Noddy.* 1950. London. Sampson Low. Little Noddy Book #2/post-ISBN prt. NF/VG+. C8. $20.00

BLYTON, Enid. *Mr Tumpy & His Caravan.* 1951. McNaughton. unp. VG/chip. M20. $25.00

BLYTON, Enid. *Noddie Has an Adventure.* nd. London. Sampson Low. 1st ed. 12mo. glazed pict brd. VG/G. C8. $25.00

BLYTON, Enid. *Noddy & His Car.* 1951. Sampson Low. Little Noddy Book #3/post-ISBN prt. lg 12mo. NF/NF. C8. $20.00

BLYTON, Enid. *Noddy & the Bumpy Dog.* 1957. London. Sampson Low. Little Noddy Book #14/post-ISBN prt. NF/NF. C8. $20.00

BLYTON, Enid. *Noddy & the Magic Rubber.* 1954. London. Sampson Low. Little Noddy Book #9/pre-ISBN prt. VG/G+. C8. $25.00

BLYTON, Enid. *Noddy at the Seaside.* 1953. London. Sampson Low. Little Noddy Book #7/post-ISBN prt. 12mo. NF/NF. C8. $20.00

BLYTON, Enid. *Noddy Gets Into Trouble.* 1954. London. Sampson Low. Little Noddy Book #8/post-ISBN prt. NF/NF. C8. $20.00

BLYTON, Enid. *Noddy Goes to School.* 1952. London. Sampson Low. Little Noddy Book #6/post-ISBN prt. NF/VG+. C8. $20.00

BLYTON, Enid. *Proud Golliwog.* ca 1953. Leicester, Eng. ils Brett. VG/pict wrp. C8. $15.00

BLYTON, Enid. *Well Done Noddy.* nd. London. Sampson Low. Little Noddy Book #5/post-ISBN prt. NF/NF. C8. $20.00

BLYTON, Enid. *You Funny Little Noddy.* 1955. London. Sampson Low. Little Noddy Book #10/pre-ISBN prt. lg 12mo. G+/G. C8. $25.00

BOADEN, James. *Maid of Bristol: Play in Three Acts.* 1803. NY. Longworth. 1st Am ed? 18mo. recent plain wrp. M1. $125.00

BOARD, John. *Horse & Pencil.* 1950. London. Christopher Johnson. 1st ed. VG/G. O3. $45.00

BOARDMAN, John. *Oxford Hist of the Classical World.* 1986. NY. Oxford. 1st ed. ils. 882p. NF/dj. M10. $27.50

BOARDMAN, John. *Parthenon & Its Sculptures.* 1985. Austin. folio. ils/photos. 256p. dj. O2. $30.00

BOARDMAN, Tom. *Science Fiction Stories.* 1979. Octopus. 1st ed. VG/VG. P3. $15.00

BOARDMAN & GRIFFIN. *Oxford History of the Classical World.* 1988. Oxford. 3rd ed. F/F. P3. $30.00

BOAS, George. *Critical Analysis of Philosophy of Emile Myerson.* 1930. Johns Hopkins. sm 8vo. 146p. russet cloth. G1. $28.50

BOAS, George. *Dominant Themes of Modern Philosophy.* 1957. NY. Ronald Pr Co. 660p. panelled bl cloth. VG/chip. G1. $38.00

BOATRIGHT, Mody C. *Mexican Border Ballads & Other Lore.* 1946. TX Folklore Soc. 1st ed. 7 essays. F. A18. $45.00

BOBINSON, Kim Stanley. *Escape From Kathmandu.* 1989. Tor. 1st ed. F/F. P3. $18.00

BOBINSON, Kim Stanley. *Planet on the Table.* 1986. Tor. 1st ed. F/F. P3. $20.00

BOBROW & JINKINS. *World's Most Extraordinary Yachts.* 1986. NY. Concepts. photos. 221p. dj. T7. $45.00

BOCCACCIO, Giovanni. *Decameron.* 1949. Garden City. 2 vol. 1/1500. ils/sgn R Kent. gilt maroon cloth. F/NF case. F1. $250.00

BOCCACCIO, John. *Three Admirable Accidents of Andrea de Piero.* 1954. Lexington, KY. Gravesend. 1/200. ils Fritz Kredel. 50p. vellum brd. F. B24. $175.00

BOCHENSKI, I.M. *Ancient Formal Logic. Issued in Studies in Logic...* 1951. North-Holland Pub. 1 fld table. 122p. prt yel cloth. VG/dj. G1. $32.50

BOCK, Carl Ernst. *Lehrbuch der Pathologischen Anatomie.* 1864. Leipzig. Wigand. 672p. orig brd. shaken/uncut. G7. $35.00

BODE, Vaughn. *Deadbone.* 1975. N Comford Communications. 1st ed. VG/VG. P3. $100.00

BODELSEN, Anders. *Straus.* 1974. Harper Row. F/F. P3. $13.00

BODEN, Margaret. *Purposive Explanation in Psychology.* 1972. Cambridge. Harvard. 408p. purple cloth. VG/dj. G1. $30.00

BODENHEIM, Maxwell. *Sardonic Arm.* 1923. Chicago. Covici McGee. 1st ed. 1/575. NF. B2. $40.00

BODERO, James. *Long Ride to Granada.* 1965. Reynal. 127p. VG/dj. N2. $7.50

BODFISH, Hartson H. *Chasing the Bowhead.* 1936. Harvard. ils. 281p. teg. T7. $110.00

BODLEY, R.V.C. *Algeria From Within.* 1927. Bobbs Merrill. 1st ed. 32 pl. G. W1. $8.00

BODLEY, Ronald. *Gertrude Bell.* 1940. Macmillan. 1st ed. 260p. bl lettered tan cloth. F/G+. M7. $70.00

BOECK & SABARTES. *Picasso.* 1959. Abrams. lg 4to. ils/fld & mc pl. pict gray cloth. VG/dj. F1. $75.00

BOEGEHOLD, Betty. *In the Castle of Cats.* 1981. Dutton. 1st ed. ils. F/G. P2. $15.00

BOEHME, Jacob. *Way to Christ.* 1949. Harper. new trans by JJ Stoudt. 254p. VG/VG. B33. $40.00

BOGART, W. *Daniel Boone & Hunters of Kentucky.* 1881. np. ils. 464p. VG. E5. $45.00

BOGEL, GOLDMAN & MARKS. *Birds & Flowers.* 1988. Brazilier. 1st ed. 91 full-p pl. 192 p. F/F. A17. $45.00

BOGEN, James. *Wittgenstein's Philosophy of Language.* 1972. London. Routledge. 244p. red cloth. VG/dj. G1. $35.00

BOGGS, Mae. *My Playhouse Was a Concord Coach...* nd (ca 1954). San Francisco. ltd ed. sgn pres. w/sgn pres booklet. VG. O3. $625.00

BOGOSIAN, Eric. *Sex, Drugs, Rock & Roll.* 1991. Harper Collins. 1st ed. sgn. F/F. B2. $45.00

BOGUE, Ronald. *Deleuze & Guattari: Critics of the 20th Century.* 1989. London. Routledge. 196p. prt blk cloth. G1. $25.00

BOHANON, Paul. *Wind & Arabella.* 1947. Oxford. 1st ed. ils Janice Holland. 69p. VG+/VG. A3. $25.00

BOHN & BOWER. *Glacier Bay Land & Science.* 1967. Sierra Club. 1st ed. VG/VG. B5. $35.00

BOHR, N. *Atomic Physics & Human Knowledge.* 1958. NY. 1st ed. 101p. dj. A13/G1. $35.00

BOICE, James M. *Romans... Vol 1 & Vol 2.* 1991 & 1992. Baker. 2 vol in 1. F/dj. B29. $25.00

BOIS, J. Samuel. *Breeds of Men.* 1970. Harper Row. 163p. M/dj. K4. $10.00

BOISGILBERT, Edmund. *Caesar's Column.* nd. Ward Lock. brd. G+. P3. $40.00

BOK, Bart J. *Astronomer's Universe.* 1958. Melbourne. 8vo. 107p. VG. K5. $10.00

BOK, Hannes. *Beauty & the Beasts.* 1978. De La Ree. 1st ed. NF/NF. P3. $45.00

BOKER, George H. *Legend of the Hounds.* 1929. Rudge. ltd ed. 1/800. VG. O3. $35.00

BOKER, George H. *Podesta's Daughter & Other Miscellaneous Poems.* 1852. Phil. Hart. 1st ed. 12mo. 156p. cloth. xl. VG. M1. $150.00

BOLDING, Amy. *Please Give a Devotion.* 1966. Baker. 99p. VG/dj. B29. $2.50

BOLEACH & FOBEL. *Big Book of Fabulous Fun-Filled Celebrations & Holiday...* 1978. np. 1st ed. cloth. VG. G2. $15.00

BOLINGBROKE, Henry St. John. *Letter to Sir William Windham II.* 1753. London. Millar. 1st ed. ils. 532p. old calf/rebacked/red morocco label. K1. $150.00

BOLITHO, William. *Murder for Profit.* 1953. London. rpt of 1926 ed. 12mo. 190p. VG. D3. $12.50

BOLLENS & SCHMANDT. *Metropolis.* 1965. Harper Row. 598p. F. K4. $10.00

BOLLIGER, Theodore P. *Hist of the First Reformed Church of Canton, OH.* ca 1916. Cleveland. 1st ed. 208p. cloth. VG. M8. $37.50

BOLSTER, Evelyn. *Hist of Diocese of Cork...to the Reformation.* ca 1972. NY. Barnes Noble. 548p. H10. $20.00

BOLT, Ben. *Sealed Envelope.* nd. Ward Lock. VG/fair. P3. $30.00

BOLT, David. *Adam.* 1960. John Day. 1st Am ed. F/wht dj. F4. $50.00

BOLTON, Herbert Eugene. *Anza's California Expeditions.* 1966. Russell. 5 vol. ils/notes/index. NF. B19. $250.00

BOLTON, Herbert Eugene. *Padre on Horseback.* 1976. Sonora. rpt. 90p. NF/wrp. B19. $20.00

BOLTON, Sarah K. *Famous Men of Science.* 1889. Crowell. 426p. cloth. VG. A10. $12.00

BOLZ, Robert. *Verztliche Mittheilungen aus Baden.* 1871. Karlsruhe. 208p. quarter cloth. G7. $65.00

BOMBECK, Erma. *I Want To Grow Hair, I Want To Grow Up, I Want To...* 1989. Harper Row. 1st ed. F/F. B3. $15.00

BONANNO, Margaret Wander. *Probe.* 1992. Pocket. Star Trek TVTI. VG/VG. P3. $19.00

BONAPARTE, Napoleon. *Confidential Correspondence of...* 1855. London. Murray. 2 vol. teg. red leather/5 raised bands. VG. H7. $85.00

BOND, Alvan. *Memoir of the Rev Pliny Fisk, American, Late Missionary...* 1828. Boston. 8vo. 437p. marbled brd/quarter brn calf/leather label. O2. $135.00

BOND, Alvan. *Young People's Illustrated Bible History.* 1874 (1872). Norwich, CT. Henry Bull. thick 4to. 584p. blk morocco/raised bands. VG. D6. $45.00

BOND, Francis. *Gothic Architecture in Eng.* 1906. Batsford/Scribner. 1st ed. 4to. 782p. G+. H1. $35.00

BOND, Gladys Baker. *Buffy Finds a Star.* 1970. Whitman. Family Affair TVTI. VG. P3. $8.00

BOND, Michael. *Paddington Bear.* 1973. Random. 1st Am ed. ils Fred Banbury. pict brd. VG+. M5. $12.00

BOND, Michael. *Paddington's Pop-Up Book.* 1977. Collins/Intervisual. 1st ed. 10p. VG. A3. $15.00

BOND, Nelson. *Exiles of Time.* 1949. Prime. 1st ed. F/NF. M2. $35.00

BOND, Nelson. *Nightmares & Daydreams.* 1968. Arkham. 1st ed. VG/VG. P3. $40.00

BOND, Nelson. *Thirty-First of February.* 1949. Gnome. 1st ed. F/dj. M2. $27.00

BOND, Nelson. *Thirty-First of February.* 1949. Gnome. 1st ed. w/sgn bookplate. F/F. T2. $55.00

BOND, William H. *Houghton Library, 1942-1967.* 1967. np. folio. 269p. F. A4. $95.00

BOND, William R. *Pickett or Pettigrew?* 1888. Weldon, NC. Hall Sledge. 1st ed. 8vo. 40p. VG/wrp. C6. $65.00

BOND & HOFFER. *Illuminated & Calligraphic Manuscripts.* 1955. Harvard. 4to. 80 pl. NF/wrp. A4. $50.00

BONDY, Louis W. *Miniature Books, Their History From the Beginnings...* 1981. London. Sheppard. 8vo. inscr. 221p. w/2 prospectuses. F/dj. B24. $150.00

BONE, David W. *Capstan Bars.* 1931. Porpoise. sgn. ils/sgn Edinburgh. 1/75. teg. T7. $85.00

BONES, Jim Jr. *Texas West of the Pecos.* 1981. TX A&M. 1st ed. ils. 136p. F/F. B19. $50.00

BONFIGLIOLI, Kyril. *Mortecai's Endgame.* 1972. Simon Schuster. 1st ed. xl. dj. P3. $6.00

BONHOEFFER, Dietrich. *Meditations on the Word.* 1986. Cambridge. 1st Eng ed. 154p. F/F. B33. $25.00

BONIFACE, Marjorie. *Murder As an Ornament.* 1940. Crime Club. 1st ed. VG. P3. $20.00

BONIFACE, Marjorie. *Wings of Death.* 1946. McBride. 1st ed. VG/VG. M15. $25.00

BONK & CARTER. *Building Library Collections.* 1964. Scarecrow. 287p. VG. A10. $12.00

BONNELL, John S. *What Are You Living For?* 1950. Abingdon Cokesbury. 188p. G. B29. $3.50

BONNELL. *Conrad Aiken: A Bibliography (1902-1978).* 1982. Huntington Lib. 303p. F/F. A4. $35.00

BONNER, Cindy. *Lily.* 1992. Algonquin. ARC/1st ed. RS. F/F. S9. $60.00

BONNER, Cindy. *Lily: A Love Story.* 1992. Algonquin. 1st ed/author's 1st book. F/F. A14. $25.00

BONNER, M.G. *Base Stealer.* 1965 (1951). Knopf. later prt. xl. G+. P8. $17.50

BONNER, Susan. *Penguin Year.* 1981. Delacorte. 1st prt. lg 8vo. M/M. C8. $30.00

BONNER, William Hallam. *Pirate Laureate.* 1947. Rutgers. 1st ed. 239p. VG+/dj. A18. $22.00

BONNET, Theodore. *Dutch.* 1955. Doubleday. 1st ed. VG/VG. P3. $20.00

BONNET, Theodore. *Mudlark.* 1949. Doubleday. 1st ed. 305p. F. H1. $5.00

BONNEY, T.G. *Mediterranean: Its Storied Cities & Venerable Ruins.* 1902. NY. Pott. 1st ed. sm 8vo. cloth. VG. W1. $30.00

BONNEY, Therese. *Europe's Children, 1939 to 1943.* (1943). NY. Bonney. 4to. 130p. F/dj. K1. $75.00

BONNEY & BONNEY. *Battle Drums & Geysers.* 1970. Swallow. ils/fld maps. xl. VG/dj. B34. $35.00

BONNIER, Gaston. *Fore Complete Illustree en Couleurs de France...* 1911-1935. Paris. 13 vol. 721 mc pl. leather or wrp. F. B26. $495.00

BONNOR, William. *Mystery of the Expanding Universe.* 1965 (1964). Macmillan. 2nd prt. VG/dj. K5. $15.00

BONO & GATLAND. *Frontiers of Space.* 1976. Macmillan. 1st Am revised ed. 279p. VG. K5. $10.00

BONSAL, Stephen. *Suitors & Suppliants: Little Nation at Versailles.* 1969. Kennikat. reprint. 301p. F. A17. $7.50

BONSAL & NILS. *Cavern of Death: A Moral Tale.* ca 1801. Baltimore. 12mo. 120p. quarter burgandy morocco/brd. K1. $200.00

BONSTELLE & DE FOREST. *Little Women: Letters From House of Alcott.* 1914. Boston. Little Brn. ils. 197p. gilt gr cloth. F. B14. $75.00

BONTEMPS, Arna. *Sad-Faced Boy.* 1937. Houghton Mifflin. 1st ed. NF/NF. very scarce. B2. $275.00

BONTEMPS & CONROY. *Slappy Hooper, the Wonderful Sign Painter.* 1946. Houghton Mifflin. 1st ed. ils Ursula Koering. F/fragment dj. B2. $100.00

BONZON, Paul Jacque. *Runaway Flying Horse.* 1976. Parents. 1st ed thus. ils Wm Pene Du Bois. M/M. C8. $35.00

BOODIN, John Eloff. *Social Mind: Foundations of Social Philosophy.* 1939. Macmillan. 594p. crimson cloth. VG. G1. $32.50

BOOKMAN & POWERS. *March to Victory.* 1986. NY. 1st ed. 340p. VG/VG. A17. $10.00

BOOLE, Mary Everest. *Collected Works...* 1931. London. Daniel. 4 vol. gr buckram. scarce. G1. $175.00

BOON, K.G. *Rembrandt: Complete Etchings.* 1963. Abrams. sm folio. 287p. terra-cotta cloth. F/VG. F1. $85.00

BOONE, Charles T. *Manual of the Law Applicable to Corporations Generally...* 1887. San Francisco. Sumner Whitney. contemporary sheep. M11. $50.00

BOONE, Lalia P. *Petroleum Dictionary.* 1952. OK U. G. N2. $7.50

BOORMAN, John. *Emerald Forest Diary.* 1985. FSG. 1st ed. MTI. F/F. P3. $15.00

BOORSTIN, Daniel J. *Image or What Happened to the American Dream.* 1962. Atheneum. 1st ed. 315p. VG/VG. A10. $15.00

BOOTH, Christopher. *Doctors in Science & Society: Essays on Clinical Scientist.* 1987. London. 1st ed. 318p. A13. $30.00

BOOTH, Martin. *Dreaming of Samarkand.* 1989. Morrow. 1st prt. 333p. gilt wht bdg. M/pict dj. M7. $19.00

BOOTH, Martin. *Very Private Gentlemen.* 1990. London. Century. 1st ed. F/F. B3. $20.00

BOOTH, Mary L. *Results of Emancipation.* 1863. Boston. 412p. O8. $27.50

BOOTH, Philip. *Letter From a Distant Land.* 1957. Viking. 1st ed. F/NF. w/card. V1. $40.00

BOOTH, Stanley. *Rythm Oil.* 1991. London. Cape. 1st ed. sm 4to. photos Eggleston. F/F. S9. $35.00

BOOTON, Kage. *Who Knows Julie Gordon?* 1980. Crime Club. 1st ed. NF/NF. P3. $13.00

BORDEAUX, Henry. *Le Visage du Maroc.* 1945. Paris. Colbert. 1st ed. 15 pl/fld map. G. W1. $8.00

BORDEN, Mrs. John. *Cruise of the Northern Light.* 1928. Macmillan. ils. 317p. T7. $45.00

BORDEN, Spencer. *Arab Horses & the Crabbet Stud.* 1973. Ft Dollins. Caballus. ltd ed. 1/1500. VG. O3. $45.00

BORDEN, W.C. *Use of the Roentgen Ray...* 1900. GPO. pl/radiographs. cloth. B14. $150.00

BORG, John. *Cacti: A Gardener's Handbook for Identification...* 1970 (1937). Poole. Dorset. 4th ed. ils. 512p. VG. B26. $31.00

BORGENICHT, Miriam. *Bad Medicine.* 1984. Macmillan. 1st ed. F/F. P3. $15.00

BORGENICHT, Miriam. *No Bail for Dalton.* 1974. Bobbs Merrill. 1st ed. VG/G. P3. $12.00

BORGES, Jorge Luis. *Labryinths.* 1962. New Directions. 1st ed. w/Ellery Queen provenance. F/NF. L3. $550.00

BORGIOTTI, Mario. *I Macchiaioli.* 1946. Florence. Arnaud Editore. 1st ed. 1/600 #d. 80 mtd mc pl/tissue guard. dj. K1. $125.00

BORING, Edwin G. *Sensation & Perception in Hist of Experimental Psychology.* 1942. Appleton Century Crofts. 613p. G. K4. $20.00

BORKO, Harold. *Computer Applications in the Behavioral Sciences.* 1962. Prentice Hall. 606p. F/dj. K4. $10.00

BORMAN, Thorleif. *Hebrew Thought Compared With Greek.* 1966. Baker. 102p. VG/dj. B29. $2.50

BORMAN & HARDY. *Aloes of the South African Veld.* 1971. Johannesburg. 297p. F/NF. quite scarce. B26. $95.00

BORN, Gerald M. *Chinese Jade: Annotated Bibliography.* 1982. Chicago. Celadon. 1st ed. maroon brd. NF. F1. $60.00

BORN, Max. *Atomic Physics.* 1963 (1935). NY. Hafner. 7th ed. 459p. G. K5. $15.00

BORNSTEIN, M. *Manual of Instruction in the Use of Dumb Bells...* 1880. NY. Bornstein. 1st ed. 18mo. 128p. cloth. xl. VG. M1. $175.00

BORRADORI, Giovanna. *Recoding Metaphysics: New Italian Philosophy.* 1988. np. 227p. prt red cloth. F. G1. $27.50

BOSANQUET, Bernard. *Logic or the Morphology of Knowledge.* 1911 (1888). Oxford. Clarendon. 2 vol. 2nd ed. emb olive cloth. VG. G1. $125.00

BOSANQUET, Bernard. *Three Lectures on Aesthetic.* 1931. London. Macmillan. 3rd prt. 12mo. 118p. crimson cloth. G1. $22.50

BOSANQUET, S.R. *New System of Logic, Development Principles of Truth...* 1839. London. Parker. 1st ed. 372p. emb mauve cloth. VG. G1. $125.00

BOSCHETTI, Anna. *Intellectual Enterprise.* 1988. Northwestern. 279p. prt blk cloth. F. G1. $28.00

BOSENTINO, Frank J. *Boehm's Birds.* 1960. Fell. 3rd prt. sgn Boehm & his wife. VG/dj. M20. $25.00

BOSSERT, H.T. *Peasant Art in Europe.* 1926. NY. Weyhe. G+. A1. $110.00

BOSTON, L.M. *Castle of Yew.* 1965. HBJ. 1st Am ed. 58p. F/VG. P2. $40.00

BOSWELL, James. *Boswell for the Defence 1769-1774.* 1960. London. 1st Eng ed. 424p. NF/dj. B18. $35.00

BOSWELL, James. *Life of Samuel Johnson, LLD.* 1807. Boston. Andrews Blake. 3 vol. 1st Am ed. contemporary marbled brd. VG. M1. $325.00

BOSWELL, James. *Life of Samuel Johnson.* 1826. Oxford. Pickering. Oxford Eng Classics. 4 vol. 8vo. teg. speckled calf. NF. F1. $300.00

BOSWELL, R. *Dancing in the Movies.* 1985. IC. 1st ed/author's 1st book. F/F. A15. $150.00

BOSWELL, Robert. *Geography of Desire.* 1989. Knopf. 1st ed. sgn. F/F. B4. $45.00

BOSWELL, Robert. *Mystery Ride.* 1993. Knopf. 1st ed. sgn. F/F. B4. $45.00

BOSWELL, Thomas. *Heart of the Order.* 1989. Doubleday. 1st ed. F/F. B3. $15.00

BOSWORTH, Clarence. *Breeding: How To Raise & Train Colts...* 1939. Derrydale. ltd ed. 1/1250. VG. O3. $60.00

BOTKIN, B.A. *Lay My Burden Down.* 1945. Chicago. ARC/probable advance bdg. 8vo. 285p. dj. H5. $100.00

BOTKIN, B.A. *Mississippi River Folklore Treasury.* 1955. NY. Crown. 1st ed. sgn pres. VG/VG. B5. $25.00

BOTKIN, B.A. *Treasury of Western Folklore.* 1951. Crown. ltd ed. sgn. 806p. G+. A8. $40.00

BOTKIN & HARLOW. *Treasury of Railroad Folklore.* 1989. NY. Bonanza. 8vo. 530p. F/F. B11. $20.00

BOTSFORD, George Willis. *Hist of the Orient & Greece for High Schools & Academies.* 1908. Macmillan. 8th prt. 383p. VG. W1. $14.00

BOTTOMS, David. *Any Cold Jordan.* 1987. Peachtree. 1st ed. VG/VG. B3. $20.00

BOUCHER, Anthony. *Best Detective Stories, 19th Series.* 1964. Dutton. 1st ed. VG/VG. P3. $25.00

BOUCHER, Anthony. *Quintessence of Queen.* 1962. Random. 1st ed. VG/VG. P3. $40.00

BOUCHER, Jonathan. *Reminiscences of an American Loyalist 1738-1739...* 1925. Boston/NY. Houghton Mifflin. 1st ed. 1/575. 201p. cloth. NF. M8. $95.00

BOUDINOT, Elias. *Star in West; or, Humble Attempt To Discover Lost Tribes...* 1816. Trenton, NJ. 1st ed. 8vo. 312p. contemporary calf. M1. $450.00

BOUDRYE, Louis Napoleon. *Hist Records of Fifth NY Cavalry, 1st IRA Harris Guard.* 1865. Albany, NY. Gray. 1st ed. 358p. cloth. VG. M8. $225.00

BOUGEANT, G.H. *Amusement Philosophique sur le Language des Bestes.* 1739. Paris. Chez Gissex. 1st ed. 12mo. contemporary mottled calf. K1. $250.00

BOULDEN, James. *American Among the Orientals.* 1855. Phil. 8vo. 178p. emb cloth. O2. $75.00

BOULE & VALLOIS. *Fossil Men.* 1957. Dryden. 535p. F. K4. $15.00

BOULLE, Pierre. *Virtue of Hell.* 1974. Vanguard. 1st ed. F/NF. F4. $20.00

BOUNDS, Sydney J. *Dimensions of Horror.* 1953. Hamilton Panther. VG/G. P3. $35.00

BOURDON, David. *Warhol.* 1989. Abrams. thick 4to. 432p. NF/VG. F1. $45.00

BOURJAILY, Vance. *Game Men Play.* 1980. Franklin Lib. 1st ed. ils Mitchell Hooks. full leather. F. B3. $30.00

BOURNE, Peter. *Flames of Empire.* 1949. Putnam. 1st ed. VG/G. P3. $18.00

BOURNE, Peter. *Twilight of the Dragon.* 1954. Putnam. 1st ed. VG/VG. P3. $20.00

BOURNE, Russell. *View From Front Street.* 1989. NY. 1st ed. 282p. F/F. A17. $20.00

BOUSSEL, Patrice. *Leonardo da Vinci.* nd. Chartwell. F/F. P3. $75.00

BOUTELL, Charles. *Heraldry, Historical & Popular.* 1864. London. 3rd ed. leather. VG. A9. $15.00

BOUTIN, Otto. *Catfish in the Bodoni: And Other Tales From Golden Age...* 1970. St Cloud, MN. 119p. F/dj. M10. $5.00

BOUVET, Francis. *Bonnard: Complete Graphic Works.* 1981. NY. VG+/VG. A1. $30.00

BOVA, Ben. *Closeup: New Worlds.* 1977. St Martin. ARC of 1st ed. RS. F/dj. F4. $30.00

BOVA, Ben. *Cyberbooks.* 1989. Tor. 1st ed. F/F. P3. $18.00

BOVA, Ben. *Dueling Machine.* 1971. Faber. 1st ed. sgn. F/F. P3. $35.00

BOVA, Ben. *First Contact.* 1990. NAL. 1st ed. VG. P3. $20.00

BOVA, Ben. *High Road.* 1981. Houghton Mifflin. 1st ed. VG. P3. $18.00

BOVA, Ben. *Kinsman.* 1979. Dial. 1st ed. F/F. P3. $20.00

BOVA, Ben. *Millenium.* 1976. Random. 1st ed. NF/NF. P3. $30.00

BOVA, Ben. *Multiple Man.* 1976. Bobbs Merrill. 1st ed. NF/NF. P3. $25.00

BOVA, Ben. *Orion in the Dying Time.* 1990. NY. Doherty. 1st ed. VG/F. B3. $15.00

BOVA, Ben. *Peacekeepers.* 1988. Tor. 1st ed. F/F. P3. $18.00

BOVA, Ben. *Peacekeepers.* 1988. Tor. 1st ed. sgn. F/dj. F4. $25.00

BOVA, Ben. *Privateers.* 1985. Tor. 1st ed. NF/NF. P3. $16.00

BOVA, Ben. *Vengeance of Orion.* 1988. Tor. 1st ed. F/F. P3. $18.00

BOVA, Ben. *Weathermakers.* 1967. Holt. 1st ed. F/dj. M2. $25.00

BOVA, Ben. *Winds of Altair.* 1973. Dutton. 1st ed. VG. P3. $13.00

BOWDEN, Charles. *Desierto.* 1991. Norton. 1st ed. F/F. B3. $30.00

BOWDEN, Charles. *Mezcal.* 1988. Tucson, AZ. 1st ed. F/F. B3. $25.00

BOWDEN, Charles. *Red Line.* 1989. Norton. 1st ed. sgn. F/F. B3. $30.00

BOWDEN, Henry Warner. *American Indians & Christian Missions: Studies...* 1981. Chicago. not 1st ed. VG/dj. N2. $10.00

BOWDEN, James. *Hist of the Society of Friends in America. Vol 1.* 1850. London. Gilpin. 1st ed. inscr. cloth. VG. M8. $45.00

BOWDEN & KREINBERG. *Street Signs Chicago: Neighborhood & Other Illusions...* 1981. Chicago Review. 1st ed. F/NF. B4. $125.00

BOWEN, Catherine D. *Yankee From Olympus.* 1944. Boston. 8th prt. 475p. cloth. NF/dj. D3. $12.50

BOWEN, Dana Thomas. *Lore of the Lakes.* 1941-1976. Cleveland/Daytona. ils. 314p. dj. T7. $25.00

BOWEN, Dana Thomas. *Shipwrecks of the Lakes.* 1952. Lakeside. 1st ed. 362p. cloth. VG. M20. $30.00

BOWEN, Elizabeth. *Heat of the Day.* 1949. np. 372p. F. S12. $10.00

BOWEN, Elizabeth. *House in Paris.* 1936. Knopf. 1st ed. VG/VG. P3. $20.00

BOWEN, John Joseph. *Strategy of Robert E Lee.* 1914. Crowell. 1st ed. 256p. bl cloth. VG. C6. $60.00

BOWEN, Marjorie. *Kecksies & Other Twilight Tales.* 1976. Arkham. 1st ed. 1/4391. F/F. T2. $10.00

BOWEN, Michael. *Can't Miss.* 1987. Harper Row. 1st ed. F/F. P8. $17.50

BOWEN, Peter. *Coyote Wind.* 1994. St Martin. 1st ed. F/F. B3. $25.00

BOWEN, Peter. *Kelley Blue.* 1991. NY. Crown. 1st ed/author's 2nd book. F/F. B3. $35.00

BOWEN, Robert Sidney. *Hawaii Five-O Top Secret.* 1969. Whitman. Hawaii Five-O TVTI. VG. P3. $10.00

BOWEN, Robert Sidney. *Man on First.* 1966. Lothrop Lee Shepard. 158p. VG/dj. M20. $20.00

BOWEN, Robert Sidney. *Player-Manager.* 1949. Grosset Dunlap. rpt. VG/F. P8. $17.50

BOWEN, Robert Sidney. *Red Randall's One-Man War.* 1946. Grosset Dunlap. last title in series. 215p. VG/chip. M20. $30.00

BOWEN, Robert Sidney. *Winning Pitch.* 1948. Lee Shepard. later prt. G+/VG. P8. $35.00

BOWER, B.M. *Flying U's Last Stand.* 1915. Little Brn. 1st ed. ftspc Anton Otto Fischer. VG. A18. $30.00

BOWER, B.M. *Lure of the Dim Trials.* nd. Grosset Dunlap. G+. P3. $10.00

BOWER, B.M. *Open Land.* 1945. Triangle. G. B34. $20.00

BOWER, B.M. *Rodeo.* 1943. Triangle. VG. P3. $15.00

BOWER, B.M. *Trail of the White Mule.* 1922. Little Brn. 1st ed. ftspc FT Johnson. F. A18. $30.00

BOWER, William Clayton. *Central Christian Church, Lexington, KY: A Hist.* 1962. St Louis. private prt. 1st ed. 192p. cloth. F. M8. $37.50

BOWERS, Dorothy. *Fear & Miss Betony.* 1942. Doubleday Crime Club. 1st Am ed. VG/VG. M15. $35.00

BOWERS, Fredson. *Principles of Bibliographical Description.* 1949. Princeton. 522p. VG. A4. $185.00

BOWERS, Janice Emily. *Mountains New Door.* 1991. AZ U. 1st ed. 147p. F/F. B19. $35.00

BOWERS, Janice Emily. *Sense of Place.* 1988. AZ U. 1st ed. ils/maps/index. 192p. F/F. B19. $25.00

BOWERS, John. *Stonewall Jackson: Portrait of a Soldier.* 1989. ils/maps/index. 367p. dj. O8. $14.50

BOWKER, Richard. *Marlborough Street.* 1987. Doubleday. 1st ed. RS. F/F. P3. $18.00

BOWLBY, John. *Personality & Mental Illness.* 1942. Emerson. 200p. G/dj. K4. $20.00

BOWLES, Charles E. *Petroleum Industry.* 1921. Schooley Stationery Prt. 1st ed. 12mo. 189p. F. H1. $15.00

BOWLES, Paul. *Days: Tangier Journal 1987-1989.* 1991. NY. Ecco. 1st ed. F/F. B3. $25.00

BOWLES, Paul. *Their Heads Are Green & Their Hands Are Blue.* 1963. Random. 1st ed. 8vo. 206p. bl-gr cloth. F/NF clip. C6. $40.00

BOWLES, Paul. *Thicket of Spring.* 1972. Blk Sparrow. 2nd sgn ltd ed. 1/200. F/acetate dj. L3. $450.00

BOWMAN, David. *Let the Dog Drive.* 1992. NY U. 1st ed/author's 1st novel. 1/1000. sgn. F/F. L3. $200.00

BOWMAN, Isaiah. *Andes of Southern Peru.* 1916. np. 1st ed. 4to. 336p. VG. F3. $25.00

BOWMAN, Martin. *B-24 Liberator 1939-45.* 1989. Great Britian. 136p. VG/dj. B18. $22.50

BOWMAN & BOWMAN. *Crusoe's Island in the Caribbean.* 1939. Bobbs Merrill. 1st ed. 8vo. 339p. gilt gr cloth. VG. B11. $25.00

BOWRA, C.M. *Greek Experience.* 1969. NY. Praeger. 210p. NF/dj. M10. $7.50

BOX 48 BRADBURY

BOX, Edgar; see Vidal, Gore.

BOYCE, Chris. *Catchworld.* 1977. Doubleday. F/F. P3. $15.00

BOYCE, William D. *Ils Africa.* 1925. np. 1st ed. sgn pres. 700p. VG. E5. $45.00

BOYD, Belle. *Belle Boyd in Camp & Prison.* 1865. NY. Blelock. 1st Am ed. 8vo. 464p. gr cloth. G+. C6. $100.00

BOYD, David French. *General WT Sherman As College President.* 1910. Baton Rouge. Ortlieb. 1st separate ed. 8vo. VG/prt wrp. C6. $20.00

BOYD, Doug. *Swami: An American's Lively Personal Exploration...* 1976. Random. G+/fair. N2. $6.50

BOYD, Elizabeth French. *First Quarter-Millenium: A Hist of Presbyterian Church...* 1976. New Brunswick. 1st ed. 127p. cloth. F/F. M8. $27.50

BOYD, Frank; see Kane, Frank.

BOYD, Hamish. *One Night of Murder.* 1958. Mystery House. VG/VG. P3. $20.00

BOYD, James. *General Ulysses S Grant, Military & Civil Life: Ils.* 1892. np. 734p. VG. E5. $45.00

BOYD, John. *Girl With the Jade Green Eyes.* 1978. Viking. 1st ed. VG/VG. P3. $25.00

BOYD, John. *Gorgon Festival.* 1972. Weybright Talley. 1st ed. VG/VG. P3. $18.00

BOYD, John. *Rakehells of Heaven.* 1969. Weybright Talley. 1st ed. VG/VG. P3. $18.00

BOYD, John. *Sex & the High Command.* 1970. Weybright Talley. 1st ed. VG/G. P3. $15.00

BOYD, Margaret. *Sew & Save Source Book.* 1984. np. VG/wrp. G2. $10.00

BOYD, Thomas. *Through the Wheat.* 1923. Scribner. 1st ed/author's 1st book. NF. B2. $35.00

BOYD, William. *Good Man in Africa.* 1981. Hamish Hamilton. 1st ed/author's 1st book. inscr/dtd 1981. F/F. B4. $850.00

BOYD, William. *On the Yankee Station.* 1984. Morrow. 1st ed/author's 3rd book. F/F. B3. $45.00

BOYER, Carl B. *Rainbow: From Myth to Mathematics.* 1987 (1959). Princeton. 8vo. ils. 376p. VG/VG. K5. $28.00

BOYER, Dwight. *Ships & Men of the Great Lakes.* 1977. Dodd Mead. 208p. dj. T7. $18.00

BOYER, Richard O. *Legend of John Brown.* 1973. Knopf. 1st ed. 627p. F/F. H1. $20.00

BOYER, Rick. *Moscow Metal.* 1988. London. Gollancz. 1st ed. F/F. S6. $20.00

BOYES, Joseph. *On the Shoulders of Giants: Notable Names in Hand Surgery.* 1976. Phil. 1st ed. 222p. A13. $200.00

BOYKIN, E. *Ghost Ship of the Confederacy: Story of the Alabama.* 1957. np. 1st ed. 400p. lib bdg. VG. E5. $28.00

BOYKIN, Edward M. *Boys & Girls Stories of the War.* 1863? Richmond. West Johnson. 32mo. 32p. VG/prt wrp. M1. $750.00

BOYLAN, Grace Duffie. *Young Folks Uncle Tom's Cabin.* 1901. Chicago. Jamieson Higgins. 1st ed. 4to. 166p. G+. D6. $100.00

BOYLE, Andrew. *Trenchard: Man of Vision.* 1962. London. Collins. 1st ed. photos/index. 768p. gilt red-orange cloth. F/NF. M7. $65.00

BOYLE, Kay. *Death of a Man.* 1936. Harcourt. 1st ed. F/NF. B2. $65.00

BOYLE, Kay. *Thirty Stories.* 1946. Simon Schuster. 1st ed. NF/NF. S9. $45.00

BOYLE, Kay. *White Horses of Vienna & Other Stories.* 1936. Harcourt Brace. 1st ed. 8vo. silvered bl cloth. G/dj. H5. $75.00

BOYLE, Patrick. *At Night All Cats Are Grey.* 1969. Grove. 1st Am ed. 256p. cloth. VG/dj. M20. $15.00

BOYLE, Robert. *Works of the Honourable Robert Boyle.* 1744. London. 5 vol. 1st ed. folio. 24 pl on 15 fld sheets. full calf. VG+. C6. $700.00

BOYLE, T. Coraghessan. *Budding Prospects.* 1984. Viking. 1st ed. F/NF. B2. $50.00

BOYLE, T. Coraghessan. *Descent of Man.* 1979. Little Brn. ARC/author's 1st book. RS. F/F. B4. $450.00

BOYLE, T. Coraghessan. *Descent of Man.* 1980. London. 1st ed/author's 1st book. F/F. A15. $60.00

BOYLE, T. Coraghessan. *Descent of Man.* 1980. London. 1st UK ed/author's 1st book. w/sgn label. F/F. A11. $75.00

BOYLE, T. Coraghessan. *East Is East.* 1990. NY. 1st ed. rem mk. F/F. A15. $20.00

BOYLE, T. Coraghessan. *East Is East.* 1990. Viking. 1st ed. sgn. F/F. S9. $45.00

BOYLE, T. Coraghessan. *Greasy Lake.* 1985. NY. 1st ed/author's 4th book. F/clip. A15. $40.00

BOYLE, T. Coraghessan. *Road to Wellville.* 1993. Viking. ARC. F/wrp. B2. $35.00

BOYLE, T. Coraghessan. *Road to Wellville.* 1993. Viking. 1st ed. F/F. B3. $30.00

BOYLE, T. Coraghessan. *Water Music.* 1981. Little Brn. 1st ed. NF/F. B3. $75.00

BOYLE, Thomas. *Brooklyn Three.* 1991. NY. Viking. UP. F/prt wrp. B3. $25.00

BOYLE, Thomas. *Cold Stove League.* 1983. Chicago. Academy Chicago. 1st ed/author's 1st book. F/NF. B3. $30.00

BOYLE, Thomas. *Only the Dead Know Brooklyn.* 1985. Stoddart. 1st ed. F/F. P3. $15.00

BOYNTON, Sandra. *A Is for Angry, an Animal & Adjective Alphabet.* 1984 (1983). London. Methuen. 1st UK ed. lg 8vo. F/NF. C8. $30.00

BRAASCH, Gary. *Photographing the Patterns of Nature.* 1990. NY. Amphoto. 1st ed. 4to. F/F. S9. $30.00

BRACE, David Kingsley. *Measuring Motor Ability: A Scale of Motor Ability Tests.* 1927. NY. Barnes. F. K4. $25.00

BRACE, Gerald Warner. *Between Wind & Water.* 1966. Norton. 1st ed. 219p. dj. T7. $22.00

BRACEWELL, Ronald N. *Paris Symposium on Radio Astronomy.* 1959. Stanford. lg 8vo. 612p. VG/VG. K5. $35.00

BRACKENRIDGE, H.H. *Modern Chivalry: Containing Adventures of a Captain...* 1813. Wilmington. 12mo. 276p. contemporary calf/leather label. M1. $125.00

BRACKETT, Hugh. *Follow the Free Wind.* 1963. Doubleday. 1st ed. F/NF. M15. $40.00

BRACKETT, Leigh. *Starmen.* 1952. Gnome. 1st ed. F/dj. M2. $125.00

BRACKMAN, Arnold C. *Search for the Gold of Tutankhamen.* 1976. Mason Charter. 1st ed. 8vo. VG/dj. W1. $16.00

BRADBURY, Edward P.; see Moore, Brian.

BRADBURY, Ray. *Death Is a Lonely Business.* 1985. Knopf. 1st ed. NF/NF. P3. $25.00

BRADBURY, Ray. *Fahrenheit 451.* 1971. Ballantine. 26th prt. lib pb bdg. P3. $5.00

BRADBURY, Ray. *Ghosts of Forever.* 1980. NY. 1st ed. folio. F/F. M9. $60.00

BRADBURY, Ray. *Graveyard for Lunatics.* 1990. Knopf. 1st ed. F/F. F4. $20.00

BRADBURY, Ray. *Green Shadows, White Whale.* 1992. Knopf. 1st ed. F/F. P3. $21.00

BRADBURY, Ray. *Haunted Computer & the Android Pope.* 1981. Knopf. stated 1st ed. VG/VG. M17. $17.50

BRADBURY, Ray. *Machineries of Joy.* 1977. Granada. F/F. P3. $25.00

BRADBURY, Ray. *S Is for Space.* 1966. Doubleday. 1st ed. G+. P3. $20.00

BRADBURY, Ray. *Something Wicked This Way Comes.* 1983. Knopf. VG/VG. P3. $25.00

BRADBURY, Ray. *Stories of Ray Bradbury.* 1980. Knopf. 1st ed. VG/G. P3. $22.00

BRADBURY, Ray. *Stories of Ray Bradbury.* 1980. NY. 1st ed. inscr. F/F. C2. $125.00

BRADBURY, Ray. *Switch on the Night.* 1993. Knopf. 1st ed. rem mk. F. B17. $8.50

BRADBURY, Ray. *Toynbee Convector.* 1988. Knopf. 1st ed. F/F. P3. $18.00

BRADBURY, Ray. *Toynbee Convector.* 1992. Turner. 1st ed. ils Anita Kunz. F/sans. B3. $20.00

BRADBURY, Ray. *When Elephants Last in the Doorway Bloomed.* 1975. Hart Davis MacGibbon. 1st ed. F/F. P3. $35.00

BRADBURY, Ray. *Where Robot Mice & Robot Men Run.* 1979. Hart Davis MacGibbon. 1st ed. VG/VG. P3. $25.00

BRADBURY, Ray. *Wonderful Ice Cream Suit.* 1973. Hart Davis MacGibbon. 1st ed. NF/NF. P3. $35.00

BRADDON, George. *Microbe's Kiss.* 1940. Faber. 1st ed. G+/dj. P3. $30.00

BRADFIELD, Scott. *Hist of Luninous Motion.* 1989. Knopf. ARC/author's 1st novel. F/pict wrp. B3. $40.00

BRADFIELD, Scott. *Secret Life of Houses.* 1988. London. Unwin Hyman. 1st ed/true 1st ed/author's 1st book. F. S9. $100.00

BRADFORD, Alden. *Hist of MA From 1764... (to 1820).* 1822, 1825 & 1829. Boston. 3 vol. 1st ed. 8vo. contemporary calf. M1. $300.00

BRADFORD, Ernie. *Companion Guide to Greek Islands.* 1963. Harper Row. 1st ed. 16 pl. NF/dj. W1. $12.00

BRADFORD, Ernie. *Paul the Traveller: St Paul's Evangelical Journeys...* 1976. Macmillan. 1st Am ed. 246p. VG/VG. B33. $20.00

BRADFORD, Perry. *Born With the Blues.* 1965. NY. Oak. 1st ed. NF/wrp. B2. $45.00

BRADLEE, Francis B.C. *Piracy in the West Indies & Its Suppression.* 1923. Salem. Exxex. 220p. T7. $115.00

BRADLEY, A.G. *Round About Wiltshire.* 1948. London. Methuen. 8th ed. VG/dj. M7. $14.00

BRADLEY, A.G. *Worcestershire.* 1909. London. Blk. 1st ed. 24 mc pl/fld map. teg. VG. H7. $35.00

BRADLEY, Alice; see Sheldon, Alice Bradley.

BRADLEY, Cuthbert. *Foxhound of the Twentieth Century.* 1914. London. Routledge. 1st ed. tall 8vo. 308p. half morocco. R2. $125.00

BRADLEY, David. *South Street.* 1975. Grossman/Viking. 1st ed. F/NF. B2. $150.00

BRADLEY, F.H. *Collected Papers.* 1935. Oxford. 2 vol. bl cloth. NF/VG. G1. $150.00

BRADLEY, John L. *Rogue's Progress...* 1965. Boston. 330p. VG. D3. $25.00

BRADLEY, Marion Zimmer. *Catch Trap.* 1979. Ballantine. 1st ed. VG/VG. P3. $23.00

BRADLEY, Marion Zimmer. *Darkover Landfall.* 1986. Severn. F/F. P3. $25.00

BRADLEY, Marion Zimmer. *Firebrand.* 1987. Simon Schuster. 1st ed. F/F. P3. $20.00

BRADLEY, Marion Zimmer. *Heirs of Hammerfell.* 1989. DAW. 1st ed. F/F. P3. $20.00

BRADLEY, Marion Zimmer. *Mists of Avalon.* nd. BC. F/F. P3. $20.00

BRADLEY, Marion Zimmer. *Star of Danger.* 1979. Gregg. 1st ed. F/sans. P3. $30.00

BRADLEY, Omar N. *Soldier's Story.* 1951. Holt. 1st ed. 618p. VG/VG. H1. $28.00

BRADLEY & LACKEY. *Rediscovery.* 1993. DAW. 1st ed. F/F. P3. $18.00

BRADSHAW, A.D. *Ecology & Design in Landscape.* 1986. Oxford. ils. 463p. F/dj. B26. $45.00

BRADSHAW, Gillian. *Hawk of May.* 1980. Simon Schuster. 1st ed. F/F. F4. $18.00

BRADSHAW, Gillian. *Horses of Heaven.* 1991. Doubleday. F/F. P3. $20.00

BRADSHAW, Gillian. *Winter's Shadow.* 1982. Simon Schuster. 1st ed. NF/NF. P3. $20.00

BRADSHAW, Jon. *Fast Company.* 1975. Harper. 1st ed. F/NF. B4. $45.00

BRADSHAW, Wesley. *Volunteer's Roll of Honor.* 1864. Phil. Barclay. 1st ed. ils. pict wrp. M1. $200.00

BRADSHAW-SMITH, Gillian. *Adventures in Toy-Making.* 1976. NY. ils/drawings/photos. 128p. F/dj. B14. $30.00

BRADY, Charles. *Seven Games in October.* 1979. Little Brn. 1st ed. F/VG. P8. $30.00

BRADY, Cyrus T. *Indian Fights & Fighters.* 1904. NY. 1st ed. inscr. G+. A1. $75.00

BRADY, Cyrus T. *Under Tops'ls & Tents.* 1901. Scribner. 1st ed. inscr to edit. VG+. A1. $50.00

BRADY, Edward Foster. *Memoir of..., Late Superintendent of Croyden School.* 1839. London. Harvey Darton. 1st ed. 16mo. 166p. lacks free ep. V3. $25.00

BRADY, Joan. *Theory of War.* 1993. Knopf. 1st Am ed. F/F. A14. $35.00

BRADY, John. *Clavis Calendaria; or, Copendious Analysis of the Calendar.* 1812. London. self pub. 2 vol. 1st ed. half calf. H10. $125.00

BRADY, John. *Unholy Ground.* 1989. Canada. Collins. 1st ed. VG/VG. P3. $20.00

BRADY, John. *Unholy Ground.* 1989. London. Constable. ARC/1st ed. RS. NF/dj. S6. $22.50

BRADY & GRISMER. *Gentleman From Mississippi.* (1909). Ogilvie. ils. 189p. cloth. VG. S11. $12.00

BRAGDON, Claude. *Beautiful Necessity.* 1922. Knopf. 1st ed. 111p. VG. B33. $28.00

BRAGDON, Claude. *Projective Ornament.* 1927. Knopf. 79p. VG. B33. $32.00

BRAGDON, Dudley A. *Billy Bounce.* 1906. Donohue. 2nd ed. ils WW Denslow. olive cloth. NF. D6. $150.00

BRAIDWOOD & HOWE. *Prehistoric Investigations in Iraqi Kurdistan...* 1972. Chicago. 3rd imp. 29 pl. VG/wrp. W1. $25.00

BRAILSFORD, H.N. *War Guilt & Peace: Crime of the Entente Allies.* 1920. NY. 185p. VG. A17. $7.50

BRAINARD, John G.C. *Poems...a New & Authentic Collection...* 1842. Hartford. Edward Hopkins. 1st ed. 12mo. 191p. cream brd/leather spine label. M1. $175.00

BRAINE, John. *Finger of Fire.* 1977. London. Eyre Methuen. 1st ed. NF/NF. B3. $15.00

BRAINE, Shelia. *Princess of Hearts.* ca 1908. Caldwell. ils Alice Woodward. 172p. VG+. P2. $65.00

BRAINERD, Eleanor Hoyt. *For Love of Mary Ellen.* 1912. Harper. 1st ed. ils. pict cloth. VG. M5. $35.00

BRAITHWAITE, Richard Bevan. *Scientific Explanation: Study of Function of Theory...* 1946. Cambridge. 376p. bl cloth. VG. G1. $28.50

BRAITHWAITE, William C. *Beginnings of Quakerism.* 1955. Cambridge. 2nd ed. 8vo. 607p. xl. scarce. V3. $50.00

BRALEY, Berton. *Sheriff of Silver Bow.* 1921. Jacobsen. poor. B34. $12.00

BRAMAH, Ernest. *Wallet of Kai Lung.* 1926. Methuen. 7th prt. VG. P3. $20.00

BRAMBLE, Forbes. *Strange Case of Deacon Brodie.* 1975. Hamish Hamilton. 1st ed. F/F. P3. $20.00

BRAMHALL, Marion. *Tragedy in Blue.* 1945. Crime Club. 1st ed. VG. P3. $18.00

BRAMLETT, Jim. *Ride for the High Points: Real Story of Will James.* 1987. Mtn Pr. 1st ed. pict ep. M/dj. A18. $30.00

BRAMWELL, J. Milne. *Hypnotism: Its History, Practice & Theory.* 1906. London. 478p. A13. $45.00

BRANCH, Edgar M. *Clemens of the Call: Mark Twain in San Francisco.* 1969. CA U. 1st ed. F/F. A18. $50.00

BRAND, Christianna. *Death in High Heels.* 1954. Scribner. 1st ed. VG/G. P3. $30.00

BRAND, Christianna. *Fog of Doubt.* 1979. Boston. Gregg. 1st ed. F/F. S6. $22.50

BRAND, Christianna. *Nurse Matilda Goes to Town.* 1968. Dutton. 2nd prt. ils. F/NF. P2. $30.00

BRAND, Max. *Fugitives' Fire*. 1991. Putnam. 1st ed. F/F. P3. $19.00

BRAND, Max. *King Bird Rides*. 1938. Hodder Stoughton. 2nd ed. VG/VG. P3. $15.00

BRAND, Max. *Lost Wolf*. 1986. Dodd Mead. 1st ed. VG/VG. P3. $15.00

BRAND, Millen. *Outward Room*. 1937. NY. 1st ed/author's 1st book. F/NF. A17. $15.00

BRANDEIS, Madeline. *Little Indian Weaver*. 1928. Grosset. lg prt. ils. VG. B34. $10.00

BRANDER, Bruce. *River Nile*. 1966. NGS. 1st ed. 8vo. 208p. VG. W1. $8.00

BRANDNER, Gary. *Hellborn*. 1988. Severn. F/F. P3. $24.00

BRANDON, John G. *Murder at the Yard*. 1936. Wright Brn. xl. VG. P3. $9.00

BRANDON, Michael. *Nonce*. 1944. Coward McCann. 1st ed. VG/dj. M2. $15.00

BRANDRETH, Henry R.T. *Unity & Reunion: A Bibliography*. 1945. London. Blk. 158p. H10. $15.00

BRANDS, Orestes M. *Lessons on the Human Body...* 1883. Boston. 255p. cloth. VG. B14. $45.00

BRANDT, Bill. *Bill Brandt: Nudes 1945-1980*. 1980. Boston. NYGS. 1st ed. 4to. 100 full-p photos. NF/NF. S9. $125.00

BRANDT, Bill. *London in the Thirties*. 1983. Pantheon. 1st ed. intro Mark Haworth-Booth. F/F. S9. $65.00

BRANDT, Nat. *Town That Started the Civil War*. 1990. Syracuse. ils/photos/map. 315p. M/M. A17. $10.00

BRANDT, Tom; see Dewey, Thomas B.

BRANLEY, Franklyn M. *Lodestar Rocket Ship to Mars*. 1951. Crowell. 1st ed. VG/VG. P3. $18.00

BRANLEY, Franklyn M. *Nine Planets*. 1978 (1958). Crowell. new revised ed. 99p. xl. K5. $6.00

BRAQUE, Georges. *Cahier de Georges Braque 1917-1947*. 1955. Paris. Maeght. 2 parts. folio. fld sheets/stiff wrp/portfolio/ties. K1. $450.00

BRASHEAR, Minnie M. *Mark Twain, Son of Missouri*. 1934. NC U. 1st ed. 294p. VG. M10. $27.50

BRASHEAR & RODNEY. *Art, Humor & Humanity of Mark Twain*. 1959. OK U. 1st ed. 423p. VG/dj. M10. $18.50

BRASHLER, William. *Bingo Long Travelling All Stars*. 1973. Harper Row. 1st ed. G/G. P8. $17.50

BRASSAI. *Brassai*. 1968. MOMA. 1st ed. inscr/dtd 1968. VG+/wrp. S9. $95.00

BRASSAI. *Les Sculptures de Picasso*. 1948. Paris. Les Editions du Chene. 218 photos. pict bdg. NF. S9. $175.00

BRAUN, Adolphe Armand. *Figures, Faces & Folds: A Practical Reference Book...* 1928. Boston. Am Photographic. 152p. VG+/G. F1. $85.00

BRAUN, Lilian Jackson. *Cat Who Ate Danish Modern*. 1967. Dutton. 1st ed. VG/dj. M15. $45.00

BRAUN, Lilian Jackson. *Cat Who Knew a Cardinal*. 1991. Putnam. 1st ed. F/F. P3. $17.00

BRAUN, Lilian Jackson. *Cat Who Sniffed Clue*. 1988. Putnam. 1st ed. VG/VG. P3. $18.00

BRAUNSTEIN, Myron L. *Depth Perception Through Motion*. 1974. Academic. 200p. F/dj. K4. $15.00

BRAUTIGAN, Richard. *Abortion: An Historical Romance*. 1966. Simon Schuster. 5th ed. VG/VG. P3. $20.00

BRAUTIGAN, Richard. *Confederate General From Big Sur*. 1964. Grove. 1st ed. F/NF. B4. $350.00

BRAUTIGAN, Richard. *Confederate General From Big Sur*. 1964. Grove. 1st ed. 8vo. 159p. bl cloth. NF/VG. C6. $200.00

BRAUTIGAN, Richard. *Dreaming of Babylon*. 1977. Delacorte. 1st ed. F/F. B3. $40.00

BRAUTIGAN, Richard. *Dreaming of Babylon*. 1977. Delacorte. 1st ed. NF/NF. P3. $30.00

BRAUTIGAN, Richard. *Hawkline Monster: A Gothic Western*. 1974. Simon Schuster. 1st ed. F/F. P3. $25.00

BRAUTIGAN, Richard. *Please Plant This Book*. 1968. San Francisco. 1st ed. w/seed packets. F. Q1/S9. $750.00

BRAUTIGAN, Richard. *Rommel Drives on Deep Into Egypt*. 1970. Delacorte. 1st ed. F/F. B4. $200.00

BRAUTIGAN, Richard. *Sombrero Fallout*. 1976. Simon Schuster. 1st ed. F/F. B3. $40.00

BRAUTIGAN, Richard. *Sombrero Fallout*. 1976. Simon Schuster. 1st ed. rem mk. 187p. NF/NF. M20/P3. $25.00

BRAUTIGAN, Richard. *Willard & His Bowling Trophies*. 1975. Simon Schuster. 1st ed. NF/NF. P3. $25.00

BRAVO, H. *Las Cactaceas de Mexico*. 1978, 1991 & 1991. Mexico. 3 vol. ils. F (vol 1) & M (vol 2 & 3). B26. $265.00

BRAY, N.N.E. *Shifting Sands*. 1934. London. Unicorn. 1st ed. ils/maps. 312p. gilt blk cloth. VG. M7. $60.00

BRAYBROOKE, Neville. *Seeds in the Wind*. 1939. London. 1st ed. 207p. gilt bdg. M. M7. $35.00

BREAKENRIDGE, William M. *Helldorado, Bringing the Law to the Mesquite*. 1928. Houghton Mifflin. M11. $65.00

BREARLEY, Joan McDonald. *Visualizations of the Standards*. 1972. Phil. Popular Dogs. 1st cloth ed. 4to. 326p. cloth. VG. R2. $20.00

BREASTED, James Henry. *Ancient Records of Egypt*. 1927. Chicago. 5 vol. 3rd prt. M. H4. $150.00

BREASTED, James Henry. *Conquest of Civilization*. 1938. Literary Guild Am. new ed. 8vo. 669p. VG/dj. W1. $15.00

BREASTED, James Henry. *Geschichte Agyptiens*. 1936. Paidon. sm 4to. 247 pl. VG. W1. $15.00

BRECHER, Irving. *Life of Riley*. 1949. Movie Reader's Lib. 1st ed. F/dj. very scarce. F4. $40.00

BRECKENRIDGE, Gerald. *Radio Boys on the Mexican Border*. 1922. Burt. VG/dj. B14. $30.00

BREE, C.R. *History of Birds of Europe*. 1866-1867. London. 4 vol. early ed. 238 full-p mc pl. red cloth. VG+. C6. $550.00

BREED, Robert S. *Sesquicentennial of the First Presbyterian Church Geneva...* ca 1950. np. 1st ed. 61p. VG/prt wrp. M8. $37.50

BREEN, John L. *Hot Air*. 1991. Simon Schuster. ARC/1st ed. sgn. RS. F/F. S6. $35.00

BREEN, John L. *Triple Crown*. 1985. Walker. 1st ed. F/F. M15. $37.50

BREESE, Louis V. *Some Unwritten Laws of Organized Foxhunting & Comments...* 1909. np. 1st ed. VG. O3. $85.00

BREHIER, Emile. *Histoire de la Philosophie*. 1944. Paris. 2 vol in 7 parts. later ed/various prt. prt wrp. G1. $100.00

BREINES & DEAN. *Book of Houses*. 1946. NY. Crown. thin 4to. photos/floor plans. tan cloth. G/dj. F1. $25.00

BREMMER, M.D.K. *Story of Dentistry: Dentistry From Dawn of Civilization...* 1946. NY. 2nd ed. 335p. A13. $75.00

BREMOND, Edouard. *Le Jedjaz Dans la Guerre Mondiale*. 1931. Paris. Payot. 1st ed. maps. 351p. VG/plain tan wrp. uncut. w/1p ad. M7. $385.00

BREMSER, Ray. *Angel*. 1967. Tompkins Sq Pr. 1/1000. F. B2. $35.00

BREMSER, Ray. *Black Is Black Blues*. 1971. Buffalo. Intrepid. 1st ed. 1/1000. F/wrp. B2. $25.00

BREMSER, Ray. *Blowing Mouth*. 1978. Cherry Valley. 1st ed. F/wrp. B2. $25.00

BRENNAN, J.H. *Shiva Accused*. 1991. Harper Collins. 1st ed. lib bdg. F/F. N3. $10.00

BRENNAN, Joseph Payne. *Adventures of Lucius Leffing.* 1990. Donald Grant. 1st ed. sgn. ils/sgn Luis Ferreira. F/F. T2. $30.00

BRENNAN, Joseph Payne. *Chronicles of Lucius Leffing.* 1977. Donald Grant. 1st ed. F/F. T2. $40.00

BRENNAN, Joseph Payne. *Sixty Selected Poems.* 1985. Amherst. New Establishment. 1st ed. F/F. T2. $18.00

BRENNAN, Louis A. *Beginner's Guide to Archaeology.* 1973. Stackpole. 1st ed. 318p. xl. dj. W1. $14.00

BRENT, Eva. *Nature in Needlepoint.* 1974. np. cloth. VG. G2. $15.00

BRENT, Peter. *TE Lawrence.* 1975. Putnam. 1st ed. 232p. gilt maroon cloth. NF/VG. M7. $35.00

BRENTANO, Frances. *Nation Under God: Religious Patriotic Anthology.* 1957. Channel Pr. 376p. VG/dj. B29. $5.50

BRENTANO, Franz. *Philosophical Investigations on Space, Time & the Continuum.* 1988. London. Croom Helm. 202p. bl cloth. VG/dj. G1. $30.00

BRENTANO, Franz. *Psychologie vom Empirischen Stadpunkt.* 1874. Leipzig. Duncker Humblot. 350p. rare. G1. $650.00

BRENTANO, Franz. *Untersuchungen des Sinnespsychologie.* 1907. Leipzig. Duncker Humblot. tall 8vo. 161p. orig wrp/modern cloth. G1. $175.00

BRERETON, C. *Mystica et Lyrica.* 1919. London. Elkin Mathews. 1st ed. 127p. blk stp brn brd. VG+. uncut. M7. $125.00

BRESLER, Fenton. *Mystery of Georges Simenon.* 1983. Beaufort. 1st ed. VG. P3. $19.00

BRESLIN, Howard. *Silver Oar.* 1954. Crowell. 1st ed. VG/VG. P3. $15.00

BRESS, Helene. *Craft of Macrame.* 1972. np. VG/wrp. G2. $6.00

BRESSON, Henri Cartier. *Face of Asia.* 1972. NY. 1st ed. VG/VG. B5. $60.00

BRETT, Jan. *Twelve Days of Christmas.* 1986. Dodd Mead. 1st ed. F/F. M5. $20.00

BRETT, Leo. *Alien Ones.* 1969. Arcadia. VG/VG. P3. $10.00

BRETT, Simon. *Amateur Corpse.* 1978. Scribner. 1st ed. VG/VG. P3. $20.00

BRETT, Simon. *Comedian Dies.* 1979. Scribner. 1st ed. VG/VG. P3. $15.00

BRETT, Simon. *Corporate Bodies.* 1992. Scribner. 1st ed. F/F. P3. $19.00

BRETT, Simon. *Dead Romantic.* 1986. Scribner. ARC/1st Am ed. sgn. RS. F/F. S6. $40.00

BRETT, Simon. *Shock to the System.* 1985. Scribner. 1st ed. NF/NF. P3. $14.00

BRETT, Simon. *Situation Tragedy.* 1981. London. Gollancz. 1st ed. F/F. S6. $35.00

BRETT, Simon. *So Much Blood.* 1976. Gollancz. 1st ed. F/F. M15. $65.00

BRETT, Thomas. *Collection of Principal Liturgies...* 1838. London. Rivington. 465p. contemporary leather. H10. $125.00

BRETT, W.H. *Indian Tribes of Guiana.* 1853. NY. Robert Carter. 12mo. ils. 352p. emb red cloth. VG. P4. $125.00

BREWER, A.T. *Hist of 61st Regiment PA Volunteers 1861-65.* 1911. Pittsburgh. 1st ed. 234p. VG. B18. $150.00

BREWER. *Anthony Burgess: A Bibliography.* 1980. np. 190p. F. A4. $35.00

BREWER. *Atlas of Breeding Birds in Michigan.* 1991. MI State. ils. 611p. F/F. A4. $40.00

BREWERTON, George Douglas. *Fitz Poodle at Newport.* 1869. Cambridge. 1st ed. emb cloth. A17. $15.00

BREWINGTON, D.E.R. *Marine Paintings & Drawings in Mystic Seaport Mus.* 1982. np. VG/VG. M17. $100.00

BREWINGTON, M.V. *American Naval Prints & Paintings.* 1959. Salem. Peabody Mus. ils. 61p. wrp. T7. $32.00

BREWINGTON & BREWINGTON. *Marine Paintings & Drawings in Peabody Museum.* 1981. np. revised ed. VG/VG. M17. $85.00

BREWSTER, David. *Stereoscope: Its History, Theory & Construction.* 1971. Hastings-on-Hudson. Morgan. facsimile. 8vo. F/F. S9. $35.00

BREYER, Siegfried. *Battleships & Battle Cruisers 1905-1970.* 1974. Doubleday. 480p. F/VG. H1. $30.00

BRIANCHANINOV, Ignatius. *On the Prayer of Jesus.* 1965. London. Watkins. 114p. VG/VG. B33. $32.00

BRICE, Tony. *Bouncing Bear.* 1945. Rand McNally Jr Elf Book 8054. K2. $8.00

BRICE, Tony. *Child's Garden of Verses.* 1942. Rand McNally Jr Elf Book 628. K2. $7.00

BRICE, Tony. *House That Jack Built.* 1942. Rand McNally Jr Elf Book 360. 64p. K2. $10.00

BRICE, Tony. *See My Toys.* 1947. Rand McNally Jr Elf Books 8092. K2. $8.00

BRICE, Tony. *Timmy Mouse.* 1959. Rand McNally Jr Elf Books 8019. K2. $6.00

BRICK, Edgar M. *Sourcebook of Orthopaedics.* 1937. Baltimore. Williams Wilkins. 376p. G7. $85.00

BRICKHILL, Paul. *Great Escape.* 1950. Norton. 1st Am ed. VG/VG. B4. $175.00

BRICKTOP & HASKINS. *Bricktop.* 1983. Atheneum. 1st ed. NF/NF. B2. $30.00

BRIDGES, Jerry. *Transforming Grace: Living Confidently...* 1991. Nav Pr. 207p. F/dj. B29. $7.00

BRIDGMAN, P.W. *Logic of Modern Physics.* 1928 (1927). Macmillan. 228p. paneled navy cloth. G. G1. $28.00

BRIDGMAN, P.W. *Way Things Are.* 1959. Cambridge. Harvard. 333p. gr brd. VG/dj. G1. $32.00

BRIDGMAN, Raymond L. *Concord Lectures on Philosophy Comprising Outlines...* 1883. Cambridge. Moses King. tall 8vo. 168p. brn cloth. G1. $150.00

BRIER, Howard. *Shortstop Shadow.* 1950. Random. 1st ed. VG+/G+. P8. $25.00

BRIGGS, Argye M. *Both Banks of the River.* 1954. Wm Eerdmans. 1st ed. 333p. F/VG. A8. $20.00

BRIGGS, L. Vernon. *History & Genealogy of the Cabot Family 1475-1927. Vol 1.* 1927. Boston. Goodspeed. thick 8vo. 465p. gilt red cloth. VG. B11. $65.00

BRIGGS, Philip. *Escape From Gravity.* 1955. Lutterworth. 1st ed. VG/VG. P3. $15.00

BRIGGS, Philip. *Silent Planet.* 1957. Lutterworth. 1st ed. VG/torn. P3. $15.00

BRIGGS, Richard. *New Art of Cookery, According to the Present Practice...* 1798. Boston. Spotswood. 2nd ed. 12mo. 444p. VG. M1. $500.00

BRIGGS, Walter. *Without Noise of Arms: 1776 Dominguez-Escalante Search...* 1976. Northland. 1st ed. ils/maps. 212p. F/VG. B19. $65.00

BRIGHAM, Clarence S. *Journals & Journeymen: Contribution to Hist...* 1950. PA U. 1st ed. 114p. F/dj. M10. $10.00

BRIGHAM, Clarence S. *Paul Revere's Engravings.* 1969. NY. Atheneum. revised ed. ils. 262p. red/bl cloth. dj. K1. $60.00

BRIGHAM. *History & Bibliography of American Newspapers 1690-1820.* 1947. Am Antiquarian Soc. 2 vol. 4to. xl. VG. A4. $350.00

BRIGHT, John. *Covenant & Promises: Prophetic Understanding...* 1976. Westminster. 202p. M/M. B29. $6.50

BRIGHT, John. *Diaries of...* 1931. Morrow. 8vo. 591p. G+. V3. $25.00

BRIGHT, John. *Speeches of John Bright, MP on the American Question.* 1865. Boston. Little Brn. 1st ed. 8vo. 278p. gilt gr cloth. VG. K1. $45.00

BRIGHT, R. *Travels From Vienna Through Lower Hungary.* 1813. Edinburgh. thick 4to. tooled leather/rebacked orig spine. C11. $300.00

BRIGHT, Robert. *Friendly Bear.* 1957. Doubleday. 1st ed. VG/dj. M20. $20.00

BRIGHTMAN, Carol. *Drawings & Digressions by Larry Rivers.* 1979. NY. VG/VG. A1. $40.00

BRIGNANO. *Black Americans in Autobiography.* 1984. np. revised ed. 204p. F. A4. $45.00

BRILLAT-SAVARIN, Jean A. *Physiology of Taste...* 1949. NY. Heritage. 471p. decor brd. F/box. B14. $125.00

BRIN, David. *Earth.* 1990. Bantam. 1st trade ed. F/F. M21. $15.00

BRIN, David. *Postman.* 1985. Bantam. 1st ed. F/F. P3. $20.00

BRIN, David. *River of Time.* 1986. Dark Harvest. ltd 1st ed. 1/400. F/dj/case. M2. $100.00

BRIN, David. *Uplift War.* 1987. Phantasia. 1st ed. F/F. M2. $75.00

BRINCKLOE, William D. *Volunteer Fire Company.* (1934). Boston. 1st ed. 144p. red cloth. VG. very scarce. H3. $150.00

BRINE, Mary D. *Grandma's Attic Treasures.* 1893. NY. Dutton. 8vo. ils/8 lithographs. 94p. aeg. F/dj. B24. $275.00

BRINIG, Myron. *Sisters.* 1937. Grosset. VG. B34. $35.00

BRINISTOOL, E.A. *Troopers With Custer.* 1952. Stackpole. revised/expanded ed. ils. F. B34. $65.00

BRINK, Andre. *Act of Terror.* 1991. Summit. 1st ed. F/F. P3. $25.00

BRINK, Andre. *States of Emergency.* 1988. Summit. 1st ed. F/NF. B3. $20.00

BRINK, Carol Ryrie. *Bad Times of Irma Baumlein.* 1972. Macmillan. 1st ed. ils Trina S Hyman. 134p. VG/G. P2. $28.00

BRINK, Carol Ryrie. *Lad With a Whistle.* 1941. Macmillan. 1st ed. 235p. VG/dj. M20. $25.00

BRINK, Carol Ryrie. *Magical Melons. More Stories About Caddie Woodlawn.* 1944. Macmillan. 3rd prt. 8vo. 193p. G/VG. A3. $7.00

BRINKLEY, J. *Elements of Plane Astronomy.* 1845. Dublin. charts. 300p. VG. E5. $65.00

BRINKMANN, David V. *Succulent Euphorbias.* 1975. Oxford. Botley. ils/photos/line drawings. pamphlet. M. B26. $7.50

BRINNIN, John Malcolm. *Beau Voyage. Life Abroad the Last Great Ships.* 1987. Dorset. 4to. 331 photos. 271p. dj. T7. $50.00

BRINNIN, John Malcolm. *Sorrows of Cold Stone.* 1951. Dodd Mead. 1st prt. 109p. VG/chip. M20. $45.00

BRINTON, Howard. *Mystic Will: Based on a Study of Philosophy of Jacob Boehme.* 1930. Macmillan. 1st ed. 12mo. 269p. G. V3. $15.00

BRION, Marcel. *World of Archaeology. Vol 2: Central Asia, Africa...* 1959. Macmillan. 1st ed. 8vo. 340p. NF/dj. W1. $15.00

BRISTED. *America & Her Resources.* 1870 (1818). np. 500p. gilt cloth. VG. E5. $22.00

BRISTOL, George. *Salute Me!* 1943. Dial. 1st ed. 172p. VG/chip. A17. $6.50

BRITE, Poppy Z. *Drawing Blood.* 1993. Delacorte/Abyss. 1st ed. F/F. T2. $20.00

BRITE, Poppy Z. *Drawing Blood.* 1993. Huntington Beach. Cahill. 1st ed. sgn. 1/274 #d. F/sans/cloth case. T2. $65.00

BRITE, Poppy Z. *Lost Souls.* 1992. Delacorte. 1st ed. M/dj. M21. $30.00

BRITTAIN, F.J. *Clock & Watchmakers Handbook, Guide & Dictionary.* 1976. Suffolk, Eng. Baron. 8vo. 388p. F/VG. A8. $30.00

BRITTON & ROSE. *Cactaceae. Descriptions & Ils of Plants of Cactus Family.* 1919-1923. WA, DC. 1st ed. 4to. 137 pl. 1068p. recent gr cloth. NF. B26. $1,695.00

BROAD, C.D. *Examination of McTaggart's Philosophy.* 1933 & 1938. Cambridge. 2 vol in 3. pebbled cloth. rare. G1. $375.00

BROAD, Lewis. *Friendships & Follies of Oscar Wilde.* 1955. Crowell. 1st ed. VG+/VG+. S9. $25.00

BROCK, A. *History of Fireworks.* 1949. London. 1st ed. VG/dj. C11. $95.00

BROCK, D. *Adventurous Crocheter.* 1972. np. VG/wrp. G2. $4.00

BROCK, Darryl. *If I Ever Get Back.* 1990. Crown. 1st ed. F/F. P8. $17.50

BROCK, Emma. *Beppo.* 1936. Whitman Jr Pr Book. 1st ed. 4to. 79p. pict bdg. VG+/G. A3. $25.00

BROCK, Emma. *Drusilla.* 1958 (1937). Macmillan. 8vo. 1290p. cloth. VG/G. A3. $15.00

BROCK, Emma. *Heedless Susan Who Sometimes Forgot To Remember.* 1939. Knopf. 1st ed. ils. 169p. G. P2. $12.50

BROCK, Emma. *Present for Auntie.* 1939. Knopf. 1st ed. sm 8vo. pict cloth. NF/VG+. C8. $45.00

BROCK, Emma. *To Market! To Market!* 1930. Knopf. 1st ed. VG. P2. $35.00

BROCK, John. *Native Plants of Northern Australia.* 1993. Chatsworth, NSW. photos/line drawings. 355p. M/dj. B26. $65.00

BROCK, Lynn. *Silver Sickle Case.* 1938. London. Collins Crime Club. 1st ed. VG/dj. M15. $95.00

BROCK, Lynn. *Slip-Carriage Mystery.* 1928. Harper. 1st ed. VG. P3. $35.00

BROCK, Ray. *Blood, Oil & Sand.* 1952. World. 1st ed. 8vo. 256p. xl. VG. W1. $16.00

BROCK, Robert Alonzo. *General Robert Edward Lee: Soldier, Citizen & Christian...* 1897. Atlanta. Hudgins. salesman's dummy 1st ed. 4to. gray cloth. VG. C6. $150.00

BROCK, Rose; see Hansen, Joseph.

BROCK & JONES. *Measurement & Prediction of Judgment & Choice.* 1968. Holden-Day. 370p. VG/dj. K4. $15.00

BROCKMAN, John. *By the Late John Brockman.* 1969. Macmillan. 1st ed. 166p. F/F. B33. $22.00

BROD, D.C. *Masquerade in Blue.* 1991. NY. Walker. ARC/1st ed. RS. F/F. S6. $22.50

BRODERICK, Therese. *Brand: A Tale of the Flathead Reservation.* 1909. Alice Harriman Co. 1st ed. ils. G. B34. $35.00

BRODIE, Benjamin. *Urinwagarnes Siukdomar...* 1839. Stockholm. Haegestron. 1st Swedish ed. 216p. half calf. G7. $35.00

BRODKEY, Harold. *First Love & Other Sorrows.* 1957. Dial. 1st ed. F/NF/cloth chemise/case. B4. $300.00

BRODKEY, Harold. *Runaway Soul.* 1991. FSG. 1st ed/author's 1st novel. F/F. B3. $20.00

BRODKEY, Harold. *Stories in an Almost Classical Mode.* 1988. Knopf. 1st ed. inscr. w/sgn letter. F/F. B2. $125.00

BRODKEY, Harold. *Women & Angels.* 1985. Phil. 1st ed. inscr. lavender brd/half cloth. F/F/case. A11. $50.00

BRODSKY, Louis Daniel. *Mississippi Vistas.* 1983. Oxford. 1st ed. pres. NF/NF. S9. $45.00

BRODSLEY, David. *LA Freeway: Appreciative Essay.* 1981. CA U. ils/notes/maps/index. 178p. F/dj. B19. $20.00

BRODY, Eugene B. *Psychoanalytic Knowledge.* 1990. Madison, CT. 2446p. russet cloth. VG/dj. G1. $22.50

BRODY, Howard. *Placebos & the Philosophy of Medicine...* 1980. Chicago. sm 8vo. 164p. gr cloth. VG/dj. G1. $25.00

BRODY, Nathan. *Personality.* 1972. London. Academic. 335p. F/dj. K4. $15.00

BROEHL, Wayne G. *Molly Maguires.* 1964. Cambridge. 1st ed. VG/VG. B5. $45.00

BROEHL, Wayne G. Jr. *Trucks...Trouble...& Triumph. The Norwalk Truck Line Co.* 1954. NY. 1st ed. photos. 226p. VG/VG. A17. $15.00

BROEZE, Frank J.A. *Merchant's Perspective: Capt Jacobus Boelen's Narrative..* 1988. Honolulu. HI Hist Soc. 1st Eng ed. 117p. gilt bdg. M/sans. P4. $24.00

BROGAN, James; see Hodder-Williams, C.

BROME, Vincent. *HG Wells: A Biography.* 1951. Longman Gr. 1st ed. NF/NF. S9. $45.00

BROME. *Six Studies in Quarrelling.* 1958. London. 207p. F/NF. A4. $55.00

BROMFIELD, Louis. *Animals & Other People.* 1955. NY. 1st ed. VG/VG. B5. $25.00

BROMFIELD, Louis. *Kenny.* 1935. NY. 1st ed. VG/VG. B5. $35.00

BROMFIELD, Louis. *Mr Smith.* 1951. Harper. 1st ed. VG/VG. P3. $29.00

BROMFIELD, Louis. *Twenty-Four Hours.* 1930. Stokes. ltd ed. sgn. 1/500. stp red cloth/wht spine. F/dj/case. B24. $250.00

BROMFIELD, Louis. *Twenty-Four Hours.* 1930. Stokes. ltd ed. sgn. 1/500. VG/VG/VG box. B5. $150.00

BROMHALL, Winifred. *Chipmunk That Went to Church.* 1952. Knopf. 1st ed. 8vo. VG/G. B17. $8.50

BRONNER, Augusta. *Manual of Individual Mental Tests & Testing.* 1932. Little Brn. 287p. reading copy. K4. $20.00

BRONOWSKI, Jacob. *Reach of Imagination.* 1967. Spring. offprint from The Am Scholar. 12p. F/wrp. B4. $225.00

BRONSON, Wilfrid. *Children of the Sea.* 1940. Harcourt Brace. 1st ed. 4to. 264p. VG. D6. $60.00

BRONTE, Charlotte. *Jane Eyre.* 1991. Courage Classics. F/F. P3. $5.00

BRONTE, Emily. *Wuthering Heights.* 1939. Triangle. 11th prt. MTI. VG/VG. P3. $25.00

BROOKE, Edward W. *Challenge of Change Crisis in Our Two-Party System.* 1966. Little Brn. 1st ed. inscr. 272p. F. B14. $75.00

BROOKE, Jocelyn. *Image of a Drawn Sword.* 1951. Knopf. 1st Am ed. F/NF. N3. $35.00

BROOKE, Keith. *Keepers of the Peace.* 1990. Gollancz. 1st ed. F/F. F4/P3. $20.00

BROOKE, Leslie. *Golden Goose Book.* nd. Warne. 32 pl. VG. P2. $100.00

BROOKE, Peggy. *What Price Freedom.* 1982. Haynes. VG. B34. $5.00

BROOKE, Rupert. *John Webster & the Elizabethan Drama.* 1915. London. Sidgwick Jackson. 1st ed. VG. Q1. $150.00

BROOKES, Owen. *Gatherer.* 1982. HRW. 1st ed. VG/VG. P3. $20.00

BROOKES, Owen. *Inheritance.* 1980. Hutchinson. 1st ed. NF/NF. P3. $25.00

BROOKES, Richard. *General Practice of Physic...4th Edition...* 1763. London. Newbery. 2 vol. contemporary polished calf. G7. $175.00

BROOKESMITH, Peter. *Against All Reason.* 1984. Orbis. 1st ed. VG. P3. $13.00

BROOKNER, Anita. *Family & Friends.* 1985. London. Cape. 1st ed. F/F. B3. $20.00

BROOKNER, Anita. *Family Romance.* 1993. London. Cape. 1st ed. F/F. B3. $20.00

BROOKNER, Anita. *Misalliance.* 1986. London. Cape. 1st ed. F/F. B3. $20.00

BROOKS, Charles S. *Chimney-Pot Papers.* 1919. Yale. 1st ed. ils Fritz Endell. VG/G. S11. $20.00

BROOKS, Cleanth. *On the Prejudices, Predilections & Firm Beliefs Wm Faulkner.* 1987. Baton Rouge. ARC/1st ed. inscr. RS. F/F. A11. $45.00

BROOKS, Cleanth. *William Faulkner: First Encounters.* 1983. New Haven. 1st ed. inscr. F/F. A11. $55.00

BROOKS, E.M. *Hist of Rocky River Baptist Church.* 1928. Albermarle, NC. self pub. 1st ed. 104p. VG/stiff prt wrp. M8. $85.00

BROOKS, Gwendolyn. *Bean Eaters.* 1960. Harper. ARC. 8vo. 71p. silvered red cloth. F/dj. H5. $500.00

BROOKS, H.C. *Compendiosa Bibliografia di Edizioni Bodoniane.* 1993 (1927). Mansfield, CT. rpt. 1/150. 357p. orange cloth. M. K1. $100.00

BROOKS, Lester. *Behind Japan's Surrender.* 1968. McGraw Hill. 1st ed. 428p. F/F. A17. $12.50

BROOKS, Noah. *Abraham Lincoln.* ca 1910. Putnam. Centennial ed. 467p. VG. M10. $10.00

BROOKS, Noah. *Our Baseball Club.* 1884. Dutton. 1st ed. intro Chadwick. team photo. pict bdg. G+/sans. P8. $550.00

BROOKS, R.T. *Ask the Bible.* 1983. Gramercy. 407p. F/F. B29. $10.50

BROOKS, Terry. *Black Unicorn.* nd. BC. VG/VG. P3. $8.00

BROOKS, Terry. *Druid of Shannara.* 1991. Ballantine. 1st ed. sgn. F/F. B3. $35.00

BROOKS, Terry. *Scions of Shannara.* 1990. Ballantine. 1st ed. VG/VG. B3. $10.00

BROOKS, Terry. *Sword of Shannara.* 1991. Ballantine. rpt. inscr. F/F. B3. $30.00

BROOKS, Terry. *Wizard At Large.* 1988. Ballantine. 1st ed. F/NF. B3. $20.00

BROOKS, Walter. *Freddy & the Baseball Team From Mars.* 1955. Knopf. 1st ed. F/VG. P8. $60.00

BROOKS, Walter. *Freddy & the Bean Home News.* 1943. Knopf. 1st ed. ils Kurt Wiese. G+. w/1st issue The Home Bean News. P2. $75.00

BROOKS, Walter. *Freddy Rides Again.* 1951. Knopf. ils. pub lib bdg. VG+. M5. $18.00

BROOKS, Walter. *Freddy the Pied Piper.* 1946. Knopf. 1st ed. 253p. VG. P2. $55.00

BROOKS, William. *Foundations of Zoology.* 1899. NY. 1st ed. 339p. xl. A13. $75.00

BROOKS & LEFLER. *Papers of Walter Clark. 2 Volumes.* 1948 & 1950. Chapel Hill. M11. $50.00

BROOKS & REINER. *2,000 Year-Old Man.* 1981. Warner. 1st ed. F/F. N3. $10.00

BROONZY & BRUYNOGHE. *Big Bill Blues.* 1955. London. Cassell. US issue. F/Grove dj. B2. $65.00

BROTHERS, Elmber D. *Medical Jurisprudence.* 1930. St Louis. 3rd ed. 309p. VG. D3. $35.00

BROTHERSON, Gordon. *Image of the New World.* 1979. London. Thames Hudson. 1st ed. 324p. VG/dj. F3. $25.00

BROUGHAM, Henry Lord. *Historical Sketches of Statesmen...in Time of George III.* 1839-1843. London. Chas Knight. 3 vol. 8vo. ils. marbled ep. teg. leather/cloth. F. F1. $350.00

BROUGHTON, Jack. *Going Downtown: War Against Hanoi & Washington.* 1988. NY. 1st ed. 300p. VG/dj. B18. $15.00

BROUGHTON, NORTHUP & PEARSALL. *Robert Browning: A Bibliography 1830-1950.* 1970. np. new ed. 462p. F. A4. $65.00

BROUN, Heywood. *Sun Field.* 1923. Putnam. 1st ed. G. P8. $75.00

BROUN, Hob. *Odditorium.* 1983. Harper Row. 1st ed. VG/VG. P8. $17.50

BROVEN, John. *South the LA: Music of the Cajun Bayous.* 1983. Gretna. Pelican. 1st ed. F/NF. B2. $35.00

BROWER, Reuben A. *On Trans. Harvard Studies in Comparative Literature #23.* 1966. Oxford. 1st pb ed. 296p. G1. $20.00

BROWER, William Leverich. *Collegiate Reformed Protestant Dutch Church of City of NY...* 1928. NY. 1st ed. 133p. cloth. VG. M8. $37.50

BROWN, Basil. *Law Sports at Gray's Inn...* 1921. NY. private prt. 1st ed. cloth/brd. VG. D3. $45.00

BROWN, Charles. *Artemus Ward: His Book.* 1862. np. 1st ed. 256p. VG. E5. $35.00

BROWN, David. *Bible Wisdom for Modern Living.* 1986. Simon Schuster. 491p. F/dj. B29. $9.50

BROWN, Dee. *Bury My Heart at Wounded Knee.* 1971. np. 8vo. 487p. F/VG. B11. $15.00

BROWN, Dee. *Creek Mary's Blood.* nd. BC. VG/G. P3. $5.00

BROWN, Dee. *Creek Mary's Blood.* 1980. Franklin Society. true 1st ed. full leather. NF. B3. $45.00

BROWN, Dee. *Hear That Lonesome Whistle Blow.* 1977. HRW. 1st ed. 8vo. 311p. VG/VG. B11. $25.00

BROWN, Dee. *Killdeer Mountain.* 1983. HRW. 1st ed. NF/NF. B3. $25.00

BROWN, Dee. *Trail Driving Days.* 1952. NY. 1st ed (A on c p). ES. w/sgn bookplate. NF/VG clip. A11. $55.00

BROWN, Esther. *Nursing for the Future: A Report Prepared for Natural Nursing...* 1948. NY. 198p. A13. $50.00

BROWN, Frances. *Granny's Wonderful Chair.* 1929 (1924). Macmillan. ils Emma Brock. 184p. VG. P2. $18.00

BROWN, Fredric. *Gibbering Night.* 1991. McMillan. 1st ed. F/F. P3. $35.00

BROWN, Fredric. *Happy Ending.* 1990. Dennis McMillan. 1st ed. 1/450. F/dj. M2. $50.00

BROWN, Fredric. *Selling Death Short. Vol 14.* 1988. McMillan. 1st ed. 1/450. sgn. F/F. S6. $50.00

BROWN, Fredric. *Water Walker.* 1990. McMillan. F/F. P3. $35.00

BROWN, Fredric. *What Mad Universe.* nd. BC. VG/VG. P3. $10.00

BROWN, Fredric. *30 Corpses Every Thursday.* 1986. McMillan. 1/375. intro/sgn Wm Campbell Gault. F/F. P3. $45.00

BROWN, George. *Old Times in Oildom.* 1909. PA. VG. A1. $20.00

BROWN, H.C. *Grandmother Brown's Hundred Years, 1827-1927.* 1931. np. ils. 369p. VG. E5. $35.00

BROWN, Harold I. *Observations & Objectivity.* 1987. Oxford. 255p. blk cloth-backed brn brd. VG/dj. G1. $25.00

BROWN, Harry. *Walk in the Sun.* 1944. Knopf. 1st ed. 187p. VG. H1. $6.00

BROWN, Henry. *Narrative of the Anti-Masonick Excitement...* 1829. Batavia, NY. Adams M'Cleary. 1st ed. 12mo. tan brd. disbound. M1. $275.00

BROWN, J. *Estimate of Manners & Principles of the Times.* 1757. London. 1st ed. VG. A15. $175.00

BROWN, J.F. *Psychology & the Social Order.* 1936. McGraw Hill. 1st ed/2nd imp. 462p. G. K4. $10.00

BROWN, J.R. *Unusual Plants: 110 Spectacular Photographs of Succulents.* 1954. Pasadena. photos. 230p. gr cloth. VG. B26. $45.00

BROWN, James Cowie. *Index to Intro Survey of Sources & Literature Scots Law.* 1939. Edinburgh. Stair Soc. sm 4to. 66p. buckram. xl. VG. D3. $25.00

BROWN, Larry. *Big Bad Love.* 1989. Chapel Hill. 1st ed. sgn. F/F. B3. $35.00

BROWN, Larry. *Facing the Music. Stories.* 1988. Chapel Hill. 1st ed/author's 1st book. sgn. F/F. A11. $65.00

BROWN, Larry. *Joe.* 1991. Chapel Hill. Algonquin. 1st ed. F/F. B3. $20.00

BROWN, Lloyd A. *Story of Maps.* 1949. Boston. Little Brn. 1st ed. 397p. gr cloth. VG/worn. P4. $45.00

BROWN, Malcolm. *Letters of TE Lawrence.* 1933. London. Dent. 1st ed. 568p. blk bdg. M. w/sgn bookplate. M7. $30.00

BROWN, Malcolm. *Touch of Genius: Life of TE Lawrence.* 1939. Paragon. 1st ed. 233p. bl cloth. M. w/sgn Brn bookplate. M7. $19.00

BROWN, Malcolm. *Writers & Their Houses.* 1993. London. Hamish Hamilton. 1st ed. 515p. blk bdg. M/dj. M7. $50.00

BROWN, Marcia. *Skipper, John's Cook.* 1956. Scribner. 2nd prt. 4to. unp. VG+/G. A3. $15.00

BROWN, Margaret Wise. *Christmas in the Barn.* 1985. Harper Collins. 1st ed thus. 12mo. unp. VG+/VG. A3. $12.95

BROWN, Margaret Wise. *Christmas in the Barn.* 1985 (1952). Crowell. 12mo. ils Barbara Cooney. F/F. B17. $10.00

BROWN, Margaret Wise. *Country Noisy Book.* 1940. Harper. ils Weisgard. VG+/VG+. C8. $30.00

BROWN, Margaret Wise. *Important Book.* 1949. Harper. late ed. ils Weisgard. F/F. C8. $25.00

BROWN, Margaret Wise. *Little Fur Family.* 1946. Harper Row. 1st ed. ils Garth Williams. rabbit fur bdg. F/NF box. P2. $1,250.00

BROWN, Margaret Wise. *Little Island.* 1946. Doubleday. 1st ed. sm 4to. NF. C8. $75.00

BROWN, Margaret Wise. *Little Lost Lamb.* 1945. Doubleday. 1st ed. sm 4to. VG. C8. $75.00

BROWN, Margaret Wise. *Noisy Book.* 1939. Harper. ils Weisgard. VG. C8. $20.00

BROWN, Margaret Wise. *Sailor Dog.* 1981 (1953). Golden/Western. 2nd prt. sm 4to. NF/VG+. C8. $27.50

BROWN, Margaret Wise. *Sea Shore Noisy Book.* 1941. Harper. ils Weisgard. lg 8vo. VG/G. C8. $25.00

BROWN, Margaret Wise. *Wait Till the Moon Is Full.* 1948. Harper. ils Williams. sm 4to. VG. C8. $25.00

BROWN, Margaret Wise. *Willie's Adventures.* 1954. NY. Wm R Scott. probable 1st ed. lg 12mo. G+. C8. $35.00

BROWN, Margaret Wise. *Wonderful Storybook.* nd. Giant Golden Book 1577-1. B ed. ils JP Miller. K2. $20.00

BROWN, Margaret Wise. *Young Kangaroo.* 1955. NY. Wm R Scott. probable 1st ed. lg 8vo. NF/NF. C8. $50.00

BROWN, Mark H. *Frontier Years.* 1955. np. 125 photos. M/M. B34. $70.00

BROWN, Mark H. *Plainsmen of the Yellowstone, Hist of Yellowstone Basin.* 1969. NE U. F. B34. $15.00

BROWN, Mary. *Unlikely Ones.* 1986. McGraw Hill. 1st ed. F/F. F4. $15.00

BROWN, Norman O. *Love's Body.* 1966. Random. 276p. russet cloth. VG/dj. G1. $22.50

BROWN, Paul. *Daffy Taffy.* 1955. Scribner. 1st ed. ils. 32p. VG/G+. A3. $40.00

BROWN, Paul. *Hi Guy, the Cinderella Horse.* 1944. Scribner. 1st ed. 60p. VG. A3. $20.00

BROWN, Paul. *Hobby Horse Hill* 1939. Doubleday Doran. 1st ed thus. 8vo. 270p. VG/G. A3. $20.00

BROWN, Paul. *Horse: His Gaits, Points & Conformation.* 1943. Scribner. later prt. VG/fair. O3. $35.00

BROWN, Paul. *Polo: A Non-Technical Explanation of the Galloping Game.* 1949. Scribner. brd. VG/G. O3. $65.00

BROWN, Paul. *Pony School.* 1950. Scribner. 1st/A ed. VG. O3. $65.00

BROWN, Paul. *Sparkie & Puff Ball.* 1956. Scribner. 3rd prt. 32p. VG/VG. A3. $27.50

BROWN, Richard Maxwell. *No Duty to Retreat: Violence & Values in Am Hist & Soc.* 1991. Oxford. 1st ed. RS. M/dj. A18. $25.00

BROWN, Rita Mae. *Sudden Death.* 1994. Bantam. 1st ed. sgn. F/F. B3. $30.00

BROWN, Rita Mae. *Venus Envy.* 1983. Bantam. 1st ed. inscr. F/F. B3. $40.00

BROWN, Robert McAfee. *Observer in Rome.* 1964. Doubleday. 271p. VG/torn. B29. $4.00

BROWN, Robert McAfee. *Spirit of Protestanism.* 1963. Oxford. 264p. G/dj. B29. $5.50

BROWN, Robert. *Explanation in Social Science.* 1963. Aldine. 193p. F/dj. K4. $10.00

BROWN, Rosellen. *Before & After.* 1992. FSG. 1st ed. F/F. T2. $16.00

BROWN, Rosellen. *Street Games.* 1974. Doubleday. 1st ed/author's 2nd book. F/NF. B2. $45.00

BROWN, Roy M. *Public Poor Relief in NC.* 1928. Chapel Hill. 1st ed. NF. B2. $40.00

BROWN, Samuel Gilman. *Works of Rufus Choate, With a Memoir of His Life. 2 Volumes.* 1862. Little Brn. cloth. G. M11. $75.00

BROWN, Slater. *Spaceward Bound.* 1955. Prentice Hall. VG. P3. $15.00

BROWN, Thomas. *Lectures on Philosophy of Human Mind.* 1831. Hallowell, MA. Glazier Masters. 2 vols. NF. G1. $100.00

BROWN, Varina Davis. *Colonel at Gettysburg & Spotsylvania.* 1931. Columbia, SC. 1st ed. 8vo. maps. 333p. F/VG. C6. $350.00

BROWN, W.R. *Horse of the Desert.* 1929. Derrydale. 1st ed after deluxe ed. 1/750. NF/fair. H4. $375.00

BROWN, Warren. *Chicago White Sox.* 1952. NY. 1st ed. sgn. VG/G+. B5. $80.00

BROWN, William. *Mind & Personality: Essay in Psychology & Philosophy.* 1926. London. 344p. ES. prt bl cloth. VG. G1. $30.00

BROWN & CASSMORE. *Migratory Cotton Pickers in AZ.* 1939. WA, DC. 1st ed. VG/wrp. B2. $25.00

BROWN & CAVE. *Touch of Genius: Life of TE Lawrence.* 1933. London. Dent. 1st ed. sgns. 233p. NF/NF. M7. $85.00

BROWN & LOVELL. *Exploration of Space by Radio.* 1957. London. Chapman Hall. sm 4to. ils. 207p. xl. VG. K5. $24.00

BROWNE, G. Waldo. *Daughter of Maryland. A Narrative of Pickett's Last Charge.* 1895. NY. Novelist Pub. 1st ed. 12mo. 179p. VG. M1. $225.00

BROWNE, Gerald A. *Green Ice.* 1978. Delacorte. 1st ed. VG/G+. P3. $17.00

BROWNE, Gerald A. *Hazard.* 1973. Arbor. VG/VG. P3. $13.00

BROWNE, Henry J. *Catholic Church & Knights of Labor.* 1949. Catholic U of Am Pr. 1st ed. 416p. VG+/wrp. B2. $45.00

BROWNE, Howard. *Halo for Satan.* 1948. Bobbs Merrill. 1st ed. VG/dj. M15. $85.00

BROWNE, Howard. *Halo in Blood.* 1988. Eng. No Exit. 1st Eng ed. F/F. S6. $35.00

BROWNE, Howard. *Paper Gun.* 1985. McMillan. F/F. P3. $35.00

BROWNE, J. Ross. *Etchings of a Whaling Cruise.* 1846. NY. Harper. 1st ed. ils. rebacked/orig cloth spine. T7. $675.00

BROWNE, J. Ross. *His Letters, Journals & Writings.* 1969. NM U. 1st ed. F. A18. $30.00

BROWNE, John. *Myographia Nove; or, Graphical Description of Muscles...* ca 1970. Medicina Rara. rpt. 1/2500. quarter calf. case. G7. $55.00

BROWNE, LUDOVICI & ROBERTS. *Abortion.* 1935. London. Allen Unwin. 1st ed. VG. V4. $15.00

BROWNE, Thomas. *Religio Medici.* 1644. Leiden. Hackius. 12mo. 235p. contemporary full vellum. G7. $895.00

BROWNE, Thomas. *Selected Writings, Edited by Sir Geoffrey Keynes.* 1968. Chicago. 1st ed. 416p. A13. $35.00

BROWNING, Robert. *Dramatis Personae.* 1910 (1864). London. Dove Pr. 1/250. 204p. vellum. case. K1. $475.00

BROWNING, Robert. *Fifine at the Fair/Red Cotton Night Cap Country/Inn Album.* 1886. Houghton Mifflin. 662p. gilt bdg. G. H1. $8.50

BROWNSON, Orestes Augustus. *Works of...* 1882-1887. Detroit. Thorndike Nouse. 20 vols. pebbled brn cloth. VG. G1. $450.00

BROXON, M.D. *Too Long a Sacrifice.* nd. BC. VG/VG. P3. $8.00

BROXON, M.D. *Too Long a Sacrifice.* 1981. Dell. SF BC. F/F. F4. $7.00

BRUCCOLI, Matthew. *Textos y Dibujos Lacadones de Naja.* 1976. Mexico. INAH. 1st ed. 1/2000. 158p. wrp. F3. $35.00

BRUCE, F.F. *Paul, Apostle of the Heart Set Free.* 1981. Eerdmans. 510p. VG/dj. B29. $9.50

BRUCE, F.F. *Peter, Stephen, James & John.* 1980. Eerdmans. 159p. VG/dj. B29. $5.50

BRUCE, F.F. *Second Thoughts on the Dead Sea Scrolls.* 1966. Eerdmans. pb. 160p. G. B29. $3.00

BRUCE, G.A. *Capture & Occupation of Richmond.* 1918. 1st ed. index. 474p. O8. $18.50

BRUCE, Harold. *Gardens of Winterthur in All Seasons.* 1968. NY. 4to. 148 photos/index. 196p. dj. B26. $19.00

BRUCE, Herbert A. *Varied Operations: Autobiography of Hon Herbert A Bruce.* 1958. Toronto. 366p. VG/worn. G7. $20.00

BRUCE, James. *Travels To Discover the Source of the Nile...1773.* 1805. Edinburgh. Constable. 7 vol+1 vol atlas. 2nd ed. contemporary calf. K1. $1,250.00

BRUCE, Jean. *Deep Freeze.* 1963. Cassell. 1st ed. VG. P3. $12.00

BRUCE, Lenny. *How To Talk Dirty.* 1965. Chicago. 1st ed. VG/VG. B5. $30.00

BRUCE, Leo. *Death in Albert Park.* 1979. Scribner. 1st Am ed. F/NF. S6. $22.50

BRUCE, Robert V. *Launching of Modern American Science 1846-1876.* 1987. Ithaca. Cornell. 446p. M. A10. $18.00

BRUCE, Robert. *National Road: Most Historic Thoroughfare in US.* 1916. Clinton. 1st ed. ils/map. 94p. VG. B5. $75.00

BRUCKMAN, John D. *City Librarians of Los Angeles.* 1973. LA Lib Assn. ils. 56p. F/sans. B19. $25.00

BRUETTE, William A. *Modern Breaking: A Book About Bird Dogs.* 1906 (1904). NY. ils. 169p. G+/wrp. R2. $45.00

BRUNELLO, Bruno. *Il Pensiero Politico Italiano Romagnosi al Croce.* 1949. Bologna. Cesare Zuffi. 258p. prt bl/wht wrp. G1. $30.00

BRUNNER, Constantin. *Science, Spirit, Superstition: New Enquiry Human Thought.* 1968. London/Toronto. Allen Unwin/Toronto U. 585p. VG/dj. G1. $37.50

BRUNNER, Emil. *Christian Doctrine of God.* 1950. Westminster. 1 vol. 361p. VG. B29. $8.00

BRUNNER, John. *Devil's Work.* 1970. Norton. 1st ed. xl. dj. P3. $20.00

BRUNNER, John. *Players at the Game of People.* nd. BC. VG/VG. P3. $8.00

BRUNNER, John. *Times Without Number.* 1974. Elmfield. VG/VG. P3. $20.00

BRUNNOW, F. *Spherical Astronomy.* 1865. London. Asher. trans from 2nd German ed. 559p. xl. K5. $100.00

BRUNO, A. *Codice Penale Per l'Esercito.* 1916. Firenza. Barbera. 16mo. 352p. VG. D3. $25.00

BRUNO, Giordano. *Expulsion of the Triumphant Beast.* 1964. New Brunswick. Rutgers. 324p. lacks half-title p. F. B33. $45.00

BRUNO, Giordano. *Heroic Frenzies.* 1964. Chapel Hill. 274p. VG/stiff paper wrp. B33. $30.00

BRUNSCHVICG, Leon. *L'Experience Humaine et la Causalite Physique.* 1949. Paris. thick 8vo. 601p. prt gr wrp. G1. $45.00

BRUNSCHWIG, Hieronymus. *Buch der Citrurgia.* ca 1970. Medicina Rara. 1/2500. quarter vellum/brd. case. w/orig prospectus. G7. $85.00

BRUNT, David. *Weather Study.* 1944 (1942). London. Nelson. 4th prt. 8vo. 215p. G/dj. K5. $12.00

BRUNVAND, Jan Harold. *Study of American Folklore.* 1968. NY. Norton. 383p. VG/dj. M10. $9.50

BRUSSO, Clifton. *Breakthru.* 1991. Vantage. 1st ed. F/F. F4. $16.00

BRUST, Steven. *Agyar.* 1993. Tor. 1st ed. F/F. P3. $19.00

BRUST, Steven. *Sun, the Moon & the Stars.* 1987. Ace. 1st ed. F/F. P3. $20.00

BRUST & LINDHOLM. *Gypsy.* 1992. Tor. 1st ed. F/F. P3. $19.00

BRUTON, Eric. *Longcase Clock.* 1986. Praeger. 1st/A ed. 146p. F/VG. A8. $22.50

BRYAN, Ashley. *All Night, All Day, a Child's First Book...* 1991. Atheneum. 1st ed. emb brd. M/M. C8. $35.00

BRYAN, Christopher. *Night of the Wolf.* 1983. Harper Row. 1st ed. F/F. F4. $16.00

BRYAN, Daniel. *Mountain Muse: Comprising Adventures of Daniel Boone...* 1813. Harrisonburg. 1st ed. 8vo. 252p. contemporary calf. K1. $200.00

BRYAN, Julien. *Julien Bryan & His Documentary Motion Pictures.* nd. NY. Paul Lovett. 1st ed. 4to. NF/ils wrp. S9. $30.00

BRYAN. *George Washington in American Literature 1775-1865.* 1970. np. 292p. VG. A4. $35.00

BRYANT, Arthur. *Turn of the Tide 1939-1943.* 1957. BOMC. biblio/index. VG/VG. A17. $9.50

BRYANT, Edward. *Among the Dead.* 1973. Macmillan. 1st ed. NF/NF. P3. $25.00

BRYANT, Edward. *Fetish.* 1991. Axotol. 1st ed. sgn. F/F. P3. $35.00

BRYANT, Edwin. *What I Saw in California.* 1985. NE U. 2nd prt. sc. M. A18. $15.00

BRYANT, Marguerite. *Heights.* 1924. Duffield. F. P3. $8.00

BRYANT, Paul. *Bear.* 1974. Boston. sgn pres. VG/VG. B5. $25.00

BRYANT, Sara Cone. *Epaminondas & His Auntie.* 1943 (1939). London. Harrap. 1st Australian ed. sm 8vo. pict brd. VG+. C8. $95.00

BRYANT, Will. *Big Lonesome.* 1971. Doubleday. 1st ed. F/dj. A18. $35.00

BRYANT, Will. *Big Lonesome.* 1971. Doubleday. 1st ed. VG. B34. $25.00

BRYCE, David. *Bhagavad Ghita.* ca 1900. Glasgow. 26x18mm. 11 ils. bl/gray wrp. F. rare. B24. $325.00

BRYCE, David. *Ghita Pancha Ratna.* ca 1900. Glasgow. 25x20mm. Sanskrit text. gilt brn roan. F. B24. $325.00

BRYCE, David. *Kordeh Avesta.* ca 1905. Glasgow. 27x18mm. aeg. gilt red roan/metal locket. F. B24. $350.00

BRYCE, David. *New Testament of Lord & Savior Jesus Christ.* 1895. Glasgow. 18x15mm. gilt bl leather/metal locket. F. B24. $350.00

BRYCE, David. *Old English, Scotch & Irish Songs, With Music.* ca 1900. Glasgow. 26x19mm. 24 orig ils/AS Boyd. 127p. M/prt rose wrp. B24. $200.00

BRYCE, David. *Witty Humorous & Merry Thoughts.* ca 1898. NY. Stokes/Bryce. 27x20mm. 127p. F/gilt roan wrp. B24. $250.00

BRYCE, James. *American Commonwealth.* 1888. London. 3 vol. 1st ed/1st issue. teg. VG. D3. $300.00

BRYSON, Charles Lee. *Woodsy Neighbors of Tan & Teckle.* 1911. Revell. 1st ed. ils. 285p. pict cloth. VG-. A3. $12.50

BUBER, Martin. *I & Thou.* 1958. Scribner. 1st Am ed. 137p. F/F. B14. $35.00

BUBER, Martin. *Men of Dialogue: Martin Buber & Albrecht Goes.* 1969. Funk Wagnall. 1st ed. 288p. VG/VG. B33. $22.00

BUCHAN, John. *Blanket of the Dark.* 1934. Nelson. 6th prt. G+. P3. $20.00

BUCHAN, John. *Castle Gay.* 1930. London. Hodder Stoughton. 1st ed. NF/dj. M15. $185.00

BUCHAN, John. *Gap in the Curtain.* 1993. Hodder Stoughton. 4th prt. VG. P3. $20.00

BUCHAN, John. *Greenmantle.* 1916. Grosset Dunlap. 345p. blk/yel stp red cloth. M7. $25.00

BUCHAN, John. *Greenmantle.* 1916. Hodder Stoughton. 1st ed. G+. P3. $40.00

BUCHAN, John. *House of the Four Winds.* 1935. Hodder Stoughton. 1st ed. VG. P3. $30.00

BUCHAN, John. *Huntingtower.* 1922. Hodder Stoughton. 1st ed. VG. P3. $40.00

BUCHAN, John. *Island of Sheep.* 1936. Hodder Stoughton. 1st ed. VG. P3. $35.00

BUCHAN, John. *Memory Hold the Door.* Nov 1940. Hodder Stoughton. 1st ed/7th prt. 327p. gilt gr cloth. VG. M7. $35.00

BUCHAN, John. *Pilgrim's Way: Autobiography of Lord Tweedsmuir.* 1940. Houghton Mifflin. 1st ed. 344p. yel cloth. VG/G. M7. $30.00

BUCHAN, John. *Prince of Captivity.* 1933. London. Hodder Stoughton. 1st ed. 8vo. 383p. gilt gr cloth. VG+. M7. $65.00

BUCHAN, John. *Sick Heart River.* 1941. Musson. 1st ed. VG. P3. $20.00

BUCHAN, William. *Domestic Medicine; or, The Family Physican.* 1993. NY. 2nd ed/facsimile of 1774 ed. 416p. full leather. A13. $60.00

BUCHAN, William. *Domestic Medicine; or, Treatise on Prevention & Cure...* 1793. Boston. Bumstead Larkin. 1st ed thus. glossary/index. 524p. calf. VG. B14. $200.00

BUCHAN, William. *Rags of Time: Fragment of Autobiography.* 1990. Southampton. Ashford Buchan Enright. 1st ed. inscr. bl cloth. M. M7. $45.00

BUCHANAN, Edna. *Contents Under Pressure.* 1992. Hyperion. 1st ed. NF/dj. M21. $20.00

BUCHANAN, Fannie. *Short Stories of American Music.* 1937. Follett. 8vo. VG. B17. $10.00

BUCHANAN, G. *Packhorse & Waterhole: 1st Overlanders to the Kimberleys.* 1933. np. 1st ed. 200+p. VG. E5. $35.00

BUCHANAN, Marie. *Dark Backward.* 1975. Hart Davis MacGibbon. 1st ed. VG/VG. P3. $20.00

BUCHANAN, Marie. *Morgana.* 1977. Doubleday. 1st ed. VG/VG. P3. $15.00

BUCHANAN, Patrick. *Sounder of Swine.* 1974. Dodd Mead. 1st ed. F/dj. F4. $16.00

BUCHWALD, Art. *I Think I Don't Remember.* 1987. Putnam. 1st prt. 350p. M/F. H1. $9.00

BUCK, Pearl S. *Gift for the Children.* 1973. John Day. 1st ed thus. sm 4to. F/NF. C8. $25.00

BUCK. *Travel & Description, 1765-1865.* 1914. np. ils. 514p. VG. A4. $85.00

BUCKE, Richard Maurice. *Cosmic Consciousness: A Study in Evolution of Human Mind.* 1970. Dutton. 384p. VG/VG. B33. $22.00

BUCKERIDGE, Anthony. *Stories for Boys.* 1957. Faber. 1st ed. VG/VG. P3. $25.00

BUCKINGHAM, Bruce. *Boiled Alive.* 1957. Michael Joseph. 1st ed. VG/VG. P3. $30.00

BUCKINGHAM, Jamie. *Into the Glory.* 1974. Logos. 249p. VG/dj. B29. $5.50

BUCKINGHAM, Nash. *De Shootinest Gent'man.* 1941. NY. 1st trade ed. photo ftspc. 24p. F/clip. A17. $95.00

BUCKINGHAM, Nash. *Tattered Coat.* 1944. Putnam. ltd ed. sgn. ils Fuller. cloth. F. B14. $165.00

BUCKLAND, C.E. *Dictionary of Indian Biography.* 1968. Haskell. rpt of 1906 ed. 494p. NF. P4. $25.00

BUCKLEY, Amelia King. *Keeneland Assn Lib: A Guide to the Collection.* 1958. KY U. John I Day's copy. VG/fair. O3. $45.00

BUCKLEY, Christopher. *Wet Work.* 1991. Knopf. UP. w/promo material. NF/wrp. B3. $25.00

BUCKLEY, Elsie Finnimore. *Children of the Dawn: Old Tales of Greece.* nd (1908). Darton. Wells Gardner. 5th imp. 24 pl. pict cloth. VG+. M5. $30.00

BUCKLEY, Francis. *History of Old English Glass.* (1925). NY. 1st ed. 4to. brn cloth. NF. C6. $65.00

BUCKLEY, J.M. *Travels in Three Continents: Europe, Africa, Asia.* 1895. NY. 8vo. ils. 614p. cloth. uncut. O2. $85.00

BUCKLEY, William F. *Saving the Queen.* 1976. Doubleday. VG/VG. P3. $13.00

BUCKLEY, William F. *Saving the Queen.* 1976. Doubleday. 1st ed. F/F. F4. $16.00

BUCKLEY, William F. *Temptation of Wilfred Malachey.* 1985. NY. Ariel. 1st ed. F/F. B3. $20.00

BUCKLEY, William F. *Who's on First.* 1980. Doubleday. 1st ed. VG/VG. P3. $20.00

BUCKLIN & PERRY. *Uncle Sam's Panama Canal & World History.* 1913. NY. Wanamaker. 8vo. 234p. gilt red brd. F. B11. $50.00

BUCKMAN, G.R. *Colorado Springs, CO & Its Famous Scenic Environs.* 1893. CO Springs. 2nd ed. 85p. B14. $125.00

BUDD, Denison. *Railroad ABC.* 1944. Franklin Watts. ils. pict brd. VG. M5. $25.00

BUDDHAGHOSA. *Path of Purification: Classic TB of Buddhist Psychology.* 1976. Berkeley. Shambhala. 2 vol. pb. VG. B33. $20.00

BUDELER, Werner. *Skylab: Has Himmelslabor.* 1973. Dusseldorf. Econ Verlag. pb. German text. ils/photos. 202p. K5. $10.00

BUDELER, Werner. *To Other Worlds: Telescopes, Rockets, Stars.* 1954. London. Burke. photos. 223p. G/remnant. K5. $25.00

BUDGE, E.A. Wallis. *Amulets & Talisman.* 1961. New Hyde Park. 1st Am ed. 543p. VG/VG. B33. $35.00

BUDGE, E.A. Wallis. *Mummy: A Handbook of Egyptian Funerary Archaeology.* 1925. Cambridge. 2nd ed. 513p. VG/worn. F1. $200.00

BUDGE, E.A. Wallis. *Papyrus of Ani; or, Book of the Dead.* 1913. London. 3 vol. 1st corrected ed. 8vo. teg. gilt bl cloth. VG. H3. $150.00

BUDGE, Frances Anne. *Annals of the Early Friends...* 1896. Phil. Henry Longstreth. 12mo. 456p. VG. V3. $16.00

BUDGE, Jane. *Glimpses of George Fox & His Friends.* 1888. London. Partridge. 1st ed. 12mo. 325p. VG. V3. $16.00

BUDGE & WALLIS. *Nile: Notes for Travelers in Egypt & Sudan.* 1912. London. ils/maps/plans. 1094p. marbled ep. gilt cloth. F. B14. $75.00

BUDINGTON, William Ives. *Hist of First Church, Charlestown, in Nine Lectures...* 1845. Boston. 1st ed. 258p. cloth. G+. M8. $45.00

BUDRYS, Algis. *Rogue Moon.* nd. BC. VG/VG. P3. $8.00

BUEL, J.W. *Great Operas.* 1809. Soc Universelle Lyrique. 5 vol. red cloth. wood case. B30. $175.00

BUEL, J.W. *Jesse & Frank James: Border Bandits.* 1893. Chicago. ils. 290p. VG. E5. $45.00

BUELL, John. *Playground.* 1976. FSG. 1st ed. VG/VG. P3. $20.00

BUELL, John. *Shewsdale Exit.* 1972. FSG. 1st ed. VG/VG. P3. $23.00

BUFORD, Bill. *Among the Thugs: Experience & Seduction of Mob Violence.* 1992. Norton. 1st ed. F/NF. B4. $45.00

BUFWACK & OERMANN. *Finding Her Voice.* 1993. Crown. ARC. F/F. S9. $30.00

BUGBEE, Willis N. *Echoes From the North.* 1946. Syracuse. photos. 168p. F. A17. $12.50

BUHLER & MASSARIK. *Course of Human Life.* 1968. Springer. 403p. F/dj. K4. $25.00

BUINING, A.F.H. *Genus Disoccatus.* nd (1980). Netherlands. ils/6 maps. 223p. sc. F. B26. $19.00

BUJOLD, Lois McMaster. *Spirit Ring.* 1992. Baen. 1st ed. F/F. P3. $17.00

BUKOWSKI, Charles. *Barfly.* 1984. Paget/Sutton West. 1/200. sgn. F/acetate. S9. $150.00

BUKOWSKI, Charles. *Confessions of a Man Insane Enough To Live With Beasts.* 1965. Bensenville. Mimeo. 1st ed (500 total). pub/sgn Blazek. F/wrp. S9. $600.00

BUKOWSKI, Charles. *Erections, Ejaculations, Exhibitions & General Tales...* 1972. San Francisco. 1st ed. inscr. VG+/8vo wrp. w/drawing. A11. $110.00

BUKOWSKI, Charles. *Factotum.* 1975. Blk Sparrow. 1/250. sgn. F/acetate. S9. $275.00

BUKOWSKI, Charles. *Screams From the Balcony.* 1993. Blk Sparrow. 1/300. sgn. w/orig silkscreen prt. F/acetate. S9. $150.00

BULATOY, M. *Nesele Pohadky a Rikadla.* 1959 (1951). Nakladatelstvi. ils J Vodrazky. 139p. VG/VG. P2. $35.00

BULAU, Alwin E. *Footprints of Assurance.* 1953. NY. Macmillan. 1st ed. 1/500. sgn Bulau/Harold V Smith. aeg. F/worn case. F1. $125.00

BULCHEV, Kirill. *Half a Life.* 1977. Macmillan. 1st ed. F/dj. F4. $22.00

BULEY & PICKARD. *Midwest Pioneer: His Ills, Cures & Doctors.* 1945. NY. ltd ed. 339p. A13. $85.00

BULFINCH, S.G. *Poems.* 1834. Charleston. James S Burges. 1st ed. 18mo. cloth. M1. $100.00

BULFINCH, Thomas. *Bulfinch's Mythology.* 1991. Harper Collins. VG. P3. $23.00

BULKELEY & CUMMINS. *Voyage to the South Seas.* 1743. London. Robinson. 8vo. 220p. full calf. T7. $875.00

BULLA, Clyde Robert. *Moon Singer.* 1969. Crowell. 1st ed. ils/inscr Hyman. F/F. C8. $40.00

BULLER, Francis. *Intro to the Law Relative to Trials at Nisi Prius...* 1806. NY. I Riley & Co Law-Booksellers. modern morocco. M11. $250.00

BULLEY, Eleanor. *Life of Edward VII, King of Great Britain & Ireland...* 1901. London. Gardner Darton. Midget Series. 76x65mm. ftspc/15 pl. F/bl box. B24. $185.00

BULLIET, C.J. *Significant Moderns & Their Pictures.* 1936. London. Allen Unwin. 1st ed. 8vo. 199p. NF. F1. $75.00

BULLOCH, James D. *Secret Service of the Confederate States in Europe.* 1884. 2 vol. 1st Am ed from 1883 London ed. ES. cloth. O8. $135.00

BULLOCK, Cynthia. *Washington & Other Poems.* 1847. NY. 108p. gr cloth. VG. M20. $40.00

BULLOCK, George. *Oeconomica Methodica Concordantiarum Scripturae Sacre.* 1572. Antwerp. Plantin. lg folio. 1214p. new ep. vellum. H10. $265.00

BULLOCK, Helen. *Williamsburg Art of Cookery...* 1942. Colonial Williamsburg. facsimile of 1742 ed. 12mo. VG. B11. $50.00

BULMER, Kenneth. *Shark North.* 1979. Severn. VG/VG. P3. $15.00

BULOVA, Joseph. *Joseph Bulova School of Watchmaking.* 1948. Bulova. 3rd ed. TB. 300p. sbdg. VG. A8. $25.00

BULOW, Ernie. *Navajo Taboos.* 1991. Gallup. 1/5 artist proofs. sgn Hillerman/Franklin/Bulow. F/case. B3. $600.00

BULWER & LYTTON. *Devereux.* 1829. NY. 1st Am ed. leather. VG. A9. $60.00

BUMPUS, T. Francis. *Cathedrals & Churches of N Italy.* 1908. Boston. Page. ils. 491p. G. M10. $7.50

BUNDY, J.M. *Life of James Abram Garfield.* 1881. NY. 274p. aeg. gilt cloth. B18. $35.00

BUNN, Thomas. *Closing Costs.* 1990. Henry Holt. 1st ed. F/F. P3. $10.00

BUNNER, H.C. *In Old Cloathes & Other Stories.* 1896. Scribner. 1st ed. 217p. G+. H1. $6.00

BUNTING, Bainbridge. *Early Architecture in NM.* 1976. NM U. 1st ed. ils/index. 122p. F/NF. B19. $40.00

BUNTING, Bainbridge. *John Gaw Meem: SW Architect.* 1983. NM U. 1st ed. ils. 177p. NF. B19. $45.00

BUNTING, Basil. *Loquitur.* 1965. London. Fulcrum. 1st ed. 1/200. Clayton Eshleman's copy. NF/dj/wrp band. B4. $150.00

BUNYAN, John. *Grace Abounding to the Chief of Sinners.* 1948. Zondervan. 117p. G. B29. $5.25

BUNYAN, John. *Pilgrim's Progress.* ca 1850. London. 1st ed thus. aeg. gilt levant morocco. NF. C6. $200.00

BUNYAN, John. *Pilgrim's Progress.* nd. Am Tract Soc. sm full leather. G. B30. $35.00

BUNYAN, John. *Pilgrim's Progress.* 1942. Heritage. ils Wm Blake. leather labels. slipcase. A17. $17.50

BUNYAN, John. *Pilgrim's Progress.* 1949. Standard Pub. Simplified ed. edit DF Foster. ils David Lamb. VG. A3. $4.00

BURBANK, Addison. *Mexican Frieze.* 1940. Coward McCann. 1st ed. 268p. VG/dj. F3. $20.00

BURCE, Leo. *Death in Albert Park.* 1979. Scribner. 1st ed. F/F. P3. $20.00

BURCH, John P. *Charles W Quantrell (sic)...His Guerrilla Warfare...* 1923. Vega, TX. 1st ed. 12mo. 266p. VG+. D3. $45.00

BURCHETT, Wilfred. *My Visit to the Liberated Zones of South Vietnam.* 1966. Hanoi. Foreign Languages Pub. 3rd ed. F/wrp/dj. B2. $45.00

BURCKHALTER, David L. *Seris.* 1976. AZ U. 1st ed. ils. 80p. NF/sans. B19. $45.00

BURCKHARDT, John L. *Travels in Nubia.* 1822. London. Murray. 4to. 3 lg maps. 498p. uncut. F. O2. $900.00

BURD, Clara M. *Child's Garden of Verses.* 1929. Saalfield. 12 ils. VG+/wrp. M5. $35.00

BURDETT, Charles. *Life of Kit Carson.* 1865. ils. 382p. O8. $21.50

BURDETTE, R. *Rise & Fall of Mustache.* 1877. Burlington. 1st ed. G. B5. $25.00

BURDICK, William. *Oration on Nature & Effects of the Art Printing.* 1802. Boston. Munroe Francis. 1st ed. 8vo. 31p. M1. $950.00

BUREN, Faber. *Color Psychology & Color Therapy.* 1950. np. 1st ed. cloth. VG. G2. $25.00

BURGER, Edward J. *Science at the White House: A Political Liability.* 1980. Baltimore. 1st ed. 180p. dj. A13. $25.00

BURGER, Nash K. *Confederate Spy: Rose O'Neale Greenhow.* 1967. 1st ed. 230p. xl. O8. $12.50

BURGESS, Anthony. *Any Old Iron.* 1989. Random. 1st ed. F/F. P3. $20.00

BURGESS, Anthony. *Clockwork Orange.* 1963. Norton. BC. VG/dj. M21. $7.50

BURGESS, Anthony. *Clockwork Testament...* 1975. Knopf. 1st ed. VG/VG. P3. $20.00

BURGESS, Anthony. *Enemy in the Blanket.* 1958. Heinemann. 1st ed. 8vo. 221p. silvered bl cloth. VG/dj. H5. $250.00

BURGESS, Anthony. *Enerby's Dark Lady.* 1984. McGraw Hill. 1st ed. NF/NF. P3. $15.00

BURGESS, Anthony. *Kingdom of the Wicked.* 1985. Arbor. 1st ed. VG/VG. P3. $20.00

BURGESS, Anthony. *Little Wilson & Big God.* 1986. Weidenfeld Nicolson. 1st ed. VG. P3. $25.00

BURGESS, Anthony. *Long Trip to Teatime.* 1976. Dempsey Squires. F/F. P3. $15.00

BURGESS, Anthony. *Pianoplayers.* 1986. Hutchinson. 1st ed. F/F. P3. $18.00

BURGESS, Anthony. *Tremor of Intent.* 1966. NY. 1st Am ed. F/F. A17. $10.00

BURGESS, Anthony. *1985.* 1978. Little Brn. 1st ed. VG/VG. P3. $18.00

BURGESS, Eric. *Frontier to Space.* 1956. Macmillan. 1st Am ed. G/worn. K5. $30.00

BURGESS, Frances Hodgson. *In Connection With the DeWilloughby Claim.* 1899. Scribner. 1st ed. 12mo. VG. B17. $20.00

BURGESS, Gelett. *Goop Tales Alphabetically Told.* 1904. Stokes. possible 1st ed. sm 4to. VG. C8. $75.00

BURGESS, Gelett. *Goops & How To Be Them.* (1900). Lippincott. 31st prt. F/NF. P2. $25.00

BURGESS, Gelett. *Little Father.* 1985. Farrar. 1st ed thus. ils Richard Egielski. F/NF. P2. $25.00

BURGESS, Jeremy. *Intro to Plant Cell Development.* 1985. Cambridge, Eng. sm 4to. ils. 246p. sc. VG. B26. $12.50

BURGESS, Thornton W. *Adventures of Baby Coon.* 1943. McClelland Stewart. VG. P3. $8.00

BURGESS, Thornton W. *Adventures of Danny Meadow Mouse.* 1959. McClelland Stewart. VG/VG. P3. $13.00

BURGESS, Thornton W. *Adventures of Johnny Chuck.* 1941 (1913). Grosset Dunlap. lg 16mo. NF/VG. C8. $25.00

BURGESS, Thornton W. *Adventures of Old Mr Toad.* 1964. Canada. Little Brn. G+. P3. $5.00

BURGESS, Thornton W. *Adventures of Paddy the Beaver.* 1945 (1917). Grosset Dunlap. lg 16mo. NF/NF. C8. $25.00

BURGESS, Thornton W. *Blacky the Crow.* 1922. Grosset Dunlap. ils Harrison Cady. bl linen. NF/dj. M5. $35.00

BURGESS, Thornton W. *Blacky the Crow.* 1922. Little Brn. Gr Forest Series. 1st ed. ils Harrison Cady. NF/VG. D6. $75.00

BURGESS, Thornton W. *Burgess Animal Book for Children.* 1950 (1920). Little Brn. 12mo. ils. pict cloth. VG. C8. $30.00

BURGESS, Thornton W. *Burgess Bird Book for Children.* 1919. Little Brn. 1st ed. gilt bl cloth/pict label. VG. M5. $75.00

BURGESS, Thornton W. *Burgess Book of Nature Lore.* 1965. Bonanza. 1st ed thus. ils Robert Candy. VG+/G+. C8. $35.00

BURGESS, Thornton W. *How Peter Cottontail Got His Name.* 1957. Wonder Book 668. K2. $7.00

BURGESS, Thornton W. *Little Peter Cottontail.* 1956. Wonder Book 641. K2. $7.00

BURGESS, Thornton W. *Littlest Christmas Tree.* 1954. Wonder Book 625. K2. $9.00

BURGESS, Thornton W. *Mother West Wind's Animal Friends.* 1912. Little Brn. 221p. VG/ragged. M20. $38.00

BURGESS, Thornton W. *Mother West Wind's Children.* 1911. Grosset Dunlap. ils George Kerr. bl line. F. M5. $15.00

BURGESS, Thornton W. *Mother West Wind When Stories.* ca 1944. Grosset Dunlap. ils Harrison Cady. VG+/VG+. C8. $15.00

BURGESS, Thornton W. *Mother West Wind Where Stories.* 1943. Grosset Dunlap. VG. P3. $13.00

BURGESS, Thornton W. *Mother West Wind Why Stories.* 1915. Grosset Dunlap. ils Harrison Cady. stp lime gr cloth. F/VG. M5. $40.00

BURGESS, Thornton W. *Old Granny Fox.* 1920. Little Brn. 1st ed. ils Harrison Cady. 202p. NF/G+. D6. $75.00

BURGESS, Thornton W. *Old Mother West Wind.* 1960 (1910). Little Brn. Golden Anniversary ed. F/F. C8. $20.00

BURGHALTER, Joel. *Fanfare on a Tin Whistle.* 1958. np. sgn. VG/wrp. M20. $20.00

BURGHEIM, Fanny Louise. *First Circus.* 1930. Platt Munk. ils. 30p. emb paper brd. A17. $9.50

BURK, Dale A. *New Interpretation.* 1969. np. VG. B34. $20.00

BURKE, Alan Dennis. *Driven to Murder.* 1986. Atlantic Monthly. 1st ed. F/F. P3. $16.00

BURKE, Edmund. *Account of European Settlements in America.* 1977. London. Dodsley. 2 vol. 6th ed. contemporary calf. K1. $175.00

BURKE, Edmund. *Letter From the Rt Honourable Edmund Burke...* 1797. London. 1st ed. 94p. contemporary drab wrp. K1. $150.00

BURKE, Edmund. *Philosophical Inquiry Into Origin of Our Ideas of Sublime...* 1806. Portland. Watts. 2nd Am ed. 12mo. 273p. contemporary calf. M1. $275.00

BURKE, James Lee. *Black Cherry Blues.* 1989. Little Brn. ARC. sgn. NF/wrp. S9. $50.00

BURKE, James Lee. *Black Cherry Blues.* 1989. Little Brn. 1st ed. F/F. B2/B34. $40.00

BURKE, James Lee. *Black Cherry Blues.* 1989. Little Brn. 1st ed. NF/NF. P3. $25.00

BURKE, James Lee. *Black Cherry Blues.* 1990. London. Century. 1st ed. sgn. F/F. B3. $50.00

BURKE, James Lee. *Convict.* 1990. Boston. 2nd ed. pres inscr. F/8vo wrp. A11. $45.00

BURKE, James Lee. *Dixie City Jam.* 1994. Hyperion. 1/1525. sgn/#d. F/case. B2. $125.00

BURKE, James Lee. *Half of Paradise.* 1965. Houghton Mifflin. 1st ed/author's 1st book. 312p. w/sgn bookblate. VG/dj. H5. $750.00

BURKE, James Lee. *Heaven's Prisoners.* 1988. Holt. 1st ed. F/F. L3. $65.00

BURKE, James Lee. *Heaven's Prisoners.* 1988. Holt. 1st ed. NF/NF. P3. $45.00

BURKE, James Lee. *In the Electric Mist With Confederate Dead.* 1993. Hyperion. ltd ed. sgn. 1/150. special bdg. F/case. Q1. $150.00

BURKE, James Lee. *In the Electric Mist With Confederate Dead.* 1993. Hyperion. 1st ed. F/F. P3. $20.00

BURKE, James Lee. *In the Electric Mist With Confederate Dead.* 1993. Hyperion. 1st ed. sgn. F/F. T2. $35.00

BURKE, James Lee. *Morning for Flamingos.* 1990. Little Brn. 1st ed. F/F. B3. $50.00

BURKE, James Lee. *Morning for Flamingos.* 1990. Little Brn. 1st ed. sgn. rem mk. F/F. T2. $25.00

BURKE, James Lee. *Morning for Flamingos.* 1990. Little Brn. 1st ed. VG/VG. P3. $25.00

BURKE, James Lee. *Neon Rain.* 1987. NY. Holt. ARC/1st ed. sgn. RS. F/F. S6. $95.00

BURKE, James Lee. *Stained White Radiance.* 1992. Hyperion. 1st ed. F/F. P3. $20.00

BURKE, James Lee. *Stained White Radiance.* 1992. Hyperion. 1st ed. sgn. F/F. F4/M15. $30.00

BURKE, Richard. *Dead Take No Bows.* 1941. Houghton Mifflin. 1st ed. F/NF. M15. $40.00

BURKETT, Charles William. *Between Two Lives.* 1914. NY. Orange Judd. sgn. cloth. F. A10. $40.00

BURKETT, Larry. *Coming Economic Earthquake.* 1991. Moody. 230p. F/F. B29. $8.00

BURKHART & STUART. *Hollywood's First Choices.* 1994. NY. Crown Trade Pbs. UP/1st ed. 220p. F/tan wrp. M7. $35.00

BURKHOLZ & IRVING. *Death Freak.* 1978. Summit. 1st ed. VG/VG. P3. $15.00

BURKS, Arthur J. *Black Medicine.* 1966. Arkham. 1st ed. NF/NF. P3. $40.00

BURL, Aubrey. *Rites of the Gods.* 1981. London. Dent. 1st ed. ils. 258p. VG/VG. B33. $32.00

BURLAND, C.A. *Magic Books From Mexico.* 1953. London. Penguin. 12mo. VG. F3. $17.50

BURLEIGH, William Henry. *Poems.* 1841. Phil. J Miller M'Kim. 1st ed. 12mo. 248p. full contemporary blk leather. M1. $175.00

BURLEY, W.J. *Charles & Elizabeth.* 1979. London. Gollancz. 1st ed. F/NF. S6. $22.50

BURLEY, W.J. *Charles & Elizabeth.* 1981. Walker. 1st ed. NF/NF. P3. $13.00

BURLINGHAME, Roger. *Of Making Many Books.* 1946. Scribner. 1st ed. pub pres. VG+. P4. $35.00

BURNE, Alfred H. *Lee, Grant & Sherman.* 1939. NY. 1st ed. ils/index/fld map. 216p. O8. $37.50

BURNET, F. *Propositions et Observations sur Diversies Maladies...* 1830. Paris. Didot Le Jeune. 16p. new stiff wrp. G7. $150.00

BURNETT, Frances Hodgson. *In the Closed Room.* 1904. McClure Phillips. 1st ed. ils JW Smith. 129p. VG+. M20. $75.00

BURNETT, Frances Hodgson. *Little Lord Fauntleroy.* 1928 (1913). Scribner. ils Reginald Birch. 246p. VG/dj. M20. $45.00

BURNETT, Frances Hodgson. *Little Lord Fauntleroy.* 1936. NY. b&w movie stills. 236p. VG/rpr. A17. $10.00

BURNETT, Frances Hodgson. *Little Princess.* 1905. Scribner. 1st ed. ils EF Betts. teg. gilt bdg. VG. D6. $85.00

BURNETT, Frances Hodgson. *Louisiana/ Pretty Sister of Jose.* 1914. Scribner. VG. P3. $15.00

BURNETT, Frances Hodgson. *Racketty-Packetty House.* 1975. Lippincott. 1st ed thus. ils Holly Johnson. 60p. VG/G. A3. $20.00

BURNETT, Frances Hodgson. *Racketty-Packetty House, As Told by Queen Crosspatch.* 1914 (1906). Century. inscr/dtd 1915. 130p. bl cloth. VG-. D6. $100.00

BURNETT, Frances Hodgson. *Sarah Crewe; or, What Happened at Miss Minchin's.* 1888. Scribner. 1st ed. 83p. gilt brn cloth. VG. M20. $40.00

BURNETT, Frances Hodgson. *Secret Garden.* 1911. Stokes. 1st ed. ils Kirk. VG+. M5. $175.00

BURNETT, Frances Hodgson. *Secret Garden.* 1949. Lippincott. 1st ed thus. ils Nora S Unwin. 284p. cloth. VG-. A3. $20.00

BURNETT, Frances Hodgson. *Spring Cleaning, As Told by Queen Crosspatch.* 1911 (1908). Century. inscr/dtd 1915. 100p. bl cloth. VG. D6. $100.00

BURNETT, Frances Hodgson. *White People.* 1917. Harper. ils Elizabeth Shippen Green. 112p. VG. M20. $35.00

BURNETT, Virgil. *Towers at the Edge of the World.* 1980. St Martin. 1st ed. F/F. P3. $15.00

BURNETT, Vivian. *Romantick Lady.* 1930 (1927). Scribner. photos. 423p. gr cloth. VG. S11. $20.00

BURNETT, W.R. *Adobe Walls.* 1953. NY. 1st ed. Kingsport Pr file copy/label. F/NF. C2. $100.00

BURNETT, W.R. *Dark Hazard.* 1933. Harper. 1st ed. VG. P3. $25.00

BURNETT, W.R. *Good-Bye, Chicago.* 1981. St Martin. 1st ed. NF/NF. P3. $18.00

BURNETT, W.R. *Iron Man.* 1930. Lincoln MacVeagh Dial. 1st ed. VG. P3. $30.00

BURNETT, W.R. *Roar of the Crowd.* 1964. Potter. 1st ed. VG. P3. $20.00

BURNETT, W.R. *Romelle.* 1946. Knopf. 1st ed. F/NF. M15. $45.00

BURNEY & CAPPS. *Colonial Georgia.* 1972. Thomas Nelson. sq 8vo. 176p. red cloth. VG/VG. B11. $15.00

BURNHAM, S.W. *Measures of Proper Motion Stars...1907 to 1912.* 1913. Carnegie. 4to. 311p. xl. wrp. K5. $80.00

BURNING, Sietze. *Purpaleanie & Other Permutations.* 1978. Orange City. 1st ed. 123p. VG/wrp. A17. $9.50

BURNO, Anthony. *Bad Moon.* 1992. Delacorte. 1st ed. sgn. F/F. M15. $27.50

BURNS, C. Delisle. *Contact Between Minds.* 1923. London. Macmillan. paneled bl cloth/gilt spine. G1. $25.00

BURNS, Emile. *Handbook of Marxism.* 1935. NY. 1088p. G. A17. $10.00

BURNS, Jim. *Youth Builders: Today's Resource...* 1988. Harvest House. 325p. VG/dj. B29. $3.50

BURNS, Olive Anne. *Cold Sassy Tree.* 1984. Ticknor Fields. 1st ed. F/NF. B3. $75.00

BURNS, Olive Anne. *Cold Sassy Tree.* 1984. Ticknor Fields. 1st ed/author's 1st book. 8vo. 391p. F/NF clip. C6. $50.00

BURNS, Rex. *Alvarez Journal.* 1975. Harper Row. 1st ed. VG/VG. P3. $20.00

BURNS, Rex. *Endangered Species.* 1992. Viking. AP. F/wrp. B2. $30.00

BURNS, Rex. *Suicide Season.* 1987. NY. Viking. 1st ed. sgn. F/F. S6. $35.00

BURNS, Tex; see L'Amour, Louis.

BURNS, Walter Noble. *Robin Hood of El Dorado.* 1932. 1st ed. 304p. O8. $21.00

BURNS, Walter Noble. *Tombstone.* 1929. NY. ils Will James. 388p. VG. A17. $15.00

BURNS, Zed. *Confederate Forts.* 1977. ils/index. 107p. dj. O8. $18.50

BUROS, Oscar K. *Educational Psychological & Personality Tests of 1936.* 1937. New Brunswick, NJ. 120p. G. K4. $50.00

BURR, Fearing. *Field & Garden Vegetables of America...* 1863. Boston. Crosby. 1st ed. ils Isaac Sprague. 674p. H10. $95.00

BURR, Frederic M. *Life & Works of Alexander Anderson...* 1893. NY. ils/pl. 210. half morocco. F. B14. $200.00

BURR, Jane. *Fourteen Radio Plays.* 1945. Hollywood. Highland. 1st ed. sgn. NF/VG. B2. $35.00

BURRAGE, Henry S. *Early English & French Voyages.* 1906. Scribner. 450p. T7. $45.00

BURROUGHS, Edgar Rice. *At the Earth's Core.* nd. BC. MTI. VG/VG. P3. $15.00

BURROUGHS, Edgar Rice. *At the Earth's Core.* 1923. Grosset Dunlap. VG. P3. $25.00

BURROUGHS, Edgar Rice. *Back to the Stone Age.* 1937. Tarzana, CA. ERB. 1st ed. 8vo. 7 pl. 381p. orange stp bl cloth. NF/cloth case. H5. $750.00

BURROUGHS, Edgar Rice. *Beasts of Tarzan.* 1917. AL Burt. NF/rpr. M2. $75.00

BURROUGHS, Edgar Rice. *Beasts of Tarzan.* 1917. AL Burt. VG. P3. $35.00

BURROUGHS, Edgar Rice. *Cave Girl.* 1926. Grosset Dunlap. VG. P3. $35.00

BURROUGHS, Edgar Rice. *Deputy Sheriff of Comanche County.* 1940. Tarzana. ERB. 1st ed. ils JC Burroughs. 312p. orange stp gray cloth. NF/NF. H5. $750.00

BURROUGHS, Edgar Rice. *Edgar Rice Burroughs Library of Illustration Vol 1.* 1976. Russ Cochran. 1st ed. F. P3. $200.00

BURROUGHS, Edgar Rice. *Escape on Venus.* 1946. ERB. 1st ed. VG/G. P3. $125.00

BURROUGHS, Edgar Rice. *Escape on Venus.* 1946. Tarzana. ERB. 1st ed. 8vo. 347p. red stp bl cloth. NF/dj/case. H5. $400.00

BURROUGHS, Edgar Rice. *Fighting Man of Mars.* 1933. John Lane/Bodley Head. 2nd ed. VG. P3. $40.00

BURROUGHS, Edgar Rice. *Girl From Hollywood.* 1923. Macaulay. 1st ed. F. P3. $75.00

BURROUGHS, Edgar Rice. *Gods of Mars.* 1935. Methuen. 6th ed. VG/G. P3. $40.00

BURROUGHS, Edgar Rice. *Jungle Girl.* 1933. Odhams. 1st ed. VG/G. P3. $75.00

BURROUGHS, Edgar Rice. *Jungle Tales of Tarzan.* 1919. McClurg. 1st ed. VG/Canon dj. M2. $150.00

BURROUGHS, Edgar Rice. *Lad of the Lion.* 1964. Canaveral. VG/VG. P3. $60.00

BURROUGHS, Edgar Rice. *Land of Terror.* 1944. Tarzana. ERB. 1st ed. 8vo. 317p. orange stp bl cloth. VG/dj. H5. $500.00

BURROUGHS, Edgar Rice. *Land That Time Forgot.* 1962. Canaveral. VG/VG. P3. $60.00

BURROUGHS, Edgar Rice. *Llana of Gathol.* 1948. ERB. NF/NF. P3. $225.00

BURROUGHS, Edgar Rice. *Master Mind of Mars.* 1929. Grosset Dunlap. VG/VG. P3. $120.00

BURROUGHS, Edgar Rice. *Monster Men.* 1962. Canaveral. VG/VG. P3. $50.00

BURROUGHS, Edgar Rice. *Moon Men.* 1962. Canaveral. NF/NF. P3. $50.00

BURROUGHS, Edgar Rice. *Mucker.* 1921. Chicago. McClurg. 1st ed. cloth. VG+/dj. S9. $3,000.00

BURROUGHS, Edgar Rice. *Mucker.* 1963. Canaveral. 1st ed. VG/VG. P3. $75.00

BURROUGHS, Edgar Rice. *Outlaw of Torn.* 1927. Chicago. McClurg. 1st ed. 8vo. 298p. gilt red cloth. NF/dj/case/fld chemise. H5. $3,000.00

BURROUGHS, Edgar Rice. *Pellucidar.* 1962. Canaveral. 1st ed. VG/VG. P3. $50.00

BURROUGHS, Edgar Rice. *Pirates of Venus.* 1934. Tarzana. ERB. 1st ed. 8vo. 314p. orange stp bl cloth. NF/gr cloth case. H5. $600.00

BURROUGHS, Edgar Rice. *Pirates of Venus.* 1940. ERB. VG/VG. P3. $150.00

BURROUGHS, Edgar Rice. *Princess of Mars.* 1965. NY. Pratt Adib. 1/500. ils/sgn Joel Rothberg. F/self wrp. B24. $125.00

BURROUGHS, Edgar Rice. *Return of Tarzan.* 1927. Grosset Dunlap. VG/G+. P3. $75.00

BURROUGHS, Edgar Rice. *Science Fiction Classics.* 1982. Castle. VG/VG. P3. $15.00

BURROUGHS, Edgar Rice. *Son of Tarzan.* 1917. Chicago. McClurg. 1st ed. 8vo. 394p. gilt gr cloth. G. H5. $200.00

BURROUGHS, Edgar Rice. *Son of Tarzan.* 1927. Grosset Dunlap. VG/G. P3. $50.00

BURROUGHS, Edgar Rice. *Swords of Mars.* 1948. ERB. VG. P3. $25.00

BURROUGHS, Edgar Rice. *Synthetic Men of Mars.* 1940. Tarzana. ERB. 1st ed. 8vo. 315p. orange stp bl cloth. VG/dj. H5. $350.00

BURROUGHS, Edgar Rice. *Synthetic Men of Mars.* 1948. ERB. F/Canon dj. M2. $20.00

BURROUGHS, Edgar Rice. *Tales of Three Planets.* 1964. Canaveral. 1st ed. F/F. P3. $75.00

BURROUGHS, Edgar Rice. *Tanar of Pellucidar.* 1962. Canaveral. NF/NF. P3. $50.00

BURROUGHS, Edgar Rice. *Tarzan, Lord of the Jungle.* 1930. Cassell. 2nd ed. VG/fair. P3. $40.00

BURROUGHS, Edgar Rice. *Tarzan & Jewels of Opar.* 1918. Chicago. 1st ed. NF. A15. $100.00

BURROUGHS, Edgar Rice. *Tarzan & the Castaways.* 1965. Canaveral. 1st ed. F/dj. M2. $125.00

BURROUGHS, Edgar Rice. *Tarzan & the City of Gold.* 1933. ERB. 1st ed. 316p. bl cloth. VG. M20. $30.00

BURROUGHS, Edgar Rice. *Tarzan & the Forbidden City.* 1948. ERB. NF/NF. P3. $80.00

BURROUGHS, Edgar Rice. *Tarzan & the Forbidden City.* 1952. Whitman. VG. P3. $8.00

BURROUGHS, Edgar Rice. *Tarzan & the Golden Lion.* 1927. Grosset Dunlap. photoplay ed. VG+. P3. $75.00

BURROUGHS, Edgar Rice. *Tarzan & the Jewels of Opar.* 1919. McClurg. 2nd ed. VG. P3. $90.00

BURROUGHS, Edgar Rice. *Tarzan & the Leopard Men.* 1948. ERB. NF/NF. P3. $75.00

BURROUGHS, Edgar Rice. *Tarzan & the Lion Man.* 1934. ERB. 1st ed. ils J Allen St John. NF/NF. Q1. $450.00

BURROUGHS, Edgar Rice. *Tarzan & the Lost Empire.* 1932. Cassell. 2nd ed. VG. P3. $35.00

BURROUGHS, Edgar Rice. *Tarzan & the Lost Safari.* 1957. Whitman. 1st ed. pict brd. VG. F4. $25.00

BURROUGHS, Edgar Rice. *Tarzan of the Apes.* 1914. AL Burt. 1st ed. VG/2nd issue dj. Q1. $250.00

BURROUGHS, Edgar Rice. *Tarzan of the Apes.* 1914. Chicago. McClurg. 1st ed/1st Tarzan book. 8vo. 401p. Sutcliffe bdg. NF. H5. $1,750.00

BURROUGHS, Edgar Rice. *Tarzan of the Apes.* 1915. AL Burt. VG+. P3. $65.00

BURROUGHS, Edgar Rice. *Tarzan's Quest.* 1936. Tarzana. ERB. 1st ed. 8vo. 318p. orange stp bl cloth. VG/rpt dj. H5. $150.00

BURROUGHS, Edgar Rice. *Tarzan the Magnificent.* 1939. ERB. 1st ed. ils John C Burroughs. NF/VG+. Q1. $300.00

BURROUGHS, Edgar Rice. *Tarzan the Terrible.* 1923. Grosset Dunlap. VG/VG. P3. $100.00

BURROUGHS, Edgar Rice. *Tarzan the Untamed.* 1920. McClelland Stewart. 1st Canadian ed. VG. P3. $125.00

BURROUGHS, Edgar Rice. *War Chief.* 1928. Grosset Dunlap. VG. P3. $40.00

BURROUGHS, Edgar Rice. *War Chief.* 1978. Gregg. 1st ed. VG/VG. P3. $40.00

BURROUGHS, Edgar Rice. *Warlord of Mars.* 1919. McClurg. VG/Canon dj. M2. $250.00

BURROUGHS, Edgar Rice. *Warlord of Mars.* 1919. McClurg. 1st ed. G+. P3. $75.00

BURROUGHS, Edgar Rice. *Warlord of Mars.* 1920. Grosset Dunlap. VG. P3. $35.00

BURROUGHS, John. *John Burroughs Talks.* 1922. Houghton Mifflin. 1st ed. 353p. VG. M20. $18.00

BURROUGHS, John. *My Dog Friends.* 1928. Houghton Mifflin. 1st ed. 104p. VG+. R2. $15.00

BURROUGHS, John. *Squirrels & Other Fur-Bearers.* 1901. Boston. 1st ed. 16 pl. 149p. gilt red cloth. F. H3. $30.00

BURROUGHS, John. *Year in the Fields.* 1896. Houghton Mifflin. 1st ed. photos. 220p. teg. gr cloth. G. S11. $15.00

BURROUGHS, Raymond Darwin. *Natural History of the Lewis & Clark Expedition.* ca 1961. MI State. 8vo. 340p. blk cloth. VG/VG. P4. $125.00

BURROUGHS, William S. *Blade Runner (A Movie).* 1979. Berkeley. Bl Wind. simultaneous wrp issue. NF. L3. $65.00

BURROUGHS, William S. *Cat Inside.* 1992. Viking. ARC. F/wrp. B2. $45.00

BURROUGHS, William S. *Cities of the Red Night.* 1981. London. Calder. 1st ed. F/F. S9. $40.00

BURROUGHS, William S. *Cities of the Red Night.* 1981. NY. 1st ed. VG/VG. B5. $25.00

BURROUGHS, William S. *Exterminator!* 1973. Viking. 1st ed. xl. dj. P3. $20.00

BURROUGHS, William S. *Four Horsemen of the Apocalypse.* 1988. Bonn. Expanded Media. 1st German ed. F/wrp. B4. $45.00

BURROUGHS, William S. *Interzone.* 1989. Viking. ARC. 8vo. 194p. NF/wrp. H5. $50.00

BURROUGHS, William S. *Nova Express.* 1964. Grove. 1st ed. F/NF. B2. $60.00

BURROUGHS, William S. *Nova Express.* 1964. Grove. 1st ed. NF/VG. S9. $50.00

BURROUGHS, William S. *Photos & Remembering Jack Kerouac.* nd (1994). Louisville. Wht Fields. 1st ed. sgn. 1/26 lettered. F/stapled wrp. B4. $125.00

BURROUGHS, William S. *Place of Dead Road.* 1983. NY. HRW. ltd ed. sgn. 1/300. F/case/pub box. A15. $100.00

BURROUGHS, William S. *Place of Dead Roads.* 1984. HRW. 1st ed. royal 8vo. 306p. brn cloth. F/dj. H5. $40.00

BURROUGHS, William S. *Port of Saints.* 1980. Berkeley. Bl Winds. 1st ed. sgn. 1/200. F/clip dj/cloth case. B4. $350.00

BURROUGHS, William S. *Queer.* 1985. NY. 1st ed. sgn. F/F. A11. $60.00

BURROUGHS, William S. *Queer.* 1985. Viking. 1st ed. 134p. NF/NF. M20. $20.00

BURROUGHS, William S. *Retreat Diaries.* 1976. NY. City Moon. 1/2000. sgn. edit James Grauerholz. F/wrp. S9. $75.00

BURROUGHS, William S. *Soft Machine.* 1966. Grove. 1st Am/1st hc ed. F/NF. L3. $100.00

BURROUGHS, William S. *Ticket That Exploded.* 1967. Grove. 1st Am/1st hc ed. F/NF. L3. $125.00

BURROUGHS, William S. *Western Lands.* 1987. Viking. 1st ed. F/F. S9. $50.00

BURROUGHS & GINSBERG. *Yage Letters.* 1963. City Lights. 1st ed. NF/wrp. B2. $50.00

BURROUGHS & MUIR. *Alaska: The Harriman Expedition 1899.* 1901. np. 2 vol. VG. E5. $35.00

BURROWS, Millar. *Dead Sea Scrolls.* 1957. Viking. 11th prt. VG/dj. W1. $10.00

BURROWS, Millar. *More Light on Dead Sea Scrolls.* 1958. Viking. 1st ed. 1 pl. 434p. VG/dj. W1. $15.00

BURRUS, Ernest J. *Mission of Sorrows: Jesuit Guevavi & Pimas 1691-1767.* 1970. AZ U. 1st ed. index/maps. 224p. F/VG. B19. $55.00

BURSTEIN, Chaya. *Joseph & Anna's Time Capsule.* 1984. Simon Schuster/Summit. 1st ed. sm 4to. F/F. C8. $35.00

BURSTEIN & CRIMP. *Many Lives of Elton John.* 1992. Birch Lane. 1st ed. F/F. P3. $20.00

BURT, Cyril. *Young Delinquent.* 1925. Appleton. 603p. reading copy. K4. $15.00

BURTCH, Robert. *Poems of W MT.* 1969. np. 1st ed. photos. VG. B34. $10.00

BURTIS, Thompson. *Daredevils of the Air.* nd. Grosset Dunlap. G+. P3. $7.00

BURTIS, Thompson. *Flying Black Birds.* nd. Grosset Dunlap. VG/rpr. P3. $13.00

BURTON, Alfred. *Adventures of Johnny Newcome in the Navy.* 1904. London. Methuen. new ed. 16 pl. 246p. T7. $95.00

BURTON, Anthony. *Josiah Wedgwood.* 1976. Stein Day. 1st ed. VG/dj. M20. $25.00

BURTON, David H. *Holmes-Sheehan Correspondence: Letters...* 1993. NY. Fordham. M11. $20.00

BURTON, John Hill. *Book-Hunter Etc.* 1862. Edinburgh/London. 392p. VG. scarce. A4. $30.00

BURTON, Katherine. *Make the Way Known: Hist of Dominican Congregation...* 1959. FSC. 1st ed. 291p. H10. $12.00

BURTON, Maria Amparo Ruiz. *Squatter & the Don. A Novel Descriptive...* 1885. San Francisco. 1st ed. 8vo. 421p. cloth. M1. $175.00

BURTON, Miles. *Hardway Diamonds Mystery.* 1930. Mystery League. 1st ed. VG. P3. $20.00

BURTON, Miles. *Secret of High Eldersham.* 1931. Mystery League. 1st ed. VG. P3. $20.00

BURTON, Peter J. *Police Court Pictures at Richmond, VA.* 1892. Richmond. 12mo. 84p. VG/wrp. D3. $35.00

BURTON, Richard F. *Jew, Gypsy & El Islam.* 1898. Chicago/NY. Stone. 1st ed. tall 8vo. 351p. teg. cloth. VG. W1. $250.00

BURTON, Richard F. *Lake Regions of Central Africa.* 1860. Harper. 1st Am ed. fld map. 472p. gilt maroon cloth. VG. P4. $450.00

BURTON, Richard F. *Letters From Battlefields of Paraguay.* 1870. London. Linsley Bros. 1st ed. 419p. teg. rebound. VG. very scarce. F3. $950.00

BURTON, Richard F. *Vikram & the Vampire.* 1893. London. Tylston Edwards. 1/200. edit Isabel Burton. ils Ernest Griset. VG. B33. $150.00

BURTON, Richard. *Arabian Nights.* 1935. Blue Ribbon. rpt. VG. M21. $5.00

BURTON, Richard. *Christmas Story.* 1964. Morrow. 2nd ed. VG/VG. P3. $10.00

BURTON, Robert. *Anatomy of Melancholy...* 1800. London. 2 vol. later bdg. G7. $295.00

BURTON, Virginia Lee. *Life Story.* 1962. Boston. Houghton Mifflin. 1st ed. VG+. C8. $20.00

BURTON, Virginia Lee. *Maybelle the Cable Car.* 1952. Houghton Mifflin. 1st ed. NF. C8. $45.00

BURTON, William. *Porcelain, a Sketch of Its Nature, Art & Manufacture.* 1906. London. Cassell. 8vo. 264p. gilt/blk stp gr cloth. G. F1. $40.00

BURTON & DRAKE. *Unexplored Syria: Visits to Libanus, the Tulul El Safa...* 1872. London. 2 vol. 1st ed. 8vo. new polished brn morocco. O2. $875.00

BURTON & MURDOCH. *Byron: An Exhibition to Commemorate 150th Anniversary...* 1974. London. folio. ils. 149p. w/card. O2. $35.00

BURTON. *Descriptive Bibliography of Civil War Manuscripts in IL.* 1966. np. 408p. F. A4. $45.00

BURWELL, Robert. *They Walked on Wings: Hist of Early Stark Co Aviation.* 1988. np. 1st ed. 4to. 160p. VG/pict wrp. B18. $19.50

BURY, G. Wyman. *Arabia Infelix; or, The Turks in Yamen.* 1915. London. 1st ed. 8vo. 213p. cloth. O2. $125.00

BURY. *Cambridge Medieval History.* 1936-1967. Cambridge. 8 vol in 9. maps. xl. VG. A4. $350.00

BUSBY, F.M. *Cage a Man.* nd. BC. VG/VG. P3. $8.00

BUSBY, F.M. *Long View.* 1974. Berkley Putnam. 1st ed. F/F. P3. $18.00

BUSBY, F.M. *Rissa Kerguelen.* 1976. Berkley Putnam. 1st ed. F/F. F4. $22.00

BUSBY, Roger. *New Face in Hell.* 1976. Collins Crime Club. 1st ed. VG/VG. P3. $20.00

BUSCEMA & LEE. *Silver Surfer.* 1988. Marvel. 1st ed. F/dj. F4. $20.00

BUSCH, Francis X. *In & Out of Court.* 1942. Chicago. 1st ed. ils. 306p. NF/dj. D3. $25.00

BUSCH, Frederick. *I Wanted a Year Without Fall.* 1971. London. Calder Boyars. 1st ed. F/NF. L3. $125.00

BUSCH, Moritz. *Travels Between the Hudson & the MS, 1851-52.* 1971. Lexington, KY. 1st ed. trans Norman H Binger. VG/dj. B18. $15.00

BUSH, Barbara. *Millie's Book.* 1990. Morrow. 1st ed. ils/photos. 141p. cloth. M/dj. R2. $20.00

BUSH, Catherine. *Minus Time.* 1993. Toronto. Harper Collins. 1st ed/author's 1st book. sgn. F/F. A14. $30.00

BUSH, Christopher. *Case of the Green Felt Hat.* 1939. Holt. VG. P3. $35.00

BUSH, Christopher. *Case of the Russian Cross.* 1958. Macmillan. 1st ed. xl. P3. $5.00

BUSH, Christopher. *Case of the Triple Twist.* 1958. Macmillan. 1st ed. VG/G. P3. $20.00

BUSH, Christopher. *Dead Man's Music.* 1937. Heinemann. VG. P3. $20.00

BUSH, Christopher. *Perfect Murder Case.* 1933. Heinemann. 5th prt. VG. P3. $13.00

BUSH, George. *Valley of Vision; or, Dry Bones of Israel Revived.* 1844. NY. Saxon Miles. 1st ed. 8vo. 60p. prt wrp. M1. $175.00

BUSH, Margaret. *Gilbert & Sullivan: Songs for Young People.* 1946. Whittlesey House. 1st prt. ils Karolyi. VG+/VG+. C8. $20.00

BUSH, Martin H. *Duane Hanson.* 1976. Wichita State. ils. 111p. VG/VG. S11. $10.00

BUSHNELL, George Herbert. *From Bricks to Books: A Miscellany.* 1949. London. Grafton. 1st ed. ils. 160p. NF/dj. M10. $7.50

BUSS, Allan R. *Psychology in Social Context.* 1979. NY. Irvington. 390p. F/dj. K4. $15.00

BUT, Paul Pui-Hay. *Hong Kong Bamboos.* 1985. Hong Kong. photos. 85p. sc. M. B26. $17.95

BUTCHER, E.L. *Things Seen in Egypt.* 1913. Dutton. 12mo. 50 pl. G. W1. $14.00

BUTCHER, S.D. *Pioneer History: Custer County, NE.* 1901. Broken Bow. 1st ed. sgn Ben Hardin. G. B5. $195.00

BUTCHER & LOMAX. *Readings in Human Intelligence.* 1972. London. Methuen. 385p. F. K4. $20.00

BUTLER, Cuthbert. *Western Mysticism...* 1924. Dutton. 344p. prt ochre cloth. F/dj. G1. $50.00

BUTLER, Ellis Parker. *Confessions of a Daddy.* 1907. Century. 1st ed. 8vo. NF. D6. $65.00

BUTLER, Ellis Parker. *Great American Pie Company.* 1907. np. 1st ed/2nd imp. 44p. VG. E5. $30.00

BUTLER, Ellis Parker. *Pigs Is Pigs.* 1907. McClure Phillips. 6th imp. 37p. VG. A3. $7.00

BUTLER, Frederick. *Farmer's Manual, Being a Plain Practical Treatise...* 1819. Hartford. Goodrich. 224p. half leather. H10. $250.00

BUTLER, Gerald. *Kiss the Blood Off My Hands.* 1946. Farrar Rinehart. 1st ed. VG/G. P3. $20.00

BUTLER, Gwendoline. *Coffin in Fashion.* 1987. London. Collins. ARC/1st ed. RS. F/F. S6. $25.00

BUTLER, Gwendoline. *Coffin on the Water.* 1986. London. Collins. 1st ed. F/F. S6. $22.50

BUTLER, Gwendoline. *Coffin on the Water.* 1986. St Martin. 1st ed. VG/VG. P3. $20.00

BUTLER, J.D. *Butleriana, Genealogica et Biographica...* 1888. Albany. rebound. xl. A9. $40.00

BUTLER, Jack. *Living in Little Rock With Miss Little Rock.* nd. Knopf. 1st ed. F/F. A14. $25.00

BUTLER, Margaret Manor. *Lakewood Story.* 1949. Stratford House. 1st ed. sgn. 263p. VG. M20. $20.00

BUTLER, Octavia E. *Dawn.* 1987. Warner. 1st ed. VG/G. P3. $13.00

BUTLER, Octavia E. *Imago.* 1989. Warner. 1st ed. F/F. P3. $20.00

BUTLER, Octavia E. *Mind of My Mind.* 1977. Doubleday. 1st ed. F/dj. M2. $50.00

BUTLER, Octavia E. *Mind of My Mind.* 1977. Doubleday. 2nd ed. NF/dj. P3. $18.00

BUTLER, Octavia E. *Survivor.* 1978. Doubleday. 1st ed. xl. dj. P3. $8.00

BUTLER, Octavia E. *Wild Seed.* 1980. Doubleday. 1st ed. F/F. P3. $30.00

BUTLER, Octavia E. *Wild Seed.* 1980. Doubleday. 1st ed. sgn. rem mk. F/F. T2. $25.00

BUTLER, Octavia E. *Xenogenesis.* nd. Guild Am. VG/VG. P3. $10.00

BUTLER, Ragan. *Captain Nash & the Wroth Inheritance.* 1976. St Martin. 1st ed. F/dj. F4. $20.00

BUTLER, Robert Olen. *Alleys of Eden.* 1981. Horizon. 1st ed. sgn. F/NF. L3. $250.00

BUTLER, Robert Olen. *On Distant Ground.* 1985. Knopf. 1st ed. sgn. F/F. B2. $75.00

BUTLER, Robert Olen. *They Whisper.* 1994. Holt. ARC. F/wrp. B2. $35.00

BUTLER & KITZINGER. *1975 Referendum.* 1976. Macmillan. 315p. NF/dj. M10. $2.50

BUTLER & PAPADOPOULOS. *Solar Terrestrial Physics: Present & Future.* 1984. NASA. 4to. ils. 445p. wrp. K5. $25.00

BUTT, Edwin. *Man Seeks the Divine.* 1957. Harper. 561p. G. B29. $4.50

BUTTERFIELD, C.W. *Hist Account of Expedition Against Sandusky...1782.* 1873. Cincinnati. Clarke. 403p. gr cloth. G. M20. $140.00

BUTTERFIELD, L.H. *Letters of Benjamin Rush.* 1951. Princeton. 2 vol. 1st ed. VG/VG. B5. $60.00

BUTTERFIELD & HYDE. *Julian P Boyd: Bibliographical Record.* 1950. np. 1/750. VG. A4. $35.00

BUTTERWORTH, Hezekiah. *In Old New England.* 1895. NY. 1st ed. 281p. emb cloth. F. A17. $12.50

BUTTERWORTH, Michael. *Remains To Be Seen.* 1990. Collins Crime Club. VG/VG. P3. $15.00

BUTTERWORTH, Michael. *Virgin on the Rocks.* 1985. Collins Crime Club. 1st ed. NF/NF. P3. $13.00

BUTTMANN, Gunther. *Shadow of the Telescope.* 1970. Scribner. 8vo. 219p. VG/dj. K5. $18.00

BUTTRICK, George Arthur. *Christ & Man's Dilemma.* 1955. Abingdon Cokesbury. 224p. xl. G. B29. $4.50

BUTZER, Karl W. *Environment & Archaeology.* 1973. Chicago. Aldine-Atherton. 703p. F/dj. K4. $20.00

BUXBAUM, Edwin C. *Collector's Guide to National Geographic Magazine.* 1956. Wilmington. 2nd ed. F. B2. $45.00

BUXTON, David. *Travels in Ethiopia.* 1957. London. Ernest Ben. 2nd ed. 8vo. 176p. VG/dj. W1. $25.00

BUXTORF, Johann. *Lexicon Chaldaicum et Syriacum...* 1622. Basel. Ex Officina Ludovici Regis. 1st ed. 640p. vellum. K1. $450.00

BUZARD, Lynn. *Freedom & Faith.* 1982. Crossway. 168p. F/F. B29. $6.50

BYFIELD, B. *Glass Harmonica.* 1967. NY. 1st ed. VG/VG. B5. $32.50

BYLES, R.S. *Dictionary of Genera & Sub-Genera of Cactacae.* 1957. Nottingham. Sherwood. 34p. VG+/heavy wrp. B26. $15.00

BYNNER, Witter. *Journey With Genius: Recollections & Reflections...* 1953. London. Peter Nevill. 1st ed. photos/index. VG/dj. A18. $30.00

BYNNER, Witter. *New Poems.* 1960. Knopf. 1st ed. sgn. 1/1750 #d. F/NF. V1. $40.00

BYNNER, Witter. *Tiger.* 1913. Mitchell Kennerley. 1st ed/author's 2nd book. 48p. VG. C6. $60.00

BYNUM & PORTER. *Living & Dying in London.* 1991. London. 1st ed. 151p. A13. $35.00

BYRD, Cecil K. *Bibliography of IL Imprints 1814-1858.* 1965. Chicago U. 601p. brn cloth. NF/soiled. P4. $95.00

BYRD, Richard E. *Big Aviation Book for Boys.* 1929. Springfield. lg 8vo. 285p. F/chip. A17. $25.00

BYRD, Richard E. *Little Am.* 1930. NY. Putnam. 3rd imp. 422p. VG. A17. $17.50

BYRD, Richard E. *Skyward.* 1937. NY. Bl Ribbon. later prt. 8vo. 359p. bl cloth. G. P2. $20.00

BYRDALL, John. *Non Compos Mentis; or, The Law Relating to Natural Fools...* 1979. NY. Garland. facsimile reissues of 1700 & 1807 eds. M11. $75.00

BYRNE, Donn. *Hangman's House.* nd. Grosset Dunlap. photoplay ed. VG. P3. $14.00

BYRNE, H.W. *Christian Education for the Local Church.* 1984. Academie. revised ed. 379p. VG/dj. B29. $7.50

BYRNE, Robert. *Tunnel.* 1977. Harcourt. 1st ed. F/dj. M2. $10.00

CABANES, Dr. *Esculape Chez les Artistes.* 1928. Paris. 1st ed. 401p. A13. $75.00

CABANIS, P.J.G. *Rapports du Physique et du Moral de l'Homme.* 1802. Paris. Crapart Caille et Revier. 2 vols. 1st separate prt. G1. $750.00

CABANIS, P.J.G. *Rapports du Physique et du Moral de l'Humme et Lettre...* 1843. Paris. Fortin Masson. 12mo. rebound modern red buckram. G1. $50.00

CABELL, James Branch. *Beyond Life.* nd. Boni Liveright/Mod Lib. VG. P3. $25.00

CABELL, James Branch. *Figures of Earth.* nd. Grosset Dunlap. VG/rpr. P3. $25.00

CABELL, James Branch. *Gallantry.* 1907. NY. 1st ed. ils H Pyle. cloth. NF. C2. $75.00

CABELL, James Branch. *Jurgen.* 1924. McBride. 15th prt. VG. P3. $15.00

CABELL, James Branch. *Jurgen: A Comedy of Justice.* 1919. McBride. 1st ed/1st issue. 368p. NF/dj/morocco case/chemise. H5. $1,000.00

CABELL, James Branch. *Music From Behind the Moon.* 1926. John Day. 1st ed. VG. M2. $75.00

CABELL, James Branch. *Silver Stallion.* 1926. McBride. 1st ed. G+. P3. $30.00

CABELL, James Branch. *Something About Eve.* 1927. NY. 1st ed. sgn. 1/850. NF. C2. $75.00

CABELL, James Branch. *There Were Two Pirates.* 1946. Farrar Straus. 1st ed. VG/G. P3. $30.00

CABELL, James Branch. *There Were Two Pirates.* 1947. London. Bodley Head. VG. P3. $20.00

CABELL, James Branch. *These Restless Heads.* 1932. Literary Guild. 2nd ed. G+. P3. $20.00

CABELL, James Branch. *Way of Ecben.* 1929. McBride. 1st ed. VG+. P3. $35.00

CABELL, Sears Wilson. *Bullodg Longstreet at Gettysburg & Chickamauga.* 1938. Atlanta. Ruralist Pr. 1st ed. 16p. NF/wrp. M8. $37.50

CABLE, George W. *Cavalier.* 1901. Scribner. 1st ed. ils Christy. 311p. VG. H1. $24.00

CABLE, George W. *Creoles of Louisiana.* 1884. Scribner. 1st ed. pict maroon cloth. VG. H4. $85.00

CABLE, George W. *Kincaid's Battery.* 1908. Scribner. 1st ed. ils Kimball. gilt cloth. VG. A17. $10.00

CABOT, W.B. *Labrador.* 1920. Boston. 1st ed. ils. 354p. VG. B5. $40.00

CADBURY, Henry J. *Peril of Modernizing Jesus.* 1937. Macmillan. 1st ed. 12mo. 216p. xl. V3. $10.00

CADE & DAVIS. *Taming of the Thunderbolts.* 1969. London. Abelard Schuman. 8vo. 176p. VG/dj. K5. $22.00

CADNUM, Michael. *Nightlight.* nd. St Martin. 3rd ed. F/F. P3. $15.00

CADY, Jack. *Man Who Could Make Things Vanish.* 1983. Arbor House. 1st ed. VG+/VG. M21. $25.00

CADY, Jack. *Well.* 1980. Arbor. 1st ed. inscr. F/dj. F4. $60.00

CAESALPINO, Dorolle M. *Caesalpin Questions Peripateticinnes.* 1929. Paris. 240p. later cloth. G7. $35.00

CAESAR, Caesar Julius. *C Julii Caesaris Quae Extant ex Emendatione Jos Scaligeri.* 1635. Leyden. Elzeviriana. 2nd prt. sm 12mo. woodcuts/fld maps. 561p. K1. $275.00

CAFFREY, Nancy. *Penny's Worth.* 1952. Dutton. 1st ed. G+. O3. $35.00

CAFFREY, Nancy. *Show Pony.* 1954. Dutton. 1st ed. ils Paul Brown. VG/G. O3. $45.00

CAGNEY, Peter. *Grave for Madam.* 1961. Herbert Jenkins. 1st ed. VG/G. P3. $18.00

CAHN, Edmond. *Moral Decision.* 1956. Bloomington, IN. 315p. F. K4. $8.50

CAHN & KETCHUM. *American Photographers & the National Parks.* 1981. Viking. 1st ed. F/VG+ case. S9. $95.00

CAIDIN, Martin. *Countdown for Tomorrow.* 1958. Dutton. 8vo. 288p. G/dj. K5. $27.00

CAIDIN, Martin. *War for the Moon.* 1959. Dutton. 1st ed. VG. P3. $20.00

CAIGER, Stephen. *Bible & Spade: Intro to Biblical Archaeology.* 1938. Oxford. 218p. G. B29. $4.50

CAILLIET, Emile. *Journey Into Light.* 1968. Zondervan. 117p. VG/dj. B29. $3.50

CAILLOU, Alan. *Journey to Orassia.* 1965. Doubleday. 1st ed. F/dj. F4. $22.00

CAIN, James M. *Baby in the Icebox.* 1981. HRW. 1st ed. F/F. P3. $18.00

CAIN, James M. *Butterfly.* 1947. Knopf. 1st ed. xl. dj. P3. $10.00

CAIN, James M. *Cain X 3.* nd. Knopf. BC. F/NF. M21. $7.50

CAIN, James M. *Cain X 3.* 1969. Knopf. 1st ed. VG. P3. $20.00

CAIN, James M. *Cloud Nine.* 1984. Mysterious. 1st ed. F/F. P3. $18.00

CAIN, James M. *Enchanted Isle.* 1985. Mysterious. 1st ed. VG/VG. P3. $16.00

CAIN, James M. *Galatea.* 1953. Knopf. 1st ed. F/NF. F4. $65.00

CAIN, James M. *Love's Lovely Counterfeit.* 1946. Tower. 3rd ed. VG/G. P3. $16.00

CAIN, James M. *Mignon.* 1962. Dial. 1st ed. NF/NF. B2. $40.00

CAIN, James M. *Mildred Pierce.* 1945. World. MTI. VG. P3. $12.00

CAIN, James M. *Our Government.* 1930. NY. 1st ed/author's 1st book. 12mo. 241p. VG. D3. $75.00

CAIN, James M. *Past All Dishonor.* 1946. Fiction BC. 5th prt. VG. P3. $8.00

CAIN, James M. *Postman Always Rings Twice.* nd. Grosset Dunlap. VG/G. P3. $20.00

CAIN, James M. *Postman Always Rings Twice.* 1946. Knopf. 11th prt. VG. P3. $15.00

CAIN, James M. *Serenade.* 1937. Knopf. 1st ed. VG. P3. $35.00

CAIN, James M. *Three Novels by James M Cain.* 1946. World. 4th ed. VG. P3. $15.00

CAIN, James M. *Two Novels by James M Cain.* 1948. Triangle. brd. VG+. P3. $15.00

CAIN, Paul. *End of the Web.* 1976. London. Gollancz. 1st ed. F/NF. S6. $25.00

CAIN, Paul. *Last Best Friend.* 1967. London. Gollancz. 1st ed. VG/VG. M15. $30.00

CAIN, Paul. *Seven Slayers.* 1988. No Exit. 1st Eng ed. F/F. S6. $35.00

CAIN, Paul. *Sleep No More.* 1966. London. Gollancz. ARC/1st ed. RS. VG/VG. M15. $45.00

CAINE, Hall. *Eternal City.* 1901. Appleton. 1st ed. 638p. VG. H1. $4.50

CAINE, Hall. *Women Thou Gavest Me.* 1913. Lippincott. 1st ed. 584p. G. H1. $8.00

CAIRNS, Alison. *New Year Resolution.* 1984. Collins Crime Club. VG/G+. P3. $15.00

CAIRNS, Bob. *Comeback Kids.* 1989. St Martin. 1st ed. VG+/F. P8. $15.00

CAIRNS, Earle E. *Christianity Through the Centuries.* 1961. Zondervan. 511p. G. B29. $5.00

CALDECOTT, Moyra. *Temple of the Sun.* 1977. Hill Wang. 1st ed. VG/VG. P3. $15.00

CALDECOTT, Randolph. *Caldecott Picture Books.* nd. London. Routledge. 8 one-shilling eds bdg in 1 vol. VG+. C8. $350.00

CALDECOTT, Randolph. *Gleanings From the Graphic.* 1889. London. Routledge. 1st ed. obl 4to. 84p. VG. D6. $100.00

CALDECOTT, Randolph. *Hey Diddle Diddle & Baby Bunting.* nd (1882). Routledge. 1st ed. ils. VG/wrp. M5. $75.00

CALDECOTT, Randolph. *Last Graphic Pictures.* 1888. London. Routledge. obl 4to. 71p. VG. D6. $135.00

CALDER, Angus. *People's War: Britain 1939-1945.* 1969. Pantheon. 1st Am ed. 656p. F/F. A17. $10.00

CALDER, Nigel. *Mind of Man.* 1971. Viking. 285p. F/dj. K4. $10.00

CALDER & CALDWELL. *Le Sacrilege D'Allan Kent.* hors d'commerce copy. 1/20. sgns. NF. A1. $5,000.00

CALDERON, W. Frank. *Animal Painting & Anatomy.* nd. Dover. ils. 336p. VG. M10. $5.00

CALDERON DE LA BARCA, Pedro. *Psalle et Sile.* 1945. Valencia, Spain. Castalia. 8vo. 1/300. 56p. gr polished mottled calf. F. K1. $75.00

CALDERWOOD, David. *Altare Damascenum Seu Ecclesiae Anglicanae Politia...* 1708. Leyden. Cornelium Boutesteyn. 4to. 782p. contemporary calf. K1. $225.00

CALDWELL, Elsie Noble. *Alaska Trail Dogs.* 1945. NY. 1st ed. 150p. photos/map. VG. A17. $17.50

CALDWELL, Erskine. *All Night Long.* 1942. DSP. 1st ed. 8vo. 283p. silvered bl cloth. VG/dj. H5. $50.00

CALDWELL, Erskine. *Bastard.* 1929. NY. Heron. 1/200. sgn. 199p. gilt pk cloth. NF. H5. $600.00

CALDWELL, Erskine. *God's Little Acre.* 1933. Viking. 1st ed. VG/poor. H4. $750.00

CALDWELL, Erskine. *In Search of Bisco.* 1965. Farrar. 1st ed. F/NF. B2. $30.00

CALDWELL, Erskine. *Jackpot: Short Stories of...* 1940. DSP. 1st ed. F/NF. B4. $125.00

CALDWELL, Erskine. *Molly Cottontail.* 1958. Boston. Little Brn. 1st ed. ils Wm Sharp. NF/NF. Q1. $175.00

CALDWELL, Erskine. *Sacrilege of Alan Kent.* 1936. Portland, ME. Falmouth. revised ed. sgn. 1/300. wht cloth/red brd. NF/case. H5. $225.00

CALDWELL, Erskine. *Say, Is This the USA?* 1941. DSP. 1st ed. ils Margaret Bourke-White. VG. F1. $65.00

CALDWELL, Erskine. *Sure Hand of God.* 1947. NY. 1st ed. VG/rpr. A17. $15.00

CALDWELL, Erskine. *Tenant Farmer.* 1935. NY. Phalanx. 1st ed. F/prt gr wrp. B24. $225.00

CALDWELL, Erskine. *Tobacco Road.* 1932. Scribner. 1st ed. inscr pres. 8vo. 241p. gilt orange cloth. VG. H5. $750.00

CALDWELL, Erskine. *Trouble in July.* 1950. NY. 1st ed. inscr. NF/NF. A11. $100.00

CALDWELL, Erskine. *We Are the Living.* 1933. Viking. 1st ed. VG/VG. S9. $60.00

CALDWELL, Erskine. *We Are the Living.* 1933. Viking. 1st trade ed. F/NF. Q1. $150.00

CALDWELL, Erskine. *When You Think of Me.* 1959. Little Brn. 1st ed. 8vo. 194p. bl cloth. F/dj. B2/H5. $35.00

CALDWELL, J.A. *Hist of Belmont & Jefferson Counties, OH...* 1880. np. 600p. VG. E5. $125.00

CALDWELL, Steven. *Aliens in Space.* 1979. Crescent. F/F. P3. $8.00

CALDWELL, Steven. *Fantastic Planet.* 1980. Crescent. F. P3. $5.00

CALDWELL, Steven. *Star Quest.* 1979. Crescent. F/F. P3. $8.00

CALDWELL, Taylor. *Balance Wheel.* 1951. Scribner. 1st ed. VG/VG. P3. $20.00

CALDWELL, Taylor. *Dear & Glorious Physician.* 1959. NY. 1st ed. VG/VG. B5. $22.50

CALDWELL, Taylor. *Grandmother & the Priests.* 1963. Doubleday. 1st ed. NF/NF. B4. $45.00

CALDWELL, Taylor. *Late Clara Beame.* 1963. Crime Club. 1st ed. VG/G. P3. $13.00

CALDWELL, Taylor. *Listener.* 1960. Doubleday. 1st ed. 8vo. gilt blk cloth. NF/dj. H5. $50.00

CALDWELL, Taylor. *On Growing Up Tough.* 1971. Greenwich. 1st ed. VG/VG. B5. $40.00

CALDWELL, Taylor. *There Was a Time.* 1947. Scribner. 1st ed. VG/VG. P3. $25.00

CALHOON, Jay W. *O'Boy.* 1945. np. 1st ed. tall 8vo. photo brd. VG. R2. $45.00

CALHOUN, Charles M. *Liberty Dethroned.* 1903. np. 1st ed. sm 4to. 379p. gilt bl cloth. NF. C6. $700.00

CALHOUN, William Lowndes. *Hist of 42nd Regiment, GA Volunteers.* 1900. Atlanta. Sisson. 1st ed. 8vo. 45p. VG/wrp/clamshell box/fld. scarce. C6. $475.00

CALISHER, Hortense. *On Keeping Women.* 1977. Arbor House. ARC. inscr. RS. w/photo & promo material. F/F. B4. $100.00

CALKINS, Frank. *Rocky Mountain Warden.* 1970. Knopf. 1st ed. F/dj. B34. $25.00

CALKINS, Robert G. *Monuments of Medieval Art.* 1979. Dutton. 1st ed. ils. 299p. VG/dj. M10. $12.50

CALL, Hughie. *Golden Fleece.* 1961 (1942). Crown. sgn. VG/torn. B34. $35.00

CALL, Hughie. *Shorn Lamb.* 1969. Houghton. 4th prt. VG/dj. B34. $25.00

CALLAGHAN, Morley. *More Joy in Heaven.* 1937. Random. 1st ed. F/NF. B2. $100.00

CALLAGHAN, Morley. *They Shall Inherit the Earth.* 1935. Random. 1st ed. F/VG. B2. $65.00

CALLAHAN, Harry. *Color. 1941-1980.* 1980. Providence. Matrix Publications. 1st ed. folio. cloth. F/case. S9. $200.00

CALLAWAY, Dorothy J. *World of Magnolias.* 1994. Portland. ils/photos. M/dj. B26. $44.95

CALLOWAY & ROLLINS. *Of Minnie the Moocher & Me.* 1976. NY. Crowell. 1st ed. sgn. 8vo. F/dj. B2/C8. $100.00

CALMIA, Estilo. *Orfebreia Prehispanica De Colombia.* 1954. Madrid. 2 vol. VG/VG/case. A1. $275.00

CALVERT, Albert F. *Spain: Hist Descriptive Account of Its Architecture...* 1924. London. Batsford. 2 vol. 2nd ed. teg. VG. W1. $125.00

CALVEZ, Jean-Yves. *Pensee de Karl Marx.* 1956. Paris. Editions Du Seuil. 662p. tan/brn wrp. G1. $30.00

CALVIN, Jack. *Sitka.* 1936. Arrowhead. 1st ed. photos. 40p. G/wrp. A17. $25.00

CALVIN, Ross. *Sky Determines: Interpretation of the SW.* 1965. NM U. revised ed. 391p. NF/VG. B19. $50.00

CALVINO, Italo. *Baron in the Trees.* 1959. Random. 1st ed. F/VG. L3. $150.00

CALVINO, Italo. *Under the Jaguar Sun.* 1988. HBJ. 1st ed. F/F. P3. $16.00

CAM, Helen M. *Year Books of Edward II. The Eyre of London... Vol 1.* 1968. London. sm 4to. Eng/Latin texts. buckram. F/dj. D3. $25.00

CAMDEN, John. *Hundredth Acre.* 1905. Turner. 1st ed. G+. P3. $20.00

CAMERON, Barbara. *Mississippi River: A Photographic Journey.* 1987. St Martin. 108 photos. 127p. dj. T7. $35.00

CAMERON, Berl. *Black Infinity.* 1952. Curtis Warren. xl. dj. P3. $20.00

CAMERON, Donald Clough. *Dig Another Grave.* 1946. Mystery House. G+. P3. $10.00

CAMERON, Donald Clough. *White for a Shroud.* nd. Boardman. VG/VG. P3. $15.00

CAMERON, John. *Researches in Craniometry.* 1928-1931. Halifax. 2 vol. pres. cloth. xl. G7. $175.00

CAMERON, Julia Margaret. *Cameron Collection.* 1975. Van Nostrand. lg 4to. NF/NF. S9. $125.00

CAMERON, Kenneth Walter. *Genesis of Christ Church, Stratford, CT...* 1972. Hartford. 1st ed. pl. 64p. cloth. VG. M8. $27.50

CAMERON, Norman. *Psychology of Behavior Disorders.* 1947. Houghton Mifflin. 598p. G. K4. $10.00

CAMERON, Owen. *Butcher's Wife.* 1954. Simon Schuster. 1st ed. VG/G+. P3. $20.00

CAMERON, Roderick. *Viceroyalities of the West.* 1968. Little Brn. 1st Am ed. 276p. VG/dj. F3. $20.00

CAMEROU, Lou. *Amphorae Pirates.* 1970. Random. 1st ed. author Joe Gores' copy. F/F. F4. $25.00

CAMMANN, Nora. *Needlepoint Designs From American Indian Art.* 1973. np. cloth. VG. G2. $18.00

CAMP, George Sidney. *Democracy.* 1859. Harper. later ed. 16mo. 249p. VG. D3. $35.00

CAMP, John. *Fool's Run.* 1989. Holt. 1st ed. NF/NF. P3. $20.00

CAMPAN, Madame. *Memoirs of Marie Antoinette.* nd. Collier. NF. P3. $15.00

CAMPBELL, Alice. *Desire To Kill.* 1934. NY. Farrar Rinehart. 1st Am ed. VG/clip. M15. $25.00

CAMPBELL, Alice. *Murder in Paris.* nd. Farrar Rinehart. VG. P3. $13.00

CAMPBELL, Bebe Moore. *Brothers & Sisters.* 1994. Putnam. 1st ed. sgn. F/F. B3. $45.00

CAMPBELL, Bebe Moore. *Sweet Summer.* 1989. Putnam. 1st ed. 8vo. F/F. S9. $50.00

CAMPBELL, Bruce F. *Ancient Wisdom Revived: A History of Theosophical Movement.* 1980. Berkeley. 249p. F/F. B33. $30.00

CAMPBELL, Bruce F. *Clue of the Marked Claw.* nd. Grosset Dunlap. VG/VG. P3. $10.00

CAMPBELL, Bruce F. *Mystery of the Plumed Serpent.* 1962. Grosset Dunlap. 1st ed. 176p. tan tweed cloth. VG/VG. M20. $100.00

CAMPBELL, George F. *Soldier of the Sky.* 1918. Chicago. 1st ed. 232p. bl cloth. G+. B18. $125.00

CAMPBELL, H.J. *Correlative Psychology of Nervous System.* 1969. Academic. 290p. F/dj. K4. $15.00

CAMPBELL, Harriet Sefton. *Pyx-BA: Just a Dog's Life.* 1928. San Diego: Frye Smith. 1st ed. sgn. cloth. F. R2. $25.00

CAMPBELL, John A. *Recollections of Evacuation of Richmond.* 1880. Baltimore. Murphy. 1st ed. 8vo. 27p. Vg/bl wrp. C6. $150.00

CAMPBELL, John Lord. *Lives of the Lord Chancellors & Keepers of Great Seal...* 1845-1847. London. 7 vol. 1st ed. gilt half calf. M11. $1,250.00

CAMPBELL, John W. *Black Star Passes.* 1953. Fantasy. 1st ed. F/dj. M2. $90.00

CAMPBELL, John W. *Cloak of Aesir.* 1952. Shasta. 1st ed. F/frayed. M2. $60.00

CAMPBELL, John W. *Mightiest Machine.* 1947. Hadley. 1st ed. F/chip. M2. $100.00

CAMPBELL, John. *Life of Africaner, a Namacqua Chief, of S Africa.* 1825. Phil. Am Sunday School Union. 1st ed. 18mo. VG/prt wrp. M1. $250.00

CAMPBELL, Julie. *Trixie Belden & the Red Trailer Mystery.* 1950. Whitman. lg 12mo. F/F. C8. $12.50

CAMPBELL, Julie. *Trixie Belden & the Secret of the Mansion.* 1948. Whitman. lg 12mo. NF/NF. C8. $12.50

CAMPBELL, Mary Mason. *Betty Crocker's Kitchen Gardens.* 1971. Scribner. ils Tasha Tudor. 170p. pict cloth. VG. A3. $50.00

CAMPBELL, Mary Mason. *New Eng Buttry Shelf Almanac.* 1970. World. 1st prt. ils Tasha Tudor. F/F. C8. $75.00

CAMPBELL, Ramsey. *Demons by Daylight.* 1973. Arkham. 1st ed. 1/3472. F/NF. T2. $35.00

CAMPBELL, Ramsey. *Height of the Scream.* 1976. Arkham. 1st ed. 1/4348. F/F. T2. $12.00

CAMPBELL, Ramsey. *Hip-Deep in Alligators.* 1987. NY. NAL. 1st ed. sgn. F/F. S6. $35.00

CAMPBELL, Ramsey. *Hungry Moon.* 1987. London. Century. 1st ed. inscr. F/F T2. $35.00

CAMPBELL, Ramsey. *Influence.* 1988. Macmillan. ARC/1st ed. RS. F/F. S6. $30.00

CAMPBELL, Ramsey. *Influence.* 1988. Macmillan. 1st ed. F/dj. F4. $18.00

CAMPBELL, Ramsey. *Night of the Claw.* 1983. St Martin. 1st ed. sgn. F/NF. F4. $30.00

CAMPBELL, Ramsey. *Parasite.* 1980. Macmillan. 1st ed. sgn. F/dj. F4. $30.00

CAMPBELL, Reau. *Campbell's New Revised Complete Guide & Descriptive Book...* 1899. Chicago. 351p. VG. F3. $30.00

CAMPBELL, Robert. *Gift Horse's Mouth.* 1990. Pocket. 1st ed. hc. sgn. F. O4. $15.00

CAMPBELL, Robert. *In La-La Land We Trust.* 1986. Mysterious. AP. F/wrp/proof dj. B2. $35.00

CAMPBELL, Robert. *Sweet La-La Land.* 1990. Poseidon. 1st ed. F/VG. O4. $15.00

CAMPBELL, Robert. *Thinning the Turkey Herd.* 1988. NAL. UP. sgn. NF. O4. $25.00

CAMPBELL, William. *Behavior Problems in Dogs.* 1975. Am Veterinary Pub. 1st ed. ils. 306p. cloth. F. R2. $20.00

CAMPE, Joachim Heinrich. *Polar Scenes, Exhibited in Voyages of Heemskirk & Barenz...* 1823. London. Harris. 12mo. 138p. red calf/prt brd. VG+. K1. $150.00

CAMPER & KIRKLEY. *Hist Record of 1st Regiment of MD Infantry.* 1871. WA, DC. Gibson. 1st ed. 312p. cloth. NF. M8. $350.00

CAMPOLO, Anthony. *How To Be Pentecostal Without Speaking in Tongues.* 1991. Word. 176p. VG/dj. B29. $6.50

CAMPOLO, Anthony. *Reasonable Faith: Responding to Secularism.* 1983. Word. 199p. VG/dj. B29. $5.50

CAMPOLO, Anthony. *Who Switched Price Tags? Search for Values...* 1986. Word. 200p. F/F. B29. $6.50

CAMUS, Albert. *La Chute.* 1956. Gallimard. 1st ed. inscr. NF/wrp/glassine dj. B4. $850.00

CAMUS, Albert. *Rebel.* 1954. Knopf. 1st Am ed. F/NF. B2. $150.00

CANDLER, Allen D. *Confederate Records of State of GA.* 1909-1911. Atlanta. Chas P Byrd. complete set. cloth. VG. M8. $1,250.00

CANFIELD, Dorothy. *Seasoned Timber.* 1939. Harcourt Brace. 485p. VG. H1. $8.00

CANIFF, Milton. *Terry & the Pirates.* 1984. Flying Buttress Classics. 12 vol. VG/VG. M17. $90.00

CANIN, Ethan. *Blue River.* 1991. Boston. 1st ed/author's 2nd book. inscr. F/F. A15. $30.00

CANIN, Ethan. *Blue River.* 1991. Houghton Mifflin. ARC/author's 2nd book. F/pict wrp. B3. $40.00

CANNAN. *Hamish.* nd. London. 4to. ils Anne Bullen. G+/wrp. R2. $10.00

CANNON, Curt; see Hunter, Evan.

CANNON, P.H. *Scream for Jeeves: A Parody.* 1994. Wodecraft. 1st ed. sgn. 1/250. ils/sgn JC Eckhardt. F/F. T2. $30.00

CANNON, William. *Amateur Printer.* 1871. NY. ils. 62p. VG. B14. $200.00

CANTINE, Marguerite. *Beggar T Bear.* 1981. Cantine Kilpatrick. photos. 62p. F/wrp. H1. $17.50

CANTOR, Louis. *Wheelin' on Beale.* 1992. Pharos. 1st ed. F/F. B2. $35.00

CANTWELL, Robert. *Land of Plenty.* 1943. NY. Farrar. 1st ed. inscr. VG. B2. $75.00

CANTWELL, Robert. *Laugh & Lie Down.* 1931. Farrar Rinehart. 1st ed. VG+. A18. $40.00

CANTWELL, Robert. *Nathaniel Hawthorn: The American Years.* 1948. Rinehart. 1st ed. photos/notes. F/chip. A18. $40.00

CAPA, Robert. *Robert Capa.* 1969. NY. Paragraphic. 1st ed. NF/wrp. S9. $35.00

CAPART & WEBROUCK. *Thebes.* 1926. London. Allen Unwin. sm folio. ils. 362p. cloth. NF. H4. $80.00

CAPEK, Karel. *Gardener's Year.* 1984 (1931). Madison. ils Josef Capek. 160p. brd/cloth spine. F. B26. $11.00

CAPGRAVE, John. *Chronicles of England.* 1858. London. 1st ed. lg 8vo. brn morocco. VG. C6. $125.00

CAPLAN, Arthur L. *Sociobiology Debate.* 1978. Harper Row. 486p. F/dj. K4. $10.00

CAPLAN, Ruth. *Psychiatry & the Community in 19th-Century America.* 1969. NY. 360p. A13. $30.00

CAPON, Brian. *Botany for Gardeners.* 1990. Portland. 121 phtos. 220p. sc. M. B26. $17.95

CAPOTE, Truman. *Breakfast at Tiffany's.* 1958. Random. 1st ed. NF/NF. Q1. $175.00

CAPOTE, Truman. *I Remember Grandpa.* 1987. Atlanta, GA. Peechtree. 1st ed. ils Moser. F/NF. E3. $45.00

CAPOTE, Truman. *In Cold Blood.* 1965. London. Hamish Hamilton. 1st ed. VG/as issued. C4. $45.00

CAPOTE, Truman. *Muses Are Heard.* 1956. Random. 1st ed. 8vo. 182p. stp blk cloth. F/NF. H5. $150.00

CAPOTE, Truman. *Music for Chameleons.* 1980. Random. ltd ed. 1/350. sgn. F/case. S9. $300.00

CAPOTE, Truman. *One Christmas.* 1983. Random. 1st ed. 1/500 #d/sgn. M/case. C4. $295.00

CAPOTE, Truman. *Thanksgiving Visitor.* 1967. Random. 1st ed. sgn. F/case. H4. $200.00

CAPP, Al. *Li'l Abner.* 1988-1991. Kitchen Sink. 12 vol. pb. VG. M17. $50.00

CAPPS, Benjamin. *Warren Wagon Train Raid.* 1974. NY. 1st ed. sgn. NF/F. A11. $60.00

CAPPS, S.R. *Geology of the Alaska Railroad Region.* 1940. GPO. photos/maps. F/prt wrp. P4. $60.00

CAPSTICK, Peter Hathaway. *Death in the Long Grass.* 1977. NY. inscr. 297p. VG/dj. B18. $22.50

CARABELLESE, Pantaleo. *Il Problema Della Filosofia da Kant Fichte.* 1939. Padua. Editore Trimarchi. prt gr wrp. G1. $40.00

CARD, Orson Scott. *Cardography.* 1987. Hypatia. 1st ed. sgn. 1/750. intro/sgn DG Hartwell. F/F/case. T2. $75.00

CARD, Orson Scott. *Memory of Earth.* 1992. Tor. 1st ed. F/dj. F4. $15.00

CARD, Orson Scott. *Prentice Alvin.* 1989. Tor. 1st ed. F/NF. N3. $15.00

CARD, Orson Scott. *Seventh Son.* 1987. Tor. 1st ed. F/F. N3. $30.00

CARD, Orson Scott. *Songmaster.* 1980. Dial. 1st ed. VG/dj. M21. $60.00

CARD, Orson Scott. *Wyrms.* 1987. Arbor. 1st ed. F/F. N3. $30.00

CARDAN, Jerome. *Book of My Life.* 1930. NY. 1st ed. 331p. A13. $40.00

CARDEW, Mirrie. *Basenji for Me.* 1986 (1979). Great Britain. ils. sgn. 48p. glossy brd. M. R2. $15.00

CARDOZO, Benjamin N. *Growth of the Law.* 1924. Yale. 2nd prt. 145p. D3. $25.00

CAREW, Thomas. *Rapture.* 1927. Golden Cockerel. 1/375. 14p. VG/dj. M20. $110.00

CAREY, A. Merwyn. *American Firearms Makers.* 1953. Crowell. 1st ed. pls. 145p. VG/dj. M20. $35.00

CAREY, Charles H. *Oregon Constitution & Proceedings & Debates...* 1926. Salem, OR. 1st ed. 543p. NF. w/sgn letter. D3. $75.00

CAREY, Henry. *Dramatick Works of...* 1743. London. only collected ed. lacks frontis. VG+. A15. $300.00

CARGILL, Morris. *Jamaica.* 1965. NY. 1st ed. 240p. VG/dj. B18. $27.50

CARKEET, David. *Greatest Slump of All Time.* 1984. Harper Row. 1st ed. F/F. P8. $20.00

CARL & PETIT. *Mountains in the Desert.* 1954. Doubleday. 1st ed. 318p. VG/worn. W1. $9.00

CARLE, Eric. *Rooster Who Set Out To See the World.* 1972. Franklin Watts. ils Eric Carle. F/VG. C8. $27.50

CARLE, Eric. *Very Quiet Cricket.* 1990. Philomel. 1st prt. lg 8vo. glazed pict brd. NF. C8. $22.50

CARLETON, Henry Guy. *Thompson Street Poker Club.* 1888. Paris. Brentano. 1st ed thus. 48p. VG. C6. $125.00

CARLIN, Jerome. *Lawyers on Their Own, a Study of Individual Practioners...* 1962. New Brunswick. Rutgers. M11. $45.00

CARLING, John R. *Weird Picture.* 1905. Little Brn. 1st ed. pict bdg. VG. F4. $50.00

CARLISLE, Bill. *Bill Carlisle, Lone Bandit.* 1946. Pasadena, CA. 1st ed. inscr. 220p. fair. B18. $37.50

CARLSON, P.M. *Bad Blood.* 1991. Doubleday. 1st ed. sgn. F/F. M15. $25.00

CARLYLE, Lilian. *Carriages at Shelburne Museum.* 1956. Shelburne. 8vo. 71p. VG/wrp. O3. $40.00

CARLYLE, Thomas. *Choice of Books.* ca 1920. NY. Crowell. 12mo. 43p. G. M10. $3.50

CARMAN & THOMPSON. *Guide to Principal Sources for Am Civilization 1800-1900.* 1962. Columbia. 676p. F/NF. A4. $65.00

CARMER, Carl. *Rebellion at Quaker Hill: Story of First Rent War.* 1954. Phil. Winston. 1st ed. 8vo. 174p. VG/torn. V3. $12.50

CARMICHAEL, Harry; see Creasey, John.

CARMONY, Neil B. *Afield With J Frank Dobie.* 1993. High-Lonesome. 265p. M. B19. $20.00

CARNAC, Nicholas. *Tournament of Shadows.* 1978. Scribner. 1st ed. F/F. F4. $16.00

CARNAP, Rudolf. *Psychologie in Physikalischer Sprache.* 1932. Leipzig. Felix Meiner. 1st separate prt. inscr. prt gr wrp. rare. G1. $125.00

CARNATION. *Fun To Cook Book.* 1955. Carnation. ils. sbdg pict brd. VG. M5. $15.00

CARNEGIE, Andrew. *Triumphant Democracy; or, Fifty Year's March of Republic.* 1888. NY. 1st ed. 516p. G. B18. $37.50

CAROTHERS, J.C. *Mind of Man in Africa.* 1972. London. Stacey. 182p. F/dj. K4. $10.00

CARPENTER, Coy. *Story of Medicine at Wake Forest University.* 1970. Chapel Hill. 1st ed. 79p. dj. A13. $20.00

CARPENTER, Don. *Hard Rain Falling.* 1966. NY. 1st ed/author's 1st novel. sgn. F/F. A11. $50.00

CARPENTER, Edward. *Drama of Love & Death.* 1912. Mitchell Kennerley. VG. N2. $15.00

CARPENTER, Edward. *Love's Coming of Age.* 1928. Vanguard. 4th ed. G+. N2. $14.00

CARPENTER, Edward. *My Days & Dreams: Being Autobiographical Notes.* 1921. Allen Unwin. 3rd ed. 344p. VG. B33. $22.00

CARPENTER, Edwin H. *Printers & Publishers in Southern California 1850-1876.* 1964. La Siesta. 1st ed. ils/index. 48p. F. B19. $50.00

CARPENTER, F.A. *Climate & Weather of San Diego.* 1913. San Diego. Chamber of Commerce. 118p. brd. B14. $75.00

CARPENTER, Frances. *Tales of a Russian Grandmother.* 1939. NY. Doubleday. ils I Bilibine. 282p. bl cloth. VG. B14. $75.00

CARPENTER, Frank C. *Baptists of Cooperstown.* 1959. Cooperstown, NY. 1st ed. 42p. NF/prt wrp. M8. $37.50

CARPENTER, Frank G. *Cairo to Kisumu: Egypt, the Sudan, Kenya Colony.* 1925. Doubleday Page. 313p. teg. G. W1. $12.00

CARPENTER, Frank G. *From Tangier to Tripoli.* 1923. Doubleday Page. 1st ed. 8vo. 277p. G. W1. $12.00

CARPENTER, Frank G. *Java & the East Indies.* 1923. NY. 1st ed. ils. 280p. pict bl cloth. VG. H3. $35.00

CARPENTER, George Rice. *John Greenleaf Whittier.* 1906. Houghton Mifflin. 12mo. 311p. VG. V4. $12.00

CARPENTER, Humphrey. *Tolkien, Authorized Biography.* 1977. Houghton Mifflin. 1st ed. 287p. F/VG. S11. $10.00

CARPENTER, J. Estlin. *Life in Palestine. When Jesus Lived.* 1915. London. Sunday School. 3rd ed. 184p. VG. W1. $9.00

CARPENTER, W. Boyd. *Spirtual Message of Dante.* 1914. London. Williams Norgate. 250p. gilt bdg. VG. B33. $24.00

CARPENTER. *Encyclopedia of the Far West.* 1991. np. 544p. F/F. A4. $40.00

CARPENTER. *History of American School Books.* 1963. PA U. 322p. F/VG. A4. $125.00

CARR, Caleb. *Devil Soldier.* 1992. Random. 1st ed/author's 3rd book. F/F. B3. $75.00

CARR, Cecil T. *Pension Book of Clement's Inn.* 1960. London. Bernard Quaritch. M11. $45.00

CARR, Charles. *Salamander War.* 1955. Ward Lock. F/F. P3. $20.00

CARR, Glynn. *Youth Hostel Murders.* 1953. Dutton. 1st ed. VG. P3. $20.00

CARR, J. Comyns. *Coasting Bohemia.* 1914. London. Macmillan. 1st ed. 281p. 8vo. VG. W1. $15.00

CARR, J. Scott. *Devil in Robes; or, Sin of Priests.* ca 1910. Aurora, MO. 472p. VG. H1. $15.00

CARR, Jayge. *Leviathan's Deep.* 1979. Doubleday. F/F. P3. $15.00

CARR, Jayge. *Rabelaisian Reprise.* 1988. Doubleday. ARC of 1st ed. RS. F/dj. F4. $20.00

CARR, John Dickson. *Below Suspicion.* 1949. Harper. 1st ed. VG/G. P3. $28.00

CARR, John Dickson. *Blind Barber.* 1974. London. Hamilton. 1st fingerprint ed. F/F. S6. $20.00

CARR, John Dickson. *Bride of Newgate.* 1950. Harper. 1st ed. VG/G. P3. $25.00

CARR, John Dickson. *Captain Cut-Throat.* 1955. Harper. 1st ed. F/F. P3. $80.00

CARR, John Dickson. *Deadly Hall.* 1971. Harper Row. 1st ed. F/NF. B2. $40.00

CARR, John Dickson. *Deadly Hall.* 1971. Harper Row. 1st ed. VG/VG. P3. $25.00

CARR, John Dickson. *Devil in Velvet.* 1951. Harper. VG/VG. P3. $20.00

CARR, John Dickson. *Door to Doom & Other Detections.* 1981. London. Hamilton. 1st Eng ed. F/F. S6. $35.00

CARR, John Dickson. *Emperor's Snuff Box.* 1942. Harper. 1st ed. G+. P3. $20.00

CARR, John Dickson. *Life of Sir Arthur Conan Doyle.* 1949. Harper. VG. P3. $35.00

CARR, John Dickson. *Most Secret.* 1964. Hamish Hamilton. 1st ed. F/F. P3. $45.00

CARR, John Dickson. *Most Secret.* 1964. Harper Row. 1st ed. VG/VG. P3. $35.00

CARR, John Dickson. *Papa La-Bas.* 1968. Harper Row. 1st ed. VG/VG. P3. $35.00

CARR, John Dickson. *Scandal at High Chimneys.* 1959. Hamish Hamilton. 1st ed. NF/NF. P3. $35.00

CARR, John Dickson. *Skeleton in the Clock.* 1948. Morrow. 1st ed. 282p. VG. H1. $18.00

CARR, John Dickson. *Sleeping Sphinx.* 1947. Harper. 1st ed. NF/NF. B2. $35.00

CARR, John Dickson. *To Wake the Dead.* 1937. Hamish Hamilton. 1st ed. VG. P3. $50.00

CARR, John Dickson. *Witch of the Low-Tide.* 1961. London. Hamish Hamilton. 1st Eng ed. F/NF. M15. $45.00

CARR, Robert Spencer. *Beyond Infinity.* 1951. Fantasy. ltd ed. sgn. 1/350. F/dj. M2. $85.00

CARR, Robert Spencer. *Beyond Infinity.* 1951. Fantasy. 1st ed. VG/VG. C8/P3. $35.00

CARR, Terry. *Best SF of the Year #6.* 1977. HRW. 1st ed. F/F. N3. $15.00

CARR, Terry. *Universe 13.* 1983. Doubleday. 1st ed. F/F. P3. $25.00

CARR, Terry. *Universe 14.* 1984. Doubleday. 1st ed. F/F. N3. $25.00

CARR, Terry. *Year's Finest Fantasy Vol 2.* 1979. Berkley Putnam. 1st ed. F/F. P3. $20.00

CARRAWAY, Gertrude Sprague. *Crown of Life Hist of Christ Church, New Bern, NC 1750-1940.* 1940. New Bern, NC. Owen Dunn. 1st ed. 245p. VG/prt wrp. M8. $37.50

CARREL & DEHILLY. *Treatment of Infected Wounds.* 1917. Hoeber. 238p. xl. fair. G7. $25.00

CARRINGTON, Grant. *Time's Fool.* 1981. Doubleday. 1st ed. F/F. P3. $13.00

CARRINGTON, Richard. *East From Tunis. Record of Travels on N Coast of Africa.* ca 1956. London. Travel Book Club. 1st ed. 8vo. VG/torn. W1. $9.00

CARROLL, Jim. *Poem, Interview, Photographs.* 1994. Louisville. Whitefields Pr. 1st ed. sgn. 1/100. F/wrp. B4. $45.00

CARROLL, Jim. *4 Ups & 1 Down.* 1970. Angel Hair Books. 1st ed/author's 1st book. 1/300. NF/stapled wrp. L3. $175.00

CARROLL, Jock. *Shy Photographer.* 1964. Stein Day. AP. sbdg. VG. S9. $45.00

CARROLL, John A. *Pioneering in Arizona.* 1964. AZ Pioneer Hist Soc. ils. 178p. F. B19. $40.00

CARROLL, John A. *Reflections of Western Historians.* 1969. AZ U. 1st ed. F/dj. A18. $20.00

CARROLL, John B. *Study of Language.* 1968. Harvard. 7th prt. 289p. M/dj. K4. $12.50

CARROLL, Jonathan. *After Silence.* 1992. MacDonald. 1st ed. F/F. P3. $30.00

CARROLL, Jonathan. *From the Teeth of Angels.* 1994. Harper Collins. 1st ed. M/dj. M21. $25.00

CARROLL, Jonathan. *Outside the Dog Museum.* 1991. MacDonald. 1st ed. F/F. P3. $30.00

CARROLL, Jonathan. *Voice of Our Shadow.* 1983. Viking. 1st ed. xl. VG+/dj. M21. $15.00

CARROLL, Lewis. *Alice in Wonderland.* 1934. Rand McNally. ils. VG. P3. $20.00

CARROLL, Lewis. *Alice in Wonderland/Through the Looking-Glass...* 1916. Rand McNally. lg 8vo. ils Milo Winter. 242p. F. B24. $100.00

CARROLL, Lewis. *Alice's Adventure in Wonderland.* nd. McKay. Newberry Classics. ils Tenniel. ftspc/bdg AL Bowley. beige cloth. VG. M5. $15.00

CARROLL, Lewis. *Alice's Adventure in Wonderland/Through the Looking-Glass.* nd. Burt. Home Lib. ils John Tenniel. gilt burgundy cloth. VG. M5. $12.00

CARROLL, Lewis. *Alice's Adventure in Wonderland/Through the Looking-Glass.* nd. Grosset Dunlap. photoplay ed. 16 pl. bl cloth. VG. M5. $45.00

CARROLL, Lewis. *Alice's Adventures in Wonderland.* 1897. Altemus. G+. P3. $12.00

CARROLL, Lewis. *Alice's Adventures in Wonderland.* 1969. Naecenas/Random. ltd ed. 1/2500 portfolios. ils/sgn Dali. M. H4. $1,000.00

CARROLL, Lewis. *Alice's Adventures in Wonderland.* 1982. Pennyroyal. ils Barry Moser. VG/VG. B30. $30.00

CARROLL, Lewis. *Alice's Adventures in Wonderland.* 1985. Chancellor. F/F. P3. $15.00

CARROLL, Lewis. *Alice's Adventures in Wonderland/Through the Looking-Glass.* 1932 & 1935. LEC. 2 vol. 1/1500. both sgn by Alice Hargreaves. F/case. A9. $1,000.00

CARROLL, Lewis. *Collected Verse.* 1933. Macmillan. 441p. VG. M20. $25.00

CARROLL, Lewis. *For the Train: Five Poems & a Tale.* 1932. London. 2nd ed. VG. M17. $22.50

CARROLL, Lewis. *Further Nonsense & Prose.* 1926. Appleton. VG. M17. $30.00

CARROLL, Lewis. *Rectory Umbrella & Misch Masch.* 1932. London. VG. M17. $25.00

CARROLL, Lewis. *Sylvie & Bruno.* 1890. Macmillan. 1st Am ed. gilt red cloth. M20. $50.00

CARROLL, Lewis. *Through the Looking-Glass.* nd. ca 1900? DeWolfe Fiske. ils Tenniel. pict cloth. G. M5. $22.00

CARROLL, Lewis. *Through the Looking-Glass.* 1972. London. stated 15th thousand. VG-. M17. $100.00

CARROLL, Lewis. *Through the Looking-Glass/What Alice Found There.* 1902. London/NY. Harper. 40 full-p pl/Peter Newell. deluxe crimson cloth. F/dj. B24. $175.00

CARROLL, Lewis. *Walt Disney's Alice in Wonderland.* 1951. Simon Schuster. Big Golden Book. 1st ed thus. slick pict brd. VG. M5. $45.00

CARROLL, Raymond. *Anwar Sadat.* 1982. Franklin Watts. 1st ed. 118p. NF/dj. W1. $15.00

CARRUTH, Hayden. *Norfolk Poems.* 1962. New Directions. 1st ed. sgn. F/F. V1. $100.00

CARRYL, Guy Wetmore. *Garden of Years.* 1904. Putnam. 1st ed. 129p. VG/G. S11. $75.00

CARSON, Blanche Mabury. *From Cairo to the Cataract.* 1909. Boston. Page. 1st ed. 8vo. 49 pl. teg. VG. W1. $15.00

CARSON, Hampton L. *Hist of Celebration of 100th Anniversary of Promulgation...* 1889. Lippincott. 2 vol. thick 4to. gilt bl cloth. VG. K1. $125.00

CARSON, Hampton L. *Supreme Court of the US: Its Hist...* 1892. Phil. 4to. 53 etched pl/tissue guards. 745p. VG. D3. $75.00

CARSON, Jane. *Bacon's Rebellion 1676-1976.* 1976. Jamestown, VA. 8vo. 91p. VG/wrp. B11. $20.00

CARSON, Jane. *Colonial Virginias at Play.* 1965. Colonial Williamsburg. 1st ed/author's personal copy. 8vo. 326p. G/wrp. B11. $25.00

CARSON, Rachel. *Silent Spring.* 1962. Houghton Mifflin. ARC. RS. F/VG. B4. $225.00

CARSON, Robert. *Waterfront Writers: Literature of Work...* 1979. Harper Row. 1st ed. VG/dj. N2. $7.50

CARTER, Angela. *Artificial Fire.* 1988. Toronto. McClelland Stewart. 1st Canadian ed. F/F. N3. $20.00

CARTER, Angela. *Fireworks.* 1981. Harper Row. 1st ed. NF/NF. P3. $30.00

CARTER, Angela. *Night at the Circus.* 1984. Hogarth. VG/VG. P3. $35.00

CARTER, Charles Franklin. *Some By-Ways of California.* 1911. Whitaker/Ray-Wiggin. 2nd ed. 199p. VG+. B19. $45.00

CARTER, Craig J.M. *Ships Annual, 1958.* 1959. London. Allen. ils. 96p. dj. T7. $30.00

CARTER, Forrest. *Vengeance Trial of Josey Wales.* 1976. Delacorte. 1st ed. F/NF. B4. $375.00

CARTER, Howard. *Tomb of Tutankhamen.* 1972. Excalibur. 4to. ils/pl. 238p. NF/dj. W1. $20.00

CARTER, Jimmy. *Outdoor Journal.* 1988. NY. 1st ed. sgn. M/dj. A9. $50.00

CARTER, John. *ABC For Book Collectors.* 1981. Knopf. 211p. VG/dj. A10. $12.00

CARTER, John. *ABC for Book Collectors.* 1995. NY. 7th ed. 224p. M/dj. B18. $25.00

CARTER, John. *Books & Book Collectors.* 1957. np. 1st Am ed. VG. A4. $35.00

CARTER, Lin. *Dreams From R'lyeh.* 1975. Arkham. 1st ed. 1/3152. F/F. T2. $35.00

CARTER, Lin. *Invisible Death.* 1975. Doubleday. 1st ed. F/F. P3. $15.00

CARTER, Lin. *Man Who Loved Mars.* 1973. Wht Lion. VG/G. P3. $17.00

CARTER, Lin. *Realms of Wizardry.* 1976. Doubleday. 1st ed. NF/NF. P3. $25.00

CARTER, Lin. *Volcano Ogre.* 1976. Doubleday. 1st ed. F/VG+. N3. $10.00

CARTER, Nick (a few); see Avallone, Mike.

CARTER, Ross. *Those Devils in Baggy Pants.* 1951. Appleton. VG/VG. B5. $40.00

CARTER, Samuel. *Riddle of Dr Mudd.* 1974. Putnam. ils. 388p. F/dj. M10. $16.50

CARTER, Sara. *Handbook of Brazilian Stitches.* 1978. np. VG/wrp. G2. $10.00

CARTER, Susan. *New Succulent Spiny Euphorbias From East Africa.* 1982. Kew. 118p. VG/wrp. B26. $10.00

CARTER, Susannah. *Frugal Housewife; or, Complete Woman Cook...* 1802. Phil. Carey. 3rd Am ed. 12mo. 2 pl. 132p. VG. M1. $500.00

CARTER, William. *Horses of the World.* 1923. NGS. paintings Edward Miner. brn cloth. VG. O3. $40.00

CARTER & KEITH. *Donkey Prince.* 1970. Simon Schuster. 1st Am ed. F/NF. B2. $100.00

CARTER & MUIR. *Printing & the Mind of Man...* 1967. London. 1st ed. 280p. NF. B14. $150.00

CARTIER, E. *Known & the Unknown.* 1977. De La Ree. NF/NF. P3. $35.00

CARTIER-BRESSON, Henri. *Beautiful Jaipur.* 1948. Bombay. Information Bureau. 1st ed. 4to. NF/NF. S9. $250.00

CARTIER-BRESSON, Henri. *Man & Machines.* 1971. NY. Viking. 1st ed. obl folio. NF/G. S9. $60.00

CARTIER-BRESSON, Henri. *Photographs of Henri Cartier-Bresson.* 1947. NY. MOMA. 1st ed. 4to. F/F. S9. $95.00

CARTLAND, F. *Southern Heroes; or, Friends in War Time.* 1895. np. 1st ed. 500p. VG. E5. $85.00

CARTWRIGHT, Peter. *Autobiography of Peter Cartwright: Backwoods Preacher...* nd (1856). np. 525p. VG. E5. $35.00

CARUS, Friedrich August. *Ideen zur Geschichte der Menschheit.* 1809. Leipzig. Bei Johann Ambrosius Barth und Karl Gotthelf Kummer. G1. $175.00

CARUS, Paul. *Gospel of Buddha.* 1937. Chicago. Open Court. 311p. VG. B33. $20.00

CARUS, Paul. *Pleroma, an Essay on the Origin of Christianity.* 1909. Chicago. Open Court. 1st ed. VG. B33. $25.00

CARUS, Paul. *Point of View: Anthology of Religon & Philosophy...* 1927. Open Court. 12mo. paneled red cloth. NF. G1. $27.50

CARVER, GALLAGHER & LE GUIN. *Dostoevsky & King Dog.* 1985. Santa Barbara. Capra. 1/200. sgns. F/pict wrp. B3. $150.00

CARVER, Jeffrey A. *Infinity Link.* 1984. Bluejay. 1st ed. sgn. F/F. P3. $25.00

CARVER, Jeffrey A. *Rapture Effect.* 1987. Tor. 1st ed. F/F. RS. P3. $20.00

CARVER, Raymond. *Fires.* 1983. Santa Barbara. 1st trade ed. sgn. F/8vo glossy wrp. A11. $45.00

CARVER, Raymond. *Glimpses.* 1985. Northampton. Basement. 1st ed. sgn. 1/15. w/author & printer materials. F. B4. $1,750.00

CARVER, Raymond. *New Path to the Waterfall.* 1989. Atlantic Monthly. ltd ed. 1/200. intro/sgn Gallagher. F/box. B4. $125.00

CARVER, Raymond. *New Path to the Waterfall.* 1989. Atlantic Monthly. 1st ed. intro Tess Gallagher. F/F clip. L3. $45.00

CARVER, Raymond. *New Path to the Waterfall.* 1989. Atlantic Montly. 1st ed. F/NF. B4. $35.00

CARVER, Raymond. *Put Yourself in My Shoes.* 1974. Santa Barbara. Capra. 1st ed. inscr. F/wrp. B4. $375.00

CARVER, Raymond. *This Water.* 1985. Concord. Ewert. 1st ed. sgn. 1/100. F. L3. $125.00

CARVER, Raymond. *Two Poems.* 1982. Scarab. 1st ed. sgn. 1/100. F/wrp. B2. $250.00

CARVER, Raymond. *Ultramarine.* 1986. Random. 1st ed. F/F. L3. $45.00

CARVER, Raymond. *What We Talk About When We Talk About Love.* 1981. Knopf. trade ed. NF/VG clip. L3. $85.00

CARVER, Raymond. *Will You Please Be Quiet, Please?* 1976. McGraw Hill. 1st ed. F/F. S9. $750.00

CARVER, Raymond. *Winter Insomnia.* 1970. Santa Cruz. Kayak. 1st ed. sgn. 1/1000. F/wrp/fld box. L3. $350.00

CARVER & GALLAGHER. *Dostoevsky.* 1985. Santa Barbara. sgns. 1/200 #d. F/12mo wrp. A11. $95.00

CARVIC, Heron. *Miss Seeton Draws the Line.* 1970. Harper Row. 1st ed. xl. dj. P3. $6.00

CARVIC, Heron. *Picture Miss Seeton.* 1968. Geoffrey Bles. 1st ed. VG/G. P3. $25.00

CARY, Gillie. *Uncle Jerry's Platform & Other Christmas Stories.* 1895. Boston. Arena. 1st ed. lg 12mo. VG. C8. $50.00

CARY, Robert. *Palaeologia Chronica.* 1677. London. Darby. folio. contemporary calf/rebacked. B14. $600.00

CASE, David. *Third Grave.* 1981. Arkham. 1st ed. F/F. F4/M2. $25.00

CASEY, John. *American Romance.* 1977. NY. 1st ed/author's 1st novel. inscr. F/F. A11. $100.00

CASEY, John. *Spartina.* 1989. NY. 1st ed. sgn. F/F. A11. $85.00

CASEY, John. *Testimony & Demeanor.* 1979. NY. 1st ed/author's 2nd book. sgn. F/F. A11. $55.00

CASEY, Robert J. *Baghad & Points East.* 1931. McBride. 8vo. 300p. VG/tattered. W1. $18.00

CASHIN. *Under Fire With the 10th US Cavalry.* 1969 (1899). np. photos. 361p. VG. E5. $45.00

CASPARI, Gertrude. *Das Lustige 1x1 fur Unsere ABC-Schutzen.* 1929. Leipzig. Hahn. 1st ed. 4to. ils brd. F/NF. B24. $485.00

CASPARY, Vera. *Weeping & the Laughter.* 1950. Little Brn. 1st ed. VG/VG. P3. $35.00

CASSADY, Ralph Jr. *Auctions & Auctioneering.* 1980. Berkeley/LA/London. 8vo. 327p. F. P4. $35.00

CASSANDRA, Kyne; see Disch, Thomas.

CASSAVETES, John. *Minnie & Moskowitz.* 1973. Blk Sparrow. 1/200. sgn. F/acetate. S9. $125.00

CASSELL, Eric. *Healer's Art: New Approach to Doctor-Patient Relationship.* 1976. Phil. pres. 240p. F/dj. G7. $20.00

CASSELS, Lavender. *Struggle for the Ottoman Empire 1717-1740.* 1967. Crowell. 1st Am ed. 226p. VG. W1. $18.00

CASSILL, R.V. *Father. And Other Stories.* 1965. NY. 1st ed/1st solo short story collection. sgn. F/F. A11. $35.00

CASSIN, J. *Mathematische und Genaue Abhand Von der Figur und Gross...* 1741. Leipsig. trans from French of 1920. full vellum. VG. C11. $175.00

CASSIRER, Ernst. *Die Philosophie der Symbolischen Formen.* 1906, 1907 & 1920. Berlin. Bruno Cassirer. 3 vol. VG. G1. $300.00

CASSIRER, Ernst. *Myth of the State.* 1946. New Haven. Yale. 304p. cream cloth. VG/dj. G1. $42.50

CASSIRER, Ernst. *Philosophy of Symbolic Forms.* 1953, 1955 & 1957. New Haven/London. Yale/Cumberledge. 3 vol. VG. G1. $125.00

CASSIRER, Ernst. *Substance & Function & Einstein's Theory of Relativity.* 1923. Chicago. Open Court. 1st Eng-language ed. 466p. paneled gr cloth. F/NF. G1. $150.00

CASSON, Lionel. *Ancient Egypt.* 1965. Time. 1st ed. 4to. ils/pl. VG. W1. $8.00

CASSON, Lionel. *Ancient Mariners.* 1968. NY. Macmillan. 286p. VG/VG. P4. $30.00

CASSON, Stanley. *Some Modern Sculptors.* 1928. Oxford. ARC/1st ed. ils. gilt bl cloth. VG/poor. F1. $75.00

CASSOU, Jean. *Jenkins.* 1963. Abrams. Modern Artist Series. VG/dj. M20. $25.00

CASSOU, LANGUI & PEVSNER. *Les Sources du Vingtieme Siecle.* 1961. Paris. Deux Mondes. sm folio. French text. ils. 364p. VG/poor. F1. $150.00

CASTANEDA, Carlos. *Fire From Within.* 1984. Simon Schuster. ne. F/F. S11. $20.00

CASTANEDA, Carlos. *Power of Silence: Further Lessons of Don Juan.* 1987. Simon Schuster. 1st ed. 286p. F/F. B33. $12.00

CASTANEDA, Carlos. *Second Ring of Power.* 1977. Simon Schuster. ne. VG/VG. S11. $20.00

CASTEL, Robert. *Regulation of Madness: Origins of Incarceration in France.* 1988. Berkeley. 1st Eng-trans ed. 297p. dj. A13. $25.00

CASTELLI, Bartolommeo. *Lexicon Medicum, Primum a Bartholomaeo Castello...* 1688. Norimbergae. Sumtibus Johannis Danielis Taubert. 939p. G7. $495.00

CASTELLI, Enrico. *Filosofia Della Storia Della Filosofia.* before 1900. Archivio di Filosofia. Organo dell'Instituto di Studi Filosofici. 276p. G1. $35.00

CASTELLI, Enrico. *Il Compito Della Fenomenologia.* 1957. Padua. Cedam. NF. G1. $35.00

CASTIGLIONI, Auturo. *Renaissance of Medicine in Italy.* 1934. Baltimore. 1st ed. tissue guard glued to title p. A13. $60.00

CASTLE, Egerton. *Young April.* 1907. Grosset Dunlap. ils. 452p. F/VG. H1. $15.00

CASTLE, Jeffery Lloyd. *Satellite E One.* 1954. Eyre Spottiswoode. VG/G. P3. $10.00

CASTLEMON, Harry. *Don Gordon's Shooting Box.* 1883. Phil. 352p. gilt emb cloth. VG. A17. $10.00

CASTLEREAGH, Frederick. *Journey to Damascus Through Egypt, Nubia, Arabia Petraea...* 1847. London. 2 vol. 8vo. rebound half red levant/raised bands. O2. $625.00

CASWELL, Helen K. *Shadows From the Singing House.* 1973. Tuttle. 3rd ed. VG/fair. P3. $10.00

CASWELL, Helen K. *Wind on the Road.* 1964. Van Nostrand. 1st ed. sm 8vo. M/M. C8. $15.00

CATHER, Willa Sibert. *Troll Garden.* 1905. McClure Phillips. 1st ed. pres. Doubleday Page imprint/2nd issue red cloth. VG. C6. $4,000.00

CATHER, Willa. *April Twilights.* 1903. Boston. Badger. 1st ed. inscr pres/dtd 1920. 52p. VG/morocco clamshell case. H5. $5,000.00

CATHER, Willa. *April Twilights.* 1923. NY. Knopf. later reissue/author's 1st book. sgn. 1/450. VG/case. Q1. $450.00

CATHER, Willa. *Collected Short Fiction, 1892-1912.* 1966. NE U. 5th prt. VG. P3. $30.00

CATHER, Willa. *My Antonia.* 1981. Franklin Lib. ltd ed. ils Hodges Soileau. gilt full leather. F. A18. $45.00

CATHER, Willa. *Old Beauty & Others.* 1948. Knopf. 1st ed. F/chip. A18. $25.00

CATHER, Willa. *Sapphira & the Slave Girl.* 1940. Knopf. 1st ed. sgn. 1/250. F/NF. B4. $350.00

CATHER, Willa. *Sapphira & the Slave Girl.* 1940. Knopf. 1st trade ed. F/dj. A18. $75.00

CATHER, Willa. *Shadows on Rock.* 1931. NY. ltd sgn ed. 1/619. VG. B5. $175.00

CATHERWOOD, John. *New Method of Curing the Apoplexy...* 1715. London. J Darby. 77p. quarter calf. VG. G7. $595.00

CATLIN, George. *Drawings of the North American Indians.* (1984). Doubleday. 1st ed. 215p. linen brd/brn buckram spine. F/F. A8. $200.00

CATLIN, George. *North American Indians. Being Letters & Notes on Manners...* 1903. Edinburgh. John Grant. 2 vol set. ils/maps. burgandy cloth. VG+. P4. $500.00

CATTELL, Ann. *Mind Juggler & Other Ghost Stories.* 1966. Exposition. 1st ed. VG/VG. P3. $15.00

CATTELL, Raymond B. *Handbook of Multivariate Experimental Psychology.* 1966. Rand McNally. 959p. F/dj. K4. $25.00

CATTELL, Raymond B. *Personality & Mood by Questionnaire.* 1973. San Francisco. Jossey-Bass. 475p. F/dj. K4. $50.00

CATTELL, Raymond B. *Scientific Use of Factor Analysis.* 1978. Plenum. 618p. F/dj. K4. $25.00

CATTELL & SCHEIER. *Meaning & Measurement of Neuroticism & Anxiety.* 1961. Ronald. 468p. F/dj. K4. $30.00

CATTON, Bruce. *Gettysburg: The Final Fury.* 1974. Doubleday. ils/maps. VG/dj/case. B18. $25.00

CATTON, Bruce. *Mr Lincoln's Army.* 1951. Doubleday. 372p. F/dj. M10. $7.50

CATTON, Bruce. *Terrible Swift Sword.* 1963. Garden City. 1st ed. 559p. VG/VG. A17. $15.00

CATTON, Bruce. *Waiting for the Morning Train.* 1972. Doubleday. 1st ed. 260p. VG/dj. M20. $25.00

CATTON, Bruce. *War Lords of WA.* 1948. Harcourt Brace. 1st ed. 313p. cloth. VG/dj. M20. $25.00

CATTON & CATTON. *Bold & Magnificent Dream.* 1978. Franklin Lib. true 1st ed. ils Dennis Lyall. full leather. F. B3. $30.00

CATULLUS, Gaius Valerius. *Complete Poetry of Gaius Catullus.* 1929. London. Fanfrolico. 1st ed. 8vo. 250p. full red-brn morocco. K1. $150.00

CAUDILL, Paul. *Broadman Comments on Internat Bible Lessons...* 1952. Broadman. 474p. F. B29. $3.50

CAUDILL, Rebecca. *Certain Sm Shepherd.* 1965. Holt Rinehart. 1st ed. inscr. ils/inscr WP DuBois. NF/NF. C8. $95.00

CAUDWELL, Sarah. *Sirens Sang of Murder.* 1989. NY. Delacorte. 1st Am ed. sgn. F/F. S6. $45.00

CAULFIELD, Anna Breiner. *Quakers in Fiction: Annotated Bibliography.* 1993. Northampton, MA. Pittenbruach. 1st ed. 12mo. sc. 169p. V3. $15.00

CAUNITZ, William J. *Black Sand.* 1989. Crown. 1st ed. VG/VG. P3. $20.00

CAUNITZ, William J. *Exceptional Clearance.* 1991. NY. Crown. 1st ed. sgn. F/F. S6. $35.00

CAUNTER & DANIELL. *Oriental Annual; or, Scenes in India.* 1835. London. Bull Churton. 263p. pict leather. NF. B14. $100.00

CAUSLEY, Charles. *Figgie Hobbin.* 1973. Walker. 1st ed. ils/inscr Hyman. NF/rpr. C8. $25.00

CAVANAH, Frances. *Louis of New Orleans.* 1941. McKay. ils Leonard Weisgard. pict brd. VG. B17. $4.50

CAVANNA, Betty. *Puppy Stakes.* 1948. Phil. 1st ed. ils. G. O3. $18.00

CAVE, Edward. *Boy Scout's Hike Book.* 1920. Doubleday Page. 243p. pict cloth. VG. A17. $25.00

CAVE, Hugh. *Cross the Drum.* 1960. Werner Laurie. VG/VG. P3. $25.00

CAVE & MACCONALD. *Birds of the Sudan.* 1955. Edinburgh. 1st ed. F/worn. very scarce. A9. $200.00

CAVENDISH, Richard. *Legends of the World.* 1982. Van Nostrand Reinhold. F/F. P3. $23.00

CAVILL, David. *All About the Spitz Breeds.* 1978. London. Pelham. 1st ed. 168p. cloth. F/F. R2. $36.00

CAWEIN, Madison. *White Snake & Other Poems.* 1895. Louisville. Morton. 1st ed. sgn. 79p. cloth. F. M1. $175.00

CECIL, Henry. *Sober As a Judge.* 1958. NY. 217p. VG/dj. D3. $15.00

CECIL, Henry. *Unlawful Occasions.* 1962. London. 1st ed. 182p. VG. D3. $15.00

CECIL, Lord Edward. *Leisure of an Egyptian Official.* 1935. Hodder Stoughton. 6th prt. 313p. G. W1. $12.00

CELINE, Louis-Ferdinand. *Rigadoon.* 1974. Delacorte. ARC/1st ed. RS. F/F. S9. $75.00

CERAM, C.W. *Gods, Graves & Scholars. Story of Archaeology...* 1951. Knopf. 1st ed. 428p. VG. W1. $12.00

CERAM, C.W. *Hands on the Past, Pioneer Archaeologists Tell Their Story.* 1966. Knopf. 1st ed. 31 pl. VG/torn. W1. $12.00

CERAM, C.W. *Secret of the Hittites, Discovery of Ancient Empire.* 1956. Knopf. 1st Am ed. 8vo. VG. W1. $15.00

CERF, Bennett. *Famous Ghost Stories.* 1946. Modern Lib. VG. P3. $18.00

CERF, Bennett. *Three Famous Murder Novels.* 1941. Modern Lib. 1st ed. VG/dj. P3. $20.00

CERF & LERNER. *Star Trek, the Truth Machine.* 1977. Random. 1st prt. 8vo. glazed pict brd. F. C8. $35.00

CERMAK & CRAIK. *Levels of Processing in Human Memory.* 1979. Lawrence Earlbaum. 479p. F/dj. K4. $25.00

CERVE, Wishar S. *Lemuria: The Lost Continent of Pac.* 1966. Amorc. 10th prt. VG/VG. P3. $14.00

CESCINSKY, Herbert. *Gentle Art of Faking Furniture.* 1967. NY. Dover. rpt. VG. A8. $10.00

CESCINSKY, Herbert. *Old English Master Clockmakers.* 1975. New Eng Pub. rpt. 182p. F. A8. $25.00

CETINTAS, Sedat. *Turk Mimari Anitlari. Osmanli Devri Bursada...* 1946 & 1952. Istanbul. 2 vol Turkish/Eng text. ils/pl. cloth brd. O2. $125.00

CH'LU-LANG & DEENEY. *Annotated Bibliography of Eng, Am & Comparative Literature.* 1975. Taiwan. 604p. F/NF. A4. $15.00

CHABER, M.E. *Bonded Dead.* 1971. HRW. 1st ed. F/F. P3. $15.00

CHABER, M.E. *Day It Rained Diamonds.* 1966. HRW. 1st ed. VG/VG. P3. $15.00

CHABER, M.E. *Green Grow the Graves.* 1970. HRW. 1st ed. F/F. P3. $15.00

CHABER, M.E. *Wanted: Dead Men.* 1965. HRW. 1st ed. VG/VG. P3. $18.00

CHABON, Michael. *Model World & Other Stories.* 1991. Morrow. 1st ed. sgn. F/F. B3. $40.00

CHACE & LOVELL. *Two Quaker Sisters: From Orig Diaries of...* 1937. NY. 1st ed. 183p. cloth. VG. M8. $75.00

CHADWICK, Lester. *Baseball Joe Around the World.* 1918. Cupples Leon. later prt. #8 in series. G. P8. $15.00

CHADWICK, Lester. *Baseball Joe at Yale.* 1913. Cupples Leon. later prt. #3 in series. VG/G. P8. $40.00

CHADWICK, Lester. *Baseball Joe in the Big League.* 1915. Cupples Leon. G+. P3. $10.00

CHADWICK, Lester. *Baseball Joe in the World Series (#7).* 1917. Cupples Leon. lists to #14. 242p. gray pict cloth. VG/dj. M20. $45.00

CHADWICK, Lester. *Baseball Joe in the World Series.* 1917. Cupples Leon. later prt. #7 in series. VG. P8. $35.00

CHADWICK, Lester. *Batting To Win.* 1911. Cupples Leon. later prt. College Sports Series. pict bdg. G+. P8. $35.00

CHAFEE, Zechariah. *State House Versus Pent House, Legal Problems...* 1937. Market Sq, Providence. Booke Shop. 165p. sewn wrp. M11. $35.00

CHAFER, Lewis S. *He That Is Spiritual.* 1918. Dunham. 193p. VG. B29. $6.50

CHAFER, Lewis S. *Major Bible Themes.* nd. Dunham. 329p. VG/dj. B29. $6.50

CHAFFEE, Allen. *Brownie...The Engineer of Beaver Brook.* 1925. Milton Bradley. 1st ed. ils Paul Bransom. cloth. VG. M5. $38.00

CHAGALL, Marc. *Ceramics & Sculptures.* 1972. Monaco. 2/orig litho. VG+/VG+. A1. $275.00

CHAGALL, Marc. *Jerusalem Windows.* 1962. NY. 1st ed. w/2 original lithographs. VG/VG. B5. $1,200.00

CHAGALL, Marc. *Lithographe III.* 1969. Boston. BBAAS. all lithos present. VG/G+. A1. $400.00

CHAGALL, Marc. *Lithographs of Chagall 1974-1979. Vol V.* 1984. NY. Crown. 1st Am ed. edit Chas Sorlier. F/dj. F1. $75.00

CHALFONT, A. *Montgomery of Alamein.* 1976. NY. Atheneum. 1st Am ed. biblio/index. 365p. F/dj. A17. $12.50

CHALKER, Jack. *Demons at Rainbow Bridge.* 1989. Ace. 1st ed. F/F. P3. $18.00

CHALKER, Jack. *Messiah Choice.* 1985. Bluejay. 1st ed. sgn. F/dj. M2. $30.00

CHALLENGER, L.G. *Description of the City of London.* ca 1960-65. London. Lilliputian Folio ed. 43x31mm. gilt morocco. F. B24. $275.00

CHALLENGER, L.G. *Heraldic Trade Emblems.* ca 1960-65. London. 3 vol. 50x40mm. ils. gilt full orange morocco. B24. $225.00

CHALLENGER, L.G. *History of Little Goody Two Shoes.* ca 1960-65. London. 48x36mm. reduced facsimile. gilt red morocco. F. B24. $275.00

CHALLINOR & RIPLEY. *Miners' Assn: A Trade Union in Age of the Chartists.* 1968. London. Lawrence Wishart. VG/dj. V4. $17.50

CHALMERS, Mary. *Come for a Walk With Me.* 1955. Harper. ils. pict brd. VG. M5. $60.00

CHALMERS, Patrick. *Horn: Hunting Novel in Verse.* 1938. Scribner. 1st ed. 4to. ils Lionel Edwards. VG/G. O3. $85.00

CHALMERS, Stephen. *Affair of the Gallows Tree.* 1930. Collins Crime Club. VG. P3. $25.00

CHALMERS, Thomas. *On the Wisdom & Goodness of God As Manifested...Nature...* 1839. London. Pickering. 2 vols. rebound red calf/gilt spine. G1. $135.00

CHALMERS-HUNT, Leonard. *Khamriyyah of Umar Ibn Al-Farid & Other Arabic Poems.* 1923. London. 1st ed. 12mo. sgn pres. VG. very scarce. W1. $45.00

CHAMALES, Tom. *Never So Few.* 1957. NY. ARC/1st ed. VG/VG. B5. $35.00

CHAMBERLAIN, George Agnew. *Great Van Suttart Mystery.* 1925. Putnam. 1st ed. VG. P3. $30.00

CHAMBERLAIN, George Agnew. *Overcoat Meeting.* 1949. NY. Barnes. 1st ed. VG/G. O3. $25.00

CHAMBERLAIN, Samuel. *Berkshires.* 1956. NY. 103p. VG/torn. B18. $15.00

CHAMBERLAIN, Samuel. *Beyond New England Thresholds.* 1937. Hastings. ils. 100p. VG. M10. $20.00

CHAMBERLAIN, Samuel. *Forty Acres: The Bishop Huntington House.* 1949. Hastings. ils. 66p. G. M10. $8.50

CHAMBERLAIN, Samuel. *New England Image.* 1963. Hastings. ils. 192p. VG/dj. M10. $12.50

CHAMBERLAIN, Sarah. *Alphabetarium.* 1982. Vienna, VA. Reisler. 63x51mm. 1/35 (total of 150). w/extra suite. F/case. B24. $450.00

CHAMBERLAIN, Sarah. *Bestiary.* 1979. Watertown. 53x58mm. 1/35 (total of 125). w/extra suite. F/chemise/case. B24. $300.00

CHAMBERLAIN & CHAMBERLAIN. *Civil War Letters of an OH Solider.* 1990. np. 67p. M/wrp. M20. $10.00

CHAMBERLAIN & NICHOLSON. *Planets, Stars & Space.* 1957. Creative Educational Soc. 4to. 223p. G. K5. $8.00

CHAMBERLAINE, William W. *Memoirs of Civil War Between N & S Sections of US of Am...* 1912. WA, DC. Byron Adams. 1st ed. sm 8vo. 138p. red cloth. F. rare. C6. $900.00

CHAMBERLAYNE, John Hampden. *Ham Chamberlayne, Virginian: Letters & Papers...* 1932. Richmond, VA. Dietz. 1st ed. 1/1000. 440p. F/NF. C6. $250.00

CHAMBERLIN, Ethel Glere. *Shoes & Ships & Sealing Wax.* 1928. Saalfield. ils Janet Laura Scott. VG. A17/B17. $8.00

CHAMBERLIN, T.C. *Origin of the Earth.* 1916. Chicago. 272p. cloth. VG. B14. $30.00

CHAMBERLIN, T.C. *Two Solar Families.* 1928. Chicago. 1st prt. 8vo. 311p. maroon cloth. VG. K5. $30.00

CHAMBERS, Andrew Jackson. *Recollections.* 1975. Ye Galleon. 1st ltd ed. 1/350. M/sans. A18. $12.50

CHAMBERS, H. *Mississippi Valley Beginnings.* 1922. NY. 1st ed. ils/maps/index. 389p. VG. B5. $30.00

CHAMBERS, Jack. *Navada Whalen, Avenger.* nd. Saalfield. G. P3. $10.00

CHAMBERS, James. *Devil's Horsemen. Mongol Invasion of Europe.* 1979. Atheneum. 1st ed. 190p. xl. G. W1. $15.00

CHAMBERS, John R. *Arctic Bush Mission.* 1970. Seattle. Superior. 1st ed. 4to. 197 photos. M/M. P4. $25.00

CHAMBERS, Julius. *Mississippi River.* 1910. NY. Putnam. ils/maps. 308p. T7. $85.00

CHAMBERS, Lenoir. *Stonewall Jackson.* 1959. Morrow. 2 vol. 1st ed/2nd prt. cloth. VG. M8. $65.00

CHAMBERS, Patrick. *Forty Nine Ladies.* 1929. Eyre Spottiswoode/Scribner. 1st ed. 4to. VG. O3. $65.00

CHAMBERS, Peter; see Phillips, Dennis.

CHAMBERS, Robert W. *Cardigan.* 1901. Harper. 1st ed. VG. M21. $15.00

CHAMBERS, Robert W. *Crimson Tide.* 1919. Appleton. 1st ed. G. N2. $8.50

CHAMBERS, Robert W. *Gay Rebellion.* 1913. Appleton. 1st ed. sgn Donald Wandrei. pict bdg. F. F4. $80.00

CHAMBERS, Robert W. *In Search of the Unknown.* 1904. Harper. 1st ed. sgn Donald Wandrei. pict bdg. F. F4. $125.00

CHAMBERS, Robert W. *Little Red Foot.* 1921. Doran. G. P3. $5.00

CHAMBERS, Robert W. *Maids of Paradise.* nd. AL Burt. VG. P3. $15.00

CHAMBERS, Robert W. *Makers of Moons.* 1896. Putnam. 1st ed. G. P3. $40.00

CHAMBERS, Robert W. *Mystery Lady.* 1925. Grosset Dunlap. VG. P3. $30.00

CHAMBERS, Robert W. *Police.* 1915. Appleton. 1st ed. VG/G+. M21. $75.00

CHAMBERS, Robert W. *Red Republic: A Romance of the Commune.* nd. AL Burt. G. N2. $5.00

CHAMBERS, Robert W. *Slayer of Souls.* 1972. Tom Stacey. 1st ed. F/F. P3. $20.00

CHAMBERS, Robert W. *Who Goes There?* nd. AL Burt. 1st ed thus. VG. M21. $30.00

CHAMBERS, Whitman. *Invasion!* 1943. Dutton. 1st ed. VG. P3. $20.00

CHAMBERS & SONNICHSEN. *San Agustin: First Cathedral Church in AZ.* 1974. AZ Hist Soc. ils/notes. 56p. F. B19. $20.00

CHAMPIE, Clark. *Cacti & Succulents of El Paso.* nd (1974). Santa Barbara. 123 photos. hc. F. B26. $20.00

CHAMPNEY, Lizzie W. *Three Vassar Girls Abroad.* 1883. Estes Lauriat. 1st ed. sq 8vo. ils. 236p. F. M1. $200.00

CHANCE, Burton. *Ophthalmology.* 1939. NY. 1st ed. 240p. A13. $75.00

CHANCE. *Book of Cats.* 1989. NY. 1st ed. 4to. 55p. brd. fair. scarce. R2. $10.00

CHANCELLOR, John. *Charles Darwin.* 1973. NY. Taplinger. 238p. VG. A10. $15.00

CHANDLEE, Edward N. *Six Quaker Clockmakers.* 1975. New Eng Pub. rpt. 8vo. 182p. F. A8. $20.00

CHANDLER, A. Bertram. *Beyond the Galactic Rim.* 1982. Allison Busby. F/F. P3. $20.00

CHANDLER, A. Bertram. *Bring Back Yesterday.* 1981. Allison Busby. 1st ed. F/F. P3. $20.00

CHANDLER, A. Bertram. *Rim of Space.* 1961. Avalon. 1st ed. F/F. P3. $45.00

CHANDLER, Anna Curtis. *Pan the Piper & Other Marvelous Tales.* 1923. Harper. 1st ed. ils. 234p. VG. P2. $18.00

CHANDLER, Raymond. *Backfire: Story for the Screen.* 1984. Teresa Pr. AP. F/wrp. B2. $30.00

CHANDLER, Raymond. *Big Sleep.* 1939. Knopf. 1st ed. 8vo. 277p. gray stp orange cloth. F/dj/clamshell case. H5. $5,000.00

CHANDLER, Raymond. *Big Sleep.* 1946. Cleveland. World. 1st ed thus. VG+. M21. $15.00

CHANDLER, Raymond. *Big Sleep.* 1986. San Francisco. Arion. 1/425. ils Lou Stoumen. reverse-litho Plexiglas bdg. F. F1. $500.00

CHANDLER, Raymond. *Farewell, My Lovely.* 1940. Knopf. 1st ed. 8vo. 275p. bl stp red cloth. VG/VG. H5. $2,500.00

CHANDLER, Raymond. *Farewell, My Lovely.* 1946. World. 3rd ed. MTI. VG/VG. P3. $25.00

CHANDLER, Raymond. *High Window.* 1942. Knopf. 1st ed. xl. VG-. P3. $125.00

CHANDLER, Raymond. *Little Sister.* 1949. Hamish Hamilton. VG. P3. $45.00

CHANDLER, Raymond. *Little Sister.* 1949. Houghton Mifflin. 1st Am ed. F/dj. M15. $350.00

CHANDLER, Raymond. *Long Goodbye.* 1953. Hamish Hamilton. VG. P3. $30.00

CHANDLER, Raymond. *Playback.* 1959. London. Hamish Hamilton. 1st ed. F/VG. M15. $85.00

CHANDLER, Raymond. *Raymond Chandler Omnibus.* 1964. Knopf. 1st ed. NF/NF. P3. $40.00

CHANDLER, Raymond. *Simple Art of Murder.* 1949. Houghton Mifflin. 1st ed. F/NF. M15. $400.00

CHANDLER & PARKER. *Poodle Springs.* 1989. Putnam. 1st ed. sgn. F/F. O4/S6. $45.00

CHANNING, Marion. *Magic of Spinning.* 1971. np. sc. VG. G2. $15.00

CHANNING, William Ellery. *Poems.* 1843. Little Brn. 1st ed/author's 1st book. 12mo. 151p. VG. M1. $250.00

CHANT, Christopher. *Space Shuttle.* 1984. NY. Exeter. 4to. 127p. VG/dj. K5. $20.00

CHANT, Joy. *Grey Mane of Morning.* 1977. Allen Unwin. 1st ed. F/F. P3. $25.00

CHANT, Joy. *High Kings.* 1983. Bantam. 1st ed. ils George Sharp. F/F. N3. $25.00

CHANT, Joy. *Red Moon & Black Mountain.* 1976. Dutton. 1st ed. VG/VG. M17. $15.00

CHAPEL, Charles Edward. *Art of Shooting.* 1960. Barnes. 416p. VG/dj. M20. $20.00

CHAPEL, Charles Edward. *Finger Printing.* 1941. Coward McCann. 2nd prt. 293p. VG/limp. M20. $25.00

CHAPEL, Charles Edward. *Guns of the Old West.* 1961. NY. 1st ed. 306p. VG/dj. B18. $22.50

CHAPEL, Charles Edward. *US Martial & Semi-Martial Single-Shot Pistols.* 1962. Coward McCann. 1st ed. VG/dj. N2. $20.00

CHAPELL, H.I. *National Watercraft Collection.* 1960. WA. 1st ed. cloth. VG. C11. $37.50

CHAPELLE, Howard Irving. *Baltimore Clipper, Its Origin & Development.* 1930. Salem. Marine Research. 4to. ils. gilt bl cloth. NF. F1. $175.00

CHAPELLE, Howard Irving. *Hist of the American Sailing Navy.* 1949. Bonanza. 558p. VG/dj. M20. $30.00

CHAPIN, Carl M. *Three Died Beside the Marble Pool.* 1936. Crime Club. 1st ed. VG. P3. $20.00

CHAPIN, Lucy Stock. *Teddie's Best Christmas Tree.* 1929. NY. ils M Farini. pict brd. VG. M5. $35.00

CHAPLIN, Arnold. *Harveian Oration on Medicine in Century Before Harvey.* 1922. London. 1st ed. 28p. A13. $25.00

CHAPLIN, Lita Grey. *My Life With Chaplin: An Intimate Memoir.* 1966. Geis. 1st ed. VG/dj. N2. $7.50

CHAPMAN, Allen. *Fred Fenton, the Pitcher.* nd. Cupples Leon. G+. P8. $17.50

CHAPMAN, Allen. *Radio Boys at Mountain Pass (#4).* 1922. Grosset Dunlap. lists to #5. 218p. VG/dj. M20. $32.00

CHAPMAN, Allen. *Radio Boys in Gold Valley.* 1927. NY. 1st ed. VG/VG. B5. $45.00

CHAPMAN, Allen. *Ralph in the Switch Tower.* 1907. Grosset Dunlap. Railroad Series #5. lists to #6. 263p. VG/dj. M20. $40.00

CHAPMAN, Frank M. *Handbook of Birds of Eastern North America.* 1895. NY. 1st ed. 421p. pict cloth. G+. B18. $35.00

CHAPMAN, Fredrik Henrik. *Achitectura Navalis Mercatoria, 1768.* 1967. NY. Sweetman. facsimile rpt. 62 pl/168 plans. loose leaf album. T7. $65.00

CHAPMAN, Lee; see Bradley, Marion Zimmer.

CHAPMAN, Olive Murray. *Across Lapland With Sledge & Reindeer.* 1932. London. 1st ed. 212p. VG. A17. $35.00

CHAPMAN, Walker. *Loneliest Continent.* 1964. NY Graphic Soc. 1st ed. 279p. VG/VG. S11. $15.00

CHAPMAN & SHIRLEY. *Tragedie of Chabot, Admiral of France.* 1639. London. 1st ed. sm thin 8vo. teg. late 19th C calf. VG. C2. $300.00

CHAPONE, Mrs. H. *Works of...* 1807. London. 4 vol set. 1st collected ed. VG+. A15. $275.00

CHAPPELL, Fred. *Dagon.* 1968. NY. 1st ed/author's 3rd novel. sgn. VG/VG. A11. $60.00

CHAPPELL, Fred. *Fred Chappel Reader.* 1986. NY. 1st ed. sgn. edit/intro/sgn Dabney Stuart. F/F. A11. $65.00

CHAPPELL, Fred. *It Is Time, Lord.* 1963. Atheneum. 1st ed/author's 1st book. 8vo. 183p. NF/dj. C6. $125.00

CHAPPELL, Fred. *More Shapes Than One.* 1991. NY. 1st ed. pres inscr. F/F. A11. $45.00

CHAPPELL, Fred. *World Between the Eyes.* 1971. Baton Rouge. 1st ed. sgn. F/F clip. C2. $45.00

CHAPPLE, Joe Mitchell. *To Bagdad & Back.* 1928. Boston. Chapple. 1st ed. inscr. 298p. VG. M10. $22.50

CHAPUIS & DROZ. *Automata: Historical & Technological Study.* 1958. Neutchatel/NY. 1st ed. sm folio. ils. VG. C11. $325.00

CHAPULS & JAQUET. *Historie et Technique de la Montre Suisse de ses Origines.* 1945. Olten, Switzerland. 1st ed. ils. 270p. red cloth. VG. H3. $200.00

CHAPULS & JAQUET. *Technique & History of the Swiss Watch.* 1970. London. Spring Books. rpt. folio. 272p. VG/G. A8. $40.00

CHAPUT, W.J. *Dead in the Water.* 1991. St Martin. 1st ed. VG/VG. P3. $16.00

CHARBONNEAU, Louis. *Way Out.* 1966. Barrie Rockliff. 1st ed. VG/VG. P3. $25.00

CHARCOT, J.M. *Lectures on Diseases of the Nervous System.* 1877. London. ils. 325p. cloth. B14. $100.00

CHARGAFF, Erwin. *Heraclitean Fire, Sketches From a Life Before Nature.* 1978. NY. 1st ed. 252p. dj. A13. $25.00

CHARLES, John. *Research & Public Health.* 1961. London. 1st ed. 114p. A13. $25.00

CHARLES, Kate. *Drink of Deadly Wine.* 1992. Mysterious. 1st Am ed. sgn. F/F. T2. $16.00

CHARLES, Ray. *Brother Ray.* 1978. Dial. 1st ed. F/NF. B2. $35.00

CHARLESWORTH, William. *Golden Retrievers.* 1952. London. Williams Norgate. 1st ed. ils. 96p. cloth. VG/G. scarce. R2. $45.00

CHARMLEY, John. *Lord Lloyd & the Decline of the British Empire.* 1987. Widenfield Nicolson. 1st ed. 294p. M/dj. M7. $25.00

CHARNAS, Suzy McKee. *Bronze King.* 1985. Houghton Mifflin. 1st ed. VG/VG. P3. $18.00

CHARNAS, Suzy McKee. *Dorothea Dreams.* 1986. Arbor. 1st ed. F/F. P3. $17.00

CHARNO. *Latin American Newspapers in United States Libraries.* 1968. TX U. 4to. 633p. xl. VG. A4. $65.00

CHARNOCK, John. *Biographia Navalis; or, Impartial Memoirs of Lives...* 1794-1796. London. R Faulder. 4 vol. ils. blk/tan cloth brd/leather label. T7. $800.00

CHARRIERE, H. *Papillon.* 1970. NY. 434p. NF. D3. $12.50

CHARTER, Samuel. *Riddle of Dr Mudd.* 1974. NY. 1st ed. ils/map ep. 380p. VG/dj. B18. $17.50

CHARTERIS, Leslie. *Saint Goes West.* 1942. Musson. 1st Canadian ed. VG/G. P3. $25.00

CHARTERIS, Leslie. *Saint in New York*. 1935. Hodder Stoughton. 1st ed. VG. P3. $60.00

CHARTERIS, Leslie. *Saint in Trouble*. 1978. Crime Club. 1st ed. VG/VG. P3. $18.00

CHARTERIS, Leslie. *Saint on Guard*. 1945. Hodder Stoughton. 1st ed. 8vo. 239p. NF/dj. H5. $300.00

CHARTERIS, Leslie. *Saint Plays With Fire*. 1951. Hodder Stoughton. VG/G. P3. $20.00

CHARTERIS, Leslie. *Saint Sees It Through*. 1947. Hodder Stoughton. 1st ed. 8vo. 256p. blk stp bl cloth. VG/dj. H5. $300.00

CHARTERIS, Leslie. *Saint Steps In*. 1943. Doubleday Doran. Crime Club. 8vo. 217p. blk stp red cloth. NF/dj. H5. $150.00

CHARTERIS, Leslie. *Saint Steps In*. 1944. Canada. Musson. VG/VG. P3. $30.00

CHARTERIS, Leslie. *Senor Saint*. 1959. Hodder Stoughton. 1st ed. VG/VG. P3. $35.00

CHARTERIS, Leslie. *Thanks to the Saint*. 1958. Hodder Stoughton. 1st ed. 8vo. 189p. gilt red cloth. F/dj. H5. $100.00

CHARTERIS, Leslie. *Vendetta for the Saint*. 1965. London. Hodder Stoughton. 1st ed. 8vo. 192p. gilt blk cloth. NF/clip. H5. $100.00

CHARTERS, Ann. *Kerouac*. 1973. Straight Arrow. 1st ed. VG/VG. P3. $40.00

CHARTERS & KUNSTADT. *Jazz: Hist of the NY Scene*. 1962. Doubleday. 1st ed. F/NF. B2. $50.00

CHARVAT, William. *Literary Pub in Am, 1790-1850*. 1959. PA U. 94p. F/VG. scarce. A4. $40.00

CHARVAT, William. *Profession of Authorship in Am 1800-1870*. 1968. OH State. 349p. F/F. A4. $45.00

CHARYN, Jerome. *Isaac Quartet*. 1984. Zomba. 1st ed. F/F. P3. $30.00

CHARYN, Jerome. *Seventh Babe*. 1979. Arbor. 1st ed. F/F. B4. $85.00

CHARYN, Jerome. *Seventh Babe*. 1979. Arbor. 1st ed. sgn. F/VG. P8. $125.00

CHASE, A. *Practical Recipes for Families, Farmers, Farriers...* 1866. np. 800 recipes. 384p. VG. E5. $45.00

CHASE, Cleveland B. *Sherwood Anderson*. 1972. Haskell House. 84p. VG. M20. $15.00

CHASE, Glen; see Fox, Gardner F.

CHASE, James Hadley. *Figure It Out for Yourself*. 1950. Robert Hale. 1st ed. VG/G. P3. $30.00

CHASE, James Hadley. *I'll Bury My Dead*. 1954. Dutton. 1st ed. VG/VG. P3. $10.00

CHASE, James Hadley. *Soft Centre*. 1975. Robert Hale. VG/G. P3. $12.00

CHASE, Mary Ellen. *Thomas Hardy From Serial to Novel*. 1927. MN U. 1st ed. NF/VG+. S9. $25.00

CHASE. *Bible & the Common Reader*. 1944. np. 316p. F/VG. A4. $25.00

CHASE-RIBOUD, Barbara. *President's Daughter*. 1994. Crown. UP. F/pict wrp. B3. $25.00

CHASE-RIBOUD, Barbara. *Sally Hemings*. 1979. Viking. 1st ed. NF/VG. B3. $25.00

CHASSEAUD, George Washington. *Druses of the Lebanon: Their Manners, Customs & History*. 1855. London. 8vo. lacks map. 422p. half cloth/brd. O2. $450.00

CHASTAIN, Thomas. *Case of Too Many Murders*. 1989. Morrow. 1st ed. F/F. P3. $15.00

CHASTAIN, Thomas. *Pandora's Box*. 1974. Mason Lipscomb. 1st ed. VG/VG. P3. $20.00

CHATALBASH, Ron. *Dr Blackfoot's Carnival Extraordinaire*. 1982. Boston. Godine. 1st ed. obl 4to. F/F. C8. $17.50

CHATHAM, Russell. *Dark Waters*. 1988. Livingston, MO. 1st ed. sgn. F/F. A11. $45.00

CHATTERJI, Mihini M. *Bhagavad Gita*. 1960. NY. Julian. 283p. VG/VG. B33. $26.00

CHATTERTON, E. Keble. *On the High Seas*. 1929. Lippincott. 1st ed. 319p. VG. M20. $25.00

CHATTERTON, E. Keble. *Ship Under Sail*. nd. Lippincott. ils/fld pl. 223p. T7. $35.00

CHATTERTON, E. Keble. *Ship-Models*. 1923. London. The Studio. 1/1000. heavy 4to. gilt bdg. VG. P4. $225.00

CHATTERTON, Pauline. *Coordinated Crafts for the Home*. 1980. np. cloth. VG. G2. $12.00

CHATWIN, Bruce. *In Patagonia*. 1977. London. Cape. 1st ed/author's 1st book. very scarce. F/dj. C2. $750.00

CHATWIN, Bruce. *In Patagonia*. 1977. Summit. 1st Am ed/author's 1st book. F/F. Q1. $150.00

CHATWIN, Bruce. *On the Black Hill*. 1982. London. Cape. 1st ed/author's 3rd book. F/F. L3. $125.00

CHATWIN, Bruce. *Songlines*. 1987. Franklin Center. 1st ed thus. sgn. leather. M. C2. $200.00

CHATWIN, Bruce. *Viceroy of Ouidah*. 1980. London. Cape. 1st ed/author's 2nd book. F/NF. L3. $125.00

CHATZIDAKIS, Manolis. *Byzantine Museum*. 1980. Athens. Ekdotike Athenon. 5th ed. VG. W1. $10.00

CHAUCER, Geoffrey. *Canterbury Tales*. 1988. NY. Lothrop. 1st ed. ils Hyman. F/NF. C8. $25.00

CHAUCER, Geoffrey. *Trolius & Cressida*. 1939. London. LEC. ils/sgn George Jones. F/case. M19. $75.00

CHAUCER, Geoffrey. *Workes of Our Antient & Learned English Poet...* 1598. London. George Bishop. 1st ed. ancient mottled calf. F. H4. $1,950.00

CHAUDHURI, Nirad C. *Autobiography of an Unknown Indian*. 1951. Macmillan. VG/worn. N2. $6.00

CHAUNDLER, Christine. *Famous Myths & Legends*. 1986. Bracken. F/F. P3. $20.00

CHAUNTLER, Samuel. *Elements of Astronomy...* 1850. London. Kendrick. revised ed. ils. 218p. aeg. gilt brn cloth. G. K5. $40.00

CHAUVEAU, C. *Historie des Maladies du Pharynx*. 1901-1905. Paris. 4 vol. orig wrp/uncut/unopened. G7. $250.00

CHAVEZ, Denise. *Last of the Menu Girls*. 1987. Houston. Arte Publico. 2nd prt/author's 1st book. pres/dtd 1988. VG/wrp. S9. $65.00

CHAYEFSKY, Paddy. *Altered States*. 1978. Harper Row. 1st ed. VG/VG. P3. $20.00

CHEEVER, John. *Some People, Places & Things That Will Not Appear...* 1961. Harper. 1st ed. F/NF. B2. $50.00

CHEEVER, John. *Stories of...* 1978. Knopf. ARC. RS. w/promo material & photo. F/NF. B4. $125.00

CHEEVER, John. *Way Some People Live*. 1943. Random. 1st ed/author's 1st book. 1/2750. VG. L3. $200.00

CHEEVER, John. *Whapshot Chronicle*. 1957. Harper. 1st ed. sgn. F/NF. B4. $400.00

CHEEVER, John. *Whapshot Chronicle*. 1957. Harper. 1st ed/author's 1st novel. sgn. VG/VG clip. L3. $350.00

CHEEVER, John. *Whapshot Scandal*. 1964. Harper Row. 1st ed. 8vo. 309p. blk/gilt stp bl cloth. NF/dj. H5. $100.00

CHEEVER, Susan. *Looking for Work*. 1979. NY. 1st ed/author's 1st book. sgn. F/F. A11. $45.00

CHEKREZI, Constantine A. *Albania Past & Present*. 1919. NY. 8vo. 2 maps. 255p. cloth. O2. $50.00

CHELTZ & RAY. *Feeding & Care of Domestic & Long-Haired Cat*. 1922. np. 1st ed. 50p. F. scarce. R2. $30.00

CHENEY, Cora. *Case of the Iceland Dogs*. 1977. Dodd Mead. 1st ed. 160p. cloth. F/G. R2. $20.00

CHENNAULT, Claire. *Way of a Fighter*. 1949. NY. 1st ed. VG. B5. $25.00

CHERNOFF & MOSES. *Elementary Decision Theory.* 1959. Wiley. 364p. G/dj. K4. $15.00

CHERRY, P.P. *Western Reserve & Early OH.* 1920. Akron, OH. Fouse. 229p. VG. M20. $50.00

CHERRYH, C.J. *Chanur's Legacy.* 1992. DAW. 1st ed. F/F. P3. $20.00

CHERRYH, C.J. *Chanur's Venture.* 1984. DAW. BC. NF/dj. M21. $5.00

CHERRYH, C.J. *Chernevog.* 1990. Ballantine. 1st trade ed. M/dj. M21. $15.00

CHERRYH, C.J. *Cuckoo's Egg.* 1985. Phantasia. 1st ed. 1/350. sgn/#d. F/F/case. P3. $40.00

CHERRYH, C.J. *Cyteen.* 1988. Warner. 1st ed. sgn. F/dj. F4. $45.00

CHERRYH, C.J. *Downbelow Station.* 1981. DAW. 1st hc ed. sgn. F/SF BC issue. F4. $22.00

CHERRYH, C.J. *Downbelow Station.* 1985. Severn. 1st ed. F/F. P3. $25.00

CHERRYH, C.J. *Faded Sun: Kutath.* 1979. Nelson Doubleday. 1st hc ed. sgn. F/SF BC issue. F4. $15.00

CHERRYH, C.J. *Foreigner.* 1994. DAW. 1st ed. F/F. P3. $20.00

CHERRYH, C.J. *Goblin Mirror.* 1992. Del Rey. 1st ed. sgn. F/F. F4. $28.00

CHERRYH, C.J. *Kif Strike Back.* 1985. Phantasia. 1st ed. 1/350. sgn/#d. F/F/case. P3. $40.00

CHERRYH, C.J. *Rusalka.* 1989. Del Rey. 1st ed. NF/NF. P3. $20.00

CHERRYH & MORRIS. *Gates of Hell.* 1986. Baen. 1st ed. F/F. N3. $15.00

CHESBRO, George C. *Bone.* 1989. Mysterious. 1st ed. F/F. P3. $18.00

CHESBRO, George C. *City of Whispering Stone.* 1978. Simon Schuster. 1st ed. rem mk. F/NF. B2. $30.00

CHESBRO, George C. *City of Whispering Stone.* 1978. Simon Schuster. 1st ed. VG/G. P3. $25.00

CHESBRO, George C. *Fear in Yesterday's Rings.* 1991. Mysterious. 1st ed. F/F. F4/P3. $20.00

CHESBRO, George C. *In the House of Secret Enemies.* 1990. Mysterious. 1st ed. sgn. F/F. M15. $25.00

CHESBRO, George C. *Incident at Bloodtide.* 1993. Mysterious. 1st ed. F/F. O4. $15.00

CHESBRO, George C. *Shadow of the Broken Man.* 1977. Simon Schuster. 1st ed. VG/VG. P3. $30.00

CHESBRO, George C. *Veil.* 1986. Mysterious. 1st ed. F/F. P3. $20.00

CHESNEY, Francis Rawdon. *Narrative of the Euphrates Expedition...1837.* 1868. London. thick 8vo. 25 full-p pl/fld maps. new brn half calf/raised bands. O2. $450.00

CHESNUTT, Helen M. *Charles Waddell Chesnutt: Pioneer of the Color Line.* 1952. Chapel Hill. 1st ed. 324p. VG. B18. $27.50

CHESTER, Samuel Hall. *Memories of Four-Score Years: An Autobiography.* 1934. Richmond, VA. 1st ed. 1/500. F/NF. M8. $75.00

CHESTERFIELD, Philip Dormer S. *Letters of..., Including Numerous Letters Now Published...* 1845. London. Bentley. 4 vol. 8vo. marbled ep. full smooth calf. NF. F1. $350.00

CHESTERTON, G.K. *Father Brown Omnibus.* nd. Dodd Mead. new ed. 661p. VG+. M21. $10.00

CHESTERTON, G.K. *Four Faultless Felons.* 1930. London. Cassell. 1st ed. VG/VG. M15. $250.00

CHESTERTON, G.K. *Paradoxes of Mr Pond.* 1937. Dodd Mead. 1st ed. VG+/dj. A18. $60.00

CHESTERTON, G.K. *Scandal of Father Brown.* 1935. London. Cassell. 1st ed. F/VG. M15. $285.00

CHESTERTON, G.K. *Tales of the Long Bow.* 1925. Tauchnitz. VG. P3. $60.00

CHESTERTON, G.K. *Thirteen Detectives.* 1987. Dodd Mead. 1st ed. F/F. T2. $16.00

CHESTNUT, Mary. *Diary From Dixie.* 1949. index. 572p. O8. $23.50

CHESTNUT, V.K. *Plants Used by the Indians of Mendocino Co, CA.* 1974 (1902). Ft Bragg, CA. rpt. ils/photos/map. sc. B26. $12.50

CHESTNUTT, Charles W. *Wife of His Youth & Other Stories of the Color Line.* 1899. Houghton Mifflin. 1st ed. 8vo. 323p. pink cloth. G. H5. $200.00

CHETWIN, Grace. *Atherling.* 1988. Tor. 1st ed. F/F. P3. $20.00

CHETWIN, Grace. *Collidescope.* 1990. Bradbury. 1st ed. F/dj. M2. $15.00

CHETWOOD, William R. *Voyages, Dangerous Adventures & Imminent Escapes...* 1720. London. Cato's Head. 1st ed. 180p. orig paneled calf. K1. $500.00

CHEW, Samuel C. *Fruit Among the Leaves: Anniversary Anthology.* 1950. Appleton Century. 1st ed. 535p. xl. VG. M10. $5.00

CHEYNE, George. *Essay on Health & Long Life.* 1724. London. 1st ed. contemporary calf. G7. $295.00

CHEYNE, George. *Philosophical Principles of Religion: Natural & Revealed.* 1715. London. Strahan. 2nd ed. contemporary paneled calf. NF. G1. $350.00

CHEYNEY, Peter. *Calling Mr Callaghan.* 1953. Todd. 1st ed. NF/dj. F4. $35.00

CHEYNEY, Peter. *Dames Don't Care.* 1936. Coward McCann. 1st ed. VG. P3. $30.00

CHEYNEY, Peter. *Dark Wanton.* 1948. Collins. VG/VG. P3. $15.00

CHEYNEY, Peter. *Ladies Won't Wait.* 1972. Collins. VG/VG. P3. $13.00

CHEYNEY, Peter. *Lady, Behave!* 1950. Collins. 1st ed. NF/NF. P3. $15.00

CHEYNEY, Peter. *Lady, Beware!* 1950. Dodd Mead. 1st Am ed. F/NF. M15. $25.00

CHEYNEY, Peter. *Meet Mr Callaghan.* 1953. London. Collins. omnibus ed. F/F. M15. $35.00

CHEYNEY, Peter. *Tough Spot for Cupid & Other Stories.* 1945. Vallancy. 1st ed. VG/VG. P3. $50.00

CHEYNEY, Peter. *Uneasy Terms.* 1958. Collins. VG/VG. P3. $18.00

CHICHESTER, Francis. *Romantic Challenge.* 1971. Coward McCann. ils/2 plans/3 maps. 255p. T7. $20.00

CHIDSEY, Donald Barr. *Captain Adam.* 1953. Crown. 1st ed. VG/VG. P3. $20.00

CHIDSEY, Donald Barr. *Panama Canal, an Informal History.* 1970. NY. Crown. ARC/1st ed. RS. F/F. B11. $30.00

CHILD, Benjamin H. *From Fredericksburg to Gettysburg.* 1895. Providence, RI. 1/250. NF/prt wrp. M11. $45.00

CHILD, Lydia Maria. *Appeal in Favor of That Class of Americans Called Africans.* 1833. Boston. Allen Ticknor. 1st ed. 12mo. 232p. bl muslin. M1. $250.00

CHILD, Lydia Maria. *Letters From NY.* 1844. np. 300p. VG. E5. $35.00

CHILD, Mary S. *Carry Away Book.* 1945. NY. ils Violet LaMont. sbdg. VG. M5. $25.00

CHILD, William Stanley. *Legal Revolution of 1902.* 1971. NY. facsimile of 1898 Chicago ed. 334p. xl. NF. D3. $15.00

CHILDE, V. Gorgon. *Dawn of European Civilization.* 1957. Routledge/Kegan Paul. 368p. G. K4. $25.00

CHILDERS, Erskine. *Common Sense About the Arab World.* 1960. Macmillan. 1st ed. 192p. F/dj. W1. $9.00

CHILDERS, James Saxon. *Way Home: Baptists Tell Their Story.* 1964. Holt Rinehart. 1st ed. sgn. 235p. VG/dj. B29. $4.50

CHILDRESS, Mark. *Tender.* 1990. Harmony/Crown. 1st ed. rem mk. NF/NF. A14. $25.00

CHILDRESS, Mark. *World Made of Fire.* 1984. Knopf. 1st ed/author's 1st book. F/F. B3. $45.00

CHILDS, Frank Hall. *Where & How To Find the Law, a Guide to Use of Law Lib.* 1923. Chicago. LaSalle Extension U. M11. $45.00

CHILDS, Marilyn. *Riding Show Horses.* 1972. NY. Arco. rpt. VG/VG. O3. $25.00

CHILDS, Mary Fairfax. *De Namin' of de Twins & Other Sketches From Cotton Land.* 1923. Macon, GA. Burke. probable 1st ed thus. pict cloth. VG. C8. $50.00

CHILTON, Charles. *Book of the West.* 1962. Bobbs Merill. 1st ed. VG/dj. B34. $20.00

CHIPIN, Anna Alice. *Eagle's Mate.* 1914. Grosset Dunlap. photoplay ed. 12mo. 300p. VG. S11. $10.00

CHIPMAN, Nathaniel. *Principles of Government: A Treatise...* 1833. Burlington, VT. royal 8vo. 330p. rebound. VG. D3. $250.00

CHIPPERFIELD, Jimmy. *My Wild Life.* 1976. Putnam. BC. F/F. O3. $18.00

CHIPPERFIELD, Joseph. *Silver Star.* nd (1960?). NY. 1st Am ed. VG/fair. O3. $35.00

CHIRARDELLI, Cornelio. *Cefalogia Fisonomica...* 1673. Bologna. Recaldini. 2nd ed. 8vo. 100 woodcuts. 662p. old vellum. K1. $600.00

CHISHOLM, Louey. *Snow Queen & Other Stories for the 5-Year Old.* nd. London. Jack. Fairyland Series. ils K Cameron. 60p. rebound. VG. M20. $75.00

CHISHOLM, Roderick M. *Perceiving: Philosophical Study.* 1957. Cornell. 204p. prt bl cloth. G1. $30.00

CHISNALL & FIELDER. *Astronomy & Spaceflight.* 1962. Harrap. 8vo. 12 pl. 230p. xl. dj. K5. $12.00

CHITTENDEN, Hiram Martin. *American Fur Trade of the Far West. Vol 3.* 1902. np. 893p. VG. E5. $35.00

CHITTENDEN, Hiram Martin. *Yellowstone National Park.* 1924. np. ils/lg fld map. 356p. O8. $18.50

CHITTENDEN, Lucius E. *Invisible Siege: Journal of April 15, 1861-July 14, 1861.* 1969. San Diego. Am Exchange. 1st ed. 1/1500. 133p. F/slipcase. A17. $15.00

CHITTY. *Woman Who Loved Black Beauty.* 1871. London. ils. 256p. F/F. R2. $20.00

CHIU, Hong-Yee. *Neutrino Astrophysics.* 1965. Gordon & Breach. 8vo. 107p. xl. VG. K5. $16.00

CHIVERS, Keith. *Shire Horse: A Hist of the Breed, the Society & the Men.* 1976. London. Allen. 1st ed. photos. 834p. VG/VG. O3. $65.00

CHOATE, Joseph H. *Trail by Jury.* 1898. np. 30p. VG/wrp. D3. $25.00

CHOATE, Pat. *Agents of Ifluence: How Japan's Lobbyists in US Manipulate.* 1990. Knopf. 1st ed. 295p. F/djc. M10. $7.50

CHOATE, Rufus. *Addresses & Orations of...* 1897. Boston. 7th ed. 529p. VG. D3. $35.00

CHOMEL & CHOMEL. *Red Cross Chapter at Work.* 1920. Indianapolis. 1st ed. 374p. A13. $40.00

CHONZ, Selina. *Snowstorm.* 1958. Walck. 1st Am ed. ils Aloris Carigiet. VG/G. P2. $25.00

CHOPER, Jesse H. *Supreme Court: Trends & Developments 1978...* 1979 & 1981. Minneapolis. 2 vol. sm 4to. wrp. D3. $45.00

CHORLTON, William. *American Grape Grower's Guide...* 1856. NY. ils. 171p. cloth. NF. B14. $75.00

CHORON, Jacques. *Suicide.* 1972. Scribner. 182p. bl cloth. VG/dj. G1. $25.00

CHRISTENSEN, Edwin O. *Index of American Design.* 1950. WA, DC. Nat Mus Art. 1st ed. ils. tan cloth. VG+. F1. $45.00

CHRISTENSEN, Paul. *Minding the Underworld.* 1991. Blk Sparrow. 1st ed. 1/150. sgn. F. B3. $50.00

CHRISTESON & CHRISTESON. *Tony & His Pals.* 1934. Whitman. 2nd prt. 144p. blk cloth. VG. M20. $35.00

CHRISTIAN, A. *Debuts de l'Imprimerie en France.* 1905. Paris. ils/woodcuts/facsimiles. half leather. K3. $50.00

CHRISTIAN, James L. *Extra-Terrestrial Intelligence.* 1976. Buffalo. Prometheus. lg 8vo. 303p. VG/chip. K5. $15.00

CHRISTIAN WOMAN'S EXCHANGE. *Creole Cookery Book. Edited by...* 1885. New Orleans. TH Thomason. 1st ed. 8vo. 223p. cloth/rebacked. M1. $375.00

CHRISTIAN. *Louis Adamic: A Checklist.* 1971. np. 211p. F. A4. $15.00

CHRISTIANSEN, V. *Les Tumeurs du Cerveau.* 1921. Paris. 337p. uncut. G7. $65.00

CHRISTIE, Agatha. *Agatha Christie Hour.* 1982. Collins. 1st ed. TVTI. VG/VG. P3. $20.00

CHRISTIE, Agatha. *Agatha Christie: An Autobiography.* 1977. Collins. 1st ed. VG. P3. $10.00

CHRISTIE, Agatha. *Appointment With Death.* 1938. Dodd Mead. 1st Am ed. VG+. B2. $25.00

CHRISTIE, Agatha. *At Bertram's Hotel.* 1965. Collins Crime Club. 1st ed. VG/VG. P3. $35.00

CHRISTIE, Agatha. *Body in the Library.* 1942. NY. 1st Am ed. NF/VG. A4. $95.00

CHRISTIE, Agatha. *By the Pricking of My Thumbs.* 1968. Dodd Mead. 1st ed. VG/G. P3. $25.00

CHRISTIE, Agatha. *Caribbean Mystery.* 1965. Dodd Mead. 1st ed. xl. dj. P3. $6.00

CHRISTIE, Agatha. *Clocks.* 1963. Dodd Mead. 1st Am ed. 276p. VG/dj. M20. $25.00

CHRISTIE, Agatha. *Dead Man's Folly.* 1956. Collins Crime Club. 1st ed. VG/rpr. P3. $30.00

CHRISTIE, Agatha. *Hercule Poirot's Christmas.* 1963. Collins Crime Club. VG/VG. P3. $13.00

CHRISTIE, Agatha. *Mousetrap & Other Plays.* 1978. Dodd Mead. 1st ed. F/F. S6. $50.00

CHRISTIE, Agatha. *Mr Parker Pyne, Detective.* 1934. Dodd Mead. 1st Am ed. F/NF. B2. $50.00

CHRISTIE, Agatha. *Murder in the Calais Coach.* 1934. Dodd Mead. 1st Am ed. VG. A4. $95.00

CHRISTIE, Agatha. *N or M?* 1941. Dodd Mead. 1st Am ed. F/NF. B2. $175.00

CHRISTIE, Agatha. *Nemesis.* 1971. Collins Crime Club. 1st ed. VG/torn. P3. $18.00

CHRISTIE, Agatha. *Ordeal by Innocence.* 1958. Collins Crime Club. 1st ed. NF/NF. P3. $40.00

CHRISTIE, Agatha. *Pale Horse.* 1961. London. Collins Crime Club. 1st ed. F/NF. M15. $45.00

CHRISTIE, Agatha. *Partners in Crime.* 1929. Dodd Mead. 1st Am ed. VG/fragmented. M15. $80.00

CHRISTIE, Agatha. *Passenger to Frankfurt.* 1970. Collins Crime Club. 2nd ed. VG/VG. P3. $15.00

CHRISTIE, Agatha. *Peril at End House.* 1932. NY. 1st Am ed. VG. A4. $40.00

CHRISTIE, Agatha. *Sleeping Murder.* 1976. Collins Crime Club. 1st ed. NF/NF. P3. $20.00

CHRISTIE, Victor J.W. *Bessie Pease Gutmann: Her Life & Works.* 1990. Wallace Homestead. 1st ed. 199p. M/M. S11. $25.00

CHRISTMAN, Henry M. *Walter P Reuther: Selected Papers.* 1961. Macmillan. 1st prt. VG/G. V4. $12.50

CHRISTMAN, Ruth C. *Soviet Science.* 1952. Baltimore. Horn-Safer Co. 2nd prt. 108p. F. K4. $12.50

CHRISTOPHER, Frederick. *Textbook of Surgery by American Authors.* 1942. Phil. Saunders. ils. 1764p. G7. $65.00

CHRISTOPHER, John R. *Capisicum.* 1980. Springville, UT. ils. 167p. sc. B26. $15.00

CHRISTOPHER, John. *Beyond the Burning Lands.* 1971. Hamish Hamilton. 1st ed. F/F. P3. $20.00

CHRISTOPHER, John. *Pendulum.* 1968. Simon Schuster. 1st ed. VG/VG. P3. $15.00

CHRISTOPHER, John. *Sword of Spirits.* 1972. Hamish Hamilton. 1st ed. F/F. P3. $15.00

CHRISTOPHER, Matt. *Diamond Champs.* 1977. Little Brn. 1st ed. F/F. P8. $17.50

CHRISTOPHERS. *George Abbot: Archbishop of Canterbury 1562-1633.* 1966. np. 235p. NF. A4. $35.00

CHRISTY, Howard Chandler. *Our Girls.* 1907. NY. 1st ed. VG. B5. $100.00

CHRYSLER, Walter P. *Life of an Am Workman.* 1950. Dodd Mead. 219p. NF/dj. A17. $14.50

CHUBB, Mary. *City in the Sand.* 1957. Crowell. 2nd prt. 213p. VG. W1. $10.00

CHUBB, Thomas. *Prt Maps in Atlases of Great Britain & Ireland...* 1966. London. Dawson. rpt. 4to. 480p. gilt gr cloth. K1. $75.00

CHURCH, Peggy Pond. *House at Otowi Bridge: Story of Edith Warner & Los Alamos.* 1960. NM U. 1st ed. F/dj. A18. $35.00

CHURCH, Peggy Pond. *Ripened Fields: Fifteen Sonnets of Marriage.* 1978. Lightening Tree. 1st ed. sgn. intro LC Powell. sc. M. A18. $17.50

CHURCH, Peggy Pond. *Wind's Trail: Early Life of Mary Austin.* 1990. NM U. 1st ed. ils/index. 215p. F/F. B19. $25.00

CHURCH OF ENGLAND. *Book of Common Prayer & Administration of Sacraments...* 1773. Oxford. Wright Gill. unp. contemporary blk paneled calf. VG. K1. $200.00

CHURCH OF ENGLAND. *Book of Common Prayer & Administration of Sacraments...* 1791. London. John Jarvis. sm 8vo. 10 engraved pl. unp. aeg. contemporary morocco. K1. $150.00

CHURCH OF ENGLAND. *Book of Common Prayer...* 1761. Cambridge. Baskerville. tall 8vo. contemporary gilt stp morocco. H10. $185.00

CHURCH OF ENGLAND. *Pictorial Edition of Book of Common Prayer...* ca 1840. London. Sangster. 771p. rebacked. xl. H10. $95.00

CHURCHILL, Winston S. *Blood, Sweat & Tears.* 1941. NY. 1st Am ed. 462p. bl/red cloth. NF. B14. $65.00

CHURCHILL, Winston S. *End of the Beginning.* 1943. Little Brn. 1st Am ed. 8vo. 322p. gilt red cloth. F/dj. H5. $225.00

CHURCHILL, Winston S. *Great Contemporaries.* 1948. Odhams. BC ed. 309p. gilt red cloth. VG/G. M7. $18.00

CHURCHILL, Winston S. *History of the English-Speaking People.* 1956-1958. London. Cassell. 4 vol. 1st ed. gilt red cloth. F/case. H5. $450.00

CHURCHILL, Winston S. *India.* 1931. London. Butterworth. 1st ed/2nd imp. sm 8vo. NF/prt gr wrp. H5. $250.00

CHURCHILL, Winston S. *London to Ladysmith via Pretoria.* 1900. Longman Gr. 1st ed. 8vo. 3 fld maps. 498p. tan cloth. NF/case. H5. $1,250.00

CHURCHILL, Winston S. *London to Ladysmith via Pretoria.* 1900. Longman Gr. 1st ed. 3 maps w/tissue gards. VG. Q1. $850.00

CHURCHILL, Winston S. *London to Ladysmith via Pretoria.* 1900. NY. 1st Am ed. 8vo. 3 fld maps. 496p. gilt red buckram. VG. H5. $750.00

CHURCHILL, Winston S. *Marlborough: His Life & Times.* 1933-1937. NY. 5 vol (lacks 6th). 1st ed. VG+. A15. $200.00

CHURCHILL, Winston S. *Onwards to Victory.* 1944. Little Brn. 1st Am ed. 8vo. 357p. blk/gilt red cloth. VG. H5. $225.00

CHURCHILL, Winston S. *River War: Historical Account of Reconquest of Soudan.* 1902. London. new/revised ed. 8vo. 381p. gilt red cloth. VG. H3. $95.00

CHURCHILL, Winston S. *Savrola.* 1900. Longman Gr. 1st ed. 8vo. 345p. gilt bl cloth. F. H5. $1,250.00

CHURCHILL, Winston S. *Second World War.* 1948-1954. London. Cassell. 6 vol. 1st Eng ed. gilt blk cloth. NF/case. H5. $450.00

CHURCHILL, Winston S. *Second World War.* 1948-1954. London. 6 vol. 1st Eng ed. VG/VG. M17. $150.00

CHURCHILL, Winston S. *Story of the Malakand Field Force.* 1898. London. Longman Gr. 1st ed/author's 1st book. gilt gr cloth. VG/case. H5. $6,000.00

CHURCHILL, Winston S. *Unrelenting Struggle.* 1942. Little Brn. 1st Am ed. 8vo. 371p. gilt red cloth. NF. H5. $225.00

CHURCHILL, Winston S. *World Crisis 1911-1918.* nd. London. 2 vol. VG. M17. $60.00

CHURCHILL, Winston S. *World Crisis.* 1923-1931. London. 6 vol. 1st ed. gilt bl cloth. F. H5. $2,000.00

CHURCHMAN, John. *Account of Gospel Labours & Christian Experiences of...* 1779. Phil. 1st ed. 255p. full calf. VG. M8. $250.00

CHURCHMAN, John. *Account of Gospel Labours & Christian Experiences of...* 1781. London. James Phillips. 3rd prt. 8vo. 351p. leather. V3. $35.00

CHURCHWARD, James. *Lost Continent of Mu.* 1926. Wm Edwin Rudge. 1st ed. VG. P3. $50.00

CIARDI, John. *Fast & Slow.* 1975. Houghton Mifflin. 2nd ed. 67p. F/F. H1. $15.00

CIARDI, John. *Man Who Sang the Sillies.* 1961. Lippincott. ils Gorey. VG. C8. $15.00

CIARDI, John. *Wish-Tree.* 1962. Crowell Collier. 1st ed. ils Louis Glanzman. VG. P2. $25.00

CIRLOT, J. E. *Dictionary of Symbols.* 1962. Philosophical Lib. 400p. NF/dj. M10. $9.50

CLAFLIN, Tennie C. *Speech on Ethics of Sexual Equality...* 1872. NY. Woodhull Claflin. 1st ed. 8vo. 24p. sewn/as issued. M1. $750.00

CLANCY, E.P. *Tides: Pulse of the Earth.* 1968. Doubleday. 8vo. 228p. bl cloth. xl. VG. K5. $15.00

CLANCY, Tom. *Cardinal of the Kremlin.* 1988. Putnam. 1st ed. VG/VG. P3. $20.00

CLANCY, Tom. *Clear & Present Danger.* 1989. Putnam. 1st ed. NF/NF. P3. $30.00

CLANCY, Tom. *Guided Tour of an Armored Cavalry Regiment.* 1994. Putnam. 1st ed. sgn. 1/150. cloth. M/case. B4. $350.00

CLANCY, Tom. *Hunt for Red October.* 1984. Annapolis. correct 1st ed/author's 1st book. F/NF. B4. $550.00

CLANCY, Tom. *Hunt of Red October.* 1984. Annapolis. Naval Inst. 1st ed. 8vo. 387p. red cloth. F/F. H5. $600.00

CLANCY, Tom. *Red Storm Rising.* 1986. Putnam. 1st ed. 8vo. 652p. gilt blk bdg. F/dj. H5. $50.00

CLANCY, Tom. *Without Remorse.* 1993. Putnam. ARC. F/wrp. B2. $35.00

CLANCY, Tom. *Without Remorse.* 1993. Putnam. ltd ed. 1/600. sgn. F/box. B3. $160.00

CLARE, John. *Dwellers in the Wood.* 1967. Macmillan. 1st ed. F/F. B3. $10.00

CLARENDON, Edward Hyde. *History of Rebellion & Civil Wars in England...* 1816. Oxford/Clarendon. 3 vol in 6. 2nd ed. folio. half red morocco. VG. C6. $750.00

CLARESON, Thomas. *Voices for the Future, Vol 3.* 1984. Bowling Gr. VG. P3. $15.00

CLARIDGE, Richard. *Tractatus Hierographicus; or, Treatise of Holy Scriptures.* 1751. London. full brn leather. G. B30. $75.00

CLARK, Ann. *Little Herder in Winter.* Jan 1942. US Dept of Interior. ils Hoke Denetsosie. Eng/Navaho text. VG+. P2. $110.00

CLARK, Arthur H. *Index to Maps of Am Revolution in Books & Periodicals...* 1974. np. 315p. F. A4. $95.00

CLARK, Arthur H. *Travels in the New South: A Bibliography.* 1962. OK U. 2 vol. VG/VG. A4. $245.00

CLARK, Arthur H. *Travels in the Old South, a Bibliography.* 1969. OK U. 3 vol. F/VG case. A4. $375.00

CLARK, Arthur H. *Venture in History, Production, Publication & Sale...* 1973. CA U. ils. 190p. F. A4. $40.00

CLARK, Carol Higgins. *Decked.* 1992. Warner. 1st ed. sgn. F/F. M15. $27.50

CLARK, Curt; see Westlake, Donald E.

CLARK, Eleanor. *Oysters of Locmariqaquer.* 1959. Pantheon. 1st ed. F/VG. H1. $35.00

CLARK, Francis E. *In Christ's Own Country.* 1914. Grosset Dunlap. 128p. VG. W1. $12.00

CLARK, Francis E. *Our Journey Around the World.* 1985. Hartford, CT. 8vo. 641p. VG. W1. $65.00

CLARK, George Rogers. *Sketches of His Campaign in IL in 1778-1779.* 1869. Cincinnati. Clarke. half gr morocco. F. H4. $125.00

CLARK, Grahame. *World Prehistory in Perspective.* 1977. London. Cambridge. 554p. F/dj. K4. $22.50

CLARK, James Hyde. *Cuba & the Fight for Freedom.* 1896. Phil. Globe Bible Pub. 12mo. 33 pl/fld map. 512p. gilt red cloth. VG. B11/H3. $40.00

CLARK, James M. *Meister Eckhart: An Intro to Study of His Works...* 1957. NY. Nelson. 1st Am ed. 267p. VG. B33. $25.00

CLARK, Jill R. *Fuchsias.* 1988. Chester, CT. photos. 144p. M/dj. B26. $20.00

CLARK, Joe. *Back Home Again.* 1981. Lynchburg, TN. obl 4to. VG/VG. A17. $15.00

CLARK, Mary Higgins. *All Around the Town.* 1992. Simon Schuster. 1st ed. F/F. O4. $15.00

CLARK, Mary Higgins. *All Around the Town.* 1992. Simon Schuster. 1st ed. sgn. F/F. T2. $22.00

CLARK, Mary Higgins. *Anastasia Syndrome & Other Stories.* 1989. Simon Schuster. ARC/1st ed. sgn. F/F. O4. $45.00

CLARK, Mary Higgins. *Anastasia Syndrome & Other Stories.* 1989. Simon Schuster. 1st ed. VG/VG. P3. $20.00

CLARK, Mary Higgins. *Aspire to the Heavens.* 1968. Meredith. 1st ed/author's 1st book. F/NF. B2. $200.00

CLARK, Mary Higgins. *Cradle Will Fall.* 1980. Simon Schuster. 1st ed. sgn. F/F clip. T2. $35.00

CLARK, Mary Higgins. *Cradle Will Fall.* 1980. Simon Schuster. 1st ed. VG/VG. O4. $20.00

CLARK, Mary Higgins. *Cry in the Night.* 1982. Simon Schuster. 1st ed. inscr/dtd. NF/F. B3. $35.00

CLARK, Mary Higgins. *Cry in the Night.* 1982. Simon Schuster. 1st ed. VG/NF. O4. $20.00

CLARK, Mary Higgins. *Cry in the Night.* 1983. Collins. 1st ed. VG/VG. P3. $20.00

CLARK, Mary Higgins. *I'll Be Seeing You.* 1993. Simon Schuster. 1st ed. sgn. F/F. T2. $22.00

CLARK, Mary Higgins. *Still-Watch.* 1984. Simon Schuster. 1st ed. sgn. F/F. O4. $25.00

CLARK, Mary Higgins. *Weep No More, My Lady.* 1987. Simon Schuster. 1st ed. VG/VG. P3. $15.00

CLARK, Mary Higgins. *Where Are the Children?* 1975. Simon Schuster. 1st ed. sgn. F/F. T2. $55.00

CLARK, Mary Higgins. *While My Pretty One Sleeps.* 1989. Simon Schuster. 1st ed. sgn. F/F. T2. $25.00

CLARK, Michael K. *Algeria in Turmoil.* 1959. Praeger. 1st ed. 466p. xl. G. W1. $8.00

CLARK, Norman. *Intro to Kant's Philosophy.* 1925. London. Methuen. 12mo. emb straight-grained gr cloth. G1. $28.50

CLARK, Peter. *Defense of the Divine Right of Infant Baptism...* 1752. Boston. Kneeland. 453p. recent cloth. H10. $135.00

CLARK, Philip. *Flight Into Darkness.* 1948. Simon Schuster. G+. P3. $10.00

CLARK, Ramsey. *Crime in America.* 1970. NY. author's 1st book. 347p. F/dj. B14. $25.00

CLARK, Ronald W. *JBS: Life & Work of JBS Haldane.* 1968. Coward McCann. 304p. F/dj. K4. $8.50

CLARK, Ronald. *Bomb That Failed.* 1969. Morrow. 1st Am ed. F/NF. N3. $15.00

CLARK, Sydney. *All the Best in Hawaii.* 1955. np. pres. 300+. VG. E5. $28.00

CLARK, Thomas D. *Off at Sunrise: Overland Journal of Charles Glass Grey.* 1976. Huntington Lib. 1st ed. map ep. M. A18. $20.00

CLARK, Thomas D. *Off at Sunrise: Overland Journey of Charles Glass Gray.* 1976. Huntington Lib. 182p. F. M10. $15.00

CLARK, Thomas F. *Hist of Myers Park Presbyterian Church 1926-1966.* ca 1966. Charlotte, NC. 1st ed. 237p. cloth. NF. M8. $37.50

CLARK, Tom. *Blue.* 1974. Blk Sparrow. 1st ed. VG+. P8. $25.00

CLARK, Tom. *Fan Poems.* 1976. N Atlantic. 1st ed. VG+. P8. $25.00

CLARK, W.J. *International Language: Past, Present & Future.* 1907. London. Dent. 205p. gilt cloth. VG. A17. $15.00

CLARK, Walter Van Tilburg. *City of Trembling Leaves.* 1945. Random. 1st ed. VG/G. P3. $25.00

CLARK, Walter Van Tilburg. *Strange Hunting.* 1985. Reno. 1/115. fwd Robert Morse Clark. M. A18. $125.00

CLARK, Walter Van Tilburg. *Watchful Gods & Other Stories.* 1950. Random. 1st ed. F/F. A18. $40.00

CLARK, Walter Van Tilburg. *Watchful Gods & Other Stories.* 1950. Random. 1st ed. VG/VG. S9. $25.00

CLARK, Walter. *Papers of Walter Clark.* 1948 & 1950. Chapel Hill. 2 vol. 1st ed. cloth. NF. M8. $125.00

CLARK, Will M. *Manual of Mechanical Movements.* 1943. Garden City. 254p. VG. H1. $9.00

CLARK & WACKERBARTH. *Red Couch.* 1985. NY. Van der Marck. 1st ed. text William Least Heat Moon. NF/VG+. S9. $65.00

CLARK. *Real Alice, Lewis Carroll's Dream Child.* 1981. London. ils. 271p. VG/VG. A4. $65.00

CLARKE, Anna. *Last Voyage.* 1982. St Martin. 1st ed. VG/VG. P3. $18.00

CLARKE, Anna. *Legacy of Evil.* 1976. Collins Crime Club. 1st ed. VG/VG. P3. $20.00

CLARKE, Arthur C. *Against the Fall of Night.* 1953. Gnome. 1st ed. VG. M2. $25.00

CLARKE, Arthur C. *Boy Beneath the Sea.* 1958. Harper. probable 1st ed. 64p. NF/VG clip. N3. $10.00

CLARKE, Arthur C. *City & the Stars.* nd. BC. VG/VG. P3. $10.00

CLARKE, Arthur C. *Earthlight.* 1972. HBJ. 1st ed. VG/VG. P3. $20.00

CLARKE, Arthur C. *Foundations of Paradise.* 1979. HBJ. 1st ed. VG/VG. P3. $25.00

CLARKE, Arthur C. *Four Great SF Novels.* 1978. Gollancz. 1st ed. F/F. P3. $30.00

CLARKE, Arthur C. *Prelude to Space.* 1954. Gnome. 1st ed. F/chip. M2. $100.00

CLARKE, Arthur C. *Prelude to Space.* 1970. HBW. NF/NF. P3. $15.00

CLARKE, Arthur C. *Reach for Tomorrow.* 1970. HBW. VG/VG. P3. $20.00

CLARKE, Arthur C. *Reefs of Taprobang.* 1957. London. 1st ed. F/worn. M2. $40.00

CLARKE, Arthur C. *Rendezvous With Rama.* 1973. Knopf. 1st ed. F/dj. w/sgn personal bookplate. F4. $90.00

CLARKE, Arthur C. *SF Hall of Fame, Vol 4.* 1981. Gollancz. 1st ed. F/F. N3. $35.00

CLARKE, Arthur C. *Songs of Distant Earth.* 1987. Del Rey. 1st ed. F/F. P3. $18.00

CLARKE, Arthur C. *Tales From the White Hart.* 1970. HBW. 1st ed. NF/NF. P3. $100.00

CLARKE, Arthur C. *1984: Spring, a Choice of Futures.* 1984. Ballantine/Del Rey. 1st ed. F/F. B3. $20.00

CLARKE, Arthur C. *1984: Spring, a Choice of Futures.* 1984. Ballantine/Del Rey. 1st ed. VG. P3. $15.00

CLARKE, Arthur C. *2010 Odyssey Two.* 1982. London. Granada. 1st ed. VG/F. B3. $40.00

CLARKE, Basil. *Mental Disorder in Earlier Britain.* 1975. Cardiff, Wales. 1st ed. 335p. A13. $50.00

CLARKE, Cyril A. *Selected Topics in Medical Genetics.* 1969. Oxford. 282p. F/dj. K4. $20.00

CLARKE, D.H. *Evolution of Singlehanders.* 1975. NY. McKay. ils. 206p. dj. T7. $24.00

CLARKE, Donald Henderson. *Alabam'.* 1946. Tower. VG/G. P3. $10.00

CLARKE, Donald Henderson. *Murderer's Holiday.* 1940. Vanguard. 1st ed. F/clip. M15. $45.00

CLARKE, H. *Longfellow's Country.* 1913. Doubleday. 242p. VG. E5. $35.00

CLARKE, H. Edwardes. *Waterloo Cup 1922-1977: Being a Detailed Account...* 1978. Surrey. Spur. 1st ed. ils. 440p. cloth. M/dj. R2. $40.00

CLARKE, H.G. *Pictorial Pot Lid Book.* 1960. London. VG/G+. A1. $50.00

CLARKE, Ida. *Men Who Wouldn't Stay Dead.* 1945. Ackerman. 1st ed. VG/dj. M2. $20.00

CLARKE, J. Harold. *Getting Started With Rhododendrons & Azaleas.* (1960). Doubleday. BC. 268p. F/VG. H1. $5.00

CLARKE, J. Jackson. *Congenital Dislocation of the Hip.* 1910. London. Bailliere Tindal. ils. 92p. G7. $175.00

CLARKE, James Freeman. *Anti-Slavery Days.* 1984. NY. H4. $30.00

CLARKE, Lindsay. *Chymical Wedding.* 1989. Knopf. 1st Am ed. F. B4. $45.00

CLARKE, Walter E. *Alaska.* 1910. Boston. lg 8vo. 207p. gilt cloth. F. A17. $30.00

CLARKE & CLARKE. *Narratives of the Sufferings of...During Captivity...* 1846. Boston. Bela Marsh. enlarged ed. 144p. H10. $45.00

CLARKE & LEE. *Ramma II.* 1989. Bantam. 1st ed. simultaneous w/Eng ed. F/F. N3. $15.00

CLARO, Joe. *Alex Gets the Business.* 1986. Weekly Reader. TVTI. VG. P3. $5.00

CLASON, Clyde B. *Exploring the Distant Stars.* 1958. Putnam. 8vo. 384p. G/dj. K5. $12.00

CLAUDY, Carl H. *Blue Grotte Terror.* 1934. Grosset Dunlap. VG. P3. $30.00

CLAUDY, Carl H. *Lion's Paw.* 1944. WA, DC. Temple Pub. inscr. G+/poor. N2. $10.00

CLAUDY, Carl H. *Mystery Men of Mars.* 1933. Grosset Dunlap. 1st ed. NF. P3. $30.00

CLAUDY, Carl H. *These Were Brethren. 24 Masonic Short Stories.* 1947. Temple Pub. N2. $7.50

CLAUSEN, Connie. *I Love You Honey But the Seasons Over.* 1961. NY. 1st ed. VG/VG. B5. $27.50

CLAVELL, James. *King Rat, a Novel.* 1962. Little Brn. 1st ed/author's 1st book. NF/VG. A4. $200.00

CLAVELL, James. *Little Samurai Thrump-O-Moto.* 1986. Hodder Stoughton. 1st ed. ils George Sharp. F/F. B3. $35.00

CLAVELL, James. *Whirlwind.* 1986. Morrow. 1st ed. NF/NF. P3. $35.00

CLAXTON, Florence. *Adventures of a Woman in Search of Her Rights...* ca 1865. London. 1st ed. obl 4to. VG. uncommon. C2. $200.00

CLAY, Beatrice. *Stories From Le Morte d'Arthur...* 1962. London. Dent. VG. P3. $15.00

CLAY, Henry. *Life & Speeches of the Hon Henry Clay.* 1853. Hartford. Andrus. 2 vol. royal 8vo. VG. D3. $75.00

CLAY, Jean. *Romanticism.* 1981. NY. Vendome. sq 4to. ils. 320p. NF/dj. F1. $75.00

CLAYMORE, Tod. *Appointment in New Orleans.* 1950. Cassell. 1st ed. VG/G. P3. $30.00

CLAYTON, Augustin S. *Office & Duty of a Justice of the Peace & Guide to Clerks...* 1819. Milledgeville, GA. Grantland. 1st ed. 8vo. 463p. disbound. M1. $750.00

CLAYTON, Horace R. *Negro Housing in Chicago.* 1940. NY. Social Action. F/wrp. B2. $35.00

CLAYTON, W.F. *Narrative of Confederate States Navy.* 1910. Weldon, NC. 1st ed. 1/100. 8vo. 116p. gray cloth. NF. C6. $900.00

CLEARY, Beverly. *Emily's Runaway Imagination.* 1961. Morrow. 1st ed. ils Beth/Joe Krush. 221p. VG/G. A3. $35.00

CLEARY, Beverly. *Emily's Runaway Imagination.* 1961. Morrow. 1st ed. 221p. ils Beth/Joe Krush. VG+. P2. $15.00

CLEARY, Beverly. *Sister of the Bride.* 1963. Morrow. 1st ed. ils Beth/Joe Krush. 288p. VG/VG. A3. $30.00

CLEARY, Beverly. *Socks.* 1973. Morrow. 1st ed. ils Beatrice Darwin. 156p. VG/G. A3. $30.00

CLEARY, Jon. *Beaufort Sisters.* 1979. Collins. 1st ed. VG/VG. P3. $23.00

CLEARY, Jon. *Dark Summer.* 1992. Harper Collins. 1st ed. F/F. P3. $25.00

CLEARY, Jon. *Golden Sabre.* 1981. Morrow. 1st ed. NF/NF. P3. $20.00

CLEARY, Jon. *Safe House.* 1975. NY. Morrow. 1st Am ed. F/NF. S6. $22.50

CLEARY, Jon. *Vortex.* 1977. Collins. 1st ed. VG/VG. P3. $25.00

CLEARY, Joy. *Strike Me Lucky.* 1962. Morrow. 1st ed. xl. dj. P3. $5.00

CLEATOR, P.E. *Intro to Space Travel.* 1961. London. Mus Pr. 1st ed. 8vo. 160p. G/worn. K5. $20.00

CLEAVELAND, Agnes. *Satan's Paradise.* 1952. Boston. 1st ed. VG/VG. B5. $25.00

CLEEVE, Brian. *Dark Blood Dark Terror.* 1965. Random. 1st ed. F/F. F4. $35.00

CLEEVE, Brian. *Death of a Painted Lady.* 1962. Hammond. 1st ed. VG/VG. P3. $25.00

CLEEVE, Brian. *Death of a Wicked Servant.* 1963. Random. 1st ed. F/dj. F4. $25.00

CLEEVE, Brian. *You Must Never Go Back.* 1968. Random. 1st ed. F/F. F4. $35.00

CLEEVES, Ann. *Killjoy.* 1993. London. Macmillan. 1st ed. F/F. S6. $25.00

CLEGG & LOVELL. *Radio Astronomy.* 1952. London. Chapman Hall. 8vo. 238p. VG/chip. K5. $18.00

CLELAND, Robert G. *Hist of CA: American Period.* Aug 1922. NY. Macmillan. 1st ed. fld map. 512p. bl cloth. F. B14. $35.00

CLELAND, T.M. *Harsh Words.* 1940. Newark, NJ. Cateret BC. 1/200. 32p. NF. M10. $25.00

CLEMENCEAU, Georges. *In the Evening of My Thought.* 1929. Boston. 2 vol. 1st ed. F/VG. A9. $40.00

CLEMENS, Clara. *My Father, Mark Twain.* 1931. Harper. 1st ed. photos. gilt bl cloth. F. F1. $75.00

CLEMENS, Susy. *Papa: Intimate Biography of Mark Twain.* 1985. Garden City. 1st ed. photos. 236p. F/F. A17. $10.00

CLEMENT, Hal. *Cycle of Fire.* 1964. Gollancz. 2nd ed. VG/VG. P3. $20.00

CLEMENT, Hal. *Mission of Gravity.* 1955. Robert Hale. 1st UK ed. sgn Clement/Stubbs. F/NF. scarce. F4. $275.00

CLEMENT, Hal. *Small Changes.* 1969. Doubleday. 1st ed. xl. dj. P3. $7.00

CLEMENT, Hal. *Still River.* 1987. Del Rey. 1st ed. sgn. F/F. P3. $25.00

CLEMENTS, William L. *William L Clements Lib of Americana at U of MI.* 1923. np. 240p. VG. A4. $25.00

CLEMMONS, Peter. *Poor Peter's Call to His Children...* 1812. Salisbury, NC. Coupee Crider. 1st ed. 153p. paper brd/leather spine. G. M8. $650.00

CLENDENIN, Kenneth W. *147th Aero Squadron Excerpts, WWI, 1918.* 1964. Parkersville, WV. 1st ed. inscr. VG/pict wrp. B18. $95.00

CLENDENING, Logan. *Behind the Doctor.* 1933. NY. 1st ed. 458p. A13. $40.00

CLENDINNEN, Inga. *Aztecs: An Interpretation.* 1991. Cambridge. 1st ed. 398p. VG/dj. F3. $35.00

CLERGUE, Lucien. *Language des Sables.* 1980. Marseille. 1/290. w/sgn prt. F/F/case. S9. $400.00

CLERGUE, Lucien. *Nude Work Shop.* 1982. Viking/The Studio. 1st ed. obl 4to. VG/NF. S9. $65.00

CLERKE, Agnes M. *Problems in Astrophysics.* 1903. London. Blk. ils/31 pl. 567p. xl. G. K5. $60.00

CLEUGH, James. *Secret Enemy: Story of a Disease.* 1954. NY. 1st ed. 273p. A13. $25.00

CLEVELAND, Grover. *Fishing & Shooting Sketches.* 1906. Outing Pub. 1st ed. 209p. cloth. VG. B14. $50.00

CLEVELAND, John. *Works of...* 1687. London. 1st complete ed. VG. A15. $285.00

CLEVENGER, S.V. *Spinal Concussion: Surgically Considered...* 1889. Phil. Davis. 359p. cloth. G7. $395.00

CLIFFORD, A.G. *Conquest of N Africa 1940-1943.* 1943. Boston. 1st ed. 450p. VG. A17. $14.50

CLIFFORD, Derek. *History of Garden Design.* 1966 (1963). NY. revised ed. photos/pl. 252p. cloth. VG. B26. $85.00

CLIFFORD, Francis. *All Men Are Lonely Now.* 1967. London. Hodder. 1st ed. NF/NF. S9. $20.00

CLIFFORD, Francis. *Wild Justice.* 1972. CMG. 1st ed. VG/VG. P3. $25.00

CLIFFORD, Martin. *Treatise on Humane Reason.* 1675. London. Henry Brome. 1st ed/2nd issue. 92p. contemporary calf. G1. $250.00

CLIFT, William. *Certain Places.* 1987. Santa Fe. 1st ed. obl 4to. F/F. S9. $175.00

CLIFTON, Lucille. *All Us Come Cross the Water.* 1973. Holt Rinehart. 1st ed. sm 4to. F/NF. C8. $45.00

CLIFTON, Lucille. *Everett Anderson's Friend.* 1976. Holt Rinehart. 1st ed. ils Grifalconi. M/F. C8. $25.00

CLIFTON, Lucille. *My Friend Jacob.* 1980. Dutton. 1st ed. ils DiGrazia. M/M. C8. $35.00

CLIFTON, Lucille. *Some of the Days of Everett Anderson.* 1972 (1970). Holt Rinehart. 2nd ed. xl. VG/VG+. C8. $17.50

CLIFTON, Lucille. *Three Wishes.* 1976. Viking. 1st ed. M/M. C8. $25.00

CLIFTON & RILEY. *They'd Rather Be Right.* 1957. Gnome. 1st ed. NF/NF. P3. $65.00

CLIFTON & RILEY. *They'd Rather Be Right.* 1957. Gnome. 1st ed. VG/VG. M17. $40.00

CLINARD, M. *Black Market. Study of White Collar Crime.* 1942. NY. 392p. VG. D3. $12.50

CLINE, C. Terry *Quarry.* 1987. NAL. 1st ed. F/dj. F4. $16.00

CLINE, C. Terry. *Mindreader.* 1981. Doubleday. 1st ed. VG/VG. P3. $20.00

CLINE, John. *Forever Beat.* 1990. Dutton. 1st ed. VG/VG. P3. $20.00

CLINE, Platt. *Mountain Campus: Story of N AZ U.* 1983. Northland. 1st ed. ils/index. 394p. F/F. B19. $35.00

CLINE, Platt. *They Came to the Mountain.* 1976. Northland. 1st ed. ils/index. 364p. F/F. B19. $35.00

CLISSOLD, Stephen. *Wisdom of the Spanish Mystics.* 1977. New Directions. 88p. F/F. B33. $17.00

CLIVE, William. *Tune That They Play.* 1973. Macmillan. 1st ed. VG/VG. P3. $15.00

CLOETE, Stuart. *Rags of Glory.* 1963. Doubleday. 1st ed. VG/dj. N2. $12.50

CLOGG & YANNOPOULOS. *Greece Under Military Rule.* 1972. NY. 8vo. 272p. cloth. O2. $25.00

CLONINGER, Claire. *Kaleidoscope: God's Patterns in Bits & Pieces of Our Lives.* 1988. Guideposts. 192p. VG/dj. B29. $4.00

CLOUD & LENTZ. *Goldilocks & the Three Bears.* 1934. Bl Ribbon. unp. VG. M20. $200.00

CLOWARD, R. *Delinquency & Opportunity.* 1961. Glencoe, IL. 220p. xl. VG. D3. $12.50

CLUNAS, Craig. *Chinese Export Watercolours.* 1984. London. Victoria/Albert Mus. 111p. glazed brd. F/dj. F1. $30.00

CLURMAN, Robert. *Nick Carter, Detective.* 1963. Macmillan. 1st ed. F/dj. F4. $27.00

CLUTTON & DANIEL. *Watches.* 1965. Viking. 1st ed. F/F. A8. $65.00

CLYNE, Geraldine. *Jolly Jump-Ups See the Circus.* 1944. McLoughlin Bros. 6 popups. NF. A3. $70.00

CLYNE, Geraldine. *Jolly Jump-Ups See the Circus.* 1944. Springfield, MA. McLaughlin Bros. VG. C8. $45.00

CLYNES, Michael. *Grail Murders.* 1993. London. Headline. ARC/1st ed. RS. F/F. S6. $30.00

COADY, John Joseph. *Appointment of Pastors.* 1929. WA. CUA. 143. wrp. H10. $15.00

COATES, Robert. *Yesterday's Burdens.* 1933. Macaulay. 1st ed. NF/NF. B2. $125.00

COATS, Alice M. *Quest for Plants.* 1969. London. photos/index. 400p. torn dj. B26. $55.00

COATSWORTH, Elizabeth. *Alice-All-By-Herself.* 1937. Macmillan. 1st ed. 181p. NF. P2. $40.00

COATSWORTH, Elizabeth. *Alice-All-By-Herself.* 1938. Harrap. 1st ed. ils M DeAngeli. VG/dj. M20. $60.00

COATSWORTH, Elizabeth. *Away Goes Sally.* 1934. Macmillan. 1st ed. 8vo. ils Helen Sewell. 122p. VG. A3. $12.50

COATSWORTH, Elizabeth. *Cat & the Captain.* 1927. Macmillan. 1st ed. ils Gertrude Kay. VG. P2. $35.00

COATSWORTH, Elizabeth. *Fair American.* 1943. Macmillan. 2nd prt. 8vo. VG. B17. $5.00

COATSWORTH, Elizabeth. *Silky.* 1953. Pantheon. 1st ed. ils John Carroll. F/VG. P2. $35.00

COATSWORTH, Elizabeth. *South Shore Town.* 1948. Macmillan. 1st ed. 200p. F/VG+. P2. $25.00

COATSWORTH, Elizabeth. *Wonderful Day.* 1946. Macmillan. 1st ed. Sally Series #5. 126p. VG-/VG. A3. $25.00

COBB, Irvin S. *Cobb's Anatomy.* 1912. Doran. 1st ed. 8vo. brn cloth. VG. D6. $45.00

COBB, Irvin S. *Cobb's Bill of Fare.* 1913. Doran. 1st ed. 8vo. 148p. VG. D6. $35.00

COBB, John B. *Christ in a Pluralistic Age.* 1975. Westminster. 287p. VG/dj. B29. $11.00

COBB, John Moser. *Hist of St Paul's Evangelical Lutheran Church Savannah, GA.* 1977. Savannah. Kennickell. 1st ed. 217p. cloth. VG. M8. $37.50

COBB, Thomas R.R. *Inquiry Into Law of Negro Slavery in USA.* 1875. NY. inscr. 155p. VG. D3. $150.00

COBB & RICKER. *Woman Into Space: Jerrie Cobb Story.* 1963. Prentice Hall. 8vo. 223p. G/worn. K5. $22.00

COBBETT, William. *Advice to Young Men...* 1831. NY. Doyle. 1st Am ed. 16mo. 268p. cloth. uncut. M1. $100.00

COBBLE, Alice D. *Wembi, the Singer of Stories.* 1959. St Louis. Bethany. sgn. ils Doris Hallas. 128p. VG/VG. A3. $12.50

COBBLEDICK, G. *Don't Knock the Rock.* 1966. Cleveland. 1st ed. VG/VG. B5. $75.00

COBHAM, Claude D. *Excerpta Cypria. Materials for History of Cyprus.* 1969. NY. rpt. sm folio. 523p. buckram. O2. $100.00

COBIA, Mark E. *Zygocactus (Schlumbergera).* 1992. Croffs Harbour, NSW. 52 mc photos. 58p. sc. M. B26. $6.95

COBLENTZ, Stanton A. *After 12,000 Years.* 1950. FPCI. 1st ed. VG/VG. P3. $25.00

COBLENTZ, Stanton A. *Moon People.* 1964. Avalon. 1st ed. F/F. M2. $25.00

COBLENTZ, Stanton A. *Under the Triple Suns.* 1955. Fantasy. 1st ed. VG/G. P3. $35.00

COBURN, Andrew. *Sweetheart.* 1985. Secker Warburg. 1st ed. VG/VG. P3. $20.00

COCHRAN, Doris M. *Poisonous Reptiles of the World: Wartime Handbook.* 1943. WA. 17 pl. 37p. orig wrp. G7. $65.00

COCHRAN, Douglas. *That's My Story.* 1938. NY. 1st ed. sgn. VG. B5. $50.00

COCHRAN, Jacqueline. *Stars at Noon.* 1954. Boston. 1st ed. VG/VG. B5. $27.50

COCHRAN & MURPHY. *Forever King.* 1992. Tor. 1st ed. F/dj. F4. $16.00

COCHRAN. *Concise Dictionary of American History.* 1962. Scribner. 4to. VG. A4. $40.00

COCKE, Sarah Johnson. *Bypaths in Dixie, Folk Tales of the South.* 1911. Dutton. 8vo. ils Duncan Smith. navy cloth. VG. D6. $25.00

COCKERELL, Douglas. *Bookbinding & the Care of Books.* 1934. np. 4th ed. 350p. F. A4. $40.00

COCTEAU, Jean. *Opium.* 1958. Grove. 1st ed. NF/glassine. B2. $75.00

CODRESCU, Andrei. *Life & Times of Involuntary Genius.* 1975. NY. Braziller. 1st ed. F/NF. B2. $35.00

COE, Tucker. *Don't Lie to Me.* nd. BC. VG/VG. P3. $8.00

COE, Tucker. *Murder Among Children.* 1967. Random. 1st ed. VG/G. P3. $20.00

COERR, Eleanor. *Jose-Fina Story Quilt.* 1986. Harper Collins. 7th prt. I Can Read Series. M/dj. A18. $14.00

COESTER. *Literary Hist of Spanish Am.* 1970. np. 2nd ed. 535p. F. A4. $35.00

COETZEE, J.M. *Age of Iron.* 1990. NY. 1st Am ed. sgn. F/F. A11. $55.00

COETZEE, J.M. *Foe.* 1986. London. 1st Eng ed (after Canadian original). sgn. F/F. A11. $60.00

COETZEE, J.M. *Life & Times of Michael K.* 1984. Viking. 1st ed. F/F. B3. $20.00

COFFEE, Frank. *Forty Years on the Pacific.* 1920. NY. Oceanic Pub. ils/maps. 375p. T7. $105.00

COFFEY, Brian; see Koontz, Dean R.

COFFEY, Frank. *Modern Masters of Horror.* 1981. CMG. 1st ed. NF/NF. P3. $20.00

COFFEY, Thomas M. *Imperial Tragedy: Japan in WWII.* 1970. Cleveland. 1st ed. 531p. VG/VG. A17. $15.00

COFFIN, Charles Carleton. *Our New Way Round the World.* 1869. Boston. 8vo. ils. 524p. cloth. O2. $55.00

COFFIN, Charles Carleton. *Our New Way Round the World.* 1876. Lovell. 1st ed. ils. 8vo. 524p. VG. W1. $25.00

COFFIN, Geoffrey; see Mason, Van Wyck.

COFFIN & COHEN. *Folklore in America: Tales, Songs, Superstitions...* 1966. Doubleday. 1st ed. 8vo. 256p. VG/VG. B11. $20.00

COFFIN. *Hist of Nantucket Island: Bibliography of Source Material...* 1970. np. 72p. NF. A4. $65.00

COFFMAN, Virginia. *From Satan, With Love.* 1983. Piatkus. F/F. P3. $15.00

COGHLAN, Richard. *Landscape Gardening in the Tropics.* 1975. London. ils/photos. 174p. F/dj. B26. $65.00

COHEN, Anthea. *Angel Without Mercy.* 1982. London. Quartet. 1st ed. NF/dj. S6. $27.50

COHEN, Barbara. *Thank You Jackie Robinson.* 1974. Lee Shepard. BC. VG. P8. $6.00

COHEN, Daniel. *Close Look at Encounters.* 1981. Dodd Mead. 1st ed. VG. P3. $15.00

COHEN, Edgar H. *Mademoiselle Libertine: Portrait of Ninon De Lanclos.* 1970. Boston. 1st ed. 329p. VG/dj. A17. $9.50

COHEN, John. *Human Robots in Myth & Science.* 1967. S Brunswick. Barnes. 1st Am ed. 156p. VG/worn. N2. $17.50

COHEN, John. *Humanistic Psychology.* 1958. Allen Unwin. 206p. F/dj. K4. $15.00

COHEN, John. *Psychological Time in Health & Disease.* 1967. Springfield, IL. Charles C Thomas. 103p. F/dj. K4. $20.00

COHEN, Julius. *Parental Authority: Community & the Law.* 1958. Rutgers. 204p. F/dj. K4. $20.00

COHEN, Lenore. *Buried Treasure in Bible Lands.* 1965. Ward Ritchie. 1st ed. 8vo. 225p. F/dj. W1. $8.00

COHEN, Leonard. *Spice-Box of Earth.* 1961. Toronto. McClelland Stewart. VG/wrp. B2. $35.00

COHEN, Leonard. *Spice-Box of Earth.* 1965. Viking. 1st Am ed. F/VG. B4. $85.00

COHEN, Lily Cohen. *Lost Spirituals.* 1928. NY. Neale. 143p. VG. M20. $35.00

COHEN, Mark Nathan. *Food Crisis in Prehistory.* 1977. Yale. 341p. M/dj. K4. $15.00

COHEN, Martin. *In Quest of Telescopes.* 1980. Cambridge. 8vo. 131p. F/F. K5. $15.00

COHEN, Morris Raphael. *Dreamer's Journey.* 1949. Beacon. 7 halftones. 318p. VG/worn. G1. $37.00

COHEN, Morris Raphael. *Intro to Logic & Scientific Method.* 1934. Harcourt Brace. 468p. bl cloth. xl. G1. $22.50

COHEN, Morris Raphael. *Reason & Nature: Essay on Meaning of Scientific Method.* 1953. Glencoe, IL. Free Pr. 2nd revised ed. 470p. red cloth. VG/dj. G1. $35.00

COHEN, Morton N. *Lewis Carroll, Photographer of Childern: 4 Nude Studies.* 1977. Phil. Rosenbach Found. thin 4to. photos. F/F. F1. $30.00

COHEN, Morton N. *Lewis Carroll & the Kitchens.* 1980. NY. Argosy Bookstore. 1/750. VG. M17. $30.00

COHEN, Octavus Roy. *Crimson Alibi.* 1929. Dodd Mead. VG. P3. $20.00

COHEN, Octavus Roy. *Dark Days & Black Knights.* 1923. Dodd Mead. 1st ed. 8vo. 335p. blk cloth. VG. C6. $30.00

COHEN, Octavus Roy. *East of Broadway.* 1938. Appleton Century. 1st ed. VG. P3. $25.00

COHEN, Stanley. *330 Park.* 1977. Putnam. 1st ed. F/F. P3. $15.00

COHEN & COHEN. *Applied Multiple Regression.* 1975. Hillsdale, NJ. Lawrence Earlbaum. 490p. F. K4. $15.00

COHN, Art. *Around the World in 80 Days Almanac.* 1956. Random. 1st ed. MTI. VG. P3. $15.00

COHN, L. *Hemingway Bibliography.* 1931. NY. 1/500. VG. A1. $150.00

COKE, Roger. *Detection of Court & State of England During 4 Last Reigns.* 1696. London. 2 vol in 1. 2nd ed corrected. recent blk calf/old red leather label. K1. $300.00

COKER, Elizabeth Boatwright. *India Allan.* 1953. Dutton. 1st ed. VG/G. P3. $15.00

COLACELLO, Bob. *Holy Terror.* 1990. Harper Collins. 1st ed. F/F. P3. $23.00

COLBECK, Norman. *Bookman's Catalogue. Norman Colbeck Collection...* 1987. U British Columbia. 2 vol. 4to. gilt bl cloth. M. F1. $165.00

COLBY, Barnard L. *New London Whaling Captains.* 1936. Mystic. ils/12 portraits. 41p. wrp. T7. $25.00

COLBY, C.B. *Moon Exploration: Space Stations, Moon Maps, Lunar Vehicles.* 1970. CMG. 4to. 48p. VG. K5. $12.00

COLBY, Merle. *Guide to Alaska.* 1950. NY. WPA. 5th prt. fld pocket map. 427p. VG. A17. $20.00

COLE, Adrian. *Place Among the Fallen.* 1987. Arbor. 1st ed. NF/NF. P3. $20.00

COLE, Alan. *Ornament in European Silks.* 1899. Phil/Westminster. 220p. half leather. VG. H4. $135.00

COLE, Babette. *Don't Go Out Tonight, a Creepy Concertina Pop-Up.* 1982. Doubleday. 1st ed. mechanical pop-up. VG+/pict wrp. C8. $30.00

COLE, Burt. *Blue Climate.* 1977. Harper Row. 1st ed. VG/VG. P3. $13.00

COLE, Burt. *Funco File.* 1969. Doubleday. 1st ed. F/NF. N3. $35.00

COLE, Burt. *Quick.* 1989. Morrow. 1st ed. NF/NF. P3. $20.00

COLE, E.B. *Philosophical Corps.* 1961. Gnome. 1st ed. F/F. P3. $30.00

COLE, Ernest. *House of Bondage.* 1967. NY. Ridge Pr. 1st ed. 4to. VG. S9. $60.00

COLE, G.L. *Civil War Eyewitnesses.* 1988. 351p. dj. M. O8. $18.50

COLE, Leslie. *Life of Noel Coward.* 1976. London. Cape. 1st ed. photos/biblio/index. 500p. silvered blk cloth. NF/VG. M7. $35.00

COLE, Robert. *Basenji Stacked & Moving.* 1987. Canada. 1st ed. ils. 187p. glossy brd. M. R2. $22.00

COLE & COLE. *Poison in a Garden Suburb.* 1929. Payson Clarke. 1st ed. G+. P3. $30.00

COLE & MALTZMAN. *Handbook of Contemporary Soviet Psychology.* 1969. Basic. 854p. F/dj. K4. $25.00

COLEMAN, J. Walter. *Molly Maguire Riots.* 1936. Richmond. GArrett Massie. NF/worn. scarce. B2. $50.00

COLEMAN, J. Winston. *Stage-Coach Days in the Bluegrass.* 1956. Lexington. 3rd prt. VG/G. O3. $125.00

COLEMAN, Robert E. *Songs of Heaven.* 1980. Revell. 159p. F/dj. B29. $4.00

COLERIDGE, Samuel Taylor. *Biographia Literaria.* 1817. London. Fenner. 2 vol. 1st ed. MacDonald bl morocco. H4. $600.00

COLERIDGE, Samuel Taylor. *Lay Sermon, Addressed to Higher & Middle Classes...* 1817. London. Fenner. 1st ed. MacDonald bl morocco. H4. $875.00

COLERIDGE, Samuel Taylor. *Rime of the Ancient Mariner.* 1863. London. 1st ed thus. ils JN Paton. full morocco. VG+. C6. $135.00

COLERIDGE, Samuel Taylor. *Rime of the Ancient Mariner.* 1929. Bristol. Cleverdon. ltd ed. 1/400. ils Jones. 38p. gilt wht bdg. NF. F1. $650.00

COLERIDGE, Samuel Taylor. *Rime of the Ancient Mariner.* 1945. NY. LEC. 1/1500. ils/sgn Edward A Wilson. ostrich hide. F/G case. S9. $150.00

COLERIDGE, Samuel Taylor. *Specimens of Table Talk of the Late Samuel Taylor Coleridge.* 1835. NY. Harper. 2 vol in 1. 1st Am ed. faint lib stp. VG. Q1. $500.00

COLERIDGE, Samuel Taylor. *Twenty-Four Negro Melodies.* 1905. Boston. Oliver Ditson. 1st ed. F/F. B2. $225.00

COLES, K. Adlard. *Sailing Years.* 1981. London. Granada. 37 pl. 212p. dj. T7. $22.00

COLES, Manning. *All That Glitters.* 1954. Doubleday Crime Club. 1st ed. 189p. VG/dj. M20. $32.00

COLES, Manning. *Basle Express.* 1956. Hodder Stoughton. 1st ed. xl. dj. P3. $10.00

COLES, Manning. *Diamonds to Amsterdam.* 1949. Doubleday Crime Club. 1st ed. RS. VG/dj. M20. $50.00

COLES, Manning. *Drink to Yesterday.* 1944. Canada. VG/VG. P3. $30.00

COLES, Manning. *No Entry.* 1958. Doubleday. 1st ed. VG. P3. $20.00

COLES, Manning. *Not for Export.* 1954. Hodder Stoughton. 1st ed. VG. P3. $25.00

COLES, Robert. *Erik H Erickson: The Growth of His Work.* 1970. Little Brn. 3rd ed. 440p. VG/VG. A10. $12.00

COLES & HALLOWELL. *Women of Crisis: Lives of Struggle & Hope.* 1978. Franklin Lib. 1st ed. ils Chet Jezierski. full leather. F. B3. $25.00

COLES & VANDERWELL. *Game & the English Landscape.* 1980. Viking/The Studio. 1st ed. 4to. VG/VG. O3. $45.00

COLETTE. *Claudine Married.* 1960. FSC. 1st Am ed. 192p. VG/VG. M20. $25.00

COLFER, Enid. *Cucumber: Story of a Siamese Cat.* 1961. Nelson. 1st ed. 98p. VG/dj. M20. $20.00

COLIN, Aubrey. *Hands of Death.* 1963. Hammond. 1st ed. VG/torn. P3. $13.00

COLLES, Christopher. *Account of the Astonishing Beauties & Operations of Nature.* 1816. NY. Wood. 44p. prt wrp. M1. $450.00

COLLETT, G. *Golf Young Players.* 1926. Boston. 1st ed. cloth. VG. C11. $65.00

COLLIE, Michael. *Henry Maudsley: Victorian Psychiatrist.* 1988. Winchester, Eng. 1st ed. 205p. dj. A13. $35.00

COLLIE & FRASER. *George Borrow: Bibliographical Study.* 1984. np. 1/750. NF/VG. A4. $65.00

COLLIER, John. *His Monkey Wife.* 1931. Appleton. 1st ed. VG. P3. $35.00

COLLIER, Katherine Brownell. *Cosmogonies of Our Fathers.* 1934. Columbia. 8vo. 500p. G/dj. K5. $85.00

COLLIER, Peter. *Fondas: A Hollywood Dynasty.* 1991. Putnam. 1st ed. NF/NF. P3. $23.00

COLLIER, Richard. *House Called Memory.* 1961. Dutton. 1st ed. VG/VG. P3. $20.00

COLLIGNON, Charles. *Miscellaneous Works of...* 1786. Cambridge. Hodson. 4to. 345p. ES. joints weak. G7. $175.00

COLLIN, Hedvig. *Wind Island.* 1945. Viking. 1st ed. ils. VG/fair. P2. $20.00

COLLINET, L.P. *Dissertation sur une Maladie du Cerveau Avec Quelques...* 1802. Paris. 75p. new brd. G7. $150.00

COLLINGS, Michael. *Naked to the Sun.* 1985. Starmont. 1st ed. F/wrp. M2. $10.00

COLLINGWOOD, Stuart Dodgson. *Life & Letters of Lewis Carroll.* 1899 (1898). Century. 429p. gilt red cloth. xl. M20. $35.00

COLLINS, Arthur. *Proceedings, Precedents & Arguments on Claims...* 1734. London. Queen's Head & 3 Daggers. folio. contemporary calf. K1. $400.00

COLLINS, Gary R. *Magnificent Mind.* 1985. Word. 262p. F/F. B29. $5.50

COLLINS, Helens. *Mutagenesis.* 1993. Tor. 1st ed. F/F. F4. $16.00

COLLINS, Hunt; see Hunter, Evan.

COLLINS, John A. *Anti-Slavery Picknick: A Collection of Speeches, Poems...* 1842. Boston. 1st ed. 12mo. 144p. stiff prt wrp. M1. $450.00

COLLINS, John S. *My Experiences in the West.* 1970. Lakeside. 252p. gilt bl cloth. VG+. M20. $25.00

COLLINS, Kenneth. *Go & Learn: International Story of Jews & Medicine...* 1988. Aberdeen. 1st ed. 193p. A13. $40.00

COLLINS, Larry. *Maze.* 1989. Simon Schuster. 1st ed. VG/VG. P3. $20.00

COLLINS, Leighton. *Air Facts Reader 1939-1941.* 1974. NY. 8vo. 240p. VG. A17. $12.50

COLLINS, Max Allan. *Million-Dollar Wound.* 1986. St Martin. 1st ed. F/F. T2. $20.00

COLLINS, Max Allan. *Nice Weekend for Murder.* 1986. Walker. 1st ed. VG/VG. P3. $16.00

COLLINS, Max Allan. *No Cure for Death.* 1983. Walker. 1st ed. VG/VG. P3. $15.00

COLLINS, Max Allan. *One Lonely Knight: Mickey Spillane's Mike Hammer.* 1984. Popular. 1st ed. ils. F/F. S6. $35.00

COLLINS, Max Allan. *Spree.* 1987. Tor. ARC/1st ed. sgn. RS. F/F. S6. $35.00

COLLINS, Michael; see Lynds, Dennis.

COLLINS, Nancy A. *Cold Turkey.* 1992. Holyoke. Crossroads. 1st ed. sgn. 1/500. ils/sgn Masztal. F/pict wrp. T2. $15.00

COLLINS, Nancy A. *Sunglasses After Dark.* 1990. London. Kinnell. 1st hc ed/author's 1st novel. sgn. F/F. T2. $45.00

COLLINS, Paul. *Alien Worlds.* 1979. Void. 1st ed. NF/NF. P3. $30.00

COLLINS, Paul. *Other Worlds.* 1978. Void. 1st ed. NF/NF. P3. $30.00

COLLINS, R.M. *Chapters From Unwritten Hist of War Between States...* 1893. St Louis. Nixon Jones. 1st ed. 8vo. 335p. gr cloth. VG+. C6. $1,650.00

COLLINS, Randall. *Case of the Philosopher's Ring.* 1980. Brighton. Harvester. 1st Eng ed. ils. F/dj. S6. $25.00

COLLINS, Wilkie. *Four Mysteries.* 1992. Folio Soc. 4 vol. dk gr cloth. VG/case. B30. $60.00

COLLINS, Wilkie. *Woman in White.* 1933. Daily Express. VG. P3. $20.00

COLLINS & GORMAN. *Jim Thompson: Killers Inside Him.* 1983. Fedora, IA. 1st prt sc orig. 1/425. F/wrp. S6. $120.00

COLLINS & LAPIERE. *Mountbatten & the Partition of India.* 1982. Bangladesh. photos/index. 191p. VG/VG. A17. $10.00

COLLINS & POMEROY. *Great Sahara Mousehunt.* 1963. Riverside. 1st Am ed. 8 pl/map ep. 200p. xl. VG. W1. $8.00

COLLINS & TIGNOR. *Egypt & the Sudan.* 1967. Englewood Cliffs. 1st ed. 180p. xl. VG. W1. $8.00

COLLIS, Maurice. *Cortes & Montezuma.* 1955. Harcourt. 1st Am ed. 256p. VG/dj. F3. $20.00

COLLODI, Carlo. *Pinocchio, the Tale of a Puppet.* nd. ca 1915? Dutton Dent. 8 mc pl. VG. M5. $40.00

COLLODI, Carlo. *Pinocchio.* 1946. Random. possible rpt. ils Lois Lenski. G+. B17. $15.00

COLLODI, Carlo. *Pinocchio.* 1946. World. 1st ed thus. ils Richard Floethe. VG/G. M5. $20.00

COLLUM, Charles R. *NY: Nude.* 1981. NY. Amphoto. 1st ed. 4to. VG/VG. S9. $75.00

COLMAN, George. *Comedies of Terence.* 1768. London. 2 vol. 2nd ed. rebound. VG. A15. $100.00

COLMAN, George. *Dramatick Works of...* 1777. London. 4 vol. only collected ed. gilt dentelles/marbled ep. VG+. A15. $300.00

COLMONT, Marie. *Up the Mountain.* 1940. Harper. stated 1st ed. ils Alexandra Exter. pict brd. F/VG. M5. $25.00

COLOMBO, John Robert. *Other Canadas.* 1979. McGraw Hill Ryerson. 1st ed. VG/G. P3. $20.00

COLT, Samuel. *Armsmear: The Home, the Arm, & the Armory.* 1866. NY. Alvord. 1/15. pres/sgn Mrs Colt. full morocco. H4. $1,500.00

COLTON, C. *Private Correspondence of Henry Clay.* 1855. np. 1st ed. 642p. VG. E5. $45.00

COLTON, Harold S. *Hopi Kachina Dolls With a Key to Their Identification.* 1964. NM U. later prt. 150p. VG/worn. P4. $45.00

COLTON, James; see Hansen, Joseph.

COLTON, Matthew. *Frank Armstrong, Captain of the Nine.* (1913). Al Burt. later prt. G. P8. $15.00

COLTON, Matthew. *Frank Armstrong's Second Term.* 1911. Hurst. 1st ed. G+. P8. $22.50

COLTON, Walter. *Land & Lee in Bosphorus & Aegean; or, Views of Athens...* 1851. NY. 8vo. ils. 366p. cloth. O2. $60.00

COLTON, Walter. *Ship & Shore, in Madeira, Lisbon & the Mediterranean.* 1851. NY. 8vo. 313p. rebound half gilt morocco. O2. $125.00

COLUM, Padraic. *King of Ireland's Son.* 1926. Macmillan. sgn. gr cloth. VG. M5. $30.00

COLUM, Padraic. *White Sparrow.* 1933. Macmillan. 1st ed. ils Lynd Ward. 46p. VG/G. P2. $45.00

COLUM, Padraic. *Wild Earth: Book of Verse.* 1907. Dublin. Maunsel. 1st ed/author's 1st book poems. inscr. 12mo. ES. NF. C6. $150.00

COLVILLE, W.J. *Studies in Thesophy: Historical & Practical.* 1890. Westport. Greenwood. rpt 1938 ed. 176p. F. B33. $40.00

COLVIN, Auckland. *Making of Modern Egypt.* ca 1900. Nelson. 12mo. 1 fld map. 384p. teg. G. W1. $10.00

COLVIN, Thomas E. *Steel Boat Building.* 1984. Camden. Internat Marine. 2 vol. ils. dj. T7. $75.00

COMAS, Ester. *Hello Stranger.* 1971. NY. 1st ed. sgn pres. NF/VG+. S9. $45.00

COMBE, William. *Tour of Doctor Syntax.* (1817). London. 3 vol. 9th ed. calf/marbled brd. NF. C2. $600.00

COMFORT, Will Levington. *Son of Power.* nd. Gundy. 1st Canadian ed. VG. P3. $10.00

COMMAGER, Henry Steele. *Blue & the Gray.* (1950). Bobbs Merrill. 2 vol. F. H1. $20.00

COMMAGER, Henry Steele. *Freedom, Loyalty, Dissent.* 1954. Oxford. M11. $35.00

COMMAGER & MORRIS. *Spirit of the Seventy Six.* 1975. Harper Row. bicentennial ed. 8vo. 1348p. F/VG. B11. $15.00

COMMONS, John R. *Trade Unionism & Labor Problems.* 1905. Ginn. F/G. V4. $25.00

COMNEUS, Demetrois. *Precis Historique de la Maison Imperiale des Comnenes...* 1784. Amsterdam. 8vo. 184p. bl wrp. O2. $150.00

COMPARETTI, Andrea. *Riscontri Medici Delle Febbri Larvate Periodiche Perniciose.* 1795. Padua. Nella Stamperia Penada. thick 8vo. recent vellum. G7. $150.00

COMPTON, D.G. *Scudder's Game.* 1988. Kerosina. 1st ed/trade issue. 1/750. F/F. N3. $25.00

COMPTON, D.G. *Windows.* 1979. Berkley Putnam. 1st ed. VG/VG. P3. $13.00

COMPTON, Herbert. *Twentieth-Century Dog.* 1904. London. Grant Richards. 1st ed. 456p. cloth. G. scarce. R2. $75.00

COMPTON, Wilson. *Organization of the Lumber Industry.* 1916. Chicago. Am Lumberman. VG. N2. $25.00

COMROE & CRANE. *Internal Medicine in Dental Practice.* 1939. Phil. 1st rpt. ils. 352p. G7. $20.00

COMSTOCK, J.L. *Elements of Chemistry.* 1850. Pratt Woodford. 32nd ed. 422p. full leather. G+. H1. $18.00

COMSTOCK, John L. *History of the Greek Revolution...* 1829. NY. 8vo. 2 fld pl. 503p. contemporary full calf. O2. $100.00

COMTE, Auguste. *Positive Philosophy of...* 1974. NY. AMS Pr. rpt of 1853 ed. VG. G1. $35.00

CONANT, Susan. *Bloodlines.* 1993. Doubleday. 1st ed. NF/NF. P3. $17.00

CONDON, Richard. *Abandoned Woman.* 1977. Dial. 1st ed. VG/VG. P3. $20.00

CONDON, Richard. *Prizzi's Family.* 1986. Putnam. 1st ed. VG/VG. P3. $18.00

CONDON, Richard. *Prizzi's Honor.* 1982. London. Michael Joseph. 1st Eng ed. NF/dj. S6. $25.00

CONDON, Richard. *Trembling Upon Rome.* 1983. Michael Joseph. 1st ed. F/F. P3. $25.00

CONDON, Richard. *Vertical Smile.* 1971. Dial. 1st ed. VG/VG. P3. $25.00

CONEY, Michael G. *Celestial Steam Locomotive.* nd. Houghton Mifflin. 2nd ed. VG/VG. P3. $15.00

CONEY, Michael G. *Gods of the Greatway.* 1984. Houghton Mifflin. 1st ed. VG/VG. P3. $16.00

CONEY, Michael G. *Hello Summer, Goodbye.* 1975. Gollancz. 1st ed. sgn. VG/VG. P3. $30.00

CONGAR, Yves M.-J. *Mystery of the Temple; or, Manner of God's Presence...* ca 1962. Westminster, MD. Newman. 1st ed. 322p. xl. VG/rpr. W1. $8.00

CONIGER, Simon. *Nature of Man in Theological & Psychological Perspective.* 1962. Harper. 264p. cloth. G1. $22.50

CONKLIN, Groff. *Omnibus of Science Fiction.* 1952. Crown. 1st ed. VG/G. P3. $35.00

CONKLIN, Groff. *Science Fiction Adventures in Mutation.* 1955. Vanguard. 1st ed. VG/VG. P3. $35.00

CONLEY, Robert J. *Dark Way.* 1993. Doubleday. AP. F/wrp. S9. $40.00

CONN, George. *Arabian Horse in America.* 1957. Woodstock. Countryman. 1st ed. VG/G. O3. $30.00

CONN, George. *Arabian Horse in Fact, Fantasy & Fiction.* 1959. NY. Barnes. 1st ed. VG/G. O3. $25.00

CONNEEN, Jane. *Wildflowers Vol I & II.* 1977 & 1981. Borrower Pr. 2 vol. 27x23mm & 20x17mm. 18 ils. gilt leather. B24. $160.00

CONNELL, Evan S. *Anatomy Lesson & Other Stories.* 1957. Viking. 1st ed/author's 1st book. inscr. NF/VG. L3. $250.00

CONNELL, Evan S. *At the Crossroads.* 1965. Simon Schuster. 1st ed. NF/VG. L3. $55.00

CONNELL, Evan S. *Diary of a Rapist.* 1986. Simon Schuster. 1st ed. F/NF. B2. $35.00

CONNELL, Evan S. *Notes From a Bottle Found on the Beach at Carmel.* 1963. NY. Viking. 1st ed. NF/chip. L3. $45.00

CONNELLY, Mark. *Souvenir From Qam.* 1965. Chicago/NY. HRW. 2nd prt. 192p. 8vo. cloth. VG/dj. W1. $12.00

CONNELLY, Michael. *Black Echo.* 1992. Little Brn. 1st ed. sgn. F/F/1st state promo band. T2. $55.00

CONNELLY, Michael. *Black Echo.* 1992. Little Brn. 1st ed. VG/VG. P3. $20.00

CONNELLY, Michael. *Black Ice.* 1993. Little Brn. 1st ed. sgn. F/F. T2. $40.00

CONNELY, Willard. *Sir Richard Steele.* 1934. Scribner. 1st ed. 462p. VG/ragged. M20. $18.00

CONNER, Howard M. *Spearhead.* 1950. WA. 1st ed. 325p. VG. B18. $125.00

CONNER, Walter T. *Christian Doctrine.* 1937. Broadman. 349p. VG. B29. $6.00

CONNER, Walter T. *Epistles of John.* 1957. Broadman. 151p. VG/dj. B29. $4.50

CONNETT, Eugene. *American Sporting Dogs.* 1948. Van Nostrand. 1st ed. lg 8vo. ils/index. rust cloth. F. K1. $100.00

CONNETT, Eugene. *Random Casts.* 1939. Derrydale. ltd sgn ed. 1/1075. VG. B5. $130.00

CONNINGHAM. *Currier & Ives Prints: Ils Checklist.* 1983. np. ils. 320p. F/NF. A4. $45.00

CONNOLLY, James Brendan. *Crested Seas.* 1907. Scribner. ils. 311p. T7. $24.00

CONOVER, David. *Finding Marilyn.* 1981. Grosset Dunlap. VG/VG. P3. $20.00

CONRAD, Jim. *On the Road to Tetlama.* 1991. NY. Walker. 1st ed. 196p. VG/dj. F3. $20.00

CONRAD, Joseph. *Joseph Conrad's Letters to RB Cunninghame Graham.* 1969. Cambridge. 1st ed. F/dj. B24. $50.00

CONRAD, Joseph. *Letters to Richard Curle.* 1928. Crosby Gaige. lg paper ed. 1/850. VG. C4. $125.00

CONRAD, Joseph. *Notes on My Books.* 1921. London. Heinemann. 1st ed. sgn. 1/250. VG. B4. $475.00

CONRAD, Joseph. *One Day More.* 1920. Doubleday Page. 1/377. 68p. quarter parchment/bl brd. NF. H5. $300.00

CONRAD, Joseph. *Secret Agent.* 1923. London. 1st ed. sgn. 1/1000 #d. NF/VG. A11. $485.00

CONRAD, Joseph. *Typhoon.* 1902. NY/London. Putnam. 1st ed (precedes Eng). 1st issue gr cloth. F. B24. $650.00

CONRAD, Joseph. *Works of...* 1938. Doubleday Doran. 21 vol. 8vo. gilt gr cloth. NF. H5. $375.00

CONRAD, Joseph. *Youth & Two Other Stories.* 1903. McClure Phillips. 1st Am ed. NF. B4. $250.00

CONROY, Frank. *Midair.* 1985. Dutton. 1st ed. F/F. B3. $25.00

CONROY, Frank. *Stop-Time.* 1967. Viking. 1st ed/author's 1st book. NF/dj. S9. $125.00

CONROY, Pat. *Boo.* 1983. Verona. McClure. 4th prt. F/F. S9. $75.00

CONROY, Pat. *Great Santini.* 1976. Houghton Mifflin. 1st ed. VG/VG. B5. $50.00

CONROY, Pat. *Great Santini.* 1976. Houghton Mifflin. 1st ed/author's 3rd book. F/F. L3. $150.00

CONROY, Pat. *Lords of Discipline.* 1980. NY. 1st ed. VG/VG. B5. $32.50

CONROY, Pat. *Water Is Wide.* 1972. Houghton Mifflin. 1st ed/author's 2nd book. 306p. red cloth. NF/dj. H5. $500.00

CONSETT, Mathew. *Tour Through Sweden, Swedish-Lapland, Finland & Denmark.* 1789. London. sm folio. 7 engravings/1 woodcut. H4. $450.00

CONSIDINE, Robert. *General Wainwright's Story.* 1946. NY. 1st ed. 314p. VG/chip. A17. $7.50

CONSTANTINE, K.C. *Rocksburg Railroad Murders.* 1972. NY. Saturday Review. 1st ed. F/clip. M15. $175.00

CONSTANTINE, K.C. *Upon Some Midnights Clear.* 1986. London. Hodder Stoughton. 1st Eng ed. NF/dj. S6. $25.00

CONWAY, Moncure Daniel. *Autobiography, Memories & Experiences of...* 1905. Houghton Mifflin. 1 vol only. 4th imp. teg. VG. H1. $8.00

CONWAY, Troy (a few); see Avallone, Mike.

COOK, A.H. *Physics of the Earth & Planets.* 1973. Wiley. 8vo. ils. 316p. VG/dj. K5. $20.00

COOK, Bob. *Disorderly Elements.* 1985. London. Gollancz. 1st ed. F/NF. S6. $20.00

COOK, Gladys Emerson. *Big Book of Cats.* 1954. NY. ils glazed pict brd. VG. M5. $18.00

COOK, Glen. *Tower of Fear.* 1989. Tor. 2nd ed. sgn. F/F. M21. $15.00

COOK, Harold R. *Intro to Christian Missions.* 1954. Moody. 287p. VG/dj. B29. $3.50

COOK, Harold R. *Missionary Life & Work.* 1972. Moody. 382p. VG/dj. B29. $4.50

COOK, Harold. *Decline of the Old Medical Regime in Stuart London.* 1986. Ithaca. 1st ed. 310p. dj. A13. $27.50

COOK, Joan Marble. *In Defense of Homo Sapiens.* 1975. FSG. 222p. cloth. VG/dj. G1. $22.50

COOK, John. *Ninth Annual Exhibition IL State Agricultural Society...* 1861. Springfield. Lanphier. 39p. VG+/wrp. A10. $40.00

COOK, Thomas. *Night Secrets.* 1990. Putnam. ARC/1st ed. w/promo material. F/F. S6. $30.00

COOK, W. Paul. *HP Lovecraft: A Portrait.* 1988. Mirage. 1st ed. VG/wrp. M2. $15.00

COOK-LYNN, Elizabeth. *Power of Horses & Other Stories.* 1990. NY. 1st ed. F/F. A17. $10.00

COOKE, Donald E. *Firebird.* 1939. Chicago. ils. gilt cloth. F. A17. $10.00

COOKE, Elliot D. *All But Me & Thee.* 1946. WA. 1st ed. 215p. G/torn. B18. $25.00

COOKE, John Esten. *Outlines From the Outpost.* 1961. Lakeside. 413p. gilt bl cloth. VG+. A18. $30.00

COOKE, John Esten. *Stonewall Jackson: A Military Biography.* 1866. NY. 1st ed. portrait/maps. 4790p. F. very rare. O8. $95.00

COOKE & COOKE. *Tale of Whoa.* 1939. McKay. ils. VG. M5. $45.00

COOLEY, A. *Handbook Perfumes, Cosmetics, Other Toilet Articles...* 1873. np. 415p. gilt bdg. VG. E5. $65.00

COOLEY, Thomas M. *Comparative Merits of Written & Prescriptive Constitutions.* 1899. Boston. 19p. brd. D3. $25.00

COOLEY, Thomas M. *Treatise on Law of Taxation.* 1886. Chicago. Callaghan. contemporary sheep. G. M11. $175.00

COOLIDGE, Calvin. *Autobiography.* 1929. NY. ltd ed. sgn. as issued. H4. $200.00

COOLIDGE, Dane. *Maverick Makers.* 1931. Dutton. 1st ed. F. A18. $25.00

COOLIDGE, Dane. *Old California Cowboys.* 1939. Dutton. ils. 148p. xl. B19. $10.00

COOLIDGE, Dane. *Wally Laughs-Easy.* 1939. Dutton. 1st ed. F/chip. A18. $40.00

COOLIDGE, Olivia E. *Egyptian Adventures.* 1954. Houghton Mifflin. 1st ed. 209p. VG. W1. $12.00

COOLING. *Era of the Civil War, 1820-1876.* 1974. np. 4to. 599p. VG. A4. $125.00

COOMARASWAMY, A.K. *Hinduism & Buddhism.* ca 1950. Philosophical Lib. 86p. VG/VG. B33. $20.00

COOMARASWAMY, A.K. *Time & Eternity.* 1947. Ascona. Artibus Asiae. 1st ed. 140p. VG/VG. B33. $45.00

COOMBS, Charles I. *Maverick.* 1959. Whitman. 1st ed. F/sans. F4. $18.00

COOMBS, Charles. *Passage to Space...* 1979. Morrow. 8vo. ils. 126p. VG/dj. K5. $8.00

COOMBS, Charles. *Young Infield Rookie.* 1954. Grosset Dunlap. rpt. VG/G. P8. $12.50

COOMBS, Clyde H. *Theory of Data.* 1964. John Wiley. 585p. F/dj. K4. $30.00

COOMBS, David. *Sport & the Countryside in English Paintings...* 1978. Oxford. Phaidon. 1st ed. sm 4to. VG/VG. O3. $65.00

COOMER, Joe. *Flatland Fable.* 1986. Texas Monthly. 1st ed. F/VG+. P8. $15.00

COON, Carleton S. *Races of Europe.* 1939. Macmillan. 652p. G. K4. $30.00

COON, Carleton S. *Seven Caves: Archaeological Explorations in Middle East.* 1957. Knopf. 1st ed. 338p. VG. W1. $18.00

COON, Carleton S. *Seven Caves: Archaeologica! Explorations in Middle East.* 1957. Knopf. 338p. G/dj. K4. $15.00

COONEY, Barbara. *Hattie & the Wild Waves, Story of Brooklyn.* 1990. Viking. 1st ed. ils Barbara Cooney. M/M. C8. $35.00

COONEY, Barbara. *Little Brother & Sister.* 1982. Doubleday. 1st ed. M/M. C8. $60.00

COONEY, Barbara. *Mother Goose in French.* 1964. Crowell. trans Hugh Latham. 44p. VG/VG. A3. $17.50

COONEY, Barbara. *Mother Goose in Spanish.* 1968. Crowell. 2nd prt. trans Alastair Reid/Anthony Kerrigan. VG/VG. A3. $17.50

COONEY, Ellen. *All the Way Home.* 1984. Putnam. 1st ed. rem mk. VG+/F. P8. $17.50

COONTS, Stephen. *Final Flight.* 1988. Doubleday. 1st ed. sgn. F/F. T2. $30.00

COONTS, Stephen. *Flight of the Intruder.* 1986. Annapolis. 1st ed. sgn. NF/clip. B3. $50.00

COONTS, Stephen. *Flight of the Intruder.* 1986. Annapolis. Naval Inst. 1st ed/ author's 1st book. F/F. M15. $45.00

COONTS, Stephen. *Minotaur.* 1989. Doubleday. 1st ed/author's 3rd novel. F/F. T2. $25.00

COONTS, Stephen. *Under Siege.* 1990. Simon Schuster. 1st ed sgn. F/NF. B3. $25.00

COOPER, Astley. *Anatomy & Surgical Treatment of Inguinal...Hernia.* 1804. London. Cox. 11 pl. 60p. rebacked. G7. $1,250.00

COOPER, Astley. *Principles & Practice of Surgery...* 1809-1810. London. folio. 157p. orig full vellum brd. G7. $1,350.00

COOPER, B.B. *Surgical Essays: Result of Clinical Observations.* 1843. London. 4 mc pl. orig brd. G7. $275.00

COOPER, Basil. *From Evil's Pillow.* 1973. Arkham. 1st ed. F/F. M21. $15.00

COOPER, Basil. *House of the Wolf.* 1983. Arkham. 1st ed. F/F. M21. $25.00

COOPER, Basil. *House of the Wolf.* 1983. Arkham. 1st ed. sgn twice/dtd. ils/sgn Stephen Fabian. F/F. F4. $45.00

COOPER, Brian. *Murder of Mary Steers.* 1964. Vanguard. M11. $25.00

COOPER, C.R. *Designs in Scarlet.* 1939. Boston. 3rd prt. 372p. NF. D3. $12.50

COOPER, C.R. *Here's to Crime.* 1937. Boston. 5th prt. 454p. NF. D3. $12.50

COOPER, Douglas. *Work of Graham Sutherland.* 1962. London. Lund Humphries. 2nd prt. tall 4to. orange/gr/blk stp wht brd. NF. F1. $65.00

COOPER, Edmund. *Kronk.* 1971. Putnam. 1st ed. VG/VG. P3. $20.00

COOPER, Edmund. *Tenth Planet.* 1973. Putnam. NF/NF. P3. $13.00

COOPER, Edmund. *Who Needs Men?* 1972. Hodder Stoughton. 1st ed. xl. dj. P3. $7.00

COOPER, Gordon. *Dead Cities & Forgotten Tribes.* 1952. NY. Philosophical Lib. 1st ed. 8vo. 160p. F/F. B11. $20.00

COOPER, Henry S.F. *Search for Life on Mars: Evolution of an Idea.* 1980. HRW. 8vo. 254p. VG/dj. K5. $15.00

COOPER, J.C. *Family.* 1991. Doubleday. 1st ed. sgn. F/F. B3. $35.00

COOPER, J.C. *Homemade Love.* 1987. St Martin. 1st ed. F/NF. B3. $25.00

COOPER, J.W. *Antebellum House of Natchez.* 1970. Natchez. 1st ed. VG/G. B5. $50.00

COOPER, James Fenimore. *American Democrat; or, Hints on Social & Civic Relations...* 1838. NY. Phinney. 1st ed. 12mo. 192p. cloth. M1. $375.00

COOPER, James Fenimore. *Deerslayer.* 1927. Scribner. ils Wyeth. 462p. G. A17. $35.00

COOPER, James Fenimore. *Home As Found.* 1838. Phil. Lea Blanchard. 2 vol. 1st ed. 12mo. cloth. M1. $250.00

COOPER, James Fenimore. *Last of the Mohicans.* 1919. Scribner. 1st ed. VG. C8. $75.00

COOPER, James Fenimore. *Last of the Mohicans: Narrative of 1757.* 1826. Phil. Cary Lea. 1st ed/1st issue. 2 vol. 12mo. w/sgn check dtd 1842. NF. C6. $25,000.00

COOPER, James Fenimore. *Leatherstocking Saga.* 1954. Pantheon. 1st ed. 34-p intro. F. A18. $25.00

COOPER, James Fenimore. *Pioneers; or, Sources of the Susquehanna...* nd. Hurst. VG. B34. $35.00

COOPER, James Fenimore. *Prairie, a Tale, by the Author of The Spy...* 1827. London. Henry Colburn. 3 vol. 1st ed. 12mo. polished calf. very scarce. M1. $350.00

COOPER, James Fenimore. *Prairie: A Tale.* 1831. Carey Lea. 2 vols. later prt. NF. A18. $80.00

COOPER, James Fenimore. *Red Rover, a Tale...in Three Volumes.* 1827. London. Henry Colburn. 3 vol. 1st Eng ed. 12mo. full gr calf. very scarce. M1. $300.00

COOPER, James Fenimore. *Spy: A Tale of the Neutral Ground...* 1822. London. Whittaker. 3 vol. 12mo. contemporary polished calf. F. rare. M1. $375.00

COOPER, Jeff (Jefferson); see Fox, Gardner F.

COOPER, John Cobb. *Explorations in Aerospace Law...* 1968. Montreal. McGill. 8vo. 480p. VG/dj. K5. $45.00

COOPER, John R. *College League Mystery.* 1953. Garden City. Mel Martin Series. G. P8. $8.00

COOPER, John R. *Fighting Shortstop.* 1953. Books Inc. rpt. Mel Martin Series. VG. P8. $17.50

COOPER, John R. *First Base Jinx.* nd. Books Inc. xl. G. P3. $4.00

COOPER, John R. *Southpaw's Secret.* 1947. Cupples Leon. Mel Martin #2. 212p. VG/dj. M20. $25.00

COOPER, John R. *Southpaw's Secret.* 1952. Garden City. VG. P3. $8.00

COOPER, Kent. *Right To Know: Exposition of the Evils News Suppression...* 1956. FSC. 1st ed. 335p. NF. M10. $7.50

COOPER, Myrtle. *From Tent Town to City...* 1981. np. sgn. ils/photos/maps. VG. B34. $25.00

COOPER, Samuel. *Memorial to Cyrus Cooper & Bertha A Cooper.* 1948. Moorestown, NJ. Cooper. 12mo. 202p. G+. V3. $14.50

COOPER, Will. *Death Has a Thousand Doors.* 1976. Bobbs Merrill. 1st ed. VG/VG. P3. $15.00

COOPER. *Bibliography & Notes on Works of Lascelles Abercrombie.* 1969. np. 166p. F/NF. A4. $25.00

COOVER, Robert. *Universal Baseball Association.* 1968. Random. 1st ed. VG+/G+. P8. $80.00

COPE, Thomas P. *Phil Merchant: Diary of Thomas P Cope, 1800-1851.* 1978. South Bend, IN. Gateway. 8vo. 628p. VG/VG. V3. $18.00

COPE, Zachary. *Royal College of Surgeons of England: A History.* 1959. London. 1st ed. 360p. A13. $60.00

COPE, Zachary. *Treatment of Acute Abdomen Operative & Post-Operative.* 1928. London. 2nd ed. 244p. G7. $30.00

COPELAND, Francis. *Land Between: The Middle East.* 1958. Abelard-Schuman. 8vo. ils/maps. xl. VG/dj. W1. $8.00

COPELAND, Paul W. *Land & People of Libya.* 1967. Lippincott. 1st ed. ils. xl. G/dj. W1. $10.00

COPELAND, R.M. *Country Life: A Handbook of Agriculture & Landscape...* 1859. Boston. 1st ed. ils. 813p. VG. H7. $120.00

COPELAND & MACMASTER. *Five George Masons: Portraits of Planters of VA & MD.* 1975. Charlottesville. 1st ed. 8vo. 341p. VG/VG. B11. $35.00

COPLAN, M.F. *Pink Lemonade.* 1945. NY. 1st ed. ils Beverly Kelley. 120p. cloth. VG. A17. $25.00

COPP & WENDELL. *Pornogrphy & Censorship.* 1983. Prometheus. 414p. cloth. G1. $28.50

COPPARD, A.E. *Collected Tales of AE Coppard.* nd. BOMC. VG/VG. P3. $10.00

COPPARD, A.E. *Fearful Pleasures.* 1946. Arkham. 1st ed. NF/NF. M2. $100.00

COPPARD, A.E. *Fearful Pleasures.* 1946. Arkham. 1st ed. 301p. VG/dj. M20. $75.00

COPPEL, Alfred. *Dragon.* 1977. HBJ. 1st ed. VG/VG. P3. $15.00

COPPEL, Alfred. *Gate of Hell.* 1967. HBJ. 1st ed. VG/VG. P3. $13.00

COPPEL, Alfred. *Show Me a Hero.* 1987. HBJ. 1st ed. F/F. P3. $17.00

COPPEL, Alfred. *Thirty-Four East.* 1976. HBJ. 1st ed. 343p. F/dj. W1. $10.00

COPPENS. *Memoris of an Erotic Bookseller...* 1969. London. 1st ed. VG/VG. A4. $65.00

COPPER, Basil. *And Afterward, the Dark.* 1977. Arkham. 1st ed. sgn. F/dj. F4. $30.00

COPPER, Basil. *From Evil's Pillow.* 1973. Arkham. 1st ed. sgn. F/F. F4. $30.00

COPPER, Basil. *From Evil's Pillow.* 1973. Arkham. 1st ed. 1/3468. F/NF. T2. $25.00

COPPER, Basil. *House of the Wolf.* 1983. Arkham. 1st ed. 1/3578. F/F. T2. $18.00

COPWAY, George. *Life, Letters & Speeches of Kah-Ge-Ga-Gah-Bowh...* 1850. NY. Benedict. 1st ed. 12mo. 224p. cloth. M1. $150.00

CORALLO, Gino. *La Pedagogia di Giovanni Dewey.* 1950. Torino. Societa Editrice Internazionale. G1. $40.00

CORBEN, Richard. *Bloodstar.* 1976. Morning Star. 1st ed. NF/NF. P3. $30.00

CORBETT, James. *Death Pool.* 1936. Herbert Jenkins. 1st ed. VG/VG. P3. $75.00

CORBETT, Jim. *Man Eaters of Jumaon.* 1955. Oxford. 1st ed. VG/VG. B5. $55.00

CORBETT, Jim. *Temple Tigers & More Man Eaters of Kumaon.* 1955. Oxford. VG/VG. B5. $35.00

CORBIN, Henry. *Creative Imagination in Sufism of Ibn 'Arabi...* 1969. Princeton. 1st ed. 8vo. 406p. VG. W1. $70.00

CORBITT & DE CARBIA. *Mexico Through My Kitchen Window.* 1961. Houghton Mifflin. 1st ed. 8vo. 236p. VG/G. B11. $20.00

CORBY, Father. *Memoirs of Chaplain Life.* 1893. Chicago. 1st ed. pres. VG. B5. $125.00

CORCOS, Loris. *Jonathan Bangs Said Nooo.* 1946. Lee Shepard. 1st ed. ils. VG/dj. P2. $28.00

CORELLI, Marie. *Ardath.* nd. AL Burt. G. P3. $5.00

CORELLI, Marie. *Barabbas.* 1896. Phil. 1st ed. silver stp cloth. VG. A17. $10.00

CORELLI, Marie. *Master-Christian.* nd. Briggs. G+. P3. $25.00

COREY, Deborah Joy. *Losing Eddie.* 1994. Algonquin. 1st ed/author's 1st novel. F/F. B3. $20.00

COREY, Paul. *Little Jeep.* Sept 1946. Cleveland. World. 1st ed. VG/G+. C8. $25.00

CORHAM, B.W. *Camp Meeting Manual, a Practical Book...* 1854. Boston. HV Degen. 1st ed. ils. cloth. M1. $200.00

CORIO, Ann. *This Was Burlesque.* 1968. NY. 1st ed. VG/VG. B5. $35.00

CORK, Barry. *Laid Dead.* 1990. London. Collins. 1st ed. F/F. S6. $25.00

CORKILL, Louis. *Fish Lane.* 1951. Bobbs Merrill. 1st ed. VG/VG. P3. $10.00

CORLE, Edwin. *Operations Santa Fe.* 1948. DSP. ils/bibliography/index. 263p. NF/NF. B19. $100.00

CORLEY & WILLMES. *Wings of Eagles.* ca 1941. Milwaukee. Bruce. 206p. H10. $17.50

CORLISS, William R. *Handbook of Unusual Natural Phenomena.* 1977. Glen Arm, MD. 8vo. 542p. xl. K5. $42.00

CORMAN, Cid. *TU: Poems.* 1983. Toothpaste Pr. ltd sgn ed. 1/500. VG+/wrp. A1. $40.00

CORMAN, Roger. *How I Made a Hundred Movies in Hollywood.* 1990. Random. 1st ed. VG/VG. P3. $20.00

CORMIER & EATON. *William J Reuther.* 1970. Prentice Hall. photos. F/G. V4. $12.50

CORNE, M.E. *Magnet for Murder.* 1939. MS Mill. xl. G. P3. $12.00

CORNELIUS, Mrs. *Young Hosekeeper's Friend.* 1863. Boston. 254p. orig blk cloth/rebacked. VG. B14. $55.00

CORNELL, Gwenda. *Pacific Odyssey.* 1985. London. Adlard Coles. 1st ed. VG/dj. N2. $7.50

CORNELL, Ralph D. *Conspicuous California Plants...* 1938. San Pasqual. 1/1500. ils TE Williams. 192p. orange/blk cloth. dj. K1. $60.00

CORNELL & HAYES. *Man & Cosmos.* 1975. Norton. 8vo. 191p. VG/dj. K5. $25.00

CORNER, George W. *Anatomy.* 1930. NY. 1st ed. 82p. A13. $60.00

CORNER, George W. *Two Centuries of Medicine.* nd. Phil. Lippincott. ils. 363p. VG/dj. G7. $45.00

CORNFELD, Gaalyahu. *Adam to Daniel: Ils Guide to Old Testament...* 1961. Macmillan. 1st prt. 559p. VG/dj. W1. $9.00

CORNICK, H.F. *Dock & Harbour Engineering. Design of Docks.* 1958. Griffin. 316p. VG/dj. M20. $35.00

CORNWELL, Anita. *Girls of Summer.* 1989. New Seed. 1st ed. M. P8. $14.50

CORNWELL, Bernard. *Crackdown.* 1990. Harper. ARC/1st ed. RS. F/F. S6. $25.00

CORNWELL, Bernard. *Crackdown.* 1990. Michael Joseph. 1st ed. NF/NF. P3. $20.00

CORNWELL, Patricia. *All That Remains.* 1992. London. Little Brn. 1st ed (prededes Am ed). sgn. F/F. M15. $50.00

CORNWELL, Patricia. *All That Remains.* 1992. Scribner. 1st ed. F/F. O4. $20.00

CORNWELL, Patricia. *Body Farm.* 1994. Scribner. ARC. sgn. F/pict wrp. B3. $45.00

CORNWELL, Patricia. *Body of Evidence.* nd. BC. VG/VG. P3. $10.00

CORNWELL, Patricia. *Body of Evidence.* 1991. Scribner. 1st ed. F/F. O4. $110.00

CORNWELL, Patricia. *Body of Evidence.* 1991. Scribner. 1st ed. sgn. F/F. L3. $150.00

CORNWELL, Patricia. *Cruel & Unusual.* 1993. Scribner. 1st ed. F/F. O4. $30.00

CORRELL & CORRELL. *Aquatic & Wetland Plants of Southwestern United States.* 1972. WA, DC. orig EPA ed. ils. 1777p. xl. VG+. B26. $115.00

CORRIGAN, Douglas. *That's My Story.* 1938. Dutton. 1st ed. ils. 221p. VG. B18. $22.50

CORRIGAN, Douglas. *That's My Story.* 1938. Dutton. 1st ed. sgn. G. B5. $42.50

CORRIGAN, Douglas. *That's My Story.* 1938. Dutton. 1st ed. sgn. 221p. VG/dj. M20. $110.00

CORRINGTON & CORRINGTON. *Civil Death.* 1987. Viking. 1st ed. F/F. S6. $22.50

CORSARO, Frank. *Love for Three Oranges, Glynbourne Version.* 1984. Farrar Straus. 1st Am ed. F/F. C8. $60.00

CORTAZAR, Julio. *End of the Game & Other Stories.* 1967. Pantheon. 1st Am ed. F/F. B4. $250.00

CORTAZAR, Julio. *End of the Game & Other Stories.* 1967. Pantheon. 1st Am ed. F/NF. L3. $200.00

CORTAZAR, Julio. *62: A Model Kit.* 1972. Pantheon. 1st ed. F/NF. B2. $40.00

CORTES, Jeronimo. *Fisonomia, y Varios Secretos de Naturaleza...* 1664. Madrid. Domingo Morras. 8vo. contemporary vellum. K1. $750.00

CORVO, Max. *OSS in Italy 1942-1945.* 1990. NY. Praeger. 1st ed. biblio/index. 324p. M/M. A17. $9.50

CORWIN, Eleanor. *Benjie Engie.* 1950. Rand McNally Jr Elf Book 8008. K2. $5.00

CORY, David. *Iceberg Express.* 1922. NY. 1st ed. VG/VG. B5. $25.00

CORY, Desmond. *Bennett.* 1977. Crime Club. 1st ed. VG/VG. P3. $15.00

CORY, Desmond. *Feramontov.* 1966. Muller. VG. P3. $8.00

CORY, Desmond. *Pilgrim at the Gate.* 1958. Washburn. G+. P3. $12.00

CORY, F.Y. *Fairy Alphabet of FY Cory.* 1991. Am/World Geographic. 1st ed. 4to. purple brd. M/dj. D6. $18.00

CORY, J. Campbell. *Cartoonist's Art.* 1912. Chicago. Tumbo. 4to. VG/ils wrp. F1. $150.00

COSELL, Howard. *Cosell.* 1973. Playboy. 1st ed. 390p. F/F. H1. $10.00

COSIO VILLEGAS, Daniel. *Historia Moderna de Mexico.* ca 1956. Mexico. Hermes. 101p. dj. F3. $35.00

COSSLETT, V. *Bibliography of Electron Microscopy.* 1950. London. 1st ed. 350p. A13. $40.00

COSTA, Peter. *Questions & Answers: Conversation With Harvard Scholars.* 1991. Cambridge. 1st ed. 262p. red cloth. F. B14. $30.00

COSTAIN, Thomas B. *Below the Salt.* 1957. Doubleday. 1st ed. VG/VG. P3. $35.00

COSTAIN, Thomas B. *High Towers.* 1949. Doubleday. 1st ed. VG/G. P3. $15.00

COSTAIN, Thomas B. *Silver Chalice.* 1952. Doubleday. pres. 533p. VG. H1. $18.00

COSTAIN, Thomas B. *Tontine.* 1955. Doubleday. 2 vol. 1st ed. VG/VG. P3. $35.00

COSTANZO & SAJEVA. *Succulents: Ils Dictionary.* 1994. Portland. 239p. M/dj. B26. $40.00

COSTELLO & HUGHES. *Jutland 1916.* 1976. HRW. 1st ed. 230p. VG/dj. M20. $20.00

COTHAM, Perry C. *Politics, Americanism & Christianity.* 1973. Baker. 335p. VG/dj. B29. $5.00

COTLOW, Lewis. *In Search of the Primitive.* 1966. Little Brn. 1st ed. 454p. VG. F3. $15.00

COTT, Nancy F. *Woman Making History: Mary Ritter Beard Through Letters.* 1991. Yale. 1st ed. 8vo. 378p. VG/VG. V3. $16.00

COTTER, Charles H. *Complete Nautical Astonomer.* 1969. NY. Elsevier. 8vo. 336p. xl. VG/dj. K5. $15.00

COTTESLOE, Gloria. *Story of the Battersea Dog's Home.* 1979. David Charles. 1st ed. ils. 175p. cloth. M/M. R2. $30.00

COTTON, Bob. *New Guide to Graphic Design.* ca 1990. Chartwell. 192p. F/F. P4. $30.00

COTTON, Nathaniel. *Visions in Verse for Entertainment & Instruction...* 1751. London. Dodsley. apparent 1st ed. contemporary leather. H10. $75.00

COTTRELL, Leonard. *Bull of Minos.* 1953. London. Evans. 1st ed. 228p. NF/dj. W1. $12.00

COTTRELL, Leonard. *Life Under the Pharaohs.* 1960. HRW. 1st ed. 8vo. ils. 255p. xl. G/dj. W1. $15.00

COTTRELL, Leonard. *Lost Pharaohs: Romance of Egyptian Archaeology.* 1951. London. Evans. 2nd prt. 33 pl. 256p. VG. W1. $16.00

COTTRELL, Leonard. *Realms of Gold.* 1963. NY Graphic Soc. 1st ed. 32 pl/2 maps. 278p. VG/torn. W1. $20.00

COUDERC, Paul. *Expansion of the Universe.* 1952. London. Faber. ils. 231p. G/dj. K5. $25.00

COUHAT, Jean Labayle. *Combat Fleets of the World 1984-85...* 1984. Annapolis. ils/index. VG/torn. B18. $45.00

COULSON, John. *Saints: Concise Biographical Dictionary.* 1958. Hawthorn. ils/pl. 496p. H10. $22.00

COULTER, M.C. *Story of the Plant Kingdom.* 1959 (1935). Chicago. revised ed. edit HJ Dittmer. cloth. VG/dj. B26. $15.00

COULTER. *Civil War & Readjustment in Kentucky.* 1926. np. later prt. 468p. NF. E5. $35.00

COULTER. *Travels in the Confederate States: A Bibliography.* 1980. np. 305p. F. A4. $85.00

COUNSELMAN, Mary Elizabeth. *Half in Shadow.* 1978. Arkham. 1st ed. 1/4288. F/F. T2. $10.00

COUPLAND, Douglas. *Shampoo Planet.* 1992. Pocket. 1st ed. rem mk. NF/NF. A14. $30.00

COURLANDER, H. *Negro Folk Music.* 1963. NY. 1st ed. ils. 324p. VG/dj. B5. $35.00

COURTIER, S.H. *Ligny's Lake.* 1971. Simon Schuster. 1st Am ed. VG+/dj. S6. $25.00

COURTOT, Claude. *Intro a la Lecture de Benjamin Peret.* 1965. Paris. Le Terrain Vague. 1st ed. F/wrp. B2. $75.00

COURVILLE, Cyril B. *Cerebral Palsy.* 1954. San Lucas. 80p. G7. $75.00

COUSENS, Marjorie. *Griffons Bruxellois.* 1960. London. Foyle. 1st ed. ils. 106p. glossy brd. VG. scarce. R2. $35.00

COUSIN, Victor. *Lestures on True, Beautiful & Good.* 1854. Appleton. 1st Eng-language ed. 391p. rebound lib buckram. VG. G1. $40.00

COUTEAU, Paul. *Observing Visual Double Stars.* 1981. MIT. 8vo. 256p. VG/dj. K5. $25.00

COVARRUBIAS, Miguel. *Indian Art Mexico.* 1957. NY. 1st ed. VG/VG. B5. $125.00

COVELLO & YOSHIMURA. *Japanese Art of Stone Appreciation: Suiseki & Its Uses...* 1984. Rutland. Tuttle. 1st ed. VG/clip. N2. $12.50

COVERT, John. *Werner Co.* 1894. Cleveland. unp. VG/wrp. B18. $37.50

COVIAN Y JUNCO, Victor. *El Tratado de Paz de Versailles y el Derecho Los Vencidos.* 1921. Madrid. 151p. VG/wrp. D3. $25.00

COVILLE, Bruce. *Jennifer Murdley's Toad.* 1992. HBJ. 1st ed. F/F. P3. $17.00

COVILLE & MACDOUGAL. *Desert Botanical Laboratory of Carnegie Institution.* 1903. WA, DC. photos/maps. 58p. brd/orig wrp bdg in. B26. $45.00

COVINGTON, Michael. *Astrophotography for the Amateur.* 1986 (1985). Cambridge. 2nd prt. VG/VG. K5. $22.00

COWAN, Sam K. *Sergeant York.* nd. Grosset Dunlap. VG/VG. P3. $20.00

COWAN. *Bibliography of History of CA, 1510-1930.* 1964. np. 4 vol in 1. 926p. VG. A4. $255.00

COWARD, Noel. *Future Indefinite.* 1954. London. Heinemann. 1st ed. 336p. gilt violet cloth. G. M7. $16.00

COWARD, Noel. *Middle East Diary.* 1944. Garden City. 1st ed. 155p. VG/torn. B18. $19.50

COWARD, Noel. *Noel Coward Song Book.* 1953. London. 1st ed. sgn pres. 4to. 312p. aeg. purple goatskin. F/box. H5. $1,250.00

COWARD, Noel. *Pomp & Circumstance.* 1960. Great Britain. VG. C4. $35.00

COWARD, Noel. *Spangled Unicorn.* 1982. Frisch. 1st prt thus. 101 p. VG/VG. A17. $10.00

COWDRY, E.V. *Arteriosclerosis: Survey of the Problem.* 1933. NY. 1st ed. 617p. A13. $150.00

COWHIG, Jerry. *Herbs & Other Medicinal Plants.* 1972. Crescent. ils. 64p. F. M10. $7.50

COWLES, Raymond B. *Zulu Journal.* 1959. CA U. 1st ed. 267p. VG/dj. A18. $25.00

COWLEY, Malcom. *Second Flowering.* 1973. NY. 1st ed. sgn. F/F. A11. $45.00

COWLEY, Stewart. *Spacecraft 2000 to 2100 AD.* 1978. Chartwell. F/F. P3. $7.00

COWPER, Richard. *Clone.* 1973. Doubleday. 1st ed. F/F. P3. $20.00

COWPER, Richard. *Tithonian Factor.* 1984. Gollancz. 1st ed. F/F. P3. $25.00

COWPER, William. *Jean Gilpin, L'Histoire Divertissante de Promenade Cheval.* 1925. Stokes. 1st ed. ils Caldecott. 79p. NF/G+. D6. $75.00

COX, Arthur. *Optics: Technique Definition.* 1961 (1943). London. Focal. 12th ed. 400p. blk cloth. G. K5. $20.00

COX, Dorothy Davis. *Karl Anderson, Am Artist.* 1981. Winesburg. 93p. NF. M20. $15.00

COX, George G. *Lindbergh: An Am Epic.* 1975. Golden Quill. 64p. VG/dj. B18. $9.50

COX, George William. *Mythology of the Aryan Nations.* 1870. London. 2 vol. 1st ed. 8vo. bl cloth. VG. C6. $125.00

COX, George. *Black Gowns & Red Coats; or, Oxford in 1834...* 1834. London. Ridgway. 6 parts in 1. contemporary red calf/marbled brd. K1. $125.00

COX, Harding. *Dogs: Part V. Bloodhounds, Dachshunds, Borzoi.* 1907. London. Fawcett. 1st ed. tipped-in pl/Maud Earl. wrp. rare. R2. $225.00

COX, J.H. *Folk Songs of the South.* 1925. Cambridge. 1st ed. ils/index/fld map. 545p. VG. B5. $60.00

COX, James. *My Native Land.* 1895. St Louis. ils. 400p. F. O8. $18.50

COX, LaWanda. *Lincoln & Blk Freedom.* 1981. SC U. 1st ed. 254p. VG. M10. $16.50

COX, Nicholas. *Gentleman's Recreation: In Four Parts.* 1706. London. Collins. 5th ed. 4 fld pl. 18th-C polished calf/rebacked. K1. $450.00

COX, Palmer. *Queer People With Wings & Stings & Their Kweeker Kapers.* 1888. Hubbard. G. M20. $50.00

COX, Palmer. *Queer Stories About Queer Animals, Told in Rhymes & Jingles.* ca 1905. Nat Pub. 8vo. ils. 48p. red/yel stp gr cloth. B24. $135.00

COX, Samuel Hanson. *Quakerism Not Christianity.* 1833. NY. D Fanshaw. 1st ed. 8vo. 686p. modern lib bdg. xl. VG. V3. $45.00

COX, Warren E. *Chinese Ivory Sculputure.* 1966. Bonanza. folio. ils/photos. 118 p. VG/VG. A17. $20.00

COX, William R. *Address on Life & Character of Major-Gen Stephen D Ramseur.* 1891. Raleigh. Uzzell. 1st ed. 8vo. 54p. rebacked. xl. C6. $175.00

COX, William R. *Big League Sandlotters.* 1971. Dodd Mead. 1st ed. F/VG. P8. $25.00

COX & GILBERT. *Oxford Book of English Ghost Stories.* 1986. Oxford. F/F. P3. $20.00

COXE, George Harmon. *Butcher, Baker, Murder-Maker.* 1954. Knopf. 1st ed. VG. P3. $25.00

COXE, George Harmon. *Fenner.* 1971. Knopf. 1st ed. NF/NF. P3. $15.00

COXE, George Harmon. *Groom Lay Dead.* 1947. Triangle. VG/VG. P3. $10.00

COXE, George Harmon. *Murder in Havana.* 1943. Knopf. 1st ed. VG. P3. $20.00

COXE, George Harmon. *One Minute Past Eight.* 1957. Knopf. 1st ed. NF/NF. P3. $25.00

COXE, George Harmon. *Silent Witness.* 1973. Knopf. 1st ed. VG/VG. P3. $20.00

COXE, John Redman. *Writings of Hippocrates & Galen...* 1846. Phil. Lindsay Blakiston. 682p. orig full sehhp. G. G7. $195.00

COXE, Richard S. *New Critical Pronouncing Dictionary of Eng Language...* 1813. Burlington, NJ. Allinson. 1st ed. thick 8vo. full contemporary sheep. G. M1. $250.00

COYLE, Harold. *Bright Star.* 1990. Simon Schuster. 1st ed. F/F. P3. $20.00

COYLE, Kathleen. *There Is a Door.* 1931. Paris. ltd ed. sgn. 1/525. teg. linen/brd. K1. $45.00

COYSH. *Collecting Bookmarkers.* 1974. np. ils. 96p. F/NF. A4. $125.00

COZZENS, Frederic S. *Father Tom & the Pope; or, A Night in the Vatican.* 1867. NY. Simpson. 1st ed. pres. brn cloth. M1. $200.00

COZZENS, Frederic S. *Sparrowgrass Papers; or, Living in the Country.* 1856. NY. Derby Jackson. 1st ed/1st state. 328p. gilt brn cloth. G. M20. $30.00

COZZENS, James Gould. *Castaway.* 1934. Random. blk cloth. VG/dj. Q1. $150.00

COZZENS, James Gould. *Just & the Unjust.* 1942. Harcourt Brace. 1st ed. VG/VG. B4. $50.00

COZZENS, James Gould. *Last Adam.* 1933. Harcourt Brace. 1st ed. xl. VG. P3. $10.00

CRABBE, George. *Borough: A Poem, in Twenty-Four Letters.* 1810. Phil. 12mo. 330p. full contemporary tree calf/leather label. M1. $150.00

CRACE, Jim. *Arcadia.* 1992. London. Cape. 1st ed. F/F. B3. $15.00

CRACE, Jim. *Continent.* 1986. London. Heinemann. 1st ed. inscr/sgn. F/F. B2. $100.00

CRACE, Jim. *Continent.* 1986. London. Heinemann. 1st ed/author's 1st book. F/F. S9. $40.00

CRADOCK, H.C. *Josephine Is Busy.* nd. Dodge. ils Honor C Appleton. 63p. VG. A3. $60.00

CRAIG, Alisa. *Grub-and-Stakers Pinch a Poke.* nd. BC. VG/VG. P3. $8.00

CRAIG, Alisa. *Grub-and-Stakers Quilt a Bee.* 1985. Doubleday. 1st ed. sgn. F/F. S6. $35.00

CRAIG, Archibald. *Golden Age.* 1956. Rindge, NH. Smith. 8vo. 140p. VG/VG. V3. $10.00

CRAIG, David Irvin. *Hist of Development of Presbyterian Church in NC.* ca 1907. Richmond, VA. Whittet Shepperson. 1st ed. cloth. VG. M8. $75.00

CRAIG, David. *Double Take.* 1972. Stein Day. 1st ed. VG/VG. P3. $15.00

CRAIG, Edward Gordon. *Woodcuts & Some Words.* 1925. Sm Maynard. 8vo. ils. brn bdg. NF. F1. $50.00

CRAIG, J. *Judging Livestock.* 1906. np. 200p. VG. E5. $35.00

CRAIG, John. *Chappie & Me.* 1979. Dodd Mead. 1st ed. F/VG. P8. $45.00

CRAIG, Patricia. *Oxford Book of English Detective Stories.* 1990. Oxford U. 1st ed. F/F. P3. $25.00

CRAIG, Richard A. *Upper Atmosphere.* 1965. Academic. 8vo. 509p. VG/dj. K5. $18.00

CRAIG. *Irish Bookbindings.* 1976. np. unp. F. A4. $20.00

CRAIGHEAD, Frank. *Track of the Grizzly.* 1979. Sierra Club. VG/dj. B34. $20.00

CRAIGIE, David. *Voyage of the Luna-1.* nd. Cadmus. lib bdg. xl. VG. P3. $8.00

CRAIS, Robert. *Monkey's Raincoat.* 1989. London. Piatkus. 1st hc ed. F/F. M15. $45.00

CRAM, Mildred. *Promise.* 1949. Knopf. 1st ed. VG/VG. P3. $30.00

CRAM, Ralph Adams. *Sins of the Fathers.* 1919. Boston. Marshall. brd. VG. N2. $17.50

CRAMER, John. *Twistor.* 1989. Morrow. 1st ed. F/F. P3. $19.00

CRAMER, Rie. *Old Songs in French & English.* 1923. Penn. 1st ed. ils. 63p. VG. P2. $75.00

CRAMER & CRAMER. *Susquehanna From NY to the Chesapeake.* 1964. Champaign. 1st ed. Rivers of the World Series. VG/VG. B5. $65.00

CRAMPTON, C. Gregory. *Land of Living Rock.* 1972. Knopf. 1st ed. ils/notes/index. 275p. F/NF. B19. $40.00

CRAMPTON, C. Gregory. *Standing Up Country: Canyon Lands of UT & AZ.* 1964. Knopf. 1st ed. ils/notes/index. 191p. F/NF. B19. $75.00

CRANDALL, Allen. *Fisher of the Antelope Hills.* 1949. Crandall. 1st ltd ed. 1/100. sc. 39p. F. A18. $100.00

CRANE, Frances. *Cinnamon Murder.* 1946. Dectective BC. VG. P3. $10.00

CRANE, Frances. *Murder in Bright Red.* 1953. Random. 1st ed. VG/VG. P3. $45.00

CRANE, Joan. *Willa Cather: A Bibliography.* 1982. Lincoln, NE. 1st ed. F/F. B2. $40.00

CRANE, Robert. *Hero's Walk.* 1954. Ballantine. F/F. P3. $35.00

CRANE, Roy. *Complete Wash Tubbs & Captain Easy.* 1987-1992. Flying Buttress. 18 vol. pb. VG. M17. $50.00

CRANE, Stephen. *Battle in Greece. Decorated by Valenti Angelo.* 1936. Mt Vernon. Peter Pauper. tall 8vo. 1/425. 30p. purple brd. slipcase. O2. $75.00

CRANE, Stephen. *Black Riders & Other Lines.* 1895. Boston. 1st ed. 12mo. F/quarter clamshell case. C2. $1,500.00

CRANE, Stephen. *Lost Poem.* 1932. Harvard. 1st ed. sgn Harvey Taylor. 1/100. F. rare. B4. $85.00

CRANE, Stephen. *Monster.* 1899. Harper. 1st ed. ils Peter Newell. VG. Q1. $200.00

CRANE, Stephen. *Open Boat.* 1898. Doubleday McClure. 1st ed. NF. B4. $375.00

CRANE, Stephen. *Pictures of War.* 1898. Heinemann. 1st ed thus. VG. Q1. $250.00

CRANE, Stephen. *Red Badge of Courage.* 1896. London. Heinemann. 1st Eng ed. gr cloth brd. VG. Q1. $250.00

CRANE, Stephen. *Red Badge of Courage.* 1944. LEC. 1/1000. ils/sgn JS Curry. pict leather. F/VG case. B4. $250.00

CRANE, Stephen. *War Is Kind.* 1899. Stokes. ils Will Bradley. blk stp gray brd. F. H4. $1,000.00

CRANE, Stephen. *War Is Kind.* 1899. Stokes. 1st ed. 8vo. 96p. NF. C6. $900.00

CRANE, Stephen. *Whilomville Stories.* 1900. Harper. 1st ed. 8vo. 198p. VG. H5. $175.00

CRANE, Walter. *Baby's Bouquet.* nd. London. Routledge. possible 1st ed. pict paper brd. VG+. C8. $200.00

CRANE, Walter. *Baby's Bouquet.* nd. London. Warne. obl 8vo. pict brd. VG+. M5. $85.00

CRANE, Walter. *Baby's Own Aesop.* 1887 (1886). London. Routledge. pict cloth. VG+. C8. $150.00

CRANE, Walter. *Bluebeard's Picture Book.* ca 1900. Bodley Head. NF/VG+. P2. $100.00

CRANE, Walter. *Legends for Lionel, in Pen & Pencil.* 1887. London. Cassell. 1st ed. pict paper brd. VG. C8. $250.00

CRANE, Walter. *Mr Michael Mouse Unfolds His Tale.* 1956. Yale. 1st ltd ed. 1/300. 8vo. gr cloth. F/dj/case. D6. $80.00

CRANEFIELD, Paul. *Science & Empire: East Coast Fever in Rhodesia & Transvaal.* 1991. Cambridge. 1st ed. 385p. A13. $35.00

CRAPANZANO, Vincent. *Fifth World of Forster Bennett: Portrait of a Navaho.* 1972. Viking. 1st ed. 8vo. 245p. F/F. B11. $25.00

CRAPSEY, Adelaide. *Verse.* 1915. Manas. 1st/posthumous ed. cloth. NF. V1. $70.00

CRAVEN, Arthur. *Borzoi As I Know It, With Hints for All...* 1930. Manchester. 1st ed. ils. 80p. wrp. very scarce. R2. $200.00

CRAVEN, Elizabeth. *Journey Through the Crimea to Constantinople...* 1800. Vienna. sm 8vo. 463p. full contemporary calf. O2. $75.00

CRAVEN, Thomas. *Treasury of American Prints.* 1939. Simon Schuster. 4to. sbdg. blk cloth/bl brd. F/G dj/case. F1. $50.00

CRAWFORD, F. Marion. *Corleone.* 1897. NY. 2 vol. 1st ed. F/rare chip djs. A15. $175.00

CRAWFORD, F. Marion. *Little City of Hope.* 1907. Macmillan. VG. P3. $10.00

CRAWFORD, F. Marion. *White Sister.* nd. Grosset Dunlap. photoplay ed. G+. P3. $10.00

CRAWFORD, J. Marshall. *Mosby & His Men: Record of Renowned Partisan Ranger...* 1867. NY. Carleton. 1st ed. 8vo. 375p. gr cloth. VG. C6. $350.00

CRAWFORD, Lewis F. *Rekindling Campfires.* 1926. Bismarck, ND. 1st ed. 324p. xl. VG. D3. $45.00

CRAWLEY, Rayburn. *Valley of Creeping Men.* 1930. Harper. 1st ed. VG. P3. $35.00

CREASEY, John. *Alibi.* 1971. Scribner. 1st ed. VG/VG. P3. $15.00

CREASEY, John. *As Merry As Hell.* 1973. Hodder Stoughton. 1st ed. VG/VG. P3. $18.00

CREASEY, John. *Baron & the Stolen Legacy.* 1967. Scribner. 1st ed. F/F. P3. $15.00

CREASEY, John. *Baron on Board.* 1968. Walker. 1st ed. F/F. P3. $15.00

CREASEY, John. *Call for the Baron.* 1976. Walker. 1st ed. VG/G. P3. $15.00

CREASEY, John. *Crime-Haters.* nd. BC. VG/VG. P3. $8.00

CREASEY, John. *Day of Fear.* 1978. HRW. 1st ed. VG/VG. P3. $15.00

CREASEY, John. *Department of Death.* 1949. Evans. 2nd ed. VG/G. P3. $20.00

CREASEY, John. *Dissemblers.* 1967. Scribner. NF/NF. P3. $15.00

CREASEY, John. *Famine.* 1968. Walker. 1st ed. F/F. P3. $15.00

CREASEY, John. *Gallows Are Waiting.* 1973. McKay. 1st ed. VG/VG. P3. $20.00

CREASEY, John. *Gideon's Drive.* 1976. Harper Row. 1st ed. VG/VG. P3. $25.00

CREASEY, John. *Gideon's Sport.* 1970. Harper Row. 1st ed. VG/VG. P3. $30.00

CREASEY, John. *Gideon's Staff.* nd. BC. VG/VG. P3. $8.00

CREASEY, John. *Hang the Little Man.* 1964. Scribner. 1st ed. VG/VG. P3. $15.00

CREASEY, John. *I Am the Withered Man.* 1973. McKay Washburn. 1st ed. NF/NF. P3. $15.00

CREASEY, John. *Inspector West Alone.* 1975. Scribner. 1st ed. VG/VG. P3. $15.00

CREASEY, John. *Killing Strike.* 1961. Scribner. 1st ed. VG/VG. P3. $15.00

CREASEY, John. *Life for a Death.* 1973. HRW. 1st ed. NF/NF. P3. $15.00

CREASEY, John. *Make-Up for the Toff.* 1956. Walker. 1st ed. 189p. cloth. NF/dj. M20. $15.00

CREASEY, John. *Man I Killed.* 1963. Macmillan. xl. dj. P3. $8.00

CREASEY, John. *Man Who Was Not Himself.* 1976. Stein Day. 1st ed. VG/G. P3. $15.00

CREASEY, John. *Murder With Mushrooms.* 1974. HRW. VG/VG. P3. $15.00

CREASEY, John. *Out of the Shadows.* 1971. World. VG/VG. P3. $16.00

CREASEY, John. *Part for a Policeman.* 1970. Scribner. 1st ed. F/F. T2. $12.00

CREASEY, John. *Rocket for the Toff.* 1960. Hodder Stoughton. 1st ed. VG/VG. P3. $25.00

CREASEY, John. *Smog.* 1971. Thriller BC. VG/VG. P3. $8.00

CREASEY, John. *So Young To Burn.* 1968. Scribner. 1st ed. VG/VG. P3. $15.00

CREASEY, John. *Take a Body.* 1972. World. VG/VG. P3. $20.00

CREASEY, John. *Toff Proceeds.* 1968. Walker. 1st ed. F/F. P3. $15.00

CREASY, E.S. *15 Decisive Battles of the World From Marathon to Waterloo.* 1851. NY. half brn leather/marbled brd. VG. B30. $65.00

CREEKMORE, Faith. *Lithos of Thomas Hart Benton.* 1990. Austin, TX. 2nd ed. biblio/index. M/M. A17. $30.00

CREELEY, Robert. *Echoes.* 1982. Toothpaste Pr. ltd ed. sgn. lettered G. VG+. A1. $125.00

CREIGHTON, Louise. *Life & Letters of Thomas Hodgkin.* 1917. London. Longman Gr. 8vo. 445p. foxed ep. V3. $16.50

CRENSHAW & WARD. *Conrnerstones: Hist of Beaumont & Methodism 1840-1968.* 1968. Beaumont, TX. 1st ed. cloth. F/dj. M8. $37.50

CRESWELL, K.A.C. *Works of Sultan Bibars Albunduqdari in Egypt.* 1926. Cairo. Imprimeri De L'Institue Francais. F. H4. $75.00

CREWS, Harry. *Car.* 1972. Morrow. 1st ed/author's 5th book. NF/NF. Q1 $175.00

CREWS, Harry. *Feast of Snakes.* 1976. NY. 1st ed. VG/VG. B5. $75.00

CREWS, Harry. *Karate Is a Thing of the Spirit.* 1971. Morrow. 1st ed/author's 3rd book. inscr. F/F. B4. $400.00

CREWS, Harry. *Karate Is a Thing of the Spirit.* 1971. NY. Morrow. 1st ed. VG/clip. Q1. $175.00

CREWS, Harry. *Knockout Artist.* 1988. Harper Row. 1st ed. 8vo. 269p. burgundy cloth. F/NF. C6. $40.00

CRICHLOW, Keith. *Time Stands Still.* 1982. St Martin. 4to. 192p. gray cloth. VG. K5. $16.00

CRICHTON, John. *Case of Need.* 1968. London. Heinemann. 1st Eng ed. VG/VG+. B4. $250.00

CRICHTON, Michael. *Andromeda Strain.* 1969. Knopf. 1st ed. F/dj. F4. $35.00

CRICHTON, Michael. *Binary.* 1972. Knopf. 1st ed. F/F. F4. $40.00

CRICHTON, Michael. *Binary.* 1972. London. Heinemann. 1st Eng ed. NF/dj. S6. $30.00

CRICHTON, Michael. *Case of Need.* 1993. Dutton. F/F. P3. $19.00

CRICHTON, Michael. *Congo.* 1980. Knopf. 1st ed. F/dj. F4. $40.00

CRICHTON, Michael. *Disclosure.* 1994. Knopf. 1st ed. F/F. P3. $24.00

CRICHTON, Michael. *Disclosure.* 1994. Knopf. 1st ed. sgn. M/M. Q1. $50.00

CRICHTON, Michael. *Great Train Robbery.* 1975. Knopf. 1st ed. NF/dj. Q1. $75.00

CRICHTON, Michael. *Great Train Robbery.* 1975. Knopf. 1st ed. VG+/dj. M21. $35.00

CRICHTON, Michael. *Great Train Robbery.* 1975. London. Cape. 1st Eng ed. VG+/dj. S6. $25.00

CRICHTON, Michael. *Jurassic Park.* nd. Quality BC. VG/VG. P3. $10.00

CRICHTON, Michael. *Jurassic Park.* 1990. Knopf. ARC. F/wrp. L3. $100.00

CRICHTON, Michael. *Rising Sun.* 1992. Franklin Lib. true 1st ed. sgn. silk marker. aeg. leather. F. L3. $150.00

CRICHTON, Michael. *Rising Sun.* 1992. Knopf. 1st ed. F/F. P3. $22.00

CRICHTON, Michael. *Sphere.* 1987. Knopf. 1st ed. F/F clip. N3. $15.00

CRICHTON, Michael. *Sphere.* 1987. London. Macmillan. 1st ed. F/F. P3. $25.00

CRICHTON, Michael. *Terminal Man.* 1972. Knopf. AP. F/wrp. B2. $85.00

CRICHTON, Michael. *Terminal Man.* 1972. Knopf. 1st ed. F/dj. F4. $45.00

CRICHTON, Michael. *Travels.* 1988. Knopf. 1st ed. F/F. B3. $25.00

CRIDER, Bill. *Evil at the Root.* 1990. St Martin. 1st ed. F/F. P3. $16.00

CRILE & LOWER. *Anoci-Association.* 1914. Phil. Saunders. 259p. xl. G7. $75.00

CRIPPS, Ernest. *Pough Court, the Story of a Notable Pharmacy 1715-1927.* 1927. London. 1st ed. 227p. A13. $25.00

CRISP, N.J. *London Deal.* 1979. St Martin. 1st ed. VG/VG. P3. $18.00

CRISP, William. *Compleat Agent.* 1984. Macmillan. 1st ed. F/F. P3. $15.00

CRISPIN, Edmund. *Fen Country.* 1979. Lodnon. Gollancz. 1st ed. F/F. S6. $30.00

CRISPIN, Edmund. *Frequent Hearses.* 1982. Walker. VG/VG. P3. $25.00

CRISPIN, Edmund. *Love Lies Bleeding.* 1981. Walker. VG/VG. P3. $20.00

CRISPIN & WEINSTEIN. *V: East Coast Crisis.* 1984. Gregg. 1st hc ed. F/F. T2. $13.00

CRISWELL, W.A. *Bible for Today's World.* 1965. Zondervan. 128p. F/F. B29. $5.00

CRISWELL, W.A. *Fifty Years of Preaching at the Palace.* 1969. Zondervan. 142p. VG/dj. B29. $4.50

CRISWELL, W.A. *These Issues We Must Face.* 1964. Zondervan. 137p. VG/dj. B29. $4.50

CROCE, Benedetto. *Aesthetic As Science of Expression & General Linguistic.* 1922. Macmillan. 2nd Eng-language ed/1st prt. 503p. bl cloth. G1. $65.00

CROCE, Benedetto. *Hist Materialism & Economics of Karl Marx.* 1915? London. Howard Latimer. 1st Eng-language ed. 188p. NF. G1. $65.00

CROCE, Benedetto. *Hist of Italy.* 1929. Oxford. Clarendon. 334p. paneled crimson cloth. VG. G1. $45.00

CROCK, Clement H. *Encyclopedia of Preaching.* ca 1955. NY. Wagner. 312p. H10. $20.00

CROCKETT, Candace. *Card Weaving.* 1973. np. cloth. VG. G2. $20.00

CROCKETT, James Underwood. *Greenhouse Gardening.* (1961). Doubleday. BC. 288p. F/F. H1. $4.50

CROCKETT, S.R. *Adventurer in Spain.* 1903. Isbister. VG. P3. $20.00

CROCKETT, S.R. *Black Douglas.* 1899. Doubleday McClure. VG. P3. $45.00

CROCKETT, W. *History of Lake Champlaign, 1609-1936.* 1936. Burlington, VG. 1st ed. ils/index/fld map. 320p. VG. B5. $35.00

CROFTS, Freeman Wills. *Pit-Prop Syndicate.* 1925. NY. Thomas Seltzer. 1st Am ed. VG/VG. M15. $100.00

CROFTS, Freeman Wills. *Sea Mystery.* 1928. Collins. 2nd ed. VG. P3. $25.00

CROFTS, Freeman Wills. *Tragedy in the Hollow.* 1939. Dodd Mead. 1st ed. VG. P3. $35.00

CROLY, George. *Tarry Thou Till I Come; or, Salathiel, Wandering Jew.* 1901. Funk Wagnall. 1st ed. 588p. VG. W1. $15.00

CROMPTON, Richard. *L' Authoritie et Iurisdiction des Courts de la Maiestie...* 1637. London. modern unlettered calf. G. M11. $650.00

CRONBACH, Lee J. *Essentials of Psychological Testing.* 1949. Harper. 475p. F. K4. $22.50

CRONBACH & DRENTH. *Mental Tests & Cultural Adaption.* 1972. Paris. Mouton. 486p. F/dj. K4. $20.00

CRONIN, Michael. *Night of the Party.* 1958. Ives Washburn. 1st ed. VG/VG. P3. $13.00

CRONIN, Vincent. *Last Migration.* 1957. Dutton. 1st ed. 343p. VG/tattered. W1. $18.00

CROOK & FARRINGTON. *Tilden Meteorites.* 1930. np. 8vo. photos/map. VG/wrp. K5. $15.00

CROOKSALL, Robert. *Interpretation of Cosmic & Mystical Experiences.* 1969. London. Clarke. 1st ed. 175p. F/VG. B33. $18.00

CROOKSHANK, F.G. *Mongol in Our Midst.* 1924. Dutton. 113p. F. K4. $15.00

CROSBY, F. *Life of Abraham Lincoln.* 1866. np. 476p. aeg. VG. E5. $45.00

CROSBY, Harry. *Mad Queen.* 1929. Blk Sun. 1st ed. 1/100 on Hollande Van Gelder Zonen. w/drawing. NF/wrp. H5. $1,250.00

CROSBY, Harry. *Tochbearer.* 1931. Paris. Blk Sun. 1st ed. 1/500 on Holland paper. F/glassine. S9. $750.00

CROSBY, John. *Company of Friends.* 1977. Stein Day. 1st ed. VG/G. P3. $13.00

CROSS, Amanda. *James Joyce Murder.* 1967. Macmillan. 2nd ed. VG/VG. P3. $10.00

CROSS, Amanda. *No Word From Winifred.* 1986. Dutton. 1st ed. NF/NF. P3. $20.00

CROSS, Amanda. *Players Come Again.* 1990. Random. 1st ed. F/F. P3. $18.00

CROSS, Gillian. *Map of Nowhere.* 1989. Holiday. 1st Am ed. F/F. F4. $15.00

CROSS, John Keir. *Best Horror Stories 2.* 1965. Faber. F/F. P3. $35.00

CROSS, Mark. *Perilous Hazard.* 1961. Ward Lock. VG/VG. P3. $15.00

CROSS, Osborne. *March of the Regiment of Mounted Riflemen to OR in 1849...* 1967. Ye Galleon. 1st ltd prt. 1/1005. M. A18. $25.00

CROSSER, Paul K. *Nihilism of John Dewey.* 1955. NY. Philisophical Lib. 238p. cloth. G1. $22.50

CROSSMAN, Carl L. *China Trade, Export Furniture, Silver & Other Objects.* 1972. Princeton. Pyne. 1st ed. 4to. 275p. gilt bl cloth. F/NF. F1. $165.00

CROSSMAN, Charles C. *Complete History of Watchmaking in America.* nd. Exter, NH. Adams Brn. 1st ed. 213p. bl cloth. G. A8. $20.00

CROTZ, Keith. *Ewaniana: Writings of Joe & Nesta Ewan.* 1989. Chillicothe. Am Botanist. 67p. cloth. M/dj. A10. $25.00

CROW & KIMURA. *Intro to Population Genetics Theory.* 1970. Harper Row. 478p. M/dj. K4. $15.00

CROWDER, Herbert. *Weatherhawk.* 1990. Putnam. 1st ed. NF/NF. P3. $20.00

CROWE, John; see Lynds, Dennis.

CROWELL, Pers. *Beau Dare: American Saddle Colt.* 1946. Whittlesey. 1st ed. 4to. VG. O3. $25.00

CROWELL, Pers. *First Horseman.* 1948. Whittlesey/McGraw Hill. 1st ed. 95p. VG/dj. A3. $15.00

CROWEN, Mrs. T.J. *Every Lady's Cook Book.* 1854. NY. Higgins Kellogg. 1st ed. 12mo. 166p. prt wrp. M1. $250.00

CROWLEY, John. *Beasts.* 1976. Doubleday. 1st ed. VG/VG. P3. $30.00

CROWN & HEINL. *Marshalls: Increasing the Tempo.* 1954. WA. 1st ed. cloth. VG. C11. $55.00

CROWNE, Douglas P. *Experimental Study in Personality.* 1979. Lawrence Erlbaum. 230p. M/dj. K4. $15.00

CROWNINSHIELD, Francis B. *Story of George Crowningshield's Yacht Cleopatra's Barge.* 1913. Boston. private prt. 40 pl. 259p. teg. gilt red cloth. T7. $250.00

CROWNINSHIELD, Mary B. *All Among the Lighthouses; or, Cruise of Golden Rod.* (1886). Boston. 1st ed. ils/pl. 392p. bl cloth. VG. H3. $50.00

CROWTHER, James G. *Francis Bacon: First Statesman of Science.* 1960. London. 362p. NF/dj. D3. $25.00

CROWTHER, Robert. *Robert Crowther's All the Fun at the Fair.* 1992. Candlewick. 1st Am ed. glazed pict brd. M. C8. $25.00

CROWTHER & FIRESTONE. *Men & Rubber: Story of Business.* 1926. Doubleday Page. 1st ed. 279p. F. H1. $16.00

CROZIER, Emmet. *Yankee Reporters 1861-1865.* 1956. map ep. 441p. O8. $12.50

CRUIKSHANK, George. *Hist of the Bottle, As Originally Published in NY Organ.* 1848. NY. Oliver. 1st ed. 8vo. 32p. M1. $200.00

CRUM, Bartley C. *Behind the Silken Curtain.* 1947. Simon Schuster. 1st ed. sgn. 297p. VG/tattered. W1. $20.00

CRUM, W.L. *Rudimentary Mathematics for Economists & Statisticians.* 1946. London/NY. McGraw Hill. 1st ed. G. K4. $10.00

CRUMLEY, James. *Dancing Bear.* 1983. Random. 1st ed. NF/F. B3. $60.00

CRUMLEY, James. *Last Good Kiss.* 1978. Random. 1st ed. sgn. F/F. B3. $125.00

CRUMLEY, James. *Mexican Tree Duck.* 1993. Mysterious. 1st ed. w/promo material. F/F. S9. $30.00

CRUMLEY, James. *Muddy Fork: A Work in Progress.* 1984. Lord John. sgn/#d. 1/200. yel paper brd/gilt brn spine. F/sans. Q1. $150.00

CRUMLEY, James. *One To Count Cadence.* 1969. Random. 1st ed/author's 1st book. F/NF. B3. $225.00

CRUMLEY, James. *Wrong Case.* 1976. London. Hart Davis. 1st Eng ed. sgn. NF/NF. S6. $275.00

CRUMP, Paul. *Burn, Killer, Burn.* 1962. Chicago. Johnson. 1st ed. F/NF. B2. $30.00

CRUTCHFIELD, James A. *Tennesseans at War.* 1987. Nashville. Rutledge Hill. 1st ed. 191p. F/F. A17. $20.00

CUDDIHY, William. *Agricultural Price Management in Egypt.* 1980. World Bank. 1st ed. 164p. VG/stiff wrp. W1. $8.00

CUDWORTH, Ralph. *True Intellectual System of the Universe: First Part...* 1678. London. Royston. folio. mottled calf/marbled brd/leather spine label. G1. $850.00

CULLEN, Countee. *Ballad of the Brown Girl.* 1927. Harper. trade ed. F/worn box. B2. $125.00

CULLEN, Countee. *Ballad of the Brown Girl.* 1927. Harper. 1st ed. 8vo. blk cloth/yel brd. F/F box. H5. $175.00

CULLEN, Countee. *Color.* 1925. NY/London. Harper. author's 1st book. sgn. buckram/brd. VG. H4. $50.00

CULLEN, Countee. *Copper Sun.* 1927. Harper. 1st ed. 8vo. 89p. blk cloth/marbled brd. VG. H5. $100.00

CULLEN, Thomas. *Early Medicine in MD.* ca 1925. np. pres. pl. 15p. G7. $20.00

CULLEY, John H. *Cattle, Horses & Men of the Western Range.* 1940. Ward Ritchie. typewritten manuscript. ils Katherine Field. 329p. VG. B3. $250.00

CULLINGFORD, Guy. *Framed for Hanging.* 1956. Lippincott. 1st Am ed. F/F. M15. $35.00

CULLINGFORD, Guy. *Touch of Drama.* 1960. London. Hammond. 1st ed. F/F. M15. $45.00

CULLMAN & GRONER. *Encyclopedia of Cacti.* 1987-1994. Portland. ils. 340p. M/dj. B26. $55.00

CULLUM, Albert. *Blackboard, Blackboard on the Wall, Who Is Fairest...* 1978. NY. Harlin Quist. 1st prt. obl 8vo. emb cloth. F/NF. C8. $40.00

CULLUM, Ridgwell. *Triumph of John Kars.* 1917. Chapman Hall. G+. P3. $10.00

CULLY, Kendig B. *Westminster Dictionary of Christian Education.* 1963. Westminster. 812p. G. B29. $4.50

CULPAN, Maurice. *Minister of Injustice.* 1966. Walker. 1st ed. VG/VG. P3. $10.00

CULPEPPER, Nicholas. *Culpepper's Family Physician...* 1825. Exeter. Scammon. 360p. full calf. G. G7. $125.00

CULPEPPER, Nicholas. *Culpepper's School of Physick; or, Experimental Practice...* 1993. NY. facsimile of 1659 ed. 361p. leather. A13. $50.00

CULVER, Timothy; see Westlake, Donald E.

CULVER & GERT. *Philosophy in Medicine: Conceptual & Ethical Issues...* 1982. Oxford. 1st ed/pb issue. 201p. VG. G1. $17.50

CULVER & GRANT. *Book of Old Ships.* 1935 (1924). Garden City. 306p. VG/tattered. M20. $35.00

CULVERWELL, R.J. *Perneiopathology: A Treatise on Venereal & Other Diseases...* 1844. NY. 100 pl. VG. H7. $125.00

CUMBERLAND, Charles. *Mexico. Struggle for Modernity.* 1968. Oxford. 1st ed. 394p. dj. F3. $10.00

CUMBERLAND, Marten. *Etched in Violence.* 1953. Hurst Blackett. 1st ed. VG/G. P3. $20.00

CUMBERLAND, Richard. *Memoirs of...* 1807. London. 2 vol. 1st ed. G+. A15. $85.00

CUMMING, Alex. *Hardy Chrysanthemums.* 1945. Doubleday Doran. revised ed. 202p. F/VG. H1. $6.00

CUMMING, E.D. *Squire Osbaldeston: His Autobiography.* 1926. Bodley Head. 1st ed. ils/fld map. beige cloth. G+. S11. $50.00

CUMMING, Kate. *Gleanings From Southland.* 1895. Birmingham. Roberts. 1st/only ed. 277p. red cloth. VG. C6. $200.00

CUMMING, Primrose. *Chestnut Filly.* nd (ca 1940). London. Blackie. G. O3. $25.00

CUMMINGS, E.E. *CIOPW.* 1931. Covici Friede. 1st ed. sgn. 1/391. rpr joint. B2. $750.00

CUMMINGS, E.E. *EE Cummings: A Miscellany.* 1958. NY. Argophile. 1st ed/ltd issue. 1/75. sgn. 8vo. gray cloth. F. H5. $300.00

CUMMINGS, E.E. *Is 5.* 1926. Boni Liveright. 1st ed. VG+. rare. V1. $125.00

CUMMINGS, E.E. *Ninety-Five Poems.* 1958. Harcourt Brace. 1st ed. sgn. 1/300. bl cloth. F/case. B24. $375.00

CUMMINGS, E.E. *No Thanks.* 1935. Golden Eagle. ltd trade ed. sgn. 1/900. F/G. V1. $120.00

CUMMINGS, E.E. *Poems 1923-1954.* 1954. Harcourt Brace. 1st ed. inscr to well-known poet. NF/VG. V1. $300.00

CUMMINGS, E.E. *Seventy-One Poems/ Xaipe.* 1950. Oxford. 1st ed. F/VG+. V1. $50.00

CUMMINGS, E.E. *Sketches & Watercolors of the Twenties & Thirties.* 1968. Profile. 1/50. w/orig sketch. F/fld/cloth chemise. H5. $225.00

CUMMINGS, E.E. *Tom (A Ballet).* 1935. NY. Arrow Eds. 1st ed. F/missing spine. V1. $100.00

CUMMINGS, E.E. *1 x 1.* 1944. Holt. 1st ed. sgn. NF/G. V1. $50.00

CUMMINGS, Parke. *Baseball Stories.* 1959. Hill Wang. 1st ed. G+/G+. P8. $20.00

CUMMINGS, Ray. *Tarrano the Conqueror.* 1930. McClurg. 1st ed. VG. P3. $50.00

CUMMINS & OWEN. *Central Readings in Hist of Modern Philosophy.* 1992. Wadsworth. 483p. G. B29. $5.50

CUMSTON, Charles. *Introduction to History of Medicine to Time of Pharaohs.* 1926. NY. 1st ed. 390p. A13. $75.00

CUNEO, John. *Air Weapon, 1914-1916.* 1947. Harrisburg, PA. 1st ed. ils. 503p. G. B18. $125.00

CUNEO, John. *Winged Mars. Vol 1.* 1942. Harrisburg, PA. ils. 338p. VG/dj. B18. $75.00

CUNLIFFE, Juliette. *All About the Lhasa Apso.* 1990. London. Pelham. 1st ed. ils. 167p. cloth. M/dj. R2. $40.00

CUNLIFFE, M. *Chattel Slavery & Wage Slavery 1830-1860.* 1979. Augusta, GA. 150p. VG. E5. $28.00

CUNLIFFE, Marcus. *American Literature to 1900.* 1986. London. Sphere. revised ed. 400p. F/F. S11. $25.00

CUNNINGHAM, Carol. *Masks.* 1983. Mill Valley. Sunflower. 60x67mm. 1/115. sgn. 60p. D'Ambrosio bdg. F/box. B24. $250.00

CUNNINGHAM, Clifford J. *Intro to Asteroids.* 1988. Richmond, VA. Willmann-Bell. 4to. 209p. pb. K5. $20.00

CUNNINGHAM, Dellwyn. *Dick Whittington & His Cat.* 1958. Wonder Books. K2. $8.00

CUNNINGHAM, Dellwyn. *What Am I?* nd. Whitman Book 832. K2. $4.00

CUNNINGHAM, E.V. *Assassin Who Gave Up His Gun.* 1969. Morrow. 1st ed. VG/VG. P3. $15.00

CUNNINGHAM, E.V. *Case of the Poisoned Eclairs.* 1979. HRW. 1st ed. VG/VG. P3. $18.00

CUNNINGHAM, E.V. *Case of the Poisoned Eclairs.* 1980. London. Deutsch. 1st Eng ed. F/F. S6. $22.50

CUNNINGHAM, E.V. *Case of the Russian Diplomat.* 1978. HRW. 1st ed. VG/VG. P3. $18.00

CUNNINGHAM, E.V. *Wabash Factor.* 1986. Delacorte. 1st ed. VG/VG. P3. $15.00

CUNNINGHAM, Imogene. *After Ninety.* 1977. Seattle. WA U. 1st ed. VG+/VG+. S9. $65.00

CUNNINGHAM, J. Morgan; see Westlake, Donald E.

CUNNINGHAM, J.V. *Doctor Drink. Poems.* 1950. Cummington. 1st ed. 1/200. ils/sgn Wrightman Williams. NF/wrp. C6. $275.00

CUNNINGHAM, J.V. *Exclusions of a Rhyme.* 1960. Denver. Alan Swallow. 1st ed. sgn. F/VG+. V1. $35.00

CUNNINGHAM, J.V. *Judge Is Fury.* 1947. Morrow/Swallow. 1st ed. sgn. F/VG. V1. $50.00

CUNNINGHAM, Jere. *Abyss.* 1981. Wyndham. 1st ed. VG/VG. P3. $20.00

CUNNINGHAM, Jere. *Visitor.* 1978. St Martin. NF/NF. P3. $20.00

CUNNINGHAM, Richard. *Place Where the World Ends: A Modern Story of Cannibalism...* 1973. Sheed Ward. VG/dj. N2. $7.50

CURIPESCHITZ, Benedict. *Yolculuk Gunsugu 1530...* 1989. Ankara. 1st ed. 8vo. VG. W1. $10.00

CURLEY, Daniel. *Marriage Bed of Procrustes. And Other Stories.* nd. np. 1st ed/author's 1st book. sgn. NF/NF. A11. $30.00

CURLEY, E.M. *Spinoza's Metaphysics: Essay in Intrepretation.* 1969. Cambridge. Harvard. 1st prt. 174p. yel cloth. VG/dj. G1. $30.00

CURRAH & PROCTOR. *Onions in Tropical Regions.* 1990. London. 18 mc photos. 232p. sc. B26. $25.00

CURRAN, Dale. *Dupree Blues.* 1948. Knopf. 1st ed. F/NF. B2. $30.00

CURRAN, Terrie. *All Booked Up.* 1987. Dodd Mead. 1st ed. NF/NF. P3. $16.00

CURRIE, Ellen. *Available Light.* 1986. Summit. 1st ed/author's 1st book. rem mk. F/F. S9. $45.00

CURRINGTON, O.J. *Break-Out.* 1978. Deutsch. 1st ed. NF/NF. P3. $18.00

CURRY, Jane. *Miss Sniff.* nd. np. Fuzzy Wuzzy Book. ils Florence Sarah Winship. VG/damaged. M5. $25.00

CURRY, Ralph L. *Stephen Leacock.* 1959. Doubleday. 1st ed. VG/VG. P3. $30.00

CURTIES, Henry. *Out of the Shadows.* 1911. Greening. brd. VG. P3. $35.00

CURTIN, Philip D. *Atlantic Slave Trade.* 1969. WI U. 296p. F/dj. K4. $10.00

CURTIS, Anna L. *Quakers Take Stock.* 1944. Island Workshop Pr. 8vo. 112p. sc. G. V3. $6.50

CURTIS, Edmund. *Calendar of Ormond Deeds. Vol 2: 1350-1413 AD.* 1934. Dublin. 403p. VG. D3. $35.00

CURTIS, George William. *Prue & I.* nd. Caldwell. 233p. G. H1. $4.50

CURTIS, George William. *Prue & I.* 1898. Harper. 1st ed. ils. 270p. VG. M10. $5.00

CURTIS, George William. *Washington Irving: A Sketch.* 1891. NY. 1st ed. 1/344. teg. gilt red calf. F/worn case. C2. $125.00

CURTIS, J. *Harvey's Views on Use of Circulation of Blood.* 1905. NY. 1st ed. ils/index. 194p. VG. B5. $90.00

CURTIS, John Gould. *Hist of Town of Brookline, MA.* 1933. Boston. Riverside. ils. 349p. F. B14. $35.00

CURTIS, William E. *From the Andes to the Ocean.* 1900. Chicago. Stone. 1st ed. 8vo. 442p. teg. pict bl brd. B11. $95.00

CURTIS, William Elroy. *Turk & His Lost Provinces. Greece, Bulgaria, Servia, Bosnia.* 1903. Chicago. 2nd ed. 8vo. 396p. pict cloth. O2. $40.00

CURTISS, Ursula. *Noonday Devil.* 1953. Eyre Spottiswode. 1st ed. VG/VG. P3. $25.00

CURWEN. *Hist of Booksellers.* 1873. London. 483p. NF. A4. $125.00

CURWOOD, James Oliver. *Barre, Son of Kazan.* nd. Grosset Dunlap. VG/G. P3. $10.00

CURWOOD, James Oliver. *Country Beyond.* 1922. Cosmopolitan. 1st ed. G+. P3. $12.00

CURWOOD, James Oliver. *Country Beyond: Romance of the Wilderness.* 1922. Cosmopolitan. 1st ed. F/VG. A18. $60.00

CURWOOD, James Oliver. *Nomads of the North.* 1926. Doubleday Page. G+. P3. $17.00

CURWOOD, James Oliver. *Plains of Abraham.* 1928. Doubleday Doran. 1st ed. VG. P3. $20.00

CURWOOD, James Oliver. *Plains of Abraham.* 1928. Doubleday Doran. 1st ed. VG/dj. A18. $25.00

CURY, Alexander R. *Cairo: How To See it.* 1928. Alexandria, Egypt. Anglo-Egyptian Supply Assoc. 8th ed. G. W1. $12.00

CURZON, Clare. *Blue-Eyed Boy.* 1990. Collins Crime Club. 1st ed. F/F. P3. $18.00

CURZON, Clare. *Blue-Eyed Boy.* 1990. London. Collins. 1st ed. sgn. F/F. S6. $22.50

CURZON, Clare. *Three-Core Lead.* 1988. Collins Crime Club. 1st ed. F/F. P3. $20.00

CURZON, George N. *Russia in Central Asia in 1889 & Anglo-Russian Question.* 1889. London. 8vo. 477p. cloth. xl. O2. $125.00

CURZON, Robert. *Armenia: Year at Erzeroom & on Frontiers of Russia...* 1854. NY. 1st Am ed. 8vo. 226p. cloth. O2. $150.00

CURZON, Robert. *Visits to Monasteries of the Levant.* 1897. London. 8vo. 307p. cloth. O2. $40.00

CUSHING, Caleb. *Treaty of Washington.* 1873. NY. 1st ed. pres. H4. $100.00

CUSHING, Harvey. *Consecratio Medici & Other Papers.* 1940. Boston. 1st ed. 276p. A13. $50.00

CUSHING, Harvey. *From a Surgeon's Journal.* 1936. Boston. 1st ed/1st prt. 534p. A13. $50.00

CUSHING, Harvey. *Life of Sir William Osler.* 1925. Oxford. 2 vol. 1st ed/2nd imp. pres. orig cloth. G7. $895.00

CUSHING, Harvey. *Medical Career & Other Papers.* 1940. Little Brn. 3rd prt. 302p. NF/dj. G7. $45.00

CUSHING, Harvey. *Pituitary Body & Its Disorders. Clinical States Produced...* 1912. Phil. 1st ed/1st ed. 341p. cloth. NF. G7. $595.00

CUSHING, Harvey. *Pituitary Body & Its Disorders. Clinical States Produced...* 1979. Birmingham. Classics of Medicine Lib. ltd ed. 341p. F. G7. $90.00

CUSHING, Harvey. *Visit to Le Puy-En-Velay.* 1986. Cleveland. Rowfant Club. 1/500. bl brd/cloth spine. M. G7. $95.00

CUSHING, M. *Story of Our Post Office.* 1893. Boston. ils/index. 1030p. VG. B5. $90.00

CUSHING & EISENHARDT. *Meningiomas: Their Classification, Regional Behaviour...* 1938. Springfield. Thomas. royal 8vo. ils. 785p. cloth. VG. G7. $895.00

CUSHMAN, Dan. *Goodbye Old Dry.* 1959. Doubleday. xl. G. B34. $10.00

CUSHMAN, Dan. *Great N Trail.* 1966. np. 1st ed. VG/torn. B34. $50.00

CUSHMAN, Dan. *Old Copper Collar.* 1957. Ballantine. 1st ed. sgn. G. B34. $55.00

CUSHMAN, Dan. *Silver Mountain.* 1957. Appleton Century Crofts. VG/dj. B34. $45.00

CUSHMAN, Robert Eugene. *Leading Constitutional Decisions. Seventh Edition.* 1940. NY. FS Crofts. worn. M11. $25.00

CUSS, Camerer. *Story of Watches.* 1952. London. MacGibbon Kee. 1st ed. 8vo. 172p. blk cloth. VG/VG. A8. $30.00

CUSSLER, Clive. *Cyclops.* 1986. Simon Schuster. 1st ed. NF/NF. P3. $20.00

CUSSLER, Clive. *Cyclops.* 1986. Simon Schuster. 1st ed. pres/dtd 1986. F/F. B3. $50.00

CUSSLER, Clive. *Dragon.* 1990. Simon Schuster. 1st ed. F/NF. B3. $15.00

CUSSLER, Clive. *Treasure.* 1988. Simon Schuster. 1st ed. F/NF. B3. $20.00

CUSTER, Elizabeth. *Boots & Saddles; or, Life in Dakota With General Custer.* 1885. np. 1st ed w/map. 312p. VG. E5. $75.00

CUSTER, Elizabeth. *Boots & Saddles; or, Life in Dakota With General Custer.* 1885. np. 1st ed. 312p. G. O8. $47.50

CUSTER, Elizabeth. *Tenting on the Plains.* 1893. NY. Webster. 403p. O8. $27.50

CUSTER, George Armstrong. *My Life on the Plains.* 1962. Citadel. edit Milo Quaife. 626p. VG. B34. $10.00

CUSTER, George Armstrong. *My Life on the Plains; or, Personal Experiences...* 1963. London. Folio Soc. 1st ed thus. intro Kenneth Fenwick. map ep. F/case. A18. $30.00

CUTHBERTSON. *Anybody's Bike Book.* 1988. Cuthbertson. ils. VG. E5. $35.00

CUTLER, Stan. *Best Performance by a Patsy.* 1991. Dutton. 1st ed. VG/G. P3. $15.00

CUTTING, E. *Jefferson Davis: Political Soldier.* 1930. 1st ed. index. 361p. O8. $18.50

CUTTING, Pauline. *Children of the Siege.* 1988. St Martin. 1st Am ed. 208p. NF/dj. W1. $18.00

CUVIER, Georges. *Essay on the Theory of the Earth.* 1818. NY. Kirk Mercein. 1st Am ed. 8 pl. contemporary calf/blk morocco label. K1. $375.00

CZWIKLITZER, Christopher. *Picasso's Posters.* 1970/71. Random. 1st Am ed. folio. 365p. blk stp bl cloth. VG+/dj. F1. $250.00

D

D'ALLEMAGNE, Henry Rene. *Decorative Antique Ironwork, a Pictorial Treasury.* 1968. NY. Dover. 4to. 415p. F/wrp. F1. $80.00

D'ALLVIELLA, Goblet. *Migration of Symbols.* 1956. University Books. hc. 277p. VG/VG. B33. $30.00

D'AMATO, Brian. *Beauty.* 1992. Delacorte. ARC from UP of 1st ed. F/pict wrp. N3. $15.00

D'ANTIGNAC, Munroe. *Georgia's Navy, 1861.* 1945. Griffin, GA. Goen. 1st ed. 8vo. 16p. NF/wrp. C6. $35.00

D'ARCY, M.C. *Meaning & Matter of Hist: Christian View.* 1959. FSC. later prt. 309p. bl cloth. VG/dj. G1. $25.00

D'AULAIRE & D'AULAIRE. *Buffalo Bill.* 1952. Doubleday. 1st ed. ils. NF/G. M5. $35.00

D'AULAIRE & D'AULAIRE. *Columbus.* 1955. Doubleday. 1st ed. 4to. VG+. C8. $30.00

D'AULAIRE & D'AULAIRE. *Conquest of the Atlantic.* 1933. Viking. 1st ed. pict cloth. VG+. C8. $40.00

D'AULAIRE & D'AULAIRE. *George Washington.* 1936. Doubleday Doran. 1st ed. 4to. pict brd. G. A3. $17.50

D'AULAIRE & D'AULAIRE. *Leif the Lucky.* 1941. Doubleday Doran. 1st ed. 4to. unp. pict brd/cloth spine. G. A3. $20.00

D'AULAIRE & D'AULAIRE. *Nils.* 1948. Doubleday Doran. 1st ed. ils. VG+. P2. $50.00

D'AULAIRE & D'AULAIRE. *Ola.* (1932). Doubleday Doran. early rpt. unp. G. A3. $10.00

D'AULAIRE & D'AULAIRE. *Ola.* 1932. Doubleday Doran. 1st ed. 4to. pict paper brd. VG+. C8. $40.00

D'AULAIRE & D'AULAIRE. *Trolls.* 1972. Doubleday. 1st ed. 4to. M/M. C8. $35.00

D'AULAIRE & D'AULAIRE. *Wings for Per.* 1944. Doubleday Doran. 1st ed. unp. VG/rpr. M20. $50.00

D'AULNOY, Marie. *D'Aulnoy's Fairy Tales.* 1923. Phil. McKay. 1st ed. 457p. teg. gilt navy cloth. NF. D6. $150.00

D'HARCOURT, Raoul. *Textiles of Ancient Peru & Their Techniques.* 1975. np. sc. VG. G2. $15.00

D'ISTRIA, Dora. *La Poesie des Ottomans.* 1877. Paris. 2nd ed. 12mo. 208p. w/prt card. O2. $75.00

D'OLIVER, Luis Nicolau. *Fray Bernardino de Sahagun.* 1987. Salt Lake City. 1st ed. 201p. VG/dj. F3. $30.00

DA VINCI, Leonardo. *Madrid Codices, Nat Lib, Madrid. Facsimile Edition.* 1976. NY. McGraw Hill. 6 vol. 1/100. gilt burgandy calf. clear Plexiglas box. G7. $1,250.00

DABNEY, Robert L. *Life & Campaigns of Lieutenant-General Thomas J Jackson.* 1866. Blelock/National. 8vo. ils. 742p. emb violet cloth. H9. $150.00

DABOLL, Nathan. *Arithmetic...With Addition of Practical Accountant...* 1825. London. S Green. 252p. calf/wood brd. G. B14. $150.00

DACEY, Philip. *Gerald Manley Hopkins Meets Walt Whitman in Heaven.* 1982. Penmaen. ltd ed. sgn. 1/75. F/sans. V1. $85.00

DACUS, J.A. *Annals of the Great Strikes in the United States.* 1877. Chicago. Palmer. ils. G. V4. $35.00

DAGLISH, E. Fitch. *Dachshund.* 1980. London. Popular Dogs. 10th ed. 256p. M/dj. R2. $10.00

DAGLISH, E. Fitch. *Dog Breeding.* 1961. London. Foyle. 1st ed. 77p. glossy brd. VG+. R2. $10.00

DAGMAR, Peter. *Alien Skies.* 1967. Arcadia. 1st ed. NF/clip. F4. $25.00

DAHL, Roald. *Going Solo.* 1986. FSG. 1st Am ed. lg 8vo. F/F. C8. $35.00

DAHL, Roald. *Gremlins, a Royal Airforce Story.* 1943. Random. author's 1st book. ils Disney Studios. VG/VG. C8. $650.00

DAHL, Roald. *Kiss Kiss.* 1960. Knopf. 1st ed. VG/dj. M2. $30.00

DAHL, Roald. *Over To You.* 1946. Reynal Hitchcock. VG. P3. $30.00

DAHL, Roald. *Switch Bitch.* 1974. Knopf. 1st ed. F/F. T2. $25.00

DAHL, Roald. *Switch Bitch.* 1974. Knopf. 1st ed. VG/VG. P3. $20.00

DAHL, Roald. *Switch Bitch.* 1974. London. Michael Joseph. 1st ed. lg 12mo. NF/NF. C8. $25.00

DAHL, Roald. *Two Fables.* 1986. Middlesex, UK. 1st ed. sm 8vo. F/F. C8. $35.00

DAHL, Roald. *Two Fables.* 1987. FSG. 1st ed. F/F. P3. $13.00

DAHL, Roald. *Witches.* 1983. FSG. 1st Am ed. NF/NF. C8. $50.00

DAHL. *Book on the Danish Writer, Hans Christian Andersen...* 1955. Copenhagen. ils. 220p. F. A4. $65.00

DAHLBERG, Edward. *Bottom Dogs.* 1930. Simon Schuster. 1st Am ed. F/NF. B2. $150.00

DAHLBERG, Gunnar. *Twin Births & Twins From Hereditary Point of View.* 1926. Stockholm. Bokforlags. 213p. G. K4. $45.00

DAHLE & JOHSHOY. *Liturgical Service of the Lutheran Church.* 1922. Augsburg. Eng/Norwegian text. 148p. G. B29. $4.50

DAHLGREN DE JORDAN, Barbro. *La Grana Cochinilla.* 1963. Mexico. Porrua. 1st ed. 4to. 327p. wrp. uncut. F3. $30.00

DAILEY, Janet. *Great Alone.* 1986. NY. 1st ed. 716p. F/F. A17. $12.50

DAILLE, Jean. *De Scriptis, Quae Sub Dionysii Areopagitae et Ignatii...* 1666. Geneva. Tournes. 4to. 501p. modern calf/marbled brd. K1. $200.00

DAIN, Norman. *Concepts of Insanity in the US 1789-1865.* 1964. New Brunswick. 1st ed. 304p. dj. A13. $60.00

DAINTITH & ISAACS. *Medical Quotes: A Thematic Dictionary.* 1989. Oxford. 1st ed. 260p. dj. A13. $35.00

DAKIN, Douglas. *British Intelligence of Events in Greece, 1824-1827.* 1959. Athens. 8vo. 184p. prt wrp. O2. $25.00

DALEY, Brian. *Han Solo's Revenge.* nd. BC. MTI. VG/VG. P3. $8.00

DALEY, Brian. *Han Solo's Revenge.* 1979. Ballantine/Del Rey. 1st ed. F/F. F4. $30.00

DALEY, Robert. *Fast One.* 1978. Crown. 1st ed. VG/VG. P3. $20.00

DALEY, Robert. *Target Blue.* 1973. Delacorte. 1st ed. VG. P3. $25.00

DALEY, Robert. *To Kill a Cop.* 1976. Crown. 1st ed. VG/VG. P3. $20.00

DALGLIESH, Alice. *Davenports & Cherry Pie.* 1949. Scribner. 1st ed. ils Flavia Gag. VG/dj. M20. $40.00

DALGLIESH, Alice. *Long Live the King.* 1937. NY. Scribner. 1st ed. NF/VG. C8. $36.00

DALGLIESH, Alice. *Ride on the wind.* 1956. NY. Scribner. 1st ed. sm 4to. pict cloth. NF/VG. C8. $20.00

DALGLISH, Doris N. *People Called Quakers.* 1938. London. Oxford. 8vo. 169p. xl. V3. $9.00

DALI, Salvadore. *Les Diners de Gala.* nd. NY. Felicie Pub Co. 1st ed. VG/G+. A1. $125.00

DALL, Anna Roosevelt. *Scamper's Christmas.* 1934. Macmillan. 1st ed. ils Marjorie Flack. VG+. C8. $60.00

DALLAS, Francis Gregory. *Papers of Francis Gregory Dallas, USN, Correspondence...* 1917. NY. Devinne. 1/700. ils. 306p. T7. $70.00

DALLAS, Oswald. *Treasures of Asshur.* 1929. World Syndicate. 1st ed. VG/dj. F4. $35.00

DALRYMPLE, Campbell. *Extracts From a Military Essay...* 1776. Phil. 1st Am ed. 8vo. 8 pl. leather. M1. $750.00

DALTON, Priscilla; see Avallone, Mike.

DALY, Carroll John. *Snarl of the Beast.* 1927. Clodd. 1st ed. VG. F4. $30.00

DALY, ELizabeth. *Wrong Way Down.* 1946. Rinehart. 1st ed. xl. VG. P3. $10.00

DALY, Louise Haskell. *Alexander Cheves Haskell: Portrait of a Man.* 1934. Plimpton. 1st ed. 1/300. 8vo. 224p. F. rare. C6. $700.00

DALY, Maureen. *Moroccan Roundabout.* 1961. Dodd Mead. 1st ed. 16 pl. xl. VG/dj. W1. $12.00

DALZIEL, Hugh. *Greyhound: Its Breeding, Training & Running.* 1928. London. Bazaar Exchange Mart. 4th revised ed. 96p. wrp. R2. $150.00

DAMASCINOS. *Oecumenical Patriarchate. The Great Church of Christ.* 1989. Athens. folio. 463 mc photos. 376p. gilt cloth. brd case. O2. $150.00

DAMP, Philip. *Dahlias.* 1987. London. ils. 96p. M/dj. B26. $17.50

DANA, Charles. *Peaks of Medical History.* 1926. NY. 1st ed. ils. 105p. A13. $50.00

DANA, Richard Henry Jr. *Two Years Before the Mast & Twenty-Four Years After.* 1980. Danbury. Grolier. Collector ed. 8vo. leatherette. M. P4. $19.95

DANA, Richard Henry Jr. *Two Years Before the Mast: A Personal Narrative...* 1947. LEC. 1/1500. ils/sgn Hans Alexander Mueller. F/case. A18. $60.00

DANA, Rose; see Ross, W.E.D.

DANBY, Mary. *Realms of Darkness.* 1988. Chartwell. VG/VG. P3. $15.00

DANCKAERTS, Jasper. *Diary of Our Second Trip From Holland to New Netherland...* 1969. Upper Saddle River. Gregg. ils. orange cloth. NF. P4. $35.00

DANE, Clemence. *Flower Girls.* 1955. Norton. 1st ed. VG. P3. $10.00

DANE & WALKER. *Mark Twain's Travels With Mr Brown...* 1940. Knopf. 1st/ltd ed. 8vo. 296p. gilt gr brd. VG. B11. $95.00

DANGELL, M.S. *Cabinet; or, Philosopher's Masterpiece, Containing...* 1824. Phil. rpt from Dublin ed/1st Am ed? 24mo. disbound. M1. $500.00

DANGERFIELD, Stanley. *Wire-Haired Fox Terrier.* 1958. London. Nicholson Watson. 1st ed. ils. 126p. F/VG+. R2. $25.00

DANIEL, David. *Ark.* 1984. St Martin/Marek. 1st ed. VG/VG. P3. $15.00

DANIEL, Elizabeth. *Our Button Book.* 1938. Rand McNally. 1st ed. photos. VG. M5. $20.00

DANIEL, William B. *Rural Sports.* 1813. London. ils/pl/index. 508p. leather. VG. B5. $275.00

DANIEL & GUNTER. *Confederate Cannon Foundries.* nd. np. ils/photos. 112p. dj. O8. $18.50

DANIELL, John Frederic. *Elements of Meteorology.* 1845. London. Parker. 2 vol. posthumous ed. F. B14. $200.00

DANIELOU, Alain. *Yoga: The Method of Re-Integration.* 1955. Universtiy Books. 1st Am ed. VG/dj. N2. $6.00

DANIELS, Cora Linn. *Bronze Buddha.* 1899. Boston. Little Brn. 1st ed. teg. bl cloth. F. M15. $50.00

DANIELS, George. *Nineteenth-Century American Science.* 1972. Evanston. Northwestern. 274p. cloth. VG. A10. $18.00

DANIELS, Les. *Black Castle.* 1978. Scribner. 1st ed. xl. dj. P3. $15.00

DANIELS, Les. *Comix: Hist of Comic Books in America.* nd. Bonanza. ils. G+/torn. N2. $10.00

DANN, Jack. *Immortal: Short Novels of the Transhuman Future.* 1978. Harper Row. 1st ed. M/dj. M21. $15.00

DANN, Jack. *Starhiker.* 1977. Harper Row. ARC. RS. F/F. T2. $20.00

DANN, Jack. *Starhiker.* 1977. Harper Row. 1st ed. F/F. N3. $15.00

DANN, Jack. *Timetipping.* 1980. Doubleday. ARC. RS. F/F. T2. $20.00

DANN, Jack. *Timetipping.* 1980. Doubleday. 1st ed. F/F. P3. $18.00

DANN & ZEBROWSKI. *Faster Than Light: An Orig Anthology...* 1977. Harper Row. 1st ed. F/F. N3. $20.00

DANOEN, Emile. *Tides of Time.* 1952. Ballantine. VG/G. P3. $30.00

DANTE, Alighieri. *Galleria Dantesca Microscopia.* 1880. Milan. Ulrico Hoepli. 54x43mm. 30 mtd photos/tissue. 400p. full morocco. B24. $1,000.00

DANTE, Alighieri. *Inferno.* nd. Collier. ils Gustave Dore. 183p. G. H1. $32.00

DANTE, Alighieri. *La Divina Commedia di Dante.* 1878. Milan. Ulrico Hoepli. 56x42mm. 1/1000. 30p. all edges red. morocco. F/case. B24. $1,500.00

DANTE, Alighieri. *Purgatory/Paradise.* nd. Collier. ils Gustave Dore. emb bdg. G. H1. $24.00

DAPPER, Olfert. *Description Exacte des Isles de l'Archipel, et de...* 1703. Amsterdam. folio. ils/fld maps/full-p pl. full old calf. O2. $4,250.00

DARBY, J.N. *Murder in the House With Blue Eyes.* 1939. Bobbs Merrill. 1st ed. VG. P3. $35.00

DARLEY, Felix. *Compositions in Outline.* 1856. NY. obl folio. 30 pl. brd/rebacked. A9. $95.00

DARLING, Abigail. *Teddy Bears' Picnic Cookbook.* 1991. Viking. 1st ed. F/F. B17. $9.00

DARLING, Esther Birdsall. *Baldy of Nome.* 1923 (1916). Penn. ils Hattie Longstreet. G+. P2. $28.00

DARLOW & MOULE. *Historical Catalogue of Printed Editions of Holy Scripture.* nd. Foreign Bible Soc. 4 vol. ltd rpt of 1903-1911 ed. 1/350 sets. F. A4. $200.00

DARNELL, J.V. *Restoration of Old American Brass Clocks.* 1972. Tampa, FL. private prt. 28p. F/wrp. A8. $5.00

DARNTON, Robert. *Business of Enlightenment: Pub Hist of Encyclopedie 1775...* 1979. Harvard. 1st ed. 624p. F/dj. M10. $18.50

DARROW, Clarence. *Farmington.* 1904. Chicago. 1st ed. VG. B5. $50.00

DARROW, Clarence. *Story of My Life.* 1932. Scribner. 1st ed. inscr to Walter White. 1/15. VG. rare. B4. $4,500.00

DARROW, Clarence. *Story of My Life.* 1932. Scribner. 1st ed/deluxe issue. 1/250. sgn. NF/VG+. S9. $1,250.00

DARWIN, Charles. *Charles Darwin 1809-1882. A Centennial Commemorative.* 1982. Wellington. Nova Pacifica. 1st ed. 1/750. 28 pl. 376p. F/case. P4. $750.00

DARWIN, Charles. *Formation of Vegetable Mould Through Action of Worms.* 1882. NY. ils. G+. M17. $45.00

DARWIN, Charles. *On the Origin of Species by Means of Natural Selection.* 1987. Birmingham, AL. facsimile of 1859 ed. 502p. full leather. A13. $60.00

DARWIN, Charles. *On the Origin of Species.* 1860. London. Murray. 2nd ed. ads/index. 502p. gilt gr cloth (bdg a variant). K1. $1,000.00

DARWIN, Charles. *On the Origin of Species.* 1966. Cambridge. Harvard. 490p. M/dj. K4. $15.00

DASKAM, Josephine. *Memoirs of a Baby.* 1904. Harper. 1st ed. ils Fanny Y Cory. bl cloth. VG. M5. $45.00

DATER, Judy. *Imogen Cunningham.* 1979. Boston. NYGS. 1st ed. 4to. NF/VG. S9. $55.00

DAUDET, Alphonse. *Port Tarascon.* 1891. Harper. 1st Am ed. 359p. teg. gilt/silver stp bl cloth. F. H1. $85.00

DAUGHERTY, James. *Walt Whitman's America.* 1964. Cleveland. World. 1st ed. pict cloth. NF/F. C8. $55.00

DAUGHERTY, James. *West of Boston.* 1956. Viking. 1st ed. inscr/dtd. F/F. C8. $75.00

DAUGHERTY, Sonia. *Ten Brave Women.* 1953. Lippincott. 1st ed. ils James Daugherty. 147p. NF/VG+. P2. $30.00

DAUGHTERY, James. *Abraham Lincoln.* 1943. Viking. 1st ed. NF/VG+. C8. $85.00

DAUGHTERY, James. *Daniel Boone.* 1939. Viking. 1st ed. sm 4to. pict cloth. F/NF. C8. $95.00

DAUGHTERY, James. *In the Beginning...* 1941. London. Oxford. 1st ed. sm 4to. NF/G+. C8. $45.00

DAUGHTERY, James. *Poor Richard.* 1941. Viking. 1st ed. VG+/VG. C8. $55.00

DAUGHTERY, Sonia. *Ten Brave Men, Makers of the Am Way.* 1951. Lippincott. 1st ed. sm 8vo. pict cloth. F/F. C8. $60.00

DAUMIER, Honore. *Lithographien: 1861-1872.* ca 1920. Munich. Albert Langen. thin folio. gilt yel/brn bdg. VG. F1. $125.00

DAUNDERS, James. *Modern Airedale.* 1929. Idle. Watmoughs. 1st ed. ils. 66p. brd. F. scarce. R2. $130.00

DAUZET, Marceline. *One Happy Day.* 1939. Saalfield. ils Janet L Scott. unp. VG. M20. $25.00

DAVENPORT, Basil. *Inquiry Into SF.* 1955. Longman Gr. 1st ed. 87p. cloth. VG/dj. M20. $25.00

DAVENPORT, Basil. *Science Fiction Novel.* 1959. Advent. 1st ed. VG. P3. $40.00

DAVENPORT, Basil. *13 Ways To Dispose of a Body.* 1966. Dodd Mead. VG/VG. P3. $13.00

DAVENPORT, Guy. *Da Vinci's Bicycle.* 1979. Johns Hopkins. 1st ed. sgn. F/NF. L3. $75.00

DAVENPORT, Guy. *Do You Have a Poem Book on EE Cummings?* 1969. Jargon. 1st ed. F/wrp. B2. $25.00

DAVENPORT, Guy. *Eclogues.* 1981. Northpoint. 1st ed. F/F. B2. $25.00

DAVENPORT, Guy. *Goldfinch Thistle Star.* 1983. Red Ozier. 1st ed. sgn. 1/45 hc. M. B4. $35.00

DAVENPORT, Homer. *Davenport's Arabians.* 1973. Ft Collins. Caballus. ltd ed. 1/2000. VG. O3. $45.00

DAVENPORT, Homer. *My Quest of the Arabian Horse.* 1909. NY. Dodge. 1st ed. sgn pres. VG. O3. $165.00

DAVENPORT, Philip. *Voyage of the Waltzing Matilda.* 1954. Dodd Mead. ils. 232p. dj. T7. $20.00

DAVENTRY, Leonard. *Man of Double Deed.* 1965. Doubleday. VG/VG. P3. $20.00

DAVEY, Jocelyn. *Capitol Offense.* 1956. Knopf. 1st Am ed. F/F. M15. $45.00

DAVEY, Jocelyn. *Dangerous Liaison.* 1988. Walker. 1st ed. F/F. P3. $18.00

DAVID, Henry. *History of the Haymarket Affair.* 1936. NY. Russell. xl. G. V4. $12.50

DAVID, J. *Weight of the Evidence.* 1968. NY. 303p. VG. D3. $12.50

DAVIDIAN, H.H. *Rhododendron Species. Vol I.* 1982. Leipotes. Timber Pr. 1st ed. ils/pl. 431p. F/VG. S11. $25.00

DAVIDSON, Avram. *Adventures in Unhistory: Conjectures on Factual Foundations.* 1993. Phil. Owlswick. 1st ed. sgn. 1/100. F/F/case. T2. $50.00

DAVIDSON, Avram. *Adventures of Doctor Eszterhazy.* 1990. Phil. Owlswick. 1st trade ed. F/F. T2. $24.00

DAVIDSON, Avram. *Best of Avram Davidson.* 1979. Doubleday. 1st ed. VG/VG. P3. $20.00

DAVIDSON, Avram. *Best of Fantasy & SF #12.* 1963. Doubleday. BC. VG/G+. M21. $2.00

DAVIDSON, Avram. *Masters of the Maze.* 1974. London. Wht Lion. 1st ed/1st hc ed. F/F clip. N3. $35.00

DAVIDSON, Avram. *Peregrine: Primus.* 1971. Walker. 1st ed. VG/VG. P3. $30.00

DAVIDSON, Avram. *Phoenix & the Mirror.* 1969. Doubleday. 1st ed. F/dj. F4. $40.00

DAVIDSON, Avram. *Reward Edward Papers.* 1978. Doubleday. 1st ed. VG/VG. P3. $20.00

DAVIDSON, Avram. *Vergil in Averno.* 1987. Doubleday. 1st ed. F/F. T2. $12.00

DAVIDSON, Basil. *Lost Cities of Africa.* 1959. Little Brn. 3rd ed. 366p. F/dj. K4. $12.50

DAVIDSON, Basil. *Lost Cities of Africa.* 1970. Little Brn/Atlantic Monthly. revised ed. NF/dj. W1. $22.00

DAVIDSON, Bill. *Cut Off.* 1972. Stein Day. 1st ed. VG/VG. P3. $15.00

DAVIDSON, Diane Mott. *Cereal Murders.* 1993. Bantam. 1st ed. F/F. B3. $30.00

DAVIDSON, Donald. *Decision Making.* 1957. Stanford. 117p. F. K4. $10.00

DAVIDSON, Donald. *Tall Men: Portrait of a Tennessean.* 1927. Houghton Mifflin. 1st ed. inscr. F/NF. B4. $285.00

DAVIDSON, Levetti. *Rocky Mountain Tales.* 1947. OK U. 1st ed. ils Skelly. VG/dj. B34. $40.00

DAVIDSON, Lionel. *Making Good Again.* 1968. Harper Row. 1st ed. F/F. P3. $20.00

DAVIDSON, Martin. *Astronomy for Everyman.* 1953. London. Dent. 8vo. 494p. G/dj. K5. $15.00

DAVIDSON, Miriam. *Convictions of the Heart: Jim Corbett & Sanctuary Movement.* 1988. AZ U. 1st ed. 187p. F/F. B19. $20.00

DAVIDSON & MOORE. *Joyleg.* 1971. Walker. 1st hc ed. F/F. N3. $20.00

DAVIE, Donald. *Ezra Pound: Poet As Sculptor.* 1965. London. 1st ed. sgn. F/NF. V1. $45.00

DAVIES, Arthur L. *Death Plays a Duet.* 1977. Exposition. 1st ed. VG/VG. P3. $10.00

DAVIES, Benajmin. *Baker's Harmony of the Gospels.* 1988. Baker. 184p. M. B29. $4.00

DAVIES, Charles. *Arithmetic Designed for Academies & Schools...* 1853. Barnes. 360p. quarter leather. fair. H1. $5.00

DAVIES, D.W. *Grant Dahlstrom & the First Fifty Years of Castle Press.* 1981. Pasadena. Castle. 1/500. ils. 77p. brn cloth. F. P4. $40.00

DAVIES, Dilys. *Alliums. Ornamental Onions.* 1992. Portland. ils/photos/drawings. M/dj. B26. $29.95

DAVIES, Frederick. *Death of a Hit-Man.* 1982. St Martin. 1st ed. xl. dj. P3. $5.00

DAVIES, J. *Legend of Hobey Baker.* 1966. Boston. 1st ed. VG/VG. B5. $40.00

DAVIES, John Paton. *Dragon by the Tail.* 1972. Norton. 1st ed. 8vo. 448p. VG/dj. W1. $18.00

DAVIES, John. *Douglas of the Forests, N Am Journals of David Douglas.* 1981. Seattle. WA U. 2nd ed. 193p. M/dj. A10. $22.00

DAVIES, L.P. *Land of Leys.* 1979. Doubleday. 1st ed. VG/VG. P3. $16.00

DAVIES, Mary Caroline. *Joy Toy Man of Joy Toy Town.* ca 1930. np. ils Queen Holden. VG/dj. M20. $75.00

DAVIES, Nigel. *Aztec Empire.* 1987. Norman. 1st ed. 342p. dj. F3. $30.00

DAVIES, Nigel. *Aztecs: A Hist.* 1974. Putnam. 1st Am ed. 363p. dj. F3. $30.00

DAVIES, Nigel. *Tolecs: Until the Fall of Tula.* 1977. Norman. 1st ed. 533p. dj. F3. $30.00

DAVIES, Nigel. *Toltec Heritage: From Fall of Tula to Rise of Tenochtitlan.* 1980. Norman. 1st ed. 401p. dj. F3. $30.00

DAVIES, P. *Dollarville.* 1989. Random. 1st ed. F/F. P3. $18.00

DAVIES, Peter. *Truth About Kent State: Challenge to American Conscience.* 1973. FSG. 2nd prt. VG/dj. N2. $12.50

DAVIES, Robertson. *Brothers in the Black Art.* 1981. Vancouver. Alcuin Soc. 1/100. F/wht stapled wrp. Q1. $175.00

DAVIES, Robertson. *Feast of Stephen.* 1970. Toronto. 1st ed. sgn. F/VG+. A11. $65.00

DAVIES, Robertson. *Intro to the 21st Toronto Antiquarian Book Fair.* 1993. Toronto. Coach House. F/stapled wrp. B4. $45.00

DAVIES, Robertson. *Lyre of Orpheus.* 1989. Viking. 1st Am ed. 8vo. 472p. gilt blk cloth/purple brd. F/dj. H5. $50.00

DAVIES, Robertson. *Masque of Mr Punch.* 1963. Toronto. Oxford U. sm star stp on rear ep. F/NF. Q1. $150.00

DAVIES, Robertson. *Mixture of Frailties.* 1979. Everest House. ARC. RS. w/promo material. F/F. B4. $175.00

DAVIES, Robertson. *Murther & Walking Spirits.* 1991. Toronto. McClelland Stewart. 1st ed. F/F. B3. $15.00

DAVIES, Robertson. *Question Time: A Play.* 1975. Toronto. 1st ed. sgn. VG+/ils wrp. A11. $45.00

DAVIES, T. *Dramatic Miscellanies.* 1785. London. 3 vol. new ed. A15. $100.00

DAVIES & HUNT. *Stories of Eng Artists From Van Dyck to Turner 1600-1851.* 1908. Chatto Windus. marbled ep. teg. full vellum. NF. F1. $150.00

DAVIS, Adelle. *Let's Cook It Right.* 1947. Harcourt Brace. 1st ed. F/VG. B4. $275.00

DAVIS, Andrew Jackson. *Free Thoughts Concerning Religion; or, Nature Vs Theology.* 1854. Boston. Bela Marsh. 1st ed. 8vo. 45p. prt wrp. M1. $125.00

DAVIS, Andrew Jackson. *Harmonial Man; or, Thoughts for the Age.* 1853. Boston. Bela Marsh. 1st ed. 8vo. 129p. prt wrp. M1. $150.00

DAVIS, Benjamin O. *American: An Autobiography.* 1991. WA. 1st ed. 442p. VG/dj. B18. $20.00

DAVIS, Berrie. *Fourth Day of Fear.* 1973. Putnam. 1st ed. VG/VG. P3. $13.00

DAVIS, Burke. *Campaign That Won America.* 1970. NY. 1st ed. 319p. VG/dj. B18. $15.00

DAVIS, Burke. *Dwelling Places.* nd. Scribner. UP/1st ed. 8vo. 237p. VG/cream wrp. C6. $20.00

DAVIS, Burke. *Gray Fox: Robert E Lee & the Civil War.* 1956. later ed. ils/maps/photos. 466p. F. O8. $12.50

DAVIS, Burke. *Jeb Stuart: The Last Cavalier.* 1992 (1957). index. 462p. dj. O8. $12.50

DAVIS, Burke. *War Bird: Life & Times of Elliott White Springs.* 1987. Chapel Hill. 1st ed. ils. 267p. F/dj. B18. $15.00

DAVIS, Carroll. *Room To Grow: Study of Parent-Child Relationships.* 1966. Toronto. 212p. F/dj. K4. $10.00

DAVIS, Charles G. *American Sailing Ships: Their Plans & Hist.* 1984 (1920). np. ils. 240p. VG. E5. $30.00

DAVIS, Charles G. *Ship Model Builder's Assistant.* 1926. Marine Research. 275p. VG/dj. M20. $85.00

DAVIS, Charles G. *Ship Models, How To Build Them.* 1925. Salem. Marine Research. ils/fld plans. gilt bl cloth. VG. F1/M20. $85.00

DAVIS, Charles G. *Ships of the Past.* 1929. Salem. Marine Research. ils/photos/plans. gilt bl cloth. VG. F1. $75.00

DAVIS, Deering. *Annapolis Houses 1700-1775.* 1947. Architec Book Pub. 1st ed. 124p. VG/VG. A17. $15.00

DAVIS, Dorothy Salisbury. *Death in the Life.* 1976. Scribner. 1st ed. VG/VG. P3. $18.00

DAVIS, Dorothy Salisbury. *Shock Wave.* 1974. Arthur Barker. 1st ed. VG/VG. P3. $18.00

DAVIS, E. Adams. *On the Night Wind's Telling.* 1946. Norman, OK. 1st ed. 276p. VG/dj. F3. $30.00

DAVIS, Frederick C. *Drag the Dark.* 1953. Crime Club. 1st ed. VG. P3. $18.00

DAVIS, G. *Moonbird.* 1986. Doubleday. 1st ed. RS. F/F. P3. $20.00

DAVIS, H.L. *Distant Music.* 1957. Morrow. 1st ed. F/dj. A18. $35.00

DAVIS, H.L. *Harp of a Thousand Strings.* 1947. Morrow. 1st ed. F/dj. A18. $35.00

DAVIS, H.L. *Honey in the Horn.* 1977. Franklin Lib. ltd ed. ils. aeg. full leather. A17. $25.00

DAVIS, H.L. *Kettle of Fire.* 1959. Morrow. 1st ed. F/dj. A18. $20.00

DAVIS, H.L. *Team Bells Woke Me & Other Stories.* 1953. Morrow. 1st ed. F/F. A18. $75.00

DAVIS, Harriet Eager. *Elmira, the Girl Who Loved Poe.* 1966. Houghton Mifflin. 1st ed. VG/VG. P3. $20.00

DAVIS, Hazel H. *General Jim.* 1958. St Louis, MO. 1st ed. 192p. VG/dj. B18. $15.00

DAVIS, J. Woodbridge. *Dynamics of the Sun.* 1981. Van Nostrand. 4to. 156p. xl. VG/wrp. K5. $80.00

DAVIS, J.A. *Samaki: Story of an Otter in Africa.* 1979. NY. 1st ed. ils. F/F. A17. $8.50

DAVIS, Jefferson. *Rise & Fall of Confederate Government.* 1881. Appleton. 2 vol. 1st ed. 8vo. pub morocco. VG. C6. $375.00

DAVIS, John Gordon. *Taller Than Trees.* 1975. Doubleday. 1st ed. F/F. P3. $15.00

DAVIS, Kathryn. *Girl Who Trod on a Loaf.* 1993. Knopf. 1st ed. NF/NF. A14. $30.00

DAVIS, Lavinia R. *Evidence Unseen.* nd. BC. VG/G. P3. $8.00

DAVIS, Lavinia R. *Sandy's Spurs.* 1951. Jr Literary Guild. VG. O3. $15.00

DAVIS, Linda. *Onward & Upward: Biography of Katharine S White.* 1989. NY. Fromm. pb. 300p. M. A10. $12.00

DAVIS, Lindsey. *Shadows in Bronze.* 1991. Crown. ARC. F/wrp. B2. $35.00

DAVIS, Lindsey. *Shadows in Bronze.* 1991. Crown. 1st Am ed. sgn. F/F. T2. $45.00

DAVIS, Mary Lee. *We Are Alaskans.* 1931. Boston. 335p. G. A17. $12.00

DAVIS, Michael. *America Organizes Medicine.* 1941. NY. 1st ed. 334p. A13. $30.00

DAVIS, Richard Harding. *Bar Sinister.* 1903. Scribner. 1st ed. 108p. cloth. VG+. R2. $60.00

DAVIS, Richard Harding. *Captain Macklin.* 1902. Scribner. 1st ed. ils WA Clark. 328p. G. H1. $12.00

DAVIS, Richard Harding. *Gallagher.* 1906. Scribner. VG. P3. $10.00

DAVIS, Richard Harding. *In the Fog.* 1901. NY. Russell. 1st ed. NF. B2. $30.00

DAVIS, Richard Harding. *Three Gringos in Venezuela & Central America.* 1896. Harper. 1st ed. 12mo. 282p. VG. B11. $40.00

DAVIS, Richard Harding. *Van Bibber & Others.* 1892. Harper. 1st ed. gilt gr cloth. VG+/case. w/sgn letter. F1. $300.00

DAVIS, Sue. *Justice Rehnquist & the Constitution.* 1989. Princeton. M11. $22.50

DAVIS, William C. *Jefferson Davis: The Man & His Hour.* 1991. NY. 1st ed. photos/biblio/index. 784p. F/F. A17. $20.00

DAVIS & PEDLER. *Dynostar Menace.* 1975. Scribner. 1st ed. F/F. P3. $10.00

DAVIS. *Horse.* 1907. London. sm 8vo. 106p. VG. R2. $25.00

DAWE, Carlton. *Live Cartridge.* 1937. Ward Lock. 1st ed. xl. VG. P3. $20.00

DAWKINS, Cecil. *Quiet Enemy.* 1963. NY. 1st Am ed. sgn. F/F. A11. $65.00

DAWKINS, R.M. *Monks of Athos.* 1936. London. Allen Unwin. 1st ed. 408p. VG/VG. B33. $50.00

DAWLEY, P.M. *Chapters in Church Hist.* 1950. Nat Council Protestant Episcopal Church. 278p. G/dj. B29. $5.50

DAWSON, Barbara. *Metal Thread Embroidery.* 1976. np. cloth. VG. G2. $14.00

DAWSON, Carol. *Waking Spell.* 1992. Algonquin. 1st ed/author's 1st novel. F/F. B3. $35.00

DAWSON, E. Yale. *New Cacti of Southern Mexico.* 1948. Los Angeles. ils/photos/map chart. wrp. scarce. B26. $26.00

DAWSON, Elmer. *Buck's Winning Hit.* 1930. Grosset Dunlap. Buck & Larry Baseball Stories #2. VG/dj. very scarce. M20. $100.00

DAWSON, Elmer. *Buck's Winning Hit.* 1930. Grosset Dunlap. 1st ed. G+. P8. $15.00

DAWSON, Elmer. *Larry's Fadeaway.* 1930. Grosset Dunlap. VG/G+. P8. $40.00

DAWSON, Elmer. *Larry's Speedball.* 1932. Grosset Dunlap. VG. P8. $20.00

DAWSON, Fielding. *Black Mountain Book.* 1970. NY. 1st ed. sgn. VG+/8vo wrp. A11. $45.00

DAWSON, Fielding. *Emotional Memoir of Franz Kline.* 1967. Pantheon. 1st ed. F/VG+. B4. $65.00

DAWSON, James. *Hell Gate.* 1971. McKay. VG/VG. P3. $10.00

DAWSON, Joseph Martin. *Brooks Takes the Long Look. Biography of SP Brooks.* 1931. Waco, TX. Baylor. sgn. VG. B11. $20.00

DAY, A. Grove. *Mark Twain's Letters From Hawaii.* 1966. Appleton Century. 1st ed. 298p. VG. M10. $15.00

DAY, Clarence M. *'96 Half-Way Book.* 1915. New Haven. Class of 1896/Yale. 1st ed/author's 2nd book. VG. B4. $85.00

DAY, Clarence. *Life With Father.* 1947. Sun Dial. VG/VG. P3. $20.00

DAY, David. *Tolkien Bestiary.* 1979. Ballantine. 1st ed. VG/VG. P3. $25.00

DAY, Donald. *Big Country: Texas.* 1947. NY. 1st ed. 326p. VG. D3. $12.50

DAY, Edgar. *In Princetown Town.* 1929. Scribner. 1st ed. F/VG. B4. $75.00

DAY, Gene. *Future Day.* 1979. Flying Buttress. 1st ed. VG. P3. $15.00

DAY, Gina. *Tell No Tales.* 1967. Hart Davis. 1st ed. F/F. P3. $15.00

DAY, Jane. *Fall of the Aztec Empire.* 1993. Rinehart. 1st ed. 4to. 128p. wrp. F3. $15.00

DAY, Jeremiah. *Inquiry Respecting Self-Determining Power of the Will...* 1838. New Haven. Herrick Noyes. pres. 200p. emb brn cloth. VG. G1. $135.00

DAY & LEE. *Castles.* 1984. Bantam. 1st ed. F/F. P3. $25.00

DAY & STURGES. *Art of the Fantastic: Latin America 1820-1987.* 1987. IN Mus of Art. 1st ed. 1/2500. 302p. wrp. F3. $45.00

DAYTON, William A. *Notes on Western Range Forbs: Equisetaceae...* 1960. WA, DC. ils/photos. 254p. maroon cloth. VG. B26. $17.50

DE ALARCON, Pedro Antonio. *Three-Cornered Hat.* 1944. NY. Bittner. 1/500. 21 hand-colored woodcuts/Kredel. 151p. F. B24. $100.00

DE ALVA IXTILXOCHITL, F. *Ally of Cortes.* 1969. El Paso, TX. W Pr. 1st ed. 141p. VG/dj. F3. $30.00

DE AMICIS, Edmondo. *Constantinople.* 1888. Putnam. 326p. cloth. VG. W1. $25.00

DE ANDREA, William. *Five O'Clock Lightning.* 1982. St Martin. 1st ed. F/VG. P8. $30.00

DE ANDREA, William. *Five O'Clock Lightning.* 1982. St Martin. 1st ed. sgn. F/F. S6. $35.00

DE ANGELI, Marguerite. *Black Fox of Lorne.* 1956. Doubleday. probable 1st ed. lg 8vo. VG+/G. C8. $40.00

DE ANGELI, Marguerite. *Bright April.* 1946. Doubleday Jr Books. inscr/dtd. VG+. C8. $45.00

DE ANGELI, Marguerite. *Bright April.* 1946. Doubleday Jr Books. 1st ed. 86p. cloth. VG/dj. A3. $40.00

DE ANGELI, Marguerite. *Copper-Toed Boots.* 1938. Doubleday Doran. 1st ed. 4to. ils. cloth. VG-/dj. A3. $50.00

DE ANGELI, Marguerite. *Door in the Wall.* 1949. Doubleday Jr Books. 1st ed. 111p. cloth. VG/G. A3. $65.00

DE ANGELI, Marguerite. *Petite Suzanne.* 1937. Doubleday. ils. pict brd/cloth spine. VG. M5. $20.00

DE ANGELI, Marguerite. *Prayers & Graces for Small Children.* 1941. NY. 8vo. ils. pict brd/cloth spine. NF/G. M5. $15.00

DE ANGELI, Marguerite. *Ted & Nina Go to the Grocery Store.* 1935. Doubleday. early rpt. 12mo. unp. pict brd. VG. A3. $25.00

DE ANGELI, Marguerite. *Thee, Hannah!* 1940. Doubleday. 1st ed. F/NF. P2. $85.00

DE ANGELI, Marguerite. *Thee, Hannah!* 1940. Doubleday. 1st ed. 8vo. G+. V3. $12.00

DE ANGELI, Marguerite. *Thee, Hannah!* 1941 (1940). Doubleday. sgn. VG/dj. M20. $70.00

DE ANGELI, Marguerite. *Turkey for Christmas.* 1949. Westminster. 1st ed. unp. VG/dj. M20. $50.00

DE AZCARATE, P. *League of Nations & National Minorities.* 1945. WA, DC. 1st ed. 216p. VG. D3. $20.00

DE BALZAC, Honore. *L'Heritier du Diable.* 1926. Paris. 1st ed thus. 1/500. morocco. F. C2. $400.00

DE BALZAC, Honore. *Napoleon, son Histoire Racontee par un Vieux Soldat...* 1927. Paris. DuCharte. folio. ils/double pl. 85p. pict brd. F. B24. $375.00

DE BALZAC, Honore. *Old Goriot.* 1948. London. LEC. ils/sgn Rene Ben Sussan. F. M19. $50.00

DE BALZAC, Honore. *Ten Droll Tales.* 1931. NY. Rarity. ils Jean De Bosschere. trans J Lewis May. F/G. H1. $15.00

DE BARTHE, Joe. *Life & Adventures of Frank Grouard.* 1958. OK U. 1st ed. ils/maps. VG/dj. B34. $80.00

DE BEAUVOIR, Simone. *Force of Circumstance.* 1965. Putnam. 1st ed. NF/NF. B2. $35.00

DE BEAUVOIR, Simone. *Les Belles Images.* 1968. Collins. 2nd ed. NF/NF. P3. $15.00

DE BEAUVOIR, Simone. *Les Bouches Inutiles.* 1946. Paris. Gallimard. 1st ed. inscr to Bill Targ. F/wrp/dj/clamshell box. B4. $850.00

DE BEAUVOIR, Simone. *Les Mandarins.* 1954. Paris. Gallimard. 1st ed. inscr. 1/100. F/F. B4. $1,250.00

DE BERG, Jeanne. *Woman's Rites.* nd. BC. VG/VG. P3. $8.00

DE BERNIERES, Louis. *Senor Vivo & the Coca Lord.* 1991. Secker Warburg. 1st ed/author's 2nd novel. sgn. F/F. L3. $150.00

DE BOUFFLERS, Stanislas Jean. *Oeuvres de Stanislas de Boufflers...* 1813. Paris. Briand. 2 vol. sm 8vo. ils. brn calf/marbled brd. K1. $150.00

DE BOURRIENNE, M. *Memoirs of Napoleon Bonaparte. By His Private Secretary.* 1836. London. 4 vol. leather/spines poor or missing. A9. $75.00

DE BRUYNE, Edgar. *L'Esthetique du Moyen Age.* 1947. Louvain. Superieur Philosophie. 12mo. 260p. prt wrp. G1. $22.50

DE CAMP, L. Sprague. *Conan Grimoire.* 1972. Mirage. 1st ed. sgn. VG/VG. P3. $65.00

DE CAMP, L. Sprague. *Conan Reader.* 1968. Mirage. 1st ed. sgn De Camp/Krenkel/Wrightson. F/dj. F4. $75.00

DE CAMP, L. Sprague. *Conan Reader.* 1968. Mirage. 1st ed. sgn. VG/VG. P3. $65.00

DE CAMP, L. Sprague. *Conan Swordbook.* 1969. Mirage. 1st ed. sgn. VG/VG. P3. $65.00

DE CAMP, L. Sprague. *Continent Makers.* 1953. Twayne. VG. P3. $25.00

DE CAMP, L. Sprague. *Dark Valley Destiny.* 1983. Bluejay. ltd ed. sgn/#d. F/F/box. P3. $80.00

DE CAMP, L. Sprague. *Demons & Dinosaurs.* 1970. Arkham. 1st ed. F/dj. M2. $300.00

DE CAMP, L. Sprague. *Honorable Barbarian.* 1989. Ballantine. 1st ed. F/dj. F4. $22.00

DE CAMP, L. Sprague. *Lest Darkness Fall.* 1941. Holt. 1st ed/author's 1st novel. F. N3. $70.00

DE CAMP, L. Sprague. *Lest Darkness Fall.* 1949. Prime. 1st ed thus. sgn. VG/dj. F4. $60.00

DE CAMP, L. Sprague. *Lost Continents.* 1954. Gnome. 1st ed. VG. P3. $40.00

DE CAMP, L. Sprague. *Lovecraft: A Biography.* 1975. London. 1st ed. F/dj. M2. $40.00

DE CAMP, L. Sprague. *Pixilate Peeress.* 1991. Ballantine. 1st ed. sgn. F/F. F4. $25.00

DE CAMP, L. Sprague. *Tales of Conan.* 1955. Gnome. 1st ed. sgn. F/NF. F4. $50.00

DE CAMP & DE CAMP. *Footprints on Sand.* 1981. Advent. 1st ed. F/F. P3. $20.00

DE CAMP & NYBERG. *Return of Conan.* 1957. Gnome. 1st ed. VG/VG. P3. $90.00

DE CAMP & PRATT. *Castle of Iron.* 1950. Gnome. 1st ed. VG/chip. P3. $75.00

DE CAMP & PRATT. *Complete Compleat Enchanter.* nd. Quality BC. VG/VG. P3. $10.00

DE CAMP & PRATT. *Tales From Gavagan's Bar.* 1978. Owlswick. 1st ed. xl. dj. P3. $10.00

DE CAMP & PRATT. *Unbeheaded King.* 1983. Del Rey. 1st ed. F/F. P3. $18.00

DE CAMP & PRATT. *Undesired Princess.* 1951. FPCI. 1st ed. VG/G. P3. $75.00

DE CAMP & PRATT. *Wheels of If.* 1948. Shasta. 1st ed. VG/G. P3. $150.00

DE CARAVA & HUGHS. *Sweet Flypaper of Life.* 1955. Simon Schuster. 1st ed. 12mo. VG+/wrp. S9. $125.00

DE CARDENAS, Juan. *Problemas y Secretos Maravillosos de las Indians.* 1945. Madrid. Cultura Hispanica. 4to. 247p. VG/wrp/dj. F3. $35.00

DE CARDONNEL, Adam. *Numismata Scotiae; or, Series of Scottish Coinage.* 1786. Edinburgh. Nicol. 20 engraved pl. old calf. K1. $250.00

DE CASSERES, Walter. *Sublime Boy: Poems of Walter De Casseres.* 1926. NY. Seven Arts. 1st ed. NF/worn. B2. $50.00

DE CASTELNAU, Michael. *Memoirs of the Reigns of Frances II & Charles IX of France.* 1724. London. full leather. G. B18. $150.00

DE CERVANTES, Miguel. *Don Quixote de la Mancha.* 1819. London. T M'Lean. ils JH Clark. 19th-C gr calf/marbled brd. K1. $250.00

DE CERVANTES, Miguel. *Don Quixote de la Mancha.* 1941. Random. trans Peter Motteux. ils HA Mueller. 567p. VG. S11. $10.00

DE CERVANTES, Miguel. *El Ingenioso Hidalgo Don Quijote de la Mancha.* 1952. Madrid. Castilla. 2 vol. 62x46mm. ils gilt kelly gr morocco. F/case. B24. $225.00

DE CHABERT, Joseph Bernard. *Voyage Fait par Ordre du Roi en 1750 et 1751...* 1753. Paris. Imprimerie Royale. 4to. 288p. contemporary mottled calf. red cloth case. K1. $200.00

DE CHAIR, Somerset. *Golden Carpet.* 1944. Faber. 1st ed. 224p. yel linen. VG. M7. $35.00

DE CHANCIE, John. *Magicnet.* 1993. Borderlands. 1st ed. sgn. 1/350. F/F. T2. $15.00

DE CHARMS, Richard. *Personal Causation: Internal Affective Determinants...* 1968. Academic. 398p. bl cloth. VG. G1. $17.50

DE CIVRIEUX, Marc. *Watunna: Orinoco Creation Cycle.* 1980. Northpoint. 1st ed. 195p. VG/dj. F3. $20.00

DE COMBRAY, Richard. *Caravansary: Alone in Moslem Places.* 1978. Doubleday. 1st ed. 179p. F/dj. W1. $8.00

DE COMINES, Philippe. *Historie of Philip de Commines: Knight, Lord of Argenton.* 1601. London. Norton. 2nd ed. sm folio. 264p. old paneled calf. K1. $450.00

DE COMINES, Philippe. *Les Memoires sur les Faicts & Gestes Abbregees Loys XI...* 1597. Anvers. Martin Nutius. 12mo. 756p. contemporary vellum. K1. $275.00

DE CONDILLAC, Etienne Bonnot. *Philosophical Writings of...* 1987. Hillsdale, NJ. Lawrence Erlbaum. 423p. prt gr cloth. VG. G1. $25.00

DE CROIX, Teodoro. *Northern Frontier of New Spain 1776-1783.* 1968. OK U. edit AB Thomas. ils/notes/index. 273p. NF/NF. B19. $25.00

DE FELICE. *Encyclopedie Ou Dictionnaire Universel Raisonne...* 1776. Yverdon. 4to. 11 fld pl. full flame calf. F. C6. $600.00

DE FELITTA, Frank. *Audrey Rose.* 1975. Putnam. 3rd ed. VG/VG. P3. $13.00

DE FELITTA, Frank. *Audrey Rose.* 1975. Putnam. 1st ed. F/VG. N3. $15.00

DE FELITTA, Frank. *Entity.* 1978. Putnam. 1st ed. G+/dj. P3. $13.00

DE FOE, Daniel. *Life & Strange Suprising Adventures of Robinson Crusoe.* 1929. London. Etchells Macdonald. 1/525. ils Kauffer. pub pres. VG. C11. $315.00

DE FONTENELLE, M. *Hist of Oracles...* 1753. Glasgow. Urie. 12mo. 144p. leather. H10. $100.00

DE FOREST, John William. *Volunteer's Adventures.* 1946. index. 237p. xl. VG. O8. $21.00

DE FOREST, Katharine. *Paris As It Is.* 1900. Paris. Brantanos. 1st ed. 188p. VG. S11. $15.00

DE FUENTES, Patricia. *Conquistadors.* 1963. NY. Orion. 1st ed. ils. 250p. VG/dj. F3. $25.00

DE GARMO, Louis. *Play Golf & Enjoy It.* 1954. NY. 95p. gray cloth. F. B14. $25.00

DE GAST, Robert. *Doors of San Miguel de Allende.* 1994. Pomegranate. 1st ed. 96p. M. F3. $17.00

DE GAULTIER, Jules. *Nietzche.* 1926. Paris. Siecle. 12mo. lib buckram. G1. $27.50

DE GEORGE, L. *La Maison Plantin a Anvers 1555 a 1589.* 1886. Paris. ils. VG. K3. $30.00

DE GORTER, Johannes. *Praxis Medicae Systema.* 1750. Hardervici. Wigmans. 2 vol in 1. sgn. quarter calf. G7. $395.00

DE GRAY, Thomas. *Compleat Horse-Man & Expert Ferrier.* 1650. London. 2 vol in 1. 3rd ed. sheepskin. B14. $1,050.00

DE GRAZIA, Ted. *DeGrazia Paints Cabeza de Vaca: 1st Non-Indian in TX, NM...* 1973. AZ U. 1st ed. ils. B19. $50.00

DE GRAZIA, Ted. *Father Junipero Serra. Sketches of His Life in CA.* (1970). Ward Ritchie/SW Mus. 1/100. w/orig sgn watercolor. F/dj/case. K1. $450.00

DE GUERIN, Basil C. *Man With Three Eyes.* 1955. Children's Pr. 1st ed. VG. P3. $15.00

DE GUERVILLE, A.B. *New Egypt.* 1906. Heinemann. 2nd ed. VG. W1. $12.00

DE HAAN, M.R. *Genesis & Evolution.* 1962. Zondervan. 152p. VG/dj. B29. $5.50

DE HAAN, M.R. *Hebrews: 26 Simple Studies in God's Pattern...* 1959. Zondervan. 192p. F/dj. B29. $5.00

DE HAAN, M.R. *Jew & Palestine in Prophecy.* 1950. Zondervan. 183p. G/dj. B29. $5.50

DE HAAN, M.R. *Portraits of Christ in Genesis.* 1966. Zondervan. 192p. F/dj. B29. $5.00

DE HARTOG, Jan. *Peaceable Kingdom.* 1972. Atheneum. 8vo. 677p. G/G. V3. $16.00

DE HERIZ, Patrick. *La Belle O'Morphi: A Brief Biography.* nd. Golden Cockeral. 1/750. 36p. bl/rose cloth. VG. S11. $25.00

DE Jong, Dola. *Whirligig of Time.* 1964. Crime Club. 1st ed. xl. dj. P3. $5.00

DE JONG, Meindert. *Far Out the Long Canal.* 1964. Harper Row. 1st ed. 231p. VG/G+. A3. $15.00

DE KAY, James. *Sketches of Turkey in 1831 & 1832 by an American.* 1833. Harper. 1st ed. 8vo. 527p. VG. W1. $145.00

DE KNIGHT, Freda. *Date With a Dish: Cookbook of American Negro Recipes.* 1948. Hermitage. 1st ed. inscr. NF. B2. $40.00

DE KOBRA, Maurice. *La Sphinx a Parle...Roman.* 1947. Paris. Baudiniere. sm 8vo. 255p. lib buckram. xl. VG. W1. $8.00

DE KOBRA, Maurice. *Serenade to the Hang Man.* 1929. Payson Clarke. 1st ed. NF/dj. F4. $65.00

DE KOVEN, Mrs. Reginald. *Sawdust Doll.* 1895. Chicago. Stone Kimball. Peacock Lib Series. Art Nouveau-style bdg. F. F1. $75.00

DE KRUIF, Paul. *Mikroben Jager. Zwiete Auf.* 1927. Zurich. 65 pl. 350p. G7. $25.00

DE LA FONTAINE, Jean. *Fables of Jean de la Fontaine.* 1930. LEC. 2 vol. ils/sgn Rudolph Ruzicka. F/case. M19. $50.00

DE LA FONTAINE, Jean. *Fables of...* 1931. Random. 2 vol. 1/525. trans/sgn Edward Marsh. ils/sgn Stephen Gooden. F/case. H4. $550.00

DE LA FOSSE, Peter H. *Trailing the Pioneers: Guide to UT's Emigrant Trails...* nd. np. sgn. maps/biblio/index. sc. M. A18. $15.00

DE LA MARE, Walter. *Ding-Dong Bell.* 1924. London. Selwyn Blount. 1st ed/1st imp. 76p. red cloth VG/VG. S11. $45.00

DE LA MARE, Walter. *Listeners & Other Poems.* 1924. London. Constable. 10th imp. 92p. aeg. bl-gr bdg. VG+. M7. $25.00

DE LA MARE, Walter. *Memoirs of a Midget.* 1921. London. Collins. 1st ed/1st imp. 365p. G/fair. S11. $45.00

DE LA MARE, Walter. *Rhymes & Verses: Collected Poems for Young People.* 1947. Holt. 1st ed. sgn. F/VG. V1. $25.00

DE LA MARE, Walter. *Three Mulla Mulgars.* 1924. Selwyn Blount. 1/260. sgn. ils JA Shepherd. 247p. unopened. VG+. P2. $175.00

DE LA MARE, Walter. *Veil & Other Poems.* 1921. London. Constable. 1/250. sgn. gray paper brd/linen spine/leather label. VG. M7. $95.00

DE LA MAZA, Francisco. *Antinoo: El Ultimo Dios Del Mundo Clasico.* 1966. Mexico. UNAM. 1st ed. Lib Congress duplicate stp. 411p. VG. F3. $15.00

DE LA MAZA, Luis Reyes. *El Teatro en Mexico Durante el Porfirismo.* 1968. Mexico. UNAM. 1st ed. 1/1500. 545p. VG/dj. F3. $25.00

DE LA PORTE, Francois. *Nature's Second Kingdom: Explorations of Vegetality...* 1982. Cambridge. MIT. 266p. M/dj. A10. $20.00

DE LA REE, Gerry. *Art of the Fantastic.* 1978. De La Ree. 1st ed. NF/NF. P3. $50.00

DE LA REE, Gerry. *Fantasy by Fabian.* 1978. De La Ree. 1st ed. NF/NF. P3. $35.00

DE LA ROCHE, Mazo. *Jalna.* 1927. Toronto. Macmillan. 1st ed. inscr. pict cloth. VG. C8. $75.00

DE LA ROCHE, Mazo. *Possession.* 1923. Toronto. Macmillan. 1st ed. inscr. pict cloth. VG. C8. $75.00

DE LA ROCHE, Mazo. *Renny's Daughter.* 1951. Little Brn. 1st ed. VG/G. P3. $18.00

DE LA ROCHE, Mazo. *Renny's Daughter.* 1951. London. Macmillan. 1st UK ed. inscr. VG+/VG. C8. $75.00

DE LA ROCHE, Mazo. *Wakefield's Course.* 1941. Little Brn. 1st ed. inscr. emb cloth. VG+/VG. C8. $75.00

DE LA ROCHE, Mazo. *White Oak Heritage.* 1940. Toronto. Macmillan. 1st ed. inscr. VG/VG. C8. $65.00

DE LA ROCHE, Mazo. *White Oaks of Jalna.* 1929. Toronto. Macmillan. 1st ed. inscr. VG+. C8. $75.00

DE LA ROQUE, J. *Voyage to Arabia the Happy...by Way of the Eastern Ocean...* 1726. London. 1st Eng ed. ils/maps. contemporary brd/new spine. O2. $425.00

DE LABRIOLLE, Pierre. *Hist & Literature of Christianity From Tertillian...* 1924. London. Kegan Paul. 555p. H10. $35.00

DE LANG, Nicholas. *Judaism.* 1986. Oxford. 156p. F/dj. B29. $6.00

DE LEEUW, H. *Crossroads of the Mediterranean.* 1953. Hanover. 1st ed. 224p. NF/dj. W1. $14.00

DE LEEUW, Hendrik. *Flower of Joy.* 1944. Willey Book. 1st ed. F/NF. B2. $35.00

DE LILLO, Don. *Americana.* 1973. NY. 1st pb ed/author's 1st novel. sgn. F. A11. $45.00

DE LILLO, Don. *Day Room.* 1987. Knopf. 1st ed. F/F. L3. $65.00

DE LILLO, Don. *End Zone.* 1973. London. 1st Eng ed/simultaneous wrp issue/2nd novel. sgn. NF. A11. $60.00

DE LILLO, Don. *Great Jones Street.* 1973. Houghton Mifflin. 1st ed/author's 3rd book. F/NF. B4. $150.00

DE LILLO, Don. *Libra.* 1988. Viking. 1st ed. F/F. P3. $20.00

DE LILLO, Don. *Ratner's Star.* 1976. Knopf. 1st ed. F/NF. B4. $125.00

DE LINT, Charles. *Cafe Purgatorium.* 1991. NY. Tor. 1st ed. F/F. T2. $20.00

DE LINT, Charles. *Dreams Underfoot.* 1993. Tor. 1st ed. sgn. F/F. P3. $30.00

DE LINT, Charles. *Ghosts of Wind & Shadow.* 1991. Axototl. Special/1st ed. sgn. F/F. P3. $45.00

DE LINT, Charles. *Little Country.* 1991. Morrow. 1st ed. VG/VG. P3. $20.00

DE LINT, Charles. *Our Lady of the Harbor.* 1991. Axolotl. Special/1st ed. sgn. F/F. P3. $45.00

DE LINT, Charles. *Riddle of the Wren.* 1994. Seattle. Hargreaves. 1st hc ed. sgn. ils/sgn Charles Vess. F/sans. T2. $55.00

DE LONG, Fred. *Guide to Bicycles & Bicycling.* 1975. Randor, PA. Chilton. ils. 278p. VG/dj. M10. $7.50

DE LONG, Thomas F. *Hist & Roster of 103rd Ammunition Train.* nd. Allentown, PA. 103rd Pub Co. 96p. VG. H1. $25.00

DE LORIA, J. *God Is Red.* 1973. NY. 1st ed. VG/VG. B5. $32.50

DE LTEIL, Joseph. *Joan of Arc.* 1926. NY. trans Malcolm Cowley. VG/dj. B18. $35.00

DE LTEIL, Loys. *Manuel de L'Amateur d'Estampes Des XIX et XX Siecles...* 1925. Paris. Dorbon-Aine. 2 vol. lg 8vo. 158 pl. pub bdg. K1. $175.00

DE MAUPASSANT, Guy. *Dark Side of Guy de Maupassant.* 1989. Carroll Graf. 1st ed. trans Arnold Kellett. F/F. T2. $20.00

DE MAUPASSANT, Guy. *Mont Oriel.* nd. St Dunstain Soc. VG. P3. $15.00

DE MILFORD, Louis Le Clerc. *Memoir; or, Cursory Glance at Different Travels...* 1956. Lakeside. 257p. VG. M20. $30.00

DE MOLIERE, Jean B.P. *Tartuffe; or, The French Puritan...* 1707. London. Wellington. 2nd appearance in Eng. sm 4to. 66p. later bdg. K1. $375.00

DE MONTHERLANT, Henry. *La Maree Du Soir.* 1972. Paris. Gallimard. 1/2300. La Collection Soleil Series. S9. $30.00

DE MONTREAL, Miguel. *Enganos de Mugeres...* 1709. Madrid. Murga. 2nd ed. 4to. 280p. vellum. K1. $450.00

DE MORGAN, Augustus. *Budget of Paradoxes.* 1915 (1872). Chicago. Open Court. 2 vol. 2nd ed. red cloth/leather label. NF. G1. $125.00

DE MUSSET, Paul. *Mr Wind & Madam Rain.* 1864. Harper. 1st Am ed. royal bl cloth. VG. M5. $150.00

DE NERVAL, Gerard. *Women of Cairo: Scenes of Life in the Orient. Vol 2.* ca 1930. Harcourt Brace. 1st ed. 402p. VG. W1. $10.00

DE NOGALES, Rafael. *Looting of Nicaragua.* 1928. McBride. 1st ed. 304p. map ep. VG. F3. $30.00

DE NOGALES, Rafael. *Memoirs of a Soldier of Fortune.* 1932. NY. 1st ed. 8vo. 380p. cloth. O2. $45.00

DE PONCINS, Gontran. *Kabloona.* 1941. NY. photos. 339p. VG/VG. A17. $9.50

DE PROROK, Byron. *Digging for Lost African Gods.* 1926. London/NY. 1st ed. 8vo. 369p. teg. VG. W1. $25.00

DE PROROK, Byron. *In Quest of Lost Worlds.* 1935. Dutton. 1st ed. 281p. VG. W1. $15.00

DE QUESADA & NORTHROP. *War in Cuba Being a Full Account of Her Great Struggle...* 1896. Liberty Pub. 8vo. ils/pl. 584p. G. B11. $45.00

DE QUEVEDO, Don Francisco. *Dog & the Fever.* 1954. Hampden, CT. Shoe String. 1st ed thus. F. E3. $35.00

DE QUILLE, Dan. *Snow-Shoe Thompson.* 1954. Los Angeles. Glen Dawson. 1/210 on Arches. linoleum block prts. brd. F. K1. $400.00

DE QUINCY, Thomas. *Confessions of an English Opium-Eater.* 1930. London. LEC. ils/sgn Zhenya Gay. VG/case. M19. $75.00

DE RO & ELDRIDGE. *Catalogue of $140,000 Jewelry, Watches & Diamonds.* 1857-1859. San Francisco. Alta Job Office. 1st ed. 12mo. 32p. prt wrp. M1. $300.00

DE ROUEN FORTH, Nevill. *Fighting Colonel of the Camel Corps.* 1991. Braunton Devon. Merlin Books. 1st ed. 201p. M/pict dj. M7. $30.00

DE ROUGEMONT, Denis. *Love in the Western World.* 1956. Pantheon. 2nd enlarged ed. 336p. VG/dj. G1. $30.00

DE ROUVIERE, Henry. *Voyage du Tour de la France.* 1713. Paris. 504p. full leather. 5. $45.00

DE SADE, Marquis. *Justine.* 1964. Castle. VG/G. P3. $8.00

DE SAINT-EXUPERY, Antoine. *Regulus vel Pueri Soli Sapiunt, qui Liber le Petit Prince...* 1961. Paris. Fernand Hazan. 1st Latin ed. 8vo. gilt tan cloth. VG/dj. D6. $25.00

DE SAINT-EXUPERY, Antoine. *Wind, Sand & Stars.* 1943. London. Heinemann. Armed Services ed. pb. G. B3. $10.00

DE SAINT-SYLVESTRE, H. *L'Arche de Noe.* nd. Paris. obl 8vo. red cloth. VG. D6. $100.00

DE SCHWEINITZ, G.E. *Diseases of the Eye: Handbook of Ophthalmic Practice...* 1896. Phil. 2nd ed. pres. 697p. cloth. G7. $125.00

DE SEGONZAC, Dunoyer. *Dunoyer DeSegonzac.* 1951. Geneva. Cailler. 1st ed. 19 pl. French text. VG+/VG+/cb wrp. S9. $200.00

DE SEGUR, Mme. La Comtesse. *Un Bon Petit Diable.* 1907. Paris. ils. aeg. Bibliotheque Rose Illustree bdg. VG. M5. $30.00

DE SPINOZA, Benedict. *Ethic, Demontrated in Geometrical Order...* 1923. London. Humphrey Milford/Oxford. 4th revised ed. r cloth. G1. $45.00

DE STAEL-HOLSTEIN, Baronne. *Reflexions sur le Suicide, Suivies Defense Reine...* 1814. Paris. Nicolle Freres. 1st combined ed. modern red morocco/marbled brd. 1. $275.00

DE TERRA, Helmut. *Man & Mammoth in Mexico.* 1957. London. Hutchinson. 1st ed. 16 pl/6 maps. 191p. map ep. VG/chip. F3. $20.00

DE TORRES, Miguel. *Vida Exemplar, y Muerte Preciosa de la Madre Barbara...* 1725. Mexico. Lupercio. 4to. ils. 528p. sm worm hole. H10. $225.00

DE TROYES, Chretien. *Complete Romances of Chretien De Troyes.* 1993. IN U. VG/VG. 3. $35.00

DE VAMATA, Sister. *Days in an Indian Monastery.* 1927. La Crescenta. Ananda Ashrama. 326p. VG/VG. B33. $20.00

DE VAUCOULEURS, Gerard. *Discovery of the Universe.* 1957. London. Faber. 8vo. s/20 pl. 328p. VG/dj. K5. $30.00

DE VAUCOULEURS, Gerard. *Reverence Catalogue of Bright Galaxies...* 1964. TX U. 1st d. 268p. VG/worn. K5. $125.00

DE VILLAR & DE VILLAR. *Where the Strange Roads Go Down.* 1953. Macmillan. 1st ed. 344p. VG/chip. F3. $20.00

DE VINNE, Theodore. *First Editor: Aldus Pius Manutius.* 1983. Targ. 1st ed. ils Antonio Frasconi. 1/250. F/case. K1. $100.00

DE VOTO, Bernard. *Across the Wide Missouri.* 1947. np. 1st ed. VG/dj. B34. $150.00

DE VOTO, Bernard. *Journals of Lewis & Clark.* 1953. Houghton Mifflin. edit ed. VG. B34. $45.00

DE VOTO, Bernard. *Mark Twain's America.* 1932. Little Brn. 1st ed. ils. 353p. VG. M10. $20.00

DE VOTO, Bernard. *Mountain Time.* 1947. Little Brn. VG/dj. B34. $20.00

DE VOTO, Bernard. *Year of Decicion: 1846.* 1943. Little Brn. VG/torn. B34. $35.00

DE VOTO, Bernard. *Year of Decision: 1846.* 1989. Houghton Mifflin. 2nd sc prt. M. A18. $12.95

DE VRIES, Leonard. *Flowers of Delight.* 1965. Pantheon. 4to. 700 woodcuts. 232p. VG. S11. $20.00

DE VRIES, Leonard. *Little Wide-Awake.* 1967. World. 1st Am ed. ils. 240p. gilt gr cloth. VG/VG. S11. $35.00

DE VRIES, Peter. *Angels Can't Do Better.* 1944. Coward. 1st ed. F/NF. B2. $350.00

DE VRIES, Peter. *No But I Saw the Movie.* 1952. Boston. 1st ed. VG/G. B5. $95.00

DE WALEFFE, Maurice. *Fair Lands of Central America.* 1911. London. John Long. 1st ed. 288p. VG. F3. $20.00

DE WARVILLE, Birissot. *New Travels in the US of Am.* 1919. Bowling Gr, OH. CS Van Tassel. 544p. VG+. M20. $30.00

DEACON, Richard. *Madoc & the Discovery of Am.* 1966. Brazillier. 1st Am ed. 269p. VG+/dj. A18. $18.00

DEAK. *Picturing America 1497-1899: Prints, Maps & Drawings.* 1988. Princeton. Vol II only. 4to. 1029 pl. F/F. A4. $135.00

DEAN, Amber. *Bullet Proof.* 1960. Crime Club. 1st ed. xl. dj. P3. $5.00

DEAN, Amber. *Wrap It Up.* 1946. Crime Club. 1st ed. VG/G. P3. $15.00

DEAN, Graham N. *Herb Kent, West Point Fullback.* 1936. Goldsmith. VG/frayed. M2. $20.00

DEAN, Joseph. *Hatred, Ridicule or Contempt: A Book of Libel Cases.* 1953. London. Constable. M11. $35.00

DEAN, Robert George. *Affair at Lover's Leap.* 1953. Crime Club. 1st ed. G/dj. P3. $18.00

DEAN, Spencer. *Murder After a Fashion.* 1960. Doubleday. 1st ed. VG/VG. P3. $25.00

DEANDREA, William L. *Killed on the Rocks.* 1990. Mysterious. 1st ed. F/F. P3. $18.00

DEANE, Norman; See Creasey, John.

DEANE, Samuel. *New England Farmer; or, Geogical Dictionary...* 1790. Worcester. Thomas. 1st ed. 335p. F. H10. $425.00

DEANE, Samuel. *New England Farmer; or, Georgical Dictionary...* 1822. Boston. Wells. 3rd ed. 532p. leather. H10. $125.00

DEAR, Ian. *Champagne Mumm Book of Ocean Racing.* 1985. Hearst Marine. 1st ed. ils. 157p. T7. $30.00

DEAR & STOWERS. *Please...Don't Kill Me.* 1989. Boston. Houghton Mifflin. 1st ed. sgn Dear. 245p. VG/dj. B18. $15.00

DEAVER, John B. *Surgical Anatomy. Vol 1.* 1899. Blakiston's Son. 4to. 151 engraved pl. 632p. leather. G. H1. $15.00

DEBASQUE, Roger. *Eastern Mediterranean Cooking.* 1973. Galahad. 1st ed. 100p. VG/dj. W1. $18.00

DEBRAY, Xavier Blanchard. *Sketch of Hist of Debray's Regiment of TX Cavalry.* 1961. Waco Village Pr. 2nd ed. 1/300. 26p. F/wp/dj. C6. $55.00

DEBREYNE, P.J.C. *Pensees d'un Croyant Catholique, Considerations...* 1840. Paris. Poussielgue-Rusand. 2nd revised ed. 496p. VG. G1. $125.00

DEBS, Eugne V. *Walls & Bars.* 1927. Chicago. Socialist Party. lg paper ed. sgn Deb's brother. F/rare tissue dj/box. B2. $200.00

DEBUS, Allen. *Medicine in Seventeenth Century England.* 1974. Berkeley. 1st ed. 485p. dj. A13. $75.00

DEEN, Edith. *All the Women of the Bible.* 1955. Harper. 410p. G. B29. $6.50

DEEPING, Warwick. *I Live Again.* 1942. Knopf. 1st ed. F/clip. F4. $25.00

DEEPING, Warwick. *Old Pybus.* 1930. Cassell. 8th prt. VG. P3. $10.00

DEERING, James H. *Code of Civil Procedure of State of CA.* 1899. San Francisco. Bancroft Whitney. contemporary sheep. M11. $50.00

DEHAAS, Arline. *Tenderloin.* 1928. Grosset. 1st ed. VG/dj. F4. $25.00

DEIGHTON, Len. *Battle of Britain.* 1980. Clarke Irwin. F/F. P3. $25.00

DEIGHTON, Len. *Berlin Game.* 1983. Hutchinson. 1st ed. F/F. P3. $18.00

DEIGHTON, Len. *Billion Dollar Brain.* 1966. London. Cape. 1st ed. VG/G. P3. $45.00

DEIGHTON, Len. *Blitzkrieg.* 1979. London. Cape. 1st ed. F/F. M15. $45.00

DEIGHTON, Len. *Blitzkrieg.* 1979. London. Cape. 1st ed. VG. P3. $20.00

DEIGHTON, Len. *Expensive Place To Die.* 1967. London. Cape. 1st Eng ed. F/F. w/transit document. M15. $85.00

DEIGHTON, Len. *Fighter: True Story of the Battle of Britain.* 1978. NY. 1st ed. 260p. VG/dj. B18. $22.50

DEIGHTON, Len. *Ipcress File.* 1963. Simon Schuster. 1st Am ed. F/NF. M15. $150.00

DEIGHTON, Len. *Len Deighton's London Dossier.* 1967. London. Cape. 1st ed. VG/VG. S11. $50.00

DEIGHTON, Len. *London Match.* 1985. Knopf. 1st ed. F/F. P3. $18.00

DEIGHTON, Len. *London Match.* 1985. London. Hutchinson. 1st ed. F/NF. B3. $20.00

DEIGHTON, Len. *Mamista.* 1991. Century. 1st ed. F/F. P3. $25.00

DEIGHTON, Len. *Spy Line.* 1989. Hutchinson. 1st ed. F/F. P3. $23.00

DEIGHTON, Len. *Spy Sinker.* 1990. Hutchinson. 1st ed. F/F. P3. $23.00

DEIGHTON, Len. *SS-GB.* 1978. Jonathan Cape. 1st ed. VG/VG. P3. $25.00

DEIGHTON, Len. *XPD.* 1981. Knopf. 1st ed. F/F. P3. $20.00

DEKKER, Carl. *Woman in Marble.* 1972. Bobbs Merrill. 1st ed. VG/VG. P3. $20.00

DEKKER, George. *James Fenimore Cooper the Novelist.* 1967. London. Routledge/Kegan Paul. 1st ed. F/clip. A18. $20.00

DEKOBRA, Maurice. *Venus on Wheels.* 1930. Macaulay. 1st ed. F/dj. F4. $70.00

DEL MARTIA, Aston; see Fearn, John Russell.

DEL REY, Judy-Lynn. *Stellar #4.* nd. BC. F/F. P3. $8.00

DEL REY, Lester. *Badge of Infamy.* 1976. Dobson. 1st ed. VG/VG. P3. $20.00

DEL REY, Lester. *Best SF Stories of the Year: 4th Annual Collection.* 1975. Dutton. 1st ed. F/NF. N3. $10.00

DEL REY, Lester. *Cave of Spears.* 1957. Knopf. 1st ed. VG. P3. $20.00

DEL REY, Lester. *Moon of Mutiny.* 1979. Gregg. 1st ed. F/F. P3. $20.00

DEL REY, Lester. *Rocket From Infinity.* 1966. HRW. 1st ed. NF/NF. P3. $30.00

DEL REY, Lester. *Year After Tomorrow.* 1954. Winston. 1st ed. 339p. VG/dj. B18. $27.50

DELAND, Margaret. *Encore.* 1907. Harper. 1st ed. ils Alice Barber Stephens. 79p. VG. M20. $20.00

DELANY, Samuel R. *Nova.* 1977. Gregg. VG. P3. $30.00

DELANY & DELANY. *Having Our Say.* 1993. Kodansha. AP. NF/wrp. B2. $35.00

DELAYEN, Gaston. *Cleopatra.* 1934. Dutton. 1st ed. 280p. VG. W1. $20.00

DELEHANTY, Elizabeth. *Arise From Sleep.* 1942. NY. 1st ed/author's 1st novel. F/F. A17. $10.00

DELEHAYA, Hippolyte. *Legends of the Saints.* 1962. Fordham. 3rd ed. 252p. VG/dj. W1. $15.00

DELESSERT & SCHMID. *Endless Party.* 1967. Harlen Quest. 1st ed. unp. VG/VG. A3. $12.50

DELEUZE, Joseph P.F. *Instruction Pratique sur le Magnetisme Animal...* 1825. Paris. Dentu. 1st ed. 472p. gr calf/gr brd. K1. $250.00

DELEUZE & FELIX. *Anti-Oedipus: Capitalism & Schizophrenia.* 1983. Minneapolis. trade pb. 400p. G1. $22.50

DELEYRE, Alexandre. *Le Genie de Montesquieu.* 1762. Amsterdam. Arkstee Merkus. 436p. contemporary mottled calf. K1. $175.00

DELL, Ethel M. *Man Under Authority.* (1926). Ryerson/Putnam. 419p. VG/F. H1. $4.50

DELL, Floyd. *King Arthur's Socks & Other Village Plays.* 1922. Knopf. 1st ed. F/NF. B2. $50.00

DELL, Floyd. *Souvenir.* 1929. Doubleday Doran. 1st ed. VG+/dj. B2. $125.00

DELLBRIDGE, John. *Unfit To Plead.* 1949. Hurst Blackett. 1st ed. VG/G. P3. $18.00

DELMAR, Vina. *Kept Woman.* 1929. Harcourt. 1st ed. F/F. B2. $35.00

DELME, Radcliffe. *Noble Science of Fox Hunting.* 1911. London. 2 vol. new ed. ils. VG. C11. $125.00

DELMORE, J. *Eucharist in the New Testament...* 1964. Baltimore. Helicon. index. 160p. H10. $15.00

DELVING, Michael. *China Expert.* 1976. Scribner. 1st ed. NF/NF. P3. $25.00

DEMARINIS, Rick. *Coming Up of the Free World.* 1988. Viking. 1st ed. F/F. B3. $25.00

DEMARINIS, Rick. *Jack & Jill.* 1979. Dutton. 1st ed. NF/VG. B3. $30.00

DEMARINIS, Rick. *Scimitar.* 1977. Dutton. 1st ed. VG/VG. P3. $25.00

DEMARINIS, Rick. *Under the Wheat.* 1986. Pittsburgh. 1st ed. sgn. F/F. B3. $45.00

DEMARINIS, Rick. *Year of the Zinc Penny.* 1989. Norton. 1st ed. VG/VG. P3. $18.00

DEMARIS, Ovid. *Brothers in Blood.* 1977. Scribner. 1st ed. VG. P3. $20.00

DEMBER, William N. *Psychology of Perception.* 1960. HRW. 402p. M/dj. K4. $15.00

DEMIJOHN, Thomas; see Disch, Thomas M

DEMING, Richard. *Assignment: Th Arranger.* 1969. Whitman. TVTI. VG. P3. $8.00

DEMING, William Edwards. *Some Theor of Sampling.* 1950. NY/London. Wiley Chapman Hall. 591p. F/dj. K4. $15.00

DEMOS, Raphael. *Philosophy of Plato.* 1939 Scribner. 406p. VG/VG. B33. $25.00

DEMPSEY, Hugh. *Crowfoot, Chief of th Blackfeet.* 1972. OK U. 1st ed. ils/maps. VG B34. $10.00

DENISON, Frederic. *Battle of Groveton* 1885. Providence, RI. 1st ed. 1/250. 35p NF/prt wrp. M8. $45.00

DENKER, Henry. *Case of Libel, a Play i Three Acts...* 1964. Random. M11. $50.00

DENKER, Henry. *Experiment.* 1976. Simo Schuster. 1st ed. F/F. P3. $10.00

DENLINGER, Milo G. *Complete Doberma Pinscher.* 1953. Richmond. 1st ed. ils. cloth VG+. R2. $50.00

DENLINGER, Milo G. *Complete Pomera nian.* 1950. Silver Spring, MD. Denlinger 1st ed. ils. 128p. cloth. F. R2. $30.00

DENNING, Alfred. *Landmarks in the Law* 1984. London. Butterworths. 394p. sew wrp. M11. $20.00

DENNING, W.F. *Telescopic Work fo Starlight Evenings.* 1891. London. Taylo Francis. 1st ed. 8vo. 361p. gilt maroon cloth G. K5. $200.00

DENNING & PHILLIPS. *Magical Philoso phy.* 1974-1978. St Paul. Llewellyn. 4 vol (c 5). 1st ed. NF. B33. $95.00

DENNIS, Amarie. *Seek the Darkness: Stor of Juana LaLoca.* 1953. Madrid, Spain VG/wrp. N2. $7.50

DENNIS, J. *Grant Wood.* 1975. Viking. 1 ed. VG/VG. B5. $50.00

DENNIS, Lane T. *Letters of Francis A Schae fer.* 1985. Crossway. 1st prt. 264p. M/N B29. $9.00

DENNIS, Patrick. *Genius.* 1962. HBW. 1 ed. 308p. F/VG. H1. $22.50

DENNIS-JONES, H. *Your Guide to Morocc* 1965. Redman. sm 8vo. 278p. VG. W1. $12.0

DENSLOW, W.W. *Denslow's Picture Boo Treasury.* 1990. Arcade. 1st ed. 4to. rem m F/F. B17. $8.00

DENT, Alan. *Bernard Shaw & Mrs Campbe Their Correspondence.* 1952. Knopf. 1st A ed. VG/dj. N2. $10.00

DENT, Lester. *Dead at the Take-Off.* 194 Cassell. G+. P3. $20.00

DENVER ART MUSEUM. *Child's Chris mas Bookbook.* 1964. Denver. ils. VG/wr scarce. M5. $20.00

DER NERSESSIAN, Sirarpie. *Aght' Amar: Church of the Holy Cross.* 1965. Cambridge. folio. 77 pl. 60p. cloth. dj. O2. $45.00

DER NERSESSIAN, Sirarpie. *Armenia & the Byzantine Empire.* 1945. Harvard. 1st ed. 8vo. 32 pl. xl. VG. W1. $30.00

DERBY, Mark. *Big Water.* 1953. Viking. 1st ed. NF/NF. P3. $30.00

DERHAM, W. *Astro-Theology; or, Demonstration of Being...of God.* 1719. London. Innys. fld pl. 246p. contemporary sheepskin. B14. $250.00

DERLETH, August. *Bright Journey.* 1940. NY. sgn. VG/VG. B5. $17.50

DERLETH, August. *Chronicles of Solar Pons.* 1973. Mycroft Moran. F/F. P3. $20.00

DERLETH, August. *Dark Mind, Dark Heart.* 1962. Arkham. 1st ed. NF/NF. P3. $45.00

DERLETH, August. *Dark Things.* 1971. Arkham. 1st ed. sgn R Block/B Lumley/B Copper. F/dj. F4. $85.00

DERLETH, August. *Empire of Fur.* 1953. Aladdin. 1st ed. VG/VG. P3. $35.00

DERLETH, August. *Hawk on the Wind.* 1938. Phil. Ritten House. 1st ed/author's 1st book poems. 8vo. gr cloth. F/NF. C6. $300.00

DERLETH, August. *Lonesome Places.* 1962. Arkham. 1st ed. VG/VG. P3. $60.00

DERLETH, August. *Mask of Cthlhu.* 1958. Arkham. VG. M17. $20.00

DERLETH, August. *Mr Conservation.* 1971. Macgregor. 1st ed. F/trade-size wrp. F4. $25.00

DERLETH, August. *New Poetry Out of Wisconsin.* 1969. Stanton Lee. 1st ed. F/F. P3. $50.00

DERLETH, August. *Night Side.* 1947. Rinehart. 1st ed. VG/VG. P3. $65.00

DERLETH, August. *Not Long for This World.* 1948. Arkham. 1st ed. F/dj. M2. $150.00

DERLETH, August. *Sleeping & the Dead.* 1947. Pellegrini Cudahy. 1st ed. NF/VG. F4. $70.00

DERLETH, August. *Someone in the Dark.* 1941. Arkham. 1st ed. VG. P3. $250.00

DERLETH, August. *Trail of Cthulhu.* 1962. Arkham. NF/NF. P3. $75.00

DERLETH, August. *Travellers by Night.* 1967. Arkham. 1st ed. F/F. P3. $50.00

DERLETH, August. *When Evil Wakes.* 1963. Souvenir. 1st ed. sgn. VG/VG. P3. $75.00

DERLETH & LOVECRAFT. *Lurker at the Threshold.* 1945. Arkham. 1st ed. inscr. F/dj. B24. $250.00

DERLETH & SCHORER. *Colonel Markesan & Less Pleasant People.* 1966. Arkham. 1st ed. NF/NF. P3. $40.00

DERMENGHEM, Emile. *Life of Mahomet.* 1930. NY. Dial. 1st ed. 353p. xl. VG. W1. $15.00

DEROSSO, H.A. *Rebel.* 1961. Whitman. TVTI. NF. P3. $20.00

DESARIO, Joseph P. *Sanctuary.* 1989. Doubleday. 1st ed. F/F. F4. $15.00

DESAULT, P.J. *Treatise on Fractures, Luxations & Other Affections...* 1805. Phil. edit X Bichat. trans C Caldwell. tree calf. VG. B14. $275.00

DESCARGUES, Pierre. *Picasso.* 1974. NY. Felicie. intro John Russell/trans Roland Balay. F/NF. F1. $75.00

DESCARTES, Rene. *Discours de la Methode.* 1947. Paris. Vrin. tall 8vo. prt gray wrp. F. G1. $50.00

DESCARTES, Rene. *Les Principles de la Philosophie.* 1698. Rouen. Besongne. 12mo. 600p. contemporary mottled calf. K1. $250.00

DESCHARNES, Robert. *World of Salvador Dali.* 1962. Atide/Crown. 1st ed. ils. 233p. VG/dj. M20. $60.00

DESCOURTILZ, J.T. *Tropical Amerian Birds.* 1960. HRW. 1st ed thus. folio. 60 pl. F/VG case. S9. $95.00

DESMOND, Bagley. *Enemy.* 1977. London. Collins. 1st ed. F/dj. S6. $30.00

DESMOND, Ray. *European Discovery of the Indian Flora.* 1992. Oxford. 32 mc pl. 355p. M/dj. B26. $119.95

DESOUTTER, D.M. *Your Book of Space Travel.* 1962. London. Faber. 8vo. ils. 72p. VG/dj. K5. $9.00

DESROCHES-NOBLECOURT, C. *Life & Death of a Pharaoh, Tutankhamen.* 1965. NY Graphic Soc. 4th prt. 312p. VG/torn. W1. $14.00

DESROCHES-NOBLECOURT, C. *Vie et Mort d'un Pharaoh Toutankhamon.* 1963. Paris. Hachette. 1st ed. 312p. VG/torn. W1. $12.00

DESSART, Gina. *Cry for the Lost.* 1959. Harper. 1st ed. VG/VG. P3. $10.00

DEUCHER & WHEELER. *Giotto Tended the Sheep.* 1938. Dutton. 1st ed. ils Dorothy Bayley. VG/VG. P2. $15.00

DEUCHLER, Florens. *Gothic Art.* 1849. Weidenfeld Nicolson. ils. 184p. NF/dj. M10. $10.00

DEUEL, Leo. *Flights Into Yesterday.* 1969. St Martin. 1st ed. 332p. NF/dj. W1. $15.00

DEUSSEN, Paul. *Erinnerungen an Friedrich Nietzsche.* 1901. Leipzig. 112p. G/worn. G1. $65.00

DEUTSCH, Babette. *Banners.* 1919. Doran. 1st ed/author's 1st book. F/NF. B4. $150.00

DEUTSCH, Babette. *Collected Poems of...* 1969. Doubleday. 1st ed. 236p. VG/dj. M20. $20.00

DEUTSCH, Babette. *Honey Out of the Rock.* 1925. Appleton. 1st ed. inscr. NF. B4. $85.00

DEUTSCH, J.A. *Structural Basis of Behavior.* 1960. Chicago U. 196p. M/dj. K4. $10.00

DEUTSCH, Mitchell F. *Doing Business With the Japanese.* 1984. NY. NAL. 1st prt. 8vo. 197p. NF/NF. P4. $12.50

DEUTSCHMAN, Deborah. *Signals.* 1978. Seaview Books. 1st ed. VG/VG. P3. $15.00

DEVAL, Jacqueline. *Reckless Appetites: Culinary Romance.* 1993. Ecco. 1st ed/author's 1st book. NF/NF. A14. $25.00

DEVERDUN, Alfred Louis. *True Mexico. Mexico-Tenochtitlan.* 1938. private prt. sgn. ils/pl. 303p. VG. B11. $85.00

DEVEREAUX, Roy. *Aspects of Algeria: Hist, Political, Colonial.* 1912. Dutton. 1st ed. 315p. VG. W1. $10.00

DEVINE, D.M. *Doctors Also Die.* 1973. Collins Crime Club. VG/VG. P3. $12.00

DEVINE, Dominic. *Sleeping Tiger.* 1968. Collins Crime Club. 1st ed. VG/VG. P3. $20.00

DEVINE, Philip E. *Ethics of Homicide.* 1978. Cornell. M11. $35.00

DEVON, Gary. *Lost.* 1986. Knopf. ARC/author's 1st book. F/pict wrp. N3. $15.00

DEVORE, Irven. *Primate Behavior.* 1965. HRW. 654p. F. K4. $12.50

DEWDNEY, Selwyn. *Wind Without Rain.* 1946. Copp Clark. VG. P3. $8.00

DEWEESE, Gene. *Adventrures of a Two-Minute Werewolf.* 1983. Weekly Reader Books. VG. P3. $8.00

DEWEESE, Jean. *Backhoe Gothic.* 1981. Doubleday. 1st ed. VG/G. P3. $13.00

DEWELL. *Black Beauty.* (1917). Phil. sm 8vo. F/F. R2. $10.00

DEWEY, John. *Problems of Men.* 1946. Philosophical Lib. 1st ed. 424p. G1. $27.50

DEWEY, John. *Psychology.* 1887. Harper. author's 1st book. 427p. prt pebbled mauve cloth. VG. G1. $250.00

DEWEY, Katharine Fay. *Star People.* 1910. Houghton Mifflin. 1st ed. 8vo. 232p. VG. D6. $25.00

DEWEY, Thomas B. *How Hard To Kill.* 1962. Simon Schuster. 1st ed. G/dj. P3. $20.00

DEWHURST, K. *Thomas Willis's Oxford Casebook.* 1981. Oxford. pres. 9 pl. 199p. F. G7. $65.00

DEWLEN, Al. *Night of the Tiger.* nd. BC. VG/G. P3. $8.00

DEXTER, Colin. *Jewel That Was Ours.* 1992. Crown. 1st ed. F/F. P3. $20.00

DEXTER, John (some); see Bradley, Marion Zimmer.

DEXTER, Pete. *Deadwood.* 1986. Random. 1st ed/author's 2nd book. F/F. B3. $45.00

DEXTER, Pete. *Paris Trout.* 1988. NY. 1st ed/author's 3rd novel. sgn. F/F. A11. $45.00

DEXTER, Peter. *God's Pocket.* 1983. Random. 1st ed/author's 1st book. sgn. rem mk. NF/NF. S9. $100.00

DEY, Mukul Chandra. *My Pilgrimages to Ajanta & Bagh.* 1925. Doran. 8vo. ils/photos. 245p. red cloth. VG. P4. $65.00

DEZOIS, Gardner. *Day in the Life...* 1972. Harper Row. 1st ed. xl. dj. P3. $10.00

DI CESNOLA, A.P. *Salaminia: History, Treasures & Antiquities...* 1882. London. 4to. ils/pl/maps. cloth. O2. $450.00

DI CESNOLA, Louis Palma. *Cyprus, Its Ancient Cities, Tombs...* 1991. Nicosia. rpt. 8vo. ils. 528p. cloth. dj. O2. $65.00

DI CESNOLA, Louis Palma. *Cyprus: Its Ancient Cities, Tombs & Temples.* 1878. NY. apparent ARC. assn pres. 456p. brn cloth/rebacked. O2. $375.00

DI MONA, Joseph. *Great Court-Martial Cases.* 1972. NY. Grosset Dunlap. M11. $35.00

DI PRIMA, Diane. *Dinners & Nightmares.* 1961. Cornith. 1st ed. NF/wrp. B2. $35.00

DI PRIMA, Diane. *Earthsong.* 1968. NY. Poets Pr. 1st ed. NF/wrp. B2. $20.00

DIAMOND, A.S. *Evolution of Law & Order.* 1973. Westport. Greenwood. M11. $35.00

DIAMOND, Solomon. *Personality & Temperment.* 1957. Harper. 426p. F/dj. K4. $10.00

DIAMONSTEIN, Barbaralee. *Visions & Images.* 1982. NY. Rizzoli. sm 4to. VG+/wrp. S9. $40.00

DIAZ DEL CASTILLO, Bernal. *Bernal Diaz Chronicles: True Story of Conquest of Mexico.* 1956. Doubleday. 1st ed. 414p. map ep. VG/dj. F3. $20.00

DIAZ DEL CASTILLO, Bernal. *Historia Verdadera de la Conquista de la Nueva Espana.* 1942. Madrid. Espasa-Calpe. 2 vol. complete. F3. $20.00

DIBBLE, R.F. *Mohammed.* 1926. Viking. 1st ed. 8vo. 257p. VG. W1. $14.00

DIBBLE, Sheldon. *Hist & General Views of Sandwich Island's Mission.* 1839. NY. Taylor Dodd. 1st ed. 12mo. 268p. dk brn cloth. K1. $350.00

DIBDIN, Michael. *Dying of the Light.* 1993. London. Faber. 1st ed. F/F. T2. $12.00

DIBDIN, Michael. *Last Sherlock Holmes Story.* 1978. Pantheon. 1st Am ed. F/F. B2. P3. $25.00

DIBDIN, Thomas Frognall. *Bibliomania; or, Book-Madness; A Biobliographical Romance.* 1875. Chatto Windus. 2 vol. new improved ed. teg. later marbled brd/leather. F. F1. $600.00

DIBELIUS, Martin. *Jesus.* 1949. Westminster. 160p. G/dj. B29. $3.50

DICK, Philip K. *Beyond Lies the Wub.* 1988. Gollancz. 1st ed. F/F. P3. $25.00

DICK, Philip K. *Broken Bubble.* 1989. Gollancz. 1st ed. F/F. P3. $30.00

DICK, Philip K. *Crack in Space.* 1989. Severn. F/F. P3. $25.00

DICK, Philip K. *Dark-Haired Girl.* 1988. Willimantic. Ziesing. 1st ed. F/F. T2. $20.00

DICK, Philip K. *Golden Man.* 1980. Berkley. SFBC. 1st hc prt (code K27). F/NF. N3. $10.00

DICK, Philip K. *Mary & the Giant.* 1988. Gollancz. 1st ed. F/F. P3. $25.00

DICK, Philip K. *Preserving Machine.* 1970. Ace/SFBC. 1st hc ed/1st prt (code 48K). F/NF. N3. $15.00

DICK, Philip K. *Puttering About a Small Planet.* 1985. Chicago. 1st ed. F/F. A9. $30.00

DICK, Philip K. *Radio Free Alemuth.* 1985. Arbor. 1st ed. F/F. P3. $20.00

DICK, Philip K. *Transmigration of Timothy Archer.* 1982. Timescape. 1st ed. F/F. P3. $25.00

DICK & DOGGETT. *Sky With Ocean Joined.* 1983. WA, DC. US Naval Observatory. 8vo. 190p. wrp. K5. $22.00

DICK & JANE READER. *Elson Gray Basic Readers-Primer.* 1936. Scott Foresman. 4 stories. VG. M5. $70.00

DICK & JANE READER. *Fun With Our Friends.* 1962. Scott Foresman. 8vo. cloth. VG. M5. $25.00

DICK & JANE READER. *Our New Friends.* 1946. Scott Foresman. 191p. VG. M20. $45.00

DICK & JANE READER. *The New Our New Friends.* 1956. Scott Foresman. 8vo. cloth. VG+. M5. $40.00

DICK & JANE READER. *The New We Come & Go.* 1956. Scott Foresman. 3rd/last primer. 8vo. VG. M5. $30.00

DICKENS, Charles. *American Notes For General Circulation.* 1842. Chapman Hall. 2 vol. 1st ed/1st issue (contents p #d xvi). VG/case. Q1. $1,350.00

DICKENS, Charles. *Barnaby Rudge.* 1987. Folio Soc. VG. P3. $30.00

DICKENS, Charles. *Bleak House.* 1953. Doubleday. ils Edward Gorey. 595p. blk/cream bdg. NF/NF. H5. $250.00

DICKENS, Charles. *Captain Boldheart.* 1927. Macmillan. 1st ed thus. ils Beatrice Pearse. cloth. VG. M5. $40.00

DICKENS, Charles. *Chimes.* 1931. London. LEC. 1st ed thus. ils/sgn Rackham. 1/1500. NF/VG case. B4. $600.00

DICKENS, Charles. *Chistmas Carol.* 1948. Heinemann. 12 pls/Rackham. VG/torn. B18. $75.00

DICKENS, Charles. *Christmas Carol.* 1914. McKay. ils Arthur Keller. gilt cloth. NF. M5. $75.00

DICKENS, Charles. *Christmas Carol.* 1987. Children's Classics. 6th prt. ils Rackham. pict brd. F. B17. $8.50

DICKENS, Charles. *Christmas Carol.* 1990. Tabori Chang. F/F. P3. $30.00

DICKENS, Charles. *Dickens Digest.* 1943. Whittlesey. G+. P3. $23.00

DICKENS, Charles. *Hard Times.* 1987. Oxford. F/F. P3. $11.00

DICKENS, Charles. *Hard Times: A Novel.* 1854. NY. Harper. 1st Am ed. yel ep. G. Q1. $250.00

DICKENS, Charles. *Life of Our Lord.* 1934. Simon Schuster. 1st ed. 12mo. VG. B17. $17.50

DICKENS, Charles. *Master Humphrey's Clock. By Boz.* 1840-41. London. Chapman Hall. 1st ed. 88 weekly parts. wrp/custom fld/solander box. C6. $2,500.00

DICKENS, Charles. *Miscellaneous Papers.* 1914. London. intro BW Matz. ils. 376p. orig buckram. VG. D3. $35.00

DICKENS, Charles. *Mystery of Edwin Drood.* 1870. London. Chapman Hall. 6 parts. gr pict wrp. morocco case. H4. $650.00

DICKENS, Charles. *Old Lamps for New Ones & Other Sketches & Essays.* (1897). New Amsterdam Book Co. w/frontis facsimile letter. F. Q1. $150.00

DICKENS, Charles. *Personal Hist & Experience of David Copperfield the Younger.* ca 1850. NY. WF Burgess. 1st Am ed? 8vo. ils JW Orr. contemporary calf. M1. $200.00

DICKENS, Charles. *Personal Hist of David Copperfield.* 1850. London. 1st ed (bdg from parts/mixed points). NF. A9. $400.00

DICKENS, Charles. *Posthumous Papers of Pickwick Club.* 1836. Chapman Hall. 1st ed. 20 orig parts in 19. 8vo. orig gr wrp/red morocco boxes. C6. $9,500.00

DICKENS, Charles. *Writings.* 1894. Boston/NY. Riverside. 32 vol. Standard Lib Ed. 8vo. teg. NF. F1. $1,600.00

DICKENSON, Luella. *Reminiscences of a Trip Across the Plains in 1846...* 1977. Ye Galleon. 1st ltd ed. 1/785. M. A18. $15.00

DICKERSON, William R. *Letters of Junius...Exposing to the Public...* 1848. Phil. 1st ed. 48p. VG/new wrp. D3. $45.00

DICKERT, D. Augustus. *Hist of Kershaw's Brigade...* 1899. Newberry, SC. Elbert H Aull. 1st ed. 10 pl. 583p. gr cloth. VG. C6. $2,500.00

DICKERT, Thomas Wilson. *Hist of St Stephens Reformed Church Reading, PA 1884-1909.* 1909. Reading, PA. 1st ed. inscr author's copy. 392p. cloth. VG. M8. $45.00

DICKEY, Christopher. *Expats: Travels in Arabia, From Tripoli to Teheran.* 1990. Atlantic Monthly. 1st ed. 228p. NF/dj. W1. $20.00

DICKEY, James. *Alnilam.* 1986. Doubleday. 1st ed. NF/VG. B3. $25.00

DICKEY, James. *Deliverance.* 1970. Houghton Mifflin. 1st ed. 8vo. 278p. gilt lettered cream cloth. G/dj. H5. $50.00

DICKEY, James. *Deliverance.* 1970. Houghton Mifflin. 1st ed/author's 1st novel. NF/NF. L3. $65.00

DICKEY, James. *Eye-Beaters, Blood, Victory, Madness, Buckhead & Mercy.* 1970. Doubleday. 1st ed. 1/250. sgn. F/F case. S9. $150.00

DICKEY, James. *Night Hurdling.* 1983. Bruccoli Clark. 1/250. sgn. F/F. B2. $40.00

DICKEY, James. *Owl-King.* 1977. NY. Red Angel. 1/100. sgn. 23p. cream buckram/bl cloth. F. H5. $125.00

DICKEY, James. *Poems 1957-1967.* nd. Wesleyan U. 1st ed. 299p. F/F. H1. $35.00

DICKEY, James. *Starry Place Between the Antlers.* 1981. Bruccoli Clark. 1st ed. 1/500 #d. VG/wrp. S9. $45.00

DICKEY, James. *Zodiac.* 1976. Doubleday. 1st ed. obl 8vo. pub pres. 62p. VG/clip. C6. $35.00

DICKINSON, Cornelius Evart. *Century of Church Life.* 1896. Marietta, OH. 1st ed. 226p. cloth. VG. M8. $45.00

DICKINSON, Emily. *Bolts of Melody: New Poems of Emily Dickinson.* 1945. Harper. 1st ed. edit pres. VG/clip. Q1. $125.00

DICKINSON, Emily. *Further Poems of Emily Dickinson.* 1929. Little Brn. 1st trade ed. 8vo. 208p. gilt gr cloth. VG. H5. $200.00

DICKINSON, Emily. *Letters of...* 1894. Roberts Bros. 2 vol. gilt gr cloth brd. VG. Q1. $350.00

DICKINSON, Emily. *Who Is the East?* 1990. Paris. 55x44mm. 1/5. ils/sgn Anne Walker. F/painted fld/case. B24. $225.00

DICKINSON, LAIRD & MAXWELL. *Voices From the SW.* 1976. Northland. 1st ed. 159p. F/F case. B19. $150.00

DICKINSON, Peter. *Annerton Pit.* 1977. Atlantic/Little Brn. 1st ed. F/F. P3. $23.00

DICKINSON, Peter. *Blue Hawk.* 1976. Little Brn. 1st ed. VG/VG. P3. $20.00

DICKINSON, Peter. *Devil's Children.* 1986. Delacorte. 1st ed. VG/VG. P3. $15.00

DICKINSON, Peter. *Flight of Dragons.* 1979. Harper Row. 1st ed. VG/VG. P3. $25.00

DICKINSON, Peter. *Lizard in the Cup.* 1972. Harper Row. 1st ed. VG/VG. P3. $20.00

DICKINSON, Peter. *Skeleton-in-Waiting.* 1989. Pantheon. 1st ed. VG/VG. P3. $17.00

DICKINSON, Terence. *Halley's Comet, Mysterious Visitor From Outer Space.* 1985. Barrington, NJ. Edmund Scientific. 125p. VG/dj. K5. $9.00

DICKINSON, Thomas A. *Aeronautical Dictionary.* 1945. NY. ils. 484p. VG. B18. $22.50

DICKS, Terrance. *Doctor Who & Planet of Spiders.* 1975. Whitman. TVTI. F/F. P3. $20.00

DICKSON, Carter. *Bowstring Murders.* 1933. Morrow. 1st Canadian ed. G+. P3. $40.00

DICKSON, Carter. *Nine & Death Makes Ten.* 1940. Morrow. 1st ed. VG. P3. $40.00

DICKSON, Carter. *White Priory Murders.* 1945. Books Inc. 3rd ed. VG/G. P3. $20.00

DICKSON, Carter; see Carr, John Dickson.

DICKSON, Gordon R. *Alien Art.* 1973. Dutton. 1st ed. F/F. P3. $25.00

DICKSON, Gordon R. *Final Encyclopedia.* 1984. Tor. 1st ed. F/F. P3. $20.00

DICKSON, Gordon R. *Forever Man.* 1986. Ace. 1st ed. NF/NF. P3. $20.00

DICKSON, Gordon R. *Iron Years.* 1980. Doubleday. 1st ed. VG/VG. P3. $15.00

DICKSON, Gordon R. *Spacepaw.* 1969. Putnam. 1st ed. VG/VG. P3. $30.00

DICKSON, Gordon R. *Star Road.* 1975. Robert Hale. 1st ed. VG/VG. P3. $15.00

DICKSON, Gordon R. *Wolf & Iron.* 1990. Tor. 1st ed. F/F. P3. $19.00

DICKSON, Grierson. *Traitor's Market.* 1936. Hutchinson. 1st ed. G+. P3. $20.00

DICKSON, H.N. *Climate & Weather.* 1923 (1912). London. Williams Norgate. 3rd prt. 4 maps. 256p. gr cloth. G. K5. $8.00

DICKSON, H.R.P. *Kuwait & Her Neighbors.* 1956. London. 1st ed. inscr by author's wife. 627p. cloth. O2. $275.00

DICKSON, Paul. *Lib in Am: Celebration in Words & Pictures.* 1986. Facts on File. 1st ed. biblio/index. 242p. F/F. A17. $20.00

DICKSON, Paul. *Out of This World: Am Space Photography.* 1977. Delacorte. 4to. 158p. VG/dj. K5. $20.00

DIDEROT, Denis. *Rameau's Nephew & Other Works.* 1926. London. Chapman Hall. 1st ed thus. VG. A17. $15.00

DIEGO, Duran. *Historia de las Indias de Nueva Espana y Islas...* 1867-1880. Mexico. 3 vol. 66 pl/atlas. very scarce. H4. $3,000.00

DIEHL, Edith. *Bookbinding: Its Background & Technique.* 1946. NY/Toronto. 2 vol. 91 pl. gilt bdg. NF/box. B14. $150.00

DIEHL, Edna Groff. *Aunt Este's Stories of the Vegetable & Fruit Children.* 1923. Whitman. A Just Right Book. 1st ed. ils Vera Stone. VG. D6. $35.00

DIEHL, William. *Primal Fear.* 1993. Villard. ARC. NF/pict wrp. B3. $15.00

DIEHL, William. *27.* 1990. Villard. 1st ed. NF/NF. P3. $20.00

DIEL, William. *Sharky's Machine.* 1978. Delacorte. 1st ed/author's 1st novel. F/F. N3. $25.00

DIELS, H. *Die Fragmente der Vorsokratiker.* 1960. Berlin. 3 vol. edit Walther Kranz. F/F. F1. $35.00

DIENES, Z.P. *Concept Formation & Personality.* 1959. Bath, Eng. Leicester. 65p. F/dj. K4. $15.00

DIETHELM, Oscar. *Etiology of Chronic Alcoholism.* 1955. Springfield. Charles Thomas. 1st ed. F/NF. B2. $45.00

DIETL, Wilhelm. *Persian Miniature Paintings.* ca 1965. Crown. 10 tipped-in pl. VG. W1. $15.00

DIETZ, August. *Postal Service of Confederate States of Am.* 1929. Richmond. Dietz. 1st ed. sgn. 8vo. 439p. gray cloth. NF. C6. $450.00

DIETZ, David. *All About Satellites & Space Ships.* nd (1958). Random. 3rd prt. G/dj. K5. $10.00

DIKE, Helen. *Stories From the Great Metropolitan Operas.* 1943. Random. 8vo. ils Tenggren. F/VG. B17. $15.00

DIKTY, T.E. *Great Science Fiction Stories About the Moon.* 1967. Frederick Fell. 1st ed. VG/VG. P3. $18.00

DILELLO, R. *Longest Cocktail Party.* 1972. Chicago. 1st ed. VG/VG. B5. $30.00

DILLARD, Annie. *American Childhood.* 1987. Harper Row. 1/250. sgn. F/case. B3. $100.00

DILLARD, Annie. *Encounters With Chinese Writers.* 1984. Wesleyan U. 1st ed. sgn. F/clip. B4. $65.00

DILLARD, Annie. *Holy the Firm.* 1977. Harper Row. 1st ed. F/F. A18. $40.00

DILLARD, Annie. *Holy the Firm.* 1977. Harper Row. 1st ed. VG/VG. B5. $35.00

DILLARD, Annie. *Living.* 1992. Harper Collins. ARC/author's 9th book. sc. F. A18. $80.00

DILLARD, Annie. *Living.* 1992. Harper Collins. 1st ltd ed. 1/300. sgn/#d. M/case. A18. $125.00

DILLARD, Annie. *Pilgrim at Tinker Creek.* 1974. Harper. 1st ed. 271p. VG/dj. M20. $40.00

DILLARD, Annie. *Pilgrim at Tinker Creek.* 1974. Harper. 1st ed/author's 1st prose. F/VG. B3. $75.00

DILLARD, Annie. *Tickets for a Prayer Wheel.* 1974. Columbia, MO. 1st ed/ author's 1st book. sgn. F/NF. C2. $500.00

DILLARD, Annie. *Writing Life.* 1990. London. Picador. 1st ed. NF/NF. B3. $30.00

DILLARD, J.M. *Star Trek: The Lost Years.* 1989. Pocket. 1st ed. NF/NF clip. N3. $10.00

DILLE, Robert C. *Collected Works of Buck Rogers in 25th Century.* 1969. Bonanza. 1st ed. lg 4to. F/F. C8. $60.00

DILLEN, Frederick G. *Hero.* 1994. S Royalton, VT. Steerforth. 1st ed/author's 1st book. F/F. B3. $20.00

DILLING, Elizabeth. *Red Network.* Sept 1936. self pub. 6th prt. 345p. VG/G. H1. $20.00

DILLMAN, Mary Alma. *Wee Folk. About the Elves in Nova Scotia.* 1956. Canada. New Brunswick. 3rd prt. 67p. pict brd/cloth spine. VG-. A3. $7.50

DILLON, Chevalier Capt. P. *Narrative & Successful Result of Voyage in South Seas...* 1972. Amsterdam/NY. N Israel/DaCapo. 2 vol set. facsimile. 8vo. M. P4. $135.00

DILLON, Richard. *Meriweather Lewis.* 1965. Coward McCann. ils/map. VG/dj. B34. $25.00

DIMENT, Adam. *Bang Bang Birds.* 1968. Dutton. 1st ed. xl. dj. P3. $6.00

DIMENT, Adam. *Dolly, Dolly Spy.* 1967. Dutton. F/F. P3. $15.00

DIMENT, Adam. *Think Inc.* 1971. Michael Joseph. 1st ed. VG/VG. P3. $18.00

DIMOCK, Edwin. *Monsieur & Madame.* 1924. Harper. ils Louis M Glackens. VG/worn. M5. $35.00

DIMSDALE, Thomas J. *Vigilantes of Montana.* 1937. np. 269p. VG. O8. $32.50

DIMSDALE, Thomas J. *Vigilantes of Montana; or, Popular Justice in Rocky Mtns.* 1950. McKee. hc. VG. B34. $45.00

DINES, Glen. *Overland Stage: Story of Famous Overland Stagecoaches...* 1961. Macmillan. 1st ed. obl 4to. VG. O3. $30.00

DINESEN, Isak. *Anecdotes of Destiny.* 1958. London. Michael Joseph. 1st ed. sgn. F/NF. w/sgn letter author Donald Windham. B4. $1,500.00

DINESEN, Isak. *Last Tales.* 1957. Random. 1st ed. 8vo. 341p. gray cloth. NF/dj. H5. $85.00

DINESEN, Isak. *On Modern Marriage.* 1986. St Martin. 1st ed. F/F. S9. $25.00

DINESEN, Isak. *Out of Africa.* 1938. Random. 1st Am ed. NF/VG. B4. $125.00

DINESEN, Isak. *Seven Gothic Tales.* 1934. Smith Haas. 1st Am ed/trade issue/ author's 1st book. NF/red case. T2. $75.00

DINESEN, Isak. *Seven Gothic Tales.* 1934. Smith Haas. 1st ed. VG/G. P3. $60.00

DINESEN, Isak. *Shadows on the Grass.* (1960). London. 1st Eng ed. F/VG. A9. $30.00

DINESEN, Isak. *Winter Tales.* 1942. NY. 1st ed. VG/VG. B5. $50.00

DINGLE, Herbert. *Science & Human Experience.* nd. Macmillan. 1st Am ed. 141p. blk cloth. VG. G1. $28.50

DINGMAN, Larry. *Booksellers Marks.* 1986. Dinkytown. ltd ed. sgn. 97p. VG. A10. $22.00

DINGMAN & NATVIG. *Surgery of Facial Fractures.* 1964. Phil. 1st ed. 380p. A13. $150.00

DINKINS, James. *Personal Recollections & Experiences in Confederate Army...* 1897. Cincinnati. Clarke. 1st ed. inscr. 280p. red cloth. VG. C6. $700.00

DINNERSTEIN, L. *Leo Frank Case.* 1968. NY. 1st ed. VG/VG. B5. $20.00

DINNING, Hector. *Nile to Aleppo.* 1920. NY. 1st ed. 288p. gilt brn linen. M7. $135.00

DIPPER, Alan. *Golden Birgin.* 1973. Walker. 1st ed. VG/VG. P3. $20.00

DISBURY, David G. *TE Lawrence of Arabia: A Collector's Booklist.* 1972. Surrey, Eng. private prt. unp. NF/tan wrp. M7. $60.00

DISCH, Thomas M. *Businessman: A Tale of Terror.* 1984. Harper Row. 1st ed. F/F. T2. $45.00

DISCH, Thomas M. *MD: A Horror Story.* 1991. Knopf. 1st ed. VG/VG. P3. $15.00

DISCH, Thomas M. *MD: A Horror Story.* 1991. Knopf. 1st ed. F/F. T2. $25.00

DISCH, Thomas M. *New Improved Sun.* 1975. Harper Row. 1st ed. VG/G. P3. $22.00

DISCH, Thomas M. *On Wings of Song.* 1979. St Martin. 1st Am ed. F/F. N3. $20.00

DISCH, Thomas M. *Silve Pillow: A Tale of Witchcraft.* 1987. Willimantic. Ziesing. 1st ed. F/F. T2. $12.00

DISNEY, Diane. *Story of Walt Disney.* 1957. NY. 1st ed. VG/VG. B5. $45.00

DISNEY, Doris Miles. *Day Miss Bessie Lewis Disappeared.* 1972. Detective BC. VG. P3. $8.00

DISNEY, Doris Miles. *Last Straw.* 1954. Crime Club. 1st ed. VG/VG. P3. $25.00

DISNEY, Dorothy Cameron. *Hangman's Tree.* 1949. Random. 1st ed. VG/fair. P3. $10.00

DISNEY STUDIOS. *Big Bad Wolf & Little Red Riding Hood.* 1934. NY. ils. 64p. VG/G. B5. $65.00

DISNEY STUDIOS. *Donald Duck & His Friends.* 1939. Heath. 1st ed. VG. B5. $25.00

DISNEY STUDIOS. *Farmyard Symphony.* 1939. Whitman. 64p. VG+. M20. $45.00

DISNEY STUDIOS. *Ferdinand the Bull.* 1938. Whitman. 12p. VG. M5. $50.00

DISNEY STUDIOS. *Here They Are.* 1940. Heath. 56p. K2. $25.00

DISNEY STUDIOS. *Mickey Mouse Presents the Golden Touch.* 1937. Racine. 1st ed. ils. VG/VG. B5. $90.00

DISNEY STUDIOS. *Mickey Never Fails.* 1939. Heath. 1st ed. VG. B5. $25.00

DISNEY STUDIOS. *Pop-Up Minnie Mouse.* 1933. Bl Ribbon. 8vo. 3 popups. unp. prt brd. VG. F1. $500.00

DISNEY STUDIOS. *Pop-Up Minnie Mouse.* 1993. Applewood. 1st ed thus. 8vo. F. B17. $10.00

DISNEY STUDIOS. *Through the Picture Frame.* 1944. Simon Schuster. 1st ed. unp. VG/dj. M20. $50.00

DISNEY STUDIOS. *Walt Disney's Cinderella, Pop-Up Movie-Go-Round Book.* 1981. Simon Schuster. lg 8vo. glazed pict paper brd. VG+. C8. $45.00

DISNEY STUDIOS. *Walt Disney's Story of Clarabelle Cow.* 1938. Whitman. 90p. VG+. M20. $40.00

DISNEY STUDIOS. *Walt Disney's Story of Minnie Mouse.* 1938. Whitman. 92p. VG. M20 $50.00

DISNEY STUDIOS. *Walt Disney's Thumper.* 1942. Grosset Dunlap. unp. VG/dj. M20. $35.00

DISNEY STUDIOS. *Water Baby Circus.* 1940. Heath. 78p. K2. $25.00

DITMARS, Raymond. *Book of Insect Oddities.* 1938. Lippincott. Jr Literary Guild. VG. B17. $6.50

DITTMAN, Elva. *White Princess.* 1945. Cupples Leon. ils Masha Nardini. 26p. cloth. VG-. A3. $10.00

DIVER, Maud. *Siege Perilous & Other Stories.* 1924. Houghton Mifflin. 1st ed. F/NF. $15.00

DIX, Morgan. *Memoirs of John Adam Dix: Am General 1798...* 1883. np. 2 vol. 800p. gilt bdg. E5. $65.00

DIX & SCOTT. *Chronicles of Krystonia.* 1987. Mildonian. 1st ed. F/F. F4. $20.00

DIXON, Alec. *Tinned Soldier. A Personal Record 1919-1926.* 1941. London. Right BC. 314p. bl cloth. VG/fair/clear plastic. M7. $65.00

DIXON, Edward. *Scenes in Practice of NY Surgeon.* 1855. np. 1st ed. 407p. G. E5. $75.00

DIXON, Franklin W. *Hardy Boys' Detective Handbook.* 1959. Grosset Dunlap. VG. P3. $10.00

DIXON, Franklin W. *Hardy Boys: Figure in Hiding (#16).* 1937. Grosset Dunlap. 212p. VG/1941 prt dj. M20. $100.00

DIXON, Franklin W. *Hardy Boys: Missing Chums (#4).* 1942 (1928). Grosset Dunlap. 214p. VG/dj. M20. $60.00

DIXON, Franklin W. *Hardy Boys: Mystery of the Chinese Junk (#39).* 1960. Grosset Dunlap. 1st ed. NF/dj. M20. $40.00

DIXON, Franklin W. *Hardy Boys: Mystery of the Desert Giant (#40).* 1961. Grosset Dunlap. 1st ed. VG/dj. M20. $40.00

DIXON, Franklin W. *Hardy Boys: Phantom Freighter (#6).* 1947. Grosset Dunlap. orange ep. tan pict buckram brd. VG+/VG. C8. $22.50

DIXON, Franklin W. *Hardy Boys: Secret of Pirates Hill (#36).* 1956. Grosset Dunlap. 1st ed. VG/dj. M20. $45.00

DIXON, Franklin W. *Hardy Boys: Secret of Skull Mountain (#27).* 1948. Grosset Dunlap. orange ep. tan tweed pict paper brd. NF/VG. C8. $22.50

DIXON, Franklin W. *Hardy Boys: Secret of the Caves (#7).* 1929. Grosset Dunlap. ils AD Scott. NF/VG. C8. $22.50

DIXON, Franklin W. *Hardy Boys: Short-Wave Mystery.* 1945. Grosset Dunlap. thin ed. lists to Secret Panel. 217p. VG/dj. M20. $25.00

DIXON, Franklin W. *Hardy Boys: What Happened at Midnight (#10).* 1933 (1931). Grosset Dunlap. A prt. 213p. VG/dj. M20. $70.00

DIXON, Franklin W. *House on the Cliff.* 1935 (1927). Grosset Dunlap. VG/dingy. M20. $150.00

DIXON, Franklin W. *Lone Eagle of the Border.* 1929. Grosset Dunlap. 1st ed. VG. M2. $20.00

DIXON, Franklin W. *Ted Scott: South of the Rio Grande.* nd. Grosset Dunlap. VG. P3. $8.00

DIXON, George. *Voyage Round the World...* 1789. London. Goulding. lg 4to. fld map/21 maps/pl (some fld). old calf. K1. $2,500.00

DIXON, Philip. *Making of the Past: Barbarian Europe.* 1976. Phaidon. ils. 151p. VG/dj. M10. $10.00

DIXON, Royal. *Human Side of Birds.* 1917. Stokes. 1st ed. ils SH Wainwright. 246p. cloth. VG. M20. $25.00

DIXON, Royal. *Signs Is Signs.* 1915. Phil. Jacobs. 1st ed. 8vo. 209p. red cloth. VG. C6. $45.00

DIXON, Thomas. *Clansman: Birth of a Nation.* 1905. NY. 1st ed thus. VG/VG. B5. $40.00

DIXON, Thomas. *Comrades: A Story of Social Adventure in California.* 1909. NY. stp Advance Pres Copy. sgn. red cloth. w/sgn card. VG. A11. $75.00

DIXON, Thomas. *Foolish Virgin.* 1915. NY. 1st ed. VG/VG. B5. $50.00

DIXON, Thomas. *Life Worth Living: A Personal Experience.* 1905. Doubleday Page. 1st ed. sgn. 140p. teg. gr brd. G. B11. $45.00

DIXON, William Hepworth. *Her Majesty's Tower.* 1869. Harper. fld map. 263p. VG. M20. $20.00

DIXON, William Hepworth. *Personal Hist of Lord Bacon.* 1861. Leipzig. Bernard Tauchnitz. contemporary half calf. M11. $125.00

DIXON, William Hepworth. *William Penn: An Historical Biography...* 1851. Phil. Blanchard Lea. 12mo. 353p. cloth. V3. $15.00

DIXON, William Scarth. *Men, Horses & Hunting.* nd (1931). NY. Wm Farquhar Payson. VG. O3. $25.00

DIXON & GODRICH. *Recording the Blues.* 1970. Stein Day. 1st Am ed. F/wrp. B2. $25.00

DIXON & GODRICH. *Recording the Blues.* 1970. Studio Vista. 1st ed (precedes Stein Day). F/F. B2. $50.00

DJELALEDDIN, Moustapha. *Les Turcs Anciens et Modernes.* 1869. Constantinople. Imprimerie de Courrier d'Orient. 364p. quarter calf. O2. $300.00

DJILAS, Milovan. *Land Without Justice.* 1958. Harcourt. 8vo. 365p. map ep. VG/dj. W1. $18.00

DJURKLOU, Baron G. *Fairy Tales From the Swedish.* 1901. London. Heinemann. 1st Eng ed. 8vo. 178p. gilt emb pk cloth. VG. D6. $135.00

DOANE, Benjamin. *Following the Sea.* 1988. Nova Scotia Mus. ils/maps. 275p. T7. $35.00

DOANE, Michael. *Six Miles to Roadside Business.* 1990. Knopf. UP. F/tan wrp. B3. $25.00

DOANE, Pelagie. *Favorite Nursery Songs.* 1941. Random. unp. VG/torn. M20. $20.00

DOANE, Pelagie. *Mary Paxton: Her Book.* 1931. Doubleday Doran. 1st ed. 98p. VG+/G+. P2. $35.00

DOBBS, Fred C. *Golden Age of BS.* 1976. Gage. 1st ed. VG/VG. P3. $15.00

DOBELL, Bertram. *Poetrical Works of William Strode.* 1907. London. 1st ed. 8vo. Francis Thomson's copy. 270p. bl-gr cloth. fair. M7. $485.00

DOBIE, J. Frank. *Apache Gold & Yaqui Silver.* 1939. Little Brn. 1st ed. ils ftspc Tom Lea. F/chip. A18. $40.00

DOBIE, J. Frank. *Cow People.* 1964. London. Hammond. 1st ed. F/dj. A18. $35.00

DOBIE, J. Frank. *Foller de Drinkin' Gou'd.* 1928. TX Folklore Soc. 1st sc ed. F. A18. $35.00

DOBIE, J. Frank. *Guide to Life & Literature of the SW.* 1943. TX U. hc. 111p. mustard cloth. VG. S11. $40.00

DOBIE, J. Frank. *Longhorns.* 1943. London. Nicholson Watson. 1st ed. ils Tom Lea. VG+/dj. A18. $40.00

DOBIE, J. Frank. *Lost Mines of the Old W: Coronado's Children.* 1960. London. Hammond. 1st ed. ils Ben Carlton Mead. F/F. A18. $50.00

DOBIE, J. Frank. *Man, Bird, & Beast.* 1930. TX Folklore Soc. 1st sc ed. F. A18. $35.00

DOBIE, J. Frank. *Mustangs.* 1952. Boston. 1st ed. lengthy sgn pres. VG/VG. B5. $65.00

DOBIE, J. Frank. *Some Part of Myself.* 1967. Little Brn. 1st ed. fwd Bertha Dobie. F/F. A18. $35.00

DOBIE, J. Frank. *Spur-of-the-Cock.* 1933. TX Folklore Soc. 1st sc ed. F. A18. $35.00

DOBIE, J. Frank. *Texan in England.* 1946. Boston. 11th prt. VG/VG. B5. $60.00

DOBIE, J. Frank. *Tone the Bell Easy.* 1932. TX Folklore Soc. 1st sc ed. F. A18. $35.00

DOBIE, J. Frank. *Tongues of the Monte: The Mexico I Like.* 1948. Hammond. 1st ed. ils Eric King. F. A18. $30.00

DOBSON, Austin. *Horace Walpole, a Memoir.* 1890. Dodd Mead. 1/425. ils Percy/Leon Moran. teg. Sutcliffe bl calf. F. F1. $300.00

DOBSON, George. *Russia's Railway Advance Into Central Asia.* 1890. London. ils/fld maps. 439p. xl. O2. $85.00

DOBSON, Margaret. *Block-Cutting & Print-Making by Hand: From Wood...* 1930. London. ils. 183p. G+. B14. $125.00

DOBY, Tibor. *Discoveries of Blood Circulation From Aristotle to...* 1963. NY. 1st ed. 285p. dj. A13. $75.00

DOBYNS, Stephen. *Concurring Beasts.* 1972. NY. 1st ed/author's 1st book. ES. F/dj. w/Lamont Price card. C2. $100.00

DOBYNS, Stephen. *Saragota Hexameter.* 1990. Viking. 1st ed. F/F. P3. $17.00

DOBYNS, Stephen. *Saratoga Longshot.* 1988. London. Century/Mysterious. ARC/1st Eng ed. RS. F/F. S6. $22.50

DOBZHANSKY, Theososius. *Evolutionary Biology. Vol 3.* 1969. NY. Meredith Corp. 293p. M/dj. K4. $35.00

DOBZHANSKY, Theososius. *Evolutionary Biology. Vol 5.* 1972. NY. Meredith Corp. 305p. M/dj. K4. $35.00

DOCKSTADER, Frederick J. *Weaving Arts of the North American Indian.* 1978. London/NY. James J Kery. 1st ed. 4to. 223p. VG/worn. P4. $65.00

DOCTOR SEUSS; see Geisel, Theodor Seuss.

DOCTOROW, E.L. *Jack London, Hemingway & the Constitution.* 1993. Random. UP/author's 1st nonfiction book. F/wrp. L3. $50.00

DOCTOROW, E.L. *Loon Lake.* 1980. Random. 1st ed. 8vo. 258p. gilt brn cloth. F/dj. H5. $30.00

DOCTOROW, E.L. *Ragtime.* 1975. Random. 1st ed. sgn. 1/150. F/NF case. B4. $450.00

DOCTOROW, E.L. *Ragtime.* 1976. London. 1st Eng ed. inscr. NF/VG+. A11. $55.00

DOCTOROW, E.L. *World's Fair.* 1986. Michael Joseph. 1st ed. NF/F. B3. $15.00

DOCZI, Gyorgy. *Power of Limits: Proportional Harmonies in Nature...* 1981. Boulder. Shambhala. pb. VG. B33. $20.00

DODD, C.H. *More New Testament Studies.* 1968. Eerdmans. 157p. G/dj. B29. $5.50

DODD, Susan. *Hell-Bent Men & Their Cities.* 1990. Viking. 1st ed. F/F. B3. $10.00

DODD, Wendy. *Puppy Book: Doggerel Puppy...* 1933. Lee Shepard. 1st ed. ils. 65p. brd. F. R2. $40.00

DODGE, David. *Angel's Ransom.* 1956. Random. 1st ed. VG/VG. M15. $30.00

DODGE, Edward N. *Who's Who in Engineering. A Biographical Dictionary...* 1964. NY/W Palm Beach. 9th ed. 8vo. 2198p. burgundy cloth. VG. P4. $19.50

DODGE, Louis. *Sandman's Mountain.* 1920. Scribner. 1st ed. 278p. VG. P2. $36.00

DODGE, Mary Mapes. *Rhymes & Jingles.* 1904. NY. 1st ed thus. ils Stilwell. pict gr cloth. VG. M5. $65.00

DODGE, Natt N. *American Southwest.* 1955. Simon Schuster. ils/maps/charts. 160p. NF/NF. B19. $20.00

DODGSON, Campbell. *Etchings of Charles Meryon.* 1921. London. The Studio. 1st ed. ils. gilt parchment/gray brd. K1. $150.00

DODRIDGE, John. *Hist Account of Ancient...Wales, Dutchy of Cornwall...* 1714. London. J Roberts in Warwick-Lane. 2nd ed. modern calf. M11. $350.00

DODSWORTH, William. *Historical Account of the Episcopal See...* 1814. Salisbury. self pub. folio. 21 pl. 240p. half leather. H10. $135.00

DODWELL, Henry. *Dissertationes Cyprianicae.* 1684. London. Sheldon. 462p. vellum. H10. $125.00

DOE, Brian. *S Arabia.* 1971. McGraw Hill. 1st ed. pls/drawings. VG/dj. W1. $45.00

DOERFLINGER, William Main. *Shantymen & Shantyboys.* 1951. Macmillan. ils. 374p. dj. T7. $50.00

DOERR, Harriet. *Consider This, Senora.* 1993. Harcourt Brace. ARC/1st ed. RS. F/F. S9. $45.00

DOGLIONI, Giovanni Nicolo. *Le Cose Notabili et Maravigliose Della Citta di Venetia...* 1675. Venice. Benetto Miloco. 12mo. 360p. old calf. K1. $150.00

DOHERTY, P.C. *Satan in St Mary's.* 1987. St Martin. ARC/1st Am ed. RS. F/F. S6. $30.00

DOHERTY, Terence. *Anatomical Works of George Stubbs.* 1975. Boston. Godine. 1st Am ed. folio. VG. O3. $95.00

DOIG, Ivan. *Dancing at the Rascal Fair.* 1987. Atheneum. ARC. RS. w/pub material & photo. F/dj. B4. $85.00

DOIG, Ivan. *Dancing at the Rascal Fair.* 1987. Atheneum. 1st ed. map. brd. F/F. A18. $25.00

DOIG, Ivan. *Ride With Me, Mariah Montana.* 1990. Atheneum. 1st ed. sgn. M/dj. A18. $40.00

DOIG, Ivan. *Sea Runners.* 1982. Atheneum. 1st ed. inscr/sgn. map/sketches. F/F. A18. $75.00

DOIG, Ivan. *This House of Sky: Landscapes of a Western Mind.* 1978. HBJ. 1st ed. VG/torn. B34. $40.00

DOIG, Ivan. *This House of Sky: Landscapes of a Western Mind.* 1978. NY. HBJ. 1st ed/author's 1st book. inscr/sgn. F/F. S9. $225.00

DOIG, Ivan. *This House of Sky: Landscapes of a Western Mind.* 1992. HBJ. 15th Anniversary ed. M/dj. A18. $25.00

DOISNEAU, Robert. *Doisneau.* 1983. Paris. Pierre Belfond. 1/2397. inscr. VG+/photo ils wrp. S9. $75.00

DOLAN, J.R. *Yankee Peddlers of Early Am.* 1964. Bramhall. 270p. NF/dj. M20. $18.00

DOLCH & DOLCH. *Circus Stories in Basic Vocabulary.* 1956. Champaign, IL. Garrard. Basic Vocabulary Reading Series. VG. C8. $12.50

DOLD, Bernard E. *TE Lawrence, Writer & Wrecker.* 1988. Roma. Herder Editore. 104p. M/wht stiff wrp. M7. $20.00

DOLINER, Roy. *Orange Air.* 1961. Scribner. 1st ed. VG/VG. P8. $45.00

DOLMETSCH, CArl. *Smart Set: A History & Anthology.* 1966. NY. 1st ed. ils. NF/VG. F1. $30.00

DOLSON, Hildegarde. *William Penn, Quaker Hero.* 1961. Random. 1st ed. 8vo. 186p. VG. V3. $8.50

DOMATILLA, John. *Last Crime.* 1981. Atheneum. 1st ed. VG/VG. P3. $20.00

DOMINGO, Placido. *My First Forty Years.* 1983. Knopf. 1st ed. VG/G+. N2. $6.00

DOMINIC, R.B. *Unexpected Developments.* 1984. St Martin. ARC/1st Am ed. RS. F/F. S6. $30.00

DOMINIC, R.B. *Unexpected Developments.* 1984. St Martin. 1st ed. VG/VG. P3. $20.00

DOMINIQUE & MORATH. *Fiesta in Pamplona.* 1957. London. Photography Magazine. 1st ed. 4to. NF/VG acetate. S9. $80.00

DONADONI, Sergio. *Egyptian Museum Cairo.* 1978. Newsweek. 4th ed. ils. 173p. VG/torn. W1. $15.00

DONAGAN, Alan. *Later Philosophy of Collingwood.* 1962. Clarendon. bl cloth. 332p. G1. $30.00

DONAHEY, Mary Dickerson. *Talking Bird/Wonderful Wishes of Jacky & Jean.* 1920. Chicago. Whitman. 1st ed. 4to. 146p. VG. D6. $45.00

DONAHEY, William. *Adventures of the Teenie Weenies.* 1920. Reilly Lee. 1st ed. 9 mc pl. cloth/pict label. VG/partial. M5. $250.00

DONAHEY, William. *Down the River With the Teenie Weenies.* 1940. Rand McNally. Junior ed. ils. pict brd. VG. M5. $60.00

DONALDSON, Frances. *PG Wodehouse: The Authorized Biography.* 1982. Weidenfeld Nicolson. 1st ed. F/F. P3. $25.00

DONALDSON, Francis. *PG Wodehouse, a Biography.* 1982. Knopf. 1st ed. NF/dj. M20. $15.00

DONALDSON, Henry Herbert. *Growth of the Brain.* 1903. NY. Scribner. 365p. G. K4. $25.00

DONALDSON, Lois. *In the Mouse's House.* 1942 (1936). Whitman. ils Mathilde Ritter. F/dj. M5. $40.00

DONALDSON, Stephen R. *Daughter of Regals.* 1984. Del Rey. 1st ed. F/F. P3. $15.00

DONALDSON, Stephen R. *Daughter of Regals.* 1984. Donald Grant. 1st ed. sgn. 1/1075. F/dj. M2. $50.00

DONALDSON, Stephen R. *Mirror of Her Dreams.* 1986. Ballantine/Del Rey. UP. sgn. NF/prt wrp. B2. $35.00

DONALDSON, Stephen R. *Mirror of Her Dreams.* 1986. Ballantine/Del Rey. 1st ed. VG/VG. P3. $25.00

DONALDSON, Stephen R. *One Dree.* 1982. Ballantine. 1st ed. NF/F. N3. $10.00

DONALDSON, Stephen R. *White Gold Wielder.* 1983. Del Rey. 1st ed. F/F. P3. $20.00

DONLEAVY, J.P. *Are You Listening Rabbi Low.* 1988. Atlantic Monthly. 1st ed. F/F. B3. $20.00

DONLEAVY, J.P. *Ginger Man.* 1956. London. Spearman. 1st Eng ed. sm 8vo. 282p. gilt bl cloth. NF/dj. H5. $150.00

DONLEAVY, J.P. *Ginger Man.* 1958. McDowell. 1st Am ed. F/NF. B4. $100.00

DONLEAVY, J.P. *Ginger Man.* 1958. Olympia. 1st Paris hc ed/author's 1st book. sgn. F/NF. Q1. $150.00

DONLEAVY, J.P. *Ginger Man.* 1958. Paris. Olympia. Traveler's Companion series. 1/500. F/F. B3. $195.00

DONLEAVY, J.P. *Leila.* 1983. Franklin Lib. 1st ed. sgn. aeg. gilt leather. F. B2. $45.00

DONLEAVY, J.P. *Onion Eaters.* 1971. Delacorte. 1st Am ed/1st prt. 306p. F/VG. H1. $20.00

DONLEAVY, J.P. *Unexpurgated Code: Complete Manual of Survival & Manners.* 1975. Delacorte. 1st ed. sgn. F/NF. B4. $125.00

DONLEY. *Atlas of California.* 1979. np. folio. 175 mc maps. 196p. F/NF. A4. $85.00

DONNE, John. *Biathanotos: Declaration of That Paradox, or Thesis...* (1644). London. Dawson. 1st ed. 4to. 218p. contemporary calf. K1. $2,750.00

DONNELLY, Joe. *Stone.* 1990. Barrie Jenkins. 1st ed. F/F. P3. $30.00

DONNELLY, Robert B. *Just Like the Flowers Dear.* 1932. NY. 1/950. sgn. 60 pl. 270p. mc brd/cloth spine. NF. B26. $37.50

DONNELLY & GULLERS. *Crewel Needlepoint World.* 1973. np. cloth. VG. G2. $15.00

DONOSO, Jose. *Charleston.* 1977. Boston. Godine. 1st ed. sgn. 1/200. F/case. L3. $125.00

DONOSO, Jose. *Coronation.* 1965. Knopf. 1st Am ed. sgn. F/NF. B4. $200.00

DONOSO, Jose. *Curfew.* 1988. London. Picador. 1st ed. F/NF. B3. $15.00

DONOVAN, John F. *Pagoda & the Cross: Life of Bishop Ford of Maryknoll.* 1967. Scribner. 1st ed. 223p. VG/dj. W1. $18.00

DONOVAN, Robert J. *PT 109: John F Kennedy in WWII.* ca 1961. McGraw Hill. BC. ils. 220p. VG. M10. $6.50

DONOVAN. *US Army Physical Exercises/ Revised for Use of Civilian.* (1902). Street Smith. ils. 130p. VG. H1. $6.50

DONTAS, Domna. *Greece & the Great Powers 1863-1875.* 1966. Thessaloniki. 8vo. 223p. w/prt card. O2. $25.00

DOODY, Margaret. *Aristotle Detective.* 1980. Harper Row. 1st ed. VG/VG. P3. $15.00

DOOLING, Richard. *Critical Care.* 1992. Morrow. 1st ed. F/F. B4. $50.00

DOOLING, Richard. *White Man's Grave.* 1994. FSG. UP. F/wrp. B4. $85.00

DOOLITTLE, Hilda. *By Avon River.* 1949. Macmillan. 1st ed. sgn. F/VG. V1. $35.00

DOOLITTLE, Hilda. *Hedylus.* 1928. Oxford. Basil Blackwell. 1/775. F/NF. Q1. $250.00

DOOLITTLE, Jerome. *Body Scissors.* 1990. Pocket. 1st ed. NF/NF. P3. $18.00

DOPAGNE, Jacques. *Dali.* 1974. Leon Amiel. 1st ed. VG/VG. P3. $15.00

DORAN, George H. *Chronicles of Barabras...1934.* 1935. Harcourt Brace. 1st Am ed. gilt bl cloth. NF/G+/clear plastic. M7. $35.00

DORAN, J. *Annals of the English Stage.* 1888. London. 3 vol set. 1st ed thus. VG. A15. $150.00

DORAN, James M. *Erroll Garner: The Most Happy Piano.* 1985. Scarecrow. 1st ed. xl. B2. $30.00

DORCUS & SHAFFER. *Textbook of Abnormal Psychology.* 1934. Baltimore, MD. Williams Wilkins. 365p. G. K4. $25.00

DORE, Helen. *William Morris.* 1990. Pyramid. 1st ed. M/dj. M21. $20.00

DORFMAN, Ariel. *Mascara.* 1988. Viking. 1st ed. F/F. B4. $45.00

DORN, Edward. *Gunslinger: Book II.* 1969. Blk Sparrow. 1st ltd ed. 1/250. sgn/#d. cloth. F/plastic. A18. $60.00

DORN, Edward. *Newly Fallen.* 1961. NY. Totem/Paterson Soc. 1st ed. F/wrp. B2. $25.00

DORR, Julia C.R. *Bermuda: An Idyl of the Summer Islands.* 1893. Scribner. 16mo. fld map. 148p. VG. B11. $35.00

DORRANCE, Ward. *Where the Rivers Meet.* 1939. NY. 1st ed. inscr. VG/VG. A11. $70.00

DORRIS, Michael. *Broken Cord.* 1989. Harper Row. 1st ed. sgn. F/F. B3. $35.00

DORRIS, Michael. *Paper Trail.* 1994. Harper Collins. 1st ed. F/F. B4. $45.00

DORRIS, Michael. *Yellow Raft in Blue Water.* 1987. Holt. AP/author's 1st book. sgn. F/pict wrp. B3. $40.00

DORRIS, Michael. *Yellow Raft in Blue Water.* 1987. NY. ARC/author's 1st novel. inscr/sgn. F/8vo wrp. A11. $55.00

DORSON, Richard. *American Beings.* 1950. Pantheon. 438p. F/worn. A10. $18.00

DOS PASSOS, John. *Easter Island: Island of Enigma.* 1971. Doubleday. 1st ed. photos. VG/clip. B4. $85.00

DOS PASSOS, John. *Facing the Chair.* 1927. Boston. Sacco Vanzetti. 1st ed. VG/wrp. B2. $60.00

DOS PASSOS, John. *Head & Heart of Thomas Jefferson.* 1954. Doubleday. 1st ed. 8vo. 422p. F/clip. C6. $45.00

DOS PASSOS, John. *John Midcentury.* 1940. London. VG. C4. $40.00

DOS PASSOS, John. *One Man's Initiation — 1917.* 1920. Allen Unwin. true 1st ed/author's 1st book. F/F. B4. $900.00

DOS PASSOS, John. *One Man's Initiation — 1917.* 1920. London. Allen Unwin. 1st ed/2nd state (line 32 on p 35 intact). VG/dj. H5. $600.00

DOS PASSOS, John. *State of the Nation.* 1944. Houghton Mifflin. 1st ed. inscr. NF/NF. L3. $550.00

DOS PASSOS, John. *42nd Parallel.* 1930. Harper. 1st ed. F/NF. B2. $150.00

DOSTOEVSKY, F. *Poor Folk.* 1894. Boston. Roberts. 1st Am ed. VG. B4. $250.00

DOSTOEVSKY, Fyodor. *Brothers Karamazov.* 1990. North Point. 2nd ed. F/F. P3. $30.00

DOSTOEVSKY, Fyodor. *Crime & Punishment.* 1992. Knopf. 1st ed. F/F. P3. $20.00

DOTTIG. *Mumpsy Goes to Kindergarten.* 1945. Rand McNally Jr Elf Book 8052. K2. $6.00

DOTY, Jean Slaughter. *Crumb.* 1976. NY. Gr Willow. 1st ed. VG/G. O3. $25.00

DOTY, Jean Slaughter. *Gabriel.* 1974. Macmillan. 1st ed. ils. 138p. xl. pict cloth. dj. very scarce. R2. $60.00

DOTY, Robert. *Am Folk Art in OH Collections.* 1976. Akron Art Inst. NF/NF. M20. $30.00

DOTY, Robert. *Photo Secession.* 1960. Eastman. 1st ed. 4to. NF/NF. S9. $125.00

DOUBLEDAY, Abner. *Reminiscences of Forts Sumter & Moultrie.* 1876. 184p. F. O8. $27.50

DOUGHTY, Charles M. *Arabisk Resa.* 1959. Stockholm. Sven-Erik Berghs Forlag. 352p. gilt brn cloth. NF/NF. M7. $85.00

DOUGHTY, Charles M. *Passages From Arabia Deserta...* 1931. London. Cape. sm 8vo. 2p map/glossary. G. W1. $15.00

DOUGHTY, Charles M. *Travels in Arabia Deserta.* July 1935. Cape/Medici Soc. 2 vol in 1. thin paper ed/2nd prt. 256p. M. M7. $125.00

DOUGHTY, Charles M. *Travels in Arabia Deserta.* nd (1937). Random. 4th ed. pocket map. 696p. tan oatmeal cloth. VG/VG. M7. $55.00

DOUGHTY, Charles M. *Travels in Arabia Deserta.* 1937. Random. 2 vol. ils/glossary. gilt/bl stp oatmeal cloth. F/plastic. M7. $200.00

DOUGHTY, Charles M. *Travels in Arabia Deserta.* 1953. LEC. 1st ed. 1/1500. brn stp natural linen. F/fld case. M7. $75.00

DOUGHTY, Charles M. *Wanderings in Arabia, Being an Abridgment of Travels...* 1927. Boni. 607p. G. M10. $15.00

DOUGHTY, Charles M. *Wanderings in Arabia.* 1926. Duckworth, UK. abridged Edward Garnett. 607p. gilt olive cloth. VG. M7. $45.00

DOUGLAS, Alfred. *Collected Poems of Lord Alfred Douglas.* 1919. London. 1/200 on Japon. sgn. 126p. VG. B14. $95.00

DOUGLAS, Amanda. *Hannah Ann.* 1899 (1897). Dodd Mead. 8vo. VG. M5. $15.00

DOUGLAS, Arthur. *Last Rights.* 1986. St Martin. 1st ed. F/F. P3. $15.00

DOUGLAS, Byrd. *Steamboatin' on the Cumberland.* 1961. TN Book Co. ils/maps. 407p. dj. T7. $45.00

DOUGLAS, Carole Nelson. *Counterprobe.* 1988. Tor. 1st ed. F/F. N3. $15.00

DOUGLAS, Carole Nelson. *Heir of Rengarth.* 1988. Tor. UP/1st ed. F/prt wrp. N3. $12.00

DOUGLAS, Carole Nelson. *Irene's Last Dance.* 1994. Tor. 1st ed. F/F. N3. $15.00

DOUGLAS, Carole Nelson. *Keepers of Edanvant.* 1987. Tor. 1st ed. sgn. F/F. F4. $25.00

DOUGLAS, D. *Huguenot.* 1954. NY. 1st ed. 387p. VG/G. B5. $25.00

DOUGLAS, David C. *Norman Achievement 1050-1100.* 1969. Berkeley/LA. 1st ed. 8vo. 271p. VG/dj. W1. $22.00

DOUGLAS, David C. *William the Conqueror: Norman Impact Upon England.* 1964. CA U. 1st ed. 476p. NF/dj. M10. $18.50

DOUGLAS, Frederick. *My Bondage & My Freedom.* 1857. NY. VG. H7. $85.00

DOUGLAS, Kirk. *Gift.* 1992. Warner. 1st ed. F/F. B3. $15.00

DOUGLAS, Laura W. *Case of the Copper Cat.* 1960. Arcadia. 1st ed. VG/G. P3. $15.00

DOUGLAS, Lloyd C. *Doctor Hudson's Secret Journal.* 1939. Riverside. 1st ed. 1/500. special bdg. VG/box. E3. $50.00

DOUGLAS, Marjory Stoneman. *Hurricane.* 1958. NY. 1st ed. VG/VG. B5. $45.00

DOUGLAS, Marjory Stoneman. *Road to the Sun.* 1952. Rinehart. 1st ed. NF/VG+. B4. $100.00

DOUGLAS, Norman. *Birds & Beasts of the Greek Anthology.* 1927. Florence. private prt. 1st ed. sgn. 1/500. VG/sans. Q1. $150.00

DOUGLAS, Norman. *Fountains in the Sand.* 1926. London. Secker. 12mo. 208p. xl. G. W1. $15.00

DOUGLAS, Norman. *Together.* 1923. NY. McBride. 1st ed. gilt bdg. M7. $55.50

DOUGLAS, Robert B. *Sophie Arnould, Actress & Wit.* 1898. Paris. Carrington. 1/500. ils Adolphe Lalauze. teg. gilt bdg. VG. F1. $80.00

DOUGLAS, Walton. *On Defining Death: Analytic Study of Concept of Death...* 1979. Montreal. McGill-Queen's U. 189p. cloth. G1. $28.50

DOUGLAS, William O. *Almanac of Liberty.* 1954. Doubleday. M11. $35.00

DOUGLAS, William O. *Justice Douglas Appeals for Rebirth of Freedom.* 1952. Phil. Am Friends Service Committee. 8 p. self wrp. M11. $45.00

DOUGLAS, William O. *My Wilderness: East to Katahdin...* 1961. NY. 1st ed. maps. F/F. B14. $35.00

DOUGLAS, William O. *My Wilderness: The Pacific West.* 1960. NY. 1st ed. ils Francis Lee Jaques. F/F. B14. $30.00

DOUGLAS, William O. *West of the Indies.* 1958. Doubleday Doran. 1st ed. 8vo. 513p. NF/dj. W1. $15.00

DOUGLAS, William. *History of Dentistry in Colorado 1859-1959.* 1959. Denver. 1st ed. 277p. A13. $20.00

DOUGLASS, Benjamin Wallace. *Every Step in Beekeeping.* 1921. Bobbs Merrill. VG. P3. $20.00

DOVE, Rita. *Through the Ivory Gate.* 1992. Pantheon. ARC. F/wrp. B2. $35.00

DOVE, Rita. *Through the Ivory Gate.* 1992. Pantheon/Random. 1st ed/author's 1st novel. NF/NF. A14. $30.00

DOW, Ethel C. *Diary of a Birthday Doll.* 1908. Barse Hopkins. ils Louise Clark Smith. 88p. gr cloth. NF/G. A3. $55.00

DOW, George Francis. *Slave Ships & Slaving.* 1927. Salem. Marine Research. 1st ed. 4to. 50 pl. 388p. F. H4. $125.00

DOWD, J.H. *Childhood.* 1936. Scribner. 1st/A ed. ils. VG/partial. M5. $75.00

DOWDEN, George. *Bibliography of Works by Allen Ginsberg.* 1971. San Francisco. 1st ed. F/NF. B2. $50.00

DOWELL, Coleman. *Silver Swanne.* 1983. Grenfell. sgn. 1/115. F. B4. $150.00

DOWN, Robert B. *Famous American Books.* 1971. McGraw Hill. 377p. VG/VG. A10. $8.00

DOWNES, Donald. *Red Rose for Maria.* 1959. Rinehart. 1st ed. VG/G. P3. $15.00

DOWNES, Randolph C. *Hist of Lake Shore OH.* 1952. Lewis Hist Pub. 3 vols. VG. M20. $125.00

DOWNES, William Howe. *John S Sargent, His Life & Work.* 1925. Little Brn. 1st ed. 4to. teg. red cloth. VG. F1. $50.00

DOWNEY, Joseph T. *Cruise of the Portsmouth 1845-1847: A Sailor's View...* 1963. New Haven/London. Yale. 246p. F. w/pub card. P4. $50.00

DOWNEY & DOWNEY. *Cabinet Portrait Gallery.* 1890. London. 2 vol. 1st ed. 4to. 72 photos. half purple calf. VG. C6. $275.00

DOWNING, Warwick. *Mountains West of Town.* nd. BC. VG/VG. P3. $8.00

DOWNS, Hugh. *Shoal of Stars. A True-Life Account of Everyman's Dream...* 1967. Doubleday. 1st ed. VG/dj. N2. $6.00

DOYLE, Arthur Conan. *Adventure of the Blue Carbuncle.* 1948. Baker Street Irregulars. ils Sidney Paget. 64p. silvered bl cloth. VG. H5. $75.00

DOYLE, Arthur Conan. *Annotated Sherlock Holmes.* 1986. Clarkson Potter. 1st 1-vol ed. ils/maps/diagrams. VG/case. B30. $60.00

DOYLE, Arthur Conan. *Boys' Sherlock Holmes.* 1936. Harper. VG. P3. $20.00

DOYLE, Arthur Conan. *Case-Book of Sherlock Holmes.* 1927. London. Murray. 1st ed. 8vo. 320p. gilt pink cloth. VG. H5. $750.00

DOYLE, Arthur Conan. *Chronicles of Sherlock Holmes.* 1981. Tarzana, CA. 46 vol. 24x18mm. 48 to 72p each in dollhouse-size bookcase. B24. $1,250.00

DOYLE, Arthur Conan. *Complete Book of Sherlock Holmes. Vol 2.* 1930. Doubleday Doran. memorial/1st ed. 462p. G. H1. $9.00

DOYLE, Arthur Conan. *Complete Works of Sherlock Holmes. Vol 1.* nd. Doubleday. 555p. NF. S12. $50.00

DOYLE, Arthur Conan. *Duet.* 1899. Appleton. 1st ed. VG. P3. $50.00

DOYLE, Arthur Conan. *Duet.* 1899. London. Grant Richards. 1st ed. inscr pres. 8vo. 330p. rebound morocco. F. H5. $650.00

DOYLE, Arthur Conan. *Hound of the Baskervilles.* 1902. McClure Phillips. 1st Am ed. VG. P3. $100.00

DOYLE, Arthur Conan. *Last Gallery.* 1911. Doubleday Page. 1st Am ed. ils NC Wyeth. F. M19. $150.00

DOYLE, Arthur Conan. *Les Chien des Baskerville.* 1976. Gallimard. F/F. P3. $20.00

DOYLE, Arthur Conan. *My Friend the Murder & Other Mysteries & Adventures.* nd. Chicago. Conkey. 288p. G. H1. $8.50

DOYLE, Arthur Conan. *Return of Sherlock Holmes.* 1987. Mysterious. 1st ed thus. 4to. F. A17. $20.00

DOYLE, Arthur Conan. *Rodney Stone.* 1896. NY. 1st Am ed. F/dj/case. C2. $850.00

DOYLE, Arthur Conan. *Rodney Stone.* 1896. NY. 1st Am ed. ftspc. ils. gilt cloth. VG. A17. $27.50

DOYLE, Arthur Conan. *Study in Scarlet.* 1891. London. Ward Lock Bowden. 2nd Eng ed. 224p. Bayntun Riviere morocco. F. H5. $1,500.00

DOYLE, Arthur Conan. *Study in Scarlet.* 1911. London. Ward Lock. 8vo. ils Hutchinson/ Greig. gilt bl cloth. VG. H5. $250.00

DOYLE, Arthur Conan. *Tales of Sherlock Holmes.* nd. Grosset Dunlap. photoplay ed. VG. P3. $35.00

DOYLE, Arthur Conan. *Vital Message.* 1919. Doran. 1st ed. VG. P3. $60.00

DOYLE, Arthur Conan. *White Company.* nd. Grosset Dunlap. ils Anders D Johansen. 391p. VG. H1. $12.00

DOYLE, Charles. *Richard Aldington.* 1990. Canada. U of Victoria. ELS Monograph Series. sgn Doyle/Crawford/Gates. 106p. M. M7. $45.00

DOYLE, Richard. *Doyle Fairy Book. Fairy Tales From All Nations.* ca 1890. Stokes. 3rd ed. 582p. VG. D6. $75.00

DOYLE, Robert O. *Long-Range Programs in Space Astronomy...* 1969. NASA SP-213. 8vo. 305p. wrp. K5. $10.00

DOYLE & DOYLE. *Knights' Wyrd.* 1992. HBJ. 1st ed. F/F. P3. $17.00

DOZOIS, Gardner. *Slow Dancing Through Time.* 1990. Ziesing. 1st ed. F/F. T2. $22.00

DOZOIS, Gardner. *Strangers.* 1978. Berkley. 1st ed. xl. F/dj. M2. $10.00

DR. SEUSS; see Geisel, Theodor Seuss.

DR. X. *Intern.* 1965. NY. 1st ed. 404p. A13. $20.00

DRABBLE, Margaret. *Radiant Way.* 1987. Weidenfeld Nicholson. 1st ed. F/F. B3. $20.00

DRACHMAN, Julian. *Studies in Literature of Natural Science.* 1930. Macmillan. 487p. cloth. xl. A10. $18.00

DRACO, F. *Devil's Church.* 1951. Rinehart. 1st ed. VG/G. P3. $30.00

DRAENOS, Stan. *Freud's Odyssey: Psychoanalysis & End of Metaphysics.* 1982. New Haven. thin 8vo. 177p. blk cloth. G1. $25.00

DRAGO, Harry Sinclair. *Canal Days in America.* 1972. Bramhall. 311p. VG/dj. M20. $30.00

DRAGO, Harry Sinclair. *Roads to Empire.* 1968. NY. 1st ed. inscr. F/F. A11. $60.00

DRAGONWAGON, Crescent. *Always, Always.* 1984. Macmillan. 1st ed. lg 8vo. M/NF. C8. $25.00

DRAGONWAGON, Crescent. *Coconut.* 1984. Harper. 1st ed. inscr. M/M. C8. $30.00

DRAGONWAGON, Crescent. *Home Place.* 1990. Macmillan. 1st ed. ils Jerry Pinkney. M/M. C8. $30.00

DRAGONWAGON, Crescent. *I Hate My Sister Maggie.* 1989. Macmillan. 1st ed. ils Leslie Morill. M/M. C8. $35.00

DRAGONWAGON, Crescent. *If You Call My Name.* 1981. Harper. 1st ed. ils David Palladine. F/F. C8. $27.50

DRAGONWAGON, Crescent. *Jemima Remembers.* 1984. Macmillan. 1st ed. ils Troy Howell. F/VG+. C8. $22.50

DRAGONWAGON, Crescent. *Katie in the Morning.* 1983. Harper. 1st ed. ils Betsy Day. M/M. C8. $35.00

DRAGONWAGON, Crescent. *Strawberry Dress Escape.* 1975. Scribner. 1st ed. lg 8vo. pict cloth. F/F. C8. $35.00

DRAGONWAGON, Crescent. *Wind Rose.* 1976. Harper. ils Ronald Himler. lg 8vo. NF/VG. C8. $25.00

DRAGONWAGON & ZINDEL. *To Take a Dare.* 1982. Harper. 1st ed. sm 8vo. F/F. C8. $35.00

DRAKE, Daniel. *Discourses Delivered Before Cincinnati Medical Lib...* 1852. Cincinnati. 93p. limp cloth. VG. B14. $175.00

DRAKE, David. *Birds of Prey.* 1984. Baen. 1st ed. F/F. P3. $22.00

DRAKE, David. *Fortress.* 1987. Tor. 1st ed. F/F. N3. $15.00

DRAKE, Samuel Adams. *Old Boston Taverns & Tavern Clubs.* 1917. Boston. new ils ed. 124p. brd. VG. B14. $75.00

DRAKE. *Alamancs of the US.* 1962. np. 2 vol. ES. F. A4. $275.00

DRANNAN, William. *31 Years on Plains & Mtns.* 1907. Chicago. VG. B5. $45.00

DRAPER, T. *84th Infantry Division BAttle of Germany.* 1946. NY. 1st ed. VG/worn. B5. $65.00

DREADSTONE, Carl; see Campbell, Ramsey.

DREIER, Thomas. *Power of Print — And Men.* ca 1936. Brooklyn. Merganthaler Linotype. 165p. half cloth. shipping box. P4. $75.00

DREISER, Theodore. *Bulwark.* 1946. Doubleday. 1st ed. 8vo. 337p. NF/poor. V3. $14.00

DREISER, Theodore. *Chains.* 1927. Boni Liveright. 1/440. sgn. box. B2. $250.00

DREISER, Theodore. *Dawn.* 1931. Liveright. 1st ed. sgn. 1/275. NF. B4. $185.00

DREISER, Theodore. *Epitaph, a Poem.* 1929. Heron. 1/700 on Keijyo Kami paper. sgn. F/case. F1. $185.00

DREISER, Theodore. *Epitaph.* 1929. NY. Heron. 1/1100. sgn author/ils Robert Fawcett. gilt blk cloth. F/case. B4. $275.00

DREISER, Theodore. *Jennie Gerhardt.* 1911. NY. Harper. 1st ed/2nd issue (is for it on p 22). inscr. VG. Q1. $600.00

DREISER, Theodore. *Letters of Theodore Dreiser.* 1959. Phil. PA U. 3 vol. 1st ed. NF/VG box. B4. $75.00

DREISER, Theodore. *Moods, Candenced & Declaimed.* 1928. Boni Liveright. 1st trade ed. F/F. B4. $275.00

DREISER, Theodore. *Moods, Candenced & Declaimed.* 1928. Boni Liveright. 1st trade ed. 8vo. 385p. F/clip. C6. $250.00

DREISER, Theodore. *Moods, Philosophic & Emotional.* 1935. Simon & Schuster. 1st ed thus. 8vo. 423p. NF/VG. C6. $35.00

DREISER, Theodore. *Symbolic Drawings of Hubert Davis for An American Tragedy...* 1930. Horace Liveright. 1/525. sgn Davis/Dreiser. folio. gilt blk cloth/brd. F/case. H5. $150.00

DREISER, Theodore. *Tragic America.* 1931. Liveright. 1st ed. F/NF. B4. $300.00

DREPPERD, Carl W. *Early American Prints.* 1930. NY. Century. 1st ed. ils. 232p. gilt bl cloth. VG. F1. $50.00

DREPPERD, Carl W. *Pioneer America, Its First Three Centuries.* 1949. Doubleday. 1st ed. 8vo. 311p. F/F/VG case. B11. $50.00

DRESSER, Norine. *American Vampires: Fans, Victims & Practioners.* 1989. Norton. 1st ed. F/F. N3. $20.00

DREYER, J.L.E. *Hist of Astronomy From Thales to Kepler.* 1953. Dover. pb. 8vo. 438p. K5. $8.00

DREYER, J.L.E. *New General Catalogue of Nebulae & Clusters of Stars...* 1971. London. Royal Astonomical Soc. sm 4to. 378p. G. K5. $75.00

DREYER, Peter. *Beast in View.* 1969. London. Deutsch. 1st ed/author's 1st novel. NF/VG. N3. $10.00

DREYFUS, John. *William Caxton & His Quincentenary.* 1976. NY. The Typophiles. 12mo. 1/700. 54p. F. M10. $22.50

DRIESCH, Hans. *Grundprobleme der Psychologie: Ihre Krisis in Gegenwart.* 1926. Leipzig. Emmanuel Reinicke. 250p. VG. G1. $40.00

DRIGGS, Howard. *Pony Express Goes Through.* 1963 (1935). Lippincott. 9 mc pl. F/F. B34. $25.00

DRIGGS & LEWINE. *Black Beauty, White Heat: Pict Hist of Classic Jazz.* 1982. Morrow. 1st ed. 360p. F/NF. B2. $150.00

DRINKA, George. *Birth of Neurosis: Myth, Malady & the Victorians.* 1984. NY. 1st ed. 431p. A13. $25.00

DRINKER, F. *Theodore Roosevelt, His Life & Work.* 1919. np. 471p. poor. B34. $8.00

DRINKER, Sophie Lewis. *Hannah Penn & the Proprietorship of PA.* 1958. Phil. private prt. 1st ed. pres. 207p. cloth. w/sgn letter & pamphlet. M8. $35.00

DROBISCH, Moritz Wilhelm. *Empirische Psychologie Nach Naturwissenschaftlicher Methode.* 1842. Leipzig. Leopold Voss. 356p. orig paper brd/leather spine label. G1. $150.00

DROST, William E. *Clocks & Watches of NJ.* 1966. Engineering Pub. ltd ed. 1/500. F/G. rare. A8. $75.00

DROULIA, Loukia. *Philhellenisme. Ouvrages Inspires par la Guerre...* 1974. Athens. tall 8vo. 314p. w/prt card. O2. $35.00

DROWER, E.S. *Book of the Zodiac.* 1949. London. Royal Asiatic Soc. 1st ed. VG. W1. $75.00

DROWN & DROWN. *Compendium of Agriculture; or, The Farmer's Guide...* 1824. Providence. Field Maxcy. 1st ed. 288p. calf. H10. $185.00

DRUMM, Chris. *An Algis Budyrs Checklist.* 1982. Polk City. Drumm. 1st ed. F. N3. $5.00

DRUMMOND, Ivor. *Frog in the Moonflower.* 1972. Macmillan. 1st ed. F/F. P3. $23.00

DRUMMOND, Walter; see Silverberg, Robert.

DRURY, Allen. *Advise & Consent.* nd. BOMC. VG/VG. P3. $10.00

DRURY, Clifford. *First White Women Over the Rockies...1836 & 1838.* 1963-1966. Arthur Clark. 3 vol. ils. F. A4. $375.00

DRURY, Victor. *Hist of the Middle Ages.* 1900. Crowell. 2nd ed. 119p. xl. G. W1. $8.00

DU BOIS, Gaylord. *Lone Ranger (#1).* 1936. Grosset Dunlap. 1st ed. 1st title in series. 218p. VG/VG. M20. $85.00

DU BOIS, Philip H. *Hist of Psychological Testing.* 1970. Boston. Allyn Bacon. 131p. F. K4. $10.00

DU BOIS, Theodora. *Death Wears a White Coat.* 1938. Houghton Mifflin. 1st ed. VG. P3. $30.00

DU BOIS, Theodora. *Listener.* 1953. Crime Club. 1st ed. VG/VG. P3. $15.00

DU BOIS, Theodora. *Travelling Toys.* 1934. Phil. Penn. ils FB Peat. orange cloth. NF. D6. $85.00

DU BOIS, W.E. Burghardt. *World & Africa.* 1947. Viking. 1st ed. F/NF. B2. $50.00

DU BOIS, William P. *Bear Party.* 1951. Viking. 1st ed. G. P2. $40.00

DU BOIS, William P. *Flying Locomotive.* 1942 (1941). Viking. 2nd prt. VG. C8. $25.00

DU BOIS, William P. *Gentleman Bear.* 1985. FSG. ARC. unbound. w/pub letter. F/VG. P2. $20.00

DU BOIS, William P. *Gentleman Bear.* 1985. FSG. 1st ed. F/F. C8. $27.50

DU BOIS, William P. *Great Geppy.* 1940. Viking. 1st ed. VG+/chip. C8. $30.00

DU BOIS, William P. *Otto at Sea.* 1958 (1936). Viking. 1st ed thus. F/VG+. C8. $35.00

DU BOISE, John Witherspoon. *General Joseph Wheeler & Army of Tennessee.* 1912. NY. Neale. 1st ed. 476p. cloth. NF. M8. $450.00

DU BOSE, Hampden C. *Memoirs of Rev John Leighton Wilson, DD...* 1895. Richmond, VA. 1st ed. 336p. orig cloth. VG. M8. $85.00

DU CANE, Peter. *High-Speed Small Craft.* ca 1951. Cambridge. Cornell Maritime. 8vo. ils/photos. 278p. VG/VG. P4. $45.00

DU CHAILLU, Paul. *Country of the Dwarfs.* 1871. Harper. 314p. gilt cloth. E5. $35.00

DU CHAILLU, Paul. *Explorations & Adventures in Equatorial Africa...* 1861. NY. Harper. 1st Am ed. 532p. rust cloth. VG. K1. $150.00

DU CHAILLU, Paul. *In African Forest & Jungle.* 1903. Scribner. 1st ed. 24 full-p pl/Victor Perard. 193p. F. B24. $100.00

DU CHAMP, Marcel. *Bride Stripped Bare by Her Bachelors Even.* nd. London. Humphries. typographic version. trans GH Hamilton. np. F. B2. $75.00

DU FRENE, Maurice. *Florilegium.* 1988. Utrecht. Catharijne Pr. 62x41mm. 1/165. ils Luce Thurkow. limp suede. F/box. B24. $350.00

DU FRENNE, Mikel. *Karl Jaspers et la Philosophie de l'Existence.* 1949. Paris. Seuil. 399p. stiff wht/bl wrp. G1. $25.00

DU MAS, Frank M. *Manifest Structure Analysis.* 1955. Missoula. 177p. G. K4. $15.00

DU MAURIER, Daphne. *Classics of the Macbre.* 1987. Doubleday. 1st ed. F/F. P3. $19.00

DU MAURIER, Daphne. *Frenchman's Creek.* 1943. Sun Dial. 310p. NF. S12. $12.00

DU MAURIER, Daphne. *House on the Strand.* 1970. World. VG/VG. P3. $10.00

DU MAURIER, Daphne. *My Cousin Rachel.* 1952. Longman. 1st ed. VG/G. P3. $18.00

DU MAURIER, Daphne. *My Cousin Rachel.* 1952. NY. Doubleday. 1st Am ed. 8vo. 348p. gr lettered beige cloth. NF/dj. H5. $200.00

DU MAURIER, Daphne. *Parasites.* 1950. Doubleday. 1st Am ed. 305p. VG/dj. M20. $25.00

DU MAURIER, Daphne. *Rebecca.* 1938. London. Gollancz. 1st ed. VG/VG. Q1. $1,250.00

DU MAURIER, Daphne. *Rendezvous & Other Stories.* 1980. Gollancz. 1st ed. VG/VG. P3. $20.00

DU MAURIER, Daphne. *Rule Britannia.* 1972. Gollancz. 1st ed. VG/VG. P3. $25.00

DU MAURIER, Daphne. *Serkkuni Raakel.* 1952. Porvoo/Helsinki. Werner Soderstrom, Osakeyhtio. 1st Finnish ed. VG. N2. $6.00

DU MAURIER, George. *Trilby.* 1894. Harper. G+. N2. $10.00

DU PONCEAU, Peter S. *Brief View of Constitution of the US, Addressed to...* 1834. Phil. EG Dorsey. contemporary sheep. VG. M11. $350.00

DU PONT, Samuel Francis. *Samuel Francis DuPont: A Selection From Civil War Letters.* 1969. Ithaca. 3 vol. 1st ed. cloth. NF. M8. $125.00

DU PONT, Sophie. *Sophie DuPont: Young Lady in America.* 1987. NY. Abrams. 1st ed. ils. 192p. gilt red cloth. M/F. P4. $35.00

DUANE, Diana. *Spock's World.* 1988. Pocket. 1st ed. TVTI. VG/VG. P3. $15.00

DUANE, Diane. *Spider-Man, the Venom Factor.* 1994. Putnam. UP. NF/prt bl wrp. B3. $20.00

DUBLEMAN, Richard. *Adventures of Holly Hoffie.* 1980. Delacorte. 1st ed. 261p. VG/dj. M20. $20.00

DUBLIN & LOTKA. *Money Value of a Man.* 1947. NY. Ronald. revised ed/2nd prt. 214p. xl. reading copy. K4. $20.00

DUBOFSKY & VAN TINE. *Labor Leaders in America.* 1987. Chicago. pb. F. V4. $8.50

DUBOIS, Gaylord. *Long Rider & Treasure/Vanished Men.* nd. Whitman. VG. P3. $10.00

DUBUS, Andre. *Blessings.* 1987. Elmwood. Ravens. 1st ed. sgn. 1/60. brd. F. S9. $75.00

DUBUS, Andre. *Lieutenant.* 1967. Dial. 1st ed/ author's 1st book. sgn. NF/VG. L3. $175.00

DUBUS, Andre. *Voices From the Moon.* 1984. Boston. 1st ed. inscr. F/F. A11. $40.00

DUBUS, Andre. *Voices From the Moon.* 1984. Boston. Godine. 1st ed. F/NF. L3. $30.00

DUBY, George. *Hist of Medieval Art, 980-1448.* 1986. NY. Skira. 3 vol in 1. 4to. ils. NF/case. M10. $50.00

DUCASSE, C.J. *CI Lewis' Analysis of Knowledge & Valuation.* 1948. np. rpt. inscr. pamphlet. G1. $35.00

DUCASSE, C.J. *Truth, Knowledge & Causation.* 1969. London. Routledge. 255p. red cloth. VG/dj. G1. $30.00

DUCKETT, Eleanor. *Wandering Saints of the Early Middle Ages.* ca 1959. Norton. 319p. xl. H10. $15.00

DUCROCQ, Albert. *Conquest of Space.* 1961. Putnam. 8vo. photos. 300p. G/dj. K5. $14.00

DUDLEY, A.T. *Great Year.* 1907. Lee Sheperd. 1st ed. pict bdg. VG. P8. $35.00

DUDLEY, A.T. *With Mask & Mitt.* 1906. Lee Shepard. 1st ed. VG+/G+. P8. $55.00

DUDLEY, David D. *Holography: A Survey.* 1973. WA, DC. NASA SP-5118. 4to. ils/diagrams. 129p. paper wrp. K5. $15.00

DUDLEY, James. *Life of Edward Grubb, 1854-1939.* 1946. London. Clarke. 1st ed. 12mo. 158p. VG/dj. V3. $14.00

DUDLEY, Mary. *Life of Mary Dudley...* 1825. Phil. Kite. 8vo. 288p. full leather. VG. V3. $32.00

DUDLEY & SHERIDAN. *What Dark Secret.* 1945. Books Inc. 2nd ed. VG/G. P3. $13.00

DUDSZUS & HENRIOT. *Dictionary of Ship Types.* 1986. London. Conway Maritime. photos. 251p. dj. T7. $60.00

DUENSING. *Type Specimen Bibliography.* 1972. Kalamazoo. private prt. ils. 54p. VG. A4. $145.00

DUERRENMATT, Friedrich. *Pledge.* 1959. NY. 1st Am ed. VG/worn. A17. $7.50

DUFFERIN, Lord. *Yacht Voyage: Letters From High Latitudes...* 1859. Boston. 406p. B14. $95.00

DUFFIELD, J.W. *Bert Wilson's Fadeaway Ball.* 1914. Sully. later prt. pict bdg. G. P8. $25.00

DUFFIELD, Kenneth Graham. *Four Little Pigs That Didn't Have Any Mother.* 1919. Altemus. 24mo. ils. 61p. NF. D6. $50.00

DUFFY, Clinton T. *Pocket Dictionary of Prison Slanguage.* 1941. np. 16mo. ils. VG/stiff wrp. D3. $35.00

DUFFY, John. *Healers: Rise of the Medical Establishment.* 1976. NY. 1st ed. 385p. dj. A13. $45.00

DUFFY, Maureen. *Occam's Razor.* 1993. London. Sinclair Stevenson. 1st ed. F/F. A14. $35.00

DUFRESNE, John. *Lethe, Cupid, Time & Love.* 1994. Candia, NH. LeBow. 1st ed. sgn. ils/sgn Dina Knapp. brd. F. B4. $85.00

DUFRESNE, John. *Way That Water Enters Stone.* 1991. Norton. 1st ed/author's 1st book. sgn. F/F. B3. $75.00

DUGAN, Thomas. *Photography Between Covers.* 1979. Rochester. Light Imp. 1st ed. silvered bl cloth. F/dj. F1. $22.50

DUGDALE, Florence E. *Book of Baby Birds.* nd. Hodder Stoughton. ils EJ Detmold. 120p. VG/G/G box. P2. $300.00

DUGDALE, Florence E. *Book of Baby Birds.* 1912. Hodder Stoughton. 4to. 19 mc pl/EJ Detmold. 120p. NF. D6. $125.00

DUGGAN, Alfred. *Lord Geoffrey's Fancy.* 1962. Pantheon. 1st ed. F/dj. F4. $20.00

DUGMORE, A. Radclyffe. *African Jungle Life.* 1928. London. Macmillan. 8 mc pl. 246p. xl. G. H1. $7.50

DUGMORE, A. Radclyffe. *Through the Sudan.* 1938. Pitman. 1st ed. 12mo. VG. W1. $15.00

DUGUID, Julian. *Green Hell: Adventures in Mysterious Jungles...* 1931. NY. Century. 1st ed. ils/maps. 339p. VG. B11. $45.00

DUHEM, Pierre. *Aim & Structure of Physical Theory.* 1954. Princeton. 1st Eng-language ed. 344p. VG/dj. G1. $50.00

DUHEME, Jacqueline. *Birthdays.* 1966. Determined Products. 1st ed. ils Jacqueline Duheme. 19p. VG/VG. A3. $30.00

DUKAS, H.H. *Albert Einstein: The Human Side.* 1969. Princeton. 167p. dj. G7. $25.00

DUKE, Basil Wilson. *Morgan's Cavalry.* 1906. NY. Neale. 1st ed thus. 441p. cloth. VG. M8. $350.00

DULAC, Edmund. *Marriage of Cupid & Psyche.* 1951. Heritage. 4to. 64p. gilt red cloth. VG+. A3. $20.00

DULANY, Harris. *One Kiss Led to Another.* 1994. Harper Collins. 1st ed/author's 1st novel. sgn. F/F. T2. $25.00

DULL, Paul S. *Battle Hist of the Imperial Japanese Navy.* 1978. Naval Inst. 433p. VG. A17. $10.00

DUMAS, Alexandre. *Chevalier d'Harmental.* 1899. Little Brn. VG. P3. $20.00

DUMAS, Alexandre. *Edmund Dantes.* 1911. Leslie Judge. VG. P3. $30.00

DUMAS, Alexandre. *Three Musketeers.* (1952). Doubleday. VG. M21. $7.50

DUMAS, Alexandre. *Three Musketeers.* 1952. Macmillan. 1st prt. inscr/twice dtd. pict cloth. F/NF. C8. $75.00

DUMAS, Alexandre. *Twenty Years After.* 1899. RF Fenno. VG. P3. $20.00

DUMAS, Claudine; see Malzberg, Barry.

DUMLAO, Rebecca. *Expectant Mother's Wardrobe Planner.* 1986. np. sc. VG. G2. $11.00

DUMMER, Jeremiah. *Defence of the New England Charters.* 1745. Boston. Gookin. 2nd Am ed. woodcuts. 44p. 19th-C brn calf. K1. $300.00

DUMONT, Jean-Paul. *Under the Rainbow.* 1976. Austin, TX. 1st ed. 178p. VG/dj. F3. $20.00

DUNAYEVSKAYA, Raya. *Philosophy & Revolution.* 1973. Delacorte. 1st ed. w/sgn card. F/NF. B2. $75.00

DUNBAR, Carl O. *Earth.* 1967. World. 235p. F/dj. K4. $10.00

DUNBAR, Janet. *Mrs GBS: A Portrait.* 1963. London. Harrap. 1st ed. 328p. F/VG/clear plastic. M7. $40.00

DUNBAR, Lady of Mochrum. *Chow.* 1924 (1914). London. Field. 3rd ed. ils. 78p. VG. R2. $80.00

DUNBAR, Lanthe. *Edge of the Desert.* ca 1920. Boston. Sm Maynard. sm 4to. ils. VG. W1. $12.00

DUNBAR, Paul Laurence. *Complete Poems of...* 1925 (1913). Dodd Mead. sm 8vo. VG. C8. $60.00

DUNBAR, Paul Laurence. *Folks From Dixie.* 1898. Dodd Mead. 1st ed. 8vo. ils EW Kemble. 263p. teg. NF. Q1. $400.00

DUNBAR, Paul Laurence. *Lyrics of Lowly Life.* 1896. Dodd Mead. 1st ed/author's 3rd book. 12mo. 208p. VG. C6. $200.00

DUNBAR, Paul Laurence. *Poems of Cabin & Field.* 1900. Dodd Mead. ils/photos. 125p. VG. B5. $80.00

DUNBAR, Willis F. *All Aboard! Hist of RR in MI.* 1969. Grand Rapids. 1st ed. 308p. NF/NF. A17. $27.50

DUNCAN, Alastair. *Fin de Siecle Masterpieces From the Silverman Collection.* 1989. Abbeville. sm folio. 192p. F/dj. F1. $45.00

DUNCAN, Andrew. *Edinburgh New Dispensatory...* 1805. Worcester. Isaiah Thomas. 6 pl. 694p. contemporary tree calf/red spine label. K1. $300.00

DUNCAN, David Douglas. *Goodbye Picasso.* nd (1974). Grosset Dunlap. folio. purple stp red cloth. NF/VG. F1. $75.00

DUNCAN, David Douglas. *Picasso's Picassos, the Treasures of La Californie.* 1961. London. Macmillan. thick 4to. ils. wht cloth. G/dj. F1. $45.00

DUNCAN, David Douglas. *Picasso's Picassos.* nd. np. tipped-in pl. VG. M17. $50.00

DUNCAN, David Douglas. *Private World of Pablo Picasso.* 1958. NY. Ridge Pr. 1st ed. 4to. VG/photo ils wrp. S9. $30.00

DUNCAN, David Douglas. *Yankee Nomad. A Photographic Odyssey.* 1967. HRW. 2nd ed. 480p. VG. W1. $45.00

DUNCAN, David James. *Brothers K.* 1992. Doubleday. 1st ed. sgn. M/M. P8. $65.00

DUNCAN, David. *Another Tree in Eden.* 1956. Heinemann. 1st ed. NF/NF. P3. $40.00

DUNCAN, David. *Dark Dominion.* 1955. Heinemann. VG/fair. P3. $35.00

DUNCAN, Dayton. *Out West, American Journey.* 1987. Viking. 1st ed. photos/maps. VG/dj. B34. $10.00

DUNCAN, Francis. *Dangerous Mr X.* 1939. Herbert Jenkins. 1st ed. VG. P3. $35.00

DUNCAN, Francis. *Murder in Man.* 1940. Herbert Jenkins. 1st ed. xl. VG. P3. $12.00

DUNCAN, Isadora. *My Life.* 1927. Boni Liveright. 1st trade ed. photos. 359p. cloth. B14. $75.00

DUNCAN, J. Garrow. *Digging Up Biblical Hist...* 1931. Macmillan. 1st ed. 275p. VG. W1. $45.00

DUNCAN, Margaret. *Witch Stone.* 1976. St Martin. 1st Am ed. F/NF. N3. $10.00

DUNCAN, Marion. *On the Farm.* 1940. McKay. photos. NF/G. M5. $20.00

DUNCAN, Robert L. *Temple Dogs.* 1977. Morrow. 1st ed. VG/VG. P3. $18.00

DUNCAN, Robert. *Derivations: Selected Poems 1950-1956.* 1968. London. Fulcrum. 1st ed. F/NF. V1. $35.00

DUNCAN, Thomas D. *Recollections of Thomas D Duncan...* 1922. Nashville. McQuiddy. 1st/only ed. 213p. NF. C6. $275.00

DUNHAM, Aileen. *Political Unrest in Upper Canada 1815-1836.* 1975. Westport. Greenwood. rpt. 210p. brn cloth. M. P4. $15.00

DUNHAM, Barrows. *Man Against Myth.* 1948. Little Brn. 316p. G. K4. $6.00

DUNLAP, Knight. *Outline of Psychobiology.* 1914. John Hopkins. 116p. G. K4. $35.00

DUNLAP, M.E. *Abridgment of Elementary Law...* 1892. St Louis. FH Thomas Law Book Co. contemporary sheep. M11. $50.00

DUNLAP, Susan. *Bohemian Connection.* 1985. St Martin. 1st ed. sgn. F/F. S6. $40.00

DUNLAP, Susan. *Death & Taxes.* 1992. Delacorte. 1st ed. sgn. F/F. M15. $27.50

DUNLAP, Susan. *Death & Taxes.* 1992. Delacorte. 2nd ed. F/F. P3. $18.00

DUNMORE, John. *Who's Who in Pacific Navigation.* 1991. Honolulu. 1st prt. 312p. M/M. P4. $36.00

DUNN, Byron A. *Last Raid.* 1914. Chicago. 1st ed. 344p. G. B18. $25.00

DUNN, Byron A. *Storming Vicksburg.* nd. np. Young Missourians Series. 1st ed. 361p. G. B18. $25.00

DUNN, E.B. *All Weather.* 1902. Dodd Mead. 1st ed. 8vo. 356p. gilt gr cloth. K5. $28.00

DUNN, H.H. *Crimson Jester. Zapata of Mexico.* 1934. NY. 8vo. ils/pl. 304p. gilt blk cloth. F/VG. H3. $30.00

DUNN, J. Allen. *Buffalo Boy.* 1929. Grosset Dunlap. 224p. cloth. VG/dj. M20. $15.00

DUNN, John. *Oregon Territory & British North American Fur Trade.* 1845. Phil. 1st Am ed. VG+. H7. $300.00

DUNN, Katherine. *Attic.* 1970. Harper Row. 1st ed/author's 1st book. F/F. L3. $300.00

DUNN, Katherine. *Geek Love.* 1989. Knopf. 1st ed/author's 3rd book. F/F. B3. $50.00

DUNN, Katherine. *Mystery Girls' Circus & College of Conundrum.* 1991. Kimberly. 1st ed. sgn. 1/125. ils Mare Blocker. cloth. F/sans. B4. $500.00

DUNN, Katherine. *Slice.* 1990. Portland. WW Pr. 1st ed. sgn. F/wrp. S9. $45.00

DUNN, Katherine. *Truck.* 1971. Harper Row. 1st ed/author's 2nd book. F/NF. N3. $150.00

DUNN, Mary Maples. *William Penn: Politics & Conscience.* 1967. Princeton. 1st ed. 8vo. 206p. VG/chip. V3. $16.50

DUNNE, Finley Peter. *Mr Dooley in Peace & in War.* 1914. Boston. Sm Maynard. pres. morocco. M11. $250.00

DUNNE, Gerald T. *Hugo Black & the Judicial Revolution.* 1977. NY. Simon Schuster. M11. $35.00

DUNNE, J.W. *Experiment With Time.* 1927. Macmillan. 1st Am ed. 208p. G+. H1. $14.00

DUNNE, Peter Masten. *Juan Antonio Balthasar, Padre Visitador to Sonora Frontier.* 1957. AZ Pioneer Hist Soc. 1st ed. 129p. NF. w/fld map. B19. $60.00

DUNNETT, Dorothy. *Dolly & the Nanny Bird.* 1982. Knopf. 1st ed. VG/VG. P3. $18.00

DUNNETT, Dorothy. *Send a Fax to the Kasbah.* 1992. HBJ. 1st Am ed. F/dj. M15. $30.00

DUNNING, H.W. *Today on the Nile.* 1905. NY. Pott. 1st ed. 8vo. pl/map. xl. VG. W1. $12.00

DUNNING, John. *Booked To Die.* 1992. Scribner. 1st ed. sgn. 1/6000. F/F. L3. $150.00

DUNNING, John. *Bookman's Wake.* 1995. Scribner. 1st ed. sgn. F/F. O4. $35.00

DUNNING, John. *Tune in Yesterday: Ultimate Encyclopedia of Old-Time Radio.* 1976. Prentice Hall. 1st ed. NF/VG. B4. $150.00

DUNPHY, Jack. *Friends & Vague Lovers.* 1952. NY. 1st ed/author's 2nd novel. sgn. NF/NF. A11. $40.00

DUNSANY, Lord. *Alexander & Three Small Plays.* 1926. Putnam. 1st ed. VG. P3. $40.00

DUNSANY, Lord. *Blessing of Pan.* 1928. Putnam. 1st ed. VG. P3. $75.00

DUNSANY, Lord. *Dreamer's Tales.* 1979. Owlswick. ne. F/dj. M2. $14.00

DUNSANY, Lord. *Fourth Book of Jorkens.* 1948. Arkham. 1st ed. F/dj. M2. $100.00

DUNSANY, Lord. *Guerrilla.* 1944. Bobbs Merrill. 1st ed. VG. P3. $30.00

DUNSANY, Lord. *Plays of Gods & Men.* 1917. Luce. 1st ed. G+. P3. $40.00

DUNSERVILLE & GARARY. *Venezuelan Orchids Ils.* 1959 & 1961. London. Deutsch. 2 vol. 1st ed. 4to. VG/G. S11. $225.00

DUNTHORNE, Gordon. *Flower & Fruit Prints of the 18th & Early 19th Centuries.* 1938. WA, DC. 1/750 for subscribers. 276p. beige linen/leather spine. K1. $375.00

DUPATHY, Charles. *Letters sur l'Italie en 1785.* 1790. Lausanne. Mourer. 2 vol. Nouvelle ed. 12mo. contemporary calf. K1. $150.00

DUPIN, Jacques. *Joan Miro, Life & Work.* 1962. Abrams. 4to. 1158 ils/46 tipped-in pl. 596p. NF/dj. F1. $250.00

DUPLAIX, Georges. *Popo the Hippopotamus.* 1935. Whitman. obl 12mo. ils. 28p. VG. D6. $40.00

DUPLAIX, Georges. *Topsy Turvy Circus.* 1940. NY. 1st ed. 4to. 40p. pict brd. G. A17. $15.00

DUPRE, Bernard. *World Treasury of Mushrooms in Color.* 1974. NY. sm 4to. 128p. dj. B26. $11.00

DUPREE, A. Hunter. *Asa Gray 1810-1888.* 1959. Cambridge. Harvard. 505p. cloth. VG. A10. $35.00

DUQUESNE, Jacques. *L'Algerie ou la Guerre Des Mythes.* 1958. Desclee de Brouwer. 12mo. xl. G. W1. $9.00

DURAN, Diego. *Historia de las Indias de Nueva Espana y Islas Tierra Firme.* 1867-1880. Mexico. 1st prt. pl/atlas vol. rebacked. H4. $3,500.00

DURANT, Will. *Caesar & Christ.* 1944. Simon Schuster. 1st ed. G. W1. $8.00

DURANT, Will. *Story of Civilization...Our Oriental Heritage.* 1942. Simon Schuster. 1049p. VG. W1. $15.00

DURANT & DURANT. *Pict Hist of American Presidents.* (1955). Barnes. 327p. VG. H1. $4.50

DURAS, Marguerite. *Yann Andrea Steiner.* 1992. Scribner. 1st ed. F/F. S9. $35.00

DURBIN, E.F.M. *Politics of Democratic Socialism.* 1954. London. Kegan Paul. VG/VG. V4. $20.00

DURBIN & SMITH. *White House Brides.* 1966. Acropolis. 1st ed. 208p. VG. H1. $6.50

DURBRIDGE, Francis. *Man Called Harry Brent.* 1970. Hodder Stoughton. 1st ed. F/F. P3. $25.00

DURBRIDGE, Francis. *Paul Temple & the Madison Case.* 1988. London. Hodder Stoughton. 1st ed. F/F. S6. $22.50

DURDEN, Charles. *Fifth Law of Hawkins.* 1990. St Martin. 1st ed. NF/NF. P3. $20.00

DURELL & SACHS. *Big Book for Peace.* 1990. Dutton. 1st ed. ils Sendak/others. F. C8. $20.00

DURHAM, David. *Hounded Down.* nd. Dectective BC. VG/G. P3. $20.00

DURHAM, Ken. *Speaking From the Heart.* 1986. Sweet. 176p. VG. B29. $3.50

DURHAM, Victor. *Submarine Boys' Lightning Cruise.* 1910. Altemus. VG. M2. $20.00

DURHAM & PORTER. *Proclamation & Presence.* 1970. John Knox. 315p. VG/dj. B29. $3.50

DURRELL, Lawrence. *Black Book.* 1960. NY. Dutton. 1st Am ed. 8vo. 250p. gilt bk cloth. NF/dj. H5. $75.00

DURRELL, Lawrence. *Deus Loci, a Poem by Lawrence Durrell.* 1950. Ischia. Di Maio Vito. 1st ed. sgn. 1/200. 10p. F/prt gray wrp. B24. $650.00

DURRELL, Lawrence. *Greek Islands.* 1978. Viking. 1st Am ed. 4to. F/NF. B4. $65.00

DURRELL, Lawrence. *Monsieur.* 1975. Viking. 1st Am ed. sgn. 8vo. 305p. gilt/blk stp blk brd. NF. H5. $85.00

DURRELL, Lawrence. *Nunquam.* 1970. Dutton. 1st Am ed. 8vo. 318p. gilt red cloth. F/dj. H5. $50.00

DURRELL, Lawrence. *Tunc.* 1968. London. Faber. 1st ed. VG/VG. B3. $20.00

DURSO, Joseph. *Casey Stengel.* 1967. NJ. 211p. F/F. A17. $15.00

DURSY, Emil. *Lehrbuch der Systematischen Anatomie.* 1863. Lahr. Schauenburg. 543p. cloth. G7. $35.00

DUTHIE, Eric. *Mystery & Adventures, Stories, Girls.* 1962. Odhams. 1st ed. VG/VG. P3. $25.00

DUTHUIT, Georges. *Les Fauves.* 1949. Geneva. Trois Collines. 1st ed. VG/wrp/dj. B2. $100.00

DUTLACK, F.M. *Australian Flying Corps in W & E Theatres of War 1914-1918.* 1984. Queensland, Australia. 1st ed thus. gilt brn bdg. M. M7. $60.00

DUTOURD, Jean. *Dog's Head.* 1951. John Lehmann. 1st ed. VG/VG. P3. $40.00

DUTTON, Joan Parry. *Flower World of Williamsburg.* 1962. Williamsburg, VA. 1st ed. 8vo. 148p. F/VG. B11. $20.00

DUTTON, Meiric K. *Historical Sketch of Bookbinding As an Art.* 1926. Norwood. Holliston. 144p. gilt top/title. red cloth. NF. B14. $125.00

DUVAL, Elizabeth M. *TE Lawrence: A Bibliography.* 1938. Arrow. 1/500 #d. 95p. F/gray case. M7. $125.00

DUVAL, Mathias. *Artistic Anatomy.* 1892. London. 6th ed. 324p. A13. $60.00

DVORNIK, Francis. *Byzantine Missions Among the Slavs...* ca 1970. Rutgers. 1st ed. 484p. H10. $35.00

DWIGGINS, W.A. *WAD: The Work of WA Dwiggins.* 1937. Am Inst Graphic Arts. exhibition catalog. F. F1. $40.00

DWIGHT, Charles Stevens. *SC Rebel's Recollections.* 1917. Columbia, SC. 1st ed. 1/150. 8vo. 18p. VG/gray wrp/fld/case. C6. $1,300.00

DWIGHT, Edwin Welles. *Toxicology.* 1904. Lea. 1st ed. 298p. G. H1. $7.50

DWYER, Deanna; see Koontz, Dean R.

DWYER, K.R.; see Koontz, Dean R.

DYER, Kate Gambold. *Turkey Trott & the Black Santa.* 1942. Platt Munk. ils Janet Robson. VG. C8. $85.00

DYER, Mary M. *Portraiture of Shakerism...* 1822. np. self pub. 446p. half leather. H10. $125.00

DYER, Walter. *Country Cousins.* 1927. Doubleday Page. 1st ed. ils CL Bull. VG/G. P2. $45.00

DYER & MARTIN. *Edison: His Life & Inventions.* 1910. NY. 2 vol. 1st ed. VG. B5. $70.00

DYKE, A.L. *Dyke's Aircraft Engine Instructor.* 1929. Chicago. 425p. G. B18. $125.00

DYKEMAN, Wilma. *French Broad.* 1955. NY. sgn pres. VG/G. B5. $45.00

DYKES, Jeff. *Billy the Kid: Bibliography of a Legend.* 1952. NM U. 186p. VG. scarce. A4. $155.00

DYKES, Jeff. *Fifty Great Western Illustrators: A Bibliographic Checklist.* 1975. Northland. 1st Collector's ed. 1/200. sgn. ils. M/case. A18. $200.00

DYMOND, Jonathan. *War: An Essay; With Introductory Words by John Bright.* nd. NY. Friends' Book & Tract. 4th ed. 88p. VG. V3. $15.00

DYSON, Anthony. *Pictures To Print.* (1984). London. Farrand. ltd ed. sm 4to. 95 ils. half brn morocco/brn cloth. K1. $125.00

DYSON, James L. *World of Ice.* 1962. NY. Knopf. 292p. VG/worn. P4. $35.00

DZIOBEK, Otto. *Mathematical Theories of Planetary Motions.* 1962 (1892). Dover. rpt. trans Harrington/Hussey. 294p. wrp. K5. $12.00

E-YEH-SHURE. *I Am a Pueblo Indian Girl.* April 1940 (Oct 1939). Morrow. 2nd prt. ils. VG. P2. $65.00

EAGER, Edward. *Magic by the Lake.* 1957. Harcourt Brace. 1st ed. 183p. VG. P2. $20.00

EALES & SULLIVAN. *Political Context of Law, Proceedings of 7th British...* 1987. London. Hambledon. M11. $35.00

EAMES, Wilberforce. *Early New England Catechisms: Bibliographical Account...* 1898. Worcester, MA. 1st ed. 111p. VG/prt wrp. M8. $85.00

EARHART, Amelia. *Fun of It.* 1932. NY. VG/poor. B5. $105.00

EARHART, Amelia. *Last Flight.* 1937. NY. 1st ed. VG/G. B5. $40.00

EARHART, Amelia. *20 Hours 40 Minutes.* 1928. NY. 1st ed. VG. B5. $125.00

EARL, John Prescott. *School Team in Camp.* 1909. Penn. later prt. pict bdg. xl. G. P8. $15.00

EARLE, Alice Morse. *Home Life in Colonial Days.* 1967. Macmillan. 8vo. ils. 470p. bl cloth. VG/VG. B11. $25.00

EARLE, Alice Morse. *Margaret Winthrop.* 1975. Corner House. 341p. F. M10. $7.50

EARLE, Alice Morse. *Sun-Dials & Roses of Yesterday.* 1902. NY. 1st ed. teg. NF. H7. $50.00

EARLE, Alice Morse. *Two Centuries of Costume in America 1650-1850.* 1903. np. 2 vol. ils. VG. M17. $50.00

EARLE, John. *Micro-Cosmographie; or, Piece of World Discovered...* 1928. Golden Cockerel. 1st ed. 4to. 73p. VG/dj. B18. $150.00

EARLE, W. Hubert. *Cacti of the Southwest.* 1980. Phoenix. revised ed. 231p. sc. F. B26. $14.00

EARLY, Jubal Anderson. *Lt-Gen Jubal Anderson Early, CSA: Autobiographical Sketch...* 1912. Lippincott. 1st ed. 496p. red cloth. NF. C6. $350.00

EARLY, Martin H. *History & Directory of Palmyra, PA.* 1898. NY. VG+. A1. $40.00

EARNEST, Adele. *Art of the Decoy.* 1965. Clarkson Potter. 208p. VG/dj. M20. $35.00

EARNEST, Adele. *Art of the Decoy: American Bird Carvings.* (1965). Bramhall. 4th ed. 208p. F/F. H1. $40.00

EARNSHAW, Brian. *Starclipper & the Song Wars.* 1985. Methuen. VG. P3. $13.00

EASON, J. Lawrence. *New Bible Survey.* 1981. Zondervan. 544p. M/F. B29. $9.00

EAST, Ben. *Bears.* 1977. Outdoor Life. F/dj. B34. $35.00

EASTLAKE, William. *Bronc People.* 1958. Harcourt Brace. 1st ed/author's 2nd book. NF/VG. L3. $175.00

EASTLAKE, William. *Bronc People.* 1958. Seven Wolves. ARC. F/prt wrp. B3. $75.00

EASTLAKE, William. *Castle Keep.* 1965. Simon Schuster. 1st ed/author's 4th book. NF/NF. L3. $50.00

EASTLAKE, William. *Long Naked Descent Into Boston.* 1977. NY. 1st ed. sgn. F/F. A11. $40.00

EASTLAKE, William. *Portrait of an Artist With 26 Horses.* 1963. Simon Schuster. 1st ed. NF/NF. L3. $75.00

EASTLAKE, William. *Portrait of an Artist With 26 Horses.* 1963. Simon Schuster. 1st ed. sgn. NF/VG. B3. $175.00

EASTMAN, Charles. *Indian Boyhood.* 1902. ils. 289p. O8. $32.50

EASTMAN, George. *Chronicles of an African Trip.* 1927. Rochester. 1st ed. photos. F/tissue dj/box. S9. $200.00

EASTMAN, Max. *Kinds of Love.* 1931. Scribner. 1st ed. F/NF. B2. $65.00

EASTMAN, Max. *Love & Revolution.* 1964. NY. 1st ed. w/sgn tipped-in p. F/NF. C2. $75.00

EASTON, M. Coleman. *Spirits of Cavern & Hearth.* 1988. St Martin. 1st ed. F/dj. M2. $25.00

EASTON, Nat. *Bill for Damages.* 1958. Roy. 1st ed. VG/VG. P3. $18.00

EATON, Allen. *Handicrafts of New Eng.* 1949. np. 1st ed. cloth. VG. G2. $25.00

EATON, Anne Thaxter. *Round Dozen Stories by Louisa May Alcott.* 1963. Viking. 1st ed. ils Tasha Tudor. NF/VG+. C8. $35.00

EATON, Charles Edward. *Countermoves.* 1962. NY. F/NF. A17. $7.50

EATON, Seymour. *Prince Domino & Muffles.* 1910. Phil. Stern. 1st ed. ils C Twelvetrees. VG. D6. $45.00

EBELING, Walter. *Subtropical Fruit Pests.* 1959. np. ils/maps/photos. 436p. B26. $29.00

EBERHART, A.G. *Everything About Dogs.* 1917. NY. Field Fancy. 3rd/final ed. ils. 295p. VG. w/prospectus. R2. $20.00

EBERHART, Mignon G. *Alpine Condo Crossfire.* 1984. Random. 1st ed. NF/NF. P3. $15.00

EBERHART, Mignon G. *Bayou Road.* 1979. Random. 1st ed. VG/VG. P3. $15.00

EBERHART, Mignon G. *Casa Madrone.* 1980. Random. 1st ed. VG/VG. P3. $15.00

EBERHART, Mignon G. *Family Affair.* 1981. Random. 1st ed. VG/VG. P3. $15.00

EBERHART, Mignon G. *Three Days for Emerald.* 1988. Random. 1st ed. F/F. P3. $15.00

EBERHART, Mignon G. *With This Ring.* 1941. Random. 1st ed. 8vo. 274p. gr stp gray cloth. VG. H5. $75.00

EBERHART, Mignon G. *With This Ring.* 1941. Random. 1st ed. G+. P3. $12.00

EBERHART, Richard. *Poems, New & Selected.* 1944. New Directions. 1st ed. 8vo. gr brd. F/NF. C6. $75.00

EBERHART, Richard. *Poems to Poets.* 1975. Penmaen. 1/300. sgn/#d/ils Michael McCurdy. cloth. F/sans. V1. $75.00

EBERLEIN & FRENCH. *Smaller Houses, Gardens...* 1926. NY. 1st ed. 4to. G. C11. $35.00

EBERS, Georg. *Elixer & Other Tales.* 1890. Gottsberger. 1st Am ed. VG. M2. $50.00

EBON, Martin. *They Knew the Unknown.* 1971. World. 1st ed. VG. P3. $15.00

EBSTEIN, Wilhelm. *Die Pest Des Thunkydides.* 1899. Stuttgart. 48p. orig wrp. G7. $35.00

EBY & FLEMING. *Case of the Malevolent Twin.* 1946. Dutton. 1st ed. G+. P3. $6.00

ECCLES, Marjorie. *Company She Kept.* 1993. London. Harper Collins. 1st ed. F/F. S6. $25.00

ECKEL, John C. *First Editions of Writings of Charles Dickens.* 1993. Mansfield, CT. Martino. rpt of 1932 ed. 1/325. ils. 272p. red cloth. M. C6. $50.00

ECKERT, Allan W. *Court Martial of Daniel Boone.* 1973. Little Brn. 1st ed. 309p. VG/dj. M20. $40.00

ECKERT, Allan W. *Crossbreed.* 1968. Little Brn. 1st ed. 242p. VG/dj. M20. $35.00

ECKERT, Allan W. *Great Auk.* 1963. Little Brn. 1st ed. sgn. 202p. cloth. VG/VG. M20. $75.00

ECKERT & KARALUS. *Owls of N America.* 1974. Garden City. 1st ed. 1/250. full leather. M/case. A9. $225.00

ECKHARDT, George. *United States Clock & Watch Patents 1790-1880.* 1960. NY. private prt. ltd ed. 8vo. 231p. VG. A8. $45.00

ECKSTEIN, Gustav. *Body Has a Head.* 1970. NY. 1st ed. 799p. dj. A13. $20.00

ECKSTEIN, Gustav. *Pet Shop.* 1944. Harper. sgn. 196p. VG/dj. M20. $25.00

ECO, Umberto. *How To Travel With a Salmon.* 1994. Harcourt Brace. UP. NF/prt salmon wrp. B3. $25.00

ECO, Umberto. *Sette Anni di Desiderio: Cronache 1977-1983.* 1983. Milano. Bompiani. 1st ed. sgn. F/F. B4. $150.00

ECO, Umberto. *Theory of Semiotics.* 1976. Bloomington. 1st ed. F/NF. B4. $175.00

EDDINGS, David. *Demon Lord of Karanda.* 1988. Del Rey. 1st ed. NF/NF. P3. $20.00

EDDINGS, David. *Domes of Fie.* 1993. Del Rey. 1st ed. F/F. P3. $22.00

EDDINGS, David. *Sorceress of Darshiva.* 1989. Ballantine. 1st ed. F/F. B3. $20.00

EDDINGTON, Arthur Stanley. *New Pathways in Science.* 1935. Macmillan. 1st Am ed. prt bl cloth. G1. $30.00

EDDINGTON, Arthur Stanley. *Philosophy of Physical Science.* 1949. Cambridge. 1st ed/rpt corrections. 230p. A13. $15.00

EDDINGTON, Arthur Stanley. *Science & the Unseen World.* 1929. Macmillan. 4th prt. 16mo. 91p. VG. V3. $12.50

EDDISON, E.R. *Worm Ouroboros.* 1926. Boni. 1st Am ed. NF/NF clip/pub promo band. L3. $450.00

EDDY, Mary Baker G. *Science & Health With Key to the Scriptures.* 1887. Boston. self pub. 29th ed. 590p. VG. H1. $38.00

EDDY, Samuel K. *Numismatic Notes & Monographs No 156.* 1967. Am Numismatic Soc. 1st ed. 133p. VG/stiff wrp. W1. $15.00

EDELSON, Marshall. *Hypothesis & Evidence in Psychoanalysis.* 1984. Chicago. 1st Am ed. 333p. prt bl cloth. VG. G1. $18.50

EDELSTEIN, J.M. *History of Science & Medicine.* 1988. NY. Swann. 284p. VG/wrp. A10. $8.00

EDEN, Dorothy. *Important Family.* 1982. Morrow. 1st ed. F/F. P3. $14.00

EDEN, Dorothy. *Time of the Dragon.* 1975. Hodder Stoughton. 1st ed. VG/VG. P3. $18.00

EDEN, Dorothy. *Whistle for the Crows.* 1962. Hodder Stoughton. 1st ed. VG/VG. P3. $25.00

EDEN, Matthew. *Murder of Lawrence of Arabia.* 1979. Crowell. 1st ed. 271p. NF/NF. M7. $25.00

EDERSHEIM, Alfred. *Life & Times of Jesus the Messiah.* 1953. Eerdmans. 2 vols. VG. B29. $17.00

EDEY, Winthrop. *French Clocks.* 1967. NY. Walker. 1st ed. 8vo. 83p. F. A8. $20.00

EDGAR, Campbell Cowan. *Zenon Papyri in the University of MI Collection.* 1931. Ann Arbor. tall 8vo. ils. 211p. gilt gr cloth. NF. F1. $150.00

EDGAR, John G. *Sea Kings & Naval Heroes: A Book for Boys.* 1866. London. Routledge. ils. 336p. T7. $50.00

EDGARTON, Linda. *London Cries Painting Book.* nd. Tuck. obl 8vo. VG/stiff wrp. M5. $45.00

EDGE, Findley B. *Greening of the Church.* 1971. Word. 195p. VG/dj. B29. $3.50

EDGERTON, Clyde. *Floatplane Notebooks.* 1988. Chapel Hill. Algonquin. AP. F. S9. $40.00

EDGERTON, Clyde. *In Memory of Junior.* 1992. Algonquin. 1st ed. F/F. B3. $20.00

EDGERTON & SNELGROVE. *British Sporting & Animal Drawings 1500-1850.* 1978. London. Tate. 23 mc pl. VG/VG. O3. $95.00

EDGHILL, Rosemary. *Speak Dagger to Her.* 1994. Foge. 1st ed. F/F. F4. $20.00

EDGLEY, Leslie. *Fear No More.* 1946. Simon Schuster. 1st ed. xl. VG. P3. $8.00

EDIB, Halide. *Turkish Ordeal. Being the Further Memoirs of...* 1928. NY. 1st ed. 8vo. 407p. gilt cloth. F. O2. $85.00

EDIE, James M. *Merleau-Ponty's Philosophy of Language.* 1987. WA, DC. 104p. prt gr cloth. F. G1. $19.00

EDIE, James M. *Phenomenology in Am: Studies in Philosophy of Experience.* 1967. Quadrangle. PBO/trade pb. 309p. G1. $22.50

EDIE, James M. *Russian Philosophy.* 1965. Quadrangle. 3 vol. cloth. G1. $75.00

EDIE, Milton. *Montana in Maps.* 1974. Big Sky Books. sbdg. VG. B34. $17.50

EDIGER, Donald. *Well of Sacrifice.* 1971. Doubleday. 1st ed. 288p. VG/chip. F3. $25.00

EDINGTON, Frank E. *Hist of NY Ave Presbyterian Church...1803-1961.* 1962. np. 1st ed. sgn. 369p. cloth. NF. M8. $30.00

EDKINS & NEWHALL. *William H Jackson.* 1974. Ft Worth. Morgan. 1st ed. VG/VG. S9. $45.00

EDMONDS, C.J. *Kurds, Turks & Arabs: Politics, Travel & Research...* 1957. London. ils/maps. 457p. cloth. scarce. O2. $50.00

EDMONDS, Charles. *TE Lawrence.* 1935. London. Peter Davis. 1st ed. 5 maps. 192p. bl cloth. G+. M7. $45.00

EDMONDS, Emma. *Nurse & Spy in the Union Army.* 1865. Hartford. 1st ed. 384p. A13. $125.00

EDMONDS, George. *Facts & Falsehoods Concerning the War on the South.* ca 1904. Memphis. Taylor. 8vo. 271p. prt gray wrp. scarce. H9. $175.00

EDMONDS, I.G. *Iron Monster Raid.* 1968. Whitman. Rat Patrol TVTI. VG. P3. $13.00

EDMONDS, Janet. *Death Has a Cold Nose.* 1993. London. Harper Collins. 1st ed. F/F. S6. $25.00

EDMONDS, Waller. *Matchlock Gun.* Oct 1941 (Sept 1941). Dodd Mead. 2nd prt. 50p. VG+. P2. $15.00

EDMUNDS, Robert. *Cold Blooded Penguin.* 1946 (1944). Simon Schuster. 2nd ed. ils Disney Studios. 24p. F/VG+. C8. $60.00

EDMUNDS, Robert. *Walt Disney's Through the Picture Frame.* 1944. NY. VG. B18. $25.00

EDMUNDS & KENDRICK. *Measurement of Human Aggressiveness.* 1980. Chichester. Ellis Horwood. 223p. G. K4. $20.00

EDSALL, F.S. *World of Psychic Phenomena.* 1958. McKay. 1st ed. VG. P3. $20.00

EDWARDES, Michael. *East-West Passage.* 1971. Taplinger. 1st ed. 8vo. xl. VG/dj. W1. $14.00

EDWARDES, Michael. *King of the World.* 1971. Taplinger. 1st Am ed. 279p. NF/dj. W1. $15.00

EDWARDS, Albert. *Barbary Coast: Sketches of French North Africa.* 1913. Macmillan. 5th ed. 312p. xl. VG. W1. $9.00

EDWARDS, Albert. *Panama: The Canal, the Country & the People.* 1911. NY. Macmillan. 1st ed. 12mo. 585p. gilt red cloth. VG. B11. $55.00

EDWARDS, Allen L. *Measurement of Personality Traits by Scales & Inventories.* 1970. HRW. 248p. F/dj. K4. $20.00

EDWARDS, Bryan. *Hist Survey of French Colony in Island of St Domingo.* 1797. London. 1st ed. 4to. early 19th C calf. VG. C6. $125.00

EDWARDS, Charles. *Pleasantries About Courts & Lawyers of the States of NY.* 1867. NY. 1st ed. 528p. VG. D3. $45.00

EDWARDS, Ernest. *Grandfather Clock.* 1980. Altringham, Eng. John Sherratt Ltd. 4th ed. VG/G. A8. $40.00

EDWARDS, Florence Dunn. *Menino.* 1940. NY. ils Mary Hellmuth. NF/partial. M5. $22.00

EDWARDS, George Wharton. *Vanished Towers & Chimes of Flanders.* 1916. Phil. 211p. xl. B18. $50.00

EDWARDS, Gladys Brown. *Arabian War Horse to Show Horse.* 1973. Covina. revised collector ed. ES. VG/VG. O3. $165.00

EDWARDS, H. *Two Runaways & Other Stories.* 1904. np. ils Kemble. 246p. VG. E5. $35.00

EDWARDS, Hugh. *Surrealism & Its Affinities. The Mary Reynolds Collection.* 1973. Art Inst Chicago. 8vo. ils. F/stiff wrp. F1. $35.00

EDWARDS, I.E.S. *Treasures of Tutankhamun.* 1977. Harmondsworth. Penguin. sm 4to. VG/stiff wrp. W1. $15.00

EDWARDS, John. *Complete Checklist of Am Clock & Watchmakers 1640-1950.* 1977. Stratford. New Eng Pub. 1st ed. 8vo. F. A8. $6.00

EDWARDS, Leo. *Andy Blake & the Pot of Gold.* 1930. Grosset Dunlap. 228p. VG/dj. scarce. M20. $85.00

EDWARDS, Leo. *Andy Blake's Comet Coaster.* 1928. Grosset Dunlap. 247p. VG. M20. $25.00

EDWARDS, Leo. *Jerry Dodd & the Flying Flapdoodle.* 1934. Grosset Dunlap. 244p. VG/tattered. M20. $40.00

EDWARDS, Leo. *Jerry Dodd Caveman.* 1932. Grosset Dunlap. 1st ed. 258p. VG/dj. M20. $85.00

EDWARDS, Leo. *Jerry Todd in the Whispering Cave.* 1927. Grosset Dunlap. lists to #10. VG/ragged. M20. $45.00

EDWARDS, Leo. *Poppy Ott & the Freckled Goldfish.* 1928. Grosset Dunlap. 1st ed. last title listed. VG/worn. M20. $45.00

EDWARDS, Leo. *Poppy Ott's Pedigreed Pickles.* 1927. Grosset Dunlap. lists to #6. VG/ragged. M20. $40.00

EDWARDS, Leo. *Tuffy Bean at Funny-Bone Farm.* 1931. Grosset Dunlap. lists to this title. VG/chip. M20. $85.00

EDWARDS, Lionel. *Getting To Know Your Pony.* nd (1948). NY. 1st Am ed. G+. O3. $35.00

EDWARDS, Lionel. *Reminiscences of a Sporting Artist.* 1947. London. Putnam. 1st ed. VG. O3. $48.00

EDWARDS, Lionel. *Seen From the Saddle.* 1937. NY. Scribner. 1st Am ed. VG. O3. $98.00

EDWARDS, Nancy Chandler. *Alphabet Book.* 1980. Boston. Bromer. 1/22 (total of 30). 32x25mm. 24p. full bl morocco. F. B24. $950.00

EDWARDS, Peter. *Blood Brothers.* 1990. Key Porter. 1st ed. VG. P3. $25.00

EDWARDS, Rem B. *Pleasures & Pains.* 1979. Cornell. sm 8vo. VG/dj. G1. $20.00

EDWARDS, Samuel. *Barbary General: Life of Wm H Eaton.* 1968. Prentice Hall. 269p. VG+/dj. M20. $15.00

EDWARDS & PAP. *Modern Intro to Philosophy.* 1973. Free Pr. 3rd ed. 868p. VG/dj. B29. $10.00

EELLS, Elsie Spicer. *Brazilian Fairy Book.* 1926. Stokes. 1st ed. 8vo. 193p. gilt gold cloth. VG+. D6. $350.00

EFFINGER, George Alec. *Bird of Time.* 1986. Doubleday. 1st ed. F/F. N3. $20.00

EFFINGER, George Alec. *Heroics.* 1979. Doubleday. 1st ed. VG/VG. P3. $20.00

EFFINGER, George Alec. *Mixed Feelings.* 1974. Harper. 1st ed. F/dj. F4. $30.00

EFFINGER, George Alec. *Nick of Time.* 1985. Doubleday. 1st ed. F/F. N3. $20.00

EFFINGER, George Alec. *Relatives.* 1973. Harper Row. 1st ed. F/NF. N3. $25.00

EFFINGER, George Alec. *What Entrophy Means to Me.* 1972. Doubleday. 1st ed. NF/NF. P3. $15.00

EGAN, Constance. *Epaminondas Helps in the Garden.* nd. London. Collins. very early ed. ils AE Kennedy. paper brd/pict label. VG. C8. $125.00

EGAN, Lesley. *Wine of Life.* 1986. Gollancz. 1st ed. F/F. P3. $22.00

EGAN, Pierce. *Life of an Actor.* 1825. London. Arnold. 1st ed. 27 mc pl. full calf. H4. $325.00

EGGER, Carl. *Im Kaukasus: Bergbesteigungen und Reiseerlebnisse...* 1915. Basel. 8vo. ils. 144p. cloth. O2. $85.00

EGGLESTON, Edward. *Circuit Rider: Tale of the Heroic Age.* 1874. JB Ford. 1st ed/1st state. NF. A18. $60.00

EGGLESTON, George. *Treasury of Christian Teaching.* 1958. Harcourt. 306p. G. B29. $3.50

EGLETON, Clive. *Missing From the Record.* 1988. St Martin. ARC/1st Am ed. RS. S6. $25.00

EGLETON, Clive. *Missing From the Record.* 1988. St Martin. 1st ed. VG/VG. P3. $17.00

EHNMARK, Anders. *Guerilla: En Antologi Redigered av Anders Enmark.* 1963. Stockholm. 1st ed. 207p. blk stp wht bdg. NF. M7. $30.00

EHRENPREIS, Marcus. *Soul of the East.* 1928. Viking. 1st Am ed. sm 8vo. 209p. xl. G. W1. $14.00

EHRENPREIS, Marcus. *Soul of the East. Experiences & Reflections.* 1928. NY. 8vo. 207p. cloth. O2. $30.00

EHRENWALD, Jan. *Telephathy & Medical Psychology.* 1948. Norton. 1st ed. 212p. F. K4. $22.50

EHRHARDT, Roy E. *Illinois Watches: Identification & Price Guide.* 1976. KS City. Heart of Am Pr. 1st ed. sc. 136p. sbdg. F. A8. $20.00

EHRHARDT, Sherry. *Vintage American & European Wristwatch Price Guide, Book I.* 1984. Heart of Am Pr. 1st ed. sc. 336p. F. A8. $20.00

EHRLICH, Arnold. *Beautiful Country: Maine to Hawaii.* 1970. Viking. ils. 175p. NF/dj. M10. $10.00

EHRLICH, Max. *Reincarnation in Venice.* 1979. Simon Schuster. 1st ed. VG/VG. P3. $15.00

EHRLICH, Max. *Shaitan.* 1981. Arbor. 1st ed. F/VG+. M21. $10.00

EHRLIGH, Gretel. *Solace of Open Spaces.* 1985. Viking. 1st ed. F/NF clip. L3. $65.00

EIBERTUS, Fra. *So Here Then Are the Preachments Entitled City of Tregaste.* 1900. Roycroft. 1/940. sgn Elbert Hubbard. half suede. VG. B18. $95.00

EIBL-EIBESFELDT, Irenaus. *Grundiss der Vergleichenden Verhaltensforschung.* 1967. Munchen. 449p. F/dj. K4. $20.00

EICHENLAUB, Val. *Weather & Climate of the Great Lakes Region.* 1979. Notre Dame. 8vo. 335p. VG. K5. $15.00

EICHLER, Alfred. *Death of an Ad Man.* 1954. Abelard Schuman. VG/VG. P3. $15.00

EICHNER. *Atlantean Chronicles.* 1971. Fantasy. 11 maps/photos. 246p. F/VG. A4. $150.00

EIDSMORE, John. *God & Caesar: Christian Faith & Political Action.* 1984. Crossway. 239p. F/dj. B29. $6.50

EIFFEL, G. *Resistance of the Air & Aviation.* 1913. London. revised 2nd ed. 4to. 26 fld pl. 242p. xl. w/emphera. B18. $295.00

EINAUDI, Mario. *Early Rousseau.* 1967. Cornell. 1st ed. 294p. index. F/F. A17. $10.00

EINCHOLZ, Georg. *Landscapes of the Bible.* ca 1963. Harper Row. 1st ed. 152p. VG/torn. W1. $9.00

EINSTEIN, Albert. *About Zionism: Speeches & Letters.* 1931. NY. Macmillan. 1st ed. G/dj. scarce. B14. $150.00

EINSTEIN, Albert. *Out of My Later Years.* 1950. Philosophical Lib. 1st ed. 282p. cloth. F. B14. $50.00

EINSTEIN, Albert. *Relativity.* nd. Crown. 13th prt. VG. P3. $10.00

EISELEY, Loren. *Francis Bacon & the Modern Dilemma.* 1962. NE U. 1st ed. F/VG. B4. $150.00

EISELEY, Loren. *Mind As Nature.* 1962. NY. Harper. 1st ed. F/F. A9. $35.00

EISELEY, Loren. *Star Thrower.* 1978. Times Books. 1st ed. ils WH Auden. F/NF. B3. $35.00

EISEN, Gustavus A. *Great Chalice of Antioch.* 1933. NY. Fahim Kouchakji. 1st ed. 22p. xl. VG. W1. $12.00

EISENBERG, Larry. *Best Laid Schemes.* 1971. Macmillan. 1st ed. F/F. P3. $20.00

EISENDSCHIML, Otto. *Civil War: The American Iliad.* 1947. 2 vol. ils. box. O8. $21.00

EISENHOWER, David. *Eisenhower at War 1943-1945.* 1986. NY. 5th prt. 977p. F/F. A17. $17.50

EISENHOWER, Dwight D. *Crusade in Europe.* 1948. Doubleday. 1st ed. 559p. F/VG. H1. $20.00

EISENHOWER, Dwight D. *Prayer of..., Preceding His Inaugural Address...1953.* 1953. NY. 12mo. 4p. F/wrp. B24. $65.00

EISENHOWER, Julie. *Mystery & Suspense.* 1976. Curtis. VG/VG. P3. $18.00

EISENSCHIML & LONG. *As Luck Would Have It: Chance & Coincidence in Civil War.* 1949. Bobbs Merrill. 1st ed. 285p. F/G. H1. $45.00

EISENSTADT, Jill. *From Rockaway.* 1987. Knopf. 1st ed/author's 1st book. F/F. A14. $45.00

EISENSTADT, Jill. *Kiss Out.* 1991. Knopf. 1st ed. F/F. A14. $25.00

EISENSTAEDT, Alfred. *Witness to Nature.* 1971. Viking. 1st ed. NF/NF. S9. $40.00

EISENSTEIN, Phyllis. *Born to Exile.* 1978. Arkham. 1st ed. xl. dj. P3. $6.00

EISENSTEIN, Phyllis. *Born to Exile.* 1978. Arkham. 1st ed. 1/4148. F/F. T2. $27.00

EISLER, Steven. *Alien World: Complete Illustrated Guide...* 1980. Crescent. F/F. P3. $13.00

EISLER, Steven. *Space Worlds & Weapons.* 1979. Crescent. F/F. P3. $6.00

EISNER, Robert. *Travellers to an Ancient Land.* 1991. Ann Arbor. 8vo. 304p. cloth. O2. $35.00

EISNER, Simon; see Kornbluth, Cyril.

EISSLER, K.R. *Searchlights on Delinquency. New Psychoanalytic Studies.* 1949. NY. 456p. VG. D3. $12.50

EISSLER, Ruth S. *Psychoanalytic Study of the Child. Vol 28.* 1973. yale. 455p. F/dj. K4. $27.50

EKKEKAKIS, G.P. *Skediasma Kritikis Bibliographias, 1499-1913.* 1990 & 1991. Rethymnon. 2 vol. ils. w/prt card. O2. $45.00

EKLUND, Gordon. *Grayspace Beast.* 1976. Doubleday. 1st ed. F/F. P3. $20.00

EKREM, Selma. *Turkey Old & New.* 1947. Scribner. 1st ed. ils. VG/torn. W1. $18.00

EKREM, Selma. *Turkish Fairy Tales.* 1964. Van Nostrand. 117p. VG/dj. W1. $20.00

EL-SAYED, Salah. *Cases in Management.* 1980. Cairo. 1st ed. 188p. VG. W1. $8.00

ELAM, Richard M. *Young Readers' Science Fiction Stories.* nd. Grosset Dunlap. VG. P3. $5.00

ELBERT & ELBERT. *Miracle Houseplants.* 1976. NY. ils. 242p. sc. B26. $12.50

ELCESAEUS, Thomas. *Series Indulgentiarum.* 1817. Rome. Arabic/Latin text. 106p. stiff wrp. K1. $125.00

ELDER, Art. *Blue Streak & Doctor Medusa.* nd. Whitman. VG. P3. $13.00

ELDRIDGE, Roger. *Shadow of the Gloom World.* 1977. Gollancz. 1st ed. F/F. P3. $15.00

ELDRIDGE & VIERECK. *Salome the Wandering Jewess.* 1934. Duckworth. 3rd ed. VG. P3. $22.00

ELEFTHERIADES, Olga. *Modern Greek Word Formation.* 1993. Minneapolis. 4to. 208p. cloth. O2. $35.00

ELGIN, Suzette Haden. *Gentle Art of Verbal Self-Defense.* nd. Dorset. 22nd prt. VG. P3. $13.00

ELGIN, Suzette Haden. *Grand Jubilee.* 1981. Doubleday. 1st ed. VG/VG. P3. $15.00

ELGOOD, P.G. *Egypt.* 1935. Bristol. Arrowsmith. 1st ed. sm 8vo. VG. W1. $9.00

ELIADE, Mircea. *From Primitives to Zen: A Thematic Sourcebook...* 1967. Harper Row. 1st Am ed. VG/VG. B33. $55.00

ELIADE, Mircea. *Symbolism, the Sacred & the Arts.* 1985. NY. Crossroad. 185p. F/F. B33. $20.00

ELIAS, Levita. *Grammatica Hebraica Absolutissima...* 1525. Basel. Froben. Latin/Hebrew text. 8vo. vellum. K1. $400.00

ELIAS, Norbert. *Power & Civility. Vol II.* 1982. Pantheon. 1st Am ed. 376p. F. K4. $12.50

ELIOT, C.W.J. *Lord Byron, Early Travelers, & Monastery at Delphi.* 1967. NY. 4to. pres to Frank Walton. disbound. O2. $15.00

ELIOT, Charles W. *Cultivated Man.* 1915. Houghton Mifflin. 1st ed. 12mo. brd. VG. M10. $5.00

ELIOT, George. *Spanish Gypsy.* 1868. Boston. 1st Am ed. gilt cloth. G. A17. $10.00

ELIOT, Marc. *Death of a Rebel.* 1989. np. 1st/revised hc ed. VG/VG. B5. $25.00

ELIOT, Porter. *In Wilderness Is the Preservation of the World.* 1962. Sierra Club. 107p. F/worn. A10. $25.00

ELIOT, Sonny. *Eliot's Ark.* 1972. Wayne State U. 1st ed. 217p. VG/VG. A17. $15.00

ELIOT, T.S. *Anabasis.* 1930. London. Faber. 1st ed. sgn. 1/350. F/VG case. B4. $650.00

ELIOT, T.S. *Ash Wednesday.* 1930. London. Faber. 1st ed. NF/dj. Q1. $200.00

ELIOT, T.S. *Classics & the Man of Letters.* 1942. London. Oxford. 1st ed. 27p. VG/lt bl wrp. H5. $200.00

ELIOT, T.S. *Cocktail Party.* 1950. Harcourt Brace. 1st Am ed. 8vo. 190p. gilt blk cloth. NF/dj. H5. $600.00

ELIOT, T.S. *Complete Plays of...* 1967. HBW. 1st Am ed. F/clip. B4. $65.00

ELIOT, T.S. *Family Reunion: A Play.* 1939. Harcourt Brace. 1st ed. F/dj. Q1. $125.00

ELIOT, T.S. *Letters of TS Eliot. Vol 1, 1898-1922.* 1988. NY/London. 1st ed. sgn Valerie Eliot. 640p. F/case. C4. $175.00

ELIOT, T.S. *Old Possum's Book of Practical Cats.* 1939. Harcourt Brace. 1st Am ed. F/NF. B4. $450.00

ELIOT, T.S. *Old Possum's Book of Practical Cats.* 1939. Harcourt Brace. 1st Am ed. 8vo. 46p. gray cloth. VG/dj. H5. $300.00

ELIOT, T.S. *Old Possum's Book of Practical Cats.* 1982 (1939). Harcourt Brace. 6th prt. ils Edward Gorey. F/F. C8. $17.50

ELIOT, T.S. *Peoms Written in Early Youth.* 1967. London. Faber. 1st Eng ed. F/F. B4/V1. $50.00

ELIOT, T.S. *Poems 1909-1925.* 1925. Faber Gwyer. 1st ed. sgn. NF. V1. $45.00

ELIOT, T.S. *Rock.* 1934. Harcourt Brace. 1st ed. 8vo. 86p. tan cloth. NF/dj. O3. $150.00

ELIOT, T.S. *Use of Poetry.* 1933. Cambridge. Harvard. 1st ed. F/F. B4. $350.00

ELIOT, T.S. *Varieties of Metaphysical Poetry.* 1994. Harcourt Brace. UP. F/prt bl wrp. B3. $35.00

ELIOT, T.S. *Waste Land.* (1922). Boni Liveright. 2nd Am ed. 1/1000. VG. Q1. $350.00

ELIOT, T.S. *Waste Land.* 1961. London. Faber. 1/300. sgn. 51p. teg. F/marbled cb case. H5. $2,500.00

ELIOT & SALKIND. *Children's Spatial Development.* 1975. Springfield, IL. Charles Thomas. 296p. F/dj. K4. $20.00

ELIOTT, E.C. *Kemlo & the Martian Ghosts.* 1954. Thomas Nelson. VG/VG. P3. $18.00

ELIOTT, E.C. *Kemlo & the Zombie Men.* 1958. Thomas Nelson. 1st ed. VG/VG. P3. $20.00

ELIS, Bret Easton. *Less Than Zero.* 1985. Simon Schuster. 1st ed/author's 1st book. F/F clip. B4. $85.00

ELISOFON, Eliot. *The Nile.* 1964. Viking. 1st ed. folio. 214 pl. VG/torn. W1. $65.00

ELKIN, Stanley. *Dick Gibson Show.* 1971. Random. 1st ed. NF/NF. B4. $75.00

ELKINS, Aaron *Curses.* nd. BOMC. F/F. P3. $10.00

ELKINS, Aaron. *Curses.* 1989. Mysterious. 1st ed. sgn. F/F. O4. $25.00

ELKINS, Aaron. *Glancing Light.* 1991. Scribner. 1st ed. F/F. O4. $15.00

ELKINS, Aaron. *Make No Bones.* 1990. Mysterious. 1st ed. sgn. F/F. O4. $25.00

ELKINS & ELKINS. *Wicked Slice.* 1989. St Martin. 1st ed. sgn. F/VG. O4. $30.00

ELLER, John. *Charlie & the Ice Man.* 1981. St Martin. 1st ed. VG/VG. P3. $13.00

ELLERY, William. *Gilgamesh.* 1974. Avon. LTC. 1/2000. ils/sgn Irving Amen. VG/VG case. B33. $85.00

ELLIN, Stanley. *Blessington Method & Other Strange Tales.* 1964. Random. 1st ed. F/dj. F4. $40.00

ELLIN, Stanley. *Dark Fantastic.* 1983. Deutsch. 1st ed. F/F. P3. $20.00

ELLIN, Stanley. *Dreadful Summit.* 1948. Simon Schuster. 1st ed. F/VG. M15. $60.00

ELLIN, Stanley. *House of Cards.* 1967. MacDonald. 1st ed. VG/torn. P3. $15.00

ELLIN, Stanley. *Key to Nicholas Street.* 1952. Simon Schuster. 1st ed. VG/VG. M15. $35.00

ELLIN, Stanley. *Star Light, Star Bright.* 1979. Random. 1st ed. NF/NF. P3. $20.00

ELLIN, Stanley. *Winter After This Summer.* 1960. Random. 1st ed. VG/VG. P3. $35.00

ELLINGTON, Mercer. *Duke Ellington in Person.* 1978. Houghton Mifflin. 1st ed. NF/NF. B2. $35.00

ELLIOT, Daniel Giraud. *North American Shore Birds.* 1895. NY. 1/100 lg paper ed. sgn. H4. $200.00

ELLIOT, Gertrude. *Stories From Mary Poppins.* 1952. Golden. 1st ed. glazed brd. F. M5. $12.00

ELLIOTT, Charles W. *Remarkable Characters & Places of the Holy Land...* 1867. Hartford. thick 8vo. 640p. aeg. cloth. O2. $50.00

ELLIOTT, Don (some); see Silverberg, Robert.

ELLIOTT, Elizabeth Shippen G. *Alliterative Alphabet Aimed at Adult Abecedarians.* 1947. McKay. 1st ed. lg 8vo. VG+/torn. scarce. M5. $35.00

ELLIOTT, H. Chandler. *Reprieve From Paradise.* 1955. Gnome. VG/VG. M17. $15.00

ELLIOTT, H. Chandler. *Reprieve From Paradise.* 1955. Gnome. 1st ed. NF/NF. P3. $35.00

ELLIOTT, Mary. *Rural Employments; or, Peep Into Village Concerns.* 1820. London. Darton. 1st ed. 24mo. gilt gr calf. VG. very scarce. D6. $350.00

ELLIS, A. Raymond. *Making a Garage.* 1913. NY. ils. cloth. VG. B14. $25.00

ELLIS, Bret Easton. *Rules of Attraction.* 1987. Simon Schuster. 1st ed. NF/NF. P3. $18.00

ELLIS, E. *Down the Mississippi.* 1886. np. 323p. G. E5. $30.00

ELLIS, Edward S. *History of Our Country From Discovery of Am to Present Time.* 1905. Indianapolis. Woolling. Vol 1 only. 8vo. ils. VG. B11. $30.00

ELLIS, Edward S. *Life & Times of Colonel Daniel Boone.* (1884). Phil. 264p. w/mc trade card. VG. B18. $20.00

ELLIS, F.S. *Syr Isambrace.* 1897. Hammersmith, Eng. Kelmscott. 1/350 on handmade. linen-backed prt brd. K1. $650.00

ELLIS, Henry. *Voyage to Hudson's Bay, by the Dobbs Galley...* 1748. London. H Whitridge. 1st ed. 8vo. 9 pl/fld map. calf. NF. H4. $1,150.00

ELLIS, John. *Short History of Guerilla Warfare.* 1975. London. Ian Allen. 1st ed. 220p. gilt brn brd. F/NF. M7. $35.00

ELLIS, Mel. *No Man for Murder.* 1973. HRW. F/F. P3. $8.00

ELLIS, Peter. *Fires of Lan-Kern.* 1980. St Martin. VG/VG. P3. $15.00

ELLIS, Peter. *Fires of Lan-Kern.* 1980. St Martin. 1st ed. sgn. F/dj. F4. $32.00

ELLIS, Peter. *Raven of Destiny.* 1984. Methuen. 1st ed. F/F. P3. $25.00

ELLIS, Richard N. *General Pope & US Indian Policy.* 1970. Albuquerque. NM U. 1st ed. 287p. mustard cloth. F/F. P4. $30.00

ELLIS, William Donohue. *Bounty Lands.* 1952. World. 1st ed. sgn. VG/VG. M20. $40.00

ELLIS, William T. *Bible Lands Today.* 1927. Appleton. 1st ed. 8vo. cloth. VG. W1. $15.00

ELLIS, William. *Majestic Rocky Mountains.* 1976. NGS. ils/maps. VG/dj. B34. $15.00

ELLISON, Harlan. *Alone Against Tomorrow.* 1971. Macmillan. 1st ed. sgn. F/F. P3. $100.00

ELLISON, Harlan. *Angry Candy.* 1988. Houghton Mifflin. 1st ed. F/F. S9. $40.00

ELLISON, Harlan. *Essential Ellison: A 35-Year Retrospective.* 1991. Beverly Hills. Morpheus. 1st ed thus. F/F. T2. $35.00

ELLISON, Harlan. *Medea: Harlan's World.* 1985. Phantasia. 1st ed. F/F. M2/T2. $45.00

ELLISON, Harlan. *Mefisto in Onyx.* 1993. Ziesing. 1st ed. F/F. T2. $25.00

ELLISON, Harlan. *Sleepless Nights in the Procrustean Bed.* 1984. San Bernardino. Borgo. 1st ed. F/wrp. N3. $20.00

ELLISON, Harlan. *Strange Wine.* 1978. Harper Row. 1st ed. sgn. F/NF. M21. $50.00

ELLISON, M.A. *Sun & Its Influence.* 1955. Macmillan. 8vo. 235p. G/dj. K5. $20.00

ELLISON, Ralph. *Going to the Territory.* 1986. Random. 1st ed. F/NF. B2. $50.00

ELLISON, Ralph. *Invisible Man.* 1952. Random. 1st ed. 8vo. 439p. blk/cream cloth. NF/dj. H5. $500.00

ELLISON, Ralph. *Shadow & Act.* 1964. Random. 1st ed. F/NF. B2. $100.00

ELLISON, Virginia H. *Pooh Get-Well Book.* 1973. Dutton. 3rd prt. ils Shepard. M/M. C8. $25.00

ELLISON, Virginia H. *Pooh Party Book.* 1971. Dutton. 1st ed. ils Shepard. F/F. C8. $30.00

ELLISON & SHAPIRO. *Writer's Experience.* 1964. Washington, DC. 1st ed. sgns. NF/thin 8vo wrp. A11. $700.00

ELLROY, James. *Blk Dahlia.* 1987. NY. Mysterious. 1st ed. sgn. F/F. S6. $45.00

ELLROY, James. *Blood on the Moon.* 1984. Mysterious. 1st ed. sgn. F/F. M15/T2. $45.00

ELLROY, James. *LA Confidential.* 1990. Mysterious. 1st ed. F/NF. B3. $25.00

ELLROY, James. *LA Confidential.* 1990. Mysterious. 1st ed. sgn. F/F. M15. $35.00

ELLROY, James. *LA Confidential.* 1990. Mysterious. 1st ed. VG/VG. P3. $20.00

ELLROY, James. *Silent Terror.* 1987. Los Angeles. Blood & Guts. 1st hc ed. 1/350. sgn. F/F. M15. $100.00

ELLROY, James. *White Jazz.* 1992. Knopf. 1st ed. F/F. P3. $22.00

ELLSBERG, Edward. *Hell on Ice.* 1938. Dodd Mead. 1st ed. 421p. VG. H1. $12.00

ELLSON, Mary. *Extensions of the Blues.* 1989. London/NY. Calder/Riverrun. 1st ed. F/NF. B2. $25.00

ELLSOWRTH, Henry Leavitt. *Washington Irving on the Prairie...* 1937. Am Book Co. 1st ed. map. A18. $35.00

ELLSWORTH, M.J. *Bath School Disaster.* 1927. Lansing. 1st ed. G/wrp. B5. $70.00

ELLUL, Jacques. *Violence.* 1969. Seabury. 179p. VG/dj. B29. $5.50

ELMSLIE, W.P. *Fifty Years of Livestock Research.* 1970. Hannibal, MO. Western Pub. VG/dj. N2. $11.50

ELON, Amos. *Herzl.* 1975. HRW. 1st ed. 448p. F/VG. H1. $20.00

ELON, Amos. *Timetable.* 1980. Doubleday. VG/VG. P3. $15.00

ELON & HASSAN. *Between Enemies: Compassionate Dialogue...* 1974. Random. 1st ed. 152p. VG. W1. $18.00

ELROD, P.N. *I, Strahd.* 1993. Lake Geneva. TSR. 1st ed. F/F. B3. $15.00

ELSDEN & ELSDEN. *Rottweiler.* 1987. London. Popular Dogs. 1st ed. 195p. M/dj. R2. $25.00

ELSON, Edward. *America's Spiritual Recovery.* 1954. Revell. intro J Edgar Hoover. 189p. G. B29. $3.50

ELTON, Packer. *Roy Rogers on the Trail of the Zeros.* 1954. Whitman. 1st ed. photos. pict brd. F/sans. F4. $12.00

ELUARD, Paul. *Anthologie des Ecrits sur L'Art.* 1972. Paris. Editions Cercle D'Art. 1/125. NF. S9. $150.00

ELUARD, Paul. *Pablo Picasso.* 1944. Geneva/Paris. Trois Collines. 1st ed. F/wrp/dj. B2. $150.00

ELWOOD, Roger. *And Walk Now Gently Through Fire.* 1972. Chilton. 1st ed. VG/VG. P3. $20.00

ELWOOD, Roger. *Continuum 4.* 1975. NY. Berkley. 1st ed. F/VG. N3. $10.00

ELWOOD, Roger. *Continuum.* 1974. Berkeley Putnam. 1st ed. VG/VG. P3. $20.00

ELWOOD, Roger. *Far Side of Time.* 1974. Dodd Mead. 1st ed. VG/VG. P3. $15.00

ELWOOD, Roger. *Future Kin.* 1974. Doubleday. 1st ed. F/F. P3. $15.00

ELWOOD, Roger. *Monster Tales.* 1973. Rand McNally. 1st ed. VG. P3. $15.00

ELWOOD, Roger. *Omega.* 1973. Walker. 1st ed. NF/dj. F4. $18.00

ELWOOD, Roger. *Showcase.* 1973. Harper. 1st ed. NF/NF. P3. $15.00

ELYTIS, Odysseas. *Ilios O Protos.* 1943. Athens. 1/600. 8vo. 38p. prt wrp/glassine dj. O2. $50.00

EMANUEL, Walter. *Dog Day, A; or, The Angel in the House.* 1919. Dutton. 1st Am ed. ils Aldin. VG. O3. $40.00

EMBERLEY, Ed. *Birthday Wish.* 1977. Little Brn. 1st ed. ils Emberley. inscr/drawing. F/F. C8. $45.00

EMBERLEY, Ed. *Ed Emberley's ABC.* 1979. London. Dent. 1st UK ed. obl 4to. pict cloth. F/F. C8. $35.00

EMBERLEY, Ed. *Klippity Klop.* 1974. Little Brn. 3rd prt. inscr/drawing. pict cloth. M/M. C8. $35.00

EMERSON, B.D. *First Class Reader: Selection for Excercises in Reading...* 1840. Claremont, NH. 276p. full leather. G. B18. $22.50

EMERSON, Earl W. *Deviant Behavior.* 1988. Morrow. 1st ed. F/F. P3. $18.00

EMERSON, Earl W. *Deviant Behavior.* 1988. Morrow. 1st ed. sgn. F/F. O4/T2. $25.00

EMERSON, Earl W. *Fat Tuesday.* 1987. Morrow. 1st ed. F/F. P3. $17.00

EMERSON, Earl W. *Fat Tuesday.* 1987. Morrow. 1st ed. sgn. F/F. S6. $35.00

EMERSON, Earl W. *Help Wanted: Orphans Preferred.* 1990. Morrow. 1st ed. VG/VG. P3. $18.00

EMERSON, Earl W. *Morons & Madmen.* 1993. Morrow. 1st ed. sgn. F/F. O4. $35.00

EMERSON, Earl W. *Yellow Dog Party.* 1991. Morrow. 1st ed. sgn. F/F. O4. $25.00

EMERSON, Haven. *Selected Papers.* 1949. Battle Creek. 1st ed. 506p. A13. $35.00

EMERSON, Jill; see Block, Lawrence.

EMERSON, Ralph Waldo. *Essay on Self-Reliance.* 1932. Los Angeles. 1/150. 56p. brn cloth/marbled brd. K1. $35.00

EMERSON, Ralph Waldo. *Essays of...* 1962. Heritage. lg 4to. box. A17. $15.00

EMERSON, Ralph Waldo. *Poems.* 1847. Boston. James Monroe. 1st Am ed/1st issue (4p ads). chemise/case. H4. $1,000.00

EMERSON, Robert M. *Judging Delinquents.* 1970. Chicago. 2nd prt. 293p. xl. VG/dj. D3. $15.00

EMERSON, Thomas. *Political & Civil Rights in the US.* 1967. Boston. 2 vol. 3rd ed. xl. VG. D3. $95.00

EMERY, Lynne Fauley. *Black Dance in the US From 1619 to 1970.* 1972. Palo Alto. Nat Pr. 1st ed. NF/VG. B2. $35.00

EMERY, R.G. *High Inside.* 1948. MacRae Smith. later prt. VG. P8. $14.00

EMLYN, Thomas. *Extracts From an Humble Inquiry Into Scriputure Account...* 1790. Boston. Hall. 1st ed. 47p. sewn. H10. $65.00

EMME, E.M. *History of Rocket Technology.* 1964. Detroit. 1st ed. VG/dj. C11. $35.00

EMMET, Dorothy. *Function, Purpose & Powers.* 1958. Macmillan. 300p. red cloth. G1. $27.50

EMMET, E.R. *Puzzles for Pleasure.* 1972. NY. Bell. 310p. F/dj. K4. $8.50

EMMIUS, Ubbo. *Graecorum Respublicae.* 1632. Leyden. Elzeviriana. 2 vol. Republics Series. 24mo. contemporary vellum. K1. $185.00

EMMONS, Della. *Leschi of the Nisquallies.* 1965. Minneapolis. TS Denison. inscr. 416p. map ep. G. B11. $45.00

EMMONS, Della. *Sacajawea of the Shoshones.* 1943. Binfords Mort. sgn. VG. B34. $80.00

EMMONS, George Thornton. *Tlingit Indians.* ca 1991. Seattle/NY. WA U/Am Mus Natural Hist. 488p. emb beige cloth. M/M. P4. $60.00

EMMOTT, Elizabeth Braithwaite. *Story of Quakerism.* 1908. London. Headley Bros. 12mo. 284p. VG. V3. $12.50

EMORY, William H. *Report of US & Mexican Boundary Survey. Vol I.* 1857. WA. 1st ed. ils/pl/maps. half calf. C6. $150.00

ENDE, Michael. *Momo.* 1985. Doubleday. 1st ed. VG/VG. M21. $15.00

ENDE, Michael. *Neverending Story.* 1983. Doubleday. UP/1st Am ed. NF. B4. $125.00

ENDE, Michael. *Neverending Story.* 1983. Doubleday. 1st ed. 398p. NF/VG+. P2. $40.00

ENDE, Michael. *Neverending Story.* 1983. London. Allen Lane. 1st Eng-language ed. trans Manheim. ils Quadflieg. F/F. T2. $85.00

ENDICOTT, Wendell. *Adventures With Rod & Harpoon Along FL Keys.* 1925. NY. ils. 271p. cloth. B14. $95.00

ENDICOTT & JENKINS. *Wrecked Among Cannibals in the Fijis.* 1923. Salem. Marine Research. ils. gilt blk cloth/bl brd. VG. F1. $75.00

ENDO, Shusku. *Samurai.* 1982. Harper. UP/1st Am ed. NF. B4. $45.00

ENDORE, Guy. *Sleepy Lagoon Mystery.* 1944. Sleepy Lagoon Defense Comm. 1st ed. NF/wrp. B2. $45.00

ENGARD, Rodney G. *Arizona Cacti & Succulents.* 1984. Tucson. ils. sc. F. B26. $9.00

ENGBERG, Robert Martin. *Dawn of Civilization.* 1940. Chicago. 384p. VG/dj. W1. $15.00

ENGEL, Frederic. *Ancient World Preserved.* 1976. NY. 1st Eng ed. 314p. VG/dj. F3. $25.00

ENGEL, Heinrich. *Japanese House, a Tradition...* 1980. Rutlland, VT. Tuttle. 9th prt. ils. 495p. blk/gray stp tan cloth. F/dj/case. F1. $75.00

ENGEL, Howard. *City Called July.* 1986. Viking. 1st ed. VG/VG. P3. $20.00

ENGEL, Howard. *Dead & Buried.* 1990. Canada. Viking. 1st ed. VG/VG. P3. $25.00

ENGEL, Howard. *Murder on Location.* 1982. St Martin. 1st ed. F/NF. B4. $35.00

ENGEL, Howard. *Ransom Game.* 1981. Clarke Irwin. 1st ed. sgn. F/F. P3. $30.00

ENGEL, Marian. *No Clouds of Glory.* 1968. Longmans Canada. 1st ed/author's 1st book. NF/VG+. B4. $350.00

ENGELS, Friedrich. *Ludwig Feuerbach & Outcome of Classical German Philosophy.* 1941. Internat Pub. later prt. thin 8vo. 96p. red cloth. VG/dj. G1. $22.50

ENGEN, Rodney K. *Randolph Caldecott, Lord of the Nursery.* 1888. London. Bloomsbury. 4to. ils Caldecott. red cloth. NF/M. D6. $25.00

ENGH, M.J. *Rainbow Man.* 1993. Tor. 1st ed. F/F. P3. $18.00

ENGLAND & MCDILL. *Agnicourt.* 1962. San Francisco. Grabhorn. M. H4. $25.00

ENGLE, Anita. *Nili Spies.* 1989. Jerusalem. Phoenix Pub. photos/index. 245p. M. M7. $27.50

ENGLE & LOTT. *Man in Flight.* 1979. Annapolis, MD. Leeward. 8vo. 396p. VG/dj. K5. $24.00

ENGSTROM, Elizabeth. *Nightmare Flower.* 1992. Tor. 1st ed. F/F. P3. $20.00

ENOCH, C. Reginald. *Mexico: Its Ancient & Modern Civilizations.* 1910. Scribner. 2nd prt. 362p. teg. VG. F3. $25.00

ENOCH, C. Reginald. *Peru: Its Former & Present Civilization...* 1910. London. Fisher Unwin. 2nd prt. 8vo. 320p. scarce. B11. $45.00

ENRIGHT, Elizabeth. *Tatsinda.* 1963. Harcourt Brace. 1st ed. F/NF. C8. $25.00

ENRIGHT, Elizabeth. *Thimble Summer.* 1938. Farrar Rinehart. NF/clip. C8. $40.00

ENSIMINGER, M. *Horses & Horsemanship.* 1969. Danville. Interstate. 4th ed. 907p. VG/fair. O3. $25.00

ENSLEIN, Kurt. *Data Acquisition & Processing in Biology & Medicine. Vol 1.* 1962. Pergamon. 191p. F/dj. K4. $25.00

ENSTROM, Robert. *Encounter Program.* 1977. Doubleday. F/F. P3. $15.00

EPICTETUS. *Golden Sayings of Epictetus.* 1903. London. Macmillan. pocket ed. 190p. VG. B33. $12.00

EPLEY, A. *Story of New Richmond Tornado.* 1900. New Richmond. 1st ed. G. C11. $37.50

EPSTEIN, Edward Jay. *Legend: Secret World of Lee Harvey Oswald.* 1978. McGraw Hill. 1st ed. VG+/VG. M21. $15.00

EPSTEIN, Sarah G. *Prints of Edvard Munch: Mirror of His Life.* 1983. Oberlin College. Allen Memorial Art Mus. 208p. F. H1. $32.50

ERDMAN, Charles R. *Revelation of John.* 1936. Westminster. 158p. VG. B29. $3.50

ERDMAN, Paul. *Panic of '89.* 1986. Deutsch. 1st ed. F/F. P3. $20.00

ERDRICH, Louise. *Beet Queen.* 1986. NY. 1st ed. inscr. F/F. A11. $90.00

ERDRICH, Louise. *Love Medicine.* 1984. HRW. 1st ed/author's 1st novel. F/F. B3. $150.00

ERDRICH, Louise. *Tracts.* 1988. NY. ARC/UP. sgn. F/ils wrp. A11. $60.00

ERDSTEIN, Erich. *Inside the Fourth Reich.* 1977. St Martin. 1st ed. VG. P3. $15.00

ERFFA, Helmut. *Paintings of Benjamin West.* 1986. Yale. VG+/VG. A1. $50.00

ERHART, Margaret. *Augusta Cotton.* 1992. Cambridge, MA. Zoland Books. 1st ed. F/F. A14. $35.00

ERICHSEN, John. *Observations on Aneurysms Selected From Works...* 1844. London. Sydenham Soc. 524p. G. G7. $125.00

ERICKSON, Eric H. *Gandhi's Truth: On the Origins of Militant Non-Violence.* 1969. Norton. 1st ed. 474p. VG/VG. B33. $20.00

ERICKSON, Millard J. *Christian Theology: Vol 1.* 1983. Baker. 477p. VG/dj. B29. $12.50

ERICKSON, Rica. *Triggerplants.* 1981. Nedlands, WA. 60 full-p pl. 229p. F/dj. B26. $29.00

ERICKSON, Steve. *Days Between Stations.* 1985. Poseidon. 1st ed/author's 1st book. NF/NF. S9. $50.00

ERICKSON, Steve. *Tours of the Black Clock.* 1989. Poseidon. 1st ed. sgn. F/F. B2. $45.00

ERIKSON, Erik. *Childhood & Society.* 1963. Norton. 2nd enlarged ed. 445p. wrp. A10. $4.00

ERIKSON, Erik. *Dimensions of a New Identity.* 1974. Norton. 125p. VG/VG. A10. $10.00

ERIKSON, Erik. *Life History & the Historical Moment.* 1975. Norton. 283p. VG/VG. A10. $10.00

ERKILLA. *Hammers on Stone: Ils Hist of Cape Ann Granite.* 1981. np. NF. E5. $35.00

ERMAN, A. *Life in Ancient Egypt.* (1894). np. later prt. 300p. VG. E5. $30.00

ERMINE, Will. *Boss of the Plains.* 1946. World. 1st prt. G. B34. $15.00

ERNEST, Edward. *Animated Animals.* 1943. Saalfield. ils Julian Wehr. mechanical pop-up. VG/dj. C8/P2. $75.00

ERNEST, Edward. *Child's First Book.* 1945. Garden City. ils Nerman. VG. P2. $20.00

ERNST & SEAGLE. *To the Pure...Study of Obscenity & Censor.* 1928. NY. 2nd prt. 336p. VG. D3. $25.00

ERSKINE, John. *Adam & Eve.* 1927. McClelland Stewart. 1st Canadian ed. VG. P3. $7.00

ERSKINE, John. *Influence of Women & Its Cure.* 1936. Bobbs Merrill. 1st ed. F/NF. B4. $50.00

ERSKINE, Laurie York. *Renfrew Flies Again.* nd. Grosset Dunlap. VG/VG. P3. $15.00

ERSKINE, Margaret. *Fatal Relations.* 1955. Hammond. 1st ed. VG. P3. $30.00

ERSKINE, Margaret. *Take a Dark Journey.* 1965. Hodder Stoughton. 1st ed. VG/VG. P3. $25.00

ERTE. *Erte Maquettes.* 1984. Hyattsville, MD. Rebecca. 72x55mm. inscr. 42 ils. blk calf/seed pearls. F/box. B24. $950.00

ERVINE, St. John. *Bernard Shaw: His Life, Work & Friends.* 1956. Morrow. 1st ed. gilt gr bdg. G+. M7. $16.50

ERWITT, Elliot. *Photographs & Anti-Photographs.* 1972. Greenwich, NYGS. 4to. NF/NF. S9. $150.00

ERWITT, Elliot. *Private Experience.* 1974. LA. Alskog. 1st ed. VG+/G. S9. $30.00

ESDAILE, Katharine A. *Eng Monumental Sculputure Since the Renaissance.* 1927. London. Soc for Promoting Knowledge. 1st ed. 179p. VG. M10. $5.00

ESHBACH, Lloyd Arthur. *Over My Shoulder: Reflections on a SF Era.* 1983. Phil. Oswald Train. 1st ed. F/F. T2. $25.00

ESHBACH, Lloyd Arthur. *Tyrant of Time.* 1955. Fantasy. 1st ed. Donald Grant bdg. M/M. P3. $20.00

ESHBACH, Lloyd Arthur. *Tyrant of Time.* 1955. Fantasy. 1st ed. F/F. M2. $18.00

ESHLEMEN, Merle W. *Africa Answers.* 1951. Scottsdale, PA. 1st ed. 179p. VG/prt wrp. M8. $37.50

ESQUEMELING, John. *Buccaneers of America.* 1893. London. Sonnerschein. ils/pl/map. 508p. VG. T7. $120.00

ESQUEMELING, John. *Buccaneers of America. A True Account...* 1893. London/NY. Swan Sonnenschein/Scribner. 508p. bl cloth. VG+. P4. $195.00

ESQUIVEL, Laura. *Like Water for Chocolate.* 1992. Doubleday. ARC. F/wrp. B2. $75.00

ESSLEMONT, J.E. *Baha 'U'llah & the New Era.* 1937. Baha'i Pub. 1st prt. 349p. VG/stiff wrp. W1. $15.00

ESSOE, Gabe. *Tarzan of the Movies.* 1968. Citadel. 1st ed. VG+/VG. M21. $30.00

ESTCOURT, Doris. *Little Elephant Comes to Town.* nd. London. Oxford. ils MK Mountain. pict cloth. G+. C8. $15.00

ESTES, Eleanor. *Lost Umbrella of Kim Chu.* 1978. NY. McElderry. 1st ed. ils Ayer. pict cloth. M/M. C8. $30.00

ESTES, Eleanor. *Rufus M.* 1943. HBJ. 1st ed. ils Louis Slobodkin. 320p. VG. P2. $30.00

ESTES, Eleanor. *Witch Family.* 1960. HBJ. 1st ed. ils Edward Ardizzone. VG. P2. $25.00

ESTLEMAN, Loren *Downriver.* 1988. Houghton. 1st ed. F/dj. F4. $17.00

ESTLEMAN, Loren *Kill Zone.* 1984. Mysterious. 1st ed. sgn. F/F. S6. $37.50

ESTLEMAN, Loren. *Bloody Season.* 1988. Bantam. 1st ed. VG/G. P3. $12.00

ESTLEMAN, Loren. *Dr Jekyll & Mr Holmes.* 1979. Doubleday. 1st ed. VG/VG. P3. $35.00

ESTLEMAN, Loren. *Kill Zone.* 1984. Mysterious. 1st ed. VG/VG. P3. $18.00

ESTLEMAN, Loren. *Lady Yesterday.* 1987. Houghton Mifflin. 1st ed. F/F. B3/P3. $25.00

ESTLEMAN, Loren. *Sweet Women Lie.* 1990. Houghton Mifflin. 1st ed. F/F. P3. $19.00

ESTRADA, Santiago. *Apuntes de Viaje del Plata a Los Andes y del Mar Pacifico...* 1872. Buenos Aires. 2nd ed. 314p. Lib of Congress duplicate. F3. $65.00

ESTY, Katherine. *Gypsies, Wanderers in Time.* 1969. Meredith. 1st ed. photos. F/VG. C8. $15.00

ETCHISON, Dennis. *Cutting Edge.* 1986. Doubleday. 1st ed. VG/VG. P3. $20.00

ETCHISON, Dennis. *Dark Country.* 1982. Scream. 1st ed. NF/dj. M2. $135.00

ETHERIDGE, Kenneth. *Viola, Furgy, Bobbi & Me.* 1989. Holiday. 1st ed. F/VG+. P8. $12.50

ETHERTON, P.T. *Across the Great Deserts.* 1948. Lutterworth. 184p. NF/dj. W1. $15.00

ETHRIDGE, Willie Snow. *There's Yeast in the Middle East.* 1962. Vanguard. 1st ed. 309p. xl. G/dj. W1. $14.00

ETS, Marie Hall. *Mr Penny's Circus.* 1961. Viking. 1st WRBC ed. lg 8vo. pict paper brd. VG. C8. $7.50

ETS, Marie Hall. *Oley the Sea Monster.* 1947. Viking. 1st ed. NF/VG. P2. $60.00

ETTINGER, M. *Psychologie und Ethik des Antisemitismus im Altherthum...* 1891. Wien. Gittkueb's Buchhandlung. 29p. VG/prt yel wrp. rare. G1. $125.00

ETTINGHOUSEN, Richard. *Turkish Miniatures.* 1965. NAL. 1st prt. 12mo. VG/stiff wrp. W1. $8.00

ETTMUELLER, Michael. *Oper Medica Theoretico-Practica...* 1708. Franfurt. 2 vol in 3. folio. full vellum. G7. $425.00

ETULAIN, Richard W. *Bibliographical Guide to Study of W Am Literature.* 1982. NE U. 1st ed. sgn. M/sans. A18. $32.50

ETULAIN, Richard W. *Writing Western Hist: Essays on Major Western Historians.* 1991. NM U. 1st sc ed. M. A18. $20.00

ETULAIN & PAUL. *Frontier & the Am West.* 1977. Goldentree Biblio Series. sc. sgn. M. A18. $20.00

EUCLID. *Euclide's Elements: The Whole 15 Books...* 1751. London. Mount Page. 9 fld pl. lacks front ep. 384p. contemporary calf. K1. $125.00

EUSTACE, J.S. *Traite d'Amitie, de Commerce et de Navigation...* 1796. Paris. Chez Desenne. 1st ed. 8vo. 68p. sewn/uncut. M1. $175.00

EUSTIS, Helen. *Fool Killer.* 1954. Doubleday. 1st ed. VG/G. P3. $20.00

EVANOVICH, Janet. *One for the Money.* 1994. Scribner. ARC. F/wrp. B2. $35.00

EVANS, A. Delbert. *Romance of British Voluntary Hospital Movement.* ca 1930. London. 1st ed. 360p. xl. A13. $70.00

EVANS, Arthur. *Anthropology & the Classics.* 1908. Oxford. 8vo. ils. 819p. NF/dj. B14. $175.00

EVANS, Bergen. *Spoor of Spooks & Other Nonsense.* 1954. Knopf. 1st ed. VG/VG. P3. $18.00

EVANS, C.B. *Another Montana Pioneer.* 1960. np. sgn. VG/dj. B34. $40.00

EVANS, C.B. *Western Pioneer Home Life.* 1965. np. photos. VG/dj. B34. $35.00

EVANS, Doris. *Saguaro.* 1980. Globe, AZ. photos/maps. 59p. sc. F. B26. $2.00

EVANS, E. Everett. *Alien Minds.* 1955. Fantasy. 1st ed. VG/VG. P3. $45.00

EVANS, Elizabeth. *Anne Tyler.* 1993. NY. 1st ed. 1/100. sgn Evans/Tyler on tipped-in p. F/F. C2. $100.00

EVANS, Eva Knox. *Araminta.* 1935. NY. Minton Balch. 6th prt. sm 8vo. pict cloth. VG. C8. $30.00

EVANS, Eva Knox. *Jerome Anthony.* 1936. Putnam. 1st ed. ils Eric Berry. VG+/VG. C8. $75.00

EVANS, Geraldine. *Dead Before Morning.* 1993. London. Macmillan. 1st ed. F/F. S6. $25.00

EVANS, Henry Oliver. *Pioneer: Henry W Oliver, 1840-1904.* 1942. np. 1st ed/2nd prt. 367p. VG. E5. $45.00

EVANS, Joan. *Flowering of the Middle Ages.* 1985. Bonanza. ils. 230p. VG/dj. M10. $16.50

EVANS, John H. *Location & Description of the Emmaus Mission.* nd. MS. 1st ed thus. VG/prt wrp. M8. $12.50

EVANS, John. *Ancient Stone Implements, Weapons & Ornaments...* 1872. London. Longman. ils/index. 640p. VG. H10. $75.00

EVANS, John. *Farmer's Receipt Book & Pocket Farrier...* 1831. Concord, NH. Fisk Chase. 12mo. 214p. half leather. H10. $125.00

EVANS, Katherine. *Little Tree, a Mexican Tale.* 1956. Bruce. 8vo. pict brd. VG. B17. $4.00

EVANS, Lawrence B. *Leading Cases on International Law.* 1917. Chicago. Callaghan. worn. M11. $45.00

EVANS, Max. *Mountain of Gold.* 1965. Norman S Berg. 1st ed. inscr/sgn. F/clip. A18. $60.00

EVANS, Max. *One-Eyed Sky.* 1974. Nash. 1st separate ed. ils. F/F. A18. $30.00

EVANS, Max. *Southwest Wind.* 1958. Naylor. 1st ed/author's 1st book. ils Evans. F/F. A18. $75.00

EVANS, Max. *Three Short Novels: One-Eyed Sky/Great Wedding/My Pardner.* 1963. Houghton Mifflin. 1st ed. F/dj. A18. $30.00

EVANS, Rosalie. *Rosalie Evans' Letters From Mexico.* 1926. Bobbs Merrill. 472p. red cloth. VG. F3. $20.00

EVANS, William. *Great Doctrines of the Bible.* 1990. Moody. 325p. M. B29. $8.50

EVANS, William. *Personal Soul Winning.* 1978. Moody. 160p. VG/dj. B29. $3.50

EVANS & FARRAR. *Bibliography of Eng Trans from Medieval Sources.* 1946. Columbia. 3839 entries. 547p. VG. A4. $95.00

EVANS-PRITCHARD, E.E. *Witchcraft, Oracles & Magic Among the Azande.* 1937. Clarendon. 1st ed. ils/pl/maps. 558p. gilt bl cloth. scarce. K1. $100.00

EVANS-WENTZ, W.Y. *Tibet's Great Yogi Milarepa.* 1963. London. Oxford. 2nd ed/3rd imp. VG. B33. $50.00

EVANS-WENTZ, W.Y. *Tibetan Book of the Dead.* 1965. Oxford. 3rd ed. 249p. NF/VG. B33. $55.00

EVATT, H.V. *Story of WA Holman & the Labour Movement.* 1942. Sydney. Angus Robertson. 2nd ed. VG/fair. V4. $7.50

EVERETT, Alexander Hill. *America; or, General Survey of Political Situation...* 1827. Phil. Carey Lea. 1st ed. 364p. rebacked. D3. $150.00

EVERETT, Charles Carroll. *Fichte's Science of Knowledge: Critical Exposition.* 1884. Chicago. 12mo. 287p. prt brn cloth. G. G1. $50.00

EVERETT, Gwen. *Li's Sis & Uncle Willie: Story Based on Life...Wm H Johnson.* 1991. Rizzoli/Smithsonian. 1st ed. F/F. C8. $25.00

EVERETT, Percival. *Suder.* 1983. Viking. 1st ed. F/VG+. P8. $25.00

EVERITT, Charles P. *Adventures of a Treasure Hunter.* 1951. Little Brn. 8vo. 264p. VG/clip. P4. $32.50

EVERS, John J. *Touching Second.* 1910. Reilly Britton. 2nd prt. 308p. VG. M20. $80.00

EVERSON, Willaim. *Waldport Poems.* 1944. Waldport, OR. 1st ed. 1/975. NF/cream wrp. C6. $100.00

EVERSON, William. *Archetype West. The Pacific Coast As Literary Region.* 1976. Berkeley. 1st ed. sgn. F/lg 8vo wrp. A11. $45.00

EVERSON, William. *In the Fictive Wish.* 1967. Oyez. ARC/ltd ed. sgn. ils/sgn Mary Fabilli. F/dj. V1. $100.00

EVERSON, William. *Pictorial Hist of the Western Film.* 1972. Secaucus. 2nd prt. 4to. VG/G. O3. $35.00

EVERSON, William. *Triptych for the Living.* 1951. Oakland, CA. Seraphim. 1st ed. 4to. 26p. full limp vellum/silk ties. F. H5. $2,250.00

EVERY, George. *Byzantine Patriarche 451-1204.* 1947. London. 8vo. ils/maps. 212p. cloth. O2. $30.00

EWAN & EWAN. *Biographical Dictionary of Rocky Mountain Naturalists.* 1981. Utrecht. 253p. cloth. M. A10. $45.00

EWELL, Jason. *Medical Companion or Family Physician...* 1827. np. 852p. full leather. VG. E5. $85.00

EWING, Cortez A.M. *Judges of the Supreme Court 1789-1937.* 1938. NM U. 12mo. 124p. VG. D3. $15.00

EWING, Juliana Horatia. *Flat Iron for a Farthing; or, Some Passages in the Life...* 1926. np. G Bell. Queen's Treasures Series. 235p. NF. D6. $25.00

EWING, Juliana Horatia. *Mill Stream. Poems of Child Life & Country Life.* 1885. London. Soc for Promoting Christian Knowledge. VG. D6. $65.00

EWING, Juliana Horatia. *Six to Sixteen. A Story for Girls.* 1910. np. G Bell. 12mo. 237p. wht lettered gr cloth. G+. D6. $25.00

EWINGS, J. Franklin. *Ancient Way: Life & Landmarks of the Holy Land.* 1964. Scribner. 1st ed. 224p. F/dj. W1. $9.00

EWLLS, Charles. *Essay on Dew & Several Appearances Connected With It.* 1838. Phil. 71p. wrp. B14. $250.00

EXLEY, Frederick. *Fan's Notes.* 1968. Harper. 1st ed. F/F. B4. $250.00

EYLER, John. *Victorian Social Medicine: Ideas & Methods of William Farr.* 1979. Baltimore. 1st ed. 262p. dj. A13. $30.00

EYSENCK, H.J. *Crime & Personality.* 1964. London. Kegan Paul. 187p. M/dj. K4. $35.00

EYSENCK, H.J. *Dynamics of Anxiety & Hysteria.* 1957. NY. Praeger. 311p. G. K4. $35.00

EYSENCK, Michael W. *Handbook of Cognitive Psychology.* 1984. London. Lawrence Erlbaum. 417p. F/wrp. K4. $15.00

FABER, Lorney. *Next Year Country.* 1975. np. 1st ed. VG/dj. B34. $30.00

FABES, Gilbert H. *John Galsworthy: His First Editions...* 1932. London. Foyle. 1st ed. 1/500. sgn. 64p. cloth. VG. A17. $30.00

FABIAN, Stephen E. *Fabian in Color.* 1980. Starmont. 1st ed. sgn. 1/800. portfolio of 8 mc pl. F. F4. $45.00

FABIAN, Stephen E. *More Fantasy by Fabian.* 1979. Gerry DeLaRee. 1st ed. F/dj. M2. $50.00

FABIAN, Stephen E. *Stephen E Fabian's Ladies & Legends.* 1993. Underwood Miller. 1st ed. F/F. T2. $25.00

FABOS, Julius G. *Frederick Law Olmsted, Sr: Founder Landscape Architecture...* 1968. Amherst. 8vo. photos. 114p. dj. B26. $47.50

FABREGA & SILVER. *Illness & Shamanistic Curing in Zinacantan.* 1973. Stanford. 1st ed. 285p. VG/dj. F3. $20.00

FABRICUS, Vicentius. *Poematum Juvenilium Libri III...* 1633. Leyden. Elzevir. 12mo. 108p. aeg. 19th-C calf. K1. $150.00

FACKENHEIM, Emil L. *Quest for Past & Future.* 1968. IN. 336p. VG/torn. B29. $3.50

FAERNO, Gabriello. *Emendationes, in Sex Fabulas Terentii.* 1565. Florence. Juntas. 8vo. 251p. 18th-C calf. K1. $500.00

FAGAN, Brian. *Aztecs.* 1984. Freeman. 1st ed. 322p. VG. F3. $25.00

FAGAN, Brian. *Rape of the Nile. Tomb Robbers, Tourists & Archaeologists...* 1975. Scribner. 1st ed. 399p. VG. W1. $30.00

FAGIN, N. Bryllion. *Histrionic Mr Poe.* 1949. Baltimore. 1st ed. inscr. NF/VG clip. A11. $45.00

FAHEY, David. *Masters of Starlight.* 1987. LA Co Mus of Art. 1st ed. 4to. NF/stiff pict wrp. S9. $25.00

FAHEY, Herbert. *Early Printing in California.* 1956. San Francisco. BC of CA. 1/400. 142p. half buckram/cloth. VG. P4. $325.00

FAIR, A.A.; see Gardner, Erle Stanley.

FAIRBAIRN, Barbara. *Little Pig Who Ate a Four-Leaf Clover.* 1928. Rand McNally. 1st ed. 102p. G+. P2. $40.00

FAIRBAIRN, Roger; see Carr, John Dickson.

FAIRBAIRN, W.E. *Get Tough! How To Win in Hand-to-Hand Fighting.* (1942). Appleton Century. sc. 120p. F/VG. H1. $7.50

FAIRBANK, John King. *Chinabound: Fifty Year Memoir.* 1982. NY. Harper Row. 1st ed. 480p. NF/dj. M10. $7.50

FAIRBANKS, Douglas. *Laugh & Live.* (1917). Britton. 2nd prt. 109p. G+. H1. $9.00

FAIRLEIGH, Runa. *Old-Fashioned Mystery.* 1983. Denys. 1st ed. VG/VG. P3. $20.00

FAIRLEY, Peter. *A-Z of Space.* 1978. St Albans, UK. Hart Davis. 2nd ed rpt. pict brd. VG. K5. $12.00

FAIRMAN, Charles E. *Art & Artists of the Capitol of the United States.* 1927. GPO. lg 4to. ils/index. 429p. O8. $18.50

FAIRMAN, Paul F. *Forgetful Robot.* 1968. HRW. 1st ed. F/F. N3. $35.00

FALCONER, D.S. *Intro to Quantitive Genetics.* 1960. Edinburgh/London. 345p. F/dj. K4. $30.00

FALCONER, Sovereign. *To Make Death Love Us.* 1987. Doubleday. RS. F/F. P3. $18.00

FALCONER, Thomas. *On Surnames & the Rules of Law Affecting Their Change.* 1862. London. Reynell. emb cloth. M11. $150.00

FALK, Lee; see Cooper, Basil; also Goulart, Ron (ghosted).

FALKLAND, Lady. *Chow-Chow: Journal Kept in India, Egypt & Syria.* 1930. London. Partridge. 408p. VG. W1. $45.00

FALKNER, Frank. *Human Development.* 1966. Phil/London. Saunders. 599p. F. K4. $25.00

FALKNER, J. Meade. *Moonfleet.* 1962. Tempo. pb lib bdg. VG. P3. $7.00

FALLON, Martin; see Patterson, Henry.

FALLOWELL, Duncan. *Drug Tales.* 1979. Hamish Hamilton. 1st ed. F/F. P3. $20.00

FALLS, Cyril. *Military Operations Egypt & Palestine...Part II.* 1930. London. index/maps/photos. gilt red cloth. G+. $90.00

FALLWELL, Gene. *Texas Indian Lore: Ils Guide to Habits, Life, Cultures...* 1959. Dallas. Boy Scouts of Am. ils/photos. VG/wrp. P4. $10.00

FALUKNER, William. *Thinking of Home.* (1992). Norton. 1/71. edit JG Watson. F/dj. Q1. $150.00

FALWELL, Jerry. *Champions for God.* 1985. Victor. pb. 132p. F. B29. $2.50

FALWELL, Jerry. *Listen America!* 1980. Doubleday. 266p. G/torn. B29. $3.50

FANGLE. *Danish Pulled Thread Embroidery.* 1977. np. sc. VG. G2. $5.00

FANNIN, Cole. *Danger at the Ranch.* 1961. Whitman. Real McCoys TVTI. VG. P3. $13.00

FANNIN, Cole. *Lucy & the Madcap Mystery.* 1963. Whitman. I Love Lucy TVTI. F. P3. $20.00

FANNIN, Cole. *Roy Rogers in River of Peril.* 1957. Whitman. G+. P3. $15.00

FANNIN, Cole. *Sea Hunt.* 1960. Whitman. Sea Hunt TVTI. F. P3. $20.00

FANNING, Edmund. *Voyages & Discoveries in the South Seas 1792-1832.* 1924. Salem. Marine Research Soc #6. ils. 335p. T7. $120.00

FANNING, Edmund. *Voyages Round the World With Selected Sketches of Voyages...* 1970. Upper Saddle River. Gregg. facsimile of 1883 ed. 8vo. 499p. VG. P4. $35.00

FANTE, John. *Wait Until Spring, Bandini.* 1938. Stackpole. 1st ed. 8vo. 265p. gr cloth. NF/dj. H5. $800.00

FANTE, John. *Wait Until Spring, Bandini.* 1983. Blk Sparrow. reissue of 1st novel. 1/26 sgn. F/dj/promo material. L3. $350.00

FANTE, John. *Wine of Youth.* 1985. Blk Sparrow. 1st ed. 1/50. sgn on tipped-in leaf. F/acetate. L3. $200.00

FANTHORPE, Lionel. *Uranium 235.* 1967. Arcadia. 1st ed. sgn. F/dj. F4. $35.00

FARAGO, Ladislas. *Abyssinia on the Eve.* 1935. Putnam. 1st ed. ils/pl/maps. 286p. VG. W1. $22.00

FARAGO, Ladislas. *Patton: Ordeal & Triumph.* 1964. NY. 1st ed. VG/VG. B5. $30.00

FARAGOH, Francis Edwards. *Pin-Wheel.* 1927. NY. John Day. 1st ed/author's 1st orig play. F/NF. B2. $45.00

FARAH, Cynthia. *Literature & Landscape: Writers of the Southwest.* 1988. TX W Pr. 1st ed. M/dj. A18. $35.00

FARBER, James. *Texas, CSA: Spotlight on Disaster.* 1947. Jackson. 1st ed. 1/1000. 8vo. 265p. VG/dj. C6. $50.00

FARBER, Marvin. *Phenomenology As Method & Philosophical Disipline.* 1928. Roswell Park Publication. 130p. prt bl wrp. scarce. G1. $125.00

FARBER, Norma. *Where's Gomer?* 1974. Dutton. 1st ed. ils Pene Du Bois. pict cloth. F/F. C8. $35.00

FARINA, Richard. *Been Down So Long It Looks Like Up to Me.* 1966. Random. 1st ed. F/NF. B4. $175.00

FARIS, El-Shidiac. *Practical Grammar of the Arabic Language...* 1866. London. Bernard Quaritch. sm 8vo. 162p. gilt bl cloth. VG. K1. $100.00

FARIS, John. *Old Roads Out of Philadelphia.* 1917. Lippincott. later prt. VG. O3. $45.00

FARIS, Lillie A. *Old Testament Stories Retold for Children.* 1938. Platt Munk. 4to. VG/G. B17. $9.00

FARJAM, Farideh. *Crystal Flower of the Sun.* 1983. Lexington, KY. Mazda. 1st ed. VG/stiff wrp. W1. $8.00

FARJEON, Eleanor. *Children's Bells.* 1960. NY. Walch. 1st Am ed. ils Fortnum. F/VG+. C8. $25.00

FARJEON, Eleanor. *More Perfect Zoo.* 1929. David McKay. 12 photos. G+. P2. $45.00

FARJEON, Eleanor. *New Book of Days.* 1961 (1941). NY. Walck. 1st Am ed. 8vo. F/F. C8. $25.00

FARJEON, Eleanor. *Prayer for Little Things.* 1945. Houghton Mifflin. Nursery Books ed. ils EO Jones. F/F. C8. $25.00

FARLEY, John. *Gametes & Spores: Ideas About Sexual Reproduction...* 1982. Baltimore. 1st ed. 299p. dj. A13. $35.00

FARLEY, Ralph Milne. *Hidden Universe.* 1950. FPCI. 1st ed. NF/NF. P3. $45.00

FARLEY, Walter. *Black Stallion Revolts.* 1953. Random. 1st ed. 62p. G+. P2. $25.00

FARLEY, Walter. *Black Stallion's Courage.* 1956. NY. Random. 1st ed. sgn. VG/fair. O3. $45.00

FARLEY, Walter. *Black Stallion's Filly.* 1952. Random. 1st ed. VG/VG. O3. $35.00

FARLEY, Walter. *Island Stallion Races.* 1955. Random. 1st prt. VG/VG. C8. $25.00

FARLEY, Walter. *Island Stallion.* 1948. Random. 1st prt. VG/G. O3. $35.00

FARLIE, Barbara. *Pennywise Boutique.* 1974. np. cloth. VG. G2. $8.00

FARLIE, Barbara. *Your House in Needlepoint.* 1976. np. cloth. VG. G2. $8.50

FARMER, Philip Jose. *Adventure of the Peerless Peer.* 1974. Aspen. 1st ed. F/dj. M2. $50.00

FARMER, Philip Jose. *Dark Design.* 1977. Berkley Putnam. 1st ed. NF/NF. P3. $20.00

FARMER, Philip Jose. *Dark Is the Sun.* 1979. Del Rey. 1st ed. F/F. P3. $20.00

FARMER, Philip Jose. *Dayworld Breakup.* 1990. Tor. 1st ed. F/NF. M21. $15.00

FARMER, Philip Jose. *Dayworld Rebel.* 1987. Putnam. 1st ed. 2nd book in Dayworld Series. F/F. N3. $15.00

FARMER, Philip Jose. *Gods of Riverworld.* 1983. Phantasia. 1st ed. sgn. 1/650 #d. F/F/case. P3. $50.00

FARMER, Philip Jose. *Love Song.* 1983. McMillan. 1/500. sgn/#d. F/F. P3. $85.00

FARMER, Philip Jose. *Magic Labyrinth.* 1980. Berkely Putnam. 1st ed. F/F. P3. $18.00

FARMER, Philip Jose. *Maker of Universes.* 1975. Garland. 1st hc ed. World of Tiers Series. F/sans. N3. $55.00

FARMER, Philip Jose. *Mother Was a Lovely Beast: A Feral Man...* 1974. Randor. Chilton. 1st ed. F/F. N3. $30.00

FARMER, Philip Jose. *Unreasoning Mask.* 1981. Putnam. 1st ed. VG/VG. P3. $20.00

FARMER & STRICKLAND. *Trumpet of Our Own.* 1981. BC of CA. 1/650. 114p. NF/sans. B19. $35.00

FARNOL, Jeffrey. *Beltaine the Smith.* 1929. Sampson Low. G+. P3. $10.00

FARNOL, Jeffrey. *Broad Highway.* 1912. Little Brn. ils. VG. P3. $25.00

FARNOL, Jeffrey. *Heritage Perilous.* 1947. Ryerson. 1st Canadian ed. VG. P3. $25.00

FARNOL, Jeffrey. *My Lady Caprice.* 1907. Dodd Mead. 1st ed. G. P3. $20.00

FARNOL, Jeffrey. *My Lord of Wrybourne.* 1948. Ryerson. 1st Canadian ed. VG/chip. P3. $15.00

FARQUHAR, Francis P. *Brief Chronology of Discovery in the Pacific Ocean...* 1943. San Francisco. Grabhorn. 1/1000. F/wrp. P4. $40.00

FARQUHAR, Francis P. *Up & Down California in 1860-1864: Journal WM H Brewer.* 1974. CA U. ils/index. 583p. NF. B19. $10.00

FARR, John; see Webb, Jack.

FARR, Robert. *Electronic Criminals.* 1975. McGraw Hill. 1st ed. VG. P3. $15.00

FARRAGUT, L. *Life & Letters of Admiral DG Farragut, 1st Admiral...* 1879. np. 1st ed. ils/maps. 740p. VG. E5. $65.00

FARRAND, Max. *Records of the Federal Convention of 1787.* 1911. New Haven. 3 vol. 1st ed. 4to. brn cloth. F. H3. $175.00

FARRAR, Geraldine. *Such Sweet Compulsion.* 1938. NY. 1st ed. pres. VG/G. w/photo & sgn letter. B5. $50.00

FARRAR, Mrs. J. *Young Ladies Friend.* 1853. np. 400p. gilt bdg. VG. E5. $35.00

FARRAR, Reginald. *On the Eaves of the World.* 1926. London. Arnold. 2 vol. 2nd imp. 64 pl. gilt bl cloth. F. K1. $125.00

FARRAR, Stewart. *Death in the Wrong Bed.* 1964. Walker. 1st ed. xl. dj. P3. $8.00

FARRE, Rowena. *Gypsy Idyll, a Personal Experience Among the Romanies.* 1962. Vanguard. possible 1st ed. VG+/VG. C8. $15.00

FARRELL, Andrew. *John Cameron's Odyssey.* 1928. Macmillan. 11 pl. 461p. T7. $25.00

FARRELL, B.A. *Experimental Psychology.* 1955. Philosophical Lib. 66p. F/dj. K4. $10.00

FARRELL, Gillian B. *Alibi for an Actress.* 1992. Pocket. 1st ed. VG/dj. N2. $5.00

FARRELL, James T. *Bernard Carr.* 1956. Paris. Bernard Grasset. 1st French ed. inscr. NF/wrp. B2. $125.00

FARRELL, James T. *Brand New Life.* 1968. Doubleday. ARC. F/F. B2. $25.00

FARRELL, James T. *La Face du Temps.* 1955. Paris. Librarie Stock. 1st French ed. inscr. NF. B2. $125.00

FARRELL, James T. *Tutto, Ma Non un Cuore.* 1957. Arnoldo Mondadori. 1st Italian ed. F/NF. B2. $125.00

FARRELL, James T. *World I Never Made.* 1936. NY. 1st ed. inscr. F/NF. A9. $150.00

FARRELL, James T. *Young Lonigan: A Boyhood in Chicago Streets.* 1932. Vanguard. 1st ed/author's 1st book. F/F. Q1. $750.00

FARRERE, Claude. *Black Opium.* 1929. NY. Nicholas Brn. 1/1250. #d. ils Alexander King. NF. B2. $75.00

FARRERE, Claude. *Useless Hands.* 1926. Dutton. 1st ed. VG. P3. $45.00

FARRINGTON, Benjamin. *Francis Bacon: Philosopher of Industrial Science.* 1949. NY. 8 pl. 202p. NF/dj. D3. $16.50

FARRINGTON, Edward J. *Gardener's Almanac.* 1946 (1939). MA Horticultural Soc. 6th revised ed. 146p. F/F. H1. $4.00

FARRINGTON, Oliver C. *Catalogue of Collection of Meteorites.* 1916. Chicago. Field Mus Natural Hist. 8vo. paper wrp. K5. $30.00

FARRINGTON, S. Kip. *Railroads of the Hour.* 1958. Coward McCann. 1st ed. sgn. 319p. VG/dj. M20. $35.00

FARRIS, John. *All Heads Turn When the Hunt Goes By.* 1977. Playboy. 1st ed. NF/dj. M2. $40.00

FARRIS, John. *Fiends.* 1990. Dark Harvest. ltd 1st ed. 1/500. M/box. M2. $45.00

FARRIS, John. *Fury.* 1976. Playboy. 1st ed. VG/fair. P3. $20.00

FARRIS, John. *Scare Tactics.* 1988. Tor. 1st ed. VG/VG. P3. $18.00

FARRIS, John. *Sharp Practice.* 1974. Simon Schuster. 1st ed. sgn. F/clip. F4. $42.00

FARRISS, N.M. *Crown & Clergy in Colonial Mexico 1759-1821.* 1968. London. Athlone. 1st ed. 288p. VG/dj. F3. $35.00

FARSHLER, Earl. *American Saddle Horse.* 1933. Louisville. Standard. 1st ed. VG. O3. $65.00

FARSON, Daniel. *Window on the Sea.* 1977. London. Michael Joseph. 1st ed. inscr/sgn. F/NF. M7. $54.00

FASANELLA, Ralph. *Fasanella's City.* 1973. Knopf. 1st ed. 4to. ils. NF/NF. S9. $45.00

FAST, Howard. *Naked God: Writer & Communist Party.* 1957. Praeger. 1st ed. NF/worn. B2. $25.00

FAST, Jonathan. *Mortal Gods.* 1978. Harper Row. 1st ed. F/F. P3. $15.00

FAST & FAST. *Picture Book Hist of the Jews.* 1942. Hebrew Pub. sm 4to. VG+/VG. C8. $15.00

FAULCONER & KEYS. *Foundations of Anesthesiology.* 1965. Springfield. 2 vol. 1st ed. A13. $250.00

FAULK, Odie B. *Destiny Road.* 1973. Oxford. 1st ed. 232p. VG/dj. M20. $25.00

FAULKNER, Georgene. *Little Peachling & Other Tales of Old Japan.* nd. Wise Parslow. ils Frederick Richardson. 91p. cloth. G+. A3. $20.00

FAULKNER, John. *Men Working.* 1941. NY. 2nd ed. VG/G. B5. $35.00

FAULKNER, William. *As I Lay Dying.* 1967. Modern lib. 1st ed thus. F/VG. B3. $20.00

FAULKNER, William. *Big Woods: Hunting Stories.* 1957. Random. 1st ed. NF/VG. B4. $75.00

FAULKNER, William. *Doctor Martino & Other Stories.* 1934. Smith Haas. 1st ed. sgn. 1/360 special bdg. VG. B2/H4. $650.00

FAULKNER, William. *Doctor Martino & Other Stories.* 1934. Smith Haas. 1st ed. sgn. 1/360. blk cloth spine. F/sans. B4. $1,200.00

FAULKNER, William. *Early Prose & Poetry.* 1962. Boston. 1st/expanded ed. sgn. NF/VG+. A11. $90.00

FAULKNER, William. *Fable.* 1954. Random. 1st ed. sgn. 1/1000. bl cloth. F/glassine wrp/cb case. H5. $750.00

FAULKNER, William. *Fable.* 1954. Random. 1st trade ed. 8vo. 437p. teal/silver stp maroon cloth. NF/dj. H5. $75.00

FAULKNER, William. *Faulkner at Nagano.* 1956. Tokyo. Kenkyusha. 1st ed. NF/VG. B4. $125.00

FAULKNER, William. *Flags in the Dust.* 1973. Random. 1st ed. F/F. B4. $100.00

FAULKNER, William. *Go Down, Moses.* 1942. Random. 1st ed. F/VG+. B4. $650.00

FAULKNER, William. *Green Bough.* 1933. NY. Smith Haas. 1st trade ed. 67p. gr cloth. NF/dj. H5. $250.00

FAULKNER, William. *Idyl in the Desert.* 1931. Random. 1st ed. sgn. 1/400. F/acetate dj. B4. $1,750.00

FAULKNER, William. *Mirrors of Chartes Street.* 1953. Minneapolis. Faulkner Studios. 1/1000. 93p. beige cloth. F/clip. H5. $400.00

FAULKNER, William. *Portable Faulkner.* 1946. NY. 1st ed. VG/VG. A11. $125.00

FAULKNER, William. *Pylon.* 1935. NY. 1st trade ed. gilt bdg. NF/1st issue. A4. $400.00

FAULKNER, William. *Pylon.* 1935. Smith Haas. 1st ed. sgn. 1/310. NF/box. B2. $650.00

FAULKNER, William. *Requiem for a Nun.* 1951. Random. 1st ed thus. 8vo. photos. 105p. gr-gray cloth. NF/dj. H5. $100.00

FAULKNER, William. *Requiem for a Nun.* 1951. Random. ltd ed. 1/750. sgn. F. H4. $700.00

FAULKNER, William. *Sartoris.* 1929. Harcourt. 1/1998. NF. B2. $250.00

FAULKNER, William. *Sartoris.* 1932. London. Chatto Windus. 1st ed. 8vo. 379p. gilt bl cloth. NF/dj. H5. $850.00

FAULKNER, William. *This Earth.* 1932. NY. Equinox Cooperative. 1st ed. 8vo. 8p. F/tan wrp. H5. $250.00

FAULKNER, William. *Town.* 1957. Random. 1st ed. 8vo. 371p. NF/dj. C6/H5. $100.00

FAULKNER, William. *Unvanquished.* 1938. Random. 1st ed. sgn. 1/250. F/sans. B4. $2,500.00

FAULKNER, William. *Wild Palms.* (1939). NY. 339p. gilt tan cloth (1st bdg). VG. H3. $75.00

FAUPEL, Charles E. *Shooting Dope.* 1991. Gainesville, FL. 1st ed. F/NF. B2. $25.00

FAURE, Raoul C. *Mister St John.* 1947. Harper. 1st ed. F/NF. F4. $20.00

FAUST, Frederick. *Notebooks & Poems of Max Brand.* 1957. Dodd Mead. 1/750. 8vo. 138p. bl cloth. F/cb case. H5. $75.00

FAWCETT, E. Douglas. *Hartmann the Anarchist.* 1893. Arnold. 1st ed. VG. scarce. P3. $200.00

FAWCETT, Raymond. *What Was Their Life? Byzantium.* ca 1960. London. Gawthorn. 1st ed. 8vo. 47p. VG/torn. W1. $10.00

FAWCETT, Raymond. *Yucatan: What Was Their Life?* nd. London. Gawthorn. ils. 42p. VG/chip. F3. $20.00

FAWCETT, William. *Saddle-Room Sayings.* 1931. NY. Richard Smith. 1st Am ed. VG/G. O3. $25.00

FAY, Charles Edey. *Mary Celeste, the Odyssey of an Abandoned Ship.* 1942. Salem. Peabody Mus. ils/facsimiles/fld map. gilt bl cloth. VG. F1. $50.00

FAY, Eli. *Rejoinder to IW Allen's Pseudo Hist of Antioch College.* 1859. Yellow Springs, OH. Longley Bros. 1st ed. 8vo. 252p. cloth. M1. $225.00

FAY, Eliot. *Lorenzo in Search of the Sun.* 1953. NY. 147p. cloth. VG. B14. $25.00

FAYEIN, Claudie. *French Doctor in Yemen.* 1957. London. 1st ed. ils. 288p. cloth. O2. $30.00

FEARING, Blanche. *In the City by the Lake.* 1892. Chicago. 1st ed. 192p. G. A17. $15.00

FEARING, Franklin. *Reflex Action, a Study in Hist of Physiological Psychology.* 1930. Baltimore. Williams Wilkins. 350p. G. K4. $35.00

FEARING, Kenneth. *Angel Arms.* 1929. Coward McCann. 1st ed/author's 1st book. F/NF. scarce. B2. $175.00

FEATHER, John. *Dictionary of Book Hist.* 1986. Oxford. 1st ed. 278p. M/F. S11. $20.00

FEATHER, Leonard. *Encyclopedia of Jazz in the Sixties.* 1966. Horizon. 1st ed. F/NF. B2. $45.00

FEATHERSTONHAUGH, George W. *Canoe Voyage Up the Minnay Sotor With Account of...* 1970. St Paul. MN Hist Soc. rpt of 1847 London ed. 2 vol. beige cloth. F/case. P4. $75.00

FEDDEN & THOMSON. *Crusader Castles.* 1957. London. 8vo. ils. 127p. cloth. dj. O2. $40.00

FEDERER, Walter T. *Experimental Design: Theory & Application.* 1955. Macmillan. 522p. K4. $30.00

FEDOSEYEV, GRigori. *Pashka of Bear Ravine.* 1967. Pantheon. 1st ed. 8vo. F/VG. B17. $4.50

FEENSTRA, Rienk M. *Ellas-Greece. A Collection of Forgeries.* 1993. Nicosia. 1/250. 4to. 128p. 4-ring binder. O2. $65.00

FEHLANDT, August. *Century of Drink Reform in the US.* 1904. Cincinnati. 1st ed. 422p. A13. $50.00

FEHLER, Gene. *Center Field Grasses.* 1991. McFarland. 1st ed. F/sans. P8. $17.50

FEIBLEMAN, James K. *Aesthetics: Study in Fine Arts in Theory & Practice.* 1949. DSP. prt russet cloth. G1. $25.00

FEIBLEMAN, James K. *Biosocial Factors in Mental Illness.* 1962. Springfield, IL. Chas C Thomas. bl cloth. F/dj. G1. $28.50

FEIBLEMAN, James K. *New Materialism.* 1970. The Hague. Martinus Nijhoff. 190p. prt bl wrp. G1. $25.00

FEIBLEMAN, James K. *Theory of Human Culture.* 1946. DSP. 362p. maroon cloth. VG/dj. G1. $25.00

FEIFEL, Herman. *Meaning of Death.* 1959. McGraw Hill. 351p. VG/VG. B33. $18.00

FEIGELSON, Naomi. *Underground Revolution: Hippies, Yippies & Others.* 1970. Funk Wagnall. F/NF. F4. $30.00

FEIGENBAUM & FELDMAN. *Computers & Thought.* 1963. McGraw Hill. 456p. F/dj. K4. $15.00

FEIGL, Herbert. *Mental & Physical: Essay & Postscript.* 1967. Minneapolis. trade pb. G1. $22.50

FEIKEMA, Feike; see Manfred, Frederick.

FEILD, Rashad. *Invisible Way: Love Story for the New Age.* 1979. Harper Row. 1st ed. 165p. VG/G. B33. $10.00

FEININGER, Andreas. *Photographic Seeing.* 1973. Englewood Cliffs. 1st ed. 8vo. NF/VG+. S9. $45.00

FEINSTEIN, Elaine. *Bessie Smith.* 1985. Viking. 1st ed. F/F. B2. $35.00

FEINSTEIN, Elaine. *Matters of Chance.* 1972. London. 1/600. sgn. F/wrp. A11. $25.00

FEIST, Raymond E. *Faerie Tale.* 1988. Doubleday. 1st ed. F/F. F4. $18.00

FEIST, Raymond E. *Prince of the Blood.* 1989. Doubleday. 1st ed. F/F. P3. $19.00

FEJES, Claire. *Villagers: Athabaskan Indian Life Along the Yukon River.* 1981. NY. Random. 2nd prt. NF/VG. P4. $45.00

FELDMAN, Annette. *Fun With Felt.* 1980. np. cloth. VG. G2. $16.00

FELDMAN, Lew David. *1975 40th-Anniversary Catalog...* 1974. NY. House of El Dieff. 1st ed. 4to. ils. 80p. NF. M10. $22.50

FELICE, Cynthia. *Downtime.* 1985. Bluejay. 1st ed. F/F. P3. $20.00

FELIX, E.H. *Television: Its Methods & Uses.* 1931. NY. 1st ed. cloth. VG. C11. $85.00

FELLER, Bob. *How To Pitch.* 1948. Ronald Pr. 90p. VG/dj. M20. $30.00

FELLIG, Arthur; See Weegee.

FELLINGS, Muriel. *Jambo Means Hello — Swahili Alphabet Book.* 1974. Dial. 1st ed. ils/sgn Tom Feelings. M/M. C8. $30.00

FENISONG, Ruth. *Widow's Plight.* 1955. Doubleday Crime Club. 1st ed. 190p. cloth. VG/dj. M20. $12.00

FENNER, Phyllis. *Crack of the Bat.* 1955. Knopf. later prt. VG/G+. P8. $17.50

FENNER, Phyllis. *Horses, Horses, Horses.* 1949. NY. Watts. ils Pers Crowell. G. O3. $12.00

FENTON, James. *You Were Marvelous: Theater Reviews From Sunday Times.* 1983. London. Cape. UP. NF. B4. $85.00

FENTON, William. *Fury & the Lone Pine Mystery.* 1957. Whitman. Fury TVTI. VG. P3. $10.00

FERBER, Edna. *American Beauty.* 1931. Doubleday Doran. 1st ed. sgn. 1/150. H3/S9. $125.00

FERBER, Edna. *Peculiar Treasure.* 1939. Doubleday Doran. 1st ed. sgn. 1/351. royal 8vo. teg. VG. H5. $150.00

FERBER & GERDTS. *New Path, Ruskin & the American Pre-Raphaelites.* 1985. Brooklyn Mus. 4to. trade pb. 288p. F. F1. $12.00

FERGUS, Charles. *Gun Dog Breeds: A Guide to Spaniels, Retrievers...* 1992. NY. Lyons Burford. 1st ed. 201p. cloth. M/dj. R2. $20.00

FERGUSON, Adam. *Essay on the History of Civil Society. Seventh Edition.* 1809. Boston. Hastings Etheridge Bliss. 1st Am ed. 8vo. calf. M1. $1,000.00

FERGUSON, Blanche Smith. *Blossoms in the Moon.* (1934). Penn. sgn. 307p. F/VG. H1. $6.00

FERGUSON, Bruce. *Shadow of His Wings.* 1987. Arbor. 1st ed/author's 1st novel. M/dj. M21. $20.00

FERGUSON, Charles. *Third of a Century in the Gold Fields.* 1888. Williams Pub. 507p. G. scarce. B34. $80.00

FERGUSON, Donald. *Chums of Scranton High or Out for the Pennant.* 1919. World. rpt. VG/VG. P8. $30.00

FERGUSON, George Oscar. *Psychology of the Negro.* 1970. Westport, CT. Negro U. rpt. 138p. F. K4. $12.50

FERGUSON, Henry. *Harpoon. Life Aboard a Norwegian Whaler.* 1936. London. Newnes. 244p. dj. T7. $40.00

FERGUSON, James. *Select Mechanical Excercises: Shewing How To Construct...* 1773. London. Cadell. 9 fld engraved pl. 272p. new ep. rebacked spine. K1. $175.00

FERGUSON, John. *Studies in Christian Social Commitment.* 1954. London. Independent Pr. 1st ed. 12mo. 128p. VG/dj. V3. $10.00

FERGUSSON, Bruce. *Mace of Souls.* 1989. Morrow. 1st ed. F/F. P3. $21.00

FERGUSSON, Bruce. *Shadow of His Wings.* 1987. Arbor. 1st ed. F/F. P3. $17.00

FERGUSSON, Erna. *Dancing Gods. Indian Ceremonials of NM & AZ.* 1931. NY. Knopf. 1st ed. sgn. 276p. G. B11. $45.00

FERGUSSON, Erna. *Dancing Gods. Indian Ceremonials of NM & AZ.* 1957. NM U. ils. 276p. red cloth. NF/worn. P4. $75.00

FERGUSSON, Erna. *Guatemala.* 1949. Knopf. 8vo. 317p. cream cloth. B11. $15.00

FERGUSSON, Harvey. *Grant of Kingdom.* 1950. Morrow. 1st ed. F/dj. A18. $75.00

FERGUSSON, Harvey. *Wolf Song.* 1927. Knopf. 1st ltd ed. 1/100. sgn. F. A18. $350.00

FERLINGHETTI, Lawrence. *Canticle of Jack Kerouac.* 1993. Limberlost. letterpress ed. sgn. 1/50 (335 total). F/wrp. L3. $45.00

FERLINGHETTI, Lawrence. *Love in the Days of Rage.* 1988. Bodley Head. 1st ed. VG/VG. B3. $20.00

FERMAN, Edward L. *Best Fantasy Stories From Fantasy & Science Fiction.* 1985. Octopus. F/F. P3. $15.00

FERMAN, Edward L. *Best From Fantasy & SF, 23rd Series.* 1980. Doubleday. 1st ed. F/NF. N3. $10.00

FERMAN, Edward L. *Magazine of Fantasy & SF: A 30 Year Retrospective.* nd. Doubleday. BC. intro Asimov. VG+/dj. M21. $5.00

FERMAN & MALZBERG. *Arena: Sports.* 1976. Doubleday. 1st ed. pres. VG/dj. N2. $5.00

FERMI, Enrico. *Thermodynamics.* 1956 (1936). Dover. rpt. pb. 160p. K5. $6.00

FERRARI, Giulio. *La Terricotta e Pavementi in Laterizio Nell'Arte Italiana.* 1928. Milano. Ulrico Hoepli. 4to. Eng/Italian text. ils. gr cloth. NF. F1. $50.00

FERRARS, Elizabeth X. *Alibi for a Witch.* 1952. Crime Club. 1st ed. VG/VG. P3. $20.00

FERRARS, Elizabeth X. *Depart This Life.* 1958. Crime Club. 1st ed. VG/VG. P3. $25.00

FERRARS, Elizabeth X. *Hunt the Tortoise.* 1950. Crime Club. 1st ed. VG/VG. P3. $15.00

FERRARS, Elizabeth X. *Last Will & Testament.* 1978. Crime Club. 1st ed. VG/G. P3. $13.00

FERRARS, Elizabeth X. *Small World of Murder.* 1973. Crime Club. 1st ed. NF/dj. F4. $18.00

FERRARS, Elizabeth X. *Smoke Without Fire.* 1990. Crime Club. 1st ed. VG/VG. P3. $18.00

FERRARS, Elizabeth X. *Thinner Than Water.* 1982. Doubleday. 1st ed. VG/VG. P3. $15.00

FERRARS, Elizabeth X. *Witness Before the Fact.* 1979. London. Collins. 1st ed. F/F. S6. $20.00

FERRE, Nels F.S. *Living God of Nowhere & Nothing.* 1966. Phil. Westminster. 1st ed. 237p. NF/dj. W1. $10.00

FERRERO, Guglielmo. *Characters & Events of Roman Hist...* 1922. Putnam. 8vo. 275p. VG. W1. $12.00

FERRI, Helen. *Watch Me, Said the Jeep.* 1944. Garden City. 1st ed. ils Tibor Gergely. VG+. C8. $30.00

FERRIERE, Adolphe. *Psychological Types & Stages of Man's Development.* 1958. Heinemann. 154p. F/dj. K4. $15.00

FERRIS, James Cody. *X-Bar-X Boys at the Round Up.* 1927. Grosset Dunlap. 1st ed. 212p. VG/dj. M20. $15.00

FERRIS, M.W. *Dawes-Gates Ancestral Lines.* 1931 & 1943. private prt. 2 vol. VG. A9. $80.00

FERRIS, Paul. *High Places.* 1977. CMG. 1st ed. VG/VG. P3. $15.00

FERRIS, Warren Angus. *Life in the Rocky Mountains, 1830-1835.* 1940. Salt Lake City. Rocky Mtn Book Shop. sq 8vo. 284p. M. H4. $85.00

FERVAL, Claude. *Cleopatra.* 1924. Garden City. 1st ed. 8vo. 321p. VG/dj. W1. $20.00

FEUCHTWANGER, Lion. *Proud Destiny.* 1947. Viking. 1st ed. VG/G. P3. $18.00

FEUER, Samuel. *Spinoza & the Rise of Liberalism.* 1958. Beadon. sm 8vo. ochre cloth. VG/dj. G1. $25.00

FEUERSTEIN, Georg. *Holy Madness: Shock Tactics & Radical Teachings...* 1991. Paragon. 296p. F/F. B33. $20.00

FEUTER, Edward Byron. *Mulatto in the US.* 1969. NY. Negro U. 417p. cloth. VG. A17. $15.00

FEWKES, J. Walter. *Archeological Field-Work on Mesa Verde National Park, CO.* 1923. Smithsonian. 8vo. VG/wrp. P4. $25.00

FICHTE, Johann Gottlieb. *Grundlage des Naturrechts Nach Principien...* 1796-1797. Jena/Leipzig. Gabler. 2 vol in 1. 1st ed. drab brd. K1. $400.00

FICHTENBAUM, Paul. *World of Major League Baseball.* 1987. Combe Books. VG/VG. P3. $10.00

FIDLER, Isaac. *Observations on Professions, Manners & Emigration in US...* 1833. np. 1st Am ed. 8vo. 247p. VG. E5. $65.00

FIEDLER, Leslie A. *Olaf Stapledon, a Man Divided.* 1983. Oxford. 1st ed. VG. P3. $20.00

FIEDLER, Maggi. *Corky's Pet Parade.* 1946. NY. lg 8vo. 32p. VG. A17. $15.00

FIELD, Edward Salisbury. *Twin Beds.* nd. Grosset Dunlap. photoplay ed. VG. P3. $20.00

FIELD, Eugene. *Favorite Poems.* 1940. NY. ils Malthe Hasselriis. VG+/dj. M5. $20.00

FIELD, Eugene. *Love Affairs of a Bibliomaniac.* 1896. Scribner. VG. N2. $20.00

FIELD, Eugene. *Wynken Blynken & Nod & Other Verses.* 1930. Saalfield. folio. ils FB Peat. F/prt wrp. F1. $50.00

FIELD, Evan. *What Nigel Knew.* 1981. Potter. 1st ed. F/F. F4. $18.00

FIELD, Henry M. *Among the Holy Hills.* 1884. Scribner. 1st ed. 243p. xl. VG. W1. $14.00

FIELD, Henry M. *Barbary Coast.* 1893. Scribner. 1st ed. xl. G. W1. $14.00

FIELD, Henry M. *From the Lakes of Killarney to the Golden Horn.* ca 1880. Scribner. 11th ed. teg. VG. W1. $18.00

FIELD, Henry M. *Gibraltar.* 1889. Scribner. ne. 8vo. xl. G. W1. $12.00

FIELD, Henry M. *Greek Islands & Turkey After the War.* 1885. NY. 8vo. 228p. gilt cloth. O2. $40.00

FIELD, James T. *Yesterday With Authors.* (1900). Houghton Mifflin. 419p. teg. gilt bl cloth. VG. S11. $20.00

FIELD, Louise A. *Peter Rabbit Goes to School.* 1917. Saalfield. ils FB Peat/Virginia Albert. VG/worn. M5. $70.00

FIELD, Mark. *Doctor & Patient in Soviet Russia.* 1957. Cambridge. 266p. A13. $40.00

FIELD, Oliver P. *Civil Service Law.* 1939. NM U. 286p. xl. VG. D3. $25.00

FIELD, Rachel. *All Through the Night.* 1940. Macmillan. 1st ed. 38p. VG/VG. A3. $10.00

FIELD, Rachel. *Bird Began To Sing.* 1932. Morrow. 1st ed. ils. 64p. NF/VG. P2. $45.00

FIELD, Rachel. *Pocket-Handkerchief Park.* 1929. Doubleday Doran. 1st ed. ils. 60p. F. P2. $35.00

FIELD, Rachel. *Yellow Shop.* 1931. Doubleday Doran. 1st ed. 62p. red plaid ep. G+. P2. $22.00

FIELD, Thomas W. *Essay Towards an Indian Bibliography.* 1951. Columbus. Long's College Book Co. 430p. bl cloth. VG. P4. $175.00

FIELDING, A. *Death of John Tait.* 1932. Kinsey. 1st ed. VG. P3. $15.00

FIELDING, Henry. *Complete Works. Memoir by T Roscoe.* ca 1860. London. ils Cruikshank. leather/brd/defective label. A15. $25.00

FIELDING, Henry. *Works of...* 1871-1872. London. 11 vol set. smooth calf/raised bands. A15. $300.00

FIELDING, T.H. *Art of Engraving. With Various Modes of Operation.* 1844. London. 8vo. 109p. VG. B14. $125.00

FIELDING, Xan. *Stronghold: Account of the Four Seasons in Wht Mtns Crete.* 1953. London. 1st ed. 8vo. 317p. cloth. dj. O2. $150.00

FIEY, J.M. *Assyrie Chretienne. Contribution a l'Etude de l'Historie...* 1965. Beyrouth. 2 vol. thick 8vo. quarter morocco. F. O2. $125.00

FIFE, George Buchanan. *Lindbergh, the Lone Eagle: His Life & Achievements.* 1927. Al Burt. VG. N2. $5.00

FIGES, Eva. *Tree of Knowledge.* 1990. London. Sinclair Stevenson. 1st ed. NF/NF. B3. $20.00

FIGUEROA, Jose. *Manifiesto to the Mexican Republic...* 1978. Berkeley. 1st prt this ed. 156p. brn cloth. P4. $30.00

FILCHNER, Wilhelm. *Hui-Hui. Asiens Islamkampfe.* 1928. Berlin. 1st ed. 8vo. 433p. G. W1. $8.00

FILORAMO, Giovanni. *History of Gnosticism.* 1990. Cambridge. Basil Blackwell. 1st ed. 269p. F/F. B33. $45.00

FILSON, Rex B. *Lichens & Mosses of Mac Robertson Land.* 1966. Burwood, Australia. Dept External Affairs. 1st ed. ils. 169p. M/M. P4. $75.00

FINCH, Christopher. *Art of Walt Disney From Mickey Mouse to Magic Kingdom.* 1973. Abrams. 1st ed. NF/VG+. C8. $175.00

FINCH, Edith. *Carey Thomas of Bryn Mawr.* 1947. London. Harper. 1st ed. 8vo. 342p. VG/dj. V3. $14.00

FINCH, J.K. *Topographic Maps & Sketch Mapping.* 1920. John Wiley. 1st ed. 175p. gr cloth. rear pocket map. VG. M20. $20.00

FINCH, Jeremiah S. *Sir Thomas Browne: A Doctor's Life of Science & Faith.* 1950. NY. 1st ed. ils/biblio/index. VG. A17. $10.00

FINCH, Jeremiah S. *Sir Thomas Browne: A Doctor's Life of Science & Faith.* 1950. NY. Schuman. 1st ed. ils. 319p. VG/VG. G7. $25.00

FINCK, William John. *Lutheran Landmarks & Pioneers in America.* 1917. Phil. 2nd ed. 200p. cloth. VG. M8. $30.00

FINDLAY & FINDLAY. *Your Rugged Constitution: What It Says...* 1952. Stanford. 282p. VG/dj. B29. $4.00

FINDLEY, Ferguson. *Waterfront.* 1951. DSP. 1st ed. VG. P3. $15.00

FINDLEY, Ferguson. *Man in the Middle.* 1952. Little Brn. 1st ed. F/NF. M15. $25.00

FINDLEY, Paul. *Abraham Lincoln: Crucible of Congress.* 1979. Crown. ils. 270p. F/dj. M10. $16.50

FINDLEY, Timothy. *Last of the Crazy People.* 1967. NY. 1st ed. sgn. F/F. A11. $125.00

FINE, Anne. *Killjoy.* 1987. Mysterious. 2nd ed. VG/VG. P3. $15.00

FINE, Benjamin. *Stranglehold of the IQ.* 1975. Doubleday. 251p. F/dj. K4. $8.50

FINE, Stephen. *Molly Dear.* 1988. St Martin. 1st ed. F/F. P3. $19.00

FINER, Steven. *Trade Catalogues.* 1990. MA. Finer. F/wrp. A10. $6.00

FINGARETTE, Herbert. *Self-Deception.* 1969. London. Routledge. 12mo. red cloth. VG/dj. G1. $25.00

FINGER, Charles. *Courageous Companions.* 1929. Longman Gr. 1st ed. ils/inscr James Daugherty. 304p. F/VG. P2. $75.00

FINGER, Stanley. *Origins of Neuroscience: A History of Explorations...* 1994. NY. 1st ed. 462p. A13. $75.00

FINK & MILLER. *Neon Signs.* 1935. NY. 1st ed. VG/dj. C11. $65.00

FINKELMAN, Paul. *Free Blacks in a Slave Society.* 1989. NY. Garland. vol 17 in series. M11. $15.00

FINLAND, Maxwell. *Harvard Medical Unit at Boston City Hospital... Vol I.* 1982. Boston. 903p. cloth. F/F. B14. $45.00

FINLAY, George. *History of Greece From Its Conquest by the Romans...* 1877. Oxford. 7 vol. 8vo. gilt cloth. scarce. O2. $625.00

FINLAY, George. *Remarks on Topography of Oropia & Diacria...* 1838. Athens. Antoniades. inscr to SG Howe. 39p. half calf. unopened. O2. $550.00

FINLAY, Virgil. *Astrology Sketchbook.* 1975. Donald Grant. 1st ed. VG. P3. $25.00

FINLAY, Virgil. *Virgil Finlay's Women of the Ages.* 1992. Underwood Miller. 1st ed. fwd LF Hernandez. F/F. T2. $25.00

FINLEY, John. *Pilgrim in Palestine.* 1920. Scribner. 8vo. 251p. VG. W1. $18.00

FINLEY, R. *Old Patchwork Quilts & Women Who Made Them.* 1929. Phil. 1st ed. VG. B5. $100.00

FINNE, K.N. *Igor Sikorsky: The Russian Years.* 1987. Eng. 1st Eng ed. 223p. VG/dj. B19. $25.00

FINNEY, Charles G. *Circus of Doctor Lao.* 1946. Abramson. 1st ed thus. F/NF. M2. $45.00

FINNEY, Charles G. *Circus of Doctor Lao.* 1984. Newark, VT. Janus. 1/150. sgn. ils/sgn VanVliet. 123p. M/clamshell box. B24. $1,500.00

FINNEY, Jack. *Body Snatchers.* 1979. Tokyo. 1st Japanese ed. inscr. F/F. A11. $55.00

FINNEY, Jack. *Night People.* 1977. Doubleday. 1st ed. VG/VG. P3. $30.00

FINNEY, Jack. *Third Level.* 1957. Rinehart. 1st ed. VG/VG. P3. $85.00

FINNIE, Richard. *Lure of the North.* 1940. McKay. ils. 227p. VG/VG. T7. $40.00

FINNIE, Richard. *Lure of the North.* 1940. Phil. photos/index. VG. A17. $25.00

FINOTTI. *Bibliographia Catholica Americana.* 1971. np. 318p. F. A4. $35.00

FIRBANK, Ronald. *Prancing Nigger.* 1924. NY. intro C VanVechten. 126p. VG. E5. $45.00

FIRBANK, Ronald. *Valmouth.* 1919. London. Grant Richards. 1st ed. inscr. NF. very rare. B4. $1,500.00

FIREMAN, Bert. *AZ: Historic Land.* 1982. Knopf. UP/author's last book. 255p. VG/wrp. B19. $15.00

FIREMAN, Judy. *Ultimate TV Book.* 1977. Workman. TVTI. VG. P3. $20.00

FIRESTONE, Harvey S. *Man on the Move: Story of Transportation.* 1967. NY. 1st ed. sgn. 318p. VG/dj. B18. $22.50

FIRMIN, Giles. *Real Christian; or, Treatise of Effectual Calling...* 1742. Boston. Edwards Blanchard. 328p. tooled leather. H10. $125.00

FIRSOFF, V.A. *Ski Track on Battlefield.* 1943. NY. 1st ed. ils. 158p. VG. B5. $35.00

FIRSOFF, V.A. *Strange World of the Moon.* 1959. Basic. 1st Am prt. 12 pl. 226p. G/dj. K5. $20.00

FISCHEL & VON BOEHM. *Modes & Manners of the 19th Century.* 1927. London. 4 vol. revised/enlarged ed. trans Edwardes. teg. morocco. VG. B18. $175.00

FISCHER, Bruno. *Quoth the Raven.* 1944. Crime Club. 1st ed. VG. P3. $25.00

FISCHER, John. *Real Christians Don't Dance!* 1988. Bethany. 191p. F/F. B29. $5.50

FISH, Robert L. *Murder League.* 1968. Simon Schuster. 1st ed. F/dj. F4. $25.00

FISH, Robert L. *Pursuit.* 1978. Doubleday. 1st ed. VG/VG. P3. $20.00

FISHBEIN, Morris. *Doctors at War.* 1945. NY. 1st ed. photos/index. 418p. G. A17. $8.50

FISHBEIN, Morris. *Medical Writing: Technic & Art.* 1938. Chicago. 1st ed. 212p. A13. $25.00

FISHER, Clay. *Big Pasture.* 1955. Houghton Mifflin. 1st ed. VG/dj. B34. $25.00

FISHER, Clay. *Brass Command.* 1955. Houghton Mifflin. 1st ed. inscr. F. A18. $175.00

FISHER, George D. *Hist & Reminiscences of the Monumental Church, Richmond...* 1880. Richmond. 1st ed. 508p. VG. M8. $45.00

FISHER, Harrison. *Hiawatha.* 1906. Indianapolis. 1st ed. VG. B5. $150.00

FISHER, Jane. *Fabulous Hoosier.* 1947. NY. 1st ed. VG/partial dj. B5. $35.00

FISHER, Leonard Everett. *Noonan.* 1978. Doubleday. 1st ed. F/VG. P8. $17.50

FISHER, Leonard Everett. *Oregon Trail.* 1990. Holiday. 1st ed. photos/maps/index. M/dj. A18. $15.00

FISHER, Lizette Andrews. *Mystic Vision.* 1966. NY. AMS Pr. facsimile 1917 ed. 148p. F. B33. $20.00

FISHER, M.F.K. *Cordiall Water: A Garland of Odd & Old Receipts...* 1958. London. 1st Eng ed of this collection. inscr/dtd 1988. F/F. A11. $115.00

FISHER, M.F.K. *Long Ago in France.* 1991. Prentice Hall. 1st ed. F/F. B3. $25.00

FISHER, M.F.K. *Serve It Forth.* 1937. NY. 1st ed/author's 1st book. inscr/dtd 1990. VG+. A11. $135.00

FISHER, M.F.K. *To Begin Again.* 1992. Pantheon. 1st ed. F/F. B3. $25.00

FISHER, M.K.F. *Here Let Us Feast.* 1946. NY. 1st ed. VG/dj. C11. $40.00

FISHER, Paul R. *Hawks of Fellheath.* 1980. Atheneum. 1st ed. VG/VG. P3. $18.00

FISHER, Richard Swainson. *Chronological History of the Civil War in America.* 1863. NY. Johnson Ward. 8vo. 8 double-p maps. 160p. H9. $550.00

FISHER, Stanley W. *English Water Colours.* 1970. London Lock. ils. 256p. NF/dj. M10. $12.50

FISHER, Steve. *Hell-Back Night.* 1970. Sherbourne. 1st ed. NF/NF. P3. $25.00

FISHER, Steve. *Saxon's Ghost.* 1969. Sherbourne. 1st ed. NF/NF. P3. $30.00

FISHER, Steve. *Take All You Can Get.* 1955. Random. 1st ed. NF/VG. F4. $27.50

FISHER, Sydney George. *William Penn: A Biography.* 1932. Lippincott. Anniversary ed. 12mo. 392p. VG. V3. $12.00

FISHER, Sydney Nettleton. *Middle East: A Hist.* 1959. Knopf. 2nd ed. 749p. VG. W1. $12.00

FISHER, Vardis. *Adam & the Serpent.* 1947. NY. 1st ed. VG/VG. B5. $60.00

FISHER, Vardis. *April: A Fable of Love.* 1937. Caxton. 1st ed. F/VG+. A18. $75.00

FISHER, Vardis. *Children of God.* 1939. Harper. 1st ed. VG/VG. P3. $45.00

FISHER, Vardis. *City of Illusion.* 1941. NY Harper. 1st ed. VG/G. B5. $35.00

FISHER, Vardis. *Darkness of the Deep.* 1943. Vanguard. 1st ed. F/dj. A18. $40.00

FISHER, Vardis. *Golden Rooms.* 1944. Vanguard. VG/G. P3. $23.00

FISHER, Vardis. *Golden Rooms.* 1944. Vanguard. 1st ed. F/dj. A18. $35.00

FISHER, Vardis. *Idaho: Guide in Word & Picture.* 1937. Caxton. 1st ed. F/F. A18. $200.00

FISHER, Vardis. *Love & Death: Complete Stories.* 1959. Doubleday. 1st ed. F/dj. A18. $50.00

FISHER, Vardis. *Neurotic Nightingale.* 1935. Casanova. 1st ed. sgn. 1/300. VG+/dj. A18. $175.00

FISHER, Vardis. *No Villain Need Be.* 1936. Caldwell. 1st ed. VG/G. B5. $75.00

FISHER, Vardis. *Passions Spin Plot.* 1934. Caxton. 1st ed. VG/VG. B5. $75.00

FISHER, Vardis. *Pemmican.* 1956. Doubleday. 1st ed. F. A18. $35.00

FISHER, Vardis. *Tale of Valor.* 1958. Doubleday. 1st ed. VG. P3. $25.00

FISHER, Vardis. *Tale of Valor.* 1958. Garden City. 1st ed. VG/VG. B5. $40.00

FISHER, Vardis. *Toilers of the Hills.* 1928. Houghton Mifflin. 1st ed. F/rpr. A18. $100.00

FISHER, W.B. *Middle East: Physical, Social & Regional Geography.* 1956. London/NY. Methuen/Dutton. 3rd ed. xl. G. W1. $10.00

FISHER & HARSHBARGER. *Flower Family Album.* 1941. Minneapolis. BC. ils. 131p. VG/dj. B26. $12.50

FISHER & LOCKWOOD. *Astronomy.* 1940. Wiley. 8vo. 205p. bl cloth. G. K5. $10.00

FISK, Nicholas. *Lindbergh the Lone Flyer.* 1968. Coward McCann. 1st Am ed. VG+/VG. C8. $17.50

FISK, Nicholas. *Space Hostages.* 1984. Kestrel. brd. VG. P3. $15.00

FISKE, John. *Darwinism & Other Essays.* 1879. London. Macmillan. sgn RG Hazard. 283p. emb pebbled bl cloth. NF. G1. $125.00

FISKE, John. *Dutch & Quaker Colonies in America.* 1899. Houghton Mifflin. 2 vol. 12mo. VG. V3. $17.50

FISKE, John. *Outlines of Cosmic Philosophy, Based on Doctrine Evolution.* 1874. London. Macmillan. 2 vols. pebbled brn cloth/gilt spine. NF. G1. $150.00

FISKE, Turbese Lummis. *Charles F Lummis: Man & His West.* 1975. OK U. ils/notes/index. 230p. NF/NF. B19. $50.00

FITCH, Brian. *Narcissistic Text: Reading of Camus' Fiction.* 1982. Toronto U. 128p. prt silver cloth. G1. $22.50

FITCH, C.G. *Handling & General Management of Thoroughbred Stallion.* nd (1947). Hutchinson. 1st ed. VG/fair. O3. $25.00

FITCH, Samuel S. *Six Lecturesx on Uses of the Lungs.* 1847. NY. Carlisle. 324p. G/wrp. A10. $40.00

FITTER, B.S. *Show & Working Whippet.* 1947. Great Britain. 1st ed. pres. 72p. wrp. very scarce. R2. $250.00

FITZGERALD, Ed. *Ballplayer.* 1957. Barnes. 1st ed. VG+/VG. P8. $40.00

FITZGERALD, Ed. *College Slugger.* 1950. Barnes. 1st ed. VG/G. P8. $40.00

FITZGERALD, Ed. *Turning Point.* 1948. Barnes. 1st ed. VG/VG. P8. $65.00

FITZGERALD, Edward. *Letters of Edward Fitzgerald to Fanny Kemble 1871-1883.* 1895. NY/London. Macmillan. 1st Am ed. cloth. VG. H4. $50.00

FITZGERALD, Edward. *Letters of...* 1894. London. Macmillan. 2 vol. 1st ed. cloth. VG. H4. $75.00

FITZGERALD, Edward. *More Letters of Edward Fitzgerald.* 1902. London. Macmillan. 1st ed. VG. H4. $35.00

FITZGERALD, Edward. *Rubaiyat of Omar Khayyam, in English Verse.* 1904. Glasgow. Bryce. 52x34mm. 59p. aeg. full red morocco. B24. $225.00

FITZGERALD, Edward. *Rubaiyat.* 1912. NY. Dodge. ils Adelaide Hanscom/Blanche Cumming. brn leather. F. F1. $200.00

FITZGERALD, Emily. *Army Doctor's Wife on the Frontier.* 1962. Pittsburgh. ils. 352p. VG/dj. B18. $9.50

FITZGERALD, F. Scott. *All the Sad Young Men.* 1926. Scribner. 1st ed/1st prt. gilt gr B cloth. F/earliest state dj. H4. $1,000.00

FITZGERALD, F. Scott. *Beautiful & Damned.* 1922. Scribner. 1st ed/1st prt. 8vo. 449p. gilt spine. F/dj/case. H5. $3,000.00

FITZGERALD, F. Scott. *Great Gatsby.* 1925. Scribner. 1st ed/1st prt. 8vo. 218p. gilt gr cloth. VG. H5. $750.00

FITZGERALD, F. Scott. *Great Gatsby.* 1948. London. Grey Walls. 1st ed. F/NF. B4. $85.00

FITZGERALD, F. Scott. *Screenplay for Three Comrads, by Erich Maria Remarque.* 1978. Carbondale, IL. edit/sgn Bruccoli. F/F. A11. $55.00

FITZGERALD, F. Scott. *Taps at Reveille.* 1935. Scribner. 1st ed/1st state (unrevised text p 349-352). F/NF. H5. $2,250.00

FITZGERALD, F. Scott. *This Side of Paradise.* April 1920. Scribner. 1st ed. lacks front ep. VG. H4. $200.00

FITZGERALD, F. Scott. *This Side of Paradise.* 1920. Scribner. 1st ed/3rd prt. 8vo. 305p. VG/case. w/sgn letter. H5. $2,000.00

FITZGERALD, F. Scott. *Vegetable; or, From President to Postman.* 1923. Scribner. 1st ed. 8vo. gilt gr cloth. NF. H5. $1,500.00

FITZGERALD, Kevin. *Quiet Under the Sun.* 1954. Little Brn. 1st ed. VG/torn. P3. $10.00

FITZGERALD, M.J. *Rope-Dancer.* 1985. Random. 1st ed/author's 2nd book. F/F. B3. $10.00

FITZHERBERT, Margaret. *Man Who Was Greenmantle.* 1983. London. John Murray. 1st ed/author's 1st book. 250p. F/NF clip. M7. $55.00

FITZHUGH, Percy Keese. *Pee-Wee Harris: As Good As His Word.* 1925. Grosset Dunlap. lists to #9. 219p. VG/chip. M20. $30.00

FITZHUGH, Percy Keese. *Skinny McCord.* 1928. Grosset Dunlap. 235p. VG/ragged. M20. $30.00

FITZSIMMONS, Cortland. *Death on the Diamond.* 1934. Stokes. 1st ed. VG. P8. $35.00

FITZSIMMONS, Cortland. *Red Rhapsody.* 1933. Stokes. 1st ed. VG. P3. $25.00

FLACELIERE, Robert. *Love in Ancient Greece.* 1962. Crown. 1st Eng ed. 224p. VG/torn. W1. $18.00

FLACH, Frederic F. *Fridericus.* 1980. Lippincott Crowell. 1st ed. VG/G. P3. $13.00

FLACK, Marjorie. *Away Goes Jonathan Wheeler.* 1944. Garden City. 1st ed. ils Marjorie Flack. F. C8. $50.00

FLACK, Marjorie. *Country Bunny & the Little Golden Shoes.* 1939. Houghton Mifflin. ils Marjorie Flack. VG+. P2. $30.00

FLACK, Marjorie. *Restless Robin.* 1937. Houghton Mifflin. unp. VG/dj. M20. $25.00

FLACK, Marjorie. *Walter the Lazy Mouse.* 1937. Doubleday Doran. ils. VG. P2. $25.00

FLACK, Marjorie. *Walter the Lazy Mouse.* 1937. Doubleday Doran. 1st ed. NF/VG+. C8. $75.00

FLAGG, Fannie. *Coming Attractions.* 1981. Morrow. 1st ed/author's 1st book. F/F. S9. $50.00

FLAGG, Fannie. *Coming Attractions.* 1981. NY. 1st ed. VG/VG. B5. $35.00

FLAGG, Fannie. *Fried Green Tomatoes at the Whistle Stop Cafe.* 1987. Random. 1st ed. sgn. F/F. T2. $65.00

FLAGG, James Montgomery. *Celebrities: A Half-Century of Caricature & Portraiture...* 1951. Watkins Glen. G+. N2. $20.00

FLAKE, Otto. *Marquis de Sade With Postscript on Restif de la Bretonne.* 1931. London. Davies. 1st ed. Colonial Ed stp. F. B2. $65.00

FLAMINA, R. *Scarlett, Rhett & a Cast of Thousands.* 1975. NY. 1st ed. VG/VG. B5. $30.00

FLAMMARION, Camille. *Popular Astronomy.* 1897. London. Chatto Windus. 8vo. 686p. bl cloth. G. K5. $9.00

FLANAGAN, Hallie. *Dynamo: Adventure in College Theatre.* 1943. DSP. 1st ed. F/NF. B2. $75.00

FLANAGAN, Richard. *Hunting Variety.* 1973. Putnam. 1st ed. F/VG. N3. $10.00

FLANDERS, Henry. *Must the War Go On?* 1863. Phil. 23p. O8. $12.50

FLANNER, Janet. *Cheri by Colette.* 1929. NY. Boni. 1st ed. ils Herman Post. cloth. VG/dj. Q1. $200.00

FLAUBERT, Gustave. *Madame Bovary.* 1950. Paris. LEC. ils/sgn Pierre Brissaud. F/G case. M19. $50.00

FLAUBERT, Gustave. *Salammbo.* 1886 (1885). London. Saxon. 1st Eng ed. gilt bl cloth. VG/ragged glassine. M20. $80.00

FLAVELL, A.J. *TE Lawrence: The Man & the Legend.* 1988. Oxford. Bodleian Lib. 113p. pict sc. M7. $25.00

FLEETWOOD, Hugh. *Painter of Flowers.* 1972. NY. 1st Am ed/author's 1st book. VG/VG. A17. $8.50

FLEETWOOD, Hugh. *Redeemer.* 1979. Hamish Hamilton. 1st ed. VG/VG. P3. $13.00

FLEETWOOD, John. *History of Medicine in Ireland.* 1951. Dublin. 1st ed. 420p. A13. $75.00

FLEISCHER, Nat. *Gene Tunney, the Enigma of the Ring.* 1931. np. sgn. 127p. cloth. VG. M20. $75.00

FLEISCHER, Nat. *How To Second & How To Manage a Boxer.* 1944. np. 2nd revised ed. 72p. VG/wrp. M20. $15.00

FLEISHMAN, Seymour. *Trip in Space.* 1968. Rand McNally Elf Book 8566. K2. $6.00

FLEISHMAN, Stanley. *Selected Obscenity Cases.* 1968. Los Angeles. 127p. NF/stiff wrp. D3. $15.00

FLEITMANN, Lida L. *Horse in Art From Primitive Times to the Present.* 1931. NY. Payson. 1st ed. sm 4to. G+. O3. $65.00

FLEMING, E. McClung. *RR Bowker: Militant Liberal.* 1952. OK U. 1st ed. 395p. F/dj. M10. $15.00

FLEMING, Ian. *Bonded Fleming.* 1965. Viking. 1st ed. VG/VG. P3. $40.00

FLEMING, Ian. *Diamond Smugglers.* 1957. London. Cape. 1st ed. 8vo. 160p. F/NF. H5. $150.00

FLEMING, Ian. *Diamonds Are Forever.* 1956. London. Cape. 1st ed. 8vo. 257p. silvered blk cloth. NF/VG. H5. $500.00

FLEMING, Ian. *Dr No.* 1958. London Cape. 1st ed. VG. P3. $60.00

FLEMING, Ian. *For Your Eyes Only.* 1960. London. Cape. 1st ed. NF/NF. Q1. $200.00

FLEMING, Ian. *From Russia, With Love.* 1957. London. Cape. 1st ed. F/NF. Q1. $500.00

FLEMING, Ian. *Gilt-Edged Bonds.* 1961. Macmillan. 1st ed thus. 256p. VG/dj. M20. $35.00

FLEMING, Ian. *Ian Fleming Introduces Jamaica.* 1965. Deutsch. 1st ed. edit M Cargill. F/VG clip. F4. $18.00

FLEMING, Ian. *Live & Let Die.* 1954. London. Cape. 1st ed. NF/VG. Q1. $1,000.00

FLEMING, Ian. *Man With the Golden Gun.* 1965. London. Cape. 1st ed. F/NF. A9. $75.00

FLEMING, Ian. *Man With the Golden Gun.* 1965. London. Cape. 1st ed. gilt blk cloth. F/F dj. B24. $100.00

FLEMING, Ian. *Man With the Golden Gun.* 1965. London. Cape. 1st ed. VG/VG. M19/P3. $50.00

FLEMING, Ian. *Man With the Golden Gun.* 1965. NAL. 1st Am ed. 183p. VG/dj. M20. $30.00

FLEMING, Ian. *Man With the Golden Gun.* 1965. NAL. 1st ed. F/dj. F4. $40.00

FLEMING, Ian. *Moonraker.* 1955. London. Cape. 1st ed. NF/NF. Q1. $1,250.00

FLEMING, Ian. *Octopussy & the Living Day-lights.* 1966. London. Cape. 1st ed. 95p. F/F. A4. $25.00

FLEMING, Ian. *Octopussy.* 1966. NAL. 1st ed. F/dj. F4. $40.00

FLEMING, Ian. *On Her Majesty's Secret Ser-vice.* 1963. London. Cape. 1st ed. 8vo. 288p. wht/silver stp dk brn cloth. F/NF. H5. $200.00

FLEMING, Ian. *Spy Who Loved Me.* 1962. Viking. 1st ed. F/clip. F4. $50.00

FLEMING, Ian. *Thrilling Cities.* 1964. NAL. 1st Am ed. lg 8vo. pict cloth. VG. C8. $20.00

FLEMING, Ian. *Thunderball.* 1961. London. Cape. 1st ed. F/F. Q1. $175.00

FLEMING, Ian. *Thunderball.* 1961. London. Cape. 1st ed. VG/G. P3. $50.00

FLEMING, Ian. *You Only Live Twice.* 1964. NAL/World. 1st ed. VG/G. P3. $35.00

FLEMING, Ian. *You Only Live Twice.* 1965. London. Cape. 1st ed. 8vo. 255p. gilt/silver stp blk cloth. NF/NF. H5. $100.00

FLEMING, Joan. *Day of the Donkey Derby.* 1978. London. Collins. 1st ed. F/NF. S6. $22.50

FLEMING, Joan. *Dirty Butter for Servants.* 1971. Hamish Hamilton. 1st ed. VG/VG. P3. $20.00

FLEMING, Joan. *Kill or Cure.* 1968. Ives Washburn. 1st ed. VG/VG. P3. $15.00

FLEMING, Peter. *Brazilian Adventure.* 1934. Scribner. 1st ed. 8vo. 412p. VG/G. B11. $15.00

FLEMING & WOLF. *Rosenbach.* 1960. World. 1st ed. 618p. VG/dj. A10. $35.00

FLETCHER, David. *Accident of Robert Luman.* 1988. London. Macmillan. 1st ed. F/F. S6. $22.50

FLETCHER, David. *Raffles.* 1977. Putnam. 1st ed. F/F. P3. $15.00

FLETCHER, Ifran Kyle. *Splendid Occasions in English History 1520-1947.* nd. London. Cassell. 1st ed. obl 4to. 138p. gilt bl cloth. dj. K1. $45.00

FLETCHER, Inglis. *Queen's Gift.* 1952. Bobbs Merrill. 1st ed. VG/VG. P3. $20.00

FLETCHER, J.S. *Murder of the Ninth Baronet.* 1932. Knopf. 1st Am ed. F/clip. M15. $45.00

FLETCHER, Lucille. *...And Presumed Dead.* 1963. Random. 1st ed. VG. P3. $10.00

FLETCHER, Sydney. *American Indian From Prehistoric Times to Present.* 1954. Grosset. VG. B34. $15.00

FLINN, John J. *Official Guide to the World's Columbian Exposition.* 1893. np. photos. VG. M17. $20.00

FLINT, Kenneth C. *Storm Shield.* 1986. Bantam. UP/1st ed. lg format. F/prt wrp. N3. $15.00

FLIPPO, C. *Your Cheatin' Heart.* 1981. NY. 1st ed. VG/VG. B5. $22.50

FLORENCE, Ronald. *Perfect Machine.* 1994. Harper Collins. 2nd prt. M/dj. K5. $27.00

FLORENCE, Ronald. *Zeppelin.* 1982. NY. 1st ed. F/F. A17. $9.50

FLORESCU, Radu. *In Search of Franken-stein.* 1975. Boston. NY Graphic Soc. 1st ed. ils. F/NF clip. N3. $25.00

FLORESCU, Radu. *In Search of Franken-stein.* 1975. NY Graphic Soc. 1st ed. VG/VG. P3. $20.00

FLORESCU & MCNALLY. *Dracula: Prince of Many Faces.* 1989. Little Brn. 1st ed. M/dj. M21. $30.00

FLORIN, Lambert. *Western Wagon Wheels.* 1970. Bonanza. photos/drawings. xl. VG/dj. B34. $18.00

FLOWER, Pat. *Vanishing Point.* 1977. Stein Day. VG/VG. P3. $10.00

FLUGEL, J.C. *Hundred Years of Psychology.* 1970. Internat U Pr. 358p. M/dj. K4. $15.00

FLYNN, Errol. *My Wicked Ways.* 1959. NY. 1st ed. VG/VG. B5. $25.00

FLYNN, Errol. *Showdown.* 1946. NY. 1st ed. VG/G. B5. $30.00

FLYNN, George L. *Vince Lombardi on Foot-ball.* 1973. NY Graphic Soc. 2 vol. ils. intro Red Smith. VG/case. B18. $45.00

FOCH, Ferdinand. *Principles of War.* 1918. NY. 9 fld pocket maps. 372p. G. A17. $15.00

FOERSTER, E. *Schiller-Gallery.* ca 1880. NY. Stroefer Kirchner. 22 mtd photos. full red leather. NF. F1. $135.00

FOKKER & GOULD. *Flying Dutchman: Life of Anthony Fokker.* 1921. NY. 1st ed. 282p. G/dj. B18. $125.00

FOLEY, Cornelia MacIntyre. *Mele & the Fire-Woman.* 1952. Honolulu. pl. cloth. F. M5. $40.00

FOLEY, J.W. *Songs of School Days.* 1906. Doubleday. 1st ed. silhouttes Katherine G Buffum. gilt gr cloth. VG. M5. $60.00

FOLEY, Rae. *Last Gamble.* 1956. Dodd Mead. 1st ed. VG/VG. P3. $29.00

FOLEY, Rae. *Trust a Woman?* 1973. Dodd Mead. 1st ed. VG/G. P3. $15.00

FOLEY & LORD. *Folk Arts & Crafts of New England.* 1965. NY. Chilton. 1st ed. 4to. 282p. F/VG. B11. $75.00

FOLLETT, Ken. *Lie Down With Lions.* 1986. Morrow. F/F. P3. $19.00

FOLLETT, Wilson. *Modern American Usage: A Guide.* 1966. Hill Wang. 1st ed. 436p. VG/dj. M10. $5.00

FOLSOM, Franklin. *Days of Anger, Days of Hope.* 1994. Niwot. 1st ed. 376p. F/F. B2. $27.50

FOLTZ, Charles S. *Surgeon of the Seas.* 1931. Indianapolis. 1st ed. ils. 350p. VG/torn. B18. $9.50

FOMON, Samuel. *Medicine & the Allied Sci-ences.* 1920. Appleton. 532p. G. H1. $8.00

FONER, Philip S. *History of Labor Move-ment in the United States...* 1947. NY. Internat Pub. VG/dj. V4. $25.00

FONER, Philip S. *Life & Writings of Freder-ick Douglas.* (1950). Internat Pub. 4 vol. pb. M/G case. H1. $45.00

FONER, Philip S. *Mark Twain, Social Critic.* 1958. Internat Pub. 335p. G/dj. M10. $12.50

FONER & MAHONEY. *House Divided: America in the Age of Lincoln.* 1990. Chicago Hist Soc. 1st ed. ils. 179p. F/dj. M10. $32.50

FONTAINE, L. *North Wind & the Sun: A Fable.* 1964. Franklin Watts. 1st Am ed. 4to. unp. VG/G. A3. $15.00

FONTANA & MATSON. *Friar Bringas Reports to the King.* 1977. AZ U. 1st ed. 177p. F/NF. B19. $35.00

FONTEYN, Margot. *Magic of Dance.* 1979. Knopf. 1st ed. sgn. F/clip. B4. $75.00

FOOSHEE, George Jr. *You Can Be Financially Free.* 1976. Revell. 127p. VG/dj. B29. $3.50

FOOTE, E.B. *Sammy Tuffs, the Boy Doctor & Sponsie, Troublesome Monkey.* 1885 (1874). Murray Hill. Science in Story Vol III. 12mo. VG. D6. $65.00

FOOTE, Horton. *Chase.* 1956. NY. 1st ed/author's 1st novel. NF/VG. A11. $95.00

FOOTE, John T. *Hoofbeats.* 1950. Grosset Dunlap. G. B34. $8.00

FOOTE, John Tainter. *Broadway Angler.* 1937. NY. 1st ed. VG/G. B5. $30.00

FOOTE, John Tainter. *Change of Idols.* 1935. NY. 1st ed. VG/VG. B5. $27.50

FOOTE, John Tainter. *Daughter of Delilah.* 1936. NY. 1st ed. sgn pres. VG/VG. B5. $40.00

FOOTE, John Tainter. *Fatal Gesture.* 1933. NY. 1st ed. VG/VG. B5. $27.50

FOOTE, Shelby. *Shiloh.* 1952. Dial. 1st ed. NF/NF clip. B4. $175.00

FOOTNER, Hulbert. *Doctor Who Held Hands.* 1929. Crime Club. 1st ed. VG. P3. $35.00

FORBES, Allan. *Story of Whaling.* 1961. Nantucket Hist Assn. ils. 28p. wrp. T7. $25.00

FORBES, Allan. *Taverns & Stagecoaches of New England.* 1953 & 1954. Boston. State St Trust. 2 vol. VG. O3. $65.00

FORBES, Colin. *Stockholm Syndicate.* 1982. Dutton. 1st ed. VG/VG. P3. $18.00

FORBES, Edgar Allen. *Leslie's Photographic Review...* 1920. Leslie Judge. photos. VG-. P3. $40.00

FORBES, Eric G. *Tobias Mayer's Opera Inedita.* 1971. Am Elsevier. 7 pl. 166p. VG/torn. K5. $34.00

FORBES, George. *Wonder & Glory of the Stars.* 1926. London. Benn. 1st ed. 16 pl. 221p. gr cloth. G. K5. $16.00

FORBES, Graham. *Boys of Columbia High on Diamond.* 1911. Grosset Dunlap. 1st ed. pict bdg. VG. P8. $20.00

FORBES, Rosita. *Secret of the Sahara: Kufara.* 1921. Doran. 1st ed. 31+2 facsimile pl. VG. W1. $8.00

FORBES, Stanton. *Grieve for the Past.* 1963. Crime Club. 1st ed. VG. P3. $10.00

FORBES, Stanton. *Terror Touches Me.* 1966. Crime Club. 1st ed. VG/VG. P3. $15.00

FORBES-LINDSAY, C.H. *Panama, the Isthmus & the Canal.* 1906. Phil. Winston. 1st ed. 12mo. 368p. G. B11. $45.00

FORBIS & SCHIMANSKI. *Royal Arabians of Egypt & the Stud of Henry B Babson.* 1976. Waco. Thoth. 1st ed. 4to. VG/G. O3. $125.00

FORBUSH, William Byron. *Fox's Book of Martyrs.* 1926. Winston. 370p. VG. B29. $6.00

FORBUSH, William Byron. *Life of Christ.* 1912. Scribner. 162p. VG. B29. $4.00

FORD, A. *John James Audubon.* 1988. index. 528p. O8. $12.50

FORD, Brian. *Single Lens, the Story of the Simple Microscope.* 1985. NY. 1st ed. 182p. dj. A13. $35.00

FORD, Corey. *Salt-Water Taffy.* 1929. Putnam. 2nd prt. 206p. VG/ragged. M20. $20.00

FORD, E.B. *Genetics for Medical Students.* 1967. London. Methuen. 211p. G. K4. $10.00

FORD, Ford Madox. *NY Essays.* 1927. NY. Rudge. sgn/#d. 1/750. orange brd/gilt blk cloth spine. VG. Q1. $200.00

FORD, Gerald. *Global Stability.* 1981. Northridge. Lord John. 75x58mm. 1/100 (of 400). sgn. quarter morocco. F/case. B24. $250.00

FORD, Hilary; see Silverberg, Robert.

FORD, Jesse Hill. *Liberation of Lord Byron Jones.* 1965. Boston. 1st ed. F/F. A17. $10.00

FORD, Lauren. *Little Book About God.* 1934. Doubleday. ils. pict brd/cloth spine. VG. M5. $20.00

FORD, Leighton. *New Man...New World.* 1972. Word. 119p. F/F. B29. $3.00

FORD, Leslie. *Bahama Murders.* 1952. Scribner. 1st ed. NF/NF. F4. $25.00

FORD, Leslie. *Date With Death.* 1949. Scribner. 1st ed. VG/torn. P3. $15.00

FORD, Leslie. *Devil's Stronghold.* 1948. NY. 1st ed. VG/VG. A17. $10.00

FORD, Leslie. *Murder in the OPM.* 1942. Scribner. 1st ed. VG. P3. $18.00

FORD, Mary. *Application of the Rorschach Test to Young Children.* 1946. Minneapolis. 96p. F/dj. K4. $18.75

FORD, Paul Leicester. *New England Primer: Hist of Its Origin & Development...* 1897. Dodd Mead. 1/425. 354p. half leather. H10. $125.00

FORD, Richard. *Chicken Catchers.* 1970. NY. ARC/hc issue. inscr. RS. VG+. A11. $65.00

FORD, Richard. *Wildlife.* 1990. Atlantic Monthly. 1st ed. sgn. NF/F. S9. $45.00

FORD & LANG. *Fighting Southpaw.* nd. Argonaut. 1st ed. VG+/G+. P8. $30.00

FORD & MARTIN. *Musical Fantasies of L Frank Baum.* 1969. Ford. ltd sgn ed. 1/1000. gilt blk cloth. F. S11. $35.00

FORD. *List of the Vernon-Wagner Manuscripts in Lib of Congress.* 1904. np. ils. 152p. VG. A4. $25.00

FOREMAN, Mrs. R.A. *Small Dog Obedience Training.* 1987. Great Britain. 1st ed. 171p. M/wrp. R2. $22.00

FOREMAN, Russell. *Long Pig.* 1958. McGraw Hill. 1st ed. F/dj. F4. $20.00

FORESTER, C.S. *Age of Flighting Sail.* 1956. Doubleday. 1st ed (precedes Eng). NF/VG+. B4. $50.00

FORESTER, C.S. *Age of Flighting Sail.* 1956. np. 1st ed. maps. 300p. VG. E5. $35.00

FORESTER, C.S. *Captain Horatio Hornblower.* 1939. Little Brn. 1st ed. ils NC Wyeth. NF/NF. B4. $150.00

FORESTER, C.S. *Captain Hornblower RN.* 1955. Michael Joseph. 14th prt. VG. P3. $10.00

FORESTER, C.S. *Hornblower During the Crisis.* 1967. Boston. 1st ed. VG/VG. B5. $35.00

FORESTER, C.S. *Hunting the Bismarck.* 1959. Michael Joseph. 1st ed. NF/NF. P3. $30.00

FORESTER, C.S. *Last Nine Days of the Bismarck.* 1959. Little Brn. 1st Am ed. F/F. B4. $50.00

FORESTER, C.S. *Nightmare.* 1954. Little Brn. 1st ed. F/NF. B2. $35.00

FORESTER, C.S. *Poo-Poo & the Dragon.* (1942). Little Brn. 2nd prt. ils Robert Lawson. 143p. VG/G. P2. $40.00

FORESTER, C.S. *Poo-Poo & the Dragon.* 1942. Little Brn. 1st ed. ils Robert Lawson. F/NF. B2. $175.00

FORESTER, C.S. *Sky & the Forest.* 1948. Michael Joseph. 1st ed. VG/VG. P3. $20.00

FORESTER, Frank. *Trouting Along the Catasauqua.* 1927. NY. 1st ed. 1/423. VG. B5. $135.00

FORGET, Jacobus. *De Vita et Scriptis Aphraatis, Sapientis Persae...* 1882. Lovanii. Excudebant Vanlinthout. 353p. VG/wrp. W1. $12.00

FORKOSCH, Morris D. *Essays in Legal Hist in Honor of Felix Frankfurter.* 1966. Bobbs Merrill. M11. $65.00

FORMAN, Charles W. *Faith for the Nations.* nd. Westminster. 94p. G/dj. B29. $2.50

FORMAN, Elizabeth Chandlee. *King of the Air & Other Poems.* 1919. Boston. RG Badger. 16mo. 119p. VG/glassine. V3. $9.50

FORMAN, H.C. *Jamestown & St Marys: Buried Cities of Romance.* 1938. Baltimore. 1st ed. VG/VG. B5. $40.00

FORMAN, James. *Sammy Younge Jr: First Black College Student to Die...* 1968. Grove. 1st ed. inscr. F/F. B2. $85.00

FORMAN & WISE. *Between the Lines: Letters & Memoranda Interchanged by...* 1945. Austin, TX. 1/525. lg 8vo. ils. gilt bl cloth. blk case. K1. $75.00

FORMAN & WOODS. *Pony Express.* 1925. Grosset. ils. G. B34. $25.00

FORRER, Eric. *From the Nets of a Salmon Fisherman.* 1973. NY. 1st ed. 158p. VG/wrp. A17. $7.50

FORREST, Richard. *Death at Yew Corner.* 1981. HRW. 1st ed. F/F. S6. $25.00

FORREST, Richard. *Death at Yew Corner.* 1981. HRW. 1st ed. VG/VG. P3. $15.00

FORRESTER, Frank H. *Fishing With Hook & Line.* ca 1850. NY. O'Kane. possible 1st ed. 64p. pict wrp. scarce. B14. $125.00

FORRESTER, Frank H. *1001 Questions Answered About the Weather.* 1981 (1957). NY. Dover. rpt. pb. K5. $10.00

FORSBERG, Malcolm. *Land Beyond the Nile.* 1958. Harper. 8vo. pl/maps. VG/dj. W1. $14.00

FORSTER, E.M. *Collected Short Stories of EM Forster.* nd (1947?). London. Sidgwick Jackson. 1st ed. 246p. aquamarine cloth. VG+. M7. $30.00

FORSTER, E.M. *Pharos & Pharillion.* 1923. Surrey. Hogarth. 1st ed. 1/900. 80p. teg. sgn 19 AB 75 on bdg. F. F1. $400.00

FORSTER, E.M. *Two Cheers for Democracy.* 1951. London. Arnold. 1st ed. 372p. VG+. M7. $55.00

FORSTER, Thomas. *Researches About Atmospheric Phaenomena.* 1815. London. Baldwin Cradock. 2nd ed. 6 mc pl. 272p. K1. $350.00

FORSTNERUS, Christoph. *Ad Libros Sex Priores Annalium C Cornelii Taciti...* 1650. Leyden. Moyardum. 12mo. 605p. contemporary vellum. K1. $150.00

FORSYTE, Charles. *Decoding of Edwin Drood.* 1980. London. Gollancz. 1st ed. NF/NF. S6. $25.00

FORSYTE, Charles. *Murder With Minarets.* 1968. Cassell. 1st ed. VG/VG. P3. $18.00

FORSYTH, Frederick. *Devil's Alternative.* 1979. Hutchinson. 1st ed. F/F. P3. $30.00

FORSYTH, Frederick. *Fourth Protocol.* 1984. London. Hutchinson. 1st ed. F/F. B3. $30.00

FORSYTH, Frederick. *No Comebacks.* 1982. London. Hutchinson. 1st ed. NF/NF. S6. $30.00

FORSYTH, Frederick. *No Comebacks.* 1982. Viking. VG/VG. P3. $25.00

FORSYTH, William. *Treatise on Culture & Management of Fruit Trees...* 1803. Albany. Whiting. 13 pl. 280p. calf. F. H10. $250.00

FORT, Charles. *Outcast Manufacturers.* 1909. Dodge. 1st ed/author's 1st book. emb red stp bdg. VG+. B2. $100.00

FORTLAGE, K. *Acht Psychologischen Vortrage.* 1869. Jena. Mauke's Verlag. contemporary cloth/marbled brd. G1. $85.00

FORTUNE, Dion. *Esoteric Philosophy of Love & Marriage.* 1967. London. Aquarian. 132p. VG/fair. B33. $12.00

FORTUNE, Dion. *Training & Work of an Initiate.* 1976. NY. Weiser. 126p. VG/VG. B33. $15.00

FORTY & FORTY. *Bovington Tanks.* 1988. Dorset. 1st UK sc ed. photos/ils/7 maps. 160p. M. M7. $25.00

FORWARD, Robert L. *Dragon's Egg.* 1980. Del Rey. 1st ed. F/F. P3. $20.00

FOSDICK, Harry Emerson. *Christianity & Progress.* 1922. Revell. 247p. xl. G. B29. $5.50

FOSDICK, Harry Emerson. *Living Under Tension.* 1941. Harper. 1st ed. 253p. G/torn. B29. $9.00

FOSDICK, Harry Emerson. *Pilgrimage to Palestine.* 1927. Macmillan. 3rd prt. xl. G1. $7.00

FOSDICK, Harry Emerson. *Twelve Tests of Character.* 1923. Assn Pr. 213p. VG. B29. $4.50

FOSS, B.M. *Determinants of Infant Behavior II.* 1963. Methuen. 248p. M/dj. K4. $20.00

FOSS, Clive. *Byzantine & Turkis Sardis.* 1976. Cambridge. 1st ed. 216p. cloth. VG. W1. $22.00

FOSS, Edward. *Memories of Westminster Hall... Vol 2.* 1874. St Louis. 14 pl. 281p. xl. VG. D3. $35.00

FOSTER, Alan Dean *Day of the Dissonance.* 1984. Phantasia. ltd ed. sgn. 1/375 #d. F/F/case. P3. $40.00

FOSTER, Alan Dean *Spoils of War.* 1993. Del Rey. 1st ed. F/F. P3. $20.00

FOSTER, Alan Dean *To the Vanishing Point.* 1988. Warner. 1st ed. NF/NF. P3. $16.00

FOSTER, Alan Dean. *Day of the Dissonance.* 1984. Phantasia. 1st ed. F/dj. M2. $17.00

FOSTER, Alan Dean. *Into the Out Of.* 1986. Warner. 1st ed. F/F. N3. $15.00

FOSTER, Alan Dean. *Star Wars.* nd. BC. MTI. VG/VG. P3. $8.00

FOSTER, Alan Dean. *Star Wars...* 1977. Ballantine. 1st trade hc ed. F/as issued. N3. $35.00

FOSTER, E.M. *EM Foster's Letters to Donald Windham.* 1975. NY/Vernona. Sandy Campbell. 1/300. inscr/dtd 1978. NF/wrp. L3. $125.00

FOSTER, E.M. *Longest Journey.* 1960. London. Oxford. 1st ed. inscr to reviewer Will Beveridge. F/VG clip. B4. $275.00

FOSTER, G. *George Washington's World.* 1946 (1941). Scribner. sgn. 344p. cloth. M20. $25.00

FOSTER, George. *Friedrich Nietzche.* 1931. Macmillan. 12mo. 249p. G. G1. $28.50

FOSTER, George. *Primitive Mexican Economy.* 1942. NY. Augustin. 1st ed. 115p. VG. F3. $20.00

FOSTER, Harry. *Combing the Caribbees.* 1929. Dodd Mead. 1st ed. 12mo. 302p. red cloth. B11. $20.00

FOSTER, Harry. *Vagabond in Barbary.* 1930. Dodd Mead. 1st ed. xl. G. W1. $15.00

FOSTER, J.J. *Dictionary of Painters of Miniatures.* 1926. London. 1st ed. cloth. VG. C11. $40.00

FOSTER, John W. *Century of American Diplomacy.* 1901. np. index. 497p. O8. $12.50

FOSTER, Marian Curtis. *Hotspur.* 1953. Lee Shepard. 1st ed. VG/VG. P2. $45.00

FOSTER, Marian Curtis. *Little Bear Learns To Read the Cookbook.* 1969. Lee Shepard. 1st ed. ils Flora McFlimsey. NF/VG. P2. $35.00

FOSTER, Marian Curtis. *Miss Flora McFlimsey's Christmas Eve.* 1949. Lee Shepard. 1st ed. 12mo. unp. VG-/G. A3. $15.00

FOSTER, Michael. *Text Book of Physiology.* 1893. NY. Macmillan. 4 vol. mixed set of 5th & 6th ed. gr cloth. G7. $250.00

FOSTER, Richard J. *Celebration of Discipline: Path to Spiritual Growth.* 1986. Harper Row. 30th prt. 8vo. 184p. G/chip. V3. $8.00

FOSTER, Robert. *Guide to Middle Earth.* 1971. Mirage. ne. F/dj. M2. $10.00

FOSTER, W. Bert. *In Alaskan Waters.* 1925. Phil. ftspc. G. A17. $9.50

FOSTER, William D. *Cottages, Manors & Other Minor Buildings of Normandy...* 1926. Architectural Book Pub. sm folio. ils/photos. gilt gr cloth. F/dj. F1. $170.00

FOSTER, William Z. *American Trade Unionism: Principles & Organization...* 1947. NY. Internat Pub. VG. V4. $15.00

FOSTER, William Z. *Toward Soviet America.* 1932. Coward McCann. 1st ed. B2/B5. $40.00

FOTHERGILL, John. *Innskeeper's Diary.* 1932. NY. Ballou. lg fld pl. 294p. cloth. worn. G7. $35.00

FOUCAULT, Michel. *Madness & Civilization: Hist of Insanity in Age of Reason.* 1965. Pantheon. 1st Eng-language ed. VG/clip. G1. $75.00

FOULKE, Joseph. *Memoirs of Jacob Ritter, a Faithful Minister...* 1844. Phil. Chapman. 16mo. 111p. marbled brd. V3. $25.00

FOUQUE, De La Motte. *Undine & Other Tales.* nd. Mershon. early rpt. VG. M21. $15.00

FOWLER, Christopher. *Bureau of Lost Souls.* 1989. London. Century. 1st ed. sgn. 1/250. aeg. F/case. F4. $65.00

FOWLER, Christopher. *Rune.* 1990. Ballantine. 1st Am ed. F/F. N3. $15.00

FOWLER, Christopher. *Rune.* 1990. London. Century. 1st ed. sgn. 1/200. F/F/box. F4. $75.00

FOWLER, Ellen T. *Sirens & Other Stories.* 1901. London. 1st ed. NF. M2. $20.00

FOWLER, John M. *Fallout: Study of Super Bombs, Strontium 90, & Survival.* 1960. NY. 2nd prt. 235p. glossary/index. F/F. A17. $15.00

FOWLER, Karen Joy. *Sarah Canary.* 1991. Holt. 1st ed/author's 1st novel. F/F. A14. $35.00

FOWLER, Kenneth. *Jackal's Gold.* 1980. VA City. 1st ed. VG/dj. B34. $20.00

FOWLER, William M. *Jack Tars & Commadores. The American Navy 1783-1815...* 1984. Houghton Mifflin. ils/maps. 318p. dj. T7. $24.00

FOWLER, William W. *Woman of the Amerian Frontier.* 1878. Hartford. VG. M17. $35.00

FOWLER & HELMFELT. *Overcomers' Bible.* 1990. np. TBN Special Ed. 8vo. 12 steps of AA/Bible scripture. 558p. gilt leatherette. A8. $12.00

FOWLES, Anthony. *Double Feature.* 1973. Simon Schuster. ARC of 1st ed. RS. F/F. F4. $27.50

FOWLES, John. *Cinderella. Adapted From Perrault's Cendrillon of 1697...* 1974. London. Cape. 1st ed. 4to. 32p. F/dj. B24. $75.00

FOWLES, John. *Enigma of Stonehenge.* 1980. Jonathan Cape. 1st ed. VG. P3. $15.00

FOWLES, John. *French Lieutenant's Woman.* 1969. Little Brn. 1st Am ed. 8vo. 467p. silver/gilt gray cloth. NF/VG. H5. $75.00

FOWLES, John. *Maggot.* 1985. Boston. Little Brn. 1st ed. F/F. N3. $15.00

FOWLES, John. *Maggot.* 1985. London. ltd. ed. 1/500. sgn. C4. $150.00

FOWLES, John. *Mantissa.* 1982. Boston. 1st ed. F/F. A17. $12.00

FOWLIE, J.A. *Genus Lycaste: Its Speciation, Distribution...* 1970. Pomona. revised ed. ils/pl/maps. 90p. VG+. B26. $37.50

FOWLIE, Wallace. *Mallarme As Hamlet.* 1949. Yonkers. 1st ed. 1/1000. ftspc Picasso. 22p. VG/wrp. A17. $20.00

FOX, Charles James. *Letter From Right Honourable Charles James Fox...* 1793. London. J Debrett. 6th ed. new wrp. D3. $85.00

FOX, Charles. *Mind & Its Body: Foundations of Psychology.* 1932. NY. Harcourt Brace. 1st Am ed. 316p. VG/dj. G1. $30.00

FOX, Frances Margaret. *Little Bear's Playtime.* 1922. Rand McNally. ils Frances Beem. pict brd. VG. M5. $25.00

FOX, Frances Margaret. *Little Toad.* 1938. Viking. 1st ed. ils Sherman Hoeflich. 79p. G. P2. $10.00

FOX, Frances Margaret. *Seven Christmas Candles.* 1909. Page. 1st ed. 192p. ils Etheldred Barry. G+. P2. $20.00

FOX, Gardner F. *Kyrik: Warlock Warrior.* 1976. Herbert Jenkins. 1st Eng/1st hc ed. F/F clip. N3. $15.00

FOX, George. *Amok.* 1978. Simon Schuster. 1st ed. VG/VG. P3. $15.00

FOX, George. *Autobiography.* 1903. Phil. Ferris Leach. 2 vol. 1st ed. 12mo. VG. V3. $22.50

FOX, George. *Journal of George Fox: Revised Ed by John L Nickalls.* 1952. Cambridge. 12mo. 789p. VG. V3. $16.00

FOX, Harold G. *Monopolies & Patents.* 1947. Toronto U. 388p. NF/dj. D3. $45.00

FOX, James M. *Operation Dancing Dog.* 1974. Walker. 1st ed. VG/torn. P3. $15.00

FOX, John. *Erskine Dale, Pioneer.* 1920. Scribner. ils FC Yohn. G. B34. $12.00

FOX, Norman A. *Roughshod.* 1951. Dodd Mead. 1st ed. lib bdg. xl. P3. $5.00

FOX, Paula. *Poor George.* 1967. NY. 1st ed/author's 1st book. sgn. F/NF. A11. $55.00

FOX, R.M. *Factory Echoes & Other Sketches.* nd. London. Daniel. 1st ed. sgn. VG/wrp. B2. $60.00

FOX, Sanford J. *Science & Justice, the MA Witchcraft Trials.* 1968. Johns Hopkins. M11. $50.00

FOX, Theodore. *Crisis in Communication... Future of Medical Journals.* 1965. London. 1st ed. 59p. dj. A13. $30.00

FOX, William Price. *Southern Fried Plus Six.* 1968. Phil. 1st hc ed/author's 1st book. inscr. F/NF. A11. $60.00

FOX & VET. *Abnormal Behavior in Animals.* 1968. Phil. Saunders. 563p. G. K4. $15.00

FOXCROFT, Frank. *War Verse.* 1918. Crowell. 4th prt. 303p. gilt gr cloth. VG. M7. $18.00

FOXX, Jack; see Pronzini, Bill.

FRADKIN, Philip L. *River No More: CO River & the West.* 1981. Knopf. 1st ed. ils. 360p. F/NF. B19. $25.00

FRADY, Marshall. *Across the Darkling Plain: American's Passage...Middle E.* 1971. Harper. 1st ed. 8vo. 199p. F/dj. W1. $8.00

FRAENKEL, Ernst. *Military Occupation & Rule of Law.* 1944. Oxford. 1st ed. 267p. NF/rpr. D3. $45.00

FRAISSE & PIAGET. *Experimental Psychology: Its Scope & Method. Vol IV.* 1964. NY. Basic. 348p. M/dj. K4. $25.00

FRANC-NOHAIN, Marie-Madeleine. *Les Malheurs de Sophie.* 1939. Tours. Maison Mame. 16 pl. pict brd. NF. M5. $125.00

FRANCE, Anatole. *At the Sign of the Queen Pedauque.* 1933. LEC. ils/sgn Sylvain Sauvage. F/M case. M19. $75.00

FRANCE, Anatole. *Honey Bee.* 1911. John Lane. 1st ed thus. ils Florence Lunborg. VG. M5. $40.00

FRANCE, Johnny. *Incident at Big Sky.* 1986. np. 1st ed. F/F. B34. $15.00

FRANCIS, Dick. *Bolt.* 1987. Putnam. 1st ed. VG/VG. P3. $18.00

FRANCIS, Dick. *Edge.* 1989. Putnam. 1st ed. F/F. P3. $18.00

FRANCIS, Dick. *High Stakes.* 1975. Harper Row. 1st ed. VG/VG. P3. $30.00

FRANCIS, Dick. *High Stakes.* 1975. London. Michael Joseph. 1st ed. F/F. M15. $75.00

FRANCIS, Dick. *Hot Money.* 1987. London. Michael Joseph. 1st ed. VG/VG. B3. $20.00

FRANCIS, Dick. *In the Frame.* 1976. Harper Row. 1st ed. F/F. B3. $45.00

FRANCIS, Dick. *In the Frame.* 1976. Michael Joseph. 1st ed. VG/VG. P3. $28.00

FRANCIS, Dick. *Knock Down.* 1974. London. Michael Joseph. 1st ed. F/F. S6. $75.00

FRANCIS, Dick. *Lester: Official Biography.* 1986. London. Michael Joseph. 1st ed. F/F. M15. $50.00

FRANCIS, Dick. *Odds Against.* 1965. London. Michael Joseph. 1st ed. F/F. M15. $250.00

FRANCIS, Dick. *Risk.* 1977. London. Michael Joseph. 1st ed. inscr. F/F. S6. $75.00

FRANCIS, Dick. *Smokescreen.* 1973. Harper Row. 1st ed. VG/VG. P3. $35.00

FRANCIS, Dick. *Straight.* 1989. London. Michael Joseph. 1st ed. sgn. F/F. S6. $50.00

FRANCIS, Dick. *Twice Shy.* 1981. London. Michael Joseph. 1st ed. inscr. F/F. S6. $60.00

FRANCIS, Dick. *Whip Hand.* nd. BC. VG/VG. P3. $8.00

FRANCIS, Dick. *Whip Hand.* 1979. Harper Row. 1st Am ed. F/F. O4. $25.00

FRANCIS, Dick. *Whip Hand.* 1979. London. 1st ed. F/F. O4. $35.00

FRANCIS, Dick. *Wild Horses.* 1984. Bristol. Scorpion. ltd sgn ed. 1/99. F/sans. O4. $175.00

FRANCIS, R. *Egypt & How To See It.* ca 1945. Cairo. 12mo. 23 pl/2 fld maps. VG. W1. $15.00

FRANCIS, Richard H. *Whispering Gallery.* 1984. Norton. 1st ed. VG/VG. P3. $15.00

FRANCIS & FRANCIS. *Summit Beach Park.* 1993. Summit Co Hist Soc. 177p. M. B18. $25.00

FRANCK, Frederick. *Days With Albert Schweitzer: A Lambarene Landscape.* 1959. NY. Holt. 1st ed. 178p. VG/VG. B33. $20.00

FRANCK, Harry A. *Fringe of the Moslem World...* 1928. Century. 1st ed. 63 pl. 426p. VG. W1. $28.00

FRANCK, Harry A. *I Discover Greece Wherein an Incurable Nomad Sets Forth...* 1929. Century. 1st ed. 8vo. 359p. xl. G. W1. $10.00

FRANCK, Harry A. *Lure of Alaska.* (1939). NY. 8vo. ils/fld map. 306p. gilt blk cloth. F/pict dj. H3. $35.00

FRANCK, Harry A. *Vagabonding Down the Andes.* 1917. Garden City, NY. Star. 12mo. 338p. VG/VG. B11. $15.00

FRANCOIS, Yves Regis. *CTZ Paradigm.* 1975. Doubleday. 1st ed. F/F. P3. $15.00

FRANK, Alan. *Galactic Aliens.* 1979. Chartwell. VG/VG. P3. $10.00

FRANK, Anne. *Diary of a Young Girl.* 1953. NY. 1st Pocket Book ed. 239p. pict bdg. VG. B14. $75.00

FRANK, Byrn. *Everyman's England.* 1984. Harper. 1st ed. 296p. F/F. S11. $10.00

FRANK, G. *An American Death: True Story of Assassination Dr ML King.* 1972. NY. 467p. D3. $12.50

FRANK, Jerome. *Courts on Trial: Myth & Reality in Am Justice.* 1949. Princeton. 441p. VG. D3. $32.50

FRANK, Larry. *Portfolio.* 1971. WA, DC. Baker-Webster Prt. 1st ed. NF/wrp. S9. $45.00

FRANK, Pat. *Mr Adam.* nd. Lippincott. 10th prt. VG. P3. $5.00

FRANK, Philip. *Modern Science & Its Philosophy.* 1949. Harvard. 324p. red cloth. VG/dj. G1. $40.00

FRANK, Robert Jr. *Harvey & the Oxford Physiologists: Scientific Ideas...* 1980. Berkeley. 1st ed. 368p. A13. $50.00

FRANKFORT, Henri. *Art & Architecture of the Ancient Orient.* 1958. Baltimore. Penguin. 2nd imp. 280p. gilt red cloth. NF/VG. F1. $35.00

FRANKFURT, Harry G. *Collection of Critical Essays.* 1972. Anchor. trade pb. 16mo. 425p. G1. $17.50

FRANKLIN, Benjamin. *Apology for Printers.* 1955. NY. Book Craftsmen Assoc. 12mo. ils John DePol. F/case. B24. $50.00

FRANKLIN, Benjamin. *Political, Miscellaneous & Philosophical Pieces...* 1779. London. Johnson. 1st ed. 1 fld table/4 pl. 568p. orig calf/rebacked. K1. $1,000.00

FRANKLIN, Benjamin. *Select Works of...,* *Including His Autobiography.* 1855 (1853). Boston. Phillips Sampson. engraved ftspc. 502p. emb cloth. NF. F1. $50.00

FRANKLIN, John. *Narrative of 2nd Expedition to Shores of Polar Sea...1827.* 1969. NY. Greenwood. rpt of 1828 ed. gilt brn cloth. M/sans. P4. $95.00

FRANKLIN, Jonathan. *Mental Science for Everyone.* 1971. London. Regency. 1st ed. 93p. VG. B33. $25.00

FRANKLIN, Wayne. *Discoverers, Explorers, Settles.* 1979. Chicago U. 1st prt. 252p. M/dj. P4. $25.00

FRANKLING, Eleanor. *Popular Dalamatian.* 1954. London. Popular Dogs. 1st ed. ils. 208p. cloth. F. R2. $20.00

FRASER, Anthea. *April Rainers.* 1989. London. Collins. ARC/1st ed. RS. NF/dj. S6. $22.50

FRASER, Anthea. *Splash of Red.* 1981. London. Weidenfeld. 1st ed. F/F. S6. $25.00

FRASER, Anthea. *Symbols at Your Door.* 1990. Collins Crime Club. 1st ed. F/F. P3. $20.00

FRASER, Antonia. *Hist of Toys.* 1966. np. Delacorte. 4to. ils. 256p. F/F. A17. $25.00

FRASER, Antonia. *Jemima Shore's First Case & Other Stories.* 1987. Norton. 1st Am ed. sgn. F/F. O4. $20.00

FRASER, Antonia. *Jemima Shore's First Case & Other Stories.* 1987. Norton. 1st ed. F/F. P3. $15.00

FRASER, Antonia. *Quiet As a Nun.* 1977. Viking. 1st Am ed. sgn. F/F. O4. $25.00

FRASER, Antonia. *Quiet As a Nun.* 1977. Viking. 1st ed. VG/VG. P3. $18.00

FRASER, George MacDonald. *Flash for Freedom!* 1972. Knopf. 1st ed. NF/NF. P3. $45.00

FRASER, George MacDonald. *Flashman & the Mountain of Light.* 1991. Knopf. 1st ed. rem mk. NF/F. B3. $15.00

FRASER, George MacDonald. *Flashman in the Great Game.* 1975. Knopf. 1st Am ed. F/NF. B4. $75.00

FRASER, George MacDonald. *Hollywood Hist of the World.* 1988. Beech Tree/Morrow. 1st Am ed. 4to. F/F. B4. $100.00

FRASER, George MacDonald. *Royal Flash.* 1970. Knopf. 1st Am ed. 257p. VG/worn. M20. $80.00

FRASER, J.T. *Of Time, Passion, & Knowledge: Reflections on...Existence.* 1975. Braziller. 530p. gray cloth. G1. $28.50

FRASER, J.T. *Study of Time III.* 1978. Springer-Verlag. lg 8vo. 727p. prt bl brd. G1. $40.00

FRASER, J.T. *Time & Mind: Interdisciplinary Issues.* 1989. Madison, CT. Internat U Pr. tall 8vo. 314p. bl-gray cloth. VG/dj. G1. $30.00

FRASER, James H. *Paste Papers of the Golden Hind Press.* 1983. Fairleigh Dickinson U. 1/70 on Fabriano paper. ils. M. B24. $350.00

FRASER, John Foster. *Panama & What It Means.* 1913. London/NY. Cassell. 2nd prt. 12mo. 291p. gilt brn cloth. B11. $35.00

FRASER, Robert W. *Kirk & the Manse.* 1857. Edinburgh. 1st ed. lg 4to. 60 full-p tinted pl. VG+. C6. $200.00

FRASER, Sylvia. *Pandora.* 1973. Little Brn. VG/VG. P3. $15.00

FRASSANITO, William A. *Grant & Lee: Virginia Campaigns 1864-1865.* 1983. Scribner. 1st ed. 442p. NF/NF. M20. $40.00

FRAYN, Michael. *Great Railway Journeys of the World.* 1981. Dutton. ils. 182p. F/F. B11. $20.00

FRAZEE, Steve. *Apache Way.* 1969. Whitman. High Chaparral TVTI. VG. P3. $8.00

FRAZEE, Steve. *High Chaparral, Apache Way.* 1969. Whitman. 1st ed. F/sans. F4. $12.00

FRAZEE, Steve. *Swiss Family Robinson.* 1960. Whitman. Disney MTI. VG. P3. $10.00

FRAZER, J. Ernest. *Manual of Embryology.* 1940. Baltimore. 2nd ed. 523p. G7. $20.00

FRAZER, James. *Golden Bough: A Study of Magic & Religion.* 1951. BC. abridged ed. 864p. VG/VG-. B33. $12.00

FRAZIER, Ian. *Dating Your Mom.* 1986. FSG. 1st ed. sgn. F/F. B4. $85.00

FRAZIER, Ian. *Great Plains.* 1989. Farrar. ils/photos. F/F. B34. $15.00

FRAZIER, J.L. *Type Lore: Popular Fonts of Today, Their Origins & Use.* 1925. Chicago. 114p. quarter cloth. G. B18. $35.00

FRAZIER, Robert Caine; see Creasey, John.

FREAS, Frank Kelly. *Art of Science Fiction.* 1977. Donning. 1st ed. F/sans. M2/P3. $35.00

FREDER, Richard. *Secret Circus.* 1967. Random. 1st ed. VG/VG. P3. $25.00

FREDERIC, Harold. *New Exodus: A Study of Israel in Russia.* 1892. NY. Putnam. 1st ed. xl. VG. H7. $75.00

FREDERICA, Queen. *Measure of Understanding.* 1971. NY. 8vo. ils. 207p. cloth. dj. O2. $25.00

FREDMAN, John. *Epitaph to a Bad Cop.* 1973. David McKay. NF/NF. P3. $15.00

FREDRICKSON, Jack M. *Cost Reduction in the Office.* 1984. NY. Am Management Assn. 278p. M/dj. P4. $20.00

FREE, Ann Cottrell. *Forever the Wild Mare.* 1943. Dodd Mead. 1st ed. VG/fair. O3. $18.00

FREE, Joseph P. *Archaeology & Bible Hist.* 1954. Van Kampen. 398p. G. B29. $4.00

FREE, Montague. *All About House Plants.* 1946. Doubleday/Am Garden Guild. 1st ed. 329p. VG/G. H1. $9.50

FREEBORN, Brian. *Good Luck Mister Cain.* 1976. St Martin. 1st ed. VG/G. P3. $12.00

FREEDMAN, Russell. *Children of the Wild West.* 1983. Clarion Books. 11th prt. photos. M/dj. A18. $16.00

FREEDMAN. *Published Works of Wm Foxwell Albright...* 1975. Am Schools for Oriental Research. 242p. NF. A4. $55.00

FREELING, Nicolas. *Cold Iron.* 1986. Viking. 1st ed. NF/NF. P3. $15.00

FREELING, Nicolas. *Tsing-Boum.* 1969. Harper Row. 1st ed. VG/VG. P3. $20.00

FREEMAN, Don. *Bearymore.* 1976. Viking. 1st ed. obl 4to. pict brd. VG-. A3. $15.00

FREEMAN, Don. *Bearymore.* 1976. Viking. 1st ed. xl. VG. C8. $12.50

FREEMAN, Don. *Dandelion.* 1964. Viking. 2nd prt. obl 4to. 48p. VG/VG. A3. $17.50

FREEMAN, Don. *Pet of the Met.* 1953. Viking. 1st ed. 63p. VG-. A3. $25.00

FREEMAN, Douglas Southall. *RE Lee: A Biography.* 1936. Scribner. 4 vol. Pulitzer Prize ed. 8vo. ils. bl fabricoid. F. H9. $250.00

FREEMAN, Douglas Southall. *South to Posterity: Intro to Writings of Confederate Hist.* 1983. np. 277p. F/F. A4. $85.00

FREEMAN, Ellis. *Social Psychology.* 1936. NY. Holt. 469p. G. K4. $10.00

FREEMAN, Frank N. *Mental Tests.* 1939. Riverside. 460p. G. K4. $20.00

FREEMAN, Frederick. *Africa's Redemption. Salvation of Our Country.* 1852. NY. D Fanshaw. 1st ed. 8vo. 383p. cloth. M1. $200.00

FREEMAN, G.L. *How To Buy & Sell Old Books.* 1965. Century. 2nd prt. 100p. gr cloth. xl. VG. S11. $10.00

FREEMAN, Kenneth J. *Schools of Hellas: Essay on Practice & Theory...* 1969. NY. Teachers College. facsimile rpt of London 1907 ed. VG/dj. G1. $25.00

FREEMAN, Larry. *Historical Prints of American Cities.* 1952. Watkins Glen. 1st ed. ils/index. 100p. VG/VG. B5. $35.00

FREEMAN, Lewis R. *In the Tracks of the Trades.* 1920. Dodd Mead. ils. 380p. worn. T7. $40.00

FREEMAN, Lewis R. *Sea-Hounds.* 1919. NY. Dodd Mead. ils. 309p. bl cloth. VG. P4. $45.00

FREEMAN, R. Austin. *Dr Thonrdyke Omnibus.* 1932. Dodd Mead. 1st ed. NF/dj. F4. $75.00

FREEMAN, R. Austin. *Mr Pottermack's Oversight.* 1930. Dodd Mead. 1st ed. VG/torn. P3. $45.00

FREEMAN, R. Austin. *Mystery of Angelina Frood.* 1928. Dodd Mead. 1st Am ed. F/NF clip. F4. $125.00

FREEMAN, R.B. *Charles Darwin: A Companion.* nd. Folkestone. rpt of 1978 ed. 309p. gr cloth. P4. $65.00

FREEMAN, R.B. *Charles Darwin: A Companion.* 1978. London. 1st ed. 309p. VG. A13. $50.00

FREEMAN, R.B. *Works of Charles Darwin: An Annotated Handlist.* 1977. Folkstone/Hamden. Dawson/Archon. 2nd ed. 8vo. 235p. VG. P4. $65.00

FREEMAN & FREEMAN. *You Will Go to the Moon.* 1959. Random. BC. 8vo. 62p. pict brd. G. K5. $8.00

FREEMANTLE, Brian. *Blind Run.* 1986. Bantam. 1st Am ed. sgn. F/F. B2. $40.00

FREEMANTLE, Brian. *Button Man.* 1992. London. Century. 1st ed. NF/dj. S6. $30.00

FREEMANTLE, Brian. *Charlie Muffin's Uncle Sam.* 1980. Jonathan Cape. 1st ed. VG/VG. P3. $25.00

FREEMANTLE, Brian. *Charlie Muffin.* 1977. London. Cape. 1st ed. F/F. S6. $60.00

FREEMANTLE, Brian. *See Charlie Run.* 1987. Bantam. 1st ed. F/F. P3. $16.00

FREEMANTLE, Brian. *Steal.* 1986. Michael Joseph. 1st ed. VG. P3. $20.00

FREEMANTLE & HASKELL. *Two Views of Gettysburg.* 1964. Lakeside. 264p. gilt bl cloth. VG. M20. $25.00

FREEMON, Frank. *Microbes & Minie Balls.* 1993. index. 253p. O8. $18.50

FREES, Harry Whittier. *Little Kitten's Nursery Rhymes.* 1956. Rand McNally. photos. glazed brd. M5. $15.00

FREES, Harry Whittier. *Snuggles.* 1958. Rand McNally. ils. pict brd. VG. M5. $15.00

FREES, Harry Whittier. *Whiskers.* 1941. Rand McNally. 8vo. photos. G. M5. $16.00

FREETH, Zahra. *Kuwait Was My Home.* 1956. Allen Unwin. 164p. VG/dj. W1. $45.00

FREGE, Gottlob. *Philosophical & Mathematical Correspondence. Vol 2.* 1980. Chicago. 1st Am ed. bl cloth. VG/dj. G1. $40.00

FREGE, Gottlob. *Trans From Philosophical Writings of...* 1952. Oxford. Basil Blackwell. thin 8vo. 244p. gr cloth. G1. $50.00

FREIBERGER & PRAGER. *Applications of Digital Computers.* 1963. NY. 321p. F/dj. K4. $15.00

FREIDSON, Eliot. *Medical Men & Their Work.* 1972. Chicago. Aldine. 1st ed. 482p. wrp. A13. $12.50

FREMONT, Jessie Benton. *Year of American Travel.* 1960. San Francisco. Plantin/BC of CA. 1/450. ils Ernest Freed. NF. P4. $95.00

FRENCH, A.P. *Einstein: Centenary Volume.* 1979. Cambridge. 331p. dj. G7. $25.00

FRENCH, Joseph Lewis. *Gallery of Old Rogues.* 1931. NY. King. 8vo. 285p. VG/G. B11. $35.00

FRENCH, Lois Meredith. *Psychiatric Social Work.* 1940. NY. 321p. F/dj. K4. $15.00

FRENCH, Richard. *From Homer to Helen Keller: Social & Educational Study...* 1932. NY. 1st ed. 298p. A13. $45.00

FRENCH, Samuel G. *Two Wars: An Autobiography.* 1901. Nashville. 1st ed. 404p. bl cloth. ES. NF. C6. $475.00

FREUD, Sigmund. *Collected Papers. Authorized Translation.* 1950. London. Hogarth. 5 vol. xl. G. G7. $100.00

FREUD, Sigmund. *General Intro to Psychoanalysis.* 1920. Liveright. 406p. cloth. G. B14. $50.00

FREVERT, Ute. *Krankheit Als Politisches Problem 1770-1880.* 1984. Gottingen. 1st ed. 496p. wrp. A13. $20.00

FREWIN, Anthony. *100 Years of SF Illustration.* 1988. Bloomsbury. VG. P3. $18.00

FREYER, Frederic. *Black Black Hearse.* 1955. St Martin. 1st ed. VG/G. P3. $25.00

FRICERO, Kate. *Little French People.* nd. Blackie. ils. brd/pict label. VG. M5. $95.00

FRICKE, Charles W. *California Criminal Law.* 1946. Los Angeles. OW Smith. M11. $20.00

FRIED, Henry B. *Electric Watch Repair Manual.* 1972. NY, NY. B Jadow. 2nd ed. 8vo. 245p. G+. A8. $20.00

FRIED, Henry B. *Repairing Quartz Watches.* 1983. Cincinnati, OH. 1st ed. 4to. 242p. F/F. A8. $35.00

FRIEDEL, Jean. *Personalite Biologique de l'Homme.* 1921. Paris. ils. 268p. half calf. G7. $35.00

FRIEDENWALD, Harry. *Jews & Medicine.* 1944. Baltimore. Hopkins. 2 vol. pres. w/sgn letter. G7. $145.00

FRIEDLANDER, Judith. *Being Indian in Hueyapan.* 1975. St Martin. 1st ed. 205p. VG/wrp. F3. $10.00

FRIEDMAN, B.H. *Circles.* nd. NY. 1st ed/author's 1st novel. sgn. scarce. A11. $60.00

FRIEDMAN, C.S. *Black Sun Rising.* 1991. NY. DAW. ARC. NF. B3. $15.00

FRIEDMAN, I.K. *Poor People.* 1900. Houghton Mifflin. 1st ed. NF. B2. $150.00

FRIEDMAN, I.K. *Radical.* 1907. Appleton. 1st ed. F. B2. $175.00

FRIEDMAN, Kinky. *Case of Lone Star.* 1987. Beech Tree. 1st ed/author's 2nd book. NF/NF. B3. $30.00

FRIEDMAN, Kinky. *Elvis, Jesus & Coca-Cola.* 1993. Simon Schuster. 1st ed. F/F. P3. $20.00

FRIEDMAN, Kinky. *Greenwich Killing Time.* 1986. NY. Beech Tree. ARC/1st ed. RS. F/F. S6. $25.00

FRIEDMAN, Kinky. *When the Cat's Away.* 1988. Beech Tree. 1st ed. F/F. B3. $25.00

FRIEDMAN, Maurice. *Martin Buber & the Eternal.* 1986. Human Sciences Pr. 192p. blk cloth. VG/dj. G1. $22.50

FRIEDMAN, Susan. *Separate Place.* 1974. Sierra Club. 1st ed. 4to. VG/NF. S9. $40.00

FRIEDMAN, Thomas L. *From Beirut to Jerusalem.* 1989. FSG. 7th prt. NF/dj. W1. $20.00

FRIEDRICH, Paul. *Agrarian Revolt in a Mexican Village.* 1970. Prentice Hall. 1st ed. 158p. VG. F3. $10.00

FRIEDRICHSEN, Carol S. *Pooh Craft Book.* 1976. Dutton. 1st ed. NF/VG. C8. $35.00

FRIEL, Arthur O. *Mountains of Mystery.* 1925. Harper. 1st ed. G+. P3. $50.00

FRIEND, Oscar. *Kid From Mars.* 1949. Frederick Fell. 1st prt. VG/G. C8. $35.00

FRIEND & MARGULIES. *From Off This World.* 1949. Merlin. 1st ed. VG/VG. P3. $50.00

FRIENDLICH, Dick. *Sweet Swing.* 1968. Doubleday. 1st ed. F/VG. P8. $45.00

FRIES & WEST. *Chemical Warfare.* 1921. NY. ils. 445p. A13. $65.00

FRISKEY, Margaret. *Johnny & the Monarch.* 1946. Chicago. Children's Pr. 1st ed. ils Katherine Evans. VG+. C8. $25.00

FRITH, Francis. *Quaker Ideal.* 1894. London. Edward Hicks. 16mo. 102p. VG. V3. $10.00

FRITZ, Jean. *Will You Sign Here John Hancock.* 1976. Coward McCann. 1st ed. ils/inscr Hyman. F/F. C8. $35.00

FRITZ & WILLIAMS. *Triumph of Culture: 18th-Century Perspectives.* 1972. Toronto. Hakkert. VG/dj. N2. $8.50

FROESCHELS, Emil. *Philosophy in Wit.* 1948. NY. Philosophical Lib. thin 8vo. red cloth/painted label. VG. G1. $22.50

FROHMAN, Charles E. *Milan & the Milan Canal...* 1976. Sandusky, OH. ils. 99p. VG. B18. $12.50

FROHMAN, Charles E. *Rebels on Lake Erie.* 1965. Columbus, OH. OH Hist Soc. 157p. cloth. M11. $60.00

FROMENTIN, Eugene. *Dominique.* 1948. London. Cresset. 1st ed thus. gilt cloth. F. A17. $12.50

FROMM, Erich. *Dogma of Christ & Other Essays on Relgion, Psychology...* 1963. Harper Row. 1st ed. 121p. VG/VG. B33. $15.00

FROMM, Erich. *Socialist Humanism: International Symposium.* 1967. Allen Lane/Penguin. 1st Eng ed. VG/dj. G1. $35.00

FROMMHOLZ, Hilda. *Sleepy Time Stories.* 1945. Whitman. 20 short stories. VG. A3. $7.00

FROST, A.B. *Stuff & Nonsense.* 1884. NY. 1st ed/author's 1st book. ils. G. C2. $100.00

FROST, Edwin Brant. *Astronomer's Life.* 1933. Houghton Mifflin. 8vo. sgn. 300p. beige cloth. G. K5. $50.00

FROST, Frances. *Fireworks for Windy Foot.* 1956. Whittlesey. 1st ed. 176p. G+/G. P2. $20.00

FROST, J.A. *Shire Horse in Peace & War.* 1915. London. Vinton. 1st ed. VG. O3. $65.00

FROST, John. *Illuminated Hist of North America From Earliest Period...* 1860. NY. ils. 725p. gilt blk leather. VG. H3. $90.00

FROST, John. *Thrilling Adventures Among the Indians.* nd. np. ils. G+. M17. $30.00

FROST, O.W. *Cross-Cultural Arts in Alaska.* 1970. AK Methodist U. photos/index. 96p. VG/wrp. A17. $10.00

FROST, Robert. *Collected Poems of Robert Frost.* 1936. NY. Holt. 6th prt. sgn. 8vo. 349p. gilt tan cloth. F/dj. H5. $250.00

FROST, Robert. *Considerable Speck.* 1939. Boston. 1st separate ed. 1/less than 100. NF. H5. $1,250.00

FROST, Robert. *In the Clearing.* 1962. HRW. 1st ed. 8vo. 101p. silvered gray cloth. F/NF. H5. $50.00

FROST, Robert. *Masque of Mercy.* 1947. Holt. 1st ed. sgn/dtd 1950. NF/VG. B4. $275.00

FROST, Robert. *Masque of Mercy.* 1947. NY. Holt. 1st trade ed. 8vo. gilt bl cloth. F/NF. H5. $60.00

FROST, Robert. *Masque of Reason.* 1945. Holt. 1st ed. inscr/sgn. bl cloth. F/dj. B24. $525.00

FROST, Robert. *New Hampshire.* 1955. Hanover, NH. 1st separate ed. sgn. 1/750. F. B24. $350.00

FROST, Robert. *New Hampshire. A Poem With Notes & Grace Notes.* 1923. NY. Holt. 1st trade ed. 8vo. 113p. gr cloth/brd. NF. H5. $125.00

FROST, Robert. *North of Boston.* 1914. London. David Nutt. 1st ed/author's 2nd book. 8vo. 143p. gr cloth. F. C6. $1,750.00

FROST, Robert. *North of Boston.* 1915. NY. 3rd ed. inscr w/1st line from Mending Wall. F. C2. $450.00

FROST, Robert. *Recognition of Robert Frost.* 1937. Holt. 25th Anniversary ed. F/VG. V1. $40.00

FROST, Robert. *Road Not Taken.* 1959. NY. 4th prt. sgn. 282p. VG/dj. B18. $175.00

FROST, Robert. *Selected Letters of Robert Frost.* 1964. HRW. ARC. RS. VG+/VG+. S9. $45.00

FROST, S. Annie. *Our West/Four Cousins/Poppet/Very Little Tales.* ca 1873. Am Tract Soc. 4 vol. 84x68mm. Marcus bookplate. ils. gilt cloth. F/wood box. B24. $500.00

FROST & FROST. *Magic Power of Witchcraft.* 1976. Parker. VG. P3. $13.00

FROUD, Brian. *Goblins.* 1983. Macmillan. 1st Am ed. NF. C8. $45.00

FRUCHT, Abby. *Snap.* 1988. Ticknor Fields. 1st ed/author's 1st novel. F/F. B3. $25.00

FRY, Clements C. *Mental Health in College.* 1942. NY. Commonwealth Fund. 353p. F/dj. K4. $15.00

FRY, Edward B. *Teaching Machines & Programmed Instruction: An Intro.* 1963. McGraw Hill. 184p. F. K4. $15.00

FRY, Henry. *History of North Atlantic Steam Navigation.* 1969. London. Cornmarket. ils/fld map. 324p. T7. $75.00

FRY, Maggie Culver. *Boy Named Will: Story of Young Will Rogers.* 1979. OK. Bluestem Pub. 1st ed. sgn. 40p. VG-/wrp. A3. $5.00

FRY, Mary. *Mary Fry's Pulled Thread Workbook.* 1978. np. VG. G2. $20.00

FRY, Roger. *Sampler of Castile.* 1923. Hogarth. 1st ed. 1/550. 4to. cloth backstrip/brd. VG. H5. $300.00

FRYE, Richard N. *Heritage of Persia.* 1963. World. 1st ed. 64 pl. NF/dj. W1. $30.00

FRYER, Jane Eayre. *Mary Frances Cookbook.* 1912. Phil. Winston. 1st ed. VG/G. B5. $150.00

FRYER, Jane Eayre. *Mary Frances Sewing Book.* 1913. Winston. 8vo. pict bdg. F/G. M5. $150.00

FRYFIELD, Frances. *Shadow Play.* 1993. London. Bantam. 1st ed. F/F. B2. $35.00

FRYXELL, Fritiof. *Tetons: Interpretations of a Mountain Landscape.* 1938. Berkeley. ils/maps/index. 77p. VG/sans. B19. $50.00

FUCHS, Emil. *With Pencil, Brush & Chisel.* 1925. Putnam. 1st ed. sgn/dtd Feb 1925. w/sgn letter & Christmas card. VG. A1. $200.00

FUCHS, Lawrence H. *John F Kennedy & American Catholicism.* 1967. Meredith. 1st ed. 271p. F/dj. M10. $7.50

FUCHS & HILARY. *Crossing of Antarctica.* 1958. Boston. 1st Am ed. 328p. F/F. A17. $17.50

FUENTES, Carlos. *Change of Skin.* 1968. London. Cape. 1st ed. 8vo. 462p. purple brd/gilt spine. F/NF. H5. $60.00

FUENTES, Carlos. *Death of Artemio Cruz.* 1964. Farrar Straus. 1st Am ed. sgn. 306p. gilt/orange stp blk brd. NF/dj. H5. $100.00

FUENTES, Carlos. *Old Gringo.* 1986. London. Deutsch. 1st ed. F/NF. B3. $25.00

FUENTES, Norberto. *Ernest Hemingway Rediscovered.* 1988. Scribner. 1st ed. 912p. F/F. B3. $75.00

FUESS, Claude M. *Life of Caleb Cushing.* 1923. Harcourt Brace. 2 vol. cloth. VG. A10. $45.00

FULANAIN. *Marsh Arab: Haji Rikkan.* 1928. Lippincott. 1st ed. 8vo. 322p. VG. W1. $24.00

FULGHUM, Robert. *It Was on Fire When I Lay Down on It.* 1989. Villard. 1st ed. 218p. M/M. H1. $18.00

FULKERSON, L. *Gynecology: Textbook of Diseases of Women.* 1929. Phil. ils. 852p. VG. G7. $25.00

FULLER, Edmund. *Affirmations of God & Man.* 1967. Assn. 156p. G/dj. B29. $3.00

FULLER, Iola. *Shining Trail.* 1946. Sun Dial. rpt. 442p. VG/dj. B34. $20.00

FULLER, John D. *Day We Bombed Utah. America's Most Lethal Secret.* 1984. NAL. 1st ed. VG/dj. N2. $7.50

FULLER, John G. *Great Soul Trail.* 1969. Macmillan. 1st ed/1st prt. 405p. F/F. H1. $18.00

FULLER, Millard. *No More Shacks!* 1986. Word. 215p. VG. B29. $3.00

FULLER, R. Buckminster. *And It Came To Pass — Not To Stay.* 1976. Macmillan. 1st ed. VG/dj. N2. $5.00

FULLER, R. Buckminster. *Synergetics.* 1975. NY. 1st ed. F/dj. A9. $40.00

FULLER, Robert. *Mesmerism & the American Cure of Souls.* 1982. Phil. 1st ed. 277p. A13. $30.00

FULLER, Roy. *Middle of a War.* 1942. London. Hogarth. 1st ed. NF/NF. B2. $35.00

FULLER, Timothy. *Harvard Has a Homicide.* 1942. Triangle. VG/G. P3. $13.00

FULLER, Timothy. *Keep Cool, Mr Jones.* 1950. Little Brn. 1st ed. F/NF. M15. $40.00

FULLER & MCCLINTOCK. *Poisonous Plants of CA.* 1986. Berkeley. photos/ils. 433p. sc. B26. $12.95

FULLER & THOMPSON. *Behavior Genetics.* 1960. Wiley. 346p. G. K4. $15.00

FULLERTON, Hugh. *Jimmy Kirkland of the Cascade College Team.* 1915. Winston. later prt. G. P8. $27.50

FULLMER, Jane. *Sir Humphry Davy's Published Works.* 1969. Cambridge. 1st ed. 112p. A13. $30.00

FULOP-MILLER, Rene. *Triumph Over Pain.* 1938. Bobbs Merrill. 1st ed. trans Eden/Cedar Paul. 438p. G+. H1. $12.00

FULTON, J.F. *Harvey Cushing: A Biography.* 1946. Springfield. 1st ed. G. G7. $65.00

FULTON, J.F. *Physiology of the Nervous System.* 1938. London. Oxford. 1st ed. 635p. cloth. G7. $250.00

FULTON, Reed. *Grand Coulee Mystery.* 1941. Doubleday. 1st ed. F/NF. F4. $21.00

FURLONG, Lawrence. *American Coast Pilot: Containing Courses & Distances...* 1798. Newburyport, MA. 2nd ed. 8vo. contemporary calf/rebacked. M1. $1,050.00

FURNAS & FURNAS. *Man, Bread & Destiny: Story of Man's Food.* 1938. London. 1st ed. 364p. A13. $45.00

FURNEAUX, Rupert. *Breakfast War.* 1958. Crowell. 1st ed. ils. 240p. VG/dj. M10. $6.50

FURNEAUX, W. *Out-Door World or Young Collector's Handbook.* 1984. London. 2nd ed. 411p. gilt cloth. VG. A17. $20.00

FURNISS, Harry. *Confessions of a Caricaturist.* 1901. London. Fisher Unwin. 2 vol. 8vo. ils. Mudie bdg. VG+. F1. $195.00

FURNIVALL, Frederick J. *Child Marriages, Divorces & Ratifications...* 1988. Millwood. Kraus. 256p. H10. $20.00

FURNIVALL. *Bibliography of Robert Browning From 1833-1881.* 1968. np. 3rd ed. 170p. F. A4. $35.00

FUSSELL, Edwin. *Frontier: Am Literature & the Am W.* 1965. Princeton. 1st ed. index. F/F. A18. $40.00

FUSSELL, Paul Jr. *Theory of Prosody in 18th-Century England.* 1954. New London. Connecticut College. 1st ed/author's 1st book. F/wrp. B2. $40.00

FUTRELLE, Jacques. *Thinking Machine.* 1907. NY. 1st ed. G+. H7. $35.00

FYFE, Andrew. *Compendium of Anatomy of Human Body.* 1810. Edinburg. 316p. half leather. G. E5. $75.00

FYFE, Thomas Alexander. *Who's Who in Dickens.* 1971. Haskell. VG. P3. $75.00

FYFIELD, Frances. *Question of Guilt.* 1988. London. Heinemann. ARC/1st ed. RS. NF/dj. S6. $30.00

FYLEMAN, Rose. *Here We Come A'Piping, Rose Fyleman's Choice of Poems...* nd. Stokes. ils J Mountfort. Art Deco bdg. VG/dj. scarce. M5. $60.00

GABRIEL, Dorothy. *Scottish Terrier: Its Breeding & Management.* 1934. Idle. Dog World. 2nd/revised/enlarged ed. 108p. VG/pict wrp. R2. $40.00

GABRIELD, Ralph E. *Elias Boudiont Cherokee & His America.* 1941. Norman, OK. 190p. VG/dj. A10. $25.00

GABRIELI, Francesco. *Arab Historians of the Crusades.* 1989. NY. Dorset. 362p. NF/dj. W1. $30.00

GABRIELI, Francesco. *Arab Revival.* 1961. London. Thames Hudson. 1st ed. 8vo. xl. VG. W1. $15.00

GADNEY, R. *Cry Hungary! Uprising 1956.* 1986. Atheneum. 1st Am ed. 183p. F/F. A17. $12.50

GAEBELEIN, Frank E. *Christian Education in a Democracy.* 1951. Oxford. 305p. G. B29. $5.50

GAEDE & GAEDE. *Camera, Spade & Pen: Inside View of SW Archaeology.* 1980. AZ U. 1st ed. ils/notes/index. 160p. NF/dj. B19. $45.00

GAER, Joseph. *Everybody's Weather.* nd (1944). Lippincott. 6th prt. 96p. gray cloth. G. K5. $8.00

GAER, Joseph. *First Round: Story of CIO Political Action Comm.* 1944. DSP. 2nd prt. ils. G/G. V4. $10.00

GAG, Wanda. *Tales From Grimm.* 1936. NY. 1st ed. inscr. NF. C2. $175.00

GAGE, Anne. *One Work: A Journey Towards the Self.* 1961. London. Vincent Stuart. 1st ed. 139p. VG/VG. B33. $35.00

GAGE, Thomas. *New Survey of the W Indies.* 1929. McBride. Argonaut Series. 407p. red cloth. VG. F3. $25.00

GAGE & GAGE. *If Wishes Were Horses: Education of a Veterinarian.* 1933. St Martin. 1st ed. VG/VG. O3. $18.00

GAGNON, Maurice. *Inner Ring.* 1985. Collins Crime CLub. 1st ed. VG/VG. P3. $18.00

GAINES, Ernest J. *Gathering of Old Men.* 1983. NY. 1st ed/author's 7th book. sgn. F/F. A11. $60.00

GAINHAM, Sarah. *Appointment in Vienna.* 1958. Dutton. 1st ed. VG/VG. P3. $15.00

GAITHER, Gloria. *Decisions: A Christian's Approach To Making Right Choices.* 1982. Word. 184p. VG/dj. B29. $3.50

GALDSTON, Iago. *Historic Derivations of Modern Psychiatry.* 1967. NY. 1st ed. 241p. dj. A13. $30.00

GALE, Gloria. *Calender Model.* 1957. Frederick Fell. 1st ed. pres. NF/NF clip. S9. $45.00

GALEN. *On the Natural Faculties.* 1916. London. 1st ed. trans Brock. 339p. A13. $100.00

GALENSON, Walter. *United Brotherhood of Carpenters: First Hunderd Years.* 1983. Harvard. VG. V4. $12.50

GALEY, John. *Sinai & Monestary of St Catherine.* 1980. Givatayim, Israel. Massada. 1st Eng ed. 191p. VG. W1. $45.00

GALLAGHER, Nancy. *Medicine & Power in Tunisia, 1780-1900.* 1983. Cambridge. 1st ed. 145p. dj. A13. $30.00

GALLAGHER, Sharon. *Medieval Art.* 1969. NY. Tudor. ils/89 pl. 40p. VG. M10. $6.50

GALLAGHER, Tess. *Instructions to the Double.* 1976. Graywolf. sgn. F/NF. V1. $35.00

GALLAGHER, Tess. *Under Stars.* 1978. Port Townsend. Graywolf. 1st ed. sgn. F/wrp. B2. $45.00

GALLAGHER, Thomas. *Doctor's Story: Commemoration of 200th Anniversary Columbia.* 1967. NY. 234p. dj. G7. $25.00

GALLANT, Roy A. *Constellations: How They Came To Be.* 1979. Four Winds. 203p. xl. dj. K5. $15.00

GALLANT, Roy A. *Man's Reach for the Stars.* 1971. Doubleday. 8vo. ils/photos. 201p. G/dj. K5. $14.00

GALLATIN & OLIVER. *Bibliography of Works of Max Beerbohm.* 1952. London. Rupert Hart Davis. 4to. ils. VG. A4. $175.00

GALLATIN. *Sir Max Beerbohm: Bibliographical Notes.* 1944. Harvard. ils. 134p. F/VG. A4. $185.00

GALLAUDET, Thomas H. *Child's Book on the Soul.* 1832. Hartford. Cooke. 2 vol. 2nd & 3rd ed. brd. M1. $250.00

GALLENKAMP, Charles. *Maya: Riddle & Rediscovery of a Lost Civilization.* 1959. McKay. 1st ed. 240p. VG/dj. F3. $25.00

GALLICO, Paul. *Boy Who Invented the Bubble Gun.* 1974. Heinemann. 1st ed. VG/VG. P3. $18.00

GALLICO, Paul. *Day Jean-Pierre Joined the Circus.* 1970 (1969). Franklin Watts. 1st Am ed. VG+/NF. C8. $30.00

GALLICO, Paul. *Man Who Was Magic.* 1966. Doubleday. 1st ed. NF/NF. P3. $20.00

GALLICO, Paul. *Man Who Was Magic.* 1966. Doubleday. 1st ed. VG/VG. A17. $9.50

GALLICO, Paul. *Manxmouse, the Mouse Who Knew No Fear.* 1968. Coward McCann. 1st Am ed. ils J & A Grahame-Johnstne. F/VG. C8. $25.00

GALLICO, Paul. *Mrs Harris Goes to NY.* Oct 1960. London. Michael Joseph. 2nd pre-pub prt. inscr/dtd Dec 1960. F/F. C8. $50.00

GALLICO, Paul. *Poseidon Adventure.* 1969. Coward McCann. 1st Am ed. F/F. N3. $25.00

GALLICO, Paul. *Scruffy.* 1963. Rpt Soc. VG/VG. P3. $8.00

GALLICO, Paul. *Small Miracle.* 1952. Doubleday. 1st ed. F/VG. C8. $40.00

GALLICO, Paul. *Snowflake.* 1952. Michael Joseph. 1st ed. pict paper brd. F/F. C8. $25.00

GALLICO, Paul. *Snowflake.* 1953. Doubleday. 1st ed. 63p. VG/VG. A3. $10.00

GALLICO, Paul. *Thomasina.* 1957. Doubleday. early ed. pict cloth. VG+/G+. C8. $22.50

GALLISON, Kate. *Death Tape.* 1987. Little Brn. 1st ed. VG/VG. P3. $15.00

GALLOIS, L. *Les Andes de Patagonie.* 1901. Paris. 18 pl. Lib of Congress bdg. VG. F3. $35.00

GALLUN, Raymond Z. *People Minus X.* 1957. Simon Schuster. 1st ed. sgn pres to Clifford Simak. NF/dj. F4. $65.00

GALLUP, George. *Guide to Public Opinion Polls.* 1944. Princeton. 1st ed. inscr. F/NF. B4. $350.00

GALLUP & POLING. *Search for America's Faith.* 1980. Abingdon. 153p. VG/dj. B29. $4.50

GALSWORTHY, John. *Addresses in America.* 1919. Scribner. 1st ed. F/NF. B4. $65.00

GALSWORTHY, John. *Annotations on Some Minor Writings of TE Lawrence.* 1935. London. Scholartis Pr. 1/500 #d. 28p. orange cloth. VG/VG. M7. $165.00

GALSWORTHY, John. *Forsyte Saga.* 1922. London. ltd ed. sgn. gr leather. VG. A1. $180.00

GALSWORTHY, John. *Forsyte Saga.* 1929. NY. 6 vol. 1/500. sgn. red morocco. F/dj/shelf holder. w/sgn letter. H4. $500.00

GALSWORTHY, John. *Four Forsythe Stories.* 1929. NY. ltd ed. sgn. 1/896. VG. C11. $35.00

GALSWORTHY, John. *Memories.* 1914. London. Heinemann. 1st ils ed. tall 8vo. cloth. VG+. R2. $40.00

GALSWORTHY, John. *Memories.* 1914. Scribner. 1st ils ed. 4to. G+. B17. $12.50

GALSWORTHY, John. *Modern Comedy.* 1929. Scribner. 1st ed. VG. P3. $30.00

GALSWORTHY, John. *Plays of...* 1929. London. Duckworth. 1/1275. 8vo. 1150p. gilt gr cloth. F/NF. H5. $200.00

GALSWORTHY, John. *Slaughter of Animals for Food.* nd (1912). London. Council Justice to Animals. F/wrp. B4. $45.00

GALSWORTHY, John. *White Monkey.* nd. London. ltd ed. sgn. G+. A1. $15.00

GALTON, Francis. *Hereditary Genius.* 1870. Appleton. 1st Am ed. 289p. cloth. G. B14. $225.00

GALUANO, Phil. *Secrets of Perfect Golf Swing.* 1961. NY. 1st ed. sgn. VG/fair. B5. $40.00

GAMOW, George. *Biography of the Earth.* 1959 (1941). Viking. revised ed. 27 pl. 242p. wrp. K5. $4.00

GANDHI, Mahatma. *Delhi Diary.* 1948. Navajivan. 1st ed. index. 406p. quarter cloth. VG/VG. A17. $25.00

GANDHI, Mahatma. *His Own Story. Edited by CF Andrews.* 1930. Macmillan. 372p. cloth. G. B14. $45.00

GANDHI, Mahatma. *Young India...* 1924. NY. Huebsch. 1200p. cloth. VG. B14. $35.00

GANDLEY, Kenneth R. *Autumn Heroes.* 1977. St Martin. 1st ed. F/dj. F4. $20.00

GANGEL, Kenneth O. *Building Leaders for Church Education.* 1981. Moody. 432p. VG/dj. B29. $5.50

GANN, Thomas. *In an Unknown Land.* 1924. Scribner. 1st ed. 263p. xl. reading copy. F3. $20.00

GANN, W.D. *Tunnel Thru the Air.* 1927. Ginancial Guardian. 1st ed. VG. P3. $40.00

GANNES, Harry. *How the Soviet Union Helps Spain.* 1936. NY. Workers Lib. 1st ed. NF/wrp. B2. $30.00

GANZEL, D. *Fortune & Men's Eyes.* nd. Collier. 1st ed. ils. F/dj. K3. $20.00

GANZFRIED, Solomon. *Code of Jewish Law.* 1927. NY. Hebrew Pub. pebbled cloth. M11. $45.00

GARBER, Lyman A. *Of Men & Not of Law, How Courts Are Usurping Political...* 1966. NY. Devin-Adair. M11. $20.00

GARBUTT, Raymond J. *Diseases & Surgery of the Dog.* 1938. Orange Judd. 1st ed. 332p. cloth. F. R2. $35.00

GARCIA MARQUEZ, Gabriel; see Marquez, Gabriel Garcia.

GARCON, Maurice. *La Justice Contemporaine 1870-1932.* 1933. Paris. 6th ed. 758p. VG/wrp. D3. $45.00

GARD, Wayne. *Chisholm Trail.* 1954. OK U. 2nd prt. VG/dj. B34. $35.00

GARDINER, Dorothy. *Great Betrayal.* 1949. Doubleday. 1st ed. VG/VG. P3. $20.00

GARDINER, Gordon. *Pattern of Chance.* 1930. Houghton Mifflin. 1st Am ed. VG/dj. M15. $25.00

GARDINER, John Rolfe. *Great Dream From Heaven.* 1974. Knopf. 1st ed. inscr. NF/F. A11. $55.00

GARDNER, Alexander. *Gardner's Photographics Sketch Book of the Civil War.* 1959. Dover. unp. F/G. H1. $35.00

GARDNER, Brian. *Allenby.* 1965. London. Cassell. 1st ed. 314p. F/NF clip. M7. $45.00

GARDNER, C.K. *Compend of the US System of Infantry Exercise...* 1819. NY. 1st ed. 20 pl. 284p. G. B18. $95.00

GARDNER, Erle Stanley. *Case of the Cautious Coquette.* nd. BC. VG/VG. P3. $8.00

GARDNER, Erle Stanley. *Case of the Grinning Gorilla.* nd. Grosset Dunlap. VG. P3. $10.00

GARDNER, Erle Stanley. *Case of the Nervous Accomplice.* nd. BC. VG/VG. P3. $8.00

GARDNER, Erle Stanley. *Hidden Heart of Baja.* 1962. NY. 1st ed. VG/VG. B5. $35.00

GARDNER, Erle Stanley. *Off the Beaten Track in Baja.* 1967. Morrow. 1st ed. inscr. NF/NF. B2. $150.00

GARDNER, Erle Stanley. *Pay Dirt.* 1983. Morrow. 1st ed. VG/VG. P3. $25.00

GARDNER, Erle Stanley. *Up for Grabs.* 1964. Morrow. 1st ed. F/NF. F4. $22.50

GARDNER, Ernest. *Fundamentals of Neurology.* 1948. Phil/London. Saunders. 303p. G. K4. $8.50

GARDNER, F.B. *Carriage Painters' Ils Manual.* 1886. NY. Fowler Wells. later prt. 12mo. VG. O3. $125.00

GARDNER, G. Peabody. *Hard Alee: Cruising Foreign.* 1977. Peabody Mus. ils. 224p. dj. T7. $28.00

GARDNER, G. Peabody. *Turkish Delight: Cruise Along the S Coast of Turkey.* 1964. Peabody Mus. 1st ed. 64p. VG. W1. $16.00

GARDNER, Howard. *Mind's New Science.* 1985. NY. Basic. 423p. F/dj. K4. $12.50

GARDNER, Jeffrey (K.); see Fox, Gardner F.

GARDNER, John. *Art of Living & Other Stories.* 1981. Knopf. 1st ed. ils Mary Azarian. 309p. gilt cream cloth. F/dj. H5. $100.00

GARDNER, John. *Brokenclaw.* 1990. Putnam. 1st ed. sgn. James Bond Series #9. F/F. T2. $20.00

GARDNER, John. *Complete State of Death.* 1969. Viking. 1st ed. sgn. Derek Torry Series #1. F/F. T2. $30.00

GARDNER, John. *Complete Works of the Gawain-Poet.* 1965. Chicago. 1st ed. inscr. F/NF. B4. $250.00

GARDNER, John. *Corner Men.* 1974. Michael Joseph. 1st ed. F/F. P3. $25.00

GARDNER, John. *Death Is Forever.* 1992. Putnam. 1st ed. sgn. F/F. T2. $20.00

GARDNER, John. *Dragon, Dragon.* 1975. Knopf. ARC. sgn. RS. F/F. B4. $275.00

GARDNER, John. *For Special Services.* 1982. CMG. 1st ed. sgn. James Bond Series #2. F/F. T2. $25.00

GARDNER, John. *For Special Services.* 1982. London. Cape. VG/VG. P3. $25.00

GARDNER, John. *For Special Services.* 1982. London. Cape/Hodder. 1st ed. F/F. S6. $35.00

GARDNER, John. *Freddy's Book.* 1980. Knopf. 1st ed. ils. 245p. gilt cream cloth. F/dj. H5. $60.00

GARDNER, John. *Icebreaker.* 1983. Jonathan Cape. 1st ed. F/F. P3. $25.00

GARDNER, John. *King's Indian: Stories & Tales.* 1974. Knopf. 1st ed. G+/dj. P3. $15.00

GARDNER, John. *King's Indian: Stories & Tales.* 1974. Knopf. 1st ed. 323p. VG/dj. M20. $30.00

GARDNER, John. *Licence Renewed.* 1981. London. Cape. 1st ed/author's 1st James Bond novel. sgn. F/F. T2. $75.00

GARDNER, John. *License Renewed.* 1981. NY. Marek. 1st ed/author's 1st James Bond novel. sgn. F/F. T2. $30.00

GARDNER, John. *Nickel Mountain.* 1973. Knopf. 1st ed. VG/VG. P3. $30.00

GARDNER, John. *No Deals, Mr Bond.* 1987. Putnam. 1st ed. sgn. F/F. T2. $25.00

GARDNER, John. *Nobody Lives Forever.* 1986. NY. 1st ed. F/F. A17. $12.50

GARDNER, John. *October Light.* 1976. Knopf. 1st ed. VG/G. P3. $20.00

GARDNER, John. *Role of Honor.* 1984. Cape/Hodder Stoughton. 1st ed. 222p. gilt blk cloth. F/dj. H5. $60.00

GARDNER, John. *Scorpius.* 1988. Putnam. 1st ed. sgn. F/F. T2. $22.00

GARDNER, John. *Secret Generations.* 1985. London. Heinemann. 1st ed. sgn. F/NF. S6. $40.00

GARDNER, John. *Stillness Shadows.* 1986. Knopf. 1st ed. M/M. B4. $30.00

GARDNER, John. *Sunlight Dialogues.* 1972. London. Cape. 1st ed. 8vo. 673p. F/dj. H5. $60.00

GARDNER, John. *Tale in the Sucide Mountains.* 1977. Knopf. 1st ed. ils Joe Servelle. F/F. C8. $75.00

GARDNER, John. *Win, Lose or Die.* 1989. Putnam. 1st ed. sgn. F/F. T2. $20.00

GARDNER, John. *Win, Lose or Die.* 1989. Putnam. 1st ed. VG/VG. P3. $14.00

GARDNER, John. *Wreckage of Agathon.* 1970. Harper. 1st ed. inscr. NF/NF. B4. $350.00

GARDNER, Leonard. *Fat City.* 1969. NY. 1st ed/author's 1st novel. sgn. F/F. A11. $65.00

GARDNER, Miriam; see Bradley, Marion Zimmer.

GARDNER, Robert G. *On the Hill: Story of Shorter College.* 1972. Rome, GA. Shorter College. 1st ed. 476p. F/NF. M8. $30.00

GARDNER, Robert W. *Parthenon: Its Science of Forms.* 1925. NY. Rudge. 1st ed. elephant folio. 1/700. VG. C6/K1. $85.00

GARDNER, Sarah M.H. *Quaker Idyls.* 1894. Holt. 16mo. 223p. lacks free ep. G. V3. $9.00

GARDNER, Will. *Covin Saga: Nantucket's Story...* 1949. Nantucket Island, MA. 8vo. 321p. VG. V3. $14.00

GARFIELD, Brian. *Death Sentence.* 1975. Evans. 1st ed. VG/VG. P3. $30.00

GARFIELD, Brian. *Deep Cover.* 1971. Delacorte. 1st ed. G+/dj. P3. $15.00

GARFIELD, Brian. *Hit.* 1970. Macmillan. 1st ed. VG/VG. P3. $23.00

GARFIELD, Brian. *Necessity.* 1984. London. Macmillan. 1st ed. sgn. F/F. S6. $35.00

GARFIELD, Brian. *Paladin.* 1980. Macmillan. 1st ed. F/F. P3. $20.00

GARFIELD, Leon. *Child O'War.* 1972. Holt Rinehart. 1st ed. F/F. C8. $20.00

GARFIELD, Leon. *Young Nick & Jubilee.* Sept 1989. Delacorte. 1st Am ed. F/F. C8. $20.00

GARIEPY, Henry. *Portraits of Perseverance.* 1989. Victor. 215p. M/dj. B29. $8.50

GARIS, Cleo. *Missing at the Marshlands.* 1934. Burt. Arden Blake #3. 249p. VG/tattered. M20. $15.00

GARIS, Howard. *Buddy & His Winter Fun.* 1929. Cupples Leon. lists 7 titles. 208p. VG/ragged. M20. $15.00

GARIS, Howard. *Buddy in Dragon Swamp.* 1942. Cupples. cloth. F/worn. M5. $15.00

GARIS, Howard. *Buddy on Floating Island.* 1933. Cupples. cloth. F/worn. M5. $15.00

GARIS, Howard. *Daddy Takes Us to the Circus.* 1914. NY. RE Fenno. ils Edyth Powers. pls. NF. C8. $25.00

GARIS, Howard. *Uncle Wiggily Longears.* 1915. Donohue. ils Edward Bloomfield. cloth/pict label. G. M5. $20.00

GARIS, Howard. *Uncle Wiggily's Apple Roast.* 1948. Whitman. 16mo. VG-. B17. $12.50

GARIS, Howard. *Uncle Wiggily's Storybook.* 1939. Platt Munk. ils Lansing Campbell. gr cloth. VG. M5. $50.00

GARIS, Lilian. *Hermit of Proud Hill.* 1940. Grosset Dunlap. last title in series. VG/ragged. M20. $32.00

GARIS, Roger. *My Father Was Uncle Wiggily.* 1966. McGraw Hill. 1st ed. 217p. cloth. VG/dj. M20. $25.00

GARITTE, Gerald. *La Prise de Jerusalem par Les Perses en 614.* 1960. Louvain. 8vo. 67p. prt wrp. O2. $35.00

GARLAND, Hamlin. *Back-Trailers From the Middle Border.* 1928. NY. 1st ed. ils Constance Garland. gilt cloth. VG. A17. $15.00

GARLAND, Hamlin. *Book of the American.* 1923. Harper. 1st ed. 35 full-p Remington pl. VG. A18. $150.00

GARLAND, Hamlin. *Captain of the Grey-Horse Troop.* 1902. Harper. 1st ed. VG+. A18. $40.00

GARLAND, Hamlin. *Companions on the Trail.* 1921. Macmillan. sgn AB Guthrie Jr. G. B34. $55.00

GARLAND, Hamlin. *Crumbling of Idols: 12 Essays on Art...* 1894. Stone Kimball. 1st ed. teg. F. A18. $75.00

GARLAND, Hamlin. *Hamlin Garland's Diaries.* 1968. Huntington Lib. 1st ed. photos/index. M/dj. A18. $20.00

GARLAND, Hamlin. *Hesper.* 1903. Harper. 1st ed. pict bdg. F. A18. $40.00

GARLAND, Hamlin. *Moccasin Ranch.* 1909. NY. 1st ed. VG. B5. $50.00

GARLAND, Hamlin. *Prairie Songs: Being Chants Rhymed & Unrhymed...* 1893. Stone Kimball. ils HT Carpenter. teg. F. A18. $75.00

GARLAND, Hamlin. *Son of Middle Border.* 1924. NY. VG/VG. B5. $35.00

GARLAND, Hamlin. *Spoil of Office: Story of the Modern West.* 1892. Arena. 1st ed. NF. A18. $80.00

GARLAND, Hamlin. *Trail-Makers of Middle Border.* 1926. Macmillan. 1st ed. ils Constance Garland. F/dj. A18. $35.00

GARLAND, Hamlin. *Wayside Courtships.* 1897. Appleton. 1st ed. F. A18. $80.00

GARLAND, Hamlin. *Witch's Gold.* 1906. Doubleday Page. 1st ed. ils. teg. VG+. A18. $40.00

GARLAND, Joseph. *Story of Medicine.* 1939. Boston. 1st ed. 259p. A13. $30.00

GARLAND. *Bibliography of Writings of Sir James Matthew Barrie.* 1928. London. 1/520. ils. 146p. NF. A4. $95.00

GARMAN, Charles Edward. *Letters & Addresses of...* 1909. Houghton Mifflin. heavy 8vo. 616p. VG. G1. $50.00

GARNER, Alan. *Elidor.* 1966. Collins. 2nd ed. xl. dj. P3. $6.00

GARNER, Alan. *Lad of Gad.* 1981. Philomel. 1st ed. F/dj. F4. $20.00

GARNER, Alan. *Red Shift.* 1973. Macmillan. 1st ed. VG/fair. P3. $13.00

GARNER, Stanton. *Civil War World of Herman Melville.* 1993. KS. 1st ed. 544p. VG/dj. B18. $17.50

GARNER, William. *Ditto, Brother Rat!* 1972. Collins. 1st ed. VG/VG. P3. $20.00

GARNETT, David. *Essential TE Lawrence.* 1951. Dutton. 1st ed. 328p. gilt maroon cloth. dj. M7. $45.00

GARNETT, David. *Essential TE Lawrence.* 1956. Harmondsworth. Penguin. 1st ed thus. 335p. red stp red/wht bdg. G. M7. $15.00

GARNETT, David. *Familiar Faces.* 1962. London. Chatto Windus. 1st ed. 252p. gilt red cloth. F/VG+ clip. M7. $55.00

GARNETT, David. *Letters of TE Lawrence.* 1939. Doubleday Doran. 1st ed. ils/2 fld maps. NF/VG. M7. $50.00

GARNETT, David. *Letters of TE Lawrence.* 1939. Doubleday Doran. 1st ed. 900p. VG. E5. $35.00

GARNETT, David. *Rabbit in the Air.* 1932. London. Chatto Windus. 1st ed. 8vo. 117p. VG/fair. M7. $75.00

GARNETT, David. *Richard Jefferies: Prose Poet of the Countryside.* 1939. Aylesbury. pamphlet. F. M7. $32.00

GARNETT, David. *Sailor's Return.* Dec 1925. NY. 1st ed/2nd prt. 189p. blk stp bl cloth. VG. M7. $25.00

GARNETT, David. *Selected Letters of TE Lawrence.* 1941. London. World. 1st ed. VG. M7. $16.00

GARNETT, David. *White/Garnett Letters.* 1968. Viking. 1st ed. F/NF clip. M7. $40.00

GARNETT, Edward. *Friday Nights.* 1922. London. Cape. 1st ed. 8vo. 377p. bl/tan bdg. VG. M7. $22.00

GARNETT, Edward. *Turgenev: A Study.* 1917. London. 1st ed. 8vo. 206p. gilt bl cloth. G+. M7. $50.00

GARNETT, Louis Ayers. *Merrymakers.* 1918. Rand McNally. 1st ed. ils James McCracken. G. P2. $30.00

GARNETT, Porter. *Stately Homes of CA.* 1915. Little Brn. 1st ed. 95p. F. B14. $60.00

GARNETT, Richard. *Twilight of the Gods.* 1924. Bodley Head. 1st ils ed. 28 pl/Henry Keen. lettered blk cloth. VG. M7. $125.00

GARNETT, Thomas. *Observations on a Tour Through the Highlands...* 1811. London. 2 vol. 4to. 52 aquatint pl/fld map. half leather. G. H3. $175.00

GARNETT & STUART-GLENNIE. *Greek Folk Poesy...Vol 1.* 1896. Guildford. 8vo. 477p. cloth. uncut. very scarce. O2. $85.00

GARNSEY & HIBBS. *Social Sciences & the Environment.* 1967. Boulder, CO. 249p. G. K4. $12.50

GARON, Paul. *Devil's Son-in-Law.* 1971. Studio Vista. 1st ed. F/NF wrp. B2. $25.00

GARRETT, Edmund H. *Victorian Songs: Lyrics of the Affections & Nature.* 1895. Little Brn. ils. 228p. teg. gilt wht cloth. VG. S11. $35.00

GARRETT, George. *King of the Mountain.* 1957. NY. 1st ed/author's 1st solo book. inscr. F/NF. A11. $75.00

GARRETT, George. *Sleeping Gypsy & Other Poems.* 1958. TX U. 1st ed. F/NF. B4. $85.00

GARRETT, George. *Writer's Voice.* 1973. NY. 1st ed. sgn. F/NF. A11. $50.00

GARRISON, Allen Ware. *Slave Songs of the US.* 1867 (1851). np. 150p. VG. E5. $35.00

GARRISON, Charles E. *Two Different Worlds.* 1988. DE U. 174p. M/M. B29. $8.00

GARRISON, Dee. *Mary Heaton Vorse: Life of American Insurgent.* 1989. Phil. Temple. 1st ed. F/F. B2. $25.00

GARRISON, Fielding. *Principles of Anatomic Ils Before Vesalius...* 1926. NY. ils. 58p. xl. G. G7. $65.00

GARRISON, Jim. *Star-Spangled Contract.* 1976. McGraw Hill. 1st ed. F/F. P3. $18.00

GARRISON, Omar. *Balboa: Conquistador.* 1971. NY. Lyle Stuart. 1st ed. 256p. VG/dj. F3. $25.00

GARRISON, Pat. *Andalusian: A Rare Breed.* 1979. Chicago. Breyer. 8vo. 28p. VG/wrp. O3. $10.00

GARRISON, Webb. *Strange Facts About Death.* 1978. Abingdon. 1st ed. VG/VG. P3. $13.00

GARRISON & MORTON. *Medical Bibliography: A Check-List of Texts...* 1943. London. Grafton. 420p. VG. A4. $150.00

GARRO, Elena. *Recollections of Things To Come.* 1969. Austin. TX U. trans Ruth LC Simms. ils Alberto Beltrain. F/F. P4. $30.00

GARROTT, Hal. *Snythergen.* 1923. McBride. 1st ed. ils DS Walker. pict cloth. VG. M5. $70.00

GARROTT, Hal. *Snythergen.* 1923. McBride. 1st ed. ils Dugald Walker. 157p. NF. P2. $75.00

GARROTT, Hal. *Squiffer.* 1924. McBride. 1st ed. 8vo. 226p. gr cloth. VG. D6. $75.00

GARSOIAN, N.G. *Armenia Between Byzantium & the Sassanians.* 1985. London. 8vo. 340p. cloth. O2. $45.00

GARTNER, Chloe. *Drums of Khartoum.* 1967. Morrow. 1st ed. 343p. VG. W1. $18.00

GARTNER, Louis. *Needlepoint Design.* 1970. np. cloth. VG. G2. $15.00

GARVE, Andrew. *Counterstroke.* 1978. Crowell. 1st ed. VG/VG. P3. $20.00

GARVE, Andrew. *Cuckoo Line Affair.* 1953. Collins Crime Club. 1st ed. VG/VG. P3. $40.00

GARVE, Andrew. *Hide & Go Seek.* 1966. Harper Row. 1st ed. VG/VG. P3. $25.00

GARVEY, Robert. *Concise Treasury of Bible Quotations.* 1974. Jonathan David. 175p. VG/dj. B29. $5.00

GARWOOD, Darrell. *Crossroads of America.* 1948. NY. 1st ed. 331p. VG. D3. $12.50

GASH, Joe. *Priestly Murders.* 1984. HRW. 1st ed. F/F. P3. $15.00

GASH, Jonathan. *Great California Game.* 1991. St Martin. 1st ed. VG/G. P3. $15.00

GASH, Jonathan. *Jade Woman.* 1989. St Martin. 1st ed. F/F. B3. $15.00

GASH, Jonathan. *Jade Woman.* 1989. St Martin. 1st ed. sgn. F/dj. F4. $25.00

GASH, Jonathan. *Moonspender.* 1986. London. Collins Crime Club. 1st ed. F/NF. M15. $40.00

GASH & LINGENFELTER. *Newspapers of Nevada: A History & Bibliography 1854-1979.* nd. NV U. photos. 337p. F/F. A4. $45.00

GASKELL, Jane. *Some Summer Lands.* 1979. St Martin. 1st ed. F/F. F4. $20.00

GASKELL, Philip. *New Introduction to Bibliography.* 1972. NY. 1st ed. 438p. A13. $35.00

GASKIN, James J. *Varieties of Irish History.* 1869. Dublin. 4 chromolithographs. VG. M17. $30.00

GASS, William H. *Fiction & Figures of Life.* 1970. Knopf. 1st ed. F/NF. B4. $65.00

GASS, William H. *In the Heart of the Heart of the Country.* 1968. NY. 1st ed/author's 2nd book. inscr. F/F. A11. $75.00

GASS, William H. *Omensetter's Luck.* 1967. London. 1st ed/author's 1st book. C4. $135.00

GASS, William H. *On Being Blue.* nd. Boston. ltd ed. sgn. 1/225 #d (precedes trade ed). F/F/F case. A11. $90.00

GASS, William H. *On Being Blue.* 1976. Boston. Godine. ARC. RS. w/pub material. F/F. B4. $100.00

GASS, William H. *Willie Masters' Lonesome Wife.* 1968. Evanston. 1st ed. sgn. 1/200. F/sans. A9. $200.00

GATACRE, Alice. *Keeshond.* 1938. London. Country Life. 1st ed. ils. 203p. cloth. G+. very scarce. R2. $260.00

GATE, Josephine Scribner. *Sunshine Annie.* 1910. Bobbs Merrill. ils Fannie Cory. 148p. G. P2. $45.00

GATENBY, Rosemary. *Fugitive Affair.* 1976. Dodd Mead. 1st ed. VG/VG. P3. $15.00

GATES, David. *Jernigan.* 1991. Knopf. UP NF. B4. $35.00

GATES, Norman T. *Richard Aldington: Autobiography in Letters.* 1992. PA State. 1st ed. 402p. blk cloth. w/sgn ES. M. M7. $49.50

GATLAND, Kenneth. *Spaceflight Today.* 1963. London. Iliffe. 8vo. 254p. G/dj. K5. $26.00

GAUBERT, H. *Moses & Joshua: Contemporary Companion to the Bible.* 1969. Hastings. 205p. VG/dj. B29. $3.50

GAULT, William Campbell. *Cat & Mouse.* 1988. St Martin. 1st ed. F/dj. F4. $20.00

GAULT, William Campbell. *Cat & Mouse.* 1988. St Martin. 1st ed. NF/NF. P3. $15.00

GAULT, William Campbell. *Out of Focus.* 1959. Random. 1st ed. F/F. M15. $30.00

GAUNT, William. *Marine Painting: Historical Survey from 16th Century...* 1975. Viking. ils. 264p. dj. T7. $55.00

GAUTER, E.-F. *Trois Heros: Le General Laperrine, le Pere de Foucauld...* 1931. Paris. Payot. 1st ed. 8vo. VG/wrp. W1. $8.00

GAUTHIER, Josie O. *Wild Flower Stories.* 1918. Cupples Leon. 30p. G-. A3. $15.00

GAUTRUCH, Petrus. *Philosophiae, AC Mathematicae Totius Institutio...* 1661. Vienna. Joannis Blaeu. 2 parts in 1. 12mo. 333p. old calf/rebacked. K1. $150.00

GAVIN, Frank. *Some Aspects of Contemporary Greek Orthodox Thought.* 1962. NY. Am Review E Orthodox. 340p. buckram. H10. $15.00

GAWRON, Jean Mark. *Apology for Rain.* 1974. Doubleday. 1st ed. F/F. P3. $15.00

GAY, John. *Fables of Mr John Gay. Complete in Two Parts...* 1806. London. Wilson Spence. 12mo. woodcuts. 252p. burgundy calf/marbled brd. K1. $150.00

GAY, John. *Shepherd's Week in Six Pastorals.* 1714. London. Burleigh. 1st ed. VG. B4. $2,500.00

GAY, Romney. *Big Picture Book.* 1947. Grosset Dunlap. 1st ed. VG/G. P2. $25.00

GAY & GAY. *Shire Colt.* 1931. Doubleday Doran. 1st ed. ils. VG/VG. P2. $60.00

GAYER, Margaruite. *Farm for Andy.* 1951. Rand McNally Elf Books. K2. $4.00

GAYLE, Addison. *Wayward Child.* 1977. Doubleday. 1st ed. F/NF. B2. $30.00

GAYLORD, James M. *Hist Reminiscences of Morgan Co.* 1984. Morgan Co Hist Soc. 92p. VG. B18. $9.50

GAYNOR, Frank. *Dictionary of Mysticism.* 1953. NY. Philosophical Lib. 1st ed. 207p. VG/G. B33. $16.00

GAZZANIGA, Michael S. *Bisected Brain.* 1970. Appleton Century Crofts. 172p. G/dj. K4. $15.00

GEACH, Peter. *Mental Acts: Their Content & Their Objects.* nd. London. Kegan Paul. 136p. F/dj. K4. $10.00

GEANAKOPLOS, Deno J. *Byzantine East & Latin West.* 1973. Hamden. 8vo. ils. 206p. cloth. O2. $30.00

GEBBIE & THOMAS. *Wolf-Rayet Stars.* 1968. Nat Bureau Standards. 8vo. ils. 277p. red cloth. G. K5. $16.00

GEDDES, Anne E. *Trends in Relief Expenditures 1910-1935.* 1937. GPO. VG/wrp. B2. $25.00

GEDGE, Pauline. *Stargate.* 1982. Macmillan. 1st ed. NF/NF. P3. $20.00

GEDYE, G.R. *Fallen Bastions: Central European Tragedy.* 1939. London. BC. 519p. VG. A17. $10.00

GEHLBACH, Frederick R. *Mountain Islands & Desert Seas.* 1981. TX A&M. 1st ed. ils/index. 298p. F/F. B19. $30.00

GEHRMAN, Henry. *New Westminster Dictionary of the Bible.* 1970. Westminster. 1027p. VG/dj. B29. $14.00

GEIGER, Maynard. *Franciscan Missionaries in Hispanic California.* 1969. San Marino. Huntington Lib. 1st ed. F/VG. P4. $45.00

GEISEL, Theodor Seuss. *Cat in the Hat Song Book.* 1968 (1957). London. Collins. 1st Eng ed. NF. C8. $32.50

GEISEL, Theodor Seuss. *Cat in the Hat.* 1956. Random possible 1st ed/early prt. VG+/VG+. C8. $95.00

GEISEL, Theodor Seuss. *King's Stilts.* 1939. Random. possible 1st ed. red lettered yel brd. VG. M5. $25.00

GEISEL, Theodor Seuss. *McElligot's Pool.* 1975. NY. special sc ed. w/sgn bookplate. NF/ils wrp. A11. $95.00

GEISEL, Theodor Seuss. *On Beyond Zebra.* 1955. Random. possible 1st ed/early prt. sm 4to. VG+/VG+. C8. $100.00

GEISEL, Theodor Seuss. *One Fish Two Fish Red Fish Blue Bish.* 1960. Random. probable 1st ed. VG/VG. C8. $75.00

GEISEL, Theodor Seuss. *Seven Lady Godivas.* 1939. Random. stated 1st ed. VG. P2. $135.00

GEISEL, Theodor Seuss. *Tough Coughs As He Ploughs the Dough.* 1987. NY. 1st ed/1st prt. sgn Dr Seuss/Geisel. F/F. A11. $195.00

GEISEL, Theodor Seuss. *You're Only Old Once! A Book for Obsolete Children.* 1986. Random. 1st ed. 4to. F/F clip. B17. $12.50

GEISER, Samuel W. *Horticulture & Horticulturists in Early Texas.* 1945. SMU. 100p. VG/wrp. A10. $40.00

GEISER, Samuel W. *Naturalists of the Frontier.* 1948. Dallas. SMU. 296p. cloth. VG/dj. A10. $45.00

GEISMAR, Maxwell. *Mark Twain: American Prophet.* 1970. Houghton Mifflin. 1st ed. 564p. VG. M10. $18.50

GEISMER & SUTER. *Very Young Verses.* 1945. Houghton Mifflin. 12mo. F/VG. B17. $6.50

GEISS & GOLDBERG. *Earth Science & Meteoritics.* 1963. Amsterdam. North-Holland. 8vo. 312p. red cloth. xl. K5. $45.00

GELDART, E.M. *Folk-Lore of Modern Greece: Tales of the People.* 1884. London. 190p. cloth. very scarce. O2. $125.00

GELDART, Mrs. Thomas. *Memorials of Samuel Gurney.* 1859. Phil. Longstreth. 12mo. 168p. VG. V3. $18.00

GELL, William. *William Gell in Italy.* 1976. London. 8vo. 182p. cloth. dj. O2. $35.00

GELLER, Michael. *Major League Murder.* 1988. St Martin. 1st ed. xl. VG/G. P8. $6.00

GELLER, Stephen. *She Let Him Continue.* 1966. NY. 1st ed/author's 1st novel. F/F. A17. $12.50

GELLHORN, Eleanor. *McKay's Guide to Bermuda, the Bahamas & the Caribbean.* 1955. NY. ils/index. 404p. VG/dj. B14. $35.00

GELLHORN, Eleanor. *McKay's Guide to the Middle East.* 1965. McKay. 1st ed. 8vo. F/dj. W1. $8.00

GELLHORN, Walter. *Ombudsmen & Others.* 1967. Harvard. 448p. xl. VG. D3. $25.00

GELLIS & FEINGOLD. *Atlas of Mental Retardation Syndromes.* nd. GPO. 167p. F. K4. $10.00

GELMAN, Steve. *Baseball Bonus Kid.* 1961. Doubleday. later prt. F. P8. $12.50

GEMMILL, W.N. *Romantic America.* 1926. Jordan Pub. 1st ed. inscr. 143p. VG. A8. $35.00

GEMMILL, W.N. *Salem Witch Trials.* 1924. Chicago. 1st ed. ils. 240p. VG. B5. $40.00

GENCO, James G. *Sound of Musketry & the Drum.* 1983. Rochester. 1st ed. 1/500. 195p. VG/VG. A17. $30.00

GENDERS, Roy. *Complete Book of the Dahlia.* 1953. London. ils. 122p. VG/dj. B26. $17.50

GENET, Jean. *Les Paravents.* 1960. Paris. L'Arbalete. 1st ed. sgn. 1/300. NF/wrp/tissue dj. B4. $350.00

GENET, Jean. *Our Lady of the Flowers.* 1963. Grove. 1st ed thus. G+. N2. $5.00

GENTHE, Arnold. *As I Remember.* 1936. NY. 1st ed. VG/G. B5. $55.00

GENTHE, Arnold. *Isadora Duncan. Twenty-Four Studies.* 1929. NY. Kennerly. folio. 24 photo pl/1 facsimile pl. gilt blk cloth. K1. $150.00

GENTLE, Mary. *Golden Witchbreed.* 1984. Morrow. 1st ed. VG/VG. P3. $20.00

GENTRY, C. *Frame-Up...Case of Tom Mooney & Warren Billings.* 1967. NY. 496p. VG. D3. $12.50

GENTRY, Curt. *Killer Mountains.* 1968. NY. 1st ed. VG/VG. B5. $27.50

GENTRY, Howard Scott. *Agaves of Continental North America.* 1982. Tucson. photos/maps. 670p. F/dj. B26. $95.00

GENUNG, John Franklin. *Stevenson's Attitude to Life: With Readings...* 1901. NY. Merrymount. 44p. VG. B14. $95.00

GEORGE, David Lloyd. *War Memoirs...1914-1917.* 1933. Boston. 4 vols. F/djs. A17. $45.00

GEORGE, Elizabeth. *Payment in Blood.* 1989. Bantam. 1st ed. F/F. M15. $30.00

GEORGE, Elizabeth. *Payment in Blood.* 1989. NY. Bantam. ARC/1st Am ed. F/wrp. B2. $35.00

GEORGE, Elizabeth. *Payment in Blood.* 1989. NY. Bantam. 1st ed. sgn. F/F. S6. $45.00

GEORGE, Leopold. *Lehrbuch der Psychologie.* 1854. Berlin. Georg Reimer. 588p. contemporary cloth/marbled brd. G1. $125.00

GEORGE, Nelson. *Blackface.* 1994. Harper Collins. 1st ed. w/promo material. F/F. S9. $25.00

GEORGIADES, Patrice. *De Freud a Platon.* 1934. Paris. Bibliotheque-Charpentier. 12mo. 192p. prt yel wrp. G1. $35.00

GERARD, Francis. *Secret Sceptre.* 1971. Tom Stacey. F/F. P3. $15.00

GERARD, James Watson. *Aquarelles; or, Summer Sketches.* 1858. NY. Stanford Delisser. 1st ed. 12mo. 95p. orange cloth. M1. $125.00

GERARD, Max. *Dali de Draeger.* 1968. Paris. Draeger. 1/1500. 4to. blk stp red cloth w/metal only melted clock. H4. $750.00

GERBAULT, Alain. *In Quest of the Sun.* 1930. Hodder Stoughton. 2nd prt. 315p. gilt bdg. VG. F3. $20.00

GERBER, Albert B. *Sex, Pornography & Justice.* 1965. NY. 349p. G. D3. $6.00

GERBER, Merrill Joan. *King of the World.* 1989. Wainscott, NY. Pushcart. 1st ed. NF/NF. A14. $30.00

GERBER & MCFADDEN. *Loren Eiseley.* 1983. NY. Unger. 183p. M/dj. A10. $10.00

GERGEN, Mary McCanney. *Feminist Thought & Structure of Knowledge.* 1988. NY U. 200p. red cloth. VG/dj. G1. $27.50

GERGMANN, Gustav. *Metaphysics of Logical Positivism.* 1954. Longman Gr. 342p. bl cloth. VG. G1. $32.00

GERNSHEIM, Helmut. *Origins of Photography.* 1982. Thames Hudson. 1st ed. 4to. F/F/F case. S9. $75.00

GERROLD, David. *Chess With a Dragon.* 1987. Walker. 1st ed. F/F. N3. $15.00

GERROLD, David. *Day for Damnation.* 1984. Timescape. 1st ed. F/F. P3. $17.00

GERROLD, David. *Man Who Folded Himself.* 1973. Random. 1st ed. inscr. F/F. N3. $10.00

GERROLD, David. *Matter for Men.* 1983. Timescape. 1st ed. inscr. F/pict wrp. N3. $15.00

GERROLD, David. *When Harlie Was One.* nd. BC. VG/VG. P3. $8.00

GERSBACH, Robert. *Training & Management of the Police Dog.* 1926. Shepherd Dog Club. 1st ed. ils. 66p. G/wrp. R2. $60.00

GERSHWIN, Ira. *Lyrics on Several Occasions.* 1959. NY. 1st ed. VG/VG. B5. $60.00

GERSON, Noel B. *Kit Carson.* 1964. Doubleday. G. B34. $15.00

GERSTER, Georg. *Sahara.* 1959. London. Barrie Rocklif. 302p. VG/torn. W1. $12.00

GERVASI, Frank. *To Whom Palestine?* 1946. Appleton Century. 1st ed. 213p. VG. W1. $10.00

GESELL, Arnold. *First Five Years of Life.* 1954. Methuen. 393p. G/dj. K4. $12.50

GESENIUS, Wilhelm. *Hebraische Grammitk.* 1854. Leipzig. Renger'sche. 8vo. 315p. xl. G. W1. $15.00

GETHERS, Peter. *Getting Blue.* 1987. Delacorte. 1st ed. VG/VG. P8. $12.00

GETHIN, David. *Dane's Testament.* 1986. London. Gollancz. 1st ed. F/F. S6. $20.00

GETZ, S. George. *Essentials of Business Law. Third Edition.* 1947. Prentice Hall. M11. $20.00

GHEERBRANT, Alain. *Incas: Royal Commentaries of Inca Carcilasco de la Vega...* 1961. Orion. 1st ed. 432p. VG/dj. F3. $35.00

GHIRSHMAN, Roman. *Persian Art, the Parthian & Sassanian Dynasties...* 1962. NY. Golden. 1st Eng-language ed. 401p. F/VG-. F1. $75.00

GHOSE, Zulfikar. *Confessions of a Native-Alien.* 1965. London. 1st ed/1st prose book. sgn. F/NF. A11. $45.00

GIANNONE, Pietro. *Civil History of the Kingdom of Naples Written in Italian...* 1729. London/Edinburgh. 2 vol. thick volio. full calf. H4. $1,500.00

GIANTURCO, Emanuele. *Istituzioni di Diritto Civile Italiano.* 1919. Firenza. Barbera. 16mo. 378p. VG. D3. $25.00

GIBB, G. *Whitesmiths of Taunton.* 1943. NY. 1st ed. VG/VG. B5. $50.00

GIBBON & SMART. *Egypt: A Picture Book To Remember Her By.* 1979. Crescent. 4to. ils. F/dj. W1. $15.00

GIBBONS, Kaye. *Charms for the Easy Life.* 1993. Putnam. 1st ed/author's 4th novel. sgn. F/F. L3. $45.00

GIBBONS, Kaye. *Virtuous Woman.* 1989. Chapel Hill. 1st ed. sgn. F/F. A9. $35.00

GIBBONS, Kaye. *Virtuous Woman.* 1989. London. Cape. 1st ed. F/clip. B3. $25.00

GIBBONS, Reginald. *Sweetbitter.* 1994. Seattle. Broken Moon. 1st ed. sgn. F/F. B3. $35.00

GIBBS, James W. *Buckeye Horology: A Review of OH Watch & Clock Makers.* 1971. Columbus, PA. 1st ed. 4to. 138p. gilt bl cloth. VG/G. A8. $40.00

GIBRAN & GIBRAN. *Kahlil Gibran: His Life & World.* 1974. NY Graphic Soc. 1st ed. 442p. VG/dj. W1. $40.00

GIBSON, Charles Dana. *Drawings by...* 1894. NY. obl folio. 120p. modern half leather. A17. $60.00

GIBSON, Charles. *Aztecs Under Spanish Rule: A History...1519-1810.* 1976. Stanford. 8vo. 657p. gray cloth. M/F. P4. $45.00

GIBSON, Hugh. *Journal From Our Legation in Belgium.* 1917. NY. 1st ed. 360p. gilt cloth. VG. A17. $10.00

GIBSON, J.T. *Hist of 78th PA Volunteer Infantry.* 1905. Pittsburgh. 1st ed. 267p. VG. B18. $150.00

GIBSON, James. *Farming the Frontier. Agricultural Opening of OR Country...* 1985. Seattle. WA U. 265p. VG/dj. A10. $25.00

GIBSON, Ralph. *L'Histoire de France.* 1991. Paris Audiovisuel. 1st ed. French text. F/F. S9. $30.00

GIBSON, Walter Murray. *Diaries of Walter Murray Gibson 1886-1887.* 1973. HI U. 1st ed. tall 8vo. 199p. F. P4. $30.00

GIBSON, Walter. *Rod Serling's Twilight Zone.* 1963. Grosset Dunlap. TVTI. VG. P3. $20.00

GIBSON, Walter. *Weird Adventure of the Shadow.* 1966. Grosset. 1st ed. inscr. F/dj. M2. $60.00

GIBSON, William Hamilton. *Eye Spy.* 1902 (1897). Harper. 264p. VG. S11. $25.00

GIBSON, William. *Count Zero.* 1986. Arbor. 1st ed. F/F. P3. $35.00

GIBSON, William. *Virtual Light.* 1993. Bantam. 8th prt. F/F. P3. $20.00

GIBSON, William. *Young Endeavour: Contributions to Science...* 1958. Springfield. 1st ed. 292p. A13. $80.00

GIBSON & GREEN. *Bibliography of A Conan Doyle.* 1984. Oxford/Soho Biblio. 8vo. 712p. gilt red cloth. M. M7. $60.00

GIBSON & HARPER. *Riddle of Jutland.* 1934. NY/London. ils/diagrams/2 pocket charts. 416p. T7. $60.00

GIBSON & JOHNSON. *Print & Privilege at Oxford to the Year 1700.* 1946. Oxford. 4to. ils. VG/worn. scarce. A4. $165.00

GIDE, Andre. *Journals of Andre Gide Vol I: 1889-1913.* 1947. NY. 1st Eng-language ed. intro/trans/inscr J O'Brien. F/NF. A11. $50.00

GIDE, Andre. *Montaigne: Essay in Two Parts.* 1929. London/NY. Blackmore/Liveright. 1st ed. sgn. 1/800. F/NF dj/box. B2. $200.00

GIDE, Andre. *Montaigne: Essay in Two Parts.* 1929. London/NY. 1st ed. sgn. 1/800. F/G. C2. $75.00

GIDE, Andre. *Oedipe. Drame en Trois Actes.* 1931. Paris. Pleiade. 1/450. royal 8vo. 125p. F/cream wrp. H5. $225.00

GIDE, Andre. *Voyage au Congo.* 1927. Paris. Gallimard. 1st ed. 1/1000. #d. ES. NF/wrp. B2. $150.00

GIECK, Jack. *Photo Album of OH's Canal Era, 1825-1913.* 1992. Kent. 2nd prt. sgn. M/dj. B18. $35.00

GIEDION, S. *Eternal Present: Beginnings of Architecture.* 1964. NY. Bollingen. ils. gilt bl cloth. NF/VG. F1. $40.00

GIEDION, S. *Eternal Present: Beginnings of Art.* 1962. NY. Bollingen. 4to. ils. gilt bl cloth. F/VG+. F1. $40.00

GIESEL. *Pocket Book of Boners.* July 1941. Pocket Books. 1st ed thus. sm 16mo. NF/pict wrp. C8. $35.00

GIESMAR, Peter. *Fanon.* 1971. NY. 1st ed. 214p. VG/VG. A17. $9.50

GIESY, J.U. *All for His Country.* 1915. Macaulay. G+. P3. $25.00

GIFFORD, Barry. *Kerouac's Town.* 1973. Santa Barbara. 1st ed/trade issue. Capra Chapbook. sgn. F/12mo wrp. $40.00

GIFFORD, Barry. *Port Tropique.* 1980. Berkeley. 1st ed. sgn. F/8vo wrp. A11. $40.00

GIFFORD, Denis. *Pictorial History of Horror Movies.* 1974. Hamlyn. 7th prt. VG/VG. P3. $20.00

GIL, Enrique. *Evolucion del Panamericanismo.* 1933. Buenos Aires. 490p. half leather/red cloth. VG. F3. $30.00

GILB, Dagoberto. *Magic of Blood.* 1993. Albuquerque. ARC/author's 1st book. sgn. NF/pict wrp. B3. $75.00

GILBERT, Anthony. *And Death Came Too.* 1977. Hamish Hamilton. VG/VG. P3. $15.00

GILBERT, Anthony. *No Dust in the Attic.* 1963. Random. 1st ed. VG/G. P3. $20.00

GILBERT, Davies. *Mount Calvary...Written in Cornish...* 1826. London. Nichols. 95p. wrp. H10. $37.50

GILBERT, James Burkhart. *Writers & Partisans.* 1968. NY. Wiley. 1st ed. F/NF. B2. $35.00

GILBERT, Katherine. *Studies in Recent Aesthetic.* 1927. Chapel Hill. 12mo. 178p. blk cloth. VG. G1. $27.50

GILBERT, Martin. *Arab-Israeli Conflict: Its Hist in Maps.* 1979. London. Weidenfeld Nicholson. 3rd ed. 115 maps. VG. W1. $18.00

GILBERT, Michael. *Games Without Rules.* 1967. Harper. 1st ed. NF/NF. B2. $50.00

GILBERT, Michael. *Night of the Twelfth.* nd. Harper Row. F/F. P3. $10.00

GILBERT, Michael. *Petrella at Q.* 1977. London. Hodder Stoughton. 1st ed. VG+/dj. S6. $25.00

GILBERT, Michael. *Young Petrella.* 1988. London. Hodder Stoughton. 1st ed. NF/dj. S6. $25.00

GILBERT, Vivian. *Romance of the Last Crusade.* 1923. NY. Appleton. 1st ed. 238p. bl cloth. VG. M7. $45.00

GILBERT, W.S. *Gilbert Without Sullivan.* 1981. Viking. 1st ed. ils LB Lubin. M/M. C8. $30.00

GILBERT & GREGG. *Love: A Diptych.* 1994. Captain's Bookshelf. 1/150. sgn authors/artist. F/wrp. V1. $125.00

GILBEY, Walter. *Early Carriages & Roads.* 1903. London. Vinton. 1st ed. VG. O3. $68.00

GILBEY, Walter. *Harness Horse.* 1898. London. Vinton. 1st ed. VG. O3. $65.00

GILBEY, Walter. *Old English War-Horse or Shire-Horse.* 1888. London. 1st ed. leather. VG. O3. $125.00

GILBO, Patrick. *American Red Cross: First Century.* 1981. NY. 300 photos. 246p. A13. $40.00

GILBRETH & GILBRETH. *Applied Motion Study: A Collection of Papers...* 1917. NY. inscr pres. 200p. VG. B14. $250.00

GILBY, Myriam. *Free Weaving.* 1976. np. cloth. VG. G2. $15.00

GILCHRIST, Ellen. *Drunk With Love.* 1986. Little Brn. 1st ed. F/F. S9. $45.00

GILCHRIST, Ellen. *In the Land of Dreamy Dreams.* 1982. London. 1st Eng ed/author's 1st book. sgn. F/F. A11. $55.00

GILCHRIST, Ellen. *In the Land of Dreamy Dreams.* 1982. London. Faber. 1st ed/author's 1st novel. F/F. S9. $45.00

GILCHRIST, Ellen. *Net of Jewels.* 1992. Little Brn. 1st ed. 360p. M/M. A17. $15.00

GILCHRIST, Ellen. *Victory Over Japan.* 1985. London. Faber. 1st ed. F/F. B3. $20.00

GILDART, Robert. *Montana's Early-Day Rangers.* 1985. MT Magazine. pb. VG. B34. $9.00

GILDER, Richard Watson. *Five Books of Song.* 1894. Century. 1st ed. 8vo. 240p. F/VG. C6. $150.00

GILES, Daphne S. *Collection of Scriptural & Miscellaneous Poems.* 1845. Ann Arbor. Cole Arnold. 1st ed. 1mo. 172p. contemporary cloth. M1. $200.00

GILES, Kenneth. *Death Among the Stars.* 1969. Walker. 1st ed. F/F. P3. $10.00

GILIGAN, Edmund. *Gaunt Woman.* 1943. Scribner. 1st ed. VG/G. P3. $20.00

GILL, B.M. *Nursery Crimes.* 1986. London. Hodder Stoughton. 1st ed. sgn. F/F. S6. $40.00

GILL, Bartholomew. *McGarr & the Method of Descartes.* 1984. Viking. 1st ed. F/F. P3. $15.00

GILL, Bartholomew. *McGarr & the Sienese Conspiracy.* 1979. London. Hale. 1st Eng ed. F/NF. S6. $25.00

GILL, Charles. *Boozer Challenge.* 1987. Dutton. 1st ed. rem mk. M/M. P8. $17.50

GILL, Elizabeth. *Crime Coast.* 1931. Crime Club. 1st ed. VG. P3. $20.00

GILL, Eric. *First Nudes.* 1954. London. Neville Spearman. 1st ed. intro Sir John Rothenstein. NF/NF. S9. $65.00

GILL, Patrick; see Creasey, John.

GILLEN, Mollie. *Wheel of Things, Biography of LM Montgomery.* 1976. Harrap. 1st ed. brd. F/VG. M5. $60.00

GILLET, R. *Pleasures of Reason; or, Hundred Thoughts...* 1809. Boston. 1st ed (from 3rd London ed). 88 p. VG. B14. $95.00

GILLETT, HOWELL & LESCHKE. *Flora of Lassen Volcanic National Park, CA.* 1961. San Francisco. inscr. photo frontis/maps. sc. VG. B26. $27.50

GILLMER, Thomas C. *Working Watercraft.* 1972. Camden. Internat Marine. ils. 184p. dj. T7. $40.00

GILLMOR, Frances. *Flute of the Smoking Mirror: Portrait Nezahualcoyotl Poet...* 1968. AZ U. ils/notes/index. 183p. F/VG. B19. $30.00

GILLMOR, Frances. *King Danced in the Market Place.* 1977. UT U. 271p. map ep. VG/wrp. F3. $10.00

GILLMOR, Frances. *Windsinger.* 1930. NY. Milton Balch. 1st ed. inscr. 218p. G. B11. $30.00

GILMAN, Bradley. *Kingdom of Coins.* 1889. Roberts. 1st ed. ils Frank T Merrill. pict brd. VG. M5. $20.00

GILMAN, Charlotte Perkins. *Herland.* 1979. Pantheon. 1st ed. xl. dj. P3. $7.00

GILMAN, Dorothy. *Maze in the Heart of the Castle.* 1983. Doubleday. 1st ed. 230p. NF/NF. P2. $25.00

GILMAN, Dorothy. *Mrs Pollifax & the Hong Kong Buddha.* 1985. Doubleday. 1st ed. F/F. P3. $15.00

GILMAN, Laselle. *Red Gate.* 1953. Ballantine. 1st ed. VG/VG. P3. $30.00

GILMAN, Robert C. *Starkahn of Rhada.* 1970. HBW. 1st ed. VG. P3. $25.00

GILMAN, William. *Our Hidden Front.* 1944. NY. 266p. VG/VG. A17. $10.00

GILMORE, Betty. *Needlepoint Primer.* 1973. np. sc. VG. G2. $8.00

GILMOUR, Pat. *Lasting Impressions: Lithography As Art.* 1988. London. Alexandria. 1st ed. F/NF. P4. $60.00

GILMOUR, William. *Undying Land.* 1985. Donald Grant. 1st ed. F/F. P3. $20.00

GILPATRICK, Guy. *Flying Stories.* 1946. NY. 1st ed. VG/G. B5. $40.00

GILPATRICK, Guy. *High Seas Over.* 1932. NY. 1st ed. VG/VG. B5. $45.00

GILROY, Frank D. *From Noon 'Til Three.* 1973. Doubleday. 1st ed. F/dj. F4. $17.00

GILSON, Etienne. *Christian Philosophy of St Thomas Aquinas.* ca 1956. Random. trans LK Shook. 502p. H10. $25.00

GILTSOFF, Natalie. *Fashion Bead Embroidery.* 1971. np. cloth. VG. G2. $7.00

GINGERICH & WELTHER. *Planetary, Lunar & Solar Positions.* 1983. Phil. Am Philosophical Soc. VG/G. K5. $20.00

GINGHER, Marianne. *Bobby Rex's Greatest Hit.* 1986. Atheneum. 1st ed/author's 1st book. RS. F/F. C6. $30.00

GINGRICH, Arnold. *Joys of Trout.* 1937. Crown. photos. NF/dj. B34. $50.00

GINGRICH, Arnold. *Well-Tempered Angler.* 1965. NY. 1st ed. VG/VG. B5. $35.00

GINNS, R. *Gymnocalyciums.* ca 1966. Morden, Surrey. photos. 44p. sc. F. B26. $9.00

GINSBERG, Allen. *Careless Love.* 1978. Madison. Red Ozier. 1/280. sgn. F/wrp. B4. $50.00

GINSBERG, Allen. *Empty Mirror.* 1961. NY. Cornith/Totem. 1st ed. sgn/dtd 1963. NF. B4. $175.00

GINSBERG, Allen. *Gates of Wrath: Rhymed Poems 1948-1952.* 1972. Grey Fox. ltd ed. sgn. 1/100 #d. F. V1. $95.00

GINSBERG, Allen. *Planet News 1961-1967.* 1970. City Lights. 2nd prt. inscr/2 drawings. NF/wrp. B4. $150.00

GINSBERG, Allen. *Planet News.* 1968. City Lights. NF/wrp. M19. $25.00

GINSBERG, Allen. *Reality Sandwiches.* 1971. City Lights. later prt. inscr. NF/wrp. B4. $150.00

GINSBERG, Allen. *To Eberhart From Ginsberg.* 1976. Penmaen. 1st ed. 1/1200. F/F. V1. $45.00

GINSBERG, Morris. *Idea of Progress: Revaluation.* 1953. Boston. Beacon. 82p. gray cloth. VG/dj. G1. $20.00

GINSBURG, Mirra. *Last Door to Aiya.* 1968. SG Phillips. 1st ed. F/F. P3. $23.00

GINZBERG, Eli. *Pattern for Hospital Care. Final Report...* 1949. NY. 1st ed. 368p. A13. $35.00

GIORGI, Amadeo. *Duquesne Studies in Phenomenology Vol 1.* 1973. Duquesne. 2nd prt/trade pb. VG. G1. $30.00

GIOVIO, Paolo. *Commentario de le Cose de Turchi...* 1544. Venice. Bernardino de Bindoni. sm 8vo. 52 leaves. antique calf. O2. $1,350.00

GIRAUD, S. Louis. *Hans Andersen's Fairy Stories.* 1934-1951. London. Strand. mechanical pop-up. VG+. C8. $100.00

GIRL SCOUTS OF AMERICA. *Girl Scout Handbook.* 1933. Girl Scouts. NF. E5. $20.00

GIRONELLA, Jose Maria. *One Million Dead.* 1963. Doubleday. trans Joan MacLean. G/G. V4. $15.00

GIRONELLA, Jose Maria. *Peace After War.* 1969. Knopf. G/G. V4. $15.00

GITTINGS, Robert. *Peach Blossom Forest.* 1951. Oxford. 1st ed. VG/VG. P3. $20.00

GIVENS, Charles G. *Jig-Time Murders.* 1936. Bobbs Merrill. 1st ed. VG. P3. $25.00

GJERTSEN, Derek. *Newton Handbook.* 1986. Kegan Paul. lg 8vo. 665p. VG/VG. K5. $28.00

GLADSTEIN, Richard. *Argument to the Jury...* nd. Civil Rights Congress. 1st ed. VG/wrp. B2. $30.00

GLADSTONE & GLADSTONE. *Needlepoint Alphabet Book.* 1973. np. cloth. VG. G2. $40.00

GLASBY, J.S. *Variable Stars.* 1969. Cambridge. Harvard. 8vo. 333p. VG/VG. K5. $30.00

GLASCOW, Ellen. *Deliverance.* 1904. Doubleday Page. 1st ed. sgn/dtd 1931. VG. B4. $100.00

GLASER, Daniel. *Effectiveness of a Prison & Parole System.* 1964. Bobbs Merrill. M11. $35.00

GLASIER, Gilson G. *Autobiography of Roujet D Marshall, Justice... 2 Vols.* 1923. Madison, WI. Democrat Prt Co. gr cloth. M11. $75.00

GLASS, David C. *Environmental Influences. Biology & Behavior.* 1968. NY. Rockefeller U. 265p. F/dj. K4. $20.00

GLASS, David C. *Genetics.* 1968. Rockefeller U. 260p. G. K4. $15.00

GLASS, David C. *Neurophysiology & Emotion.* 1967. Rockefeller. 234p. cloth. F. B14. $45.00

GLASS, Justine. *Story of Biochemistry.* 1964. NY. 1st ed. 232p. A13. $50.00

GLASSCOCK, C.B. *War of the Copper Kings.* 1966 (1962). Grosset. VG/dj. B34. $55.00

GLATTHAAR, J.T. *Forged in Battle.* 1990. ils/index. 370p. dj. O8. $12.50

GLAZE, Harold. *Merry Piper; or, Magical Trip of the Sugar Bowl Ship.* 1925. Longman. 1st ed. 8 mc pl. cloth. VG. M5. $85.00

GLAZER, Nathan. *Remembering the Answers.* 1970. NY. NF/dj. D3. $15.00

GLAZNER, Greg. *From the Iron Chair.* 1992. Norton. 1st ed. F/F. B3. $20.00

GLEASON, Ralph. *Jam Session: Anthology of Jazz.* 1958. Putnam. VG. N2. $17.50

GLEASON, Robert W. *Yahweh: God of the Old Testament.* 1964. Prentice Hall. 124p. VG/dj. B29. $3.00

GLEICK, James. *Chaos: Making a New Science.* 1988 (1987). Viking. 11th prt. 8 mc pl/photos/diagrams. 352p. VG/VG. K5. $20.00

GLEN, Douglas. *In the Steps of Lawrence of Arabia.* 1939. London. Rich Cowan. 1st ed. 320p. gilt cloth. VG+/G. M7. $65.00

GLEN, W. Cunningham. *Treatise on the Law of Highways.* 1860. London. Butterworth. 1st ed. VG. O3. $145.00

GLENN, John H. Jr. *PS I Listened To Your Heart Beat: Letters to John Glenn.* 1964. World Book Encyclopedia. 8vo. 248p. G/torn. K5. $14.00

GLENN, Lois. *Charles WS Williams: Checklist.* 1975. Kent State. 128p. VG. A17. $12.50

GLIMCHER, Arnold B. *Louise Nevelson.* 1972. Praeger. 1st ed. ils. NF/NF. S9. $35.00

GLOAG, John. *English Tradition in Design.* 1947. London. Penguin. ils. 72p. brd. VG. M10. $5.00

GLOAG, John. *Englishman's Castle.* 1944. London. Eyre Spottiswode. 176p. VG/G. S11. $15.00

GLUBB, John Bagot. *Empire of the Arabs.* 1965. Prentice Hall. 8vo. 384p. VG. W1. $30.00

GLUBB, John Bagot. *Short History of the Arab Peoples.* 1988. Dorset. 2nd prt. 318p. gilt bl cloth. M. M7. $9.00

GLUBB, John Bagot. *Soldier With the Arabs.* 1957. NY. Harper. 1st Am ed. 23 pl. 458p. VG/torn. W1. $22.00

GLUCK, Louise. *House on Marshland.* 1975. Ecco. 1st ed. NF/VG clip. L3. $40.00

GLUECK, Nelson. *Deities & Dolphins.* 1965. FSG. 1st prt. 650p. VG/dj. W1. $45.00

GLUECK, Nelson. *River Jordan.* 1968. McGraw Hill. 1st ed. 235p. VG/dj. W1. $22.00

GLUECK, Nelson. *Rivers in the Desert.* 1959. FSC. 2nd prt. 302p. VG/dj. W1. $22.00

GLUECK & GLUECK. *Delinquents & Nondelinquents in Perspective.* 1968. Harvard. 4to. 268p. xl. VG. D3. $12.50

GLUECK & GLUECK. *One Thousand Juvenile Delinquents...* 1970. NY. rpt of 1934 ed. 341p. buckram. NF. D3. $15.00

GLYN, Elinor. *Philosophy of Love.* 1923. Auburn. Author's Pr. 251p. VG/worn. A17. $8.50

GMELIN, C.G. *Versuche Ueber die Wirkungen des Raryts...* 1824. Tuebingen. H Laupp. 96p. VG/wrp. B14. $350.00

GNOLI, Domenico. *Orestes; or, The Act of Smiling No 611.* 1961. Simon Schuster. 1st ed. 71p. VG-. A3. $60.00

GOBINEAU, J.-A. *World of the Persians.* 1971. Geneva. Minerva. 1st ed. ils. VG/dj. W1. $20.00

GOBLE, Neil. *Asimov Alalyzed.* 1972. Mirage. 1st ed. F/dj. M2. $10.00

GOBLE, Neil. *Asimov Analyzed.* 1972. Mirage. 1st ed. sgn Asimov. F/F. F4. $35.00

GOCEK, Fatma M. *East Encounters West: France & the Ottoman Empire...* 1987. NY. ils. 192p. cloth. O2. $25.00

GOCKEL, Herman W. *Answer to Anxiety.* 1961. Concordia. 179p. G/dj. B29. $3.50

GODDARD, John. *Kayaks Down the Nile.* 1979. Provo, UT. 8vo. 318p. VG. W1. $8.00

GODDARD, Ken. *Prey.* 1992. NY. Tor. 1st ed. F/F. B3. $10.00

GODDEN, Rumer. *Candy Floss.* 1960. Viking. 1st ed. 8vo. VG/G. A3. $35.00

GODDEN, Rumer. *Diddakoi.* 1972. Viking. 1st ed. pict paper brd. M/M. C8. $30.00

GODDEN, Rumer. *Dolls' House.* 1948. Viking. 1st ed. ils Dana Saintsbury. VG/G. A3. $40.00

GODDEN, Rumer. *Fairy Doll.* 1967. Viking. 7th prt. ils Adrienne Adams. 67p. VG/VG. A3. $10.00

GODDEN, Rumer. *Impunity Jane.* 1954. Viking. 1st ed. 8vo. 47p. VG/G. A3. $35.00

GODDEN, Rumer. *Story of Holly & Ivy.* 1985. Viking Kestrel. 1st ed thus. ils/inscr Barbara Cooney. M/M. C8. $75.00

GODEY, John. *Fatal Beauty.* 1984. Irwin. 1st ed. G+/dj. P3. $15.00

GODFRAY, Hugh. *Elementary Treatise on the Lunar Theory.* 1981. NY. Arno. rpt of 3rd revised 1871 ed. beige cloth. VG. K5. $30.00

GODIN, Gabriel. *Analysis of Tides.* 1972. Toronto U. 4to. 264p. VG/VG. K5. $30.00

GODWIN, Felix. *Exploration of the Solar System.* 1960. London. Chapman Hall. sm 4to. ils. 200p. bl cloth. G. K5. $25.00

GODWIN, Gail. *Southern Family.* 1987. London. Heinemann. 1st ed. NF/VG. B3. $15.00

GODWIN, Parke. *Firelord.* 1980. Doubleday. 1st ed. VG/G. P3. $18.00

GODWIN, Tom. *Survivors.* 1958. Gnome. 1st ed. VG/dj. M2. $45.00

GODWIN & KAYE. *Wintermind.* 1982. Doubleday. 1st ed. F/F. P3. $15.00

GOEBEL, Julius Jr. *King's Law & Local Custom in 17th-Century New Eng.* nd. np. 448p. VG/wrp. D3. $17.50

GOELL, Milton J. *Wall That Is My Skin.* 1945. NY. Wendell Mailliet. 1st ed. F/NF. B2. $35.00

GOERNER, Fred. *Search for Amelia Earhart.* 1966. Doubleday. 1st ed. sgn. VG/VG clip. S11. $18.00

GOESII, Wilelmi. *Rei Agrarie Auctores Legesque Variae...* 1674. Waesberge. Janssonium. ils/fld table. rebacked. H10. $185.00

GOETZMANN & SLOAN. *Looking Far North: Harriman Expediiton to Alaska 1899.* 1983. Princeton. Viking. 1st ed. pb. 244p. M. P4. $12.00

GOFF, John S. *AZ Territorial Officials I: Supreme Court Justices...1912.* 1975. Blk Mtn. 1st ed. ils. 199p. F/sans. B19. $25.00

GOFF, John S. *George WP Hunt & His AZ.* 1973. Socio-Technical Pub. index/notes. 286p. F/NF. B19. $45.00

GOFFSTEIN, Brooke. *Our Prairie Home, a Picture Album.* 1988. Harper. 1st ed. M/F. C8. $25.00

GOGARTY, Oliver St. John. *Elbow Room.* 1942. DSP. 1st ed. NF/G. V1. $45.00

GOHN, Jack B. *Kingsley Amis: A Checklist.* 1976. Kent State. 230 p. cloth. VG. A17. $10.00

GOING, Maud. *Field, Forest & Wayside Flowers.* 1899. NY. 102 photos/drawings. 411p. cloth. B26. $25.00

GOLD, Douglas. *Schoolmaster With the Blackfeet Indians.* 1963. NY. Caxton. 1st ed. 8vo. 287p. VG/VG. B11. $25.00

GOLD, E.J. *Joy of Sacrifice.* 1978. IDHHB. 1st ed. 246p. VG. B33. $20.00

GOLD, Fay. *Louie: Story of a Yorkshire Terrier.* 1971. NY. 18p. stapled wrp. scarce. R2. $30.00

GOLD, H.L. *Fourth Galexy Reader.* 1959. Doubleday. 1st ed. VG/VG. P3. $30.00

GOLD, H.L. *Old Die Rich.* 1965. Dobson. 1st ed. VG/VG. P3. $45.00

GOLD, Herbert. *Prospect Before Us.* 1954. Cleveland. 1st ed/author's 2nd novel. inscr. F/NF. A11. $60.00

GOLD, Michael. *Hollow Men.* 1941. Internat. 1st hc ed. NF/NF. B2. $50.00

GOLD, Michael. *120 Million.* 1929. Internat. 1st ed. NF. B2. $45.00

GOLDBERG, B.Z. *Sacred Fire: Story of Sex & Religion.* 1930. np. 1st ed. 386p. A13. $35.00

GOLDBERG, Hyman. *Our Man in the Kitchen.* (1964). Odyssey. ils Wm Hogarth. 386p. F/VG. H1. $7.50

GOLDBERG, Isaac. *Tin Pan Alley: A Chronicle of Am Popular Music Racket.* 1930. NY. John Day. ils. 340p. purple cloth. VG. B14. $50.00

GOLDBERG, Rube. *Is There a Doctor in the House?* 1930. John Day. 3rd prt. inscr/dtd 1931. VG. B4. $85.00

GOLDBERG, Rube. *Rube Goldberg Vs the Machine Age.* 1968. Hastings House. 1st ed. NF/VG. B3. $20.00

GOLDEN, Francis Leo. *Laughter Is Legal.* 1951. NY. 4th prt. 280p. VG. D3. $15.00

GOLDEN & ROLAND. *Sir William Osler: Annotated Bibliography With Ils.* 1988. San Francisco. 1st ed. 214p. dj. A13. $125.00

GOLDIN, Gullie B. *Coming Peace Settlement With Germany.* 1943. NY. Reklam. M11. $35.00

GOLDIN, Stephen. *Assault on the Gods.* 1977. Doubleday. 1st ed. F/F. P3. $15.00

GOLDING, Louis. *Goodbye to Ithaca.* 1955. London. Hutchinson. 1st ed. NF/F. B4. $100.00

GOLDING, M.P. *Nature of Law: Readings in Legal Philosophy.* 1966. NY. 376p. VG. D3. $10.00

GOLDING, William. *Close Quarters.* 1987. FSG. 1st ed. F/F. B3. $15.00

GOLDING, William. *Egyptian Journal.* 1985. London. Faber. 1st ed. royal 8vo. 207p. F/NF. H5. $50.00

GOLDING, William. *Nobel Lecture.* 1984. Lemington Spa, Eng. Sixth Chamber. 1/50 #d. sgn. F/marbled cb case. H5. $300.00

GOLDING, William. *Paper Men.* 1984. FSG. 1st ed. F/F. P3. $15.00

GOLDING, William. *Temple of Gold.* 1957. Knopf. 1st ed/author's 1st book. 277p. NF/NF. H5. $200.00

GOLDMAN, Elliott. *Clarence Williams Discography.* nd. London. Jazz Music Books. 28p. VG/wrp. B2. $50.00

GOLDMAN, Emma. *Anarchism & Other Essays.* 1910. Mother Earth. F/VG. V4. $100.00

GOLDMAN, Emma. *Anarchism & Other Essays.* 1950s. Indore. Modern Pub. 1st ed. VG. B2. $45.00

GOLDMAN, Emma. *Philosophy of Atheism & Failure of Christianity.* 1916. Mother Earth. 1st ed. F/wrp. scarce. B2. $175.00

GOLDMAN, Emma. *Syndicalism: Modern Menace to Capitalism.* 1913. Mother Earth. 1st ed. NF/wrp. B2. $175.00

GOLDMAN, Emma. *Truth About the Boylsheviki.* nd. Mother Earth. 1st ed. F/wrp. B2. $150.00

GOLDMAN, Lawrence Louis. *Tiger by the Tail.* 1946. McKay. VG/G. P3. $15.00

GOLDMAN, Nathan C. *American Space Law: Internat & Domestic.* 1988. IA State U. 8vo. 374p. blk cloth. G. K5. $20.00

GOLDMAN, William. *Color of Light.* 1984. Warner. 1st ed. VG/VG. P3. $18.00

GOLDMAN, William. *Father's Day.* 1971. HBJ. 1st ed. F/VG+. N3. $10.00

GOLDMAN, William. *Father's Day.* 1971. Michael Joseph. 1st ed. VG. P3. $10.00

GOLDMAN, William. *Marathon Man.* 1974. Delacorte. 1st ed. VG/VG. P3. $30.00

GOLDMAN, William. *Princess Bride.* 1973. Harcourt Brace. 1st ed. F/F. Q1. $375.00

GOLDMAN, William. *Soldier in the Rain.* 1960. NY. 1st ed. 308p. VG/dj. B18. $22.50

GOLDMAN, William. *Temple of Gold.* 1957. NY. 1st ed/author's 1st book. sgn. NF/NF. A11. $110.00

GOLDMAN & SAUNDERS. *Directory of Unpublished Experimental Mental Measures.* 1974. NY. Behavorial Pub. 213p. G. K4. $14.00

GOLDMARK, Josephine. *Fatigue & Efficiency: Study in Industry.* 1912. Russell Sage Found. 3rd ed. pres. 326p. H1. $16.00

GOLDMSITH, Joel S. *Conscious Union With God.* 1974. University Books. 253p. VG/VG. B33. $15.00

GOLDMSITH, Joel S. *Living the Infinite Way.* 1988. Harper Row. revised ed. 128p. VG/VG. B33. $10.00

GOLDSBOROUGH, Robert. *Death on Deadline.* 1989. London. Collins. 1st Eng ed. sgn. F/dj. S6. $35.00

GOLDSBOROUGH, Robert. *Murder in E Minor.* 1986. Bantam. 1st ed. F/F. P3. $15.00

GOLDSCHEIDER, Ludwig. *Ghiberti.* 1949. NY. lg folio. 120 pl. VG/VG. A17. $25.00

GOLDSCHMIDT, Arthur Jr. *Concise Hist of the Middle East.* nd. Boulder/Cairo. Westview/Cairo U. 2nd ed. 8vo. 13 maps. G. W1. $12.00

GOLDSCHMIDT, Walter. *Sebei Law.* 1967. CA U. ils/maps. 303p. xl. VG. D3. $15.00

GOLDSEN, Joseph M. *Outer Space in World Politics.* 1963. London. Pall Mall. 8vo. 180p. G/dj. K5. $18.00

GOLDSMITH, Donald E. *Scientists Confront Velikovsky.* 1977. Cornell. 8vo. 183p. VG/dj. K5. $15.00

GOLDSMITH, Oliver. *Goody Two Shoes.* 1924. Macmillan. Little Lib. 1st ed thus. ils Alice Woodward. cloth. F/G. M5. $38.00

GOLDSMITH, Oliver. *Miscellaneous Works of...* 1850. Putnam. rpt of 1837 (1st) London ed. G. H1. $28.00

GOLDSMITH, Oliver. *Vicar of Wakefield.* nd (ca 1900). London/NY. 224p. aeg. pict cloth. G. B18. $22.50

GOLDSMITH, Oliver. *Vicar of Wakefield.* ca 1905. London. Frowde. 55x47mm. 584p. aeg. red morocco. B24. $200.00

GOLDSMITH, Oliver. *Vicar of Wakefield.* 1929. Harrap. 1st ed. 24 full-p Rackham pl. VG. Q1. $175.00

GOLDSMITH, Oliver. *Vicar of Wakefield.* 1929. McKay. 1st ed. 4to. ils Rackham. teg. VG/G. B17. $100.00

GOLDSTEIN, Leon J. *Historical Knowing.* 1976. Austin/London. TX U. 242p. tan cloth. VG/dj. G1. $25.00

GOLDSTEIN, Lisa. *Dream Years.* 1985. Bantam. 1st ed. F/F. P3. $15.00

GOLDSTEIN. *Bioethics. A Guide to Information Sources.* 1982. np. 384p. xl. VG. A4. $65.00

GOLDTHWAIT, John T. *Value, Language & Life.* 1985. Prometheus. 336p. F/dj. K4. $15.00

GOLDWATER, Barry. *Face of Arizona.* 1964. np. 1/100. sgn. F. H4. $300.00

GOLDWATER, Barry. *Speeches of Henry Fountain Ashurst of AZ.* nd. np. 1st ed. inscr. 110p. C6. $45.00

GOLDWURM, Caspar. *Kirchen Calendar: In Welchem Nach Ordnung Gemeiner...* 1588 (1559). Frankfurt. Christian Egenolffs Erben. 8vo. woodcuts. 346p. vellum. K1. $1,000.00

GOLENBOCK, Peter. *Teammates.* 1990. Harcourt Brace. 2nd prt. ils Paul Bacon. M/M. C8. $20.00

GOLLER, Nicholas. *Tomorrow's Silence.* 1979. Macmillan. 1st ed. VG/VG. P3. $15.00

GOLLOMB, Joseph. *Curtain of Storm.* 1933. Macmillan. 1st ed. F/VG. M15. $35.00

GOLOMBEK, Harry. *Chess, a History.* 1976. np. 4to. ils. 256p. F/VG. A4. $30.00

GOLYNETS. *Ivan Bilibin.* 1981. np. 4to. 227p. F/F. A4. $85.00

GOMME, George. *Princess's Story Book.* 1901. London. Constable. ils Helen Stratton. 443p. teg. gilt pict bdg. VG. P2. $65.00

GOMPERTZ, Heinrich. *Psychologische Beobachtungen Griechischen Philosophen.* 1924. Leipzig. Internationaler Psychoanalytischer. 92p. VG. G1. $37.50

GONZALES, Laurence. *Jambeaux.* 1979. HBJ. 1st ed/author's 1st novel. rem mk. NF/F dj/wrp band. B4. $85.00

GOOCH, Fanny Chambers. *Face to Face With the Mexicans.* 1887. NY. Fords Howard. 1st ed. 584p. pict cloth. G. F3. $75.00

GOOCH, G. *Frederick the Great: Ruler, Writer, Man.* 1947. np. 1st ed. 400p. VG. E5. $28.00

GOOD, John Mason. *Patologia: A New Encyclopedia...* 1813. London. 12 vol. 8vo. 370 full-p pl. full flame calf. C6. $500.00

GOODALL, Daphne M. *Seventh Continent.* ca 1969. Royston. Priory. ils. 74p. VG/VG clip. P4. $30.00

GOODBLATT, Morris S. *Jewish Life in Turky in the XVth Century...* 1952. NY. 1st ed. 8vo. 240p. cloth. O2. $40.00

GOODELL, William. *Forty Years in the Turkish Empire; or, Memoirs...* 1876. NY. 1st ed. inscr pres. 489p. cloth. O2. $100.00

GOODENOUGH, Erwin R. *Psychology of Religious Experiences.* 1965. Basic Books. 192p. VG/VG. B33. $15.00

GOODENOUGH, Florence L. *Mental Testing: Its Hist, Principles & Applications.* 1949. Rinehart. 592p. G. K4. $8.50

GOODHART, A.L. *Essays in Jurisprudence & the Common Law.* 1931. Cambridge. 1st ed/author's 1st book. 295p. VG. D3. $45.00

GOODHART, A.L. *Precedents in Eng & Continental Law.* 1934. London. Stevens Ltd. M11. $65.00

GOODIS, David. *Dark Passage.* 1946. Julian Messner. VG. P3. $45.00

GOODIS, David. *Retreat From Oblivion.* 1939. Dutton. 1st ed/author's 1st book. F/NF dj/custom case. B4. $2,500.00

GOODMAN, Eric. *In Days of Awe.* 1991. Knopf. 1st ed. F/F. P8. $15.00

GOODMAN, Frances. *Embroidery of Mexico & Guatemala.* 1976. np. cloth. VG. G2. $20.00

GOODMAN, Henry Nelson. *Fact, Fiction & Forecast.* 1955. Cambridge. Harvard. sm 8vo. 126p. orange cloth. NF/dj. G1. $36.50

GOODMAN, Henry Nelson. *Problems & Projects.* 1972. Bobbs Merrill. 463p. red brd. VG/dj. G1. $30.00

GOODMAN, Paul. *Ceremonial Stories 1936-1940. Vol II.* 1978. Blk Sparrow. 1/200. 8vo. 273p. Earle Gray bdg. F. H5. $75.00

GOODMAN, W. *Percentage of the Take.* 1971. NY. 226p. VG/dj. D3. $12.50

GOODMAN, William. *Breakup of Our Camp.* 1978. Blk Sparrow. 1st trade ed. 1/750. F/acetate. S9. $25.00

GOODMAN, William. *Marathon Man.* 1974. Delacorte. AP. NF/wrp. S9. $40.00

GOODRICH, Charles A. *Universal Traveller: Designed To Introduce Readers...* 1836. Hartford. 8vo. 610p. contemporary calf. O2. $75.00

GOODRICH, Lloyd. *Max Weber.* 1949. NY. 1st ed. 58p. VG/dj. B18. $17.50

GOODRICH, Lloyd. *Reginald Marsh.* nd. Abrams. 1st ed. VG+/VG+. A1. $175.00

GOODSPEED, Bernice. *Mexican Tales: Compilation of Mexican Stories & Legends...* 1937. Mexico. 1st ed. inscr. 227p. VG/wrp. F3. $20.00

GOODSPEED, Charles. *Angling in America.* 1939. Boston. 1st ed. sgn. 1/795. VG/orig glassine/box. B5. $300.00

GOODSPEED, E.J. *Hist of Great Fires of Chicago & the West.* 1871. Goodspeed. 676p. gilt gr cloth. VG. M20. $50.00

GOODSPEED, Edgar J. *How To Read the Bible.* 1947. Winston. 244p. G. B29. $3.50

GOODSPEED, Edgar J. *Story of the New Testament.* 1946. Chicago. 150p. VG. B29. $3.00

GOODSPEED, Thomas Wakefield. *Hist of U of Chicago.* 1916. Chicago. xl. F. B14. $95.00

GOODWIN, William B. *Spanish & English Ruins in Jamaica.* 1946. Boston. Meador. 239p. F/VG. B11. $75.00

GOOKIN, Frederick William. *Japanese Colour-Prints & Their Designers.* 1913. NY. Japan Soc. tall 4to. ils. cloth/brd. reading copy. F1. $65.00

GORBATSKII, V.G. *Exploding Stars & Galaxies.* 1970. Jerusalem. 8vo. 49 photos. 121p. paper wrp. K5. $15.00

GORDIMER, Nadine. *Burger's Daughter.* 1979. Viking. 1st ed. NF/F. B3. $25.00

GORDIMER, Nadine. *Occasion for Loving.* 1963. London. Gollancz. 1st ed. NF/VG+. B4. $125.00

GORDIMER & GOLDBLATT. *Lifetimes: Under Apartheid.* 1986. Knopf. 1st ed. sgn. F/F. L3. $225.00

GORDON, Anna A. *Beautiful Life of Francis E Willard.* 1898. Womens Temperance Pub. Memorial ed. lg 8vo. 416p. gilt gray cloth. G. A8. $20.00

GORDON, Benjamin Lee. *Medicine Throughout Antiquity.* 1949. Phil. Davis. 157 ils. 818p. G7. $95.00

GORDON, Cyrus H. *Before Columbus... Ancient America.* 1971. NY. F/F. B14. $25.00

GORDON, Dorothy. *Sing in Yourself.* 1928. Dutton. ils Alida Conover. VG. P2. $15.00

GORDON, Dudley. *Charles F Lummis: Crusader in Corduroy.* 1972. Cultural Assets. 1st ed. 344p. NF/VG. B19. $45.00

GORDON, Elizabeth. *Billy Bunny's Fortune.* 1919. Volland. Sunny Book Series. 40p. brd/cloth spine. G+. A3. $17.50

GORDON, Elizabeth. *Billy Bunny's Fortune.* 1936 (1919). Algonquin. ils MW Enright. VG. P2. $30.00

GORDON, Elizabeth. *Bird Children, Little Playmates of the Flower Children.* 1912. Volland. 11th ed. 8vo. 96p. G+. D6. $50.00

GORDON, Elizabeth. *Buddy Jim.* 1935. Wise Parslow. 4to. 109p. G+. A3. $25.00

GORDON, Elizabeth. *Loraine & the Little People of Summer.* 1936 (1920). Rand McNally. ils James McCracken. 64p. VG. P2. $20.00

GORDON, Elizabeth. *Loraine & the Little People.* 1915. Rand McNally. 1st ed. ils MT Ross. cloth/pict label. VG+. M5. $75.00

GORDON, Elizabeth. *More Really So Stories.* nd. Wise Parslow. rpt. 8vo. VG. B17. $8.00

GORDON, Elizabeth. *More Really So Stories.* 1929. Volland. probable 1st ed. ils Jane Priest. VG+. C8. $20.00

GORDON, G.E.C. *Clockmaking Past & Present.* 1978. W Yorkshire, Eng. EP Pub. rpt. 8vo. 232p. VG/VG. A8. $20.00

GORDON, Jan. *Modern French Painters.* 1929. London. Bodley Head. 3rd prt. lg 8vo. ils. tan cloth/gr spine label. VG+. F1. $25.00

GORDON, Jesse E. *Handbook of Clinical & Experimental Hypnosis.* 1967. Collier Macmillan. 640p. F. K4. $20.00

GORDON, John F. *All About the Boxer.* 1976 (1970). London. Pelham. 2nd imp. 164p. cloth. M/dj. R2. $8.00

GORDON, John F. *Dandie Dinmont Terrier.* 1957. London. Nicholson Watson. 1st ed. 148p. cloth. F. R2. $36.00

GORDON, John F. *Miniature Schnauzers.* 1986 (1966). London. Foyle. 66p. glossy brd. M. R2. $15.00

GORDON, Karen Elizabeth. *Transitive Vampire: Handbook of Grammar for the Innocent...* 1984. Time Books. not 1st ed. VG/dj. N2. $7.50

GORDON, Richard. *Doctor & Son.* 1959. Michael Joseph. 1st ed. VG/VG. P3. $30.00

GORDON, Richard. *Doctor in the Swim.* 1962. Michael Joseph. 1st ed. VG/VG. P3. $20.00

GORDON, Stuart. *Two Eyes.* 1975. Sidgwick Jackson. 1st ed. VG/VG. P3. $20.00

GORDON, William. *Separation of the Jewish Tribes After Death of Solomon.* 1777. Boston. Gill. 1st ed. 8vo. 37p. M1. $600.00

GORDON & TATE. *House of Fiction.* 1950. NY. 1st ed. contributors sgns. NF/NF. C2. $500.00

GORDON. *William Makepeace Thackeray: Exhibition...* 1947. NY Public Lib. 4to. 39p. VG/wrp. A4. $35.00

GORE, J.E. *Scenery of the Heavens.* 1890. London. Roper Drowley. 8vo. ils/pl. 320p. bl leather/raised bands. VG. K5. $85.00

GORES, Joe. *Final Notice.* nd. BC. VG/VG. P3. $8.00

GOREY, Edward. *Amphigory Also.* 1983. NY. Congdon Weed. 1st ed. ils Gorey. F/NF. F1. $85.00

GOREY, Edward. *Amphigory.* 1972. NY. 1st ed. VG/fair. B5. $50.00

GOREY, Edward. *Blue Aspic.* 1968. Meredith. 1st ed. obl 12mo. M/M. C8. $60.00

GOREY, Edward. *Eclectic Abecedarium.* 1983. Boston. Bromer. 27x34mm. 1/100 (total of 400). sgn. morocco-edged brd. F/case. B24. $500.00

GOREY, Edward. *Fletcher & Zenobia.* 1967. Meredith. 1st ed. ils VC Chess. F/F. C8. $60.00

GOREY, Edward. *Limerick.* 1973. Dennis. Salt-Works Pr. 1st ed. sgn. F/prt brn wrp. B24. $185.00

GOREY, Edward. *Listing Attic.* 1954. DSP. 1st ed/author's 2nd book. ils. pict brd. F/F. B24. $250.00

GOREY, Edward. *Prune People.* 1983. Albondocani. 1st ed. sgn. 16mo. 1/426. F/pict orange wrp. H5. $60.00

GOREY, Edward. *Red Riding Hood, Retold in Verse...* 1972. Atheneum. 1st ed. pict cloth. M/F. C8. $60.00

GOREY, Edward. *Willowdale Handcar.* 1962. NY. 1st ed. VG/VG. B5. $30.00

GORGAS, Josiah. *Civil War Diary of General Josiah Gorgas...* 1947. AL U. 1st ed. 208p. cloth. VG/dj. M8. $175.00

GORKY, Maxim. *Reminiscences of Leo Nikolaevich Tolstoy.* 1920. NY. Huebsch. 1st Am ed. authorized trans Koteliansky/Woolf. 86p. VG. C6. $50.00

GORLAEUS, Abraham. *Dactyliothecae Pars Secunda seu Variarum Gemmarum... Vol II.* 1695. Leyden. Vander. ils. vellum. H10. $50.00

GORMAN, Ed. *Cry of Shadows.* 1990. St Martin. 1st ed. sgn. F/F. T2. $20.00

GORMAN, Ed. *Death Ground.* 1988. NY. Evans. 1st ed. sgn. F/F. T2. $20.00

GORMAN, Ed. *Guild.* 1987. Evans. 1st ed. F/F. P3. $15.00

GORMAN, Ed. *Murder on the Aisle.* 1987. St Martin. 1st ed. sgn. F/F. T2. $22.00

GORMAN, Ed. *Prisoners & Other Stories.* 1992. Baltimore. CD Pub. 1st ed. F/F. T2. $22.00

GORMAN, Ed. *Stalkers.* 1989. Dark Harvest. 1st ed. contributors sgn. 1/750 #d. F/F/case. P3. $90.00

GORMAN, T.M. *Christian Psychology: Soul & Body in Correlation...* 1875. London. Longman Gr. 1st ed. 502p. calf. H10. $125.00

GORNICK, Vivian. *In Search of Ali Mahmoud.* 1973. Dutton. 1st ed. 8vo. VG. W1. $10.00

GORWILL, Sylvia G. *Hairless Dogs of the World.* 1987. Great Britain. 1st ed. ils. 71p. M/wrp. R2. $25.00

GOSHEN, Charles E. *Documentary Hist of Psychiatry.* 1967. Philosophical Lib. G+/fair. N2. $10.00

GOSS, Fred. *Memories of a Stag Harbourer...* 1931. London. Witherby. 1st ed. sgn. VG. O3. $65.00

GOSS, Warren Lee. *Recollections of a Private.* 1890. NY. 354p. new cloth spine/ep. G. B18. $35.00

GOSS, Warren Lee. *Soldier's Story of His Captivity at Andersonville...* 1868 (1866). Boston. ils Thos Nast. gr cloth. VG. w/Nast's sgn cancelled check. A11. $55.00

GOSTELOW, Mary. *Complete Guide to Needlework, Techniques & Materials.* 1982. np. cloth. VG. G2. $20.00

GOSTELOW, Mary. *Cross Stitch Book.* 1982. np. cloth. VG. G2. $17.50

GOTLIEB, Phyllis. *Heart of Red Iron.* 1989. St Martin. 1st ed. VG/VG. P3. $16.00

GOTTFRIDSON & GOTTFRIDSON. *Swedish Mitten Book.* 1984. np. sc. VG. G2. $9.00

GOTTLIEB, Gay. *Hungarian Vizsla.* 1985. London. Nimrod. 1st ed. ils. 272p. F/F. R2. $60.00

GOTTLIEB, Samuel Hirsh. *Overbooked in Arizona.* 1994. Scottsdale. Camelback Gallery. 1st hc ed. sgn. F/F. T2. $25.00

GOUDEY, Alice E. *Day We Saw the Sun Come Up.* 1961. Scribner. 1st ed. ils Adrienne Adams. unp. VG+/G. A3. $30.00

GOUDGE, Elizabeth. *Little White Horse.* 1947. Coward McCann. 1st Am ed. 8vo. gilt bl cloth. VG/G+. D6. $40.00

GOUDGE, Elizabeth. *Lost Angel.* 1971. Coward McCann. 1st Am ed. NF/VG+. C8. $20.00

GOUDGE, Elizabeth. *White Witch.* 1958. Coward McCann. 1st ed. NF/NF. P3. $25.00

GOUDGE, T.A. *Ascent of Life.* 1961. Toronto. trade pb. 236p. G1. $17.50

GOUDY, Frederic. *Bertha M Goudy: Recollections by One Who Knew Her Best.* 1939. Marlboro, NY. Village. 1/300. 33p. VG. A4. $135.00

GOUGH, Lawrence. *Death on a No 8 Hook.* 1988. Gollancz. 1st ed. F/F. P3. $20.00

GOUGH, Lawrence. *Serious Crimes.* 1990. London. Gollancz. 1st ed. F/F. S6. $25.00

GOUGH, Mary. *Travel Into Yesteday.* 1954. Doubleday. 1st ed. 12 pl. 305p. VG/dj. W1. $25.00

GOULART, Ron. *Chameleon Corps & Other Shape Changers.* 1972. Macmillan. 1st ed. F/F. N3. $20.00

GOULART, Ron. *Death in Silver.* 1975. Golden. brd. F. P3. $8.00

GOULART, Ron. *Graveyard of My Own.* 1985. Walker. ARC of 1st ed. F/F. w/promo letter. F4. $25.00

GOULART, Ron. *Graveyard on My Own.* 1985. Walker. 1st ed. xl. dj. P3. $7.00

GOULART, Ron. *Island of Dr Moreau.* nd. BC. VG/VG. P3. $5.00

GOULART, Ron. *Wisemann Originals.* 1989. Walker. 1st ed. F/F. N3. $15.00

GOULD, Heywood. *Glitterburn.* 1981. St Martin. 1st ed. xl. dj. P3. $6.00

GOULD, L. *Manipulators.* 1966. NY. 3rd prt. 276p. NF. D3. $12.50

GOULD, Polly. *Lines Composed by...a Few Days Before Her Death.* 1827. Hudson, NY. Ashbel Stoddard. 18mo. 8p. M1. $150.00

GOULD, Stephen Jay. *Hen's Teeth & Horse's Toes.* 1983. NY. 1st ed. 413p. dj. A13. $30.00

GOULD & PYLE. *Anomalies & Curiosities of Medicine.* 1956. NY. facsimile of 1896 ed. 968p. G7. $45.00

GOULDEN, Joseph C. *Death Merchant.* 1984. Simon Schuster. 1st ed. 8 pl. NF/dj. W1. $18.00

GOULDSBURY, C.E. *Tigerland: Reminiscences of 40 Years' Sport & Adventure...* 1916. NY. ils. 261p. VG/torn. B18. $20.00

GOUSCHEV & VASSILIEV. *Russian Science in the 21st Century.* 1960. McGraw Hill. VG. N2. $7.50

GOVER, Robert. *One Hundred Dollar Mis-understanding.* 1962. Grove. 1st ed. F/2 djs. B2. $45.00

GOVERNMENT PRINTING OFFICE. *Abstract of Infantry Tactics.* 1853. Phil. Dept of War. ils. 135p. O8. $32.50

GOVERNMENT PRINTING OFFICE. *Bank's Expedition.* 1863. 318p. F/new wrp. O8. $9.50

GOVERNMENT PRINTING OFFICE. *Battle of Antietam.* 1862. 2 vol. 1st ed. index. O8. $32.50

GOVERNMENT PRINTING OFFICE. *Battle of Chancelorsville.* 1889. 1st ed. index. 975p. blk cloth. O8. $14.50

GOVERNMENT PRINTING OFFICE. *Campaign of Bristoe & Mine Run.* 1890. Official Records of the Armies Vol 24. 1100p. O8. $14.50

GOVERNMENT PRINTING OFFICE. *Campaigns in Northern Virginia. Official Records Vol 12.* covers March to Sept of 1862. index. 900+p. O8. $18.50

GOVERNMENT PRINTING OFFICE. *Chickamauga Campaign.* 1890. Official Records of Armies. O8. $18.50

GOVERNMENT PRINTING OFFICE. *Message From President of US (Regarding Civil Strife KS).* 1856. GPO. 900p. VG. E5. $65.00

GOVERNMENT PRINTING OFFICE. *Operations Against Franklin & Nashville, TN.* 1894. Official Records Vol 45. 1st ed. 1300p. O8. $18.50

GOVERNMENT PRINTING OFFICE. *Operations in Louisiana.* 1886. Official Record Vol 15. 1st ed. F. O8. $18.50

GOVERNMENT PRINTING OFFICE. *Operations in Missouri With General Price.* 1893. Official Records Vol 41. index. 1100p. O8. $18.50

GOVERNMENT PRINTING OFFICE. *Price's Missouri Expedition.* 1893. 1st ed. 1000+p. blk cloth. F. O8. $14.50

GOVERNMENT PRINTING OFFICE. *Report of the Secretary of the Interior.* 1870. 937p. O8. $18.50

GOVERNMENT PRINTING OFFICE. *War of the Rebellion: Official Records Union/Confederate...* 1881. GPO. Series 1. Vol 5. 1200p. VG. E5. $85.00

GOWERS, William Richard. *Diagnosis of Diseases of Brain & Spinal Cord.* 1885. NY. Wood. 293p. Wood Lib bdg. G7. $250.00

GOYEN, William. *New Work & Work in Progress.* 1983. Palemon. 1st ed. sgn. 1/200. F. A9. $100.00

GRABB, John R. *Canal: Its Rise & Fall in Ross County...* nd. np. sgn. 48p. VG/wrp. B18. $10.00

GRABBE, Christian-Dietrich. *Comedy, Satire, Irony & Deeper Meaning.* 1955. London. Gaberbocchus. 1st ed thus. VG/dj. A17. $20.00

GRABER, Ralph. *Baseball Reader.* 1951. Barnes. 1st ed. VG/G. P8. $35.00

GRABHORN, Robert. *Short Account of Life & Work of Wynkyn de Worde...* 1949 (1527). Grabhorn/BC of CA. 1/375. folio. ils. brn cloth/brd. K1. $350.00

GRAE, Ida. *Nature's Colors. Dyes From Plants.* 1974. NY. 41 mc photos. 229p. dj. B26. $22.50

GRAEME, Bruce. *Cherchez la Femme.* 1951. Hutchinson. 1st ed. VG/VG. P3. $30.00

GRAF, Alfred Byrd. *Exotic House Plants.* (1973). Roehrs. 9th ed. 176p. F/G. H1. $18.00

GRAF, Pablo. *Luis Vives Como Apologetica...* 1943. Madrid. 1st Spanish-language ed. 158p. VG/wrp. G1. $30.00

GRAFTON, Sue. *A Is for Alibi.* 1982. HRW. 1st ed. inscr/dtd 1989. F/F. Q1. $750.00

GRAFTON, Sue. *A Is for Alibi.* 1982. London. Macmillan. 1st Eng ed. F/F. O4. $275.00

GRAFTON, Sue. *B Is for Burglar.* 1985. HRW. 1st ed. sgn. F/F. O4/Q1. $600.00

GRAFTON, Sue. *C Is for Corpse.* 1986. HRW. 1st ed. F/F. B2. $225.00

GRAFTON, Sue. *D Is for Deadbeat.* 1987. HRW. 1st ed. F/F. B2. $125.00

GRAFTON, Sue. *E Is for Evidence.* 1988. Holt. 1st ed. F/F. B2. $100.00

GRAFTON, Sue. *F Is for Fugitive.* 1988. Holt. 1st ed. F/F. M15. $35.00

GRAFTON, Sue. *G Is for Gumshoe.* 1990. Holt. 1st ed. F/F. B2. $40.00

GRAFTON, Sue. *G Is for Gumshoe.* 1990. NY. Holt. 1st ed. sgn. F/F. L3. $45.00

GRAFTON, Sue. *H Is For Homicide.* 1991. NY. Holt. 1st ed. 8vo. 256p. quarter blk cloth/gray brd. M/M. H5. $50.00

GRAFTON, Sue. *I Is for Innocent.* 1992. Holt. 1st ed. F/F. B4. $45.00

GRAFTON, Sue. *J Is for Judgement.* 1993. Holt. 1st ed. F/F. B4. $35.00

GRAFTON, Sue. *J Is for Judgement.* 1993. Holt. 1st ed. sgn. F/F. L3. $45.00

GRAFTON, Sue. *K Is for Killer.* 1994. Holt. 1st ed. F/F. O4. $20.00

GRAFTON, Sue. *Keziah Dane.* 1967. Macmillan. 1st ed. G+/dj. O4. $300.00

GRAFTON, Sue. *Keziah Dane.* 1967. Macmillan. 1st ed/author's 1st book. F/F. B4. $850.00

GRAHAM, Bessie. *Bookman's Manual: Guide to Literature.* 1925 (1921). Bowker. revised/enlarged ed. 627p. G+. S11. $15.00

GRAHAM, Billy. *Hope for the Troubled Heart.* 1991. Word. 230p. F/F. B29. $5.50

GRAHAM, Billy. *Storm Warning.* 1992. Word. 318p. VG/dj. B29. $4.50

GRAHAM, Caroline. *Killings at Badger's Drift.* nd. BC. VG/VG. P3. $8.00

GRAHAM, Caroline. *Murder at Madingly Grange.* 1990. London. Century. 1st ed. F/F. M15. $45.00

GRAHAM, George Edward. *Schley & Santiago: Historical Account of the Blockade...* 1902. Chicago. WB Conkey. 1st ed. 4to. 484p. gilt bl cloth. G. B11. $85.00

GRAHAM, GROUNDS & RAMM. *Is God Dead?* 1966. Zondervan. 120p. VG/dj. B29. $6.50

GRAHAM, Harry. *Misrepresentative Women.* 1906. Duffield. 1st ed. ils DS Grosebeck. 120p. G. S11. $20.00

GRAHAM, James; see Patterson, Henry.

GRAHAM, John Alexander. *Babe Ruth Caught in a Snowstorm.* 1973. Houghton Mifflin. 1st ed. F/VG. P8. $60.00

GRAHAM, John. *Crowd of Cows.* 1968. HBJ. 1st ed. ils Feodor Rojankovsky. F/VG. P2. $35.00

GRAHAM, Jorie. *Hybrids of Plants & of Ghosts.* 1980. Princeton. 1st ed/author's 1st book. F/NF. V1. $85.00

GRAHAM, L. *Niagara Country. American Folkways.* 1949. NY. 1st ed. sgn. VG/G. B5. $25.00

GRAHAM, Lorenz. *John Brown: Cry for Freedom.* 1980. Crowell. 1st ed. sgn. F/NF. B2. $30.00

GRAHAM, Mary Nancy. *Fifty Songs for Boys & Girls.* 1935. Whitman. ils Janet Laura Scott. 60p. NF. D6. $20.00

GRAHAM, R.B. Cunninghame. *Brought Forward.* 1916. London. Duckworth. 1st ed. 8vo. gilt russet cloth. VG. M7. $40.00

GRAHAM, R.B. Cunninghame. *Mogreb-el-Acksa: A Journey in Morocco.* 1930. NY. 1st Am ed. 8vo. map ep. gilt blk cloth. F/VG. H3. $30.00

GRAHAM, R.B. Cunninghame. *Mogreb-el-Acksa: A Journey in Morocco.* 1930. Viking. 1st ed. 358p. VG. W1. $12.00

GRAHAM, R.B. Cunninghanme. *S Am Sketches of...* 1978. Norman, OK. 1st ed. 304p. VG/dj. F3. $20.00

GRAHAM, Robert; see Haldeman, Joe.

GRAHAM, Shirley. *There Was Once a Slave. Heroic Story of Frederick Douglass.* 1947. Messner. 1st ed. NF/NF. B2. $30.00

GRAHAM, Tom; see Lewis, Sinclair.

GRAHAM, Thomas. *Elements of Chemistry. Vol 2.* 1858. London. Bailliere. 2nd ed. 804p. xl. VG. H1. $8.00

GRAHAM, W.A. *Story of the Little Big Horn.* 1959. Bonanza. 5th prt. F/F. B34. $45.00

GRAHAM, William. *Reno Court of Inquiry.* 1954. Harrisburg. 1st ed. VG/VG. B5. $75.00

GRAHAM, Winston. *Angell, Pearl & Little God.* 1970. Literary Guild. VG/fair. P3. $10.00

GRAHAM, Winston. *Merciless Ladies.* 1979. Bodley Head. 1st ed. VG/VG. P3. $20.00

GRAHAME, Elspeth. *First Whisper of the Wind in the Willows.* 1944. London. Methuen. 1st ed. 12mo. ils/photos. VG/G+. C8. $65.00

GRAHAME, Kenneth. *Cambridge Book of Poetry for Children.* 1916. Putnam. 1st ed. 8vo. ils Maud Fuller. 288p. NF. D6. $40.00

GRAHAME, Kenneth. *Fun O'the Fair.* 1929. Dent. Aldine Chapbook. 30p. VG. M20. $50.00

GRAHAME, Kenneth. *Golden Age.* 1900 (1899). London. Bodley Head. 1st ed thus. 18 Parrish pl. VG. Q1. $175.00

GRAHAME, Kenneth. *Headswoman.* 1921. Bodley Head. 1/75. sgn on limitation p. 8vo. 8 pl. F. H5. $750.00

GRAHAME, Kenneth. *Wind in the Willows.* 1966. Cleveland. Collins. ils/sgn Tasha Tudor. 255p. gr cloth. VG/VG. A3. $100.00

GRAHAME, Kenneth. *Wind in the Willows.* 1980. Ariel. 1st ed. ils Michael Hague. F/G. B17. $15.00

GRAHAME, Kenneth. *Wind in the Willows.* 1983. Holt Rinehart. 1st ed. ils Babette Cole. mechanical pop-up. NF. C8. $25.00

GRAM & KLEMKE. *Ontological Turn: Studies in Philosophy of Gustav Bergmann.* 1974. IA U. 314p. gr plastic brd. G1. $32.00

GRAMATKY, Hardie. *Little Toot.* 1939. Putnam. 2nd prt. 90p. VG. P2. $30.00

GRAND, Gordon. *Silver Horn.* 1932. Derrydale. ltd ed. 1/950. VG+. O3. $275.00

GRANDVAL, Gilbert. *Ma Mission au Maroc.* 1956. Paris. Plon. 1st ed. 273p. G. W1. $10.00

GRANGER, Bill. *El Murders.* 1987. Holt. 1st ed. F/F. P3. $17.00

GRANGER, Bill. *Man Who Heard Too Much.* 1989. Warner. 1st ed. F/F. P3. $19.00

GRANIT, Ragnar. *Purposive Brain.* 1977. MIT. 215p. M/dj. K4. $12.50

GRANT, Arthur. *Grey Shrines of England.* nd. ca 1920? London. Chambers. N2. $6.00

GRANT, Campbell. *Rock Art of the Am Indian.* 1967. Promotory. 178p. NF/dj. M20. $20.00

GRANT, Charles L. *Dark Cry of the Moon.* 1985. Donald Grant. 1st ed. F/F. M2. $15.00

GRANT, Charles L. *Dark Cry of the Moon.* 1985. Donald Grant. 1st ed. sgn. F/F. T2. $24.00

GRANT, Charles L. *Fire Mask.* 1991. Bantam. 1st ed. F/F. T2. $12.00

GRANT, Charles L. *Pet.* 1986. Tor. 1st ed. sgn. F/F. T2. $25.00

GRANT, Charles L. *Ravens of the Moon.* 1978. Doubleday. 1st ed. VG/VG. P3. $20.00

GRANT, Charles L. *Shadows 2.* 1979. Doubleday. 1st ed. NF/NF. P3. $25.00

GRANT, Charles L. *Shadows 9.* 1986. Doubleday. 1st ed. xl. dj. P3. $8.00

GRANT, Charles L. *Tales From the Nightside.* 1981. Arkham. 1st ed. 1sgn. 1/4121. F/F. T2. $44.00

GRANT, Donald. *Talbot Mundy: Messenger of Destiny.* 1983. Donald Grant. 1st ed. F/dj. M2. $20.00

GRANT, Linda. *Love Nor Money.* 1991. NY. Scribner. ARC/1st ed. sgn. F/F. S6. $35.00

GRANT, Maxwell (house name); see Davis, Robert Hart; Dent, Lester; Gibson, Walter; Lynds, Dennis.

GRANT, Michael. *Classical Greeks.* 1989. Scribner. F/F. P3. $27.00

GRANT, Michael. *Dawn of the Middle Ages.* 1986. Bonanza. ils. 224p. F/dj. M10. $16.50

GRANT, Roderick. *Private Vendetta.* 1978. Scribner. 1st ed. F/F. P3. $15.00

GRANT, Ulysses S. *Personal Memoirs of US Grant. Vol 2.* 1886. Webster. 1st ed. gilt gr cloth. G. H1. $12.00

GRANT, Ulysses S. *Personal Memoirs...* 1885-1886. NY. 2 vol. 1st ed. VG. A9/A15. $100.00

GRANT, Vernon. *Tinker Tim the Toy-Maker.* 1934. Whitman. ils. pict brd/rebacked spine. VG. M5. $65.00

GRANTLAND, Keith; see Beaumont, Charles.

GRANVILLE, George. *Works in Verse & Prose.* 1736. London. 3 vol. G+. A15. $75.00

GRAPHIC ENTERPRISES. *Easy Art of Flower Crochet.* 1972. np. sc. VG. G2. $4.00

GRASNICK, M. *Das Alphabet.* ca 1930-40. Berlin. Karich. 8vo. German text. F/self wrp. B24. $275.00

GRASS, Gunter. *Dog Years.* 1965. HBW. 1st Am ed. trans Manheim. 570p. gilt/peach stp blk cloth. VG/dj. H5. $75.00

GRASS, Gunter. *Flounder.* 1985. NY. 3 vol. 1/1000. sgns. obl 4to. trans Manheim. eelskin bdg. F/case. B24. $750.00

GRASS, Gunter. *Kopfgeburten Oder die Deutschen Sterben Aus.* 1980. Darmstadt. Luchterhand. correct 1st ed. F/F. B2. $45.00

GRASS, Gunther. *Die Blechtrommel.* 1959. Darmstadt. Hermann Luchterhand. 1st ed. F/F. B4. $450.00

GRASSET, J. *Des Localisations Dans Les Maladies Cerebrales. 2nd Edition.* 1878. Paris. 138p. new brd. G7. $395.00

GRASSUS, Beneventius. *De Oculis, Eorumque Egritudinibus et Curis...* 1929. Stanford. 5 manuscript facsimiles. 104p. gray/wht cloth. case. K1. $100.00

GRATTEN & SINGER. *Anglo-Saxon Magic & Medicine.* 1952. London. 1st ed. 234p. A13. $125.00

GRAU, Shirley Ann. *Black Prince. And Other Stories.* 1955. NY. 1st ed/author's 1st book. sgn. F/NF. A11. $90.00

GRAU, Shirley Ann. *Condor Passes.* 1971. Knopf. 1st ed. F/F. M21. $25.00

GRAU, Shirley Ann. *Condor Passes.* 1971. Knopf. 1st ed/author's 5th book. NF/NF. B3. $20.00

GRAUMONT & WENSTROM. *Fisherman's Knots & Nets.* 1948. NY. Cornell Maritime. ils/77 pl. 224p. T7. $30.00

GRAVE, S.A. *Scottish Philosophy of Common Sense.* 1960. Oxford. 262p. bl cloth. VG/clip. G1. $38.00

GRAVES, A.P. *Railroad Man.* 1900. Phil. 1st ed. 207 p. gilt cloth. VG. A17. $25.00

GRAVES, John. *From a Limestone Ledge: Some Essays & Other Ruminations...* 1980. Knopf. 1st ed. sgn. ils Glenn Wolff. F/dj. A18. $35.00

GRAVES, John. *Goodbye to a River.* 1960. NY. 1st ed. VG/VG. B5. $50.00

GRAVES, Richard Perceval. *Lawrence of Arabia & His World.* 1976. London. 1st ed. 127p. gilt olive cloth. F/NF. M7. $65.00

GRAVES, Richard. *Spiritual Quixote.* 1774. London. 3 vol. 2nd ed. VG. A15. $125.00

GRAVES, Robert. *Adam's Rib & Other Anomalous Elements in Hebrew Creation...* 1955. London. Trianon. 1st ed. 1/26 lettered. red cloth. F/NF/cb case/morocco case. H5. $550.00

GRAVES, Robert. *Anger of Achilles. Homer's Iliad.* 1959. NY. 1st ed. 383p. VG. A17. $10.00

GRAVES, Robert. *Another Future of Poetry.* 1926. Hogarth. 1st ed. VG+/blk prt wht wrp. Q1. $200.00

GRAVES, Robert. *Assault Heroic 1895-1926.* 1987. Viking. 1st ed. index/notes/biblio. 387p. M. M7. $19.00

GRAVES, Robert. *Big Green Book.* 1962. Crowell Collier. 1st ils ed. ils Sendak. F. B24. $85.00

GRAVES, Robert. *Big Green Book.* 1968 (1962). Crowell Collier. reformatted ed. ils Maurice Sendak. F/F. C8. $40.00

GRAVES, Robert. *Gladius the God.* 1935. Smith Haas. 1st ed. G+. P3. $25.00

GRAVES, Robert. *Golden Ass. By Lucius Apuleius.* 1951. Harmondsworth. 1st/special hc ed. sgn. 1/200 #d. teg. F/VG+/pub case. A11. $145.00

GRAVES, Robert. *Good-Bye to All That.* Oct 1969. London. BC Associates. 4th ed/2nd imp. red imitation leather. NF. M7. $25.00

GRAVES, Robert. *Greek Myths.* 1981. London. ils ed. 224p. F/NF. M7. $40.00

GRAVES, Robert. *Hercules, My Shipmate.* 1945. Creative. 1st ed. 464p. VG/VG. M20. $45.00

GRAVES, Robert. *I, Claudius.* 1977. London. BC Associates. BC ed. 482p. F/F. M7. $25.00

GRAVES, Robert. *Isles of Unwisdom.* 1950. Cassell. 1st ed. VG/G. P3. $20.00

GRAVES, Robert. *Lars Porsena; or, Future of Swearing & Improper Language.* 1927. London. Kegan Paul. 1st ed. 12mo. 94p. VG. C6. $100.00

GRAVES, Robert. *Lawrence & the Arabian Adventure.* 1928. Doubleday Doran. 24 pl. 400p. map ep. gilt brn linen. VG. M7. $35.00

GRAVES, Robert. *Lawrence & the Arabs.* 1927. Jonathan Cape. 1st ed. ils Eric Kennington. yel-orange bdg. VG+. M7. $35.00

GRAVES, Robert. *Lawrence & the Arabs.* 1927. Jonathan Cape. 1st ed. ils Kennington. 4 maps/H Perry. rebound leather. M7. $125.00

GRAVES, Robert. *Lawrence & the Arabs.* 1935. London. Cape. concise ed. 288p. lacks front ep. G. W1. $9.00

GRAVES, Robert. *Long Week-End.* 1950. London. Faber. 1st ed/2nd imp. 455p. gilt brn cloth. VG+/VG. M7. $30.00

GRAVES, Robert. *Man Does Woman Is.* 1964. London. 1st ed. sgn. F/NF. V1. $45.00

GRAVES, Robert. *More Deserving Cases.* 1962. Marlborogh College. 1st ed. 1/750. sgn. teg. reddish-brn morocco. F. C6. $175.00

GRAVES, Robert. *My Head! My Head!* 1925. London. Secker. 1st ed. G. M7. $63.00

GRAVES, Robert. *Penny Fiddle.* 1960. Doubleday. 1st ed. ils Ardizzone. VG/dj. M20. $20.00

GRAVES, Robert. *Poems 1965-1968.* 1969. Doubleday. 1st ed. 97p. VG/dj. M20. $25.00

GRAVES, Robert. *Twelve Caesars: Gaius Suetonius Tranquillus.* (1962). London. Cassell. 2nd UK/1st hc ed. NF/NF. Q1. $175.00

GRAVES, Valerie; see Bradley, Marion Zimmer.

GRAY, A.W. *Bino.* 1988. Dutton. 1st ed/author's 1st book. F/F. M15. $30.00

GRAY, A.W. *Defense of Judges.* 1990. Dutton. 1st ed. VG/VG. P3. $20.00

GRAY, A.W. *Size.* 1989. Dutton. 1st ed. F/F. M15. $25.00

GRAY, Alasdair. *Fall of Kelvin Walker.* 1986. Braziller. 1st ed. F/NF. B4. $35.00

GRAY, Asa. *Elements of Botany for Beginners & for Schools.* 1887. Am Book Co. revised ed. ils. 760p. G7. $35.00

GRAY, Berkeley. *Lost World of Everest.* 1952. TC Pr. 1st ed. VG/dj. F4. $40.00

GRAY, Don. *Traces.* 1980. Bear Willow Pub. ltd ed. sgn all 3 artists. VG. B34. $90.00

GRAY, Dulcie. *Dark Calypso.* 1978. London. MacDonald. 1st ed. F/F. S6. $22.50

GRAY, Edward. *William Gray, of Salem Merchant.* 1914. Houghton Mifflin. 1/500 #d. NF/VG case. S9. $125.00

GRAY, Elizabeth Janet. *Adam of the Road.* 1942. Viking. 1st ed. ils Robert Lawson. VG+/VG. C8. $45.00

GRAY, Elizabeth Janet. *Cheerful Heart.* 1959. Viking. 3rd ed. 8vo. 176p. VG. V3. $7.50

GRAY, Elizabeth Janet. *Young Walter Scott.* 1953. Viking. 10th prt. 239p. NF/VG. A3. $7.50

GRAY, Francine Du Plessix. *Divine Disobedience: Profiles in Catholic Radicalism.* 1970. Knopf. 322p. H10. $14.00

GRAY, George W. *Frontier Flight: Story of NASA Research.* 1948. NY. 1st ed. 362p. VG/dj. B19/C11. $45.00

GRAY, Harold Studley. *Character Bad: Story of a Conscientious Objector.* 1934. Harper. inscr. VG. V4. $25.00

GRAY, Harold. *Pop-Up Little Orphan Annie & Jumbo the Circus Elephant.* 1935. Pleasure Books. 3 pop-ups. unp. VG. M20. $300.00

GRAY, Henry. *Anatomy, Descriptive & Surgical.* 1883. Phil. 1023p. xl. G7. $85.00

GRAY, Justin. *Inside Story of the Legion.* 1948. NY. Boni Gaer. 1st ed. F/NF. B2. $45.00

GRAY, Martin. *For Those I Loved.* 1972. Boston. photos/maps. 351p. VG/rpr. A17. $9.50

GRAY, Mike. *Angle of Attach.* 1992. Norton. 1st prt. VG/VG. K5. $22.00

GRAY, Thomas. *Elegy Written in a Country Churchyard.* 1911. Glasgow. Midget Series. 19x14mm. 93p. aeg. gilt wrp. B24. $450.00

GRAY, Thomas. *Poems & Letters.* 1867. London. Chiswick. 1st ed. 4 mtd photos. 416p. calf. K1. $200.00

GRAY, W. Forbes. *Books That Count.* 1912. London. Blk. 12mo. gilt red cloth. G+. S11. $15.00

GRAYSON, Richard. *Death en Voyage.* 1985. Gollancz. 1st ed. NF/NF. P3. $20.00

GREAVES, Dod. *Me & Dod.* 1924. London. Jenkins. 1st ed. ils. 158p. cloth. F. scarce. R2. $30.00

GREAVES, Margaret. *Lucky Coin.* 1989. Steward Tabori Chang. ils Liz Underhill. VG. B17. $9.00

GREBER, Judith. *Mendocino.* 1988. Crown. 1st ed. sgn. rem mk. NF/F. B3. $20.00

GREEBEM A. *Yankee Among the Nullifiers.* 1870 (1833). np. 143p. VG. E5. $27.00

GREELEY, Andrew M. *God Game.* 1986. Warner. 1st ed. F/F. P3. $17.00

GREELEY, Horace. *American Conflict: History of the Great Rebellion. Vol 1.* 1865. Hartford. leather. fair. B11. $35.00

GREELEY, Horace. *Hints Toward Reforms in Lectures, Addresses...Writings.* 1850. NY. 1st ed. 400p. cloth. G. A17. $30.00

GREELY, A.W. *Handbook of Polar Discoveries.* 1910. Boston. 5th ed. 336p. cloth. G. A17. $30.00

GREELY, A.W. *Reminiscences of Adventure & Service.* 1927. NY/London. Scribner. 1st ed. inscr. photos. 356p. gilt red cloth. VG+/chip. P4. $400.00

GREELY, Aldlpius L. *Three Years of Arctic Service.* 1886. London. 2 vol. ils/maps. VG. M17. $175.00

GREEN, Anna Katharine. *Chief Legatee.* 1906. NY. 1st ed. ils Frank Merrill. VG. A17. $10.00

GREEN, Ben K. *Horse Tradin'.* 1967. Knopf. 1st ed. ils Bjorklund. F/dj. A18. $40.00

GREEN, Bert F. *Digital Computers in Research.* 1963. NY. McGraw Hill. 300p. F/dj. K4. $12.50

GREEN, Christine. *Death in the Country.* 1993. London. Macmillan. 1st ed. F/dj. S6. $25.00

GREEN, Edith Pinero. *Rotten Apples.* nd. BC. VG/VG. P3. $8.00

GREEN, Fitzhugh. *Dick Byrd: Air Explorer.* 1928. London/NY. Putnam. later prt. 8vo. 282p. red cloth. VG. P4. $25.00

GREEN, G. Gilbert. *Cacti for Everyone.* 1957. London. 1st ed. photos. 108p. orange cloth. F/NF. B26. $25.00

GREEN, George Dawes. *Caveman's Valentine.* 1994. Warner. 1st ed/author's 1st book. F/F. B3. $25.00

GREEN, Gerald. *Stones of Zion.* 1971. Hawthorn. 1st ed. 386p. F/dj. W1. $10.00

GREEN, Gerald. *To Brooklyn With Love.* 1967. Trident. BC. F/F. P8. $8.50

GREEN, Henry. *Back: A Novel.* 1946. Hogarth. 1st ed. NF/NF. Q1. $150.00

GREEN, Honor. *Chow Chow.* 1975. Great Britain. 1st ed. ils. 100p. F/F. R2. $40.00

GREEN, Horace. *Treatise on Diseases of the Air Passages.* 1846. Wiley Putnam. 272p. cloth. B14. $275.00

GREEN, Joseph. *Conscience Interplanetary.* 1973. Doubleday. 1st ed. F/F. P3. $15.00

GREEN, Martin. *Earth Again Redeemed.* 1977. Basic. 1st ed. F/NF. N3. $15.00

GREEN, Paul E. *Mathematical Tools for Applied Multivariate Analysis.* 1976. Academic. 376p. F. K4. $30.00

GREEN, Robert Alan. *Jewelers Trade Cards.* 1989. Sutherland. 1st ed. 286p. M/wrp. S11. $10.00

GREEN, Terence M. *Barking Dogs.* 1988. St Martin. 1st ed. VG/VG. P3. $16.00

GREEN, Thomas J. *Flowered Box.* 1980. Beaufort. 1st ed. VG/VG. P3. $15.00

GREEN, Thomas. *John Woolman: A Study for Young Men.* 1885. Manchester. Brook Chrystal. 16mo. 126p. xl. G+. V3. $10.50

GREEN & GREEN. *Baby.* 1985. Simon Schuster. 1st ed. pict brd. F. F4. $15.00

GREEN & LANE. *Particulate Clouds.* 1964. Van Nostrand. 2nd ed. 471p. G/dj. K5. $20.00

GREEN & MURRAY. *Book of Kantela.* 1985. Bluejay. 1st ed. sgn Roland Green. F/dj. F4. $15.00

GREEN & WYATT. *Atomic & Space Physics.* 1965. Reading, MA. Addison Wesley. 8vo. 619p. gray cloth. G. K5. $25.00

GREENAWAY, Kate. *A Apple Pie.* ca 1940. Frederick Warne. obl 4to. 45p. pict brd. VG/G+. A3. $28.00

GREENAWAY, Kate. *Almanack for 1884.* 1884. London. Routledge. 1st ed. 16mo. gilt faux morocco wrp. F. F1. $165.00

GREENAWAY, Kate. *Almanack for 1886.* 1886. London. Routledge. 1st ed. 16mo. prt glossy brd/cloth spine. VG+. F1. $150.00

GREENAWAY, Kate. *Almanack for 1892.* 1892. London. Routledge. 1st ed. 16mo. prt glossy brd/yel cloth spine. NF. F1. $155.00

GREENAWAY, Kate. *Almanack for 1894.* 1894. London. Routledge. 1st ed. 16mo. prt glossy brd/tan cloth spine. VG. F1. $135.00

GREENAWAY, Kate. *Almanacks 1883-1897.* 1882-1896. London. Routledge. 14 vols. 1st ed. NF or better/F custom case. C8. $4,500.00

GREENAWAY, Kate. *Greenaway's Babies.* 1907. Saalfield. pirate ed. G. M5. $45.00

GREENAWAY, Kate. *Kate Greenaway's Birthday Book.* 1970s. Warne. rpt. 16mo. F/F. B17. $20.00

GREENAWAY, Kate. *Mother Goose.* nd. Warne. pict brd. VG. M5. $35.00

GREENAWAY, Kate. *Mother Goose; or, Old Nursery Rhymes.* nd. London. Rutledge. later prt of 1st ed. VG. Q1. $150.00

GREENBERG, Eric Rolfe. *Celebrant.* 1983. Everest. 1st ed. F/VG+. P8. $85.00

GREENBERG, Joseph H. *Universals of Language.* 1963. Cambridge. MIT. 270p. ES. red cloth. VG. G1. $22.50

GREENBERG, Martin. *Coming Attractions.* 1957. Gnome. 1st ed. VG/VG. M17. $15.00

GREENBERG, Martin. *On the Diamond.* 1987. Bonanza. 1st ed. F/F. P8. $20.00

GREENBERG, Martin. *Robot & the Man.* 1953. Gnome. 1st ed. VG. P3. $25.00

GREENBERG & ROARK. *Interseller Grains.* 1967. NASA SP-140. 8vo. 269p. bl cloth. VG. K5. $25.00

GREENBERG & SCHMIDT. *Unknown Worlds: Tales From Beyond.* 1988. Galahad. 1st ed. F/F. P3. $15.00

GREENBERG & SILVERBERG. *Worlds Imagined.* 1989. Avenel. VG/VG. P3. $15.00

GREENBLATT, Robert. *Search the Scriptures.* 1965. Lippincott. 127p. fair/dj. B29. $3.50

GREENBURG, Dan. *Nanny.* 1987. Macmillan. 1st ed. F/F. N3. $15.00

GREENE, Felix. *Divorce Trial in China.* 1961. Ann Arbor. Radical Education Project. 13p. stapled wrp. M11. $15.00

GREENE, Graham. *Bear Fell Free.* 1935. London. 1st ed. 1/250. sgn. NF/NF. C2. $1,000.00

GREENE, Graham. *Brighton Rock & End of the Affair.* 1987. Peerage Books. F/F. P3. $15.00

GREENE, Graham. *Brighton Rock.* 1938. London. Heinemann. 1st ed. 8vo. 361p. gilt red cloth. VG. H5. $250.00

GREENE, Graham. *Complaisant Lover.* 1959. London. Heinemann. 1st ed. inscr to Dorothy Craigie. NF/NF. B4. $950.00

GREENE, Graham. *End of the Affair.* 1951. Viking. 1st ed. NF/NF. P3. $100.00

GREENE, Graham. *Getting To Know the General.* 1984. Denys. 1st ed. VG/VG. P3. $15.00

GREENE, Graham. *Getting To Know the General.* 1984. Simon Schuster. UP. VG/prt yel wrp. B3. $30.00

GREENE, Graham. *Honorary Consul.* 1973. London. Bodley Head. 1st ed. F/F. B3. $30.00

GREENE, Graham. *Journey Without Maps.* 1953. London. Heinemann. rpt. inscr. NF. B4. $1,750.00

GREENE, Graham. *Loser Takes All.* 1955. London. Heinemann. 1st ed. inscr. NF. B4. $1,500.00

GREENE, Graham. *Monsignor Quixote.* 1982. Denys. 1st ed. G+/dj. P3. $15.00

GREENE, Graham. *Potting Shed.* 1958. London. Heinemann. 1st ed. inscr to Mercia Ryhiner. F/NF. B4. $1,750.00

GREENE, Graham. *Quick Look Behind.* 1983. Sylvester Orphanos. 1/330. sgn. 8vo. F/cloth case. H5. $200.00

GREENE, Graham. *Visit to Morin.* 1959. London. Heinemann. 1st ed. inscr to Ian Fleming. 1/250. NF/VG. B4. $3,750.00

GREENE, Graham. *Weed Among the Flowers.* 1990. Sylvester Orphanos. 1st ed. 74x74mm. 1/330. sgns. 47p. F/box. B24. $275.00

GREENE, Harry A. *Measurement & Evaluation in Secondary School.* 1944. Longman Gr. 651p. reading copy. K4. $20.00

GREENE, Jacob W. *Greene Brothers' Clinical Course in Dental Prosthesis.* 1910. Chillicothe, MO. self pub. 210p. G+. H1. $20.00

GREENE & GREENE. *Penguin Book of Victorian Vilanies.* 1991. Bloomsbury. F/F. P3. $15.00

GREENFIELD, Eloise. *Daydreamers.* 1981. NY. Dial. 1st prt. sgn. ils/sgn Tom Feelings. M/M. C8. $75.00

GREENFIELD, Eloise. *Grandmama's Joy.* 1980. NY. Wm Collins. 1st ed. inscr. ils Carole Byard. M/M. C8. $55.00

GREENHILL, Basil. *Quayside Camera, 1845-1917.* 1975. Middletown, CT. Wesleyan U. ils. 112p. dj. T7. $30.00

GREENLEAVES, Winifred. *Trout Inn Mystery.* 1929. Lincoln MacVeagh. 1st ed. NF. P3. $35.00

GREENWALD, Norman. *Mideast in Focus.* 1960. WA, DC. Public Affairs. 1st ed. 8vo. VG. W1. $12.00

GREENWOOD, D.M. *Idol Bones.* 1993. London. Headline. 1st ed. F/F. S6. $25.00

GREENWOOD, Grace. *Haps & Mishaps of Tour in Europe.* 1854. np. 1st ed. 437p. E5. $35.00

GREENWOOD, L.B. *Sherlock Holmes & Case of Sabrina Hall.* 1988. Simon Schuster. 1st ed. VG/VG. P3. $20.00

GREENWOOD, L.B. *Sherlock Holmes & the Thistle of Scotland.* 1989. Simon Schuster. ARC/1st ed. RS. F/dj. S6. $27.50

GREENWOOD, Walter. *Love on the Dole: Tale of Two Cities.* 1935. London. Cape. G. V4. $7.50

GREENWOOD. *CA Imprints, 1833-1862.* 1961. np. 1/750. 524p. F/NF. A4. $185.00

GREER, Germaine. *Female Eunuch.* 1970. London. MacGibbon Kee. 1st ed. F/VG clip. B4. $125.00

GREG, Richard. *Memoria Technica; or, New Method of Artifical Memory...* 1730. London. 1st ed. 120p. contemporary paneled calf. K1. $650.00

GREGG, Cecil Freeman. *Inspector Higgins Goes Fishing.* 1951. Methuen. 1st ed. VG. P3. $20.00

GREGG, Leah. *Scarface Al: Amazing Career or Al Capone.* nd. Girard. Haldeman Julius. Little Bl Book 1723. F/wrp. B2. $30.00

GREGG, Linda. *Too Bright To See.* 1981. Graywolf. 1st ed. sgn. F/NF. V1. $135.00

GREGG, Willis Ray. *Aeronautical Meteorology.* 1925. NY. Ronald. 8vo. ils. 144p. gray cloth. G. K5. $18.00

GREGOR, Elmer Russell. *Red Arrow.* 1915. Harper. ils Norman Rockwell. cloth. VG. M5. $25.00

GREGORICH, Barbara. *She's On First.* 1987. Contemporary. 1st ed. F/F. P8. $40.00

GREGORY, Jackson. *Case for Mr Paul Savoy.* 1933. Scribner. 1st ed. VG. P3. $20.00

GREGORY, Lady. *Kincora, a Drama in Three Acts.* 1905. NY. John Quinn. 1st Am ed. sgn. 1/50. F/prt gray wrp. B24. $850.00

GREGORY, Richard. *My Daughter, a Poem.* 1816. Phil. Charles. woodcut ils. wrp. very rare. B14. $275.00

GREGSON, J.M. *Stranglehold.* 1993. London. Collins. 1st ed. F/F. S6. $25.00

GREIMAS, Algirdas Julien. *Narrative Semiotics & Cognitive Discourses.* 1990. London. Pinter. 197p. blk cloth. F/F. G1. $25.00

GREMLI, A. *Flora of Switzerland.* 1888. Zurich. 5th ed. 454p. VG. B26. $32.50

GRENDON, Stephen; see Derleth, August.

GRENE, Marjorie. *Toward a Unity of Knowledge.* 1969. Internat U Pr. 302p. prt wrp. G1. $25.00

GRENFELL, W. *Labrador Log Book.* 1938. Boston. 1st ed. VG/VG. B5. $27.50

GRENFELL, W. *Labrador.* 1913. NY. 1st revised ed. VG. B5. $40.00

GRESHAM, William Lindsay. *Book of Strength. Body Building the Safe, Correct Way.* 1961. John Day. 1st ed. NF/VG+. B2. $30.00

GRESHAM, William Lindsay. *Nightmare Alley.* 1946. NY. Rinehart. 1st ed/author's 1st book. 8vo. 275p. VG/dj. H5. $50.00

GRESHOFF, J. *Harvest of the Lowlands: An Anthology...* 1945. NY. Querido. 626p. G+. N2. $6.00

GRESSINGER, A.W. *Charles D Poston: Sunland Seer.* 1961. Dale Stuart King Pub. 1st ed. ils/index. 212p. F/NF. B19. $35.00

GRESSWELL & GRESSWELL. *Equine Hospital Prescriber.* 1904. Toronto. Carveth. 3rd ed. free front ep missing. VG. O3. $40.00

GREW, David. *Buckskin Colt.* 1967. NY. Grosset Dunlap. pict brd. VG. O3. $15.00

GREW, Joseph C. *Report From Tokyo.* 1942. NY. 88p. VG/VG. A17. $8.50

GREY, Zane. *Captives of the Desert.* ca 1950. Grosset Dunlap. 12mo. F/F. C8. $22.50

GREY, Zane. *Forlorn River.* 1927. Harper. 1st ed. VG. A18. $25.00

GREY, Zane. *Heritage of the Desert.* nd. Grosset Dunlap. photoplay ed. VG/fair. P3. $15.00

GREY, Zane. *Horse Heaven Hill.* 1959. Harper. 1st ed. F/dj. A18. $65.00

GREY, Zane. *Ken Ward in the Jungle.* 1912. Harper. 1st ed. 309p. pict cloth. F. B14. $150.00

GREY, Zane. *Last of the Plainsmen.* 1936 (1908). Grosset Dunlap. VG/VG. C8. $22.50

GREY, Zane. *Nevada.* 1928. Harper. 1st ed. VG. P3. $40.00

GREY, Zane. *Ranger & Other Stories.* 1960. Harper. 1st ed. F/dj. A18. $65.00

GREY, Zane. *Robber's Roost.* ca 1940s. Grosset Dunlap. wartime ed. 12mo. VG+/partial. C8. $20.00

GREY, Zane. *Robber's Roost.* 1932. Harper. 1st ed. VG/G. B5. $80.00

GREY, Zane. *Shadow on the Trail.* 1946. Harper. 1st ed. F/NF. B4. $125.00

GREY, Zane. *Shortstop.* nd. Grosset Dunlap. 12mo. VG/VG. B17. $15.00

GREY, Zane. *Shortstop.* 1909. McClurg. 2nd prt. VG. P8. $25.00

GREY, Zane. *Spirit of the Border Retold for Young Readers.* 1950. Whitman. lg 12mo. pict cloth. F/VG. C8. $22.50

GREY, Zane. *Spirit of the Border.* ca 1950. Grosset Dunlap 12mo. F/VG+. C8. $22.50

GREY, Zane. *Spirit of the Border.* 1943. Triangle. 18th prt. VG/VG. P3. $13.00

GREY, Zane. *Stairs of Sand.* 1945. Musson. VG. P3. $12.00

GREY, Zane. *Tales of Fishing Virgin Seas.* 1925. Harper. A-A prt. 216p. gr cloth. VG. M20. $125.00

GREY, Zane. *Tales of Fresh-Water Fishing.* (1928). Grosset Dunlap. 277p. VG. E5. $45.00

GREY, Zane. *Tales of Fresh-Water Fishing.* April 1928. Harper. 1st ed. inscr/dtd 1929. 277p. G. B14. $650.00

GREY, Zane. *Tales of Fresh-Water Fishing.* 1928. Harper. 1st ed. 277p. gilt gr cloth. NF/dj. H5. $450.00

GREY, Zane. *Tales of Lonely Trails.* 1922. Harper. 394p. G. M20. $45.00

GREY, Zane. *Tales of S Rivers.* 1924. Grosset Dunlap. 249p. cloth. VG. M20. $75.00

GREY, Zane. *Tales of Swordfish & Tuna.* 1927. Harper. 1st ed. inscr. 203p. cloth. G. B14. $650.00

GREY, Zane. *Tales of the Angler's Eldorado, New Zealand.* 1926. London. Harper. 1st ed. Zane Grey's copy. morocco/marbled brd. H4. $1,250.00

GREY, Zane. *To the Last Man.* 1922. Harper. VG. P3. $20.00

GREY, Zane. *Twin Sombreros.* 1940. Harper. 1st ed. VG/VG. B5. $100.00

GREY, Zane. *Under the Tonto Rim.* 1926. Harper. 1st ed. VG/G. B5. $80.00

GREY, Zane. *Vanishing American.* 1925. Canada. Musson. 1st ed. VG/G. P3. $35.00

GREY, Zane. *Wanderer of the Wasteland.* (1923). Grosset Dunlap. wartime prt. 12mo. VG+/VG. C8. $22.50

GREY, Zane. *Young Forester.* 1910. Harper. 1st ed. pict brn cloth. VG. M20. $120.00

GREY, Zane. *Young Pitcher.* 1911. Harper. 248p. pict gr cloth. VG. M20. $90.00

GREY, Zane. *Young Pitcher.* 1939. Grosset Dunlap. rpt. VG/G. P8. $20.00

GREY, Zane. *Zane Gray Fishing Library.* 1990-1991. Derrydale. 10 vol. 1/2500 sets. sgn Loren Grey. leather. M. A18. $450.00

GRIBBIN, John. *Whence & How the Universe?* 1928. Baltimore, MD. St Mary's Seminary Pr. 8vo. ils. 631p. maroon cloth. G. K5. $12.50

GRIBBIN & ORGILL. *Sixth Winter.* 1979. Simon Schuster. 1st ed. VG/VG. P3. $15.00

GRIBBLE, Frances. *Romance of the Oxford Colleges.* 1910. London. Mills Boon. G+. N2. $7.50

GRIDER, Doorthy. *Busy Bulldozer.* 1952. Rand McNally Elf Book 8375. 20p. K2. $4.00

GRIDLEY, Marion. *Indians of Yesterday.* 1940. Donohue. folio. ils Lone Wolf. VG/VG. B17. $14.00

GRIEPENKERL, Major-General. *Letters on Applied Tactics.* 1914. KS City. 2 vol. 4th ed. 343p. VG. B18. $25.00

GRIER, Mary C. *Oceanography of the North Pacific Ocean, Bering Sea...* 1969. NY. Greenwood. prt. 8vo. 290p. gray cloth. VG. P4. $45.00

GRIERSON, Francis D. *Murder in the Garden.* 1933. Collins Crime Club. 6th prt. G+. P3. $10.00

GRIESE, Arnold A. *Way of Our People.* 1975. NY. Crowell. 1st ed. 8vo. 82p. M/torn. P4. $25.00

GRIFFIN, Harold. *Alaska & the Canadian Northwest.* 1944. NY. Norton. 221p. VG. A17. $15.00

GRIFFITH, A. Leonard. *Ephesians: Positive Affirmation.* 1975. Word. 173p. VG/dj. B29. $4.50

GRIFFITH, C.J. *Romance of the Sky.* ca 1907. London. Routledge. 8vo. 166p. pict red cloth. G. K5. $32.00

GRIFFITH, Leonard. *God in Man's Experience.* 1969. Word. 192p. VG/dj. B29. $3.50

GRIFFITH, Peggy. *New Klondike.* 1926. Jacobsen Hodgkinson. 1st ed. photos from movie. VG. P8. $145.00

GRIFFITHS, John. *Loyal & Dedicated Servant.* 1981. Playboy. 1st ed. VG/VG. P3. $18.00

GRIFFITHS, Maurice. *Swatchways & Little Ships.* 1971. London. Allen Unwin. ils/1 chart. 192p. T7. $27.50

GRIFFITHS, Philip Jones. *Vietnam Inc.* 1971. NY. Collier. 1st ed. 4to. photos. F/wrp. S9. $275.00

GRIFFITHS & THOMPSON. *Cacti.* 1929. WA, DC. ils/photos/pl. 25p. wrp. B26. $14.00

GRIGGS, R. *Valley of 10,000 Smokes.* 1922. WA. 1st ed. G. B5. $50.00

GRIMES, Martha. *Deer Leap.* 1985. Little Brn. ARC/1st ed. RS. F/F. S6. $30.00

GRIMES, Martha. *Deer Leap.* 1985. Little Brn. 1st ed. F/F. P3. $16.00

GRIMES, Martha. *Five Bells & Bladebone.* 1987. Little Brn. 1st ed. VG/VG. P3. $15.00

GRIMES, Tom. *Stone of the Heart.* 1990. 4 Walls 8 Windows. 1st ed. F/VG+. P8. $15.00

GRIMM, Mary. *Left to Themselves.* 1993. Random. UP/author's 1st book. F/wrp. L3. $30.00

GRIMM, Wilhelm. *Dear Mili.* 1988. FSG. 1st ed. ils Sendak. F/F. B17. $10.00

GRIMM & GRIMM. *Bear & the Kingbird: A Tale From the Brothers Grimm.* 1979. FSG. 1st ed. ils Chris Conover. 31p. VG/VG. A3. $12.50

GRIMM & GRIMM. *Fairy Tales by the Brothers Grimm.* 1931. LEC. 1/1500. ils/sgn Kredel. F/F case. C8. $150.00

GRIMM & GRIMM. *Grimm's Fairy Tales.* 1920. Ward Lock. G+. P3. $10.00

GRIMM & GRIMM. *Grimm's Fairy Tales.* 1945 (1944). Pantheon. ils Josef Scharl. F/dj/case. M5. $20.00

GRIMM & GRIMM. *Snow White & the Seven Dwarfs. A Tale From Brothers Grimm.* 1972. FSG. 1st ed. trans Randall Jarrell. ils Nancy E Burkert. VG/G. A3. $37.50

GRIMM & ROY. *Human Interest Stories of 3 Days' Battles at Gettysburg.* 1927. Time & News Pub. 4to. ils. 62p. VG/wrp. N2. $7.50

GRIMSHAW, Anne. *Horse: A Bibliography of British Books 1851-1976.* 1982. London. Lib Assn. 1st ed. sgn. 1/1000. F/F. O3. $85.00

GRIMWOOD, Ken. *Breakthrough.* 1976. Doubleday. 1st ed. VG/VG. P3. $25.00

GRIMWOOD, Ken. *Replay.* 1986. Arbor. 1st ed. F/F. T2. $25.00

GRINKER, Roy R. *Neurology With Assistance of Norman A Levey.* 1944. Springfield. Thomas. 1136p. cloth. G7. $35.00

GRINKER, Roy R. *Toward a Unified Theory of Human Behavior.* 1956. Basic. 361p. F/dj. K4. $15.00

GRINSPOON, Lester. *Cocaine: Drug & Its Social Evolution.* 1976. NY. 1st ed. 308p. A13. $25.00

GRISHAM, John. *Chamber.* 1994. Doubleday. 1st ed. sgn. F/F. L3. $50.00

GRISHAM, John. *Client.* 1993. Doubleday. 1st ed. F/NF. B4. $50.00

GRISHAM, John. *Client.* 1993. Doubleday. 1st ed. sgn. F/F. L3. $100.00

GRISHAM, John. *Firm.* 1991. Doubleday. 1st ed. F/F. M15. $75.00

GRISHAM, John. *Pelican Brief.* 1992. Doubleday. 1st ed. VG/VG. P3. $25.00

GRISS, Henry. *New Soviet Psychic Discoveries.* 1979. Souvenir. 1st ed. VG. P3. $20.00

GRISWOLD, Erwin N. *5th Amendment Today.* 1955. Harvard. 82p. VG. D3. $15.00

GRISWOLD, John. *Fuels, Combustion & Furnaces.* 1946. McGraw Hill. 1st ed/3rd imp. 496p. VG. H1. $15.00

GRISWOLD, Mac. *Pleasures of the Garden: Images From NY Metropolitian Mus...* 1987. Abrams. 160p. VG/dj. A10. $25.00

GRMEK, Mirko. *History of Aids: Emergence & Origin of Modern Pandemic.* 1990. Princeton. 1st ed. 279p. A13. $30.00

GRODIN, Joseph R. *In Pursuit of Justice, Reflections of State Supreme Court...* 1989. Berkeley. pres. fwd Wm J Brennan Jr. M11. $35.00

GROGAN, Emmett. *Ringolevio.* 1972. Little Brn. 1st ed. F/VG. B2. $45.00

GROHMANN, Will. *Kandinsky.* nd. Abrams. VG/VG. A1. $100.00

GROHMANN, Will. *Paul Klee.* nd (1955). NY. Abrams. lg 4to. ils. 448p. F/NF. F1. $175.00

GROMACKI, Robert G. *Modern Tongues Movement.* 1967. P&R. 165p. G/dj. B29. $4.50

GROMACKI, Robert G. *New Testament Survey.* 1987. Baker. 432p. M/dj. B29. $11.50

GROOM, Winston. *Better Times Than These.* 1978. NY. 1st ed/author's 1st book. sgn. rem mk. NF/NF. C2. $75.00

GROOMS, Steve. *Modern Pheasant Hunting.* 1984. Stackpole. 2nd prt. pb. 222p. F. H1. $6.00

GROS, Johann Daniel. *Natural Principles of Rectitude for Conduct of Man...* 1795. NY. Swords. 456p. contemporary calf/leather spine label. G1. $200.00

GROSBY, Ruth. *Mystery at Mountain View.* 1940. Grosset Dunlap. Barbara Ann #2. 243p. VG/dj. M20. $20.00

GROSE, Parlee C. *Five Fairies.* 1915. Fifth Ave Pub. 223p. VG/dj. M20. $12.50

GROSECLOSE, Elgin. *Ararat.* 1939. NY. Carrick. 1st ed. 482p. cloth. VG/dj. W1. $20.00

GROSS, Louis S. *Redefining the American Gothic.* 1989. UMI Research. 1st ed. VG. P3. $35.00

GROSS, Samuel W. *Practical Treatise on Tumors of the Mammary Gland.* 1880. NY. ils. 246p. VG. B14. $450.00

GROSSBERG, Stephen. *Studies of Mind & Brain: Neural Principles of Learning...* 1982. Dordrecht. D Reidel Pub. 662p. VG/dj. G1. $37.50

GROSSER, Lewis. *Fabulous Fifty.* 1990. Atheneum. 1st ed. F/F. P8. $15.00

GROSSMAN, James. *James Fenimore Cooper.* 1949. Stanford. 1st ed. ftspc. F. A18. $20.00

GROSSMAN, Sebastian P. *Textbook of Physiological Psychology.* 1967. Wiley. 932p. G/dj. K4. $25.00

GROSSMAN & TANENHAUS. *Frontiers of Judicial Research.* 1969. NY. 492p. NF. D8. $35.00

GROSVENOR, Charles. *Portraits of TE Lawrence.* 1975. Otterden Pr. 1st ed. sgn. 1/200 #d. M. M7. $95.00

GROTH, John. *Studio: Europe.* 1945. NY. ils. 283p. cloth. VG. A17. $12.50

GROTIUS, Hugo. *De Jure Belli Ac Pacis Livri Tres...* 1702. Amsterdam. Apud Henricum Westenium. contemporary calf/ rebacked. G. M11. $350.00

GROUARD, Frank. *Life & Adventures of...* 1982 (1894). De Bartle. facsimile. 545p. VG. E5. $35.00

GROUP, Harold E. *House-of-the-Month Book of Small Houses.* 1946. Garden City. thin 4to. drawings/floor plans. cloth. VG. F1. $20.00

GROUT, A.J. *Mosses With a Hand-Lens.* 1924. NY. 3rd ed. ils. 339p. VG. B26. $27.50

GROUT, Lewis. *Zulu-Land; or, Life Among the Zulu-Kafirs of Natal...* (1864). Phil. 1st ed. ils/fld map. 351p. gr cloth. VG. scarce. H3. $150.00

GROVER, Eulalie Osgood. *Mother Goose.* 1915. Donohue. 1st revised ed. pict brd. VG. M5. $75.00

GROVER, Eulalie Osgood. *Overall Boys in Switzerland.* 1916. Rand McNally. 8vo. beige cloth. 158p. NF. D6. $55.00

GROVER, Eulalie Osgood. *Sunbonnet Babies Book.* 1928. Rand McNally. ils Bertha Corbett. 105p. cloth. VG. A3. $35.00

GROVER, Eulalie Osgood. *Sunbonnet Babies in Holland.* 1915. Rand McNally. 8vo. 150p. VG. D6. $55.00

GROVER, Eulalie Osgood. *Sunbonnet Babies in Mother Goose Land.* 1928 (1927). Rand McNally. ils Bertha Corbett Melcher. 115p. G. P2. $60.00

GROVES, J. Percy. *With the Green Jackets.* ca 1890s. Bretanos. ils. VG. M5. $10.00

GROWDEN, Gordon A. *Freighters & Tankers of the US Merchant Marine.* 1954. Putnam. obl format. ils. unp. T7. $22.00

GRUBB, Davis. *Ancient Lights.* 1982. Viking. 1st ed. F/dj. M2. $95.00

GRUBB, Davis. *Night of the Hunter.* 1953. NY. 1st ed. VG/G. B5. $50.00

GRUBB, Davis. *Shadow of My Brother.* 1966. Hutchinson. 1st ed. NF/NF. P3. $25.00

GRUBB, Davis. *Watchman.* 1961. NY. 1st ed. VG/VG. B5. $35.00

GRUBB, Edward. *Social Aspects of the Quaker Faith.* 1899. London. Headley Bros. 12mo. 252p. xl. V4. $8.50

GRUBER, Frank. *Laughing Fox.* 1943. Tower. VG/VG. P3. $20.00

GRUBER, Ruth. *I Went to the Soviet Arctic.* 1939. Simon Schuster. 1st ed. 333p. map ep. NF/worn. P4. $35.00

GRUELLE, Johnny. *Beloved Belindy.* 1926. Donohue. ils. pict brd. NF. M5. $95.00

GRUELLE, Johnny. *Cheery Scarecrow.* 1929. Donohue. Sunny Books Series. 40p. VG-. A3. $30.00

GRUELLE, Johnny. *Friendly Fairies.* 1919. Donohue. 8vo. pict paper brd. VG+. C8. $85.00

GRUELLE, Johnny. *Friendly Fairies.* 1960 (1949). Bobbs Merrill. rpt. 8vo. pict cloth. F/F. C8. $85.00

GRUELLE, Johnny. *Little Brown Bear.* 1920. Volland. Sunny Book Series. 12mo. G. C8. $35.00

GRUELLE, Johnny. *Little Sunny Stories.* nd (1919). Donohue. VG. P2. $25.00

GRUELLE, Johnny. *Old-Fashioned Raggedy Ann & Andy ABC Book.* 1975. NY. Windmill Books/Simon Schuster. 1st ed. 32p. VG. A3. $12.50

GRUELLE, Johnny. *Raggedy Andy Stories.* 1920. Donohue. early ed. 8vo. pict paper brd. NF/VG+. C8. $125.00

GRUELLE, Johnny. *Raggedy Ann & Marcella's First Day at School.* 1952. Wonder Book 588. K2. $12.00

GRUELLE, Johnny. *Raggedy Ann & the Hoppy Toad.* 1943. McLoughlin. ils Justin Gruelle. pict brd. F/VG. M5. $75.00

GRUELLE, Johnny. *Raggedy Ann in Cookie Land.* 1931. Volland. 1st ed. 95p. VG. P2. $85.00

GRUELLE, Johnny. *Raggedy Ann's Magical Wishes.* (1928). Chicago. Donohue. early rpt of Volland ed w/logo. NF/VG+. C8. $125.00

GRUELLE, Johnny. *Raggedy Ann's Magical Wishes.* 1928. Volland. 1st ed. 8vo. pict paper brd. VG+. C8. $100.00

GRUELLE, Johnny. *Raggedy Ann's Magical Wishes.* 1928. Volland. 1st ed. 94p. G. P2. $40.00

GRUELLE, Johnny. *Raggedy Ann's Wishing Pebble.* 1925. Volland. 14th prt. pict brd. VG. M5. $75.00

GRUELLE, Johnny. *Raggedy Ann Stories.* 1961. Bobbs Merrill. ils. yel cloth/pict label. VG+/dj. M5. $55.00

GRUELLE, Johnny. *Raggedy Ann Stories.* 1993. Derrydale. reissue. 8vo. F/F. B17. $12.00

GRUMBACH, Doris. *Spoil of the Flowers.* 1962. NY. 1st ed/author's 1st novel. inscr/dtd 1962. NF/NF. A11. $135.00

GRUNBAUM, Adolf. *Foundations of Psychoanalysis: Philosophical Critique.* 1984. Berkeley. CA U. pres. gray cloth. VG/dj. G1. $37.50

GRUNBAUM, Adolf. *Geometry & Chromoetry in Philosophical Perspective.* 1968. Minnesota U. 378p. VG/dj. G1. $25.00

GRUNBAUM, Adolf. *Validation in Clinical Theory of Psychoanalysis.* 1993. Madison, CT. Internat U Pr. blk cloth. VG/dj. G1. $37.50

GUARE, John. *Six Degrees of Separation.* 1990. Random. 1st ed. NF/dj. B4. $85.00

GUARINI, Giovanni Battista. *Lettere...* 1596. Venice. Ciotti. 3 parts in 1. 4to. contemporary vellum. K1. $350.00

GUEDALLA, Philip. *Middle East 1940-1942.* 1944. Hodder Stoughton. 1st prt. 8vo. 237p. VG. W1. $15.00

GUENTHER, William C. *Analysis of Variance.* 1964. Prentice Hall. 199p. F/dj. K4. $10.00

GUERDAN, Rene. *Byzantium: Its Triumphs & Tragedy.* 1957. Putnam. 1st Am ed. 228p. VG/clip. W1. $25.00

GUERINI, V. *Hist of Dentistry from Most Ancient Times...* 1909. Phil. 1st ed. ils/pls. 355p. G. G7. $175.00

GUERTIK, H. *Des Oiseux (Birds).* ca 1945. np. sq 8vo. G/wrp. A17. $17.50

GUICCIARDINI, Francesco. *Historie of Guicciardin: Containing Warres of Italie...* 1618. London. Richard Field. folio. 821p. contemporary paneled calf. K1. $350.00

GUIGNEBERT, Charles. *Christ.* 1968. University Books. VG/VG. B33. $22.00

GUILD, Vera. *Creative Use of Stitches.* 1964. np. cloth. VG. G2. $7.00

GUILES, Fred L. *Norman Jean.* 1969. McGraw. 1st ed. VG/G. S11. $15.00

GUILEY, Rosemary Ellen. *Moonscapes.* 1991. Prentice Hall. ils. 192p. F/F. K5. $13.00

GUILFORD & HOEPFNER. *Analysis of Intelligence.* 1971. McGraw Hill. 361p. F/dj. K4. $10.00

GUILLEMIN, Amedee. *Le Ciel: Notions d'Astronomie a l'Usage des Gens du Monde...* 1865. Paris. Hatchette. 2nd ed. 4to. 626p. gilt leather/cloth. G. K5. $300.00

GUINESS, Alec. *Blessings in Disguise.* 1986. Knopf. 6th prt. 238p. purple cloth. F/NF. M7. $26.50

GULLETT, Henry Somer. *Australian Imperial Force in Sinai & Palestine 1914-1918.* 1934. Queensland, Australia. 1st ed thus. ils/photos/maps. M/pict dj. M7. $60.00

GULLETT, Henry Somer. *Australian Imperial Force in Sinai & Palestine 1914-1918.* 1938. Sydney. Angus Robertson. 6th ed. ils/photos/maps. G. M7. $40.00

GULLEY, Norman. *Plato's Theory of Knowledge.* 1962. London. Methuen. 204p. red cloth. VG/dj. G1. $27.50

GULLIVER, Sam. *Vulcan Bulletins.* 1973. Simon Schuster. F/dj. F4. $17.00

GUMHAILL, P.W. *Investing in Clocks & Watches.* 1967. Clarkson Potter. 4to. ils. 159p. VG/G. A8. $25.00

GUMMERE, Francis B. *Old English Ballads.* 1894. Boston. Ginn. G+. N2. $12.50

GUMMERMAN, Jay. *We Find Ourselves in Moontown.* 1989. Knopf. 1st ed. F/F. P8. $12.00

GUMPERT, Martin. *Dunant: Story of the Red Cross.* 1938. NY. 323p. A13. $30.00

GUNN, F.W. *Master of the Gunnery. Memorial of FW Gunn by His Pupils.* 1887. NY. folio. photo. VG. A9. $50.00

GUNN, James E. *Breaking Point.* 1972. NY. Walker. 1st ed. F/F. N3. $15.00

GUNN, James E. *End of the Dreams.* 1975. Scribner. 1st ed. F/F. P3. $15.00

GUNN, James E. *Some Dreams Are Nightmares.* 1974. Scribner. 1st ed. F/F. P3. $15.00

GUNN, James E. *This Fortress World.* 1955. Gnome. 1st ed. NF/dj. M2. $40.00

GUNN & WILLIAMSON. *Star Bridge.* 1955. Gnome. 1st ed. VG. P3. $40.00

GUNTHER, Hans F.K. *Racial Elements of European Hist.* 1970. Kennikat. trans from 1927 German ed. 279p. VG. A17. $15.00

GURGANUS, Allan. *Blessed Assurance.* 1990. Rocky Mtn, NC. ARC/1st ed. sgn. RS. gilt maroon cloth. F/sans. A11. $45.00

GURGANUS, Allan. *Country Ahead of Us, Country Behind.* 1989. Harper Row. 1st ed/author's 1st book. sgn. F/F. B3. $125.00

GURGANUS, Allan. *Good Help.* 1988. Rocky Mtn, NC. 1/1000. inscr/sgn. F/wrp. A15. $45.00

GURGANUS, Allan. *Oldest Living Confederate Widow Tells All.* 1989. Knopf. 1st ed. NF/NF clip. A14. $50.00

GURGANUS, Allan. *Practical Heart.* 1993. Rocky Mtn, NC. 1/1000. sgn. F/sans. B3. $30.00

GURGANUS, Allan. *Snow Falling on Cedars.* 1994. Harcourt Brace. 1st ed. sgn. F/F. B3. $35.00

GURGANUS, Allan. *White People: Stories & Novellas.* 1991. Knopf. 1st ed. F/F. A14. $25.00

GURGANUS, Allan. *White People: Stories & Novellas.* 1991. Knopf. 1st ed/author's 2nd novel. sgn. F/F. L3. $50.00

GURNEY, Gene. *Space Technology Spinoffs.* 1979. Franklin Watts. sm 4to. 88p. blk cloth. VG. K5. $12.00

GURNEY, Joseph John. *Familiar Letters to Henry Clay of KY...* 1840. NY. Mahlon Day. 8vo. 203p. V3. $85.00

GURNEY, Joseph John. *Observation on Distinguishing Views & Practices...Friends.* 1856. NY. Wood. 2nd Am ed from 7th London ed. 8vo. 338p. full leather. $45.00

GURVITCH, Georges. *Les Tendances Actuelles de la Philosophie Allemande.* 1949. Paris. rpt 1930 ed. prt gray wrp. G1. $25.00

GURWITSCH, Aron. *Theorie du Champ de la Conscience.* 1957. Paris. Desclee De Brouwer. 347p. F/wrp. G1. $35.00

GUSDORF, Georges. *De l'Histoire des Sciences a l'Historie de la Pensee.* 1966. Paris. Payot. 336p. NF/prt wrp. G1. $25.00

GUSTAFSON, Donald F. *Essays in Philosophical Psychology.* 1964. Anchor. PBO. 16mo. 412p. G1. $22.00

GUSTAFSON, Scott. *Night Before Christmas.* 1992. Knopf. 10th prt. rem mk. F/VG. B17. $8.00

GUTERSON, David. *Snow Falling on Cedars.* 1994. Harcourt Brace. 1st ed/author's 1st novel. sgn. F/F. L3. $75.00

GUTHRIE, A.B. *Big It.* 1960. Houghton. 2nd prt. F/F. B34. $40.00

GUTHRIE, A.B. *Big Sky, Fair Land: Environmental Essays.* 1988. Northland. 1st ed. sgn. M/M. A18. $100.00

GUTHRIE, A.B. *Big Sky.* 1947. Wm Sloane. 1st ed. F/F. B34. $60.00

GUTHRIE, A.B. *Big Sky.* 1947. Wm Sloane. 1st ed. VG+. A18. $30.00

GUTHRIE, A.B. *Big Sky.* 1964. NY. 1st Time Reading Program ed. sgn. NF/stiff wrp. A11. $60.00

GUTHRIE, A.B. *Fair Land, Fair Land.* 1982. Houghton Mifflin. 1st ed. F/F. B34. $40.00

GUTHRIE, A.B. *Fair Land, Fair Land.* 1982. Houghton Mifflin. 1st ed. sgn. map ep. M/dj. A18. $60.00

GUTHRIE, A.B. *Field Guide to Writing Fiction.* 1991. Harper Collins. 1st ed. M/dj. A18. $16.00

GUTHRIE, A.B. *Genuine Article.* 1977. Houghton Mifflin. 1st ed. F/F. S6. $30.00

GUTHRIE, A.B. *Murder in the Cotswolds.* 1989. Houghton Mifflin. 1st ed. 5th/last in Chick Charleston Series. M/dj. A18. $30.00

GUTHRIE, A.B. *Playing Catch-Up.* 1985. Houghton Mifflin. 1st ed. F/NF. B3. $35.00

GUTHRIE, A.B. *Way West.* 1949. Wm Sloane. 1st ed. w/sgn bookplate. F/NF. A11. $125.00

GUTHRIE, A.B. *Way West.* 1949. Wm Sloane. 1st prt. VG. B34. $35.00

GUTHRIE, A.B. *Way West.* 1979. Franklin Lib. 1st ed. full leather. NF. B3. $35.00

GUTHRIE, A.B. *Wild Pitch.* 1973. Houghton Mifflin. later prt. VG/VG. P8. $15.00

GUTHRIE, W.K.C. *Socrates.* 1988. Cambridge. trade pb. 200p. G1. $22.50

GUTHRIE, William. *Socialism Before the French Revolution.* 1907. Macmillan. 1st ed. NF. B2. $45.00

GUTTERIDGE, Lindsay. *Cold War in a Country Garden.* 1971. Putnam. VG/VG. P3. $15.00

GUTTMANN, Allen. *Games Must Go On: Avery Brundage & the Olympic Movement.* 1984. Columbia. 1st ed. ils. 317p. F/dj. M10. $7.50

GUTTMANN, Paul. *Handbook of Physical Diagnosis Comprising Throat, Thorax...* 1880. NY. Wood. Wood Lib ed. 344p. NF. G7. $75.00

GUTTRIDGE, Roger. *Ten Dorset Mysteries.* 1989. Southampton, Eng. Ensign Pub. 1st ed. M/pict wrp. M7. $30.00

GUTZKE, Manford G. *Help Thou My Unbelief.* 1974. Nelson. pb. 124p. VG. B29. $2.00

GUYOT, Charles. *Le Printemps sur la Neige et d'Autres Contes du Bon Vieux...* 1922. Paris. H Piazza. 1/300 (extra suite pl). 4to. ils Rackham. NF/pict wrp. F1. $1,250.00

H

H.H.; see Jackson, Helen Hunt.

HAACK, Hermann. *Echte Temppiche. Einfuhrung in Die Orientteppichkunde.* 1957. Munich. sm 4to. ils/fld map. 95p. cloth. O2. $50.00

HAAG, Earl C. *PA German Anthology.* 1988. Susquehanna. 1st ed. 352p. F/F. A17. $12.50

HAAR, Charles M. *Golden Age of American Law.* 1965. Braziller. M11. $45.00

HAAS, Ernst. *Creation.* 1971. Viking. 1st ed. NF/VG+. S9. $75.00

HAAS, Ernst. *In America.* 1975. Viking. 1st ed. NF/VG. S9. $65.00

HAAS, Robert Bartlett. *Muybridge: Man in Motion.* 1976. Berkeley. CA U. 1st ed. sq 4to. F/F. S9. $45.00

HAAS, William S. *Iran.* 1946. Columbia. 273p. VG. W1. $15.00

HABBERTON, John. *Helen's Babies: Some Account of Their Ways...* ca 1908. Grosset Dunlap. ils Tod Dwiggins. 244p. pict cloth. VG. B10. $18.00

HACHIYA. *Hiroshima Diary: Journal of a Japanese Physician...* 1955. NC U. 249p. VG/VG. A4. $65.00

HACK, Mary Pryor. *Mary Pryor: Life Story of a Hundred Years Ago.* nd. Phil. Longstreth. 12mo. 160p. xl. V3. $10.00

HACKETT, J. *History of the Orthodox Church in Cyprus...* 1901. London. ils/maps. 8vo. 720p. uncut. O2. $250.00

HACKETT, John. *Third World War.* 1978. Sidgwick Jackson. 1st ed. VG/VG. P3. $20.00

HADDAD, C.A. *Academic Factor.* 1980. Harper Row. 1st ed. F/dj. M15. $25.00

HADDAD, Robert M. *Syrian Christians in Muslim Society...* 1970. Princeton. 1st ed. 118p. H10. $20.00

HADDOCK, J.A. *Souvenir of Thousand Islands of St Lawrence River.* 1896. Alexandria Bay, NY. ils. 256p. T7. $90.00

HADER & HADER. *Little Appaloosa.* 1949. Macmillan. 1st ed. 4to. unp. VG. A3. $25.00

HADER & HADER. *Little White Foot.* 1952. Macmillan. 1st ed. ils. F/VG. P2. $40.00

HADER & HADER. *Picture Book of Travel.* 1928. Macmillan. 2nd prt. 63p. VG. B10. $15.00

HADER & HADER. *Rainbow's End.* 1945. Macmillan. 8vo. NF/VG. C8. $25.00

HADER & HADER. *Reindeer Trail.* 1959. Macmillan. 1st ed. ils. F/VG. P2. $45.00

HADFIELD, John. *Chamber of Horrors of the Macabre in Words & Pictures.* 1965. Little Brn. 1st Am ed. 320p. F/VG. N3. $15.00

HADLEY, Arthur T. *Education & Government.* 1935. Yale. 2nd prt. 210p. xl. VG. D3. $25.00

HAECKEL, Ernst. *Evolution of Man: Popular Exposition of Principle Points...* 1896 & 1897. Appleton. 2 vol. marbled brd. G. H1. $22.50

HAEFNER, Dick. *How To Judge Your Personality by the Dog You Own.* 1980. NY. Ashley. 1st ed. 188p. cloth. M/dj. R2. $45.00

HAEGER, Knut. *Illustrated History of Surgery.* 1988. NY. 200 ils. 288p. dj. A13. $30.00

HAFEN, LeRoy R. *Mountain Men & the Fur Trade of the Far West.* 1965-1972. Glendale. Arthur Clark. 10 vol set. inscr in 1st vol. F/plain djs. P4. $2,750.00

HAFEN & HAFEN. *Handcarts to Zion: Story of W Migration 1856-1860.* 1992. NE U. 1st Bison Book prt. M/M. A18. $25.00

HAFEN & HAFEN. *Utah Expedition 1857-1858. A Documentary Account...* 1958. Glendale. Arthur H Clark. 1st ed. 8vo. ils/fld map. 375p. gr cloth. VG. P4. $95.00

HAFEN & YOUNG. *Fort Laramie: 1834-1890.* 1938. Glendale. 1st ed. VG+. A15. $125.00

HAFLZ. *Teachings of Haflz.* 1985. London. Octagon. trans Gertrude Bell. 186p. F/F. B33. $20.00

HAGAN, Orville R. *Beauty & Watches From the Past.* nd. Hagans Clock Manor. 1st ed. 8vo. 11p. VG/wrp. A8. $2.00

HAGEL, Bob. *Game Loads & Practical Ballistics for the American Hunter.* 1978. Knopf. 1st ed. 315p. VG/G. S11. $10.00

HAGEN, Richard. *Bio-Sexual Factor.* 1979. NY. Doubleday. 279p. dj. K4. $8.50

HAGER & HAGER. *Hist Society of S CA, Bibliography All Pub Works 1884-1957.* 1958. Hist Soc S CA. 183p. F/dj. B19. $50.00

HAGGARD, H. Rider. *Ayesha: The Return of She.* 1905. Doubleday Page. 1st ed. G+. P3. $40.00

HAGGARD, H. Rider. *Classic Adventures.* 1986. New Orchard. 1st ed. F/F. P3. $20.00

HAGGARD, H. Rider. *Farmer's Year.* 1899. London. 1st ed. VG. M2. $125.00

HAGGARD, H. Rider. *Heu-Heu; or, The Monster.* 1924. Doubleday Page. 1st ed. VG. P3. $65.00

HAGGARD, H. Rider. *Jess.* 1896. Smith Elder. G+. P3. $60.00

HAGGARD, H. Rider. *Montezuma's Daughter.* 1905. Longman Gr. 7th ed. G+. P3. $20.00

HAGGARD, H. Rider. *People of the Mist.* 1919. Longman Gr. VG. P3. $25.00

HAGGARD, H. Rider. *She & Allan.* 1921. Longman Gr. 1st ed. G+. P3. $30.00

HAGGARD, Howard. *Devils, Drugs & Doctors.* (1929). Bl Ribbon. 405p. G+. H1. $15.00

HAGGARD, Howard. *Doctor in History.* 1934. New Haven. 408p. VG. A13. $65.00

HAGGARD, William. *Arena.* 1961. Washburn. 1st ed. VG/G. P3. $15.00

HAGGARD, William. *Hard Sell.* 1966. Ives Washburn. 1st ed. VG/VG. P3. $18.00

HAGGARD, William. *Notch on the Knife.* 1973. Walker. 1st ed. VG/VG. P3. $15.00

HAGGERTY, James J. *1964 US Aircraft, Missiles & Spacecraft.* 1964. WA, DC. Nat Aerospace Research Council. 4to. 168p. wrp. K5. $24.00

HAGUE, Kathleen. *Legend of the Veery Bird.* 1985. HBJ. 1st ed. ils Michael Hague. F/F. B17. $20.00

HAGUE, Kathleen. *Out of the Nursery, Into the Night.* 1986. Holt. 1st ed. 8vo. F/G. B17. $10.00

HAGUE, Michael. *Child's First Book of Prayers.* 1985. NY. Holt. 3rd ed. 4to. 28p. NF/NF. D6. $100.00

HAGUE, Michael. *Deck the Halls.* 1991. Holt. 1st ed. ils. rem mk. F/F. B17. $8.00

HAGUE, Michael. *Favourite Hans Christian Andersen Fairy Tales.* 1981. HRW. 1st ed. F/NF. B3. $25.00

HAGUE, Michael. *Jingle Bells.* 1990. Holt. 1st ed. ils. rem mk. F/F. B17. $8.00

HAHN & HANRAHAN. *What Do you Get...Pop-Up Book of Riddles.* nd. Random. ils Paul Taylor. VG. C8. $20.00

HAIBLUM, Isidore. *Tsaddik of the Seven Wonders.* 1981. Doubleday. VG/VG. P3. $15.00

HAIBLUM, Isidore. *Wilk Are Among Us.* 1975. Doubleday. 1st ed. VG/VG. P3. $15.00

HAIG-BROWN, Roderick L. *Measure of the Year.* 1950. Toronto. Collins. 1st Canadain. VG/dj. A18. $50.00

HAIG-BROWN, Roderick L. *Return to the River: Story of the Chinook Run.* 1946. Toronto. McClelland Stewart. 1st Canadian ed. F/chip. A18. $40.00

HAIG-BROWN, Roderick L. *Western Angler: Account of Pacific Salmon & Western Trout.* 1991. Derrydale. 2 vol. 1/2500 sets. aeg. full leather. M. A18. $100.00

HAIG-BROWN, Roderick L. *Whale People.* 1962. London. Collins. 1st ed. ils Mary Weiler. F/F. A18. $40.00

HAIG-BROWN, Roderick. *Fisherman's Fall.* 1964. NY. 1st ed. VG/VG. B5. $40.00

HAIG-BROWN, Roderick. *Fisherman's Spring.* 1951. NY. 1st ed. VG/VG. B5. $45.00

HAIG-BROWN, Roderick. *Primer of Fly Fishing.* 1964. NY. 1st ed. VG/VG. B5. $50.00

HAIG-BROWN, Roderick. *River Never Sleeps.* 1946. NY. 1st ed. VG/VG. B5. $45.00

HAIG-BROWN, Roderick. *Western Angler.* 1947. NY. 1st ed. VG/G. B5. $75.00

HAILBLUM, Isidore. *Mutants Are Coming.* 1984. Doubleday. 1st ed. F/F. P3. $20.00

HAINES, Charles G. *Role of the Supreme Court in Am Government & Politics...* 1944. CA U. 1st ed. 679p. NF/dj. D3. $45.00

HAINES, Francis. *Nez Perces, Tribesmen of Columbia Plateau.* 1955. OK U. 1st ed. F/F. B34. $125.00

HAINES, Gail Kay. *Explosives.* 1976. Morrow. 1st lib ed. unp. F/G. B10. $10.00

HAINES, Joseph E. *History of Friends' Central School.* 1938. Overbrook, PA. Friends Central School. ltd ed. 12mo. VG. V3. $14.00

HAINES, Max. *True Crime Stories Book III.* 1989. Toronto. Sun. 1st ed. VG. P3. $20.00

HAINES & STAFFORD. *North by West: Collection of Poetry.* 1975. Spring Rain. 1st ed. sc. F. A18. $20.00

HAINING, Peter. *Art of Mystery & Detective Stories.* 1986. Chartwell. F/F. P3. $20.00

HAINING, Peter. *Dead of Night: Horror Stories From Radio, Television...* 1983. Stein Day. 1st Am ed. F/NF. N3. $10.00

HAINING, Peter. *Deadly Nightshade.* 1978. Taplinger. 1st ed. F/F. P3. $23.00

HAINING, Peter. *Eyewitness to the Galaxy.* 1985. London. 4to. 221p. VG/dj. K5. $26.00

HAINING, Peter. *Ghouls.* nd. BC. MTI. VG/VG. P3. $10.00

HAINING, Peter. *Great British Tales of Terror: 1765-1840.* 1972. London. 1st ed. F/dj. M2. $25.00

HAINING, Peter. *Hollywood Nightmare.* 1970. MacDonald. 1st ed. VG/VG. P3. $15.00

HAINING, Peter. *Pictorial History of Horror Stories.* 1985. Treasure. 1st revised ed. 175p. F/dj. F4. $25.00

HAINING, Peter. *Sherlock Holmes Scrapbook.* 1974. NY. Potter. 1st Am ed. ils. F/NF. S6. $30.00

HAINWORTH, Henry. *Collector's Dictionary.* 1981. London. Routledge. 119p. VG/dj. A10. $6.00

HAJNAL, Peter I. *Seven-Power Summit, Documents of Summits...1975-1989.* 1989. Millwood. Kraus Internat Pub. 1st comprehensive collection. M11. $42.00

HALBERSTAM, David. *One Very Hot Day.* 1967. Houghton Mifflin. pres. VG/dj. N2. $10.00

HALDEMAN, Joe. *All My Sins Remembered.* 1977. St Martin. 1st ed. F/F. P3. $23.00

HALDEMAN, Joe. *Dealing in Futures.* 1985. Viking. 1st ed. F/F. P3. $17.00

HALDEMAN, Joe. *Hemingway Hoax.* 1990. Morrow. 1st ed. inscr/sgn. F/dj. F4. $45.00

HALDEMAN, Joe. *Worlds...* 1981. Viking. 1st ed. F/F. N3. $20.00

HALE, D.E. *Great Dane.* 1933. Chicago. Judy. 1st ed. ils. 103p. cloth. VG. R2. $15.00

HALE, John R. *Age of Exploration.* 1966. Time Books. 1st ed. 4to. VG. W1. $8.00

HALE, Lucretia. *Peterkin Papers.* (1924). Houghton Mifflin. later rpt. ils Harold Brett. F/G. B17. $6.50

HALE, Matthew. *Historia Placitorum Coronae. Hist of Pleas of the Crown...* 1736. London. Nutt Gosling. 2 vol. modern crimson morocco. M11. $850.00

HALE, Sarah Josepha. *Biography of Distinguished Women...* 1876. NY. 3rd ed. 230p. 918p. VG. F1. $50.00

HALEY, Alex. *Different Kind of Christmas.* 1988. Doubleday. 1st ed. 12mo. 101p. VG/VG. V3. $12.00

HALEY, Alex. *Roots.* 1976. Doubleday. 1st ed. 8vo. 587p. blk cloth/tan brd. VG/dj. H5. $100.00

HALEY, Alex. *Roots.* 1976. Doubleday. 1st ed. 1/500. sgn. 587p. full leather. F/cb case. H5. $450.00

HALEY, Gail. *Go Away, Stay Away.* 1977. Scribner. 1st ed. 32p. F/VG. P2. $25.00

HALEY, J.E. *George Littlefield, Texan.* 1943. OK. 1st ed. F/dj. A15. $100.00

HALEY, James. *Stoker Bush.* 1926. Macmillan. 1st Am ed. F/NF. B2. $50.00

HALKETT, Sarah Phelps Stokes. *Aunt Sadie's Rhymes & Rhyme Stories.* ca 1916. Dutton. inscr pres. 114p. VG. B10. $25.00

HALL, Adam. *Mandarin Cypher.* 1975. Doubleday. 1st Am ed. F/F. M15. $25.00

HALL, Adam. *Peking Target.* 1982. Playboy. 1st ed. VG. P3. $10.00

HALL, Adam. *Warsaw Document.* 1971. Heinemann. 1st ed. VG/G. P3. $25.00

HALL, Alexander. *Universalism Against Itself...* 1846. St Clairsville, OH. Heaton Gressinger. 1st ed. full calf/morocco label. VG. M8. $150.00

HALL, Basil. *Extracts From a Journal Written on Coasts of Chili...* 1824. Edinburgh. Constable. 2 vol. 8vo. fld map. marbled brd/ep/edges. VG. F1. $185.00

HALL, C.E. *Field Notes of Delaware County.* 1885. Harrisburg. 2nd Geological Soc. 8vo. ils/photos. 128p. G. B11. $35.00

HALL, Charles Frances. *Arctic Researches & Life Among the Esquimauz...* 1866. NY. sgn. F. H4. $300.00

HALL, Clarence. *Flowers of the Islands in the Sun.* 1966. London. Yoseloff. 1st ed. sq 4to. 143p. VG/dj. F3. $35.00

HALL, David. *Mercenary's Guide to the Rare Coin Market.* 1987. Am Bureau Econ Research. inscr. 417p. F/F. S11. $10.00

HALL, David. *Some Brief Memoirs of Life of...* 1758. London. Luke Hinde. 1st ed. 12mo. 222p. worn leather. V3. $48.00

HALL, Donald. *Life Work.* 1993. Boston. Beacon. 1st ed. F/F. B3. $25.00

HALL, Donald. *Man Who Lived Alone.* 1984. Godine. 1st ed. sgn. ils/sgn Mary Azarian. 35p. M/dj. B24. $85.00

HALL, Donald. *Riddle Rat.* 1977. NY. Warne. 1st ed. inscr. ils Mort Gerberg. red brd. F/pict dj. B24. $75.00

HALL, Edward T. *Beyond Culture.* 1976. Anchor. 1st ed. 256p. VG/VG. A10. $15.00

HALL, Edward T. *Dance of Life: The Other Dimension of Time.* 1983. Anchor. 232p. VG/VG. A10. $15.00

HALL, Edward T. *Hidden Dimension.* 1966. Doubleday. 201p. VG/VG. A10. $15.00

HALL, Eliza Calvert. *Aunt Jane of Kentucky.* 1907. Little Brn. 283p. VG. M10. $5.00

HALL, Eliza Calvert. *Land of Long Ago.* 1909. Little Brn. 1st ed. ils Nelson/Strong. 295p. VG. H1. $7.50

HALL, George. *Grant: In Memoriam.* 1885. Dover, NH. 15p. G/wrp. O8. $9.50

HALL, J.K. *One Hundred Years of American Psychiatry.* 1944. NY. 649p. A13. $125.00

HALL, James B. *Us He Devours.* 1964. NY. New Directions. 1st ed/hc issue. pres/sgn twice. F/NF. A11. $35.00

HALL, James B. *Yates Paul, His Grand Flights, His Tootings.* 1964. London. 1st UK ed/author's 1st novel. sgn. F/NF. A11. $50.00

HALL, James Norman. *Kitchener's Mob.* 1916. Boston. 1st ed/author's 1st book. VG+. A9. $35.00

HALL, James W. *Paper Products.* 1990. Norton. 1st ed. F/F. M15. $25.00

HALL, James W. *Paper Products.* 1990. Norton. 1st ed. NF/NF. P3. $20.00

HALL, John F. *Psychology of Learning.* 1966. Lippincott. 633p. F/dj. K4. $15.00

HALL, Josef Washington. *Eminent Asians.* 1929. Appleton. 1st ed. 8vo. 511p. VG. W1. $14.00

HALL, Katherine Stanley. *Children at Play in Many Lands, a Book of Games.* 1912. NY. Missionary Education Movement US/Canada. NF. D6. $25.00

HALL, Kermit L. *Comprehensive Bibliography of Am Constitutional...Hist...* 1984-1991. Millwood. Kraus Internat Pub. 7 vol. M11. $150.00

HALL, Leland. *Salah & His American.* 1935. Knopf. 2nd ed. 8vo. 200p. VG. W1. $9.00

HALL, Lynn. *New Day for Dragon.* 1975. Chicago. Follett. 1st ed. brd. VG. O3. $22.00

HALL, Manly P. *Old Testament Wisdom: Keys to Bible Interpretation.* 1957. Los Angeles. Philosophical Research Soc. 312p. VG/VG. B33. $45.00

HALL, Manly P. *Self-Unfoldment by Disciplines of Realization.* 1977. Los Angeles. 221p. VG/VG. B33. $14.00

HALL, Marshall. *Descriptive, Diagnostic & Practical Essay...Digestive...* 1823. Keene, NH. 2nd ed. 142p. brd. uncut. G7. $95.00

HALL, Mrs. Marshall. *Memoirs of Marshall Hall, MD, FRS...by His Widow.* 1861. London. Bentley. 518p. Victorian cloth. G. G7. $195.00

HALL, O.M.; see Hall, Oakley.

HALL, Oakley. *Apaches.* 1986. Simon Schuster. 1st ed. F/F. B4. $35.00

HALL, Oakley. *Lullaby.* 1982. Atheneum. 1st ed. F/NF. F4. $17.00

HALL, Oakley. *Murder City.* 1950. London. 1st Eng ed/author's 1st book. inscr. VG+/VG. A11. $60.00

HALL, Oakley. *So Many Doors.* 1950. NY. 1st ed. sgn. F/NF. A11. $55.00

HALL, Oakley. *Warlock.* 1958. Viking. 1st ed. F/VG. F4. $25.00

HALL, Parnell. *Client.* 1990. Donald Fine. 1st ed. F/F. P3. $19.00

HALL, Pearl Crist. *Long Road to Freedom: One Person's Discovery of Death.* 1978. Richmond, IN. Friends United Pr. 12mo. 138p. VG. V3. $8.00

HALL, R. Cargill. *Lightning Over Bougainville.* 1991. WA. 1st ed. 220p. VG/dj. B18. $15.00

HALL, Robert Lee. *Exit Sherlock Holmes: Great Detective's Final Days.* 1977. London. Murray. 1st Eng ed. F/dj. S6. $27.50

HALL, Rosalyn. *Baker's Man.* ca 1954. Lippincott. inscr. unp. VG/G. B10. $15.00

HALL, S.C. *Royal Gallery of Art: Ancient & Modern.* ca 1875. London. Virtue. 2 vol. 1st ed. 144 engravings. NF. C6. $375.00

HALL, Sharlot. *Cactus & Pine.* 1924. AZ Republican Prt Shop. 1st ed. 250p. NF/ragged. B19. $45.00

HALL, Sharlot. *Poems of a Ranch Woman.* 1953. Sharlot Hall Hist Soc of AZ. 1st ed. 144p. NF/G. B19. $45.00

HALL, Sharlot. *Sharlot Hall on the AZ Strip: A Diary of a Journey...* 1975. Northland. 1st ed. edit CG Crampton. 97p. F/F. B19. $35.00

HALL, Sharlot. *Sharlot Herself: Selected Writings.* 1992. Sharlot Hall Mus Pr. ils/notes/index. 105p. F/wrp. B19 $15.00

HALL, Tom T. *How To Write Songs.* 1976. NY. 1st ed. VG/VG. B5. $25.00

HALL, Trowbridge. *Egypt in Silhouette.* 1928. Macmillan. 1st ed. 8vo. 278p. VG. W1. $12.00

HALL, William H. *Near East: Crossroads of the World.* 1920. Interchurch Pr. 1st ed. 12mo. 230p. VG. W1. $18.00

HALLAHAN, William. *Catch Me, Kill Me.* 1978. London. Gollancz. 1st Eng ed. F/NF. S6. $25.00

HALLAM, Elizabeth. *Four Gothic Kings.* 1987. Weidenfeld Nicolson. 1st ed. ils. 314p. VG/dj. M20. $25.00

HALLAM, Henry. *View of State of Europe During the Middle Ages.* ca 1860. Harper. 1st Am ed. VG. W1. $10.00

HALLAS, Richard. *You Play the Black & the Red Comes Up.* 1980. Boston. Gregg. 1st ed thus. new intro. F/F. B4. $45.00

HALLE, Louis. *Transcaribbean. Travel Book of Guatemala, El Salvador...* 1936. NY. Longman Gr. 1st ed. ils. 311p. VG. F3. $20.00

HALLECK, Seymour L. *Psychiatry & the Dilemmas of Crime.* 1967. Harper/Hoeber. 1st ed. F/F. B2. $25.00

HALLER, John. *American Medicine in Transition, 1840-1910.* 1981. Chicago. 1st ed. 457p. A13. $30.00

HALLETT, Charles. *Furniture Decoration Made Easy.* 1952. Boston. Bradford. 1st ed. 4to. ils. 146p. G/torn. M10. $5.00

HALLEY, Henry. *Halley's Bible Handbook.* 1965. Zondervan. 850p. VG. B29. $4.50

HALLEY, Henry. *Pocket Bible Handbook.* 1954. Halley 768p. G/dj. B29. $4.50

HALLGREN, Mauritz. *All About Stamps: Their Hist & Art of Collecting Them.* 1940. Knopf. 1st ed. ils. sc. VG. M10. $5.00

HALLIBURTON, Richard. *Flying Carpet.* 1932. Bobbs Merrill. 352p. VG. W1. $12.00

HALLIBURTON, Richard. *New Worlds To Conquer.* 1929. Bobbs Merrill. 8vo. 368p. map ep. brn cloth. VG/VG. B11. $30.00

HALLIBURTON, Richard. *Seven League Boots.* 1935. Bobbs Merrill. 1st ed. 8vo. 62 pl. VG. W1. $20.00

HALLIDAY, Brett. *Date With a Dead Man.* 1959. Dodd Mead. 1st ed. VG/VG. P3. $25.00

HALLIDAY, Brett. *Date With a Dead Man.* 1959. Torquil. 1st ed. F/dj. F4. $45.00

HALLIDAY, Brett. *Die Like a Dog.* 1959. Torquil. 1st ed. F/NF. F4. $45.00

HALLIDAY, Brett. *Fit To Kill.* 1958. Dodd Mead. 1st ed. xl. lacks front ep. dj. P3. $10.00

HALLIDAY, Brett. *Fit To Kill.* 1958. Torquil. 1st ed. F/dj. F4. $50.00

HALLIDAY, Brett. *Homicidal Virgin.* 1960. Torquil. 1st ed. VG/VG. P3. $25.00

HALLIDAY, Brett. *Murder & the Wanton Bride.* 1958. Torquil. 1st ed. F/dj. F4. $50.00

HALLIDAY, Brett. *Pay-Off in Blood.* 1962. Torquil. 1st ed. F/NF. F4. $40.00

HALLIDAY, Brett. *Target, Mike Shayne.* 1959. Dodd Mead. 1st ed. VG/G. P3. $15.00

HALLIDAY, F.E. *Cult of Shakespeare.* 1960. NY. 1st ed. 218 p. NF/torn. A17. $9.50

HALLIDAY, Fred. *Ambler.* 1983. Simon Schuster. 1st ed. VG/VG. P3. $14.00

HALLINAN, Timothy. *Everything but the Squeal.* 1990. NAL. 1st ed. sgn. F/F. P3. $28.00

HALLINAN, Timothy. *Incinerator.* 1992. Morrow. 1st ed. sgn. F/F. M15. $27.50

HALLINAN, Vincent. *Lion in Court.* 1963. Putnam. M11. $35.00

HALLIWELL, Leslie. *Dead That Walk.* 1988. Continuum. 1st ed. VG. P3. $25.00

HALPER, Albert. *Chicago Sideshow.* 1932. np. 1st ed/1st book. sgn. 1/100 #d. F/gr 8vo wrp. very scarce. A11. $245.00

HALSALL, Eric. *Gael: Sheepdog of the Hills.* 1985. Great Britain. Patrick Stevens. 1st ed. 224p. M/dj. R2. $30.00

HALSEY. *Forgotten Books of the American Nursery.* 1911. Goodspeed. 1/700. 255p. xl. VG. scarce. A4. $75.00

HALSMAN, Phillippe. *Jump Book.* 1959. Simon Schuster. 1st ed. 8vo. VG/VG. S9. $50.00

HALSTEAD, Maurice H. *Machine-Independent Computer Programming.* 1962. WA, DC. Spartan. 150p. F/dj. K4. $12.50

HALSTEAD, Murat. *Hist of Am Expansion.* 1898. np. photos/maps/mc pl. 712p. G. A17. $12.50

HALSTEAD, Murat. *Our Country in War & Relations With All Nations.* 1898. United Subscription. 8vo.ils/pl/maps. 648p. pict gray-gr cloth. B11. $45.00

HAMAKER & WEAVER. *Survival of Civilization: Solving Problems of Co2...* 1982. MI. Authors. 218p. A10. $9.00

HAMBLY, Barbara. *Those Who Hunt the Night.* 1988. Del Rey. 1st ed. F/F. P3. $20.00

HAMILTON, Allan M. *Types of Insanity: Ils Guide in Physical Diagnosis...* 1883. NY. 4to. 10 pl. wrp/portfolio. very scarce. B14. $450.00

HAMILTON, Anthony. *Fairy Tales & Romances.* 1849. London. Henry Bohn. 1st ed. trans M Lewis/HT Ryde/C Kenney. 562p. NF. D6. $135.00

HAMILTON, Bob. *Gene Autry & the Red-wood Pirates.* 1946. Whitman. ils Erwin Hess. G. B34. $15.00

HAMILTON, David. *Monkey Gland Affair.* 1986. London. 1st ed. 155p. A13. $40.00

HAMILTON, Edmond. *City at World's End.* 1951. Frederick Fell. 1st ed. F/dj. F4. $75.00

HAMILTON, Edmond. *Haunted Stars.* nd. BC. VG/VG. P3. $10.00

HAMILTON, Edward John. *Human Mind: Treatise in Mental Philosophy.* 1883. NY. Carter. author's 1st book. sgn. 720p. brn cloth. VG. G1. $100.00

HAMILTON, Elizabeth. *Put Off Thy Shoes: Journey to Israel & Jordan.* 1957. London. Deutsch. 1st ed. 8vo. 192p. xl. VG/dj. W1. $12.00

HAMILTON, Franklin; see Silverberg, Robert.

HAMILTON, Henry W. *Aftermath of War.* 1982. Dayton. Morningside. 1st ed. 257p. cloth. VG. A17. $20.00

HAMILTON, Ian. *In Search of JD Salinger.* 1988. Random. 1st prt. 222p. F/F. S11. $10.00

HAMILTON, J. *Gentle Thoughts.* ca 1835. Phil. Hamilton. 30x27mm. aeg. F/gilt red cloth wrp. B24. $350.00

HAMILTON, James McClellan. *From Wilderness to Statehood.* 1957. np. 620p. VG/dj. B34. $70.00

HAMILTON, James. *Arthur Rackham: A Biography.* 1990. Arcade. 1st Am ed. folio. ils. F/F. B17. $37.50

HAMILTON, James. *Arthur Rackham: A Biography.* 1990. NY. 1st Am ed. 199p. M/M. A17. $45.00

HAMILTON, Jane. *Map of the World.* 1994. Doubleday. ARC. NF/pict wrp. B3. $75.00

HAMILTON, Jane. *Map of the World.* 1994. Doubleday. 1st ed. sgn. F/F. S9. $75.00

HAMILTON, Jean. *Playing Cards in the Victoria & Albert Museum.* 1988. ils. 79p. M. O8. $12.50

HAMILTON, Lord Frederick. *More About PJ: Secret Service Boy.* nd. Nelson. ils HM Brock. 330p. G. B10. $20.00

HAMILTON, Virginia. *All Jahdu Story Book.* 1991. Harcourt Brace. 1st ed. sm 4to. M/M. C8. $75.00

HAMILTON, Virginia. *Bells of Christmas.* 1989. Harcourt Brace. 1st ed. inscr. ils Lambert Davis. M/M. C8. $75.00

HAMILTON, William R. *Memorandum on Subject of the Earl of Elgin's Pursuits...* 1811. London. 2nd ed. 8vo. 77p. new quarter calf/marbled brd. O2. $275.00

HAMILTON. *Correspondence of Commodore Hamiltion During Greek War...* 1930. London. 8vo. intro Joannes Gennadius. 26p. prt wrp. O2. $30.00

HAMLIN, C. *Life & Times of Hannibal Hamlin.* 1899. Cambridge. 1st ed. ils/index. 627p. VG. B5. $50.00

HAMLIN & HOWARD. *European & Japanese Gardens.* 1902. Phil. 1st ed. VG. C11. $40.00

HAMLYN, D.W. *Psychology of Perception: A Philosophical Examination...* 1957. London. Routledge. 12mo. 120p. red cloth. VG/dj. G1. $22.50

HAMM, Charles. *Music in the New World.* 1983. Norton. 1st ed. 722p. VG/dj. F3. $20.00

HAMMACHER, A.M. *Evolution of Modern Sculpture.* nd. Abrams. lg 4to. 383p. silvered bl cloth. F/VG. F1. $85.00

HAMMETT, Dashiell. *Big Knockover.* nd. BOMC. VG/fair. P3. $10.00

HAMMETT, Dashiell. *Big Knockover.* 1966. Random. 1st ed. F/F. M15. $65.00

HAMMETT, Dashiell. *Creeps by Night.* 1931. John Day. VG. P3. $250.00

HAMMETT, Dashiell. *Glass Key.* 1931. Knopf. 1st Am ed. 8vo. 282p. maroon/dk gr stp gr cloth. VG/dj. H5. $3,000.00

HAMMETT, Dashiell. *Maltese Falcon.* nd. Grosset Dunlap. VG/fair. P3. $15.00

HAMMETT, Dashiell. *Woman in the Dark.* 1988. NY. Knopf. 1st hc ed. intro/sgn Robert B Parker. F/F. S6. $40.00

HAMMETT, Dashiell. *Woman in the Dark. A Novel of Dangerous Romance.* 1988. London. 1st Eng ed. sgn. F/F. A11. $55.00

HAMMETT, Samuel Adams. *Wonderful Adventures of Captain Priest.* 1855. NY. Long. 299p. cloth. B14. $150.00

HAMMIL, Joel. *Limbo.* 1980. Arbor. 1st ed. VG/VG. P3. $13.00

HAMMOND, C.S. *Hammond's Ils Atlas for Young America.* ca 1956. Hammond. ils/maps. 96p. pict bdg. G+. B10. $10.00

HAMMOND, Gerald. *Cousin Once Removed.* 1984. London. Macmillan. 1st ed. NF/dj. S6. $20.00

HAMMOND, Kenneth. *Teaching Comprehensive Medical Care.* 1959. Harvard. 573p. F/dj. K4. $20.00

HAMMOND, Natalie. *New Adventures in Needlepoint Design.* 1973. np. cloth. VG. G2. $9.00

HAMMOND, Ralph. *Antebellum Mansions of AL.* 1951. Bonanza. 196p. VG/dj. M20. $20.00

HAMMOND & HOLDER. *Intro to the Statistical Method.* 1963. Knopf. 412p. G. K4. $10.00

HAMMONDS, Michael. *Gathering of Wolves.* 1975. Doubleday. 1st ed. VG/VG. P3. $12.00

HAMNER, Laura. *Short Grass & Longhorns.* 1943. OK. 1st ed. VG+. A15. $30.00

HAMPTON, Taylor. *Nickle Plate Road.* 1947. Cleveland. 1st ed. 366p. buckram. VG/laminated dj. B18. $37.50

HAMRICK, R. Hubbard. *Hist of the First Baptist Church of Shelby, NC.* 1969. Shelby, NC. 1st ed. 167p. cloth. NF. M8. $37.50

HANCOCK, H. Irving. *Dave Darrin After the Mine Layers.* 1919. Altemus. 1st ed. VG/frayed. M2. $25.00

HANCOCK, H. Irving. *Square Dollar Boys Smash the Ring.* 1912. Altemus. VG. M20. $30.00

HANDFORTH, Thomas. *Faraway Meadow.* 1939. Doubleday Doran. 1st ed thus. lg 4to. unp. VG-/G. A3. $35.00

HANDFORTH, Thomas. *Mei Li.* 1938. Doubleday Doran. 1st ed. G+/G+. P2. $75.00

HANDLER, Milton. *Cases & Other Materials on Trade Regulation.* 1937. Chicago. Foundation Pr. M11. $35.00

HANDLIN, Oscar. *Harvard Guide to American History.* 1954. Cambridge. 1st ed. 8vo. 689p. VG. B11. $20.00

HANDY & PUKUI. *Polynesian Family System in Ka-u, HI.* 1972. Rutland. Tuttle. rpt of 1958 ed. VG/dj. N2. $10.00

HANF, Walter. *Mexico.* 1967. Rand McNally. 1st ed. sq 4to. 136p. VG/dj. F3. $20.00

HANFF, Helene. *Duchess of Bloomsbury Street.* 1973. Lippincott. 1st ed. 137p. VG/G. S11. $20.00

HANFF, Helene. *Q's Legacy.* 1985. Little Brn. 1st ed. 177p. VG/G. S11. $15.00

HANFF, Helene. *84, Charing Cross Road.* 1970. Grossman. 1st ed. NF/NF. B4. $85.00

HANHAM, H.J. *19th-Century Constitution 1814-1914.* 1969. Cambridge. 486p. xl. NF. D3. $25.00

HANKINS, Phillip. *Southpay From San Francisco.* 1948. Morrow. 1st ed. VG. P8. $20.00

HANKINS, Samuel W. *Simple Story of a Soldier.* 1912. Nashville, TN. 1st ed. pl. 63p. VG/prt wrp. M11. $950.00

HANKS, Keith. *Falk.* 1972. Cassell. 1st ed. NF/NF. P3. $20.00

HANLEY, Hope. *Needlepoint in America.* 1979. np. cloth. VG. G2. $12.95

HANLEY, Hope. *Needlepoint.* 1975. np. cloth. VG. G2. $9.00

HANLEY, James. *Boy.* 1931. London. Boriswood Ltd. 1st ed. 271p. F/NF. M7. $250.00

HANLEY, James. *German Prisoner.* nd (1930). Muswell Hill. private prt. 1/500. blk buckram. NF/clear plastic. M7. $250.00

HANLEY, James. *Men in Darkness. Five Stories by James Hanley.* 1932. Knopf. 1st ed. 293p. gray linen. NF/VG+. M7. $80.00

HANLY & LAZEROWITZ. *Psychoanalysis & Philosophy.* 1970. NY. Internat U Pr. 362p. gray cloth. VG/dj. G1. $30.00

HANNA, Phil Townsend. *CA Through Four Centuries: A Handbook...* 1935. Farrar Rinehart. 1st ed. 212p. VG. B19. $40.00

HANNA, Phil Townsend. *Libros Californianos; or, Five Feet of CA Books.* 1932. Primavera. 1st ed. 74p. NF. B19. $50.00

HANNAH, Barry. *Captain Maximus.* 1985. NY. 1st ed. inscr. F/F. A15. $50.00

HANNAH, Barry. *Geronimo Rex.* 1972. NY. 1st ed/author's 1st book. inscr. xl. scarce. A15. $75.00

HANNAH, Barry. *Ray: A Novel.* 1980. NY. 1st ed/author's 4th book. sgn. F/F. A11. $40.00

HANNAN, Jerome Daniel. *Canon Law of Wills, an Hist Synopsis & Commentary.* 1935. Phil. Dolphin. M11. $50.00

HANNAY, David. *Short History of the Royal Navy 1217-1815.* 1898. London. Methuen. 2 vol. T7. $130.00

HANNON, Ezra; see Hunter, Evan.

HANNUM, A. *Roseanna McCoy.* 1947. NY. 1st ed. sgn. VG/G. B5. $20.00

HANNUM, Alberta. *Spin a Silver Dollar: Story of a Desert Trading Post.* 1945. Viking. 1st ed. 175p. VG/G. B10. $25.00

HANO, Arnold. *Big Out.* 1951. Grosset Dunlap. rpt. Famous Sports Stories Series. VG/G. P8. $25.00

HANSEL, Tim. *Hidden Adventure.* 1987. Guideposts. 198p. F/dj. B29. $3.50

HANSEN, Joseph. *Bohannon's Book: Five Mysteries.* 1988. Woodstock, VT. Foul Play. 1st ed. sgn. F/F. O4. $25.00

HANSEN, Joseph. *Death Claims.* 1973. Harper Row. 1st ed. sgn. NF/VG. O4. $85.00

HANSEN, Joseph. *Early Graves.* 1987. Mysterious. 1st prt. F/F. H1. $25.00

HANSEN, Joseph. *Fadeout.* 1972. London. Harrap. 1st Eng ed. F/NF. S6. $45.00

HANSEN, Joseph. *Gravedigger.* 1982. HRW. 1st ed. sgn. F/F. O4. $25.00

HANSEN, Joseph. *Little Dog Laughed.* 1986. Holt. 1st ed. sgn. F/F. O4. $25.00

HANSEN, Joseph. *Man Everybody Was Afraid Of.* 1978. HRW. ARC/1st ed. RS. F/F. M15. $40.00

HANSEN, Joseph. *Man Everybody Was Afraid Of.* 1978. NY. HRW. 1st ed. sgn. F/F. S6. $40.00

HANSEN, Joseph. *Obedience.* 1988. Mysterious. 1st ed. sgn. F/F. O4. $30.00

HANSEN, Joseph. *Obedience.* 1988. Mysterious. 1st ed. VG/VG. P3. $20.00

HANSEN, Joseph. *Skinflick.* 1979. HRW. 1st ed. F/F. P3. $15.00

HANSEN, Joseph. *Skinflick.* 1979. HRW. 1st ed. sgn. NF/VG. O4. $30.00

HANSEN, Joseph. *Smile in His Lifetime.* 1981. HRW. 1st ed. sgn. F/F. O4. $25.00

HANSEN, Robert P. *Back to the Wall.* 1957. Mill Morrow. 1st ed. VG/torn. P3. $15.00

HANSEN, Robert P. *Trouble Comes Double.* 1954. Mill Morrow. 1st ed. VG/G. P3. $20.00

HANSEN, Ron. *Desperadoes.* 1979. Knopf. 1st ed. NF/clip. B3. $45.00

HANSEN, Ron. *Desperadoes.* 1979. Knopf. 1st ed. sgn. F/NF. L3. $125.00

HANSEN, Ron. *Nebraska.* 1989. Atlantic Monthly. 1st ed. F/F. B4. $65.00

HANSEN, Thorkild. *Arabia Felix: Danish Expedition of 1761-1767.* 1962. Harper Row. 1st ed. ils/maps. 381p. VG/dj. W1. $35.00

HANSEN, Woodrow James. *Search for Authority in California.* 1960. Oakland. Biobooks. 1st ed thus. 1/750. 192p. gr cloth. F. P4. $35.00

HANSON, Charles H. *Land of Greece Described & Ils.* 1886. London. sm 4to. 400p. F. scarce. O2. $185.00

HANSON, Ole. *Americanism Versus Bolshevism.* 1920. NY. 1st ed. 299p. G. A17. $7.50

HANSON, Willis Tracy Jr. *Hist of St George's Church in City of Schenectady.* 1919. Schenectady. 2 vol. 1st ed. 1/600. paper brd/cloth spine. NF. M8. $85.00

HARALSON, Carol. *Native American Art at Philbrook.* 1980. Philbrook Art Center. ils. 96p. VG/wrp. B19. $20.00

HARANG, L. *Aurorae.* 1951. NY. Wiley. 8vo. 166p. bl cloth. xl. K5. $30.00

HARASZTY, Eszter. *Embroiderer's Portfolio of Flower Designs.* 1981. np. VG. G2. $25.00

HARCOURT, Palma. *Shadows of Doubt.* 1983. London. Collins. 1st ed. NF/dj. S6. $25.00

HARCOURT, Robert H. *Elementary Forge Practice...* 1920. Peoria. Manual Arts Pr. 2nd ed. VG. O3. $28.00

HARDEN, Maximilian. *Word Portraits: Character Sketches of Famous Men & Women.* 1911. Edinburgh. 1st ed. trans from German. 425p. gilt cloth. VG. A17. $15.00

HARDIN, Garrett. *Population, Evolution, Birth Control.* 1964. San Francisco/London. Freeman. 337p. F/dj. K4. $8.50

HARDIN, James W. *Poisonous Plants of North Carolina.* 1961. Raleigh. photos. 128p. sc. VG. B26. $14.00

HARDIN, Philomelia Ann Maria. *Every Body's Cook & Receipt Book...* 1842. Cleveland. private prt. 1st ed. 12mo. 108p. cloth. M1. $1,250.00

HARDING, Arthur M. *Astronomy: Splendor of the Heavens Brought Down to Earth.* 1935. Garden City. 4to. 418p. bl cloth. G. K5. $12.00

HARDING, Paul. *Nightingale Gallery.* 1991. Morrow. 1st ed. F/F. P3. $20.00

HARDING, Todd; see Reynolds, Mack.

HARDMAN, Francis. *Frontier Life; or, Scenes & Adventures in South West.* 1857. NY. 376p. G. O8. $65.00

HARDWICK, Elizabeth. *Ghostly Lover.* 1945. NY. 1st ed/author's 1st novel. sgn. VG+/VG+ clip. A11. $85.00

HARDWICK, Michael. *Private Life of Dr Watson.* 1983. NY. Dutton. 1st ed. F/dj. S6. $30.00

HARDWICK, Michael. *Revenge of the Hound.* 1987. Villard. 1st ed. F/F. P3. $20.00

HARDWICK, Michael. *Sherlock Holmes Companion.* 1962. John Murray. 1st ed. VG. P3. $40.00

HARDY, A.C. *Everyman's History of the Sea War, 1939-1946.* 1948-1955. London. Nicholson Watson. 2 vol. ils. dj. T7. $110.00

HARDY, Adam; see Bulmer, Kenneth.

HARDY, James D. *Physiological Problems in Space Exploration.* 1964. Springfield, IL. Charles Thomas. 8vo. 333p. VG/VG. K5. $25.00

HARDY, Phil. *Encyclopedia of Western Movies.* 1983. Woodbury. 1st ed. MTI. VG/VG. P3. $45.00

HARDY, Thomas. *Dynasts.* 1927. London. Macmillan. 3 vol. sgn. 1/525 sets. quarter vellum/brd. H4. $600.00

HARDY, Thomas. *Human Shows Far Phantasies, Songs & Trifles.* 1925. Macmillan. 1st ed. 279p. VG/dj. M20. $50.00

HARDY, Thomas. *Human Shows Far Phantasies, Songs & Trifles.* 1925. NY. Macmillan. 1st ed. F/NF. Q1. $175.00

HARDY, Thomas. *Jude the Obscure.* 1896. Harper. 1st Am ed. 12 pl. 488p. gilt cloth. K1. $75.00

HARDY, Thomas. *Jude the Obscure.* 1896. London. Osgood McIlvaine. 1st ed/1st issue. map. teg. VG. H4. $100.00

HARDY, Thomas. *Old Mrs Chundle: A Short Story.* 1929. NY. Crosby Gaige. 1st ed. 1/700. 8vo. H4. $150.00

HARDY, Thomas. *Selected Poems of Thomas Hardy.* 1921. London. Medici Soc. Riccardi Pr book. 1/1025. bl brd/tan buckram spine. NF. Q1. $250.00

HARDY, W.G. *Alberta Golden Jubilee Anthology.* 1955. Toronto. McClelland Stewart. 1st ed. ils. 470p. G. M10. $5.00

HARDY, W.G. *Alberta: A Natural Hist.* 1967. Edmonton, Alberta. Hurtig. ils. 343p. VG/dj. M10. $7.50

HARDYMENT, Christina. *Dream Babies: Child Care From Locke to Spock.* 1983. London. 1st ed. 334p. A13. $40.00

HARGRAVE, John. *At Sulva Bay, Being Notes & Sketches of Scenes...* 1916. London. 1st ed. pres. 181p. pict cloth. B18. $35.00

HARGREAVES, H.A. *North by 2000.* 1975. Peter Martin. 1st ed. RS. F/F. P3. $25.00

HARGREAVES, Mathew D. *Anne Inez McCAffrey: Forty Years of Publishing.* 1992. Seattle. Hargreaves. 1st ed. sgn Hargreaves/McCaffrey. 1/500 #d. F/sans. T2. $55.00

HARING, J.V. *Hand of Hauptman.* 1937. Palinfield, NJ. 1st ed. VG/VG. B5. $37.50

HARINGTON, Donald. *Cockroaches of Stay More.* 1989. HBJ. 1st ed. F/F. P3. $20.00

HARKER, L. Allan. *Vagaries of Tod & Peter.* 1923. Scribner. 1st Am ed? 300p. VG. B10. $12.00

HARKNESS. *Career of Samuel Butler: A Bibliography.* 1968. np. facsimile of 1955 ed. 154p. NF. A4. $45.00

HARLAN, Robert D. *Chapter Nine: Vulgate Bible & Other Unfinished Projects...* 1982. NY. The Typophiles. 12mo. 76p. F. M10. $27.50

HARLAND, Marion. *Carringtons of High Hill.* 1919. NY. 1st ed. 308p. cloth. G+. R2. $40.00

HARLAND, Marion. *House & Home: Complete Housewife's Guide.* 1889. np. royal 8vo. 532p. gilt bdg. VG. E5. $45.00

HARLAND, Marion. *Under the Flag of the Orient.* 1897. Phil. Hist Pub. sm 4to. 446p. VG. W1. $35.00

HARLOW, A.F. *Brass Pounders.* 1962. 159p. O8. $9.50

HARLOW, Frederick Pease. *Making of Sailor; or, Sea Life Aboard Yankee Square-Rigger.* 1928. Salem. Marine Research Soc #17. 26 pl. 377p. T7. $70.00

HARLOW, Frederick Pease. *Making of Sailor; or, Sea Life Aboard Yankee Square-Rigger.* 1928. Salem. Marine Research. ils gilt bl cloth. NF. F1. $100.00

HARMON & SHUMWAY. *Sons of the Admiral: Story of Diego & Fernado Columbus.* 1940. Page. 1st ed. 373p. VG. B10. $12.00

HARMSEN, Tyrus G. *Forty Years of Book Collecting.* 1985. Tiger. 24p. F/wrp. B19. $25.00

HARNACK, Curtis. *Persian Lions, Persian Lambs.* 1965. HRW. 1st ed. 279p. NF/worn. W1. $14.00

HARNED, J. *Wild Flowers of Alleghanies.* 1931. Oakland, MD. 1st ed. ils. 670-. VG. B5. $35.00

HARNESS, Charles L. *Krono.* 1988. Watts. 1st ed. F/F. P3. $20.00

HAROLD, Childe. *Child's Book of Abridged Wisdom.* 1905. San Francisco. Paul Elder/Tamoye. plain brd/4 twine cords. F/NF. F1. $85.00

HARPER, E.A. *Eighteenth Amendment: Its Validity, Public Opinion.* 1928. Westerville. Am Issue Pub Co. 21p. stapled wrp. M11. $15.00

HARPER, George W. *Gypsy Earth.* 1982. Doubleday. F/F. P3. $15.00

HARPER, Henry. *Merely the Patient.* 1930. NY. 1st ed. 95p. A13. $30.00

HARPER, Robert J. C. *Cognitive Processes: Readings.* 1964. Prentice Hall. 700p. G/dj. K4. $8.50

HARPER, Robert S. *Lincoln & the Press.* 1951. McGraw Hill. 1st ed. 418p. VG/dj. M10. $27.50

HARPER, Theodore A. *Mushroom Boy.* 1925. Harper. 1st ed. 4 mc pl. cloth. VG. M5. $40.00

HARPER, Wilhelmina. *Brownie of the Circus & Other Stories of Today.* 1941. McKay. 1st ed. ils Vera Neville. VG. B17. $8.00

HARRADEN, Beatrice. *Little Rosebud or Things Will Take a Turn.* nd. Burt. ils Anne Merriman Peck. 285p. G. B10. $15.00

HARRAP, Elizabeth. *Dachshund.* 1977. Edinburgh. Bartholomew. 1st ed. 96p. F/wrp. R2. $12.00

HARRE, T. Everret. *Behold the Woman!* 1916. Lippincott. 5th ed. pres to Donald Wandrei. VG/dj. F4. $45.00

HARRINGTON, Alan. *Apple & the Cactus.* 1984. NY. manuscript photocopy. 200p. NF. B3. $75.00

HARRINGTON, H. Nazeby. *Engraved Work of Sir Francis Seymour Haden...* 1910. Liverpool. 1st ed. sgn. 1/75. 108 pl. morocco/cloth. NF. C6. $450.00

HARRINGTON, H.D. *Edible Native Plants of the Rocky Mountains.* 1991 (1967). Albuquerque. ils Y Matsumura. sc. M. B26. $14.95

HARRINGTON, M.R. *How To Build a CA Adobe.* 1948. Ward Ritchie. 1st ed. ils. 57p. NF. B19. $35.00

HARRINGTON, Mildred P. *Ring-A-Round.* 1930. Macmillan. 1st ed. ils Corydon Bell. gray cloth. VG. M5. $30.00

HARRIS, Albert J. *How To Increase Reading Ability.* 1970. NY. McKay. 512p. F/dj. K4. $8.50

HARRIS, Albert. *Blood of the Arab: World's Greatest War Horse.* 1941. Chicago. 1st ed. 4to. VG. O3. $125.00

HARRIS, Albert. *Hist of Arabian Horse Club Registry of Am, Inc 1908-1950.* 1950. Chicago. 1st ed. VG. O3. $38.00

HARRIS, Alfred. *Baroni.* 1975. Putnam. 1st ed. VG/VG. P3. $15.00

HARRIS, Eddy. *Mississippi Solo.* 1988. Nick Lyons. 1st ed. F/F. L3. $25.00

HARRIS, F. McCready. *Bible Scenes & Stories for Young People.* ca 1920. Cassell. ils Gustave Dore. 176p. G. W1. $15.00

HARRIS, Frank. *Bernard Shaw.* 1931. Gollancz. 2nd ed. VG. P3. $18.00

HARRIS, Frank. *Mad Love.* 1920. NY. 1st ed. sgn pres. VG/wrp. A17. $20.00

HARRIS, Geraldine. *Children of the Wind.* 1982. Greenwillow. 1st ed. VG/G. P3. $13.00

HARRIS, Geraldine. *Seventh Gate.* 1983. Greenwillow. 1st ed. VG/G. P3. $13.00

HARRIS, H.G. *Handbook of Watch & Clock Repairs.* 1974. Emmerson Books. 1st ed/3rd prt. VG. A8. $20.00

HARRIS, Hyde. *Kyd for Hire.* 1977. London. Gollancz. 1st Eng/1st hc ed. VG+/dj. S6. $35.00

HARRIS, J. *Peregrine Falcon in Greenland.* 1979. Columbia, MO. 1st ed. ils/index. 255p. VG/VG. B5. $25.00

HARRIS, Joel Chandler. *Bishop & the Boogerman.* 1909. NY. Doubleday Page. 1st ed. 8vo. 184p. gilt gr cloth. VG. H5. $75.00

HARRIS, Joel Chandler. *Daddy Jake the Runaway & Short Stories Told After Dark.* 1889. NY. Century. 1st ed. 145p. pict brd. G. H5. $300.00

HARRIS, Joel Chandler. *Little Union Scout.* 1904. McClure Phillips. 1st ed. ils George Gibbs. pict cloth. G+. C8. $100.00

HARRIS, Joel Chandler. *Nights With Uncle Remus.* Oct 1917. Houghton Mifflin. probable 1st ed thus. NF. C8. $65.00

HARRIS, Joel Chandler. *On the Plantation.* 1892. NY. Appleton. 1st ed. 8vo. 233p. mustard cloth. VG. H5. $200.00

HARRIS, Joel Chandler. *Plantation Pageants.* 1899. Westminster. 1st UK ed. ils E Boyd Smith. VG. C8. $75.00

HARRIS, Joel Chandler. *Told by Uncle Remus: New Stories of Old Plantation.* 1905. McClure Phillips. 1st ed. 295p. gilt bdg. VG. P2. $90.00

HARRIS, Joel Chandler. *Uncle Remus, His Songs & His Sayings.* 1881. Appleton. 1st ed/3rd state. 8vo. 231p. bl cloth. VG. C6. $275.00

HARRIS, Joel Chandler. *Uncle Remus, His Songs & His Sayings.* 1905 (1881). NY. Appleton. new/revised ed. teg. pict cloth. VG+. C8. $75.00

HARRIS, Joel Chandler. *Uncle Remus & His Friends.* 1899. Houghton Mifflin. ils AB Frost. VG. B17. $35.00

HARRIS, Joel Chandler. *Uncle Remus Stories.* nd. London. Collins. ils Wm Blackhouse. VG+/VG+. C8. $25.00

HARRIS, Joel Chandler. *Wally Wanderoon & His Story-Telling Machine.* 1903. McClure Phillips. 1st ed/probable 1st state. 294p. pict tan cloth. VG+. C6. $150.00

HARRIS, Joel Chandler. *Walt Disney's Uncle Remus Stories.* 1947. Giant Golden Book. stated 1st prt. ils. VG. M5. $60.00

HARRIS, Ken. *Index to the Journals of Continental Congress.* 1976. National Archives. 429p. O8. $21.00

HARRIS, Leon. *Upton Sinclair: American Rebel.* 1975. Crowell. 1st ed. F/F clip. S9. $20.00

HARRIS, Louise Dyer. *Visions of St Nick in Action.* 1950. Phillips Pub. 5 fld scenes. pict brd/vinyl spine. VG. A3. $25.00

HARRIS, MacDonald. *Little People.* 1986. Morrow. 1st ed. F/F. N3. $25.00

HARRIS, Mark. *Bang the Drum Slowly.* 1956. Knopf. 1st ed. Henry Wiggins Series #2. VG/G. P8. $135.00

HARRIS, Mark. *City of Discontent.* 1952. Indianapolis. 1st ed/author's 2nd book. inscr. NF/VG+. A11. $60.00

HARRIS, Mark. *Southpaw.* 1953. Bobbs Merril. 1st ed. Henry Wiggens Series #1. G+/G+. hard to find. P8. $175.00

HARRIS, Mark. *Ticket for a Seamstich.* 1957. Knopf. 1st ed. Henry Wiggens Series #3. VG/VG. P8. $45.00

HARRIS, Thaddeus Mason. *Journal of Tour in Territory NW of Allegheny Mountains.* 1805. Boston. 1st ed. 1st separate map of OH. H4. $375.00

HARRIS, Thaddeus William. *Treatise on Some Insects Injurious to Vegetation...* 1862. Boston. 8 mc pl. 640p. NF. H10. $145.00

HARRIS, Thomas. *Black Sunday.* 1975. Putnam. 1st ed/author's 1st novel. NF/NF. M15. $75.00

HARRIS, Thomas. *Red Dragon.* 1981. Putnam. 1st ed. NF/clip. M21. $40.00

HARRIS, Thomas. *Red Dragon.* 1981. Putnam. 1st ed/author's 2nd book. F/dj. F4/N3. $50.00

HARRIS, Thomas. *Silence of the Lambs.* 1988. St Martin. 1st ed. F/NF. N3. $45.00

HARRIS, Thomas. *Silence of the Lambs.* 1988. St Martin. 1st ed. VG/VG. P3. $30.00

HARRIS, W.R. *Catholic Church in Utah.* 1909. Salt Lake City. Intermountain Catholic Pr. lg 8vo. 350p. gilt gr cloth. K1. $75.00

HARRIS, W.S. *Capital & Labor.* 1907. Harrisburg. Minter Co. 1st ed. 331p. F. B2. $50.00

HARRIS, W.S. *Complete Index to Thought & Teachings of Christ.* 1939. Cokesbury. 191p. VG/dj. B29. $4.50

HARRIS, W.S. *Life in a Thousand Worlds.* (1905). Am Pub. ils. 344p. G. H1. $7.00

HARRIS, Walter B. *Journey Through the Yemen & Some General Remarks...* 1893. Edinburgh. 8vo. ils/pl/maps. 385p. cloth. O2. $275.00

HARRIS, William H. *Keeping the Faith.* 1977. Urbana. ils. F. V4. $12.50

HARRIS, Wilson. *Da Vilva da Silva's Cultivated Wilderness & Genesis...* 1977. London. Faber. 1st ed. F/F. B2. $30.00

HARRIS & HARRIS. *Plant Identification Terminology.* 1994. Spring Lake, UT. ils. 198p. sc. M. B26. $18.00

HARRIS & HARRIS. *Tony & Toinette in the Topics.* 1939. Whitman. 90p. VG/VG. B10. $15.00

HARRIS & VELPEAU. *Elementary Treatise on Midwifery; or, Principles...* 1845. Phil. 3rd ed. 8vo. 600p. full calf. G. H3. $65.00

HARRISON, C.S. *Gold Mine in Front Yard & How To Work It.* 1905. St paul. photos. 279p. cloth. F. B26. $29.00

HARRISON, Chip; See Block, Lawrence.

HARRISON, Earle. *Panama Canal Illustrated by Color Photography...* 1913. NY. Moffat Yard. slim 8vo. 34p. VG. B11. $65.00

HARRISON, Eugene. *How To Win Souls.* 1952. Scripture Pr. 155p. G/dj. B29. $3.50

HARRISON, Everett F. *Intro to the New Testament.* 1982. Eerdmans. 507p. VG/dj. B29. $8.50

HARRISON, F. *Painted Glass of York: Account of Medieval Glass...* 1927. London. Soc for Promoting Christian. 1st ed. VG/dj. M10. $22.50

HARRISON, H. *Sacco-Vanzetti Anthology of Verse.* 1927. NY. Henry Harrison. 1st ed. VG/wrp. B2. $85.00

HARRISON, Harry. *Ahead of Time.* 1972. Doubleday. VG. P3. $13.00

HARRISON, Harry. *Mechanismo.* 1978. Reed. 1st ed. VG/VG. P3. $25.00

HARRISON, Harry. *One Step From Earth.* nd. BC. VG/VG. P3. $8.00

HARRISON, Harry. *Stainless Steel Rat Gets Drafted.* 1987. Bantam. 1st Am ed. F/F. M21. $15.00

HARRISON, Harry. *Tunnel Through the Deeps.* 1972. Putnam. 1st ed. F/F. T2. $15.00

HARRISON, Harry. *Winter in Eden.* 1986. Bantam. 1st ed. sgn. F/F. P3. $25.00

HARRISON, Helen Redett. *Modern Meditations for Women...* 1971. Vantage. 70p. VG/VG. B29. $2.00

HARRISON, Jack. *Famous Saddle Horses & Distinguised Horsemen.* 1933. Columbia. 1st ed. G. O3. $325.00

HARRISON, Jim. *Dalva.* 1988. Dutton/Lawrence. 1st ed. F/F. L3. $40.00

HARRISON, Jim. *Farmer.* 1976. NY. 1st ed. VG/VG. B5. $75.00

HARRISON, Jim. *Farmer.* 1976. Viking. 1st ed. sgn. F/NF. B4. $200.00

HARRISON, Jim. *Good Day To Die.* 1973. NY. 1st ed. VG/VG. B5. $125.00

HARRISON, Jim. *Just Before Dark.* 1991. Livingston. Clark City. 1/250. sgn. F/case. B3. $150.00

HARRISON, Jim. *Legends of the Fall.* 1979. Delacorte. 1st ed. VG/VG. B5. $75.00

HARRISON, Jim. *Legends of the Fall.* 1979. Delacorte. 1st ed. 3 vol set. rem mk. NF/case. B3. $225.00

HARRISON, Jim. *Legends of the Fall.* 1980. London. Collins. 1st ed. VG. C4. $45.00

HARRISON, Jim. *Legends of the Fall.* 1980. London. Collins. 1st Eng ed. F/F. B4. $85.00

HARRISON, Jim. *Letters to Yesinin & Returning to Earth.* 1979. Los Angeles. Sumac. 1st ed thus. sgn. F/pict wrp. B3. $35.00

HARRISON, Jim. *Locations.* 1968. Norton. 1st ed. inscr to William Meredith. F/wrp. B4. $250.00

HARRISON, Jim. *New & Selected Poems.* 1981. Delacorte. 1st ed. sgn. 1/250 special bdg. F/case. B2. $200.00

HARRISON, Jim. *Returning to Earth.* 1977. Berkeley. Ithaca. 1st ed. F/stapled wrp. L3. $450.00

HARRISON, Jim. *Sundog.* 1984. Dutton. 1st ed. sgn. F/NF. B2. $85.00

HARRISON, Jim. *Theory & Practice of Rivers.* 1986. Seattle. Winn. ltd ed. sgn. F/case. B4. $125.00

HARRISON, Jim. *Theory & Practice of Rivers.* 1989. Livingston. Clark City. 1st ed. sgn. F/F. B3. $35.00

HARRISON, Jim. *Warlock.* 1981. Delacorte. 1st ed. sgn. rem mk. NF/F. B3. $110.00

HARRISON, Jim. *Warlock.* 1981. Delacorte. 1st ed. sgn. 1/250 special bdg. F/case. B2. $150.00

HARRISON, Jim. *Woman Lit by Fireflies.* 1990. Houghton Mifflin. 1st ed. sgn. F/F. B3. $45.00

HARRISON, Joseph T. *Story of the Dining Fork.* 1927. Cincinnati. inscr. ils. 370p. VG. B18. $55.00

HARRISON, Juanita. *My Great Wide Beautiful World.* 1936. Macmillan. 1st ed. F/NF. B2. $40.00

HARRISON, M. John. *Centauri Device.* 1974. Doubleday. 1st ed. F/F. P3. $20.00

HARRISON, M. John. *Viriconium Nights.* 1985. Gollancz. 1st ed. sgn. F/F. P3. $25.00

HARRISON, Michael. *Exploits of Chevalier Dupin.* 1968. Arkham. 1st ed. F/dj. M2. $65.00

HARRISON, Michael. *I, Sherlock Holmes.* 1977. Morrow. 1st ed. VG/VG. P3. $30.00

HARRISON, R.K. *Intro to the Old Testament.* 1979. Eerdmans. 1324p. VG/dj. B29. $17.00

HARRISON, Ray. *Murder in Petticoat Square.* 1993. London. Constable. 1st ed. F/F. S6. $25.00

HARRISON, Robert A. *New Municipal Manual for Upper Canada...* 1859. Toronto. Maclear. contemporary sheep/rebacked. M11. $250.00

HARRISON, Russell. *Against the American Dream.* 1994. Blk Sparrow. 1/100. sgn. F/F. S9. $35.00

HARRISON, Stanley. *Gentlemen: The Horse!* 1951. Lexington. Thoroughbred Pr. 1st ed. VG/G. O3. $25.00

HARRISON, Sue. *Brother Wind.* 1994. Morrow. 1st ed. sgn. F/F. B3. $25.00

HARRISON, Whit; see Whittington, Harry.

HARRISON, William. *In a Wild Sanctuary.* 1969. NY. 1st ed/author's 2nd novel. sgn. F/F. A11. $45.00

HARRISON, William. *Roller Ball Murder.* 1974. Morrow. 1st ed. NF/NF. P3. $18.00

HARRISON, William. *Roller Ball Murder.* 1974. Morrow. 1st ed/13 short stories. sgn. F/F. A11. $45.00

HARRISON & STOVER. *Stonehenge.* 1972. Scribner. 1st ed. sgn. F/NF clip. F4. $45.00

HARROD, R.F. *Foundations of Inductive Logic.* 1956. London. Macmillan. 290p. red cloth. VG/dj. G1. $25.00

HARRY. *Paperback Writers: Hist of Beatles in Print...* 1984. London. 192p. F/wrp. A4. $20.00

HART, Carolyn G. *Danger: High Explosives.* 1972. NY. Evans. 1st ed. sgn. rem mk. F/dj. M15. $35.00

HART, Carolyn G. *Southern Ghost.* 1992. Bantam. 1st ed. sgn. F/F. S6. $35.00

HART, Clive. *Prehistory of Flight.* 1985. Berkeley. 1st ed. ils. F. B18. $47.50

HART, Francis Russell. *Admirals of the Caribbean.* 1922. Boston. Houghton Mifflin. ne. inscr/dtd 1923. half cloth/paper spine label. VG. P4. $60.00

HART, George. *Violin & Its Music.* 1977 (1881). np. 484p. gilt bdg. VG. E5. $45.00

HART, Herbert. *Tour Guide to Old Forts of Montana, Wyoming...* 1980. Boulder, CO. Pruett. ils/maps. VG. B34. $5.00

HART, Hornell. *Chart for Happiness.* 1940. Macmillan. 185p. F/dj. K4. $15.00

HART, Ivor. *Makers of Science: Mathematics, Physics, Astronomy.* 1923. London. 1st ed. 320p. A13. $15.00

HART, James D. *Companion to California.* 1978. NY. Oxford. 2nd prt. maps. 504p. gilt bl cloth. M/F. P4. $30.00

HART, Josephine. *Damage.* 1991. London. Chatto Windus. AP/author's 1st book. F/wrp. S9. $100.00

HART, Josephine. *Damage.* 1991. London. Chatto Windus. 1st ed/author's 1st book. NF/NF. A14. $75.00

HART, Josephine. *Sin.* 1992. Knopf. 1st Am ed. rem mk. NF/NF. A14. $25.00

HART, Liddell. *Colonel Lawrence: Man Behind the Legend.* 1934. Dodd Mead. 4th prt. 382p. VG. W1. $32.00

HART, Roy. *Remains To Be Seen.* 1989. London. Macmillan. ARC/1st ed. RS. F/F. S6. $27.50

HART & TOLLERIS. *Big-Time Baseball.* 1950. NY. ils Sydney Weiss. ils/photos. 192p. VG. A17. $20.00

HARTE, Bret. *East & West Poems.* 1871. Osgood. 1st ed. F. A18. $50.00

HARTE, Bret. *Luck of Roaring Camp.* 1870. Fields Osgood. 1st ed. 8vo. 238p. VG/fld/case. C6. $600.00

HARTE, Bret. *Poems.* 1871. Fields Osgood. 1st ed/1st state. F. A18. $90.00

HARTE, Bret. *She Woke to Darkness.* 1954. Torquil. 1st ed. NF/dj. P3. $20.00

HARTE, Bret. *Tales of the Gold Rush.* 1944. Heritage. 8vo. 223p. marbled brd/cream cloth spine. F/VG case. B11. $20.00

HARTE, Bret. *Wild West. Stories by Bret Harte.* 1930. Harrison of Paris. 1/36 on Japan vellum. embroidered grass cloth. F/case. B24. $450.00

HARTE, Bret. *Works of...* 1882-1907. Collier. Argonaut ed. 25 vol. gilt dark gr cloth. F. A18. $150.00

HARTHAN, John. *Hist of the Ils Book: The Western Tradition.* 1981. London. Thames Hudson. 1st ed. ils. 288p. VG/VG. S11. $55.00

HARTLEY, Marsden. *Androscoggin.* 1940. Falmouth Pub. 1st ed. inscr. VG/dj. B4. $1,250.00

HARTLEY, Norman. *Quicksilver.* 1979. Atheneum. 1st ed. VG/VG. P3. $15.00

HARTLEY, Oliver. *Hunting Dogs.* 1909. Columbus, OH. Harding. 1st ed. ils. 251p. cloth. G. R2. $25.00

HARTLEY. *Ladies Hand Book of Fancy & Ornamental Works...* 1860. np. 240p. VG. E5. $65.00

HARTMANN, Klaus. *Sartre's Ontology: Study in Being & Nothingness...* 1980. Evanston. 2nd prt. 166p. bl cloth. G1. $21.50

HARTMANN, Nicolai. *Ethics.* 1932. London. Allen Unwin. 3 vol. 1st Eng-language ed. VG. G1. $100.00

HARTMANN, PHILLIPS & TAYLOR. *Origin of the Moon.* 1986. Houston, TX. Lunar & Planetary Inst. 781p. xl. VG. K5. $60.00

HARTMANN, Richard. *Die Krisis des Islam.* 1928. Leipzig. Hinrich'she. 8vo. VG/wrp. W1. $8.00

HARTON, F.P. *Elements of Spiritual Life...* ca 1939. London. SPCK. 344p. H10. $17.00

HARTRIDGE, Jon. *Earthjacket.* 1970. Walker. 1st ed. VG/G. P3. $15.00

HARTSHORNE, Charles. *Philosophy & Psychology of Sensation.* 1934. Chicago. 288p. russet cloth. VG. G1. $30.00

HARTUNG, Marion T. *First Book of Carnival Glass...Tenth Book of Carnival Glass.* 1962-1973. Emporia, KS. self pub. 10 vol. 100 patterns per book. sbdg. VG. H1. $175.00

HARTWELL, Henry. *Present State of Virginia & the College.* 1940. Colonial Williamsburg. 1st ed. 8vo. 105p. G/G. B11. $35.00

HARUF, Kent. *Tie That Binds.* 1984. HRW. 1st ed/author's 1st novel. F/F. B3. $30.00

HARVARD, William C. *Henry Sidgwick: Later Utilitarian Political Philosophy.* 1959. Gainesville, FL. 197p. gr cloth. G1. $27.50

HARVESTER, Simon. *Bamboo Screen.* 1968. Walker. 1st ed. NF/NF. P3. $15.00

HARVESTER, Simon. *Zion Road.* 1968. Walker. 1st ed. NF/NF. P3. $15.00

HARVEY, A. McGehee. *Research & Discovery in Medicine.* 1981. Baltimore. 1st ed. 322p. dj. A13. $40.00

HARVEY, Henry. *History of the Shawnee Indians From Year 1681 to 1854...* 1855. Cincinnati. Ephraim Morgan. 16mo. 316p. cloth. V3. $80.00

HARVEY, John. *Rough Treatment.* 1990. NY. Holt. ARC/1st Am ed. sgn. RS. F/F. S6. $35.00

HARVEY, M. Elayn. *Warhaven.* 1987. Franklin Watts. 1st ed. F/F. P3. $16.00

HARVEY, Samuel. *History of Memostasis.* 1929. NY. 1st ed. 128p. A13. $50.00

HARVEY, Virginia. *Macrame: Art of Creative Knotting.* 1967. np. VG/wrp. G2. $4.00

HARVEY, William. *Anatomical Exercises of Dr William Harvey.* 1928. London. Nonesuch. 1/1450. fld pl. 202p. Niger morocco. G7. $175.00

HARVEY, William. *De Motu Locali Animalium, 1627.* 1959. Cambridge. ltd ed. 4to. 163p. dj. A13. $100.00

HARVEY, William. *Exercitatio Anatomica De Motv Cordis Sangvinis Animalibvs.* 1928. Florence. Lier. quarter linen. F. G7. $75.00

HARVEY, William. *Movement of the Heart & Blood in Animals.* 1957. Springfield. ltd ed. trans KJ Franklin. 209p. dj. A13. $60.00

HARWELL, Richard. *Confederate Hundred: Bibliophilic Selection...* 1982. np. 2nd ed. 85p. F. A4. $45.00

HARWELL, Richard. *Cornerstones of Confederate Collecting.* 1982. np. 3rd ed. 1/500. 55p. F. A4. $45.00

HARWELL, Richard. *More Confederate Imprints.* 1957. Richmond. 2 vol. ils. F/wrp. A4. $85.00

HARWIG. *Battle of Antietam & Maryland Campaign of 1862.* 1990. np. 120p. F. A4. $65.00

HASAN BIN TALAL, Crown Prince. *Search for Peace: Politics of Middle Ground of Arab E.* 1984. St Martin. 1st Am ed. 8vo. 152p. NF/dj. W1. $12.00

HASEGAWA, Nyozekan. *Japanese Character: A Cultural Profile.* 1970. Tokyo. Kodansha. VG/dj. N2. $10.00

HASELTINE, John W. *Descriptive Catalogue of Confederate Notes & Bonds...* 1876. Phil. Bavis Pennypacker. 1st ed. royal 8vo. 36p. prt wrp. M1. $350.00

HASELTON, Scott E. *Epiphyllum Handbook.* 1951 (1946). Pasadena. ils/photos/pl. 231p. maroon cloth. VG/dj. B26. $35.00

HASHIZUME, T. *Epiphyllums & Other Related Genera. Parts 1 & 2.* 1982 & 1985. Japan. 2 vol. Japanese text. photos. F/dj. B26. $95.00

HASKELL. *Massachusetts, a Bibliography of Its History.* 1893. New Eng U. corrected ed. NF. A4. $70.00

HASKETT, Edyth Rance. *Grains of Pepper: Folk Tales From Liveria.* 1967. John Day. 1st ed. inscr. ils Musu Miatta. F/F. B2. $50.00

HASKIN, Frederic J. *Panama Canal.* 1913. Doubleday Page. 386p. VG. M20. $25.00

HASKIN, Leslie L. *Wild Flowers of the Pacific Coast.* 1934. Portland. 1st ed. 407p. VG/dj. B26. $25.00

HASLAM, Gerald. *Western Writing.* 1974. Albuquerque. 1st ed. sgn Haslam/Stegner. VG+/8vo wrp. A11. $45.00

HASLAM & HOUSTON. *California Heartland: Writing From Great Central Valley.* 1978. Capra. 1st ed. M/dj. A18. $20.00

HASLIP, Joan. *Crown of Mexico.* 1971. NY. Holt. BC. 531p. VG/dj. F3. $10.00

HASLIP, Joan. *Sultan: Life of Abdul Hamid II, 1842-1918.* 1972. NY. 1st Am ed. 8vo. 309p. cloth/brd. dj. O2. $20.00

HASSAN, Sana. *Enemy in the Promised Land: Egyptian Woman's Journey...* 1986. Pantheon. 1st ed. 335p. NF/dj. W1. $20.00

HASSLER, Kenneth W. *Dream Squad.* 1970. Lenox Hill. 1st ed. VG/VG. P3. $13.00

HASSRICK, Royal. *History of Western American Art.* 1987. London. Bison. 4to. ils. F/F. B11. $20.00

HASTINGS, Howard L. *Top Horse of Crescent Ranch.* 1942. Cupples Leon. 1st ed. VG/G. O3. $20.00

HASTINGS, Macdonald. *Jesuit Child.* 1977. St Martin. 1st ed. VG/VG. P3. $20.00

HASTINGS, Macdonald. *Search for the Little Yellow Men.* 1956. Knopf. VG. P3. $10.00

HASWELL, Charles H. *Mechanics' Tables.* 1866. Harper. ils/2 pocket ship plans. 82p. T7. $135.00

HASWELL, Jock. *D-Day: Intelligence & Deception.* 1980. Times Books. 1st ed. F/F. P3. $15.00

HATCHER, Harlan. *Lake Erie.* 1945. Bobbs Merrill. 1st ed. sgn. 404p. VG/ragged. M20. $30.00

HATHAWAY, Katharine Butler. *Mr Muffet's Cat & Her Trip to Paris.* 1934. Harper. 1st ed. ils. VG/poor. B10. $12.00

HATHERELL. *Romeo & Juliet.* nd. NY. 4to. 22 mtd mc pl. VG. M5. $28.00

HATTERAS, Owen; see Mencken, H.L.

HATTLE, Jack. *Wayward Winds.* 1972. Salisbury. Longman Rhodesia. pb. photos/diagrams. 138p. K5. $8.00

HAUGAARD, Erik Christian. *Messenger for Parliament.* 1976. Houghton Mifflin. 1st ed. VG/VG. B10. $10.00

HAUPT, Georg. *Rudolf Koch der Schrieber.* 1936. Weimar. Gesellschaft der Bibliophilen. 8vo. 115p. F. B24. $200.00

HAUSER, Thomas. *Beethoven Conspiracy.* 1986. London. MacDonald. 1st Eng hc ed. F/F. S6. $22.50

HAUSMAN, Patricia. *Right Dose.* 1987. Rodale. 1st ed. VG/VG. P3. $25.00

HAVELL, E.B. *Art Heritage of India.* 1964. Bombay. Taraporevala. revised ed. ils. 199p. VG/dj. F1. $30.00

HAVEN, Erastus Otis. *Legal Profession in America...* 1866. Ann Arbor. 1st ed. inscr. 19p. VG/wrp. D3. $35.00

HAVEN, Joseph. *Mental Philosophy: Intellect, Sensibilities & Will.* 1862 (1857). Boston. Gould Lincoln. 12mo. rebound. NF. G1. $35.00

HAVER. *David O Selznick's Hollywood.* 1980. NY. 1st ed. folio. F/NF. M9. $40.00

HAVERSTOCK, Mary Sayre. *American Bestiary.* 1979. Abrams. ils. 248p. orange cloth. M/M. P4. $45.00

HAVIARAS, Stratis. *When the Tree Sings.* 1979. NY. 1st ed. inscr. F/F. A11. $40.00

HAVIGHURST, W. *Upper Mississippi.* 1937. NY. 1st ed. Rivers of Am Series. VG/VG. B5. $40.00

HAVIGHURST, Walter. *Masters of the Modern Short Story.* 1959. Gage. 1st ed. VG. P3. $15.00

HAVILAND, Virginia. *Favorite Fairy Tales Told in Greece.* ca 1970. Little Brn. 1st ed. lib bdg. VG. B10. $45.00

HAVOC, June. *Early Havoc.* 1959. NY. 1st ed. pres. VG/VG. B5. $30.00

HAVOC, June. *More Havoc.* 1980. NY. 1st ed. pres. VG/VG. B5. $30.00

HAWES, J. *Religion of the East, With Impressions of Foreign Travel.* 1845. Hartford. 8vo. 215p. gilt cloth. O2. $75.00

HAWGOOD, John A. *America's Western Frontiers.* 1967. NY. 1st Am ed. 440p. VG/dj. B18. $20.00

HAWK, John. *House of Sudden Sleep.* 1930. Mystery League. 1st ed. VG/G. P3. $25.00

HAWKES, Alex D. *Wild Flowers of Jamaica.* 1974. np. ils. 96p. glossy photo brd. VG. B26. $14.00

HAWKES, Charles Boardman. *Dark Frigate.* ca 1923. Atlantic Monthly. 247p. pict gold cloth. VG. B10. $35.00

HAWKES, Clarence. *Dapples of the Circus, Story of a Shetland Pony & a Boy.* nd. Platt Munk. 12mo. pict cloth. VG+. C8. $12.50

HAWKES, Clarence. *Dapples of the Circus: Story of a Shetland Pony & a Boy.* 1923. Lothrop Lee Shepard. 1st ed. G. O3. $15.00

HAWKES, E. *Pioneers of Wireless.* 1927. London. 1st ed. teg. leather spine. C11. $100.00

HAWKES, Ellison. *Stars Shown to the Children.* nd. London. Jack. 49 pl. 119p. pict cloth. G. K5. $12.00

HAWKES, Jacquette. *Land.* 1951. Random. 1st ed. 248p. VG/dj. W1. $15.00

HAWKES, John. *Beetle Leg.* 1951. New Directions. 1st ed. NF/NF. B2. $65.00

HAWKES, John. *Cannibal.* 1949. New Directions. ARC. RS. NF/NF. B4. $225.00

HAWKES, John. *Innocent Party: Four Short Plays.* 1966. New Directions. ARC. inscr. w/pub material. F/F. B4. $200.00

HAWKES, John. *Passion Artist.* 1979. NY. 1st ed. sgn. NF/F. A11. $30.00

HAWKING, Stephen. *Stephen Hawking's Brief Hist of Time.* 1992. Bantam. 194p. VG/VG. K5. $20.00

HAWKINS, B. Waterhouse. *Comparative View of the Human & Animal Frame.* 1859. London. Chapman Hall. AP. folio. 10 engraved pl. 27p. cloth. G7. $495.00

HAWKINS, Gerald S. *Splendor in the Sky.* 1969 (1961). Harper Row. revised ed. ils. 292p. G/torn. K5. $8.00

HAWKINS, Stephen W. *Briefly Hist of Time: From Big Bang to Blk Holes.* 1988. Bantam. 1st ed. M/silver-bl dj. B4. $300.00

HAWKS, Ellison. *Astronomy.* 1924. London. Jack. 24 pl. 295p. ils cloth. G. K5. $20.00

HAWTHORNE, Hildegarde. *California's Missions.* 1942. Appleton Century. 1st ed. VG. P3. $35.00

HAWTHORNE, Julian. *Rumpty-Dudget's Tower.* 1925 (1924). Stokes. ils George W Hood. 72p. VG. M20. $45.00

HAWTHORNE, Julian. *Spanish America.* 1899. Collier. 1st ed. 491p. VG. F3. $15.00

HAWTHORNE, Nathaniel. *Eight Works in Eleven Vol Set of Complete Literary Prose.* 1865-1866. Ticknor Fields. 11 vol. 1st collected ed? 12mo. gilt brn cloth. F. M1. $1,250.00

HAWTHORNE, Nathaniel. *Hawthorne's Lost Notebook, 1835-1941.* 1978. PA State. ils. 203p. F/VG. A4. $65.00

HAWTHORNE, Nathaniel. *Life of Franklin Pierce.* 1852. Boston. 1st ed. VG. A9. $125.00

HAWTHORNE, Nathaniel. *Scarlet Letter, a Romance.* 1850. Ticknor Reed Fields. 1st ed. 8vo. 322p. pub ads dtd March 1850. VG. C6. $3,500.00

HAWTHORNE, Nathaniel. *Tanglewood Tales.* 1897. Crowell. VG. P3. $30.00

HAWTHORNE, Nathaniel. *Twice-Told Tales.* 1873. Boston. 1st ed (4p ads in front/16p at rear). VG/case. C2. $2,000.00

HAWTHORNE, Nathaniel. *Wonder Book for Girls & Boys.* 1893. Houghton Mifflin. 1st ed. ils Walter Crane. cloth. fair. M5. $20.00

HAWTHORNE, Nathaniel. *Writings on...* (1900). Boston. Old Manse ed. 22 vol. red cloth. F. A9. $225.00

HAY, Binnie. *Titine: A Dream Romance.* 1914. Scotland. Andrew Elliot. 1st ed. inscr. NF. F4. $38.00

HAY, Clarence. *Maya & Their Neighbor.* 1962. UT U. rpt 1940 ed. 606p. VG. F3. $35.00

HAY, Elizabeth. *Sambo Sahib: Story of Little Black Sambo & Helen Bannerman.* 1981. Barnes Noble. 1st ed. 8vo. 194p. NF/M. D6. $35.00

HAY, Helen. *Verses for Jock & Joan.* 1905. NY. Duffield. 1st ed. folio. ils Charlotte Harting. VG+. D6. $175.00

HAY, John. *Pike County Ballads.* 1912. Houghton Mifflin. 1st ed. thus. ils Wyeth. VG. B17. $150.00

HAY, Thomas Robson. *Confederate Leadership at Vicksburg.* 1925. np. 1st ed. G. M8. $25.00

HAY & NICOLAY. *Abraham Lincoln: A History.* 1914. Century. 10 vol set. G. B5. $200.00

HAYCOX, Ernest. *Canyon Passage.* 1945. Little Brn. 1st ed. F/dj. A18. $25.00

HAYCOX, Ernest. *Deep West.* 1937. Little Brn. ne. VG+. A18. $20.00

HAYCOX, Ernest. *Earthbreakers.* 1952. Little Brn. 1st ed. VG/VG. P3. $35.00

HAYCOX, Ernest. *Whispering Range.* 1930. Doubleday Doran. 1st ed. F/dj. A18. $35.00

HAYDEN, C.A. *Capen Family.* 1929. Minneapolis. revised ed. VG. A9. $40.00

HAYDOCK, Roger. *Collection of Christian Writings, Labours, Travels...* 1700. London. T Sowle. 16mo. 223p. fair. V3. $95.00

HAYEK, F.A. *Sensory Order.* 1952. London. Kegan Paul. G. K4. $25.00

HAYES, Alfred. *Welcome to the Castle.* 1950. Harper. 1st ed. sgn. w/p of review notes. F/NF. V1. $25.00

HAYES, Harry. *Anthology of Plastic Surgery.* 1986. Rockville, MD. 1st ed. ils. 388p. A13. $125.00

HAYES, John H. *Intro to the Bible.* 1971. Westminster. 515p. M/dj. B29. $6.00

HAYES, John Russell. *Old Quaker Meeting-Houses.* 1909. Phil. Biddle. 8vo. unp. VG+. V3. $20.00

HAYFORD, Jack W. *Worship His Majesty.* 1987. Word. 238p. M/M. B29. $7.50

HAYGOOD, Atticus G. *New South: Gratitude Amendment, Hope. A Thanksgiving Sermon.* 1880. Oxford, GA. 1st ed. 8vo. 16p. prt wrp. very rare. M1. $375.00

HAYMAN, Max. *Alcoholism, Mechanism & Management.* 1966. Charles C Thomas. 8vo. inscr to Bill Weikert. 315p. F/F. A8. $25.00

HAYMON, S.T. *Very Particular Murder.* 1989. Constable. 1st ed. F/F. P3. $20.00

HAYNE, Coe. *Red Men on the Bighorn.* 1929. Judson Pr. 2nd prt. VG. B34. $40.00

HAYNES, Gideon. *Pictures From Prison Life.* 1869. Boston. Lee Shepard. 1st ed. 290p. cloth. VG. B2/B14. $100.00

HAYNES, Herbert. *Emperor's Doom; or, Patriots of Mexico.* 1898. T Nelson. VG. N2. $7.50

HAYNES, William. *Airedale.* 1911. NY. Outing. 1st ed. 102p. cloth. VG. R2. $35.00

HAYNES, William. *Practical Dog Keeping.* 1922 (1913). Macmillan. 160p. cloth. F. R2. $18.00

HAYS, Donald. *Dixie Association.* 1984. Simon Schuster. 1st ed. F/F. P8. $17.50

HAYS, Wilma Pitchford. *Little Horse That Raced a Train.* 1959. Little Brn. 1st ed. ils Wesley Dennis. pict cloth. VG/VG. C8. $25.00

HAYTER, Sparkle. *What's a Girl Gotta Do.* 1994. NY. Soho. 1st ed. F/F. B4. $35.00

HAYTER. *About Prints.* 1962. Oxford. 4to. 65 pl. 187p. VG/VG. A4. $75.00

HAYWARD, Charles. *Automobile Ignition, Starting & Lighting.* 1927. Chicago. ils/diagrams. blk leatherette. G. A17. $25.00

HAYWARD, John. *Book of Religions.* 1843. Boston. full brn leather. VG. B30. $65.00

HAYWOOD. *Modern Arabic Literature 1800-1970...* 1972. np. 319p. F/NF. A4. $35.00

HAZARD, Caroline. *Narragansett Ballads.* 1894. Houghton Mifflin. 1st ed. 16mo. 107p. G+. V3. $14.00

HAZARD, Lucy Lockwood. *Frontier in American Literature.* 1927. Crowell. 1st ed. NF. A18. $30.00

HAZARD, Paul. *Books, Children & Men.* 1944. Horn Book. 1st ed. 1/3000. 176p. VG/VG. S11. $25.00

HAZARD, Rowland G. *Language: Its Connection With Present Condition & Future.* 1836. Providence. Marshall Brn. 12mo. 153p. very scarce. G1. $125.00

HAZARD, Thomas R. *Miscellaneous Essays & Letters.* 1883. Phil. Collins. 12mo. 384p. G+. V3. $15.00

HAZARD & SHAPIRO. *Soviet Legal System.* 1962. Dobbs Ferry. Oceana Pub. M11. $25.00

HAZEL, Paul. *Wealdwife's Tale.* 1993. AvoNova. ARC of 1st ed. F/F. M21. $25.00

HAZEL, Paul. *Yearwood.* 1980. Atlantic/Little Brn. 1st ed. F/F. P3. $20.00

HAZEN, Barbara Shook. *Step on It, Andrew.* 1980. Atheneum. 1st ed. VG/VG. B10. $10.00

HEAD, Henry. *Studies in Neurology.* 1920. Oxford. 2 vol. 4to. lib stp on title. new cloth. G7. $275.00

HEAD, Matthew. *Accomplice.* 1947. Simon Schuster. 1st ed. VG/VG. P3. $20.00

HEADLEY, P.C. *Island of Fire.* (1874). Boston. ils. 357p. decor cloth. F. B14. $45.00

HEALD, Jean Sadler. *Picturesque Panama, Panama Railroad, Panama Canal.* 1928. Chicago. Curt Teich. 8vo. ils/fld map. 126p. pict gr cloth. VG. B11. $50.00

HEALD, Tim. *Brought to Book.* 1988. Crime Club. 1st ed. VG/VG. P3. $13.00

HEALD, Tim. *Red Herrings.* 1985. London. Macmillan. 1st ed. VG+/dj. S6. $20.00

HEALEY, Ben. *Terrible Pictures.* 1967. Harper Row. 1st ed. VG/VG. P3. $13.00

HEALEY, Ben. *Vespucci Papers.* 1972. Lippincott. 1st ed. VG/VG. P3. $15.00

HEALY, William. *Structure & Meaning of Psychoanalysis...* 1930. Knopf. 480p. reading copy. K4. $15.00

HEANEY, Seamus. *After Summer.* 1978. Deerfield/Gallery. ltd ed. sgn. 1/250. F/NF. V1. $170.00

HEANEY, Seamus. *Death of a Naturalist.* 1966. Oxford. 1st ed/author's 1st book. F/NF. V1. $140.00

HEARD, H.F. *Dopplegangers.* 1947. Vanguard. 1st ed. F/chip. M2. $22.00

HEARD, H.F. *Taste for Honey.* 1941. Vanguard. xl. VG. P3. $20.00

HEARD, H.F. *Weird Tales of Terror & Detection.* nd. Sun Dial. rpt. F/NF. M21. $10.00

HEARN, Lafcadio. *Gombo Zhebes: Little Dictionary of Creole Proverbs...* 1885. NY. Coleman. 1st ed. sm 4to. 42p. blk/gilt stp gr cloth. VG. H5. $500.00

HEARN, Lafcadio. *Japanese Lyrics.* 1915. Riverside. presumed 2nd prt (title p integral). VG/stiff wrp/gr dj. Q1. $75.00

HEARN, Lafcadio. *Kotto.* 1902. London/NY. Macmillan. 1st ed. 8vo. 251p. olive cloth. NF. C6. $900.00

HEARN, Lafcadio. *Kwaidan. Jikininki. Yuki-Onna.* 1969. Tustin, CA. Garden View. 57x52mm. ils Batchelder. 56p. w/prospectus. F/case. B24. $225.00

HEARN, Lafcadio. *Romance of the Milky Way & Other Stories.* 1905. Houghton Mifflin. apparent early ed. 8vo. 209p. yel stp gr cloth. VG. H5. $75.00

HEARN, Lafcadio. *Some Chinese Ghosts.* 1887. Boston. Roberts. 1st ed. 8vo. 185p. red cloth. VG. C6. $400.00

HEARN, Lafcadio. *Writings...* 1922. Boston/NY. 16 vol. lg paper ed. sgn Mrs Hearn. w/sgn manuscript p. F. H4. $1,500.00

HEARNER, Vicki. *Bandit: Dossier of a Dangerous Dog.* 1991. Harper Collins. UP. 304p. M/wrp. R2. $22.00

HEARON, Shelby. *Armadillo in the Grass.* 1968. Knopf. 1st ed. inscr/dtd 1968. F/VG. B4. $125.00

HEARTMAN. *Bibliography of Writings of Hugh Henry Brackenridge...* 1968. np. 37p. F. A4. $20.00

HEAT-MOON, William Least. *Prairyeth.* 1991. Houghton Mifflin. 1st ed. inscr. F/NF. B3. $40.00

HEATLEY, D.P. *Dipomacy & the Study of International Relations.* 1919. Oxford. 1st ed. 12mo. 292p. VG. D3. $35.00

HEATON, Peter. *Singlehanders.* 1976. Hastings. 1st Am ed. ils. VG/dj. N2. $7.50

HEBARD, Grace. *Sacajawea, Guide of Lewis & Clark Expedition.* 1957. Arthur H Clark. 340p. VG. B34. $120.00

HEBB, D.O. *Organization of Behavior.* 1949. London. Chapman Hall. 303p. F. K4. $10.00

HEBDEN, Juliet. *Pel Picks Up the Pieces.* 1993. London. Constable. 1st ed. F/F. S6. $25.00

HEBDEN, Mark. *Pel & the Paris Mob.* 1986. London. Hamilton. 1st ed. F/F. S6. $25.00

HEBDEN, Mark. *Pel & the Prowler.* 1986. Walker. 1st ed. F/F. P3. $16.00

HEBERT, Anne. *Children of the Black Sabbath.* 1977. Musson. 1st ed. VG/VG. P3. $20.00

HECHT, Ben. *Humpty Dumpty.* 1924. Boni Liveright. 1st ed. F/NF. B2. $125.00

HECHT, Ben. *Perfidy.* 1961. NY. Messner. 3rd prt. G. N2. $7.50

HECHT & STEERE. *Essays in Evolution & Genetics in Honor of...Dobzhansky.* 1970. Appleton Century Crofts. 539p. M/dj. K4. $25.00

HECKELMEN. *Big Valley.* 1966. Whitman. 1st ed. pict brd. F/sans. F4. $15.00

HECKER, J.F.C. *Epidemics of the Middle Ages.* 1846. London. 1st Eng-trans ed. trans BG Babington. 380p. A13. $150.00

HECKLINGER. *Hecklinger's Dress & Cloak Cutter.* (1883). NY. 2 vol. 1st ed. folio. fld patterns. VG. C11. $165.00

HECKSTALL-SMITH, Anthony. *Tobruk: Story of a Siege.* 1960. NY. 1st Am ed. 255p. F/F. A17. $9.50

HEDGES, Doris. *Dumb Spirit: Novel of Montreal.* 1952. Arthur Barker. 1st ed. VG/G. P3. $40.00

HEDGES, F.A.M. *Battles With Giant Fish.* 1924. Boston. VG. A9. $60.00

HEEREN, A.H.L. *Hist Researches Into Politics, Intercourse & Trade...* 1838. Oxford. Talboys. vol 2 only. xl. VG. W1. $15.00

HEERMANS, Forbes. *Thirteen Stories of the Far West.* 1887. NY. Bardeen. 1st ed. 12mo. 263p. VG. D3. $125.00

HEGAB, Sayed. *New Egyptian: Autobiography of a Young Arab.* 1971. Praeger. 1st ed. 8vo. 160p. F/dj. W1. $9.00

HEGEL, G.W.F. *Wissenschaft der Logik.* 1812, 1813 & 1816. Schrag. 3 vol. contemporary bdg. VG/clamshell case. B4. $7,500.00

HEGEL, Georg Wilhelm F. *Logic of Hegel.* 1892 (1874). Oxford. Clarendon. 2nd English-language ed. 12mo. VG. G1. $75.00

HEGEMANN, Elizabeth Compton. *Navaho Trading Days.* 1963. NM U. 1st ed. photos. 388p. photo ep. VG/worn. P4. $95.00

HEGGEN, Thomas. *Mister Roberts.* 1946. Houghton Mifflin. 1st ed. 221p. G. B14. $50.00

HEGGEN & LOGAN. *Mister Roberts. A Play.* 1948. Random. 1st ed. 8vo. 162p. gilt bl cloth. NF/NF. H5. $125.00

HEGLAND, Martin. *Problems of Young Christians.* 1946. Augsburg. 185p. VG. B29. $3.50

HEICK, Otto. *Hist of Christian Thought.* 1976. Fortress. 509p. VG/dj. B29. $8.50

HEIDEGGER, Martin. *Sein und Zeit.* 1960 (1927). Tubingen. Max Niemeyer. 7th ed. 436p. paneled tan cloth. VG/dj. G1. $30.00

HEIER & LOTZ. *Banjo on Record.* 1993. Westport. Greenwood. 1st ed. F/sans. B2. $45.00

HEIKAL, Mohamed. *Autumn of Fury: Assassination of Sadat.* 1983. Random. 1st ed. 290p. NF/dj. W1. $20.00

HEIKAL, Mohamed. *Cairo Documents.* 1973. Doubleday. 1st ed. 8vo. 16 pl. VG/dj. W1. $18.00

HEIKAL, Mohamed. *Road to Ramadan.* 1975. Quadrangle/NY Times. 1st Am ed. 8vo. 285p. G. W1. $8.00

HEILBUT, Ivan. *Francisco & Elizabeth.* 1942. Pantheon. inscr. ils R Busoni. 24p. G. B10. $12.00

HEIM, A.W. *Appraisal of Intelligence.* 1954. London. Methuen. 165p. G/dj. K4. $10.00

HEIM, Ralph D. *Harmony of the Gospels.* 1947. Fortress. VG/dj. B29. $5.00

HEINDEL, Max. *Complete Index of Books by Max Heindel.* 1950. Oceanside. Rosicrucian Fellowship. 278p. VG. B33. $18.00

HEINECCIUS, Johann Gottlieb. *Antiquitatium Romanarum Jusrisprudentiam...* 1977. Chalmot & Romar. Editio Quinta. 8vo. 750p. rebacked. VG. D3. $450.00

HEINEMANN, Larry. *Paco's Story.* 1986. FSG. 1st ed. 209p. VG/dj. M20. $20.00

HEINEMANN, Lillian. *Scoundrel Time.* 1976. Little Brn. 1st ed. 155p. VG/dj. M20. $20.00

HEINEMANN, Margot. *Adventurers.* 1961. NY. Marzani Munsell. pb. VG. V4. $15.00

HEINLEIN, Robert A. *Assignment in Eternity.* 1953. Reading, PA. 1st ed/1st state. gilt bl variant bdg. F/F. C2. $250.00

HEINLEIN, Robert A. *Cat Who Walks Through Walls.* 1985. Putnam. 1st ed. NF/NF. P3. $20.00

HEINLEIN, Robert A. *Cat Who Walks Through Walls.* 1985. Putnam. 1st ed. sgn. 1/350. blk cloth. F/case. B24. $185.00

HEINLEIN, Robert A. *Friday.* 1982. HRW. 1st ed. VG/VG. P3. $15.00

HEINLEIN, Robert A. *Grumbles From the Grave.* 1990. Del Rey. 1st ed. VG. P3. $20.00

HEINLEIN, Robert A. *Pass Through Tomorrow.* 1967. Putnam. BC. F/VG+. M21. $10.00

HEINLEIN, Robert A. *Past Through Tomorrow Book 2.* 1977. NEL. 1st ed. NF/NF. P3. $35.00

HEINLEIN, Robert A. *Podkayne of Mars.* 1977. NEL. 1st UK ed. F/F. T2. $45.00

HEINLEIN, Robert A. *Revolt in 2100.* 1953. Chicago. Shasta. 1st ed. sgn. 1/500. F/NF. B4. $850.00

HEINLEIN, Robert A. *Rolling Stones.* 1952. Scribner. 1st ed. F/clip. Q1. $350.00

HEINLEIN, Robert A. *Starman Jones.* 1953. Scribner. 1st ed. NF/dj. M2. $225.00

HEINRICHS, E. *My Little Friends.* 1892 (1891). Lee Shepard. 71 photos. leather-like brd. VG. M5. $75.00

HEINTZ, Calvin W. *Coppacaw Story: Hist of Cuyahoga Falls, OH.* 1962. Cuyahoga Falls. 92p. VG/pict wrp. B18. $15.00

HEISENFELT, Kathryn. *Jane Withers & the Swamp Wizard.* 1944. Whitman. VG/torn. P3. $12.00

HEISENFELT, Kathryn. *Shirley Temple & Spirit of Dragonwood.* 1945. Whitman. VG. P3. $13.00

HEITMAN, Ernestine Beckwith. *Rosy the Skunk.* 1952. Pageant. 1st ed. ils Al Kilgore. VG/G. B17. $4.00

HEIZER, Robert F. *Languages, Territories & Names of California Indian Tribes.* 1966. Berkeley/Los Angeles. 5 maps. 62p. NF/NF. P4. $65.00

HEIZER & WHIPPLE. *California Indians: A Source Book.* 1971. Berkeley. 2nd ed. 8vo. 619p. gilt gr cloth. M. P4. $15.00

HELD, John Jr. *Gods Were Promiscuous.* 1937. Vanguard. 1st ed. sgn. VG/VG. Q1. $150.00

HELD, Peter; see Vance, Jack.

HELFER, Jacques. *Trees & Tree-Like Shrubs of Mendocino Coast.* 1966. Ukiah. ils/drawings. sc. VG. B26. $14.00

HELIAS, Pierre-Jakes. *Horse of Pride. Life in a Breton Village.* 1979. New Haven/London. Yale. 3rd prt. 8vo. photos. NF/NF. P4. $25.00

HELLER, Joseph. *Catch-22.* 1961. Simon Schuster. 1st ed. sgn. VG/VG+. B4. $1,150.00

HELLER, Keith. *Man's Illegal Life.* 1984. London. Collins. 1st ed. sgn. F/F. S6. $35.00

HELLER, Rhinhold. *Hildegard Auer, a Yearning for Art.* 1987. NY. Assoc Faculty Pr. sq 4to. ils. 214p. linen/blk spine titles. F/NF. F1. $50.00

HELLER, Ruth. *Chickens Aren't The Only Ones.* 1984. Grosset Dunlap. VG. B10. $10.00

HELLERSBERG, Elizabeth F. *Individual's Relation to Reality in Our Culture.* 1950. Springfield, IL Chas C Thomas. 128p. blk cloth. G1. $22.50

HELLMAN, Lillian. *Maybe.* 1980. Little Brn. 1st ed. F/F. B3. $20.00

HELLMAN, Lillian. *Unfinished Woman.* 1969. Little Brn. 1st ed/special reserved for friends. ils. F/sans. S9. $25.00

HELM, Thomas Monroe. *Desert Ghost.* 1977. Doubleday. 1st ed. VG/VG. P3. $12.00

HELME, Eleanor. *Mayfly: The Gray Pony.* 1931. Scribner. 1st Am ed. ils. VG. O3. $25.00

HELMREICH, Paul C. *From Paris to Sevres: Partition of Ottoman Empire...* 1974. Columbus. 376p. xl. VG/dj. W1. $35.00

HELMS, Randel. *Tolkien & the Silmarils.* 1981. Houghton Mifflin. 1st ed. F/NF. T2. $14.00

HELMS, Randel. *Tolkien's World.* 1974. Houghton Mifflin. 1st ed. VG. P3. $25.00

HELPER, Hinton Rowan. *Impending Crises of the South.* 1857. NY. Burdick. 50th thousand. 418p. VG. M20. $75.00

HELPRIN, Mark. *Soldier of the Great War.* 1991. HBJ. 1st ed. F/F. N3. $15.00

HELVETIUS, Claude Adrien. *De l'Homme, de ses Facultes et de Son Education.* 1774. Liege. 2 vols. later ed. orig calf. G. G1. $125.00

HELWIG & SMITH. *Liquor: The Servent of Man.* 1940. Little Brn. 1st ed/6th prt. 8vo. 46p bibliography. red cloth. VG. A8. $10.00

HEMINGWAY, Ernest. *Across the River & Into the Trees.* 1950. Scribner. 1st Am ed. 8vo. 308p. gilt blk cloth. F/yel prt dj. H5. $150.00

HEMINGWAY, Ernest. *Collected Poems of Ernest Hemingway.* ca 1955. np. 1st ed. 8vo. 24p. NF/self wrp. C6. $200.00

HEMINGWAY, Ernest. *Dangerous Summer.* 1985. Scribner. 1st ed. 8vo. 228p. bl cloth/brd. F/clip. H5. $50.00

HEMINGWAY, Ernest. *Death in the Afternoon.* 1932. Scribner. 1st ed. F/VG. B4. $1,000.00

HEMINGWAY, Ernest. *Death in the Afternoon.* 1932. Scribner. 1st ed. royal 8vo. 81 photos. 517p. gilt blk cloth. VG/dj. H5. $500.00

HEMINGWAY, Ernest. *Ernest Hemingway: By-Line.* 1968. London. 1st ed. C4. $50.00

HEMINGWAY, Ernest. *Farewell to Arms.* 1929. Scribner. 1st ed. NF/VG. Q1. $1,250.00

HEMINGWAY, Ernest. *Farewell to Arms.* 1929. Scribner. 1st ed. pub device on copyright p. without disclaimer. VG. H5. $750.00

HEMINGWAY, Ernest. *Fifth Columm & First Forty-Nine Stories.* 1938. Scribner. 1st ed. 8vo. 597p. blk/gilt stp red cloth. VG/clip. H5. $450.00

HEMINGWAY, Ernest. *For Whom the Bell Tolls.* 1940. Scribner. 1st ed. F/NF. B4. $550.00

HEMINGWAY, Ernest. *Garden of Eden.* 1986. Scribner. 1st ed. 247p. VG/dj. M20. $20.00

HEMINGWAY, Ernest. *Gattorno.* 1935. Havana. 1st ed. 1/460. 38 reproductions. NF/wrp. H5. $350.00

HEMINGWAY, Ernest. *God Rest Ye Merry Gentlemen.* 1933. NY. House of Books. 1st ed. 1/300 #d. gilt cloth. F/VG glassine. S9. $875.00

HEMINGWAY, Ernest. *Green Hills of Africa.* 1935. NY. Scribner. 1st ed. VG+/VG+. B4. $600.00

HEMINGWAY, Ernest. *In Our Time.* nd (1978). Bruccoli Clark. ARC/facsimile of 1924 1st ed. F/NF. w/promo material. B4. $135.00

HEMINGWAY, Ernest. *Men at War, Best War Stories of All Time.* 1942. NY. 1st ed. 82 war stories. NF/VG. A4. $165.00

HEMINGWAY, Ernest. *Moveable Feast.* 1964. Scribner. 1st ed. photos. F/NF. Q1. $75.00

HEMINGWAY, Ernest. *Old Man & the Sea.* 1953. London. Cape. 1st Eng ed. F/F variant dj. B4. $750.00

HEMINGWAY, Ernest. *Short Stories of...* nd. BOMC. VG. P3. $10.00

HEMINGWAY, Ernest. *Spanish Earth.* 1938. Cleveland. JB Savage. 1st ed/2nd issue. 1/1000 #d. VG+/sans. Q1. $500.00

HEMINGWAY, Ernest. *Spanish War.* 1938. London. FACT. 12mo. 97p. NF/wrp. H5. $200.00

HEMINGWAY, Ernest. *Sun Also Rises.* 1926. Scribner. 1st ed/2nd issue. VG. Q1. $200.00

HEMINGWAY, Ernest. *To Have & Have Not.* 1937. Scribner. 1st ed. 8vo. 262p. blk cloth. VG/dj. H5. $600.00

HEMINGWAY, Ernest. *Today Is Friday.* 1962. Englewood, NJ. As Stable Pub. 1st ed. sgn. 1/300. F/envelope/case. B24. $4,000.00

HEMINGWAY, Ernest. *Torrents of Spring.* 1926. Scribner. 1st ed. F/dj. B24. $3,250.00

HEMINGWAY, Ernest. *Uber den Fluss und in Die Walder.* 1964. Berlin. Deutsch Buch Gemeninschaft. VG. N2. $10.00

HEMINGWAY, Ernest. *Winner Take Nothing.* 1933. Scribner. 1st ed. G+/dj. Q1. $400.00

HEMINGWAY, Ernest. *Winner Take Nothing.* 1933. Scribner. 1st ed. 8vo. 244p. blk cloth/gold paper labels. NF/dj. H5. $500.00

HEMMENWAY, Moses. *Discourse Concerning the Church...* 1792. Boston. Thomas Andrews. 123p. sewn. H10. $50.00

HEMMINGS, F.W.J. *Bauderlaire: The Damned.* 1982. Scribner. 1st ed. photos. NF/NF. S9. $25.00

HEMPHILL, Essex. *Earth Life.* 1985. Be Bop. 1st ed. inscr. F/wrp. L3. $25.00

HEMPHILL, Paul. *Long Gone.* 1979. Viking. 1st ed. VG+/G+. P8. $25.00

HENDERLY, Brooks. *YMCA Boys on Bass Island.* 1916. Cupples Leon. VG. M20. $25.00

HENDERSON, Alexander Roy. *Hist of Castle Gate Congregational Church, Nottingham...* 1905. London. 1st ed. pres. 263p. cloth. VG. M8. $37.50

HENDERSON, Elliott Blaine. *Soliloquy of Satan & Other Poems.* 1907. Springfield, OH. self pub. B2. $150.00

HENDERSON, Elsie. *Mary's Little Lamb.* 1941. WPA New Reading Project. ils Jean Oliver. 32p. F/glassine wrp. B10. $20.00

HENDERSON, G.F.R. *Civil War: Soldier's View.* 1958. Chicago. 1st ed. 323p. w/map. F. A17. $18.50

HENDERSON, G.F.R. *Stonewall Jackson & the American Civil War.* 1927. 2 vol. ils/maps/plans/index. O8. $27.50

HENDERSON, James D. *Miniature Books, by the Scrivener of News-Letter of LXIV...* 1930. Leipzig. Tondeur Sauberlich. 16mo. 1/260. striped brd. F. B24. $200.00

HENDERSON, James D. *News-Letters of the LXIVMOs.* 1927-1929. Woodstock, VT. Lilliputter. 8vo. 1/500. complete run. 102p+index. F. B24. $150.00

HENDERSON, John. *West Indies.* 1905. London. Blk. 1st ed. ils AS Forrest. teg. VG. B11. $120.00

HENDERSON, LeGrand. *How Baseball Began in Brooklyn.* 1958. Abingdon. 1st ed. VG. P8. $25.00

HENDERSON, Lois T. *Hagar.* 1978. Christian Herald. 1st ed. F/F. P3. $10.00

HENDERSON, M.R. *If I Should Die.* 1985. Doubleday. 1st ed. VG/VG. P3. $15.00

HENDERSON, Marjorie Buell. *Fun With Little Lulu.* 1944. Phil. David McKay. ils Marge. pict paper brd. VG. C8. $17.50

HENDERSON, Marjorie Buell. *Little Lulu & the Organ Grinder Man.* 1946. McLoughlin. ils. pict brd. F/G. M5. $50.00

HENDERSON, Marjorie Buell. *Little Lulu at Grandma's Farm.* 1946. McLoughlin Bros. ils Marge. pict cloth. VG. C8. $25.00

HENDERSON, Marjorie Buell. *Little Lulu Plays Pirate.* 1946. McLoughlin. pict brd. F/G. M5. $50.00

HENDERSON, Marjorie Buell. *Little Lulu: Her Train Ride to Grandma's.* 1946. McLoughlin. ils Marge. pict cloth. VG+. C8. $25.00

HENDERSON, Marjorie Buell. *Oh, Little Lulu!* 1943. Phil. McKay. 8vo. ils. pict brd. NF/VG. D6. $50.00

HENDERSON, Mrs. L.R.S. *Magic Aeoroplane: A Fairy Tale.* 1911. Reilly Britton. ils Emile A Nelson. 96p. G. P2. $135.00

HENDRICK, Burton J. *Bulwark of the Republic.* 1937. Little Brn. 1st ed. 8vo. G. B11. $20.00

HENDRICKS, Garland A. *Biography of a Country Church.* 1950. Nashville. Broadman. 1st ed. 137p. F/VG. M8. $30.00

HENDRICKSON, Paul. *Looking for the Light: Hidden Life & Art of Marion Wolcott.* 1992. Knopf. 1st ed. sgn. F/F. S9. $20.00

HENDRIKSEN, William. *Gospel of John, Vol 1 & Vol 2.* 1952 & 1954. Baker. VG/dj. B29. $15.00

HENDRYX, James B. *Corporal Downey Takes the Trail.* 1931. NY. 1st ed. VG/VG. B5. $45.00

HENELY, William Ernest. *Lyrica Heroica: Book of Verse for Boys.* 1907 (1891). London. Nutt. 9th lib ed. 8vo. 366p. NF. D6. $35.00

HENIGHAN, Tom. *Well of Time.* 1988. Collins. 1st ed. sgn. F/F. P3. $25.00

HENISSART, Paul. *Winter Spy.* 1976. Simon Schuster. 1st ed. VG/VG. P3. $15.00

HENKEL, Socrates. *Hist of Evangelical Lutheran Tennessee Synod...* 1890. New Market, VA. Henkel. 1st ed. 275p. cloth. VG. M8. $150.00

HENKIN, Harmon. *Fly Tackle.* 1976. Phil. 1st ed. VG/VG. B5. $20.00

HENRICK, Burton. *Statesmen of the Lost Cause.* 1939. 1st ed. ils. 439p. O8. $12.50

HENRIQUES, Robert D.Q. *Death by Moonlight: Account of Darfur Journey.* ca 1935. Morrow. 353p. VG. W1. $24.00

HENRY, Carl F.H. *Pacific Garden Mission.* 1942. Zondervan. intro HA Ironside. 142p. G. B29. $4.00

HENRY, Carl F.H. *Revelation & the Bible.* 1976. Baker. 413p. G. B29. $8.50

HENRY, Marguerite. *Album of Horses.* 1951. Rand McNally. 1st/A ed. cloth. F/damaged. M5. $25.00

HENRY, Marguerite. *Auno & Tauno: Story of Finland.* 1944. Whitman. 4th prt. pict bl cloth. VG. A3. $12.50

HENRY, Marguerite. *Birds at Home.* 1942. Donohue. ils Jacob B Abbott. 88p. pict brd. VG/G+. A3. $20.00

HENRY, Marguerite. *Black Gold.* 1957. Rand McNally. later prt. VG/VG. O3. $18.00

HENRY, Marguerite. *Brightly of the Grand Canyon.* 1958. Rand McNally. ils Wesley Dennis. 222p. VG/VG. B10. $15.00

HENRY, Marguerite. *Gaudenzia, Pride of the Palio.* ca 1960. Rand McNally. 1st ed. 237p. VG/G. B10. $35.00

HENRY, Marguerite. *Geraldine Belinda.* ca 1942. Platt Munk. unp. VG/fair. B10. $15.00

HENRY, Marguerite. *Geraldine Belinda.* 1942. Platt Munk. 1st ed. 32p. VG. scarce. A17. $15.00

HENRY, Marguerite. *Ils Marguerite Henry...* 1980. Chicago. Rand McNally. 1st ed. 4to. brd. VG. O3. $45.00

HENRY, Marguerite. *King of the Wind.* 1948. Rand McNally. G+. O3. $15.00

HENRY, Marguerite. *King of the Wind.* 1977. Rand McNally. 25th prt. inscr. VG. B10. $75.00

HENRY, Marguerite. *Little Fellow.* 1945. Phil. Winston. 2nd prt. VG. O3. $18.00

HENRY, Marguerite. *Misty of Chincoteague.* 1947. Rand McNally. inscr/Misty's hoofprint. 173p. VG/VG. B10. $125.00

HENRY, Marguerite. *Misty of Chincoteague.* 1947. Rand McNally. 1st ed. 173p. VG/G. P2. $25.00

HENRY, Marguerite. *Pictured Geography: W Indies in Story & Pictures.* 1943. Chicago. ils Kurt Wiese. cloth. F/F. B14. $50.00

HENRY, Marguerite. *San Domingo.* 1972. Rand McNally. 1st ed. F. M5. $10.00

HENRY, Marguerite. *Sea Star Orphan of Chincoteague.* ca 1949. Rand McNally. 1st ed. ils Wesley Dennis. 172p. VG/dj. B10. $25.00

HENRY, Marguerite. *White Stallion of Lipizza.* ca 1964. Rand McNally. 1st ed. sgn. ils/sgn Wesley Dennis. VG. B10. $45.00

HENRY, O; See O Henry.

HENRY, Ralph C. *People of MT: Study of MT Government.* 1958. Helena. State Pub. xl. poor. B34. $12.00

HENRY, Ralph C. *Treasure State, Story of Montana.* 1962. np. F. B34. $25.00

HENRY, Stephen. *Whistling Stallion.* nd. Grosset Dunlap. Famous Horse Stories Series. pict brd. VG. O3. $15.00

HENRY, Thomas R. *Wht Continent: Story of Antarctica.* 1950. NY. 212p. VG/VG. A17. $8.50

HENRY, Will. *Who Rides With Wyatt.* 1955. Random. 1st ed. F/dj. A18. $40.00

HENRY & DENNIS. *Benjamin West & His Cat Grimalkin.* ca 1947. Bobbs Merrill. 1st ed. 147p. G. B10. $15.00

HENSCHEN, Folke. *History & Geography of Diseases.* 1966. NY. 1st Eng-trans ed. 344p. A13. $50.00

HENSLEY, Joe L. *Color Him Guilty.* 1987. NY. Walker. 1st ed. F/F. S6. $22.50

HENSLEY, Joe L. *Outcasts.* 1981. Crime Club. 1st ed. VG/VG. P3. $15.00

HENSON, Josiah. *Father Henson's Story of His Own Life.* 1858. Boston. Jewett. 1st ed. intro HB Stowe. VG. H7. $175.00

HENTY, G.A. *By Conduct & Courage.* 1905. London/Toronto. presumed 1st ed/variant prt. pl. red cloth. NF. H4. $35.00

HENTY, G.A. *By Pike & Dike.* nd. Burt. ils. VG. M5. $10.00

HENTY, G.A. *Redskin & Cow-Boy: Tale of the Western Plains.* 1891. Scribner. 1st ed. ils Alfred Pearse. VG. A18. $40.00

HENTY, G.A. *Under Drake's Flag.* nd. Coates. ils. VG. M5. $10.00

HEPHER, Cyril. *Fruits of Silence: Being Further Studies...of Prayer...* 1917. London. Macmillan. 5th prt. 12mo. 222p. VG+. V3. $12.00

HEPPER, F. Nigel. *Pharaoh's Flowers.* 1990. London. ils. sc. M. B26. $22.95

HERBER, William. *Live Bait for Murder.* 1955. Lippincott. 1st ed. F/NF. F4. $27.50

HERBERG, Will. *Four Existentialist Theologians: A Reader...* 1958. Doubleday. 1st ed. 346p. VG/VG. B33. $25.00

HERBERMANN, Erik. *Dressage Formula.* 1989. London. Allen. 2nd ed. VG/VG. O3. $18.00

HERBERT, A.P. *Laughing & Other Poems.* 1926. Doubleday Page. 1st ed. ils. 118p. VG. M10. $7.50

HERBERT, Brian. *Garbage Chronicles.* 1985. WH Allen. 1st ed. VG/VG. P3. $20.00

HERBERT, Brian. *Sudanna, Sudanna.* 1985. Putnam. 1st ed. F/F. P3. $16.00

HERBERT, Frank. *Capterhouse: Dune.* 1985. Putnam. 1st ed. F/F. P3. $25.00

HERBERT, Frank. *Dragon in the Sea.* 1956. Doubleday. 1st ed. VG/G. P3. $175.00

HERBERT, Frank. *Dune Messiah.* 1969. Putnam. 2nd ed. NF/NF. P3. $20.00

HERBERT, Frank. *God Makers.* 1972. Putnam. 1st ed. VG/VG. P3. $35.00

HERBERT, Frank. *Heretics of Dune.* 1984. Putnam. 1st ed. VG/VG. P3. $25.00

HERBERT, Frank. *Santaroga Barrier.* 1970. Rapp Whiting. 1st ed. NF/NF. P3. $35.00

HERBERT, Ivor. *Queen Mother's Horses.* 1967. London. Pelham. 1st ed. VG. O3. $25.00

HERBERT, James. *Magic Cottage.* 1987. NAL. 1st ed. F/F. P3. $18.00

HERBERT, James. *Sepulchre.* 1987. Hodder Stoughton. 1st ed. F/F. P3. $25.00

HERBERT, W. *Fighting Joe Hooker.* 1944. Indianapolis. 1st ed. VG/G. B5. $40.00

HERBERT, Wally. *Noose of Laurels.* 1989. NY. 1st ed. 395p. M/M. A17. $14.50

HERBERTSON, Agnes Grozier. *Tinkler Johnny.* nd. London. Blackie. 12mo. ils Florence Harrison. sage gr cloth. NF. D6. $75.00

HERDER, Johann Gottfried. *Ideen zur Philosophie der Geschichte der Menschheit.* 1965 (1784). Berlin/Weimar. Aufbau-Verlag. sm 8vo. 523p. VG/dj. G1. $45.00

HERFORD, Oliver. *Rubaiyat of the Persian Kitten.* 1904. Scribner. 1st ed. unp. fair. B10. $12.00

HERGESHEIMER, Joseph. *Berlin.* 1932. Knopf. 1st ed. sgn. 1/125. gr/pk stp blk cloth. NF/glassine wrp. H5. $150.00

HERGESHEIMER, Joseph. *Sheridan: A Military Narrative.* 1931. Houghton Mifflin. 1st ed. 382p. cloth. NF/VG. M8. $85.00

HERGESHEIMER, Joseph. *Swords & Roses.* 1929. NY. 327p. ils cloth. G/dj. B18. $42.50

HERING, D.W. *Lure of the Clock.* 1963. Crown. revised ed. 121p. G/G. A8. $30.00

HERITEAU & VIETTE. *American Horticultural Society Flower Finder.* 1992. NY. photos. 317p. M/dj. B26. $37.50

HERLIHY, James Leo. *All Fall Down.* 1960. NY. 1st ed. VG/VG. A17. $20.00

HERLIHY, James Leo. *Midnight Cowboy.* 1965. Simon Schuster. 1st ed. 8vo. 253p. gilt bl cloth. NF/dj. H5. $150.00

HERLIHY, James Leo. *Sleep of Baby Filbertson. And Other Stories.* 1959. NY. 1st ed/author's 1st book. inscr. ils Tom Keogh. NF/VG+. A11. $60.00

HERMANN, Binger. *Louisiana Purchase & Our Title West of Rocky Mountains...* 1900. WA, DC. 1st corrected ed. 4 fld maps. 87p. gilt blk cloth. VG. H3. $250.00

HERMANN, Eva. *On Parade.* 1929. Coward McCann. 1st ed. 4to. edit Erich Posselt. VG. B4. $85.00

HERMANN, Imre. *Psychoanalyse und Logik: Individuell-Logische...* 1924. Leipzig. Internationaler Psychoanalytischer. 110p. G1. $50.00

HERNDON & GIBBON. *Exploration of the Valley of the Amazon.* 1854. WA, DC. 2 vol. 417p. VG. F3. $75.00

HERNTON, Calvin. *Scarecrow.* 1974. Doubleday. 1st ed. VG/VG. L3. $45.00

HERON, Roy. *Sporting Art of Cecil Aldin.* 1990. London. Sportsmans. 1st ed. ils. 126p. cloth. M/dj. scarce. R2. $75.00

HERR & WELLS. *Bodies & Souls.* 1961. CRime CLub. 1st ed. VG/VG. P3. $25.00

HERRERA, Velino. *Papago Indians of AZ & Their Relatives the Pima.* nd. US Bureau Indian Affairs. 1st ed. ils. NF/wrp. B19. $20.00

HERRICK, Robert. *One Hundred & Eleven Poems.* 1955. Golden Cockerel. 1/550. ils Wm R Flint. 127p. gilt cream/bl bdg. F/case. F1. $350.00

HERRICK, William. *Itinerant.* 1967. NY. 1st ed/author's 1st novel. sgn. NF/VG+. A11. $45.00

HERRIMAN, George. *Krazy Kat.* 1946. NY. 1st ed. VG. B5. $40.00

HERRIN, Lamar. *Rio Loja Ringmaster.* 1977. Viking. 1st ed. VG+/G+. P8. $40.00

HERRIOT, James. *Blossom Comes Home.* 1988. St Martin. 4to. F/VG. B17. $7.50

HERRIOT, James. *Vets Might Fly.* 1976. Michael Joseph. 1st ed. VG/VG. P3. $20.00

HERRON, Shaun. *Whore-Mother.* 1973. Evans. 1st ed. VG/VG. P3. $23.00

HERSEY, John. *Hiroshima.* 1946. Harmondsworth. 1st Eng ed/PBO. sgn. NF/wrp. A11. $100.00

HERSEY, John. *Men on Bataan.* 1942. Knopf. 1st ed. NF/VG. B4. $150.00

HERSEY, John. *War Lover.* 1959. Knopf. 1st ed. NF/clip. B4. $45.00

HERSHLAG, Z.Y. *Turkey: Economy in Transition.* ca 1958. The Hague. Uitgeverij Van Keulen. 1st ed. VG/dj. W1. $45.00

HERTL, Michael. *Das Gesicht Des Kranken Kindes Physiognomisch-Mimische...* 1962. Berlin. 11 pl/139 ils. 266p. G7. $35.00

HERTRICH, William. *Palms & Cycads.* 1960 (1951). San Marino, CA. 2nd prt. 141p. VG/chip. B26. $59.00

HERTZLER, Arthur. *Horse & Buggy Doctor.* 1938. Harper. 1st ed. 322p. G/dj. B34. $15.00

HERVEY, Harry. *School for Eternity.* 1941. Putnam. 1st ed. F/VG. F4. $25.00

HERZBERG, Frederick. *Motivation To Work.* 1959. Wiley/Chapman Hall. 139p. F. K4. $10.00

HERZOG, Arthur. *Heat.* 1977. Simon Schuster. 1st ed. F/dj. F4. $20.00

HERZOG, Arthur. *IQ 83.* 1978. Simon Schuster. 1st ed. F/F. P3. $15.00

HERZOG, Arthur. *IQ 83.* 1978. Simon Schuster. 1st ed. sgn. F/dj. F4. $27.50

HESKY, Olga. *Sequin Syndicate.* 1969. Dodd Mead. 1st ed. VG. P3. $6.00

HESS, Earl. *German in the Yankee Fatherland.* 1983. ils/maps/diagrams/index. 169p. O8. $12.50

HESS, Fjeril. *Magic Switch.* 1929. Macmillan. 1st ed. ils Neva Kanaga Brn. 74p. cloth. VG/dj. A3. $19.50

HESS, Fjeril. *Toplofty.* 1939. Macmillan. 1st ed. 304p. VG/dj. M20. $18.00

HESS, Joan. *Death by the Light of the Moon.* 1992. St Martin. 1st ed. sgn. F/F. M15. $27.50

HESS, Joan. *Mischief in Maggody.* 1988. St Martin. 1st ed. F/F. B3. $10.00

HESS, Joan. *Poisoned Pins.* 1993. Dutton. AP. F/wrp. B2. $25.00

HESS, Joan. *Really Cute Corpse.* nd. BC. VG/VG. P3. $8.00

HESS & KAPLAN. *Ungentlemanly Art.* 1968. Macmillan. 1st ed. sgn Hess. NF/NF. B2. $35.00

HESSE, Erich. *Narcotics & Drug Addiction.* 1946. Philosophical Lib. 1st ed. F/NF. B2. $50.00

HESSE, Herman. *Beneath the Wheel.* 1968. NY. 1st ed. NF/clip. S9. $30.00

HESSELTINE, WIlliam B. *Lincoln & the War Governors.* 1955. 1st ed. index. 405p. dj. O8. $12.50

HESSELTINE, William B. *Pioneer's Mission: Story of Lyman Copeland Draper.* 1954. Madison, WI. State Hist Soc of WI. 1st ed. 384p. VG/dj. M10. $12.50

HESSING, Siegfried. *Speculum Spinozanum 1677-1977.* 1977. London. Routledge. 8 halftones. 590p. blk cloth. VG/dj. G1. $50.00

HETHERINGTON, A.L. *Early Ceramic Wares of China.* 1922. Scribner. 4to. 100 pl. 160p. gilt tan cloth/beveld brd. VG. F1. $150.00

HEUER, Kenneth. *Rainbows, Halos & Other Wonders.* nd (1978). Dodd Mead. 4th prt. xl. dj. K5. $16.00

HEUMAN, William. *Custer, Man & Legend.* 1968. NY. ils. VG/dj. B18. $17.50

HEWENS, Frank E. *Murder of the Dainty-Footed Model.* 1968. Macmillan. 1st ed. F/F. P3. $18.00

HEWES, Agnes Danforth. *Boy of the Lost Crusade.* 1951. Houghton Mifflin. 8vo. 279p. VG. W1. $8.00

HEWETT, Edgar. *Ancient Andean Life.* 1939. Bobbs Merrill. 1st ed. 336p. VG/dj. F3. $50.00

HEWETT, Edgar. *Ancient Life in Mexico & Central America.* 1936. Bobbs Merrill. 1st ed. 364p. map ep. VG. F3. $50.00

HEWITT, Edward. *Hewitt's Nymph Fly Fishing.* 1934. NY. 1st ed. VG/wrp. B5. $35.00

HEYER, Georgette. *Black Moth.* 1961. Heinemann. 18th prt. VG/VG. P3. $18.00

HEYER, Georgette. *Cousin Kate.* 1968. Dutton. 1st Am ed. 318p. VG/dj. M20. $23.00

HEYER, Georgette. *Why Shoot the Butler?* 1973. Dutton. VG/dj. P3. $20.00

HEYERDAHL, Thor. *Aku-Aku.* 1958. Rand McNally. 1st ed. 62 mc photos. 384p. VG/G. S11. $12.00

HEYERDAHL, Thor. *American Indians in the Pacific.* 1953. Chicago. 1st ed. VG/VG. B5. $100.00

HEYERDAHL, Thor. *Art of Easter Island.* 1975. Doubleday. 4to. 336 mc pl. 350p. gr linen. dj. K1. $150.00

HEYLINGER, William. *Bartley, Freshman Pitcher.* 1911. Appleton. 1st ed. pict bdg. G+. P8. $65.00

HEYLINGER, William. *Big Leaguer.* 1936. Goldsmith. 1st ed. VG/G. P8. $12.50

HEYLYN, Peter. *Cyprianus Angicus; or, Hist of Life & Death of Wm Laud...* 1719. Dublin. Hyde Owne. folio. tooled calf. H10. $95.00

HEYLYN, Peter. *Hist of the Sabbath in Two Books.* 1636. London. Seile. 2 vol in 1. tooled calf. H10. $150.00

HEYMAN, Ken. *Willie.* 1963. NY. Ridge Pr. 1st ed. 4to. VG+/sans. S9. $55.00

HEYMANN, C. David. *Woman Named Jackie: Intimate Biography...* 1989. Lyle Stuart. ils. 715p. F/dj. M10. $5.00

HEYWARD, Du Bose. *Porgy.* 1925. Doran. 1st ed. inscr. 196p. blk cloth. NF. C6. $200.00

HEYWOOD, E.H. *Hard Cash: An Essay To Show Financial Monopolies Hinder...* 1875. Princeton. Co-Operative. 3rd ed (20th Thousand on title p). 8vo. 24p. prt wrp. M1. $125.00

HIAASEN, Carl. *Double Whammy.* 1987. Putnam. 1st ed. NF/F. B3. $50.00

HIAASEN, Carl. *Strip Tease.* 1993. Knopf. 1st ed. F/F. F4. $20.00

HIATT, Ben. *Fish Poems.* 1968. Sacramento. Runcible Spoon. 1/200. 12mo. 10p. VG/wrp. A17. $20.00

HIBBEN, Thomas. *Sons of Vulcan: Story of Metals.* ca 1940. Lippincott/Jr Literary Guild. VG/fair. B10. $15.00

HICHBORN, Franklin. *Story of the Session of CA Legislature of 1921.* 1922. San Francisco. James H Barry. M11. $25.00

HICHENS, Robert. *Dweller on the Threshold.* 1911. Century. 1st ed. VG. P3. $40.00

HICKERINGILL, Edmond. *Curse ye Moroz; or, The Fatal Doom. In a Sermon...* 1680. London. Williams. 4to. 38p. H10. $85.00

HICKEY, James C. *Introducing the Universe.* 1952. Eyre Spottiswoode. 8vo. 18 pl. 159p. brn cloth. G. K5. $8.00

HICKMAN, William. *Treatise on the Law & Practice of Naval Courts-Martial.* 1851. London. John Murray/Albemarle Street. contemporary calf. M11. $450.00

HICKMAN & WIES. *Serpent Mage.* 1992. Bantam. 1st ed. VG/VG. P3. $20.00

HICKOCK, Laurens P. *Rational Psychology; or, Sujective Idea & Objective Law...* 1849. Derby Miller. 717p. emb Victorian cloth. VG. rare. G1. $300.00

HICKS, Granville. *Only One Storm.* 1942. Macmillan. ARC. RS. F/NF. B2. $40.00

HICKS, Jimmie. *WW Robinson: A Biography & a Bibliography.* 1970. Los Angeles. Zamorano. 8vo. 83 p. gilt gr cloth. F/case. P4. $75.00

HIDY, R. *Timber & Men.* 1963. NY. 1st ed. VG/VG. B5. $30.00

HIEB, Louis A. *Tony Hillerman: A Bibliography.* 1990. Tucson. Pr of Gigantic Hound. ltd sgn ed. 1/1000. F/sans. O4. $40.00

HIELSCHER, Kurt. *Deutschland Baukunst und Landschaft.* 1927. Berlin. 304 full-p sepia pl. G. A17. $27.50

HIGBEE, Edward. *American Oasis: Land & Its Uses.* 1957. Knopf. 269p. VG. A10. $18.00

HIGDON, Hal. *Horse That Played Center Field.* 1969. HRW. 1st ed. pict bdg. F. P8. $10.00

HIGGINBOTHAM, Charles T. *Precision Time Measures.* 1952. Chicago. N Am Watch Tool. revised ed. 12mo. 345p. F. A8. $15.00

HIGGINS, C.A. *To CA: Over the Santa Fe Trail.* 1905. Passenger Dept/SF RR. revised ed. ils. 207p. VG/wrp. B19. $45.00

HIGGINS, Frances Lowry. *Sweeper of the Skies: Story of Life of Caroline Herschel...* 1967. Chicago. Follett. 8vo. 127p. VG/dj. K5. $15.00

HIGGINS, George V. *Choice of ENemies.* 1984. Knopf. 1st ed. VG/VG. P3. $18.00

HIGGINS, George V. *City on a Hill.* 1975. Knopf. 1st ed. VG/VG. P3. $35.00

HIGGINS, George V. *Imposters.* 1986. Holt. 1st ed. VG/VG. P3. $17.00

HIGGINS, George V. *Judgement of Deke Hunter.* 1976. Little Brn. 1st ed. VG/VG. P3. $20.00

HIGGINS, George V. *Victories.* 1990. Holt. 1st ed. M/M. P8. $12.50

HIGGINS, George V. *Wonderful Years, Wonderful Years.* 1988. Holt. 1st ed. VG/VG. P3. $20.00

HIGGINS, Jack; see Patterson, Henry.

HIGGINS, Vera. *Cactus Growing for Beginners.* 1971 (1935). London. revised ed. photos. M. B26. $7.50

HIGGINSON, A. Henry. *Hunting in the US & Canada.* 1928. Garden City. ltd ed. 1/450. sgns. 367p. NF. H4. $250.00

HIGGINSON, A. Henry. *Old Sportsman's Memories 1876-1951.* 1951. Berryville, VA. Bl Ridge. 1st ed. 4to. G. O3. $45.00

HIGGINSON, Henry H. *Letters From an Old Sportsman to a Young One.* 1929. Doubleday/Merrymount. 1st ed. 1/201. ils/sgn Lionel Edwards. peach cloth. F. B24. $200.00

HIGH, Philip E. *These Savage Futurians.* 1969. Dobson. F/F. P3. $25.00

HIGH, Philip E. *Time Mercenaries.* 1969. Dobson. 1st ed. NF/NF. P3. $25.00

HIGHAM, Robin. *Civil Wars in the Twentieth Century.* 1972. Lexington. F/VG. V4. $10.00

HIGHSMITH, Patricia. *Glass Cell.* 1964. Crime Club. 1st ed. xl. VG. P3. $5.00

HIGHSMITH, Patricia. *Plotting & Writings Suspense Fiction.* 1966. Boston. The Writer. 1st ed. NF/NF. B2. $65.00

HIGHSMITH, Patricia. *Ripley Under Ground.* 1971. London. 1st Eng ed. sgn. F/F. A11. $60.00

HIGHSMITH, Patricia. *Slowly, Slowly in the Wind.* 1979. Mysterious. 1st Am ed. 8vo. 177p. gilt gr cloth. rem mk. F. H5. $45.00

HIGHSMITH, Patricia. *Tales of Natural & Unnatural Castrophes.* 1989. NY. 1st Am ed. F/F. A17. $9.50

HIGHWATER, Jamake. *Kill Hole.* 1992. Grove. UP. F/pict wrp. B3. $25.00

HIGHWATER, Jamake. *Mick Jagger. The Singer Not the Song.* 1973. NY. 1st ed/PBO. sgn. NF/wrp. A11. $50.00

HIGHWATER, Jamake. *Sun He Dies.* 1980. NY. 1st ed. sgn. F/F. A11. $50.00

HIJUELOS, Oscar. *Fourteen Sisters of Emilio Montez O'Brien.* 1993. FSG. 1st ed. inscr. F/F. S9. $40.00

HIJUELOS, Oscar. *Mambo Kings Pay Songs of Love.* 1989. NY. 1st ed. inscr. F/F. A11. $50.00

HIJUELOS, Oscar. *Our House in the Last World.* 1983. NY. Persea. AP. w/promo material. F/wrp. B2. $250.00

HIJUELOS, Oscar. *Our House in the Last World.* 1983. NY. Persea. 1st ed/author's 1st book. inscr. F/F. B4. $175.00

HIJUELOS, Oscar. *Our House in the Last World.* 1987. London. 1st Eng ed/PBO. inscr. F/ils wrp. A11. $40.00

HILGARD, Ernest R. *Divided Consciousness: Multiple Controls in Human Thought...* 1977. Wiley. 256p. G. K4. $15.00

HILGARD & MARQUIS. *Conditioning & Learning.* 1940. Appleton Century. 336p. reading copy. K4. $8.50

HILGARTNER, Beth. *Necklace of Fallen Stars.* 1979. Little Brn. 1st ed. F/F. P3. $13.00

HILL, D. *Football Through the Years.* (1940). NY. 1st ed. sgn. VG/dj. C11. $40.00

HILL, Douglas. *Exiles of Colsec.* 1984. Gollancz. 1st ed. F/F. P3. $18.00

HILL, Douglas. *Galactic Warlord.* 1979. Gollancz. 1st ed. F/F. P3. $25.00

HILL, Ernestine. *Kabbarli: Personal Memoir of Daisy Bates.* 1973. Sydney. Angus Robertson. 1st ed. F/F. B14. $40.00

HILL, F. Warner. *Labradors.* 1966. Arco. 1st ed. ils. 85p. glossy brd. M. R2. $10.00

HILL, G.C. *Daniel Boone.* ca 1900. Chicago. Donohue. 273p. pict cloth. G. A17. $15.00

HILL, Grace Livingston. *War Romance in the Salvation Army.* 1919. Phil. 1st ed. VG/VG. B5. $35.00

HILL, John C. *Love Songs & Heroines of Robert Burns.* 1961. London. Dent. 1st ed. F/NF. B3. $35.00

HILL, John; see Koontz, Dean R.

HILL, Lorna. *Little Dancer.* 1957. Thomas Nelson. 1st Am ed. 151p. VG/dj. M20. $14.00

HILL, Norman Alan. *Florida Cruise.* 1945. Baltimore. George King. 1st ed. 1/1000. 430p. brn brd. VG/G. B11. $120.00

HILL, Reginald. *Blood Sympathy.* 1993. London. Harper Collins. 1st ed. F/F. S6. $35.00

HILL, Reginald. *Clubbable Woman.* 1984. Foul Play. NF/NF. P3. $20.00

HILL, Reginald. *Fairly Dangerous Thing.* 1983. Foul Play. 1st Am ed. F/F. S6. $25.00

HILL, Reginald. *Killing Kindness.* 1980. Pantheon. 1st ed. VG/VG. P3. $20.00

HILL, Reginald. *Pinch of Snuff.* 1978. Harper Row. 1st ed. VG/VG. P3. $18.00

HILL, Reginald. *Ruling Passion.* 1977. Harper Row. 1st ed. VG/G. P3. $18.00

HILL, W.C. Osman. *Comparative Anatomy & Taxonomy Primates.* 1953-1960. Edinburgh. 4 vol. lg 8vo. djs. G7. $125.00

HILL & MAXWELL. *When Marius Was Ten.* 1937. Macmillan. 1st ed. ils. 163p. VG/fair. B10. $12.00

HILL & STEPP. *Mirror of the War.* 1961. ils/index. 378p. F. O8. $12.50

HILL & WILLIAMS. *Supernatural.* ca 1970. Hawthorn. ils. 351p. VG. M10. $8.50

HILLARY, Edmund. *Boys' Book of Exploration.* 1957. Cassell. 1st ed. 196p. VG/fair. B10. $12.00

HILLER, L. *Surgery Through the Ages: A Pictorial Chronicle.* 1944. NY. 1st ed. 177p. A13. $75.00

HILLERMAN, Tony. *Best of the West: Anthology of Classic Writing...* 1991. Harper Collins. 1st ed. 142 stories. M/dj. A18. $25.00

HILLERMAN, Tony. *Blessing Way.* 1989. Mysterious. ne. F/dj. M2. $20.00

HILLERMAN, Tony. *Boy Who Made Dragonfly.* 1972. Harper Row. 1st ed. sgn. F/VG. O4. $450.00

HILLERMAN, Tony. *Coyote Waits.* nd. Quality BC. F/F. P3. $10.00

HILLERMAN, Tony. *Coyote Waits.* 1990. Harper Row. ltd 1st ed. sgn. 1/500. F/sans/F case. M15. $75.00

HILLERMAN, Tony. *Coyote Waits.* 1991. London. Michael Joseph. 1st Eng ed. F/F. S6. $40.00

HILLERMAN, Tony. *Dance Hall of the Dead.* 1973. London. Pluto. 1st Eng ed. sgn. F/F. O4. $175.00

HILLERMAN, Tony. *Dance Hall of the Dead.* 1991. Armchair Detective Lib. 1st trade ed thus. sgn. M/dj. A18. $75.00

HILLERMAN, Tony. *Dark Wind.* 1982. Harper Row. ltd ed. sgn. F/F/F case. M15. $400.00

HILLERMAN, Tony. *Dark Wind.* 1982. Harper Row. 1st ed. sgn. F/F. O4. $165.00

HILLERMAN, Tony. *Ghostway.* 1985. Harper Row. 1st trade ed. sgn. F/F. L3. $200.00

HILLERMAN, Tony. *Great Taos Bank Robbery.* 1973. Albuquerque. NM U. 1st ed. sgn. F. O4. $250.00

HILLERMAN, Tony. *Indian Country.* 1987. Flagstaff. Northland. 1st ed. ils Bela Kaufman. NF/clip. M15. $100.00

HILLERMAN, Tony. *Jim Chee Mysteries: 3 Classic Hillerman Mysteries...* 1990. Harper Collins. 1st ed. sgn. M/dj. A18. $75.00

HILLERMAN, Tony. *Leaphorn & Chee.* 1992. Harper Collins. 1st ed. F/F. B3. $30.00

HILLERMAN, Tony. *Listening Woman.* 1979. London. Macmillan. 1st ed. F/F. A18. $80.00

HILLERMAN, Tony. *Mysterious West.* 1994. Harper Collins. ARC. RS. F/F. B3. $30.00

HILLERMAN, Tony. *NM, Rio Grande, & Other Essays.* 1992. Graphic Arts Center. 1st ed. photos David Muench/Robert Reynolds. M/M. A18. $35.00

HILLERMAN, Tony. *People of Darkness.* 1980. Harper Row. 1st ed. F/NF. L3. $400.00

HILLERMAN, Tony. *Rio Grande.* 1975. Portland. Charles H Belding. 1st ed. lg format. F/F. M15. $200.00

HILLERMAN, Tony. *Sacred Clowns.* 1993. Harper Collins. 1st ed. sgn. F/F. T2. $55.00

HILLERMAN, Tony. *Sacred Clowns.* 1993. Harper Collins. 1st ltd ed. 1/500. sgn/#d. M/case. A18. $100.00

HILLERMAN, Tony. *Talking God.* 1989. Harper Row. 1st ed. F/F. P3. $20.00

HILLERMAN, Tony. *Talking Mysteries. A Conversation With Tony Hillerman.* 1991. NM U. 1st ed. sgn. 8vo. 135p. khaki cloth. F/F. H5. $100.00

HILLERMAN, Tony. *Thief of Time.* 1988. Harper Row. ARC. F/pict wrp. B3. $60.00

HILLERMAN, Tony. *Thief of Time.* 1988. Harper Row. 1st ed. sgn. F/F. T2. $55.00

HILLERMAN, Tony. *Words, Weather & Wolfmen.* 1989. Gallup. Southwesterner. 1st ed. 1/350. sgn Hillerman/Bulow/Franklin. F/F. M15. $125.00

HILLIARD, O.M. *Compositae.* 1977. Pietermaritzburg. 659p. map ep. M/dj. B26. $24.95

HILLIER, Bevis. *Decorative Arts of the Forties & Fifties.* 1975. NY. Potter. 4to. 200p. F/F. F1. $30.00

HILLIER & SHINE. *Walt Disney's Mickey Mouse Memorabilia, Vintage Years...* 1986. Abrams. 4to. 235 ils. 180p. F/F. A4. $60.00

HILTON, James. *Nothing So Strange.* 1947. Little Brn. 1st ed. VG/VG. P3. $23.00

HILTON, John Buxton. *Death of an Alderman.* 1968. Cassell. 1st ed. VG/VG. P3. $30.00

HILTON, John Buxton. *Playground of Death.* 1981. London. Collins. 1st ed. F/NF. S6. $22.50

HILTON, John. *On Rest & Pain: Course of Lectures... Second Edition.* 1879. Wood. 299p. xl. G7. $35.00

HILU, Virginia. *Beloved Prophet.* 1981. Knopf. 7th prt. VG/torn. W1. $20.00

HIMES, Chester. *Case of Rape.* 1980. NY. Targ. 1st ed. sgn. 1/350. F/F tissue. M15/S9. $125.00

HIMES, Chester. *Cotton Comes to Harlem.* 1965. Putnam. 1st Am ed. F/NF. M15. $85.00

HIMES, Chester. *If He Hollers Let Him Go.* 1947. London. 1st ed. NF/clip. Q1. $200.00

HIMES, Chester. *Pinktoes.* 1965. Putnam/Stein Day. 1st ed. VG/VG. P3. $40.00

HIMES, Chester. *Une Affaire de Viol.* 1963. Paris. Yeux Ouverts. correct 1st ed. F/wrp. B2. $65.00

HIMES, Gustavus. *Wild Life in Oregon: Being a Stirring Recital...* ca 1881. NY. R Worthington. Franklin ed. 437p. red cloth. VG. P4. $50.00

HIMMEL, Richard. *23rd Web.* 1977. Random. 1st ed. F/F. P3. $15.00

HINDE, Edmund Cavileer. *Journal of Edmond Cavileer Hinde.* 1983. Ye Galleon. 1st ed. M/sans. A18. $12.00

HINDE, Thomas. *Bird.* 1970. Hodder Stoughton. 1st ed. VG/VG. B4. $45.00

HINDE, Thomas. *Village.* 1966. Hodder Stoughton. 1st ed. VG/VG. B4. $45.00

HINDLE, Brooke. *Material Culture of Wooden Age.* 1981. Tarrytown. Sleepy. 394p. VG/dj. A10. $25.00

HINE, Robert. *American West.* 1973. Little Brn. 1st prt. VG. B34. $25.00

HINES, Gustavus. *Life on the Plains of the Pacific. Oregon: Its Hist...* 1851. Buffalo, NY. Derby. 2nd ed. 8vo. 437p. cloth. VG. M1. $175.00

HINKLE, Thomas. *Black Tiger.* nd. NY. Grosset Dunlap. VG. O3. $12.00

HINKLE, Thomas. *Tornado Boy.* nd. Grosset Dunlap. VG/G. O3. $15.00

HINKLE, Thomas. *VIC: A Famous Hinkle Dog Story.* nd. Grosset Dunlap. VG/fair. O3. $15.00

HINMAN, Charlton. *Printing & Proof-Reading of the First Folio of Shakespeare.* 1963. Oxford. 2 vol. ils. xl. VG. scarce. A4. $250.00

HINSHAW, David. *Herbert Hoover: American Quaker.* 1950. Farrar Straus. ltd ed. 1/1500 #d. 8vo. 469p. VG/box. V3. $27.00

HINSHAW, Seth Bennett. *Walk Cheerfully, Friends: Essential Optimism...* 1978. NC Yearly Meeting. 8vo. pb. 152p. NF. V3. $8.00

HINSON, William H. *Solid Living in a Shattered World.* 1985. Abingdon. 158p. VG/dj. B29. $4.00

HINTON, C. Howard. *Fourth Dimension.* 1951. Allen Unwin. 270p. VG. B33. $15.00

HINTON, S.E. *Tex.* 1979. Delacorte. 1st ed. cloth. RS. NF. M20. $15.00

HINTZ, Naomi A. *You'll Like My Mother.* nd. Putnam. 2nd ed. VG/VG. P3. $10.00

HINXMAN, Margaret. *Night They Murdered Chelsea.* 1984. Collins Crime Club. 1st ed. VG/VG. P3. $13.00

HINZ, Christopher. *Anachronisms.* 1988. St Martin. 1st ed. F/F. P3. $18.00

HINZ, Christopher. *Ash Ock: The Paratwa Saga — Book Two.* 1989. St Martin. 1st ed. F/F. F4. $18.00

HINZ, Earl. *Sail Before Sunset.* 1979. NY. McKay. photos. 244p. dj. T7. $20.00

HIPPOCRATES. *On Intercourse & Pregnancy.* 1952. NY. 1st Eng-trans ed. 128p. A13. $100.00

HIRAO, Hiroshi. *Colour Encyclopaedia of Cacti.* 1979. Tokyo. Japanese text. photos. sc. F. B26. $75.00

HIRDMAN, Arne. *With Adventure in My Sucksack.* 1957. London. Jarrolds. 1st ed. 8vo. 16 pl. gr cloth. VG/VG. B11. $45.00

HIRSCH, Edward. *Night Parade.* 1989. Knopf. UP. F/wrp. L3. $35.00

HIRSCH, Jerry. *Behavior-Genetic Analysis.* 1967. McGraw Hill. 435p. F/dj. K4. $10.00

HIRSH, Marilyn. *Rabbi & the 29 Witches, a Talmudic Legend.* 1976. Holiday House. 1st ed. inscr. ils Hirsh. VG+/VG+. C8. $20.00

HIRTH, Georg. *Dreitaufend Kunstblatter der Munchner Jugend Ausgewahlt...* 1909. Munich. sm 4to. ils. 407p. Art Nouveau-style cloth. VG. F1. $150.00

HISCOCK, Eric C. *Atlantic Cruise in Wanderer III.* 1968. London. Oxford. 68 ils/7 charts. 159p. dj. T7. $25.00

HISLOP, Alexander. *Two Babylons or the Papal Worship.* 1959. Loizeaux. 330p. VG/dj. B29. $5.50

HISLOP & SKEAPING. *Steeplechasing.* nd (1953). Dutton. 1st Am ed. VG/G. O3. $20.00

HITCHCOCK, Alfred. *Daring Detectives.* 1969. Random. 1st ed. VG/VG. P3. $20.00

HITCHCOCK, Alfred. *Ghostly Gallery.* 1962. Random. VG. P3. $15.00

HITCHCOCK, Alfred. *Portraits of Murder.* 1988. Galahad. 1st ed. F/F. P3. $15.00

HITCHCOCK, Alfred. *Spellbinders in Suspense.* 1967. Random. VG/VG. P3. $20.00

HITCHCOCK, Alfred. *Stories Not for the Nervous.* 1966. Reinhardt. 1st ed. VG/VG. P3. $25.00

HITCHCOCK, Alfred. *Stories That Go Bump in the Night.* 1977. Random. 1st ed. VG/VG. P3. $18.00

HITCHCOCK, Alfred. *Stories To Be Read w/Doors Locked.* 1975. Random. 1st ed. F/NF. N3. $15.00

HITCHCOCK, Alfred. *Supernatural Tales of Terror & Suspicion.* 1973. Random. VG. P3. $15.00

HITCHCOCK, Alfred. *Witch's Brew.* 1977. Random. 1st ed. VG. P3. $15.00

HITCHCOCK, C.H. *Geology of New Hampshire.* 1874, 1877 & 1878. Concord. 3 vol. 1st ed. teg. gilt half leather. F. H3. $350.00

HITCHCOCK, F.H.J. *Building of a Book, Articles by Experts.* 1929. Bowker. 315p. red cloth. VG. B14. $60.00

HITCHCOCK, Roswell. *Hitchcock's Topical Bible.* 1956. Baker. 685p. G. B29. $8.50

HITCHENS, Dolores. *Baxter Letters.* 1971. Putnam. 1st ed. xl. dj. P3. $5.00

HITCHENS, Dolores. *Fools' Gold.* 1958. Crime Club. 1st ed. VG/VG. P3. $25.00

HITCHENS & HITCHENS. *One-Way Ticket.* 1956. Crime Club. 1st ed. VG/VG. P3. $40.00

HITE, Shere. *Women & Love.* nd. Knopf. 992p. F/dj. K4. $15.00

HITT, Orrie. *Lion's Den.* 1957. Key. 1st ed. F/dj. F4. $45.00

HITT, Russell T. *Jungle Pilot: Life & Witness of Nate Saint.* 1959. NY. ils. 303p. VG/dj. B18. $17.50

HITTI, Philip K. *Arabs: Short Hist.* 1960. Macmillan. 4th revised prt. xl. VG/dj. W1. $12.00

HITTI, Philip K. *Near East in Hist: A 5,000 Year Story.* 1961. Van Nostrand. 1st rpt. 574p. xl. VG/dj. W1. $35.00

HIX, Charles. *Man Alive, Dressing the Free Way.* 1984. Simon Schuster. 1st ed. 232p. VG/VG. S11. $10.00

HIXSON, Richard F. *Isaac Collins: A Quaker Printer in 18th-Century America.* 1968. Rutgers. 8vo. 241p. VG/VG. V3. $16.00

HJORT, James William. *Ebon Roses, Jewelled Skulls.* 1980. Buffalo. Weirdbook. 1st ed. 1/250. F/F. T2. $16.50

HJORTSBERG, William. *Alp.* 1969. Simon Schuster. 1st ed/author's 1st book. inscr/dtd 1974. F/F. L3. $150.00

HJORTSBERG, William. *Falling Angel.* 1978. HBJ. 1st ed. inscr/dtd 1978. F/F gold foil. L3. $125.00

HJORTSBERG, William. *Toro! Toro! Toro!* 1974. Simon Schuster. 1st ed. inscr. F/F. L3. $100.00

HOAGLAND, Edward. *African Calliope: A Journey to the Sudan.* 1979. NY. Random. 2nd prt. 239p. NF/VG. P4. $20.00

HOAGLAND, Edward. *Cat Man.* 1956. Houghton Mifflin. 1st ed/author's 1st book. F/G. B4. $85.00

HOAGLAND, Edward. *Circle Home.* 1960. Crowell. 1st ed/author's 2nd book. F/NF. L3. $150.00

HOAGLAND, Edward. *Courage of Turtles.* 1970. NY. 1st ed/author's 1st book essays. inscr. F/VG+. A11. $65.00

HOAGLAND, Edward. *Tugman's Passage.* 1982. NY. 1st ed. sgn. F/F. A11. $50.00

HOAGLAND, Edward. *Walking the Dead Diamond River.* 1973. Random. 1st ed. F/F. L3. $85.00

HOBAN, Lillian. *Tales of Fuzzy Mouse. 6 Cozy Stories for Bedtime.* 1988. Golden/Western Pub. 1st ed. 45p. glossy pict brd. VG. A3. $7.00

HOBAN, Russell. *Baby Sister for Frances.* ca 1964. Harper Row. unp. VG. B10. $15.00

HOBAN, Russell. *Flight of the Bumbel Rudzuk.* ca 1982. Methuen. 1st ed. unp. VG. B10. $10.00

HOBAN, Russell. *Medusa Frequency.* 1987. Atlantic Monthly. 1st ed. F/F. P3. $20.00

HOBAN, Russell. *Pilgermann.* 1983. Summit. 1st ed. VG/VG. P3. $18.00

HOBAN, Tana. *Wonder of Hands.* 1970. Parents Magazine Pr. 1st ed. 4to. VG. S9. $20.00

HOBART, Vere Henry. *On Capital Punishment for Murder: An Essay.* 1861. London. Parker. 35p. disbound. clean. M11. $125.00

HOBBES, Thomas. *Treatise on Human Nature & That on Liberty & Necessity.* 1812. London. Johnson. 1/250. 12mo. blk calf/marbled brd. K1. $100.00

HOBBIE, Holly. *Art of Holly Hobbie.* 1986. Random. 1st ed. pict cloth. NF/NF. C8. $75.00

HOBBIE & HOBBIE. *Art of Holly Hobbie, Drawing on Affection.* 1986. np. 1st collected ed. 100 mc pl. 127p. F/F. A4. $35.00

HOBBS, W. *Exploring About North Pole of the Winds.* 1930. NY. 1st ed. VG. B5. $35.00

HOBBS & WHALLEY. *Beatrix Potter: The Victoria & Albert Collection.* nd. London. ils. 240p. F/F. A4. $125.00

HOBE, Phyllis. *Never Alone.* 1986. Macmillan. 125p. VG. B29. $2.50

HOBHOUSE, L.T. *Development & Purpose: Essay Towards Philosophy Evolution.* 1913. London. Macmillan. 383p. crimson cloth. G1. $65.00

HOBHOUSE, L.T. *Mind in Evolution.* 1926 (1901). London. Macmillan. 3rd ed. VG. G1. $35.00

HOBSON, Geary. *Remembered Earth: Anthology of Contemporary Native Am...* 1981. NM U. 1st prt. M/dj. A18. $20.00

HOBSON, W. *World Health & History.* 1963. Bristol, Eng. 1st ed. ils. 252p. A13. $30.00

HOCH, Edward D. *Best Detective Stories 1981.* 1981. Dutton. 1st ed. F/F. P3. $25.00

HOCHWALT, A.F. *Working Dog & His Education.* 1921. Cincinnati. Sportsmen Review Pub. 1st ed. 116p. VG. R2. $35.00

HOCKING, Anne. *Death Disturbs Mr Jefferson.* 1951. Geoffrey Bles. 1st ed. VG/VG. P3. $25.00

HOCKNEY, David. *China Diary.* 1982. Abrams. 1st ed. sm 4to. F/F. S9. $50.00

HODDER-WILLIAMS, Christopher. *Chain Reaction.* 1959. Hodder Stoughton. 1st ed. VG/VG. P3. $20.00

HODDER-WILLIAMS, Christopher. *Prayer Machine.* 1976. St Martin. 1st Am ed. F/F. N3. $20.00

HODGE, Paul W. *Concepts of Contemporary Astronomy.* 1974. NY. McGraw Hill. sm 4to. 547p. red cloth. xl. K5. $10.00

HODGE & Kress. *Social Semiotics.* 1988. Cornell. 286p. blk cloth. G1. $30.00

HODGELL, P.C. *Dark of the Moon.* nd. BC. VG/VG. P3. $8.00

HODGES, Charles Clement. *Guide to Priory Church of St Andrew, Hexham.* 1913. Hexham. 1st ed. 112p. cloth. VG. M8. $22.50

HODGES, George. *When the King Came: Stories From the Four Gospels.* ca 1923. Houghton Mifflin. ils Frank C Pape. 399p. fair. B10. $20.00

HODGES, George. *William Penn.* 1901. Houghton Mifflin. 16mo. 140p. VG. V3. $10.00

HODGES, Margaret. *Persephone & the Springtime.* ca 1973. Little Brn. ils Arvis Stewart. VG/VG. B10. $10.00

HODGES, Margaret. *St Jerome & the Lion.* 1991. Orchard Books. 1st ed thus. F/F. B17. $10.00

HODGKIN, A.E. *Archer's Craft.* 1951. London. 1st ed. VG. C11. $35.00

HODGKIN, James B. *Southland Stories.* 1903. Manassas, VA. Journal Pr. 1st ed. 12mo. 175p. gr cloth. VG. C6. $60.00

HODGKINS, Louise Manning. *Guide to the Study of 19th-Century Authors.* 1890 (1888). DC Heath. 12mo. 101p. VG. S11. $10.00

HODGSON, Fred T. *Practical Carpentry.* 1883. Industrial Pub Co. 144p. VG. M20. $20.00

HODGSON, N. Barrie. *Grasses, Sedges, Rushes & Ferns of British Isles.* 1949. London. pl. 93p. VG/rpr. B26. $12.50

HODGSON, Shadworth H. *Theory of Practice: Ethical Inquiry in Two Books.* 1870. London. Longman Gr Reader Dyer. 2 vols. cream cloth. G1. $185.00

HODGSON, William Hope. *Carnacki, the Ghost-Finder.* 1947. Mycroft Moran. VG. P3. $50.00

HODGSON, William. *Select Historical Memoirs of Religious Society of Friends.* 1844. Phil. self pub. 1st ed. 12mo. 420p. fair. V3. $26.00

HOEHLING, A.A. *Lonely Command.* 1957. London. 181p. VG/dj. B18. $22.50

HOEHLING, Mary. *Thaddeus Lowe: Am's One-Man Air Corps.* 1958. Chicago. 1st ed. 189p. VG/VG. A17. $15.00

HOFFA, James R. *Hoffa: The Real Story.* 1975. Stein Day. 1st ed. photos. F/F. V4. $15.00

HOFFDING, H. *Hist of Modern Philosophy: Sketch of Hist...* 1915 (1900). London. Macmillan. 2 vol. 3rd prt. brn cloth. G. G1. $40.00

HOFFER, Frank William. *Presbyterian Churches of Roanoke, VA.* ca 1936. Roanoke, VA. 1st ed. 65p. NF/prt wrp. M8. $37.50

HOFFMAN, Abby. *Steal This Book.* 1971. NY. pirate ed/author's 1st book. inscr. VG+/wrp. A11. $135.00

HOFFMAN, Alice. *Angel Landing.* 1980. NY. Putnam. 1st ed. F/F. B4. $85.00

HOFFMAN, Alice. *Angel Landing.* 1982. London. Sevren. 1st ed/author's 3rd book. F/F. B3. $45.00

HOFFMAN, Alice. *At Risk.* 1988. Putnam. 1st ed. F/VG. B3. $20.00

HOFFMAN, Alice. *Illumination Night.* 1987. Putnam. UP. NF. B4. $85.00

HOFFMAN, Alice. *Second Nature.* 1994. Putnam. 1st ed. sgn. F/F. B4. $65.00

HOFFMAN, Charles Fenno. *Winter in the West.* 1966. np. 2 vol. rpt of 1835 ed. VG. B18. $25.00

HOFFMAN, E.T.A. *Nutcracker.* 1984. Crown. 1st ed. ils Maurice Sendak. 102p. NF/NF. M20. $25.00

HOFFMAN, Eleanor. *Realm of the Evening Star.* 1965. Chilton. 1st ed. tall 8vo. 307p. VG/dj. W1. $20.00

HOFFMAN, Felix. *King Thrushbeard.* 1970. HBJ. 1st Am ed. ils. VG/VG. P2. $25.00

HOFFMAN, Heinrich. *Mountain Bounder.* 1967. NY. Macmillan. 1st Am prt. F/NF. C8. $35.00

HOFFMAN, Heinrich. *Slovenly Peter.* nd. Winston. ils. beige cloth. VG. M5. $60.00

HOFFMAN, Lee. *Fox.* 1976. Doubleday. 1st ed. VG/VG. P3. $12.00

HOFFMAN, Malvina. *Sculpture Inside & Out.* (1939). Norton. 330p. G. H1. $18.00

HOFFMAN, Melita. *Pearls of Ferrara.* 1943. Dutton. 1st ed. sgn. 213p. VG/dj. M20. $35.00

HOFFMAN, Nina Kiriki. *Courting Disasters.* 1991. Wildside. 1st ed. sgn. 1/250 #d. M/sans. P3. $65.00

HOFFMAN, Professor. *Modern Magic.* nd. Phil. VG. M17. $40.00

HOFFMAN, Professor. *More Magic.* nd. McKay. brd. NF. P3. $30.00

HOFFMAN, Robert V. *Revolutionary Scene in New Jersey.* 1942. Am Hist Co. sgn. 383p. G. B11. $75.00

HOFFMAN, Wilbur. *Sages of Old Western Travel & Transport.* 1980. Howell North. 1st ed. F/NF. B34. $25.00

HOFFMAN & HOFFMAN. *Little Arab Ali.* ca 1941. Lippincott. VG/VG. B10. $25.00

HOFFMAN & HOFFMAN. *Our Arabian Nights.* 1940. Carrick Evans. 8vo. ils. 307p. xl. G. W1. $15.00

HOFFMAN & HOFFMAN. *Review of Child Development Research.* 1966. Russell Sage Found. 2 vol. F/djs. K4. $20.00

HOFFMAN & SIMON. *Run Run Run: Lives of Abbie Hoffman.* 1994. Tarcher/Putnam. 1st ed. F/F. B4. $35.00

HOFFMANN, Adolph. *Holzsculpturen und Mobel in Rococo. Zweite Serie.* 1896. Berlin. Bruno Hessling. portfolio of 30 loose pl. VG. F1. $150.00

HOFFMANN, Adolph. *Wood Carvings & Furniture in Style of Louis XV.* ca 1895. NY. Hessling Spielmeyer. 30 loose heliotype pl in portfolio. VG. F1. $150.00

HOFFMANN, Friedrich. *Fundamenta Medicinae.* 1971. London. 1st Eng-trans ed. 142p. A13. $40.00

HOFFNER, Eric. *Passionate State of Mind.* 1955. Harper Row. 151p. VG/G. B33. $16.00

HOFFNER, Eric. *Working & Thinking on the Waterfront.* 1969. Harper Row. 1st ed. pres. 180p. F/VG. B33. $25.00

HOFLAND, Barbara. *Young Cadet; or, Henry Delamere's Voyage to India...* 1828. NY. Roorbach. 12mo. ils. 206p. maroon calf/gr brd. K1. $100.00

HOGAN, Inez. *Kangaroo Twins.* nd. London. Dent. 12mo. pict brd. F/NF. C8. $55.00

HOGAN, Inez. *Monkey Twins, They Saw It All!* Aug 1944. Dutton. 2nd prt. NF. C8. $30.00

HOGAN, Inez. *Mule Twins.* 1939. Dutton. NF/NF. C8. $60.00

HOGAN, Inez. *Nicodemus & the Newborn Baby.* 1940. Dutton. 1st ed. 12mo. VG+. C8. $100.00

HOGAN, Inez. *Runaway Toys.* 1950. Dutton. 1st ed. VG/G. C8. $45.00

HOGAN, Inez. *Twin Deer.* April 1943. Dutton. 2nd prt. 12mo. G+. C8. $27.50

HOGAN, James P. *Code of the Lifemaker.* 1983. Del Rey. 1st ed. F/F. P3. $20.00

HOGAN, James P. *Endgame Enigma.* 1987. Bantam. 1st ed. F/F. P3. $17.00

HOGARTH, Burne. *Dynamic Anatomy.* 1984. Watson Guptill. 11th ed. F/F. P3. $20.00

HOGARTH, D.G. *Hejaz Before World War I.* 1978. Cambridge. 1st ed thus. 155p. M. M7. $30.00

HOGARTH, D.G. *Life of Charles M Doughty.* 1928. Oxford. tall 8vo. 216p. uncut. O2. $75.00

HOGARTH, D.G. *Wandering Scholar in the Levant.* 1896. London. 1st ed. 8vo. 206p. cloth. O2. $150.00

HOGARTH, Grace Allen. *Australia: Island Continent.* 1943. Houghton Mifflin. 1st ed. NF/G+. C8. $20.00

HOGARTH, William. *Complete Works of...* ca 1875. London. ils. aeg. VG. A15. $100.00

HOGARTH, William. *Complete Works of...* ca 1880. London. lg 4to. 151 steel engravings. half levant morocco. NF. C6. $250.00

HOGBEN, Lancelot. *Astronomer Priest & Ancient Mariner.* 1973. St Martin. 4to. 110p. VG/dj. K5. $25.00

HOGBEN, Lancelot. *Pigmentary Effector System.* 1924. Edinburgh. ils. 152p. G7. $35.00

HOGBEN, Lancelot. *Wonderful World of Energy.* 1957. Garden City. 1st ed. 69p. VG. B10. $10.00

HOGBEN, Lancelot. *Wonderful World of Mathematics.* 1955. Garden City. 1st Am ed 69p. VG. B10. $10.00

HOGG, Edward. *Visit to Alexandria, Damascus & Jerusalem.* 1835. London. 2 vol. 8vo. gilt tan half calf. O2. $600.00

HOGG, Gary. *Malta: Bl-Water Island.* 1968. Barnes. 1st Am ed. 16 pl. VG. W1. $18.00

HOGNER, Dorothy Childs. *Our Am Horse.* 1944. Nelson. ils Nils Hogner. 114p. VG. B10. $12.00

HOGREFE, Pearl. *Sir Thomas Moore Circle: Program of Ideas...* 1959. Urbana. index. 360p. H10. $20.00

HOGROGIAN, Nonny *Renowned Hist of Little Red Riding Hood.* 1967. Crowell. 2nd prt. F/F. C8. $25.00

HOKE, Helen. *Demons Within: And Other Disturbing Tales.* 1977. Taplinger. 1st ed. F/F. N3. $15.00

HOKE, Helen. *Major & the Kitten.* 1941. Franklin Watts. ils Diane Thorne. pict ep. G/G. P2. $22.50

HOKE & HOKE. *Horrifying & Hideous Hauntings.* 1986. Dutton. 1st ed. F/F. N3. $10.00

HOLABIRD, Katherine. *Angelina & the Princess.* 1984. CN Potter. 1st Am ed. M/M. C8. $20.00

HOLABIRD, Katherine. *Angelina at the Fair.* 1985. CN Potter. 1st ed. ils Helen Craig. M/M. C8. $20.00

HOLABIRD, Katherine. *Angelina Ballerina.* 1983. CN Potter. 1st Am ed. M/M. C8. $20.00

HOLBERG, Ruth Langland. *Hester & Timothy Pioneers.* 1937. Doubleday Doran. 1st ed. ils Richard Holberg. VG/fair. B10. $15.00

HOLBERG, Ruth Langland. *Tansy for Short.* 1951. Doubleday. 1st ed. 208p. VG/fair. B10. $15.00

HOLBERG, Ruth Langland. *Tibby's Venture.* ca 1943. Doubleday Doran. 1st ed. 122p. VG/fair. B10. $15.00

HOLBROOK, S.H. *Golden Age of Quackery.* 1959. NY. 302p. A13. $35.00

HOLBROOK, S.H. *Little Annie Oakley & Other Rugged People.* 1948. Macmillan. 1st ed. G+. N2. $6.00

HOLBROOK, S.H. *Wonderful West.* ca 1963. Doubleday. 8vo. ils. 154p. VG. P4. $10.00

HOLDEN, G.P. *Steamcraft.* 1919. Cincinnati. 1st ed. VG. B5. $45.00

HOLDEN, Jane. *Bonnell Site.* 1952. Lubbock. TX Archeological & Paleontological Soc. VG/wrp. P4. $15.00

HOLDER, C.F. *Along the Florida Reef.* 1892. Appleton. ils. 273p. pict cloth. B14. $55.00

HOLDER, C.F. *Marvels of Animal Life.* 1885. Scribner. 1st ed. 240p. pict cloth. B14. $75.00

HOLDER, C.F. *Treasure Divers.* 1898. Dodd Mead. 1st ed. 207p. pict cloth. VG. B14. $55.00

HOLDING, Elisabeth Sanxay. *Too Many Bottles.* nd. BC. VG/G. P3. $8.00

HOLDREDGE, H. *Mammy Pleasant.* 1953. NY. ARC/1st ed. VG/VG. w/photo. B5. $55.00

HOLLAND, Cecelia. *Two Ravens.* 1977. Knopf. 1st ed. F/F. N3. $15.00

HOLLAND, Henry. *Travels in Ionian Isles, Albania, Thessaly, Macedonia...* 1971. NY. tall 8vo. 551p. cloth. O2. $45.00

HOLLAND, Isabelle. *Kilgaren.* 1974. Weybright Talley. 1st ed. VG/VG. P3. $20.00

HOLLAND, Rupert Sargent. *Historic Railroads.* 1927. Phil. Macrae Smith. probable 1st ed. NF. C8. $60.00

HOLLAND, Rupert Sargent. *Historic Ships.* (1926). Grosset Dunlap. rpt. NF/VG. C8. $45.00

HOLLANDER, Edwin P. *Principles & Methods of Social Psychology.* 1971. Oxford. 2nd ed. 628p. F. K4. $10.00

HOLLERAN, O.C. *Holly, His Book.* 1924. Chicago. private prt. pres. cloth. VG. C11. $85.00

HOLLIDAY, Joe. *Dale of the Mounted, Atomic Plot.* 1959. Allen. VG/G. P3. $18.00

HOLLIDAY, Joe. *Dale of the Mounted, Dew Line Duty.* 1957. Allen. 159p. VG/ragged. M20. $15.00

HOLLIDAY, Joe. *Dale of the Mounted, in Hong Kong.* 1962. Allen. 160p. VG/dj. M20. $15.00

HOLLIDAY, Joe. *Dale of the Mounted, Pursuit on the St Lawrence.* 1960. Allen. 160p. VG/dj. M20. $15.00

HOLLIDAY, Michael; see Creasey, John.

HOLLING, Holling C. *Book of Cowboys.* 1936. Platt Munk. orange pict cloth. F/VG. C8. $65.00

HOLLING, Holling C. *Book of Indians.* ca 1935. Platt Munk. 125p. VG/G. B10. $35.00

HOLLING, Holling C. *Book of Indians.* 1935. Platt Munk. F/NF. C8. $65.00

HOLLING, Holling C. *Paddle to the Sea.* (1941). Houghton Mifflin. 17th prt. 4to. VG/VG. B17. $10.00

HOLLING, Holling C. *Paddle to the Sea.* 1941. Houghton Mifflin. unp. pict cloth. VG. B18. $20.00

HOLLING, Holling C. *Pagoo.* 1957. Houghton Mifflin. probable 1st ed. VG+/G+. C8. $20.00

HOLLING, Holling C. *Seabird.* 1948. Houghton Mifflin. 1st ed. ils. G/G. P2. $25.00

HOLLING, Holling C. *Tree in the Trail.* (1942). Houghton Mifflin. early rpt. G-. A3. $4.50

HOLLING, Holling C. *Tree in the Trail.* 1942. Houghton Mifflin. 1st ed. ils. F/VG. P2. $45.00

HOLLINGHURST, Alan. *Folding Star.* 1994. Pantheon. 1st ed. F/F. B3. $25.00

HOLLINGS, Patsy. *All About the Weimaraner.* 1992. London. Pelham. 1st ed. ils. 168p. cloth. M/dj. R2. $30.00

HOLLINSWORTH, Brian. *Railways of the World.* 1979. NY. Gallery. 4to. ils. 350p. F/F. B11. $30.00

HOLLISTER, Ovando J. *CO Volunteers in NM, 1862.* 1962. Lakeside. 309p. gilt bl cloth. VG+. M20. $35.00

HOLLISTER, U.S. *Navaho & His Blanket.* 1953. Denver. sgn. F/Jan Sabota solander case. H4. $275.00

HOLLON, W. Eugene. *Great American Desert.* 1966. Oxford. ils/notes/index. 284p. NF/VG. B19. $27.50

HOLLY, H.W. *Carpenter's & Joiner's Handbook.* 1883 (1863). Wiley. revised ed. cloth. VG. M20. $15.00

HOLLY, J. Hunter. *Encounter.* 1959. Avalon. 1st ed. sgn. VG/VG. P3. $45.00

HOLMAN, Felice. *At the Top of My Voice & Other Poems.* 1970. Norton. 1st ed. ils Gorey. M/M. C8. $60.00

HOLMAN, Felice. *Murderer.* ca 1978. Scribner. 1st ed. 151p. F/VG. B10. $10.00

HOLMAN, Felice. *Witch on the Corner.* 1966. Norton. 1st ed. ils Arnold Lobel. VG/dj. M20. $22.00

HOLMAN, Hugh. *Slay the Murderer.* 1946. MS Mill. 1st ed. VG/G. P3. $25.00

HOLMAN, Hugh. *Trout in the Milk.* 1945. MS Mill. 1st ed. VG/VG. P3. $30.00

HOLMAN, John. *Squabble.* 1990. Ticknor Fields. 1st ed. F/F. B3. $20.00

HOLME, Bryan. *Kate Greenaway Book.* 1976. Gallery. ils Greenaway. 144p. VG/VG clip. S11. $20.00

HOLME, Charles. *Modern Etching & Engraving.* 1902. London. The Studio. 4to. lib bdg/orig wrp bdg in. F. F1. $60.00

HOLME, Timothy. *Assisi Murders.* 1985. London. Macmillan. 1st ed. NF/dj. S6. $22.50

HOLME, Timothy. *At the Lake of Sudden Death.* 1987. Detective BC. VG. P3. $8.00

HOLME, Timothy. *Devil & the Dolce Vita.* 1988. Walker. VG/VG. P3. $18.00

HOLMES, Clellon. *Go.* 1952. Scribner. 1st ed. F/NF. B4. $850.00

HOLMES, David C. *Search for Life on Other Worlds.* nd (1966). Sterling. 8vo. photos. 240p. G. K5. $14.00

HOLMES, Grace W. *Student Protest & the Law.* 1969. Ann Arbor. Inst of Continuing Legal Education. M11. $35.00

HOLMES, James William. *Voyaging. Fifty Years on the Seven Seas in Sail.* 1972. Dodd Mead. 8vo. 207p. NF/VG. P4. $25.00

HOLMES, John Clellon. *Get Home Free.* 1966. London. 1st Eng ed/PBO. sgn. VG/wrp. A11. $65.00

HOLMES, John Clellon. *Horn.* 1958. Random. 1st ed. F/NF. B2. $60.00

HOLMES, John Clellon. *Nothing More To Declare.* 1967. NY. 1st ed/1st nonfiction book. author's copy. F/NF. A11. $115.00

HOLMES, Kenneth L. *Covered Wagon Women: Diaries & Letters...1840-1890.* 1983-1993. Arthur H Clark. 11 vols (6 1st prt). M. A18. $350.00

HOLMES, Oliver Wendell. *Autocrat of the Breakfast Table.* 1858. Phillips Samson. 1st ed/1st state. 373p. brn pebble cloth. G. G7. $95.00

HOLMES, Oliver Wendell. *Autocrat of the Breakfast Table/Every Man His Own Boswell.* 1858. Boston. 1st ed. 373p. VG. A13. $150.00

HOLMES, Oliver Wendell. *Collected Legal Papers.* 1920. Harcourt Brace. orig ed. 316p. xl. NF. D3. $20.00

HOLMES, Oliver Wendell. *Collected Works...* ca 1890s. Boston. Riverside. 14 vol. collected ed. red cloth/leather label. G7. $95.00

HOLMES, Oliver Wendell. *Intro Lecture Delivered Before Medical Class of Harvard...* 1867. Boston. Clapp. 45p. VG/wrp. B14. $125.00

HOLMES, Oliver Wendell. *Mechanism in Thought & Morals...* 1871. Boston. Osgood. 12mo. prt gr cloth. NF. G1. $125.00

HOLMES, Oliver Wendell. *Poems.* 1836. Boston. Otis Broaders. 1st ed/author's 1st book. emb gr cloth. w/clip sgn. F. B24. $575.00

HOLMES, Oliver Wendell. *Poetical Works.* 1882. Houghton Mifflin. 2 vol. inscr. later prt. aeg. limp leather. VG. B4. $150.00

HOLMES, Oliver Wendell. *Professor at the Breakfast Table.* 1860. Ticknor Fields. 1st ed/1st issue. 410p. brn pebble cloth. G. G7. $95.00

HOLMES, Prescott. *Young People's History of the War With Spain.* nd. Phil. Altemus. 16mo. 184p. pict brn cloth. VG. B11. $25.00

HOLMES, R.R. *Windsor.* 1908. London. Blk. 20 mc pl. teg. VG. H7. $30.00

HOLMES, Sarah Katherine. *Brokenburn: Journal of Kate Stone, 1861-1868.* 1955. Baton Rouge. 1st ed. 400p. cloth. VG/dj. M8. $65.00

HOLMES, Thomas J. *Increase Mather, His Works.* 1930. Cleveland. For Private Distribution. lg 8vo. 60p. gr morocco. K1. $100.00

HOLMES & PITKIN. *On the Wings of the Wind.* 1955. McBride. 8vo. 204p. VG/dj. K5. $10.00

HOLMSTROM, J.G. *Drake's Modern Blacksmithing & Horshoeing.* 1972. NY. Drake. VG. O3. $25.00

HOLMYARD, E.J. *British Scientists.* 1951. London. Dent. 8vo. 88p. xl. G. K5. $10.00

HOLROYD, Michael. *Lytton Strachey: A Critical Biography.* 1967. HRW. 2 vol. 1st ed. VG/dj. M10. $15.00

HOLT, Florrie B. *Antique Turpin Dolls.* 1961. Cinncinatti. inscr twice. VG/VG. A1. $40.00

HOLT, George Edmund. *Morocco the Bizarre; or, Life in Sunset Land.* 1914. McBride Nast. 242p. xl. G. W1. $12.00

HOLT, Guy. *Bibliography of James Branch Cabell.* 1924. Phil. Centaur Book Shop. 1/500. VG+. A1. $35.00

HOLT, Hazel. *Shortest Journey.* 1992. London. Macmillan. 1st ed. F/F. S6. $25.00

HOLT, Hazel. *Uncertain Death.* 1993. London. Macmillan. 1st ed. F/F. S6. $25.00

HOLT, Henry. *Call Out the Flying Squad.* 1933. Crime Club. 2nd ed. VG/G. P3. $20.00

HOLT, Henry. *Freudian Wish & Its Place in Ethics.* 1915. Holt. later prt. 12mo. bl cloth. G1. $22.50

HOLT, Lee E. *Samuel Butler.* 1964. Twayne. 1st ed. xl. VG/dj. M21. $7.50

HOLT, Samuel; see Westlake, Donald E.

HOLT, Tom. *Flying Dutch.* 1991. Orbit. 1st ed. F/F. P3. $26.00

HOLT, Tom. *Who's Afraid of Beowulf?* nd. BC. VG/VG. P3. $8.00

HOLT, Vesta. *Keys of Identification of Wild Flowers, Ferns, Trees...* 1962 (1955). Palo Alto. revised ed/2nd prt. 174p. sc. B26. $14.00

HOLTON, Leonard. *Devil To Play.* 1974. Dodd Mead. 1st ed. VG. P8. $45.00

HOLTON, Leonard. *Out of the Depths.* nd. BC. VG/VG. P3. $8.00

HOLTON, Leonard. *Touch of Jonah.* 1968. Dodd Mead. 1st ed. VG/VG. P3. $15.00

HOLTZMAN, Jerome. *Fielder's Choice.* 1979. HBJ. 1st ed. sgn. VG/VG. P8. $50.00

HOLZER, Hans. *Beyond Medicine.* 1973. Henry Regnery. VG. P3. $15.00

HOLZER, Hans. *Haunted Hollywood.* nd. Bobbs Merrill. 2nd ed. VG/G. P3. $13.00

HOME, John. *History of Rebellion in Year 1745.* 1802. London. 1st ed. 4to. raised spine bands. A15. $125.00

HOMER, Winslow. *Life & Works of...* (1911). np. rpt. edit Downes. 464p. VG. E5. $35.00

HOMER. *Iliad & the Odyssey.* ca 1956. Simon Schuster. ils Provensen. 96p. G. B10. $15.00

HOMER. *Iliad.* 1976. Franklin Lib. leather. F. P3. $35.00

HOMER. *Odyssey of Homer.* 1990. CA U. 1st ed. F/F. P3. $25.00

HOMER. *Odyssey.* 1976. Franklin Lib. leather. F. P3. $30.00

HOMER. *Odyssey.* 1991. Oxford. F/F. P3. $25.00

HOMES, A.M. *In a Country of Mothers.* 1993. Knopf. 1st ed. NF/NF. A14. $25.00

HOMES, A.M. *In a Country of Mothers.* 1993. Knopf. 1st ed. sgn. F/F. L3. $40.00

HOMES, Geoffrey. *Man Who Murdered Goliath.* 1938. Morrow. 1st ed. VG/VG. M15. $85.00

HOMES, Geoffrey. *Then There Were Three.* 1944. Books Inc. VG. P3. $10.00

HONEY, W.B. *Dresden China.* 1946. NY. Tudor. 8vo. 223p. silvered bl cloth. VG/G. F1. $40.00

HONEYWELL, Roy J. *Chaplains of the US Army.* 1948. WA. 1st ed. biblio/index. 376p. F. A17. $20.00

HONIG, Donald. *Last Great Season.* 1979. Simon Schuster. 1st ed. F/G+. P8. $15.00

HONROS, John L. *Occupation & Resistance. The Greek Agony 1941-1944.* 1983. NY. 8vo. 340p. cloth. dj. O2. $30.00

HOOBLER & WETANSON. *Hunters.* 1978. Doubleday. 1st ed. F/F. P3. $13.00

HOOD, J.B. *Advance & Retreat.* 1880. New Orleans. 1st ed. leather. G. B5. $150.00

HOOD, R. *Gashouse Gang.* 1976. NY. 1st ed. VG/VG. B5. $20.00

HOOD, Thomas. *Poems by Thomas Hood, Illustrated by Birket Foster.* 1871. London. Moxon. lg paper ed. 4to. 109p. aeg. morocco. F. B24. $300.00

HOOD, Thomas. *Poems of Thomas Hood.* 1870. Cassell/Peter Galpin. folio. 58p. aeg. F. B24. $150.00

HOOK, Donald D. *Madmen of History.* 1976. Jonathan David. VG/VG. P3. $18.00

HOOK, Sidney. *Common Sense & the 5th Amendment.* 1957. NY. 160p. VG/dj. D3. $15.00

HOOK, Sidney. *Dimensions of the Mind: A Symposium.* 1960. NY U. 282p. blk cloth. VG/dhip. G1. $27.50

HOOK, Sidney. *From Hegel to Marx: Studies in Intellectual Development...* 1958. Humanities Pr. 2nd ed. 336p. blk cloth. G1. $25.00

HOOKER, Forrestine. *Garden of the Lost Key.* 1929. Doubleday Doran. 1st ed. 288p. VG. P2. $20.00

HOOKER, Richard. *M*A*S*H Goes to Maine.* 1972. Morrow. TVTI. VG/VG. P3. $15.00

HOOKER, Thomas. *Poor Doubting Christian Drawn to Christ...* 1743. Boston. Henchman. 16mo. 143p. H10. $125.00

HOOPES, Penrose. *Connecticut Clockmakers of the 18th Century.* 1975. New Eng Pub. rpt. 8vo. 178p. cloth. VG. A8. $20.00

HOOVER, Herbert. *Memoirs of Herbert Hoover: Years of Adventure, 1874-1920.* 1951. Macmillan. 2nd ed. 8vo. 496p. VG/dj. V3. $16.00

HOOVER, Matt. *Wild Ginger.* 1909. NY. 1st ed. sgn pres. VG. B5. $75.00

HOPE, Brian; see Creasey, John.

HOPE, James. *Memoir of Late James Hope, MD...* 1842. London. 358p. G7. $95.00

HOPE, Laura Lee. *Bobbsey Twins at Mystery Mansion.* nd. Grosset Dunlap. rpt. VG+/G. C8. $17.50

HOPE, Laura Lee. *Bobbsey Twins at School (#4).* 1941. Grosset Dunlap. NF/NF. C8. $15.00

HOPE, Laura Lee. *Bobbsey Twins at School.* 1913. Grosset Dunlap. lists to #15. 216p. VG/dj. M20. $35.00

HOPE, Laura Lee. *Bobbsey Twins at the County Fair (#15).* 1922. Grosset Dunlap. 1st ed. 216p. VG/dj. M20. $50.00

HOPE, Laura Lee. *Bobbsey Twins at the Seashore (#3).* 1950. Grosset Dunlap. NF/NF. C8. $15.00

HOPE, Laura Lee. *Bobbsey Twins in the Country.* nd. Grosset Dunlap. rpt. VG+/VG. C8. $12.50

HOPE, Laura Lee. *Bobbsey Twins in Washington.* 1919. Grosset Dunlap. gr cloth/pict label. VG. M5. $15.00

HOPE, Laura Lee. *Bobbsey Twins on a Ranch (#28).* 1935. Grosset Dunlap. 12mo. VG/VG. C8. $15.00

HOPE, Laura Lee. *Bobbsey Twins on an Airplane Trip (#26).* 1933. Grosset Dunlap. VG/VG. C8. $35.00

HOPE, Laura Lee. *Bobbsey Twins Treasure Hunting.* 1920. Grosset Dunlap. thicker ed w/paper dolls on dj. VG/VG. M20. $20.00

HOPE, Laura Lee. *Story of a Plush Bear.* ca 1921. Grosset Dunlap. ils Harry L Smith. 120p. G. B10. $10.00

HOPE, Laura Lee. *Story of a White Rocking Horse.* 1920. Grosset Dunlap. lists 12 titles. VG/dj. M20. $18.00

HOPKINS, Budd. *Intruders.* 1987. Random. 1st ed. 224p. F/F. S11. $10.00

HOPKINS, Budd. *Missing Time: Documented Study of UFO Abductions.* 1981. NY. Marek. 1st ed. F/F. T2. $15.00

HOPKINS, Ernest J. *Financing the Frontier: 50 Year Hist of Valley Nat Bank.* 1950. private prt. 1st ed. 276p. NF/VG. B19. $30.00

HOPKINS, Harry. *Egypt the Crucible.* 1970. Houghton Mifflin. 1st Am ed. 8vo. 533p. VG/dj. W1. $10.00

HOPKINS, John. *Attempt.* 1967. Viking. 1st ed. F/NF. F4. $20.00

HOPKINS, Jospeh R. *Hamiltoniad; or, Effects of Discord.* Aug 3, 1804. Phil. self pub. 1st ed. 8vo. M1. $375.00

HOPKINS, Kenneth. *She Is My Bright & Smiling & Shy Dear. Poems by...* 1985. Easthampton, MA. 1/75. sgn poet/ils/prt. 63p. tan brd. F. B24. $325.00

HOPKINS, William John. *She Blows! And Sparm at That!* 1922. Houghton Mifflin. ils. 317p. T7. $35.00

HOPLEY, George; see Woolrich, Cornell.

HOPPE. *Bibliography of Writings of Samuel Butler...* 1925. np. 1/500. ils. 201p. NF. A4. $145.00

HOPPER, James. *Coming Back With the Spitball.* 1914. Harper. 1st ed. pict bdg. VG+. P8. $70.00

HOPWOOD, Derek. *Russian Presence in Syria & Palestine 1843-1914.* 1969. Oxford. 8vo. 232p. cloth. O2. $30.00

HORACE. *Opera.* 1733-1737. London. Joahnnes Pine. 2 vol. 2nd state vol 2. morocco. H4. $750.00

HORAN, James D. *Across the Cimarron.* 1956. Crown. 1st ed. 301p. VG/dj. M20. $30.00

HORAN, James D. *McKenney-Hall Portrait Gallery of Am Indians.* 1972. NY. Crown. 4to. ils. 373p. VG/dj. M10. $35.00

HORAN, James D. *Out in the Boon Docks.* 1943. NY. 1st ed. VG/VG. B5. $40.00

HORGAN, Paul. *Distant Trumpet.* 1960. FSC. 1st ed. sgn. F/dj. A18. $60.00

HORGAN, Paul. *Lamp of the Plains.* 1937. Harper. 1st ed. F/NF. A18. $75.00

HORGAN, Paul. *Return of the Weed.* 1980. Flagstaff. Northland. Southwestern Classic Series #1. F/NF. S9. $35.00

HORGAN, Paul. *Rome Eternal.* 1959. FSC. 1st ltd ed. 1/350. sgn/#d. photos Vadala. NF/case. A18. $100.00

HORGAN & USTINOV. *On the Arts.* 1968. Cleveland. Inst of Music. 1st ed. F. A18. $35.00

HORLER, Sydney. *Curse of Doone.* 1930. Mystery League. 1st ed. VG/VG. P3. $20.00

HORLER, Sydney. *False Face.* 1926. Doran. 1st ed. VG. P3. $20.00

HORLER, Sydney. *False Purple.* 1933. Mystery League. 1st ed. VG/VG. P3. $30.00

HORLER, Sydney. *Man Who Stayed to Supper.* 1941. Herbert Jenkins. 1st ed. VG/VG. P3. $30.00

HORLER, Sydney. *Tiger Standish Comes Back.* 1970. John Long. NF/NF. P3. $18.00

HORN, Calvin. *University in Turmoil & Transition.* 1981. Albuquerque. Rocky Mtn Pub. 1st ed. sgn. VG/G. B11. $15.00

HORN, Holloway. *Murder at Linpara.* 1931. Collins. 1st ed. VG. P3. $25.00

HORN, Madeline Darrough. *Farm on the Hill.* 1936. Scribner. 1st ed. ils Grant Wood. 78p. G+. B10. $100.00

HORN, Madeline Darrough. *Farm on the Hill.* 1939. Scribner. ils/sgn Grant Wood. ils ep. bl stp tan cloth. F/dj. F1. $325.00

HORN, Maurice. *Women in Comics.* 1977. Chelsea House. 1st ed. VG/VG. P3. $15.00

HORNADAY, William T. *Campfires on Desert & Lava.* 1908. Scribner. 1st ed. ils/index/maps. NF. B19. $95.00

HORNADAY, William T. *Our Vanishing Wild Life: Its Extermination & Preservation.* 1913. NY Zoological Soc. 1st ed. ils/maps/index. F. A18. $75.00

HORNER, Tom. *All About the Bull Terrier.* 1978 (1973). London. Pelham. 2nd ed. 144p. cloth. F/F. R2. $30.00

HORNIG, Doug. *Hardball.* 1986. London. Macmillan. 1st Eng ed. F/F. S6. $25.00

HORNSBY, Sarah. *Who I Am in Jesus.* 1986. Chosen. unp. F/F. B29. $3.50

HORNSBY, Wendy. *Half a Mind.* 1990. NAL. 1st ed. inscr. F/F. T2. $32.00

HORNSBY, Wendy. *Nine Sons.* 1992. Royal Oak/Mission Viejo. 1st ed/trade ed. sgn. 1/200. ils/sgn Phil Parks. F/wrp. T2. $12.00

HORNSBY, Wendy. *No Harm.* 1987. Dodd Mead. 1st ed. inscr. F/F. T2. $40.00

HORNSBY, Wendy. *Telling Lies.* 1992. NY. Dutton. ARC/1st ed. sgn. RS. F/F. S6. $35.00

HORNUNG, Clarence. *Handbook of Early American Advertising Art.* 1953. Dover. 2 vol. 2nd ed. 4to. silver/red stp bl cloth. VG+/dj. F1. $200.00

HORNUNG, Clarence. *Treasury of American Antiques.* 1977. Abrams. 1st ed. 4to. 175p. gilt bl cloth. VG/VG. S11. $15.00

HORNUNG, Clarence. *Treasury of American Design.* 1976. Abrams. 1st ed. VG/G. S11. $25.00

HORNUNG, E.W. *Crime Doctor.* 1914. Bobbs Merrill. VG. P3. $30.00

HORNUNG, E.W. *Mr Justice Raffles.* 1909. Scribner. 1st Am ed. gilt cloth. G. A17. $20.00

HORNUNG, E.W. *Mr Justice Raffles.* 1909. Scribner. 1st ed. VG. P3. $40.00

HORODISCH, Abraham. *Uber Bucher Kleinsten Formats.* 1978. Frankfurt. Sonderdruck. 1/100. 12mo. 44p. F/cream wrp. B24. $100.00

HOROWITZ, Caroline. *Boy's Treasury of Things-To-Do.* ca 1946. Hart. ils. 93p. VG/fair. B10. $10.00

HOROWITZ, Irving Louis. *Professing Sociology: Studies in Life Cycle Social Science.* 1968. Chicago. Aldine. 354p. F/dj. K4. $15.00

HORRAX, Gilbert. *Neurosurgery: Hist Sketch.* 1952. Springfield. Thomas. sgn. 135p. NF/dj. G7. $135.00

HORSLEY, Samuel. *Nine Sermons.* 1815. London. full brn leather. G. B30. $75.00

HORST, Kay. *Official Record of Show Horse Sires & Dams. Vol 1 & 2.* 1951 & 1952. Lexington. 2 vols. VG. O3. $325.00

HORTON, Clarence. *These Storied Walls: Brief Hist of Olivet United Methodist.* ca 1984. np. 1st ed. 14p. NF/prt wrp. M8. $17.50

HORTON, George. *Home of the Nymph & Vampires.* 1929. Bobbs Merrill. 1st ed. 319p. VG. W1. $35.00

HORTON, George. *In Argolis.* 1902. Chicago. Merrymount. 8vo. 226p. cloth/linen spine. O2. $40.00

HORTON, Michael. *Agony of Deceit: What Some TV Preachers Are Really Teaching.* 1990. Moody. 284p. VG/VG. B29. $7.00

HORTON. *Cleaning & Preserving Bindings & Related Materials.* 1967. Am Lib Assn. 4to. 95p. VG/wrp. A4. $45.00

HORWITZ, Julius. *Inhabitants.* 1960. Cleveland. 1st ed. F/F. A17. $9.50

HORWOOD, William. *Duction Wood.* 1980. McGraw Hill. 1st Am ed. VG/VG. M21. $25.00

HOSKINS, Halford Lancaster. *Modern Egypt.* 1932. Open Court. 1st ed. 8vo. ils. VG/stiff wrp. W1. $8.00

HOSMER, George L. *Practical Astronomy: A TB for Engineering Schools...* 1963 (1910). NY. Wiley. 4th ed/8th prt. ils. 355p. G. K5. $20.00

HOSMER, Margaret. *Ten Years of a Lifetime.* 1866. M Doolady. 1st ed. 422p. gilt gr cloth. G. S11. $20.00

HOSOE, Eikoh. *Aperture 79.* 1977. Millerton. Aperture. 1st ed. NF/wrp. S9. $25.00

HOSSENT, Harry. *Movie Treasury: Gangster Movies.* 1974. Octopus. VG/VG. P3. $18.00

HOSTETTER, D. *Hostetter's United States Almanac.* 1861. Pittsburgh. Singerly. 36p. wrp. $25.00

HOTCHKISS, Bill. *Medicine Calf.* 1981. Norton. 1st ed. M/dj. A18. $25.00

HOTTES, Alfred C. *Climbers & Ground Covers.* 1947. NY. photos/drawings. VG. B26. $22.50

HOU-TEIN, Cheng. *Chinese New Year.* ca 1976. Holt. 4th prt. unp. F/F. B10. $10.00

HOUGH, Clara. *Leif the Lucky.* 1926. Century. 1st ed. VG. M2. $15.00

HOUGH, Emerson. *Firefly's Light.* 1916. Trow. 1st ed. 23p. VG. S11. $35.00

HOUGH, Emerson. *Law of the Land.* 1904. Bobbs Merrill. 1st ed. ils Arthur I Keller. F. A18. $40.00

HOUGH, Emerson. *Mother of Gold.* 1924. Appleton. 1st ed. VG. A18. $30.00

HOUGH, Emerson. *Sagebrusher.* 1919. Appleton. 1st ed. VG. A18. $30.00

HOUGH, Emerson. *Way to the West...Lives of...Boone, Crockett, Carson.* 1903. np. 1st ed. ils Frederick Remington. F. A18. $60.00

HOUGH, Emerson. *54-50 or Fight.* 1909. Bobbs Merrill. 1st ed. ils Arthur I Keller. F. A18. $50.00

HOUGH, Henry Beetle. *Martha's Vineyard.* 1970. NY. sq 4to. 96 p. VG/chip. A17. $15.00

HOUGH, Henry Beetle. *Martha's Vineyard.* 1970. NY. 1st ed. 96p. VG/dj. B18. $27.50

HOUGH, Richard. *Blind Horn's Hate.* 1971. Norton. 1st ed. 336p. xl. dj. F3. $10.00

HOUGH, Richard. *Fighting Ships.* 1969. Putnam. ils/pl. 304p. dj. T7. $35.00

HOUGH, Richard. *Wings of Victory.* 1980. Morrow. 1st ed. F/F. P3. $13.00

HOUGH, S.B. *Bronze Perseus.* 1962. Walker. VG/G. P3. $10.00

HOUGH, S.B. *Dear Daughter Dead.* 1966. Walker. 1st ed. G+/dj. P3. $10.00

HOUGH, S.B. *Fear Fortune, Father.* 1974. London. Gollancz. 1st ed. F/NF. S6. $25.00

HOUGHLAND, Mason. *Gone Away.* nd (1933). Berryville, VA. Bl Ridge. sm 4to. VG. O3. $65.00

HOUGHTON, Claude. *This Was Ivor Trent.* 1935. Heinemann. 1st ed. VG. P3. $12.00

HOUGHTON, Norris. *Moscow Rehearsals.* 1936. Harcourt Brace. 1st ed. inscr. 291p. G. H1. $8.50

HOULIHAN & HOULIHAN. *Lummis in the Pueblos.* 1986. Northland. 1st ed. ils. 155p. F/NF. B19. $100.00

HOURANI, A.H. *Syria & Lebanon: A Political Essay.* 1946. Oxford. 8vo. 402p. cloth. dj. O2. $20.00

HOUSE, E.H. *Japanese Episodes.* 1881. Boston. 1st ed. VG. scarce. A9. $60.00

HOUSE, Kay Seymour. *Cooper's Americans.* 1965. OH State. 1st ed. F/F. A18. $25.00

HOUSEHOLD, Geoffrey. *Arabesque.* 1948. Atlantic/Little Brn. 3rd ed. VG/G. P3. $15.00

HOUSEHOLD, Geoffrey. *Dance of the Dwarfs.* 1968. Atlantic/Little Brn. 1st ed. VG/VG. P3. $20.00

HOUSEHOLD, Geoffrey. *Sending.* 1980. Little Brn. 1st Am ed. F/F. T2. $45.00

HOUSEHOLD, Geoffrey. *Summon the Bright Water.* 1981. Atlantic/Little Brn. 1st ed. VG/VG. P3. $18.00

HOUSEHOLD, Geoffrey. *Thing To Love.* 1972. Wht Lion. VG/VG. P3. $15.00

HOUSEHOLD, Geoffrey. *Three Sentinels.* 1972. Little Brn. 1st ed. xl. dj. P3. $6.00

HOUSEHOLD, Geoffrey. *Watcher in the Shadows.* 1960. London. Michael Joseph. 1st ed. VG+/VG+. S6. $25.00

HOUSEMAN, A.E. *Shropshire Lad.* 1935. Heritage. 1st ed. gilt pigskin. F/case. B2. $100.00

HOUSTON, Andrew Jackson. *Texas Independence.* 1938. np. ltd ed. sgn. full leather. VG. M17. $50.00

HOUSTON, Edwin J. *Wonder Book of Magnetism.* 1908. Stokes. 1st ed. ils. 325p. F/G. H1. $8.50

HOUSTON, Gloria. *Year of Perfect Christmas Tree.* 1988. NY. Dial. 1st ed. ils Barbara Cooney. M/M. C8. $22.00

HOUSTON, Neal B. *Ross Santee.* 1968. Steck-Vaughn. 1st ed. 44p. NF/wrp. B19. $15.00

HOUSTON, Pam. *Cowboys Are My Weakness.* 1992. Norton. ARC. M/wrp. B4. $250.00

HOUSTON, Pam. *Cowboys Are My Weakness.* 1992. Norton. 1st ed/author's 1st book. F/F. A14/L3. $150.00

HOUSTON, Ralph. *White Jade.* 1950. Great Pyramid. ils Reeda Seldon. VG/G. B17. $5.00

HOUSTON, Robert. *Fourth Codex.* 1988. Houghton Mifflin. 1st ed. VG/VG. P3. $18.00

HOUSTON, Robert. *Nation Thief.* 1984. Pantheon. 1st ed. F/NF. B4. $45.00

HOUSTON, Robert. *Nation Thief.* 1984. Pantheon. 1st ed. inscr. F/F. A11. $50.00

HOUTS, M. *Where Death Delights.* 1967. NY. 317p. VG. D3. $15.00

HOVEYDA, Fereydoun. *Fall of the Shah.* 1980. NY. Wyndham. 1st ed. 221p. VG/dj. W1. $22.00

HOVING, Thomas. *Secular Spirit: Life & Art at the End of the Middle Ages.* 1975. Dutton. 1st ed. ils. 287p. F/dj. M10. $22.50

HOWARD, Alice Woodbury. *Ching-Li & the Dragons.* 1931. Jr Literary Guild. 1st ed. VG+. C8. $45.00

HOWARD, Clark. *Doomsday Squad.* 1970. Weybright Talley. 1st ed. VG/VG. P3. $15.00

HOWARD, Constance. *Design for Embroidery From Traditional English Sources.* 1956. np. VG/wrp. G2. $22.95

HOWARD, Constance. *Embroidery & Colour.* 1976. np. cloth. VG. G2. $15.00

HOWARD, Constance. *Textile Crafts.* 1978. np. cloth. VG. G2. $25.00

HOWARD, Edward. *Remarks on New Philosophy of Des-Cartes in Four Parts...* 1701 (1700). London. Ballard. later issue. contemporary calf. G1. $375.00

HOWARD, Harry N. *Turkey: The Straits & US Policy.* 1974. Baltimore. 8vo. 337p. cloth. O2. $25.00

HOWARD, Hartley. *Treble Cross.* 1975. Collins Crime Club. 1st ed. VG/VG. P3. $15.00

HOWARD, J. Woodford. *Mr Justice Murphy, a Political Biography.* 1968. Princeton. M11. $35.00

HOWARD, Joseph K. *Montana High, Wide & Handsome.* 1951. Yale. 1st ed. F/dj. B34. $60.00

HOWARD, Joseph K. *Montana Margins, a State Anthology.* 1946. Yale. VG. B34. $60.00

HOWARD, Lady Winefred. *Journal of a Tour in the US, Canada & Mexico.* 1897. London. Sampson Low. 35 pl/tissue guard. 355p. modern calf/marbled brd. F. P4. $225.00

HOWARD, Leslie Ruth. *Quite Remarkable Father.* 1959. NY. Harcourt Brace. 1st ed. 307p. VG+/VG. M7. $25.00

HOWARD, Robert E. *Alurmic.* 1975. Donald Grant. 1st ed. VG/VG. P3. $20.00

HOWARD, Robert E. *Black Colussus.* 1979. Donald Grant. 1st ed. F/F. M2. $30.00

HOWARD, Robert E. *Coming of Conan.* 1953. Gnome. 1st ed. F/NF. M2. $95.00

HOWARD, Robert E. *Conan the Barbarian.* 1954. NY. Gnome. 1st ed. 8vo. 224p. blk stp red coth. NF/dj. H5. $250.00

HOWARD, Robert E. *Conan the Conqueror.* 1950. Gnome. VG/VG. P3. $75.00

HOWARD, Robert E. *Hour of the Dragon.* 1977. Berkley Putnam. 1st ed. edit/sgn KE Wagner. F/F. F4. $35.00

HOWARD, Robert E. *Iron Man.* 1976. Donald Grant. 1st ed. VG/VG. P3. $25.00

HOWARD, Robert E. *Kull.* 1985. Donald Grant. 1st ed. F/F. P3. $25.00

HOWARD, Robert E. *Mayhem on Bear Creek.* 1979. Donald Grant. 1st ed. F/F. P3. $25.00

HOWARD, Robert E. *People of the Black Circle.* 1974. Donald Grant. 1st ed. NF/NF. P3. $40.00

HOWARD, Robert E. *People of the Black Circle.* 1977. Berkley Putnam. 1st ed. F/dj. F4. $25.00

HOWARD, Robert E. *Red Nails.* 1975. Donald Grant. 1st ed. F/F. M2. $45.00

HOWARD, Robert E. *Red Shadows.* 1968. Donald Grant. VG/G+. P3. $75.00

HOWARD, Robert E. *Skull-Face Omnibus.* 1974. Neville Spearman. NF/NF. P3. $35.00

HOWARD, Robert E. *Swords of Shahrazar.* 1976. Starmont. 1st ed. F/dj. M2. $25.00

HOWARD, Robert E. *Tigers of the Sea.* 1974. Donald Grant. 1st ed. F/F. M2/P3. $20.00

HOWARD, Robert E. *Vultures.* 1973. Fictioneer. 1st ed. F/F. P3. $35.00

HOWARD, Robert W. *Great Iron Trail...* 1962. Bonanza. VG/dj. B34. $30.00

HOWARD, Robert W. *This Is the West.* 1957. NAL. 1st prt. 12mo. 240p. VG. D3. $15.00

HOWARD & LUPOFF. *Return of Skull-Face.* 1977. FAX. 1st ed. F/F. P3. $25.00

HOWARD & SMITH. *Red Blades of Black Cathay.* 1971. Donald Grant. 1st ed. NF/NF. P3. $75.00

HOWARTH, David. *Desert King: Life of Ibn Saud.* 1964. London. Collins. 1st ed. gilt brn tweed cloth. VG+/VG+. M7. $45.00

HOWARTH, O.J.R. *London & Advancement of Science by Various Authors.* 1931. London. 1st ed. 321p. A13. $30.00

HOWAT, John K. *Hudson River & Its Painters.* 1972. NY. 1st ed. VG/VG+. A1. $30.00

HOWATSON, M.C. *Oxford Companion to Classical Literature.* 1989. Oxford. 2nd ed. F/F. P3. $45.00

HOWAY, Frederic W. *List of Trading Vessels in the Maritime Fur Trade 1785-1825.* 1972. Kingston. Limestone. 8vo. 208p. VG/bl wrp. P4. $65.00

HOWAY, Frederic W. *Voyages of the Columbia to the Northwest Coast 1787...1793.* 1941. MA Hist Soc. Updike/Merrymount. 518p. T7. $175.00

HOWBERT, Abraham R. *Reminiscences of the War.* 1884. Springfield, OH. 1st ed. 388p. cloth. VG. M8. $125.00

HOWE, Donald W. *Quabbin: The Lost Valley.* 1951. Ware, MA. ils. VG/VG. M17. $75.00

HOWE, E.W. *Plain People.* 1929. 317p. xl. O8. $18.50

HOWE, E.W. *Story of a Country Town.* 1883. Atchison. Howe. 1st issue (no name of binder on spine). VG. w/ephemera. Q1. $175.00

HOWE, Henry. *Historical Collections of Ohio.* 1848. Cincinnati. ils/map. 599p. G. E5. $125.00

HOWE, Henry. *Historical Collections of the Great West.* 1857. NY. 2 vol in 1. mc pl. 527p. very scarce. O8. $65.00

HOWE, Irving. *Sherwood Anderson.* 1951. Sloane. 1st prt. 271p. VG/worn. M20. $25.00

HOWE, James. *Celery Stalks at Midnight.* 1983. Atheneum. 1st ed. 111p. NF/dj. M20. $30.00

HOWE, Julia Ward. *Reminiscences 1819-1899.* 1899. Boston. 8vo. ils. 465p. cloth. O2. $75.00

HOWE, Samuel G. *Hist Sketch of the Greek Revolution.* 1828. NY. Wht Galleher. 1st ed. 8vo. contemporary calf. G. W1. $65.00

HOWELLS, W.D. *Between the Dark & Daylight.* 1907. Harper. 1st ed. 8vo. 185p. red cloth. M1. $150.00

HOWELLS, W.D. *Familiar Spanish Travels.* 1913. Harper. 1st ed. 8vo. 32 pl. VG. W1. $15.00

HOWELLS, W.D. *Hazard of New Fortunes.* 1890. NY. Harper. 2 vol. 1st ed thus. inscr/dtd Feb 1890. red cloth. VG. C6. $400.00

HOWELLS, W.D. *Kentons.* 1902. Harper. 1st ed. 317p. VG. M20. $25.00

HOWELLS, W.D. *Leatherwood God.* 1916. Century. 1st ed. ils. VG/pc missing. A17. $45.00

HOWELLS, W.D. *New Leaf Mills.* 1913. Harper. inscr. 154p. cloth. VG. A10. $45.00

HOWELLS, W.D. *Poems.* 1886. Boston. 1st ed. pub vellum. VG. scarce. A9. $50.00

HOWELLS, W.D. *Register.* 1899. Houghton Mifflin. later prt. 16mo. 91p. decor dk gr cloth. F. C6. $85.00

HOWELLS, W.D. *Rise of Silas Lapham.* 1951. Modern Lib. 1st ed. VG/VG. P3. $10.00

HOWELLS, W.D. *Shadow of a Dream.* 1890. Harper. 1st Am ed. 8vo. 218p. VG. C6. $150.00

HOWELLS, W.D. *Undiscovered Country.* 1880. Houghton Mifflin. 1st ed. sgn. 1st state bdg (letters on front). NF. Q1. $200.00

HOWELLS, W.D. *Venetian Life.* 1907. Cambridge. 2 vol. Autograph ed. 1/550. ils/sgn EH Garrett. F/case. C6. $450.00

HOWES, Barbara. *From the Green Antilles.* 1966. NY. 1st ed. sgn. F/VG+. A11. $80.00

HOWES, Royce. *Murder at Maneuvers.* 1938. Crime Club. 1st ed. VG. P3. $17.00

HOWORTH, Henry H. *Golden Days of Early English Church...* 1917. Dutton. 3 vol. ils/index. H10. $125.00

HOY, Ken. *Land, Life & Nature Pop-Up.* 1990. Ideals. 1st ed. ils Mike Peterkin. F. B17. $11.00

HOYLE, Fred. *Black Cloud.* nd. BC. VG/VG. P3. $8.00

HOYLE, Fred. *Element 79.* 1967. NAL. 1st ed. VG/G. P3. $20.00

HOYLE, Fred. *Galaxies, Nuclei & Quasars.* 1965. Harper. 8vo. 160p. G/G. K5. $20.00

HOYLE, Fred. *Man in the Universe.* 1966. Columbia. 8vo. 81p. VG/G. K5. $14.00

HOYLE, Fred. *Nicolaus Coperniucs, Essay on His Life & Work.* 1973. Heinemann. 8vo. ils. 84p. VG/dj. K5. $25.00

HOYLE, Fred. *Some Recent Researches in Solar Physics.* 1949. Cambridge. 8vo. ils. 134p. red cloth. G. K5. $40.00

HOYLE, Trevor. *Last Gasp.* 1983. Crown. 1st ed. VG/VG. P3. $18.00

HOYLE & HOYLE. *Molecule Men.* nd. BC. NF/NF. P3. $8.00

HOYLE & WICKRAMASINGHE. *Space Travellers: Bringers of Life.* 1981. Cardiff, Wales. 8vo. 197p. VG/VG. K5. $19.00

HOYT, E.P. *Gentleman of Broadway.* 1964. Little Brn. 1st ed. VG/VG. S11. $10.00

HOYT, E.P. *Horatio's Boys. Life & Works of Horatio Alger Jr.* 1974. Chilton. 1st ed. ils. 263p. VG/VG. S11. $12.00

HOYT, Edwin J. *Bucksin Joe.* 1966. NE U. edit Glenn Shirley. 185p. VG+/dj. M20. $45.00

HOYT, Richard. *Head of State.* 1985. Tor. 1st ed. F/F. P3. $15.00

HOYT, Richard. *Trotsky's Run.* 1982. NY. Morrow. 1st ed. F/F. S6. $30.00

HSU, Leonard Shihlien. *Political Philosophy of Confucianism...* 1975. London. Curzon. rpt 1932 ed. brn cloth. F/F. G1. $25.00

HUANG & LYNCH. *Thinking Body, Dancing Mind.* 1992. Bantam. 1st ed. VG/dj. N2. $5.00

HUBBARD, Bernard R. *Mush, You Malemutes!* 1932. NY. Am Pr. 1st ed. 81 pl/2 maps. map ep. 97p. VG. P4. $30.00

HUBBARD, Elbert. *Elbert Hubbard's Scrapbook.* 1928 (1923). Roycroft. 228p. VG. H1. $18.00

HUBBARD, L. Ron. *Alien Affair.* 1986. Bridge. 1st ed. F/F. P3. $25.00

HUBBARD, L. Ron. *Battlefield Earth...* 1982. St Martin. 1st ed. F/F. N3. $30.00

HUBBARD, L. Ron. *Black Genesis.* 1986. Bridge. 1st ed. F/F. P3. $25.00

HUBBARD, L. Ron. *Buckskin Brigades.* 1977. Theta. 1st ed thus. F/dj. M2. $50.00

HUBBARD, L. Ron. *Buckskin Brigades.* 1987. Jameson Books. 1st ed. F/F. P3. $20.00

HUBBARD, L. Ron. *Child Dianetics.* 1982. Bridge. VG. P3. $15.00

HUBBARD, L. Ron. *Dianetics.* 1950. NY. 1st ed. VG/VG. B5. $250.00

HUBBARD, L. Ron. *Disaster.* 1987. Bridge. 1st ed. F/F. P3. $25.00

HUBBARD, L. Ron. *Doomed Planet.* 1987. Bridge. 1st ed. F/F. P3. $25.00

HUBBARD, L. Ron. *Enemy Within.* 1986. Bridge. 1st ed. F/F. P3. $25.00

HUBBARD, L. Ron. *Final Blackout.* 1975. Garland. F. P3. $60.00

HUBBARD, L. Ron. *Fortune of Fear.* 1986. Bridge. 1st ed. F/F. P3. $25.00

HUBBARD, L. Ron. *From Death to the Stars.* 1948. Fantasy. 1st ed. VG/worn. M2. $400.00

HUBBARD, L. Ron. *Hymns of Asia: An Eastern Poem.* 1974. Church Scientology of CA. 1st ed. gilt emb cloth. F/sans. N3. $35.00

HUBBARD, L. Ron. *Problems of Work.* 1983. Bridge. VG. P3. $15.00

HUBBARD, L. Ron. *Slaves of Sleep.* 1948. Chicago. 1st ed. NF/dj. A15. $200.00

HUBBARD, L. Ron. *Typewriter in the Sky/Fear.* 1951. Gnome. 1st ed. NF/dj. M2. $275.00

HUBBARD, L. Ron. *Typewriter in the Sky/Fear.* 1951. Gnome. 1st ed. VG/VG. P3. $250.00

HUBBARD, L. Ron. *Villainy Victorious.* 1987. Bridge. 1st ed. F/F. P3. $25.00

HUBBARD, L. Ron. *Voyage of Vengeance.* 1987. Bridge. 1st ed. F/F. P3. $25.00

HUBBARD, Margaret Ann. *Murder at St Denis.* 1952. Bruce. 1st ed. VG/VG. P3. $20.00

HUBBARD, Margaret Ann. *Step Softly on My Grave.* 1966. Bruce. 1st ed. NF/NF. P3. $18.00

HUBBELL, Alvin. *Development of Ophthalmology in America, 1800-1870.* 1908. Chicago. 1st ed. 197p. xl. A13. $175.00

HUBERT, Margaret. *One-Piece Knits That Fit.* 1978. np. cloth. VG. G2. $15.95

HUBERT, Renee Riese. *Surrealism & the Book.* 1988. CA U. 1st ed. 8vo. 358p. blk stp ochre cloth. F/dj. F1. $50.00

HUBIN, Allen J. *Bibliography of Crime Fiction 1749-1975.* 1979. Pub Inc. F. P3. $75.00

HUBIN, Allen J. *Crime Fiction 1749-1980.* 1980. Garland. F. B2. $45.00

HUC, Abbe. *High Road in Tartary.* 1948. NY. 1st ed thus. 219p. G+/dj. B18. $15.00

HUCK, Virginia. *Brand of the Tartan.* 1955. Appleton Century. G+. N2. $6.50

HUDGENS, Betty L. *Kurt Vonnegut Jr: A Checklist.* 1972. Gale/Bruccoli Clark. 1st ed. F/sans. scarce. B2. $45.00

HUDSON, Jan; see Smith, George.

HUDSON, Tom. *West Is My Home.* 1956. Laguna House. ltd ed. ils Ralph Love. 12mo. 221p. F/fair. A8. $35.00

HUDSON, W.H. *Birds in London.* 1898. Longman Gr. 1st ed. ils. teg. gilt gr cloth. VG. Q1. $175.00

HUDSON, W.H. *Far Away & Long Ago.* 1918. London. 1st ed. VG. A9. $35.00

HUDSON, W.H. *Green Mansions.* nd. Books Inc. early rpt. VG. M21. $10.00

HUDSON, W.H. *Green Mansions.* 1904. London. 1st ed/2nd issue. NF. C2. $125.00

HUDSON, W.H. *Purple Land.* 1921. Dutton. 355p. gilt purple cloth. VG/dj. F3. $15.00

HUDSON & REED. *Stratosphere: Present & Future.* 1979. NASA 1049. 4to. ils. 432p. wrp. K5. $20.00

HUEBNER, Rudolf. *Hist of Germanic Private Law.* 1918. Boston. 1st ed. trans from German. 785p. NF. D3. $75.00

HUESTON, Ethel. *Prudence Says So.* ca 1916. Bobbs Merrill. ils Arthur William Brown. G. B10. $15.00

HUEY, F.B. Jr. *Yesterday's Prophets for Today's World.* 1980. Broadman. 174p. F/F. B29. $4.00

HUGGETT, Frank. *Carriages at Eight.* 1980. NY. Scribner. 1st Am ed. 4to. VG/VG. O3. $45.00

HUGGINS, M.A. *History of North Carolina Baptists 1727-1932.* 1967. Raleigh, NC. General Brd Baptist State Convention. 454p. VG/VG. B11. $50.00

HUGHART, Barry. *Story of the Stone.* 1988. Doubleday. 1st ed. F/dj. M2. $18.00

HUGHES, Charles Evans. *Conditions of Progress in Democratic Government.* 1910. Yale. 1st ed. 122p. navy cloth. xl. NF. D3. $75.00

HUGHES, Colin; see Creasey, John.

HUGHES, Dorothy B. *Blackbirder.* 1943. DSP. 1st ed. VG. P3. $15.00

HUGHES, H. Stuart. *Hist As Art & As Science: Twin Vistas on the Past.* 1964. Harper. 12mo. VG/dj. G1. $22.50

HUGHES, James. *Ends.* 1971. Knopf. 1st ed. F/NF. N3. $10.00

HUGHES, Ken. *High Wray.* 1952. John Gifford. 1st ed. VG/VG. P3. $20.00

HUGHES, Langston. *Ask Your Mama.* 1961. Knopf. 1st ed. obl 8vo. 92p. cream cloth. NF/VG clip. H5. $100.00

HUGHES, Langston. *Jim Crow's Last Stand.* 1943. NY. Negro Pub Soc of Am. 8vo. 30p. F/prt wrp. H5. $350.00

HUGHES, Langston. *Langston Hughes Reader.* 1958. Braziller. 1st ed. 8vo. 501p. F/NF. C6. $75.00

HUGHES, Langston. *Shakespeare in Harlem.* 1942. Knopf. 1st ed. 8vo. 124p. blk/orange cloth. F/NF. C6. $300.00

HUGHES, Langston. *Simple's Uncle Sam.* 1965. Hill Wang. 1st ed. 8vo. 180p. yel cloth. F/NF. C6. $100.00

HUGHES, Langston. *Simple Speaks His Mind.* 1950. Simon Schuster. 1st ed. 8vo. 231p. F/NF. C6. $200.00

HUGHES, Langston. *Songs to the Dark Virgin.* 1941. NY. G Shirmer. 1st ed. inscr. VG/wrp. C6. $1,100.00

HUGHES, Langston. *Weary Blues.* 1945. Knopf. 10th prt/author's 1st book. sgn. 109p. F. C6. $250.00

HUGHES, Monica. *Guardian of Isis.* 1981. Hamish Hamilton. 1st ed. sgn. F/F. P3. $25.00

HUGHES, R. *Complete Detective Life...Cases of Raymond Schindler...* 1950. NY. inscr Schindler. 319p. VG. D3. $15.00

HUGHES, Robert. *Barcelona.* 1992. Knopf. 1st ed/3rd prt. 575p. VG/dj. W1. $25.00

HUGHES, Robert. *Fatal Shore.* 1987. NY. Knopf. 4th prt. 688p. gray cloth. M/dj. P4. $24.95

HUGHES, Rupert. *She Goes to War.* nd. Grosset Dunlap. photoplay ed. VG. P3. $20.00

HUGHES, Ted. *Hawk in the Rain.* 1957. London. Faber. 1st ed. NF/dj. Q1. $200.00

HUGHES, Ted. *River, New Poems.* 1984. Harper Row. ARC. w/photo. F/F. B3. $25.00

HUGHES, Therle. *Prints for the Collector. British Prints From 1500-1900.* 1971. Praeger. 8vo. ils. 216p. F/VG. F1. $30.00

HUGHES, Thomas. *Memoir of a Brother.* 1873. Boston. Osgood. VG. H1. $20.00

HUGHES, Thomas. *Tom Brown's School Days.* nd. Grosset. VG. B34. $10.00

HUGO, Hermannus. *De Militia Equestri Antiqua et Nova...Libri Quinque.* 1630. Antwerp. ils/pl/engravings. vellum. F. B30. $500.00

HUGO, Richard. *Death & the Good Life.* 1981. St Martin. 1st ed. rem mk. F/NF clip. L3. $85.00

HUGO, Victor. *Hunchback of Notre Dame.* nd. AL Burt. photoplay ed. VG. P3. $30.00

HUGO, Victor. *Notre-Dame de Paris.* 1888. Estes Lauriat. trans AL Alger. 431p. teg. bl cloth. VG. S11. $15.00

HUGO, Victor. *Notre-Dame de Paris.* 1928. NY. Ives Washburn. 583p. teg. VG/worn case. B18. $45.00

HUGO, Victor. *Notre-Dame de Paris.* 1930. Paris. LEC. 2 vol. 1/1500. ils/sgn Masereel. VG+/cb fld box. S9. $125.00

HUGO, Victor. *Notre-Dame de Paris.* 1955. LEC. ils/sgn Bernard LaMotte. F/case. M19. $50.00

HUGO. *Bewick Collector: Descriptive Catalog of Works...* 1968. np. rpt of 1866 ed. VG. A4. $55.00

HUIE & METZL. *Seabee Road to Victory.* 1944. Dutton. sgn Metzl. 1/400. sbdg. F. B2. $200.00

HUIZINGA, Johan. *Homo Ludens: Study of Play Element in Culture...* 1939. Pantheon Akademische. 1st German-language ed. NF/buff wrp/glassine wrp. G1. $100.00

HULBERT, Archer Butler. *Forty Niners.* 1931. Little Brn. 1st ed. 8vo. F/F. B11. $45.00

HULBERT, Homer B. *Face in the Mist.* ca 1926. Milton Bradley. ils Henry Hintermeister. 245p. VG. B10. $12.00

HULL, Richard. *Murder Isn't Easy.* 1936. Putnam. 1st Am ed. F/NF. M15. $100.00

HULL, Robert Charlton. *Search for Adele Parker.* 1974. Libra. 188p. VG/dj. M20. $20.00

HULL, William I. *William Penn & the Dutch Quaker Migration to Pennsylvania.* 1970. Baltimore. Genealogical Pub. rpt. 8vo. 445p. VG. V3. $30.00

HULME, Keri. *Bone People.* 1983. Spiral/Hodder Stoughton. 1st ed. F/F. B4. $200.00

HULSE, Olive M. *Salads: Two Hundred Recipes for Making Salads...* 1910. Chicago. Hopewell. 94p. F. H1. $6.00

HULSTED, Helen. *Timothy Taylor: Ambassador of Goodwill.* ca 1941. Coward McCann. 3rd imp. inscr pres. unp. VG. B10. $15.00

HUME, David. *Baron David Hume's Lectures 1786-1822. Vol 1.* 1939. Edinburgh. Stair Soc. sm 4to. 390p. buckram. VG. D3. $25.00

HUME, David. *Essays & Treatises on Several Subjects.* 1784 (1753). London. Cadell Donaldson Creech. 2 vols. 2nd ed. Gl. $275.00

HUME, David. *You'll Catch Your Death.* 1940. Collins. 1st ed. VG/G+. P3. $35.00

HUME, Fergus. *Tales of Fairyland: Chronicles of Fairyland.* 1911. Lippincott. 8vo. red cloth. VG. D6. $45.00

HUME, H. *Hollies.* 1953. NY. 1st ed. VG. C11. $40.00

HUMMELCHEN & ROHWER. *Chronology of the War at Sea 1939-1945.* 1972. NY. Arco. 2 vol. revised ed. 150 photos. T7. $60.00

HUMPHREY, George M. *Old Age, the Results of Information...* 1889. Macmillan. 216p. w/3 orig photos. VG. B14. $100.00

HUMPHREY, Laurence. *Joannis Juelli Angeli.* 1573. London. Day. 369p. rebound. xl. H10. $250.00

HUMPHREY, Maude. *Bride's Book.* 1900. NY. 1st ed. ils. VG. B5. $175.00

HUMPHREY, Robert R. *Boojum & Its Home.* 1974. Tucson. ils/tables/maps. 214p. bl buckram. F. B26. $24.00

HUMPHREY, Robert R. *90 Years & 535 Miles: Vegetation Changes...Mexican Border.* 1987. NM U. 1st ed. ils/index. 448p. F/dj. B19. $50.00

HUMPHREY, William. *Collected Stories.* 1985. Delacorte. 1st ed. rem mk. F/F. B4. $45.00

HUMPHREYS, Robin A. *Evolution of Modern Latin America.* 1973. NY. Cooper Sq Pub. 8vo. index/maps. gr cloth. VG. P4. $17.50

HUMPHRYES, Charles. *Field, Camp, Hospital & Prison.* 1918. Boston. 428p. scarce. O8. $32.50

HUNEKER, James Gibbons. *Steeplejack.* 1922. NY. ils/index. gilt cloth. VG. A17. $10.00

HUNGERFORD, Edward. *Transport for War.* 1943. Dutton. 1st ed. 272p. cloth. VG/ragged. M20. $20.00

HUNKEN, J. *Botany for All Ages.* 1989. Chester, CT. 126 activities/experiments. sc. M. B26. $12.95

HUNNEWELL, J.F. *Historical Monuments of France.* 1884. Boston. 1st ed. cloth. VG. C11. $45.00

HUNNISETT, Basil. *Illustrated Dictionary of British Steel Engravers.* 1989. London. 2nd ed. 190p. dj. A13. $90.00

HUNT, Aurora. *Kirby Benedict, Frontier Federal Judge...1853-1874.* 1961. Glendale. Arthur H Clark. M11. $35.00

HUNT, Charles Havens. *Life of Edward Livingston.* 1864. NY. Appleton. gr cloth. M11. $175.00

HUNT, David. *Cities Cactaceae Checklist.* 1992. Kew. 190p. sc. NF. B26. $17.50

HUNT, Edwin S. *Safari.* 1955. Evanston. Men's Club Covenant Methodist Church. 186p. NF/dj. W1. $8.00

HUNT, Howard. *Murder in State.* 1990. St Martin. 1st ed. VG/VG. P3. $15.00

HUNT, J. *Personality & Behavior Disorders.* 1944. Ronald. 2 vol. reading copy. K4. $30.00

HUNT, Kyle; see Creasey, John.

HUNT, Leigh. *Captain Sword & Captain Pen.* 1835. London. Knight. 1st ed. sm 8vo. 112p. gr cloth. K1. $100.00

HUNT, Linda. *Secret Agenda: US Government, Nazi Scientists...* 1991. St Martin. 1st prt. 8vo. 340p. VG/dj. K5. $30.00

HUNT, Mabel Leigh. *Johnny-Up & Johnny-Down.* 1962. Lippincott. Weekly Reader BC/1st ed thus. 8vo. 94p. G. V3. $8.50

HUNT, Mabel Leigh. *Matilda's Buttons.* 1948. Lippincott. 1st ed. ils Elinore Blaisdell. VG. M5. $12.00

HUNT, Mabel Leigh. *Peddlar's Clock.* 1943. NY. Story Parade Picture Book. ils EO Jones. F/G. M5. $16.00

HUNT, Marsha. *Joy.* 1991. Dutton. AP. NF/wrp. B2. $35.00

HUNT, Violet. *Tiger Skin.* 1924. Heinemann. 1st ed. VG. P3. $30.00

HUNT & KNOWLES. *Cloud's Hill: Dorset.* 1992. Dorset. private prt. 1/1000. ils/photos/facsimile letters. ES. M. M7. $35.00

HUNTER, Alan. *Death of the Broadlands.* 1984. Walker. 1st ed. F/F. P3. $15.00

HUNTER, Alan. *Landed Gently.* 1957. CAssell. 1st ed. VG/torn. P3. $20.00

HUNTER, Archibald M. *Message of the New Testament.* 1954. Westminster. 122p. VG/torn. B29. $3.50

HUNTER, Dard. *Making of Books.* 1987. Chillocothe. Mtn House. 4 vol. 48x33mm. 1/50. F/morocco case. B24. $500.00

HUNTER, Dard. *My Life With Paper.* 1958. Knopf. 1st ed. 237p. F/dj. B24. $175.00

HUNTER, Dard. *Paper-Making in the Classroom.* 1931. Peoria. Manual Arts. 1st ed. inscr. ils. tan cloth. NF. B24. $250.00

HUNTER, Dard. *Papermaking in Pioneer America.* 1981. Garland. rpt of 1952 ed. ils. 178p. brn cloth. F. B24. $40.00

HUNTER, Dard. *Papermaking in Pioneer America.* 1981. NY. Garland. 181p. VG. A10. $25.00

HUNTER, Dard. *Papermaking: History & Technique of an Ancient Craft.* 1947. Knopf. 2nd ed. 8vo. ils/fld map. 611p. F. B24. $175.00

HUNTER, Evan. *Beauty & the Beast.* 1983. HRW. 1st ed. sgn. F/F. O4. $30.00

HUNTER, Evan. *Beauty & the Beast.* 1983. HRW. 1st ed. VG/VG. P3. $15.00

HUNTER, Evan. *Bread.* 1974. Random. 1st ed. F/F. F4. $30.00

HUNTER, Evan. *Calypso.* 1979. Viking. 1st ed. sgn. VG/VG. O4. $20.00

HUNTER, Evan. *Chisholms.* 1976. Harper Row. 1st ed. F/F. P3. $25.00

HUNTER, Evan. *Cinderella.* 1986. HRW. 1st ed. VG/VG. P3. $20.00

HUNTER, Evan. *Every Little Crook & Nanny.* 1972. Doubleday. 1st ed. NF/dj. F4. $20.00

HUNTER, Evan. *Evil Sleep!* 1952. NY. 1st ed/PBO/author's 1st adult fiction. sgn. F. rare. A11. $175.00

HUNTER, Evan. *Find the Feathered Serpent.* 1952. Phil. Winston. 1st ed/author's 1st book. F/NF. B4. $100.00

HUNTER, Evan. *Ghosts.* 1980. Viking. 1st ed. F/F. M15. $25.00

HUNTER, Evan. *Heat.* 1981. Viking. 1st ed. inscr. F/F. S6. $40.00

HUNTER, Evan. *Horse's Head.* 1967. Delacorte. 1st ed. F/dj. F4. $28.00

HUNTER, Evan. *House That Jack Built.* 1988. Holt. 1st ed. F/F. F4. $20.00

HUNTER, Evan. *Jack & the Bean-Stalk.* 1984. HRW. 1st ed. NF/F. B3. $20.00

HUNTER, Evan. *Kiss.* 1992. Morrow. 1st ed. sgn. F/F. O4. $30.00

HUNTER, Evan. *Lizzie.* 1984. Arbor. 1st ed. F/NF. F4. $20.00

HUNTER, Evan. *Love, Dad.* 1981. Crown. 1st ed. VG/VG. P3. $20.00

HUNTER, Evan. *Lullaby.* 1989. Morrow. 1st ed. F/dj. F4. $18.00

HUNTER, Evan. *McBain Brief.* 1982. Arbor. 1st ed. sgn. F/F. O4. $20.00

HUNTER, Evan. *McBain's Ladies.* 1988. Mysterious. 1st ed. F/dj. F4. $18.00

HUNTER, Evan. *Mugger.* 1956. Permabooks. early PBO. sgn. VG/wrp. B4. $50.00

HUNTER, Evan. *Nobody Knew They Were There.* 1971. Doubleday. 1st ed. VG/G. P3. $23.00

HUNTER, Evan. *Poison.* 1987. Arbor. 1st ed. F/F. F4. $20.00

HUNTER, Evan. *Sadie When She Died.* 1972. Doubleday. 1st ed. VG/VG. P3. $35.00

HUNTER, Evan. *Second Ending.* 1956. Simon Schuster. 1st ed. NF/NF. P3. $75.00

HUNTER, Evan. *So Long As You Both Shall Live.* 1976. Random. 1st ed. sgn. rem mk. VG/VG. O4. $30.00

HUNTER, Evan. *Trick.* 1987. Arbor. 1st ed. F/F. F4. $20.00

HUNTER, Evan. *Widows.* 1991. Morrow. 1st ed. F/clip. F4. $17.00

HUNTER, George Leland. *Tapestries: Their Origin, History & Renaissance.* 1913. np. ltd ed. inscr. ils. VG/G case. M17. $50.00

HUNTER, Henry C. *How Eng Got Its Merchant Marine 1066-1776.* 1935. Nat Council Am Shipbuilders. 369p. VG/dj. M20. $35.00

HUNTER, J.A. *Hunter's Tracks.* 1957. Appleton Century. 1st ed. 240p. F/VG. H1. $48.00

HUNTER, J.A. *Tales of African Frontier.* 1954. NY. 1st ed. VG/VG. B5. $35.00

HUNTER, P. Hay. *James Inwick, Ploughman & Elder.* 1896. NY. 1st ed. glossary. gilt cloth. VG. A17. $10.00

HUNTER, Sam. *George Segal.* 1984. NY. Rizzolio. VG/VG. A1. $40.00

HUNTER, William S. *Hunter's Eastern Townships Scenery, Canada East.* 1860. Montreal. John Lovell. 1st ed. lg 4to. 36p. cloth. M1. $1,750.00

HUNTIN, Serge. *History of Alchemy.* 1962. Walker Sun. brd. F. P3. $18.00

HUNTING, Gardner. *Vicarion.* 1927. Unity. VG. P3. $8.00

HUNTING, William. *Art of Horse-Shoeing: A Manual for Farriers & Veterinarians.* 1920. Chicago. Am Verterinary Pub. later prt. VG. O3. $35.00

HUNTLEY, Chet. *Generous Years, Remembraces of a Frontier Boyhood.* 1968. Random. 1st ed. F/dj. B34. $30.00

HURD, Clement. *Goodnight Noon Room, a Pop-Up Book.* 1984. Harper Collins. rpt. 12mo. F/sans. B17. $10.00

HURD, Edith Thacher. *Day the Sun Danced.* ca 1965. Harper Row. ils Clement Hurd. unp. VG. B10. $12.00

HURLEY, Vic. *Arrows Against Steel.* 1975. NY. 1st ed. VG/G. B5. $25.00

HURLIMANN, Bettina. *Three Centuries of Children's Books in Europe.* 1968. Cleveland. World. 1st Am ed. lg 8vo. 297p. NF/NF. D6. $35.00

HURLIMANN, Martin. *Frankreich Landschaft Und Baukunst.* 1931. Berlin-Zurich. 1st ed. 304 full-p photos. gilt cloth. VG. A17. $35.00

HURRELL, F.G. *John Lillibud.* 1935. Kendall Sharp. 1st ed. VG. P3. $10.00

HURST, Mark. *Golden Man.* 1980. Berkley. SF BC. 1st hc ed. F/F. T2. $12.00

HURST, Willard. *Law in the US.* 1960. Phil. Am Philosophical Soc. rpt. 9p. M11. $35.00

HURSTON, Zora Neale. *Man of the Mountain.* 1939. Lippincott. 1st ed. 8vo. 351p. VG/VG. H5. $750.00

HURWITZ, Johanna. *Baseball Fever.* 1981. Morrow. 1st ed. xl. G+/G+. P8. $6.00

HUSAIN, Muhammad Ashraf. *Guide to Fatepur Sikri.* 1937. Delhi. 1st ed. 77p. G. W1. $12.00

HUSEN, Torsten. *Talent, Opportunity & Career.* 1969. Stockholm. 270p. F/dj. K4. $15.00

HUSSEY, C. *Tait McKenzie, Sculptor of Youth.* 1930. Phil. 1st ed. VG/G. B5. $45.00

HUSSEY, N.W. *Pests of Protected Cultivation.* 1969. NY. 1st Am ed. ils/photos. 404p. VG/dj. B26. $35.00

HUTCHENS, John K. *One Man's Montana.* 1964. Lippincott. 3rd prt. F/dj. B34. $30.00

HUTCHINGS, Margaret. *Toys From Alice in Wonderland.* 1979. London. Mills Boon. 1st ed. sm 4to. F/F. C8. $40.00

HUTCHINGS & WAUD. *Papillon Butterfly Dog.* 1985. Great Britain. 1st ed. ils. 300p. cloth. M/dj. R2. $60.00

HUTCHINS, Jere C. *Jere C Hutchins: A Personal Story.* 1938. Detroit. private prt. sgn. ils. 372p. G/G. B11. $45.00

HUTCHINSON, A.S.M. *Book of Simon.* 1930. Little Brn. 1st ed. F/worn. M5. $40.00

HUTCHINSON, Frederick Wintrop. *Men Who Found America.* ca 1909. Barse Hopkins. later prt. 158p. fair. B10. $12.00

HUTCHINSON, H.G. *Golf.* 1895. London. new ed. cloth. VG. C11. $185.00

HUTCHINSON, W.F. *Under the Southern Cross.* 1891. Providence. ils. 231p. gilt red cloth. VG. B14. $30.00

HUTCHINSON, W.H. *California: Two Centuries of Man, Land, & Growth...* 1969. Am W Pub. 1st ed. ils John Barr Tompkins. F/dj. A18. $20.00

HUTCHINSON, W.H. *Gene Autry & the Big Valley Grab.* 1952. Whitman. VG. P3. $10.00

HUTCHINSON, W.H. *Gene Autry & the Golden Ladder Gang.* 1950. Whitman. Authorized ed. F. A18. $25.00

HUTCHINSON, W.H. *Gene Autry & the Golden Ladder Gang.* 1950. Whitman. VG. P3. $18.00

HUTCHINSON, W.H. *Notebook of the Old West.* 1947. Bob Hurst. 1st ed. sc. VG. A18. $50.00

HUTCHINSON, W.M.L. *Golden Porch.* 1925. Longmans. 1st ed thus. ils DS Walker. VG. M5. $40.00

HUTCHINSON, W.T. *Cyrus Hall McCormick Harvest 1856-1884.* 1935. NY. 1st ed. ils. VG/VG. B5. $45.00

HUTCHINSON & PICARD. *Horrors: A History of Horror Movies.* 1983. Royce. VG/VG. P3. $20.00

HUTTER, Heribert. *Medieval Stained Glass.* 1964. Crown. ils. 30p. VG/dj. M10. $4.50

HUTTON, Clarke. *Country ABC.* ca 1940. NY. Oxford. 4to. 52p. cloth. VG. A17. $30.00

HUTTON, Clarke. *Picture Hist of Britain.* 1946. Houghton Mifflin. 1st Am ed. 62p. G. B10. $12.00

HUTTON, Clarke. *Picture Hist of Great Discoveries.* 1945. Oxford. 1st ed. pict brd. F/dj. M5. $25.00

HUTTON & ROONEY. *Story of the Stars & Stripes.* 1946. NY. 1st ed. 240p. VG/VG. A17. $9.50

HUXLEY, Aldous. *After Many a Summer Dies the Swan.* 1953. Vanguard. G+. P3. $10.00

HUXLEY, Aldous. *Beyond the Mexique Bay.* 1934. Chatto Windus. ltd ed. sgn. 1/210. 30 pl. 319p. teg. NF/case. H5. $400.00

HUXLEY, Aldous. *Brave New World Revisited.* 1958. Harper. 1st Am ed. F/NF. B4. $75.00

HUXLEY, Aldous. *Brave New World Revisited.* 1958. Harper. 1st ed. VG/G. S11. $10.00

HUXLEY, Aldous. *Brave New World Revisited.* 1959. Chatto Windus. 2nd ed. VG. P3. $25.00

HUXLEY, Aldous. *Brave New World.* 1932. Chatto Windus. 1st trade ed. 8vo. 306p. bl cloth. VG/dj. C6. $500.00

HUXLEY, Aldous. *Brave New World.* 1932. Chatto Windus. 1st ed. 8vo. 306p. gilt bl cloth. G/dj/cloth clamshell case. H5. $650.00

HUXLEY, Aldous. *Brave New World.* 1932. Doubleday Doran. 1st Am ed. sgn. 1/250. NF/sans. B4. $950.00

HUXLEY, Aldous. *Brief Candles. Stories.* 1930. London. Chatto Windus. 1st ed. 324p. gilt red cloth. prt dj. K1. $50.00

HUXLEY, Aldous. *Crows of Pearblossom.* 1967. Random. BC. 8vo. VG. B17. $5.00

HUXLEY, Aldous. *Defeat of Youth & Other Poems.* 1918. Oxford. Blackwell. 1st ed. inscr/dtd 1945. 8vo. 48p. NF/morocco case. H5. $450.00

HUXLEY, Aldous. *Essays New & Old.* 1927. Doran. 1st Am ed. pub sample copy. NF. B4. $75.00

HUXLEY, Aldous. *Eyeless in Gaza.* (1936). Harper. 7th ed. VG. P3. $15.00

HUXLEY, Aldous. *Island.* 1962. Chatto Windus. 1st ed. NF/dj. Q1. $100.00

HUXLEY, Aldous. *Olive Tree & Other Essays.* 1936. Chatto Windus. 1st ed. sgn. 1/160. 303p. gilt gr cloth. VG/case. H5. $400.00

HUXLEY, Aldous. *On the Margin.* 1923. Chatto Windus. 1st ed. NF/G. B4. $250.00

HUXLEY, Aldous. *Perennial Philosophy.* 1945. Harper. 3rd ed. 312p. VG. B33. $14.00

HUXLEY, Aldous. *Proper Studies.* 1927. Chatto Windus. 1/260. sgn. 299p. maroon cloth/marbled brd. NF/case/chemise. H5. $350.00

HUXLEY, Aldous. *Those Barren Leaves.* 1926. Chatto Windus. 1st ed. NF/NF. B4. $250.00

HUXLEY, Elspeth. *African Poison Murders.* nd. BOMC. VG/VG. P3. $10.00

HUXLEY, Elspeth. *New Earth: An Experiment.* 1960. Chatto Windus. 1st ed. VG. P3. $20.00

HUXLEY, Julian. *From an Antique Land.* 1966. Harper Row. 1st ed. 8vo. 55 pl. VG. W1. $16.00

HUXLEY, Julian. *Humanist Frame.* 1961. London. Allen Unwin. 432p. gr cloth. VG/clip. G1. $28.50

HUXLEY, Julian. *Humanist Frame.* 1961. NY. 1st ed. 432p. NF/rpr. D3. $25.00

HUXLEY, Julian. *Soviet Genetics & World Science.* 1949. London. 1st ed. 245p. dj. A13. $25.00

HUXLEY, Thomas H. *Hume: With Helps to the Study of Berkeley.* 1894. London. Macmillan. 12mo. crimson cloth. G1. $50.00

HUXLEY, Thomas H. *Hume: With Helps to the Study of Berkeley.* 1897. Appleton. authorized ed. 319p. quarter leather/marbled brd. VG. B33. $45.00

HUXLEY, Thomas H. *On Our Knowledge of Causes of Phenomena of Organic Nature.* 1863. London. 1st ed. 156p. A13. $100.00

HUYGEN, Will. *Gnomes.* 1977. Abrams. VG/VG. P3. $30.00

HUYGHE, Rene. *Art & Mankind. Larousse Encyclopedia of Prehistoric...Art.* 1962. NY. Prometheus. thick 4to. 414p. blk cloth. VG/dj. F1. $25.00

HUYGHE, Rene. *Delacroix ou le Combat Solitaire.* 1964. Paris. Hachette. 1st ed. 371 pl. F/NF. S9. $100.00

HUYSMANS, J.K. *Against the Grain.* 1924. NY. 331p. VG/dj. B18. $20.00

HUYSMANS, J.K. *Down There.* 1958. University Books. xl. VG. P3. $10.00

HYDE, Christopher. *Wave.* 1979. McClelland Stewart. 1st ed. VG/VG. P3. $15.00

HYDE, E.A. Watson. *Little Sisters to the Campfire Girls...* 1918. Rand McNally. 64p. G. B18. $12.50

HYDE, Harford Montgomery. *Solitary in the Ranks.* 1977. London. Constable. 1st ed. 288p. NF/NF clip. M7. $55.00

HYDE, Harford Montgomery. *Solitary in the Ranks.* 1978. Atheneum. 1st ed. 291p. gilt bl linen. F/F/clear plastic. M7. $50.00

HYER, Richard. *Riceburner.* 1986. Scribner. 1st ed/author's 1st novel. F/F. P3/T2. $17.00

HYLANDER, Carl. *Deep Well.* 1970. St Martin. 1st Am ed. 210p. VG/dj. F3. $15.00

HYMAN, Jackie. *Eyes of a Stranger.* 1987. St Martin. 1st ed. VG/VG. P3. $18.00

HYMAN, Jane. *Gumby Book of Shapes.* 1986. Doubleday. VG. P3. $4.00

HYMAN, Mac. *Take Now Thy Son.* 1965. Random. 1st ed/author's 2nd book. 8vo. 240p. VG/dj. C6. $50.00

HYMAN, Ray. *Nature of Psychological Inquiry.* 1964. Prentice Hall. 116p. VG/dj. G1. $16.50

HYMAN, Tony. *Handbook of Cigar Boxes.* 1979. Arnot Art Mus. ltd 1st ed. sgn. 166p. VG/dj. M20. $45.00

HYMAN, Trina Schart. *Ghost Eye.* 1992. Scholastic. 1st ed. ils. 92p. F/F. A3. $12.95

HYMAN, Trina Schart. *Mechanical Doll.* 1979. Houghton Mifflin. 1st ed. sq 8vo. 45p. VG/VG. A3. $20.00

HYMAN & THORPE. *Tales of the Diamond.* 1991. Woodford. 1st ed. M/M. P8. $32.00

HYMES, Dell. *Use of Computers in Anthropology.* 1965. London. Mouton. 503p. M/dj. K4. $25.00

HYMOFF, Edward. *Space Centers.* 1992. Smithmark. 4to. 100 mc photos. 57p. F/F. K5. $14.00

HYNE, C.J. Cutliffe. *Lost Continent.* 1974. Oswald Train. F/F. P3. $20.00

HYSLOP, Beatrice Fry. *French Nationalism in 1789 According to General Cahiers.* 1934. Columbia. VG. N2. $10.00

I

IACONE, Salvatore J. *Pleasures of Book Collecting.* 1976. Harper. 1st ed. 303p. VG/VG. S11. $20.00

IAMS, Jack. *Do Not Murder Before Christmas.* 1949. Morrow. 1st ed. VG/dj. M15. $35.00

IBSEN, Henrik. *Doll's House.* 1890. Appleton. 1st Am ed. cloth. VG. B4. $150.00

ICEBERG SLIM; see Beck, Robert.

ICHENHAUSER, Julius. *Ils Catalogue of Hist & World-Renowned Collection Torture...* 1893. NY. VG/wrp. N2. $15.00

IDES, E. Ysbrandt. *Three Years Travels From Moscow Over-Land to China...* 1706. London. Freeman. 1st Eng ed. 4to. 210p. contemporary paneled calf. K1. $2,000.00

IDZERDA, Stanley J. *Lafayette in the Age of the American Revolution.* 1977-1983. Ithaca/London. Cornell. 5 vol set. 1st ed. NF/VG. P4. $200.00

IGNATIUS OF LOYOLA, Saint. *Constitutions of Society of Jesus.* 1970. St Louis. Inst Jesuit Sources. 1st ed. 420p. H10. $27.50

IINO, Norimoto. *Seven-Hued Rainbow.* 1967. Philosophical Lib. 127p. VG/VG. B33. $20.00

IKBAL ALI SHAH, Sirdar. *Oriental Caravan: Revelation of Soul & Mind of Asia.* 1974. Tucson. Omen. 2nd ed. 331p. VG/stiff wrp. W1. $7.00

IKEDA & INOUE. *Letters of Four Seasons.* 1980. Tokyo. 1st ed. fwd Burton Watson. 123p. F/F. A17. $10.00

IKIN, Van. *Australian SF.* 1984. Academy. 1st Am ed. dj. F4. $22.00

ILIFF, Flora Gregg. *People of the Blue Water.* ca 1954. Harper. 8vo. 271p. bl cloth/blk spine. VG. P4. $20.00

ILLICH, Ivan. *Gender.* 1982. Pantheon. 192p. F/dj. K4. $10.00

ILLINGWORTH, Ronald S. *Normal Child.* 1964. London. Churchill. 331p. G/dj. K4. $15.00

INCE, Mabel. *Our Ups & Downs.* nd. London. Castel. late 19th C. 24mo. VG/wrp. C8. $30.00

INCH & SCHULTZ. *Interpreting the Word of God.* 1976. Moody. 218p. VG/dj. B29. $5.50

ING, Dean. *Big Lifers.* 1988. Tor. 1st ed. F/F. T2. $17.00

ING, Dean. *Ransom of Black Stealth One.* 1989. St Martin. 1st ed. F/F. P3. $19.00

INGALLS, Albert G. *Amateur Telescope Making.* 1935 (1926). Munn. 4th ed. 8vo. 499p. G. K5. $30.00

INGARDEN, Roman. *Cognition of Literary Work of Art.* 1973. Evanston. 1st Eng-language ed. prt gr cloth. G1. $30.00

INGARDEN, Roman. *Literary Work of Art.* 1973. Evanston. 1st Eng-language ed. 436p. prt gr cloth. G1. $30.00

INGE, M. Thomas. *Frontier Humorists: Critical Views.* 1975. Archon. 1st ed. F/dj. A18. $17.50

INGE, William Ralph. *Lay Thoughts of a Dean.* 1926. Putnam. 1st ed. 366p. VG. B33. $18.00

INGERSOL, Jared. *Diamond Fingers.* 1970. Robert Hale. 1st ed. xl. dj. P3. $5.00

INGERSOLL, Charles Jared Jr. *Fears for Democracy...* 1875. Lippincott. 1st ed. royal 8vo. 297p. VG. D3. $50.00

INGHAM, H. Lloyd. *Bury Me Deep.* 1963. Hammond. VG. P3. $8.00

INGLEE, C. *Sporting Dogs & Hounds.* 1935. Am Kennel Club. 1st ed. VG/VG. B5. $50.00

INGLIS, John. *Yachtsman's Holidays.* 1879. London. Pickering. 2nd ed. 151p. T7. $95.00

INGOLDSBY, Thomas. *Knight & the Lady.* ca 1885. London. Eyre Spottiswoods. ils EM Jessop. 19p. F. H1. $28.00

INGPEN & WILKINSON. *Encyclopedia of Mysterious Places.* 1990. Dragon's World. 1st ed. F/F. P3. $25.00

INGRAHAM, Corinne. *Peacock & the Wishing Fairy & Other Stories.* 1922. London. Brentano. 4to. ils ep. 44p. NF/rpr. D6. $50.00

INGRAHAM, Henry. *American Trout Streams.* 1926. NY. 1/150. sgn. VG/box. B5. $350.00

INN, Henry. *Chinese Houses & Gardens.* 1940. Honolulu. Fong Inn's Ltd. 140p. VG/tattered. F1. $65.00

INNERST, Stuart. *China Gray, China Green.* nd. Davis, CA. Almena Innerst Neff. 8vo. sc. 89p. M. V3. $10.00

INNES, Brian. *Book of Spies.* 1966. Grosset Dunlap. VG. P3. $20.00

INNES, Clive. *Complete Handbook of Cacti & Succulents.* 1981 (1977). NY. correct ed. photos. 224p. sc. F. B26. $15.00

INNES, Hammond. *Angry Mountain.* 1950. Collins. 1st ed. VG/VG. P3. $23.00

INNES, Hammond. *Big Footprints.* 1977. Collins. 1st ed. NF/NF. P3. $25.00

INNES, Hammond. *Conquistadors.* 1969. Knopf. 1st Am ed. 4to. 336p. VG/dj. F3. $25.00

INNES, Hammond. *Doomed Oasis.* 1960. Collins. 1st ed. VG/VG. P3. $20.00

INNES, Hammond. *Golden Soak.* 1973. Collins. 1st ed. NF/NF. P3. $23.00

INNES, Hammond. *Hammond Innes.* 1984. Peerage Books. F/F. P3. $15.00

INNES, Hammond. *Levkas Man.* 1971. Collins. 1st ed. F/F. P3. $30.00

INNES, Hammond. *Solomon's Seal.* 1980. Collins. 1st ed. VG/VG. P3. $18.00

INNES, Hammond. *Strode Venturer.* 1965. Collins. 1st ed. VG/VG. P3. $25.00

INNES, Michael; see Stewart, John Innes M.

INNES, William T. *Exotic Aquarium Fishes.* 1951. Phil. Innes. 13th ed. 512p. G. H1. $6.00

INNIS, Pauline. *Ice Bird: Christmas Legend.* ca 1965. Western Prt. ils Wesley Dennis. unp. VG/G. B10. $12.00

INWARDS, Richard. *Weather Lore.* 1950. London. Rider. 4th ed. 8vo. ils. 251p. VG/dj. K5. $35.00

IONESCO, Eugene. *Ionesco: La Cantatrice Chauve.* 1972. Paris. Gallimard. 1/2200. French text. F/NF. S9. $45.00

IONESCO, Eugene. *Journeys Among the Dead.* 1987. LEC. 1st ed. 1/1000. ils/sgn Ionesco. NF/NF. E3. $500.00

IONESCO, Eugene. *Present Past Past Present.* 1971. NY. Grove. 1st Am ed. F/NF. B4. $45.00

IPAR, Dahlov. *Bug City.* 1975. NY. Holiday House. 1st ed. 8vo. yel cloth. NF/M. D6. $30.00

IPCAR, Dahlov. *Dark Horn Blowing.* 1978. Viking. 1st ed. VG/VG. P3. $15.00

IQBAL. *Iqbal: Poet of the East.* ca 1962. np. Nisar Art Pr. 1st ed. 36 tipped-in pl. 302p. F/dj/case. W1. $350.00

IQBAL. *Prophet's Diplomacy: Art of Negotiation...* 1975. Cape Cod, MA. Stark. 1st ed. 142p. F/dj. W1. $7.00

IRELAND, Alexander. *Booklover's Enchiridion.* 1888. London. 2 vol. 5th ed. extra ils. aeg. Tout morocco. NF. B18. $495.00

IRESON, Barbara. *April Witch & Other Strange Tales.* 1978. Scribner. 1st ed. NF/NF. P3. $20.00

IRISH, William; see Woolrich, Cornell.

IRONS, Peter. *Courage of Their Convictions: 16 Americans Who Fought...* 1988. NY. Free Pr. M11. $22.50

IRVINE, Robert. *Gone To Glory.* 1990. St Martin. 1st ed. F/VG+. P8. $27.50

IRVING, John Treat Jr. *Indian Sketches, Taken During Expedition to Pawnee Tribes...* (1835). OK U. 1st prt. 8vo. ils. F. A8. $30.00

IRVING, John Treat Jr. *Indian Sketches, Taken During Expedition to Pawnee Tribes...* 1835. Carey Lea Blanchard. 2 vol. 1st ed. cloth. scarce. H4. $195.00

IRVING, John. *Hotel New Hampshire.* 1981. Dutton. 1st ed. VG/VG. P3. $25.00

IRVING, John. *Hotel New Hampshire.* 1981. Dutton. 1/550. sgn. 8vo. 401p. teg. gilt full leather. F/case. H5. $150.00

IRVING, John. *Setting Free the Bears.* 1968. Random. 1st ed. NF/NF. B4. $250.00

IRVING, John. *Water-Method Man.* 1972. Random. 1st ed. F/clip. Q1. $175.00

IRVING, John. *World According to Garp.* 1978. Dutton. 1st ed. F/F. B3. $75.00

IRVING, John. *World According to Garp.* 1978. NY. 1st ed. w/sgn bookplate. F/F. A11. $90.00

IRVING, John. *158-Pound Marriage.* 1993. Bloomsbury. 1st ed. NF/F. B3. $25.00

IRVING, Washington. *Chronicle of the Conquest of Granada.* 1893. Putnam. 2 vol. ils. gilt wht cloth. bl cloth djs. K1. $85.00

IRVING, Washington. *Journal of...& Miscellaneous Notes on Moorish Legend...* 1937. Am Book Co. VG/G. N2. $15.00

IRVING, Washington. *Legend of Sleepy Hollow.* 1928. London. Harrap. 1/250. ils/sgn Rackham. ils ep. gilt full vellum. F. F1. $1,500.00

IRVING, Washington. *Legend of Sleepy Hollow.* 1983. Hyattsville, MD. Rebecca. 60x74mm. 1/35 (of 150). fore-edge painting. F/case. B24. $850.00

IRVING, Washington. *Legends of the Alhambra.* 1909. Lippincott. 1st ed thus. ils George Hood. G+. M20. $50.00

IRVING, Washington. *Rip Van Winkle.* 1870. NY. Putnam/Henry Hinton. thin 8vo. ils. 32p. gr cloth/beveled brd. w/ad bill. NF. F1. $300.00

IRVING, Washington. *Rip Van Winkle.* 1921. Phil. McKay. 4to. 7 mc pl/NC Wyeth. 86p. gilt brn cloth. NF. D6. $85.00

IRVING, Washington. *Rip Van Winkle.* 1969. Abingdon. lg 4to. ils Frank Aloise. music Gant. 40p. VG/dj. A17. $9.50

IRVING, Washington. *Salagundi; or, Whim Whams & Opinions...* 1835. Harper. 2 vol. 1st ed/1st imp. 12mo. brn cloth. fair. S11. $75.00

IRVING, Washington. *Sketch Book.* 1882. Lippincott. Cabinet ed. gilt tooled bdg. G+. M21. $20.00

IRVING, Washington. *Sketch Book.* 1882. Putnam. VG. P3. $75.00

IRVING, Washington. *Tour on the Prairies.* 1835. London. John Murray. 1st ed/precedes Am ed. brd/cloth/spine label. VG. A18. $450.00

IRVING. *Tour on the Prairies.* 1835. London. Murray. 1st ed (precedes Am). orig brd/cloth/label. VG. A18. $500.00

IRWIN, J.A. *Hydrotherapy on Saratoga: Treatise Natural Mineral Waters.* 1892. NY. 1st ed. 270p. xl. A13. $60.00

IRWIN, W. *History of Union League Club of NYC.* (1952). NYC. 1st ed. VG/dj. C11. $30.00

ISAAC, Issac S. *Friday Night: A Selection of Tales Ils Hebrew Life.* 1870. NY. Office of The Jewish Messenger. 1st ed. 12mo. cloth. M1. $175.00

ISAACS, George. *Burlesque of Frankenstein; or, The Man-Gorilla.* 1989. Sydney. 1st ed. F/sans. M2. $30.00

ISHAKAWA, Takuboku. *Ichiaku-No-Suna (A Handful of Sand).* 1980. Tokyo. Bijou Hoshino. 29x30mm. 1/44. 160p. teg. goatskin/bezel ruby. F/case. B24. $525.00

ISHAKAWA, Takuboku. *Kanashiki-Gangu (Melancholy Toy).* 1982. Tokyo. Bijou Hoshino. 24x21mm. 1/30. goatskin/bezel emerald. F/case. B24. $525.00

ISHAM, Giles. *Guide to California & the Mines.* 1972. Ye Galleon. 1st ltd ed. 1/402. M/sans. A18. $15.00

ISHERWOOD, Christopher. *Down There on a Visit.* 1962. Simon Schuster. 1st ed. 318p. VG/dj. M20. $30.00

ISHERWOOD, Christopher. *Ramakrishna & His Disciples.* 1965. Simon Schuster. 1st ed. 348p. VG/VG. B33. $20.00

ISHERWOOD, Christopher. *Sally Bowles.* 1937. London. Hogarth. 1st ed. F/NF. Q1. $500.00

ISHIGURO, Kazuo. *Artist of Floating World.* 1986. London. Faber. corrected proof/author's 2nd novel. NF/wrp. B4. $450.00

ISHIGURO, Kazuo. *Artist of the Floating World.* 1986. London. Faber. 1st ed. F/NF. Q1. $100.00

ISHIGURO, Kazuo. *Artist of the Floating World.* 1986. Putnam. 1st Am ed/author's 2nd novel. F/F. L3. $125.00

ISHIGURO, Kazuo. *Pale View of the Hills.* 1982. Putnam. 1st Am ed/author's 1st book. rem mk. F/NF clip. B4. $125.00

ISHIGURO, Kazuo. *Pale View of the Hills.* 1982. Putnam. 1st Am ed/author's 1st novel. F/F. L3. $250.00

ISLEY, Reymoure Keith. *Strange Code of Justice.* 1974. Bobbs Merrill. 1st ed. VG/VG. P3. $15.00

ISMAEL, Tareq Y. *UAR in Africa: Egypt's Policy Under Nasser.* 1971. Evanston, IL. 1st ed. 4to. 8 maps. VG. W1. $25.00

ISON, Graham. *Confirm or Deny.* 1989. London. Macmillan. ARC/1st ed. sgn. RS. F/F. S6. $40.00

ISRAEL, J.I. *Race, Class & Politics in Colonial Mexico 1610-1670.* 1975. Oxford. 1st ed. 305p. VG/dj. F3. $25.00

ISRAEL, Peter. *French Kiss.* 1976. Crowell. 1st ed. VG/VG. P3. $15.00

ISRAEL, Peter. *If I Should Die Before I Die.* 1989. Mysterious. 1st ed. VG/VG. P3. $18.00

ISRAEL, Peter. *Stiff Upper Lip.* 1978. NY. Crowell. 1st ed. F/NF. S6. $25.00

ITURBIDE, Agustin. *Memoirs of Agustin de Iturbide.* 1971. Documentary Pub. 1/500. 157p. VG. F3. $20.00

IVALL, T.E. *Electronic Computers: Principles & Applications.* 1956. NY. Philosophical Lib. 159p. VG. K4. $15.00

IVERSON, Genie. *Louis Armstrong.* 1976. Harper. 2nd prt. lg 8vo. F/F. C8. $35.00

IVES, A.G.L. *British Hospitals.* 1948. London. 1st ed. 50p. A13. $20.00

IVES, Morgan; see Bradley, Marion Zimmer.

IVES, Ruth. *Cinderella.* 1954. Wonder Book 640. K2. $6.00

IVEY, Paul Wesley. *Pere Marquette RR Co.* 1970. Blk Letter. facsimile 1919 ed. M/M. A17. $20.00

IVINS, Dan. *God's People in Transition.* 1981. Broadman. 153p. M/M. B29. $3.25

IVRY, Alfred L. *Al-Kindi's Metaphysics.* 1974. Albany. 1st ed. 207p. cloth. VG. W1. $45.00

IWAHASHI, Takeo. *Light From Darkness.* 1933. Phil. Winston. 12mo. 103p. VG. V3. $12.00

IWAMIYA, Takeji. *Japanese Garden.* 1978. Zokeisha. 2nd prt. NF/NF. S9. $80.00

IZARD, Carroll E. *Human Emotions.* 1977. NY/London. Plenum. 452p. F/dj. K4. $25.00

IZZEDDIN, Nejla. *Arab World: Past, Present & Future.* 1953. Chicago. Regnery. 1st ed. 16pl. cloth. NF/dj. W1. $20.00

IZZI, Eugene. *Prowlers.* 1991. Bantam. 1st ed. sgn. F/F. T2. $16.00

IZZI, Eugene. *Prowlers.* 1991. NY. Bantam. ARC/1st ed. RS. w/promo photo. F/F. S6. $25.00

IZZI, Eugene. *Take.* 1987. St Martin. 1st ed/author's 1st novel. F/F. T2. $22.00

J

JAASTAD & WOODWARD. *Man of the W: Reminiscences of George Washington Oaks...* 1956. AZ Pioneer Hist Soc. 1st ed. F/wrp. B19. $50.00

JABER, William. *Tree Houses: How To Build Your Own Tree House.* ca 1975. Weathervane. 1st ed. 81p. G. B10. $10.00

JABLOKOV, Alexander. *Carve the Sky.* 1991. Morrow. 1st ed. F/F. T2. $25.00

JABLOKOV, Alexander. *Nimbus.* 1993. Avonova Morrow. 1st ed. F/F. P3. $22.00

JABOBI, Charles T. *Printing: A Practical Treatise on Art of Typography.* 1898. London. 2nd ed. 322p. w/14 paper samples. B14. $125.00

JACKH, Ernst. *Kiderlen-Wachter Der Staatsmann Und Mensch.* 19225. Berlin. 2 vols. VG. A17. $20.00

JACKMAN, Stuart. *Davidson Affair.* 1966. Eerdmans. VG/VG. P3. $13.00

JACKS, L.P. *Last Legend of Smokeover.* 1939. Hodder Stoughton. VG/VG. P3. $30.00

JACKSON, Basil. *Epicenter.* 1971. Norton. 2nd ed. NF/NF. P3. $10.00

JACKSON, C. Paul. *Little Leaguer's First Uniform.* 1952. Crowell. 1st ed. VG/G+. P8. $20.00

JACKSON, C. Paul. *Pennant Stretch Drive.* 1969. Hastings. 1st ed. F/VG+. P8. $25.00

JACKSON, Charles James. *English Goldsmiths & Their Marks.* 1921. Los Angeles. Borden. 2nd ed. thick 4to. 747p. maroon/gilt bl cloth. NF. F1. $85.00

JACKSON, Charles. *Being & Race.* 1970. Bloomington, IN. 1st ed/author's 1st nonfiction book. sgn. F/F. A11. $70.00

JACKSON, Charles. *Lost Weekend.* 1960. NY. Noonday. 1st ed. pb. inscr/dtd 1965. VG/8vo wrp. A11. $35.00

JACKSON, Charles. *Outer Edges.* 1948. NY. 1st ed. 240p. F/chip. A17. $15.00

JACKSON, Charles. *Second-Hand Life.* 1967. NY. 1st ed. sgn. F/NF. A11. $40.00

JACKSON, Edgar. *Three Rebels Write Home...* 1955. Franklin, VA. News Pub. 1st ed. 1/150. VG/prt wrp. M8. $300.00

JACKSON, Everett. *Burros & Paintbrushes.* 1985. TX A&M. 1st ed. 5 mc pl. 151p. VG/dj. F3. $15.00

JACKSON, George. *Soledad Brother.* 1970. NY. 1st ed. VG/VG. B5. $22.50

JACKSON, Helen Hunt. *California & the Missions.* 1902. Boston. 1st ed. VG. C11. $25.00

JACKSON, Helen Hunt. *Century of Dishonor: A Sketch...* 1881. Harper. 1st ed. gilt bdg. NF. A18. $150.00

JACKSON, Helen Hunt. *Ramona.* 1939. Boston. 1st ed. ils Wyeth. VG/G. B5. $80.00

JACKSON, Helen Hunt. *Ramona.* 1945. Little Brn. late rpt. 8vo. ils NC Wyeth. VG. B17. $12.50

JACKSON, Helen Hunt. *Ramona: A Story.* 1884. Roberts Bros. 1st ed. gilt cloth. F. A18. $500.00

JACKSON, Helen Hunt. *Ramona: A Story.* 1900. Little Brn. 2 vol. ils. NF. B19. $95.00

JACKSON, Holbrook. *Platitudes in the Making.* 1911. London. Rider. 1st ed. inscr. 92p. G. B18. $22.50

JACKSON, James. *Memoir on Last Sickness of General Washington...* 1860. Boston. 31p. brd. VG. B14. $175.00

JACKSON, John A. *Blind Pig.* 1978. Random. 1st ed. F/F. M15. $30.00

JACKSON, Joseph Henry. *Tintypes in Gold, Four Studies in Robbery.* 1939. NY. Macmillan. 1st prt. inscr/dtd 1939. 181p. red cloth. NF/VG. P4. $45.00

JACKSON, Kathryn. *Golden Circus: A Fuzzy Golden Book.* 1950. Simon Schuster. probable 1st ed. VG+/VG. C8. $50.00

JACKSON, Margaret. *Extracts From Letters & Other Pieces Written by...* 1825. Phil. Kite. 16mo. 95p. leather. VG. V3. $18.00

JACKSON, Percival E. *Wisdom of the Supreme Court.* 1962. Norman. orig cloth. M11. $25.00

JACKSON, Richard. *Occupied With Crime.* 1967. NY. 310p. F/dj. D3. $15.00

JACKSON, Robert. *Systematic View of Formation, Discipline...Armies.* 1804. London. 347p. contemporary brd. rebacked. uncut. G7. $325.00

JACKSON, Shirley. *Life Among the Savages.* nd. BC. VG/VG. P3. $8.00

JACKSON, Shirley. *Lottery.* 1949. Farrar Straus. 1st ed. author Wm Targ's copy. VG/poor. B4. $125.00

JACKSON, Shirley. *Road Through the Wall.* 1948. Farrar. 1st ed/author's 1st book. F/NF. Q1. $250.00

JACKSON, Shirley. *Sundial.* 1959. FSG. 1st ed. VG/VG. M15. $30.00

JACKSON, Shirley. *We Have Always Lived in the Castle.* 1962. Viking. 1st ed. NF/NF. S9. $35.00

JACKSON, T.W. *On a Slow Train Through Arkansaw...* 1903. Chicago. Jackson. G+. B5. $32.50

JACKSON, T.W. *On a Slow Train Through Arkansaw...* 1903. Chicago. Jackson. 12mo. ils. 96p. xl. reading copy. B11. $25.00

JACKSON, T.W. *On a Slow Train Through Arkansaw...* 1903. Chicago. Jackson. 12mo. VG/pict wrp. C8. $60.00

JACKSON, Tony. *Hunter Pointer Retriever: The Continental Gundog.* 1989. Great Britain. 1st ed. ils. 151p. cloth. M/dj. R2. $28.00

JACKSON & JACKSON. *Quanah Parker: Last Chief of the Comanches.* 1963. NY. Exposition. 1st ed. 184p. red cloth. VG/chip. P4. $35.00

JACKSON & WOOD. *Sierra Madre.* 1975. Time Life. 4to. ils/maps/index. 184p. VG. F3. $10.00

JACKSON. *Bird Etchings: Illustrators & Their Books 1655-1855.* 1985. Cornell. 4to. 80 pl. 297p. F/wrp. A4. $35.00

JACOB, Caroline N. *Builders of the Quaker Road, 1652-1952.* 1953. Chicago. REgnery. 1st ed. 8vo. 233p. VG/chip. V3. $16.00

JACOB, Caroline N. *Road to Our Meeting House.* 1951. Friends Bookstore. 2nd ed. 12mo. 133p. sc. VG. V3. $10.00

JACOB, Heinrich Eduard. *Felix Mendelssohn & His Times.* 1963. Prentice Hall. 1st Am ed. 343p. cloth. VG/dj. M20. $15.00

JACOB, Naomi. *Prince China.* 1955. London. Hutchinson. 1st ed. 159p. cloth. VG/VG. R2. $25.00

JACOBI, Carl. *Disclosures in Scarlet.* 1972. Arkham. 1st ed. 1/3127. F/F. T2. $30.00

JACOBI, Carl. *Revelations in Black.* 1947. Arkham. VG/VG. P3. $65.00

JACOBI, Elizabeth P. *Adventures of Andris.* 1929. Macmillan. 1st ed. ils Kata Benedek. 124p. VG. B10. $12.00

JACOBI, Mary Putnam. *Question of Rest for Women During Menstruation.* 1877. Putnam. 282p. cloth. B14. $125.00

JACOBS, Flora Gill. *Toy Shop Mystery.* ca 1960. Coward McCann. ils Sofia. 96p. VG/VG. B10. $12.00

JACOBS, Harvey. *Egg of the Glak & Other Stories.* 1969. NY. 1st ed. F/F. A17. $10.00

JACOBS, Jane. *Death & Life of Great American Cities.* 1961. Random. 1st ed. 458p. dj. A10. $8.00

JACOBS, Lynn. *Waste of the West.* 1991. private prt. ils/index/maps. 602p. F/wrp. B19. $30.00

JACOBS, Michael. *Notes on the Rebel Invasion of MD & PA & Battle Gettysburg.* 1864. Phil. Lippincott. 12mo. fld chromolithograph battle plan. 47p. brn cloth. H9. $295.00

JACOBS, Ruth Harriet. *We Speak for Peace: An Anthology.* 1992. Manchester, CT. 8vo. sc. V3. $15.50

JACOBS, T.C.H. *Appointment With the Hangman.* 1936. Macaulay. 1st ed. VG. P3. $30.00

JACOBS, T.C.H. *Scorpion's Trail.* 1934. Macaulay. VG. P3. $25.00

JACOBS, W.W. *Lady of the Barge.* 1902. Dodd Mead. 1st ed. 8vo. 300p. pict cloth. NF. H5. $225.00

JACOBSEN, H. *Lexicon of Succulent Plants.* 1974. London. German ed. 200 pl. 664p. F/dj. B26. $92.50

JACOBSEN, H. *Succulent Plants.* 1955 & 1959. London. 4th/5th prt. photos. 293p. VG/chip. B26. $56.00

JACOBSEN & MUELLER. *Testament of Samuel Beckett.* 1964. NY. Hill Wang. PBO/Jacobsen's 4th book. sgns. VG+/wrp. A11. $40.00

JACOBSON, Edmund. *Biology of Emotions.* 1967. Springfield, IL. Charles Thomas. 211p. M/dj. K4. $15.00

JACQUARD, Albert. *In Praise of Difference: Genetics in Human Affairs.* 1984. Columbia. 187p. M/dj. K4. $15.00

JACQUAT, Christiane. *Plants From the Markets of Thailand.* 1990. Bangkok. ils/photos. 251p. F/sleeve. B26. $35.00

JACQUEMARD, Simonne. *Night Watchman.* 1964. HRW. 1st ed. VG. P3. $13.00

JACQUEMARD-SENECAL. *Eleventh Little Indian.* 1979. NY. Dodd Mead. 1st Am ed. F/F. S6. $25.00

JACQUES, John. *Catechism for Children...* 1877. Salt Lake City. 25th thousand. 74p. B18. $25.00

JAFFAR, S.M. *Education in Muslim India.* 1973. Delhi. Idarah-i-Adabiyat-i Delli. 2nd ed. xl. VG/dj. W1. $15.00

JAFFE, Leonard. *Communications in Space.* 1966. HRW. 8vo. 176p. xl. G/wrp. K5. $14.00

JAFFE, Rona. *Mazes & Monsters.* 1981. Delacorte. 1st ed. VG/VG. P3. $20.00

JAFFE, Susanne. *Other Anne Fletcher.* 1980. NAL. VG/VG. P3. $15.00

JAFFEE, Bernard. *Crucibles: Lives & Achievements of Great Chemists.* (1934). Tudor. 3rd prt. 377p. VG. H1. $9.00

JAFFREY, Sheldon. *Arkham House Companion.* 1989. Starmont. 1st ed. F/wrp. M2. $40.00

JAGOW, G.V. *Eng Und Der Kriegsausbruch.* 1925. Berlin. 82p. VG. A17. $7.50

JAGUER, E. *Permanence du Regard Surrealiste.* 1981. Elac de Lyon. 1st ed. 1/500. F/wrp/dj. B2. $75.00

JAHODA, G. *River of Golden Ibis.* 1973. NY. 1st ed. VG/VG. B5. $27.50

JAIN & KALIA. *Bibliography of Bibliographies on India.* 1975. Delhi. 204p. xl. VG. A4. $45.00

JAKES, John. *Devil Has Four Faces.* 1958. Mystery House. 1st ed. F/dj. F4. $65.00

JAKES, John. *Secrets of Stardeep.* 1972. Westminster. 1st ed. F/NF. F4. $17.00

JAKUBOWSKI, Maxim. *New Crimes 2.* 1991. NY. Carroll Graf. ARC/1st Am ed. RS. sgn Melville/Pronzini/Vachss. F/F. S6. $35.00

JAKUBOWSKI, Maxim. *New Crimes 3.* 1991. Carroll Graf. F/F. P3. $19.00

JAMES, Alfred Proctor. *Writings of General John Forbes...* 1938. Menasha, WI. rpt. 316p. G. B18. $15.00

JAMES, Arthur. *Potters & Potteries of Chester County, PA.* 1978. PA. ltd sgn ed. leatherette. VG. A1. $25.00

JAMES, Bill. *Astride a Grave.* 1991. London. Macmillan. 1st ed. F/F. S6. $25.00

JAMES, Bill. *Short Hist of Jericho Church of Christ, July 24, 1872...* 1982. np. 1st ed. orig typescript. 38p. VG. M8. $22.50

JAMES, Edward. *Franks.* 1988. Oxford. Basil Blackwell. ils. 265p. F/dj. M10. $12.50

JAMES, George Wharton. *Grand Canyon of AZ: How To See It.* 1911. Fisher Unwin. ils/index. 265p. NF. B19. $50.00

JAMES, George Wharton. *In & Around the Grand Canyon.* 1913. Little Brn. ils. 351p. VG+. B19. $50.00

JAMES, George Wharton. *New Mexico: Land of Delight Makers.* 1920. Boston. 1st ed. VG/VG. B5. $125.00

JAMES, George Wharton. *Wonders of the CO Desert.* 1911. Little Brn. ils Carl Eytel. 547p. VG+. B19. $45.00

JAMES, Henry. *Daisy Miller: A Study.* 1879. Harper. 1st ed. 18mo. 116p. 12 ad p. VG/prt tan wrp. M1. $3,500.00

JAMES, Henry. *German Subs in Yankee Waters, First World War.* 1940. NY. Gotham. 1st ed. 208p. T7. $40.00

JAMES, Henry. *Spoils of Poynton.* 1897. Houghton Mifflin. 1st Am ed. VG. Q1. $200.00

JAMES, Henry. *Terminations.* 1895. NY. 1st ed. F. A9. $85.00

JAMES, Henry. *Travelling Companions.* 1919. Boni Liveright. 1st ed. 309p. VG. M20. $30.00

JAMES, J. *Life of George Rogers Clark.* 1929. np. 1st ed. 534p. VG. E5. $45.00

JAMES, Lawrence. *Golden Warrior.* 1990. Weidenfeld Nicolson. 1st ed. 404p. F/F. M7. $65.00

JAMES, Lawrence. *Imperial Warrior.* 1993. Weidenfeld Nicolson. 1st ed. w/inscr bookplate. M. M7. $45.00

JAMES, M.R. *Best Ghost Stories of Mr James.* 1946. Tower. 5th ed. VG/VG. P3. $20.00

JAMES, Marquis. *Cherokee Strip.* 1945. Viking. 1st ed. VG/worn. M20. $20.00

JAMES, Martha. *My Friend Jim: Story of Real Boys & for Them.* 1901. Lee Shepard. 1st ed. ils FT Merrill. 212p. G. B10. $12.00

JAMES, Martin S. *War Reminiscences.* 1911. Providence. 1st ed. 1/250. NF/prt wrp. M8. $45.00

JAMES, P.D. *Children of Men.* 1993. Knopf. 1st Am ed. sgn. F/F. O4. $40.00

JAMES, P.D. *Cover Her Face.* 1962. Scribner. 1st Am ed/author's 1st book. F/NF. Q1. $200.00

JAMES, P.D. *Death of an Expert Witness.* 1977. London. Faber. 1st ed. F/F. M15. $90.00

JAMES, P.D. *Devices & Desires.* 1990. Knopf. 1st ed. sgn. F/F. O4. $35.00

JAMES, P.D. *Innocent Blood.* nd. BOMC. VG/VG. P3. $10.00

JAMES, P.D. *Innocent Blood.* 1980. London. Faber. 1st ed. inscr. NF/dj. S6. $55.00

JAMES, P.D. *Maul & the Pear Tree.* 1986. Mysterious. 1st ed. VG. P3. $18.00

JAMES, P.D. *Mind To Murder.* 1976. Hamish Hamilton. F/F. P3. $15.00

JAMES, P.D. *Skull Beneath the Skin.* 1982. Lester/Orpen Denys. 1st ed. VG/VG. P3. $17.00

JAMES, P.D. *Taste for Death.* 1986. Knopf. 1st Am ed. sgn. F/F. O4. $40.00

JAMES, P.D. *Taste for Death.* 1986. Knopf. 1st ed. F/F. P3. $19.00

JAMES, P.D. *Taste for Death.* 1986. London. Faber. 1st ed. F/F. M15. $65.00

JAMES, P.D. *Unnatural Causes.* 1967. Scribner. 1st ed. F/dj. Q1. $150.00

JAMES, P.D. *Unsuitable Job for a Woman.* 1972. Scribner. 1st Am ed. sgn. NF/VG. O4. $150.00

JAMES, Peter. *Possession.* 1988. Doubleday. 1st ed. NF/NF. P3. $18.00

JAMES, Peter. *Prophecy.* 1992. Gollancz. 1st ed. sgn. F/F. F4. $35.00

JAMES, Professor. *Therapeutics of the Respiratory Passages.* 1884. NY. Wood. Wood Lib ed. 23 woodcuts. 316p. G7. $35.00

JAMES, Will. *Cowboys North & South.* 1925. Scribner. author's 1st book. pres. H4. $200.00

JAMES, Will. *Dark Horse.* 1939. Scribner. 1st ed. VG+/VG+. C8. $100.00

JAMES, William. *Letters of...* 1920. London. Longman Gr. 1st ed. bl cloth. G1. $65.00

JAMES, William. *Meaning of Truth: Sequel to Pragmatism.* 1909. Longman Gr. 298p. G1. $125.00

JAMES, William. *On Some of Life's Ideals.* 1900. NY. Holt. later prt. 16mo. xl. VG. G1. $17.50

JAMES, William. *Pluralistic Universe: Hibbert Lectures at Manchester...* 1909. Longman Gr. 404p. VG. G1. $100.00

JAMES, William. *Pragmatism. Works of Wm James Vol 1.* 1975 (1907). Harvard. 316p. blk cloth. VG/dj. G1. $40.00

JAMES, William. *Principles of Psychology.* 1890. NY. Holt. 2 vol. 1st prt. thick 8vo. olive cloth. G1. $1,500.00

JAMES, William. *Varieties of Religious Experience: Study in Human Nature.* 1902. Longman Gr. 534p. gr-gray cloth. VG. scarce. G1. $750.00

JAMES & JAMES. *Hoffa & the Teamsters.* 1965. Princeton. Van Nostrand. VG/G. V4. $12.50

JAMES & LANGE. *Emotions.* 1967. NY. Hafner. facsimile 1922 ed. red cloth. G1. $30.00

JAMESON, J. Franklin. *History of Historical Writing in America.* 1969 (1891). Greenwood. 160p. VG. A10. $8.00

JAMIESON, M.M. *Little Redskins.* nd. London/NY. Nister/Dutton. 1st ed. ils Susan Jeffers. M/M. C8. $35.00

JAMISON, Leland. *Light for the Gentiles: Paul & the Growing Church.* 1961. Westminster. 91p. xl. VG. B29. $3.25

JAMISON, Mrs. C.V. *Thistledown.* 1903. Century. 1st ed thus. ils W Benda. 269p. VG. B10. $15.00

JAMME, W.F. *Sabaean Inscriptions From Mahram Bilqis.* 1962. Johns Hopkins. 4to. ils. 480p. VG+/dj. F1. $65.00

JANCE, J.A. *Failure To Appear.* 1993. Morrow. 1st ed. sgn. F/F. O4. $25.00

JANCE, J.A. *Hour of the Hunter.* 1991. Morrow. 1st ed. sgn. F/F. T2. $35.00

JANCE, J.A. *Tombstone Courage.* 1994. Morrow. 1st ed. sgn. F/F. O4. $25.00

JANCE, J.A. *Without Due Process.* 1992. Morrow. 1st ed. F/F. P3. $20.00

JANCE, J.A. *Without Due Process.* 1992. Morrow. 1st ed. inscr. F/F. O4. $25.00

JANE, Cecil. *Spanish Voyage to Vancouver & the NW Coast of Am...1792...* 1930. London. Argonaut. 1/525. ils/fld maps. 156p. vellum. VG+. P4. $500.00

JANET, Paul. *Histoire de la Science Politique...* 1887. Paris. F Alcan. 2 vol. Triosieme ed. new cloth/pattern brd. D3. $150.00

JANEY, Russell. *Miracles of the Bells.* 1946. McLeod. G+/dj. P3. $8.00

JANIFER, Laurence. *Reel.* 1983. Doubleday. 1st ed. RS. F/F. P3. $20.00

JANNEY, Samuel MacPherson. *Life of George Fox...* 1853. Lippincott Grambo. 8vo. 499p. modern cloth. VG. V3. $32.00

JANNEY, Samuel MacPherson. *Memoris of...* 1881. Phil. 1st ed. 309p. cloth. VG. M8. $75.00

JANSON, W.H. *History of Art, 4th Edition.* 1991. Abrams. F/F. P3. $50.00

JANSSENS, Herman F. *L'Entretien de la Sagesse.* 1937. Paris. Librairie E Droz. 378p. VG. G1. $40.00

JANSSON, Tove. *Finn Family Moomintroll.* 1950. London. Benn. 1st Eng ed. trans Elizabeth Portch. gr cloth. VG. D6. $75.00

JANSSON, Tove. *Moominland Midwinter.* 1958. NY. Henry Walck. 1st Am ed. trans Warburton. 165p. NF/G+. D6. $40.00

JANVIER, Thomas A. *Aztec Treasure-House.* nd. Harper. VG. P3. $25.00

JAQUET, Eugene. *History of the Self-Winding Watch 1730-1931.* 1956. Neuchatel, Switzerland. 1st/A ed. w/special pres p. gilt gr cloth. F. A8. $150.00

JAQUET, Eugene. *Technique & History of the Swiss Watch.* 1970. London. Spring Books. VG/G+. A1. $100.00

JARDIN, Rex. *Devil's Mansion.* 1931. Fiction League. G+. P3. $10.00

JARMAN, Thomas. *Treatise on Wills. In Two Volumes.* 1855. Little Brn. contemporary sheep. M11. $85.00

JARRELL, Randall. *Blood for a Stranger.* 1942. Harcourt Brace. 1st ed/1st individual book of poetry. F/NF. V1. $275.00

JARRELL, Randall. *Losses.* 1948. Harcourt Brace. 1st ed. NF/VG. V1. $115.00

JARRELL, Randall. *Pictures From an Institution.* 1954. Knopf. 1st ed. sgn. NF/VG. L3. $450.00

JARRELL, Randall. *Sad Heart at the Supermarket.* 1962. Atheneum. 1st ed. F/NF. B4. $100.00

JARRETT, James L. *Educational Theories of the Sophists.* 1969. NY. Teachers College Pr. 12mo. 232p. red cloth. VG/dj. G1. $25.00

JARVIS, C.S. *Arab Command.* 1943. London. Hutchinson. 3rd imp. gilt bl cloth. reading copy. M7. $12.00

JARVIS, C.S. *Three Deserts.* 1937. Dutton. 1st ed. 313p. VG. W1. $12.00

JARVIS, Sharon. *Inside Outer Space SF Professionals Look at Their Craft.* 1985. NY. Ungar. 1st ed. F/NF. N3. $20.00

JASON, Leon. *Heckle & Jeckle.* 1957. Wonder. TVTI. VG. P3. $8.00

JASPERS, Karl. *De la Psychotherapie: Etude Critique.* 1956. Paris. 1st Eng-language ed. 80p. bl cloth. VG/dj. G1. $25.00

JASPERS, Karl. *Die Atombombe und die Zukunft des Menschen...* 1957. Munchen. Piper. 26p. VG/red wrp. G1. $37.50

JASPERS, Karl. *Hoffnung und Sorge: Schriften zur Deutschen Politik...* 1965. Munchen. Piper. 370p. bl cloth. VG/dj. G1. $50.00

JASPERS, Karl. *Nietzsche: Einfuhrung Verstandnis Seines Philosophierens.* 1936. Berlin. Gruyter. 437p. cream wrp. G1. $175.00

JASPERS, Karl. *On Max Weber.* 1989. Paragon. 216p. gray cloth. VG/dj. G1. $25.00

JASPERS, Karl. *Philosophy Is for Everyman: Short Course...* 1967 (1956). NY. Wolff Book. 1st Eng-language ed. 126p. bl cloth. VG/dj. G1. $22.50

JASPERS, Karl. *Truth & Symbol.* 1959. Twayne. 1st Eng-language ed. bl cloth. VG/dj. G1. $25.00

JAST, L. Stanley. *Reincarnation & Karma: Spiritual Philosophy Applied...* 1944. NY. Bernard Ackerman. 190p. VG/VG. B33. $14.00

JASTRO, Morris. *Study of Religion.* 1902. London. Walter Scott. 451p. VG. B33. $18.00

JASTROW, Robert. *Journey to the Stars.* 1989. Bantam. 1st ed. VG. P3. $20.00

JAY, Charlotte. *Arms for Adonis.* 1960. Collins Crime Club. 1st ed. VG/VG. P3. $25.00

JAYME, Erik. *Inter Nationes, Festschrift fur Stefan Riesenfeld...* 1983. Heidelberg. CF Muller. M11. $45.00

JEANES & STACEY. *Desert Beauty: Story of Cacti.* 1962. Chicago. 4to. photos. 32p. pict brd. F. B26. $9.00

JEANS, James. *Mysterious Universe.* 1930. NY. 1st ed. 163p. A13. $25.00

JEBB, Richard C. *Tragedies of Sophocles.* 1928. Cambridge, Eng. 376p. VG. M10. $3.50

JEFFERIES & NICHOLS. *Safe Counsel; or, Practical Eugenics.* (1922). Naperville, IL. Nicols. 36th ed. ils. 512p. VG. H1. $5.00

JEFFERS, H. Paul. *Adventure of the Stalwart Companions.* 1978. Harper. 1st ed. F/NF. S9. $25.00

JEFFERS, H. Paul. *Rubout at the Onyx.* 1981. Ticknor Fields. 1st ed. NF/NF. P3. $15.00

JEFFERS, John Robinson. *Flagons & Apples.* 1912. LA. Grafton. 1st ed/author's 1st book. 46p. cream/brn bdg. VG. H5. $850.00

JEFFERS, Leroy. *Call of the Mountains.* 1923. Dodd Mead. 2nd prt. ils. VG. B34. $40.00

JEFFERS, Robert H. *Friends of John Gerard.* 1967. Falls Village. ils. 99p. F/dj. B26. $24.00

JEFFERS, Robinson. *Be Angry at the Sun.* 1941. Random. 1/100. sgn. 8vo. 156p. cream cloth/marbled brd. F/case. H5. $500.00

JEFFERS, Robinson. *Cawdor & Other Poems.* 1928. Liveright. 1st ed. F/NF. B4. $200.00

JEFFERS, Robinson. *Cawdor & Other Poems.* 1928. Liveright. 1st ed. sgn. 1/375 special bdg. F/VG+ box. B2. $250.00

JEFFERS, Robinson. *Cawdor.* 1983. Yolla Bolly. 1/240. folio. sgn James Houston/ Mark Livingston. F/F case. S9. $275.00

JEFFERS, Robinson. *Dear Judas & Other Poems.* 1929. Liveright. 1st ed. 8vo. 129p. gilt blk/purple bdg. NF/dj. H5. $150.00

JEFFERS, Robinson. *Descent to the Dead: Poems Written in Ireland...* 1931. Random. ARC/1st ltd ed. sgn. 1/50. fancy brd/vellum spine. VG+. A18. $300.00

JEFFERS, Robinson. *Give Your Heart to the Hawks.* 1933. Random. 1st ed. VG/VG. S9. $75.00

JEFFERS, Robinson. *Hungerfield & Other Poems.* 1954. Random. 1st ed. F/VG+. V1. $75.00

JEFFERS, Robinson. *Medea.* 1946. Random. 1st ed. sgn. F/VG. V1. $85.00

JEFFERS, Robinson. *Solstice & Other Poems.* 1935. Random. 1/320. VG+/custom case. S9. $250.00

JEFFERS, Robinson. *Themes in My Poems.* 1956. San Francisco. BC of CA. 1st ed. 1/350. ils Mallette Dean. F/case. Q1. $300.00

JEFFERS, Robinson. *Thurso's Landing & Other Poems.* 1932. Liveright. 1st ed. F. A18. $35.00

JEFFERS, Robinson. *Women at Point Sur.* 1927. Liveright. 1st ed. sgn. F/F/ chemise/case. B4. $600.00

JEFFERS, Susan. *Baby Animals.* 1989. Random. 1st ed. 4to. rem mk. VG/VG. B17. $10.50

JEFFERSON, Charles Edward. *Character of Paul.* 1924. Macmillan. 381p. VG. B33. $20.00

JEFFERSON, Joseph. *Autobiography.* (1890). NY. 1st ed. vellum. VG+. A9. $45.00

JEFFERSON, Joseph. *Rip Van Winkle.* 1903. Dodd Mead. photoplay ed. 199p. G. S11. $20.00

JEFFERSON, Thomas. *Notes of the State of Virginia.* 1825. Phil. Carey Lea. 344p. calf/brd. VG. B14. $150.00

JEFFERSON, Thomas. *Notes on the State of Virginia.* 1825. Carey Lea. early ed. 16mo. 344p. half calf. lacks map. H4. $85.00

JEFFERY, George. *Brief Description of the Holy Sepulchre...* 1919. Cambridge. 8vo. 233p. cloth. uncut. O2. $45.00

JEFFREY, Grant R. *Messiah: War in the Middle East & Road to Armageddon.* 1991. Frontier. 332p. M. B29. $7.50

JEFFREYS, J.G. *Suicide Most Foul.* 1981. Walker. 1st ed. VG/VG. P3. $15.00

JEFFREYS, Julius. *Views Upon Statics of Human Chest, Animal Heat...* 1843. London. Longman. 233p. cloth. G. G7. $75.00

JEFFRIES, Roderic. *Dead Against the Lawyers.* 1966. Dodd Mead. 1st ed. VG/VG. P3. $15.00

JEFFRIES, Roderic. *Murder Confounded.* 1993. Harper Collins. 1st ed. F/F. S6. $22.50

JEFFRIES, Roderic. *Police Dog.* 1965. NY. Harper. 1st ed. brd. VG/G. O3. $18.00

JEFFRIES, Roderic. *Two-Faced Death.* 1976. Collins Crime Club. 1st ed. VG/VG. P3. $20.00

JEKYLL, Gertrude. *Color Schemes for the Flower Garden.* 1986 (1936). Woodbridge, Suffolk. Antique Collector rpt. 8th ed. ils. 326p. M/dj. B26. $19.00

JENKINS, Cecil. *Message From Sirius.* 1961. Collins Crime Club. 1st ed. F/F. P3. $30.00

JENKINS, Cecil. *Twist of Sand.* 1959. Collins. 1st ed. VG/VG. P3. $20.00

JENKINS, Cecil. *Watering Place of Good Peace.* 1960. Collins. 1st ed. NF/NF. P3. $30.00

JENKINS, David. *Works of That Grave & Learned Lawyer-Judge Jenkins...* 1648. London. I Gyles. contemporary sheep. M11. $275.00

JENKINS, Peter. *Walk Across Am.* 1979. NY. 1st ed. photos. F/F. A17. $10.00

JENKINS, Rolland. *Mediterranean Cruise.* 1923. Putnam. 1st ed. 40 pl. 279p. VG. W1. $10.00

JENKINS, Romilly. *Dilessi Murders.* 1961. London. 1st ed. 8vo. 190p. cloth. O2. $25.00

JENKINS, Will F. *Forgotten Planet.* 1984. Crown. 1st ed. F/F. P3. $13.00

JENKINS, Will F. *Murder Madness.* 1949. Fantasy. 1st prt thus. NF/NF. N3. $15.00

JENKINS, Will F. *Operation Outer Space.* 1954. Fantasy. 1st ed. 2nd bdg. F/dj. M2. $50.00

JENKINS, Will F. *Outlaw Sheriff.* 1934. King. 1st ed. VG. P3. $40.00

JENKINS & SCHROEDER. *Brief Hist of NM.* 1974. NM U. 1st ed. ils. 89p. VG/wrp. B19. $15.00

JENNER, Janann V. *Sandeagozu.* 1986. Harper Row. 1st ed. F/F. N3. $20.00

JENNES, J. *Isles of Shoals.* 1884. Boston. VG. B5. $45.00

JENNINGS, Al. *Through the Shadows With O Henry.* 1921. NY. HK Fly Co. G+. N2. $15.00

JENNINGS, Dean; see Fox, Gardner F.

JENNINGS, Gary. *Killer Storms: Hurricanes, Typhoons & Tornadoes.* 1970. Lippincott. 8vo. photos. 207p. VG/dj. K5. $16.00

JENNINGS, George Henry. *Anecdotal Hist of the British Parliament...* 1881. Appleton. 530p. VG. D3. $45.00

JENNINGS, John. *Banners Against the Wind.* 1954. Little Brn. 1st ed. VG/VG. P3. $15.00

JENNINGS, John. *Chronicle of the Calypso...* 1955. Little Brn. 1st ed. VG/VG. P3. $15.00

JENNINGS, John. *Pepper Tree.* 1950. Little Brn. 1st ed. VG/VG. P3. $15.00

JENNINGS, Ronald C. *Christians & Muslims in Ottoman Cyprus & Mediterranean...* 1993. NY. 8vo. 416p. cloth. O2. $65.00

JENSEN, Arthur R. *Genetics & Education.* 1972. Harper Row. 335p. F/dj. K4. $25.00

JENSEN, Oliver. *American Heritage History of Railroads in America.* 1981. Heritage. 4to. ils. 320p. VG/VG. B11. $25.00

JEPPSON, J.O. *Last Immortal.* 1980. Houghton Mifflin. 1st ed. F/F. N3. $15.00

JEPSEN, Dee. *Women: Beyond Equal Rights.* 1984. Word. 238p. M/M. B29. $5.00

JEPSON, Selwyn. *Black Italian.* 1954. London. Collins Crime Club. 1st ed. inscr. VG/clip. M15. $45.00

JEPSON, Selwyn. *Golden Dart.* 1949. Crime Club. 1st ed. VG. P3. $15.00

JEPSON, Selwyn. *Keep Murder Quiet.* 1941. Doubleday Crime Club. 1st ed thus. VG/G. M21. $15.00

JEPSON, Selwyn. *Man Dead.* 1951. Doubleday. 1st ed. VG. P3. $18.00

JERNIGAN, Muriel Molland. *Forbidden City.* nd. BC. VG/G. P3. $8.00

JERNINGHAM, Arthur W. *Remarks on Means of Directing Fire of Ship's Broadsides.* 1851. London. Parker Furnivall. 10 fld pl. rebacked. T7. $225.00

JEROME, J.K. *Paul Kelver.* 1902. NY. 1st ed. VG. A17. $10.00

JERROLD, Walter. *Highways & Byways in Middlesex.* 1909. London. Macmillan. 1st ed. fld map. 400p. G. S11. $35.00

JERSILD, P.C. *Animal Doctor.* 1975. Pantheon. 1st Am ed. F/F. N3. $15.00

JESSEE, F. Tennyson. *Murder & Its Motives.* 1952. London. Harrap. 271p. G. K4. $8.50

JESSOP, S. *Yorkshire Terrier.* ca 1910s. Manchester. Our Dogs. revised ed. 34p. limp cloth. VG+. rare. R2. $120.00

JESSUP, M.K. *Case for the UFO*. 1955. NY. 1st ed. VG/G. B5. $20.00

JESSUP, M.K. *Expanding Case for the UFO*. 1957. London. 1st ed. VG/G. B5. $25.00

JESSUP, Richard. *Recreation Hall*. 1967. Little Brn. 1st ed. F/NF. F4. $20.00

JESSUP, Richard. *Threat*. 1981. London. Gollancz. 1st Eng ed. F/F. S6. $22.50

JESSUP, Ronald. *Wonderful World of Archeology*. 1956. Garden City. unp. VG. B10. $15.00

JETER, K.W. *Death Arms*. 1987. Morrigan. 1st ed. F/F. P3. $30.00

JETER, K.W. *Farewell Horizontal*. 1989. St Martin. 1st ed. F/F. P3. $17.00

JETER, K.W. *Madlands*. 1991. St Martin. 1st ed. F/F. P3. $19.00

JEVONS, William Stanely. *Principles of Science: Treatise on Logic...* 1892 (1874). London. Macmillan. 2nd corrected ed. 12mo. VG. G1. $50.00

JEWETT, John Howard. *Toy Bearkins Christmas Tree*. nd. Nister Dutton. ils Rosa C Petherick. VG. M5. $175.00

JEWETT, Paul. *New England Farrier...* 1822. Exeter. Williams. enlarged 2nd ed. 12mo. incomplete brd. H10. $85.00

JEWETT, Sarah Orne. *Life of Nancy*. 1895. Houghton Mifflin. Riverside. 1st ed. gr cloth. NF. Q1. $150.00

JEWETT, Sarah Orne. *Native of Winby & Other Tales*. 1893. Houghton Mifflin. 1st ed. VG+. Q1. $200.00

JEWETT, Sarah Orne. *Queen's Twin*. 1899. Houghton Mifflin/Riverside. 1st ed. gilt bdg. F. Q1. $125.00

JEWETT, Sarah Orne. *Tales of New Eng.* 1895. Houghton Mifflin. later prt. 8vo. 276p. NF. C6. $25.00

JEWETT, Sarah Orne. *White Heron*. 1963. London. Constable Young. 1st UK prt. lg 8vo. F/VG+. C8. $35.00

JHABVALA, Ruth Prawer. *Backward Glance*. 1965. Norton. 1st ed. inscr. F/F. B4. $200.00

JHABVALA, Ruth Prawer. *In Search of Love & Beauty*. 1983. London. Murray. 1st ed. F/F. B4. $85.00

JHABVALA, Ruth Prawer. *Nature of Passion*. 1956. London. Allen Unwin. 1st ed/author's 2nd novel. F/clip. Q1. $150.00

JHABVALA, Ruth Prawer. *Out of India*. 1986. Morrow. uncorrected bound galleys. NF/prt wrp. B3. $40.00

JHABVALA, Ruth Prawer. *Stronger Climate*. 1968. Norton. 1st Am ed. F/NF. B4. $85.00

JHABVALA, Ruth Prawer. *Three Continents*. 1987. London. Murray. 1st ed. F/F. B3. $20.00

JIMENEZ, Mary Ann. *Changing Faces of Madness: Early American Attitudes...* 1987. Hanover, NH. 1st ed. 219p. dj. A13. $35.00

JIRKU, A. *Die Altere Kupfer-Steinzeit Palastinas...* 1941. Berlin. De Gruyter. 1st ed. G/stiff wrp. W1. $9.00

JOBSON, Hamilton. *Exit to Violence*. 1979. London. Collins. 1st ed. F/F. S6. $25.00

JOBSON, Hamilton. *Shadow That Caught Fire*. 1972. Scribner. 1st ed. F/F. P3. $15.00

JOELS & KENNEDY. *Space Shuttle Operator's Manual*. 1982. Ballantine. pb. ils. 154p. VG. K5. $10.00

JOERG, W.L.G. *Brief Hist of Polar Exploration Since Intro of Flying*. 1930. NY. Am Geog Soc. Special Pub No 11. maps. 50p. VG/wrp. P4. $50.00

JOERNS, Consuelo. *Midnight Castle*. ca 1983. Lee Shepard. 1st ed. unp. VG/VG. B10. $10.00

JOFFE, Patricia. *Impossible Enchantment*. 1978. Cambridge, MA. Ephemera Designs. 76x53mm. 1/500. 80p. F/case. B24. $350.00

JOHANSON & SHREEVE. *Lucy's Child: Discovery of a Human Ancestor*. 1989. Morrow. 1st ed. 318p. VG/dj. F3. $15.00

JOHANSON & SHREEVE. *Lucy: Beginnings of Humankind*. 1981. Simon Schuster. BC. 409p. VG. F3. $10.00

JOHN, Augustus. *Chiaroscuro, Fragments of Autobiography*. 1952. Pellegrini Cudahy. ARC/1st ed. ils. F/VG. F1. $75.00

JOHNER, Dominic. *New School of Gregorian Chant...* 1925. NY. Pustet. 363p. H10. $22.00

JOHNS, C.A. *Flowers of the Field*. 1911. London. 4th imp. 378p. beveled brd. VG. B26. $32.50

JOHNS, Jeanne Rowett. *All About the Basset Hound*. 1973. London. Pelham. 1st ed. ils. 151p. M/dj. R2. $14.00

JOHNS, Marston. *Beyond Time*. 1966. Arcadia. VG/VG. P3. $15.00

JOHNS, W.E. *Biggles Cuts It Fine*. 1954. Hodder Stoughton. 1st ed. VG/VG. P3. $15.00

JOHNS, W.E. *Biggles Flies East*. 1943. Canada. Oxford. 1st ed. VGVG. P3. $20.00

JOHNS, W.E. *Biggles in the Blue*. 1953. Brock Books. 1st ed. VG/G. P3. $15.00

JOHNS, W.E. *Man Who Vanished Into Space*. nd. Children's BC. VG/VG. P3. $10.00

JOHNS, W.E. *Orchids for Biggles*. nd. Children's BC. VG/VG. P3. $8.00

JOHNS, W.E. *Outer Space*. 1957. Hodder Stoughton. 1st ed. VG/G. P3. $20.00

JOHNS, W.E. *Worrals Goes East*. 1944. Hodder Stoughton. 1st ed. VG/fair. P3. $15.00

JOHNSHOY, J. Walter. *Apaurak in Alaska. Social Pioneering Among the Eskimos*. nd. np. 8vo. ils. 325p. blk cloth. F/wht pict dj. H3. $35.00

JOHNSON, Alfred J. *Golden Playbook, Comprising The Golden Alphabet...* 1886. London. Warene. 4to. ils. aeg. unp. NF. D6. $300.00

JOHNSON, Alvin. *Touch of Color & Other Tales*. 1963. NY. 1st ed. F/F. A17. $9.50

JOHNSON, B.S. *Travelling People*. 1963. Hertfordshire. Constable. 1st ed/author's 1st book. F/NF. B4. $250.00

JOHNSON, Burges. *Little Book of Necessary Nonsense*. 1929. Harper. 1st ed. ils Elizabeth MacKinstry. VG/G. P2. $35.00

JOHNSON, Burges. *Rubaiyat of Omar Ki-Yi*. 1938. Putnam. 1st ed. ils Morgan Dennis. 39p. VG. R2. $40.00

JOHNSON, Burges. *Sonnets From the Pekingese*. 1935. Macmillan. 2nd imp. ils Edwina. 40p. F/VG. R2. $25.00

JOHNSON, C. Pierpont. *British Wild Flowers*. 1876. London. rpt. 90 mc pl/John E Sowerby. H4. $100.00

JOHNSON, Christopher N. *Seven Churches of Asia*. 1916. London. Blk. 8vo. pres. 176p. cloth. O2. $60.00

JOHNSON, Clarence R. *Constantinople Today; or, Pathfinder Survey...* 1922. NY. 8vo. ils/maps. 418p. cloth. O2. $40.00

JOHNSON, Clifton. *Highways & Byways of Florida*. 1918. NY. Macmillan. 1st ed. photos. 264p. VG. B14. $45.00

JOHNSON, Cuthbert William. *Life of Sir Edward Coke...Two Volumes*. 1837. London. marbled ep. gilt diced morocco. M11. $350.00

JOHNSON, Cuthbert. *Farmer's & Planter's Encyclopaedia of Rural Affairs*. 1851. np. 1st ed. royal 8vo. ils. 1200p. VG. E5. $65.00

JOHNSON, Denis. *Angels*. 1983. NY. 1st ed/author's 1st novel. sgn. F/F. A11. $40.00

JOHNSON, Denis. *Resuscitation of a Hanged Man*. 1991. London. Faber. 1st ed. NF/F. B3. $25.00

JOHNSON, Denis. *Stars at Noon*. 1986. Knopf. 1st ed. F/VG. B3. $15.00

JOHNSON, Diane. *Dashiell Hammett: A Life*. 1983. Random. 1st ed. NF/NF. P3. $20.00

JOHNSON, Don. *Hummers, Knucklers & Slow Curves*. 1991. U of IL. 1st ed. M/M. P8. $32.00

JOHNSON, Doris Miller. *Golden Prologue to Future: Hist of Highland Park Methodist*. 1966. Nashville. 1st ed. 143p. F/dj. M8. $37.50

JOHNSON, Dorothy M. *Beulah Bunny Tells All.* 1942. Morrow. 1st ed. F. A18. $60.00

JOHNSON, Dorothy M. *Bloody Bozeman.* 1971. np. Am Trails Series. 1st ed. F/dj. B34. $60.00

JOHNSON, E. Richard. *Mongo's Back in Town.* 1970. Macmillan. 1st ed. F/F. P3. $20.00

JOHNSON, E.C. *On the Track of the Crescent.* 1885. London. 8vo. ils/fld map. gilt cloth. O2. $75.00

JOHNSON, Edward A. *History of Negro Soldiers in the Spanish-American War...* 1899. Raleigh, NC. Capital Prt. 1st ed. 228p. gilt/blk stp bl-gr cloth. K1. $125.00

JOHNSON, Emeroy. *Eric Norelius: Pioneer, Midwest Pastor & Churchman.* 1954. Rock Island, IL. 1st ed. 255p. F/F. M8. $37.50

JOHNSON, Fenton. *Scissors, Paper, Rock.* 1993. Pocket. 1st ed. F/F. A14. $25.00

JOHNSON, Gerald W. *America Is Born, America Grows Up, America Moves Forward.* 1959, 1960 & 1960. Morrow. 3 vol set. 1st ed. VG/VG. P2. $50.00

JOHNSON, Gerald W. *America's Silver Age.* 1939. NY. 1st ed. VG/G. B5. $20.00

JOHNSON, Hannibal Augustus. *Sword of Honor, From Captivity to Freedom.* 1903. Providence. 1st ed. 1/250. NF/prt wrp. M8. $45.00

JOHNSON, Herschel. *Visit to the Country.* 1989. Harper. 1st ed. ils Romare Bearden. F/F. C8. $25.00

JOHNSON, Jack. *Jack Johnson Is a Dandy.* 1969. Chelsea House. 1st ed. F/NF. B2. $45.00

JOHNSON, James L. *Coming Back.* 1979. Springhouse. 128p. VG/dj. B29. $3.50

JOHNSON, James Weldon. *Fifty Years & Other Poems.* 1917. Boston. Cornhill Co. ARC. pub card. gilt blk cloth. F. Q1. $200.00

JOHNSON, Joyce. *Minor Characters.* 1983. Boston. 1st ed. VG/dj. N2. $15.00

JOHNSON, L.D. *Israel's Wisdom: Learn & Live.* 1975. Broadman. 128p. VG. B29. $2.75

JOHNSON, Lee. *Heads for Death.* 1966. John Gifford. 1st ed. VG/G. P3. $15.00

JOHNSON, Lyndon Baines. *Vantage Point: Perspectives of the Presidency 1963-1969.* 1971. HRW. 1st ed. 636p. F/VG+. H1. $25.00

JOHNSON, M.L.; see Malzberg, Barry.

JOHNSON, Marg. *Dixie Dobie.* 1945. NY. 1st ed. 90p. G+. R2. $35.00

JOHNSON, Marg. *Miss Kelly.* 1947. NY. 1st ed. 125p. F/F. R2. $30.00

JOHNSON, Marjorie P. *Concise Encyclopedia of Favorite Flowers.* (1953). BC. 256p. F/VG. H1. $4.50

JOHNSON, Martin. *Time, Knowledge & Nebulae.* 1945. London. Faber. 8vo. 189p. blk cloth. xl. K5. $20.00

JOHNSON, Mary. *To Have & To Hold.* 1900. Sun Dial. 310p. NF. S12. $12.00

JOHNSON, Mel; see Malzberg, Barry.

JOHNSON, Owen. *Hummingbird.* 1910. Baker Taylor. 1st ed. VG. P8. $100.00

JOHNSON, Owen. *Tennessee Shad.* 1911. NY. Baker Taylor. 1st ed. NF/VG+. B4. $300.00

JOHNSON, Owen. *Varmint.* 1910. Baker Taylor. 3rd prt. G+. P8. $40.00

JOHNSON, Patricia H. *Meet the Horse.* 1972. Grosset Dunlap. VG/VG. O3. $10.00

JOHNSON, Paul. *Civilizations of the Holy Land.* 1979. Atheneum. 1st Am ed. xl. VG. W1. $18.00

JOHNSON, Peter. *Sail Magazine Book of Sailing.* 1989. NY. Knopf. photos. 351p. dj. T7. $40.00

JOHNSON, Raynor. *Imprisoned Splendour.* 1953. Harper Row. 424p. VG/VG. B33. $20.00

JOHNSON, Rich. *Central AZ Project, 1918-1968.* 1977. AZ U. 1st ed. ils/index. 242p. F/F. B19. $40.00

JOHNSON, Robert Clyde. *Meaning of Christ.* 1958. Westminster. 95p. xl. VG/dj. B29. $2.50

JOHNSON, Ronald. *Book of Greens.* 1966. Norton. 1st ed. sgn. F/VG. V1. $50.00

JOHNSON, Rossiter. *Campfires & Battlefields: Pict Hist of Civil War.* 1967. NY. 9th prt. 532p. F/dj. A17. $25.00

JOHNSON, Samuel. *Dictionary of English Language.* 1818. London. Longman Hurst. 4 vol. lg 4to. brn calf/rebacked. K1. $400.00

JOHNSON, Samuel. *Letters of...1731-1784.* 1992-1994. Princeton. 5 vol set. F/F. A4. $125.00

JOHNSON, Samuel. *Rambler.* nd. London. 3 vol. G. B18. $95.00

JOHNSON, SAYERS & SICKLES. *Anthology of Children's Literature.* 1959. Houghton Mifflin. 3rd ed. ils Fritz Eichenberg. 1239p. VG-. A3. $12.50

JOHNSON, Stanley. *Doomsday Deposit.* 1980. Dutton. F/F. P3. $13.00

JOHNSON, Thomas H. *Final Harvest: Emily Dickinson's Poems.* (1961). Little Brn. ARC. w/pub promo letter. F/NF. Q1. $75.00

JOHNSON, Vernon E. *I'll Quit Tomorrow.* 1973. Harper Row. 1st ed. 8vo. VG/G+ clip. A8. $10.00

JOHNSON, Victor. *May Clinic: It's Growth & Progress.* 1984. Bloomington, MN. 1st ed. 369p. dj. A13. $20.00

JOHNSON, Victor. *Too Late! Too Late! The Maiden Cried.* 1975. Putnam. 1st ed. VG/VG. P3. $15.00

JOHNSON, W. *Whatta Gal.* 1977. Boston. 1st ed. VG/VG. B5. $25.00

JOHNSON, Warren. *Muddling Toward Frugality.* 1978. Sierra Club. 1st ed. 252p. 12mo. F/F. A17. $14.50

JOHNSON, Wendell. *People in Quandaries: Semantics of Personal Adjustment.* 1946. Harper. later prt. 532p. blk cloth. G1. $22.50

JOHNSON, William Ernest. *Logic.* 1921, 1922 & 1924. Cambridge. 3 vol. olive cloth. VG. G1. $125.00

JOHNSON, William S. *Lafcadio Hearn: Selected Writings 1872-77.* 1979. Woodruff. 1st ed. 1/750. biblio. 226p. F/F. A17. $25.00

JOHNSON, William Weber. *Baja California.* 1972. Time Life. 4to. ils/maps/index. 184p. VG. D3. $10.00

JOHNSON, William. *Still Point, Relfections on Zen & Christian Mysticism.* 1970. Fordham. 1st ed. 193p. F/VG. B33. $18.00

JOHNSON & JOHNSON. *Memory of Dragons.* 1986. Atheneum. 1st ed. F/F. N3. $10.00

JOHNSON & JOHNSON. *Roman Collar Detective.* 1956. Bruce. 2nd ed. VG/VG. P3. $13.00

JOHNSON & JOHNSON. *Yankee Sails the Nile.* 1966. Norton. 1st ed. 8vo. 256p. NF/dj. W1. $10.00

JOHNSON & NEWKIRK. *Ceramic Arts.* 1942. NY. 1st ed. 4to. 158p. VG/worn. A17. $20.00

JOHNSON & PECK. *Runaway Balboa.* 1938. NY. Harper. 1st ed. 4to. G. B11. $15.00

JOHNSON & WEBBER. *What Christians Believe: Biblical & Hist Summary.* 1989. Zondervan. 480p. VG/torn. B29. $13.00

JOHNSON & WINTER. *Route Across the Rocky Mountains With Description of OR...* 1982. Ye Galleon. 1st ed thus. ils/maps/index. M/sans. A18. $15.00

JOHNSON. *Checklist of New London, CT Imprints, 1709-1800.* 1978. np. ils. 535p. NF. A4. $95.00

JOHNSTON, Angus Anthony. *Hist of the Catholic Church in E Nova Scotia...* 1960. Antigonish. St Francis Xavier U. 2 vol. index. H10. $45.00

JOHNSTON, Annie Fellows. *For Pierre's Sake.* 1934. Page. 1st ed/author's last book. 200p. pict bl cloth. M20. $40.00

JOHNSTON, Annie Fellows. *Old Mammy's Torment.* 1897. Boston. Page. 1st ed. 12mo. 118p. pict cloth. VG. C6. $40.00

JOHNSTON, Annie Fellows. *Travelers Five Along Life's Highway.* 1911. Boston. 1st ed. ils Garrett. 199p. G. A17. $10.00

JOHNSTON, Charles H.L. *Famous Scouts, Including Trappers, Pioneers & Soldiers...* 1918. Page. 8th imp. xl. poor. B34. $15.00

JOHNSTON, Denis Foster. *Analysis of Sources of Information on Population of Navaho.* 1966. GPO. 7 maps. olive cloth. VG+. P4. $35.00

JOHNSTON, Frances B. *Hampton Album.* 1966. NY. MOMA. 1st ed. phtos. brd. VG/sans. S9. $20.00

JOHNSTON, George. *Basset Hound.* 1974 (1968). London. Popular Dogs. 4th ed. ils. 228p. M/dj. R2. $12.00

JOHNSTON, Harry. *Gay-Dombeys.* 1920. Chatto Windus. 6th ed. VG. P3. $13.00

JOHNSTON, Joe. *Adventures of Teebo.* 1984. Random. 1st ed. Star Wars tie-in. VG. P3. $10.00

JOHNSTON, Lucile. *Celebrations of a Nation: Early Am Holidays.* 1987. Johnston Bicentennail Found. 165p. M. B29. $4.50

JOHNSTON, M.F. *Coronation of a King; or, Ceremonies, Pageants...* 1902. London. 24 pl. 279p. VG. D3. $35.00

JOHNSTON, Mary. *Audrey.* 1902. Houghton Mifflin. 1st ed. ils Yohn. gilt cloth. NF. A17. $15.00

JOHNSTON, Otta Taggart. *Picture Book of Houses Around the World.* 1934. Harter Pub. 1st ed. photos. unp. VG. B10. $15.00

JOHNSTON, Stanley. *Queen of Flat-Tops.* 1942. Dutton. 1st ed. sgn. 280p. VG/ragged. M20. $18.50

JOHNSTON, T.T. *Early Architecture of NC.* ca 1965. Chapel Hill. 2nd ed. frontis photo. gr/tan cloth. VG/case. C6. $200.00

JOHNSTON, Terry. *Carry the Wind.* 1982. np. M/M. B34. $15.00

JOHNSTON, Terry. *One-Eyed Dream.* 1988. np. M/M. B34. $15.00

JOHNSTON, Velda. *Etruscan Smile.* nd. Quality BC. VG/VG. P3. $8.00

JOHNSTON, Velda. *Frenchman.* 1976. Dodd Mead. 1st ed. VG/VG. P3. $20.00

JOHNSTON, Velda. *I Came to a Castle.* 1969. Dodd Mead. 1st ed. VG/VG. P3. $20.00

JOHNSTON, Velda. *People on the Hill.* 1971. Dodd Mead. 2nd ed. VG/torn. P3. $8.00

JOHNSTON, Velda. *Room With Dark Mirrors.* 1975. Dodd Mead. 1st ed. VG/VG. P3. $15.00

JOHNSTON, William G. *Overland to California.* 1948. Biobooks. 1st ed thus. 1/1000. fld map. F. A18. $40.00

JOHNSTON, William. *Barney.* 1970. Random. 1st ed. VG/G. P3. $13.00

JOHNSTON, William. *Dr Kildare: The Magic Key.* 1964. Whitman. Dr Kildare TVTI. VG. P3. $8.00

JOHNSTON, William. *F Troop, the Indian Uprising.* 1967. Whitman. 1st ed. F/sans. F4. $10.00

JOHNSTON, William. *Great Indian Uprising.* 1964. Whitman. F Troop TVTI. F. P3. $10.00

JOHNSTON, William. *Munsters: The Last Resort.* 1966. Whitman. 1st ed. pict bdg. NF/sans. F4. $18.00

JOHNSTON, William. *Picture Frame Frame-Up.* 1969. Whitman. Ironside TVTI. VG. P3. $10.00

JOHNSTON, William. *Who's Got the Button?* 1968. Whitman. Monkees TVTI. VG. P3. $13.00

JOHNSTONE, J.H.S. *Horse Book.* 1908. Chicago. Sanders. G. O3. $25.00

JOHNSTONE, Pauline. *Guide to Greek Island Embroidery.* 1972. London. 1st ed. 110p. NF/stiff wrp. W1. $14.00

JOLAS, Eugene. *Transition Workshop.* 1940. NY. 1st ed. VG. A17. $20.00

JOLIVET, Regis. *Les Doctrines Existentialistes de Kiekegaard a J-P Sartre.* 1948. Paris. Fontenelle. 372p. NF/prt stiff tan wrp. G1. $37.50

JONAS, Gerald. *On Doing Good: The Quaker Experiment.* 1971. Scribner. 8vo. 177p. VG/chip. V3. $14.00

JONAS, Walter. *Les Bucoliques de Virgile.* 1942. Zurich. Conzett Huber. Latin/French text. inscr/dtd 1943. F/prt wrp/chemise. B24. $500.00

JONES, Anson. *Memoranda & Official Correspondence Relating to...Texas...* 1859. NY. Appleton. 1st ed/1st issue. cloth. NF. H4. $185.00

JONES, Aubrey. *Mathematical Astronomy With a Pocket Calculator.* 1978. Wiley. 8vo. 254p. VG/VG. K5. $26.00

JONES, Billy. *Health-Seekers in the South-west, 1871-1900.* 1967. Norman, OK. 1st ed. 254p. A13. $25.00

JONES, Courtway. *In the Shadow of the Oak King.* 1991. Pocket. 1st ed. F/F. N3. $15.00

JONES, D.F. *Xeno.* 1979. British SF BC. VG/VG. P3. $10.00

JONES, Dan Burne. *Prints of Rockwell Kent, a Catalogue Raisonne.* 1975. Chicago. 1st ed. sgn. M/dj. F1. $125.00

JONES, David. *Anathemata.* nd. NY. Chilmark. VG/clip. N2. $12.50

JONES, David. *Epoch & Artist: Selected Writings.* 1959. Chilmark. 1st Am ed. F/NF dj/NF overjacket. B4. $45.00

JONES, Diana Wynne. *Fire & Hemlock.* 1985. Greenwillow. F/F. P3. $15.00

JONES, Diana Wynne. *Howl's Moving Castle.* 1986. Greenwillow. 1st ed. VG/VG. P3. $15.00

JONES, DuPre. *Adventures of Gremlin.* 1966. Phil. 1st ed. VG+. C8. $15.00

JONES, E. Stanley. *Christ of the Am Road.* 1944. Abingdon. 255p. VG/dj. B29. $3.50

JONES, E. Stanley. *Song of Ascents.* 1968. Abingdon. 400p. VG. B29. $5.50

JONES, Franklin D. *Igenious Mechanisms for Designers & Inventors.* 1944. Industrial Pr. 2 vol. F. H1. $22.50

JONES, Frederic W. *Unscientific Excursions.* 1934. London. 1st ed. 207p. A13. $50.00

JONES, George Henry. *Account of Murder of Late Mr William Weare.* 1824. London. Nichols. tall 8vo. ils/4 pl/2 fld plans. 344p. pink brd. uncut. K1. $150.00

JONES, George Neville. *Flowering Plants & Ferns of Mt Rainier.* 1938. Seattle. later prt. 192p. sc. B26. $12.50

JONES, George. *Excursions to Cairo, Jerusalem, Damascus & Balbec...* 1836. NY. 8vo. half calf/brd. O2. $250.00

JONES, George. *Sketches of Naval Life...* 1829. New Haven. 2 vol. 8vo. new quarter calf. O2. $450.00

JONES, H. Spencer. *General Astronomy.* 1934 (1922). London. Arnold. 2nd ed. 8vo. 437p. bl cloth. G. K5. $18.00

JONES, Helen L. *Robert Lawson, Illustrator: A Selection...* 1972. Little Brn. 1st ed. 121p. VG/dj. M10. $18.50

JONES, Hugh. *Present State of Virginia From Whence Is Inferred...* 1956. Chapel Hill. 1st ed. inscr. 10 pl. 295p. F/F. B11. $75.00

JONES, Ian. *Australian Light Horse.* 1987. Time Life. Sydney. 1st ed. ils/photos. M/clear plastic. M7. $45.00

JONES, James. *From Here to Eternity.* 1951. Scribner. 1st ed/author's 1st book. inscr. 8vo. 861p. NF/dj. H5. $350.00

JONES, James. *From Here to Eternity.* 1951. Scribner. 1st ed/author's 1st book. 8vo. 861p. VG. H5. $100.00

JONES, James. *Go to the Widow-Maker.* 1967. Delacorte. 1st prt. 618p. F/VG. H1. $28.00

JONES, James. *Some Came Running.* 1957. Scribner. 1st ed. NF/NF. B4. $100.00

JONES, James. *Spirit & the World.* 1975. Hawthorn. 158p. VG/dj. B29. $5.50

JONES, James. *Whistle.* 1978. Franklin Lib. 1st ed. F. B3. $35.00

JONES, John B. *Readings in Descriptive Bibliography.* 1974. Kent State. 1st ed. 208p. VG. A10. $20.00

JONES, John Beauchamp. *Rebel War Clerk's Diary at Confederate States Capital*. 1982. Time Life. 2 vol. rpt of 1866 ed. full leather. F. M8. $50.00

JONES, John William. *Life & Letters of Robert E Lee: Soldier & Man*. 1906. NY/WA. Neale. 1st ed. 486p. cloth. VG+. M8. $175.00

JONES, Joseph. *Explorations of Aboriginal Remains of Tennessee*. 1876. WA. 171p. lacking front wrp. uncut/unopened. G7. $75.00

JONES, Kenneth Glyn. *Messier's Nebulae & Star Clusters*. 1968. London. Faber. sm 4to. 480p. VG/VG. K5. $50.00

JONES, Kenneth. *Harley Harris Bartlett Diaries*. 1975. Ann Arbor. Jones. ltd ed. sgn. 1/200. 323p. cloth. A10. $25.00

JONES, LeRoi. *Baptism & the Toilet*. 1967. NY. ARC/1st ed. sgn as Amiri Baraka. sbdg. RS. NF. A11. $75.00

JONES, LeRoi. *Home. Social Essays*. 1966. NY. Morrow. 1st ed. 8vo. 252p. wht lettered blk/gray bdg. NF/dj. H5. $75.00

JONES, LeRoi. *Raise Race Rays Raze*. 1971. Random. 1st ed. sgn/dtd 1979. 8vo. 169p. yel cloth. NF/dj. H5. $75.00

JONES, N.E. *Squirrel Hunters in OH*. 1898 (1897). Cincinnati. Clarke. 363p. gr cloth. VG. M20. $100.00

JONES, Peter. *Collection of Ojebway & English Hymns For Use...* nd. Toronto. Methodist Missionary Soc. 16mo. 234p. VG. scarce. H4. $75.00

JONES, R.W. *Cop Out*. 1987. St Martin. 1st ed. VG/VG. P3. $17.00

JONES, Raymond F. *Cybernetic Brains*. 1962. Avalon. 1st ed. F/F. N3. $25.00

JONES, Raymond F. *Planet of Light*. 1953. Phil. Lippincott. 1st ed. NF/NF. B4. $85.00

JONES, Raymond F. *Renaissance*. 1951. Gnome. 1st ed. VG/VG. P3. $60.00

JONES, Raymond F. *Son of the Stars*. 1952. Winston. 1st ed. VG. P3. $25.00

JONES, Raymond F. *Voyage to the Bottom of the Sea*. 1965. Whitman. TVTI. VG. P3. $10.00

JONES, Raymond F. *Voyage to the Bottom of the Sea*. 1965. Whitman. 1st ed. pict brd. F/sans. F4. $20.00

JONES, Richard Glyn. *Solves!* 1987. BOMC. VG/VG. P3. $10.00

JONES, Rufus. *Call To What Is Vital*. 1948. Macmillan. 1st ed. 12mo. 143p. VG/chip. V3. $12.50

JONES, Rufus. *Trail of the Middle Years*. 1934. Macmillan. 1st ed. 8vo. 250p. VG. V3. $12.50

JONES, Rupert F. *Our Church: Its Heritage & Achievements*. 1940. Winchester, MA. 1st ed. 190p. cloth. F. M8. $37.50

JONES, Stephen. *Flann O'Brien Reader*. 1978. Viking. 1st ed. NF/F. B2. $40.00

JONES, Stephen. *Hard Life*. 1962. Pantheon. 1st ed. F/F. B2. $60.00

JONES, Terry. *Nicobobinus*. 1986. Peter Bedrick. 8vo. rem mk. F/F. B17. $10.00

JONES, Thomas. *Pugilist at Rest*. 1993. Little Brn. 1st ed/author's 1st collection stories. F/F. S9. $45.00

JONES, Tristan. *Heart of Oak*. 1984. St Martin. 282p. dj. T7. $18.00

JONES, Tristan. *Steady Trade: Boyhood at Sea*. 1982. St Martin. BC. VG/dj. N2. $5.00

JONES, Virgil Carrington. *Eight Hours Before Richmond*. 1957. NY. Holt. 1st ed/2nd prt. 180p. cloth. NF/VG. M8. $45.00

JONES, Virgil Carrington. *Gray Ghosts & Rebel Raiders*. 1958. photos/index. 431p. xl. VG. O8. $18.50

JONES, Virgil Carrington. *Ranger Mosby*. 1944. NC U. 3rd prt. 347p. xl. VG. H1. $8.00

JONES, William. *Dissertations & Miscellaneous Pieces Relating to History...* 1793. Dublin. 643p. full tree calf/red leather label. VG. H7. $150.00

JONES, William. *Grammar of the Persian Language*. 1775. London. 2nd ed. 4to. 147p. rebound calf. O2. $250.00

JONES & JONES. *There Was a Little Man*. 1948. Random. 1st ed. VG/VG. P3. $30.00

JONES & SUTTON. *Best Horror From Fantasy Tales*. 1990. Carroll Graf. 1st ed. F/F. P3. $18.00

JONG, Erica. *Any Woman's Blues*. 1990. Harper Row. 1st ed. sgn. F/VG. B3. $30.00

JONG, Erica. *At the Edge of the Body*. 1979. HRW. 1st ed. sgn. F/F clip. B4. $85.00

JONG, Erica. *Fruits & Vegetables*. 1971. Holt. 1st ed. inscr. NF/wrp. B3. $25.00

JORDAC, George. *Voice of Human Justice*. 1987. Islamic Seminary Pub. 2nd ed. 508p. VG. W1. $12.00

JORDAN, Charlotte Brewster. *Tuckaway House*. 1935. Doubleday Doran. ils Bernice Oehler. 313p. G/fair. B10. $12.00

JORDAN, David K. *Gods, Ghosts & Ancestors: Folk Religion Taiwanese Village*. 1967. CA U. Formosan pirated ed. VG/dj. N2. $10.00

JORDAN, David. *Nile Green*. 1973. John Day. 1st ed. VG/VG. P3. $13.00

JORDAN, Fritz. *Escape. Trans From the Hebrew by Niusia Indursky*. 1970. S Brunswick. 8vo. 278p. cloth. dj. O2. $25.00

JORDAN, Joe. *Bluegrass Horse Country*. 1940. Lexington. Transylvania. 1st trade ed. VG/G. O3. $65.00

JORDAN, Kate. *Happifats & the Grouch*. 1917. Dutton. 1st ed. VG. M5. $75.00

JORDAN, Mildred. *Asylum for the Queen*. 1948. np. 409p. NF. S12. $6.00

JORDAN, Robert. *Fires of Heaven*. 1993. NY. Tor. 1st ed. F/F. B3. $15.00

JORDAN & MANSON. *Tales From Alfred Hitchcock...* 1988. Morrow. 1st ed. NF/NF. P3. $15.00

JORDAN & STOKES. *From Major Jordan's Diaries*. 1952. NY. 284p. VG/wrp. B18. $7.50

JORDAN-SMITH, Paul. *Road I Came*. 1960. Caxton. 474p. F/VG. scarce. A4. $65.00

JORDANOFF, Assen. *Through the Overcast. Weather & Art of Instrument Flying*. 1938. NY. revised ed. 356p. VG/dj. B18. $19.50

JORDANOFF, Assen. *Your Wings*. 1943. NY. revised/enlarged ed. 294p. VG/dj. B18. $22.50

JORGENSEN, Christine. *Love To Die For*. 1994. Walker. 1st ed. sgn. F/NF. B3. $20.00

JORGENSEN, H.R. *Red Lacquer Case*. 1933. World Syndicate. VG. P3. $20.00

JORGENSON, Nels Leroy. *Dave Palmer's Diamond Mystery*. 1954. Cupples Leon. 1st ed. VG. P8. $12.50

JOSCELYN, Archie. *Golden Bowl*. 1931. Internat Fiction Lib. VG. P3. $10.00

JOSEPH, Franz. *Star Fleet Technical Manual*. 1975. Ballantine. 1st ed. Star Trek TVTI. F. P3. $50.00

JOSEPHS, Herbert. *Diderot's Dialogue of Language & Gesture...* 1969. OH State. 228p. brn brd. VG/dj. G1. $30.00

JOSEPHSON, Hannah. *Golden Threads*. 1949. DSP. 1st ed. VG/fair. V4. $17.50

JOSEPHSON, Matthew. *Union House, Union Bar*. 1956. Random. 1st ed. photos. VG/dj. V4. $15.00

JOSEPHUS, Flavius. *Whole Genuine & Complete Works...* 1792-1794. NY. Durrell. issued in 60 parts then bdg. folio. calf. H10. $325.00

JOSEPHUS, Flavius. *Works of..., Learned & Authentic Jewish Historian...* nd. Coates. sm 4to. trans Wm Whiston. 105p. brn cloth. F. H1. $30.00

JOSEPHUS, Flavius. *Works of..., To Which Is Added, Christopher Noldius' Hist...* 1754. London. 1st ed thus. folio. modern blk cloth. VG. C6. $225.00

JOSEPHUS, Flavius. *Works of...: Jewish Historian & Celebrated Warrior*. 1844. np. 648p. full leather. VG. E5. $65.00

JOSEPHY, Alvin. *American Heritage Book of Indians*. 1961. NY. ils. 424p. VG/dj. F3. $25.00

JOSEPHY, Alvin. *Indian Heritage of America.* 1986. Knopf. F/dj. B34. $20.00

JOSHI, S.T. *HP Lovecraft Annotated Bibliography.* 1981. Kent State. VG. P3. $30.00

JOSHI, S.T. *Weird Tale.* 1990. Austin. 1st ed. F/F. T2. $18.00

JOSLIN, Elliott P. *Diabetic Manual for Use of Doctor & Patient.* 1918. Phil. 1st ed. 187p. B14. $150.00

JOSLIN, Elliott P. *Treatment of Diabetes Mellitus...* 1917. Phil. 559p. cloth. G7. $65.00

JOSLIN, Sesyle. *Doctor George Owl.* ca 1970. Houghton Mifflin. 1st prt. ils Lisl Weil. F/VG. B10. $10.00

JOSSELYN, John. *New England's Rarities.* 1865. Boston. Beazie. 1st ed. pub sgn. 1/75. 170p. gilt blk cloth. F. K1. $125.00

JOUFFROY, Theodore Simon. *Melange Philosophiques.* 1833. Paris. Paulin. 491p. modern red leather. NF. G1. $185.00

JOULE, James Prescott. *Scientific Papers.* 1884. London. Taylor Franics. 2 vol. 1st ed. rebound gilt blk leather. H4. $400.00

JOURDAIN, M. *English Interiors in Smaller Houses From Restoration...* 1923. London. Batsford. tall 4to. ils. 202p. G+. F1. $85.00

JOVANOVICH, William. *Now, Barabbas.* 1964. Harper Row. 1st ed. 228p. F/dj. M10. $7.50

JOY, Charles R. *Music in the Life of Albert Schweitzer.* 1951. Harper Row. 1st ed. 300p. VG. B33. $16.00

JOY, Thomas. *Mostly Joy, a Bookman's Story.* 1971. London. ils. 206p. F/NF. A4. $65.00

JOYANT & TOULOUSE-LAUTREC. *Art of Cuisine.* 1966. HRW. 1st ed. 164p. VG/dj. M20. $75.00

JOYCE, James. *Anna Livia Plurabelle.* 1928. NY. Crosby Gaige. 1st ed. sgn. 1/800. teg. gilt brn buckram. F. B24. $1,500.00

JOYCE, James. *Anna Livia Plurabelle.* 1930. London. Faber. 1st ed. Ralph Block's copy. VG. Q1. $200.00

JOYCE, James. *Dubliners.* 1969. Modern Lib. VG/VG. P3. $13.00

JOYCE, James. *Finnegan's Wake.* 1939. London. Faber. 1st ed. 8vo. 628p. gilt red cloth. NF/dj. H5. $1,500.00

JOYCE, James. *Finnegan's Wake.* 1939. Viking. 1st ed (simultaneously w/Eng ed). F/NF. S9. $750.00

JOYCE, James. *Haveth Childers Everywhere.* 1930. Paris. Babou Kahane. 1st ed. F/F wax paper/F case. B2. $800.00

JOYCE, James. *Imagist Anthology 1930. New Poetry by the Imagists.* 1930. Covici Friede. 1st ed. 1/1000. 229p. NF/VG. C6. $275.00

JOYCE, James. *Letters of...* 1957. London. Faber. 1st ed. edit Stuart Gilbert. VG+/VG+ clip. S9. $50.00

JOYCE, James. *Pomes Penyeach.* 1927. Paris. Shakespeare. 1st ed. 16mo. gr brd. NF. C6. $350.00

JOYCE, James. *Pomes Penyeach.* 1933. London. Faber. 1st ed. VG/stiff wrp. M7. $115.00

JOYCE, James. *Portrait of the Artist As a Young Man.* 1916. NY. BW Huebsch. 1st Am ed. Ralph Block's copy. VG. Q1. $1,250.00

JOYCE, James. *Storiella As She Is Syung.* 1937. London. Corvinus. 1st ed. 1/150. 4to. teg. gilt orange vellum. F. H5. $3,000.00

JOYCE, James. *Ulysses.* 1934. Random. 1st authorized Am ed. 767p. VG/dj. B18. $175.00

JOYCE, John Alexander. *Jewels of Memory.* 1895. Gibson. 1st ed. 245p. cloth. NF. M8. $150.00

JOYCE, William. *Day With Wilbur Robinson.* 1990. Harper Row. 1st ed. F/F. B3. $20.00

JOYCE, William. *Dinosaur Bob & His Adventures With the Family Lazardo.* nd. Harper Row. 5th prt. 8vo. rem mk. F/F. B17. $9.00

JOYCE, William. *Nicholas Cricket.* 1989. Harper Row. 1st ed. trans Joyce Maxner. F/F. B3. $25.00

JUDD, Alex. *Tango.* 1990. Summit. 1st ed. F/F. F4. $17.00

JUDD, Cyril. *Gunner Cade.* 1952. Simon Schuster. 1st ed. xl. dj. P3. $10.00

JUDD, Frances K. *Sunken Garden.* nd. Books Inc. VG. P3. $10.00

JUDD, Laura Fish. *Honolulu.* 1966. Lakeside. 379p. VG+. M20. $25.00

JUDGE, William O. *Echoes From Orient: Broad Outline of Theosophical Doctrine.* 1918. Los Angeles. Magazine Theosophy. 64p. VG. B33. $15.00

JUDSON & JUDSON. *Your Holiday in Cuba.* 1952. NY. Harper. 1st ed. 8vo. 306p. VG. B11. $25.00

JUGAKU. *Bibliographical Study of Wm Blake's Note-Book.* 1971. np. 175p. F. A4. $35.00

JUGIE, Martin. *Le Schisme Byznatin Apercu Historique et Doctrinal.* 1941. Paris. Lethielleux. 487p. lib bdg. H10. $27.50

JULIAN, Philippe. *Triumph of Art Nouveau. Paris Exhibition 1900.* 1974. NY. Larousse. 4to. ils. bl cloth. F/dj. F1. $55.00

JUNG, C.G. *Basic Writings of CG Jung.* 1959. Modern Lib. intro Violet S deLaszlo. 522p. F/F. H1. $12.00

JUNG, C.G. *Modern Man in Search of a Soul.* 1936. London. Keagan Paul. 282p. VG. B33. $22.00

JUNG-STILLING, Johann H. *Theory of Pneumatology, in Reply to Question.* 1851. NY. Redfield. 1st Am ed. 12mo. 286p. VG. G1. $135.00

JUNKINS, Donald. *And Sandpipers She Said.* 1970. MA U. 1st ed. 62p. VG/dj. M10. $5.00

JUPO. *Wishing Shoe.* ca 1946. Collins. ils. unp. VG. B10. $10.00

JUST, Ward. *Ambition & Love.* 1994. Houghton Mifflin. ARC. F/wrp. w/promo material. F/wrp. L3. $30.00

JUSTER, Norton. *Otter Nonsense.* 1982. Philomel. possible 1st ed. F/VG+. C8. $27.50

JUSTICE, Keith L. *Science Fiction, Fantasy & Horror Reference.* 1989. McFarland. 1st ed. VG. P3. $35.00

JUSTINIANUS I, Emperor. *Institutionum Libri IV...* 1642. Blaeu. 12mo. 648p. contemporary vellum. K1. $150.00

JUSTINUS, Marcus Junianus. *Trogi Pompeii Historiarum Philippicarum Epitoma...* 1581. Paris. Dionysium du Val. 2 parts in 1. sm 8vo. old calf/rebacked. K1. $350.00

JUSTUS, May. *House in No-End Hollow.* 1938. Doubleday Doran. 1st ed. 286p. VG. B10. $20.00

JUSTUS, May. *Jumping Johnny & Skedaddle.* 1958. Evanston, IL. Row Peterson. 1st ed. VG+/G. C8. $25.00

JUVENAL. *Satires of Juvenal...* 1807. London. Payne Mackinlay. lg 4to. 572p. gilt contemporary red morocco. K1. $175.00

K

KABIR, Humayun. *Muslim Politics 1906-1947.* 1969. Calcutta. Mukhopadhyay. 1st ed. VG/dj. W1. $14.00

KADEN, Vera. *Ils of Plants & Gardens 1500-1850.* 1982. London. ils/pl. sc. M. B26. $15.00

KAFKA, Franz. *Amerika.* 1927. Muchen. Woolf. 1st ed. VG/wrp. B4. $1,500.00

KAFKA, Franz. *Castle.* 1969. Modern Lib. VG/VG. P3. $15.00

KAFKA, Franz. *Diaries.* 1948. London. 2 vol. 1st Eng ed. NF/VG. C2. $90.00

KAFKA, Franz. *Trial.* 1960. Knopf. rpt. VG/poor. N2. $6.00

KAHIN & LEWIS. *United States in Vietnam.* 1967. Dell. 465p. M11. $10.00

KAHL, Virginia. *Droopsi.* 1958. Scribner. 1st ed. VG+/G. C8. $40.00

KAHLENBERG, Mary H. *Navajo Blanket.* 1972. NY. Praeger. 1st ed. VG+/VG+. A1. $45.00

KAHLER, Erich. *Man the Measure: New Approach to History.* 1956 (1943). Braziller. 1st ed thus. 700p. VG/VG. G1. $25.00

KAHN, Herman. *On Thermonuclear War.* 1960. NJ. 1st ed. 651p. G/dj. B18. $25.00

KAHN, James. *Timefall.* 1987. St Martin. 1st ed. RS. F/F. P3. $20.00

KAHN, Joan. *Edge of the Chair.* nd. BOMC. VG/G. P3. $10.00

KAHN, Joan. *Hanging by a Thread.* 1969. Houghton Mifflin. 1st ed. VG/G. P3. $15.00

KAHN, Peggy. *Christmastime at Santa's Workshop.* 1990s. Random. 8vo. 6 popups. F. B17. $7.00

KAHN, Roger. *Seventh Game.* 1982. NAL. 1st ed. F/VG+. P8. $12.50

KAINS, Josephine; see Goulart, Ron.

KAISER, R.B. *RFK Must Die! Hist of Robert Kennedy Assassination...* 1970. NY. 1st ed. ils/pls. 634p. NF. D3. $12.50

KAJENCKI, Francis. *Star on Many a Battlefield.* 1980. ils/index. 280p. map ep. dj. O8. $12.50

KAKONIS, Tom. *Criss Cross.* 1990. St Martin. 1st ed. VG/VG. P3. $20.00

KAKONIS, Tom. *Michigan Roll.* 1988. St Martin. 1st ed/author's 1st book. sgn. F/F. L3. $75.00

KALCHURI, Bhau. *Avatar of the Age: Meher Baba Manifesting.* 1985. N Myrtle Beach. Manifestation. 222p. F/F. B33. $20.00

KALLEN, Horace Meyer. *League of Nations Today & Tomorrow.* 1919. Boston. Marshall Jones. 1st ed. 181p. xl. G. W1. $15.00

KALLEN, Lucille. *Tanglewood Murder.* 1989. Wyndham. 1st ed. F/F. P3. $15.00

KALLETT, Arthur. *Counterfeit.* 1935. Vanguard. 1st ed. ils. 96p. VG/G. S11. $10.00

KALLIR, Otto. *Grandma Moses.* 1973. Abrams. 1st ed. obl folio. ils/135 pl. 356p. gr/wht cloth. F/F. H3. $65.00

KALTCHAS, Nicholas. *Intro to Constitutional Hist of Modern Greece.* 1970. AMS. 1st ed. 187p. xl. VG. W1. $8.00

KAMIN, Leon J. *Science & Politics of IQ.* 1974. Potomac, MD. Lawrence Erlbaum. 178p. F/dj. K4. $12.50

KAMINSKY, Stuart M. *Cold Red Sunrise.* 1988. NY. Scribner. ARC/1st ed. w/promo material. F/F. S6. $30.00

KAMINSKY, Stuart M. *Cold Red Sunrise.* 1988. Scribner. 1st ed. F/F. M15. $45.00

KAMINSKY, Stuart M. *Man Who Walked Like a Bear.* 1990. Scribner. 1st ed. VG/VG. P3. $17.00

KAMINSKY, Stuart M. *Man Who Walked Like a Bear.* 1991. London. Heinemann. 1st ed. F/F. B3. $10.00

KAMINSKY, Stuart M. *Murder on the Yellow Brick Road.* 1977. St Martin. 1st ed. sgn. F/F. B2. $85.00

KAMINSKY, Stuart M. *Red Chameleon.* 1985. NY. Scribner. 1st ed. F/F. M15. $35.00

KAMINSKY, Stuart M. *Tomorrow Is Another Day.* 1995. Mysterious. ARC. F/wrp. B2. $30.00

KAMM, Minnie Watson. *Second Two Hundred Pattern Glass Pitchers.* 1940. Detroit. Motschall. 1st ed. 135p. sbdg. VG. H1. $27.50

KAMPFFMEYER, Georg. *Ignaz Krackovskij.* 1929. Berlin. Deutsche. 1st ed. 8vo. VG. W1. $10.00

KANAVEL, Allen. *Infections of the Hand... Second Edition...* 1914. Phil. 496p. VG. G7. $65.00

KANE, Art. *Paperdolls.* 1984. Melrose. 1st ed. F/NF. S9. $45.00

KANE, Bob. *Batman: The Dailies 1943-46.* 1990. Kitchen Sink. 1st ed. F/box. B3. $55.00

KANE, Frank. *Red Hot Ice.* 1955. Ives Washburn. VG. P3. $25.00

KANE, H. *Louisiana Hayride.* 1941. NY. sgn. VG/VG. B5. $20.00

KANE, Harnett T. *Amazing Mrs Bonaparte.* 1963. Doubleday. 1st ed. sgn. VG/dj. M20. $25.00

KANE, Harnett T. *Gentlemen, Swords & Pistols.* 1951. Morrow. 1st ed. VG/VG. P3. $20.00

KANE, Harnett T. *Queen New Orleans.* 1949. Morrow. 1st ed. sgn. 366p. VG+/dj. M20. $25.00

KANE, Henry. *Hang by Your Neck.* 1949. Simon Schuster. 1st ed. VG/VG. P3. $20.00

KANE, Henry. *Operation Delta.* 1967. Michael Joseph. 1st ed. VG/VG. P3. $25.00

KANE, Henry. *Report for a Corpse.* 1948. Simon Schuster. 1st ed. 245p. VG/dj. M20. $15.00

KANE, Joe. *Running the Amazon.* 1989. Knopf. ils. 278p. VG/dj. F3. $15.00

KANT, Immanuel. *Anthropologie in Pragmatischer Hinsicht.* 1800. Konigsburg. 2nd revised ed. bl wrp. G1. $275.00

KANT, Immanuel. *Critique of Pur Reason & Other Works on Theory of Ethics.* 1873. London. Longman Gr. 6th ed. cloth. G1. $24.00

KANT, Immanuel. *Die Metaphysik der Sitten.* 1797. Konigsburg. Friedrich Nicolovius. orig drab bl wrp. G1. $1,000.00

KANT, Immanuel. *Kant's Kritik of Judgment.* 1892. London. Macmillan. 1st Eng-language ed. 430p. ruled crimson cloth. VG. G1. $100.00

KANT, Immanuel. *Kritik der Reinen Vernunft.* 1781. Riga. Johann Friedrich Hartnoch. 12mo. 856p. G1. $7,500.00

KANTOR, MacKinlay. *Missouri Bittersweet.* 1969. Doubleday. 1st ed. 324p. G/dj. B18. $19.50

KANTOR, MacKinlay. *Spirit Lake.* 1961. Cleveland. World. 1st ed. dj. N2. $14.00

KANTOR, MacKinley. *Diversey.* 1928. Coward McCann. 1st ed/author's 1st book. VG. B2. $35.00

KANTOR, MacKinley. *God & My Country.* 1954. World. 1st ed. inscr. F/F. B4. $125.00

KANTOR, McKinlay. *Andersonville.* 1955. 760p. dj. O8. $12.50

KANTOROVITCH, Haim. *Towards Socialist Reorientation.* nd. NY. ASQ Rpts. No 1 in Rpt Series. NF/wrp. B2. $40.00

KAPLAN, Marshall H. *Space Shuttle: America's Wings to the Future.* 1978. Fallbrook, CA. Aero. 4to. 215p. VG/torn. K5. $16.00

KAPP, Edmond X. *Reflections. A Second Series of Drawings.* 1922. London. Cape. ltd ed. 1/50. 24 tipped-in pl. F. F1. $50.00

KAPUSCINSKI, Ryszard. *Shah of Shahs.* 1985. San Diego/NY/London. HBJ. 1st Am ed. 8vo. VG/dj. W1. $18.00

KARAGEORGHIS, Vassos. *Salamis: Recent Discoveries in Cyprus.* 1969. McGraw Hill. 1st ed. 212p. xl. VG/dj. W1. $35.00

KARIER, Clarence. *Scientists of the Mind, Intellectual Founders...* 1986. Chicago. 1st ed. 356p. dj. A13. $35.00

KARINTHY, F. *Journey Round My Skull.* 1939. NY. 288p. G7. $15.00

KARL, Frederick R. *William Faulkner: Am Writer.* 1989. NY. 1st ed. photos/biblio/index. 1131p. F/F. A17. $20.00

KARLOFF, Boris. *And the Darkness Falls.* 1946. World. 1st ed. G/rpr. M2. $40.00

KARR, Charles. *Remington Handguns.* 1960. Stackpole. 4th ed. G/G. A1. $20.00

KARSH, Yousuf. *Karsh Portrait.* 1976. Boston. NYGS. 1st ed. 4to. F/F. S9. $125.00

KARSON, Marc. *American Labor Unions & Politics, 1900-1918.* 1958. Carbondale. M. V4. $12.50

KARST, Kenneth. *Evolution of Law in the Barrios of Caracas.* 1973. Los Angeles. 125p. VG. D3. $15.00

KASHER, Asa. *Cognitive Aspects of Language Use.* 1989. Amsterdam. Elsevier Science Pub. 298p. F. G1. $50.00

KASPER, Walter. *Faith & the Future.* 1982. Crossroad. 140p. M/M. B29. $4.50

KASS, Philip. *Children of Wonder.* nd. BC. VG/VG. P3. $15.00

KASSEBAUM, G. *Prison Treatment & Parole Survival.* 1971. NY. 380p. VG. D3. $12.50

KASTLE, Herbert. *Cross-Country.* 1975. WH Allen. 1st ed. VG/VG. P3. $20.00

KASTNER, Erich. *Animals Conference.* 1955. London. Collins. probable 1st UK ed. VG+/VG. C8. $65.00

KASTNER, Erich. *Baron Munchhousen.* 1957. NY. Messner. 1st ed thus. trans Winston. VG+/chip. C8. $27.50

KASTNER, Erich. *Simpletons.* 1957 (1954). Messner. 1st Am ed. NF/VG. C8. $65.00

KASTNER, Joseph. *World of Naturalists.* 1977. London. Murray. 350p. cloth. M/dj. A10. $22.00

KATAEV, Valentine. *Embezzlers.* 1929. NY. Dial. 1st ed. NF/NF. B2. $35.00

KATES, Brian. *Murder of a Shopping Bag Lady.* 1985. Harcourt. ARC/1st ed. RS. F/F. S6. $25.00

KATIBAH, H.I. *Other Arabian Nights.* 1928. Scribner. 1st ed. 8vo. 266p. G. W1. $14.00

KATKOV, George. *Russia 1917: February Revolution.* 1967. NY. Harper Row. F/F. V4. $20.00

KATZ, David. *Psychological Atlas.* 1948. Philosophical Lib. 137p. G/dj. K4. $30.00

KATZ, Michael J. *Murder Off the Glass.* 1987. Walker. 1st ed. NF/NF. P3. $16.00

KATZ, Richard. *Schnaps, Kokain und Lamas.* 1931. Berlin. 1st ed. 251p. G/dj. F3. $15.00

KATZ, Robert. *Ziggurat.* 1977. Houghton Mifflin. 1st ed. NF/NF. P3. $17.00

KATZ, S. *Freud: On War, Sex & Neurosis.* 1947. Arts & Science Pr. 276p. G. K4. $15.00

KATZ. *Teacher's Guide to American Negro History.* 1971. np. 2nd ed/revised. 192p. xl. VG. A4. $35.00

KAUFFMAN, Donald. *Dictionary of Religious Terms.* 1967. Revell. 445p. VG/torn. B29. $6.50

KAUFFMAN, Janet. *Collaborators.* 1986. Knopf. 1st ed. F/F. B3. $20.00

KAUFFMAN, Reginald Wright. *Spanish Dollars...* 1925. Penn Pub. 1st ed. 299p. VG. B10. $20.00

KAUFFMAN, Reginald. *Puss-In-Boots. A Ballad-Arrangement for Young Children.* 1922. Altemus. 16mo. 29 mc ils. red cloth. VG. D6. $25.00

KAUFMAN, Stuart B. *Samuel Gompers Papers Vol I: Making of a Union Leader...* 1986. Chicago. VG/VG. V4. $17.50

KAUFMANN, Walter. *Discovering the Mind Vol 3.* 1980. McGraw Hill. 494p. VG/clip. G1. $40.00

KAUFMANN, Walter. *Faith of a Heretic.* 1961. Doubleday. 432p. gr cloth. NF/chip. G1. $35.00

KAUTSKY, Karl. *High Cost of Living, Changes in Gold Production...* 1915. Kerr. VG. B34. $50.00

KAVANAGH, Dan. *Duffy.* 1980. London. 1st ed/author's 2nd book & 1st crime novel. sgn. F/NF. A11. $75.00

KAVANAGH, Dan. *Fiddle City.* 1981. London. Cape. 1st ed. VG+/dj. S6. $30.00

KAVANAGH, Dan. *Flaubert's Parrot.* 1985. Knopf. 1st Am ed. F/F. B4. $75.00

KAVANAGH, Dan. *Talking It Over.* 1991. London. Cape. 1st ed. F/F. B4. $45.00

KAVANAUGH, Patrick. *Spiritual Lives of the Great Composers.* 1992. Sparrow. 119p. VG/dj. B29. $6.50

KAVEN, Anna. *House of Sleep.* 1947. Doubleday. 1st ed. NF/VG. B4. $85.00

KAVENEY, Roz. *Tales From the Forbidden Planet.* 1987. Titan. 1st ed. F/F. P3. $25.00

KAWABETA, Yasunari. *Izu Dancer.* 1981. Tokyo. Bijou Hoshino. 28x30mm. 1/44. teg. blk morocco/onlays. F/case. B24. $325.00

KAWAKAMI, K.K. *Jokichi Takamine: A Record of His American Achievements.* 1918. Rudge. 1st ed. 73p. VG. M10. $7.50

KAWATA, Yasuyo. *Prisoner of Conscience, Chen Yu-Hsi.* 1975. Honolulu. 21st Century Books. 228p. M11. $25.00

KAY, Gertrude Alice. *Adventures in Geography.* ca 1930. Volland. ils. 157p. VG. B10. $35.00

KAY, Gertrude Alice. *Friends of Jimmy.* 1926. Volland. 5th prt. ils. VG. P2. $38.00

KAY, Gertrude Alice. *Us Kids & the Circus.* 1928. Saalfield. unp. VG. M20. $70.00

KAY, Helen. *Cats on Pier 56.* 1961. Reilly Lee. ils Ralph E Rickets. unp. VG/G. B10. $12.00

KAY, Susan. *Phantom.* 1991. Delacorte. 1st ed. F/F. T2. $17.00

KAY, Ted. *Hazel Jubilee.* 1959. Dutton. 1st ed. 4to. F/VG clip. B4. $50.00

KAY, Terry. *To Dance With the White Dog.* 1990. Atlanta, GA. Peach Tree. 1st ed. F/F. B3. $30.00

KAYE, M.M. *Death in Zanzibar.* 1983. Allen Lane. 1st ed. VG/VG. P3. $15.00

KAYE, M.M. *Ordinary Princess.* 1984. Doubleday. 1st ed. 8vo. 112p. VG/VG. A3. $20.00

KAYE, M.M. *Trade Wind.* 1981. St Martin. 1st ed. VG+/VG+. M21. $20.00

KAYE, Marvin. *Lively Game of Death.* 1974. Arthur Barker. VG/VG. P3. $20.00

KAYSEN, Susanna. *Girl, Interrupted.* 1993. Turtle Bay Books. ARC. F/wrp. S9. $30.00

KAZANTZAKIS, Nikos. *Report to Greco.* 1965. Simon Schuster. 2nd prt. 512p. F/dj. W1. $15.00

KAZANTZAKIS, Nikos. *Zorba the Greek.* 1952. London. Lehmann. 1st Eng trans. 8vo. 319p. pk brd. VG/dj. H5. $300.00

KEANE, Christopher. *Crossing.* 1978. Arbor. 1st ed. F/F. F4. $12.00

KEARNEY, Julian; see Goulart, Ron.

KEARNEY, Patrick J. *Hist of Erotic Literature.* 1982. London. Macmillan. 1st ed. 192p. VG/VG. S11. $40.00

KEARNEY & KUTLER. *Super Soaps.* 1977. Grosset Dunlap. 1st ed. F/F. P3. $20.00

KEASEY, Merritt S. *Saguaro Book.* 1981. Dubuque. photos. 48p. sc. F. B26. $8.00

KEATING, B. *Alaska.* 1969. WA. NGS. ils/index. VG/VG. A17. $10.00

KEATING, Edward. *Story of Labor: 33 Years on Rail Worker's Fighting Front.* 1953. WA, DC. Darby. pres. photos. VG/G. V4. $25.00

KEATING, H.R.F. *Body in the Billiard Room.* 1987. Hutchinson. 1st ed. F/F. P3. $20.00

KEATING, H.R.F. *Crime & Mystery: 100 Best Books.* 1987. London. Xanadu. 1st ed. F/F. w/promo material. S6. $35.00

KEATING, H.R.F. *Man Who...* 1992. London. Macmillan. 1st ed. sgn contributor Symons. F/F. S6. $45.00

KEATING, H.R.F. *Murder Must Appetize.* 1981. Mysterious. 1st ed. F/sans. M2. $10.00

KEATING, H.R.F. *Rich Detective.* 1993. London. Macmillan. 1st ed. F/F. S6. $25.00

KEATING, James. *Function of Philosopher in Am Pragmatism.* 1953. Catholic U of Am Pr. 36p. VG/wrp. G1. $30.00

KEATON, Buster. *Wonderful World of Slapstick.* 1960. NY. 1st ed. VG/VG. B5. $30.00

KEATS, Ezra Jack. *Goggles!* 1970. Macmillan. 2nd prt. unp. G. B10. $10.00

KEATS, John. *Poetical Works & Other Writings of..* 1938. Scribner. 8 vol. 1/1050. Hamstead ed. sgn John Masefield/MB Foreman. M/box. H4. $650.00

KEATS, John. *Two Odes.* 1926. San Francisco. 1/160. F/wrp. A9. $30.00

KEATS, John. *You Might As Well Live.* 1970. Simon Schuster. 1st ed. F/F. S9. $30.00

KEAY, R.W.J. *Trees of Nigeria.* 1989. Oxford. ils. 486p. M. B26. $99.00

KEEBLE, John. *Broken Ground.* 1987. Harper Row. 1st ed. sgn. F/F. A11. $30.00

KEEBLE, John. *Broken Ground.* 1987. Harper Row. 1st ed. VG/VG. P3. $18.00

KEEBLE, John. *Crab Canon.* 1971. NY. 1st ed. inscr. F/VG. A11. $55.00

KEEGAN, John. *Churchill's Generals.* 1991. NY. 1st Am ed. 368p. M/M. A17. $12.50

KEEL, John A. *Jadoo.* 1957. Messner. 1st ed. VG. P3. $20.00

KEEL, John A. *Jadoo.* 1957. Messner. 1st ed. VG+/VG. M21. $40.00

KEELE, W.C. *Provincial Justice; or, Magistrate's Manual...* 1851. Toronto. H Rowsell. 3rd ed. modern quarter calf. G. M11. $350.00

KEELEY, Gertrude. *Story of the Birds for Young People With Bird Alphabet.* ca 1914. Hurst. unp. fair. B10. $15.00

KEELING, Jill. *Old English Sheepdog.* 1961. London. Foyle. 1st ed. 94p. glossy brd. G+. R2. $35.00

KEEN, A.M. *Sea Shells of Tropical West America.* 1958. Stanford. NF/dj. F1. $30.00

KEEN, Benjamin. *Aztec Image in W Thought.* 1971. Rutgers. 1st ed. 667p. VG/dj. F3. $35.00

KEENE, Carolyn. *Dana Girls: By the Light of the Study Lamp.* 1934. Grosset Dunlap. early thick ed. lists 4 titles. VG/ragged. M20. $90.00

KEENE, Carolyn. *Dana Girls: Haunted Lagoon (#21).* 1959. Grosset Dunlap. lists to Bamboo Bird. VG/dj. M20. $25.00

KEENE, Carolyn. *Dana Girls: Mysterious Fireplace.* nd. Grosset Dunlap. VG. P3. $8.00

KEENE, Carolyn. *Dana Girls: Mystery at the Crossroads.* 1954. Grosset Dunlap. gr bdg. VG. P3. $8.00

KEENE, Carolyn. *Dana Girls: Mystery of the Locked Room (#7).* 1938. Grosset Dunlap. lists to #11. 218p. VG/dj. M20. $30.00

KEENE, Carolyn. *Dana Girls: Portrait in the Sand.* nd. Grosset Dunlap. 12mo. NF/VG. C8. $22.50

KEENE, Carolyn. *Dana Girls: Portrait in the Sand.* 1943. Grosset Dunlap. lists to this title. 216p. VG/dj. M20. $60.00

KEENE, Carolyn. *Dana Girls: Secret at Lone Tree Cottage.* nd. Grosset Dunlap. bl bdg. VG. P3. $12.00

KEENE, Carolyn. *Dana Girls: Secret at the Hermitage (#5).* 1936. Grosset Dunlap. lists to this title. 218p. NF/NF. M20. $250.00

KEENE, Carolyn. *Dana Girls: Secret of the Jade Ring.* 1953. Grosset Dunlap. NF/VG. C8. $22.50

KEENE, Carolyn. *Nancy Drew Cookbook.* 1973. Grosset Dunlap. 1st ed. red ep. 159p. VG. M20. $28.00

KEENE, Carolyn. *Nancy Drew: Bungalow Mystery (#3).* ca 1955. Grosset Dunlap. bl tweed pict brd. VG+/G+. C8. $20.00

KEENE, Carolyn. *Nancy Drew: Bungalow Mystery (#3).* 1931 (1930). Grosset Dunlap. B prt. 204p. bl cloth. VG/dj. M20. $350.00

KEENE, Carolyn. *Nancy Drew: Clue in the Diary.* 1934 (1932). Grosset Dunlap. thick ed/A prt. 202p. bl cloth. VG/dj. M20. $250.00

KEENE, Carolyn. *Nancy Drew: Clue in the Jewel Box.* nd. Grosset Dunlap. brd. VG. P3. $4.00

KEENE, Carolyn. *Nancy Drew: Clue of the Broken Locket (#11).* ca 1937. Grosset Dunlap. orange decor bl pict cloth. VG/G+. C8. $45.00

KEENE, Carolyn. *Nancy Drew: Clue of the Broken Locket (#11).* 1934. Grosset Dunlap. thick ed/B prt. 219p. bl cloth. VG/dj. M20. $225.00

KEENE, Carolyn. *Nancy Drew: Clue of the Tapping Heels (#16).* ca 1950. Grosset Dunlap. VG/VG. C8. $30.00

KEENE, Carolyn. *Nancy Drew: Hidden Staircase (#2).* ca 1937. Grosset Dunlap. orange decor bl cloth. VG/G+. C8. $45.00

KEENE, Carolyn. *Nancy Drew: Hidden Window Mystery.* nd. Grosset Dunlap. VG/VG. P3. $10.00

KEENE, Carolyn. *Nancy Drew: Hidden Window Mystery.* 1956. Grosset Dunlap. 1st ed. lists 18 titles. 214p. bl tweed cloth. VG/dj. M20. $35.00

KEENE, Carolyn. *Nancy Drew: Message in the Hollow Oak (#12).* ca 1952 (1935). Grosset Dunlap. VG/G. C8. $30.00

KEENE, Carolyn. *Nancy Drew: Message in the Hollow Oak (#12).* 1936 (1935). Grosset Dunlap. thick ed/B prt. lists to this title. 218p. VG/dj. M20. $145.00

KEENE, Carolyn. *Nancy Drew: Mystery at the Moss-Covered Mansion.* 1941. Grosset Dunlap. thick ed C (3rd) prt. 215p. bl cloth. VG/dj. M20. $150.00

KEENE, Carolyn. *Nancy Drew: Mystery of Brass Bound Trunk (#17).* ca 1953. Grosset Dunlap. bl tweed pict brd. VG+/VG. C8. $25.00

KEENE, Carolyn. *Nancy Drew: Mystery of Ivory Charm (#13).* ca 1953. Grosset Dunlap. bl tweed pict brd. VG+/G. C8. $25.00

KEENE, Carolyn. *Nancy Drew: Mystery of Lilac Inn (#4).* ca 1953. Grosset Dunlap. bl tweed pict paper brd. VG. C8. $15.00

KEENE, Carolyn. *Nancy Drew: Mystery of the Tolling Bell.* 1946. Grosset Dunlap. C (3rd) prt. 213p. bl cloth. VG/dj. M20. $30.00

KEENE, Carolyn. *Nancy Drew: Nancy's Mysterious Letter.* 1934. Grosset Dunlap. A prt. 209p. bl cloth. VG/dj. M20. $250.00

KEENE, Carolyn. *Nancy Drew: Password to Larkspur Lane (#10).* ca 1953. Grosset Dunlap. bl tweed pict brd. VG. C8. $15.00

KEENE, Carolyn. *Nancy Drew: Password to Larkspur Lane (#10).* 1937 (1933). Grosset Dunlap. B prt. 220p. VG/dj. M20. $75.00

KEENE, Carolyn. *Nancy Drew: Password to Larkspur Lane (#10).* 1960 (1933). Grosset Dunlap. NF/NF. C8. $25.00

KEENE, Carolyn. *Nancy Drew: Ringmaster's Secret (#31).* 1957. Grosset Dunlap. F/NF. C8. $30.00

KEENE, Carolyn. *Nancy Drew: Secret at Shadow Ranch (#5).* ca 1949. Grosset Dunlap. VG/VG. C8. $30.00

KEENE, Carolyn. *Nancy Drew: Secret at Shadow Ranch (#5).* 1931. Grosset Dunlap. 1st ed. 203p. bl cloth. G. M20. $50.00

KEENE, Carolyn. *Nancy Drew: Secret in the Old Attic.* 1944. Grosset Dunlap. 1st ed. 216p. bl cloth. VG/dj. M20. $55.00

KEENE, Carolyn. *Nancy Drew: Secret of the Old Clock (#1).* ca 1932. Grosset Dunlap. 10 ad p. orange prt bl cloth. VG. C8. $75.00

KEENE, Carolyn. *Nancy Drew: Secret of the Old Clock (#1).* 1941. Grosset Dunlap. medium thick ed/C prt. 210p. bl cloth. NF/dj. M20. $75.00

KEENE, Carolyn. *Nancy Drew: Sign of the Twisted Candles.* 1935 (1933). Grosset Dunlap. thick ed/B prt. 217p. VG/dj. M20. $225.00

KEENE, Carolyn. *Nancy Drew: Whispering Statue (#14).* ca 1937. Grosset Dunlap. orange decor bl cloth. VG+/VG. C8. $50.00

KEENE, Carolyn. *Nancy Drew: Whispering Statue (#14).* 1938 (1937). Grosset Dunlap. A (2nd) prt. VG/ragged. M20. $90.00

KEENE, Carolyn. *Picture Book: Mystery of the Lost Dogs.* 1977. Grosset Dunalp. ils T Sullivan. VG. B17. $12.00

KEEP, Rosalind. *Fourscore Years. A History of Mills College.* 1931. Mills College. ltd ed. sgn. 143p. VG. B11. $35.00

KEER, James. *Clinic.* nd. BC. VG/VG. P3. $8.00

KEFAUVER, Estes. *Crime in Am.* 1951. NY. 1st ed. photos/index. 333p. F/F. A17. $15.00

KEHOE, S.M. *Indian Club Exercise. With Explanatory Figures & Positions.* 1866. NY. Dick & Fitzgerald. 1st ed. lg 4to. ils. cloth. VG. M1. $275.00

KEIDEL, George Charles. *Catonsville Lutheran Church: Sketch of Its Origin.* 1919. WA, DC. 1st ed. 12mp. NF/prt wrp. M8. $27.50

KEIFITZ, Norman. *Sensation.* 1975. Atheneum. 1st ed. F/VG. P8. $15.00

KEILL, John. *Introductio ad Veram Astronomiam...* 1721. London. Strahan. 2nd ed. Latin text. 2 fld pl of moon. 513p. leather. K5. $420.00

KEILLIN, David. *History of Cell Respiration & Cytochrome.* 1966. Cambridge. 1st ed. 416p. A13. $100.00

KEITH, Agnes Newton. *Children of Allah.* 1966. Little Brn. 1st ed. 467p. xl. VG. W1. $14.00

KEITH, Brandon. *Affair of the Gentle Saboteur.* 1966. Whitman. Man From UNCLE TVTI. VG. P3. $13.00

KEITH, Brandon. *Message From Moscow.* 1966. Whitman. I Spy TVTI. VG. P3. $10.00

KEITH, Carlton. *Taste of Sangria.* 1968. Crime Club. 1st ed. VG. P3. $10.00

KEITH, David. *Matter of Accent.* 1943. Dodd Mead. VG. P3. $25.00

KELEMEN, Pal. *Medieval American Art.* 1956. Macmillan. 1 vol ed. 4to. 414p. silvered blk cloth. G. F1. $60.00

KELLAND, Clarence B. *Mark Tidd in the Backwoods.* 1914. Harper. ils. F. M5. $20.00

KELLAND, Clarence B. *Mark Tidd's Citadel.* 1916. Harper. ils. F. M5. $20.00

KELLAND, Clarence B. *Mark Tidd.* 1913. Harper. 1st ed. sgn. 317p. VG. M20. $80.00

KELLAWAY, G.P. *Map Projections.* 1949 (1946). Methuen. 2nd ed. 8vo. 127p. G/dj. K5. $18.00

KELLEAM, Joseph E. *When the Red King Woke.* 1966. Avalon. 1st ed. F/F. P3. $20.00

KELLER, David H. *Folsom Flint.* 1969. Arkham. 1st ed. F/F. P3. $30.00

KELLER, David H. *Life Everlasting.* 1947. Avalon. 1st ed. NF/dj. w/M bibliography. M2. $90.00

KELLER, David H. *Solitary Hunters & the Abyss.* 1948. New Era. 1st ed. sgn ils/pub. NF/dj. M2. $60.00

KELLER, Frances R. *Contented Little Pussy Cat.* 1949. Platt Munk. ils Adele Werber/Doris Laslo. 53p. cloth. G. A3. $7.00

KELLER, Fred S. *Definition of Psychology.* 1973. Appleton Century Crofts. 144p. F. K4. $10.00

KELLER, Harry. *Official Detective Omnibus.* 1948. DSP. 1st ed. VG. P3. $20.00

KELLER, Helen. *Story of My Life.* 1903. Doubleday Page. 1st ed. VG. B2. $50.00

KELLER, Katherine Southwick. *Dog Days.* 1944. Nelson. 1st ed. unp. brn cloth. VG/dj. B10. $10.00

KELLER, Werner. *Bible As Hist: Confirmation of Book of Books.* 1956. Morrow. 1st ed. 8vo. VG/dj. W1. $10.00

KELLERMAN, Faye. *Quality of Mercy.* 1989. Morrow. 1st ed. F/F. T2. $25.00

KELLERMAN, Faye. *Sacred & Profane.* 1987. Arbor. 1st ed. F/F. T2. $22.00

KELLERMAN, Faye. *Sacred & Profane.* 1987. Arbor. 1st ed. sgn. F/F. S6. $35.00

KELLERMAN, Jonathan. *Blood Test.* 1986. Atheneum. 1st ed. VG/VG. P3. $30.00

KELLERMAN, Jonathan. *Blood Test.* 1986. Atheneum. 1st ed/author's 2nd novel. F/F. T2. $40.00

KELLERMAN, Jonathan. *Butcher's Theater.* 1988. Bantam. 1st ed. F/F. T2. $30.00

KELLERMAN, Jonathan. *Over the Edge.* 1992. Bantam. 1st ed. F/F. T2. $22.00

KELLERMAN, Jonathan. *Silent Partner.* 1989. Bantam. 1st ed. F/F. T2. $20.00

KELLERMAN, Jonathan. *Silent Partner.* 1989. London. MacDonald. 1st ed (precedes Am). sgn. F/F. S6. $35.00

KELLERMAN, Jonathan. *Time Bomb.* 1990. Bantam. 1st ed. NF/NF. P3. $20.00

KELLERMAN, Jonathan. *When the Bough Breaks.* 1985. Atheneum. 1st ed/author's 1st novel. F/F. M15. $85.00

KELLEY, Dean. *Why Conservative Churches Are Growing.* 1972. Harper. 184p. VG/torn. B29. $4.00

KELLEY, Hall J. *Narrative of Events & Difficulties in Colonization of OR...* 1852. Boston. 1st ed. 8vo. 92p. xl. F/prt wrp/clamshell case. M1. $2,500.00

KELLEY, Leo P. *Luke Sutton: Outrider.* 1984. Doubleday. 1st ed. RS. F/F. P3. $13.00

KELLEY, Leo P. *Time 110100.* 1972. Walker. 1st ed. F/F. P3. $15.00

KELLEY, Louis Read. *Some Little Folks That I Know.* ca 1900. Ashtabula, OH. Standard Pub. photos. brd. worn. scarce. M5. $35.00

KELLNER, Bruce. *Biblio of Work of Carl Van Vechten.* 1980. Westport. index. 258p. VG. A17. $15.00

KELLOGG, Charles. *Driving the Horse in Harness.* 1980. Brattleboro. Greene. later prt. VG/wrp. O3. $15.00

KELLOGG, M. Bradley. *Wave & the Flame.* 1987. Gollancz. 1st ed. VG/VG. P3. $20.00

KELLOGG & KNAPP. *College of Agriculture: Science in Public Service.* 1966. McGraw. 237p. cloth. VG. A10. $20.00

KELLOGG'S. *Kellogg's Funny Jungleland Moving Pictures.* 1932. Kellogg's. mechanical pop-up. unp. G+. M20. $30.00

KELLY, Frederick Joseph. *Man Before God: Thomas Merton on Social Responsibility.* 1974. Doubleday. 1st ed. 287p. H10. $16.50

KELLY, Harold C. *Practical Course in Horology.* 1944. Manual Arts Pr. 1st ed. 12mo. 192p. VG. A8. $30.00

KELLY, Howard. *Snakes of Maryland.* 1936. Baltimore. 1st ed. 103p. wrp. A13. $100.00

KELLY, J.F. *Early Connecticut Meeting Houses.* 1948. NY. 2 vol. 1st ed. park service stps. VG. C11. $75.00

KELLY, James Patrick. *Look Into the Sun.* 1989. Tor. 1st ed. M/dj. M21. $15.00

KELLY, June. *Brisbane Is a Garden.* 1988 (1982). Buderim, Queensland. 4th ed. ils. VG/rpr. B26. $9.00

KELLY, Mary. *Girl in the Alley.* 1974. Walker. 1st ed. VG/VG. P3. $15.00

KELLY, Regina Z. *Beaver Trail.* ca 1955. Lee Shepard. ils Carl S Junge. 237p. VG/G. B10. $10.00

KELLY, Robert. *Lectiones.* 1965. Placitas. Duende. 1st ed. VG+/wrp. B2. $35.00

KELLY, Walt. *Pogo Stepmother Goose.* 1954. Simon Schuster. 1st prt. 4to. unp. VG-/wrp. A3. $30.00

KELLY & HOFFMANOWA. *Girl Who Would Be Queen: Story & Diary of...Kransinka.* 1939. McClurg. 1st ed. ils Vera Bock. 201p. VG/G. B10. $15.00

KELLY. *John Berryman: A Checklist.* 1972. np. 141p. F. A4. $15.00

KELMAN, John. *Road, a Study of John Bunyan's Pilgrim's Progress.* 1911-1912. London. Anderson Ferrier. 2 vol. ils. teg. cloth/vellum. VG+. F1. $60.00

KELSEY, Albert. *Yucatecan Scenes & Sounds.* 1919. Phil. 4to. 40p. VG. F3. $45.00

KELSEY, Alice Geer. *Ricardo's White Horse.* 1948. NY. Longman Gr. 1st ed. VG/G. O3. $18.00

KELSEY, Alice Geer. *Thirty Gilt Pennies.* ca 1968. Abingdon. ils Gordon Laite. 64p. VG/G. B10. $10.00

KELSEY, Morton. *Encounter With God.* 1972. Bethany. 281p. VG/dj. B29. $7.00

KELSEY, V. *Red River Runs North.* 1951. NY. 1st ed. VG/VG. B5. $27.50

KELSO, A.J. *Physical Anthropology.* 1970. Lippincott. 331p. F. K4. $8.50

KEMBLE. *History of CA Newspapers, 1846-1858.* 1962. np. 1/750. 398p. F/NF. A4. $125.00

KEMELMAN, Harry. *Saturday the Rabbi Went Hungry.* 1966. Crown. 1st ed. VG/VG. P3. $40.00

KEMELMAN, Harry. *Someday the Rabbi Will Leave.* 1985. Morrow. 1st ed. F/F. P3. $16.00

KEMENY, John G. *Philosopher Looks at Science.* 1959. Princeton. Van Nostrand. 273p. RS. VG/dj. G1. $35.00

KEMP, Charles. *Campaigning With Crook & Stories of Army Life.* 1890. Harper. ils. VG. extremely scarce. B34. $100.00

KEMP, Tage. *Prostitution.* 1936. London. Heinemann. 247p. G. K4. $50.00

KEMPIS. *De Imitatione Christi. Auctore Thoma a Kempis.* 1869. Casterman. 57x42mm. 493p. brn cloth. F. B24. $550.00

KEMPLEY, Walter. *Probability Factor.* 1972. Saturday Review. 1st ed. F/dj. F4. $16.00

KEMPTON, Murray. *Part of Our Time.* 1955. NY. 1st ed. VG/worn. A17. $15.00

KENDALL, Charles Wye. *Private Men of War.* 1932. NY. ils. VG. M17. $45.00

KENDALL, E. *Phantom Prince.* 1981. NY. 1st ed. VG/VG. B5. $15.00

KENDALL, John. *Recollections of a Confederate Officer.* 1946. LA Hist Soc. index. 362p. prt self wrp. O8. $14.50

KENDALL & KOEHLER. *Radio Simplified...* 1923. Chicago. Winston. 1st ed. 302p. pict cloth. F. B14. $50.00

KENDRAKE, Carleton; see Gardner, Erle Stanley.

KENDREW, W.G. *Climates of the Continents.* 1942 (1922). Oxford. 3rd ed. ils. 473p. bl cloth. G. K5. $16.00

KENDRICK, Baynard. *Flames of Time.* 1948. Scribner. 1st ed. VG/G. P3. $35.00

KENEALLY, Thomas. *Blood Red, Sister Rose.* 1974. London. Collins. 1st ed. F/NF. B4. $100.00

KENEALLY, Thomas. *Confederates.* 1979. Harper. 1st Am ed. F/NF. B4. $85.00

KENEALLY, Thomas. *Fear.* 1965. Australia. 1st ed. NF/VG+. B4. $350.00

KENEALLY, Thomas. *Flying Hero Glass.* 1991. Time Warner. 1st ed. sgn. NF/F. B4. $85.00

KENEALLY, Thomas. *Gossip From the Forest.* 1975. London. Collins. 1st ed. F/F clip. B4. $125.00

KENEALLY, Thomas. *Gossip From the Forest.* 1976. HBJ. 1st ed. VG/NF. B3. $25.00

KENEALLY, Thomas. *Passenger.* 1979. London. Collins. 1st ed. F/NF. B4. $100.00

KENEALLY, Thomas. *Schindler's List.* 1982. Simon Schuster. 1st ed. F/VG. B3. $200.00

KENEALLY, Thomas. *Survivor.* 1970. Viking. 1st ed/author's 3rd novel. NF/NF. L3. $65.00

KENEALLY, Thomas. *Three Cheers for the Paraclete.* 1969. Angus Robertson. 1st ed. F/F. B4. $225.00

KENEALLY, Thomas. *Woman of the Inner Sea.* 1993. Doubleday. 1st ed. F/NF. B4. $100.00

KENFIELD, Scott Dix. *Akron & Summit Co, OH, 1825-1928.* 1928. Chicago/Akron. 3 vol. VG. B18. $75.00

KENNA, Michael. *Elkhorn Slough & Moss Landing.* 1994. Elkhorn Slough Found. 2nd prt. F/prt wrp. S9. $20.00

KENNAN, George. *Campaigning in Cuba.* 1899. NY. Century. 8vo. 269p. G. B11. $75.00

KENNARD, J.S. *Italian Theatre: From Its Beginning to Close 17th Century.* 1932. NY. 2 vol. 1st ed. inscr. NF/G. C2. $100.00

KENNEALY, Jerry. *Polo's Ponies.* 1988. St Martin. 1st ed. F/dj. F4. $16.00

KENNEDY, Adam. *Just Like Humphrey Bogart.* 1978. Viking. 1st ed. VG/VG. P3. $15.00

KENNEDY, Adrienne. *People Who Led to My Plays.* 1987. np. 4to. 125p. F/F. A4. $35.00

KENNEDY, D. James. *Evangelism Explosion: Coral Ridge Program for Lay Witness.* 1974. Tyndale. 187p. VG. B29. $3.50

KENNEDY, Edward. *Critical Condition: Crisis in America's Health Care.* 1972. NY. 1st ed. 254p. A13. $25.00

KENNEDY, Gerald. *For Preachers & Other Sinners.* 1964. Harper. 110p. VG/dj. B29. $3.50

KENNEDY, Gerald. *Fresh Every Morning.* 1966. Harper. 194p. VG/VG. B29. $4.50

KENNEDY, Gerald. *Have This Mind.* 1948. Harper. 210p. VG. B29. $3.00

KENNEDY, Gerald. *Preacher & the New Eng Bible.* 1972. Oxford. 183p. G/torn. B29. $4.00

KENNEDY, J.M. *Gospel of Superman.* 1910. Foulis. 1st Eng trans. 1/2000. VG. S11. $85.00

KENNEDY, Janet. *Friends of Jesus.* 1954. Rand McNally Jr Elf Book 8022. K2. $3.00

KENNEDY, John F. *Profiles in Courage.* 1964. Harper Row. memorial ed. 8vo. VG/VG. B11. $15.00

KENNEDY, John F. *Profiles in Courage.* 1967. NY. special ed. pres from Shrivers. bl marbled ep. full bl leather/case. H4. $250.00

KENNEDY, John F. *Strategy of Peace.* 1960. Harper. 1st ed. inscr to Sen J Larkins. 8vo. 233p. F/morocco case. H5. $2,750.00

KENNEDY, John. *New Method of Stating & Explaining the Scripture Chronology.* 1751. London. 2 fld tables. 432p. calf. K1. $125.00

KENNEDY, Lucy. *Sunlit Field.* 1950. Crown. 1st ed. VG/fair. P8. $20.00

KENNEDY, Mary. *Surprise to the Children.* 1933. Doubleday Doran. 1st ed. 88p. VG. B10. $15.00

KENNEDY, Michael S. *Cowboys & Cattlemen.* 1964. NY. 1st ed. VG/VG. B5. $45.00

KENNEDY, R. Emmet. *Mellows: Chronicle of Unknown Singers.* 1925. NY. 4to. xl. lib bdg. A17. $15.00

KENNEDY, Robert F. *Robert Kennedy in His Own Words.* 1988. Bantam. 1st ed. VG/VG clip. S11. $10.00

KENNEDY, Robert F. *Thirteen Days: Memoir of the Cuban Missile Crisis.* 1969. Norton. BOMC. ils. 224p. VG/dj. M10. $5.00

KENNEDY, Robert F. *To Seek a Newer World.* 1967. Doubleday. 1st ed. inscr. NF/NF. B4. $400.00

KENNEDY, Thomas E. *Andre Dubus: A Study of Short Fiction.* 1988. Twayne. AP. VG+. S9. $30.00

KENNEDY, W.S. *Henry W Longfellow.* 1882. Moses King. 3rd ed. 368p. G. S11. $20.00

KENNEDY, William. *Billy Phelan's Greatest Game.* 1978. NY. 1st ed. VG/VG. B5. $50.00

KENNEDY, William. *Cotton Club.* 1983. Astoria, NY. revised shooting script. sgn. 124p. unbound. H5. $175.00

KENNEDY, William. *Hurrah for Life of a Sailor!* 1900. Edinburgh. Blackwood. ils/47 pl/maps. 456p. T7. $75.00

KENNEDY, William. *Ironweed.* 1983. Viking. 1st ed. F/VG+. P8. $125.00

KENNEDY, William. *Legs.* 1975. NY. CMG. 1st ed. F/NF. Q1. $150.00

KENNEDY, William. *Quinn's Book.* 1988. Viking. 1st ed. sgn. 1/500. F/F case. S9. $75.00

KENNEDY & NICHOLS. *Hints on Drawing & Painting & Use of Paints.* 1860. Auburn. 1st ed. 12mo. 46p. prt wrp. scarce. M1. $175.00

KENNERLY, W.C. *Persimmon Hill. Narrative of Old St Louis.* 1948. OK. 1st ed. NF/dj. A15. $40.00

KENNINGTON, Eric. *Drawing the RAF. A Book of Portraits.* 1942. London. Oxford. 1st ed. 144p. gilt bl cloth. VG/G. M7. $65.00

KENNY, Kathryn. *Trixie Belden & Black Jacket Mystery.* 1961. Whitman. VG. P3. $8.00

KENNY, Kathryn. *Trixie Belden & Mystery of Blinking.* 1963. Whitman. VG. P3. $8.00

KENRICK, Tony. *Two for the Price of One.* 1974. Michael Joseph. 1st ed. F/F. S6. $35.00

KENSEY, Nina. *Nineteen Years With an Alcoholic.* 1954. Vantage. ne. 8vo. 208p. G. A8. $7.00

KENT, A. *Sloop of War.* 1972. NY. 1st ed. VG/dj. B5. $40.00

KENT, Charles. *Charles Dickens As a Reader.* 1872. Lippincott. 1st Am ed. 12mo. 271p. bevelled cloth. VG. D3. $45.00

KENT, Edward. *Revolution & the Rule of Law.* 1917. Englewood Cliffs. 181p. VG/stiff wrp. D3. $15.00

KENT, Henry Watson. *What I Am — Call My Education.* nd. Grollier. ltd ed. VG. K3. $15.00

KENT, J.C. *Northborough History.* 1921. Newton. VG. A9. $45.00

KENT, Karlene. *Little Black Eyes.* 1927. Macmillan. 1st ed. 134p. VG/fair. B10. $25.00

KENT, Kate Peck. *Pueblo Indian Textiles.* 1983. School Am Research. ils/bibliography/index. 118p. F/F. B19. $45.00

KENT, Louis, Andrews. *Two Children of Tyer.* 1932. Jr Literary Guild. 1st ed. 8vo. 234p. VG. W1. $14.00

KENT, Rockwell. *Bookplates & Marks of Rockwell Kent...* 1929. Random. 1/1250. 8vo. 79p. F/dj. B24. $250.00

KENT, Rockwell. *It's Me O Lord. Autobiography of Rockwell Kent.* 1955. Dodd Mead. 1st ed. F/dj. B24. $150.00

KENT, Rockwell. *It's Me O Lord. Autobiography of Rockwell Kent.* 1955. Dodd Mead. 1st ed. VG. B5. $75.00

KENT, Rockwell. *Later Bookplates & Marks of Rockwell Kent.* 1937. NY. Pynson. author's copy. sgn. gilt rose cloth. F. w/prospectus. P4. $600.00

KENT, Rockwell. *Moby Dick.* 1930. NY. 1st ed. VG. B5. $45.00

KENT, Rockwell. *N by E.* 1930. Random. 1st ed. 1/900. ils/sgn Rockwell Kent. silvered bl cloth. F/case. F1. $300.00

KENT, Rockwell. *Of Men & Mountains, Being Account of European Travels...* 1959. Ausable Forks. Asgaard. 1/250. ils/sgn Kent. F/glassine. B24. $450.00

KENT, Rockwell. *Rockwell Kent, an Anthology of His Work.* 1982. Knopf. 1st ed. folio. edit Fridolf Johnson. F/F. F1. $120.00

KENT, Rockwell. *Voyaging: Southward From Strait of Magellan.* 1924. Putnam. 1st ed. inscr. 4to. VG. B4. $350.00

KENT, Rockwell. *What Is an American?* 1936. Los Angeles. Plantin. 1st ed. F/prt wrp. B24. $285.00

KENT, Rockwell. *Wilderness: A Journal of Quiet Adventure in Alaska.* 1970. Los Angeles. 1/1550. lg 8vo. sgn. 49 pl. aqua cloth/pict label. F/case. K1. $100.00

KENT, Rockwell. *World-Famous Paintings.* (1939). NY. Wise. 4to. 100 mc pl. unp. VG. H1. $35.00

KENWORTHY, Leonard S. *Quakerism: A Study Guide on Religious Society of Friends.* 1981. Kennett Sq, PA. Quaker Pub. 12mo. 215p. V3. $7.50

KENYON, Frederic G. *Books & Readers in Ancient Greece & Rome.* 1951. Oxford. 2nd ed. 8vo. 136p. cloth. O2. $30.00

KENYON, Michael. *May You Die in Ireland.* 1965. Morrow. 2nd ed. F/F. P3. $12.00

KENYON, Timothy. *Utopian Communism & Political Thought in Early Modern Eng.* 1989. London. Pinter. 286p. VG/dj. G1. $25.00

KEPES, Gyorgy. *Sign Image Symbol.* 1966. Braziller. 1st ed. F/NF. B2. $75.00

KEPES, Juliet. *Five Little Monkeys.* 1942. Houghton Mifflin. 1st ed. ils. VG/VG. P2. $30.00

KEPHART. *Captives Among the Indians.* 1915. np. 240p. VG. E5. $25.00

KER, Donald. *African Adventure.* 1957. Stackpole. 200 photos. 256p. F/VG. A4. $45.00

KER-SEYMER, Vere. *Idle But Happy.* 1930. London. Chapman Hall. 1st ed. 8vo. 16 pl. VG. W1. $9.00

KERAN, Don W. *David W Davies: A Bibliography.* 1973. Orangerie Pr. 1st ed. 39p. F/sans. w/ephemera. B19. $20.00

KEREKES, Tibor. *Arab Middle East & Muslim Africa.* 1961. Praeger. 1st ed. 8vo. 126p. xl. G. W1. $8.00

KERENYI, C. *Religion of the Greeks & the Romans.* 1962. Dutton. ils. 303p. NF/dj. M10. $20.00

KERFOOT, J.B. *Am Pewter.* 1942 (1924). Crown. 2nd prt. 236p. VG/dj. M20. $40.00

KERMAN, Cynthia Earl. *Creative Tension: Life & Thought of Kenneth Boulding.* 1974. Ann Arbor, MI. 1st ed. 8vo. 380p. M/M. V3. $18.00

KERN, Gregory; see Tubb, E.C.

KEROFILAS, C. *Eleftherios Venizelos: His Life & Work.* 1915. NY. 8vo. 178p. cloth. O2. $45.00

KEROUAC, Jack. *Big Sur.* 1962. NY. FSG. 1st ed. 8vo. 241p. gilt blk cloth/bl brd. F/NF. H5. $250.00

KEROUAC, Jack. *Excerpts From Visions of Cody.* 1960. New Directions. 1st ed. sgn. 1/750. 128p. prt cream brd/purple spine. VG/dj. C6. $550.00

KEROUAC, Jack. *On the Road.* 1957. Viking. 1st ed. VG+/dj. Q1. $850.00

KEROUAC, Jack. *On the Road.* 1957. Viking. 1st ed/author's 2nd novel. F/F. L3. $2,000.00

KEROUAC, Jack. *Two Early Stories.* 1973. London. Aloe. 1st ed. 1/175. F/wrp. C2. $100.00

KEROUAC, Jack. *Visions of Gerard.* 1963. NY. 1st ed. 151p. VG/dj. B18. $125.00

KEROUAC, John. *Town & the City.* 1950. Harcourt Brace. 1st ed. F/NF. B4. $60.00

KERR, Ben; see Ard, William.

KERR, Philip. *March Violets.* 1989. Viking. 1st ed. NF/NF. P3. $18.00

KERR, W.A. *Practical Horsemanship/Riding For Ladies.* 1891. London. Bohn's Lib of Sports & Games. G+. O3. $85.00

KERR & YASSIN. *Rich & Poor States in the Middle East.* 1982. Boulder, CO/Cairo. 1st ed. 482p. VG. W1. $20.00

KERROD, Robin. *Space Shuttle.* 1985 (1984). Gallery Books. 4to. 71p. VG/VG. K5. $12.00

KERSH, Gerald. *Fowler's End.* 1957. Simon Schuster. 1st ed. NF/dj. F4. $35.00

KERSH, Gerald. *Night & the City.* 1948. World Forum. 2nd ed. VG. P3. $10.00

KERSH, Gerald. *Song of the Flea.* 1948. Reginald Saunders. 1st Canadian ed. VG. P3. $20.00

KERTESZ, Andre. *Andre Kertesz.* 1987. Budapest. Szentendre. miniature ltd ed. 160 sm pl. red velvet bdg. F. S9. $250.00

KERTESZ, Andre. *Lifetime of Perception.* 1982. Abrams. 1st ed. 4to. F/NF. S9. $95.00

KERTESZ, Andre. *On Reading.* 1971. NY. Grossman. 1st ed. 8vo. F/clip. S9. $50.00

KESEY, Ken. *Day After Superman Died.* 1980. Lord John. 1st ed. sgn. 1/50. 48p. gilt bl cloth/marbled brd. F. H5. $150.00

KESEY, Ken. *Kesey's Garage Sale.* 1973. Viking. 1st pb ed. sgn. F. S11. $35.00

KESEY, Ken. *Kesey's Garage Sale.* 1973. Viking. 1st ed. 283p. 2-toned bl cloth. NF/clip. H5. $50.00

KESEY, Ken. *Sometimes a Great Notion.* 1964. NY. Viking. 1st ed/author's 2nd novel. NF/G. L3. $125.00

KESSEL, Dmitri. *Splendors of Christendom. Great Art & Architecture...* 1964. Switzerland. Edita Luasanne. sq folio. ils. VG. F1. $45.00

KESSEL, John. *Good News From Outer Space.* 1989. Tor. 1st ed. F/F. T2. $17.00

KESSELL, John L. *Friars, Soldiers & Reformers.* 1976. AZ U. 1st ed. ils/index. 347p. F/NF. B19. $50.00

KESSELL, John L. *Remote Beyond Compare: Letters of Don Diego de Vargas...* 1989. NM U. 1st ed. 596p. NF/sans. B19. $30.00

KESTEN, Hermann. *Copernicus & His World.* 1945. London. Secker Warburg. 8vo. 408p. G/worn. K5. $30.00

KESTERTON, David. *Darkling.* 1982. Arkham. 1st ed/author's 1st novel. 1/3126. F/F. P3/T2. $13.00

KETCHUM, Philip. *Death in the Night.* 1939. Phoenix. 1st ed. F/F. M15. $65.00

KETCHUM, Philip. *Wyatt Earp.* 1956. Whitman. VG. P3. $15.00

KETTELL, Samuel. *Specimens of American Poetry.* 1829. Boston. Goodrich. 3 vol. 1st ed. 8vo. tan brd/purple spine. F. C6. $600.00

KETTERER, Bernadine. *Manderley Mystery.* 1937. Eldon. 1st ed. VG. P3. $20.00

KETTERER, David. *New Worlds for Old.* 1976. IN U. 3rd ed. VG/VG. P3. $20.00

KEY, Alexander. *Red Eagle: Being the Adventures of Two Young Flyers.* nd. Wise Parslow. 120p. G. B10. $12.00

KEY, Astley Cooper. *Narrative of the Recovery of HMS Gorgon...1844.* 1847. London. Smith Elder. 8vo. maps/fld chart. 114p. gilt emb bl cloth. VG. P4. $295.00

KEY, Ted. *Phyllis.* 1957. Dutton. 1st ed. F/VG. P8. $25.00

KEYES, Daniel. *Flowers for Algernon.* 1966. HBW. 1st ed. xl. VG/VG. M21. $65.00

KEYES, E.D. *From West Point to California.* 1950. CA Biobooks #24. 8vo. 90p. bl cloth. F. P4. $30.00

KEYES, F. Parkinson. *Cook Book.* 1955. NY. 1st ed. VG/fair. B5. $45.00

KEYES, Nelson B. *America's National Parks.* 1957. Doubleday. photos/maps. G/dj. B34. $10.00

KEYNES, Geoffrey. *Bibliography of Sir Thomas Browne.* 1968. Oxford. 2nd ed. 4to. xl. dj. G7. $135.00

KEYNES, Geoffrey. *Jane Austen: Bibliography by G Keynes.* nd. London. Nonesuch. 1st ed. 1/875. F/NF. C2. $150.00

KEYNES, Geoffrey. *Portraiture of William Harvey. The Thomas Vicary Lecture.* 1985. London. Keynes. 1/300. F. G7. $65.00

KEYS, Thomas E. *Hist of Surgical Anesthesia.* 1945. Schuman. 191p. G7. $75.00

KEYSTONE, Oliver. *Arsenic for the Teacher.* 1950. Phoenix. VG. P3. $10.00

KHALIFA, Ali Mohammed. *United Arab Emirates: Unity & Fragmentation.* 1979. Boulder. 8vo. 235p. cloth. O2. $25.00

KHALILI, Khalilullah. *Quatrains of...* 1981. London. Octagon. 1st imp. 82p. NF/dj. W1. $15.00

KHAYAAM, Omar. *Original Rubaiyat of Omar Khayaam.* 1968. Doubleday. 1/500. trans/sgn Robert Graves/Omar Ali-Sah. F/case. F1. $150.00

KHERDIAN, David. *I Sing the Song of Myself.* 1978. Greenwillow. 1st ed. sgn. M/dj. A18. $30.00

KHERDIAN, David. *Nonny Poems.* 1974. Macmillan. 1st ed. inscr. 50p. F. M10. $12.50

KHERDIAN, David. *Settling Am: Ethnic Expression of 14 Contemporary Poets.* 1974. Macmillan. 1st ed. 50p. F/dj. M10. $12.50

KHERDIAN, David. *Six Poets of the San Francisco Renaissance.* 1967. Giligia. 1st ed. sgn. F. A18. $35.00

KHYAAYAM, Omar; see Fitzgerald, Edward (trans).

KIDD, John. *On Adaption External Nature to Physical Condition of Man...* 1833. London. Pickering. 375p. contemporary bl cloth. G1. $135.00

KIDD, Mary M. *Wild Flowers of the Cape Peninsula.* 1950. Cape Town. 94 full-p pl. VG. B26. $37.50

KIDDER, Alfred. *Rediscovering America.* 1964. NY. Am Heritage. maps/photos. hc. F. P4. $15.00

KIDDER, Tracy. *House.* 1985. Houghton Mifflin. 1st ed. NF/VG. B3. $20.00

KIDWELL, Art. *Ambush: Story of Bill Keys.* 1979. Pioneer. 1st ed. inscr. 184p. F/VG. A8. $50.00

KIEFER, Hermann. *Liberty Writings.* 1917. NY. 1st ed. 513p. VG. A17. $10.00

KIEFER, Monica. *American Children Through Their Books, 1700-1835.* 1948. PA U. 1st ed. 25 pl. 289p. F/F. A4. $65.00

KIEFER, Warren. *Outlaw.* 1989. Donald Fine. UP. F/pict wrp. B3. $20.00

KIEHI. *American Art Posters of the 1890s.* 1984. Metropolitian Mus Art. ils. 200p. F/F. A4. $95.00

KIEL, Hanna. *Antique Chinese Portraits.* 1972. Milan. 1st ed. folio. 10 portraits on silk. M/silk tray case. H3. $300.00

KIENZLE, William X. *Shadow of Death.* 1983. Andrews McMeel. 1st ed. VG/VG. P3. $15.00

KIERKEGAARD, Soren. *Fear & Trembling.* 1939. London. Oxford. 1st Eng-language ed. 192p. blk cloth. VG/dj. G1. $37.50

KIERKEGAARD, Soren. *Frygt og Baeven: Dialektist Lyrik.* 1843. Kjobenhavn. Reitzel. 135p. emb red cloth/gilt spine. VG. rare. G1. $1,000.00

KIERKEGAARD, Soren. *Kierkegaard's the Concept of Dread.* 1967. Princeton. 2nd Eng-language ed/3rd prt. 154p. maroon cloth. VG/dj. G1. $25.00

KIERKEGAARD, Soren. *Philosophiski Smuler Eller en Smule Philosophi.* 1844. Kjobenhavn. Reitzel. sm 8vo. 164p. blk cloth. G1. $485.00

KIJEWSKI, Karen. *Kat's Cradle.* 1992. Doubleday. 1st ed. sgn. F/F. M15. $30.00

KIJEWSKI, Karen. *Katwalk.* 1989. St Martin. 1st ed/author's 1st novel. F/F. M15. $75.00

KILBOURN, William. *Pipeline.* 1970. Clarke Irwin. VG/G. P3. $15.00

KILGORE, Starnell. *Against Tomorrow.* 1964. Garrett Massie. 1st ed. 260p. VG/G. B10. $12.00

KILIAN, Crawford. *Icequake.* 1979. Douglas McIntyre. 1st ed. NF/NF. P3. $30.00

KILLENS, John Oliver. *And Then We Heard the Thunder.* 1963. NY. 1st ed/author's 2nd novel. inscr. F/NF. A11. $95.00

KILPATRICK, Christopher H. *Kirkmouse.* ca 1979. McLean, VA. ils Jeff MacNelly. VG. B10. $10.00

KILWORTH, Garry. *In Solitary.* 1977. Faber. 1st ed. F/F. P3. $20.00

KIM, Yong Choon. *Oriental Thought: An Intro to Philosophical & Religious...* 1973. Totowa. Rowman Littlefield. 192p. VG. B33. $16.00

KIMBALL, David Tenney. *Sketch of Ecclesiastical Hist of Ipswitch.* 1823. Haverhill, MA. 1st ed. 44p. VG/prt wrp. M8. $37.50

KIMBALL, Fiske. *Domestic Architecture of the American Colonies...* 1922. NY. photos. VG. M17. $50.00

KIMBALL, Horace. *American Naval Battles.* 1848. Concord, NH. Roby. 273p. T7. $95.00

KIMBALL, Spencer L. *Hist Intro to the Legal System.* 1966. St Paul. W Pub. sm 4to. NF. D3. $35.00

KIMBROUGH & SKINNER. *Our Hearts Were Young & Gay.* 1942. Dodd Mead. 1st ed. 247p. F/VG. H1. $22.50

KINCAID, Jamaica. *At the Bottom of the River.* 1983. FSG. 1st ed. F/F. L3. $75.00

KINDER, Gary. *Light Years.* 1987. Atlantic Monthly. 1st ed. VG. P3. $19.00

KING, Alexander. *Peter Altenberg's Evocation of Love.* 1960. Simon Schuster. 1st prt. 174p. F/case. H1. $22.50

KING, Charles. *Daughter of the Sioux.* 1903. Hobart. 1st ed. ils Remington/Deming. teg. pict bdg. F. A18. $50.00

KING, Clive. *Town That Went South.* 1959. Macmillan. 1st prt. 118p. VG/G. B10. $10.00

KING, Edna K. *Doll's Family Album.* 1937. Chicago. Whitman. inscr/sgn. G+. A1. $40.00

KING, Ernest J. *Fleet Admiral King: A Naval Record.* 1952. Norton. 1st ed. VG/fair. N2. $10.00

KING, Francis. *Voices in an Empty Room.* 1984. Hutchinson. 1st ed. VG/VG. P3. $15.00

KING, Frank. *Skeezix & Pal.* 1925. Reilly Lee. 4to. 105p. pict blk cloth. VG+. A3. $60.00

KING, Gertrude Louise Besse. *Alliances for the Mind.* 1924. Harcourt Brace. 154p. bl cloth. G. scarce. G1. $100.00

KING, Gordon. *Herodotus, the First European Historian.* 1929. Doubleday Doran. 1st ed. 274p. xl. VG. W1. $14.00

KING, Henry C. *History of the Telescope.* 1979 (1955). Dover. rpt. photos/diagrams, 456p. bl cloth. VG. K5. $50.00

KING, Henry C. *World of the Moon.* 1966. London. Barrie Rockliff. 8vo. 125p. G/dj. K5. $16.00

KING, Joe M. *Hist of SC Baptists.* 1964. Columbia, SC. Bryan. 1st ed. 494p. cloth. NF/VG. M8. $37.50

KING, Julia. *Flowering of Art Nouveau Graphics.* 1990. Salt Lake City. 1st ed. 144 p. F/F. A17. $17.50

KING, Lawrence J. *Weeds of the World.* 1966. NY. ils/pl. VG. B26. $72.50

KING, Lester. *Growth of Medical Thought.* 1963. Chicago. 1st ed. 254p. A13. $50.00

KING, Louise W. *Pekingese Trifle.* 1979. CT. Lapin. 1st ed. 1/850. M/wrp. R2. $40.00

KING, Magda. *Heidegger's Philosophy: Guide to His Basic Thought.* 1966. NY. Delta. 1st pb ed. sm 8vo. VG. G1. $15.00

KING, Marian. *Sean & Sheela.* 1937. Whitman Jr Pr Book. 1st ed. ils Emma Brock. 134p. VG. A3. $15.00

KING, Martin Luther Jr. *Stride Toward Freedom.* 1958. NY. Harper. 1st ed/author's 1st book. F/clip. Q1. $175.00

KING, Rufus. *Case of the Dowager's Etchings.* 1944. Doubleday Crime Club. 1st ed. 8vo. 178p. gray cloth. F/NF. H5. $100.00

KING, Rufus. *Case of the Dowager's Etchings.* 1944. Doubleday Crime Club. 1st ed. VG. P3. $15.00

KING, Rufus. *Diagnosis Murder.* 1941. Doubleday Crime Club. 1st ed. VG/dj. M15. $55.00

KING, Rufus. *Murder in the Willett Family.* 1931. Doubleday Crime Club. 1st ed. NF/clip. N15. $75.00

KING, Rufus. *Somewhere in This House.* 1930. Doubleday Crime Club. 1st ed. VG. P3. $30.00

KING, Stephen. *Bare Bones.* 1989. London. NEL. 1st ed. F/F. B3. $30.00

KING, Stephen. *Carrie.* nd. BC. VG/VG. P3. $10.00

KING, Stephen. *Carrie.* 1974. Doubleday. 1st ed. xl. poor. P3. $75.00

KING, Stephen. *Carrie.* 1983. Viking. 1st ed. VG/VG. P3. $60.00

KING, Stephen. *Christine.* 1983. Viking. 1st ed. F/F. M2. $60.00

KING, Stephen. *Cujo.* 1981. Viking. 1st trade ed. NF/dj. F4. $25.00

KING, Stephen. *Cujo.* 1981. Viking. 4th prt. NF/NF. P3. $15.00

KING, Stephen. *Cujo.* 1981. Viking. 1st ed. 8vo. 381p. blk cloth/tan brd. F/F. H5. $50.00

KING, Stephen. *Cycle of the Werewolf.* 1983. Westland. Land of Enchantment. 1st ed/trade copy. 1/7500. F/F. T2. $100.00

KING, Stephen. *Dark Tower II: Drawing of the Three.* 1987. Donald Grant. 1st ed. F/F. F4. $55.00

KING, Stephen. *Dark Tower II: Drawing of the Three.* 1987. W Kingston. Donald Grant. ltd ed. sgn King/Hale. 1/100. F/F/case. T2. $750.00

KING, Stephen. *Dark Tower III: The Wastelands.* 1991. Donald Grant. 1st ed. F/F. P3. $45.00

KING, Stephen. *Dark Tower: The Gunslinger.* 1982. Donald Grant. 1st ed. sgn. 1/500. ils/sgn Michael Whelan. F/F/case. T2. $1,250.00

KING, Stephen. *Dark Tower: The Gunslinger.* 1982. Donald Grant. 1st ed. VG/VG. P3. $450.00

KING, Stephen. *Dead Zone.* 1979. Viking. 1st ed. F/F. S9. $60.00

KING, Stephen. *Delores Claiborne.* 1993. Viking. 1st ed. F/F. P3. $24.00

KING, Stephen. *Different Seasons.* 1982. Viking. 1st ed. VG/VG. P3. $75.00

KING, Stephen. *Dolan's Cadillac.* 1989. Northridge. Lord John. 1/250 #d. quarter leather/marbled brd. F/F case. S9. $500.00

KING, Stephen. *Dolan's Cadillac.* 1989. Northridge. Lord John. 1st ed. sgn pres. 1/100. F/sans/case. T2. $650.00

KING, Stephen. *Eyes of the Dragon.* 1987. Viking. 1st ed. F/F. P3. $40.00

KING, Stephen. *Eyes of the Dragon.* 1987. Viking. 1st trade ed. VG+/dj. M21. $17.50

KING, Stephen. *Firestarter.* 1980. Viking. 1st trade ed. F/NF clip. N3. $25.00

KING, Stephen. *Four Past Midnight.* 1990. Viking. 1st ed. NF/NF. P3. $23.00

KING, Stephen. *Four Past Midnight.* 1990. Viking. 1st trade ed. rem mk. M/dj. M21. $12.00

KING, Stephen. *Gerald's Game.* 1992. Viking. ltd ed distributed at 1992 ABA convention. F/box. B2. $100.00

KING, Stephen. *Gerald's Game.* 1992. Viking. 1st ed. F/F. P3. $23.00

KING, Stephen. *Insomnia.* 1994. Viking. 1st trade ed. sgn. F/F. T2. $75.00

KING, Stephen. *Insomnia.* 1994. Ziesing. 1st ed. 1/3750. F/F/case. T2. $95.00

KING, Stephen. *Insomnia.* 1994. Ziesing. 1st ed. 1/1250. sgn King/Hale/Fenner. F/F/tray case. T2. $395.00

KING, Stephen. *It.* 1986. Viking. 1st ed. G+/dj. P3. $20.00

KING, Stephen. *Langoliers From Four Past Midnight.* 1990. Time Life. F/F. P3. $15.00

KING, Stephen. *Misery.* 1987. Viking. 1st ed. NF/NF. P3. $40.00

KING, Stephen. *Misery.* 1987. Viking. 1st ed. VG+/dj. M21. $20.00

KING, Stephen. *Misery*. 1987. Viking. 1st ed. 310p. M/M. A17. $45.00

KING, Stephen. *Nightmares in the Sky*. 1988. Viking Studio Books. 2nd ed. VG/VG. P3. $30.00

KING, Stephen. *Pet Sematary*. 1983. Doubleday. 1st ed. F/F. P3. $35.00

KING, Stephen. *Rage*. 1977. NY. 1st ed/PBO. sgn. NF/ils wrp. A11. $165.00

KING, Stephen. *Shining*. 1977. Doubleday. 1st ed. F/dj. B24. $250.00

KING, Stephen. *Skeleton Crew*. 1985. Putnam. 1st ed. F/F. P3. $60.00

KING, Stephen. *Tommyknockers*. 1987. Putnam. 1st ed. VG/VG. P3. $25.00

KING, T.S. *White Hills: Their Legends, Landscape & Poetry*. 1864. Boston. 403p. teg. purple cloth. VG. H7. $65.00

KING, Tabitha. *Caretakers*. 1984. Methuen. 1st ed. F/F. P3. $50.00

KING, Thomas. *Green Grass, Running Water*. 1993. Houghton Mifflin. UP. F/pict wrp. B3. $35.00

KING, W.J. Harding. *Mysteries of the Libyan Desert*. 1925. London. Seeley Service. 1st ed. 8vo. 16pl. xl. VG. W1. $45.00

KING, Willis J. *Negro in American Life*. 1926. NY. 1st ed. 154p. gray cloth. VG. B14. $25.00

KING & MILLBURN. *Geared to the Stars*. 1978. Toronto. 4to. ils/photos/diagrams. 442p. bl cloth. VG. K5. $200.00

KING & POLIKARPUS. *Down Town*. 1985. Arbor. 1st ed. F/F. P3. $20.00

KING & STRAUB. *Talisman*. 1984. Viking. 1st ed. NF/NF. P3. $40.00

KING & STUART. *House of Warne: One Hundred Years of Publishing*. 1965. London/NY. Warne. 107p. NF. P4. $50.00

KINGMAN, LeRoy Wilson. *Early Owego*. 1987. Owego, NY. Tioga Co Hist Soc. rpt 1907 ed. 300p. VG. M10. $15.00

KINGMAN. *Authenticated Contemporary Portrait of Shakespeare*. 1932. Rudge. 4to. ils. 87p. VG. A4. $65.00

KINGSBURY, Donald. *Courtship Rite*. 1982. Timescape. 1st ed. F/NF. N3. $45.00

KINGSBURY, Donald. *Moon Goddess & the Son*. 1986. Baen. 1st ed. F/F. P3. $20.00

KINGSFORD-SMITH, Charles. *My Flying Life*. 1937. London. 1st ed. 284p. VG/dj. B18. $95.00

KINGSLEY, Charles. *Heroes; or, Greek Fairy Tales for My Children*. 1856. Boston. 8vo. ils. 320p. cloth. O2. $60.00

KINGSLEY, Charles. *Water Babies*. nd. London. Jack. 8 mc pl. 246p. NF. P2. $75.00

KINGSLEY, Charles. *Water Babies*. nd. Ward Lock. ils Harry Theaker. pict brd. VG. M5. $65.00

KINGSLEY, Charles. *Water Babies*. 1928 (1885). London. Macmillan. 1st ed thus. ils Sambourne. 280p. VG. P2. $75.00

KINGSLEY, Charles. *Water Babies: Fairy Tale for a Land Baby*. nd. Little Brn. ils Ethel F Everett. 243p. G+. B10. $25.00

KINGSLEY, Charles. *Westward, Ho!* 1857. Cambridge. 3rd ed. half leather/marbled brd. VG. B30. $60.00

KINGSLEY, Charles. *Westward Ho!* 1930. Scribner. ils NC Wyeth. 413p. reading copy. B10. $15.00

KINGSOLVER, Barbara. *Another America: Otra America*. 1992. Seattle. Seal. 1st ed. sgn. trans Cartes. F/F. B3/S9. $45.00

KINGSOLVER, Barbara. *Bean Trees*. 1988. Harper Row. 1st ed. sgn. NF/VG. B3. $150.00

KINGSOLVER, Barbara. *Holding the Line: Women in the Great AZ Mine Strike of 1983*. 1989. Cornell. ILR Pr. 1st ed/author's only non-fiction book. sgn. F/sans. B3. $75.00

KINNEAR, John Gardiner. *Cairo, Petra, & Damascus in 1839 With Remarks...* 1841. London. 8vo. 348p. cloth. O2. $750.00

KINNELL, Galway. *Body Rags*. 1968. np. ARC/1st ed. sgn. RS. F/F. V1. $145.00

KINNELL, Galway. *Lackawanna Elegy*. 1970. Sumac. 1/26. sgn. F/sans. C2. $200.00

KINNELL, Galway. *Two Poems, by Galway Kinnell*. 1979. Newark, VT. Janus. 1/185. sgn. ils Claire VanVliet. brn cloth. F. B24. $150.00

KINNEY, Charles; see Gardner, Erle Stanley.

KINNEY, Thomas. *Devil Take the Foremost*. 1947. Crime Club. 1st ed. VG. P3. $10.00

KINROSS, Lord. *Ataturk: Biography of Mustafa Kemal...* 1965. NY. 8vo. 613p. cloth. dj. O2. $25.00

KINROSS, Lord. *Turkey*. 1959. Viking Studio Book. 1st ed. 4to. VG. W1. $35.00

KINSELLA, W.P. *Born Indian*. 1981. np. 1st ed. inscr. F/ils wrp. A11. $60.00

KINSELLA, W.P. *Chapter One of a Work in Progress*. 1988. Hoffer. ltd ed. sgn. 1/300. M. P8. $85.00

KINSELLA, W.P. *Dance Me Outside: More Tales From Ermineskine Reserve*. 1986. Boston. Godine. 1st ed. inscr. F/F. B2. $75.00

KINSELLA, W.P. *Iowa Baseball Confederacy*. 1986. NY. 1st ed/author's baseball novel. sgn. F/F. A11. $55.00

KINSELLA, W.P. *Moccasin Telegraph & Other Tales*. 1984. NY. 1st Am/1st hc ed. sgn as Bill Kinsella. F/F. A11. $65.00

KINSELLA, W.P. *Shoeless Joe Jackson Comes to Iowa*. 1980. Canada. Oberon. simultaneous wrp issue. NF. L3. $85.00

KINSELLA, W.P. *Shoeless Joe*. 1982. Houghton Mifflin. 1st ed. sgn. F/VG+. P8. $200.00

KINSELLA, W.P. *Thrill of the Grass*. 1984. Hoffer. ltd ed. sgn. 1/300. M. P8. $110.00

KINSLEY, D.A. *Favor the Bold, Custer the Civil War Years*. 1967. Promontory. F/VG. B34. $30.00

KIPLING, Rudyard. *Animal Stories*. 1953. Macmillan. VG. P3. $20.00

KIPLING, Rudyard. *Barrack-Room Ballads*. 1892. London. Methuen. 1st ed. w/sgn inscr. VG. Q1. $250.00

KIPLING, Rudyard. *Complete Works in Prose & Verse*. 1941. Doubleday Doran. 26 vol. Burwash ed. sgn. teg. red cloth. NF. H4. $950.00

KIPLING, Rudyard. *Elephant's Child*. 1968. CBS Records. 48p. VG/G. A3. $5.00

KIPLING, Rudyard. *France at War*. 1915. Doubleday Page. 1st Am ed. sgn. VG/VG. B4. $650.00

KIPLING, Rudyard. *Just So Stories*. 1912. Doubleday. 1st ed thus. ils Joseph Gleeson. VG+. M5. $150.00

KIPLING, Rudyard. *Just So Stories*. 1978. Weathervane. 2nd ed. VG/VG. P3. $10.00

KIPLING, Rudyard. *Kim*. 1901. NY. 1st ed/1st issue. 10 ils. 460p. gilt cloth. NF. A17. $60.00

KIPLING, Rudyard. *Kim*. 1962. LEC. 1/1500. ils/sgn Robin Jacques. F/VG+ case. S9. $45.00

KIPLING, Rudyard. *Kipling Stories & Poems Every Child Should Know*. 1911. Doubleday Page. 1st ed. 8vo. ils JM Gleason/CL Bull. 361p. NF. D6. $55.00

KIPLING, Rudyard. *Out of India*. 1895. NY. Dillinham. 1st Am ed. tan cloth. VG. Q1. $150.00

KIPLING, Rudyard. *Puck of Pooks Hill*. 1916. Doubleday. 12mo. ils Rackham. G+. B17. $15.00

KIRALY, Sherwood. *California Rush*. 1990. Macmillan. ARC. RS. F/F. P8. $15.00

KIRBY, Joshua. *Dr Brook Taylor's Method of Perspective Made Easy...* 1755. Ipswich. Craighton. 4to. 84p. rebound modern cloth/brd. modern case. F1. $300.00

KIRBY, R.S. *Inventors & Engineers of Old New Haven*. 1939. New Haven. 1st ed. cloth. VG. C11. $25.00

KIRCHBERGER, Claire. *Coasts of the Country: Anthology of Prayer...* ca 1944. Chicago. Regnery. 266p. VG/VG. B33. $26.00

KIRCHMANN, Johannes. *Du Funeribus Romanorum...* 1625 (1603). Lubeck. Samuel Jauch. 2 parts in 1. 737p. contemporary vellum. K1. $250.00

KIRIAKOPOULOS, G.C. *Ten Days to Destiny: Battle for Crete.* 1985. NY. 8vo. 408p. cloth. dj. O2. $25.00

KIRK, Daniel. *Santa Claus the Movie Pop-Up Panorama Book.* 1985. Grosset Dunlap. 1st prt. VG. C8. $15.00

KIRK, George E. *Short Hist of the Middle East.* 1964. Praeger. 7th revised ed. cloth. xl. VG. W1. $10.00

KIRK, Michael. *Cut in Diamonds.* 1986. Doubleday Crime Club. 1st ed. NF/NF. P3. $13.00

KIRK, R.G. *White Monarch & the Gas-House Pup.* 1917. Little Brn. 1st ed. 113p. cloth. F. scarce. R2. $60.00

KIRK, Russell. *Creature of the Twilight.* 1966. Fleet. 1st ed. VG/G. P3. $35.00

KIRK, Russell. *Princess of All Lands.* 1979. Arkham. 1st ed. 1/4120. F/F. T2. $45.00

KIRK, Russell. *Watchers at the Strait Gate: Mystical Tales.* 1984. Arkham. 1st ed. 1/3459. F/F. T2. $15.00

KIRKBRIDE, Alec Seath. *Crackle of Thorns: Experiences in Middle East.* 1956. London. 1st ed. 8vo. 201p. cloth. dj. O2. $25.00

KIRKBRIDGE, Ronald. *Winds, Blow Gently.* 1945. Frederick Fell. 1st ed. VG/VG. P3. $20.00

KIRKBRIDE, Thomas S. *On Construction, Organization...Hospitals for Insane.* 1880. Phil. 2nd ed. 320-. B14. $95.00

KIRKEBY, Ed. *Ain't Misbehavin'. Story of Fats Waller.* 1966. Dodd Mead. 1st ed. F/NF. B2. $45.00

KIRKHAM, Stanton Davis. *In the Open: Intimate Studies & Appreciation of Nature.* 1908. San Francisco. Paul Elder. cloth. NF. B4. $125.00

KIRKPATRICK. *Bibliography of Edmund Bluden.* 1979. np. 11 pl. 756p. F/F. A4. $125.00

KIRKUS, A. Mary. *Robert Gibbings, a Bibliography.* 1962. London. Dent. 1st ed. 1/975. ils. edit Patience Empson/John Harris. F/VG. F1. $125.00

KIRKWOOD, James. *Amerian Grotesque.* 1970. Simon Schuster. 1st ed. VG/VG. S11. $10.00

KIRN, Walter. *My Hard Bargain.* 1990. Knopf. 1st ed/author's 1st book. F/F. A14. $25.00

KIRN, Walter. *My Hard Bargain.* 1990. Knopf. 1st ed/author's 1st book. inscr. F/F. B4. $65.00

KIRN, Walter. *She Needed Me.* 1992. Pocket. 1st ed/author's 1st novel. inscr. F/F. B4. $45.00

KIRSCH & MURPHY. *West of the West: Witness to CA Experience 1542-1906.* 1967. EP Dutton. 1st ed. ils/index. 526p. F/NF. B19. $20.00

KIRSHENBAUM, Sandra. *Fine Print, Review for Arts of the Book.* 1975-1990. San Francisco. complete (63 issues). 4to. F/wrp. A4. $630.00

KIRST, Hans Hellmut. *Heroes for Sale.* 1982. Collins. 1st ed. F/F. P3. $20.00

KIRST, Hans Helmut. *Party Games.* 1979. Simon Schuster. 1st ed thus. rem mk. F/F. M21. $10.00

KIRT, Michael. *Cut in Diamonds.* 1986. Doubleday. 1st Am ed. F/F. S6. $25.00

KISER, Clyde V. *Trends & Variations in Fertility in the US.* 1968. Harvard. 338p. F/dj. K4. $15.00

KISH, George. *Source Book in Goegraphy.* 1978. Cambridge/London. 453p. M/NF. P4. $30.00

KITAHARA, Michio. *Tragedy of Evolution: Human Animal Confronts Modern Soc.* 1991. NY. Praeger. 192p. prt red cloth. G1. $20.00

KITCHEN, E.A. *Birds of the Olympic Peninsula.* 1949. Port Angeles. sgn. 258p. cloth. VG. M20. $15.00

KITCHIN, C.H.B. *Crime at Christmas.* 1969. Hamish Hamilton. 1st ed. VG/G. P3. $20.00

KITE, Thomas. *Selections From the Letters of Thomas Kite to His Daughter.* nd. Phil. 16mo. 35p. cloth. G. V3. $14.00

KITT, Eartha. *Thursday's Child.* 1956. Duell Sloan. 1st ed. w/sgn letter. F/NF. B2. $75.00

KITTEREDGE, George Lyman. *Witchcraft in Old & New England.* 1956. NY. Russell & Russell. 373p. F/dj. K4. $15.00

KITTERIDGE, William. *Hole in the Sky.* 1992. Knopf. 1st ed. F/F. S9. $45.00

KITTERIDGE, William. *We Are Not in This Together.* 1984. Graywolf. ltd ed. sgn Kittredge/Ray Carver. 1/50. F/F. S9. $350.00

KITTERIDGE, William. *We Are Not in This Together.* 1984. Port Townsend. Graywolf. 1st ed. sgn. F/F. L3. $125.00

KIZZIA, Tom. *Wake of the Unseen Object.* 1991. NY. 1st ed. 278p. M/M. A17. $10.00

KLAAR. *Language-Teaching Bibliography, Second Edition.* 1972. Cambridge. 252p. xl. VG. A4. $45.00

KLAMKIN, Charles. *Weathervanes: Hist, Design & Manufacture of Am Folk Art.* 1973. Hawthorn. 1st ed. 350 photos. 209p. F/G. H1. $28.00

KLAUSMEIR, Herbert J. *Learning & Human Abilities.* 1961. Harper. 550p. F. K4. $10.00

KLAVIN, Andrew. *Don't Say a Word.* 1991. Pocket. 1st ed. VG/VG. P3. $20.00

KLEIN, Chaim H. *Second Million: Israel Tourist Industry...* 1973. Tel Aviv. Amir. 1st Eng ed. 300p. VG/dj. W1. $10.00

KLEIN, D.B. *Hist of Scientific Psychology: Its Origins...* 1970. Basic Books. thick 8vo. 907p. olive cloth. VG/dj. G1. $50.00

KLEIN, Daniel M. *Embryo.* 1980. Doubleday. 1st ed. F/NF. N3. $10.00

KLEIN, Dave. *Great Infielders of the Major League.* 1972. Random. VG. P3. $8.00

KLEIN, Milton M. *Independent Reflector; or, Weekly Essays...* 1963. Cambridge. Harvard. M11. $45.00

KLEIN, Viola. *Feminine Character. Hist of an Ideology.* 1948. NY. Internat U. 182p. F/dj. K4. $15.00

KLEIN, William. *William Klein.* 1991. Tokyo. 1st ed. obl 4to. VG+/wrp. S9. $25.00

KLEIN, Zachary. *Still Among the Living.* 1990. Harper Row. 1st ed. F/F. P3. $19.00

KLEINFIELD, S. *Biggest Company on Earth.* 1981. NY. 1st ed. VG/VG. B5. $20.00

KLEINLEIN, Walter J. *Practical Balance & Hair Spring Work.* 1925. private prt. 1st ed. aeg. gilt red leatherette. F/plastic wrp. A8. $30.00

KLEINLEIN, Walter J. *Rules & Practice for Adjusting Watches.* 1940. private prt. 2nd ed. 16mo. 133p. aeg. blk leatherette. F/plastic wrp. A8. $30.00

KLEITMAN, N. *Sleep Characteristics.* 1937. Chicago. 86p. G. K4. $25.00

KLIMOWICZ, Barbara. *When Shoes Eat Socks.* 1971. Nashville, TN. Abingdon. 1st ed. obl 8vo. NF/VG+. C8. $25.00

KLINE, Fred. *I, Dodo: A Poem Cycle.* 1968. San Francisco. 1st ed. 16mo. VG/wrp. A17. $7.50

KLINE, Mary Jo. *Guide to Documentary Editing.* 1987. Johns Hopkins. 228p. cloth. VG. A10. $20.00

KLINE, Morris. *Mathematics in Western Culture.* 1960. Oxford. 7th prt. 484p. M/dj. K4. $10.00

KLINE, Otis Adelbert. *Outlaws of Mars.* 1961. Avalon. 1st ed. F/clip. F4. $40.00

KLINE, Otis Adelbert. *Outlaws of Mars.* 1961. Avalon. 1st ed. VG/VG. P3. $30.00

KLINE, Otis Adelbert. *Tam, Son of the Tiger.* 1962. Avalon. 1st ed. F/clip. F4. $40.00

KLINE, Paul. *Fact & Fantasy in Freudian Theory.* 1972. London. Methuen. 359p. F/dj. K4. $20.00

KLINE, Penny. *Dying To Help.* 1993. London. Macmillan. 1st Am ed. F/F. S6. $22.50

KLINEFELTER, Walter. *Third Display of Old Maps & Plans: Study Postal Cartography.* 1973. LaCrosse, WI. Sumac. 1st ed. ils. 77p. NF/dj. M10. $18.50

KLINEFELTER. *Fortas Bibliohoax, Revised & Newly Annotated...* 1986. Evanston. Ward Schori. 1/378. 95p. F. A4. $165.00

KLINGEL, Gilbert. *Ocean Island.* 1940. Dodd Mead. 1st ed. 8vo. 385p. blk cloth. VG/VG. B11. $40.00

KLINGER, Eric. *Structure & Functions of Fantasy.* 1971. Wiley-Interscience. 379p. M/dj. K4. $15.00

KLINKOWITZ, Jerry. *Short Season & Other Stories.* 1988. Johns Hopkins. 1st ed. F/VG+. P8. $17.50

KLOTS, Allen T. *Mental Illness & Due Process.* 1962. Cornell. 303p. F/dj. K4. $20.00

KLUCKHOHN, Clyde. *To the Foot of the Rainbow.* 1927. Century. 1st ed/author's 1st book. 276p. gr cloth. dj. K1. $75.00

KLUGE, Carl A.F. *Versuch Einer Darstellung des Animalischen Magestismus.* 1811. Berlin. 503p. G7. $495.00

KLUGER, Steve. *Changing Pitches.* 1984. St Martin. 1st ed. F/VG+. P8. $17.50

KLUTCH, M.S. *Mr 2 of Everything.* ca 1946. Coward McCann. ils Kurt Wiese. unp. VG/G. B10. $35.00

KNAPP, Robert. *Shakespeare, the Theatre & the Book.* 1989. Princeton. 269p. F/F. A4. $25.00

KNEALE, Nigel. *Year of the Sex Olympics.* 1976. Ferret Fantasy. 1st ed. F/F. P3. $20.00

KNEBEL, Fletcher. *Trespass.* 1969. Doubleday. 1st ed. VG/VG. P3. $20.00

KNEE, Ernest. *Mexico: Laredo to Guadalajara.* 1961. Hastings. 1st ed. ils. map ep. 96p. VG/dj. F3. $15.00

KNEELAND, George. *Commercialized Prostitution in NY City.* 1913. NY. 1st ed. 334p. A13. $50.00

KNIGHT, C. Morley. *Hints on Driving.* 1976. London. Allen. rpt. VG/VG. O3. $12.00

KNIGHT, Charles. *Working-Man's Companion.* 1831. Leavitt Allen. 3 vol in 1. 1st Am ed. 12mo. cloth. M1. $325.00

KNIGHT, Clayton. *Hist of the Wings Club, 1942-1967.* 1967. The Wings Club. 307p. VG. B18. $35.00

KNIGHT, Clifford. *Affair of the Fainting Butler.* 1943. Dodd Mead. 1st ed. NF/VG. B2. $45.00

KNIGHT, Clifford. *Affair of the Scarlet Crab.* 1937. Dodd Mead. 1st ed. VG. P3. $20.00

KNIGHT, Damon. *Best From Orbit.* 1975. Berkley Putnam. 1st ed. VG/VG. P3. $18.00

KNIGHT, Damon. *Best of Damon Knight.* 1978. Taplinger. VG/VG. P3. $20.00

KNIGHT, Damon. *Century of Science Fiction.* 1962. Simon Schuster. VG/VG. P3. $30.00

KNIGHT, Damon. *Dimension X.* 1970. Simon Schuster. 1st ed. VG/G. P3. $20.00

KNIGHT, Damon. *One Side Laughing.* 1991. St Martin. F/F. P3. $17.00

KNIGHT, Damon. *Orbit 18.* 1976. Harper Row. 1st ed. F/worn. N3. $10.00

KNIGHT, Damon. *Reasonable World.* 1991. Tor. 1st ed. F/F. P3. $18.00

KNIGHT, David C. *32 Moons: Natural Satellites of Our Solar System.* 1974. Morrow. 8vo. 96p. xl. G/dj. K5. $6.00

KNIGHT, David. *Natural Science Books in English 1600-1900.* 1972. NY. Praeger. VG. A10. $25.00

KNIGHT, Eric. *Flying Yorkshireman.* 1938. Harper. 1st ed. VG/VG. P3. $15.00

KNIGHT, Hilary. *Circus Is Coming.* 1978. Golden. 2nd prt. F. C8. $17.50

KNIGHT, John Alden. *Moon Up Moon Down.* 1942. NY. 1st ed. VG/VG. B5. $30.00

KNIGHT, Ronald D. *TE Lawrence: His Orders, Decorations & Medals.* 1939. Dorset. 1st ed. 38p. M/prt wrp. M7. $18.00

KNIGHTLEY, Phillip. *First Casualty: From Crimea to Vietnam...* 1975. HBJ. BC ed. F/NF clip. M7. $15.00

KNIGHTLEY & SIMPSON. *Lawrence av Arabien.* 1969. Stockholm. Nordstedt Soners. 1st ed. 318p. F/clear plastic. M7. $75.00

KNIGHTLEY & SIMPSON. *Secret Lives of Lawrence of Arabia.* 1969. London. Nelson. 1st ed. NF/VG+. M7. $45.00

KNIGHTLEY & SIMPSON. *Secret Lives of Lawrence of Arabia.* 1970. McGraw Hill. 1st Am ed. 334p. VG. W1. $22.00

KNIPPEL, Dolores. *Poems for the Very Young Child.* 1932. Whitman. 1st ed. 122p. G+. P2. $18.00

KNOBEL, Elizabeth. *When Little Thoughts Go Rhyming.* 1939. Rand McNally. ils MW Enright. 61p. VG. A3. $17.50

KNOBLAUCH, H.C. *State Agricultural Experiment Stations.* 1962. USDA. 262p. cloth. VG. A10. $12.00

KNORR, L.C. *Handbook of Citrus Diseases in Florida.* 1957. Gainesville. ils/photos. 157p. sc. B26. $14.00

KNOTT, Leonard L. *Children's Book of the Saguenay.* 1945. Montreal. Edit Assn Ltd. 1st ed. 32p. G. A3. $6.00

KNOTTS, Raymond. *And the Deep Blue Sea.* 1944. Farrar Rinehart. 1st ed. VG/VG. P3. $30.00

KNOWLAND, Helen. *Madame Baltimore.* 1949. Dodd Mead. 1st ed. VG. P3. $10.00

KNOWLES, Charles N. *Care of Horse's Legs & Corrective Horseshoeing.* 1963. San Luis Obispo. CA State Polytechnic. 26p. VG. O3. $25.00

KNOWLES, Elizabeth. *Gertrude, by Herself.* 1974. Great Britain. 1st ed. 2321p. sbdg. M. R2. $10.00

KNOWLES, John. *Separate Peace.* 1960. Macmillan. 1st ed. VG/VG clip 2nd issue. L3. $200.00

KNOWLES, Richard T. *Human Development & Human Possibility.* 1986. Lanham. U Pr of Am. 208p. F/prt bl wrp. G1. $22.50

KNOWLTON, Helen M. *Art-Life of William Morris Hunt.* 1900. Boston. Little Brn. 219p. gilt cloth. VG. B14. $45.00

KNOX, Bill. *Draw Batons!* 1973. Doubleday Crime Club. 1st ed. NF/NF. P3. $15.00

KNOX, Calvin; see Silverberg, Robert.

KNOX, D. Edward. *Making of a New Eastern Question...* 1981. WA, DC. Catholic U. 1st ed. 219p. VG/torn. W1. $20.00

KNOX, Patty. *New Directions in Fair Isle Knitting.* 1985. np. cloth. VG. G2. $30.00

KNOX, Ronald A. *Footsteps at the Lock.* 1928. London. Methuen. 1st ed. VG. M15. $35.00

KNUDTSON, Violet Emslie. *Landmark of a Century Hist 1st United Church San Diego, CA.* 1969. San Diego. 1st ed. 154p. cloth. F. M8. $37.50

KOCAOGLU, O. Maummer. *Standardisation des Boyaux en Turquie.* 1975. Istanbul. 1st ed. lg 8vo. sgn pres. VG. W1. $14.00

KOCH, Carl. *Die Zeichnungen Hans Baldung Griens.* 1941. Berlin. 1st ed. folio. 283 pl. gilt gr cloth. K1. $150.00

KOCH, Charles R.E. *Hist of Dental Surgery.* 1910. Ft Wayne. 4to. orig brd. xl. G7. $295.00

KOCH, Christopher W. *History of the Revolutions in Europe...* 1838. Middletown. 2 vol in 1. 8vo. 389p. full contemporary gilt calf. O2. $75.00

KOCH, Helen L. *Twins & Twin Relations.* 1966. London/Chicago. Chicago U. 200p. F/dj. K4. $45.00

KOCH, Stephen. *Night Watch.* 1969. NY. 1st ed. sgn twice. F/NF. A11. $35.00

KOCH, Theodore W. *Tales for Bibliophiles.* nd. Caxton. 1/300. VG. K3. $30.00

KOCH, Vivienne. *William Carlos Williams.* 1950. New Directions. 1st ed. sgn Williams. F/NF. V1. $55.00

KOCHER, Paul H. *Master of the Middle Earth.* 1972. Houghton Mifflin. 1st ed. 247p. VG/G. S11. $10.00

KOCHER, Theodor. *Textbook of Operative Surgery. Third Eng Edition...* 1911. NY. Macmillan. ils. 723p. xl. G7. $125.00

KOCHMAN, Karl. *Gustav Becker Story.* 1976. Antique Clock Pub. revised ed. sc. 8vo. 80p. G+. A8. $20.00

KOCHMAN, Karl. *Junghans Story.* ca 1976. Antique Clock Pub. 2nd ed. sc. 8vo. 208p. G+. A8. $20.00

KOEBEL, W.H. *Central American, Guatemala, Nicaragua, Costa Rica...* 1917. London. Fisher Unwin. 1st ed. thick 8vo. 24 pl. G. B11. $35.00

KOECHLIN & MIGEON. *Oriental Art: Ceramics, Fabrics & Carpets.* 1930. np. 4to. 100 pl. xl. rare. E5. $65.00

KOEGAN, Terry. *Heavy Horse: Its Harness & Harness Decoration.* 1974. Barnes. 1st Am ed. VG/VG. O3. $45.00

KOESTLER, Arthur. *Act of Creation.* 1964. Macmillan. 752p. gray cloth. VG/dj. G1. $40.00

KOESTLER, Arthur. *Case of the Midwife Toad.* 1971. Random. 1st Am ed. sm 8vo. red cloth. VG/dj. G1. $27.50

KOESTLER, Arthur. *Lotus & the Robot.* 1961. Macmillan. 1st Am ed. 296p. blk cloth. VG/dj. G1. $25.00

KOESTLER, Arthur. *Sleepwalkers: Hist of Man's Changing Vision of the Universe.* 1959. Macmillan. 624p. blk cloth. VG. G1. $28.50

KOGAN & WENDT. *Give the Lady What She Wants.* 1952. Rand McNally. 1st ed. pres. 384p. VG/VG. B11. $45.00

KOHAK, Erazin V. *Idea & Experience: Edmund Hursserl's Project...* 1978. Chicago. 249p. bl cloth. F/F. G1. $27.50

KOHS, S.C. *Intelligence Measurement.* 1923. NY. Macmillan. 294p. G. K4. $25.00

KOIZUMI, Yagumo. *Kwaidan.* 1978. Bijou Hoshino. 28x30mm. 1/150. Japanese/ English texts. teg. F/case. B24. $300.00

KOLB, E.L. *Through the Grand Canyon From Wyoming to Mexico.* 1958. Macmillan. 8vo. 76 pl. 344p. pict bl brd. B11. $45.00

KOLB, Leon. *Woodcuts of Jakob Steinhardt.* 1962. PA. 1st trade ed. VG/VG. A1. $125.00

KOLLONTAY, Alexandra. *Tyovaen Kommunisti-Puolueessa.* 1920. Duluth. Workers Socialist Pub. 1st ed. Finnish text. NF/wrp. B2. $100.00

KOLLONTAY, Alexandra. *Women Workers Struggle for Rights.* 1973. Bristol, Great Britian. 3rd ed. pamphlet. VG. V4. $8.00

KOLLWITZ, Johannes. *Mosaics.* 1954. Germany. Herder. ils. 30p. VG/dj. M10. $7.50

KOLUPAEV, Victor. *Hermit's Swing.* 1980. Macmillan. 1st ed. VG/VG. P3. $15.00

KOLUPAILA. *Bibliography of Hydrometry.* 1961. Notre Dame. 998p. xl. VG. scarce. A4. $200.00

KOMAN, Victor. *Jehovah Contract.* 1987. Watts. 1st ed. VG/VG. P3. $20.00

KOMROFF, Manuel. *Grace of Lambs.* 1925. NY. 1st ed. inscr w/musical quotation. A1. $40.00

KOMROFF, Manuel. *Voice of Fire.* 1927. London. Blk Manikin. inscr. ils Polia Chentoff. VG. A1. $100.00

KONEFSKY, Samuel J. *Chief Justice Stone & the Supreme Court.* 1946. Macmillan. M11. $35.00

KONIGSBURG, E.L. *About the B'nai Bagels.* 1969. Atheneum. later prt. VG/VG. P8. $12.50

KONORSKI, J. *Conditioned Reflexes & Neuron Organization.* 1948. London. Cambridge. 260p. G. K4. $25.00

KONVITZ, Jeffrey. *Sentinel.* 1974. Simon Schuster. 1st ed. pres. F/F. M21. $55.00

KONYT & REICHMANN. *White Rider: My 60 Years As a Circus Equestrian.* 1961. Barrington. Hill & Dale. 1st ed. sgn Reichmann. VG/G. O3. $58.00

KOOIKER, Leonie. *Legacy of Magic.* 1981. Morrow. 1st Eng-language ed. F/F clip. N3. $15.00

KOONTZ, Dean R. *Bad Place.* 1990. NY. Putnam. 1st ed. F/F. T2. $20.00

KOONTZ, Dean R. *Bad Place.* 1990. Putnam. 1st trade ed. sgn. F/F. F4. $35.00

KOONTZ, Dean R. *Blood Risk.* 1973. Bobbs Merrill. 1st ed. F/NF. M15. $150.00

KOONTZ, Dean R. *Cold Fire.* 1991. Putnam. 1st ed. F/F. F4/T2. $20.00

KOONTZ, Dean R. *Dance With the Devil.* 1972. NY. 1st ed/PBO. w/sgn card. F/wrp. A11. $115.00

KOONTZ, Dean R. *Dark Rivers of the Heart.* 1994. Knopf. 1st trade ed. sgn. F/F. T2. $45.00

KOONTZ, Dean R. *Dragon Tears.* 1993. Putnam. 1st ed. VG/VG. P3. $23.00

KOONTZ, Dean R. *Face of Fear.* 1977. Bobbs Merrill. 2nd ed. xl. dj. P3. $30.00

KOONTZ, Dean R. *Funhouse.* 1980. Doubleday. 1st hc ed. sgn. F/F. F4. $30.00

KOONTZ, Dean R. *Hideaway.* 1992. Putnam. 1st ed. F/F. N3. $15.00

KOONTZ, Dean R. *House of Thunder.* 1988. Dark Harvest. 1st Am ed. sgn. F/F. F4. $50.00

KOONTZ, Dean R. *How To Write Best-Selling Fiction.* 1981. Cincinnati. Writers Digest. 1st ed. F/F. T2. $125.00

KOONTZ, Dean R. *Lightning.* 1988. Putnam. 1st ed. F/F. T2. $30.00

KOONTZ, Dean R. *Midnight.* 1989. London. Headline. 1st ed. F/F. T2. $55.00

KOONTZ, Dean R. *Midnight.* 1989. Putnam. 1st ed. VG/VG. P3. $25.00

KOONTZ, Dean R. *Night Chills.* 1976. Atheneum. 1st ed. F/F. P3. $300.00

KOONTZ, Dean R. *Oddkins: A Fable of All Ages.* 1988. London. Headline. 1st ed. ils Phil Parks. F/pict wrp. T2. $16.00

KOONTZ, Dean R. *Servants of Twilight.* nd. Quality BC. VG/VG. P3. $15.00

KOONTZ, Dean R. *Shadowfires.* 1990. Dark Harvest. F/F. P3. $45.00

KOONTZ, Dean R. *Shattered.* 1973. Random. 1st ed. xl. dj. P3. $30.00

KOONTZ, Dean R. *Strangers.* 1986. Putnam. 1st ed. F/F clip. N3. $25.00

KOONTZ, Dean R. *Strangers.* 1986. Putnam. 1st ed. F/F. T2. $45.00

KOONTZ, Dean R. *Surrounded.* 1974. Bobbs Merrill. 1st ed. VG/VG. P3. $275.00

KOONTZ, Dean R. *Trapped.* 1993. Eclipse Books. 1st ed. F/F. T2. $25.00

KOONTZ, Dean R. *Twilight Eyes.* 1985. Land of Enchantment. ltd ed. sgn. 1/250 #d. F/F case. P3. $300.00

KOONTZ, Dean R. *Twilight Eyes.* 1985. Plymouth. Land of Enchantment. 1st ed. sgn. F/F. T2. $75.00

KOONTZ, Dean R. *Watchers.* 1987. Putnam. 1st ed. F/F. T2. $55.00

KOONTZ, Dean R. *Whispers.* 1980. Putnam. BC. VG+/dj. M21. $7.50

KOONTZ, Dean R. *Whispers.* 1980. Putnam. 1st ed. VG/VG-. P3. $90.00

KOONTZ, Dean R. *Winter Moon.* 1994. London. Headline. 1st/hc ed. F/F. T2. $68.00

KOOPMAN, Harry Lyman. *Miniature Books.* 1968. Los Angeles. Dawson. 49x33mm. 1/400. 103p. F/stiff cream wrp. B24. $200.00

KOPAL, Zdenek. *Of Stars & Men, Reminiscences of an Astronomer.* 1986. Bristol, UK. Adam Hilger. 8vo. photos. 486p. VG/VG. K5. $52.00

KOPP, Sheldon. *Guru: Metaphors From a Psychotherapist.* 1971. Palo Alto. Science Behavior Books. 180p. VG/VG. B33. $15.00

KORDA, Michael. *Charmed Lives: A Personal Romance.* 1979. Random. BC. 498p. gilt maroon cloth. VG. M7. $18.00

KOREIN, Julius. *Brain Death: Interrelated Medical & Social Issues.* 1978. NY Academy of Sciences. 454p. prt bl wrp. G1. $42.00

KORNBLUH, Joyce. *Rebel Voices.* 1964. Ann Arbor. 1st ed. G/VG. B2. $25.00

KORNBLUTH, C.M. *Best of CM Kornbluth.* 1977. Taplinger. 1st ed. F/F. P3. $15.00

KORNBLUTH, C.M. *Mile Beyond the Moon.* 1958. Doubleday. 1st ed. F/NF. N3. $55.00

KORNBLUTH, C.M. *Takeoff.* 1952. Doubleday. 1st ed. VG/G. P3. $60.00

KORNBLUTH, Jesse. *Pre-Pop Warhol.* 1988. Panche/Random. 1st ed. intro Tina Fredericks. F. F1. $45.00

KORNBLUTH & POHL. *Space Merchants.* 1953. Ballantine. 1st ed. NF/NF. N3. $45.00

KORNGOLD, Ralph. *Citizen Toussaint.* 1944. Boston. Little Brn. 1st ed. inscr. F/NF. B2. $65.00

KORNS & MORGAN. *West From Ft Bridger...Immigrant Trails Across UT 1846-1850.* nd. np. revised/sgn Bagley & Schindler. M/M. A18. $30.00

KORTRIGHT, Francis H. *Ducks, Geese & Swans of North America.* 1943. Am Wildlife Assn. 2nd ed. 476p. VG. S11. $10.00

KORZYBSKI, Alfred. *Science & Sanity: Intro to Non-Aristotelian Systems...* 1948 (1933). Lakeville, CT. Internat Non-Aristotelian Lib Pub. 3rd ed. G1. $35.00

KOSINSKI, Jerzy. *Blind Date.* 1977. Houghton Mifflin. 1st ed. F/F. B3. $20.00

KOSINSKI, Jerzy. *Devil Tree.* 1973. HBJ. 1st ed. F/F. B3. $25.00

KOSINSKI, Jerzy. *Notes of the Arthur on the Painted Bird.* 1967. Scientia-Factum. 3rd ltd ed. inscr. F/wrp. B2. $45.00

KOSINSKI, Jerzy. *Passion Play.* 1979. St Martin. 1st ed. VG/VG. P3. $30.00

KOSINSKI, Jerzy. *Passion Play.* 1979. St Martin. 1/500. sgn. 271p. gilt blk cloth. F/glassine wrp/cb box. H5. $100.00

KOSKOFF, David E. *Joseph P Kennedy: A Life & Times.* 1974. Englewood Cliffs. Prentice Hall. 1st ed. ils. 643p. VG/dj. M10. $7.50

KOTKER, Norman. *Earthly Jerusalem.* 1969. Scribner. 1st ed. 16 pl. 307p. xl. VG/dj. W1. $12.00

KOTZWINKLE, William. *Christmas at Fontaine's.* 1982. Putnam. 1st ed. F/F. M2. $15.00

KOTZWINKLE, William. *Christmas at Fontaine's.* 1982. Putnam. 1st ed. F/NF. N3. $10.00

KOTZWINKLE, William. *Hermes 3000.* 1972. Pantheon. 1st ed. store stp. F/NF. B2. $25.00

KOTZWINKLE, William. *Jack-in-the-Box.* 1980. Putnam. 1st ed. VG/torn. P3. $13.00

KOTZWINKLE, William. *Midnight Examiner.* 1957. Houghton Mifflin. 1st ed. F/F. P3. $18.00

KOVALEVSKY, Jean. *Intro to Celestial Mechanics.* 1967. Springer-Verlag. sm 4to. 126p. G. K5. $27.00

KOWAL, Charles T. *Asteroids: Their Nature & Utilization.* 1988. Chichester, UK. Ellis Horwood. 8vo. 152p. pict brd. K5. $23.00

KOZOL, Jonathan. *Night Is Dark & I Am Far Away From Home.* 1975. Boston. 1st ed. sgn. F/F. B14. $25.00

KRACAUER, Siegfried. *Hist: The Last Things Before the Last.* 1969. NY. Oxford. sm 8vo. 269p. blk cloth. G1. $27.50

KRAELING, Emil G. *Rand McNally Bible Atlas.* 1956. Rand McNally. 485p. VG/dj. B29. $10.50

KRAEMER, J. Hugo. *Trees of the Western Pacific Region.* 1951. W Lafayette. ils. 436p. VG. B26. $37.50

KRAFT, Julius. *Von Husserl zu Heidegger: Kritik der Phanomenologischen...* 1957 (1932). Frankfurt am Main. Offentliches Leben. 2nd ed. 146p. VG/dj. G1. $22.00

KRAFT & SLOAN. *John Sloan in Santa Fe.* 1981. Smithsonian. ils. 72p. NF/wrp. B19. $10.00

KRAMER, Jack. *Cacti & Other Succulents.* 1977. NY. 188 ;photos. sc. B26. $17.50

KRAMER, Samuel Noah. *Great Ages of Man: Hist of World's Cultures.* 1967. Time Inc. 1st ed. 182p. ils. xl. VG. W1. $15.00

KRAMISH, Arnold. *Griffin: The Greatest Untold Espionage Story of WWII.* 1986. Boston. 1st ed. biblio/index. F/F. A17. $9.50

KRANTZ, John. *Historical Medical Classics Involving New Drugs.* 1974. Baltimore. 1st ed. 129p. A13. $50.00

KRASILOVSKY, Phyllis. *Cow Who Fell Into the Canal.* 1957. Doubleday. 1st ed. ils. NF/VG. P2. $40.00

KRASILOVSKY, Phyllis. *First Tulips in Holland.* 1982. Doubleday. 1st ed. ils Schindler. F/F. C8. $85.00

KRASINSKI, Zygmunt. *Un-Divine Comedy.* ca 1921. London. fwd Chesterton. trans Kennedy/Uminska. 112p. VG. A17. $12.50

KRASNER, William. *Death of a Minor Poet.* 1984. NY. Scribner. 1st ed. F/F. S6. $22.50

KRASNER, William. *Stag Party.* 1957. Harper. 1st ed. VG/VG. P3. $20.00

KRASNEY, Samuel. *Homicide West.* 1961. Morrow. 1st ed. F/dj. F4. $24.00

KRASSNER, Albert. *Journey To Be.* 1983. WA. Veridon. 1st ed. 133p. VG/VG. B33. $20.00

KRAUS, George. *High Road to Promontory.* 1969. Am W. 310p. VG/dj. M20. $30.00

KRAUS, Helen. *International Relief in Action, 1914-1943.* 1944. Phil. Research Center. 8vo. 248p. VG. V3. $16.00

KRAUS, Joe W. *Hist of Way & Williams With Biblio of Their Publications...* 1984. Phil. MacManus. 1/500. F/sans. B2. $45.00

KRAUS, John Louis. *John Locke: Empiricist, Atomist, Conceptualist & Agnostic.* 1968. Philosophical Lib. 202p. blk cloth VG/chip. G1. $25.00

KRAUS, Michelle P. *Allen Ginsberg: Annotated Bibliography.* 1980. Metuchen. Scarecrow. 1st ed. F/sans. B2. $30.00

KRAUS, Ruth. *Monkey Day.* 1957. Harper. sgn. ils Phyllis Roward. VG. P2. $30.00

KRAUS & KRAUS. *Detective of London.* ca 1978. Windmill Dutton. 1st Am ed. unp. VG/G. B10. $10.00

KRAUSE, Herbert. *Oxcart Trail.* 1954. Bobbs Merrill. ltd Minnesota ed. inscr/sgn twice. F/dj. A18. $50.00

KRAUSE, Herbert. *Wind Without Rain.* 1939. Bobbs Merrill. 1st ed/author's 1st book. inscr. VG+/dj. A18. $60.00

KRAUSE. *Custer's Prelude to Glory.* 1974. ils/index. 279p. O8. $23.50

KRAUSS, Bob. *Exceptional View of Life. The Easter Seal Story.* 1977. Honolulu. 1st ed. sq 4to. 64p. VG/VG. A17. $12.50

KRAUSS, Helen K. *Geraniums for Home & Garden.* (1955). Macmillan. BC. 194p. F/VG. H1. $4.50

KRAUSS, Ruth. *Mama, I Wish I Was Snow — Child, You'd Be Very Cold.* 1962. Atheneum. 1st ed. F/rpr. C8. $45.00

KRAUSZ, Sigmund. *Street Types of Great American Cities.* 1896. Werner. 1st ed thus. 46 photos. cloth. VG. M5. $65.00

KREMENTZ, Jill. *Sweet Pea, a Black Girl Growing Up in Rural South.* 1969. Harcourt Brace. 1st ed. VG/VG. C8. $30.00

KREMENTZ, Jill. *Writer's Image.* 1980. Boston. Godine. 1st ed. 4to. NF/VG+. S9. $35.00

KREMPIN, Jack. *Palms & Cycads Around the World.* 1993 (1990). Broadbeach Waters. revised ed. 4to. photos. 276p. M/dj. B26. $50.00

KRENKEL, Roy G. *Cities & Scenes From the Ancient World.* 1974. Owlswick. 1st ed. ils. F/F. T2. $30.00

KRENSKY, Stephen. *Castles in the Air & Other Tales.* 1979. Atheneum. 1st ed. ils Warren Lieberman. 66p. VG/VG. B10. $10.00

KRESS, Nancy. *Alien Light.* 1988. Arbor. 1st ed.d F/NF. N3. $15.00

KRESS, Nancy. *Aliens of Earth.* 1993. Arkham. 1st ed. ils Jane Walker. F/F. T2. $22.00

KRESS, Nancy. *Beggars in Spain.* 1991. Axolotl. Deluxe Leather ed. 1/75. sgn. M. M21. $90.00

KRESS, Nancy. *Golden Grove.* 1984. Bluejay. 1st ed. F/F. P3. $20.00

KREYMBORG, Alfred. *Funnybone Alley.* 1927. Macauley. 1st ed. ils Boris Artzybasheff. VG+. M5. $95.00

KREYMBORG, Alfred. *Others: Anthology of New Verse.* 1916. Knopf. 1st ed. inscr/dtd 1916. 152p. NF/VG. C6. $500.00

KRIEGER, Michael J. *Tramp. Sagas of High Adventure in Vanishing World...* 1986. Chronicle. obl 4to. 142p. dj. T7. $35.00

KRIGER, Malcolm D. *Peaceable Kingdom.* 1983. Rosywick. 1st ed. lg 8vo. ils. 192p. cloth. F/F. R2. $35.00

KRIKORIAN, Yervant H. *Naturalism & the Human Spirit.* 1944. Columbia. 397p. ochre cloth. VG/chip. G1. $30.00

KRISTEVA, Julia. *About Chinese Women.* 1977. NY. Urizen. 1st ed. F/NF. B2. $30.00

KRISTEVA, Julia. *Powers of Horror: Essay on Abjection.* 1982. Columbia. 220p. beige cloth. VG/dj. G1. $25.00

KRIVATSY, Peter. *Catalogue of 17th-Century Printed Books in Nat Lib Medicine.* 1989. Bethesda. 4to. 1315p. rubber stp front ep. NF. G7. $50.00

KROCHMAL & KROCHMAL. *Gardening in the Carolinas.* 1975. Garden City. ils. VG/dj. B26. $24.00

KROEBER, A.L. *Anthropology Today.* 1953. Chicago. 966p. F/dj. K4. $22.50

KROEBER, A.L. *Handbook of the Indians of California.* 1953. CA Book Co. rpt of 1925 ed. ils/fld map/tables. NF. A8. $100.00

KROEBER, A.L. *Roster of Civilizations & Culture.* 1962. Chicago. Aldine. 1st ed. 96p. cloth. NF/dj. W1. $14.00

KROLL, Harry Harrison. *Darker Grows the Valley.* 1947. Bobbs Merrill. 1st ed. VG/G. P3. $10.00

KROLL, Harry Harrison. *Their Ancient Grudge.* 1946. Bobbs Merrill. 1st ed. VG/VG. P3. $20.00

KRONICK, David. *Literature of the Life Sciences.* 1985. Phil. 1st ed. 219p. A13. $25.00

KRONINGER, Robert H. *Sarah & Her Senator.* 1964. Howell North. VG/clip. N2. $7.50

KROPOTKIN, Peter. *Ethics: Origin & Development.* nd. NY. Tudor. later prt. red cloth. VG/dj. G1. $22.50

KROPOTKIN, Peter. *Memoirs of a Revolutionist.* 1899. Houghton Mifflin. 1st Am ed. inscr/dtd 1901. NF. B4. $1,000.00

KRUGER, Paul. *Finish Line.* 1968. Simon Schuster. 1st ed. VG/VG. P3. $20.00

KRUMAN, Marc W. *Parties & Politics in NC 1836-1865.* 1983. LSU. biblio/index/maps. M/M. A17. $15.00

KRUMGOLD, Joseph. *Henry 3.* 1967. Atheneum. 1st ed. 268p. F/NF. P2. $30.00

KRUMGOLD, Joseph. *Sweeny's Adventure.* ca 1942. Random. ils Tibor Gergely. VG/G. B10. $12.00

KRUSE, H.D. *Integrating the Approaches to Mental Disease.* 1958. Hoeber-Harper. 393p. G/dj. K4. $20.00

KRUTCH, Joseph Wood. *Grand Canyon: Today & All Its Yesterdays.* 1958. Sloane. 1st ed. 276p. NF/NF. B19. $45.00

KRUTCH, Joseph Wood. *Voice in the Desert: Naturalist's Interpretation.* 1955. Sloane. 1st ed. 223p. VG+/worn. B19. $30.00

KUBASTA, V. *Am Indian Camp.* 1962. London. Bancroft. 1 pop-up. pict brd. VG+. C8. $75.00

KUBASTA, V. *Circus Life.* 1961. London. Bancroft. mechanical pop-up. pict brd. VG. C8. $20.00

KUBASTA, V. *Moko & Koko in the Jungle.* 1961. London. Bancroft. mechanical pop-up. pict brd. VG+. C8. $75.00

KUBASTA, V. *Red Riding Hood.* 1961. London. Bancroft. lg 8vo. mechanical pop-up. VG/wrp. C8. $30.00

KUBE-MCDOWELL, Michael P. *Quiet Pools.* 1990. Ace. 1st ed. F/F. P3. $18.00

KUBLER, George A. *New Hist of Stereotyping.* 1941. NY. Dry Mat. 362p. VG. RS. A10. $40.00

KUBLER, George A. *Short Hist of Stereotyping.* 1927. NY. Eagle/Dry Mat. 93p. VG. A10. $30.00

KUBLER-ROSS, Elisabeth. *Working It Through: An Elisabeth Kubler-Ross Workshop...* 1982. Macmillan. 1st ed. 144p. VG/VG. B33. $15.00

KUHLMAN, C. *Legend Into History.* 1952. Harrisburg. 2nd ed. G/chip. B5. $45.00

KUIST. *Nicols File of Gentleman's Magazine...* 1982. WI U. 4to. 344p. F. A4. $95.00

KUKLICK, Bruce. *Josiah Royce: Intellectual Biography.* 1985. Hackett Pub. revised ed. 8vo. red cloth. F. G1. $20.00

KUMIN, Maxine. *Looking for Luck.* 1992. Norton. 1st ed. NF/NF. B3. $25.00

KUMIN, Maxine. *Nightmare Factory.* 1970. Harper Row. 1st ed. inscr. NF/NF. B3. $50.00

KUMIN, Maxine. *Why Can't We Live Together Like Civilized Human Beings.* 1981. Viking. 1st ed. F/VG. B3. $30.00

KUMMER, Frederic Arnold. *First Days of Knowledge.* 1923. Doran. 1st ed. VG. P3. $20.00

KUNDERA, Milan. *Book of Laughter & Forgetting.* 1980. Knopf. 1st Am ed. F/F clip. B4. $85.00

KUNDERA, Milan. *Unbearable Lightness of Being.* 1984. Harper. 1st Am ed. F/NF. B4. $85.00

KUNG, Hans. *Does God Exist?* 1980. Doubleday. index/notes. 839p. H10. $15.00

KUNG, Hans. *On Being a Christian.* 1976. Doubleday. 720p. G. B29. $8.50

KUNZ, George F. *Curious Lore of Precious Stones.* 1938. Halcyon. 7th ed. 406p. VG/VG. B33. $45.00

KUPPER, Walter. *Das Kakteenbuch.* 1929. Berlin-Westend. German text. ils/pl. 201p. yel cloth. B26. $62.00

KURCHAREK, Casimir. *Sacramental Mysteries: A Byzantine Approach.* 1976. Ontario. Alleluia. 415p. VG/VG. B33. $30.00

KURLAND, Philip B. *Supreme Court Review 1969.* 1969. Chicago. M11. $25.00

KURTEN, Bjorn. *Dance of the Tiger: A Novel of the Ice Age.* 1980. Pantheon. 1st Am ed/author's 1st novel. F/F. N3. $25.00

KURTZ, Charles M. *Official Ils From Art Gallery of World's Columbian Expo.* 1893. Phil. Barrie. 1st ed. 8vo. 383p. G. B11. $75.00

KURTZ, John Henry. *TB of Church Hist.* 1892. Lippincott. 1002p. xl. B29. $12.50

KURTZ, Katherine. *Bishop's Heir.* 1984. Century. 1st ed. F/F. F4. $18.00

KURTZ, Katherine. *Harrowing of Gwynedd.* 1989. Del Rey. 1st ed. F/F. P3. $18.00

KURTZ, Kenneth. *Literature of the Am SW: Selective Bibliography.* 1956. Occidental College. 1st ed. 63p. F/sans. B19. $30.00

KUSHNER, Ellen. *Thomas the Rhymer.* 1990. Morrow. 1st ed. F/F. M21. $40.00

KUSHNER, Harold S. *When Bad Things Happen to Good People.* 1981. Schoken Books. 148p. VG/dj. B29. $4.25

KUTAK, Rosemary. *I Am the Cat.* 1948. Farrar Straus. 1st ed. RS. VG/dj. M20. $15.00

KUTTNER, Henry. *As You Were.* ca 1952-55. Sidney. Malian. Am SF Magazine. 1st separate prt. NF/pict wrp. N3. $35.00

KUTTNER, Henry. *Man Drowning.* 1952. Harper. 1st ed. VG/torn. P3. $25.00

KWITNY, Jonathan. *Shakedown.* 1977. Putnam. 1st ed. VG/VG. P3. $15.00

KYD, Stewart. *Treatise on the Law of Bills of Exchange & Promissory Notes.* 1800. Albany. Loring Andrews. contemporary sheep. M11. $500.00

KYLE, David. *Pictorial Hist of SF.* 1976. Hamlyn. 1st ed. F/dj. M2. $18.00

KYLE, Duncan. *Black Camelot.* 1978. Collins. 1st ed. F/F. P3. $15.00

KYLE, Duncan. *Honey Ant.* 1988. London. Collins. 1st ed. NF/dj. S6. $22.50

KYLE, Louisa Venable. *Hist of Eastern Shore Chapel & Lynhaven Parish 1642-1969.* 1970. Norfolk, VA. 1st ed/2nd prt. 121p. cloth. NF/VG. M8. $27.50

KYLE, Melvin Grove. *Excavating Kirjath-Sepher's Ten Cities.* 1934. Grand Rapids, MI. 1st ed. 203p. VG. W1. $65.00

KYNE, Peter B. *Enchanted Hill.* 1924. Cosmopolitan. 1st ed. ils Dean Cornwell. F/reinforced. A18. $50.00

KYNE, Peter B. *Kindred of the Dust.* 1920. Cosmopolitan. 1st ed. ils. VG. A17. $9.50

KYNE, Peter B. *Never the Twain Shall Meet.* 1923. Copp Clark. 1st Canadian ed. VG. P3. $20.00

KYNE, Peter B. *Never the Twain Shall Meet.* 1923. Cosmopolitan. 1st ed. ils Dean Cornwell. F/dj. A18. $35.00

KYNE, Peter B. *They Also Serve.* 1927. Cosmopolitan. 1st ed. ils CL Bainbridge. F/dj. A18. $40.00

L

L'AMOUR, Louis. *Comstock Lode.* 1981. Bantam. UP. sc. pict bdg. VG. A18. $40.00

L'AMOUR, Louis. *Education of a Wandering Man.* 1989. Bantam. 1st ed. intro DJ Boorstin. F/dj. A18. $20.00

L'AMOUR, Louis. *Education of a Wandering Man.* 1989. Bantam. 1st ed. VG/VG. P3. $17.00

L'AMOUR, Louis. *Fair Blows the Winds.* 1978. Dutton. 1st ed. F/dj. F4. $30.00

L'AMOUR, Louis. *Hondo.* 1983. Bantam. 1st deluxe ed. aeg. leather. F. A18. $60.00

L'AMOUR, Louis. *Jubal Sackett.* 1985. Bantam. AP. F/prt wrp. S9. $25.00

L'AMOUR, Louis. *Outlaws of the Mesquite.* 1990. Bantam. 1st ed. VG/VG. P3. $17.00

L'AMOUR, Louis. *Sackett's Land.* 1974. Dutton. 1st ed. F/VG. A18. $80.00

L'AMOUR, Louis. *Shamelady.* 1966. Heinemann. 1st ed. VG. P3. $10.00

L'AMOUR, Louis. *To the Far Blue Mountains.* 1976. Dutton. 1st ed. F/F. A18. $80.00

L'AMOUR, Louis. *Walking Drum.* 1984. Bantam. ARC. sc. F. A18. $50.00

L'ENGLE, Madeleine. *Camillia Dickinson.* 1951. Simon Schuster. 1st prt. VG/G+. C8. $65.00

L'ENGLE, Madeleine. *Intergalactic PS3.* 1970. Children's Book Council. pamphlet. F/wrp. C8. $22.50

L'ENGLE, Madeleine. *Many Waters.* 1986. FSG. 1st ed. F/F. B3. $35.00

L'ENGLE, Madeleine. *Ring of Endless Light.* 1980. FSG. 1st prt. inscr. F/F. C8. $85.00

L'ENGLE, Madeleine. *Summer of the Great-Grandmother.* 1974. FSG. 4th ed. rem mk. F/F. B17. $8.00

L'ENGLE, Madeleine. *Swiftly Tilting Planet.* 1978. FSG. 1st prt. NF/VG+. C8. $50.00

L'ENGLE, Madeleine. *Wind in the Door.* 1973. FSG. 1st prt. F/F. C8. $65.00

L'ENGLE, Madeline. *Swiftly Tilting Planet.* 1978. FSG. 1st ed. 278p. VG/VG. P2. $40.00

L'ESTRANGE, Roger. *Fables of Aesop & Other Eminent Mythologists...* 1714. London. Sare Churchill. 6th ed. sm 8vo. 550p. full leather. VG. D6. $275.00

L'HOMMEDIEU, Dorothy K. *Little Black Chaing.* 1958. NY. Ariel Books. 1st ed. ils. unp. cloth. F/dj. scarce. R2. $60.00

L'HOMMEDIEU, Dorothy K. *Nipper, the Little Bull Pup.* 1957. London. Robert Hale. 1st ed. ils Marguerite Kirmse. cloth. F/F. P2/R2. $45.00

L'HOMMEDIEU, Dorothy K. *Tinker, the Little Fox Terrier.* 1942. Lippincott. ils Marguerite Kirmse. 62p. VG. P2. $35.00

L'HOMMEDIEU, Dorothy K. *Tyke, the Little Mutt.* 1949. Lippincott. 1st ed. ils Kirmse. VG+/dj. M5. $25.00

LA FARGE, Oliver. *Enemy Gods.* 1927. Boston. 1st ed. NF/tape rpr. A17. $22.50

LA FARGE, Oliver. *Laughing Boy.* 1929. Cambridge. 1st ed. VG/VG. B5. $95.00

LA FARGE, Oliver. *Pict Hist of the American Indian.* 1958. London. Deutsch. 1st ed. photos/ils. VG+. A18. $60.00

LA FARGE, Oliver. *Pictorial History of the American Indian.* 1956. Crown. 1st ed. 4to. xl. G. A8. $25.00

LA FOLLETTE JENSEN, Amy. *White House. And It's Thirty-Four Families.* 1965. NY. McGraw Hill. revised ed. 4to. VG/G. B11. $15.00

LA GRANGE & LA GRANGE. *Clipper Ships of Am & Great Britain 1833-1869.* 1938. NY. Putnam. trade ed. ils. 381p. beige cloth. VG. P4. $95.00

LA HAYE, Tim. *Your Temperment: Discover Its Potential.* 1984. Tyndale. 351p. F/F. B29. $5.00

LA MOTT, Ellen. *Opium Monopoly.* 1920. NY. 1st ed. 84p. A13. $45.00

LA PIERRE, Janet. *Grandmother's House.* 1991. Scribner. 1st ed. F/F. T2. $16.00

LA PIERRE, Janet. *Unquiet Grave.* 1987. St Martin. 1st ed. sgn. F/F. T2. $45.00

LA PRADE, Ernest. *Alice in Orchestralia.* 1927. Doubleday Page. not 1st ed. VG. N2. $10.00

LA VARRE, William. *Southward Ho! A Treasure Hunter in South America.* 1940. Doubleday Doran. 8vo. 15 pl. 301p. G/G. B11. $15.00

LAAR, Clemens. *Kampf in der Wuste.* 1941. Berlin. Franz Eher Nahs. rpt. ils. 235p. brn bdg. VG. M7. $65.00

LABRADOR RETRIEVER CLUB. *Labrador Retriever Club 1945-1946.* 1947. np. ils. 79p. cloth. F/tissue wrp. R2. $25.00

LACEY, Robert. *Kingdom.* 1981. HBJ. 8vo. NF/torn. W1. $16.00

LACHENMEYER, Charles W. *Essence of Social Research: Copernican Revolution.* 1973. Free Pr. 309p. cloth. VG/dj. G1. $22.50

LACKER & LACKER. *Elvis, Portrait of a Friend.* 1979. Wimmer. 1st prt. sgns. 1/5000. 316p. VG/G. S11. $85.00

LACKEY, Mercedes. *Winds of Change.* 1992. DAW. 1st ed. F/F. P3. $20.00

LACKINGTON, James. *Confessions of James Lackington, Late Bookseller...* 1898. NY. 2nd Am ed. 12mo. 189p. contemporary calf. K1. $150.00

LACKLAND, William. *Meteors, Aerolites, Storms & Atmospheric Phenomena.* 1886. Scribner. 8vo. 324p. gilt cloth. G. K5. $42.00

LACOUTURE & LACOUTURE. *Egypt in Transition.* 1958. Criterion. 1st ed. ils/maps. xl. VG. W1. $9.00

LACY, Ed. *Hotel Dwellers.* 1966. Harper Row. 1st ed. NF/NF. P3. $25.00

LACY, Ed. *Room To Swing.* 1957. Harper. 1st ed. VG/VG. P3. $25.00

LADBURY, Ann. *Practical Sewing.* 1978. np. cloth. VG. G2. $15.00

LADBURY, Ann. *Sewing Book.* 1985. np. cloth. VG. G2. $12.95

LADD, George Trumbull. *Knowledge, Life & Reality: Essay on Systematic Philosophy.* 1918 (1909). np. 549p. gr cloth. VG. G1. $35.00

LADD, George Trumbull. *Phycology Descriptive & Explanatory...* 1894. Scribner. 8vo. 676p. VG. G1. $50.00

LADD, George Trumbull. *Theory of Reality...* 1899. Scribner. heavy 8vo. 556p. VG. G1. $50.00

LADD, Horatio. *History of the War With Mexico.* 1911. Dodd Mead. 12mo. 328p. gr cloth. G. B11. $25.00

LADD, Richard S. *Descriptive List of Treasure Maps & Charts.* 1964. WA, DC. GPO/Map Division. 4to. wrp. T7. $15.00

LADO, Robert. *Language Testing.* 1961. NY. McGraw Hill. 389p. G/dj. K4. $10.00

LADREYT, Casimir. *Nouvelle Arithmetique Raisonnee...* 1836. Montreal. Compte de l'Auteur. 120p. calf/bl-gray brd. K1. $100.00

LAFFERTY, R.A. *Does Anyone Else Have Something To Add?* 1974. Scribner. 1st ed. F/F. P3. $20.00

LAFFERTY, R.A. *Mischief Malicious...Murder Most Strange.* 1991. Weston, Ont. United Mythologies. 1st ed. F/wrp. N3. $15.00

LAFFERTY, R.A. *Not to Mention Camels.* 1976. Bobbs Merrill. 1st ed. F/F. P3. $20.00

LAFFERTY, R.A. *Okla Hannali.* 1972. Doubleday. 1st ed. F/VG+. N3. $25.00

LAFFERTY, R.A. *Serpent's Egg.* 1987. Morrigan. 1st ed. F/F. P3. $30.00

LAGERKVIST, Par. *Eternal Smile & Other Stories.* 1954. Random. 1st ed. F/F. L3. $75.00

LAGERLOF, Selma. *Further Adventures of Nils.* 1915 (1911). Doubleday. ils Astri Heiberg. cloth. VG. M5. $18.00

LAGERLOF, Selma. *Wonderful Adventures of Nils.* 1913. Doubleday Page. 1st ed thus. 24 mc pl. 263p. VG. P2. $95.00

LAING, Alexander. *Cadaver of Gideon Wyck.* 1942. Triangle. VG/VG. P3. $20.00

LAING, Alexander. *Dr Scarlett.* 1936. Farrar Rinehart. 1st ed. 338p. VG/dj. M20. $15.00

LAING, Alexander. *Great Ghost Stories of the World.* 1941. Blue Ribbon. G+. P3. $20.00

LAING, Donald A. *Roger Fry: Annotated Bibliography of Pub Writings.* 1979. NY. Garland. 1st ed. F/sans. B2. $40.00

LAIRD, Carobeth. *Encounter With an Angry God.* 1975. Banning, CA. Malki Mus. 1st ed. VG+/VG+. S9. $30.00

LAIRD, Carobeth. *Encounter With an Angry God.* 1975. Malki Mus. 1st ed. 190p. F/NF. B19. $35.00

LAIRD, John. *Study in Realism.* 1920. Cambridge. 228p. ruled red cloth. G1. $46.50

LAIT, Jack. *Big House.* nd. Grosset Dunlap. MTI. VG P3. $25.00

LAKE, David J. *Fourth Hemisphere.* 1980. Victoria, Australia. Void. 1st ed. 1/250. F/F. N3. $50.00

LAKE, Simon. *Submarine in War & Peace.* 1918. Lippincott. ils. 301p. T7. $120.00

LAKE, Veronica. *Veronica.* 1971. NY. 1st ed. VG/VG. B5. $50.00

LAKE. *No Symbols Where None Indended.* 1984. TX U. ils. 185p. F. A4. $35.00

LAMB, A. *Horse Facts: A Study of the Points of the Horse...* 1946. London. Hurst Blackett. 3rd prt. VG/G. O3. $22.00

LAMB, Charles M. *Land Use Politics & Law in the 1970s.* 1975. WA, DC. 85p. wrp. D3. $15.00

LAMB, Charles. *Dream-Children & the Child Angel.* 1929. Dent. 1st ed. 28p. VG. B10. $20.00

LAMB, Dana. *Enchanted Vagabonds.* 1938. Harper. 1st ed. 415p. VG. F3. $20.00

LAMB, Dana. *Green Highlanders Pink Ladies.* 1971. Barre. 1/1500. VG/box. B5. $75.00

LAMB, David. *Arabs: Journeys Beyond the Mirage.* 1987. NY. Random. 1st ed. 333p. VG/dj. W1. $24.00

LAMB, E. *Flowering Your Cacti.* 1948 (1943). Worthing. 21 photos. 56p. prt brd. VG. B26. $20.00

LAMB, E. *Ils Reference on Cacti & Other Succulents. Vol 1.* 1958 (1955). London. photos. 311p. VG/fair. B26. $27.50

LAMB, Elizabeth. *Hist Sketch of Hay St Methodist Episcopal Church...* 1934. Fayetteville, NC. 1st ed. 96p. VG/prt wrp. scarce. M8. $75.00

LAMB, H.H. *Changing Climate.* 1968 (1966). London. Methuen. 2nd prt. 8vo. 236p. VG/VG. K5. $20.00

LAMB, Harold. *Durandal.* 1981. Donald Grant. 1st ed. F/F. P3. $15.00

LAMB, Harold. *March of Barbarians.* 1940. Doubleday Doran. 1st ed. 8vo. 389p. G. W1. $15.00

LAMB, Harold. *Nur Mahl.* 1935. Doubleday Doran. 8vo. 325p. xl. VG. W1. $12.00

LAMB, Harold. *Three Palladins.* 1977. Donald Grant. 1st ed. VG/G. P3. $15.00

LAMB, Hugh. *Cold Fear.* 1978. Taplinger. 1st ed. F/F. P3. $25.00

LAMB, Hugh. *Return From the Grave.* 1977. Taplinger. 1st Am ed. F/F clip. N3. $20.00

LAMB, Martha J. *History of City of NY.* 1877 & 1880. NY. 2 vol. 1st ed. ils/maps. VG. B5. $200.00

LAMB, Martha J. *Homes of America.* 1879. NY. Appleton. ils. 256p. gr cloth/beveled brd. VG. F1. $125.00

LAMB, Wally. *She's Come Undone.* 1992. Pocket. 1st ed/author's 1st book. F/F. A14. $25.00

LAMB & LAMB. *Popular Exotic Cacti in Color.* 1975. Poole, Dorset. sgns. 100 mc photos. 176p. F/dj. B26. $16.00

LAMBERT, Derek. *Chase.* 1987. London. Hamilton. 1st ed. NF/dj. S6. $20.00

LAMBERT, Derek. *Golden Express.* 1984. Stein Day. 1st ed. VG/VG. P3. $15.00

LAMBERT, Harold. *Infectious Disease Ils.* 1982. Phil. folio. mc pl. G7. $35.00

LAMBERT, Janet. *Dreams of Glory.* 1942. Dutton. 6th prt. sgn. 252p. VG/dj. M20. $25.00

LAMBERT, Janet. *One for the Money.* 1946. Grosset Dunlap. brd. VG/G. M5. $10.00

LAMBERT, Janet. *Up Goes the Curtain.* 1946. Grosset Dunlap. brd. VG/G. M5. $10.00

LAMBERT, Mercedes. *Dogtown.* 1991. Viking. 1st ed. F/F. M15. $25.00

LAMBERT, Mercedes. *El Nino.* 1990. Viking. 1st ed. sgn. F/F. M15. $40.00

LAMBETH, Joseph A. *Lambeth Method of Cake Decoration & Practical Pastries.* 1936. London. Virtue. 1st ed. 4to. ils. 308p. gilt/emb maroon bdg. F. F1. $300.00

LAMBOURNE, Lionel. *Ernest Griset.* 1979. London. Thames Hudson. ils. 88p. VG/wrp. S11. $15.00

LAMOND, Henry G. *Kilgour's Mare.* 1943. NY. Morrow. 1st ed. VG. O3. $18.00

LAMORISSE, Albert. *White Mane...Taken From the Film.* 1954. Dutton. 1st ed. G/G. O3. $9.00

LAMOTT, K. *Who Killed Mr Crittenden?* 1963. NY. 305p. NF. D3. $12.50

LAMPELL, Millard. *Wall.* 1961. NY. 1st ed. sgn. photos. F/NF. A11. $95.00

LAMPLUGH, Lois. *Shadowed Man: Henry Williamson 1895-1977.* 1991. Somerset. Exmoor. 2nd UK ed. photos. 202p. gilt bdg. M. M7. $35.00

LAMPRECHT, Karl. *Einfuhrung in Das Historische Denken.* 1912. Leipzig. Voigtlander. sq 8vo. 9 pl. gray linen. G1. $30.00

LANARD, Thomas S. *One Hundred Years With the State Fencibles.* 1913. Phil. 1st ed. teg. VG. B18. $95.00

LANCASTER, Bruce. *Phantom Fortress.* 1950. Little Brn. 1st ed. VG/G. P3. $13.00

LANCASTER, Graham. *Nuclear Letters.* 1979. Atheneum. 1st ed. VG/VG. P3. $15.00

LANCASTER. *French Tragedy in the Reign of Louis XVI & Early Years...* 1953. Johns Hopkins. 191p. F. A4. $45.00

LANCOUR, Gene. *Lerios Mecca.* 1973. Doubleday. 1st ed. VG/VG. P3. $20.00

LANDACRE, Paul. *Landacre & Quince.* 1989. Laguna Verde. Ward Ritchie. 74x56mm. 1/50. 28p. blk cloth. F. B24. $375.00

LANDAU, Ergy. *Aujourd'Hui la Chine.* 1955. Lausanne. Editions Clairefontaine. 1st ed. 4to. VG/wrp. S9. $70.00

LANDAU, Ergy. *Horoldamba.* 1957. Paris. Camann-Levy. 1st ed. 4to. G/wrp. S9. $40.00

LANDAU, Jacob M. *Word Count of Modern Arabic Prose.* 1959. Hebrew U. 453p. VG/wrp. W1. $15.00

LANDAU, Ron. *Islam & the Arabs.* 1959. Macmillan. 1st ed. F/VG. B33. $20.00

LANDER, David. *History of the Lander Family of VA & KY.* 1926. Chicago. Regan. sgn. ils. 213p. G. B11. $50.00

LANDER & LANDER. *Journal of Expedition To Explore Course...Niger...* nd. NY. Harper. 2 vol set. ils/maps. cloth. VG+. P4. $200.00

LANDERS, Lynda Stone. *Season To Remember.* 1989. Avalon. 1st ed. M/M. P8. $12.50

LANDHAM, Edwin. *Wind Blew West.* 1935. Longman Gr. 1st ed. inscr. VG/dj. Q1. $200.00

LANDHEER, Bart. *Mind & Society: Epistemological Essays on Sociology.* 1952. The Hague. 112p. wrp. G1. $17.50

LANDING, James E. *American Essence.* 1969. Kalamazoo. ils. 244p. F/dj. B26. $25.00

LANDIS, C.S. *.22 Caliber Varmint Rifles.* 1947. Samworth. VG/VG. A1. $60.00

LANDIS, H.R.M. *Hist of Development of Medical Science in Am...* 1901. Phil. ils. 24p. orig prt wrp. G7. $35.00

LANDOR, A. *Explorer's Adventures in Tibet.* 1910. Harper. 1st ed. 276p. pict cloth. VG. B14. $55.00

LANDOR, Walter Savage. *Classical (Imaginary) Conversations: Greek, Roman, Modern.* 1901. NY. Dunne. 418p. VG. M10. $3.50

LANDOR, Walter Savage. *Imaginary Conversations.* 1936. LEC. ils/sgn Hans Mardersteig. F/VG/case. M19. $50.00

LANDSTROM, Bjorn. *Ships of the Pharaohs.* 1970. Doubleday. folio. ils. VG/dj. T7. $60.00

LANE, Edward. *Look Unto Jesus; or, Ascent to Holy Mount To See Jesus...* 1663. London. self pub. 1st ed. 4to. later leather. H10. $145.00

LANE, Maggie. *Needlepoint by Design: Variations on Chinese Themes.* 1970. np. cloth. VG. G2. $18.00

LANE, Margaret. *Tale of Beatrix Potter, a Biography.* 1946. Warne. 1st Am ed. 20 pl. cloth. VG+/tattered. M5. $15.00

LANE, Mark. *Citizens Dissent.* 1968. NY. 1st ed. VG/VG. B5. $22.50

LANE, Samuel A. *Fifty Years & Over of Akron & Summit Co.* 1892. Akron. 1167p. rebound. VG. B18. $125.00

LANE. *British Racing Prints, 1700-1940.* 1990. London. 4to. 126 pl. 216p. F/F. A4. $85.00

LANES, Selma G. *Art of Maurice Sendak.* 1980. Abrams. 1st ed. lg sq 4to. ils. cloth. glassine wrp. F1. $125.00

LANES, Selma G. *Art of Maurice Sendak.* 1984. Abradale. ils. 278p. F/VG. S11. $45.00

LANES, Selma G. *Down the Rabbit Hole.* 1971. Atheneum. 1st ed. RS. VG/dj. M20. $22.00

LANG, Andrew. *All Sorts of Stories by Mrs Lang.* 1911. Longman Gr. 1st ed. NF. C8. $200.00

LANG, Andrew. *Angling Sketches.* 1891. London. ils. 176p. VG. B5. $175.00

LANG, Andrew. *Ballads & Verses Vain.* 1884. Scribner. probable 1st ed. VG. C8. $35.00

LANG, Andrew. *Book of Romance.* 1902. Longman Gr. 1st ed. 8vo. 384p. VG. D6. $110.00

LANG, Andrew. *Brown Fairy Book.* 1904. Longman Gr. 1st ed. ils Ford. VG. M5. $150.00

LANG, Andrew. *Chronicles of Pantouflia.* 1981. Boston. Godine. 1st ed thus. F/VG+. C8. $27.50

LANG, Andrew. *Chronicles of Pantouflia.* 1981. Godine. VG/VG. P3. $15.00

LANG, Andrew. *Disentanglers.* 1902. London. Longman Gr. 1st ed. ils HJ Ford. 418p. G. S11. $25.00

LANG, Andrew. *Orange Fairy Book.* 1906. Longman Gr. 1st ed. 12mo. VG. C8. $140.00

LANG, Andrew. *Pink Fairy Book.* 1897. Longman Gr. 1st ed. pict cloth. VG. C8. $75.00

LANG, Andrew. *Prince Prigio & Prince Ricardo.* 1961. Dent Dutton. F/F. P3. $23.00

LANG, Andrew. *Prince Prigio.* 1942. Little Brn. 1st ed. ils Robert Lawson. 110p. VG. P2. $25.00

LANG, Andrew. *Red Fairy Book.* 1924. Phil. McKay. 1st ed. ils Gustaf Tenggren. 85p. VG. D6. $195.00

LANG, Andrew. *Red Fairy Book.* 1948. Longman Gr. 1st prt thus. VG. C8. $20.00

LANG, Andrew. *Red Romance Book.* 1905. Longman Gr. 1st ed. 8vo. 366p. gilt red cloth. VG. D6. $110.00

LANG, Andrew. *Violet Fairy Book.* 1951. Longman Gr. revised ed. VG/VG. C8. $30.00

LANG, Andrew. *Yellow Fairy Book.* ca 1900. AL Burt. 12mo. VG+. C8. $65.00

LANG, Don. *Strawberry Roan.* nd. NY. Famous Horse Stories Series. pict brd. VG. O3. $12.00

LANG, Iain. *Background of the Blues.* 1943. London. Workers Music Assn. 1st ed. VG/wrp. B2. $60.00

LANG, Jean. *Book of Myths.* ca 1920. Nelson. ils Helen Stratton. bl cloth/mc pl. VG. M5. $60.00

LANG, Mrs. *Book of Princes & Princesses.* 1908. Longman Gr. 1st ed. 361p. aeg. VG. B10. $65.00

LANG, R. Hamilton. *Cyprus: Its History, Its Present Rescources...* 1878. London. 8vo. 370p. cloth. very scarce. O2. $125.00

LANG, W. *Hist of Seneca County.* 1880. Springfield. xl. VG. M20. $75.00

LANGART, Darrell T. *Anything You Can Do.* nd. BC. VG/VG. P3. $10.00

LANGE, Friedrich Albert. *Hist of Materialism & Criticism...* 1877-1880. London. Trubner. 3 vols. 1st Eng-language ed. 398p. bl cloth. VG. G1. $175.00

LANGE, John; see Crichton, Michael.

LANGER, Susanne. *Cruise of the Little Dipper & Other Fairy Tales.* 1923. NY. Norcross. ils Helen Sewell. pict cloth. VG+. C8. $40.00

LANGER, Susanne. *Intro to Symbolic Logic.* 1937. London. Allen Unwin. 363p. VG/dj. G1. $85.00

LANGEVELD, M.J. *Columbus: Picture Analysis of Growth Towards Maturity.* 1969. NY. Basel. 72p. F. K4. $35.00

LANGEWIESCHE, Karl Robert. *Der Stille Garten.* 1940. Verlag/Konigstein. 128p. VG/VG. S11. $10.00

LANGFORD, N.P. *Vigilante Days & Ways, Pioneers of the Rockies.* 1912. Burt. VG. B34. $45.00

LANGLEY, Batty. *Practical Geometry Applied to Useful Arts of Building...* 1726. London. Innys Osborn. folio. ils. 136p. paneled calf/rebacked. VG. K1. $1,250.00

LANGLEY, Lee. *Persistent Rumors.* 1994. Milkweed. UP/1st Am ed. F/F. B4. $45.00

LANGLEY, Samuel Pierpont. *New Astronomy.* 1887 (1884). Houghton Mifflin. 4th prt. ils. 260p. maroon cloth. G. K5. $80.00

LANGSTAFF, J.B. *Dr Bard of Hyde Park.* 1932. NY. ils. 398p. dj. G7. $25.00

LANGTON, Jane. *God in Concord.* 1992. Viking. 1st ed. sgn. F/F. M15. $27.50

LANGTON, Jane. *Good & Dead.* 1986. St Martin. 1st ed. F/F. M15. $25.00

LANGTON, Jane. *Memorial Hall Murder.* 1990. London. Gollancz. 1st Eng ed. F/F. S6. $25.00

LANGTON, Jane. *Paper Chains.* 1977. Harper Row. 1st ed. VG/VG. P3. $20.00

LANGWELL, Lyndesay. *Index to Musical Wind-Instrument Makers.* 1962. Edinburgh. 2nd ed. 202p. VG/torn. B14. $225.00

LANGWORTHY, John Luther. *Aeroplane Boys on the Wing; or, Aeroplane Chums in Tropics.* 1912. Donohue. ftspc. pict cloth. VG. A17. $10.00

LANHAM, Edwin. *Iron Maiden.* 1954. Harcourt Brace. 1st ed. VG/VG. P3. $18.00

LANIER, Sidney. *Boy's King Arthur: Sir Thomas Malory's History...* 1946. Scribner. early rpt. pict blk cloth. VG+. A3. $40.00

LANIER, Sidney. *Poems.* 1877. Lippincott. 1st ed/author's 1st book poems. 94p. F. C6. $450.00

LANKER, J.N. *Lutherans in All Lands.* 1893. Milwaukee. 8vo. ils. 383p. VG+. M9. $35.00

LANSDALE, Joe R. *Act of Love.* 1992. Baltimore. CD Pub. 1st hc ed. sgn. 1/750. F/F. T2. $50.00

LANSDALE, Joe R. *Savage Season.* 1990. Ziesing. sgn. F/F. P3. $35.00

LANSING, Elisabeth Hubbard. *Seeing NY.* ca 1938. Crowell. ils Syd Browne. 237p. VG/G. B10. $20.00

LANSING, Robert. *Peace Negotiations: A Personal Narrative.* 1921. Houghton Mifflin. 1st ed. photos/index. 328p. VG. A17. $8.50

LANTERI-LAURA, Georges. *Histoire de la Phrenologie.* 1970. Paris. 1st ed. 264p. wrp. A13. $30.00

LANTZ, Walter. *Easy Way To Draw.* 1958. Racine. 1st ed. VG. B5. $25.00

LANZONE, John A. *Horse, Next to Woman, God's Greatest Gift to Man...* 1970. San Antonio. 1st ed. VG. O3. $68.00

LAPIDES, Adelson. *Lodz Ghetto: Inside a Cummunity Under Siege.* 1989. np. 1st ed. photos. 550p. F/dj. E5. $28.00

LAPIN, Mark. *Pledge of Allegiance.* 1991. Dutton. 1st ed. rem mk. M/M. P8. $15.00

LAPP, John A. *Important Federal Laws.* 1917. Indianapolis. Bowen. M11. $35.00

LAPP, Ralph E. *Man & Space: The Next Decade.* 1961. Harper. 1st ed. photos. 183p. G/torn. K5. $14.00

LAPPE & MORISON. *Ethical & Scientific Issues Posed by Human Uses Genetics.* 1976. NY Academy Sciences. 208p. prt bl wrp. G1. $22.50

LAQUEUR, Walter Z. *Middle East in Transition. Studies in Contemporary Hist.* 1958. Praeger. 1st ed. 513p. VG/torn. W1. $10.00

LAQUEUR, Walter. *Guerilla Reader.* 1977. Meridan/NAL. 1st prt thus. sc. VG+. M7. $25.00

LARDNER, Dionysius. *Popular Astronomy, First Series.* ca 1873. London. Lockwood. 8vo. 469p. bl cloth. G. K5. $47.00

LARDNER, Ring. *Bib Ballads.* 1915. Volland. 1st ed. ils Fontaine Fox. gilt brn cloth. F. Q1. $350.00

LARDNER, Ring. *Ecstasy of Owen Muir.* 1954. London. correct 1st ed/author's 1st book. inscr. F/NF clip. A11. $85.00

LARDNER, Ring. *How I & the Mrs Go to NY To See Life & Get Katie a Husband.* 1921. Bobbs Merrill. 1st ed. ils May Wilson Preston. VG. Q1. $150.00

LARDNER, Ring. *Lardners. My Family Remembered.* 1976. NY. 1st ed. sgn. F/NF. A11. $55.00

LARDNER, Ring. *Love Nest & Other Stories.* 1926. NY. 1st ed. F/VG. C2. $125.00

LARDNER, Ring. *Own Your Own Home.* 1919. Bobbs Merrill. 1st ed. ils Fontaine Fox. pict brd. VG. Q1. $350.00

LARDNER, Ring. *Round Up.* 1929. Scribner. 1st ed. VG. P8. $35.00

LARDNER, Ring. *Some Champions.* 1976. NY. 1st ed. sgn. edit Bruccoli/Layman. F/NF clip. A11. $65.00

LARDNER, Ring. *Symptoms of Being 35.* 1921. Bobbs Merrill. 1st ed. ils HE Jacoby. pict bdg. G+. Q1. $250.00

LARDNER, Ring. *Treat 'Em Rough.* 1918. Bobbs Merrill. 1st ed. G+. P8. $100.00

LARDNER, Ring. *You Know Me Al.* 1925. Scribner. later prt. F. P8. $25.00

LARIAR, Lawrence. *Stone Cold Blonde.* 1951. Crown. 1st ed. F/VG. F4. $30.00

LARKIN, David. *Fantastic Kingdom.* 1974. Ballantine. ils. VG+/wrp. S11. $10.00

LARNED, J.N. *Talk About Books.* 1897. Buffalo, NY. Peter Paul Book Co. 12mo. 36p. G. M10. $3.50

LARNED, W.T. *American Indian Fairy Tales.* 1921. Volland. 32nd ed. ils John Rae. VG+. M5. $75.00

LARNER & TEFFERTELLER. *Addict in the Street.* 1964. NY. 1st ed. sgn Larner. NF/NF. A11. $55.00

LARRIMORE, Lida. *Blossoming of Patricia-the-Less.* 1942. Penn. 1st ed. ils Hattie L Price. 253p. VG. M20. $30.00

LARSON, Bruce. *My Creator, My Friend: Genesis of a Relationship.* 1986. Word. 194p. F/F. B29. $3.50

LARSON, Charles R. *Academia Nuts; or, Collected Works of Clara Lepage.* 1977. Bobbs Merrill. 1st ed. ils. 177p. VG. M10. $20.00

LARSON & OSBORNE. *Emerging Church.* 1970. Word. 170p. VG/dj. B29. $3.50

LARTIQUE, J.H. *Boyhood Photos of JH Lartigue.* (1966). Ami Guichard. obl 4to. ils/mtd photos. 128p. gilt maroon cloth. F. K1. $300.00

LARTIQUE, J.H. *Les Femmes Aux Cigarettes.* 1980. NY. Viking/The Studio. 1st ed. sq 16mo. 80 photos. F/F. S9. $40.00

LASAGNA, Louis. *Life, Death, & the Doctor.* 1968. NY. 1st ed. 322p. A13. $20.00

LASDUN, James. *Silver Age.* 1985. London. Cape. 1st ed/author's 1st book. F/F clip. L3. $65.00

LASDUN, James. *Three Evnings & Other Stories.* 1992. FSG. 1st Am ed. rem mk. F/F. L3. $25.00

LASH, Jospeh P. *From Diaries of Felix Frankfurter.* 1975. Norton. M11. $35.00

LASKEY, Muriel. *Aunt Mathilda & the Lost Cheese.* 1946. Pied Piper. ils Doris Stolberg. VG/VG. B17. $6.50

LASKI, Harold J. *Studies in Law & Politics.* 1969. Archon. 299p. F/dj. M10. $7.50

LASKIN & LECHEVALIER. *Handbook of Microbiology.* 1974. Cleveland, OH. CRC. condensed ed. F. K4. $10.00

LASKY, Kathryn. *Night Journey.* 1981. NY. Warne. 1st ed. ils/inscr Hyman. M/M. C8. $40.00

LASKY, Victor. *JFK: The Man & the Myth.* 1963. Macmillan. 653p. VG/torn. M10. $4.50

LASSAIGNE & WEELEN. *Vieira da Sliva.* nd (1979). Barcelona. Poligrafa. sq 4to. 343p. blk stp wht cloth. F/F. F1. $50.00

LASSWELL, M. *Mrs Rasmussen's One-Arm Cookery.* 1946. Boston. VG/VG. B5. $30.00

LATCH, Jean. *Plusieurs Tres-Bons Cases, come ils Estoyent Adjudgees...* 1661. London. Twyford Dring Place. modern quarter calf. fair. M11. $250.00

LATHAM, Jean Lee. *This Dear-Bought Land.* 1957. Harper. 1st ed. 8vo. 46p. VG/G+. A3. $15.00

LATHAN, Lenn. *Let God In.* 1961. Guideposts. 176p. G/dj. B29. $3.50

LATHEN, Emma. *Ashes to Ashes.* 1971. Simon Schuster. 1st ed. VG/VG. P3. $15.00

LATHEN, Emma. *Ashes to Ashes.* 1971. Simon Schuster. 1st ed. xl. dj. P3. $5.00

LATHEN, Emma. *Double, Double, Oil & Trouble.* 1979. London. Gollancz. 1st Eng ed. F/dj. S6. $35.00

LATHEN, Emma. *Longer the Thread.* 1971. Simon Schuster. 1st ed. VG/VG. P3. $15.00

LATHEN, Emma. *When in Greece.* 1969. Simon Schuster. 1st ed. F/dj. M15. $45.00

LATHROP, Dorothy. *Dog in the Tapestry Garden.* 1963 (1962). Macmillan. 2nd prt. 42p. cloth. F/G. R2. $75.00

LATHROP, Dorothy. *Fairy Circus.* 1942 (1931). NY. Macmillan. 5th ed. 8vo. 66p. NF/VG. D6. $100.00

LATHROP, Dorothy. *Snail Who Ran.* 1934. Stokes. 1st ed. 57p. VG. scarce. P2. $40.00

LATHROP, Dorothy. *Sung Under the Silver Umbrella. Poems for Young Children.* 1936. Macmillan. 2nd prt. 8vo. VG. A3. $12.50

LATHROP, Elise. *Historic Houses of Early Am.* 1936. NY. reprint. 464p. F/F. A17. $25.00

LATHROP, Jo Anna. *Willa Cather: A Checklist of Her Pub Writing.* 1975. Lincoln, NE. 1st ed. 118p. F/wrp. B2. $25.00

LATTIMORE, Deborah Nourse. *Flame of Peace.* 1987. Harper Row. 1st ed. ils. VG/VG. B17. $5.00

LAU, Josephine Sanger. *Cheeky, a Prairie Dog.* 1937. Whitman. 1st ed. ils Kurt Wiese. 64p. NF/G+. P2. $40.00

LAUBER, John. *Making of Mark Twain: A Biography.* 1985. Am Heritage. 298p. F/dj. M10. $12.50

LAUBIN. *American Indian Archery.* 1980. np. 200p. NF/dj. E5. $35.00

LAUGHLIN, James. *Random Essays, Recollections of a Publisher.* 1989. New Directions. ils. 286p. F/F. A4. $20.00

LAUGHLIN, S.B. *Beyond Dilemmas: Quakers Look at Life.* 1937. Lippincott. 1st ed. 8vo. 306p. VG. V3. $15.00

LAUMER, Keith. *Glory Game.* 1973. Doubleday. 1st ed. VG/VG. P3. $20.00

LAUMER, Keith. *Night of Delusions.* 1972. Putnam. 1st ed. VG/VG. P3. $25.00

LAUMER, Keith. *Time Trap.* 1970. Putnam. 1st ed. F/F. N3. $85.00

LAUMER, Keith. *World Shuffler.* 1970. Putnam. 1st ed. F/dj. F4. $30.00

LAUNAY, Pierre-Jean. *Greece.* 1961. Hastings. 1st ed. 8vo. 126p. VG/dj. W1. $12.00

LAUREMBERG, Johann. *Graecia Antiqua. Editit Samuel Pufendorf.* 1969. Amsterdam. rpt. 8vo. 31 pl. prt gilt brd. O2. $50.00

LAURENCE, D.R. *Quantitative Methods in Human Pharmacology... Vol 3.* 1959. Pergamon. 253p. F/dj. K4. $25.00

LAURENCE, Janet. *Death & the Epicure.* 1993. London. Macmillan. 1st ed. F/F. S6. $25.00

LAURENT, Peter Edmund. *Recollections of a Classical Tour...Greece, Turkey, Italy...* 1822. London. 2 vol. 8vo. rebound quarter tan calf. O2. $325.00

LAURIE, Bruce. *Artisans Into Workers. Labor in 19th Century America.* 1989. Hill Wang. 1st ed. M/M. V4. $10.00

LAURY, Jean Ray. *Applique Stitchery.* 1966. np. VG/wrp. G2. $10.00

LAURY, Jean Ray. *Treasury of Needlecraft Gifts for the New Baby.* 1976. np. cloth. VG. G2. $15.00

LAUSANNE, Edita. *Great Tapestries: Web of Hist From 12th to 20th Century.* 1965. np. cloth. VG. G2. $75.00

LAUT, A.C. *Pathfinders of the West.* 1927. np. ils. xl. poor. scarce. B34. $40.00

LAVELL, Cecil Fairfield. *Biography of Greek People.* 1934. Houghton Mifflin. 1st ed. 297p. VG. W1. $8.00

LAVENDER, David. *Land of Giants.* 1958. NY. 468p. NF. D3. $15.00

LAVENDER, David. *Westward Vision: Story of the Oregon Trail.* 1963. McGraw Hill. 1st ed. ils Marian Ebert. F/clip. A18. $30.00

LAVENDER, David. *Westward Vision: Story of the Oregon Trail.* 1963. NY. 1st ed. American Trails Series. VG/VG. B5. $25.00

LAVRIN, Janko. *Russian Writers: Their Lives & Their Literature.* 1954. NY. biblio/index. 363p. F/F. A17. $15.00

LAVRIN, Janko. *Tolstoy.* 1946. Macmillan. 1st ed. NF/VG+. S9. $25.00

LAW, Alexander. *To an Easy Grave.* 1986. St Martin. 1st ed. VG/VG. P3. $15.00

LAWLEY & MAXWELL. *Factor Analysis As a Statistical Method.* 1963. London. Butterworths. 101p. F/dj. K4. $10.00

LAWRENCE, A.W. *Captives of Tipu.* 1929. London. Cape. navy lettered beige cloth. VG+. M7. $30.00

LAWRENCE, A.W. *Oberst Lawrence: Geschildert Von Seinen Freunden.* 1938. Leipzig. Paul List. 1st German ed. 332p. gilt blk cloth. VG. M7. $45.00

LAWRENCE, A.W. *TE Lawrence by His Friends.* Aug 1963. McGraw Hill. 2nd Am/1st ed thus. 397p. VG. M7. $50.00

LAWRENCE, A.W. *TE Lawrence by His Friends.* 1937. London. Cape. 1st ed. 595p. gilt wine red cloth. F/NF. M7. $185.00

LAWRENCE, Bruce B. *Defenders of God: Fundamentalist Revolution...* 1989. Harper Row. 1st ed. 306p. NF/dj. W1. $22.00

LAWRENCE, D.H. *Assorted Articles.* 1930. London. Martin Secker. 1st ed. 8vo. 215p. gilt red cloth. NF/dj. H5. $125.00

LAWRENCE, D.H. *England My England.* 1922. NY. Seltzer. 1st ed (precedes Eng ed). bl cloth. F/NF. B24. $650.00

LAWRENCE, D.H. *Fantasia of the Unconscious.* 1922. NY. Thomas Seltzer. 1st ed. 8vo. 297p. gilt lettered bl cloth. G. H5. $75.00

LAWRENCE, D.H. *Kangaroo.* 1923. NY. Thomas Selzer. 1st Am ed. 8vo. 421p. gilt bl cloth. VG. H5. $75.00

LAWRENCE, D.H. *Lady Chatterly's Lover.* 1928. Florence. private prt. 1st ed. sgn. 1/1000. 8vo. 365p. NF/clamshell case. H5. $4,000.00

LAWRENCE, D.H. *Man Who Died.* 1931. London. Martin Secker. 1st Eng ed. 1/2000. 8vo. 97p. gilt gr cloth. NF/dj. H5. $300.00

LAWRENCE, D.H. *My Skirmish With Jolly Roger.* 1929. Random. 1st ed. 1/600. 8vo. gray brd/gray prt label. VG. H5. $60.00

LAWRENCE, D.H. *Plumed Serpent.* 1989. London. Grafton. 1st Cambridge ed. F/dj. A18. $20.00

LAWRENCE, D.H. *Rainbow.* 1916. NY. BW Huebsch. 1st ed. Ralph Block's copy. VG. Q1. $175.00

LAWRENCE, D.H. *St Mawr/The Princess.* 1925. London. Martin Secker. 1st ed. 8vo. 238p. brn cloth. NF/NF. H5. $100.00

LAWRENCE, D.H. *Story of a Marriage by Brenda Maddox.* 1994. Simon Schuster. UP. F/prt yel wrp. B3. $35.00

LAWRENCE, D.H. *Story of Dr Manente.* 1929. Florence. Orioli. 1st ed. 1/1000 #d. 119p. H5. $100.00

LAWRENCE, D.H. *Virgin & the Gipsy.* 1930. London. Martin Secker. 1st Eng ed. 8vo. 191p. brn cloth. F. H5. $100.00

LAWRENCE, D.H. *We Need One Another.* 1933. Equinox. 1st ed. ils John P Heins. F/NF. B4. $250.00

LAWRENCE, D.H. *White Peacock.* 1911. Heinemann's Colonial Lib. 1st UK ed. Ralph Block's copy. blk cloth. VG. Q1. $500.00

LAWRENCE, D.H. *Woman Who Rode Away.* 1928. NY. Knopf. 1st Am ed. VG/VG. Q1. $100.00

LAWRENCE, Frieda. *Not I, But the Wind...* 1934. Santa Fe. Rydal. 1/100. sgn. 311p. cream buckram/gray brd. VG. H5. $250.00

LAWRENCE, J. *Plain Thoughts on Secret Societies.* 1852. Circleville, OH. 222p. VG. E5. $65.00

LAWRENCE, John. *Good Babies, Bad Babies.* 1986. Fullerton, CA. Lorson/Whittington. 63x49mm. 1/175. F/box. B24. $375.00

LAWRENCE, Josephine. *Man in the Moon Stories Told Over the Radiophone.* 1922. Cupples Leon. 1st ed. ils Johnny Gruelle. 121p. VG. D6. $65.00

LAWRENCE, Josephine. *Next Door Neighbors.* ca 1926. Cupples Leon. 311p. VG. B10. $25.00

LAWRENCE, M.R. *Home Letters of TE Lawrence & His Brothers.* 1954. NY. Macmillan. 1st ed. photos/index. 731p. gilt bl cloth. F/F. M7. $165.00

LAWRENCE, Margery. *Daughter of the Nile.* 1956. Robert Hale. 1st ed. VG/G. P3. $20.00

LAWRENCE, Margery. *Number Seven, Queer Street.* 1969. Mycroft Moran. 1st ed. 1/2000. F/dj. F4. $90.00

LAWRENCE, Richard Moore. *On Localized Galvanism...* 1858. London. Renshaw. 164p. VG/wrp. B14. $85.00

LAWRENCE, Robert. *Boris Godunoff.* 1944. Grosset Dunlap. ils Alexander Serebriakoff. VG+/G. C8. $22.50

LAWRENCE, Robert. *Carmen.* 1938. Grosset Dunlap. lg 8vo. VG. C8. $22.50

LAWRENCE, Robert. *Faust.* 1942. Grosset Dunlap. ils paul Kinear. VG+/G+. C8. $22.50

LAWRENCE, Robert. *Gondoliers.* 1940. Grosset Dunlap. ils Sheilah Beckett. NF/VG. C8. $22.50

LAWRENCE, Robert. *Hansel & Gretel: Story of Humperdinck's Opera.* ca 1938. Grosset Dunlap. ils Mildred Boyle. G/fair. B10. $12.00

LAWRENCE, Robert. *Hansel & Gretel: Story of Humperdinck's Opera.* 1938. Grosset Dunlap. lg 8vo. VG+/VG. C8. $22.50

LAWRENCE, Robert. *Petrouchka: A Ballet.* 1940. Random. ils Serebriakoff. VG+/VG. C8. $22.50

LAWRENCE, Robert. *Primitive Psycho-Therapy & Quackery.* 1910. London. 1st Eng ed. 276p. A13. $100.00

LAWRENCE, Robert. *Three-Cornered Hat.* 1940. Random. ils Serebraikoff. NF/VG. C8. $17.50

LAWRENCE, T.E. *Crusader Castles.* 1936. Golden Cockerel. 2 vol. 1st ed. 1/1000. gilt red morocco/cream buckram. F/dj. M7. $1,250.00

LAWRENCE, T.E. *Diary of TE Lawrence MCMXI.* 1993. Garnet/Folio Archive Lib. 1st ed thus. 79p. gilt blk brd. M. M7. $45.00

LAWRENCE, T.E. *Men in Print.* 1940. Golden Cockerel. 1st UK ed. 1/500. teg. wht brd/bl spine. VG/cb box. M7. $575.00

LAWRENCE, T.E. *Mint.* 1955. Cape. 1st ed. 1/2000. 206p. teg. bl buckram/bl pigskin spine. VG/case/plastic. M7. $275.00

LAWRENCE, T.E. *Mint.* 1962. Panther. 1st ed thus. 192p. VG. M7. $45.00

LAWRENCE, T.E. *Odyssey of Homer.* 1940. Oxford. 1st ed thus. Hesperides Series. 1/2500. teg. gilt brn cloth. VG. M7. $50.00

LAWRENCE, T.E. *Oriental Assembly.* 1939. London. Williams Norgate. 1st ed. 76 pl. 291p. maroon cloth. xl. VG/clear plastic. M7. $75.00

LAWRENCE, T.E. *Revolt in the Desert.* 1927. Doran. 1st Am trade ed. 8vo. 335p. mauve cloth. F/NF. C6. $150.00

LAWRENCE, T.E. *Revolt in the Desert.* 1927. NY. George H Doran. 1st Am ed. 1/250. 335p. gilt bl cloth. F/pub cb case. H5. $1,250.00

LAWRENCE, T.E. *Revolte Dans le Desert.* 1930. Paris. Payot. 1st French ed/3rd imp. 463p. unpolished tan cloth. G. M7. $45.00

LAWRENCE, T.E. *Selections From Seven Pillars of Wisdom.* 1940. London. Methuen. 1st ed thus. 2 maps. 148p. brn stp yel cloth. VG. M7. $50.00

LAWRENCE, T.E. *Seven Pillars of Wisdom.* 1973. London. BC Associates. 7th Eng ed. 8 pl/4 maps. 700p. brn brd. F/VG+. M7. $35.00

LAWRENCE, T.E. *Then & Now.* 1935. London. Cape. 1st ed. 229p. G/wrp. M7. $50.00

LAWRENCE, T.E. *Wilderness of Zin.* 1914. London. 1st ed. 37 pl/fld plan/index. 154p. VG. M7. $650.00

LAWRENCE, T.E. *Wilderness of Zin.* 1936. Scribner. 1st ed. 40 pl. 166p. brick red buckram. NF. M7. $150.00

LAWRENCE & MAYBEE. *Barbie, Midge & Ken.* 1964. Random. 181p. VG. M20. $12.00

LAWS, Stephen. *Ghost Train.* 1985. Beaufort. 1st ed. VG/VG. P3. $20.00

LAWSON, Elizabeth. *Reign of Witches: Struggle Against Alien & Sedition Laws...* 1952. NY. Civil Rights Congress. 64p. stapled wrp. M11. $25.00

LAWSON, John Howard. *Loud Speaker.* 1927. Macaulay. 1st ed. F/NF. B2. $100.00

LAWSON, Marie. *Hail Columbia: Life of a Nation.* 1931. Doubleday Doran. 1st ed. 387p. G. B10. $20.00

LAWSON, Robert. *Capt Kidd's Cat.* 1956. Little Brn. 1st ed. ils. 152p. VG/G. P2. $50.00

LAWSON, Robert. *Country Colic, the Weeder's Digest.* 1944. Little Brn. 1st ed. VG+/VG+. C8. $95.00

LAWSON, Robert. *Fabulous Flight.* 1949. Little Brn. 1st ed. ils Lawson. VG+/VG. C8. $40.00

LAWSON, Robert. *Great Wheel.* 1964. Viking. 4th prt. VG+/VG+. C8. $20.00

LAWSON, Robert. *Mr Revere & I.* 1953. Little Brn. 1st ed. sm 8vo. NF/VG. C8. $100.00

LAWSON, Robert. *Mr Wilmer.* 1945. Little Brn. 1st ed. lg 12mo. VG+/G. C8. $45.00

LAWSON, Robert. *Mr Wilmer.* 1945. Little Brn. 1st ed. xl. VG. P3. $15.00

LAWSON, Robert. *Rabbit Hill.* (1944). Viking. 3rd prt. VG. B10. $15.00

LAWSON, Robert. *Rabbit Hill.* (1944). Viking. 6th prt. 8vo. F/G. B17. $19.50

LAWSON, Robert. *Rabbit Hill.* 1944. Viking. 1st Am ed. VG/VG. C8. $125.00

LAWSON, Robert. *Watchwords of Liberty.* 1943. Little Brn. 1st ed. ils. 115p. G. P2. $15.00

LAWTON, Charles. *Clarkville Battery.* 1937. Cupples Leon. 2nd prt. VG/G. P8. $20.00

LAWTON, Charles. *Home Run Hennessey.* 1941. Cupples Leon. later prt. VG/G+. P8. $20.00

LAWTON, Harry. *Willie Boy.* 1960. Paisano. 1st prt. 224p. VG+/dj. M20. $20.00

LAWTON, Thomas. *Century of Carpet & Rug Making in America.* 1925. NY. Bigelow Hartford Carpet Co. leather. G+. A1. $65.00

LAY & TAUBENFELD. *Law Relating to Activities of Man in Space.* 1970. Chicago U. M11. $50.00

LAYHEW, Jane. *Rx for Murder.* 1946. Lippincott. 1st ed. VG/VG. P3. $20.00

LAYMON, Richard. *Alarms.* 1992. Ziesing. 1st trade ed. F/F. T2. $25.00

LAYMON, Richard. *Good, Secret Place.* 1993. Deadline. 1st ed. sgn. ils/sgn Larry Mori. intro/sgn Ed Gorman. F/F. P3. $35.00

LAYMON, Richard. *Stake.* 1991. St Martin. 1st Am ed. F/F. T2. $24.00

LAYMON, Richard. *Tread Softly.* 1987. London. Allen. 1st hc ed. sgn. F/F. T2. $65.00

LAYNE, J. Gregg. *Western Wayfaring: Routes of Exploration...* 1954. Auto Club S CA. ils/index. 63p. NF/sans. B19. $120.00

LAZARON, Morris S. *Olive Trees in Storm.* 1955. NY. Am Friends of the ME. 1st ed. 8vo. 111p. VG. W1. $20.00

LAZARUS, A.L. *Best of George Ade.* 1985. IN U. 1st ed. inscr. NF/NF. S9. $25.00

LE BARON, Anthony; see Laumer, Keith.

LE BLANC, Maurice. *Memoirs of Arsene Lupin.* 1925. NY. Macaulay. 1st Am ed. VG/VG. M15. $125.00

LE CARRE, John. *Call for the Dead.* 1962. 1st Am ed/author's 1st book. F/VG. A4. $400.00

LE CARRE, John. *Deadly Affair.* 1966. Harmondsworth. 1st movie ed/1st as this title. w/sgn bookplate. NF. A11. $65.00

LE CARRE, John. *Honorable Schoolboy.* 1977. Franklin Lib. correct 1st ed. full leather. F. O4. $75.00

LE CARRE, John. *Honorable Schoolboy.* 1977. Knopf. 1st Am trade ed. F/F. O4. $15.00

LE CARRE, John. *John LeCarre.* 1979. Heinemann/Octopus. 1st ed. F/F. P3. $15.00

LE CARRE, John. *LeCarre Omnibus.* 1964. London. 1st omnibus ed. inscr. NF/VG+. A11. $425.00

LE CARRE, John. *Little Drummer Girl.* 1983. Hodder Stoughton. 1st ed. VG/VG. O4. $30.00

LE CARRE, John. *Little Drummer Girl.* 1983. Hodder Stoughton. 1st Eng ed. F/F. M15. $60.00

LE CARRE, John. *Little Drummer Girl.* 1983. Knopf. special ed for Book of Month Club. sgn. 429p. F/case. H5. $150.00

LE CARRE, John. *Little Drummer Girl.* 1983. Knopf. 1st ed. 8vo. 429p. silvered maroon cloth. F/NF. H5. $75.00

LE CARRE, John. *Looking-Glass War.* 1965. London. Heinemann. 1st ed. inscr. F/F. M15. $250.00

LE CARRE, John. *Looking-Glass War.* 1965. London. Heinemann. 1st ed. VG/VG. O4. $75.00

LE CARRE, John. *Naive & Sentimental Lover.* 1971. London. Hodder Stoughton. 1st ed. F/F. O4. $100.00

LE CARRE, John. *Naive & Sentimental Lover.* 1972. Knopf. 1st ed. VG/VG. P3. $75.00

LE CARRE, John. *Night Manager.* 1993. Hodder Stoughton. 1st ed. sgn. F/F. O4. $75.00

LE CARRE, John. *Perfect Spy.* 1986. Hodder Stoughton. 1st ed. F/F. O4. $50.00

LE CARRE, John. *Perfect Spy.* 1986. Hodder Stoughton. 1st ed. inscr/sgn. F/F. M15. $200.00

LE CARRE, John. *Perfect Spy.* 1986. Knopf. 1st Am ed. F/F. O4. $15.00

LE CARRE, John. *Secret Pilgrim.* 1991. Hodder Stoughton. 1st ed. sgn. F/F. M15. $100.00

LE CARRE, John. *Secret Pilgrim.* 1991. Knopf. 1st ed. F/F. P3. $22.00

LE CARRE, John. *Small Town in Germany.* 1968. London. Heinemann. 1st ed. VG/VG. O4. $120.00

LE CARRE, John. *Small Town in Germany.* 1968. NY. Coward. 1st Am ed. F/NF. B2. $30.00

LE CARRE, John. *Smiley's People.* 1980. Hodder Stoughton. 1st ed. sgn. F/NF. L3. $175.00

LE CARRE, John. *Smiley's People.* 1980. Knopf. 1st ed. VG/VG. M21/O4. $15.00

LE CARRE, John. *Spy Who Came in From the Cold.* 1963. London. Gollancz. 1st ed. VG/VG. O4. $600.00

LE CARRE, John. *Spy Who Came in From the Cold.* 1963. London. Gollancz. 1st ed/author's 3rd book. NF/NF. L3. $750.00

LE CORBEAU, Adrien. *Forest Giant.* 1924. London. Cape. 1st ed. 158p. gray-olive brd. VG/clear plastic. M7. $145.00

LE CORBUSIER. *Towards a New Architecture.* nd. NY. Brewer Warren. trans from 13th French ed. VG. F1. $75.00

LE FANU, J. Sheridan. *Green Tea.* 1945. Arkham. 1st ed. F/dj. M2. $185.00

LE FANU, J. Sheridan. *Purcell Papers.* 1975. Arkham. 1st ed. 1/4288. F/F. T2. $10.00

LE FONTAINE, Joseph. *Handbook for Booklovers.* 1988. Prometheus. 612p. VG/VG. A10. $12.00

LE GALLIENNE, Eva. *Seven Tales by HC Andersen.* 1959. Harper. 1st ed. ils Maurice Sendak. F/G. M5. $60.00

LE GALLIENNE, Richard. *Maker of Rainbows & Other Fairy Tales & Fables.* 1912. Harper. ils. 104p. VG. B10. $55.00

LE GALLIENNE, Richard. *Romance of Perfume.* 1928. NY/Paris. Richard Hudnut. ils George Barbier. M/G case. H4. $100.00

LE GRAND, Edy. *Two Brothers of Different Sex.* 1955. Rodale. 1st ed. 51p. F/G+ glassine. P2. $25.00

LE GUIN, Ursula K. *Always Coming Home.* 1985. Harper Row. 1st ed. F/box. B3. $20.00

LE GUIN, Ursula K. *Beginning Place.* 1980. Harper Row. 1st ed. F/F. N3. $20.00

LE GUIN, Ursula K. *Buffalo Gals & Other Animal Presence.* 1990. Gollancz. 1st ed. F/F. P3. $28.00

LE GUIN, Ursula K. *Buffalo Gals & Other Animal Presences.* 1987. Santa Barbara. Capra. 1st ed. F/F. B3. $20.00

LE GUIN, Ursula K. *Compass Rose.* 1982. Harper Row. 1st ed. NF/NF. P3. $30.00

LE GUIN, Ursula K. *Compass Rose.* 1982. Underwood Miller. 1st ed. sgn. 1/550. F/dj. M2. $60.00

LE GUIN, Ursula K. *Fisherman of the Inland Sea: SF Stories.* 1994. Harper Prism. 1st ed. 1/1500. F/sans. T2. $25.00

LE GUIN, Ursula K. *Tehanu.* 1990. Atheneum. 1st ed. sgn. F/dj. F4. $27.00

LE MAIR, H. Willebeek. *Little Songs of Long Ago.* 1912. Augener-McKay. 30 mc pl. VG+. M5. $95.00

LE MARCHAND, Elizabeth. *Cyanide With Compliments.* 1972. London. McGibbon. 1st ed. NF/dj. S6. $25.00

LE MARCHLAND, Elizabeth. *Unhappy Returns.* 1977. Hart Davis/MacGibbon. 1st ed. VG/VG. P3. $20.00

LE MAY, Alan. *Searchers.* 1954. Harper. 1st ed. NF/dj. A18. $40.00

LE MAY, Alan. *Winter Range.* 1932. Farrar Rinehart. 1st ed. pict ep. VG. A18. $30.00

LE QUEUX, William. *Golden Three.* 1931. Fiction League. VG. P3. $20.00

LE ROY, Georges. *La Psychologie de Condillac.* 1937. Paris. Boivin. 231p. F/stiff gray wrp. G1. $30.00

LE STRANGE, G. *Don Juan of Persia.* 1926. NY. 1st Eng-language ed. 8vo. 355p. cloth. O2. $35.00

LE TOUMELIN, Jacques Yves. *Kurun: Around the World.* 1955. NY. Dutton. ils/maps/plans. 300p. T7. $25.00

LEA, H.C. *History of Aurocular Confession in Latin Church.* 1896. Phil. 3 vol set. 1st ed. VG. B5. $175.00

LEA, Tom. *Art of Tom Lea.* 1989. TX A&M. 1st ed. intro WW Johnson. M/dj. A18. $50.00

LEA, Tom. *Brave Bulls.* 1949. Little Brn. 1st ed. F. A18. $30.00

LEA, Tom. *Hands of Cantu.* 1964. Little Brn. 1st ed. sgn. F/NF. B2. $100.00

LEA, Tom. *King Ranch.* 1957. Little Brn. 2 vol. 1st ed. beige/rust cloth. VG. P4. $85.00

LEA, Tom. *Wonderful Country.* 1952. Little Brn. 1st ed. ils. F. A18. $25.00

LEA, Tom. *Wonderful Country.* 1952. Little Brn. 1st ed. VG. B34. $15.00

LEACH, A.F. *Schools of Medieval England.* 1969. Barnes Noble. rpt 1915 ed. 356p. bl cloth. G1. $40.00

LEACH, Alison. *Big Book for Greedy Cooks.* ca 1983. London. Macmillan. 1st ed. 32p. VG. B10. $25.00

LEACH, E.W. *Racine County Militant.* 1915. Racine. 1st ed. ils. 394p. VG. B5. $75.00

LEACH, Maria. *How the People Sang the Mountain Up.* ca 1967. Viking. 1st ed. 159p. VG/G. B10. $25.00

LEACOCK, Stephen. *Iron Man & the Tin Woman.* 1929. Dodd Mead. 1st ed. VG. P3. $60.00

LEADABRAND, Russ. *Secret of Drake's Bay.* 1969. Ward Ritchie. lib ed. 45p. VG/VG. B10. $15.00

LEADBITTER & SLAVEN. *Blues Records 1943-1966.* 1968. London/NY. 1st ed. F/Oak dj. B2. $125.00

LEAF, Ann Sellers. *Aesop's Fables.* 1952. Rand McNally Elf Book 8615. K2. $4.00

LEAF, Ann Sellers. *Emperor's New Clothes.* 1958. Rand McNally Elf Book 8567. K2. $4.00

LEAF, Munro. *Being an American Can Be Fun.* ca 1964. Lippincott. 1st ed. ils. VG/fair. B10. $18.00

LEAF, Munro. *Ferdinandus Taurus, Latin Version of Story of Ferdinand.* 1962. Hamish Hamilton. 1st Eng ed. F/F. C8. $30.00

LEAF, Munro. *John Henry Davis.* 1940. NY. Stokes. 1st ed. VG/G. C8. $40.00

LEAF, Munro. *Story of Ferdinand.* 1936. Viking. 1st ed. 8vo. ils. 72p. gray cloth. F/dj. H5. $1,850.00

LEAF, Munro. *War-Time Handbook for Young Americans.* 1942. Stokes. probable 1st ed. F. C8. $45.00

LEAF, Munro. *Wee Gillis.* 1938. Viking. 1st ed. sgn. ils R Lawson. G/G. B5. $40.00

LEAF, Munro. *Wee Gillis.* 1938. Viking. 2nd prt. sm 4to. VG/VG. C8. $35.00

LEAF, Munro. *Wishing Pool.* 1960. Lippincott. inscr/orig drawing. 63p. VG/G. P2. $45.00

LEAKE, William M. *Topography of Athens With Some Remarks on Its Antiquities.* 1821. London. tall 8vo. rebacked/orig label. uncut. O2. $300.00

LEAKEY, Mary. *Disclosing the Past: An Autobiography.* 1984. Doubleday. 1st ed. F/F. P3. $16.00

LEAR, Edward. *Edward Lear in Greece.* 1971. Meriden. obl 8vo. ils. 87p. pict wrp. O2. $20.00

LEAR, Edward. *Jumblies.* 1968. NY. Young Scott Books. 1st separate ed. obl 8vo. unp. NF/clip. H5. $100.00

LEAR, Edward. *Quangle Wangle's Hat, by Edward Lear, 1877.* 1988. Berkeley. Poole. 70x52mm. 1/75. inscr. wood engravings. F/hat-formed case. B24. $200.00

LEAR, Edward. *Views in the Seven Ionian Islands.* 1980 (1853). (London). rpt/ltd ed. atlas folio. gilt brd. brd case. O2. $175.00

LEAR, Peter; see Lovesey, Peter.

LEARY, Lewis Gaston. *Syria, the Land of Lebanon.* 1914. McBride Nast. 2nd prt. 225p. VG. W1. $45.00

LEARY, Timothy. *Flashbacks.* 1983. Los Angeles. Tarcher. 1st ed. F/NF. B2. $45.00

LEARY, Timothy. *High Priest.* 1968. World/NAL. 1st ed. F/F. B2. $65.00

LEARY, Timothy. *Psychedelic Prayers.* 1966. New Hyde Park. 2nd ed. NF/yellow wrp. B2. $30.00

LEARY & WEIL. *Psychedelic Reader.* 1965. U Books. VG/VG. P3. $30.00

LEASOR, James. *Green Beach.* 1975. Heinemann. 1st ed. F/F. P3. $18.00

LEASOR, James. *Passport to Peril.* 1966. Heinemann. 1st ed. VG/G. P3. $20.00

LEATHER, Edwin. *Duveen Letter.* 1980. Macmillan. 1st ed. VG/VG. P3. $15.00

LEAVITT, David. *Family Dancing.* 1984. Knopf. 1st ed/author's 1st book. F/F. S9. $45.00

LEAVITT, Robert G. *Outlines of Botany.* 1901. NY. ils. 272p. VG. B26. $12.50

LEAVITT & MCDOWELL. *Kings of Capital & Knights of Labor.* 1885. NY. Wiley. 1st ed. gilt tan cloth. NF. B2. $125.00

LEAVY, Jane. *Squeeze Play.* 1990. Doubleday. 1st ed. F/F. P8. $15.00

LEBEDOFF, David. *21st Ballot: Political Party Struggle in MN.* 1969. MN U. 1st ed. sgn. NF/NF. B2. $30.00

LECERF, Jean. *Litterature Arabe Moderne et l'Enseignement...* 1931. Alger. Carbonel. 1st ed. pres. w/sgn letter. VG. W1. $12.00

LECHLITNER, Ruth. *Shadow on the Hour.* 1956. Iowa City. Prairie Pr. 1st ed. F/NF. B2. $40.00

LECHNER & LECHNER. *World of Salt Shakers.* 1976. Collector Books. 1st ed. 127p. F. H1. $17.50

LECKY, W.E.H. *Hist of European Morals From Augustus to Charlemagne.* 1955. Braziller. 2 vol in 1. 468p. VG/dj. G1. $35.00

LECLER, Rene. *Sahara.* 1954. Hanover. 1st ed. 280p. VG/tattered. W1. $8.00

LECLER, Rene. *World Without Mercy. Story of the Sahara.* 1954. London. Laurie. 1st ed. 223p. F/dj. W1. $14.00

LEDBETTER, Rosanna. *Hist of the Malthusian League 1877-1927.* 1976. OH State. VG/dj. N2. $10.00

LEDERER, FLorence. *Wisdom of the East: Secret Rose of Sa'd ud din Mahmud ...* 1920. London. Murray. 1st ed. 92p. VG. W1. $14.00

LEDYARD, Gleason H. *And to the Eskimos.* 1962. Chicago. 4th prt. 254p. F/F. A17. $15.00

LEE, Albert. *Weather Wisdom.* 1976. Doubleday. 8vo. ils. 180p. VG/dj. K5. $15.00

LEE, Frederick George. *Directorium Anglicanum...* 1865. London. Bosworth. 2nd ed. 4to. 15 pl. vellum. H10. $95.00

LEE, Gus. *China Boy.* 1991. Dutton. 1st ed/author's 1st book. F/F. A14. $45.00

LEE, Gus. *Honor & Duty.* 1994. Knopf. ARC. sgn w/author's chop. RS. F/F. S9. $45.00

LEE, H. *History of the Campbell Family.* 1920. NY. Maxwell Famous Old Families Series. VG+. F1. $20.00

LEE, Harper. *To Kill a Mockingbird.* 1960. Lippincott. 1st ed/author's only book. NF/G 1st issue. L3. $2,500.00

LEE, Harper. *To Kill a Mockingbird.* 1960. Lippincott. AP. 8vo. 296p. F/wrp/morocco clamshell case. H5. $2,250.00

LEE, John S. *Sacred Cities: Narrative, Descriptive, Historical.* 1878. Cincinnati. Williamson Cantwell. 5 pl. G. W1. $15.00

LEE, John. *Memorial for Bible Societies in Scotland...* 1824. Edinburgh Bible Soc. 2 pl. brd. H10. $125.00

LEE, Laurie. *I Can't Stay Long.* 1975. Deutsch. 1st ed. 230p. VG/dj. M20. $22.00

LEE, Rawdon. *Collie or Sheepdog in His British Varieties.* 1890. London. Cox. 1st trade ed. ils Arthur Wardle. cloth. R2. $250.00

LEE, Robert C. *Iron Arm of Michael Glenn.* 1965. Little Brn. 1st ed. F/VG+. P8. $30.00

LEE, Robert Edson. *From West to East: Studies in Literature of Am West.* 1966. IL U. 1st ed. F/F. A18. $25.00

LEE, Robert Edson. *From West to East: Studies in Literature of Am West.* 1966. IL U. 1st ed. 172p. VG/dj. M10. $12.50

LEE, Russell. *Physician.* 1973. NY. 1st ed. 200p. A13. $20.00

LEE, Ruth Webb. *Antique Fakes & Reproductions.* (1950). Lee Pub. enlarged/revised 7th ed. 317p. F/G. H1. $45.00

LEE, Ruth Webb. *Sandwich Glass Handbook.* 1947. self pub. 3rd prt. 227p. VG/wrp. H1. $15.00

LEE, Ruth Webb. *19th-Century Art Glass.* Sept 1957. Barrows. 3rd prt. 128p. F/F. H1. $35.00

LEE, Sally. *Hurricanes.* 1993. Franklin Watts. pb. 63p. F. K5. $5.00

LEE, Stan. *Dunn's Conundrum.* 1984. Harper Row. 1st ed. F/F. P3. $15.00

LEE, Tanith. *Book of the Beast: Secret Books of Paradys II.* 1991. Overlook. 1st Am/1st hc ed. F/F. T2. $20.00

LEE, Tanith. *Book of the Damned.* 1990. Woodstock. Overlook. 1st hc ed. F/F. T2. $20.00

LEE, Tanith. *Book of the Mad: Secret Books of Paradys IV.* 1993. Overlook. 1st ed. F/F. T2. $20.00

LEE, Tanith. *Dreams of Dark & Light.* 1986. Arkham. 1st ed. 1/3957. F/F. T2. $55.00

LEE, Tanith. *Secret Books of Paradys I & II.* 1988. Guild America. 1st compilation ed. F/dj. F4. $12.00

LEE, Tanith. *Silver Metal Lover.* nd. BC. NF/NF. P3. $8.00

LEE, Tanith. *Unsilent Night.* 1981. NESFA. 1st e. 1/1000. F/dj. M2. $20.00

LEE, W. Storrs. *Great California Deserts.* 1963. Putnam. 1st ed. ils Edward Sanborn. VG/G. A8. $25.00

LEE, W.F. *Stan Kenton, Artistry in Rhythm.* 1980. LA. 1st ed. sgn. VG/VG. B5. $70.00

LEE, Wayne C. *Bat Masterson.* 1960. Whitman. TVTI. VG. P3. $15.00

LEE, William; see Burroughs, William S.

LEE & DEVORE. *Man the Hunter.* 1968. Chicago. Aldine. 415p. G/dj. K4. $12.50

LEEDER, S.H. *Desert Gateway: Biskra & Thereabouts.* 1912. London. Cassell. 2nd prt. 272p. VG. W1. $12.00

LEEDS, Marc. *Vonnegut Encyclopedia.* 1994. Greenwood. F/F. P3. $75.00

LEEDY, Loreen. *Dragon Halloween Party. A Story & Activity Book.* 1986. Holiday House. 1st ed. 32p. VG/VG. A3. $6.00

LEEMING, David Adams. *World of Myth.* 1990. Oxford. 1st ed. F/F. P3. $25.00

LEES, James. *Masting & Rigging of English Ships of War, 1625-1860.* 1979-1984. Annapolis. Naval Inst. ils/figures. 196p. T7. $45.00

LEESE, Oliver. *Cacti.* 1973. London. ils/photos. 144p. F/dj. B26. $15.00

LEESER, Isaac. *Twenty-Four Books of the Holy Scriptures Carefully Trans...* 1854. Phil. 1st ed. thick 4to. marbled ep. full contemporary roan. M1. $1,800.00

LEFEBURE, Molly. *Murder With a Difference.* 1958. Heinemann. 1st ed. VG. P3. $20.00

LEGARET, Jean. *Tightrope.* 1968. Little Brn. 1st ed. xl. dj. P3. $5.00

LEGG, Rodney. *Lawrence of Arabia in Dorset.* 1988. Dorset/Wincanton. 1st UK ed. photos/maps/index. M/wrp. M7. $25.00

LEGG, Rodney. *Literary Dorset.* 1990. Dorset. 1st Eng ed. photos. 192p. gilt blk bdg. M. M7. $25.00

LEHMAN, John H. *Standard Hist of Stark Co, OH.* nd. Chicago. 3 vol. half leather. fair. B18. $95.00

LEHMANN, Karl. *Samothrace.* 1966. Locust Valley, NY. Augustin. 3rd ed. 119p. VG/stiff wrp. W1. $12.00

LEHNIG, Beverly. *Your Silky Terrier.* 1972. Fairfax, VA. Denlinger. 1st ed. ils. 128p. cloth. VG-. R2. $20.00

LEHNINGER, Albert L. *Mitochondrion.* 1965. NY/Amsterdam. WA Benjamin. 252p. F. K4. $11.00

LEIBER, Fritz. *Big Time.* 1976. London. 1st ed. sgn. F/dj. M2. $50.00

LEIBER, Fritz. *Big Time.* 1976. Severn House. 1st ed. F/F. P3. $25.00

LEIBER, Fritz. *Knight & Knave of Swords.* 1988. Morrow. 1st ed. inscr. F/dj. F4. $40.00

LEIBER, Fritz. *Night's Black Agents.* 1980. Gregg. 1st ed. VG. P3. $25.00

LEIBLING, A.J. *Sweet Science.* 1956. NY. 1st ed. VG/G. B5. $45.00

LEIBNIZ, Gottfried Wilhelm. *Discourse on Metaphysics.* 1961. Manchester. later prt. 12mo. orange cloth. VG/dj. G1. $20.00

LEIBOVITZ, Annie. *Photographs 1970-1990.* 1991. Harper Collins. 1st ed. sgn. 1/326. F/NF case. S9. $250.00

LEIF, Alfred. *Harvey Firestone.* 1951. NY. 1st trade ed. 324p. VG/dj. B18. $12.50

LEIGH, Robert. *Girl With the Bright Head.* 1982. Macmillan. 1st ed. VG/VG. P3. $18.00

LEIGHTON, Clare. *Sometime-Never.* 1939. NY. 1st ed. ils. pict paper brd. VG. A17. $15.00

LEIGHTON, Robert. *Olaf, the Glorious.* 1929. Macmillan. 1st ed. 208p. VG. B10. $20.00

LEIGHTON, Robert. *Rules & Instruction for a Holy Life.* 1835. London. Hamilton Adams. 62x40mm. 60+1 ad p. bl watered-silk bdg. F. B24. $285.00

LEINSTER, Murray; see Jenkins, Will F.

LEIRIS, Michael. *Brisees: Broken Branches.* 1989. Northpoint. 1st Am ed. trans from French. 266p. M/M. A17. $9.50

LEIS, H. Spencer. *Symbolic Prophesy of the Great Pyramid.* 1961. San Jose, CA. Rosicrucian Pr. 7th ed. 207p. VG. W1. $15.00

LEISY, James F. *Folk Song Acecedary.* 1966. NY. Hawthorn. 8vo. 391p. orange cloth. VG. B11. $20.00

LEITCH, R.P. *Course of Water Colour Painting.* ca 1872. London. 36 mtd mc ils. B14. $125.00

LEITER, Alfred. *Die Uhr Zeitmesser und Schmuck in Funf Jahrhunderten.* 1967. W Germany. 1st ed. ils. 359p. G+/fair. A8. $25.00

LEITER, Robert D. *Musicians & Petrillo.* 1953. Bookman. 2nd prt. sgn Petrillo. F/NF. B2. $45.00

LEITHAUSER, Brad. *Hence.* 1989. Knopf. 1st ed. F/F. P3. $18.00

LEJARD, Andre. *Matisse: Seize Peintures 1939-1943.* 1943. Paris. Du Chene. 1st ed. 16 tipped-in mc pl. G/wrp. A17. $35.00

LELAND, Charles Godfrey. *Estruscan Magic & Occult Remedies.* 1963. University Books. 385p. VG/VG. B33. $50.00

LELAND, John. *Kykneion Asma. Cygnea Cantio.* 1545. London. Herford. 4to. old half calf. H10. $125.00

LELAND, Mrs. W. *Master of Precision, Henry Leland.* 1966. Detroit. 1st ed. ils/index. 266p. VG/G. B5. $40.00

LELCHUK, Alan. *Brooklyn Boy.* 1990. McGraw Hill. 1st ed. F/F. P8. $15.00

LEM, Stanislaw. *Flasco.* 1987. HBJ. 1st ed. F/F. P3. $18.00

LEM, Stanislaw. *Invincible.* 1973. Seabury. 1st Eng-language ed. F/VG clip. N3. $10.00

LEM, Stanislaw. *Memoirs of a Space Traveler.* 1982. Harcourt. 1st ed. F/F. P3. $15.00

LEM, Stanislaw. *More Tales of Pirx the Pilot.* 1982. HBJ. 1st ed. F/F. P3. $15.00

LEM, Stanislaw. *Perfect Vacuum.* 1978. HBJ. 1st Eng-language ed. F/F. N3. $20.00

LEM, Stanislaw. *Solaris.* 1970. Walker. 1st Eng-language ed. NF/NF. N3. $45.00

LEMAIRE, Charles. *Iconographie Descriptive des Cactees.* 1993. Mill Valley. facsimile. 1/300. folio. 16 mc pl. M/dj. B26. $175.00

LEMAITRE, Solange. *Ramakrishna & the Vitality of Hinduism.* 1969. Funk Wagnall. 244p. VG/VG. B33. $8.00

LEMAN, Rhoda. *Book of the Night.* 1984. HRW. 1st ed. F/NF. M21. $25.00

LEMMING, Joseph. *Fun With Magic.* ca 1943. Lippincott. 5th ed. 86p. cloth. G. B10. $15.00

LEMOISNE, Paul Andre. *Gavarni, Peintre et Lithographie.* 1924-1928. Paris. Floury. 2 vol. 4to. half red morocco. K1. $350.00

LENBURG, J. *Peekaboo.* 1983. NY. 1st ed. VG/VG. B5. $35.00

LENCE, Karen V. *Hist of W Books Exhibition: If They've Got To Flap...* 1978. Rounce Coffin Club. 1st ed. 94p. F/sans. B19. $20.00

LENGYEL, Emil. *Dakar: Outpost of Two Hemispheres.* 1943. Garden City. 1st ed. 8vo. 3 pl/map ep. VG. W1. $14.00

LENGYEL, Emil. *Siberia.* 1943. NY. ils/index. 416p. cloth. F. B14. $45.00

LENNON, Florence Baker. *Victoria Through the Looking Glass.* 1945. Simon Schuster. 1st ed. cloth. VG. M5. $18.00

LENNON, Florence Becker. *Lewis Carroll: A Biography.* 1947. London. Cassell. 1st ed. ils. VG+/VG+ clip. S9. $25.00

LENS, Sidney. *Futile Crusade: Anti-Communism As American Credo.* 1964. Quadrangle. 1st ed. F/NF. B2. $35.00

LENSKI, Lois. *At Our House. A Read & Sing Book.* 1959. NY. Henry Walck. music by Clyde Robert Bulla. VG+. A3. $10.00

LENSKI, Lois. *Bayou Suzette.* 1943. Lippincott. 3rd prt. 208p. VG/G. P2. $28.00

LENSKI, Lois. *Blue Ridge Billy.* ca 1946. Lippincott. 1st ed. 203p. G+. B10. $20.00

LENSKI, Lois. *Cotton in My Sack.* 1949. Lippincott. 1st ed. 191p. VG. P2. $50.00

LENSKI, Lois. *High-Rise Secret.* 1966. Lippincott. 1st ed. VG+. C8. $22.50

LENSKI, Lois. *Little Fire Engine.* 1946. NY. Oxford. 1st ed. VG+. C8. $40.00

LENSKI, Lois. *Papa Pequeno/Papa Small.* 1961 (1951). NY. Walck. 1st ed thus. bilingual text. F/F. C8. $40.00

LENSKI, Lois. *Songs of Mr Small.* 1954. Oxford. 1st ed. music Clyde Robert Bulla. 40p. F/VG+. P2. $28.00

LENSKI, Lois. *We Are Thy Children.* 1952. Crowell. 1st ed. music Clyde Bulla. NF/VG. C8. $35.00

LENSKI, Lois. *We Live in the Southwest.* 1962. Lippincott. 2nd prt. 128p. VG/G+. A3. $10.50

LENTILHON, E. *40 Years Beagling in US.* 1921. NY. 1st ed. VG/fair. B5. $40.00

LENTZ, Harold. *Jack the Giant Killer.* 1932. Bl Ribbon. 4 pop-ups. G+. C8. $100.00

LENTZ, Harold. *Mother Goose.* 1934. Bl Ribbon. 3 popups. VG. P2. $250.00

LEON-PORTILLA, Miguel. *Broken Spears.* 1962. Beadon. 1st ed. ils. 168p. VG. F3. $15.00

LEONARD, Charles L. *Treachery in Trieste.* 1951. Crime Club. 1st ed. VG/torn. P3. $10.00

LEONARD, Elmore. *Bandits.* 1987. Arbor. 1st ed. sgn. F/F. O4. $30.00

LEONARD, Elmore. *Bandits.* 1987. Arbor. 1st ed. VG/VG. P3. $18.00

LEONARD, Elmore. *Cat Chaser.* 1982. Arbor. 1st ed. F/NF. M15. $25.00

LEONARD, Elmore. *City Primeval.* 1980. Arbor. 1st ed. sgn. F/F. O4. $85.00

LEONARD, Elmore. *Freaky Deaky.* 1988. Arbor/Morrow. 1st ed. sgn. F/dj. F4. $30.00

LEONARD, Elmore. *Freaky Deaky.* 1988. Arbor/Morrow. 1st ed. xl. dj. P3. $8.00

LEONARD, Elmore. *Freaky Deaky.* 1988. London. Viking. 1st Eng ed. sgn. F/F. S6. $40.00

LEONARD, Elmore. *Get Shorty.* 1990. Delacorte. 1st ed. sgn. F/F. O4. $30.00

LEONARD, Elmore. *Glitz.* 1985. Arbor. 1st ed. inscr/sgn. F/F. S9. $45.00

LEONARD, Elmore. *Glitz.* 1985. Arbor. 1st ed. sgn. F/F. O4. $35.00

LEONARD, Elmore. *Killshot.* 1989. Arbor. 1st ed. sgn. F/F. O4. $30.00

LEONARD, Elmore. *Split Images.* 1981. Arbor. 1st ed. F/F. M15. $40.00

LEONARD, Elmore. *Stick.* 1983. Arbor. 1st ed. sgn. F/F. O4. $35.00

LEONARD, Elmore. *Swag.* 1976. Delacorte. 1st ed. VG/F. B3. $50.00

LEONARD, Elmore. *Touch.* 1987. Arbor. 1st ed. F/F. P3. $18.00

LEONARD, Elmore. *Touch.* 1987. Arbor. 1st ed. sgn. F/F. O4. $25.00

LEONARD, Neil. *Jazz & the White Americans.* 1962. Chicago. 1st ed. 206p. cloth. VG/dj. M20. $30.00

LEOPOLD, A. *San Country Almanac.* 1949. NY. 1st ed. VG/VG. B5. $50.00

LEOPOLD, A. Carl. *Plant Growth & Development.* 1964. NY. ils. 466p. VG. B26. $19.00

LERMAN, Rhoda. *Call Me Ishtar.* 1973. HRW. ARC/1st ed/author's 2nd novel. inscr. RS. F/F. B4. $65.00

LERNER, Alan Jay. *Street Where I Live.* 1978. Norton. 1st ed. sgn. VG/VG. S11. $10.00

LERNER, Max. *Mind & Faith of Justice Holmes, His Speeches, Essays...* 1989. New Brunswick. Transaction Pub. M11. $15.00

LERNER, Max. *Ted & the Kennedy Legend: A Study in Character & Destiny.* 1980. St Martin. ils. 218p. F/dj. M10. $4.50

LERNER, Michael I. *Population Genetics & Animal Improvement.* 1950. Cambridge. 302p. G. K4. $15.00

LEROUX, Gaston. *Machine To Kill.* 1935. Macaulay. 1st Am ed. 254p. VG/poor. M20. $35.00

LEROUX, Gaston. *Man of a Hundred Faces.* 1930. MacAulay. 1st ed. VG. P3. $35.00

LEROUX, Gaston. *Phantom of the Opera.* 1911. Grosset Dunlap. photoplay ed. G. B5. $35.00

LESCROART, John T. *13th Juror.* 1994. Donald Fine. ARC. sgn. 1/310. F/wrp/band. B2. $35.00

LESLIE, Charles. *Theological Works...* 1721. London. Bowyer. 2 vol. 1st ed. folio. old ornate calf. H10. $185.00

LESLIE, Craig. *River Song.* 1989. Houghton Mifflin. 1st ed. M/dj. A18. $19.00

LESLIE, Craig. *Winterkill.* 1984. Houghton Mifflin. 1st ed. F/clip. A18. $60.00

LESLIE, J.A.K. *Survye of Dar Es Salaam.* 1963. London/NY/Nairobi. Oxford. 1st ed. 305p. VG/dj. W1. $22.00

LESLIE, Jean. *Intimate Journal of Warren Winslow.* 1952. Crime Club. 1st ed. NF/dj. F4. $25.00

LESSER, Milton. *Earthbound.* 1952. Winston. 1st ed. VG. P3. $25.00

LESSER, Milton. *Looking Forward.* 1953. Beechhurst. 1st ed. F/NF. F4. $32.00

LESSER, Milton. *Star Seekers.* 1943. Winston. 1st ed. F/frayed. M2. $65.00

LESSER, Robert. *Celebration of Comic Art & Memorabilia.* 1975. Hawthorne. 1st ed. ils 292 p. VG/VG. M20. $30.00

LESSING, Doris. *Four-Gated City.* 1969. Knopf. 1st Am ed. F/NF. B4. $45.00

LESSING, Doris. *Golden Notebook.* 1962. Simon Schuster. 1st Am ed. VG/VG. L3. $175.00

LESSING, Doris. *Good Terrorist.* 1985. Jonathan Cape. 1st ed. NF/NF. P3. $20.00

LESSING, Doris. *Habit of Loving.* 1957. London. MacGibbon Kee. 1st ed. VG/VG. L3. $100.00

LESSING, Doris. *Temptation of Jack Orkney & Other Stories.* 1972. Knopf. 1st Am ed. 8vo. 308p. gilt gr cloth. NF/clip. H5. $75.00

LESTER, Reginald M. *Observer's Book of Weather.* 1970 (1955). London. Warne. photos. 152p. VG/dj. K5. $9.00

LETCHFORD, Albert. *Series 70 Orig Ils to Capt Sir RF Burton's Arabian Nights...* 1897. London. Nichols. 1st ed. sm 4to. 71 pl. teg. VG. W1. $125.00

LETHABY, W.R. *Bookbinding & the Care of Books.* 1916. ils/index. 342p. O8. $12.50

LETHWIDGE, Arnold. *Bookbindings of Ralph Randolph Adams.* 1904. NY. private prt. 24p. orig prt wrp. K1. $45.00

LEVASSEUR, H. *La Pendule Francais, Part II.* 1976. Paris. Tarday. 1st ed. sc. 279p. G. A8. $40.00

LEVENE, Malcolm. *Carder's Paradise.* 1968. Hart Davis. 1st ed. inscr pres. F/dj. F4. $35.00

LEVENE, Malcolm. *Carder's Paradise.* 1969. Walker. 1st Am ed. F/dj. N3/P3. $15.00

LEVER, Charles. *Davenport Dunn; or, Man of Day.* 1857-1859. London. Chapman Hall. 22 parts in 21. 42 pl by Phiz. prt wrp/gr cloth case. K1. $600.00

LEVERELL, Roland Q. *Evangelism: Christ's Imperative Commission.* 1951. Broadman. 234p. G. B29. $3.50

LEVERTOV, Denise. *Summer Poems.* 1970. Oyez. 1/150. hc. sgn. F/sans. V1. $110.00

LEVERTOV, Denise. *With Eyes at the Back of Our Heads.* 1959. New Directions. 1st ed. sgn. F/worn. V1. $55.00

LEVI, Peter. *Grave Witness.* 1985. St Martin. 1st ed. F/F. P3. $13.00

LEVILLIER, Roberto. *Don Francisco del Toledo.* 1935. Buenos Aires. 2 vols. G. F3. $30.00

LEVIN, Betty. *Sword of Culann.* 1973. Macmillan. 1st ed. VG/VG. P3. $18.00

LEVIN, Ira. *Boys From Brazil.* 1976. Random. 1st ed. F/NF. T2. $20.00

LEVIN, Ira. *Silver.* 1991. Bantam. 1st ed. F/F. T2. $15.00

LEVIN, Meyer. *Citizens.* 1940. Viking. 1st ed. G. V4. $10.00

LEVIN, Meyer. *Citizens.* 1940. Viking. 1st ed. VG/dj. B2. $35.00

LEVIN, Sis. *Beirut Diary: Husband Held Hostage & Wife Determined...* 1989. Downers Grove, IL. InterVarsity Pr. 1st ed. VG/tattered. W1. $18.00

LEVINE, Paul. *Night Vision.* 1991. NY. Bantam. 1st ed. sgn. F/F. S6. $35.00

LEVINE, Philip. *Not This Pig.* 1968. Wesleyan. 1st ed. sgn. NF/stiff wrp. V1. $65.00

LEVINE, Rhoda. *Herbert Situation.* ca 1969. Harlin Quist. 1st ed. unp. VG. B10. $10.00

LEVINSON, Abraham. *Pioneers of Pediatrics.* 1936. NY. 1st ed. 112p. scarce. A13. $100.00

LEVINSON, Edward. *I Break Strikes! Technique of Pearl L Bergoff.* 1935. NY. McBride. 1st ed. photos. fair. V4. $20.00

LEVITAS, G.B. *World of Psychology.* 1965. Braziller. 2 vol. 4th prt. M. K4. $20.00

LEVITIN, Sonia. *Sound To Remember.* 1979. Harcourt Brace. 1st ed. ils Lisowski. F/F. C8. $20.00

LEVITSKY, Ronald. *Love That Kills.* 1991. Scribner. 1st ed. sgn. F/F. T2. $20.00

LEVITT, I.M. *Space Traveler's Guide to Mars.* nd. Holt. 1st ed. 8vo. 175p. G/dj. K5. $14.00

LEVITT & LEVITT. *Tissue of Lies: Nixon Vs Hiss.* 1970. McGraw Hill. M11. $25.00

LEVY, Bill. *Three Yards & a Cloud of Dust.* 1966. World. 487p. VG/dj. M20. $25.00

LEVY, Edward. *Came a Spider.* 1978. Arbor. 1st ed/author's 1st novel. F/F. T2. $9.00

LEVY, Elizabeth. *Something Queer at the Ballpark.* 1975. Delacorte. BC. VG+. P8. $8.00

LEVY, H. *Man Against Musky.* 1962. Harrisburg. 1st ed. VG/G. B5. $50.00

LEVY, Juliette de Bairacli. *Gypsy in NY.* 1962. London. Faber. 1st ed. sm 8vo. NF/VG. C8. $15.00

LEVY, Melvin. *Gold Eagle Guy.* 1935. Random. 1st ed. NF/NF. B2. $85.00

LEVY, Melvin. *Last Pioneers.* 1934. NY. Alfred H King. 1st ed. F/chip. B2. $50.00

LEVY, Mervyn. *Whistler Lithographs, an Ils Catalogue Raisonne.* 1975. London. Jupiter. 1st ed. sm 4to. ils. F/dj. F1. $45.00

LEVY, Reuben. *Persian Literature: An Intro.* 1936. London. Milford. 3rd ed. 112p. xl. VG. W1. $10.00

LEWES, G.H. *Female Characters of Goethe.* ca 1880. NY. Stroefer Kirchner. 22 mtd photos. full red leather. NF. F1. $135.00

LEWIN, Elyse. *Child Photography.* 1981. NY. Amphoto. 1st ed. VG/VG+. S9. $20.00

LEWIN, Ira. *Stepford Wives.* 1972. Random. 1st ed. NF/F. B3. $25.00

LEWIN, Michael Z. *Called by a Panther.* 1991. Mysterious. F/F. P3. $18.00

LEWIN, Michael Z. *Enemies Within.* 1974. London. Hamilton. 1st Eng ed. F/NF. S6. $22.50

LEWIN, Michael Z. *Night Cover.* 1976. Hamish Hamilton. 1st ed. VG/VG. P3. $20.00

LEWIS, Alfred H. *Apaches of NY.* 1912. NY. 1st ed. ils. 272p. VG. D3. $25.00

LEWIS, Alfred H. *Confessions of a Detective.* 1906. Barnes. 1st ed. VG. B2. $30.00

LEWIS, Alfred H. *Treasure in the Andes.* ca 1952. Abingdon Cokesbury. ARC/1st ed. 127p. VG/VG. B10. $45.00

LEWIS, Anthony. *Make No Law, the Sullivan Case & the First Amendment.* 1991. Random. M11. $25.00

LEWIS, Archibald. *Northern Seas: Shipping & Commerce in N Europe 300-1100.* 1978. Octagon. 498p. NF. M10. $12.50

LEWIS, Arthur H. *Copper Beeches.* 1971. Trident. 1st ed. xl. dj. P3. $20.00

LEWIS, C.S. *Abolition of Man; or, Reflections on Education...* 1947. Macmillan. 1st ed. F/clip. A18. $50.00

LEWIS, C.S. *Beyond Personality: Christian Idea of God.* 1944. London. Bles. 1st ed. F/clip. A18. $60.00

LEWIS, C.S. *Beyond the Bright Blur.* 1963. HBW. 1st ed/ltd prt. pres. F. A18. $40.00

LEWIS, C.S. *Chronicle of Narnia.* 1994. Harper Collins. 1st ed thus. 7 vols. M/case. A18. $105.00

LEWIS, C.S. *Eng Literature in 16th Century Excluding Drama.* 1954. London. Oxford. 1st ed. F/clip. A18. $90.00

LEWIS, C.S. *Experiment in Criticism.* 1961. London. Cambridge. 1st ed. F/clip. A18. $50.00

LEWIS, C.S. *Four Loves.* 1960. London. Bles. 1st ed. 160p. VG/VG. B33. $30.00

LEWIS, C.S. *Great Divorce: A Dream.* 1945. London. Bles. 1st ed. F/chip. A18. $60.00

LEWIS, C.S. *Joyful Christian: 127 Readings From CS Lewis.* 1977. Macmillan. 1st ed. F/F. A18. $25.00

LEWIS, C.S. *Letters of CS Lewis.* 1966. London. Bles. 1st ed. photos. NF/chip. A18. $40.00

LEWIS, C.S. *Letters to an American Lady.* 1967. Grand Rapids. 1st ed. F/VG. F1. $30.00

LEWIS, C.S. *Letters to Children.* 1985. Macmillan. 1st ed. M/M. C8. $17.50

LEWIS, C.S. *Letters to Malcolm: Chiefly on Prayer.* 1964. London. Bles. 1st ed. F/VG. A18. $40.00

LEWIS, C.S. *Lion, Witch & the Wardrobe.* 1950. Macmillan. 1st Am ed. ils Pauline Baynes. 154p. NF/VG. rare. P2. $900.00

LEWIS, C.S. *Magician's Nephew.* 1935. Bodley Head. 1st ed. 8vo. 183p. NF/dj. H5. $750.00

LEWIS, C.S. *Miracles.* 1947. Macmillan. 2nd prt. 220p. VG/G. B33. $16.00

LEWIS, C.S. *Miracles: Preliminary Study.* 1947. London. Bles. 1st ed. F/VG. A18. $75.00

LEWIS, C.S. *Of Other Worlds: Essays & Stories.* 1967. HBW. 1st ed. F/clip. A18. $40.00

LEWIS, C.S. *Pilgrim's Regress: Allegorical Apology...* 1935. Sheed Ward. 1st Am ed. map ep. F/NF. A18. $250.00

LEWIS, C.S. *Reflections on the Psalms.* 1958. NY. Harcourt Brace. 1st Am ed. 151p. VG/VG. B33. $28.00

LEWIS, C.S. *Screwtape Letters.* 1945. Reginald Saunders. 1st Canadian ed. VG. P3. $18.00

LEWIS, C.S. *Silver Chair.* 1953. Macmillan. 1st Am ed. ils Pauline Baynes. 208p. VG/poor. P2. $75.00

LEWIS, C.S. *Surprised by Joy: Shape of My Early Life.* 1956. Harcourt Brace. 1st ed. F/chip. A18. $50.00

LEWIS, Carroll. *Novelty & Romancement: A Story.* 1925. Boston. Brimmer. 1st ed. intro Randolph Edgar. VG/dj. Q1. $150.00

LEWIS, Cecil. *Sagittaurias Rising.* 1936. NY. ARC/1st ed. sgn. VG/G. B5. $75.00

LEWIS, Charles. *Cain Factor.* 1975. Harwood Smart. 1st ed. F/F. P3. $13.00

LEWIS, Clarence Irving. *Collected Papers of Clarence Irving Lewis.* 1970. Stanford. gold cloth. VG/dj. G1. $30.00

LEWIS, Clarence Irving. *Mind & the World-Order: Outline of Theory of Knowledge.* 1929. Scribner. 446p. ribbed bl cloth. G1. $50.00

LEWIS, David. *Icebound in Antarctica.* 1988. Norton. 1st ed. ils/2 maps. 242p. F/F. S11. $20.00

LEWIS, Deborah; see Grant, Charles L.

LEWIS, Edwin. *Philosophy of Christian Revelation.* 1940. Harper. 356p. G. B29. $5.50

LEWIS, Florence Jay. *Climax.* 1944. Books Inc. VG. P3. $15.00

LEWIS, Geoffrey. *Turkey.* 1955. London. Benn. 1st ed. lg fld map. VG/dj. W1. $14.00

LEWIS, Georgina King. *John Greenleaf Whittier.* nd. London. Headley Bros. 8vo. 221p. fair. V3. $12.50

LEWIS, H.H. *Gunner Aboard the Yankee From Diary of Number Five...* 1898. Doubleday McClure. 8vo. 312p. gilt dk gr cloth. VG. B11. $120.00

LEWIS, Isabel M. *Astronomy for Young Folks.* 1922 (1921). Duffield. 8vo. 267p. bl cloth. G. K5. $15.00

LEWIS, J. *Brandeis: An Intimate Biography...* 1983. Prentice Hall. M11. $35.00

LEWIS, Janet. *Ghost of Monsieur Scarron.* 1959. Garden City. 1st ed/author's 6th novel. sgn. NF/NF. A11. $60.00

LEWIS, LEWIS & RIGDON. *Four Men: Living the Revolution, an Oral History...Cuba.* 1977. Urbana. photos. F/F. V4. $8.00

LEWIS, Lloyd. *Captain Sam Grant.* 1950. Little Brn. 1st ed. 484p. VG/ragged. M20. $20.00

LEWIS, M.G. *Journal of a West India Proprietor 1815-1817.* 1929. np. ils. VG/G+. M17. $35.00

LEWIS, Myra. *Great Balls of Fire: Jerry Lee Lewis Story.* 1982. NY. 1st ed. lg sc. VG. B5. $30.00

LEWIS, Naomi. *Once Upon a Rainbow.* 1981. London. Cape. 1st ed. ils Gabriele Eichenauer. VG/VG. A3. $15.00

LEWIS, Oscar. *Hearn & His Biographers.* 1930. Westgate/Grabhorn. 1/350. NF. M19. $200.00

LEWIS, Oscar. *Lola Montez. Mid-Victorian Bad Girl in California.* 1938. San Francisco. 1/750. sgn. red brd. VG+/sans case. A11. $50.00

LEWIS, Oscar. *Uncertain Journey.* 1945. Knopf. 253p. VG/G. B19. $15.00

LEWIS, Peter. *John LeCarre.* 1985. NY. Unger. 1st ed. F/F. S6. $25.00

LEWIS, Roy. *Antiquarian Books: An Insider's Account.* 1978. London. David & Charles. 1st ed. 200p. F/VG. S11. $20.00

LEWIS, Roy. *Bloodeagle.* 1993. London. Collins. 1st ed. F/F. S6. $22.50

LEWIS, Roy. *Death in Verona.* 1989. np. 188p. F/F. A4. $25.00

LEWIS, Roy. *Error of Judgment.* 1971. Collins Crime Club. 1st ed. NF/NF. P3. $20.00

LEWIS, Roy. *Salamander Chill.* 1988. Collins Crime Club. 1st ed. NF/NF. P3. $18.00

LEWIS, Roy. *Where Agents Fear To Tread.* 1984. NY/London. St Martin/Hale. 1st ed. F/F. S6. $30.00

LEWIS, Shari. *Shari Lewis Puppet Book.* 1958. Citadel. 1st prt. ils Leipzig/photos Lurin. VG+/VG+. C8. $35.00

LEWIS, Sinclair. *Ann Vickers.* 1933. NY. 1st ed. 1/2350. VG/VG. B5. $150.00

LEWIS, Sinclair. *Babbitt.* 1946. Bantam. 1st pb ed. 408p. VG/dj. M20. $40.00

LEWIS, Sinclair. *Dodsworth.* 1929. Harcourt Brace. 1st ed. 377p. VG/chip. M20. $225.00

LEWIS, Sinclair. *Elmer Gantry.* 1927. Harcourt Brace. 1st ed/1st state (C not G on spine). VG/dj. M20. $200.00

LEWIS, Sinclair. *From Main Street to Stockholm, Letters...1919-1930.* 1952. Harcourt Brace. 1st ed. VG/dj. M20. $15.00

LEWIS, Sinclair. *Hike & the Aeroplane.* 1912. Stokes. author's 1st book (written as Tom Graham). very scarce. M20. $2,200.00

LEWIS, Sinclair. *It Can't Happen Here.* nd. Sun Dial. VG. P3. $25.00

LEWIS, Sinclair. *Kingsblood Royal.* 1947. Random. 1st prt. 384p. G. H1. $16.00

LEWIS, Sinclair. *Man From Main Street.* 1953. Random. 1st prt. 371p. cloth. VG/worn. M20. $15.00

LEWIS, Sol. *Sand Creek Massacre, a Documentary History.* 1973. rpt of GPO document. 1/500. 8vo. bl cloth. F. A8. $75.00

LEWIS, W. Bevan. *Human Brain, Histological & Coarse Methods of Research.* 1882. London. 8vo. 4 mtd albumin pl. 163p. VG. B14. $375.00

LEWIS, Walker. *Without Fear or Favor, Biography of Chief Justice...Taney.* 1965. Houghton Mifflin. G/dj. M11. $35.00

LEWIS, Wyndham. *Apes of God.* 1932. NY. McBride. 1st Am ed. VG/dj. Q1. $225.00

LEWIS, Wyndham. *Tarr.* 1918. Knopf. 1st Am ed (precedes UK ed). Ralph Block's copy. VG. Q1. $275.00

LEWIS & MANLEY. *Bewitched Beings.* 1974. Lee Shepard. 1st ed. F/F. P3. $30.00

LEWIS & SCHARY. *Storm in the West.* (1963). NY. 1st ed. F/VG. A9. $25.00

LEWISOHN, Ludwig. *Israel.* 1925. Boni Liveright. 3rd prt. 280p. VG. W1. $15.00

LEY, Willy. *Dawn of Zoology.* 1967. Englewood. ils. 280p. G7. $25.00

LEY, Willy. *On Earth & in the Sky.* 1967. Doubleday. 1st ed. F/NF. M2. $75.00

LEYDET, Francois. *Time & the River Flowing: Grand Canyon.* 1964. Sierra Club. 1st ed. F/VG+. S9. $60.00

LEYEL, Mrs. C.F. *Magic of Herbs.* 1932 (1926). London. 320p. VG/dj. B26. $27.50

LEYLAND, Eric. *Smugglers of the Skies.* 1958. Edmund Ward. VG/G. P3. $15.00

LEYNER, Mark. *Et Tu, Babe.* 1992. NY. Harmony. 1st ed. F/F. B4. $30.00

LICHTENBERG, Jacqueline. *Mahogany Trinrose.* 1981. Doubleday. 1st ed. F/F. P3. $20.00

LICHTENBERG, Jacqueline. *Unto Zeor, Forever.* 1978. Doubleday. 1st ed. VG/rpr. P3. $15.00

LICHTENBERG & LORRAH. *First Channel.* 1980. Doubleday. 1st ed. F/NF. N3. $20.00

LICHTENBERG & LORRAH. *First Channel.* 1980. Doubleday. 1st ed. VG/G. P3. $13.00

LIDA. *Cuckoo.* 1942. Harper. 1st ed. unp. VG/G. B10. $65.00

LIDE, Alice Alison. *Thord Firetooth.* 1937. Lee Shepard. 1st ed. ils Henry Pitz. VG/VG. B10. $25.00

LIEB, F. *Pittsburgh Pirates.* 1948. NY. Putnam. 1st ed. sgn. VG/VG. B5. $75.00

LIEBENAU, Jonathan. *Medical Science & Medical Industry.* 1987. London. 1st ed. 207p. A13. $25.00

LIEBER, Francis. *Manual of Political Ethics...* 1892 (1874). Lippincott. 2 vol. 2nd revised ed/later prt. blk cloth. VG. G1. $65.00

LIEBER, Lillian R. *Einstein Theory of Relativity...* 1966 (1945). NY. HRW. 13th prt. 8vo. 324p. VG/dj. K5. $27.00

LIEBERT & SPIEGLER. *Personality.* 1970. Georgetown, Ontario. Irvin Dorsey. 404p. F. K4. $10.00

LIEBICH, Hayat Salam. *L'Art Islamique.* 1983. Paris. Flammarion. 1st ed. ils. 63p. VG/wrp. W1. $10.00

LIEBIG, Justus. *Organic Chemistry in Its Application to Agriculture...* 1841. Cambridge. 1st Am ed. 435p. paper label. VG. B14. $125.00

LIEBKNECHT, Karl. *Future Belongs to the People.* 1918. Macmillan. NF. B2. $60.00

LIEBKNECHT, Karl. *Militarism.* 1917. NY. Huebsch. 1st ed. VG. V4. $25.00

LIEBLING, A.J. *Between Meals.* 1962. Simon Schuster. 1st ed. VG/VG. S9. $45.00

LIEBLING, A.J. *Chicago: Second City.* 1952. Knopf. 1st ed. ils Steinberg. F/NF. B2. $65.00

LIEBLING, R. *Time Line of Culture in Nile Valley...* 1979. Metropolitan Mus Art. 2nd prt. VG/case. W1. $15.00

LIEBOW, Ely M. *Dr Joe Bell: Model for Sherlock Holmes.* 1982. Popular. 1st ed. ils. F/F. S6. $30.00

LIEF, Erwin. *Der Arzt und Seine Sendung.* 1927. Munich. 4th ed. 174p. worn dj. G7. $20.00

LIEUWEN & VALDES. *Cuban Revolution: A Research-Study Guide 1959-1969.* 1971. NM U. 242p. xl. VG. A4. $45.00

LIFTON, Betty Jean. *Cock & the Ghost Cat.* 1967. Atheneum. 3rd prt. 32p. VG/VG. B10. $10.00

LIGHTFOOT, J.B. *St Paul's Epistle to the Colossians & to Philemon.* 1987. Hendrickson. 430p. M. B29. $10.00

LIGHTNER, A.M. *Space Olympics.* 1967. Norton. 1st ed. brd. VG. P3. $15.00

LIGHTNER, A.M. *Star Circus.* 1977. Dutton. 1st ed. M/M. C8. $20.00

LIGHTON, Conrad. *Cape Floral Kingdom.* 1973. Cape Town. 221p. VG/dj. B26. $32.50

LIGNELL & PRINCEHORN. *Three Japanese Mice & Their Whiskers.* 1934. Farrar Rinehart. 1st ed. sgns. NF/VG. P2. $100.00

LIGOTTI, Thomas. *Grimscribe: His Lives & Works.* 1991. London. Robinson. 1st ed/author's 1st novel. F/F. T2. $45.00

LIGOTTI, Thomas. *Songs of a Dead Dreamer.* 1990. Carroll Graf. 1st hc ed. F/F. T2. $20.00

LILEY, Alison. *Craft of Embroidery.* 1961. np. cloth. VG. G2. $9.75

LILIENTHAL, Albert H. *There Goes the Middle East.* 1957. NY. Devin Adair. 1st ed. 12 pl. 300p. VG. W1. $12.00

LILIUS, Aleko. *Turbulent Tangier.* 1956. London. Elek. 1st ed. 179p. VG/dj. W1. $12.00

LILJENCRANTZ, Ottilie A. *Thrall of Leif the Lucky.* 1902. Chicago. 1st ed. ils Kinney. 354p. gilt emb cloth. G. A17. $7.00

LILLARD, Richard G. *Desert Challenge: Interpretation of Nevada.* 1942. NY. Knopf. 1st ed. 388p. beige cloth. VG+/worn. P4. $65.00

LILLIBRIDGE, Will. *Quercus Alba: Veteran of the Ozarks.* 1910. Chicago. McClurg. 49p. G/G case. N2. $5.00

LILLIE, Ralph S. *General Biology & Philosophy of Organism.* 1945. Chicago. tan cloth. VG/worn. G1. $25.00

LILLY, John. *Center of the Cyclone.* 1972. Julian. 222p. VG/VG. B33. $20.00

LILLY, John. *Modern Entries: Being Collection of Select Pleadings...* 1741. London. Henry Linton. contemporary calf. M11. $250.00

LILLY, John. *Simulations of God.* 1975. Simon Schuster. 1st ed. 288p. VG/VG. B33. $18.00

LILLY & LILLY. *Dyadic Cyclone: Autobiography of a Couple.* 1976. Simon Schuster. 287p. VG/VG. B33. $25.00

LIMERICK, Patricia Nelson. *Legacy of Conquest: Unbroken Past of the American West.* 1987. Norton. 1st ed. photos/notes/index. F/dj. A18. $35.00

LIMPUS, L. *History of New York Fire Dept.* 1940. NY. 1st ed. 380p. VG/worn. B5. $35.00

LINAKIS, Steven. *In the Spring the War Ended.* 1965. NY. 1st ed/author's 1st novel. F/F. A17. $15.00

LINCOLN, Abraham. *Collected Poetry...* 1971. Springfield. private prt. 1st ed. marbled paper brd. F. Q1. $40.00

LINCOLN, Abraham. *Lincoln's Gettysburg Address.* 1947. Whitman. 1st ed. ils James Daugherty. NF/VG. P2. $90.00

LINCOLN, Abraham. *Proclamation of Emancipation by President of United States.* 1863. Boston. JM Forbes. 1st complete book ed. 84x56mm. 8p. NF/prt peach wrp. B24. $1,500.00

LINCOLN, Abraham. *Writings of...* 1905. NY. Lamb. 8 vol. intro Theodore Roosevelt. F. O8. $45.00

LINCOLN, C. Eric. *Avenue, Clayton City.* 1988. Morrow. UP. VG/prt gray wrp. B3. $25.00

LINCOLN, C. Eric. *Black Muslims in America.* 1961. Boston. Beacon. 1st ed. red cloth. VG/dj. B14. $35.00

LINCOLN, Joe. *Cape Cod Ballads.* 1902. Trenton. 1st ed. VG. B5. $85.00

LINCOLN, Joseph C. *Great-Aunt Lavinia.* 1936. Appleton Century. 1st ed. 339p. G. H1. $9.00

LINCOLN, Joseph C. *Thankful's Inheritance.* nd. Al Burt. rpt. 383p. pict bdg. F. H1. $6.00

LINCOLN, Mrs. D.A. *Mrs Lincoln's Cook Book. What To Do & What Not To Do...* 1884. Boston. Roberts Bros. 1st ed. 8vo. 534p. pub half cloth/brd. M1. $1,500.00

LINCOLN, W. Bruce. *In War's Dark Shadow: Russians Before the Great War.* 1983. NY. 1st prt. 557p. F/F. A17. $10.00

LINCOLN & LINCOLN. *Blair's Attic.* 1929. Coward McCann. 1st ed. 369p. G. H1. $7.50

LIND, J. *Muskie.* 1964. Chicago. 1st ed. VG/VG. B5. $45.00

LIND, L.R. *Studies in Pre-Vesalian Anatomy, Biography, Trans...* 1975. Phil. lg 4to. 344p. M/dj. G7. $65.00

LINDAUER, Martin S. *Psychological Study in Literature.* 1974. Chicago. Nelson Hall. 254p. G/dj. K4. $12.50

LINDBARGER, Paul. *Psychological Warfare.* 1948. WA. Infantry Journal. 1st ed. 251p. F/dj. K4. $15.00

LINDBERGH, Anne Morrow. *Earth Shine.* 1969. HBW. photos. 73p. VG/dj. K5. $10.00

LINDBERGH, Anne Morrow. *Gift From the Sea.* March 1955. Pantheon. 4th prt. 127p. F/G. H1. $6.00

LINDBERGH, Charles A. *We.* July 1927. Putnam. 3rd prt. photos. 318p. G. H1. $8.00

LINDER, Leslie. *Journal of Beatrix Potter.* 1966. London. Warne. rpt. 448p. gilt gr cloth. VG/VG. S11. $25.00

LINDERMAN, Frank Bird. *Recollections of Charley Russell.* 1963. OK U. 1st ed. edit HG Merriam. F/dj. A18. $30.00

LINDGREN, Astrid. *Cherry Time at Bullerby.* (1961). London. Methuen. 1st Eng ed. M/M. C8. $30.00

LINDGREN, Astrid. *Karlsson-on-the-Roof.* 1971. Viking. 1st Am ed. NF/NF. C8. $25.00

LINDGREN, Astrid. *Runaway Sleigh Ride.* 1984. Viking. 1st Am ed. M. C8. $20.00

LINDGREN, Astrid. *Skrallan & the Pirates.* ca 1967. Doubleday. 1st ed. 48p. VG/VG. B10. $15.00

LINDGREN, Linda Lee. *Home Decorating With Needlecrafts.* 1985. np. VG/wrp. G2. $122.95

LINDMAN, M. *Flicka, Ricka, Dicka & the Girl Next Door.* 1945 (1940). Whitman. 6th prt. 12 mc pl. 24p. NF. D6. $45.00

LINDMAN, M. *Snipp, Snapp, Snurr & the Big Farm.* 1946. Whitman. 1st ed. 4to. VG/poor. M5. $24.00

LINDMAN, M. *Snipp, Snapp, Snurr & the Gingerbread.* 1932. Whitman. 1st ed. 4to. 10 special mc pl. brn cloth. VG+. D6. $100.00

LINDMAN & MCINTYRE. *Mentally Disabled & the Law.* 1961. Chicago. 368p. F/dj. K4. $30.00

LINDSAY, David Moore. *Voyage to the Arctic in the Whaler Aurora.* 1911. Boston. Estes. ils. 223p. pict brd. T7. $75.00

LINDSELL & WOODBRIDGE. *Handbook of Chritian Truch.* 1953. Revell. 351p. M/VG. B29. $7.00

LINDSEY, Bessie M. *American Historical Glass.* 1967. Tuttle. 2nd prt. 541p. F/F. H1. $60.00

LINDSEY, David L. *Cold Mind.* 1983. Harper Row. 1st ed. NF/NF. P3. $25.00

LINDSEY, David L. *Heat From Another Sun.* 1984. Harper Row. 1st ed. F/F. M15. $35.00

LINDSEY, David L. *In the Lake of the Sun.* 1988. Atheneum. 1st ed. F/F. M15. $30.00

LINDSEY, Gene. *Saudi Arabia.* 1991. Hippocrene. 1st ed. maps. 368p. NF/dj. W1. $24.00

LINEBARGER, Paul. *Best of Cordwainer Smith.* nd. BC. F/F. P3. $10.00

LINEBARGER, Paul. *Rediscovery of Man.* 1988. Gollancz. 1st ed. F/F. P3. $30.00

LINEBARGER, Paul. *Ria.* 1947. DSP. 1st ed. F/NF. P3. $200.00

LINES, Kathleen. *Four to Fourteen.* 1950. London. Cambridge. 12mo. 204p. VG/VG. S11. $20.00

LING, Nicholas. *Politeuphuia, Withs Common-Wealth.* nd (1620?). London. Smethwicke. 12mo. 513p. old calf. K1. $250.00

LINGS, Martin. *Moslem Saint of the Twentieth Century.* 1961. Macmillan. 1st Am ed. 224p. VG. W1. $35.00

LINGS, Martin. *Sufi Saint of the Twentieth Century.* 1971. Berkeley. 8vo. 242p. VG. W1. $35.00

LININGTON, Elizabeth. *Date With Death.* 1966. Harper Row. 1st ed. xl. dj. P3. $8.00

LININGTON, Elizabeth. *Felony Report.* 1984. Crime Club. 1st ed. xl. dj. P3. $5.00

LININGTON, Elizabeth. *Proud Man.* 1955. Viking. 1st ed. VG/torn. P3. $30.00

LINKLATER, Eric. *Northern Garrisons.* 1941. London. 1st ed. 72p. G/wrp. B18. $7.50

LINKLATER, Eric. *Private Angelo.* 1957. London. McCorquodale. 1/2000. 12mo. VG. A17. $9.50

LINKSY, Leonard. *Referring.* 1967. London. Routledge. 139p. red cloth. VG/dj. G1. $30.00

LINSDAY, David. *Sphiny.* 1988. Carroll Graf. 1st ed. F/F. P3. $18.00

LINTON & LINTON. *We Gather Together. The Story of Thanksgiving.* 1949. Schuman. 1st ed. 8vo. 100p. VG/G. B11. $25.00

LINZEE, David. *Belgravia.* 1979. Seaview. 1st ed. VG/VG. P3. $15.00

LION, Jindrich. *Prague Ghetto.* nd. London. Artia for Spring Books. 4to. gilt blk cloth. VG/dj. B14. $50.00

LIPE, Karen S. *More Boat Canvas.* 1984. Newport. Seven Seas. ils/photos. sbdg. T7. $18.00

LIPMAN, Jean *Rufus Porter, Yankee Pioneer.* 1968. NY. Potter. 1st ed. 4to. 202p. G/G. B11. $50.00

LIPPINCOTT, David. *Savage Ransom.* 1978. Rawson Assoc. 1st ed. VG/VG. P3. $20.00

LIPPINCOTT, Horace Mather. *Portraiture of the People Called Quakers.* 1915. Phil. Jenkins. 8vo. 116p. G. V3. $12.00

LIPPMAN, Walter. *Preface to Morals.* 1929. Macmillan. 348p. blk cloth. G1. $27.50

LIPSEY, Roger. *Art of Our Own: Spiritual in Twentieth Century Art.* 1988. Shambhala. 1st ed. ils. 518p. F/F. B33. $55.00

LIPSITT & SPIKER. *Advances in Child Development & Behavior. Vol 1.* 1963. Academic. 373p. F/dj. K4. $15.00

LIPSKY, Eleazar. *People Against O'Hara.* 1950. Doubleday Crime Club. 1st ed. RS. 247p. VG/dj. M20. $18.00

LIPSYTE, Robert. *Jack & Jill.* 1982. Harper Row. 1st ed. F/VG+. P8. $12.50

LIPTON, Benjamin H. *Aim for a Job in Watchmaking.* 1967. NY. Richard Rosen Pr. 1st ed. 8vo. 125p. F/VG. A8. $10.00

LIPTON, Lawrence. *Holy Barbarians.* 1959. Messner. 1st ed. VG/VG+. S9. $25.00

LISH, Gordon. *Zimzum.* 1993. Pantheon/Random. 1st ed. F/F. A14. $25.00

LISSNER, Ivar. *Man, God & Magic.* 1961. Putnam. 1st ed. VG. P3. $25.00

LIST, Herbert. *Junge Manner.* 1988. Altadena, CA. Twin Palms. 1st ed. 4to. gray linen. F/F. F1. $50.00

LISTER, Lord. *Third Huxley Lecture.* 1907. London. 58p. VG. B14. $200.00

LITCHFIELD, Frederick. *Ils Hist of Furniture: From Earliest to Present Time.* 1892. London. Truslove Shirley. 2nd ed. 4to. teg. gilt brn brd. VG+. F1. $85.00

LITCHFIELD, Frederick. *Pottery & Porcelain: A Guide to Collectors.* 1925. London. Blk. 4th ed. thick 8vo. 464p. gilt red cloth. F/VG. F1. $85.00

LITTELL, Robert. *Debriefing.* 1979. Harper Row. 1st ed. VG/VG. P3. $20.00

LITTELL, Robert. *Sisters.* 1986. London. Cape. 1st Eng ed. F/F. S6. $25.00

LITTLE, Bentley. *Revelation.* 1990. St Martin. 1st ed/author's 1st novel. sgn. F/F. T2. $45.00

LITTLE, Frances. *House of the Misty Star.* 1915. McClelland Goodchild. VG. P3. $20.00

LITTLE, George. *American Cruisers Own Book.* 1859. Phil. JB Smith. ils Billings. 384p. emb cloth. VG. P4. $75.00

LITTLE, Nina Fletcher. *Some Old Brookline Houses Built...Before 1825...* 1949. Brookline. ils. 160p. bl cloth. F. B14. $55.00

LITTLE, Tom. *Modern Egypt.* 1967. NY/WA. Praeger. 1st ed. fld map. 281p. NF/dj. W1. $15.00

LITTLE & LITTLE. *Black Shrouds.* 1942. Triangle. G+/dj. P3. $20.00

LITTLEFAIR, Duncan E. *Sin Corners of Age.* 1975. Westminster. 191p. VG/dj. B29. $3.50

LITTLEFIELD, Bill. *Prospect.* 1989. Houghton Mifflin. 1st ed. F/VG+. P8. $12.50

LITTLEFIELD & PARINS. *American Indian & Alaska Native Newspapers & Periodicals...* 1986. NY. Greenwood. 1st ed. 8vo. 609p. gray cloth. M. P4. $35.00

LITTLETON, Thomas. *Les Tenures de Monsieur Littleton...* 1604. Londoni. In Aedibus Tho Wright. 32mo. VG. D3. $450.00

LITZEL, Otto. *Darkroom Magic.* 1969. Amphoto. 3rd prt. 143 p. VG/VG. A17. $12.50

LIU, Yeh-Ching. *Colored Ils of Important Trees in Taiwan.* 1971 (1970). ROC. ils/photos. 538p. F. B26. $59.00

LIVERANI, G. *Five Centuries of Italian Majolica.* 1960. McGraw Hill. VG+/VG+/case. A1. $100.00

LIVERMAN, Alexander. *Art & Technique of Color Photography.* 1951. Simon Schuster. 1st ed. folio. F/F. F1. $60.00

LIVINGSTON, George. *Twenty-Four Ivans: Russian Folk Tale.* ca 1946. Pied Piper Books. unp. G+. B10. $15.00

LIVINGSTON, Jack. *Hell-Bent for Election.* 1988. St Martin. 1st ed. NF/NF. P3. $17.00

LIVINGSTON, Nancy. *Incident at Parga.* 1987. London. Gollancz. 1st ed. F/F. S6. $25.00

LIVINGSTON, Walter. *Mystery of Villa Sineste.* 1931. Mystery League. 1st ed. VG/torn. P3. $18.00

LIVINGSTONE, David. *Adventures...Herald-Stanley Expedition.* 1872. Hubbard. 598p. VG. M20. $50.00

LIVINGSTONE, David. *Livingstone's Africa. Perilous Adventures...* 1872. Phil. Hubbard. 8vo. ils. 598p. gilt half leather. VG. F1. $150.00

LIVINGSTONE, Richard. *Plato & Modern Education.* 1944. Cambridge. 12mo. bl-gr brd. G1. $25.00

LJONE, Oddm. *Green Light for Adventure.* 1957. London. Allen Unwin. 1st ed. 8vo. 252p. VG/VG. B11. $20.00

LLEWELLYN, Richard. *Flame for Doubting Thomas.* 1953. Macmillan. 1st ed. VG/VG. P3. $25.00

LLEWELYN, Sam. *Blood Orange.* 1989. NY. Summit. ARC/1st Am ed. w/promo material & photos. F/F. S6. $25.00

LLOYD, Ann. *Good Guys, Bad Guys.* 1983. Orbis Great Movies. 1st ed. VG. P3. $15.00

LLOYD, Ann. *Wild & Young.* 1983. Orbis Great Movies. 1st ed. VG/VG. P3. $15.00

LLOYD, G.E.R. *Aristotle: Growth & Structure of His Thought.* 1968. Cambridge. 324p. bl cloth. VG/dj. G1. $27.50

LLOYD, H.H. *Lloyd's Battle History of the Great Rebellion.* 1883. US Army Chief Engineers. atlas folio. 18 litho battle plans. half morocco. H9. $3,750.00

LLOYD, Henry Demarest. *Country Without Strikes.* 1900. Doubleday Page. 1st ed. inscr. NF. B2. $100.00

LLOYD, Hugh. *Copperhead Trail Mystery.* 1931. Grosset Dunlap. Hal Keen #3. orange cloth. VG/dj lists 6 titles. M20. $80.00

LLOYD, Hugh. *Mysterious Arab.* 1931. Grosset Dunlap. 237p. cloth. VG/dj lists 7 titles. M20. $100.00

LLOYD, Selwyn. *Suez 1956: A Personal Account.* 1978. Mayflower. 1st Am ed. ils/pl/map. 282p. NF/dj. W1. $18.00

LLOYD, Seton. *Early Highland Peoples of Anatolia.* 1967. NY. 8vo. 144p. cloth. dj. O2. $25.00

LLOYD, Seton. *Foundations in the Dust.* 1947. London/NY/Toronto. Oxford. 1st ed. 237p. VG. W1. $20.00

LO, Steven C. *Incorporation of Eric Chung.* 1989. Algonquin. 1st ed/author's 1st book. F/F. A14. $30.00

LOBAY, Halyna. *Rudolph Ruzicka & His Contributions...Am Fine Book.* 1971. self pub. 4to. 232p. w/sgn letter. NF. M10. $45.00

LOBEL, Arnold. *On Market Street.* ca 1981. Greenwillow. unp. G. B10. $10.00

LOBEL, Arnold. *On the Day Peter Stuyvesant Sailed Into Town.* 1971. Harper. 1st ed. NF. C8. $25.00

LOBEL, Arnold. *Owl at Home.* ca 1975. Harper Row. 1st ed. VG/VG. B10. $15.00

LOBELL, Nathan D. *Shadow & the Blot.* 1949. Harper. 1st ed. VG/dj. M21. $15.00

LOBSACK, Theo. *Earth's Envelope.* 1959. London. Collins. trans Rewald. photos/diagrams. 256p. bl cloth. G. K5. $14.00

LOCH, Joyce Nankievell. *Fringe of Blue: An Autobiography.* 1968. NY. 1st Am ed. 8vo. 243p. cloth. dj. O2. $35.00

LOCH, S. *Athos: The Holy Mountain.* 1957. NY. 1st Am ed. 8vo. 264p. cloth. dj. O2. $45.00

LOCHER, A. *With Star & Crescent.* 1889. Phil. 1st ed. 634p. pict cloth. G. B18. $37.50

LOCHER, A. *With Star & Crescent.* 1889. Phil. 8vo. 634p. cloth. VG. O2. $55.00

LOCHHEAD. *Preliminary Checklist of 19th Century Canadian Poetry...* 1976. New Brunswick. Mt Allison U. 4to. 184p. VG/wrp. A4. $95.00

LOCHTE, Dick. *Blue Bayou.* 1992. NY. Simon Schuster. ARC/1st ed. sgn. RS. F/F. S6. $35.00

LOCHTE, Dick. *Blue Bayou.* 1992. Simon Schuster. 1st ed. sgn. F/F. M15. $27.50

LOCK, Stephen. *Difficult Balance: Editorial Peer Review in Medicine.* 1985. Phil. 1st ed. 172p. A13. $35.00

LOCKE, David R.; see Nasby, Petroleum.

LOCKE, John. *Some Thoughts Concerning Education...* 1900? London. Nat Soc Depository. new ed. 12mo. 364p. VG. G1. $30.00

LOCKE, John. *Some Thoughts Concerning Education...* 1699 (1692). London. Churchill. 4th ed. 12mo. 380p. reading copy. G1. $125.00

LOCKEY, Joseph Byrne. *Essays in Pan-Americanism.* 1939. CA U. 1st ed. 174p. NF/dj. D3. $25.00

LOCKRIDGE, Norman. *Bachelor's Quarters.* 1946. Herald Pub. 1st ed. NF/NF. F4. $45.00

LOCKRIDGE, Norman. *Waggish Tales of the Czechs.* 1947. Candide. 1st ed. VG/worn. A17. $15.00

LOCKRIDGE, Richard. *Death on the Hour.* 1974. Lippincott. 1st ed. VG/VG. P3. $20.00

LOCKRIDGE, Richard. *Die Laughing.* nd. BC. VG/VG. P3. $10.00

LOCKRIDGE, Richard. *Something Up a Sleeve.* 1972. Lippincott. 1st ed. F/F. P3. $15.00

LOCKRIDGE & LOCKRIDGE. *Death by Association.* 1952. Lippincott. VG. M21. $5.00

LOCKRIDGE & LOCKRIDGE. *Death Has a Small Voice.* nd. BC. VG/VG. P3. $10.00

LOCKRIDGE & LOCKRIDGE. *Distant Clue.* nd. BC. VG/VG. P3. $10.00

LOCKRIDGE & LOCKRIDGE. *First Come, First Kill.* 1962. Lippincott. 1st ed. G+/dj. P3. $20.00

LOCKRIDGE & LOCKRIDGE. *Murder Has Its Points.* nd. BC. VG/VG. P3. $10.00

LOCKRIDGE & LOCKRIDGE. *Night of Shadows.* nd. BC. VG/VG. P3. $10.00

LOCKRIDGE & LOCKRIDGE. *Practice To Deceive.* nd. BC. VG/VG. P3. $10.00

LOCKRIDGE & LOCKRIDGE. *With One Stone.* nd. BC. VG/VG. P3. $10.00

LOCKWOOD, Douglas. *I, the Aboriginal.* 1962. Rigby. 2nd imp. sgn. 240p. VG/dj. M20. $15.00

LOCKWOOD, E.H. *Book of Curves.* 1961. Cambridge. 199p. F/dj. K4. $20.00

LOCKWOOD, Frank C. *With Padre Kino on the Trail.* 1934. AZ U. ils/fld map. 142p. NF/wrp. B19. $45.00

LOCKWOOD, Sarah M. *Antiques.* 1930. Doubleday Doran. 161p. VG. H1. $18.00

LOCKYER, Herbert. *All the Apostles of the Bible.* 1972. Zondervan. 278p. VG/dj. B29. $9.00

LOCKYER, Herbert. *All the Promises of the Bible.* 1977. Zondervan. 351p. VG. B29. $8.50

LOCKYER, J. Norman. *Elements of Astronomy.* 1878. NY. Appleton. 8vo. 312p. quarter leather/cloth. G. K5. $22.00

LOCY, William. *Biology & Its Makers.* 1936. Holt. 477p. xl. A10. $12.00

LODDIGES, Conrad. *Botanical Cabinet Consisting of Coloured Delineations...* 1817-1821. London. 6 vol. sm 4to. 600 floral pl. full morocco. C6. $1,000.00

LODGE, Edmund. *Portraits of Illustrious Personages of Great Britain.* 1823-1828.. London. 32 parts in 8 vol. folio. w/160 proofs on India. VG+. C6. $275.00

LODIN, Johannes Gustavus. *Dissertatio Chirurgica de Tumoribus Salivalibus.* 1785. Upsaliae. 4to. 24p. G7. $35.00

LODS, Adolphe. *Israel From Its Beginnings to Middle of 8th Century.* 1953. Knopf. 1st ed. 512p. xl. VG. W1. $15.00

LOEB, Anton. *Wizard of Oz for Ages 5-9.* 1950. Random. K2. $6.00

LOEB, Jacques. *Mechanistic Conception of Life.* 1912. Chicago. 1st ed. pres. H4. $50.00

LOEB, Robert H. *Nip Ahoy: The Picture Bar Guide.* 1954. NY. ils Joel King. 96p. F/F. B14. $30.00

LOENGARD, John. *Pictures Under Discussion.* 1987. Amphoto. 1st ed. inscr to Joan Rivers. VG+/VG+. S9. $50.00

LOENING, Grover. *Air Road Will Widen!* 1969. NY. ils. 41p. VG. B18. $35.00

LOEWENBERG, Robert J. *Equality on the OR Frontier: Jason Lee & Methodist Mission.* 1976. Seattle/London. WA U. 1st ed. 8vo. 287p. blk cloth. M/dj. P4. $30.00

LOEWINSOHN, Ron. *Sea, Around Us.* 1968. Blk Sparrow. 1st ed. sgn. 1/250. F/sewn wrp. B2. $35.00

LOFTING, Hugh. *Doctor Dolittle, a Treasury.* 1967. Lippincott. 3rd prt. 4to. 246p. NF/case. D6. $30.00

LOFTING, Hugh. *Doctor Dolittle's Caravan.* 1926. Stokes. 1st ed. VG+. M5. $75.00

LOFTING, Hugh. *Doctor Dolittle's Circus.* 1924. Stokes. 1st ed. 4to. ils. bl stp cloth. 379p. NF. D6. $70.00

LOFTING, Hugh. *Doctor Dolittle's Garden.* 1927. Stokes. 1st ed. 327p. VG+. P2. $75.00

LOFTING, Hugh. *Doctor Dolittle's Zoo.* nd. Lippincott. 23rd prt. 8vo. 338p. VG/G. A3. $15.00

LOFTING, Hugh. *Dr Dolittle's Birthday Book.* 1935. Stokes. 1st ed. 16mo. gilt bl cloth. VG. D6. $70.00

LOFTING, Hugh. *Twilight of Magic.* 1930. Stokes. 1st ed. 8vo. purple cloth. NF/G. D6. $90.00

LOFTS, Norah. *Hauntings: Is There Anybody There?* 1975. Doubleday. 1st Am ed. F/NF. N3. $15.00

LOGAN, Jeffrey. *Complete Book of Outer Space.* 1953. NY. Maco Magazine Corp. sm 4to. 144p. yel cloth. VG. K5. $25.00

LOGAN, John. *Ghosts of the Heart.* 1960. Chicago. inscr/dtd 1960. F/NF. V1. $45.00

LOGUEN, J.W. *Rev JW Loguen, As a Slave & As a Freeman. A Narrative...* 1859. NY. JGK Truair. 1st ed. 8vo. 451p. cloth. M1. $275.00

LOKVIG, Tor. *Star Trek the Motion Picture Pop-Up Book.* 1980. Wanderer. 1st ed. MTI. VG. P3. $15.00

LOMAX, Beatrice. *Pigs Have a Party.* nd. Pitkin. ils Hilda Boswell. G. B10. $35.00

LOMBARDI, Frank. *Gypsy Blood.* 1972. Poughkeepsie, NY. Davison. possible 1st ed. VG/wrp. C8. $12.00

LOMBARDO, Thomas J. *Reciprocity of Perceiver & Environment.* 1987. Hillsdale, NJ. 396p. prt laminated brd. G1. $37.50

LONDON, Charmain. *Our Hawaii.* 1917. NY. Macmillan. 1st ed. photos. gilt bl cloth. NF. H5. $250.00

LONDON, Darryl. *Man of Respect.* 1986. Lyle Stuart. VG/fair. P3. $10.00

LONDON, Ephraim. *World of Law, Law in Literature, Law As Literature.* 2 Vols. 1960. Simon Schuster. M11. $85.00

LONDON, Jack. *Apostate.* 1906. Girard, KS. Appeal to Reason. 1st separate ed. 16p. complete. H5. $175.00

LONDON, Jack. *Before Adam.* 1907. Macmillan. 1st ed. VG. P3. $80.00

LONDON, Jack. *Before Adam.* 1917. Review of Reviews Co. rpt. G+. M21. $5.00

LONDON, Jack. *Cruise of the Snark.* 1911. NY. Macmillan. 1st ed. 8vo. 340p. gilt bl cloth. NF. H5. $600.00

LONDON, Jack. *Daughters of the Rich: A Play.* 1971. Holmes Book Co. 1st ed thus. sc. 24p. M. A18. $20.00

LONDON, Jack. *Dutch Courage & Other Stories.* 1922. Macmillan. 1st ed. NF/VG. B2. $2,000.00

LONDON, Jack. *Dutch Courage & Other Stories.* 1922. NY. Macmillan. 1st ed. 8vo. 180p. blk/gilt stp red cloth. NF/case. H5. $2,750.00

LONDON, Jack. *Faith of Men & Other Stories.* 1904. NY. Macmillan. 1st ed. 8vo. 286p. bl cloth. VG/morocco case. H5. $500.00

LONDON, Jack. *Game.* 1905. NY. Macmillan. 1st ed/2nd issue (rubber stp copyright p). teg. VG. H5. $200.00

LONDON, Jack. *God of His Fathers & Other Stories.* 1901. McClure Phillips. 1st ed. 8vo. 299p. gilt bl cloth. G/case. H5. $500.00

LONDON, Jack. *Hearts of Three.* 1920. Macmillan. 1st ed. 8vo. 373p. red cloth. maroon cloth/case. H5. $200.00

LONDON, Jack. *House of Pride & Other Stories.* 1912. Macmillan. 1st ed. 8vo. 232p. pict gr cloth. G. H5. $300.00

LONDON, Jack. *Klondike Trilogy.* 1983. Santa Barbara. Neville. 1/300. 4to. 41p. cream buckram. F. H5. $75.00

LONDON, Jack. *Little Lady of the Big House.* 1916. Macmillan. 1st ed. pict cloth. NF. A18. $60.00

LONDON, Jack. *Love of Life & Other Stories.* 1907. NY. Macmillan. 1st ed. 8vo. gilt bl cloth. VG. H5. $300.00

LONDON, Jack. *Michael, Brother of Jerry.* 1917. NY. Macmillan. 1st ed. 8vo. 344p. VG. H5. $150.00

LONDON, Jack. *Moon Face & Other Stories.* 1906. NY. 1st ed. 273p. cloth. G. B18. $135.00

LONDON, Jack. *Mutiny of the Elsinore.* 1914. NY. Macmillan. 1st ed. 8vo. 378p. stp yel cloth. NF/NF. H5. $2,000.00

LONDON, Jack. *Scarlet Plague.* 1915. NY. Macmillan. 1st ed. 8vo. 181p. stp maroon cloth. NF. H5. $350.00

LONDON, Jack. *Sea Sprite & the Shooting Star.* Nov 1932. private prt. 1st ed. F. H5. $150.00

LONDON, Jack. *Smoke Bellew.* 1912. NY. Century. 1st ed. 8vo. 385p. pict bl cloth. VG. H5. $200.00

LONDON, Jack. *Son of the Wolf.* 1900. Houghton Mifflin. 1st ed. 8vo. 251p. silvered gray cloth. NF. H5. $850.00

LONDON, Jack. *Sun-Dog Trail.* 1951. World. 1st ed. VG. P3. $25.00

LONDON, Jack. *Valley of the Moon.* nd. Grosset Dunlap. G+. P3. $15.00

LONDON, Jack. *White Fang.* 1906. NY. 1st ed. ils. 327p. pict cloth. G. B18. $150.00

LONDON, Jack. *White Fang.* 1906. NY. Macmillan. 1st ed. 327p. Sangorski Sutcliffe/Zaehnsdorf bdg. F. H5. $375.00

LONG, A.L. *Memoirs of Robert E Lee.* 1887. NY. Stoddart. 707p. VG. H7. $65.00

LONG, Esmond. *History of Pathology.* 1928. Baltimore. 1st ed. 291p. A13. $125.00

LONG, Frank Belknap. *Horror From Hills.* 1963. Arkham. 1st ed/1st issue. F/F. T2. $95.00

LONG, Frank Belknap. *In Mayan Splendor.* 1977. Arkham. 1st ed. F/F. w/sgn & dtd 1937 postcard. F4. $65.00

LONG, Frank Belknap. *It Was the Day of the Robot.* 1964. Dobson. 1st ed. VG/VG. P3. $30.00

LONG, Frank Belknap. *Rim of the Unknown.* 1972. Arkham. 1st ed. 1/3650. F/F. T2. $65.00

LONG, Haniel. *If He Can Make Her So.* 1968. Frontier. 1st ed. 85p. F/NF. B19. $50.00

LONG, Haniel. *Pinon Country.* 1941. DSP. 3rd ed. 327p. NF/ragged. B19. $25.00

LONG, Harmon. *Silverface.* nd. Rich Cowan. VG/G. P3. $20.00

LONG, Huey P. *Every Man a King.* 1933. Nat Book Co. 1st ed. F/NF. B2. $75.00

LONG, Jeff. *Duel of Eagles: Mexican & US Fight for the Alamo.* 1990. NY. BOMC. 431p. F/F. A17. $10.00

LONG, John Davis. *Journal of...* 1923. np. 1st/only ed. 250p. VG. E5. $35.00

LONG, Julius. *Keep the Coffins Coming.* 1947. Messner. 1st ed. VG/VG. P3. $25.00

LONG, Lyda Belknap; see Long, Frank Belknap.

LONG, Margaret. *Shadow of the Arrow.* 1950. Caxton. revised ed. ils/maps. F/NF. B34. $75.00

LONG, Max Freedom. *Growing Into the Light.* 1955. Santa Monica, CA. DeVorss. 177p. F. H1. $45.00

LONG, Max Freedom. *Huna Code in Religions.* (1965). Vista, CA. Huna Research Pub. 306p. F/G. H1. $55.00

LONG, Paul. *Training Pointing Dogs: All Answers to All Your Questions.* 1985 (1974). NY. Lyons Burford. 98p. ils. M/wrp. R2. $12.00

LONG, Stephen. *From Pittsburgh to the Rocky Mountains...1819-1820.* 1988. Golden. Fulcrum. 8vo. ils. 410p. burgundy cloth. M/M. P4. $20.00

LONG, William J. *School of the Woods.* 1902. Ginn. 1st ed. ils Charles Copeland. 361p. VG. M20. $35.00

LONGFELLOW, Henry Wadsworth. *Aftermath.* 1873. Boston. Osgood. 1st ed. sgn/dtd 1873. cloth. VG. B4. $2,000.00

LONGFELLOW, Henry Wadsworth. *Divine Tragedy.* 1871. Boston. Osgood. 1st ed. 12mo. 150p. G. H1. $25.00

LONGFELLOW, Henry Wadsworth. *Evangeline.* 1909. Reilly Britton. ils John Rea Neill. 172p. VG. M10. $50.00

LONGFELLOW, Henry Wadsworth. *Hyperion, a Romance.* 1845. Boston. Ticknor Fields. 1st ed. gilt emb purple bdg. VG. E5. $35.00

LONGFELLOW, Henry Wadsworth. *New Eng Tragedies.* 1868. Boston. Ticknor Fields. 1st ed. 179p. red cloth. VG. M20. $30.00

LONGFELLOW, Henry Wadsworth. *Poems by...* 1901. James Pott. Vignette ed. ils Charles H Johnson. 523p. gilt bdg. VG. S11. $18.00

LONGFELLOW, Henry Wadsworth. *Song of Hiawatha.* 1855. Ticknor Fields. 1st Am ed/1st prt (Dove on p96). w/sgn letter. VG. C6. $2,500.00

LONGFELLOW, Henry Wadsworth. *Song of Hiawatha.* 1911. Houghton Mifflin. 1st ed. ils Parrish/Remington/Wyeth. 142p. VG. rare. D6. $350.00

LONGFELLOW, Henry Wadsworth. *Voices of the Night.* 1839. Cambridge. Owen. 1st ed/author's 1st book. 144p. VG. B14. $150.00

LONGFORD, Lord. *Abraham Lincoln.* 1975. Putnam. 1st Am ed. ils. 231p. F/dj. M10. $15.00

LONGLAND, Julia. *Clear Round! Interviews by...* 1978. NY. Mayflower. 1st Am ed. VG/VG. O3. $25.00

LONGLEY, Pearl Dorr. *Rebirth of Venkata Reddi.* 1946. Judson. 2nd ed. VG. P3. $8.00

LONGSTREET, James. *From Manassas to Appomattox.* 1991. rpt of 1880s ed. 690p. dj. O8. $12.50

LONGYEAR, Barry B. *City of Barboo.* 1980. Berkley Putnam. 1st ed. sgn. F/F. P3. $25.00

LONGYEAR, Barry B. *Sea of Glass.* 1987. St Martin. 1st ed. sgn. F/F. P3. $25.00

LOOFBOUROW, Leonidas Latimer. *In Search of God's Gold: Story of Christian Pioneering...* 1950. San Francisco. 1st ed. 313p. cloth. F/dj. M8. $37.50

LOOMES, Brian. *Watchmakers & Clockmakers of the World.* 1976. London. NAG Pr. 1st ed. 8vo. 263p. F/F. A8. $20.00

LOOMIS, A. *Figure Drawing for All Its Worth.* 1960. Viking. VG/VG. B5. $75.00

LOOMIS, Alfred F. *Fair Winds in the Far Baltic.* 1928. NY/London. ils. 265p. T7. $24.00

LOOMIS, Elias. *Treatise on Algebra.* 1879 (1869). Harper. revised ed. 384p. leather. H1. $8.00

LOOS, Anita. *Kiss Hollywood Good-By.* Vol 2. 1974. NY. 1st ed. inscr. 16p photos. VG/NF. A11. $35.00

LOPEZ, Barry. *Arctic Dreams: Imagination & Desire in a Northern Landscape.* 1986. Scribner. 1st ed. sgn. F/F. A18/B3. $75.00

LOPEZ, Barry. *Crossing Open Ground.* 1987. Scribner. 1st ed. sgn. F/F. A18. $35.00

LOPEZ, Barry. *Crow & Weasel.* 1993. Harper Perennial. 1st ed thus. sgn. ils Tom Pohrt. M. A18. $17.50

LOPEZ, Barry. *Desert Notes.* 1976. Sheed Andrews McMeel. 1st ed/author's 1st book. sgn. F/F. L3. $550.00

LOPEZ, Barry. *Field Notes: Grace Note of the Canyon Wren.* 1994. Knopf. 1st ed. sgn. M/M. A18. $35.00

LOPEZ, Barry. *Giving Birth to Thunder, Sleeping With His Daughter...* 1977. Sheed Andrews McMeel. 1st ed/author's 2nd book. inscr. F/F. B4. $300.00

LOPEZ, Barry. *Of Wolves & Men.* 1978. Scribner. 1st ed/author's 3rd book. F/F. L3. $250.00

LOPEZ, Barry. *Rediscovery of N America.* 1990. Lexington, KY. 1st ed. sgn. F/F. L3. $85.00

LOPEZ, Barry. *River Notes: Dance of Herons.* 1979. Andrews McMeel. 1st ed. sgn. F/VG. A18. $60.00

LOPEZ, Barry. *Winter Count.* 1981. Scribner. 1st ed. F/clip. B3. $125.00

LOPEZ DE GOMARA, Francisco. *Cortes.* 1965. Berkeley. 2nd prt. 425p. VG. F3. $25.00

LORAC, E.C.R. *Screen for Murder.* 1948. Crime Club. 1st ed. xl. dj. P3. $13.00

LORAIN, Peter. *Clandestine Operations.* 1983. NY. 1st ed. 185p. F/F. A17. $15.00

LORAINE, Philip. *Crackpot.* 1993. London. Harper Collins. 1st ed. F/F. S6. $22.50

LORAINE, Philip. *WIL One to Curtis.* 1967. Random. 1st ed. F/F. P3. $15.00

LORANT, Stefan. *Lincoln: Picture Story of His Life.* 1952. Harper. 256p. F/G. H1. $20.00

LORANT, Stefan. *Lincoln: Picture Story of His Life.* 1952. ils/photos. 256p. VG. O8. $18.50

LORANT, Stefan. *Pittsburgh: Story of an American City.* 1964. Doubleday. 2nd prt. 520p. VG/G+. N2. $15.00

LORCA, Frederico. *Lorca.* 1949. Paris. 1/995. French text. NF/wrp. S9. $125.00

LORD, Arthur Hardy. *Eliot Church of Newton, MA: Hist of 100 Years 1845-1945.* ca 1945. np. 1st ed. 50p. cloth. VG. M8. $27.50

LORD, Garland. *Murder's Little Helper.* 1941. Doubleday. 1st ed/author's 1st book. F/NF. B4. $75.00

LORD, Glenn. *Last Celt.* 1976. Donald Grant. 1st ed. VG/VG. P3. $30.00

LORD, Henry. *Displaye of Two Forraigne Sects in East Indias...* 1630. London. Constable. 2 parts in 1. 4to. old leather/rebacked suede. H10. $425.00

LORD, John P. *Maine Townsman; or, Laws for Regulation of Towns.* 1844. Boston. Lewis Potter. contemporary sheep. M11. $150.00

LORD, Phillips. *Aboard the Seth Parker.* 1934. Dayton, OH. Frigidaire Sales. pamphlet. photos. unp. T7. $12.00

LORD, Walter. *Blue & White Devils.* 1984. Battery Pr. 1st ed. inscr. 173p. VG/VG. S11. $18.00

LORD, Walter. *Freemantle Diary.* 1954. np. 1st ed. 304p. map ep. O8. $18.50

LORD, Walter. *Incredible Victory.* 1967. NY. index. 331p. VG/VG. A17. $8.50

LORD & SPRAGUE. *Cases on the Law of Admiralty.* 1926. St Paul. West Pub. buckram. M11. $50.00

LORENZ, Adolf. *My Life & Work: Search for a Missing Glove.* 1936. NY. pres. 352p. w/sgn letter. G7. $75.00

LORENZ, D.E. *New Mediterranean Traveler.* 1925. Revell. 11th revised ed. 357p. xl. VG. W1. $16.00

LORENZ, D.E. *Round the World Traveler.* 1925. Revell. 3rd ed. 464p. VG. W1. $10.00

LORIMER, Norma. *By the Waters of Egypt.* ca 1910. Stokes. 1st ed. ils/maps. 314p. G. W1. $12.00

LORING, Rosamond B. *Marbled Papers: Address Delivered...* Nov 16 1932. Boston. author's 1st book. 1/149. M/case. B14. $295.00

LORTZ, Richard. *Lovers Living, Lovers Dead.* 1977. Putnam. 1st ed. NF/NF. P3. $25.00

LORUS & MILNE. *Nature of Life: Earth, Plants, Animals, Man...* 1972. Crown. 4to. ils. 316p. F/dj. M10. $7.50

LOSSKY, Vladimir. *Mystical Theology of the Eastern Church.* 1973. Cambridge. James Clark. 3rd imp. 252p. VG/VG. B33. $35.00

LOTH, J.T. *Tourist's Conversational Guide in English, French, German...* ca 1895-1900. Glasgow. Bryce. Mite Series. 28x20mm. 126p. gilt red roan. F. B24. $425.00

LOTHROP, Eaton S. Jr. *Century of Cameras.* 1973. Dobbs Ferry. Morgan. 1st ed. 8vo. F/F. S9. $40.00

LOTT, Milton. *Dance Back the Buffalo.* 1959. Houghton Mifflin. 1st ed. F/F. B34. $40.00

LOTT, Milton. *Last Hunt.* 1979. Gregg. 1st prt/author's 1st novel. M/M. B34. $40.00

LOTTINVILLE, Savoie. *Rhetoric of Hist.* 1976. OK U. 1st ed. M/dj. A18. $20.00

LOTTMAN, Herbert R. *How Cities Are Saved.* 1976. Universe Books. VG/dj. N2. $7.50

LOTTMAN, Herbert R. *Petain: Hero or Traitor.* 1985. NY. 1st ed. 444p. F/F. A17. $10.00

LOTZE, Rudolf Hermann. *Outlines of Psychology Dictated Portions of Lectures of...* 1973. NY. Arno. 150p. prt gray cloth. G1. $30.00

LOUDON, J.C. *Encyclopedia of Cottage, Farm & Villa Architecture...* 1839. London. new ed. thick 8vo. ils. contemporary bdg. C6. $200.00

LOUIE, David Wong. *Pangs of Love: Stories.* 1991. Knopf. 1st ed/author's 1st book. F/F. A14. $30.00

LOUIS, Pierre Charles A. *Recherches Anatomico-Pathologiques sur La Phithisie.* 1825. Paris. Chez Gabon. 1st ed. half title. 560p. rebound. uncut/foxed. G7. $595.00

LOULIS, John C. *Greek Communist Party, 1940-1944.* 1982. London. 8vo. 224p. cloth. dj. O2. $30.00

LOUNSBURY, Thomas. *James Fenimore Cooper.* 1883. Houghton Mifflin. 1st ed. VG. A18. $25.00

LOUNSBURY, Thomas. *Pro-Slavery Overthrown & True Principles of Abolitionism...* 1847. NY. Henry B Bennett. 16mo. 155p. cloth. M1. $150.00

LOUSLEY, J.E. *Wild Flowers of Chalk & Limestone.* 1950. London. photos/maps/diagrams. 254p. F/dj. B26. $29.00

LOVALLO & SANDERS. *Agatha Christie Companion, Complete Guide...* 1984. Delacorte. 1st ed. 550p. F/F. A4. $40.00

LOVE, Edmund G. *Hourglass: Hist of 7th Infantry Division in WWII.* 1950. Infantry Journal. 1st ed. photos/maps. 496p. VG. A17. $30.00

LOVE, John. *Geodaesia; or, Art of Surveying & Measuring of Land...* 1760. London. Rivington. 7th ed. 196p. old leather. H10. $100.00

LOVE, Robertus. *Poems All the Way From Pike.* 1904. St Louis. Pan-American Pr. VG. N2. $7.50

LOVECRAFT, H.P. *At the Mountains of Madness.* 1964. Arkham. 1st ed. F/NF. M2. $125.00

LOVECRAFT, H.P. *Dagon.* 1965. Arkham. 1st ed. F/NF. M2. $120.00

LOVECRAFT, H.P. *Dark Brotherhood.* 1966. Arkham. 1st ed. F/dj. F4. $120.00

LOVECRAFT, H.P. *History of the Necromomicon.* 1977. W Warwick. Necronomicon. 2nd ed. 1/500. F/wrp. scarce. T2. $75.00

LOVECRAFT, H.P. *Horror in the Museum.* 1970. Arbor. 1st ed. F/F. P3. $45.00

LOVECRAFT, H.P. *Tales of the Ctlulhu Mythos.* 1990. Arkham. 1st ed thus. F/F. T2. $35.00

LOVECRAFT, H.P. *Watchers Out of Time & Others.* 1974. Arkham. 1st ed/1st prt. 1/5070. F/F. T2. $45.00

LOVELL, Bernard. *Out of the Zenith, Jodrell Bank 1957-1970.* 1973. Harper Row. lg 8vo. ils. VG/dj. K5. $18.00

LOVELL, Marc. *How Green Was My Apple.* 1984. NY. Doubleday. 1st Am ed. F/F. S6. $20.00

LOVELL, Marc. *Imitation Thieves.* 1971. Crime Club. 1st ed. VG/VG. P3. $15.00

LOVELL, Mary S. *Sound of Wings: Life of Amelia Earhart.* 1989. NY. 1st ed. 420p. F/F. A17. $10.00

LOVESEY, Peter. *Bertie & the Tinman.* 1987. Bodley Head. 1st ed. F/F. P3. $20.00

LOVESEY, Peter. *Butchers & Other Stories of Crime.* 1985. Mysterious. 1st Am ed. sgn. F/F. O4. $15.00

LOVESEY, Peter. *Case of Spirits.* 1975. London. Macmillan. 1st ed. F/F. M15. $45.00

LOVESEY, Peter. *Keystone.* 1983. Pantheon. 1st ed. F/F. O4/P3. $15.00

LOVESEY, Peter. *Last Detective.* 1991. Doubleday. 1st Am ed. sgn. F/F. M15. $27.50

LOVESEY, Peter. *Last Detective.* 1991. Doubleday. 1st ed. F/F. P3. $18.00

LOVESEY, Peter. *Last Detective.* 1991. London. Scribner. 1st ed. F/F. S6. $30.00

LOVESEY, Peter. *On the Edge.* 1989. London. Mysterious/Century. 1st ed. sgn. F/F. S6. $40.00

LOVESEY, Peter. *Rough Cider.* 1986. Mysterious. 1st ed. sgn. F/F. O4. $15.00

LOVESEY, Peter. *Spider Girl.* 1980. London. Cassell. 1st ed. F/F. M15. $35.00

LOVESEY, Peter. *Swing, Swing Together.* 1976. Dodd Mead. 1st Am ed. F/NF. B2. $35.00

LOVESEY, Peter. *Waxwork.* 1978. London. Macmillan. 1st ed. sgn. F/F. M15. $50.00

LOVETT, C.S. *Dealing With the Devil.* 1967. Personal Christianity. 158p. VG. B29. $4.00

LOVETT, Charlie. *Everybody's Guide to Book Collecting.* 1993. Overland Park, KS. Write Brain Pub. 1st ed. 8vo. 80p. M. D6. $9.00

LOVETT, Lois. *Little Lost Kitten.* ca 1962. Random. unp. VG. B10. $10.00

LOVETT, Sarah. *Dangerous Attachments.* 1995. Villard. ARC. NF/wrp. B2. $30.00

LOW, David. *Cartoon Hist of Our Times.* 1939. NY. 173p. VG. B14. $125.00

LOW, James G. *Memorials of Church of St John the Evangelist...* 1891. Montrose. 1st ed. 208p. cloth. VG. M8. $37.50

LOW, Sidney. *Egypt in Transition.* 1914. Macmillan. 1st ed. 8vo. 316p. VG. W1. $9.00

LOWE, Kenneth. *Haze of Evil.* 1953. Crime Club. 1st ed. VG. P3. $12.00

LOWELL, James Russell. *Anti-Slavery Papers of...* 1902. Boston. 2 vol set. 1st ed. 1/525. F. C2. $150.00

LOWELL, James Russell. *Courtin', by Lowell.* 1938. Collingswood, NJ. private prt. 21x20mm. 1/49. ils J Streeter. brn calf. B24. $750.00

LOWELL, James Russell. *Latest Literary Essays & Addresses.* 1892. Houghton Mifflin. Clarence Darrow's copy. calf. M11. $1,500.00

LOWELL, James Russell. *Poems.* 1844. London. CE Mudie. 1st UK ed. 12mo. gilt brn cloth. VG+. Q1. $175.00

LOWELL, Robert. *Land of Unlikeness.* 1944. Cummington Pr. 1st ed/author's 1st book. 1/250. prt bl brd. NF. C6. $3,000.00

LOWELL, Robert. *Life Studies.* 1959. NY. 1st ed. sgn. NF/NF clip. C2. $275.00

LOWELL, Robert. *Life Studies.* 1959. NY. 1st ed. VG/VG. B5. $60.00

LOWELL, Robert. *Lord Weary's Castle.* 1946. Harcourt Brace. VG/dj. scarce. H4. $150.00

LOWELL, Robert. *Old Glory.* 1965. NY. 1st ed. F/F. A17. $35.00

LOWELL, Robert. *Voyage & Other Version of Poems by Baudelaire.* 1968. London. Faber. 1/200. sgns. 8 mc pl. gilt bl/purple bdg. F/purple case. H5. $400.00

LOWENTHAL, James. *Hidden Sun: Solar Eclipses & Astro-Photography.* 1984. NY. Avon. ils/photos. 107p. pb. K5. $6.00

LOWIE, Robert H. *Culture & Ethnology.* 1929. NY. Peter Smith. 189p. xl. K4. $12.50

LOWITH, Karl. *Meaning in Hist.* 1958. Chicago. Phoenix. 257p. wrp. G1. $17.50

LOWNDES, I. *Modern Greek & English Lexicon...Modern Greek Grammar.* 1837. Corfu. thick 8vo. 671p. new quarter calf/brd. O2. $650.00

LOWREY, Janette Sebring. *Annunciata & the Shepherds.* ca 1938. Gentry Pr. ils Willard Clark. VG. B10. $25.00

LOWRY, Malcolm. *October Ferry to Gabriola.* 1970. NY. 1st ed. F/wrinkled. A17. $20.00

LOWRY, Malcolm. *Under the Volcano.* 1947. Reynal Hitchcock. 1st ed. 8vo. 375p. red lettered gray cloth. VG/dj. H5. $750.00

LOWRY, Robert. *Bad Girl Marie.* 1942. Cincinnati. 1/100 #d. sgn Lowry/Flora. NF/labeled wrp. A11. $65.00

LOWRY, Robert. *Casualty.* 1946. NY. 1st ed/author's 1st novel. sgn. F/VG+. A11. $55.00

LT. WOODARD, M.D. see Silverberg, Robert.

LUBBOCK, Basil. *Adventures by Sea From Art of Old Time.* 1925. London. The Studio. 1/1750. 22 mtd mc pl/93 halftones. teg. VG. T7. $215.00

LUBBOCK, Basil. *Bully Hayes: South Sea Pirate.* 1931. Boston. photos. VG. M17. $50.00

LUBBOCK, Basil. *Log of the Cutty Sark.* 1924. Lauriat. 422p. VG/dj. M20. $80.00

LUBBOCK, Basil. *Round the Horn Before the Mast.* 1928 (1902). Dutton. 375p. VG/tattered. M20. $25.00

LUBBOCK, Percy. *Earlham.* 1930. London. Cape. 12th prt. 16mo. 253p. G+. V3. $12.00

LUBKE, Wilhelm. *Ecclesiastical Art in Germany During Middle Ages.* 1873. Edinburgh. Jack. 299p. H10. $22.50

LUCAS, C.P. *Historical Geography of the British Colonies, Vol II.* 1905. London. Oxford. 2nd ed. 12mo. 348p. VG. B11. $45.00

LUCAS, Cary. *Unfinished Business.* 1947. Simon Schuster. 1st ed. VG. P3. $10.00

LUCAS, E.V. *Book of Queen's Dolls' House/...Queen's Dolls' House Lib.* 1924. London. Methuen. 2 vol. 1/1500. b&w ils. linen-backed bl brd. F. B24. $675.00

LUCAS, E.V. *Wanderer Among Pictures.* (1924). Garden City. 289p. F. H1. $8.00

LUCAS, E.V. *Wanderer in London.* 1906. Methuen. 1st ed. gilt bl cloth. VG+. M5. $20.00

LUCAS, F.L. *Woman Clothed With the Sun & Other Stories.* 1938. Simon Schuster. 1st ed. VG. M2. $15.00

LUCAS, George; see Foster, Alan Dean.

LUCAS, John. *Basic Jazz on Long Play.* 1954. Northfield. Carleton Jazz Club. 1st ed. 104p. NF/wrp. B2. $30.00

LUCAS & MORROW. *What a Life!* 1975. NY. 1st Am ed. intro/sgn John Ashbery. F/8vo wrp. A11. $50.00

LUCE, Helen. *In the Midst of Death.* 1980. Macmillan. 1st ed. NF/NF. P3. $15.00

LUCE, R. Duncan. *Readings in Mathematical Psychology. Vol II.* 1965. Wiley. F. K4. $20.00

LUCE, Robert B. *Day the Bicycles Disappeared.* ca 1969. np. inscr pres. 61p. VG. B10. $12.00

LUCHETTI, Cathy. *Under God's Spell: Frontier Evangelists 1772-1915.* 1989. HBJ. 1st ed. obl 4to. F/F. A17. $20.00

LUCIE-SMITH, Edward. *Holding Your Eights Hands.* 1969. Doubleday. 1st ed. NF/pict wrp. N3. $5.00

LUCKHARDT, Mildred Corell. *Brave Journey: Launching of the US.* ca 1975. Abingdon. ils Tom Armstrong. VG/fair. B10. $10.00

LUCKINGHAM, Bradford. *Urban SW: Profile Hist of Albuquerque, El Paso, Phoenix...* 1982. TX W Pr. ils/notes/index. 161p. NF/wrp. B19. $10.00

LUDLUM, Robert. *Aquitaine Progression.* 1984. Random. 1st ed. VG/VG. P3. $35.00

LUDLUM, Robert. *Bourne Identity.* 1980. Richard Marak. 1st ed. sgn. VG/VG. O4. $35.00

LUDLUM, Robert. *Bourne Supremacy.* 1986. Franklin Lib. 1st ed. sgn. leather. VG+. A1. $30.00

LUDLUM, Robert. *Bourne Supremacy.* 1986. Random. 1st ed. F/F. P3. $25.00

LUDLUM, Robert. *Bourne Ultimatum.* 1990. Random. 1st ed. sgn. 1/350. F/F. M15. $75.00

LUDLUM, Robert. *Chancellor Manuscript.* 1977. NY. 1st ed. VG/VG. B5. $25.00

LUDLUM, Robert. *Cry of the Halidon.* 1974. Delacorte. 1st ed. VG/VG. O4. $40.00

LUDLUM, Robert. *Gemini Contenders.* 1976. Dial. 1st ed. sgn. VG/NF. O4. $30.00

LUDLUM, Robert. *Osterman Weekend.* 1972. World. 1st ed. sgn. VG/G. O4. $65.00

LUDLUM, Robert. *Parsifal Mosaic.* 1982. NY. Random. 1st ed. incr. F/F. S6. $75.00

LUDLUM, Robert. *Road to Omaha.* 1992. Random. 1st ed. F/F. P3. $24.00

LUDLUM, Robert. *Trevayne.* 1973. Delacorte. 1st ed. NF/NF. B2. $100.00

LUDMERER, Kenneth. *Genetics & American Society: Historical Appraisal.* 1972. Baltimore. 1st ed. 222p. A13. $35.00

LUDWIG, Coy. *Maxfield Parrish.* 1975. Watson Guptill. 3rd prt. 223p. VG/VG. S11. $35.00

LUDWIG, Emil. *Nile, the Life Story of a River.* 1939. Garden City. trans MH Lindsay. tall 8vo. VG. W1. $12.00

LUDWIG, Emil. *Wilhelm Der Zweite.* 1926. Berlin. German text. 495p. gilt cloth. VG. A17. $12.50

LUEDERS, Edward. *Writing Natural Hist: Dialogues With Authors.* 1989. UT U. 1st ed. sgn. sc. A18. $20.00

LUIJPEN, William A. *Phenomenology & Metaphysics.* 1965. Pittsburgh. Duquesne. 202p. VG. B33. $20.00

LUKACS, Georg. *Die Theorie des Romans.* 1920. Berlin. Paul Cassirer. true 1st ed. paper brd. F. B4. $600.00

LUKEMAN, Tim. *Rajan.* 1979. Doubleday. 1st ed. F/F. P3. $15.00

LUKENS, Adam. *Conquest of Life.* 1960. Avalon. 1st ed. F/F. M2. $15.00

LUKENS, Adam. *Sea People.* 1959. Avalon. 1st ed. F/F. P3. $25.00

LUKENS, John. *Adders Abounding.* 1954. Hodder Stoughton. 1st ed. VG. P3. $20.00

LUMEIJ, J.L. *Methods of Psychology & Psychiatry.* 1957. Netherlands. Van Gorcum. 243p. G. K4. $25.00

LUMLEY, Brian. *Beneath the Moors.* 1974. Arkham. 1st ed. F/F. P3. $40.00

LUMLEY, Brian. *Blood Brothers.* 1992. Tor. 1st ed. sgn. F/dj. F4. $35.00

LUMLEY, Brian. *Burrowers Beneath.* 1988. Buffalo. Ganley. 1st hc ed. F/F. T2. $22.50

LUMLEY, Brian. *Caller of the Black.* 1971. Arkham. 1st ed. F/F. P3. $45.00

LUMLEY, Brian. *Compleat Khash: Vol One. Never a Backward GLance.* 1991. Buffalo. Ganley. 1st ed/deluxe issue. sgn. 1/300. F/F. T2. $40.00

LUMLEY, Brian. *Deadspeak.* 1990. London. Kinnell. 1st ed. F/F. T2. $20.00

LUMLEY, Brian. *Elysia: The Coming of Cthulhu.* 1989. Buffalo. Ganley. 1st ed. F/F. T2. $25.00

LUMLEY, Brian. *Hero of Dreams.* 1986. Buffalo. Ganley. 1st ed. sgn. F/F. T2. $30.00

LUMLEY, Brian. *Horror at Oakdeene & Others.* 1977. Arkham. 1st ed. sgn. F/F. T2. $45.00

LUMLEY, Brian. *Mad Moon of Dreams.* 1987. Buffalo. Ganley. 1st ed. F/F. P3/T2. $22.00

LUMLEY, Brian. *Ship of Dreams.* 1986. Buffalo. Ganley. 1st ed. F/F. T2. $22.00

LUMLEY & PANOFSKY. *Structure of Atmospheric Turbulence.* 1964. NY. Interscience. 8vo. 239p. gray cloth. VG. K5. $20.00

LUMMIS, Charles F. *Letters From the SW: Sept 20, 1884 to March 14, 1885.* 1989. AZ U. 1st ed. ils James W Byrkit. 309p. F/NF. B19. $40.00

LUMMIS, Charles F. *Some Strange Corners of Our Country.* 1892. Century. 1st ed. ils. F. A18. $75.00

LUMPKIN, Katharine DuPre. *Emancipation of Angelina Grimke.* 1974. Chapel Hill. 8vo. 265p. M. V3. $15.00

LUNAN, Duncan. *Man & the Stars.* 1974. London. Souvenir. 8vo. 13 pl. 324p. VG/G. K5. $25.00

LUND, Johannes. *Die Alten Judischen Heiligthumer...* 1738. Hamburg. Christian Wilhelm Brand. 5 books in 1. pigskin. K1. $1,500.00

LUPICA, Mike. *Extra Credits.* 1988. Villard. 1st ed. F/F. P3. $16.00

LUPICA, Mike. *Limited Partner.* 1990. Villard. 1st ed. F/F. P8. $15.00

LUPOFF, Richard A. *Barsoom: Edgar Rice Burroughs...* 1976. Mirage. 1st ed. VG. P3. $15.00

LUPOFF, Richard A. *Countersolar.* 1987. Arbor. 1st ed. F/F. N3/P8. $15.00

LUPOFF, Richard A. *Forever City.* 1987. Walker. 1st ed. F/F. T2. $20.00

LUPOFF, Richard A. *Lovecraft's Book.* 1985. Sauk City. 1st ed. F/F. T2. $16.00

LUPOFF, Richard A. *Triune Man.* 1976. Berkley Putnam. 1st ed. F/F. N3. $20.00

LUPOFF, Richard A. *Triune Man.* 1976. Berkley Putnam. 1st ed. sgn. F/dj. F4. $30.00

LURAY, Howard. *Strobe: The Lively Light.* 1949. Camera Craft. ils/biblio. 128 p. F/F. A17. $10.00

LURIA & YUDOVICH. *Speech & Development of Mental Processes in the Child.* 1959. London. Staples. 123p. F/dj. K4. $20.00

LURIE, Alison. *Foreign Affairs.* 1984. Franklin Lib. 1st ed. sgn. ribbon marker. aeg. leather. F. L3. $100.00

LURIE, Alison. *Only Children.* 1979. Random. 1st ed. F/NF. B3. $15.00

LUSTGARTEN, Edgar. *Business of Murder.* 1968. Scribner. 1st ed. F/F. F4. $25.00

LUSTGARTEN, Edgar. *One More Unfortunate.* 1947. Scribner. 1st ed. F/NF. F4. $50.00

LUSTGARTEN, Edgar. *Turn the Light Out As You Go.* 1978. London. Elek. 1st ed. NF/dj. S6. $25.00

LUTHER, D. Martin. *Die Heilige Schrift.* 1930. Stuttgart. Wurttembergilche. F. S12. $200.00

LUTHER, Tal. *Custer High Spots.* ca 1972. Old Army Pr. ils Byron Wolfe. intro Don Russell. 99p. VG. S11. $25.00

LUTYENS, Emily. *Candles in the Sun: Story of Spiritual Ferment.* 1957. Lippincott. 196p. VG/VG. B33. $20.00

LUTZ, Hermann. *Lord Gray & the World War.* 1928. NY. 1st Am ed. trans from German. 346p. VG. A17. $8.50

LUTZ, John. *Bloodfire.* 1991. Holt. 1st ed. NF/NF. P3. $18.00

LUTZ, John. *Lazarus Man.* 1979. NY. Morrow. 1st ed. inscr. F/F. S6. $45.00

LUTZ, John. *Ride the Lightning.* 1987. St Martin. 1st ed. sgn. F/F. F4. $22.00

LUTZ, John. *Tropical Heat.* 1986. NY. Holt. 1st ed. sgn. F/F. S6. $35.00

LUTZ, Otto. *Zoologia, Para Las Escuelas Hispano-Americans.* 1921. Koehler Volckmar. 192p. VG. S11. $10.00

LUYS, Jules. *Brain & Its Function.* 1897. NY. Appleton. 327p. emb cloth. G7. $85.00

LYALL, Gavin. *Crocus List.* 1986. Viking. 1st ed. VG/VG. P3. $16.00

LYALL, Gavin. *Secret Servant.* 1980. NY. Viking. 1st Am ed. F/NF. S6. $25.00

LYLE, Evelyn. *Search for the Royal Road.* 1966. London. Vision. 1st ed. 8vo. 216p. F/dj. W1. $12.00

LYLE, R.C. *Brown Jack.* 1934. London. Putnam. 2nd prt. VG. O3. $45.00

LYLES, William H. *Putting Dell on the Map.* 1983. Greenwood. 1st ed. F. P3. $40.00

LYMAN, George D. *John Marsh, Pioneer.* 1930. np. 1st ed. ils. 394p. O8. $32.50

LYMINGTON, John. *Voyage of the Eighth Mind.* 1980. Hodder Stoughton. 1st ed. F/F. P3. $18.00

LYNCH, Hannah. *French Life in Town & Country.* 1901. London. Newnes. 2nd ed. 261p. VG. S11. $20.00

LYNCH, Jeremiah. *Three Years in the Kondike.* 1967. Lakeside. 375p. VG+. M20. $25.00

LYNCH, Nancy. *Old-Fashioned Garden.* 1987. Rizzoli. probable 1st ed. 4 lg popups. F. B17. $12.00

LYNDS, Dennis. *Blue Death.* nd. BC. VG/VG. P3. $8.00

LYNDS, Dennis. *Crime, Punishment & Resurrection.* 1992. Donald Fine. 1st ed. sgn. F/F. M15. $27.50

LYNDS, Dennis. *Deadly Innocents.* 1986. Walker. 1st ed. F/F. P3. $15.00

LYNDS, Dennis. *Falling Man.* 1970. Random. 1st ed. xl. dj. P3. $5.00

LYNDS, Dennis. *Here To Die.* 1971. Random. 1st ed. VG/VG. P3. $20.00

LYNDS, Dennis. *Man Who Dreamt of Lobsters.* 1993. Random. 1st Am ed. sgn. NF/NF. A14. $35.00

LYNDS, Dennis. *Mission to Mars.* 1990. Grove Weidenfeld. 1st prt. 8vo. 307p. VG/VG. K5. $25.00

LYNDS, Dennis. *Night of the Toads.* 1972. London. Hale. 1st ed. F/NF. B3. $25.00

LYNDS, Dennis. *Nightrunners.* 1978. NY. Dodd Mead. 1st ed. inscr. F/F. S6. $45.00

LYNDS, Dennis. *Silent Scream.* 1973. Dodd Mead. 1st ed. VG/VG. P3. $25.00

LYNDS, Dennis. *Slasher.* 1980. NY. Dodd Mead. 1st ed. inscr. F/F. S6. $45.00

LYNE, Michael. *Parson's Son: Sporting Artist.* 1974. London. Allen. ltd sgn ed. 1/750. obl 4to. VG. O3. $150.00

LYNN, Elizabeth A. *Silver Horse.* 1984. Bluejay. 1st ed. F/F. P3. $18.00

LYON, Benjamin. *Manuscript Shoemaker's Ledger.* 1753-1797. Dorchester (Boston), MA. sm 4to. 338p. orig vellum w/ties. M1. $2,000.00

LYON, Ralph A. *Mocking Bards.* 1905. Ridgeville. 1st ed. 12mo. VG. S11. $15.00

LYON, W. *First Aid Hints for the Horse Owner.* 1966. London. Collins. later prt. VG/G. O3. $15.00

LYONS, Arthur. *As the Hands of Another.* 1983. HRW. 1st ed. VG/VG. P3. $20.00

LYONS, Arthur. *Dead Are Discreet.* 1974. NY. Mason Lipscomb. 1st ed. VG/dj. M15. $100.00

LYONS, Arthur. *Fast Fade.* 1987. Mysterious. 1st ed. sgn. F/F. S6. $40.00

LYONS, Dorothy. *Golden Soverign.* 1946. Harcourt. later prt. VG. O3. $35.00

LYONS, J.B. *James Joyce & Medicine.* 1973. Dublin. Dolmen. 255p. dj. G7. $30.00

LYONS & LYONS. *Someone Is Killing the Great Chefs of Europe.* 1976. HBJ. 1st ed. F/NF. B3. $35.00

LYTLE, Andrew. *Bedford Forrest.* 1939. Eyre Spottiswoode. 1st Eng ed. 402p. cloth. NF/VG. M8. $350.00

LYTLE, Andrew. *Long Night.* 1936. Indianapolis. 1st ed. VG/G. B5. $175.00

LYTLE, Andrew. *Reflections of a Ghost.* 1980. Dallas. 1st ed. sgn. 1/300 #d. red stp blk cloth. F/sans/wrp. A11. $45.00

LYTLE, Andrew. *Wake for the Living: A Family Chronicle.* 1975. NY. 1st ed. sgn. NF/NF. A11. $75.00

LYTLE, Horace. *No Hunting?* 1928. Field Sports Pub. 1st ed. VG/VG. P3. $30.00

LYTLE, William M. *Merchant Steam Vessels of the US 1807-1868.* 1952. Mystic. 1/1000. 294p. T7. $95.00

LYTTELTON, George. *Works of...* 1776. London. 3 vol. 3rd ed. VG. A15. $150.00

LYTTLETON, Raymond. *Modern Universe.* 1956. Hodder Stoughton. 8vo. ils. 207p. G/dj. K5. $10.00

LYTTON, Bulwer. *Last Days of Pompeii.* 1926. Scribner. 1st ed. ils FC Yohn. 425p. VG/dj. M20. $100.00

LYTTON, Robert Lord. *Athens: Its Rise & Fall.* 1874. London. Routledge. 8vo. 550p. VG. W1. $8.00

LYTTON, Robert Lord. *Lucile.* 1860. London. Chapman Hall. 1st ed. red morocco. F. H4. $85.00

LYTTON, Robert Lord. *Wanderer.* 1876. London. Chapman Hall. Poetical Works #4. morocco. M/case. H4. $100.00

M'CABE, John Collins. *Scraps.* 1835. Richmond, VA. JC Walker. 1st ed. 12mo. 192p. cloth/leather label. M1. $225.00

M'COLLESTER, Sullivan Holman. *Round the Globe in Old & New Paths.* 1909. Boston. Universalist Pub. 354p. G. W1. $8.00

M'ILVAINE, William. *Sketches of Scenery & Notes of Personal Adventure in CA...* 1951. San Francisco. Grabhorn. 1/400. ils. half cloth/marbled cloth. NF. P4. $250.00

MAAS, Carl. *Common Sense in Home Decoration.* 1945. World. 1st rpt ed. photos. 350p. F. H1. $12.00

MAASS, Edgar. *World & Paradise.* 1950. Scribner. 1st ed. VG/VG. P3. $20.00

MABILLE, Pierre. *Le Merveilleux.* 1946. Paris. Quatre Vents. F/wrp B2. $75.00

MABRO, Robert. *Egyptian Economy 1952-1972.* 1974. Oxford. 1st ed. sm 8vo. xl. VG. W1. $15.00

MABRY, Caroline. *Castles in Spain.* ca 1933. Whitman. 1st ed. inscr. 127p. VG/poor. B10. $18.00

MACARTHUR, Wilson. *Desert Watches.* 1954. Bobbs Merrill. 1st ed. 8vo. xl. VG. W1. $9.00

MACARTNEY, Clarence E. *Grant & His Generals.* 1953. ils/index. map ep. 352p. dj. O8. $14.50

MACARTNEY, Clarence E. *Mr Lincoln's Admirals.* 1956. np. 1st ed. ils/index. 335p. xl. O8. $12.50

MACAVOY, R.A. *King of the Dead.* 1991. Morrow. 1st ed. VG. P3. $19.00

MACAVOY, R.A. *Tea With the Black Dragon.* 1987. Hypatia. 1st hc ed. sgn MacAvoy/McCaffrey/Newcomer. 1/750. F/F/case. T2. $55.00

MACBETH, George. *Seven Witches.* 1978. WH Allen. 1st ed. VG/VG. P3. $15.00

MACBRIDE, J. Francis. *Autumn Flowers & Fruits.* 1924. Chicago. photos. wrp. B26. $12.50

MACCARGO, J.T.; see Rabe, Peter.

MACCLOSKEY, Monro. *Alert the Fifth Force.* 1969. NY. Richard Rosens. 1st ed. 190p. VG. A17. $15.00

MACCORKLE. *Some Southern Questions: Negro & Intelligence...* 1908. np. 1st ed. 318p. VG/dj. E5. $35.00

MACCOUN, Townsend. *Holy Land in Geography & Hist Vol 1.* 1897. Revell. 1st ed. 12mo. 53 maps. VG. W1. $28.00

MACDONALD, Betty. *Plague & I.* 1948. Phil. 1st ed. sgn. VG/G. B5. $35.00

MACDONALD, George. *At the Back of the North Wind.* nd. AL Burt. 371p. VG/G. B10. $15.00

MACDONALD, George. *At the Back of the North Wind.* 1919. Phil. David McKay. 1st ed thus. ils JW Smith. VG+. C8. $175.00

MACDONALD, George. *At the Back of the North Wind.* 1924. Macmillan. 1st ed thus. ils FD Bedford. 376p. F. P2. $85.00

MACDONALD, George. *At the Back of the North Wind.* 1964. Franklin Watts. 1st Am ed thus. ils Mozley. 278p. VG. B10. $35.00

MACDONALD, George. *Princess & Curdie.* 1908. Lippincott. ils Maria Kirk. gilt red pict cloth. G. M5. $20.00

MACDONALD, George. *Princess & the Goblin.* 1926. Macmillan. 1st ed thus. ils FD Bedford. 267p. VG+. P2. $55.00

MACDONALD, George. *Princess & the Goblin.* 1927. Saalfield. G+. P3. $20.00

MACDONALD, Golden; see Brown, Margaret Wise.

MACDONALD, J. Ramsay. *Parliament & Revolution.* 1920. NY. 1st ed. 12mo. 180p. VG. D3. $35.00

MACDONALD, J. Ramsay. *Wanderings & Excursions.* 1925. London. Cape. 2nd imp. 319p. VG. W1. $15.00

MACDONALD, John D. *Barrier Island.* 1986. Knopf. 1st ed. VG/VG. P3. $18.00

MACDONALD, John D. *Cinnamon Skin.* 1982. Harper. 1st ed. F/F. B2. $25.00

MACDONALD, John D. *Condominium.* nd. BOMC. VG/VG. P3. $10.00

MACDONALD, John D. *Condominium.* 1977. London. Hale. 1st Eng ed. F/F. S6. $30.00

MACDONALD, John D. *Crossroads.* 1959. Simon Schuster. 1st ed. VG/G+. P3. $125.00

MACDONALD, John D. *Deadly Shade of Gold.* 1974. Lippincott. 1st Am hc ed. F/F. M15. $250.00

MACDONALD, John D. *Empty Copper Sea.* 1978. Lippincott. 1st ed. VG/VG. P3. $40.00

MACDONALD, John D. *Free Fall in Crimson.* 1981. Harper Row. 1st ed. VG/VG. P3. $30.00

MACDONALD, John D. *Green Ripper.* 1979. Lippincott. 1st ed. F/F. P3. $25.00

MACDONALD, John D. *House Guests.* 1965. Doubleday. 1st ed. F/F. B2. $75.00

MACDONALD, John D. *Key to the Suite.* 1989. Mysterious. 1st ed. F/F. P3. $18.00

MACDONALD, John D. *No Deadly Drug.* 1968. Doubleday. 1st ed. F/F. F4. $40.00

MACDONALD, John D. *One More Sunday.* 1984. Knopf. 1st ed. VG/VG. P3. $20.00

MACDONALD, John D. *Please Write for Details.* 1959. Simon Schuster. 1st ed. F/NF. B2. $65.00

MACDONALD, John D. *Purple Place for Dying.* 1976. Lippincott. 1st Am hc ed. rem mk. F/NF. M15. $150.00

MACDONALD, John D. *Tan & Sandy Silence.* 1979. Lippincott. 1st Am hc ed. F/NF. M15. $125.00

MACDONALD, John D. *Turquoise Lament.* 1973. Lippincott. 1st ed. NF/VG. B4. $85.00

MACDONALD, John Ross; see Millar, Kenneth.

MACDONALD, L. *Somme.* 1989. NY. 8vo. 366p+photo sections. M/wrp. A17. $9.50

MACDONALD, Patricia J. *Little Sister.* nd. BC. VG/VG. P3. $8.00

MACDONALD, Philip. *Choice.* 1931. Collins. VG. P3. $30.00

MACDONALD, Philip. *Death & Chicanery.* 1963. Herbert Jenkins. VG/VG. P3. $30.00

MACDONALD, Philip. *Link.* 1930. Doubleday Crime Club. 1st Am ed. F/dj. M15. $100.00

MACDONALD, Philip. *Man Out of the Rain & Other Stories.* 1957. London. Jenkins. 1st ed. F/F. M15. $75.00

MACDONALD, Ross; see Millar, Kenneth.

MACDONALD, William Colt. *Cartridge Carnival.* 1945. Doubleday. 1st ed. xl. G+. P3. $7.00

MACDONALD & ROWAN. *Friendship.* 1986. Knopf. 1st ed. F/F. F4. $20.00

MACDONALD & WRIGHT. *Fact, Science & Morality: Essays on AJ Ayer's Language...* 1987. NY. Blackwell. 1st Am ed. bl cloth. VG/dj. G1. $25.00

MACE, Elisabeth. *Out There.* 1977. Greenwillow. VG/VG. P3. $13.00

MACE, Elisabeth. *Under Siege.* 1990. Orchard. 1st Am ed. F/F. N3. $10.00

MACE, Tony. *Notactus.* 1975. np. 1st ed. photos/maps/drawings. 87p. cbdg. F. B26. $11.00

MACEWEN, Gwendolyn. *TE Lawrence Poems.* 1983. Canada. Mosaic. 2nd prt. 70p. M/pict wrp. M7. $20.00

MACFALL, Haldane. *Aubrey Beardsley the Clown, Harlequin, Pierrot of His Age.* 1927. Simon Schuster. 1st ed. ils. gilt blk cloth. VG+. F1. $115.00

MACGIBBON & THOMAS. *Ecclesiastical Architecture of Scotland to 17th Century.* 1896-1897. Edinburgh. 3 vol. 1st ed. lg 8vo. bl cloth. NF. C6. $200.00

MACGOWAN, John. *Life of Joseph, Son of Israel, in Eight Books.* 1800. Dover, NH. Bragg. 195p. calf. VG. B14. $125.00

MACGRATH, Harold. *Voice in the Fog.* nd. Grosset Dunlap. G. P3. $7.00

MACH, Ernst. *Die Analyse der Empfindungen und das Verhaltniss...* 1902. Jena. 3rd ed. 8vo. 286p. half leather. VG. B14. $150.00

MACH, Ernst. *Erkenntnis und Irrtum: Skizzen zur Psychologie Forschung.* 1905. Leipzig. Johann Ambrosius Barth. 461p. G. scarce. G1. $350.00

MACHEN, Arthur. *Anatomy of Tobacco.* 1926. Knopf. 1st Am ed. VG/worn. M2. $75.00

MACHEN, Arthur. *Fantastic Tales.* 1923. Carbonnek. 1/1050 #d. G+. A1. $30.00

MACHEN, Arthur. *Far Off Things.* 1923. Knopf. 1st ed. VG. P3. $40.00

MACHEN, Arthur. *Memoirs of Casanova.* ca 1960. BOMC. 6 vols. VG/djs. A17. $35.00

MACHEN, Arthur. *Memoirs of Jacques Casanova de Seingalt.* nd. Putnam. 6 vol. ils. VG/dj. B30. $45.00

MACHEN, Arthur. *Memoirs of Jacques Casanova.* 1932. Boni. 2 vol. 1st ed thus. NF. w/sgn card. F4. $185.00

MACHETANZ, Frederick. *On Arctic Ice.* 1940. NY. 1st ed. sgn. 105p. pict cloth. VG. A17. $12.00

MACINNES, Helen. *Above Suspicion.* 1941. Triangle. MTI. VG/VG. P3. $18.00

MACINNES, Helen. *Ride a Pale Horse.* 1984. HBJ. 1st ed. VG/VG. P3. $20.00

MACINNES, J. Watson. *Guard Dogs: Alstians, Boxers, Bull Mastifs (sic)...* 1949. London. Williams Norgate. 1st ed. 128p. cloth. F/VG. R2. $60.00

MACISAAC, Fred. *Vanishing Professor.* 1927. Whitman. 1st ed. VG. P3. $35.00

MACK, Ebenezer. *Cat-Fight: A Mock Heroic Poem.* 1824. NY. 1st ed. 12mo. 276p. calf/marbled brd. M1. $475.00

MACK, John E. *Prince of Our Disorder: Life of TE Lawrence.* 1976. Little Brn. 1st ed. photos/maps. gilt red cloth. NF/G. M7. $55.00

MACK, John E. *Prince of Our Disorder: Life of TE Lawrence.* 1976. Little Brn. 1st ed. 8vo. 560p. VG/dj. W1. $25.00

MACK, Willard. *Old Clothes: Sequel to the Ragman.* 1925. Jacobsen Hodgkinson. 1st ed. movie photos. NF/wrp. B4. $100.00

MACKAY, F.F. *Art of Acting.* 1913. NY. 1st ed. sgn pres. 296p. half leather/cloth. VG. B14. $55.00

MACKAY, John Henry. *Anarchists: Picture of Civilization Close of 19th Century.* 1891. Boston. Tucker. 1st ed. NF. B2. $200.00

MACKAY-SMITH, Alexander. *Race Horses of America 1832-1872: Portraits...* 1981. Nat Mus of Racing. ltd ed. 1/1500. sgn/#d. ils. VG/sans. O3. $125.00

MACKELLAR, William. *Mound Menace.* 1969. Follett. 1st ed. F/VG+. P8. $27.50

MACKENZIE, Clinton. *New Design in Crochet.* 1972. np. cloth. VG. G2. $6.00

MACKENZIE, Colin. *Mackenzie's 5000 Recipes in All Useful & Domestic Art.* 1831. np. 456p. VG. E5. $75.00

MACKENZIE, Compton. *Gallipoli Memories.* 1929. London. 1st ed. map. 406p. gilt blk cloth. VG. M7. $35.00

MACKENZIE, Donald. *Cool Sleeps Balabam.* 1964. Houghton Mifflin. 1st ed. xl. dj. P3. $4.00

MACKENZIE, Donald. *Raven Settles a Score.* 1979. London. Macmillan. 1st ed. F/F. S6. $22.50

MACKENZIE, Donald. *Sleep Is for the Rich.* 1971. Macmillan. 1st ed. VG/VG. P3. $18.00

MACKINNON, Captain. *Atlantic & Transatlantic: Sketches Afloat & Ashore.* 1852. Harper. 324p. T7. $75.00

MACKINSTRY, Elizabeth. *Alladin & the Wonderful Lamp.* 1935. Macmillan. 1st ed. gr cloth. NF/G. M5. $60.00

MACLAGAN, T.J. *Rheumatism: Its Nature, Its Pathology &...Treatment.* 1886. NY. Wood. Wood Lib ed. 277p. cloth. G7. $95.00

MACLAINE, Shirley. *You Can't Get There From Here.* 1975. Norton. 1st ed. sgn. F/VG clip. S11. $20.00

MACLAREN, Ian. *Bonnie Brier Bush.* 1895. np. inscr pres. 300p. VG. E5. $35.00

MACLAURIN, C. *Mere Mortals: Medico-Historical Essays.* 1925. NY. 1st ed. 291p. A13. $30.00

MACLAY, E.S. *History of American Privateers.* 1899. NY. VG. M17. $45.00

MACLAY, E.S. *History of the Navy.* 1901. NY. 3 vol. 1st ed. gilt bdg. VG. C11. $145.00

MACLAY, John. *Mindwarps.* 1991. Baltimore. 1st ed. sgn. 1/500. F/F. T2. $10.00

MACLAY, John. *Nukes: Four Horror Writers on the Ultimate Horror.* 1986. Baltimore. Maclay. 1st ed. sgn. F/pict wrp. T2. $5.00

MACLAY, John. *Other Engagements.* 1987. BC. VG/VG. P3. $20.00

MACLAY, John. *Other Engagements.* 1987. Madison. Dream House. 1st ed. sgn. 1/1000. F/sans. T2. $10.00

MACLAY, William. *Journal of William Maclay.* 1890. NY. royal 8vo. 438p. teg. VG. D3. $45.00

MACLEAN, A.D. *Winters Tales 26.* 1980. Macmillan. 1st ed. NF/NF. P3. $18.00

MACLEAN, Alistair. *Bear Island.* 1971. Collins. 1st ed. VG/VG. P3. $25.00

MACLEAN, Alistair. *Captain Cook.* 1972. Garden City. 1st ed. photos/maps/index. 192 p. F/F. A17. $17.50

MACLEAN, Alistair. *Floodgate.* 1983. Collins. 1st ed. F/F. P3. $20.00

MACLEAN, Alistair. *Lawrence of Arabia.* 1962. Random. BC. 177p. gilt tan cloth. F/F. M7. $30.00

MACLEAN, Alistair. *Partisans.* 1982. London. Collins. 1st ed. F/F. S6. $30.00

MACLEAN, Alistair. *Santorini.* 1986. Collins. 1st ed. F/F. P3. $20.00

MACLEAN, Charles. *Watcher.* 1982. London. Allen Lane. 1st ed. F/NF. B3. $35.00

MACLEAN, Katherine. *Missing Man.* 1975. Berkley Putnam. 1st ed. VG/VG. P3. $15.00

MACLEAN, Norman. *River Runs Through It & Other Stories.* 1990. London. Pan Books. 1st ed. intro David Profumo. F/F. A18. $60.00

MACLEAN, Norman. *Young Men & Fire.* 1992. Chicago. 1st ed. photos/map. M/M. A18. $40.00

MACLEOD, Charlotte. *Astrology for Skeptics.* 1972. Macmillan. 1st ed. VG. P3. $20.00

MACLEOD, Charlotte. *Plain Old Man.* 1985. Crime Club. 1st ed. VG/VG. P3. $15.00

MACLEOD, Mary. *King Arthur & His Knights.* 1950. Rainbow Classics. F/F. P3. $20.00

MACLEOD, Murdo. *Spanish Central America.* 1973. Berkeley. 1st ed. 554p. VG/dj. F3. $25.00

MACLURE, William. *Opinions on Various Subjects, Dedicated to Industrious...* 1831, 1837 & 1838. New Harmony, IN. 3 vol. 1st complete ed. 8vo. calf. M1. $3,000.00

MACMAHON & MACPHERSON. *Ten Commandments.* 1924. Grosset Dunlap. 236p. VG/chip. M20. $20.00

MACMAHON. *Elizabeth Bishop: A Bibliography 1927-1979.* 1980. np. 246p. F/F. A4. $35.00

MACMANUS, Seamus. *Ballads of a Country Boy.* 1905. Dublin. Gill. 100p. G. H1. $30.00

MACMANUS, Seamus. *Woman of Seven Sorrows.* 1905. Dublin. 1st ed. sgn. F/wrp. C2. $150.00

MACMICHAEL, William. *Gold-Headed Cane. Second Edition.* 1828. London. Murray. pl. 267p. brd/rebacked orig label. uncut. G7. $150.00

MACMILLAN, Donald B. *Four Years in the White North.* 1918. NY/London. Harper. 8vo. ils. 426p. brick-red cloth. VG. P4. $75.00

MACMILLAN, Harold. *Reconstruction: Plea for a National Policy.* 1933. London. 1st ed. sg/dtd 1933. 128p. VG. D3. $75.00

MACNAUGHTON, William R. *Mark Twain's Last Years As a Writer.* 1979. MO U. 1st ed. 254p. F/dj. M10. $12.50

MACNEICE, Louis. *Astrology.* nd. NY. Doubleday. sm 4to. 351p. G. K5. $15.00

MACNEICE, Louis. *Poems 1925-1940.* 1940. Random. 1st ed. sgn. F/VG. V1. $45.00

MACNEICE, Louis. *Poems.* 1937. Random. 1st ed. different content from 1935 title. sgn. F/G. V1. $75.00

MACNEIL, Neil; see Ballard, W.T.

MACON, T.J. *Life's Gleanings.* 1913. Richmond. 101p. F. scarce. O8. $32.50

MACQUARRIE, John. *Dictionary of Christian Ethics.* 1967. Westminster. 366p. VG/dj. B29. $5.50

MACQUEEN, John Fraser. *Chief Points in the Laws of War & Neutrality...* 1863. Richmond. Johnson. 102p. prt bl wrp. K1. $150.00

MACQUITTY, William. *Abu Simbel.* 1965. Putnam. 1st ed. 189p. VG/dj. M20. $25.00

MACQUITTY, William. *Tutankhamun: The Last Journey.* 1978. NY. Quartet. 3rd prt. VG/dj. W1. $18.00

MACQUOID, Katherine S. *In the Ardennes.* 1881. Chatto Windus. 1st ed. ils Macquoid. 351p. teg. gilt olive cloth. VG. S11. $50.00

MACROW, Brenda G. *Field Folk.* ca 1958. Blackie. unp. VG/fair. B10. $12.00

MACURDY, Grace Harriet. *Troy & Paeonia With Glimpses of Ancient Balkan History...* 1925. Columbia. 8vo. 259p. cloth. unopened. O2. $30.00

MACVEY, John W. *Journey to Alpha Centauri.* 1968. Macmillan. 3rd prt. 8vo. 256p. G/G. K5. $30.00

MACVICAR, Angus. *Lost Planet.* 1960. Burke. VG-/dj. P3. $10.00

MACY, John. *Story of the World's Literature.* 1930. Liveright. ils. 610p. fair. M10. $6.50

MADDAMS, W.F. *Interesting Newer Mammillarias.* nd. np. Mammillaria Soc. orig ed. photos. 39p. brn cloth. F. B26. $17.50

MADDEN, David. *Beautiful Greed.* 1961. NY. 1st ed. pres. F/NF. A11. $60.00

MADDEN, David. *Cheaters & the Cheated. A Collection of Critical Essays.* 1973. Delano, FL. 1st ed. inscr. F/sans. A11. $55.00

MADDEN, Henry Miller. *Xantus: Hungarian Naturalist in Pioneer West.* 1949. Books of the West. ils/notes. 312p. NF. B19. $50.00

MADDEN, Joe Markee. *Back Room.* 1937. NY. 1st ed. sgn. VG/VG. B5. $30.00

MADDEN, R.R. *Shrines & Sepulchres of the Old & New World...* 1831. London. 2 vol. 8vo. pres. cloth. O2. $125.00

MADDEROM, Gary. *Four-Chambered Villain.* 1971. Macmillan. 1st ed. F/F. P3. $13.00

MADDI, Salvatore R. *Personality Theories.* 1968. Nobleton, Ontario. Irwin Dorsey. 461p. F/dj. K4. $15.00

MADDOCK, Reginald. *Time Maze.* 1960. Thomas Nelson. 1st ed. VG-/VG. P3. $15.00

MADDOCK, Stephen. *Danger After Dark.* 1934. Collins. 1st ed. VG-. P3. $7.00

MADGE, Charles. *Society in the Mind: Elements of Social Eidos.* 1964. NY. Free Pr. 158p. cloth. G1. $22.50

MADISON, Charles A. *Owl Among Colophons: Henry Holt As Publisher & Editor.* 1966. HRW. 1st ed. 197p. M10/S11. $10.00

MADISON, Charles. *Emma Goldman: Biographical Sketch.* 1960. Libertarian BC. 1st ed. 32p. NF/wrp. B2. $45.00

MADISON, Dolly. *Memoirs & Letters of...* 1886. Houghton Mifflin. 12mo. 210p. VG. V3. $14.00

MADSEN, Axel. *Borderlines.* 1975. Macmillan. 1st ed. VG/VG. P3. $15.00

MADSEN, David. *Black Plume.* 1980. Simon Schuster. 1st ed. F/F. M15. $35.00

MADSEN, David. *USSA.* 1989. Morrow. 1st ed/author's 2nd book. sgn. F/F. S6. $40.00

MADSEN & MADSEN. *North to Montana!* 1980. UT Pr. 1st ed. M/M. B34. $85.00

MAETERLINCK, Maurice. *Blue Bird.* 1911. Dodd Mead. 1st Am ed thus. ils F Cayley Robinson. gilt bdg. G+. P2. $75.00

MAETERLINCK, Maurice. *Blue Bird: A Fairy Play in 6 Acts.* 1911. Dodd Mead. 1st/deluxe ed. sm 4to. 25 tipped-in pl. 211p. NF. D6. $125.00

MAETERLINCK, Maurice. *Brian Wildsmith: Maurice Maeterlinck's Blue Bird.* 1976. NY. Franklin Watts. 1st ed. 4to. 37p. F/F. D6. $35.00

MAETERLINCK, Maurice. *Great Beyond.* 1947. Philosophical Lib. trans Marta Meufeld/Renee Spodheim. VG/G. B33. $15.00

MAETERLINCK, Maurice. *Hours of Gladness.* 1912. London. Allen. 1st ed. 4to. gilt wht cloth. VG. C8. $225.00

MAETERLINCK, Maurice. *Monna Vanna.* 1904 (1903). Harper. trans Alexis Coleman. 144p. VG. H1. $6.50

MAGDOL, Edward. *Antislavery Rank & File: A Social Profile...* 1986. Greenwood Pr. 1st ed. 8vo. 172p. M. V3. $12.00

MAGGIOLO, Marcio Veloz. *Arqueologia de Punta de Garza.* 1977. San Pedro de Marcoris. 1st ed. 241p. Lib of Congress bdg. F3. $20.00

MAGIDOFF, Robert. *Russian SF 1969.* 1969. NY U. 1st ed. F/F. N3. $20.00

MAGNER, Dennis. *Classic Encyclopedia of the Horse.* 1980. NY. Bonanza. rpt. 644p. VG/VG. O3. $25.00

MAGNER, Lois. *History of Medicine.* 1992. NY. 1st ed. 393p. A13. $40.00

MAGNUS, Philip. *Kitchner: Portrait of an Imperialist.* 1959. Dutton. 1st ed. 410p. VG/torn. W1. $15.00

MAGNUSON, James. *Rundown.* 1977. Dial. 1st ed. F/VG+. P8. $35.00

MAGNUSSON, David. *Test Theory.* 1966. Reading, MA. Addison Wesley. 246p. F/dj. K4. $15.00

MAGOUN, F. Alexander. *Frigate Constitution & Other Historic Ships.* 1928. Salem. Marine Research. sm folio. ils. gilt bl cloth. VG. F1. $225.00

MAGRIEL, P. *Backgammon.* 1977. WA. F/F. B5. $50.00

MAHAFFY, J.P. *Rambles & Studies in Greece.* 1900. Phil. Coates. 30 pl/fld map. VG. W1. $9.00

MAHAN, A.T. *Influence of Sea Power Upon History 1660-1805.* 1980. Prentice Hall. ils/halftones. 256p. dj. T7. $45.00

MAHAN, A.T. *Life of Nelson.* 1899. Boston. 2nd ed. F. A9. $50.00

MAHAN, A.T. *Types of Naval Officers Drawn From Hist of British Navy.* 1901. Little Brn. 1st ed. 500p. cloth. NF. B14. $125.00

MAHER, Brendan A. *Progress in Experimental Personality Research. Vol 1.* 1964. NY/London. Academic. 343p. F/dj. K4. $35.00

MAHMUD, S.F. *Story of Islam.* 1959. Karachi/London/Dacca. Oxford. 1st ed. 354p. xl. G/dj. W1. $10.00

MAHOT, H. *De La Paralysie Pseudo-Hypertrophique.* 1877. Paris. inscr. 56p. orig wrp. G7. $35.00

MAHY, Margaret. *Pirates' Mixed-Up Voyage, Dark Doings in Thousand Islands.* 1983. London. Dent. 1st ed. M/M. C8. $25.00

MAHY, Margaret. *Princess & the Clown.* 1971. Franklin Watts. ils Carol Barker. 28p. VG/VG. A3. $8.50

MAIER, Franz G. *Cyprus From the Earlist Time to the Present Day.* 1968. London. 8vo. 176p. dj. O2. $35.00

MAIER, Paul. *First Easter: True & Unfamiliar Story.* 1973. Harper. 128p. F/F. B29. $47.50

MAILER, Norman. *Advertisements for Myself.* 1959. Putnam. 1st ed. VG/VG. B3. $50.00

MAILER, Norman. *Ancient Evenings.* 1983. Little Brn. AP. F/NF. B2. $60.00

MAILER, Norman. *Ancient Evenings.* 1983. Little Brn. ltd ed. sgn. 1/350. F/F case. S9. $150.00

MAILER, Norman. *Deaths for the Ladies.* 1962. NY. 1st ed. sgn. NF/wrp. A9. $50.00

MAILER, Norman. *Fight.* 1975. Little Brn. 1st ed. inscr. F/F. A11. $55.00

MAILER, Norman. *Fight.* 1975. Little Brn. 1st ed. NF/NF. S9. $45.00

MAILER, Norman. *Harlot's Ghost.* 1991. Random. 1st ed. sgn. F/F. O4. $75.00

MAILER, Norman. *Marilyn.* 1973. Grosset Dunlap. ltd ed. sgn. photos Schiller. 270p. bl stp wht cloth. F/case. H5. $250.00

MAILER, Norman. *Marilyn.* 1974. Grosset Dunalp. VG/VG. P3. $20.00

MAILER, Norman. *Naked & the Dead.* 1948. Rinehart. 1st ed. VG/VG. M21. $90.00

MAILER, Norman. *Of a Fire on the Moon.* 1970. Little Brn. ARC. sgn. RS. F/F. w/sgn card & photo. B4. $175.00

MAILER, Norman. *Tough Guys Don't Dance.* nd. BC. VG/VG. P3. $8.00

MAILLOL, Aristide. *Woodcuts of..., a Complete Catalogue With 176 Ils.* 1951. NY. Pantheon. edit John Rewald. gilt brn cloth. F/VG. F1. $65.00

MAILLY, William. *National Convention of the Socialist Party.* 1904. Chicago. 1st ed. 338p. VG/wrp. B2. $100.00

MAINE, Charles Eric. *Isotope Man.* nd. BC. VG/VG. P3. $8.00

MAINE, Henry. *Village Communities in the East & West.* 1881. London. Murray. 8vo. 413p. VG. D3. $250.00

MAINGOT, Rodney. *Abdominal Operations.* 1940. NY. Appleton. 2 vol. G7. $45.00

MAIR, George B. *Miss Turquoise.* 1965. Random. 1st ed. VG/VG. P3. $15.00

MAJOR, Howard. *Domestic Architecture of the Early American Republic.* 1926. Lippincott. 4to. ils/photos. F/VG+. F1. $100.00

MAJOR, Ralph. *Fatal Partners, War & Disease.* 1941. NY. 1st ed. 342p. A13. $50.00

MAJORS, Simon; see Fox, Gardner F.

MAKAL, Mahmut. *Village in Anatolia.* 1954. London. 1st ed. 8vo. ils/maps. 190p. cloth. dj. O2/W1. $25.00

MAKSIMOVIC, Desanka. *Little Shaggy Dog.* 1938. Faber. 1st ed. unp. VG. B10. $10.00

MALAMUD, Bernard. *God's Grace.* 1982. FSG. 1st ed. NF/NF. B3. $25.00

MALAMUD, Bernard. *God's Grace.* 1982. FSG. ltd ed. 1/300. sgn. 223p. dk gr/silver stp gr cloth. F/case. H5/L3. $150.00

MALAMUD, Bernard. *Natural.* 1963. Eyre Spottiswode. 1st ed. F/VG+. P8. $550.00

MALAMUD, Bernard. *Rembrandt's Hat.* 1973. FSG. 1st ed. 8vo. 204p. F/F. C6. $30.00

MALAMUD, Bernard. *Stories of Bernard Malamud.* 1983. FSG. 1/300. sgn. 349p. gilt bl/gr cloth. F/case. H5. $250.00

MALCOLM, John. *Sheep, Goats & Soap.* 1991. London. Collins. 1st ed. F/F. S6. $30.00

MALCOLM, John. *Whistler in the Dark.* 1986. London. Collins. 1st ed. F/F. S6. $35.00

MALCOLM, Norman. *Ludwig Wittgenstein: A Memoir.* 1958. London. Oxford. 99p. blk cloth. VG/dj. G1. $37.50

MALCOLMSON, Anne. *Yankee Doodle's Cousins.* ca 1941. Houghton Mifflin. 16th prt. inscr pres. 268p. VG/G. B10. $12.00

MALCOLMSON, Anne. *Yankee Doodle's Cousins.* 1941. Houghton Mifflin. 1st ed. ils Robert McCloskey. pict cloth. VG. B11/C8. $20.00

MALCOMSON, David. *London: Dog Who Made the Team.* 1963. DSP. 1st ed. VG/G. P8. $27.50

MALEFIJT, Annemarie De Waal. *Images of Man.* 1974. Knopf. 347p. F/dj. K4. $10.00

MALET, Andre. *Thought of Rudolf Bultmann.* 1969. Doubleday. 440p. VG/torn. B29. $8.50

MALIK, Charles. *Christ & Crisis.* 1962. Eerdmans. 101p. G/dj. B29. $3.50

MALINE, Sarah. *Lawrence, Jarry, Zukofsky: A Tripych.* 1987. Austin. ils. 182p. F. M7. $16.50

MALING, Arthur. *Koberg Link.* 1979. Harper Row. 1st ed. VG/VG. P3. $15.00

MALING, Arthur. *Rheingold Route.* 1979. London. Gollancz. 1st Eng ed. F/F. S6. $25.00

MALING, Arthur. *Schroeder's Game.* 1977. Harper Row. 1st ed. xl. dj. P3. $5.00

MALINOWSKI, Bronislaw. *Argonauts of the Western Pacific.* 1932. London. 2nd imp. photos. 527p. VG. F1. $100.00

MALINOWSKI, Bronislaw. *Sexual Life of Savages in NW Menanesia.* 1929. Eugenics Pub. 572p. reading copy. K4. $10.00

MALKIEL, Theresa. *Woman & Freedom.* nd. Socialist Literature Co. NF/wrp. B2. $100.00

MALKIN, Michael R. *Traditional & Folk Puppets of the World.* 1977. NY. Barnes. photos/4 mc pl. 194p. VG/dj. A17. $15.00

MALL, Thomas. *Hist of the Martyrs Epitomised.* 1747. Boston. Rogers Fowle. 1st Am ed. 2 vol in 1. contemporary calf. K1. $350.00

MALLAN, Lloyd. *Men, Rockets & Space Rats.* 1955. NY. Messner. 8vo. ils. 335p. G/dj. K5. $30.00

MALLOCH, Douglas. *Little Hop-Skipper.* 1926. Doran. 8vo. 99p. cloth. G+. A3. $10.00

MALLON, Thomas. *Arts & Sciences.* 1988. NY. 1st ed. F/F. A17. $10.00

MALLORY, Drew. *Target Manhattan.* 1975. Putnam. 1st ed. VG/VG. P3. $15.00

MALMSTROM, Christiam. *Dissertatio Anatomico Pathologica de Insolita Costarum...* 1807. Lundae. fld engraved pl. G7. $45.00

MALO, Charles. *Les Capitales de l'Europe.* ca 1850. Paris. 16mo. 36p. brd. O2. $75.00

MALO, Vincent Gaspard. *And Why Not?* 1958. Arthur Barker. 1st ed. NF/NF. P3. $25.00

MALONE, Michael. *Uncivil Seasons.* 1983. Delacorte. 1st ed. F/F. M15. $45.00

MALONE, Thomas F. *Compendium of Meteorology.* 1960 (1951). Boston. Am Meteorological Soc. 3rd prt. 1334p. bl cloth. G. K5. $60.00

MALOT, Hector. *Adventures of Perrine.* 1936 (1932). Rand McNally. Windemere Classic. ils Milo Winter. F/chip. M5. $35.00

MALOT, Hector. *Adventures of Remi.* ca 1925. Rand McNally. 492p. VG. B10. $15.00

MALOT, Hector. *Nobody's Boy.* 1916. Cupples Leon. ils Gruelle. gilt gr cloth. VG+. M5. $60.00

MALOT, Hector. *Nobody's Boy.* 1916. Cupples Leon. 272p. G. B10. $35.00

MALOUF, David. *Johnno.* 1975. Queensland. correct 1st ed/author's 1st novel. NF/NF. L3. $150.00

MALRAUX, Andre. *Anti-Memoirs.* 1968. HRW. 1st ed. 420p. VG/VG. M7. $15.00

MALTHUS, Thomas Robert. *Essay on Principle of Population.* 1826. London. Murray. 2 vol. 6th ed. calf/brd. G. B14. $450.00

MALVERN & MALVERN. *Land of Surprise.* 1938. McLoughlin. unp. VG. M20. $40.00

MALVEZZI, Virgilio. *Il Davide Persequitato. David Persecuted.* 1647. London. Humphrey. 12mo. 164p. rebacked. K1. $125.00

MALZ & RITCHIE. *My Glimpse of Eternity/Return From Tomorrow.* 1978. Guideposts. VG/dj. B29. $3.50

MALZBERG, Barry. *Beyond Apollo.* 1975. Readers Union. VG/VG. P3. $10.00

MALZBERG, Barry. *Herovit's World.* 1973. Random. 1st ed. F/F. N3. $30.00

MALZBERG, Barry. *Herovit's World.* 1973. Random. 1st ed. VG/VG. P3. $20.00

MALZBERG, Barry. *Screen.* 1970. Olympia. 1st Am hc ed. F/dj. F4. $15.00

MALZBERG & PRONZINI. *Dark Sins, Dark Dreams.* 1978. Doubleday. 1st ed. VG/VG. P3. $18.00

MAMBOURY, Ernest. *Les Iles de Princes. Banlieu Maritime d'Istanbul.* 1943. Istanbul. 8vo. ils/5 fld maps. 94p. cloth. O2. $30.00

MAMET, David. *Some Freaks.* 1989. NY. 1st ed/author's 2nd book of essays. sgn. F/F. A11. $45.00

MANCHESTER, William. *Death of a President.* 1967. BOMC. 710p. VG/dj. M10. $4.50

MANCHESTER, William. *Goodbye, Darkness: Memoir of the Pacific War.* 1980. Boston. 1st ed. 401p. VG/rpr. A17. $10.00

MANCHESTER, William. *One Brief Shining Moment: Remembering Kennedy.* 1983. Little Brn. ils. 280p. F/dj. M10. $10.00

MANDEL, Bernard. *Samuel Gompers: A Biography.* 1963. Yellow Springs. 1st ed. F/torn. B2. $25.00

MANDEL, George. *Flee the Angry Strangers.* 1952. Bobbs Merrill. 1st ed. F/F. L3. $100.00

MANDELBAUM, Maurice. *Problem of Hist Knowledge: Answer to Relativism.* 1967. NY. Harper Torchbooks. 1st pb ed. 338p. G1. $22.50

MANDELBAUM, Maurice. *Purpose & Necessity in Social Theory.* 1987. Johns Hopkins. 198p. gr cloth. VG/dj. G1. $25.00

MANDOLFO, Rodolfo. *Problemi del Pensiero Antico.* 1936. Bologna. Nicola Zanichelli. 276p. VG/wrp. G1. $30.00

MANEK & STOTZ. *Albanesische Bibliographie.* 1909. Vienna. 8vo. cloth/brd. O2. $125.00

MANFRED, Frederick. *Arrow of Love.* 1961. Denver. 1st ed. inscr. 1/500. NF/NF. A11. $95.00

MANFRED, Frederick. *Carnal Knowledge.* 1971. FSG. 1st ed. F/F. B4. $125.00

MANFRED, Frederick. *King of Spades.* 1966. Trident. 1st ed. sgn. F/chip. A18. $35.00

MANFRED, Frederick. *Milk of Wolves.* 1976. Avenue Victor Hugo. 1st ed. sgn. sc. pict bdg. F. A18. $15.00

MANFRED, Frederick. *No Fun on Sunday.* 1990. OK U. 1st ed. F/F. P8. $15.00

MANFRED, Frederick. *This Is the Year.* 1947. Garden City. 1st ed/author's 3rd novel. sgn. NF/VG+. A11. $75.00

MANGELSDORF, Paul C. *Corn: Its Origin, Evolution & Improvement.* 1974. Cambridge. ils/photos/tables. 262p. VG/torn. B26. $21.00

MANGO, Cyril. *Materials for the Study of Mosaics of St Sophia...* 1962. WA. 4to. ils/fld diagrams/pl. cloth. dj. O2. $100.00

MANKOWITZ, Wolf. *Mazeppa: Lives, Loves & Legends of Adah Isaacs Menken.* 1982. Stein Day. 1st Am ed. VG/VG. O3. $25.00

MANN, E.A. *Portals.* 1974. Simon Schuster. 1st ed. NF/VG. F4. $25.00

MANN, E.B. *Killer's Range.* 1943. Triangle. VG/VG. P3. $6.00

MANN, Horace. *Demands of the Age on Colleges.* 1857. NY. 1st ed. 86p. VG/prt wrp. M8. $27.50

MANN, John. *Cacti Naturalized in Australia & Their Control.* 1970. Brisbane. photos/fld maps. 128p. cloth. VG+. B26. $35.00

MANN, S.E. *Arabian Literature: Outline of Prose, Poetry & Drama.* 1955. London. 8vo. 121p. cloth. dj. O2. $25.00

MANN, Sally. *Still Time.* 1988. Clifton Forge. Alleghany Highlands Arts & Crafts Center. F/wrp. S9. $30.00

MANN, Sylvia. *Collecting Playing Cards.* 1973 (1966). London. Howard Baker. photos/ils. 215p. F/VG. H1. $35.00

MANN, Thomas. *Beloved Returns.* 1940. Knopf. 1st Am ed. sgn. NF/NF. L3. $450.00

MANN, Thomas. *Holy Sinner.* 1951. Knopf. VG. P3. $20.00

MANN, Thomas. *Letters to Paul Amann 1915-1952.* 1960. Middletown, CT. Wesleyan U. VG. N2. $10.00

MANN, Thomas. *Nocturnes.* 1934. NY. Equinox. 1st Am ed. 1/1000. ils Lynd Ward. bl cloth. NF/remnant box. H5. $250.00

MANN, Thomas. *Stories of Three Decades.* 1936. Knopf. VG/VG. P3. $35.00

MANN & VON KAHLER. *Blatter der Thomas Mann Gesell-Schaft.* 1970. Zurich. pres. 68p. NF. B2. $85.00

MANNERS, David X. *Dead to the World.* 1947. David McKay. xl. dj. P3. $5.00

MANNHEIM, Grete. *Veterinarian's Children.* ca 1971. Knopf. 43p. VG/G. B10. $10.00

MANNIN, Ethel. *Woman & the Revolution.* 1939. Dutton. 1st ed. NF/tattered. B2. $45.00

MANNING, Frederic. *Scenes & Portraits.* 1909. London. Murray. 1st ed. VG. M7. $63.00

MANNING, Marie. *Judith of the Plains.* 1903. Harper. 1st ed. poor. B34. $10.00

MANNING, Russ. *Tarzan in the Land That Time Forgot.* 1974. Treasure House. 1st ed. pict brd. F/sans. F4. $30.00

MANNING, Samuel. *Palestine Ils by Pen & Pencil.* ca 1890. NY. sm folio. 198p. aeg. pict cloth. O2. $65.00

MANOR, Jason. *Too Dead To Run.* 1953. Viking. 1st ed. VG/VG. P3. $18.00

MANOS, Constantine. *Greek Portfolio.* 1972. Viking. 1st ed. 112 pl. VG+/VG. S9. $100.00

MANSEL, Henry Longueville. *Limits of Religious Thought Examined in 8 Lectures...* 1860. Boston. Gould Lincoln. 12mo. 364p. G. G1. $75.00

MANSFIELD, Jared. *Essays, Mathematical & Physical...* (1801). New Haven. Wm Morse. 1st ed. 13 fld copper-engraved pl. mottled calf. K1. $200.00

MANSFIELD, Peter. *History of the Middle East.* 1991. Viking Penguin. 1st ed. 373p. M. M7. $19.00

MANSO, Peter. *Mailer: His Life & Times.* 1985. NY. 1st ed. photos/index. 718p. F/F. A17. $15.00

MANSON, Richard. *Theory of Knowledge of Giambattista Vico.* 1969. Archon Books. sm 8vo. 83p. bl cloth. F/dj. G1. $25.00

MANTEGAZZZA, Paolo. *Sexual Relations of Mankind.* 1932. Anthropological Pr. 258p. gilt bdg. F. H1. $40.00

MANTLEY, John. *27th Day.* nd. BC. VG/VG. P3. $8.00

MANVTII, Pavlli. *Apophthegmatvm EX. Optimis Vtivsque. Lingvae Scriptoribus...* 1604. Venetiis. Ex Officina Damiani Zenari. 706p. full old vellum. G. G7. $150.00

MANZINI, Gianna. *L'Opera Complete del Greco.* 1969. Rizzoli. 1st ed. Italian text. VG. P3. $15.00

MAPES, Mary A. *Surprise!* 1944. np. Howell Soskin. ils David Fredenthal. sbdg. VG. A17. $10.00

MAPLES, William R. *Dead Men Do Tell Tales: Strange & Fascinating Cases...* 1994. Doubleday. 1st ed. F/F. T2. $23.00

MAPPLETHORPE, Robert. *Certain People.* 1985. Pasadena. Twelvetrees. 1/5000. NF/NF. S9. $150.00

MARA, Bernard; see Moore, Brian.

MARASCO, Robert. *Burnt Offerings.* nd. BC. VG/VG. P3. $8.00

MARASCO, Robert. *Burnt Offerings.* 1973. Delacorte. 1st ed/author's 1st novel. F/NF. T2. $25.00

MARASCO, Robert. *Burnt Offerings.* 1973. Delacorte. 1st ed/author's 1st novel. NF/VG+. N3. $10.00

MARBARGER, John P. *Space Medicine: Human Factor in Flights Beyond Earth.* 1951. IL U. 8vo. 83p. VG/dj. K5. $50.00

MARCEAU, Marcel. *Story of Bip.* 1976. Harper. 1st ed. NF/VG+. C8. $40.00

MARCH, Harold. *Gide & the Hound of Heaven.* 1952. Phil. PA U. 1st ed. VG/worn. A17. $12.50

MARCH, Joseph Moncure. *Wild Party.* 1947. Sylvan. ils. 123p. VG. M10. $10.00

MARCH, William. *Bad Seed.* 1954. Rinehart. 1st ed. NF/NF. O4. $100.00

MARCH & TAMBINUTTU. *TS Eliot: A Symposium.* 1949. Chicago. 1st ed. 259p. F/F. A17. $35.00

MARCHAJ, C.A. *Seaworthiness.* 1986. Camden. Internat Marine. ils. 371p. dj. T7. $35.00

MARCHINI, G. *Italina Stained Glass Windows.* (1956). NY. Abrams. 93 mtd pl/18 diagrams. 264p. gilt bl cloth. dj. K1. $100.00

MARCINKO, Richard. *Red Cell: Rogue Warrior.* 1994. Pocket. ARC. RS. F/F. S9. $35.00

MARCONI, Degna. *My Father, Marconi.* 1962. London. Muller. 8vo. photos. 306p. VG. K5. $25.00

MARCOSSON, Isaac. *Anaconda.* 1957. Dodd Mead. ils. VG/dj. B34. $25.00

MARCUCCUI & MICHELETTI. *Medieval Painting.* 1960. Viking. ils. 207p. F/dj. M10. $30.00

MARCUSE, Herbert. *Eros & Civilization.* 1966 (1955). Boston. Beacon. 277p. VG/dj. G1. $27.50

MARCUSE, Herbert. *Reason & Revolution.* 1941. Humanities Pr. 2nd enlarge ed. 429p. VG/chip. G1. $30.00

MARCUSE, Ludwig. *Obscene: Hist of an Indignation.* 1965. London. 327p. NF. D3. $25.00

MARCY, Mary. *Nepszuru Gazdasagtan.* 1920. Chicago. 1st ed. NF. scarce. B2. $85.00

MARCY, Mary. *Rhymes of Early Jungle Folk.* 1922. Chicago. Kerr. 1st ed. G. B2. $35.00

MARDEN, William. *Exile of Ellendon.* 1974. Doubleday. 1st ed. F/F. F4. $16.00

MAREK, George R. *Eagles Die: Franz Joseph, Elisabeth & Their Austria.* 1974. NY. photos/ils/maps. F/F. A17. $8.50

MARGE; see Henderson, Marjorie Buell.

MARGENAU, Heny. *Nature of Physical Reality: Philosophy of Modern Physics.* 1950. McGraw Hill. blk cloth. G1. $40.00

MARGOLIES, Joseph. *Strange & Fantastic Stories.* 1946. Whittlesey. 1st ed. F/dj. M2. $30.00

MARGOLIN, Phillip. *Gone, But Not Forgotten.* 1993. Doubleday. 1st ed. F/F. T2. $22.00

MARGOLIN, Phillip. *Last Innocent Man.* 1981. Little Brn. 1st ed. F/F. T2. $20.00

MARGOLIS, John D. *Joseph Wood Krutch.* 1980. TN U. 1st ed. 254p. F/F. B19. $55.00

MARGOTTA, Roberto. *Story of Medicine.* 1968. NY. 1st ed. 4to. 319p. dj. A13. $50.00

MARGUILES, Leo. *Baseball Round-Up.* 1948. Cupples Leon. 1st ed. VG/G+. P8. $20.00

MARIANA; see Foster, Marian Curtis.

MARIETTE, Auguste. *Catalogue General des Mouments D'Abydos Decouverts...* 1880. Paris. L'Imprimerie Nationale. folio. half vellum. F. H4. $225.00

MARION, J.H. *Notes of Travel Through Territory of AZ.* 1965. AZ U. map/notes/bibliography. 62p. F/sans. B19. $45.00

MARITAIN, Jacques. *Art & Scholasticism...* 1943. Scribner. later prt. sm 8vo. 232p. purple cloth. G. G1. $17.50

MARITAIN, Jacques. *Art et Scolastique.* 1927. Paris. 2nd revised ed. 352p. cream wrp. G1. $35.00

MARITAIN, Jacques. *Christianity & Democracy.* 1944 (1943). Scribner. 1st Eng-language ed. sm 8vo. blk cloth. VG/dj. G1. $25.00

MARITAIN, Jacques. *Dream of Descartes Together With Some Other Essays.* 1944. Philosophical Lib. 1st Eng-language ed. 220p. tan cloth. G. G1. $25.00

MARITAIN, Jacques. *Existence & Existent.* 1948. Pantheon. 1st Eng-language ed. 148p. gr cloth. G. G1. $17.50

MARITAIN, Jacques. *Freedom in the Modern World.* 1936. Scribner. 1st Am ed. 223p. VG/defective. G1. $27.50

MARITAIN, Jacques. *Intro to Philosophy.* 1930. Sheed Ward. sm 8vo. 272p. G. G1. $20.00

MARITAIN, Jacques. *Man & the State.* 1951. Chicago. 219p. bl cloth. VG/dj. G1. $27.50

MARITAIN, Jacques. *Person & the Common Good.* 1947. Scribner. 1st Eng-language ed. bl cloth. VG/dj. G1. $25.00

MARITAIN, Jacques. *Preface to Metaphysics: Seven Lessons on Being.* 1939. London. Sheed Ward. 1st Eng-language ed. sm 8vo. VG/chip. G1. $25.00

MARITAIN, Jacques. *Questions de Conscience: Essais et Allocutions.* 1938. Paris. Desclee De Brouwer & Cie. 279p. prt buff wrp. G1. $46.50

MARITAIN, Jacques. *Ransoming the Time.* 1941. Scribner. 322p. gray cloth. VG/dj. G1. $27.50

MARITAIN, Jacques. *Science & Wisdom.* 1940. Scribner. 1st Eng-language ed. 241p. blk cloth. VG/dj. G1. $30.00

MARITAIN, Jacques. *Things That Are Not Caesar's.* 1930. Scribner. 1st Am ed. sm 8vo. 228p. bl cloth. G1. $27.50

MARITAIN, Jacques. *True Humanism.* 1954. London. Bles. later prt. blk cloth. 304p. VG. G1. $22.50

MARITAIN, Jacques. *Twilight of Civilization.* 1943. Sheed Ward. 1st Eng-language ed. 65p. gr cloth. VG/dj. G1. $27.50

MARIUS, Richard. *Bound for the Promised Land.* 1976. Knopf. 1st ed/author's 3rd book. F/F. B4. $125.00

MARIVAUX. *Seven Comedies by Marivaux.* 1968. Cornell. 366p. VG/dj. M20. $15.00

MARK, Davis. *Sheep of the Lal Bagh.* 1967. Parents Magazine Pr. ils Lionel Kalish. 41p. G+. A3. $6.00

MARK, Jan. *Ennead.* 1978. Crowell. 1st ed. F/dj. N3/P3. $10.00

MARK, Kathleen. *Meteorite Craters.* 1987. Tucson. 8vo. 288p. VG/VG. K5. $25.00

MARKHAM, Beryl. *West With the Night.* 1987. San Francisco. 261p. F/F. A17. $12.50

MARKHAM, Clements R. *Threshold of the Unknown Regions.* 1876. Sampson Low. ils/10 charts/maps. 463p. VG. T7. $75.00

MARKHAM, Edwin. *CA the Wonderful: Her Romantic Hist, People, Wild Shores...* 1923. Markham. ils/notes/index. 400p. VG. B19. $45.00

MARKHAM, Robert. *Colonel Sun.* 1968. Harper Row. 1st ed. VG/VG. P3. $35.00

MARKHAM, S.F. *Climate & the Energy of Nations.* 1947. Oxford. 2nd Am ed. 240p. bl cloth. G. K5. $12.00

MARKLE, Gladys Jones. *Presbyterian Church of Hazelton: Hist of 1st Hundred Yrs.* 1938. Hazelton. 1st ed. 1/250. 244p. F/case. M8. $45.00

MARKS, David. *Life of David Marks to 26th Year of His Age by Himself.* 1831. Limerick, ME. 1st ed. 396p. sheep. VG. B14. $150.00

MARKS, J.; see Highwater, Jamake.

MARKS, Jeannette. *Geoffrey's Window.* 1921. Milton Bradley. ils Clara Burd. 236p. VG/ragged. M20. $40.00

MARKS-HIGHWATER, J.; see Highwater, Jamake.

MARKSON, David. *Ballad of Dingus Magee.* 1965. Indianapolis. 1st ed/1st hc novel. inscr. NF/VG+. A11. $55.00

MARKSON, David. *Going Down.* 1970. NY. 1st ed. sgn. NF/F. A11. $55.00

MARKSON, David. *Malcolm Lowry's Volcano. Myth/Symbol/Meaning.* 1978. NY. 1st ed. sgn. F/NF. A11. $50.00

MARKSTEIN, George. *Cooler.* 1974. Souvenir. 1st ed. F/F. P3. $20.00

MARKUS, Julia. *La Mora.* 1976. Washington, DC. 1st ed/author's 1st novel. sgn. 1/1000. F/silver wrp. A11. $60.00

MARKWARD, Frank. *Swing Dat Fiddle Bow.* 1920. KS City, MO. Burton. ltd ed. 1/500. pict cloth. VG+. C8. $35.00

MARLOWE, Christopher. *Passionate Shepherd to His Love.* 1984. Fullerton. Ampersand. 55x41mm. 1/20. sgn/printer W Voss & ils C Voss. M/case. B24. $200.00

MARLOWE, Christopher. *Twelve Flowers, Arranged According to the Month...* 1983. Fullerton. Ampersand. 70x48mm. 1/35. sgns/printers Gray & Voss. w/portfolio. B24. $165.00

MARLOWE, George Francis. *Coaching Roads of Old New England.* 1945. Macmillan. 2nd prt. VG. O3. $30.00

MARLOWE, Hugh; see Patterson, Henry.

MARLOWE, John. *Arab Nationalism & British Imperialism.* 1961. NY. Praeger. 1st ed. 8vo. 236p. G. W1. $8.00

MARLOWE, Piers. *Knife for Your Heart.* 1966. Gifford. VG/VG. P3. $13.00

MARLOWE, Steven. *Man With No Shadow.* 1974. Prentice Hall. 1st ed. VG/VG. P3. $15.00

MARLOWE, Steven. *Search for Bruno Heidler.* 1967. Boardman. 1st ed. NF/NF. P3. $20.00

MARMER, H.A. *Tide.* 1926. Appleton. 282p. VG/dj. M20. $35.00

MARON, Margaret. *Death of a Butterfly.* 1984. Doubleday Crime Club. 1st ed. F/F. M15. $20.00

MARPLES, Theo. *Sealyham Terrier.* 1922. Manchester. Our Dogs. ils. 67p. limp cloth. G+. R2. $60.00

MARQUAND, John P. *HM Pulham, Esquire.* 1941. Little Brn. 1st ed. VG/G. P3. $30.00

MARQUAND, John P. *HM Pulham, Esquire.* 1941. Little Brn. 1st trade ed. 431p. VG. H1. $8.00

MARQUAND, John P. *Mr Moto Is So Sorry.* 1938. Little Brn. 1st ed. M15/Q1. $350.00

MARQUAND, John P. *Thank You, Mr Moto.* 1973. Tom Stacey. VG/G. P3. $10.00

MARQUAND, John P. *Think Fast, Mr Moto.* 1937. Little Brn. 1st ed. VG/VG. scarce. Q1. $350.00

MARQUAND, John P. *Wickford Point.* 1939. Little Brn. 1st ed. sgn. NF/VG. B4. $125.00

MARQUEZ, Gabriel Garcia. *Clandestine in Chile.* 1987. NY. Holt. 1st Am ed. 8vo. 116p. red lettered tan cloth/cream brd. F/dj. H5. $75.00

MARQUEZ, Gabriel Garcia. *General in His Labyrinth.* nd. BOMC. VG/VG. P3. $10.00

MARQUEZ, Gabriel Garcia. *General in His Labyrinth.* 1990. Knopf. ltd 1st Am ed. sgn. 1/300. full leather. F/case. C2. $300.00

MARQUEZ, Gabriel Garcia. *General in His Labyrinth.* 1990. Knopf. 1st Am ed. 8vo. 285p. gilt/blk stp gr cloth. F/NF. H5. $50.00

MARQUEZ, Gabriel Garcia. *General in His Labyrinth.* 1991. London. Cape. UP. F/pict wrp. B3. $75.00

MARQUEZ, Gabriel Garcia. *In Evil Hour.* 1979. NY. 1st Am ed. F/clip. A15. $45.00

MARQUEZ, Gabriel Garcia. *Innocent Erendira & Other Stories.* 1978. Harper. 1st Am ed. F/F. A15. $50.00

MARQUEZ, Gabriel Garcia. *Innocent Erendira & Other Stories.* 1978. Harper. 1st ed. mottled cloth. VG/VG. L3. $35.00

MARQUEZ, Gabriel Garcia. *La Hojarasca.* 1986. Mexico City. Diana. 1st ed thus. inscr/dtd 1993. F/F. L3. $450.00

MARQUEZ, Gabriel Garcia. *Los Funerales de la Mama Grande.* 1962. Xalapa. Universidad Veracruzana. 1st ed. rebound leather. F. L3. $500.00

MARQUEZ, Gabriel Garcia. *Los Funerales de la Mama Grande.* 1987. Madrid. Mondadori. 1st Spanish ed. inscr. F/F. B4. $450.00

MARQUEZ, Gabriel Garcia. *Love in the Time of Cholera.* 1988. Knopf. 1st Am ed. inscr. F/F. B4. $850.00

MARQUEZ, Gabriel Garcia. *One Hundred Years of Solitude.* 1970. Harper. 1st Am ed. inscr/sgn. F/NF. B4. $3,500.00

MARQUEZ, Gabriel Garcia. *One Hundred Years of Solitude.* 1970. Harper. 1st ed/all 1st issue points. F/F. S9. $750.00

MARQUEZ, Gabriel Garcia. *Story of the Shipwrecked Sailor.* 1986. Knopf. 1st Am ed. inscr. F/F. L3. $750.00

MARQUEZ, Gabriel Garcia. *Strange Pilgrims.* 1993. Knopf. 1st ed. F/F. B3. $15.00

MARQUIS, Don. *Archy Does His Part.* 1935. Doubleday Doran. 2nd ed. VG/VG. P3. $20.00

MARRIC, J.J.; see Creasey, John.

MARRILL, Alvin H. *Samuel Goldwyn Presents.* 1967. Barnes. VG/VG. P3. $35.00

MARRIN, Albert. *Aztecs & Spaniards.* 1986. Atheneum. 1st ed. 212p. dj. F3. $15.00

MARRIN, Albert. *War Clouds in the West. Indians & Calvarymen 1860-1890.* 1984. Atheneum. 1st ed. 8vo. ils. 220p. F/F. B11. $15.00

MARRIOTT, Charles. *Modern Movements in Painting.* nd. Scribner. 8vo. ils. wht stp bl cloth. VG. F1. $35.00

MARRYAT, F. *Children of the New Forest.* April 1930. Macmillan. 1st ed thus. VG/G+. C8. $80.00

MARRYAT, F. *Children of the New Forest.* 1927. Scribner. 1st ed. 9 mc pl. 372p. VG/G. P2. $75.00

MARRYAT, Frederick. *Peter Simple.* 1895. Little Brn. 2 vol. 1st ed. 1/750 on handmade paper. F. B2. $50.00

MARSDEN, C. *Mammillaria.* 1957. London. photos. 407p. F/dj. B26. $41.00

MARSDEN, George. *Reforming Fundamentalism.* 1988. Eerdmans. 319p. VG. B29. $7.50

MARSH, E.A. *Evolution of Automatic Machinery As Applied to...* 1896. Chicago. Hazlitt. ils. 150p. gilt bl cloth. K1. $100.00

MARSH, Geoffrey. *Patch of the Odin Soldier.* 1987. Doubleday. 1st ed. VG/VG. P3. $18.00

MARSH, Herbert. *Hist of Politicks of Great Britain & France...* 1800. London. John Stockdale. 2 vol. contemporary full tree calf. K1. $150.00

MARSH, Ngaio. *Artists in Crime.* nd. Grosset Dunlap. VG. P3. $12.00

MARSH, Ngaio. *Clutch of Constables.* 1969. Little Brn. 1st ed. 244p. VG/dj. M20. $20.00

MARSH, Ngaio. *Collected Short Fiction of Nagio Marsh.* nd. Quality BC. F/F. P3. $10.00

MARSH, Ngaio. *Death & the Dancing Footman.* 1941. Little Brn. 1st ed (precedes Eng ed). F/VG. M15. $85.00

MARSH, Ngaio. *False Scent.* 1960. Collins. 1st ed. VG/VG. P3. $25.00

MARSH, Ngaio. *Hand in Glove.* 1962. Collins Crime Club. 1st ed. VG/torn. P3. $20.00

MARSH, Ngaio. *Hand in Glove.* 1962. Little Brn. 1st Am ed. F/F. M15. $25.00

MARSH, Ngaio. *Killer Dolphin.* 1946. Little Brn. 1st ed. VG/VG. P3. $40.00

MARSH, Ngaio. *Light Thickens.* 1982. London. Collins Crime Club. 1st ed. F/clip. M15. $25.00

MARSH, Ngaio. *Scales of Justice.* 1955. Collins Crime Club. 1st ed. VG/G. P3. $30.00

MARSH, Ngaio. *Scales of Justice.* 1955. Little Brn. 1st ed. VG/VG. S9. $45.00

MARSH, Ngaio. *When in Rome.* 1971. Little Brn. 1st ed. VG/G. P3. $20.00

MARSH & PINNEY. *Millennial Harp: New Collection of Scriptural Hymns...* 1851. Rochester. Advent Harbinger Office. 1st ed. thick 8vo. 511p. M1. $425.00

MARSHALL, Alan; see Westlake, Donald E.

MARSHALL, Catherine. *Best of Peter Marshall.* 1983. Guideposts. 338p. F/F. B29. $4.50

MARSHALL, Catherine. *Helper.* 1978. Guideposts. 221p. VG/dj. B29. $4.50

MARSHALL, Edison. *Dian of the Lost Land.* 1966. Chilton. VG/VG. P3. $30.00

MARSHALL, Edison. *Sleeper of the Moonlit Ranges.* 1925. NY. 1st ed. NF. A17. $15.00

MARSHALL, Edward. *Fox All Week.* 1984. Dial. 1st ed. ils James Marshall. M/M. C8. $40.00

MARSHALL, Emma. *Tower on the Cliff.* 1886. Dutton. 1st ed. VG. M2. $12.00

MARSHALL, Henry Rutgers. *Consciousness.* 1909. London. Macmillan. 1st ed. inscr. 685p. bl cloth. G1. $75.00

MARSHALL, James. *George & Martha, Back in Town.* 1984. Houghton Mifflin. 1st ed. inscr w/drawing. M/M. C8. $60.00

MARSHALL, James. *George & Martha, Encore.* 1973. Houghton Mifflin. 1st prt. M/M. C8. $40.00

MARSHALL, James. *It's So Nice To Have a Wolf Around the House.* 1977. Doubleday. 1st ed. inscr w/drawing. M/M. C8. $60.00

MARSHALL, James. *Miss Dog's Christmas Treat.* 1973. Houghton Mifflin. 1st prt. ils Marshall. VG. C8. $15.00

MARSHALL, James. *Old Mother Hubbard & Her Wonderful Dog.* 1991. FSG. 1st ed. sm 4to. M/M. C8. $30.00

MARSHALL, James. *Portly McSwine.* 1979. Houghton Mifflin. 1st ed. inscr w/drawing. M/M. C8. $50.00

MARSHALL, James. *Rapscallion Jones.* 1983. Viking. 1st ed. sm 4to. M/M. C8. $40.00

MARSHALL, James. *Summer in the South.* 1977. Houghton Mifflin. 1st ed. inscr w/drawing. F/F. C8. $55.00

MARSHALL, James. *Three Little Pigs.* 1989. Dial. stated 1st ed. M/M. C8. $30.00

MARSHALL, James. *Willis.* 1974. Houghton Mifflin. 1st prt. inscr w/drawing. M/M. C8. $60.00

MARSHALL, John. *Life of George Washington: Commander in Chief...* 1807. np. 1st ed. tall 8vo. full calf. VG. E5. $65.00

MARSHALL, Logan. *Story of the Panama Canal.* 1913. Phil. Ziegler. sample copy. 8vo. fld map. red cloth. VG. B11. $75.00

MARSHALL, Paule. *Brown Girl, Brownstones.* 1959. NY. Random. 1st ed/author's 1st book. F/NF. Q1. $200.00

MARSHALL, Peter. *Mr Jones, Meet the Master.* 1951. Revell. 192p. G/dj. B29. $3.50

MARSHALL, Raymond. *In a Vain Shadow.* 1951. Jarrolds. 1st ed. VG/VG. P3. $25.00

MARSHALL, Rosamond. *Kitty.* 1945. Forum. 3rd ed. VG/G. P3. $18.00

MARSHALL, S.L.A. *Ambush.* 1969. NY. 1st ed. ils. 242p. VG/dj. B18. $22.50

MARSHALL, William. *Far Away Man.* 1984. NY. Holt. 1st Am ed. sgn. F/F. S6. $35.00

MARSHALL, William. *Frogsmouth.* 1987. Mysterious. 1st ed. F/dj. F4. $16.00

MARSHALL, William. *Hatchet Man.* 1976. HRW. 1st Am ed. F/F. O4. $35.00

MARSHALL, William. *Out of Nowhere.* 1988. Mysterious. UP. NF/prt yel wrp. B3. $20.00

MARSHALL, William. *Out of Nowhere.* 1988. Mysterious. 1st ed. F/F. F4/P3. $16.00

MARSHALL, William. *Roadshow.* 1985. HRW. 1st Am ed. F/F. O4. $15.00

MARSHALL, William. *Sci-Fi.* 1981. HRW. ARC/1st Am ed. F/F. O4. $25.00

MARSHALL, William. *War Machine.* 1977. Mysterious. 1st Am ed. sgn. F/F. S6. $35.00

MARSON, G.F. *Ghosts, Ghouls & Gallows.* 1946. Rider. 1st ed. VG/torn. P3. $25.00

MARSTEN, Richard; see Hunter, Evan.

MARSTON, R.B. *Walton & Earlier Fishing Writers.* 1894. London. VG. B5. $175.00

MARSZALEK, John. *Sherman: A Soldier's Passion for Orders.* 1993. index. 635p. dj. O8. $14.50

MARTEL, Suzanne. *City Under Ground.* 1964. Viking. 1st ed. G+/dj. P3. $20.00

MARTI-IBANEZ, Felix. *Ariel: Essays on the Arts & History & Philosophy Medicine.* 1962. NY. 1st ed. 292p. A13. $30.00

MARTIN, Dahris. *I Know Tunisia.* 1943. NY. Washburn. 1st ed. 271p. xl. G. W1. $7.00

MARTIN, David. *Final Harbor.* 1984. HRW. 1st ed. VG/VG. P3. $25.00

MARTIN, Edward Sandford. *Luxury of Children & Some Other Luxuries.* 1904. NY. 1st ed. 8 mc pl. gr cloth/pl. VG. M5. $95.00

MARTIN, Eva. *Reincarnation: Ring of Return.* 1963. University Books. 1st Am ed. 306p. VG/VG. B33. $24.00

MARTIN, George Madden. *Emmy Lou: Her Book & Heart.* 1903. McClure Phillips. 7th imp. G+. B10. $20.00

MARTIN, George R.R. *Armageddon Rag.* 1983. Poseidon. 1st ed. F/dj. M2. $25.00

MARTIN, George R.R. *Fevre Dream.* 1982. Poseidon. 1st ed. inscr. F/F. T2. $50.00

MARTIN, George R.R. *Songs the Dead Men Sing.* 1985. Gollancz. 1st ed. sgn. F/F. P3. $35.00

MARTIN, George R.R. *Turf Voyaging.* 1986. Baen. 1st ed. F/F. T2. $12.00

MARTIN, George Victor. *Bells of St Mary's.* 1946. Grosset Dunlap. MTI. VG/VG. P3. $20.00

MARTIN, H.B. *Great Golfers in the Making.* 1932. NY. 1st ed. cloth. VG. C11. $65.00

MARTIN, H.B. *50 Years of American Golf.* 1966 (1936). NY. rpt. cloth. VG. C11. $65.00

MARTIN, Isaac. *Journal of Life, Travels, Labours & Religious Exercises...* 1834. Phil. 1st ed. 160p. orig full leather. VG. M8. $75.00

MARTIN, Jack; see Etchison, Dennis.

MARTIN, John. *God's Dark & Other Bedtime Verses & Songs.* 1927. Doran. 1st ed. inscr. ils Harold Sichel. VG. C8. $75.00

MARTIN, Joseph Plumb. *Yankee Doodle Boy: Young Soldier's Adventures...* ca 1964. Scott. 191p. F/VG. B10. $10.00

MARTIN, Kingsley. *Harold Laski (1893-1950).* 1953. NY. 278p. xl. VG. D3. $15.00

MARTIN, L'Abbe. *Actes Du Brigandage d'Ephese.* 1874. Amiens. 1st ed. 183p. VG. W1. $10.00

MARTIN, Marty. *Gertrude Stein.* 1980. Random. BC. NF/NF. E3. $10.00

MARTIN, Mary. *Mary Martin's Needlepoint.* 1969. np. cloth. VG. G2. $16.00

MARTIN, Patricia Preciado. *Songs My Mother Sang to Me: Oral Hist of Mexican-Am Women.* 1992. AZ U. 1st ed. ils/index. 224p. F/F. B19. $20.00

MARTIN, Robert. *Killer Among Us.* 1958. Detective BC. VG. P3. $8.00

MARTIN, Scott. *Medieval Europe.* 1964. McKay. 463p. F/dj. M10. $10.00

MARTIN, Thomas. *Conveyancers; Recital-Book: With Explanatory Intro & Notes.* 1834. London. Stevens. contemporary brd/rebacked. M11. $250.00

MARTIN, Valerie. *Alexandra.* 1979. FSG. 1st ed. F/F. T2. $12.00

MARTIN, Valerie. *Consolation of Nature & Other Stories.* 1988. Houghton Mifflin. 1st ed. F/F. T2. $15.00

MARTIN, Valerie. *Mary Reilly.* 1990. Doubleday. 1st ed. inscr. F/F. B4. $100.00

MARTIN & TUTTLE. *Windhaven.* 1981. Timescape. 1st ed. sgn Martin. F/F. P3. $40.00

MARTINEAU, Harriet. *Feats on the Fiord.* 1924. Macmillan. 1st ed. ils Artzybasheff. gilt blk/bl pict bdg. VG. P2. $60.00

MARTINEAU, Harriet. *Feats on the Fiord.* 1928. Macmillan. later prt. ils Artzybasheff. VG. B10. $20.00

MARTINEAU, James. *Types of Ethical Theory.* 1885. Clarendon. 2 vol. paneled bl cloth. VG. G1. $85.00

MARTINEK, Frank V. *Don Winslow & Scorpion's Stronghold.* 1946. Whitman. ils. VG. P3. $8.00

MARTINEZ, Al. *Jigsaw John.* 1975. Tarcher. 1st ed. VG. P3. $15.00

MARTINEZ, Jose Longinos. *Journal of Jose Longinos Matinez...CA & the S Coast...1792.* 1961. San Francisco. Howell. 1/1000. 3 maps. 144p. gr cloth. F. P4. $85.00

MARTINGDALE, T. *Hunting in the Upper Yukon.* 1913. Phil. 1st ed. ils. 320p. VG. B5. $95.00

MARTINS, Mildred. *Martins of Gunbarrel.* 1959. Caxton. author's only book. F/VG. B34. $35.00

MARTINUCCI, Pio. *Manuale Sacrarum Caeremoniarum in Libros Octo Digestum.* 1879. Rome. Cecchini. 2 vol in 1. 320p. xl. H10. $25.00

MARTY, Martin E. *Health & Medicine in the Lutheran Tradition.* 1986. Crossroad. 178p. G/dj. B29. $7.00

MARURG, Theodore. *Draft Convention for League of Nations.* 1918. NY. 12mo. 46p. xl. VG. D3. $25.00

MARVELL, Andrew. *Garden.* 1981. Mill Valley. Sunflower. 70x73mm. 1/55. sgn printer Cunningham. floral bdg. F. B24. $200.00

MARWIL, Jonathan. *Frederick Manning: An Unfinished Life.* 1988. Sydney. Angus Robertson. 1st ed. F/F. M7. $35.00

MARX, Groucho. *Beds.* 1930. NY. Farrar Rinehart. 1st ed (pub colophon copyright p). pict brd. NF/dj. Q1. $375.00

MARX, Groucho. *Groucho Letters.* 1967. NY. 1st ed. sgn. F/NF. C2. $200.00

MARX, K.F.H. *Zur Erinnerung der Arztlichen Wirksamkeit Herman Conring's.* 1872. Gottingen. 4to. 51p. brd/orig wrp laid down. unopened. G7. $45.00

MARX, Robert F. *Port Royal Rediscovered.* 1973. Doubleday. 1st ed. 8vo. 304p. VG/VG. B11. $30.00

MARYSTONE, Cyril. *Grave & Urgent Warnings From Heaven.* ca 1978. np. 1st ed. 418p. VG/stiff wrp. W1. $14.00

MASAEUS. *Loves of Hero & Leander.* 1747. London. 1s ed thus. trans Bally. quarter cloth. gilt bdg. C2. $300.00

MASCART, Jean. *Impressions et Observations Dans un Voyage a Tenerife.* ca 1912. Paris. Flammarion. 1st ed. ils. 366p. xl. G/wrp. W1. $12.00

MASEFIELD, John. *Right Royal.* 1920. London. ltd ed. sgn. 1/500. VG. A1. $20.00

MASEFIELD, John. *Sea Life in Nelson's Time.* 1925. Macmillan. ils. 218p. T7. $45.00

MASEFIELD, John. *Water Poems & Ballads.* 1916. np. 160+p. gilt cloth. NF. E5. $35.00

MASHA. *Bedtime Stories.* 1946. Wonder Book 507. K2. $15.00

MASJUTIN, Wassilij. *Ruslan und Ludmilla.* 1922. Munich. Orchis. 1/100. sgn. pochoir ils brd/vellum spine. NF. B24. $750.00

MASKELL, Alfred. *Ivories.* 1905. NY. Connoisseurs Lib. 88 pl. 443p. G. B5. $95.00

MASKELL, Alfred. *Ivories.* 1986. Rutland. Tuttle. 2nd prt of 1905 rpt. 551p. F/dj/cb case. F1. $35.00

MASLOW & MITTELMANN. *Principles of Abnormal Psychology.* 1941. Harper. 546p. reading copy. K4. $10.00

MASON, A.E.W. *House in Lordship Lane.* 1946. Dodd Mead. xl. VG. P3. $10.00

MASON, A.E.W. *They Wouldn't Be Chessmen.* 1935. Doubleday Doran. 1st ed. VG. P3. $35.00

MASON, Alpheus Thomas. *Brandeis: A Free Man's Life.* 1956. Viking. VG/worn. M11. $35.00

MASON, Bobbie Ann. *Feather Crowns.* 1993. Harper Collins. 1st trade ed. sgn. F/F. L3. $45.00

MASON, Bobbie Ann. *In Country.* 1985. Harper Row. 1st ed. F/F. B3. $35.00

MASON, Bobbie Ann. *In Country.* 1985. Harper Row. 1st ed. sgn. F/F. C2. $50.00

MASON, Bobbie Ann. *Jazz.* nd. Larkspur. 1st ed. 32p. VG. C4. $30.00

MASON, Bobbie Ann. *Shiloh & Other Stories.* 1982. Harper Row. 1st ed. F/F. L3. $65.00

MASON, Bobbie Ann. *Shiloh & Other Stories.* 1982. Harper Row. 1st ed/1st hc/1st fiction book. inscr. F/NF. A11. $115.00

MASON, Clifford. *Case of the Ashanti Gold.* 1985. NY. St Martin. 1st ed. F/NF. M15. $25.00

MASON, Douglas R. *Phaeton Condition.* 1973. Putnam. 1st ed. F/F. P3. $15.00

MASON, Erskine. *God's Hand in Human Events.* 1850. NY. Craighead. 1st ed. 19p. VG/prt wrp. M8. $22.50

MASON, John. *Papermaking As an Artistic Craft.* 1963. Leicester. Twelve by Eight. 8vo. ils R Graham. F/wrp. B24. $175.00

MASON, John. *Papermaking As an Artistic Craft.* 1963. Leicester. Twelve by Eight. revised ed. 96p. w/sgn note. K1. $200.00

MASON, Lisa. *Arachne.* 1990. Morrow. 1st ed. F/F. T2. $20.00

MASON, Newell Ormsbee. *Hist of Cavalry Episcopal Church in Summit, NJ 1854-1954.* 1954. np. 1st ed. 86p. cloth. VG. M8. $37.50

MASON, Paule. *Man in the Garden.* 1969. McKay Washburn. 1st ed. VG/VG. P3. $15.00

MASON, Phillips. *X of Psychology: Essay on Problem of Science of Mind.* 1940. Cambridge. Harvard. 216p. paneled crimson cloth. VG. G1. $28.50

MASON, Van Wyck. *Blue Hurricane.* 1955. Jarrolds. 1st ed. VG/rpr. P3. $8.00

MASON, Van Wyck. *Deadly Orbit Mission.* 1968. Doubleday. 1st ed. VG/VG. P3. $23.00

MASON, Van Wyck. *Rio Casino Intrigue.* 1941. Reynal Hitchcock. 1st ed. VG/VG. M15. $30.00

MASPERO, Gaston. *Popular Stories of Ancient Egypt.* 1967. New Hyde Park. revised ed. 316p. VG. W1. $30.00

MASPERO, Gaston. *Struggle of Nations.* 1897. NY. Appleton. 1st Am ed. 794p. xl. VG. W1. $40.00

MASSEY, Marilyn. *Above & Below Ground: Jack Russell Terrier in North Am.* 1985. VA. Woodluck. 1st ed. sgn. 187p. cloth. F/F. R2. $60.00

MASSEY, William T. *How Jerusalem Was Won.* 1919. London. Constable. 1st ed. 8vo. 295p. gilt bl cloth. G+. M7. $75.00

MASSIE, Allan. *One Night in Winter.* 1984. Bodley Head. 1st ed. F/F. P3. $15.00

MASSIN. *Letter & Image.* 1970. Van Nostrand Reinhold. 1st ed. 4to. 287p. red/wht stp blk cloth. F/F. F1. $45.00

MASSMANN, Robert. *Dard Hunter on Papyrus.* 1971. New Britain, CT. Art Pr. 41x52mm. 1/50. 16p/frenchfold. sarcophagus-formed wrp. B24. $285.00

MASSMANN, Robert. *Dard Hunter: Miscellaneous Thoughts & Reflections...* 1984. New Britain, CT. 2 vol. 60x53mm & 55mm diameter. F/cb model of paper mill case. B24. $300.00

MASSMANN, Robert. *Legendary History of the Cross.* 1965. New Britain. 66x59mm. 1/50. inscr. 11 fld pl. formed as Maltese Cross. F. B24. $450.00

MASSON, Gustave. *Mediaeval France: From Reign of Hugues Capet...* 1888. London/NY. 1st ed. 354p. G. W1. $15.00

MASSOTH, Ray. *Book of Christmas.* 1991. Ashfield. 51x46mm. 1/26 lettered. ils Suzanne Moore. damask. F/sleeve. B24. $285.00

MAST, Isaac. *Gun, Saddle & Rod: 9 Months in California.* 1875. Phil. 1st ed. VG. B5. $50.00

MASTERMAN, Walter S. *Crime of the Reckaviles.* 1934. Methuen. 3rd ed. VG. P3. $18.00

MASTERS, Anthony. *Natural Hist of the Vampire.* 1972. Putnam. 1st ed. ils. 259p. VG/VG. S11. $20.00

MASTERS, David. *Romance of Excavation.* 1923. Dodd Mead. 1st ed. 8vo. VG. W1. $12.00

MASTERS, E.L. *Across Spoon River.* 1946. NY. later ed. sgn pres. VG/VG. B5. $30.00

MASTERS, E.L. *Mitch Miller.* 1920. Macmillan. ils. G+. B10. $20.00

MASTERS, John. *Now, God Be Thanked.* 1979. Franklin Lib. 1st ed. ils Francis Golden. full leather. F. B3. $40.00

MASTERSON, Whit. *Evil Come, Evil Go.* nd. BC. VG/VG. P3. $8.00

MASTERSON, Whit. *Gravy Train.* 1971. Dodd Mead. 1st ed. VG/VG. P3. $20.00

MASTERSON, Whit. *Why She Cries, I Do Not Know.* 1972. Dodd Mead. VG/VG. P3. $18.00

MASTERTON, Graham. *Mirror.* 1988. Tor. 1st ed. F/F. P3. $19.00

MASTON, T.B. *Conscience of a Christian.* 1971. Word. 157p. VG/torn. B29. $3.25

MASUR, Harold Q. *Attorney.* 1973. Random. 1st ed. VG/VG. P3. $18.00

MATHER, Berkely. *Springers.* 1968. London. Collins. 1st ed. F/NF. S6. $22.50

MATHER, Cotton. *Essay To Do Good, Addressed to All Christians...* 1815. NY. Asa Child. 12mo. 196p. orig calf/blk spine. K1. $100.00

MATHESON, Richard. *Born of Man & Woman.* 1954. Chamberlain. 1st ed. F/chip. M2. $200.00

MATHESON, Richard. *Earthbound.* 1989. Robinson. F/F. P3. $30.00

MATHESON, Richard. *Hell House.* 1971. Viking. 1st ed. VG/NF. B2. $85.00

MATHESON, Richard. *Somewhere in Time/What Dreams May Come.* 1991. Los Angeles. Dream. 1st combined ed. sgn. F/F. T2. $65.00

MATHESON & TABACHNICK. *Images of Lawrence.* 1988. Cape. photos. gilt brn cloth. M/dj. M7. $35.00

MATHESON & TABACHNICK. *Images of Lawrence.* 1991. Tokyo. 1st Japanese ed. sgn Tabachnick. gray brd. M. M7. $39.00

MATHEWS, Basil. *Life of Jesus.* 1931. Smith. 1st ed. 519p. VG. W1. $9.00

MATHEWS, D.L. *Very Welcome Death.* 1961. HRW. 1st ed. VG. P3. $8.00

MATHEWS, F. Schuyler. *Familiar Flowers of Field & Garden.* 1898 (1895). NY. 4th ed. ils/index/floral calendar. gilt cloth. VG. B26. $16.00

MATHEWS, George. *Account of the Trial...Reverend Thomas Emlyn...* 1839. Belfast/Dublin. W M'Comb. modern quarter calf. G. M11. $275.00

MATHEWS, Kevin; see Fox, Gardner F.

MATHEWSON, Christy. *Catcher Craig.* 1915. Grosset Dunlap. rpt. Matty Books Series #2. VG/G. P8. $55.00

MATHEWSON, Christy. *First Base Faulkner.* 1916. Dodd Mead. 1st ed. Matty Books Series #3. G. P8. $65.00

MATHEWSON, Christy. *Pitching in a Pinch.* 1912. NY. Boy Scout ed. photos. VG. B5. $40.00

MATHIAS, Fred. *Amazing Bob Davis: His Last Vagabond Journey.* 1944. NY. Longman. 1st ed. 326p. VG/dj. F3. $15.00

MATHIESON, Elizabeth. *Complete Book of Crochet.* 1977. np. cloth. VG. G2. $12.50

MATHIS, Edward. *From a High Place.* nd. BC. VG/VG. P3. $8.00

MATHIS, Edward. *September Song.* 1991. NY. Scribner. ARC/1st ed. RS. F/F. S6. $25.00

MATHISON, Richard. *Eternal Search: Story of Man & His Drugs.* 1959. London. Muller. 1st ed. 308p. VG/G. B33. $17.00

MATHUR, Y.B. *Muslims & Changing India.* 1972. New Delhi. Trimurti. 8vo. VG/torn. W1. $12.00

MATISSE, Henri. *Henri Matisse, Roman.* 1971. Paris. Gallimard. 2 vol. 1st ed. French text. F/F/F cloth case. S9. $250.00

MATISSE, Henri. *Matisse, 50 Years of His Graphic Art.* 1956. NY. Braziller. sm 4to. wht/red stp blk cloth. VG/dj. F1. $35.00

MATSCHAT, Cecile Hulse. *American Butterflies & Moths.* 1942. Random. ils Rudolf Freund. VG. B17. $8.00

MATSUMURA, Masko. *Bird's Wedding.* ca 1982. Faber. 1st ed. trans Lucy Meredith. VG. B10. $12.00

MATTES, Merrill J. *Great Platte River Road: Covered Wagon Mainline...* 1987. NE U. 3rd sc ed. M. A18. $17.00

MATTES, Merrill J. *Platte River Road Narratives: Descriptive Bibliography...* 1988. IL U. lg format. 632p. M. A18. $95.00

MATTES. *Platte River Road Narratives, a Descriptive Bibliography...* 1988. IL U. maps. 647p. F/sans. A4. $95.00

MATTHEW, Donald. *Atlas of Medieval Europe.* 1983. Facts on File. ils. 240p. VG/dj. M10. $27.50

MATTHEW, Donald. *Atlas of Medieval Man.* ca 1980. Crescent. ils. 256p. NF/dj. M10. $18.50

MATTHEWS, Anthony. *Swinging Murder.* 1969. Walker. 1st ed. VG/VG. P3. $15.00

MATTHEWS, Greg. *Further Adventures of Huckleberry Finn.* 1983. Crown. 1st ed. VG/VG. P3. $16.00

MATTHEWS, Greg. *Further Adventures of Huckleberry Finn.* 1983. NY. 1st Am ed. F/wrinkled. A17. $15.00

MATTHEWS, I.G. *Religious Pilgrimage of Israel.* 1947. Harper. 1st ed. 304p. G/dj. B29. $8.00

MATTHEWS, Jack. *Booking in the Heartland.* 1986. Johns Hopkins. 1st ed. 161p. VG/VG. S11. $10.00

MATTHEWS, Jack. *Memoirs of a Bookman.* 1990. Athens. 1st ed. F/F. B3. $10.00

MATTHEWS, Kevin; see Fox, Gardner F.

MATTHEWS, L. Harrison. *Natural History of the Whale.* 1978. NY. Columbia. 1st ed/3rd prt. ils/pl. 219p. M/dj. P4. $35.00

MATTHEWS, Patricia. *Unquiet.* 1991. Severn. 1st ed. NF/NF. P3. $20.00

MATTHEWS, Thomas. *Stories of the World's Great Operas.* 1968. Golden. ils Robert Shore. F/NF. C8. $25.00

MATTHIAE, Paolo. *Ebla: Empire Rediscovered.* 1980. Hodder Stoughton. 1st Eng ed. 237p. NF/dj. W1. $25.00

MATTHIESSEN, Peter. *African Silences.* 1991. Random. 1st ed. F/F. B3. $15.00

MATTHIESSEN, Peter. *In the Spirit of Crazy Horse.* 1983. NY. 1st ed. NF/NF. C2. $150.00

MATTHIESSEN, Peter. *In the Spirit of Crazy Horse.* 1983. NY. 1st ed. VG/VG. A9. $75.00

MATTHIESSEN, Peter. *Indian Country.* 1984. Viking. 1st ed. F/F. L3. $100.00

MATTHIESSEN, Peter. *Killing Mr Watson.* 1989. NY. AP. F/wrp. C2. $75.00

MATTHIESSEN, Peter. *Men's Lives.* 1988. London. 1st ed. VG. C4. $55.00

MATTHIESSEN, Peter. *Nine-Headed Dragon River: Zen Journals 1969-1982.* 1986. Viking. 1st ed. 288p. VG/VG. B33. $24.00

MATTHIESSEN, Peter. *On the River Styx & Other Stories.* 1989. NY. AP. F/wrp. C2. $60.00

MATTHIESSEN, Peter. *Oomingmak.* 1967. NY. 1st ed. sgn. F/F. A11. $60.00

MATTHIESSEN, Peter. *Partisans.* 1956. London. Secker Warburg. 1st Eng ed/author's 2nd book. VG/VG. L3. $125.00

MATTHIESSEN, Peter. *Race Rock.* 1954. Harper. 1st ed/author's 1st novel. bl cloth/blk brd. NF/NF. L3. $325.00

MATTHIESSEN, Peter. *Sand Rivers.* 1981. NY. Viking. 1st ed. F/VG. B3. $30.00

MATTHIESSEN, Peter. *Snow Leopard.* 1978. Viking. 338p. VG/VG. B33. $20.00

MATTINGLY, Garrett. *Armada.* 1959. Houghton Mifflin. BC. 443p. VG/fair. B11. $15.00

MATTINGLY, Garrett. *Armada.* 1959. Houghton Mifflin. ils/maps. VG/VG. T7. $25.00

MATUDA & PINA. *Las Plantas Mexicanas del Genero Yucca.* 1980. Toluca. photos/maps. 145p. sc. F. B26. $56.00

MATZ, Friedrich. *Art of Early Crete & Early Greece.* 1962. NY. Graystone. 1st ed. 258p. VG/dj. W1. $25.00

MAUDER, Bruno. *Ornamente.* ca 1900. Plauen. Christian Stroll. folio. unbound as issued. F/lacks 1 ribbon tie. B24. $850.00

MAUDSLEY, Henry. *Body & Will: Being Essay...* 1884. Appleton. 1st Am ed. ruled gr cloth. G. G1. $100.00

MAUER, M. *Air Force Combat Units of WWII.* 1963. NY. 1st ed. ils/index. 506p. VG/VG. B5. $65.00

MAUGHAM, Robin. *Wrong People.* 1971. McGraw Hill. 1st ed. F/F. B3. $25.00

MAUGHAM, W. Somerset. *Ashenden; or, The British Agent.* 1928. Doubleday Doran. 1st ed. VG+/dj. Q1. $750.00

MAUGHAM, W. Somerset. *Catalina.* 1948. Doubleday. 1st ed. VG/VG. P3. $30.00

MAUGHAM, W. Somerset. *Making of a Saint.* 1898. Boston. Page. 1st Am ed/mixed state (1st issue ads/later spine). NF. B4. $400.00

MAUGHAM, W. Somerset. *Princess September & the Nightingale.* 1939. London. Oxford. 1st ed thus. ils RC Jones. F/VG. C8. $50.00

MAUGHAM, W. Somerset. *Princess September.* ca 1969. HBW. 1st ed thus. unp. VG/G. B10. $18.00

MAULDIN, Bill. *Mud, Mules & Mountains.* nd (1944). np. 1st ed. cartoons. VG/pict wrp. Q1. $125.00

MAULDIN, Bill. *Up Front.* 1945. Holt. 4th prt. 228p. cloth. F/F. B14. $100.00

MAULE, Harry E. *Fall Roundup.* 1955. Random. ARC of 1st ed. 17 stories. F/dj. A18. $20.00

MAUNDER, E.W. *Sir William Huggins & Spectorscopic Astronomy.* ca 1914. London. Jack. 94p. gr cloth. G. K5. $30.00

MAUNOIR, J.-P. *Memoires Physiologiques et Pratiques sur l'Aneurisme...* 1802. Geneva. half title. 2 fld engraved pl. 130p. contemporary brd. G7. $195.00

MAURICE, Frederick Denison. *Conscience: Lectures on Casuistry...* 1872. London. Macmillan. 2nd ed. 12mo. G. G1. $35.00

MAURICE, Henry. *Vindication of Primitive Church & Diocesan Episcopany...* 1682. London. Moses Pitt. 1st ed. 567p. calf. rpr hinge. H10. $95.00

MAUROIS, Andre. *Chelsea Way.* 1930. London. Mathews Marrot. 1/530 #d. trans Hamish Miles. VG+/VG+. S9. $75.00

MAUROIS, Andre. *Illusions.* 1968. Columbia. sm 8vo. 101p. mottled gr-gray cloth. VG/dj. G1. $25.00

MAUROIS, Andre. *Lafayette in America.* 1960. Houghton Mifflin. 184p. VG/G. B10. $10.00

MAUROIS, Andre. *Memoirs 1885-1967.* 1970. Harper. 1st Am ed. 440p. red cloth. VG/dj. G1. $25.00

MAVITY, Nancy Barr. *Tule Marsh Murder.* 1929. Crime Club. 1st ed. VG. P3. $20.00

MAWSON, Thomas H. *Art & Craft of Garden Making.* 1912. NY. 5th ed. rebacked gr leather. H4. $165.00

MAXIM, John R. *Time Out of Mind.* 1986. Houghton Mifflin. 1st ed. VG/VG. P3. $18.00

MAXWELL, A.E. *Art of Survival.* 1989. Doubleday. 1st ed. VG/VG. P3. $18.00

MAXWELL, A.E. *Jut Another Day in Paradise.* 1985. Doubleday. 1st ed. sgn. F/F. M15. $45.00

MAXWELL, Herbert. *Chronicle of Lanercost, 1272-1346.* 1913. Glasgow. 1st ed thus. 1/100. half vellum/red brd. VG. C6. $150.00

MAXWELL, James. *Level & Trend of National Intelligence.* 1961. London. 75p. F/dj. K4. $20.00

MAXWELL, Lilian. *'Round New Brunswick Roads.* 1951. Ryerson. VG. P3. $15.00

MAXWELL, Thomas. *Kiss Me Twice.* 1988. Mysterious. 1st ed. VG/VG. P3. $18.00

MAXWELL, William. *Chateau.* 1961. Knopf. 1st ed. F/NF. B2. $40.00

MAXWELL, William. *Heavenly Tenants.* 1946. NY. 1st ed/1st & only children's book. inscr. F/VG-. A11. $75.00

MAXWELL, William. *Over by the River.* 1977. Knopf. 1st ed. F/F. B2. $40.00

MAXWELL, William. *So Long, See You Tomorrow.* 1988. London. 1st ed. intl inscr. F/F. A11. $45.00

MAXWELL, William. *So Long, See You Tomorrow.* 1988. London. Secker Warburg. ARC. F/F. L3. $65.00

MAXXE, Robert; see Rosenblum, Robert.

MAY, Barbara. *Buckle Horse.* 1956. NY. Holt. 1st ed. VG. O3. $30.00

MAY, Gerald G. *Addiction & Grace.* 1988. Harper. 200p. F/dj. B29. $7.50

MAY, Julian. *Golden Torc.* 1982. Houghton Mifflin. 1st ed. inscr. F/NF. F4. $22.00

MAY, Julian. *How We Are Born.* 1969. Follett. 1st ed. NF. N3. $10.00

MAY, Julian. *Many-Colored Land.* 1981. Houghton Mifflin. sgn. F/dj. F4. $25.00

MAY, Julian. *Pliocene Companion.* 1985. Collins. 1st Eng ed. F/F. M21. $20.00

MAY, Lini S. *Iqbal: His Life & Times.* 1974. Lahore. Ashraf. 1st ed. 8vo. xl. G/dj. W1. $10.00

MAY, Rollo. *Paulus: Reminiscences of a Friendship.* 1973. Harper Row. 1st ed. 113p. VG/VG. B33. $30.00

MAY, Stella Burke. *Men, Maidens & Mantillas.* 1923. Century. 362p. VG. F3. $20.00

MAYER, B. *Tah-Gah-Jute; or, Logan & Cresap.* 1867. Albany. enlarged ed. G. C11. $100.00

MAYER, M. *Met: 100 Years of Grand Opera.* 1983. NY. ltd special bdg 1st ed. sgn. NF. B5. $95.00

MAYER, Mercer. *Ah-Choo.* 1976. Dial. 1st prt. ils Mercer Mayer. glazed pict brd. RS. M/M. C8. $50.00

MAYER, Mercer. *Hiccup.* 1976. Dial. 1st ed. ils. VG/VG. P2. $18.00

MAYER, Robert. *Grace of Shortstops.* 1984. Doubleday. 1st ed. F/VG+. P8. $20.00

MAYER & PRIDEAUX. *Never To Die.* 1938. Viking. 1st ed. 224p. VG/G. S11. $30.00

MAYHAR, Ardath. *Warlock's Gift.* 1982. Doubleday. 1st ed. VG/VG. P3. $15.00

MAYHEW, Aubrey. *Medals, Coins & Tokens: Ils Standard Reference...* 1966. Morrow. 4to. ils. 197p. VG/torn. M10. $20.00

MAYHEW, Augustus. *Paved With Gold.* 1858. London. Chapman Hall. 24 full-p ils. 408p. Birdsall bdg. K1. $125.00

MAYHEW, Phyllis M. *Tibetan Spaniel.* 1971. Great Britain. 1st ed. 104p. VG/wrp. R2. $60.00

MAYNARD & MILES. *William S Burroughs: A Bibliography 1953-1973.* 1978. np. 1/2000. 265p. F. A4. $35.00

MAYNE, Peter. *Alleys of Marrakesh.* 1954. London. Travel Book Club. 1st ed. 172p. VG. W1. $12.00

MAYNE, William. *Green Book of Hob Stories.* 1984. Philomel. 1st Am ed. ils. F/F. P2. $20.00

MAYNE, William. *Ravensgill.* 1970. Dutton. 1st ed. 174p. VG/ils Edward Gorey. M20. $12.50

MAYO, Jim; see L'Amour, Louis.

MAYOR, A. Hyatt. *Popular Prints of the Americas.* 1973. NY. Crown. folio. ils. gilt gr cloth. F/VG+. F1. $35.00

MAZAR & MOSHE. *Ils Hist of the Jews.* 1963. Harper. 1st ed. 414p. VG/tattered. W1. $12.00

MAZOWER, Mark. *Inside Hitler's Greece. Experience of Occupation 1941-44.* 1993. New Haven. 8vo. ils. 437p. cloth. dj. O2. $32.50

MAZZEI, Filippo. *Recherches Historiques et Politiques sur les Etats-Unis...* 1788. Paris. 4 vol. 1st ed. 12mo. full gilt speckled calf/leather labels. F. M1. $825.00

MCADOO, William Gibbs. *Challenge: Liquor & Lawlessness Vs Constitutional...* 1928. NY. 1st ed. inscr. 305p. cloth/brd. VG. D3. $75.00

MCALEER, John J. *Theodore Dreiser.* 1968. NY. Barnes Noble. 1st ed. 8vo. red cloth/brd. F. S9. $25.00

MCALEER, Neil. *Earthlove.* 1978. Strawberry Hill. 1st ed. sgn. F/wrp. M2. $10.00

MCALISTER, Hugh. *Flaming River: Story of an Intrepid Boy...* ca 1930. Saalfield. 252p. G. B10. $10.00

MCALISTER, Hugh. *Flight of the Silver Ship.* 1930. Saalfield. 1st ed. VG/VG. P3. $30.00

MCALLISTER, Hayden. *War Stories.* 1984. Octopus. 1st ed/4th prt. 352p. VG+. M7. $28.50

MCALPINE, Gordon. *Joy in Mudville.* 1989. Dutton. 1st ed. rem mk. F/F. P8. $12.50

MCALPINE, William Henry. *Catalogue of Law Lib at Hartwell House, Buckinghamshire.* 1968. London. Palmer. 2nd revised ed. M11. $450.00

MCALPINE & MCALPINE. *Japanese Tales & Legends.* 1959. Walck. 1st ed. ils. VG/dj. B18. $15.00

MCARTHUR, Dan. *We Carry On.* nd. London. ILP Guild of Youth. NF/wrp. B2. $45.00

MCBAIN, Ed; see Hunter, Evan.

MCBRIDE, Bill. *Pocket Guide to Indentification of First Editions.* 1989. McBride. 4th ed. sgn. sc. M. A18. $7.95

MCBRIDE, W.H. *Rifleman Went to War.* 1935. Plantersville Samworth. 1st ed. VG/VG. B5. $75.00

MCCABE, James. *National Encyclopedia of Business & Social Forms...* 1879. ils/index. 846p. leather. O8. $21.50

MCCABE, Joseph. *Wonders of the Stars.* 1923. Putnam. sm 8vo. 134p. ils/diagrams. brn cloth. G. K5. $14.00

MCCABE, Patrick. *Butcher Boy.* 1993. NY. Fromm Internat. 1st Am ed of 1992 Pan ed. F/F. A14. $60.00

MCCAFFREY, Anne. *Coelura.* 1987. Tor. 1st ed. F/F. P3. $15.00

MCCAFFREY, Anne. *Cooking Out of This World.* 1992. Wayside. 1st hc ed. sgn. 1/250. F/dj. M2. $45.00

MCCAFFREY, Anne. *Damia.* 1994. Ace/Putnam. 1st ed. F/NF. N3. $10.00

MCCAFFREY, Anne. *Dolphins of Pern.* 1994. Ballantine. 1st ed. F/F. N3. $15.00

MCCAFFREY, Anne. *Girl Who Heard Dragons.* 1994. Tor. 1st ed. F/F. N3. $15.00

MCCAFFREY, Anne. *Nerilka's Story.* 1986. Del Rey. 1st ed. F/F. P3. $18.00

MCCAFFREY, Anne. *Renegades of Pern.* 1989. Del Rey. 1st ed. VG/VG. P3. $20.00

MCCAFFREY, Anne. *Ship Who Sang.* 1969. Walker. 1st ed. F/F. N3. $195.00

MCCAFFREY, Donald W. *Golden Age of Sound Comedy.* 1973. Barnes. 202p. VG/dj. M20. $20.00

MCCAFFREY & NYE. *Death of Sleep.* 1991. Orbit. F/F. P3. $30.00

MCCAIG, Robert. *Danger Trail.* 1975. Doubleday. 1st ed. VG/VG. P3. $20.00

MCCAIN & MURRAY. *Books.* 1962. Simon Schuster. 12mo. ils. 30p. VG/dj. M10. $5.00

MCCALL, Anthony; see Kane, Henry.

MCCALL, Dan. *Beecher.* 1979. Dutton. 1st ed. F/F. B3. $20.00

MCCALL, Dan. *Example of Richard Wright.* 1969. HBW. 1st ed. VG/G clip. L3. $75.00

MCCAMMON, Robert R. *Mystery Walk.* nd. HRW. 2nd ed. VG/VG. P3. $15.00

MCCAMMON, Robert R. *Mystery Walk.* 1983. HRW. 1st ed/author's 1st hc book. NF/dj. F4. $45.00

MCCAMMON, Robert R. *Usher's Passing.* 1984. Holt. 1st ed. F/dj. F4. $40.00

MCCANN, E. Armitage. *Ship Model Making. Vol 1.* 1926. Norman Henley. 129p. VG/chip. M20. $30.00

MCCANN, Edson. *Preferred Risk.* 1955. Simon Schuster. 1st ed. VG. P3. $20.00

MCCARRY, Charles. *Miernik Dossier.* 1973. Saturday Review. 1st ed. NF/NF. P3. $25.00

MCCARRY, Charles. *Second Sight.* 1991. Dutton. ARC. F/wrp. B2. $30.00

MCCARTHY, Cormac. *All the Pretty Horses.* 1993. London. Picador. 1st ed. F/F. S9. $75.00

MCCARTHY, Cormac. *Blood Meridian.* 1985. Random. ARC/author's 5th book. F/F. L3. $850.00

MCCARTHY, Cormac. *Blood Meridian; or, The Evening Redness in the West.* 1985. Random. 1st ed. rem mk. F/dj. Q1. $300.00

MCCARTHY, Cormac. *Child of God.* 1973. Random. 1st ed. F/clip. Q1. $750.00

MCCARTHY, Cormac. *Child of God.* 1973. Random. 1st ed/author's 3rd book. 8vo. 197p. VG/clip. C6. $500.00

MCCARTHY, Cormac. *Child of God.* 1975. Chatto Windus. 1st ed. F/F. B3. $450.00

MCCARTHY, Cormac. *Crossing.* 1994. Knopf. AP. F. M19. $200.00

MCCARTHY, Cormac. *Stonemason.* 1994. Ecco. 1st ed. F/F. B4. $45.00

MCCARTHY, Cormac. *Stonemason.* 1994. Hopewell. Ecco. ltd ed. sgn. F/box. B3. $295.00

MCCARTHY, Cormac. *Suttree.* 1979. Random. 1st ed. 8vo. 471p. NF/dj. C6. $450.00

MCCARTHY, Denis. *Afghan Hound.* 1982 (1977). Edinburgh. Bartholomew. ils. 95p. M/wrp. R2. $10.00

MCCARTHY, Denis. *Cocker Spaniel.* 1982 (1980). Edinburgh. Bartholomew. ils. 96p. M/mc wrp. R2. $10.00

MCCARTHY, Gary. *First Sheriff.* 1979. Doubleday. 1st ed. VG/VG. P3. $10.00

MCCARTHY, Justin Huntly. *Proud Prince.* 1903. Harper. 1st ed. 275p. VG. M20. $15.00

MCCARTHY, Justin. *Dryad.* 1905. Harper. 1st ed. VG. M2. $20.00

MCCARTHY, Mary. *Cannibals & Missionaries.* 1979. HBJ. 1st ed. VG/VG. P3. $15.00

MCCARTHY, Mary. *Ideas & the Novel.* 1980. NY. 1st ed. sgn. F/F. A11. $45.00

MCCARTHY, Mary. *Oasis.* 1949. London. 1st ed/author's 1st novel. sgn. NF/8vo wrp. A11. $75.00

MCCARTHY, Ralph F. *Moon Princess.* 1993. Kodansha Internat. 1st ed. ils Kancho Oda. F/F. B17. $8.00

MCCARTHY, Shawna. *Isaac Asimov's Fantasy.* 1985. Dial. ARC. RS. F/F. P3. $15.00

MCCARTY, Doran. *Teilhard de Chardin.* 1976. Word Books. 149p. cloth. VG/chip. G1. $18.00

MCCAULEY, Kirby. *Dark Forces.* 1980. Viking. 1st ed. F/F. N3. $75.00

MCCAULEY & POLITO. *Fireworks: Lost Writings of Jim Thompson.* 1988. NY. Donald Fine. 1st ed. F/F. S6. $40.00

MCCLANE, Kenneth A. *To Hear the River.* 1981. Cambridge. W End. 1st ed. inscr/dtd 1982. F/wrp. L3. $35.00

MCCLARY, Thomas Calvert. *Three Thousand Years.* 1954. Fantasy. 1st ed. VG/VG. P3. $40.00

MCCLELLAN, George B. *McClellan's Own Story.* 1887. NY. 1st ed. index. 678p. VG. O8. $21.00

MCCLELLAND, Doug. *Golden Age of B Movies.* 1981. Bonanza. VG/VG. P3. $15.00

MCCLELLAND, Nancy. *Young Decorators.* 1928. Harper. 1st ed. ils Rudolph Stanley-Brown. VG/dj. M5. $60.00

MCCLINTOCK, Michael. *Instruments of Statecraft: US Guerrilla Warfare...* 1992. Pantheon. 1st ed. 604p. F/dj. M10. $12.50

MCCLINTON, Katharine. *Chromolithographs of Louis Prang.* 1973. NY. Potter. 1st ed. 4to. 246p. red cloth/blk brd. NF/dj. F1. $40.00

MCCLINTON, Katherine. *Antiques of American Childhood.* nd (1970). Bramhall. 380 ils. 351p. F/F. H1. $37.50

MCCLOSKEY, Burr. *He Will Stay Till You Come: Rise & Fall of Skinny Walker.* 1978. Durham, NC. F/VG. V4. $7.50

MCCLOSKEY, Robert. *Burt Dow Deep-Water Man.* 1963. Viking. 1st ed. ils. VG/VG. P2. $65.00

MCCLOSKEY, Robert. *Make Way for Ducklings.* 1969 (1941). Viking. renewed ed. inscr. M/M. C8. $60.00

MCCLOY, C.H. *Appraising Physical Status: Methods & Norms.* 1938. IA City. 260p. F. K4. $35.00

MCCLOY, Helen. *Changeling Conspiracy.* 1976. Dodd Mead. 1st ed. F/F. P3. $23.00

MCCLOY, Helen. *Question of Time.* 1971. Dodd Mead. 1st ed. F/F. P3. $20.00

MCCLUNG, C.E. *Handbook of Microscopical Technique.* 1929. NY. Hoeber. 495p. cloth. worn. G7. $65.00

MCCLURE, James. *Artful Egg.* 1984. London. Macmillan. 1st ed. F/F. S6. $30.00

MCCLURE, James. *Snake.* 1976. Harper Row. 1st ed. F/F. P3. $20.00

MCCLUSKEY, John. *Mr America's Last Season Blues.* 1983. Baton Rouge. LSU. 1st ed. F/NF. B2. $25.00

MCCOAN, J.C. *Egypt.* 1900. Collier. xl. VG. W1. $12.00

MCCOLLUM, Kenneth G. *Nelson Algren: A Checklist.* 1973. Gale/Bruccoli-Clark. 1st ed. F/sans. B2. $65.00

MCCOLLUM, Lee. *Our Sons At War.* 1940. Chicago. ils. 216p. VG. A17. $7.50

MCCONKEY, Harriet E. Bishop. *Dakota War Whoop.* 1965. Lakeside. 377p. gilt bl cloth. VG+. M20. $25.00

MCCONNELL, Lela Grace. *Pauline Ministry in KY Mtns; or, Brief Account...* nd. Louisville, KY. 7th ed. 200p. cloth. VG. M8. $37.50

MCCONNOR, Vincent. *Paris Puzzle.* 1981. Macmillan. 1st ed. VG/VG. P3. $18.00

MCCONVILLE, Michael. *Small War in the Balkans.* 1986. London. 8vo. ils/maps. 336p. cloth. dj. O2. $25.00

MCCOOK, Henry C. *Quaker Ben: A Tale of Colonial Pennsylvania...* 1911. Phil. George W Jacobs. 1st ed. 8vo. 336p. VG. V3. $12.00

MCCORD & MCCORD. *Origins of Crime: New Evaluation Cambridge-Somerville...* 1959. NY. Columbia. M11. $25.00

MCCORKLE, Jill. *Crash Diet.* 1992. Algonquin. ARC. RS. F/F. B3. $35.00

MCCORKLE, Jill. *Crash Diet.* 1992. Algonquin. 1st ed. F/F. S9. $25.00

MCCORKLE, Jill. *Ferris Beach.* 1990. Algonquin. UP. w/promo material. F/prt yel wrp. B3. $60.00

MCCORMICK, Donald. *Master Book of Spies.* 1973. Hodder Causton. 1st ed. VG. P3. $20.00

MCCORMICK, Donald. *Who's Who in Spy Fiction.* 1977. London. Elm Tree. 1st ed. F/NF. S6. $25.00

MCCORMICK, Washington. *Colors From an Old Montana Sluice Boy.* 1980. np. sc. VG. B34. $15.00

MCCORMICK, Wilfred. *Bases Loaded.* 1950. Grosset Dunlap. rpt. pict bdg. VG. P8. $17.50

MCCORMICK, Wilfred. *Bluffer.* 1961. McKay. 1st ed. VG+/VG. P8. $35.00

MCCORMICK, Wilfred. *Flying Tackle.* 1949. Grosset Dunlap. rpt. Bronc Burnett Series #4. VG. P8. $10.00

MCCORMICK, Wilfred. *Legion Tourney.* 1956. Grosset Dunlap. rpt. Bronc Burnett Series #2. VG+/VG. P8. $22.50

MCCORMICK, Wilfred. *Wild on the Bases.* 1965. DSP. 1st ed. F/VG+. P8. $60.00

MCCOSH, James. *Examination of Mr JS Mill's Philosophy...* 1869. NY. Carter. 2nd enlarged ed. paneled mauve cloth. G. G1. $135.00

MCCOSH, James. *Intuitions of Mind Inductively Investigated.* 1860. London. Murray. 504p. emb mauve cloth. VG. G1. $125.00

MCCOSH, James. *Realistic Philosophy Defended in Philosophic Series.* 1887. Scribner. 2 vol. 12mo. VG. scarce. G1. $100.00

MCCOSTER, M.J. *Historical Collection of Insurance Co of North America.* 1945. Phil. ICNA. 1st ed. ils. 173p. VG. T7. $35.00

MCCOSTER, M.J. *Historical Collection of Insurance Co of North America.* 1945. Phil. 1st ed. 173p. gilt terra-cotta cloth. w/fire marks pamphlet. F. F1. $75.00

MCCOUSLAND, H. *Old Sporting Characters & Occasions.* 1948. London. 1st ed. VG/dj. C11. $25.00

MCCOY, Melvyn H. *Ten Escape From Tojo.* 1944. Farrar Rinehart. 1st ed. F/F. P3. $25.00

MCCOY, Neely. *Jupie Follows His Tale.* 1928. Macmillan. 1st ed. ils. 106p. G. P2. $12.50

MCCRACKAN, W.D. *Italian Lakes.* 1907. Page. 1st ed. ils. 362p. teg. gr cloth. G. S11. $15.00

MCCRACKAN, W.D. *New Palestine: Authoritative Account...* 1922. Boston. Page. 392p. cloth. xl. VG. W1. $45.00

MCCRACKEN, Harold. *Biggest Bear on Earth.* 1934. Stokes. 1st ed. ils. 114p. G+. P3. $20.00

MCCRACKEN, Harold. *Frederic Remington's Own West.* 1960. Dial. 1st trade ed. 254p. VG/dj. M20. $25.00

MCCRACKEN, Harold. *Frederic Remington's Own West: Written & Ils by Remington.* 1960. NY. Dial. BC. VG/G. O3. $20.00

MCCRACKEN, Harold. *Roughnecks & Gentlemen, Memoirs of a Maverick.* 1968. Doubleday. 1st ed. VG/dj. B34. $45.00

MCCRUM, Robert. *In the Secret State.* 1980. Simon Schuster. 1st ed. VG/VG. P3. $15.00

MCCRUMB, Sharyn. *Hangman's Beautiful Daughter.* 1992. Scribner. 1st ed. sgn. F/F. T2. $22.00

MCCRUMB, Sharyn. *MacPherson's Lament.* 1992. Ballantine. F/F. P3. $17.00

MCCRUMB, Sharyn. *Windsor Knot.* 1990. Ballantine. 1st ed. sgn. F/F. T2. $17.00

MCCUE, Andy. *Baseball by the Books.* 1991. Wm C Brn. 1st ed. pict bdg. M/sans. P8. $20.00

MCCULLERS, Carson. *Collected Stories...* 1987. Boston. 392p. VG/wrp. A17. $10.00

MCCULLEY, Johnston. *Black Star.* 1921. Chelsea. 1st ed. VG/VG. P3. $50.00

MCCULLEY, Johnston. *Range Cavalier.* 1930. G Howard Watt. 1st ed. xl. VG. P3. $15.00

MCCULLOUGH, Colleen. *First Man in Rome.* 1990. Morrow. 1st ed. F/F. M21. $15.00

MCCULLOUGH, David Willis. *City Sleuths & Tough Guys.* 1989. Houghton Mifflin. 1st ed. VG/VG. P3. $20.00

MCCULLOUGH, E. *Good Old Coney Island.* 1957. NY. 1st ed. VG/G. B5. $22.50

MCCURDY, Harold. *Personal World.* 1961. HBW. 581p. F. K4. $10.00

MCCUTCHAN, Philip. *Bright Red Businessmen.* 1969. London. Harrap. 1st ed. F/F. S6. $25.00

MCCUTCHAN, Philip. *Halfhyde & the Chain Gangs.* 1986. St Martin. 1st ed. F/F. F4. $14.00

MCCUTCHAN, Philip. *Poulter's Passage.* 1967. Harrap. 1st ed. NF/NF. P3. $18.00

MCCUTCHAN, Philip. *Skyprobe.* 1967. John Day. 1st ed. F/clip. F4. $20.00

MCCUTCHEON, George Barr. *Brewster's Millions.* nd. Grosset Dunlap. photoplay ed. red cloth. G+. H1. $7.50

MCCUTCHEON, George Barr. *Her Weight in Gold.* 1912. Dodd Mead. 1st ed. ils HD Welsh. 120p. G+. H1. $12.00

MCCUTCHEON, George Barr. *Husbands of Edith.* 1908. Dodd Mead. 1st ed. ils Harrison Fisher. 126p. VG. M20. $25.00

MCCUTCHEON, George Barr. *Mr Bingle.* 1915. Dodd Mead. 1st ed. ils JM Flagg. 357p. G. H1. $6.00

MCCUTCHEON, George Barr. *Purple Parasol.* 1905. Dodd Mead. 1st ed. ils Harrison Fisher. VG. M20. $20.00

MCCUTCHEON, John Elliott. *Hartley Colliery Disaster, 1862.* 1963. Seaham, Eng. McCutcheon. photos. F/VG. V4. $15.00

MCDADE. *Annals of Murder: Bibliography of Books & Pamphlets...* 1961. OK U. 400p. NF/NF. A4. $145.00

MCDANIEL, R. *Vinegarroon.* 1936. Kingsport. 1st ed. VG/VG. B5. $27.50

MCDERMID, Finlay. *Ghost Wanted.* 1945. Tower. 1st ed. VG-/dj. P3. $13.00

MCDERMOTT, John Francis. *George Caleb Bingham, River Portraitist.* 1959. Norman. lg 8vo. ils. 454p. gilt brn cloth. F/VG. F1. $65.00

MCDONALD, Archibald. *Peace River, Canoe Voyage From Hudson's Bay to Pacific.* 1971. Tuttle. 1st ed thus. VG/dj. B34. $25.00

MCDONALD, Gregory. *Fletch, Too.* 1987. London. Gollancz. 1st hc ed. F/F. M15. $30.00

MCDONALD, Gregory. *Fletch & the Widow Bradley.* 1981. London. Gollancz. 1st Eng/1st hc ed. F/F. S6. $35.00

MCDONALD, Gregory. *Fletch Won.* 1985. Warner. 1st ed. VG/VG. P3. $15.00

MCDONALD, Gregory. *Who Took Roby Rinaldi?* 1980. Putnam. 1st ed. VG/VG. P3. $18.00

MCDONALD, Ian. *Broken Land.* 1992. Bantam. 1st ed. F/F. P3. $23.00

MCDONNELL, Killian. *Charismatic Renewal & the Churches.* 1976. Seabury. 202p. VG/dj. B29. $5.50

MCDONNELL, Philip. *First Book of the Congo.* ca 1960. Franklin Watts. ils Edna Mason Kaula. VG/fair. B10. $10.00

MCDONNELL, Virginia. *Accident.* 1975. Whitman. TVTI. VG. P3. $5.00

MCDONNELL & HEALY. *Gold-Tooled Bookbindings Commissioned by Trinity College...* (1987). Irish Georgian Soc. folio. 106 full-p pl. bl cloth. dj. K1. $100.00

MCDONNOLD, Benjamin Wilburn. *Hist of Cumberland Presbyterian Church.* 1888. Nashville. 2nd ed. 687p. cloth. VG. M8. $85.00

MCDONOUGH, Mary Lou. *Poet Physicians: Anthology of Medical Poetry...* 1945. Springfield. Thomas. 2nd ed. 210p. G7. $65.00

MCDOWELL, Bart. *American Cowboy in Life & Legend.* 1972. NGS. ils/maps. VG. B34. $25.00

MCDOWELL, Bart. *Gypsies, Wanderers of the World.* 1970. NGS. possible 1st ed. ils Dale Bruce. NF. C8. $12.00

MCELROY, Joseph. *Plus.* 1977. NY. 1st ed/wrp issue. inscr. F. A11. $45.00

MCEVOY, J.P. *Bam Bam Clock.* 1936. Altonquin. ils. pict brd. VG+. M5. $30.00

MCEWAN, Graham J. *Freak Weather.* 1991. London. Hale. 8vo. 192p. F/F. K5. $15.00

MCEWAN, Ian. *Child in Time.* 1987. Houghton Mifflin. 1st Am ed. sgn. F/F. B4. $85.00

MCEWAN, Ian. *First Love, Last Rites.* 1975. Random. 1st Am ed/author's 1st book. NF/NF. L3. $85.00

MCFARLAND, J. Horace. *How To Grow Roses.* 1946 (1937). Harrisburg, PA. 21st ed. ils. 192p. VG. H1. $6.50

MCFARLAND, John. *Exploding Frog & Other Fables From Aesop.* 1981. Little Brn. 1st ed. ils James Marshall. NF. C8. $25.00

MCFARLAND & NICHOLS. *Norman McLean.* 1988. Confluence Pr. 1st ed. M/dj. A18. $18.00

MCFARLANE, Leslie. *Ghost of the Hardy Boys.* 1976. Methuen. 1st ed. 211p. VG/ragged. M20. $65.00

MCFEE, William. *Life of Sir Martin Frobisher.* 1928. NY. 1st ed. 276p. VG/chip. A17. $35.00

MCGAVIN, E. Cecil. *Mormon Pioneers.* 1947. Salt Lake City. Stevens Wallis. 8vo. 234p. VG. B11. $30.00

MCGAVRAN, Donald. *Eye of the Storm: Great Debate in Mission.* 1972. Word. 293p. VG/dj. B29. $3.50

MCGAW. *Most Wonderful Machine, Mechanization & Social Change...* 1987. Princeton. ils. 454p. F/F. A4. $35.00

MCGEE & MOONEY. *Seri Indians: Calendar History of the Kiowa.* 1898. WA. GPO. 1st ed. 468p. olive cloth. reading copy. P4. $75.00

MCGILLIGAN, Patrick. *Double Life: George Cukor.* 1991. NY. 1st ed. photos. 404 p. F/F. A17. $10.00

MCGINLEY, Patrick. *Goosefoot.* 1982. Dutton. 1st Am ed. F/NF. S6. $20.00

MCGIVERN, William P. *Caper of the Golden Bulls.* 1966. Dodd Mead. 1st ed. VG/VG. P3. $25.00

MCGLASHAN, C.F. *Hist of the Donner Party: Tragedy of the Sierra.* 1980. Stanford. fwd Hinkle. photos/index. M/dj. A18. $20.00

MCGOVERN, G. *Great Coalfield War.* 1972. Boston. 1st ed. VG/VG. B5. $45.00

MCGOVERN, John P. *Appreciations, Reminiscenes & Tributes...* 1980. Houston. 1/800. ils. 680p. G7. $25.00

MCGOVERN, Walter. *Shall We Reform the Criminal Procedure of CA?* 1927. np. 11p. prt stapled self wrp. M11. $25.00

MCGOVERN, William Montgomery. *Jungle Paths & Inca Ruins.* 1927. Grosset Dunlap. 8vo. 7 pl. 526p. gr brd. G. B11. $10.00

MCGOWN, Jill. *Murder at the Old Vicarage.* nd. BC. VG/VG. P3. $8.00

MCGRATH, P.T. *Newfoundland in 1911.* 1911. London. ils. 271p. G. B5. $125.00

MCGRATH, Patrick. *Spider.* 1990. Poseidon. 1st ed. F/F. P3. $19.00

MCGRATH & SCOBEY. *Do-It-All-Yourself Needlepoint, Essandess Special Edition.* 1971. np. cloth. VG. G2. $9.00

MCGREGOR, Mary. *Stories of King Arthur's Knights Told To the Children.* nd. Dutton. ils Katherine Cameron. Art Nouveau bdg. VG+. M5. $32.00

MCGREW, Fenn. *Taste of Death.* 1953. Rinehart. 1st ed. VG. P3. $10.00

MCGUANE, Thomas. *Keep the Change.* 1989. Houghton Mifflin. 1st ed. F/F. B3. $25.00

MCGUANE, Thomas. *Missouri Breaks.* 1976. NY. 1st/only ed. sgn. NF/wrp. A11. $75.00

MCGUANE, Thomas. *Ninety-Two in the Shade.* 1973. FSG. 1st ed/author's 3rd book. F/F. L3. $150.00

MCGUANE, Thomas. *To Skin a Cat.* 1986. Dutton. 1st ed. 8vo. 212p. wht cloth/blk brd. F/dj. H5. $50.00

MCGUIRE, Patrick O. *Fiesta for Murder.* 1962. Hammond. 1st ed. VG/VG. P3. $20.00

MCHARGUE, Georges. *Horseman's World.* 1981. Delacorte. 1st ed. VG/VG. O3. $22.00

MCHARGUE, Georges. *Hot & Cold Running Cities.* 1974. Holt. 1st ed. F/F. P3. $15.00

MCHOY, Peter. *Getting the Best From Chalky Gardens.* 1989. London. 128p. M. B26. $12.50

MCHUGH, Paul. *Prostitution & Victorian Social Reform.* 1980. London. 1st ed. 306p. A13. $35.00

MCILVAINE, Charles. *Earnest Word From Bishop McIlvaine in Behalf...* 1843. NY. Wm Osborn. 1st ed. 8p. VG/prt wrp. M8. $45.00

MCILVAINE, Charles. *Outdoors, Indoors & Up the Chimney.* 1906. np. poor. B34. $5.00

MCINERNEY, Jay. *Story of My Life.* 1988. Atlantic Monthly. 1st ed. F/F. P3. $20.00

MCINERNEY, Ralph. *Second Vespers.* 1980. Vanguard. 1st ed. NF/NF. P3. $18.00

MCINTOSH, David Gregg. *Campaign of Chancellorsville.* 1915. Richmond, VA. 1st ed. 59p. NF/prt wrp. M8. $350.00

MCINTOSH, J.T. *Born Leader.* 1955. Mus Pr. 1st ed. NF/NF. P3. $50.00

MCINTOSH, J.T. *One in Three Hundred.* 1954. Doubleday. 1st ed. VG/VG. P3. $50.00

MCINTOSH, J.T. *World Out of Mind.* 1955. Mus Pr. 1st ed. VG/VG. P3. $50.00

MCINTOSH & MURRAY. *Solar Activity: Observations & Preditions.* 1972. MIT. 8vo. 444p. VG/worn. K5. $32.00

MCINTYRE, Anna Theresa. *Blue Bells & Silver Chimes.* ca 1935. Nat Pub. ils EP Pyle. 61p. VG. B10. $18.00

MCINTYRE, Elisabeth. *Jane Likes Pictures.* ca 1959. Collins. 1st ed. unp. VG/VG. B10. $12.00

MCINTYRE, Elisabeth. *Puck in Pasture.* 1925. Doubleday Page. 79p. G. B10. $25.00

MCINTYRE, Vonda N. *Barbary.* 1986. Houghton. 1st ed. F/dj. F4. $17.00

MCINTYRE, Vonda N. *Enterprise. The First Adventure.* nd. BC. VG/VG. P3. $10.00

MCINTYRE, Vonda N. *Fireflood...* 1979. Houghton Mifflin. 1st ed. inscr. F/NF. N3. $15.00

MCINTYRE, Vonda N. *Star Trek IV: The Voyage Home.* 1986. Pocket. 1st hc ed. sgn Robin Curtis (Lt Saavik). F/F SF BC issue. F4. $25.00

MCINTYRE, Vonda N. *Superluminal.* 1983. Houghton Mifflin. 1st ed. F/NF. N3. $10.00

MCINTYRE, Vonda N. *Superluminal.* 1983. Houghton Mifflin. 1st ed. sgn. F/F. T2. $20.00

MCISAAC, F.J. *Tony Sarg Marionette Book.* 1921. Huebsch. 1st ed. ils. VG. P2. $25.00

MCKAY, Amanda. *Death on the River.* 1983. London. Gollancz. 1st Eng ed. F/F. S6. $22.50

MCKAY, Claude. *Banjo.* 1929. NY. 1st ed. F/pict dj. C2. $400.00

MCKAY, Claude. *Harlem Glory.* 1990. Chicago. Kerr. 1st ed. 8vo. 112p. F/wrp. H5. $30.00

MCKEARIN & MCKEARIN. *Two Hundred Years of American Blown Glass.* 1962. Crown. 10th prt. 382p. F/VG. H1. $65.00

MCKELVEY, John Jay. *Handbook of the Law of Evidence, Fourth Edition.* 1932. St Paul. W Pub. orig buckram. M11. $35.00

MCKELWAY, S. *True Tales From the Annals of Crime & Rascality.* 1950. NY. 339p. VG. D3. $12.50

MCKENNA, Richard. *Casey Agonistes.* 1973. Harper Row. 1st ed. NF/NF. P3. $20.00

MCKENNEY, Kenneth. *Moonchild.* 1978. Simon Schuster. 1st ed. F/NF. F4. $22.50

MCKENZIE, Alexander. *Lectures on Hist of First Church in Cambridge.* 1873. Boston. 1st ed. 289p. cloth. VG. M8. $45.00

MCKENZIE, John L. *Power & the Wisdom: Interpretation of New Testament.* 1965. Milwaukee, WI. Bruce. 1st ed. 8vo. 300p. xl. VG/dj. W1. $8.00

MCKEOWN, Martha F. *Alaska Silver.* 1951. Macmillan. 1st ed. map ep. VG/chip. A17. $12.50

MCKEOWN, Martha F. *Trail Led North: Monty Hawthorne's Story.* 1948. NY. 1st ed. map. 222p. VG/dj. A17. $15.00

MCKERNAN, Victoria. *Osprey Reef.* 1990. Carroll Graf. 1st ed. F/F. P3. $18.00

MCKERROW, Ronald. *Intro to Bibliography for Literary Students.* 1928. Oxford. 2nd imp. 374p. VG. A4. $75.00

MCKERROW, Ronald. *Intro to Bibliography for Literary Students.* 1962. Clarendon. 359p. VG/dj. A10. $20.00

MCKIERNAN, Dennis L. *Dark Tide.* 1984. Doubleday. 1st ed. VG/VG. P3. $18.00

MCKIERNAN, Dennis L. *Dark Tide/Darkest Day/Shadows of Doom.* 1984. Doubleday. 3 vol Iron Tower Trilogy. 1st ed. F/F. N3. $40.00

MCKILLIP, Patricia A. *Fool's Run.* 1987. Warner. 1st ed. F/F. N3. $15.00

MCKILLIP, Patricia A. *Harpist in the Wind.* 1979. Atheneum. 1st ed. xl. dj. P3. $7.00

MCKIMMEY, James. *Man With the Gloved Hand.* 1972. Random. 1st ed. VG/VG. P3. $20.00

MCKINLEY, Charles Jr. *Harriet.* 1946. Viking. 1st ed. ils Wm Pene Du Bois. VG/VG. C8. $40.00

MCKINLEY, Claire. *Amos Learns To Talk.* 1950. Rand McNally Elf Book 8352. K2. $5.00

MCKINLEY, Claire. *Chester the Little Pony.* 1951. Rand McNally Elf Book 8731. 20p. K2. $7.00

MCKINLEY, D.W.R. *Meteor Science & Engineering.* 1961. McGraw Hill. 309p. beige cloth. VG. K5. $40.00

MCKINNEY, E.L. *King of Indoor Sports.* 1963. Chicago. Petit Oiseau. 48x38mm. 1/50. 21p. bl brd. F. B24. $175.00

MCKINSTRY, E. Richard. *Trade Catalogues at Wintethur.* 1984. Garland. 438p. cloth. F. A10. $20.00

MCKISSACK, Patricia C. *Million Fish More or Less.* 1992. Knopf. 1st ed. ils Dena Schutzer. M/M. C8. $22.50

MCKUEN, Rod. *Come to Me in Silence.* 1973. NY. ltd sgn ed. F/F. M9. $15.00

MCLACHLAN, Ian. *Seventh Hexagram.* 1976. Macmillan. 1st ed. NF/NF. P3. $15.00

MCLANATHAN, Richard. *Art in America: A Brief History.* 1973. HBJ. ils. sc. 216p. G. M10. $2.50

MCLANATHAN, Richard. *Art of Marguerite Stix.* 1977. Abrams. 1st ed. NF/NF. S9. $100.00

MCLANATHAN, Richard. *Pageant of Medieval Art & Life.* 1966. Phil. Westminster. 4to. ils. 127p. F/dj. M10. $7.50

MCLAREN, R. Keith. *Bluenose & Bluenose II.* 1981. Willowdale, Ontario. Hounslow. 8 mc photos/58 monochrome ils. unp. dj. T7. $40.00

MCLAUGHLIN, C.H. *Space Age Dictionary.* 1963 (1959). Van Nostrand Reinhold. revised 2nd ed. 8vo. 246p. VG/dj. K5. $15.00

MCLAUGHLIN, Dean. *Hawk Among the Sparrows.* 1983. Doubleday. 1st ed. RS. F/F. P3. $20.00

MCLAUGHLIN, J. Fairfax. *American Cyclops, Hero of New Orleans, Spoiler of Silver...* 1868. Baltimore. Kelly Piet. 1st ed. 8vo. 12 pl. cloth. worn. M1. $250.00

MCLEAN, Rauri. *Victorian Publishers' Book-Bindings in Paper.* 1983. London. Gordon Fraser. 1st ed. 4to. 1129p. gilt bl cloth. F/glassine. F1. $120.00

MCLEAN, Ruari. *George Cruikshank.* 1948. London. Art & Technics. 1st ed. ils John Tenniel. NF/VG. C8. $36.00

MCLEAN, Ruari. *Victorian Publishers' Bookbindings in Paper.* 1983. Berkeley/Los Angeles. 1st Am ed. 112p. bl cloth. M/dj. P4. $65.00

MCLEARY, Robert. *Call Me Doctor! Cartoon Memories of a Medical Student.* 1946. Baltimore. 1st ed. A13. $30.00

MCLEAVE, Hugh. *Under the Icefall.* 1987. London. Gollancz. ARC/1st ed. RS. F/F. S6. $22.50

MCLENNAN, William. *In Old France & New.* 1899. Harper. 1st ed. ils. 319p. VG. S11. $35.00

MCLEOD, Donald. *History of Wiskonsan.* 1846. Buffalo. 1st ed. 4 pl/lg fld map. VG. H7. $600.00

MCLINTOCK, David. *Companion to Flowers.* 1968 (1966). London. BC. ils. 254p. VG/dj. B26. $14.00

MCLINTON, Katherine Morrison. *Antiques of Am Childhood.* 1970. NY. 380 ils. biblio/index. F/F. A17. $22.50

MCLOUGHLIN BROTHERS. *Aladdin & the Wonderful Lamp.* 1940. McLoughlin. Little Color Classics 838. ils Corinne Malvern. K2. $18.00

MCLOUGHLIN BROTHERS. *Alphabet of Country Scenes.* 1899. McLoughlin. 4to. 16p. VG/gilt chromolithograph wrp. D6. $75.00

MCLOUGHLIN BROTHERS. *Brownie, the Little Bear Who Liked People.* 1939. McLoughlin. Little Color Classics 824. K2. $18.00

MCLOUGHLIN BROTHERS. *Comical Pets ABC Book.* 1899. McLoughlin. 16p. VG/wrp. M5. $38.00

MCLOUGHLIN BROTHERS. *Duck of Dingle Dell & Other Stories.* 1941. McLoughlin. Little Color Classics 848. K2. $12.00

MCLOUGHLIN BROTHERS. *Eine ABC Geschichte.* 1905. McLoughlin. German ed for Am schools. sm 4to. VG. M5. $70.00

MCLOUGHLIN BROTHERS. *Great Big ABC.* ca 1870. McLoughlin. ils JH Howard. VG. M5. $48.00

MCLOUGHLIN BROTHERS. *Great Big ABC.* nd. McLoughlin. 12mo. ils JH Howard. G. M5. $22.00

MCLOUGHLIN BROTHERS. *Jack & the Beanstalk.* 1938. McLoughlin. Little Color Classics 808. K2. $10.00

MCLOUGHLIN BROTHERS. *King of the Golden River & Robinson Crusoe.* 1939. McLoughlin. unp. pict brd/cloth spine. VG. A3. $7.00

MCLOUGHLIN BROTHERS. *Little Child's Home ABC.* 1899. McLoughlin. prt entirely on glazed linen. F. M5. $50.00

MCLOUGHLIN BROTHERS. *Little Red Riding Hood.* 1899. McLoughlin. 6 mc pl. VG/wrp. M5. $85.00

MCLOUGHLIN BROTHERS. *Little Snowdrop.* ca 1902. McLoughlin. ils. 12mp. fair. B10. $25.00

MCLOUGHLIN BROTHERS. *Menagerie & Arab Show.* 1890. McLoughlin. 16p. VG. M5. $65.00

MCLOUGHLIN BROTHERS. *Mother Goose.* nd. NY. McLoughlin. new ed. mc w/sage gr ils. VG/wrp. M5. $75.00

MCLOUGHLIN BROTHERS. *Mother Hubbard & Her Dog.* 1890. McLoughlin. Pleasewell Series. 6 pl. stiff pict wrp. B24. $75.00

MCLOUGHLIN BROTHERS. *Peter Pig & His Airplane Trip.* 1943. McLoughlin. Little Color Classics 875. K2. $16.00

MCLOUGHLIN BROTHERS. *Puss in Boots.* 1941. McLoughlin. Little Color Classics 886. K2. $14.00

MCLOUGHLIN BROTHERS. *Rip Van Winkle.* 1941. McLoughlin. Little Color Classics 887. K2. $14.00

MCLOUGHLIN BROTHERS. *Rock-a-Bye Stories.* 1940. McLoughlin. Little Color Classics 833. ils Geraldine Clyne. K2. $12.00

MCLOUGHLIN BROTHERS. *Rusty, the Pup Who Wanted Wings.* 1939. McLoughlin. Little Color Classics 821. K2. $14.00

MCLOUGHLIN BROTHERS. *Simple Simon & Bo-Peep.* 1896. McLoughlin. 16p. VG+. M5. $70.00

MCLOUGHLIN BROTHERS. *Sing a Song of Sixpence.* ca 1890. McLoughlin. Dame Trot Series. 8vo. F/self wrp. B24. $50.00

MCLOUGHLIN BROTHERS. *Sunny Tales.* 1942. McLoughlin. Little Color Classics 894. K2. $14.00

MCLOUGHLIN BROTHERS. *Toy Shop.* 1943. McLoughlin. Little Color Classics 874. K2. $12.00

MCLUBAN, Marshall. *Understanding Media: The Extensions of Man.* 1964. McGraw Hill. 3rd prt. VG/dj. N2. $6.50

MCMAHON, Jim. *McMahon!* 1986. Warner. 1st ed. VG/VG. S11. $10.00

MCMAHON, Jo. *Dennie Folks & Friends of Theirs.* 1925. Volland. Fairy Books. 7th ed. ils John Gee. VG+. M5. $60.00

MCMAHON, Thomas Patrick. *Cornered at Six.* 1972. Simon Schuster. 1st ed. VG. P3. $6.00

MCMANAWAY. *Joseph Quincy Adams: Memorial Studies.* 1948. Folger Shakespeare Lib. 818p. F. A4. $65.00

MCMANUS, James. *Chin Music.* 1985. Crown. 1st ed. rem mk. F/VG. P8. $15.00

MCMEEKIN, McLennan. *First Book of Horses.* ca 1949. Franklin Watts. 9th prt. VG. B10. $10.00

MCMEEKIN, McLennan. *First Book of Horses.* 1949. Franklin Watts. 11th prt. VG/G+. A3. $7.50

MCMILLAN, Terry. *Disappearing Acts.* 1989. Viking. 1st ed/author's 2nd novel. sgn. F/F. L3. $75.00

MCMILLAN, Terry. *Mama.* 1987. London. Cape. AP/author's 1st book. NF/prt wrp. S9. $150.00

MCMILLAN, Terry. *What We've Lost.* 1992. Anaheim. ABA. 1st ed. F/wrp. B2. $35.00

MCMULLEN, Mary. *But Nellie Was So Nice.* 1979. Crime Club. VG/VG. P3. $15.00

MCMULLEN, Mary. *Man With Fifty Complaints.* 1978. Crime Club. 1st ed. VG/VG. P3. $15.00

MCMURRAY, Donald L. *Coxey's Army.* 1929. Little Brn. 1st ed. 330p. NF. B2. $50.00

MCMURRAY, George. *Jose Donoso.* 1979. Boston. Twayne. 1st prt. biblio/index. 178p. xl. A17. $7.50

MCMURRY & ROBERTSON. *Rank & File.* 1976. 164p. O8. $9.50

MCMURTRIE, D.C. *Bibliography of Chicago Imprints 1835-1850.* 1944. np. 4th revised ed. 1/200. 227p. NF. A4. $225.00

MCMURTRIE, D.C. *Golden Book: Story of Fine Books & Bookmaking.* 1934. Covici-Friede. VG/dj. N2. $35.00

MCMURTRIE, D.C. *Gutenberg Documents, With Trans of Texts Into English.* 1941. Oxford. 1/900. 8240p. F/VG. A4. $155.00

MCMURTRIE, D.C. *The Book: Story of Printing & Bookmaking.* 1965. Oxford. NF/torn. A15. $45.00

MCMURTRY, Larry. *All My Friends Are Going To Be Strangers.* 1972. Simon Schuster. 1st ed. sgn. F/NF. Q1. $200.00

MCMURTRY, Larry. *Anything for Billy.* 1988. Simon Schuster. 1st ed. VG. P3. $22.00

MCMURTRY, Larry. *Anything for Billy. A Novel.* 1988. NY. 1st ed. sgn. F/F. A11. $65.00

MCMURTRY, Larry. *Buffalo Girls.* 1990. NY. AP. F/wrp. C2. $50.00

MCMURTRY, Larry. *Buffalo Girls.* 1990. Simon Schuster. 1st ed. NF/NF. P3. $20.00

MCMURTRY, Larry. *Buffalo Girls.* 1990. Simon Schuster. 1st ed. sgn. F/F. T2. $40.00

MCMURTRY, Larry. *Cadillac Jack.* 1982. Simon Schuster. 1st ed. sgn. F/F clip. L3. $150.00

MCMURTRY, Larry. *Cadillac Jack.* 1982. Simon Schuster. 1st ed. sgn. 1/250 #d. F/case. Q1. $275.00

MCMURTRY, Larry. *Desert Rose.* 1983. Simon Schuster. ltd ed. sgn. 1/250 #d. gilt rose cloth. F/case. Q1. $250.00

MCMURTRY, Larry. *Desert Rose.* 1983. Simon Schuster. 1st ed. 8vo. 254p. gilt purple/gray bdg. F/dj. H5. $75.00

MCMURTRY, Larry. *Evening Star.* 1992. Simon Schuster. 1st ed. sgn. F/F. T2. $35.00

MCMURTRY, Larry. *Horseman, Pass By.* 1961. Harper. 1st ed/author's 1st book. F/F. S9. $1,500.00

MCMURTRY, Larry. *In a Narrow Grave.* 1968. NM U. 177p. F/wrp. B19. $10.00

MCMURTRY, Larry. *Last Picture Show.* 1966. NY. 1st ed. VG/VG. B5. $175.00

MCMURTRY, Larry. *Lonesome Dove.* 1985. Simon Schuster. 1st ed. 8vo. 843p. gilt blk bdg. NF/clip. H5. $225.00

MCMURTRY, Larry. *Pretty Boy Floyd.* 1994. Simon Schuster. 1st ed. sgn. F/F. T2. $40.00

MCMURTRY, Larry. *Some Can Whistle.* 1989. Simon Schuster. 1st ed. sgn. F/F. T2. $35.00

MCMURTRY, Larry. *Somebody's Darling.* 1978. Simon Schuster. 1st ed. 8vo. 347p. gilt bl cloth. F/dj. H5. $100.00

MCMURTRY, Larry. *Streets of Laredo.* 1993. Simon Schuster. 1st ed. sgn. F/F. T2. $35.00

MCMURTRY, Larry. *Tendres Passions.* 1984. Paris. France Loisirs. 1st French ed. sgn. F/VG. B3. $30.00

MCMURTRY, Larry. *Terms of Endearment.* 1975. Simon Schuster. 1st ed. inscr. F/F. Q1. $250.00

MCMURTRY, Larry. *Texasville.* 1987. Simon Schuster. 1st ed. NF/NF. P3. $25.00

MCNABB, Vincent. *Faith & Prayer.* 1953. London. Blackfriars. 215p. xl. H10. $16.50

MCNABB, Vincent. *Geoffrey Chaucer: A Study in Genius & Ethics.* 1934. London. 1/300 #d on handmade. 12mo. F/glassine wrp. B24. $150.00

MCNALLY, Dennis. *Desolate Angel.* 1979. Random. 1st ed. 400p. VG/VG. S11. $20.00

MCNALLY, T.M. *Until Your Heart Stops.* 1993. Villard/Random. 1st ed/author's 1st novel. F/F. A14. $30.00

MCNAMARA, Brooks. *Step Right Up: Ils History of the American Medicine Show.* 1976. Garden City, NY. 1st ed. 233p. A13. $40.00

MCNEER, May. *John Wesley.* 1951. Abington Cokesbury. 1st ed. ils Lynd Ward. VG+/VG. C8. $35.00

MCNEER, May. *Martin Luther.* 1953. Abington Cokesbury. 1st ed. ils Lynd Ward. F/F. C8. $35.00

MCNEER, May. *Prince Bantam, Being Adventures of Yoghitsune the Brave...* 1929. Macmillan. 1st ed. ils Lynd Ward. F/NF. C8. $65.00

MCNEER, May. *Prince Bantam, Being Adventures of Yoghitsune the Brave...* 1929. Macmillan. 229p. VG. B10. $45.00

MCNEER, May. *Story of the Southern Highlands.* ca 1945. Harper. unp. xl. G. B10. $12.00

MCNEER, May. *Wolf of Lambs Lane.* 1967. Houghton Mifflin. ils Lynd Ward. 64p. VG/G. B10. $15.00

MCNEIL, Everett. *With Kit Carson in the Rockies. A Tale of Beaver Country.* 1909. Dutton. 8vo. VG. B17. $6.50

MCNEIL, John. *Spy Game.* 1980. CMG. 1st ed. VG/VG. P3. $15.00

MCNEILE, H.C. *Guardians of the Treasure.* 1934. Doubleday Doran. VG. P3. $18.00

MCNEILE, H.C. *Temple Tower.* 1929. Crime Club. 1st Am ed. F/VG+. F4. $65.00

MCNEILL, William. *Plagues & Peoples.* 1976. Garden City, NY. 1st ed. 369p. A13. $25.00

MCNELIS, Sarah. *Copper King at War.* 1968. MT U. 1st ed. ils. VG/dj. B34. $85.00

MCNICHOLS, Charles. *Crazy Weather.* 1944. Macmillan. VG/G. B34. $12.00

MCNICKLE, D'Arcy. *Wind From an Enemy Sky.* 1978. Harper. 1st ed. F/F. B2. $40.00

MCPARTLAND, John. *No Down Payment.* nd. Simon Schuster. 2nd ed. VG/G. P3. $15.00

MCPHAIL, David. *Bear's Toothache.* 1972. Little Brn. 1st ed. 8vo. 32p. VG/VG. A3. $10.00

MCPHARLIN, P. *Puppet Theatre in America From 1524.* 1949. NY. 1st ed. ils/index. 506p. VG/G. B5. $45.00

MCPHEE, John. *Control of Nature.* 1989. NY. 1st ed. sgn. F/F. A11. $30.00

MCPHEE, John. *Crofter & the Laird.* 1970. FSG. 1st ed. F/F. B4. $150.00

MCPHEE, John. *Giving Good Weight.* 1979. FSG. 1st ed. 8vo. 261p. mustard cloth. VG/dj. H5. $50.00

MCPHEE, John. *Pine Barrens.* 1968. NY. 1st ed/author's 4th book. inscr. F/NF. A11. $50.00

MCPHEE, John. *Pine Barrens.* 1981. NY. 1st ed. photos. VG/VG. B5. $22.50

MCPHEE, John. *Survival Bark Canoe.* 1975. NY. 1st ed. VG/VG. B5. $60.00

MCPHEE, John. *Table of Contents.* 1985. FSG. 1/150 #d. sgn. F/F case. S9. $125.00

MCPHERSON, James Alan. *Elbow Room.* 1977. Atlantic/Little Brn. 1st ed. F/NF. B2. $85.00

MCPHERSON, James M. *Abraham Lincoln & the Second American Revolution.* 1990. Oxford. 1st ed. 173p. F/F. M10. $14.50

MCPHERSON, James. *Battle Cry for Freedom: The Civil War Era.* 1988. NY. ils/biblio/index. F/wrp. A17. $10.00

MCQUADE, James. *Cruise of the Montauk to Bermuda, West Indies & Florida.* 1885. NY. Knox. 1st ed. 8vo. 441p. VG. B11. $100.00

MCQUEEN, Ian. *Sherlock Holmes Detected.* 1974. David Charles. 1st ed. VG/VG. P3. $30.00

MCRAE, Wallace. *Cowboy Curmudgeon & Other Poems.* 1992. Penegrine. 1st ed. sgn. sc. F. B34. $15.00

MCROBERTS, Duncan. *While China Bleeds.* MCMXLIII. Zondervan. 162p. VG. B29. $3.50

MCROYD, Allan. *Death in Costume.* 1940. Graystone. 1st ed. VG. P3. $30.00

MCSHANE, Mark. *Lashed But Not Leashed.* 1976. Crime Club. 1st ed. VG/VG. P3. $15.00

MCTAGGART & MCTAGGART. *Nature of Existence.* 1921. Cambridge. 2 vol. gr cloth. F. scarce. G1. $150.00

MCTAGGART & MCTAGGART. *Some Dogmas of Religion.* 1906. London. Arnold. 300p. gr cloth. G. G1. $75.00

MCTAGGART & MCTAGGART. *Studies in Hegelian Dialectic.* 1896. Cambridge. 260p. gr cloth. VG. G1. $85.00

MCTAGGART & MCTAGGART. *Studies in Hegelian Dialectic.* 1922. Cambridge. 2nd ed. 256p. gr cloth. NF. G1. $65.00

MCVICKER, Mary Louise. *Writings of J Frank Dobie: Bibliography.* 1968. Mus of Great Plains. 1st trade ed. intro HL Ransom. F/VG. B19. $35.00

MCWADE, Robert M. *Uncrowned King...Charles Stewart Parnell.* 1891. Edgwood Pub. 1st ed. 448p. gr cloth. VG. B2. $125.00

MCWATTERS, George S. *Knots United; or, Ways & Byways Hidden Life Am Detectives.* 1872 (1871). Hartford. Burr Hyde. 665p. G+. M20. $40.00

MCWHINNIE, Alexina Mary. *Adopted Children: How They Grow Up.* 1967. London. Humanities Pr. 269p. F/dj. K4. $20.00

MEACHAM, Beth. *Terry's Universe.* 1988. Tor. 1st ed. F/F. N3. $15.00

MEAD, Arthur Raymond. *Supervised Student-Teaching.* 1930. Richmond. Johnson. 868p. G. K4. $10.00

MEAD, D.M. *History of the Town of Greenwich, Fairfield County, CT.* 1857. NY. 1st ed. VG. H7. $100.00

MEAD, Donald C. *Growth & Structural Change in Egyptian Economy.* 1967. Homewood. 1st ed. 414p. NF/dj. W1. $15.00

MEAD, Frank S. *Who's Who in the Bible.* 1973. Galahad. 250p. F. B29. $5.00

MEAD, G.R.S. *Fragments of Faith Forgotten...* 1906 (1900). London/Benares. Theosophical Pub House. 2nd ed. prt gr cloth. VG. G1. $75.00

MEAD, G.R.S. *Thrice Greatest Hermes. Studies in Hellenistic Theosophy...* 1992. York Beach. Weiser. 3 vol in 1. 819p. F/F. B33. $50.00

MEAD, Margaret. *People & Places.* (1959). Cleveland. World. 1st ed. pres. 318p. yel cloth. dj. K1. $125.00

MEAD, Matthew. *Vision of the Wheels Seen by Prophet Ezekiel...* 1689. London. Parkhurst. 1st ed. 112p. H10. $185.00

MEAD, Richard. *Medica Sacra: Sive, De Morbis Insignioribus...* 1759. London. half title. 108p. contemporary full calf. G7. $195.00

MEAD, Shepherd. *'Er.* 1970. Harrap. 1st ed. VG/G. P3. $15.00

MEAD, Sidney E. *Lively Experiment: Shaping of Christianity in America.* 1963. Harper. 220p. VG/dj. B29. $6.50

MEAD & WOLFENSTEIN. *Childhood in Contemporary Cultures.* (1955). Chicago. pres. 28 pl. 474p. bl cloth. K1. $125.00

MEADE, L.T. *Frances Kane's Fortune.* nd.. Donohue. G. B10. $10.00

MEADER, Stephen. *Red Horse Hill.* 1930. Harcourt Brace. later prt. VG. O3. $12.00

MEADOW, A.J. *Science & Controversy: A Biography of Sir Norman Lockyer.* 1972. MIT. 8vo. 331p. VG/dj. K5. $60.00

MEADOWCROFT, E.L. *Along the Erie Towpath.* 1940. Crowell. 1st ed. 227p. VG/VG. P2. $25.00

MEADOWCROFT, E.L. *By Wagon & Flatboat.* 1938. Crowell. 1st ed. sgn. 170p. VG/dj. M20. $20.00

MEADOWCROFT, E.L. *China's Story.* (1946). Crowell. ils. 92p. F/dj. H1. $4.00

MEADOWS, Denis. *Saint & a Half: New Interpretation of Abelard...* 1963. NY. Devin Adair. 209p. xl. H10. $15.00

MEARNS, Martha. *HMS Pinafore.* 1967 (1966). Franklin Watts. 1st Am ed. ils Jonstone. F/VG. C8. $15.00

MEARNS, Martha. *Yeoman of the Guard.* 1967 (1966). Franklin Watts. 1st Am ed. ils Johnstone. NF/VG+. C8. $17.50

MEASELES, Evelyn Brack. *Lee's Ferry: Crossing on the CO.* 1981. Pruett. 1st ed. ils/notes/index. 130p. F/NF. B19. $25.00

MECKLENBURG, George. *Last of the Old West.* 1927. 1st ed. 149p. O8. $21.00

MEDAWAR, Peter B. *Limits of Science.* 1984. Harper. bl cloth. G1. $17.50

MEE, A.J. *Book About Weather.* 1946. Worcester, UK. Littlebury. 8vo. ils. 147p. red cloth. G. K5. $9.00

MEE, Jon. *Three Little Frogs.* 1924. Volland. 1st ed. ils John Rae. G+. P2. $45.00

MEE & THOMPSON. *Book of Knowledge, the Children's Encyclopedia.* 1911. NY. Grolier. 20 vol. 4to. gilt bl cloth. VG. D6. $125.00

MEEK, M.R.D. *Mouthful of Sand.* 1988. London. Collins. 1st ed. F/F. S6. $27.50

MEEK, M.R.D. *Split Second.* 1985. London. Collins. 1st ed. F/F. S6. $30.00

MEEK, S.P. *Frog: The Horse That Knew No Master.* 1946. NY. Knopf. later prt. VG/G. O3. $25.00

MEEK, Wilbur. *Exchange of Colonial Mexico.* 1948. King's Crown. 114p. VG/wrp. F3. $15.00

MEEKS, Esther K. *Fireman Casey & the Fireboat 999.* 1949. Wilcox Follet. unp. G. B18. $20.00

MEEKS, S.P. *Drums of Tapajos.* 1961. Avalon. 1st ed. NF/NF. P3. $25.00

MEERPOLOL & MEERPOLOL. *We Are Your Sons: Legacy of Ethel & Julius Rosenberg.* 1975. Houghton Mifflin. inscr. M11. $25.00

MEGARGEE, Edwin. *Dog Dictionary.* 1954. Cleveland. World. 1st ed. tall 8vo. 104p. cloth. F. scarce. R2. $40.00

MEGRUE, Roi Cooper. *Under Cover.* 1914. Little Brn. 1st ed. G+. P3. $20.00

MEHDEVI, Anne Sinclair. *Persian Adventure.* 1962. Knopf. 4th prt. 8vo. xl. VG/dj. W1. $12.00

MEHRBIAN, Albert. *Analysis of Personality Theories.* 1968. Prentice Hall. 184p. F/dj. K4. $8.50

MEIGS, Cornelia. *As the Crow Flies.* 1927. Macmillan. 1st ed. 299p. VG/VG. P2. $28.00

MEIGS, Cornelia. *Crooked Apple Tree.* 1929. Boston. 1st ed. ils Helen Grose. pict cloth. VG. A17. $12.50

MEIGS, Cornelia. *Louisa May Alcott & the American Family Story.* 1970. London. Bodley Head. 1st ed. lg 12mo. F/VG. C8. $30.00

MEIGS, Cornelia. *Two Arrows.* 1949. Macmillan. 1st prt. VG+/VG+. C8. $35.00

MEIGS, J. Forsyth. *Hist of 1st Quarter of 2nd Century of PA Hospital...* 1877. Phil. Collins. 2 pl. 145p. orig brd. worn. G7. $95.00

MEIGS, Peveril. *Geography of Coastal Deserts.* 1966. Belgium. 1st ed. 4to. VG/wrp. W1. $8.00

MEIKLE, James. *Traveller; or, Meditations on Various Subjects.* 1811. NY. Dodge. 1st Am ed. 12mo. 360p. calf/blk spine label. K1. $100.00

MEINE, Franklin. *John McCutcheon's Book.* 1948. Chicago. Caxton. sm folio. 1/1000. F. A9. $65.00

MEINERTZHAGEN, Richard. *Middle East Diary 1917-1956.* 1960. NY. rpt. 8vo. 376p. cloth. O2. $45.00

MEIR, Golda. *My Life.* 1975. Putnam. 1st Am ed. 480p. F/F. H1. $18.00

MELDEN, A.I. *Free Action.* 1961. London. Routledge. cloth. VG/dj. G1. $22.50

MELENDY, Mary Ries. *Science of Eugenics & Sex Life.* 1917. Vansant. ils. 596p. gilt bdg. F. H1. $9.00

MELETZIS & PAPADAKIS. *Delphi.* 1968. Munich/Zurich. Schnell Steiner. 4th ed. 8vo. VG/stiff wrp. W1. $14.00

MELINGO, P.V. *Griechenland in Unseren Tagen.* 1892. Off Vienna. 8vo. 223p. cloth/brd. O2. $35.00

MELLERSH, H.E.L. *Destruction of Knossos: Rise & Fall of Minoan Crete.* 1993. Barnes Noble. 1st ed. 8vo. 205p. NF/dj. W1. $20.00

MELLIN, Jeanne. *Horses Across the Ages.* 1954. Dutton. 1st ed. obl 4to. VG/VG. O3. $48.00

MELTZER, David. *Ragas.* 1959. San Francisco. Discovery. 1st ed. NF. B2. $35.00

MELTZER, David. *We All Have Something To Say to Each Other.* 1962. San Francisco. Auerhan. 1/750. sgn/drawing. F/wrp. B2. $30.00

MELVILLE, Herman. *Benito Cereno.* 1926. London. 1/1650. tall 4to. 123p. red buckram. F/dj. B24. $150.00

MELVILLE, Herman. *Collected Poems.* 1947. Chicago. Packard. 1st ed. edit HP Vincent. VG/VG. Q1. $100.00

MELVILLE, Herman. *Confidence Man.* 1954. Hendricks. VG. P3. $20.00

MELVILLE, Herman. *Encantadas; or, Enchanted Isles.* 1940. Burlinghame, CA. Wreden. 1st separate ed. 1/550. 118p. VG. C6. $225.00

MELVILLE, Herman. *Israel Potter: His Fifty Years of Exile.* 1855. Putnam. 3rd ed. 12mo. 276p. morocco. M1. $775.00

MELVILLE, Herman. *Journal of Visit to Europe & the Levant...1857* 1955. Princeton. 1st ed thus. 8vo. 299p. brn cloth. VG/clip. C6. $60.00

MELVILLE, Herman. *Moby Dick.* nd. Grosset Dunlap. MTI. water damage. P3. $10.00

MELVILLE, Herman. *Moby Dick.* 1942. Dodd Mead. ils Mead Schaeffer. G/G. P2. $20.00

MELVILLE, Herman. *Moby Dick; or, The White Whale.* 1923. Dodd Mead. 540p. G. B10. $350.00

MELVILLE, Herman. *Omoo: A Narrative of Adventures in the South Seas.* 1847. Harper. 5th ed/2 parts. 12mo. 389p. prt wrp. M1. $300.00

MELVILLE, Herman. *Selected Poems of...* 1943. London. Hogarth. 1st ed. 8vo. 52p. aqua brd. VG. C6. $150.00

MELVILLE, Herman. *Typee: A Peep at Polynesian Life.* 1846. Wiley Putnam/Murray. 1st Am book ed/author's 1st book. 2 vol in 1. G. C6. $250.00

MELVILLE, James. *Bogus Buddha.* 1990. London. Headline. 1st ed. F/F. S6. $27.50

MELVILLE, James. *Bogus Buddha.* 1990. London. Headline. 1st ed. sgn. F/F. S6. $40.00

MELVILLE, James. *Death Ceremony.* 1985. London. Secker. 1st ed. sgn. NF/NF. S6. $35.00

MELVILLE, James. *Death of a Daimyo.* 1984. St Martin. 1st Am ed. inscr. F/F. M15. $35.00

MELVILLE, James. *Imperial Way.* 1986. Andre Deutsch. 1st ed. VG/VG. P3. $25.00

MELVILLE, James. *Reluctant Ronin.* 1988. London. Headline. 1st ed. F/F. M15. $30.00

MELVILLE, Jennie. *Making Good Blood.* 1989. St Martin. 1st ed. F/F. P3. $18.00

MELVILLE, Robert. *Henry Moore: Sculpture & Drawings 1921-1969.* ca 1970. Abrams. 4to. 846 ils. brn cloth. dj. VG. K1. $125.00

MENCKEN, H.L. *American Language.* 1919, 1921 & 1923. 3 vol set. 1st prt. VG. A9. $200.00

MENCKEN, H.L. *American Language: Supplement I.* 1945. Knopf. 2nd ed. 739p. VG. M10. $5.00

MENCKEN, H.L. *Artist.* 1912. Boston. John W Luce. 1st ed. 12mo. 32p. pict brd. NF. H5. $300.00

MENCKEN, H.L. *Book of Burlesques.* 1916. John Lane. 1st ed. fld genealogical chart. VG. Q1. $175.00

MENCKEN, H.L. *In Defense of Women.* 1918. Goodman. 1st ed. inscr/dtd 1918. NF. B4. $300.00

MENCKEN, H.L. *Men Vs the Man: A Correspondence.* 1910. Holt. 1st ed. F. B4. $450.00

MENCKEN, H.L. *Pistols for Two.* 1917. NY. Knopf. 1st ed. F/blk prt red wrp. Q1. $250.00

MENCKEN, H.L. *Prejudices, Fourth Series.* 1924. Knopf. 1st ed. 1/110 on rag paper. sgn. F/rpr case. B24. $525.00

MENDELSON, Lee. *Charlie Brown & Charlie Schulz: ...20th-Anniversary Peanuts.* ca 1970. World. 1st prt. F/VG. B10. $25.00

MENDELSSOHN, Kurt. *Riddle of the Pyramids.* 1975. BC. 224p. F/dj. W1. $12.00

MENDELSSOHN, Sidney. *South African Bibliography.* 1993. Cambridge. 2 vol. rpt of 1910 ed. 1/175. M. F1. $175.00

MENDOZA, George. *And Amedeo Asked, How Does One Become a Man?* 1959. Braziller. probable 1st (SD) ed. ils Ali Forberg. NF/VG. C8. $30.00

MENDOZA, George. *Gillygoofang.* 1968. Dial. 1st ed. ils Mercer Mayer. F/VG+. P2. $35.00

MENDOZA, George. *Marcel Marceau Alphabet Book.* 1970. Doubleday. 1st ed. photos Milton Green. NF/NF. C8. $30.00

MENDOZA, George. *Norman Rockwell's Americana ABC.* 1975. Dell/Abrams. probable 1st ed. NF. C8. $30.00

MENDOZA, George. *World From My Window.* 1969. Hawthorn. 1st ed. VG+/VG. C8. $30.00

MENEN, Aubrey. *Cities in the Sand.* 1973. Dial. 1st ed. 272p. F/dj. W1. $15.00

MENGARINI, G. *Recollections of the Flathead Mission.* 1977. Glendale. 1st ed. cloth. VG. C11. $40.00

MENGERT, William. *History of the American College of Obstetricians...1970.* 1971. Chicago. 1st ed. 154p. A13. $35.00

MENNINGER, Karl. *Theory of Psychoanalytic Technique.* 1958. Basic. 179p. F/dj. K4. $15.00

MENOTTI, Gian-Carlo. *Amahl & the Night Visitors.* ca 1952. Whittlesey. ils Roger Duvoisin. VG/VG. B10. $15.00

MERA, H.P. *Pueblo Designs: 176 Ils of the Rainbird.* 1970. Dover. rpt. ils Tom Lea. 113p. NF/wrp. B19. $10.00

MERANI, Shambhu T. *Turks of Istanbul.* 1980. Macmillan. 1st ed. 196p. NF/dj. W1. $18.00

MERCER, A.S. *Banditti of the Plains; or, Cattlemen's Invasion of WY...* 1954. OK U. 2nd prt. 12mo. 1195p. NF/dj. D3. $15.00

MERCER, F.H.F. *Spaniel & Its Training.* 1890. NY. Forest Stream. 1st ed. ils. 143p. cloth. R2. $75.00

MERCHAN, Rafael M. *Free Cuba: Her Oppression, Struggle for Liberty...* 1896. np. salesman's copy. 8vo. 60 pl. VG. B11. $45.00

MERCHANT, Paul; see Ellison, Harlan.

MEREDITH, Owen. *Lucile.* 1868. Ticknor Fields. 8vo. ils Gene DuMaurier. aeg. gilt bdg. G. H1. $8.50

MEREDITH, Roy. *Face of Robert E Lee.* 1947. NY. 1st ed. VG/G. B5. $32.50

MEREDITH, Roy. *Mr Lincoln's Camera Man: Mathew B Brady.* 1946. NY. 1st ed. 135 photos. 368p. VG. A17. $27.50

MEREDITH, Scott. *Bar I: Round-Up of Best W Stories.* 1942. London. Andrew Dakers. 1st ed. F/chip. A18. $25.00

MERIVALE, Margaret. *Furnishing the Small Home.* 1946. London. The Studio. new/revised ed. gilt yel cloth. VG. F1. $25.00

MERKLEY, Christopher. *Biography of Christopher Merkley.* 1887. Salt Lake City. JH Parry. VG/wrp. P4. $125.00

MERLE, Robert. *Ahmed Ben Bella.* 1967. Walker. 1st Am ed. 8vo. 160p. F/dj. W1. $14.00

MERLEAU-PONTY, Maurice. *Adventures of the Dialectic.* 1973. Evanston. Northwestern. 1st Eng-language ed. 237p. bl cloth. G1. $20.00

MERLEAU-PONTY, Maurice. *Phenomenologie de la Perception.* 1949 (1945). Paris. Librairie Gallimard. 531p. F/prt cream wrp. G1. $25.00

MERLIN, O. *Tresors d'Art de Yougoslavie.* 1967. Arthaud. VG+/VG. A1. $55.00

MERREDITH, Richard C. *No Brother, No Friend.* 1976. Doubleday. 1st ed. F/F. F4. $24.00

MERRELL, Jean. *Shan's Lucky Knife: Burmese Folk Tale.* nd. Wm Scott. unp. VG/G. B10. $12.00

MERRICK, Leonard. *Position of Peggy.* 1911. Mitchell Kennerly. 1st ed. 309p. F. H1. $6.00

MERRICK, William. *Packard Case.* 1961. Random. 1st ed. G+. P3. $18.00

MERRILL, Arch. *Land of the Senacas.* 1964. Statford. 4th ed. sgn. VG/poor. N2. $7.50

MERRILL, Judith. *Beyond Human Ken.* 1952. Random. 1st ed. VG/VG. P3. $35.00

MERRILL, Judith. *SF 12.* 1968. Delacorte. 1st ed. F/VG. N3. $10.00

MERRILL, Judith. *SF 57.* 1957. Gnome. 1st ed. VG/torn. P3. $25.00

MERRILL, Judith. *Shadow on the Hearth.* 1950. Doubleday. 1st ed/author's 1st book. F/VG+. N3. $15.00

MERRILL, Judith. *Shadow on the Hearth.* 1953. Sidgwick Jackson. 1st ed. RS. VG/chip. P3. $30.00

MERRILL, Judith. *Shadow on the Hearth.* 1968. Doubleday. 1st ed. F/dj. M2. $25.00

MERRILL, Selah. *Ancient Jerusalem.* 1908. Revell. ils. 419p. xl. G. M10. $30.00

MERRILL & MERRILL. *Among the Nudists.* 1933. Garden City. VG/VG. H7. $25.00

MERRITT, A. *Dwellers in the Mirage.* 1932. Liveright. 1st ed. NF. P3. $200.00

MERRITT, A. *Face in the Abyss.* 1931. Liveright. 1st ed. G+. P3. $90.00

MERRITT, A. *Face of the Abyss.* 1931. Liveright. 1st ed. 343p. VG. B14. $95.00

MERRITT, A. *Moon Pool.* 1919. Liveright. NF/NF. P3. $175.00

MERRITT, A. *Reflections in the Moon Pool.* 1985. Oswald Train. ltd ed. 399 p. NF/NF. M20. $35.00

MERRITT, A. *Ship of Ishtar.* 1949. Borton. VG/VG. P3. $40.00

MERRITT, A. *Story Behind the Story.* 1942. private prt. 1st ed. sgn. hc. F/sans. F4. $110.00

MERRYMAN, Richard. *Andrew Wyeth.* 1969. Houghton Mifflin. 1st ed. obl folio. brn cloth. F/VG. H4. $300.00

MERTON, Robert K. *Sociology Today: Problems & Prospects.* 1959. Basic. 623p. reading copy. K4. $10.00

MERTON, Thomas. *Ascent of Truth.* 1951. Harcourt Brace. 1st ed. 342p. xl. VG. B33. $15.00

MERTON, Thomas. *Disputed Questions.* 1960. FSC. 497p. VG. B33. $14.00

MERTON, Thomas. *Life & Holiness.* 1963. BC. 162p. VG/VG. B33. $10.00

MERTON, Thomas. *Man in the Divided Sea.* 1946. New Directions. 1st ed/author's 2nd book. blk cloth. F. B24. $185.00

MERTON, Thomas. *Seven Story Mountain.* 1949. Harcourt Brace. 429p. VG. B33. $14.00

MERTON, Thomas. *Spiritual Direction & Meditation.* 1960. Collegeville. Liturgical Pr. 99p. VG/G. B33. $20.00

MERTON, Thomas. *What Are These Wounds. Life of a Cistercian Mystic.* 1950. Milwaukee. Bruce. 191p. VG. B33. $10.00

MERTZ, Barbara Gross. *Annie, Come Home.* 1968. Meredity. 1st ed. sgn. VG/VG. O4. $25.00

MERTZ, Barbara Gross. *Crying Child.* 1971. Dodd Mead. 1st ed. xl. dj. P3. $10.00

MERTZ, Barbara Gross. *Die for Love.* 1984. Congdon Weed. 1st ed. sgn. F/F. O4. $25.00

MERTZ, Barbara Gross. *House of Stone.* 1993. Simon Schuster. 1st ed. sgn. F/F. T2. $32.00

MERTZ, Barbara Gross. *Jackal's Head.* 1968. Meredith. 1st ed. F/NF. M15. $100.00

MERTZ, Barbara Gross. *Jackal's Head.* 1968. Meredith. 1st ed. VG/dj. P3. $40.00

MERTZ, Barbara Gross. *Last Camel Died at Noon.* 1991. Warner. 1st ed. sgn. F/F. T2. $25.00

MERTZ, Barbara Gross. *Legend in Green Velvet.* 1976. Dodd Mead. 1st ed. NF/NF. P3. $50.00

MERTZ, Barbara Gross. *Lion in the Valley.* 1986. Atheneum. 1st ed. F/F. P3. $20.00

MERTZ, Barbara Gross. *Love Talker.* 1980. Dodd Mead. 1st ed. sgn. F/F. O4. $40.00

MERTZ, Barbara Gross. *Master of Blacktower.* 1966. Appleton Century. 1st ed. VG/VG. P3. $40.00

MERTZ, Barbara Gross. *Mummy Case.* 1985. NY. Congdon. 1st ed. sgn. F/F. S6. $40.00

MERTZ, Barbara Gross. *Murders of Richard III.* 1974. Dodd Mead. 1st ed. lF/F. M15. $85.00

MERTZ, Barbara Gross. *Night Train to Memphis.* 1994. Warner. 1st ed. sgn. F/F. O4. $30.00

MERTZ, Barbara Gross. *Search the Shadows.* 1987. Atheneum. ARC/1st ed. sgn. w/promo material. F/F. S6. $40.00

MERTZ, Barbara Gross. *Seventh Sinner.* 1985. London. Severn House. 1st Eng hc ed. inscr. F/F. M15. $40.00

MERTZ, Barbara Gross. *Shattered Silk.* 1986. Atheneum. 1st ed. F/F. P3. $16.00

MERTZ, Barbara Gross. *Smoke & Mirrors.* 1989. Simon Schuster. 1st ed. sgn as by Barbara Michaels. F/F. T2. $23.00

MERTZ, Barbara Gross. *Snake, Crocodile & the Dog.* 1992. Warner. 1st ed. sgn. F/F. T2. $25.00

MERTZ, Barbara Gross. *Sons of the Wolf.* 1967. Meredith. 1st ed. F/F. M15. $100.00

MERTZ, Barbara Gross. *Sons of the Wolf.* 1967. Meredith. 1st ed. VG/VG. P3. $40.00

MERTZ, Barbara Gross. *Temples, Tombs & Hieroglyphs.* 1964. Delta. 4th ed. 349p. G. W1. $7.00

MERTZ, Barbara Gross. *Trojan Gold.* 1987. Atheneum. ARC. sgn. stp Not For Resale. F/F. O4. $35.00

MERTZ, Barbara Gross. *Vanish With the Rose.* 1992. Simon Schuster. 1st ed. sgn. F/F. O4. $25.00

MERTZ, Barbara Gross. *Wizard's Daughter.* 1980. Dodd Mead. 1st ed. F/NF. M15. $40.00

MERWIN, Sam. *House of Many Worlds.* 1951. Doubleday. 1st ed. F/NF. M2. $30.00

MERWIN, Sam. *Killer To Come.* 1953. Abelard. 1st ed. xl. dj. P3. $15.00

MERWIN, W.S. *Green With Beasts.* 1956. Knopf. 1st ed. NF/dj. Q1. $150.00

MESERVE & SANDBURG. *Photographs of Abraham Lincoln.* 1944. Harcourt Brace. 1st ed. photos. 126p. F/VG. H1. $75.00

MESERVEY, A.B. *Meservey's Book-Keeping, Single & Double Entry.* 1882. Boston. Thompson Brn. 222p. tan cloth. VG. B14. $35.00

MESSERLI. *Djuna Barnes: A Bibliography.* 1975. Stinehour. 1/500. ils. F. A4. $85.00

MESSICK, Dale. *Brenda Starr, Girl Reporter.* 1943. Whitman. VG/VG. P3. $15.00

METCALF, Paul. *Genoa.* 1965. Highlands, NC. 1st ed. sgn. F/NF. A11. $135.00

METCALFE, John. *Feasting Dead.* 1954. Arkham. 1st ed. F/dj. M2. $175.00

METCHNIKOFF, Elie. *Nature of Man.* 1903. NY. 1st Am ed. VG. A9. $50.00

METZGAR, Judson D. *Adventures in Japanese Prints.* (1943). Grabhorn. 1/300. folio. 10 mc pl. linen-backed gr brd. K1. $300.00

METZGER, Berta. *Tales Told in HI.* 1929. Stokes. 1st ed. 116p. G. B10. $15.00

METZGER, Bruce. *New Tastament: Its Background, Growth & Content.* 1978. Abingdon. 288p. VG/dj. B29. $10.00

METZGER, Charles H. *Catholics & the American Revolution: A Study...* 1962. Loyola. 306p. xl. H10. $20.00

METZNER, Sheila. *Objects of Desire.* 1986. NY. Potter. 1st ed. 4to. VG/VG. S9. $75.00

MEULEN, John M. Vander. *Faith of Christendom: Series of Studies on Apostles' Creed.* 1936. Presbyterian Comm of Pub. 285p. G/dj. B29. $4.50

MEW, Charlotte. *Farmer's Bride.* 1929. London. Poetry Bookshop. 3rd ed. blk stp bl brd. VG. M7. $85.00

MEYER, Enno. *Shepherd or Police Dog.* 1928 (1924). Cincinnati. Sportsmans Digest. 81p. cloth. scarce. R2. $25.00

MEYER, Ernest L. *Hey! Yellowbacks! War Diary of Conscientious Objector.* 1930. John Day. G/VG. V4. $20.00

MEYER, Franz. *Marc Chagall.* nd. Abrams. 1st ed. VG+/VG+. A1. $85.00

MEYER, Harold J. *Hanging Sam.* 1990. Denton. 1st ed. biblio/index. VG/wrp. A17. $8.50

MEYER, Marvin. *Secret Teachings of Jesus.* 1984. Random. 1st ed. 129p. F/F. B33. $22.00

MEYER, Nicholas. *Seven-Per-Cent Solution Being a Reprint From Reminiscences.* 1974. Dutton. 1st ed. 253p. VG/VG. H1. $27.50

MEYER, Nicholas. *Seven-Per-Cent Solution.* 1975. Hodder Stoughton. 1st ed. NF/VG+. N3. $10.00

MEYER, Nicholas. *West End Horror.* 1976. Dutton. 1st ed. VG/VG. P3. $25.00

MEYER, William E. *Sailor on Horseback.* 1912. Providence. 1st ed. 1/250. 71p. NF/prt wrp. M8. $45.00

MEYER. *Treasury of the Great Children's Book Illustrators.* 1983. Abrams. 4to. 272p. NF/NF. A4. $95.00

MEYEROWITZ, Joel. *Wild Flowers.* 1983. Little Brn. 1st ed. VG+/VG+. S9. $35.00

MEYERS, Annette. *Big Killing.* 1989. Bantam. 1st ed. sgn. F/F. T2. $15.00

MEYERS, Annette. *Tender Death.* 1990. Bantam. 1st ed. sgn. F/F. T2. $16.00

MEYERS, Barlow. *Have Gun, Will Travel.* 1959. Whitman. TVTI. G+. P3. $6.00

MEYERS, Barlow. *Janet Lennon at Camp Calamity.* 1962. Whitman. TVTI. VG. P3. $9.00

MEYERS, Jeffrey. *Wounded Spirit.* 1989. St Martin. 1st ed. 239p. gilt bl bdg. M. M7. $35.00

MEYERS, Manny. *Last Mystery of Edgar Allan Poe.* 1978. Lippincott. 1st ed. VG. P3. $18.00

MEYERSON, Emile. *Du Cheminement de la Pensee.* 1931. Paris. Felix Alcan. 3 vol. cloth. VG. G1. $100.00

MEYNELL, Laurence. *Bluefeather.* 1972. Tom Stacey. VG/VG. P3. $15.00

MEYRAN & PINA. *Cactaceas y Otras Suculentas del Estado de Mexico.* 1986. Toluca. photos/maps. 135p. sc. M. B26. $14.95

MEZIES, William W. *Understanding the Times of Christ.* 1969. Gospel Pub. 125p. M. B29. $3.75

MEZZROW, M. *Really the Blues.* 1946. NY. 1st ed. VG/VG. B5. $35.00

MEZZROW & WOLFE. *Really the Blues.* 1946. Random. 1st ed. NF/worn. B2. $45.00

MIALL & MAILL. *Victorian Nursery Book.* 1980. Pantheon. 1st Am ed. 192p. VG/VG. S11. $20.00

MICHAELS, Barbara; see Mertz, Barbara Gross.

MICHAELS, Carolyn C. *Children's Book Collecting.* 1993. Hamden, CT. Lib Professional Pub. 1st ed. royal 8vo. M/M. D6. $35.00

MICHAELS, Leonard. *Going Places.* 1969. FSG. ARC/author's 1st book. F. L3. $75.00

MICHAELS & ORDE. *Night They Stole Manhattan.* 1980. Putnam. 1st ed. F/F. P3. $15.00

MICHALOWSKI, Kazimierz. *Art of Ancient Egypt.* 1968. NY. M. H4. $125.00

MICHALS, Duane. *Album. Portraits of Duane Michals 1958-1988.* 1988. Pasadena. Twelvetrees. 1st ed. folio. NF/NF. S9. $125.00

MICHALS, Duane. *Real Dreams.* 1976. Addison House. 1st ed. photos. w/promo material. F/F. S9. $200.00

MICHAUX, F.A. *Travels to the West of the Allegheny Mountains.* 1805. London. 2nd ed. map. H4. $400.00

MICHEL, Louis. *Eilshemius.* 1978. NY. VG/VG. A1. $75.00

MICHEL, Virgil. *Liturgy of the Church According to Roman Rite.* 1937. Macmillan. 369p. H10. $16.50

MICHENER, James A. *Bridge at Andau.* 1957. Random. 1st ed. NF/NF. B2. $50.00

MICHENER, James A. *Drifters.* 1971. Random. 1st ed. sgn. 1/500. F/glassine dj/case. B4. $350.00

MICHENER, James A. *Eagle & the Raven.* 1990. Austin, TX. State House. 1/350. sgns. 214p. faux leather/cloth. F/case. H5. $125.00

MICHENER, James A. *Fires of Spring.* 1949. NY. 1st ed. pres. F/sans. scarce. A15. $190.00

MICHENER, James A. *Floating World.* 1954. NY. 1st ed. VG/G. B5. $80.00

MICHENER, James A. *Hawaii.* (1959). NY. 1st ed. F/F. A9. $125.00

MICHENER, James A. *James Michener's USA.* 1981. Crown. 1st ed. 342p. F/F. H1. $35.00

MICHENER, James A. *Japanese Prints.* 1963. Rutland. 1st ed/4th prt. VG/VG/VG box. B5. $125.00

MICHENER, James A. *Legacy.* 1987. Random. 1st ed. 8vo. 176p. gilt red cloth. F/dj. H5. $45.00

MICHENER, James A. *Literary Reflections.* 1993. Austin. State House. 1/200. sgn. F/case. B3. $150.00

MICHENER, James A. *Michener Miscellany.* 1973. Random. 1st ed. F/NF. B2. $45.00

MICHENER, James A. *My Lost Mexico.* 1992. Austin. State House. 1st ed. sgn. F/F. B3. $35.00

MICHENER, James A. *Presidential Lottery.* 1969. NY. 1st ed. VG/VG. B5. $45.00

MICHENER, James A. *Sayonara.* 1954. Random. 1st ed. F/clip. Q1. $150.00

MICHENER, James A. *Sayonara.* 1954. Random. 1st ed. 8vo. 243p. half blk cloth/brn brd. VG/dj. H5. $150.00

MICHENER, James A. *South Pacific.* 1992. San Diego. HBJ. 1st ed thus. ils Michael Hague. F/F. B3. $20.00

MICHENER, James A. *Texas.* 1985. Random. 1st ed. 8vo. 1096p. gilt bl cloth. F/NF. H5. $50.00

MICHENER, James A. *Watermen.* 1979. Random. 1st ed. sm 4to. F/F. S9. $25.00

MICKELESEN, A. Berkeley. *Interpreting the Bible.* 1984. Eerdmans. 425p. G. B29. $6.50

MICKLE, William English. *Well-Known Confederate Veterans & Their War Records.* 1907. New Orleans. Mickle. 74p. cloth. VG. M8. $500.00

MICKS, Marianne. *Intro to Theology.* 1964. Seabury. 203p. G/dj. B29. $4.50

MICZAIKA & SINTON. *Tools of the Astronomer.* 1961. Cambridge. 8vo. 294p. xl. G. K5. $18.00

MIDDLETON, C. *Free Inquiry Into Miraculous Powers in Christian Church.* 1749. London. 1st ed. calf. G. A15. $100.00

MIDDLETON, Don. *Roy Rogers & the Gopher Creek Gunman.* 1945. Whitman. ils Erwin L Hess. VG. P3. $10.00

MIDDLING, T. *Johnny Appleseed's Rhymes.* 1894. St Louis. VG. A9. $45.00

MIDLER, Bette. *Saga of Baby Divine.* 1983. NY. 1st ed. F/F. B5. $25.00

MIEL, Jan. *Pascal & Theology.* 1985. Johns Hopkins. 215p. VG/dj. G1. $18.50

MIERS, Earl. *Monkey Shines.* 1952. World. 1st ed. VG+/VG. P8. $30.00

MIGEON, Gaston. *Les Arts Musulmans.* 1926. Paris/Bruxelles. Nat d'Art & d'Histoire. 1st ed. 64 pl. disbound. W1. $12.00

MIGHELS, Philip Verrill. *Bruvver Jim's Baby.* 1904. Harper. 1st ed. 265p. cloth. VG. B10. $10.00

MIGOT, Andre. *Lonely South.* 1956. London. Hart Davis. photos/maps. 206p. T7. $35.00

MIJATOVICH, Chedomil. *Constantine Palaeologus. Last Emperor of the Greeks...1453.* 1968. Chicago. 8vo. 239p. cloth. O2. $35.00

MIKESH, Robert C. *Japan's World War II Balloon Bomb Attacks on N America.* 1973. WA, DC. ils. 85p. VG/wrp. B18. $22.50

MILAN, Victor. *Cybernetic Samurai.* 1985. Arbor. 1st ed. F/F. N3. $15.00

MILES, George C. *Hoard of Kakwayhid Dirhems.* 1966. np. 1st ed. tall 8vo. VG/missing wrp. W1. $10.00

MILES, Henry Downes. *English Country Life.* ca 1960. London. McKenzie. 4to. 52 engraved pl. 524p. half leather. G. H1. $150.00

MILES, John. *Blackmailer.* 1974. Bobbs Merrill. 1st ed. VG/VG. P3. $15.00

MILES, Keith; see Tralins, Bob.

MILHAN, Willis L. *Time & Timekeepers.* 1942. Imperial. rpt. ils. 609p. bl cloth. VG/G. A8. $25.00

MILHOUS, Katherine. *Herodia, the Lovely Puppet.* 1942. Scribner. 8vo. ils. 193p. VG/dj. A3. $20.00

MILL, John Stuart. *Considerations on Representative Government.* 1860. London. Parker Bourn. 340p. emb gold cloth. G1. $450.00

MILL, John Stuart. *Letters of John Stuart Mill.* 1910. Longman Gr. 2 vol. 7 pl. maroon cloth. worn. G1. $125.00

MILL, John Stuart. *Nature, the Utility of Religion, Theism.* 1874. London. Longman Gr Reader Dyer. pebbled buckram. VG. G1. $125.00

MILL, John Stuart. *Subjection of Women.* 1869. London. Longman Gr Reader Dyer. emb gold cloth. VG. G1. $350.00

MILL, John Stuart. *System of Logic, Ratiocinative & Inductive...* 1846. London. Parker. 2 vol. 2nd ed. mauve cloth/paper spine label. G1. $300.00

MILL, John Stuart. *System of Logic...* 1865. London. Longman Gr. 2 vol. 6th ed. gr morocco/gilt spine/raised bands. G1. $125.00

MILLAIS, John Guille. *Life & Letters of Sir John Everett Millais.* 1899. NY. Stokes. 2 vol. 1st Am ed. maroon cloth. VG+. F1. $75.00

MILLAR, Kenneth. *Barbarous Coast.* 1956. Knopf. 1st ed. F/NF. M15. $500.00

MILLAR, Kenneth. *Blue Hammer.* 1976. Knopf. 1st ed. 8vo. 269p. gilt blk/bl bdg. F/dj. H5. $50.00

MILLAR, Kenneth. *Far Side of the Dollar.* 1965. Knopf. 1st ed. F/NF. B2. $150.00

MILLAR, Kenneth. *Goodbye Look.* 1969. Knopf. 1st ed. F/NF. B2. $50.00

MILLAR, Kenneth. *Instant Enemy.* 1968. Knopf. 1st ed. F/F. M15. $100.00

MILLAR, Kenneth. *On Crime Writing.* 1973. Santa Barbara. 1st ed. sgn. 1/250. brd. F. A11. $90.00

MILLAR, Kenneth. *Sleeping Beauty.* 1973. Knopf. 1st ed. NF/VG. B3. $30.00

MILLARD, Oscar. *Missing Person.* 1972. McKay Washburn. 1st ed. VG/VG. P3. $15.00

MILLAY, Edna St Vincent. *Conversation at Midnight.* 1937. Harper. 1st ed. 126p. VG/G. S11. $15.00

MILLAY, Edna St. Vincent. *Buck in the Snow.* 1928. Harper. 1st ed. sgn. 1/515. 69p. wht cloth/gr brd. F. H5. $275.00

MILLAY, Edna St. Vincent. *Collected Sonnets.* 1941. Harper. 1st ed. 161p. VG+. H1. $32.00

MILLAY, Edna St. Vincent. *Make Bright the Arrows.* 1940. Harper. 1st prt. 65p. F. H1. $18.50

MILLER, A. Austin. *Climatology.* 1947. London. Methuen. 5th ed. 325p. bl cloth. G. K5. $12.00

MILLER, Agnes. *Linger-Nots & the Valley Feud.* 1928. Cupples Leon. 210p. pict cloth. VG/ragged. M20. $20.00

MILLER, Albert G. *Fury & the White Mare.* nd. Grosset Dunlap. pict brd. VG. O3. $12.00

MILLER, Andrew. *Illinois Horology.* 1977. Chicago. NAWCC. 8vo. 64p. F. A8. $10.00

MILLER, Arthur. *After the Fall.* 1964. Viking. 1st ed. sgn. 1/999. 129p. gilt/red stp tan cloth. F/wrp/case. H5. $250.00

MILLER, Arthur. *Price.* 1968. Viking. 1st ed. 116p. F/VG. S11. $25.00

MILLER, Arthur. *View From the Bridge.* 1955. Viking. 1st ed. 160p. VG/G. S11. $35.00

MILLER, Denning. *Wind, Storm & Rain.* 1952. Coward McCann. 8vo. 177p. pict cloth. G. K5. $10.00

MILLER, Edward. *Prince of Librarians: Life & Times of Antionio Panizzi.* 1967. London. Deutsch. 356p. NF/dj. M10. $12.50

MILLER, Florence Hazen. *Memorial Album of Revolutionary Soldiers.* 1958. Crete, NE. 406p. VG/dj. M20. $25.00

MILLER, Genevieve. *Adoption of Inoculation for Smallpox in England & France.* 1957. Phil. 1st ed. 355p. A13. $50.00

MILLER, George A. *Psychology*. 1962. Harper Row. 345p. F/dj. K4. $20.00

MILLER, H.S. *General Biblical Intro From God to Us*. 1954. Word-Bearer. 422p. G. B29. $6.50

MILLER, Helen Hill. *Bridge to Asia: Greeks in E Mediterranean*. 1967. Scribner. 1st ed. sm 4to. F/dj. W1. $12.00

MILLER, Henry. *Crazy Cock*. 1991. Grove Weidenfeld. 1st ed. F/F. B3. $15.00

MILLER, Henry. *Henry Miller Miscellanea*. 1945. Bern Porter. 1/500. w/sgn holograph postcard. NF/sans. B2. $200.00

MILLER, Henry. *Henry Miller's Book of Friends*. 1976. Capra. 1st trade ed/1st issue. 138p. orange cloth. NF/dj. H5. $75.00

MILLER, Henry. *Het Heelal van de Dood: Een Studie Over Lawrence...* ca 1941. Holland. Agris Occupatis. 1/200. trans Jacques den Haan. F/wrp. B24. $325.00

MILLER, Henry. *Insomnia; or, The Devil at Large*. 1974. Doubleday. 1st trade ed. sgn. NF/VG clip. L3. $250.00

MILLER, Henry. *Mother, China & the World Beyond*. 1977. Santa Barbara. 1st ed. sgn. F/ils orange wrp. A11. $60.00

MILLER, Henry. *Order & Chaos Chez Hans Reichel*. 1966. Tucson. Loujon. 1/1399. F/case. S9. $300.00

MILLER, Henry. *Reunion in Barcelona*. 1959. Scorpion. 1st ed. sgn. 1/50. F/wrp. B2. $250.00

MILLER, Henry. *Tropic of Capricorn*. 1939. Paris. Obelisk. 1st ed. ES. F/wrp. B24. $1,750.00

MILLER, Henry. *World of Lawrence*. 1980. Santa Barbara. Capra. 1st ed. 1/250. M/sans. S9. $100.00

MILLER, Hugh. *Echo of Justice*. 1990. London. Gollancz. ARC/1st ed. RS. F/F. S6. $25.00

MILLER, Hugh. *Testimony of Rocks; or, Geology in Its Bearings...* 1853. Boston. ils. cloth. B14. $85.00

MILLER, J. Roscoe. *Childcraft*. 1954. Chicago. Field Enterprise. 15 vol. 4to. orange cloth. NF. D6. $175.00

MILLER, J.P. *House That Jack Built*. 1973 (1954). Golden/Western. mechanical pop-up. glazed paper brd. M. C8. $40.00

MILLER, J.P. *Skook*. 1985. Hutchinson. F/F. P3. $20.00

MILLER, Joaquin. *Baroness of NY*. 1877. Carleton. 1st ed. NF. A18. $50.00

MILLER, Joaquin. *How I Became Chief of the Scalplocks*. 1970. private prt. 1/200. 8p. F/wrp. B19. $17.50

MILLER, Joaquin. *Memorie & Rime*. 1884. NY. 1st ed. w/sgn card. VG/wrp. A11. $125.00

MILLER, Joaquin. *Songs of the Sierras*. 1871. Roberts Bros. 1st ed. teg. gilt bdg. NF. A18. $75.00

MILLER, John C. *Origins of the American Revolution*. 1943. Atlantic Monthly. 1st ed. 8vo. 419p. VG. B11. $15.00

MILLER, Joseph. *AZ Indians: People of the Sun*. 1941. Hastings. ils. 59p. NF/NF. B19. $25.00

MILLER, Joseph. *Monument Valley & the Navajo Country...* nd. Hastings. ils. 96p. NF/dj. B19. $15.00

MILLER, Joseph. *NM: Guide to the Colorful State*. 1962. Hastings. rpt. edit Henry G Alsberg. 472p. NF/VG. B19. $35.00

MILLER, Keith. *Scent of Love*. 1983. Word. 252p. F/dj. B29. $4.00

MILLER, Kenneth. *Blue Hammer*. 1976. Knopf. 1st ed. VG/VG. P3. $35.00

MILLER, Kenneth. *Moving Target*. 1986. Allen Busby. 1st ed. F/F. P3. $23.00

MILLER, Kenneth. *Underground Man*. 1971. Detective BC. VG. P3. $8.00

MILLER, L.H. *Trails Along the Musselshell*. 1986. Central MT Pub. 1st ed. sgn. sc. VG. B34. $10.00

MILLER, Leo. *In the Wilds of S Am*. 1918. Scribner. 1st ed. 4to. 424p. VG. F3. $45.00

MILLER, Madeleine S. *Footprints in Palestine Where the East Begins*. 1936. Revell. 1st ed. 8vo. 223p. xl. VG. W1. $12.00

MILLER, Marc. *Death Is a Liar*. 1959. Arcadia. 1st ed. VG/VG. P3. $15.00

MILLER, Max. *I Cover the Waterfront*. 1932. Dutton. 1st ed. sgn. F/VG. B4. $200.00

MILLER, Maxine Adams. *Bright Blue Beads: Am Family in Persia*. 1965. Caxton. 4th prt. 11 pl. VG. W1. $12.00

MILLER, Merle. *Gay & Melancholy Sound*. 1961. NY. 1st ed. inscr/dtd 1961. VG+/VG+. A11. $40.00

MILLER, Naomi. *Heavenly Caves: Reflections on Garden Grotto*. 1982. London. ils/plans/index. 141p. VG/dj. B26. $22.50

MILLER, Olive Beaupre. *Engines & Brass Bands*. 1933. Doubleday Doran. 1st ed. 376p. VG/fair. B10. $18.00

MILLER, Olive Beaupre. *Little Pictures of Japan*. ca 1925. Book House for Children. ils Katharine Sturges. 181p. VG. B10. $25.00

MILLER, Olive Beaupre. *My Book of Hist: Picturesque Tale of Progress*. ca 1933. Book House for Children. 512p. VG. B10. $25.00

MILLER, Olive Beaupre. *My Bookhouse*. 1925 (1920). Chicago. Bookhouse for Childern. 6 vol. 12th ed. sm 4to. VG. D6. $150.00

MILLER, Olive Beaupre. *Tales From Holland*. ca 1926. Book House for Children. ils Petersham. VG. B10. $25.00

MILLER, P. Schuyler. *Alicia in Blunderland*. 1983. Oswald Train. 1st ed. F/F. M2/P3. $10.00

MILLER, P. Schuyler. *Alicia in Blunderland*. 1983. Phil. Oswald Train. 1st ed. pub copy. F/F. T2. $20.00

MILLER, P. Schuyler. *Titan*. 1952. Fantasy. ltd ed. sgn. 1/350. F/Bok dj. M2. $125.00

MILLER, R. *Bare-Faced Messiah*. 1987. London. 1st ed. VG/VG. B5. $22.50

MILLER, Samuel M. *Have Faith in God...He Answers Prayer*. 1952. Augustana. 156p. G/torn. B29. $3.00

MILLER, Thomas. *Flowers of Affection: Original Poetry*. 1848. London. Harris. 50x34mm. 97p. ornate gilt burgandy morocco. F. B24. $275.00

MILLER, Wade. *Calimity Fair*. 1950. Unicorn Mystery BC. G+. P3. $10.00

MILLER, Wade. *Devil on Two Sticks*. 1949. Farrar Straus. 1st ed. F/F. M15. $45.00

MILLER, Walter M. *Beyond Armageddon*. 1985. NY. Donald Fine. 1st ed. F/F. N3. $15.00

MILLER, Walter M. *Canticle for Leibowitz*. 1960. Lippincott. 2nd ed. G+/dj. P3. $30.00

MILLER, Warren H. *Boy Explorers & Ape-Man of Sumatra*. 1923. Harper. 1st ed. brd. G+. P3. $10.00

MILLER & MILLER. *In Russia*. 1969. NY. Studio/Viking. 1st ed. sgns. M. H4. $125.00

MILLER & WRIGHT. *Ecumenical Dialogue at Harvard...* 1964. Harvard. 385p. H10. $15.00

MILLER. *Negro in America, a Bibliography*. 1968. np. 207p. F. A4. $45.00

MILLER. *Paul Bowles: A Descriptive Bibliography*. 1986. Blk Sparrow. 28 pl. 351p. F/F. A4. $125.00

MILLETT, Kate. *Sita*. 1977. FSG. 1st ed. F/F. S9. $25.00

MILLHISER, Marlys. *Mirror*. 1978. Putnam. 1st ed. F/VG+. N3. $45.00

MILLIS, W. *American Military Thought*. 1966. Bobbs Merrill. biblio/index. 554p. F/chip. A17. $10.00

MILLIS, W. *Martial Spirit: Study of Our War With Spain*. 1931. Houghton Mifflin. 1st ed. 8vo. 427p. VG/VG. B11. $40.00

MILLIS, W. *Road to War: America 1914-1917*. 1935. Boston. 1st ed. 466p. VG/VG. A17. $10.00

MILLIS, W. *Spy Under the Common Law of War*. 1926. Detroit. sgn. 24p. VG/wrp. D3. $25.00

MILLS, Alfred. *Costumes of Different Nations.* 1814. London. Darton Harvey. 67x60mm. 47 pl. 96p. gilt red morocco. NF. B24. $350.00

MILLS, Arthur. *Intrique Island.* 1930. Collins. 1st ed. VG/torn. P3. $50.00

MILLS, Enos. *Bird Memories of the Rockies.* 1931. Boston. 1st ed. VG. B5. $27.50

MILLS, Enos. *Wild Life on the Rockies.* 1909. Boston. 1st ed/author's 1st book. VG+. A15. $45.00

MILLS, H.R. *Positional Astronomy & Astro-Navigation Made Easy.* 1978. Wiley. sm 4to. 267p. xl. VG. K5. $20.00

MILLS, James. *Report to the Commissioner.* 1972. FSG. 1st ed. VG/rpr. P3. $14.00

MILLS, John. *Up the Clouds, Gentlemen Please.* 1981. New Haven/NY. 1st ed. 290p. yel cloth. NF/NF. M7. $25.00

MILLS, Woosnam. *Phantom Scarlet.* 1940. Hodder Stoughton. 1st ed. VG/fair. P3. $25.00

MILNE, A.A. *Autobiography.* 1939. Dutton. 1st ed. VG/G+. C8. $40.00

MILNE, A.A. *Birthday Party.* 1948. Dutton. 1st ed. NF/VG. C8. $50.00

MILNE, A.A. *By Way of Introduction.* 1929. London. Methuen. 1st ed. 8vo. lavender cloth. NF/VG+. D6. $50.00

MILNE, A.A. *Fourteen Songs From When We Were Very Young.* 1924. London. Methuen. 14th ed. music H Fraser-Simson. VG/G+. C8. $60.00

MILNE, A.A. *House at Pooh Corner.* 1928. Dutton. 1st ed. sgn Milne/EH Shepard. 1/250 #d. VG+. Q1. $750.00

MILNE, A.A. *House at Pooh Corner.* 1928. London. Methuen. 1st ed. 8vo. 178p. gilt shrimp cloth. VG. D6. $225.00

MILNE, A.A. *House at Pooh Corner.* 1928. Methuen. 1st ed. 8vo. 178p. aeg. pict ep. deluxe full gray calf. F/cb box. H5. $950.00

MILNE, A.A. *King's Breakfast.* 1925. Methuen. 1st ed. ils Ernest Shepard. pict brd. VG. M5. $75.00

MILNE, A.A. *Now We Are Six.* 1927. London. Methuen. 1st Eng ed. ils Shepard. pict maroon cloth. VG+. C8. $200.00

MILNE, A.A. *Once on a Time.* 1922. Putnam. 1st ed thus. ils. pict red cloth. VG+. M5. $45.00

MILNE, A.A. *Pooh's Counting Book.* 1982. Dutton. 1st ed. ils Shepard. NF. C8. $20.00

MILNE, A.A. *Prince Rabbit & the Princess Who Could Not Laugh.* 1966. Dutton. 1st ed. ils Mary Shepard. 72p. VG/VG. P2. $50.00

MILNE, A.A. *Red House Mystery.* 1965. Dutton. 22nd prt. VG/VG. P3. $15.00

MILNE, A.A. *Teddy Bear & Other Songs.* 1926. Dutton. 1st Am ed. ils H Frazer-Simpson/EH Shepard. 43p. G/G. P2. $75.00

MILNE, A.A. *Toad of Toad Hall. A Play...* 1929. London. Methuen. 1st ed. 8vo. 167p. gilt bl cloth. NF/partial. D6. $100.00

MILNE, A.A. *When We Were Very Young.* 1924. Dutton. 1st Am ed/2nd issue. 8vo. gilt red cloth. VG. D6. $75.00

MILNE, A.A. *When We Were Very Young.* 1928. Dutton. rpt. 12mo. gilt red cloth. F. B17. $15.00

MILNE, A.A. *Year In, Year Out.* 1952. London. Methuen. 1st ed. ils Shepard. cloth. VG+/VG+. C8. $50.00

MILNE, John. *Dead Birds.* 1987. Viking. 1st ed. NF/NF. P3. $15.00

MILNER, George. *Leave-Taking.* 1966. Dodd Mead. 1st ed. VG/VG. P3. $13.00

MILNER, Viscount. *England & Egypt.* 1903. London. Arnold. 10th ed. 8vo. VG. W1. $10.00

MILTON, John. *Areopagitica: A Speech of Mr John Milton...* 1927. NY. Payson Clarke. facsimile of 1644 ed. prt brd. uncut. dj. M11. $125.00

MILTON, John. *Conversations With Frank Waters.* 1971. Swallow. 1st ed. 90p. F/NF. B19. $30.00

MILTON, John. *Novel of the American West.* 1980. NE U. 1st ed. bibliography/index. M/dj. A18. $30.00

MILTON, John. *Paradise Lost.* nd. Thompson Thomas. ils Gustave Dore. 311p. G. H1. $15.00

MILTON, John. *Paradise Lost: Poem in Twelve Books...* 1759. Birmingham. Baskerville. 4to. 416p. rebound. K1. $400.00

MILTON, John. *Poetical Works.* 1794, 1795 & 1799. London. Bulmer. 3 vol. aeg. gilt gr morocco. F. F1. $1,450.00

MILTON, John. *Pro Populo Anglicano Defensio...* 1652. London. Du Gardianis. 12mo. 192p. old paneled calf/rebacked. K1. $150.00

MILWARD-OLIVER, Edward. *Len Deighton Companion.* 1987. London. Grafton. 1st ed. F/F. S6. $30.00

MIMAR. *Architecture in Development.* 1985. Singapore. Concept Media. VG/dj. W1. $12.00

MINAHAN, John. *Face Behind the Mask.* 1986. Norton. 1st ed. F/F. P3. $15.00

MINARIK, Else Holmelund. *What If?* 1987. Greenwillow. 1st ed. ils MB Graham. F/F. C8. $35.00

MINES, Samuel. *Best From Starling Stories.* 1953. Holt. 1st ed. VG. P3. $25.00

MINKOFF, George Robert. *Bibliography of the Black Sun Press.* 1970. NY. GR Minkoff. 1st ed. 1/1250. 4to. 60p. gilt blk cloth. F. H5. $60.00

MINKOWSKI, Eugene. *Lived Time: Phenomenological & Psychopathological Studies.* 1970. Evanston. 1st Eng-language ed. purple cloth. VG. G1. $37.50

MINKOWSKI, Eugene. *Temps Vecu: Etudes Phenomenologiques et Psychologiques.* 1933. Paris. Collection de l'Evolution Psychiatrique. VG. G1. $85.00

MINNERY, Tom. *Pornography: Human Tragedy.* 1986. Tyndale. 340p. F/dj. B29. $6.50

MINNIGERODE, Meade. *Some Personal Letters of Herman Melville...* 1922. Hackett/Brick Row Book Shop. 1st ed. 1/1500. VG/dj. C6. $150.00

MINOT, Susan. *Lust & Other Stories.* 1989. Houghton Mifflin. 1st ed. F/F. A14. $20.00

MINTER, John Easter. *Chagres, River of Westward Passage.* 1948. NY. Rinehart. 1st ed. 8vo. 418p. xl. B11. $20.00

MIRANDA, Eve. *Fragrant Flowers of the South.* 1991. Sarasota. ils. 127p. sc. M. B26. $14.95

MIRBEAU, Ken; see Weiss, Joseph.

MIRGELER, Albert. *Mutations of Western Christianity.* 1964. NY. Herder. 158p. xl. H10. $15.00

MISCHEL, Walter. *Personality & Assessment.* 1968. Wiley. 301p. F. K4. $15.00

MISHA. *Red Spider White Web.* 1990. Lancaster. Morrigan. 1st ed/author's 1st novel. F/F. T2. $25.00

MISHIMA, Yukio. *Sun & Steel.* 1971. London. Secker Warburg. 1st Eng ed. 8vo. 104p. gilt blk brd. NF/clip. H5. $100.00

MISKELLA, W.J. *Practical Auto Lacquering.* 1928. Chicago. 1st ed. ils. VG. C11. $95.00

MISS FRANCES. *Baby Chipmunk.* nd. Ding Dong School Books 208. A prt. K2. $7.00

MISS FRANCES. *Robin Family.* nd. Ding Dong School Books 215. A prt. K2. $7.00

MISS FRANCES. *Suitcase With a Surprise.* nd. Ding Dong School Books 202. A prt. K2. $9.00

MISS FRANCES. *Your Friend the Policeman.* nd. Ding Dong School Books 200. K2. $8.00

MISS MULOCK. *Little Lame Prince/Adventures of a Brownie/Poor Prin.* 1918. Lippincott. ils Maria Kirk. 280p. gilt red cloth. VG. M20. $25.00

MITCHAM, Gilroy. *Man From Bar Harbour.* 1958. Dobson. 1st ed. NF/NF. P3. $30.00

MITCHELL, Carleton. *Winds Call: Cruises Near & Far.* 1971. Scribner. 1st ed. 280p. VG/dj. W1. $20.00

MITCHELL, Charles A. *Expert Witness &...Human Identification...* 1923. NY. 1st Am ed. VG. D3. $35.00

MITCHELL, Don. *Souls of Lambs, a Fable.* 1979. Houghton Mifflin. 12mo. ils Georgann Schroeder. F/VG. B17. $4.50

MITCHELL, Donald. *Wet Days at Edgewood.* 1865. Scribner. 324p. cloth/rebacked. A10. $45.00

MITCHELL, Gladys. *Rising of the Moon.* 1984. St Martin. 1st Am ed. F/F. S6. $25.00

MITCHELL, Gladys. *Speedy Death.* 1929. NY. MacVeagh/Dial. 1st Am ed/author's 1st mystery. F/NF. M15. $350.00

MITCHELL, Gladys. *Uncoffin'd Clay.* 1982. St Martin. 1st ed. NF/NF. P3. $15.00

MITCHELL, J.B. *Decisive Battles of the Civil War.* 1955. np. 1st ed. ils/index. 226p. O8. $12.50

MITCHELL, James. *Smear Job.* 1975. Hamish Hamilton. 1st ed. VG/VG. P3. $25.00

MITCHELL, John. *Organized Labor.* 1903. Phil. Am Book & Bible House. 436p. VG+. B2. $100.00

MITCHELL, Joseph. *Old Mr Flood.* 1948. NY. 1st ed. sgn. VG/G. B5. $35.00

MITCHELL, L. *Here, Tricks, Here!* 1923. Cupples Leon. 1st ed. ils. cloth. VG+. R2. $10.00

MITCHELL, Margaret A. *Gone With the Wind.* 1936. 1st ed/1st issue. VG/1st state dj. A15. $2,050.00

MITCHELL, Margaret A. *Gone With the Wind.* 1936. NY. Macmillan. NF. S12. $1,500.00

MITCHELL, Margaret A. *Margaret Mitchell & Her Novel, Gone With the Wind.* 1936. Macmillan. promotional pamphlet. NF/wrp. B2. $100.00

MITCHELL, Mary. *Hist of United Church of New Haven...* 1942. New Haven. 1st ed. 286p. cloth. NF. M8. $37.50

MITCHELL, S. Weir. *Autobiography of a Quack & Other Stories.* 1905. NY. Century. Author's Definitive Ed. 8vo. 311p. VG. V3. $15.00

MITCHELL, S. Weir. *Red City: Novel of 2nd Administration of Pres Washington.* 1908. NY. Century. 1st book ed. 421p. cloth. VG. G7. $25.00

MITCHELL, S. Weir. *Talk About Nurses & Nursing.* 1892. Phil. Billstein. inscr. 15p. VG/wrp. B14. $125.00

MITCHISON, Naomi. *Blessing.* 1951. Random. 1st Canadian ed. VG. P3. $8.00

MITFORD, Bertram. *Heath Hover Mystery.* 1911. London. Ward Locke. 1st ed. NF. M15. $45.00

MITFORD, Jessica. *American Way of Birth.* 1992. London. 1st ed. 237p. dj. A13. $35.00

MITFORD, Jessica. *Poison Penmanship: Gentle Art of Muckraking.* 1979. Knopf. 1st ed. 277p. VG. M10. $5.00

MITFORD, John. *Adventures of Johnny Newcome in the Navy.* 1919. London. 2nd ed. 20 pl/C Williams. rebound. H4. $325.00

MITRA, S.K. *Upper Atmosphere.* 1952. Calcutta. Asiatic Soc. 2nd ed. 714p. xl. VG. K5. $35.00

MITSUMASA, Anno. *Anno's Counting Book.* 1977. Crowell. 1st Am ed. ils. VG/dj. M20. $28.00

MITTELHOLZER, Edgar. *Old Blood.* 1958. Doubleday. 1st ed. VG/VG. P3. $30.00

MITTLER, Peter. *Psychological Assessment of Mental & Physical Handicaps.* 1970. London. Methuen. 826p. F/dj. K4. $20.00

MIX, Paul. *Life & Legends of Tom Mix.* 1972. NY. 1st ed. VG/VG. B5. $22.50

MIYAO, Shigeo. *Twelve Months in Edo.* nd. np. Iseya. 75x65mm. Japanese text. woodcuts. NF/sewn wrp. B24. $165.00

MIZENER, Arthur. *Far Side of Paradise.* 1951. Houghton Mifflin. 1st ed. 362p. VG/dj. M20. $35.00

MIZMURA, Kazue. *If I Were a Cricket.* ca 1973. Crowell. 1st ed. unp. VG/G. B10. $10.00

MOATS & MOATS. *Off to Mexico.* 1940. Scribner. 2nd prt. 172p. VG/dj. F3. $20.00

MOCKET, Richard. *God & the King; or, A Dialogue, Shewing...* 1663. London. 4to. 40p. old calf. K1. $200.00

MODEL, Lisette. *Lisette Model.* 1979. Aperture. 1st ed. folio. rem mk. VG+/VG+. S9. $100.00

MODI & SHAMS-UL-ULAMA. *King Akabar & the Persian Trans of Sanskrit Books.* 1925. Poona. Aryabhushan Pr. 1st ed. 25p. G/wrp. W1. $10.00

MODIANO, Collette. *Turkish Coffee & the Fertile Crescent.* 1974. London. Michael Joseph. 1st ed. 190p. NF/NF. M7. $35.00

MOE, Virginia. *Animal Inn.* 1946. Houghton Mifflin. 1st ed. ils Milo Winter. 174p. VG/tattered. M20. $25.00

MOEBIUS. *Metallic Memories.* 1992. Epic. 1st ed. F/sans. F4. $18.00

MOEBS, Thomas T. *US Reference-Iana: 1481-1899.* 1989. Williamsburg. Moebs. 830p. VG/VG. A10. $75.00

MOELLER & MOELLER. *Oregon Trail: Photographic Journey.* 1985. Beautiful Am Pub. 1st ed. map. M/dj. A18. $35.00

MOFFAT, Gwen. *Over the Sea to Death.* 1976. Scribner. 1st ed. VG/VG. P3. $15.00

MOFFAT, Gwen. *Raptor Zone.* 1990. London. Macmillan. 1st ed. sgn. F/F. S6. $40.00

MOFFATT, James. *Everyman's Life of Jesus.* 1925. Doran. 242p. G/rpr. B29. $8.50

MOFFIT, Ella B. *Elias Vail Trains Gund Dogs.* 1937. Orange Judd. 1st ed. 219p. cloth. VG+. R2. $10.00

MOFFITT, John. *New Charter for Monasticism...* 1970. Notre Dame. 335p. H10. $20.00

MOFFITT, Virginia May. *Great Horse: A Forest Pony of Long Ago.* 1938. NY. Winston/Jr Literary Guild. VG/G. O3. $15.00

MOFFORD, Juliet Haines. *Hist of N Parish Church of N Andover...* 1975. N Andover, MA. 1st ed. 326p. cloth. VG. M8. $30.00

MOHAMMAD REZA PAHLAVI, Shah. *Answer to Hist: Shah of Iran.* 1980. Stein Day. 3rd ed. 8vo. 204p. NF/dj. W1. $12.00

MOHLENBROCK, Robert H. *Where Hall All the Wildflowers Gone?* 1983. NY. ils/photos. 239p. M/dj. B26. $15.00

MOHR, J. *Diaries of a Northern Family in the Civil War: Cormandy.* 1982. Pittsburgh. ils. 624p. VG. E5. $35.00

MOHR, Louise. *Egyptians of Long Ago.* 1926. Rand McNally. 1st ed. sm 8vo. ils. cloth. VG. W1. $15.00

MOHR, Nicolaus. *Excursion Through Am.* 1973. Lakeside. 398p. gilt bl cloth. VG+. M20. $32.00

MOHR & SLOANE. *Celebrated American Caves.* 1955. New Brunswick. ils/photos. gray cloth. F. B14. $30.00

MOISE, Lusius Clifton. *Biography of Isaac Harby...* ca 1931. Columbia, SC. 1st ed. 145p. cloth. VG. M8. $85.00

MOITESSIER, Bernard. *First Voyage of the Joshua.* 1973. Morrow. 1st Am ed. dj. N2. $7.50

MOJTABAI, A.G. *Mundome.* 1974. NY. 1st ed. sgn. F/VG+. A11. $55.00

MOLE, William. *You Pay for Pity.* 1958. Dodd Mead. 1st ed. VG/VG. P3. $18.00

MOLESWORTH, Mrs. *Cuckoo Clock.* ca 1914. Lippincott. 4th ed. 282p. VG. B10. $20.00

MOLESWORTH, Mrs. *Little Miss Peggy: Only a Nursery Story.* nd. AL Burt. 8vo. 260p. stp bl cloth. G+. A3. $12.50

MOLL, Robert C. *Hist of Bethany Reformed Church.* 1916. Bethleham, PA. 1st ed. 197p. cloth. VG. M8. $37.50

MOLLOY, Paul. *Pennant for the Kremlin.* 1954. Doubleday. 1st ed. VG/G+. P8. $25.00

MOLLOY, Robert. *Pride's Way.* 1945. Macmillan. 1st ed. 312p. VG. H1. $4.50

MOLNAR, Ferenc. *Days of Ferenc Molnar.* (1929). Vanguard. 1/400. sgn. 824p. gilt bl cloth. K1. $125.00

MOLTMANN, Jurgen. *Power of the Powerless.* 1983. Harper. 166p. F/F. B29. $4.00

MOMADAY, N. Scott. *House Made of Dawn.* 1968. Harper. later prt. inscr/dtd 1969. NF/NF. B4. $100.00

MOMADAY, N. Scott. *In the Presence of the Sun: Stories & Poems 1961-1991.* 1992. St Martin. UP. sc. NF. A18. $50.00

MOMADAY, N. Scott. *Owl in the Cedar Tree.* 1975. Northland. ils. 116p. F/NF. B19. $25.00

MONACHAN, John; see Burnett, W.R.

MONACO, Richard. *Final Quest.* 1980. Putnam. 1st ed. F/dj. M2. $20.00

MONAGHAN, David. *Smiley's Circus: A Guide to Secret World of John LeCarre.* 1986. St Martin. 1st Am ed. F/F. O4. $15.00

MONAGHAN. *Lincoln Bibliography 1839-1939.* 1943 & 1945. np. 2 vol. VG. A4. $165.00

MONBODDO, James Burnett. *Antient Metaphysics; or, Science of Universals.* 1779. Edinburgh. Balfour. 1 vol. 556p. G1. $250.00

MONCRIEFF, A.R. Hope. *Romance & Legend of Chivalry.* 1986. Crescent. 1st ed. F/F. P3. $20.00

MONCRIEFF, Anthony. *Suez: Ten Years After.* 1967. Random. 1st Am ed. 160p. VG. W1. $12.00

MONETA, Daniela P. *Charles F Lummis: Centennial Exhibition...* 1985. SW Mus. ils/notes. 82p. F/sans. B19. $30.00

MONETTE, Paul. *Half-Way Home.* 1991. Crown. 1st ed. F/wrp. B4. $35.00

MONRO, Harold. *Strange Meetings.* 1917. London. Poetry Bookshop. 1st ed. NF/wrp. B2. $40.00

MONROE, Marilyn. *My Story.* 1974. Stein Day. 1st ed. VG/VG. P3. $25.00

MONROE, Paul. *Cyclopedia of Education.* 1911-1913. Macmillan. 5 vol. 4to. 86 full-p pl. gilt red cloth. K1. $175.00

MONSARRAT, Nicholas. *Master Mariner Book 2: Darken Ship.* 1980. Cassell. 1st ed. VG/VG. P3. $17.00

MONSARRAT, Nicholas. *Richer Than All His Tribe.* 1968. Cassell. 1st ed. VG/VG. P3. $20.00

MONSARRAT, Nicholas. *Time Before This.* 1962. Cassell. 1st ed. VG/VG. P3. $25.00

MONSON, Arllys. *What Now, Mom?* 1984. np. VG/wrp. G2. $6.00

MONTAGU, Mary Wortley. *Works...* 1803. London. Richard Phillips. 5 vol. 1st ed. sm 8vo. Bayntun bdg. VG+. F1. $450.00

MONTAGU, Walter. *Miscellanea Spiritualia; or, Devout Essaies.* 1648-1654. London. Lee Pakeman Bedell. 2 vol. 4to. 20th-C calf. K1. $125.00

MONTAGUE, Ashley. *On Being Human.* 1957. London. Abelard Schuman. 1st ed. 125p. VG/VG. B33. $20.00

MONTAGUE, Edward P. *Narrative of the Late Expedition to the Dead SEa.* 1849. Phil. 8vo. 336p. cloth. O2. $55.00

MONTAGUE, Gilbert H. *Rise & Progress of Standard Oil Co.* 1904. NY. Harper. 143p. gr cloth. VG. B14. $20.00

MONTANUS, Arnoldus. *Ambassades de la Compagnie Hollandois des Indes d'Orient...* 1686. Leyden. Drummond. 2 vol. 12mo. contemporary calf. K1. $750.00

MONTE, Evelyn. *Pet Brittany Spaniel.* 1956. WI. All Pets. 1st ed. ils. 64p. VG/wrp. scarce. R2. $15.00

MONTEILHET, Hubert. *Perfect Crime, or Two.* 1971. Simon Schuster. 1st ed. VG/VG. P3. $16.00

MONTEITH, James. *Manual of Geography.* (1868). Barnes. ils. 124p. G. H1. $9.50

MONTELEONE, Thomas F. *Blood of the Lamb.* 1992. Tor. 1st ed. F/F. T2. $25.00

MONTER, E. William. *Studies in Genevan Government (1536-1605).* 1964. Geneve. Librairie Droz. pres. M11. $35.00

MONTESSORI, Maria. *Montessori Method.* 1912. NY. Stokes. 1nd ed. G+. N2. $14.00

MONTET, Pierre. *Isis.* 1977. Editions Ferni. 1st ed. VG. P3. $15.00

MONTGOMERY, D. Bruce. *Solenoid Magnet Design.* 1980. Huntington, NY. Krieger. 312p. gray cloth. F. P4. $30.00

MONTGOMERY, Elizabeth. *Land Divided.* 1938. London. Hutchinson. 1st ed. 8vo. cloth. VG. W1. $12.00

MONTGOMERY, Frances Trego. *Billy Whiskers in the South.* 1917. Saalfield. 148p. G. uncommon. P2. $55.00

MONTGOMERY, Frances Trego. *Billy Whiskers in Town.* ca 1913. Saalfield. 193p. G. B10. $45.00

MONTGOMERY, Frances Trego. *Billy Whiskers Jr & His Chum.* 1907. Akron. 124p. pict cloth. G. B18. $15.00

MONTGOMERY, Frances Trego. *Billy Whiskers Jr.* ca 1904. Saalfield. 140p. G. B10. $45.00

MONTGOMERY, John. *Jack Kerouac: A Memoir.* 1970. Fresno. 1st ed. 1/200. cloth. F/sans. C2. $125.00

MONTGOMERY, L.M. *Further Chronicles of Avonlea.* 1956. Ryerson. 2nd ed. xl. dj. P3. $8.00

MONTGOMERY, L.M. *Golden Road.* 1913. Boston. 1st ed. VG. B5. $45.00

MONTGOMERY, L.M. *Golden Road.* 1926. Burt. cloth. VG. M5. $10.00

MONTGOMERY, L.M. *Rilla of Ingleside.* 1921. Stokes. 1st ed. pict bdg. VG. M5. $65.00

MONTGOMERY, L.M. *Rilla of Ingleside.* 1923. Al Burt. ftspc Maria Kirk. VG. M5. $25.00

MONTGOMERY, L.M. *Road to Yesterday.* 1974. Toronto. McGraw Hill Ryerson. 1st ed. NF/VG+. C8. $45.00

MONTGOMERY, L.M. *Story Girl.* 1911. Page. ils George Gibbs. 2nd imp. gilt cloth/pict label. VG. M5. $50.00

MONTGOMERY, Ruth. *Searth for the Truth.* 1967. Morrow. 3rd ed. VG/G. P3. $13.00

MONTGOMERY, Rutherford. *Hill Ranch.* 1951. Doubleday. 1st ed. ils Barbara Cooney. VG/dj. B17. $15.00

MONTI, Franco. *Precolumbian Terracottas.* 1965. London. Hamlyn. 1st ed. 158p. VG/dj. F3. $20.00

MONTORTUEIL, Georges. *Three Apprentices of Moon Street.* 1895. Crowell. 1st Am ed. 316p. G. P2. $20.00

MOODIE, Roy. *Antiquity of Disease.* 1923. Chicago. 1st ed. 148p. A13. $50.00

MOODY, Anne. *Mr Death. Four Stories.* 1975. NY. 1st ed/author's 1st fiction book. inscr. F/NF clip. A11. $45.00

MOODY, Dale. *Letters of John.* 1970. Word. 136p. VG. B29. $4.50

MOODY, Minnie Hite. *Long Meadows.* 1941. NY. 1st ed. sgn pres. VG/VG. B5. $35.00

MOODY, Ralph. *Home Ranch.* 1956. Norton. 1st ed. ils Shenton. VG/dj. B34. $25.00

MOODY, Ralph. *Man of the Family.* ca 1951. Norton. 1st ed. ils Edward Shenton. VG. B10. $15.00

MOODY, Susan. *Penny Dreadful.* 1984. London. Macmillan. 1st ed. F/F. S6. $35.00

MOODY, Susan. *Penny Saving.* 1990. London. Michael Joseph. 1st ed. F/F. S6. $30.00

MOODY, Susan. *Takeout Double.* 1993. London. Headline. ARC/1st ed. RS. F/F. S6. $30.00

MOON, Eric. *Book Selection & Censorship in the Sixties.* 1969. Bowker. xl. VG. N2. $12.50

MOON, Grace. *Arrow of Tee May.* 1931. Doubleday Doran. 1st ed. 284p. G+. P2. $20.00

MOON, Grace. *Chi-Wee: Adventures of a Little Indian Girl.* ca 1925. Doubleday. ils Carl Moon. VG/VG. B10. $35.00

MOON, Grace. *Magic Trail.* 1929. Doubleday. stated 1st ed. ils Carl Moon. VG. M5. $50.00

MOON, Grace. *Missing Katchina.* 1930. Doubleday. 1st ed. ils Carl Moon. VG. M5. $45.00

MOON, Grace. *Nadita (Little Nothing).* 1927. Doubleday. 1st ed. ils Carl Moon. VG. M5. $50.00

MOON, James H. *Why Friends Do Not Baptize With Water.* 1909. Fallsington, PA. Moon. 16mo. 70p. G+. V3. $14.00

MOON, Jay. *Chancellor of Mars.* 1978. Hicksville. Exposition. 1st ed. F/VG. N3. $10.00

MOON, Sarah. *Improbable Memories.* 1981. Paris. Matrix/Delpire. 1st ed. inscr. 94 pl. F/F. S9. $150.00

MOON, Sarah. *Souvenirs Improbables.* 1981. Paris. Delpire. 1st ed. 4to. F/F. S9. $100.00

MOONEY, Harry John Jr. *Fiction & Criticism of Katherine Anne Porter.* 1957. Pittsburgh. 1st ed. VG. S9. $25.00

MOORCOCK, Michael. *Before Armagedon.* 1975. WH Allen. 1st ed. F/F. P3. $20.00

MOORCOCK, Michael. *Behold the Man.* 1969. London. 1st ed. w/inscr label. F/F. A11. $60.00

MOORCOCK, Michael. *End of All Songs.* 1976. Harper Row. 1st ed. F/VG. N3. $10.00

MOORCOCK, Michael. *England Invaded.* 1977. London. 1st ed. F/dj. M2. $25.00

MOORCOCK, Michael. *Eternal Champion.* 1978. Harper Row. 1st ed. NF/NF. P3. $30.00

MOORCOCK, Michael. *Hollow Lands.* 1974. Harper Row. 1st ed. F/NF clip. N3. $10.00

MOORCOCK, Michael. *Land Leviathan.* 1974. Doubleday. 1st ed. F/F. P3. $15.00

MOORCOCK, Michael. *Letters From Hollywood.* 1986. London. Harrap. 1st ed. F/NF clip. N3. $15.00

MOORCOCK, Michael. *Mother London.* 1988. Harmony. 1st ed. F/F. P3. $20.00

MOORCOCK, Michael. *Oak & the Ram...* 1973. London. Allison Busby. 1st ed. F/NF. N3. $20.00

MOORCOCK, Michael. *Retreat From Liberty. Erosion of Democracy...* 1983. Zomba. 1st ed. F/wrp. N3. $15.00

MOORCOCK, Michael. *Russian Intelligence.* 1980. Manchester. 1st ed. NF/pict wrp. N3. $6.00

MOORCOCK, Michael. *Vanishing Tower.* 1981. Archival. 1st ed. F/case. M2. $35.00

MOORE, Alan. *Sailing Ships of War, 1800-1860.* 1926. London. Halton Truscott Smith. 4to. 1/1500. 90 pl. T7. $220.00

MOORE, Austin. *Birds of the Night.* 1931. NY. Richard Smith. 1st Am ed. F/VG. B4. $50.00

MOORE, Brian. *Black Robber.* 1985. London. Cape. 1st ed. F/F. B3. $50.00

MOORE, Brian. *Cold Heaven.* 1983. McClelland Stewart. 1st ed. VG/VG. P3. $20.00

MOORE, Brian. *Color of Blood.* 1987. McClelland Stewart. 1st ed. VG/VG. B3. $25.00

MOORE, Brian. *Emperor of Ice-Cream.* 1965. NY. 1st ed. sgn. F/F. A11. $135.00

MOORE, Brian. *Fergus.* 1970. HRW. 1st ed (precedes UK ed). 228p. VG/dj. M20. $22.50

MOORE, Brian. *Great Victorian Collection.* 1974. NY. 1st ed. sgn. F/F. A11. $125.00

MOORE, Brian. *Great Victorian Collection.* 1975. Toronto. McClelland Stewart. 1st ed. F/F. B3. $30.00

MOORE, Brian. *Mangan Inheritance.* 1979. FSG. 1st ed. F/dj. F4. $35.00

MOORE, Brian. *Mangan Inheritance.* 1979. FSG. 1st ed. VG/VG. P3. $20.00

MOORE, C.L. *Doomsday Morning.* 1957. Doubleday. 1st ed. F/dj. M2. $65.00

MOORE, C.L. *Judgment Night.* 1952. Gnome. 1st ed. F/NF. M2. $85.00

MOORE, C.L. *Scarlet Dream.* 1981. Donald Grant. 1st ed. F/F. P3. $19.00

MOORE, Charlotte E. *Atomic Lines in the Sun-Spot Spectrum.* 1933. Princeton U Observatory. 4tol 47p. xl. wrp. K5. $20.00

MOORE, Christopher. *Coyote Blue.* 1994. Simon Schuster. 1st ed. rem mk. F/F. A14. $25.00

MOORE, Christopher. *Practical Demon Keeping.* 1992. St Martin. 1st ed. F/F. B3. $30.00

MOORE, Clement C. *Night Before Christmas.* nd. Lippincott. 1st Am ed. ils Rackham. 36p. NF/G+. P2. $185.00

MOORE, Clement C. *Night Before Christmas.* 1981. Holt. 8th prt. 6 popups/ils Michael Hague. VG. B17. $9.50

MOORE, Clement C. *Twas the Night Before Christmas.* 1992. Derrydale. 16mo. ils JW Smith. F/sans. B17. $5.00

MOORE, Colleen. *Enchanted Castle.* 1935. Garden City. inscr pres. ils Marie A Lawson. 63p. G. B10. $35.00

MOORE, Colleen. *Enchanted Castle.* 1935. Garden City. 1st ed. NF. C8. $45.00

MOORE, Doris Langley. *E Nesbit: A Biography.* 1966. Chilton. 1st Am ed. 315p. G/G. S11. $20.00

MOORE, Elaine. *Winning Your Spurs.* 1954. Little Brn. 1st ed. 4to. VG/fair. O3. $25.00

MOORE, F. *Wrecked on Cannibal Island.* 1931. Cupples Leon. Jerry Ford Wonder Stories #1. lists 4 titles. VG/worn. M20. $32.00

MOORE, Frederick. *Passing of Morocco.* 1908. Boston/NY. 1st ed. 12 pl/fld map. xl. VG. W1. $15.00

MOORE, George. *In Single Strictness.* 1922. London. ltd ed. sgn. 1/1030 #d. VG/G+. A1. $30.00

MOORE, Howard Parker. *Life of General John Stark of NH.* 1949. NY. self pub. 8vo. ils. 539p. VG. B11. $20.00

MOORE, J. Hamilton. *Young Gentleman & Lady's Monitor & Eng Teacher's Assistant.* 1792. NY. Durrell. 12mo. 406p. contemporary calf. K1. $125.00

MOORE, James. *Kilpatrick & Our Cavalry.* 1865. NY. Widdleton. 1st ed. pl. 245p. cloth. VG. M8. $150.00

MOORE, John Trotwood. *Uncle Was: His Stories.* 1910. Winston. 1st ed thus. VG+. C8. $45.00

MOORE, John Wheeler. *Roster of NC Troops in the War Between the States.* 1882. Raleigh. Ashe Gatling. 4 vol. 1st ed. cloth. recased. G. M8. $1,500.00

MOORE, Laurie. *Like Life.* 1990. Knopf. 1st ed. sgn. F/F. B2. $45.00

MOORE, Lilian. *Just Right.* 1968. Parents Magazine. ils Aldren Watson. 40p. VG-. A3. $5.00

MOORE, Lorrie. *Who Will Run the Frog Hospital?* 1994. Knopf. 1st ed. F/F. S9. $40.00

MOORE, Marianne. *O To Be a Dragon.* 1959. NY. Viking. 1st ed. 8vo. 37p. silvered gray cloth/brd. F/NF. H5. $75.00

MOORE, Marianne. *Observations.* 1924. Dial. 1st ed. VG. Q1. $200.00

MOORE, Merrill. *More Clinical Sonnets.* 1953. Twayne. 1st ed. 8vo. 72p. bl cloth. VG/dj. C6. $35.00

MOORE, N. Hudson. *Old China Book.* 1937. Tudor. rpt. 300p. VG/poor. H1. $15.00

MOORE, Norman. *Harveian Oration.* 1901. London. 1st ed. 59p. A13. $35.00

MOORE, Patrick. *Conquest of the Air: Story of the Wright Brothers.* 1968 (1961). London. Lutterworth. 2nd imp. 8vo. 94p. G/dj. K5. $12.00

MOORE, Patrick. *Next Fifty Years in Space.* 1976. London. Scientific BC. 4to. 144p. VG/VG. K5. $16.00

MOORE, Patrick. *Stargazing: Astronomy Without a Telescope.* 1985. Woodbury, NY. Barron's Educational Series. 4to. 176p. xl. dj. K5. $14.00

MOORE, Patrick. *Survey of the Moon.* 1963 (1953). NY. Norton. 8vo. 333p. xl. G/dj. K5. $20.00

MOORE, Patrick. *Wheel in Space.* 1956. Lutterworth. 1st ed. VG. P3. $15.00

MOORE, Robin. *Fifth Estate.* 1973. Doubleday. 1st ed. VG/VG. P3. $18.00

MOORE, Suzanne. *Christmas ABC et XYZ.* 1991. Ashfield. 51x46mm. 1/26. sgn. 26p. teg. purple silk brocade. F/sleeve. B24. $285.00

MOORE, Suzanne. *Transplanted New England Gardener's Alphabetical Delirium.* 1985. Ashfield. 58x47mm. 1/26. sgn. accordian-fld ABC. F/fld/gr ribbon. B24. $375.00

MOORE, Thomas H. *Bibliography of Henry Miller.* 1961. Henry Miller Literay Soc. 1st ed. 1/1000. F/wrp. w/addendum sheet. B2. $45.00

MOORE, Thomas. *Poetical Works of Late Thomas Little.* 1801. London. Carpenter. crude paper over brd. NF/full morocco solander case. H4. $350.00

MOORE, Warren. *Spurling Sail & Steam.* 1980. Grosset Dunlap. ils/50 mc pl/map. 175p. dj. T7. $110.00

MOORE, Willis L. *Descriptive Meteorology.* 1910. Appleton. 1st ed. 8vo. 344p. G. K5. $22.00

MOORE & NICOLSON. *Black Holes in Space.* 1974. Norton. 8vo. 126p. xl. dj. K5. $8.00

MOORE & ROBIN. *Studies in Philosophy of Chas Sanders Pierce Second Series.* 1964. Amherst. 525p. brn cloth. VG/dj. G1. $65.00

MOOREHEAD, Alan. *Blue Nile.* 1962. Harper Row. 1st ed. ils/maps. 308p. cloth. xl. VG. W1. $8.00

MOOREHEAD, Alan. *White Nile.* 1960. Hamish Hamilton. 1st ed. 8vo. ils/maps. VG. W1. $10.00

MOORES, Charles W. *Life of Abraham Lincoln for Boys & Girls.* ca 1909. Houghton Mifflin. 132p. G. B10. $10.00

MOORHEAD, Alan. *Eclipse.* 1968. Harper Row. 1st ed thus. 319p. VG/VG. A17. $10.00

MOORHEAD, Alan. *March to Tunis: N African War 1940-1943.* 1965. NY. 1st Am ed 592p. F/F. A17. $10.00

MOORHOUSE, Geoffrey. *Fearful Void.* 1974. Phil/NY. Lippincott. 288p. VG. W1. $14.00

MOORMAN. *Arthurian Dictionary.* 1978. MS U. 143p. xl. VG. scarce. A4. $65.00

MORA, Gilles. *Walker Evans Havana 1933.* 1989. NY. Pantheon. 1st Am ed. 111p. M/M. A17. $20.00

MORAN, Richard. *Knowing Right From Wrong, Insanity Defense D McNaughtan.* 1981. NY. Free Pr. M11. $25.00

MORAWIETZ & WEIER. *Alaskan Props.* 1988. London. Osprey. sq 8vo. 128p color photo study. F/wrp. A17. $10.00

MOREHOUSE, Marion. *Adventures in Value: 50 Photographs by Marion Morehouse.* 1962. HBW. 1st ed. sgn. VG/VG. S9. $70.00

MORELAND, Arthur. *Dickens Landmarks in London.* 1931. London. 1st ed. 82p. pict brd. VG/dj. D3. $75.00

MORELEY, Christopher. *I Know a Secret.* 1927. Doubleday. 1st ed. 235p. G. B10. $12.00

MORELEY, W.M. *Staffordshire Bull Terrier.* 1983 (1982). Newton Abbot. 2nd imp. ils. 176p. M/dj. R2. $30.00

MORGADO, Martin J. *Junipero Serra's Legacy.* 1987. Pacific Grove. Mt Carmel. 1st ed/2nd prt. 251p. M/dj. P4. $45.00

MORGAN, Al. *Essential Man.* 1977. Playboy. 1st ed. F/F. P3. $15.00

MORGAN, Alfred P. *Boy Electrician.* 1914. Boston. 1st ed. 394p. gilt pict cloth. VG. A17. $20.00

MORGAN, Barbara. *Martha Graham.* 1941. DSP. 1st ed. 4to. VG/sans. S9. $150.00

MORGAN, Barbara. *Skeptic's Search for God.* 1947. Harper. 1st ed. 248p. G. B29. $2.75

MORGAN, Dan J. *Hist Lights & Shadows of OH Penitentiary.* 1896. Columbus. revised ed. 150p. fair/pict wrp. B18. $25.00

MORGAN, Dan. *Concrete Horizon.* 1976. Millington. 1st ed. F/F. P3. $15.00

MORGAN, Edmund M. *Intro to Study of Law.* 1926. Chicago. Callaghan. bl cloth. M11. $35.00

MORGAN, G. Campbell. *Crisis of the Christ.* 1989. Power. 477p. M. B29. $7.00

MORGAN, G. Campbell. *Gospel According to Luke.* 1981. Revell. 284p. M/dj. B29. $9.00

MORGAN, G. Campbell. *Gospel According to Mark.* 1977. Revell. 350p. M/dj. B29. $7.50

MORGAN, Howard K. *Industrial Training & Testing.* 1945. McGraw Hill. 1st ed. 216p. G. K4. $15.00

MORGAN, John Medford; see Fox, Gardner F.

MORGAN, Lewis H. *Houses & House: Life of the American Aborigines.* 1881. part of US G&G Survey Rocky Mtns. 1st ed. VG. A8. $110.00

MORGAN, Rod; see Fox, Gardner F.

MORGAN, Seth. *Homeboy.* 1990. London. Chatto Windus. 1st ed/author's 1st (& last) book. NF/NF. S9. $40.00

MORGAN, William. *American College of Physicians: Its First Quarter Century.* 1940. Phil. 1st ed. 275p. A13. $25.00

MORGAN & STRIKLAND. *AZ Memories.* 1984. AZ U. 1st ed. index. 353p. F/F. B19. $45.00

MORGANSTEIN, Gary. *Man Who Wanted To Play Centerfield for NY Yankees.* 1983. Atheneum. 1st ed. VG/VG. P8. $12.50

MORGANSTEIN, Gary. *Take Me Out to the Ballgame.* 1980. St Martin. 1st ed. F/VG+. P8. $35.00

MORGENTHAU, Henry. *Ambassador Morgenthau's Story.* 1979. NY. 8vo. 407p. w/prt card. O2. $25.00

MORI, Ougai. *Sanshou-Dayu.* 1982. Bijou Hoshino. 28x28mm. 1/140 (340 total). 192p. teg. morocco/onlay. F/case. B24. $475.00

MORI, Tamezo. *Coloured Butterflies From Korea.* 1934. np. 4to. 30 pl. 86p text/23p bibliography/index. VG. H4. $65.00

MORICE, Anne. *Publish & Be Killed.* 1986. St Martin. 1st ed. VG/VG. P3. $13.00

MORICE, Anne. *Treble Exposure.* 1988. St Martin. ARC/1st Am ed. RS. F/F. S6. $25.00

MORIER, James. *Adventures of Hajji Baba, of Ispahan, in England.* 1828. NY. Harper. 2nd Am ed/author's 1st novel. 2 vols. 8vo. VG. C6. $250.00

MORIER, James. *Adventures of Hajji Baba of Ispahan.* 1937. Random. 1st ed. 404p. VG/dj. W1. $14.00

MORIER, James. *Journey Through Persia, Armenia & Asia Minor...* 1812. London. 1st ed. folio. 438p. full contemporary calf. O2. $800.00

MORISON, Sameul Eliot. *Maritime Hist of MA 1783-1860.* 1921. Houghton Mifflin. 6th prt. 400p. VG/dj. M20. $35.00

MORISON, Samuel Eliot. *By Land & By Sea.* 1966. Knopf. 8vo. VG/VG. B11. $15.00

MORISON, Samuel Eliot. *Samuel De Champlain: Father of New France.* 1972. Boston. 1st ed. VG/G. B5. $30.00

MORISON, Sanuel Eliot. *Introduction to Whaler Out of New Bedford.* 1962. New Bedford. Old Dartmouth Hist Soc. ils. unp. wrp. T7. $20.00

MORLEY, Christopher. *Seacoast of Bohemia.* 1929. Doubleday. ARC. RS. F/NF. B2. $50.00

MORLEY, John. *Edmund Burke: Hist Study.* 1867. London. Macmillan. 312p. leather. VG. H1. $55.00

MORLING, G.H. *Quest for Serenity.* 1989. Word. 96p. F/dj. B29. $3.50

MORO, Cesar. *Amour a Mort.* 1973. TVRT. 1st ed. trans Frances LeFevre. F/wrp. B2. $45.00

MORPURGO, J.E. *Their Majesties' Royal College, William & Mary...* 1976. Hennage Creative Prt. 1st ed. 4to. 247p. VG/G. B11. $45.00

MORRELL, David. *Blood Oath.* 1982. St Martin/Marek. 1st ed. F/NF. N3. $60.00

MORRELL, David. *Fireflies.* 1988. Dutton. 1st ed. F/F. F4. $15.00

MORRELL, David. *Fireflies.* 1988. Dutton. 1st ed. rem mk. VG+/dj. M21. $12.00

MORRELL, David. *First Blood.* 1972. Evans. 1st ed. VG/VG. P3. $50.00

MORRELL, David. *First Blood.* 1972. Evans. 1st ed/author's 1st book. xl. VG/dj. M21. $15.00

MORRELL, David. *League of Night & Fog.* 1987. Dutton. 1st ed. F/F. N3. $15.00

MORRELL, David. *Testament.* 1975. NY. Evans. 1st ed. F/VG. N3. $35.00

MORRELL, David. *Totem.* 1979. Evans. 1st ed. sgn. F/dj. F4. $75.00

MORRELL, David. *Totem: Complete & Unaltered.* 1994. Donald Grant. 1st ed. sgn Morrell/Canty. 1/1000. F/F/fld tray case. T2. $100.00

MORRESSY, John. *Frostworld & Dreamfire.* 1977. Doubleday. 1st ed. F/F. P3. $15.00

MORRILL, Claire. *Taos Mosaic: Portrait of NM Village.* 1973. NM U. 1st ed. ils/notes. 176p. F/NF. B19. $100.00

MORRIS, Alice Talwin. *Elephant's Apology.* nd. London. Blackie. sm 8vo. ils Alice B Woodward. 152p. aeg. red cloth. NF. D6. $95.00

MORRIS, Ann. *Digging in Yucatan.* 1937. Doubleday. 279p. VG/dj. F3. $25.00

MORRIS, Bill. *Motor City.* 1992. Knopf. ARC. NF/wrp. B3. $30.00

MORRIS, Donald R. *Washing of the Spears: Hist of Rise of the Zulu Nation...* 1965. Simon Schuster. 1st ed. VG. N2. $15.00

MORRIS, E. Joy. *Notes of Tour Through Turkey, Greece, Egypt & Arabia...* 1843. London. 8vo. 142p. new sark bl quarter calf. O2. $140.00

MORRIS, F.O. *Hist of British Moths.* 1903. London. Nimmo. 4 vol. 6th ed. 132 mc pl. gilt gr cloth. K1. $375.00

MORRIS, George Ford. *Portraitures of Horses.* 1952. Shrewsbury. Fordacre. 1st ed. obl folio. VG. O3. $595.00

MORRIS, George P. *Little Frenchman & His Water Lots...* 1839. Phil. Lea Blanchard. 1st ed. 8vo. 155p. cloth. M1. $175.00

MORRIS, Ivan. *World of the Shining Prince. Court Life in Ancient Japan.* 1964. Knopf. 1st Am ed. 336p. VG/dj. M20. $25.00

MORRIS, J. Wesley. *Christ Church Cincinnati 1817-1967.* 1967. Cincinnati. 1st ed. 196p. NF/VG. M8. $37.50

MORRIS, J.H.C. *Thank You, Wodehouse.* 1981. Weidenfeld Nicolson. 1st ed. NF/NF. P3. $20.00

MORRIS, James. *Islam Inflamed: Middle East Picture.* 1957. Pantheon. 1st ed. 8vo. VG/dj. W1. $15.00

MORRIS, James. *Preachers.* 1973. St Martin. 418p. VG. B29. $9.00

MORRIS, James. *Sultan in Oman.* 1957. Pantheon. 1st ed. 8vo. VG/torn. W1. $35.00

MORRIS, Janet. *Beyond Sanctuary.* 1985. Baen. 1st ed. F/F. P3. $20.00

MORRIS, Janet. *Earth Dreams.* 1982. Putnam. 1st ed. F/dj. F4. $16.00

MORRIS, Jim. *Sheriff of Purgatory.* 1979. Doubleday. 1st ed. F/NF. N3. $35.00

MORRIS, Jim. *Sheriff of Purgatory.* 1979. Doubleday. 1st ed. VG/VG. P3. $15.00

MORRIS, Jim. *War Story.* 1979. Sycamore Island. 1st ed. 342p. VG/dj. M20. $18.00

MORRIS, John. *Candywine Development.* 1971. Citadel. 1st ed. VG/VG. P3. $18.00

MORRIS, Paul C. *American Sailing Coasters of the North Atlantic.* 1973. Chardon. Bloch Osborn. 224p. map ep. bl cloth. NF. P4. $60.00

MORRIS, Phyllis. *Adventures of Willy & Nilly.* 1921. John Lane. 134p. cloth. fair. B10. $15.00

MORRIS, W. Meredith. *British Violin Makers: Biographical Dictionary...* 1920. London. 2nd ed. 318p. scarce. B14. $250.00

MORRIS, William. *Poems by the Way.* 1891. Kelmscott. Golden type (2-color prt) ed. sm 4to. stiff vellum. F. H4. $6,500.00

MORRIS, Wright. *Cloak of Light: Writing My Life.* 1985. Franklin Lib. Sgn 1st Ed Soc. sgn. gilt navy leather. M. A18. $50.00

MORRIS, Wright. *Inhabitants.* 1972. NY. 2nd ed. VG/VG. B5. $45.00

MORRIS, Wright. *Love Affair — A Venetian Journal.* 1972. NY. 1st ed. pres. w/intl inscr slip. F/F. A11. $65.00

MORRIS, Wright. *Man Who Was There.* 1945. Scribner. 1st ed. F/NF. B2. $125.00

MORRIS & MORRIS. *Threshold.* 1990. NY. ROC. 1st ed. F/F. N3. $15.00

MORRIS & RASKIN. *Lawrence of Arabia: 30th-Anniversary Pict Hist.* 1992. Doubleday. 1st ed. 237p. gilt blk cloth. M/dj. M7. $40.00

MORRISON, Alex. *Better Golf Without Practice.* 1940. NY. 1st ed. VG/G. B5. $30.00

MORRISON, Gertrude W. *Girls of Central High on Lake Luna (#2).* 1914. Grosset Dunlap. 204p. pict cloth. VG/mc dj. M20. $15.00

MORRISON, Robert. *Grammar of the Chinese Language.* 1815. Sermapore. Mission Pr. 1st ed. 4to. 280p. cloth. F. M1. $1,250.00

MORRISON, Toni. *Beloved.* 1987. Knopf. 1st ed. F/F. B2. $75.00

MORRISON, Toni. *Bluest Eye.* 1970. HRW. 1st ed/author's 1st book. 8vo. 164p. F/VG. C6. $1,000.00

MORRISON, Toni. *Jazz.* 1992. Franklin Lib. 1st ed. sgn. F. L3. $150.00

MORRISON, Toni. *Jazz.* 1992. London. Chatto Windus. 1st ed. sgn. F/F. S9. $75.00

MORRISON, Toni. *Jazz.* 1992. NY. 1st trade ed. sgn. F/F. A11. $75.00

MORRISON, Toni. *Song of Solomon.* 1977. Knopf. 1st ed. NF/VG. B3. $100.00

MORRISON, Toni. *Tar Baby.* 1981. Chatto Windus. UP/1st UK ed. F/salmon wrp. Q1. $200.00

MORRISON, Toni. *Tar Baby.* 1981. Franklin Center. 1st ed. ils Walt Spitzmiller. full leather. NF. B3. $125.00

MORRISON, Toni. *Tar Baby.* 1981. Knopf. 1st ed/author's 4th book. inscr. F/NF. L3. $275.00

MORRISON, Toni. *Tar Baby.* 1981. Knopf. 1st trade ed. sgn. 305p. F/F. C6. $150.00

MORRISON, William. *Mel Oliver & Space Rover on Mars.* 1954. Gnome. 1st ed. G. M2. $8.00

MORROW, Elizabeth. *Rabbit's Nest.* 1940. Macmillan. 1st ed. ils Howard Willard. 43p. NF/VG. P2. $30.00

MORROW, James. *City of Truth.* 1990. Legend. 1st ed. F/F. P3. $25.00

MORROW, James. *Wine of Violence.* 1981. Holt. 1st ed/author's 1st book. F/dj. F4. $20.00

MORSE, Elizabeth. *Siamese Cat.* ca 1929. Dutton. ils Ruth Seymour. F/G. B10. $10.00

MORSE, Peter. *Jean Charlot's Prints. A Catalogue Raisonne.* (1976). Honolulu. 1/200. special ed. w/orig sgn Charlot etching. case. K1. $300.00

MORSE, Samuel French. *Time of Year.* 1943. Cummington. 1st ed/1st book poems. intro Wallace Stevens. F/torn. V1. $130.00

MORTENSEN, William. *Model. A Book on Problems of Posing.* 1937. San Francisco. Camera Craft. 5th prt. 8vo. VG/VG. S9. $65.00

MORTENSEN, William. *Mortensen on the Negative.* 1949. Simon Schuster. 5th prt. 8vo. VG. S9. $60.00

MORTIMER, John. *Answer Yes or No.* 1950. London. Bodley Head. 1st ed/author's 3rd novel. NF/NF. B4. $275.00

MORTIMER, John. *Art of Husbandry, Part II.* 1712. London. Mortlock. 1st ed. 266p. new half leather. H10. $125.00

MORTIMER, John. *Charade.* 1986. Viking. F/F. P3. $20.00

MORTIMER, John. *Like Men Betrayed.* 1953. London. Collins. 1st ed/author's 4th novel. F/NF clip. B4. $200.00

MORTON, H.V. *In the Steps of St Paul.* 1936. Dodd Mead. 499p. H10. $13.50

MORTON, H.V. *In the Steps of the Master.* (1934). Dodd Mead. 20th prt. 448p. VG. B29. $4.00

MORTON, H.V. *Through Lands of the Bible.* 1928. London. Methuen. 1st ed. 400p. VG/VG. M7. $35.00

MORTON, Harry A. *Wind Commands: Sailors & Sailing Ships in the Pacific.* 1975. Wesleyen U. ils/64 pl. 498p. dj. T7. $40.00

MORTON, Julia F. *Fruits of Warm Climates.* 1987. Miami. ils/photos. 559p. M. B26. $80.00

MORTON, Leslie T. *Garrison & Morton: Medical Bibliography...* 1954. London. Grafton. 655p. NF/dj. G7. $75.00

MORTON, Louis. *Robert Carter of Nomini Hall.* 1945. Colonial Williamsburg. 2nd ed. 8vo. 332p. VG/fair. B11. $25.00

MORTON, Michael. *Herder & the Poetics of Thought.* 1989. University Park/London. PA State. 186p. crimson cloth. F/F. G1. $22.50

MORTON, Robert. *Southern Antiques & Folk Art.* 1976. Oxmoor. 1st ed. 251p. beige sailcloth. VG. S11. $15.00

MORTON, Rosalie Slaughter. *Doctor's Holiday in Iran.* 1940. Funk Wagnall. revised ed. 8vo. 335p. VG/dj. W1. $15.00

MOSELEY, Dana. *Dead of Summer.* 1953. Abelard. 1st ed. VG/VG. P3. $20.00

MOSER, Barry. *An Alphabet.* 1986. Pennyroyal. ltd ed. sgn. 1/150. gilt full red leather. M. E3. $550.00

MOSER, Barry. *Appalachia.* 1991. San Diego. HBJ. 1st ed. ils. F/F. B3. $15.00

MOSER, Barry. *Messiah.* 1992. NY. Willa Perlman. 1st ed. inscr/dtd Moser. F/F. S9. $60.00

MOSER, Don. *Central American Jungles.* 1977. Time Life. 4to. ils/maps/index. 184p. VG. F3. $10.00

MOSER, Gunther. *Kakteen.* 1985. Kufstein. 224 photos/2 full-p mc maps. stiff sc. F/dj. B26. $24.00

MOSER & WELTY. *Robber Bridegroom.* 1987. Pennyroyal. 1/150 #d. sgns. full leather. F. S9. $750.00

MOSES, Anna Mary Robertson. *Grandma Moses Storybook for Boys & Girls.* ca 1961. Random. 141p. VG. B10. $45.00

MOSES, Henry. *Gallery of Pictures Painted by Benjamin West...* 1811-1816. London. Henry Moses. 2nd ed. folio. 12 pl. contemporary calf. M1. $500.00

MOSKOWITZ, Sam. *A Merritt: Reflections in the Moon Pool.* 1985. Oswald Train. 1st ed. F/F. T2. $20.00

MOSKOWITZ, Sam. *Strange Horizons: Spectrum of SF.* 1976. NY. Scribner. 1st ed. F/NF. T2. $12.00

MOSKOWITZ, Sam. *Under the Moons of Mars.* 1970. HRW. 1st ed. VG/VG. P3. $55.00

MOSLEY, Leonard. *Marshall: Hero of Our Times.* 1982. NY. 1st ed. 570p. VG/dj. B18. $15.00

MOSLEY, Leonard. *On Borrowed Time: How WWII Began.* 1969. BOMC. 509p. VG/VG. A17. $10.00

MOSLEY, Walter. *Black Beauty.* 1994. Norton. 1st ed. sgn. F/F. O4. $35.00

MOSLEY, Walter. *Black Betty.* 1994. Norton. ARC. F/wrp. B2. $35.00

MOSLEY, Walter. *Devil in a Blue Dress.* 1990. Norton. 1st ed. sgn. F/F. T2. $60.00

MOSLEY, Walter. *White Butterfly.* 1992. Norton. 1st ed. F/F. T2. $65.00

MOSLEY, Walter. *White Butterfly.* 1992. Norton. 1st ed. sgn. F/F. B3. $75.00

MOSS, Sidney P. *Poe's Major Crisis: His Libel Suit & NY's Literary World.* 1970. Duke U. VG/dj. N2. $10.00

MOSS, W.S. *War of Shadows.* 1952. London. 8vo. ils. 240p. cloth. O2. $35.00

MOSS & THURLOW. *Chinese Snuff Bottles From the Collection...Marques Exeter.* 1974. London. Hugh Moss. 8vo. 162p. gilt brn cloth. F. F1. $35.00

MOSSHAMER, Ottalie. *Priest & Womanhood.* 1965. Westminster. Newman. 388p. xl. H10. $18.50

MOSSIKER, Frances. *Pocahontas: The Life & the Legend.* 1976. Knopf. 1st ed. 8vo. ils. 383p. F/VG. B11. $18.00

MOST, Konrad. *Training Dogs.* 1955. Coward McCann. 1st Am ed. 230p. cloth. VG. very scarce. R2. $60.00

MOSTAFA, Mohamed. *Museum of Islamic Art: A Short Guide.* 1979. Cairo. 3rd ed. fld map. VG. W1. $10.00

MOSTOFSKY, David I. *Attention: Contemporary Theory & Analysis.* 1970. Appleton Century Crofts. 431p. F. K4. $10.00

MOTHERWELL, Robert. *Modern Artists in America.* 1951. NY. ils. blk brd. NF. F1. $100.00

MOTT, Valentine. *Travels in Europe & the East.* 1842. NY. Harper. 452p. cloth. G7. $150.00

MOUNTFORT, Guy. *Portrait of a Desert.* 1965. Houghton Mifflin. 1st Am ed. pl. VG/dj. W1. $30.00

MOUNTJOY, Henry. *Minister of Police.* 1912. Bobbs Merrill. 1st ed. VG/dj. M15. $35.00

MOURAVIEFF, A.N. *History of the Church of Russia.* 1842. Oxford. trans RW Blackmore. 448p. cloth. O2. $60.00

MOUROT, F. *Bernard Buffet: Lithographs 1952-1966.* 1967. Paris. 1/125 #d. 2 orig sgn lithographs. case. C11. $1,500.00

MOUSA, Suleiman. *Lawrence & the Arabs.* 1992. Amman. Ministry Culture, Hashemite Kingdom. 1st ed. sgn. M. M7. $25.00

MOUSA, Suleiman. *TE Lawrence, an Arab View.* 1966. Oxford. 1st ed. 301p. brn stp yel cloth. F/VG clip/clear plastic. M7. $65.00

MOWAT, Farley. *Boat Who Wouldn't Float.* 1973. Boston. Atlantic Monthly. 1st ed. NF/VG. B3. $35.00

MOWAT, Farley. *Whale for the Killing.* 1972. Toronto. McClelland Stewart. 1st ed. NF/VG+. S9. $45.00

MOWAT, Farley. *Woman in the Mists.* 1988. London. MacDonald. 1st ed. NF/F. B3. $15.00

MOWRY, Jess. *Six Out Seven.* 1993. FSG. 1st ed. F/F clip. A14. $30.00

MOWRY, Jess. *Way Past Cool.* 1992. FSG. 1st ed. NF/F. A14. $35.00

MOXLEY, F. Wright. *Red Snow.* 1930. Simon Schuster. 2nd ed. G+. P3. $20.00

MOXON, Joseph. *Mechanick Excercises on the Whole Art of Printing.* 1962. Oxford. 2nd ed. ils. 545p. F/NF. A4. $185.00

MOYES, Patricia. *Many Deadly Returns.* 1970. HRW. 1st ed. VG. P3. $10.00

MOYES, Patricia. *Night Ferry to Death.* 1985. London. Collins. 1st ed. sgn. F/F. S6. $45.00

MOYES, Patricia. *Season of Snows & Sins.* 1971. HRW. 1st ed. VG. P3. $10.00

MOYNIHAN, Elizabeth B. *Paradise As Garden in Persia & Mughal India.* 1979. Braziller. 1st ed. 168p. VG. W1. $18.00

MOZANS, H.J. *Up the Orinoco & Down the Magdalena.* 1910. Appleton. 1st ed. 439p. VG. scarce. F3. $45.00

MOZART. *Letters of Mozart & His Family.* 1989. Norton. 2nd ed. F/F. P3. $75.00

MOZINGO, Hugh N. *Shrubs of the Great Basin: A Natural Hist.* 1987. NV U. 1st ed. ils/index. 342p. F/NF. B19. $45.00

MRACEK, Franz. *Atlas of Diseases of the Skin...* 1990. Phil. 62 mc pl/39 half-tone ils. G. G7. $45.00

MRAZEK, James E. *Fighting Gliders of WWII.* 1977. NY. 1st Am ed. 207p. VG/dj. B18. $22.50

MUCH, Hans. *Hippodrates der Grosse.* 1926. Stuttgart. 162p. dj. G7. $30.00

MUCK, Otto. *Secret of Atlantis.* 1978. Canada. Collins. VG. P3. $18.00

MUDWINKLE, H.J. *Study of Dinosaurs on the Comparative Method...* 1988. Lorson/Whittington. 64x50mm. ils P Forster. 20p. w/extra suite. F/box. B24. $275.00

MUELLER, Hans Alexander. *Woodcuts & Wood Engravings: How I Make Them.* 1939. np. ils. VG/VG. M17. $85.00

MUELLER, Joseph. *Fatherhood of St Joseph.* 1952. St Louis. Herder. 238p. xl. H10. $15.00

MUGGERIDGE, Malcolm. *Jesus Rediscovered.* 1969. Doubleday. 217p. xl. G/dj. B29. $3.50

MUIR, Augustus. *Shadow on the Left.* 1928. Methuen. 1st ed. VG. P3. $20.00

MUIR, John S. *Geology of Tampico Region of Mexico.* 1936. Tulsa. Am Assn Petroleum Geologists. 1st ed. 280p. VG/VG. B5. $150.00

MUIR, John. *Climb the Mountains.* 1965. Pasadena. Dawson. 46x38mm. 28p. Bela Blau bdg. F. B24. $350.00

MUIR, John. *Cruise of the Corwin: Journal of Arctic Expedition of 1881.* 1917. Houghton Mifflin. 1st ed. aeg. F. A18. $125.00

MUIR, John. *Mountains of CA.* 1988. Fulcrum. ils/index. 291p. F/NF. B19. $20.00

MUIR, John. *My First Summer in the Sierra.* 1988. Sierra Club. 1st ed. ils Michael McCurdy. M/dj. A18. $35.00

MUIR, John. *Our National Parks.* 1901. Houghton Mifflin. 1st ed. inscr pres/dtd 1907. 12 pl. 370p. NF/morocco case. H5. $2,000.00

MUIR, John. *Stickeen.* 1910. Houghton Mifflin. 8th imp. inscr. VG/dj. Q1. $250.00

MUIR, Marcie. *Bibliography of Australian Children's Books.* 1970. np. ils. 1038p. F/NF. A4. $125.00

MUIR, Percy. *English Children's Books 1600 to 1900.* 1985 (1954). London. BT Batsford. 4th ed. 4to. NF/NF. D6. $30.00

MUIR, Percy. *Victorian Ils Books.* 1989. London. rpt. F/F. A4. $55.00

MUIRDEN, James. *How To Use an Astronomical Telescope.* 1985. NY. Linden. lg 8vo. 397p. VG/VG. K5. $18.00

MUKHERJEE, Bharati. *Jasmine.* 1990. London. Virago. 1st ed. F/NF. B3. $20.00

MUKHERJEE, Bharati. *Middleman & Other Stories.* 1988. Grove. 1st ed. F/F. B3. $20.00

MULFORD, Charles E. *Bar-20 Three.* 1973. Tom Stacey. VG/VG. P3. $15.00

MULFORD, Charles E. *Bar-20.* nd. Grosset Dunlap. VG. P3. $15.00

MULFORD, Charles E. *Coming of Hopalong Cassidy.* nd. Grosset Dunlap. VG/G. P3. $12.00

MULFORD, Clarence E. *Hopalong Cassidy.* 1910. Grosset Dunlap. 6th ed. NF/VG. C8. $30.00

MULHOLLAND, St. Clair A. *Military Order Congress Medal of Honor Legion of the US.* 1905. Phil. 1st ed. 4to. ils. 694p. teg. gilt half leather. VG. H3. $175.00

MULJI, Karsandas. *Hist of Sect of Mah'ra'jas; or, Vallabha'cha'ryas...* 1865. London. Trubner. 2 parts in 1. 184p. half maroon/red cloth. K1. $200.00

MULLALLY, Frederic. *Assassins.* 1965. Walker. 1st ed. NF/NF. P3. $10.00

MULLANY, Katherine F. *Augustine of Hippo.* 1930. NY. Pustet. 196p. xl. H10. $15.00

MULLEN, Kevin J. *Let Justice Be Done.* 1989. NV U. 313p. F/dj. D3. $12.50

MULLEN, Thomas J. *Renewal of the Ministry.* 1963. Abingdon. 12mo. inscr. 143p. VG/dj. V3. $12.00

MULLER, Dan. *Chico of the + Up Ranch.* ca 1938. Reilly Lee. ils. 249p. VG. B10. $15.00

MULLER, Herbert J. *Thomas Wolfe.* 1947. New Directions. 1st ed. 12mo. cloth. VG. A17. $15.00

MULLER, John E.; see Fanthorpe, Lionel.

MULLER, Marcia. *Cavalier in White.* 1986. NY. St Martin. UP. sgn. RS. F/wrp. S6. $35.00

MULLER, Marcia. *Dark Star.* 1989. St Martin. 1st ed. F/F. M15. $25.00

MULLER, Marcia. *Leave a Message for Willie.* 1984. St Martin. 1st ed. VG/VG. P3. $20.00

MULLER, Marcia. *Shape of Dread.* 1989. Mysterious. 1st ed. sgn. F/F. O4. $20.00

MULLER, Marcia. *There Hangs the Knife.* 1988. St Martin. 1st ed. sgn. F/VG. O4. $20.00

MULLER, Max. *Sacred Books of the East.* 1965. Delhi. Motilal Benarsidass. 50 vol. VG. B33. $530.00

MULLER, Orrie. *Orientalisches Tagebuch.* 1932. Bremen. Leumer. 1st ed. 8vo. 171p. G/torn. W1. $12.00

MULLER & PRONZINI. *Chapter & Hearse: Suspense Stories About World of Books.* 1985. np. F/F. A4. $30.00

MULLER & PRONZINI. *1001 Midnights.* 1986. NY. Arbor. 1st ed. inscr/sgn both authors. F/F. S6. $110.00

MULLET, Charles. *Public Baths & Health in England, 16th-18th Century.* 1946. Baltimore. 1st ed. 85p. wrp. A13. $35.00

MULLINS, Richard. *Most Valuable Player.* 1962. Funk Wagnall. later prt. F/VG. P8. $25.00

MULLINS & REED. *Union Bookshelf: Selected Civil War Bibliography.* 1982. np. 17 pl. 107p. F. A4. $75.00

MULLINS. *Rocking Horse, a History of Moving Toy Horses.* 1992. np. lg 4to. photos. 376p. F/F/NF case. A4. $135.00

MULOCK, Dinah Maria. *Adventures of a Brownie.* ca 1929. Winston. ils EJ Prittie. VG/fair. B10. $35.00

MULOCK, Miss. *Little Lame Prince & His Traveling Cloak.* nd. Burt. 155p. G. B10. $10.00

MUMEY, Nolie. *Evolution of Flight.* 1931. Denver. Kendrick Bellamy. 1st ed. sgn. 1/200. 123p. G+. B18. $125.00

MUMFORD, John Kimberly. *Oriental Rugs.* 1902. NY. ils. VG. M17. $50.00

MUMFORD, Lewis. *City in History.* 1961. HBW. 657p. VG/dj. A10. $15.00

MUMFORD, Lewis. *Culture of Cities.* 1969. HBW. 586p. xl. VG/dj. A10. $10.00

MUMFORD, Lewis. *Myth of the Machine.* 1967. HBW. 342p. VG. A10. $20.00

MUMFORD, Lewis. *Story of Utopias.* 1922. NY. 1st ed/author's 1st book. 8vo. buckram. NF. D3. $150.00

MUNDY, Ethel. *Popular Yorkshire Terrier.* 1958. London. Popular Dogs. 1st ed. 160p. cloth. F/VG. R2. $20.00

MUNDY, Talbot. *Nine Unknown.* 1924. Bobbs Merrill. VG. P3. $75.00

MUNDY, Talbot. *Queen Cleopatra.* 1929. Bobbs Merrill. 1st ed. VG/VG. P3. $60.00

MUNK, Joseph Amasa. *Activities of a Lifetime.* 1924. Times-Mirror. 1st ed. ils. 221p. B19. $40.00

MUNN, Henry Toke. *Tales of the Eskimo.* nd. London. VG/VG. A17. $40.00

MUNN, Norman L. *Evolution & Growth of Human Behavior.* 1965. Houghton Mifflin. 2nd ed. 571p. G. K4. $10.00

MUNRO, Alice. *Friend of My Youth.* 1990. Knopf. AP. sgn. F/case. B2. $50.00

MUNRO, Alice. *Friend of My Youth.* 1990. Knopf. ARC. sgn. NF/wrp/pub fld box. L3. $75.00

MUNRO, Alice. *Friend of My Youth.* 1990. Knopf. UP. sgn. F. B3. $35.00

MUNRO, Donald. *Treatment of Injuries to the Nervous System.* 1952. Phil. Saunders. 284p. G7. $35.00

MUNRO, Hugh. *Clutha Plays a Hunch.* 1959. Ives Washburn. 1st ed. VG/VG. P3. $15.00

MUNRO, James. *Man Who Sold Death.* 1964. Hammond. 1st ed. VG/fair. P3. $20.00

MUNZ, Philip A. *California Spring Wildflowers.* 1961. Berkeley. ils/photos/2 maps. cloth. VG. B26. $15.00

MURAKAMI, Haruki. *Wild Sheep Chase.* 1989. Tokyo. Kodansha. 1st Eng-language ed/author's 1st book. F/NF. B2. $40.00

MURBARGER, Nell. *Sovereigns of the Sage.* 1958. Desert Magazine Pr. 1st ed. inscr. 342p. VG+. A8. $60.00

MURCHISON, Carl. *Handbook of Social Psychology.* 1935. NY. Russell & Russell. 2 vol. F. K4. $150.00

MURCOCH, Iris. *Book & the Brotherhood.* 1987. London. Chatto Windus. 1st ed. VG/NF. B3. $25.00

MURCOCH, Iris. *Philosopher's Pupil.* 1983. London. Chatto Windus. 1st ed. F/clip. B3. $30.00

MURDIN & MURDIN. *Supernovae.* 1985. Cambridge. revised ed. 185p. F/F. K5. $25.00

MURDOCH, W.B. Burn. *From Edinburgh to the Antarctic: An Artist's Notes...* 1984. Bungay. Bluntisham. rpt of 1894 ed. 8vo. 364p. bl cloth. M. P4. $55.00

MURDOCK, Eugene Converse. *Patriotism Limited 1862-1965.* 1967. Kent, OH. 1st ed. 270p. VG. B18. $20.00

MURDOCK, George. *Our Primitive Contemporaries.* 1938. Macmillan. ils/photos. VG. B34. $35.00

MURE, G.R.G. *Study in Hegel's Logic.* 1950. Oxford. Clarendon. 376p. F/dj. G1. $60.00

MURIE, Adolph. *Wolves of Mt McKinley.* 1944. WA, DC. photos/index. 238p. G/wrp. A17. $20.00

MURNEEK & WHYTE. *Vernalization & Photoperiodism.* 1948. Waltham, MA. Chronica Botanica. 196p. brd. VG. A10. $45.00

MURPHY, Clyde. *Glittering Hill.* 1944. World. VG/dj. B34. $35.00

MURPHY, Gardner. *Personality.* 1947. Harper. 927p. G. K4. $10.00

MURPHY, Gloria. *Blood Ties.* 1987. NY. Donald Fine. 1st ed. F/F. N3. $15.00

MURPHY, Gloria. *Playroom.* 1987. Donald Fine. 1st ed. VG/VG. P3. $18.00

MURPHY, Haughton. *Murder & Acquisitions.* 1988. London. Collins. ARC/1st Eng ed. RS. F/F. S6. $25.00

MURPHY, Haughton. *Murder for Lunch.* 1986. Simon Schuster. 1st ed. F/F. P3. $15.00

MURPHY, Marguerite. *Dangerous Legacy.* 1962. Avalon. 1st ed. xl. dj. P3. $5.00

MURPHY, Robert F. *Robert H Lowie.* 1972. NY. Columbia. 1st ed. 179p. M/chip. P4. $17.50

MURPHY, Shirley Rousseau. *Castle of Hape.* 1990. Atheneum. 1st ed. F/F. P3. $15.00

MURPHY, Shirley Rousseau. *Ivory Lyre.* 1987. Harper Row. 1st ed. F/F. P3. $13.00

MURPHY, Thomas. *One Hundred Years of the Presbyterian Church of Frankford.* 1872. Phil. 1st ed. 167p. cloth. VG. M8. $45.00

MURRAY, A.A. *Blanket.* 1957. Vanguard. dj. N2. $5.00

MURRAY, Albert. *Omni-Americans.* 1970. Outerbridge Dienstfrey. 1st ed/author's 1st book. F/NF. B2. $35.00

MURRAY, Albert. *Stomping the Blues.* 1976. McGraw. 1st ed. VG+. B2. $25.00

MURRAY, Cromwell. *Day of the Dead.* 1946. McKay. 1st ed. VG/VG. P3. $20.00

MURRAY, Francis Edwin. *Bibliography of Austin Dobson.* 1968 (1900). Franklin. 174p. gr cloth. F. S11. $12.00

MURRAY, Frank B. *Impact of Piagetian Theory on Education, Philosophy...* 1979. Baltimore. University Park Pr. 232p. blk cloth. VG/dj. G1. $25.00

MURRAY, Henry A. *Explorations in Personality.* 1938. Oxford. 742p. reading copy. K4. $15.00

MURRAY, John Ogden. *Immortal Six Hundred: A Story of Cruelty...* 1905. Winchester, VA. Eddy Pr. 1st ed. 274p. cloth. VG+. M8. $250.00

MURRAY, Lindley. *Some Account of the Life & Religious Labours of Sarah Grubb.* 1795. Trenton. Collins. 12mo. 418p. brn calf/red leather spine label. K1. $150.00

MURRAY, Ruth S. *Valiant for the Truth.* 1880. Cambridge. 12mo. 236p. VG. V3. $20.00

MURRAY, William H. *Adventures in the Wilderness; or Camp Life in Adirondacks.* 1869. Boston. pl. 236p. cloth. VG. B14. $95.00

MURRAY, William. *Getaway Blues.* 1990. Bantam. ARC/1st ed. inscr/dtd 1990. RS. w/promo material. F/F. S9. $30.00

MURRAY, William. *Getaway Blues.* 1990. Bantam. 1st ed. F/F. P3. $18.00

MURROW, Edward R. *This Is London.* 1941. NY. 1st ed. VG/VG. B5. $30.00

MURRY, Colin. *Golden Valley.* 1958. Hutchinson. 1st ed. xl. dj. P3. $25.00

MURRY, Margaret. *Genesis of Religion.* 1963. London. Kegan Paul. 88p. VG/VG. B33. $10.00

MURTAUGH, Janet. *Wonder Tales of Giants & Dwarfs.* 1945. Random. ils Florian. pict brd. VG. A3. $10.00

MUSIL, Robert. *Man Without Qualities.* 1953-1960. London. 3 vol. 1st Eng ed. NF/NF. C2. $400.00

MUSSELMAN, M.M. *Get a Horse! Story of the Automobile in Am.* 1950. Phil. 1st ed. 304p. F/G. A17. $12.50

MUSSEN, Paul Henry. *Child Development & Personality.* 1963. Harper Row. 2nd ed. 607p. G. K4. $8.50

MUSSER, H.B. *Turf Management.* 1950. NY. 1st ed. VG/VG. B5. $50.00

MUSTO, David. *American Disease: Origins of Narcotic Control.* 1973. New Haven. 1st ed. 354p. A13. $35.00

MUYBRIDGE, Eadweard. *Human Figure in Motion.* 1955. NY. Dover. 4to. 195 pl. gilt cloth. G+. F1. $25.00

MUZZEY, A.B. *Reminiscences & Memorials of Men of the Revolution.* 1883. Boston. ils/index. 424p. O8. $14.50

MYER, Albert J. *Manual of Signals.* 1868. Van Nostrand. new enlarged ed. 30 pl. 417p. rebound. T7. $95.00

MYER, William Edward. *Indian Trails of the Southeast.* 1971. Nashville. Bl Gray. 1st book ed. 1/1000. 132p. gilt gr buckram. F. B11. $50.00

MYERS, Amy. *Murder Makes an Entree.* 1992. London. Headline. 1st ed. F/F. S6. $25.00

MYERS, Gary. *House of the Worm.* 1975. Arkham. 1st ed. F/F. P3. $20.00

MYERS, Gustavus. *Hist of Supreme Court of the US.* 1912. Chicago. Chas H Kerr. 1st ed. bl cloth. G. M11. $25.00

MYERS, John M. *Deaths of the Bravos.* 1962. Little Brn. 1st ed. VG/VG. P3. $40.00

MYERS, John Myers. *Saga of Hugh Glass.* 1963. Bison. sc. VG. B34. $6.00

MYERS, Robert J. *Cross of Frankenstein.* 1975. Lippincott. 1st ed. VG/VG. P3. $25.00

MYERS, Robert Manson. *Children of Pride: True Story of Georgia & Civil War.* 1972. New Haven/London. Yale. 1st ed. thick 8vo. 1845p. gray cloth. VG. B11. $75.00

MYERS, Robert Manson. *From Beowulf to Virginia Woolf.* 1952. Bobbs Merrill. ils. 75p. VG/VG clip. S11. $10.00

MYERS, Robin. *Bibliographica: Papers on Books, Their Hist & Art 1895-1897.* 1979. Private Lib. 3rd Series/vol 2. NF. A4. $25.00

MYERSON. *Ralph Waldo Emerson, a Descriptive Bibliography.* 1982. Pittsburgh. ils. 821p. F. A4. $110.00

MYKEL, A.W. *Salamandra Glass.* 1983. St Martin. 1st ed. NF/NF. P3. $20.00

MYRES, J.L. *Dawn of History.* 1911. Holt/Butterworth. 1st ed. 12mo. 256p. VG/dj. W1. $10.00

N

NABB, Magdalen. *Death of a Dutchman.* 1983. NY. Scribner. 1st Am ed. F/F. S6. $25.00

NABHAN, Gary Paul. *Desert Smells Like Rain.* 1982. Northpoint. 1st ed. 148p. F/NF. B19. $35.00

NABHAN, Gary Paul. *Gathering the Desert.* 1985. AZ U. 1st ed. sgn. ils/sgn Paul Mirocha. 209p. F/F. B19. $50.00

NABHAN, Gary Paul. *Saguaro: View of Saguarao Nat Monument & Tucson Basin.* 1986. SW Parks Monuments Assn. ils. 74p. F/wrp. B19. $10.00

NABOKOV, Vladimir. *Bend Sinister.* 1947. Holt. 1st ed. NF/dj. Q1. $200.00

NABOKOV, Vladimir. *King, Queen, Knave.* 1968. McGraw Hill. 1st ed. G+. P3. $12.00

NABOKOV, Vladimir. *Lectures on Don Quixote.* 1983. NY. 1st ed. 219 p. F/F. A17. $15.00

NABOKOV, Vladimir. *Look at the Harlequins!* 1974. McGraw Hill. 1st ed. F/NF clip. B4. $50.00

NABOKOV, Vladimir. *Nabokov's Quartet.* 1966. Phaedra. 1st ed. F/VG clip. B3. $50.00

NADAR; see Tournachon, Gaspard-Felix.

NADEAU, Maurice. *Hist of Surrealism.* 1965. Macmillan. 1st ed. F/NF. B2. $45.00

NADER, George. *Chrome.* 1978. Putnam. 1st ed. VG/VG. P3. $15.00

NAGEL, Ernest. *Structure of Science: Problems in Logic...* 1961. HBW. 618p. prt gray-gr cloth. G1. $25.00

NAGEL, Hanna. *Die Sternenprinzessin.* nd (1950s). Oldenburg. ils. pict brd. VG. M5. $35.00

NAGEL, Robert F. *Constitutional Cultures: Mentality & Consequence...* 1989. Berkeley. CA U. M11. $20.00

NAIPAUL, V.S. *Among the Believers: An Islamic Journey.* 1981. NY. Knopf. 1st ed. NF/VG. E3. $40.00

NAIPAUL, V.S. *Area of Darkness.* 1964. London. Deutsch. 1st ed/author's 2nd book. VG/VG. L3. $250.00

NAIPAUL, V.S. *Congo Diary.* 1988. Los Angeles. 1st ed. sgn. 1/300. stp red cloth. F/sans. A11. $75.00

NAIPAUL, V.S. *Guerillas.* 1975. London. 1st ed. w/sgn label. F/F. A11. $125.00

NAIPAUL, V.S. *Middle Passage.* 1962. London. Deutsch. 1st ed/author's 5th book. VG/VG. L3. $350.00

NAIPAUL, V.S. *Million Mutinies Now.* 1991. Viking. AP. F/wrp. B2. $35.00

NAIPAUL, V.S. *Way in the World.* 1994. Knopf. AP. NF/wrp. B2. $85.00

NAIPAUL, V.S. *Way in the World.* 1994. Knopf. ARC. sgn. F/case. B2. $100.00

NAKAYA, U. *Snow Crystals, Natural & Artificial.* 1954. Boston. 1st ed. VG/dj. C11. $50.00

NANI, Battista. *History of the Affairs of Europe in This Present Age...* 1673. London. 4to. contemporary tree calf. O2. $650.00

NANSEN, Fridtjof. *Farthest North Westminster.* 1897. UK. 2 vol. ils. VG. M17. $175.00

NANSEN, Fridtjof. *Ski Over Growland.* 1890. Kristiania. inscr pres. Danish text. H4. $200.00

NAOKI, Sanjugo. *Man Who Was Revenged.* 1987. Bijou Hoshino. 35x32mm. 1/50 (200 total). teg. leather/inlay. F/case. B24. $475.00

NAPHEGYI, G. *Ghardaia; or, Ninety Days Among the B'ni Mozab.* 1871. NY. 348p. VG. F1. $100.00

NAPIER, John. *Bigfoot.* 1972. London. Cape. UP. photos. 230p. VG. S11. $10.00

NAPIER, John. *Roots of Mankind.* 1970. Smithsonian. 221p. F/dj. K4. $10.00

NAPJUS, James. *Trouble on the Infield.* 1967. Van Nostrand. 1st ed. F/VG. P8. $30.00

NARANJO, Claudio. *Healing Journey: New Approaches to Consciousness.* 1973. Pantheon. 1st ed. 235p. F/F. B33. $25.00

NARING, H. Jr. *Sinister Researches of CP Ransom.* 1954. Doubleday. 1st ed. VG/VG. P3. $35.00

NASBY, Petroleum V. *Diverse Views, Opinions & Prophecies of...* 1867. np. 424p. VG. E5. $35.00

NASBY, Petroleum V. *Ekkoes From Kentucky.* 1868. Boston. 1st ed. ils/sgn Thos Nast. w/F sgn slip & cancelled check. VG. A11. $110.00

NASBY, Petroleum V. *Nasby in Exile; or, Six Months of Travel.* 1882. np. 1st ed. 672p. VG. E5. $35.00

NASH, Charles Edgar. *Lure of Long Beach.* 1936. Long Meach Brd of Trade. ils. 170p. T7. $30.00

NASH, Cyril. *Yours Faithfully: Autobiography of a Schnauzer.* 1938. London. Longman Gr. 1st ed. ils John Nicholson. 180p. VG. R2. $60.00

NASH, Ogden. *Christmas That Almost Wasn't.* 1957. Little Brn. 1st ed. VG+/VG. C8. $25.00

NASH, Ogden. *Family Reunion.* 1950. Little Brn. 1st ed. 146p. cloth. VG/ragged. M20. $20.00

NASH, Ogden. *Four Prominent So & So's.* 1934. Simon Schuster. 1st separate/unexpurgated ed. VG/tan stapled wrp. Q1. $175.00

NASH, Ogden. *Versus.* nd. Little Brn. VG/VG. P3. $15.00

NASH, Ronald. *New Evangelism.* 1963. Zondervan. 183p. VG. B29. $5.50

NASHE, Thomas. *Pierce Penilesse, His Supplication.* 1924. Bodley Head. VG. P3. $35.00

NASR, Seyyed Nossein. *Islamic Studies, Essays on Law & Society...* 1967. Beirut. 1st ed. 155p. VG/dj. W1. $35.00

NASR, Seyyed Nossein. *Persia: Bridge of Turquoise...* 1975. NY Graphic Soc. 1st ed. 367p. NF/dj. W1. $145.00

NASR, Seyyed Nossein. *Sufi Essays.* 1973. Albany. 1st Am ed. 184p. VG/dj. W1. $35.00

NATANSON, Maurice. *Edmund Husserl: Philosopher of Infinite Tasks.* 1973. Evanston. 228p. prt bl cloth. VG. G1. $27.50

NATANSON, Maurice. *Philosphy of the Social Sciences: A Reader.* 1963. Random. 560p. emb red cloth. VG/worn. G1. $25.00

NATHAN, George Jean. *Theatre of the Moment.* 1936. Knopf. 1st ed. 309p. G. H1. $18.00

NATHAN, John. *Mishima: A Biography.* 1974. Little Brn. 1st ed. VG/dj. N2. $8.50

NATHAN, Robert. *Mr Whittle & the Morning Star.* 1947. Knopf. 1st ed. VG/G. P3. $20.00

NATHANSON, Jerome. *John Dewey: Reconstruction of Democratic Life.* 1951. Scribner. sm 8vo. 127p. blk cloth. VG/chip. G1. $17.50

NATION, Carry A. *Use & Need of Life of Carry A Nation, Written by Herself.* 1908. Eureka Springs. self pub. revised ed. 1/10,000. F. B2. $50.00

NATIONAL GEOGRAPHIC SOCIETY. *Book of Dogs.* 1957. NGS. 1st ed. ils. 430p. cloth. F/G. R2. $40.00

NATSUKI, Shizuko. *Murder on Mt Fuji.* 1984. St Martin. ARC/1st Am ed. RS. F/F. S6. $27.50

NATSUME, Soseki. *Dreams Ten Nights.* 1987. Tokyo. Bijou. 40x33mm. 1/50 (total of 200). 127p. teg. F/case. B24. $475.00

NAUCKE, Wolfgang. *Uber die Juristische Relevanz der Sozialwissenschaften.* 1972. Frankfurt am Main. German text. 72p. NF/stiff wrp. D3. $25.00

NAUGHTON, Jim. *My Brother Stealing Second.* 1989. Harper Row. 1st ed. VG+/VG+. P8. $12.50

NAUROY, Charles. *Bibliographie des Impressions Microscopiques.* 1881. Paris. Charavay Freres. 1/250. 12mo. 125p. prt wrp. B24. $450.00

NAVE, Oriville J. *Nave's Topical Bible: Digest of the Holy Scriptures.* 1974. Moody. 1376p. F. B29. $12.00

NAWROCKI & PAPA. *Atmospheric Processes.* 1961. Bedford, MA. Geophysics Corp of Am. 4to. 699p. gray cloth. VG. K5. $25.00

NAYLER, J.L. *Advances in Space Technology.* 1962. London. Newnes. 8vo. 215p. G/torn. K5. $30.00

NAYLOR, James Ball. *Witch Crow & Barney Bylow.* 1906. Saalfield. 1st ed. ils CB Williams. 118p. G+. D6. $30.00

NAYLOR, Phyllis Reynolds. *Amish Family.* 1974. Chicago. O'Hara. 1st prt. inscr. ils George Armstrong. NF/NF. C8. $45.00

NAYLOR, Phyllis Reynolds. *Dark of the Tunnel.* 1985. Atheneum. 1st ed. F/F. P3. $12.00

NAYLOR, Phyllis Reynolds. *Night Cry.* 1984. Atheneum. 1st ed. 8vo. M/M. C8. $20.00

NAYLOR, Phyllis Reynolds. *String of Chances.* 1982. Atheneum. 1st ed. F/F. C8. $30.00

NEALE, John Mason. *Hist of the Holy Eastern Church.* 1850. London. Masters. 2 vol. ils/index. buckram. H10. $100.00

NEALE, W.T. *Cacti & Other Succulents.* 1935. Newhaven, Sussex. photos. 200p. red buckram. F. B26. $29.00

NEARING, Scott. *Free Born. Unpublished Novel.* 1932. NY. Urquhart. 1st ed. sgn. VG. B2. $275.00

NEARING, Scott. *Russia Turns East.* 1926. NY. Social Science Pub. 1st ed. F/wrp. B2. $35.00

NEATE, W.R. *Mountaineering & Its Literature.* 1980. Mountaineers. photos/maps. F/wrp. S11. $10.00

NEEDHAM, Joseph. *Within the Four Seas.* 1969. Allen Unwin. 228p. F/dj. K4. $12.50

NEEDLEMAN, Jacob. *Heart of Philosophy.* 1982. Knopf. 1st ed. 237p. VG/VG. B33. $24.00

NEEDLEMAN, Jacob. *Lost Christianity: Journey of Rediscovery...* 1980. Doubleday. 1st ed. 228p. VG/VG. B33. $24.00

NEEDLEMAN, Jacob. *New Religions.* 1970. Doubleday. 1st ed. 245p. VG/VG. B33. $25.00

NEEL, James. *Changing Perspectives on Genetic Effects of Radiation.* 1963. Springfield. 1st ed. 97p. dj. A13. $40.00

NEEL, S. *Medical Support of the US Army in Vietnam 1965-1970.* 1973. WA. ils. 196p. G7. $25.00

NEELY, Richard. *Accidental Woman.* 1981. HRW. 1st ed. F/F. P3. $20.00

NEELY, Tom. *Queen Fussy.* ca 1973. Phoenix. Ten Publications. unp. VG. B10. $12.00

NEELY. *Confederate Image, Prints of the Lost Cause.* 1987. NC U. ils. 287p. F/F. A4. $165.00

NEEPER, Cary. *Place Beyond Man.* 1975. Scribner. 1st ed. F/NF. N3. $10.00

NEIDER, Charles. *Beyond Cape Horn: Travels in Antarctic.* 1980. San Francisco. 1st ed. 385p. VG/VG. A17. $15.00

NEIDER, Charles. *Comic Mark Twain Reader.* 1977. Doubleday. 1st ed. 489p. F/dj. M10. $8.50

NEIDER, Charles. *Great West.* 1958. np. VG/dj. B34. $45.00

NEIDER, Charles. *Plymouth Rock & the Pilgrims & Other Salutary Platform...* 1984. Harper Row. 1st ed. 344p. VG/dj. M10. $20.00

NEIHARDT, John G. *Poetic Values: Their Reality & Our Need of Them.* 1925. Macmillan. 1st ed. NF. A18. $60.00

NEIHARDT, John G. *Songs of the Indian Wars.* 1925. Macmillan. 1st ed. sgn. 1/500. ils Allen True. brn brd/bl spine. F. Q1. $400.00

NEIL, Ewell. *Upper & the Lower: Simplified Full Denture Imp Procedure.* 1941. Chicago. Cal Technical Lib/Coe Laboratories. 152p. VG. H1. $6.00

NEIL, William. *Rediscovery of the Bible.* 1954. Harper. 255p. VG. B29. $4.50

NEILL, John R. *Land of Oz, Jr Edition.* 1939. Rand McNally Jr Elf Book 299. 62p. K2. $18.00

NEILL, John R. *Lucky Bucky in Oz.* (1942). Reilly Lee. not 1st ed. blank ep. F. B17. $75.00

NEILL, John R. *Lucky Bucky in Oz.* 1942. Reilly Lee. 1st ed. ils. 289p. G+. P2. $185.00

NEILL, John R. *Scalawagons of Oz.* 1941. Reilly Lee. G. P3. $50.00

NEILL, John R. *Scalawagons of Oz.* 1941. Reilly Lee. later prt. 309p. VG. M20. $90.00

NEILL, John R. *Scarecrow of Oz.* 1940. Reilly Lee. 4to. 288p. red cloth. G. A3. $30.00

NEILL, John R. *Three Little Pigs.* nd. McKay. ils. VG/fair. P2. $45.00

NEILL, John R. *Wonder City of Oz.* 1940. Reilly Lee. not 1st ed. pict ep. pict tan cloth. VG. B17. $100.00

NEILL & SCHMANDT. *Hist of the Catholic Church.* 1965. Milwaukee. Bruce. 696p. xl. H10. $16.50

NEILSON, Francis. *Old Freedom.* 1919. NY. Huebsch. 1st ed. NF. B2. $40.00

NELIGAN & SEYMOUR. *True Irish Ghost Stories.* 1992. Galahad. F/F. P3. $15.00

NELSEN, Donald. *Sam & Emma.* 1971. NY. Parents. probable 1st ed. ils Edward Gorey. F. C8. $17.50

NELSON, C.M. *Barren Harvest.* 1949. Crime Club. 1st ed. G+. P3. $6.00

NELSON, Christopher. *Mapping the Civil War, Featuring Rare Maps...* 1992. np. Starwood. 1st ed. ils. cloth. F/F. M8. $45.00

NELSON, Daniel. *Am Rubber Workers & Organized Labor, 1900-1941.* 1988. Princeton, NJ. ils. 339p. F/F. B18/V4. $15.00

NELSON, Earl. *Life & the Universe.* 1953. London. Staples. 8vo. ils. 223p. G/dj. K5. $12.00

NELSON, Edna. *O'Higgins & Don Bernardo.* 1954. Dutton. 1st ed. 384p. VG/dj. F3. $15.00

NELSON, Horatio. *Dispatches & Letters of Vice-Admiral Lord Viscount Nelson.* 1844-1846. London. Colburn. 7 vol. ils/plans. bl cloth. F. T7. $950.00

NELSON, Hugh Lawrence. *Dead Giveaway.* 1950. Rinehart. 1st ed. VG. P3. $13.00

NELSON, Nina. *Tunisia.* nd. Hastings. 1st ed. 183p. F/dj. W1. $9.00

NELSON, Ozzie. *Ozzie.* 1973. NY. 1st ed. sgn pres. VG/VG. B5. $25.00

NELSON, R.H. *Pyrethrum Flowers.* 1975. Minneapolis. 3rd ed. ils. VG/dj. B26. $34.00

NELSON, Truman. *Old Man: John Brown at Harper's Ferry.* 1973. HRW. 1st ed. VG/dj. N2. $12.50

NELSON & WRIGHT. *Tomorrow's House, a Complete Guide for the Home-Builder.* 1945. Simon Schuster. 2nd prt 4to. red stp tan brd. G/dj. F1. $30.00

NEMEROV, Howard. *Homecoming Game.* 1957. NY. 1st ed. w/sgn bookplate. NF/NF. A11. $60.00

NEMETH, Laszlo. *Revulsion.* 1965. NY. 1st Am ed. trans from Hungarian. F/F. A17. $12.50

NERUDA, Pablo. *Bestiary/Bestiario.* 1965. HBW. 1/300. ils/printer/sgn Joseph Blumenthal. NF/VG case. S9. $200.00

NERUDA, Pablo. *Memoirs.* 1977. FSG. 1st Am ed. F/NF. B4. $45.00

NERUDA, Pablo. *Twenty Poems.* 1967. Sixties Pr. 1st ed. NF/wrp. B2. $50.00

NESBIT, E. *New Treasure Seekers; or, Bastable Children in Search...* 1904. NY. Stokes. 8vo. 328p. gilt dk gr cloth. VG. D6. $60.00

NESBIT, E. *Nine Unlikely Tales for Children.* 1901. London. Fisher Unwin. 8vo. 297p. red cloth. D6. $95.00

NESBIT, E. *Railway Children.* Sept 1906. Macmillan. 1st Am ed. pict cloth. G+. C8. $50.00

NESBIT, E. *Winter Snow.* nd. Dutton. 12mo. ils H Bellingham Smith. VG. D6. $20.00

NESBIT, Wilber D. *As Children Do.* 1929. Volland. 1st ed. ils Ellery Friend. VG. B10/M5. $35.00

NESBITT, L.M. *Hell-Hole of Creation: Exploration of Abyssinian Danakil.* 1935. Knopf. 3rd prt. 382p. VG. W1. $15.00

NESS, Elliot. *Untouchables.* 1957. NY. 1st ed. VG/G. B5. $25.00

NESVADBA, Josef. *Lost Face.* 1971. Taplinger. 1st ed. VG/VG. P3. $15.00

NETTER, Frank H. *CIBA Collection of Medical Ils. Vol I, Nervous System.* 1967. NY. 122 mc pl. cloth. F/dj. B14. $75.00

NEUBERGER, Richard L. *Lewis & Clark Expedition.* 1951. Random. lg prt. ils. VG/dj. B34. $10.00

NEUGEBOREN, Jay. *Sam's Legacy.* 1974. HRW. 1st ed. F/VG. P8. $35.00

NEUHAUS, E. *San Diego Garden Fair: Personal Impressions of Architecture.* 1916. Paul Elder. 1st ed. ils. 81p. uncut. B19. $55.00

NEUMANN, Carl Friedrich. *Versuch Einer Geschichte der Armenischen Literatur...* 1836. Leipzig. 8vo. 308p. new cloth. O2. $125.00

NEUMEYER, Peter F. *Why We Have Day & Night.* 1970. NY. Young Scott. 1st ed. ils Gorey. M/M. C8. $60.00

NEUNHEUSER, B. *Bapteme et Confirmation...* 1966. Paris. DuCerf. 249p. buckram. xl. H10. $25.00

NEURDENBURY & RADHAM. *Old Dutch Pottery & Tiles.* 1923. London. Benn Bros Ltd. VG. A1. $75.00

NEVIL, Susan R. *Picture Story of the Middle East.* 1956. McKay. 1st ed. 52p. xl. G. W1. $8.00

NEVILL, Ralph. *Days & Nights in Montmartre & the Latin Quarter.* 1927. Doran. 1st ed. VG. H7. $25.00

NEVILL, Ralph. *Old English Sporting Books.* 1924. London. The Studio. ltd ed. 1/1500. 23 mc pl. VG. O3. $195.00

NEVILLE, A.W. *Red River Valley: Then & Now.* 1948. Paris, TX. Hertzog. inscr. ils/sgn Jose Cisneros. F/VG. P4. $150.00

NEVILLE, Henry. *Plato Redivivus; or, Dialogue Concerning Government...* 1681. London. 1st ed. sm 8vo. 272p. rebacked. K1. $500.00

NEVILLE, Margot. *Murder of a Nymph.* 1950. Detective BC. VG. P3. $8.00

NEVINS, Allan. *Burden & Glory: Hopes & Purposes of Kennedy...* 1964. BOMC. F/dj. M10. $3.50

NEVINS, ROBERTSON & WILEY. *Civil War Books: Critical Bibliography.* 1969 & 1970. np. 2 vol. 4to. F/NF. A4. $225.00

NEVIUS, Blake. *Cooper's Landscapes: Essay on Picturesque Vision.* 1976. CA U. 1st ed. ils/index. F/F. A18. $20.00

NEWBERRY, Clare Turlay. *Cats & Kittens, a Portfolio of Drawings.* 1956. Harper. 16 prt. F/VG+ portfolio. C8. $100.00

NEWBERRY, Clare Turlay. *Drawing a Cat.* 1941. The Studio. 3rd imp. ils. G/F. B10. $25.00

NEWBERRY, Clare Turlay. *Kitten's ABC.* ca 1946. Harper. early prt. unp. VG. B10. $35.00

NEWBIGIN, Marion I. *Footprints in Spain.* 1922. Methuen. 1st ed. sm 8vo. 248p. VG. W1. $14.00

NEWBY, P.H. *Barbary Light.* 1962. London. 1st ed. inscr. NF/NF. A11. $45.00

NEWBY, P.H. *Guest & His Going.* 1960. London. 1st ed. w/sgn label. VG+/VG+. A11. $45.00

NEWCOMB, Covelle. *Secret Door.* 1946. Dodd Mead. 1st ed. ils Addison Burbank. 162p. VG/dj. M20. $40.00

NEWCOMB, Franc Johnson. *Hosteen Klah.* 1964. Norman. 227p. F/NF. P4. $45.00

NEWCOMB, R. *Our Lost Explorers: Jeannette Arctic Expedition.* 1883. np. ils/maps. 479p. VG-. B5. $75.00

NEWCOMB, Simon. *Popular Astronomy.* 1883. London. Macmillan. 2nd ed. 112 text ils/5 fld star maps. 579p. gr cloth. G. K5. $80.00

NEWELL, Gordon. *Ocean Liners of the 20th Century.* 1963. Superior. 1st ed. 192p. VG/VG. S11. $25.00

NEWELL, H.M. *Hardhats.* 1955. Houghton Mifflin. BC. VG/G. V4. $7.50

NEWELL & NEWELL. *Struggle for Afghanistan.* 1981. Cornell. 1st ed. 236p. NF/dj. W1. $18.00

NEWGEON, Walter. *Rhesa.* 1922. Raymond Pub. 1st ed. VG. M2. $12.00

NEWHALL, Beaumont. *History of Photography.* 1964. MOMA. 4to. VG. S9. $55.00

NEWLIN. *Life & Writings of Hugh Henry Brackenridge.* 1932. Princeton. 334p. VG. A4. $45.00

NEWMAN, Arnold. *One Mind's Eye.* 1974. Boston. NYGS. inscr to Robert Sobieszek (wrote intro). VG+/wrp. S9. $225.00

NEWMAN, Daisy. *Golden String.* 1986. Harper Row. BC. 8vo. 185p. VG/VG. V3. $9.00

NEWMAN, Daisy. *I Take Thee, Serenity.* 1982. Houghton Mifflin. BC. 8vo. 314p. VG/chip. V3. $9.50

NEWMAN, Elmer S. *Lewis Mumford: A Bibliography 1914-1970.* 1971. HBJ. 1st ed/5th prt. 167p. VG/VG. A10. $25.00

NEWMAN, Ernest. *Stories of the Great Operas.* (1930). Garden City. 371p. VG. H1. $18.00

NEWMAN, Frances. *Hard-Boiled Virgin.* 1926. Boni Liveright. 1st ed/author's 1st novel. 285p. VG/rpr. C6. $200.00

NEWMAN, George. *Interpreters of Nature.* 1927. NY. 1st ed. 296p. dj. A13. $25.00

NEWMAN, George. *Quaker Profiles.* 1946. Bannisdale. 1st ed. 12mo. 134p. G+. V3. $12.00

NEWMAN, Gertrude. *Story of Delicia, a Rag Doll.* 1937 (1935). Rand McNally. photos. VG. M5. $15.00

NEWMAN, John Henry. *Apologia Pro Vita Sua: Being Reply to a Pamphlet...* 1864. London. Longman. 1st ed. rebacked/orig spine. H10. $100.00

NEWMAN, John Henry. *Fine Gold of Newman Collected From His Writings...* 1931. Macmillan. edit Joseph Reilly. 245p. H10. $12.50

NEWMAN, Kim. *Night Mayor.* 1989. Simon Schuster. 1st ed. F/F. T2. $25.00

NEWMAN, Kim. *Night Mayor.* 1989. Simon Schuster. 1st ed. sgn. F/F. P3. $30.00

NEWMAN, Paul S. *Showdown on Front Street.* 1969. Whitman. Gunsmoke TVTI. VG. P3. $8.00

NEWMAN, Richard Brinsley. *Belle Islers.* 1908. Boston. 1st ed. ils. VG. A17. $12.50

NEWMAN, Sharan. *Death Comes As Epiphany.* 1993. Tor. 1st ed. sgn. F/F. T2. $30.00

NEWMARK, Nathan. *Law of Sales of Personal Property...* 1887. San Francisco. Bancroft Whitney. contemporary sheep. M11. $50.00

NEWPORT, David. *Pleasures of Home.* 1884. Lippincott. 1st ed. 12mo. 99p. VG. V3. $10.00

NEWSON & NEWSON. *Infant Care in an Urban Community.* 1963. Allen Unwin. 240p. F/dj. K4. $15.00

NEWTON, A. Edward. *Amenities of Book Collecting & Kindred Affections.* 1918. Atlantic Monthly. ils. 373p. G. M10. $6.50

NEWTON, A. Edward. *Amenities of Book Collecting.* 1924. Boston. ils/index. 373p. VG. O8. $9.50

NEWTON, A. Edward. *Amenities of Book Collecting.* 1935. Modern Lib. 1st ed. ils. 373p. VG. S11. $15.00

NEWTON, A. Edward. *End Papers.* 1933. Little Brn. 1st ed. ils. 223p. VG. S11. $20.00

NEWTON, A. Edward. *Magnificnet Farce.* 1970. Libraries Pr. rpt. ils. 267p. VG. S11. $10.00

NEWTON, H.W. *Face of the Sun.* 1958. Harmondsworth, UK. Penquin. pb. 208p. VG. K5. $6.00

NEWTON, Isaac. *Philosophiae Naturalis Principia Mathematica...* 1713. Cambridge. 2nd ed. 4to. 484p. contemporary paneled calf. K1. $6,000.00

NEXO, Martin Andersen. *Days in the Sun.* 1929. Coward McCann. 1st ed. F/NF. B2. $40.00

NEXO, Martin Anderson. *Days in the Sun.* 1929. NY. 1st Am ed. trans from Danish. 297p. G/dj. B18. $25.00

NG, Fae Myenne. *Bone.* 1993. NY. Hyperian. 1st ed/author's 1st book. F/F. B3. $20.00

NIALL, Ian. *Country Blacksmith.* 1966. London. Heinemann. 1st ed. VG/VG. O3. $45.00

NICHIREN. *Selected Writings of Nichiren.* 1990. NY. Columbia. 1st ed. 8vo. 508p. wht cloth. NF/VG. P4. $20.00

NICHIREN. *Selected Writings of...* 1990. NY. Columbia. 1st ed. 508p. F/F. B33. $45.00

NICHOLS, Beverly. *The Fool Hath Said.* 1936. London. Cape. later prt. 317p. VG. A10. $20.00

NICHOLS, Frances S. *Index to Schoolcraft's Indian Tribes of the US.* ca 1954. GPO. Bulletin 152. 257p. F/wrp. P4. $35.00

NICHOLS, J.L. *Business Guide; or, Safe Methods of Business.* 1891 (1886). Naperville, IL. Nichols. 26th ed. ils. 251p. G. H1. $8.00

NICHOLS, James M. *Perry's Saints.* 1886. Boston. VG. M17. $45.00

NICHOLS, John. *American Blood.* 1987. Holt. 1st ed. F/NF. B3. $15.00

NICHOLS, John. *Ghost in the Music.* 1979. HRW. 1st ed. sgn. VG/G. B3. $25.00

NICHOLS, John. *Literary Anecdotes of the 18th Century.* 1812-1815. London. 11 vol set. gilt dentelles/marbled p. VG+. A15. $350.00

NICHOLS, John. *Nirvana Blues.* 1981. HRW. 1st ed. sgn. F/dj. B3/L3. $65.00

NICHOLS, John. *Nirvana Blues.* 1981. HRW. 1st ed. sgn. VG+/VG+. S9. $50.00

NICHOLS, John. *Sterile Cuckoo.* 1965. David McKay. 1st ed/author's 1st book. NF/VG+. A18. $80.00

NICHOLS, Leigh; see Koontz, Dean R.

NICHOLSON, Irene. *Firefly in the Night.* 1959. Grove. 1st ed. 231p. VG/dj. F3. $30.00

NICHOLSON, Joan. *Canvas Work Simplified.* 1973. np. cloth. VG. G2. $5.95

NICHOLSON, John. *Farmer's Assistant.* 1814. Albany. Southwick. 1st ed. 336p. calf. H10. $185.00

NICHOLSON, John. *Space Ship to Venus.* 1948. London. 1st ed. F/dj. M2. $25.00

NICHOLSON, Joyce. *Our First Overlander.* 1956. Sydney. Shakespeare Head. ils Penglase. VG. B10. $15.00

NICHOLSON, Meredith. *Blacksheep, Blacksheep!* 1920. NY. 1st ed. F/NF. A15. $60.00

NICHOLSON, Reynold Alleyne. *Studies in Islamic Mysticism.* 1967. Cambridge. 2nd ed. 8vo. VG. W1. $45.00

NICKLAUS, Jack. *Jack Nicklaus Plays the NCR South.* 1969. Dayton. NCR Country Club. sgn. gr cloth. F. B4. $100.00

NICOL, Eric. *Say Uncle.* 1961. Harper. VG/VG. P3. $10.00

NICOLAI, Rudolf. *Gerschichte der Neugriechischen Literatur.* 1876. Off Leipzig. 8vo. quarter calf. O2. $45.00

NICOLAY, H. *Lincoln's Secretary.* 1949. NY. 1st ed. VG/VG. B5. $25.00

NICOLL, M.J. *Three Voyages of a Naturalist.* 1909. London. Witherby. 2nd ed. 8vo. 246p. VG. B11. $65.00

NIEBUHR, Alta D. *Herbs of Greece.* 1970. Athens. 120 mc photos. 140p. VG/wrp. B26. $17.50

NIEHAUS, James J. *Guide to Watch Holders.* 1978. St Marys, OH. Hunter Prt. 1st ed. ils. 37p. F/wrp. A8. $8.00

NIELSEN, Kay. *East of the Sun & West of the Moon, Old Tales From North.* nd (1921). NY. Doran. 8vo. 25 tipped-in pl. ils ep. red stp tan cloth. F/dj. F1. $550.00

NIELSEN, Torben. *Gallowsbird's Song.* 1976. Collins Crime Club. 1st ed. VG/VG. P3. $15.00

NIELSON, Helen. *Killer in the Street.* 1967. Morrow. 1st ed. VG. P3. $13.00

NIEMOELLER, A.F. *Complete Guide to Bust Culture.* 1944. Harvest House. 160p. gray cloth. VG. B14. $20.00

NIETZ, John A. *Old Textbooks.* 1961. Pittsburgh. 364p. VG. A10. $25.00

NIETZCHE, Friedrich. *Works of Friedrich Nietzche.* 1931. NY. Tudor. 340p. VG. B33. $30.00

NIETZEL, M. *Crime & Its Modification...* 1979. NY. 301p. VG. D3. $12.50

NIGHBERT, David. *Strikezone.* 1989. St Martin. 1st ed. M/M. P8. $11.50

NIGHBERT, David. *Timelapse.* 1988. St Martin. 1st ed. NF/NF. P3. $18.00

NIJINSKY, Romola. *Nijinsky.* 1934. Simon Schuster. 9th prt. sgn. 447p. VG/dj. M20. $35.00

NILES, Blair. *Black Haiti, a Biography of Africa's Eldest Daughter.* 1926. NY. Putnam. 1st ed. photos R Niles. VG. C8. $45.00

NILES, Blair. *Peruvian Pageant.* 1937. Bobbs Merrill. 1st ed. 311p. VG/dj. F3. $20.00

NILES, James N. *View of South America & Mexico by a Citizen of the US.* 1826. NY. Huntington. 2 vol in 1. gilt calf. VG. B14. $95.00

NIMOY, Leonard. *I Am Not Spock.* 1975. Millbrae. Celestial Arts. 1st ed. F/pict wrp. T2. $25.00

NIN, Anais. *DH Lawrence: Unprofessional Study.* 1932. Paris. Edward Titus. 1st ed/author's 1st book. 1/550. 146p. blk cloth. NF/VG. C6. $350.00

NIN, Anais. *Four-Chambered Heart.* 1986. San Diego. HBJ. 1st ed. octavo. 274p. quarter bl cloth/cream brd. F. H5. $50.00

NIN, Anais. *Nuances.* 1970. Sans Souci. 1/99 #d. F/acetate. S9. $175.00

NIN, Anais. *Spy in the House of Love.* 1954. NY. British Book Centre. 1st Am ed/variant issue. bl bdg/no pub imprint. F. L3. $150.00

NININGER, H.H. *Find a Falling Star.* 1972. NY. Paul Eriksson. 8vo. 254p. pb. K5. $15.00

NININGER, H.H. *Out of the Sky.* 1952. Denver. lg 8vo. 336p. G/dj. K5. $70.00

NISBET, Jim. *Death Puppet.* 1989. Blk Lizard. 1st ed. F/F. P3. $20.00

NISBET, Robert A. *Social Change & Hist: Aspects of W Theory of Development.* 1969. Oxford. 336p. blk clth. VG/dj. G1. $28.50

NISENSON & PARKER. *Minute Biographies: Intimate Glimpses Into Lives...* ca 1931. Grosset Dunlap. ils. 160p. cloth. G. B10. $12.00

NISSEN, Claus. *Botanische Prachtwerke Die Blutezeit der Pflanzenillustion.* 1933. Wein. Reichner. 44p. wrp/protective dj. A10. $45.00

NISSEN, Claus. *Die Botanische Buch-Illustration.* 1994 (1950). Mansfield, CT. rpt. 1/225. 324p. red cloth/blk spine label. K1. $100.00

NISTER, Ernest. *Children's Express.* nd. London. Nister. ils Stuart Hardy. 12p. G+. D6. $75.00

NISTER, Ernest. *Nister's Panorama Pictures. Novel Colour Book for Children.* nd (1894). London. Nister. folio. 36 pl/5 popups. VG. D6. $600.00

NISTER, Ernest. *Rainbow Round About, Dimensional Reproduction...* 1992. World. 5 popups. F. B17. $8.50

NISTER, Ernest. *Warriors Brave, a Story of the Little Lead Soldiers.* nd. London. Nister. 32mo. 56p. G+. D6. $55.00

NISTER, Ernest. *Wild Animal Stories.* 1988. Philomel. facsimile. 5 popups. F. B17. $8.50

NISWANDER, Adam. *Charm.* 1993. Integra. 1st ed. F/dj. M2. $22.00

NISWANDER, Adam. *Charm.* 1993. Pheonix. Integra. 1st ed. sgn. F/F. T2. $25.00

NITTI, Francesco. *Decadence of Europe.* 1923. NY. 1st ed. 302p. w/sgn letter. VG. A17. $20.00

NIVEDITA, Sister. *Cradle Tales of Hinduism.* 1955. Calcutta. Advaita Ashrama. 300p. VG/VG. B33. $20.00

NIVEN, Larry. *Integrel Trees.* 1984. Del Rey. 1st ed. VG/VG. P3. $15.00

NIVEN, Larry. *N Space.* 1990. Tor. 1st ed. F/F. M21. $15.00

NIVEN, Larry. *Niven's Laws.* 1984. Phil. PSFS/Owlswick. 1st ed. F/sans. T2. $12.00

NIVEN, Larry. *Playgrounds of the Mind.* 199. Tor. 1st ed. F/F. P3. $23.00

NIVEN, Larry. *Smoke Ring.* 1987. Del Rey. 1st ed. F/F. P3. $18.00

NIVEN, Larry. *Time of the Warlock.* 1984. Steel Dragon. 1st ed. 1/800. F/F. T2. $20.00

NIVEN & POURNELLE. *Lucifer's Hammer.* 1977. Playboy. 1st ed. NF/VG+. N3. $15.00

NIXON, Alan. *Attack on Vienna.* 1972. St Martin. 1st ed. F/F. P3. $13.00

NIXON, Alfred. *Hist of Daniel's Evangelical Lutheran & Reformed Churches...* 1969. Lincoln, NC. Lincoln Co Hist Assn. 44p. VG/wrp. M8. $27.50

NIXON, Richard. *Six Crises.* 1962. Doubleday. stated 1st ed. G+. N2. $7.50

NIZER, Louis. *Jury Returns.* 1966. Doubleday. 1st ed. sgn. F/NF. B2. $75.00

NIZER, Louis. *My Life in Court.* 1961. Garden City. 1st ed. 524p. VG. D3. $15.00

NOAKES, Aubrey. *Sportsmen in a Landscape.* 1954. Lippincott. 1st trade ed. VG/VG. O3. $45.00

NOBLE, Hollister. *One Way to Eldorado.* 1954. Doubleday. VG. B34. $5.00

NOCK, O.S. *Encyclopedia of Railways.* 1977. London. Octopus. 4to. 480p. VG/VG. B11. $35.00

NOCK, O.S. *Railways Then & Now. A World History.* 1975. NY. Crown. 4to. ils. 215p. F/VG. B11. $25.00

NODIER, Charles. *Luck of the Bean-Rows.* nd (1921). London. O'Connor. ils CL Fraser. G+. B10. $25.00

NODIER, Charles. *Woodcutter's Dog.* 1921. London. O'Connor. 18p. NF. B10. $20.00

NOEL, Ruth S. *Mythology of Middle Earth: Study of Tolkien's Mythology...* 1977. Houghton Mifflin. 1st ed. NF. N2. $10.00

NOLAN, Alan T. *Iron Brigade.* 1983. Berrien Springs. 3rd ed. F/F. A17. $25.00

NOLAN, Frederick. *Kill Petrosino!* 1975. Barker. 1st ed. VG/VG. P3. $20.00

NOLAN, J.C. *Treason at the Point.* ca 1944. Messner. ils/sgn Pitz. 224p. VG/G. B10. $35.00

NOLAN, Jeannette Covert. *Sudden Squall.* 1955. Ives Washburn. 1st ed. sgn. 185p. cloth. VG/dj. M20. $25.00

NOLAN, William F. *Black Mask Boys: Masters of Hard-Boiled School Detective...* 1985. NY. Morrow. 1st ed. sgn Nolan. F/F. S6. $45.00

NOLAN, William F. *Black Mask Murders.* 1994. St Martin. 1st ed. sgn. F/F. T2. $22.00

NOLAN, William F. *Human Equation.* 1971. Sherbourne. 1st ed. F/VG. N3. $10.00

NOLAN, William F. *Logan: A Trilogy.* 1986. Baltimore. Maclay. 1st combined/hc ed. sgn. F/F. T2. $20.00

NOLAN. *Ray Bradbury Companion...Comprehensive Checklist...* 1975. np. ils. 352p. F/VG case. scarce. A4. $135.00

NOLL, Arthur. *From Empire to Republic.* 1970. St Martin. 1st ed. 336p. VG. F3. $15.00

NOLTHENIUS, Helene. *Duecento: The Late Middle Ages in Italy.* 1968. McGraw Hill. 1st ed. ils. 268p. VG/dj. M10. $8.50

NOMACHI, Kazuyoshi. *Sahara.* 1978. Grosset Dunlap. 1st ed. NF/NF clip. S9. $50.00

NOONAN, John. *Contraception, a History of Its Treatment by Catholic...* 1965. Cambridge. 1st ed. 561p. A13. $40.00

NOONE, Edwina; see Avallone, Mike.

NOONE, John. *Man With the Chocolate Egg.* 1966. NY. 1st ed/author's 1st book. F/F. A17. $10.00

NORBORG, C. Sverre. *Christ on Main Street.* 1959. Denison. 400p. VG/dj. B29. $4.50

NORDAN, Lewis. *Music of the Swamp.* 1991. Algonquin. 1st ed/author's 3rd book. F/F. B3. $45.00

NORDAU, Max. *Degeneration.* 1895. London. Heinemann. 1st Eng-language ed. 560p. w/24p catalog. G1. $50.00

NORDEN, Pierre. *Conan Doyle: A Biography.* 1967. Holt. 1st Am ed. ils. F/F. S6. $25.00

NORDFORS, Jill. *Needle Lace & Needle Weaving.* 1974. Van Nostrand. 1st ed. lg 8vo. 160p. F/F. A17. $10.00

NORDHOFF, Walter. *Journey of the Flame.* 1955. Houghton Mifflin. ils. 295p. NF. B19. $35.00

NORDON, Pierre. *Conan Doyle.* 1966. John Murray. 1st ed. VG/VG. P3. $30.00

NORELLI-BACHELET, Patrizia. *Symbols & the Question of Unity.* 1974. Holland. Servire. 1st ed. 157p. F/F. B33. $35.00

NORFOLK, Lawrence. *Lempriere's Dictionary.* 1991. London. Sinclair Stevenson. 1st ed/author's 1st book. F/F. A14. $40.00

NORFOLK, Lawrence. *Lempriere's Dictionary.* 1991. NY. Harmony/Crown. 1st Am ed. F/F. A14. $25.00

NORFOLK, William; see Farmer, Philip Jose.

NORMAN, A. *Operation Overlord.* 1952. Harrisburg. 1st ed. VG/VG. B5. $35.00

NORMAN, Dorothy. *Alfred Stieglitz.* 1960. NY. 1st ed. sgn. VG/VG. B5. $45.00

NORMAN, Dorothy. *Alfred Stieglitz: An American Seer.* 1973. Random. 1st ed. VG+/VG+. S9. $60.00

NORMAN, Frank. *Too Many Crooks Spoil the Caper.* 1979. St Martin. 1st ed. VG/dj. P3. $15.00

NORMAN, Howard. *How Glooskap Outwits the Ice Giants.* 1989. Little Brn. 1st ed. F/F. L3. $75.00

NORMAN, Howard. *Kiss in the Hotel Joseph Conrad.* 1989. Summit. 1st ed/1st collection short stories. sgn. F/F. B4. $150.00

NORMAN, Howard. *Northern Lights.* 1987. Summit. 1st ed/author's 1st novel. sgn. F/F. L3. $250.00

NORMAN, Philip. *Elton John: The Biography.* 1991. Harmony. 1st ed. VG/VG. P3. $23.00

NORMAN, Rick. *Fielder's Choice.* 1991. August House. ARC. RS. M/M. P8. $22.50

NORMAN & POTTINGER. *English Weapons & Warfare 449-1660.* 1979. Prentice Hall. 224p. F/F. H1. $12.00

NORRIS, Frank. *McTeague: Story of San Francisco.* 1982. Franklin Lib. photos from Greed. aeg. silk ep. gilt gr leather. M. A18. $40.00

NORRIS, Frank. *Moran of the Lady Letty.* 1898. Doubleday McClure. 1st ed/author's 1st novel. VG. Q1. $175.00

NORRIS, Frank. *Third Circle.* 1909. NY. 1st ed. NF. A9. $50.00

NORRIS, Kathleen. *Corner of Heaven.* (1943). Collier. Palo Alto ed. 290p. F. H1. $5.00

NORRIS, Kathleen. *Maiden Voyage.* 1934. Collier. Palo Alto ed. 334p. G. H1. $2.50

NORRIS, Kathleen. *Secret of the Marshbanks.* 1940. Collier. Palo Alto ed. 304p. F. H1. $5.00

NORRIS, Kathleen. *Venables.* 1941. Collier. Palo Alto ed. 462. F. H1. $5.00

NORRIS, L. Bull. *Monolithic Axe Found in Connecticut.* 1931. Hartford. 22p. VG/stiff wrp. N2. $10.00

NORSE, Harold. *Beat Hotel.* 1983. San Diego. 1st Am ed. sgn. F/ils wrp. A11. $40.00

NORTH, Andre; see Norton, Andre Alice.

NORTH, Anthony; see Koontz, Dean R.

NORTH, Eric. *Ant Men.* 1955. Winston. 1st ed. VG. P3. $25.00

NORTH, Howard. *Expressway.* 1973. Collins. 1st ed. VG/G. P3. $15.00

NORTH, Marianne. *Vision of Eden, the Life & Work Of.* 1980. Exeter. Webb Bower. 240p. VG/VG. A10. $35.00

NORTH, Robert Carver. *Bob North With Tog Team & Indians.* 1929. NY. 1st ed. 170p. F. B14. $25.00

NORTH, Sterling. *Little Rascal.* ca 1975. Dutton. 1st ed thus. ils Carl Burger. VG/fair. B10. $10.00

NORTH, Sterling. *Midnight & Jeremiah.* 1943. Winston. 1st ed. ils Kurt Wiese. 125p. F/NF. M20. $35.00

NORTHCOTE, James. *Fables, Original & Selected.* 1833. London. 2nd series. 1st ed. cloth. VG. A9. $50.00

NORTHEND, Mary Harrod. *American Glass.* 1936. NY. Tudor. ils. gilt purple cloth. F/VG. F1. $25.00

NORTHROP, F.S.C. *Logic of the Sciences & Humanities.* 1948 (1947). Macmillan. 2nd prt. 402p. red cloth. G1. $28.50

NORTHROP, Henry D. *Armenian Massacres; or, Sword of Mohammed.* 1896. WA. 8vo. ils. 512p. gr cloth. O2. $60.00

NORTHRUP, Marguerite. *Christmas Story From Gospel of Matthew & Luke.* 1966. NYGS. 4to. VG/VG. B17. $6.50

NORTON, Andre Alice. *Androids at Arms.* 1971. Harcourt. 1st ed. VG/NF. M2. $60.00

NORTON, Andre Alice. *Forerunner: The Second Venture.* 1985. Tor. 1st ed. NF/NF. P3. $15.00

NORTON, Andre Alice. *Grayphon in Glory.* 1981. Atheneum. 1st ed. F/F. N3. $35.00

NORTON, Andre Alice. *Iron Cage.* 1974. Viking. 1st ed. F/F. P3. $35.00

NORTON, Andre Alice. *Moon of Three Rings.* 1966. Viking. 1st ed. lib bdg. F/NF. N3. $55.00

NORTON, Andre Alice. *Operation Time Search.* 1967. HBW. 1st ed. xl. dj. P3. $13.00

NORTON, Andre Alice. *Plague Ship.* 1956. Gnome. 1st ed. F/NF. M2. $100.00

NORTON, Andre Alice. *Secret of the Lost Race.* 1978. Gregg. 1st Am hc ed. F/NF. N3. $20.00

NORTON, Andre Alice. *Tales of the Witch-world 2.* 1988. Tor. 1st ed. VG/VG. P3. $17.00

NORTON, Andre Alice. *Victory on Janus.* 1966. HBW. 1st ed. 224p. VG/VG. M20. $75.00

NORTON, Andre Alice. *Ware Hawk.* 1983. Atheneum. 1st ed. F/F. F4. $35.00

NORTON, Andrews. *Inaugural Discourse, Delivered...University in Cambridge...* 1819. Cambridge. Hilliard Metcalf. 1st ed. 48p. wrp. H10. $85.00

NORTON, Donna E. *Through the Eyes of a Child.* 1987. Merrill. 2nd ed/3rd prt. 691p. pict brd. F. S11. $18.00

NORTON, Mary. *Borrowers Afloat.* 1959. London. Dent. 1st ed. 176p. VG/later state. M20. $45.00

NORTON, Mary. *Borrowers Afloat.* 1959. NY. Harcourt Brace. 1st Am ed. 191p. VG/dj. M20. $35.00

NORTON, Mary. *Borrowers.* 1952. London. 1st ed. ils Diana Stanley. VG. M5. $30.00

NORTON, Mary. *Borrowers.* 1953. Harcourt Brace. 1st ed. ils Krush. pict cloth. G+/G+. C8. $35.00

NORTON, Olive. *Corpse-Bird Cries.* 1971. Cassell. 1st ed. VG/VG. P3. $18.00

NORTON, Thomas. *Ordinal of Alchemy.* 1975. London. Oxford. 125p. VG/VG. B33. $30.00

NORVELL, Anthony. *Mind Cosmology.* 1972. Parker. 3rd ed. VG. P3. $15.00

NORVIL, Manning; see Bulmer, Kenneth.

NORWAY, G. *True Cornish Maid.* nd. Blackie. 288p. G/fair. B10. $10.00

NOTCUTT, Bernard. *Psychology of Personality.* 1953. London. Methuen. 235p. F/dj. K4. $10.00

NOTH, Martin. *Hist of Israel.* 1958. Harper. 479p. G/dj. B29. $10.00

NOTLEP, Robert. *Autograph Collector.* 1968. ils/index. 240p. dj. O8. $9.50

NOTT, Stanley Charles. *Chinese Jade Throughout the Ages.* 1969. Rutland. Tuttle. 6th prt. tall 4to. terra-cotta cloth. NF/dj. F1. $50.00

NOTT, Stanley Charles. *Ils Annotation of the Working & Dating of Chinese Jades.* 1941. St Augustine, FL. sgn pres. gilt gr cloth. F. F1. $75.00

NOURSE, Alan E. *Mercy Men.* nd. BC. VG/VG. P3. $8.00

NOVARR, David. *Lines of Life: Theories of Biography 1880-1970.* 1986. Purdue. 202p. gray cloth. F/F. G1. $20.00

NOVITCH, Miriam. *Passage of the Barbarians.* 1898. Hull. 176p. cloth. dj. O2. $25.00

NOY, William. *Principal Grounds & Maxims, With Analysis...Ninth Edition...* 1821. London. S Sweet. contemporary calf. G. M11. $350.00

NOYES, Alfred. *Watchers of the Sky.* 1922. NY. Stokes. 8vo. 281p. ils cloth. G. K5. $40.00

NOYES, James O. *Roumania: Border Land of the Christian & the Turk...* 1857. NY. 8vo. ils. 520p. cloth. O2. $45.00

NOYES & RAY. *Little Plays for Little People.* 1910. Ginn. ils. G. M5. $15.00

NOZICK, Robert. *Anarchy, State & Utopia.* 1974. Basic Books. 367p. brn cloth. VG/dj. G1. $30.00

NUNN, Kem. *Tapping the Source.* 1984. Delacorte. 1st ed. F/NF. L3. $45.00

NUNN, Kem. *Tapping the Source.* 1984. Delacorte. 1st ed. inscr/sgn. F/F. A11. $65.00

NURBAKHSH, Javad. *Divani Nurbakhsh: Sufi Poetry.* 1980. NY. Khaniqahi-Nimatullahi. 265p. w/photo. F/VG. B33. $20.00

NUSBAUM, Rosemary. *Tierra Dulce: Reminiscences From Jesse Nusbaum Papers.* 1980. Sunstone. 1st ed. ils. 96p. VG/wrp. B19. $15.00

NUTT, Frederic. *Complete Confectioner; or, Whole Art of Confectionary...* 1807. NY. rpt for Richard Scott/1st Am ed. 12mo. 91p. calf. M1. $525.00

NUTTALL, Thomas. *Journal of Travels Into the AR Territory During Year 1819.* 1980. Norman, OK. 361p. gray cloth. M/M. P4. $30.00

NUTTING, Anthony. *No End of a Lesson: Inside Story of Suez Crisis.* 1967. Potter. 1st Am ed. 8vo. 205p. VG/dj. W1. $12.00

NUTTING, Wallace. *American Windsors.* (1917). Framingham. 1st ed. VG. C11. $125.00

NUTTING, Wallace. *Connecticut Beautiful.* 1984. Boston. Godine. 4to. ils. VG/dj. N2. $20.00

NUTTING, Wallace. *Massachusetts Beautiful.* 1935. Garden City. VG. N2. $22.50

NUTTING, Wallace. *Nutting's Biography.* 1936. np. VG. M17. $35.00

NUTTING, Wallace. *Pennsylvania Beautiful (Eastern).* (1924). Bonanza. rpt. 302p. F/F. H1. $18.00

NYANAPONIKA, Bhikku. *Abhidhamma Studies: Researches in Buddhist Psychology.* 1949. Frewin. 86p. VG. G1. $40.00

NYE, Bud. *Stay Loose.* 1959. Doubleday. 1st ed. F/VG. P8. $30.00

NYE, Edgar Wilson. *Bill Nye's Red Book.* 1906. Thompson Thomas. 1st ed. ils JH Smith. 389p. G. H1. $7.00

O'BRIAN, Jack. *Rip Darcy, Adventurer.* 1938. Winston. 8vo. VG. B17. $6.50

O'BRIAN, Patrick. *Desolation Island.* 1979. Stein Day. 1st Am ed. F/F. L3. $300.00

O'BRIAN, Patrick. *Mauritius Command.* 1978. Stein Day. 1st Am ed. F/F clip. L3. $450.00

O'BRIEN, Dan. *In the Center of the Nation.* 1991. Atlantic. 1st ed. F/F. S9. $25.00

O'BRIEN, David M. *Storm Center, Supreme Court in Am Politics.* 1986. Norton. M11. $25.00

O'BRIEN, Edna. *Lonely Girl.* 1962. London. Cape. 1st ed. NF/NF. B2. $75.00

O'BRIEN, Flann. *Dalkey Archive.* 1964. London. MacGibbon Kee. 1st ed. F/NF. L3. $250.00

O'BRIEN, Flann. *Hard Life.* 1962. Pantheon. 1st ed. F/F. B2. $60.00

O'BRIEN, Flann. *Poor Mouth.* 1941. Dublin. An Press Naisunta. 1st ed. Gaelic text. VG+/wrp. rare. B4. $1,250.00

O'BRIEN, Flann. *Poor Mouth.* 1974. Viking. 1st ed. F/NF. B2. $30.00

O'BRIEN, Flann. *Stories & Plays.* 1976. Viking. 1st ed. F/NF. B2. $35.00

O'BRIEN, Kate. *English Diaries & Journals.* 1947. London. Collins. 3rd ed. 8vo. 48p. VG/chip. V3. $12.00

O'BRIEN, Michael J. *Irish at Bunker Hill.* 1968. np. VG/VG. M17. $12.50

O'BRIEN, Sharon. *Willa Cather: The Emerging Voice.* 1987. Oxford. 1st ed. F/F. P3. $30.00

O'BRIEN, Tim. *In the Lake of the Woods.* 1994. Houghton Mifflin. 1st ed. sgn. F/F. B3. $40.00

O'BRIEN, Tim. *Nuclear Age.* 1985. Knopf. UP/author's 4th book. F/wrp. L3. $100.00

O'CALLAGHAN, Jeremiah. *Holy Bible Authenticated: Baptism & Matrimony...* 1858. NY. self pub. 1st ed. 12mo. 244p. cloth. M1. $175.00

O'CASEY, Sean. *Green Crow.* 1956. Braziller. 1st ed. F/F. S9. $100.00

O'CASEY, Sean. *Windfalls: Stories, Poems & Plays.* 1934. Macmillan. 1st Am ed. F/NF. B2. $40.00

O'CONNELL, D.P. *Influence of Law on Sea Power.* 1975. Annapolis. Naval Inst. M11. $45.00

O'CONNER, Philip F. *Old Morals, Small Continents, Darker Times.* 1971. Iowa City. ARC/author's 1st book. pres. NF/prt wht wrp. A11. $55.00

O'CONNOR, Flannery. *Complete Stories.* 1971. Farrar. 1st ed. NF/NF. B2. $125.00

O'CONNOR, Flannery. *Habbit of Being: Letters of...* 1979. FSG. 1st ed. F/NF. B4. $125.00

O'CONNOR, Harvey. *World Crisis in Oil.* 1962. Monthly Review. 1st ed. 433p. VG/dj. W1. $25.00

O'CONNOR, Jack. *Game in the Desert.* 1939. Derrydale. 1/950. M. H4. $425.00

O'CONNOR, Philip F. *Stealing Home.* 1979. Knopf. 1st ed. 308p. VG/dj. M20. $20.00

O'CONNOR, Richard. *Ambrose Bierce: A Biography.* 1968. Gollancz. VG/VG. P3. $25.00

O'CONNOR, V.C. Scott. *Vision of Morocco.* 1923. London. Butterworth. 1st ed. 32 pl/map. 382p. VG. W1. $15.00

O'CONOR, Pierce. *Terriers for Sport.* 1926. Manchester. Our Dogs. 1st ed. ils. 47p. F/wrp. R2. $135.00

O'CORK, Shannon. *End of the Line.* 1981. St Martin. 1st ed. F/F. F4. $17.00

O'DANIEL, Victor Francis. *Dominicans in Early Florida.* 1930. NY. 1st ed. 230p. cloth. VG. M8. $37.50

O'DELL, Scott. *Hawk That Dare Not Hunt by Day.* 1975. Houghton Mifflin. 1st ed. F/F. B17. $10.00

O'DELL, Scott. *Sarah Bishop.* 1980. Houghton Mifflin. UP. 211p. NF/wrp. P2. $20.00

O'DELL, Scott. *Sing Down the Moon.* 1970. Houghton Mifflin. 1st ed. 137p. cloth. VG/VG. A3. $25.00

O'DONNELL, Barrett; see Malzberg, Barry.

O'DONNELL, Bernard. *Old Bailey & Its Trials.* 1950. London. 1st ed. 9 pl. 226p. VG. D3. $25.00

O'DONNELL, K.M.; see Malzberg, Barry.

O'DONNELL, Lillian. *Casual Affairs.* 1985. Putnam. 1st ed. F/F. P3. $17.00

O'DONNELL, Lillian. *Wicked Designs.* 1980. Putnam. 1st ed. VG/VG. P3. $13.00

O'DONNELL, Michael. *Long Walk Home.* 1984. NY. St Martin. ARC/1st Am ed. RS. F/F. S6. $22.50

O'DONNELL, Peter. *I, Lucifer.* 1967. Souvenir. 1st ed. VG/VG. P3. $60.00

O'DONNELL, Peter. *Modesty Blaise.* 1963. London. Souvenir. 1st ed. F/F. M15. $45.00

O'DONNELL, Terence. *Lenore. Maritime Chronicle of a China Clipper...* 1926. Houghton Mifflin. ils 325p. T7. $45.00

O'DONNELL & POWERS. *Johnny, We Hardly Knew Ye.* 1972. Little Brn. 1st ed. 434p. VG/dj. M10. $6.50

O'FLAHERTY, Liam. *Informer.* 1925. Knopf. 1st Am ed. xl. NF. B2. $40.00

O'FLAHERTY, Liam. *Tourist's Guide to Ireland.* nd. London. Mandrake. 1st ed. sgn. 16mo. blk cloth. NF/dj. H5. $200.00

O'HARA, John. *Appointment in Samarra.* 1934. Harcourt Brace. author's 1st book. 301p. cloth. ES. F/F. B14. $350.00

O'HARA, John. *Files on Parade.* 1939. Harcourt Brace. 1st ed. VG+/clip. Q1. $200.00

O'HARA, John. *Rage To Live.* 1949. Random. 1st ed. VG/VG. P3. $60.00

O'HARA, John. *Sermons & Soda-Water.* 1961. London. Cresset. 3 vol. 1/525 sets. sgn. F/cb case. H5. $150.00

O'HARA, Kenneth. *Death of a Moffy.* 1987. Doubleday. ARC/1st Am ed. RS. F/F. S6. $25.00

O'HARA, Kevin. *Exit & Curtain.* 1952. Hurst Blackett. 1st ed. xl. VG. P3. $10.00

O HENRY. *Four Million.* 1906. McClure Phillips. 1st ed. gilt red cloth. F. Q1. $150.00

O HENRY. *Heart of the West.* 1907. McClure. 1st ed. VG+. A18. $50.00

O HENRY. *Stories of...* 1965. LEC. 1st ed. 40 stories. gilt leather spine. F/case. A18. $60.00

O'KEEFE, J.A. *Tektites & Their Origin.* 1976. Amsterdam. Elsevier. Developments in Petrology Series. ils. 254p. VG/dj. K5. $75.00

O'MALLEY & SAUNDERS. *Leonardo Da Vinci on the Human Body.* 1982. NY. facsimile of 1952 ed. 504p. A13. $60.00

O'MEARA, John. *Charter of Christendom: Significance of City of God.* 1961. Macmillan. 120p. H10. $15.00

O'MEARA, Walter. *Minnesota Gothic.* 1956. Holt. 1st ed. 314p. VG/VG. A17. $12.50

O'NEAL, Lulu Rasmussen. *Peculiar Piece of Desert.* 1957. Lib Desert Magazine. ltd 1st ed. 1/450. F/VG plastic. A8. $50.00

O'NEIL, Denny. *Stacked Deck: The Greatest Joker Story.* 1990. Longmeadow. 1st ed. aeg. leather. F. P3. $60.00

O'NEIL, W.M. *Early Astronomy: From Babylonia to Copernicus.* 1986. Sydney, Australia. 8vo. ils. 214p. VG/VG. K5. $21.00

O'NEILL, Charles. *Wild Train: Story of Andrews Raiders.* 1956. Random. 1st ed. w/sgn leaf. NF/VG. M8. $60.00

O'NEILL, Elizabeth. *War, 1916: Hist & an Expiation for Boys & Girls.* nd. Stokes. ils. 96p. VG. B10. $25.00

O'NEILL, Eugene. *Ah, Wilderness!* 1933. Random. 1st ed. 8vo. 159p. pict ep. gilt bl cloth. VG/dj. H5. $125.00

O'NEILL, Eugene. *All God's Chillun Got Wings.* 1924. NY. Boni Liveright. 1st ed. NF/dj. Q1. $350.00

O'NEILL, Eugene. *Days Without End.* 1934. Random. 1st ed. 8vo. 157p. gilt bl cloth. VG/dj. H5. $75.00

O'NEILL, Eugene. *Last Will & Testament of an Extremely Distinguised Dog.* 1972. Worcester, MA. St Onge. miniature/1st ed thus. 1/1000. 26p. aeg. leather. R2. $60.00

O'NEILL, Eugene. *Moon for the Misbegotten.* 1952. Random. 1st ed. 8vo. 177p. brn/bl/gray bdg. NF/clip. H5. $75.00

O'NEILL, Hester. *Young Patriots.* ca 1948. Nelson. ils Richard Floethe. 256p. VG/fair. B10. $10.00

O'NEILL, John. *Clyfford Still.* 1979. Metropolitan Mus Art. 217p. VG/dj. M20. $25.00

O'NEILL, John. *Prodigal Genius.* 1968. London. 1st ed. VG/VG. B5. $40.00

O'REILLY, Bernard. *True Womanhood.* 1899. NY. 466p. O8. $18.50

O'REILLY, Edward. *Irish-English Dictionary.* 1821. Dublin. 1st ed thus. thick 4to. full polished calf. VG+. scarce. C6. $175.00

O'REILLY, Henry. *Settlement in the West. Sketches of Rochester...* 1838. Rochester, NY. Wm Alling. 1st ed. 8vo. ils. 416p. orig cloth. M1. $200.00

O'REILLY, John. *Glob.* 1952. Viking. 1st ed. ils Walt Kelly. VG/fair. B10. $25.00

O'ROURKE, Frank. *Flashing Spikes.* 1948. Barnes. 1st ed. VG+/G+. P8. $35.00

O'ROURKE, Frank. *Heavenly World Series & Other Stories.* 1952. Barnes. 1st ed. xl. G+/G+. P8. $15.00

O'ROURKE, Frank. *Team.* 1949. Barnes. 1st ed. VG. P8. $17.50

O'SHEA, Sean; see Tralins, Bob.

OAKLEY, Violet. *Holy Experiment: Our Heritage From William Penn.* 1950. Phil. Cogslea. ltd ed. sgn. 158p. bl cloth/brn spine. B11. $75.00

OAN. *Tales of Oan.* 1986. Bijou Hoshino. 40x31mm. 1/75 (225 total). leather/coin inlay. F/case/box. B24. $350.00

OATES, Joyce Carol. *Angel of Light.* 1981. Dutton. 1st ed. sgn. 434p. gilt beige/tan bdg. VG/clip. H5. $75.00

OATES, Joyce Carol. *Black Water.* 1992. London. Macmillan. AP. F/wrp. S9. $25.00

OATES, Joyce Carol. *Bloodsmoor Romance.* 1982. Dutton. 1st ed. sgn. NF/NF. B3. $25.00

OATES, Joyce Carol. *By the North Gate.* 1963. NY. Vanguard. 1st ed/author's 1st book. F/F. B24. $350.00

OATES, Joyce Carol. *Goddess & Other Women.* 1974. Vanguard. 1st ed. VG/VG. P3. $30.00

OATES, Joyce Carol. *Hungry Ghosts.* 1974. Blk Sparrow. 1/350 #d. sgn. F/acetate. S9. $50.00

OATES, Joyce Carol. *Marya. A Life.* 1986. Dutton. 1st trade ed. sgn. 8vo. 310p. gilt cream cloth/bl brd. F/dj. H5. $75.00

OATES, Joyce Carol. *Miracle Play.* 1974. Blk Sparrow. 1/350 #d. F/acetate. S9. $45.00

OATES, Joyce Carol. *Oates in Exile.* 1990. Toronto. Exile Eds. ARC. RS. F/F. B4. $125.00

OATES, Joyce Carol. *On Boxing.* 1987. Garden City. 1st ed. inscr. F/F. A11. $65.00

OATES, Joyce Carol. *Raven's Wing.* 1986. Dutton. 1st ed. sgn. VG/NF. B3. $25.00

OATES, Joyce Carol. *Sentimental Education.* 1980. Dutton. 1st ed. sgn. F/VG. B3. $25.00

OATES, Joyce Carol. *Soul/Mate.* 1989. Dutton. 1st ed. VG/VG. P3. $20.00

OATES, Joyce Carol. *Where Are You Going, Where Have You Been?* 1979. Logan, IA. 1st separate ed. sgn. F/ils wrp. A11. $25.00

OATES, Joyce Carol. *Women Whose Lives Are Food, Men Whose Lives Are Money.* 1978. LSU. 1st ed. F/F. B4. $125.00

OATES, Wayne. *Psychology of Religion.* 1973. Word. 291p. VG. B29. $4.50

OATES, Whitney J. *Stoic & Epicurean Philosophers: Complete Extant Writings...* 1940. Random. 6th prt. bl cloth. G1. $35.00

OBERG, James E. *Mission to Mars.* 1982. Harrisburg, PA. 8vo. 221p. xl. K5. $15.00

OBERG, James E. *Red Star in Orbit.* 1981. Random. 2nd prt. photos 272p. VG/VG. K5. $25.00

OBERLING, Pierre. *Road to Bellapais. Turkish Cypriot Exodus to N Cyprus.* 1982. NY. ils/maps. 256p. dj. O2. $30.00

OBLIGADO, George. *Magic Butterfy & Other Fairy Tales of Central Europe.* 1963. Golden/Western. 1st prt. VG+. C8. $30.00

OBOLER, Arch. *House of Fire.* 1969. Bartholomew. 1st ed. F/VG+. N3. $20.00

OBOLER, Eli M. *Fear of the Word: Censorship & Sex.* 1974. Metuchen, NJ. Scarecrow. 1st ed. 362p. NF. M10. $7.50

OCHARTE, Pedro. *Cartilla Para Ensenar a Leer.* 1935. Los Angeles. Ward Ritchie. 1/125. VG/chip. P4. $100.00

ODUM, Howard W. *Race & Rumors of Race.* 1943. Chapel Hill. 1st ed. F/worn. B2. $30.00

ODUM, Howard W. *Wings on My Feet.* 1929. Bobbs Merrill. 1st ed. F/NF. B2. $100.00

OEHSER, Paul. *Sons of Science.* 1949. NY. Schuman. 220p. cloth. VG. A10. $25.00

OEMLER, Marie Conway. *Woman Named Smith.* 1920. NY. 1st ed. cloth. G. A17. $7.50

OFFICER, James E. *Hispanic AZ 1536-1856.* 1987. AZ U. 1st ed. ils/notes/index. 463p. F/F. B19. $45.00

OFFILL, Cecile Cox. *...And Thy Neighbor: Sam Shoemaker Talks...* 1967. Word 200p. VG/dj. B29. $3.50

OFFNER, Max. *Guy Montrose Whipple: Mental Fatigue.* 1911. Baltimore. Warwick York. 121p. G. K4. $20.00

OFFUTT, A.J. *Black Sorceror of the Black Castle.* 1976. Hall. 1st ed. F/wrp. M2. $10.00

OGBURN, Charlton Jr. *Marauders.* 1959. NY. 1st ed. 307p. VG/chip. A17. $10.00

OGBURN, Charlton. *Adventure of Birds.* 1976. Morrow. 1st prt. 381p. VG/VG. S11. $10.00

OGILVIE, Lloyd John. *Bush Is Still Burning.* 1983. Word. 257p. G/torn. B29. $4.50

OGILVIE, Lloyd John. *Making Stress Work for You.* 1984. Word. 216p. F. B29. $4.00

OGLE, Lucille. *Work & Play the Healthy Way, Reading, Coloring, Cutting...* 1937. NY. Artist/Writers Guild. folio. 60p. VG. D6. $30.00

OGNYOV, N. *Diary of a Communist Schoolboy.* 1929. Payson Clarke. 1st ed. trans Alexander Werth. NF. B2. $65.00

OGRIZEK, Dore. *L'Arique du Nord.* 1952. Paris. Ode. 12mo. VG. W1. $15.00

OHANIAN, Phyllis. *Songs To Sing With the Very Young.* 1966. Random. ils Marjorie Torrey. pict brd. VG. M5. $20.00

OHRELIUS, Bengt. *Vasa: The King's Ship.* 1963. Phil. Chilton. 1st Am ed. VG/dj. N2. $10.00

OHRENSCHALL, Helen E. *Tom Tit Tales... Bedtime Stories for Children by Gilly Bear.* 1915. np. 12 mc pl. front ep missing. pict bl cloth. VG. M5. $45.00

OKAKURA, Tenshin. *Book of Tea.* 1988. Tokyo. Bijou. 45x37mm. 1/50 (total of 200). 159p. full brn morocco. M/box. B24. $450.00

OKINSHEVICH, Leo. *Latin America in Soviet Writings.* 1966. John Hopkins. 1st ed. 257p. VG/dj. F3. $35.00

OLBY, Robert. *Origins of Mendelism.* 1966. NY. 204p. A13. $25.00

OLCOTT, Frances Jenkins. *Adventures of Haroun er Raschid & Other Tales...* 1923. Holt. 1st ed. ils Willy Pogany. 363p. VG. M20. $75.00

OLCOTT, Julia. *Happy Surprises.* 1929. Whitman. 1st ed. ils Eleanore Mineah Hubbard. VG. M5. $35.00

OLCOTT & PUTNAM. *Field Book of the Skies.* 1936. Putnam. 3rd revised ed/7th imp. 534p. VG/worn. K5. $70.00

OLDENBURG, Claes. *Drawings & Prints.* 1969. Chelsea. 1st ed. intro Gene Baro. 274p. F/dj. F1. $150.00

OLDHAM, John. *Works...* 1692. London. raised bands/no spine label. A15. $150.00

OLDS, Helen D. *Krista & the Frosty Packages.* ca 1952. Messner. inscr. ils Ursula Koering. 60p. VG/G. B10. $12.00

OLDS, Irving S. *Bits & Pieces of American History...* 1951. NY. Olds. 1/500. ils. 463p. beige-gray cloth. F. P4. $350.00

OLGIATO, Francesco. *L'Idealismo di Giorgio Berkeley ed suo Significato Storico.* 1926. Milano. Societa Editrice Vita e Pensiero. 221p. VG. G1. $40.00

OLIPHANT, L. *Narrative of the Earl of Elgin's Mission to China & Japan...* 1960. NY. 1st Am ed. VG. C11. $55.00

OLIPHANT, Laurence. *Haifa; or, Life in Modern Palestine.* 1887. Edinburgh. 8vo. 369p. new quarter morocco/marbled brd. O2. $125.00

OLIVER, Anthony. *Elberg Collection.* 1985. Doubleday. 1st Am ed. F/F. S6. $25.00

OLIVER, Chad. *Mists of Dawn.* 1979. Gregg. VG/G. P3. $15.00

OLIVER, Chad. *Shores of Another Sea.* 1984. Crown. 1st ed. F/F. P3. $13.00

OLIVER, Edmund H. *Tracts for Difficult Times.* 1933. Round Table. 212p. VG/worn. B29. $3.50

OLIVER, Elizabeth Murphy. *Black Mother Goose Book.* 1969. MD Pub Co. 1st ltd ed. ils Aaron Sopher. 48p. NF. D6. $45.00

OLIVER, Ian. *Growing South African Succulents.* 1993. Claremont, Cape. ils. 54p. sc. M. B26. $8.95

OLIVER, Jerome. *Khan, Phantom Emperor.* 1934. Reklar. 1st ed. VG. M2. $30.00

OLIVER, Maria Rosa. *Geografia Argentina.* ca 1939. Edit Sudamericana. unp. VG. B10. $25.00

OLIVER, Paul. *Savannah Syncopators. African Retentions in the Blues.* 1970. Studio Vista. 1st ed. F/NF. B2. $25.00

OLIVER, Paul. *Story of the Blues.* 1969. Chilton. 1st Am ed. F/NF. B2. $85.00

OLIVIER, Charles P. *Meteors.* 1925. Baltimore. Williams Wilkins. 276p. gilt bl cloth. VG. K5. $105.00

OLIVIER, Robert L. *Tidoon: Story of the Cajun Teche.* 1972. Pelican. 83p. VG/VG. B10. $12.00

OLLIVANT, Alfred. *Bob, Son of Battle.* 1898. Doubleday McClure. 1st ed/author's 1st book. 8vo. 356p. NF/dj. H5. $450.00

OLLIVANT, Alfred. *Boxer & Beauty: A Tale of Two Cart-Horses.* 1989. Southampton. Ashford. VG/wrp. O3. $6.00

OLLIVANT, Alfred. *Danny.* 1902. Doubleday Page. 1st ed. 425p. cloth. G. R2. $35.00

OLMSTEAD, Frederick Law. *Journey Through Texas; or, Saddle-Trip on SW Frontier...* 1857. NY. Dix Edwards. 1st ed. pl/map. cloth. VG. H4. $75.00

OLNEY, Ross R. *Americans in Space.* 1973. Nashville. Nelson. revised rpt. 8vo. 188p. VG/dj. K5. $16.00

OLSEN, D.B. *Cat Wears a Noose.* 1944. Doubleday Crime Club. 1st ed. F/clip. M15. $45.00

OLSON, Charles. *Distances.* 1960. Grove. 1st ed. F/wrp. B2. $30.00

OLSON, Charles. *In Cold Hell, in Thicket.* 1953. Dorchester, MA. 1st ed. VG/wht dj/pub band. Q1. $125.00

OLSON, Charles. *Maximus Poems.* 1960. Jargon/Cornith. 1st trade ed. VG/wrp. L3. $75.00

OLSON, Roberta J.M. *Fire & Ice: Hist of Comets in Art.* 1985. Smithsonian. pb. fwd Isaac Asimov. 134p. VG. K5. $14.00

OLSSON, Bengt. *Memphis Blues.* 1970. London. Studio Vista. 1st ed. F/wrp. B2. $25.00

OLSZOWY, Damon R. *Horticulture for the Disabled & Disadvantaged.* 1978. Springfield, IL. 228p. F/dj. B26. $27.50

OMAN, Lela Kiana. *Ghost of the Kingikty & Other Eskimo Legends.* ca 1967. Ken Wray's Prt Shop. 2nd prt. inscr. 45p. VG. B10. $20.00

OMWAKE, John. *Conestoga Six-Horse Bell Teams of Eastern PA 1750-1850.* 1930. Cincinnati. sm 4to. sgn pres. VG. O3. $235.00

ONDAATJE, Michael. *Collected Works of Billy the Kid.* 1974. NY. 1st Am ed/author's 3rd book. sgn. ES. F/NF clip. A11. $65.00

ONDAATJE, Michael. *English Patient.* 1992. Knopf. UP. w/promo mateial. F/prt beige wrp. B3. $125.00

ONDAATJE, Michael. *In the Skin of the Lion.* 1987. Knopf. UP. NF/prt beige wrp. B3. $60.00

ONDAATJE, Michael. *In the Skin of the Lion.* 1987. NY. 1st Am ed. sgn. F/F. C2. $50.00

ONDAATJE, Michael. *Running in the Family.* 1982. NY. correct 1st ed. sgn. F/F. A11. $55.00

ONG, Walter J. *Fighting for Life: Contest, Sexuality & Consciousness.* 1981. Cornell. 231p. bl cloth. VG/dj. G1. $22.50

OPIE, John Newton. *Rebel Cavalryman With Lee, Stuart & Jackson.* 1899. Chicago. WB Conkey. 1st ed. 336p. cloth. VG+. M8. $450.00

OPIE & OPIE. *Nursery Companion.* 1980. Oxford. 1st ed. 128p. F/F. S11. $30.00

OPPENHEIM, E. Philips. *Great Prince Shan.* 1922. Little Brn. 1st ed. VG. M2. $20.00

OPPENHEIM, E. Phillips. *Battle of Basinghall Street.* 1935. McClelland Stewart. 1st Canadian ed. VG/chip. P3. $30.00

OPPENHEIM, E. Phillips. *Dumb Gods Speak.* 1937. McClelland Stewart. 1st Canadian ed. VG/chip. P3. $30.00

OPPENHEIM, E. Phillips. *Floating Peril.* 1936. Little Brn. 3rd ed. VG. P3. $13.00

OPPENHEIM, E. Phillips. *Man Who Changed His Plea.* 1942. Little Brn. 1st ed. VG. P3. $20.00

OPPENHEIM, E. Phillips. *Pulpit in the Grill Room.* 1939. Little Brn. 1st ed. VG. P3. $20.00

OPPENHEIM, E. Phillips. *Shy Plutocrat.* 1941. Little Brn. 1st ed. F/NF. F4. $42.00

OPPENHEIM, E. Phillips. *Zeppelin's Passenger.* 1918. Little Brn. 1st ed. G+. P3. $10.00

OPPENHEIMER, Joel. *Poems 1962-1968.* 1969. Indianapolis. VG/VG. A17. $9.50

OPPENHEIMER, Joel. *Wrong Season.* 1973. Bobbs Merrill. 1st ed. sgn. NF/NF. L3. $75.00

OPPENHEIMER, M. *Urban Guerrilla.* 1969. Chicago. 188p. NF/dj. D3. $12.50

OPTIC, Oliver. *Charades & Pantomines.* ca 1850. np. 150p. VG. E5. $20.00

OPTIC, Oliver. *Haste & Waste.* 1866. np. 1st ed. poor. B34. $10.00

ORCUTT, William Dana. *Princess Kalisto & Other Tales of the Fairies.* 1911 (1902). Harper. 1st ed thus. ils Herriette Amsden. VG. D6. $75.00

ORCZY, Baroness. *By the Gods Beloved.* 1910. Greening. G+. P3. $45.00

ORCZY, Baroness. *Petticoat Government.* 1911. Hutchinson. VG. P3. $20.00

ORCZY, Baroness. *Skin O' My Tooth.* 1928. Doubleday Crime Club. 1st Am ed. F/VG. M15. $65.00

ORDWAY, Donald. *Sicily, Island of Fire.* 1930. National Travel Club. 27 pl. 269p. VG. W1. $15.00

ORFIELD, Lester B. *Criminal Procedure From Arrest to Appeal.* 1947. London/NY. royal 8vo. 614p. buckram. NF/dj. D3. $45.00

ORGILL, Douglas. *Lawrence.* 1973. Ballantine. 1st prt. 158p. VG. M7. $45.00

ORGILL, Douglas. *Man in the Dark.* 1980. Ian Henry. VG/dj. P3. $20.00

ORIOL, Laurence. *Short Circuit.* 1967. MacDonald. 1st ed. VG/dj. P3. $15.00

ORKIN, Ruth. *World Through My Window.* 1978. Harper Row. 1st ed. sgn. F/F. S9. $95.00

ORLANDINI, P. *Le Medecin Nomade. Traduction de Juliette Bertrand.* 1948. Paris. 348p. G7. $25.00

ORLANDO, Jordan. *Object Lesson.* 1993. Simon Schuster. 1st ed/author's 1st book. rem mk. F/F. A14. $25.00

ORLANS, Harold. *Lawrence of Arabia, Strange Man of Letters.* July 1993. Dickinson U. 1st ed. 336p. gilt blk cloth. w/inscr bookplate. M. M7. $47.50

ORMEROD, Roger. *Dead Ringer.* 1985. London. Constable. 1st ed. NF/dj. S6. $20.00

ORMOND, Alexander Thomas. *Foundations of Knowledge.* 1900. London. Macmillan. 1st Eng ed. xl. 528p. pebbled russet cloth. VG. G1. $36.50

ORMOND, Brande. *American Primitives in Needlepoint.* 1977. np. cloth. VG. G2. $12.95

ORMOND, Clyde. *Bear!* 1961. Stackpole. 291p. VG/dj. M20. $18.00

ORMOND, Clyde. *Complete Book of Outdoor Lore.* 1966. Harper. 4th prt. ils E Barth. VG. B34. $15.00

ORMSBY, Clifford A. *Staffordshire Terrier.* 1956. NY. Owen. 1st ed. sgn. 48p. cloth. F/VG+. R2. $200.00

ORMSBY, Waterman L. *Butterfield Overland Mail.* 1962. San Marino. Huntington Lib. later prt. VG/VG. O3. $58.00

ORNITZ, Samuel. *Yankee Passional.* 1927. Boni. 1st ed. F/NF. B2. $45.00

ORNSTEIN, Martha. *Role of the Scientific Societies in 17th Century.* 1913. NY. pres. 322p. new cloth. G7. $85.00

ORNSTEIN, Robert. *Physchology of Consciousness.* 1974. Viking. 247p. VG/VG. B33. $20.00

ORR, A. *World in Amber.* 1985. Bluejay. 1st ed. VG/dj. P3. $20.00

ORR, Douglas. *Health Insurance With Medical Care, the British Experience.* 1938. NY. 1st ed. 271p. A13. $40.00

ORR, James L. *Smithville Days.* 1922. Smithville, OH. 1st ed. ils. 128p. VG. B18. $35.00

ORTEGA Y GASSET, Jose. *Hist As System of Other Essays Toward Philosophy of Hist.* 1961. Norton. later prt. 269p. blk cloth. VG/dj. G1. $25.00

ORTEGA Y GASSET, Jose. *On Love: Aspects of a Single Theme.* 1958. Greenwhich Eds. 2nd prt. 204p. VG/VG. B33. $24.00

ORTLOFF, Henry Stuart. *Garden Bluebook of Annuals & Biennia.* 1931. Nelson Doubleday. VG. P3. $8.00

ORWELL, George. *Animal Farm.* 1945. London. Secker Warburg. 1st ed. VG/dj. Q1. $750.00

ORWELL, George. *Animal Farm.* 1946. NY. Harcourt Brace. 1st Am ed/1st issue. blk cloth. NF/dj. Q1. $150.00

ORWELL, George. *Homage to Catalonia.* 1952. Harcourt Brace. 1st Am ed. 232p. gr stp yel cloth. NF/dj. H5. $150.00

ORWELL, George. *Nineteen Eighty-Four.* 1949. London. Secker Warburg. 1st ed. 8vo. 312p. red stp gr cloth. VG/dj. H5. $850.00

OSBORN, Marjorie Noble. *Jolly Times Cook Book.* 1935 (1934). Rand McNally. ils Clarnece Biers. VG. M5. $32.00

OSBORNE, Arthur. *Future Is Now: Significance of Precognition.* 1961. New Hyde Park. 1st ed. 254p. VG/VG. B33. $30.00

OSBORNE, Charles. *Life & Crimes of Agatha Christie.* 1982. Collins. 1st ed. F/F. P3. $25.00

OSBORNE, Margaret. *Popular Collie.* 1957. London. Popular Dogs. 1st ed. 239p. cloth. F/VG. r2. $25.00

OSBORNE, Newell Yost. *Select School: Hist of Mt Union College...* 1967. Mt Union College. 1st ed. ils. 645p. VG/dj. B18. $17.50

OSBORNE, Reuben. *Freud & Marx: Dialectical Study.* 1937. London. Gollancz. 285p. blk cloth. G. G1. $30.00

OSBOURNE, Katharine D. *Robert Louis Stevenson in California.* 1911. Chicago. McClurg. 1st ed. 113p. F. P4. $60.00

OSBUN, Albert G. *To California & the South Seas.* 1966. San Marino. Huntington Lib. 1st ed. 233p. VG/soiled. P4. $47.50

OSGOOD, Frances S. *Poetry of Flowers & Flowers of Poetry...* 1841. NY. Riker. 1st ed. 8vo. 276p. pict brd/rebacked. F. B24. $450.00

OSLER, William. *Aequanimitas & Other Addresses.* 1905. Phil. 1st ed/2nd prt. 389p. A13. $150.00

OSLER, William. *Aequanimitas & Other Addresses.* 1932. Phil. 3rd ed. 453p. A13. $35.00

OSLER, William. *Growth of Truth As Ils Discovery of Circulation of Blood.* 1906. London. 1st ed. 44p. brd. A13. $250.00

OSLER, William. *Lectures on Diagnosis of Abdominal Tumors.* 1900. London. 1st ed. VG. A9. $100.00

OSLER, William. *Men & Books. Collected & Rpt From Canadian Medical Assn...* 1959. Pasadena. 1st ed. 1/200. intro/sgn Earl F Nation. 67p. A13. $150.00

OSLER, William. *Old Humanities & New Science.* 1919. London. Murray. 32p. VG/wrp. B14. $100.00

OSLER, William. *Principles & Practice of Medicine. 5th Edition.* 1905. Appleton. 1182p. orig brd/rebacked. G7. $75.00

OSLER, William. *Principles & Practice of Medicine...* 1892. NY. Appleton. 1st ed/2nd issue. rebound. G7. $495.00

OSMAN, Ahmed. *Stranger in Valley of the Kings.* 1988. Harper Row. 1st Am ed. 171p. VG/dj. W1. $20.00

OSMOND, Humphrey. *Understanding Understanding.* 1974. Harper. 223p. cloth. VG/dj. G1. $22.50

OSOFSKY, Gilbert. *Puttin' on Ole Massa.* 1969. Harper Row. 1st ed. 409p. F/F. H1. $18.00

OSSENDOWSKI, Ferdinand. *Oasis & Simoon.* 1927. Dutton. 1st Am ed. 306p. VG. W1. $10.00

OSTENSO, Martha. *Wild Geese.* nd. Grosset Dunlap. ils. 356p. F/VG. H1. $10.00

OSTER, Jerry. *Club Dead.* 1988. Harper Row. 1st ed. F/F. P3. $16.00

OSTER, Jerry. *Rancho Maria.* 1986. Harper Row. 1st ed. F/F. P3. $15.00

OSTER, Jerry. *Sweet Justice.* 1985. NY. Harper. 1st ed. F/F. S6. $25.00

OSTOVAR, Pat. *Great Danes in Canada.* 1982. Denlingers. 1st ed. folio. ils. 96p. VG/wrp. R2. $12.00

OSTRANDER, Fannie E. *Baby Goose, His Adventures.* 1900. Chicago. Laird Lee. obl 4to. ils. glossy brd. worn. F1. $125.00

OSTRANDER, Shelia. *Psychic Discoveries Behind the Iron.* nd. Laffont. VG. P3. $15.00

OSTROGORSKY, George. *Hist of the Byzantine State.* 1957. New Brunswick, NJ. Rutgers. 40 pl/map ep. VG. W1. $14.00

OTIS, James. *Tim & Tip; or, Adventures of a Boy & Dog.* 1883. Harper. 1st ed. 16mo. 179p. NF. D6. $65.00

OTIS, James. *Toby Tyler; or, Ten Weeks With the Circus.* 1923. Harper. VG/dj. P3. $15.00

OTIS, Philo Adam. *First Presbyterian Church: Hist of Oldest Organization...* 1900. Chicago. 1st ed. pres. 179p. cloth. NF. M8. $45.00

OTTAVIANI, Alaphridus. *Institutiones Iuris Publici Ecclesiastici.* 1958. Romae. Polyglottis Vaticanis. 2 vol. wrp. H10. $25.00

OTTLEY, Roi. *New World A-Coming: Inside Black America.* 1943. Boston. 364p. VG. A17. $9.50

OTTLEY & WEATHERBY. *Negro in NY: Informal Social Hist.* 1967. NY/Dobbs Ferry. NYPL & Oceana. 1st ed. F/NF. B2. $50.00

OTTO, Whitney. *How To Make an American Quilt.* 1991. NY. Villard/Random. 1st ed/author's 1st book. NF/NF. A14. $45.00

OTTUM, Bob. *See the Kid Run.* 1978. Simon Schuster. 1st ed. F/F. P3. $15.00

OUIMET, Francis. *Game of Golf: A Book of Reminiscence.* 1963. Boston. private prt. inscr. gr cloth. F/F. B14. $150.00

OURSLER, Fulton. *String of Blue Beads.* 1956. Doubleday. 1st ed. 32p. VG/G+. A3. $15.00

OURSLER, Will. *Narcotics: America's Peril.* 1952. Doubleday. 1st ed. VG. P3. $25.00

OURSLER, Will. *Trial of Vincent Doon.* 1941. Simon Schuster. 1st ed. F/F. M15. $45.00

OURSLER & SMITH. *Marijuana: The Facts. The Truth.* 1968. NY. Ericksson. F/NF. B2. $35.00

OUSBY, Ian. *Bloodhounds of Heaven/Detective in English Fiction...* 1976. Harvard. 1st ed. F/VG. F4. $20.00

OUTHWAITE & RENTOUL. *Little Green Road to Fairyland.* nd (1922). Dutton. 4to. 102p. gr cloth. G+. D6. $150.00

OUTLAND, Charles. *Stagecoaching on El Camino Real...* 1973. Glendale. Arthur Clarke. 1st ed. xl. VG/VG. scarce. O3. $45.00

OVENDEN, Charles T. *Marvels in the World of Light.* 1904. London. 1st ed. ils. teg. gray cloth. K5. $40.00

OVERMAN, Frederick. *Mechanics for the Millwright, Machinist, Engineer...* 1851. Lippincott. 1st ed. ils. 420p. VG. M10. $16.50

OVERTON, Grant. *American Nights Entertainment.* 1923. Appleton Doran. 1st ed. VG. P3. $35.00

OVERTON, Grant. *Cargoes for Crusoes.* 1924. Appleton. 1st prt. photos. bl cloth. VG. S11. $10.00

OVERTON, Mark. *Jack Winters' Baseball Team.* 1919. Donohue. probable later prt. G+/G. P8. $40.00

OVINGTON, Roy. *Tactics on Trout.* 1969. Knopf. 1st ed. F. B34. $30.00

OWEN, David Dale. *Report of Geological Survey of WI, IA & MN...* 1852. Lippincott Grambo. lg 4to. ils/maps/plans. 638p. gilt burgundy cloth. VG. K1. $300.00

OWEN, Dean; see McGaughy, Dudley.

OWEN, John. *Enquiry Into Orig, Nature, Instit, Power, Order...Churches.* 1681. London. Ponder Lee. 4to. 365p. old calf. H10. $125.00

OWEN, Meredith; see Lytton, Robert Lord.

OWEN, Robert L. *Russian Imperial Conspiracy 1892-1914.* 1927. NY. Boni. 1st ed. 212p. w/sgn card & letter. VG. A17. $15.00

OWENS, Mary Beth. *Caribou Alphabet.* 1988. Dog Ear. 1st ed. ils. F/F. P2. $20.00

OWENS, William A. *TX Folk Songs.* 1950. TX Folklore Soc. 1st ed. F/dj. A18. $75.00

OXENHORN, Harvey. *Tuning the Rig: Journey to the Arctic.* 1990. NY. Harper. 281p. M/wrp. A17. $10.00

OZICK, Cynthia. *Trust.* 1955. NAL. 1st ed/author's 1st book. VG/G. L3. $125.00

PAALEN, Wolfgang. *Form & Sense.* 1945. NY. Wittenborn. ARC/1st ed. 64p. F/prt wrp. F1. $35.00

PABOR, William E. *Colorado As an Agricultural State: Its Farms, Fields...* 1883. Orange Judd. 213p. cloth. M. A10. $100.00

PACE, Mildred Mastin. *Early American: Story of Paul Revere.* 1940. Scribner. 1st ed. 140p. VG. B10. $12.00

PACK, Arthur Newton. *We Called It Ghost Ranch.* 1965. Ghost Ranch. 1st ed. 148p. F/NF. B19. $25.00

PACKARD, Francis. *Guy Patin & the Medical Profession in Paris in XVIIth C.* 1925. NY. 1st ed. sgn. 334p. xl. A13. $30.00

PACKARD, Frank L. *Pawned.* 1921. Copp Clarke. 1st Canadian ed. VG. P3. $20.00

PACKARD, Frank L. *Tiger Claws.* 1928. Copp Clarke. 1st ed. VG. P3. $25.00

PACKARD, S.S. *Packard's New Manual of Book-Keeping & Correspondence.* 1887. NY. 158p. gilt gr cloth. VG. B14. $35.00

PACKE, Michael St. John. *Life of John Stuart Mill.* 1954. Macmillan. 567p. russet cloth. VG/worn. G1. $40.00

PACKER, Eleanor. *Charlie McCarthy...So Help Me Mr Bergen.* 1938. Grosset Dunlap. 1st ed. ils Henry Valley. F/NF. B4. $150.00

PACKER, Eleanor. *Story of Our Gang, Romping Through Hal Roach Comedies.* 1929. Whitman. 8vo. VG. B17. $25.00

PADDLEFORD, Clementine. *How America Eats.* 1960. Scribner 1st ed. sgn. VG/dj. M20. $15.00

PADEN, Irene D. *Prairie Schooner Detours.* 1949. Macmillan. 1st ed. F/VG. A18. $30.00

PADGETT, Lewis. *Mutant.* 1953. Gnome. 1st ed. VG/VG. P3. $100.00

PADGETT, Lewis. *Robots Have No Tails.* 1952. Gnome. 1st ed. NF/dj. P3. $150.00

PADILLA, Victoria. *Bromeliads in Color & Their Culture.* 1966. Los Angeles. photos/drawings. VG/worn. B26. $49.00

PADILLA, Victoria. *Bromeliads. A Descriptive Listing...* 1977 (1973). NY. photos. 134p. F/dj. B26. $25.00

PADOVER, Saul. *Letters of Karl Marx.* 1979. Englewood Cliffs. 1st ed. 576p. F/F. A17. $17.50

PAETOW, Louis John. *Guide to Study of Medieval Hist.* 1931. Crofts. 8vo. cloth. xl. VG. W1. $14.00

PAGE, Elizabeth. *Wild Horses & Gold.* 1932. Farrar Rinehart. 1st ed. VG. O3. $30.00

PAGE, Emma. *Cold Light of Day.* 1984. Walker. 1st ed. VG/dj. P3. $18.00

PAGE, Francis. *Confucious Comes to Broadway.* 1940. Wisdom House. 1st ed. F/dj. M2. $35.00

PAGE, Gerald W. *Nameless Places.* 1975. Arkham. 1st ed. F/F. P3. $15.00

PAGE, J.M. *Old Buckingham by the Sea.* 1936. Phil. 1st ed. VG/G. B5. $45.00

PAGE, Jake. *Stolen Gods.* 1993. Ballantine. 1st ed/author's 1st novel. F. B3. $40.00

PAGE, Jesse. *John Bright, the Man of the People.* nd. Fleming Revell. 12mo. 160p. VG. V3. $14.00

PAGE, Thomas Nelson. *Two Little Confederates.* 1953. Scribner. ils JW Thomason Jr. 189p. VG. B10. $15.00

PAGE, Thomas Nelson. *Two Prisoners.* 1903. Russell. ils Virginia Keep. 82p. VG. B10. $25.00

PAGE, Victor W. *Modern Aircraft: Basic Principles, Operation, Application...* 1929. NY. ils/charts/diagrams. 859p. G. B18. $95.00

PAGE & PAGE. *Beyond the Milky Way.* 1969. NY. Macmillan. 8vo. 336p. VG/chip. K5. $20.00

PAGET, Stephen. *Pasteur & After Pasteur.* 1914. London. 1st ed. 152p. A13. $40.00

PAGET-FREDERICKS, J. *Miss Pert's Christmas Tree.* 1929. Macmillan. 1st ed. 24p. VG/VG. A3. $50.00

PAIGE, Richard; see Koontz, Dean R.

PAIN, Barry. *Stories & Interlude.* 1892. Harper. VG-. P3. $100.00

PAINE, Albert Bigelow. *Hollow Tree & Deep Woods Book.* ca 1938. Harper. ils JM Conde. 271p. VG/G. B10. $25.00

PAINE, Albert Bigelow. *Hollow Tree.* 1901 (1899). NY. Russell. 2nd prt. 8vo. VG+. D6. $40.00

PAINE, Albert Bigelow. *How Mr Rabbit Lost His Tail.* 1910. Harper. ils JM Conde. cloth/paper label. VG. M5. $18.00

PAINE, Albert Bigelow. *Lure of the Mediterranean.* 1921. Harper. 8vo. 394p. VG. W1. $18.00

PAINE, Albert Bigelow. *Tent Dwellers.* 1908. Outing Pub. 1st ed. VG. B34. $30.00

PAINE, Albert Bigelow. *Tent Dwellers.* 1921. Harper. 279p. gr cloth. VG/worn. M20. $30.00

PAINE, Albert Bigelow. *Thomas Nast.* 1974. index. 483p. dj. O8. $14.50

PAINE, Albert Bigelow. *Thomas Nast: His Period & His Pictures.* 1904. NY. ils. VG. M17. $75.00

PAINE, Martyn. *Discourse on Soul & Instinct...* 1849 (1848). NY. Fletcher. 2nd enlarged ed. 230p. emb Victorian cloth. G1. $85.00

PAINE, Ralph D. *Ships & Sailor of Old Salem.* 1923-1927. Boston. Lauriat. ils. 471p. teg. T7. $50.00

PAINE, Thomas. *Rights of Man.* 1961. NY. ils Lynd Ward. lg 4to. slipcase. VG. A17. $15.00

PAIR, Claude H. *Irrigation.* 1986 (1983). Arlington, VA. 5th ed/2nd prt. ils. 686p. F. B26. $24.00

PAKENHAM, Valerie. *Out in the Noonday Sun: Edwardians in the Tropics.* 1985. NY. Random. 2nd ed. ils/photos/map. 255p. M/M. P4. $25.00

PAL, Mrinal Kanti. *Catalogue of Folk Art in Asutosh Mus. Part I.* 1962. Calcutta. Asutoch Mus. 8vo. 41p. bl stp red cloth. VG. F1. $30.00

PALERM, Angel. *Obras Hidraulicas Prehispanicas en el Sistema Lacustre...* 1973. Mexico. INAH. 1st ed. maps. 246p. wrp. F3. $15.00

PALLOTTINO, Massimo. *Etruscan Painting.* 1952. Skira. 1st ed. 4to. 140p. red stp gr cloth. VG. F1. $30.00

PALMER, Adelaide. *Blacky Daw: Story of a Pet Crow.* ca 1930. Chicago. Beckley Cardy. 128p. VG. B10. $20.00

PALMER, Arnold. *Situation Golf.* 1970. NY. 1st ed. sgn. VG/VG. B5. $60.00

PALMER, Brooks. *Book of American Clocks.* 1974. NY. Macmillan. 1st ed/12th prt. 318p. F/VG. A8. $45.00

PALMER, Drew; see Lucas, Mark.

PALMER, Frank. *Bent Grasses.* 1993. London. Constable. 1st ed. F/F. S6. $25.00

PALMER, Frederick. *So a Leader Came.* 1932. Ray Long/Richard Smith. 1st ed. VG. P3. $40.00

PALMER, Harold. *Philosophy of Psychiatry: Psychiatric Prolegomena.* 1952. NY. 70p. cloth. VG/chip. G1. $22.50

PALMER, Herriott Clare. *First Presbyterian Church of Franklin, IN.* 1946. Franklin. 1st ed. 515p. cloth. NF. M8. $45.00

PALMER, J.A.B. *Georgius de Hungaria & Tractatus de Moribus...* 1951. Manchester. 1st ed. tall 8vo. VG/wrp. W1. $10.00

PALMER, Joel. *Journal of Travels Over the Rocky Mountains.* 1983. Ye Galleon. 1st ed thus. ils. M/sans. A18. $20.00

PALMER, Ralph F. *Doctor on Horseback.* 1975. private prt. 1st ed. ils. 168p. F/F. B19. $25.00

PALMER, Robert C. *Eng Law in Age of Blk Death, 1348-1381...* 1993. Chapel Hill. M11. $45.00

PALMER, William. *Patriarch & the Tsar.* 1871-1873. London. Trubner. 3 vol. lib buckram. H10. $125.00

PALTSITS, Victor Hugo. *Exhibition of Bibles of Ancient & Modern Times.* 1923. NY Pub Lib. 1st ed thus. 18p. VG/prt wrp. M8. $45.00

PANAGOS & VOUZAS. *Mythology & Hist of Delphi.* 1965. Athens. sm 8vo. ils. VG/wrp. W1. $8.00

PANASSIE, Hugues. *Hot Jazz.* 1934. NY. Witmark. 1st ed. NF/NF. scarce. B2. $250.00

PANASSIE, Hugues. *Real Jazz.* 1942. Smith Durrell. 1st Am ed. VG. B2. $25.00

PANATI, Charles. *Links.* 1978. Houghton Mifflin. 1st ed. VG/G. P3. $10.00

PANGBORN, Edgar. *Davy.* 1964. St Martin. 1st ed. VG/VG. P3. $60.00

PANGBORN, Edgar. *Trial of Callista Blake.* 1961. St Martin. 1st ed. VG/G+. P3. $40.00

PANIZZI, Anthony. *Stories From Italian Writers With Literal Interlinear Trans.* 1832. Phil. Carey Lea. 1st Am ed. 12mo. contemporary calf. M1. $175.00

PANSHIN, Alexei. *Farewell to Yesterday's Tomorrow.* 1975. Berkley Putnam. 1st ed. VG/VG. P3. $18.00

PANSHIN, Alexei. *Transmutations.* 1982. Elephant Books. 1st ed. sgn. 1/150. F/dj. M2. $30.00

PANSHIN, Alexei. *World Beyond the Hill.* 1989. Jeremy Tarcher. F/F. P3. $60.00

PANSY; see Alden, Isabella M.

PANTIN, C.F.A. *Relations Between the Sciences.* 1959. Cambridge. 205p. NF/chip. G1. $24.00

PAPADAKI, Stamo. *Le Corbusier, Architect, Painter, Writer.* 1948. Macmillan. sm 4to. ils. 152p. red stp tan cloth. VG/dj. F1. $75.00

PAPAGIANNIS, Michael D. *Eighth Texas Symposium of Relativistic Astrophysics.* 1977. NY Academy Sciences. 8vo. pb. 689p. K5. $20.00

PAPAZOGLOU, Orania. *Sanctity.* 1986. Crown. 1st ed. VG/VG. P3. $17.00

PAPER, Herbert H. *Judeo-Persian Deverbativesin...* 1967. The Hague. Mouton. 8vo. VG/stiff wrp. W1. $8.00

PARACHEK, Ralph E. *Desert Architecture.* 1967. Parr of AZ. 1st ed. 93p. F/sans. B19. $35.00

PARADIS, Adrian A. *Gold: King of Metals.* ca 1970. Hawthorn. 1st ed. 80p. VG/VG. B10. $12.00

PARADISE, Scott H. *Hist of Printing in Andover, MA 1798-1931.* 1931. Andover. 8vo. leather. VG. B14. $60.00

PARANJPE, A.C. *Theoretical Psychology, the Metting of East & West.* 1984. Plenum. 344p. F/dj. K4. $25.00

PARDIES, Ignace Gaston. *Dell'Anima Delle Bestie, e sue Funzioni.* 1694. Venezia. Andrea Poletti. sm 8vo. 187p. contemporary vellum. G1. $185.00

PARE, Madeline Ferrin. *AZ Pageant: Short Hist of the 48th State.* 1970. AZ Hist Found. ils/index. 336p. F/sans. B19. $15.00

PARES, B. *Krylov's Fables.* 1926. London. 1st ed. VG. C11. $40.00

PARET, J. Parmly. *Methods & Players of Modern Lawn Tennis.* 1915. NY. Am Lawn Tennis. 1st ed. lg 8vo. ils. 296p. red cloth. K1. $75.00

PARETO, Vilfredo. *Mind & Society.* 1935. Harcourt Brace. 4 vol. 1st Eng-language ed. blk cloth. VG/worn. G1. $150.00

PARETSKY, Sara. *Bitter Medicine.* 1987. London. Gollancz. ARC/1st Eng ed. sgn. RS. F/F. S6. $50.00

PARETSKY, Sara. *Bitter Medicine.* 1987. Morrow. 1st ed. sgn. F/F. M15. $100.00

PARETSKY, Sara. *Blood Shot.* 1988. Delacorte. 1st Am ed. F/F. M15. $35.00

PARETSKY, Sara. *Deadlock.* 1984. Dial. 1st ed. NF/NF. P3. $250.00

PARETSKY, Sara. *Deadlock.* 1984. Dial. 1st ed. rem mk. F/NF. B2. $150.00

PARETSKY, Sara. *Guardian Angel.* 1992. Delacorte. 1st ed. F/F. F4. $22.00

PARETSKY, Sara. *Killing Orders.* 1985. Morrow. 1st ed. F/F. B2. $100.00

PARETSKY, Sara. *Killing Orders.* 1985. Morrow. 1st ed. VG/VG. P3. $75.00

PARGETER, Edith Mary. *Confession of Brother Haluin.* 1988. London. Headline. 1st ed. sgn. NF/NF. O4. $65.00

PARGETER, Edith Mary. *Confession of Brother Haluin.* 1989. NY. Mysterious. 1st Am ed. F/F. S6. $30.00

PARGETER, Edith Mary. *Devil's Novice.* 1984. Detective BC. VG. P3. $8.00

PARGETER, Edith Mary. *Excellent Mystery.* 1985. Morrow. 1st Am ed. NF/NF. O4. $40.00

PARGETER, Edith Mary. *Hermit of Eyton Forest.* 1988. Mysterious. 1st Am ed. sgn. F/F. O4. $40.00

PARGETER, Edith Mary. *Holy Thief.* 1993. Mysterious. 1st Am ed. inscr. F/F. T2. $18.00

PARGETER, Edith Mary. *Nice Derangement of Epitaphs.* 1965. London. Collins. 1st ed. sgn. VG/VG. O4. $250.00

PARGETER, Edith Mary. *One Corpse Too Many.* 1980. Morrow. 1st Am ed. rem mk. F/NF. M15. $50.00

PARGETER, Edith Mary. *Potter's Field.* 1990. Mysterious. 1st Am ed. sgn. F/F. O4. $30.00

PARGETER, Edith Mary. *Rare Benedictine.* 1988. Mysterious. 1st Am ed. sgn. F/F. O4. $30.00

PARGETER, Edith Mary. *Raven in the Forgate.* 1986. NY. Morrow. 1st Am ed. F/F. S6. $30.00

PARGETER, Edith Mary. *Sanctuary Sparrow.* 1983. NY. Morrow. 1st Am ed. F/F. S6. $65.00

PARGETER, Edith Mary. *St Peter's Fair.* 1981. Morrow. 1st Am ed. F/F. M15. $50.00

PARGETER, Edith Mary. *Virgin in the Ice.* 1983. Morrow. 1st ed. F/F. M15. $35.00

PARISH, James Robert. *Hollywood Character Actors.* 1978. Arlington House. 1st ed. VG/VG. P3. $35.00

PARK, Bertram. *World of Roses.* 1962. NY. photos. VG/dj. B26. $22.50

PARK, Jordon; see Kornbluth, C.M.

PARK, Paul. *Coelestis.* 1993. Harper Collins. 1st ed. F/F. P3. $30.00

PARK, Roswell. *Epitome of Hist of Medicine. 2nd Edition.* 1899. Phil. 370p. G7. $35.00

PARK, Roswell. *Selected Papers, Surgical & Scientific.* 1914. Buffalo. 1st ed. 383p. A13. $150.00

PARK, Ruth. *Witch's Thorn.* 1952. Houghton Mifflin. 1st ed. VG/VG. P3. $35.00

PARKER, Arthur C. *Skunny Wundy & Other Indian Tales.* 1930. Doubleday Doran. ils Will Crawford. 262p. VG. B10. $25.00

PARKER, Charles H. *Civil Practice Act of the State of CA...* 1863. San Francisco. contemporary sheep. M11. $250.00

PARKER, Dorothy. *Not So Deep a Well: Collected Poems.* 1936. Viking. 1st ed. sgn. 1/485. VG/case. E3. $150.00

PARKER, Franklin. *Travels in Central Am 1821-1840.* 1970. Gainesville, FL. 1st ed. 340p. VG/dj. F3. $35.00

PARKER, George S. *Mysterious Yangtze: A Travelog.* 1937. private prt. sgn. 19 photos. 94p. VG. B33. $22.00

PARKER, George. *Elementary Nervous System.* 1919. Phil. ils. 229p. G7. $65.00

PARKER, George. *Smell, Taste & Allied Senses in the Vertebrates.* 1922. Phil. 192p. cloth. G. G7. $30.00

PARKER, Gilbert. *Donovan Pasha.* 1902. Appleton. 1st ed. 392p. F. H1. $15.00

PARKER, John Henry. *Glossary of Terms Used in Grecian, Roman, Italian...* 1850. Oxford. Parker. 3 vol. 5th ed. 8vo. full leather. VG. F1. $325.00

PARKER, John Lloyd. *Unmasking Wall Street.* 1933 (1932). Boston. 2nd ed. 233p. F/G. H1. $15.00

PARKER, John P. *Sails of the Maritimes: Story of...Schooners...* 1961-1969. London. Hazell Watson Vinney. ils/fld maps. 226p. dj. T7. $50.00

PARKER, M. *Arcana of Arts & Sciences...* 1824. WA, PA. Grayson. 1st ed. 348p. full leather. G. B18. $250.00

PARKER, R. *Yankee Saint.* 1935. NY. 1st ed. VG/VG. B5. $30.00

PARKER, Robert B. *Catskill Eagle.* 1985. Delacorte. 1st ed. sgn. F/F. F4. $25.00

PARKER, Robert B. *Catskill Eagle.* 1985. Delacorte. 1st ed. VG/VG. P3. $18.00

PARKER, Robert B. *Ceremony.* 1982. Delacorte/Lawrence. 1st ed. sgn. F/F. M15/T2. $45.00

PARKER, Robert B. *Ceremony.* 1982. London. Piatkus. 1st Eng ed. sgn. F/F. O4. $30.00

PARKER, Robert B. *Crimson Joy.* 1988. Delacorte. 1st ed. sgn. F/F. T2. $20.00

PARKER, Robert B. *Early Autumn.* 1981. Delacorte. 1st ed. NF/dj. P3. $45.00

PARKER, Robert B. *Early Autumn.* 1981. NY. Delacorte. 1st ed. inscr/sgn. F/F. S6. $55.00

PARKER, Robert B. *God Save the Child.* 1974. Houghton Mifflin. 1st ed/author's 2nd Spenser novel. VG/VG. P3. $40.00

PARKER, Robert B. *Judas Goat.* 1978. Houghton Mifflin. 1st ed. F/F. B2. $75.00

PARKER, Robert B. *Judas Goat.* 1978. Houghton Mifflin. 1st ed. sgn. F/F. T2. $85.00

PARKER, Robert B. *Judas Goat.* 1982. London. Deutsch. 1st ed. sgn. F/F. T2. $55.00

PARKER, Robert B. *Looking for Rachel Wallace.* 1980. Delacorte/Lawrence. 1st prt. sgn. F/F. T2. $85.00

PARKER, Robert B. *Looking for Rachel Wallace.* 1981 (1980). Delacorte/Lawrence. 3rd ed. NF/NF. P3. $20.00

PARKER, Robert B. *Love & Glory.* 1983. Delacorte/Lawrence. 1st ed. sgn. F/F. T2. $60.00

PARKER, Robert B. *Pale Kings & Princes.* 1987. Delacorte. 1st ed. F/F. P3. $16.00

PARKER, Robert B. *Pale Kings & Princes.* 1987. Delacorte. 1st ed. sgn. F/F. O4. $30.00

PARKER, Robert B. *Paper Doll.* 1993. London. Viking. 1st Eng ed. F/F. S6. $30.00

PARKER, Robert B. *Playmates.* 1989. Putnam. 1st ed. VG/VG. P3. $18.00

PARKER, Robert B. *Savage Place.* 1981. Delacorte. 1st ed. inscr/sgn. F/F. S6. $75.00

PARKER, Robert B. *Savage Place.* 1981. Delacorte/Lawrence. 1st prt. sgn. rem mk. F/F. T2. $40.00

PARKER, Robert B. *Taming a Sea Horse.* 1986. Delacorte. 1st ed. sgn. F/F. P3. $25.00

PARKER, Robert B. *Valediciton.* nd. BC. VG/VG. P3. $8.00

PARKER, Robert B. *Valediction.* 1984. Delacorte. 1st ed. sgn. F/F. O4. $25.00

PARKER, Robert B. *Widening Gyre.* 1983. Delacorte. 1st ed. sgn. F/F. O4. $25.00

PARKER, T. Jefferson. *Little Saigon.* 1988. St Martin. 1st ed. F/F. P3. $19.00

PARKER, Wayne. *Bridewell Site.* ca 1982. Crosbyton. Crosby Co Pioneer Memorial. VG+/cbdg. P4. $25.00

PARKER, William. *Homosexuality Bibliography: Second Supplement 1976-1982.* 1985. Scarecrow. 8vo. 395p. gray cloth. F. P4. $35.00

PARKER & WHEELER. *John Singleton Copley, American Portraits in Oil...* 1938. Boston. Mus Fine Arts. 1st ed. 130 pl. 284p. gilt bl cloth. VG+/G. F1. $150.00

PARKER & WINFIELD. *Winfield: A Player's Life.* 1988. Norton. 1st ed. F/F. P3. $17.00

PARKES, James. *Hist of Palestine...* 1949. Oxford. 1st ed. 8vo. 391p. VG/dj. W1. $25.00

PARKES, Oscar. *British Battleships, 1860-1950.* 1970-1973. London. Seeley Service. new revised ed. photos/450 plans. 701p. dj. T7. $120.00

PARKINSON, C. Northcote. *Devil To Pay.* 1973. Houghton Mifflin. 1st ed/author's 1st novel. F/dj. F4. $30.00

PARKINSON, C. Northcote. *Fireship.* 1975. Houghton Mifflin. 1st ed. F/NF. F4. $20.00

PARKINSON, Thomas. *Casebook on the Beat.* 1961. Crowell. 1st ed. NF/wrp. B2. $30.00

PARKINSON, Virginia. *Pointers for Little Persons Book 2.* 1943. NY. JL Schilling. ils Marjorie Wells. NF/dj. A17. $17.50

PARKMAN, Francis. *Discovery of the Great West.* 1869. Little Brn. 1st ed. gilt gr cloth. F. A18. $150.00

PARKMAN, Francis. *Oregon Trail & the Conspiracy of Pontiac.* 1991. Lib of Am. 1st ed thus. M/dj. A18. $35.00

PARKMAN, Francis. *Oregon Trail.* 1994. NE U. 1st ed thus. 293p. M. A18. $22.50

PARKS, Aileen. *Bedford Forrest: Boy on Horseback.* 1952. Bobbs Merrill. 1st ed. ils Paul Laune. VG/G. O3. $15.00

PARKS, Gordon. *Arias in Silence.* 1994. Bulfinch/Little Brn. 1st ed. sgn. F/NF. S9. $75.00

PARKS, Gordon. *Learning Tree.* 1963. Harper. 1st ed. sgn/dtd 1963. F/NF. F4. $35.00

PARKS, Gordon. *To Smile in Autumn.* 1979. Norton. 1st ed. inscr. F/S. S9. $50.00

PARKS, Joseph Howard. *General Leonidas Polk, CSA: The Fighting Bishop.* 1962. Louisiana State. 1st ed. 408p. cloth. NF/NF. M8. $125.00

PARKS, S. *Chymical Catechism Withe Variety of Amusing Experiment.* 1807. np. 300p. full leather. G. E5. $35.00

PARKS, Tim. *Juggling the Stars: A Novel of Menace.* 1992. Grove. ARC. F/pict wrp. B3. $25.00

PARKS. *CT: A Bibliography of Its Hist.* 1986. np. 4to. 633p. VG. A4. $75.00

PARRISH, Anne. *Floating Island.* 1930. NY. Harper. 1st ed. 265p. fuchsia cloth. NF. D6. $75.00

PARRISH, Frank. *Bird in the Net.* 1988. Harper Row. 1st ed. VG/VG. P3. $16.00

PARRISH, Maxfield. *Arabian Nights. Their Best-Known Tales.* 1930. Scribner. edit KD Wiggin/Nora Smith. 339p. pict blk cloth. VG-. A3. $75.00

PARRISH, Maxfield. *Maxfield Parrish Poster Book.* 1974. NY. Crown. probable 1st ed. NF/VG+. C8. $75.00

PARRISH, Randall. *Beth Novell: Romance of the West.* 1907. McClurg. 1st ed. ftspc NC Wyeth. F. A18. $75.00

PARRISH, Randall. *Bob Hampton of Placer.* 1906. McClurg. 1st ed. ils Arthur I Keller. pict bdg. VG. A18. $25.00

PARRISH, Randall. *When Wilderness Was King: Tale of IL Country.* 1904. McClurg. 1st ed. ils Kinney. VG+. A18. $25.00

PARRISH & PARRISH. *Dream Coach: Fare Forty Winks, Coach Leaves Every Night...* 1924. Macmillan. 1st ed. 8vo. bl cloth. VG. D6. $50.00

PARRY, Edwin Satterthwaite. *Betsy Ross, Quaker Rebel.* 1930. Phil. Winston. 1st ed. 8vo. 252p. VG. V3. $12.00

PARRY, Leonard. *Trail of Dr Smethurst.* 1931. Edinburgh/London. Hodge. 4 pl. 259p. xl. VG. D3. $25.00

PARRY & SHERLOCK. *Short History of the West Indies.* 1956. London. Macmillan. 1st ed. 8vo. 316p. VG/VG. B11. $45.00

PARSONS, C.G. *Inside View of Slavery; or, Tour Among the Planters.* 1855. Boston. 1st ed. intro Harriet B Stowe. 318p. gilt bl cloth. G. H3. $75.00

PARSONS, Edwin C. *I Flew With the Lafayette Escadrille.* 1963. IN. Seale. sepia photos. 335p. F/NF. A17. $22.50

PARSONS, Robert. *Sermon Preached at Funeral of Rt Hon John Earl of Rochester.* 1680. Oxford. Davis Bowman. 1st ed. 48p. H10. $125.00

PARSONS, Thomas W. *Poems.* 1854. Ticknor Fields. 1st ed/3rd issue. 12mo. brn cloth. VG. M1. $200.00

PARSONS, Thomas W. *Seventeen Cantos of the Inferno of Dante Alighieri.* 1865. Boston. Wilson. 1st ed. wide 8vo. 104p. VG. M1. $150.00

PARSONS, Usher. *Directions for Making Anatomical Preparations...* 1831. Phil. Carey Lea. 1st ed. 4 pl. rebound. K1. $150.00

PARTRIDGE, Bellamy. *Country Lawyer.* 1939. Whittlesey House. 12th prt. VG/dj. B34. $25.00

PARTRIDGE, Eric. *Gentle Art of Lexiography As Pursued by the Addict.* 1963. Macmillan. 119p. F. M10. $10.00

PASCAL, Blaise. *Pensees de M Pascal sur Religion Quelques Autres Sujets...* 1683 (1669). Paris. Chez Guillaume Desprez. 356p. contemporary calf. G1. $285.00

PASHLEY, Robert. *Travels in Crete.* 1837. London. 2 vol. 8vo. ils/fld map. half crushed red levant. O2. $750.00

PATCH, Blanche. *Thirty Years With GBS.* Jan 1951. London. Gollancz. 3rd imp. 256p. VG/G. M7. $18.00

PATCHEN, Kenneth. *Before the Brave.* 1936. Random. 1st ed/author's 1st book. NF/NF. B2. $175.00

PATCHEN, Kenneth. *Love Poems of Kenneth Patchen.* 1960. City Lights. 1st ed. VG/wrp. L3. $35.00

PATCHEN, Kenneth. *Red Wine & Yellow Hair.* 1949. New Directions. 1st ed. sgn. F/torn. V1. $65.00

PATCHEN, Kenneth. *Teeth of the Lion.* 1942. New Directions. 1st ed. NF/wrp. L3. $65.00

PATCHEN, Kenneth. *They Keep Riding Down All the Time.* 1946. NY. Padell. 1st ed. 8vo. 32p. VG/wht wrp/pict dj. C6. $35.00

PATCHETT, M.E. *Kidnappers of Space.* 1953. Lutterworth. 1st ed. VG-/dj. P3. $15.00

PATELIDIS, Veronica S. *Arab World. Libraries & Librarianship 1960-1976.* 1979. London. Mansell. 1st ed. 100p. VG/stiff wrp. W1. $12.00

PATENT, Greg. *More Big Sky Cooking.* 1980. Mtn Prt Co. 2nd prt. photos/recipes. VG. B34. $15.00

PATER, Walter. *Studies in Hist of Renaissance.* 1873. London. Macmillan. 12mo. bl-gr cloth. VG. G1. $150.00

PATER, Walter. *Works...* 1900-1901. London. Macmillan. 9 vol. 1/775 sets. 8vo. teg. Riviere bdg. F. F1. $1,500.00

PATERNO, Joe. *Football My Way.* 1971. NY. 1st ed. sgn. VG/VG. B5. $35.00

PATERSON, A.B. (Banjo). *Sign of the Chrysanthemum.* 1973. Crowell. 1st ed. inscr. ils Peter Landa. M/M. C8. $50.00

PATERSON, John. *Praises of Israel. Studies Literary & Religious in Pslams.* 1950. Scribner. 1st ed. 256p. VG. W1. $12.00

PATON, Alan. *Too Late the Phalarope.* 1953. Scribner. 1st ed. 8vo. 276p. yel/bl stp gray-bl cloth. VG/dj. H5. $50.00

PATRIS, Rene. *Guirlande de l'Iran.* 1948. Paris. Flammarion. 1st ed. sm 4to. VG/dj. W1. $15.00

PATTEN, Gilbert. *Frank Merriwell's Father.* 1964. OK U. 1st ed. 324p. VG/VG. M20. $27.00

PATTEN, Gilbert. *Rival Pitchers of Oakdale.* 1911. Hust. 1st ed. pict bdg. G+. P8. $20.00

PATTEN, Lewis B. *Gene Autry & the Ghost Riders.* 1955. Whitman. VG-. P3. $12.00

PATTERSON, Harry; see Patterson, Henry.

PATTERSON, Henry. *Cold Harbor.* 1990. Simon Schuster. 1st ed. F/F. M21. $15.00

PATTERSON, Henry. *Day of Judgment.* 1978. Collins. 1st ed. VG/VG. P3. $20.00

PATTERSON, Henry. *Eye of the Storm.* 1992. Putnam. 1st ed. F/F. P3. $20.00

PATTERSON, Henry. *Luciano's Luck.* 1981. London. Collins. 1st ed. F/F. S6. $40.00

PATTERSON, Henry. *Prayer for the Dying.* 1974. HRW. 1st ed. VG/VG. P3. $22.00

PATTERSON, Henry. *Season in Hell.* 1989. Simon Schuster. 1st ed. NF/NF. M21. $12.00

PATTERSON, Henry. *Solo.* 1980. Collins. 1st ed. VG/VG. P3. $15.00

PATTERSON, Howard. *Captain of the Rajah.* 1890. NY. Union Sq Pub. ils. 155p. T7. $36.00

PATTERSON, J.H. *In the Grip of the Nyika in British East Africa.* 1909. London. ils/map. 389p. VG. F1. $125.00

PATTERSON, James. *Along Came a Spider.* 1993. Little Brn. 4th ed. F/dj. M21. $5.00

PATTERSON, James. *Black Market.* 1986. Simon Schuster. 1st ed. NF/NF. P3. $20.00

PATTERSON, James. *Kiss the Girls.* 1994. Little Brn. ARC. F/wrp. B3. $25.00

PATTERSON, James. *Midnight Club.* 1989. Little Brn. 1st ed. F/F. T2. $15.00

PATTERSON, James. *Virgin.* 1980. McGraw Hill. 1st ed. F/F. T2. $15.00

PATTERSON, R.M. *Dangerous River.* ca 1954. NY. Wm Sloane. 8vo. 314p. half gr cloth/yel paper brd. VG. P4. $30.00

PATTERSON, Richard North. *Outside Man.* 1981. Little Brn. 1st ed/author's 2nd book. F/VG. B3. $50.00

PATTON, Lucia. *Prayers for Little Children.* 1944. Rand McNally Jr Elf Book 277p. 64p. K2. $10.00

PATTOU, Edith. *Hero's Song.* 1991. HBJ. 1st ed. F/F. P3. $17.00

PAUCK & PAUCK. *Paul Tillich: His Life & Thought. Vol 1: Life.* 1976. Harper Row. 1st ed. 340p. F/VG. B33. $20.00

PAUL, Barbara. *But He Was Already Dead When I Got There.* 1986. Scribner. 1st ed. F/F. P3. $14.00

PAUL, Elliot. *Fracas in the Foothills.* 1940. Random. 436p. G/dj. rare. B34. $50.00

PAUL, Elliot. *Ghost Town on the Yellowstone.* 1948. Random. 2nd prt. VG/dj. B34. $25.00

PAUL, Elliot. *Linden on the Saugus Branch.* 1947. Random. 1st prt. 401p. VG. H1. $12.00

PAUL, F.W.; see Fairman, Paul.

PAULL, H.M. *Literary Ethics: Study in Growth of Literacy Conscience.* 1928. London. 1st ed. 358p. VG/dj. D3. $35.00

PAVEY, Gina. *Cacti & Succulents.* 1979. NY. unp. F/dj. B26. $12.50

PAVLOV, Ivan Petrovich. *Die Arbeit der Verdauungsdrusen.* 1898. Wiesbaden. JF Bergmann. 1st trans from Russian. 199p. VG. G7. $2,500.00

PAVLOV, Ivan Petrovich. *Work of the Digestive Glands. 2nd Eng Edition.* 1910. London. 266p. perforated lib stp on title. new cloth. G7. $115.00

PAXTON, June LeMert. *My Life on the Mojave.* 1957. Vantage. 1st ed. inscr. 168p. VG. A8. $40.00

PAYER, Julius. *New Lands Within the Arctic Circle.* 1877. NY. Appleton. 1st Am ed trans from German. 92 woodcuts. cloth. VG. H4. $125.00

PAYNE, Laurence. *Malice in Camera.* 1983. Crime Club. 1st ed. F/F. P3. $15.00

PAYNE, Robert. *Journey to Persia.* 1952. Dutton. 1st ed. 15 pl. 256p. VG/dj. W1. $20.00

PAYNE, Robert. *Lawrence of Arabia.* Jan 1962. Pyramid. 1st prt. 190p. NF. M7. $40.00

PAYNE, Robert. *Three Worlds of Albert Schweitzer.* 1959. NY. Nelson. 252p. VG/VG. B33. $15.00

PAYNE, Will. *Scarred Chin.* 1920. Dodd Mead. 1st ed. F/NF. M15. $45.00

PAYSON, Seth. *Proofs of Real Existence & Dangerous Tendency of Illuminism.* 1802. Charlestown. self pub. 290p. leather. H10. $57.50

PAZ, Octavio. *Essays on Mexican Art.* 1993. Harcourt Brace. 1st Eng trans. 303p. rem mk. G/dj. F3. $20.00

PEABODY, F. *Religio Medical Masquerade.* 1915. Chicago. 1st ed. 197p. VG. B5. $25.00

PEACOCK, Lawrence K. *Dahlia. A Practical Treatise on Its Habits, Characteristics.* 1931. NY. 20 sepia halftones. 124p. VG. B26. $19.00

PEAKE, Mervyn. *Titus Groan.* 1946. Reynal Hitchcock. 1st ed. NF/NF. P3. $250.00

PEALE, Norman Vincent. *Power of Positive Thinking for Young People.* 1955. Prentice Hall. 214p. VG/dj. B29. $3.00

PEALE, Norman Vincent. *Sin, Sex & Self-Control.* 1965. Guideposts. 207p. F/dj. B29. $3.00

PEALE, Norman Vincent. *Unlock Your Faith-Power.* 1957. Guideposts. 307p. VG/dj. B29. $3.00

PEARCE, F.B. *Zanzibar: Island Metropolis of E Africa.* 1920. Dutton. 1st ed. sm 4to. xl. VG. W1. $125.00

PEARCE, Michael. *Mamur Zapt & the Donkey-Vous.* 1990. London. Collins Crime Club. F/F. M15. $50.00

PEARL, Jack. *Dam of Death.* 1967. Whitman. TVTI. VG. P3. $8.00

PEARL, Jack. *Invaders: Dam of Death.* 1967. Whitman. sgn. pict brd. F. F4. $35.00

PEARS, D.F. *Bertrand Russell & the British Tradition of Philosophy.* 1967. Random. 1st Am ed. inscr. 283p. bl cloth. VG/chip. G1. $150.00

PEARSALL, Ronald. *Conan Doyle: A Biological Solution.* 1977. London. Weidenfeld. 1st ed. ils. F/dj. S6. $22.50

PEARSON, Hesketh. *Bernard Shaw: His Life & Personality.* 1948. Rpt Soc. rpt of 1942 Collins ed. yel buckram/gr leather spine. G. M7. $7.00

PEARSON, John. *James Bond: The Authorized Biography of 007.* 1973. Morrow. 1st ed. F/F. P3. $50.00

PEARSON, John. *Kindness of Dr Avicenna.* 1982. HRW. 1st ed. F/F. P3. $15.00

PEARSON, John. *Life of Ian Fleming.* 1966. London. Cape. 1st ed. ils. VG+/dj. S6. $35.00

PEARSON, Michael. *Beauty of Clocks.* 1978. NY. Crescent. 1st ed. folio. ils. 96p. VG/G. A8. $20.00

PEARSON, Ridley. *Probable Cause.* 1990. St Martin. 1st ed. F/NF. B3. $20.00

PEARSON, Ridley. *Seizing of Yankee Green Mall.* 1987. St Martin. 1st ed. sgn. F/F. T2. $20.00

PEARSON, Ridley. *Undercurrents.* 1988. St Martin. 1st ed. VG/VG. P3. $18.00

PEARSON, Virginia. *Everything But Elephants.* 1947. Whittlesey House. 1st ed. ils. 211p. VG. F3. $10.00

PEARSON, William. *Chessplayer.* 1984. Viking. 1st ed. VG/VG. P3. $15.00

PEASE, Howard. *Jungle River.* 1938. Doubleday Doran. pict black cloth. VG/dj. M20. $15.00

PEASE, Josephine Van Dolzen. *Book of Food.* 1938. Grosset Dunlap. 1st Experience in Reading Series. K2. $12.00

PEASE, Josephine Van Dolzen. *Book of Heat & Light.* 1938. Grosset Dunlap. 1st Experiences in Reading. K2. $12.00

PEASE, Josephine Van Dolzen. *Book of Houses.* 1938. Grosset Dunlap. 1st Experiences in Reading Series. K2. $12.00

PEASE, Sharon. *Down Beat's 88 Keys to Fame.* 1943. NY. Leeds. 1st ed. F/wrp. B2. $40.00

PEAT, Fern Bisel. *Mother Goose, Her Best-Known Rhymes.* 1933. Saalfield. VG+. C8. $75.00

PEAT, Fern Bisel. *Mother Goose.* 1934. Saalfield #992. VG+/pict wrp. C8. $40.00

PEAT, Fern Bisel. *Rags.* 1929. Saalfield. lg 4to. G+/wrp. C8. $20.00

PEAT, Fern Bisel. *Three Little Kittens, They Lost Their Mittens.* 1931. Saalfield. 12p. VG/stiff wrp. M5. $30.00

PEAT, Frank Edwin. *Christmas Carols.* 1937. Saalfield. ils Fern Bisel Peat. 45p. VG/dj. M20. $50.00

PEAT, Harold R. *Inexcusable Lie.* 1923. Chicago. Donnelley. 1st ed. sgn. 186p. VG. A17. $7.50

PEATTIE, Donald Culross. *Almanac for Moderns.* 1938. LEC. ils/sgn Asa Cheffetz. F/G case. M19. $50.00

PEATTIE, Donald Culross. *Audubon's America.* 1940. Houghton Mifflin. 1st ed. 328p. VG. H1. $45.00

PEATTIE, Donald Culross. *Immortal Village.* 1945. Chicago. sgn. ils/sgn Landacre. 202p. mc dj/case. K1. $175.00

PEATTIE, Roderick. *Black Hills.* 1952. Vanguard. 320p. cloth. VG. A10. $25.00

PEATTIE, Roderick. *Pacific Coast Ranges.* 1946. Vanguard. 1st ed. 402p. NF/NF. B19. $45.00

PECK, Anne Merriman. *Belgium.* 1940. Harper. 1st ed. ils Serebriakoff. unp. G. B10. $12.00

PECK, Anne Merriman. *Rene & Patou.* 1938. Chicago. Whitman. 1st ed. ils. 64p. mc brd. VG/G+. R2. $22.00

PECK, George Bacheler. *Recruit Before Petersburg.* 1880. Providence. 1st ed. 1/250. NF/prt wrp. M8. $45.00

PECK, J.M. *Guide for Emigrants, Containing Sketches of IL, MO...* 1837. Boston. Gould Kendall Lincoln. 2nd ed. 381p. cloth. F. M1. $250.00

PECK, John James. *Sign of the Eagle.* 1970. San Diego. Copley. 1st ed. ils/maps. 170p. VG/dj. F3. $45.00

PECK, Robert Newton. *Last Sunday.* 1977. Doubleday. 1st ed. VG/VG. P8. $12.00

PECK, Walter Edwin. *Shelley, His Life & Work.* 1927. Houghton Mifflin. 1st ed. 2 vols. 532p. VG. M20. $40.00

PECKHAM, Howard H. *Narratives of Colonial Am 1704-1765.* 1971. Lakeside. 314p. gilt bl cloth. VG+. M20. $25.00

PEDLER, Margaret. *Splendid Folly.* (1921). Grosset Dunlap. 288p. F/G. H1. $8.00

PEEBLES, P.J.E. *Principles of Physical Cosmology.* 1993. Princeton. 8vo. 718p. VG/VG. K5. $40.00

PEEL, Colin D. *Flameout.* 1976. St Martin. 1st ed. F/F. P3. $15.00

PEEL, H.M. *Pilot the Hunter.* 1962. Franklin Watts. 1st Am ed. VG/G. O3. $15.00

PEELER, Margaret. *Yesterday's Harvest.* 1926. np. G. S12. $10.00

PEET, Bill. *Caboose Who Got Loose.* 1971. Houghton Mifflin. 1st ed. ils. G+. P2. $15.00

PEET, Bill. *Keeks of Kookatumdee.* 1985. Houghton Mifflin. 1st ed. ils Bill Peet. F/F. C8. $25.00

PEET, Bill. *Pinkish, Purplish, Bluish Egg.* 1963. Houghton Mifflin. 5th prt. inscr. VG+. C8. $25.00

PEIXOTTO, Ernest. *Pacific Shores From Panama.* 1913. Scribner. 1st ed. 8vo. 285p. VG/VG. B11. $65.00

PELL, Franklyn. *Hangman's Hill.* 1946. Dodd Mead. 1st ed. VG/VG. P3. $23.00

PELL, Herbert Claiborne. *Glimpses of Eng Hist.* ca 1967. Barnes. ils OB Pell. 60p. VG/G. B10. $12.00

PELLEGRIN, Arthur. *L'Islam Dans de Monde.* 1937. Paris. Payot. 1st ed. 8vo. 182p. VG/wrp. W1. $12.00

PELLEGRINO, Charles. *Unearthing Atlantis.* 1991. Random. 1st ed. VG. p3. $23.00

PELLETIER, Cathie. *Marriage Made at Woodstock.* 1994. Crown. UP. NF/prt wrp. B3. $15.00

PELLY, David. *Faster! Faster! Quest for Sailing Speed.* 1984. NY. Hearst Marine Books. 1st ed. VG/dj. N2. $5.00

PELTIER, Leslie C. *Starlight Nights: Adventures of a Star-Gazer.* 1967. London. Macmillan. 1st ed. inscr/sgn twice. 236p. VG/VG. K5. $200.00

PEMBERTON, Max. *Diamond Ship.* 1907. Appleton. 1st ed. VG. M2. $45.00

PENDER, Lydia. *Useless Donkeys.* ca 1979. Warne. unp. VG. B10. $8.00

PENELHUM, Terence. *Butler.* 1985. London/Boston/Henley. 222p. edit Ted Honderich. ochre cloth. VG/dj. G1. $30.00

PENFIELD, Frederic Courtland. *East of Suez: Ceylon, India, China & Japan.* 1912. Century. 8vo. 54 pl. VG. W1. $15.00

PENFIELD, Frederic Courtland. *Present-Day Egypt.* 1899. Century. 1st ed. 8vo. 54 pl. teg. xl. VG. W1. $10.00

PENFIELD, Thomas. *Lost Treasure Trails.* 1954. Grosset Dunlap. ils Robert Glaubke. VG/G. B17. $10.00

PENFIELD, Wilder. *Mystery of the Mind.* 1975. Princeton. 123p. cloth. VG/dj. G1. $35.00

PENFIELD, Wilder. *No Other Gods.* 1954. Boston. 1st ed. 340p. dj. A13. $40.00

PENICK, B. *Empire Strikes Back: A Pop-Up Book.* 1980. Random. VG. P3. $15.00

PENKOWER. *Federal Writer's Project: A Study in Government Patronage...* 1977. IL U. 278p. F/VG. A4. $45.00

PENN, Irving. *Inventive Paris Clothes 1909-1939.* 1977. Viking. 1st ed. inscr. F/F. S9. $300.00

PENN, Irving. *Moments Preserved.* 1960. NY. Simon Schuster. 1st ed. folio. F/VG case. S9. $275.00

PENN, John. *Deadly Sickness.* 1985. Scribner. 1st ed. F/F. P3. $14.00

PENN, John. *Feast of Death.* 1989. London. Collins. 1st ed. F/F. S6. $30.00

PENN, John. *Haven of Danger.* 1993. London. Harper Collins. 1st ed. F/F. S6. $30.00

PENN, William. *Journal of William Penn, While Visiting Holland & Germany...* 1878. Friends Bookstore. 16mo. 189p. VG. V3. $20.00

PENN, William. *Primitive Christianity Revived in Faith & Practice...* 1877. Phil. Longstreth. 16mo. 89p. VG. V3. $20.00

PENN, William. *Tender Counsel & Advice, by Way of Epistle...* 1793. Phil. Enoch Story. 1st Am ed. 12mo. 49p. VG/plain wrp. M1. $250.00

PENNINGTON, Alicia. *Royal Toy Spaniels.* 1989. Great Britain. Ringpress. 1st ed. 126p. cloth. M/dj. R2. $32.00

PENNINGTON, Campbell. *Tepehaun of Chihuahua.* 1969. Salt Lake City. 1st ed. 413p. VG/dj. F3. $25.00

PENNINGTON, M. Basil. *Centering Prayer: Renewing Ancient Christian Prayer.* 1980. Doubleday. 222p. H10. $15.00

PENNOCK, J. Roland. *Limits of Law.* 1974. NY. 1st ed. 276p. NF. D3. $35.00

PENROSE, Roland. *Man Ray.* 1975. Boston. NYGS. 1st ed. 4to. F/F. S9. $75.00

PENTECOST, J. Dwight. *Design for Living.* 1975. Moody. 208p. VG/dj. B29. $5.50

PENZER. *Annotated Bibliography of Sir Richard Francis Burton.* 1923. London. 1/500. sgn. 4to. 367p. VG. A4. $450.00

PEPITONE, Lena. *Marilyn Monroe Confidential.* 1979. Simon Schuster. 1st ed. VG/VG. S11. $10.00

PEPLOW, Edward H. *Taming of the Salt.* 1970. Salt River Project. ils. 143p. NF/sans. B19. $30.00

PEPPER, Charles. *Panama to Patagonia.* 1906. McClurg. 1st ed. 398p. VG. F3. $25.00

PEPPER, George Wharton. *Phil Lawyer: An Autobiography.* 1944. Lippincott. 1st ed. 407p. F/sm tears. H1. $5.00

PEPYS, Samuel. *Great Fire of London. Six Days of Conflagration...* 1985. Berkeley. Poole. 74x56mm. 1/35 (100 total). 7 pl. 49p. F/half leather case. B24. $165.00

PERCEVAL, Don. *From Ice Mountain: Indian Settlement of the Americas.* 1979. Northland. 1st ed. ils. 65p. F/NF. B19. $25.00

PERCY, Walker. *Lancelot.* 1977. FSG. 1st ed. 8vo. 257p. gilt orange cloth. F/dj. H5. $60.00

PERCY, Walker. *Lancelot.* 1977. FSG. 1st ed/Canadian issue. RS. orange cloth. NF/clip. C6. $40.00

PERCY, Walker. *Last Gentleman.* 1966. FSG. 1st ed/author's 2nd book. 8vo. 409p. F/NF. C6. $120.00

PERCY, Walker. *Love in the Ruins.* 1971. FSG. 1st ed/2nd prt. sgn. 8vo. 403p. blk cloth. VG/dj. C6. $95.00

PERCY, Walker. *Message in the Bottle.* 1975. FSG. 1st ed/1st issue. Anne Rice provenance. F/NF clip. L3. $75.00

PERCY, Walker. *Movie-Goer.* 1963. Eyre Spottiswoode. 1st Eng ed/author's 1st book. VG/VG. L3. $350.00

PERCY, Walker. *Thanatos Syndrome.* 1987. Franklin Lib. true 1st ed. sgn. F/as issued. C4. $150.00

PERCY, Walker. *Thanatos Syndrone.* 1987. FSG. VG/G. P3. $15.00

PERCYVALL, Richard. *Dictionary In Spanish & English...Now Enlarged & Amplified.* 1623. London. Haveland/Lownes. 3 parts in 1. folio. rebound full tan calf. K1. $650.00

PEREK, Lubos. *Highlights of Astronomy.* 1968. Dordrecht, Holland. Reidel. 4to. 548p. VG/VG. K5. $40.00

PERELMAN, S.J. *Rising Gorge.* 1961. Simon Schuster. 1st prt. 287p. F/F. H1. $25.00

PERETZ, Don. *Middle East Today.* 1964. HRW. 8vo. 483p. G. W1. $12.00

PERETZ, I.L. *Magician.* 1973. Macmillan. 1st ed. ils Shulevitz. F/F. C8. $30.00

PEREZ-GUERRA, Anne. *Poppy, the Adventures of a Fairy.* 1942. Rand McNally. 1st ed thus. ils Betty Barclay. pict brd. VG. M5. $40.00

PERINN, Vincent L. *Ayn Rand: First Descriptive Bibliography.* 1990. Quill & Brush. 1st ed. 8vo. 92p. gilt red cloth. M/dj. F1. $29.95

PERKINS, John. *To the Ends of the Earth.* 1981. Pantheon. 1st ed. 4to. VG+/VG+. S9. $50.00

PERKINS, Joshua Newton. *Hist of the Parish of Incarnation, NYC 1852-1912.* 1912. Poughkeepsie. 1st ed. 293p. cloth. VG. M8. $37.50

PERKINS, Justin. *Residence of Eight Years in Persia...* 1843. Andover. 8vo. 27 pl/fld map. 512p. cloth. O2. $325.00

PERKINS, Lucy Fitch. *American Twins of the Revolution.* 1926. Houghton Mifflin. Clear Type ed. VG+. C8. $25.00

PERKINS, Lucy Fitch. *American Twins of 1812.* 1925. Houghton Mifflin. lg 12mo. G+. C8. $20.00

PERKINS, Lucy Fitch. *Belgian Twins.* 1917. Houghton Mifflin. 1st ed. NF. C8. $42.50

PERKINS, Lucy Fitch. *Cave Twins.* Oct 1916. Houghton Mifflin. 1st ed. VG+/VG+. C8. $45.00

PERKINS, Lucy Fitch. *Colonial Twins of Virginia.* 1924. Houghton Mifflin. probable 1st ed. F/VG. C8. $45.00

PERKINS, Lucy Fitch. *Filipino Twins.* 1923. Houghton Mifflin. probable 1st ed. VG. C8. $25.00

PERKINS, Lucy Fitch. *Indian Twins.* (1930). Houghton Mifflin. later prt. NF/VG+. C8. $16.00

PERKINS, Lucy Fitch. *Irish Twins.* ca 1913. Houghton Mifflin. 205p. G. B10. $25.00

PERKINS, Lucy Fitch. *Italian Twins.* 1920. Houghton Mifflin. 1st ed. VG. C8. $25.00

PERKINS, Lucy Fitch. *Japanese Twins.* 1912. Houghton Mifflin. ne. VG. C8. $30.00

PERKINS, Lucy Fitch. *Mexican Twins.* Nov 1915. Houghton Mifflin. 1st ed. NF. C8. $35.00

PERKINS, Lucy Fitch. *Pickaninny Twins.* 1931. Houghton Mifflin. 1st ed. 8vo. 153p. VG+. D6. $100.00

PERKINS, Lucy Fitch. *Pioneer Twins.* 1927. Houghton Mifflin. 1st ed. VG. C8. $35.00

PERKINS, Lucy Fitch. *Puritan Twins.* 1921. Houghton Mifflin. ne. VG+. C8. $30.00

PERKINS, Lucy Fitch. *Scotch Twins.* 1919. Houghton Mifflin. ne. F/VG. C8. $45.00

PERKINS, Lucy Fitch. *Swiss Twins.* 1922. Houghton Mifflin. ne. VG+/rpr. C8. $40.00

PERL, Lila. *Mexico: Crucible of the Americas.* 1978. Morrow. 1st ed. 159p. VG/dj. F3. $15.00

PEROT, Ross. *United We Stand: How We Can Take Back Our Country.* 1992. Hyperion. PBO/2nd prt. sgn. F/wrp. B4. $20.00

PEROTTI, Viola Andersen. *Important Firsts in MO Imprints 1808-1858.* 1967. KS City. RF Perotti. 1/500. 21 pl. 51p. red cloth. NF. P4. $135.00

PEROWNE, Barry. *Singular Conspiracy.* 1974. Bobbs Merrill. 1st ed. F/F. P3. $15.00

PEROWNE, Stewart. *Jerusalem & Bethlehem.* 1965. Barnes. 1st ed. 78p. VG/torn. W1. $9.00

PERPER, Hazel. *Avocado Pit Grower's Indoor How-To Book.* 1965. NY. ils. 63p. B26. $9.00

PERRAIVOS, Christophoros. *History of Suli & Parga.* 1990. Athens. rpt. 334p. w/prt card. O2. $20.00

PERRAULT, Charles. *New History of Blue Beard, Written by Black Beard...* 1804. Phil. John Adams. 32p. 31p. F/buff wrp. B24. $200.00

PERRIN, Leslie. *Keeping a Corgi.* 1958. London. Rockcliff. 1st ed. 131p. ils. cloth. M/G-. R2. $25.00

PERRINS, C.W. Dyson. *Italian Book-Illustrations & Early Printing.* 1914. Oxford. Quaritch. rpt. 1/250. 4to. 256p. gray cloth. K1. $185.00

PERRONE, Ionnes. *Praelectiones Theologicae...* 1872. Taurini. Hyacinth Marietti. 2 vol. leather. H10. $20.00

PERRY, Anne. *Belgrave Square.* 1992. NY. Fawcett Columbine. 1st Am ed. sgn. F/F. M15. $27.50

PERRY, Anne. *Bluegate Fields.* 1992. London. Souvenir. 1st Eng ed. F/F. S6. $25.00

PERRY, Anne. *Sudden, Fearful Death.* 1993. Fawcett Columbine. 1st ed. sgn. VG/dj. N2. $8.50

PERRY, Bliss. *Life & Letters of Henry Lee Higginson.* 1921. Boston. index. 557p. O8. $12.50

PERRY, Ralph Barton. *In the Spirit of Wm James.* 1938. New Haven. Yale. gr cloth. G1. $50.00

PERRY, Richard. *Mexico's Fortress Monasteries.* 1992. Santa Barbara. Espadana. 1st ed. sgn. 224p. VG/wrp. F3. $20.00

PERRY, Ritchie. *Fall Guy.* 1972. Houghton Mifflin. 1st ed. VG/VG. P3. $18.00

PERRY, Thomas A. *Bibliography of Am Literature Trans Into Roumanian.* 1984. Philosophical Lib. 331p. VG/dj. N2. $15.00

PERRY, Thomas. *Big Fish.* 1985. Scribner. 1st ed. F/F. B4. $45.00

PERRY, Thomas. *Big Fish.* 1985. Scribner. 1st ed. VG/VG. P3. $20.00

PERRY, Thomas. *Island.* 1987. Putnam. 1st ed. sgn. F/F. T2. $20.00

PERRY, Thomas. *Sleeping Dogs.* 1992. Random. 1st ed. sgn. F/F. T2. $18.00

PERRY, Vincent G. *Skitch: Message of the Roses.* 1975. Denlinger. 1st ed. 190p. brd. VG. R2. $25.00

PERRY, William B. *Our Sammies in the Trenches.* ca 1918. Saalfield. ils Clare Angell. 380p. G. B10. $10.00

PERRY & PERRY. *Maya Missions: Exploring Spanish Colonial Churches...* 1988. Santa Barbara. Espadana. 1st ed. sgn. 249p. VG/wrp. F3. $15.00

PERRY & STOCKBRIDGE. *Florida in the Making.* 1926. De Bower. 351p. G+. H1. $6.00

PERSE, St. John. *Anabasis.* 1949. Harcourt Brace. 3rd ed. F/VG. H4. $35.00

PERSE, St. John. *Eloges & Other Poems.* 1956. NY. Bollingen. bilingual text. NF/VG. F1. $20.00

PERSE, St. John. *Letters.* 1979. Princeton. trans AJ Knodel. F/VG+. F1. $25.00

PERSE, St. John. *Winds.* 1953. NY. Bollingen 34. bilingual text. NF/dj. F1. $35.00

PERSICO, Joseph E. *Piercing of the Reich.* 1979. Viking. 1st ed. VG/VG. P3. $18.00

PERTWEE, Roland. *Hell's Loose.* 1929. Houghton Mifflin. VG. P3. $8.00

PERUGINI, Kate. *Comedy of Charles Dickens.* 1906. London. 1st Series. 1st ed. 542p. VG. D3. $35.00

PERUGINI, Mark E. *Victorian Days & Ways.* nd. London. rpt. 12mo. 288p. G. D3. $15.00

PESOTTA, Rose. *Bread Upon the Waters.* 1944. Dodd Mead. 1st ed. NF/dj. B2. $40.00

PETAJA, Emil. *As Dream & Shadow.* 1972. Sisu. 1st ed. F/F. P3. $30.00

PETAJA, Emil. *Hannes Bok Memorial Showcase of Fantasy Art.* 1974. San Francisco. Sisu. 1st ed. F/pict wrp. T2. $55.00

PETERJOHN, Bruce G. *Birds of OH.* 1989. Bloomington. 49 mc pl. M/dj. B18. $27.50

PETERKIN, Julia. *Plantation Christmas.* 1934. Houghton Mifflin. 12mo. VG/VG. B17. $12.00

PETERKIN, Julia. *Roll, Jordan, Roll.* 1933. Bobbs Merrill. 8vo. photos Doris Ulmann. 251p. G. B11. $75.00

PETERKIN, Julia. *Roll, Jordan, Roll.* 1934. London. Cape. 1st ed. 8vo. 251p. brn cloth. VG+. C6. $150.00

PETERS, Ed. *Mountaineering: Freedom of the Hills.* 1982. np. 4th ed. F/dj. B34. $35.00

PETERS, Elizabeth; see Mertz, Barbara Gross.

PETERS, Ellis; see Pargeter, Edith Mary.

PETERS, Harry T. *Currier & Ives: Printmakers to the American People.* 1929-1931. NY. 2 vol set. #457/501. VG. A1. $450.00

PETERS, Ludovic. *Tarakian.* 1963. Abelard Schuman. 1st ed. VG/G. P3. $20.00

PETERS, Stephen. *Park Is Mine.* 1981. Doubleday. 1st ed. F/dj. F4. $18.00

PETERSEN, E.J. *North of Saginaw Bay.* 1952. Tall Timbers. 241p. VG/dj. M20. $15.00

PETERSEN, Herman. *Covered Bridge.* 1950. Crowell. 1st ed. VG/VG. P3. $20.00

PETERSEN, Peter. *Wilhelm Wundt und Seine Zeit.* 1925. Stuttgart. sm 8vo. 306p. G1. $30.00

PETERSEN, Wilhelm. *Totentanz in Polen.* 1940. Hamburg. obl folio. ils. VG. A9. $200.00

PETERSEN, William J. *Steamboating on the Upper MS.* 1968. IA City. rpt. 575p. map ep. B18. $35.00

PETERSHAM & PETERSHAM. *Ark of Father Noah & Mother Noah.* 1940 (1930). Doubleday Doran. ils. G. P2. $20.00

PETERSHAM & PETERSHAM. *Circus Baby.* 1950. Macmillan. early ed. F/NF. C8. $25.00

PETERSHAM & PETERSHAM. *Get-a-Way & Harry Janos.* 1933. Viking. 1st ed. ils. unp. orange spine/pict brd. VG. D6. $95.00

PETERSHAM & PETERSHAM. *Moses.* 1958. Macmillan. 1st ed thus. cloth. F/VG-. M5. $10.00

PETERSHAM & PETERSHAM. *Silver Mace: Story of Williamsburg.* 1956. Macmillan. 1st prt. VG+/VG+. C8. $25.00

PETERSON, Charles S. *Take Up Your Mission: Mormon Colonizing Along Little CO...* 1973. AZ U. ils/notes/bibliography/index. 309p. F/F. B19. $25.00

PETERSON, Esther Allen. *Penelope Gets Wheels.* ca 1982. Crown. 1st ed. unp. F/F. B10. $10.00

PETERSON, Harold. *Pageant of the Gun.* 1967. Doubleday. not 1st ed. VG/dj. N2. $12.50

PETERSON, Roger Tory. *Field Guide to Birds of TX.* 1960. Boston. 1st ed. 304p. VG/dj. B18. $22.50

PETERSON. *Magazines in the Twentieth Century.* 1964. IL U. 2nd ed. 497p. VG/VG. A4. $40.00

PETIEVICH, Gerald. *Earth Angels.* 1989. NAL. 1st ed. NF/NF. P3. $18.00

PETIEVICH, Gerald. *Paramour.* 1991. Dutton. AP. F/wrp. B2. $30.00

PETIEVICH, Gerald. *Shakedown.* 1988. Simon Schuster. 1st ed. F/F. P3. $17.00

PETRADAKIS, M.S. *Postal History of the Aegean.* 1991. Athens. 2 vol. 4to. w/card. O2. $45.00

PETRAKIS, Harry Mark. *Waves of Night & Other Stories.* 1969. NY. 8vo. 230p. cloth. O2. $15.00

PETRAN, Tabitha. *Syria: Nation of the Modern World.* 1972. London. Benn. 1st ed. 8vo. 16pl. 284p. NF/dj. W1. $18.00

PETRIE, Glen. *Dorking Gap Affair: A Mycroft Holmes Adventure.* 1989. London. Bantam. 1st ed. F/F. S6. $30.00

PETRO, F. *American Quilts & Coverlets.* 1949. NY. 1st ed. VG/poor. B5. $45.00

PETRY, Ann. *Country Place.* 1947. Houghton Mifflin. 1st ed. 8vo. 266p. gr/blk stp gray cloth. NF/clip. H5. $85.00

PETRY, Ann. *Narrows.* 1953. Houghton Mifflin. 1st ed/author's 2nd novel. NF/VG. L3. $250.00

PETTEE, F.M. *Palgrave Mummy.* 1929. Payson Clarke. 1st ed. VG. P3. $30.00

PETTERSON, Alan Rune. *Frankenstein's Aunt.* 1980. Little Brn. 1st Am ed. F/NF clip. F4. $20.00

PETTINGILL, Amos. *White-Flower-Farm Garden Book.* 1977 (1966). Boston. ils Nils Hogner. 372p. sc. B26. $10.00

PETTUS, Daisy Caden. *Rosalie Evans' Letters From Mexico.* 1926. Bobbs Merrill. 12mo. 472p. gilt red cloth. VG. B11. $15.00

PEVSNER, Stella. *And You Give Me a Pain, Elaine.* 1978. Seabury. 1st ed. 182p. F/F. P2. $30.00

PFEIFFER, Charles F. *Dead Sea Scrolls & the Bible.* 1969. Weathervane. 152p. VG/dj. B29. $3.00

PFEIFFER, Charles F. *Old Testament Hist.* 1973. Canon Pr. 640p. VG/dj. B29. $15.00

PFEIFFER, G.S.F. *Voyages & 5 Years' Captivity in Algers...* 1836. Harrisburg, PA. Winebrenner. 1st ed. 398p. G. W1. $30.00

PFEIFFER, Ida. *Journey to Iceland & Travels in Sweden & Norway.* 1852. NY. 1st ed. 273p. VG. A17. $65.00

PFEIFFER, John. *Emergence of Man.* 1969. Harper Row. 1st ed. 477p. VG/dj. F3. $15.00

PFEIFFER, John. *Emergence of Society.* 1977. McGraw Hill. 1st ed. 515p. VG/dj. F3. $15.00

PFLEIDERER, Otto. *Philosophy of Religion on Basis of Its Hist.* 1886. London. Williams Norgate. 4 vols. G. G1. $100.00

PFLUGER, Eduard. *Ueber das Hemmungs-Nervensystem fur die Peristaltischen...* 1857. Berlin. 75p. lacks orig wrp. G7. $65.00

PHELAN, John. *Kingdom of Quito in 17th Century.* 1967. Madison, WI. 1st ed. 432p. VG/dj. F3. $30.00

PHELAN, Nancy. *Welcome the Wayfarer: Traveller in Modern Turkey.* 1965. Macmillan/St Martin. 1st ed. 8vo. 243p. xl. VG/dj. W1. $14.00

PHELPS, William Lyon. *City of the Great King & Other Places in the Holy Land.* 1926. Cosmopolitan. 2nd ed. 116p. G. W1. $14.00

PHILBROOK, Clem. *Magic Bat.* 1954. Macmillan. 1st ed. VG. P8. $25.00

PHILBY, H. St. John B. *Arabian Days.* 1948. London. Hale. 2nd prt. 8vo. 49 pl. 336p. VG. W1. $120.00

PHILIP, A.P.W. *On the Influence of Minute Doses of Mercury...* 1834. Washington. 60p. new antique-style cloth. G7. $65.00

PHILIP, Kenneth R. *John Collier's Crusade for Indian Reform 1920-1954.* 1977. AZ U. 1st ed. 304p. F/NF. B19. $25.00

PHILIPS, Judson. *Champagne Killer.* 1972. Dodd Mead. 1st ed. VG/VG. P3. $20.00

PHILIPS, Judson. *Deadly Trap.* 1978. Dodd Mead. 1st ed. NF/NF. P3. $15.00

PHILIPS, Judson. *Escape a Killer.* 1971. Dodd Mead. 1st ed. VG/VG. P3. $20.00

PHILIPS, Judson. *Murder Goes Round & Round.* 1988. Dodd Mead. 1st ed. VG/dj. P3. $16.00

PHILIPS, Judson. *Power Killers.* 1974. Dodd Mead. 1st ed. VG/G+. P3. $13.00

PHILIPS, Judson. *Wings of Madness.* 1966. Dodd Mead. 1st ed. F/NF. M15. $35.00

PHILLIPS, Alan. *Living Legend: Story of the Royal Canadian Mounted Police.* 1957. Boston. 328p. NF. D3. $15.00

PHILLIPS, Alexander M. *Mislaid Charm.* 1947. Prime. 1st ed. VG/2nd state gr dj. P3. $25.00

PHILLIPS, Conrad. *Empty Cot.* 1958. Arthur Barker. 1st ed. VG/VG. P3. $25.00

PHILLIPS, D.L. *Letters From California.* 1877. Springfield. VG. A9. $80.00

PHILLIPS, Deane. *Horse Raising in Colonial New England.* 1922. Ithaca. Cornell. 52p. VG/wrp. O3. $45.00

PHILLIPS, Duncan. *Collection in the Making, a Survey of Problems...* 1926. NY. Weyhe. tall 4to. 112p. gilt bl cloth. VG+. F1. $120.00

PHILLIPS, Edward. *New World of Words; or, Universal English Dictionary.* 1706. London. folio. unp. contemporary paneled calf/rebacked. K1. $375.00

PHILLIPS, Ethel Calvert. *Little Rag Doll.* 1930. Houghton Mifflin. 1st ed. ils Lois Lenski. cloth. VG. M5. $60.00

PHILLIPS, Ethel Calvert. *Little Sally Waters.* 1926. Houghton Mifflin. 1st ed. ils Edith F Butler. 143p. G/poor. P2. $15.00

PHILLIPS, Ethel Calvert. *Peter Peppercorn.* 1939. Houghton Mifflin. 1st ed. 148p. F/G. B10. $20.00

PHILLIPS, George. *Versuch Einer Darstellung der Geschichte...* 1825. Gottingen. 1st ed. 8vo. 272p. contemporary morocco. VG. D3. $150.00

PHILLIPS, Harlan B. *Felix Frankfurter Reminisces, Recorded in Talks...* 1960. Reynal. M11. $25.00

PHILLIPS, J.B. *Plain Christianity.* 1956. Macmillan. 87p. G. B29. $3.00

PHILLIPS, J.B. *Young Church in Action.* 1958. Macmillan. 103p. VG/dj. B29. $4.00

PHILLIPS, Jayne Anne. *Fast Lanes.* 1984. NY. Vehicle. 1st ed. sgn. 1/2000. F/wrp. L3. $85.00

PHILLIPS, Jayne Anne. *Machine Dreams.* 1984. Dutton. 1st ed/author's 1st novel. sgn. F/F. L3. $75.00

PHILLIPS, Jill M. *Walford's Oak.* 1990. Citadel. 1st ed. F/F. M21. $25.00

PHILLIPS, John. *Exploring Romans.* 1969. Moody. 286p. G/torn. B29. $6.50

PHILLIPS, Keith. *Making of a Disciple.* 1981. Revell. 157p. F/dj. B29. $4.00

PHILLIPS, Lance. *Yonder Comes the Train.* 1965. Barnes. ils. 395p. VG/dj. M20. $30.00

PHILLIPS, Roger. *Trees of North America & Europe.* 1978. NY. photos. 224p. sc. B26. $15.00

PHILLIPS, W.S. *Indian Tales for Little Folks.* 1928. Platt Munk. 4to. 80p. ils brd. F/remnant. B24. $125.00

PHILLIPS, Wendell. *Quataban & Sheba.* 1955. Harcourt. 1st ed. ils. 362p. xl. VG. W1. $12.00

PHILLIPS, Wendell. *Unknown Oman.* 1966. McKay. 1st Am ed. sgn pres. 319p. NF/dj. W1. $35.00

PHILLPOTTS, Eden. *Clue From the Stars.* 1932. Macmillan. 1st ed. VG. M2. $12.00

PHILPOTTS, Adelaide E. *Camillus & the Schoolmaster, a Play in One Act.* 1923. London/Glasgow. Gowans Gray. 12mo. 23p. F/parchment wrp. B24. $30.00

PHIPPS, Constantine John. *Voyage Towards the North Pole Undertaken...1773.* 1774. London. J Nourse. 4to. ils/maps. 253p. rebacked. custom box. P4. $1,500.00

PIAGET, Jean. *Behavior & Evolution.* 1978. Pantheon. 165p. M/dj. K4. $15.00

PIAGET, Jean. *Child's Conception of Physical Causality.* 1930. Harcourt Brace. 1st Eng-language ed/later issue. 309p. NF. G1. $100.00

PIAGET, Jean. *Insights & Illusions of Philosophy.* 1971. World. 1st Eng-language ed. 232p. blk cloth. VG/dj. G1. $25.00

PIAGET, Jean. *Intro a l'Epistemologie Genetique.* 1950. Paris. Presses Universitaires de France. 3 vol. F. G1. $200.00

PIAGET, Jean. *Logic & Psychology.* 1970. London. Routledge. 1st Eng-language ed. 8vo. 98p. F/F. G1. $30.00

PIAGET, Jean. *Psychology of Intelligence.* 1951. Keagan Paul. 173p. VG/dj. K4. $10.00

PICART, Bernard. *Ceremonies & Religious Customs of Various Nations... Vol 3.* 1734. London. 1st ed. folio. 45 full-p pl. full calf. C6. $750.00

PICART, Bernard. *Ovid's Metamorphoses. In Latin & Eng, Hist Explications...* 1732. Amsterdam. 2 vol in 1. 1st ed thus. 125 pl. full flame calf. C6. $300.00

PICASSO, Pablo. *Les Memines 1957.* 1959. Paris. Galerie Louise Leiris Catalogue No 10. F1. $100.00

PICKARD, Nancy. *Crossbones.* 1990. London. Macmillan. ARC/1st Eng ed. sgn. RS. F/F. S6. $35.00

PICKARD, Nancy. *Marriage Is Murder.* 1987. Scribner. 1st ed. F/F. P3. $15.00

PICKARD, Samuel T. *Whittier-Land: A Handbook of North Essex...* 1904. Houghton Mifflin. 4th ed. 16mo. 160p. VG. V3. $15.00

PICKEN, Mary Brooks. *Sewing Materials.* 1924. Scranton, PA. Women's Inst Domestic Arts & Sciences. 267p. VG. H1. $22.50

PICKERING, Ernest. *Architectural Design.* 1941. Wiley. 2nd ed. 4to. ils. 329p. VG. F1. $40.00

PICKERING, William. *Quintus Horatius Flaccus.* 1820. London. Pickering. 85x48mm. 185p. aeg. fore-edge painting. F. B24. $850.00

PID, Mr.; see Luce, Robert B.

PIDGIN, C.F. *Blennerhassett.* 1901. Boston. 1st ed. ils. emb pict cloth. F. A17. $10.00

PIENKOWSKI, Jan. *Haunted House.* 1979. Dutton. mechanical popups. NF. C8. $35.00

PIENKOWSKI, Jan. *Robot.* 1981. Dell. 1st Am ed. 7 moveables/popups. F. B17. $22.00

PIEPER, Josef. *End of Time: Mediation on Philosophy of Hist.* 1954. London. Faber. 1st Eng-language ed. 157p. purple cloth. VG/dj. G1. $25.00

PIER, G. *Hanit the Enchantress.* 1921. Dutton. 1st ed. G. M2. $10.00

PIERCE, Bob. *Untold Korean Story.* nd. Zondervan. 89p. xl. G. B29. $2.75

PIERCE, James W. *Story of Turkey & Armenia.* 1896. Baltimore. 8vo. 500p. pict cloth. O2. $45.00

PIERCE. *Iron in the Pines, the Story of NJ's Ghost Towns & Bog Iron.* 1957. Rutgers. ils. 253p. VG/VG. A4. $35.00

PIERCY, Marge. *Breaking Camp.* 1968. Weslyan. 1st ed/author's 1st book of poetry. sgn. F/F. V1. $65.00

PIERCY, Marge. *He, She & It.* 1991. Knopf. 1st ed. VG/dj. P3. $22.00

PIERON, Henri. *Thought & Brain.* 1927. Harcourt Brace. 262p. VG. B33. $24.00

PIERS, Anthony. *Adventures of Kelvin Rud, Across the Frames.* 1991. Guild Am Books. 1st compilation ed. F/F. F4. $15.00

PIERSOL, George. *Textbook of Normal Histology.* 1896. Phil. 4th ed. 439p. worn sheep. G7. $20.00

PIKE, Christopher. *Sati.* 1990. St Martin. 1st ed. F/F. B3. $15.00

PIKE, Nicolas. *Abridgement of New & Complete System of Arithmetick...* 1795. Worcester. Thomas. 348p. leather. H10. $65.00

PIKE, Robert. *Tall Trees, Tough Men.* 1967. NY. 1st ed. VG/VG. B5. $22.50

PILBEAM, John W. *First Fifty Haworthias.* 1970. Morden, Surrey. ils. sc. VG. B26. $9.00

PILBOROUGH, Geoffrey D. *History of RAF Marine Craft 1918-1939.* 1986. Eng. Canipex. sc. M/clear plastic. M7. $25.00

PILCHER, Verona. *Searcher.* 1929. London. Heinemann. 1st ed. 1/1000. VG/dj. C6. $125.00

PILKINGTON, William T. *Harvey Fergusson.* 1975. Twayne. F. A18. $15.00

PILKINGTON, William T. *My Blood's Country: Studies in SW Literature.* 1973. TX Christian U. 1st ed. 211p. VG/wrp. B19. $15.00

PILLSBURY, Dorothy L. *Adobe Doorways.* 1953. NM U. 1st ed/2nd prt. sgn. 197p. VG. A8. $30.00

PIM, Paul. *Telling Tommy About the Things We Use.* ca 1946. Cupples Leon. ils. VG/G. B10. $12.00

PINART, Alphonse. *Journey to Arizona in 1876.* 1962. Los Angeles. Zamorano. 1/500. fld map. 47p. NF. P4. $65.00

PINCHER, Chapman. *Not With a Bang.* 1965. NAL. 1st ed. G+. P3. $4.00

PINCKNEY, Darryl. *High Cotton.* 1992. FSG. 1st ed. F/F. B2. $50.00

PINCKNEY, Darryl. *High Cotton.* 1992. FSG. 1st ed/author's 1st book. NF/NF clip. A14. $45.00

PINCUS, Arthur. *Terror in Cuba.* 1936. NY. Workers Defense. intro Dos Passos. NF/wrp. B2. $40.00

PINDAR. *Ta Tou Pindarou Sesosmena.* 1754. Glasgow. Foulis. 83x53mm. 158p. aeg. fore-edge painting. early full leather. F. B24. $650.00

PINGET, Robert. *Inquisitory.* 1967. Grove. ARC. RS. F/F. B2. $35.00

PINI, Wendy. *Elfquest Book 1.* 1981. Donning. ltd ed. sgn. #d. F/box. P3. $225.00

PINI, Wendy. *Elfquest Book 2.* 1982. Donning. ltd 3d. sgn. #d. F/box. P3. $150.00

PINI, Wendy. *Elfquest Book 3.* 1983. Donning. ltd ed. sgn. #d. F/box. P3. $100.00

PINI, Wendy. *Elfquest Book 4.* 1984. Donning. ltd ed. sgn. #d. F/box. P3. $75.00

PINIUS, Joanne. *Tractatus Historico — Chronoloicus, ad Tomun VI Julii...* 1729. Antwerp. DuMoulin. folio. tooled calf. H10. $98.00

PINKERTON, Allan. *Bucholz & the Detectives.* 1880. Carleton. 1st ed. 341p. VG. M20. $30.00

PINKERTON, John. *Medallic Hist of England.* 1802. London. Harding. folio. 40 copper-engraved pl. 112p. brn polished calf. K1. $375.00

PINKERTON, Robert E. *Canoe: Its Selection, Care & Use.* 1916. NY. Outing. ils. 162p. VG. P4. $20.00

PINNELL, Lois M. *French Creek Presbyterian Church...* 1971. Parsons, WV. 1st ed. 249p. cloth. VG. M8. $37.50

PINNER, David. *Ritual.* 1967. New Authors Ltd. 1st ed. F/F. P3. $13.00

PIPER, David. *Genius of British Painting.* 1975. Morrow. VG/VG. A1. $20.00

PIPER, Watty. *Animal Story Book.* ca 1954. Platt Munk. ils Wesley Dennis. unp. VG. B10. $25.00

PIPER, Watty. *Brimful Book: A Collection of Mother Goose Rhymes...* 1939. Platt Munk. folio. ils Eulaile/Burd/Haumann. VG. B17. $17.50

PIPER, Watty. *Bumper Book. A Harvest of Stories & Verses.* 1969. Platt Munk. ils Eulalie. 63p. pict yel cloth. VG-. A3. $22.50

PIPER, Watty. *Folk Tales Children Love.* 1943. Platt Munk. VG. M19. $45.00

PIPER, Watty. *Little Engine That Could.* 1930. Platt Munk. ils Lenski. unp. pict red cloth. G/G. A3. $17.50

PIPER, Watty. *Little Engine That Could.* 1930. Platt Munk. ils Lois Lenski. VG. B17. $20.00

PIPER, Watty. *Little Folks of Other Lands.* ca 1929. Platt Munk. ils Holling. unp. G. B10. $25.00

PIPER, Watty. *Once Upon a Time Fairy Tales.* ca 1922. Platt Munk. unp. fair. B10. $10.00

PIPER, Watty. *Tales From Storyland.* ca 1941. Platt Munk. unp. VG/fair. B10. $35.00

PIPER, Watty. *Tales From Storyland.* 1949. Platt Munk. VG. M19. $45.00

PIPINELIS, M.P. *Caitiff Bulgaria.* ca 1944. Hutchinson. 12mo. 61p. VG. W1. $14.00

PIPPERT, Wesley G. *Land of Promise, Land of Strife: Israel at Forty.* 1988. Word. 273p. VG/torn. B29. $7.50

PIQUER, D. Andre. *Tratado de Calenturas.* 1788. Madrid. D Blas Roman. sm 4to. 304p. vellum. K1. $125.00

PIRONE, Pascal P. *Diseases & Pests of Ornamental Plants.* 1978 (1943). NY. 5th ed. ils. F/dj. B26. $44.00

PISTON, Donald S. *Meteorology.* 1931. Phil. Blakiston. 8vo. ils/13 maps. gr cloth. G. K5. $18.00

PISTORIUS, Anna. *What Bird Is It?* ca 1944. Wilcox Follett. unp. G. B10. $10.00

PITARD, M.C.J. *Exploration Scientifique du Maroc Organisee...* 1913. Paris. Masson. 1st ed. 4to. 9 pl. VG. W1. $15.00

PITCHER, George. *Philosophy of Wittgenstein.* 1964. Prentice Hall. 340p. blk cloth. VG/dj. G1. $30.00

PITMAN, Mrs. E.R. *Elizabeth Fry.* 1886. Boston. Roberts Bros. 12mo. 269p. VG. V3. $12.50

PITTENGER, Peggy. *Back-Yard Horse.* 1973. NY. Arco. rpt. VG/VG. O3. $15.00

PITTMAN, Philip. *Present State of the European Settlements on the Mississipi.* 1906. Cleveland. Arthur Clark. ltd ed. 1/500. F. H4. $125.00

PITTS, Charles Frank. *Chaplains in Gray: Confederate Chaplains' Story.* 1957. Nashville. Broadman. 1st ed. 166p. cloth. NF. M8. $35.00

PITZ, Henry C. *Tale of the Warrior Lord.* 1930. Longman Gr. 1st ed. 156p. VG/VG. P2. $35.00

PITZ, Henry. *King Arthur & His Noble Knights.* 1949. Lippincott. 1st imp. 8vo. F/VG. B17. $6.50

PITZ, Henry. *Practice of Illustration.* 1947. Watson Guptill. 1st ed. lg 4to. 146p. cloth. VG. A17. $35.00

PLACE, Marian T. *Copper Kings of Montana.* 1961. Random. ils Ernest Barth. VG/dj. B34. $25.00

PLAIDY, Jean. *Prince of Darkness.* 1978. Hale. 1st ed. VG/VG. P3. $12.00

PLANTE, David. *Ghost of Henry James.* 1970. NY. 1st Am ed. inscr. F/VG+. A11. $65.00

PLANTE, David. *Slides.* 1971. Gambit. ARC/1st Am ed/author's 2nd book. inscr. F/F. B4. $150.00

PLANTIN, Christopher. *Psalterion Prophetou kai tou David.* 1584. Antwerp. Plantini. 85x56mm. 391p. old full calf/raised bands. B24. $550.00

PLANTON, Nicholas. *Zakros: Discovery of a Lost Place of Ancient Crete.* 1971. Scribner. 1st Am ed. 345p. VG/dj. W1. $45.00

PLANTOS, Ted. *Heather Hits Her First Home Run.* 1989. Blk Moss. 1st ed. ils Heather Collins. 24p. M. P8. $6.00

PLATH, Sylvia. *Ariel.* nd. London. Faber. 1st ed. sgn. F/VG. V1. $85.00

PLATH, Sylvia. *Two Poems.* 1980. Knotting. Sceptre Pr. 1/300. F/stapled wrp. L3. $85.00

PLATT, Charles. *Planet of the Voles.* 1971. Putnam. 1st ed. NF/dj. P3. $20.00

PLATT, Colin. *Medieval England: A Social Hist & Archaelogy...* 1978. Scribner. 1st ed. ils. 282p. NF/dj. M10. $18.50

PLATT, Kin. *Body Beautiful Murder.* 1976. Random. 1st ed. VG/G+. P3. $18.00

PLATT, Kin. *Giant Kill.* 1974. Random. ARC of 1st ed. inscr to Joe Gores. F/dj. F4. $40.00

PLATT, Kin. *Screwball King Murder.* 1978. Random. 1st ed. F/VG+. P8. $30.00

PLAUTUS. *Ex Fide, Atque Actoritate. Compilum Librorum...* 1577. Paris. 1st ed thus. folio. full polished calf/rebacked. VG. C6. $400.00

PLAYNE, Beatrice. *St George for Ethiopia.* 1954. London. Constable. 1st ed. sm 4to. 200p. VG. W1. $65.00

PLEASANTS, W. Shepard. *Stingaree Murders.* 1932. Mystery League. 1st ed. VG. P3. $15.00

PLEASANTS, William J. *Twice Across the Plains 1849 & 1856.* 1981. Ye Galleon. 1st ed. ils. M/dj. A18. $12.00

PLESSNER, Helmuth. *Laughing & Crying: Study of Limits of Human Behavior.* 1970. Evanston. Northwestern. 172p. VG. G1. $25.00

PLIMPTON, George. *Bogey Man.* 1968. NY. Harper Row. 1st ed. 306p. gr cloth. VG. B14. $35.00

PLIMPTON, George. *Curious Case of Sidd Finch.* 1987. Macmillan. 1st ed. F/F. P8. $20.00

PLOMER, Henry R. *Robert Wyer: Printer & Bookseller.* 1897. London. Bibliographical Soc. 11 pl. brn calf/purple cloth. K1. $50.00

PLOMLEY, N.J.B. *Word-List of the Tasmanian Aboriginal Languages.* 1976. np. 1st ed. 1/1000. 486p. beige cloth. M/dj. P4. $50.00

PLOOS VAN AMSTEL, Cornelis. *Aanleiding tot de Kennis der Anatomie...* 1783. Amsterdam. J Yntema. 27 engraved pl. 114p. half vellum. G7. $595.00

PLOWHEAD, Ruth Gipson. *Josie & Joe.* 1938. Caxton. 1st ed thus. 8vo. 262p. VG/G. A3. $15.00

PLOWRIGHT, Teresa. *Dreams of an Unseen Planet.* 1986. Arbor. 1st ed. RS. F/F. P3. $18.00

PLUMMER, D. Brian. *Fell Terrier.* 1989. London. Boydell Brewer. 243p. cloth. M/dj. R2. $40.00

PLUMMER, Frank Everett. *Gracia: Social Tragedy.* 1900. Chicago. Charles Kerr. 1st ed. VG. B2. $45.00

POCHIN MOULD, Daphne. *Angels of God: Their Rightful Place in Modern World.* 1963. NY. Devin Adair. 177p. H10. $17.50

POE, Edgar Allan. *Cask of Amontillado.* 1981. Boston. Bromer. 65x51mm. 1/35 (total of 150). full blk morocco. F/box. B24. $550.00

POE, Edgar Allan. *Complete Tales & Poems.* 1989. Dorset. 4th ed. F/NF. M21. $20.00

POE, Edgar Allan. *Mask of the Red Death.* 1969. Baltimore. Aquarius. 1/500. ils/sgn Frederico Castellon. F/case. F1. $250.00

POE, Edgar Allan. *Masque of the Red Death.* 1932. Halcyon. 1st ed thus. 1/175. 170p. F. C6. $500.00

POE, Edgar Allan. *Poe: Stories & Poems.* 1986. NJ. ils Greg Hildebrandt. VG. B18. $15.00

POE, Edgar Allan. *Two Poems, by Edgar Allan Poe.* 1984. Utrecht. Catharijne. 41x63mm. 1/100. inscr by printer. full blk morocco. F. B24. $175.00

POGANY, Willy. *Frenzied Prince. Heroic Stories of Ancient Ireland.* 1943. Phil. 1st ed. ils P Colum. VG/G. B5. $65.00

POGANY, Willy. *My Poetry Book.* 1957. Winston. 2nd prt of revised ed. red cloth. VG. M5. $28.00

POGANY, Willy. *Peterkin.* 1940. Phil. McKay. 1st ed. NF/VG. C8. $50.00

POGANY, Willy. *Twilight & Dawn in Birdland, a Talking Book.* 1919. NY. ils. w/2 78-rpm records. VG. M5. $80.00

POHL, Frederik. *Chernobyl.* 1987. Bantam. 1st ed. VG/G+. P3. $15.00

POHL, Frederik. *Cook War.* 1981. Del Rey. 1st ed. VG/VG. P3. $15.00

POHL, Frederik. *Drunkard's Walk.* 1960. Gnome. VG/G+. M17. $20.00

POHL, Frederik. *Drunkard's Walk.* 1960. Gnome. 1st ed. F/dj. M2. $35.00

POHL, Frederik. *Eleventh Galaxy Reader.* 1969. Doubleday. 1st ed. VG/VG. P3. $25.00

POHL, Frederik. *Gateway Trip: Tales & Vignettes of the Heechee.* 1990. Ballantine. 1st ed. M/dj. M21. $15.00

POHL, Frederik. *Heechee Rendezvous.* 1984. Del Rey. 1st ed. F/F. P3. $20.00

POHL, Frederik. *Jem.* 1978. St Martin. 1st ed. F/F. P3. $20.00

POHL, Frederik. *Jem.* 1979. London. Gollancz. 1st ed. F/F. N3. $15.00

POHL, Frederik. *Merchant's War.* 1984. St Martin. 1st ed. F/F. N3. $15.00

POHL, Frederik. *Ninth Galaxy Reader.* 1966. Doubleday. 1st ed. NF/VG clip. N3. $20.00

POHL, Frederik. *Outnumbering the Dead.* 1990. Legend. 1st ed. F/F. P3. $25.00

POHL, Frederik. *Second If Reader of SF.* 1968. Doubleday. 1st ed. VG/VG. P3. $25.00

POHL, Frederik. *Starburst.* 1982. Del Rey. 1st ed. VG/VG. P3. $15.00

POHL, Frederik. *Way the Future Was: A Memoir.* 1978. Ballantine. 1st ed. F/NF. N3. $10.00

POHL, Frederik. *Years of the City.* 1984. Timescape. 1st ed. F/F. P3. $20.00

POHL, P. Alfredus. *Historia Populi Israel...* 1933. Rome. Apud Pont. 194p. xl. H10. $17.50

POINSETT, Joel Roberts. *Notes on Mexico Made in 1822...* 1969. NY. Praeger. VG. N2. $12.50

POINTER, Michael. *Public Life of Sherlock Holmes.* 1975. Newton Abbot. 1st ed. ils. F/F. S6. $35.00

POINTER, Priscilla. *How To Draw Children.* 1943. The Studio. 1st Am ed. brd. VG+/worn. M5. $30.00

POLE, David. *Later Philosophy of Ludwig Wittgenstein...* 1958. London. U of London/Athlone. thin 8vo. 132p. VG/clip. G1. $35.00

POLING, Daniel A. *Romance of Jesus: Favorite Telling of the Favorite Story.* 1953. Assn Pr. 236p. G/worn. B29. $3.50

POLIT, Manuel Maria Espinosa. *Perfect Obedience: Commentary on the Letter...St Ingatius...* 1947. Westminster. Newman. 331p. H10. $25.00

POLITI, Leo. *At the Palace Gates.* 1967. Viking. 7th prt. 64p. VG/VG. A3. $15.00

POLITI, Leo. *Juanita.* 1948. Scribner. 1st ed. inscr/sgn/dtd 1952. 4to. cloth. VG/G. A3. $100.00

POLITI, Leo. *Mr Fong's Toy Shop.* 1978. Scribner. 1st ed. ils. F/VG. P2. $55.00

POLITI, Leo. *Piccolo's Prank.* 1965. Scribner. 1st ed. ils. F/VG. P2. $75.00

POLK, William R. *United States & the Arab World.* 1965. Cambridge. 1st ed. 320p. xl. VG. W1. $12.00

POLK. *Island of CA: History of the Myth.* 1991. np. 398p. F/F. A4. $95.00

POLLACK, J.H. *Dr Sam: An American Tragedy.* 1972. Chicago. 1st ed. VG/VG. B5. $22.50

POLLARD, Edward A. *First Year of the War.* 1863 (1862). NY. Richardson. 368p. gilt gr cloth. VG. M20. $75.00

POLLARD, Edward A. *Lost Cause.* 1866. 1st ed. 752p. O8. $85.00

POLLARD, Josephine. *Life of George Washington in Words of One Syllable.* early 20th century. McLoughlin. 120p. pict cloth. VG+. B14. $60.00

POLLEN, Anne. *Mother Mabel Digby...* 1914. Longman Gr. ils. 404p. H10. $16.50

POLLEY, Robert L. *America the Beautiful in Words of John F Kennedy.* 1964. Elm Grove, WI. Country Beautiful Foundation. 4to. 98p. VG. M10. $5.00

POLLITT, Levin Irving. *Hist of Brn Memorial Presbyterian Church 1870-1945.* 1945. Baltimore. 1st ed. 166p. cloth. VG. M8. $37.50

POLLITZ, Edward A. *Forty-First Thief.* 1975. Delacorte. 1st ed. VG/VG. P3. $15.00

POLLOCK, J.C. *Faith of Russian Evangelicals.* 1964. McGraw Hill. 190p. VG/dj. B29. $4.50

POLLOCK, J.C. *Mission MIA.* 1982. Crown. 1st ed. F/F. P3. $16.00

POLLOK, Robert. *Course of Time: A Poem.* 1850. NY. Clark Austin. 328p. cloth. G. H1. $16.00

POLO, Marco. *Travels of Marco Polo.* 1954. LEC. 2 vol. ils/sgn Nikolai Lapshin. F/case. M19. $50.00

POLTARNEES, Welleran. *All Mirrors Are Magic Mirrors.* 1972. Gr Tiger. ils/pl. 61p. VG/wrp. S11. $20.00

POLZER, Charles. *Rules & Precepts of Jusuit Missions of NW New Spain.* 1976. AZ U. index/bibliography. 141p. F/F. B19. $25.00

POMERANZ, Gary. *Out at Home.* 1985. Houghton Mifflin. ARC. sgn. RS. F/F. P8. $30.00

POMEROY, Vivian. *Enchanted Children.* 1925. Houghton Mifflin. 1st ed. ils HI Bacharach. VG/G. P2. $20.00

POMET, Pierre. *Historie Generale des Drogues, Simples et Composees...* 1735. Paris. Estienne Ganeau. 1 vol only. 55 engraved pl. 306p. G7. $150.00

PONDOEV, G.S. *Notes of a Soviet Doctor.* 1959. NY. 238p. VG. G7. $25.00

PONSAT, Georges. *Romance of the River.* nd. Dodd Mead. 8vo. ils EJ Detmold. 290p. VG. D6. $25.00

PONSONBY, D.A. *Dogs in Clover.* 1954. London. Hutchinson. 1st ed. 192p. cloth. F/F. R2. $35.00

PONSOT, Marie. *Chinese Fairy Tales.* 1973. Golden. 1st revised ed. glazed brd. VG. M5. $20.00

PONSOT, Marie. *Chinese Fairy Tales.* 1973 (1960). Golden/Western. 1st revised ed. NF. C8. $35.00

PONSOT, Marie. *Fairy Tale Book.* 1958. Simon Schuster. 1st/A ed. ils Adrienne Segur. glazed brd. VG. scarce. M5. $50.00

POOLE, John. *Hamlet Travestie: In 3 Acts With Burlesque Annotations...* 1812. London. Richardson. 4th ed. inscr to famous Eng actor. VG. B4. $475.00

POOR, Henry Varnum. *Artist Sees Alaska.* 1945. NY. ils. 279p. VG. A17. $14.50

POORTVLIET, R. *Dutch Treat.* 1981. NY. 1st ed. VG/VG. B5. $50.00

POPE, Alexander. *Correspondence of...* 1956. Oxford. 5 vol. 1st ed. edit George Sherburn. NF/NF. C2. $125.00

POPE, Alexander. *Selecta Poemata Italorum.* 1740. London. 2 vol. 1st ed. raised bands. A15. $200.00

POPE, Gustavus. *Journey to Mars.* 1974. Hyperion. rpt of 1894 ed. F/dj. M2. $15.00

POPE, John. *Report of Major General John Pope.* 1863. GPO. 8vo. lg fld map (removed). 256p. H9. $250.00

POPPER, Karl R. *Logic of Scientific Discovery.* 1959. Basic Books. 1st Eng-language ed/1st Am prt. 479p. cloth. VG/dj. G1. $50.00

POPPER, Karl R. *Phantasien Eines Realisten.* 1909 (1899). Dresden/Leipzig. Carl Reissner. revised ed. prt gr brd. G1. $75.00

PORAZINSKA, Janina. *Enchanted Book, Tale From Krakow.* 1987. NY. Harcourt Brace. 1st ed. trans Bozena Smith. M/M. C8. $22.50

PORGES, Irwin. *Edgar Rice Burroughs.* 1975. Bringham Young U. 1st ed. VG. P3. $25.00

PORTENS, Stanley D. *Maze Test & Mental Differences.* 1933. Vineland, NJ. Smith. 192p. G. K4. $25.00

PORTER, Burton P. *Old Canal Days.* 1942. Columbus, OH. 1st ed. 469p. VG. B18. $65.00

PORTER, E. *Fall River Tragedy.* 1985. Portland. facsimile of 1893 ed. VG. B5. $35.00

PORTER, Eliot. *Intimate Landscapes.* 1979. Metropolitan Mus Art. 1st ed. hc. mc pl. F. S9. $125.00

PORTER, Eliot. *Nature's Chaos.* 1990. Viking. 1st ed. F/F. B3. $30.00

PORTER, Gene Stratton. *Harvester.* 1911. Grosset Dunlap. 564p. NF. S12. $30.00

PORTER, Gene Stratton. *Keeper of the Bees.* 1925. Doubleday Page. 1st ed. brd. G. P3. $25.00

PORTER, Gene Stratton. *Laddie.* nd. Grosset Dunlap. 401p. F/G. H1. $20.00

PORTER, Gene Stratton. *Laddie: A True Blue Story.* 1913. Doubleday Page. 1st ed. brd. G+. P3. $30.00

PORTER, Hoah. *Elements of Moral Science, Theoretical & Practical.* 1887. Scribner. 575p. paneled pebbled cloth. G1. $30.00

PORTER, Hoah. *Human Intellect With Intro Upon Psychology & the Soul.* 1890 (1868). Scribner. 4th ed/later prt. 673p. Victorial cloth. G1. $28.50

PORTER, Horace. *Campaigning With Grant.* 1897. NY. morocco/brd. H4. $40.00

PORTER, Horace. *Our Young Aeroplane Scouts in Russia...* 1915. NY. Al Burt. 1st ed? 8vo. 252p. VG. W1. $15.00

PORTER, Joyce. *Dover & the Unkindest Cut of All.* 1967. Scribner. 1st Am ed. F/F. S6. $25.00

PORTER, Joyce. *Dover Beats the Band.* 1991. Woodstock. Foul Play. ARC/1st Am ed. F/wrp. B2. $25.00

PORTER, Joyce. *Dover One.* 1964. Scribner. 1st ed. VG/VG. P3. $40.00

PORTER, Katherine Anne. *Christmas Story.* 1967. Delacorte. ARC/1st ed. inscr. RS. gilt brd. F/dj. B24. $250.00

PORTER, Katherine Anne. *Flowering Judas & Other Stories.* 1940. NY. Modern Lib. 1st ed. sgn. NF/VG+. A11. $65.00

PORTER, Katherine Anne. *Hacienda.* 1934. Harrison of Paris. 1/895. F/F case. w/prospectus. B2. $100.00

PORTER, Mark. *Duel on the Cinders.* 1960. Simon Schuster. 1st ed. Win Hadley #6. 218p. VG/dj. M20. $10.00

PORTER, Mark. *Winning Pitcher.* 1960. Simon Schuster. 1st ed. VG/VG. P8. $22.50

PORTER. *Negro in the United States, a Selected Bibliography.* 1970. Lib of Congress. 327p. VG. A4. $75.00

PORTIS, Charles. *True Grit.* 1968. Simon Schuster. 1st ed/author's 2nd book. NF/NF. L3. $75.00

POST, Alfred C. *Observations on Cure of Strabismus.* 1841. NY. 7 Nathaniel Currier lithos. 67p. limp cloth. B14. $300.00

POST, C.C. *Ten Years a Cowboy.* 1896. np. 471p. emb gilt bdg. VG. E5. $35.00

POST, Melville D. *Methods of Uncle Abner.* 1974. Boulder. Aspen Pr. 1st collected ed. F/F. M15. $35.00

POST, Melville D. *Mountain School Teacher.* 1922. NY. Appleton. 1st ed. VG. M15. $45.00

POSTELLO, Gulielmo. *De Magistratibus Atheniensium Liber, ad Intelligendam...* 1551. Basileae. early vellum. M11. $500.00

POSTON, Charles D. *Building a State in Apache Land.* 1963. Aztec. ils/notes/index. 174p. NF/NF. B19. $30.00

POSY, Arnold. *Israeli Tales & Legends.* 1948. Block. ils Morgan. VG/G. B17. $4.00

POTOK, Chaim. *Chosen.* 1967. Simon Schuster. later prt. VG+/VG. P8. $10.00

POTOK, Chaim. *Promise.* 1969. Knopf. 1st ed. 358p. F/clip. H1. $18.00

POTTER, Ambrose George. *Bibliography of Rubaiyat of Omar Khayyam...* 1929. London. Ingpen Grant. 1st ed. 1/300. 8vo. 314p. VG. $350.00

POTTER, Beatrix. *Pie & Patty-Pan.* 1905. Warne. early prt. 52p. tan cloth/pict label. M20. $100.00

POTTER, Beatrix. *Tailor of Gloucester.* 1903. London. Warne. 1st trade ed. inscr/dtd 1904. 27 mc pl. VG+. D6. $1,000.00

POTTER, Beatrix. *Tale of Mr Toad.* 1912. London. Warne. 3rd prt. earliest ep. gr stp gray brd. G. M5. $75.00

POTTER, Beatrix. *Tale of Peter Rabbit.* ca 1920. Saalfield #1172. 10p muslin cloth/bdg. G. A3. $10.50

POTTER, Beatrix. *Tale of Peter Rabbit.* 1932. Platt Munk. pirated ed. 12p. VG/wrp. M5. $22.00

POTTER, David. *Debating in the Colonial Chartered Colleges 1642-1900.* 1944. Columbia. 158p. worn wrp. A10. $15.00

POTTER, Dennis. *Pennies From Heaven.* 1981. London. 1st ed. inscr. NF/glossy 8vo wrp. scarce. A11. $65.00

POTTER, Dennis. *Sufficient Carbohydrate.* 1983. London. Faber. PBO. inscr. F/wrp. A11. $50.00

POTTER, Henry H. *Catechism of Health; or, Plain & Simple Rules...* 1831. Phil. Journal of Health. 5th ed. 12mo. broken leather. H10. $65.00

POTTER, Israel R. *Life & Remarkable Adventures of Israel R Potter.* 1824. Providence. Trumbull. 1st ed. 12mo. 108p. old calf. K1. $150.00

POTTER, Jeremy. *Death in the Forest.* 1977. Constable. 1st ed. F/F. P3. $18.00

POTTER, Miriam Clark. *Pinafore Pocket Story Book.* 1922. Dutton. ils Sophia Balcom. 360p. VG. P2. $25.00

POTTER, Russell. *Little Red Ferry Boat.* ca 1947. Holt. 50p. VG. B10. $10.00

POTTER, Samuel O.L. *Compend of Materia Medica Therapeutics & Prescription...* 1908. Blakiston's Son. 7th ed. 292p. G+. H1. $10.00

POTTER, Theodore Edgar. *Autobiography of...* 1978. Berrien Springs. facsimile of 1913 ed. 228p. F. A17. $17.50

POTTLE, F. *Boswell in Holland 1763-1764.* 1952. NY. 1st ed. ils. 433 p. F/dj. A17. $15.00

POTTLE, F. *Literary Career of James Boswell...* 1929. np. 379p. F/F/NF case. A4. $350.00

POUCHELLE, Marie. *Body & Surgery in the Middle Ages.* 1990. New Brunswick. 1st ed. 277p. dj. A13. $35.00

POUCHET, F.A. *Universe.* nd. London. 13th ed. ils/pl. VG. M17. $35.00

POULSSON, Emilie. *Finger Plays.* 1893. Boston. Lothrop. 1st ed. sm 4to. 72p. F. D6. $75.00

POUND, Arthur. *The Penns of Pennsylvania & England.* 1932. NY. Macmillan. 1st ed. 8vo. 349p. VG. V3. $17.50

POUND, Ezra. *Cantos of Ezra Pound.* 1933. NY. Farrar Rinehart. 8vo. 22p. F/prt wrp. H5. $250.00

POUND, Ezra. *Canzoni.* 1911. London. Elkin Mathews. 1st ed/2nd issue bdg (no author on spine). brn brd. VG. C6. $400.00

POUND, Ezra. *Cathay.* 1915. London. 1st ed. NF/NF. C2. $350.00

POUND, Ezra. *Lustra With Earlier Poems.* 1917. Knopf. 1st ed. Ralph Block's copy. bl prt yel brd. VG+. Q1. $200.00

POUND, Ezra. *Lustra.* 1917. Knopf. 1st Am trade ed. 8vo. 202p. orig yel brd. NF/dj. C6. $850.00

POUND, Ezra. *Personae.* 1909. London. Elkin Mathews. 1st ed/author's 3rd book poems/1st hc. 59p. VG. C6. $600.00

POUND, Ezra. *Poems Selected From Personae, Exultations & Canzoniere.* (1910). Sm Maynard. 2nd imp. gr prt tan brd. F/NF. Q1. $750.00

POUND, Ezra. *Prolegomena I: How To Read.* 1932. Toulon. Cabasson. 1st ed thus. 8vo. 159p. VG/prt wrp. C6. $150.00

POUND, Ezra. *Provenca.* 1910. Sm Maynard. 1st ed/1st Am book poems. 12mo. 84p. tan brd. NF/dj. C6. $750.00

POUND, Ezra. *Translations of Ezra Pound.* (1953). London. Faber. 1st ed. intro Hugh Kenner. NF/dj. Q1. $150.00

POUND, Ezra. *Umbra: Early Poems of Ezra Pound.* 1920. London. Elkin Mathews. 1st ed. 1/1000. 128p. gray brd/beige spine. VG. C6. $350.00

POUND, Reginald. *Scott of the Antarctic.* 1967. NY. Coward McCann. 1st Am ed/2nd imp. VG/dj. P4. $35.00

POUND, Roscoe. *Contemporary Juristic Theory.* 1940. Ward Ritchie. 1st ed. 83p. NF/remnant. D3. $35.00

POURADE, Richard F. *Anaza Conquers the Desert.* 1971. Copley. 1st ed. ils/index. F/NF. B19. $45.00

POURNELLE, Jerry. *Step Farther Out.* 1980. WH Allen. 1st ed. VG. p3. $20.00

POWELL, A. Van Buren. *Mystery of the 15 Souls.* 1938. Goldsmith. 1st ed. F/dj. M2. $30.00

POWELL, Agnes Baden. *Handbook for Girl Scouts.* 1917. NY. 1st ed. ils/index. 154p. linen. G. B5. $60.00

POWELL, Anthony. *Fisher King.* 1986. Heinemann. 1st ed. sgn. F/F clip. L3. $150.00

POWELL, Anthony. *Hearing Secret Harmonies.* 1975. London. Heinemann. 1st ed. sgn. NF/NF. L3. $250.00

POWELL, Anthony. *O, How the Wheel Becomes It!* 1983. London. Heinemann. 1st ed. sgn. F/NF. L3. $150.00

POWELL, Anthony. *Question of Upbringing.* 1951. Scribner. 1st Am ed. NF/NF. B2. $175.00

POWELL, Calvin. *Poems, Hymns, & Divine Songs.* 1832. Dansville, NY. self pub. 1st ed. 12mo. contemporary calf. M1. $175.00

POWELL, E. Alexander. *By Camel & Car to the Peacock Throne.* 1923. Century. 1st ed. 392p. VG. W1. $18.00

POWELL, E. Alexander. *In Barbary, Tunisia, Algeria, Morocco & the Sahara.* 1926. London/NY. Century. 1st ed. 8vo. 65 pl. G. W1. $9.00

POWELL, Fay Ellen. *That Kitty Colette.* 1988. Saltbush. 1/200. ils. F/sans. B19. $10.00

POWELL, Gordon. *Happiness Is a Habit & Release From Guilt & Fear.* 1961. Guidebosts. G. B29. $3.50

POWELL, J.W. *Lands of the Arid Region of the US.* 1983. Harvard Common. ils/maps/charts. NF/wrp. B19. $17.50

POWELL, J.W. *Sixth Annual Report of the Bureau of Ethnology.* 1888. WA. 669p. olive cloth. G+. M20. $95.00

POWELL, Lawrence Clark. *Alchemy of Books.* 1954. Ward Ritchie. 1st ed. 263p. NF/sans. B19. $95.00

POWELL, Lawrence Clark. *AZ: A Hist.* 1976. Norton. ils/index. F/F. B19. $25.00

POWELL, Lawrence Clark. *Bibliographers of the Golden State.* 1967. CA U. 1st ed. NF/wrp. B19. $35.00

POWELL, Lawrence Clark. *Books in My Baggage.* 1960. World. 257p. NF/VG. B19. $50.00

POWELL, Lawrence Clark. *Books West Southwest: Essays on Writers...* 1957. Ward Ritchie. 1st ed. 157p. VG+. B19. $75.00

POWELL, Lawrence Clark. *California Classics.* 1989. Capra. ils/index. 393p. M/wrp. B19. $12.00

POWELL, Lawrence Clark. *El Morro.* 1984. Capra. 129p. NF. B19. $30.00

POWELL, Lawrence Clark. *Eucalyptus Fair: Memoir in Form of a Novel.* 1992. Books W Southwest. 1st ltd ed. 1/50. sgn Powell/Ritchie. M/case. A18. $150.00

POWELL, Lawrence Clark. *From the Heartland: Profiles of People & People...* 1976. Northland. 1st ed. ils Bettina Steinke. F/dj. A18. $40.00

POWELL, Lawrence Clark. *Islands of Books.* 1991. Dawson. sgn. 111p. M. B19. $10.00

POWELL, Lawrence Clark. *Land of Fact.* 1992. Hist Soc S CA. ltd ed. sgn. 1/150. F. B19. $100.00

POWELL, Lawrence Clark. *Land of Fact: Companion to Land of Fiction.* 1992. Hist Soc S CA. ltd ed. 1/500. M. A18. $30.00

POWELL, Lawrence Clark. *Land of Fiction: 32 Novels About S CA...* 1991. Hist Soc S CA. 1st prt. 1/100. sgn. M. A18. $40.00

POWELL, Lawrence Clark. *My Haydn Commonplace Book.* 1983. private prt. F. B19. $25.00

POWELL, Lawrence Clark. *Mysterious Transformation.* 1993. Books W Southwest. 1st ltd ed. 1/50. sgn Powell/Ritchie/Sanders. M/case. A18. $150.00

POWELL, Lawrence Clark. *Passion for Books.* 1958. World. special ltd ed. sgn. 1/975. F/NF case. B19. $110.00

POWELL, Lawrence Clark. *Portrait of My Father.* 1986. Capra. 1st ed. sgn. 111p. NF. B19. $25.00

POWELL, Lawrence Clark. *River Between.* 1979. Capra. sgn. 107p. VG. B19. $20.00

POWELL, Lawrence Clark. *Robinson Jeffers: Man & His Work.* 1934. Los Angeles. 1st ed/author's 2nd book. 1/750. VG/VG. Q1. $250.00

POWELL, Lawrence Clark. *Southwestern Book Trials: A Reader's Guide...* 1964. Horn Wallace. revised ed. 1/1000. NF/NF. B19. $65.00

POWELL, Richard. *Blues Aesthetic: Blk Culture & Modernism.* 1989. WA, DC. WA Project for the Arts. 104p. F/wrp. B2. $25.00

POWELL, Talmadge. *Cellar Team.* 1972. Whitman. 1st ed. pict bdg. VG. P8. $4.00

POWELL, Talmage. *Mission: Impossible.* 1970. Whitman. 1st ed. pict brd. F/sans. F4. $15.00

POWELL, Talmage. *Smasher.* 1959. Macmillan. 1st ed. w/sgn label. VG/VG. P3. $35.00

POWELL, Thomas Reed. *Current Current of Commerce Clause & State Taxation...* 1940. Columbia. National Tax Assn. stapled wrp. M11. $10.00

POWELL, William S. *St Luke's Episcopal Church 1753-1953.* 1953. Salisbury, NC. St Luke Episcopal Church. 1st ed. 76p. VG/prt wrp. M8. $37.50

POWELL. *North Carolina Fiction, 1734-1957.* 1958. NC U. ils. 207p. NF. A4. $85.00

POWELSON, Jack. *Dialogue With Friends.* 1988. Horizon. 1st ed. pb. 164p. VG. V3. $8.00

POWER, D'Arcy. *Portraits of Dr William Harvey.* 1913. Oxford. 20 pl. 49p. brd. G7. $135.00

POWERS, Alfred. *Long Way to Frisco.* 1951. Little Brn. 1st ed. ils James Daugherty. VG+/VG. P2. $35.00

POWERS, J.F. *Look How the Fish Live.* 1975. London. Hogarth. PBO. sgn. F/wrp. A11. $30.00

POWERS, J.F. *Morte D'Urban.* 1962. Garden City. 1st ed/author's 1st novel. sgn. F/VG+ clip. A11. $60.00

POWERS, Richard. *Prisoner's Dilemma.* 1988. Morrow. 1st ed/author's 2nd book. F/F. B4. $85.00

POWERS, Richard. *Three Farmers on Their Way to a Dance.* 1985. London. Weidenfeld Nicolson. F/F. S9. $75.00

POWERS, Robert M. *Shuttle: World's First Spaceship.* 1979. Stackpole. pb. ils. 255p. G. K5. $5.00

POWERS, Samuel A. *Variola.* 1882. Boston. 21 pl. cloth. B14. $95.00

POWERS, Tim. *Anubis Gates.* 1989. Shingletown. Ziesing. 1st Am hc ed. F/F. T2. $25.00

POWERS, Tim. *Dinner at Deviant's Place.* 1985. Ace. 1st hc ed. sgn. F/SF BC issue. F4. $18.00

POWERS, Tim. *Drawing of the Dark.* 1991. Hypatia. 1st hc ed. sgn Powers/Jeter/Blaylock. 1/300. leather. F. T2. $75.00

POWERS, Tim. *Last Call.* 1992. Morrow. 1st ed. sgn. F/F. T2. $115.00

POWERS, Tim. *On Stranger Tides.* 1987. Ace. 1st ed. sgn. F/F. T2. $45.00

POWERS, Tim. *Skies Discrowned.* 1993. Huntington Beach. Cahill. 1st hc ed. sgn Powers/Blaylock/Parks. 1/300. F/F. T2. $75.00

POWERS, Tom. *Scotch Circus.* 1934. Houghton Mifflin. 1st ed. ils Lois Lenski. wht-dotted red cloth. VG. P2. $60.00

POWYS, John Cowper. *Dorothy M Richardson.* 1931. London. Joiner Steele. 1st ed. F/NF. B2. $100.00

POWYS, John Cowper. *Three Fantasies.* 1986. Carcanet. UP. F/prt bl wrp. B3. $25.00

POWYS, Llewelyn. *Now That the Gods Are Dead.* 1932. NY. Equinox. 1/400. sgn Powys/Lynd Ward. bl-striped cloth. NF. F1. $325.00

POYER, David C. *Stepfather Bank.* 1987. St Martin. 1st ed. F/dj. P3. $10.00

POYER, Joe. *Contract.* 1978. Atheneum. 1st ed. VG. P3. $10.00

POYNTER, F.N.L. *Medicine & Culture.* 1969. London. 1st ed. 322p. A13. $40.00

POYNTER, F.N.L. *Selected Writings of William Clowes 1544-1604.* 1948. London. 8 pl. 279p. dj. G7. $25.00

POYS, T.F. *Fred My Swine.* 1926. London. ltd ed. sgn. 1/100. VG/wrp. fragile. A1. $50.00

PRADINES, Maurice. *Philosophie de la Sensation...* 1928. London. Oxford. 280p. VG/gray wrp. G1. $40.00

PRAG, Hugo Steiner. *Designs for a Machzor.* 1963. NY. folio-sized loose plates. VG+/orig binder. A1. $300.00

PRAGER, Arthur. *Rascals at Large.* 1971. Doubleday. 1st ed. VG/VG. P3. $25.00

PRATCHETT, Terry. *Strata.* 1994. Eng. Doubleday. ltd ed. sgn. 1/500. F/F. P3. $45.00

PRATER, Arnold. *Release From Phoniness.* 1968. World. 123p. G/dj. B29. $2.75

PRATHER, Richard S. *Amber Effect.* 1986. Tor. 1st ed. F/F. P3. $13.00

PRATHER, Richard S. *Three's a Shroud.* 1973. Gold Lion. VG/dj. P3. $20.00

PRATT, Anne. *Flowering Plants, Grasses, Sedges & Ferns...* ca 1874. London. ils/pl. 2119p. aeg. gilt gr cloth. B26. $475.00

PRATT, Fletcher. *Alien Planet.* 1962. Avalon. 1st ed. F/dj. M2. $30.00

PRATT, Fletcher. *Double in Space.* 1951. Doubleday. 1st ed. NF/dj. P3. $40.00

PRATT, Fletcher. *Night Work.* 1946. Holt. 1st ed. VG. P3. $30.00

PRATT & PRATT. *Guide to Early Am Houses South.* 1956. NY. 227p. VG/worn. A17. $15.00

PREISS, Byron. *Planets.* 1985. Bantam. 1st ed. F/F. N3. $25.00

PREISS, Byron. *Raymond Chandler's Philip Marlowe.* 1988. Knopf. 1st ed. F/F. P3. $19.00

PREISS, R. *Ultimate Dracula.* 1991. Dell. 1st hc ed. F/dj. F4. $15.00

PRELINGER & ZIMET. *Ego-Psychological Approach to Character Assessment.* 1964. NY. Free Pr of Glencoe. 211p. F. K4. $10.00

PREMINGER, Alex. *Princeton Encyclopedia of Poetry & Poetics.* 1974. Princeton. enlarged/2nd ed. 992p. F/NF. B2. $35.00

PRESCOT, Dray; see Bulmer, Kenneth.

PRESCOTT, H.F.M. *Once to Sinai. Further Pilgrimage of Friar Felix Fabri.* 1958. Macmillan. 1st prt. 310p. VG/dj. W1. $12.00

PRESCOTT, William H. *Hist of Conquest of Mexico.* 1892. McKay. 3 vol. VG. H1. $30.00

PRESCOTT, William H. *World of the Incas.* 1974. Tudor. ils. 156p. VG. F3. $15.00

PRESCOTT, William H. *World of the Incas.* 1989. Minerva. photos. F. P4. $15.00

PRESTON, A. *Battleships of World War I.* 1972. NY. Galahad. ils. 260p. dj. T7. $35.00

PRESTON, Raymond. *Chaucer.* 1952. London. Sheed Ward. 1st ed. ftspc. 325p. VG/VG. A17. $9.50

PRESTON, Richard. *Hot Zone.* 1994. Random. 1st ed. F/F. T2. $35.00

PRESTON-MAFHAM, Ken. *Cacti & Succulents in Habitat.* 1994. NY. photos. M/dj. B26. $24.95

PREUSS, Paul. *Starfire.* 1988. Tor. 1st ed. F/F. P3. $18.00

PRICE, Anthony. *Gunner Kelly.* 1984. Doubleday. 1st Am ed. F/F. S6. $27.50

PRICE, Anthony. *October Men.* 1973. London. Gollancz. 1st ed. F/F. M15. $90.00

PRICE, E. Hoffman. *Far Lands Other Days.* 1975. Carcosa. 1st ed. F/F. P3. $60.00

PRICE, E. Hoffman. *Strange Gateways.* 1967. Arkham. 1st ed. 1/2007. F/F. scarce. T2. $100.00

PRICE, Edwin. *Extracts From the Papers of Edwin Price...* 1820. Phil. Kite. 24mo. 82p. leather. G. V3. $15.00

PRICE, Emerson. *Inn of That Journey.* 1939. Caldwell. 1st ed/author's 1st book. fwd Jack Conroy. F/F. A17. $20.00

PRICE, Eugenia. *Early Will I Seek Thee.* 1985. Guideposts. 238p. VG/dj. B29. $4.75

PRICE, Ira Maurice. *Dramatic Story of Old Testament Hist.* 1935. Revell. 471p. VG. B29. $6.50

PRICE, Lucien. *Dialogues of Alfred North Whitehead.* 1956. Little Brn. 396p. VG/VG clip. B33. $25.00

PRICE, Nancy. *Sleeping With the Enemy.* 1987. Simon Schuster. 1st ed. F/dj. F4. $45.00

PRICE, Nancy. *Tails & Tales.* 1945. London. Gollancz. 1st ed. 135p. cloth. F. R2. $25.00

PRICE, Reynolds. *Blue Calhoun.* 1992. Atheneum. 1st ed. F/NF. B2. $30.00

PRICE, Reynolds. *Clear Pictures.* 1989. Atheneum. 1st ed. F/F. B4. $45.00

PRICE, Reynolds. *Country Mouse, City Mouse.* 1981. NC Wesleyan College. 1st ed. 1/500. F/wrp. C6. $35.00

PRICE, Reynolds. *Foreseeable Future.* 1991. Atheneum. 1st ed. F/F. B4. $45.00

PRICE, Reynolds. *Foreseeable Future.* 1991. Atheneum. 1st ed. sgn. F/F. B2. $50.00

PRICE, Reynolds. *Generous Man.* 1967. Chatto Windus. 1st ed. VG/VG. B3. $25.00

PRICE, Reynolds. *Good Hearts.* 1988. Atheneum. 1st ed. NF/NF. E3. $20.00

PRICE, Reynolds. *Good Hearts.* 1988. Atheneum. 1st ed. sgn. F/F. B2. $60.00

PRICE, Reynolds. *Long & Happy Life.* 1962. Atheneum. 1st ed/author's 1st book. 8vo. 195p. brn cloth. NF/dj. C6. $125.00

PRICE, Reynolds. *Love & Work.* 1968. Atheneum. 1st ed. F/F. B2. $40.00

PRICE, Reynolds. *New Music.* 1990. NY. Dramatists Play Service. 3 vol. 1st separate ed. F/wrp. C6. $45.00

PRICE, Reynolds. *Private Contentment.* 1984. Atheneum. 1st ed. 8vo. 136p. F/dj. C6. $40.00

PRICE, Reynolds. *Things Themselves.* 1972. Atheneum. 1st ed/author's 1st book nonfiction. 269p. F/F. C6. $55.00

PRICE, Richard. *Wanderers.* 1974. Boston. Houghton Mifflin. 1st ed/author's 1st book. VG/VG. S9. $50.00

PRICE, Richard. *Wanderers.* 1974. Boston. 1st ed/author's 1st book. sgn. F/F. A11. $65.00

PRICE, Richard. *Wanderers.* 1974. Houghton Mifflin. UP/author's 1st book. VG/wrp. L3. $250.00

PRICE, Robert M. *Tales of the Lovecraft Mythos.* 1992. Minneapolis. Fedogan Bremer. 1st ed. F/F. N3. $20.00

PRICE, Robert. *Black Forbidden Things.* 1992. Starmont. F. M2. $12.00

PRICE, Willard. *Roving South: Rio Grande to Patagonia.* 1948. John Day. 1st ed. ils/maps. 373p. VG/dj. F3. $15.00

PRICHARD, H. Hesketh. *Through the Heart of Patagonia.* 1902. NY. Appleton. 1st Am ed. 8vo. 346p. gilt red cloth. VG. P4. $175.00

PRIDE, Nigel. *Butterfly Sings to Picaya: Travels in Mexico...* 1978. London. Constable. 1st ed. 367p. VG/dj. F3. $20.00

PRIEST, Christopher. *Anticipations.* 1978. Faber. 1st ed. M/dj. M21. $15.00

PRIEST, Christopher. *Glamour.* 1984. Jonathan Cape. 1st ed. sgn. F/F. P3. $30.00

PRIEST, Christopher. *Space Machine.* 1976. Harper Row. 1st ed. VG/VG. P3. $20.00

PRIEST, Josiah. *American Antiquities & Discoveries in the West.* 1833. Albany. 400p. full leather. B18. $95.00

PRIEST, Josiah. *Anti-Universalist; or, Hist of Fallen Angels of Scriptures.* 1837. Albany, NY. Munsell. 1st ed. 8vo. 420p. contemporary calf/leather labels. M1. $275.00

PRIEST, Josiah. *Slavery, As It Relates to the Negro, or African Race.* 1844. Albany. 2nd ed. G. H7. $75.00

PRIESTLEY, Heather. *All About the Beagle.* 1973. London. Pelham. 1st ed. ils. 140p. cloth. M/dj. R2. $12.00

PRIESTLEY, Herbert Ingram. *Diary of Pedro Fages: CO River Campaign 1781-1782.* 1913. CA U. 1st ed. 101p. NF/wrp. B19. $40.00

PRIESTLEY, J.B. *Festival at Farbridge.* 1951. Heinemann. 1st ed. VG. P3. $30.00

PRIESTLEY, J.B. *Good Companions.* 1929. Harper. 1st Am ed. 640p. G. H1. $12.00

PRIESTLEY, J.B. *Good Companions.* 1929. Harper. 1st ed. VG. P3. $35.00

PRIESTLEY, J.B. *Lost Empires.* 1966. Rpt Soc. VG/VG. P3. $8.00

PRIESTLEY, J.B. *Man & Time.* 1964. Doubleday. 4to. 319p. VG/VG. A8. $20.00

PRIESTLEY, J.B. *Town Major of Miracourt.* 1930. London. Heinemann. 1/525. sgn. 31p. teg. gilt full vellum. F/cb case. H5. $250.00

PRIESTLEY, Joseph. *Comparison of Instit of Moses With Those of the Hindoos...* 1799. Northumberland. self pub. 1st ed. 428p. calf. H10. $350.00

PRIESTLEY, Joseph. *Discourses on Evidence of Revealed Religion.* 1795. Boston. Spotswood. 2nd ed. 275p. leather. H10. $95.00

PRIME, E.D.G. *Around the World: Sketches of Travel Through Many Lands...* 1872. NY. 8vo. ils. 455p. cloth. O2. $60.00

PRIME, Samuel I. *Alhambra & the Kremlin.* (1873). NY. 12mo. ils. 482p. gilt gr cloth. VG. H3. $35.00

PRIME, Samuel I. *Travels in Europe & the East: Year in England, Scotland...* 1864. NY. 2 vol. emb cloth. F. O2. $110.00

PRIME, William C. *Pottery & Porcelain of All Times & Nations.* 1879. Harper. 3rd ed. thick 8vo. 531p. gilt gr cloth/rebacked. F1. $95.00

PRINCE & PRINCE. *Pomological Manual; or, Treatise on Fruits... Vol II.* 1831. NY. 1st ed. quarter cloth. F. H10. $85.00

PRINGLE, David. *Modern Fantasy, the Hundred Best Novels.* 1989. Peter Bedrick. 1st ed. F/F. P3. $18.00

PRINGLE, Patrick. *Jolly Roger: Story of Great Age of Piracy.* 1953. NY. Norton. ils. 294p. T7. $36.00

PRINGLE, Patrick. *Modern Adventurers Under the Sea.* ca 1959. Franklin Watts. 240p. VG/VG. B10. $12.00

PRINGLE-PATTISON, A. Seth. *Partly Studies in Philosophy of Religion.* 1930. Clarendon. 256p. bl cloth. G1. $40.00

PRISHVIN, M. *Treasure Trove of the Sun.* 1952. Viking. 1st ed. 79p. G+. B10. $25.00

PRITCHARD, Alan. *Alchemy: A Bibliography of Eng-Language Writings.* 1980. London. Routledge/Paul. 1st prt. 439p. F/F. B33. $85.00

PRITCHARD, James B. *Gibeon Where the Sun Stood Still.* nd. Princeton. 1st ed. 8vo. 176p. VG/dj. W1. $15.00

PRITCHARD, James B. *Hebrew Inscriptions & Stamps From Gibeon.* 1959. Phil. 1st ed. 32p. G/wrp. W1. $12.00

PRITCHETT, V.S. *Marching Spain.* 1928. London. Benn. 1st ed/author's 1st book. NF/NF. B4. $550.00

PRITCHETT, V.S. *When My Girl Comes Home.* 1961. NY. 1st Am ed. F/F. A17. $20.00

PRITZKE, Herbert. *Bedouin Doctor: Adventures of a German in the Middle East.* 1957. London. Weidenfeld Nicolson. 2nd imp. cloth. VG/tattered. W1. $25.00

PROAL, L. *Passion & Criminality: A Legal & Literary Study.* nd. Paris. 679p. buckram. VG. D3. $35.00

PROCTER, Maurice. *His Weight in Gold.* 1966. Harper Row. 1st ed. F/F. P3. $18.00

PROCTER, Maurice. *Rogue Running.* 1966. Harper Row. 1st ed. F/F. P3. $18.00

PROCTER. *Horse.* 1885. London. 2nd ed. 306p. cloth. G+. R2. $20.00

PROCTOR, F.B. *Treasury of Quotations on Religious Subjects.* 1977. Kregel. 816p. VG/dj. B29. $10.50

PROCTOR, L.B. *William H Seward As a Lawyer.* 1887. Albany, NY. 1st ed. 16mo. 30p. VG/new wrp. D3. $25.00

PROCTOR, Richard A. *Other Suns Than Ours.* 1908 (1887). Longman Gr. Silver Lib ed/new imp. sm 8vo. 419p. VG. K5. $35.00

PRODDOW, Penelope. *Demeter & Persephone: Homeric Hymn #2.* 1972. Doubleday. 1st ed. VG+. C8. $22.50

PROKOFIEFF, Serge. *Peter & the Wolf.* 1968. Franklin Watts. 2nd prt. F/F. C8. $22.50

PROKOSCH, Frederic. *Ballad of Love.* 1960. FSC. 1st ed. 311p. VG/dj. M20. $30.00

PROLMAN, Marilyn. *Story of the Constitution.* ca 1969. Children's Pr. 5th prt. xl. VG. B10. $10.00

PRONZINI, Bill. *Arbor House Treasury of Detective...* 1983. Arbor. 1st ed. VG/VG. P3. $20.00

PRONZINI, Bill. *Bindlestiff.* 1983. St Martin. 1st ed. F/F. T2. $15.00

PRONZINI, Bill. *Bindlestiff.* 1983. St Martin. 1st ed. sgn. F/F. O4. $40.00

PRONZINI, Bill. *Cat's Paw.* 1983. Richmond. Waves. 1st ed. sgn. 1/150. F/wrp/dj. M15. $45.00

PRONZINI, Bill. *Deadfall.* 1986. St Martin. 1st ed. sgn. F/F. O4. $25.00

PRONZINI, Bill. *Demons.* 1993. Delacorte. 1st ed. F/F. P3. $20.00

PRONZINI, Bill. *Dragonfire.* 1982. St Martin. 1st ed. F/F. M15. $25.00

PRONZINI, Bill. *Games.* 1976. Putnam. 1st ed. sgn. VG/VG. O4. $30.00

PRONZINI, Bill. *Graveyard Plots.* 1985. St Martin. 1st ed. NF/dj. P3. $25.00

PRONZINI, Bill. *Gun in Cheek.* 1982. CMG. 1st ed. sgn. F/F. O4. $30.00

PRONZINI, Bill. *Gun in Cheek: A Study in Alternative Crime Fiction.* 1982. CMG. 1st ed. F/F. T2. $22.00

PRONZINI, Bill. *Masques.* 1981. Arbor. 1st ed. F/F. T2. $15.00

PRONZINI, Bill. *Masques.* 1981. Arbor. 1st ed. sgn. F/F. O4. $25.00

PRONZINI, Bill. *Nightshades.* 1984. St Martin. 1st ed. F/F. F4. $25.00

PRONZINI, Bill. *Panic!* 1972. Random. 1st ed. VG/VG. P3. $40.00

PRONZINI, Bill. *Scattershot.* 1982. St Martin. 1st ed. F/F. P3. $30.00

PRONZINI, Bill. *Shackles.* 1988. St Martin. 1st ed. F/NF. M15. $22.50

PRONZINI, Bill. *Small Felonies.* 1988. St Martin. 1st ed. F/F. P3. $20.00

PRONZINI, Bill. *Stalker.* 1971. Random. 1st ed. sgn. F/F. M15. $60.00

PRONZINI, Bill. *Stalker.* 1971. Random. 1st ed/author's 1st book. sgn. F/NF. S6. $50.00

PRONZINI, Bill. *Undercurrent.* 1973. Random. 1st ed. F/F. M15. $30.00

PRONZINI, Bill. *Voodoo!* 1980. Arbor. 1st ed. NF/dj. F4. $15.00

PRONZINI & MULLER. *Kill or Cure.* 1985. Macmillan. 1st ed. sgns. F/F. O4. $30.00

PROSE, Francine. *Glorious Ones.* 1974. Atheneum. ARC/author's 2nd novel. inscr. RS. F/F. B4. $150.00

PROSKAUER, Julien J. *Dead Do Not Talk.* 1946. Harper. 1st ed. G+. N2. $10.00

PROTESTANT EPISCOPAL CHURCH. *Book of Common Prayer...* 1843. NY. Hewett. 1st ed. 105p. emb leather. H10. $165.00

PROUD, Robert. *Hist of Pennsylvania in North America.* 1797. Phil. 1st ed. full leather. G. E5. $150.00

PROUDHON, P.-J. *Qu'est-ce Que la Propriete?* 1873. Paris. Lacroix. Nouvelle ed. marbled paper brd/leather backstrip. worn. B2. $75.00

PROUDHON, P.-J. *Si Les Traites de 1815 ont Cesse d'Exister?* 1863. Paris. Dentu. 1st ed. lacks front wrp. B2. $125.00

PROULX, E. Annie. *Shipping News.* 1992. Scribner. UP. w/promo material. F/prt bl wrp. B3. $250.00

PROULX, E. Annie. *Shipping News.* 1993. Scribner. AP. F/prt wrp. S9. $350.00

PROUST, Marcel. *Jean Santeuil.* 1956. Simon Schuster. 1st Am ed. VG/dj. M20. $15.00

PROUTY. *Stella Dallas.* 1923. NY. 1st ed. VG/VG. B5. $25.00

PROVOL, W. Lee. *Pack Peddler.* 1933. np. 1st ed. 314p. VG. E5. $35.00

PRYCE-JONES, David. *Face of Defeat: Palestinian Refugees & Guerrillas.* 1973. HRW. 8vo. 2 full-p maps. 179p. xl. VG/dj. W1. $12.00

PRYOR, William Clayton. *Train Book: Photographic Picture Book With a Story.* ca 1933. Harcourt Brace. photos. G. B10. $12.00

PRYSE, James M. *Apocalypse Unsealed: Being Interpretation...* 1910. Los Angeles. 222p. VG. B33. $37.00

PSEUDOMAN, Akkad. *Zero to Eighty.* 1937. Scientific Pub. 1st ed. VG/VG. P3. $35.00

PSOMIADES & THOMADAKIS. *Greece, the New Europe & the Changing International Order...* 1993. NY. 8vo. 439p. O2. $20.00

PUCH, John. *Treatise on Science of Muscular Action.* ca 1970. Editions Medicina Rara. rpt of 1794 Dilly ed. 15 pl. half calf/linen. case. G7. $85.00

PUDNEY, John. *Suez: De Lesseps' Canal.* 1979. Praeger. 2nd prt. ils. 242p. NF/dj. W1. $7.00

PUFFER, Ethel D. *Psychology of Beauty.* 1905. Houghton Mifflin. 286p. prt pebbled crimson cloth. G1. $35.00

PUHARICH, Andrija. *Sacred Mushroom.* 1959. Doubleday. 1st ed. F/NF. B2. $60.00

PULLEN, J. *20th Maine.* 1957. Phil. 1st ed. sgn pres. VG/VG. B5. $85.00

PULLEN, J. *20th Maine.* 1957. Phil. 1st ed. VG/VG. B5. $60.00

PUMPIAN-MINDLIN, E. *Psychoanalysis As Science...* 1956. Basic Books. 2nd prt. 174p. yel cloth. G1. $28.50

PUNSHON, E.R. *Blue John Diamond.* 1929. Clode. 1st ed. VG. P3. $35.00

PUNSHON, E.R. *Crossword Murder.* 1934. Knopf. 1st Am ed. F/NF. M15. $35.00

PUPIN, Michael. *From Emmigrant to Inventor.* Oct 1924. Scribner. ils. 396p. G. H1. $6.00

PURDY, James. *Eustace Chisholm & the Works.* 1967. NY. 1st ed. F/F. A17. $17.50

PURDY, James. *Lessons & Complaints.* 1978. Nadja. 1/525. sgn. 8vo. 8p. F/stiff wrp. unopened. H5. $50.00

PURDY, James. *63: Dream Palace.* 1956. NY. 1st ed/author's 1st novel. sgn. F/wht wrp. A11. $135.00

PURDY, Susan. *Halloween Cookbook.* ca 1977. Franklin Watts. 2nd prt. 96p. VG. B10. $10.00

PURSER, Philip. *Four Days to the Fireworks.* 1965. Walker. 1st ed. VG/VG. P3. $13.00

PURVINE, Mary B. *Mary B Purvine, Pioneer Doctor.* 1958. Santa Barbara. 1/100. 4 photo pl. brn morocco. K1. $100.00

PURYEAR, Vernon J. *International Economics & Diplomacy in the Near East.* 1935. Stanford. 8vo. 264p. dj. O2. $35.00

PUSATERI, Samuel J. *Flora of Our Sierran National Parks...* 1963. Three Rivers. ils/photos. VG/dj. B26. $44.00

PUSHKIN, Alexander. *Boris Godunov.* 1985. Sixth Chamber. 1st ed this trans. trans/sgn DM Thomas. F. C6. $40.00

PUSHKIN, Alexander. *Golden Cockerel.* ca 1962. Obolensky. 1st prt. ils/inscr pres Rosalie Richards. VG/VG. B10. $15.00

PUSHKIN, Alexander. *Golden Cockerel.* 1938. NY. Nelson. 1st ed. ils Pogany. NF/VG. C8. $60.00

PUSSEY, W. *Syphilis As a Modern Problem.* 1915. np. 1st ed. 129p. A13. $75.00

PUTNAM, David Binney. *David Goes to Greenland.* 1928. NY. 11th imp. 167p. F/G. A17. $15.00

PUTNAM, George H. *Memories of My Youth 1844-1865.* 1914. 1st ed. ils/index. 447p. O8. $18.50

PUTNAM, George H. *Prisoner of War in Virginia.* 1912. 1st ed. 127p. O8. $32.50

PUTNAM, Mrs. William Lowell. *On Growing Old.* 1929. Rudge. 1/500. 35p. VG. M10. $6.50

PUTNAM, Robert. *Early Sea Charts.* 1983. Abbeville. folio. 76 mc pl. 142p. dj. T7. $50.00

PUXLEY, W.L. *Samoyeds.* 1947 (1934). London. Williams Norgate. 2nd ed. 80p. F/VG. R2. $38.00

PUZO, Mario. *Fools Die.* 1978. Putnam. 1st ed. VG/G+. P3. $25.00

PYLE, Ernie. *Here Is Your War.* 1943. NY. 1st ed. F/F. B14. $20.00

PYLE, Ernie. *Home Country.* nd. Wm Sloane. BC. VG/G. M21. $2.50

PYLE, Howard. *Otto of the Silver Hand.* 1916 (1888). Scribner. 170p. VG+. M20. $50.00

PYLE, Howard. *Otto of the Silver Hand.* 1925. Scribner. 8vo. VG. B17. $20.00

PYLE, Katherine. *Careless Jane & Other Tales.* 1902. Dutton. 1st ed thus. ils. 110p. G. P2. $35.00

PYLE, Katherine. *Once Upon a Time in Rhode Island.* 1914. Doubleday Page. ils Helen B Mason. 204p. VG. P2. $20.00

PYNCHON, Thomas. *Gravity's Rainbow.* 1973. Viking. 1st ed. 8vo. 750p. orange cloth. NF/dj. C6. $500.00

PYNCHON, Thomas. *Slow Learner.* 1984. Little Brn. fld/gathered sheets for review. RS. F/proof dj. rare. B4. $2,000.00

PYNCHON, Thomas. *Slow Learner.* 1984. Little Brn. 1st ed. F/NF. S9. $40.00

PYNCHON, Thomas. *Vineland.* 1990. Little Brn. 1st ed. F/F. L3. $35.00

PYNE, Mable. *Little Geography of the US.* 1941. Houghton Mifflin. 1st ed. G. B10. $10.00

PYRNELLE, Louise-Clarke. *Diddie, Dumps & Tot; or, Plantation Child-Life.* nd. Grosset Dunlap. rpt Harper 1882 ed. 240p. xl. VG/G. B10. $15.00

PYRNELLE, Louise-Clarke. *Diddie, Dumps & Tot; or, Plantation Child-Life.* 1882. Harper. 1st ed. 12 pl. olive-gr cloth. rebacked old cloth. M5. $275.00

QIRIAZI, Gjerasim. *Captured by Brigands.* nd. Wrexham. 12mo. 129p. O2. $20.00

QUAIFE, Milo Milton. *Chicago's Highways Old & New.* 1923. Chicago. Keller. 1st ed. VG. O3. $58.00

QUAIFE, Milo Milton. *Development of Chicago 1674-1914...* 1916. Chicago. Caxton. 1/175 on Italian-made paper. gilt vellum/gray brd. F. F1. $300.00

QUAIFE, Milo Milton. *Personal Narrative of James O Pattie of KY.* 1930. Lakeside. ils/index. 428p. F/sans. B19. $45.00

QUAIN, B. *Fijian Village.* 1948. Chicago. 1st ed. VG/G. B5. $40.00

QUARRINGTON, Paul. *Home Game.* 1983. Doubleday. 1st ed. F/VG+. P8. $30.00

QUARRY, Nick; see Albert, Marvin H.

QUATERMAIN, James. *Diamond Hostage.* 1975. Constable. 1st ed. VG/VG. P3. $20.00

QUAYLE, Eric. *Collector's Book of Books.* 1971. NY. ils/14 mc pl. 144p. F/F. A17. $20.00

QUEBBEMAN, Frances. *Medicine in Territorial Arizona.* 1966. Phoenix. 424p. A13. $40.00

QUEBEDEAUX, Richard. *By What Authority.* 1982. Harper. 204p. VG/dj. B29. $6.50

QUEBEDEAUX, Richard. *New Charismatic: Origins, Development & Significance...* 1976. Doubleday. 252p. VG/dj. B29. $6.50

QUEBEDEAUX, Richard. *Worldly Evangelicals.* 1978. Harper. 189p. F/dj. B29. $4.25

QUEEN, Ellery. *Calamity Town.* 1942. Boston. Little Brn. 1st ed. F/F. M15. $250.00

QUEEN, Ellery. *Calamity Town.* 1942. Little Brn. 1st ed. VG/clip. Q1. $175.00

QUEEN, Ellery. *Cat of Many Tails.* 1949. Little Brn. 1st ed. F/F. M15. $100.00

QUEEN, Ellery. *Chinese Orange Mystery.* 1934. Gollancz. 1st ed. VG-. P3. $35.00

QUEEN, Ellery. *Devil To Pay.* 1938. Stokes. 1st ed. F/NF. M15. $400.00

QUEEN, Ellery. *Door Between.* 1937. Stokes. 1st ed. F/NF. M15. $400.00

QUEEN, Ellery. *Dutch Shoe Mystery.* 1931. Stokes. 1st ed. VG. M15. $45.00

QUEEN, Ellery. *Dutch Shoe Mystery.* 1940. Triangle. 2nd ed. VG/VG. P3. $10.00

QUEEN, Ellery. *Ellery Queen's Awards, Tenth Series.* 1966. Little Brn. 1st ed. VG. P3. $20.00

QUEEN, Ellery. *Ellery Queen's Scenes of the Crime.* 1979. Dial. sgn Ruth Rendell on p of her story. F/VG. O4. $25.00

QUEEN, Ellery. *Four of Hearts.* 1946. Tower. 1st ed. VG. P3. $10.00

QUEEN, Ellery. *Halfway House.* 1936. Stokes. 1st ed. F/NF. M15. $450.00

QUEEN, Ellery. *King Is Dead.* 1952. Little Brn. 1st ed. F/F. M15. $100.00

QUEEN, Ellery. *Murderer Is a Fox.* 1945. Little Brn. 1st Am ed. 8vo. 231p. purple stp yel cloth. VG/dj. H5. $100.00

QUEEN, Ellery. *Player on the Other Side.* 1963. Gollancz. 1st ed. VG/VG. P3. $35.00

QUEEN, Ellery. *Sporting Blood.* 1942. Little Brn. 1st ed. 8vo. 360p. blk stp red cloth. NF/dj. H5. $85.00

QUEEN, Ellery. *There Was an Old Woman.* 1943. Little Brn. 1st ed. VG. P3. $30.00

QUENNELL, Peter. *Byron in Italy.* 1941. Viking. 1st ed. VG+/VG+. S9. $25.00

QUENTIN, Patrick. *Follower.* 1950. Simon Schuster. 1st ed. F/F. M15. $40.00

QUENTIN, Patrick. *Follower.* 1950. Simon Schuster. 1st ed. VG/VG. P3. $15.00

QUENTIN, Patrick. *Man With Two Wives.* 1955. Gollancz. 1st ed. VG/VG. P3. $20.00

QUENTIN, Patrick. *Puzzle for Pilgrims.* 1947. Simon Schuster. 1st ed. F/NF. F4. $30.00

QUERRY, Ronald B. *Growing Old at Willie Nelson's Picnic.* 1983. College Station. 1st ed. sgn. F/F. B3. $75.00

QUEST, Rodney. *Cerberus Murders.* 1970. McCall. 1st ed. VG/VG. P3. $18.00

QUICK, Armand. *Bleeding, Drugs, Vitamins: Their Impact on History.* 1976. Milwaukee. 1st ed. 80p. A13. $45.00

QUIGLEY, Jarold S. *From Versailles to Locarno.* 1927. MN U. inscr. 170p. VG. D3. $25.00

QUIGLEY, Martin. *Original Colored House of David.* 1981. Houghton Mifflin. 1st ed. F/VG+. P8. $25.00

QUIGLEY, Martin. *Today's Game.* 1965. Viking. 1st ed. VG/G+. P8. $20.00

QUILLER-COUCH, Arthur. *Twelve Dancing Princesses.* ca 1913. Doran. 16 mc pl/Kay Nielsen. 244p. gilt pict bed. NF/VG. P2. $450.00

QUILLER-COUCH, Arthur. *Twelve Dancing Princesses.* 1988. NY. Portland House. 1st prt. ils Kay Nielsen. F/F. C8. $40.00

QUINE, Willard Van Orman. *Methods of Logic.* 1959. NY. Holt. revised ed. 272p. ochre cloth. VG/dj. G1. $30.00

QUINE, Willard Van Orman. *Roots of Reference.* 1973. La Salle. Open Court. 151p. bl cloth. VG/dj. G1. $27.50

QUINE, Willard Van Orman. *System of Logistic.* 1934. Cambridge. Harvard. 204p. russet cloth. VG. G1. $150.00

QUINN, Charles Russell. *Christmas Journey Into the Desert.* 1959. Downey, CA. 61p. F/sans. B19. $45.00

QUINN, Seabury. *Phantom-Fighter.* 1966. Arkham. 1st ed. VG/VG. P3. $60.00

QUINN, Seabury. *Roads.* 1948. Arkham. 1st hc ed. F/NF. F4. $160.00

QUINN, William P. *Shipwrecks Along the Atlantic Coast.* 1988. Orleans, MA. Parnassus. ils. 232p. dj. T7. $36.00

QUIRK, R.E. *Affair of Honor: Woodrow Wilson & Occupation of Vera Cruz.* 1964. NY. 8vo. 184p. VG/wrp. A17. $5.00

QUIROGA, Horacio. *South American Jungle Tales.* 1923. London. Methuen. 1st ed. 8vo. 166p. bl brd. G. B11. $10.00

QUIROS & YOUNG. *World of Cactus & Succulents & Other Water-Thirsty Plants.* 1977. San Francisco. photos. gr cloth. F. B26. $16.00

R

RABAN, Jonathan. *Arabia: Journey Through the Labyrinth.* 1979. Simon Schuster. 1st ed. 344p. cloth. VG/torn. W1. $20.00

RABAN, Jonathan. *Huckleberry Finn.* 1968. NY. Woodbury. 1st Am ed. inscr. NF/ils wrp. A11. $75.00

RABELAIS, Francois. *Complete Works of Dr Francois Rabelais.* 1927. Bodley Head. 2 vol. 1st ed. 1/4000. G. S11. $45.00

RABELAIS, Francois. *Gargantua & Panta-gruel.* 1990. Norton. 2nd ed. F/F. P3. $30.00

RABKIN, Eric S. *Fantastic Worlds.* 1979. Oxford. 1st ed. VG/VG. P3. $20.00

RABORE, Paul. *Mechanized Might.* 1942. NY. 1st ed. VG/G. B5. $25.00

RACK & RACK. *Macrame Advanced Technique & Design.* 1972. np. VG/wrp. G2. $4.00

RACKHAM, Arthur. *Greek Heroes.* 1910. Cassell. 1st ed. 12mo. G. B17. $25.00

RACKHAM, Arthur. *Queen's Gift Book.* nd. Hodder Stoughton. 8vo. ils. G+. B17. $25.00

RACKHAM, Arthur. *Ringegold & the Valkyrie.* 1939. Garden City. early rpt. VG/G. B17. $45.00

RACKHAM, Arthur. *Wind in the Willows.* 1959 (1940). Heritage. 12 mc pl. cloth. F/G. M5. $35.00

RACY, John. *Psychiatry in the Arab East.* 1970. Copenhagen. 1st ed. sgn. 171p. A13. $45.00

RADBILL, Samuel X. *Bibliography of Medical Ex Libris Literature.* 1951. Los Angeles. Hilprand. 15 pl. 40p. brick red cloth. VG. K1. $50.00

RADCLIFFE, Talbot. *Spaniels for Sport.* 1988. NY. Boydell/Howell. ils. 136p. cloth. F/F. R2. $25.00

RADCLIFFE, Walter. *Milestones in Midwifery & the Secret Instrument.* 1989. Norman. ils. G7. $75.00

RADDALL, Thomas H. *Wings of Night.* 1956. Doubleday. 1st ed. VG/VG. P3. $20.00

RADEK, Karl. *Portraits & Pamphlets.* nd. NY. McBride. 1st ed. 306p. NF. B2. $25.00

RADIGUET, Raymond. *Count's Ball.* 1929. NY. Norton. VG/VG. Q1. $175.00

RADLEY, Sheila. *Fate Worse Than Death.* 1986. NY. Scribner. ARC/1st ed. RS. F/F. S6. $25.00

RADLEY, Sheila. *Who Saw Him Die?* 1987. London. Constable. 1st ed. F/F. M15. $30.00

RADLEY, Sheila. *Who Saw Him Die?* 1987. Scribner. 1st ed. VG/VG. P3. $15.00

RADZINOWICZ, L. *History of English Criminal Law.* 1948-1956. London. 3 vol. 1st ed. F/dj. A15. $30.00

RAE, Hugh C. *Harkfast.* 1976. St Martin. 1st ed. F/F. P3. $20.00

RAE, John. *Lucy Locket, the Doll With the Pocket.* 1928. Saalfield. ils. VG. M5. $45.00

RAFIZADEH, Mansur. *Witness: From Shah to Secret Arms Deal, Insider's Account...* 1987. Morrow. 1st ed. 12 pl. 396p. NF/dj. W1. $18.00

RAHBAR, Muhammad Daud. *Cup of Jamshid: Collection of Orig Ghazal Poetry.* 1974. Cape Cod, MA. Stark. 1st ed. 199p. cloth. NF/dj. W1. $7.00

RAHEB, Barbara. *Creation. Illustrations by Edward Burne-Jones.* 1981. Tarzana, CA. 43x31mm. 1/100. sgn. full blk morocco/ribbon bookmark. F. B24. $275.00

RAHEB, Barbara. *Golden Age.* 1982. Tarzana, CA. Pennyweight. 48x34mm. 1/100. sgn. 10 pl/tissue guards. silk ep. F. B24. $350.00

RAHEB, Barbara. *Russian Fairy Tales.* 1982. Tarzana, CA. Pennyweight. 48x33mm. 1/100. sgn. 4 tipped-in pl. gilt morocco. F. B24. $450.00

RAHEB, Barbara. *Saint George & the Dragon.* nd. Tarzana, CA. Pennyweight. 32x35mm. ltd ed. 5 3-D popups. gilt blk leather. F. B24. $250.00

RAHEB, Barbara. *Stamp Album. The Finest & Most Complete Album Published.* 1977. Tarzana. Littlest Lib. 28x21mm. ltd ed. full red leather. F. B24. $375.00

RAHMAN, Fazlur. *Islam.* 1966. HRW. 1st ed. 8vo. 38 pl. VG. W1. $20.00

RAINE, Katharine. *All About the Dachshund.* 1980. London. Pelham. 2nd ed. ils. 160p. cloth. M/dj. R2. $15.00

RAINE, Richard. *Corder Index.* 1967. Harcourt. 1st ed/author's 1st book. F/dj. F4. $22.00

RAINE, William MacLeod. *.45-Caliber Law: Way of Life of Frontier Peace Officer.* 1941. Evanston, IL. 1st ed. ils. pict cloth. xl. VG. D3. $15.00

RAINE, William MacLeod. *Border Breed.* 1944. Triangle. 4th prt. VG. P3. $6.00

RAINE, William MacLeod. *Famous Sheriffs & Western Outlaws.* 1929. Doubleday Doran. 1st ed. F/chip. A18. $75.00

RAINE, William MacLeod. *For Honor & Life.* 1933. Houghton Mifflin. 1st ed. F/chip. A18. $35.00

RAINE, William MacLeod. *Hell & High Water.* 1973. Tom Stacey. VG/VG. P3. $15.00

RAINE, William MacLeod. *Pirate of Panama.* nd. Grosset Dunlap. G+. P3. $10.00

RAINES, Robert A. *Secular Congregation.* 1968. Harper Row. 144p. VG/dj. B29. $3.50

RALLI, Paul. *Nevada Lawyer.* 1949. Culver City, CA. 2nd ed. 320p. VG. D3. $25.00

RALPHS. *Cat in Russian Literature & Folklore.* 1984. Edinburgh. 1st ed. sgn. 79p. M. R2. $20.00

RALPHSON, G. Harvey. *Boy Scouts on Motorcycles; or, With the Flying Squadron.* 1912. Donohue. pict cloth. VG. A17. $10.00

RAM, James. *Treatise on Facts As Subjects of Inquiry by a Jury.* 1873. NY. Baker Voorhis. contemporary sheep. M11. $150.00

RAMDAS. *World Is God.* 1955. India. Anandashram. 1st ed. 316p. VG/VG. B33. $30.00

RAMIREZ, Jose F. *Historia de las Indias de Nueva-Expana y Islas Tierra Firme.* 1867-1880. Mexico. 3 vol. Spanish text/atlas. 4to. VG-. H4. $4,000.00

RAMM, Bernard. *Protestant Biblical Interpretations.* 1975. Baker. 298p. VG. B29. $4.50

RAMM, Bernard. *Rapping About the Spirit.* 1974. Word. 176p. VG/dj. B29. $2.75

RAMON Y CAJAL, Sanitago. *Studies on Cerebral Cortex Trans from Spanish...* 1955. Chicago. VG. G7. $75.00

RAMPLING, Anne; see Rice, Anne.

RAMSAY, Jay; see Campbell, Ramsey.

RAMSAY, W.M. *Letters to the Seven Churches of Asia & Their Place...* 1905. NY. 8vo. ils/16 pl/map. 446p. cloth. uncut. O2. $75.00

RAMSBOTTOM, John. *Mushrooms & Toadstools.* 1954 (1953). London. New Naturalist #7. photos. VG/dj. B26. $19.00

RAMSDEN, Charles. *French Bookbinders 1789-1848.* 1989. London. Batsford. rpt. 228p. M/M. P4. $85.00

RAMSEY, Frederic Jr. *Chicago Documentary: Portrait of Jazz Era.* 1944. London. Jazz Music Books. VG+/wrp. B2. $75.00

RAMSEY, G.C. *Agatha Christie: Mistress of Mystery.* 1967. Dodd Mead. VG/VG. P3. $20.00

RAMSEY, L.G.G. *Connoisseur Year Book.* 1956. London. The Connoisseur. 4to. gilt bl cloth. VG. F1. $20.00

RAMSLAND, Katherine. *Prism of the Night.* 1991. Dutton. 1st ed. F/F. P3. $23.00

RAMSLAND, Katherine. *Prism of the Night.* 1991. Dutton. 1st ed. sgn. sgn biography of Anne Rice. F/F. L3. $50.00

RAMSLAND, Katherine. *Vampire Companion.* 1993. Ballantine. 1st ed. F/F. P3. $30.00

RANCE, Adrian. *Fast Boats & Flying Boats.* 1989. Ensign Pub. sgn. 192p. gilt tan brd. M/dj. M7. $30.00

RAND, Ayn. *Analysis of Extremism & Racism.* 1964. NY. Objectivist. rpt. NF/wrp. B2. $30.00

RAND, Ayn. *Atlas Shrugged.* 1957. Random. 1st ed. 8vo. 1168p. gilt/blk stp gr cloth. VG/dj. H5. $225.00

RAND, Ayn. *Atlas Shrugged.* 1957. Random. 1st ed. VG. M19. $75.00

RAND, Ayn. *For the New Intellectual.* 1961. Random. 1st ed. VG/VG. B2. $85.00

RAND, Ayn. *Night of January 16th.* 1968. NY. World. definitive ed. intro Rand. F/NF. Q1. $75.00

RAND, Benjamin. *Berkeley's Am Sojourn.* 1932. Cambridge. Harvard. 79p. tan cloth. G1. $37.50

RAND, Thomas. *Pocket History of the Presidents, & Information About US.* ca 1904. NY. Lentilhon. revised ed. 71x60mm. lettered red cloth. B24. $185.00

RANDALL, Bob. *Fan.* 1977. Random. 1st ed. VG/VG. P3. $18.00

RANDALL, D.A. *Dukedom Large Enough.* 1969. Random. 1st ed. ils. 368p. NF/dj. M10. $12.50

RANDALL, D.A. *Handwriting of God in Egypt, Sinai & the Holy Land...* 1862. Columbus, OH. 1st ed. 8vo. 355p. aeg. VG. W1. $75.00

RANDALL, G.A. *Saddle Up!* 1941. Dutton. 1st ed. ils. cloth. VG. M5. $20.00

RANDALL, J.G. *Civil War & Reconstruction.* 1953. Boston. ils/maps/charts/index. 971p. O8. $21.50

RANDALL, J.G. *Lincoln, the Liberal Statesman.* 1947. Dodd Mead. 1st ed. 266p. VG/dj. M10. $12.50

RANDALL, Janet. *Buffalo Box.* 1969. McKay. G. B34. $12.00

RANDALL, Jarrell. *Animal Family.* 1976 (1965). London. Rupert Hart-Davis. 1st ed. ils Sendak. F/F. C8. $45.00

RANDALL, John Herman. *Nature & Hist Experience.* 1959. Columbia. 2nd prt. gr cloth. VG/dj. G1. $27.50

RANDALL, L.W. *Footprints Along the Yellowstone.* 1961. Naylor. 1st ed. photos. VG. B34. $60.00

RANDALL, Marta. *Sword of Winter.* 1983. Timescape. 1st ed. VG/VG. P3. $20.00

RANDALL, Robert. *Dawning Light.* 1959. Gnome. 1st ed. VG/VG. M17. $17.50

RANDALL, Robert. *Shrouded Planet.* 1957. Gnome. 1st ed. VG/VG. M17. $17.50

RANDALL & WINTERICH. *Primer of Book Collecting.* 1966. Bell. 3rd revised ed. 228p. VG/dj. A10. $12.00

RANDAU & ZUGSMITH. *Visitor.* 1945. Tower. 1st ed. NF/NF. P3. $20.00

RANDISI, Robert. *Ham Reporter: Bat Masterson in NY.* 1986. Doubleday. 1st ed. inscr. F/F. M15. $35.00

RANDISI, Robert. *Separate Cases.* 1990. NY. Walker. ARC/1st ed. sgn. F/F. S6. $35.00

RANDLE, Burt. *Friendship.* ca 1940s. AR. 5x4mm. leather/clasp. author won Ripley's Believe It or Not contest. F. B24. $375.00

RANDLE, Burt. *Lincoln Messages.* 1940. AR. 12x10mm. bl leather/wire clasp. F/glass tube/wood insert. B24. $375.00

RANDLE, Burt. *Tiniest Book of All.* ca 1940s. AR. 2x2mm. 10p. bl leather/wire clasp. F/corked glass tube/BB shot. B24. $375.00

RANDOLPH, Bernard. *Present State of the Islands in the Archipelago...* 1983 (1687). Oxford. rpt. 2 lg fld maps. 108p. O2. $25.00

RANGER, Robin. *Antelopes.* 1866. NY. Carlton Porter. 54p. gilt red cloth. F. w/10p Carlton Porter ads. B14. $150.00

RANIVER, M.L. *Etude Anatomique des Glandes Connues Sous les Noms...* 1886. Paris. rpt from Arch Physiol. 34p. uncut/unopened. G7. $75.00

RANKE, Leopold. *Ottoman & the Spanish Empires...* 1845. Phil. Lee Blanchard. 138p. 8vo. modern quarter calf. VG. W1. $135.00

RANKIN, David. *David Rankin, Farmer.* 1906. Ashe. 80 p. wrp. A10. $20.00

RANKIN, Hugh F. *American Revolution.* 1964. Putnam. 1st Am ed. inscr. 282p. VG/VG. B11. $35.00

RANKIN & SCHEER. *Rebels & Redcoats: Living Story of an American Revolution.* 1967. World. 1st ed. inscr Rankin. 572p. F/F. B11. $50.00

RANKINE, John. *Never the Same Door.* 1967. Dobson. 1st ed. F/F. P3. $20.00

RANKINE, John. *One Is One.* 1968. Dobson. 1st ed. VG/VG. P3. $35.00

RANSHOFF, Joseph. *Under the Northern Lights & Other Stories.* 1921. Cincinnati. 166p. xl. G7. $50.00

RANSOM, Caroline L. *Tomb of Perneb.* 1919. Metropolitan Mus Art. 1st ed. 79p. VG/wrp. W1. $18.00

RANSOM, Harry Hunt. *Other TX Frontier.* 1984. TX U. 1st ed. ils. 72p. F/NF. B19. $20.00

RANSOM, John Crowe. *Poems About God.* 1919. NY. 1st ed/author's 1st book. VG. C2. $200.00

RANSOM, Will. *Private Presses & Their Books.* 1929. NY. Bowker. 1st ed. 8vo. 293p. gilt terra-cotta cloth. VG. F1. $225.00

RANSOME, Stephen. *Alias His Wife.* 1965. Dodd Mead. 1st ed. VG/G+. P3. $15.00

RANSOME, Stephen. *Frazer Acquittal.* 1955. Crime Club. 1st ed. VG/VG. P3. $20.00

RANSOME, Stephen. *Trap #6.* 1971. Crime Club. 1st ed. xl. VG/VG. P3. $8.00

RAPAPORT, David. *Organization & Pathology of Thought.* 1951. Columbia. 730p. G. K4. $15.00

RAPPAPORT, Doreen. *Be the Judge, Be the Jury: The Alger Hiss Trial.* 1993. NY. Harper Trophy. 184p. M11. $20.00

RASCOE, Burton. *Joys of Reading: Life's Greatest Pleasure.* 1937. Doubleday. 1st ed. 12mo. 186p. VG. M10. $4.50

RASHDALL, Hastings. *Theory of Good & Evil.* 1907. Clarendon. 2 vol. paneled bl cloth/gilt spine. VG. G1. $100.00

RASMUSSEN, Waldo. *Latin Am Artists of the 20th Century.* 1993. NY. Abrams/MOMA. 1st ed. lg 4to. 424p. dj. F3. $35.00

RASWAN, Carl. *Arab & the Horse.* nd (1955). W Des Moines. 3rd ed. VG/VG. O3. $45.00

RASWAN, Carl. *Drinkers of the Wind.* 1942. NY. Creative Age. 1st ed. VG/fair. O3. $58.00

RATHBONE, Basil. *In & Out of Character.* 1962. NY. 1st ed. F/F. A9. $75.00

RATHBONE, Julian. *Carnival!* 1976. Michael Joseph. 1st ed. VG/VG. P3. $20.00

RATHBONE, Julian. *Watching the Detectives.* 1983. Pantheon. 1st ed. VG/VG. P3. $14.00

RATHBUN, Carole. *Village in the Turkish Novel & Short Story 1920 to 1955.* 1972. Paris. 8vo. 192p. cloth. dj. O2. $20.00

RATHJEN, Carl Henry. *Land of the Giants.* 1969. Whitman. 1st ed. sgn by series star/Gary Conway. pict brd. F. F4. $35.00

RATTIGAN, Terence. *Ross: A Dramatic Portrait.* 1962. Random. 1st prt. 180p. gray brd/blk spine. F/NF. M7. $35.00

RATTRAY, Jeannette Edwards. *Perils of the Port of New York.* 1973. Dodd Mead. ils. 302p. dj. T7. $45.00

RAU, Jack. *Discovering Lost Maya Cities...* 1960. NY. Pre-Columbian Pr. 1st ed. sgn. 1/500. VG. F3. $45.00

RAUCH, Frederick Augustus. *Psychology; or, View of the Human Soul...* 1841. NY. MW Dodd. 2nd revised ed. emb cloth. VG. G1. $200.00

RAUCH, Frederick Augustus. *Psychology; or, View of the Human Soul...* 1846. NY. MW Dodd. 4th revised ed. 12mo. emb Victorian cloth. G. G1. $75.00

RAUCHER, Herman. *Maynard's House.* 1980. Putnam. 1st ed. F/dj. F4. $50.00

RAUH, Werner. *Bettrag Zur Kenntnis der Peru-anischen Kakteenvegetation.* 1958. Heidelberg. sgn. ils. 542p. bl buckram. F. B26. $175.00

RAUH, Werner. *Die Grossartige Welt der Sukkulenten.* 1967. Hamburg. German text. 700 photos/96 pl/maps. F/dj. B26. $50.00

RAUH, Werner. *Wonderful World of Succulents.* 1984. WA, DC. 2nd ed. photos/pl/maps. VG/dj. B26. $75.00

RAVEN, John Howard. *Old Testament Intro: General & Special.* 1910. Revell. 363p. G. B29. $4.00

RAVID, Joyce. *Here & There: Photographs.* 1993. Knopf. 1st ed. 103 hc photos. F/F. A17. $17.50

RAWE, Rolf. *Succlents in the Veld.* 1968. Cape Town. 104p. F/dj. B26. $45.00

RAWLINGS, A.L. *Science of Clocks & Watches.* 1974. Rawlings. 2nd ed. 8vo. 303p. F/VG. A8. $25.00

RAWLINGS, Margerie Kinnan. *Cross Creek Cookery.* 1942. NY. 1st ed. VG/missing pieces. B5. $70.00

RAWLINGS, Margerie Kinnan. *Yearling.* 1967. Scribner. late rpt. ils NC Wyeth. F/VG. B17. $14.00

RAWLINGS, Marjorie Kinnan. *Sojourner.* 1953. Scribner. 1st ed. VG/VG. P3. $40.00

RAWLINGS, Marjorie Kinnan. *Yearling.* 1939. Scribner. ltd ed. sgn. 1/750. ils/sgn NC Wyeth. 400p. gr-bl cloth. F/wrp/case. H5. $1,100.00

RAWLINGS, Maurice. *Beyond Death's Door...* 1978. Nelson. 173p. VG/dj. B29. $4.50

RAWLINS, Ray. *Stein & Day Book of World Autographs.* 1977. Stein Day. ils. 244p. F/dj. O8. $21.00

RAWLINSON, A. *Adventures in the Near East 1918-1922.* 1923. London. 8vo. 377p. cloth. O2. $60.00

RAWN, Melanie. *Dragon Token.* 1992. DAW. 1st ed. F/F. P3. $20.00

RAWSON, T. *Analysis of a Murder. I Want To Live!* 1958. NY. 12mo. 142p. VG/wrp. D3. $12.50

RAY, Anthony. *English Delftware Pottery.* 1968. Boston. 1st ed. VG/VG. A1. $50.00

RAY, David A. *Where Are You, God?* 1970. Revell. 160p. G/dj. B29. $3.25

RAY, Gordon N. *HG Wells & Rebecca West.* 1974. Yale. ARC. RS. NF/NF. S9. $25.00

RAY, Gordon N. *Illustrator & the Book in England From 1790-1914.* 1976. London/NY. lg 4to. ils. gilt bl cloth. F. B14. $125.00

RAY, Irene. *Kay Darcy & the Mystery Hideout.* 1937. Whitman. Big Little Book. 282p. VG. M20. $35.00

RAY, Man. *Man Ray: Self Portrait.* 1963. Boston. 1st ed. 398 p. F/sm tear. A17. $85.00

RAY, Robert J. *Murdock for Hire.* 1987. St Martin. 1st ed. sgn. F/F. S6. $35.00

RAY, Tom. *Yellowstone Red.* 1984. Dorrance. 1st ed. sgn. VG/VG. P3. $30.00

RAY & RAY. *Twice Sold, Twice Ransomed.* 1926. Chicago. Free Methodist. 1st ed. 320p. NF. P4. $50.00

RAYER, F.G. *Tomorrow Sometimes Comes.* 1951. Home/Van Thal. 1st ed. VG. P3. $15.00

RAYMOND, Evelyn. *Quaker Maiden: A Story of Girls.* 1923. Phil. Penn Pub. 8vo. 324p. worn. V3. $9.00

RAYMOND, Louise. *Child's Book of Prayers.* 1941. Random. ils Masha. 36p. pict brd/cloth spine. VG. A3. $7.00

RAYMOND, Louise. *Child's Story of the Nativity.* 1943. Random. ils. pict brd. VG+. M5. $28.00

RAYMOND, M. *God Goes to Murderer's Row.* 1951. Bruce. VG/VG. P3. $10.00

RAYMOND, Marcel. *From Baudelaire to Surrealism.* 1950. NY. Wittenborn Schultz. 1st ed. NF/wrp. B2. $65.00

RAYMOND, Rossiter W. *Statistics of Mines & Mining in the States & Territories...* 1873. GPO. 8vo. 550p. blk cloth. VG. P4. $95.00

RAYTER, Joe. *Stab in the Dark.* 1955. Morrow. 1st ed. VG-/dj. P3. $15.00

RAYTER, Joe. *Stab in the Dark.* 1955. NY. Morrow. 1st ed. F/NF. M15. $22.50

REA, Amadeo M. *Once a River: Bird Life & Habitat Changes on Middle Gila.* 1983. AZ U. ils/index/maps/charts. 385p. F/F. B19. $30.00

READ, B.E. *Gleanings From Old Chinese Medicine.* 1926. np. rpt. G7. $15.00

READ, David. *Sons of Anak: Gospel & Modern Giants.* 1964. Scribner. 208p. VG/dj. B29. $4.00

READ, Herbert. *Forms of Things Unknown. Essays...* 1960. NY. Horizon. 1st ed. ils. 248p. red stp blk cloth. NF/F. F1. $30.00

READ, Herbert. *Green Child.* 1935. London. 1st ed. VG. M2. $20.00

READ, Herbert. *Limits of Permissiveness in Art.* 1968. Puerto Rico. 1/1000. bilingual text. F/wrp. B2. $50.00

READ, J.R. *Case of Rudolf Hess, a Problem in Diagnosis...* 1948. Norton. dj. M11. $45.00

READ, Robert W. *Genus Thrinax.* 1975. WA, DC. Smithsonian. photos. 98p. VG/stiff wrp. B26. $29.00

READE, Brian. *Aubrey Beardsley.* 1967. London. Victoria/Albert Mus. VG/wrp. F1. $20.00

READE, Charles. *Christie Johnstone: A Novel.* 1855. Boston. Ticknor Fields. 1st Am ed. 12mo. 310p. gilt gr cloth. K1. $85.00

READE, Hamish. *Comeback for Stark.* 1968. Putnam. NF/dj. P3. $10.00

READY, Alma. *Very Small Place: AZ's Santa Cruz Co Book List.* 1989. Alto. index. 80p. NF/wrp. B19. $20.00

REAGAN, H.C. *Legend of the Grand Canyon of the Yellowstone.* 1925. Boston. Cristopher. 43p. cloth. VG. B14. $35.00

REAGAN, Ronald. *Speaking My Mind.* 1989. Simon Schuster. 1st ed. F/F. S11. $10.00

REAVEY, George. *Colours of Memory.* 1955. Grove. 1st ed. sgn. 1/250. F/NF. B4. $85.00

REBELE, Otto. *Come to My Party & Wear a Fancy Hat.* 1950. Duenewald. ils Steffie E Lerch. unused novelty. F. M5. $55.00

RECKLESS, W. *Crime Problem.* 1950. NY. 537p. cloth. VG. D3. $12.50

RECLUS, Elisee. *Earth & Its Inhabitants.* 1886-1895. NY. Appleton. 19 vol. 4to. ils/maps. contemporary gr calf/buckram. K1. $750.00

RECTOR, Frank. *Health & Medical Service in Am Prisons & Reformatories.* 1929. NY. 1st ed. 282p. A13. $90.00

RED, W.S. *History of Presby Church in Texas.* (1936). np. VG. C11. $40.00

RED FOX, Chief. *Memoirs of Chief Red Fox.* 1971. McGraw Hill. 1st ed. 8vo. F/F. B11. $20.00

REDDING, David. *New Immorality.* 1967. Revell. 156p. VG/dj. B29. $3.50

REDDING, M. Wolcott. *Antiquities of the Orient Unveiled...* 1875. NY. Temple. 421p. recent buckram. VG. W1. $65.00

REDFIELD, Robert. *Folk Culture of Yucatan.* 1941. Chicago. 1st ed. 416p. VG. F3. $35.00

REDFIELD, Robert. *Primitive World & Its Transformations.* 1967. Ithaca. 9th prt. 185p. VG. F3. $15.00

REDFORD, Bruce. *Letters of Samuel Johnson, 1731-1784.* 1992-1994. Princeton. 4 vol. ils. F/F. A4. $125.00

REDGROVE, H. Stanley. *Alchemy: Ancient & Modern.* 1910. Phil. ils. 141p. cloth. VG. B14. $95.00

REDIER, Antoine. *Comrads in Courage.* 1918. NY. 1st Am ed. trans from French. 260p. VG. A17. $7.50

REDMAN, J.L. *Isles in Summer, Beautiful Bermuda.* 1913. NY. 1st ed. ils. 242p. VG. B5. $32.50

REDMOND, Louis. *What I Know About Boys/What I Know About Girls.* 1952. NY. 2 vol. photos. brd. VG. M5. $50.00

REDPATH, James. *Public Life of Capt John Brown.* 1860. Boston. 406p. O8. $18.50

REED, Charles B. *Four Way Lodge.* 1924. np. 1st ed. 28p. VG. E5. $45.00

REED, George. *Dark Sky Legacy.* 1989. NY. Prometheus. 8vo. 199p. VG/VG. K5. $22.00

REED, Ishmael. *Free-Lance Pallbearers.* 1967. Doubleday. 1st ed/author's 1st book. F/F clip. S9. $150.00

REED, Ishmael. *Last Days of Louisiana Red.* 1974. Random. 1st ed. 8vo. 179p. gilt red cloth. F/clip. H5. $50.00

REED, Ishmael. *Reckless Eyeballing.* 1986. St Martin. 1st ed. inscr. F/F. L3. $100.00

REED, Ishmael. *Yellow Back Radio Broke-Down.* 1969. Doubleday. 1st ed/author's 2nd book. inscr/dtd 1974. NF/NF. L3. $200.00

REED, John. *Ten Days That Shook the World.* 1934. NY. Modern Lib. ils. VG/chip. V4. $12.50

REED, Kit. *Fat.* 1971. Bobbs Merrill. 1st ed. VG/VG. P3. $15.00

REED, Robert C. *Train Wrecks.* 1968. Bonanza. 183p. NF/dj. M20. $15.00

REED, Robert. *Harmone Jungle.* 1987. Donald Fine. 1st ed. F/F. P3. $20.00

REED, Rowena. *Combined Operations in the Civil War.* 1978. np. index. 468p. dj. O8. $12.50

REED, W. *John Clymer.* 1975. Flagstaff. 1st ed. VG/dj. C11. $75.00

REES, Leslie. *Story of Koonaworra the Black Swan.* nd. Sydney. John Sands. ne. ils Margaret Senior. VG+. C8. $25.00

REES, Leslie. *Story of Kurri Kurri the Kookaburra.* nd. Sydney. John Sands. ne. ils Margaret Senior. VG. C8. $25.00

REES, Leslie. *Story of Sarli the Barrier Reef Turtle.* nd. Sydney. John Sands. ne. NF/NF. C8. $25.00

REES, Leslie. *Story of Shy the Platypus.* nd. Sydney. John Sands. ils Walter Cunningham. F/F. C8. $25.00

REES, Leslie. *Two-Thumbs the Koala.* nd. Sydney. John Sands. ne. ils Margaret Senior. F/F. C8. $25.00

REES, Ronald. *Interior Landscape.* 1993. Baltimore. ils/photos. 190p. VG. B26. $25.00

REES-MOGG, William. *How To Buy Rare Books: Practical Guide...* 1985. London. Phaidon. 1st ed. ils. 159p. F/VG. S11. $35.00

REESE, John. *Sunblind Range.* 1968. Doubleday. 1st ed. VG/VG. P3. $15.00

REEVE, Arthur B. *Craig Kennedy Listens In.* (1923). Grosset Dunlap. NF/VG. F4. $35.00

REEVE, Arthur B. *Craig Kennedy Listens In.* 1923. Harper. 1st ed. VG/fair. P3. $45.00

REEVE, Arthur B. *Gold of Gods.* 1915. McClelland Goodchild. 1st Canadian ed. VG. P3. $11.00

REEVE, Frank D. *New Mexico: A Short, Ils Hist.* 1964. Sage. 1st ed. ils. 112p. NF. B19. $20.00

REEVE, J. Stanley. *Foxhunting Formalities.* 1930. Derrydale. 1/99 lg paper copies. 8vo. 54p. morocco. H4. $750.00

REEVE, J. Stanley. *Red Coats in Chester County.* 1940. Derrydale. 1/570. NF. H4. $125.00

REEVES, James. *Blackbird in the Lilac. Poems for Children.* 1967 (1952). London. Oxford. 8vo. ils Ardizzone. 95p. VG/VG. A3. $8.00

REEVES, James. *How the Moon Began.* 1971. Abelard-Schuman. 1st Am ed. ils Ardizzone. NF/dj. M20. $30.00

REEVES, John. *Death in Prague.* 1988. Canada. Doubleday. 1st ed. F/F. P3. $20.00

REEVES & ROBINSON. *Decade of Champions.* 1980. NY. Fine Arts. 1st ed. sgn pres. obl folio. VG/VG. O3. $295.00

REEVES-STEVENS, Garfield. *Nighteyes.* 1989. Doubleday. 1st ed. F/F. P3. $19.00

REFORMED CHURCH IN AMERICA. *Constitution of Reformed Dutch Church in US of Am.* 1793. NY. Durrell. 1st ed. 354p. leather. VG. H10. $125.00

REGAL, Philip J. *Anatomy of Judgment.* 1990. Minneapolis. trade pb. 368p. VG. G1. $12.50

REGAN, Tom. *All That Dwell Therein.* 1982. CA U. 1st ed. VG/VG. P3. $10.00

REGINALD, R. *SF & Fantasy Literature: Checklist 1700-1974/SF Authors II.* 1979. Detroit. Gale. 2 vol. 1st ed. NF. B2. $125.00

REGISTER, Alvaretta Kenan. *Everitt/Everitt Family: A Geneaological History.* nd. np. 8vo. 520p. F. B11. $40.00

REGLER, Gustav. *Owl of Minerva.* 1960. NY. 1st ed. 375p. F/F. A17. $10.00

REHWINKEL, Alfred M. *Planned Parenthood & Birth Control...* 1959. Concordia. 120p. VG. B29. $3.50

REICH, Wilhelm. *Character-Analysis.* 1945. NY. Orgone Inst. 2nd ed. 324p. VG. K4. $15.00

REICHARD, Gladys A. *Dezba: Woman of the Desert.* 1939. NY. Augustin. 1st ed. lg 8vo. 161p. map ep. beige cloth. VG. P4. $65.00

REICHEN, Charles Albert. *Hist of Physics.* 1968. Hawthorn. 2nd prt. 4to. 112p. gr cloth. VG. K5. $15.00

REICHENBACH, Hans. *From Copernicus to Einstein.* 1942. Philosophical Lib. thin 8vo. 123p. VG. G1. $35.00

REICHENBACH, William. *Sixguns & Bullseyes.* 1936. Samworth. VG+/VG+. A1. $40.00

REICHLER, Joseph. *Baseball's Great Moments.* 1985. Bonanza. VG/VG. P3. $10.00

REICHLER, Joseph. *Inside the Majors.* 1952. Hart. 192p. VG. A17. $20.00

REICHMAN, Edith. *Busy Children. With Two Pop-Ups. A Bonnie Book.* 1949. John Martin's House. pict brd. VG. M5. $25.00

REICYN, Nina. *La Pedagogie de John Locke.* 1941. Paris. Hermann. 229p. VG. G1. $37.50

REID, Ed. *Green Felt Jungle.* 1964. NY. rpt of 1963 ed. 244p. VG/wrp. D3. $12.50

REID, J.H. Stewart. *Mountains, Men & Rivers.* 1954. Ryerson. 1st ed. VG/VG. P3. $25.00

REID, John Phillip. *Chief Justice, Judicial World of Charles Doe.* 1967. Cambridge. Harvard. M11. $45.00

REID, John. *Turkey & the Turks: Present State of the Ottoman Empire.* 1840. London. author's copy. 8vo. 2 maps/5 (of 6) pl. gilt cloth. O2. $1,200.00

REID, Thomas. *Essays on Intellectual Powers of Man.* 1785. London. Bell Robinson. 4to. 766p. modern buckram. VG. G1. $850.00

REID, Whitelaw. *Careers for the Coming Men.* 1904. Saalfield. 1st ed. 245p. teg. VG. S11. $15.00

REIF, Jane. *Tibetan Terrier Book.* 1984. Southfarm. 1st ed. ils. 256p. M/wrp. R2. $20.00

REIFF, Robert. *Indian Miniatures: Rajput Painters.* 1959. Tuttle. 12 pl. VG. W1. $15.00

REIGER, George. *Zane Grey: Outdoorsman.* 1972. Prentice Hall. 1st ed. xl. VG/dj. M21. $7.50

REIGER & REIGER. *Zane Grey Cookbook.* 1976. Prentice Hall. 1st ed. pict ep. F/F. A18. $40.00

REIK, Theodor. *Listening With the Third Ear.* 1949. Farrar Straus. 514p. F/dj. K4. $9.00

REIK, Theodor. *Pagan Rites in Judaism.* 1964. Farrar Straus. 1st ed. 206p. VG/VG. B33. $20.00

REIK, Theodor. *Ritual Psycho-Analytic Studies.* 1958. NY. new prt. 367p. xl. G7. $30.00

REILLY, Helen. *Death Demands an Audience.* 1941. Dial. VG. P3. $20.00

REILLY, Helen. *Follow Me.* 1960. Random. 1st ed. NF/NF. P3. $25.00

REISMAN, John M. *Hist of Clinical Psychology.* 1976. NY. Irvington. 420p. G. K4. $15.00

REITMEISTER, Louis A. *Philosophy of Freedom.* 1970. NY. 753p. F/dj. D3. $35.00

REITMEISTER, Louis A. *Philosophy of Time.* 1962. Citadel. 452p. VG/dj. G1. $25.00

REMARQUE, Erich Maria. *All Quiet on the Western Front.* 1929. Little Brn. 1st ed. 291p. cloth. VG. B14. $45.00

REMARQUE, Erich Maria. *Der Weg Zuruck.* 1931. Berlin. 1st ed. VG. A17. $20.00

REMBAR, Charles. *End of Obscenity.* 1968. NY. 528p. NF. B18. $15.00

REMENHAM, John. *Peacemaker.* 1947. MacDonald. 1st ed. VG/rpr. P3. $15.00

REMINGTON, Frederic. *Drawings.* 1897. NY. 1/250. sgn. full suede. H4. $2,250.00

REMINGTON & ROOSEVELT. *Ranch Life in the Far West.* 1985. Northland. M/M. B34. $14.00

REMMERS, H.H. *Growth, Teaching & Learning.* 1957. Harper. 555p. G. K4. $10.00

RENAULT, Mary. *King Must Die.* 1958. Pantheon. 1st ed. F/NF. B2. $45.00

RENAULT, Mary. *Mask of Apollo.* 1966. Pantheon. 1st ed. 371p. VG/VG. M20. $30.00

RENAULT, Paul. *Manuel de Tracheotomie...* 1887. Paris. Steinheil. 120p. quarter leather/marbled brd. very scarce. G7. $195.00

RENAY, Liz. *My Face for the World To See.* 1971. NY. 455p. NF. D3. $12.50

RENDELL, Ruth. *Bridesmaid.* 1989. Doubleday. 1st ed. F/F. P3. $18.00

RENDELL, Ruth. *Bridesmaid.* 1989. London. Hutchinson. 1st ed. sgn. F/F. O4. $50.00

RENDELL, Ruth. *Collected Stories.* 1987. Pantheon. 1st Am ed. sgn. F/F. O4. $40.00

RENDELL, Ruth. *Crocodile Bird.* 1993. Crown. 1st Am ed. F/F. O4. $15.00

RENDELL, Ruth. *Crocodile Bird.* 1993. Crown. 1st Am ed. sgn. F/F. B2/L3. $45.00

RENDELL, Ruth. *Crocodile Bird.* 1993. London. Hutchinson. ltd sgn ed. 1/150. F/sans. O4. $150.00

RENDELL, Ruth. *Dark-Adapted Eye.* 1986. London. Viking. 1st ed. sgn. F/F. O4. $40.00

RENDELL, Ruth. *Dark-Adapted Eye.* 1986. Viking. 1st ed. VG/VG. P3. $15.00

RENDELL, Ruth. *Death Notes.* 1981. Pantheon. 1st Am ed. sgn. F/F. O4. $35.00

RENDELL, Ruth. *Face of Trespass.* 1974. Doubleday Crime Club. 1st Am ed. F/F. M15. $70.00

RENDELL, Ruth. *Fever Tree.* 1982. Pantheon. 1st Am ed. F/VG. O4. $35.00

RENDELL, Ruth. *Going Wrong.* 1990. London. Hutchinson. 1st ed. F/F. B3. $30.00

RENDELL, Ruth. *House of Stairs.* 1988. London. Viking. 1st ed. F/F. O4. $40.00

RENDELL, Ruth. *Killing Doll.* 1984. London. Hutchinson. 1st ed. F/F. S6. $45.00

RENDELL, Ruth. *Lake of Darkness.* 1980. Doubleday. 1st Am ed. sgn. F/NF. O4. $35.00

RENDELL, Ruth. *Live Flesh.* 1986. Hutchinson. 1st ed. NF/NF. P3. $25.00

RENDELL, Ruth. *Live Flesh.* 1986. London. Hutchinson. 1st ed. sgn. F/F. O4. $65.00

RENDELL, Ruth. *Master of the Moor.* (1982). Pantheon. BC. F/F. M21. $5.00

RENDELL, Ruth. *Master of the Moor.* 1982. London. Hutchinson. 1st ed. F/F. M15. $65.00

RENDELL, Ruth. *Means of Evil.* 1979. Doubleday. 1st Am ed. sgn. VG/VG. O4. $40.00

RENDELL, Ruth. *New Lease of Death.* 1967. Doubleday. 1st Am ed. sgn. VG/G+. O4. $60.00

RENDELL, Ruth. *Shake Hands Forever.* 1975. London. Hutchinson. 1st ed. sgn. F/clip/pub wrp band. M15. $150.00

RENDELL, Ruth. *Sleeping Life.* (1978). Doubleday. BC. VG+/dj. M21. $5.00

RENDELL, Ruth. *Talking to Strange Men.* 1987. Pantheon. 1st Am ed. sgn. F/F. O4. $35.00

RENDELL, Ruth. *Talking to Strange Men.* 1987. Pantheon. 1st ed. F/F. P3. $17.00

RENDELL, Ruth. *Veiled One.* 1988. London. Hutchinson. 1st ed. F/F. P3. $18.00

RENDELL, Ruth. *Veiled One.* 1988. Pantheon. 1st Am ed. sgn. F/F. O4. $40.00

RENEN, Ernest. *Saint Paul.* 1869. NY. Carlton. 1st ed. 422p. xl. G. B33. $18.00

RENICK, Marion. *Dooley's Play Ball.* 1949. Scribner. later prt. G. P8. $5.00

RENICK & RENICK. *Tommy Carries the Ball.* 1940. Scribner. rpt. 12mo. ils Machetanz. VG/VG. B17. $4.00

RENIER, G.J. *Oscar Wilde.* 1933. London. Peter Davies. 1st ed. 1/500. sgn. gilt wht cloth/beveled brd. F. F1. $150.00

RENO, Philip. *Taos Pueblo.* 1963. Sage. 1st ed. ils. 36p. NF/wrp. B19. $5.00

RENOIR, Jean. *Notebooks of Captain Georges.* 1966. Boston. 1st ed. VG/VG. A17. $10.00

RENOUF, P. Le Page. *Elementary Grammar of Ancient Egyptian Language.* 1905. London. Bagster. 4th ed. Archaic Classics Series. gilt blk cloth. VG. F1. $40.00

RENSCH & RENSCH. *Hist Spots in CA: The S Counties.* 1938. Stanford. 2nd prt. 267p. VG. D3. $35.00

RENSTROM. *Wilbur & Orville Wright: A Bibliography.* 1968. np. 193p. NF/wrp. A4. $65.00

REPOGLE, Justine. *Auden's Poetry.* 1969. WA U. 1st ed. F/NF. V1. $25.00

REPP, Ed Earl. *Radium Pool.* 1949. FPCI. 1st ed. sgn. F/clip. F4. $60.00

RESCHER, Nicholas. *Distributive Justice: Constructive Critique...* 1966. Bobbs Merrill. sm 8vo. 166p. gray cloth. VG/dj. G1. $22.50

RESCHER, Nicholas. *Limits of Science.* 1984. Berkeley. 226p. beige cloth. VG/dj. G1. $25.00

RESLINGER, G. *Final Solution.* 1953. NY. 1st ed. VG/G. B5. $45.00

RESNICK, Mike. *Eros at Zenith.* 1984. Phantasia. 1st ed. sgn. 1/300. F/case. P3. $50.00

RESNICK, Mike. *Ivory.* 1988. Tor. 1st ed. F/F. P3. $18.00

RESNICK, Mike. *Paradise.* 1989. Tor. 1st ed. F/F. N3. $20.00

RESNICOW, Herbert. *Gold Gamble.* 1988. St Martin. 1st ed. VG/VG. P3. $18.00

RESNICOW & SEAVER. *Beanball.* 1989. Morrow. 1st ed. VG/VG. P3. $17.00

REUTHER, Victor G. *Brothers Reuther & the Story of the UAW.* 1976. Houghton Mifflin. sgn. photos. VG/G. V4. $20.00

REVERE, Paul. *Cleveland in the War With Spain.* 1900. Cleveland. 1st ed. 4to. 285p. G. B18. $85.00

REVKIN, Andrew. *Burning Season: Muscle of Chico Mendes...Amazon Rain Forest.* 1990. Houghton Mifflin. M/M. V4. $10.00

REVONS, E.C. *Sayings of Sages; or, Selections...* 1863. NY. Carlton Porter. 294p. VG. M10. $12.50

REX, Stella. *Choice Hooked Rugs.* 1953. np. cloth. VG. G2. $30.00

REXROTH, Kenneth. *Collected Longer Poems.* 1968. New Directions. 1st ed. F/NF. V1. $35.00

REXROTH, Kenneth. *Collected Shorter Poems.* 1966. New Directions. 1st ed. sgn. F/NF. V1. $35.00

REY, H.A. *Feed the Animals.* 1944. Houghton Mifflin. apparent 1st ed. mc moveable flap book. VG. M5. $75.00

REY, H.A. *Where's My Baby?* 1943. Houghton Mifflin. apparent 1st ed. mc moveable flap book. VG. scarce. M5. $60.00

REYNAUD, Leonce. *Memoir Upon the Illumination & Beaconage of Coast of France.* 1876. GPO. folio. 39 pl. 226p. xl. half calf. T7. $175.00

REYNOLDS, Clay. *Taking Stock: A Larry McMurtry Casebook.* 1989. S Methodist U. 1st ed. M/dj. A18. $17.00

REYNOLDS, John Lawrence. *Whisper Death.* 1991. Viking. 1st ed. F/F. P3. $19.00

REYNOLDS, John. *His Own Times.* 1855. Bellvue, IL. 1st ed. old half leather. A9. $150.00

REYNOLDS, Mack. *Star Trek Mission to Horatius.* 1968. Whitman. TVTI. G+. P3. $15.00

REYNOLDS, Maxine; see Reynolds, Mack.

REYNOLDS, Quentin. *Fiction Factory; or, From Pulp Row to Quality Street.* 1955. NY. 1st ed. ils/photos. 283p. VG/dj. B18. $35.00

REYNOLDS, William J. *Things Invisible.* 1989. Putnam. 1st ed. F/F. P3. $19.00

REYNOLDS & TAMPION. *Double Flowers. A Scientific Study.* 1983. NY. ils/photos/ drawings. 183p. M. B26. $12.50

REZANOV, Nikolai Petrovich. *Rezanov Reconnoiters California, 1806.* 1972. San Francisco. BC of CA. 1/450. 74p. F. P4. $115.00

REZNIKOFF, Charles. *By the Waters of Manhattan.* 1930. NY. Boni Paper Book. F. B14. $55.00

RHINEHART, Luke. *Dice Man.* 1971. Morrow. 1st ed. VG/VG. P3. $30.00

RHODE, John. *Dead of the Night.* 1942. Dodd Mead. 1st ed. xl. G+. P3. $15.00

RHODE, John. *Death Takes a Partner.* 1959. Dodd Mead. 1st Am ed. F/F. M15. $65.00

RHODE, John. *Secret Meeting.* 1951. London. Bles. 1st ed. F/NF. B2. $45.00

RHODE, John. *Venner Crime.* 1933. London. Odham. 1st ed. VG/dj. M15. $65.00

RHODES, Eugene Manlove. *Best Novels & Stories of Eugene Manlove Rhodes.* 1949. Houghton Mifflin. 1st ed. map ep. F. A18. $30.00

RHODES, Eugene Manlove. *Brave Adventure.* 1971. Clarendon. 1st appearance in book form. 49p. NF. w/emphera. B19. $50.00

RHODES, Eugene Manlove. *Desire of the Moth.* 1916. NY. 1st ed. 149p. pict cloth. G. scarce. A17. $25.00

RHODES, Eugene Manlove. *Little World Waddies.* 1946. Hertzog. 1st ltd ed. 1/1000. edit/sgn Hutchinson. ils Harold Bugbee. F. A18. $175.00

RHODES, Eugene Manlove. *Once in the Saddle & Paso for Aqui.* 1927. Houghton Mifflin. 1st ed. pict ep. F. A18. $90.00

RHODES, H. *Alphonse Bertillon.* 1956. London. ils. 238p. VG. D3. $12.50

RHODES, Henry J. *Art of Lithography... Planographic Printing.* 1924. London. 2nd revised/enlarged ed. 328 p. VG. A17. $28.00

RHODES, John H. *Gettysburg Gun.* 1892. Providence. 1st ed. 1/250. NF/prt wrp. M8. $45.00

RHODES, Richard. *Last Safari.* 1980. Doubleday. UP. NF/prt red wrp. B3. $25.00

RICARD, P. *Algeria & Tunisia...* 1926. Paris/London. Hachette. 12mo. 340p. G. W1. $8.00

RICCI, Elisa. *Old Italian Lace.* 1913. Heinemann/Lippincott. 2 vol. 1st ed. 1/300. teg. gilt cloth. F. B24. $850.00

RICCIOTTI, Giuseppe. *Life of Christ.* 1951. Milwaukee, WI. Bruce. 5th prt. 703p. VG. W1. $10.00

RICE, Anne. *Beauty's Punishment.* 1984. Dutton. 1st ed. F/F. B2. $150.00

RICE, Anne. *Beauty's Punishment.* 1984. Dutton. 1st ed. sgn as Anne Rice. F/F. L3. $350.00

RICE, Anne. *Beauty's Release.* 1985. Dutton. 1st ed. F/F. Q1. $125.00

RICE, Anne. *Beauty's Release.* 1985. Dutton. 1st ed. sgn. F/F. B4. $300.00

RICE, Anne. *Belinda.* 1986. Arbor House. 1st ed. sgn. F/F. L3. $150.00

RICE, Anne. *Claiming of Sleeping Beauty.* 1983. Dutton. 1st ed. sgn as Anne Rice. F/F. L3. $350.00

RICE, Anne. *Cry to Heaven.* 1982. Knopf. 1st ed. VG/VG. P3. $45.00

RICE, Anne. *Cry to Heaven.* 1982. Knopf. 1st ed/author's 3rd book. sgn. F/NF. B4. $150.00

RICE, Anne. *Exit to Eden.* 1985. Arbor. 1st ed. sgn. F/F. L3. $125.00

RICE, Anne. *Feast of All Saints.* 1979. Simon Schuster. 1st ed. F/NF. N3. $75.00

RICE, Anne. *Feast of All Saints.* 1979. Simon Schuster. 1st ed/author's 2nd novel. sgn. rem mk. F/F. L3. $200.00

RICE, Anne. *Interview With the Vampire.* 1976. NY. 1st ed/author's 1st book. F/NF. A15. $600.00

RICE, Anne. *Lasher.* 1993. Knopf. 1st ed. sgn. F/F. B4. $100.00

RICE, Anne. *Memnoch the Devil.* 1995. Knopf/BE Trice. 1st ed. 1/425. F/sans/ case. T2. $150.00

RICE, Anne. *Mummy.* 1989. Ballantine. 1st ed. sgn. NF/wrp. L3. $100.00

RICE, Anne. *Queen of the Damned.* 1988. Knopf. 1st ed. VG/VG. P3. $25.00

RICE, Anne. *Tale of the Body Thief.* 1992. Knopf. 1st ed. inscr. F/F. B2. $65.00

RICE, Anne. *Taltos.* 1994. Knopf. ltd 1st ed. sgn. 1/500. linen. w/photo. F/sans/case. T2. $150.00

RICE, Anne. *Witching Hour.* 1990. Knopf. 1st ed. VG/VG. P3. $25.00

RICE, Craig. *Having Wonderful Crime.* 1944. Simon Schuster. 2nd ed. VG. p3. $15.00

RICE, Craig. *Knocked for a Loop.* 1957. Simon Schuster. 1st ed. G+. P3. $15.00

RICE, Craig. *Lucky Stiff.* 1947. Cleveland. World/Tower. 1st ed thus. sgn. NF/worn. B2. $85.00

RICE, Craig. *Mother Finds a Body.* 1942. Simon Schuster. 1st ed. F/NF. M15. $65.00

RICE, Craig. *Thursday Turkey Murders.* 1943. Simon Schuster. 1st ed. F/VG. M15. $45.00

RICE, Craig. *Thursday Turkey Murders.* 1943. Simon Schuster. 1st ed. VG. P3. $20.00

RICE, Cyprian. *Persian Sufis.* 1964. London. Allen Unwin. 1st ed. 104p. F/F. B33. $30.00

RICE, Damon. *Season's Past.* 1976. Praeger. 1st ed. F/VG+. P8. $50.00

RICE, David Talbot. *Islamic Art.* 1965. Praeger Art Series. sm 8vo. 249p. VG/stiff wrp. W1. $14.00

RICE, Edward. *Captain Sir Richard Francis Burton.* 1990. NY. Scribner. 1st ed/4th prt. ils/maps. 522p. M/dj. P4. $35.00

RICE, Elizabeth. *Gee Whillikins.* 1950. Steck Vaugh. later rpt. ils Adda Mai Sharp. VG/VG clip. B17. $5.00

RICE, Elmer. *Voyage to Purilla.* 1930. Cosmopolitan. 1st ed. VG. N3. $10.00

RICE, John R. *Why Our Churches Do Not Win Souls.* 1968. Sword of the Lord. 178p. VG. B29. $4.50

RICE, Laura W. *Cacti & Succulents for Modern Living.* 1976. Kalamzoo. 147 photos. sc. M. B26. $5.95

RICE, R. Talbot. *Icons.* nd. London. Batchworth. 1st ed. folio. 65 pl. Eng/German/ French text. VG/VG. S9. $100.00

RICE, Robert. *Business of Crime.* 1956. FSC. 1st ed. VG. P3. $15.00

RICE, W.G. *Carillons of Belgium & Holland.* 1914. NY. ils. VG. F1. $35.00

RICE & RICE. *Icons & Their History.* 1974. Woodstock, NY. Overlook. 4to. ils. 192p. F/dj. M10. $18.50

RICH, Frank. *Theatre Art of Boris Aronson.* 1987. NY. 1st ed. VG/VG. A1. $40.00

RICHARD, Dennis. *Fantastic Art of Clark Ashton Smith.* 1973. Mirage. 1st ed. F/wrp. M2. $35.00

RICHARD, James Robert. *Club Team.* 1950. Lee Shepard. 1st ed. VG/G+. P8. $25.00

RICHARDS, Allen. *To Market to Market.* 1961. Macmillan. 1st ed. VG/VG. P3. $15.00

RICHARDS, Eva Alvey. *Arctic Mood.* 1949. Caldwell. 1st ed. photos/maps. 282p. VG/VG. A17. $15.00

RICHARDS, Gregory B. *SF Movies.* 1984. Bison Books. 1st ed. VG/VG. P3. $15.00

RICHARDS, John. *Stagecoach: Real Story of Coaching Across the Land...* 1976. Watmoughs Ltd. 96p. G+/wrp. O3. $40.00

RICHARDS, Laura E. *Nautilus.* 1895. Estes Lauriat. probable 1st ed. 120p. G+. P2. $25.00

RICHARDS, Lawrence. *Theology of Christian Education.* 1975. Zondervan. 324p. VG/dj. B29. $8.50

RICHARDS, Linda. *Reminiscences of Linda Richards...* 1915. Boston. ils. cloth. VG. B14. $40.00

RICHARDS, Mark. *Fishboy.* 1993. Doubleday. UP/author's 2nd book. F/wrp. B4. $45.00

RICHARDS, Milton. *Dick Kent, Fur Trader.* 1927. Saalfield. ils. F/F. A17. $8.50

RICHARDS, Vyvyan. *Portrait of TE Lawrence.* April 1967. Scholastic Book. 2nd prt. 148p. VG/paper wrp/clear plastic. M7. $25.00

RICHARDS, Vyvyan. *TE Lawrence.* 1954. London. Duckworth. 4th imp. gilt cloth. G/VG. M7. $35.00

RICHARDSON, Albert D. *Our New States & Territories.* 1866. NY. 1st ed. ils. wrp. O8. $100.00

RICHARDSON, Benjamin. *Ministry in Health & Other Addresses.* 1879. NY. 1st Am ed. 354p. A13. $40.00

RICHARDSON, Charles F. *Choice of Books.* 1881. Am Book Exchange. 12mo. 94p. VG. M10. $3.50

RICHARDSON, Clive. *Driving: The Development & Use of Horse-Drawn Vehicles.* 1985. London. Batsford. 1st ed. VG/VG. O3. $28.00

RICHARDSON, E.H. *Forty Years With Dogs.* 1931 (1929). London. Hutchinson. 3rd ed. 288p. cloth. VG. R2. $80.00

RICHARDSON, E.H. *Watch Dogs: Their Training & Management.* 1923. London. Hutchinson. 1st ed. ils. 271p. cloth. VG. R2. $65.00

RICHARDSON, Evelyn M. *B...Was for Butter & Enemy Craft.* 1976. Halifax. 4th prt. 122p. VG/wrp. A17. $7.50

RICHARDSON, Frances. *Hark Back With Love.* 1970. Phil. Dorrance. 8vo. 205p. VG/chip. V3. $12.00

RICHARDSON, Harry J. *A Selection of Dialect Poems Written on the Rail...* 1884. Boston. Travellers Pub. 1st ed. ils Chivers. prt pict wrp. G. M1. $175.00

RICHARDSON, James H. *For the Life of Me: Memoirs of a City Edit.* 1954. NY. 312p. VG. D3. $12.50

RICHET, Charles. *Melanges Biologiques. Livre Dedie a Charles Richet.* 1912. Paris. pres. 541p. orig prt wrp. uncut/unopened. G7. $395.00

RICHLER, Mordecai. *Hunting Tigers Under Glass.* 1968. Toronto. McClelland Stewart. 1st ed. NF/VG. B3. $20.00

RICHLER, Mordecai. *Shovelling Trouble.* 1973. London. Quartet. ARC. RS. F/F. B3. $30.00

RICHMOND, Grace S. *On Christmas Day in the Morning.* 1910. Doubleday. ils Charles M Relyea. VG+. M5. $18.00

RICHMOND, Grace S. *Red Pepper Returns.* 1931. Doubleday Doran. 1st ed. 321p. G. H1. $3.00

RICHTER, Ada. *Play & Sing. Favorite Songs in Easy Arrangement.* 1939. Bryn Mawr. obl 4to. 55p. G/wrp. A17. $6.00

RICHTER, Conrad. *Early Americana & Other Stories.* 1936. Knopf. 1st ed. VG. A18. $35.00

RICHTER, Conrad. *Free Man.* 1943. Knopf. 1st ed. inscr/sgn. F/dj. A18. $90.00

RICHTER, Conrad. *Tacey Cromwell.* 1942. Knopf. 1st ed. F/reinforced. A18. $40.00

RICHTER, Conrad. *Tacey Cromwell.* 1942. Knopf. 1st ed. VG/VG. B5. $25.00

RICHTER, Conrad. *Trees.* 1940. Knopf. 1st ltd advance ed. pub pres. 1/255. F/VG case. A18. $125.00

RICHTER, Gisela M. *Handbook of Greek Art.* 1965. London. Phaidon. ils. 421p. VG/dj. M10. $12.50

RICHTER, Gisela M. *Kouroi, Archaic Greek Youths. A Study of Development...* 1960. London. Phaidon. 1st ed. 4to. 342p. gilt gray-brn cloth. F/dj/case. F1. $185.00

RICHTER, Hans. *Dreams That Money Can Buy.* nd. Films Internat. 1st ed. F/prt gr wrp. B2. $65.00

RICHTER, Melvin. *Essays in Theory & Hist: Approach to Social Sciences.* 1970. Harvard. bl cloth. G1. $25.00

RICKARDS, Maurice. *Collecting Printed Ephemera.* 1988. Phaidon. 1st ed. 224p. M/M. S11. $25.00

RICKARDS, Maurice. *Public Notice.* 1973. NY. Clarkson. 128p. VG/dj. A10. $15.00

RICKETTS, Viva Leone. *Pet Pomeranian.* 1956 (1954). Fond du Lac, WI. All Pets. 2nd ed. 64p. VG/wrp. R2. $15.00

RICKEY, D. *Forty Miles a Day on Beans & Hay.* 1963. Norman. 1st ed. VG/VG. B5. $45.00

RICKOFF, Jean. *Writing About the Frontier: Mark Twain.* 1961. Chicago. Britannica. 191p. VG/dj. M10. $12.50

RICOEUR, Paul. *Oneself As Another.* 1992. Chicago. 1st Eng-language ed. gray cloth. F/dj. G1. $25.00

RIDDLE, James. *Animal Lore & Disorder, a Riddle Book.* nd. London. Falcon. mechanical pop-up. VG+. C8. $30.00

RIDGAWAY, H.B. *Lord's Land. A Narrative of Travels in Sinai...* 1876. NY. 1st ed. 743p. ils/map. G+. F1. $75.00

RIDLEY, Nicholas. *Way to Peace Amongst All Protestants...* 1688. London. Baldwin. 1st ed. H10. $85.00

RIDPATH, Ian. *Hamlyn Encyclopedia of Space.* 1981. London. Hamlyn. 4to. 160p. VG/VG. K5. $25.00

RIDPATH, Ian. *Star Tales.* 1988. NY. Universe. 8vo. ils. 161p. F/F. K5. $25.00

RIEFENSTAHL, Leni. *Last of the Nuba.* 1973. np. 1st Am ed. M/clip. H4. $100.00

RIEMAN, Terry. *Vamp Till Ready.* 1954. Harper. 1st ed. NF/NF. P3. $15.00

RIESE, Walther. *History of Neurology.* 1959. NY. 1st ed. 223p. A13. $75.00

RIESMAN, David. *Faces in the Crowd.* 1952. Yale. 741p. G. K4. $15.00

RIFKIN, Jeremy. *Algeny.* 1983. Viking. 298p. VG/VG. A10. $15.00

RIFKIN, Jeremy. *Beyond Beef: Rise & Fall of Cattle Culture.* 1992. Dutton. 353p. F/F. A10. $20.00

RIFKIN, Jeremy. *Biosphere Politics. Cultural Odyssey From Middle Ages...* 1992. Harper. 388p. VG. A10. $10.00

RIFKIN, Jeremy. *Entrophy.* 1980. Viking. inscr. 305p. VG/VG. A10. $20.00

RIFKIN & HOWARD. *Emerging Order: God in the Age of Scarcity.* 1979. Putnam. 303p. VG/VG. A10. $15.00

RIFLIN, Shepard. *Murderer Vine.* 1970. Dodd Mead. 1st ed. VG/VG. P3. $15.00

RIGBY, Reginald. *Miss ToTo of Pooh-Pooh Town.* nd. London. Seigle Hill. ils May Gladwin. 64p. sage gr brd. NF. D6. $75.00

RIGELSFORD, Adrian. *Doctor Who: The Monsters.* 1992. Doctor Who Books. TVTI. F/dj. P3. $25.00

RIGGS, Lynn. *Green Grow the Lilacs.* 1954. LEC. 1/1500. ils/sgn TH Benton. emb buckram. F/glassine/case. B24. $250.00

RIHANI, Ameen F. *Quatrians of Abu'l-Ala.* 1904. London. Grant Richards. VG. N2. $17.50

RIHBANY, Abraham Mitrie. *Far Journey.* 1914. Boston/NY. Houghton Mifflin. 2nd ed. 352p. VG. W1. $14.00

RIIS, Jacob A. *Battle With the Slum.* 1902. NY. 1st ed. ils. teg. 465p. gilt bl cloth. VG. H3. $45.00

RIIS, Jacob A. *Making of an American.* 1904. Macmillan. later prt. inscr. G. S9. $40.00

RIIS, Jacob A. *Old Town.* 1909. NY. 1st ed. cloth. VG. C11. $40.00

RIKER, Ben. *Pony Wagon Town.* 1948. Bobbs Merrill. 1st ed. VG/G. O3. $65.00

RIKHOFF, Jim. *Hunting the African Elephant.* 1985. Clinton. 1/1000. sgn. ils. 688p. VG/case. B18. $27.50

RILEY, Athelstan. *Athos or the Mountain of the Monks.* 1887. London. 8vo. ils/pl/map. 409p. gilt cloth. F. O2. $450.00

RILEY, Elhu Samuel. *Stonewall Jackson: A Thesaurus of Anecdotes & Incidents...* 1920. Annapolis, MD. 1st ed. 203p. cloth. NF. M8. $450.00

RILEY, Frank L. *Bible of Bibles.* 1928. Los Angeles, CA. Rowny Pr. sgn. 432p. cloth. VG/dj. W1. $14.00

RILEY, James Whitcomb. *Boy Lives on Our Farm.* 1908. Bobbs Merrill. ils Ethel F Betts. 28p. bl cloth. VG+. D6. $75.00

RILEY, James Whitcomb. *Child-World.* 1897. Bowen Merrill. 1st ed/later prt. 209p. red cloth. NF. M20. $60.00

RILEY, James Whitcomb. *Love Lyrics.* 1899. Bobbs Merrill. ils Wm B Dyer. pict gr cloth. VG. M5. $15.00

RILEY, James Whitcomb. *Morning.* 1907. Bobbs Merrill. 1st ed. 162p. VG. M20. $40.00

RILEY, James Whitcomb. *Old Sweetheart of Mine.* 1902. Bobbs Merrill. ils HC Christy. gilt cloth. NF/dj. M20. $50.00

RILEY, James Whitcomb. *Old Sweetheart of Mine.* 1902. Bobbs Merrill. ils HC Christy. VG. N2. $25.00

RILEY, James Whitcomb. *Riley Love: Lyrics With Life Pictures by Wm B Dyer.* (1899). Bowen Merrill. 190p. gilt pict bdg. VG+. H1. $15.00

RILEY, James. *Authentic Narrative of Loss of Am Brig Commerce...* 1833. Andrus Judd. 8vo. 271p. G. W1. $45.00

RILING, R. *Union & Dress of Army & Navy of Confederate States of Am.* 1960. Phil. ltd ed. 4to. intro Harwell. VG/torn glassine. C11. $150.00

RILKIE, Rainer Maria. *Selected Poems.* 1981. LEC. ltd ed. sgn/lithographer Robert Kipniss. F/case. V1. $85.00

RIMEL, Duane W. *Curse of Caine.* 1945. McKay. 1st ed. VG/VG. P3. $25.00

RIMMER, Robert H. *Zolotov Affair.* 1967. Sherbourne Pr. 1st ed. F/NF. F4. $30.00

RIMMER, William. *Elements of Design. Book First. For Use of Parents...* 1864. Boston. Wilson. 1st ed. 8vo. 36 full-p pl. M1. $200.00

RINE, Josephine Z. *Ideal Boston Terrier.* 1932. Orange Judd. 1st ed. ils. 192p. cloth. F/VG. R2. $65.00

RINEHARD, Mary R. *Through Glacier Park.* 1916. Houghton Mifflin. 1st ed. ils. VG. scarce. B34. $75.00

RINEHART, Mary Roberts. *Album.* 1933. Farrar Rinehart. 1st ed. G+. P3. $30.00

RINEHART, Mary Roberts. *Dangerous Days.* 1919. Doran. VG. P3. $20.00

RINEHART, Mary Roberts. *Great Mistake.* 1940. Farrar Rinehart. 1st ed. F/NF. M15. $45.00

RINEHART, Mary Roberts. *Lost Ecstasy.* nd. Grosset Dunlap. photoplay ed. VG. P3. $20.00

RINEHART, Mary Roberts. *Lost Ecstasy.* 1927. Doran. 1st ed. 372p. orange cloth. VG. S11. $10.00

RINEHART, Mary Roberts. *My Story.* 1931. NY. Farrar. 1st ed. NF/torn. B2. $45.00

RINEHART, Mary Roberts. *Red Lamp.* 1925. Doran. 1st ed. VG-. P3. $20.00

RINEHART, Mary Roberts. *Red Lamp.* 1925. Doran. 1st ed. VG/VG. M15. $45.00

RINEHART, Mary Roberts. *Street of Seven Stars.* 1914. Houghton Mifflin. 1st ed. 377p. VG. M20. $25.00

RINEHART, Mary Roberts. *Yellow Room.* 1945. Farrar Rinehart. 1st ed. VG. P3. $15.00

RING, B. *Peik.* 1932. Little Brn. 1st ed. ils Robert Lawson. 268p. VG. P2. $55.00

RING, Douglas; see Prather, Richard.

RING, Ray. *Arizona Kiss.* 1991. Little Brn. 1st ed. F/F. P3. $18.00

RINGE, Donald A. *James Fenimore Cooper.* 1962. Twayne. 1st ed. F/VG+. A18. $20.00

RINK, Evald. *Printing in Delaware 1761-1800: A Checklist.* 1969. Wilmington, DE. 1st ed. 8vo. 214p. NF/VG. V3. $17.50

RIPLEY, Clements. *Devil Drums.* 1930. London. 1st ed. VG. M2. $15.00

RIPLEY, Mary Churchill. *Oriental Rug Book.* 1904. NY. ils. VG. M17. $50.00

RIPLEY, Robert. *Believe It or Not!* 1929. Simon Schuster. 4th prt. inscr/dtd 1929. 172p. red stp gr cloth. G. H5. $250.00

RIPLEY, Sherman. *Raggedy Animals.* 1935. Rand McNally. ils Harrison Cady. 62p. pict bdg. G+. A3. $25.00

RIPPON, Angela. *Badminton: A Celebration.* 1987. Topsfield. Salem House. 1st Am ed. VG+/VG+. O3. $25.00

RISENHOOVER, C.C. *White Heat.* 1992. Bakerville. 1st ed. F/VG+. P8. $35.00

RISTEEN, M.L. *MT Gold.* 1951. Cupples Leon. 1st ed. ils. G. B34. $28.00

RITCH, Johnny. *Horse Feathers.* 1940. Helena, MT. private prt. F. B34. $45.00

RITCHIE, Ward. *Guide to the Hand Press.* 1989. W Yorkshire. Fleece. 73x55mm. 1/200. 38p. gilt blk calf. F/linen case. B24. $650.00

RITCHIE, Ward. *Harold Action: A Bibliography.* 1984. np. 1/500. F/F. A4. $85.00

RITCHIE, Ward. *Story of the SW Mus.* 1960. Ward Ritchie. sgn. 50p. NF/wrp. B19. $35.00

RITCHIE, Ward. *Years Touched With Memories.* 1992. AB Bookman. 1st ed. 171p. F/sans. B19. $75.00

RITTENHOUSE, Jack. *American Horse-Drawn Vehicles.* 1948. NY. Bonanza. rpt. 4to. VG/VG. O3. $40.00

RITZ, David. *Man Who Brought the Dodgers Back to Brooklyn.* 1981. Simon Schuster. 1st ed. F/VG+. P8. $25.00

RIVERA, Diego. *Frescoes of Diego Rivera.* 1929. Harcourt Brace. ARC/1st ed. intro Ernestine Evans. 144p. gilt cloth. F. F1. $250.00

RIVES, Reginald. *Coaching Club: Its Hist, Records & Activities.* 1935. Derrydale. ltd ed. 1/350. folio. VG+. O3. $925.00

RIVET, Paul. *Maya Cities.* 1960. London/NY. 1st ed. 234p. VG. F3. $60.00

RIVIERE, B.B. *Retrievers.* 1947. London. Faber. 1st ed. 73p. VG/tattered. R2. $40.00

RIVIERE, Lazare. *Arcana...* 1696. Venice. Joannes La Nou. 4to. 476p. 20th-C brn calf/marbled brd. K1. $375.00

RIZK, Salom. *Syrian Yankee.* 1954. Doubleday. 1st ed. sgn twice. cloth. VG/dj. W1. $18.00

RIZVI, Maulana Syed Saeed. *Elements of Islamic Studies.* 1989. Bloomfield, NJ. Pyam-e-Aman. 1st revised Am ed. VG/stiff wrp. W1. $8.00

ROAD, Alan. *Doctor Who: Making of a TV Series.* 1982. Andre Deutsch. TVTI. NF. P3. $20.00

ROBACK, A.A. *Personality in Theory & Practice.* 1950. Cambridge, MA. Sci-Art Pub. 347p. F/dj. K4. $25.00

ROBACK, A.A. *Present-Day Psychology.* 1955. NY. Philosophical Lib. G/dj. K4. $15.00

ROBB, David M. *Art of the Illuminated Manuscript.* 1973. Barnes. 345p. VG/rpr. M20. $30.00

ROBBINS, Archibald. *Journal of Loss of Brig Commerce of Hartford...* 1821. Hartford. 275p. full leather. missing map. E5. $65.00

ROBBINS, Archibald. *Journal of Loss of Brig Commerce of Hartford...* 1842. Hartford. gr leather. VG. M17. $60.00

ROBBINS, James J. *Government of Labor Relations in Sweden.* 1942. Chapel Hill. bl cloth. M11. $35.00

ROBBINS, Thomas. *Diary..., 1796-1854...* 1886-1887. Boston. Beacon. 2 vol. 1st ed. VG. H10. $125.00

ROBBINS, Tod. *Spirit of the Town.* 1912. Ogilvie. 1st ed. VG. M2. $100.00

ROBBINS, Tom. *Another Roadside Attraction.* 1971. Doubleday. 1st ed/author's 1st novel. NF/NF. L3. $675.00

ROBBINS, Tom. *Even Cowgirls Get the Blues.* 1976. Houghton Mifflin. 1st ed/author's 2nd novel. NF/F. B4. $350.00

ROBBINS, Tom. *Even Gowgirls Get the Blues.* 1976. Houghton Mifflin. UP. F/prt bl wrp. B3. $500.00

ROBBINS, Tom. *Jitterbug Perfume.* 1984. Bantam. 1st ed. VG/VG. P3. $16.00

ROBBINS, Tom. *Still Life With Woodpecker.* 1980. Bantam. 1st ed. sgn. F/VG. B3. $100.00

ROBER, P. *La Noblesse de France aux Croisades.* 1845. Paris. DeRache Dumoulin. ils/pl. 399p. cloth. H10. $27.50

ROBERTS, Charles G.D. *In the Morning of Time.* 1922. McClelland Stewart. 1st ed. VG-. P3. $35.00

ROBERTS, Dan. *Wyoming Showdown.* 1969. Arcadia. G/dj. B34. $10.00

ROBERTS, David E. *Psychotherapy & the Christian View of Man.* 1950. Scribner. 161p. G/dj. B29. $4.00

ROBERTS, David. *DVs: Cattle Breeds & Origin.* 1916. WI. 177p. gr cloth. VG. M20. $36.00

ROBERTS, Elizabeth. *Buried Treasure.* 1931. Viking. dj. N2. $10.00

ROBERTS, Elizabeth. *Under the Tree.* 1922. NY. 1st ed. NF/NF. C2. $250.00

ROBERTS, Gillian. *Caught Dead in Philadelphia.* 1987. Scribner. 1st ed. F/F. M15. $45.00

ROBERTS, James. *Grant & Validity of British Patents for Inventions.* 1903. NY. 1st Am ed ils. 647p. VG. D3. $45.00

ROBERTS, Keith. *Anita.* 1990. Owlswick. 1st Am hc ed. ils SE Fabian. F/F. T2. $20.00

ROBERTS, Keith. *Kaeti on Tour.* 1992. Sirius Book Co. 1st ed. F/F. P3. $30.00

ROBERTS, Keith. *Kiteworld.* 1985. Gollancz. 1st ed. F/F. P3. $25.00

ROBERTS, Keith. *Kiteworld.* 1985. Gollancz. 1st ed. sgn. F/F. T2. $32.00

ROBERTS, Keith. *Kiteworld.* 1986. Arbor. 1st Am ed. F/F. N3. $15.00

ROBERTS, Kenneth. *Boon Island.* 1956. Doubleday. 1st ed. NF/VG. B3. $35.00

ROBERTS, Kenneth. *Lydia Bailey.* 1947. Doubleday. 1st ed. 488p. VG. H1. $8.50

ROBERTS, Kenneth. *Northwest Passage.* 1937. Doubleday Doran. 709p. VG/dj. B34. $30.00

ROBERTS, Kenneth. *Northwest Passage.* 1940. Doubleday Doran. 709p. map ep. VG+. P4. $12.00

ROBERTS, Lee; see Martin, Robert.

ROBERTS, Les. *Carrot for the Donkey.* 1989. St Martin. 1st ed. F/F. P3. $17.00

ROBERTS, Les. *Not Enough Horses.* 1988. St Martin. 1st ed. sgn. F/F. S6. $35.00

ROBERTS, Ned H. *Muzzle-Loading Cap Lock Rifle.* 1958. Stackpole. 5th prt. 308p. VG/dj. M20. $45.00

ROBERTS, Norman C. *Baja California Plant Field Guide.* 1989. La Jolla. 2 maps/295 mc photos. 309p. M. B26. $22.95

ROBERTS, Patricia. *Tender Prey.* 1983. Doubleday. 1st ed. VG/VG. P3. $15.00

ROBERTS, Paul. *Hoof Prints on Forest Ranges.* 1963. San Antonio. sgn. photos. VG/dj. B26. $21.00

ROBERTS, Susan. *Magician of the Golden Dawn.* 1978. Contemporary Books. VG/VG. P3. $20.00

ROBERTS, W. Adolphe. *Brave Mardi Gras.* 1946. Bobbs Merrill. 1st ed. VG/G+. P3. $15.00

ROBERTS, W. Adolphe. *Lands of the Inner Sea. The West Indies & Bermuda.* 1948. Coward McCann. 8vo. 301p. G. B11. $20.00

ROBERTS, William. *Essay on Wasting Palsey.* 1858. London. 4 pl. 210p. VG. scarce. B14. $750.00

ROBERTS, William. *Treatise on Construction of the Statues...* 1825. Hartford. Oliver D Cooke. contemporary sheep. M11. $125.00

ROBERTS, Windsor Hall. *Hist of College Baptist Church 1855-1955.* ca 1955. np. 1st ed. 64p. VG/prt wrp. M8. $27.50

ROBERTSON, A.H. *European Inst, Co-Operation, Integration, Unification.* 1958. NY. Praeger. M11. $45.00

ROBERTSON, A.T. *Harmony of the Gospels.* 1950. Harper. 305p. M/dj. B29. $7.00

ROBERTSON, Bruce. *Air Aces of the 1914-1918 War.* 1959. Letchworth. 1st ed. ils. G/dj. B18. $45.00

ROBERTSON, Bruce. *Aircraft Camouflage & Markings 1907-1954.* 1959. Letchworth. 1st ed. 212p. G. B18. $45.00

ROBERTSON, Charles Franklin. *Early Days of the Church in KS City.* 1883. KS City, MO. Wimbush Powell. 1st ed. 14p. ES. NF/prt wrp. M8. $150.00

ROBERTSON, Don. *River & the Wilderness.* 1962. Doubleday. 1st ed. VG/VG. M20. $15.00

ROBERTSON, E. Arnot. *Sign Post.* 1944. Canada. Macmillan. 1st ed. VG. P3. $13.00

ROBERTSON, E. Arnot. *Spanish Town Papers.* 1959. London. Cressent. ils. 199p. dj. T7. $40.00

ROBERTSON, J. Drummond. *Evolution of Clockwork.* 1972. SR Pub Ltd. 2nd ed. 8vo. red cloth. VG/VG. A8. $30.00

ROBERTSON, John Kellock. *Intro to Physical Optics.* 1935. London. Chapman Hall. 2nd ed. 8vo. 471p. maroon cloth. G. K5. $22.00

ROBERTSON, John M. *Letters on Reasoning.* nd. London. Watts. 174p. G. K4. $8.50

ROBERTSON, John W. *Francis Drake & Other Early Explorers Along Pacific Coast.* 1927. San Francisco. Grabhorn. 1/1000. 28 maps. 290p. VG+. P4. $350.00

ROBERTSON, Pat. *New Millennium: 10 Trends That Will Impact You...* 1990. Word. 322p. F. B29. $6.50

ROBERTSON, Terence. *Crisis: Inside Story of Suez Conspiracy.* 1965. Atheneum. 1st Am ed. 8vo. NF/NF. W1. $14.00

ROBERTSON, W. Graham. *Blake Collection of W Graham Robertson.* 1952. London. Faber. ils. blk stp red cloth. VG/dj. F1. $55.00

ROBERTSON, Wilfrid. *Coaster's Mate.* 1961. Collins. 1st ed. VG/VG. P3. $13.00

ROBESON, Kenneth; see Goulart, Ron.

ROBINS, Elizabeth. *Under the Southern Cross.* 1907. Stokes. 1st ed. 4 mc pl. cloth. VG+. M5. $30.00

ROBINSON, B.W. *Persian Miniatures.* nd. Citadel. 1st ed. 12mo. 20 color pl. cloth. VG. W1. $15.00

ROBINSON, Brooks. *Third Base Is My Home.* 1974. Waco. 2nd prt. photos. 202p. VG/VG. A17. $9.50

ROBINSON, Cecil. *With the Ears of Strangers.* 1971. AZ U. ils/notes/index. 338p. VG/wrp. B19. $10.00

ROBINSON, Charles N. *Old Naval Prints: Their Artists & Engravers.* 1924. London. The Studio. 1/1500. 4to. 96 text pl+24 tipped-in pl. gilt bl cloth. P4. $650.00

ROBINSON, Charles. *Prince Babillon or the Little White Rabbit by Nella.* ca 1912. Kennerley. ils. 131p. gilt/red pict wht vellum. G+. P2. $85.00

ROBINSON, Edward Arlington. *Amaranth.* 1934. Macmillan. 1st ed. 105p. VG/dj. M20. $25.00

ROBINSON, Edward Arlington. *Edward Arlington Robinson & His Manuscripts.* 1944. Colby College Lib. ltd ed. 1/250. 36p. VG. A4. $55.00

ROBINSON, Fay. *Mexico & Her Military Chieftains.* 1970. Rio Grande Pr. facsimile of 1847 ed. fld map. 353p. VG. F3. $20.00

ROBINSON, H. *Great Fur Land: Sketches of Life in Hudson's Bay Territory.* 1879. np. 348p. VG. E5. $45.00

ROBINSON, Henry. *Stout Cortez.* 1931. NY. Century. 1st ed. 347p. VG/dj. F3. $20.00

ROBINSON, Irene B. *Beasts of the Tar Pits.* 1949. Ward Ritchie. ils. 45p. G. B19. $20.00

ROBINSON, Jackie. *Little League Baseball Book.* 1972. NY. 1st ed. VG/VG. B5. $50.00

ROBINSON, James. *Phil Directory for 1807.* 1807. Phil. 1st ed. 16mo. old calf brd. M1. $475.00

ROBINSON, Kim Stanley. *Gold Coast.* 1988. St Martin. 1st ed. F/F. T2. $35.00

ROBINSON, Kim Stanley. *Pacific Edge.* 1990. Tor. 1st Am ed. F/F. N3. $15.00

ROBINSON, Kim Stanley. *Planet on the Table.* 1986. Tor. 1st ed. inscr. F/F. T2. $35.00

ROBINSON, Kim Stanley. *Remaking History.* 1991. Tor. 1st ed. sgn. F/F. T2. $25.00

ROBINSON, Kim Stanley. *Short, Sharp Shock.* 1990. Ziesing. 1st ed. sgn. F/F. T2. $25.00

ROBINSON, Lewis. *General Goes Too Far.* 1936. Putnam. 1st Am ed. F/NF. M15. $45.00

ROBINSON, Marilynne. *Housekeeping.* 1980. FSG. 1st ed/author's 1st book. F/F. S9. $75.00

ROBINSON, Maude. *South Down Farm in the Sixties.* 1947. London. Bannisdale. 2nd ed. 8vo. 78p. VG/dj. V3. $14.00

ROBINSON, Maude. *Time of Her Life & Other Stories.* nd. London. Swarthmore. 12mo. 261p. G. V3. $16.00

ROBINSON, N.F. *Monasticism in the Orthodox Churches.* 1916. London. 8vo. ils. 175p. cloth. O2. $35.00

ROBINSON, P.C. *Willa: Life of Willa Cather.* 1983. Doubleday. 1st ed. F/dj. A18. $25.00

ROBINSON, P.F. *Designs for Ornamental Villas...Scenic Views...* 1836. London. 3rd ed. 4to. 96 full-p pl. gr cloth. C6. $250.00

ROBINSON, Peter. *Dedicated Man.* 1991. Scribner. 1st Am ed. sgn. F/F. T2. $20.00

ROBINSON, Peter. *Gallows View.* 1990. Scribner. ARC/1st Am ed. sgn. RS. F/F. S6. $40.00

ROBINSON, Peter. *Necessary End.* 1989. Canada. Viking. 1st ed. VG/VG. P3. $25.00

ROBINSON, S.T.L. *Kansas: Its Interior & Exterior Life.* 1857. Boston. 366p. F. O8. $28.50

ROBINSON, Spider. *Kill the Editor.* 1991. Axolotl. sgn. F/F. P3. $50.00

ROBINSON, Spider. *Time Pressure.* 1987. Ace. 1st ed. F/F. P3. $20.00

ROBINSON, Stanford. *Celtic Illuminative Art in Gospel Books of Durrow...* 1908. Dublin. Hodges Figgis. 1st ed. folio. 51 pl. unp. cloth. H10. $100.00

ROBINSON, Tom. *Greylocks & the Robins.* 1946. Viking. 1st ed. VG+. C8. $35.00

ROBINSON, Victor. *Victory Over Pain: History of Anesthesia.* 1946. NY. 1st ed. 338p. A13. $35.00

ROBINSON, W. Heath. *Don Quixote.* 1925. Dodd Mead. 1st ed thus. ils. red cloth. VG. M5. $20.00

ROBINSON & SHAVER. *Measures of Social Psychological Attitudes.* 1973. Survey Research Center. 744p. G. K4. $15.00

ROBISON, S.R. *Can Delinquency Be Measured?* 1936. NY. 277p. VG. D3. $12.50

ROCHE, Ruth A. *Bobby's Diary.* 1944. NY. Action Play Books. 1st prt. 34p. VG/rpr. A17. $12.50

ROCHLIN & ROCHLIN. *Pioneer Jews.* 1984. Houghton Mifflin. 1st ed. 243p. NF/NF. B19. $35.00

ROCK, Pat. *Lakeland Terrier.* 1984. np. 1st ed. ils. 89p. sbdg. M. R2. $22.00

ROCKWELL, Anne. *Gypsy Girl's Best Shoes.* 1966. Parents. probable 1st ed. VG. C8. $10.00

ROCKWELL, Carey. *Sand by for Mars!* 1952. Grosset Dunlap. VG/VG. P3. $20.00

ROCKWELL, Charles. *Sketches of Foreign Travel & Life at Sea...* 1842. Boston. 2 vol. 8vo. cloth. O2. $275.00

ROCKWELL, F.F. *Flower Arrangement in Color.* (1940). Wise. 238p. F/VG. H1. $14.00

ROCKWELL, F.F. *Gladiolus.* 1932 (1927). Macmillan. Home Garden Handbook Series. 79p. F. H1. $5.00

ROCKWELL, F.F. *10,000 Garden Questions Answered by 20 Experts.* 1959. Doubleday BC. 2 vol. F/F. H1. $10.00

ROCKWELL & ROCKWELL. *Willie Was Different. Tale of an Ugly Thrushling.* 1969. Funk Wagnall. 1st ed. sgns. 41p. M/dj. B24. $225.00

ROCKWOOD, Roy. *Bomba & the Lost Explorers.* nd. Grosset Dunlap. VG/fair. P3. $12.00

ROCKWOOD, Roy. *Bomba the Jungle Boy in Abandoned City.* 1927. Cupples Leon. 1st ed. VG. M2. $15.00

ROCKWOOD, Roy. *Bomba the Jungle Boy: Jaguar Island.* 1953 (1927). Grosset Dunlap. VG+/VG+. C8. $12.50

ROCKWOOD, Roy. *Lost on the Moon.* 1911. Cupples Leon. Great Marvel #5. lists to #9. VG/torn. M20. $45.00

ROCKWOOD, Roy. *Through Space to Mars.* 1910. Cupples Leon. NF. M2. $20.00

ROCQ, Margaret Miller. *CA Local Hist: Bibliography & Union List of Lib Holdings.* 1970. np. 2nd revised ed. brn cloth. A4/P4. $85.00

RODAHL, Kaare. *Last of the Few.* 1963. NY. 1st ed. 208p. VG. A17. $9.50

RODD, Ralph. *Midnight Murder.* 1931. Collins Crime Club. 1st ed. VG. P3. $20.00

RODD, Rennell. *Princes of Achaia & the Chronicles of Morea.* 1907. London. 2 vol. 8vo. cloth. xl. O2. $225.00

RODEN, H.W. *Too Busy To Die.* 1944. Detective BC. VG. P3. $10.00

RODEN & WELLER. *Life & Times of Sherlock Holmes.* 1992. Crescent. F/F. P3. $20.00

RODMAN, Selden. *Lawrence: The Last Crusade — A Poem of Three Lives...* 1937. Viking. 1st ed. maps/notes. VG/G clear plastic. M7. $45.00

RODNEY, Robert M. *Mark Twain International: A Bibliography...* 1982. Westport, CT. 1st ed. 275p. F. M10. $27.50

ROE, Clifford G. *Great War on White Slavery; or, Fighting for Protection...* 1911. np. 8vo. 32 engravings. 448p. B11/B34. $40.00

ROE, E.P. *Brave Little Quakeress & Other Stories.* 1892. Dodd Mead. 16mo. 214p. worn bdg. V3. $8.50

ROE, F. Gordon. *Sporting Prints of Eighteenth & Early Nineteenth Centuries.* 1927. Payson Clarke. 1st Am ed. 48 mc pl. VG. O3. $125.00

ROE, Frank Gilbert. *Indian & the Horse.* 1962. Norman. VG/G. O3. $35.00

ROE, Wellington. *Tree Falls South.* 1937. Putnam. 1st ed. sgn. F/NF. B2. $75.00

ROEDER, Helen. *Ordeal of Captain Roeder.* 1960. London. 1st ed. 248p. VG/dj. B18. $12.50

ROEMER, Paul. *Textbook of Ophthalmology in Form of Clinical Lectures...* 1912. NY. Rebman. 3 vol. 1st Eng ed. sm 4to. G7. $75.00

ROESSEL, Ruth. *Navajo Livestock Reduction.* 1974. Navajo Community College. ils. 224p. F/sans. B19. $35.00

ROETHKE, Theodore. *Open House: A Volume of Poems.* 1941. Knopf. 1st ed. 1/1000 #d. VG+/dj. Q1. $300.00

ROFFMAN, Jan. *Walk in the Dark.* 1970. Crime Club. 1st ed. VG/VG. P3. $15.00

ROGER, Andrew Denny. *Noble Fellow, William Starling Sullivant.* 1940. Putnam. 361p. VG/dj. A10. $35.00

ROGERS, Alan. *New Life for the Dead.* 1991. Wildside. 1st ed. sgn. 1/250. F/dj. M2. $40.00

ROGERS, Alva. *Requiem for Astounding.* 1964. Advent. 1st ed. VG/dj. P3. $45.00

ROGERS, Cameron. *Trodden Glory.* 1949. Santa Barbara. ils. 130p. VG/dj. B26. $27.50

ROGERS, Dale Evans. *Angel Unaware, Dearest Debbie, Salute to Sandy.* 1967. Revell. 117p. VG/dj. B29. $4.00

ROGERS, Dale Evans. *Angel Unaware.* 1953. Revell. 63p. VG/torn. B29. $2.25

ROGERS, Dale Evans. *Only One Star: Cure for Celebrity Syndrome.* 1988. Word. 165p. M/M. B29. $6.50

ROGERS, Dale Evans. *Where He Leads.* 1974. Revell. 126p. F/dj. B29. $3.00

ROGERS, Dale Evans. *Woman, Be All You Can Be.* 1980. Revell. 127p. xl. VG/dj. B29. $3.00

ROGERS, Dale Evans. *Woman at the Well.* 1970. Guideposts. 191p. VG/dj. B29. $4.50

ROGERS, Edward. *Some Account of Life & Opinions of 5th Monarchy Man...* 1867. London. Longman. 1st ed. 4to. 343p. morocco. H10. $85.00

ROGERS, Felicity. *All About the Shetland & Sheepdog.* 1980. London. Pelham. 2nd revised ed. 112p. cloth. M/dj. R2. $22.00

ROGERS, Fred. *Healing Art: History of Medical Society of New Jersey.* 1966. Trenton. 1st ed. 4to. 346p. dj. A13. $25.00

ROGERS, G. *Memoranda of the Experience, Labors & Travels...* 1845. Cincinnati. full calf/leather spine label. VG. A9. $50.00

ROGERS, Horatio. *Personal Experiences of the Chancellorsville Campaign.* 1881. Providence. 1st ed. 1/250. 33p. prt wrp. M8. $45.00

ROGERS, Mary Eliza. *Domestic Life in Palestine.* 1869. Cincinnati. 8vo. 436p. cloth. O2. $50.00

ROGERS, Samuel. *Italy, a Poem.* 1830. London. Cadell. 1st revised ed. full bl sheepskin. w/sgn letter. H4. $385.00

ROGERS, Will. *Autobiography of Will Rogers.* 1949. Houghton Mifflin. front ep removed. G+/dj. P3. $18.00

ROGERS, Will. *How We Elect Our Presidents.* 1952. Little Brn. 1st ed. edit/sgn Donald Day. 175p. blk lettered gr cloth. F. H5. $125.00

ROGERS, Will. *Illiterate Digest.* 1924. NY. Boni. ils. 351p. F/F. B14. $55.00

ROGERS, Will. *Illiterate Digest.* 1924. NY. Boni. 351p. VG. E5. $35.00

ROGERS, Will. *Letters of a Self-Made Diplomat to His President.* 1926. NY. Boni. 1st ed. 8vo. 263p. dk brn stp brn cloth. NF/dj. H5. $250.00

ROGERS, Will. *On How We Elect Our Presidents.* 1952. Boston. 1st ed. VG/VG. B5. $25.00

ROGERS & WARD. *August Reckoning.* 1973. LSU. 1st ed. 195p. cloth. VG+/dj. M20. $15.00

ROHDE, Eleanour S. *Story of the Garden.* 1936. Boston. 3rd prt. 325p. G7. $25.00

ROHMER, Sax. *Bat Wing.* 1931. Cassell. 3rd ed. VG. P3. $20.00

ROHMER, Sax. *Book of Fu Manchu.* 1927. MacBride. 1st ed. G+. M21. $10.00

ROHMER, Sax. *Brood of the Witch Queen.* 1924. Doubleday Page. 1st ed. G+. P3. $45.00

ROHMER, Sax. *Daughter of Fu Manchu.* 1931. Doubleday Doran. 1st ed. poor. P3. $15.00

ROHMER, Sax. *Devil Doctor.* 1973. Tom Stacey. F/F. P3. $20.00

ROHMER, Sax. *Dope.* 1919. AL Burt. 1st ed thus. VG. M21. $20.00

ROHMER, Sax. *Dope.* 1931. Cassell. VG. P3. $20.00

ROHMER, Sax. *Emperor Fu Manchu.* 1959. London. Herbert Jenkins. 1st ed. 8vo. 221p. blk stp red brd. F/dj. H5. $75.00

ROHMER, Sax. *Emperor of America.* 1935. Cassell. 3rd ed. VG. P3. $35.00

ROHMER, Sax. *Fu Manchu's Bride.* 1933. Crime Club. 1st ed. front free ep removed. VG. P3. $40.00

ROHMER, Sax. *Green Eyes of Bast.* 1920. McBride. 1st ed. VG. P3. $75.00

ROHMER, Sax. *Hangover House.* 1949. Random. 1st ed. VG. P3. $45.00

ROHMER, Sax. *Island of Fu Manchu.* 1941. Doubleday Crime Club. 1st ed. F/NF. M15. $450.00

ROHMER, Sax. *President Fu Manchu.* 1936. Crime Club. 1st ed. VG. P3. $50.00

ROHMER, Sax. *Return of Dr Fu Manchu.* nd. McKinlay Stone MacKenzie. VG. P3. $20.00

ROHMER, Sax. *Return of Dr Fu Manchu.* 1916. McBride. 1st ed. VG. Q1. $200.00

ROHMER, Sax. *Sinister Madonna.* 1956. Herbert Jenkins. 1st ed. sgn. VG/dj. P3. $85.00

ROHMER, Sax. *White Velvet.* 1936. Doubleday Doran. 1st ed. F/NF. M15. $250.00

ROHMER, Sax. *Yellow Claw Mystery.* 1924. Methuen. 11th prt. VG/fair. P3. $25.00

ROHMER, Sax. *Yu'An Hee See Laughs.* (1932). Collier. 1st ed thus. VG+. M21. $15.00

ROHMER, Sax. *Yu'an Hee See Laughs.* 1932. Doubleday Crime Club. 1st ed. F/NF. M15. $450.00

ROJANKOVSKY, Feodor. *Tall Book of Mother Goose.* 1942. Harper/Artists & Writers Guild. 120p. pict brd. G+. A3. $20.00

ROJAS, Mariano. *Estudios Gramaticales del Idioma Mexicano.* 1935. Salvador. 84p. gilt bdg. VG. F3. $25.00

ROLAND, Charles. *Sir William Osler, 1849-1919.* 1982. Toronto. 1st ed. 116p. dj. A13. $30.00

ROLFE, Edwin. *Collected Poems.* 1993. Urbana. 1st ed. F/F. B2. $35.00

ROLLESTON, Humphrey. *Internal Medicine.* 1930. NY. 1st ed. 92p. A13. $60.00

ROLLESTON, T.W. *Celtic Myths & Legends.* 1986. Bracken Books. 1st ed. VG. P3. $25.00

ROLLIN, M. *Histoire des Egyptiens, des Carthaginois, de Assyriens...* 1739. Paris. Estienne. Nouvelle ed. 18mo. contemporary calf. VG. W1. $20.00

ROLLINS, Mark. *Mental Imagery: On Limits of Cognitive Science.* 1989. np. 170p. tan cloth. VG/dj. G1. $18.50

ROLLS, Sam Cottington. *Settel Chariots of the Desert.* 1937. London. Cape. 1st ed. photos/2 maps. rebound half leather. F. M7. $250.00

ROLLYSON, Carl. *Lillian Hellman: Her Legend & Her Legacy.* 1988. St Martin. 1st ed. 613p. F/F. A17. $15.00

ROLSTON, Holmes. *Faces About the Christ.* 1959. John Knox. 215p. VG/dj. B29. $4.50

ROLT-WHEELER, Francis. *Book of Cowboys.* 1921. Lothrop Lee. 1st ed. ils. F/torn. A18. $60.00

ROLVAAG, O.E. *Boat of Longing.* 1933. Harper. 1st ed. trans Nora O Solum. F/dj. A18. $50.00

ROLVAAG, O.E. *Their Fathers' God.* 1931. Harper. 1st ed. trans TM Ager. F/chip. A18. $50.00

ROMANES, George J. *Mind & Motion & Monism.* 1895. Longman Gr. 1st Am ed. 12mo. paneled gr cloth. VG. G1. $50.00

ROMANN & WEINGROD. *Living Together Separately: Arabs & Jews...* 1991. Princeton. 1st ed. 8vo. maps. 259p. NF/dj. W1. $20.00

ROMAYNE, Nicolaus. *Dissertatio Inauguralis, de Puris Generatione.* 1780. Edinburgh. Balfour Smellite. pres. 48p. half cloth/marbled brd. G7. $500.00

ROME, Margaret. *Chateau of Flowers.* 1976. Harlequin. VG. P3. $5.00

ROME & ROME. *Life of Incas in Ancient Peru.* 1987. Italy. Liber. ils. 139p. laminated brd. VG. F3. $10.00

ROMERO, Orlando. *Nambe — Year One.* 1976. Tonatiuh. 1st ed. 172p. NF/wrp. B19. $35.00

ROMERO & SPARROW. *Dawn of the Dead.* nd. BC. VG/VG. P3. $8.00

ROMERO & SPARROW. *Dawn of the Dead.* 1978. St Martin. 1st ed. NF/dj. F4. $25.00

RONALDS, A. *Fly Fisher's Entomology.* 1901. NY. 10th ed. 20 mc pl. VG. B5. $80.00

RONNE, Finn. *Antarctic Command.* 1961. Bobbs Merrill. 1st ed. 8vo. 272p. VG/VG. P4. $30.00

RONNS, Edward; see Aarons, Edward S.

ROOK, Arthur. *Cambridge & Its Contribution to Medicine.* 1971. London. 1st ed. 289p. dj. A13. $40.00

ROOKE, Daphne. *Mittee.* 1952. Boston. 1st ed. VG. A17. $7.50

ROOKE, Daphne. *New Zealand Twins.* 1956. London. Cape. 1st ed. ils Shirley Scarlett. VG/VG. C8. $20.00

ROOKE, Leon. *Fat Woman.* 1981. Knopf. 1st ed. F/F. B3. $35.00

ROOME, Annette. *Real Shot in the Arm.* 1989. Crown. 1st ed. NF/NF. P3. $18.00

ROONEY, Andrew. *Fortunes of War.* 1962. Boston. 1st ed. VG/VG. B5. $30.00

ROONEY, James. *Mechanics of the Horse.* 1981. Huntington. Krieger. 1st ed. VG. O3. $38.00

ROOS, Carl. *Nietzche und das Labyrinth.* nd. Copenhagen. Gyldendal. 148p. VG/prt orange wrp. G1. $40.00

ROOS, Kelley. *Bad Trip.* 1971. Dodd Mead. 1st ed. VG/VG. P3. $20.00

ROOS, Kelley. *Requim for a Blonde.* 1958. Dodd Mead. 1st ed. VG/dj. P3. $25.00

ROOS & ROOS. *Few Days in Madrid.* 1968. Andrew Deutsch. 1st ed. VG/VG. P3. $18.00

ROOSEVELT, Anna. *Parmana.* 1980. Academic. 1st ed. 320p. VG. F3. $24.00

ROOSEVELT, Eleanor. *Christmas, Story by Eleanor Roosevelt.* 1940. Knopf. 1st ed. ils Fritz Kredel. M/M. C8. $60.00

ROOSEVELT, Eleanor. *On My Own.* 1958. NY. ARC/1st ed. sgn. M. H4. $185.00

ROOSEVELT, Elliott. *Murder at the Palace.* nd. BC. VG/VG. P3. $8.00

ROOSEVELT, Franklin Delano. *My Friends: 28 History-Making Speeches.* 1945. Foster Stewart. 2nd prt. 157p. VG. H1. $5.00

ROOSEVELT, Theodore. *An Autobiography.* 1913. NY. 1st ed. VG+. A9. $50.00

ROOSEVELT, Theodore. *Book-Lover's Holidays in the Open.* 1920. Scribner. 373p. VG. B19. $15.00

ROOSEVELT, Theodore. *Outdoor Pastimes of an American Hunter.* 1925. Scribner. ils. 409p. VG. B34. $75.00

ROOSEVELT, Theodore. *Ranch Life & the Hunting Trail.* 1978. Bonanza. rpt of 1888 ed. VG/VG. B11. $25.00

ROOSEVELT, Theodore. *Ranch Life & the Hunting Trail.* 1978. Bonanza. 1st ed thus. ils Remington. F/dj. B34. $35.00

ROOSEVELT, Theodore. *Ranch Life in the Far West.* 1968. Northland. ils. 89p. NF/dj. B19. $35.00

ROOT, A.I. *ABC of Bee Culture.* 1895. Medina, OH. 62nd thousand. 428p. VG. M20. $75.00

ROOTH, Signe A. *Seeress of the Northland. Fredrika Bremer's Am Journey...* 1955. Am Swedish Hist Found. 1st ed. inscr/dtd 1955. ils/notes. 327p. NF/worn. P4. $35.00

ROQUELAURE, A.N.; see Rice, Anne.

RORSCHACH, Hermann. *Psychodiagnostics.* 1942. Berne, Switzerland. Verlag Hans Huber. 216p. VG. K4. $45.00

ROSBOROUGH, E.H. *Tying & Fishing Fuzzy Nymphs.* 1969. Manchester, VT. Ornis. 1st ed. VG/VG. B5. $50.00

ROSCOE, Thomas. *Pleasant History of Reynard the Fox.* 1873. London. Sampson Low. ils AT Elwes/John Jellico. 136p. half morocco. F. B24. $65.00

ROSE, Barbara. *Claes Oldenburg.* 1970. MOMA. obl 4to. ils. 221p. limp paded vinyl. NF. F1. $250.00

ROSE, Dixie E. *Utah's Intermountain Wildflowers.* 1979. Salt Lake City. inscr. photos. sc. B26. $12.50

ROSE, Ethne. *Toys & Puppets.* 1979. np. cloth. VG. G2. $8.95

ROSE, Gilbert J. *Power of Form: Psychoanalytic Approach to Aesthetic Form.* 1980. Internat U Pr. 234p. gr cloth. F/chip. G1. $24.00

ROSE, H. Townshend. *English Local Government Law...* 1938. London. H Emerson Smith. 4th revised ed. xl. VG. D3. $35.00

ROSE, Hugh James. *New General Biographical Dictionary...* 1853. London. Fellowes. 12 vol. gilt full leather. H10. $245.00

ROSE, Robert R. *Advocates & Adversaries.* 1977. Lakeside. 328p. gilt bl cloth. M20. $30.00

ROSE, William. *Surgical Treatment of Neuralgia of the 5th Nerve.* 1892. London. Bailliere. 85p. orig cloth/new spine. G7. $295.00

ROSE & SOUCHON. *New Orleans Jazz.* 1967. LSU. 1st ed. inscr both authors. VG. B2. $35.00

ROSE. *Authors & Owners: Invention of Copyright.* 1993. Harvard. 186p. F/F. A4. $35.00

ROSELER, David. *Lawrence, Prince of Mecca.* 1927. Sydney, Australia. Cornstalk. 1st ed. 227p. blk stp red cloth. xl. G. M7. $55.00

ROSEN, Edward. *Nicholas Copernicus, on the Revolutions.* 1978. London. Macmillan. 4to. 450p. G/tattered. K5. $125.00

ROSEN, George. *Preventive Medicine in the US, 1900-1975: Trends...* 1977. NY. 1st ed. 94p. wrp. A13. $25.00

ROSEN, Ismond. *Pathology & Treatment of Sexual Deviation.* 1964. Oxford. 510p. NF/dj. G7. $25.00

ROSEN, R.D. *Strike Three, You're Dead.* nd. Walker. 2nd ed. VG/dj. P3. $20.00

ROSEN, Richard. *Fadeaway.* 1986. Harper Row. 1st ed. F/F. P3. $16.00

ROSEN, Richard. *Fadeaway.* 1986. Harper Row. 1st ed. sgn. F/F. S6. $35.00

ROSEN, Richard. *Saturday Night Dead.* 1988. Viking. 1st ed. VG/VG. P3. $17.00

ROSEN, Sidney. *My Voice Will Go With You.* 1982. Norton. F/dj. K4. $10.00

ROSENBERG, Joel. *Hero.* 1990. NY. ROC. 1st ed. F/F. N3. $15.00

ROSENBERG, Joel. *Not for Glory.* 1988. NAL. 1st ed. F/F. P3. $17.00

ROSENBERG, Samuel. *Naked Is the Best Disguise.* 1975. London. Arlington. 1st Eng ed. VG/dj. N2. $6.50

ROSENBLUETH, Arturo. *Mind & Brain: Philosophy of Science.* 1970. MIT. sm 8vo. 128p. bl cloth. VG/dj. G1. $25.00

ROSENBLUM, Robert. *Arcade.* 1984. Doubleday. 1st ed. F/NF. F4. $15.00

ROSENBLUM, Robert. *Good Thief.* 1975. Hart Davis/MacGibbon. VG/VG. P3. $20.00

ROSENBLUM, Robert. *Sweetheart Deal.* 1976. Putnam. 1st ed. F/F. P3. $15.00

ROSENKRANTZ, Barbara. *Public Health & the State: Changing Views in MA, 1842-1936.* 1972. Cambridge. 1st ed. 259p. A13. $35.00

ROSENSTONE, Robert A. *Crusade of the Left: Lincoln Battalion in Spanish Civil War.* 1969. NY. Pegasus. 1st ed. photos. F/F. V4. $10.00

ROSENTHAL, Bernard G. *Images of Man.* 1971. London/NY. Basic. 238p. M/dj. K4. $10.00

ROSENTHAL, Eric. *Gold! Gold! Gold! The Journal of Hannesburg Gold Rush.* ca 1970. Macmillan. 1st prt. 8vo. 372p. gilt brn cloth. VG. P4. $30.00

ROSENTHAL, Franz. *Humor in Early Islam.* 1956. Phil. 1st ed. 8vo. 11 pl. 154p. cloth. dj. O2. $30.00

ROSENTHAL, M.L. *William Carlos Williams Reader.* 1966. New Directions. sgn Williams. F/NF. V1. $45.00

ROSENTHAL, Michael. *Character Factory: Baden-Powell's Boy Scouts...* 1986. Pantheon. VG/dj. N2. $10.00

ROSENTHAL & ZACHARY. *Jazzways.* 1947. Greenberg. 1st ed. VG. B2. $45.00

ROSETT, Joshua. *Intercortical Systems of the Human Cerebrum.* 1933. NY. Columbia. ils. 132p. G7. $45.00

ROSS, Alexander. *View of All Religions in the World...* 1655. London. Saywell. 2 parts. 8vo. old calf. K1. $375.00

ROSS, David D. *Argus Gambit.* 1989. St Martin. 1st ed. F/F. P3. $19.00

ROSS, Diana. *Little Red Engine Gets a Name.* ca 1940. London. Faber. obl 8vo. 32p. VG/VG. A17. $15.00

ROSS, Edward. *South of Panama.* 1921. Century. ils/map. 396p. VG. F3. $10.00

ROSS, Frank Jr. *Space, Science & You.* 1970. Lothrop Lee Shepard. 4to. 190p. xl. VG. K5. $12.00

ROSS, Frank. *Sleeping Dogs.* 1978. Atheneum. 1st ed. VG/VG. P3. $18.00

ROSS, Isabel. *Margaret Fell: Mother of Quakerism.* 1949. Longman Gr. 1st ed. 8vo. 421p. VG. V3. $15.00

ROSS, Ivan T. *Requiem for a Schoolgirl.* 1961. Heinemann. 1st ed. VG/VG. P3. $28.00

ROSS, Lawrence Sullivan. *Personal Civil War Letters of General Lawrence Sullivan...* 1994. Austin. Morrison. 1st ed. 1/500. cloth. M. M8. $40.00

ROSS, Margaret. *Tiger Island.* nd. London. Gawthorn. ils Margaret Ross. pict cloth. VG. C8. $30.00

ROSS, Nancy Wilson. *I, My Ancestor.* 1950. Random. 1st ed. VG/VG. P3. $15.00

ROSS, W. Donald. *Aristotle.* 1923. London. Methuen. thick 8vo. 300p. emb bl cloth. NF. G1. $75.00

ROSS, W. Gillies. *Arctic Whalers, Icy Seas.* 1985. Tor. 1st ed. photos/maps. F/F. A17. $25.00

ROSS, Wallace. *Sail Power.* 1978. Knopf. ils. 492p. dj. T7. $25.00

ROSSE, Lillian. *Takes.* 1983. NY. 1st ed. VG/torn. A17. $7.50

ROSSELAND, Svein. *Pulsation Theory of Variable Stars.* 1949. Oxford. Clarendon. 8vo. 152p. VG/chip. K5. $70.00

ROSSELLINI, Roberto. *War Trilogy.* 1973. Grossman. 1st ed. 467p. NF/dj. A17. $15.00

ROSSI, Flippo. *Chefs-d'Oeuvre de l'Orfevrerie.* 1956. France. Arts Et Metiers Graphiques. gilt brd. VG+/dj/case. F1. $65.00

ROSSIS, L. *William Withering: Intro to Digitalis.* 1936. NY. 131p. G7. $25.00

ROSSITER, Oscar. *Tetrasomy Two.* 1974. Doubleday. 1st ed. F/F. P3. $13.00

ROSTAND, Robert. *D'Artagnan Signature.* 1976. Putnam. 1st ed. VG/torn. P3. $13.00

ROSTAND & TETRY. *Atlas of Human Genetics.* 1964. London. Hutchinson Scientific & Technical. 102p. F/dj. K4. $20.00

ROSTEN & SHAW. *Marilyn Among Friends.* 1987. Bloomsbury. VG/VG. P3. $20.00

ROSTOV, Mara. *Night Hunt.* 1979. Putnam. 1st ed. F/F. P3. $18.00

ROSZAK, Theodore. *Dreamwatcher.* 1985. Doubleday. 1st ed. F/dj. M2. $16.00

ROTH, Charlene. *Art of Making Cloth Toys.* 1974. np. cloth. VG. G2. $12.50

ROTH, Charlene. *Driving the Light Horse.* 1984. Prentice Hall. 4to. 210p. VG. O3. $25.00

ROTH, Gunter D. *System of Minor Planets.* nd. Van Nostrand. trans Alex Helm. 128p. VG/dj. K5. $25.00

ROTH, Henry. *Nature's First Green.* 1979. NY. 1st ed. sgn. 1/350. gr linen. F/sans. A11. $45.00

ROTH, Holly. *Content Assignment.* nd. BC. VG. P3. $3.00

ROTH, Holly. *Sleeper.* 1955. Simon Schuster. 1st ed. VG/torn. P3. $10.00

ROTH, Philip. *Breast.* 1972. HRW. 1st ed. VG/VG. M20. $25.00

ROTH, Philip. *Great American Novel.* 1973. HRW. 1st ed. F/VG+. P8. $35.00

ROTH, Philip. *Great American Novel.* 1973. HRW. 1st ed. royal 8vo. 382p. gilt navy cloth. F/dj. H5. $50.00

ROTH, Philip. *Portnoy's Complaint.* 1969. Random. 1st ed. sgn. 1/600. F/case. B24. $250.00

ROTH, Philip. *When She Was Good.* 1967. Random. ARC/author's 3rd book. RS. F/F. B4. $150.00

ROTH & WILLIS. *Medical & Veterinary Importance of Cockroaches.* 1957. WA, DC. Smithsonian. 7 pl. 147p. VG/wrp. B14. $45.00

ROTHBERG, Abraham. *Sword of the Golem.* 1970. McCall. 1st ed. F/dj. F4. $15.00

ROTHENSTEIN, John. *Summer's Lease.* 1965. HRW. 1st ed. ils/index. 260p. bl-gr cloth. F/VG. M7. $25.00

ROTHENSTEIN, William. *Since Fifty. Men & Memories 1922-1938.* 1940. NY. Macmillan. 1st ed. 352p. gilt bl linen. NF/VG clear plastic. M7. $95.00

ROTHMAN, David. *Conscience & Convenience: Asylum & Its Alternatives...* 1980. Boston. 1st ed. 484p. A13. $35.00

ROTHWELL, H.T. *Dive Deep for Danger.* 1966. Roy. VG. P3. $10.00

ROTHWELL, H.T. *Duet for Three Spies.* 1967. Roy. 1st ed. F/F. P3. $16.00

ROTSLER, William. *Hidden Worlds of Zandra.* 1983. Doubleday. 1st ed. F/VG+. N3. $10.00

ROTTENSTEINER, Franz. *Fantasy Book: Ils Hist From Dracula to Tolkien.* 1978. Collier. 1st ed. ils. 160p. VG. S11. $10.00

ROTTENSTEINER, Franz. *SF Book: Ils Hist.* 1975. Seabury. 4to. 160p. VG/VG. S11. $30.00

ROUECHE, Berton. *Feral.* 1974. Harper Row. 1st ed. VG/VG. P3. $18.00

ROUECHE, Berton. *Neutral Spirit.* 1960. Little Brn. 1st ed. xl. VG. P3. $5.00

ROUILLE, Guillaume. *Promptuarii Iconum Insigniorum a Seculo Hominum...* 1553. Lyon. Gulielmum Rouillium. 2 parts in 1. 4to. early vellum. K1. $650.00

ROUMAIN, Jacques. *Masters of the Dew.* 1947. Reynal Hitchcock. 1st ed. 8vo. 180p. blk stp bl cloth. NF/NF. H5. $75.00

ROUS, Peyton. *Modern Dance of Death. Linacre Lecture 1929.* 1929. Cambridge. 51p. G7. $30.00

ROUSE, Francis. *Academia Coelestis: Heavenly Universtiy...* 1702. London. Sowle. 3rd ed. sm 12mo. 170p. H10. $100.00

ROUSE, Parke Jr. *Cows on Campus: Williamsburg in Bygone Days.* 1973. Richmond. Dietz. 1st ed. sgn. 219p. VG/VG. B11. $40.00

ROUSSEAU, Jean Jacques. *Emilius; or, Essay on Education.* 1763. London. Nourse Vaillant. 2 vols. 1st ed thus. uncommon. G1. $575.00

ROUSSEL, Raymond. *Locus Solus.* 1914. Paris. Lemerre. 1st ed/lg paper copy on Japon. inscr. NF/wrp/dj/case. B4. $5,500.00

ROUTH, E.M.G. *Tangier: England's Lost Altantic Outpost 1661-1684.* 1912. London. Murray. ils. 388p. gilt bl cloth. K1. $75.00

ROUX, Antoine. *Ships & Shipping. A Collection of Pictures...* 1925. Salem. Marine Research. trans Alfred Johnson. gilt red cloth. F. F1. $150.00

ROUX, P.J. *Nouveau Elemens de Medecine Operatoire.* 1813. Paris. fld table. half leather. B14. $500.00

ROUX & ROUX. *Greece.* 1965. NY. Orion. 1st ed. pls. cloth. G. W1. $15.00

ROWAN, Archibald Hamilton. *Report of Trial of Archibald Hamilton...* 1794. NY. Tiebout O'Brien. 152p. disbound. K1. $150.00

ROWAN, Richard Wilmer. *Pinkertons: Detective Dynasty.* 1931. Little Brn. 1st ed. NF. B2. $25.00

ROWAN, Richard Wilmer. *Terror in Our Time: Secret Service of Surprise Attack.* 1941. NY/Tornoto. Longman Gr. 1st ed. maps/index. 438p. NF/G. M7. $25.00

ROWE, John. *Long Live the King.* 1984. Stein Day. VG/dj. P3. $15.00

ROWE, William Hutchinson. *Shipbuilding Days & Tales of the Sea...* 1927. Portland. Marks Prt House. ils. 145p. T7. $110.00

ROWLAND, Benjamin. *Art & Architecture of India: Buddhist, Hindu, Jain.* 1967. Penguin. 3rd ed/revised. 4to. ils. 314p. NF/dj/prt case. F1. $35.00

ROWLAND, Johns. *Jock: The King's Pony.* 1936. Dutton. stated 1st ed. VG/G. O3. $45.00

ROWLANDSON, Thomas. *Dance of Life.* 1817. London. Ackermann. all pl present. full tan leather. VG. A1. $425.00

ROWLANDSON, Thomas. *Medical Caricatures.* 1971. Medicina Rara. 1/2500. clamshell box. G7. $200.00

ROWLEY, Gordon D. *Adenium & Pachypodium Handbook.* 1983. Botley, Oxford. ils/photos. 95p. F. B26. $7.50

ROWNTREE, John Stephenson. *Quakerism, Past & Present: Being an Inquiry...* 1860. Phil. Longstreth. 12mo. 191p. VG. V3. $15.00

ROY & TAYLOR. *Making a Monster.* 1980. Crown. F/F. P3. $20.00

ROYAL, Brian James. *My Turn To Die.* 1958. Citadel. 1st ed. VG/dj. P3. $20.00

ROYAL, Brian James. *Star Chase.* 1979. Elsevier/Nelson. 1st ed. VG/VG. P3. $15.00

ROYCE, Josiah. *CA From Conquest in 1846 to 2nd Vigilance Committee...* 1886. Houghton Mifflin. 12mo. 513p. pebbled olive cloth. VG. G1. $150.00

ROYCE, Josiah. *Feud of Oakfield Creek: Novel of CA Life.* 1887. Houghton Mifflin. 1st ed. F. A18. $90.00

ROYCE, Josiah. *Sources of Religious Insight.* 1923 (1912). Scribner. later prt. 12mo. 298p. VG. G1. $27.50

ROYCE, Josiah. *War & Insurance.* 1914. Macmillan. 2nd prt. 12mo. russet cloth. G1. $28.50

ROYCE, Josiah. *World & the Individual.* 1900 & 1901. NY. Macmillan. 2 vol. thick 8vo. paneled pebbled olive cloth. G1. $85.00

ROYCE, Josiah. *World & the Individual.* 1959. Dover. facsimile. 588p. G1. $25.00

ROYLE, Edwin. *Squaw Man.* 1906. Harper. 1st ed. ils. G. B34. $10.00

RUARK, Robert C. *Grenadine Etching: Her Life & Loves.* 1947. Doubleday. 1st ed/ author's 1st book. 8vo. 270p. VG/dj. C6. $450.00

RUARK, Robert. *Horn of Hunter.* 1953. NY. 1st ed. VG/VG. B5. $105.00

RUARK, Robert. *Old Man & Boy.* 1957. NY. 1st ed. 303p. VG/dj. B18. $45.00

RUARK, Robert. *Old Man's Boy Grows Older.* 1961. NY. 1st ed. VG/VG. B5. $47.50

RUARK, Robert. *Something of Value.* 1955. NY. 1st ed. VG/VG. A4. $30.00

RUARK, Robert. *Use Enough Gun.* 1966. NY. 1st ed. F/F. A17. $40.00

RUBBENS, Antoine. *Le Pouvoir, l'Organisation, et la Competence Judiciaires.* 1970. Kinshasa/Bruxelles. 340p. NF/stiff wrp. D3. $25.00

RUBIE, Peter. *Werewolf.* 1991. Longmeadow. 1st ed. sgn. F/F. F4. $25.00

RUBIN, Barry. *Paved With Good Intentions: Am Experience & Iran.* 1980. Oxford. 1st ed. sm 8vo. NF/dj. W1. $20.00

RUBIN, William. *Matta.* (1957). MOMA. Bulletin Vol 25/No 1. ils. 36p. G/wrp. H1. $9.00

RUBINGER, Michael. *I Know an Astronaut.* 1972. Putnam. 47p. xl. dj. K5. $5.00

RUBINSTEIN, Gillian. *Beyond the Labyrinth.* 1990. NY. Orchard. 1st Am ed. F/F. N3. $10.00

RUBLE, Kenneth D. *Flight to the Top.* 1986. Viking. 271p. cloth. VG. A17. $18.50

RUCHES, P.J. *Albanian Historical Folksongs 1716-1943.* 1967. Chicago. 1st collected ed. 8vo. 126p. dj. O2. $35.00

RUCKER, Wilbur. *History of the Opthalmoscope.* 1971. Rochester. 1st ed. sgn. 127p. A13. $100.00

RUCKHABER, Erich. *Des Daseins und Denkens Mechanik und Metamechanik.* 1910. Hirschberg in Schlesien. inscr to Wm James. 626p. bl-gray cloth. G. G1. $125.00

RUDAUX, Lucien. *Larousse Encyclopedia of Astronomy.* 1967. Prometheus. 2nd ed. xl. dj. P3. $15.00

RUDHYAR, Dane. *Astrological Houses.* 1972. Doubleday. 1st ed. P3. $10.00

RUDORFF, Raymond. *House of the Brandersons.* 1973. Arbor. VG-/dj. P3. $20.00

RUFFERT, George R. *Great Pyramid Proof of God.* 1935. Detroit. 3rd ed. fld diagram. 233p. G. B33. $15.00

RUGGLES, E.A. *Small Stone Houses of the Cotswold District.* 1931. Cleveland. Jansen. folio. 143p. gilt bl cloth. VG. F1. $195.00

RUGGLES, R. *One Rose (Rose O'Neill).* 1964. Oakland. 1st ed. sgn. VG/VG. B5. $95.00

RUGOFF, Milton. *Beechers.* 1981. NY. 1st ed. 653p. VG/VG. A17. $15.00

RUITENBEEK, Hendrik M. *Psychoanalysis & Existential Philosophy.* 1962. Dutton. PBO. 16mo. 262p. G1. $17.50

RUMAKER, Michael. *Gringos & Other Stories.* nd (1967). NY. 1st Am ed/author's 2nd book. inscr. F/F. A11. $45.00

RUMBELOW, Donald. *Complete Jack the Ripper.* nd. BC. VG. P3. $8.00

RUMER, Thomas A. *Emigrating Company: 1844 OR Trail Journal of Jacob Hammer.* 1991. Arthur H Clark. 1st ltd ed. 1/750. M/dj. A18. $36.00

RUMFORD, Benjamin. *Essays: Political, Economical & Philosophical. Vol II.* 1799. Boston. West. 1st Am ed. 496p. sheep. H10. $65.00

RUNCIMAN, Stephen. *Fall of Constantinople 1453.* 1965. Cambridge. 1st Am ed. fld map. 256p. cloth. O2. $30.00

RUNCIMAN, Stephen. *Great Church in Captivity. A Study in Patriarchate...* 1968. Cambridge. 1st ed. 8vo. 455p. cloth. O2. $55.00

RUNES, D. *Diary & Sundry Observations of Thomas Alva Edison.* 1948. NY. photos/index. 247p. F/F. A17. $20.00

RUNNING, Theodore R. *Graphical Mathematics.* 1927. London. Chapman Hall. 89p. F. K4. $10.00

RUOFF, Antonio. *Lehr-Reiche Predigen Aus Alle Sonn und Feyrtag...* 1749. Munich. Gastels. sm folio. 820p. tooled pigskin. H10. $125.00

RUPORT, Arch. *Art of Cockfighting.* 1949. Devin Adair. 1st ed. 211p. VG/dj. M20. $65.00

RUSBY, Henry H. *Manual of Structural Botany.* 1911. Phil. ils. 248p. VG+. B26. $19.00

RUSCH, Kristine. *Gallery of His Dreams.* nd. Pulphouse. 1/300. sgn. M/sans. M21. $35.00

RUSCH, Kristine. *Gallery of His Dreams.* 1991. Axolotl. sgn. F/F. P3. $35.00

RUSCHA, Edward. *Crackers.* 1969. Hollywood. Heavy Industry Pub. 1st ed. sgn. F/stiff wrp/dj. S9. $300.00

RUSCHA, Edward. *Every Building on Sunset Strip.* 1966. np. ne. 12mo. F/F foil case. S9. $200.00

RUSCHA, Edward. *Gucamole Airlines & Other Drawings.* 1980. Abrams. 1st ed. obl 4to. rem mk. NF/NF. S9. $175.00

RUSH, Norman. *Mating.* 1991. Knopf. 1st ed. inscr. F/F. B2. $65.00

RUSH, Norman. *Whites. Short Stories.* 1986. London. 1st Eng ed/author's 1st book. sgn. F/F. A11. $50.00

RUSH, William Marshall. *Wild Animals of the Rockies...* 1947. Halcyon House. 16p. F/dj. B34. $30.00

RUSHDIE, Salman. *East, West.* 1994. London. Cape. 1st ed. sgn. F/F. L3. $200.00

RUSHDIE, Salman. *Grimus.* 1979. Woodstock. Overlook. 1st Am ed/author's 1st book. rem mk. F/F. B2. $85.00

RUSHDIE, Salman. *Haround & the Sea of Stories.* 1991. NY. Granta. UP of 1st Am ed. sgn. F/wrp. L3. $100.00

RUSHDIE, Salman. *Imaginary Homelands.* 1991. Viking. AP. w/sgn bookplate. F/wrp. B2. $45.00

RUSHDIE, Salman. *Midnight's Children.* 1981. Knopf. 1st Am ed. F/F. scarce. B4. $250.00

RUSHDIE, Salman. *Shame.* 1983. Jonathan Cape. 4th ed. F/F. P3. $18.00

RUSHING, James Fowler. *Men & Things I Saw in Civil War Days.* 1914. NY. 1st ed. inscr. 420p. VG/glassine wrp. B18. $125.00

RUSHKOPF, Douglas. *Cyberia: Life in the Trenchs of Hyper.* 1994. San Francisco. Harper. 1st ed. F/F. P3. $22.00

RUSHMORE, Jane P. *Further Footsteps Along the Quaker Way.* 1954. Phil Yearly Meeting. 12mo. 55p. VG. V3. $10.00

RUSHO, W.L. *Everett Ruess: A Vagabond for Beauty.* 1983. Gibbs Mith. 1st ed. ils/notes/index. 226p. F/NF. B19. $50.00

RUSHTON, William. *WG Grace's Last Case.* 1984. London. Methuen. 1st ed. ils. F/dj. S6. $30.00

RUSINOW, Irving. *Camera Report on El Cerrito: Typical Spanish-Am Community...* 1942. USDA. ils. NF/wrp. B19. $40.00

RUSKIN, Arthur. *Classics in Arterial Hypertension.* 1956. Springfield. 1st ed. 358p. A13. $125.00

RUSKIN, John. *King of the Golden River.* nd. Homewood. G. P3. $7.00

RUSKIN, John. *Notes on Samuel Prout & William Hunt.* 1880. London. ils. VG. M17. $35.00

RUSKIN, John. *Poems.* 1882. Wiley. 12mo. 233p. G. H1. $15.00

RUSKIN, John. *Seven Lamps of Architecture.* 1880. Wiley. 14 pl. 206p. gilt gr cloth. G. H1. $18.00

RUSKIN, John. *Studies in Both Arts: Being 10 Subjects Drawn & Described.* 1895. London. 1st ed. folio. 10 chromolithograph pl. cloth. VG. C6. $150.00

RUSS, Joanna. *Extra (Ordinary) People.* 1984. St Martin. 1st ed. F/F. P3. $25.00

RUSS, Joanna. *Two of Them.* 1978. Berkley Putnam. 1st ed. F/F. P3. $25.00

RUSS, Joanna. *Zanzibar Cat.* 1983. Arkham. 1st ed. F/dj. M2/T2. $55.00

RUSSELL, A.J. *Devalino Caper.* 1975. Random. 1st ed. VG/VG. P3. $15.00

RUSSELL, Alan Kingsley. *Book of the Sleuth.* 1986. New Orchard. 1st ed. VG/VG. P3. $20.00

RUSSELL, Alan Kingsley. *Rivals of Sherlock Holmes.* 1981. Castle Books. VG/VG. P3. $15.00

RUSSELL, Belden A. *Hist of Cayuga Baptist Assn.* 1851. Auburn, NY. Derby Miller. BC. 214p. VG. M10. $8.50

RUSSELL, Bertrand. *Analysis of Mind.* 1921. London. Allen Unwin. 310p. paneled crimson cloth. F. G1. $125.00

RUSSELL, Bertrand. *Autobiography of...* 1967, 1968 & 1969. Atlantic Monthly/Little Brn. 3 vol. 1st Am ed. VG/dj. G1. $50.00

RUSSELL, Bertrand. *Human Knowledge: Its Scope & Limits.* 1948. Simon Schuster. 2nd Am prt. orange cloth. VG/worn. G1. $25.00

RUSSELL, Bertrand. *Justice in War Time.* 1916. Open Court. later prt (lacks portrait photo). 244p. bl cloth. G1. $50.00

RUSSELL, Bertrand. *Justice in War Time.* 1917. Chicago. 2nd ed. 229p. xl. VG. D3. $45.00

RUSSELL, Bertrand. *Unpopular Essays.* 1950. London. Allen Unwin. 224p. bl cloth. F. G1. $25.00

RUSSELL, Charles Edward. *Charlemagne: First of the Moderns.* 1930. Houghton Mifflin. 1st ed. ils. 305p. VG. M10. $18.50

RUSSELL, Charles Edward. *Why I Am a Socialist.* 1910. Doran. 1st ed. F/NF. B2. $75.00

RUSSELL, Charles M. *Trails Plowed Under.* 1978 (1927). np. NF/VG. B34. $60.00

RUSSELL, Charlotte Murray. *Between Us & Evil.* 1950. Crime Club. 1st ed. front free ep removed. VG. P3. $10.00

RUSSELL, Dorothy S. *Histological Technique for Intracranial Tumors.* 1939. London. Oxford. pl. 69p. cloth. G7. $35.00

RUSSELL, Eric Frank. *Dreadful Sanctuary.* 1972. Dobson. VG/VG. P3. $40.00

RUSSELL, Eric Frank. *Sinister Barrier.* 1948. Fantasy. 1st ed. VG/G. P3. $60.00

RUSSELL, Fox. *Horse-Keeping for Amateurs: A Practical Manual...* nd (1888). London. Gill. 1st ed. VG. O3. $35.00

RUSSELL, G.W. *Sketches of Physicians of Hartford in 1820...* 1890. Hartford. 64p. G7. $35.00

RUSSELL, George. *Tour Through Sicily in Year 1815.* 1819. London. Sherwood Neely Jones. 1st ed. half morocco. F. H4. $400.00

RUSSELL, M. *Polynesia; or, Hist Account of Principal Islands of S Sea...* 1845. Harper. fld map. 362p. cloth. VG. B14. $95.00

RUSSELL, Martin. *Darker Side of Death.* 1985. Collins Crime Club. 1st ed. VG/VG. P3. $15.00

RUSSELL, Martin. *Daylight Robbery.* 1978. London. Collins. 1st ed. F/F. S6. $22.50

RUSSELL, Ray. *Absolute Power.* 1992. Baltimore. Maclay. 1st ed. sgn. 1/500. F/sans/case. T2. $45.00

RUSSELL, Ray. *Bishop's Daughter.* 1981. Houghton Mifflin. 1st ed. F/F. T2. $45.00

RUSSELL, Ray. *Colony.* 1969. Sherbourne. 1st ed. VG/VG. P3. $20.00

RUSSELL, Ray. *Haunted Castles.* 1985. Maclay. 1st ed. F/dj. M2. $10.00

RUSSELL, Ray. *Incubus: A Novel of Sexual Possession.* 1976. Morrow. 1st ed. F/F. T2. $100.00

RUSSELL, Ray. *Incubus: A Novel of Sexual Possession.* 1976. Morrow. 1st ed. VG/VG. P3. $25.00

RUSSELL, Ray. *Princess Pamela.* 1979. Houghton Mifflin. 1st ed. F/dj. F4. $15.00

RUSSELL, Ray. *Sardonicus & Other Stories.* 1961. NY. Ballantine. 1st ed/PBO/author's 1st book. sgn. NF. A11. $45.00

RUSSELL, Ross. *Bird Lives! High Life & Hard Times of Charlie Parker.* 1973. NY. 1st ed. VG/VG. B5. $55.00

RUSSELL, W. Clark. *British Seas.* 1892. London. Seeley. 12 pl/41 text vignettes. 88p. aeg. gilt brd. T7. $135.00

RUSSELL, William. *Scientific Horseshoeing for Leveling & Balancing...* 1899. Cincinnati. Robert Clarke. 4th ed. VG. O3. $65.00

RUSSO, Richard. *Bibliography of George Ade, 1866-1944.* 1947. np. ils. 329p. NF. A4. $75.00

RUSSO, Richard. *Mohawk.* 1986. Vintage/Random. 1st ed/author's 1st book. rem mk. NF/ils wrp. A14. $20.00

RUSSO, Richard. *Nobody's Fool.* 1993. Random. ARC/author's 3rd book. F/wrp. L3. $45.00

RUSSO, Richard. *Risk Pool.* 1988. Random. 1st ed. NF/NF. A14. $40.00

RUST, Brian. *Jazz Records 1897-1942.* 1970. London. Storyville. 2 vol. revised ed. gilt red cloth. NF. B2. $175.00

RUST, Zad. *Teddy Bare: Last of the Kennedy Clan.* 1971. Boston. Western Islands. hc. N2. $6.00

RUTH, Babe. *Home Run King.* 1920. Burt. rpt. pict bdg. G. P8. $30.00

RUTH, Mrs. Babe. *Babe & I.* 1959. NJ. 2nd prt. photos/index. 215p. VG/VG. A17. $10.00

RUTHERFORD, Douglas. *Black Leather Murders.* 1966. Walker. 1st ed. VG/VG. P3. $15.00

RUTHERFORD, Douglas. *Collision Course.* 1978. Macmillan. 1st ed. NF/NF. P3. $16.00

RUTHERFORD, Douglas. *Turbo.* 1980. Macmillan. 1st ed. NF/NF. P3. $15.00

RUTHERFORD, Ernest. *Radioactive Substances & Their Radiations.* 1913. Cambridge. 1st ed. 699p. G. H1. $45.00

RUTHERFORD, Michael. *Infinite Kingdoms.* 1990. Owlswick. 1st ed/author's 1st book of fiction. F/F. T2. $24.00

RUTHVEN, Malise. *Divine Supermarket: Shopping for God in America.* 1989. Morrow. 317p. F. B29. $8.50

RUTHVEN, Malise. *Satanic Affair: Salman Rushdie & Rage of Islam.* 1990. London. Chatto Windus. 1st ed, index. 184p. NF/NF clear plastic. M7. $25.00

RUTKOW, I.M. *Hist of Surgery in the US 1775-1900.* 1988. San Francisco. Norman. 515p. M/dj. G7. $145.00

RUTLEDGE, Archibald. *World Around Hampton.* 1960. Indianapolis. 1st ed. VG/VG. B5. $27.50

RUTLEDGE, Nancy. *Easy to Murder.* 1951. Crime Club. 1st ed. VG. P3. $20.00

RUTLEDGE, Nancy. *Preying Mantis.* 1947. Crime Club. 1st ed. VG/G+. P3. $20.00

RUTMAN, Darret B. *Old Dominion: Essays on Thomas Perkins Abernethy.* 1964. Charlottesville. 1st ed. 200p. VG/G tissue. B11. $45.00

RUTTER, Owen. *Passion Fruit.* nd. Readers Lib. VG/VG. P3. $15.00

RUZIC, Neil P. *Case for Going to the Moon.* 1965. Putnam. fwd Arthur C Clarke. photos. 240p. VG/dj. K5. $14.00

RUZIC, Neil P. *Where the Winds Sleep.* 1970. Doubleday. 8vo. 236p. VG/dj. K5. $16.00

RYAN, Alan. *Cast a Cold Eye.* 1984. Dark Harvest. 1st ed. F/dj. M2. $60.00

RYAN, Alan. *Penguin Book of Vampire Stories.* 1991. Bloomsbury. F/F. P3. $20.00

RYAN, Alan. *Perpetual Light.* 1982. Warner. hc ed. F/F SF BC issue. F4. $10.00

RYAN, Alan. *Vampires.* nd. BC. NF/NF. P3. $13.00

RYAN, Cornelius. *Across the Space Frontier.* 1952. London. Sidgwick Jackson. 1st ed. ils Chesley Bonestell. NF/worn. N3. $20.00

RYAN, Cornelius. *Bridge Too Far.* nd. Simon Schuster. 2nd ed. VG/VG. P3. $13.00

RYAN, John Fergus. *Redneck Bride.* 1982. Little Rock. 1st ed/author's 1st novel. inscr. w/orig drawing. F/NF. A11. $85.00

RYAN, Marah Ellis. *My Quaker Maid.* (1906). Rand McNally. 254p. G. H1. $12.00

RYAN, Stella. *Death Never Weeps.* 1946. Coward McCann. 1st ed. VG/VG. P3. $23.00

RYAN, Thomas Arthur. *Work & Effort.* 1947. Ronald. 312p. F. K4. $20.00

RYBKA, Eugeniusz. *Four Hundred Years of the Copernican Heritage.* 1964. Cracow. Jagellonian U. 8vo. 235p. VG/wrp/chip dj. K5. $26.00

RYCAUT, Paul. *History of the Turkish Empire From Year 1623 to 1677...* 1680 (1679). London. folio. 336p. cloth. O2. $850.00

RYDER, Jonathan; see Ludlum, Robert.

RYLE, Gilbert. *Dilemmas. The Tanner Lectures 1953.* 1954. Cambridge. 129p. bl cloth. VG/dj. G1. $30.00

RYLE, J.C. *Expository Thoughts on the Gospels.* 1990. Baker. 4 vol. F. B29. $54.00

RYMAN, Geoff. *Child Garden.* nd. BOMC. VG/VG. P3. $10.00

RYMAN, Geoff. *Was...* 1992. Harper Collins. 1st ed. F/F. P3. $25.00

RYRIE, Charles C. *Biblical Theology of the New Testament.* 1959. Moody. 384p. VG/dj. B29. $6.50

RYRIE, Charles C. *Dispensationalism Today.* 1965. Moody. 221p. VG/dj. B29. $10.00

RYRIE, Charles C. *Holy Spirit.* 1965. Moody. VG. B29. $2.75

RYRIE, Charles C. *Transformed by His Glory.* 1990. Victor. 144p. VG. B29. $6.50

SA'EDI, Gholam-Hossein. *Dandil: Stories From Iranian Life...* 1981. Random. 1st ed. 8vo. 239p. NF/dj. W1. $15.00

SAARINEN, Eliel. *City: Its Growth, Its Decay, Its Future.* 1943. Reinhold. 8vo. inscr. ils. 380p. VG/dj. F1. $75.00

SAAVEDRA, Miguel de Cervantes; see De Cervantes, Miguel.

SABATINI, Rafael. *Bardelys the Mignificent.* 1931. McClelland Stewart. VG. P3. $10.00

SABATINI, Rafael. *Captain Blood.* 1922. Grosset Dunlap. photoplay ed. 356p. VG/dj. M20. $20.00

SABATINI, Rafael. *Carolinian.* nd. Phoenix Book Co. leather. G+. P3. $15.00

SABATINI, Rafael. *Justice of the Duke.* 1926. Stanley Paul. 13th prt. G+. P3. $12.00

SABATINI, Rafael. *Mistress Wilding.* 1924. Houghton Mifflin. VG. P3. $10.00

SABERHAGEN, Fred. *Berserker Throne.* 1985. Simon Schuster. 1st ed. F/F. P3. $20.00

SABERHAGEN, Fred. *Complete Book of Swords.* nd. BC. VG/VG. P3. $10.00

SABERHAGEN, Fred. *Fifth Book of Lost Swords: Coinspinner's Story.* 1989. NY. Tor. 1st ed. F/F. N3. $15.00

SABERHAGEN, Fred. *Matter of Taste.* 1990. Tor. 1st ed. F/F. T2. $17.00

SABERHAGEN, Fred. *Second Book of Lost Swords: Sightbinder's Story.* 1987. NY. Tor. 1st ed. F/F. N3. $15.00

SABERHAGEN, Fred. *Third Book of Swords.* 1988. Tor. 1st ed. F/F. P3. $16.00

SABIN, Edwin. *City of the Sun.* 1924. Jacobs. 1st ed. VG. M2. $35.00

SABIN, Elbridge H. *Magical Man of Mirth.* 1910. Jacobs. 1st ed. ils EP Abbott/HA Knipe. ils ep. VG. M5. $75.00

SABINI, John. *Armies in the Sand: Struggle for Mecca & Medina.* 1981. Thames Hudson. 1st ed. 8vo. 223p. NF/dj. W1. $22.00

SABIR, Hussein. *Geology & Mineralogy of the Polymetallic Sulfide...* 1981. Jiddah. Ministry Mineral Resources. 1st ed. VG/wrp. W1. $20.00

SABLE, Martin H. *Exobiology: A Research Guide.* 1978. Gr Oak. inscr/sgn. 324p. gr cloth. VG. K5. $18.00

SABLJAK, Mark. *Bloody Legacy.* 1992. Gramercy. 1st ed. VG. P3. $15.00

SABLOFF, Jeremy A. *Cities in Ancient Mexico. Reconstructing a Lost World.* 1989. Thames Hudson. 1st ed. 224p. VG/wrp. F3. $20.00

SABLOFF, Jeremy A. *Cities of Ancient Mexico. Reconstructing a Lost World.* 1989. NY. Thames Hudson. 8vo. 224p. F/VG. B11. $25.00

SACKVILLE-WEST, Edward. *Inclinations: Studies in 3 Literatures.* 1949. Scribner. 1st Am ed from Eng sheets. VG/VG. B4. $45.00

SADLER, Mark; see Lynds, Dennis.

SADLER, William A. *Existence & Love: New Approach in Existential Phenomenology.* 1969. Scribner. 427p. gr cloth. VG/dj. G1. $30.00

SADOVSKY & SCHUETZ. *Die Gattung Astrophytum.* 1979. Arten. German text. ils/photos. 247p. F. B26. $34.00

SAFIRE, William. *Full Disclosure.* 1977. Doubleday. 1st ed. VG/VG. P3. $15.00

SAGAN, Carl. *Broca's Brain.* 1978. Random. 1st ed. VG/VG. S11. $10.00

SAGAN, Carl. *Contact.* nd. BOMC. VG/VG. P3. $10.00

SAGAN, Carl. *Dragons of Eden.* 1977. Random. 1st ed. VG/VG. S11. $10.00

SAGAN, Francoise. *Heart-Keeper.* 1968. Dutton. 1st ed. NF/NF. P3. $15.00

SAGAN, Francoise. *Those Without Shadows.* 1957. NY. 1st ed. F/chip. A17. $10.00

SAGAN, Francoise. *Wonderful Clouds.* 1961. London. Murray. 1st ed. trans Anne Green. F/VG. B3. $25.00

SAGE, Brian. *Arctic & Its Wildlife.* 1986. NY. Facts on File. 1st ed. rem mk. F/F. P4. $25.00

SAGE, Dana. *22 Brothers.* 1950. Simon Schuster. VG-/dj. P3. $20.00

SAGHAPHI, Mirza Mahmoud Khan. *In the Imperial Shadow.* 1928. Doubleday Doran. 1st ed. 8vo. 403p. cloth. G. W1. $16.00

SAHA, Arthur W. *Year's Best Fantasy Stories: 13.* nd. BC. F/F. P3. $8.00

SAHAKIAN, William S. *Hist of Psychology.* 1968. Itasca, IL. Peacock. 559p. G/dj. K4. $15.00

SAHINOGLU, Metin. *Anadolu Selcuklu Mimarsinde Yazinin Dekoratif...* 1977. Istanbul. APA Offset. 79p. VG/stiff wrp. W1. $15.00

SAID, Hakim. *Diseases of the Liver: Greco-Arab Concepts.* 1982. Karachi, Pakistan. 1st ed. 131p. dj. A13. $50.00

SAID, K.A. Mohyeldin. *Modeling the Mind.* 1990. Oxford. 216p. blk cloth. VG/dj. G1. $27.50

SAILLE, Olaf. *Troubadour of the Stars.* 1940. NY. Oskar Piest. trans JA Galston. 8vo. 344p. G/chip. K5. $25.00

SAINSBURY, Noel. *Bill Bolton & the Hidden Danger.* 1933. Goldsmith. G. M2. $5.00

SAINSBURY, Noel. *Billy Smith Mystery Ace (#3).* 1932. Cupples Leon. lists to this title. 199p. NF/rpr. M20. $25.00

SAINSBURY, Noel. *Billy Smith: Secret Service Ace.* 1932. Cupples Leon. VG. P3. $10.00

SAINSBURY, Noel. *Cracker Stanton.* 1934. Cupples Leon. 1st ed. VG/VG. P8. $15.00

SAINT, H.F. *Memoirs of an Invisible Man.* nd. BOMC. VG/VG. P3. $10.00

SAINT-CLAIR, William. *Lord Elgin & the Marbles.* 1967. London. 8vo. ils. 309p. O2. $45.00

SAINT-GAUDENS, Homer. *American Artist & His Times.* 1941. Dodd Mead. 1st ed. 323p. VG/dj. M20. $20.00

SAINT-JOHNS, Adela Rogers. *Final Verdict.* 1962. NY. inscr. 512p. cloth. VG. D3. $15.00

SAINT-JOHNS, Adela Rogers. *Honeycomb.* 1969. Doubleday. 1st ed. sgn. 598p. VG/dj. M20. $20.00

SAJER, Guy. *Forgotten Soldier.* 1967. NY. 1st ed. VG/G. B5. $45.00

SAKEL, Manfred. *Schizophrenia.* 1958. Philosophical Lib. 334p. F/dj. K4. $10.00

SAKSENA, J. *Art of Rajasthan.* 1979. Delhi. 1st ed. VG. C11. $65.00

SALAH, Said. *Medal of Magnanimity.* ca 1965. Dhahran. IPA. 1st ed. 4to. VG. W1. $20.00

SALAMAN, Malcolm C. *Old English Mezzotints.* 1910. London. The Studio. sm volio. ils/pl. gilt bronze cloth. NF. F1. $50.00

SALAMAN & WHITMAN. *Print Collector's Handbook.* 1918. np. ils/index. 376p. O8. $18.50

SALBOM, Johanne. *Dissertatio Medica, Exhibins Spiritus Corporis Humani...* 1691. Dorpati. 4to. sewn as issued. G7. $75.00

SALE, Edith. *Historic Gardens of Virginia.* 1923. Richmond. ltd ed. 1/1000. VG. H7. $45.00

SALE, Medora. *Murder in a Good Cause.* 1990. Viking. 1st ed. NF/NF. P3. $23.00

SALE, Richard. *Not Too Narrow...Not Too Deep.* 1943. Tower. VG/torn. P3. $20.00

SALE, Richard. *White Buffalo.* 1975. Simon Schuster. 1st ed. VG/VG. P3. $23.00

SALINGER, J.D. *Boy in France. In Post Stories 1942-1945.* (1946). NY. 1st ed. F/F. A9. $25.00

SALINGER, J.D. *Catcher in the Rye.* 1951. Little Brn. 1st ed/author's 1st book. VG/VG. B5. $1,200.00

SALINGER, J.D. *Kitbook for Soldiers, Sailors & Marines.* 1943. Chicago. Consolidated. 1st ed/2nd issue. Salinger's 1st book appearance. VG. C6. $100.00

SALINGER, J.D. *Raise High the Roof Beam, Carpenters, & Seymour: An Intro.* 1963. Little Brn. 1st ed/3rd state. 8vo. 248p. gilt gray bdg. VG/clip. H5. $75.00

SALINGER, Pierre. *Am Held Hostage: Secret Negotiations.* 1981. Doubleday. 1st ed. 349p. NF/dj. W1. $18.00

SALISBURY & SALISBURY. *Two Captains West.* 1950. Superior. 1st ed. ils. F/VG. B34. $35.00

SALK, Jonas. *Anatomy of Reality: Merging of Intuition & Reason.* 1983. Columbia. 1st ed. sgn. F/VG. B33. $35.00

SALLANDER. *Bibliotheca Walleriana: Books Ils History of Medicine...* nd. 2 vol. rpt of 1955 ed. 1/400 sets. F. A4. $145.00

SALLUSTIUS, G. Crispus. *De Coniuratione Catilinae et de Bello Iugurthinae Historiae.* 1656. Venice. Bonelli. 4to. 162p. lacks final blank. early limp vellum. B24. $375.00

SALMI, Mario. *Masaccio.* nd. Milan. Amilcare Pizza. mtd/matted mc pl. cloth portfolio. F. F1. $65.00

SALSBURY, Frank B. *Flowering Process.* 1963. Oxford. ils/drawings/charts. F/torn. B26. $21.00

SALTEN, Felix. *Fairy Tales From Near & Far.* 1946. Philosophical Lib. 4to. VG/G. B17. $6.50

SALTER, Andrew. *What Is Hypnosis?* 1946. NY. Smith. 82p. G/dj. K4. $10.00

SALTER, James. *Dusk.* 1988. San Francisco. 1st ed/author's 6th book. sgn. F/F. A11. $45.00

SALTER, James. *Sheridan Lord 1926-1994.* 1995. Kelly Winterton. sgn. 1/200. F/saddlestiched wrp. B4. $75.00

SALTER, James. *Sport & Pastime.* 1967. Doubleday/Paris Review. 1st ed. F/NF. B2. $60.00

SALTER, Lord. *Memoirs of a Public Servant.* 1945. London. Faber. 1st ed. 356p. blk lettered bl cloth. VG/G. M7. $35.00

SALVATORE, R.A. *Legacy.* 1992. Lake Geneva. TSR. 1st ed. F/F. P3. $16.00

SALVATORE, R.A. *Siege of Darkness.* 1994. Lake Geneva. TSR. 1st ed. F/F. N3. $15.00

SALVATORE, R.A. *Starless Night.* 1993. Lake Geneva. TSR. UP of 1st ed. F/prt wrp. N3. $10.00

SALVINI, Robert. *Medieval Sculpture.* 1969. NY Graphic Soc. ils. 368p. F/dj. M10. $16.50

SALWAY, Lance. *Peculiar Gift.* 1976. London. Kestrel. 1st ed. ils. 573p. F/VG. S11. $25.00

SAMJANOVA. *Sweden-Bulgaria, Voices From 7 Centuries: Slavonic...* 1980. Stockholm. State Hist Mus. 4to. 144p. F/VG. A4. $125.00

SAMPSON, Emma Speed. *Miss Minerva Broadcasts Billy.* 1925. Reilly Lee. 329p. VG/clip. M20. $25.00

SAMPSON, Emma Speed. *Miss Minerva Goin' Places.* 1931. Reilly Lee. 327p. pict red cloth. VG/torn. M20. $20.00

SAMPSON, Emma Speed. *Miss Minerva's Baby.* 1920. Chicago. Reilly Lee. 12mo. VG. C8. $30.00

SAMPSON, Emma Speed. *Miss Minerva's Baby.* 1920. Reilly Lee. 1st ed. cloth. G. M5. $20.00

SAMPSON, Emma Speed. *Miss Minerva's Neighbors.* 1929. Reilly Lee. 327p. red cloth. VG/dj. M20. $25.00

SAMPSON, Emma Speed. *Miss Minerva's Problem.* 1936. Reilly Britton. VG+/VG. C8. $45.00

SAMPSON, Martin. *Good Giant.* 1928. Houghton Mifflin. ils Hilton. VG. B17. $6.50

SAMPSON, William. *Catholic Question in America...* 1813. NY. Edward Gillespy. 1st ed. 138p. later full leather. NF. M8. $250.00

SAMTER, Max. *Excerpts From Classics in Allergy.* 1969. Columbus. ils. 117p. G7. $30.00

SAMUELS, Samuel. *From the Forecastle to the Cabin: 50 Years at Sea...* 1887. Harper. ils. 308p. T7. $55.00

SAMUELS & SAMUELS. *Samuels' Encyclopedia of Artists of American West.* 1985. Secaucus. Castle. 322p. M/F. P4. $30.00

SANAI, Hakim. *Walled Garden of Truth.* 1989. London. Octagon. 77p. F/F. B33. $16.00

SANBORN, M. *The American.* 1974. NY. Rivers of America Series. 1st ed. VG/VG. B5. $35.00

SANBOURN, Ruth Burr. *Murder on the Aphrodite.* 1935. Macmillan. 1st ed. xl. G+. P3. $12.00

SANCHEZ, Ramon Diaz. *Cumboto.* nd. Austin/London. TX U. 273p. VG. P4. $20.00

SANCHEZ, Thomas. *Zoot-Suit Murders.* 1978. Dutton. 1st ed. inscr. F/NF. S9. $75.00

SAND, George. *Cesarine Dietrich.* 1987. Osgood. 1st ed. trans Edward Stanwood. VG. S11. $25.00

SAND, George. *Handsome Lawrence.* 1871. Osgood. 1st ed. trans Carroll Owen. G. S11. $20.00

SANDBURG, Carl. *Abraham Lincoln. One-Vol Edition.* 1954. Harcourt Brace. 762p. VG. H1. $12.00

SANDBURG, Carl. *Abraham Lincoln: The War Years.* 1939. 4 vol. photos/cartoons/index. O8. $55.00

SANDBURG, Carl. *Always the Young Strangers.* 1953. NY. 1st ed. inscr/dtd 1953. turquoise cloth. VG+. A11. $45.00

SANDBURG, Carl. *Carl Sandburg Miscellany.* 1977. NY. Appletree Books. 1/290. 4to. 32p. F/yel wrp. H5. $50.00

SANDBURG, Carl. *Chicago Race Riots.* 1919. Harcourt. 1st ed. VG/wrp. B2. $100.00

SANDBURG, Carl. *Civil War Centennial Address.* 1961. Lib of Congress. 1/1000. F/sans. V1. $45.00

SANDBURG, Carl. *Lincoln Collector.* 1960. np. ils. 344p. O8. $14.50

SANDBURG, Carl. *Poems of the Midwest.* 1946. Cleveland. 1st ed. 267p. VG. E5. $35.00

SANDBURG, Carl. *Rootabaga Stories.* 1988. HBJ. 1st ed. 4to. ils Michael Hague. F/VG. B17. $15.00

SANDBURG, Carl. *Sandburg Range.* 1957. Harcourt Brace. 1st ed. VG+/VG+. S9. $25.00

SANDBURG, Carl. *Steichen the Photographer.* 1929. Harcourt Brace. 1st ed. 1/925. ils/photos. sgn Sandburg/Steichen. H4. $1,000.00

SANDERS, Dori. *Clover.* 1990. Algonquin. 1st ed. rem mk. F/F. L3. $30.00

SANDERS, Dori. *Her Own Place.* 1993. Algonquin. 1st ed. NF/NF clip. A14. $35.00

SANDERS, George. *Stranger at Home.* 1946. Simon Schuster. 1st ed. VG/chip. P3. $45.00

SANDERS, Hope. *Photo Maxima IV.* 1961. NY. Photo Maxima. sm 4to. photos. unp. wht stp red cloth. NF. F1. $35.00

SANDERS, Joe. *Science Fiction Fandom.* 1994. Greenwood. F/sans. P3. $55.00

SANDERS, Lawrence. *Capital Crimes.* 1989. Putnam. 1st ed. F/F. P3. $20.00

SANDERS, Lawrence. *Fourth Deadly Sin.* 1985. Putnam. 1st ed. NF/NF. P3. $25.00

SANDERS, Lawrence. *Passion of Molly T.* 1984. Putnam. 1st ed. VG/VG. P3. $20.00

SANDERS, Lawrence. *Timothy Files.* 1987. Putnam. 1st ed. F/F. P3. $19.00

SANDERS, Nicholas. *People of the Jaguar.* 1989. Souvenir. 1st ed. 276p. VG/dj. F3. $25.00

SANDERS, Ronald. *Lost Tribes & Promised Lands.* 1978. Little Brn. 1st ed. 443p. xl. VG/dj. F3. $10.00

SANDERS, Sol. *Mexico: Chaos on Our Doorstep.* 1986. Lanham. Madison Books. 8vo. 222p. red cloth. M/M. P4. $30.00

SANDERS, Ti. *Weather Is Front Page News...* 1983. South Bend, IN. Icarus. pb. photos. 207p. K5. $10.00

SANDERS. *Agatha Crhistie Companion: Complete Guide...* 1984. Delacorte. 1st ed. F/F. A4. $40.00

SANDERSON, Edmund L. *Waltham Industries.* 1957. Waltham Hist Soc. 1st ed. 8vo. 164p. blk cloth. VG. A8. $35.00

SANDERSON, Patrick. *Antiquities of the Abbey or Cathedral Church of Durham.* 1767. Durham. Sanderson. 12mo. leather. H10. $80.00

SANDFORD, John. *Empress File.* 1991. Holt. 1st ed. F/F. T2. $15.00

SANDFORD, John. *Fool's Run.* 1989. Holt. 1st ed/author's 1st novel. F/F. T2. $15.00

SANDFORD, John. *Shadow Prey.* 1990. Putnam. 1st ed/author's 2nd book. F/F. B3. $35.00

SANDFORD, John. *Silent Prey.* 1992. Putnam. 1st ed. F/F. M21/T2. $20.00

SANDFORD, John. *Winter Prey.* 1993. Putnam. 1st ed. F/F. P3. $22.00

SANDLER, Martin W. *Story of American Photography.* 1979. Boston. 1st ed. 318 p. VG. A17. $17.50

SANDLIN, Tim. *Sex & Sunsets.* 1987. London. Collins. 1st ed/author's 1st book. F/F. S9. $30.00

SANDLIN, Tim. *Sex & Sunsets.* 1987. NY. Holt. 1st ed/author's 1st book. F/F. B3. $40.00

SANDLIN, Tim. *Skipped Parts.* 1991. Holt. 1st ed. F/F. B3. $20.00

SANDOZ, Mari. *Beaver Men.* 1964. NY. 1st ed. VG/VG. B5. $35.00

SANDOZ, Mari. *Buffalo Hunters: Story of the Hide Men.* 1954. Hastings. 1st issue (Bismark misspelled)F/rpr. A18. $110.00

SANDOZ, Mari. *Cattlemen, From the Rio Grande Across the Far Miles.* 1958. Hastings. 1st ed. VG/dj. B34. $70.00

SANDOZ, Mari. *Cheyenne Autumn.* 1953. NY. 1st ed. VG/VG. B5. $45.00

SANDOZ, Mari. *Crazy Horse: Strange Man of the Oglalas.* 1955. NY. inscr pres/sketch. H4. $75.00

SANDOZ, Mari. *Horsecatcher.* 1957. Westminster. 1st ed. 192p. w/sgn note. VG. P2. $40.00

SANDOZ, Mari. *Old Jules Country.* 1965. Hastings House. VG/VG. P3. $15.00

SANDOZ, Mari. *Old Jules.* 1935. Little Brn. 1st ed/1st issue (cover sketch present). inscr/sgn. NF. A18. $90.00

SANDS, B.F. *Reports on the Total Solar Eclipse of August 7, 1869.* 1870. WA, DC. US Naval Observatory. 4to. 217p. G. K5. $150.00

SANDWELL, Helen B. *Valley of Color Days.* 1924. Little Brn. 1st ed. ils Alice Bolam Preston. cloth. VG+. M5. $60.00

SANFORD, John. *Seventy Times Seven.* 1939. Knopf. 1st ed. F/NF. B2. $35.00

SANGER, Richard H. *Where the Jordan Flows.* 1963. WA. Middle E Inst. 1st ed. 397p. G/dj. W1. $8.00

SANGSTER, Jimmy. *Snowball.* 1986. Holt. 1st ed. F/F. T2. $16.00

SANSOVINO, Francesco. *Delle Orationi Volgarmente Scritte da Molti Huomini...* 1575. Venice. Al Segno della Luna. sm 4to. 2 parts in 1. vellum. K1. $375.00

SANTAYANA, George. *Realm of Matter: Book of Second of Realms of Being.* 1930. Scribner. 1st ed. 209p. VG. B33. $30.00

SANTAYANA, George. *Sense of Beauty: Being Outlines of Aesthetic Theory.* 1955. Modern Lib. 268p. VG/VG. B33. $16.00

SANTAYANA, George. *Works of...* 1936. Scribner. 15 vol. Triton ed. 1/940. sgn. F/box. H4. $545.00

SANTEE, Ross. *Bar X Golf Course.* 1933. Farrar Rinehart. 1st ed. ils. F. A18. $40.00

SANTEE, Ross. *Cowboy.* 1928. Cosmopolitan. 1st ed. ils. pict bdg. VG. A18. $40.00

SANTEE, Ross. *Cowboy.* 1964. Hastings. ils. 257p. NF/VG. B19. $25.00

SANTEE, Ross. *Dog Days.* 1955. Scribner. 1st ed. ils. F/dj. A18. $60.00

SANTEE, Ross. *Rummy Kid Goes Home & Other Stories of the Southwest.* 1965. Hastings. 1st ed. ils. F/dj. A18. $40.00

SANTEE, Ross. *Wranglers & Rounders: Cowboy Lore.* 1981. Northland. 1st ed. ils. 69p. F/F. B19. $35.00

SANTESSON, Hans Stefan. *Fantastic Universe Omnibus.* nd. BC. VG/G. P3. $8.00

SANTESSON, Hans Stefan. *Fantastic Universe Omnibus.* 1960. Prentice Hall. F. M21. $5.00

SANTILLANA & VON DECHEND. *Hamlet's Mill: Essay on Myth & Frame of Time.* 1969. Boston. Gambit. 505p. VG/dj. G1. $27.50

SANTINI, Piero. *Forward Impulse.* 1936. NY. Huntington. ltd ed. 1/950. VG. O3. $65.00

SAPERSTEIN, Alan. *Mom Kills Kids & Self.* 1979. Macmillan. 1st ed/author's 1st book. sgn. F/dj. F4. $25.00

SAPPER. *Black Gang.* 1950. Hodder Stoughton. 51st prt. VG/VG. P3. $20.00

SAPPER. *Bull-Dog Drummond at Bay.* 1939. Hodder Stoughton. 6th prt. VG/G. P3. $18.00

SAPPER. *Jim Maitland.* 1934. Doubleday Doran. VG. P3. $15.00

SAPPER. *Tiny Cartert.* 1932. Musson/Hodder Stoughton. NF. P3. $15.00

SARASON, Seymour B. *Psychological Problems in Mental Deficiency.* 1949. Harper. 336p. F. K4. $10.00

SARBER, Mary A. *Charles F Lummis: A Bibliography.* 1977. AZ U. 71p. F/wrp. B19. $10.00

SARG & STODDARD. *Book of Marionette Plays.* 1927. Greenberg. 1st ed. sgn/dtd/ drawing Sarg. VG+. C8. $175.00

SARGANT, Jane Alice. *Two Letters to the Queen & an Address to Females of Britain.* 1820. Maidenhead. Wetton. 8th ed. 32p. orig purple cloth/marbled brd. rare. K1. $150.00

SARGEANT, Harold. *Garden Trees & Shrubs in Australasia.* 1952. Melbourne. 2nd revised ed. ils/photos. 256p. VG/dj. B26. $21.00

SARGENT, Herbert H. *Campaign of Santiago de Cuba.* 1914. Chicago. McClurg. 3 vol. 1st ed. 12mo. VG. B11. $150.00

SARGENT, Lucious M. *Seed Time & Harvest Founded on Fact.* 1835. Boston. Damrell & Gould. 1st ed. 24p. VG/wrp. B14. $150.00

SARGENT, Pamela. *Golden Space.* 1982. Timescape. 1st ed. F/F. P3. $20.00

SARGENT, Pamela. *Golden Space.* 1982. Timescape. 1st ed. rem mk. F/dj. M21. $7.50

SARGENT, Pamela. *Venus of Shadows.* 1988. Doubleday. 1st ed. F/F. P3. $20.00

SARKISSIAN, Karekin. *Witness of the Oriental Orthodox Churches...* 1970. Lebanon. Antelias. 2nd ed. ils. 91p. H10. $25.00

SARLAT, N. *America's Cities of Sin.* 1951. NY. 12mo. 128p. VG/wrp. D3. $12.50

SAROYAN, William. *Razzle-Dazzle; or, Human Ballet, Opera & Circus...* 1942. Harcourt Brace. 1st ed. F. A18. $40.00

SAROYAN, William. *Saroyan Special.* 1948. Harcourt Brace. 1st ed. 8vo. ils Don Freeman. 368p. F/dj. H5. $175.00

SARRANTONIO, Al. *Campbell Wood.* 1986. Doubleday. 1st ed. RS. F/F. P3. $18.00

SARTON, George. *Hist of Science: Hellenistic Science & Culture...* 1952. Cambridge. Harvard. 554p. bl cloth. VG/worn. G1. $35.00

SARTON, George. *History of Science & the New Humanism.* 1937. Cambridge. 1st ed. 196p. A13. $30.00

SARTON, George. *Six Wings: Men of Science in the Renaissance.* 1957. Bloomington. 318p. G7. $35.00

SARTON, George. *Third Preface to Vol XXXIII of Busbecq, 1522-1592.* 1942. Isis. 18p. wrp/stiff cardboard. A10. $20.00

SARTON, May. *Magnificent Spinster.* 1985. Norton. 1st ed. F/VG. B3. $25.00

SARTON, May. *Reconing.* 1978. NY. 1st ed. pres. F/VG. H4. $35.00

SARTRE, Jean-Paul. *Existentialism & Human Emotions.* 1957. NY. Philosophical Lib. 1st ed. 96p. bl cloth. VG/dj. G1. $17.50

SARTRE, Jean-Paul. *Nausea.* nd. New Directions. New Classic Series. 238p. VG/tattered. M20. $25.00

SARTRE, Jean-Paul. *Philosophy of...* 1965. Random. 491p. blk cloth. VG/dj. G1. $25.00

SARTRE, Jean-Paul. *Psychology of Imagination.* 1948. Philosophical Lib. 1st Eng-language ed. blk cloth. G1. $30.00

SARTRE, Jean-Paul. *Search for a Method: A Sartrean Approach to Sociology...* 1963. Knopf. 1st Am ed. 181p. VG/VG. B33. $28.00

SARZANO, Frances. *Sir John Tenniel.* 1948. London. Art & Technics. 1st ed. ils Tenniel. NF/VG. C8. $36.00

SASEK, M. *This Is Paris.* 1959. Macmillan. 1st ed. pict brd. VG+/dj. M5. $45.00

SASLOW, James M. *Poetry of Michelangelo.* 1991. Yale. 1st ed. F/F. P3. $45.00

SASSON, Jean P. *Princess: True Story Life Behind the Veil in Saudi Arabia.* 1992. Morrow. 1st ed. 288p. cloth. VG/dj. W1. $20.00

SASSOON, Siegfried. *Memoirs of a Fox-Hunting Man.* 1929. Coward McCann. 1st ed. NF/dj. Q1. $100.00

SASSOON, Siegfried. *Memoirs of a Fox-Hunting Man.* 1971. Folio Soc. 2nd imp. ils Lynton Lamb. 290p. NF/cardboard case. M7. $40.00

SASSOON, Siegfried. *Memoirs of an Infantry Officer.* 1930. London. Faber. 1st ils UK ed. ils Barnett Freedman. 311p. VG. M7. $35.00

SASSOON, Siegfried. *Sassoon's Long Journey.* 1933. London. Faber. 1st ed. 100 ils. 180p. as new. M7. $16.50

SASSOON, Siegfried. *Siegfried's Journey 1916-1920.* 1945. London. Faber. 1st ed. gilt coral cloth. VG+/VG. M7. $55.00

SATO, Shozo. *Art of Arranging Flowers.* 1965. NY. thick 4to. 366p. silk bdg. H4. $75.00

SATO, Teruo. *Japanese Crane.* 1990. Tokyo. Graphic-Sha. 1st ed. Japanese text. 80p. F/F. S9. $35.00

SATTELMEYER. *Thoreau's Reading: A Study in Intellectual History.* 1988. Princeton. 348p. F. A4. $35.00

SATTERTHWAIT, Walter. *Ease With the Dead.* 1991. London. Collins. 1st ed. F/F. T2. $20.00

SATTERTHWAIT, Walter. *Wilde West.* 1991. St Martin. 1st ed. sgn. F/F T2. $25.00

SAUCIER, Ted. *Bottoms Up.* 1951. NY. 1st ed. VG/VG. B5. $50.00

SAUERS. *Gettysburg Campaign, June 3-August 1, 1863: ...Bibliography.* 1982. np. 294p. F/sans. A4. $40.00

SAUL, John. *Creature.* 1989. Bantam. 1st ed. F/dj. M21. $8.00

SAUNDERS, Clare Casler. *Design for Treachery.* nd. Collier. VG. P3. $15.00

SAUNDERS, Doris E. *Cyclamen. A Gardener's Guide to the Genus.* 1975 (1959). np. revised ed. photos/drawings. sc. VG. B26. $11.00

SAUNDERS, Frederick. *Salad for the Social by the Author of Salad for Solitary.* 1856. NY. De Witt Davenport. 8vo. 15 engravings. 401p. G. D6. $30.00

SAUNDERS, Frederick. *Salad for the Solitary by an Epicure.* 1853. London. Lamport Blakeman Law. 6th thousand. 344p. VG. D6. $40.00

SAUNDERS, Harold N. *All the Astrolabes.* 1984. Oxford, UK. Senecio. 4to. 102p. VG/VG. K5. $40.00

SAUNDERS, John Monk. *Wings.* 1927. Grosset Dunlap. 1st ed. photos. F/NF. Q1. $75.00

SAUNIER, Claudis. *Treatise on Modern Horology.* 1952. London. Foyle. 8vo. 844p. bl cloth. VG/VG. A8. $90.00

SAURAT, Dennis. *Three Conventions: Metaphysical Dialogues.* 1926. Dial. 1st ed. 128p. VG/VG. B33. $50.00

SAUVETER, Jean Claude. *Narrow Path, Part One.* 1993. Vantage. 1st ed. F/F. F4. $18.00

SAVAGE, Blake. *Assignment in Space With Rip Foster.* 1958. Whitman. VG. P3. $10.00

SAVAGE, Ernest. *Two If By Sea.* 1982. NY. Scribner. 1st ed. NF/dj. S6. $22.50

SAVAGE, Kim. *Hellion.* 1951. NY. 1st ed. VG/VG. A17. $10.00

SAVAGE, Les. *Silver Street Woman.* 1954. Hanover House. 1st ed. VG/VG. P3. $20.00

SAVAGE, Marc. *Flamingos.* 1992. Doubleday. 1st ed. sgn. F/F. T2. $30.00

SAVAGE, Marc. *Paradise.* 1993. Doubleday. 1st ed. sgn. F/F. T2. $25.00

SAVAGE, Raymond. *Allenby of Armageddon. A Record of the Career & Campaigns...* 1926. Bobbs Merrill. pref DL George. map. 353p. tan cloth. VG. M7. $45.00

SAVARY, Jacques. *Universal Dictionary of Trade & Commerce.* 1757. London. Knapton. 2 vol. 2nd ed. folio. fld talbes. new gr leather. H10. $350.00

SAVCHENKO, Vladimir. *Self-Discovery.* 1979. Macmillan. 1st ed. VG/VG. P3. $15.00

SAVILLE, Malcom. *Saucers Over the Moor.* nd. Children's BC. VG/VG. P3. $8.00

SAVITT, Sam. *Wild Horse Running.* 1973. Dodd Mead. 1st ed. VG. O3. $25.00

SAVORY, Teo. *Gunter Eich.* 1971. Santa Barbara. Unicorn German Series. 1st ed. 56p. VG/wrp. A17. $15.00

SAVOY, Gene. *On the Trail of the Feathered Serpent.* 1974. Bobbs Merrill. 1st prt. 8vo. 32 pl. map ep. VG/VG. B11. $25.00

SAWER, Geoffrey. *Australian Federal Politics & Law 1901-1929.* 1956. Melbourne. 1st ed. 350p. NF/dj. D3. $20.00

SAWYER, Franklin. *Military Hist of 8th Regiment OH Volunteer Infantry.* 1994. Huntington, WV. rpt of 1881 ed. M/dj. B18. $30.00

SAWYER, Jesse. *Studies in American Indian Languages.* 1973. Berkley. CA U. gilt gr cloth. M/sans. P4. $42.50

SAWYER, Ruth. *Cottage for Betsy.* 1954. Harper. 1st ed. ils Vera Bock. 120p. VG/G. P2. $25.00

SAWYER, Ruth. *Joy to the World.* 1966. Little Brn. 1st ed thus. cloth. F/VG. M5. $35.00

SAWYER, Ruth. *Maggie Rose: Her Birthday Christmas.* 1952. Harper. 1st ed. ils Sendak. VG. C8. $135.00

SAXON, Gladys Relyea. *California Camel Adventure.* 1955. Caxton. 1st ed. 183p. F/G+. P2. $15.00

SAXON, Lyle. *Fabulous New Orleans.* 1930. np. ils EH Suydam. 300p. VG. E5. $28.00

SAYERS, Dorothy L. *Busman's Honeymoon.* 1955. Gollancz. 16th prt. NF/NF. P3. $20.00

SAYERS, Dorothy L. *Devil To Pay.* 1939. Canterbury. 1st ed. sgn. 63p. wrp/case. C2. $350.00

SAYERS, Dorothy L. *Hangman's Holiday.* 1954. Gollancz. 18th prt. NF/NF. P3. $20.00

SAYERS, Dorothy L. *Mind of the Maker.* 1941. Methuen. 2nd ed. VG/VG. P3. $35.00

SAYERS, Dorothy L. *Nine Tailors.* 1939. Gollancz. 11th ed. VG/VG. P3. $20.00

SAYERS, Dorothy L. *Strong Poison.* 1930. Brewer Warren. 2nd ed. xl. G+. P3. $10.00

SAYERS, Dorothy L. *Strong Poison.* 1930. NY. Brewer Warren. 1st Am ed. VG/VG. Q1. $650.00

SAYERS, Dorothy L. *Treasury of Sayers Stories.* 1958. Gollancz. VG/G+. P3. $35.00

SAYERS, Dorothy L. *Zeal of Thy House.* 1937. Harcourt Brace. 1st ed. F/poor. A18. $50.00

SAYLES, G.O. *Select Cases of the Court of King's Bench Under Richard II.* 1971. London. Bernard Quaritch. Vol VII only. M11. $45.00

SAYLES, John. *Anarchists' Convention.* 1979. Atlantic/Little Brn. 1st ed. inscr. F/NF. B2. $65.00

SAYLES, John. *Union Dues.* 1977. Little Brn. 1st ed/author's 2nd book. F/F. S9. $50.00

SAYLES, Mary Buell. *Substitute Parents: A Study of Foster Families.* 1936. NH. 1st ed. 309p. cloth. VG. B14. $35.00

SAYRE, Nora. *Running Time. Films of the Cold War.* 1982. Dial. ARC. w/promo photo. F/F. B2. $25.00

SAYRE & VILLANI. *Pig Iron SF.* 1982. Pig Iron. 1st ed. F/wrp. M2. $10.00

SCAFFE, W.L. *John A Brashear.* 1924. NY. 1st ed. VG. C11. $55.00

SCARBOROUGH, Dorothy. *From a Southern Porch.* 1919. Putnam. 1st ed. VG+. A18. $40.00

SCARBOROUGH, Elizabeth Ann. *Healer's War.* 1988. Doubleday. 1st ed. rem mk. F/F. M21. $10.00

SCARBOROUGH, Elizabeth. *Healer's War.* 1988. Doubleday. 1st ed. F/F. P3. $18.00

SCHAAP, Dick. *Bridge to the Seven Seas.* 1973. McKay. 4to. ils. 120p. dj. T7. $30.00

SCHACHNER, Nathan. *Space Lawyer.* 1953. Gnome. 1st ed. F/NF. M2. $60.00

SCHACHNER, Nathan. *Sun Shines West.* 1943. Appleton Century. 1st ed. VG/VG. P3. $23.00

SCHACHT, Al. *Clowning Through Baseball.* 1941. NY. Barnes. 189p. G. A17. $10.00

SCHACKLETON, Robert. *Book of Chicago.* 1920. Penn Pub. 1st ed. ils Herbert Pullinger. 354p. G+. H1. $9.00

SCHAEBERLE, J.M. *Terrestrial Atmospheric Absorption of Photographic Rays...* 1893. Sacramento. CA U. 8vo. 89p. blk cloth. xl. G. K5. $35.00

SCHAEFER, Jack. *American Bestiary.* 1975. Houghton Mifflin. 1st ed. fwd James Findley. ils Linda Powell. F/dj. A18. $30.00

SCHAEFER, Jack. *Great Endurance Horse Race.* 1963. Stagecoach. 1st ltd ed. 1/750. RS. F/F. A18. $200.00

SCHAEFER, Jack. *Heroes Without Glory.* 1966. London. Deutsch. 1st ed. F/clip. A18. $45.00

SCHAEFER, Jack. *Out West: Anthology of Stories.* 1955. Houghton Mifflin. 1st ed. F. A18. $25.00

SCHAEFFER, Francis A. *How Should We Then Live?* 1976. Revell. 287p. VG/dj. B29. $7.00

SCHAEFFER, Franky. *Sham Pearls for Real Swine.* 1990. Wolgenmuth. 290p. M/M. B29. $7.50

SCHAEFFER, J. Parsons. *Morris' Human Anatomy.* 1942. Phil/Toronto. Blakiston. 10th ed. 1515p. G. K4. $20.00

SCHAEFFER, O. *Anatomical Atlas of Obstetrics...* 1901. np. ils. 300p. VG. E5. $45.00

SCHAEFFER, Susan Fromberg. *Granite Lady.* 1974. Macmillan. ARC. inscr. RS. F/F. B4. $85.00

SCHAFF, Adam. *Intro to Semantics.* 1962. Pergamon. 1st Eng-language ed. cream linen. VG. G1. $35.00

SCHALDACH, William. *Currents & Eddies.* 1944. NY. 1st ed. VG/G. B5. $45.00

SCHALLER, Michael. *Douglas MacArthur: Far-Eastern General.* 1989. NY. 1st ed. 320p. F/F. A17. $15.00

SCHAMA, Simon. *Dead Certainties.* 1991. Knopf. 1st ed. NF/NF. A14/P3. $20.00

SCHATZBERG, Walter. *Relations of Literature & Science.* 1987. Modern Language Assn. 458p. cloth. M. A10. $25.00

SCHAUINGER, J. Herman. *William Gaston, Carolinian.* 1949. Milwaukee. inscr. 242p. NF/dj. D3. $25.00

SCHEDEL, Hartman. *Das Buch der Chroniken.* 1966. NY. folio. facsimile on rag paper. 1/1350. NF/VG. F1. $85.00

SCHEICK, William J. *Critical Response to HG Wells.* 1995. Greenwood. 1st ed. F/sans. P3. $55.00

SCHEINFELD, Amram. *You & Heredity.* 1939. Stokes. 407p. G. K4. $10.00

SCHEINFELD, Amram. *Your Heredity & Environment.* 1965. Lippincott. 728p. F. K4. $25.00

SCHELE, Linda. *Maya Glyphs.* 1982. Austin, TX. 1st ed. 4to. 427p. VG. F3. $40.00

SCHENCK, Hilbert. *Chronosequence.* 1988. Tor. 1st ed. F/F. P3. $18.00

SCHENCK, Hilbert. *Rose for Armageddon.* 1984. London. Allison Busby. 1st Eng/1st hc ed. F/F. N3. $20.00

SCHERF, Margaret. *To Cache a Millionaire.* 1972. Detective BC. VG. P3. $8.00

SCHERMAN, Katherine. *Slave Who Freed Haiti: Story of Toussaint Louverture.* 1954. Random. ils Adolf Dehn. VG+/VG. C8. $15.00

SCHEYER, Amram. *Laurens Hamered Bamidrar Ul'Acharav.* 1972. v'Hotsa'at Sheba. 1st Israeli ed. Hebrew text. 133p. yel paper brd. G. M7. $65.00

SCHICKEL, Richard. *Disney Version.* 1968. NY. biblio/index. 382p. F/VG. A17. $7.00

SCHIDDEL, Edmund. *Swing.* 1975. Simon Schuster. 1st ed. F/dj. F4. $22.00

SCHIFF, Stuart David. *Whispers III.* 1981. Doubleday. 1st ed. F/F. P3. $25.00

SCHIFF, Stuart David. *Whispers.* 1977. Doubleday. 1st ed. F/F. P3. $40.00

SCHIFFER, Michael. *Ballpark.* 1982. Simon Schuster. 1st ed. rem mk. F/VG. P8. $15.00

SCHIFFMAN, Jack. *Uptown: Story of Harlem's Apollo Theatre.* 1971. NY. Cfowles. 1st ed. F/NF. B2. $40.00

SCHILLIP, Paul Arthur. *Albert Einstein: Philosopher-Scientist.* 1949. Evanston. 1st trade ed. thick 8vo. 781p. bl buckram. G1. $50.00

SCHISGALL, Oscar. *Devil's Daughter.* 1932. Fiction League. 1st ed. VG. P3. $25.00

SCHLARMAN, Joseph H. *Catechetical Sermon-Aides.* 1942. St Louis. Herder. 540p. xl. H10. $11.00

SCHLEE, Susan. *On Almost Any Wind.* 1978. Ithaca. Cornell. 1st ed. photos/charts/index. 301p. F/NF. P4. $25.00

SCHLENFIELD, Alan. *Dark Kingdoms.* 1975. Morrow. 1st ed. 194p. VG/VG. A18. $14.00

SCHLESINGER, Arthur M. *Robert Kennedy & His Times. Vol II.* ca 1978. Houghton Mifflin. BC. ils. VG. M10. $2.50

SCHLESINGER, Arthur M. Jr. *Thousand Days: John F Kennedy in the White House.* 1965. Houghton Mifflin. 1st ed. 1087p. G. M10. $4.50

SCHLESINGER, G. *Confirmation & Confirmability.* 1974. Clarendon. 109p. cloth. VG/dj. G1. $16.50

SCHLISSEL, Lillian. *Women's Diaries of the Westward Journey.* 1992. Schochen Books. photos/index. sc. M. A18. $14.00

SCHLOSS, Albert. *English Bijou Almanac for 1839.* 1838. London. Schloss. 20x15mm. 64p. gilt gr morocco/onlay. F/morocco sleeve/case. B24. $875.00

SCHMALENBACH, Werner. *Fernand Leger.* 1976. Abrams. 1st ed. Lib of Great Painters Series. ils. bl cloth. F/dj. F1. $75.00

SCHMALENBACH, Werner. *Noble Horse: A Journey Through the History of Art.* 1962. London. Allen. 1st Eng-language ed. fwd Lionel Edwards. VG/G. O3. $25.00

SCHMECKEBIER, Laurence E. *Modern Mexican Art.* 1939. NM U. 1st ed. 4to. 190p. NF. A17. $35.00

SCHMIDT, Dana Adams. *Journey Among Brave Men.* 1964. Little Brn. 1st ed. 298p. xl. VG. W1. $22.00

SCHMIDT, Dana Adams. *Yemen the Unknown War.* 1968. HRW. 1st ed. 8vo. 16 pl/maps. cloth. VG/dj. W1. $20.00

SCHMIDT, Karl Patterson. *Home & Habits of Wild Animals.* 1934. Donohue. ils Walter Alois Weber. 64p. VG. A3. $12.50

SCHMIDT, Margaret Fox. *Passion's Child...Life of Jane Digby.* 1976. Harper Row. 8vo. ils. 329p. VG/torn. W1. $18.00

SCHMIDT, Nathaniel. *Prophet of Nazareth.* 1905. Macmillan. 1st ed. 422p. G. W1. $12.00

SCHMIDT, Oscar. *Doctrine of Descent & Darwinism.* 1875. NY. ils. 334p. cloth. B14. $100.00

SCHMIDT, Raymond. *Die Philosophie der Genenwart in Selstdarstellungen.* 1923. Leipzig. Felix Meiner. 2nd revised ed. 243p. VG. G1. $25.00

SCHMIDT, Stanley. *Analog's Children of the Future.* 1982. Dial. 1st ed. VG/VG. P3. $15.00

SCHMIDT, Stanley. *Analog's Expanding Universe.* 1986. Longmeadow. 1st ed. F/VG+. N3. $10.00

SCHMIDT, Stanley. *From Mind to Mind.* 1984. Doubleday. 1st ed. RS. F/F. P3. $18.00

SCHMIDT, Stanley. *From Mind to Mind...* 1984. NY. Dial. 1st ed. NF/NF. N3. $10.00

SCHMIDT, Stanley. *Tweedlioop.* 1986. NY. Tor. 1st ed. F/F. N3. $20.00

SCHMITZ, James H. *Agent of Vega.* 1960. Gnome. 1st ed/author's 1st book. F/dj. M2. $40.00

SCHMITZ, James H. *Eternal Frontiers.* 1973. Putnam. 1st ed. F/F. N3. $30.00

SCHMITZ, James H. *Pride of Monsters.* 1970. Macmillan. 1st ed. F/F. P3. $35.00

SCHMOLZ, Hugo. *Fotografierte Architektur 1924-1937.* 1982. Munich. Mahnert-Lueg. 1st ed. German text. F/F. S9. $175.00

SCHNAPPER, Edith. *Inward Oddyssey: Concept of the Way in Great Religions...* 1965. London. Allen Unwin. ils. 237p. VG/G. B33. $20.00

SCHNECK, Jerome. *History of Psychiatry.* 1960. Springfield. 1st ed. 196p. dj. A13. $45.00

SCHNEIDER, Isadore. *Comrade Mister.* 1934. Equinox. 1st ed. 1/500. NF. B2. $45.00

SCHNEIDER, Isadore. *Temptation of Anthony.* 1928. Boni Liveright. 1st ed. F/NF. B2. $100.00

SCHNELLER, H. *Katalog und Ephemeriden Veranderlicher Sterne Fur 1940.* 1939. Berlin. 8vo. 261p. G/wrp. K5. $25.00

SCHOFIELD, Susan Clark. *Refugio, They Named You Wrong.* 1991. Algonquin. 1st ed/author's 1st book. NF/B. B3. $25.00

SCHOLES, Robert. *Structural Fabulation.* 1975. Notre Dame. 1st ed. F/F. P3. $25.00

SCHOLZ, Jackson. *Batter Up.* 1949. Comet. 1st ed. G+. P8. $9.00

SCHOLZ, Jackson. *Fielder From Nowhere.* 1948. Morrow. 1st ed. xl. G+/G+. P8. $8.00

SCHOLZ, Jackson. *Sparkplug at Short.* 1966. Morrow. 1st ed. VG/VG. P8. $15.00

SCHONFIELD, Hugh J. *Passover Plot: New Interpretation of Life & Death of Jesus.* 1965. NY. Gies. 5th ed. G+/worn. N2. $7.50

SCHOOLCRAFT, Henry Rowe. *Algic Researches Comprising Inquires...N American Indians.* 1839. Harper. 2 vol. 1st ed. orig bdg. G/box. B5. $450.00

SCHORER, Mark. *William Blake: The Politics of Vision.* 1946. Holt. 1st ed. VG/dj. Q1. $75.00

SCHOTT, Max. *Murphy's Romance.* 1980. NY. 1st ed/author's 2nd book (1st novel). sgn. NF/F. A11. $45.00

SCHOW, David J. *Kill Riff.* 1988. Tor. 1st ed. F/F. P3. $18.00

SCHREIBER & SCHREIBER. *Vanished Cities.* 1957. Knopf. 1st ed. 344p. xl. VG. W1. $15.00

SCHREINER, Olive. *Woman & Labor.* 1911. Stokes. 1st ed. NF. B2. $65.00

SCHREINER-YANTIS, Netti. *Genealogical & Local History Books in Print.* 1981. Springfield, VA. Genealogical Books. 3rd ed. 8vo. 1000p. F. B11. $65.00

SCHRIBER, Fritz. *Complete Carriage & Wagon Painter.* 1905. NY. Richardson. later prt. VG. O3. $95.00

SCHRIER, A.M. *Behavior of Non-Human Primates. Vol I & Vol II.* 1965. Academic. 2 vol. 595p. F/dj. K4. $65.00

SCHRIER & STORY. *Russian Looks at America, Journey of Aleksandr B Lakier...* 1979. Chicago. ils. 345p. F/F. A4. $65.00

SCHROEDER, Doris. *Annette Sierra Summer.* 1960. Whitman. TVTI. G+. P3. $6.00

SCHROEDER, Doris. *Annie Oakley in Danger at Diablo.* 1955. Whitman. TVTI. NF. P3. $20.00

SCHROEDER, Doris. *Forbidden Valley.* 1959. Whitman. Lassie TVTI. G+. P3. $10.00

SCHROEDER, Doris. *Saga of Wildcat Creek.* 1963. Whitman. Beverly Hillbillies TVTI. VG. P3. $10.00

SCHROEDER, George W. *Church Brotherhood Guidebook.* 1960. Broadman. 192p. G. B29. $2.00

SCHROEDER, John Frederick. *Life & Times of Washington: Containing Particular Account...* (1857). NY. Johnson Fry. 2 vol. ils Alonzo Chappel. full leather. VG. H1. $125.00

SCHROEDER, John H. *Shaping a Maritime Empire.* 1985. Westport, CT. 1st ed. 229p. F. A17. $15.00

SCHROEDER, Theodore. *Obscene Literature & Constitutional Law, Forensic Defense...* 1911. NY. Private Prt for Forensic Uses. cloth. M11. $125.00

SCHULLIAN, Dorothy. *Baglivi Correspondence From Lib of Sir Wm Osler.* 1974. Ithaca. sm 4to. 531p. F. G7. $45.00

SCHULMAN, J. Neil. *Alongside Night.* 1979. Crown. 1st ed. F/F. N3. $15.00

SCHULMAN, J. Neil. *Rainbow Cadenza.* 1983. Simon Schuster. 1st ed. F/F. N3. $15.00

SCHULT, Joachim. *Curious Yachting Inventions.* 1974. NY. Taplinger. ils/photos. 139p. dj. T7. $25.00

SCHULTZ, James Willard. *Bear Chief's War Shirt.* 1984. Mtn Pr. 1st ed. F/dj. A18. $35.00

SCHULTZ, James Willard. *My Life As an Indian: Story of Red Woman & White Man...* 1935. Houghton Mifflin. ils GB Brinnell. VG. B34. $75.00

SCHULTZ, James Willard. *With the Indians in the Rockies.* 1912. Houghton Mifflin. ils George Varian. NF. B34. $125.00

SCHULTZ, James Willard. *With the Indians in the Rockies.* 1960. Houghton Mifflin. 1st ed thus. ils Bjorklund. F/dj. A18. $40.00

SCHULTZ, Mark. *Cadillacs & Dinosaurs.* 1989. Kitchen Sink. 1st ed. sgn. F. P3. $25.00

SCHULZ, Charles. *Charlie Brown Christmas.* 1965. World. 1st prt. 8vo. F/VG. B17. $18.50

SCHULZ, Charles. *Charlie Brown's All-Stars.* 1966. World. 1st ed. pict bdg. VG. P8. $12.50

SCHULZ, Charles. *Sandlot Peanuts.* 1977. HRW. 1st ed. VG. P8. $17.50

SCHULZ, Charles. *Snoopy & the Red Baron.* 1966. HRW. 1st ed. 8vo. F/F. B17. $15.00

SCHULZ, Charles. *We're Right Behind You Charlie Brown.* 1964. HRW. 1st ed. VG. P8. $10.00

SCHULZ, Charles. *You Can Do It Charlie Brown.* 1963. HRW. 1st ed. VG. P8. $15.00

SCHULZ, H.C. *Monograph on the Italian Choir Book.* 1941. Grabhorn. 1/75. folio. ils Valenti Angelo. tan/red linen. K1. $1,200.00

SCHUMANN, Karl. *Bluhende Kakteen.* 1982 (1905). Thungen (Neudamm). ltd/German rpt. folio. 84p. sc. M. B26. $179.00

SCHUR, Nathan. *Jerusalem in Pilgrim's Accounts.* 1980. Jerusalem. 4to. 151p. cloth. O2. $30.00

SCHURE, Edouard. *Pythagoras & the Delphic Mysteries.* ca 1915. London. Rider. revised ed. 180p. VG. B33. $45.00

SCHURHAMMER, George. *Shin-To: Way of the Gods of Japan.* 1923. Bonn/Leipzig. ils. 210p. cloth/brd. B14. $150.00

SCHURZ, Carl. *Reminiscences of...* 1907. NY. 3 vol. portraits/drawings/index. F. O8. $45.00

SCHUTZ, Benjamin M. *All the Old Bargains.* 1985. Bluejay. 1st ed. F/F. F4. $15.00

SCHUTZ, Benjamin M. *All the Old Bargains.* 1985. Bluejay. 1st ed. sgn. F/F. P3. $25.00

SCHUYLER, Henry C. *Mary, Mother Most Admirable.* 1935. Phil. Reilly. 173p. H10. $10.00

SCHUYLER, James. *What's for Dinner.* 1978. Blk Sparrow. 1st trade ed. F/acetate. S9. $25.00

SCHUYLER, Keith. *Bow Hunting for Big Game.* 1974. Stackpole. xl. B34. $10.00

SCHWARTZ, Alvin. *Ten Copycats in a Boat & Other Riddles.* 1980. Harper. 1st ed. ils Marc Simont. NF/NF. C8. $20.00

SCHWARTZ, Delmore. *I Am Cherry Alive, the Little Girl Sang.* 1979. Harper. 1st ed. ils Barbara Cooney. NF/NF. C8. $40.00

SCHWARTZ, Delmore. *Summer Knowledge: New & Selected Poems 1938-1958.* 1959. Doubleday. 1st ed. sgn. F/VG+. V1. $45.00

SCHWARTZ-NOBEL, Loretta. *Engaged to Murder.* 1987. Viking. 2nd ed. P3. $15.00

SCHWEITZER, Albert. *Goethe: Two Addresses.* 1948. NY. Beacon. 1st ed. 75p. VG/VG. B33. $18.00

SCHWEITZER, Albert. *Indian Thought & Its Development.* 1954. Boston. Beacon. 1st Am ed. 272p. VG/VG. B33. $30.00

SCHWEITZER, Albert. *Mysticism of Paul the Apostle.* 1955. Macmillan. 411p. VG/VG. B33. $25.00

SCHWEITZER, Albert. *Out of My Life & Thought: An Autobiography.* 1949. Holt. 4th ed. VG/dj. N2. $6.00

SCHWEITZER, Darrell. *Pathways to Elfland: Writings of Lord Dunsany.* 1989. Phil. Owlswick. 1st ed. F/F. T2. $25.00

SCHWEITZER, Darrell. *Tom O'Bedlam's Night Out & Other Strange Excursions.* 1985. Buffalo. Ganley. 1st ed. ils SE Fabian. F/F. T2. $20.00

SCHWEITZER, Darrell. *White Isle.* 1989. Owlswick. 1st ed. F/F. P3. $19.00

SCHWIMMER, Rosika. *Tiza Tales.* 1928. Doubleday. 1st ed. ils Pogany. VG. C8. $45.00

SCITHERS, George. *Isaac Asimov's Marvels of SF.* 1979. Dial. 1st ed. VG/VG. P3. $15.00

SCITHERS, George. *On Writing SF.* 1981. Owlswick. 1st ed. F/dj. M2. $20.00

SCOFIELD, Samuel. *Practical Treatise on Vaccinia or Cowpox.* 1810. NY. Southwick Pelsue. 139p. tree sheepskin. VG+. B14. $200.00

SCORTIA, Thomas N. *Best of Thomas N Scortia.* 1981. Doubleday. 1st ed. NF/NF. P3. $20.00

SCORTIA, Thomas N. *Strange Bed Fellows: Sex & SF.* 1972. Random. 1st ed. F/VG+. N3. $10.00

SCOTT, A. MacCallum. *Barbary: Romance of the Nearest East.* 1921. London. Butterworth. 1st ed. 222p. G. W1. $12.00

SCOTT, Alastair. *Tracks Across Alaska: A Dog Sled Journey.* 1990. NY. 1st Am ed. 247p. M/M. A17. $9.50

SCOTT, Anna M. *Day Dawn in Africa; or, Progress of the Prot Epis Mission...* 1858. NY. 1st ed. pl/fld map. 314p. cloth. VG. M8. $150.00

SCOTT, C.A. Dawson. *Haunting.* 1985. Tabb House. NF/NF. P3. $20.00

SCOTT, E.B. *Saga of Lake Tahoe.* 1957. Lake Tahoe. 1st revised ed. VG/G. B5. $50.00

SCOTT, Evelyn. *Background in TN.* 1937. McBride. 1st ed. NF. B2. $100.00

SCOTT, Evelyn. *Wave.* 1929. Cape Smith. 1st ed. F/NF. B2. $100.00

SCOTT, Everett. *Third Base Thatcher.* 1923. Dodd Mead. 1st ed. Matty Books Series. VG. scarce. P8. $70.00

SCOTT, Genio C. *Fishing in Am Waters.* 1869. Harper. 1st ed. 484p. cloth. NF. B14. $75.00

SCOTT, Hugh. *In the High Yemen.* 1947. London. 2nd ed. 8vo. 260p. dj. F. O2. $85.00

SCOTT, Jack S. *Corporal Smithers Deceased.* 1983. London. Gollancz. 1st ed. F/F. S6. $25.00

SCOTT, Jack S. *Local Lads.* 1983. Dutton. 1st ed. F/dj. F4. $15.00

SCOTT, Jack S. *Time of Fine Weather.* 1984. Gollancz. xl. dj. P3. $8.00

SCOTT, James Brown. *Hague Conventions & Declarations of 1899 & 1907...* 1915. NY. 2nd ed. 303p. xl. VG. D3. $35.00

SCOTT, M.W. *Old Richmond Neighborhoods.* 1950. Richmond. 1st ed. sgn. VG/G. B5. $60.00

SCOTT, Mark. *Krystonian Adventures.* 1987. Mildonian. 1st ed. F/F. F4. $15.00

SCOTT, Melissa. *Burning Bright.* 1993. Tor. 1st ed. F/F. P3. $22.00

SCOTT, Melissa. *Mighty Good Road.* 1990. Baen. 1st hc ed. F/SF BC issue. F4. $8.00

SCOTT, Morgan; see Patten, Gilbert.

SCOTT, Nathan A. *3 American Moralists: Mailer, Bellow, Trilling.* 1973. Notre Dame. ARC/1st ed. RS. F/F. S9. $25.00

SCOTT, Robert. *Analytical Digest of Military Laws of the US.* 1873. np. index. 510p. O8. $32.50

SCOTT, Walter. *Complete Poetical & Dramatic Works.* 1883. Rutledge. 8vo. ils Wm B Scott. 640p. marbled brd. G+. H1. $20.00

SCOTT, Walter. *Ivanhoe.* 1950. Heritage. VG/case. P3. $45.00

SCOTT, Walter. *Letters on Demonology & Witchcraft.* 1830. London. 1st ed. 24mo. rebound cloth. NF. C2. $100.00

SCOTT, Walter. *Letters on Demonology & Witchcraft...Second Edition.* 1831. London. John Murray. gilt quarter blk calf. M11. $275.00

SCOTT, Walter. *Schottishe Lieder und Balladen von Walter Scott.* 1817. Leipzig/Altenburg. Brochhaus. trans Schubart. rebound. VG. H1. $28.00

SCOTT-STOKES, Henry. *Life & Death of Yukio Mishima.* 1974. Farrar. 1st ed. F/F. B2. $25.00

SCOVILLE, Warren C. *Revolution in Glassmaking: Entrepreneurship...* 1948. Harvard. 1st ed. photos. 398p. F/VG. H1. $35.00

SCROGGS, William. *Practice of Courts-Leets & Courts-Baron...* 1728. London. Nutt Gosling. 4th ed. 8vo. contemporary calf. VG. D3. $350.00

SCUBRING, Paul. *Die Kunst der Hochrenaissance in Italien.* 1926. Berlin. Im Propylaen. 1st ed. 54 mtd pl. 615p. F. F1. $185.00

SCULL, William Ellis. *Sometime Quaker: An Autobiography.* 1939. Winston. 8vo. 219p. VG. V3. $20.00

SCULLY, Vincent. *American Architecture & Urbanism.* 1969. NY. Praeger. sm 4to. 275p. yel stp gray cloth. F/dj. F1. $40.00

SCULLY, Vincent. *Earth, the Temple, & the Gods.* 1962. Yale. 1st ed. 257p. VG. M20. $45.00

SCUPOLI, Lawrence. *Spiritual Combat & Treatise on Peace of the Soul.* 1950. Westminster. Newman. 240p. xl. H10. $15.00

SEABORN, Bill. *Bromeliads. Tropical Air Plants.* 1976. Laguna Hills. photos. 41p. sc. VG. B26. $7.50

SEABORNE, E.A. *Detective in Fiction.* 1960. Clarke Irwin. G+. P3. $10.00

SEABROOK, W.B. *Adventures in Arabia Among Bedouins, Druses...* 1930. Bl Ribbon. 6th prt. 8vo. cloth. VG. W1. $14.00

SEABROOK, W.B. *Magic Island.* 1929. Literary Guild. ils. 336p. VG/dj. F3. $10.00

SEABY, Allen W. *Sheltie: Story of a Shetland Pony.* 1939. London. Black. 1st ed. ils Allen W Seaby. NF/NF. C8. $25.00

SEAGER, Richard B. *Explorations in the Island of Mochlos.* 1912. Boston. Am School Classical Studies. 4to. cloth. O2. $75.00

SEAMAN, Augusta Huiell. *Disappearance of Anne Shaw.* 1928. Doubleday. 1st ed. 262p. VG/tattered. M20. $25.00

SEAMAN, Augusta Huiell. *Mystery at Linden Hall.* 1939. Grosset Dunlap. ils Manning de V Lee. VG/dj. M5. $20.00

SEAMAN, Augusta Huiell. *Sally Sims Adventures It.* 1942 (1924). Appleton Century. 226p. VG/dj. M20. $30.00

SEARLE, John R. *Speech Acts: Essay in Philosophy of Language.* 1969. Cambridge. blk cloth. VG/clip. G1. $100.00

SEARLE, S.A. *Environment & Plant Life.* 1973. London. 48 pl/12 figures/14 tables. F/dj. B26. $29.00

SEARLES, Baird. *Films of SF & Fantasy.* 1988. Afi/Abrams. 1st ed. VG. P3. $75.00

SEARLS, Hank. *Pentagon.* 1971. Bernard Geis. 1st ed. F/NF. F4. $18.00

SEARLS, Hank. *Pilgrim Project.* nd. BC. VG/VG. P3. $8.00

SEAVER, George. *Albert Schweitzer: Christian Revolutionary.* 1944. Harper. 130p. VG/VG. B33. $14.00

SEAVER, SOUTHERN & TROCCHI. *Writers in Revolt: An Anthology.* 1963. NY. Frederick Fell. VG/dj. N2. $7.50

SECHRIST, Elsie. *Dreams: Your Magic Mirror.* nd. BC. VG. P3. $3.00

SECKLER-HUDSON, Catheryn. *Statelessness: With Special Reference to the US.* 1934. WA, DC. 1st ed. 332p. VG. D3. $30.00

SECORD & WURTS. *Honored & Betrayed: Irangate, Covert Affairs...* 1992. John Wiley. 1st ed. 8vo. 405p. NF/dj. W1. $20.00

SEDIRA, Belkassem Ben. *Dialogues Francais-Arabes.* 1905. Jourdan. 4th ed. 12mo. G. W1. $12.00

SEDWICK, Henry. *Cortes the Conqueror.* 1926. Bobbs Merrill. 390p. VG. F3. $15.00

SEDYCH, Andrei. *This Land of Israel.* 1967. Collier Macmillan. 1st ed. 244p. NF/dj. W1. $8.00

SEE, Carolyn. *Blue Money.* 1974. McKay. 1st ed/author's 1st book. F/NF. B4. $100.00

SEE, Carolyn. *Making History.* 1991. Houghton Mifflin. 1st ed. F/F. B3. $15.00

SEEBOHM & SEEBOHM. *Private Memoirs.* 1873. London. Provost. 12mo. 442p. V3. $24.00

SEELEY, Mabel. *Listening House.* 1944. Triangle. 2nd ed. VG/VG. P3. $15.00

SEELEY, Mabel. *Stranger Beside Me.* 1951. Doubleday. 1st ed. VG/VG. P3. $23.00

SEELEY, Mabel. *Woman of Property.* 1947. Doubleday. 1st ed. VG/G+. P3. $23.00

SEELIG, G. *Medicine: Hist Outline. 2nd Edition.* 1931. Baltimore. pres. 205p. VG/worn. G7. $35.00

SEELYE, John. *Kid.* 1972. NY. 1st ed/author's 2nd novel. inscr. F/NF clip. A11. $65.00

SEELYE, John. *Mark Twain in the Movies: A Meditation With Pictures.* 1977. Viking. 177p. F/dj. M10. $12.50

SEESE, Mildred Parker. *Tower of the Lord in the Land of Goshen: A Hist...* 1945. Goshen. 1st ed. 146p. cloth. VG. M8. $37.50

SEGAL, Erich. *Roman Laughter: Comedy of Plautus.* 1968. Cambridge. Harvard. 1st ed. inscr. F/NF. B4. $125.00

SEGAL & SENDAK. *Juniper Tree & Other Tales From Grimm.* 1973. FSG. 2 vol. 1st ed. 8vo. gilt brn cloth. F/dj/case. F1. $75.00

SEGOVIA, L. *Wisdom of Bernard Shaw.* 1913. NY. 1st ed. sgn Archibald Henderson bookplate. G. B5. $35.00

SEGRE, Alfredo. *Mahogany.* 1944. NY. 1st ed. F/F. A17. $10.00

SEGUR, Adrienne. *Il Etait une Fois.* 1951. Flammarion. 8 pl. 227p. VG+/G+. P2. $75.00

SEIDE, Katherine. *Paul Felix Warburg Union Catalog of Arbitration...* 1974. Rowman Littlefield. 3 vol. M11. $95.00

SEIDENSTICKER, Edward. *Kafu the Scribbler.* 1965. Stanford. 1st ed. NF/NF. M20. $15.00

SEIDMAN, Joel. *Intro to Labor Problems.* 1937. Detroit. UAW Education Dept. revised ed. VG/wrp. B2. $35.00

SEIDMAN, Joel. *Needle Trades.* 1942. Farrar Rinehart. 1st ed. VG/dj. V4. $17.50

SEIGEL, Robert. *Alpha Centauri.* 1980. Cornerstone. 2nd ed. F/F. P3. $10.00

SEIGER & VON DEWITZ. *Complete German Short-Haired Pointer.* 1951. Denlingers. 1st ed. 128p. 304p. cloth. F/tattered. R2. $50.00

SELA, Owen. *Exchange of Eagles.* 1977. Pantheon. 1st ed. VG/VG. P3. $15.00

SELBY, Hubert Jr. *Demon.* 1976. Playboy. 2nd ed. VG/VG. P3. $15.00

SELBY, Hubert Jr. *Last Exit to Brooklyn.* 1964. Grove. 1st ed/author's 1st book. NF/NF. S9. $125.00

SELBY, Hubert Jr. *Room.* 1972. Calder Boyars. 2nd ed. F/F. P3. $40.00

SELBY-LOWNDES. *Circus Train.* 1957. Abelard-Schuman. 240p. VG/chip. A17. $7.50

SELDEN, Georges. *Chester Cricket's Pigeon Ride.* 1981. Farrar Straus. 1st ed. F/F. C8. $35.00

SELDES, George. *Witness To a Century: Encounters...* 1987. Ballantine. VG/clip. N2. $7.50

SELDES, George. *You Can't Do That.* 1938. Modern Age. 1st ed. F/wrp/dj. B2. $25.00

SELF, Will. *Cock & Bull.* 1992. Atlantic Monthly. 1st ed/author's 2nd book. F/F. B3. $30.00

SELF, Will. *My Idea of Fun.* 1994. Atlantic Monthly. ARC/1st Am ed. F/wrp. B2. $35.00

SELIGMANN, Kurt. *History of Magic.* 1948. Pantheon. ils. 504p. VG/VG. B33. $20.00

SELIGO, Hans. *Morocco.* 1966. Munich. Andermann. 30 mc pl. 60p. NF. W1. $10.00

SELLARS, Roy Wood. *Philosophy of Physical Realism.* 1932. Macmillan. 488p. prt bl cloth. VG/dj. G1. $50.00

SELLERS, A. *Loeb Leopold Case.* 1926. Brunswick, GA. 1st ed. VG. B5. $75.00

SELLINGS, Arthur. *Quy Effect.* 1966. Dobson. 1st ed. VG/VG. P3. $28.00

SELLTIZ, Claire. *Research Methods in Social Relations.* 1959. Holt. 487p. F. K4. $8.50

SELSAM, Millicent E. *Stars, Mosquitoes & Crocodiles.* 1962. Harper Row. 8vo. 170p. pict brd. VG/VG. B11. $20.00

SELTZER, Carl C. *Contributions to Racial Anthropology of Near East...* 1969. Kraus. rpt. tall 8vo. VG/stiff wrp. W1. $12.00

SELTZER, Charles Alden. *Land of the Free.* 1927. Gundy. 1st ed. VG. P3. $30.00

SELTZER, Charles Alden. *Open Range Omnibus.* 1937. Grosset. 311p. G. B34. $15.00

SELTZER, Charles Alden. *So Long, Sucker.* 1941. Doubleday Doran. 1st ed. G+. P3. $20.00

SELTZER, Charles Alden. *Treasure Ranch.* 1940. Doubleday Doran. 1st ed. G+. P3. $20.00

SELTZER, L. *Financial History of Automobile Industry.* 1928. Boston. 1st ed. tables/charts/index. 297p. VG/G. B5. $90.00

SELWAY, N.C. *Golden Age of Coaching & Sport.* 1972. Leigh-on-Sea. ltd ed. 1/500. 4to. yel bdg. VG. O3. $265.00

SELWAY, N.C. *Regency Road.* 1957. London. Faber. 1st ed. VG/VG. O3. $245.00

SELZER, Richard. *Imagine a Woman & Other Stories.* 1990. Random. 1st ed. F/F. B3. $15.00

SEMAK, Michael. *Michael Semak Monograph.* 1974. Toronto. Impressions. 1st ed. w/orig photo & business note. S9. $275.00

SEMEONOFF & TRIST. *Diagnostic Performance Tests.* 1958. London. Tavistock. 115p. F/dj. K4. $12.50

SENCOURT, Robert. *St Paul: Envoy of Grace.* 1948. London. Hollis Carter. 256p. xl. H10. $10.50

SENDAK, Maurice. *Caldecott & Co: Notes on Books & Pictures.* 1988. Farrar Straus. 1st ed. 214p. F/F. S11. $25.00

SENDAK, Maurice. *Posters by Maurice Sendak.* 1976. Harmony Books. 1st ed. M/M. C8. $75.00

SENDAK, Maurice. *Some Swell Pup; or, Are You Sure You Want a Dog?* 1976. Farrar Straus. 1st ed. F/NF. C8. $65.00

SENDAK, Maurice. *Very Far Away.* 1957. Harper. 1st ed. F/VG. B2. $150.00

SENDAK, Maurice. *Where the Wild Things Are.* 1988. Harper Collins. 25th-anniversary ed. sgn. F/F. L3. $45.00

SENN, Nicholas. *Tahiti, the Island Paradise.* 1906. Chicago. Conkey. ils. 254p. T7. $40.00

SENOUR, Caro. *Master St Elmo: Autiobiography of a Celebrated Dog.* 1904. Chicago. Juvenile Book. 1st ed. ils/photos. 153p. scarce. R2. $45.00

SENTER, Ruth. *Startled by Silence: Finding God in Unexpected Places...* 1986. Guideposts. VG/dj. B29. $4.75

SERAFIN, David. *Port of Light.* 1987. London. Gollancz. 1st ed. F/F. S6. $22.50

SEREDY, Kate. *Brand-New Uncle.* 1961. Viking. 1st ed. NF/VG. C8. $35.00

SEREDY, Kate. *Chestry Oak.* 1948. Viking. 1st ed. 236p. VG/dj. M20. $35.00

SEREDY, Kate. *Good Master.* 1935. Viking. 3rd prt. sgn. 210p. VG/dj. M20. $50.00

SEREDY, Kate. *Gypsy.* 1951. Viking. 1st ed. ils. NF/NF. A17. $25.00

SEREDY, Kate. *Open Gate.* 1943. Viking. 1st ed. VG+. C8. $25.00

SEREDY, Kate. *White Stag.* 1937. Viking. 1st ed. 94p. VG/G+. P2. $75.00

SERGEANT, George. *Hist of the First Presbyterian Church of Dallas, TX.* 1943. Dallas. 1st ed. 145p. cloth. NF. M8. $37.50

SERGEANT, Lewis. *New Greece.* ca 1880. Cassell/Peter Galpin. 1st ed. 8vo. 423p. xl. G. W1. $15.00

SERGI, Sergio. *Crania Habessinica Contributo All'Antropologia...* 1912. Rome. Loescher. ils/fld tables. 598p. orig wrp. G7. $125.00

SERLING, Robert. *Air Force One Is Haunted.* 1985. St Martin. VG/VG. P3. $15.00

SERLING, Robert. *From the Captain to the Colonel.* 1980. NY. 1st ed. 535p. VG/dj. B18. $12.50

SERLING, Robert. *Probable Cause.* 1960. NY. 1st ed. VG/G. B5. $27.50

SERLING, Robert. *Something's Alive on the Titanic.* 1990. St Martin. 1st ed. F/F. T2. $20.00

SERLING, Rod. *From the Twilight Zone.* nd. BC. VG/torn. P3. $10.00

SERPEIRI, Paolo. *Morbus Gravis.* 1986. Darguad. 1st ed. pict brd. F. F4. $40.00

SERVAN-SCHREIBER, J.-J. *Lieutenant in Algeria.* 1957. Knopf. 1st Am ed. 235p. G/torn. W1. $10.00

SERVICE, Robert W. *Complete Poetical Works.* (1921). NY. 1st collected ed. F/dj/box. A9. $45.00

SERVICE, Robert W. *Rhymes of a Red Cross Man.* 1916. Barse Hopkins. 1st Am ed. 8vo. 192p. gilt gr cloth. VG. M20. $45.00

SERVICE, Robert W. *Songs of a Sourdough.* 1909. Wm Briggs. leather. G+. P3. $15.00

SERVISS, Garrett P. *Moon Metal.* 1972. Starmont. ne. F/sans. M2. $15.00

SERVISS, Garrett P. *Round the Year With the Stars.* 1910. Harper. 1st prt. 147p. VG. K5. $23.00

SETH, Vikram. *Mappings.* 1980. np. 1st ed. sgn. 1/150. F/stapled wrp. L3. $575.00

SETON, Ernest Thompson. *Bannertail.* 1922. Scribner. 1st ed. ils. 265p. cloth. VG. M20. $60.00

SETON, Ernest Thompson. *Lives of the Hunted.* 1901. Scribner. 1st ed. NF. B2. $85.00

SETON, Ernest Thompson. *Trail of the Sandhill Stag.* 1899. Scribner. 6th prt. 12mo. VG. B17. $12.50

SETON, Ernest Thompson. *Two Little Savages.* 1903. Doubleday Page. 1st ed. ils. gilt gr cloth. VG. M20. $50.00

SETON, Ernest Thompson. *Woodmyth & Fable.* 1905. NY. Century. 1st ed. 8vo. 181p. gilt/gr stp red cloth. H5. $100.00

SETTLE, Mary Lee. *Know Nothing.* 1960. Viking. 1st ed. inscr. NF/NF. L3. $275.00

SETTLE, Mary Lee. *Prisons.* 1973. Putnam. 1st ed. inscr. F/F. L3. $200.00

SEVERIN, Tim. *Jason Voyage: Quest for the Golden Fleece.* ca 1985. NY. Simon Schuster. BC. 8vo. 263p. half cloth. VG. P4. $25.00

SEVERIN, Tim. *Sinbad Voyage.* 1983. NY. Putnam. 1st Am ed. VG/dj. P4. $25.00

SEWARD, C.A. *Metal Pl Lithography.* 1931. NY. 1/3000. full-p pl. 69p. G. A17. $28.00

SEWARD, Desmond. *Henry V: The Scourge of God.* 1988. Viking. 251p. NF/dj. M10. $6.50

SEWARD, F.W. *Reminiscences of a War-Time Statesman & Diplomat.* 1916. 1st ed. ils/index. 489p. O8. $12.50

SEWEL, William. *History of Rise, Increase & Progress of...Quakers.* nd. Friends Bookstore. 2 vol in 1. 8vo. VG. V3. $45.00

SEWEL, William. *History of Rise, Increase & Progress of...Quakers.* 1722. London. Sowle. 1st ed. folio. broken front hinge. H10. $125.00

SEWELL, Anna. *Black Beauty.* 1990. FSG. VG/VG. O3. $18.00

SEWELL, S. *History of Woburn.* 1868. Boston. 1st ed. w/separate index/contents. VG. A9. $75.00

SEXTON, Anne. *Selected Poems of Anne Sexton.* 1988. Houghton Mifflin. 1st ed. F/F. B3. $25.00

SEXTON, S.W. *American Public Buildings of Today.* 1931. NY. 1st ed. VG/VG. B5. $125.00

SEYMOUR, Charles. *Intimate Papers of Colonel House. Vol 3: Into World War...* (1928). Houghton Mifflin. 453p. F/G. H1. $12.00

SEYMOUR, Flora Warren. *Story of the Red Man.* 1929. Longman Gr. 1st ed. sgn. ils. 421p. blk cloth. VG. B11. $40.00

SEYMOUR, Gerald. *Glory Boys.* 1976. Random. 1st ed. VG/VG. P3. $25.00

SEYMOUR, Henry. *Infernal Idol.* 1967. Thriller BC. VG/dj. P3. $10.00

SEYMOUR, Henry. *Intrigue in Tangier.* 1958. Gifford. 1st ed. VG/VG. P3. $18.00

SEYMOUR-SMITH, Martin. *Robert Graves: His Life & Work.* 1932. HRW. 1st ed. notes/biblio/index. 609p. F/F. M7. $25.00

SHAARA, Michael. *Killer Angels.* 1974. McKay. ARC/1st ed. RS. F/NF. B4. $1,000.00

SHACKELFORD, George G. *George Wythe Randolph & the Confederate Elite.* 1988. GA U. index. 235p. dj. O8. $12.50

SHACKELFORD, L.T. *As I See It...Story Drawings of Life in the Army.* 1943. Knopf. 1st ed. oblong 8vo. NF/VG. B4. $85.00

SHACOCHIS, Bob. *Easy in the Islands.* 1985. NY. Crown. 1st ed/author's 1st book. NF/NF. B3. $40.00

SHACOCHIS, Bob. *Easy in the Islands. Stories.* 1985. NY. ARC/1st ed. RS. F/F. A11. $65.00

SHAFEI, A.Z. *Common Endemic Diseases in Egypt.* 1958. Cairo. pres. ils. cloth. VG. G7. $35.00

SHAFER, Y.G. *Cosmic Rays & Problems of Space Physics.* 1967. Jerusalem. Israel Program for Scientific Trans. 8vo. 311p. G/wrp. K5. $20.00

SHAFFER, Hiram. *Treatise on Baptism.* 1851. Cincinnati. 251p. full leather. G. B5. $25.00

SHAH, Idries. *Hundred Tales of Wisdom.* 1978. London. Octagon. hc. 159p. VG/VG. B33. $15.00

SHAHN, Ben. *Haggadah for Passover.* 1966. Paris. Trianon. 1/16 (292 total). w/extra suite pl. F/stiff wrp. B24. $5,000.00

SHAHN, Ben. *November Twenty Six Nineteen Hundred Sixty Three.* 1964. NY. Braziller. ltd ed on Fabriano. sgns. linen brd. F/case. B24. $225.00

SHAKESPEARE, William. *Antony & Cleopatra.* 1979. Guilford, Eng. 1/355. ils/sgn Ronald King. unbound. chemise. H4. $1,200.00

SHAKESPEARE, William. *Plays of Shakespeare in Nine Volumes.* 1825. London. Pickering. 9 vol. Diamond Classics. 87x53mm. 37 pl/tissue guards. F. B24. $1,500.00

SHAKESPEARE, William. *Shall I Die? Shall I Fly?* 1986. Boston. 62x40mm. 1/35 (total of 160). ils Suzanne Moore. F/red case. B24. $325.00

SHAKESPEARE, William. *Tragedy of Hamlet, Prince of Denmark.* 1933. LEC. 1/1500. ils/sgn Eric Gill. full pigskin. F/case. F1. $375.00

SHAKESPEARE, William. *Twelfth Night.* nd. London. Hodder Stoughton. 40 mtd pl. gilt gr cloth. F/dj. F1. $450.00

SHAKESPEARE, William. *Works of...* 1868. NY. Women's Edition. edit Mary Cowden Clarke. ils. aeg. full leather. VG. H3. $100.00

SHAMES, Deborah. *Freedom With Reservation: Menominee Struggle...* 1972. Madison. Nat Comm To Save Menominee. NF/wrp. B2. $30.00

SHAMES, Laurence. *Florida Straits.* 1992. Simon Schuster. 1st ed. F/F. B3. $45.00

SHANE & SHANE. *New Baby.* 1948. Simon Schuster. Golden. 1st ed thus. ils Eloise Wilkin. cloth. F. M5. $60.00

SHANGE, Ntozake. *Betsey Brown.* 1985. St Martin. 1st ed. NF/NF. S9. $35.00

SHANK, Robert. *Life in the Son.* 1979. Wescott. 380p. VG. B29. $6.50

SHANKS, William F. *Personal Recollections of Distinguished Generals.* 1866. NY. 1st ed. H4. $40.00

SHANNAHAN, J.H.K. *Tales of Old Maryland.* 1907. Baltimore. VG. A1. $25.00

SHANNON, Dell. *Chance To Kill.* 1967. Morrow. 1st ed. VG/VG. P3. $16.00

SHANNON, Dell. *Chaos of Crime.* 1985. NY. Morrow. 1st ed. F/F. S6. $20.00

SHANNON, Dell. *Streets of Death.* nd. BC. VG/VG. P3. $8.00

SHAPIRO, Karl. *Auden (1907-1973): A Poem.* 1974. Davis Putah Creek Pr. 1st ed. 1/175. sgns. F/tan wrp. B24. $150.00

SHAPIRO, Robert. *Human Blueprint: Race to Unlock the Secrets...* 1991. NY. 1st ed. 412p. dj. A13. $25.00

SHARKEY, Jack. *Death for Auld Lang Syne.* 1962. Holt. 1st ed. VG/dj. M2. $22.00

SHARKEY, Jack. *Murder, Maestro Please.* 1960. Abelard-Schuman. 1st ed. F. A17. $10.00

SHARP, Andrew. *Ancient Voyages in Polynesia.* 1964. Berkeley, CA. VG/dj. N2. $15.00

SHARP, Ann Pearsall. *Little Garden People & What They Do.* 1938. Saalfield. ils Marion Bryson. pict brd. VG. M5. $30.00

SHARP, Cecil J. *Nursery Songs From the Appalachian Mountains.* nd. London. Novello. ils MacKinnon. VG+. C8. $75.00

SHARP, John K. *Our Preaching: Characteristics of Sermon Types...* 1936. Phil. Dolphin. 279p. xl. H10. $12.00

SHARP, Margery. *Britannia Mews.* 1946. Little Brn. 1st ed. VG/VG. P3. $30.00

SHARP, Margery. *Miss Bianca in the Salt Mines.* 1966. Little Brn. 1st ed. ils Garth Williams. 148p. VG/dj. M20. $45.00

SHARP, Margery. *Stone of Chastity.* 1945. Tower. 2nd ed. VG. P3. $10.00

SHARP, Margery. *Turret.* 1963. Little Brn. 1st ed. 138p. VG/clip. M20. $75.00

SHARP, Marilyn. *Sunflower.* 1979. Marek. 1st ed. F/F. P3. $15.00

SHARP, William. *Dante Gabriel Rossetti: A Record & Study.* 1882. London. Macmillan. 8vo. 432p. gilt gr cloth/recased. scarce. F1. $85.00

SHARPE, R.B. *Analytical Index to Works of Late John Gould.* 1994. Mansfield, CT. Martino. ltd ed. 1/125. 375p. gilt gr cloth. F. F1. $90.00

SHARPE, Tom. *Great Pursuit.* 1978. Harper. 1st ed. F/F. P3. $20.00

SHARPLESS, Isaac. *Quaker Experiment in Government.* 1898. Phil. Ferris. 1st ed. 12mo. 280p. G. V3. $14.00

SHARTLE, Carroll L. *Occupational Information.* 1946. Prentice Hall. 321p. G. K4. $10.00

SHATNER, William. *Tek/Lords.* 1991. Ace/Putnam. 1st ed. F/F. T2. $15.00

SHATNER, William. *Tek/War.* 1989. Ace/Putnam. 1st ed. F/F. T2. $20.00

SHATNER, William. *Tek/War.* 1989. Phantasia. ltd ed. sgn. 1/475. F/dj. M2. $100.00

SHATRAW, Milton. *Thrashin' Time: Memories of a MT Boyhood.* 1970. Am W Pub. M/VG. B34. $50.00

SHATTUCK, George Burbank. *Bahama Islands.* 1905. Macmillan. 93 pl/maps/diagrams. VG. T7. $135.00

SHAW, Andrew; see Block, Lawrence.

SHAW, Bernard. *Intelligent Woman's Guide to Socialism & Capitalism.* 1928. Brentano. 1st ed. G. V4. $12.50

SHAW, Bob. *Cosmic Kaleidoscope.* 1976. Gollancz. 1st ed. F/F. P3. $35.00

SHAW, Bob. *Dark Night in Toyland.* 1989. Gollancz. 1st ed. F/F. P3. $25.00

SHAW, Bob. *Medusa's Children.* nd. BC. VG/VG. P3. $8.00

SHAW, Bob. *Wooden Spaceships.* 1988. Gollancz. 1st ed. F/F. P3. $25.00

SHAW, Clifford R. *Brothers in Crime.* 1938. Chicago. worn. M11. $50.00

SHAW, George Bernard. *Apple Cart.* 1930. London. Constable. 69th thousand. 80p. gilt apple gr cloth. NF. M7. $35.00

SHAW, George Bernard. *Everybody's Political What's What?* 1944. London. Constable. 1st ed. gilt coral linen. VG. M7. $25.00

SHAW, George Bernard. *Prefaces by...* 1934. London. 1st ed. sm 4to. 802p. VG. D3. $75.00

SHAW, George Bernard. *Prefaces by...* 1934. London. 1st ed. 4to. VG+/G. F1. $85.00

SHAW, George. *Naturalist's Miscellany.* 1789-1813. London. 18 vol in 9. 1st ed. 773 mc pl. full morocco. VG+. C6. $3,000.00

SHAW, Irwin. *In the Company of Dolphins.* 1964. NY. 1st ed. 8vo. 154p. cloth. O2. $10.00

SHAW, Mary L. *Ottoman Empire From 1720 to 1734.* 1944. Urbana. tall 8vo. 165p. prt wrp. O2. $20.00

SHAW, Thomas. *Travels; or, Observations Relating to Several Parts Barbary.* 1738. Oxford. folio. ils/maps. paneled calf/rebacked. O2. $700.00

SHAW, Verno. *Dogs for Hot Climates.* 1895. London. Thacker. 1st ed. 172p. cloth. scarce. R2. $125.00

SHAW, W.B. Kennedy. *Long Range Desert Group.* 1945. London. Collins. 1st ed. ils/maps/appendices/index. 256p. gilt bl linen. VG/G. M7. $45.00

SHAWN, Frank S.; see Goulart, Ron.

SHAY, Felix. *Elbert Hubbard of East Aurora.* 1926. Wm Wise. ils. 553p. VG. A4. $45.00

SHAYNE, Mike; see Halliday, Brett.

SHCHAPOV, Yaroslav N. *State & Church in Early Russia.* 1993. New Rochelle. 8vo. 252p. cloth. O2. $50.00

SHEA, John Gilmary. *Hist of the Catholic Church in the US...1808...1843. Vol 3.* 1890. Shea. ils. 734p. xl. H10. $35.00

SHEA, Michael. *I, Said the Fly.* 1993. Seattle. Silver Salamander. 1st ed. sgn Shea/Tritten. 1/300. F/F. T2. $40.00

SHEA, Michael. *Polyphemus.* 1987. Arkham. 1st ed. F/F. T2. $55.00

SHEA, Michael. *Tomorrow's Men.* 1982. Weidenfeld Nicolson. 1st ed. F/F. P3. $20.00

SHEA & TROYER. *Oriental Literature; or, The Dabistan.* 1937. Tudor. 1st ed. 411p. cloth. G. W1. $9.00

SHEA. *Perils of the Ocean & Wilderness.* 1856. Brn. later prt. 200p. VG. E5. $27.00

SHEAR, Jack. *Four Marines & Other Portraits.* 1985. Pasadena. Twelvetrees. 1/2000. NF/dj. S9. $125.00

SHEARDOWN, Frank. *Working Longdog.* 1989. Great Britain. Dickson Price. 1st ed. ils. 153p. M/dj. R2. $35.00

SHECKLEY, Robert. *Alchemical Marriage of Alistair Crompton.* 1978. London. Michael Joseph. 1st ed. F/F. N3. $40.00

SHECKLEY, Robert. *Crompton Divided.* 1978. HRW. 1st ed. xl. dj. P3. $8.00

SHECKLEY, Robert. *Victim Prime.* 1987. Methuen. 1st ed. F/F. P3. $20.00

SHEED, Frank. *Church & I.* 1974. Doubleday. 383p. H10. $10.50

SHEED, Wilfrid. *Muhammad Ali.* 1975. Crowell. VG/VG. P3. $15.00

SHEEHAN, Neil. *Bright Shining Lie.* 1988. Random. AP. VG/prt wrp. S9. $65.00

SHEEHAN, Perley Poore. *Abyss of Wonders.* 1953. Polaris. ltd 1st deluxe ed. F/box. P3. $65.00

SHEFFIELD, Charles. *Divergence.* 1991. Del Rey. 1st ed. F/F. P3. $17.00

SHEFFIELD, Charles. *Summertide.* 1990. Del Rey. F/F. P3. $17.00

SHEFFIELD, J. *Duke of Buckingham, Works of...* 1729. London. 2 vol. 2nd ed. VG+. A15. $150.00

SHEFFIELD, Robyn. *Killing Term.* 1993. London. Harper Collins. 1st ed. F/F. S6. $22.50

SHEFNER, Vadim. *Unman/Kovrigin's Chronicles.* 1980. Macmillan. 1st ed. VG/VG. P3. $15.00

SHEHADEH, Raja. *Third Way: Journal of Life in W Bank.* 1982. Quartet. 1st ed. 8vo. 143p. NF/dj. W1. $12.00

SHEK, Madame Chaing Kai. *Selected Speeches 1958-1959.* 1959. Taipei. sgn. VG+/VG. A1. $100.00

SHELDON, Alice Bradley. *Brighness Falls From the Air.* 1985. Tor. 1st ed. F/F. P3. $20.00

SHELDON, Alice Bradley. *Brightness Falls From the Air.* 1985. Tor. 1st ed. NF/dj. F4. $14.00

SHELDON, Alice Bradley. *Byte Beautiful.* 1985. Doubleday. 1st ed. F/NF. N3. $15.00

SHELDON, Alice Bradley. *Her Smoke Rose Up Forever: Great Years of James Tiptree Jr.* 1990. Arkham. 1st ed. ils Andrew Smith. F/F. T2. $26.00

SHELDON, Alice Bradley. *Tales of the Quintana Roo.* 1986. Arkham. 1st ed. as issued. M2/T2. $12.00

SHELDON, Alice Bradley. *Up the Walls of the World.* nd. BC. VG/VG. P3. $8.00

SHELDON, Charles M. *In His Steps.* 1982. Putnam. 242p. M/M. B29. $4.75

SHELDON, Frederick. *Minstrels of the English Border.* 1st ed. London. Longman Br. 1st ed. 432p. teg. NF. B2. $125.00

SHELDON, Lee. *Doomed Planet.* 1967. Avalon. 1st ed. xl. dj. P3. $6.00

SHELDON, Lord; see Block, Lawrence.

SHELDON, Margaret. *Clipping Your Poodle.* 1962 (1960). London. Foyle. 96p. brd. M. R2. $5.00

SHELDON, Roy. *House of Entrophy.* 1953. Hamilton Panther. G+/G+. P3. $35.00

SHELDON, Sidney. *Rage of Angels.* 1980. Morrow. 1st ed. VG/G+. P3. $20.00

SHELDON, W.H. *Varieties of Human Physique.* 1940. Harper. 299p. G. K4. $25.00

SHELLEY, Bruce. *Call to Christian Character.* 1970. Zondervan. F/F. B29. $6.00

SHELLEY, Frederick. *Aaron Dodd Crane, an American Original.* 1987. Colum, PA. NAWCC Pub. 1st ed. 4to. sc. VG. A8. $5.00

SHELLEY, Mary W. *Frankenstein; or, The Modern Prometheus.* ca 1930. Grosset Dunlap. 1st photoplay ed. 8vo. 240p. aeg. Sutcliffe bdg. F. H5. $950.00

SHELLEY, Percy Bysshe. *Complete Works of...* 1927. Scribner. 10 vol. edit Ingpen/Peck. teg. vellum/cloth. M/case. H4. $275.00

SHELLEY, Percy Bysshe. *To a Skylark.* 1953. Chicago. Petit Oiseau. 1/100. 22p. bl/wht pattered brd. NF. B24. $185.00

SHELLEY, Percy Bysshe. *Zastrozzi: A Romance.* 1955. London. Golden Cockerel. 1/200 total (this 1/60). w/special suite pl. F/case. K1. $350.00

SHELTON, Frederick W. *Trollopiad; or, Travelling Gentlemen in America.* 1837. Providence. Shepard Tingley. 1st ed. 12mo. 151p. cloth. M1. $225.00

SHEPARD, Birsa. *Cat Next Door.* 1943. Oxford. 1st ed. ils pelagie Doane. VG/G. P2. $18.00

SHEPARD, J.W. *Christ of the Gospels.* 1954. Eerdmans. 650p. G. B29. $10.00

SHEPARD, Lucius. *Ends of the Earth.* 1991. Arkham. 1st ed. sgn. F/F. T2. $45.00

SHEPARD, Lucius. *Golden.* 1993. Shingletown. Ziesing. 1st ed. sgn. F/F. T2. $55.00

SHEPARD, Lucius. *Jaguar Hunter.* 1987. Arkham. 1st ed. F/F. T2. $75.00

SHEPARD, Lucius. *Jaguar Hunter.* 1988. Kerosina. 1st ed. F/F. P3. $30.00

SHEPARD, Lucius. *Kalimantan.* 1990. Legend. ltd ed. sgn. 1/300. aeg. deluxe bdg. F/case. F4. $75.00

SHEPARD, Lucius. *Kalimantan.* 1990. Legend. 1st ed. F/F. P3. $27.00

SHEPARD, Lucius. *Life During Wartime.* 1988. London. Grafton. 1st hc ed. F/F. T2. $30.00

SHEPARD, Odell. *Lore of the Unicorn.* nd. Avenel. 5th ed. VG/VG. P3. $13.00

SHEPARD, Sam. *Operation Sidewinder.* 1970. Bobbs Merrill. 1st ed. 8vo. 126p. metallic gr stp gray cloth. F/dj. H5. $100.00

SHEPHARD, Kevin. *Sufi Matriarch: Hazrat Babajan.* 1986. London. Anthropographia. 1st ed. 78p. VG/VG. B33. $25.00

SHEPHERD, Michael; see Ludlum, Robert.

SHEPHERD, Shep; see Whittington, Harry.

SHEPPARD, Tad. *Pack & Paddock.* 1938. Derrydale. ltd ed. 1/950. VG/case. O3. $125.00

SHEPPARD, William. *Touch-Stone of Common Assurances...The Fifth Edition.* 1784. London. Strahan Woodfall. modern quarter leather. G. M11. $350.00

SHERER, Lorraine M. *Clan System of the Fort Mojave Indians.* 1965. Hist Soc S CA. ils/notes. F. B19. $20.00

SHERIDAN, P.H. *Personal Memoirs of PH Sheridan.* 1888. Webster. 2 vol. 1st ed. gilt gr cloth. G. H1. $18.00

SHERIDAN, Richard Brinsley. *School for Scandal.* nd. Hodder Stoughton. ils Hugh Thomson. 196p. VG. P2. $85.00

SHERIDAN, Richard. *Plays & Poems of Richard Brimsley Sheridan.* 1933. Oxford. 3 vol. 1st ed. F/VG. C2. $150.00

SHERIDAN, Thomas E. *Los Tucsonenses: Mexican Community in Tucson 1854-1941.* 1986. AZ U. 1st ed. ils/notes/index. 327p. F/F. B19. $40.00

SHERLOCK, Christopher. *Night of the Predator.* 1991. London. Heinemann. 1st ed/author's 2nd book. F/F. S6. $22.50

SHERMAN, Dan. *Dynasty of Spies.* 1980. Arbor. 1st ed. VG/VG. P3. $20.00

SHERMAN, Harold M. *Batter Up!* 1930. Grosset Dunlap. Home Run Series. 304p. VG/dj. M20. $20.00

SHERMAN, Harold M. *Down the Ice.* 1932. Goldsmith. 1st ed. F/dj. M2. $20.00

SHERMAN, Harold M. *Flashing Steel.* 1929. Grosset Dunlap. VG/fair. P8. $15.00

SHERMAN, Harold M. *Holt That Line!* 1930. Grosset Dunlap. 253p. G+/dj. M20. $20.00

SHERMAN, Harold M. *Strike Him Out.* 1931. Goldsmith. later prt. VG/VG. P8. $15.00

SHERMAN, James. *Memoir of William Allen, FRS.* ca 1851. Phil. Henry Longstreth. 8vo. 530p. VG. V3. $26.00

SHERMAN, John H. *Sherman Directory, Alphabetical Listing...* 1991. np. 4 vol. 59p genealogy listing. 2874p. F. A4. $250.00

SHERMAN, William Tecumseh. *Memoirs..., Written by Himself, With an Appendix...* 1891. NY. Webster. 2 vol. 4th ed. gr cloth/shoulder strap insignia spine. M8. $150.00

SHERRINGTON, Charles. *Integrative Action of the Nervous System.* 1911. London. Constable. 1st ed/2nd issue. later cloth. G7. $395.00

SHERROD, Robert. *History of the Marine Corps Aviation in WWII.* 1952. WA. Combat Forces Pr. 1st ed. ils. 496p. T7. $45.00

SHERRY, Edna. *Survial of the Fittest.* 1960. Dodd Mead. 1st ed. VG/G+. P3. $13.00

SHERSTON, George. *Shersto's Progress.* 1974. Folio Soc. 1st imp. 171p. tan cloth. F/cardboard case. M7. $35.00

SHERWOOD, Jane. *Post-Mortem Journal. Communications of TE Lawrence.* 1964. London. Neville Spearman. 1st ed. blk stp yel cloth. VG/VG clip. M7. $75.00

SHERWOOD, John. *Flowers of Evil.* nd. BC. VG/VG. P3. $8.00

SHERWOOD, John. *Sunflower Plot.* 1990. London. Macmillan. 1st ed. F/F. S6. $22.50

SHERWOOD, Martin. *Maxwell's Demon.* 1976. NEL. 1st ed. F/F. P3. $15.00

SHERWOOD, Mary Martha. *Fairchild Family.* 1902. NY. Stokes. 8vo. ils Florence M Rudland. 470p. G+. D6. $45.00

SHERWOOD, Robert E. *There Shall Be No Night.* 1941. NY. 1st ed. F/F. A17. $20.00

SHEW, Spencer. *Second Companion to Murder.* 1961. Knopf. 1st ed. VG. P3. $25.00

SHIEL, M.P. *Prince Zaleski & Cummings King Monk.* 1977. Mycroft Moran. 1st ed. F/F. P3. $20.00

SHIEL, M.P. *Purple Cloud.* 1946. World. NF/NF. P3. $30.00

SHIELDS, Carol. *Happenstance.* 1991. London. 4th Estate. 1st ed. sgn. F/F. B3. $75.00

SHIELDS, Carol. *Mary Swann.* 1990. London. 4th Estate. 1st ed. sgn. F/F. B3. $85.00

SHIELDS, Carol. *Small Ceremonies.* 1976. McGraw Hill Ryerson. 1st ed/author's 1st book. F/NF. B4. $350.00

SHIELDS, Carol. *Swan: A Mystery.* 1987. Toronto. Stoddart. true 1st ed/author's 5th book. F/F. B4. $125.00

SHIELDS, G.O. *Hunting in the Great West.* 1885. Caxton. ils. 306p. VG. rare. B34. $80.00

SHINE, Deborah. *Ghost Stories.* 1980. Octopus. brd. VG. P3. $15.00

SHINER, Lewis. *Deserted Cities of the Heart.* 1988. Doubleday. 1st ed. F/F. P3. $18.00

SHINGLETON, R.G. *Sea Ghost of the Confederacy.* 1979. np. index. 242p. O8. $12.50

SHIPHERD, Jacob R. *Hist of the Oberlin-Wellington Rescue.* 1859. Boston. 1st ed. 433p. VG/dj. B18. $50.00

SHIPTON, Eric. *Mt Everest Reconnaissance Expedition.* 1953. Dutton. 2nd prt. 128p. VG/dj. N2. $25.00

SHIPWAY, Verna Cook. *Decorative Design in Mexican Homes.* 1966. Architectural Book Pub. 1st ed? 249p. NF/NF. B19. $30.00

SHIRAS, Wilmar H. *Children of the Atom.* 1953. Gnome. 1st ed. VG/VG. P3. $65.00

SHIRER, William L. *Collapse of the 3rd Republic.* 1969. Simon Schuster. 1st prt. 1082p. F/F. A17. $18.00

SHIRLEY, John. *Heatseeker.* 1989. Scream. 1st ed. F/F. T2. $35.00

SHIRLEY, John. *Wetbones.* 1991. Ziesing. 1st trade ed. F/F. T2. $25.00

SHIROKOGOROFF, S.M. *Psychomental Complex of the Tungus.* 1935. London. Kegan Paul. folio. 470p. tan cloth. xl. K1. $150.00

SHIVKUMAR, K. *King's Choice: A Folktale From India.* 1961. Parents Magazine Pr. sm 4to. ils Yoko Mitsuhashi. 37p. cloth. VG. A3. $7.50

SHOBERL, Frederick. *Persia: Containing Description of a Country...* 1845. Phil. Grigg Elliot. 1st ed. 12mo. 12 pl. 181p. new cloth. VG. D3. $150.00

SHOBIN, David. *Seeding.* 1982. Linden. 1st ed. F/F. P3. $18.00

SHOHAM, Giora S. *Sex As Bait: Eve, Casanova & Don Juan.* 1983. NY. Queensland. 226p. blk cloth. VG/dj. G1. $25.00

SHORE, Henry N. *Smuggling Days & Smuggling Ways. Story of a Lost Art.* 1892. London. Cassell. 2nd ed. ils/plans. 286p. VG. T7. $95.00

SHORT, Christopher. *Blue-Eyed Boy.* 1966. Dodd Mead. 1st ed. VG/VG. P3. $20.00

SHORT, Luke. *Saddle by Starlight.* 1952. Houghton Mifflin. 1st ed. NF/NF. P3. $35.00

SHORTALL, Leonard. *Peter in Grand Central Station.* 1969. Morrow. 1st ed. VG+/VG. C8. $25.00

SHOUMATOFF, Alex. *In Southern Light.* 1986. Simon Schuster. 1st ed. 239p. VG/dj. F3. $15.00

SHREVE, Susan Richards. *Country of Strangers.* 1989. Morrow. 1st ed. F/VG. B3. $20.00

SHRIBER, Ione Sandberg. *Never Say Die.* 1950. Rinehart. 1st ed. VG/VG. P3. $25.00

SHRINER, Charles A. *Wit, Wisdom & Foibles of the Great.* 1918. Funk Wagnalls. 1st ed. sm 4to. 698p. VG. H1. $12.00

SHTEMENKO, S.M. *Last Six Months.* 1977. NY. 1st ed. 436p. VG. B18. $17.50

SHUB, Elizabeth. *Seeing Is Believing.* 1979. Greenwillow. 1st ed. inscr. ils/inscr. glazed brd. F. C8. $60.00

SHUGART, Cooksey. *Complete Guide to American Pocket Watches.* 1981. Overstreet. 1st ed. sc. 253p. VG. A8. $10.00

SHULMAN, H.M. *Slums of New York.* 1938. NY. 1st ed. 394p. VG/rpr. D3. $25.00

SHULMAN, Irving. *Children of the Dark.* 1956. Holt. 1st ed. F/NF. F4. $50.00

SHUMWAY, Nehemiah. *American Harmony: Containing...Rules of Singing...* 1793. Phil. John M'Culloch. 1st ed. obl 8vo. 212p. M1. $375.00

SHUMWAY, Nina Paul. *Your Desert & Mine.* 1979. ETC Pub. 1st ed. sgn. ils. 337p. F/G. A8. $40.00

SHURCLIFF, S. *Jungle Islands.* 1930. NY. 1st ed. VG/G. B5. $85.00

SHURCLIFF, W.A. *Bombs at Bikini: Official Report of Operation Crossroads.* 1947. NY. Wise. 1st ed. 32 pl. 212p. cloth. G. A17. $25.00

SHURKIN, Joel N. *Jupiter: The Star That Failed.* 1979. Phil. Westminster. 8vo. 110p. pict cloth. VG. K5. $8.00

SHUSTER, W. Morgan. *Strangling of Persia.* 1912. NY. 1st ed. 8vo. 423p. gilt cloth. O2. $30.00

SHUTE, Clarence. *Psychology of Aristotle: Analysis of the Living Being.* 1941. Columbia. 148p. ochre cloth. G1. $27.50

SHUTE, Nevil. *Beyond Black Stump.* 1956. NY. ARC/1st ed. VG/VG. B5. $35.00

SHUTE, Nevil. *Chequer Board.* 1947. McClelland Stewart. 1st ed. VG/G+. P3. $25.00

SHUTE, Nevil. *Kindling.* 1938. NY. 1st ed. sgn. VG/G. B5. $85.00

SHUTE, Nevil. *No Highway.* 1951. Heinemann. 7th ed. VG. P3. $15.00

SHUTE, Nevil. *On the Beach.* 1957. Morrow. 4th ed. VG/VG. P3. $20.00

SHUTE, Nevil. *Pastoral.* 1944. Morrow. 1st ed. F/F. S9. $50.00

SHYROCK, Patricia Roberts. *All About Collies.* 1961. Orange Judd. 1st ed. sgn. 152p. F/F. R2. $45.00

SHYROCK, Richard. *Medicine & Society in America, 1660-1860.* 1960. NY. 1st ed. 182p. dj. A13. $40.00

SIBLEY, Celestine. *Malignant Heart.* 1958. Crime Club. 1st ed. VG/VG. P3. $17.00

SIBLEY, Celestine. *Small Blessings.* 1977. Doubleday. 184p. F/F. B29. $3.00

SICK, Gary. *All Fall Down.* 1985. Random. 1st ed. 366p. NF/dj. W1. $18.00

SIDDIQUI, Kalim. *Issues in the Islamic Movement.* 1984. Open Pr. 1st prt. 8vo. VG/stiff wrp. W1. $8.00

SIDGWICK, Alfred. *Use of Words in Reasoning.* 1901. London. Blk. 370p. paneled crimson cloth. VG. G1. $125.00

SIDGWICK, J.B. *Amateur Astronomer's Handbook.* 1961 (1955). London. Faber. 2nd ed. 8vo. 580p. VG. K5. $20.00

SIDNEY, Margaret. *Five Little Peppers & How They Grew.* 1909. Lee Shepard. 16mo. VG/VG. B17. $10.00

SIDNEY, Sylvia. *Sylvia Sidney Needlepoint Book.* 1968. np. cloth. VG. G2. $12.95

SIEBENHELLER, Norma. *PD James.* 1981. NY. Unger. 1st ed. F/NF. S6. $27.50

SIEBER, Roy. *African Textiles & Decorative Arts.* 1974. MOMA. ils. 4to. VG/wrp. F1. $20.00

SIEDEL, Frank. *OH Story.* 1950. World. 4th prt. sgn. VG/dj. M20. $15.00

SIEGAL, Aranka. *Upon the Head of the Goat: Childhood in Hugary 1939-1944.* 1981. FSG. 1st prt. inscr. M/M. C8. $75.00

SIEGEL, Jack. *Squeegee.* 1965. Horizon. 1st ed/author's 1st book. NF/dj. F4. $28.00

SIEGEL, Mark. *World According to Evan Mecham.* 1987. Blue Sky. 1st ed. ils. 95p. NF/wrp. B19. $10.00

SIEGEL, R.E. *Galen on Sense Perception: His Doctrines, Observations...* 1970. Basel. Karger. 216p. NF/dj. G7. $75.00

SIGERIST, Henry. *Amerika und die Medizin.* 1933. Leipzig. 1st ed. sgn. 352p. A13. $150.00

SIGERIST, Henry. *University at the Crossroads.* 1946. NY. 1st ed. 162p. A13. $40.00

SIGOURNEY, Mrs. L.H. *Select Poems.* 1848. Phil. 6th ed. 8vo. 338p. aeg. cloth. O2. $30.00

SIH, Paul K.T. *Decision for China: Communism or Christianity.* 1959. Chicago. Regnery. 262p. xl. H10. $10.00

SILBERER, Herbert. *Problems of Mysticism & Its Symbolism.* 1917. Moffat Yard. 1st English-language ed. 452p. red cloth. G1. $125.00

SILITCH, Clarissa M. *Mad & Magnificent Yankees.* 1973. Dublin, NH. Yankee Magazine. 1st ed. 8vo. F/G. B11. $15.00

SILKO, Leslie Marmon. *Almanac of the Dead.* 1991. Simon Schuster. 1st ed. F/dj. A18. $25.00

SILKO, Leslie Marmon. *Almanac of the Dead.* 1991. Simon Schuster. 1st ed/author's 2nd novel. sgn. F/F. L3. $45.00

SILKO, Leslie Marmon. *Ceremony.* 1977. NY. 1sd ed. F/VG. C2. $150.00

SILKO, Leslie Marmon. *Storyteller.* 1981. Grove. 1st ed. NF/VG. B3. $75.00

SILKO, Leslie Marmon. *Storyteller.* 1981. Grove. 1st ed. obl 8vo. F/F. C2. $100.00

SILLER, Van. *Lonely Breeze.* 1965. Crime Club. 1st ed. VG/VG. P3. $20.00

SILLER, Van. *Somber Memory.* 1945. Doubleday. 1st ed. VG/dj. rare. B34. $25.00

SILONE, Ignazio. *Bread & Wine.* 1937. Harper. 1st ed. F/VG. A17. $10.00

SILVA, Joseph; see Goulart, Ron.

SILVERBERG, Robert. *Androids Are Coming.* 1979. Elsevier/Nelson. 1st ed. sgn. sgn/contributor Simak. F/dj. F4. $50.00

SILVERBERG, Robert. *Beyond Control.* 1972. Thomas Nelson. 1st ed. xl. dj. P3. $5.00

SILVERBERG, Robert. *Beyond the Safe Zone.* 1986. Donald Fine. 1st ed. F/F. P3. $20.00

SILVERBERG, Robert. *Calibrated Alligator.* 1969. HRW. 1st ed. NF/NF. P3. $25.00

SILVERBERG, Robert. *Conglomeroid Cocktail Party.* 1984. Arbor. 1st ed. F/F. P3. $15.00

SILVERBERG, Robert. *Desert of Stolen Dreams.* 1981. Underwood Miller. 1st ed. xl. dj. P3. $8.00

SILVERBERG, Robert. *Explorers of Space.* 1975. Thomas Nelson. ARC. unbdg signatures. F/F. N3. $20.00

SILVERBERG, Robert. *Gate of Worlds.* 1978. Gollancz. 1st ed. F/F. P3. $17.00

SILVERBERG, Robert. *Infinite Jests.* 1974. Chilton. 1st ed. F/F. P3. $18.00

SILVERBERG, Robert. *Invaders From Space...* 1972. Hawthorn. 1st ed. F/NF. N3. $10.00

SILVERBERG, Robert. *Letters From Atlantis.* 1990. Atheneum. 1st ed. F/F. P3. $15.00

SILVERBERG, Robert. *Morning of Mankind.* 1967. NY Graphic Soc. 1st ed. 233p. VG/dj. M20. $25.00

SILVERBERG, Robert. *New Dimensions 10.* 1980. Harper Row. 1st ed. F/F. P3. $20.00

SILVERBERG, Robert. *New Springtime.* 1990. Warner. 1st Am ed. M/M. M21. $15.00

SILVERBERG, Robert. *No Mind of Man.* 1973. Hawthorn. 1st ed. F/VG+. N3. $10.00

SILVERBERG, Robert. *Other Dimensions.* 1973. Hawthorne. 1st ed. F/VG+. N3. $5.00

SILVERBERG, Robert. *Project Pendulum.* 1987. Walker. 1st ed. sgn. F/F. P3. $25.00

SILVERBERG, Robert. *Queen of Springtime.* 1989. Gollancz. 1st ed. F/F. P3. $27.00

SILVERBERG, Robert. *Sarnia.* 1974. Hamish Hamilton. 1st ed. NF/NF. P3. $20.00

SILVERBERG, Robert. *Shores of Tomorrow.* 1976. Nelson. 1st ed. F/F. P3. $20.00

SILVERBERG, Robert. *Star of Gypsies.* 1986. Donald Fine. 1st ed. F/F. P3. $20.00

SILVERBERG, Robert. *Starman's Quest.* 1958. Gnome. 1st ed. VG/VG. M17. $45.00

SILVERBERG, Robert. *Stochastic Man.* 1975. Harper. 1st ed. sgn. F/dj. F4. $25.00

SILVERBERG, Robert. *Thebes of the Hundred Gates.* 1991. Axolotl. Deluxe Leather ed. 1/75. sgn. M/sans. M21. $45.00

SILVERBERG, Robert. *To the Stars...* 1971. NY. Hawthorn. 1st ed. F/NF. N3. $10.00

SILVERBERG, Robert. *Tom O'Bedlam.* 1985. Donald Fine. 1st ed. F/F. P3. $17.00

SILVERBERG, Robert. *Treasures Beneath the Sea.* 1960. Whitman. 1st ed. brd. F. P3. $30.00

SILVERBERG, Robert. *Winter's End.* 1988. Warner. 1st ed. F/dj. M2. $18.00

SILVERBERG, Robert. *Wonders of Ancient Chinese Science.* 1969. Hawthorn. 1st ed. ils. 126p. F/dj. M10. $7.50

SILVERBERG, Robert. *World Inside.* 1976. Millington. F/F. P3. $23.00

SILVERMAN, Jerry. *Folk Blues.* 1958. Macmillan. 1st ed. photos Julius Lester. F/F. B2. $100.00

SILVERMAN, Jonathan. *For the World To See: Life of Margaret Bourke-White.* 1983. Viking. 1st ed. 4to. F/VG+. S9. $35.00

SILVERMAN, Kenneth. *Edgar A Poe: Mournful & Never-Ending Romance.* 1991. Harper Collins. 1st ed. NF/NF. P3. $28.00

SILVERMAN, Kenneth. *Edgar A Poe: Mournful & Never-Ending Romance.* 1991. NY. Harper Collins. 1st ed. 564p. VG/VG. A17. $15.00

SILVERS, Phil. *This Laugh Is on Me.* 1972. Prentice Hall. 1st ed. VG/torn. P3. $15.00

SILVERSTEIN, Mira. *Bargello Pluss.* 1973. np. cloth. VG. G2. $12.95

SILVERSTEIN, Shel. *Missing Piece.* 1976. Harper Row. 1st ed. 8vo. VG/VG. B17. $12.50

SILVESTER, Hans. *Tsiganes et Gitans.* 1974. Paris. Chene. 1st ed. 4to. w/1974 catalog from Toulouse exhibition. F/wrp. S9. $125.00

SILVESTRINI, Guisseppe. *Contribuzione Allo Studio Della Pathologia Cerebrale.* 1881. Nell Emilia. 4 pl. 100p. new brd. G7. $125.00

SIMAK, Clifford D. *Brother & Other Stories.* 1986. Severn House. 1st ed. F/F. P3. $25.00

SIMAK, Clifford D. *City.* 1952. Gnome. 1st ed. F/dj. M2. $450.00

SIMAK, Clifford D. *Cosmic Engineers.* 1950. Gnome. 1st ed. VG/VG. P3. $125.00

SIMAK, Clifford D. *Fellowship of the Talisman.* 1978. Del Rey. 1st ed. F/F. P3. $20.00

SIMAK, Clifford D. *Heritage of Stars.* 1977. Berkley Putnam. 1st ed. F/clip. F4. $25.00

SIMAK, Clifford D. *Heritage of Stars.* 1978. British SF BC. VG/VG. P3. $10.00

SIMAK, Clifford D. *Highway of Eternity.* 1986. Del Rey. 1st ed. sgn author file copy. F/dj. F4. $40.00

SIMAK, Clifford D. *Our Children's Children.* 1974. Putnam. 1st ed. sgn. F/clip. F4. $35.00

SIMAK, Clifford D. *Out of Their Minds.* 1970. Putnam. 1st ed. NF/NF. P3. $50.00

SIMAK, Clifford D. *Project Pope.* 1981. Del Rey. 1st ed. F/F. P3. $20.00

SIMAK, Clifford D. *Special Deliverance.* 1982. Del Rey. 1st ed. VG/VG. P3. $20.00

SIMAK, Clifford D. *Time & Again.* 1951. Simon Schuster. 1st ed. NF/NF. P3. $90.00

SIMAK, Clifford D. *Time Is the Simplest Thing.* 1962. Gollancz. VG/VG. P3. $45.00

SIMAK, Clifford D. *Visitors.* 1980. Del Rey. 1st ed. VG/VG. P3. $20.00

SIMAK, Clifford D. *Where the Evil Dwells.* 1982. Del Rey. 1st ed. F/F. P3. $20.00

SIMAK, Clifford D. *Where the Evil Dwells.* 1982. Del Rey. 1st ed. sgn author file copy. F/dj. F4. $40.00

SIME, Sidney. *Beasts That Might Have Been.* 1974. Ferret Fantasy. 1st ed. VG/wrp. M2. $17.00

SIMENON, Georges. *Betty.* 1975. HBJ. VG/VG. P3. $15.00

SIMENON, Georges. *First-Born.* 1947. Reynal Hitchcock. 1st ed. F/NF. B2. $30.00

SIMENON, Georges. *Five Times Maigret.* 1964. HBW. 1st ed. VG/VG. P3. $28.00

SIMENON, Georges. *Girl With a Squint.* 1978. HBJ. 1st ed. NF/NF. P3. $20.00

SIMENON, Georges. *Magician & the Widow: Two Novels.* 1955. Doubleday. 1st ed. VG/VG. P3. $30.00

SIMENON, Georges. *Maigret & the Black Sheep.* 1976. Hamish Hamilton. 1st ed. VG/VG. P3. $18.00

SIMENON, Georges. *Maigret & the Black Sheep.* 1976. London. Hamish Hamilton. 1st ed. F/F. M15. $35.00

SIMENON, Georges. *Maigret & the Bum.* 1973. Detective BC. VG. P3. $8.00

SIMENON, Georges. *Maigret & the Madwoman.* 1972. HBJ. 2nd ed. VG/VG. P3. $10.00

SIMENON, Georges. *Maigret & the Spinster.* 1977. London. Hamish Hamilton. 1st ed. F/F. M15. $30.00

SIMENON, Georges. *Maigret to the Rescue.* 1941. NY. Harcourt. 1st Am ed. cloth. F. B14. $35.00

SIMENON, Georges. *Rich Man.* 1971. HBJ. 1st ed. xl. dj. P3. $6.00

SIMENON, Georges. *Shadow Falls.* 1945. Harcourt Brace. 1st Am ed. 371p. yel stp bl cloth. NF/dj. H5. $100.00

SIMENON, Georges. *When I Was Old.* 1971. HBJ. 1st ed. NF/NF. P3. $25.00

SIMMONDS, Jean Daniels. *Ils Shetland Sheepdog Standard.* 1974. US issue/3rd prt. ils. 47p. M/stiff cb wrp. R2. $12.00

SIMMONDS, Jude. *Complete Bernese Mountain Dog.* 1989. Great Britain. 1st ed. ils. 160p. cloth. M/dj. R2. $25.00

SIMMONDS. *William March: An Annotated Checklist.* 1988. AL U. 215p. F. A4. $55.00

SIMMONS, Andre. *Arab Foreign Aid.* 1981. E Brunswick, NJ. Assoc U Pr. 1st ed. 196p. G/dj. W1. $12.00

SIMMONS, Dan. *Carrion Comfort.* 1989. Dark Harvest. 1st ed. inscr. F/dj. F4. $80.00

SIMMONS, Dan. *Children of the Night.* nd. Quality BC. VG/VG. P3. $10.00

SIMMONS, Dan. *Children of the Night.* 1992. Putnam. 1st ed. F/F. B3. $20.00

SIMMONS, Dan. *Hollow Man.* 1992. Bantam. 1st ed. F/F. P3. $20.00

SIMMONS, Dan. *Lovedeath.* 1993. Warner. ARC. F/wrp. B2. $45.00

SIMMONS, Diane. *Let the Bastards Freeze in the Dark.* 1980. Wyndham. 1st ed. VG/VG. P3. $15.00

SIMMONS, Ernest. *Checkhov.* 1962. Atlantic. Little Brn. 1st ed. RS. F/VG+. S9. $30.00

SIMMONS, Geoffrey. *Adam Experiment.* 1978. Arbor. 1st ed. F/F. P3. $15.00

SIMMONS, Marc. *Albuquerque: Narrative Hist.* 1982. NM U. 1/200. sgn. ils/notes/index. 443p. F/F. B19. $150.00

SIMMONS, Marc. *Sena Family: Blacksmiths of Santa Fe.* 1981. Pr of Palace Governors. 1st ed. 15p. F. B19. $35.00

SIMMONS, Paula. *Spinning & Weaving With Wool.* 1977. np. VG/wrp. G2. $15.00

SIMMONS, Samuel. *Elements of Anatomy & Animal Economy.* 1775. London. Wilie. 1st ed. 396p. ES. old quarter calf. G7. $75.00

SIMMONS, William Scranton. *Catantowwit's House.* 1970. Brown U. 1st ed. 172p. VG/dj. M20. $18.00

SIMMS, Colin. *Brough Superior SS100.* 1934. Somerset, UK. Haynes. 1st ed. photos. 56p. laminated bdg. M. M7. $22.50

SIMON, Carly. *Amy the Dancing Bear.* 1989. Doubleday. 1st ed/author's 1st children's book. NF/F. B3. $25.00

SIMON, Ellen. *Critter Book.* 1940. Holiday. 1st ed. ils. VG/VG. P2. $25.00

SIMON, James F. *Antagonists, Hugo Blk, Felix Frankfurter & Civil Liberties.* 1989. NY. Simon Schuster. M11. $17.50

SIMON, Leonard. *Irving Solution.* 1977. Arbor. 1st ed. F/F. P3. $15.00

SIMON, Michael A. *Matter of Life: Philosophical Problems of Biology.* 1971. Yale. sm 8vo. bl cloth. VG/dj. G1. $27.50

SIMON, Roger L. *California Roll.* 1985. Villard. 1st ed. F/F. O4. $15.00

SIMON, Roger L. *Heir.* 1968. Macmillan. 1st ed/author's 1st novel. F/NF. F4. $25.00

SIMON, Roger L. *Peking Duck.* 1979. London. Deutsch. 1st Eng ed. sgn. NF/NF. S6. $40.00

SIMON, Roger L. *Raising the Dead.* 1988. Villard. 1st ed. NF/NF. P3. $16.00

SIMON, Roger L. *Straight Man.* 1986. Villard. 1st ed. NF/F. O4. $20.00

SIMON, Roger L. *Wild Turkey.* 1974. Straight Arrow. 1st ed. F/NF. O4. $20.00

SIMON, Ted. *Burning Sorrow.* 1991. Toronto. Random. 1st ed. F/F. B3. $15.00

SIMON, Ted. *River Stops Here.* 1994. Random. ARC/1st ed. RS. F/F. S9. $25.00

SIMON & SIMON. *Educational Psychology in the USSR.* 1963. Routledge. 279p. F/dj. K4. $15.00

SIMONDS, Frank H. *Hist of the World War.* 1917-1919. NY. 5 vols. 1st ed. gilt cloth. VG. A17. $50.00

SIMONDS, Jessee Rupert. *Hist of the First Church & Soc of Banford, CT, 1644-1919.* 1919. New Haven. 1st ed. 191p. cloth. NF. M8. $37.50

SIMONE, Andre. *Men of Europe.* 1941. NY. 330p. VG. A17. $7.50

SIMONSON, Harold P. *Beyond the Frontier: Writers, Western Regionalism...* 1989. TX Christian U. 1st ed. M/dj. A18. $16.00

SIMONT, Marc. *Afternoon in Spain.* 1965. Morrow. 1st ed. ils. VG/G+. P2. $35.00

SIMPSON, Charles. *Life in the Mines.* 1898. Thomas W Jackson Pub. ils H DeLay. poor. B34. $25.00

SIMPSON, Dorothy. *Close Her Eyes.* 1984. Scribner. 1st ed. F/F. P3. $18.00

SIMPSON, Dorothy. *Dead by Morning.* 1989. Scribner. UP. F/prt bl wrp. B3. $30.00

SIMPSON, Dorothy. *No Laughing Matter.* 1993. London. Michael Joseph. 1st ed. F/F. S6. $30.00

SIMPSON, Dorothy. *Suspicious Death.* 1988. Michael Joseph. 1st ed. VG/dj. P3. $20.00

SIMPSON, George Gaylord. *Attending Marvels. A Patagonian Journal.* 1934. Macmillan. 1st ed. 8vo. 295p. VG. B11. $35.00

SIMPSON, James Young. *Remarks on Superinduction of Anaesthesia...* 1848. Boston. pub inscr pres. 48p. VG/wrp. B14. $325.00

SIMPSON, John L. *Holiday in Wartime & Other Stories.* 1956. np. 1st ed. lg 8vo. cloth. VG. A17. $10.00

SIMPSON, Louis. *Revolution in Taste.* 1978. Macmillan. 1st ed. RS. NF/VG+. S9. $25.00

SIMPSON, Mona. *Lost Father.* 1992. Knopf. ARC/author's 2nd novel. sgn. F/wrp/fld box. L3. $65.00

SIMPSON, Mona. *Lost Father.* 1992. Knopf. 1st ed. NF/NF. A14. $30.00

SIMPSON, Theodore R. *Space Station: An Idea Whose Time Has Come.* 1985. NY. IEEE. 8vo. 295p. VG/dj. K5. $20.00

SIMS, George; see Cain, Paul.

SIMS, Newell L. *Problem of Social Change.* 1939. Crowell. 453p. F. K4. $8.50

SIMSOVA, Sylva. *Tibetan & Related Dog Breeds: A Guide to Their History.* 1979. Tibetan Terrier. 1st ed. typed manuscript/card wrp. scarce. R2. $45.00

SINCLAIR, Andrew. *Jack: Biography of Jack London.* 1977. NY. 1st ed. photos. 297 p. F/F. A17. $12.00

SINCLAIR, Andrew. *Project.* 1960. Simon Schuster. 1st ed/author's 2nd book. A17/P3. $10.00

SINCLAIR, Angus. *Conditions of Knowing: Essay Towards Theory of Knowledge.* 1951. Harcourt Brace. 260p. G1. $28.00

SINCLAIR, John. *Guitar Army: Street Writings, Prison Writings.* 1972. Douglas Book Corp. 1st ed. sgn. F/F. B2. $50.00

SINCLAIR, Upton. *Another Pamela.* 1950. Viking. 1st ed. VG. P3. $10.00

SINCLAIR, Upton. *Boston: A Novel.* 1928. Boni. 2 vol. 1st ed. 8vo. gr cloth. F/djs. C6. $85.00

SINCLAIR, Upton. *Captain of Industry: Being Story of a Civilized Man.* 1906. Girard, KS. Appeal to Reason. 1st ed. VG. B4. $100.00

SINCLAIR, Upton. *Fliver King.* 1937. Detroit/Pasadena. UAW/Sinclair. VG/wrp. B2. $50.00

SINCLAIR, Upton. *It Happened to Didymus.* 1958. Sagamore. 1st ed. F/NF. B2. $35.00

SINCLAIR, Upton. *Jungle.* 1906. Jungle Pub. 1st ed. NF. B2. $200.00

SINCLAIR, Upton. *Overman.* 1907. Doubleday Page. 1st ed. 90p. gr cloth. NF. C6. $50.00

SINCLAIR, Upton. *Prince Hagen: A Phantasy.* 1903. Boston. Page. 1st ed. 8vo. 249p. bl cloth. NF. C6. $95.00

SINCLAIR. *NJ & the Negro: A Bibliography 1715-1966.* 1967. np. 196p. VG. A4. $85.00

SINGER, Bant. *Don't Slip, Delaney.* 1954. Collins. 1st ed. VG/VG. P3. $25.00

SINGER, Berthold. *Patent Laws of the World.* 1930. WB Conkey. M11. $35.00

SINGER, Charles. *From Magic to Science: Essays on Scientific Twilight.* 1928. Boni Liveright. ils/14 mc pl. 253p. G7. $95.00

SINGER, Charles. *Studies in Hist & Method of Science.* 1917-1921. Clarendon. 2 vol. royal 8vo. ils. xl. G7. $375.00

SINGER, Dorothea Waley. *Giordano Bruno: His Life & Thought...* 1950. NY. Schuman. 11 halftones. blk cloth. VG. G1. $45.00

SINGER, Dorothea. *Selections From Works of Ambroise Pare...* 1924. London. 1st ed. 241p. A13. $100.00

SINGER, Isaac Bashevis. *Collected Stories.* nd. BOMC. VG/VG. P3. $15.00

SINGER, Isaac Bashevis. *Conversations With...* 1985. Doubleday. 1st ed. VG/VG. C8 $20.00

SINGER, Isaac Bashevis. *Elijah the Slave.* 1970. FSG. 1st ed. ils Frasconi. F/VG. P2. $40.00

SINGER, Isaac Bashevis. *Fools of Chelm & Their Hist.* 1973. FSG. 1st prt. xl. VG+/VG+. C8. $25.00

SINGER, Isaac Bashevis. *Friend of Kafka.* 1970. FSG. 1st ed. F/F. B4. $85.00

SINGER, Isaac Bashevis. *Golem.* 1983. Deutsch. 1st Eng ed. 84p. F/F. P2. $30.00

SINGER, Isaac Bashevis. *Joseph & Koza or the Sacrifice to the Vistula.* 1970. FSG. 1st ed. ils Symeon Shimin. F/VG. P2. $50.00

SINGER, Isaac Bashevis. *Power of Light.* 1983. London. Robinson. 1st Eng ed. F/F. C8. $25.00

SINGER, Isaac Bashevis. *Shosha.* 1978. FSG. 1st ed. 277p. VG/VG. M20. $25.00

SINGER, Isaac Bashevis. *When Shlemiel Went to Warsaw & Other Stories.* 1968. FSG. 1st prt. ils Margot Zemach. VG+/VG. C8. $20.00

SINGER, Isaac Bashevis. *Wicked City.* 1972. FSG. 1st prt. ils Fisher. VG/VG. C8. $20.00

SINGER, Isaac Bashevis. *Yentl the Yeshiva Boy.* 1983. FSG. 1st ed. ils Frasconi. M/F. C8. $30.00

SINGER, Kurt. *Spy Stories From Asia.* 1955. Wilfred Funk. VG/VG. P3. $30.00

SINHA, Chris. *Language & Representation.* 1988. NY U. 236p. bl cloth. VG/dj. G1. $25.00

SINHA, Jadunath. *Indian Psychology Vol 2.* 1961. Calcutta. Sinha Pub House. 568p. VG/dj. G1. $30.00

SINYARD, Neil. *Directors: The All-Time Greats.* 1985. Gallery Books. 1st ed. VG/VG. P3. $12.00

SIODMAK, Curt. *City in the Sky.* 1975. Barrie Jenkins. 1st ed. F/F. P3. $18.00

SIODMAK, Curt. *Third Ear.* 1971. Putnam. 1st ed. NF/NF. P3. $18.00

SIRAISI, Nancy. *Taddeo Alderotti & His Pupils.* 1981. Princeton. 1st ed. 462p. dj. A13. $35.00

SITWELL, Sacheverell. *Cupid & the Jacaranda.* 1952. London. 1st ed. VG. A17. $15.00

SITWELL, Sacheverell. *Poltergeists.* 1959. NY. ARC/1st ed. VG/VG. H7. $20.00

SIU, R.G.H. *Man of Many Qualities: Legacy of I Ching.* 1968. Cambridge. MIT. 463p. VG/G. B33. $18.00

SIVARAMAMURTI, C. *Indian Sculpture.* 1961. Bombay. Allied Pub. 1st ed. 8vo. 48 pl. 164p. VG/dj. F1. $25.00

SJOWALL & WAHLOO. *Abominable Man.* 1972. Pantheon. 1st ed. F/NF. B2. $30.00

SJOWALL & WAHLOO. *Locked Room.* nd. BOMC. VG/VG. P3. $10.00

SJOWALL & WAHLOO. *Terrorists.* 1976. Pantheon. 1st ed. VG/VG. P3. $23.00

SKAF, Robert. *Story of the Planet Candy.* 1990. Vantage. 1st ed. sgn. VG/VG. P3. $15.00

SKELTON, R.A. *Vinland Map & the Tartar Relation by RA Skelton...* 1965. New Haven. Yale. 4to. ils/19 pl. 291p. dj. T7. $50.00

SKINNER & SKINNER. *Child's Book of Modern Stories.* 1935. Dial. 1st ed. ils JW Smith. 341p. VG. D6. $75.00

SKINNER & SKINNER. *Skinner's Hist Stories of New Baltimore.* 1979. New Baltimore Pub Lib. rpt of 1951 ed. VG. B18. $27.50

SKOGLUND, Sandy. *Sandy Skoglund.* 1992. Paris Audiovisuel. 1st ed. 4to. hc. F/F. S9. $35.00

SKOLNICK, Jerome H. *Justice Without Trial, Law Enforcement in Democratic Soc.* 1966. John Wiley. M11. $35.00

SKUTCH, Alexander. *Naturalist on a Tropical Farm.* 1980. Berkeley. 1st ed. ils Dana Gardner. 397p. VG/dj. F3. $20.00

SKVORECHY, Josef. *Miss Silver's Past.* 1974. NY. 1st Eng-language ed. inscr. NF/NF. A11. $135.00

SKY, Gino August. *Ball Tournament Specialist.* 1973. Placitas. Duende. 1/1000. F/stapled wrp. L3. $75.00

SLABA, Rudolf. *Ils Guide to Cacti.* 1992. NY. ils/drawings. 224p. M/dj. B26. $15.00

SLADE, Gurney. *Led by Lawrence.* nd (1934?). London. Warne. 1st ed. red cloth. G/fair pict dj/clear plastic. M7. $95.00

SLADE, Michael. *Ghoul.* 1987. Morrow. 1st ed. F/F. P3. $20.00

SLADEK, John. *Bugs.* 1989. London. Macmillan. 1st ed. sgn. F/F. T2. $28.00

SLADEK, John. *Invisible Green.* 1979. Walker. 1st ed. VG/VG. P3. $25.00

SLADEK, John. *Lunatics of Terra.* 1984. London. Gollancz. 1st ed. F/F. T2. $20.00

SLADEK, John. *Reproductive System.* 1968. Gollancz. 1st ed. VG/VG. P3. $65.00

SLATER, Henry. *Ship of Destiny.* 1951. Crowell. ne. VG/dj. M2. $10.00

SLATER, Philip. *How I Saved the World.* 1985. Dutton. VG/VG. P3. $17.00

SLATTERY, Margaret. *New Paths Through Old Palestine.* 1921. Pilgrim. 1st ed. 26p. cloth. VG/dj. W1. $12.00

SLATTERY, Marty. *Diamonds Are Trumps.* 1990. St Lukes. 1st ed. F/F. P8. $12.50

SLATZER, Robert F. *Life & Curious Death of Marilyn Monroe.* 1975. WH Allen. VG/VG. P3. $20.00

SLAUGHTER, Philip. *Hist of Bristol Parish, VA, With Genealogies of Families...* 1879. Richmond. 2nd ed. 237p. cloth. VG. M8. $85.00

SLAUSON, H.W. *Everyman's Guide to Motor Efficency.* 1920. Leslie-Judge. 1st ed. 290p. limp leatherette. VG. A17. $30.00

SLAVIN, Neal. *When Two or More Are Gathered Together.* 1976. FSG. 1st ed. inscr/dtd 1976. F/F. S9. $65.00

SLAVITT, David R. *Agent.* 1986. Doubleday. 1st ed. VG/VG. P3. $15.00

SLESINGER, Tess. *Time, the Present.* 1935. Simon Schuster. 1st ed. NF/VG. B2. $40.00

SLOANE, Eric. *Legacy.* 1979. Funk Wagnall. 1st ed. ils. F/NF. C8. $22.50

SLOANE, Eric. *Return to Taos.* 1960. NY. 1st ed. sgn. VG/VG. B5. $150.00

SLOANE, Eric. *Weather Book.* 1952 (1949). DSP/Little Brn. 4to. ils. 90p. gray cloth. VG. K5. $15.00

SLOANE, William. *Edge of Running Water.* nd. BC. VG/VG. P3. $10.00

SLOANE & WHITE. *Stapelieae.* 1933. Pasadena. 1st ed. ils/fld map. 206p. xl. NF. B26. $110.00

SLOBODKIN, Louis. *Big Circus April 1st.* 1953. Macmillan. 1st ed. ils. VG+/VG. C8. $28.00

SLOBODKIN, Louis. *Gogo the French Seagull.* 1960. Macmillan. 1st ed. lib bdg. F/VG. P2. $25.00

SLOBODKIN, Louis. *Our Friendly Friends.* 1951. NY. ils. pict brd. VG/worn. M5. $15.00

SLOCOMBE, George. *Dangerous Sea: Mediterranean & Its Future.* 1937. Macmillan. 1st ed. 8vo. map ep. VG. W1. $22.00

SLOCUM, Joshua. *Sailing Alone Around the World & Voyage of the Liberdade.* 1948-1950. London. Hart Davis. ils/maps. 384p. T7. $24.00

SLOCUM, Victor. *Capt Joshua Slocum.* 1950. NY. Sheridan. 1st ed. 8vo. 384p. NF/clip. P4. $36.00

SLOSSER, Bob. *Changing the Way America Thinks.* 1989. Word. 220p. F/dj. B29. $7.50

SLOTE, Alfred. *Finding Buck McHenry.* 1991. Harper Collins. 1st ed. F/F. P8. $12.50

SLOTE, Alfred. *Stranger on the Ball Club.* 1970. Lippincott. 1st ed. F/VG+. P8. $12.50

SLUNG, Michele. *I Shudder at Your Touch.* 1991. Roc. 1st ed. F/F. M2/P3. $20.00

SLUSSER, George Edgar. *Bridges to Fantasy.* 1982. IL U. 1st ed. VG/VG. P3. $25.00

SMALL, Austin J. *Mystery Maker.* 1930. Crime Club. 1st ed. G+. P3. $20.00

SMALL, George G. *Bachelor's Love Scrapes.* 1883. NY. Frank Tousey. 1st ed. ils. 54p. wrp. M1. $125.00

SMART, Borlase. *Technique of Seascape Painting.* 1957. London. 77 mtd mc pl. 129p. T7. $65.00

SMEDLEY, Agnes. *Daughter of Earth.* 1929. Coward McCann. 1st ed. F/NF. B2. $250.00

SMEDLEY, H.H. *Fly Patterns & Their Origins.* 1943. Muskegon. 1st ed. sgn. G. B5. $85.00

SMEE, Alfred. *Instinct & Reason: Deduced From Electro-Biology.* 1850. London. Reeve Benham. 10 litho pl. 320p. emb ochre cloth. scarce. G1. $250.00

SMEETON, Miles. *Sea Was Our Village.* 1973. Sidney, BC. Grays Pub. ils. 224p. dj. T7. $24.00

SMILEY, Jane. *Age of Grief.* 1987. Knopf. 1st ed. sgn. F/F. B2. $150.00

SMILEY, Jane. *Catskill Crafts: Artisans of Catskill Mountains.* 1988. Crown. 1st ed. F/F. B2. $40.00

SMILEY, Jane. *Duplicate Keys.* 1984. Knopf. 1st ed. F/F. S9. $200.00

SMILEY, Jane. *Greenlanders.* 1988. Knopf. AP. w/leter from edit. NF/prt gr wrp. S9. $125.00

SMILEY, Jane. *Greenlanders.* 1988. Knopf. ARC. VG. B3. $40.00

SMILEY, Jane. *Greenlanders.* 1988. Knopf. 1st ed. sgn. NF/F. B2. $60.00

SMILEY, Jane. *Thousand Acres.* 1991. Knopf. 1st ed. F/clip. B4. $125.00

SMITH, A. Croxton. *About Our Dogs: The Breeds & Their Management.* 1931. London. Ward Lock. 1st ed. 448p. cloth. R2. $200.00

SMITH, Andre. *Scenewright.* 1926. Macmillan. 1st ed. ils. 135p. VG. H1. $6.00

SMITH, Anthony. *Blind White Fish in Persia.* 1953. Allen Unwin. 3rd prt. 8vo. 231p. G. W1. $12.00

SMITH, April. *North of Montana.* 1994. Knopf. ARC. F/wrp. B2. $35.00

SMITH, Basil A. *Scallion Stone.* 1980. Whispers. 1st ed. sgn. 1/250. F/dj/box. M2. $30.00

SMITH, Benjamin T. *Private Smith's Journal: Recollections of the Late War.* 1963. Lakeside. 1st ed. 253p. cloth. VG. M8. $45.00

SMITH, Bruce Lannes. *Propaganda, Communication & Public Opinion.* 1946. Princeton. 435p. xl. VG. D3. $35.00

SMITH, C. Raimer. *Physician Examines the Bible.* 1950. Philosophical Lib. 394p. NF/dj. G7. $25.00

SMITH, Canon Basil A. *Scallion Stone.* 1980. Whispers. 1st ed. F/F. P3. $20.00

SMITH, Charles M. *From Andersonville to Freedom.* 1894. Providence. 1st ed. 1/250. 74p. NF/prt wrp. M8. $45.00

SMITH, Charles Merrill. *How To Talk to God When You Aren't Feeling Religious.* 1971. Word. 223p. VG/dj. B29. $4.00

SMITH, Clark Ashton. *Black Book of Clark Ashton Smith.* 1979. Arkham. 1st ed. 1/2588. F/prt wrp. T2. $65.00

SMITH, Clark Ashton. *Genius Loci.* 1948. Arkham. NF/NF. P3. $175.00

SMITH, Clark Ashton. *Genius Loci.* 1972. Spearman. 1st ed. F/dj. M2. $35.00

SMITH, Clark Ashton. *Other Dimensions.* 1970. Arkham. 1st ed. NF/dj. M2. $85.00

SMITH, Clark Ashton. *Rendezvous in Averoigne.* 1988. Arkham. 1st ed. 1/5025. F/F. T2. $23.00

SMITH, Cordwainer; see Linebarger, Paul.

SMITH, Cornelius C. *Fort Huachuca: Story of Frontier Post.* 1978. private prt. ils/index/bibliography. 417p. NF/wrp. B19. $25.00

SMITH, Cornelius C. *Tanque Verde: Story of a Frontier Rance, Tucson, AZ.* nd. private prt. ils/notes/index. 187p. F. B19. $25.00

SMITH, D.I. *Western Journals of John May.* (1961). Cincinnati. 1st ed. VG. C11. $35.00

SMITH, D.J. *Discovering Horse-Drawn Carriages.* 1985. Aylesbury. Shire. 8vo. 80p. VG/wrp. O3. $10.00

SMITH, D.M. *Serious Crimes.* 1987. London. Macmillan. ARC/1st ed. RS. NF/NF. S6. $25.00

SMITH, D.W. *Silver Spoon Murders.* 1988. Lyle Stuart. 1st ed. VG/VG. P3. $16.00

SMITH, Dennis. *Glitter & Ash.* 1980. Dutton. 1st ed. VG/VG. P3. $13.00

SMITH, Don. *China Coaster.* 1953. Holt. 1st ed. NF/dj. F4. $20.00

SMITH, Dwight L. *John D Young & the Colorado Gold Rush.* 1969. Chicago. Lakeside Classic. 1st ed. bl cloth. F. P4. $40.00

SMITH, E. Boyd. *Railroad Book: Bob & Betty's Summer on the Railroad.* Oct 1913. Houghton Mifflin. 1st ed. ils EB Smith. VG+. C8. $150.00

SMITH, E.E. *Copy Shop.* 1985. Doubleday. 1st ed. F/F. N3. $12.00

SMITH, Edgar Newbold. *American Naval Broadsides.* 1974. Phil Maritime Mus. 1st ed. 117 pl. 225p. VG. P4. $55.00

SMITH, Edgar W. *Profiles by Gaslight.* 1944. Simon Schuster. 1st ed. 312p. VG. H1. $130.00

SMITH, Edmund Ware. *Further Adventures of One-Eyed Poacher.* 1947. NY. 1st ed. VG/VG. B5. $55.00

SMITH, Edmund Ware. *Tall Tales & Short.* 1938. Derrydale. 1/950. ils Milton Wieler. F. H4. $150.00

SMITH, Edward E. *Children of the Lens.* 1954. Fantasy. ltd ed. sgn. 1/500. F/dj. M2. $250.00

SMITH, Edward E. *Gray Lensman.* 1961. Gnome. 1st ed. VG/VG. P3. $20.00

SMITH, Edward E. *Skylark of Space.* 1946. Hadley. 1st ed. G+. P3. $40.00

SMITH, Edward E. *Vortex Blaster.* 1960. Gnome. 1st ed. VG/VG. P3. $40.00

SMITH, Edwin Ware. *Up River & Down.* 1965. NY. 1st ed. VG/VG. B5. $32.50

SMITH, Elias. *Sermons, Containing Ils of the Prophecies...* 1808. Exeter. self pub. 300p. leather. H10. $165.00

SMITH, Evelyn E. *Miss Melville Regrets.* nd. BC. VG/VG. P3. $8.00

SMITH, F. Berkeley. *In London Town.* 1906. Funk Wagnall. ils. 272p. VG. S11. $15.00

SMITH, Frank. *Corpse in Handcuffs.* 1969. Canada. Macmillan. 1st ed. F/F. P3. $15.00

SMITH, Frank. *Yazoo.* 1954. NY. 1st ed. Rivers of Am Series. VG/VG. B5. $45.00

SMITH, Frederick. *Early Hist of Veterinary Literature...* 1976. London. Allen. 4 vol. rpt. F/sans. O3. $85.00

SMITH, George O. *Path of Unreason.* 1958. Gnome. 1st ed. VG/G. P3. $25.00

SMITH, George O. *Path of Unreason.* 1958. Gnome. 1st ed. VG/VG. M17. $30.00

SMITH, George O. *Venus Equilaterial.* 1947. Prime. 1st ed. inscr. F/frayed. M2. $50.00

SMITH, George. *Assyrian Discoveries...* 1875. NY. Scribner Armstrong. 4th ed. ils. 461p. VG. W1. $75.00

SMITH, Graham. *Disciples of Light.* 1990. Getty Mus. ARC/1st ed. 4to. F/F. S9. $50.00

SMITH, Gregory Blake. *Divine Comedy of John Venner.* 1992. Poseidon/Simon Schuster. 1st ed. rem mk. F/F. A14. $25.00

SMITH, H. Allen. *Age of the Tail.* 1955. Little Brn. 1st ed. F/NF clip. N3. $10.00

SMITH, H. Allen. *Desert Island Decameron.* 1945. Doubleday. VG/VG. P3. $20.00

SMITH, H. Allen. *Rhubarb.* 1946. Doubleday. 1st ed. VG/G. P8. $25.00

SMITH, H. Maynard. *Inspector Frost in the City.* 1930. Doubleday. 1st ed. VG. P3. $28.00

SMITH, H.H. *Jeb Stuart: A Character Sketch.* 1933. Ashland. 1st ed. 16mo. VG/wrp. C11. $65.00

SMITH, Harry. *Harry Smith: Magic Moments.* 1981. LA. Stephen White. 1st ed. intro Anita Ventura Mozley. F/F. S9. $35.00

SMITH, Henry Nash. *Virgin Land: American West As Symbol & Myth.* 1950. Harvard. 1st ed. F/dj. A18. $40.00

SMITH, Homer V. *Kamongo.* 1932. NY. 167p. dj. G7. $35.00

SMITH, Janet Adam. *Children's Ils Books.* 1948. London. Collins. Britain in Pictures Series. ils. 50p. VG/G. S11. $25.00

SMITH, Janet Adam. *John Buchan: A Biography.* 1965. London. Rupert Hart-Davis. 1st ed. VG/G clip. M7. $25.00

SMITH, Jessie Willcox. *Child's Garden of Verses.* 1905. Scribner. 1st ed. ils ep. teg. VG. M5. $95.00

SMITH, John Chabot. *Alger Hiss: The True Story.* 1976. Holt. 1st ed. 485p. F/F. A17. $10.00

SMITH, John. *Benny Hill Story.* 1988. St Martin. 1st Am ed. fwd Bob Hope. F/dj. F4. $18.00

SMITH, Joseph. *Bibliotheca Anti-Quakeriana; or, A Catalogue of Books...* 1968. NY. Kraus Rpt Co. rpt. 8vo. 474p+32p ads. V3. $20.00

SMITH, Karl U. *Perception & Motion.* 1962. Phil/London. 322p. G. K4. $20.00

SMITH, Kay Nolte. *Mind Spell.* 1983. Morrow. 1st ed. NF/NF. N3. $15.00

SMITH, Kay Nolte. *Watcher.* 1980. CMG. 1st ed/author's 1st novel. F/NF. N3. $45.00

SMITH, L. Neil. *Crystal Empire.* 1986. Tor. 1st ed. F/F. P3. $18.00

SMITH, L.P. *Weathercraft.* 1960. London. Blanford. 8vo. photos/diagrams. 86p. G/dj. K5. $12.00

SMITH, Laurence Dwight. *G-Men in Jeopardy.* 1938. Grosset Dunlap. 1st ed. F/NF. F4. $30.00

SMITH, Laurence Dwight. *G-Men Trap the Spy Ring.* 1939. Grosset Dunlap. 218p. yel cloth. VG/dj. M20. $30.00

SMITH, Lee. *Appalachian Portraits.* 1993. Jackson, MS. 1st ed. 1/1500. 108p. maroon cloth. M/dj/swrp. C6. $45.00

SMITH, Lee. *Black Mountain Breakdown.* 1980. NY. Putnam. 1st ed. sgn. F/F. A11. $85.00

SMITH, Lee. *Cakewalk.* 1981. Putnam. 1st ed. sgn/dtd July 1984. 256p. cream/bl brd. M/dj. C6. $85.00

SMITH, Lee. *Cakewalk.* 1981. Putnam. 1st ed/author's 5th book. rem mk. NF/F. L3. $45.00

SMITH, Lee. *Devil's Dream.* 1992. Putnam. 1st ed. F/F. L3. $35.00

SMITH, Lee. *Fair & Tender Ladies.* 1988. Putnam. AP. F/wrp. B2. $35.00

SMITH, Lee. *Fair & Tender Ladies.* 1988. Putnam. 1st ed. F/F. B3. $15.00

SMITH, Lee. *Family Linen.* 1985. Putnam. 1st ed. inscr/dtd 1989. 272p. bl brd. F/NF. C6. $50.00

SMITH, Lee. *Something in the Wind*. 1971. Harper Row. 1st ed/author's 2nd book. sgn. F/NF. L3. $200.00

SMITH, Linell. *And Miles To Go: Biography of a Great Arabian Horse...* 1967. Little Brn. 1st ed. VG/G+. O3. $45.00

SMITH, Lyman B. *Bromeliaceae of Brazil*. 1977 (1955). Baltimore. rpt. 290p. sc. M. B26. $7.50

SMITH, Malcolm. *British Reptiles & Amphibia*. 1949. King Penguin. VG. P3. $10.00

SMITH, Marie. *Entertaining in the White House*. 1967. Acropolis. 1st ed. inscr. 320p. F/G. H1. $15.00

SMITH, Mark. *Death of the Detective*. 1974. Knopf. UP. NF/tall wrp. very scarce. L3. $100.00

SMITH, Martin Cruz. *Gorky Park*. 1981. Random. 1st ed. VG/VG. P3. $25.00

SMITH, Martin Cruz. *Gypsy in Amber*. 1971. Putnam. BC. VG+/VG. C8. $10.00

SMITH, Martin Cruz. *Nightwing*. 1977. Norton. 1st ed. F/F. T2. $25.00

SMITH, Martin Cruz. *Polar Star*. 1989. Random. 1st ed. sgn. F/F. T2. $20.00

SMITH, Martin Cruz. *Stallion Gate*. 1986. Random. 1st ed. VG/VG. P3. $18.00

SMITH, Matthew Hale. *Sunshine & Shadow in NY*. 1868. Hartford. Burr. 1st ed. royal 8vo. 712p. cloth. VG. D3. $75.00

SMITH, Milton. *To Go On*. 1973. Shawnee Mission. 1st ed. inscr. NF/stapled wrp. L3. $35.00

SMITH, Mitchell. *Daydreams*. 1987. McGraw Hill. 1st ed. NF/NF. P3. $18.00

SMITH, Mrs. John. *Confessions of a House-keeper*. 1851. Lippincott Grambo. 1st ed. 12mo. 213p. old calf. M1. $450.00

SMITH, Nathan. *Medical & Surgical Memoirs*. 1831. Baltimore. 374p. ES. calf brd/rebacked. G7. $175.00

SMITH, Nora Archibald. *Kate Douglas Wiggin As Her Sister Knew Her*. 1925. Houghton Mifflin. 1st ed. 383p. gilt gr cloth. VG. M20. $35.00

SMITH, Nora Archibald. *Old, Old Tales From the Old, Old Book*. 1916. Doubleday Page. 1st ed. 484p. G. W1. $15.00

SMITH, Peter. *Design & Construction of Stables*. 1973. London. Allen. later prt. VG/G. O3. $22.00

SMITH, Philip. *Mineral Industry of Alaska in 1940*. 1942. WA. lg mc pocket map. VG/wrp. A17. $8.50

SMITH, Richard M. *Light to the Ancient Greeks*. 1889. Nashville. 1st ed. 34p. G+/prt wrp. M8. $27.50

SMITH, Robert D. *Mark of Holiness*. 1961. Westminster. Newman. 323p. H10. $11.50

SMITH, Robert. *Universal Directory, for Taking Alive & Destroying Rats...* 1812. London. Walker. 4th ed. fld pl. 150p. later half cloth. H10. $95.00

SMITH, Rosamond; see Oates, Joyce Carol.

SMITH, Rosemary. *Big Book of Animal Stories*. 1946. Kenosha. b&w ils. 118p. F/F. A17. $25.00

SMITH, Roy L. *It All Happened Once Before*. 1944. Abingdon Cokesbury. 136p. G/torn. B29. $3.50

SMITH, Seba. *John Smith's Letters...* 1839. NY. Samuel Colman. 1st ed. 8vo. 139p. cloth. M1. $325.00

SMITH, Shelley. *Game of Consequences*. 1978. Macmillan. 1st ed. F/F. P3. $20.00

SMITH, Stanley W.C. *Bird Dogs of the World*. 1989. Great Britain. Nimrod. 1st ed. ils. 182p. M/dj. R2. $30.00

SMITH, Steve. *Years & the Wind & the Rain*. 1984. np. 1st ed. M/M. B34. $22.50

SMITH, T. Lynn. *Fundamentals of Population Study*. 1960. Lippincott. 542p. reading copy. K4. $8.50

SMITH, T.C. *Jesus in the Gospel of John*. 1959. Broadman. 198p. G/dj. B29. $3.50

SMITH, Thomas R. *Walking Swiftly*. 1992. Ally Pr. 1st ed. F/F. S9. $30.00

SMITH, Thorne. *Night Life of the Gods*. 1939. Sun Dial. MTI. VG/VG. P3. $35.00

SMITH, Thorne. *Topper*. 1926. McBride. 1st ed. VG+. B2. $125.00

SMITH, Thorne. *Turnabout*. 1936. Doubleday Doran. VG. P3. $18.00

SMITH, Timothy. *RA Canton & the Fortune Press*. 1983. London. Bertram Rota. photos. 607 entries. 100p. F/NF. A4. $65.00

SMITH, W. Spooner. *Travel Notes of an Octogenerian*. 1914. Boston. Gorham. 1st ed. 8vo. 215p. xl. G. W1. $15.00

SMITH, W.H.B. *Mauser Pistols & Rifles*. 1947. PA. 2nd ed. G/G. A1. $25.00

SMITH, Walker C. *Everett Massacre*. 1918. Chicago. 1st ed. F. B2. $85.00

SMITH, Wesley. *Hippocratic Tradtion*. 1979. Ithaca. 1st ed. 264p. A13. $35.00

SMITH, Wilbur. *Burning Shore*. 1985. Stoddart. VG/VG. P3. $20.00

SMITH, Wilbur. *Hungry As the Sea*. 1978. Heinemann. 1st ed. VG/VG. P3. $25.00

SMITH, Willard K. *Bowery Murders*. 1929. NY. 1st ed. VG. A17. $10.00

SMITH, William. *Hist of Greece...* 1855. Boston. Hickling Swan Brn. 1st ed. 670p. G. W1. $12.00

SMITH & WIGGIN. *Hour With the Fairies*. *Pleasant Hour Series*. 1911. Doubleday Page. ils MacKinstry. 59p. pict brd. VG. A3. $25.00

SMITH. *Monitor & the Merrimac: A Bibliography*. 1968. UCLA. 4to. ils. VG/wrp. A4. $55.00

SMITH. *War Story Guide: Annotated Bibliography Military Fiction...* 1980. np. 449p. F. A4. $55.00

SMITH-NASH, Susan. *Inside the Veil*. 1992. Norman, OK. Texture Pr. 1/26. 24p. M/stiff paper wrp. M7. $5.00

SMITHCORS, J.P. *Evolution of the Veterinary Art*. 1957. KS City, MO. Veterinary Medicine Pub. 1st ed. VG. O3. $65.00

SMOLAN, Rick. *Day in the Life of Australia*. 1982. Abrams. 1st ed. folio. F/F. S9. $65.00

SMOLLETT, Tobias. *Adventures of Peregrine Pickle*. 1751. London. Wilson. 4 vol. 1st ed. 8vo. F/morocco & cloth box. B24. $2,500.00

SMOLLETT, Tobias. *Expedition of Humphrey Clinker*. 1793. London. 2 vol in 1. ils Rowlandson. tree calf. VG. C2. $220.00

SMULDERS, Piet. *Design of Teilhard de Chardin...* 1967. Westminster. Newman. 310p. H10. $12.00

SMYTH, Frank. *Ghost & Poltergeists*. 1976. Doubleday. 1st ed. VG. P3. $15.00

SMYTHE, Frank S. *Valley of Flowers*. 1949. NY. ils/photos. VG. B26. $25.00

SNAITH, J.C. *Araminta*. 1923. McLeod. 1st ed. VG. P3. $20.00

SNAPPER, I. *Maladies Osseuses*. 1938. Paris. 1st ed. photos. VG. C11. $100.00

SNEAD-COX, J.G. *Life of Cardinal Vaughan*. 1912. London. Burns Oates. 2 vol. xl. H10. $22.00

SNEDEKER, Caroline. *Town of the Fearless*. 1931. Doubleday Doran. 1st ed. ils Manning de V Lee. 351p. VG. P2. $20.00

SNELGROVE, Dudley. *British Sporting & Animal Prints 1658-1874*. 1981. London. Tate. 4to. ils. 257p. VG+/VG+. O3. $95.00

SNELL, Edmund. *Yellow Seven*. 1923. Century. 1st ed. VG. M2. $15.00

SNELL, Roy J. *Hour of Enchantment*. 1933. Reilly Lee. sgn. 252p. VG/dj. M20. $25.00

SNELL, ROY J. *Jane Withers & the Phantom Violin*. nd. Whitman. NF/NF. P3. $18.00

SNELL, T.L. *Wild Shores: America's Beginnings*. 1974. NGS. ils Walter Edwards/Louis Glanzman. xl. F/G. B34. $10.00

SNIDER, Frank W. *First Church Davidson Co: A Hist of Pilgrim Evangelical...* 1957. Lexington, NC. FO Sink Prt. 1st ed. 94p. VG/stiff wrp. M8. $45.00

SNODGRASS, Melinda. *Very Large Array.* 1987. NM U. 1st ed. F/F. P3. $23.00

SNODGRASS, R.E. *Principals of Insect Morphology.* 1935. McGraw Hill. 1st ed. 623p. VG. M20. $30.00

SNOECK, A. *Confession & Pastoral Psychology.* 1961. Westminster. Newman. 183p. xl. H10. $12.00

SNOW, C.P. *Coat of Varnish.* 1979. Scribner. 1st ed. F/NF. B3. $20.00

SNOW, C.P. *Variety of Men.* 1967. Scribner. 1st ed. 270p. VG/VG. S11. $10.00

SNOW, Dorothea. *Secret of the Summer.* 1958. Whitman. Lassie TVTI. F. P3. $20.00

SNOW, Edward Rowe. *Great Atlantic Adventures.* 1970. Dodd Mead. ils. 272p. dj. T7. $20.00

SNOW, Elliot. *Sea, Ship & Sailor, Tales of Adventure From Log Books...* 1925. Salem. Marine Research. ils. gilt bl cloth. VG. F1. $75.00

SNOW, Glenna. *Glenna Snow's Cook Book.* 1944. NY. 2nd ed. 480p. G. B18. $20.00

SNOW, Jack. *Who's Who in Oz.* 1954. Chicago. 1st ed. VG/chip. A9. $100.00

SNYDER, Gary. *Back Country.* 1967. London. Fulcrum. 1st ed. F/heavy wrp. A18. $30.00

SNYPP, Wilbur. *Buckeyes.* 1974. Strode. 308p. cloth. VG/dj. M20. $20.00

SOANE, E.B. *To Mesopotamia & Kurdistan in Disguise.* 1912. Boston. 8vo. ils/fld map. 410p. uncut. O2. $125.00

SOBEL, Bernard. *Pict Hist of Vaudeville.* 1961. Citadel. 224p. cloth. VG/dj. M20. $20.00

SOBIN, Harris J. *Florence Townsite.* 1977. private prt. ils/maps/notes/index. 359p. F/F. B19. $100.00

SOFIA, S. *Variations of the Solar Constant.* 1981. NASA. Conference Pub 2191. 4to. 296p. wrp. K5. $24.00

SOHL, Jerry. *Altered Ego.* 1954. Rinehart. 1st ed. VG. P3. $13.00

SOHL, Jerry. *Costigan's Needle.* 1953. Rinehart. 1st ed. F/clip. w/sgn label. F4. $50.00

SOHL, Jerry. *Prelude to Peril.* 1957. Rinehart. 1st ed. VG/VG. P3. $30.00

SOHL, Jerry. *Spun Sugar Hole.* 1971. Simon Schuster. 1st ed. F/F. P3. $15.00

SOHM, Rudolph. *Institutes.* 1907. Oxford. 3rd ed. 605p. VG. D3. $45.00

SOKOLOFF, Boris. *Story of Penicillin.* 1945. Chicago. 1st ed. 167p. A13. $30.00

SOLEM, Elizabeth. *Anaghalook, Eskimo Girl.* 1947. Encyclopedia Brittanica. lg 8vo. 40p. VG/wrp. A17. $9.50

SOLOMITA, Stephen. *Piece of the Action.* 1992. Putnam. 1st ed. sgn. F/F. M15. $30.00

SOLOVYOV, Vladimir. *Solovyov Anthology.* 1950. Scribner. 1st Am ed. 256p. red cloth. VG/dj. G1. $27.50

SOMERS, Jane; see Lessing, Doris.

SOMERVILLE, John. *Communist Trials & the American Tradition.* 1956. NY. inscr. 256p. VG. D3. $25.00

SOMERVILLE, Martha. *Personal Recollections, From Early Life to Old Age...* 1874. London. Murray. 8vo. 377p. purple cloth. G. K5. $125.00

SOMMERHOFF, G. *Logic of the Living Brain.* 1974. Wiley. 413p. F/dj. K4. $40.00

SOMTOW, S.P.; see Sucharitkul, Somtow.

SONDERN, Frederic. *Brotherhood of Evil: The Mafia.* 1959. FSC. VG. P3. $15.00

SONENSCHER. *Hatters of 18th Century France.* 1987. np. 200p. VG. E5. $27.00

SONNEBORN, T.M. *Control of Human Heredity & Evolution.* 1965. Macmillan. 127p. VG/dj. K4. $10.00

SONNICHSEN, C.L. *Ambidextrous Historian: Historical Writers & Writing...* 1981. OK U. 1st ed. F/dj. A18. $25.00

SONNICHSEN, C.L. *From Hopalong to Hud: Thoughts on W Fiction.* 1978. TX A&M. 1st ed. F/F. A18. $40.00

SONNICHSEN, C.L. *SW in Life & Literature.* 1962. Devin-Adair. 1st ed. 554p. NF/worn. B19. $50.00

SONNINI, C.S. *Voyage en Grece et en Turquie.* 1801. Paris. pl vol only. folio. lacks 1 pl. O2. $600.00

SONTAG, Susan. *Benefactor.* 1963. Farrar. 1st ed. F/NF. B2. $60.00

SONTAG, Susan. *Benefactor.* 1963. Farrar. 1st ed/author's 1st book. sgn. NF/NF. A11. $65.00

SOOTHILL, William Edward. *Analects; or, Conversations of Confucius...* 1937. London. Oxford. 254p. bl cloth. VG. B33. $15.00

SOPHOCLES. *Odipus der Tyrann.* 1919. Tolz. Bremer. 1/270. 94p. vellum/marbled brd. K1. $300.00

SORACCO, Sin. *Low Bite.* 1989. Blk Lizard. 1st ed. F/F. P3. $20.00

SORANUS. *Soranus' Gynecology. Trans With Intro by Owei Temkin.* 1956. Baltimore. 1st Eng-trans ed. 258p. A13. $175.00

SOREL, Georges. *Reflections on Violence.* 1950. Free Pr. 1st Eng-language ed. prt gray cloth. VG/dj. G1. $32.00

SORENSEN, Robert C. *Adolescent Sexuality in Contemporary America.* 1973. NY. World. 376p. F/dj. K4. $20.00

SORENSON, Theodore C. *Kennedy.* 1965. Harper. BOMC. VG/dj. M10. $5.00

SORLIER, Charles. *Chagall's Posters: A Catalogue Raisonne.* 1975. NY. Crown. 4to. ils. wht stp bl cloth. F/dj. F1. $175.00

SORRENTINO, Gilbert. *Darkness Surrounds Us.* 1960. Jarjon. Penlands. 1st ed/author's 1st book. sgn. F/wrp. B2. $40.00

SORRENTINO, Gilbert. *Perfect Fiction.* 1968. Norton. 1st ed. F/NF. B2. $30.00

SOTO, Gary. *Baseball in April & Other Stories.* 1990. HBJ. 1st ed. F. P8. $6.00

SOUCHAL, Francoiis. *Art of the Early Middle Ages.* 1968. Abrams. ils. 263p. VG. M10. $15.00

SOURDEL, Dominque. *Islam.* 1962. Walker. 1st ed. 8vo. 155p. cloth. VG. W1. $10.00

SOUSTELLE, Jacques. *Four Suns.* 1971. NY. Grossman. 8vo. 256p. bl cloth. NF/NF. P4. $20.00

SOUSTIEL, Joseph. *L'Art Turc. Ceramiques Tapis Etoffes Velours Broderies.* 1952. Paris. pres. 32p. prt wrp. O2. $40.00

SOUTHARD, C.Z. *Evolution of Trout & Trout Fishing in America.* 1928. NY. 1st ed. VG/worn. B5. $60.00

SOUTHERN, Terry. *Flash & Filigree.* 1958. Coward McCann. VG/VG. P3. $35.00

SOUTHERN, Terry. *Red-Dirt Marijuana.* 1967. NAL. 1st ed. F/F. S9. $50.00

SOUTHERN, Terry. *Red-Dirt Marijuana.* 1967. NAL. 1st ed. VG/VG. P3. $45.00

SOUTHERNE, T. *Plays.* 1774. London. 3 vol set. 1st collected ed. calf. A15. $150.00

SOUTHMAYD & SMITH. *Small Community Hospitals.* 1944. NY. 1st ed. 182p. dj. A13. $20.00

SOWERBY, E. Millicent. *Rare People & Rare Books.* 1987. Williamsburg. Bookpress. 248p. VG/VG. A10. $22.00

SOWERS, Robert. *Language of Stained Glass.* 1981. Forest Grove, OR. 1st ed. 4to. 206p. VG/VG. A17. $20.00

SOYER, Abraham. *Adventures of Yemina.* 1979. Viking. 1st ed. ils/trans Soyer. M/M. C8. $35.00

SPACKMAN, W.M. *Heyday.* 1953. Ballantine. 1st ed/author's 1st book. NF/NF. L3. $150.00

SPAETH, Sigmund. *Barber Shop Ballads & How To Sing Them.* 1940. NY. 2nd prt. 125p. pict cloth. G. A17. $17.50

SPALDING, George B. *Discourses on Occasion of Death of President Garfield.* 1881. Dover. 24p. G/wrp. B18. $17.50

SPARGO, J. *Early American Pottery & China.* 1926. NY. 1st ed. ils. 393p. G. B5. $50.00

SPARGO, J. *Potters & Potteries of Bennington.* 1926. Boston. ltd ed. 1/800. VG-. B5. $95.00

SPARGO, John. *Spiritual Significance of Modern Socialism.* 1908. NY. Huebsch. 1st ed. F/NF. B2. $35.00

SPARK, Muriel. *Hothouse by the E River.* 1973. London. McMillan. 1st ed. VG/VG. B3. $20.00

SPARK, Muriel. *Mandelbaum Gate.* 1965. London. McMillan. 1st ed. VG/clip. B3. $20.00

SPARK, Muriel. *Prime of Miss Jean Brodie.* 1961. London. 1st ed. sgn. NF/VG+. A11. $175.00

SPARK, Muriel. *Very Fine Clock.* 1969. London. Macmillan. 1st ed. obl 8vo. M/M. C8. $60.00

SPARK, Muriel. *Voices at Play.* 1961. London. 1st ed. inscr. F/NF. A11. $70.00

SPARKS, George F. *Many-Colored Toga: Diary of Henry Fountain Ashurst.* 1962. AZ U. 1st ed. 416p. F/F. w/ephemera. B19. $50.00

SPARKS, Jared. *Catalogue of Lib of...* 1871. Cambridge. Riverside. 230p. H10. $75.00

SPARROW, Anthony. *Collection of Articles...Church of England...* 1684. London. Blanch Pawlet. 4th ed. 4to. 406p. rebacked. H10. $150.00

SPARROW, Walter Shaw. *British Sporting Artists From Barlow to Herring.* 1964. London. Spring. rpt of 1922 ed. 249p. orange cloth. NF. F1. $45.00

SPEAKMAN, Harold. *Hilltops in Galilee.* 1923. NY/Cincinnati. Abingdon. 1st ed. 8vo. 259p. VG. W1. $15.00

SPEARMAN, C. *Abilities of Man.* 1927. Macmillan. 415p. reading copy. K4. $12.50

SPEARMAN, C. *Nature of Intelligence & Principles of Cognition.* 1927. London. Macmillan. 355p. G. K4. $20.00

SPEARMANN, Anders. *Voyage Round the World With Capt James Cook...* 1944. Golden Cockerel. 1/350. tall 4to. 281p. orig gr cloth. K1. $650.00

SPEIR, Jerry. *Ross MacDonald.* 1978. Ungar. 1st ed. NF/dj. F4. $20.00

SPEKKE, A. *History of Latvia.* 1951. Stockholm. 60 pl/17 maps. 436p. VG+. H7. $25.00

SPENCE, Janet T. *Elementary Statistics.* 1976. Prentice Hall. 282p. F. K4. $8.50

SPENCE, Joseph. *Polymetis; or, Enquiry Concerning Agreement Between Works...* 1747. London. 1st ed. folio. aeg. gilt morocco. VG. C6. $225.00

SPENCE, Joseph. *Polymetis; or, Enquiry Concerning Agreement...* 1755. London. 2nd ed. 37 full-p/4 double-p pl. folio. full calf. C6. $100.00

SPENCE, Sydney A. *Antarctic Miscellany: Books, Periodicals & Maps...* 1980. Surrey. Simper. 220p. M/sans. P4. $85.00

SPENCER, Elizabeth. *Light in the Piazza.* 1960. NY. 1st ed. sgn. F/F. A11. $65.00

SPENCER, Herbert. *Autobiography.* 1904. Appleton. 2 vol. 1st Am ed. thick 8vo. VG. G1. $45.00

SPENCER, Herbert. *Data of Ethics.* 1879. London. Williams Norgate. 288p. VG. G1. $135.00

SPENCER, Herbert. *Education: Intellectual, Moral & Physical.* 1898. Appleton. 283p. mauve cloth/gilt spine. G1. $27.50

SPENCER, Herbert. *First Principles.* 1900. Appleton. 4th revised ed/later prt. 612p. gr cloth. VG. G1. $25.00

SPENCER, Herbert. *Principles of Psychology. Synthetic Philosophy Vol 45.* 1897. Appleton. 2 vol. 3rd revised ed/later prt. ruled mauve cloth. G1. $65.00

SPENCER, John. *Paranormal: A Modern Perspective.* 1992. Hamlyn. VG. P3. $15.00

SPENCER, O.M. *Indian Captivity: A True Narrative of Capture of...* ca 1860. Carlton Porter. 8th ed. 4 pl. G. H7. $35.00

SPENCER, Ross H. *Kirby's Last Circus.* 1987. Donald Fine. 1st ed. F/F. P8. $11.50

SPENCER, Ross H. *Monastery Nightmare.* 1986. Mysterious. 1st ed. F/F. P3. $20.00

SPENCER, Scott. *Preservation Hall.* 1976. Knopf. 1st ed. F/F. L3. $45.00

SPENCER, William. *Land & People of Tunisia.* 1967. Lippincott. 1st ed. ils. xl. VG. W1. $8.00

SPENDER, Stephen. *Destructive Element.* 1936. Houghton Mifflin. 1st ed. sgn/dtd 1943. NF/G. V1. $65.00

SPENDER, Stephen. *Poems of Dedication.* 1947. Random. 1st ed. inscr/dtd 1948. F/VG. V1. $100.00

SPENDER, Stephen. *WH Auden.* 1975. Macmillan. 1st Am ed. 255p. VG/VG. S11. $10.00

SPENSER, Edmund. *Faerie Queen...Together With Other Works...* 1611. Mathew Lownes. 1st collected/1-vol ed. aeg. Riviere mottled calf. H4. $2,500.00

SPENSER, Edmund. *Spenser's Faerie Queen.* 1897. London. George Allen. 6 vol. 1/100 on handmade paper. ils W Crane. F. F1. $1,800.00

SPERBER, Manes. *Achilles Heel.* 1959. London. Deutsch. 1st ed. gilt brn brd. dj. M7. $65.00

SPERRY, Armstrong. *Call It Courage.* 1940. Macmillan. 30th prt. 8vo. F/VG. B17. $7.00

SPERRY, Armstrong. *One Day With Tuktu, an Eskimo Boy.* 1937 (1935). Winston. ils. inscr. VG. P2. $40.00

SPERRY, Armstrong. *River of the W. Story of the Boston Men.* 1952. Phil. 1st ed. ills Henry Pitz. 102p. F/F. A17. $7.50

SPERRY, Raymond. *Larry Dexter & the Ward Diamonds.* 1927. Garden City. lists 8 titles. 212p. NF/pict wrp. M20. $30.00

SPEWACK, Samuel. *Skyscraper Murder.* 1928. MacAulay. 1st ed. G+. P3. $15.00

SPHYROERAS, Vasilis. *Maps & Map-Makers of the Aegean.* 1985. Athens. sm folio. 263p. cloth. O2. $85.00

SPICER, Bart. *Act of Anger.* 1962. Atheneum. 1st ed. F/F. M15. $45.00

SPICER, Bart. *Burned Man.* 1987. London. Barker. 1st ed. NF/NF. S6. $25.00

SPICER, Bart. *Kellogg Junction.* 1969. Atheneum. 1st ed. F/F. M15. $45.00

SPICER, Edward H. *People of Pascua.* 1988. AZ U. 1st ed. ils/notes/bibliography/index. 331p. F/F. B19. $50.00

SPICER, Henry. *Judicial Dramas: or, Romance of French Criminal Law.* 1872. London. 1st ed. 423p. VG. D3. $35.00

SPICER, Michael. *Cotswold Mistress.* 1992. London. Constable. ARC/1st ed. RS. F/F. S6. $27.50

SPIEGELBERG, Flora. *Princess Goldenhair & the Wonderful Flowers.* 1932. World Syndicate. ils Milo Winter. 176p. cloth. VG. M20. $40.00

SPIELBERG, Steven. *Close Encounters of the Third Kind.* 1977. Delacorte. 1st ed. F/F. F4. $50.00

SPIELMANN, Percy Edwin. *Catalogue of the Library of Miniature Books...* 1961. London. Edward Arnold. 1/500. 8vo. 289p. F/chip. B24. $400.00

SPIER, Peter. *Of Dikes & Windmills.* 1969. Doubleday. 1st ed. 187p. VG/VG. P2. $35.00

SPIER, Peter. *Star-Spangled Banner.* 1973. Doubleday. 1st ed. ils Spier. M/M. C8. $35.00

SPIER, Peter. *We the People, the Constitution of the US.* 1987. Doubleday. 1st ed. F/VG+. C8. $30.00

SPIESMAN, M.G. *Essentials of Clinical Proctology.* 1946. NY. Grune Stratton. 238p. cloth. F. B14. $35.00

SPIESS, Eliot B. *Genes in Populations.* 1977. Wiley. 671p. F/dj. K4. $35.00

SPILLANE, Mickey. *Deep.* 1961. Dutton. 1st ed. VG/VG. P3. $60.00

SPILLANE, Mickey. *Girl Hunters.* 1962. Dutton. 1st ed. sgn. VG/VG. P3. $90.00

SPILLANE, Mickey. *Hammer Strikes Again.* 1989. Avenel. 1st ed. F/F. P3. $15.00

SPILLANE, Mickey. *Killing Man.* 1989. Dutton. 1st ed. F/F. P3. $18.00

SPILLANE, Mickey. *Tomorrow I Die.* 1984. Mysterious. 1st ed. sgn. 1/250. 234p. gilt maroon cloth. F/dj/case. H5. $125.00

SPILLANE, Mickey. *Twisted Thing.* 1966. Dutton. 1st ed. VG/VG. P3. $40.00

SPILLANE, Mickey. *Vintage Spillane.* 1974. WH Allen. 1st ed. VG/VG. P3. $25.00

SPILLER, Robert E. *Fenimore Cooper: Critic of His Time.* 1931. Minton Balch. 1st ed. ils/biblio. F/F. A18. $30.00

SPINA, Lillian. *Fire in the Louvre.* 1979. Swamp Pr. ltd ed. sgn. 1/65. ils Jon Vlakos. F. V1. $125.00

SPINOZA. *Oeuvres Completes.* 1954. Paris. 1st ed thus. 16mo. NF/NF. S9. $25.00

SPINRAD, Norman. *Agent of Chaos.* 1988. Watts. 1st ed. NF/NF. P3. $17.00

SPINRAD, Norman. *Songs From the Stars.* 1980. Simon Schuster. 1st ed. F/F. P3. $20.00

SPIRIDONAKIS, B.G. *Essays on the Historical Geography of the Greek World...* 1977. Thessaloniki. 8vo. 171p. cloth. O2. $30.00

SPITZER, Lyman Jr. *Physical Processes in the Interseller Medium.* 1978. John Wiley. 8vo. 318p. VG/G. K5. $35.00

SPOEHR, Herman A. *Essays on Science: A Selection...* 1956. Stanford. 220p. VG/dj. A10. $40.00

SPOERL, Karl. *Alt-Gera 24 Kunstdrucke Mit Erlauterndem Text.* ca 1920. Germany. 24 mtd photo repos. orig wrap-around box. A17. $25.00

SPOOR, Jack. *Heat Sink Applications Handbook.* 1974. np. Aham Inc. 180p. VG. P4. $10.00

SPOTO, Donald. *Dark Side of Genius: Life of Alf.* 1983. Little Brn. 1st ed. VG/VG. P3. $20.00

SPRADLING, Charles T. *Liberty & the Great Libertarians.* 1913. Golden. 1st ed. inscr. VG. B2. $100.00

SPRATLING, William. *File on Spratling.* 1967. Little Brn. 1st ed. NF/VG+. B4. $65.00

SPRATT, T.A.B. *Travels & Researches in Crete.* 1865. London. 2 vol. 8vo. cloth. O2. $850.00

SPRINGER, John S. *Forest Life & Forest Trees...* 1851. NY. Harper. 1st ed. ils. 259p. pict cloth. H10. $125.00

SPRINGS, Elliot White. *War-Birds. Diary of an Unknown Aviator.* 1929. London. Hamilton. 2nd ed/3rd prt. bl cloth. VG. M7. $55.00

SPROAT, Iain. *Wodehouse at War.* 1981. Ticknor Fields. 1st ed. NF/NF. P3. $20.00

SPRUNGMAN, Ormal I. *Photography Afield.* 1951. Stackpole. 1st ed. 449 p. VG. A17. $15.00

SPUHLER, J.N. *Genetic Diversity & Human Behavior.* 1967. Chicago. Aldine. 278p. F/dj. K4. $20.00

SPURR, Howard W. *Paul Revere Album.* 1897. Boston. Howard Spurr Coffee Co. 8vo. 43p. VG. B11. $40.00

SPURZHEIM, J.G. *Anatomy of the Brain...* 1834. Boston. Marsh Capen Lyon. 1st Am ed. 244p. cloth. B14. $150.00

SPYKMAN, Nicholas John. *America's Strategy in World Politics...* 1942. Harcourt Brace. 1st ed. 8vo. cloth. xl. VG. W1. $8.00

SPYRI, Johanna. *Heidi.* nd. McKay. Golden Books for Children. 8 mc pl. gilt gr cloth. M5. $25.00

SPYRI, Johanna. *Heidi.* nd. Whitman. ils Alice Carsey. 240p. pict cloth. NF. B14. $35.00

SPYRI, Johanna. *Heidi.* 1919. Lippincott. ils Maria Kirk. 319p. gilt bdg. VG. P2. $65.00

SQUAREMAN, Clarence. *My Book of Outdoor Games.* nd. Whitman. ils/photos. cloth. VG. M5. $25.00

SQUIER, E. George. *Peru: Incidents of Travel & Exploration in Land of Incas.* 1877. Harper. 8vo. 599p. VG. P4. $250.00

STABLEFORD, Brian M. *Empire of Fear.* 1988. Simon Schuster. 1st ed. sgn. F/dj. F4. $47.50

STABLEFORD, Brian M. *Man in a Cage.* 1975. John Day. 1st ed. VG/VG. P3. $20.00

STABLEFORD, Brian M. *Paradise Game.* 1976. London. Dent. 1st hc/1st Eng ed. F/F. N3. $35.00

STABLEFORD, Brian M. *Promised Land.* 1975. Dent. 1st ed. sgn. F/F. P3. $25.00

STACEY, C.P. *Records of the Nile Voyageurs 1884-1885...Gordon Relief...* 1959. Toronto. Champlain Soc. 1/600. gilt red cloth. NF. P4. $125.00

STACEY, Susannah. *Knife at the Opera.* 1988. Summit. 1st ed. F/F. P3. $18.00

STACHEY, Lytton. *Elizabeth & Essex.* 1928. NY. 1st ed. sgn. 1/1060. NF. C2. $50.00

STACKPOLE, Edouard A. *Sea-Hunters: Great Age of Whaling.* 1953. Lippincott. ils. 510p. VG/VG. P4. $35.00

STACKPOLE, Edouard A. *Small Craft at Mystic Seaport...* 1959. Mystic. 82p. wrp. T7. $22.00

STACKPOLE, Edward J. *Fredericksburg Campaign.* 1957. ils/index. 297p. dj. O8. $18.50

STACKPOLE, Edward J. *They Met at Gettysburg.* 1959. stated 1st ed but probable 2nd ed. index. 342p. F. O8. $14.50

STACY & WAXMAN. *Computers in Biomedical Research.* 1965. NY. Academic. 2 vol. F. K4. $30.00

STAFFORD, Jean. *Boston Adventure.* 1944. Harcourt. ARC/author's 1st book. VG/wrp. B2. $150.00

STAFFORD, Jean. *Collected Stories.* 1969. FSG. 1st ed. F/NF. B4. $100.00

STAFFORD, Jean. *Elephi the Cat With the High IQ.* 1962. Farrar. 1st ed. F/F. B2. $65.00

STAFFORD, Kim R. *Having Everything Right: Essays of Place.* 1986. Confluence. 1st ed. sgn. cloth. M/dj. A18. $25.00

STAFFORD, Muriel. *X Marks the Dot.* 1943. DSP. 1st ed. VG. P3. $25.00

STAFFORD, William. *Allegiances.* 1970. Harper Row. 1st ed. sgn. F/NF. V1. $40.00

STAFFORD, William. *Life of Harman Blenner Hassett.* 1850. Chillicothe. 1st ed. VG. B5. $75.00

STAFFORD, William. *Listening Deep.* 1984. Penmaen. ltd ed. sgn. ils/sgn Michael McCurdy. F/glassine. V1. $150.00

STAGGE, Jonathan. *Death's Old Sweet Song.* nd. Collier. VG. P3. $15.00

STALLMAN, Robert. *Beast.* 1990. London. Kinnell. 1st hc ed. ils/inscr/sgn Don Maitz. F/F. T2. $35.00

STALLMAN, Robert. *Captive.* 1989. London. Kinnell. 1st hc ed. F/F. T2. $25.00

STALLMAN, Robert. *Orphan.* 1989. London. Kinnell. 1st hc ed. inscr. F/F. T2. $35.00

STAM & YACHNIN. *Turgenev in English: A Checklist of Works...* 1962. NY Public Lib. 55p. VG/wrp. A4. $45.00

STANDISH, Burt L. *Courtney of the Center Garden.* 1915. Barse Hopkins. 1st ed. Big League Series #7. G+. P8. $20.00

STANDISH, Burt L. *Frank Merriwell's Victories.* 1900. McKay. 319p. khaki pict cloth. VG/dj. M20. $35.00

STANDISH, Burt L. *Making of a Big Leaguer.* 1915. Barse Hopkins. 1st ed. Big League Series #6. VG. P8. $20.00

STANDLEE, Mary. *Great Pulse. Japanese Midwifry & Obstetrics Through Ages.* 1959. Tokyo. ils. 192p. VG/dj. G7. $45.00

STANFILL, Francesca. *Wakefield Hall.* 1993. Villard/Random. 1st ed. F/F. A14. $30.00

STANFORD, Alfred. *Force Mulberry: Planning & Installation...* 1951. NY. 1st ed. ils/map ep. 240p. G/dj. B18. $45.00

STANHOPE, Leicester. *Greece in 1823 & 1824; Being a Series of Letters...* 1824. London. 5 facsimile letters. 368p. polished calf/rebacked. O2. $525.00

STANHOPE, P.D. *Miscellaneous Works of...* 1778. London. 2 vol. 4to. G+. A15. $225.00

STANISLAVSKI, Constantin. *Actor Prepares.* 1984. NY. Thearte Arts Books. 295p. VG/VG. B33. $20.00

STANLEY, Arthur Penrhyn. *Sinai & Palestine in Connection With Their History.* 1871. London. John Murray. 560p. emb cloth. P4. $40.00

STANLEY, Charles. *Eternal Security.* 1990. Nelson. 194p. F/F. B29. $4.50

STANLEY, Henry M. *How I Found Livingstone: Travels, Adventures, Discoveries...* 1873. np. 700p. lib bdg. VG. E5. $45.00

STANLEY, Louis T. *Collecting Staffordshire Pottery.* 1963. Doubleday. 1st ed. 215p. VG/dj. M20. $25.00

STANLEY, O. *History of the Fighting 41st 1899-1901.* nd (1944-1945). np. 1st ed. VG. C11. $35.00

STANLEY, Paul. *Plants of Glacier National Park.* 1926. GPO. ils. sc. G. B34. $45.00

STANLEY, Thomas. *Pythagoras: His Life & Teachings.* 1970. Los Angels. Philosophical Research Soc. facsimile. 95p. B33. $45.00

STANTON, Carey. *Island Memoir.* 1984. Zamorano Club. ils. 38p. F/sans. B19. $45.00

STANWELL, Theodora. *Driftwood Valley.* 1947. Little Brn. ils. G. B34. $15.00

STANWOOD, Brooks. *Glow.* 1979. McGraw Hill. 1st ed. F/F. P3. $25.00

STANWOOD, Brooks. *Seventh Child.* 1981. Linden. 1st ed. F/F. N3. $20.00

STANWOOD, James Rindge. *Direct Ancestry of Late Jacob Wendell.* 1882. Boston. David Clapp. 1st ed. tall 8vo. 60p. gilt gr cloth. F. K1. $35.00

STAPLEDON, Olaf. *Death Into Life.* 1946. Methuen. 1st ed. VG. P3. $45.00

STAPLEDON, Olaf. *Far Future Calling.* 1979. Oswald Train. 1st ed. F/F. P3. $20.00

STAPLEDON, Olaf. *Nebula Maker & Four Encounters.* 1983. Dodd Mead. 1st Am/1st combined ed. NF/VG. N3. $10.00

STAPLEDON, Olaf. *Nebula Maker.* 1976. Bran's Head Books. ltd 1st ed. F/F. F4. $25.00

STAPLETON. *Sir John Betjeman: Bibliography of Writings...* 1974. np. 148p. F. A4. $15.00

STAR & SWEENEY. *Forward: History of 2nd/14th Light Horse.* 1989. Queensland, Australia. 1st ed. 230p. M/dj. M7. $40.00

STARCKE, Anna. *Survival: Taped Interviews With S Africa's Power Elite.* 1978. Cape Town, S Africa. Tafelberg. 1st ed. 217p. VG/dj. M10. $5.00

STARK, Freya. *Baghdad Sketches.* 1938. Dutton. 1st ed. 8vo. 42 pl. 269p. VG. W1. $30.00

STARK, Freya. *Lycian Shore.* 1956. Harcourt Brace. 1st ed. ils. 204p. VG. W1. $20.00

STARK, Freya. *Perseus in the Wind.* June 1949. London. Murray. ils Reynolds Stone. VG/VG. E3. $20.00

STARK, Freya. *Riding to the Tigris.* 1959. Harcourt Brace. 1st Am ed. 114p. xl. VG. W1. $18.00

STARK, Richard; see Westlake, Donald E.

STARKELL, Don. *Paddle to the Amazon.* 1989. Rocklin, CA. Prima. 1st ed. 8vo. ils. 318p. F/F. B11. $10.00

STARKIE, Walter. *In Sara's Tent.* 1953. Dutton. possible 1st ed. NF/VG. C8. $25.00

STARNES, Richard. *Another Mug for the Bier.* 1950. Lippincott. 1st ed. VG/VG. P3. $30.00

STAROSCIAK, Kenneth. *JD Salinger: A Thirty Years Bibliography. 1938-1968.* nd. Croixside. 1st ed. F. S9. $40.00

STARR, M. Allen. *Atlas of Nerve Cells.* 1896. NY. Columbia. 53 pl/13 diagrams. 77p. orig brd/rebacked. G7. $295.00

STARR, Roland. *Operation Omina.* 1970. Lenox Hill. 1st ed. NF/dj. F4. $25.00

STARRETT, Agnes. *Darlington Memorial Lib U of Pittsburgh.* 1938. University Pr. fld map. 28p. cloth. M. A10. $35.00

STARRETT, Vincent. *Books & Bipeds.* 1947. Argus. 1st ed. 268p. VG/dj. M10. $12.50

STARRETT, Vincent. *Books Alive.* 1940. Random. 3rd prt. 360p. VG. S11. $10.00

STARRETT, Vincent. *Great All Star Animal League Ball Game.* 1957. NY. 1st ed. ils Wiese. VG/G. B5. $30.00

STARRETT, Vincent. *Seaports in the Moon.* 1928. Doubleday. 1st ed. VG/dj. M2. $40.00

STARZYNSKI, Juliusz. *Aleksander Gierymski.* 1971. Warsaw. 1st ed. 189 full-p/24 tipped-in mc pl. F/F. A17. $50.00

STASHEFF, Christopher. *Company of Stars.* 1991. Del Rey. 1st ed. F/F. P3. $19.00

STASHEFF, Christopher. *Houses Without Doors.* 1990. Dutton. 1st ed. rem mk. F/F. M21. $7.50

STASHEFF, Christopher. *Wizard in Bedlam.* 1979. Doubleday. 1st ed. VG/G. P3. $15.00

STASZ, Clarice. *American Dreamers: Charmain & Jack London.* 1988. St Martin. 1st ed. photos/notes/index. M/dj. A18. $20.00

STAVEACRE & SUMMERHAYS. *In Praise of the Arabian Horse.* 1954. London. photos. 60p. VG/wrp. O3. $45.00

STAVELEY, Ronald. *Notes on Modern Bibliography.* 1954. London. Lib Assn. 111p. VG. M10. $7.50

STCHUR, John. *Down on the Farm.* 1987. St Martin. 1st ed. F/F. P3. $16.00

STEADMAN, Ralph. *I, Leonardo.* 1983. Summit. 1st ed. 4to. ils. NF/NF. S9. $35.00

STEARNS, Martha. *Homespun & Blue.* 1988. np. cloth. VG. G2. $25.00

STEATFEILD, Noel. *Party Frock.* 1964. London. Collins. probable 1st ed. ils Anna Zinkeisen. 255p. VG/G. P2. $25.00

STEBBING, L. Susan. *Logical Positivism & Analysis.* 1933? np. thin 8vo. 35p. prt gray wrp. G1. $25.00

STEBBINS, G.B. *Facts & Opinions Touching the Real Origin & Opinions...* 1853. Boston. Jewett. 1st ed. 8vo. 224p. cloth. M1. $200.00

STEBBINS, Theodore E. *American Master Drawings & Watercolors.* 1976. Harper. 1st ed. 4to. ils. 464p. F/VG+. F1. $65.00

STEBEL, S.L. *Spring Thaw.* 1989. Walker. 1st ed. inscr. F/F. N3. $20.00

STEED, Neville. *Tinplate.* 1986. London. Weidenfeld. 1st ed/author's 1st book. sgn. F/F. S6. $40.00

STEEGMANN, Mary G. *Book of Divine Consolation of Blessed Angels of Folignop.* 1966. Cooper Sq Pub. Medieval Lib Series. 265p. F. B33. $16.00

STEEGMULLER, Francis. *Cocteau: A Biography.* 1970. Boston. 1st ed. 583p. VG/VG. A17. $25.00

STEEGMULLER, Francis. *Stories & True Stories.* 1972. Boston. 1st ed. F/NF. A17. $10.00

STEEL, David. *Elements & Practice of Rigging & Seamanship.* 1978. London. Comfort. 2 vol. facsimile of 1794 1st ed. 1/500. 95 fld pl. box. T7. $650.00

STEEL, Flora Annie. *Tales of the Punjab.* 1983. Greenwich House. 1st ed. F/F. P3. $15.00

STEELE, Adison; see Lupoff, Richard A.

STEELE, Arthur R. *Flowers for the King.* 1964. Durham. ils/2 maps. xl. VG/dj. B26. $32.50

STEELE, James W. *Frontier Army Sketches.* 1969. Albuquerque. NM U. rpt of 1883 ed. 329p. olive/tan cloth. F/VG. P4. $35.00

STEELE, Mary Q. *First of the Penguins.* 1973. Macmillan. 1st ed. F/NF. N3. $10.00

STEELE, Matthew Forney. *American Campaigns Vol 1.* 1909. WA, DC. Adams. 1st ed. 731p. VG. H1. $22.50

STEERE, William C. *Fifty Years of Botany Golden Jubilee of Botanical Soc...* 1958. McGraw Hill. 638p. VG. A10. $40.00

STEFANIK. *John Berryman: Descriptive Bibliography*. 1974. Pittsburgh. 314p. F. A4. $45.00

STEFANSSON, Evelyn. *Here Is Alaska*. 1959. NY. revised. sgn pres. VG/VG. A17. $17.50

STEFANSSON, Vilhjalmur. *Adventure of Wrangel Island*. 1925. NY. 1st ed. photos/maps. 424p. new ep. VG. A17. $40.00

STEFANSSON, Vilhjalmur. *Adventure of Wrangel Island*. 1925. NY. Macmillan. 1st ed. inscr/dtd 1960. 424p. gilt bl cloth. VG. P4. $195.00

STEFANSSON, Vilhjalmur. *Friendly Arctic: Story of 5 Years in Polar Regions*. 1939. NY. later prt. pocket map. 784p. VG. A17. $45.00

STEFANSSON, Vilhjalmur. *Northward Course of Empire*. 1924. NY. 2nd ed. fld map. 274p. VG. A17. $22.50

STEFANSSON & WEIGERT. *Compass of the World*. 1945. NY. 2nd prt. 466p. VG/VG. A17. $16.50

STEFFEN, Jack. *Firm Hand on the Rein*. 1961. NY. Longman Gr. 1st ed. VG. O3. $15.00

STEGNER, Wallace. *All the Little Live Things*. 1967. Viking. 1st ed. F/VG. A18. $50.00

STEGNER, Wallace. *Angle of Repose*. 1971. Doubleday. 1st ed. VG/G. B5. $50.00

STEGNER, Wallace. *Angle of Repose*. 1971. London. Heinemann. 1st ed. NF/NF. S9. $75.00

STEGNER, Wallace. *Collected Stories*. 1990. Random. 2nd prt. sgn. F/dj. A18. $25.00

STEGNER, Wallace. *Conversations With...* 1983. UT U. 1st ed. sgn Stegner/Etulain. F/F. A18. $125.00

STEGNER, Wallace. *Crossing to Safety*. 1987. Franklin Lib. 1st ed. sgn. aeg. gilt navy leather. F. A18/C4. $125.00

STEGNER, Wallace. *Discovery!* 1971. Beruit, Lebanon. Middle E Export Pr. 1st ed. NF/wrp. B4. $100.00

STEGNER, Wallace. *Four Protraits & One Subject: Bernard De Voto*. 1963. Houghton Mifflin. 1st ed. NF/NF. A18. $80.00

STEGNER, Wallace. *Gathering of Zion: Story of the Mormon Trail*. 1992. NE U. 1st sc ed. ils/index. M. A18. $12.95

STEGNER, Wallace. *Mormon Country*. 1942. DSP. 1st ed. sgn. map ep. F. A18. $100.00

STEGNER, Wallace. *Mormon Country*. 1942. DSP. 2nd prt. NF/NF. B4. $85.00

STEGNER, Wallace. *On the Teaching of Creative Writing*. 1988. New Eng U. 1st ed. sgn. 72p. brd. M/sans. A18. $45.00

STEGNER, Wallace. *Recapituation*. 1979. Franklin Lib. 1st ed. ils Walter Crane. gilt red leather. F. A18. $80.00

STEGNER, Wallace. *Recapitulation*. 1979. Doubleday. 1st ed. F/NF. L3. $85.00

STEGNER, Wallace. *Spectator Bird*. 1976. Franklin Lib. 1st ed. gilt leather. F. A18. $80.00

STEGNER, Wallace. *Stanford Short Stories 1950*. 1950. Stanford. 1st ed. sgn. F/dj. A18. $30.00

STEGNER, Wallace. *Uneasy Chair: Biography of Bernard De Voto*. 1974. Doubleday. 1st ed. RS. F/VG. A18. $75.00

STEGNER, Wallace. *Wolf Willow: A History...* 1967. Toronto. Macmillan. 1st Canadian ed. sgn. VG+. A18. $30.00

STEICHEN, Edward. *Life in Photography*. 1963. Doubleday. 1st ed. VG/VG clip. S9. $125.00

STEIG, Jeanne. *Consider the Lemming*. 1988. FSG. ils William Seig. M. C8. $20.00

STEIG, William. *Abel's Island*. 1976. FSG. 1st ed. F/VG+. C8. $40.00

STEIG, William. *Amazing Bone*. 1989 (1976). FSG. 6th prt. F/F. C8. $20.00

STEIG, William. *Brave Irene*. 1978. FSG. 1st ed/3rd prt. M/M. C8. $50.00

STEIG, William. *Rotten Island*. 1984. Boston. Godine. 4to. ils. VG/dj. N2. $5.00

STEIG, William. *Shrek!* 1990. FSG. 1st ed. glazed pict brd. M. C8. $20.00

STEIG, William. *Tiffky Doofky*. 1978. FSG. 1st ed. F/VG. C8. $40.00

STEIN, Aaron Marc. *Chill Factor*. 1978. Crime Club. 1st ed. VG/VG. P3. $15.00

STEIN, Aaron Marc. *We Saw Him Die*. 1947. Doubleday. 1st ed. VG/G. P3. $20.00

STEIN, Ben. *Croesus Conspiracy*. 1978. Simon Schuster. 1st ed. NF/NF. P3. $10.00

STEIN, Edith. *Science of the Cross: A Study of St John of the Cross...* 1960. London. Burns Oates. 243p. H10. $25.00

STEIN, Gertrude. *Brewsie & Willie*. 1946. Random. 1st ed. 8vo. 114p. blk stp beige cloth. NF/dj. H5. $65.00

STEIN, Gertrude. *Elucidation*. April 1927. Transition. 1st separate ed. NF/wrp. B2. $125.00

STEIN, Gertrude. *Geography & Plays*. 1922. Boston. 4 Seas. 1st ed. 8vo. 419p. gray brd/bl spine. VG. w/sgn letter. C6. $1,400.00

STEIN, Gertrude. *Last Operas & Plays*. 1949. Rinehart. 1st ed. VG/VG. E3. $45.00

STEIN, Gertrude. *Making of Americans*. 1934. Harcourt Brace. 1st Abridged ed. pres. NF. H4. $385.00

STEIN, Gertrude. *World Is Round*. 1939. NY. 1st ed. sgn Stein/Clement Hurd. VG/box. B5. $500.00

STEIN, Harry. *Hoopla*. 1983. Knopf. 1st ed. F/VG+. P8. $30.00

STEIN, Henri. *Archers D'Autrefois: Archers D'Aujourd'Hui*. 1925. Paris. DA Longuet. 1st ed. ils Leon Laugier. 1/1200. prt wrp. K1. $175.00

STEIN, Maurice R. *Identity & Anxiety*. 1960. Glencoe, IL. Free Pr. 632p. reading copy. K4. $8.50

STEIN, Morris I. *Thematic Appreception Test*. 1948. Cambridge, MA. Addison Wesley. 91p. G. K4. $15.00

STEIN, Sol. *Touch of Treason*. 1985. St Martin. 1st ed. VG/VG. P3. $15.00

STEIN, William. *Hualcan: Life in Highlands of Peru*. 1961. Ithaca. 1st ed. 383p. VG. F3. $20.00

STEINBECK, John. *Burning Bright*. 1950. NY. Viking. 1st ed. sm 8vo. 159p. orange stp gray cloth. F/NF. H5. $200.00

STEINBECK, John. *Cannery Row*. 1945. Viking. 1st ed. NF/VG. A9. $150.00

STEINBECK, John. *Cup of Gold*. 1929. NY. McBride. 1st ed/1st issue/author's 1st book. 269p. NF/clip. H5. $3,750.00

STEINBECK, John. *Cup of Gold*. 1936. NY. Covici. 1st ed. VG/VG. B5. $50.00

STEINBECK, John. *East of Eden*. 1952. Viking. 1st ed. sgn. 1/1500. 8vo. 602p. gilt/brn stp gr bdg. F/cb case. H5. $1,250.00

STEINBECK, John. *Grapes of Wrath*. April 1939. Viking. 1st ed/1st prt. 8vo. 619p. pict beige cloth. F/NF clip. C6. $2,200.00

STEINBECK, John. *Grapes of Wrath*. 1939. London. Heinemann. 1st ed. F/NF. A18. $300.00

STEINBECK, John. *Of Mice & Men*. 1937. NY. Covici Friede. 1st ed/1st issue. sm 8vo. 186p. beige cloth. VG/dj. H5. $450.00

STEINBECK, John. *Pearl*. 1947. Viking. 1st ed. F/NF 1st issue. Q1. $250.00

STEINBECK, John. *Red Pony*. 1937. NY. Covici Friede. 1st ed. sgn. 1/699. 81p. beige cloth. F/cb case. H5. $1,250.00

STEINBECK, John. *Sea of Cortez*. 1941. NY. 1st ed. VG/VG. B5. $350.00

STEINBECK, John. *Short Reign of Pippin IV: A Fabrication*. 1957. London. Heinemann. 1st ed. F/chip. A18 $35.00

STEINBECK, John. *Sweet Thursday*. 1954. Viking. 1st ed. VG/VG. P3. $65.00

STEINBERG, S.H. *Encyclopedia of the World*. 1963. St Martin. Centenary ed. 1728p. VG/dj. W1. $10.00

STEINBERG, S.H. *Stateman's Yearbook*. 1963. St Martin. sm 8vo. 8 fld pl. VG/dj. W1. $10.00

STEINBRUNNER, Chris. *Cinema of the Fantastic.* 1972. Saturday Review. 1st ed. G+. P3. $20.00

STEINEL, Alvin. *History of Agriculture in Colorado.* 1926. Ft Collins. State Agricultural College. 659p. VG. A10. $85.00

STEINER, Charlotte. *Copycat Colt.* 1951. Wonder Book 545. K2. $10.00

STEINER, Edward A. *From Alien to Citizen.* 1914. NY. Revell. 1st ed. F/NF. B2. $40.00

STEINER, M.J. *Inside Pan-Arabia.* 1947. Chicago. Packard. 1st ed. sgn. VG/dj. W1. $20.00

STEINHARDT, Jacob. *Woodcuts.* ca 1955. Jerusalem Art Pub Soc. lg 4to. intro F Schiff. sbdg. F/poor. F1. $200.00

STEINHARDT, Jacob. *Woodcuts.* 1959. Israel. ltd ed. 57 woodcuts. VG+/VG/brn cardboard case. A1. $450.00

STELMASIAK, M. *Anatomical Atlas of the Human Brain & Spinal Cord.* 1956. Warsaw. ils/pl. 227p. cloth. G7. $65.00

STEMMLE, R. *Jugendkriminalitat.* 1967. Munchen. Der Neue Pitaval Series. 12mo. 260p. NF/dj. D3. $15.00

STENHOUSE, David. *Evolution of Intelligence.* 1973. Barnes Novle. 338p. F/dj. K4. $10.00

STEPHANE, Roger. *TE Lawrence.* 1960. Gallimard. 1st French ed. VG. M7. $60.00

STEPHANE, Roger. *Theatre de Destin.* 1953. Paris. 1st French ed. 282p. VG. M7. $60.00

STEPHANS, Ian. *Horned Moon.* 1955. IN U. 8vo. pl/maps. 288p. xl. VG/worn. W1. $12.00

STEPHEN, David. *Bodach the Badger.* 1983. St Martin. 1st ed. VG/VG. P3. $11.00

STEPHEN, David. *String Lug the Fox.* 1952. Little Brn. 1st ed. VG. O3. $20.00

STEPHEN, F.G. *Catalogue of Prints & Drawings in British Museum.* 1877. London. 2 vol. VG. A15. $100.00

STEPHENS, Henry. *Journeys & Experiences in Argentina, Paraguay & Chile.* 1920. NY. 1st ed. inscr. ils. 520p. VG. F1. $75.00

STEPHENS, J.W. *Blackwater Fever: Hist Survey & Summary of Observations...* 1937. Liverpool. 727p. G7. $75.00

STEPHENS, James. *Irish Fairy Tales.* 1920. Macmillan. 1st ed. 8vo. ils Rackham. VG-. B17. $85.00

STEPHENS, James. *Julia Elizabeth: A Comedy in One Act.* 1929. Crosby Gaige. 1/861. sgn/#d. NF. B2. $85.00

STEPHENS, John Lloyd. *Incidents of Travel in Greece, Turkey, Russia & Poland.* 1839. NY. 7th ed. 2 vol. 8vo. cloth. O2. $110.00

STEPHENSON, Dorothy. *Night It Rained Toys.* 1963. Follett. 1st ed. ils John E Johnson. 32p. VG/VG. P2. $15.00

STEPHENSON, Geoffrey M. *Development of Conscience.* 1966. Humanities Pr. 1st Am ed. 134p. VG/dj. G1. $14.00

STEPHENSON, Jessie Bane. *From Old Stencils to Silk Screening.* 1953. Scribner. ils. 239p. VG/dj. M10. $7.50

STEPHENSON, Nathaniel W. *Nelson W. Aldrich.* 1971. Kennikat. rpt. 496p. F. A17. $9.50

STEPHENSON, Ray. *Sedums. Cultivated Stonecrops.* 1994. Portland. photos/drawings. 356p. M/dj. B26. $49.95

STEPHENSON & STEPHENSON. *Railway Revolution.* 1962. St Martin. 1st Am ed. 342p. VG/ragged. M20. $25.00

STERLING, Bruce. *Crystal Express.* 1990. Legend. 1st ed. F/F. P3. $25.00

STERLING, Stewart. *Too Hot To Handle.* 1961. Random. 1st ed. VG. P3. $18.00

STERLING, Tom. *Amazon.* 1975. Time Life. 4to. ils/maps/index. 184p. pict brd. F3. $10.00

STERN, August. *USSR Vs Dr Mikhail Stern: Only Tape Recording of a Trial...* 1977. NY. Urizen. M11. $35.00

STERN, Axel. *Science of Freedom: Essay in Applied Philosophy.* 1969. London. Longman. 142p. VG/VG. B33. $14.00

STERN, Bernhard. *Medical Services by Government: Local, State & Federal.* 1946. NY. 1st ed. 208p. A13. $40.00

STERN, Bill. *Favorite Boxing Stories.* 1949. Bl Ribbon. VG. P3. $10.00

STERN, Curt. *Principles of Genetics.* 1949. San Francisco/London. 733p. G. K4. $10.00

STERN, George. *Methods in Personality Assessment.* 1956. Glencoe, IL. Free Pr. 254p. F/dj. K4. $10.00

STERN, Norton B. *California Jewish History.* 1967. Glendale. Arthur Clark. 1st ed. 8vo. 175p. M/plain dj. P4. $22.50

STERN, Philip Van Doren. *Drums of Morning.* 1942. Doubleday Doran. 1st ed. VG/G. P3. $20.00

STERN, Philip Van Doren. *Robert E Lee: Man & the Soldier.* 1963. McGraw Hill. 1st ed. 256p. F/F. H1. $40.00

STERN, Rene B. *Book Trails.* 1946. Chicago. Child Development. 8 vol. 4to. faux red leather. NF. D6. $125.00

STERN, Richard Martin. *Flood.* 1979. Doubleday. 1st ed. VG/VG. P3. $20.00

STERN, Richard Martin. *I Hide, We Seek.* 1965. Scribner. 1st ed. VG/VG. P3. $17.00

STERN, Roger. *Death & Life of Superman.* 1993. Bantam. 1st ed. F/F. N3/P3. $20.00

STERN. *CA Jewish Hist.* 1967. Arthur Clark. 175p. F/F. A4. $35.00

STERNBERG, Robert J. *Advances in Psychology of Human Intelligence. Vol 3.* 1986. Lawrence Erlbaum. 382p. G. K4. $20.00

STERNE. *Sentimental Journey Through France & Italy.* 1936. LEC. 1/1500. 142p. VG. A4. $200.00

STERRE, Douglas V. *Work & Contemplation.* 1957. Harper. 1st ed. 12mo. 148p. VG/VG. V3. $12.00

STETSON, Charlotte Perkins. *In This Our World.* 1893. Oakland, CA. McCombs Vaughn. 1st ed. 12mo. contemporary cloth. M1. $3,000.00

STETTINIUS, E.R. *Roosevelt & the Russians: The Yalta Conference.* 1949. Doubleday. 1st ed. 367p. F/G. H1. $22.50

STEUART, Henry. *Planter's Guide; or, Practical Essay...* 1832. NY. Thorburn. 1st Am ed. 4 pl. 422p. contemporary cloth. xl. H10. $135.00

STEUART, R.H.J. *Diversity in Holiness.* 1937. Sheed Ward. 221p. xl. H10. $15.00

STEUBEN, John. *Labor in Wartime.* 1940. Internat. 1st ed. NF/NF. B2. $30.00

STEUBEN, John. *Strike Strategy.* 1950. NY. Gaer Assoc. VG/G. V4. $20.00

STEVEN, Shane. *Anvil Chorus.* 1985. Delacorte. 1st ed. F/F. F4. $25.00

STEVENS, Carla. *Trouble for Lucy.* 1979. Clarion Books. 11th prt. ils Ronald Himler. M/sans. A18. $14.00

STEVENS, Dorothy. *Missionary Education in a Baptist Church.* 1953. Judson. 208p. G/torn. B29. $3.50

STEVENS, Francis. *Heads of Cerberus.* 1952. Polaris. NF/dj/case. P3. $45.00

STEVENS, H.L. *House That Jack Built.* 1865. Hurd Houghton. ils. 16p. brd. VG. B14. $250.00

STEVENS, Henry. *Recollections of Mr James Lenox of NY...* 1886. London. 211p. half cloth. VG. B14. $200.00

STEVENS, James. *Big Jim Turner.* 1948. Doubleday. 1st ed. G. B34. $5.00

STEVENS, John. *Marathon Monks of Mount Hiel.* 1988. Boston. Shambhala. photos. 158p. VG. B33. $22.00

STEVENS, M. *Meet Mr Grizzly.* 1943. Albuquerque. 1st ed. VG. B5. $50.00

STEVENS, Reba Mahan. *Old Town Clock.* 1931. Lee Shepard. ils Florence Liley Young. VG. B17. $7.50

STEVENS, Shane. *By Reason of Insanity.* 1979. Simon Schuster. 1st ed. F/NF. F4. $30.00

STEVENS, Shane. *Dead City.* 1973. Holt. 1st ed. F/dj. F4. $50.00

STEVENS, Shane. *Go Down Dead.* 1966. Morrow. 1st ed/author's 1st novel. F/F. M15. $55.00

STEVENS, Wallace. *Auroras of Autumn.* 1950. Knopf. 1st ed. 8vo. 193p. gilt bl cloth. F/dj. H5. $300.00

STEVENS, Wallace. *Auroras of Autumn.* 1952. Knopf. 2nd prt. sgn. F/NF. V1. $45.00

STEVENS, Wallace. *Esthetique du Mal.* 1945. Cummington, MA. 1st ed. 1/300. blk quarter morocco/gr brd. NF. C6. $750.00

STEVENS, Wallace. *Mattino Domenicale.* 1954. Guilo Einaudi. sgn. NF/stiff wrp. V1. $55.00

STEVENS, Wallace. *Parts of a World.* 1942. Knopf. 1st ed. F/NF. Q1. $350.00

STEVENS, Wallace. *Parts of a World.* 1942. Knopf. 1st ed. sgn. NF/VG. V1. $225.00

STEVENS, Wallace. *Selected Poems.* 1953. London. Faber. 1st UK ed. F/NF. Q1. $125.00

STEVENS, William Oliver. *Charleston: Hist City of Gardens.* 1939. NY. 1st ed. 331p. xl. VG. B18. $9.50

STEVENSON, Adlai. *Adlai Stevenson's Veto 1949.* 1971. Amsterdam. 1/30 (of 250 total). 48x48mm. gilt brn leather. F. B24. $475.00

STEVENSON, Charles G. *But As Yesterday: Early Life & Times of St Ann's Church...* 1967. np. 1st ed. 169p. cloth. VG. M8. $27.50

STEVENSON, D. Alan. *World's Lighthouses Before 1820.* 1959. London. Oxford. 199 ils/7 maps. 310p. teg. dj. T7. $120.00

STEVENSON, D.E. *Shoulder the Sky.* 1951. Rinehart. 1st ed. 275p. VG/VG. M20. $12.00

STEVENSON, James. *No Need for Money.* 1987. Greenwillow. 1st ed. M/M. C8. $20.00

STEVENSON, Robert Louis. *Aes Triplex.* 1898. np. prt for US subscribers. 1st ed. 1/160. VG/wrp. C2. $100.00

STEVENSON, Robert Louis. *Amateur Emigrant & the Silverado Squatters.* 1991. London. Folio Soc. 1st ed. thus. M/case. A18. $35.00

STEVENSON, Robert Louis. *Child's Garden of Verses.* nd. Donohue. early ed. ils Myrtle Sheldon. NF/VG. C8. $30.00

STEVENSON, Robert Louis. *Child's Garden of Verses.* 1902. Rand McNally. 1st ed thus. ils E Mars/MH Squire. VG. M5. $15.00

STEVENSON, Robert Louis. *Child's Garden of Verses.* 1919. Rand McNally. ils Ruth Mary Hallock. 96p. VG+. M20. $60.00

STEVENSON, Robert Louis. *Child's Garden of Verses.* 1921. Phil. Altemus. lg 32mo. ils Hoppes. VG. C8. $25.00

STEVENSON, Robert Louis. *Child's Garden of Verses.* 1926. NY. Sears. 1st ed. ils Eva Noe. VG+. C8. $35.00

STEVENSON, Robert Louis. *Child's Garden of Verses.* 1940. Saalfield. ils FB Peat. pict brd. F/torn. M5. $65.00

STEVENSON, Robert Louis. *Child's Garden of Verses.* 1943. Saalfield #2925. ils FB Peat. VG+/pict wrp. C8. $30.00

STEVENSON, Robert Louis. *Child's Garden of Verses.* 1947. Henry Walck. ils Tasha Tudor. 118p. cloth. VG/VG. A3. $25.00

STEVENSON, Robert Louis. *Child's Garden of Verses.* 1947. Oxford. 1st ed. ils Tasha Tudor. F/VG. P2. $185.00

STEVENSON, Robert Louis. *Child's Garden of Verses.* 1947 (1945). Kenosha, WI. John Martin. ils Peter Mabie. NF/VG. C8. $25.00

STEVENSON, Robert Louis. *Child's Garden of Verses.* 1951. Golden Pr. ils Provensen. VG. B17. $10.00

STEVENSON, Robert Louis. *Child's Garden of Verses.* 1957. Grosset Dunlap. ils Gyo Fujikawa. VG+. C8. $25.00

STEVENSON, Robert Louis. *Child's Garden of Verses.* 1985. Childrens Classics. rpt. ils JW Smith. F/F. B17. $9.00

STEVENSON, Robert Louis. *Dr Jekyll & Mr Hyde.* 1923. Everleigh Nash/Grayson. VG/fair. P3. $35.00

STEVENSON, Robert Louis. *Essays in Art of Writing.* 1905. London. Chatto Windus. 1st ed. VG. Q1. $150.00

STEVENSON, Robert Louis. *Island Nights' Entertainments.* 1893. Cassell. 1st UK ed/1st issue (price correction in list). VG. Q1. $200.00

STEVENSON, Robert Louis. *Kidnapped.* 1941. Scribner Classic. later rpt. ils NC Wyeth. VG. B17. $40.00

STEVENSON, Robert Louis. *Master of Ballantrae.* 1911. London. Cassell. 8vo. ils Paget. VG. B17. $8.00

STEVENSON, Robert Louis. *Memories & Portraits.* 1908. London. 182p. vellum/cloth. B14. $95.00

STEVENSON, Robert Louis. *Silverado Squatters.* 1972. Osborne. rpt. F/wht paper dj. B19. $40.00

STEVENSON, Robert Louis. *Stevenson Song Book, Verses From a Child's Garden...* 1915 (1987). Scribner. VG. C8. $50.00

STEVENSON, Robert Louis. *Treasure Island.* 1933. Scribner. early rpt. ils Wyeth. pict blk cloth. VG. A3. $40.00

STEVENSON, Robert Louis. *Treasure of Franchard.* 1954. Emmaus, PA. ils. 4to. VG/worn slipcase. A17. $10.00

STEVENSON, Robert Louis. *Virginibus Puerisque.* nd. Putnam. Ariel Booklet Series. 102p. NF. H1. $16.00

STEVERS, Martin. *Steel Trails: The Epic of the Railroad.* 1933. Grosset. ils. VG. B34. $25.00

STEWARD, Edgar. *Custer's Luck.* 1955. Gilcrease Inst of Am. 2nd prt. VG/dj. B34. $45.00

STEWART, Anna Bird. *Two Young Corsicans: A Boy & His Colt.* 1944. Lippincott. 1st ed. 254p. VG/G. P2. $25.00

STEWART, Basil. *Subjects Portrayed in Japanese Colour-Prints.* 1922. London. Kegan Paul. 1st ed. folio. 382p. tan line/bl brd/blk morocco label. K1. $450.00

STEWART, Cal. *Uncle Josh Weatheby's Punkin Center Stories.* 1905. Chicago. 1st ed. VG. B5. $35.00

STEWART, D.J. *New Historical Atlas of Senaca Co, OH.* 1874. Phil. 55p. VG. M20. $200.00

STEWART, Desmond. *Arab World.* nd (1964). Netherlands. Time Life Internat. 160p. pict brd. VG. M7. $30.00

STEWART, Desmond. *Middle East: Temple of Janus.* 1971. Doubleday. 1st ed. 414p. cloth. VG. W1. $12.00

STEWART, Desmond. *TE Lawrence: A New Biography.* 1977. London. Hamish Hamilton. 1st ed. 352p. F/F. M7. $55.00

STEWART, Desmond. *TE Lawrence: A New Biography.* 1977. NY. 1st ed. 352p. F/F. M7. $35.00

STEWART, Dugald. *Elements of Philosophy of Human Mind. Second Vol.* 1818. NY. Eastburn. 420p. G. G1. $75.00

STEWART, Dugald. *Elements of Philosophy of the Human Mind.* 1822. Albany. Rosford. 2 vol in 1. worn sheep. G7. $75.00

STEWART, Dugald. *Works of...* 1829. Cambridge. Hilliard Brn. 7 vol. pebbled gr cloth. VG. G1. $575.00

STEWART, Fred Mustard. *Star Child.* 1974. Arbor. 1st ed. VG/VG. P3. $20.00

STEWART, George R. *California Trail.* 1962. McGraw Hill. 1st ed. F/clip. A18. $35.00

STEWART, George R. *California Trail.* 1962. McGraw Hill. 1st ed. ils/index. 339p. VG/dj. O8. $18.50

STEWART, George R. *California Trail: An Epic With Many Heroes.* 1983. NE U. 3rd sc prt. M. A18. $10.00

STEWART, George R. *Doctor's Oral.* 1939. Random. 1st ed. pict ep. F/dj. A18. $50.00

STEWART, Ian. *Peking Payoff.* 1975. Macmillan. 1st ed. F/F. P3. $15.00

STEWART, James Innes M. *Ampersand Papers.* 1978. Gollancz. 1st ed. F/F. P3. $20.00

STEWART, James Innes M. *Appleby File.* 1975. Gollancz. 1st ed. F/F. P3. $15.00

STEWART, James Innes M. *Bridge at Arta.* 1981. NY. Norton. 1st ed. F/VG. B3. $15.00

STEWART, James Innes M. *Carson's Conspiracy.* 1984. Gollancz. 1st ed. F/F. P3. $18.00

STEWART, James Innes M. *Christmas at Candleshoe.* 1953. Dodd Mead. 1st Am ed. VG/dj. M15. $25.00

STEWART, James Innes M. *Daffodil Affair.* 1942. Dodd Mead. 1st Am ed. F/VG. M15. $75.00

STEWART, James Innes M. *Gay Phoenix.* 1976. Gollancz. 1st ed. F/F. P3. $20.00

STEWART, James Innes M. *Honeybath's Haven.* 1977. Dodd Mead. 1st Am ed. F/F. M15. $30.00

STEWART, James Innes M. *Lament for a Maker.* 1938. Dodd Mead. 1st Am ed. NF/NF. M15. $100.00

STEWART, James Innes M. *Money From Home.* 1964. Gollancz. 1st ed. VG/VG. P3. $45.00

STEWART, James Innes M. *Secret Vanguard.* 1972. Gollancz. F/F. P3. $20.00

STEWART, James Innes M. *Sheiks & Adders.* 1982. Dodd Mead. 1st ed. F/F. P3. $15.00

STEWART, Janet Ann. *AZ Ranch Houses.* 1974. AZ Hist Soc. 1st ed. inscr. 121p. F/wrp. B19. $45.00

STEWART, Katie. *Pooh Cook Book.* 1971. London. Methuen. 1st Eng ed. ils Shepard. glazed pict brd. NF/NF. C8. $27.50

STEWART, Mary. *Gabriel Hounds.* 1967. Hodder Stoughton. 1st ed. VG/VG. P3. $30.00

STEWART, Mary. *Wicked Day.* 1983. Hodder Stoughton. 1st ed. F/F. P3. $20.00

STEWART, R.J. *Book of Merlin.* 1987. Blanford. 1st ed. F/F. P3. $25.00

STEWART, Roy. *Turner Ranch.* 1961. OK City. 1st ed. VG/VG. B5. $20.00

STEWART, Will; see Williamson, Jack.

STEWART, William Drummond. *Edward Warren.* 1986. Mtn Pr. 1st ed thus. M/dj. A18. $27.00

STEWART, William M. *Reminiscences of Senator Wm M Stewart of Nevada.* 1908. NY/WA. Neale. 1st ed. 358p. cloth. NF/dj. M8. $250.00

STEWART & STEWART. *I Have a Book.* 1940. NY. Stewart. 1st ed. ils. 63p. VG/dj. M10. $6.50

STICKLES, William. *Spirituals: Time-Honored Songs of the Negro People.* 1953. Chas H Hansen Music Co. Red Book ed. VG+/wrp. C8. $20.00

STIEGLITZ, Alfred. *Twice a Year. A Book of Literature, Arts & Civil Liberties.* Fall/Winter 1946-1947. photos. VG. S9. $45.00

STIER, Johann. *Praecepta Doctrinae Logicae, Ethicae, Physicae...* 1671. London. Redmayne. 7th ed. 6 parts in 1. 4to. calf/marbled brd. K1. $375.00

STILES, Henry Reed. *Bundling: Its Origin, Progress & Decline in America.* 1934. NY. Book Collectors Assn. 12mo. red brd. G. B11. $15.00

STILLMAN, Jacob D.B. *Around the Horn to California in 1849.* 1967. Lewis Osborne. 1st ltd/#d ed. ils. F. A18. $40.00

STILLWELL, M.B. *Incunabula & Americana 1450-1800...Bibliographical Study.* 1931. Columbia. 4to. 501p. NF. scarce. A4. $185.00

STILWELL, H. *Fishing in Mexico.* 1948. NY. 1st ed. VG/G. B5. $30.00

STIMSON, D. *Sarton on Hist of Science...* 1962. Cambridge. 383p. dj. G7. $30.00

STINE, G. Harry. *Man & Space Frontier.* 1962. Knopf. 8vo. ils Lewis Zacks. 149p. VG/VG. K5. $12.00

STIREWALT, Jerome Paul. *Brief Hist of Rader's Lutheran Church...to April 11, 1921.* 1922. New Market, VA. Henkel. 1st ed. 81p. cloth. NF. M8. $85.00

STIRLING, Matthew. *Indians of the Americas.* 1955. NGS. 1st ed. 431p. VG/dj. F3. $30.00

STIRLING, Walter Francis. *Safety Last.* Jan 1954. London. Hollis Carter. 4th imp. 251p. F/NF. M7. $45.00

STITES, Lord. *Intimate Acrobatics.* 1927. McBride. 1st ed. 208p. VG/VG. M20. $22.50

STITZEL, Mrs. H.V. *What Came of It.* 1878. George H Himes. 1st ed. 320p. gilt bl cloth. G. S11. $25.00

STIX, Thomas Howard. *Theory of Plasma Waves.* nd (1962). McGraw Hill. 8vo. 283p. VG/dj. K5. $30.00

STOBE, Donald B. *Faith Under Fire.* 1969. Word. 182p. VG/dj. B29. $4.00

STOCKTON, Bayard. *Phoenix With a Bayonet.* 1971. Ann Arbor. 8vo. ils. 306p. cloth. dj. O2. $20.00

STOCKTON, Frank R. *Griffin & the Minor Canon.* 1963. HRW. 1st ed. 56p. VG/G+. P2. $75.00

STOCKTON, Frank. *Ting Ling Tales.* 1882. Scribner. 1st ed thus. ils EB Bonsell. 187p. VG. P2. $65.00

STODDARD, Dwight L. *Steel Square Pocket Book.* 1917. McKay. 2nd ed. 24mo. 159p. G. H1. $7.50

STODDARD, H. *Bobwhite Quail.* 1936. NY. VG. B5. $80.00

STODDARD, John L. *Constantinople, Jerusalem, Egypt.* 1909. Boston. Balch. 334p. VG. W1. $20.00

STODDARD, John. *Remarks on Local Scenery & Manners in Scotland...1799-1800.* 1801. London. 2 vol. 32 aquatint pl/fld map. marbled brd. red leather. G. H3. $85.00

STODDARD, Lothrop. *New World of Islam.* 1922. Scribner. 362p. VG. W1. $12.00

STODDARD, W.O. *Little Smoke: Story of Sioux Indians.* 1892. Appleton. ils. 295p. gilt cloth. VG. B14. $40.00

STODDARD, W.O. *Long Bridge Boys.* 1904. Lothrop Lee Shepard. 1st ed. 344p. cloth. VG/tattered. M20. $12.50

STODDARD, Whitney S. *Monastery & Cathedral in France: Medieval Architecture...* 1966. Wesleyan. 1st ed. 4to. ils. 412p. VG/dj. M10. $35.00

STODDARD, William. *Sufism: Mystical Doctrines & Methods of Sufism.* 1976. NY. Weiser. 1st ed. 91p. VG/VG. B33. $15.00

STODDART, Anna M. *Elizabeth Pease Nichol.* 1899. London. Dent. 8vo. 314p. xl. fair. V3. $10.00

STOHLER, Betty J. *Kiss for the Desert.* 1978. Desert Prt. 1st ed. inscr. ils. 205p. F. A8. $25.00

STOIANOVICH, Traian. *Between East & West. Vol 2.* 1992. New Rochelle. 4to. ils/maps. 192p. cloth. dj. O2. $85.00

STOIKO, Michael. *Soviet Rocketry: Past, Present & Future.* 1970. HRW. 1st ed. 8vo. 272p. VG/dj. K5. $30.00

STOKELY, Edith Keeley. *Bubbleloon.* 1926. NY. Doran. 1st ed. ils Porter. VG. C8. $35.00

STOKER, Bram. *Dracula.* nd. Grosset Dunlap. photoplay ed. VG. P3. $50.00

STOKER, Bram. *Dracula: The Rare Text of 1901.* 1994. Transylvania Pr. 1st hc ed. 1/500. F/sans/case. T2. $65.00

STOKES, Donald. *Appointment With Fear.* 1950. Coward McCann. 1st ed. VG/G. P3. $18.00

STOKES, Hazel. *What Flower Is That?* 1969. Cape Town. ils. 78p. VG. B26. $11.00

STOKES, Michael C. *One & Many in Presocratic Philosophy.* 1971. WA, DC. 355p. yel cloth. F. G1. $28.50

STOKESBURY, James L. *Short Hist of Air Power.* 1986. London. 313p. VG+/dj. B18. $25.00

STOLBERG, Benjamin. *Tailor's Progress: Story of a Famous Union...* 1944. NY. Doubleday Doran. photos. VG/fair. V4. $10.00

STOLBERG, Doris. *Look Who I Am!* 1952. NY. novelty doll dresses by turning p. sbdg. VG+. M5. $60.00

STOLBOV, Bruce. *Last Fall.* 1987. Doubleday. 1st ed. F/F. P3. $13.00

STOLZ, Mary. *Belling the Tiger.* 1961. Harper. ARC. ils Beni Montresor. 64p. F/NF. P2. $45.00

STOMMEL, Henry. *Gulf Stream.* 1958. CA U. 82 figures/tables/graphs. 202p. dj. T7. $24.00

STONE, David. *Yank Brown, Pitcher.* 1924. Barse Hopkins. 1st ed? VG/G. P8. $60.00

STONE, E.M. *History of Beverly.* 1843. Boston. 1st ed. cloth. VG. A9. $50.00

STONE, Hampton. *Babe With the Twistable Arm.* 1962. Simon Schuster. 1st ed. F/VG. F4. $8.00

STONE, Hampton. *Kid Who Came Home With a Corpse.* 1972. Simon Schuster. 1st ed. VG/VG. P3. $15.00

STONE, Herbert Stuart. *First Editions of American Authors.* 1893. Cambridge. Stone Kimball. Lg Paper ed. 1/50. sgn pub. 224p. lavender cloth. K1. $450.00

STONE, I.F. *Trial of Socrates.* 1988. Little Brn. M11. $25.00

STONE, Irving. *Love Is Eternal.* 1954. Doubleday. 1st ed. 468p. VG/VG. M20. $15.00

STONE, Irving. *They Also Ran.* 1944 (1943). Doubleday Doran. 389p. VG/dj. M20. $25.00

STONE, Josephine Rector. *Green Is for Galanx.* 1980. Atheneum. 1st ed. RS. VG/VG. P3. $18.00

STONE, Leslie F. *Out of the Void.* 1967. Avalon. 1st ed. F/dj. M2. $20.00

STONE, R.H. *Aviation Stories for Boys.* 1936. Cupples Leon. 1st ed. 836p. VG/tattered. M10. $18.00

STONE, R.W. *Pennsylvania Caves.* 1932. Harrisburg. 143p. G/wrp. H7. $20.00

STONE, Robert. *Children of Light.* 1986. Knopf. ARC. inscr. RS. w/photo & promo material. F/F. B4. $100.00

STONE, Robert. *Children of Light.* 1986. Knopf. 1st ed. 8vo. 258p. purple cloth/bl brd. F/dj. H5. $75.00

STONE, Robert. *Children of Light.* 1986. Knopf. 1st ed. rem mk. NF/F. B3. $50.00

STONE, Robert. *Children of Light.* 1986. London. Deutsch. true 1st ed/author's 4th novel. F/F. L3. $125.00

STONE, Robert. *Outerbridge Reach.* 1992. Franklin Lib. true 1st ed. sgn. aeg. leather. F. L3. $200.00

STONE, Robert. *Outerbridge Reach.* 1992. Tichnor Fields. 1st ed. sgn. F/F. B2. $45.00

STONE, Stuart. *Kingdom of Why.* 1913. Bobbs Merrill. probable 1st ed. ils Peter Newell. 275p. G. Scarce. P2. $85.00

STONE, Ted. *13 Canadian Ghost Stories.* 1988. Prairie Books. 1st ed. F/F. P3. $20.00

STONE, Wilbur Macey. *Divine & Moral Songs of Isaac Watts...* 1918. Triptych. 1/250. w/prospectus & 4p typescript. H10. $145.00

STONE, Wilbur Macey. *Gigantick Histories of Thomas Boreman.* 1933. Portland, ME. Southworth. 1/250. sgn. cloth/marbled brd. F. B24. $225.00

STONE, Wilbur Macey. *Snuff-Boxful of Bibles.* 1926. Newark. Carteret BC. 1/200. 12mo. ils. 99p. cloth/label. F. B24. $225.00

STONE, Wilbur Macey. *Some Children's Book-Plates.* 1901. Bros of the Book. 1/350. gray brd. VG+. M5. $125.00

STONE, Wilbur Macey. *Thumb Bible of John Taylor.* 1928. Brookline. The LXIVMOS. 1/100. 12mo. 9 ils. 68p. 2 ES. cloth. F. B24. $250.00

STONE, William S. *Ship of Flame. Saga of the South Seas.* 1945. Knopf. 1st ed. inscr/dtd 1959. 164p. VG/chip. P4. $75.00

STONEHOUSE, Bernard. *North Pole. South Pole. A Guide to Ecology & Resources...* 1990. London. Prion. 1st ed. 216p. photo ep. M/M. P4. $35.00

STONELEY, Peter. *Mark Twain & the Feminine Aesthetic.* 1992. Cambridge. 205p. F/dj. M10. $18.50

STONERIDGE, M.A. *Horse of Your Own.* 1968. Doubleday. revised ed/3rd prt. 508p. NF. H1. $16.00

STONG, Phil. *High Water.* 1937. Dodd Mead. 1st ed. ils Kurt Wiese. 78p. VG. P2. $45.00

STONG, Phil. *Young Settler.* 1938. Dodd Mead. 1st ed. ils Kurt Wiese. VG. M5. $38.00

STORKE, Thomas M. *California Editor.* 1958. Los Angeles. Westernlore. 489p. brn cloth. VG/worn. P4. $20.00

STORM, Hyemeyohsts. *Seven Arrows.* 1972. Harper. 1st ed. NF/F. B2. $75.00

STORRING, Gustav. *Die Erkenntnistheorie von Tetens...* 1901. Leipzig. Wilhelm Engelmann. inscr. later gr linen. G. G1. $50.00

STORRS, Ronald. *Lawrence of Arabia.* June 1940. Penguin. 1st prt. 96p. VG. M7. $45.00

STORRS, Ronald. *Orientations.* 1939. Readers Union. 558p. VG. M7. $19.50

STORY, Jack Trevor. *Mix Me a Person.* 1960. Macmillan. 1st ed. VG/VG. P3. $25.00

STORY, Joseph. *Commentaries on Laws of Bills of Exchange, Foreign & Inland.* 1843. London. A Maxwel. emb cloth/rebacked. M11. $650.00

STOTT, John. *What Christ Thinks of the Church.* 1990. Harold Shaw. 127p. F/dj. B29. $7.50

STOTTER, James. *Beauty Unmasked.* 1936. NY. 1st ed. 141p. A13. $45.00

STOUGHTON. *Books of CA: Intro to Hist & Heritage...* 1968. np. ils. 270p. F/F. A4. $55.00

STOUT, Peter. *Nicaragua: Past, Present & Future...* 1859. Phil. John Potter. 1st ed. 372p. rebound. xl. F3. $35.00

STOUT, Rex. *Death of a Doxy.* 1966. Viking. 1st ed. VG/VG. P3. $50.00

STOUT, Rex. *Doorbell Rang.* 1965. Viking. 1st ed. VG/G+. P3. $40.00

STOUT, Rex. *Double for Death.* 1939. Farrar Rinehart. 1st ed. VG/VG. M15. $125.00

STOUT, Rex. *Mother Hunt.* 1963. Viking. 1st ed. VG. P3. $20.00

STOUT, Rex. *Mountain Cat.* 1939. Farrar. 1st ed. xl. VG. B2. $25.00

STOUT, Rex. *Plot It Yourself.* 1959. Viking. 1st ed. F/F. M15. $140.00

STOUT, Rex. *Prisoner's Base.* 1952. Viking. 1st ed. 8vo. 186p. blk stp gr brd. NF/clip. H5. $150.00

STOUT, Rex. *Right To Die.* 1964. Viking. 1st ed. VG/G. P3. $40.00

STOUT, Rex. *Silent Speaker.* 1946. Viking. 1st ed. F/NF. S9. $150.00

STOUT, Rex. *Silent Speaker.* 1946. Viking. 1st ed. VG/VG. M15. $85.00

STOUT, Rex. *Three Men out.* 1953. Viking. BC. VG/G. P8. $15.00

STOVER, Ron. *Alice in Wonderland.* 1983. Honey Bear Giant Pop-Up Book. VG. P3. $10.00

STOW, Marietta Lois. *Probate Chaff; or, Beautiful Probate...* 1879. np. self pub. gilt pict brn cloth. NF. M11. $175.00

STOWE, Harriet Beecher. *Men of Our Times; or, Leading Patriots of the Day...* 1868. Hartford. salesman's sample. 18 portraits. 3 bdg styles in 1. M1. $200.00

STOWE, Harriet Beecher. *My Wife & I; or, Harry Henderson's History.* 1871. NY. Ford. 1st ed. ils. 474p. G. H1. $9.00

STOWE, Harriet Beecher. *Pink & White Tyranny.* 1871. Roberts. 1st ed. 331p. brn cloth. G+. M20. $60.00

STOWE, Harriet Beecher. *Uncle Tom's Cabin.* ca 1915. Donohue. Young Folks ed. F. H1. $30.00

STOWE, Harriet Beecher. *Uncle Tom's Cabin; or, Life Among the Lowly.* 1879. Boston. Houghton Osgood. new ed. inscr. 529p. pict gray-brn cloth. NF/box. C6. $1,100.00

STRACHAN. *Artist & the Book in France, 20th-Century Livre d'Artiste.* 1969. London. 4to. 181 pl. 368p. F/F. A4. $125.00

STRACHEY, Lytton. *Queen Victoria.* 1921. Harcourt Brace. 434p. VG. H1. $8.00

STRACHEY, Marjorie. *Nightingale.* nd (1925). Longman Gr. 305p. G. H1. $5.00

STRACZYNSKI, J. Michael. *Demon Night.* 1988. Dutton. 1st ed. F/F. N3. $20.00

STRAHAN, Kay Cleaver. *Footprints.* 1929. Crime Club. 1st ed. G+. P3. $20.00

STRAIGHT, Susan. *I Been in Sorrow's Kitchen & Licked Out All the Pots.* 1992. NY. 1st ed. inscr. F/F. A11. $45.00

STRAND, Paul. *Retrospective Monograph of Years 1915-1946 & 1950-1968.* 1972. NY. Aperture. 2 vol. 4to. blk stp tan cloth. NF/dj. F1. $175.00

STRANDNESS, T.B. *Samuel Sewall: Puritan Portrait.* 1967. MI State. 234p. cloth. VG/dj. A10. $15.00

STRANG, Mrs. Herbert. *What Baby Reads.* nd. Hodder Stoughton. 12mo. ils Millicent Sowerby. 32p. VG. D6. $40.00

STRANG, Ruth. *Counseling Technics in College & Secondary Schools.* 1946. Harper. 248p. G/dj. K4. $10.00

STRANGE, John Stephen. *Strangler Fig.* 1930. Doubleday Crime Club. 1st ed. F/NF. M15. $75.00

STRANGE, John Stephen. *Strangler Fig.* 1930. Doubleday Crime Club. 1st ed. VG. P3. $30.00

STRASBERG, Lee. *At the Actors' Studio.* 1965. NY. 1st ed. VG/VG. B5. $30.00

STRATTON, William. *Incidents in Montana, Old Vintage.* 1954. Pageant. 1st ed. VG/torn. B34. $22.50

STRAUB, Peter. *Floating Dragon.* 1983. Collins. 1st ed. F/F. P3. $35.00

STRAUB, Peter. *Ghost Story.* 1979. CMG. 1st ed. VG/VG. P3. $45.00

STRAUB, Peter. *Houses Without Doors.* 1990. Dutton. 1st ed. F/F. M2/P3. $20.00

STRAUB, Peter. *Mystery.* 1990. Dutton. 1st ed. sgn. F/F. F4. $35.00

STRAUS, Edwin. *Phenomenology of Memory.* 1970. Duquesne. sm 8vo. 206p. gr cloth. VG/dj. G1. $32.50

STRAUSS, Leon. *Natural Right & Hist.* 1953. Chicago. 327p. xl. VG. D3. $12.50

STRAUSS, Theodore. *Moonrise.* 1946. Viking. 1st ed. F/NF. B2. $20.00

STRAWSON, P.F. *Individuals: Essay in Descriptive Metaphysics.* 1959. London. Methuen. 256p. gr cloth. VG/dj. G1. $75.00

STREATFEILD, Noel. *Circus Shoes.* 1939. NY. Random. Ils Richard Floethe. VG+. C8. $22.50

STREATFIELD, F.N. *Sporting Recollections of an Old'Un.* 1913. London. 1st ed. VG. C11. $100.00

STREBEIGH, Barbara. *Pet Airedale Terrier.* 1963. Fond du Lac, WI. 1st ed. sgn. 94p. VG+. R2. $25.00

STREET, Donald M. Jr. *Cruising Guide to the Lesser Antilles.* 1966. Dodd Mead. 1st ed. 8vo. 242p. G/G. B11. $20.00

STREET, George Edmund. *Some Account of Gothic Architecture in Spain.* 1914. London. Dent. 2 vol. index/ils. H10. $45.00

STREET, James. *Gauntlet.* 1945. Doubleday. 1st ed. VG/VG. P3. $13.00

STREETER, Daniel W. *Camels!* 1927. Putnam. 1st ed. 31 pl. VG. W1. $12.00

STRETE, Craig. *Death Chants.* 1988. Doubleday. 1st ed. VG/VG. P3. $20.00

STRETE, Craig. *If All Else Fails.* 1980. Doubleday SF. 1st ed. VG/G. B3. $15.00

STRETTELL & SYLVA. *Legends From River & Mountain.* 1896. London. Allen. ils TH Robinson. 328p. teal-bl cloth. VG. D6. $45.00

STRIBLING, T.S. *Sound Wagon.* 1935. Garden City. 1st ed. sgn. 1/250. VG+/VG+. A11. $55.00

STRICKER, Thomas P. *Calendar of the Francis Bret Harte Letters...* 1942. CA Hist Records Project. 1st ed. w/pres letter. sc. F. A18. $50.00

STRICKLAND, W.P. *Pioneers of the West.* 1856. np. 403p. VG. E5. $65.00

STRIEBER, Whitley. *Billy.* 1990. Putnam. 1st ed. sgn. F/F. T2. $25.00

STRIEBER, Whitley. *Black Magic.* 1982. Morrow. 1st ed. F/F. T2. $45.00

STRIEBER, Whitley. *Cat Magic.* 1986. Tor. 1st ed. F/F. T2. $15.00

STRIEBER, Whitley. *Hunger.* 1981. Morrow. 1st ed. sgn. F/dj. F4. $40.00

STRIEBER, Whitley. *Hunger.* 1981. Morrow. 1st ed/author's 2nd novel. F/F. B3. $15.00

STRIEBER, Whitley. *Majestic.* 1989. Putnam. 1st ed. F/F. P3. $19.00

STRIEBER, Whitley. *Majestic.* 1989. Putnam. 1st ed. NF/VG. B3. $15.00

STRIEBER, Whitley. *Night Church.* 1983. Simon Schuster. 1st ed. sgn. F/dj. F4. $40.00

STRIEBER, Whitley. *Transformation: The Breakthrough.* 1988. Morrow. 1st ed. VG. P3. $19.00

STRIEBER, Whitley. *Wolfen.* 1978. Morrow. 1st ed. F/F. T2. $60.00

STRIKER, Fran. *Lone Ranger & the Gold Robbery (#3).* 1939. Grosset Dunlap. lists to #7. VG/ragged. M20. $35.00

STRIKER, Fran. *Lone Ranger & the Outlaw Stronghold (#4).* 1939. Grosset Dunlap. 1st ed. lists 3 titles. 214p. cloth. VG/dj. M20. $40.00

STRIKER, Fran. *Lone Ranger Rides & the Outlaw Stronghold.* 1939. Grosset Dunlap. F/VG+. C8. $20.00

STRIKER, Fran. *Lone Ranger Rides Again (#8).* 1943. Grosset Dunlap. thick ed. lists to this title only. 214p. VG/dj. M20. $35.00

STRIKER, Fran. *Lone Ranger Rides at the Haunted Gulch.* 1941. Grosset Dunlap. F/G+. C8. $20.00

STRIKER, Fran. *Lone Ranger Rides North.* 1946. Grosset Dunlap. F/VG. C8. $20.00

STRIKER, Fran. *Lone Ranger Traps the Smugglers (#7).* 1941. Grosset Dunlap. 1st ed. 214p. VG/dj. M20. $45.00

STRIKER, Fran. *Lone Ranger.* 1938. Grosset Dunlap. VG/G+. C8. $15.00

STRIKER, Fran. *Lone Ranger: Mystery Ranch.* 1938. Grosset Dunlap. NF/NF. C8. $15.00

STRIKER, Fran. *Mystery of the Timber Giant.* 1955. Clover. VG. p3. $8.00

STRINDBERG, August. *Getting Married.* 1972. NY. 1st ed in Eng. 384p. F/F. A17. $17.50

STRODE, Hudson. *Jefferson Davis: American Patriot 1808-1861.* 1955. Harcourt Brace. 1st ed. 8vo. G/G. B11. $20.00

STROMHOLM, Stig. *Legal Science Today.* 1978. Uppsala. 71p. NF/wrp. D3. $12.50

STRONG, Anna Louise. *Chinese Conquer China.* 1949. Girard. Haldeman Julius. 1st ed thus. inscr. VG+. B2. $65.00

STRONG, Anna Louise. *New Lithuania.* 1941. Workers Lib. 1st ed. F/wrp. B2. $45.00

STRONG, Charles. *Story of American Sailing Ships.* 1957. Grosset Dunlap. ils Gordon Grant/HB Vestal. VG/VG. B17. $5.00

STRONG, Edward K. *Vocational Interests of Men & Women.* 1945. London. Oxford. 716p. G. K4. $40.00

STRONG, Kendrick. *All the Master's Men: Patterns for Modern Discipleship.* 1978. Christian Herald. 220p. VG/dj. B29. $4.00

STRONG, L.A.G. *All Fall Down.* 1944. Doubleday Crime Club. 1st Am ed. F/NF. M15. $45.00

STRONG, L.A.G. *All Fall Down.* 1944. Doubleday Crime Club. 1st ed. VG. P3. $18.00

STRONG, Leah A. *Joseph Hopkins Twichell, Mark Twain's Friend & Pastor.* 1966. GA U. 182p. VG. M10. $15.00

STRONG, Nathan. *Hartford Selection of Hymns...* 1802. Hartford. Cooke. 2nd ed. 24mo. 357p. leather. H10. $45.00

STROUD, Carsten. *Sniper's Moon.* 1990. Bantam. 1st ed. VG/VG. P3. $19.00

STROUD, Robert. *Diseases of Canaries.* 1933. KS City. Canary Pub. 1st ed. F/sans. scarce. B4. $225.00

STROUP, Thomas B. *Humanities & Understanding of Reality.* 1966. Lexington. thin 8vo. 84p. red cloth. VG/dj. G1. $25.00

STRUCHEN, Jeanette. *What Do I Do Now, Lord?* 1971. Revell. 120p. VG/dj. B29. $2.75

STRUGATSKY & STRUGATSKY. *Definitely Maybe.* 1978. Macmillan. 1st ed. F/F. P3. $20.00

STRUGATSKY & STRUGATSKY. *Hard To Be a God.* 1973. Seabury. 1st ed. VG/VG. P3. $25.00

STRUIK, Dirk. *Yankee Science in the Making.* 1948. Little Brn. 430p. cloth. VG. A10. $20.00

STRYK, Samuel. *Examen Juris Feudalis...* 1716. Francofurti. German/Latin text. 32mo. 530p. contemporary vellum. G. D3. $350.00

STUART, Anthony. *Russian Leave.* 1981. Arbor. 1st ed. VG/VG. P3. $15.00

STUART, Gene. *Mighty Aztecs.* 1981. NGS. 1st ed. 8vo. ils. VG/VG. B11. $10.00

STUART, Gordon. *Boy Scouts of the Air in the Northern Wilds.* 1912. Chicago. 1st ed. ils Norman P Hall. pict cloth. VG. A17. $12.50

STUART, Graham H. *Internat City of Tangier.* 1955. Stanford. 2nd ed. sgn. 270p. VG. W1. $12.00

STUART, James. *Three Years in North America.* 1833. Edinburgh. Cadell. 2 vol. 2nd ed. half leather/marbled brd. G+. P4. $85.00

STUART, Jesse. *Man With the Bull-Tongue Plow.* 1934. NY. 1st ed. NF/worn. C2. $375.00

STUART, Jesse. *Seven by Jessie.* 1970. Terre Haute. IN Council of Teachers of Eng/ISU. F/wrp. B2. $50.00

STUART, Jesse. *World of Jesse Stuart: Selected Poems.* 1975. NY. 1st ed. F/NF clip. C2. $50.00

STUART, Sidney; see Avallone, Michael.

STUART, William L. *Dead Lie Still.* 1945. Farrar Rinehart. 1st ed. xl. dj. P3. $10.00

STUART & STUART. *Calvin B West of the Umpqua.* 1961. Stockton. 1/250. 115p. gilt beige cloth. F. P4. $125.00

STUBBS, Jean. *Dear Laura.* 1973. Macmillan. 1st ed. VG/fair. P3. $13.00

STUBBS, Stanley A. *Bird's-Eye-View of the Pueblos.* 1950. OK U. 1st ed. 122p. F/VG. B19. $50.00

STUCK, Hudson. *Voyages on the Yukon & Its Tributaries...Alaska.* 1917. Scribner. 8vo. 397p. bl cloth. VG. P4. $195.00

STUCKEY & STUCKEY. *Lithographs of Stow Wengenroth 1931-1972.* 1974. np. VG/VG. M17. $70.00

STUKELEY, William. *Itinerarium Curiosum; or, Account of Antiquities...* 1776. London. 2 vol in 1. 2nd ed. folio. 206 full-p pl/fld map. C6. $500.00

STURGEON, Theodore. *Godbody.* 1986. Donald Fine. 1st ed. VG/VG. P3. $20.00

STURGEON, Theodore. *Player on the Other Side (as by Ellery Queen).* 1963. Random. 1st ed. NF/VG clip. w/sgn card. F4. $40.00

STURGEON, Theodore. *Without Sorcery.* 1948. Prime. 1st ed. F/NF. M2. $80.00

STURUP, G. *Treating the Untreatable.* 1968. Baltimore. 266p. VG. D3. $12.50

STYKER, Lloyd. *Courts & Doctors.* 1932. NY. 1st ed. 236p. A13. $40.00

STYRON, William. *Darkness Visible. Memoir of Madness.* 1990. NY. 1st ed. sgn. F/NF. A11. $40.00

STYRON, William. *Inheritance of Night.* 1933. Durham/London. Duke. 1st trade ed. 4to. 139p. red cloth. F/dj. C6. $20.00

STYRON, William. *La Proie des Flammes.* 1962. Paris. Gallimard. 1/4100. La Collection Soleil Series. S9. $45.00

STYRON, William. *Lie Down in Darkness.* 1951. Indianapolis. 1st ed/author's 1st book. VG/VG+. A1. $250.00

STYRON, William. *Quiet Dust & Other Writings.* 1982. Random. VG/dj. N2. $5.00

STYRON, William. *Set This House on Fire.* 1960. Random. 1st ed. 8vo. 507p. red/gilt/gray stp blk cloth. F/NF. H5. $75.00

STYRON, William. *Set This House on Fire.* 1960. Random. 1st ed. 8vo. 507p. blk cloth. VG/dj. C6. $40.00

STYRON, William. *Set This House on Fire.* 1961. London. Hamish Hamilton. 1st ed. F/NF clip. L3. $85.00

STYRON, William. *Sophie's Choice.* 1979. London. Cape. 1st ed. VG/VG. B3. $30.00

STYRON, William. *Tidewater Morning.* 1993. NY. Random. 1st ed. F/F. B4. $35.00

SUBIK, Rudolf. *Cacti & Succulents.* 1985 (1968). London. 96 full-p pl. 266p. F. B26. $11.00

SUBLETT, Jessee. *Boiled in Concrete.* 1992. NY. Viking. ARC/1st ed. sgn. RS. F/F. S6. $35.00

SUCHARITKUL, Somtow. *Moon Dance.* 1989. Tor. 1st ed. F/F. P3. $25.00

SUCHARITKUL, Somtow. *Shattered Horse.* 1986. NY. Tor. 1st ed. F/F. N3. $15.00

SUCHARITKUL, Somtow. *Vampire Junction.* 1984. Donning Starblaze. 1st ed. F/dj. F4. $45.00

SUCHER, Jaime J. *Shetland Sheepdogs.* 1990. NY. Barrons. 1st ed. ils. 79p. M/wrp. R2. $8.00

SUDEK, Josef. *Photographie der Moderne in Prag 1900-1925.* 1991. Frankfurt. German text. photos. F/F. S9. $40.00

SUDEK, Josef. *Sudek.* 1978. NY. Potter. 1st ed 4to. F/F. S9. $250.00

SUDWORTH, George B. *Poplars, Principal Tree Willows & Walnuts...* 1934. WA, DC. ils. 112p. wrp. scarce. B26. $17.50

SUGARMAN, Sidney. *Garland of Legends.* 1992. Eng. 1st ed. gilt maroon cloth. M. w/pub prospectus. M7. $35.00

SUGDEN. *Tecumseh's Last Stand: Old Northwest Territory.* 1985. np. ils/maps. 300+p. NF. E5. $36.00

SULEIMAN, Ezra N. *Private Power & Centralization in France...* 1987. Princeton U. M11. $17.50

SULEIMAN, Hamid. *Miniatures of Babur-Namah.* 1978. Tashkent. Uzbek/Russian/Eng text. folio. 96 pl. NF/torn. W1. $65.00

SULLIVAN, Alan. *In the Beginning.* 1927. Dutton. 1st Am ed. VG. M2. $20.00

SULLIVAN, Edward. *Book of Kells.* 1933. NY. 24 tipped-in pl. VG/VG. B5. $90.00

SULLIVAN, Edward. *Chaplin Vs Chaplin.* 1965. Hollywood, CA. 1st ed. thick 12mo. VG/wrp. D3. $25.00

SULLIVAN, Louis H. *Kindergarten Chats on Architecture, Education & Democracy.* 1934. Scarab Fraternity Pr. 1st ed. 8vo. 256p. VG+/dj. F1. $350.00

SULLIVAN, Robert R. *Political Hermeneutics: Early Thinking Hans-Georg Gadamer.* 1989. PA State. 206p. gray cloth. G1. $22.50

SULLIVAN, Walter. *Quest for a Continent.* 1957. NY. 372p. F/worn. A17. $12.00

SULLIVAN. *GK Chesterton: A Bibliography.* 1958. U London. ils. 215p. VG/VG. A4. $175.00

SULLOWAY, Frank J. *Freud: Biologist of the Mind.* 1979. Basic. 503p. M/dj. K4. $15.00

SULLY, James. *Human Mind: TB of Psychology.* 1892. London. Longman G.r 2 vol. 1st ed/2nd issue. emb brn cloth. G1. $100.00

SULZBERGER, C.L. *Tooth Merchant.* 1973. Quadrangle. 1st ed. G+/dj. P3. $10.00

SUMMERS, Alex. *Brand Book in Number Five: San Diego Corral of Westerners...* 1978. San Diego. 1/450. 206p. F/F case. B19. $75.00

SUMMERS, Ian. *Tomorrow & Tomorrow.* 1978. Workman. 1st ed. NF/NF. P3. $25.00

SUMMERS, Montague. *Geography of Witchcraft.* 1958. U Books. VG. P3. $15.00

SUMMERS, Montague. *Gothic Quest.* nd. London. Fortune. 1/910. VG. B2. $125.00

SUMNER, William Graham. *Earth-Hunger & Other Essays.* 1914. Yale. 2nd prt. 377p. VG. D3. $25.00

SUNDMAN, Per Olof. *Flight of the Eagle.* 1970. NY. 1st Am ed. trans Mary Sandbach. VG/dj. B18. $15.00

SUNSET BOOKS. *Crochet Techniques & Projects.* 1975. np. VG/wrp. G2. $4.95

SUPREE, Burton. *Bear's Heart, Scenes From the Life of a Cheyenne Artist...* 1977. Lippincott. 1st ed. 8vo. F/G. B17. $25.00

SURBURG, Raymond. *Intro to the intertestamental Period.* 1975. Concordia. 197p. VG/dj. B29. $6.50

SURING & WEGENER. *Moedebeck/ Taschenbuch fur Flugtechniker und Luftschiffer.* 1923. Berlin. 4th revised ed. 920p. G+. B18. $75.00

SURREY, Stanley S. *Pathways to Tax Reform: Concept of Tax Expenditures.* 1973. Cambridge. Harvard. M11. $35.00

SUSKIND, Patrick. *Perfume: Story of a Murderer.* 1986. Knopf. 1st Am ed. trans JE Woods. F/F. T2. $35.00

SUSKIND, Patrick. *Pigeon.* 1988. Knopf. 1st Am ed. F/F. T2. $15.00

SUTCLIFF, Rosemary. *Little Dog Like You.* 1987. London. Orchard. 1st ed. ils. 46p. cloth. M. R2. $25.00

SUTCLIFF, Rosemary. *Sword & the Circle.* 1981. Bodley Head. 1st ed. F/F. P3. $20.00

SUTCLIFFE, Edmund F. *Old Testament & the Future Life.* 1949. London. Burns Oates. 201p. xl. H10. $12.50

SUTERMEISTER, Edwin. *Story of Papermaking.* 1954. Boston. 100th-Anniversary SD Warren Co. 209p. VG+. B18. $17.50

SUTHERLAND, Douglas. *Mad Hatters: Great Sporting Eccentrics of 19th Century.* 1987. London. Robert Hall. 1st ed. F/F. O3. $35.00

SUTHERLAND, Lane V. *Obscenity: The Court, the Congress & President's Commission.* 1975. WA, DC. 127p. NF/wrp. D3. $15.00

SUTIN, Lawrence. *In Persuit of Valis: Selections From the Exegesis.* 1991. Underwood Miller. 1st ed. F/F. T2. $40.00

SUTTON, Adah L. *Mr Bunny: His Book.* 1900. Saalfield. 4to. 110p. VG. D6. $95.00

SUTTON, George Miksch. *Eskimo Year: Naturalist's Adventures in Far North.* 1934. Macmillan. 1st ed. pres. 321p. VG/fair. H1. $42.50

SUTTON, George P. *Rocket Propulsion Elements: Intro to Engineering Rockets.* 1963. Wiley. 3rd ed. 464p. F/VG. H1. $12.00

SUTTON, George. *Mexican Birds.* 1951. Norman. 1st ed. 282p. xl. VG/dj. F3. $15.00

SUTTON, H. Eldon. *Intro to Human Genetics.* 1965. NY. HRW. 252p. F. K4. $15.00

SUTTON, Henry. *Vector.* 1970. Bernard Geis. 2nd ed. VG/VG. P3. $10.00

SUTTON, Margaret. *Haunted Road.* 1954. Grosset Dunlap. Judy Bolton #25. lists to Hidden Clue. VG. M20. $60.00

SUTTON, Margaret. *Living Portrait.* 1947. Grosset Dunlap. 1st ed. Judy Bolton #18. lists 17 titles. VG/dj. M20. $25.00

SUTTON, Willie. *Where the Money Was.* 1976. Viking. 1st ed. VG/VG. P3. $20.00

SUVAK. *Memoirs of Am Prisons: Annotated Bibliography.* 1979. np. 235p. F. A4. $45.00

SUZUKI, D.T. *Miscellany on Shin Teaching of Buddhism.* 1949. Kyot. 1st ed. 151p. VG/VG. B33. $50.00

SUZUKI, D.T. *Mysticism: Christian & Buddhist.* 1957. Harper. World Perspective Series. 214p. VG/VG. B33. $35.00

SVERIN, Timothy. *Tracking Marco Polo.* 1964. London. author's 1st book. VG/VG. M17. $35.00

SWADESH, Morris. *Origin & Diversification of Language.* 1971. Chicago. Aldine Atherton. 330p. F/dj. K4. $15.00

SWAIN, Henry. *Civics for MT Students.* 1912. Scott Foresman. not xl. G. B34. $40.00

SWALLOW, Alan. *Wild Bunch.* 1966. Sage Books. 1st ed. F/dj. A18. $50.00

SWAN, Gladys. *On the Edge of the Desert.* 1979. Urbana, IL. 1st ed/author's 1st book. sgn. F/wrp. A11. $40.00

SWAN, Hoard. *Music in the SW: 1825-1950.* 1952. Huntington Lib. 1st ed. ils/notes/ index. 316p. F/dj. B19. $45.00

SWAN, Joseph R. *Treatise on Law Relating to Powers & Duties of Justices...* 1837. Columbus, OH. Isaac N Whiting. 1st ed. full sheep. M11. $450.00

SWANBERTG, W. *Rector & the Rogue.* 1968. NY. ils. 168p. NF. D3. $12.50

SWANN, Barbara Beaumont. *Versitile Border Collie.* 1988. Great Britain. Nimorod. 1st ed. 168p. M/wrp. R2. $25.00

SWANN, Francis. *Brass Key.* 1964. Simon Schuster. 1st ed. VG/VG. P3. $20.00

SWANSON, Logan; see Matheson, Richard.

SWANSON, Neil H. *Unconquered.* 1947. Doubleday. 1st ed. VG/G. P3. $15.00

SWANSON, Walter S.J. *Deepwood.* 1981. Little Brn. 1st ed. 323p. VG/VG. M20. $15.00

SWANWICK, Michael. *Gravity's Angels.* 1991. Arkham. 1st ed. F/F. P3/T2. $22.00

SWANWICK, Michael. *Griffin's Egg.* 1991. Legend. 1st ed. F/F. P3. $25.00

SWARBRECK, S.D. *Sketches in Scotland.* 1839. London. 1st ed. elephant folio. gr cloth/morocco back. VG. C6. $500.00

SWARTZBAUGH, Constance H. *Episcopal Church in Fulton Co, IL 1835-1959.* 1959. Canton, IL. 1st ed. 187p. NF. M8. $37.50

SWAW, Frank S.; see Goulart, Ron.

SWEDENBORG, Emanuel. *Christian Religion, Containing Universal Theology...* 1856. NY. trans from Latin. 8vo. 576p. VG. B14. $175.00

SWEDENBORG, Emanuel. *Doctrine of Life for the New Jerusalem.* 1913. London. Swedenborg. 74p. VG. B33. $14.00

SWEDENBORG, Emanuel. *Swedenborg's Works.* ca 1930. Houghton Mifflin. 32 vol. 8vo. teg. gilt bl cloth. K1. $500.00

SWEENEY, J. Gray. *Masterpieces of Western American Art.* 1991. Mallard. 239 ils. M/M. B34. $40.00

SWEENEY, James B. *Pictorial History of Oceanographic Submersibles.* 1971. NY. Crown. ils. 308p. dj. T7. $30.00

SWEENEY, James J. *Joan Miro.* 1941. MOMA. 1st ed. 87 p. paper brd. VG. A17. $20.00

SWEENEY, James J. *Three Young Rats & Other Rhymes.* 1946. MOMA. 2nd ed. ils. 132p. red cloth. VG. S11. $25.00

SWEET, Bill. *They Call Me Mr Airshow.* 1972. Milwaukee. 1st ed. sgn pres. VG/VG. B5. $45.00

SWEET, Melissa. *Garden Companion.* 1984. Boston. Bromer. 63x48mm. 1/30. aeg. gilt alphabet on full maroon morocco. F/box. B24. $850.00

SWEETEN, Margaret O. *Second Bull Terrier Book.* 1967. Great Britain. 1st ed. ils. 128p. cloth. VG. R2. $350.00

SWEETMAN, Jack. *US Naval Academy: Ils Hist...* 1979. Annapolis. Naval Inst. ils. 289p. M. H1. $17.50

SWEM, E.G. *Brothers of the Spade.* 1957. Barre, MA. Barre Gazette. 8vo. 196p. gr cloth. VG/G. B11. $50.00

SWEM, E.G. *Jamestown 350th-Anniversary Historical Booklets.* 1957. Williamsburg, VA. complete set of 23 booklets. VG/wrp/VG case. B11. $75.00

SWENSON & SWENSON. *Something About Kierkegaard.* 1941. Augsburg. 173p. G. B29. $5.50

SWIFT, David E. *Joseph John Gurney: Banker, Reformer & Quaker.* 1962. Middletown, CT. Wesleyan U. 1st ed. 8vo. 304p. VG. V3. $14.00

SWIFT, Jonathan. *Anti-Longin, Oder die Kunst in der Poesie zu Kriechen...* 1734. Leipzig. JG Loewe. 8vo. 208p. contemporary vellum. K1. $350.00

SWIFT, Jonathan. *Gulliver's Travels to Lilliput & Brobdingnag.* nd. Garden City. ils RG Mossa. VG/G. B17. $6.50

SWIGART, Rob. *Portal.* 1988. St Martin. 1st ed. F/F. P3. $20.00

SWIHART, Thomas L. *Astrophysics & Stellar Astronomy.* 1968. NY. Wiley. 8vo. 299p. bl cloth. VG. K5. $20.00

SWINBOURNE, Robert F.G. *Sansevieria in Cultivation in Australia.* 1979. Adelaide. 32 full-p ils. 48p. VG/stapled photo wrp. B26. $7.50

SWINBURNE, Algernon Charles. *Laux Veneris.* 1866. NY. Author's Ed. gilt cloth. VG. A17. $20.00

SWINBURNE, Algernon Charles. *Lesbia Brandon.* 1952. Falcon. 1st ed. 583p. VG/dj. M20. $20.00

SWINBURNE, Algernon Charles. *Poems & Ballads.* 1866. London. 1st ed/2nd issue. half gr morocco/orig bdg. F. H4. $175.00

SWINDLER, William F. *Court & Constitution in 20th Century.* 1970 & 1974. Bobbs Merrill. 2 vols. M11. $45.00

SWINFEN, Averil. *Donkeys Galore.* 1976. Newton Abbott. David & Charles. 1st ed. VG/G+. O3. $25.00

SWING, Raymond Gram. *Forerunners of American Fascism.* 1935. Messner. VG. N2. $10.00

SWINTON, George. *Sculpture of the Eskimo.* 1972. Toronto. McClelland Stewart. ils. F/VG. F1. $65.00

SWOPE, Martha. *Baryshnikov At Work: Mikhail Baryshnikov Discusses His Work.* 1976. Knopf. 1st ed. 252p. F/F. A17. $15.00

SWORDS & WALWER. *Costs & Resources of Legal Education.* 1974. Columbia. M11. $35.00

SYDENHAM, Thomas. *Opera Medica; In Hae Novissima Editione Variis Variorum...* 1762. Venice. 1 fld pl. 438p. contemporary calf. K1. $175.00

SYKES, Christopher. *Nancy: Life of Lady Astor.* 1972. Harper Row. 1st ed. photos. ES. gilt brick cloth. F/F. M7. $28.00

SYKES, John. *Mountain Arabs: Window in the Middle East.* 1968. Phil. Chilton. 1st ed. 12mo. xl. VG/dj. W1. $12.00

SYLVA & VACARESCO. *Bard of Dimbo Vitza.* nd. Harper. new/enlarged ed. 8vo. 271p. gilt gr cloth. VG. D6. $25.00

SYLVESTER, Martin. *Dangerous Age.* 1988. Villard. 1st Am ed. F/F. M15. $25.00

SYLVESTER, Martin. *Rough Red.* 1990. Villard. 1st Am ed. rem mk. F/F. M15. $22.50

SYME, James. *Principles of Surgery. 2nd Edition.* 1837. Edinburgh. John Carfrae. 460p. contemporary half sheep/marbled brd. G. G7. $275.00

SYMONDS, John Addington. *Renaissance in Italy.* 1882-1887. NY. 7 vol. VG. F1. $100.00

SYMONDS, John Addington. *Short Hist of the Renaissance in Italy.* 1966. NY. Cooper Sq Pub. 8vo. 335p. gr cloth. VG. P4. $20.00

SYMONDS, John Addington. *Webster & Tourneur.* ca 1980. London. Unwin. Mermaid Series. 432p. VG. M10. $4.50

SYMONDS, R.W. *Book of English Clocks.* 1950. King Penguin. 2nd ed. VG/VG. P3. $20.00

SYMONS, Arthur. *Art of Aubrey Beardsley.* 1918. Modern Lib. 16mo. ils. flexible gr cloth. G. S11. $10.00

SYMONS, Julian. *Blackheath Poisonings.* 1978. London. Collins. 1st ed. F/F. S6. $30.00

SYMONS, Julian. *Horatio Bottomley.* 1955. Cresset. 1st ed. VG. P3. $15.00

SZALAI, Alexander. *Philosophische Grundprobleme der Psychoanalytischen...* 1936. Zurich. Octava Verlag. thin 8vo. 63p. F/gray-gr wrp. G1. $65.00

SZE, Mai-Mai. *Tao of Painting: Study of Ritual Disposition...* 1956. NY. Pantheon. Bollingen Series XLIX. 2 vol. ils. F/VG/case. F1. $175.00

SZEKELY, Sari. *Marika.* 1939. Whitman. 1st ed. ils Barbara Gabor. VG. M19. $35.00

SZILAGYI, Steve. *Photographing Fairies.* 1992. Ballantine/Random. 1st ed/author's 1st book. rem mk. F/F. A14. $25.00

SZULC, Tad. *Fidel: A Critical Portrait.* 1986. Morrow. 1st ed. 703p. VG/dj. F3. $20.00

SZYK, Arthur. *Ten Commandments.* 1947. Phil. Winston. ltd ed. sgn. 1/1000. ils cloth. F. F1. $475.00

T

TABACHNICK, Stephen E. *ET Lawrence P*U*Z*Z*L*E.* 1984. GA U. 1st ed. sgn Tabachnick/O'Brien. silvered gr cloth. M. M7. $35.00

TABER, Gladys. *First Book of Dogs.* 1949. Franklin Watts. ils Bob Kuhn. 45p. VG/dj. M20. $25.00

TABER, Gladys. *Harvest at Stillmeadow.* 1940. Little Brn. 1st ed. F/VG. B4. $100.00

TABER, Gladys. *Harvest of Yesterdays.* 1976. Lippincott. 1st ed. 224p. F/F. H1. $18.00

TABER, Gladys. *Stillmeadow Sampler.* 1959. Lippincott. 1st ed. 282p. NF/NF. M20. $25.00

TABORI, Paul. *Companions of the Unseen.* 1968. U Books. VG/VG. P3. $12.00

TABORIN, Glorina. *Norman Rockwell's Counting Book.* 1977. Abrams. probable 1st ed. VG+. C8. $25.00

TAFFT, Henry Spurr. *Reminiscences of the Signal Service in the Civil War.* 1899. Providence. 1st ed. 1/250. 41p. NF/prt wrp. M8. $45.00

TAFT, Lorado. *Modern Tendencies in Sculpture.* 1928. Chicago. 8vo. ils. 152p. gilt gr cloth. F. F1. $95.00

TAFT, Philip. *Organized Labor in American History.* 1964. Harper Row. VG/G. V4. $25.00

TAFT, Robert. *Artists & Ils of the Old W: 1850-1900.* 1953. Scribner. 1st ed. 91 pl. 133 p. map ep. F. A18. $50.00

TAGG, Lawrence V. *Harold Bell Wright: Storyteller to Am.* 1986. Westernlore. 1st ed. 197p. F/F. B19. $20.00

TAGGART, Donald G. *Hist of the Third Infantry Division in WWII.* 1947. WA. 1st ed. ils/map ep. VG. B18. $135.00

TAINE, John. *Forbidden Garden.* 1947. Fantasy. 1st ed. VG. P3. $18.00

TAINE, John. *Gold Tooth.* 1927. Dutton. 1st ed. G+. M2. $20.00

TALFORD, Thomas N. *Ion, a Tragedy in Five Acts.* nd (1835). London. 2nd ed. 8vo. cloth/rebacked. O2. $65.00

TALLANT, Edith. *David & Patience.* 1940. Lippincott. sgn. ils Dorothy Bayley. 166p. VG/tattered. M20. $25.00

TALLANT, Edith. *Girl Who Was Marge.* 1939. Lippincott. sgn. ils Dorothy Bayley. 267p. VG/ragged. M20. $25.00

TALMAGE, T. DeWitt. *From Manger to Throne, Embracing New Life of Jesus...* 1893. Christian Herald. 8vo. ils. cloth. G. W1. $12.00

TALMAN, Charles Fitzhugh. *Book About the Weather.* 1931 (1925). Bl Ribbon. rpt. 8vo. 318p. G/dj. K5. $16.00

TAMINIAUX, Jacques. *Dialectic & Difference: Finitude in Modern Thought.* 1985. Atlantic Highlands, NJ. Humanities Pr. 178p. bl cloth. VG/dj. G1. $30.00

TAN, Amy. *Kitchen God's Wife.* 1991. Putnam. UP/author's 2nd book. F/wrp. L3. $100.00

TANIZAKI, Junichiro. *Some Prefer Nettles.* 1955. Knopf. 1st ed. NF/NF. L3. $65.00

TANNAHILL, Reay. *Flesh & Blood.* 1975. Hamish Hamilton. 1st ed. VG/VG. P3. $20.00

TANNAHILL, Reay. *Food in History.* 1973. NY. 1st ed. 448p. A13. $25.00

TANNAHILL, Reay. *Sex in History.* 1980. Hamish Hamilton. 1st ed. 480p. VG/dj. M20. $20.00

TANNER, George Clinton. *Fifty Years of Church Work in Dioces of MN 1857-1907...* 1909. St Paul. 1st ed. 516p. cloth. NF. M8. $45.00

TANNER & VANN. *Samuel Beckett: Checklist of Criticism.* 1969. np. 91p. F. A4. $20.00

TAPIE, Victor. *Age of Grandeur, Baroque & Classicism in Europe.* 1960. London. Weidenfeld. 1st Eng-language ed. tall 8vo. 305p. VG. F1. $35.00

TAPIERO, E. *Le Dogme et les Rites de l'Islam.* 1957. Paris. Llinchsieck. 1st ed. Arabic/French text. VG. W1. $8.00

TAPPLY, William G. *Dead Meat.* nd. BC. VG/VG. P3. $8.00

TAPPLY, William G. *Dead Meat.* 1987. Scribner. 1st ed. F/F. T2. $20.00

TAPPLY, William G. *Dead Winter.* 1989. Delacorte. 1st ed. F/F. O4. $15.00

TAPPLY, William G. *Death at Charity's Point.* 1984. Scribner. 1st ed. F/NF. M15. $100.00

TAPPLY, William G. *Follow the Sharks.* 1985. Scribner. 1st ed. F/F. P8. $35.00

TARASOV, S.V. *Technology of Watch Production.* 1964. Smithsonian. 1st ed. 8vo. 446p. VG. A8. $30.00

TARBELL, F.B. *Hist of Greek Art With Intro Chapter on Art in Egypt...* 1922. Macmillan. sm 8vo. 295p. VG. W1. $15.00

TARBELL, Ida M. *In the Footsteps of the Lincolns.* 1924. Harper. ils. 418p. VG. M10. $9.50

TARDIEU, Jean. *Jours Petriefies 1943-1944 Poemes.* 1947. Paris. Gallimard. 1/126. 4to. unp. F/VG case. S9. $375.00

TARG, William. *American West: Treasury of Stories, Legends...* 1946. World. 1st ed. F. A18. $20.00

TARG, William. *Bibliophile in the Nursery.* 1969 (ca 1957). Metuchen, NJ. Scarecrow. 8vo. xl. NF. D6. $18.00

TARG, William. *Bibliophile in the Nursery.* 1957. World. 503p. VG/dj. M20. $60.00

TARG, William. *Bouillabaisse for Bibliophiles.* 1955. World. 1st ed. 506p. VG/dj. M20. $70.00

TARG, William. *Modern English First Editions & Their Prices.* 1932. Chicago. Blk Archer. VG. N2. $10.00

TARKINGTON, Booth. *Beasley's Christmas Party.* 1909. Harper. ils Ruth Sypherd Clements. 99p. gilt red cloth. VG. A3. $30.00

TARKINGTON, Booth. *Gentleman From Indiana.* 1899. McClure. 1st ed/author's 1st book. 8vo. 384p. F/case/chemise. H5. $225.00

TARKINGTON, Booth. *Guest of Quesnay.* 1917. Scribner. VG. P3. $10.00

TARKINGTON, Booth. *Image of Josephine.* 1945. Doubleday Doran. 1st ed. 275p. G. H1. $6.00

TARKINGTON, Booth. *Midlander.* 1923. Doubleday Page. 1st ed. sgn. 1/377. 493p. NF/dj. C6. $125.00

TARKINGTON, Booth. *Penrod, His Complete Story.* 1931. Doubleday. 1st ed thus. ils Gordon Grant. VG. M5. $30.00

TARKINGTON, Booth. *Penrod & Sam.* 1916. Grosset Dunlap. photoplay ed. 356p. G/ragged. M20. $15.00

TARKINGTON, Booth. *Penrod.* 1914. Doubleday Page. 1st ed/2nd state (sence changed to sense p 19). VG. P2. $50.00

TARKINGTON, Booth. *Seventeen.* 1916. Harper. 1st ed. 329p. gilt cloth. VG. M20. $100.00

TARKINGTON, Booth. *Your Amicable Uncle.* 1949. Bobbs Merrill. 1st ed. 192p. VG/G. H1. $18.00

TARRANT, John. *Clauberg Trigger.* 1979. Atheneum. 1st ed. F/F. P3. $15.00

TARRANT, Margaret. *Songs the Letters Sing.* nd. London. Grant Educational. sm 12mo. VG. C8. $25.00

TARSOULI, Athina. *Iles Blanches.* 1939. Athens. sq 8vo. 3 mtd aquatints. 153p. cloth. O2. $40.00

TARTT, Donna. *Secret Hist.* 1992. Knopf. ARC/author's 1st novel. NF/wrp. L3. $45.00

TARTT, Donna. *Secret Hist.* 1992. Knopf. 1st ed. sgn. F/F. B2. $65.00

TASCHER, Harold. *Maggie & Montana.* 1954. np. F/dj. B34. $20.00

TASHIRO, Haruo. *Turfgrass Insects of the US & Canada.* 1992 (1987). Ithaca. photos/figures. 391p. M/dj. B26. $45.00

TASHJIAN, Dickran. *Skyscraper Primitives, Dada & the American Avant-Garde...* 1975. Middleton, CT. Wesleyan. 1st ed. lg 8vo. 382p. gilt/brn stp tan cloth. F/F. F1. $45.00

TATE, Allen. *Collected Poems 1919-1976.* 1977. NY. 1st ed. w/sgn bookplate. F/F. A11. $45.00

TATE, Allen. *Reason in Madness: Ctitical Essays.* 1941. Putnam. 1st ed. 8vo. 230p. gr cloth. NF/dj. C6. $200.00

TATE, Allen. *Selected Poems.* 1937. Scribner. 1st ed. F/VG. V1. $45.00

TATE, James. *Build a Model of the Flying Cloud.* 1934. Moddel Ship Supply. ils. 51p. wrp. T7. $20.00

TATE, James. *Lost Pilot.* 1967. New Haven/London. Yale. 1st ed/author's 1st book. 8vo. 72p. NF/dj. C6. $150.00

TATE, Joyce L. *Cactus Cook Book.* 1971. Succulent Cookery Internat. sgn. 128p. gr buckram. F. B26. $12.50

TATE, Peter. *Faces in the Flames.* 1976. Doubleday. 1st ed. VG/VG. P3. $13.00

TATE, Sally. *Gingerbread Man. A Fuzzy Wuzzy Book.* 1944. Whitman. 28p. pict brd. VG/VG. A3. $20.00

TATHAM. *Prints & Printmakers of NY State, 1825-1940.* 1986. Syracuse. 4to. ils. 287p. F/VG. A4. $35.00

TATSIOS, Theodore G. *Megali Idea & the Greek-Turkish War of 1897...* 1984. NY. 8vo. 302p. cloth. O2. $45.00

TATTERSAL, C.E.C. *History of British Carpets.* 1934. London. 1st ed. VG. A1. $100.00

TATTERSFIELD, D. *Halley's Comet.* 1985 (1984). NY. Blackwell. 8vo. 176p. VG/VG. K5. $10.00

TATTERSFIELD, D. *Physics Problems in Astronautics.* 1966. London. 8vo. 94p. xl. VG. K5. $14.00

TAUBER, Eliezer. *Arab Movements in WWI.* 1993. London. 1st ed. 322p. M/stiff wrp. M7. $32.50

TAVOULAREAS, William. *Fighting Back: Story...Pres of Mobil Took on WA Post...* 1985. NY. Simon Schuster. M11. $25.00

TAWIL, Raymonda Hawa. *My Home, My Prison.* 1979. HRW. 1st ed. 265p. NF/dj. W1. $18.00

TAX, Sol. *Evolution of Life. Vol 1.* 1960. Chicago. 629p. G/dj. K4. $15.00

TAYLER, William Lonsdale. *Federal States & Labor Treaties.* 1935. NY. 171p. prt sewn wrp. M11. $35.00

TAYLOR, Alfred S. *On Poisons in Relation to Medical Jurisprudence & Medicine.* 1859. Phil. 2nd Am ed (from revised London ed). 755p. VG. B14. $150.00

TAYLOR, Andrew. *Caroline Minuscule.* 1982. London. Gollancz. 1st ed. F/NF. S6. $35.00

TAYLOR, Anne. *Laurence Oliphant 1829-1888.* 1982. Oxford. 8vo. 306p. cloth. dj. O2. $25.00

TAYLOR, Bayard. *Central Asia. Travels in Cashmere, Little Tibet...* 1883. NY. 8vo. 365p. gilt cloth. O2. $25.00

TAYLOR, Bayard. *Lands of the Saracen; or, Pictures of Palestine...* 1867. Putnam. 8vo. 451p. VG. W1. $35.00

TAYLOR, Bayard. *Poems of the Orient.* 1855. Boston. 8vo. 203p. emb cloth. O2. $50.00

TAYLOR, Bernard. *Reaping.* 1980. Souvenir. 1st ed. NF/NF. P3. $20.00

TAYLOR, C. Clark. *Updike: A Bibliography.* 1968. Kent State. 1st ed. cloth. F/sans. B4. $75.00

TAYLOR, Charles. *Mechanical Treatment of Angular Curvature...* 1863. NY. Bailliere. ils. 48p. VG/prt wrp. B14. $60.00

TAYLOR, Don Alonzo. *Old Sam: Thoroughbred Trotter.* 1955. Chicago. Follett. VG. O3. $10.00

TAYLOR, Edwin. *Hist of City of Bismarck, ND...* 1972. Bismarck Centennial Assn. F/VG. B34. $40.00

TAYLOR, Franc C. *Alberta Hunter: Celebration in Blues.* 1987. McGraw Hill. 1st ed. F/F. B2. $35.00

TAYLOR, Frederic Winslow. *Principles d'Organisation Scientifique des Usines.* 1911. Paris. H Dunod et E Pinat. 1st French ed. 149p. H4. $300.00

TAYLOR, Gabriele. *Price, Shame & Guilt.* 1985. Oxford. Clarendon. 144p. blk cloth. VG/dj. G1. $25.00

TAYLOR, Hannis. *Science of Jurisprudence...* 1908. NY. 1st ed. 676p. teg. VG. D3. $50.00

TAYLOR, Herman E. *Faulkner's Oxford. Recollections & Reflections.* 1990. Nashville. 1st ed. inscr. F/F. A11. $40.00

TAYLOR, Ida Scott. *Year Book of American Authors.* 1894. Caldwell. 13 author portraits. 372p. VG. S11. $15.00

TAYLOR, Isaac. *Origin of the Aryans.* 1898. London. ils. 339p. F. B14. $35.00

TAYLOR, Jeremy. *Credenda; or, What Is To Be Believed.* ca 1850. London. Simpkin Marshall. 57x40mm. 36p. aeg. full gray-bl calf. F/case/cloth wrp. B24. $250.00

TAYLOR, John Russell. *Hitch.* 1978. Pantheon. 1st ed. VG/VG. P3. $20.00

TAYLOR, John W.R. *Combat Aircraft of the World.* 1969. Putnam. VG/G. P3. $20.00

TAYLOR, John. *Identity of Junius With Distinguished Living Character...* 1818. NY. Kirk Mercein. 1st Am ed. 300p. VG. D3. $150.00

TAYLOR, John. *Pondoro, Last of Ivory Hunters.* 1955. NY. 1st ed. VG+. A15. $35.00

TAYLOR, Joseph. *Complete Weather Guide...Drawn From Plants, Animals...* 1812. London. Harding. fld pl. 160p. later calf. H10. $125.00

TAYLOR, Joshua C. *William Page: The American Titian.* 1957. Chicago U. 1st ed. ils. 294p. cloth. F1/K1. $60.00

TAYLOR, Louis. *Bits: Their Hist, Use & Misuse.* 1966. Harper Row. 1st ed. VG/VG. O3. $48.00

TAYLOR, Louis. *Horse American Made.* 1944. Louisville. 1st ed. VG. O3. $65.00

TAYLOR, Louis. *Horse American Made: Story of Am Saddle Horse.* 1961. NY. Harper. stated 1st but is 1st trade ed. VG/G. O3. $35.00

TAYLOR, Marvin J. *Religious Education: Comprehensive Survey...* 1960. Abingdon. 446p. G/worn. B29. $3.50

TAYLOR, Nigel P. *Genus Echinocereus.* 1985. Portland. ils/maps. 172p. M/dj. B26. $22.50

TAYLOR, Norman. *Cinchona in Java: Story of Quinne.* 1945. NY. 1st ed. 87p. A13. $30.00

TAYLOR, P. Walker. *Murder in the Game Reserve.* 1947. Butterworth. 1st ed. VG. P3. $35.00

TAYLOR, Peter. *Collected Stories of...* 1969. FSG. 1st ed. F/VG. B4. $85.00

TAYLOR, Peter. *In the Miro District.* 1977. Knopf. 1st ed. 204p. blk cloth. F/NF. C6. $50.00

TAYLOR, Peter. *In the TN Country.* 1994. Knopf. AP. F/wrp. B2. $50.00

TAYLOR, Peter. *Miss Leonora When Last Seen.* 1963. Obolensky. 1st ed. sgn. 398p. VG/dj. C6. $250.00

TAYLOR, Peter. *Miss Leonora When Last Seen.* 1963. Obolensky. 1st ed. inscr to author Cleanth Brooks. w/sgn card. F/VG+. B4. $500.00

TAYLOR, Peter. *Observing the Sun.* 1991. Cambridge. ils/photos/diagrams. 159p. VG/VG. K5. $25.00

TAYLOR, Peter. *Oracle at Stoneleigh Court.* 1993. Knopf. ARC/author's last book. 1/650. F/wrp/case. L3. $75.00

TAYLOR, Peter. *Woman of Means.* 1950. Harcourt Brace. 1st ed/author's 2nd book. 8vo. 160p. VG/dj. C6. $400.00

TAYLOR, Phoebe Atwood. *Going, Going, Gone.* 1943. Norton. 1st ed. VG. P3. $35.00

TAYLOR, Phoebe Atwood. *Left Leg.* 1940. Norton. 1st ed. F/NF. M15. $150.00

TAYLOR, Phoebe Atwood. *Proof of the Pudding.* 1945. Norton. 1st ed. F/NF. M15. $50.00

TAYLOR, Phoebe Atwood. *Six Iron Spiders.* 1942. Norton. 1st ed. F/F. M15. $125.00

TAYLOR, R.L. *Weeds of Roadsides & Waste Ground in New Zealand.* 1981. Upper Moutere. Nelson. 300 photos. 177p. sc. B26. $17.50

TAYLOR, Rebecca N. *Earth People & Other Verse.* nd. London. Stockwell. 12mo. 32p. VG/dj. V3. $9.50

TAYLOR, Robert Lewis. *Center Ring.* 1956. Doubleday. 1st ed. 222p. VG/dj. M20. $12.00

TAYLOR, Robert Lewis. *Winston Churchill: An Informal Study of Greatness.* 1952. Doubleday. BC. 433p. VG/VG. M7. $12.00

TAYLOR, Samuel W. *Grinning Gismo.* 1951. AA Wyn. 1st ed. VG/VG. P3. $35.00

TAYLOR, Silas. *Hist of Gavel-Kind.* 1970. Los Angeles. 210p. F. D3. $35.00

TAYLOR, William. *California Life Illustrated.* 1858. np. 1st ed. 348p. complete reading copy. E5. $35.00

TAYLOR, William. *Landlord & Peasant in Colonial Oaxaca.* 1972. Stanford. 1st ed. 287p. VG. F3. $20.00

TAYLOR, William. *Landlord & Peasant in Colonial Oaxaca.* 1972. Stanford. 1st ed. 8vo. 287p. red cloth. M/M. P4. $30.00

TAYLOR, William. *Letters to a Quaker Friend on Baptism.* 1880. NY. Phillips Hunt. 12mo. 163p. VG. V3. $16.00

TAYLOR. *Lewis Carroll at TX: Warren Weaver Collection...* 1985. TX U. 233p. F. A4. $35.00

TAYLOR. *Thomas Chatterton's Art, Experiments in Imagined Hist.* 1978. Princeton. 343p. F/F. A4. $30.00

TEALE, Edwin Way. *Audubon's Wildlife.* 1964. Viking. 1st ed. F/clip. B3. $40.00

TEARLE. *Mrs Piozzi's Tall Young Beau, William Augustus Conway.* 1991. Fairleigh Dickinson. ils 252p. F/F. A4. $35.00

TEASDALE, Sara. *Biography of Margaret Haley Carpenter.* 1960. Schulte Pub. 1st ed. NF/VG. V1. $25.00

TEASDALE, Sara. *Stars Tonight.* 1930. Macmillan. 1st ed. ils Dorothy Lathrop. cloth. VG/G. M5. $85.00

TEBBEL, John. *Between Covers.* 1987. Oxford. 1st prt. 514p. F/F. S11. $15.00

TEBBEL, John. *Inheritors: Study of Am's Great Fortunes & What Happened...* 1962. Putnam. 2nd imp. 310p. F. H1. $10.00

TEDLOCK, Dennis. *Popol Vuh.* 1985. Simon Schuster. 1st ed. 380p. VG/dj. F3. $20.00

TEETERS, N. *Challenge of Delinquency.* 1950. NY. ils. 819p. VG. D3. $12.50

TEGGART, Frederick J. *Academy of Pacific Coast Hist Publications.* 1910-1911. Berkeley. 2 vol. 9 pl. contemporary blk calf/buckram. K1. $100.00

TEGNER, Henry. *White Foxes of Gorfenletch.* 1954. Morrow. 1st ed. VG/dj. N2. $7.50

TEILHARD DE CHARDIN, Pierre. *Future of Man.* 1964. London. Harper. 1st Eng-language ed. VG/chip. G1. $22.50

TEMPLE, WIlliam F. *Martin Magnus on Mars.* 1956. Muller. 1st ed. VG/VG. P3. $35.00

TENGGREN, Gustaf. *Tenggren's Story Book.* 1944. Simon Schuster. 1st ed. 87p. pict brd. VG. A3. $17.50

TENNEY, Merrill C. *Galatians: Charter of Christian Liberty.* 1989. Eerdmans. pb. 216p. M. B29. $8.50

TENNYSON, Alfred Lord. *Alfred Lord Tennyson: A Memoir by His Son.* 1897. Macmillan. 2 vol. VG. M10. $15.00

TENNYSON, Alfred Lord. *Poems by...* 1905. Glasgow. Stokes. 55x35mm. 1472p. silvered red cloth. NF. B24. $225.00

TENNYSON, Hallam. *Jack & the Beanstalk.* 1886. London. Macmillan. 1st ed. ils Caldecott. 70p. NF. D6. $80.00

TENSEN, Ruth M. *Come to the Farm.* 1949. Reilly Lee. 3rd prt. photos. pict brd. 2 school stp. G. M5. $10.00

TEONGE, Henry. *Diary of..., Chaplain on Board His Majesty's Ships...* 1825. London. Chas Knight. 1st ed. 8vo. 327p. marbled ep. modern bdg. P4. $200.00

TEONGE, Henry. *Diary of..., Chaplain on Board His Majesty's Ships...* 1927. NY. 8vo. 328p. cloth. O2. $35.00

TEPPER, Sheri S. *Grass.* 1989. Doubleday. F/F. P3. $19.00

TEPPER, Sheri S. *Plague of Angels.* nd. Bantam Spectra. ARC of 1st ed. hc. F/proof. M21. $35.00

TERENCE. *Publius Terentius Afer.* 1824. London. Pickering. 83x49mm. ils Visconti. 220p. fore-edge painting. F. B24. $750.00

TERHUNE, Albert Payson. *Book of Famous Dogs.* 1937. Doubleday Doran. 1st ed. ils Robert Dickey. 300p. F/VG. R2. $80.00

TERHUNE, Albert Payson. *Bruce.* 1920. Dutton. 4th prt. 204p. cloth. G+. R2. $40.00

TERHUNE, Albert Payson. *Heart of a Dog.* 1924. Doran. ils Marguerite Kirmse. cloth/mc pl. VG. M5. $40.00

TERHUNE, Albert Payson. *How To Box To Win.* ca 1935. np. rpt. F/wrp. R2. $40.00

TERHUNE, Albert Payson. *My Friend the Dog.* 1926. Harper. 1st ed. 11 pl. 317p. G+. M20. $75.00

TERHUNE, Albert Payson. *Return of Peter Grimm.* 1912. NY. 1st ed. ils. 344p. G+. R2. $30.00

TERHUNE, Albert Payson. *Story of Damon & Pythias.* 1915. Grosset Dunlap. photoplay ed. VG/torn. P3. $35.00

TERHUNE, Albert Payson. *Syria From the Saddle.* 1897. Boston. 1st ed/author's 1st book. 8vo. 318p. cloth. uncut. O2. $55.00

TERHUNE, Albert Payson. *Terhune Omnibus.* 1945. World. 1st/rpt ed. VG/VG. B5. $30.00

TERHUNE, Albert Payson. *Way of a Dog.* 1932. Harper. 1st ed. ils. 334p. cloth. R2. $35.00

TERHUNE, Anice. *Dutch Ditties for Children.* 1910. NY. folio. F. scarce. R2. $25.00

TERHUNE, Mary. *Helping Hand Cook Book.* 1912. NY. 1st ed. ils. 340p. xl. G. R2. $20.00

TERHUNE, Mary. *Housekeepers Week.* 1908. Indianapolis. 1st ed. ils. 439p. VG. R2. $40.00

TERHUNE, Mary. *Long Lane.* 1915. NY. 1st ed. 363p. G+. R2. $20.00

TERHUNE, Mary. *Looging Westward.* 1914. NY. 1st ed. 28p. G+. R2. $12.00

TERHUNE, Mary. *Not Pretty But Precious.* 1887. MA. 1st ed. 308p. VG. scarce. R2. $15.00

TERHUNE, Mary. *When Grandmamma Was 14.* 1905. Boston. 1st ed. 359p. G+. R2. $12.00

TERHUNE & THORNE. *True Dog Stories.* 1936. Akron, OH. 1st ed. ils. 61p. R2. $25.00

TERKEL, Studs. *Giants of Jazz.* 1957. Crowell. 1st ed. inscr. F/NF. B2. $125.00

TERRACE, Vincent. *Complete Encyclopedia of TV 1947-1976. Vol 2.* 1976. Barnes. TVTI. VG/VG. P3. $20.00

TERRALL, Robert. *They Deal in Death.* 1944. Books Inc. VG. P3. $18.00

TERRELL, John Upton. *War for the CO River.* 1965. Arthur Clark. 2 vol. F/NF. B19. $90.00

TERRILLON, O. *Du Role de l'Action Musculaire Dans les Luxations...* 1875. Paris. Doin. 104p. G7. $115.00

TERZIAN, James P. *Caravan From Ararat.* 1959. Phil. Muhlenberg. 1st ed. 8vo 239p. VG/dj. W1. $18.00

TESSIER, Thomas. *Finishing Touches.* 1986. Atheneum. 1st ed. F/F. T2. $18.00

TESSIER, Thomas. *Nightwalker.* 1979. Macmillan. 1st ed. VG/VG. P3. $20.00

TESSIER, Thomas. *Shockwaves.* 1983. Severn House. 1st ed. VG/VG. P3. $25.00

TESTA, Fulvio. *Land Where the Ice Cream Grows.* 1979. Doubleday. 1st Am ed. F. C8. $25.00

TETLEY, Nigel. *Trimaran Solo. Story of Victress...* 1970. Lymington. Nautical Pub. 12 pl/10 maps. 176p. dj. T7. $20.00

TETREAULT, Mary Ann. *Organization of Arab Petroleum Exporting Countries...* 1981. Greenwood. 1st ed. xl. VG. W1. $18.00

TEVIS, Walter. *Queen's Gambit.* nd. BOMC. VG/VG. P3. $10.00

TEVIS, Walter. *Steps of the Sun.* 1983. Doubleday. 1st ed. RS. F/F. P3. $20.00

THACHER, James. *American New Dispensatory...* 1817. Boston. Wait. 3rd ed. 724p. old leather. H10. $95.00

THACKER, May Dixon. *Strange Death of President Harding From Diaries...* nd. London. John Hamilton. VG. N2. $5.00

THACKERAY, William Makepeace. *Four Georges.* 1861. Smith Elder. 1st Eng ed/2nd issue (Dec ads). inscr pres. F/2 cases. H4. $850.00

THACKERAY, William Makepeace. *Hist of Henry Esmond.* 1905. Macmillan. 1st ed thus. ils Hugh Thompson. aeg. gilt cloth. VG+. M5. $60.00

THACKERAY, William Makepeace. *Vanity Fair.* 1947-1948. London. Bradbury Evans. 1st ed/1st issue. woodcut. brn morocco. H4. $2,000.00

THANE, Eric. *High Border Country.* 1942. DSP. 1st ed. VG. B34. $20.00

THANE, Eric. *High Border Country.* 1942. DSP. 1st ed. VG/VG. B5. $40.00

THANE, Eric. *Majestic Land, Peaks, Parks & Prevaricators of Rockies...* 1950. np. 1st ed. VG/dj. B34. $45.00

THARAUD & THARAUD. *Les Mille et un Jours de l'Islam.* 1925. Paris. Plon. 1st ed. 259p. G. W1. $8.00

THAW, Harry K. *Traitor: Being the Untampered With, Unrevised Account...* 1926. Phil. Dorrance. 1st ed. 12mo. 271p. VG. D3. $12.50

THAYER, Charles W. *Life World Lib: Russia.* 1961. Time Books. ils. 176p. brd. F. M10. $2.50

THAYER, Emma H. *Wild Flowers of the Pacific Coast.* 1887. NY. folio. ils. 64p. floral ep. aeg. gilt pict cloth. B26. $165.00

THAYER, James Bradley. *Western Journey With Mr Emerson.* 1980. BC of CA. rpt. 1/600. F/sans. B19. $20.00

THAYER, James Stewart. *Hess Cross.* 1977. Putnam. 1st ed. F/F. P3. $15.00

THAYER, Jane. *Part-Time Dog.* 1965. Morrow. 12mo. VG/G. B17. $5.00

THAYER, John. *Discourse, Delivered at Roman Catholic Church in Boston...* 1798. Boston Hall. 2nd ed. 31p. H10. $165.00

THAYER, Tiffany. *Three Musketeers.* 1946. Citadel. 13th prt. VG/VG. P3. $15.00

THAYER, William Roscoe. *Life & Letters of John Hay.* 1940. 2 vol. index. O8. $18.50

THAYER, William Roscoe. *Life & Times of Cavour.* 1911. Houghton Mifflin. 2 vols. gilt cloth. VG. A17. $15.00

THAYER, William. *Marvels of the New West.* 1890. Henry Bill Pub. 6 books in 1 vol. poor. rare. B34. $80.00

THAYER, William. *Murfreesboro to Fort Pillow.* 1865. 336p. O8. $14.50

THEOCRITUS. *Eidyllia Triginta Sex, Latino Carmine Reddita...* 1545. Frankfurt. Brubacchii. 1st ed. 8vo. vellum/gilt tooled spine. H10. $145.00

THEODORAKIS, Mikis. *Journal of Resistance.* 1973. NY. 1st Am ed. 8vo. 334p. cloth. dj. O2. $15.00

THEODORE, Mary. *Heralds of Christ the King: Missionary Record...1878.* 1939. NY. Kenedy. 273p. H10. $35.00

THEOTEKNI, Sister. *Meteora: Rocky Forest of Greece.* 1984. Athens. Meteora. 1st ed. sm 8vo. 238p. VG/stiff wrp. W1. $14.00

THEROUX, Paul. *Christmas Card.* 1978. Houghton Mifflin. 1st ed. 8vo. 84p. cloth. VG/G. A3. $12.50

THEROUX, Paul. *Dr De Marr.* 1990. London. Hutchinson. 1st ed. F/NF. B3. $25.00

THEROUX, Paul. *London Snow. A Christmas Story.* 1979. London. sgn. 1/450 #d. w/bookseller prospectus. F/glassine. A11. $70.00

THEROUX, Paul. *O-Zone.* 1986. Putnam. 1st ed. F/F. P3. $20.00

THEROUX, Paul. *Old Patagonian Express. By Train Through the Americas.* 1979. Houghton Mifflin. 8vo. 404p. VG/G. B11. $15.00

THEROUX, Paul. *Picture Palace.* 1978. Houghton Mifflin. 1st ed. VG/VG. P3. $20.00

THESIGER, Wilfred. *Arabian Sands.* 1959. Dutton. 1st ed. 326p. VG. W1. $28.00

THESIGER, Wilfred. *Last Nomad: One Man's Forty Year Adventure...* 1980. Dutton. 1st Am ed. 4to. VG. W1. $45.00

THIAN, Raphael P. *Legislative Hist of the Great Staff of the US...* 1901. WA. 800p. VG. B18. $125.00

THIBAULT, J.T. *Application de la Perspective Lineaire aux Arts...* 1827. Paris. Thibault. folio. ils. 168p. brd. VG/modern case. F1. $150.00

THIELICKE, Helmut. *Ethics of Sex.* 1964. Harper. 1st ed. 338p. G/dj. B29. $8.50

THIERRY, James. *Adventure of the Eleven Cuff Buttons.* 1979. Aspen. 1st ed. F/wrp. M2. $10.00

THIESSEN, Grant. *SF Collector Vol 1.* 1980. Pandora. 1/400 #d. sgn. F. P3. $35.00

THIONOT, Leon. *Medico-Legal Aspects of Moral Offenses.* 1930. Phil. 487p. VG. D3. $45.00

THIRGOOD, J.Y. *Cyprus. Chronicle of Its Forests, Land & People.* 1987. Vancouver. 8vo. 371p. cloth. dj. O2. $45.00

THOMAS, Alan G. *Great Books & Book Collectors.* 1988. London. Spring. rpt. lg 4to. 280p. F/F. A17. $25.00

THOMAS, Alan G. *Pleasures & Treasures: Fine Books.* 1967. Putnam. 120p. VG/dj. A10. $12.00

THOMAS, Alexander. *Behavioral Individuality in Early Childhood.* 1963. NY U. 94p. F/dj. K4. $20.00

THOMAS, Alfred Barnaby. *Forgotten Frontiers.* 1969. Norman. 2nd prt. 8vo. 420p. bl cloth. VG/VG. P4. $30.00

THOMAS, Alfred Barnaby. *Teodoro de Croix & the N Frontier of New Spain 1776-1783.* 1968. OK U. ils/notes/index. 273p. F/clip. B19. $35.00

THOMAS, Bertha. *George Sand.* 1883. Roberts. 1st ed. 278p. VG. S11. $20.00

THOMAS, Bertram. *Araberna.* 1939. Stockholm. 1st ed. pl/fld map. 311p. NF. M7. $65.00

THOMAS, Craig. *Firefox Down.* 1983. Michael Joseph. 1st ed. VG/VG. P3. $30.00

THOMAS, Craig. *Sea Leopard.* 1981. Michael Joseph. 1st ed. F/F. P3. $25.00

THOMAS, D.M. *Flute Player.* 1979. Dutton. 1st Am ed. VG/dj. M20. $18.00

THOMAS, D.M. *Swallow.* 1984. Toronto. Lester & Orphen Dennys. 1st ed. F/NF. B3. $20.00

THOMAS, Daniel. *Outlines of Australian Art. Joseph Brown Collection.* 1989. Abrams. expanded 3rd ed. lg sq 4to. ils. gilt tan cloth. F/F. F1. $45.00

THOMAS, Donald. *Ripper's Apprentice.* 1989. St Martin. 1st Am ed. F/F. T2. $16.00

THOMAS, Donna. *Story of the Tree Keeper's Wisdom.* 1985. Santa Cruz. Good Book Pr. 64x48mm. 1/19 (200 total). gilt full vellum. F/case. B24. $375.00

THOMAS, Dylan. *Adventures in the Skin Trade.* 1955. London. Putnam. 1st Eng ed. 8vo. gilt blk brd. F/dj. H5. $150.00

THOMAS, Dylan. *Adventures in the Skin Trade.* 1955. New Directions. 1st ed. VG/VG. M20. $60.00

THOMAS, Dylan. *Conversation About Christmas.* 1954. New Directions. 1st ed. F/wht stapled wrp. Q1. $125.00

THOMAS, Dylan. *Portrait of the Artist As a Young Dog.* 1940. New Directions. 1st ed. 1/1000. F/F. S9. $300.00

THOMAS, Dylan. *Quite Early One Morning.* 1954. New Directions. 1st ed. 239p. VG/dj. M20. $40.00

THOMAS, Frank J. *Circus Wagons.* 1972. Los Angeles. 62x62mm. 1/150. sgn author/printer. F/paper case. B24. $165.00

THOMAS, Henry. *Stories of the Great Dramas & Their Authors.* ca 1958. Garden City. 481p. NF/dj. M10. $4.50

THOMAS, Ianthe. *Lordy, Aunt Hattie.* 1973. Harper. 1st ed. M/M. C8. $20.00

THOMAS, Isaiah. *History of Printing in America.* 1970. NY. Weathervane. 650p. VG/VG. A10. $15.00

THOMAS, J.A. *Archaeology & the Pre-Christian Centuries.* 1959. Eerdmans. 139p. G. B29. $3.00

THOMAS, John J. *Am Fruit Culturist.* 1871 (1867). NY. Wm Wood. 511p. gr cloth. VG. M20. $30.00

THOMAS, Joseph B. *Hounds & Hunting Through the Ages.* 1928. Derrydale. 1st ed. 1/750. ils/tissue guards. 272p. aeg. cloth. R2. $300.00

THOMAS, Lately. *Debonair Scoundrel.* 1962. San Francisco. 1st ed. NF/dj. D3. $15.00

THOMAS, Leslie. *Man With the Power.* 1972. Eyre Methuen. VG/VG. P3. $15.00

THOMAS, Leslie. *Man With the Power.* 1972. Harper Row. 1st ed. VG/VG. P3. $15.00

THOMAS, Lewis. *Fragile Species.* 1992. Scribner. 1st ed. F/F. B3. $15.00

THOMAS, Louis. *Good Children Don't Kill.* 1968. Dodd Mead. 1st ed. F/F. P3. $15.00

THOMAS, Lowell. *Good Evening Everybody From Cripple Creek to Samarkand.* 1976. Morrow. 2nd prt. 349p. NF/NF. M7. $16.00

THOMAS, Lowell. *Med Lawrence I Arabien.* 1926. Stockholm. 1st ed. 256p. wht pict bdg. VG. M7. $75.00

THOMAS, Lowell. *Old Gimlet Eye.* 1939. NY. sgn Thomas/Smedley Butler. VG. B5. $40.00

THOMAS, Lowell. *Out of This World: Across the Himalays to Forbidden Tibet.* 1950. Greystone. 1st ed. 320p. VG/VG. B33. $20.00

THOMAS, Lowell. *With Lawrence in Arabia.* nd. London. Hutchinson. 132nd thousand. VG/G pict dj. M7. $50.00

THOMAS, Lowell. *With Lawrence in Arabia.* nd. NY. Century. 1st ed. 408p. NF. M7. $65.00

THOMAS, Lowell. *With Lawrence in Arabia.* 1924. Garden City. 15 pl. 408p. VG. W1. $14.00

THOMAS, Lowell. *With Lawrence in Arabia.* 1964. London. 2nd prt. 256p. VG+. M7. $35.00

THOMAS, Martha B. *Katy Cricket Plays the Fiddle.* 1929. NY. ils. VG. M5. $30.00

THOMAS, Norman. *Mr Chairman, Ladies & Gentlemen...* 1955. Hermitage. ARC. RS. F/F. B2. $35.00

THOMAS, P. *Epics, Myths & Legends of India.* nd. Bombay. 11th ed. ils. VG+/dj. F1. $25.00

THOMAS, Ross. *Backup Men.* 1971. Hodder Stoughton. 1st ed. F/F. B2. $45.00

THOMAS, Ross. *Briarpatch.* 1984. Simon Schuster. 1st ed. F/F. P3. $30.00

THOMAS, Ross. *Cast a Yellow Shadow.* 1967. Morrow. 1st ed. sgn. F/NF. M15. $150.00

THOMAS, Ross. *Eighth Dwarf.* 1979. Simon Schuster. 1st ed. F/F. P3. $65.00

THOMAS, Ross. *Fools in Town Are On Our Side.* 1971. Morrow. 1st Am ed. NF/NF. B2. $85.00

THOMAS, Ross. *Fourth Durango.* 1989. Mysterious. 1st ed. VG/VG. P3. $20.00

THOMAS, Ross. *Highbinders.* 1974. Morrow. 1st eed. F/F. F4. $30.00

THOMAS, Ross. *Missionary Stew.* 1982. Simon Schuster. 1st ed. F/NF. M15. $35.00

THOMAS, Ross. *Porkchoppers.* 1972. Morrow. 1st ed. F/F. F4. $50.00

THOMAS, Ross. *Porkchoppers.* 1974. London. Hamilton. ARC/1st Eng ed. sgn. RS. F/NF. S6. $60.00

THOMAS, Ross. *Seersucker Whipsaw.* 1967. Morrow. 1st ed. NF/NF. P3. $250.00

THOMAS, Ross. *Seersucker Whipsaw.* 1968. Hodder Stoughton. 1st ed. VG/fair. P3. $80.00

THOMAS, Ross. *Yellow-Dog Contract.* 1977. Morrow. 1st ed. VG/VG. P3. $100.00

THOMAS, Stephen N. *Formal Mechanics of Mind.* 1978. Cornell. 325p. ochre cloth. VG/dj. G1. $25.00

THOMAS, T. Gaillard. *Abortion & Its Treatment.* 1895 (1890). Appleton. 112p. burgandy cloth. VG. S11. $40.00

THOMAS, Thomas Ebenezer. *Correspondence of... Relating to Anti-Slavery Conflict...* 1909. np. 1st ed. 137p. cloth. G. scarce. M8. $150.00

THOMAS, Verlin. *Successful Physician.* 1923. np. 1st ed. 303p. A13. $75.00

THOMASON, J. *Jeb Stuart.* 1930. NY. VG. A15. $25.00

THOMASON, John W. *Fix Bayonets!* 1970. NY. 1st ed thus. 523p. VG/dj. B18. $15.00

THOMPSON, Blanche Jennings. *Silver Pennies: A Collection of Modern Poems...* May 1945. Macmillan. ils Bromhall. pict cloth. F/VG. C8. $40.00

THOMPSON, Blanche Jennings. *Silver Pennies: A Collection of Modern Poems...* 1925. Macmillan. 1st ed. ils Winifred Bromhall. pict bl cloth. VG. very scarce. M5. $125.00

THOMPSON, Blanche Jennings. *Silver Pennies: A Collection of Modern Poems...* 1929. Macmillan. early rpt. 138p. gr cloth. VG. A3. $17.50

THOMPSON, C.J.S. *Lure & Romance of Alchemy: A History of Secret Link...* 1990. NY. Bell. 248p. F/F. B33. $18.00

THOMPSON, D'Arcy. *On Growth & Form.* 1961. Cambridge. 346p. M/dj. K4. $10.00

THOMPSON, Edwin Porter. *Hist of the Orphan Brigade.* 1973. Dayton, OH. Morningside Bookshop. facsimile of 1898 ed. VG. M8. $65.00

THOMPSON, Gene. *Lupe.* 1977. Random. ARC of 1st ed. VG/pict wrp. N3. $10.00

THOMPSON, George. *Thompson in Africa; or, Account of Missionary Labors...* 1852. NY. private prt. 2nd ed/1st Am ed. sgn author's son. 356p. cloth. VG. F1. $75.00

THOMPSON, Harlan. *Outcast: Stallion of Hawaii.* 1957. Doubleday. 1st ed. sgn pres. VG/G. O3. $35.00

THOMPSON, Harold W. *Body, Boots & Britches.* 1940. Lippincott. 8vo. 430p. G. B11. $15.00

THOMPSON, Hunter S. *Fear & Loathing in Las Vegas.* 1971. Random. 1st ed. 8vo. 206p. blk cloth. F/dj. H5. $200.00

THOMPSON, Hunter S. *Hell's Angels: Strange & Terrible Saga.* 1967. Random. 1st ed/author's 1st book. F/clip. B4. $500.00

THOMPSON, Hunter S. *Screwjack.* 1991. Santa Barbara. Neville. 1st ed. sgn. 1/300. F/sans. L3. $175.00

THOMPSON, J. *Six Seconds in Dallas.* 1967. NY. 1st ed. VG/G. B5. $50.00

THOMPSON, J. Eric. *Catalogue of Maya Hieroglyphs.* 1976. Norman, OK. 3rd prt. 458p. VG/dj. F3. $35.00

THOMPSON, J. Eric. *Maya Archaeologist.* 1963. Norman, OK. 1st ed. 284p. VG/dj. F3. $20.00

THOMPSON, J. Eric. *Thomas Gage's Travels in New World.* 1958. Norman, OK. 1st ed. 379p. VG/dj. F3. $35.00

THOMPSON, J.A. *Bible & Archaeology.* 1962. Grand Rapids, MI. Eerdmans. 468p. NF/dj. W1. $22.00

THOMPSON, Jim. *Heed the Thunder.* 1946. Greenberg. 1st ed. VG/VG. P3. $500.00

THOMPSON, Jim. *Heed the Thunder.* 1991. Armchair Detective Lib. F/F. P3. $25.00

THOMPSON, Jim. *Killer Inside Me.* 1989. Los Angeles. 1st hc ed. contributor/sgn Stephen King. F/F/F case. A11. $175.00

THOMPSON, Jim. *Now & on Earth.* 1986. Denis McMillan. 1st ed. 1/400. intro/sgn Stephen King. F/dj. M2. $100.00

THOMPSON, Julius E. *Black Pr in MS 1865-1985: A Directory.* 1988. W Cornwall. Locust Hill. 144p. F. B2. $25.00

THOMPSON, June. *Dying Fall.* 1986. Crime Club. 1st ed. VG/VG. P3. $18.00

THOMPSON, Kay. *Eloise at Christmas Time.* 1958. Random. 1st ed. ils Hilary Knight. VG. D6. $115.00

THOMPSON, Kay. *Eloise at Christmas Time.* 1959 (1958). London. Reinhardt. 1st ed. sm 4to. F/F. C8. $200.00

THOMPSON, Kay. *Eloise in Moscow.* 1959. Random. 1st ed. VG/VG. B5. $120.00

THOMPSON, Kay. *Eloise in Moscow.* 1959. Random. 1st ed. 4to. orange brd. G/G. D6. $100.00

THOMPSON, Kay. *Eloise in Moscow.* 1960 (1959). London. Reinhart. 1st Eng ed. ils Hilary Knight. NF/NF. C8. $175.00

THOMPSON, Kay. *Eloise in Paris.* 1958. London. Reinhart. 1st Eng ed. ils Hilary Knight. F/F. C8. $175.00

THOMPSON, Kay. *Eloise: A Book for Precocious Grown-Ups.* 1955. Simon Schuster. 9th prt. ils Hilary Knight. NF/VG+. C8. $40.00

THOMPSON, Lawrence. *Robert Frost: Early Years: 1874-1915.* 1966. HRW. 1st ed. NF. B4. $75.00

THOMPSON, Leroy. *All Americans, the 82nd Airborne.* 1988. Great Britian. 192p. VG/dj. B18. $15.00

THOMPSON, Mary Lou. *Voices of the New Feminism.* 1970. Beacon. F/G. V4. $8.50

THOMPSON, Morley K. *Climatological Atlas of Canada.* 1953. Ottawa. Dept Transport. 256p. G/sbdg. K5. $20.00

THOMPSON, Paul D. *Gases & Plasmas.* 1966. Lippincott. 8vo. 168p. beige cloth. xl. G. K5. $9.00

THOMPSON, Richard L. *Vedic Cosmography & Astronomy.* 1989. Los Angeles. Bhaktivedanta Book Trust. 8vo. 242p. pb. K5. $16.00

THOMPSON, Ruth Plumly. *Captain Salt in Oz.* 1936. Reilly Lee. 2nd or latter issue. fair. M5. $18.00

THOMPSON, Ruth Plumly. *Cowardly Lion of Oz.* 1923. Reilly Lee. 1st ed. ils JR Neill. 291p. gr cloth. VG. D6. $175.00

THOMPSON, Ruth Plumly. *Lost King of Oz.* 1925. Reilly Lee. 1st ed. ils JR Neill. bl cloth. VG. D6. $175.00

THOMPSON, Ruth Plumly. *Princess of Cozytown.* 1922. Chicago. 1st ed. VG. B5. $150.00

THOMPSON, Steven L. *Recovery.* 1980. Warner. VG/VG. P3. $15.00

THOMPSON, Valerie M. *Not a Suitable Hobby for an Airman.* 1986. Orchard Books. 1st ed. sgn. rebound half leather. F. M7. $75.00

THOMPSON, Walter. *Federal Centralization: A Study & Criticism...* 1923. Harcourt Brace. bl cloth. xl. M11. $25.00

THOMPSON, William. *William Butterfield, Victorian Architect.* 1971. Cambridge. MIT. ils. gilt/red stp gray cloth. F/VG. F1. $35.00

THOMSON, E.H. *Harvey Cushing.* 1950. NY. ils. 374p. G7. $35.00

THOMSON, John. *Enquiry, Concerning the Liberty, & Licentiousness of Press.* 1801. NY. Johnson Stryker. 1st ed. 8vo. 84p. sewn plain wrp. M1. $550.00

THOMSON, June. *Secret Files of Sherlock Holmes.* 1990. London. Constable. 1st ed. sgn. F/F. M15. $45.00

THOMSON, Richard. *Antique American Clocks & Watches.* 1976. Galahad. rpt. 192p. VG/VG. A8. $12.00

THOMSON, W.M. *Land & the Book; or, Biblical Ils Drawn From Manners...* 1860. Harper. 1 of 2 vol only. sm 8vo. 560p. xl. G. W1. $10.00

THOMSON, William. *Outline of Laws of Thought.* 1842. London. Pickering. 12mo. full paneled calf. VG. scarce. G1. $250.00

THORBECKE, Ellen. *Promised Land.* 1947. Harper. 1st ed. 171p. VG. W1. $14.00

THOREAU, Henry David. *Cape Cod.* 1865. Tichnor Fields. 1st ed/1st prt. 8vo. 1/2000. F. w/24p pub catalog. B24. $500.00

THOREAU, Henry David. *Early Spring in MA.* 1881. Houghton Mifflin. 1st ed. teg. gilt gr cloth. VG. Q1. $350.00

THOREAU, Henry David. *Excursions.* 1863. Tichnor Fields. 1st ed/1st prt. 1/1500. ftspc. gr cloth. F. B24. $500.00

THOREAU, Henry David. *Letters to Various Persons.* 1865. Ticknor Fields. 1st ed/1st prt. 8vo. 229p. purple cloth. F. B24. $850.00

THOREAU, Henry David. *Maine Woods.* 1864. Ticknor Fields. 1st ed/1st prt. 8vo. 1/1450. 328+23 ad p. F. B24. $600.00

THOREAU, Henry David. *Men of Concord.* 1936. Boston. 1st ed thus. 10 mc pl. VG. A17. $45.00

THOREAU, Henry David. *Walden; or, Life in the Woods.* 1854. Ticknor FIelds. 1st ed/1st prt. 8vo. 1/2000. 252+8 ad p. F. B24. $8,000.00

THOREAU, Henry David. *Week on the Concord & Merrimack Rivers.* 1849. Boston. 1st ed/author's 1st book. recased. gr cloth case. C2. $2,000.00

THOREAU, Henry David. *Week on the Concord & Merrimack Rivers.* 1849. Boston/Cambridge. Munroe. 1st ed/author's 1st book. 412p. F/box/leather label. C6. $16,000.00

THOREAU, Henry David. *Winter Walk.* 1991. Bangor, ME. Theodore Pr. 1/140. sgn ils/prt/binder. linen boards. M. B24. $325.00

THOREAU, Henry David. *Yankee in Canada, With Anti-Slavery & Reform Papers.* 1866. Ticknor Fields. 1st ed. 8vo. 286p. A bdg. VG. C6. $650.00

THORNBURG, Newton. *Black Angus.* 1978. Little Brn. 1st ed. VG/VG. P3. $23.00

THORNBURG, Opal. *Earlham: Story of the College, 1847-1962.* 1963. Earlham College. 8vo. 484p. VG/chip. V3. $20.00

THORNDIKE, Lynn. *Sphere of Sacrobosco & Its Commentators.* 1949. Chicago. 8vo. 496p. VG. K5. $85.00

THORNDIKE, Russell. *Master of the Macabre.* 1946. London. 1st ed. F/chip. M2. $35.00

THORNE, D. *Peter the Goat.* 1940. McKay. ils. VG/G. P2. $25.00

THORNE, D. *Your Dogs & Mine.* 1932. NY. Loring Massey. ils. 115p. cloth. G. R2. $30.00

THORNE, Paul. *Murder in the Fog.* 1929. Penn. 1st ed. VG. P3. $40.00

THORNE, Wynne. *Land & Water Use.* 1963. WA, DC. ils/index. 364p. xl. B26. $15.00

THORNE & MORAN. *Chips: Story of a Cocker Spaniel.* 1945 (1944). Phil. Winston. 4th prt. unp. VG. R2. $30.00

THOROLD, W.J. *Near the Throne.* 1899. Meyer. 290p. blk stp gr cloth. VG. S11. $12.00

THORP, N. Howard. *Pardner of the Wind: Story of the SW Cowboy.* 1945. Caxton. 1st ed. photos/index. VG. A18. $50.00

THORPE, Edward. *Chandlertown: Los Angeles of Philip Marlowe.* 1984. St Martin. 1st Am ed. ils. F/F. S6. $30.00

THRASHER, L.L. *Cat's Paw, Inc.* 1991. Tulsa. Council Oaks. 1st ed. F/F. B3. $15.00

THROWER, S.L. *Hong Kong Lichens.* 1988. Hong Kong. ils/photos. 193p. sc. M. B26. $34.95

THURBER, James. *My Life & Hard Times.* 1933. NY. 4th prt. inscr/sgn author & wife. 153p. G/fair. w/ephemera. B18. $450.00

THURBER, James. *White Deer.* Sept 1945. Harcourt Brace. NF/VG. C8. $30.00

THURBER, James. *Wonderful O.* 1957. Simon Schuster. 1st ed. 72p. VG/dj. M20. $30.00

THURBER, James. *Wonderful O.* 1957. Simon Schuster. 1st prt. NF/NF. C8. $42.00

THURSTON, Robert. *Alicia II.* 1978. Putnam. 1st ed. F/F/wrp band. P3. $10.00

THURSTONE, L.L. *Measurement of Values.* 1959. Chicago. 322p. M/dj. K4. $40.00

TIBBLES, Thomas Henry. *Buckskin & Blanket Days.* 1957. Doubleday. 1st ed. 336p. VG/dj. M20. $20.00

TICE, George A. *Seacoast Maine: People & Places by Martin Dibner.* 1973. Doubleday. 1st ed. sgn. F/NF. S9. $100.00

TICKELL, John. *History of the Town & Country of Kingston Upon Hull.* 1796. Hull, Eng. 1st ed. 18 pl/2 maps. full calf. C6. $300.00

TIELE, C.P. *History of the Egyptian Religion.* 1882. London. Trubner. 8vo. 230p. trans Ballingal. gilt orange cloth. VG. F1. $45.00

TIELKE, Johann Gottlieb. *Vertrage Fur Kriegs-Kunst und Geschichte des Krieges...* 1786. Frieburg. sm 4to. 332p. early full calf. VG. F1. $350.00

TIEMANN & TIEMANN. *Boy Named John.* 1948. Platt Munk. ils Rebus. brd. F. M5. $25.00

TIFFANY, Francis. *This Goodly Frame the Earth...* 1900. Houghton Mifflin. 5th ed. 364p. cloth. G. W1. $14.00

TIGAR, Michael E. *Law & Rise of Capitalism.* 1977. NY. Monthly Review. fwd Thomas I Emerson. M11. $35.00

TILDEN, Josephine E. *Algae & Their Life Relations.* 1935. Minneapolis. ils. 550p. B26. $37.50

TILLETT, Leslie. *American Needlework 1776-1976...* 1975. np. cloth. VG. G2. $15.00

TILLEY, Patrick. *Cloud Warrior.* 1984. WH Allen. 1st ed. VG/VG. P3. $18.00

TILLICH, Paul. *Future of Religions.* 1966. Harper Row. 94p. VG/VG. B33. $24.00

TILMAN, H.W. *Mischief Among the Penguins.* 1961. London. Hart Davis. ils/maps/diagrams. 192p. dj. T7. $28.00

TILTON, George Fred. *Cap'n George Fred.* 1929 (1928). Doubleday Doran. 295p. gilt bl cloth. VG/chip. M20. $35.00

TIMBS, John. *Curiosities of London...* 1867. London. Virtue. new ed. sm 4to. 871p. VG. D3. $75.00

TIME LIFE. *Mountains. Life Nature Lib.* 1971. Time Life. ils. VG. B34. $5.00

TIMROD, Henry. *Poems of Henry Timrod.* 1899. Houghton Mifflin. Memorial ed/1st prt. 193p. bl cloth. VG. C6. $35.00

TINBERGEN, N. *Social Behavior in Animals.* 1953. Methuen/Wiley. 139p. G. K4. $10.00

TINGLE, Dolli. *Valiant Little Tailor.* 1946. WI. John Martin. ils. unp. pict brd/sbdg. VG/VG. A3. $13.00

TINKER, Ben. *Mexican Wilderness & Wildlife.* 1978. Austin, TX. 1st ed. 131p. VG/dj. F3. $20.00

TINKLE, Don. *American Original: Life of J Frank Dobie.* 1978. Little Brn. 1st ed. photos/bibliography/index. F/F. A18. $25.00

TINKLE, Lon. *J Frank Dobie: Makings of an Ample Mind.* 1968. Encino. 1/850. sgn. F/VG case. B19. $50.00

TINLING & WRIGHT. *William Byrd of Virginia: London Diary 1717-1721.* 1958. Oxford. 8vo. 647p. bl cloth. VG/G. B11. $40.00

TIPPETT, Tom. *When Southern Labor Stirs.* 1931. Cape Smith. 1st ed. 2nd tan cloth bdg. NF/NF. B2. $40.00

TIPPETT, Tom. *When Southern Labor Stirs.* 1931. NY. Cape Smith. 1st ed. VG/fair. V4. $25.00

TIPTREE, James; see Sheldon, Alice Bradley.

TIRMIZI, S.A.I. *Persian Letters of Ghalib.* 1969. New Delhi. Ghalib. 1st ed. 122p. VG/dj. W1. $10.00

TISSANDIER, Gaston. *Livres Minuscules. La Plus Grande Bibliotheque...* 1894. Paris. Masson. 8vo. 7 wood engravings. 20p. F/prt wrp. B24. $350.00

TITMUSS, Richard. *Gift Relationship: From Human Blood to Social Policy.* 1971. NY. 1st ed. 339p. A13. $30.00

TITTLE, Walter. *First Nantucket Tea Party.* 1907. Doubleday. 1st ed. cloth/mc pl. NF. M5. $45.00

TOBIE, Edward P. *History of the First Maine Cavalry.* 1887. Boston. 1st ed. index. 732p. O8. $275.00

TOBIN, A.I. *Frank Harris.* 1931. Madelaine Mendelsohn. 1st ed. 1/1000. F/VG. F4. $85.00

TODD, Mabel Loomis. *Tripoli the Mysterious.* 1912. Boston. Sm Maynard. 8vo. 214p. teg. xl. VG. W1. $35.00

TODD, Robert B. *Clinical Lectures on Certain Acute Diseases.* 1860. London. 487p. cloth. G7. $95.00

TOESCA, Pietro. *La Pittura Fiorentina del Trecento.* 1929. Verona. Pantheon. 1st ed. 119 pl. gilt quarter morocco/cloth. K1. $200.00

TOGAWA, Masako. *Lady Killer.* 1986. NY. Dodd Mead. 1st Am ed. trans Simon Grove. F/F. S6. $30.00

TOIBIN, Colm. *South.* 1991. NY. Viking/Penguin. 1st Am ed. F/F. A14. $25.00

TOKLAS, Alice B. *Staying on Alone.* 1973. Liveright. 1st ed. RS. NF/NF. S9. $30.00

TOKLAS, Alice B. *What Is Remembered.* 1963. HRW. 1st Am ed. F/F. H4. $45.00

TOKLAS, Alice B. *What Is Remembered.* 1963. HRW. 1st ed. VG/VG. S11. $15.00

TOKLAS, Alice B. *What Is Remembered.* 1963. NY. HRW. 1st ed. NF/VG+. E3. $35.00

TOLKIEN, J.R.R. *Adventures of Tom Bombadil & Other Verses From the Red Book.* 1963. Houghton Mifflin. 8th prt. 63p. VG-. A3. $6.00

TOLKIEN, J.R.R. *Adventures of Tom Bombadil.* 1963. Houghton Mifflin. 1st Am ed. 63p. pict brd. F/clip. H5. $100.00

TOLKIEN, J.R.R. *Farmer Giles of Ham.* 1950. Houghton Mifflin. 1st Am ed. 8vo. 78p. blk stp bl cloth. F/dj. H5. $250.00

TOLKIEN, J.R.R. *Film Book of Lord of the Rings.* 1978. Ballantine. 1st ed. VG/lg closed tears. P3. $40.00

TOLKIEN, J.R.R. *Finn & Hengest.* 1983. Houghton Mifflin. 1st ed. 12mo. F/F. S11. $20.00

TOLKIEN, J.R.R. *Hobbit.* nd. Houghton Mifflin. 35th ed. VG+/dj. M21. $7.50

TOLKIEN, J.R.R. *Hobbit.* 1938. Houghton Mifflin. 1st Am ed/2nd state (Pan on title p). 310p. G+. P2. $285.00

TOLKIEN, J.R.R. *Letters of JRR Tolkien.* 1981. Houghton Mifflin. 1st ed. VG/VG. P3. $20.00

TOLKIEN, J.R.R. *Lord of the Rings.* 1993. London. Folio Soc. 3rd prt thus. ils Ingahild Grathmer. 3 vols. M/case. A18. $150.00

TOLKIEN, J.R.R. *Mr Bliss.* 1983 (1982). Houghton Mifflin. 1st Am ed. NF/VG+. C8. $35.00

TOLKIEN, J.R.R. *Return of the King.* 1956. Houghton Mifflin. 1st Am ed. 416p. VG/G. P2. $250.00

TOLKIEN, J.R.R. *Return of the Shadow.* 1988. Houghton Mifflin. 1st ed. VG/VG. P3. $20.00

TOLKIEN, J.R.R. *Silmarillion.* 1977. Allen Unwin. 1st ed. F/F. P3. $25.00

TOLKIEN, J.R.R. *Silmarillion.* 1977. Houghton Mifflin. 1st Am ed/1st ed. F/F. T2. $16.00

TOLKIEN, J.R.R. *Sir Gawain & the Gr Knight, Pearl, Sir Orfeo.* 1975. Houghton Mifflin. 1st ed thus. F/NF. S9. $35.00

TOLKIEN, J.R.R. *Two Towers.* 1967. Houghton Mifflin. 1st ed/1st prt revised ed. F/F. N3. $15.00

TOLLES, Fredrick B. *Meeting House & Courting House.* 1948. Chapel Hill. 1st ed. 8vo. 292p. xl. G. V3. $10.00

TOLTEN, Hans. *Enchanting Wilderness. Adventures in Darkest South Am.* 1936. London. Selwyn Blount. 1st ed. 8vo. 17 bl. blk cloth. VG/VG 2nd prt. B11. $45.00

TOMALIN, Claire. *Katherine Mansfield.* 1988. NY. 1st ed. 283p. F/F. A17. $10.00

TOMKINS, Calvin. *Lewis & Clark Trail.* 1965. Stewart Udall. 1st ed. photos/maps. F/VG. B34. $35.00

TOMLIN, E.W.F. *RG Collingwood. Writers & Their Work No 42.* 1953. Longman Gr. 40p. VG. G1. $25.00

TOMLINSON, Everett. *Pennant.* 1912. Barse Hopkins. rpt. G. P8. $20.00

TOMLINSON, H.M. *Brown Owl.* 1928. Garden City. 1st ed. sgns. 1/107. 12mo. patterned brd. NF/glassine. C2. $150.00

TOMLINSON, P.B. *Structural Biology of Palms.* 1990. Oxford. ils/pl/bibliography/index. 477p. M. B26. $119.95

TOMPKINS, Jane. *Porcupine Twins.* 1954. Lippincott. 1st ed. ils Kurt Wiese. 121p. G/G. P2. $15.00

TOMPKINS, John Barr. *Voyage of Pleasure: Log of Bernard Gilboy...* 1956. Cornell Maritime Pr. sgn. 2 fld plans. 64p. VG/worn. P4. $45.00

TOMPKINS, Peter. *Italy Betrayed.* 1966. Simon Schuster. 1st prt. 341p. VG/dj. M20. $10.00

TOMPKINS, Peter. *Murder of Admiral Darlan.* 1965. Simon Schuster. 1st prt. 287p. F/G. A17. $8.50

TOMPKINS, Peter. *Mysteries of the Mexican Pyramids.* 1976. Harper Row. 1st ed. ils. 427p. VG/VG. B11. $30.00

TONEYAMA, Kajin. *Popular Arts of Mexico.* 1974. Weatherhill/Heibonsha. 2nd prt. 225p. dj. F3. $95.00

TOOLE, K. Ross. *Hist Essays on Montana & Northwest.* 1957. np. 1/2000. sc. VG. B34. $40.00

TOOLE, K. Ross. *Montana, an Uncommon Land.* 1973. OK U. 6th prt. VG/dj. B34. $35.00

TOOLE, K. Ross. *Rape of the Great Plains, NW Am, Cattle & Coal.* 1976. np. 1st ed. NF/VG. B34. $55.00

TOOLE, K. Ross. *20th-Century Montana, State of Extremes.* 1972. OK U. 2nd prt. NF/dj. B34. $35.00

TOOLEY, R.V. *Maps & Map-Makers.* 1952. London. Batsford. ils. 140p. T7. $55.00

TOOMER, Jean. *Essentials.* 1931. Chicago. 1st ed. 1/1000. 8vo. 72p. F/VG. C6. $1,100.00

TOPHAM, John. *Traditional Crafts of Saudi Arabia.* 1981. London. Stacey. 1st ed. ils. VG/G. O3. $65.00

TOPOR, Roland. *Tenant.* 1966. WH Allen. 1st ed. VG/G. P3. $18.00

TORBET, Robert. *Hist of the Baptists.* 1965. Judson. 553p. G/dj. B29. $8.00

TORBET, Robert. *Venture of Faith.* 1955. Judson. 634p. VG/dj. B29. $7.50

TORGOVNICK, Marianna. *Gone Primitive.* 1990. Chicago. 1st ed. F/F. P3. $25.00

TORRES, Luis Maria. *Los Primitivos Habitantes del Delta del Parana.* 1911. Buenos Aires. 4to. 617p. rebound. F3. $95.00

TOSCHES, Nick. *Cut Numbers.* 1988. Harmony. 1st ed. F/NF. F4. $15.00

TOURGEE, Albion W. *Bricks Without Straw.* 1880. Fords Howard Hulbert. 1st ed. 521p. ES. G. H1. $25.00

TOURGEE, Albion W. *Figs & Thistles.* 1879. Fords Howard Hulbert. 1st ed. 538p. G. H1. $12.00

TOURNACHON, Gaspard-Felix. *Nadar: 50 Photographies de ses Illustres Contemporains.* 1975. Paris. Tresors De La Photogrphie. 1st ed. 4to. F/NF. S9. $75.00

TOURON, Antoine. *Histoire des Hommes Illustres de l'Ordre de Saint Dominique.* 1743-1749. Paris. Babuty. 6 vol. 1st ed. 4to. mottled calf. H10. $275.00

TOUSEY, Sanford. *Chinky Joins the Circus.* 1941 (1938). Doubleday. ils Sanford Tousey. G+. C8. $20.00

TOVEY, Eloyde. *Guide to the New Am Poetry: San Francisco Bay Scene 1918-60.* 1985. private prt. 1st ed. sgn. plain buckram. F. B2. $50.00

TOWLER, J.M.D. *Silver Sunbeam.* 1969. Hastings-on-Hudson. Morgan. facsimile/1st prt. 8vo. F. S9. $35.00

TOWNSEND, C.H. *US Albatross in Lower California Sea Cruise of 1911.* 1925. NY. Am Mus. 1st ed. VG. B5. $175.00

TOWNSEND, G.W. *Memorial Life of Wm McKinley.* nd. np. ils. 520p. marbled foredge. VG. H1. $18.00

TOWNSEND, John K. *Narrative of a Journey Across the Rocky Mountains...* 1839. Phil. brd/lacks backstrip. A1. $300.00

TOWNSEND, Kim. *Sherwood Anderson.* 1987. Houghton Mifflin. UP. 358p. VG/orange wrp. M20. $12.00

TOY, Barbara. *Way of the Chariots: Niger River...* 1964. London. Murray. 1st ed. sm 8vo. VG. W1. $18.00

TOYE, Randall. *Agatha Crhistie Who's Who.* 1990. Canada. Collins. VG/VG. P3. $20.00

TOYNBEE, Arnold J. *Study of Hist.* 1947. Oxford. 7th prt. sm 8vo. xl. W1. $10.00

TOYNBEE, J.M.C. *Roman Art Treasures From Temple of Mithras.* 1986. London/Middlesex. broad 8vo. 69p. VG/stiff wrp. W1. $7.00

TRACY, Jack. *Encyclopedia of Sherlockiana.* 1977. NY. 1st ed. 411 p. F/F. A17. $17.50

TRAIN, Arthur. *Hermit of Turkey Hollow.* 1921. Scribner. 1st ed. VG. P3. $25.00

TRAIN, Arthur. *Lost Gospel.* 1925. Scribner. 1st ed. VG. M2. $30.00

TRAIN, Arthur. *True Stories of Crime From District Attorney's Office.* 1926. NY. Scribner. orig cloth. M11. $35.00

TRAIN, Arthur. *Yankee Lawyer: Autobiography of Ephraim Tutt.* 1943. Scribner. 1st ed. G/worn. M11. $35.00

TRALINS, Bob. *Green Murder.* 1991. London. MacDonald. 1st ed. F/F. S6. $25.00

TRAPIER, Paul. *Incidents in My Life.* 1954. Charleston, SC. 1st ed. 66p. NF/prt wrp. M8. $27.50

TRAPP, Carolyn. *Cacti of Zion National Park.* 1969. np. ils/map. 21p. F/wrp. B26. $7.50

TRAPP, Dan L. *Encyclopedia of Frontier Biography.* 1990. Arthur H Clark. 3 vol. 2nd prt. M/dj. A18. $175.00

TRAPROCK, Walter E. *Sarah of the Sahara: Romance of Nomads' Land.* 1923. Putnam. 1st ed. 224p. VG. W1. $15.00

TRAUX, Rhoda. *Joseph Lister: Father of Modern Surgery.* 1944. Indianapolis. 283p. G7. $20.00

TRAVEN, B. *Cotton-Pickers.* 1969. Hill Wang. 1st ed. F/clip. B3. $60.00

TRAVEN, B. *White Rose.* 1979. Westport. Lawrence Hill. 1st ed. F/NF. B3. $30.00

TRAVER, Robert. *Laughing Whitefish.* 1965. McGraw Hill. 1st ed. VG/VG. P3. $25.00

TRAVER, Robert. *Laughing Whitefish.* 1965. NY. 1st ed. F/F. A17. $65.00

TRAVER, Robert. *Small Town DA.* 1954. NY. 1st ed. 253p. brd. NF/dj. D3. $75.00

TRAVERS, Hugh. *Madame Aubry Dines With Death.* 1967. Harper Row. 1st ed. VG/VG. P3. $10.00

TRAVERS, P.L. *Mary Poppins Come Back.* 1935. Reynal Hitchcock. 1st Am ed. ils Mary Shepard. 268p. VG/fair. P2. $50.00

TRAVIS, Elizabeth. *Under the Influence.* 1989. np. 263p. F/NF. A4. $30.00

TRAYNOR, Roger J. *Riddle of Harmless Error.* 1970. OH State. M11. $65.00

TREATT, Stella Court. *Cape to Cairo: Record of Hist Motor Journey.* 1927. Little Brn. 1st ed. 8vo. 56 (of 62) pl. xl. G. W1. $12.00

TREECE, Henry. *Queen's Brooch.* 1967. Putnam. 1st ed. VG. P3. $10.00

TREMAIN, Henry Edwin. *Last Hours of Sheridan's Cavalry.* 1904. Bonnell Silver Bowers. 1st ed. 563p. cloth. VG+. M8. $150.00

TREMAYNE, Peter; see Ellis, Peter.

TRENCH, Richard C. *Notes on the Parables of Our Lord.* 1955.. Baker. 211p. VG/dj. B29. $5.50

TRENDLEBURG, Adolf. *Logische Untersuchungen.* 1862. Leipzig. Hirzel. 2 vol in 1. 2nd enlarged ed. leather brd. VG. G1. $150.00

TRENT, Robbie. *To Church We Go.* 1956. Follet. ils EO Jones. VG/VG. B17. $4.00

TRENTO, Joseph J. *Prescription for Disaster: From Glory of Apollo...* 1987. NY. Crown. 1st prt. VG/VG. K5. $20.00

TRESS, Arthur. *Dream Collector.* 1972. Richmond. Westover. 1st ed. sgn. NF/VG. S9. $150.00

TRESS, Arthur. *Shadow.* 1975. Avon. 1st ed. sgn. VG+/wrp. S9. $125.00

TREVANIAN. *Loo Sanction.* 1973. Crown. 1st ed. F/dj. F4. $18.00

TREVELYAN, Humphrey. *Middle East in Revolution.* 1970. Boston. Gambit. 1st ed. 8vo. 275p. VG/dj. W1. $14.00

TREVES, Frederick. *Cradle of the Deep.* 1908. London. Smith Elder. 8vo. 40 pl/4 maps. teg. bl brd. G. B11. $75.00

TREVINO, Lee. *Call Me Super Mex.* 1982. NY. 1st ed. sgn. VG/VG. B5. $35.00

TREVOR, Elleston. *Place for the Wicked.* 1968. Doubleday. 1st ed. NF/NF. P3. $35.00

TREVOR, William. *Family Sins.* 1990. Bodley Head. 1st ed. sgn. NF/NF. B3. $30.00

TREVOR, William. *Night at the Alexandra.* 1987. London. Hutchinson. 1st ed. ils Paul Hogarth. F/F. B3. $15.00

TREVOR-BATTYE, Aubyn. *Ice-Bound on Kolguev.* 1895. Westminster. Constable. 3rd ed. 453p. gr cloth. VG+. P4. $100.00

TREW, Antony. *Bannister's Chart.* 1985. St Martin. 1st Am ed. F/NF. M15. $25.00

TRIENENS. *Pioneer Imprints From Fifty States.* 1973. Lib of Congress. 4to. ils. 95p. VG. A4. $45.00

TRIGG, Elwood B. *Gypsy Demons & Divinities: Magic & Religion of Gypsies.* 1973. Secaucus, NY. Citidel. 1st ed. F/F. C8. $25.00

TRIMBLE, Albert C. *Modern Porcelain.* 1962. Harper. 1st ed. 224p. VG/dj. M20. $15.00

TRIMMER, Sarah. *Easy Intro to Knowledge of Nature...* 1796. Boston. West. 12mo. 147p. leather spine/lacks brd. H10. $100.00

TRIMMER, Sarah. *Series of Prints Designed to Ils the Scripture Hist.* 1821. London. Baldwin Craddock. rpt of 1786 ed. 15mo. 32 copper pl. contemporary calf. K1. $75.00

TRIMPEY, Alice Kent. *Becky, My First Love...* 1946. Baraboo, WI. Remington. 1st ed. inscr. photos EB Trimpey. NF/NF. C8. $60.00

TRIPP, Miles. *Death of Man-Tamer.* 1987. St Martin. 1st ed. VG/VG. P3. $15.00

TROGUS POMPEIUS. *Justini in Historias...Accutante Matthia Berneccero...* 1631. Argentoratum. Zetzneri. orig prt this ed. 12mo. 572p. vellum. H10. $125.00

TRONCHE, Anne. *Ljuba.* 1981. NY. Alpine Fine Arts. trans I Mark Paris. ils. F/F. F1. $75.00

TROTT, Harold W. *Santa Claus in Santa Land.* 1943. Grosset Williams. 1st ed. ils Ben/Ruby Easton. 95p. cloth. VG/dj. A3. $17.50

TROTZKY, Leon. *Bolshevicki & World Peace.* 1918. Boni Liveright. 1st ed. F/NF. B2. $50.00

TROTZKY, Leon. *Real Situation in Russia.* 1928. Harcourt. 1st ed. trans Max Eastman. F/NF. B2. $200.00

TROUT, Kilgore; see Farmer, Philip Jose.

TROW, Charles. *Old Shipmasters of Salem.* 1905. Putnam. ils. 337p. T7. $70.00

TROY, Simon. *Drunkard's End.* 1961. Walker. 1st ed. VG/VG. P3. $15.00

TROYAT, Henri. *Ivan the Terrible.* 1984. NY. Dutton. 1st Am ed. 283p. F/F. B14. $20.00

TRUDEAU, Noah. *Bloody Roads South: Wilderness to Cold Harbor.* 1989. ils/index. 354p. dj. O8. $12.50

TRUEBLOOD, Elton. *Company of the Committed.* 1961. Harper. 113p. F/dj. B29. $4.00

TRUEBLOOD, Elton. *Future of the Christian.* 1971. Harper. 1st ed. 102p. VG/dj. B29. $3.50

TRUEBLOOD, Elton. *Humor of Christ: Significant But Often Unrecognized Aspect.* 1964. Harper Row. sgn. 125p. F/F. B33. $25.00

TRUEBLOOD, Elton. *New Man for Our Time.* 1970. Harper Row. 12mo. 126p. VG/G. V3. $10.00

TRUMAN, Ben C. *Occidental Sketches.* 1881. San Francisco News Co. 1st ed. pres. 212p/12p ads. gilt brn cloth. VG+. P4. $150.00

TRUMAN, Harry S. *Memoirs... Vol 1: Year of Decisions.* 1955. Doubleday. 1st ed. 596p. VG/G. H1. $16.00

TRUMAN, Margaret. *Murder at the FBI.* 1985. Arbor. 1st ed. VG/VG. P3. $15.00

TRUMAN, Margaret. *Murder at the Kennedy Center.* 1985. Random. 1st ed. F/F. P3. $18.00

TRUMBO, Dalton. *Eclipse.* 1935. London. Lovat Dickson. 1st ed/author's 1st book. F/VG. B4. $300.00

TRUMBO, Dalton. *Washington Jitters.* 1936. Knopf. 1st ed. 287p. bl stp yel cloth. VG/dj. H5. $125.00

TRUMP, Elizabeth. *Every Child's Pet Book.* 1941. Lothrop. 1st ed. ils Carroll C Snell. pict brd. VG+/dj. M5. $20.00

TRUSS, Seldon. *Doctor Was a Dame.* 1953. Crime Club. 1st ed. VG/VG. P3. $20.00

TRUSS, Seldon. *Turmoil at Brede.* 1931. Mystery League. 1st ed. VG. P3. $18.00

TRUX, Jon. *Space Race: From Sputnik to Shuttle.* 1985. Sevenoaks, UK. NEL. ils. 160p. VG/VG. K5. $25.00

TRYON, Thomas. *Harvest Home.* 1979. Knopf. 7th ed. VG/VG. P3. $12.00

TSCHIFFELY, A.F. *Coricancha.* 1943. London. 2nd prt. 220p. VG. F3. $10.00

TSCHIFFELY, A.F. *Tale of Two Horses.* 1935. Simon Schuster. 1st ed. VG. O3. $40.00

TUBB, E.C. *Rogue Planet.* 1977. Barker. 1st ed. Space: 1999 TVTI. NF/NF. P3. $18.00

TUCHMAN, Barbara. *Distant Mirror.* 1978. Franklin Lib. 1st ed. full leather. F. B3. $40.00

TUCHMAN, Barbara. *Stilwell & the American Experience in China 1911-45.* 1971. NY. 1st ed. 621p. VG/dj. B18. $19.50

TUCK, Raphael. *Friends in the Country.* ca 1907-1910. Tuck. pict brd. VG. M5. $70.00

TUCK, Raphael. *Jack the Giant Killer.* ca 1900. Tuck. 4 mc pl. VG/stiff wrp. M5. $60.00

TUCKER, Glenn. *High Tide at Gettysburg.* 1958. index. 462p. dj. O8. $23.50

TUCKER, Irving F. *Adjustment: Models & Mechanisms.* 1970. Academic. 472p. F/dj. K4. $10.00

TUCKER, Wilson. *Ice & Iron.* 1974. Doubleday. 1st ed. VG/VG. P3. $25.00

TUCKER, Wilson. *Ice & Iron.* 1975. London. Gollancz. 1st ed. inscr. F/F. T2. $25.00

TUCKER, Wilson. *Witch.* 1971. Doubleday. 1st ed. VG/VG. P3. $30.00

TUCKMAN, B. *Zimmerman Telegram.* 1958. NY. 1st ed. VG/VG. B5. $35.00

TUDOR, B. *Drawn From New England.* 1979. Cleveland. 1st ed. VG/VG. B5. $32.50

TUDOR, Tasha. *A Is for Annabelle.* 1954. Oxford. 1st ed. F/VG+. P2. $185.00

TUDOR, Tasha. *A Is for Annabelle.* 1954. Oxford. 1st ed. obl 8vo. gilt gr cloth. NF/NF. D6. $225.00

TUDOR, Tasha. *And It Was So.* 1958. Phil. Westminster. 1st ed. 48p. gr cloth. VG/VG. A3. $95.00

TUDOR, Tasha. *Bas ·: of Herbs: A Book of American Sentiments.* 1983. Stephen Green. 2nd prt. 12mo. F/F. B17. $55.00

TUDOR, Tasha. *Book of Christmas, a Three-Dimensional Book.* 1979. Philomel. 3rd prt. 4to. 6 popups/advent calendar. F. B17. $32.50

TUDOR, Tasha. *Christmas Village, a Three-Dimensional Advent Calendar.* 1984. Philomel. F/orig envelope. $50.00

TUDOR, Tasha. *Favorite Stories.* 1965. Lippincott. 1st ed. NF/NF. C8. $75.00

TUDOR, Tasha. *First Delights, a Book About the Five Senses.* 1991. Platt Munk. sgn. F/F. B17. $50.00

TUDOR, Tasha. *First Delights.* 1966. Platt Munk. early prt ($2.50 dj price). VG+/VG. P2. $50.00

TUDOR, Tasha. *First Poems of Childhood.* 1967. Platt Munk. pict brd. NF/VG+. C8. $35.00

TUDOR, Tasha. *More Prayers.* 1967. NY. Walck. cloth. NF/F. C8. $45.00

TUDOR, Tasha. *Mother Goose: Seventy-Seven Verses With Pictures by...* ca 1944. Oxford. 1st ed. sm 8vo. gr cloth. VG/dj. D6. $100.00

TUDOR, Tasha. *Rosemary for Remembrance.* 1981. Philomel. 1st ed. F. C8. $35.00

TUDOR, Tasha. *Springs of Joy.* 1979. Rand McNally. late rpt. folio. F/sans. B17. $18.50

TUDOR, Tasha. *Take Joy: Tasha Tudor Christmas Book.* 1966. World. 2nd ed. sm obl 4to. NF/VG+. C8. $30.00

TUDOR, Tasha. *Tale for Easter.* 1941. Oxford. 1st ed. VG/G. P2. $145.00

TUDOR, Tasha. *Tale for Easter.* 1989. Random. 16mo. rem mk. F/dj. B17. $7.50

TUDOR, Tasha. *Tasha Tudor Book of Fairy Tales.* 1969. Platt Munk. folio. F. B17. $15.00

TUDOR, Tasha. *Tasha Tudor's Favorite Christmas Carols.* 1978. NY. McKay. 2nd prt. F/NF. C8. $30.00

TUDOR, Tasha. *Tasha Tudor's Sampler: A Tale for Easter, Pumpkin Moonshine.* nd. David McKay. 2nd prt. unp. VG/G. A3. $17.50

TUDOR, Tasha. *Time To Keep.* 1977. Rand McNally. 1st prt. NF. C8. $30.00

TUDOR, Tasha. *Twenty Third Psalm.* 1965. Achille J St Onge. miniature ed. aeg. polished gr calf. F/F. B17. $35.00

TUER, Andrew W. *Pages & Pictures From Children's Books...* 1968. NY. Benjamin Blom. reissue. 8vo. 510p. bl cloth. NF. D6. $22.00

TUER, Andrew W. *Quads Within Quads. Quads for Authors, Editors & Devils.* 1884. London. Field Tuer. 2 vol. 146p+16p glossary/94 p larger version. F. B24. $1,000.00

TUER, Andrew W. *Stories From Old-Fashioned Children's Books.* 1989. Bracken. 8vo. F/F. B17. $6.50

TUKE, Daniel Hack. *Ils of Influence of Mind Upon Body in Health & Disease.* 1872. London. 444p. cloth. B14. $100.00

TUKE, Samuel. *Selections From Epistles of George Fox.* 1879. Cambridge, MA. Obadiah Brn Benevolent Fund. 12mo. 312p. G. V3. $16.00

TUKER, Francis. *Pattern of War.* 1948. London. 1st ed. 159p. VG. A17. $12.50

TUKEY, H.B. *XVIth International Horticultural Congress.* 1962. Belgium. Duculot. 5 vol (1st paper/others cloth). A10. $25.00

TULL, Jethro. *Horse-Hoeing Husbandry; or, Treatise...Tillage...* 1829. London. Cobbett. 466p. pub cloth. H10. $150.00

TUNIS, John R. *All American.* 1942. HBW. 1st ed. G+. P8. $12.50

TUNIS, John R. *Highpockets.* 1948. Morrow. 1st ed. VG/G+. P8. $40.00

TUNIS, John R. *Keystone Kids.* 1943. Harcourt. 1st ed. G+/G+. P8. $30.00

TUNIS, John R. *Kid Comes Back.* 1946. Morrow. 1st ed. VG+/VG. P8. $40.00

TUOHY, Frank. *Fingers in the Door.* 1970. NY. 1st ed. sgn title p. inscr front ep. F/NF. A11. $35.00

TURBERVILLE, A.S. *Johnson's England: Account of Life & Manners of His Age.* 1933. Oxford. 2 vol. 1st ed. NF/djs. D3. $75.00

TURBEVILLE, Deborah. *Unseen Versailles.* 1981. Doubleday. 1st ed. sgn. intro Louis Auchincloss. F/F. S9. $200.00

TUREK, Leslie. *Noreascon Proceedings Sept 3-6, 1971.* 1976. Nesfa. 1st ed. F/F. P3. $75.00

TUREVILLE, Deborah. *Wallflowers.* 1978. NY. Congreve. 1st ed. NF/VG+. S9. $80.00

TURKI, Fawaz. *Disinherited: Journal of Palestinian Exile.* 1972. Monthly Review. 1st ed. 8vo. cloth. NF/dj. W1. $18.00

TURNBULL, Andrew. *Thomas Wolfe.* 1967. Scribner. 1st ed. inscr/dtd 1968. 8vo. 374p. blk cloth. VG/poor. C6. $95.00

TURNBULL, Coulson. *Life & Teachings of Giordano Bruno.* 1913. San Diego. Gnostic. 8vo. 100p. VG/chip. K5. $40.00

TURNBULL, Ralph. *Baker's Dictionary of Practical Theology.* 1982. Baker. 469p. VG/dj. B29. $10.50

TURNER, Arlin. *George W Cable.* 1956. Duke. 1st ed. 372p. VG/dj. M20. $22.00

TURNER, E.S. *History of Courting.* 1954. London. 1st ed. 290p. A13. $35.00

TURNER, E.S. *Phoney War.* 1962. NY. 1st ed. 311p. VG/VG. A17. $9.50

TURNER, Edward. *Elements of Chemistry.* 1835. Phil. DeSilver Thomas. 5th Am ed from 5th London ed. 682p. ES. full leather. H1. $24.00

TURNER, J.M.W. *Liber Studiorum of JMW Turner.* 1882. London. Cheswick. 3 vol in 1. 1st ed thus. obl folio. aeg. VG. C6. $200.00

TURNER, Merle B. *Realism & Explanation of Behavior.* 1971. Appleton Century Crofts. 257p. cloth. VG. G1. $32.50

TURNER, Nancy Byrd. *When It Rained Cats & Dogs.* 1946. Lippincott. 1st ed. ils Timor Gergely. VG/VG. P2. $25.00

TURNER, Robert Y. *Shakespeare's Apprenticeship.* 1974. Chicago. 1st ed. RS. F/F. S9. $25.00

TURNER, Robert. *Gunsmoke.* 1958. Whitman. Gunsmoke TVTI. VG. P3. $20.00

TURNER, Theresa. *People of Fort Lowell.* 1982. Pimo Co Ft Lowell Hist District Brd. 67p. F/wrp. B19. $20.00

TURNILL, Reginald. *Language of Space: Dictionary of Astronautics.* 1970. London. Cassell. 8vo. 165p. bl cloth. VG. K5. $25.00

TUROW, Scott. *Pleading Guilty.* 1993. FSG. 1st ed. F/F. P3. $24.00

TUROW, Scott. *Presumed Innocent.* 1987. FSG. 1st ed. F/F. M15. $40.00

TURTLEDOVE, Harry. *Agent of Byzantium.* 1987. Congdon Weed. 1st ed. F/dj. M2. $25.00

TURTLEDOVE, Harry. *Different Flesh.* 1988. Congdon Weed. 1st ed. F/F. P3. $17.00

TUSKA, Jon. *Am West in Film: Critical Approaches to the Western.* 1985. Greenwood. 1st ed. photos/biblio/index. M. A18. $25.00

TUSKA, Jon. *Films of Mae West.* 1973. Citadel. 1st ed. VG/VG. P3. $20.00

TUSSER, Thomas. *Tusser Revivus...Mr Tusser's 500 Points of Husbandry...* 1710. London. Morphew. 1st ed this form. modern brd. H10. $325.00

TUTE, Warren. *Tarnham Connection.* 1971. Dent. 1st ed. NF/NF. P3. $22.00

TUTTLE, Charles R. *Alaska: Its Meaning to the World...* 1914. Seattle. Shuey. ils. 318p. T7. $45.00

TUTTLE, Lisa. *Gabriel.* 1987. Severn. 1st ed. F/F. P3. $25.00

TUTTLE, W.C. *Bluffer's Luck.* 1936. Collins. 4th ed. VG. P3. $15.00

TUTTLE, W.C. *Valley of Twisted Trails.* 1931. Boston. 1st ed. VG. A17. $10.00

TUTUOLA, Amos. *My Life in the Bush of Ghosts.* 1954. Grove. 1st Am ed. F/F. B2. $40.00

TWAIN, Mark. *Adam's Diary.* nd. Salisbury, CT. Lime Rock. 59x52mm. 1/125 total. ils/sgn Catryna Ten Eyck. F/case. B24. $200.00

TWAIN, Mark. *Adventures of Huckleberry Finn With 174 Ils.* 1885. NY. Webster. 1st Am ed. 3rd state ftspc/title p. 8vo. pict cloth. F. M1. $1,850.00

TWAIN, Mark. *Adventures of Huckleberry Finn.* 1884. London. Chatto Windus. 1st ed (precedes 1st Am ed). gilt red cloth. VG. Q1. $2,500.00

TWAIN, Mark. *Adventures of Huckleberry Finn.* 1885. Webster. 1st Am ed/1st issue. pict gr cloth. F/chemise/case. C6. $7,500.00

TWAIN, Mark. *Adventures of Huckleberry Finn.* 1885. Webster. 1st ed. ils. 366p. pict gr cloth. G. B18. $1,500.00

TWAIN, Mark. *Adventures of Huckleberry Finn.* 1885 (1884). NY. 1st ed/early issue. orig dk gr cloth. F. H4. $2,000.00

TWAIN, Mark. *Adventures of Huckleberry Finn.* 1985. CA U. ils Barry Moser. 417p. F/dj. M10. $20.00

TWAIN, Mark. *Adventures of Tom Sawyer.* 1876. Toronto. Belford Bros. 1st Canadian ed. 12mo. 4 ad p. lacks rear wrp. M1. $4,500.00

TWAIN, Mark. *Adventures of Tom Sawyer.* 1931. Winston. ils NC Wyeth. VG. B17. $8.00

TWAIN, Mark. *Adventures of Tom Sawyer.* 1939. LEC. NF. A9. $100.00

TWAIN, Mark. *American Claimant.* 1892. NY. 1st ed. 277p. pict cloth. VG. B18. $125.00

TWAIN, Mark. *Celebrated Jumping Frog & Other Stories.* 1992. Reader's Digest. VG. P3. $15.00

TWAIN, Mark. *Celebrated Jumping Frog of Calavras County & Other Sketches.* 1867. NY. Webb. 1st ed/2nd prt. sm 8vo. 198p. bl cloth. G. C6. $400.00

TWAIN, Mark. *Christian Science.* 1907. NY. 1st ed/1st issue. VG+. A9. $40.00

TWAIN, Mark. *Christian Science.* 1986. Buffalo, NY. Prometheus. 196p. F/dj. M10. $12.50

TWAIN, Mark. *Double-Barrelled Detective Story.* 1902. NY. Harper. 1st ed. ils. 179p. VG. M10. $50.00

TWAIN, Mark. *Following the Equator: Journey Around the World.* 1897. Hartford, CT. Am Pub. 1st ed/1st state. ils. 712p. VG. M10. $200.00

TWAIN, Mark. *Gilded Age.* 1873. Hartford. 1st ed/1st state except repeating lines. rare. A9. $200.00

TWAIN, Mark. *Horse's Tale.* 1907. Harper. 1st ed. ils Lucius Hitchcock. 153p. red cloth. VG. M20. $100.00

TWAIN, Mark. *Innocents Abroad.* 1869. Hartford. 1st ed/1st issue. 651p. G. B18. $250.00

TWAIN, Mark. *Life on the MS.* 1883. Boston. Osgood. 1st ed/intermediate state. 8vo. 624p. half morocco. NF. C6. $750.00

TWAIN, Mark. *Mark Twain Compliments the President's Wife.* 1984. Boston. Bromer. 61x47mm. 1/50 (total of 200). ils Rez Lingen. brn morocco. F. B24. $325.00

TWAIN, Mark. *Mark Twain's Notebook.* 1935. NY. 1st ed. F/VG. A9. $80.00

TWAIN, Mark. *Old Times on the Mississippi.* 1876. Toronto. Belford. 1st ed. 12mo. 157p. purple cloth. M1. $300.00

TWAIN, Mark. *Prince & the Pauper.* 1937. Chicago. Winston. 1st ed thus. ils Robert Lawson. NF. C8. $40.00

TWAIN, Mark. *Prince & the Pauper.* 1964. Heritage. ils. 221p. VG/case. M10. $12.50

TWAIN, Mark. *Punch, Brothers, Punch!* 1878. Clote Woodman. correct 1st ed. 12mo. 140p. decor bl cloth. VG. C6. $175.00

TWAIN, Mark. *Roughing It.* 1872. Hartford, CT. 1st ed/1st issue. ils. 591p. poor bdg. M10. $50.00

TWAIN, Mark. *Saint Joan of Arc.* 1919. Harper. 1st ed/1st state. sm 8vo. 32p. gilt blk cloth. F. D6. $125.00

TWAIN, Mark. *Tom Sawyer Abroad. By Huck Finn. Edit by Mark Twain.* 1894. Webster. 1st ed. 8vo. 219p. pict tan cloth/B bdg. NF. C6. $800.00

TWAIN, Mark. *Tragedy of Pudd'nhead Wilson.* 1894. Hartford. Am Pub. 1st Am ed/1st prt. 8vo. 432p. brn cloth. NF. C6. $500.00

TWAIN, Mark. *Tramp Abroad.* 1880. Hartford, CT. Am Pub. 1st ed. ils. 631p. fair. M10. $25.00

TWAIN, Mark. *Wit & Wisecracks.* 1961. Peter Pauper. ils 61p. F/dj. M10. $4.50

TWAIN, Mark. *Yankee at the Court of King Arthur.* 1889. London. Chatto Windus. 1st UK ed. red cloth. VG/gr cloth dj/gr cloth case. Q1. $400.00

TWENEY, George H. *Washington 89.* 1989. Morongo Valley. Sagebrush. ltd 1st ed. 1/890. 98p. M. P4. $45.00

TWIFORD, William Richard. *Sown in Darkness.* 1940. Tremayne. 1st ed. F/dj. M2. $75.00

TWIGG, Ena. *Ena Twigg: Medium.* 1972. Hawthorn. F/G. H1. $6.00

TWINING, Louisa. *Symbols & Emblems of Early & Mediaeval Christian Art.* 1852. London. Longman Gr. tall 4to. 93 pl. morocco. H10. $95.00

TWINING, T. *Travels in India 100 Years Ago With a Visit to the US.* 1893. London. 1st ed. pres. VG. C11. $100.00

TYLER, Anne. *Breathing Lessons.* 1988. Franklin Center. true 1st ed. sgn. F. L3. $125.00

TYLER, Anne. *Breathing Lessons.* 1988. Knopf. 1st trade ed. 8vo. 327p. gilt gr cloth/cream brd. F/F. H5. $50.00

TYLER, Anne. *Clock Winder.* 1972. Knopf. 1st ed. w/inscr card. VG/NF clip. L3. $650.00

TYLER, Anne. *Earthly Possessions.* 1977. Knopf. 1st ed. F/F. B4. $250.00

TYLER, Anne. *If Morning Ever Comes.* 1964. Knopf. 1st ed/author's 1st book. F/clip. C2. $1,250.00

TYLER, Anne. *If Morning Ever Comes.* 1964. Knopf. 1st ed/author's 1st book. F/F. S9. $2,000.00

TYLER, Anne. *Morgan's Passing.* 1980. Knopf. 1st ed. 8vo. 311p. brn cloth/cream brd. F/clip. H5. $100.00

TYLER, Anne. *Saint Maybe.* 1991. Franklin Lib. 1st trade ed. sgn. F/F. L3. $85.00

TYLER, Anne. *Saint Maybe.* 1991. Knopf. 1st ed. sgn. F/F. B2. $85.00

TYLER, Donald H. *Old Lawrenceville.* 1965. np. ltd ed. inscr. ils/maps. F. B14. $25.00

TYLER, E.J. *Clocks & Watches.* 1974. Golden. 1st ed. 4to. 80p. G. A8. $12.00

TYLER, E.J. *Craft of the Clockmaker.* 1973. Beekman House. 1st ed. 8vo. 192p. F/VG. A8. $20.00

TYLER, Helen E. *Where Prayer & Purpose Meet.* 1949. Signal. 311p. VG. B29. $5.00

TYLER, J.E.A. *Tolkien Companion.* 1976. St Martin. 1st ed. 531p. NF/dj. M20. $25.00

TYLER, Mabs. *Big Book of Soft Toys.* 1972. np. cloth. VG. G2. $9.00

TYLER, Maston W. *Recollections of the Civil War.* 1912. 1st ed. ils/maps. 379p. dj. O8. $32.50

TYLER, Parker. *Divine Comedy of Pavel Tchelitchew.* 1967. NY. Fleet. thick 8vo. ils. 504p. blk cloth. G. F1. $25.00

TYLER, Ron. *Alfred Jacob Miller: Artist on the OR Trail.* 1982. Amon Carter Museum. 1st ed. M/dj. A18. $45.00

TYLER, W.T. *Ants of God.* 1981. NY. 1st ed. F/F. A17. $10.00

TYNAN, Kathleen. *Agatha.* 1978. Ballantine. 1st ed. VG/VG. P3. $18.00

TYNDALE, Walter. *Below the Cataracts.* 1907. Lippincott/Heinemann. 1st ed. 60 pl. 271p. VG. W1. $65.00

TYRRELL, Henry. *History of the War With Russia.* ca 1856. London/NY. 3 vol. 1st ed. 4to. half red levant morocco. VG+. C6. $125.00

UDALL, Stewart. *In Coronado's Footsteps.* 1984. AZ Highways. ils. 50p. NF/sans. B19. $35.00

UDRY, Janice May. *Moon Jumpers.* 1979 (1959). London. Bodley Head. 1st Eng ed. ils Sendak. M. C8. $60.00

UELSMANN, Jerry N. *Jerry N Uelsmann.* 1973. NY. Aperture. revised/enlarged ed. NF/wrp. S9. $35.00

UHLAN, Edward. *Rogue of Publisher's Row: Confessions of a Publisher.* 1960. Exposition. 254p. VG/dj. M10. $6.50

UHNAK, Dorothy. *Bait.* 1968. Simon Schuster. 1st ed. VG/VG. P3. $30.00

UHNAK, Dorothy. *False Witness.* 1981. Simon Schuster. 1st ed. VG/G. P3. $10.00

UHNAK, Dorothy. *Victims.* 1985. Simon Schuster. 1st ed. F/F. F4. $15.00

ULANOFF, Stanley. *Ils Guide to US Missiles & Rockets.* 1959. Doubleday. ils. 128p. blk cloth. K5. $20.00

ULANOV, Barry. *Incredible Crosby.* 1948. NY. 1st ed. VG/VG. B5. $40.00

ULICH, Robert. *Three Thousand Years of Educational Wisdom.* 1954. Cambridge. Harvard. 2nd ed. reading copy. K4. $10.00

ULLMAN, B.L. *Ancient Writing & Its Influence.* 1963. NY. Cooper Sq. 1st ed. 12mo. 234p. VG/dj. M10. $7.50

ULLMAN, James Michael. *Neon Haystack.* nd. BC. VG/VG. P3. $8.00

ULLOM, Judith C. *Folklore of the North American Indians.* 1969. Lib of Congress. 8vo. ils/map. 126p. cloth. VG. P4. $32.50

ULMAN, James Ramsey. *Americans on Everest: Official Account of Ascent...* 1964. Lippincott. BC. G+/worn. N2. $7.50

ULMAN, James Ramsey. *Kingdom of Adventure: Everest.* 1947. NY. Wm Sloane. VG/dj. N2. $7.50

ULMAN, James Ramsey. *Straight Up: Life & Death of John Harlin.* 1968. Doubleday. VG. N2. $8.50

ULMANN, Doris. *Darkness & the Light.* 1974. Aperture. 1st ed. 4to. VG/VG. S9. $45.00

ULPH, Owen. *Fiddleback: Lore of the Linecamp.* 1981. Dream Garden. 1st ed. ils T Pat Leary. F/F. A18. $35.00

ULPH, Owen. *Leather Throne.* 1984. Dream Garden. 1st ed. F/F. A18. $40.00

UMEDA, Haruo. *Amuse for Collection.* 1983. Tokyo. Bijou. 28x32mm. 1/40 (total of 190). gr goatskin/mc inlay. F/case. B24. $400.00

UMEDA, Haruo. *Ants, the Smallest Book in the World.* 1980. Tokyo. Bijou. 2 vol. 27x27mm. 1/200. gilt gr goatskin. F/case/glass. B24. $475.00

UMEN, Samuel. *World of the Mystic.* 1988. NY. Philosophical Lib. 200p. F/F. B33. $16.00

UNCLE MERRY. *Merry's Gems of Prose & Poetry.* 1860. NY. H Dayton. 1st ed. 8vo. 240p. navy ribbed cloth. VG. D6. $35.00

UNDERHILL, Evelyn. *Man & the Supernatural.* 1927. London. Methuen. 275p. G. B33. $16.00

UNDERHILL, F.C. *Driving for Pleasure: Harness, Stable & Its Appointments.* 1897. NY. 4to. half leather/suede. VG. C11. $250.00

UNDERHILL, Harold A. *Deep Water Sail.* 1969. Glasgow. Brn Ferguson. 2nd ed. 100 pl/99 photos. dj. T7. $60.00

UNDERHILL, Ruth M. *First Penthouse Dwellers of Am.* 1946. Laboratory of Anthropology. ils. 141p. NF. B19. $45.00

UNDERHILL, Ruth M. *Indians of Southern California.* 1941. Lawrence. US Office Indian Affairs. ils. 73p. tan wrp. B19/P4. $25.00

UNDERWOOD, E. Ashworth. *Boerhaave's Men at Leyden & After.* 1977. Edinburgh. 1st ed. 227p. dj. A13. $40.00

UNDERWOOD, Geoffrey. *Strategies of Information Processing.* 1978. Academic. 455p. VG/dj. K4. $20.00

UNDERWOOD, Michael. *Man Who Killed Too Soon.* 1968. MacDonald. 1st ed. xl. dj. P3. $10.00

UNDERWOOD, Michael. *Unprofessional Spy.* 1964. Crime Club. 1st ed. VG/VG. P3. $20.00

UNDERWOOD, Peter. *Haunted London.* 1974. Harrap. 2nd ed. VG. P3. $15.00

UNDERWOOD, Tim. *Bare Bones.* 1988. McGraw Hill. 1st ed. F/F. P3. $18.00

UNGER, Gottfried. *Die Grossen Kugelkakteen Nordamerikas.* 1992. Graz. photos. 467p. F/dj. B26. $165.00

UNGER, Peter. *Ignorance: Case for Scepticism.* 1975. Clarendon. 324p. blk cloth. G1. $30.00

UNGERER, Tomi. *Emile.* 1960. Harper. 4to. pict brd. VG. B17. $8.00

UNITED STATES CONSTITUTION. *Constitution of the United States, With Amendments.* 1845. Albany. Pocket ed. 80x56mm. 32p. F/prt sage-gr wrp. B24. $550.00

UNRUH, John D. Jr. *Plains Across: Overland Emigrants & Trans-Mississippi West.* 1993. IL U. 33p biblio. M. A18. $50.00

UNSCHULD, Paul. *Medicine in China: History of Pharmaceutics.* 1986. Berkeley. 1st ed. 4to. 367p. A13. $65.00

UNSOLD, A. *Physik der Sternatmospharen.* 1948 (1938). Ann Arbor. rpt. German text. 500p. yel cloth. K5. $32.00

UNSWORTH, Barry. *Sacred Hunger.* 1992. London. Hamish Hamilton. ARC. sgn. NF/wrp. L3. $175.00

UNTERMEYER, Louis. *Kitten Who Barked.* 1962. Golden. 1st ed. ils Lilian Obligado. NF/NF. P2. $30.00

UNTERMEYER, Louis. *Pour Toi.* 1966 (1961). Golden. ils Anglund. paper brd. F/dj. M5. $20.00

UNWIN, Stanley. *Truth About Publishing.* 1927. Houghton Mifflin. 311p. VG. M10. $5.00

UNZELMAN, Gail. *Wine & Gastronomy. New Short-Title Bibliography...* 1990. Nomis. 1/390. 346p. dj. G7. $85.00

UP DE GRAFF, F.W. *Head Hunters of the Amazon.* nd. Garden City. early rpt of 1923 ed. ils. VG/dj. F3. $15.00

UPCHURCH, Boyd. *Slave Stealer.* 1968. Weybright Talley. 1st ed. VG/G. P3. $20.00

UPDEGRAFF, Allan. *Native Soil.* 1930. NY. 1st ed. VG/worn. A17. $8.50

UPDIKE, John. *Bech Is Back.* 1982. Knopf. 1st ed. VG/VG. P3. $20.00

UPDIKE, John. *Brazil.* 1994. Knopf. ARC. F/wrp. B2. $50.00

UPDIKE, John. *Carpentered Hen.* 1982. Knopf. 1st ed thus. F/NF. B3. $15.00

UPDIKE, John. *Collected Poems 1953-1993.* 1993. Knopf. 1st ed. sgn. F/F. L3. $65.00

UPDIKE, John. *Coup.* 1978. NY. 1st ed. sgn. F/F. A11. $45.00

UPDIKE, John. *Five Poems.* 1980. Cleveland. Bits Pr. 1st ed. sgn. 1/50 on handmade paper. F/wrp. B4. $350.00

UPDIKE, John. *Hoping for a Hoopoe.* 1959. London. Gollancz. 1st ed/author's 1st book. 8vo. 82p. blk brd. VG/dj. C6. $150.00

UPDIKE, John. *In the Day's Work.* 1924. Harvard/Merrymount. 70p. VG. A4. $75.00

UPDIKE, John. *Marry Me.* 1976. Knopf. 1st trade ed. 8vo. 303p. gilt/silver stp bl cloth. F/dj. H5. $125.00

UPDIKE, John. *Midpoint & Other Poems.* 1969. Knopf. 1st ed. 8vo. 98p. gilt beige cloth. F/dj. H5. $50.00

UPDIKE, John. *Picked Up Pieces.* 1975. Knopf. 1/250 #d. F/VG+ case. S9. $175.00

UPDIKE, John. *Poorhouse Fair/Rabbit, Run.* 1965. Modern Lib. 1st ed thus. new intro. F/NF. B4. $65.00

UPDIKE, John. *Rabbit at Rest.* 1990. Knopf. 1st trade ed. sgn. F/F. Q1. $60.00

UPDIKE, John. *Rabbit Redux.* 1971. Knopf. 1st ed. F/F. B2. $25.00

UPDIKE, John. *Rabbit Redux.* 1971. Knopf. 1st ed. NF/NF. H7/P3. $20.00

UPDIKE, John. *Roger's Version.* 1986. NY. 1st ed. F/clip. A17. $15.00

UPDIKE, John. *Self-Consciousness.* 1989. London. Deutsch. 1st ed. F/NF. B3. $25.00

UPDIKE, John. *Trust Me.* 1987. Knopf. 1st trade ed. 8vo. 302p. bl cloth/brd. F/F. H5. $75.00

UPDIKE, John. *Warm Wine: An Idyll.* 1973. Albondocani. 1st ed. sgn. 1/250. 8vo. 20p. F/French marbled wrp. C6. $150.00

UPDIKE, John. *Witches of Eastwick.* 1984. Knopf. 1st ed. VG/VG. P3. $20.00

UPDIKE, John. *Witches of Eastwick.* 1984. Knopf. 1st trade ed. NF/dj. M21. $25.00

UPDYKE, James; see Burnett, W.R.

UPFIELD, Arthur W. *Journey to the Hangman.* 1959. Doubleday Crime Club. 1st ed. NF/VG. F4. $55.00

UPFIELD, Arthur W. *Venom House.* 1952. Doubleday Crime Club. 1st ed. VG/rpr. P3. $25.00

UPHAM, Charles Wentorth. *Life, Explorations & Public Services of John Chas Fremont.* 1856. Boston. Ticknor Fields. 356p. gr cloth. VG. M20. $50.00

UPHAM, Edward. *History of the Ottoman Empire From Its Establishment...* 1833. Phil. 1st Am ed. 8vo. gilt cloth. O2. $75.00

UPHAM, Elizabeth. *Little Brown Bear.* 1942. Platt Munk. ils Marjorie Hartwell. red brd. VG+. M5. $25.00

UPHAM, Thomas C. *Elements of Intellectual Philosophy...* 1827. Portland. Hyde. 504p. lacks paper spine label. G1. $375.00

UPHAM, Thomas C. *Elements of Mental Philosophy Embracing...Intellect...* 1828. Portland. 2nd ed. 576p. contemporary calf. G1. $125.00

UPHAM, Thomas C. *Outlines of Imperfect & Disordered Mental Action.* 1840. Harper. 16mo. 400p. pebbled brn cloth. G1. $85.00

UPSON, Theodore Frelinghuysen. *With Sherman to the Sea: Civil War Letters, Diaries...* 1958. Bloomington, IN. IU. 1st ed thus. 181p. VG/VG. M8. $65.00

UPSON, William H. *Keep Em Crawling.* 1943. NY. 1st ed. VG/G. B5. $35.00

UPTON, Joe. *Alaska Blues: Fisherman's Journal.* 1977. Anchorage. AK NW Pub. 4to. 236p. VG/worn. P4. $25.00

UPTON, Robert. *Golden Fleecing.* 1979. St Martin. 1st ed. F/F. P3. $13.00

UPTON, Robert. *Killing in Real Estate.* 1990. Dutton. 1st ed. NF/NF. P3. $18.00

URBAN, Greg. *Discourse-Centered Approach to Culture.* 1911. Austin, TX. 1st ed. 215p. VG/dj. F3. $20.00

URIS, Leon. *Topaz.* 1967. McGraw Hill. 1st ed. F/clip. B3. $40.00

URIS, Leon. *Trinity.* 1976. Franklin Lib. 1st ed. full leather. F. B3. $50.00

URMSON, J.O. *Philosophical Analysis: Its Development...* 1960. Oxford. Clarendon. later prt. 12mo. 202p. bl cloth. VG. G1. $22.50

URQUHART, Fred. *Seven Ghosts in Search.* 1983. Wm Kimber. 1st ed. VG/VG. P3. $20.00

US DEPARTMENT OF INTERIOR. *Fading Trails.* 1942. Macmillan. 1st ed. VG/torn. B34. $35.00

USHIMARU, Procius Yasuo. *Bishop Innocent: Founder of Am Orthodoxy.* 1964. Bridgeport. biblio/photos/map. 44p. VG/wrp. A17. $7.50

UTLEY, Robert. *Lance & the Shield, Life & Times of Sitting Bull.* 1993. np. 1st ed. M/M. B34. $20.00

UTLEY & WASHBURN. *Indian Wars.* 1977. NY. American Heritage. 352p. VG/dj. B18. $15.00

UTTAL, William R. *Psychobiology of Mind.* 1978. Lawrence Erlbaum. 785p. F/dj. K4. $16.00

UTTAL, William R. *Taxonomy of Visual Processes.* 1981. Hillsdale, NJ. Lawrence Erlbaum. 1097p. F. K4. $60.00

UTTLEY, Alison. *Fuzzypeg's Brother.* 1971. London. Collins. 1st ed. ils Wigglesworth. VG+. C8. $20.00

UTTLEY, Alison. *Grey Rabbit & the Circus.* 1983 (1961). London. Collins. 1st ed. VG/VG. C8. $30.00

UTTLEY, Alison. *Grey Rabbit & the Wandering Hedgehog.* 1967 (1948). London. Collins. 8th prt. VG. C8. $30.00

UTTLEY, Alison. *Grey Rabbit Finds a Shoe.* 1960. London. Collins. probable 1st ed. pict brds. G+. C8. $25.00

UTTLEY, Alison. *Grey Rabbit's May Day.* 1963. Collins. VG/VG. C8. $30.00

UTTLEY, Alison. *Hare & Guy Fawkes.* 1986 (1956). London. Collins. F. C8. $20.00

UTTLEY, Alison. *Little Grey Rabbit Makes Lace.* May 1962. London. Collins. 5th prt. pict brd. VG. C8. $22.50

UTTLEY, Alison. *Little Grey Rabbit's Pancake Day.* 1967. London. Collins. 1st ed. ils Margaret Tempest. G+. C8. $22.50

UTTLEY, Alison. *Little Grey Rabbit's Valentine.* 1955. London. Collins. 2nd prt. VG/VG. C8. $25.00

UTTLEY, Alison. *Sam Pig Storybook.* 1965. London. Faber. 1st ed. ils Cecil Leslie. NF/VG+. C8. $20.00

UTTLEY, Alison. *Six Tales of Sam Pig.* 1957. London. Collins. 7th prt. VG. C8. $25.00

UTTLEY, Alison. *Speckled Hen.* Aug 1957. London. Collins. ils Margaret Tempest. F. C8. $22.50

UTTLEY, Alison. *Story of Fuzzypeg the Hedgehog.* June 1948. London. Heinemann. ils Margaret Tempest. VG. C8. $25.00

UTTLEY, Alison. *Wise Owl's Story.* Feb 1954. London. Collins. lg 12mo. VG. C8. $20.00

UTTLEY, Alison. *Yours Ever, Sam Pig.* 1954. London. Faber. 2nd prt. F/NF. C8. $32.50

UTZ, Arthur-Fridolin. *Sozialethik mit Internationaler Bibliographie...* 1963. Heidelberg. German text. 409p. NF. D3. $45.00

VACALOPOULOS, Apostolos E. *Origins of the Greek Nation.* 1970. New Brunswick. 8vo. 401p. cloth. O2. $30.00

VACHSS, Andrew. *Blossom.* 1990. Knopf. 1st ed. F/F. S6. $25.00

VACHSS, Andrew. *Blossom.* 1990. Knopf. 1st ed. inscr. F/F. B2. $40.00

VACHSS, Andrew. *Blossom.* 1990. Knopf. 1st ed. VG/VG. P3. $18.00

VACHSS, Andrew. *Blue Belle.* 1988. Knopf. 1st ed. sgn. F/F. B2. $50.00

VACHSS, Andrew. *Flood.* 1985. NY. Donald Fine. 1st ed/author's 1st book. F/NF. S6. $35.00

VACHSS, Andrew. *Hard Candy.* 1989. Knopf. 1st ed. inscr. F/F. B2. $40.00

VACHSS, Andrew. *Sacrifice.* 1991. Knopf. UP. F/wrp. L3. $45.00

VACHSS, Andrew. *Strega.* 1987. Knopf. 1st ed. inscr. F/F. B2. $50.00

VAGTS, Alfred. *Hist of Militarism: Civilian & Military.* 1959. London. revised ed. 542p. VG. A17. $10.00

VAIL. *Voice of the Old Frontier.* 1949. PA U. 503p. NF. A4. $165.00

VAILLANT, George. *Aztecs of Mexico.* 1941. Doubleday. 1st ed. 340p. VG. F3. $20.00

VAKA, Demetra. *Constantine: King & Traitor.* 1918. London. 8vo. 300p. uncut. O2. $65.00

VAKA, Demetra. *Unveiled Ladies of Stamboul.* 1923. Boston. 1st ed. 8vo. 261p. cloth. O2. $30.00

VALENTIN, Jacques. *Monks of Mount Athos.* 1960. London. 8vo. 191p. cloth. dj. O2. $30.00

VALENTINE, C.W. *Experimental Psychology of Beauty.* 1962. London. Methuen. 423p. F/dj. K4. $20.00

VALENTINE, Edward Uffington. *Hecla Sandwith.* 1905. Bobbs Merrill. 1st ed. 8vo. 433p. VG. V3. $12.00

VALENTINE, Jean. *Dream Barker.* 1965. Yale. 1st ed/author's 1st book. sgn. NF/sm tear. V1. $45.00

VALENTINE, Willard L. *Experimental Foundations of General Psychology.* 1938. Farrar Rinehart. 369p. reading copy. K4. $8.50

VALENZUELA, Louisa. *Lizard's Tail.* 1983. NY. 1st Eng-language ed. sgn. NF/NF. A11. $45.00

VALERIANI, Richard. *Travels With Henry.* 1979. Houghton Mifflin. 1st ed. sgn. F/VG. S11. $10.00

VALIN, Jonathan. *Dead Letter.* 1981. Dodd Mead. 1st ed. VG/VG. P3. $30.00

VALIN, Jonathan. *Life's Work.* 1986. Delacorte. 1st ed. sgn. F/F. P3. $30.00

VALIN, Jonathan. *Second Chance.* 1975. Dutton. 1st ed. VG/VG. P3. $20.00

VALLE, Ronald S. *Metaphors of Consciousness.* 1981. NY. Plenum. 522p. VG/dj. G1. $28.50

VALLENTIN, Antonia. *El Greco.* 1955. Garden City. 1st ed. ils/biblio/index. 316p. F/F. A17. $15.00

VALLENTINE, Foy. *Cross in the Marketplace.* 1966. Word. 122p. G. B29. $3.50

VALSECCHI, Ambrogio. *Controversy: Birth Control Debate 1968.* 1968. WA. 1st Eng-trans ed. 235p. A13. $25.00

VALSINER, Jaan. *Developmental Psychology in the Soviet Union.* 1988. Bloomington, IN. 398p. F/dj. K4. $25.00

VAMBERY, Arminius. *Travels in Central Asia From Teheran Across Turkoman Desert.* 1865. NY. fld pocket map. 493p. VG. F1. $175.00

VAN ABEELEN, J.H.F. *Genetics of Behavior.* 1974. Am Elsevier/Holland Pub. 430p. F/dj. K4. $30.00

VAN AITZEMA, Lieuwe. *Historia Pacis, a Foederatis Belgis.* 1966. Leyden. Elsevier. 4to. 872p. K1. $375.00

VAN ALLSBURG, Chris. *Just a Dream.* 1990. Houghton Mifflin. 3rd prt. VG/VG. B17. $9.00

VAN ALLSBURG, Chris. *Wretched Stone.* 1991. Houghton Mifflin. 1st ed. rem mk. F/F. B17. $11.00

VAN ASH, Cay. *Fires of Fu Manchu.* 1987. Harper Row. 1st ed. F/F. P3. $20.00

VAN BRUGGEN, Theodore. *Vascular Plants of South Dakota.* 1976. Ames. 4 maps. 538p. sc. VG+. B26. $27.50

VAN BURINESSEN, Martin. *Agha, Shaikh & State: Social & Political Structure...* 1992. Atlantic Highlands. 8vo. 400p. w/card. O2. $35.00

VAN BUSKIRK, William R. *Saviors of Mankind.* 1929. Macmillan. 537p. xl. VG. B33. $22.00

VAN CAMPEN, Heilner. *Salt-Water Fishing.* 1953. NY. 2nd ed. intro E Hemingway. VG/dj. B5. $75.00

VAN CAUWENBERGH, Etienne. *Les Pelerinages Expiatoires et Judiciatres...* 1922. Louvain. 244p. new wrp. D3. $35.00

VAN CREVELD, Martin. *Command in War.* 1985. Harvard. 1st ed. 339p. VG/VG. A17. $10.00

VAN DE HULST, H.C. *Light Scattering by Small Particles.* 1957. NY. Wiley. 8vo. inscr. 470p. bl cloth. G. K5. $40.00

VAN DE HULST, H.C. *Radio Astronomy.* 1957. Cambridge. 4to. ils. 409p. xl. K5. $30.00

VAN DE WETERING, Janwillem. *Blond Baboon.* 1978. Houghton Mifflin. 1st ed. VG/VG. P3. $20.00

VAN DE WETERING, Janwillem. *Blond Baboon.* 1978. London. Heinemann. 1st Eng ed. NF/dj. S6. $22.50

VAN DE WETERING, Janwillem. *Butterfly Hunter.* 1982. Houghton Mifflin. 1st ed. F/F. B2. $25.00

VAN DE WETERING, Janwillem. *Hard Rain.* 1986. Pantheon. 1st ed. sgn. F/NF. B2. $40.00

VAN DE WETERING, Janwillem. *Inspector Saito's Sm Satori.* 1985. Putnam. 1st ed. sgn. F/NF. B2. $40.00

VAN DE WETERING, Janwillem. *Rattle-Rat.* 1985. Pantheon. 1st ed. sgn. F/NF. B2. $45.00

VAN DE WETERING, Janwillem. *Sergeant's Cat & Other Stories.* 1987. Pantheon. 1st ed. NF/NF. P3. $18.00

VAN DE WETERING, Janwillem. *Sergeant's Cat & Other Stories.* 1987. Pantheon. 1st ed. sgn. F/F. B2. $40.00

VAN DE WIELE, Annie. *West in My Eyes.* 1956. Dodd Mead. ils/maps/plans. 288p. dj. T7. $24.00

VAN DEN BERGH, G. *Astronomy for the Millions.* 1937. Dutton. 2nd prt. bl cloth. G. K5. $14.00

VAN DEN BOOGAART, E. *Johan Maurits Van Nassausiegen 1604-1679.* 1979. The Hague. The John Maurits van Nassau Stichting. ils. brn linen. K1. $85.00

VAN DER MEER, F. *Augustine the Bishop: Life & Work of a Father of the Church.* 1961. London. Sheed Ward. 1st Eng-language ed. VG/chip. G1. $35.00

VAN DEVIER, Roy B. *Son of Michigan.* 1949. Akron. 47p. VG/wrp. B18. $4.50

VAN DINE, S.S. *Bishop Murder Case.* 1929. Scribner. 1st ed. VG. P3. $20.00

VAN DINE, S.S. *Casino Murder Case.* 1934. Scribner. 1st ed. F/NF. M15. $175.00

VAN DINE, S.S. *Dragon Murder Case.* 1933. Scribner. 1st ed. VG. P3. $35.00

VAN DINE, S.S. *Greene Murder Case.* 1928. Scribner. 1st ed. VG. P3. $25.00

VAN DINE, S.S. *Kennel Murder Case.* 1933. Scribner. 1st ed. VG/VG. M15. $100.00

VAN DINE, S.S. *Scarab Murder Case.* 1930. Scribner. 1st ed. F/NF. M15. $150.00

VAN DINE, S.S. *Scarab Murder Case.* 1930. Scribner. 1st ed. G+. P3. $30.00

VAN DOREN, Carl. *Benjamin Franklin.* 1938. Viking. 1st trade ed. 845p. VG. H1. $20.00

VAN DOREN, Carl. *Secret Hist of the American Revolution.* 1941. Viking. 2nd prt. G+. N2. $6.00

VAN DOREN, Mark. *Careless Clock.* 1947. Wm Sloane. 1st ed. sgn. ils/sgn Waldo Pierce. F/NF. V1. $45.00

VAN DOREN STERN, Philip. *Prehistoric Europe.* 1969. NY. 1st ed. 383p. F/dj. K4. $10.00

VAN DRESSER, Jamine Stone. *Little Pink Pig & the Big Road.* 1935 (1924). Rand McNally. ils Clarence Biers. 64p. VG+. P2. $35.00

VAN DYKE, H.B. *Physiology & Pharmacology of the Pituitary Body.* 1936. Chicago. 1st ed. 577p. NF. G7. $75.00

VAN DYKE, Henry. *Calling of Dan Matthews.* 1909. AL Burt. 364p. NF. S12. $30.00

VAN DYKE, Henry. *Companionable Books.* 1922. Scribner. 1st ed. 391p. bl cloth. VG. S11. $15.00

VAN DYKE, Henry. *Eyes of the World.* 1914. Book Supply. ils. 464p. NF. S12. $30.00

VAN DYKE, Henry. *Ruling Passion.* 1901. Scribner. NF. S12. $15.00

VAN DYKE, Henry. *White Bees & Other Poems.* 1909. Scribner. 1st ed. 12mo. 105p. F. H1. $20.00

VAN DYKE, John C. *Desert: Further Studies in Natural Appearances.* 1901. Scribner. 1st ed. VG. A18. $25.00

VAN DYKE, John C. *Grand Canyon of CO: Recurrent Studies...* 1920. Scribner. 1st ed. photos/map. VG+. A18. $50.00

VAN DYKE, John C. *In Egypt: Studies & Sketches Along the Nile.* 1931. Scribner. 1st ed. 206p. VG. W1. $22.00

VAN DYKE, John C. *Rembrandt Drawings & Etchings.* 1927. NY/London. Scribner. 1st ed. 1/1200. NF. F1. $50.00

VAN DYNE, Edith. *Flying Girl.* 1911. Reilly Britton. 1st ed/1st state. 4 ils. VG/VG. B5. $750.00

VAN EVERY, Edward. *Sins of NY As Exposed by the Police Gazette.* 1930. NY. 299p. VG. D3. $25.00

VAN GEHUCHTEN, A. *Contributions a l'Etude Des Ganglions Cereb Ro-Spinaux.* 1892. Bruxelles. author's offprint. pres. 40p. uncut/unopened. G7. $65.00

VAN GENNEP, Arnold. *Rites of Passage.* 1960. Chicago. trans Vizedom/Caffee. 194p. F. K4. $15.00

VAN GIESON, Judith. *Lies That Bind.* 1993. Harper Collins. 1st ed. sgn. F/F. T2. $30.00

VAN GIESON, Judith. *Raptor.* 1990. Harper Row. 1st ed. F/F. M15. $30.00

VAN GIESON, Judith. *Wolf Path.* 1992. NY. Harper Collins. ARC/1st ed. sgn. RS. F/F. S6. $45.00

VAN GULIK, Robert. *Chinese Maze Murders.* 1956. Hague/Bandung. 1st ed. 19 pl. F/F. Q1. $400.00

VAN GULIK, Robert. *Chinese Maze Murders.* 1956. The Hague. W VanHoeve. 1st Eng-language ed. NF/clip. M15. $325.00

VAN GULIK, Robert. *Chinese Nail Murders.* 1961. Harper. 1st Am ed. F/F. B2. $75.00

VAN GULIK, Robert. *Given Day.* 1984. Denis McMillan. 1st Am ed. 1/300. F/dj. M2. $50.00

VAN LAREN, A.J. *Succulents Other Than Cacti.* 1934. Los Angeles. ltd ed. 1/1000. 145 tipped-in pl. NF. B26. $125.00

VAN LAREN, A.J. *Vetplanten.* 1932. Zaandam. Dutch text. ils. 101p. VG+. B26. $62.50

VAN LINH, Eric. *Police Your Planet.* 1956. Avalon. 1st ed. xl. VG/dj. M2. $10.00

VAN LOAN, Charles. *Score by Innings.* 1919. Doran. 1st ed. VG. P8. $35.00

VAN LOON, Hendrik Wilhelm. *Last of the Troubadours.* 1939. NY. 1st ed. VG/VG. B5. $25.00

VAN LOON, Hendrik Wilhelm. *Lives.* 1942. NY. ils. 886p. F/F. A17. $10.00

VAN LOON, Hendrik Wilhelm. *Van Loon's Geography.* 1932. NY. 1st ed. VG/fld map dj. A17. $17.50

VAN LUSTBADER, Eric. *Black Heart.* 1983. Evans. 1st ed. VG/VG. P3. $20.00

VAN LUSTBADER, Eric. *Black Heart.* 1983. NY. Evans. 1st ed. NF/dj. M21. $25.00

VAN LUSTBADER, Eric. *Dai-San.* 1978. Doubleday. 1st ed. F/dj. F4. $28.00

VAN LUSTBADER, Eric. *Sirens.* 1981. Evans. 1st ed. VG/VG. P3. $20.00

VAN LUSTBADER, Eric. *Sunset Warrior.* 1977. Doubleday. 1st ed. VG/dj. N2. $7.50

VAN MILLINGEN, Alexander. *Byzantine Constantinople: Walls of the City...* 1899. London. 8vo. 361p. cloth. O2. $250.00

VAN NESS, Martha. *Cacti & Succulents Indoors & Outdoors.* 1971. NY. sgn. photos/drawings. 112p. VG/dj. B26. $12.50

VAN NUYS, Kelvin. *Science & Cosmic Purpose.* 1949. NY. Harper. 1st ed. sgn. 256p. VG/VG. B33. $15.00

VAN PAASSEN, Pierre. *Days of Our Years 1903-1938.* 1939. Hillman-Curl Inc. 5th prt. F/fair/clear plastic. M7. $10.50

VAN PAASSEN, Pierre. *Earth Could Be Fair.* 1946. Dial. 1st ed. 509p. F. H1. $8.00

VAN PAASSEN, Pierre. *Forgotten Ally.* 1944. Dial. 5th ed. 343p. VG. W1. $15.00

VAN PATTEN, Joan F. *Collector's Encyclopedia of Nippon Porcelain: 2nd Series.* 1982. Collector Books. ils. 239p. F. H1. $16.00

VAN PATTEN, Nathan. *Catalog of Memorial Lib of Music, Stanford U.* 1950. Stanford. 4to. 310p. red cloth. VG/tan dj. P4. $75.00

VAN RAVENSWAAY, Charles. *Arts & Architecture of German Settlements in Missouri.* 1977. Columbia. MO U. 4to. 600+ photos. 536p. gilt bl cloth. dj. K1. $85.00

VAN RJNDT, Philippe. *Blueprint.* 1977. Putnam. 1st ed. VG/VG. P3. $18.00

VAN RJNDT, Philippe. *Tetramachus Collection.* 1976. Lester Orphen. 1st ed. VG/VG. P3. $20.00

VAN SCYOC, Sydney J. *Cloud Cry.* 1977. Berkley Putnam. 1st hc ed. F/F. F4. $11.00

VAN SICKLE, Dirck. *Montana Gothic.* 1979. HBJ. 1st ed. VG/VG. P3. $20.00

VAN SINDEREN, Adrian. *Best Indoor Game.* 1957. Syracuse. 1/250. brd. NF. M10. $22.50

VAN SINDEREN, Adrian. *Our Home in the Countryside.* 1957. NY. private prt. ltd ed. 1/700. VG. O3. $45.00

VAN STOCKUM, Hilda. *Penengro.* 1972. FSG. 1st ed. 212p. NF/VG. P2. $35.00

VAN TASSEL, C.S. *Book of OH. Vol 2.* nd. Bowling Gr, OH. 996p. VG. M20. $225.00

VAN TASSEL, David D. *Recording America's Past...1607-1884.* 1960. Chicago. 222p. F/dj. M10. $7.50

VAN TELLINGEN, Ruth T. *Bunny Blue.* 1946. Rand McNally Jr Elf Book 8023. K2. $5.00

VAN THAL, Herbert. *James Agate: An Anthology.* 1961. Hill Wang. 1st ed. VG/G. P3. $25.00

VAN URK, J. Blan. *Story of the Rolling Rock.* 1950. NY. Scribner. ltd ed. 1/750. sgn pres. VG. O3. $325.00

VAN VECHTEN, Carl. *Nigger Heaven.* nd. Grosset Dunlap. VG/G. P3. $30.00

VAN VOGT, A.E. *Book of Ptath.* 1947. Fantasy. 1st ed. F/VG. F4. $90.00

VAN VOGT, A.E. *Empire of the Atom.* nd. BC. VG/VG. P3. $10.00

VAN VOGT, A.E. *Empire of the Atom.* 1956. Shasta. 1st ed. sgn. F/NF. F4. $85.00

VAN VOGT, A.E. *House That Stood Still.* 1950. Greenberg. 2nd ed. VG/VG. P3. $25.00

VAN VOGT, A.E. *Masters of Time.* 1950. Fantasy. 1st ed. F/dj. M2. $75.00

VAN VOGT, A.E. *Slan.* 1951. Simon Schuster. 2nd ed. VG/VG. P3. $35.00

VAN VOGT, A.E. *Van Vogt Omnibus 2.* 1971. Sidgwick Jackson. 1st ed. F/F. P3. $22.00

VAN VOGT, A.E. *Voyage of the Space Beagle.* 1950. Simon Schuster. 1st ed. VG/VG. P3. $125.00

VAN VOGT, A.E. *Weapon Makers.* 1952. Greenberg. VG/G+. M17. $15.00

VAN WINKLE, D. *Old Bergen: History & Reminiscences With Maps & Ils.* 1902. Jersey City. VG. H7. $40.00

VAN WINKLE, William Mitchell. *Henry William Herbert.* 1936. ME. Southworth Anthoesen. 1st ed. 189p. cloth. G+. R2. $75.00

VAN ZILE, Edward S. *Perkins, the Fakeer.* 1903. Smart Set. 1st ed. VG. M2. $72.00

VANCE, Ethel. *Escape.* 1939. Little Brn. 1st ed. 428p. F. H1. $9.00

VANCE, Jack. *Big Planet.* 1957. Avalon. 1st ed. F/F. M2. $200.00

VANCE, Jack. *Languages of Pao.* 1958. Avalon. 1st ed. F/F. P3. $450.00

VANCE, Jack. *Maske: Thaery.* 1976. Putnam. 1st ed. xl. dj. P3. $12.00

VANCE, Jack. *Wyst.* 1984. Underwood Miller. 1st hc ed. F/dj. M2. $25.00

VANCE, John Holbrook. *Deadly Isles.* 1969. Bobbs Merrill. 1st ed. F/VG. O4. $250.00

VANCE, John Holbrook. *Fox Valley Murders.* 1966. Bobbs Merrill. 1st ed. NF/NF. P3. $175.00

VANCE, John Holbrook. *Fox Valley Murders.* 1966. Bobbs Merrill. 1st ed. sgn. F/F. O4. $250.00

VANCE, John Holbrook. *Man in the Cage.* 1960. Random. 1st ed. sgn. F/VG. O4. $250.00

VANCE, Louis Joseph. *Alias the Lone Wolf.* 1921. Doubleday Page. 1st ed. VG/VG. M15. $45.00

VANCE, Randolph. *Down in the Oller.* 1953. Norman. 1st ed. VG/VG. B5. $35.00

VANCOURT, Raymond. *La Phenomenologie et la Foi.* 1953. Tournai. Desclee et Cie Editeurs. 12mo. 126p. gray wrp. G1. $27.50

VANDE VELDE, Vivian. *Hidden Magic.* 1985. Crown. 1st ed. ils Kyman. M/M. C8. $30.00

VANDE VELDE, Vivian. *User Unfriendly.* 1991. HBJ. 1st ed. F/F. P3. $17.00

VANDENBERG, Philipp. *Golden Pharaoh.* 1980. Macmillan. 1st Am ed. 8vo. 328p. VG/dj. W1. $15.00

VANDENBURG, Arthur H. *Private Papers of Senator Vandenburg.* 1952. Boston. 599p. VG. A17. $10.00

VANDERBILT, William K. *Fifteen Thousand Miles Cruise With ARA.* 1928. NY. private prt. ils/maps. 261p. teg. T7. $230.00

VANDERCOOK, John W. *Caribee Cruise: Book of the West Indies.* 1938. NY. Reynal Hitchcock. 349p. VG/VG. B11. $30.00

VANDERCOOK, John W. *Murder in Trinidad.* 1941. Triangle. 2nd ed. G+. P3. $5.00

VANDERSLOOT, Samuel. *True Path of Gospel Temperance.* 1878. Chicago. J Fairbanks. 1st ed. 12mo. 642p. bl cloth. G. A8. $20.00

VANDERVEER, Helen. *Little Sally Mandy Story Book.* 1935. Platt Munk. 4to. ils. VG. M5. $25.00

VANDERVEER, Helen. *Little Slam Bang.* 1928. Volland. 1st ed. ils Fletcher Cranson. pict brd. VG. M5. $40.00

VANDEWATER, John. *Street of Forgotten Men.* nd. Grand Rapids. Eerdmans/Reformed. NF. B2. $45.00

VANDIVER, Frank E. *Mighty Stonewall.* 1957. ils/index. 547p. scarce. O8. $21.00

VANDIVER, Frank E. *Southwest: South or West?* 1975. TX A&M. 1st ed. ils Jo Alys Downs. 48p. F/dj. V19. $20.00

VANDIVER, Frank E. *Texas & the Confederate Army's Meat Problem.* ca 1944. np. 1st ed thus. NF/prt wrp. M8. $40.00

VANGHELI, Spiridon. *Meet Guguze.* 1978 (1977). Addison-Wesley. 2nd prt. ils/inscr Hyman. F/F. C8. $40.00

VARDON, H. *Complete Golfer.* 1905. NY. 1st ed. Edward MacDowell bookplate. VG. C11. $150.00

VARDRE, Leslie. *Nameless Ones.* 1967. John Long. VG/VG. P3. $15.00

VARILLAS, Antoine. *Les Anecdotes de Florence, ou l'Histoire Secrete...* 1685. The Hague. Armout Leers. 1st ed. 12mo. 324p. contemporary vellum. K1. $250.00

VARLEY, John. *Ophiuchi Hotline.* 1977. Dial. 1st ed. VG/VG. P3. $20.00

VARLEY, John. *Steel Beach.* 1992. Ace/Putnam. 1st ed. NF/NF. P3. $23.00

VARLEY, John. *Titan.* 1979. Berkley. 1st ed. sgn. NF/dj. M2. $50.00

VARLEY, John. *Wizard.* 1980. Berkley Putnam. 1st ed. 2nd of Gaen Series. F/F. F4. $50.00

VARLO, Charles. *New System of Husbandry...* 1785. NY. self pub. 2 vol. calf. cracked hinges. H10. $175.00

VARMA, Devendra P. *Voices From the Vaults.* 1987. Key Porter Books. 1st ed. F/F. P3. $23.00

VASARELY, Victor. *Octal, par Michel Butor.* 1972. Munich. Studio Bruckmann. 1st ed. 1/850. sgns. 9 lithographs. blk cloth. F/wrp. B24. $1,000.00

VASSILIEV, M. *Sputnik into Space.* 1958. Dial. 8vo. 181p. G/worn. K5. $30.00

VAUGHAN, J.W. *With Crook at Rosebud.* 1956. Harrisburg. 1st ed. VG/VG. B5. $65.00

VAUGHAN, Keith. *Journal & Drawings 1939-1965.* 1966. London. 1st ed. 4to. F/F. S9. $60.00

VAUGHAN, Matthew. *Discretion of Dominick Ayres.* 1976. Atlantic/Little Brn. 1st ed. VG/VG. P3. $18.00

VAUGHAN, Sam. *Who Ever Heard of Kangaroo Eggs?* 1957. Doubleday. 1st ed. ils Leonard Weisgard. VG/VG. P2. $25.00

VAUGHAN, Thomas. *Magical Writings of Thomas Vaughan.* 1888. London. Redway. 1st ed. 164p. NF/dj. B33. $350.00

VAUGHAN, Thomas. *Works of Thomas Vaughan: Mystic & Alchemist.* 1968. New Hyde Park. University Books. facsimile 1919 ed. 498p. VG/VG. B33. $25.00

VAUGHN, Robert. *Only Victims: Study of Show Business Blacklisting.* 1972. Putnam. 1st ed. F/NF. B2. $50.00

VAUX, Calvert. *Villas & Cottages.* 1857. London. ils/plans. G+. M17. $150.00

VAVRA, Robert. *Lion & Blue.* 1974. NY. Reynal. 1st ed. ils Fleur Cowles. NF/VG+. C8. $35.00

VAVRA, Robert. *Romany Free.* 1977. London. Collins. 1st ed. NF/NF. C8. $20.00

VAWTER, Bruce. *Path Through Genesis.* 1956. Sheed Ward. 1st ed. 8vo. 308p. xl. G. W1. $8.00

VAWTER, Clara. *Of Such Is the Kingdom.* 1899. Bowen Merrill. 8vo. 192p. cloth. VG. A3. $20.00

VAYDA, Andrew P. *Peoples & Cultures of the Pacific.* 1968. Natural Hist Pr. 537p. dj. N2. $7.50

VAZQUEZ, Pedro Ramirez. *National Mus of Anthropology, Mexico.* 1968. Abrams. 4to. 258p. NF/VG. F1. $35.00

VEATCH, Robert M. *Theory of Medical Ethics.* 1981. Basic Books. 387p. cloth. VG/dj. G1. $28.50

VEBLEN, T. *Vested Interests & State of the Industrial Arts.* 1919. NY. 1st ed. VG. C11. $35.00

VECORS. *You Shall Know Them.* 1953. McClelland Stewart. 1st ed. NF/NF. P3. $15.00

VEDDER, Henry. *Short Hist of the Baptists.* 1954. Am Baptist. 431p. G/rpr. B29. $7.00

VEGLAHN, Nancy. *Dance of the Planets.* 1979. CMG. 63p. VG/worn. K5. $8.00

VEITH, Ilaz. *Hysteria: History of a Disease.* 1965. Chicago. 1st ed. 301p. A13. $40.00

VELIE, Alan R. *Four American Indian Literary Masters...* 1982. OK U. 1st ed. M/dj. A18. $25.00

VELIKOVSKY, Immanuel. *Ages in Chaos.* 1952. Doubleday. 1st ed. 350p. F/fair. H1. $30.00

VELIKOVSKY, Immanuel. *Oedipus & Akhnaton.* (1960). Doubleday. 209p. F/VG. H1. $30.00

VELIKOVSKY, Immanuel. *Peoples of the Sea.* 1977. Doubleday. 2nd prt. 261p. F/F. H1. $20.00

VELIKOVSKY, Immanuel. *Worlds in Collision.* 1950. Macmillan. 1st ed. VG/VG. B5. $35.00

VELIKOVSKY, Immanuel. *Worlds in Collision.* 1950. Macmillan. 2nd prt. 401p. G. H1. $12.00

VENABLE, C. *Fleet Fin.* 1925. Chicago. 1st ed. VG/VG. B5. $32.50

VENABLES, Hubert. *Frankenstein Diaries.* 1980. Viking. 1st ed. VG/VG. P3. $20.00

VENDIKOV, Ivan. *Bulgaria's Treasures From the Past.* ca 1970. np. 4to. ils. 200p. VG/torn. M10. $7.50

VENK, Ernest. *Complete Outboard Boating Manual.* 1958. Chicago. photos/index. 281p. VG/chip. A17. $15.00

VENN, John. *Logic of Chance: Essay on...Probability...* 1888. London. Macmillan. 3rd revised/enlarged ed. 12mo. 508p. cloth. G1. $85.00

VENN, John. *Principles of Empirical or Inductive Logic.* 1889. London. Macmillan. 594p. mauve cloth. G. G1. $250.00

VENNING, Frank D. *Cacti: A Golden Guide.* 1974. NY. 12mo. ils. 160p. sc. B26. $6.00

VEQUIN, Capini. *Ghosts of My Friends.* 1938. Stokes. G. K4. $10.00

VER BECK, Frank. *Donkey Child.* 1917. Oxford. Milford. 1st ed. VG+/wrp. C8. $27.50

VER BECK, Frank. *Little Black Sambo & the Baby Elephant.* 1925. Altemus. 24mo. ils. NF. D6. $85.00

VERBRUGGE, Frank. *Whither Thou Goest: Life Story of Jacobus & Maria Verbrugge.* 1979. Minneapolis. private prt. sgn. 102p. gr cloth. F. B11. $30.00

VERDERY, Katherine. *Dixie Doll.* 1930. Indianapolis. Bobbs Merrill. 1st ed. ils Bromhall. VG+/G+. C8. $35.00

VERDERY, Katherine. *Little Dixie Captain.* 1930. Bobbs Merrill. 1st ed. ils Bromhall. VG+/VG. C8. $35.00

VERGA, Giovanni. *House by the Medlar Tree.* 1890. NY. 1st ed in Eng. trans Mary Craig. emb cloth. VG. A17. $10.00

VERGILIUS MARO, Publius. *Opera.* 1632. Leiden. Elzevir. 12mo. index/fld map. 411p. full leather. NF. F1. $250.00

VERGILIUS MARO, Publius. *Opera.* 1744. London. Brindley. 12mo. 324p. aeg. 18th-C red morocco/blk spine label. K1. $75.00

VERLAINE, Paul. *Forty Poems.* 1948. London. 1st ed. trans Gant/Apcher. F/F. A17. $15.00

VERLAINE, Paul. *Selected Poems.* 1948. Berkeley. 1st ed thus. trans CF MacIntyre. 228p. VG. A17. $15.00

VERLET, Pierre. *Book of Tapestry, Hist & Technique.* 1965. np. cloth. VG. G2. $35.00

VERLET, Pierre. *Great Tapestries, the Web of Hist From 12th to 20th Century.* 1965. Switzerland. Lausanne. thick folio. ils/pl. 278p. F/VG+/case. F1. $60.00

VERNAM, Glenn. *Men on Horseback: Story of Mounted Man From Scythians...* 1965. Harper Row. 1st ed. VG/VG. O3. $48.00

VERNE, Jules. *Adventures in Land of the Behemoth.* 1874. Boston. Shepard. 1st Am ed. 190p. cloth. G. M20. $50.00

VERNE, Jules. *Dr Ox's Experiment.* 1963. Macmillan. 1st prt. F/VG+. C8. $45.00

VERNE, Jules. *Floating City.* 1964. Assoc Booksellers. 2nd ed. VG/VG. P3. $15.00

VERNE, Jules. *Secret of the Island.* 1914. Dent. 3rd ed. VG. P3. $30.00

VERNE, Jules. *Voyage au Centre de la Terre.* 1974. La Galaxie. French text. F. P3. $10.00

VERNE, Jules. *20,000 Leagues Under the Sea.* 1940. Book League of Am. G+. P3. $20.00

VERNEUIL, A.A. *Systeme Veineux.* 1853. Paris. 175p. G7. $75.00

VERNON, Edward Johnston. *Guide to the Anglo-Saxon Tongue.* nd. London. Reeves Turner. VG. N2. $15.00

VERNON, M.D. *Backwardness in Reading.* 1960. Cambridge. 97p. F/dj. K4. $12.50

VERNON, Philip E. *Personality Tests & Assessments.* 1953. Methuen. 206p. reading copy/dj. K4. $12.50

VERRA, Valerio. *FH Jacobi: Dall'Illuminismo all'Idealismo.* 1963. Torino. lg 8vo. 381p. stiff bl wrp. G1. $37.50

VERRAL, Charles Spain. *Rin Tin Tin & the Hidden Treasure.* 1958. Golden Pr. TVTI. VG. P3. $10.00

VERRAL, Charles Spain. *Robert Goddard: Father of the Space Age.* 1966. Prentice Hall. 4th prt. 79p. xl. G. K5. $12.00

VERRILL, A. Hyatt. *Boys' Book of Buccaneers.* 1927. Dodd Mead. G+. P3. $12.00

VERRILL, A. Hyatt. *Bridge of Light.* 1950. Fantasy. 1st ed. VG. M2. $15.00

VERRILL, A. Hyatt. *Great Conquerors of S & Central America.* nd. New House Lib. ne. F/dj. M2. $15.00

VERRILL, A. Hyatt. *Harper's Aircraft Book. Why Aeroplanes Fly...* 1913. NY. Harper. sm 8vo. ils/photos. 245p. gilt bl cloth. VG. F1. $45.00

VERRILL, A. Hyatt. *Strange Customs, Manners & Beliefs.* 1946. LC Page. 1st imp. ils. 302p. F/G. H1. $17.50

VERRILL, H. Hyatt. *Great Conquerors of S & Central Am.* 1943. NY. New Home Lib. ils/bibliography. 398p. VG. F3. $15.00

VERSAND, Kenneth. *Polyglot's Lexicon 1943-1966.* 1973. NY. Links. 1st prt. 468p. VG/wrp. A17. $12.50

VERZANDVOORT, E. *History of Reynard the Fox.* 1991. Zuilichem. Catharijne. 66x55mm. 1/15 (total of 190). w/extra ftspc. M/box. B24. $350.00

VESEY-FITZGERALD, Brian. *Gypsies of Britain, Intro to Their Hist.* 1946. London. Chapman Hall. 2nd prt. VG. C8. $20.00

VESTAL, Stanley. *Big Foot Wallace.* 1942. Boston. 1st ed. VG/VG. B5. $75.00

VESTAL, Stanley. *Fandango.* 1927. Boston. 1st ed. VG/VG. B5. $125.00

VESTAL, Stanley. *Missouri.* 1945. Farrar. ils/maps. G. B34. $20.00

VESTAL, Stanley. *Sitting Bull, Champion of the Sioux.* 1932. OK U. new ed/1st prt. VG/dj. B34. $60.00

VEVIS, William W. *Ten Tough Trips: Montana Writers & the West.* 1990. WA U. 1st ed. 12 essays. M/dj. A18. $25.00

VIAN, Boris. *Round About Close to Midnight.* 1988. Quartet. 1st ed. trans/edit Mike Zwerin. NF/NF. M20. $20.00

VIAUD, Gaston. *Intelligence Its Evolution & Forms.* 1960. Harper. 127p. G. K4. $8.50

VIBERT, Charles. *Precis de Medecine Legale...* 1896. Paris. ils. 912p. old brd/later rebacking. G7. $45.00

VICKER, Ray. *Kingdom of Oil: The Middle East...* 1974. Scribner. 1st ed. 8vo. 264p. VG/dj. W1. $15.00

VICKERS, Roy. *Best Police Stories.* 1966. Faber. 1st ed. VG. P3. $15.00

VICKERY, W.F. *Advanced Gunsmithing.* 1940. Samworth. VG/VG. A1. $35.00

VICTOR, Frances Fuller. *River of the West.* 1974. Brooks Sterling. ltd ed. 1/1500. maroon buckram. M. A18. $25.00

VICTOR, Metta V. *Maum Guinea & Her Plantation Children...* 1861. London. 44 Paternoster Row. 1st ed? 12mo. 215p. cloth. M1. $550.00

VIDA, Marci Hieronymi. *Christiados Libri Sex.* 1535. Cremona. Lodovic. 8vo. 155 leaves. quarter vellum. H10. $250.00

VIDAL, Gore. *In the Yellow Wood.* 1947. Dutton. 1st ed/author's 2nd book. 8vo. 216p. VG/dj. C6. $125.00

VIDAL, Gore. *Myron.* 1974. Random. 1st ed. VG/VG. P3. $15.00

VIDAL, Gore. *Myron.* 1975. London. Heinemann. 1st ed. F/NF. B4. $35.00

VIDAL, Gore. *Two Sisters.* 1970. Little Brn. 1st ed. VG/VG. P3. $30.00

VIEMEISTER, Peter E. *Lightning Book.* 1972 (1961). MIT. pb. ils. 316p. K5. $15.00

VIERGE, Daniel. *Pen & Ink Drawings.* 1931. Cleveland. Jansen. portfolio of 63 (lacks 1) loose pl. cloth fld. VG. H4. $37.50

VIETS, Henry R. *Myasthenia Gravis. 2nd Internat Symposium Proceedings.* 1961. Springfield. 707p. cloth. xl. G7. $25.00

VIGNES, Jacques. *Rage To Survive.* 1976. NY. Morrow. 12 photos. 215p. dj. T7. $20.00

VILLA, Jose Garcia. *Have Come, Am Here.* 1942. Viking. 1st ed/author's 1st book. inscr. NF. V1. $95.00

VILLANO, Anthony. *Brick Agent.* 1977. Quadrangle. 1st ed. VG. P3. $15.00

VILLAR CORDOVA, Pedro Eduardo. *Las Culturas Pre-Hispanicas del Departamento de Lima.* 1935. Lima. 2 fld pl. 432p. G. F3. $20.00

VILLASENOR, Edmundo. *Macho!* 1973. NY. Bantam. PBO/author's 1st novel. inscr. F/ils wrp. very scarce. A11. $55.00

VILLASENOR, Victor. *Rain of Gold.* 1991. Houston. Arte Publico. 1st ed. F/F. S9. $50.00

VILLIERS, Alan. *Whalers of the Midnight Sun.* 1934. Scribner. 1st ed. ils. 285p. T7. $30.00

VILLOLDO, Albert. *Four Winds: Shaman's Odyssey Into the Amazon.* 1990. Harper. 1st ed. 265p. VG/dj. F3. $20.00

VINCENT, Clovis. *Meningites Chroniques Syphilitiques...* 1910. Paris. Steinheil. 104p. NF. G7. $395.00

VINCENT, George. *Theodore W Miller: Rough Rider, Hist Diary As Soldier...* 1899. Akron. private prt. 179p. bl cloth. F. B14. $125.00

VINCENT, Harry. *Sea Fish of Trinidad Port of Spain.* 1910. np. photos. VG. M17. $35.00

VINCENT, Jerry Fox. *Cabin Grows: Hist of the Church.* ca 1949. Dayton, OH. 1st ed. 113p. cloth. VG. M8. $37.50

VINCENT, Marvin R. *Vincent's Word Studies of the New Testament.* nd. Hendrickson. 4 vol. VG. B29. $28.00

VINCIGUERRA, Mario. *Croe: Ricordi e Pensieri.* 1957. Napoli. Vajro. 104p. F/stiff wrp. G1. $27.50

VINES, Sydney H. *Elementary TB of Botany.* 1898. NY/London. 397 ils. 611p. VG. B26. $11.00

VINGE, Joan D. *Return of the Jedi Storybook.* 1983. St Michael. MTI. VG. P3. $15.00

VINGE, Joan D. *World's End.* 1984. Bluejay. 1st ed. VG/VG. P3. $20.00

VINGE, Vernor. *Fire Upon the Deep.* 1992. Tor. 1st ed. F/F. T2. $125.00

VINGE, Vernor. *Marooned in Real Time.* 1986. Blue Jay. 1st ed. F/F. T2. $25.00

VINGE, Vernor. *Peace War.* 1984. Bluejay. 1st ed. F/F. P3. $20.00

VINGE, Vernor. *Witling.* 1976. Dobson. 1st ed. F/F. P3. $35.00

VINING, Elizabeth. *I, Roberta.* 1967. Lippincott. 2nd ed. 8vo. 224p. NF/dj. V3. $9.50

VINING, Elizabeth. *Take Heed of Loving Me. Novel About John Donne.* 1963. Lippincott. 1st ed. sgn. F/NF. B2. $35.00

VIOLA. *National Archives of the United States.* 1986. Abrams. 4to. ils. 282p. F/NF. A4. $65.00

VIOUX, Marcelle. *Au Sahara. Autor du Grand Erg.* 1930. Paris. Fasquelle 1st ed. sm 8vo. G. W1. $8.00

VIPONT, Elfrida. *Lark on the Wing.* 1951. Bobbs Merrill. 8vo. 255p. NF/tattered. V3. $12.00

VIPONT, Elfrida. *Lift Up Your Lamps.* 1930. Manchester. 16mo. 47p. NF. V3. $12.00

VIPONT, Elfrida. *Story of Quakerism.* 1955. London. Bannisdale. 3rd prt. 312p. VG/VG. V3. $20.00

VIRCHOW, Rudolf. *Alttrojanische Graber und Schadel.* 1882. Berlin. 1st ed. 152p. A13. $100.00

VIRCHOW, Rudolf. *Die Krankhaften Geschulste.* 1863-1867. Berlin. 3 vol. 1st ed. 243 woodcuts. xl. G. very rare. G7. $1,250.00

VIRGIL. *The Aeneid.* 1991. Donald Grant. 1/500. sgn trans/ils Luis Ferreira. F/dj. M2. $40.00

VIRGINIA STATE LIBRARY. *More Virginia Broadsides Before 1877.* 1975. index. 76p. prt wrp. O8. $18.50

VISNIAC, Roman. *Vanished World.* 1983. FSG. 1st ed. folio. F/F. S9. $125.00

VISSERING, Harry. *Zeppelin: Story of Great Achievement.* 1922. Chicago. 1st ed. VG. B18. $175.00

VITRY, Alexis. *L'Oeuvre Francaise en Tunisie.* 1900. Compiegne. Leveziel. 211p. quarter morocco. xl. fair. W1. $8.00

VITRY, Paul. *French Sculpture During the Reign of St Louis 1226-1270.* 1938. Florence. Pantheon. 1st ed. 90 pl. gray cloth. F/dj. K1. $250.00

VIVAS, Julie. *Nativity.* 1986. Harcourt Brace. 1st ed. F/VG. C8. $25.00

VIVES, Joseph Calasanctio. *Comendium Theologiae Ascetico-Mysticae...* 1907. Rome. Pustet. 750p. H10. $15.00

VIZETELLY, Henry. *Four Months Among the Gold Finders of CA.* 1870 (1849). np. 200p. VG. E5. $27.00

VIZETELLY, Henry. *History of Champagne With Notes on Other Sparkling Wines...* 1980 (1888). np. rpt of 1888 London ed. lg 4to. gilt cloth. G7. $95.00

VLADISLAV, Jan. *Italian Fairy Tales.* 1971. Hamlyn. VG. P3. $12.00

VLASTO, J.A. *Popular Pekingese.* 1924. London. Popular Dogs. 1st ed. 144p. VG. scarce. R2. $65.00

VOGAN, Sara. *In Shelly's Leg.* 1981. Knopf. 1st ed. F/F. P8. $27.50

VOGEL, Virgil. *American Indian Medicine.* 1977. Norman. 1st ed. 584p. A13. $90.00

VOGT, Gregory. *Space Shuttle: Projects for Young Scientists.* 1983. Franklin Watts. 8vo. 122p. xl. dj. K5. $10.00

VOIGHT, Cynthia. *Solitary Blue.* 1983. Atheneum. 1st ed. 189p. F/F. P2. $35.00

VOIGHT, F.A. *Greek Sedition.* 1949. London. Hollis Carter. 1st ed. 258p. VG. W1. $20.00

VOIGT, Cynthia. *Solitary Blue.* 1984. Atheneum. 3rd prt. 8vo. VG/VG. B17. $6.50

VOISIN, Felix. *Causes Morales et Physiques des Maladies Mentales...* 1826. Paris. Bailliere. 418p. prt wrp. uncut/unopened. G7. $250.00

VOLKER, Joseph F. *AZ Medical School Study.* 1962. AZ U. notes/charts. 258p. F/NF. B19. $15.00

VOLLMAN, William. *Thirteen Stories & Thirteen Epitaphs.* 1991. London. Deutsch. 1st ed. NF/F. B2. $100.00

VOLLMAN, William. *Whores for Gloria.* 1991. Pantheon. 1st Am ed. F/F. L3. $35.00

VOLOSINOV, V.N. *Freudianism: A Marxist Critique.* 1976. NY. Academic. trans IR Titunik. 248p. F/dj. K4. $12.50

VOLTAIRE. *Candide.* 1928. Random. ltd ed. colored/sgn Rockwell Kent. 112p. gilt bdg. F/case. B24. $2,000.00

VOLTAIRE. *L'Esprit de Monsieur de Voltaire.* 1760. np. 12mo. 298p. orig calf/gilt spine label. K1. $125.00

VON BAMBERGER, Heinrich. *Lehrbuch der Krankheiten des Herzens.* 1857. Vienna. 459p. orig marbled brd/rebacked calf. G7. $595.00

VON BREYDENBACH, Bernhard. *Die Reise ins Heilige Land.* 1977. Wiesbaden. 1/1000. folio. 56p. cloth. dj. O2. $90.00

VON BULOW, Bernhard. *Imperial Germany.* 1914. NY. 1st ed. trans from German. 342p. gilt cloth. VG. A17. $10.00

VON CANSTATT, Heinrich S. *Durch des Gartens Kleine Wunderwelt.* 1890. Frankfurt. Trowitzsch. 472p. VG. A10. $30.00

VON DANIKEN, Erich. *According to the Evidence.* 1977. Souvenir. 1st ed. VG. P3. $20.00

VON DICKHUTH-HARRACH, Gustaf. *Im Felde Unbesiegt, der Weltdrieg in 29 Einzeldarstellingen.* 1921. Muenchen. 2nd ed. 330p. G. B18. $45.00

VON DRYGALSKI, Erich. *Southern Ice-Continent: German South Polar Expedition...* 1989. Cambridgeshire. Bluntisham. 1st Eng ed. 4to. M/sans. P4. $125.00

VON GOETHE, J.W. *Story of Reynard the Fox.* 1954. LEC. 1/1500. ils/sgn Eichenberg. patterned brd. F/case. B24. $100.00

VON GRUNEBAUM, Gustave E. *Medieval Islam: A Study in Cultural Orientation.* 1947. Chicago. 2nd prt. 8vo. 365p. cloth. dj. O2. $35.00

VON HAGEN, Victor. *Desert Kingdoms of Peru.* 1965. NY Graphic Soc. 1st Am ed. 191p. VG/dj. F3. $35.00

VON HAGEN, Victor. *Maya Explorer: John Lloyd Stephens & Lost Cities...* 1967. Norman, OK. 8vo. ils. 324p. gilt gr cloth. VG/VG. B11. $18.00

VON HAGEN, Victor. *Maya Explorer: John Lloyd Stephens...* 1948. Norman, OK. 2nd prt. 324p. VG/dj. F3. $20.00

VON HAGEN, Victor. *Off With Their Heads.* 1937. McMillan. 1st ed. 220p. VG. F3. $25.00

VON HAMMER, Joseph. *History of the Assassins.* 1835. London. Smith Elder. sm 8vo. 240p. later blk calf/marbled brd. K1. $85.00

VON HARTSEN, F.A. *Untersuchungen Uber Psychologie.* 1869. Leipzig. Theodor Thomas. 124p. VG/prt buff wrp. G1. $75.00

VON HOBBS, H. *Irish Setter Reflections.* 1974. Exposition. 1st ed. ils. 212p. F/VG. R2. $25.00

VON HOFFMAN, Nicholas. *Citizen Cohn: Life & Times of Roy Cohn.* 1988. Doubleday. 1st ed. VG/G+. N2. $7.50

VON KAHLER, Erich. *Form und Entformung.* 1965. Koln. Kiepenheuer Witsch. inscr. F. B2. $60.00

VON KANOWSKI, Johannes. *Der Suezkanal: Geschichte, Land und Leute.* ca 1930. Berlin. Schonfeld. 8vo. 49 pl. VG/torn. W1. $9.00

VON KLEIST, Heinrich. *Robert Guiskard Herzog der Normanner.* 1919. Tolz. Bremer. 1/270. vellum/marbled brd. VG. K1. $250.00

VON LEWINSTI, Anna Liese. *Weilst de Wieviel Sternlein Stehen?* nd. Schreiber. mc pl. pict brd. NF. M5. $50.00

VON LINSINGEN, F.W.B. *Pressure Gauge Murder.* 1930. Dutton. VG. P3. $25.00

VON LIPPMANN, Edmund. *Entstehung und Ausbreitung der Alchemie.* 1919. Berlin. 1st ed. 742p. A13. $250.00

VON LOHER, Franz. *Cyprus: Historical & Descriptive...* 1878. NY. 8vo. ils/maps. 324p. cloth. O2. $100.00

VON MACH, Edmund. *Greek Sculpture, Its Spirit & Principles.* 1903. Boston. Ginn. 1st ed. 72 pl. 357p. VG. W1. $15.00

VON MANSTEIN, Field Marshall. *Lost Victories.* 1958. Chicago. 1st ed. VG/VG. B5. $55.00

VON MARTENS, Georg Friedrich. *Grundriss des Handelsrechts.* 1798. Gottingen. Johann Christian Dieterich. calf. M11. $125.00

VON MEYER, Ernst. *Hist of Chemistry.* 1906. London. 1st ed. 691p. B13. $75.00

VON MIKUSCH, Dagobert. *Gasi Mustafa Kemal Zwischen Europa un Asien.* 1929. Leipzig. 8vo. fld map. 335p. cloth. O2. $40.00

VON NELL-BREUNING. *Reorganization of Social Economy...* ca 1936. Milwaukee. Bruce. 451p. xl. H10. $20.00

VON SECKENDORF, Viet Ludwig. *History of the Reformation & Dr Martin Luther...* 1728. Delft. 3 vol. tall folio. German text. pl/fld table. full vellum. H3. $550.00

VON TEMPSKI, Armine. *Born in Paradise.* 1968. Hawthorn. G+/dj. N2. $7.50

VON WITZLEBEN, Elizabeth. *Stained Glass in French Cathedrals.* 1968. NY. VG/VG. A1. $150.00

VON WOLFF, Christian. *Psychologia Rationalis Methodo Scientifica Pertracta...* 1734. Francofurti/Lipsiae. Rengeriana. 4to. modern leather. G1. $850.00

VON WOLFF, Christian. *Psychologica Empirica Methodo Scientifica Pertracta...* 1779 (1732). Veronae. Apud Haeredes Marci Moroni. sm folio. 411p. G1. $285.00

VON WRIGHT, Georg Henrik. *Form & Content in Logic.* 1949. Cambridge. 16mo. prt stiff brn wrp. G1. $27.50

VON WRIGHT, Georg Henrik. *Treatise on Induction & Probability.* 1951. London. Routledge/Kegan Paul. 310p. w/catalog. VG/dj. G1. $37.50

VON WRIGHT, Georg Henrik. *Varieties of Goodness.* 1964. London. Routledge. 2nd prt. VG/chip. G1. $32.00

VON ZIEMSSEN, Hugo. *Acute Infectious Diseases.* 1874. NY. 2 vol. 1st Eng-trans ed. full leather. A13. $125.00

VON ZUMBUSCH, Ludwig. *Unser Liederbuch, Die Beliebtesten Kinderlieder...* 1902. Schott's Sohne. lg obl 8vo. 44p. ils ep. cloth. F. B24. $85.00

VONNEGUT, Kurt. *Between Time & Timbuktu or Prometheus-5.* 1972. Delacorte. 1st ed. F/F. B4. $650.00

VONNEGUT, Kurt. *Breakfast of Champions.* (1973). Delacorte. 5th ed. F/F. P3. $10.00

VONNEGUT, Kurt. *Breakfast of Champions.* 1973. Delacorte. ARC. sgn. RS. F/F. L3. $250.00

VONNEGUT, Kurt. *Deadeye Dick.* 1982. Delacorte. 1st ed. sgn. 1/350. 240p. gilt maroon cloth. F/case. H5. $150.00

VONNEGUT, Kurt. *Hocus Pocus.* 1990. Putnam. 1st ed. VG/VG. P3. $22.00

VONNEGUT, Kurt. *Jailbird.* 1979. Delacort. 1st ed. VG/VG. P3. $30.00

VONNEGUT, Kurt. *Mother Night.* 1966. Harper Row. 1st hc ed. 8vo. 202p. blk/red bdg. F/dj. C6. $100.00

VONNEGUT, Kurt. *Nothing Is Lost Save Honor.* 1984. Jackson, MS. Nouveau. 1/300. sgn. 8vo. 48p. gilt brn cloth/marbled brd. F. H5. $175.00

VONNEGUT, Kurt. *Player Piano.* 1952. Scribner. 1st A ed/author's 1st book. 295p. gr brd. VG/dj. H5. $350.00

VONNENGUT, Kurt. *Fates Worse Than Death.* 1991. Putnam. 1st ed. F/F. B3. $20.00

VONNENGUT, Kurt. *Slapstick.* 1976. Delacorte. 1st ed. NF/NF. P3. $40.00

VONNENGUT, Kurt. *Slapstick; or, Lonesome No More!* 1976. Franklin Lib. 1st ed. full leather. F. B3. $35.00

VOORHIS, Jerry. *American Cooperatives.* 1961. Harper. 1st ed. inscr. F/NF. B2. $40.00

VORLANDER, Karl. *Geschichte der Philosophie.* 1932. Berlin. Gustav Kiepenheller. 490p. reading copy. K4. $15.00

VORONOFF, Serge. *Greffe Animale Applications Utilitaires au Cheptel.* 1925. Paris. pres. 59 pl. 100p. wrp. G7. $95.00

VORSE, Mary Heaton. *Footnote to Folly.* 1935. NY. 1st ed. VG/VG. B5. $45.00

VROMAN, Leo. *Blood.* 1967. Natural Hist Pr. 169p. F/dj. K4. $8.50

VRYONIS, Speros Jr. *Byzantium & Europe.* 1967. NY. 8vo. 216p. cloth. dj. O2. $30.00

VRYONIS, Speros Jr. *Greeks & the Sea.* 1993. New Rochelle. 4to. ils. 234p. cloth. O2. $65.00

VULLIAMY, C.E. *English Letter Writers.* 1946. London. Collins. 2nd imp. ils. NF/VG. M7. $35.00

VYNER, Robert. *Notitia Venatica: Treatise on Fox-Hunting...* nd. np. 6th revised ed. 8 mc pl/fld kennel plan. VG. O3. $85.00

VYSE, Michael. *Overworld.* 1980. Faber. F/F. P3. $20.00

WACH, Joachim. *Types of Religious Experience: Christian & Non-Christian.* 1951. Chicago. 275p. VG. B33. $18.00

WADD, William. *Nugae Chirurgicae; or, Biographical Miscellany...* 1824. London. Nichols. 276p. recent cloth. uncut. G7. $195.00

WADDELL, H. *Mediaeval Latin Lyrics.* 1929. London. 1st ed. cloth. VG. C11. $65.00

WADDELL, H. *Wandering Scholars.* 1932. London. 6th ed. coth. VG. C11. $50.00

WADE, Henry. *Litmore Snatch.* 1957. London. Constable. 1st ed. NF/clip. M15. $45.00

WADE, Henry. *Litmore Snatch.* 1957. Macmillan. 1st ed. NF/NF. P3. $23.00

WADE, Jonathan. *Back to Life.* 1961. Pantheon. F/F. P3. $13.00

WADE, Mary. *Our Little Armenian Cousin.* 1905. Boston. May. 1st ed. ils. pict cloth. F. B14. $50.00

WADE, Mary. *Our Little Japanese Cousin.* Dec 1906. Boston. ils Bridgman. pict cloth. VG. B14. $45.00

WADSWORTH, William. *Complete Works...With Descriptions of Country...N Eng.* 1844. np. 8vo. edit H Reed. 550p. VG. E5. $35.00

WAGENKNECHT, E. *Marilyn Monroe, a Composite View.* 1969. NY. 1st ed. VG/VG. B5. $30.00

WAGENKNECHT, Edward. *Six Novels of the Supernatural.* 1944. Viking. 1st ed. VG. P3. $35.00

WAGNER, Henry R. *Collecting. Especially Books.* 1968. np. Zamorano Club. 1/400. 25p. F. P4. $65.00

WAGNER, Henry R. *One Rare Book.* 1956. Zamorano Club. 1/250. NF. B19. $75.00

WAGNER, Henry R. *Plains & Rockies: Critical Biblio of Exploration...* 1982. John Howell. ils/biblio/index. 765p. M. A18. $150.00

WAGNER, Henry R. *Sir Francis Drake's Voyage Around the World.* 1926. San Francisco. Howell. 4to. ils. gilt maroon cloth. VG+. F1. $325.00

WAGNER, Henry R. *Spanish Voyages to the NW Coast of America in 16th Century.* 1966. Amsterdam. N Israel. facsimile of 1929 ed. 571p. M. P4. $95.00

WAGNER, Jane. *Search for Signs of Intelligent Life in the Universe.* 1986. NY. 1st ed. sgn Wagner/Lily Tomlin. F/F. A11. $65.00

WAGNER, Karl Edward. *Book of Kane.* 1985. Donald Grant. 1st ed. F/dj. M2. $20.00

WAGNER, Karl Edward. *Echoes of Valor II.* 1989. Tor. 1st ed. M/dj. M21. $15.00

WAGNER, Karl Edward. *Why Not You & I?* 1987. Dark Harvest. F/VG+. M21. $25.00

WAGNER, Linda. *William Carlos Williams: A Critical Study.* 1964. Wesleyan. 1st ed. sgn Williams. F/NF. V1. $45.00

WAGNER, Richard. *Ring of the Niblung.* 1939. NY. lg 8vo. 24 full-p pl. VG. A17. $35.00

WAGONER, David. *Road to Many a Wonder.* 1974. NY. 1st ed. sgn. F/F. A11. $45.00

WAGONER, Jay J. *AZ Territory 1863-1912.* 1970. AZ U. ils/index. 587p. F/NF. B19. $55.00

WAGONER, Jay J. *Early AZ: Prehistory to Civil War.* 1975. AZ U. ils/notes/index. 547p. F/NF. B19. $45.00

WAHL, Jan. *Carrot Nose.* 1978. FSG. 1st ed. ils/inscr James Marshall. M/M. C8. $60.00

WAHL, Jan. *Cobweb Castle.* 1968. Holt Rinehart. 1st ed. ils Gorey. F/clip. C8. $60.00

WAHL, Jan. *Cucumber Princess.* 1981. Owings Mills, MD. Stemmer. 1st ed. ils Caraway. M/M. C8. $25.00

WAHL, Jan. *Grandpa Gus's Birthday Cake.* 1981. Prentice Hall. 1st ed. F/F. C8. $25.00

WAHL, Jan. *How the Children Stopped the Wars.* 1969. FSG. ARC. RS. VG/dj. M20. $22.00

WAHLENBERG, Anna. *Old Swedish Fairy Tales.* 1925. NY. Hampton. 8vo. 296p. pict label/red cloth. F. B24. $100.00

WAHLOO, Peter. *Assignment.* 1966. Knopf. 1st ed. VG/VG. P3. $25.00

WAINER, Cord; see Dewey, Thomas B.

WAINWRIGHT, John. *Man Who Wasn't There.* 1989. St Martin. 1st ed. VG/G. P3. $13.00

WAINWRIGHT, John. *Medical Knowledge of William Shakespeare...* 1915. NY. 1st ed/4th prt. 81p. A13. $150.00

WAITE, Arthur Edward. *Book of Ceremonial Magic.* 1961. New Hyde Park. 337p. VG/VG. B33. $40.00

WAITE, Arthur Edward. *Lamps of Western Mysticism. Essays on Life of Soul in God.* 1923. Knopf. 1st Am ed. 334p. gilt/gr stp bl cloth. B33. $110.00

WAITT, Alden H. *Gas Warfare: Chemical Weapon, Its Use & Protection Against.* 1942. DSP. 1st ed. pres. 327p. F. H1. $15.00

WAKEFIELD, H. Russell. *Strayers From Sheol.* 1961. Arkham. 1st ed. F/dj. F4. $70.00

WAKEFIELD, H. Russell. *They Return at Evening.* 1928. Appleton. 1st ed. VG. P3. $100.00

WAKEMAN, Fredric. *Hucksters.* 1946. Rinehart. 1st ed. VG/G. M21. $15.00

WAKOSKI, Diane. *Coins & Coffins.* 1962. NY. Hawks Well. 1st ed. NF/wrp. B2. $85.00

WAKOSKI, Diane. *Lament of the Lady Bank Dick.* 1969. Sans Souci. 1/99. 8vo. 34p. blk lettered blk cloth/wht brd. F. H5. $75.00

WALCOTT, Derek. *Selected Poems.* 1964. Farrar. 1st ed. F/F. B2. $85.00

WALCOTT, Derek. *Star-Apple Kingdom.* 1979. FSG. 1st ed. NF/NF. V1. $65.00

WALCOTT & WALCOTT. *Chats About Miniature Books.* 1932. Boston. Thomas Todd. 1/250. 30p. F/stiff wrp/matching case. B24. $300.00

WALDEN, Amelia. *Play Ball, McGill.* 1972. Westminster. 1st ed. VG/VG. P8. $15.00

WALDMAN, Frank. *Bonus Pitcher.* 1951. Houghton Mifflin. 1st ed. VG/G+. P8. $27.50

WALDO, Frank. *Elementary Meteorology.* nd (1896). NY. Am Book Co. 8vo. photos/diagrams. 373p. G. K5. $20.00

WALDROP, Frank C. *MacArthur on War.* 1942. DSP. 1st ed. 419p. F/chip. A17. $15.00

WALDROP, Howard. *Dozen Tough Jobs.* 1989. Ziesing. 1st ed. F/F. P3. $16.00

WALDROP, Keith. *Poem From Memory.* 1975. Providence. 1st ed. 1/500. ils Linda Lutes. VG/silkscreen wrp. A17. $10.00

WALDSTEIN. *Evolution of Modern Hebrew Literature 1850-1912.* 1916. Columbia. 134p. NF. A4. $65.00

WALES, Hubert. *Wife of Colonel Hughes.* 1910. Stuyvesant. 1st ed. VG. H1. $5.00

WALEWSKI, Stefan Colonna. *System of Caucasian Yoga.* 1955. Indian Hills. 1st ed. 127p. VG/VG. B33. $100.00

WALEY, Arthur. *Three Ways of Thought in Ancient China.* 1953. Allen Unwin. 275p. VG/VG. B33. $22.00

WALKER, Alan. *Breakthrough: Rediscovery of the Holy Spirit.* 1969. Abingdon. 92p. VG/dj. B29. $3.00

WALKER, Alice. *Her Blue Body Everything We Know.* 1990. HBJ. 1st ed. rem mk. VG/F. B3. $30.00

WALKER, Anne Kendrick. *Tuskegee & the Black Belt.* 1944. Richmond. Dietz. 2nd prt. NF/NF. S9. $25.00

WALKER, Anne. *Coming Into Our Own, by Edward Kessler.* 1989. Paris. Ann Walker. 1/3 in manuscript form. sgns. brd. M/box. B24. $650.00

WALKER, Ardis M. *Francisco Garces: Pioneer Padre of Kern.* 1946. Kern Co Hist Soc. ils. 99p. NF/worn. B19. $30.00

WALKER, Barbara. *Little House Cookbook: Frontier Foods...* 1979. Harper. 1st ed. ils Garth Williams. NF/NF. C8. $30.00

WALKER, Benjamin. *Hindu World: Encyclopedic Survey of Hinduism.* 1968. NY. 2 vol. 1st Am ed. NF/VG. F1. $30.00

WALKER, David. *Lord's Pink Ocean.* 1972. Houghton Mifflin. 1st ed. F/F. P3. $15.00

WALKER, Don D. *Clio's Cowboys: Studies in Historiography of Cattle Trade.* 1981. NE U. 1st ed. M/dj. A18. $25.00

WALKER, Donald. *British Manly Exercises: In Which Rowing & Sailing...* 1836. Phil. Thomas Wardle. 1st Am ed. 16mo. 285p. cloth. M1. $275.00

WALKER, Frank. *Jack.* 1976. CMG. 1st Am ed. ils. 183p. cloth. F/dj. R2. $20.00

WALKER, Franklin. *Jack London & the Klondike.* 1966. Bodley Head. 1st ed. photos/notes/index. F/dj. A18. $35.00

WALKER, Franklin. *Literary Hist of S CA.* 1950. CA U. 1st ed. inscr. ils/photos. F. A18. $50.00

WALKER, Franklin. *San Francisco's Literature Frontier.* 1939. Knopf. 1st ed. F/VG. A18. $40.00

WALKER, Fred M. *Song of the Clyde.* 1985. NY. Norton. ils. 232p. dj. T7. $35.00

WALKER, Henry. *Wagonmasters: High Plains Freighting...* 1968. Norman. 2nd prt. F/F. O3. $45.00

WALKER, Ira. *Man in the Driver's Seat.* 1964. Abelard Schuman. 1st ed. VG/VG. P3. $15.00

WALKER, Jacqueline. *Equator South, Equator North.* nd. San Francisco. 1st ed. sgn. 207p. gilt cloth. F3. $20.00

WALKER, Jeremy D.B. *Study of Ferge.* 1965. Cornell. 202p. gray cloth. VG/dj. G1. $25.00

WALKER, L. Edna. *Mother Goose Nursery Tales.* 1923. London. Blk. 1st ed. ils Folkard/Hartley. 219p. VG+. P2. $75.00

WALKER, Max; see Avallone, Michael.

WALKER, Mort. *Backstage at the Strips.* 1975. NY. 1st ed. VG/VG. B5. $45.00

WALKER, Robert J. *Algebraic Curves.* 1966. Princeton. 2nd prt. 201p. F/dj. K4. $15.00

WALKER, Ronald. *Infernal Paradise.* 1978. CA U. 1st ed. 391p. VG/dj. F3. $15.00

WALKER, Stella A. *Sporting Art, England 1700-1900.* 1972. London. Studio Vista. tall 4to. ils. F/VG. F1. $25.00

WALKER, Todd. *Portfolio of Eighteen Reproductions of Photographs.* 1968. Thumbprint Pr. 1/500. 4to. F/NF fld. S9. $125.00

WALKER, Walter. *Appearance of Impropriety.* 1993. Pocket. 1st ed. F/F. P3. $20.00

WALKER, Warren S. *Leatherstocking & the Critics.* 1965. Scott Foresman. 30 essays. sc. VG. A18. $15.00

WALKER, William. *War in Nicaragua.* 1860. Mobile. Goetzel. 1st ed. lg fld map. 432p. brn cloth. very scarce. K1. $300.00

WALKER, Williston. *Hist of the Christian Church.* 1918. Scribner. 624p. G. B29. $4.00

WALKER. *Letters From Aubrey Beardsley to Leonard Smithers.* 1937. London. 1st Ed Club. ils. 260p. NF. A4. $125.00

WALL, Dorothy. *Blinky Bill: The Quaint Little Australian.* 1940. Sydney. Angus Robertson. 1st ed. VG. C8. $125.00

WALL, James W. *Hist of First Presbyterian Church of Mocksville, NC...* 1963. Salisbury, NC. Rowan Prt. 1st ed. 136p. cloth. NF. M8. $37.50

WALL, R.J. *Dictionary of Photography.* 1889. NY. 1st ed. pres. weak hinges. C11. $35.00

WALLACE, Anthony F.C. *Men & Cultures.* 1960. Phil. PA U. 810p. G/dj. K4. $25.00

WALLACE, Archer. *Adventures in the Air.* 1932. Ryerson. sgn. VG. P3. $20.00

WALLACE, Bruce. *Topics in Population Genetics.* 1968. NY. ils. 481p. dj. B26. $20.00

WALLACE, D. Mackenzie. *Egypt & the Egyptian Question.* 1883. Macmillan. 1st ed. 521p. xl. VG. W1. $45.00

WALLACE, Dillon. *Lure of the Labrador Wild.* 1905. NY. Revell. ils/photos/pocket map. 339p. T7. $60.00

WALLACE, Dillon. *Story of Grenfell of Labrador.* 1922. NY. 1st ed. VG/G. B5. $17.50

WALLACE, Edgar. *Day of Uniting.* 1930. Mystery League. 1st ed. VG/torn. P3. $25.00

WALLACE, Edgar. *Feathered Serpent.* 1928. Crime Club. G+. P3. $20.00

WALLACE, Edgar. *Fightened Lady.* 1933. Musson. 1st Canadian ed. VG. P3. $20.00

WALLACE, Edgar. *Flying Squad.* 1929. Crime Club. 1st ed. VG. P3. $18.00

WALLACE, Edgar. *Four Just Men.* 1905. Tallis. 1st ed. xl. P3. $75.00

WALLACE, Edgar. *Governor of Chi-Foo.* 1933. World Syndicate. 1st ed. VG. P3. $60.00

WALLACE, Edgar. *Gunman's Bluff.* 1929. Crime Club. 1st ed. VG. P3. $30.00

WALLACE, Edgar. *Law of the Three Just Men.* 1931. Crime Club. VG. P3. $35.00

WALLACE, Edgar. *Mammoth Mystery Book.* 1929. Doubleday Crime Club. omnibus ed. VG/clip. M15. $65.00

WALLACE, Edgar. *Man at the Carlton.* 1931. Musson. 1st Canadian ed. VG. P3. $10.00

WALLACE, Edgar. *Square Emerald.* 1932. Musson. 1st Canadian ed. VG. P3. $20.00

WALLACE, Edgar. *Stretelli Case.* 1930. Internat Fiction Lib. G+. P3. $12.00

WALLACE, Edgar. *Thief in the Night.* nd. World Wide. 1st Am ed. VG/VG. M15. $75.00

WALLACE, Edgar. *Traitor's Gate.* 1927. Doubleday Page. 13th prt. VG/G. P3. $20.00

WALLACE, Edgar. *White Face.* 1932. Musson. 1st Canadian ed. VG. P3. $20.00

WALLACE, F.L. *Address: Centauri.* 1955. Gnome. 1st ed. VG/G+. M17. $20.00

WALLACE, Francis. *Big Game.* 1936. Grosset Dunlap. 220p. VG/dj. M20. $20.00

WALLACE, Ian. *Deathstar Voyage.* 1972. Dobson. 1st ed. F/F. P3. $13.00

WALLACE, Irving. *Pigeon Project.* 1979. Simon Schuster. 1st ed. F/F. P3. $15.00

WALLACE, Irving. *R Document.* 1976. Simon Schuster. 1st ed. F/F. P3. $18.00

WALLACE, Lew. *Ben-Hur, a Tale of the Christ.* 1880. Harper. S12. $1,500.00

WALLACE, Lew. *Ben-Hur.* 1906 (1899). Harper. 2 vol. ils WM Johnson. teg. gilt brn/bl decor gr cloth. VG. S11. $45.00

WALLACE, Lew. *Fair God; or, The Last of the 'Tzins.* 1889. Houghton Mifflin. 12mo. 586p. gilt brn bdg. VG. B11. $35.00

WALLACE, Lew. *Prince of India.* 1893. Harper. 2 vol. 1st ed/2nd issue. VG. H1. $45.00

WALLACE, Robert. *Seven Men Are Murdered.* 1930. Fiction League. VG. P3. $25.00

WALLACE, Susan E. *Repose in Egypt.* 1891. Nims Knight. 18 pl. VG. W1. $15.00

WALLACH, Ira. *Hopalong, Freud & Other Modern Literary Characters...* 1953. George Price. 134p. F/dj. B14. $40.00

WALLER, Fats. *Fats Waller's Orig Piano Conceptions.* 1932? Mills Music. 32p. VG/rpr wrp. B2. $35.00

WALLER, Robert James. *Bridges of Madison County.* 1992. NY. Warner. 1st ed. 171p. silver stp gr cloth/tan brd. F/dj. H5. $250.00

WALLERSTEIN, James. *Demon's Mirror.* 1951. Harbinger. 1st ed. NF/dj. M2. $15.00

WALLEY, Dean. *Raggedy Ann & the Daffy Taffy Pull.* 1972. Bobbs Merrill/Hallmark. ils Marianne Smith. 14p. pict brd. VG. A3. $15.00

WALLING, R.A.J. *Corpse With the Dirty Face.* 1939. Triangle. 2nd ed. VG. P3. $10.00

WALLIS, Dave. *Only Lovers Left Alive.* 1964. Dutton. 1st ed. VG/VG. P3. $20.00

WALLIS, George. *Art of Preventing Diseases & Restoring Health...* 1793. London. Robinson. 850p. full tree calf. G7. $125.00

WALLIS, J.H. *Murder by Formula.* 1932. Jarrolds. 1st ed. inscr. G+. P3. $45.00

WALLIS, Mrs. *Life in Feejee; or, Five Years Among the Cannibals.* 1967. Ridgewood. Gregg. rpt of 1851 ed. 8vo. 422p. F. P4. $35.00

WALLMANN, Jeffrey M. *Judas Cross.* 1974. Random. 1st ed. sgn. G+. P3. $16.00

WALLOP, Douglas. *Year the Yankees Lost the Pennant.* 1954. Norton. BC. F. P8. $7.00

WALNE, Shirley. *Poodle.* 1977. Edinburgh. Bartholomew. 1st ed. ils. 96p. M/mc wrp. R2. $10.00

WALSDORF, John. *William Morris in Private Presses & Limited Editions...* 1983. Phoenix. Oryx. sm 4to. sgn. fwd Sir Basil Blackwell. 602p. F/case. F1. $120.00

WALSER, Richard. *Thomas Wolfe Undergraduate.* 1977. Duke. 1st ed. inscr. 8vo. 166p. bl cloth. NF/dj. C6. $60.00

WALSH, Helen. *Starting Right With Milk Goats.* 1947. NY. Macmillan. 1st ed. 138p. cloth. VG. B14. $25.00

WALSH, Jill Paton. *Wyndham Case.* 1993. London. Hodder Stoughton. 1st ed. F/F. S6. $25.00

WALSH, P.G. *Letters of St Paulinus of Nola... Vol 1.* 1966. Westminster. Newman. 277p. H10. $15.00

WALSH, W.H. *Reason & Experience.* 1947. Clarendon. 260p. blk cloth. VG/dj. G1. $40.00

WALTER, Elizabeth. *In the Mist.* 1979. Arkham. 1st ed. F/F. P3. $15.00

WALTER, Nehemiah. *Discourses on Whole LVth Chapter of Isaiah...* 1755. Boston. Fowle. only ed. 412p. worn calf. H10. $150.00

WALTER, Richard. *Canary Island Venture.* 1956. Dutton. 1st ed. 8vo. 255p. xl. G. W1. $12.00

WALTERS, Helen B. *Wernher Von Braun: Rocket Pioneer.* 1964. Macmillan. 8vo. ils. 187p. xl. K5. $20.00

WALTERS, Minette. *Scold's Bridle.* 1994. Scorpion. ltd sgn ed. 1/75. F/sans. O4. $225.00

WALTERS, Minette. *Sculptress.* 1993. St Martin. 1st Am ed. sgn. F/F. O4. $50.00

WALTON, George A. *Quaker of the Future Time.* 1916. Phil. Jenkins. 12mo. 49p. VG/wrp. V3. $7.50

WALTON, Izaak. *Compleat Angler; or, Contemplative Man's Recreation...* ca 1900. London. Frowde. 61x49mm. 586p. gilt full red calf. F. B24. $400.00

WALTON, Izaak. *Complete Angler; or, Contemplative Man's Recreation...* nd. Peter Pauper. ils. linen-backed pict brd. G7. $75.00

WAMBAUGH, Joseph. *Black Marble.* 1978. Delacorte. 1st ed. inscr. VG/VG. O4. $30.00

WAMBAUGH, Joseph. *Blooding.* 1989. Perigord. 1st ed. VG. P3. $20.00

WAMBAUGH, Joseph. *Blue Knight.* 1972. Atlantic/Little Brn. 1st ed. inscr. VG/VG. O4. $25.00

WAMBAUGH, Joseph. *Glitter Dome.* 1981. Morrow. 1st ed. inscr. F/F. O4. $20.00

WAMBAUGH, Joseph. *Golden Orange.* 1990. Perigord/Morrow. 1st ed. VG/VG. P3. $20.00

WAMBAUGH, Joseph. *Onion Field.* 1973. Delacorte. 1st ed. F/F. M15. $35.00

WAMBAUGH, Joseph. *Secrets of Harry Bright.* 1985. Morrow. 1st ed. inscr. F/F. O4. $30.00

WANDREI, Donald. *Dark Odyssey.* 1931. Webb. 1st ed. sgn. 1/400. F/dj. M2. $250.00

WANGER, E.D. *Art & Decoration Book of Successful Houses.* 1940. McBride. 112p. cloth. VG. A10. $20.00

WANGERIN, Walter Jr. *Book of Sorrows.* 1985. Harper Row. 1st ed. F/F. P3. $16.00

WANKLYN, Joan. *Bobtail Shawn.* 1949. London. Warne. 1st ed. G. O3. $15.00

WANNER, Irene. *Sailing to Corinth.* 1988. Owl Creek. 1st ed. M/NF. A17. $7.50

WARBASSE, James P. *Surgical Treatment: Practical Treatise...* 1920. Phil. 3 vol. 3rd prt. ils. G7. $45.00

WARBURG, Fredric. *All Authors Are Equal.* 1973. London. 1st ed. 310 p. VG/VG. A17. $12.50

WARD, Amy. *Paper Furniture for Paper Dolls.* 1857. NY. Clark Austin Smith. 1st ed. sq 12mo. red cloth. M1. $400.00

WARD, Edward. *Sahara Story.* 1962. Norton. 1st ed. 8vo. cloth. NF/dj. W1. $8.00

WARD, Hortense Warner. *Century of Missionary Effort: Church of the Good Sheperd...* 1960. Austin. 1st ed. 1/100. F/case. M8. $45.00

WARD, Jonas (some); see Ard, William.

WARD, Kenneth. *Boy Volunteers With the British Artillery.* 1917. NY Book Co. NF. M2. $20.00

WARD, Lynd. *Silver Pony: Story in Pictures.* 1973. Houghton Mifflin. 1st prt. F/F. C8. $200.00

WARD, Lynd. *Song Without Words. Book of Engravings on Wood.* 1936. Random. 1/1250. sgn. copper foil brd. F/case. F1. $295.00

WARD, Lynd. *Vertigo.* 1937. Random. 1st ed. woodcuts. bl cloth. VG. F1. $250.00

WARD, Lynd. *Wild Pilgrimage.* 1932. NY. Smith Haas. 1st ed. 8vo. orange cloth. VG. F1. $275.00

WARD, Lynd. *Wolf of Lambs Lane.* 1967. Houghton Mifflin. 1st ed. ils Lynd Ward. M/M. C8. $40.00

WARD, Mrs. Humphrey. *Testing of Diana Mallory.* 1908. Harper. 1st ed. 549p. VG. M20. $20.00

WARD, Philip. *Cambridge Street Literature.* 1978. Cambridge. ils. 64p. NF. A4. $20.00

WARE, Charles Crossfield. *Roundtree Chronicles 1827....* 1947. Wilson, NC. 1st ed. 64p. VG/prt wrp. M8. $37.50

WARE, Joseph E. *Emigrants' Guide to CA.* 1972. Da Capo. rpt of 1932 Princeton ed. F. A18. $30.00

WARGA, Wayne. *Hardcover.* 1985. Arbor. 1st ed. F/F. B2. $25.00

WARING, Joseph. *History of Medicine in South Carolina, 1825-1900.* 1967. Columbia, SC. 1st ed. 366p. A13. $40.00

WARING, P. Alston. *Peacock Country.* 1948. Day. 1st ed. 8vo. VG. W1. $15.00

WARKWORTH, Lord. *Notes From a Diary in Asiatic Turkey.* 1898. London. 4to. 31 full-p pl/lg fld map. 267p. cloth. uncut. O2. $350.00

WARMAN, Cy. *Snow on the Headlight.* 1899. Appleton. 1st ed. NF. B2. $75.00

WARMAN, Edwin G. *American Cut Glass: Pattern Book of Brilliant Period 1895...* 1954. Warman. 1st ed. ils Don Maust. 115p. F. H1. $17.50

WARNER, Charles Dudley. *My Winter on the Nile.* 1881. Houghton Mifflin. revised new ed. 496p. G. W1. $9.00

WARNER, Charles Dudley. *Roundabout Journey.* 1891. Houghton Mifflin. 8th ed. 360p. VG. W1. $12.00

WARNER, Charles Dudley. *Their Pilgrimage.* 1893 (1886). Harper. ils CS Reinhart. 363p. G. S11. $20.00

WARNER, Deborah Jean. *Alvan Clark & Sons.* 1968. Smithsonian. 8vo. 12mo. gilt bl cloth. VG. K5. $200.00

WARNER, Langdon. *Craft of the Japanese Sculptor.* 1936. NY. 1st ed. VG. A17. $45.00

WARNER, Marina. *Alone of All Her Sex: Myth & Cult of the Virgin Mary.* 1976. Knopf. BC. 1st Am ed. VG/VG. B33. $20.00

WARNER, Marina. *Indigo or Mapping the Waters.* 1992. Simon Schuster. 1st Am ed. rem mk. F/F. A14. $25.00

WARNER, Marina. *Queen Victoria's Sketchbook.* 1979. Crown. 1st ed. 224p. VG/G. S11. $10.00

WARNER, Mignon. *Crown Jewels.* 1951. King Penguin. 1st ed. VG/VG. P3. $20.00

WARNER, Mignon. *Death in Time.* 1982. Crime Club. 1st ed. F/F. P3. $13.00

WARNER, Sylvia Townsent. *Kingdoms of Elfin.* 1977. Viking. 1st ed. NF/NF. P3. $18.00

WARNER, Ted J. *Dominguez-Escalante Journal: Their Expedition...CO, UT...* 1976. Bringham Young U. edit Ted J Warner. 203p. F/wrp. B19. $20.00

WARREN, Austin. *New Eng Conscience.* 1967. Ann Arbor. 231p. VG/dj. G1. $22.50

WARREN, Edward. *Epitome of Practical Surgery for Field & Hospital.* 1989. Norman. facsimile rpt. G7. $65.00

WARREN, Edward. *Life of John Collins Warren, MD...* 1860. Ticknor Fields. 2 vol. ils. orig cloth. VG. G7. $175.00

WARREN, Francis A. *Rocket Propellants.* 1958. Reinhold. 218p. F. H1. $8.00

WARREN, Henry White. *Recreations in Astronomy.* 1886. NY. Chautauqua. 8vo. 284p. G. K5. $32.00

WARREN, James. *Disappearing Corpse.* 1958. Washburn. 1st ed. VG/VG. P3. $20.00

WARREN, John C. *Physical Education & Preservation of Health.* 1846. Boston. 1st ed. 90p. A13. $200.00

WARREN, Robert Penn. *Eleven Poems on the Same Theme.* 1942. Norfolk, CT. 1st ed. w/sgn bookplate. F/gray dj. A11. $75.00

WARREN, Robert Penn. *Jefferson Davis Gets His Citizenship Back.* 1980. Lexington. KY U. 1st ed. sgn. 8vo. 114p. bl cloth. F/dj. C6. $100.00

WARREN, Robert Penn. *New & Selected Essays.* 1989. Random. UP. F/wrp. B4. $125.00

WARREN, Robert Penn. *Robert Penn Warren Talking. Interviews 1950-1978.* 1980. NY. 1st ed. sgn. F/NF. A11. $50.00

WARREN, Robert Penn. *Selected Essays.* 1958. Random. 1st ed. F/clip. B4. $100.00

WARREN, Robert Penn. *Selected Poems 1923-1943.* 1944. Harcourt Brace. 1st ed. sgn. F/G. V1. $95.00

WARREN, Robert Penn. *Selected Poems 1923-1975.* 1976. Random. 1st trade ed. inscr. 325p. blk cloth/yel brd. F/dj. C6. $125.00

WARREN, Robert Penn. *Selected Poems: New & Old, 1923-1966.* 1966. Random. 1st ed. 1/250. 300p. beige cloth. F/dj/case. C6. $250.00

WARREN, Winslow. *How a Protectionist Became a Free Trader.* 1889. Boston. lg 8vo. 40p. tan prt wrp. K1. $30.00

WARREN & WARREN. *Victorian Architecture of the Rocky Mountain West.* 1989. Flagstaff. Northland. VG/wrp. N2. $5.00

WARRICK, Patricia S. *Mind in Motion.* 1987. S IL U. 1st ed. F/F. P3. $25.00

WASHBURN, William Lewis. *Blue Bells & Thistles. A Bouquet of Scotch Jokes...* 1942. Haddon Hgts, NJ. 45x42mm. 1/99. 42p/frenchfold. sgn. gilt bl morocco. F/box. B24. $650.00

WASHBURN, William Lewis. *Caxton Doll's Prymer. For a Litel Childe's Delyte.* 1939. Haddon Hgts, NJ. 32x25mm. 1/39. ils ABC. mottled calf. F/cb box. B24. $1,250.00

WASHBURN, William Lewis. *Chess: The Game of Life. Showing Different Versions...* 1939. Collingswood, NJ. 73x53mm. 1/64 on Japan. 46p. F/Japanese wrp/envelope. B24. $650.00

WASHBURN, William Lewis. *Colonial Courting. Being Extracts...* 1940. Haddon Hgts, NJ. 69x52mm. 1/72. ftspc portrait. subscriber listing. F. B24. $650.00

WASHBURN, William Lewis. *Last Will of the Elder John White, One of First Settlers...* 1933. Collingswood, NJ. 63x38mm. w/prospectus. brn calf. F. B24. $750.00

WASHBURN, William Lewis. *Poems of LiPo, the Chinese Poet.* 1941. Haddon Hgts, NJ. 60x50mm. 1/27. trans/sgn Akenbrand. 2 pl. full calf. F. B24. $850.00

WASHBURN, William Lewis. *Pots: A Cry to God.* 1935. Collingswood. 71x57mm. 1/17 (64 total). vellum. F/vellum wrp/silk ties. B24. $950.00

WASHBURN, William Lewis. *Wolf-King; or, Little Red Riding-Hood.* 1940. Haddon Hgts, NJ. 48x48mm. 1/64. ftspc Hy Gage. red cloth/paper label. F. B24. $450.00

WASHBURN & COMPANY. *Amateur Cultivator's Guide to Flower & Kitchen Garden.* 1868. Boston. Washburn. ils/pl. 144p. H10. $125.00

WASHINGTON, Brooker T. *Story of the Negro.* 1909. NY. 2 vol. 1st ed. VG. C11. $115.00

WASHINGTON, Brooker T. *Up From Slavery.* 1907. Burt. sgn author's son. 330p. VG/dj. M20. $45.00

WASHINGTON, George. *Diaries of...,* 1748-1799. 1971 (1925). 4 vol. edit John C Fitzpatrick. M. O8. $65.00

WASHINGTON, George. *Journal of Major George Washington...1754.* 1959. Colonial Williamsburg. facsimile 1754 ed. 12mo. VG/VG. B11. $45.00

WASHINGTON, George. *Washington, His Farewell Address.* 1932. Kingsport. 21x15mm. 142p. full dk bl leather/gilt stars. F/case. B24. $400.00

WASSERMANN, Gerhard D. *Neurobiological Theory of Pshychological Phenomena.* 1978. Baltimore. U Park Pr. 219p. F/dj. K4. $12.50

WATANABE, John. *Maya Saints & Souls in a Changing World.* 1992. Austin, TX. 1st ed. 280p. VG/wrp. F3. $15.00

WATANABE, Sylvia. *Talking to the Dead.* 1992. Doubleday. UP. F/prt bl wrp. B3. $25.00

WATERHOUSE, Keith. *Billy Liar.* 1960. Norton. 1st Am ed. 191p. VG/VG. M20. $40.00

WATERLOO, Stanley. *Story of a Strange Career.* 1902. Appleton. 1st ed. VG. M2. $25.00

WATERMAN. *Practical Stock Doctor: Common Sense Ready Reference...* 1912. np. 300 recipes/remedies. 800+p. VG. E5. $35.00

WATERS, Ethel. *His Eye Is on the Sparrow.* 1951. Doubleday. ARC. RS. F/worn. B2. $40.00

WATERS, Frank. *Dust Within the Rock.* 1940. Liveright. 1st ed. F. A18. $90.00

WATERS, Frank. *Earp Brothers of Tombstone. Story of Mrs Virgil Earp.* 1960. NY. 1st ed. sgn. F/NF. A11. $65.00

WATERS, Frank. *Flight From Fiesta.* 1986. Santa Fe. Rydal. ltd ed. sgn. F/box. B3. $125.00

WATERS, Frank. *Man Who Killed the Deer.* 1942. Sage Books. 1st prt. sgn. F/clip. A18. $40.00

WATERS, Frank. *Man Who Killed the Deer.* 1965. Northland. ltd ed. sgn. ils Don Perceval. brd. F/case. A18. $175.00

WATERS, Frank. *People of the Valley.* 1941. Farrar Rinehart. 1st ed. inscr. VG+. A18. $50.00

WATERS, Frank. *Yogi of Cockroach Court.* 1947. NY. 1st ed. inscr. NF/NF. A11. $55.00

WATERS, Thomas A. *Lost Victim.* 1973. Random. ARC of 1st ed. RS. F/dj. F4. $25.00

WATKINS, Harold. *Time Counts: Story of the Calendar.* 1954. London. Neville Spearman. 1st ed. G+/fair. N2. $15.00

WATKINS, Ivor. *Demon.* 1983. MacDonald. 1st ed. VG/fair. P3. $13.00

WATKINS, Vera H. *Saluki: Companion of Kings.* 1974. Great Britain. Fenrose. 1st ed. ils. 95p. M/dj. scarce. R2. $65.00

WATKINS, William Jon. *God Machine.* 1973. Doubleday. 1st ed. VG/VG. P3. $20.00

WATSON, Aldren A. *Village Blacksmith.* 1968. NY. Crowell. 1st ed. 125p. VG/VG. O3. $35.00

WATSON, Art. *Devil Man With a Gun.* 1967. np. VG/dj. B34. $35.00

WATSON, Deek. *Story of the Ink Spots.* 1967. Vantage. 1st ed. NF/VG. B2. $50.00

WATSON, Delmar. *Quick Watson, the Camera.* 1975. LA. Hollywood. 1st ed. inscr/dtd 1976. NF/NF. S9. $60.00

WATSON, Frederick. *Hunting Pie.* 1931. Derrydale. ltd ed. 1/750. VG. O3. $125.00

WATSON, Graham. *Book Society: Reminiscences of a Literary Agent.* 1980. NY. 1st Am ed. 164p. blind-stp ep. F/F. A17. $9.50

WATSON, Harold Francis. *Sailor in English Fiction & Drama 1550-1800.* 1931. Columbia. 241p. T7. $40.00

WATSON, Helen Orr. *Black Horse of Culver.* 1950. Houghton Mifflin. 1st ed. VG. O3. $20.00

WATSON, Helen Orr. *Fools Over Horses.* 1952. Houghton Mifflin. 1st ed. ils Wesley Dennis. VG/fair. O3. $25.00

WATSON, I. *Silvertail: Story of a Lyrebird.* nd. Sydney. John Sands. ils Walter Cunningham. F/F. C8. $25.00

WATSON, Ian. *Book of Ian Watson.* 1985. Ziesing. 1st ed. sgn Watson/Shea. F/F. T2. $35.00

WATSON, Ian. *Flies of Memory.* 1990. Gollancz. 1st ed. sgn. F/F. P3. $30.00

WATSON, Ian. *Queenmagic, Kingmagic.* 1986. Gollancz. 1st ed. sgn. F/F. P3. $30.00

WATSON, Ian. *Queenmagic, Kingmagic.* 1988. St Martin. 1st ed. F/dj. F4. $18.00

WATSON, Ian. *Very Slow Time Machine.* 1979. Gollancz. 1st ed. F/F. P3. $30.00

WATSON, James. *Dog Book.* 1906. Double Page. 2 vol. 1st ed. cloth. G. R2. $200.00

WATSON, John. *Kant & His English Critics: Comparison...Philosophy.* 1881. Glasgow. Maclehose. 402p. w/catalog. VG. G1. $100.00

WATSON, Larry. *Montana 1948.* 1993. Milkweed. 1st ed. F/F. A14. $100.00

WATSON, Lawrence. *In a Dark Time.* 1980. Scribner. 1st ed/author's 1st novel. F/F. B4. $250.00

WATSON, Robert Grant. *Spanish & Portuguese South America During Colonial Period.* 1884. London. Trubner. 2 vol. lg fld map. gilt tan cloth. K1. $100.00

WATSON, Robert I. *Great Pshychologists.* 1968. Phil/NY. Lippincott. 581p. F. K4. $12.50

WATSON, Robert. *Paper Horse.* 1962. Atheneum. 1st ed/author's 1st book. 8vo. 87p. VG/prt wrp. C6. $30.00

WATSON, S.H. *Folio of Old Songs.* 1912. TX Division. 1st ed. 152p. cloth. NF. M8. $150.00

WATSON, Samuel N. *Those Paris Years.* 1937. Revell. ltd ed. sgn. w/photo dtd 1936. bl cloth. NF. S9. $40.00

WATSON, Tom. *Rules of Golf.* 1980. NY. 1st ed. sgn. VG/lg wrp. B5. $25.00

WATSON, W. *Cactus Culture for Amateurs.* 1899 (1889). London. ils/fld frontis. 270p. cloth. VG-. B26. $75.00

WATT, Lauchlan Maclean. *Advocate's Wig.* 1932. Herbert Jenkins. 1st ed. VG. P3. $30.00

WATT, R.A. Watson. *Through the Weather House...* 1935. London. Davis. sm 8vo. 192p. G/dj. K5. $15.00

WATTERS, Frank. *Hist of the Idylwood Presbyterian Church.* 1974. Falls Church, VA. 1st ed. 103p. NF/stiff prt wrp. M8. $22.50

WATTERS, Philip. *Prayers of the Bible.* 1959. Baker. 334p. G/dj. B29. $5.50

WATTS, Alan. *Beyond Theology: Art of Godmanship.* 1964. NY. Pantheon. 1st ed. 236p. VG/VG. B33. $26.00

WATTS, Alan. *Reading the Weather.* nd. Dodd Mead. 4to. 208p. VG/dj. K5. $15.00

WATTS, C.B. *Marginal Zone of the Moon.* 1963. Nautical Almanac Office. 4to. 951p. VG. K5. $30.00

WATTS, Isaac. *Doctrine of Passions Explained & Improved...* 1795. NY. 1st Am ed. 32mo. G. scarce. G1. $200.00

WATTS, Isaac. *Horae Lyricae...* 1722. London. Clarke. 4th ed. 299p. contemporary half leather. H10. $195.00

WATTS, Niki. *Greek Folk Songs.* 1988. Bristol. 8vo. 104p. cloth. O2. $25.00

WAUCHOPE, Robert. *Indian Background of Latin Am Hist.* 1970. Knopf. 1st ed. 211p. VG/dj. F3. $20.00

WAUCHOPE, Robert. *Lost Tribes & Sunken Continents.* 1970. Chicago/London. Chicago U. 155p. beige cloth/red spine titles. VG/dj. P4. $40.00

WAUGH, Albert A. *Sundials: Theory & Construction.* 1973. Dover. 1st ed. sc. 1228p. VG. A8. $6.00

WAUGH, F.A. *Landscape Gardening.* 1913 (1899). NY. 2nd ed. ils. 156p. B26. $27.50

WAUGH, Hillary. *Madman at My Door.* 1978. Doubleday. 1st ed. VG/G. P3. $16.00

WAVELL, A.P. *Allenby in Egypt...* 1944. Oxford. 161p. VG. W1. $12.00

WAVELL, A.P. *Palestine Campaigns.* 1928. London. Constable. 1st ed. 20 maps. 260p. VG. M7. $65.00

WAXELL, Sven. *Am Expedition.* 1952. London. Wm Hodge. 236p. F/F. A17. $22.50

WAY, Frederick. *Allegheny.* 1942. np. ltd ed. sgn. VG/VG. B5. $75.00

WAY, Frederick. *Inland River Record, 1959.* 1959. Sewickley, PA. 330p. T7. $35.00

WAY, Wayne. *Body Betrays.* 1949. Phoenix. 1st ed. NF/dj. F4. $22.00

WAYMAN, John Hudson. *Doctor on the California Trail.* 1971. Denver. Old W Pub. 1st ed. 4to. fld map. 136p. F. P4. $39.00

WAYNE, Joseph. *By Gun & Spur.* 1952. Dutton. 1st ed. VG. P3. $10.00

WEAR, Terri A. *Horse Stories: Annotated Bibliography of Books for All Ages.* 1987. Metuchen. Scarecrow. 1st ed. VG. O3. $35.00

WEARNER, Edythe. *Tigers of Como Zoo.* 1961. Viking. 1st ed. ils. VG/VG. P2. $18.00

WEATHERLY, Frederic E. *Rhymes & Roses.* ca 1890. London/NY. ils St Clair Simmons/ Ernest Wilson. pict brd. VG. M5. $125.00

WEATHERMAN, Hazel Marie. *Price Trends 1978.* 1978. self pub. 112p. VG/wrp. H1. $8.00

WEATHERWAX, Rudd. *Lassie Method: Raising & Training Your Dog With Patience...* 1971. Cooper Sales Assn. 1st ed. 126p. G/wrp. R2. $18.00

WEAVER, Gordon. *Eight Corners of the World.* 1988. Chelsea Gr. 1st ed. F/F. P8. $20.00

WEAVER, Michael D. *Mercedes Nights.* 1987. St Martin. 1st ed. F/F. P3. $17.00

WEAVER, Muriel Porter. *Aztecs, Maya & Their Predecessors.* 1972. Seminar. 1st ed. 347p. VG. F3. $30.00

WEAVER, Robert A. *Up From Muttontown.* 1965. Nantucket, MA. 1st ed. 95p. VG. B18. $27.50

WEAVER, Robert. *Nice Guys Go Home.* 1968. Harper Row. 1st ed. F/VG+. P8. $30.00

WEBB, George Ernest. *Three Rings & Telescopes.* 1983. Tucson. lg 8vo. 242p. VG/dj. K5. $33.00

WEBB, Jack. *Badge.* 1958. Prentice Hall. 2nd ed. VG/G. P3. $14.00

WEBB, Jack. *Make My Bed Soon.* 1963. HRW. 1st ed. VG/VG. P3. $25.00

WEBB, James. *Fields of Fire.* 1978. Prentice Hall. 1st ed/author's 1st book. 344p. VG/VG. M20. $35.00

WEBB, James. *Flight From Reason.* 1971. MacDonald. 1st ed. VG/VG. B33. $35.00

WEBB, Walter Prescott. *Texas Rangers in the Mexican War.* 1975. Jenkins Garrett. 1st ed. maps/notes/index. M/glassine. A18. $40.00

WEBB, Walter Prescott. *Texas Rangers.* 1935. Boston. 1st ed. inscr. NF/chip. A9. $125.00

WEBB, Wilse B. *Profession of Psychology.* 1962. HRW. 291p. reading copy/dj. K4. $10.00

WEBBE, Elizabeth. *Children That Lived in a Shoe.* 1951. Rand McNally Elf Book 8391. K2. $5.00

WEBBE, Elizabeth. *God Is Good.* 1955. Rand McNally Jr Elf Book 8018. K2. $3.00

WEBBER, F.R. *Church Symbolism.* 1971. Detroit. Gale. 2nd ed/facsimile 1938 ed. F. B33. $20.00

WEBBER, John M. *Yuccas of the Southwest.* 1953. WA, DC. ils/72 pl. VG/wrp. B26. $47.50

WEBER, Bruce. *Calvin Klein Jeans.* nd. np. 1st ed. 4to. NF/wrp. S9. $75.00

WEBER, Carl J. *Thousand & One Fore-Edge Paintings.* 1949. Waterville, ME. Colby College. 1st ed. 1/1000. buckram. F/dj. B24. $475.00

WEBER, Francis J. *Bibliography of CA Bibliographies.* 1968. Ward Ritchie. 1/500. 47p. F/NF case. A4. $55.00

WEBER, Francis J. *CA Missions.* 1986. np. revised ed. 1/500. 171p. F/F. A4. $45.00

WEBER, Francis J. *Peninsular California Missions 1808-1880.* 1979. Los Angeles. 1/300. gilt bl cloth. F. P4. $65.00

WEBER, Francis J. *SmallPAXweber: The Last of the Mission Shelties.* 1989. San Diego. Ash Ranch. 1/26 (total of 128). gilt b&w leather. F/clamshell box. B24. $225.00

WEBER, Nicholas. *Art of Babar, the Work of Jean & Laurent DeBrunhoff.* 1989. Abrams. 4to. F/F. B17. $25.00

WEBER, Nicholas. *Patron Saints: 5 Rebels Who Opened Am to New Art 1928-43.* 1992. Knopf. 1st ed. VG/clip. N2. $10.00

WEBER, Shirley H. *Schliemann's First Visit to America, 1850-1851.* 1942. Harvard. sm 4to. 112p. bl cloth/bl prt brd. VG. K1. $75.00

WEBSTER, Daniel. *Works of Daniel Webster.* 1890. Little Brn. 6 vol. 20th ed. 8vo. gilt bl cloth. K1. $125.00

WEBSTER, Frank V. *Harry Watson's High School Days.* 1912. Cupples Leon. 1st ed. pict bdg. G+. P8. $10.00

WEBSTER, George V. *Something Wrong.* 1918. Plimpton. 1st ed. 88 p. VG. S11. $10.00

WEBSTER, H.T. *Best of HT Webster.* 1953. Simon Schuster. 1st ed. VG/G. P3. $35.00

WEBSTER, Hutton. *Early European Hist.* 1917. Heath. 1st ed. ils. 753p. VG. W1. $10.00

WEBSTER, Jean. *Daddy-Long-Legs.* 1912. Grosset Dunlap. 12mo. 304p. red/blk stp gr cloth. G. S11. $10.00

WEBSTER, John W. *Description of Island of St Michael...* 1821. Boston. Williams. 3 pl/2 fld maps. 244p. brn cloth. worn. very scarce. K1. $150.00

WEBSTER, Joseph A. *Brief Hist of Presbyterian Church of S Salem, NY 1752-1902.* ca 1902. Elizabeth, NJ. 1st ed. 74p. cloth. VG. M8. $37.50

WEBSTER, Noah. *Am Speller, Adaptation Noah Webster's Blue-Backed Speller.* 1960. NY. Crowell. 1st ed. 8vo. pict cloth. F/F. C8. $40.00

WEBSTER, Noah. *Dictionary of English Language.* 1832. London. 2 vol. 1st Eng ed. spine of vol 1 gone. A9. $350.00

WEBSTER, Noah. *Pay-Off in Switzerland.* 1977. Crime Club. 1st ed. VG/VG. P3. $15.00

WECHSBERG, J. *Glory of the Violin.* 1973. NY. 1st ed. VG/VG. B5. $35.00

WECHSLER, Herbert. *Nationalization of Civil Liberties & Civil Rights.* 1970. Austin, TX. 61p. NF. D3. $5.00

WEDDELL, Elizabeth Wright. *St Paul's Church Richmond, VA: Its Hist Years & Memorials.* 1931. Richmond. 2 vol. 1st ed. cloth. NF. M8. $45.00

WEDECK, Harry. *Dictionary of Aphrodisiacs.* 1961. NY. 1st ed. 256p. A13. $50.00

WEEDMAN, Jane B. *Women Worldwalkers: New Dimensions of SF & Fantasy.* 1985. Lubbock. TX Tech Pr. 1st ed. F/F. T2. $20.00

WEEGEE. *Naked City.* nd. Essential Books. 246p. VG/dj. M20. $175.00

WEEGEE. *Naked City.* 1945. NY. 1st ed. royal 8vo. photos. 246p. photo ep. buckram. NF. D3. $100.00

WEEGEE. *Weegee.* 1977. Knopf. 1st ed. 4to. F/NF. S9. $65.00

WEEKS, Alvin G. *Massasolt.* (1920). private prt. 1st ed. 270p. emb cloth. A8. $75.00

WEEKS, Genevieve C. *Oscar Carleton McCulloch 1843-1891...* 1976. Indianapolis. 1st ed. 248p. cloth. NF. M8. $30.00

WEEKS, John. *Men Against Tanks: Hist of Anti-Tank Warfare.* 1975. NY. BC. 189p. VG/VG. A17. $7.00

WEEMS, John Edward. *Peary the Explorer & the Man.* ca 1987. Los Angeles. photos/biblio/index. M/wrp. A17. $8.50

WEEMS, M.L. *God's Revenge Against Murder; or, The Drown'd Wife...* 1808. Phil. self pub. 4th ed. 8vo. 4op. uncut. M1. $225.00

WEEMS, P.V.H. *Air Navigation.* (1943). McGraw Hill. 3rd ed/2nd imp. 406p. G. H1. $6.00

WEES, Frances Shelley. *Country of the Strangers.* 1960. Doubleday. 1st ed. RS. VG/VG. P3. $20.00

WEHR, Julian. *Animated Animals.* 1943. Saalfield. pict brd/sbdg. VG/VG. A3. $12.50

WEHRMANN, Stephen. *Lhasa Apsos.* 1990. NY. Barrons. 1st ed. 71p. M/wrp. R2. $8.00

WEIDENFELD, S.R. *First Lady's Lady: With the Fords at the White House.* 1979. NY. 1st ed. inscr. F/F. B14. $35.00

WEIDER, Arthur. *Contributions Toward Medical Psychology.* 1953. NY. Ronald. 2 vol. G/djs. K4. $40.00

WEIGALL, Arthur. *Echnaton, Konig Von Agypten und Seine Zeit.* 1923. Basel. Schwabe. 1st ed. 25 pl. xl. VG. W1. $15.00

WEIGALL, Arthur. *Life & Times of Cleopatra, Queen of Egypt...* 1926. Putnam. revised ed. lg 8vo. 445p. xl. G. W1. $15.00

WEIGALL, Arthur. *Tutankhamen & Other Essays.* 1923. Butterworth. 1st ed. VG. P3. $45.00

WEIGER, Del. *Cacti of Texas & Neighboring States.* 1984. Austin. photos. 356p. sc. M. B26. $22.95

WEIGER, Del. *Cacti of the Southwest.* ca 1970. Austin, TX. photos. 249p. F/dj. scarce. B26. $89.00

WEIL, Lisl. *Candy Egg Bunny.* 1975. Holiday House. 32p. VG. A3. $5.00

WEIL, Lisl. *If Eggs Had Legs, Nonsense & Some Sense.* 1976. Doubleday. 1st ed. ils. VG+/VG+. C8. $25.00

WEIL, Simone. *Notebooks of...* 1956. London. 1st ed in Eng. 2 vols. F/djs. A17. $45.00

WEILL, E. *Traite Clinique des Maladies du Coer Chez les Infants.* 1895. Paris. Doin. 390p. orig wrp/lib buckram. xl. G7. $75.00

WEILL, Gus. *Bonnet Man.* 1978. Macmillan. 1st ed. F/NF. M21. $10.00

WEIMER, Walter B. *Notes on Methodology of Scientific Research.* 1979. Hillsdale, NJ. Halsted Pr Division of Wiley. 258p. VG/dj. G1. $35.00

WEINBAUM, Stanley. *Black Flame.* 1948. Fantasy. 1st ed. 1/500. pl. F/dj. M2. $150.00

WEINBERG, Arthur. *Attorney for the Damned (Clarence Darrow).* 1957. NY. Simon Schuster. M11. $35.00

WEINBERG, George. *Numberland.* 1987. St Martin. 1st ed. F/F. P3. $10.00

WEINBERG, Robert. *Armageddon Box.* 1991. Wayside. 1st ed. sgn. 1/400. F/dj. M2. $40.00

WEINBERG, Robert. *Devil's Auction.* 1988. Owlswick. 1st ed. F/F. P3. $20.00

WEINBERG, Robert. *Devil's Auction.* 1988. Owlswick. 1st ed. inscr. F/dj. F4. $25.00

WEINBERG, Robert. *Far Below & Other Horrors.* 1974. Starmont. 1st ed. F/dj. M2. $30.00

WEINBERGER, B.W. *Dental Bibliography.* 1929. NY. 2nd ed. 183p. G7. $75.00

WEINBERGER, Harry. *Liberty of the Press.* 1934. Berkeley Hgts, NJ. Oriole. 38p. brd. G. M10. $9.50

WEINER, Irving B. *Psychodiagnosis in Schizophrenia.* 1966. Wiley. 573p. G. K4. $12.50

WEINER, M. *Matters of Felony.* 1967. NY. 204p. cloth. VG+. D3. $12.50

WEINER, Melissa Ruffner. *Prescott: A Pict Hist.* 1981. Donning. 1st ed. ils/bibliography/index. 208p. F/sans. B19. $45.00

WEINTRAUB, Stanley. *Private Shaw & Public Shaw.* 1963. Brazillier. 3rd prt. 302p. VG/VG. M7. $40.00

WEIR, R.C. *Wonderful Plane Ride.* 1949. Chicago. Rand McNally Elf Book. G. B18. $7.50

WEIR & WEIR. *Hostage Bound. Hostage Free.* 1987. Westminster. 1st ed. 8vo. 183p. NF/dj. W1. $10.00

WEIR. *Our Cats.* 1889. Boston. 1st Am ed. 248p. NF. scarce. R2. $85.00

WEIRMAN, Irving. *Virgil's Ghost.* 1989. Fawcett Columbine. 1st ed. 340p. F/dj. M10. $5.00

WEISBORD, Albert. *Conquest of Power.* 1937. Covici Friede. 2 vol. 1st ed. F/dj. B2. $150.00

WEISBORD, Vera Buch. *Radical Life.* 1977. Bloomington. IN U. 1st ed. inscr. F/F. B2. $45.00

WEISER, William J. *Space Guidebook.* 1960. Coward McCann. 8vo. 322p. G/dj. K5. $15.00

WEISGARD, Leonard. *Circus Animals.* 1958. Penn Prts. VG. A3. $50.00

WEISGARD, Leonard. *Plymouth Thanksgiving.* 1967. Doubleday. 4to. ils. 61p. VG/VG. A3. $15.00

WEISMAN, Alan. *La Frontera: US Border With Mexico.* 1986. HBJ. sgn. ils/bibliography/index. 200p. cloth. NF/VG. B19. $55.00

WEISNER, David. *Tuesday.* 1991. Clarion. 1st ed. 8vo. F/F. B17. $25.00

WEISS, Egon. *Design of Lettering.* 1932. Pencil Points. 4to. ils. 174p. red lettered blk cloth. F/VG. F1. $150.00

WEISS, Joseph. *Studies in Eastern European Jewish Mysticism.* 1985. Harvard. 272p. F/F. B33. $30.00

WEISS, Kenneth M. *Demographic Models for Anthropology.* 1973. Soc Am Archeology. 25 tables. F/prt wrp. P4. $15.00

WEISS, Paul H. *Reality.* 1938. Princeton/London. 314p. orange cloth. G1. $35.00

WEISS-ROSMARIN, Trude. *Jerusalem.* 1950. Philosophical Lib. 1st ed. ils/fld map. 51p. VG/dj. W1. $10.00

WELBURN, Ron. *Peripheries.* 1972. Greenfield Review. 1st ed. inscr/dtd 1976. NF/wrp. L3. $35.00

WELCH, Anthony. *Artists for the Shah.* 1976. Yale. 1st ed. 233p. VG/dj. W1. $45.00

WELCH, Anthony. *Calligraphy in the Arts of the Muslim World.* 1979. Anthony, NY. The Asia Soc. 4to. ils. 216p. NF. M10. $22.50

WELCH, E. Parl. *Philosophy of Edmund Hussel...* 1941. Columbia. 337p. ruled gray cloth. NF. G1. $50.00

WELCH, Holmes. *Parting of the Way: Lao Tzu & Taoist Movement.* 1957. Boston. Beacon. sm 8vo. 204p. orange cloth. VG/dj. G1. $32.50

WELCH, James. *Fools Crow.* 1986. np. 1st ed. F/dj. B34. $30.00

WELCH, James. *Indian Lawyer.* 1990. Norton. F/dj. B34. $15.00

WELCH, James. *Indian Lawyer.* 1990. Norton. 1st ed. sgn. F/F. A18. $50.00

WELCH, James. *Riding the Earthboy 40: Poems.* 1971. World. 1st ed. F/dj. A18. $125.00

WELCH, James. *Winter in the Blood.* 1974. Harper. 1st ed. inscr/sgn. F/dj. A18. $90.00

WELCH, Kenneth F. *History of Clocks & Watches.* 1972. Drake Pub. 1st ed. 8vo. 120p. F/F. A8. $18.00

WELCH, Oliver. *American Arithmetic...* 1812. Exeter. Norris. 231p. lacks front ep. leather. H10. $35.00

WELCH, Stuart Cary. *Persian Painting.* 1976. Braziller. 1st ed. 4to. 48 pl. 127p. NF/wrp. W1. $20.00

WELCOME, John. *Best Crime Stories.* 1964. Farber. 1st ed. NF/NF. P3. $30.00

WELCOME, John. *Sporting World of RS Surtees.* 1982. Oxford. 1st ed. VG/fair. O3. $25.00

WELDON, Fay. *...And the Wife Ran Away.* 1968. McKay. 1st Am ed/author's 1st book. F/NF. B2. $75.00

WELFORD, A.T. *Fundamentals of Skill.* 1968. London. Methuen. 426p. F/dj. K4. $20.00

WELLES, Orson. *Cradle Will Rock.* 1994. Santa Barbara. Santa Teresa. 1/1000. F/F. B2. $35.00

WELLINGTON. *Economic Theory of Location of Railways.* 1887. np. ils/maps/charts. VG. E5. $45.00

WELLMAN, Manly Wade. *After Dark.* 1980. Doubleday. 1st ed. VG/VG. P3. $25.00

WELLMAN, Manly Wade. *Cahena.* 1986. Doubleday. ARC. RS. F/dj. F4. $22.00

WELLMAN, Manly Wade. *Dark Destroyers.* 1959. Avalon. VG/VG. P3. $50.00

WELLMAN, Manly Wade. *Lost & the Lurking.* 1981. Doubleday. 1st ed. rem mk. F/dj. F4. $20.00

WELLMAN, Manly Wade. *Old Gods Waken.* 1979. Doubleday. 1st ed. VG/VG. P3. $25.00

WELLMAN, Manly Wade. *Voice of the Mountain.* 1984. Doubleday. 1st ed. F/F. F4. $20.00

WELLMAN, Manly Wade. *Worse Things Waiting.* 1973. Chapel Hill. 1st ed. F/F. T2. $100.00

WELLMAN, Paul. *Ride the Red Earth.* 1958. NY. 1st ed. VG/VG. B5. $45.00

WELLS, Anna Mary. *Sin of Angels.* 1948. Simon Schuster. 1st ed. G+. P3. $15.00

WELLS, Carolyn. *Patty & Azalea.* nd. Grosset Dunlap. VG. P3. $15.00

WELLS, Carolyn. *Spooky Hollow.* 1923. Phil. 1st ed. VG. A17. $8.50

WELLS, Carolyn. *Such Nonsense, an Anthology: Wit & Nonsense in Words...* 1918. NY. Doran. 1st ed. 8vo. 249p. F/G+. D6. $35.00

WELLS, Carveth. *Let's Do the Mediterranean.* 1928. Doubleday Doran. 1st ed. 262p. VG. W1. $20.00

WELLS, Gabriel. *These Three.* 1932. NY. Wm E Rudge. 1/750. 12mo. 91p. NF. M10. $22.50

WELLS, Gordon Lynn. *Vertebrate Eye & Its Adaptive Radiation.* 1942. Bloomfield. 785p. cloth. VG. B14. $125.00

WELLS, H. Gideon. *Die Chemischen Anschauungen Uber Immunitatsvorgange.* 1927. Jena. 1st German ed. 288p. cloth. G7. $35.00

WELLS, H.G. *Anatomy of Frustration.* 1936. Macmillan. 1st ed. VG. P3. $30.00

WELLS, H.G. *Experiment in Autobiography.* 1934. Macmillan of Canada. 1st ed. VG. P3. $35.00

WELLS, H.G. *Experiment in Autobiography.* 1934. NY. 1st ed. inscr/dtd 1940. beige buckram. VG+. M7. $75.00

WELLS, H.G. *Joan & Peter.* 1918. Macmillan. 1st ed. G+. P3. $12.00

WELLS, H.G. *Mr Britling Sees It Through.* 1916. Macmillan. 1st ed. VG. P3. $40.00

WELLS, H.G. *Sea Lady.* 1902. Appleton. 1st Am ed. VG. M2. $250.00

WELLS, H.G. *Secret Places of the Heart.* 1922. Macmillan. 287p. gilt red cloth. VG. S11. $12.00

WELLS, H.G. *Shape of Things To Come.* 1933. Canada. Macmillan. 1st ed. VG. P3. $75.00

WELLS, H.G. *Time Machine.* 1931. Random. VG/case. P3. $30.00

WELLS, H.G. *Undying Fire.* 1919. Macmillan. 1st Am ed. G+. M21. $15.00

WELLS, H.G. *War in the Air.* 1908. NY. Macmillan. 1st Am ed. 8vo. 395p. stp gray cloth. G. H5. $300.00

WELLS, H.G. *War of the Worlds.* 1898. London. Heinemann. 1st ed. 8vo. 303p. blk lettered gray cloth. NF. H5. $1,500.00

WELLS, H.G. *World of William Clissold.* 1926. London. Benn. 3 vol. 1st ed/deluxe issue. 1/198. gr cloth. F/case. C6. $450.00

WELLS, Helen. *Cherry Ames, Senior Nurse.* nd. Grosset Dunlap. VG/VG. P3. $8.00

WELLS, Helen. *Doctor Betty.* 1969. Messner. xl. 190p. VG/dj. M20. $30.00

WELLS, Helen. *Vicki Finds an Answer.* nd. Grosset Dunlap. VG/VG. P3. $8.00

WELLS, Rosemary. *Benjamin & Tulip.* 1973. NY. Dial. 1st prt. NF/VG+. C8. $40.00

WELLS, Rosemary. *Fritz & the Mess Fairy.* 1991. Dial. 1st ed. 4to. F/VG. B17. $12.50

WELLS, Rosemary. *Peabody.* 1983. Dial. 1st ed. 8vo. F/VG. B17. $7.50

WELLS, S.M. *Electropathic Guide.* 1886. La Crosse. 8th ed. cloth. VG. C11. $55.00

WELLS, Tobias. *Matter of Love & Death.* 1966. Crime Club. 1st ed. VG/VG. P3. $18.00

WELSH, Stanley L. *Common Utah Plants.* 1965. Provo. 2nd ed. ils/line drawings. 312p. VG. B26. $24.00

WELSMAN, Ernest. *Your Holiday in Greece.* 1960. Taplinger. 2nd ed. 24 pl/11 maps. 240p. VG. W1. $14.00

WELTY, Eudora. *Bride of the Innisfallen.* 1955. Harcourt Brace. 1st issue. remnant RS. F/NF. B4. $450.00

WELTY, Eudora. *Delta Wedding.* 1946. Harcourt Brace. 1st ed/author's 4th book. NF/VG. L3. $150.00

WELTY, Eudora. *Henry Green: Novelist of the Imagination.* 1961. offprint (TX Quarterly). 1/50. VG/wrp. C2. $300.00

WELTY, Eudora. *Ida M'Toy.* 1979. Urbana. 1/350. sgn. 4to. 40p. gilt red cloth. F. H5. $200.00

WELTY, Eudora. *Losing Battles.* 1970. Random. 1st ed. 436p. gr cloth. NF/dj. C6. $45.00

WELTY, Eudora. *One Writer's Beginnings.* 1984. Cambridge. Harvard. 1/350 #d. F/F case. S9. $250.00

WELTY, Eudora. *Photographs.* 1989. Jackson, MS. 1/52. sgn. leather. w/original photo. F/F custom box. S9. $1,000.00

WELTY, Eudora. *Ponder Heart.* 1982. Jackson, MS. New Stage Theatre. 1st prt. 4to. F/wrp. C6. $65.00

WELTY, Eudora. *Robber Bridegroom.* 1987. Hatfield, MA. Pennyroyal. ltd ed. 1/150. sgn Welty/Moser. red leather. E3. $550.00

WELTY, Eudora. *White Fruitcake.* 1980. Albondocani. 1st ed. 1/450. sgn. pub/sgn George Bixby. F/wrp. S9. $125.00

WELTY, Eudora. *Wide Net.* (1947). Harcourt Brace. early prt. bl brd. VG. E3. $15.00

WELYKYJ, Athanasius G. *Documenta Pontificum Romanorum Historiam Ucrainae...* 1953-1954. Romae. Basiliani. 2 vol. xl. H10. $85.00

WENDT, Herbert. *In Search of Adam: Story of Man's Quest for Truth...* 1956. Houghton Mifflin. 1st Am ed. 540p. VG/torn. W1. $15.00

WENSLEY, F. *Forty Years of Scotland Yard.* 1931. NY. 312p. VG. D3. $20.00

WENTWORTH, M.P. *Forged in Strong Fires.* 1948. Caldwell. ltd ed. sgn. 1/1000. 373p. F/VG ltd ed & trade djs. P4. $50.00

WENTWORTH, Marion Craig. *War Brides.* 1915. Century. 12mo. photos. 71p. VG. S11. $10.00

WENTWORTH, Patricia. *Blind Side.* 1975. Wht Lion. xl. dj. P3. $8.00

WENTWORTH, Patricia. *Case Is Closed.* 1950. Hodder Stoughton. 3rd ed. VG. P3. $15.00

WERDERMANN, E. *Brazil & Its Columnar Cacti.* 1942. Pasadena. photos/map. 121p. VG. B26. $65.00

WERFEL, Franz. *Forty Days of Musa Dagh.* 1934. Viking. 1st ed. VG+. P3. $20.00

WERFEL, Franz. *Forty Days of Musa Dagh.* 1934. Viking. 1st ed. 8vo. map ep. VG. W1. $18.00

WERFEL, Franz. *Star of the Unborn.* 1946. Viking. 1st ed. F/dj. M2. $35.00

WERKMEISTER, W.H. *Intro to Critical Thinking.* 1948. Lincoln, NE. 657p. G. K4. $8.50

WERNER, C.A. *Tobaccoland.* 1922. NY. 1st ed. VG+. A15. $25.00

WERNER, Jane. *Child's Book of Bible Stories.* 1944. NY. 1st ed. ils Masha. 54p. VG/VG. A17. $20.00

WERNER, Jane. *Child's Book of Bible Stories.* 1944. Random. ils Masha. 53p. VG. A3. $15.00

WERNER, Jane. *Giant Golden Book of Elves & Fairies.* 1951. Simon Schuster. 1st/A ed. ils Garth Williams. pict brd. VG. M5. $95.00

WERNER, Jane. *Great Golden Story Book of Elves & Fairies.* 1953. Sydney. Golden. ils Garth Williams. VG. C8. $250.00

WERT, J. *From Winchester to Cedar Creek.* 1987. ils/index. 324p. dj. O8. $14.50

WERT, J. *John W Mosby: Legendary Leader of Mosby's Rangers.* 1990. np. 400p. NF/dj. E5. $20.00

WERTH, Alexander. *Moscow War Diary.* 1942. Knopf. 297p. VG/VG. A17. $9.50

WERTHAM, F. *Seduction of Innocent.* 1954. NY. 1st ed. VG/G. B5. $50.00

WERTHAM, Fred. *Show of Violence.* 1949. NY. 1st ed. 279p. cloth. VG. D3. $12.50

WESCHER, Herta. *Collage.* (1979). Abrams. 4to. 418p. blk stp yel cloth. F/dj. K1. $200.00

WESCOTT, Cynthia. *Gardener's Bug Book.* 1946. Doubleday/Am Garden Guild. 1st ed. 590p. G/G. H1. $16.00

WESLEY, John. *Works of the Reverand John Wesley.* 1835. np. 1st ed. full leather. VG. E5. $45.00

WESLEY. *Works of... Vol II.* nd. Zondervan. Standard ed. M/plastic wrp. B29. $13.00

WESSELLS, Katherine Tyler. *Golden Song Book.* 1945. Simon Schuter. 1st prt. ils Gertrude Elliott. VG+. C8. $27.50

WEST, Edwin; see Westlake, Donald E.

WEST, Geoffrey. *Charles Darwin: A Portrait.* 1938. Yale. 359p. dj. A10. $20.00

WEST, James E. *Lone Scout of the Sky.* 1928. Phil. ils/photos. 275p. VG/dj. B18. $45.00

WEST, Jerry. *Happy Hollisters at Pony Hill Farm.* 1956. Garden City. VG/G. O3. $15.00

WEST, Jessamyn. *Collected Stories.* 1986. HBJ. 1st ed. 8vo. 490p. rem mk. VG/VG. V3. $10.50

WEST, Jessamyn. *Friendly Persuasion.* 1945. Harcourt Brace. 8vo. 214p. NF/chip. V3. $8.50

WEST, Levon. *Making an Etching.* 1932. London. The Studio. tall 8vo. ils/photos. 79p. NF. F1. $65.00

WEST, Morris L. *Cassidy.* 1986. Doubleday. 1st ed. VG/G+. P3. $15.00

WEST, Morris L. *Harlequin.* 1974. Morrow. 1st ed. F/F. P3. $23.00

WEST, Nathanael. *Day of the Locust.* 1939. Random. 1st ed/author's last book. 8vo. 238p. red cloth. VG/dj. C6. $650.00

WEST, Oliver. *Field Guide to the Aloes of Rhodesia.* 1974. Salisbury. photos. 96p. sc. F. B26. $9.00

WEST, Owen; see Koontz, Dean R.

WEST, Pamela. *Yours Truly, Jack the Ripper.* nd. BC. VG/VG. P3. $10.00

WEST, Paul. *Alley Jaggers.* 1966. NY. 1st ed/author's 3rd novel. sgn. NF/NF. A11. $55.00

WEST, Paul. *Sheer Fiction.* 1946. McPherson. 1st ed. F/F. L3. $40.00

WEST, Ray B. *Rocky Mountain Cities.* 1949. Norton. 1st ed. 320p. VG/G. B19. $25.00

WEST, Samuel. *On Granular Kidney & Physiological Albuminuria...* 1900. London. Glaisher. 197p. G. G7. $30.00

WEST, Victor C. *Guide to Shipwreck Sites Along the Oregon Coast.* 1984. North Bend, OR. Wells West. ils/maps. 75p. wrp. T7. $10.00

WEST, Wallace. *Bird of Time.* 1959. Gnome. 1st ed. F/dj. M2. $30.00

WEST, Wallace. *Bird of Time.* 1959. Gnome. 1st ed. VG/VG. P3. $25.00

WEST, Wallace. *Outposts in Space.* 1962. Avalon. 1st ed. NF/NF. P3. $30.00

WESTBROOK, Robert. *Lady Left.* 1990. Crown. 1st ed. NF/NF. P3. $18.00

WESTCOTT, Cynthia. *Anyone Can Grow Roses.* 1954. Toronto. 2nd ed. 159p. VG+/dj. B26. $12.50

WESTCOTT, Jan. *Hepburn.* 1950. Crown. 1st ed. VG/VG. P3. $15.00

WESTERMAN, Percy F. *Rival Submarines.* ca 1920. London. Partridge. ils. 432p. brd. T7. $16.00

WESTERMEIER, Clifford P. *Who Rush to Glory: Cowboy Volunteers on 1898...* 1958. Caldwell. Caxton. 1st ed. ils. 272p. red cloth. F/G. B11. $60.00

WESTHEIMER, David. *Magic Fallacy.* 1950. NY. 1st ed. inscr. NF/VG. A11. $40.00

WESTHEIMER, Ruth. *All in a Lifetime: An Autobiography.* 1990. London. 1st Eng ed. VG/dj. N2. $5.00

WESTLAKE, Donald E. *Baby, Would I Lie?* 1994. Mysterious. 1st ed. NF/NF. P3. $20.00

WESTLAKE, Donald E. *Damsel.* 1967. Macmillan. 1st ed. VG/VG. P3. $75.00

WESTLAKE, Donald E. *Don't Ask.* 1993. Mysterious. 1st ed. sgn. F/F. O4. $30.00

WESTLAKE, Donald E. *Drowned Hopes.* 1990. Mysterious. 1st ed. sgn. F/F. S6. $40.00

WESTLAKE, Donald E. *Good Behavior.* 1985. Mysterious. 1st ed. sgn. F/F. O4. $20.00

WESTLAKE, Donald E. *Green Eagle Score.* 1986. Allison Busby. 1st ed. NF/NF. P3. $20.00

WESTLAKE, Donald E. *Handle.* 1985. London. 1st ed. sgn. F/F. O4. $25.00

WESTLAKE, Donald E. *High Adventure.* 1985. Mysterious. 1st ed. F/clip. F4. $15.00

WESTLAKE, Donald E. *Humans.* 1992. Mysterious. 1st ed. F/F. T2. $20.00

WESTLAKE, Donald E. *I Know a Trick Worth Two of That.* 1986. Tor. 1st ed. VG/G. P3. $15.00

WESTLAKE, Donald E. *Jugger.* 1986. London. Allison. 1st Eng hc ed. NF/NF. S6. $27.50

WESTLAKE, Donald E. *Justice Ends at Home.* 1977. NY. Viking. 1st ed. edit John McAleer. F/F. S6. $35.00

WESTLAKE, Donald E. *Killing Time.* 1961. Random. 1st ed/author's 2nd novel. NF/VG. B4. $85.00

WESTLAKE, Donald E. *Killy.* 1963. Random. 1st ed. VG/G. P3. $75.00

WESTLAKE, Donald E. *Levine.* 1984. Mysterious. 1st ed. VG/VG. P3. $15.00

WESTLAKE, Donald E. *Point Blank.* 1984. Allison Busby. 1st ed. F/F. P3. $25.00

WESTLAKE, Donald E. *Rare Coin Score.* 1984. London. Allison. 1st Eng hc ed. sgn. F/F. S6. $40.00

WESTLAKE, Donald E. *Slay-Ground.* 1984. London. Allison Busby. 1st ed. sgn. F/F. O4. $20.00

WESTLAKE, Donald E. *Spy in the Ointment.* 1966. Random. 1st ed. sgn. G/NF. O4. $30.00

WESTLAKE, Donald E. *Too Much.* 1975. NY. Evans. 1st ed. sgn. VG/VG. O4. $30.00

WESTLAKE, Donald E. *Trust Me on This.* 1988. Mysterious. 1st ed. F/F. T2. $17.00

WESTLAKE, Donald E. *What I Tell You Three Times Is False.* 1987. Tor. 1st ed. F/F. F4. $22.00

WESTLEY, William A. *Violence & the Police.* 1970. Cambridge. VG/dj. D3. $12.50

WESTMAN, Johannes. *Dissertatione Medicae de Hydrope.* 1742. Upsalie. sm 4to. 20p. G. G7. $25.00

WESTON, Edward. *Edward Weston. The Flame of Recognition.* 1975. Aperture. 4to. VG/wrp. S9. $30.00

WESTON, Garnett. *Hidden Portal.* 1946. Crime Club. 1st ed. VG/VG. P3. $20.00

WESTON, Peter. *Andromeda 2.* 1977. Dobson. 1st ed. F/F. P3. $20.00

WESTOVER, Russ. *Tillie the Toiler.* 1928. NY. sq 8vo. all ils. 48p. pict wrp/cloth spine. F. H3. $50.00

WESTPAHALL, Victor. *Merceder Reales: Hispanic Land Grants of Upper Rio Grande...* 1983. NM U. 1st ed. 8vo. index/notes/maps. 356p. bl cloth. M/dj. P4. $30.00

WESTRATE, Bruce C. *Araba Bureau: British Policy in the Middle East...* 1992. PA State. 1st ed. 240p. gilt red cloth. M/dj. M7. $35.00

WESTROPP, M.S. *Irish Glass. An Account of Glass-Making in Ireland...* 1921. Phil. Present Day. 1st ed. 4to. gr cloth. NF. C6. $60.00

WESTWOOD, J.N. *History of Russian Railways.* 1964. London. 1st ed. VG/dj. C11. $35.00

WESTWOOD, John. *Art of Illuminated Manuscripts, Ils Sacred Writings...* 1988. np. rpt of 1843-45 ed. thick folio. F/F. A4. $45.00

WESTWOOD, John. *Pictorial History of Railways.* 1988. NY. Gallery. sm folio. ils. 208p. F/F. B11. $25.00

WETMORE, Helen Cody. *Buffalo Bill, Last of the Great Scouts.* 1965. Bison Books. sc. VG. B34. $10.00

WETMORE, Helen Cody. *Last of the Great Scouts: Life Story of Col Wm F Cody.* 1899. Duluth, MN. 1st ed. 267p. VG. D3. $60.00

WETMORE, Prosper. *Lexington With Other Fugitive Poems.* 1830. NY. Carvill. 1st ed. 8vo. 87p. F. M1. $175.00

WETZEL, George. *Gothic Horror & Other Weird Tales.* 1978. Ganley. 1st ed. F/dj. M2. $30.00

WEVERKA, Robert. *One Minute to Eternity.* 1968. Morrow. VG/VG. P3. $13.00

WEYGAND, James Lamar. *Action on the North Atlantic.* 1988. Nappanee, IN. Maestro. 68x48mm. 1/about 50. 21p+insert. bl brd. F. B24. $200.00

WEYGAND, James Lamar. *Girls Will Be Girls.* nd. Nappanee, IN. 68x48mm. 1/about 40. 26p. w/card. prt orange brd. F. B24. $200.00

WEYGAND, James Lamar. *Issue of Tissue.* 1983. Nappanee. Pr of IN Kid. 80x62mm. 1/about 65. 24p/frenchfold. lavender brd. F. B24. $250.00

WEYGAND, James Lamar. *Printer's Meeting 1822. A Slight Case of Price Fixing.* nd. Nappanee. Pr of IN Kid. 66x48mm. 14p+foldout. w/facsimile report. ils brd. F. B24. $200.00

WEYGAND, James Lamar. *Twain's 1601.* 1974. Pr of IN Kid. 68x48mm. 1/40 on gray paper. woodcut title p. bl brd. F. B24. $200.00

WEYMOUTH, R.F. *New Testament in Modern Speech.* nd. Pilgrim Pr. 3rd ed. 734p. aeg. leather. G. B29. $5.00

WHALEN, Grover. *Trip to the NY World's Fair With Bobby & Betty.* 1938. Dodge. 1st ed. photos. pict cloth. VG+. M5. $22.00

WHALEN, Philip. *Highgrade.* 1966. Coyote's Journal. 1st ed. F/wrp. B2. $35.00

WHALEN, Philip. *Like I Say.* 1960. Totem. 1st ed. F/wrp. B2. $25.00

WHALEY, Elizabeth J. *Forgotten Hero: General James B McPherson.* 1955. Exposition. 1st ed. 203p. VG/dj. M20. $45.00

WHARTON, Edith. *Buccaneers.* 1993. Viking. ARC. F/wrp. B2. $30.00

WHARTON, Edith. *Children.* 1928. Appleton. 1st prt. 346p. VG/dj. M20. $80.00

WHARTON, Edith. *Fruit of the Tree.* 1907. Scribner. 1st ed. 633p. VG. M20. $45.00

WHARTON, Edith. *Italian Villas & Their Gardens.* 1904. NY. 1st ed. ils Parrish. VG+. B5. $425.00

WHARTON, Edith. *Reef.* 1912. NY. Syndicate. 1st ed. VG/VG. B5. $20.00

WHARTON, Joseph. *Red Roan Pony.* 1951. Lippincott. 1st ed thus. ils CW Anderson. F/poor. M5. $25.00

WHARTON, William. *Dad.* 1981. NY. 1st ed. F/clip. A17. $10.00

WHARTON, William. *Last Lovers.* 1991. FSG. 1st ed. F/F. L3. $30.00

WHARTON, William. *Pride.* 1985. Knopf. 1st ed. F/F. L3. $35.00

WHEAT, Carl I. *Mapping the Transmississippi West 1540-1861.* 1957-1963. San Francisco. Inst Hist Cartography. 5 vol in 6. F/djs/cartons. P4. $4,950.00

WHEAT, Carl I. *Pioneer Press of California.* 1948. Oakland, CA. Grabhorn/Biobooks. 1/450. folio. woodcuts. K1. $125.00

WHEATCROFT, Andrew. *Ottomans.* 1993. Viking. 1st ed. 8vo. 322p. NF/dj. W1. $25.00

WHEATLEY, Dennis. *Bill for Use of a Body.* 1964. Hutchinson. 1st ed. G+/dj. P3. $15.00

WHEATLEY, Dennis. *Dark Secret of Josephine.* 1955. Hutchinson. 1st ed. VG/VG. P3. $30.00

WHEATLEY, Dennis. *Haunting of Toby Jugg.* 1951. Hutchinson. 3rd ed. G+/dj. P3. $25.00

WHEATLEY, Dennis. *Man Who Killed the King.* 1965. NY. 1st Am ed. VG/dj. A17. $7.50

WHEATLEY, Dennis. *Murder Off Miami.* 1986. Michael Joseph. brd. F. P3. $25.00

WHEATLEY, Dennis. *Sultan's Daughter.* 1963. Hutchinson. 1st ed. VG/G. P3. $25.00

WHEATLEY, Dennis. *To the Devil — a Daughter.* 1972. Edito-Service. VG. P3. $10.00

WHEATSTONE, Charles. *Scientific Papers.* 1879. London. Taylor Francis. 1st ed. rear pocket w/pl. rebound bl leather. H4. $450.00

WHEELER, B. *Yankee From the West.* 1962. Doubleday. 1st ed. 436p. VG/dj. B34. $20.00

WHEELER, C.H. *Ten Years on the Euphrates; or, Primitive Missionary...* 1868. Boston. 8vo. ils/2 fold map. cloth. O2. $100.00

WHEELER, Daniel. *Memoir of Daniel Wheeler With an Account of His Gospel...* 1859. Phil. 24mo. 259p. xl. V3. $36.00

WHEELER, Edward W. *Report of Joint New England Railroad Committee.* June 1923. np. fld maps. full leather. VG. M17. $75.00

WHEELER, Guy. *Year 'Round: A Perennial Miscellany for Foxhunters.* 1968. WA. Luce. VG/case. O3. $25.00

WHEELER, J.B. *Elements of Field Fortications.* 1889. NY. ils. 295p. O8. $55.00

WHEELER, Joseph. *Santiago Campaign 1898.* 1898. NY. Lamson Wolffe. 1st ed. 8vo. 369p. bl cloth. F. B11. $120.00

WHEELER, Mark. *Half-Baked Alaska.* 1972. Ketchikan. 1st ed. 160p. VG/wrp. A17. $8.50

WHEELER, Opal. *HMS Pinafore Adapted From Gilbert & Sullivan.* 1946. Dutton. 1st ed. ils Fritz Kredel. VG/G+. C8. $22.50

WHEELER, Opal. *Sing for America.* 1944. Dutton. 1st ed. ils Gustav Tenggren. 127p. VG/G. A17. $30.00

WHEELER & WHITED. *Oil From Prospect to Pipeline.* 1958. Gulf Pub. 8th prt. 8vo. VG/dj. W1. $12.00

WHELEN, Townsent. *Wilderness Hunting & Wildcraft.* 1927. np. 1st ed. 338p. VG. E5. $35.00

WHENWELL, William. *Hist of Inductive Sciences...* 1857 (1837). London. Parker. 3 vol. 3rd revised ed. sm 8vo. emb orange cloth. F. G1. $350.00

WHIPPLE, Sidney B. *Lindbergh Crime.* (1935). NY. rpt. 341p. ES. cloth. VG. D3. $25.00

WHISNANT, Luke. *Watching TV With the Red Chinese.* 1992. Algonquin. 1st ed/author's 1st book. F/F. A14. $75.00

WHISTLER, W. Arthur. *Tongan Herbal Medicine.* 1992. Honolulu. ils/photos. sc. M. B26. $12.95

WHITAKER, Herman. *Probationer.* 1905. Harper. 1st ed. 392p. gilt gr cloth. VG. M20. $20.00

WHITAKER & WHITAKER. *Rhineland: Battle to End the War.* 1989. NY. 1st ed. 422p. VG/dj. B18. $15.00

WHITCOMB, Jon. *Coco, the Far-Out Poodle.* 1963. Random. 1st prt. VG/VG. B17. $10.00

WHITE, Anne Terry. *Lost Worlds: Romance of Archaeology.* 1941. Random. 1st ed. 8vo. 316p. VG. W1. $14.00

WHITE, Colin. *World of the Nursery.* 1984. Dutton. 1st ed. 224p. VG/VG. S11. $35.00

WHITE, Dan. *Crosscurrents in Quiet Water.* 1987. Dallas, TX. Taylor. 4to. 150+ photos. 203p. dj. T7. $45.00

WHITE, E.B. *Charlotte's Web.* 1952. Harper. stated 1st ed. ils Garth Williams. C8/M5. $80.00

WHITE, E.B. *Fox of Peapack.* 1938. Harper. 1st ed. VG/G clip. L3. $125.00

WHITE, E.B. *Stuart Little.* 1945. Harper. 1st ed. ils Garth Williams. VG. C8. $50.00

WHITE, E.B. *Trumpet of the Swan.* 1970. Harper. early later prt. inscr. F/NF. B4. $100.00

WHITE, Edmund. *Beautiful Room Is Empty.* 1988. Knopf. 1st ed. VG/VG. P3. $18.00

WHITE, Edmund. *Caracole.* 1985. Dutton. 1st ed. 342p. F/F. H1. $18.00

WHITE, Edward Stewart. *African Camp Fires.* 1913. NY. 1st ed. VG. B5. $37.50

WHITE, Eliza Orne. *House Across the Way.* 1940. Houghton Mifflin. 1st ed. ils Lois Maloy. cloth. F/partial. M5. $15.00

WHITE, Herbert C. *Peking the Beautiful.* nd. Shanghai. Commercial Pr Ltd. folio. embroidered bl silk. F. rare. H4. $400.00

WHITE, J. *Horsecars, Cable Cars & Omnibuses...* (1888). np. facsimile. NF. E5. $35.00

WHITE, James. *Watch Below.* 1966. Whiting Wheaton. 1st ed. VG/VG. P3. $75.00

WHITE, John W. *White's Mt Vernon Directory & City Guide...* 1876. Mt Vernon, OH. ils. 160p. G. B18. $95.00

WHITE, Kay. *Boxer.* 1984 (1977). Edinburgh. Bartholomew. ils. 96p. M/mc wrp. R2. $10.00

WHITE, Lionel. *To Find a Killer.* 1954. Dutton. 1st ed. VG/VG. P3. $40.00

WHITE, Mrs. E.G. *Desire of the Ages.* 1898. Oakland, CA. Pacific. 866p. cloth. VG. W1. $10.00

WHITE, Patrick. *Vivisector.* 1970. Viking. 1st ed. VG/NF. B3. $30.00

WHITE, R. Clyde. *Administration of Public Welfare.* 1940. Am Book Co. 507p. G. K4. $10.00

WHITE, R.E.O. *Open Letter to Evangelicals.* 1964. Eerdmans. 276p. VG/dj. B29. $5.00

WHITE, Richard. *It's Your Misfortune & None of My Own.* 1991. OK U. 1st ed. photos/maps/tables. M/dj. A18. $40.00

WHITE, Richard. *Middle Ground. Indians, Empires & Republics of Great Lakes.* 1991. Cambridge. 1st ed. 8vo. 544p. gilt brn cloth. M/sans. P4. $70.00

WHITE, Ruth. *Yankee From Sweden.* 1960. NY. Holt. 1st ed. 8vo. 299p. dj. T7. $25.00

WHITE, Stephen. *Privileged Information.* 1991. Viking. 1st ed. sgn. F/F. T2. $20.00

WHITE, Stewart Edward. *AZ Nights.* 1907. McClure. 1st ed. 345p. VG. B19. $65.00

WHITE, Stewart Edward. *Conjuror's House.* 1903. McClure Phillips. 1st ed. sgn. ils CS Chapman. VG. A18. $75.00

WHITE, Stewart Edward. *Gray Dawn.* 1915. Doubleday Page. 1st ed. ils Thomas Fogarty. F. A18. $35.00

WHITE, Stewart Edward. *Killer.* 1921. Doubleday Page. 1st ed. 346p. VG. B19. $35.00

WHITE, Stewart Edward. *Long Rifle.* 1990. Mtn Pr. 1st ed. M/dj. A18. $25.00

WHITE, Stewart Edward. *Old California in Picture & Story.* 1937. Doubleday Doran. 1st ed. ils. F/dj. A18. $40.00

WHITE, Stewart Edward. *Wild Geese Calling.* 1940. Doubleday Doran. 1st ed. sgn. F/chip. A18. $75.00

WHITE, T.H. *Once & Future King.* 1958. Internat Collectors Lib. 1st ed. G+. M21. $5.00

WHITE, T.H. *Sword in the Stone.* 1938. London. Collins. 1st ed. 8vo. 338p. blk cloth. VG/dj. H5. $650.00

WHITE, T.H. *Sword in the Stone.* 1939. Putnam. 1st ed. front free ep removed. VG. P3. $30.00

WHITE, T.H. *Witch in the Wood.* 1939. Putnam. 1st ed. F/NF. S9. $150.00

WHITE, Teri. *Thursday's Child.* 1991. Mysterious. 1st ed. NF/NF. P3. $19.00

WHITE, Trumbull. *Our New Possessions.* 1898. Chicago. Internat Pub. VG. N2. $15.00

WHITE, Trumbull. *United States in War With Spain & History of Cuba.* 1898. Chicago. Internat Pub. ils. 566p. gilt brn cloth. G. B11. $35.00

WHITE, William Allen. *Real Issues.* 1896. Way Williams. 1st ed/1st separate book. 16mo. teg. VG. A17. $25.00

WHITE, William. *Edwin Arlington Robinson: Supplementary Bibliography.* 1971. Kent State. 1st ed. 168p. VG. A17. $12.50

WHITEFIELD, George. *Ten Sermons Preached on Various Important Subjects...* 1797. Portsmith. Larkin. 206p. old leather. H10. $85.00

WHITEFORD, Mike. *How To Talk Baseball.* 1983. NY. ils. 144p. VG/wrp. M10. $2.50

WHITEHEAD, Alfred North. *Dialogues of Alfred North Whitehead...* 1954. Atlantic Monthly. 396p. bl cloth. G1. $22.50

WHITEHEAD, Alfred North. *Process & Reality: Essay in Cosmotology.* 1929. Macmillan. 1st Am ed. 546p. cloth. G1. $50.00

WHITEHEAD, George. *Memoirs of George Whitehead...Written by Himself.* 1832. Phil. Kite. 2 vol in 1. 12mo. cloth. worn. V3. $30.00

WHITEHEAD, Henry. *West India Lights.* 1946. Arkham. 1st ed. F/dj. F4. $100.00

WHITEHEAD. *This Solemn Mockery: Art of Literary Forgery.* 1973. London. ils. 181p. F/VG. A4. $55.00

WHITEHOUSE, Arch. *Tank: Story of Their Battles & the Man Who Drove Them...* 1960. Garden City. 1st ed. ils. 383p. G/worn. B18. $12.50

WHITEHOUSE, Arch. *Zeppelin Fighters.* 1966. Garden City. 1st ed. 290p. VG/dj. B18. $45.00

WHITELAW, Alex. *Book of Scottish Ballads.* 1851. Glascow. Blackie. 1st ed. gilt stp leather. NF. B2. $75.00

WHITELEY & WHITELEY. *Permissive Morality.* 1964. London. Methuen. 12mo. 141p. bl cloth. VG/dj. G1. $22.50

WHITEMAN, Maxwell. *Mankind & Medicine: A History...* 1966. Phil. 1st ed. 269p. A13. $25.00

WHITFIELD, Christopher. *Together & Alone.* 1945. London. Golden Cockerel. 1/100 (500 total). sgn author/ils. 109p. teg. F. B24. $450.00

WHITFIELD, Raoul. *Green Ice.* 1988. Eng. No Exit. 1st ed. F/F. S6. $35.00

WHITFIELD, Raoul. *Virgin Kills.* 1988. Eng. No Exit. 1st Eng ed. F/F. S6. $35.00

WHITING, Charles. *Bloody Aachen.* 1976. NY. BC. maps/photos. VG/VG. A17. $6.00

WHITING, Lilian. *Athens, the Violet-Crowned.* 1913. Little Brn. 1st ed. 32 pl. 361p. teg. VG. W1. $15.00

WHITLATCH, M. *Golf for Beginners & Others.* 1910. NY. 1st ed. cloth. VG. C11. $60.00

WHITLOCK, Brand. *Her Infinite Variety.* 1904. Bobbs Merrill. 1st ed. ils HC Christy. gilt silk cloth. F. M5. $35.00

WHITMAN, Edmund S. *Those Wild West Indies.* 1938. NY. Sheridan. 1st ed. inscr. 316p. G/G. B11. $40.00

WHITMAN, Walt. *Criticism: An Essay.* 1913. Newark. 1st ed. 1/100. NF. C2. $125.00

WHITMAN, Walt. *Leaves of Grass.* nd (1943). Peter Pauper. 1/1000. folio. ils Boyd Hanna. half morocco/prt brd. F/case. F1. $295.00

WHITMAN, Walt. *There Was a Child Went Forth.* 1943. Harper. stated 1st ed. ils Zhenya Gay. pict brd. VG. M5. $60.00

WHITMAN, Walt. *Wound Dresser.* 1898. Boston. Sm Maynard. 1st ed. 8vo. 201p. red cloth. NF. C6. $250.00

WHITMORE, Charles. *Winter's Daughter.* 1984. Timescape. 1st ed. VG/VG. P3. $15.00

WHITNEY, Helen Hay. *Bed-Time Book.* 1907. NY. Duffield. 1st ed. ils JW Smith. 32p. rust cloth. VG. D6. $350.00

WHITNEY, Janet. *Geraldine S Cadbury: 1865-1941.* 1948. London. Harrap. 1st ed. 8vo. 200p. VG/VG. V3. $12.50

WHITNEY, Janet. *Judith.* 1943. NY. Morrow. 1st ed. 8vo. 340p. VG. V3. $9.50

WHITNEY, Leon F. *How To Breed Dogs.* 1937. Orange Judd. 1st ed. 338p. cloth. VG. R2. $35.00

WHITNEY, Leon F. *Natural Method of Dog Training.* 1964. London. Nicholas Vane. 1st ed. ils. 128p. F/VG+. R2. $25.00

WHITNEY, Mary. *Cowleses Across America.* 1986. Ottisville, PA. ltd ed. 8vo. bl brd. F. B11. $25.00

WHITNEY, Phyllis A. *Black Amber.* 1965. Robert Hale. 1st ed. VG/G. P3. $25.00

WHITNEY, Phyllis A. *Feather on the Moon.* 1988. Doubleday. 1st ed. F/F. P3. $18.00

WHITNEY, Phyllis A. *Poinciana.* 1980. Doubleday. 1st ed. G+/dj. P3. $12.00

WHITNEY, Phyllis A. *Sea Jade.* 1964. Appleton Century. 1st ed. VG/VG. P3. $15.00

WHITNEY, William Dwight. *Century Dictionary & Cyclopedia.* 1900. NY. Century. 10 vol. early prt. 4to. rebound brn buckram. F. G1. $275.00

WHITROW, G.J. *Time in Hist: Views of Time From Prehistory to Present Day.* 1989. Oxford. 220p. blk cloth. VG/dj. G1. $22.50

WHITSON. *Luther Burbank: His Methods & Discoveries.* 1914-1915. London. Burbank. 12 vol. tipped-in pl. gilt bl bdg. H4. $250.00

WHITTAKER, Frederick. *Complete Life of General George A Custer.* 1876. NY. 1st ed. ils. 648p. pict cloth. B18. $150.00

WHITTEMORE, Thomas. *Mosaics of St Sophia at Istanbul.* 1933. Oxford. 4to. ils/tables. O2. $35.00

WHITTENMORE, Reed. *Fascination of the Abomination: Poems, Stories & Essays.* 1963. Macmillan. 1st ed. VG/dj. N2. $10.00

WHITTIER, John Greenleaf. *Among the Hills & Other Poems.* 1869. Boston. Fields Osgood. 1st ed. 12mo. 100p. gr cloth. G+. V3. $35.00

WHITTIER, John Greenleaf. *At Sundown.* 1892. Houghton Mifflin. 1st trade ed. gilt cloth. teg. VG. A17. $20.00

WHITTIER, John Greenleaf. *At Sundown.* 1892. Houghton Mifflin. 1st trade ed. 12mo. 70p. G+. V3. $10.50

WHITTIER, John Greenleaf. *Ballads of New England.* 1870. Fields Osgood. 8vo. 92p. G. V3. $12.00

WHITTIER, John Greenleaf. *Miriam & Other Poems.* 1871. Boston. Fields Osgood. gr cloth. G+. N2. $12.50

WHITTINGTON, Harry. *Strangers on Friday.* 1959. Abelard Schuman. 1st ed. VG/G. P3. $60.00

WHITTINGTON, Harry. *Wild Oats.* 1953. Universal. 1st ed. NF/digest-size wrp. scarce. F4. $65.00

WHITTLE, Tyler. *Some Ancient Gentlemen.* 1966. NY. ils/photos. 244p. VG+/dj. B26. $25.00

WHITTON, Blair. *Paper Toys of the World.* 1986. Hobby House. obl 8vo. F/F. B17. $25.00

WHYMPER, Edward. *Travels Amongst the Great Andes of the Equator.* 1892. NY. ils/fld pocket map. 456p. NF. F1. $55.00

WHYTE, James C. *History of the British Turf, From Earliest Period...* 1840. London. 2 vol. 1st ed. 8vo. ils. teg. marbled brd/leather. VG. H3. $125.00

WIBBERLEY, Leonard. *Mouse That Saved the West.* 1981. Morrow. 1st ed. F/F. F4. $15.00

WICHMANN, Louis J. *True Hist of Assassination of Abraham Lincoln...* 1975. Knopf. 1st ed. 498p. NF/dj. M20. $30.00

WICKERSHAM, James. *Old Yukon Tales, Trails, Trials.* 1973. St Paul. photos/index. 514p. F. A17. $30.00

WICKES, George. *Henry Miller & the Critics.* 1963. Carbondale. 1st ed. NF/NF. S9. $30.00

WICKSTEED, Joseph H. *Blake's Innocence & Experience.* 1928. Dent/Dutton. sq 8vo. 301p. VG. F1. $80.00

WICKWARE, Francis Sill. *Dangerous Ground.* nd. Doubleday. VG. P3. $8.00

WIDDENMER, Margaret. *Gallant Lady.* nd. Grosset Dunlap. 306p. F/G. H1. $4.00

WIDDER, William J. *Fiction of L Ron Hubbard.* 1994. Bridge. 1st ed. F. P3. $50.00

WIEAND, Albert Cassel. *New Harmony of the Gospels.* 1984. Eerdmans. 268p. M/dj. B29. $12.00

WIEBE, Rudy. *Blue Mountains of China.* 1970. Erdman. 1st ed. sgn. F/dj. A18. $35.00

WIEBE, Rudy. *Peace Shall Destroy Man.* 1962. McClelland Stewart. 1st Canadian ed. sgn. F/dj. A18. $60.00

WIENER, Philip P. *Dictionary of Hist of Ideas: Studies of Selected Ideas.* 1973 (1968). Scribner. 4 vol. 1st pb ed. VG/case. G1. $100.00

WIENER, Philip P. *Readings in Philosophy of Science...* 1953. Scribner. later prt. 646p. gray cloth. VG. G1. $27.50

WIENER, Philip P. *Roots to Scientific Thought...* 1957. Basic Books. later prt. thick 8vo. blk cloth. VG. G1. $32.00

WIENER, Willard. *Four Boys & a Gun.* 1944. Dial. 1st ed. F/NF. F4. $52.50

WIENERS, John. *Ace of Pentacles.* 1964. Carr Wilson. 1st ed. NF. B2. $35.00

WIENERS, John. *Nerves.* 1970. Grossman. 1st ed. F/F. B2. $25.00

WIENERS, John. *Selected Poems.* 1972. Grossman. 1st ed. F/F. B2. $50.00

WIESE, Kurt. *Karoo the Kangaroo.* 1929. Coward McCann. 1st ed. ils. VG/fair. P2. $30.00

WIGGIN, Kate Douglas. *Birds' Christmas Carol.* ca 1930. Grosset Dunlap. ils Helen Mason Grose. 74p. VG/G. A3. $10.50

WIGGIN, Kate Douglas. *My Garden of Memory: An Autobiography.* (1923). Houghton Mifflin. 11th imp. 465p. G+. H1. $22.50

WIGGIN, Kate Douglas. *New Chronicles of Rebecca.* 1907. Houghton Mifflin. 1st ed. ils FC Yohn. pict cloth. VG. M5. $40.00

WIGGIN, Kate Douglas. *Old Peabody Pew.* 1907. Boston. 1st ed. ils Alice Stephens. 143p. gilt cloth. G. A17. $10.00

WIGGIN, Kate Douglas. *Story of Patsy.* 1917. Houghton Mifflin. ils. VG/VG. A3. $27.50

WIGGIN, Kate Douglas. *Summer in Canon: California Story.* 1889. Houghton Mifflin. 1st ed. ils. pict bdg. VG+. A18. $60.00

WIGGIN, Kate Douglas. *Susanna & Sue.* 1909. Houghton Mifflin. 1st ed. ils Wyeth. pict cloth. VG. A17. $16.50

WIGGIN, Kate Douglas. *Timothy's Quest.* (1894). Grosset Dunlap. photoplay ed. blk stp red cloth. VG. S11. $10.00

WIGGIN, Kate Douglas. *Village Watch-Tower.* 1895. Houghton Mifflin. 1st ed. 12mo. 218p. VG. D6. $65.00

WIGGINS, Florence. *Where the Heart Is.* 1976. Christian Herald. 131p. VG/dj. B29. $3.00

WIGLEY, Mrs. W.H. *Our Home Work: Manual of Domestic Economy.* ca 1870. np. 401p. gilt emb bdg. E5. $45.00

WIJNGAARDS, John. *Handbook to the Gospels.* 1979. Servant Books. 301p. F/dj. B29. $7.50

WILBER, Donald N. *Persepolis.* 1969. Crowell. 1st ed. 120p. VG/dj. M20. $18.00

WILBER, Richard. *Bestiary: Fourth Estate.* 1993. London. 1st ed. ils Alexander Calder. 77p. M. M7. $28.00

WILBERT, Johannes. *Folk Literature of the Yamana Indians.* 1977. Berkeley. 1st ed. 308p. VG/dj. F3. $25.00

WILBERT, Johannes. *Navigators of the Orinoco.* 1980. Los Angeles. 1st ed. 4to. VG/wrp. F3. $15.00

WILBUR, Earl Morse. *Hist of First Unitarian Church of Portland, OR...* 1893. Portland. 1st ed. 95p. VG. scarce. M8. $45.00

WILBUR, Richard. *Beautiful Changes & Other Poems.* 1947. Reynal Hitchcock. 1st ed/author's 1st book. 8vo. beige cloth. NF/clip. C6. $300.00

WILBUR, Richard. *Bestiary.* 1955. Pantheon. 1st ed. 1/800. sgn. ils/sgn Calder. 74p. F/case. C6. $375.00

WILBUR, Susan. *Egypt & the Suez Canal.* 1927. Chicago. Wheeler. 404p. xl. G. W1. $9.00

WILCOX, Collin. *Bernhardt's Edge.* 1988. Tor. 1st ed. NF/NF. P3. $18.00

WILCOX, James. *Modern Baptists.* 1983. Garden City. 1st ed/author's 1st novel. sgn twice/inscr. F/NF. A11. $65.00

WILCOX, R.T. *Mode in Furs.* 1951. NY. 1st ed. VG/VG. B5. $45.00

WILCOX, Richard. *Of Men & Battle.* 1944. NY. ils David Fredenthal. 125p. cloth. VG. A17. $15.00

WILCOX, Willa Wheeler. *Maurine & Other Poems.* 1888. WB Conkey. gilt bdg. S12. $200.00

WILD, Doris. *Holy Icons in the Religious Art of Eastern Church.* 1965. Berne. Hallwag. 12mo. 22 pl. VG. W1. $8.00

WILDE, Irma. *Snow White & the Seven Dwarfs.* 1959. Rand McNally Jr Elf Book 8028. K2. $5.00

WILDE, Oscar. *Lady Windemere's Fan.* 1903. Paris. pirated ed. 1/250. NF. C2. $175.00

WILDE, Oscar. *Poems.* 1892. London. Mathews Lane. 1/220. sgn. F. H4. $4,000.00

WILDE, Oscar. *Salome.* 1938. LEC. 2 vol. 1/1500 sets. ils/sgn Andre Derain. F/case. B24. $200.00

WILDE, Oscar. *Salome. Drame en un Acte.* 1923. Paris. Cres. ils Alastair. new bdg/orig wrp bdg in. F. F1. $325.00

WILDE, Oscar. *Selfish Giant & Other Tales.* 1986. Mitchell. 1st ed. VG. P3. $20.00

WILDE, Oscar. *Teacher of Wisdom.* 1994. Oregon House, CA. Petrarch. 1/200 on Magnani Vergata. ils Roosje Penfold. B33. $55.00

WILDER, Alec. *Lullabies & Night Songs.* 1969 (1965). London. Bodley Head. 1st Eng ed. NF/VG. C8. $100.00

WILDER, Billy Diamond. *Apartment & the Fortune Cookie.* 1971. Praeger. 1st ed. sq 12mo. F/F. A17. $10.00

WILDER, F.L. *Sporting Prints.* 1974. Viking/ The Studio. 1st ed. 4to. VG/G. O3. $65.00

WILDER, Laura Ingalls. *By the Shores of Silver Lake.* April 1947. Harper. ils Helen Sewell. VG+/G+. C8. $50.00

WILDER, Laura Ingalls. *Little House in the Big Woods.* 1932. Harper. ils Helen Sewell. 172p. VG/G. P2. $80.00

WILDER, Laura Ingalls. *West From Home. Letters of Laura Ingalls Wilder...* 1915. Family Bookshelf Ed. 124p. VG/VG. A3. $6.00

WILDER, Thornton. *Alcestiad; or, Life in the Sun.* 1977. Franklin Lib. 1st ed. ils Daniel Maffia. full leather. F. B3. $35.00

WILDER, Thornton. *Bridge at San Luis Rey.* 1929. Boni. 1st ils ed. sgn. 4to. ils/sgn Rockwell Kent. VG. B4. $150.00

WILDER, Thornton. *Our Town.* 1974. Avon, CT. ltd ed. 1/2000. sgn. ils/sgn RJ Lee. F/case. B24. $150.00

WILDES, Harry Emerson. *William Penn: A Biography.* 1975. Macmillan. 2nd ed. 8vo. 469p. VG/dj. V3. $15.00

WILDING, Suzanne. *Book of Ponies.* 1965. St Martin. 1st ed. ils Wesley Dennis. VG/G. P2. $25.00

WILDMON, Donald E. *Home Invaders.* 1985. Victor. 192p. M. B29. $5.50

WILDSMITH, Brian. *Circus.* 1970. Franklin Watts. 1st Am ed. sgn. F/G. P2. $35.00

WILDSMITH, Brian. *Circus.* 1970. Franklin Watts. 1st Am ed. VG+. C8. $17.50

WILDSMITH, Brian. *Mother Goose.* 1965. Franklin Watts. 1st Am ed. 80p. VG/VG. P2. $30.00

WILDSMITH, Brian. *Pelican.* 1982. Random. 1st Am ed. ils. M/M. C8. $25.00

WILENSKI, R.H. *Modern Movement in Art.* 1926. NY. Stokes. ARC/1st ed. ils. gilt red ribbed cloth. F/chip. F1. $75.00

WILEY, Bell. *Life of Johnny Reb, Life of Billy Yank.* 1943. Indianapolis. 2 vol. VG/box. B5. $50.00

WILEY, Bell. *Life of Johnny Reb, Life of Billy Yank.* 1971. 2 vol. F/dj/box. O8. $12.50

WILEY, Richard. *Fool's Gold.* 1988. Knopf. 1st ed/author's 2nd novel. F/F. L3. $30.00

WILEY, Richard. *Indigo.* 1992. Dutton. ARC/1st ed. w/sgn edit letter. F/F. A14. $25.00

WILEY, Richard. *Soldiers in Hiding.* 1986. Boston. 1st ed/author's 1st novel. inscr. F/F. A11. $70.00

WILHELM, Kate. *Clewiston Test.* 1976. FSG. 1st ed. VG/VG. P3. $15.00

WILHELM, Kate. *Dark Door.* 1988. St Martin. 1st ed. 248p. F/F. H1. $15.00

WILHELM, Kate. *Hamlet Trap.* 1987. St Martin. 1st ed. NF/NF. P3. $16.00

WILHELM, Kate. *Sense of Shadow.* 1981. Houghton Mifflin. 1st ed. NF/NF. P3. $20.00

WILHELM, Kate. *Somerset Dreams & Other Fictions.* 1978. Harper Row. 1st ed. F/dj. F4. $20.00

WILHELM, Richard. *Lectures on the I Ching: Constancy & Change.* 1979. Princeton. 1st ed. 182p. F/F. B33. $30.00

WILHELM, Richard. *Soul of China.* 1928. Harcourt Brace. 382p. VG. B33. $20.00

WILK, Christopher. *Marcel Breuer, Furniture & Interiors.* 1981. MOMA. sm 4to. 192p. F/wrp. F1. $30.00

WILKERSON, David. *Little People.* 1966. REvell. 157p. G/torn. B29. $3.25

WILKERSON, David. *Suicide.* 1978. Revell. 123p. VG. B29. $3.50

WILKERSON, Don. *Gutter & the Ghetto.* 1969. Word. 179p. VG/dj. B29. $3.50

WILKERSON & WILKERSON. *Untapped Generation.* 1971. Zondervan. 256p. VG/dj. B29. $3.50

WILKES, T. *General View of the Stage.* 1759. London. 1st ed. scarce. A15. $275.00

WILKIN, Eloise Burns. *Baby's Golden Childhood.* 1929. Donohue. 8vo. 32p. pict brd. NF/VG box. D6. $85.00

WILKIN, Eloise Burns. *Big Circus.* nd. USA. Miller Bros Concession. folio. 24p. VG. D6. $20.00

WILKINS, H.T. *Flying Saucers on Attack.* 1954. NY. 1st ed. VG/G. B5. $20.00

WILKINS, Hubert. *Under North Pole: Wilkins Ellsworth Submarine Expedition.* 1931. Brewer Warren Putnam. deluxe ed. 1/275. sgn. ES. F. H4. $275.00

WILKINS, Simon. *Works of Sir Thomas Browne.* 1836. London. Pickering. 4 vol. ils. orig full tree calf. G7. $350.00

WILKINS-FREEMAN, Mary E. *Collected Ghost Stories.* 1974. Arkham. 1st ed. VG/G. P3. $15.00

WILKINSON, J. Gardner. *Popular Account of Ancient Egyptians. Vol 2.* 1854. London. Murray. abridged ed. sm 8vo. 438p. G. W1. $10.00

WILKINSON, Tate. *Memoirs of His Own Life.* 1790. York. 4 vol. 1st ed. half morocco/ marbled brd. VG+. rare. A15. $550.00

WILLARD, George O. *Hist of the Providence Stage, 1762-1891.* 1891. Providence. 1st ed. 8vo. 298p. cloth. M1. $125.00

WILLARD, James Field. *Parliamentary Taxes on Personal Property.* 1970. NY. rpt of 1934 ed. 357p. NF. D3. $25.00

WILLARD, John Ware. *Simon Willard & His Clocks.* 1968. NY. Dover. 1st ed. ils. 133p. VG. A8. $10.00

WILLARD, John. *CMR Book.* 1970. Superior Pub. 1st ed. ils. gilt leather. F/dj. A18. $75.00

WILLARD, N. *Voyage of the Ludgate Hill.* 1987. Harcourt Brace. 1st ed. ils Provensen. F/F. B17. $12.50

WILLARD, Nancy. *East of the Sun & West of the Moon.* 1989. Harcourt Brace. 1st ed thus. ils Barry Moser. F/F. B17. $15.00

WILLARD, Nancy. *Sister Water.* nd. Knopf. bdg proof of 1st ed. hc. F/F. M21. $25.00

WILLARD, T.A. *Bride of the Rain God.* 1930. Burrows. 1st ed. inscr. G. M2. $25.00

WILLEFORD, Charles. *Dead Calm.* 1963. Viking. 1st ed. F/NF. M15. $50.00

WILLEFORD, Charles. *Everybody's Metamorphosis.* 1988. Dennis McMillan. ltd sgn ed. 1/400. F/F. O4. $125.00

WILLEFORD, Charles. *Guide for the Undehemorrhoided.* 1977. Miami. 1st ed. inscr. F/F. A11. $165.00

WILLEFORD, Charles. *Kiss Your Ass Goodbye.* 1987. Dennis McMillan. ltd sgn ed. 1/400. F/F. O4. $140.00

WILLEFORD, Charles. *Off the Wall.* 1980. Montclair. Pegasus Rex. 1st ed. F/F. M15. $100.00

WILLEFORD, Charles. *Proletarian Laughter.* 1948. Alicat Bookshop. 1st ed/author's 1st poetry book. 1/1000. F/pict wrp. M15. $125.00

WILLEFORD, Charles. *Scorpion Reef.* 1955. Macmillan. 1st ed. F/NF. M15. $85.00

WILLEFORD, Charles. *Sideswipe.* 1987. St Martin. 1st ed. F/F. T2. $25.00

WILLEFORD, Charles. *Sideswipe.* 1987. St Martin. 1st ed. VG/VG. P3. $23.00

WILLEFORD, Charles. *Something About a Soldier.* 1986. Random. 1st ed. F/F. F4. $20.00

WILLEFORD, Charles. *Way We Die Now.* 1988. Random. 1st ed. F/F. L3/O4. $35.00

WILLEFORD, Charles. *Way We Die Now.* 1988. Ultramarine. 1st ed. sgn. 1/99. quarter leather/marbled brd. B4. $350.00

WILLEFORD, Charles. *Way We Die Now.* 1989. Gollancz. 1st ed. F/F. P3. $25.00

WILLEMSE, C. *Behind the Green Lights.* (1931). Garden City. rpt. 364p. D3. $10.00

WILLETT, Hurd C. *Descriptive Meteorology.* 1944. NY. Academic. 8vo. fld maps. 310p. bl cloth. G. K5. $15.00

WILLEY, Gordon. *Essay in Maya Archaeology.* 1987. Albuquerque. 1st ed. 245p. VG/wrp. F3. $15.00

WILLEY, Gordon. *New World Archaeology & Culture Hist.* 1990. Albuquerque. 1st ed. ils. 3436p. VG. F3. $30.00

WILLIAMS, A.C. *Dictionary of Trout Flies.* 1949. London. Blk. 1st ed. pl. VG. B5. $40.00

WILLIAMS, Alan. *Shah-Mak.* 1976. CMG. 1st ed. F/F. P3. $18.00

WILLIAMS, Alonzo. *Investment of Ft Pulaski.* 1887. Providence. 1st ed. 1/250. 59p. NF/wrp. M8. $45.00

WILLIAMS, Ben Ames. *House Divided.* 1947. map ep. 1514p. O8. $9.50

WILLIAMS, Charles H. *Last Tour of Duty at the Seige of Charleston.* 1882. Providence. 1st ed. 1/250. NF/prt wrp. M8. $45.00

WILLIAMS, Charles J.B. *Rational Exposition of Physical Signs of Diseases...* 1834. Phil. 1st ed. 3 pl/tables. 203p. brd. VG. B14. $200.00

WILLIAMS, Charles. *Place of the Lion.* 1931. London. Gollancz. 1st ed. sc. F. A18. $75.00

WILLIAMS, Charles. *Sailcloth Shroud.* 1960. Viking. 2nd ed. VG/VG. P3. $25.00

WILLIAMS, David. *Copper, Gold & Treasure.* 1982. St Martin. 1st ed. VG/rpr. P3. $10.00

WILLIAMS, David. *Murder for Treasure.* 1980. London. Collins. 1st ed. sgn. F/F. S6. $35.00

WILLIAMS, David. *Treasure by Degrees.* 1977. Collins Crime Club. 1st ed. NF/NF. P3. $20.00

WILLIAMS, Dorian. *Master of One: An Autobiography.* 1978. London. Dent. 1st ed. VG/VG. O3. $25.00

WILLIAMS, Douglas E. *Truth, Hope & Power.* 1989. Toronto. 237p. bl cloth. VG/dj. G1. $27.50

WILLIAMS, E.W. *Child of the Sea: Life Among the Mormons.* (1905). np. later prt. 239p. wrp. E5. $45.00

WILLIAMS, Edward H. *Opiate Addiction: Its Handling & Its Treatment.* 1922. NY. 1st ed. 12mo. 194p. VG. D3. $50.00

WILLIAMS, Edward. *Doctor in Court.* 1930. Baltimore. 298p. A13. $45.00

WILLIAMS, Edwin T. *Graecum Pomarium; or, Key to the Greek Verg.* 1847. Phil. 1st ed. 110p. G. H3. $45.00

WILLIAMS, Elsa. *Joy of Stitching.* 1978. np. VG. G2. $12.00

WILLIAMS, Garth. *Rabbits' Wedding.* 1960 (1958). London. Harper. 1st Eng ed. NF/VG. C8. $100.00

WILLIAMS, George Walton. *Catalogue of Lib of Reverend James Warley Miles.* 1955. Charleston, SC. 1st ed. 33p. NF/wrp. M8. $20.00

WILLIAMS, George. *Holy City; or, Hist & Topographical Notices of Jerusalem.* 1845. London. 8vo. ils/maps. 512p. blind-stp cloth. O2. $185.00

WILLIAMS, Gordon. *Hazel Plays Solomon.* 1975. Walker. 1st ed. NF/NF. P3. $13.00

WILLIAMS, Gordon. *Ravens & Crows.* 1966. Los Angeles. Wm Cheney. 25x17mm. 20p. F/ils stiff brn wrp. B24. $225.00

WILLIAMS, Gordon. *Siege of Trencher's Farm.* 1969. Morrow. 1st Am ed. F/F. M15. $40.00

WILLIAMS, H.W. *Travels in Italy, Greece & Ionian Islands....* 1820. Edinburgh. 2 vol. 20 pl. contemporary paneled calf. O2. $550.00

WILLIAMS, Harry Lee. *Hist of Craighead Co, AR.* 1930. Parke Harper. 648p. gr cloth. VG+. M20. $35.00

WILLIAMS, Henry Smith. *Historians' History of the World.* 1905. NY. 25 vol. dk red half leather. G. B30. $150.00

WILLIAMS, J. Paul. *What Americans Believe & How They Worship.* 1952. Harper. 400p. G. B29. $4.00

WILLIAMS, J. Rodman. *Renewal Theology.* 1988 & 1990. Academie Books. 2 vol. VG+/djs. B29. $24.00

WILLIAMS, J.R. *Redrawn by Request.* 1955. Garden City. 1st ed. VG/G. B5. $35.00

WILLIAMS, Jay. *Battle for the Atlantic.* 1959. NY. 1st prt. 178p. VG. A17. $6.00

WILLIAMS, Jay. *Stage Left.* 1974. Scribner. 1st ed. F/F. B2. $30.00

WILLIAMS, John Hoyt. *Great & Shining Road: Epic Story of Transcontinental RR.* 1988. Time. 1st ed. 8vo. rem mk. F/F. B11. $12.00

WILLIAMS, John. *Butcher's Crossing.* 1960. Macmillan. 1st ed. F/dj. A18. $40.00

WILLIAMS, Joseph J. *Voodoos & Obeahs: Phases of W India Witchcraft.* July 1933. Dial. 4th prt. 257p. F/VG. H1. $75.00

WILLIAMS, Kenneth Powers. *Lincoln Finds a General: A Military Study of Civil War.* 1949-1959. Macmillan. 5 vol. mixed prt. pres inscr in vol 1. cloth. VG. M8. $150.00

WILLIAMS, Kit. *Masquerade.* 1980. Schocken. 1st Am ed. F/VG+. M5. $12.00

WILLIAMS, M. *Velveteen Rabbit.* 1983. Holt. 13th prt. ils Michael Hague. F/VG. B17. $9.00

WILLIAMS, Martin. *Where's the Melody?* 1966. Pantheon. 1st ed. F/NF. B2. $45.00

WILLIAMS, Mary Roslin. *Advanced Labrador Breeding.* 1988. London. Witherby. 1st ed. 151p. cloth. M/dj. R2. $45.00

WILLIAMS, Moyra. *Riding Is My Hobby.* 1963. Newton, MA. Branford. 1st Am ed. VG/VG. O3. $25.00

WILLIAMS, Neville. *Chronology of the Modern World 1763-1965.* 1975. Harmondsworth. Penguin. pb. 1019p. VG. P4. $12.50

WILLIAMS, Nigel. *Black Magic.* 1988. Hutchinson. 1st ed. F/F. P3. $12.00

WILLIAMS, Philip Lee. *Final Heat.* 1992. Turtle Bay/Random. 1st ed. F/F. A14. $25.00

WILLIAMS, Ralph C. *US Public Health Service 1798-1950.* nd. np. thick 4to. 890p. NF. G7. $95.00

WILLIAMS, Roger. *Bloudy Tenent of Persecution for Cause of Conscience...* 1848. London. Hanserd Knollys. 439p. leather/gilt spine. H10. $65.00

WILLIAMS, S.E. *Stories of Mathematics.* 1963. London. Evans. 6th imp. 8vo. ils. 79p. red cloth. xl. G. K5. $12.00

WILLIAMS, Samuel H. *Voodoo Roads.* 1949. Vienna. Jugend Volk. 1st ed. Eng text. VG. B2. $50.00

WILLIAMS, Tad. *Dragonbone Chair.* 1988. DAW. 1st ed. F/F. P3. $20.00

WILLIAMS, Tennessee. *Cat on a Hot Tin Roof.* 1957. London. Secker Warburg. 1st UK movie ed. 197p. bl cloth. VG/dj. H5. $75.00

WILLIAMS, Tennessee. *I Rise in Flame, Cried the Pheonix: Play About DH Lawrence.* 1951. New Directions. 1st ed. sgn. 1/300. pub bookplate. F/VG case. B4. $1,500.00

WILLIAMS, Tennessee. *Letters to Donald Windham.* 1976. NY. Sandy Campbell. 1/500. F/wrp/case. S9. $125.00

WILLIAMS, Tennessee. *Moise & World of Reason.* 1975. Simon Schuster. 1st ed/2nd prt. inscr. 8vo. 190p. blk brd. NF/dj. C6. $100.00

WILLIAMS, Tennessee. *Roman Spring of Mrs Stone.* 1950. New Directions. 1st trade ed. 148p. yel stp blk cloth. F/dj. H5. $125.00

WILLIAMS, Tennessee. *Rose Tattoo.* 1954. London. Secker Warburg. 1st Eng ed. 8vo. 143p. red cloth. VG/dj. C6. $50.00

WILLIAMS, Tennessee. *Suddenly Last Summer.* (1958). NY. 1st ed. VG+/VG+. A9. $45.00

WILLIAMS, Tennessee. *Summer & Smoke.* 1948. New Directions. 1st ed. photos. 130p. VG/G. S11. $80.00

WILLIAMS, Thomas. *Whipple's Castle.* 1968. Random. 1st ed. F/F. L3. $45.00

WILLIAMS, Tom. *Post-Traumatic Stress Disorders of the Vietnam Veteran.* 1980. DAV. 8vo. 140p. G/wrp. A8. $5.00

WILLIAMS, Valentine. *Clock Ticks On.* nd. Collier. VG. P3. $15.00

WILLIAMS, W. Ewart. *Applications of Interferometry.* 1950 (1930). London. Methuen. 4th ed. 104p. VG/dj. K5. $14.00

WILLIAMS, Walter Jon. *Angel Station.* 1989. Tor. 1st ed. sgn twice. ES. F/F. T2. $28.00

WILLIAMS, Walter Jon. *Facets.* 1990. Tor. 1st ed. sgn. F/F. T2. $24.00

WILLIAMS, Walter Jon. *Hardwired.* 1986. Tor. 1st ed. sgn. F/F. T2. $28.00

WILLIAMS, Walter Jon. *Wall, Stone, Craft.* 1993. Axolotl. 1st ed. sgn. 1/300. F/F. T2. $50.00

WILLIAMS, William Carlos. *Autobiography...* 1951. Random. 1st ed. 8vo. 402p. bl cloth. VG/rpr. C6. $50.00

WILLIAMS, William Carlos. *Build-Up.* 1952. Random. 1st ed. 335p. NF/clip. C6. $60.00

WILLIAMS, William Carlos. *Collected Later Poems.* 1950. New Directions. sgn. F/piece missing. V1. $50.00

WILLIAMS, William Carlos. *Great Am Novel.* 1923. Paris. 3 Mtns. 1st ed/author's 1st book prose. 1/300 on Rives. VG. H5. $650.00

WILLIAMS, William Carlos. *Journey to Love.* 1955. Random. 1st ed. F/NF clip. L3. $65.00

WILLIAMS, William Carlos. *Knife of the Times & Other Stories.* 1932. NY. Dragon. 1st ed/1st collection short stories. 1/500. F/2 djs. C6. $900.00

WILLIAMS, William Carlos. *Kora in Hell: Improvisations.* 1920. Boston. 4 Seas. 1st ed/author's 4th book. 1/1000. 86p. VG. C6. $250.00

WILLIAMS, William Carlos. *Life Along the Passaic River.* 1938. New Directions. ltd ed. sgn. 1/1006. F. Q1. $200.00

WILLIAMS, William Carlos. *Pink Church.* 1949. Golden Goose. 1st ed. sgn. 1/400. F/bl wrp. B24. $425.00

WILLIAMS, William Carlos. *Voyage to Pagany.* 1928. Macaulay. 1st ed/author's 1st novel. 338p. brn cloth. VG/dj. C6. $300.00

WILLIAMS & WILLIAMS. *Redeemed Captive Returning to Zion: A Faithful History...* 1853. Northampton. 1st ed thus. VG. H7. $85.00

WILLIAMSON, Chet. *Reign.* 1990. Dark Harvest. ltd 1st ed. 1/425. F/dj/box. M2. $40.00

WILLIAMSON, Harold E. *American Petroleum Industry: Age of Energy 1899-1959.* 1963. Northwestern. 928p. F/G. H1. $16.00

WILLIAMSON, Henry. *Genius of Friendship: TE Lawrence.* 1941. London. Faber. 1st ed. 1/2000. 78p. VG. M7. $85.00

WILLIAMSON, Henry. *Pen & Plough.* 1993. Henry Williamson Soc. 1st ed. 1/50. quarter morocco. M. M7. $65.00

WILLIAMSON, J.N. *Masques IV.* 1991. MacLay. 1st ed. VG. P3. $20.00

WILLIAMSON, J.N. *Masques.* 1984. MacLay. 1st ed. sgn. F/F. P3. $25.00

WILLIAMSON, J.N. *New Devil's Dictionary: Creepy Cliches & Sinister Synonyms.* 1985. Buffalo. Ganley. 1st ed. F/F. T2. $15.00

WILLIAMSON, Jack. *Brother to Demons, Brother to Gods.* 1979. Bobbs Merrill. 1st ed. F/F. P3. $18.00

WILLIAMSON, Jack. *Firechild.* 1986. Bluejay. 1st ed. F/F. T2. $15.00

WILLIAMSON, Jack. *HG Wells: Critic of Progress.* 1973. Mirage. 1st ed. F/dj. M2. $25.00

WILLIAMSON, Jack. *Humanoids.* 1949. Simon Schuster. 1st ed. VG/VG. P3. $40.00

WILLIAMSON, Jack. *Legion of Space.* 1947. Fantasy. 1st ed. sgn. VG/dj. M2. $65.00

WILLIAMSON, Jack. *Legion of Time.* 1952. Fantasy. 1st ed. F/NF. A4. $35.00

WILLIAMSON, W.N. *Cat Spring Story.* 1956. Cat Spring. 166p. cloth. M. A10. $20.00

WILLIAMSON & WILLIAMSON. *Car of Destiny.* 1907. NY. 1st ed. ils Armand Both. emb cloth. VG. A17. $12.50

WILLINGHAM, Calder. *End As a Man.* 1947. NY. 1st ed/author's 1st novel. inscr. VG+/VG+. A11. $85.00

WILLIS, Bailey. *Yanqui in Patagonia.* 1947. Stanford. 1st ed. 152p. map ep. VG. F3. $20.00

WILLIS, Beth Goe. *Peter Rabbit Story Book.* 1935. Platt Munk. Beatrix Potter imitation. orange brd. VG. M5. $48.00

WILLIS, Fritz. *Muffin.* 1945. Cherokee Pr. 4to. ils. 18p. brd. G. A3. $7.00

WILLIS, George. *Bottle Fighters.* 1963. Random. 8vo. 310p. VG/G. A8. $18.00

WILLIS, Hugh E. *Intro to Anglo-American Law.* 1926. IN U. 234p. VG/stiff wrp. D3. $25.00

WILLIS, James F. *Bibliophily or Booklove.* 1921. Houghton Mifflin. 1st ed. 83p. brd/cloth spine. G+. S11. $15.00

WILLIS, N.P. *American Scenery.* 1840. London. 2 vol. 1st ed. half purple morocco. NF. C6. $600.00

WILLIS, N.P. *Pencillings by the Way.* 1842. London. 8vo. ils/pl. rebacked calf/leather label. O2. $85.00

WILLIS, R. *William Harvey: A Hist of Discovery of Circulation of Blood.* 1878. London. Kegan Paul. 1st ed. VG. scarce. H7. $65.00

WILLIS, Ted. *Man-Eater.* 1977. Morrow. 1st ed. VG/dj. P3. $15.00

WILLIS, William. *Journals of Rev Thomas Smith & Rev Samuel Deane...* 1849. Portland. Bailey. 483p. H10. $85.00

WILLISON, Charles A. *Reminiscences of Boy's Service With the 76th Ohio...* 1995. Huntington, WV. rpt of 1908 ed. M/dj. B18. $22.95

WILLISON, G.O. *Bearded Collie.* 1971. London. Foyle. 1st ed. 66p. F. scarce. R2. $35.00

WILLMINGTON, Harold L. *Willmington's Complete Guide to Bible Knowledge.* 1991. Tyndale. 502p. M/dj. B29. $13.00

WILLOCK, Franklin J. *Dalmatian.* 1927. NY. Derrydale. 1st ed. 1/200. ils. 44p. F. rare. R2. $800.00

WILLOUGHBY, V.E. *Cream of Pointerdom 1900-1945.* 1946. OK U. 1st ed. ils. 382p. scarce. R2. $250.00

WILLS, Garry. *Kennedy Imprisonment: Meditation on Power.* 1982. Little Brn. 1st ed. ils. 310p. F/dj. M10. $5.00

WILMERDING, John. *History of American Marine Painting.* 1968. Salem. Peabody Mus. 18 mc pl/168 halftones. 279p. dj. T7. $100.00

WILMINGTON, N.C. *Let There Be Light: God's Story Through Stained Glass...* 1990. Tabor City, NC. Atlantic Pub. 1st ed. 135p. F/NF. M8. $45.00

WILMOT, Robert Patrick. *Death Rides a Painted Horse.* 1954. Lippincott. 1st ed. VG/VG. P3. $30.00

WILSON, Charles. *Ambassadors in White: Story of American Tropical Medicine.* 1942. NY. 1st ed. 372p. A13. $40.00

WILSON, Colin. *Dark Dimensions.* 1977. Everest. 1st ed. VG/VG. P3. $15.00

WILSON, Colin. *Outsider.* Aug 1956. Gollancz. 9th imp. 288p. VG+/VG. M7. $35.00

WILSON, Colin. *Outsider.* 1956. Gollancz. 1st ed. VG. P3. $75.00

WILSON, Colin. *Outsider.* 1956. Gollancz. 3rd prt. 288p. cloth. VG. G1. $22.50

WILSON, Colin. *Philosopher's Tone.* 1971. Crown. 1st ed. VG/VG. P3. $50.00

WILSON, Colin. *Religion & Rebel.* 1967. London. Gollancz. 1st ed. 236p. VG+. M7. $45.00

WILSON, Colin. *Ritual in the Dark.* 1960. Gollancz. 2nd ed. VG/G. P3. $35.00

WILSON, Colin. *Ritual in the Dark.* 1960. Houghton Mifflin. 1st Am ed. F/NF. B2. $50.00

WILSON, Colin. *Space Vampires.* 1976. Random. 1st ed. F/F. T2. $50.00

WILSON, Craig. *Index to Samuel A Lane's 50 Years & Over in Akron...* 1987. Akron. 192p. M. B18. $16.00

WILSON, Daniel. *Memorials of Edinburgh in Olden Time.* 1848. London. 2 vol in 1. 1st ed. 4to. contemporary blk morocco. VG. C6. $75.00

WILSON, David M. *Vikings & Their Origins.* 1980. A & W Visual Lib. ils. 96p. F. M10. $8.50

WILSON, Dixie. *Pinky Pup/The Empty Elephant.* (1922 & 1928). Volland. revised ed. sm 4to. pict brd/blk cloth spine. VG. D6. $135.00

WILSON, Dorothy Clarke. *Bright Eyes: Story of Suzette La Lesche, Omaha Indian.* 1974. McGraw Hill. 1st ed. VG/dj. N2. $10.00

WILSON, Edmund. *American Earthquake.* 1958. NY. 1st ed. F/F. A17. $25.00

WILSON, Edmund. *Letters on Literature & Politics.* 1977. NY. 1st ed. photos/index. F/F. A17. $17.50

WILSON, Edmund. *Night Thoughts.* 1961. FSC. 1st ed. NF/dj. E3. $25.00

WILSON, Edmund. *Note-Books of Night.* 1945. Secker Warburg. 2nd Eng ed. inscr. blk cloth. VG/dj. C6. $100.00

WILSON, Edmund. *Upstate.* 1971. NY. 1st ed. F/F. A17. $20.00

WILSON, Edward L. *In Scripture Lands. New Views in Sacred Places.* 1895. NY. 8vo. ils. 386p. cloth. O2. $45.00

WILSON, Edward L. *Photographic Mosaics...* 1887. NY. 192p. VG/wrp. B14. $35.00

WILSON, Edward. *Birds of the Antarctic.* 1967. London. ils. VG/VG. M17. $65.00

WILSON, Edward. *Exciting Days of Arizona.* 1966. Santa Fe. Stagecoach. 1/750. 62p. VG/VG. A17. $20.00

WILSON, Erica. *Crewel Embroidery.* 1962. np. cloth. VG. G2. $15.00

WILSON, Erica. *More Needleplay.* 1979. np. cloth. VG. G2. $12.50

WILSON, F. Paul. *Black Wind.* 1988. Tor. 1st ed. F/F. P3. $30.00

WILSON, F. Paul. *Black Wind.* 1988. Tor. 1st ed. sgn. F/dj. F4. $35.00

WILSON, F. Paul. *Keep.* 1981. Morrow. 1st ed. F/F. T2. $40.00

WILSON, F. Paul. *Keep.* 1981. Morrow. 1st ed/author's 1st horror novel. sgn. F/dj. F4. $50.00

WILSON, F. Paul. *Reborn.* 1990. Dark Harvest. ltd ed. 1/500. sgn. M/box. M2. $40.00

WILSON, F. Paul. *Sibs.* 1991. Dark Harvest. 1st ed. sgn. 1/400. F/F/case. T2. $45.00

WILSON, F. Paul. *Touch.* 1986. Putnam. 1st ed. F/F. T2. $55.00

WILSON, Gahan. *Everybody's Favorite Duck.* 1988. Mysterious. 1st ed. F/dj. M2. $18.00

WILSON, Gahn. *Everybody's Favorite Duck.* 1988. Mysterious. 1st ed. VG/VG. P3. $16.00

WILSON, H.W. *With the Flag to Pretoria: A Hist of Boer War of 1899-1900.* 1900. London. 2 vol in 1. 1st ed. lg 4to. ils/fld map. VG. C6. $200.00

WILSON, Helen Van Pelt. *Geraniums Pelargontiums for Windows & Gardens.* 1946. NY. 1st prt. ils NT Davis. 248p. F/NF. B26. $14.00

WILSON, J.G. *Thackeray in the US.* 1904. London. 2 vol. 1st ed. ils. F. A9. $50.00

WILSON, James C. *Treatise on Continued Fevers...* 1881. NY. Wood. Wood Lib ed. 365p. F. G7. $65.00

WILSON, James Harrison. *Under the Old Flag: Recollections of Military Operations...* 1912. NY. Appleton. 2 vol. 1st ed. orig cloth. VG+. M8. $275.00

WILSON, James. *Missionary Voyage to the Southern Pacific Ocean...* 1799. London. Chapman. 1st ed. 4to. 420p. subscriber list. later bdg. NF. F1. $925.00

WILSON, Jeremy. *TE Lawrence: Lawrence of Arabia.* 1988. London. Nat Gallery Pub. 248p. M. M7. $55.00

WILSON, John Cook. *Statement & Inference With Other Philosophical Papers.* 1926. Clarendon. 2 vol. F. G1. $100.00

WILSON, John Fleming. *Master Key.* nd. Grosset Dunlap. photoplay ed. VG. P3. $20.00

WILSON, John Fleming. *Master Key.* nd (1915). Grosset Dunlap. photoplay ed. 21 photos. 312p. G. H1. $7.50

WILSON, John. *Cruise of the Gipsy.* 1991. Fairfield, WA. Ye Galleon. ils/5 maps. 404p. T7. $45.00

WILSON, L.A. *Darkling Plain.* 1993. Vantage. 1st ed. F/dj. M2. $16.00

WILSON, Laura. *Watt Matthews of Lambshead.* 1989. TX State Hist Assn. 1st ed. 139p. F/F. B19. $50.00

WILSON, Ralph Pinder. *Islamic Art.* 1957. Macmillan. 4to. 100 pl. gilt gr cloth. F/dj. F1. $45.00

WILSON, Richard. *Girls From Planet 5.* 1955. Ballantine. 1st ed. VG/G. P3. $60.00

WILSON, Robert C. *Gypsies.* 1989. Doubleday. 1st ed. F/F. P3. $17.00

WILSON, Robert C. *Icefire.* 1984. Putnam. 1st ed. F/dj. F4. $20.00

WILSON, Robert E. *Aideen MacLennon: Story of a Rebel.* 1952. Fellowship Pub. 8vo. 253p. NF. V3. $10.00

WILSON, Robert Forrest. *Living Pageant of the Nile.* 1924. Bobbs Merrill. 2nd ed. 240p. VG. W1. $9.00

WILSON, Robert. *Crooked Tree.* 1980. Putnam. 1st ed. 350p. VG/dj. M20. $15.00

WILSON, Robert. *Modern Book Collecting.* 1980. np. ils. 286p. F/NF. A4. $45.00

WILSON, Selden L. *Recollections & Experiences During the Civil War 1861-1865.* 1913. WA. 1st ed. 168p. VG+/prt wrp. M8. $450.00

WILSTACH, Paul. *Islands of the Mediterranean: A Holiday.* 1926. Bobbs Merrill. 1st ed. 8vo. 31 pl/map ep. VG. W1. $25.00

WILSTACH, Paul. *Tidewater Maryland.* 1938. Blue Ribbon. 3rd prt. 383p. VG. H1. $12.00

WILTON, George. *Fingerprints: Hist, Law & Romance.* 1938. London. 1st ed. fwd Robert Heindl. 317p. NF. D3. $75.00

WILTSE, David. *Close to the Bone.* 1992. Putnam. 1st ed. F/F. P3. $22.00

WILTSEE, Ernest A. *Truth About Fremont: An Inquiry.* 1936. San Francisco. Henry Nash. half cloth. F/F. P4. $95.00

WILTZ, Chris. *Diamond Before You Die.* 1987. Mysterious. 1st ed. VG/VG. P3. $16.00

WIMBER, John. *Power Evangelism.* 1986. Harper. 201p. M/dj. B29. $8.50

WIMHURST, C.G.E. *Complete Book of Toy Dogs.* 1969. Putnam. 1st Am ed. 254p. F/VG. R2. $30.00

WINCH, Robert F. *Identification & Its Familial Determinants.* 1962. Bobbs Merrill. 151p. G. K4. $12.50

WINCHESTER, Clarence. *Shipping Wonders of the World.* 1936-1937. London. Amalgamated. 2 vol. 28 mc pl/40 ship plans/2000+ photos. T7. $120.00

WINCKLER, Paul A. *Reader in the Hist of Books & Printing.* 1978. Englewood. ils. 406p. NF. M10. $8.50

WINDELBAND, Wilhelm. *Hist of Philosophy With Special Reference...* 1901. Macmillan. 2nd Eng-language ed/later prt. 726p. G1. $30.00

WINDHAM, Donald. *Footnote to a Friendship.* 1983. Verona. 1st ed. sgn. 1/400. F/wrp. A11. $75.00

WINFREY, Guy. *Bunny Bearskin.* 1926. Milton Bradley. ils Louise Tessin. VG. P2. $75.00

WINGE, Joan D. *Summer Queen.* Nov 1991. Warner. 1st ed. NF/NF. M21. $12.50

WINGERT, P. *Sculpture of Negro Africa.* 1950. NY. 1st ed. 118 pl. 96p. VG. B5. $35.00

WINGET. *Anecdotes of Buffalo Bill That Never Appeared in Print.* 1927. Chicago. photos. 280p. VG. A4. $45.00

WINKS, Robin. *Frederick Billings: A Life.* 1991. NY. Oxford. 1st ed. 398p. F/F. A17. $15.00

WINKS, Robin. *Historian As Detective.* 1969. Harper. 1st ed. 543p. VG/VG. A10. $12.00

WINN, Patrick. *Colour of Murder.* 1965. Robert Hale. 1st ed. VG/G. P3. $15.00

WINOGRAND, Garry. *Stock Photographs: Ft Worth Fat Stock Show & Rodeo.* 1980. Austin, TX. 1st ed. F/NF. S9. $40.00

WINSHIP, George Parker. *Cabot Bibliography With Introductory Essay...* (1900). np. rpt. 232p. F. A4. $40.00

WINSHIP, George Parker. *John Carter Brown Lib: A History.* 1914. Providence. Merrymount. pres. 101p. NF. A4. $95.00

WINSLOW, Forbes. *On Obscure Diseases of the Brain & Disorders of the Mind.* 1860. Blanchard Lea. 1st Am ed. 576p. brd. G7. $250.00

WINSLOW, Pauline Glen. *Brandenburg Hotel.* 1976. Detective BC. VG. P3. $8.00

WINSOR, Frederick. *Space Child's Mother Goose.* 1958. Simon Schuster. 1st ed. unp. cloth. VG. A3/P2. $35.00

WINSOR, Justin. *Memorial History of Boston. Including Suffolk County, MA...* (1880). Boston. 4 vol. 1st ed. 4to. ils. half tan leather. F. H3. $400.00

WINSPEAR, Alban Dewes. *Genesis of Plato's Thought.* 1940. Dryden. 348p. orange cloth brd. G. G1. $30.00

WINSTON, Joan. *Making of the Trek Conventions.* 1977. Doubleday. 1st ed. P3. $30.00

WINSTON, John C. *Story Book of Corn.* ca 1936. np. ils/sgn Maud & Miska Petersham. VG. B10. $25.00

WINSTON, John C. *Story Book of Oil.* ca 1936. np. ils/sgn Maud & Miska Petersham. unp. VG. B10. $25.00

WINSTONE, H.V.F. *Woolley of Ur: Life of Sir Leonard Woolley.* 1990. London. Secker Warburg. 1st ed. inscr. 314p. F/F. M7. $65.00

WINTER, Amelia. *School Belles.* 1925. Gibson. photos. VG. M5. $22.00

WINTER, Donald E. *Soul of the Wobblies.* 1985. Westport. Greenwood. 1st ed. F/sans. B2. $30.00

WINTER, Douglas E. *Prime Evil.* 1988. Donald Grant. 1st ed. 15 contributors sgn. 1/1000. M/box. M2. $350.00

WINTER, Douglas E. *Prime Evil.* 1988. NAL. 1st ed. NF/NF. P3. $19.00

WINTER, Douglas E. *Prime Evil.* 1988. NAL. 1st ed. sgn. F/dj. M2. $25.00

WINTER, Douglas E. *Stephen King: Art of Darkness.* 1984. NAL. 1st ed. photos. 252p. F/VG. S11. $25.00

WINTER, Milo. *Aesop for Children.* 1960. Rand McNally. VG/VG. A3. $7.50

WINTER, Milo. *Ils Bible Story Book.* 1923. Rand McNally. folio. VG. B17. $12.50

WINTER, Nevin. *Mexico & Her People of Today.* 1910. Boston. Page. 3rd prt. 405p. VG. F3. $25.00

WINTERBOTHAM, F.W. *Nazi Connection.* 1978. Harper Row. 1st ed. VG/VG. P3. $15.00

WINTERBOTHAM, F.W. *Ultra Secret: How the British Broke the German Code...* 1974. Harper Row. VG/dj. N2. $6.50

WINTERBOTHAM, Russ. *Joyce of the Secret Squadron.* nd. Whitman. VG/VG. P3. $20.00

WINTERBOTHAM, Russ. *Lord of Nardos.* 1966. Avalon. 1st ed. F/F. M2. $15.00

WINTERNITZ, Milton Charles. *Collected Studies on Pathology of War Gas Poisoning.* 1920. New Haven. 4to. 41 pl. NF/dj. G7. $125.00

WINTERS, Yvor. *Diadems & Fagots. Two Sonnets & Two Fragments by...* 1921. Santa Fe. private prt. 1st ed/trans 1st book. 1/about 50. inscr. F/sewn wrp. B24. $950.00

WINTERS, Yvor. *Giant Weapon.* 1943. New Directions. 1st ed. sgn. NF/NF. V1. $50.00

WINTERS, Yvor. *Magpie's Shadow.* 1922. Chicago. Musterbookhouse. 1st ed/author's 2nd book. inscr. F/prt wrp. B24. $500.00

WINTERSON, Jeanette. *Passion.* 1988. Atlantic Monthly. 1st ed. F/F. B3. $30.00

WINTERSON, Jeanette. *Sexing the Cherry.* 1989. London. Bloomsbury. 1st ed. F/F. S9. $100.00

WINTERSON, Jeanette. *Sexing the Cherry.* 1989. NY. Atlantic. 1st ed. F/F. S9. $40.00

WINTHROP, James. *Attempt to Trans Prophetic Part of Apocalypse of St John...* 1794. Boston. self pub. 1st ed. 79p. ES. uncut. H10. $95.00

WINTHROP, Theodore. *Canoe & the Saddle of Klalam & Klickatat...* 1913. Tacoma. JH Williams. 8vo. 16 pl. 332p. burgundy cloth. xl. VG. P4. $125.00

WINTHROP, Theodore. *Canoe & the Saddle.* 1862. NY. 1st ed. 375p. O8. $55.00

WINTON, Tim. *Cloudstreet.* 1992. Graywolf. 1st Am ed. F/F. A14. $25.00

WINWAR, Frances. *Haunted Place.* 1959. Harper. 1st ed. F/NF. M2. $35.00

WINWARD, Walter. *Fives Wild.* 1976. Atheneum. 1st ed. VG/VG. P3. $15.00

WIPRUD, Theodore. *Business Side of Medical Practice.* 1938. Phil. 1st ed. 177p. A13. $40.00

WIRT, Mildred A. *Vanishing Houseboat.* 1939. Cupples Leon. VG/VG. P3. $20.00

WIRTH, E. *German Geographical Research Overseas.* 1988. Bonn. Deutsche. sm 4to. 172p. VG/stiff wrp. W1. $8.00

WISDOM, Charles. *Chorti Indians of Guatemala.* 1940. Chicago U. 8vo. photos/map. 490p. bl cloth. VG. P4. $50.00

WISDOM, John Oulton. *Foundations of Inference in Natural Science.* 1952. London. Methuen. 242p. red cloth. VG/chip. G1. $42.00

WISE, Arthur. *Who Killed Enoch Powell?* 1971. Harper Row. 1st ed. VG/VG. P3. $20.00

WISE, D. *Young Man's Counselor, Duties & Dangers.* 1863. np. 258p. gilt bdg. VG. E5. $35.00

WISE, George. *Hist of 17th Virginia Infantry.* 1870. Baltimore. Kelly Piet. 1st ed. 312p. cloth. VG. scarce. M8. $450.00

WISE, John S. *End of an Era.* 1902. index. 474p. O8. $14.50

WISE, Thomas J. *Ashley Library: A Catalogue.* 1922-1930. London. private prt. 10 vol. 1/200 sets. lg 8vo. inscr pres in vol 2. H4. $2,100.00

WISEMAN, B. *Morris & Boris at the Circus.* 1988. Harper. 1st ed. M. C8. $12.50

WISEMAN, Thomas. *Day Before Sunrise.* 1976. HRW. 1st ed. F/F. P3. $15.00

WISER, William. *Disappearances.* 1980. NY. 1st ed. inscr. F/F. A11. $55.00

WISER, William. *K.* 1971. Garden City. 1st ed/author's 1st novel. inscr. F/NF. A11. $90.00

WISLIZENUS, A. *Memoir of a Tour to Northern Mexico.* 1969 (1848). Glorieta, NM. rpt. 141p. VG. B26. $36.00

WISLOFF, Fredrik. *I Believe in the Holy Spirit.* 1949. Augsburg. 272p. G. B29. $3.50

WISTAR, Caspar. *System of Anatomy...* 1817. Phil. Dobson. 2 vol. 2nd Am ed. 13 engraved pl. calf. G7. $125.00

WISTER, Fanny Kemble. *Owen Wister Out West.* 1958. Chicago U. 269p. xl. G. S11. $10.00

WISTER, Owen. *Journey in Search of Christmas.* 1904. Harper. 1st ed. ils Remington. teg. F. A18. $100.00

WISTER, Owen. *Lady Baltimore.* 1906. Macmillan. 1st ed. 406p. G. H1. $16.00

WISTER, Sarah. *Journal & Occasional Writings.* 1987. Rutherford, NJ. Fairleigh Dickinson. 8vo. 149p. M/M. V3. $15.00

WITHERING, William. *Account of Scarlet Fever & Sore Throat...* 1793. Birmingham. 2nd ed. 127p. modern leather/brd. B14. $600.00

WITKIN, H.A. *Psychological Differentiation.* 1962. Wiley. 389p. G. K4. $15.00

WITKIN, Joel Peter. *Forty Photographs.* 1985. San Francisco. Mus Modern Art. exhibition catalog. VG+/wrp. S9. $35.00

WITTGENSTEIN, Ludwig. *Notebooks 1914-1916.* 1961. Oxford. Blackwell. Eng/German text. navy cloth. G1. $75.00

WITTGENSTEIN, Ludwig. *On Certainty/Uber Gewissheit.* 1969. Oxford. Blackwell. German/Eng text. blk cloth. NF/dj. G1. $50.00

WITTGENSTEIN, Ludwig. *Preliminary Studies for Philosophical Investigations.* 1960 (1958). Oxford. Blackwell. 2nd prt. sm 8vo. NF/dj. G1. $45.00

WITTGENSTEIN, Ludwig. *Tractatus Logico-Philosophicus.* 1933 (1922). London/NY. Kegan Paul/Harcourt Brace. 2nd corrected prt. scarce. G1. $350.00

WITTGENSTEIN, Ludwig. *Zettel.* 1967. Oxford. Blackwell. German/Eng text. 248p. blk cloth. NF/dj. G1. $45.00

WITTLICH, Peter. *Art Nouveau Drawings.* 1974. London. Octopus. ils. gilt bl cloth. VG/VG. F1. $35.00

WITTMAN, George. *Matter of Intelligence.* 1975. Macmillan. 1st ed. F/F. P3. $15.00

WITTMAN, William. *Travels in Turkey, Asia-Minor, Syria & Across the Desert...* 1803. London. 1st ed. 4to. 595p. recent full morocco. xl. O2. $1,500.00

WITTMER, M. *Floreana Adventure.* 1961. NY. 1st ed. VG/VG. B5. $25.00

WITWER, H.C. *Fighting Back.* nd. Grosset Dunlap. photoplay ed. VG. P3. $18.00

WODEHOUSE, P.G. *Bachelors Anonymous.* 1974. Simon Schuster. 1st Am ed. 8vo. 186p. silvered bl cloth. F/dj. H5. $60.00

WODEHOUSE, P.G. *Big Money.* 1931. McClelland Stewart. 1st Canadian ed. VG. P3. $60.00

WODEHOUSE, P.G. *Bring on the Girls.* 1953. Simon Schuster. 1st ed. G+. P3. $40.00

WODEHOUSE, P.G. *Catnappers.* 1974. Simon Schuster. 2nd ed. VG/dj. M21. $12.50

WODEHOUSE, P.G. *Century of Humor.* 1934. Hutchinson. VG+. P3. $50.00

WODEHOUSE, P.G. *Eggs, Beans & Crumpets.* 1940. Longman Gr. 1st ed. VG/G. P3. $60.00

WODEHOUSE, P.G. *Full Moon.* 1947. Doubleday. 1st ed. VG. P3. $40.00

WODEHOUSE, P.G. *Hot Water.* 1932. McClelland Stuart. 1st Canadian ed. VG. P3. $50.00

WODEHOUSE, P.G. *Leave It to Psmith.* 1924. Doran. 1st ed. VG. P3. $60.00

WODEHOUSE, P.G. *Luck of the Bodkins.* 1935. McClelland Stewart. 1st Canadian ed. VG/VG. P3. $75.00

WODEHOUSE, P.G. *Luck of the Bodkins.* 1936. NY. 1st ed. F/VG. A9. $125.00

WODEHOUSE, P.G. *Mating Season.* 1949. Didier. 2nd ed. rebacked. G. M21. $10.00

WODEHOUSE, P.G. *Money for Nothing.* 1928. Doubleday Doran. 1st ed. VG. P3. $60.00

WODEHOUSE, P.G. *Much Obliged, Jeeves.* 1971. Barrie Jenkins. 1st ed. VG/VG. P3. $20.00

WODEHOUSE, P.G. *Mulliner Omnibus.* 1935. Herbert Jenkins. 1st ed. G+. P3. $35.00

WODEHOUSE, P.G. *Quick Service.* 1941. Longman Gr. VG/G. P3. $50.00

WODEHOUSE, P.G. *Sam the Sudden.* 1925. Methuen. 1st ed. VG. P3. $75.00

WODEHOUSE, P.G. *Uncle Fred in the Springtime.* 1939. Doubleday Doran. 1st ed. xl. VG. M21. $15.00

WODEHOUSE, P.G. *Uncle Fred in the Springtime.* 1939. Herbert Jenkins. 1st ed. VG. P3. $60.00

WODEHOUSE, P.G. *White Feather.* 1972. Souvenir. F/F. P3. $13.00

WODEHOUSE, P.G. *World of Mr Mulliner.* 1972. Barrie Jenkins. 1st ed. VG/VG. P3. $25.00

WOELFEL, Barry. *Through a Glass, Darkly.* 1921. Robert Scott. 1st ed. NF/NF. P3. $20.00

WOENS, Rochelle. *Joe 82 Creation Poems.* 1974. Blk Sparrow. 1st ed. 1/200. sgn. cloth. F/F. B2. $25.00

WOENS, Rochelle. *Not Be Essence That Cannot Be.* 1961. Trobar. 1st ed. F/wrp. B2. $50.00

WOGLOM, W.H. *Discoveries for Medicine.* 1949. London. 229p. brd. G7. $25.00

WOITITZ, Janet G. *Adult Children of Alcoholics.* 1983. Health Communications. BC. 118p. VG/VG. A8. $5.00

WOIWODE, Larry. *Born Brothers.* 1988. FSG. 1st ed. F/F. B3. $25.00

WOLD, Allen. *Star God.* 1980. St Martin. 1st ed. F/dj. F4. $15.00

WOLD, Allen. *V: Persuit of Diana.* 1984. Gregg. 1st hc ed. F/F. T2. $13.00

WOLDERING, Imgaard. *Art of Egypt: Time of the Pharaohs.* 1963. Greystone. 1st Eng ed. 256p. VG. W1. $10.00

WOLF, Blue. *Dwifa's Curse: Tale of the Stone Age.* 1921. Robert Scott. NF. P3. $60.00

WOLF, Edmund Jacob. *Lutherans in Am.* 1890. NY. 1st ed. 544p. cloth. VG. M8. $45.00

WOLF, Eric. *Sons of the Shaking Earth.* 1959. Chicago. 1st ed. 303p. VG. F3. $20.00

WOLF, Gary. *Resurrectionist.* 1979. Doubleday. 1st ed. F/NF. N3. $15.00

WOLF, Gary. *Who P-p-p-plugged Roger Rabbit?* 1991. Villard. 1st ed. F/F. O4. $20.00

WOLF, George D. *William Warren Scranton: PA Statesman.* 1981. PA State U. 220p. M/M. H1. $8.50

WOLF, John B. *Barbary Coast: Algeria Under the Turks...* 1979. Norton. 1st ed. 8vo. 364p. cloth. VG/dj. W1. $20.00

WOLF, Josef. *Dawn of Man.* 1978. Abrams. 219p. F/dj. K4. $15.00

WOLF, Ralph F. *India Rubber Man: Story of Charles Goodyear.* 1939. Caxton. 291p. VG. H1. $15.00

WOLF & WOLF. *World, Flesh & the Holy Ghosts.* 1933. Caxton. 1st ed. sgns. VG. B18. $22.50

WOLF. *William Blake, 1757-1827: Descriptive Catalog...* 1939. Phil Mus of Art. ils. 194p. VG/wrp. A4. $85.00

WOLFE, Aaron; see Koontz, Dean R.

WOLFE, Don. *Freshman & His World.* 1954. Stackpole. 585p. G. K4. $15.00

WOLFE, Don. *Purple Testament: Life Stories of Disabled Veterans.* 1946. Stackpole. 1st ed. 361p. VG/chip. A17. $8.00

WOLFE, Gene. *Castleview.* 1990. Tor. 1st ed. F/F. N3. $45.00

WOLFE, Gene. *Citadel of the Autarch.* 1983. Timescape. 1st ed. w/sgn label. F/F. P3. $60.00

WOLFE, Gene. *Claw of the Conciliator.* 1981. Timescape. 1st ed. F/F. P3. $50.00

WOLFE, Gene. *Endangered Species.* 1989. Tor. 1st ed. F/NF. N3. $10.00

WOLFE, Gene. *Fifth Head of Cerberus.* 1972. Scribner. 1st ed. F/NF. N3. $30.00

WOLFE, Gene. *Pandora by Holly Hollander.* 1990. Tor. 1st ed. F/F. F4. $18.00

WOLFE, Gene. *Peace.* 1975. Harper Row. 1st ed. F/F. P3. $35.00

WOLFE, Gene. *Stories From the Old Hotel.* 1992. Tor. 1st Am ed. F/F. F4. $18.00

WOLFE, Gene. *There Are Doors.* 1988. Tor. 1st ed. F/F. N3. $20.00

WOLFE, Gene. *Turnips to T-Bone.* 1977. Sultana. 1st ed. inscr. 297p. F/F. A8. $40.00

WOLFE, Gene. *Urth of the New Sun.* 1987. Gollancz. 1st ed. F/F. P3. $30.00

WOLFE, Louis. *Adventures on Horseback.* 1954. Dodd Mead. 1st ed. VG/fair. O3. $35.00

WOLFE, Martin. *Green Light.* 1989. Phil. 1st ed. 498p. VG/dj. B18. $22.50

WOLFE, Thomas. *Face of a Nation.* 1939. Literary Guild. 1st ed (pub simultaneously w/Scribner ed). VG/VG. A17. $20.00

WOLFE, Thomas. *From Death to Morning.* 1935. Scribner. 1st ed. 8vo. 304p. gilt purple cloth. VG/dj. H5. $200.00

WOLFE, Thomas. *Mannerhouse: A Play in Prologue & 3 Acts.* 1948. NY. 1st ed. 1/500 #d. w/12p facimile letter. VG/dj/case. H4. $175.00

WOLFE, Thomas. *Story of a Novel.* 1936. NY. ARC. 93p. VG/dj. B18. $125.00

WOLFE, Thomas. *Story of a Novel.* 1936. Scribner. 1st ed. 93p. rose cloth. VG/dj. C6. $100.00

WOLFE, Thomas. *Web & the Rock.* 1939. Harper. 1st ed. 8vo. 695p. gilt/red stp bl cloth. NF/dj. H5. $150.00

WOLFE, Tom. *A La Mode.* 1973. NY. Seabury. 1st ed. VG+/VG+. S9. $30.00

WOLFENDALE, A.W. *Cosmic Rays.* 1963. NY. Philosophical Lib. 8vo. 222p. VG/dj. K5. $16.00

WOLFERSTAN, Bertram. *Catholic Church in China From 1860-1907.* 1909. London. Sands. bibliography/index. lacks fld map. 470p. H10. $22.50

WOLFERT, Ira. *Battle for the Solomons.* 1943. Boston. 1st ed. 200p. VG/VG. A17. $9.50

WOLFF, Fritz. *Avesta: Die Heiligen Bucher...* 1960. Strassburg. Trubner. rpt 1910 ed. VG. W1. $45.00

WOLFF, Geoffrey. *Sightseer.* 1973. NY. 1st ed/author's 2nd novel. sgn. F/F. A11. $55.00

WOLFF, Joseph. *Researches & Missionary Labours Among Jews...* 1837. Phil. 8vo. 338p. brd. scarce. O2. $75.00

WOLFF, Miles Jr. *Season of the Owl.* 1980. Stein Day. 1st ed. F/VG. P8. $30.00

WOLFF, Philippe. *Cultural Awakening.* 1968. Pantheon. 314p. VG/dj. M10. $7.50

WOLFF, Robert Lee. *Strange Stories.* 1971. Gambit. 1st ed. VG/VG. P3. $25.00

WOLFF, Tobias. *Back in the World.* 1985. Houghton Mifflin. 1st ed. F/NF. L3. $40.00

WOLFF, Tobias. *In Pharaoh's Army: Memories of the Lost War.* 1994. Knopf. ARC. sgn. F/case. B2. $45.00

WOLFF, Werner. *Personality of the Preschool Child.* 1947. NY. Grune Stratton. 302p. G/dj. K4. $15.00

WOLFSON, Harry Austryn. *Hallevi & Maimonides on Prophecy.* 1942. Phil. VG/stiff wrp. W1. $8.00

WOLKSTEIN, Diane. *Red Lion.* 1977. Crowell. 1st ed. ils Ed Young. pict cloth. F/F. C8. $25.00

WOLLE, Murie Sibell. *Bonanza Trail...* 1958. Bloomington, IN. 3rd prt. sgn. ils. 510p. G/dj. B18. $22.50

WOLLETT, Donald H. *Labor Relations & Federal Law.* 1949. WA U. 148p. VG. D3. $20.00

WOLLOCOMBE, John B. *Tetcott Hunt Week: Antecedents & Consequences...* 1895. London. Skeffington. VG. O3. $25.00

WOLMAN, Benjamin B. *Dictionary of Behavioral Science.* 1973. NY. 1st ed. 478p. dj. A13. $40.00

WOLMAN, Benjamin B. *Handbook of General Psychology.* 1973. Prentice Hall. 958p. G/dj. K4. $25.00

WOLMAN, Benjamin B. *Historical Roots of Contemporary Psychology.* 1968. Harper Row. 367p. F. K4. $10.00

WOLO. *Amanda.* 1941. Morrow. 1st ed. 4to. 41p. G/worn. A3. $15.00

WOLTER, Allan B. *Book of Life: Explanation of Rule of 3rd Order...* 1954. NY. Franciscan Inst. 1st ed. index. 148p. H10. $22.00

WOMACK, Jack. *Ambient.* 1987. Weidenfeld Nicolson. 1st ed/author's 1st book. M/dj. M21. $25.00

WOOD, Alexander. *Thomas Young: Natural Philosopher 1773-1829.* 1954. Cambridge. 4 pl. 356p. bl cloth. VG/chip. G1. $36.50

WOOD, Alfred C. *History of the Levant Company.* 1964. London. 8vo. 267p. cloth. dj. O2. $30.00

WOOD, B. *Slavery in Colonial Georgia 1730-1775.* 1984. GA U. ils. 264p. VG. E5. $35.00

WOOD, Bari. *Light Source.* 1984. NY. NAL. 1st ed. F/F. N3. $15.00

WOOD, Bari. *Tribe.* 1981. NAL. 1st ed. VG/VG. P3. $15.00

WOOD, C.F. *Yachting Cruise in the South Seas.* 1875. London. King. 221p. T7. $70.00

WOOD, Charles Erskine Scott. *Too Much Government.* 1931. Vanguard. 1st ed. F/NF. B2. $40.00

WOOD, Christina. *Safari S Am.* 1973. Taplinger. 1st ed. 224p. VG/dj. F3. $15.00

WOOD, Christopher. *Taiwan.* 1981. Michael Joseph. 1st ed. VG/VG. P3. $15.00

WOOD, Clement. *Double Jeopardy.* 1947. NY. Arcadia. 1st ed. F/NF. M15. $30.00

WOOD, E. Lindley. *Smooth Fox Terrier.* 1974. London. Foyle. 3rd revised ed. ils. glossy brd. M. R2. $12.00

WOOD, H. *Intellectual Pup, Extracts From His Diary.* 1908. Dillingham. 12mo. G+. B17. $6.00

WOOD, Horatio. *Therapuetics: Its Principles & Practice. The 7th Edition.* 1888. Phil. 908p. orig worn sheep. G7. $25.00

WOOD, James. *Hound, Bay Horse & Turtle Dove.* 1963. Pantheon. Thoreau for Young Readers. 172p. VG/VG. S11. $10.00

WOOD, John A. *Solar System.* 1979. Englewood Cliffs. 8vo. 196p. pb. K5. $15.00

WOOD, Lawson. *Mr Trunk.* nd (1916). Warne. ils. VG/wrp. M5. $75.00

WOOD, Lawson. *Mrs Polly.* nd (1920). Warne. ils. VG/wrp. M5. $75.00

WOOD, Michael. *In Search of the Dark Ages.* 1987. Facts on File. 1st ed. 4to. ils. 250p. VG/dj. M10. $15.00

WOOD, Richard G. *Stephen Harriman Long: 1784-1864...* 1966. Arthur H Clark. 1st ed. 8vo. 292p. gilt bl cloth. NF. P4. $50.00

WOOD, Ted. *Live Bait.* 1985. Canada. Collin Macmillan. 1st ed. F/F. P3. $15.00

WOOD, Thomas. *Institute of Laws of England...* 1734. London. Nutt Gosling. sm folio. 633p. full calf. D3. $250.00

WOOD, Wallace. *Wizard King.* 1978. self pub. 1st ed. sgn. F/F. P3. $45.00

WOOD, William. *Manual of Physical Excercises...* 1867. NY. 316 ils. 316p. emb cloth. worn. G7. $85.00

WOODBERRY, E. George. *North Africa & the Desert: Scenes & Moods.* 1914. Scribner. 1st ed. 8vo. teg. xl. VG. W1. $15.00

WOODBURY, David O. *Battlefronts of Industry: Westinghouse in WWII.* 1948. NY. 1st ed. 342p. VG. A17. $10.00

WOODBURY, David O. *Outward Bound for Space.* 1961. Little Brn. 8vo. ils Henry Kane. 178p. G/dj. K5. $15.00

WOODBURY, George. *Great Days of Piracy in the West Indies.* 1951. NY. Norton. 1st ed. VG/VG. B11. $25.00

WOODCOCK, Percy. *Weather Warnings for the Novice.* 1942. London. Muller. 72p. G/G. K5. $10.00

WOODCOTT, Keith; see Brunner, John.

WOODFORD, Frank B. *Father Abraham's Children.* 1961. Detroit. 1st ed. 305p. VG/dj. B18. $27.50

WOODHAM-SMITH, Cecil. *Reason Why.* 1953. NY. 4th prt. 287p. VG/dj. B18. $12.50

WOODHOUSE, Barbara. *Talking to Animals.* 1955. Norton. 1st Am ed. VG/G. O3. $25.00

WOODHOUSE, Martin. *Mama Doll.* 1972. CMG. VG/G. P3. $12.00

WOODRELL, Daniel. *Under the Bright Lights.* 1986. Holt. 1st ed. F/F. M15. $30.00

WOODRUFF, Hiram. *Trotting Horse of America.* 1869. NY. leather. G+. M17. $30.00

WOODRUFF, Samuel. *Journal of a Tour to Malta, Greece, Asia Minor, Carthage...* 1831. Hartford. 8vo. engraved ftspc. 283p. brd. O2. $175.00

WOODS, Robert Archey. *English Social Movements.* 1891. Scribner. 1st ed. inscr. NF. B2. $150.00

WOODS, Sara. *Knives Have Edges.* 1968. HRW. 1st ed. NF/NF. P3. $15.00

WOODS, Sara. *Naked Villainy.* 1987. Macmillan. 1st ed. VG/VG. P3. $20.00

WOODS, Stuart. *Deep Lie.* 1986. Norton. 1st ed. F/F. M15. $30.00

WOODS, Stuart. *Grass Roots.* 1989. Simon Schuster. 1st ed. F/F. M15. $25.00

WOODS, Stuart. *Grass Roots.* 1989. Simon Schuster. 1st ed. F/NF. B3. $20.00

WOODS, Stuart. *Grass Roots.* 1989. Simon Schuster. 1st ed. sgn. F/F. T2. $30.00

WOODS, Stuart. *Santa Fe Rules.* 1992. Harper Collins. ARC. w/pub materials. F/F. B3. $40.00

WOODS, Stuart. *White Cargo.* 1988. Simon Schuster. 1st ed. F/F. B3. $25.00

WOODS & WOODWARD. *Urban Disease & Mortality in 19th-Century England.* 1984. NY. 1st ed. 255p. A13. $25.00

WOODSON, Robert E. *Rauwolfia: Botany, Pharmacognosy, Chemistry...* 1957. Boston. ils. 149p. VG+/dj. B26. $36.00

WOODWARD, J.J. *Medical & Surgical Hist of War of Rebellion 1861-1865.* 1870-1888. WA, DC. 6 vol. mixed eds. lg 4to. mixed bdg. VG. G7. $1,500.00

WOODWARD, J.J. *Outlines of Chief Camp Diseases in the US Armies.* 1964. Hafner. rpt of Phil 1863 ed. G7. $25.00

WOODWARD, John. *Treatise on Ecclesiastical Heraldry.* 1894. Edinburgh. Johnstone. 36 pl. 580p. morocco. H10. $145.00

WOODWARD, Walter Carleton. *Timothy Nicholson, Master Quaker.* 1927. Richmond, IN. 1st ed. 252p. cloth. NF. M8. $45.00

WOOLCOTT, Alexander. *Letters of...* 1944. NY. F/F. A17. $7.50

WOOLCOTT, Alexander. *Long, Long Ago.* 1943. Viking. 1st ed. 280p. gilt red cloth. VG/G. S11. $10.00

WOOLEY, C. Leonard. *Hist Unearthed.* 1962. Praeger. ils/pl. 176p. VG. W1. $9.00

WOOLEY, C. Leonard. *Ur of the Chaldees: Record of 7 Years of Excavation.* 1930. Scribner. 1st Am ed. xl. VG. W1. $12.00

WOOLEY, C. Leonard. *Ur: The First Phases.* 1946. Penguin. sm 8vo. pl. VG. W1. $9.00

WOOLEY, C. Leonard. *Vor 5,000 Jahren.* ca 1932. Stuttgart. Franckch'she. 118p. xl. VG. W1. $12.00

WOOLF, Douglas. *Wall to Wall.* 1962. Grove. 1st ed. NF/NF. B2. $35.00

WOOLF, Leonard. *Barbarians at the Gate.* 1939. London. BC/Gollancz. 1st ed. NF/sans. B2. $25.00

WOOLF, Leonard. *Quack, Quack!* 1935. Harcourt Brace. 1st ed. NF/dj. Q1. $125.00

WOOLF, Virginia. *Moment & Other Essays.* 1948. Harcourt Brace. 1st Am ed. 8vo. 240p. gilt red cloth. F/dj. H5. $100.00

WOOLF, Virginia. *Mr Bennett & Mrs Brown.* 1924. London. Hogarth. 1st ed. F/wht wrp. H4. $150.00

WOOLF, Virginia. *Mrs Dalloway.* 1925. Harcourt Brace. 1st Am ed. VG. Q1. $150.00

WOOLF, Virginia. *Three Guineas.* 1938. Longon. Hogarth. 1st ed. 329p. fair. M10. $50.00

WOOLF, Virginia. *Years.* 1937. Harcourt Brace. 1st Am ed. NF/G clip. L3. $85.00

WOOLFE, Raymond Jr. *Steeplechasing.* 1983. Viking/The Studio. 1st ed. obl 4to. VG. O3. $40.00

WOOLFOLK, William. *President's Doctor.* 1975. Playboy. 1st ed. VG/VG. P3. $20.00

WOOLLEY, Persia. *Queen of the Summer Stars.* 1990. Poseidon. 1st ed. VG/VG. P3. $20.00

WOOLRICH, Cornell. *After-Dinner Story.* 1944. Lippincott. 1st ed. VG/dj/case. B4. $950.00

WOOLRICH, Cornell. *Best of William Irish.* nd. BC. VG. P3. $5.00

WOOLRICH, Cornell. *Black Curtain.* 1941. Simon Schuster. 1st ed. VG/VG. M15. $275.00

WOOLRICH, Cornell. *Blue Ribbon.* 1949. Lippincott. 1st ed. NF/NF. M15. $200.00

WOOLRICH, Cornell. *Deadline at Dawn.* 1944. Lippincott. 1st ed. VG/VG. M15. $150.00

WOOLRICH, Cornell. *Into the Night.* 1987. Mysterious. 1st ed. sgn. F/F. S6. $40.00

WOOLRICH, Cornell. *Phantom Lady.* 1944. Tower. MTI. VG/G. P3. $25.00

WOOLRICH, Cornell. *Rendezvous in Black.* 1979. Gregg. 1st ed. VG/VG. P3. $30.00

WORCESTER, Samuel. *Watts & Select Hymns.* 1845. Boston. 776p. full leather. G. O8. $9.50

WORDEN, Felice. *Sketchbook of Dogs.* 1945. NY. Ackerman. 1st ed. unp. cloth. M. R2. $30.00

WORDSWORTH, William. *Memorials of a Tour on the Continent, 1820.* 1822. London. Longman Hurst Rees Orme Brn. 1st ed. H4. $650.00

WORK, James C. *Prose & Poetry of the American West.* 1990. NE U. 1st sc ed. 733p. M. A18. $25.00

WORKMAN, Boyle. *City That Grew...* 1936. Los Angeles. Author Autograph ed. 3rd prt. 430p. VG. D3. $25.00

WORKMAN, Karen Wood. *Alaskan Archaeology: A Bibliography.* 1974. Anchorage. AK Division of Parks. 2nd ed. 46p. VG. P4. $20.00

WORMELEY, K. Prescott. *Other Side of War With the Army of the Potomac.* 1889. Boston. index. 210p. scarce. O8. $32.50

WORSFOLD, W. Basil. *Redemption of Egypt.* 1899. London. Allen. sm 4to. 333p. VG. W1. $45.00

WORSHAM, William Johnston. *Old Nineteenth Tennessee Regiment, CSA, June, 1861-Apr 1865.* 1902. Knoxville, TN. Pr of Paragon Prt. 1st ed. 235p. cloth. VG. M8. $450.00

WORTHAM, Louis J. *History of Texas From Wilderness to Commonwealth.* 1924. np. 5 vol. leather. VG. M17. $85.00

WORTIS, Joseph. *Recent Advances in Biological Psychiatry. Vol IX.* 1967. Plenum. 377p. G. K4. $20.00

WORTMAN, Sterling. *Plant Studies in People's Republic of China.* 1975. WA, DC. Nat Academy Science. 206p. wrp. A10. $15.00

WORVILL, Roy. *Exploring Space.* 1964. Loughborough, UK. Ladybird Books. revised ed. 8vo. 51p. G. K5. $8.00

WOYWOD, Stanislaus. *Practical Commentary on Code of Canon Law.* 1932. NY. Wagner. 2 vol. 1st ed. H10. $18.95

WOZENCRAFT, Kim. *Rush.* 1990. Random. 1st ed/author's 1st book. rem mk. F/F. A14. $30.00

WPA WRITERS PROGRAM. *Canada: New Member of the Pan Am Front.* nd. IL Writers Progam. mimeo. F. B2. $45.00

WPA WRITERS PROGRAM. *Copper Camp, Stories of World's Greatest Mining Town...* 1943. Hastings. 1st ed. NF/VG. B34. $125.00

WPA WRITERS PROGRAM. *Copper Camp, Stories of World's Greatest Mining Town...* 1945. np. 4th prt. ils. G. B34. $45.00

WPA WRITERS PROGRAM. *Drums & Shadows: Stuvival Studies Among GA Coastal Negroes.* 1940. Athens. 1st ed. NF/VG. B2. $125.00

WPA WRITERS PROGRAM. *Idaho: Guide in Word & Picture.* 1950. NY. revised 2nd ed. 300p. VG/dj. B18. $35.00

WPA WRITERS PROGRAM. *Indiana: Guide to the Hoosier State.* 1961. NY. 548p. VG/dj. B18. $22.50

WPA WRITERS PROGRAM. *Massachusetts.* 1937. Boston. 1st ed/later prt. ils/map ep. 675p. VG/torn. B18. $25.00

WPA WRITERS PROGRAM. *Minnesota: State Guide.* 1938. NY. 1st ed. 523p. VG/torn. B18. $47.50

WPA WRITERS PROGRAM. *Montana: Profile in Pictures.* 1941. GPO. VG. B34. $15.00

WPA WRITERS PROGRAM. *Nebraska.* 1939. NY. 1st ed. pocket map. VG/G. B5. $55.00

WPA WRITERS PROGRAM. *New Jersey.* 1939. NY. 1st ed. w/pocket map. VG. B5. $45.00

WPA WRITERS PROGRAM. *New Orleans City Guide.* 1938. Boston. 430p. G/torn. B18. $27.50

WPA WRITERS PROGRAM. *North Carolina.* 1939. Chapel Hill. 1st ed. pocket map. VG/VG. B5. $60.00

WPA WRITERS PROGRAM. *Wyoming: Guide to Its Hist, Highways & People.* 1941. NY. 1st ed. 490p. VG/dj. B18. $125.00

WRAGG, David W. *Helicopters at War.* 1983. NY. 1st Am ed. 283p. VG/dj. B18. $25.00

WREN, P.C. *Beau Sabreur.* nd. Grosset Dunlap. photoplay ed. VG. P3. $15.00

WREN, P.C. *Snow White & Rose Red.* 1989. Tor. 1st ed. inscr. F/dj. F4. $25.00

WRIGHT, Anna A. *More Truth Than Poetry.* 1884. Chicago. WS Battis. 1st ed. 12mo. 237p. cloth. M1. $100.00

WRIGHT, Beatrice A. *Psychology & Rehabilitation.* 1959. WA, DC. Am Psychological Assn. 105p. F. K4. $10.00

WRIGHT, Chauncey. *Letters of Chauncy Wright...* 1878. Cambridge. John Wilson. 392p. blind-blocked gr cloth. scarce. G1. $225.00

WRIGHT, D.G. *Southern Girl in '61.* 1905. NY. 1st ed. VG. A15. $50.00

WRIGHT, Danforth P. *Seaman's Medical Guide...* 1834. Boston. Russell Odiorne Metcalf. 168p. cloth. VG. B14. $85.00

WRIGHT, Dare. *Doll & the Kitten.* 1960. Doubleday. 4to. 55p. pict brd/cloth spine. G+. A3. $25.00

WRIGHT, Dare. *Holiday for Edith & the Bears.* 1958. Doubleday. 4to. pict brd/cloth spine. G+. A3. $25.00

WRIGHT, Dare. *Lona: A Fairy Tale.* 1963. Random. 1st ed. unp. pict brd. VG/G. A3. $40.00

WRIGHT, Dudley. *Book of Vampires.* 1973. Causeway. 1st ed. VG. P3. $20.00

WRIGHT, E.O. *Politics of Punishment.* 1973. NY. 349p. VG/pict wrp. D3. $10.00

WRIGHT, Edward Needles. *Chestnut Bur Lions.* 1977. Whimsie. 1st ed. M/sans. P8. $15.00

WRIGHT, Eric. *Death by Degrees.* 1993. London. Harper Collins. 1st Eng ed. F/F. S6. $25.00

WRIGHT, Eric. *Death in the Old Country.* 1985. Collins Crime Club. 1st ed. VG/VG. P3. $18.00

WRIGHT, Eric. *Night Gods Smiled.* 1983. Collins Crime Club. 1st ed. VG/VG. P3. $18.00

WRIGHT, Esmond. *Hist of the World: Prehistory to the Renaissance.* ca 1985. Bonanza. ils. 648p. F/dj. M10. $18.50

WRIGHT, Eugene. *Great Horn Spoon.* 1928. Bobbs Merrill. 2nd ed. 8vo. G. W1. $9.00

WRIGHT, Frank Lloyd. *Future of Architecture.* 1953. Horizon. 1st ed. gilt red/tan cloth. F/NF. F1. $150.00

WRIGHT, Frank Lloyd. *Natural House.* 1954. Horizon. 1st ed. 8vo. 223p. red/blk stp tan linen. VG+. F1. $175.00

WRIGHT, Harold Bell. *Calling of Dan Matthews.* 1909. Chicago Book Supply. VG. N2. $15.00

WRIGHT, Harold Bell. *Exit.* 1930. NY. 1st ed. VG/G. B5. $60.00

WRIGHT, Harold Bell. *Eyes of the World.* 1914. Book Supply. 1st ed. 464p. G. H1. $18.00

WRIGHT, Harold Bell. *Mine With the Iron Door.* 1923. Appleton. 1st ed. 338p. VG/dj. M20. $60.00

WRIGHT, Harold Bell. *Re-Creation of Brian Kent.* 1919. Chicago Book Supply. G+. N2. $10.00

WRIGHT, Harold Bell. *Their Yesterdays.* 1912. Book Supply. 1st ed. ils FG Cootes. 310p. F. H1. $22.50

WRIGHT, Harold Bell. *Uncrowned King.* 1910. Chicago. 1st ed. gilt red cloth. F. B5. $50.00

WRIGHT, Harold Bell. *When a Man's a Man.* 1916. AL Burt. 1st ed. photos. VG/G. B5. $27.50

WRIGHT, Harold Bell. *When a Man's a Man.* 1916. Chicago Book Supply. G+. N2. $10.00

WRIGHT, Harold Bell. *When a Man's a Man.* 1916. Chicago Book Supply. 1st ed. 348p. VG. H1. $18.00

WRIGHT, Helen. *Sweeper in the Sky.* 1949. NY. Macmillan. 1st prt. 8vo. 253p. VG/chip. K5. $60.00

WRIGHT, Helena. *Sex & Society.* 1968. WA U. 122p. F/dj. K4. $8.50

WRIGHT, Henrietta Christian. *Children's Stories in Am Hist.* 1886. London. Bickers. 1st ed. ils JS Davis. 356 p. gilt leather. NF. A17. $35.00

WRIGHT, Jack. *Scout Patrol Boys at Circle U Ranch.* nd. World. ne. F/dj. M2. $20.00

WRIGHT, Joseph. *Old English Grammar.* 1925. London. Humphrey Milford. 3rd ed. VG/poor. N2. $10.00

WRIGHT, Keith. *Addressed To Kill.* 1993. London. Constable. 1st ed. F/F. S6. $22.50

WRIGHT, Kenneth. *Mysterious Planet.* 1953. Winston. 1st ed. F/dj. M2. $125.00

WRIGHT, L.R. *Fall From Grace.* 1991. Viking. AP. F/NF wrp. B2. $25.00

WRIGHT, L.R. *Love in the Temperate Zone.* 1988. Viking. 1st ed. VG/VG. P3. $18.00

WRIGHT, L.R. *Sleep While I Sing.* 1986. Canada. Doubleday. 1st ed. F/F. P3. $20.00

WRIGHT, Louis B. *First Gentlemen of Virginia: Intellectual Qualities...* 1940. Huntington Lib. 8vo. 373p. brn cloth. G. B11. $25.00

WRIGHT, Louis B. *Of Books & Men.* 1976. SC U. 202p. F/VG. A4. $35.00

WRIGHT, Marcus J. *Official & Illustrated War Record.* 1898. WA, DC. ils/maps/rosters. 560p. H1. $35.00

WRIGHT, Marie Robinson. *Picturesque Mexico.* 1897. Lippincott. 1st ed. folio. 445p. cracked hinges. F3. $45.00

WRIGHT, Milton. *Getting Along With People.* 1935. McGraw Hill. 285p. reading copy. K4. $8.50

WRIGHT, Olgivana Lloyd. *Struggle Within.* 1955. NY. 1st ed. VG/VG. B5. $65.00

WRIGHT, Orville. *How We Invented the Airplane.* 1988. np. ils. 96p. VG. E5. $30.00

WRIGHT, Paul. *New & Complete Life of Our Blessed Lord & Savior...* (1803?). NY. Durrell. folio. ils. 380p. calf. H10. $75.00

WRIGHT, Richard. *Black Boy: Record of Childhood & Youth.* 1945. Harper. later prt. inscr. 228p. VG/dj. C6. $225.00

WRIGHT, Richard. *Lawd Today.* 1963. Walker. 1st ed/posthumously pub. F/NF. Q1. $75.00

WRIGHT, Richard. *Native Son.* 1940. Harper. 1st ed. 359p. bl cloth. G/fair. H1. $12.00

WRIGHT, Richard. *Outsider.* 1953. Harper. 1st ed. gray lettered blk cloth. NF/dj. H5. $75.00

WRIGHT, Richard. *White Man, Listen!* 1957. Doubleday. 1st ed. 8vo. 190p. blk cloth. VG/dj. H5. $125.00

WRIGHT, Richardson. *Forgotten Ladies.* 1928. np. 1st ed. ils. 307p. O8. $12.50

WRIGHT, Richardson. *Hawkers & Walkers in Early America.* 1927. Lippincott. 1st ed. 317p. VG. A10. $25.00

WRIGHT, S. Fowler. *Deluge.* 1928. Cosmopolitan. 1st ed. VG. P3. $25.00

WRIGHT, S. Fowler. *Deluge.* 1928. NY. 1st ed. cloth. G. A17. $9.50

WRIGHT, S. Fowler. *Island of Captain Sparrow.* 1928. Cosmopolitan. 1st Am ed. VG. M21. $12.50

WRIGHT, Stephen. *M31: A Family Romance.* 1988. Harmony. 1st ed. F/F. P3. $20.00

WRIGHT, T.M. *Strange Seed.* 1978. Everest. 1st ed. VG/VG. P3. $20.00

WRIGHT, Thomas. *Life of William Blake.* 1969 (1929). NY. Burt Franklin. rpt. 2 vol in 1. 192p. VG. B33. $40.00

WRIGHT, W. Aldis. *Bacon's Essays & Colours of Good & Evil.* 1891. London. Macmillan. 1/250. gilt contemporary calf. M11. $150.00

WRIGHT, Willard. *Forty Years of Tropical Medicine Research: A History...* 1970. WA. 1st ed. 426p. A13. $30.00

WRIGHT, William. *Black Bear.* 1910. NY. 1st ed. VG. B5. $65.00

WRIGHT, William. *Pictorial History of the Locomotive.* 1899. Chicago. Pneumatic Tool Co. sq 4to. 81p. pict blk cloth. VG. F1. $125.00

WRIGHT. *American Fiction, 1774-1850.* 1969. San Marino. Huntington Lib. 429p. F/F. A4. $40.00

WRIGHTMAN, W.P.D. *Growth of Scientific Ideas.* 1953. Yale. 496p. russet cloth. VG/chip. G1. $25.00

WROTH, Lawrence C. *William Parks, Printer & Journalist of Eng & Colonial Am...* 1926. Richmond. Wm Parks Club. 1/300. 1 facsimile. 70p. full gilt red calf. K1. $75.00

WU, William F. *Hong on the Range.* 1989. NY. Walker. 1st ed. F/F. N3. $15.00

WUAMETT, Victor. *Teardown.* 1990. St Martin. 1st ed. F/F. P3. $17.00

WUEST, Kenneth S. *New Testament: Expanded Trans.* 1962. Eerdmans. 624p. VG/dj. B29. $8.50

WULF, Maurice. *Mediaeval Philosophy Ils From System of Thomas Aquinas.* 1924. Cambridge. Harvard. thin 8vo. 151p. ruled maroon cloth. VG. G1. $32.00

WULFFEN, Erich. *Woman As a Sexual Criminal.* 1935. Falstaff Pr. ils. 528p. VG. D3. $45.00

WUNDERLICH, Carol Reinhold A. *Das Verhalten der Eignewarme in Krakheiten.* 1868. Leipzig. Wigand. orig brd/recently recased. G7. $1,995.00

WUNDERLICH, Hans Georg. *Secret of Crete.* 1974. Macmillan. tall 8vo. 367p. VG. W1. $10.00

WUNDT, Wilhelm. *Einleitung in die Philosophie.* 1901. Leipzig. Wilhelm Engelmann. 466p. bl cloth. VG. G1. $100.00

WUNDT, Wilhelm. *Logik: Eine Untersuchung der Prinzipien der Erkenntnis...* 1880 & 1883. Stuttgart. Ferdinand Enke. 2 vol. VG. G1. $250.00

WUORINEN, John H. *Hist of Finland.* 1965. Columbia. G+/dj. N2. $10.00

WURF, Karl. *To Serve Man: A Cookbook for People.* 1976. Phil. Owlswick. 1st ed. ils Jack Bozzi. F/F. T2. $10.00

WURLITZER, Rudolph. *Nog.* 1968. Random. 1st ed/author's 1st book. F/F. B2. $60.00

WURM, Michael. *Apokeryxis, Abdicatio und Exheredatio.* 1972. Munchen. German/Latin/Greek text. 108p. NF/stiff wrp. D3. $25.00

WYATT, David. *Fallen Into Eden.* 1986. Cambridge. 1st ed. notes/index. 280p. F/NF. B19. $30.00

WYATT, James Cromar. *Examples of Greek & Pompeian Decorative Work.* 1897. London. 1st ed. lg folio. 60 full-p pl. gr cloth. VG+. C6. $150.00

WYATT, Joan. *Middle-Earth Album.* 1979. Simon Schuster. 1st ed. VG/VG. P3. $30.00

WYCHERLEY, William. *Posthumous Works of...* 1728. London. 1st ed. scarce. A15. $150.00

WYCOFF. *Bibliography Relating to Floras...* 1911-1914. Cincinnati. 13 parts in 1. 522p. VG. A4. $85.00

WYDEN, Peter. *Bay of Pigs, the Untold Story.* 1979. Simon Schuster. 1st ed. 8vo. map ep. VG/VG. B11. $20.00

WYDEN, Peter. *Hired Killers.* 1963. NY. 236p. cloth/brd. VG. D3. $10.00

WYETH, Betsy. *Stray.* 1979. NY. 1st ed. VG/VG. B5. $45.00

WYETH, Jamie. *Jamie Wyeth.* 1980. Boston. 1st ed. VG/VG. B5. $35.00

WYETH, N.C. *Men of Concord & Some Others As Portrayed in Journal...* 1936. Houghton Mifflin. 1st ed thus. sm 4to. ils NC Wyeth. gr cloth. F/dj. B24. $200.00

WYETH, N.C. *Yearling.* 1939. Scribner. ils NC Wyeth. 400p. pict yel cloth. VG. A3. $25.00

WYKES, Alan. *Pen-Friend.* 1950. Duckworth. 1st ed. VG/VG. P3. $30.00

WYLDE, James. *Circle of the Sciences.* late 1800s. London. 4 vol. wood engravings. marbled edges/ep. half leather. G. B18. $150.00

WYLER, Rose. *Exploring Space: True Story About the Rockets of Today...* 1958. Simon Schuster. 8vo. 21p. G. K5. $4.00

WYLIE, C.C. *Our Starland.* 1938. Chicago. Lyons Carnahan. sm 8vo. 378p. bl cloth. G. K5. $14.00

WYLIE, James. *Sign of Dawn.* 1981. Viking. 1st ed. F/NF. B2. $35.00

WYLIE, Philip. *Essay on Morals.* 1947. Rinehart. sm 8vo. 204p. gray cloth. G1. $22.50

WYLIE, Philip. *Gladiator.* 1930. Knopf. 1st ed. xl. VG. P3. $15.00

WYLIE, Philip. *Sons & Daughters of Mom.* 1971. Doubleday. 1st ed. VG/VG. P3. $20.00

WYLIE, Philip. *They Both Were Naked.* 1965. NY. 1st ed. F/VG. A17. $15.00

WYLIE, Philip. *Tomorrow!* 1954. Rinehart. 1st ed. F/NF. B3. $40.00

WYLIE, Ruth C. *Self-Concept. Vol 2.* 1979. Lincoln/London. NE U. revised ed. 701p. M/dj. K4. $22.50

WYLLIE, John. *Pocket Full of Dead.* 1978. Crime Club. 1st ed. VG/G. P3. $13.00

WYLLIE, John. *Tumours of the Cerebellum.* 1908. London. Lewis. 109p. brd. VG. G7. $295.00

WYMALEN. *Riding for Children.* nd. London. 4to. ils Michael Lyne. G/wrp. R2. $10.00

WYMAN, A.L. *Los Angeles Times Prize Cook Book.* 1923. Los Angeles. Times Mirror. 340p. pict brd. B14. $50.00

WYMAN, Barry. *Behind the Mask of Tutankhamen.* 1972. Souvenir Pr. 1st ed. 203p. F/dj. W1. $12.00

WYMAN, L.P. *Lakewood Boys in Montana.* 1927. AL Burt. G. B34. $15.00

WYNDHAM, John. *Midwich Cuckoos.* 1958. Ballantine. 1st ed. VG/VG. P3. $35.00

WYNDHAM, John. *Seeds of Time.* 1956. London. 1st ed. VG. M2. $25.00

WYNNE, James. *Private Libraries of NY.* 1860. NY. French. 417p. uncut/unopened. G7. $135.00

WYNNE, John Huddlestone. *Tales for Youth; in Thirty Poems: To Which Are Annexed...* 1794. London. Newbery. 8vo. ftspc/30 vignettes. 158p. contemporary calf. B24. $750.00

XYZ

XILINAS, Elephteri M. *These: Le Nil, Son Limon et la Terre Egyptienne.* 1936. Cairo. Noury. 1st ed. 192p. xl. NF. W1. $12.00

YAGODA, Ben. *Will Rogers: A Biography.* 1993. Knopf. ARC/1st ed. RS. F/F. S9. $40.00

YALE, William. *Near East: Modern Hist.* 1958. Ann Arbor. 1st ed. tall 8vo. VG. W1. $22.00

YAN, Mo. *Garlic Ballads.* 1995. Viking. AP. F/wrp. B2. $30.00

YANCEY, Becky. *My Life With Elvis.* 1977. St Martin. 1st ed. VG/VG. S11. $10.00

YANCEY, Philip. *Where Is God When It Hurts?* 1977. Zondervan. 187p. VG/dj. B29. $5.50

YANEZ, Agustin. *Edge of the Storm.* 1969. TX U. 3rd ed. 8vo. 332p. gray cloth. F/F. P4. $30.00

YARBOROUGH, Ralph W. *Frank Dobie: Man & Friend.* 1967. np. Pontomac Corral of Westerners. 1st ed. VG. B19. $50.00

YARBRO, Chelsea Quinn. *Crusader's Torch.* 1988. Tor. 1st ed. F/dj. F4. $20.00

YARBRO, Chelsea Quinn. *False Dawn.* 1978. Doubleday. 1st ed. F/F. P3. $18.00

YARBRO, Chelsea Quinn. *Flame in Byzantium.* 1987. Tor. 1st ed. F/dj. F4/N3. $20.00

YARBRO, Chelsea Quinn. *Four Horses for Tishtry.* 1985. Harper. 1st ed. F/dj. F4. $25.00

YARBRO, Chelsea Quinn. *Locadio's Apprentice.* 1984. Harper Row. 1st ed. F/F. P3. $15.00

YARBRO, Chelsea Quinn. *Palace.* 1978. St Martin. 1st ed. F/dj. F4. $25.00

YARBRO, Chelsea Quinn. *Signs & Portents.* 1984. Dream. 1st ed. F/sans. M2. $25.00

YARBRO, Chelsea Quinn. *Time of the Fourth Horseman.* 1976. Doubleday. 1st ed/author's 1st SF book. F/NF. N3. $15.00

YARDLEY, Michael. *Backing Into the Limelight.* 1985. London. Harrap. 1st ed. gilt blk cloth. F/F. M7. $55.00

YARDLEY, Michael. *TE Lawrence: A Biography.* 1987. Stein Day. index/notes. 267p. M/dj. M7. $21.50

YARNALL, Elizabeth Biddle. *Addison Hutton: Quaker Architect, 1834-1916.* 1974. Phil. Art Alliance. 1st ed. 4to. 78p. VG/VG. V3. $24.00

YARROW, Philip. *Fighting the Debauchery of Our Girls.* 1923. Yarrow. G. P3. $15.00

YARWOOD, Edmund. *Vselod Garshin.* 1981. Twayne. 1st prt. 147p. xl. A17. $7.50

YATES, Dornford. *Blind Corner.* 1927. Hodder Stoughton. 3rd ed. VG. P3. $20.00

YATES, Dornford. *She Fell Among Thieves.* 1949. Ward Lock. 13th ed. VG/VG. P3. $15.00

YATES, Elizabeth. *Howard Thurman: Portrait of a Practical Dreamer.* 1964. John Day. 1st ed. F/VG. B2. $30.00

YATES, Haydie. *70 Miles From a Lemon.* 1947. Houghton Mifflin. ils. VG/dj. B34. $60.00

YATES, Raymond F. *Boys' Book of Rockets.* 1950. London. T Werner Laurie. sm 8vo. 131p. VG/dj. K5. $30.00

YATES, Richard. *Easter Parade.* 1976. Delacorte. 1st ed. F/F. B2. $40.00

YATES, Richard. *Easter Parade.* 1976. Delacorte/Lawrence. UP. NF/tall wrp. L3. $75.00

YATES, Richard. *Revolutionary Road.* 1961. Atlantic/Little Brn. ARC/author's 1st book. RS. F/F. B4. $275.00

YATES, W. Ross. *Joseph Wharton: Quaker Industrial Pioneer.* 1987. Bethlehem. Lehigh U. 1st ed. 8vo. 413p. M/M. V3. $22.00

YAVNO, Max. *Story of Wine in California.* 1962. Berkeley. 1st ed. 4to. NF/VG+. S9. $60.00

YEAGER, Chuck. *Yeager: An Autobiography.* 1985. Bantam. 8vo. 342p. VG/dj. K5. $12.00

YEARDLEY, John. *Memoir & Diary of John Yeardley, Minister of Gospel.* 1859. London. Bennett. 8vo. 456p. VG. V3. $35.00

YEATMAN, Christopher. *Plant Genetic Resources.* 1984. Boulder, CO. ils. 164p. VG. B26. $19.00

YEATS, Jack B. *La La Noo.* 1943. Dublin. Cuala. 1st ed. 1/250 #d. F/glassine. B24. $185.00

YEATS, William Butler. *Cutting of an Agate.* 1912. Macmillan. 1st Am ed. Ralph Block's copy. VG. Q1. $250.00

YEATS, William Butler. *Death of Synge & Other Passages From an Old Diary.* 1928. Dublin. Cuala. 1/400. 8vo. 34p. beige cloth/gray brd. NF/wrp. H5. $500.00

YEATS, William Butler. *King's Threshold. A Play in Verse.* 1904. NY. private prt. 1st ed. 1/100. sgn. 8vo. 58p. F/glassine dj/case. B24. $3,000.00

YEATS, William Butler. *On the Boiler.* 1939. Dublin. Cuala. 2nd ed. sm 4to. 46p. VG/prt bl wrp. C6. $150.00

YEATS, William Butler. *Poems of...* 1970. LEC. 1/1500. ils/sgn Robin Jacques. leather. F/F case. L3. $150.00

YEATS, William Butler. *Poems.* 1901. London. Fisher. 3rd ed. 304p. bl cloth. VG. C6. $150.00

YEATS, William Butler. *Responsibilities & Other Poems.* 1916. Macmillan. 1st Am ed. 8vo. 188p. pict gray brd. VG. C6. $250.00

YEATS, William Butler. *Shadowy Waters.* 1900. Hodder Stoughton. 1st ed. 4to. 57p. bl cloth. VG. C6. $200.00

YEATS, William Butler. *Stories of Red Hanrahan/Secret Rose/Rosa Alchemica.* 1914. Macmillan. 1st Am ed. NF/NF. L3. $550.00

YEATS, William Butler. *Where There Is Nothing.* 1903. London. AH Bullen. 1st ed. Forrest Reid's copy/sgn. 129p. NF. C6. $200.00

YEATS-BROWN, Francis. *Bengal Lancer.* 1930. London. Gollancz. 1st ed. 288p. VG+. M7. $50.00

YEATS-BROWN, Francis. *Lancer at Large.* 1937. Viking. 1st ed. 323p. VG+. M7. $45.00

YEE, Lee. *New Realism: Writings From China After Cultural Revolution.* 1983. NY. Hippocrene. 349p. NF/dj. M10. $6.50

YEE, Min S. *Melancholy Hist of Soledad Prison.* 1970. NY. 268p. NF/dj. D3. $15.00

YEE, Warren. *Lychee in Hawaii.* 1979. Honolulu. ils. 24p. sc. VG. B26. $12.50

YEFSKY, S. *Law Enforcement Science & Technology.* 1967. NY. 985p. xl. VG. D3. $35.00

YELLEN, Samuel. *American Labor Struggles.* 1936. Harcourt Brace. ils/photos. G/fair. V4. $17.50

YENNE, Bill. *Atlas of the Solar System.* 1987. NY. Exeter. obl 4to. 192p. VG/dj. K5. $16.00

YEO, Eileen. *Unknown Mayhew.* 1971. Pantheon. 1st Am ed. ils. F/VG. V4. $7.00

YEOMANS, Frank C. *Proctology: Treatise on Malformations, Injuries & Diseases.* 1936. Appleton. ils. 661p. G7. $35.00

YEP, Laurence. *Child of the Owl.* 1977. Harper Row. VG/VG. P3. $15.00

YEP, Laurence. *Rainbow People.* 1989. Harper Row. 1st ed. lib bdg. F/F. N3. $15.00

YEP, Laurence. *Seademons.* 1977. Harper Row. 1st ed. VG/VG. P3. $13.00

YERBY, Frank. *Bride of Liberty.* 1954. Doubleday. 1st ed. VG/VG. P3. $20.00

YERBY, Frank. *Griffin's Way.* 1962. Dial. 1st ed. dj. N2. $5.00

YERFREMOV, Ivan. *Andromeda.* 1959. Foreign Languages Pub. 1st ed. VG/VG. P3. $30.00

YERGIN, Daniel. *Prize: Epic Quest for Oil, Money & Power.* 1991. Simon Schuster. 2nd ed. 877p. NF/dj. W1. $20.00

YEVTUSHENKO, Yevgeny. *Precocious Autobiography.* 1963. NY. 1st ed. photos. VG/VG. A17. $7.50

YGLESIAS, Rafael. *Fearless.* 1993. Random. 1st ed. F/F. A14. $30.00

YIANNIAS, John J. *Byzantine Tradition After the Fall of Constantinople.* 1991. Charlottesville. 8vo. 354p. cloth. dj. O2. $50.00

YLLA. *Dogs by...* 1949. London. Harvill. tall 8vo. 96p. VG/worn. R2. $15.00

YODER, Dale. *Personnel Management & Industrial Relations.* 1942. Prentice Hall. 805p. reading copy. K4. $8.50

YOEMAN, R.S. *Guide Book of US Coins.* 1948. Racine. 3rd ed. ils. 254p. gilt red cloth. VG. H3. $75.00

YOLEN, Jane. *All in the Woodland Early.* 1979. Collins. 1st ed. ils James Breskin Zalbern. VG/G+. P2. $20.00

YOLEN, Jane. *Bird of Time.* 1971. Crowell. 1st ed. F/F. C8. $30.00

YOLEN, Jane. *Dove Isabeau.* 1989. HBJ. B prt. ils Dennis Nolan. F/F. B17. $7.50

YOLEN, Jane. *Friend: Story of George Fox & the Quakers.* 1972. Seabury. 8vo. 179p. VG/dj. V3. $12.50

YOLEN, Jane. *Girl Who Cried Flowers & Other Tales.* 1947. Crowell. 1st ed. ils David Palladine. VG/G+. P2. $25.00

YOLEN, Jane. *Merlin's Booke.* 1986. Minneapolis. Steel Dragon. 1st hc ed. ils Thomas Canty. F/F. T2. $17.00

YOLEN, Jane. *Sister Light, Sister Dark.* 1988. Tor. 1st ed. F/F. T2. $18.00

YOLEN, Jane. *Stone Silenus.* 1984. Philomel. 1st ed. VG/VG. P3. $15.00

YOLEN, Jane. *White Jenna.* 1989. NY. Tor. 1st ed. F/F. N3. $20.00

YONGE, Charlotte M. *Lances of Lynwood.* 1929. Macmillan. 1st ed. ils M DeAngeli. 217p. VG/dj. M20. $35.00

YONGE, James. *Journal of James Yonge (1647-1721), Plymouth Surgeon.* 1963. London. Longman Gr. 8vo. 247p. bl cloth. VG/worn. P4. $45.00

YOORS, Jan. *Gypsies.* 1967. Simon Schuster. 2nd prt. VG+/VG. C8. $15.00

YOORS, Jan. *Only One New York.* 1965. Simon Schuster. 1st ed. sgn/dtd 1965. VG. S9. $75.00

YORK, Andrew. *Captivator.* 1974. Crime Club. 1st ed. VG. P3. $10.00

YORK, Jeremy; see Creasey, John.

YORK, Thomas. *America's Great Railroads.* 1987. London. Bison. 4to. ils. 192p. F/F. B11. $20.00

YORKE, Margaret. *Come-On.* 1979. Harper. 1st ed. NF/NF. P3. $15.00

YORKE, Margaret. *Hand of Death.* 1981. St Martin. 1st ed. VG/VG. P3. $13.00

YOSHIMOTO, Banana. *Kitchen.* 1993. Grove. ARC/1st Am ed. F/wrp. B4. $45.00

YOST, Edna. *American Women of Science.* 1943. Phil. 1st ed. 232p. VG/dj. B18. $25.00

YOUATT, William. *Horse.* 1843. Phil. ils. rebound. VG. M17. $60.00

YOUNG, Barbara. *This Man From Lebanon: A Study of Kahlil Gibran.* 1961. Knopf. ils. 188p. VG/VG. B33. $20.00

YOUNG, Calvin M. *Little Turtle (Me-She-Kin-No-Quah): Great Chief of Miami...* 1917. np. 1st ed. 8vo. ils. 249p. G. B11. $45.00

YOUNG, Collier; see Bloch, Robert.

YOUNG, Edgerton R. *My Dogs in the Northland.* 1902. Revell. 1st ed. 285p. G+. R2. $60.00

YOUNG, Edward J. *My Servants the Prophets.* 1978. Eerdmans. 231p. VG. B29. $3.50

YOUNG, Ernest. *North American Excursion.* 1947. London. Edward Arnold. 1st ed. inscr. 302p. red cloth. F. P4. $25.00

YOUNG, Felicity. *Dorset Mysteries.* 1992. Cornwall. 2nd imp. 96p. pict sc. M7. $20.00

YOUNG, Hubert. *Independent Arab.* 1933. London. Murray. 1st ed. 3 fld maps. 346p. VG. M7. $125.00

YOUNG, J. Harvey. *Medical Messiahs: Social History of Health Quackery...* 1967. Princeton. 1st ed. 460p. A13. $50.00

YOUNG, J.Z. *Doubt & Certainty in Science.* 1950. BBC Reith Lectures. 163p. G/dj. K4. $10.00

YOUNG, J.Z. *Intro to the Study of Man.* 1971. Oxford. 719p. F/dj. K4. $30.00

YOUNG, James. *What Price Sex in Hollywood?* 1932. NY. 1st ed. VG/worn & tape rpr. A17. $12.50

YOUNG, John Sacret. *Weather Tomorrow.* 1981. Random. 1st ed/author's 1st novel. sgn. F/NF. B4. $100.00

YOUNG, John. *Thief of Dreams.* 1991. Viking. AP. F/wrp. B2. $30.00

YOUNG, Lot D. *Reminiscences of a Soldier in the Orphan Brigade.* 1922. Louisville, KY. Courier-Journal Job Prt Co. 1st ed. 99p. VG+/prt wrp. M8. $95.00

YOUNG, Louise B. *Earth's Aura.* 1977. Knopf. lg 8vo. photos. 305p. VG/dj. K5. $10.00

YOUNG, Lyman. *Pop-Up Tim Tyler in the Jungle.* 1935. Chicago. Pleasure Books. mechanical pop-up. NF. C8. $95.00

YOUNG, Marguerite. *Angel in the Forest.* 1966. London. Owen. 331p. F/dj. A10. $25.00

YOUNG, Mary Elizabeth. *Redskins, Ruffleshirts & Rednecks.* 1961. OK U. 1st ed. 217p. VG/tattered. M20. $25.00

YOUNG, Mrs. S. Glen. *Life & Exploits of S Glen Young.* 1924. Herrin, IL. 1st ed. VG. B5. $150.00

YOUNG, Pauline V. *Social Treatment in Probation & Delinquency.* 1952. NY. McGraw Hill. 2nd e. 518p. G/dj. K4. $10.00

YOUNG, Perry Deane. *God's Bullies: Power, Politics & Religious Tyranny.* 1982. HRW. 1st ed. 356p. VG/dj. B29. $7.50

YOUNG, Philip. *Ernest Hemingway.* 1952. NY. 1st ed/author's 1st book. inscr. VG+/VG. A11. $65.00

YOUNG, Robert W. *Political Hist of the Navajo Tribe.* 1978. Navajo Community College. 1st ed. ils. 174p. NF/sans. B19. $35.00

YOUNG, T. Cuyler. *Near Eastern Culture & Society.* 1951. Princeton. 1st ed. 8vo. 250p. cloth. dj. O2. $30.00

YOUNG, Waldemar. *Birds of Rhiannon.* 1930. Grabhorn. 1/1500. M/as issued. H4. $10.00

YOUNGSON, A.J. *Scientific Revolution in Victorian Medicine.* 1979. London. 1st ed. 237p. dj. A13. $22.50

YOUNT, John. *Trapper's Last Shot.* 1973. Random. 1st ed. NF/NF. B2. $30.00

YOUNT, John. *Wolf at the Door.* 1967. NY. 1st ed/author's 1st novel. sgn. F/NF clip. A11. $75.00

YOURCENAR, Marguerite. *Dark Brain of Piranesi & Other Essays.* 1984. FSG. 1st ed. F/F. S9. $40.00

YOUTZ, Philip Newell. *Journey by Ponycart From the Finger Lakes...* 1985. NY. Johnnycake. 75x65mm. 1/50. ils/sgn David Marshall. gilt goatskin. F. B24. $200.00

YU, Beongcheon. *Ape of Gods: The Art & Thought of Lafcadio Hearn.* 1964. Wayne State. 1st ed. 346p. VG/worn. A17. $15.00

YUILL, P.B.; see Williams, Gordon.

YUNGBLUT, John R. *Gentle Art of Spiritual Guidance.* 1991. Rockport, MA. Element. 12mo. pb. 148p. M. V3. $9.00

YURICK, Sol. *Richard A.* 1981. Arbor. 1st ed. F/F. F4. $18.00

YURICK, Sol. *Warriors.* 1965. HRW. 1st ed. VG/VG. P3. $35.00

YUSHINBO. *Tannisho.* 1989. Bijou Hoshino. 50x41mm. 1/50 (200 total). brd/gold plaque onlay. F/case/box. B24. $400.00

ZACCHI, Mario. *Neapolitan Mastiff.* 1987 (1983). Great Britain. LaMoye. 1st Eng-trans ed. 190p. cloth. M/dj. R2. $60.00

ZACHARIAS, Ellis M. *Behind Closed Doors: Secret Hist of the Cold War.* 1950. NY. 3rd imp. 367p. VG/worn. A17. $7.50

ZACKEL, Fred. *Cocaine & Blue Eyes.* 1978. CMG. 1st ed. VG/VG. P3. $20.00

ZAEHNSDORF, Joseph W. *Art of Bookbinding: A Practical Treatise.* 1900. London. Bell. ils/pl. gr cloth. VG. B14. $85.00

ZAFFO, George. *Big Book of Real Airplanes.* 1951. NY. ils. VG. M5. $25.00

ZAFFO, George. *Tommy on the Train.* 1946. Saalfield. F/VG. C8. $95.00

ZAHN, Timothy. *Cascade Point & Other Stories.* 1986. Bluejay. 1st ed. F/F. N3. $15.00

ZAHN, Timothy. *Dark Force Rising.* 1992. Bantam. 1st ed. VG/VG. P3. $19.00

ZAHN, Timothy. *Heir to the Empire.* 1991. Bantam. 1st ed. F/F. P3. $15.00

ZAIDENBERG, Arthur. *Emotional Self.* 1934. NY. Claude Kendall. 4to. ils. 105p. NF/dj. F1. $85.00

ZALCMAN, Moshe. *Joseph Epstein Alias Colonel Giles.* 1984. La Digitale. 1st ed. trans into French from Yiddish. F/wrp. B2. $40.00

ZALCMAN, Moshe. *Veridique Histoire de Moshe Ouvrier Juif et Communiste...* 1977. Fontenay-sous-Bois. Recherches. 1st ed. inscr. NF/wrp. B2. $40.00

ZANGWILL, Israel. *King of Schorees.* 1894. London. 1st ed. VG. M2. $75.00

ZARBIN, Earl A. *Roosevelt Dam: A Hist to 1911.* 1984. Salt River Project. 1st ed. ils/maps/index. 254p. F/F. B19. $50.00

ZEBROWSKI, George. *Macrolife.* 1979. Harper Row. 1st ed. F/F. P3. $15.00

ZEBROWSKI, George. *Macrolife.* 1979. Harper Row. 1st ed. sgn pres. 1/250. F/dj. M2. $30.00

ZEBROWSKI, George. *Sunspacer.* 1978. Harper Row. 1st ed. F/F. P3. $15.00

ZEISLER, Sigmund. *Reminiscences of the Anarchist Case.* 1927. Chicago Literary Club. 1st ed. NF/wrp. B2. $125.00

ZELAZNY, Roger. *Blood of Amber.* 1986. Arbor. 1st ed. F/F. P3. $20.00

ZELAZNY, Roger. *Blood of Amber.* 1986. Arbor. 1st ed. sgn. F/F. F4. $25.00

ZELAZNY, Roger. *Courts of Chaos.* 1978. Doubleday. 1st ed. F/F. P3. $35.00

ZELAZNY, Roger. *Eye of Cat.* 1982. Timescape. 1st ed. NF/NF. P3. $20.00

ZELAZNY, Roger. *Illustrated Roger Zelazny.* 1978. Baronet. 1st ed. sgn. F/sans. P3. $60.00

ZELAZNY, Roger. *Jack of Shadows.* 1971. Walker. 1st ed. VG/VG. P3. $45.00

ZELAZNY, Roger. *Roadmarks.* 1979. Del Rey. 1st ed. F/F. P3. $25.00

ZELAZNY, Roger. *Sign of Chaos.* 1987. Arbor. 1st ed. F/F. N3. $20.00

ZELAZNY, Roger. *Trumps of Doom.* 1985. Arbor. 1st ed. F/F. P3. $25.00

ZELAZNY, Roger. *Unicorn Variations.* 1983. Timescape. 1st ed. F/F. N3. $25.00

ZELL, Franz. *Bauren-Mobel & Dem Bayerischen Hochland.* 1899. Frankfurt. Heinrich Keller. folio. 30 loose pl in portfolio. VG. F1. $150.00

ZELLER, Eduard. *Aristotle & Earlier Peripatics...* 1897. Longman Gr. 2 vol. 1st English-language ed. 12mo. emb mauve cloth. G. G1. $75.00

ZELLER, Edward. *Socrates & the Socratic Schools.* 1877. London. Longman Gr. 408p. VG. B33. $50.00

ZELTZER, Moshe. *Aspects of Near East Society.* 1962. Bookman. 1st ed. 276p. cloth. VG. W1. $15.00

ZELUCO. *Various Views of Human Taken From Life & Manners.* 1790. NY. 2 vol. full leather. VG. E5. $35.00

ZEMACH, Harve. *Salt: A Russian Tale.* 1977 (1965). FSG. 1st ed thus. ils Margot Zemach. M/F. C8. $25.00

ZENKERT, Charles A. *Flora of the Niagara Frontier Region.* 1934. Buffalo. photos/fld mc map. 328p. cloth. B26. $24.00

ZERBI, Gabriele. *Gerontocomia: On Care of Aged & Maximanius...* 1988. Phil. 1st ed. trans LR Lind. 346p. A13. $40.00

ZERLENTOS, Perikleous. *Letters of the Western Dukes of the Aegean 1438-1565.* 1985. Athens. 8vo. 126p. w/prt card. O2. $12.00

ZERVOS, Christian. *L'Art de la Crete Neolithique et Minoenne.* 1956. Paris. Cahiers d'Art. folio. ils/photos. 524p. NF/dj. F1. $95.00

ZERVOS, Christian. *L'Art de la Mosopotamie.* 1935. Paris. Cahiers D'Art. lg 4to. rebound. xl. A17. $40.00

ZHDANOV, Aleksandr I. *Shadow of Peril.* 1963. Doubleday. 1st ed. VG/VG. P3. $25.00

ZIEGLER, Ernest. *Text-Book of General Anatomy & Pathogenesis...* 1883. NY. Wood Lib ed. 117 woodcuts. 370p. G7. $45.00

ZIEGLER, Philip. *Omdurman.* 1974. Knopf. 1st Am ed. 240p. NF/dj. W1. $30.00

ZIEMANN, Hans Heinrich. *Accident.* 1979. St Martin. 1st ed. F/F. P3. $15.00

ZIEMER, Gregor. *Education for Death: Making of the Nazi.* 1943 (1941). London. 5th prt. 209p. VG. A17. $6.50

ZIENKOWICZ, Leon. *Les Costumes du Peuple Polonais...* 1841. Paris. Polonaise. lg 4to. 39 pl. 2 leaves lithographed music. red calf. K1. $2,500.00

ZIEROLD, Norman. *Skyscraper Doom.* 1972. Lenox Hill. 1st ed. F/NF. N3. $10.00

ZIESING, Mark V. *Mark V Ziesing Bibliography 1982-1993.* 1993. Royal Oak/Mission Viejo. 1st ed. 1/200 #d. sgn all contributors. F/wrp. T2. $12.00

ZIFF, William B. *Coming Battle of Germany.* 1942. NY. biblio. 280p. VG. A17. $7.50

ZIGROSSER, Carl. *Ars Medica: Collection of Medical Prints...* 1959. Phil. 1st ed. 91p. wrp. A13. $25.00

ZIGROSSER, Carl. *Kaethe Kollwitz.* 1946. NY. Bittner. 1st ed. 4to. brn stp tan cloth. VG/VG. F1. $80.00

ZIM, Herbert S. *Comets.* 1957. NY. Morrow. 8vo. 64p. xl. dj. K5. $6.00

ZIM, Herbert S. *Rockets & Jets.* 1945. Harcourt Brace. 8vo. 326p. red cloth. G. K5. $45.00

ZIM, Jacob. *My Shalom, My Peace. Paintings & Poems...* 1975. McGraw Hill. 96p. NF/dj. W1. $10.00

ZIMMER, Henry. *Hindu Medicine.* 1948. Baltimore. 1st ed. 203p. xl. A13. $50.00

ZIMMERMAN, John Lee. *Where the People Sing: Green Land of the Maoris.* 1946. Knopf. 1st ed. 8vo. 234p. bl-gr cloth. VG/worn. P4. $25.00

ZIMROTH, Peter L. *Perversions of Justice.* 1974. Viking. 1st ed. NF/NF. B2. $25.00

ZINDEL, Paul. *Pigman.* 1968. Harper. 1st ed. F/NF. B2. $50.00

ZINDEL, Paul. *When Darkness Falls.* 1984. Bantam. VG/G. P3. $13.00

ZINN, Johann Gottried. *Descriptio Anatomica Oculi Humani.* 1755. Gottingen. Vandenhoeck. 1st ed. 7 fld engraved pl. 272p. calf. G7. $2,500.00

ZINSSER, William K. *Search & Research: Collections & Uses of NY Public Lib.* 1961. NY Pub Lib. 1st ed. 4to. ils. 46p. NF. M10. $12.50

ZIPES, Jack. *Spells of Enchantment.* nd. BC. VG/VG. P3. $15.00

ZOCHERT, Donald. *Man of Glass.* 1981. HRW. 1st ed. VG/VG. P3. $13.00

ZOLA, Emile. *Stories for Ninon.* 1898. NY. GH Richmond. NF. A9. $30.00

ZOLOTAREV, V.A. *Russko-Turetskaia Voina, 1877-1878...* 1978. Moscow. Nauka. 1st ed. sm 8vo. VG/wrp. W1. $10.00

ZOLOTOW, Charlotte. *It's Not Fair.* 1976. Harper. 1st ed. ils Wm Pene Du Bois. M/M. C8. $40.00

ZOLOTOW, Charlotte. *Someone New.* 1978. Harper. 1st ed. ils Eric Belgvad. NF/NF. C8. $30.00

ZOLOTOW, Maurice. *It Takes All Kinds.* 1952. Random. 1st prt. VG/VG. C8. $30.00

ZOMLEFER, Wendy B. *Guide to Flowering Plant Families.* 1994. Chapel Hill. ils. 430p. sc. M. B26. $27.50

ZONIS, Marvin. *Majestic Failure.* 1991. Chicago. 1st ed. 350p. NF/dj. W1. $25.00

ZOSS, Joel. *Greatest Moments in Baseball.* 1987. Bison Books. 1st ed. VG/VG. P3. $10.00

ZUALDI, Felix. *Sacred Ceremonies of Low Mass...* 1911. NY. Benziger. 207p. H10. $15.00

ZUBRO, Mark Richard. *Simple Suburban Murder.* 1990. St Martin. 1st ed. F/VG+. P8. $20.00

ZUCHMAYER, Carl. *Carnival Confession.* 1961. Methuen. 1st ed. VG/VG. P3. $20.00

ZUCKERMAN, Solly. *Functional Affinities of Man, Monkeys & Apes...* 1933. London. 1st ed. 24 pl/11 tables. 203p. NF/dj. G7. $95.00

ZUGSMITH, Leane. *All Victories Are Alike.* 1929. Payson Clarke. 1st ed. F. B2. $35.00

ZULLIGER, Hans. *Einfuhrung in Den Behn-Rorschach-Test.* 1946. Hans Huber. 320p. reading copy. K4. $40.00

ZUMWALT, Elmo R. Jr. *On Watch.* 1976. NY. 1st ed. photos/maps/index. 568p. VG/tape rpr. A17. $10.00

ZUROY, Michael. *Second Death.* 1992. Walker. 1st ed. F/F. P3. $20.00

ZUSNE, Leonard. *Names in the Hist of Psychology: Biographical Source Book.* 1975. Hemisphere Pub. 489p. F/dj. K4. $25.00

ZUURDEEG, Willem F. *Analytical Philosophy of Religion.* 1958. NY. Abingdon. 320p. VG/worn. G1. $25.00

ZWEMER, S.M. *Arabia: Cradle of Islam.* 1900. NY. 8vo. 434p. pict cloth. O2. $55.00

ZWEMER, S.M. *Cross Above the Crescent.* 1941. Grand Rapids. 8vo. 292p. cloth. dj. O2. $30.00

ZWEMER, S.M. *Islam: Challenge to Faith.* 1907. NY. 1st ed. 8vo. ils/maps/fld charts. 295p. cloth. O2. $75.00

ZWINGER, Ann Haymond. *John Xantus: Fort Tejon Letters 1857-1859.* 1986. AZ U. 1st ed. ils/notes. 255p. F/F. B19. $35.00

ZWINGER, Ann Haymond. *John Xantus: Fort Tejon Letters 1857-1859.* 1986. Tucson. AZ U. 1st ed. F/NF. B3. $30.00

ZWINGER, Ann Haymond. *Mysterious Land: Naturalist Explores 4 Great Deserts...* 1989. Dutton. 1st ed. ils/notes/index. 388p. F/F. B19. $35.00

ZWINGER, Ann Haymond. *Run, River, Run: A Naturalist's Journey...* 1984. AZ U. ils/notes/index. 317p. F/wrp. B19. $15.00

ZWINGER, Ann Haymond. *Wind in the Rock.* 1978. Harper Row. 1st ed. sgn. F/NF. B3. $30.00

PSEUDONYMS

Listed below are pseudonyms of many paperback and hardcover authors. This information was shared with us by some of our many contributors, and we offer it here as a reference for our readers. This section is organized alphabetically by the author's actual name (given in bold) followed by the pseudonyms he or she has been known to use. (It is interesting to note that 'house names' were common with more than one author using the same name for a particular magazine or publishing house.)

If you have additional information (or corrections), please let us hear from you so we can expand this section in future editions.

Aarons, Edward S.
Ayres, Paul; Ronns, Edward

Albert, Marvin H.
Conroy, Albert;
Jason, Stuart; Quarry, Nick;
Rome, Anthony

Ard, William
Kerr, Ben; Ward, Jonas (some)

Auster, Paul
Benjamin, Paul

Avallone, Mike
Carter, Nick (a few);
Conway, Troy (a few); Dalton, Priscilla;
Jason, Stuart; Noone, Edwina;
Stuart, Sidney; Walker, Max

Ballard, W.T.
Hunter, D'Allard; MacNeil, Neil;
Shepherd, John

Ballinger, Bill
Sanborn, B.X.

Barnard, Robert
Bastable, Bernard

Barnes, Julian
Kavanagh, Dan; Seal, Basil

Blake, Roger
Sade, Mark

Blassingame, Lurton
Duncan, Peter

Beaumont, Charles
Grantland, Keith

Beck, Robert
Iceberg Slim

Bedford-Jones, H.
Feval, Paul; Pemjion, L.

Bloch, Robert
Young, Collier

Block, Lawrence
Ard, William; Emerson, Jill;
Harrison, Chip; Lord, Sheldon;
Morse, Benjamin, M.D.; Shaw, Andrew

Bradley, Marion Zimmer
Chapman, Lee; Dexter, John (some);
Gardner, Miriam; Graves, Valerie;
Ives, Morgan

Brunner, John
Woodcott, Keith

Bulmer, Kenneth
Hardy, Adam; Norvil, Manning;
Prescot, Dray

Burnett, W.R.
Monachan, John; Updyke, James

Burroughs, William S.
Lee, William

Byrne, Stuart
Bloodstone, John

Cain, Paul
Sims, George

Campbell, Ramsey
Dreadstone, Carl; Ramsay, Jay

Carr, John Dickson
Dickson, Carter; Fairbairn, Roger

Cooper, Basil
Falk, Lee

Cooper, Clarence
Chestnut, Robert

Creasey, John
Ashe, Gordon; Carmichael, Harry;
Deane, Norman; Frazier, Robert Caine;
Gill, Patrick; Holliday, Michael;
Hope, Brian; Hughes, Colin; Hunt, Kyle;
Marric, J.J.; York, Jeremy

Crichton, Michael
Lange, John

Cross, David
Chesbro, George B.

Daniels, Norman
Daniels, Dorothy; Wade, David

Davidson, Avram
Queen, Ellery (about 2 titles only)

Derleth, August
Grendon, Stephen

Dewey, Thomas B.
Brandt, Tom; Wainer, Cord

Disch, Thomas
Demijohn, Thomas;
Cassandra, Knye (both with John Sladek)

Ellis, Peter
Tremayne, Peter

Ellison, Harlan
Merchant, Paul

Etchison, Dennis
Martin, Jack

Fairman, Paul
Paul, F.W.

Fanthorpe, Lionel
Muller, John E.

Farmer, Philip Jose
Norfolk, William; Trout, Kilgore

Fearn, John Russell
Del Martia, Aston

Foster, Alan Dean
Lucas, George

Fox, Gardner F.
Chase, Glen; Cooper, Jefferson;
Gardner, Jeffrey; Gardner, Matt;
Gray, James Kendricks; Jennings, Dean;
Majors, Simon; Matthews, Kevin;
Morgan, John Medford; Morgan, Rod;
Summers, Bart

Gardner, Erle Stanley
Fair, A.A.; Kendrake, Carleton;
Kinney, Charles

Garrett, Randall
Bupp, Walter; Gordon, David;
1/2 of Mark Phillips and Robert Randall

Geis, Richard
Owen, Robert; Swenson, Peggy

Geisel, Theodor Seuss
Dr. Seuss

Gibson, Walter B.
Brown, Douglas; Grant, Maxwell

Goulart, Ron
Falk, Lee; Kains, Josephine;
Kearney, Julian; Robeson, Kenneth;
Shaw(n), Frank S.; Silva, Joseph

Grant, Charles L.
Andrew, Felicia; Lewis, Deborah

Haas, Ben
Meade, Richard

Haldeman, Joe
Graham, Robert

Hall, Oakley
Hall, O.M.

Halliday, Brett
Shayne, Mike

Hansen, Joseph
Brock, Rose; Colton, James

Harknett, Terry
Hedges, Joseph; Stone, Thomas H.

Harris, Timothy
Hyde, Harris

Highwater, Jamake
Marks, J.; Marks-Highwater, J.

Hochstein, Peter
Short, Jack

Hodder-Williams, C.
Brogan, James

Holt, John Robert
Giles, Elizabeth; Giles, Raymond

Hunt, E. Howard
St. John, David

Hunter, Evan
Cannon, Curt; Collins, Hunt;
Hannon, Ezra; Marsten, Richard;
McBain, Ed

Jacks, Oliver
Gandley, Kenneth R.

Jakes, John
Ard, William; Payne, Alan; Scotland, Jay

Jenkins, Will F.
Leinster, Murray

Jones, H. Bedford
Pemjean, Lucien

Kane, Frank
Boyd, Frank

Kane, Henry
McCall, Anthony

Kavanagh, Dan
Barnes, Julian

Kent, Hal
Davis, Ron

King, Stephen
Bachman, Richard

Klass, Philip
Tenn, William

Knowles, William
Allison, Clyde; Ames, Clyde

Koontz, Dean R.
Axton, David; Coffey, Brian;
Dwyer, Deanna; Dwyer, K.R.; Hill, John;
Nichols, Leigh; North, Anthony;
Paige, Richard; West, Owen; Wolfe, Aaron

Kornbluth, Cyril
Eisner, Simon; Park, Jordan

Kosinski, Jerzy
Somers, Jane

Kubis, P.
Scott, Casey

Kurland, Michael
Plum, Jennifer

L'Amour, Louis
Burns, Tex; Mayo, Jim

Lariar, Lawrence
Knight, Adam

Laumer, Keith
LeBaron, Anthony

Lesser, Milton
Marlowe, Stephen

Lessing, Doris
Somers, Jane

Lewis, Alfred Henry
Quinn, Dan

Linebarger, Paul
Smith, Cordwainer

Long, Frank Belknap
Long, Lydia Belknap

Lovesey, Peter
Lear, Peter

Lucas, Mark
Palmer, Drew

Ludlum, Robert
Ryder, Jonathan; Shepherd, Michael

Lupoff, Richard
Steele, Adison

Lynds, Dennis
Collins, Michael; Crowe, John;
Grant, Maxwell (some); Sadler, Mark

Malzberg, Barry
Berry, Mike; Dumas, Claudine;
Johnson, Mel; Johnson, M.L.;
O'Donnell, Barrett; O'Donnell, K.M.

Manfred, Frederick
Feikema, Feike

Marshall, Mel
Tayler, Zack

Martin, Robert
Roberts, Lee

Mason, Van Wyck
Coffin, Geoffrey

Masterton, Graham
Luke, Thomas

Matheson, Richard
Swanson, Logan

McGaughy, Dudley
Owen, Dean

Meaker, Marijane
Aldrich, Ann;
Packer, Vin

Menken, H.L.
Hatteras, Owen

Mertz, Barbara Gross
Michael, Barbara; Peters, Elizabeth

Millar, Kenneth
MacDonald, Ross; MacDonald, John Ross

Moorcock, Michael
Bradbury, Edward P.; Barclay, Bill

Moore, Brian
Michael, Bryan; Mara, Bernard

Morris, James
Morris, Jan (after sex change)

Nasby, Petroleum
Locke, David R.

Norton, Andre Alice
North, Andrew; Norton, Alice;
Norton, Andre

Nuetzel, Charles
Augustus, Albert Jr.; Davidson, John;
English, Charles; Rivere, Alec

Oates, Joyce Carol
Smith, Rosamond

Offutt, Andrew
Cleve, John; Giles, Baxter;
Williams, J.X. (some)

Pargeter, Edith Mary
Peter, Ellis

Patterson, Henry
Fallon, Martin; Graham, James;
Higgins, Jack; Patterson, Harry;
Marlowe, Hugh

Philips, James Atlee
Atlee, Philip

Phillips, Dennis
Chambers, Peter; Chester, Peter

Phillips, Judson
Pentecost, Hugh

Posner, Richard
Foster, Iris; Murray, Beatrice; Todd, Paul

Prather, Richard
Knight, David; Ring, Douglas

Pronzini, Bill
Foxx, Jack

Rabe, Peter
MacCargo, J.T.

Radford, R.L.
Ford, Marcia

Rawson, Clayton
Towne, Stuart

Rendell, Ruth
Vine, Barbara

Reynolds, Mack
Belmont, Bob; Harding, Todd;
Reynolds, Maxine

Rice, Anne
Rampling, Anne; Roquelaure, A.N.

Rosenblum, Robert
Maxxe, Robert

Ross, W.E.D.
Dana, Rose; Daniels, Jan;
Ross, Clarissa; Ross, Dan; Ross, Dana;
Ross, Marilyn

Rossi, Jean-Baptiste
Japrisot, Sebastien

Sellers, Con
Bannion, Della

Sheldon, Alice Bradley
Bradley, Alice; Sheldon, Raccoona;
Tiptree, James

Silverberg, Robert
Beauchamp, Loren;
Burnett, W.R. (some only);
Drummond, Walter; Elliott, Don (some);
Ford, Hilary; Hamilton, Franklin;
Knox, Calvin; Lt. Woodard, M.D.

Smith, George H.
Deer, J.M.; Hudson, Jan; Jason, Jerry;
Knerr, M.E.; Summers, Diana

Stacton, David
Clifton, Bud

Sturgeon, Theodore
Ewing, Frederick R.;
Ellery Queen (1 book only)

Thomas, Ross
Bleeck, Oliver

Tracy, Don
Fuller, Roger

Tralins, Bob
Miles, Keith; O'Shea, Sean

Tubb, E.C.
Kern, Gregory

Vance, Jack
Held, Peter; Queen, Ellery (some/few)

Vidal, Gore
Box, Edgar

Wager, Walter
Tiger, John; Walker, Max

Ward, Harold
Zorro

Webb, Jack
Farr, John

Weiss, Joe
Anatole, Ray; Dauphine, Claude;
Mirbeau, Ken

Westlake, Donald E.
Allan, John B.; Clark, Curt;
Culver, Timothy; Cunningham, J. Morgan;
Holt, Samuel; Marshall, Alan;
Stark, Richard; West, Edwin

Williams, Gordon
Yuill, P.B

Whittington, Harry
Harrison, Whit; Shepherd, Shep

Williamson, Jack
Stewart, Will

Wollheim, Don
Grinnell, David

Woolrich, Cornell
Hopley, George; Irish, William

Worts, George F.
Brent, Loring

BOOKBUYERS

In this section of the book we have listed buyers of books and related material. When you correspond with these dealers, be sure to enclose a self-addressed stamped envelope if you want a reply. Do not send lists of books for appraisal. If you wish to sell your books, quote the price you want or send a list and ask if there are any on the list they might be interested in and the price they would be willing to pay. If you want the list back, be sure to send a SASE large enough for the listing to be returned. When you list your books, do so by author, full title, publisher and place, date, edition, and condition, noting any defects on cover or contents.

Advance Review Copies
Paperbacks
The American Dust Co.
47 Park Ct.
Staten Island, NY 10301
718-442-8253

Adventure
The Silver Door
P.O. Box 3208
Redondo Beach, CA 90277
310-379-6005

African-American
Children's Book Adoption Agency
P.O. Box 643
Kensington, MD 20895-0643
310-565-2834 or Fax 301-585-3091

Fran's Bookhouse
6601 Greene St.
Phil., PA 19119
215-438-2729 or Fax 215-438-8997

Alaska
Artis Books
201 N Second Ave.
P.O. Box 822
Alpena, MI 49707
517-354-3401

Albania
W.B. O'Neill-Old & Rare Books
11609 Hunters Green Ct.
Reston, VA 22091
703-860-0782 or Fax 703-620-0153

Alcoholics Anonymous
The Book Baron
1236 S Magnolia Ave.
Anaheim, CA 92804
714-527-7022 or Fax 714-527-5634

1939-1954
Paul Melzer Fine Books
12 E Vine St.
Redlands, CA 92373
902-792-7299

Americana
Amaranth Books
P.O. Box 421
Wilmette, IL 60091-0421
708-328-2939

The Book Inn
6401 University
Lubbock, TX 79413

The Bookseller, Inc.
521 W Exchange St.
Akron, OH 44302
216-762-3101

Bowie & Co. Booksellers, Inc.
314 First Ave. S
Seattle, WA 98104
206-624-4100 or Fax 206-223-0966

Woodbridge B. Brown
P.O. Box 445
Turners Falls, MA 01376
413-772-2509 or 413-773-5710

The Captain's Bookshelf, Inc.
P.O. Box 2258
Asheville, NC 28802-2258
704-253-6631

Chapel Hill Rare Books
P.O. Box 456
Carrboro, NC 27510
919-929-8351

Duck Creek Books
Jim & Shirley Richards
P.O. Box 203
Caldwell, OH 43724
614-732-4856 (10 am to 10 pm)

Terry Harper, Bookseller
P.O. Box 312
Vergennes, VT 05491-0312
802-877-9262

Susan Heller, Pages for Sages
22611 Halburton Rd.
Beachwood, OH 44122-3939
216-283-2665 or Fax 216-991-2665

Jim Hodgson Books
908 S Manlius St.
Fayetteville, NY 13066
315-637-6264

M & S Rare Books, Inc.
P.O. Box 2594, E Side Sta.
Providence, RI 02906
401-421-1050 or Fax 401-272-0831
(attention M & S)

Parmer Books
7644 Forrestal Rd.
San Diego, CA 92120-2203
619-287-0693 or Fax 619-287-6135
Internet: ParmerBook@aol.com

Randall House
835 Laguna St.
Santa Barbara, CA 93101
805-963-1909 or Fax 805-963-1650

18th & 19th C
Gordon Totty
Scarce Paper Americana
347 Shady Lake Pky.
Baton Rouge, LA 70810
504-766-8625

Yesterday's Books
229 Riverview Dr.
Parchment, MI 49004
616-345-1011

Anarchism
Nutmeg Books
354 New Litchfield St. (Rte. 202)
Torrington, CT 06790
203-482-9696

Angling
Book & Tackle Shop
29 Old Colony Rd.
P.O. Box 114
Chestnut Hill, MA 02167
617-965-0459 (winter) or
401-596-0700 (summer)

Anthropology
The King's Market Booksellers
P.O. Box 709
Boulder, CO 80306-0709
303-447-0234

Anthologies

Cartoonists from 1890-1960
Craig Ehlenberger
Abalone Cove Rare Books
7 Fruit Tree Rd.
Portuguese Bend, CA 90275

Antiquarian

A.B.A.C.U.S.®
Phillip E. Miller
343 S Chesterfield St.
Aiken, SC 29801
803-648-4632

Antiquarian Book Arcade
110 W 25th St., 9th Floor
New York, NY 10001

Fine & hard-to-find books
Arnold's of Michigan
511 S Union St.
Traverse City, MI 49684

The Book Baron
1236 S Magnolia Ave.
Anaheim, CA 92804
714-527-7022 or Fax 714-527-5634

Pre-1900 leatherbound, any subject
Arthur Boutiette
410 W 3rd St., Ste. 200
Little Rock, AR 72201

Bowie & Co. Booksellers, Inc.
314 First Ave. S
Seattle, WA 98104
206-624-4100 or Fax 206-223-0966

Children's Book Adoption Agency
P.O. Box 643
Kensington, MD 20895-0643
310-565-2834 or Fax 301-585-3091

Terry Harper, Bookseller
P.O. Box 312
Vergennes, VT 05491-0312
802-877-9262

Murray Hudson
Antiquarian Books & Maps
The Old Post Office
109 S Church St.
P.O. Box 163
Halls, TN 38040
901-836-9057 or 800-748-9946

Jeffrey Lee Pressman, Bookseller
3246 Ettie St.
Oakland, CA 94608
510-652-6232

Robert Mueller Rare Books
8124 W 26th St.
N Riverside, IL 60546
708-447-6441

Scribe Company
Attn: Bonnie Smith
P.O. Box 1123
Flippin, AR 72634

Printed before 1800
Gordon Totty
Scarce Paper Americana
347 Shady Lake Pky.
Baton Rouge, LA 70810
504-766-8625

Antiques & Reference

Antique & Collectors Reproduction News
Box 17774-OB
Des Moines, IA 50325
515-270-8994

Bohemian Bookworm
110 W 25th St., 9th Floor
New York, NY 10001
212-620-5627

Collector's Companion
Perry Franks
P.O. Box 24333
Richmond, VA 23224

Galerie De Boicourt
6136 Westbrooke Dr.
W Bloomfield, MI 48322
810-788-9253

Henry H. Hain III
Antiques & Collectibles
2623 N Second St.
Harrisburg, PA 17110
717-238-0534

Appraisals

J. Sampson Antiques & Books
107 S Main
Harrodsburg, KY 40330
606-734-7829

Lee & Mike Temares
50 Hts. Rd.
Plandome, NY 11030
516-627-8688

Arabian Horses

Worldwide Antiquarian
P.O. Box 391
Cambridge, MA 02141
617-876-6220 or Fax 617-876-0939

The Arabian Nights

Worldwide Antiquarian
P.O. Box 391
Cambridge, MA 02141
617-876-6220 or Fax 617-876-0939

Archaelogy

Flo Silver Books
8442 Oakwood Ct. N
Indianapolis, IN 46260
317-255-5118

Architecture

Cover to Cover
P.O. Box 687
Chapel Hill, NC 27514

Armenia

W.B. O'Neill-Old & Rare Books
11609 Hunters Green Ct.
Reston, VA 22091
703-860-0782 or Fax 703-620-0153

Art

AL-PAC
Lamar Kelley Antiquarian Books
2625 E Southern Ave., C-120
Tempe, AZ 85282
602-831-3121 or Fax 602-831-3193

Bohemian Bookworm
110 W 25th St., 9th Floor
New York, NY 10001
212-620-5627

Book & Tackle Shop
29 Old Colony Rd.
P.O. Box 114
Chestnut Hill, MA 02167
617-965-0459 (winter) or
401-596-0700 (summer)

Books West Southwest
J.E. Reynolds, Bookseller
2452 N Campbell Ave.
Tucson, AZ 85719
602-326-3533

The Captain's Bookshelf, Inc.
P.O. Box 2258
Asheville, NC 28802-2258
704-253-6631

Fine & applied
L. Clarice Davis Art Books
P.O. Box 56054
Sherman Oaks, CA 91413-1054
818-787-1322

Galerie De Boicourt
6136 Westbrooke Dr.
W Bloomfield, MI 48322
810-788-9253

Edison Hall Books
5 Ventnor Dr.
Edison, NJ 08820
908-548-4455

Heritage Book Shop, Inc.
8540 Melrose Ave.
Los Angeles, CA 90069
213-659-3674

David Holloway, Bookseller
7430 Grace St.
Springfield, VA 22150
703-659-1798

Significant Books
3053 Madison Rd.
P.O. Box 9248
Cincinnati, OH 45209
513-321-7567

Lee & Mike Temares
50 Hts. Rd.
Plandome, NY 11030
516-627-8688

Xanadu Records, Ltd.
3242 Irwin Ave.
Kingsbridge, NY 10463
212-549-3655

Arctic
Artis Books
201 N Second Ave.
P.O. Box 822
Alpena, MI 49707
517-354-3401

Parmer Books
7644 Forrestal Rd.
San Diego, CA 92120-2203
619-287-0693 or Fax 619-287-6135
Internet: ParmerBook@aol.com

Arthurian
Camelot Books
Charles E. Wyatt
P.O. Box 2883
Vista, CA 92083
619-940-9472

Astronomy
Knollwood Books
Lee & Peggy Price
P.O. Box 197
Oregon, WI 53575
608-835-8861 or Fax 608-835-8421

Atlases
Murray Hudson
Antiquarian Books & Maps
The Old Post Office
109 S Church St.
P.O. Box 163
Halls, TN 38040
901-836-9057 or 800-748-9946

Before 1870
Gordon Totty
Scarce Paper Americana
347 Shady Lake Pky.
Baton Rouge, LA 70810
504-766-8625

Atomic Bomb
Key Books
P.O. Box 58097
St. Petersburg, FL 33715
813-867-2931

Autobiography
Wellerdt's Books
3700 S Osprey Ave. #214
Sarasota, FL 34239
813-365-1318

Autographs
Ads Autographs
P.O. Box 8006
Webster, NY 14580
716-671-2651

Michael Gerlicher
1375 Rest Point Rd.
Orono, MN 55364

Susan Heller, Pages for Sages
22611 Halburton Rd.
Beachwood, OH 44122-3939
216-283-2665 or Fax 216-991-2665

Heritage Book Shop, Inc.
8540 Melrose Ave.
Los Angeles, CA 90069
213-659-3674

Key Books
P.O. Box 58097
St. Petersburg, FL 33715
813-867-2931

McGowan Book Co.
P.O. Box 16325
Chapel Hill, NC 27516
919-968-1121 or Fax 919-968-1169

Paul Melzer Fine Books
12 E Vine St.
Redlands, CA 92373
909-792-7299

Randall House
835 Laguna St.
Santa Barbara, CA 93101
805-963-1909 or Fax 805-963-1650

Autobiographies
Herb Sauermann
21660 School Rd.
Manton, CA 96059

Aviation
The Bookseller, Inc.
521 W Exchange St.
Akron, OH 44302
216-762-3101

Cover to Cover
P.O. Box 687
Chapel Hill, NC 27514

Baedeker Handbooks
W.B. O'Neill-Old & Rare Books
11609 Hunters Green Ct.
Reston, VA 22091
703-860-0782 or Fax 703-620-0153

Baseball
Brasser's
8701 Seminole Blvd.
Seminole, FL 34642

R. Plapinger, Baseball Books
P.O. Box 1062
Ashland, OR 87520
503-488-1200

Bibliography
About Books
6 Sand Hill Ct.
P.O. Box 5717
Parsippany, NJ 07054
201-515-4591

Books West Southwest
J.E. Reynolds, Bookseller
2452 N Campbell Ave.
Tucson, AZ 85719
602-326-3533

Big Little Books
Jay's House of Collectibles
75 Pky. Dr.
Syosset, NY 11791

Biographies
Herb Sauermann
21660 School Rd.
Manton, CA 96059

Black Americana
A\K\A Fine Used Books
4142 Brooklyn Ave., NE
Seattle, WA 98107
206-632-5870

History & literature
David Holloway, Bookseller
7430 Grace St.
Springfield, VA 22150
703-569-1798

Mason's Bookstore, Rare Books
& Record Albums
115 S Main St.
Chambersburg, PA 17201
717-261-0541

Black Fiction & Literature
Almark & Co.-Booksellers
P.O. Box 7
Thornhill, Ontario
Canada L3T 3N1
phone/Fax 905-764-2665

Black Hills
James F. Taylor
515 Sixth St.
Rapid City, SD 57701
605-341-3224

Book Search Service
Authors of the West
191 Dogwood Dr.
Dundee, OR 97115
503-538-8132

Avonlea Books
P.O. Box 74, Main Station
White Plains, NY 10602
914-946-5923

Bookingham Palace
Rosan Van Wagenen &
Eileen Layman
52 North 2500 East
Teton, ID 83451
209-458-4431

Heritage Book Shop, Inc.
8540 Melrose Ave.
Los Angeles, CA 90069
310-659-3674 or Fax 310-659-4872

Hilda's Book Search
Hilda Gruskin
199 Rollins Ave.
Rockville, MD 20852
301-948-3181

Passaic Book Center
594 Main Ave.
Passaic, NJ 07055
201-778-6646 or Fax 201-778-6738

The Silver Door
P.O. Box 3208
Redondo Beach, CA 90277
310-379-6005

Especially children's out-of-print books
Treasures from the Castle
Connie Castle
1720 N Livernois
Rochester, MI 48306
810-651-7317

Books About Books
About Books
6 Sand Hill Ct.
P.O. Box 5717
Parsippany, NJ 07054
201-515-4591

Books West Southwest
J.E. Reynolds, Bookseller
2452 N Campbell Ave.
Tucson, AZ 85719
602-326-3533

Bowie & Co. Booksellers, Inc.
314 First Ave. S
Seattle, WA 98104
206-624-4100 or Fax 206-223-0966

First Folio
1206 Brentwood
Paris, TN 38242
phone/Fax 901-644-9940

Susan Heller, Pages for Sages
22611 Halburton Rd.
Beachwood, OH 44122-3939
216-283-2665 or Fax 216-991-2665

Key Books
P.O. Box 58097
St. Petersburg, FL 33715
813-867-2931

Randall House
835 Laguna St.
Santa Barbara, CA 93101
805-963-1909 or Fax 805-963-1650

George H. Tweney
16660 Marine View Dr. SW
Seattle, WA 98166
206-243-8243

Botany
Brooks Books
Philip B. Nesty
P.O. Box 21473
1343 New Hampshire Dr.
Concord, CA 94521
510-672-4566 or Fax 510-672-3338

Bottles
Homebiz Books & More
2919 Mistwood Forest Dr.
Chester, VA 23831-7043

Breweries of Germany
Mike Geffers
1615 Doty St.
Oshkosh, WI 54901

Charles Bukowski
Ed Smith Books
P.O. Box 66
Oak View, CA 93022
805-649-2844 or FAX 805-649-2863
email: EdsBooks@aol.com

California
Books West Southwest
J.E. Reynolds, Bookseller
2452 N Campbell Ave.
Tucson, AZ 85719

Paul Melzer Fine Books
12 E Vine St.
Redlands, CA 92373
909-792-7299

Cartography
Overlee Farm Books
P.O. Box 1155
Stockbridge, MA 01262
413-637-2277

Cartoon Art
Jay's House of Collectibles
75 Pky. Dr.
Syosset, NY 11791

Catalogs
Glass, pottery, furniture, doll, toy, jewelry, general merchandise, fishing tackle
Bill Schroeder
P.O. Box 3009
Paducah, KY 42002-3009

Antiques or other collectibles
Antique & Collectors Reproduction News
Box 17774-OB
Des Moines, IA 50325
515-270-8994

Hillcrest Books
Rt. 3, Box 479
Crossville, TN 38555-9547
phone/Fax 615-484-7680

Celtic
Camelot Books
Charles E. Wyatt
P.O. Box 2883
Vista, CA 92083
619-940-9472

Central America
Flo Silver Books
8442 Oakwood Ct. N
Indianapolis, IN 46260
317-255-5118

Marc Chagall
Paul Melzer Fine Books
12 E Vine St.
Redlands, CA 92373
909-792-7299

Children's Illustrated
Noreen Abbot Books
2666 44th Ave.
San Francisco, CA 94116
415-664-9464

Book & Tackle Shop
29 Old Colony Rd.
P.O. Box 114
Chestnut Hill, MA 02167
617-965-0459 (winter) or
401-596-0700 (summer)

Books of the Ages
Gary Overmann
4764 Silverwood Dr.
Batavia, OH 45103
513-732-3456

Bromer Booksellers
607 Boylston St.
Boston, MA 02116
617-247-2818 or Fax 617-247-2975

Uncle Wiggily, circa 1912 – 1948
Audrey V. Buffington
2 Old Farm Rd.
Wayland, MA 01778
508-358-2644

19th & 20th C
Children's Book Adoption Agency
P.O. Box 643
Kensington, MD 20895-0643
301-565-2834 or Fax 301-585-3091

Ursula Davidson
Children's & Illustrated Books
134 Linden Ln.
San Rafael, CA 94901
414-454-3939 or Fax 415-454-1087

Drusilla's Books
859 N Howard St.
Baltimore, MD 21201
401-225-0277

Edison Hall Books
5 Ventnor Dr.
Edison, NJ 08820
908-548-4455

Circa 1850s through 1970s
Encino Books
Diane Yaspan
5063 Gaviota Ave
Encino, CA 91436
818-905-711 or Fax 818-501-7711

First Folio
1206 Brentwood
Paris, TN 38242
phone/Fax 901-644-9940

Fran's Bookhouse
6601 Greene St.
Phil., PA 19119
215-438-2729 or Fax 215-438-8997

Glo's Children's Series Books
906 Shadywood
Southlake, TX 76092

Susan Heller, Pages for Sages
22611 Halburton Rd.
Beachwood, OH 44122-3939
216-283-2665 or Fax 216-991-2665

Illustrated before 1940; also Uncle Wiggily, Raggedy Ann & Andy
Jacquie Henry
Antique Treasures & Toys
P.O. Box 17
2240 Academy St.
Walworth, NY 14568
315-968-1424

Especially by Raphael Tuck or McLoughlin Brothers
Melanie Hewitt
2101 Beechwood
Little Rock, AR 72202

Johnny Gruelle's Raggedy Ann
Carole Jemison
Rt. 1, Box 73
Wann, OK 74083
918-534-2129

Ilene Kayne
1308 S Charles St.
Baltimore, MD 21230

Bob Lakin
3021 Lavita Ln.
Dallas, TX 75234
214-247-3291

Marvelous Books
P.O. Box 1510
Ballwin, MO 63022
314-458-3301

Much Ado
Seven Pleasant St.
Marblehead, MA 01945
617-639-0400

Nerman's Books
410-63 Albert St.
Winnipeg, Manitoba
Canada R3B 1G4
Fax 204-947-0753

Page Books
HCR 65, Box 233
Kingston, AR 72472
501-861-5831

Jo Ann Reisler, Ltd.
360 Glyndon St., NE
Vienna, VA 22180
703-938-2967 or Fax 703-938-9057

Scribe Company
Attn: Bonnie Smith
P.O. Box 1123
Flippin, AR 72634

Barbara Smith Books
P.O. Box 1185
Northampton, MA 01061
413-586-1453

Nancy Stewart, Books
1188 NW Weybridge Way
Beaverton, OR 97006
503-645-9779

Yesterday's Books
229 Riverview Dr.
Parchment, MI 49004
616-345-1011

Treasures from the Castle
Connie Castle
1720 N Livernois
Rochester, MI 48306
810-651-7317

Children's Series
Bobbsey Twins
Audrey V. Buffington
2 Old Farm Rd.
Wayland, MA 01778
508-358-2644

Children's Book Adoption Agency
P.O. Box 643
Kensington, MD 20895-0643
301-565-2834 or Fax 301-585-3091

Circa 1900s through 1970s
Encino Books
Diane Yaspan
5063 Gaviota Ave
Encino, CA 91436
818-905-711 or Fax 818-501-7711

Ilene Kayne
1308 S Charles St.
Baltimore, MD 21230

Bob Lakin
3021 Lavita Ln.
Dallas, TX 75234
214-247-3291

Nerman's Books
410-63 Albert St.
Winnipeg, Manitoba
Canada R3B 1G4
Fax 204-947-0753

Scribe Company
Attn: Bonnie Smith
P.O. Box 1123
Flippin, AR 72634

Bob & Gail Spicer
R.D. 1 Ashgrove Rd., Box 82
Cambridge, NY 12816
518-677-5139

Gloria Stobbs
906 Shadywood
Southlake, TX 76092

Lee & Mike Temares
50 Hts. Rd.
Plandome, NY 11030
516-627-8688

Yesterday's Books
229 Riverview Dr.
Parchment, MI 49004
616-345-1011

Christian Faith
Books Now & Then
Dennis Patrick
P.O. Box 337
Stanley, ND 58784
701-628-2084

Christmas
Especially illustrated antiquarian
Drusilla's Books
859 N Howard St.
Baltimore, MD 21201
410-225-0277

Sir W.S. Churchill
Chartwell Booksellers
55 E 52nd St.
New York, NY 10055
212-308-0643

Robert L. Merriam
Rare, Used & Old Books
Newhall Rd.
Conway, MA 01341
413-369-4052

Cinema, Theatre & Films
Cinemage Books
105 W 27th St.
New York, NY 10001
212-243-4919

Xanadu Records, Ltd.
3242 Irwin Ave.
Kingsbridge, NY 10463
212-549-3655

Civil War
The Book Corner
Michael Tennero
728 W Lumsden Rd.
Brandon, FL 33511
813-684-1133

Brasser's
8701 Seminole Blvd.
Seminole, FL 34642

Chapel Hill Rare Books
P.O. Box 456
Carrboro, NC 27510
919-929-8351

Elder's Book Store
2115 Elliston Pl.
Nashville, TN 37203
615-327-1867

Rick Harmon
Military Books & Relics
910 Sullivan Dr.
Belvidere, IL 61008
815-547-7580

Jim Hodgson Books
908 S Manlius St.
Fayetteville, NY 13066
315-637-6264

Mason's Bookstore, Rare Books
& Record Albums
115 S Main St.
Chambersburg, PA 17201
717-261-0541

K.C. Owings
P.O. Box 19
N Abington, MA 02351
617-857-1655

Also ephemera before 1900
Gordon Totty
Scarce Paper Americana
347 Shady Lake Pky.
Baton Rouge, LA 70810
504-766-8625

Cobb, Irvin S.
Always paying $3.00 each plus shipping. Send for immediate payment:
Bill Schroeder
5801 KY Dam Rd.
Paducah, KY 42003

Collectibles
Henry H. Hain III
Antiques & Collectibles
2623 N Second St.
Harrisburg, PA 17110
717-238-0534

Color Plate Books
Bowie & Co. Booksellers, Inc.
314 First Ave. S
Seattle, WA 98104
206-624-4100 or Fax 206-223-0966

Drusilla's Books
859 N Howard St.
Baltimore, MD 21201
410-225-0277

Worldwide Antiquarian
P.O. Box 391
Cambridge, MA 02141
617-876-6220 or Fax 617-876-0839

Comics
Passaic Book Center
594 Main Ave.
Passaic, NJ 07055
201-778-6646 or Fax 201-778-6738

Cookery & Cookbooks
Book & Tackle Shop
29 Old Colony Rd.
P.O. Box 114
Chestnut Hill, MA 02167
617-965-0459 (winter) or
401-596-0700 (summer)

The Book Corner
Mike Tennero
728 W Lumsden Rd.
Brandon, FL 33511
813-684-1133

RAC Books
R.R. #2
P.O. Box 296
Seven Valleys, PA 17360
717-428-3776

Barbara Smith Books
P.O. Box 1185
Northampton, MA 01061
413-586-1453

Crime
The Silver Door
P.O. Box 3208
Redondo Beach, CA 90277
310-379-6005

Cyprus
W.B. O'Neill-Old & Rare Books
11609 Hunters Green Ct.
Reston, VA 22091
703-860-0782 or Fax 703-620-0153

Decorative Arts
Robert L. Merriam
Rare, Used & Old Books
Newhall Rd.
Conway, MA 01341
413-369-4052

Detective
First editions
Karl M. Armens
740 Juniper Dr.
Iowa City, IA 52245

Mordida Books
P.O. Box 79322
Houston, TX 77279
713-467-4280 or Fax 713-467-4182

Roman Noir
440 E 79th St. #16B
New York City, NY 10021
212-737-8004 or Fax 212-737-3743

Thomas Books
P.O. Box 14036
Phoenix, AZ 85063
602-247-9289

The Silver Door
P.O. Box 3208
Redondo Beach, CA 90277
310-379-6005

Charles Dickens
Harold B. Diamond
Box 1193
Burbank, CA 19507
818-846-0342

Emily Dickinson
Robert L. Merriam
Rare, Used & Old Books
Newhall Rd.
Conway, MA 01341
413-369-4052

Disney
Cohen Books & Collectibles
Joel J. Cohen
P.O. Box 810310
Boca Raton, FL 33481
407-487-7888

Jay's House of Collectibles
75 Pky. Dr.
Syosset, NY 11791

Documents
McGowan Book Co.
P.O. Box 16325
Chapel Hill, NC 27516
919-968-1121 or Fax 919-968-1169

Dogs
Kathleen Rais & Co.
211 Carolina Ave.
Phoenixville, PA 19460
610-933-1388

Thomas Edison
Edison Hall Books
5 Ventnor Dr.
Edison, NJ 08820
908-548-4455

Ephemera
Antique valentines
Kingsbury Productions
4555 N Pershing Ave., Ste. 33-138
Stockton, CA 95207
209-467-8438

The Mulberry Cat
Yvonne Davis
Jan Davis Martel
P.O. Box 3573
Boone, NC 28607
704-963-7693

Espionage
Roman Noir
440 E 79th St. #16B
New York City, NY 10021
212-737-8004 or Fax 212-737-3743

The Silver Door
P.O. Box 3208
Redondo Beach, CA 92077
310-379-6005

Estate Libraries
The Book Collector
2347 University Blvd.
Houston, TX 77005
713-661-2665

Exhibition Catalogs
L. Clarice Davis Art Books
P.O. Box 56054
Sherman Oaks, CA 91413-1054
818-787-1322

Exploration
Western
Terry Harper, Bookseller
P.O. Box 312
Vergennes, VT 05491-0312
802-877-9262

Heritage Book Shop, Inc.
8540 Melrose Ave.
Los Angeles, CA 90069
213-659-3674

Key Books
P.O. Box 58097
St. Petersburg, FL 33715
813-867-2931

Paul Melzer Fine Books
12 E Vine St.
Redlands, CA 92373
909-792-7299

Flo Silver Books
8442 Oakwood Ct. N
Indianapolis, IN 46260
317-255-5118

Fantasy
The Book Baron
1236 S Magnolia Ave.
Anaheim, CA 92804
714-527-7022 or Fax 714-527-5634

Camelot Books
Charles E. Wyatt
P.O. Box 2883
Vista, CA 92083
619-940-9472

Farming
First editions
Karl M. Armens
740 Juniper Dr.
Iowa City, IA 52245

Also gardening
Hurley Books
1752 Rt. 12
Westmoreland, NH 03467-4724
603-399-4342 or Fax 603-399-8326

Henry Lindeman
4769 Bavarian Dr.
Jackson, MI 49201
517-764-5728

Fiction
Late 20th C
Kacey Kowars
425 Buckingham Dr.
Indianapolis, IN 46208
317-921-9408

Bob Lakin
3021 Lavita Ln.
Dallas, TX 75234
214-247-3291

19th & 20th-C American
Mason's Bookstore, Rare Books
& Record Albums
115 S Main St.
Chambersburg, PA 17201
717-261-0541

Fine Bindings & Books
The Book Collector
2347 University Blvd.
Houston, TX 77005
713-661-2665

Bromer Booksellers
607 Boylston St.
Boston, MA 02116
617-247-2818 or Fax 617-247-2975

Heritage Book Shop, Inc.
8540 Melrose Ave.
Los Angeles, CA 90069
310-659-3674 or Fax 310-659-4872

Terry Harper, Bookseller
P.O. Box 312
Vergennes, VT 05491-0312
802-877-9262

Kenneth Karimole, Bookseller, Inc.
P.O. Box 464
509 Wilshire Blvd.
Santa Monica, CA 94001
310-451-4342 or 310-458-5930

Mason's Bookstore, Rare Books
& Record Albums
115 S Main St.
Chambersburg, PA 17201
717-261-0541

Paul Melzer Fine Books
12 E Vine St.
Redlands, CA 92373
909-792-7299

Also sets
Randall House
835 Laguna St.
Santa Barbara, CA 93101
805-963-1909 or Fax 805-963-1650

Fine Press
Susan Heller, Pages for Sages
22611 Halburton Rd.
Beachwood, OH 44122-3939
216-283-2665 or Fax 316-991-2665

Heritage Book Shop, Inc.
8540 Melrose Ave.
Los Angeles, CA 90069
310-659-3674 or Fax 310-659-4872

Randall House
835 Laguna St.
Santa Barbara, CA 93101
805-963-1909 or Fax 805-963-1650

Firearms
Melvin Marcher, Bookseller
6204 N Vermont
Oklahoma City, OK 73112

First Editions
After 1937
A.B.A.C.U.S.®
Phillip E. Miller
343 S Chesterfield St.
Aiken, SC 29801
803-648-4632

Hyper-modern
Almark & Co.-Booksellers
P.O. Box 7
Thornhill, Ontario
Canada L3T 3N1
phone/Fax 905-764-2665

Modern or signed
AL-PAC
Lamar Kelley Antiquarian Books
2625 E Southern Ave., C-120
Tempe, AZ 85282
602-831-3121 or Fax 602-831-3193

Amaranth Books
P.O. Box 421
Wilmette, IL 60091-0421
708-328-2939

Karl M. Armens
740 Juniper Dr.
Iowa City, IA 52245

Modern
Bella Luna Books
P.O. Box 260425
Highlands Ranch, CO 80126-0425
800-497-4717 or Fax 303-794-3135

Between the Covers
132 Kings Hwy. E
Haddonfield, NJ 08033

The Book Baron
1236 S Magnolia Ave.
Anaheim, CA 92804
714-527-7022 or Fax 714-527-5634

Modern
Chapel Hill Rare Books
P.O. Box 456
Carrboro, NC 27510
919-929-8351

Edison Hall Books
5 Ventnor Dr.
Edison, NJ 08820
908-548-4455

Literary
Janet Egelhofer
36 Fairfield Ave.
Holyoke, MA 01040
413-532-1295

Modern
Susan Heller, Pages for Sages
22611 Halburton Rd.
Beachwood, OH 44122-3939
216-283-2665 or Fax 216-991-2665

Modern
David Holloway, Bookseller
7430 Grace St.
Springfield, VA 22150
703-569-1798

Heritage Book Shop, Inc.
8540 Melrose Ave.
Los Angeles, CA 90069
310-659-3674 or Fax 310-659-4872

Modern
Ken Lopez, Bookseller
51 Huntington Rd.
Hadley, MA 01035
413-584-4827 or Fax 413-584-2045

Much Ado
Seven Pleasant St.
Marblehead, MA 01945
617-639-0400

Robert Mueller Rare Books
8124 W 26th St.
N Riverside, IL 60546
708-447-6441

Jeffrey Lee Pressman, Bookseller
3246 Ettie St.
Oakland, CA 94608
510-652-6232

American & British
Quill & Brush
Box 5365
Rockville, MD 20848
301-460-3700 or Fax 301-871-5425

Modern
Ed Smith Books
P.O. Box 66
Oak View, CA 93022
805-646-2844 or Fax 805-649-2863
email: EdsBooks@aol.com

Scribe Company
Attn: Bonnie Smith
P.O. Box 1123
Flippin, AR 72634

Harrison Fisher
Parnassus Books
218 N 9th St.
Boise, ID 83702

Fishing
Artis Books
201 N Second Ave.
P.O. Box 208
Alpena, MI 49707
517-354-3401

Edison Hall Books
5 Ventnor Dr.
Edison, NJ 08820
908-548-4455

Jim Hodgson Books
908 S Manlius St.
Fayetteville, NY 13066
315-637-6264

Melvin Marcher, Bookseller
6204 N Vermont
Oklahoma City, OK 73112

Mason's Bookstore, Rare Books
& Record Albums
115 S Main
Chambersburg, PA 17201
717-261-0541

Yesterday's Books
229 Riverview Dr.
Parchment, MI 49004
616-345-1011

Florida
Brasser's
8701 Seminole Blvd.
Seminole, FL 34642

Football
Brasser's
8701 Seminole Blvd.
Seminole, FL 34642

Fore-Edge Painting Books
Susan Heller, Pages for Sages
22611 Halburton Rd.
Beachwood, OH 44122-3939
216-283-2665 or Fax 316-991-2665

Freemasonry
Mason's Bookstore, Rare Books
& Record Albums
115 S Main St.
Chambersburg, PA 17201
717-261-0541

Gambling & Gaming
Gambler's Book Shop
630 S Eleventh St.
Las Vegas, NV 89101
800-634-6243

Especially on cheating
John A. Greget-Magic Lists
2631 E Claire Dr.
Phoenix, AZ 85032-4932
602-971-5497

Games
Card or board
Bill Sachen
927 Grand Ave.
Waukegan, IL 60085
708-662-7204

Gardening
The American Botanist Booksellers
P.O. Box 532
Chillicothe, IL 61523
309-274-5254

The Book Corner
Mike Tennero
728 W Lumsden Rd.
Brandon, FL 33511
813-684-1133

Brooks Books
Philip B. Nesty
P.O. Box 21473
1343 New Hampshire Dr.
Concord, CA 94521
510-672-4566 or Fax 510-672-3338

The Captain's Bookshelf, Inc.
P.O. Box 2258
Asheville, NC 28802-2258
704-253-6631

Gazetteers
Murray Hudson
Antiquarian Books & Maps
The Old Post Office
109 S Church St.
P.O. Box 163
Halls, TN 38040
901-836-9057 or 800-748-9946

Genealogy
Elder's Book Store
2115 Elliston Pl.
Nashville, TN 37203
615-327-1867

General Out-of-Print
Thomas C. Bayer
85 Reading Ave.
Hillsdale, MI 49242
517-439-4134

Best-Read Books
122 State St.
Sedro-Wooley, WA 98284
206-855-2179

Bicentennial Book Shop
820 S Westnedge Ave.
Kalamazoo, MI 49008
616-345-5987

The Book Baron
1236 S Magnolia Ave.
Anaheim, CA 92804
714-527-7022 or Fax 714-527-5634

Book Den South
2249 First St.
Ft. Myers, FL 33901
813-332-2333

The Bookseller, Inc.
521 W Exchange St.
Akron, OH 44302
216-762-3101

Cinemage Books
105 W 27th St.
New York, NY 10001

Edison Hall Books
5 Ventnor Dr.
Edison, NJ 08820
908-548-4455

Fran's Bookhouse
6601 Greene St.
Phil., PA 19119
215-438-2729 or Fax 215-438-8997

Grave Matters
P.O. Box 32192-08
Cincinnati, OH 45232
phone/Fax 513-242-7527

McGowan Book Co.
P.O. Box 16325
Chapel Hill, NC 27516
919-968-1121 or Fax 919-968-1169

Robert L. Merriam
Rare, Used & Old Books
New Hall Rd.
Conway, MA 01341
413-369-4052

The Mulberry Cat
Yvonne Davis
Jan Davis Martel
P.O. Box 3573
Boone, NC 28607
704-963-7693

Passaic Book Center
594 Main Ave.
Passaic, NJ 07055
201-778-6646 or Fax 201-778-6738

RAC Books
R.R. #2
P.O. Box 296
Seven Valleys, PA 17360
717-428-3776

J. Sampson Antiques & Books
107 S Main
Harrodsburg, KY 40330
606-734-7829

Significant Books
3053 Madison Rd.
P.O. Box 9248
Cincinnati, OH 45209
513-321-7567

Tuttle Antiquarian Books, Inc.
P.O. Box 541
26 S Main St.
Rutland, VT 05701
802-773-8229

A.A. Vespa
P.O. Box 637
Park Ridge, IL 60068
708-692-4210

Genetics
The King's Market Booksellers
P.O. Box 709
Boulder, CO 80306-0709
303-447-0234

Geographies
Murray Hudson
Antiquarian Books & Maps
The Old Post Office
109 S Church St.
P.O. Box 163
Halls, TN 38040
901-836-9057 or 800-748-9946

Overlee Farm Books
P.O. Box 1155
Stockbridge, MA 01262
413-637-2277

Golf
Brasser's
8701 Seminole Blvd.
Seminole, FL 34642

David Goodis
The American Dust Co.
47 Park Ct.
Staten Island, NY 10301
718-442-8253

The Great Lakes
Artis Books
201 N Second Ave.
P.O. Box 822
Alpena, MI 49707
517-354-3401

Sue Grafton
Thomas Books
P.O. Box 14036
Phoenix, AZ 85063
602-247-9289

Greece
W.B. O'Neill-Old & Rare Books
11609 Hunters Green Ct.
Reston, VA 22091
703-860-0782 or Fax 703-620-0153

Herbals
The American Botanist Booksellers
P.O. Box 352
Chillicothe, IL 61523
309-274-5254

Brooks Books
Philip B. Nesty
P.O. Box 21473
1343 New Hampshire Dr.
Concord, CA 94521
510-672-4566 or Fax 510-672-3338

Heritage Press
Lee & Mike Temares
50 Hts. Rd.
Plandome, NY 11030
516-627-8688

History
Science & medicine
Amaranth Books
P.O. Box 421
Wilmette, IL 60091-0421
708-328-2939

Camelot Books
Charles E. Wyatt
P.O. Box 2883
Vista, CA 92083
619-940-9472

Harold B. Diamond
Box 1193
Burbank, CA 91507
818-846-0342

Early American &Indian
Duck Creek Books
Jim & Shirley Richards
P.O. Box 203
Caldwell, OH 43724
614-732-4856 (10 am to 10 pm)

Postal & postal artifacts
McGowan Book Co.
P.O. Box 16325
Chapel Hill, NC 27516
919-968-1121 or Fax 919-968-1169

Local & regional
Significant Books
3053 Madison Rd.
P.O. Box 9248
Cincinnati, OH 45209
513-321-7567

Hollywood
Cinemage Books
105 W 27th St.
New York, NY 10001
212-243-4919

Horticulture
The American Botanist Booksellers
P.O. Box 532
Chillicothe, IL 61523
309-274-5254

Ornamental
Brooks Books
Philip B. Nesty
P.O. Box 21473
1343 New Hampshire Dr.
Concord, CA 94521
510-672-4566 or Fax 510-672-3338

Woodbridge B. Brown
P.O. Box 445
Turners Falls, MA 01376
413-772-2509 or 413-773-5710

Horror
The Book Baron
1236 S Magnolia Ave.
Anaheim, CA 92804
714-527-7022 or Fax 714-527-5634

Kai Nygaard
19421 Eighth Place
Escondido, CA 92029
619-746-9039

Pandora's Books, Ltd.
P.O. Box BB-54
Neche, ND 58265
204-324-8548 or Fax 204-324-1628

L. Ron Hubbard
AL-PAC
Lamar Kelley Antiquarian Books
2625 E Southern Ave., C-120
Tempe, AZ 85282
602-831-3121 or Fax 602-831-3193

Humanities
Reprint editions
Dover Publications
Dept. A 214
E Second St.
Mineola, NY 11501

Hunting
Artis Books
201 N Second Ave.
P.O. Box 822
Alpena, MI 49707
517-354-3401

Edison Hall Books
5 Ventnor Dr.
Edison, NJ 08820
908-548-4455

Jim Hodgson Books
908 S Manlius St.
Fayetteville, NY 13066
315-637-6264

Melvin Marcher, Bookseller
6204 N Vermont
Oklahoma City, OK 73112

Yesterday's Books
229 Riverview Dr.
Parchment, MI 49004
616-345-1011

Idaho
Parnassus Books
218 N 9th St.
Boise, ID 83702

Illustrated
Noreen Abbot Books
2666 44th Ave.
San Francisco, CA 94116
415-664-9464

Bowie & Co. Booksellers, Inc.
314 First Ave. S
Seattle, WA 98104
206-624-4100 or Fax 206-223-0966

Books of the Ages
Gary Overmann
4764 Silverwood Dr.
Batavia, OH 45103
513-732-3456

Bromer Booksellers
607 Boylston St.
Boston, MA 02116
617-247-2818 or Fax 617-247-2975

Old or new; may subjects
Gary R. Smith
517 Laurel Ave.
Modesto, CA 95351

Barbara Smith Books
P.O. Box 1185
Northampton, MA 01061
413-586-1453

Randall House
835 Laguna St.
Santa Barbara, CA 93101
805-963-1909 or Fax 805-963-1650

Irvin S. Cobb
Always paying $3.00 each plus shipping. Send for immediate payment to:
Bill Schroeder
5801 KY Dam Rd.
Paducah, KY 42003

Indians
Wars
K.C. Owings
P.O. Box 19
N Abington, MA 02351
617-857-1655

Plains, Black Hills, etc.
Flo Silver Books
8442 Oakwood Ct. N
Indianapolis, IN 46260
317-255-5118

Iowa
Karl M. Armens
740 Juniper Dr.
Iowa City, IA 52245

Jazz
Chartwell Booksellers
55 E 52nd St.
New York, NY 10055
212-308-0643

James Joyce
Paul Melzer Fine Books
12 E St.
Redlands, CA 92373
909-792-7299

John Deere
Henry Lindeman
4769 Bavarian Dr.
Jackson, MI 49201
517-764-5728

Judaica
Harold B. Diamond
Box 1193
Burbank, CA 91507
818-846-0342

Stanley Schwartz
1934 Pentuckett Ave.
San Diego, CA 92104-5732
619-232-5888 or Fax 619-233-5833

Juvenile
Cover to Cover
P.O. Box 687
Chapel Hill, NC 27514

Edison Hall Books
5 Ventnor Dr.
Edison, NJ 08820
908-548-4455

Susan Heller, Pages for Sages
22611 Halburton Rd.
Beachwood, OH 44122-3939
216-283-2665 or Fax 216-991-2665

Page Books
HRC 65, Box 233
Kingston, AR 72472
501-861-5831

Jo Ann Reisler, Ltd.
360 Glyndon St., NE
Vienna, VA 22180
703-938-2967 or Fax 703-938-9057

Nancy Stewart, Books
1188 NW Weybridge Way
Beaverton, OR 97006
503-645-9779

Lee & Mike Temares
50 Hts. Rd.
Plandome, NY 11030
516-627-8688

Kentucky Authors
Bill Schroeder
P.O. Box 3009
Paducah, KY 42002-3009

Kentucky History
Bill Schroeder
P.O. Box 3009
Paducah, KY 42002-3009

Labor
A\K\A Fine Used Books
4124 Brooklyn Ave. NE
Seattle, WA 98107

Volume I Books
1 Union St.
Hillsdale, MI 49242
517-437-2228

Landscape Architecture
The American Botanist Booksellers
P.O. Box 532
Chillicothe, IL 61523
309-274-5254

Brooks Books
Philip B. Nesty
P.O. Box 21473
1343 New Hampshire Dr.
Concord, CA 94521
510-672-4566 or Fax 510-672-3338

Latin American Literature
Almark & Co.-Booksellers
P.O. Box 7
Thornhill, Ontario
Canada L3T 3N1
phone/Fax 905-764-2665

Flo Silver Books
8442 Oakwood Ct. N
Indianapolis, IN 46260
317-255-5118

Harold B. Diamond
Box 1193
Burbank, CA 91507
818-846-0342

Law & Crime
Harold B. Diamond
Box 1193
Burbank, CA 91507
818-846-0342

T.E. Lawrence
Denis McDonnell, Bookseller
653 Park St.
Honesdale, PA 18431
717-253-6706 or Fax 717-253-6785
e-mail:
denis.mcdonnell@microserve.com

Lawrence of Arabia
Denis McDonnell, Bookseller
653 Park St.
Honesdale, PA 18431
717-253-6706 or Fax 717-253-6785
e-mail:
denis.mcdonnell@microserve.com

Lebanon
W.B. O'Neill-Old & Rare Books
11609 Hunters Green Ct.
Reston, VA 22091
703-860-0782 or Fax 703-620-0153

Lewis & Clark Expedition
George H. Tweney
16660 Marine View Dr. SW
Seattle, WA 98166
206-243-8243

Limited Editions
Scribe Company
Attn: Bonnie Smith
P.O. Box 1123
Flippin, AR 72634

Lee & Mike Temares
50 Hts. Rd.
Plandome, NY 11030
516-627-8688

Literature
Amaranth Books
P.O. Box 421
Wilmette, IL 60091-0421
708-328-2939

In translation
Almark & Co.-Booksellers
P.O. Box 7
Thornhill, Ontario
Canada L3T 3N1
phone/Fax 905-764-2665

First editions
Karl M. Armens
740 Juniper Dr.
Iowa City, IA 52245

18th & 19th-C English
The Book Collector
2347 University Blvd.
Houston, TX 77005
713-661-2665

First editions
Bromer Booksellers
607 Boylston St.
Boston, MA 02116
617-247-2818 or Fax 617-247-2975

African-American
Between the Covers
132 Kings Hwy. E
Haddonfield, NJ 08033

By the Way Books
P.O. Box 23359
Columbia, SC 29924
803-788-7447 or Fax 803-736-9566

The Captain's Bookshelf, Inc.
P.O. Box 2258
Asheville, NC 22802-2258
704-253-6631

Chapel Hill Rare Books
P.O. Box 456
Carrboro, NC 27510
919-929-8351

Harold B. Diamond
Box 1193
Burbank, CA 91507
818-846-0342

Southern
Elder's Book Store
2115 Elliston Pl.
Nashville, TN 37203
615-327-1867

Susan Heller, Pages for Sages
22611 Halburton Rd.
Beachwood, OH 44122-3939
216-283-2665 or Fax 216-991-2665

Ken Lopez, Bookseller
51 Huntington Rd.
Hadley, MA 01035
413-584-4827 or Fax 413-584-2045

Mason's Bookstore, Rare Books
& Record Albums
115 S Main St.
Chambersburg, PA 17201
717-261-0541

Much Ado
Seven Pleasant St.
Marblehead, MA 01945
617-639-0400

Randall House
835 Laguna St.
Santa Barbara, CA 93101
805-963-1909 or Fax 805-963-1650

Wellerdt's Books
3700 S Osprey Ave. #214
Sarasota, FL 34239
813-365-1318

Xanadu Records, Ltd.
3242 Irwin Ave.
Kingsbridge, NY 10463
212-549-3655

Little Leather Library
Gary R. Smith
517 Laurel Ave.
Modesto, CA 95351

Magazines
Mystery only
Grave Matters
P.O. Box 32192-08
Cincinnati, OH 45232

Robert A. Madle
4406 Bestor Dr.
Rockville, MD 20853
301-460-4712

The Magazine Baron
1236 S Magnolia Ave.
Anaheim, CA 92804
714-527-0358 or Fax 714-527-5634

Relating to decorative arts
Mordida Books
P.O. Box 79322
Houston, TX 77279
713-467-4280 or Fax 713-467-4182

Passaic Book Center
594 Main Ave.
Passaic, NJ 07055
201-778-6646 or Fax 201-778-6738

Magic
Especially tricks
John A. Greget-Magic Lists
2631 E Claire Dr.
Phoenix, AZ 85032
602-971-5497

Manuscripts
Susan Heller, Pages for Sages
P.O. Box 2219
Beachwood, OH 44122-3939
216-283-2665 or Fax 216-991-2665

Heritage Book Shop, Inc.
8540 Melrose Ave.
Los Angeles, CA 90069
310-659-3674 or Fax 310-659-4872

Key Books
P.O. Box 58097
St. Petersburg, FL 33715
813-867-2931

Asiatic languages
Worldwide Antiquarian
P.O. Box 391
Cambridge, MA 02141
617-876-6220 or Fax 617-876-0839

Randall House
835 Laguna St.
Santa Barbara, CA 93101
805-963-1909 or Fax 805-963-1650

Maps
State, pocket-type, ca 1800s
The Bookseller, Inc.
521 W Exchange St.
Akron, OH 44302
216-762-3101

Bowie & Co. Booksellers, Inc.
314 First Ave. S
Seattle, WA 98104
206-624-4100 or Fax 206-223-0966

Pre-1900 Florida
Brasser's
8701 Seminole Blvd.
Seminole, FL 34642

Elegant Book & Map Company
815 Harrison Ave.
P.O. Box 1302
Cambridge, OH 43725
614-432-4068

Maritime
Book & Tackle Shop
29 Old Colony Rd.
P.O. Box 114
Chestnut Hill, MA 02167
617-965-0459 (winter) or
401-596-0700 (summer)

Overlee Farm Books
P.O. Box 1155
Stockbridge, MA 01262
413-637-2277

J. Tuttle Maritime Books
1806 Laurel Crest
Madison, WI 53705
608-238-SAIL (7245)

Martial Arts
Nutmeg Books
354 New Litchfield St. (Rte. 202)
Torrington, CT 06790
203-482-9696

Masonic History
Mason's Bookstore, Rare Books
& Record Albums
115 S Main St.
Chambersburg, PA 17201
717-261-0541

Mathematics
Significant Books
3053 Madison Rd.
P.O. Box 9248
Cincinnati, OH 45209
513-321-7567

Medicine
Amaranth Books
P.O. Box 421
Wilmette, IL 60091-0421
708-328-2939

Book & Tackle
29 Old Colony Rd.
P.O. Box 114
Chestnut Hill, MA 02167
617-965-0459 (winter) or
401-596-0700 (summer)

Key Books
P.O. Box 58097
St. Petersburg, FL 33715
813-867-2931

M & S Rare Books, Inc.
P.O. Box 2594, E Side Sta.
Providence, RI 02906
401-421-1050 or Fax 401-272-0831
(attention M & S)

Smithfield Rare Books
20 Deer Run Trail
Smithfield, RI 02917
401-231-8225

Medieval
Camelot Books
Charles E. Wyatt
P.O. Box 2883
Vista, CA 92083
619-940-9472

Metaphysics
AL-PAC
Lamar Kelley Antiquarian Books
2625 E Southern Ave., C-120
Tempe, AZ 85282
602-831-3121 or Fax 602-831-3193

Meteorology
Knollwood Books
Lee & Peggy Price
P.O. Box 197
Oregon, WI 53575
608-835-8861 or Fax 608-835-8421

Mexico
Flo Silver Books
8442 Oakwood Ct. N
Indianapolis, IN 46260
317-255-5118

Michigan
Artis Books
201 N Second Ave.
P.O. Box 822
Alpena, MI 49707
517-354-3401

Yesterday's Books
229 Riverview Dr.
Parchment, MI 49004
616-345-1011

Middle Eastern Countries
Denis McDonnell, Bookseller
653 Park St.
Honesdale, PA 18431
717-253-6706 or Fax 717-253-6785
e-mail:
denis.mcdonnell@microserve.com

Worldwide Antiquarian
P.O. Box 391
Cambridge, MA 02141
617-876-6220 or Fax 617-876-0839

Militaria
The Book Corner
Mike Tennero
728 W Lumsden Rd.
Brandon, FL 33511
813-684-1133

The Bookseller, Inc.
521 W Exchange St.
Akron, OH 44302
216-762-3101

Brasser's
8701 Seminole Blvd.
Seminole, FL 34642

Edison Hall Books
5 Ventnor Dr.
Edison, NJ 08820
908-548-4455

Rick Harmon
Military Books & Relics
910 Sullivan Dr.
Belvidere, IL 61008
815-547-7580

Robert L. Merriam
Rare, Used & Old Books
Newhall Rd.
Conway, MA 01341
413-369-4052

Significant Books
3053 Madison Rd.
P.O Box 9248
Cincinnati, OH 45209
513-321-7567

Before 1900
Gordon Totty
Scarce Paper Americana
347 Shady Lake Pky.
Baton Rouge, LA 70810
504-766-8625

Histories
Tryon County Bookshop
2071 State Hwy. 29
Johnstown, NY 12905
518-762-1060

Volume I Books
1 Union St.
Hillsdale, MI 49242
517-437-2228

Miniature Books
Bromer Booksellers
607 Boylston St.
Boston, MA 02116
617-247-2818 or Fax 617-247-2975

Foreign atlases
Murray Hudson
Antiquarian Books & Maps
The Old Post Office
109 S Church St.
P.O. Box 163
Halls, TN 38040
901-836-9057 or 800-748-9946

Hurley Books
1752 Rt. 12
Westmoreland, NH 03467-4724
603-399-4342 or Fax 603-399-8326

Gary R. Smith
517 Laurel Ave.
Modesto, CA 95351

Miscellaneous
Bridgman Books
906 Roosevelt Ave.
Rome, NY 13440
315-337-7252

Montana
Nancy C. May
Bygone Books 'n Things
1720-C S Peaceable Rd.
McAlester, OK 74501

Movies
Cinemage Books
105 W 27th St.
New York, NY 10001
212-243-4919

Mystery
Karl M. Armens
740 Juniper Dr.
Iowa City, IA 52245

First editions
Island Books
P.O. Box 19
Old Westbury, NY 11568

Kacey Kowars
425 Buckingham Dr.
Indianapolis, IN 46208
317-921-9408

Mordida Books
P.O. Box 79322
Houston, TX 77279
713-467-4280 or Fax 713-467-4182

Roman Noir
440 E 79th St. #16B
New York City, NY 10021
212-737-8004 or Fax 212-737-3743

Pandora's Books, Ltd.
P.O. Box BB-54
Neche, ND 48265
204-324-8548 or Fax 204-324-1628

RAC Books
R.R. #2
P.O. Box 296
Seven Valleys, PA 17360
717-428-3776

The Silver Door
P.O. Box 3208
Redondo Beach, CA 90277
310-379-6005

Napoleonic Memorabilia
The Book Collector
2347 University Blvd.
Houston, TX 7005
713-661-2665

Narcotics
Nutmeg Books
354 New Litchfield St. (Rte. 202)
Torrington, CT 06790
203-482-9696

Natural History
Thomas C. Bayer
85 Reading Ave.
Hillsdale, MI 49242
517-439-4134

Bohemian Bookworm
110 W 25th St., 9th Floor
New York, NY 10001
212-620-5627

Woodbridge B. Brown
P.O. Box 445
Turners Falls, MA 01376
413-772-2509 or 413-773-5710

Noriko I. Ciochon
Natural History Books
1025 Keokut St.
Iowa City, IA 52240
319-354-4844

Melvin Marcher, Bookseller
6204 N Vermont
Oklahoma City, OK 73112

Nautical
Much Ado
Seven Pleasant St.
Marblehead, MA 01945
617-639-0400

Overlee Farm Books
P.O. Box 1155
Stockbridge, MA 01262
413-637-2277

Needlework
Stanley Schwartz
1934 Pentuckett Ave.
San Diego, CA 92104-5732
619-232-5888 or Fax 619-233-5833

Neuroscience
John Gach Books
5620 Waterloo Rd.
Columbia, MD 21045
410-465-9023 or Fax 410-465-0649

New England
Book & Tackle
29 Old Colony Rd.
P.O. Box 114
Chestnut Hill, MA 02167
617-965-0459 (winter) or
401-596-0700 (summer)

Non-Fiction
Pre-1950
Brasser's
8701 Seminole Blvd.
Seminole, FL 34642

Novels
The Silver Door
P.O. Box 3208
Redondo Beach, CA 90277
310-379-6005

Occult
AL-PAC
Lamar Kelley Antiquarian Books
2625 E Southern Ave., C-120
Tempe, AZ 85282
602-831-3121 or Fax 602-831-3193

Ohio
The Bookseller, Inc.
521 W Exchange St.
Akron, OH 44302
216-762-3101

Omar Khayyam
Worldwide Antiquarian
P.O. Box 391
Cambridge, MA 02141
617-876-6220 or Fax 617-876-0839

Original Art
By children's illustrators
Kendra Krienke
230 Central Park W
New York, NY 10024
201-930-9709 or 201-930-9765

Paperbacks
The American Dust Co.
47 Park Ct.
Staten Island, NY 10301
718-442-8253

For Collectors Only
2028B Ford Pky. #136
St. Paul, MN 55116

Michael Gerlicher
1375 Rest Point Rd.
Orono, MN 55364

Vintage
Grave Matters
P.O. Box 32192-08
Cincinnati, OH 45232

Modern Age Books
P.O. Box 325
E Lansing, MI 48826
517-351-9334

Originals
Mordida Books
P.O. Box 79322
Houston, TX 77279
713-467-4280 or Fax 713-467-4182

Olde Current Books
Daniel P. Shay
356 Putnam Ave.
Ormond Beach, FL 32174
904-672-8998 or
e-mail: PEAKMYSTER@aol,com

Pandora's Books, Ltd.
P.O. Box BB-54
Neche, ND 58265
204-324-8548 or Fax 204-324-1628

Tom Rolls
540 E Seminary #2
Greencastle, IN 46135

Robert B. Parker
Thomas Books
P.O. Box 14036
Phoenix, AZ 85063
502-247-9289

Pennsylvania
Mason's Bookstore, Rare Books
& Record Albums
115 S Main
Chambersburg, PA 17201
717-261-0541

Performing Arts
Bowie & Co. Booksellers, Inc.
314 First Ave. S
Seattle, WA 98104
206-624-4100

Philosophy
The Book Corner
Mike Tennero
728 W Lumsden Rd.
Brandon, FL 33511
813-684-1133

By the Way Books
P.O. Box 23359
Columbia, SC 29924
803-788-7447 or Fax 803-736-9566

John Gach Books
5620 Waterloo Rd.
Columbia, MD 21045
410-465-9023 or Fax 410-465-0649

Photography
Cary Loren
The Captain's Bookshelf, Inc.
P.O. Box 2258
Asheville, NC 28802-2258
704-253-6631

Significant Books
3053 Madison Rd.
P.O. Box 9248
Cincinnati, OH 45209
513-321-7567

19th-C Middle & Far East Countries
Worldwide Antiquarian
P.O. Box 391
Cambridge, MA 02141
617-876-6220 or Fax 617-876-0839

Playing Cards
Bill Sachen
927 Grand Ave.
Waukegan, IL 60085
708-662-7204

Poetry
Edison Hall Books
5 Ventnor Dr.
Edison, NJ 08820
908-548-4455

Janet Egelhofer
36 Fairfield Ave.
Holyoke, MA 01040
413-532-1295

Ed Smith Books
P.O. Box 66
Oak View, CA 93022
805-649-2844 or Fax 805-649-2863
email: EdsBooks@aol.com

VERSEtility Books
P.O. Box 1366
Burlington, CT 06013-1366
203-675-9338

Polar Explorations & Ephemera
Alaskan Heritage Bookshop
174 S Franklin, P.O. 22165
Juneau, AK 99802

Parmer Books
7644 Forrestal Rd.
San Diego, CA 92120-2203
619-287-0693 or Fax 619-287-6135
Internet: ParmerBook@aol.com

Political
Radical
A\K\A Fine Books
4142 Brooklyn Ave. NE
Seattle, WA 98107

Gossip, memoirs or histories
Herb Sauermann
21660 School Rd.
Manton, CA 96059

Radical
Volume I Books
1 Union St.
Hillsdale, MI 49242
517-437-2228

Post Cards
Book & Tackle Shop
29 Old Colony Rd.
P.O. Box 114
Chestnut Hill, MA 02167
617-965-0459 (winter) or
401-596-0700 (summer)

Posters
The Mulberry Cat
Yvonne Davis
Jan Davis Martel
P.O. Box 3573
Boone, NC 28607
704-963-7693

Pre-Colombian Art
Flo Silver Books
8442 Oakwood Ct. N
Indianapolis, IN 46260
317-255-5118

Press Books
Heritage Book Shop, Inc.
8540 Melrose Ave.
Los Angeles, CA 90069
213-659-3674

Randall House
835 Laguna St.
Santa Barbara, CA 93101
805-963-1909 or Fax 805-963-1650

Prints
The Mulberry Cat
Yvonne Davis
Jan Davis Martel
P.O. Box 3573
Boone, NC 28607
704-963-7693

Private Presses
American
Richard Blacher
209 Plymouth Colony, Alps Rd.
Branford, CT 06405

First Folio
1206 Brentwood
Paris, TN 34842
phone/Fax 901-644-9940

Susan Heller, Pages for Sages
22611 Halburton Rd.
Beachwood, OH 44122-3939
216-283-2665 or Fax 216-991-2665

Promoters of Paper, Ephemera & Book Fairs
Kingsbury Productions
Katherine & David Kreider
4555 N Pershing Ave., Ste. 33-138
Stockton, CA 95207
209-467-8438

Psychedelia
Nutmeg Books
354 New Litchfield St. (Rte. 202)
Torrington, CT 06790
203-482-9696

Psychiatry
John Gach Books
5620 Waterloo Rd.
Columbia, MD 21045
410-465-9023 or Fax 410-465-0649

Psychoanalysis
Also related subjects
John Gach Books
5620 Waterloo Rd.
Columbia, MD 21045
410-465-9023 or Fax 410-465-0649

Psychology
John Gach Books
5620 Waterloo Rd.
Columbia, MD 21045
410-465-9023 or Fax 410-465-0649

The King's Market Booksellers
P.O. Box 709
Boulder, CO 80306-0709
303-447-0234

Pulps
Science fiction & fantasy before 1945
Robert A. Madle
4406 Bestor Dr.
Rockville, MD 20853
301-460-4712

Quaker
Vintage Books
117 Concord St.
Framingham, MA 01701

Also Shakers, Christians & Collectivists
Duck Creek Books
Jim & Shirley Richards
P.O. Box 203
Caldwell, OH 43724
614-732-4856 (10 am to 10 pm)

Quilt Books
Bill Schroeder
P.O. Box 3009
Paducah, KY 42002-3009

Galerie De Boicourt
980 Chester
Birmingham, MI 48009
313-540-0166

Arthur Rackham
Books of the Ages
Gary Overmann
4764 Silverwood Dr.
Batavia, OH 45103
513-732-3456

Railroading
Mason's Rare & Used Books
115 S Main St.
Chambersburg, PA 17201
717-261-0541

Rare & Unusual Books
First Folio
1206 Brentwood
Paris, TN 38242
phone/Fax 901-644-9940

Susan Heller, Pages for Sages
22611 Halburton Rd.
Beachwood, OH 44122-3939
216-283-2665 or Fax 216-991-2665

Kenneth Karmiole, Bookseller, Inc.
P.O. Box 464
509 Wilshire Blvd.
Santa Monica, CA 94001
310-451-4342 or 310-458-5930

M & S Rare Books, Inc.
P.O. Box 2594, E Side Sta.
Providence, RI 02906
401-421-1050 or Fax 401-272-0831
(attention M & S)

Reprint editions
Dover Publications
Dept. A 214
E Second St.
Mineola, NY 11501

Terry Harper, Bookseller
P.O. Box 312
Vergennes, VT 05491-0312
802-877-9262

Heritage Book Shop, Inc.
8540 Melrose Ave.
Los Angeles, CA 90069
213-659-3674

Paul Melzer Fine Books
12 E Vine St.
Redlands, CA 92373
909-792-7299

Reference
About Books
6 Sand Hill Ct.
P.O. Box 5717
Parsippany, NY 07054
201-515-4591

Religion
Also Theology, Mysticism, The Spiritual Life, Gurdjieff/Ouspensky & The Fourth Way
By the Way Books
P.O. Box 23359
Columbia, SC 29924
803-788-7447 or Fax 803-736-9566

Chimney Sweep Books
419 Cedar St.
Santa Cruz, CA 94060-4304
408-458-1044

Reptiles
Mason's Bookstore, Rare Books
& Record Albums
115 S Main St.
Chambersburg, PA 17201
717-261-0541

Revolutionary War
K.C. Owings
P.O. Box 19
N Abington, MA 02351
617-857-1655

Roycroft Press
Richard Blacher
209 Plymouth Colony, Alps Rd.
Branford, CT 06405

Rubaiyats
Harold B. Diamond
Box 1193
Burbank, CA 91507
818-846-0342

Scholarly Books
Reprint editions
Dover Publications
Dept. A 214
E Second St.
Mineola, NY 11501

Science & Technology
Thomas C. Bayer
85 Reading Ave.
Hillsdale, MI 49242
517-439-4134

Book & Tackle Shop
29 Old Colony Rd.
P.O. Box 114
Chestnut Hill, MA 02167
617-965-0459 (winter) or
401-596-0700 (summer)

Key Books
P.O. Box 58097
St. Petersburg, FL 33715
813-867-2931

M & S Rare Books, Inc.
P.O. Box 2594, E Side Sta.
Providence, RI 02906
401-272-0831 or Fax 401-272-0831
(attention M & S)

Smithfield Rare Books
20 Deer Run Trail
Smithfield, RI 02917
401-231-8225

Science Fiction
AL-PAC
Lamar Kelley Antiquarian Books
2625 E Southern Ave., C-120
Tempe, AZ 85282
602-831-3121 or Fax 602-831-3193

Karl M. Armens
740 Juniper Dr.
Iowa City, IA 52245

First editions
Island Books
P.O. Box 19
Old Westbury, NY 11568
516-759-0233

Horror & Occult
Bob Lakin
3021 Lavita Ln.
Dallas, TX 75234
214-247-3291

Robert A. Madle
4406 Bestor Dr.
Rockville, MD 20853
301-460-4712

Also fantasy
Kai Nygaard
19421 Eighth Place
Escondido, CA 92029
619-746-9039

Pandora's Books, Ltd.
P.O. Box 54
Neche, ND 58265
204-324-8548 or Fax 204-324-1628

Also fantasy
Xanadu Records, Ltd.
3242 Irwin Ave.
Kingsbridge, NY 10463
212-549-3655

Sciences
Cover to Cover
P.O. Box 687
Chapel Hill, NC 27514

Harold B. Diamond
Box 1193
Burbank, CA 91507
818-846-0342

Reprint editions
Dover Publications
E Second St.
Mineola, NY 11501

Significant Books
P.O. Box 9248
3053 Madison Rd.
Cincinnati, OH 45209
513-321-7567

Series Books
Glo's Children's Series Books
906 Shadywood
Southlake, TX 76092

Set Editions
Arthur Boutiette
410 W 3rd St., Suite 200
Little Rock, AR 72201

Surveying
Also tools, instruments & ephemera
David & Nancy Garcelon
10 Hastings Ave.
Millbury, MA 01527-4314
508-754-2667

Set Editions
Bowie & Weatherford, Inc.
314 First Ave. S
Seattle, WA 98104
206-624-4100

Shakespeare
Harold B. Diamond
Burbank, CA 91507
818-846-0342

Sherlockiana
The Silver Door
P.O. Box 3208
Redondo Beach, CA 90277
310-379-6005

Ships & Sea
Book & Tackle Shop
29 Old Colony Rd.
P.O. Box 114
Chestnut Hill, MA 02167
617-965-0459 (winter) or
401-596-0700 (summer)

Parmer Books
7644 Forrestal Rd.
San Diego, CA 92120-2203
619-287-0693 or Fax 619-287-6135
Internet: ParmerBook@aol.com

J. Tittle Maritme Books
1806 Laurel Crest
Madison, WI 53705
608-238-SAIL

Signed Editions
Chapel Hill Rare Books
P.O. Box 456
Carrboro, NC 27510
919-929-8351

Janet Egelhofer
36 Fairfield Ave.
Holyoke, MA 01040
413-532-1295

Dan Simmons
Thomas Books
P.O. Box 14036
Phoenix, AZ 85063
602-247-9289

Socialism
Volume I Books
1 Union St.
Hillsdale, MI 49242
517-437-2228

South America
Flo Silver Books
8442 Oakwood Ct. N
Indianapolis, IN 46260
317-255-5118

South Dakota
Also any pre-1970 Western-related books
James F. Taylor
515 Sixth St.
Rapid City, SD 57701
605-341-3224

Space Exploration
Knollwood Books
Lee & Peggy Price
P.O. Box 197
Oregon, WI 53575
608-835-8861 or Fax 608-835-8421

Speciality Publishers
Arkham House, Gnome, Fantasy, etc.
Robert A. Madle
4406 Bestor Dr.
Rockville, MD 20853
301-460-4712

Sports
Adelson Sports
13610 N Scottsdale Rd. #10
Scottsdale, AZ 85254
602-596-1913 or Fax 602-598-1914

Randall House
835 Laguna St.
Santa Barbara, CA 93101
805-963-1909 or Fax 805-963-1650

Statue of Liberty
Mike Brooks
7335 Skyline
Oakland, CA 94611

Robert Louis Stevenson
1890s, especially Scribners
Chris Jankus
214 Alcott Rd.
Brookhaven, PA 19015

Technology
Cover to Cover
P.O. Box 687
Chapel Hill, NC 27514

Significant Books
3053 Madison Rd.
P.O. Box 9248
Cincinnati, OH 45209
513-321-7567

Tennessee History
Elder's Book Store
2115 Elliston Pl.
Nashville, TN 37203
615-327-1867

Tennis
Brasser's
8701 Seminole Blvd.
Seminole, FL 34642

Texana Fiction & Authors
Bob Lakin
3021 Lavita Ln.
Dallas, TX 75234
214-247-3291

Textiles
Galerie De Boicourt
980 Chester
Birmingham, MI 48009
313-540-0166

Stanley Schwartz
1934 Pentuckett Ave.
San Diego, CA 92104-5732
619-232-5888 or Fax 619-233-5833

Theology
Chimney Sweep Books
419 Cedar St.
Santa Cruz, CA 94060-4304
408-458-1044

Hurley Books
1752 Rt. 12
Westmoreland, NH 03467-4724
603-399-4342 or Fax 603-399-8326

Jim Thompson
The American Dust Co.
47 Park Ct.
Staten Island, NY 10301
718-442-8253

Thrillers
Kacey Kowars
425 Buckingham Dr.
Indianapolis, IN 46208
317-921-9408

Time-Life Books
Gary R. Smith
517 Laurel Ave.
Modesto, CA 95351

Trades & Crafts
19th C
Cover to Cover
P.O. Box 687
Chapel Hill, NC 27514

Hillcrest Books
Rt. 3, Box 479
Crossville, TN 38555-9547
phone/Fax 615-484-7680

Travel
Bohemian Bookworm
110 W 25th St., 9th Floor
New York, NY 10001
212-620-5627

Also exploration
Duck Creek Books
Jim & Shirley Richards
P.O. Box 203
Caldwell, OH 43724
614-732-4856 (10 am to 10 pm)

Terry Harper, Bookseller
P.O. Box 312
Vergennes, VT 05491-0312
802-877-9262

Heritage Book Shop, Inc.
8540 Melrose Ave.
Los Angeles, CA 90069
213-659-3674

Jim Hodgson Books
908 S Manlius St.
Fayetteville, NY 13066
315-637-6264

Flo Silver Books
8442 Oakwood Ct. N
Indianapolis, IN 46260
317-255-5118

Discoveries before 1900
Gordon Totty
Scarce Paper Americana
347 Shady Lake Pky.
Baton Rouge, LA 70810
504-766-8625

Turkey
W.B. O'Neill-Old & Rare Books
11609 Hunters Green Ct.
Reston, VA 22091
703-860-0782 or Fax 703-620-0153

Tasha Tudor
Books of the Ages
Gary Overmann
4764 Silverwood Dr.
Batavia, OH 45103
513-732-3456

UFO
AL-PAC
Lamar Kelley Antiquarian Books
2625 E Southern Ave., C-120
Tempe, AZ 85282
602-831-3121 or Fax 602-831-3193

Vargas
Parnassus Books
218 N 9th St.
Boise, ID 83702

Vietnam War
A\K\A Fine Used Books
4124 Brooklyn Ave. NE
Seattle, WA 98107
206-632-5870

Rick Harmon
Military Books & Relics
910 Sullivan Dr.
Belvidere, IL 61008
815-547-7580

Voyages, Exploration & Travel
Chapel Hill Rare Books
P.O. Box 456
Carrboro, NC 27510
919-929-8351

Terry Harper, Bookseller
P.O. Box 312
Vergennes, VT 05491-0312
802-877-9262

Heritage Book Shop, Inc.
8540 Melrose Ave.
Los Angeles, CA 90069
213-659-3674

Jim Hodgson Books
908 S Manlius St.
Fayetteville, NY 13066
315-637-6264

Key Books
P.O. Box 58097
St. Petersburg, FL 33715
813-867-2931

Overlee Farm Books
P.O. Box 1155
Stockbridge, MA 01262
413-627-2277

George H. Tweney
16660 Marine View Dr. SW
Seattle, WA 98166
206-243-8243

Weapons
All edged types
Knife Readables
115 Longfellow Blvd.
Lakeland, FL 33810
813-666-1133

Western Americana
Bowie & Co. Booksellers, Inc.
314 First Ave. S
Seattle, WA 98104
206-624-4100

Harold B. Diamond
Box 1193
Burbank, CA 91507
818-846-0342

Terry Harper, Bookseller
P.O. Box 312
Vergennes, VT 05491-0312
802-877-9262

K.C. Owings
P.O. Box 19
N Abington, MA 02351
617-857-1655

Scribe Company
Attn: Bonnie Smith
P.O. Box 1123
Flippin, AR 72634

George H. Tweney
16660 Marine View Dr. SW
Seattle, WA 98166
206-243-8243

Charles Willeford
The American Dust Co.
47 Park Ct.
Staten Island, NY 10301
718-442-8253

Walt Whitman
By the Way Books
P.O. Box 23359
Columbia, SC 29924
803-788-7447 or Fax 803-736-9566

Women's History
Volume I Books
1 Union St.
Hillsdale, MI 49242
517-437-2228

World War I
The Book Corner
Mike Tennero
728 W Lumsden Rd.
Brandon, FL 33511
813-684-1133

Denis McDonnell, Bookseller
653 Park St.
Honesdale, PA 18431
717-253-6706 or Fax 717-253-6785
e-mail:
denis.mcdonnell@microserve.com

World War II
Cover to Cover
P.O. Box 687
Chapel Hill, NC 27514

BOOKSELLERS

This section of the book lists names and addresses of used book dealers who have contributed the retail listings contained in this edition of *Huxford's Old Book Value Guide*. The code (A1, S7, etc.) located before the price in our listings refers to the dealer offering that particular book for sale. (When more than one dealer has the same book listing their code is given alphabetically before the price.) Given below are the dealer names and their codes.

Many book dealers issue catalogs, have open shops, are mail order only, or may be a combination of these forms of business. When seeking a book from a particular dealer, it would be best to first write (enclose SASE) or call to see what type of business is operated (open shop or mail order).

A1
A-Book-A-Brac Shop
6760 Collins Ave.
Miami Beach, FL 33141
305-865-0092

A2
Aard Books
31 Russell Ave.
Troy, NH 03465
603-242-3638

A3
Noreen Abbot Books
2666 44th Ave.
San Francisco, CA 94116
415-664-9464

A4
About Books
6 Sand Hill Ct.
P.O. Box 5717
Parsippany, NJ 07054
201-515-4591

A5
Adelson Sports
13610 N Scottsdale Rd. #10
Scottsdale, AZ 85254
602-596-1913 or Fax 602-596-1914

A6
Ads Autographs
P.O. Box 8006
Webster, NY 14580
716-671-2651

A7
Avonlea Books Search Service
P.O. Box 74, Main Sta.
White Plains, NY 10602
914-946-5923
Fax 914-946-5924 (allow 6 rings)

A8
AL-PAC
Lamar Kelley Antiquarian Books
2625 E Southern Ave., C-120
Tempe, AZ 85282
602-831-3121 or Fax 602-831-3193

A9
Amaranth Books
P.O. Box 421
Wilmette, IL 60091-0421
708-328-2939

A10
The American Botanist
P.O. Box 532
Chillicothe, IL 61523

A11
The American Dust Co.
47 Park Ct.
Staten Island, NY 10301
718-442-8253

A12
Antiquarian Book Arcade
110 W 25th St., 9th Floor
New York, NY 10001

A13
Antiquarian Medical Books
W. Bruce Fye
1607 N Wood Ave.
Marshfield, WI 54449
Fax 715-389-2990

A14
Almark & Co.-Booksellers
P.O. Box 7
Thornhill, Ontario
Canada L3T 3N1
phone/Fax 905-764-2665

A15
Karl M. Armens
740 Juniper Dr.
Iowa City, IA 52245
319-337-7755

A16
Arnold's of Michigan
218 S Water St.
Marine City, MI 48039
313-765-1350

A17
Artis Books
201 N Second Ave.
P.O. Box 822
Alpena, MI 49707-0822
517-354-3401

A18
Authors of the West
191 Dogwood Dr.
Dundee, OR 97115
503-538-8132

A19
Aplin Antiques & Art
HC 80, Box 793-25
Piedmont, SD 57769
605-347-5016

B1
Thomas C. Bayer
85 Reading Ave.
Hillsdale, MI 49242
517-439-4134

B2
Beasley Books
1533 W Oakdale, 2nd Floor
Chicago, IL 60657
312-472-4528 or Fax 312-472-7857

B3
Bela Luna Books
P.O. Box 260425
Highlands Ranch, CO 80126-0425
800-497-4717 or Fax 303-794-3135

B4
Between the Covers
132 Kings Hwy. E
Haddonfield, NJ 08033
609-354-7665 or Fax 609-354-7695
e.mail-BetweenCov@aol.com

B5
Bicentennial Book Shop
820 S Westnedge Ave.
Kalamazoo, MI 49008
616-345-5987

B6
Bibliography of the Dog
The New House
216 Covey Hill Rd.
Havelock, Quebec
Canada J0S 2C0
514-827-2717 or Fax 514-827-2091

B7
Best-Read Books
122 State St.
Sedro-Woolley, WA 98284
206-855-2179

B8
Bohemian Bookworm
110 W 25th St., 9th Floor
New York, NY 10001
212-620-5627

B9
The Book Baron
1236 S Magnolia Ave.
Anaheim, CA 92804
714-527-7022 or Fax 714-527-5634

B10
Book Broker
310 E Market St.
Charlottesville, VA 22902
804-296-2194

B11
The Book Corner
Michael Tennero
728 W Lumsden Rd.
Brandon, FL 33511
813-684-1133

B12
The Book Emporium
235 Glen Cove Ave.
Sea Cliff, LI, NY 11579
516-671-6524

B13
The Book Inn
6401-D University
Lubbock, TX 79413

B14
Book & Tackle Shop
29 Old Colony Rd.
P.O. Box 114
Chestnut Hill, MA 02167
617-965-0459 (winter) or
401-596-0700 (summer)

B15
Book Treasures
P.O. Box 121
E Norwich, NY 11732

B16
The Book Den South
Nancy Costello
2249 First St.
Ft. Myers, FL 33901
813-332-2333

B17
Books of the Ages
Gary J Overmann
Maple Ridge Manor
4764 Silverwood Dr.
Batavia, OH 45103
513-732-3456

B18
The Bookseller, Inc.
521 W Exchange St.
Akron, OH 44302
216-762-3101

B19
Books West Southwest
2452 N Campbell Ave.
Tucson, AZ 85719
602-326-3533

B20
Bowie & Co. Booksellers, Inc.
314 First Ave. S
Seattle, WA 98104
206-624-4100 or Fax 206-223-0966

B21
Brasser's
8701 Seminole Blvd.
Seminole, FL 34642

B22
Bridgman Books
906 Roosevelt Ave.
Rome, NY 13440
315-337-7252

B23
British Stamp Exchange
12 Fairlawn Ave.
N Weymouth, MA 02191

B24
Bromer Booksellers
607 Boylston St.
Boston, MA 02116
617-247-2818 or Fax 617-247-2975

B25
Mike Brooks
7335 Skyline
Oakland, CA 9461

B26
Brooks Books
Philip B. Nesty
1343 New Hampshire Dr.
P.O. Box 21473
Concord, CA 94521
510-672-4566 or Fax 510-672-3338

B27
The Bookstall
570 Sutter St.
San Francisco, CA 94102
Fax 415-362-1503

B28
Woodbridge B. Brown
312 Main St.
P.O. Box 445
Turner Falls, MA 01376
413-772-2509 or 413-773-5710

B29
Books Now & Then
Dennis Patrick
P.O. Box 337
Stanley, ND 58784
701-628-2084

B30
Burke's Bookstore
1719 Poplar Ave.
Memphis, TN 38104-6447
901-278-7484

B32
Richard Blacher
209 Plymouth Colony, Alps Rd.
Branford, CT 06405

B33
By the Way Books
P.O. Box 23359
Columbia, SC 29224
803-788-7447 or Fax 803-736-9566

B34
Bygone Books 'n Things
Nancy C. May
1720-C S Peaceable Rd.
McAlester, OK 74501

C1
Camelot Books
Charles E. Wyatt
P.O. Box 2883
Vista, CA 92083
619-940-9472

C2
The Captain's Bookshelf, Inc.
Cary Loren
P.O. Box 2258
Asheville, NC 22802-2258
704-253-6631

C3
Cattermole
20th-C Children's Books
9880 Fairmount Rd.
Newbury, OH 44065

C4
Bev Chaney, Jr. Books
73 Croton Ave.
Ossining, NY 10562
914-941-1002

C5
Chimney Sweep Books
419 Cedar St.
Santa Cruz, CA 95060-4304
408-458-1044

C6
Chapel Hill Rare Books
P.O. Box 456
Carrboro, NC 27510
919-929-8351

C7
Chartwell Booksellers
55 E 52nd St.
New York, NY 10055
212-308-0643

C8
Children's Book Adoption Agency
P.O. Box 643
Kensington, MD 20895-0643
301-565-2834 or Fax 301-585-3091

C9
Cinemage Books
105 W 27th St.
New York, NY 10001
212-243-4919

C10
Cohen Books & Collectibles
Joel J. Cohen
P.O. Box 810310
Boca Raton, FL 33481
407-487-7888

C11
Cover to Cover
P.O. Box 687
Chapel Hill, NC 27514

C12
Noriko I. Chichon
Natural History Books
1025 Keokut St.
Iowa City, 52240
319-354-4844

C13
Creatures of Habit
403 Jefferson
Paducah, KY 42001
502-442-2923

D1
Ursula Davidson
Children's & Illustrated Books
134 Linden Ln.
San Rafael, CA 94901
415-454-3939 or Fax 415-454-1087

D2
L. Clarice Davis
Fine & Applied Art Books
P.O. Box 56054
Sherman Oaks, CA 91413-1054
818-787-1322

D3
Harold B. Diamond, Bookseller
Box 1193
Burbank, CA 91507
818-846-0342

D4
Carol Docheff, Bookseller
1390 Reliez Vly. Rd.
Lafayette, CA 94549
510-935-9595

D5
Dover Publications
Dept. A 214
E Second St.
Mineola, NY 11501

D6
Drusilla's Books
859 N Howard St.
P.O. Box 16
Baltimore, MD 21201
410-225-0277

D7
Duck Creek Books
Jim & Shirley Richards
P.O. Box 203
Caldwell, OH 43724
614-732-4856

E1
The Early West
P.O. Box 9292
College Sta., TX 77842
409-775-6047

E2
Edison Hall Books
5 Ventnor Dr.
Edison, NJ 08820
908-548-4455

E3
Janet Egelhofer
36 Fairfield Ave.
Holyoke, MA 01040
413-532-1295

E4
Elder's Book Store
2115 Elliston Pl.
Nashville, TN 37203
615-327-1867

E5
Elegant Book & Map Company
815 Harrison Ave.
P.O. Box 1302
Cambridge, OH 43725
614-432-4068

F1
First Folio
1206 Brentwood
Paris, TN 38242-3804
phone/Fax 910-944-9940

F2
Fisher Books & Antiques
345 Pine St.
Williamsport, PA 17701

F3
Flo Silver Books
8442 Oakwood Ct. N
Indianapolis, IN 46260
317-255-5118

F4
For Collectors Only
2028B Ford Pky. #136
St. Paul, MN 55116

F5
Fran's Bookhouse
6601 Greene St.
Phil., PA 19119
215-438-2729 or Fax 215-438-8997

F6
Frontier America
P.O. Box 9193
Albuquerque, NM 87119-9193

G1
John Gach Fine & Rare Books
5620 Waterloo Rd.
Columbia, MD 21045
800-376-4775 or Fax 410-465-0649
e.mail-biblionet@clark.net

G2
Galerie De Boicourt
6136 Westbrooke Dr.
W Bloomfield, MI 48322
810-788-9253

G3
Gambler's Book Shop
630 S Eleventh St.
Las Vegas, NV 89101
800-634-6243

G4
David & Nancy Garcelon
10 Hastings Ave.
Millbury, MA 01527-4314

G5
Michael Gerlicher
1375 Rest Point Rd.
Orono, MN 55364

G6
Glo's Children's Series Books
Gloria Stobbes
906 Shadywood
Southlake, TX 76092

G7
James Tait Goodrich
Antiquarian Books & Manuscripts
214 Everett Place
Englewood, NJ 07631
201-567-0199 or Fax 201-567-0433

G8
Grave Matters
P.O. Box 32192-08
Cincinnati, OH 45232
phone/Fax 513-242-7527

G9
John A. Greget-Magic Lists
2631 E Claire Dr.
Phoenix, AZ 85032
602-971-5497

H1
Henry F. Hain III
Antiques & Collectibles
2623 N Second St.
Harrisburg, PA 17110
717-238-0534

H2
Rick Harmon
Military Books & Relics
910 Sullivan Dr.
Belvidere, IL 61008
815-547-7580

H3
Terry Harper, Bookseller
P.O. Box 312
Vergennes, VT 05491-0312
802-877-9262

H4
Susan Heller, Pages for Sages
22611 Halburton Rd.
Beachwood, OH 44122-3939
216-283-2665 or Fax 216-991-2665

H5
Heritage Book Shop, Inc.
8540 Melrose Ave.
Los Angeles, CA 90069
310-659-3674 or Fax 310-659-4872

H6
Hillcrest Books
Rt. 3, Box 479
Crossville, TN 38555-9547
phone/Fax 615-484-7680

H7
Jim Hodgson Books
908 S Manlius St.
Fayetteville, NY 13066
315-637-6264

H8
Homebiz Paper
2919 Mistwood Forest Dr.
Chester, VA 23831-7043

H9
Murray Hudson
Antiquarian Books & Maps
The Old Post Office
109 S Church St.
P.O. Box 163
Halls, TN 38040
901-836-9057 or 800-748-9946

H10
Hurley Books/Celtic Cross Books
1753 Rt. 12
Westmoreland, NH 03467
603-399-4342 or Fax 603-399-8326

I1
Island Books
P.O. Box 19
Old Westbury, NY 11586
516-759-0233

J1
Jay's House of Collectibles
75 Pky. Dr.
Syosset, NY 11791

K1
Kenneth Karmiole, Bookseller, Inc.
P.O. Box 464
509 Wilshire Blvd.
Santa Monica, CA 90401
310-451-4342 or Fax 310-458-5930

K2
Ilene Kayne
1308 S Charles St.
Baltimore, MD 21230

K3
Key Books
P.O. Box 58097
St. Petersburg, FL 33715-8097

K4
The King's Market Booksellers
P.O. Box 709
Boulder, CO 80306-0709
303-447-0234

K5
Knollwood Books
Lee & Peggy Price
P.O. Box 197
Oregon, WI 53575-0197
608-835-8861 or Fax 608-835-8421

K6
Kendra Krienke
230 Central Park West
New York, NY 10024
201-930-9709 or 201-930-9765

L1
Bob Lakin
3021 Lavita Ln.
Dallas, TX 75234
214-247-3291

L2
Henry Lindeman
4769 Bavarian Dr.
Jackson, MI 49201
517-764-5728

L3
Ken Lopez, Bookseller
51 Huntington Rd.
Hadley, MA 01035
413-584-4827 or Fax 413-584-2045

L4
Liberty Historic Manuscripts, Inc.
300 Kings Hwy. E
Haddonfield, NJ 08033

M1
M & S Rare Books, Inc.
P.O. Box 2594, E Side Sta.
Providence, RI 02806
401-421-1050 or
Fax 401-272-0831 (attention M & S)

M2
Robert A. Madle
4406 Bestor Dr.
Rockville, MD 20853
301-460-4712

M3
The Magazine Baron
1236 S Magnolia Ave.
Anaheim, CA 92804
714-527-0358 or Fax 714-527-5634

M4
Melvin Marcher, Bookseller
6204 N Vermont
Oklahoma City, OK 73112

M5
Marvelous Books
P.O. Box 1510
Ballwin, MO 63022
314-458-3301

M6
Mason's Bookstore, Rare Books
& Record Albums
115 S Main St.
Chambersburg, PA 17201
717-261-0541

M7
Denis McDonnell, Bookseller
653 Park St.
Honesdale, PA 18431
717-253-6706 or Fax 717-253-6786

M8
McGowan Book Co.
P.O. Box 16325
Chapel Hill, NC 27516
919-968-1121 or Fax 919-968-1169

M9
Paul Melzer Fine & Rare Books
12 E Vine St.
Redlands, CA 92373
909-792-7299

M10
Robert L. Merriam
Rare & Used Books
39 Newhall Rd.
Conway, MA 01341-9709
413-369-4052

M11
Meyer Boswell Books, Inc.
2141 Mission St.
San Francisco, CA 94110
415-255-6400 or Fax 415-255-6499

M12
Frank Mikesh
1356 Walden Rd.
Walnut Creek, CA 94596
510-934-9243

M13
Ken Mitchell
710 Conacher Dr.
Willowdale, Ontario
Canada M2M 3N6
416-222-5808

M14
Modern Age Books
P.O. Box 325
E Lansing, MI 48826
517-351-9334

M15
Mordida Books
P.O. Box 79322
Houston, TX 77279
713-467-4280 or Fax 713-467-4182

M16
The Mulberry Cat
Yvonne Davis
Jan Davis Martel
P.O. Box 3573
Boone, NC 28607
704-963-7693

M17
Much Ado
Seven Pleasant St.
Marblehead, MA 01945
617-639-0400

M18
Robert Mueller Rare Books
8124 W 26th St.
N Riverside, IL 60546
708-447-6441

M19
My Book Heaven
2406 Lincoln Ave.
P.O. Box 2715
Alameda, CA 94501
510-521-1683

M20
My Bookhouse
27 S Sandusky St.
Tiffin, OH 44883
419-447-9842

M21
Brian McMillan, Books
1429 L Ave.
Traer, IA 60575
319-478-2360 (Mon.-Sat., 9 am to
9pm CDT)

N1
Nerman's Books
410-63 Albert St.
Winnipeg, Manitoba
Canada R3B 1G4
Fax 204-947-0753

N2
Nutmeg Books
354 New Litchfield St. (Rte. 202)
Torrington, CT 06790
203-482-9696

N3
Roman Noir
440 E 79th St. #16B
New York City, NY 10021
212-737-8004 or Fax 212-737-3743

N3
Kai Nygaard
19421 Eighth Pl.
Escondido, CA 92029
619-749-9039

O1
David L. O'Neal, Antiquarian
Bookseller
234 Clarendon St.
Boston, MA 02116

O2
W.B. O'Neill
Old & Rare Books
11609 Hunters Green Ct.
Reston, VA 22091
703-860-0782 or Fax 703-620-0153

O3
October Farm
2609 Branch Rd.
Raleigh, NC 27610
919-772-0482

O4
The Old London Bookshop
111 Central Ave.
P.O. Box 922
Bellingham, WA 98227-0922
206-733-RARE or Fax 206-647-8946

O5
The Old Map Gallery
Paul F. Mahoney
1746 Blake St.
Denver, CO 80202
303-296-7725

O6
Old Paint Lick School Antique
Mall
Raymond P. Mixon
11000 Hwy. 52 West
Paint Lick, KY 40461
606-925-3000 or 606-792-3000

O7
Overlee Farm Books
P.O. Box 1155
Stockbridge, MA 01262
413-637-2277

O8
K.C. Owings
P.O. Box 19
N Abington, MA 02351
617-857-1655

O9
Olde Current Books
Daniel P. Shay
356 Putnam Ave.
Ormond Beach, FL 32174
904-672-8998 or e-mail:
PEAKMYSTER@aol,com

P1
Pacific Rim Books
Michael Onorato
P.O. Box 2575
Bellingham, WA 98227-2575
206-676-0256

P2
Page Books
H.C.R. 65, Box 233
Kingston, AR 72472
501-861-5831

P3
Pandora's Books Ltd.
P.O. Box 54
Neche, ND 58265
204-324-8548 or Fax 204-324-1628

P4
Parmer Books
7644 Forrestal Rd.
San Diego, CA 92120-2203
619-287-0693 or Fax 619-287-6135
Internet: ParmerBook@aol.com

P5
Parnassus Books
218 N 9th St.
Boise, ID 83702

P6
Passaic Book Center
594 Main Ave.
Passaic, NJ 07055
201-778-6646 or Fax 201-778-6738

P7
Pauper's Books
206 N Main St.
Bowling Green, OH 43402-2420
419-352-2163

P8
R. Plapinger, Baseball Books
P.O. Box 1062
Ashland, OR 97520
503-488-1220

P9
Prometheus Books
59 John Glenn Dr.
Buffalo, NY 14228-2197
716-691-0133 or Fax 716-691-0137

Q1
Quill & Brush
Patricia & Allen Ahearn
Box 5365
Rockville, MD 20848
301-460-3700 or Fax 301-871-5425

R1
Raintree Books
432 N Eustis St.
Eustis, FL 32726
904-357-7145

R2
Kathleen Rais & Co.
Rais Place Cottage
211 Carolina Ave.
Phoenixville, PA 19460
610-933-1388

R3
Randall House
835 Laguna St.
Santa Barbara, CA 93101
805-963-1909 or Fax 805-963-1650

R4
Reference Books
C. Scott Hall
P.O. Box 7076
Salem, OR 97305
503-399-6185

R5
Jo Ann Reisler, Ltd.
360 Glyndon St., NE
Vienna, VA 22180
703-938-2967 or Fax 703-938-9057

R6
Wallace Robinson Books
RD #6, Box 574
Meadville, PA 16335
800-653-3280 or 813-823-3280
814-724-7670 or 814-333-9652

R7
Tom Rolls
640 E Seminary #2
Greencastle, IN 46135

R8
RAC Books
R.R. #2
P.O. Box 296
Seven Valleys, PA 17360
717-428-3776

S1
Bill Sachen
927 Grand Ave.
Waukegan, IL 60085-3709
708-662-7204

S2
J. Sampson Antiques & Books
107 S Main
Harrodsburg, KY 40330
606-734-7829

S3
Stanley Schwartz
1934 Pentuckett Ave.
San Diego, CA 92104-5732
619-232-5888 or Fax 619-233-5833

S4
Scribe Company
Attn: Bonnie Smith
P.O. Box 1123
Flippin, AR 72634
501-453-7387

S5
Significant Books
3053 Madison Rd.
P.O. Box 9248
Cincinnati, OH 45209
513-321-7567

S6
The Silver Door
P.O. Box 3208
Redondo Beach, CA 90277
310-379-6005

S7
K.B. Slocum Books
P.O. Box 10998 #620
Austin, TX 78766
800-521-4451 or Fax 512-258-8041

S8
Barbara Smith Books
P.O. Box 1185
Northampton, MA 01061
413-586-1453

S9
Ed Smith Books
P.O. Box 66
Oak View, CA 93022
805-649-2844 or Fax 805-649-2863
email: EdsBooks@aol.com

S10
Smithfield Rare Books
20 Deer Run Trail
Smithfield, RI 02917
401-231-8225

S11
Nancy Stewart, Books
1188 NW Weybridge Way
Beaverton, OR 97006
503-645-9779

S12
Sweet Memories
Sharyn Laymon
400 Mulberry St.
Loudon, TN 37774
615-458-5044

T1
Lee & Mike Temares
50 Hts. Rd.
Plandome, NY 11030
516-627-8688

T2
Thomas Books
4425 W Olive, Ste. 168
Glendale, AZ 85302
602-435-5055 (10 am to 5 pm) or
602-247-9289 (after hours)

T3
Gordon Totty
Scarce Paper Americana
347 Shady Lake Pky.
Baton Rouge, LA 70810
504-766-8625

T4
Trackside Books
8819 Mobud Dr.
Houston, TX 77036
713-772-8107

T5
Treasures From the Castle
Connie Castle
1720 N Livernois
Rochester, MI 48306
810-651-7317

T6
H.E. Turlington Books
P.O. Box 190
Carrboro, NC 27510

T7
J. Tuttle Maritime Books
1806 Laurel Crest
Madison, WI 53705
608-238-SAIL (7245)

T8
George H. Tweney
16660 Marine View Dr. SW
Seattle, WA 98166
206-243-8243

T9
Typographeum Bookshop
The Stone Cottage
Bennington Rd.
Francestown, NH 03043

V1
VERSEtility Books
P.O. Box 1366
Burlington, CT 06013-1366
203-675-9338

V2
A.A. Vespa
P.O. Box 637
Park Ridge, IL 60068
708-692-4210

V3
Vintage Books
Nancy & David Haines
181 Hayden Rowe St.
Hopkinton, MA 01748
508-435-3499

V4
Volume I Books
1 Union St.
Hillsdale, MI 49242
517-437-2228

W1
Worldwide Antiquarian
P.O. Box 391
Cambridge, MA 02141
617-876-6220 or Fax 617-876-0839

W2
William P. Wreden, Books &
Manuscripts
P.O. Box 56
Palo Alto, CA 94302-0056
415-325-6851

Y1
Yesterday's Books
229 Riverview Dr.
Parchment, MI 49004
616-345-1011

X1
Xanadu Records, Ltd.
3242 Irwin Ave.
Kingsbridge, NY 10463
718-549-3655

Reach **Thousands** with Your **Free Listing** in Our Next Edition!

☞ *Book Sellers!* If you publish lists or catalogs of books for sale, take advantage of this *free* offer. Put us on your mailing list right away so that we can include you in our next edition. We'll not only list you in our Bookbuyers section under the genre that best represents your special interests (please specify these when you contact us), but each book description we choose to include from your catalog will contain a special dealer code that will identify you as the book dealer to contact in order to buy that book. Please send your information and catalogs or lists right away, since we're working on a first-come, first-served basis. Be sure to include your current address, just as you'd like it to be published. You may also include a fax number or an e-mail address. Our dealers tell us that this service has been very successful for them, both in buying and selling.

Send your listings to:

Huxford's Old Book Value Guide
1202 Seventh Street
Covington, IN 47932

Schroeder's
ANTIQUES
Price Guide

. . . is the #1 best-selling antiques & collectibles value guide on the market today, and here's why . . .

Schroeder's
ANTIQUES
Price Guide

OUR #1 BEST SELLER!

Identification & Values Of Over 50,000 Antiques & Collectibles

8½ x 11, 608 Pages, $14.95

• *More than 300 advisors, well-known dealers, and top-notch collectors work together with our editors to bring you accurate information regarding pricing and identification.*

• *More than 45,000 items in almost 500 categories are listed along with hundreds of sharp original photos that illustrate not only the rare and unusual, but the common, popular collectibles as well.*

• *Each large close-up shot shows important details clearly. Every subject is represented with histories and background information, a feature not found in any of our competitors' publications.*

• *Our editors keep abreast of newly developing trends, often adding several new categories a year as the need arises.*

If it merits the interest of today's collector, you'll find it in *Schroeder's*. And you can feel confident that the information we publish is up to date and accurate. Our advisors thoroughly check each category to spot inconsistencies, listings that may not be entirely reflective of market dealings, and lines too vague to be of merit. Only the best of the lot remains for publication.

Without doubt, you'll find
SCHROEDER'S ANTIQUES PRICE GUIDE
the only one to buy for
reliable information and values.